Icon	Name
	Arabic
	Canada
	Cyrillic
	Cyrillic transliterated
	Denmark
	Faeroe Islands
	Germany
	Hebrew
	Japanese Katakana
	Japanese Romaji
	Korean
	Netherlands, period decimal separator (previously NL.)
	Netherlands, comma decimal separator
	Roman (U.S.)
	Spain
	Swiss French
	Swiss German
	Swiss Italian
	Turkey
	Turkish, U.S. modified
	United Kingdom (previously GB)
	United States

Color Plate I. Examples of keyboard icons

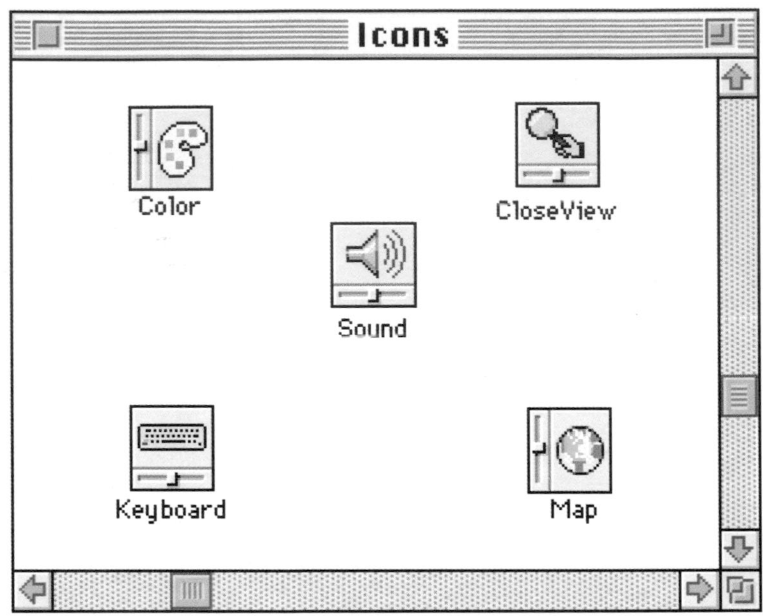

Color Plate II. A colorized window

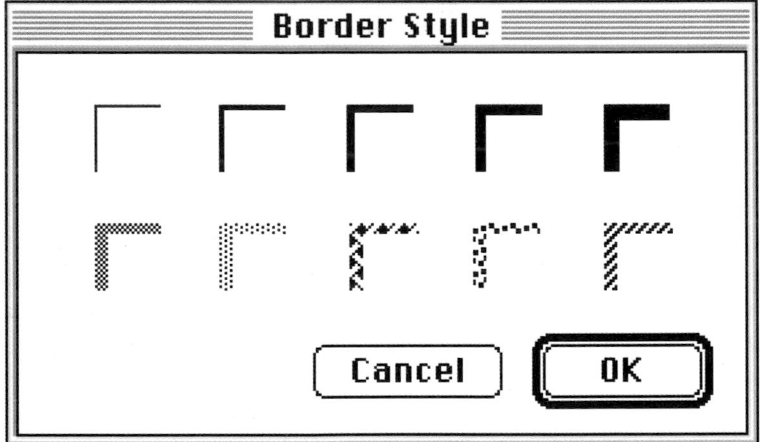

Color Plate III. A colorized movable modal dialog box

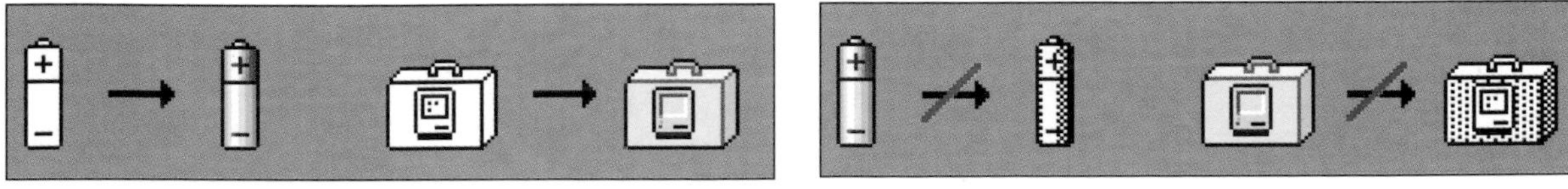

Color Plate IV. Design for black-and-white monitors first

Color Plate V. Don't mimic color effects in black-and-white designs

Color Plate VI. Use light colors for large areas

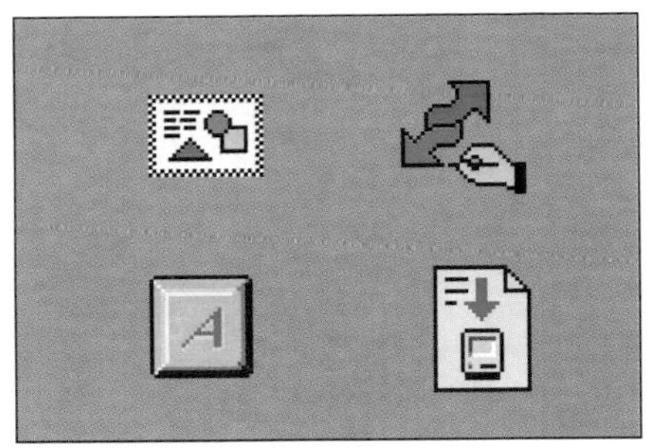

Color Plate VII. Don't use bright colors for large areas

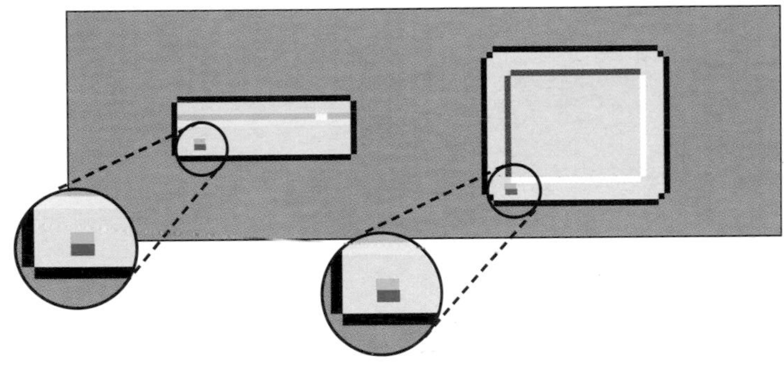

Color Plate VIII. Use bright colors for details (enlarged for detail)

Color Plate IX. A consistent light source (enlarged for detail)

Color Plate X. Inconsistent light sources (enlarged for detail)

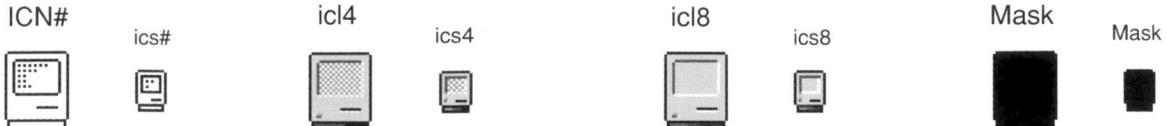

Color Plate XI. An icon family

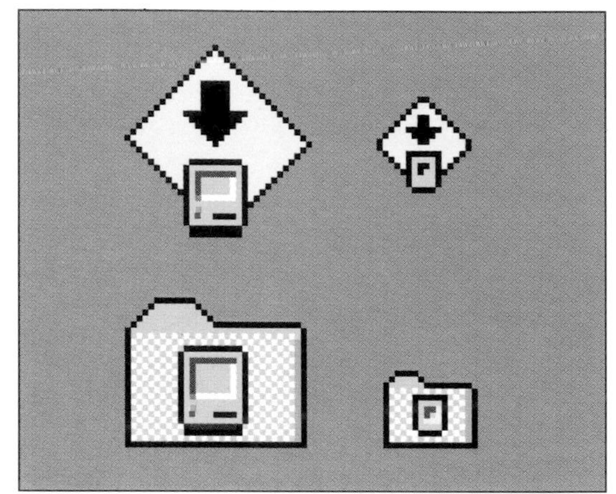

Color Plate XII. Consistently designed small icons (enlarged for detail)

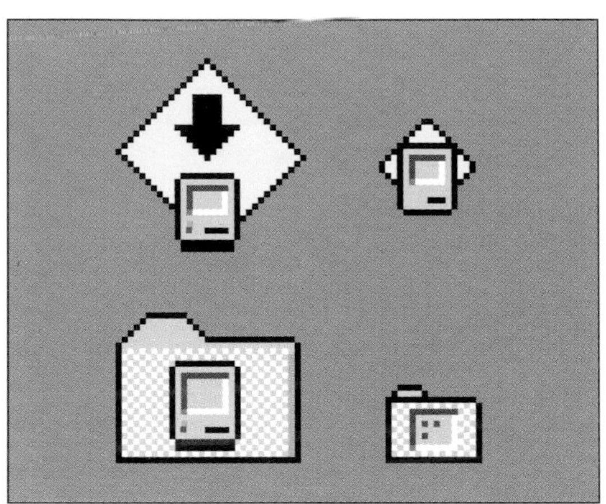

Color Plate XIII. Inconsistently designed small icons (enlarged for detail)

Color Plate XIV. Icons with a black outline (enlarged for detail)

Color Plate XV. Icons without a black outline (enlarged for detail)

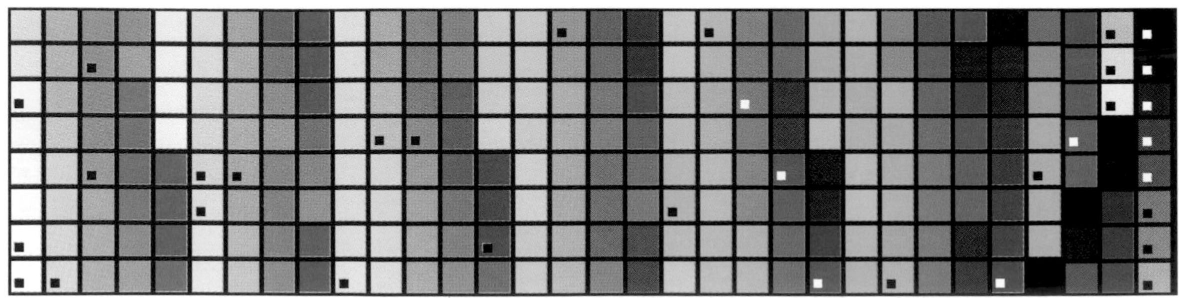

Color Plate XVI. Apple icon colors (as marked)

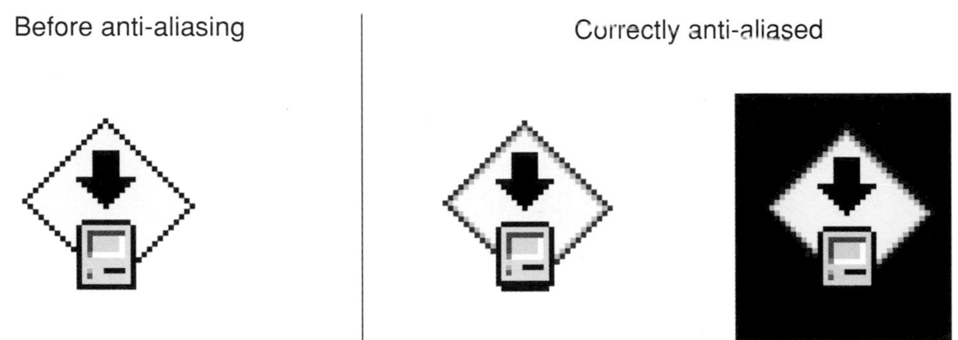

Color Plate XVII. Correct anti-aliasing (enlarged for detail)

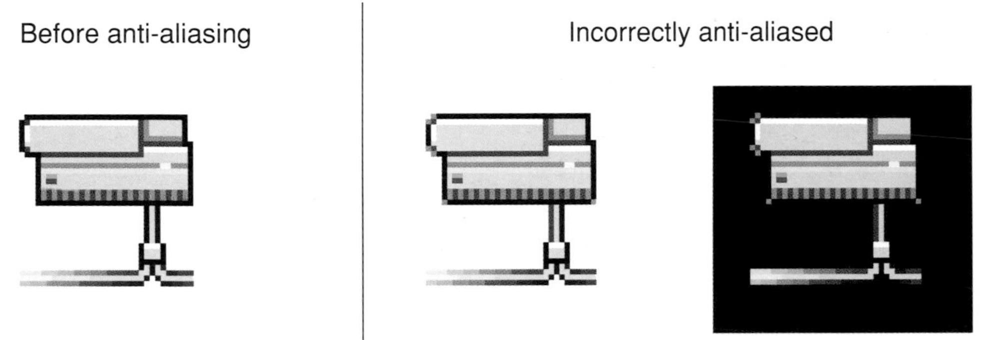

Color Plate XVIII. Incorrect anti-aliasing (enlarged for detail)

Color Plate XIX. Consistent use of icon elements (enlarged for detail)

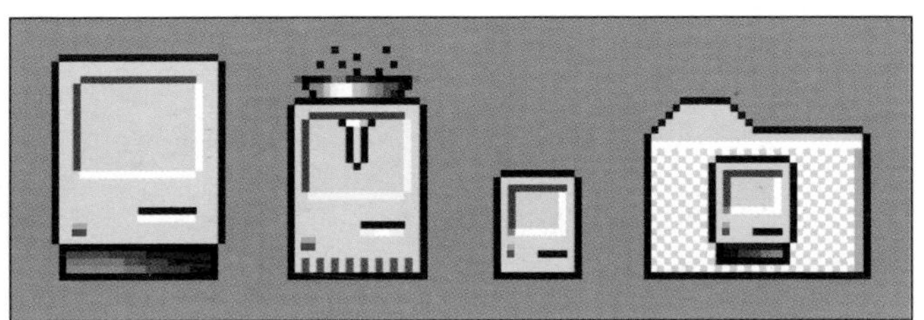

Color Plate XX. Inconsistent use of icon elements (enlarged for detail)

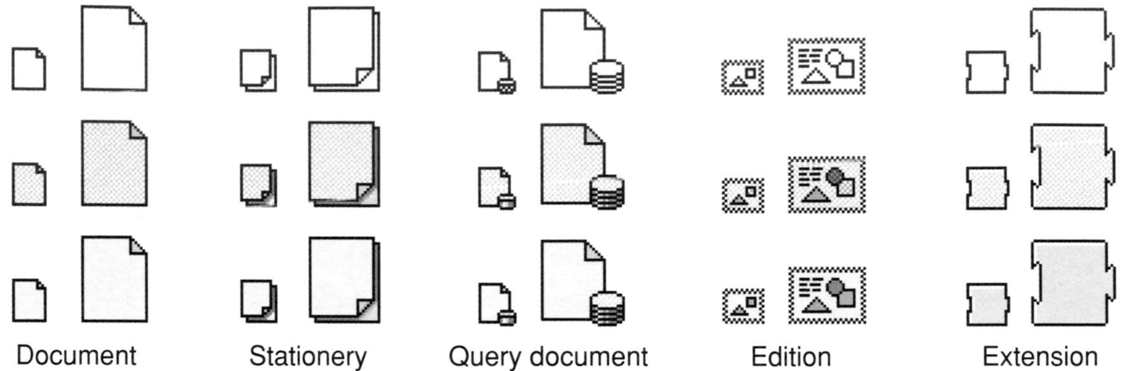

Color Plate XXI. Default system icon families

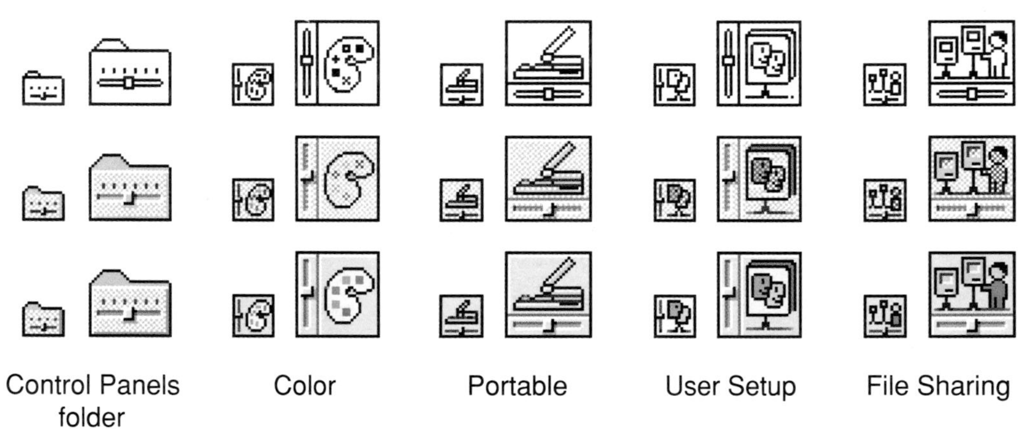

Color Plate XXII. Examples of control panel icons

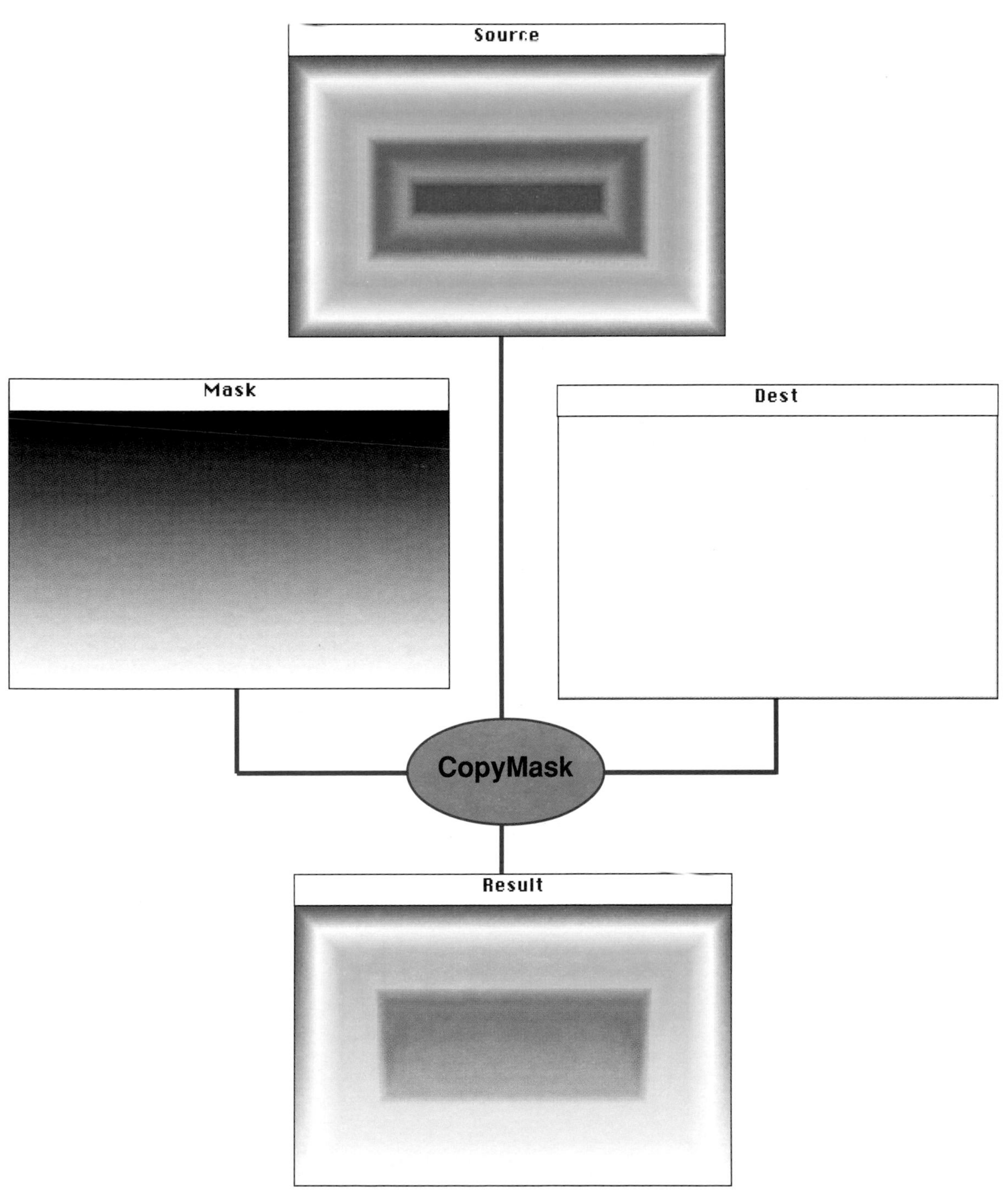

Color Plate XXIII. Copying with a pixel map as a mask

Color Plate XXIV. Colorizing

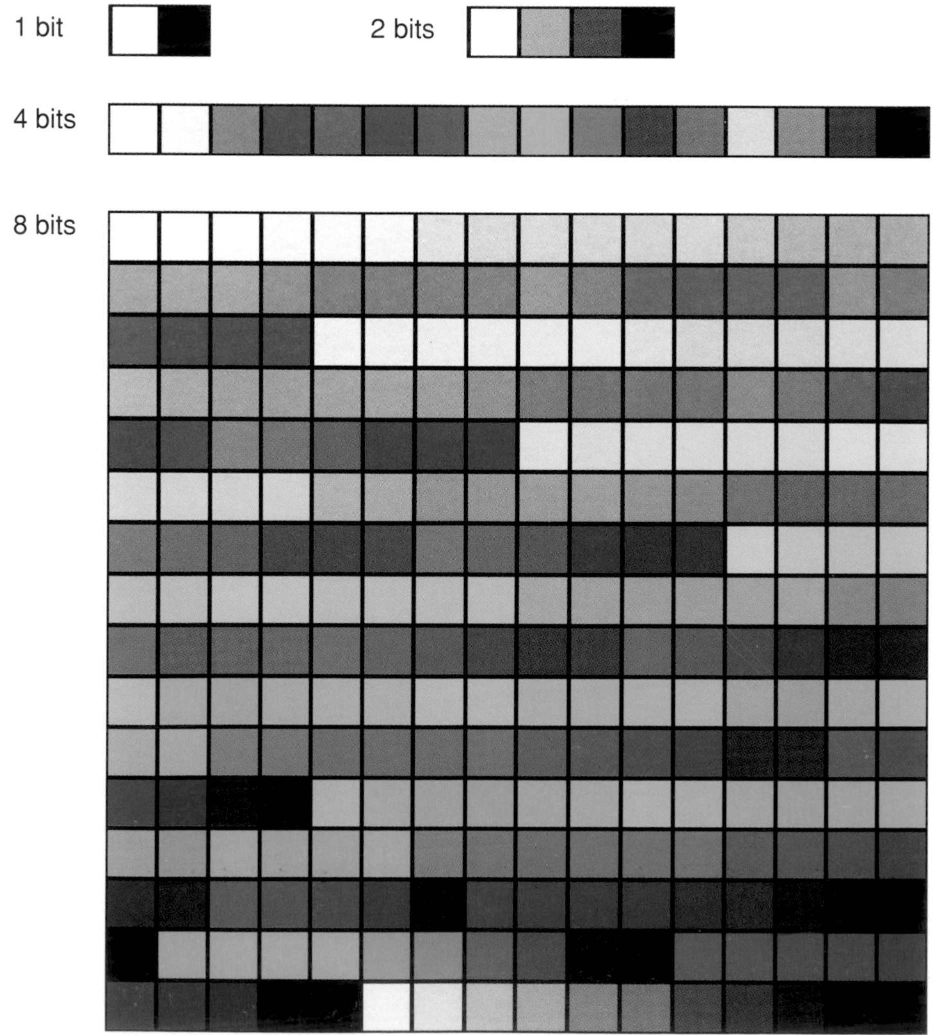

Color Plate XXV. Default color tables

Inside Macintosh®
Volume VI

®

Addison-Wesley Publishing Company, Inc.

Reading, Massachusetts   Menlo Park, California   New York
Don Mills, Ontario   Wokingham, England   Amsterdam
Bonn   Sydney   Singapore   Tokyo   Madrid
Paris   Seoul   Milan   Mexico City   Taipei   San Juan

APPLE COMPUTER, INC.

20525 Mariani Avenue
Cupertino, CA 95014-6299
(408) 996-1010

Simultaneously published in the United States and Canada.

ISBN 0-201-57755-0 (book)
ISBN 0-201-57776-3 (boxed edition)
2 3 4 5 6 7 8 9 10 - MU - 94939291
Second printing, June 1991

Inside Macintosh
Volume VI

Limited Warranty on Media and Replacement

ALL IMPLIED WARRANTIES ON THIS MANUAL, INCLUDING IMPLIED WARRANTIES OF MERCHANTABILITY AND FITNESS FOR A PARTICULAR PURPOSE, ARE LIMITED IN DURATION TO NINETY (90) DAYS FROM THE DATE OF THE ORIGINAL RETAIL PURCHASE OF THIS PRODUCT.

Even though Apple has reviewed this manual, **APPLE MAKES NO WARRANTY OR REPRESENTATION, EITHER EXPRESS OR IMPLIED, WITH RESPECT TO THIS MANUAL, ITS QUALITY, ACCURACY, MERCHANTABILITY, OR FITNESS FOR A PARTICULAR PURPOSE. AS A RESULT, THIS MANUAL IS SOLD "AS IS," AND YOU, THE PURCHASER, ARE ASSUMING THE ENTIRE RISK AS TO ITS QUALITY AND ACCURACY.**

IN NO EVENT WILL APPLE BE LIABLE FOR DIRECT, INDIRECT, SPECIAL, INCIDENTAL, OR CONSEQUENTIAL DAMAGES RESULTING FROM ANY DEFECT OR INACCURACY IN THIS MANUAL, even if advised of the possibility of such damages.

THE WARRANTY AND REMEDIES SET FORTH ABOVE ARE EXCLUSIVE AND IN LIEU OF ALL OTHERS, ORAL OR WRITTEN, EXPRESS OR IMPLIED. No Apple dealer, agent, or employee is authorized to make any modification, extension, or addition to this warranty.

Some states do not allow the exclusion or limitation of implied warranties or liability for incidental or consequential damages, so the above limitation or exclusion may not apply to you. This warranty gives you specific legal rights, and you may also have other rights which vary from state to state.

Contents

Contents

8 The Data Access Manager

9 The Finder Interface

11 The Help Manager

12 The Font Manager

22 The Sound Manager

25 The File Manager

26 The Standard File Package

27 The Alias Manager

28 Memory Management

Figures, Tables, and Listings

Color Plates

Color plates are immediately preceding the title page.

Preface

1 Introduction to the System Software Version 7.0 Environment

2 User Interface Guidelines

3 Compatibility Guidelines

5 The Event Manager

6 The Apple Event Manager

7 The Program-to-Program Communications Toolbox

8 The Data Access Manager

15 TextEdit

16 Graphics Overview

17 Color QuickDraw

26 The Standard File Package

27 The Alias Manager

28 Memory Management

29 Process Management

30 The Slot Manager

31 The Power Manager

PREFACE

ABOUT *INSIDE MACINTOSH*

Inside Macintosh is a six-volume set of books that describes how to write an application for the Apple® Macintosh® family of computers. *Inside Macintosh* is the definitive guide and reference for anyone writing software for the Macintosh computer. The first two volumes describe the routines in the Macintosh User Interface Toolbox and the Macintosh Operating System. The third volume is a summary of the Pascal interfaces for all routines described in Volumes I and II. The fourth and fifth volumes describe features and routines introduced with the Macintosh Plus, Macintosh SE, and Macintosh II computers. Volume VI describes the managers and features available in system software version 7.0.

Volume I contains the original user interface guidelines for Macintosh applications and an introduction to memory management and assembly language. It also describes QuickDraw™, the Resource Manager, the Event Manager, the Font Manager, the Window Manager, the Menu Manager, the Dialog Manager, TextEdit, and other routines relating to the user interface that you can use in your application.

Volume II describes the Macintosh Operating System, including the routines that perform file I/O, device I/O, memory management, and interrupt handling. It covers the File Manager, the Device Manager, the Printing Manager, the AppleTalk® Manager, and various drivers and utilities.

Volume III describes the Finder™ interface, provides an overview of the hardware of the Macintosh 128K and Macintosh 512K computers, and contains summaries of the Pascal interfaces for all routines described in Volumes I and II.

Volume IV describes routines introduced with the Macintosh Plus and Macintosh 512K enhanced computers. It introduces the Hierarchical File System, the SCSI Manager, the Time Manager, and the List Manager. The volume also describes changes to various managers and drivers and presents an overview of the Macintosh Plus hardware.

Volume V describes routines introduced with the Macintosh SE and Macintosh II computers. It describes Color QuickDraw, the Palette Manager, the Script Manager, the Sound Manager, the Slot Manager, the Apple Desktop Bus™, and changes made to various managers to support color. The volume also includes additional user interface guidelines and compatibility guidelines. It explains how to add color to menus, windows, and dialog boxes. It also discusses hierarchical, scrolling, and pop-up menus.

This volume, Volume VI, describes the system software version 7.0 environment, new managers available with version 7.0, new routines and data structures, new user interface guidelines, and how to take advantage of the version 7.0 environment.

Inside Macintosh, Volume VI, is also available in an on-line edition. The on-line edition provides a navigational model that lets you browse through information and it provides a search capability to quickly locate routines, data structures, and other text.

The *Inside Macintosh X-Ref* provides a comprehensive, integrated index for Volumes I through VI of *Inside Macintosh,* as well as *Programmer's Introduction to the Macintosh Family; Technical Introduction to the Macintosh Family; Designing Cards and Drivers for the Macintosh Family,* second edition; and *Guide to the Macintosh Family Hardware*, second edition. All these books are available from Addison-Wesley.

The Development Environment

The User Interface Toolbox and Macintosh Operating System routines are available using Pascal, C, or assembly-language interfaces. How you access these routines depends on the development environment you are using. This volume shows all routines in their Pascal interface using the Macintosh Programmer's Workshop (MPW®). All sample code listings are shown in MPW Pascal, with a few examples shown in assembly language.

The MPW development environment includes these books: *Macintosh Programmer's Workshop Development Environment,* Volume 1; *Macintosh Programmer's Workshop Development Environment,* Volume 2; *MPW Pascal: Macintosh Programmer's Workshop Pascal; MPW C: Macintosh Programmer's Workshop C;* and *MPW Assembler: Macintosh Programmer's Workshop Assembler.* These books are available from APDA® (Apple Programmers and Developers Association).

The code listings and other code in this volume were developed using MPW 3.0. They show methods of using various routines and illustrate techniques for accomplishing particular tasks. All code listings have been compiled and, in many cases, tested. However, Apple does not intend that you use these code samples in your application.

If you are programming in assembly language, pay attention to the assembly-language notes and trap macro notes. These notes provide information about saving and restoring registers, details of what each register must contain on entry to Operating System routines, what the routines return in the registers, and other information you might find helpful.

If you are programming in Pascal or C only, you can skip over the assembly-language information.

This volume occasionally uses *SurfWriter, WipeOut, store data, display data, send and receive, make memo,* and *spell quick* as names of sample programs for illustrative purposes; these are not actual products of Apple Computer, Inc.

APDA offers worldwide access to a broad range of programming products, resources, and information for anyone developing on Apple platforms. You'll find the most current versions of Apple and third-party development tools, debuggers, compilers, languages, and technical references for all Apple platforms. To establish an APDA account, obtain additional ordering information, or find out about site licensing and developer training programs, contact

APDA
Apple Computer, Inc.
20525 Mariani Avenue, M/S 33-G
Cupertino, CA 95014-6299

Telephone: 800-282-2732 (United States)
800-637-0029 (Canada)
408-562-3910 (elsewhere in the world)
Fax: 408-562-3971
Telex: 171-576

If you provide commercial products and services, call 408-974-4897 for information on the developer support programs available from Apple.

For information on registering signatures, file types, Apple events, and other technical information, contact

Macintosh Developer Technical Support
Apple Computer, Inc.
20525 Mariani Ave., M/S 75-3T
Cupertino, CA 95014-6299

The System Software Environment

Inside Macintosh Volume VI focuses on system software version 7.0; however, many of the chapters in this volume contain information that is also relevant to system software version 6.0 and later. See the Compatibility Guidelines chapter for information on developing applications that can run in both system software version 6.0 and system software version 7.0.

If the Gestalt function is available, you should use it instead of the SysEnvirons and Environs routines. You can use the Gestalt function to determine whether all the features your application requires are present on a particular Macintosh computer. You should not rely on the ROM version, since later system software versions can override routines in ROM. See the Compatibility Guidelines chapter for details on how to use the Gestalt function.

The Format of a Typical Chapter

Almost all chapters in Volume VI have a standard structure. For example, the Edition Manager chapter contains these sections:

- "About This Chapter" This section describes the information you can find in the chapter and includes references to related chapters.
- "About the Edition Manager" This section provides an overview of the features provided by the Edition Manager.
- Additional sections describe concepts related to the Edition Manager.
- "Using the Edition Manager" This section describes the tasks you can accomplish using the routines provided by the Edition Manager. It describes how to use the most common routines, gives related user interface information, provides code samples, and supplies additional information.
- "Edition Manager Routines" This section lists Edition Manager routines in version 7.0, with routine declarations and descriptions of every parameter for each routine.
- "Summary of the Edition Manager" This section provides the Edition Manager's Pascal interface for version 7.0 constants, data structures, routines, and result codes, as well as relevant assembly-language information.

The Conventions Used in This Volume

This volume uses elements such as assembly-language notes, trap macro notes, note boxes, and warning boxes to set off important information. Trap macro notes and assembly-language notes are useful only if you are programming in assembly language.

All routines (with a few exceptions) have both a Pascal and assembly-language form. The summary at the end of each chapter first lists the constants, data structures, and routines provided with the MPW Pascal interface files, and then lists equivalent assembly-language information for data structures and routines for use with the MPW Assembler interface files. The constants for the MPW Assembler interface files are the same as their Pascal equivalents, so the constant names are shown only in the Pascal section of the summary. (The constants, data structure names, and routine names in the MPW C interface files are also the same as their Pascal equivalents.)

When appropriate, the declaration for a procedure or function includes relevant assembly-language information in the form of a trap macro note that immediately follows the declaration. The trap macro that corresponds to a Pascal interface routine begins with an underscore character (_) followed by the Pascal routine name. Trap macro notes appear in this form:

Trap macro	For register-based routines, this shows the trap macro name and describes the parameters that must be in the registers on entry to the routine and describes the values returned in the registers. For stack-based routines, this shows the name of the trap macro if it is different from the Pascal interface name.

Assembly-language notes appear in this form:

Assembly-language note: This gives information of interest only if you are programming in assembly language.

If you are programming in Pascal or C only, you can skip over the information in trap macro notes and assembly-language notes.

Important information is often called out in a note box:

> **Note:** Text set off in this way presents reminders or notes related to the topic.

Information that you need to pay special attention to is shown in a warning box:

> ▲ **Warning:** Warnings like this alert you to situations in which you could damage software or lose data. ▲

Words that appear in **boldface** are key terms or concepts and are defined in the Glossary

All code listings use the Courier font (`this is Courier`) to indicate code from a sample program that can be compiled. The summary listings and set-off code in text also use Courier for the actual data structure names, field names, constant names, and routine names that match the names used in the MPW Pascal interface files.

Many Toolbox and Operating System routines accept a pointer to a parameter block as a parameter. For these routines, the routine description includes a list of the fields in the parameter block that are used by the routine.

A typical parameter block description looks like this:

Parameter block

[in/out]	[offset]	[field name]	[size]	[description]
→	0	input1	long	This is an input parameter
←	4	ouput1	word	This is an output parameter
↔	6	inAndOut	long	This is an input/output parameter
→	10	reqCount	long	Requested number of files to send
→	14	buffer	long	Pointer to data buffer
←	18	accCount	long	Actual number of files sent

The arrow in the first column indicates whether the field is an input parameter, output parameter, or both. You must supply values for all input parameters and input/output parameters. The routine returns values in output parameters and input/output parameters.

The second column indicates the offset and is useful only if you are programming in assembly language or debugging your code. The offset value is the offset in bytes from the beginning of the parameter block for each field within the structure.

The third column shows the field name as defined in the MPW Pascal interfaces, and the fourth column shows the size of that field. The size is given in bytes or indicated as *word* or *long* (for long word). Long indicates a field that occupies 4 bytes; word indicates a field that occupies 2 bytes. The size is provided for your information and is more useful if you are programming in assembly language. The final column provides a short description of the field.

Other Documentation

For specific hardware information about the Macintosh family, see *Guide to the Macintosh Family Hardware,* second edition, and *Designing Cards and Drivers for the Macintosh Family,* second edition; for additional software information, see previous volumes of *Inside Macintosh.* Also see *Macintosh Worldwide Development: Guide to System Software* for a complete description of all components of the worldwide system software. See *Human Interface Guidelines: The Apple Desktop Interface* for a complete description of the Apple human interface.

AN OVERVIEW OF THE CHAPTERS IN VOLUME VI

The following sections describe the content of each chapter in this volume and tell where to find additional information in previous volumes. Figure P-1 (at the end of the Preface) lists the chapters in Volume VI and shows which other volumes cover those topics.

Introduction to the System Software Version 7.0 Environment

The first chapter in this volume provides an overview of the features of system software version 7.0. It describes the operating environment for applications that run in version 7.0.

User Interface Guidelines

The User Interface Guidelines chapter in Volume VI reviews the user interface design principles and gives new guidelines for system software version 7.0. The chapter discusses windows, dialog boxes and movable modal dialog boxes, additions to the standard menus, terminology, and user feedback. It also gives guidelines for developing worldwide software and for designing color icons and windows.

The Finder Interface chapter in this volume provides related information on the user interface presented by the Finder. Individual chapters address specific issues related to the user interface features provided by a particular manager.

The User Interface Guidelines chapter in Volume I describes the various components of a Macintosh application and discusses the use of menus, windows, dialog boxes, scroll bars and other controls.

The User Interface Guidelines chapter in Volume IV discusses use of the arrow keys, reserved keyboard equivalents, window zooming, and the standard close box.

The User Interface Guidelines chapter in Volume V briefly discusses the use of color in your application. The chapter describes features of the standard and extended keyboards, and discusses using sound, hierarchical menus, and scrolling menus in your application.

For more information on the Apple human interface, see the *Human Interface Guidelines: The Apple Desktop Interface.*

Compatibility Guidelines

The Compatibility Guidelines chapter describes issues relating to compatibility for various managers in system software version 7.0. It also includes details on pop-up menus, movable modal dialog boxes, new routines for manipulating dialog items in a dialog box, and discusses menu access when an application displays a modal dialog box.

The chapter also shows you how to call Gestalt, the new function for determining various attributes, versions, and features of the system software.

The chapter gives guidelines you should follow to help ensure that your application is compatible across the Macintosh family of computers. It also provides information on how to make your application compatible with A/UX® (Apple's version of the UNIX® operating system) and presents a brief overview of how to write software that can be easily localized for use in other regions.

The Edition Manager

The Edition Manager chapter describes how you can let users publish and subscribe data among many documents. The Edition Manager is part of the interapplication communications (IAC) architecture in version 7.0. See the Edition Manager chapter for sample code that shows how to add publish and subscribe capabilities to your application.

The Event Manager

The Event Manager chapter in Volume VI includes information on all events, including suspend and resume events. The chapter incorporates information from *Programmer's Guide to MultiFinder* and replaces the information found there. The Event Manager chapter in this volume also describes how to send and receive high-level events.

For specific information on keyboard events, the modifier flags field of the event record, reading the keyboard and keypad, and responding to mouse events or disk-inserted events, see the Toolbox Event Manager chapter in Volume I.

You also may want to read about the Operating System Event Manager, described in Volume II. The Operating System Event Manager handles low-level, hardware-related events. The Operating System Event Manager chapter also describes how your application can post its own events in the event queue. You usually use the Event Manager to send and retrieve events. For information on the PPostEvent function, see the Operating System Event Manager chapter in Volume IV.

For information on standard keyboards, an addition to the modifier flags field in the event record, and the KeyTrans function, see the Toolbox Event Manager chapter in Volume V.

The Apple Event Manager

The Apple Event Manager chapter describes Apple events and how your application can receive and process the required set of Apple events. It also describes how to create and send Apple events.

The Program-to-Program Communications Toolbox

The Program-to-Program Communications (PPC) Toolbox chapter describes how your application can exchange message blocks with other applications. The PPC Toolbox provides low-level control of communication and is generally more suitable for code that is not event-based or desk accessories or applications that are closely integrated.

The Data Access Manager

The Data Access Manager chapter describes how your application can communicate with a database application or other data source running on a remote computer. The chapter describes how your application can use high-level or low-level routines to initiate communication with a remote data server, send commands or data to the server, and, after the server executes the commands, retrieve any requested data from the server.

The Finder Interface

The Finder Interface chapter in this volume describes how to create bundles, file references, and icons, including small icons and color icons. Code listings show how to set up the resources the Finder needs to start up your application and display your application's icons on the desktop.

The chapter also describes changes to the Finder interface—for example, the new aliases and stationery documents. It shows how to find special folders, such as the Preferences folder and Temporary Items folder. In addition, the chapter describes how fonts and sounds are visible on the desktop and how the user installs fonts and sounds by moving their icons to the System Folder icon.

The Finder Interface chapter describes the Desktop Manager, a new manager that lets your application add or remove information from the desktop database.

The Finder Interface chapter in this volume replaces the Finder Interface chapters in Volumes III and IV.

Control Panels

The Control Panels chapter in this volume describes the new behavior of control panels in system software version 7.0. If you develop video cards, you can also use the information in the chapter to create an Options dialog box for the Monitors control panel.

The Control Panel chapter in Volume V describes how to write a control panel. Read the information in the Control Panels chapter in this volume for additional information on writing a control panel in system software version 7.0. Control panels written for earlier versions of system software are compatible with version 7.0.

The Help Manager

The Help Manager chapter discusses how you can provide help balloons that supply your users with information that describes the actions, behaviors, or properties of elements of your application. The chapter explains how to create help balloons for menus, windows, icons, controls, and other elements of the user interface of your application.

The Font Manager

The Font Manager chapter in Volume VI describes how your application can take advantage of TrueType™ fonts.

The Font Manager chapter in Volume I describes how the Font Manager works with QuickDraw to draw characters. It discusses font numbers, character styles, font size, scaling factors, the ascent line, the base line, the descent line, and leading. The chapter also describes the format of a bitmapped font.

The Font Manager chapter in Volume IV discusses bitmapped fonts (of resource type 'FONT' or 'NFNT') and font families (of resource type 'FOND'). It describes a few data structures, like the font family record.

The Font Manager chapter in Volume V includes information on fractional character widths, the font search algorithm (how the Font Manager looks for a particular font), and how to specify colors for a font.

The Resource Manager

The Resource Manager chapter in Volume VI lists the standard resource types in version 7.0. The chapter also describes routines that you can use to read or write part of a resource.

The Resource Manager chapter in Volume I describes how you can store menus, fonts, icons, and other data as resources. It gives definitions and descriptions of resource files, resource forks, and data forks. It describes how to create and open resource files, how to read resources from a resource file, and how to add, remove, update, and write resources to a resource file.

The Resource Manager chapter in Volume IV describes a few routines that search only the current resource file (these routines have the numeral 1 in their routine name). It also describes two advanced functions, RsrcMapEntry and OpenRFPerm.

The Resource Manager chapter in Volume V describes the RGetResource function and lists resource types, ROM resources, and resources in the System file.

Worldwide Software Overview

The Worldwide Software Overview chapter provides an introduction to scripts and script systems. It can help you design your application so that it is compatible with Macintosh computers throughout the world.

See the Worldwide Software Overview chapter for an introduction to worldwide issues, and see the User Interface Guidelines chapter for guidelines about developing your application for use around the world. See the International Utilities Package chapter in Volume I for information on displaying numbers, currency, time, and dates in the correct format for various countries around the world. *Macintosh Worldwide Development: Guide to System Software* (available from APDA) replaces the Script Manager chapter in Volume V and provides a more complete description of all components of the worldwide system software.

TextEdit

The TextEdit chapter in this volume describes how TextEdit provides support for working with different script systems. It describes how you can use TextEdit to let the user edit and display text in multiple scripts and styles when a non-Roman script system is in use. TextEdit automatically handles text that uses more than one script, style, or direction.

The TextEdit chapter in Volume I introduces TextEdit and explains how your application can use TextEdit routines for basic text formatting and editing.

The TextEdit chapter in Volume IV describes how TextEdit supports automatic scrolling of text.

The TextEdit chapter in Volume V explains how TextEdit lets you vary text attributes such as size, style, and font. It also describes the style record that stores the style information.

Graphics Overview

The Graphics Overview chapter provides an introduction to graphics on the Macintosh computer. The system software provides a rich set of routines that support quick drawing of objects such as circles, rectangles, and text. The Graphics Overview chapter introduces many of the concepts and data structures explained in greater detail in the chapters on Color QuickDraw, the Picture Utilities Package, the Color Picker Package, the Palette Manager, and the Graphics Devices Manager.

Color QuickDraw

The Color QuickDraw chapter in Volume VI describes how version 7.0 supports both indexed and direct specification of color. It also describes changes to the pixel map record and the PICT2 file format, and it describes a routine that lets you convert a bitmap record into a region. The information in the Color QuickDraw chapter in this volume supplements the QuickDraw chapter in Volume I and the Color QuickDraw chapter in Volume V.

The QuickDraw chapter in Volume I introduces the basic concepts of QuickDraw, including descriptions of the mathematical foundation of QuickDraw and the graphics environment that QuickDraw provides. It also describes QuickDraw routines.

The Color QuickDraw chapter in Volume V describes how Color QuickDraw provides support for drawing objects using a large number of different colors.

The Picture Utilities Package

The Picture Utilities Package chapter describes routines you can use to examine the contents of pictures and pixel maps.

The Color Picker Package

The Color Picker Package chapter in this volume describes how to present users with a standard user interface for selecting a color. This chapter replaces the Color Picker Package chapter in Volume V.

The Palette Manager

The Palette Manager chapter in this volume describes palettes, the default color tables, and how to create and use a palette to control the color environment. This chapter replaces the Palette Manager chapter in Volume V.

The Graphics Devices Manager

The Graphics Devices Manager chapter describes how you can prepare offscreen graphics and move them quickly into view. It also provides useful information if you are developing a graphics-intensive application. This chapter replaces the Graphics Devices chapter in Volume V.

The Sound Manager

The Sound Manager chapter in this volume completely replaces any previous information in *Inside Macintosh* regarding the Sound Manager. The Sound Manager chapter in Volume VI is the complete reference and guide for the use of sound. It provides an introduction to sound and describes sound synthesizers, sound channels, sound commands, sound resources, and sound files.

The chapter also describes how your application can use the Sound Manager to create and play sounds, mix and synchronize multiple channels of sound, expand and compress sound data, and play sounds continuously from disk.

See the Sound Manager chapter in this volume if you want to use any kind of sound in your application, even if you only want to use the SysBeep procedure.

The Time Manager

The Time Manager chapter in this volume describes the original Time Manager, the revised Time Manager (available in system software version 6.0.3 and later), and the extended Time Manager (available in system software version 7.0). It completely replaces the Time Manager chapter in Volume IV.

The chapter describes how to schedule a routine for later execution, how to schedule a routine to execute at periodic intervals, and how to compute elapsed time. It also describes other time-related services, such as those provided by the TickCount and Delay functions, and the Vertical Retrace Manager.

The Notification Manager

The Notification Manager chapter describes how to notify users of significant occurrences relating to your application when your application is running in the background. Device drivers, VBL tasks, Time Manager tasks, completion routines, startup code, desk accessories, and applications can use the Notification Manager.

The Notification Manager chapter in this volume replaces the information in Appendix D of the *Programmer's Guide to MultiFinder*.

The File Manager

The File Manager chapter in this volume describes how to create a file specification to identify a file, folder, or volume. It also describes how you can use the File Manager to search for and quickly find files.

The File Manager chapter in Volume IV describes the file system, including the Macintosh File System (MFS) and Hierarchical File System (HFS). The chapter provides descriptions of File Manager data structures and routines.

The chapter on File Manager Extensions in a Shared Environment in Volume V presents routines that allow your application to more easily execute in a shared environment.

The Standard File Package

The Standard File Package chapter in this volume describes the StandardGetFile and StandardPutFile procedures available in version 7.0. You can use these two procedures to present the standard user interface when a user opens or saves a file. The chapter also describes the two new procedures CustomGetFile and CustomPutFile, which let your application exercise more control over the user interface when opening and saving files.

The Standard File Package chapter in Volume I describes the original procedures that present the standard user interface for opening and saving files in earlier system software. The Standard File Package chapter in Volume IV describes modifications to the original procedures for use with the Hierarchical File System.

The Alias Manager

The Alias Manager chapter describes how to create and resolve alias records—a new data structure that describes a file, folder, or volume.

You can use alias records instead of conventional file specifications to store file or directory information. If you create an alias record, your application can use the Alias Manager to locate the file or directory when needed—even if the user has renamed it, copied it, restored it from backup, or moved it. The chapter describes the routines you can use to manage the information in alias records.

Memory Management

The Memory Management chapter in Volume VI describes 32-bit addressing, virtual memory, and routines that let your application use available temporary memory. The chapter replaces the discussion of temporary memory in Chapter 3 of the *Programmer's Guide to MultiFinder.*

The Memory Manager chapter in Volume II describes the system heap zone and application heap zone, how to allocate memory blocks, and how to avoid memory fragmentation. It also discusses dereferencing a handle, lists general-purpose data types, shows the organization of memory, and gives an overview of the stack and the heap. The routine descriptions discuss how to set the heap zone size, create handles and pointers, allocate relocatable and nonrelocatable blocks, and how to free memory in the heap.

The Memory Manager chapter in Volume IV describes improvements to Memory Manager routines that are largely transparent to your application. It also describes routines that let your application set or clear flags that the Memory Manager associates with each relocatable block.

Process Management

The Process Management chapter describes how the Process Manager schedules applications for execution and manages access to shared resources. It describes routines that let your application get information about any or all running applications. The chapter replaces the discussion of launching applications found in the *Programmer's Guide to MultiFinder.*

The Slot Manager

The Slot Manager chapter in this volume describes how version 7.0 supports 32-bit addressing of NuBus™ cards. The Slot Manager chapter in Volume V gives an overview of the firmware of a slot card, explains the slot parameter block, and describes Slot Manager routines.

The Power Manager

The Power Manager chapter describes a manager used only with the Macintosh Portable in system software version 6.0.4 and later. This information is useful only if you are writing a device driver or application that might be affected when power for the various subsystems of the Macintosh Portable is shut off.

The AppleTalk Manager

The AppleTalk Manager chapter in this volume describes how version 7.0 supports various link access protocols (for example, the LocalTalk® Link Access Protocol and the EtherTalk® Link Access Protocol) that can be used for AppleTalk communication. It describes the AppleTalk Data Stream Protocol (ADSP), a new protocol your application can use to exchange information between two equal entities.

The chapter explains how you can request that your program receive notification each time another routine opens or closes the .MPP driver or whenever another routine is about to close the .MPP driver.

The chapter also discusses how the LAP Manager lets your application control communication over non-LocalTalk networks, such as Ethernet. In addition, it provides information you can use to write your own protocol handler for Ethernet or 802.3.

The AppleTalk Manager chapters in Volumes II, IV, and V provide additional information on the device drivers and protocols associated with AppleTalk.

A ROAD MAP TO VOLUME VI

Figure P-1 shows each chapter in this volume. If you need to read related chapters in earlier volumes of *Inside Macintosh* for additional information, those other volumes are also shown. For each chapter, the volumes are shown in the order in which you should read them; the volumes shown are the only ones you need to read for information on that topic.

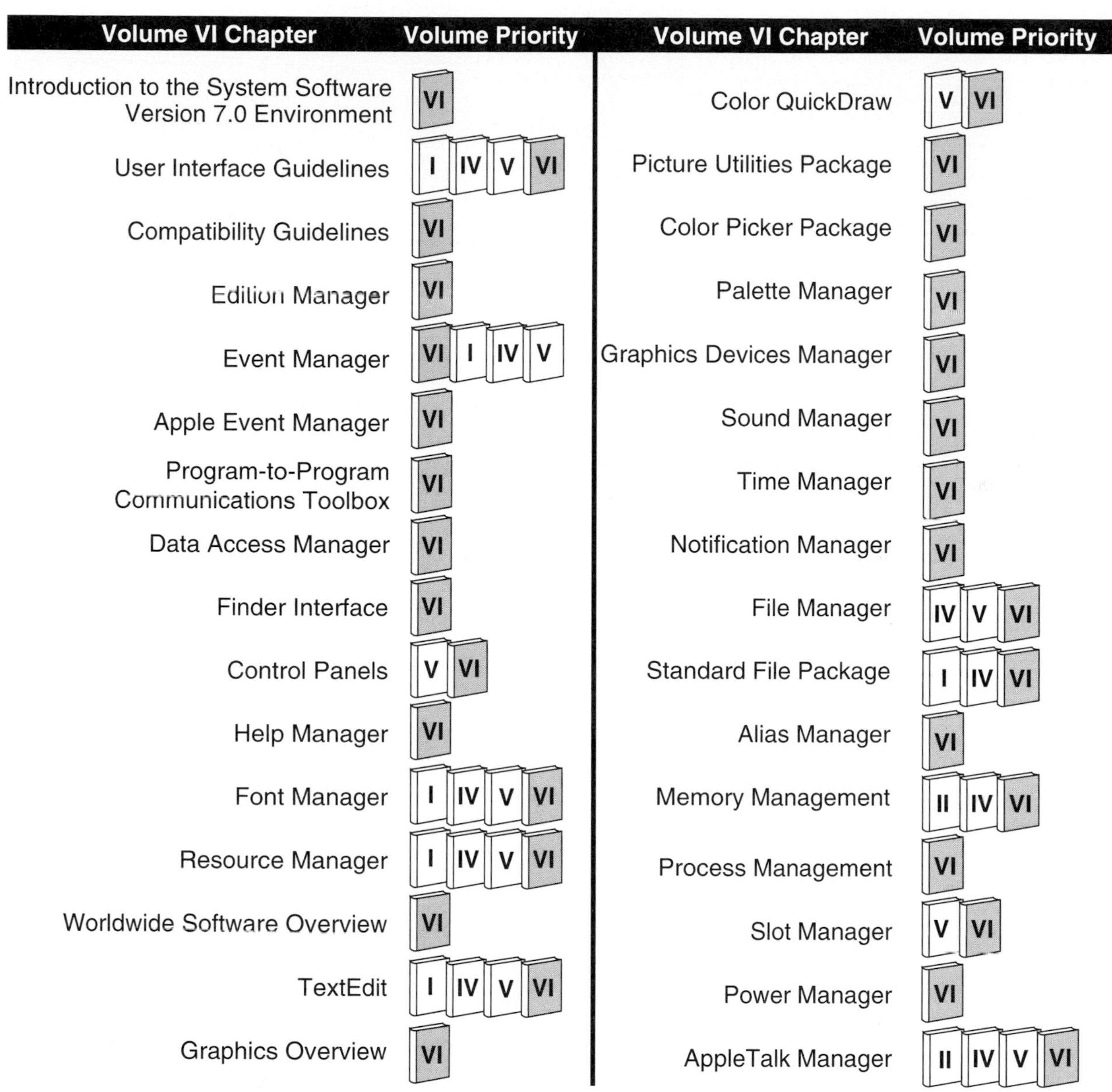

Volume VI Chapter	Volume Priority	Volume VI Chapter	Volume Priority
Introduction to the System Software Version 7.0 Environment	VI	Color QuickDraw	V VI
User Interface Guidelines	I IV V VI	Picture Utilities Package	VI
Compatibility Guidelines	VI	Color Picker Package	VI
Edition Manager	VI	Palette Manager	VI
Event Manager	VI I IV V	Graphics Devices Manager	VI
Apple Event Manager	VI	Sound Manager	VI
Program-to-Program Communications Toolbox	VI	Time Manager	VI
Data Access Manager	VI	Notification Manager	VI
Finder Interface	VI	File Manager	IV V VI
Control Panels	V VI	Standard File Package	I IV VI
Help Manager	VI	Alias Manager	VI
Font Manager	I IV V VI	Memory Management	II IV VI
Resource Manager	I IV V VI	Process Management	VI
Worldwide Software Overview	VI	Slot Manager	V VI
TextEdit	I IV V VI	Power Manager	VI
Graphics Overview	VI	AppleTalk Manager	II IV V VI

Figure P-1. A road map to Volume VI

1 INTRODUCTION TO THE SYSTEM SOFTWARE VERSION 7.0 ENVIRONMENT

ABOUT THIS CHAPTER

This chapter describes the operating environment for applications that run in system software version 7.0. It also provides general information about the features available to you when you design an application to run in the system software version 7.0 environment.

Read this chapter for an overview of how your application can use the Macintosh® User Interface Toolbox and Macintosh Operating System routines in system software version 7.0 to

- share data with other applications using the Edition Manager
- communicate with other applications using the Event Manager, Apple® Event Manager, or the Program-to-Program Communications (PPC) Toolbox
- access data from other sources, including remote databases, using the Data Access Manager
- play sounds using the Sound Manager
- keep track of specific files using the Alias Manager
- perform quick searches for specific files using the File Manager
- provide on-line assistance for users with the Help Manager
- draw TrueType™ fonts using the Font Manager
- use direct devices for graphics applications using Color QuickDraw™
- function in worldwide markets using the Script Manager, International Utilities Package, and TextEdit

This chapter discusses the features and managers new to version 7.0. In addition, see the Preface, where "A Road Map to Volume VI" shows each manager discussed in this volume and illustrates a pathway through related information in previous volumes of *Inside Macintosh.*

Although Volume VI focuses on system software version 7.0, many of its chapters contain information that is also relevant to system software version 6.0 and later. See the Compatibility Guidelines chapter in this volume for information on developing applications that can run in both system software version 6.0 and system software version 7.0.

ABOUT THE SYSTEM SOFTWARE VERSION 7.0 ENVIRONMENT

System software version 7.0 extends the environment of the Macintosh computer by providing even greater support for cooperation between applications. The user interface continues to build on solid design principles and provides additional benefits; for example, in version 7.0 users can more directly manipulate icons on the desktop and users can customize the Apple menu. The Finder™, the Macintosh Operating System, and the User Interface Toolbox provide and maintain this environment.

The Finder is the system application that lets users organize and manage applications, documents, folders, and disks on the desktop. Users can choose commands from the Finder menu bar or use the mouse to perform various tasks. Because the Finder presents the standard interface that the user becomes familiar with, you need to make sure that your application performs in an expected manner in the Finder environment.

Macintosh users also expect certain standard behavior from Macintosh applications; for example, all applications should provide File and Edit menus. Macintosh applications that follow the user interface guidelines provide consistency and let users determine what action to take to perform a particular task.

In earlier Macintosh computers a user ran one application at a time. Today's Macintosh model recognizes that a user often wants to run many applications at once. System software version 7.0 provides this cooperative environment.

In system software versions 5.0 and 6.0, the MultiFinder® option provided a cooperative multitasking environment. In system software version 7.0, the features of MultiFinder are integrated into the Macintosh Operating System.

The Macintosh Operating System lets the user have several applications open at the same time and lets the user switch between them. The Operating System also gives the user constant access to the Finder. This lets a user move among open documents and applications without having to save or quit the previous document or application. This environment also allows applications to run in the background. For example, the Finder can copy files while the user is working on another task in the foreground.

The cooperative environment of the Macintosh allows multiple applications to share the CPU and other resources. You need to understand how this environment can affect your application. The next section, "The Cooperative Multitasking Environment," explains this in more detail.

An important aspect of system software version 7.0 is **interapplication communication (IAC),** a new collection of features that help applications work together.

Copy and paste is a simple way in which Macintosh applications work together by sharing data. In system software version 7.0, applications can provide automated copy and paste features (that is, your application can automatically update the data that the user pastes into a document when the original source of information changes). Applications can extend this concept by using high-level events to request that other applications perform a particular task or return requested information. Applications and drivers that require close integration with each other can also extend this concept by reading and writing low-level message blocks.

Apple Computer, Inc. has defined a protocol for high-level events called the Apple Event Interprocess Messaging Protocol. High-level events that adhere to this protocol are called Apple events. You can help ensure effective communication with other applications by using this protocol.

Macintosh applications in system software version 7.0 can respond to incoming high-level events from other applications as well as events generated by the user, and they can also send high-level events to other applications. Better cooperation and communication between applications help users to get the most out of any one application or to use the best features from many applications—in effect, combining the features of many applications to achieve the desired result.

By including the features provided by IAC in your application, you give the users of your application even greater power, ease of use, and flexibility in accomplishing their tasks.

Figure 1-1 highlights the general areas for which system software version 7.0 provides routines. The next sections describe these topics in greater detail.

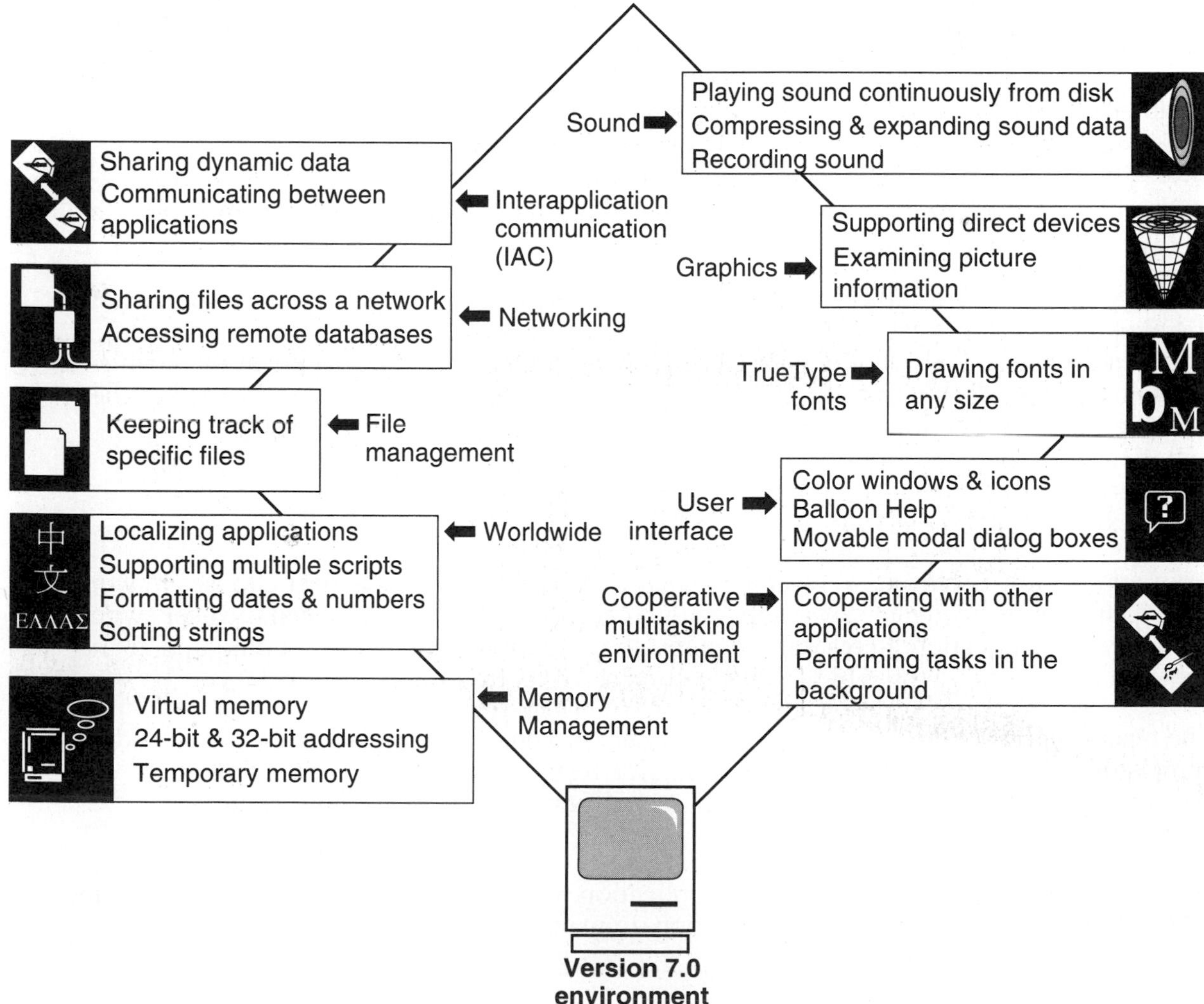

Figure 1-1. Features of the system software version 7.0 environment

The Cooperative Multitasking Environment

The cooperative multitasking environment is a standard part of system software version 7.0. The Macintosh Operating System and the Finder work together to provide this environment. MultiFinder is now transparent to the user; the user always has the capability to run more than one application at a time. Because the user may choose to run other applications in addition to your application, your application needs to be capable of existing in a shared environment.

The Operating System schedules the processing of all applications and desk accessories. When a user opens a document or application, the Operating System loads the application code into memory and schedules the application to run. The application runs at the next available opportunity. The next available opportunity usually means when the current process or application gives up the CPU. In most cases, the application runs immediately (or appears to the user to run immediately).

Once an application is executing, the CPU is available only to that application. The application can only be interrupted by hardware interrupts, and these are transparent to the application. However, to allow the user to interact with your application and others, you must periodically relinquish the CPU using the WaitNextEvent or EventAvail function. Using these event routines in your application lets the user interact with your application and also with other applications.

Although the user can have a number of open documents and applications, only one application is the active application. The **active application** is the application currently interacting with the user; its icon appears in the right side of the menu bar. The active application displays its menu bar and is responsible for highlighting the controls of its frontmost window.

When your application is the active application and the user switches to another application (by clicking in the window of a document belonging to another application, for example), the Operating System sends your application a suspend event. When your application receives a suspend event, it should prepare to suspend processing, allowing the user to switch to the other application. For example, in response to a suspend event, your application should remove the highlighting from the controls of its frontmost window and take any other necessary actions. The suspension actually occurs the next time your application calls WaitNextEvent or EventAvail.

Your application also needs to be able to resume processing when the user chooses to work with your application again. Your application receives a resume event when the user switches back to your application. In response to a resume event, your application should update the contents of its windows and highlight the controls of its frontmost window.

The Operating System preserves the environment of your application when it is suspended and restores that environment before sending it a resume event. Your application does not need to preserve or restore the operating environment in response to suspend or resume events.

When you perform user testing of your application, you might want to observe people using other applications as well as your application, to make sure that your application works well in a cooperative environment.

See the Compatibility Guidelines and the Event Manager chapters in this volume for specific information on how your application can handle suspend and resume events and how your application can take advantage of the cooperative multitasking environment.

Interapplication Communication

The interapplication communications architecture provides support for

- automated copy and paste between applications
- sending and receiving events between applications
- reading and writing blocks of data between applications

The Edition Manager, Apple Event Manager, Event Manager, and PPC Toolbox provide these features, and Figure 1-2 shows their relationships.

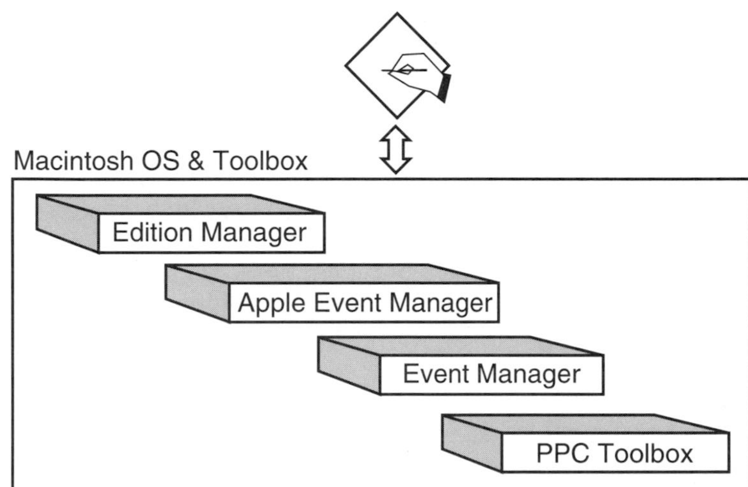

Figure 1-2. The managers constituting the interapplication communications architecture

The IAC architecture is built on communication and cooperation between applications. Apple has defined important standards to help ensure that communication between applications is effective. Using the Clipboard, applications can share static data by allowing the user to copy and paste data between documents. Using the Edition Manager, applications can support dynamic data sharing and allow users to perform automatic copy and paste between documents. Applications that support dynamic data sharing allow users to copy data from one document to another and receive automatic updating of the information when the data in the original document changes. The verbs *publish* and *subscribe* describe this form of dynamic data sharing.

You can let users publish and subscribe among many documents by using the Edition Manager and implementing the Create Publisher and Subscribe To menu commands. This is a form of high-level communication between applications; actually, the communication is indirect, as the Edition Manager provides the interface that allows applications to share dynamic data.

Your application can publish and subscribe with applications and documents on a local disk or across a network. In general, anything that you allow the user to copy or paste you should also allow the user to publish or subscribe to. See "Sharing Data Among Applications" later in this chapter for more information on using the publish and subscribe features in your application.

Using the Apple Event Manager, applications can send Apple events to each other to request services or information. These types of events are often the result of a user request, or they can be specific events that your application sends to another application. Apple events provide a standard way in which your application can communicate with many other applications. Other high-level events are for applications that choose to use a protocol other than the Apple Event Interprocess Messaging Protocol (AEIMP). Applications can use the Event Manager to send high-level events that follow their own protocol.

The Program-to-Program Communications (PPC) Toolbox is a set of low-level routines that allow applications to communicate on the local computer or over a network. Using the PPC Toolbox, applications can exchange blocks of data with each other by reading and writing low-level message blocks. The PPC Toolbox provides a method of communication between applications that is more useful for applications that are closely integrated, specifically designed to work together, or dependent on each other for information. The PPC Toolbox is typically more useful for code that is not event-based.

Your application can use the PPCBrowser function to allow the user to choose another application to which to send high-level events or low-level message blocks. The PPCBrowser function provides a standard user interface for choosing an application to communicate with, much like the Standard File Package provides a standard user interface for opening a file.

All these forms of interapplication communication are based on the premise that applications cooperate with each other. Both the application sending the high-level event or low-level message block and the application receiving it must agree on the protocol of communication.

Figure 1-3 shows that your application can use the Edition Manager to publish and subscribe data. Your application can use the Apple Event Manager to send and process Apple events and the Event Manager to send and receive high-level events. Your application can use the PPC Toolbox to read and write low-level message blocks. Your application can use any of these methods to communicate with other applications located on the same computer or across a network.

As Figure 1-3 shows, managers in the IAC architecture can use the services of other managers. For example, the Apple Event Manager uses the communication services of the Event Manager. The Event Manager in turn uses the PPC Toolbox on behalf of applications.

Figure 1-4 shows how two different applications can use the Edition Manager to publish and subscribe, and how they can use the routines provided by the Apple Event Manager, the Event Manager, or the PPC Toolbox to communicate with each other.

The next sections describe the three parts of the IAC architecture: the Edition Manager, the Apple Event Manager and Event Manager, and the PPC Toolbox.

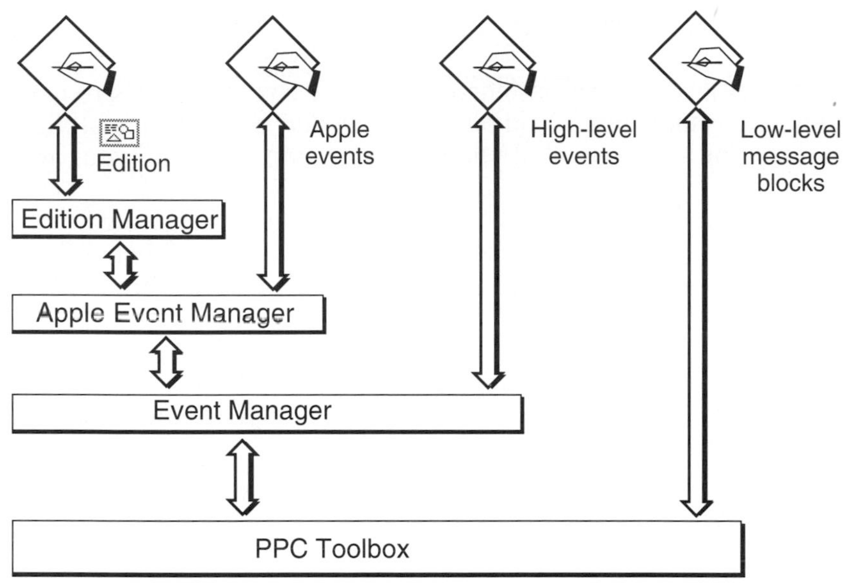

Figure 1-3. Using interapplication communication

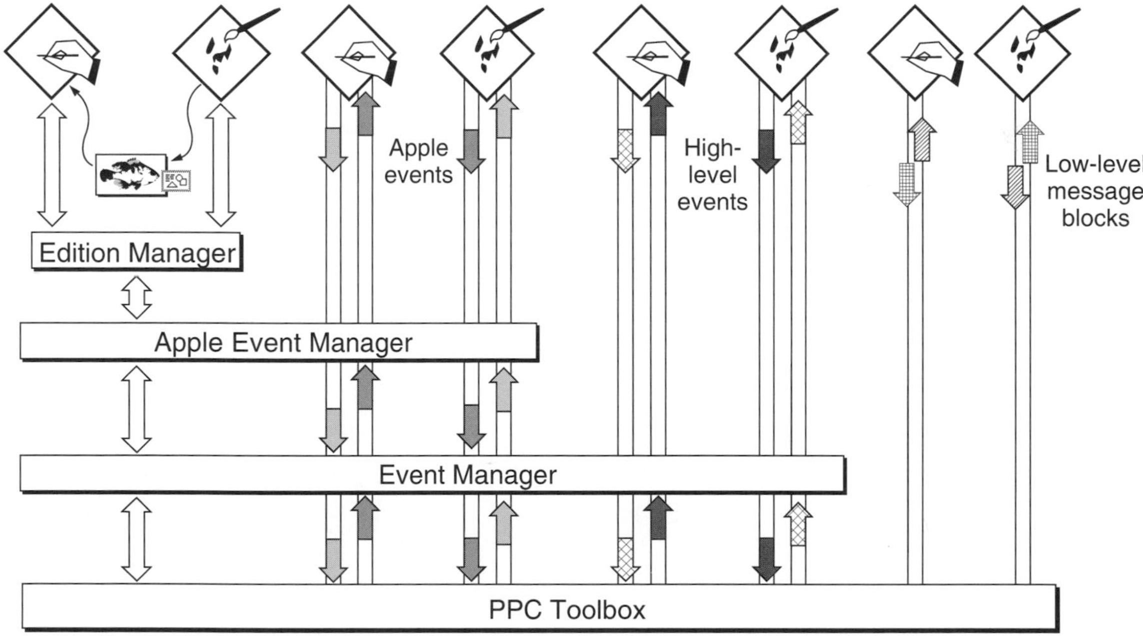

Figure 1-4. Applications using interapplication communication

Sharing Data Among Applications

The Edition Manager lets applications share dynamic data at the user's request. (The Clipboard lets applications share static data.) You build publish and subscribe capabilities into your application in much the same way that you build copy and paste into your application.

Using the Edition Manager, you can let a user publish data by selecting a portion of text, graphics, or other data within a document and choosing Create Publisher from the Edit menu. When the user performs this action, your application saves the selected information in a separate file. The information that is stored in a separate file is referred to as an **edition.** You can also let a user subscribe to data in an edition by choosing Subscribe To from the Edit menu; when the user chooses an edition, your application includes the information from the edition in the current document. The information in an edition can be shared by many documents.

A **publisher** is a portion of a document that is made available to other documents through an edition. A **subscriber** is a portion of a document that receives the information from an edition.

Figure 1-5 shows a document containing a publisher, a file containing an edition, and a document containing a subscriber. The bottom fish in the Fishes of the World document is a publisher. The information from this publisher is made available to other documents through the Illustration edition. The Aquarium poster document contains a subscriber that gets its information from the Illustration edition. Note that when a user selects a publisher or subscriber within a document, your application should display a border surrounding the publisher or subscriber.

In general, when a user modifies the contents of a publisher and saves the document, your application should write the new data to the edition. The Edition Manager then informs all open applications with documents that subscribe to the edition that the edition contains updated information. These applications can then automatically update the subscribers in

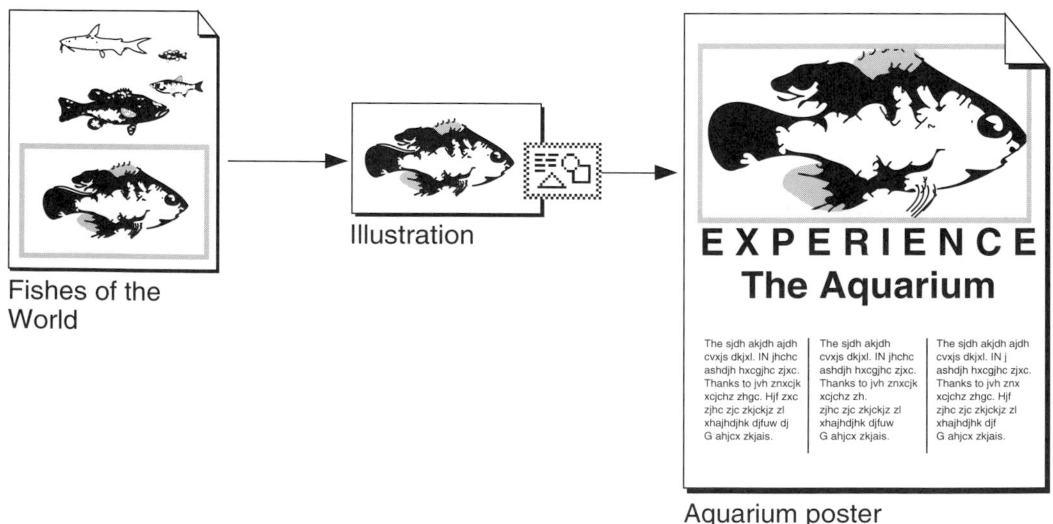

Figure 1-5. A publisher, an edition, and a subscriber

the documents. For example, in Figure 1-5, if the user changes the color of the fish in the Fishes of the World document and then saves the document, the change can be automatically made in the Illustration edition and the Aquarium poster document.

Figure 1-6 shows how a user might create a poster by using information from other documents. For example, the user could subscribe to separate editions containing an illustration created by a graphics designer, text created by a writer, and a headline created by an editor.

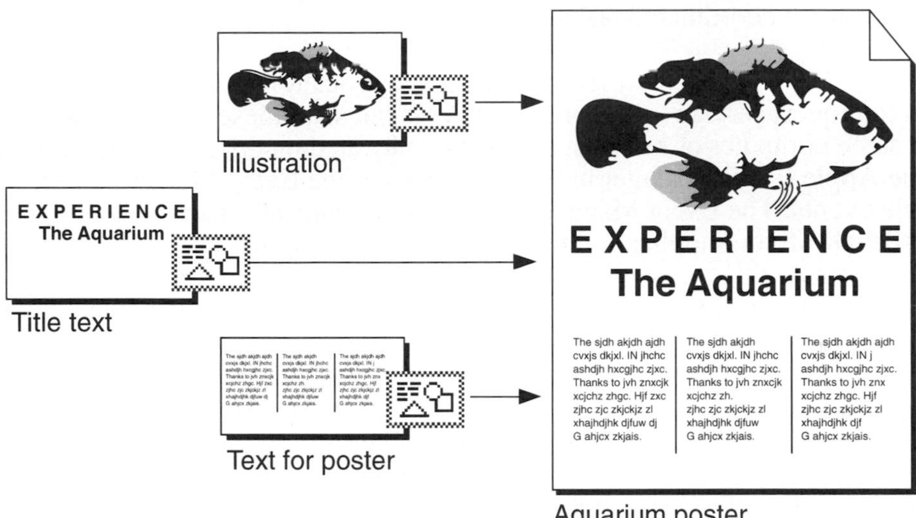

Figure 1-6. Sharing dynamic data with other applications

Your application should save the new information in the edition whenever the user edits the publisher and saves the document that contains the publisher—unless the user has indicated that the information should be saved in the edition on request only. Saving new information in an edition replaces the previous contents of the edition.

When the information in an edition changes, the Edition Manager informs your application. Your application should then update any subscribers with the new information from the edition (unless the user has indicated that updates should be incorporated on request only).

For example, a user might open a word-processing document called My Stocks that accesses information from an edition called Stock Report. The Stock Report edition might be updated twice a day by an on-line database. As the information in the edition changes, the My Stocks document can receive automatic updates with the latest information.

You can implement publish and subscribe capabilities in your application by using the routines provided by the Edition Manager and supporting the required set of Apple events. See the Edition Manager chapter for sample code that shows how to add these features to your application.

Sending Events Between Applications

The Macintosh Operating System provides routines that allow your application to send and receive events using the Apple Event Manager and Event Manager. The Event Manager provides a general method for communication between applications. The Apple Event Manager provides a standard method of communication between applications using the Apple Event Interprocess Messaging Protocol. (The PPC Toolbox can be used to read and write low-level message blocks and is more useful for applications that are closely integrated or perform coordinated tasks.)

Using the Apple Event Manager or Event Manager, applications can send events to other applications to request services or information. You can send these events between applications on the same computer or between applications located on different computers on a network. The Apple Event Manager uses the services of the Event Manager to send and receive Apple events. The Event Manager uses the communication services of the PPC Toolbox on behalf of your application to send and receive events.

For high-level events and Apple events, the applications involved must agree on what they can ask each other and on the action that should be taken in each situation. Both the application sending the event and the application receiving the event must agree on the protocol of communication.

Your application should support at least the required set of Apple events sent by the Operating System. If you plan to implement publish and subscribe capabilities, your application should also support the Apple events sent by the Edition Manager. You can also implement other common Apple events or design your own customized Apple events. In addition, sets of Apple events exist for many specific categories of applications (for example, word processors or spreadsheets).

If your application acts on an Apple event, it should perform the standard action requested by that event. This helps ensure that other applications (and eventually users) can send an event to a particular type of application and expect the other application to understand and act on the event in a standard way.

In most cases, you should use Apple events to communicate with other applications. However, if necessary, you can implement your own protocol for high-level events. Figure 1-7 shows how two applications might use high-level events. For example, a user might need to update the telephone numbers of everyone in the marketing department. To accomplish this, the user might use a word-processing application to send a high-level event with the new telephone numbers across a network to a directory application running on a Macintosh computer at the company's headquarters. When the telephone directory application receives the high-level event, it updates its directory with the new telephone numbers.

See the Event Manager chapter in this volume for information on how to send and receive high-level events. See the Apple Event Manager chapter for information on the Apple Event Interprocess Messaging Protocol.

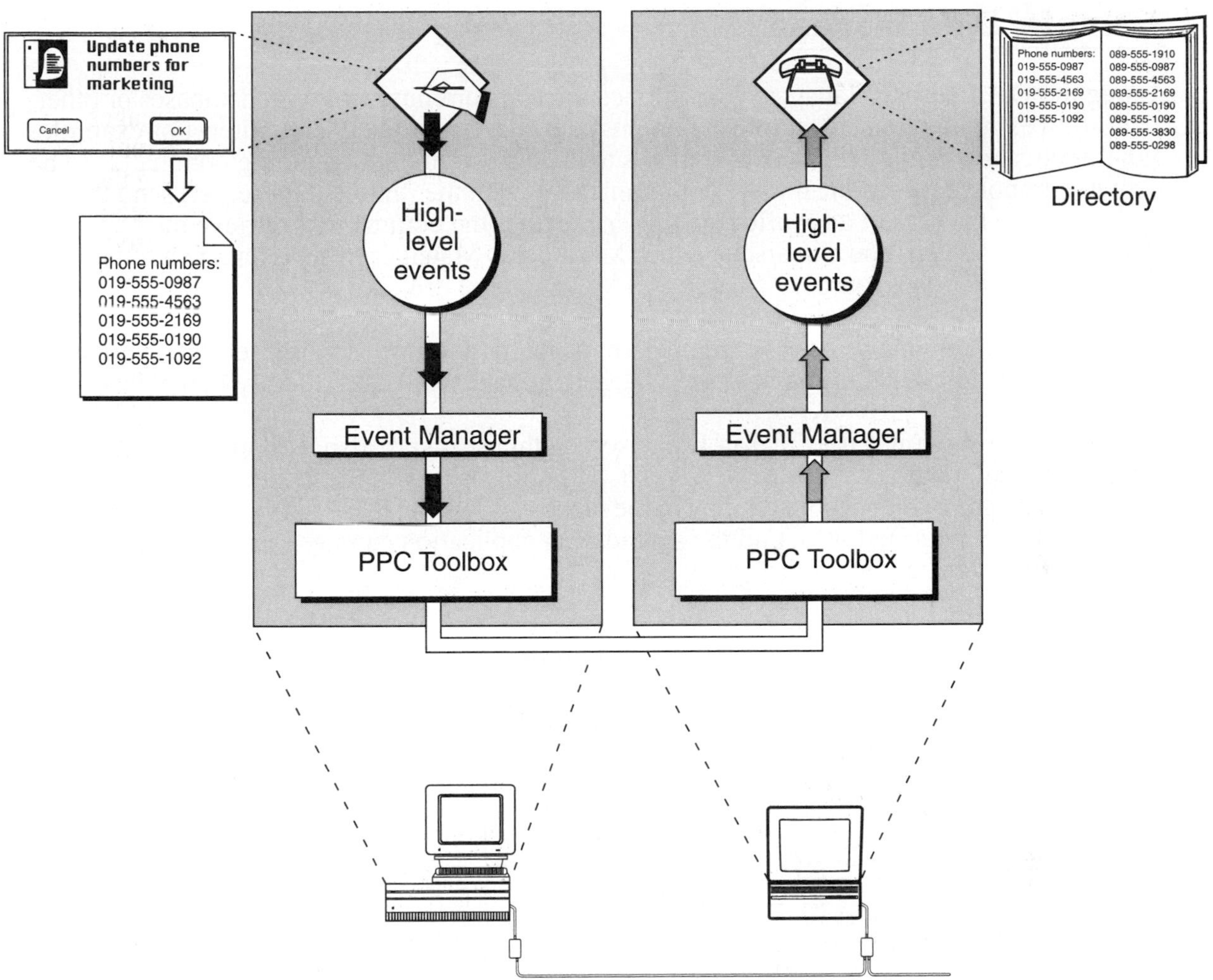

Figure 1-7. Sending events to other applications

Exchanging Message Blocks Between Programs

Using the Event Manager or Apple Event Manager to send events should meet the needs of most applications for program-to-program communication. However, for low-level control or to get services not provided by the Event Manager or Apple Event Manager, you can use the PPC Toolbox. The PPC Toolbox lets you send larger amounts of data to other applications located on the same computer or across a network. The PPC Toolbox can also be used by pieces of code that are not event-driven. The PPC Toolbox is usually called by the Operating System; device drivers, desk accessories, or other code modules can also use it.

Using the PPC Toolbox to send data between programs requires that both your program and the program you're communicating with are open at the same time. To initiate communication, one program opens a port and requests a session with another program. The target program must also open a port and accept the request. Once a session is established, the two programs can read and write low-level message blocks.

See the Program-to-Program Communications Toolbox chapter in this volume for information on reading and writing low-level message blocks between programs.

Remote Data Access

Using the Data Access Manager, your application can communicate with databases or other data sources running on a Macintosh computer or on a remote host computer. For example, your application can use high-level routines to open a document containing commands to be sent to a remote data server; initiate communication with the remote data server; send the commands to the server; and (after the server executes the commands) retrieve the requested data from the server. You can also use the Data Access Manager to send data to a remote database or other data source.

If your application knows how to create commands for a remote data server, then your application can use low-level routines to send these commands and data directly to the data server.

Figure 1-8 shows how a user in San Francisco might use a spreadsheet application to request data from a company database in New York. The spreadsheet application can use the Data Access Manager to request the data from the database. The database application in New York sends back the requested data, and the spreadsheet application can use this data to generate a graph of the information.

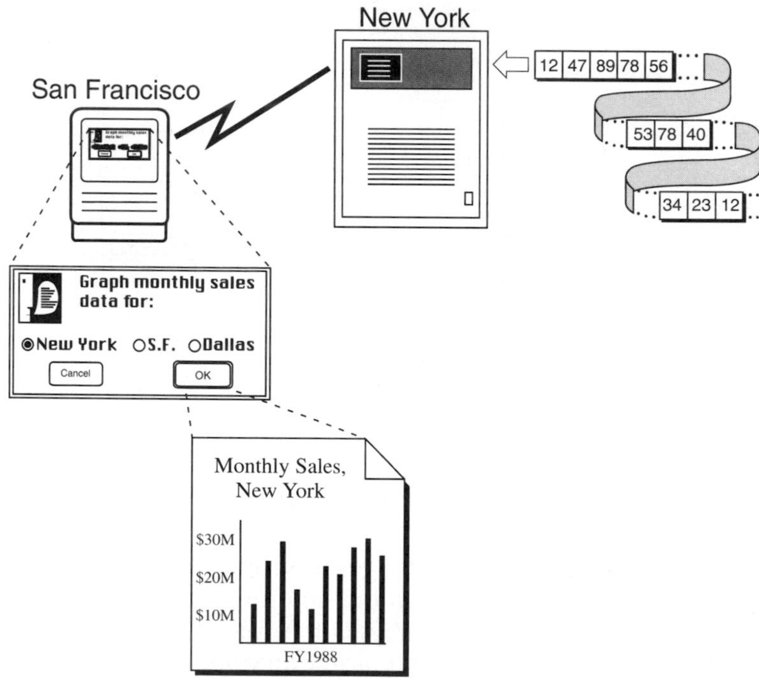

Figure 1-8. Requesting data from a remote database

See the Data Access Manager chapter for information on sending and retrieving information from a remote database or other data source.

Enhanced User Interface

The user interface for system software version 7.0 contains noticeable improvements, such as support for movable modal dialog boxes, and several new features. The Apple menu can now contain applications, documents, folders, or other Finder objects. You can supply small icons that the Finder displays in the Apple menu for your application and documents created by your application. Names of open applications now appear in the Application menu, a new menu to the right of all other menus. The Finder displays the small icon for your application in the right side of the menu bar whenever your application is active.

The structure of the System Folder has changed, including the addition of new folders that reside inside the System Folder. You can now store preference files in the Preferences folder and temporary files in the Temporary Items folder.

The Control Panels folder, which is inside the System Folder, replaces the Control Panel desk accessory. Control panels now appear as individual documents in the Control Panels folder. The user can open the Control Panels folder from the Finder or the Apple menu. In addition, if you develop video cards, you can create an Options dialog box that is used with the Monitors control panel.

In version 7.0, fonts, desk accessories, keyboards, international resource collections, and sounds are represented as icons on the desktop. The user installs fonts and sounds by dragging their icons to the System Folder icon. The user can store desk accessories in the Apple Menu Items folder within the System Folder or anywhere in the volume. You can now distribute fonts and desk accessories as movable resource files with separate icons.

The Finder now lets you create one or more icons for a single document or other desktop object; one of the icons represents the real object, and the others are aliases that point to the object. Aliases can give convenient access to documents that are nested within many folders or that reside on a file server.

The Finder can display help balloons with descriptive text when the user moves the cursor to certain elements of the Finder user interface while help is activated. In addition, if you use standard windows in your application, the Help Manager automatically displays help balloons for standard elements of the window, like the title bar and close box. You can use the features of the Help Manager to display help balloons for other elements of the user interface of your application. For example, you can create help balloons for menus, dialog boxes, and controls used by your application.

See the Control Panels, Finder Interface, Help Manager, and User Interface Guidelines chapters in this volume for information on these user interface features.

Sound

Your application can create and play sounds, mix and synchronize multiple channels of sound, expand and compress sound data, record sound, and play sounds continuously from disk using the Sound Manager.

The Sound Manager provides a rich set of routines for producing sounds, from playing a single sound to playing a set of digitally recorded sounds. You can also compress sound data for efficient storage of sound data on disk, and expand compressed sound data in real time.

See the Sound Manager chapter in this volume for complete information on using sound in your application.

TrueType Fonts

System software version 7.0 provides support for TrueType fonts. The Font Manager uses equations (instead of bitmaps) to define the appearance of glyphs in TrueType fonts. After using the equation to define a specific glyph in a particular font, the Font Manager translates the outline to a bitmap for display on the screen.

The advantage of TrueType fonts is that a single TrueType font can be used to generate glyphs at any size. The TrueType font includes instructions that fine-tune the image of the font at different sizes. TrueType fonts are also resolution independent; the same TrueType font can generate glyphs on a 72 dpi device or a 300 dpi device.

Your application can immediately take advantage of TrueType fonts if they are supported by the user's system software. However, the Font Manager still supports bitmapped fonts, and gives preference to bitmapped fonts over TrueType fonts if both are available for a specific typeface at a particular size.

To offer full support for TrueType fonts, your application can provide a menu command (such as Size or Other) to let the user choose any size of a TrueType font. Your application can also request that the Font Manager always choose TrueType fonts over bitmapped fonts.

Figure 1-9 shows an example of on-screen glyphs generated using a TrueType font and a bitmapped font. The left side of the figure shows glyphs in a TrueType font that is rendered at 12, 16, 19, 24, 31, 37, and 45 points. The right side of the figure shows glyphs in a bitmapped font scaled at the same sizes.

See the Font Manager chapter for an introduction to TrueType fonts and for information on using TrueType fonts in your application.

Graphics

The Macintosh User Interface Toolbox provides a rich set of routines that support graphics. Using the Toolbox routines, your application can provide fast and high-quality graphics and visual display to the user.

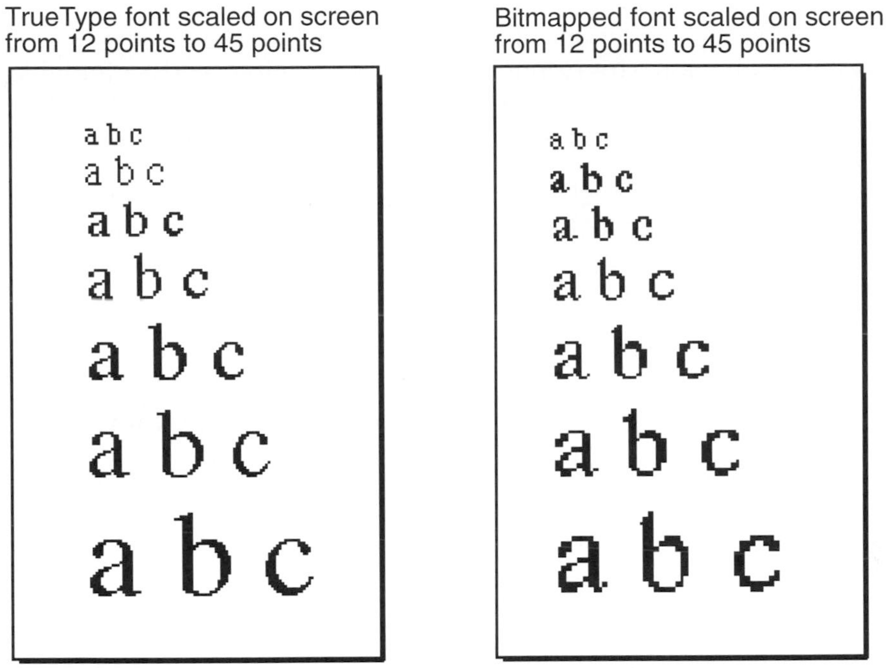

TrueType font scaled on screen from 12 points to 45 points

Bitmapped font scaled on screen from 12 points to 45 points

Figure 1-9. Comparison of TrueType and bitmapped fonts

You can use the routines provided by QuickDraw to draw text, straight lines, ovals, rectangles, or any variety of shapes. QuickDraw lets you define multiple drawing environments (ports)—each with its own coordinate system, location on the screen, and other characteristics. QuickDraw also performs automatic clipping of drawing environments—preventing another application from drawing in the drawing environment used by your application. QuickDraw manages all drawing to the screen and provides a flexible set of routines your application can use to perform most graphics operations.

Color QuickDraw provides support for gray-scale and color devices. In addition, users can connect multiple monitors of different sizes, depths, and color capabilities. Color QuickDraw automatically draws to the appropriate screen and takes advantage of the special characteristics of that device.

Color QuickDraw in version 7.0 supports both indexed and direct devices. Indexed devices typically have a color look-up table with 256 entries, meaning that up to 256 different colors can be displayed at once on the screen. The user's video card and monitor determine the number of bits per pixel and the number of colors that can be displayed on the screen. For indexed devices, Color QuickDraw supports 1, 2, 4, or 8 bits of information per pixel.

Direct devices do not use a color look-up table; instead, the video card contains enough RAM to directly store color information for each pixel. This allows direct devices to display up to 16 million colors. For direct devices, Color QuickDraw supports 32 bits of information per pixel (although only 24 are actually used). See the Graphics Overview chapter in this volume for a comparison of indexed and direct devices.

Using the Palette Manager, you can create palettes for your application. A palette is a convenient way to group collections of colors. You can also use palettes if your application makes special uses of color—for example, if your application needs color table animation. See the Palette Manager chapter in this volume for information on the default color tables supplied with version 7.0 and for information on how to set up and maintain palettes.

You can use the Color Picker Package to offer users a standard dialog box for choosing a color. The user can choose any color from the entire range the available device can display. See the Color Picker Package chapter in this volume for information on how to display the Color Picker dialog box and for a description of the various color models used by the Color Picker Package.

You can examine the contents of pictures and pixel maps using the Picture Utilities Package. See the Picture Utilities Package chapter in this volume for more information.

You can use offscreen graphics to prepare images in a graphics environment you create and then move the images quickly into view. The Graphics Devices Manager lets your application get information about particular graphics devices and provides routines your application can use if it needs exacting control of the graphics environment.

For an introduction to graphics on the Macintosh computer, see the Graphics Overview chapter in this volume. If you're developing a graphics-intensive application, see the Color QuickDraw, Palette Manager, and Graphics Devices Manager chapters in this volume for information on routines that provide advanced graphics features.

System software version 7.0 also provides support for color icons. See the Finder Interface chapter in this volume for information on how you can create color icons for your application and the documents it creates.

File Management

Your application can easily locate the files it needs by using alias records. An alias record is a data structure that identifies a file, folder, or volume. Whenever your application needs to store the location of a file or directory that it might need later, you can record the location and other identifying information in an alias record. The next time your application needs the file or directory, you can use the alias record to locate it, even if the user has renamed it, copied it, restored it from backup, or moved it. You can also use alias records to identify objects on other volumes, including AppleShare® volumes. The Alias Manager provides routines for managing the information in alias records.

Note that the Finder creates alias objects that are visible to the user, while your application usually creates alias records when it needs to store identifying information about a file or directory that it uses internally.

You can also quickly search a disk for particular files using File Manager routines. You can search for one or more files that match certain criteria that your application specifies. For example, your application can search for all files that have a modification date later than June 15, 1991, and the File Manager returns to your application a list of all files that match this specification.

In version 7.0, individuals can share files with other users. A user can make all files within one or more of the folders on a local disk available over a network. This increases the chance that documents created by your application are used in a shared environment.

The File Manager provides a new standard format for identifying files. You can use this standard format in File Manager routines, and other managers also accept files specified in the new format.

The user interface for opening and saving a file is enhanced in version 7.0. The Standard File Package provides two new procedures, StandardGetFile and StandardPutFile, that your application can use to display the standard user interface for choosing a file. To customize the user interface for choosing a file, you can use the new CustomGetFile and CustomPutFile procedures.

See the File Manager chapter in this volume for information on identifying and locating files on a volume, see the Standard File Package chapter for information on letting the user choose a file, and see the Alias Manager chapter for information on using alias records.

Memory Management

The Macintosh Operating System manages the loading of applications, desk accessories, and other code into and out of memory. Applications must share the amount of memory available. Without virtual memory, if an application needs a greater amount of memory than is currently free for application use in the user's system, the user must free up some memory. With virtual memory, the Operating System can store elsewhere the contents of memory in use by other applications in order to make room for the active application.

Virtual memory extends the available memory beyond the limits of physical RAM by using part of the available secondary storage (such as a hard disk) to hold portions of programs and data not currently in use. When an application needs portions of memory stored on disk, the Operating System brings those portions back into physical memory by swapping them with other unused portions of memory.

The operation of virtual memory is mostly transparent to your application. The user sets options in the Memory control panel to control various features of virtual memory. The user chooses whether virtual memory is turned on and, if so, how much virtual memory is available. The main benefit of virtual memory is that it allows users to run more applications at once and work with larger amounts of data.

See the Memory Management chapter in this volume for further information on using virtual memory.

Temporary Memory

Your application can allocate temporary memory if it needs additional memory for short-term purposes. Your application is not always guaranteed the desired amount of memory, so it should work correctly even if it does not get the requested memory. For example, you might allocate a small buffer in your application heap to copy data, and request additional temporary memory. If the temporary memory is available, your application can use it to copy large amounts of data more quickly. If the temporary memory is not available, your application should still be able to perform the copy, although it might take a little longer. As soon as your application finishes using the temporary memory, you should release it so that the memory can be made available to other applications.

See the Memory Management chapter for further information on using temporary memory.

24-Bit and 32-Bit Addressing

For Macintosh computers that support 32-bit addressing, the Memory Manager in version 7.0 uses all 32 bits of a memory address when the 32-bit addressing setting in the Memory control panel is on. Earlier versions of system software use 24-bit addressing, in which only the first 24 bits of a memory address are significant, and the upper 8 bits are ignored. For compatibility, all machines that support 32-bit addressing also support 24-bit addressing.

Macintosh computers that support 32-bit addressing can run with either 32-bit addressing or 24-bit addressing, but not both at the same time. The user chooses 32-bit addressing or 24-bit addressing by changing the setting in the Memory control panel and restarting the computer.

Applications that use the upper 8 bits of a memory address do not work correctly in 32-bit addressing mode. Applications that strip the upper 8 bits of a memory address or rely on the structure of the Memory Manager heap also do not work correctly in 32-bit addressing mode. Therefore, your application should not directly manipulate the bits in a memory address. If your application can operate correctly in 32-bit addressing mode, you can indicate this to the Operating System by setting a flag in your application's 'SIZE' resource. See the Event Manager chapter for a discussion of the 'SIZE' resource.

If you use your own customized window definition functions or customized control definition functions, see the Memory Management chapter for guidelines on avoiding memory address violations. The Memory Management chapter also provides further guidelines on how to write an application that works with 32-bit addressing.

Process Management

System software version 7.0 provides support for process management. Your application can get information about any currently running process, including your own. For example, for a specified process, you can find the application's name, type and signature; the number of bytes in the process partition, the number of free bytes in the application heap, the application that launched the process, and other information. Your application can also launch other applications and desk accessories.

When a user opens a desk accessory in version 7.0, the Operating System launches the desk accessory in its own partition. When a desk accessory is open, the Finder puts the name of the desk accessory in the list of open applications in the Application menu, and also gives the active desk accessory its own About command in the Apple menu that includes the name of the desk accessory. This makes the user interface for desk accessories more consistent with the user interface of small applications.

You can achieve greater control over other applications using the Process Manager routines. You can bring an application to the front, get information about other applications, and launch other applications without terminating your own application. Your application can also receive notification if any application that it has launched terminates.

System software version 7.0 provides greater support for launching applications and documents at startup. All desktop objects in the Startup Items folder are automatically opened at startup. All background applications in the Extensions folder are launched early in the startup sequence before the Finder is started. Background applications generally perform a specific task and are invisible to the user. The Startup Items folder and Extensions folder are located inside the System Folder.

See the Process Management chapter in this volume for information on launching other applications and getting information on currently running processes.

Timing Services

You can schedule routines to execute at a later time using the Time Manager. The Time Manager provides a hardware-independent method of performing time-related tasks.

You can schedule routines to run periodically or after a specified delay. Time delays can be specified in milliseconds or microseconds in version 7.0. You can achieve a maximum resolution of 20 microseconds. This gives you greater accuracy in coordinating sound, multimedia, and other events that require precise timing.

See the Time Manager chapter in this volume for information on how to schedule a routine for later execution and how to compute elapsed time.

Compatibility

You can determine what features are available on a Macintosh computer using the Gestalt function. The Gestalt function provides information about various attributes, versions, and features of particular software and hardware available on the currently running system.

The Compatibility Guidelines chapter in this volume discusses guidelines you should follow to ensure that your application is compatible with previous versions of Macintosh system software as well as with new releases of Macintosh system software.

These guidelines can help you develop your application so that it is compatible across the Macintosh family of computers. The guidelines also provide information on how to make your application compatible with A/UX® and how to design your application so that it can be easily localized for use in other regions.

Worldwide Development

As you develop applications for worldwide markets, you need to consider differences in scripts, languages, and regions. The Macintosh system software presents one of the most flexible architectures for developing applications that can support more than one script.

A script, such as Roman, Kanji, or Arabic, is a writing system for a human language such as English, Japanese or Arabic. Scripts have different characteristics; for example, they can differ in the direction in which their characters and lines run and in the number of characters in their character sets. The way in which you need to input, display, render, and edit text may change depending on the script in use.

A script system is a collection of software facilities that provides for basic differences between writing systems. Script systems include character sets, fonts, keyboards, and routines for text collation and word breaks. Examples of script systems are Roman, Japanese, Arabic, Hebrew, Thai, Devanagari, and Korean. A script system can also be localized for a particular language, region, or country. For example, the Roman script system has been localized for French, British, Italian, and U.S. users (among others). The system software of all Macintosh computers includes the Roman script system. If another script system is required, it is also customized for the particular language or region. You can use the Script Management System to help you display text in the correct format for various scripts.

Worldwide system software consists of the Macintosh Script Management System (that is, the Script Manager and one or more Macintosh script systems) and related components (including the International Utilities Package, the international resources, and keyboard resources).

Measurement systems often differ from country to country, as do currency, sorting order, word boundaries, and the formatting of dates and times. The International Utilities Package handles formats for the presentation of numbers, currency, time, and dates in countries around the world. The international resources and several of the keyboard resources also contain region-specific or language-specific information, such as date and time formats.

TextEdit also provides support for working with different script systems. You can use TextEdit to let the user edit and display text in multiple scripts and styles when a non-Roman script system is in use. TextEdit automatically handles text with more than one script, style, and direction. For example, TextEdit supports mixing English text (a left-to-right directional script) with Arabic text (a right-to-left directional script) in the same line.

You should use resources to store text for menus, dialog boxes, and other parts of the user interface of your application. This lets a translator localize your application for a particular language, region, or country without requiring modification of your code. In addition, by using routines provided by the Macintosh Script Management System, you can write your application so that it works independently of the particular script in use.

Figure 1-10 shows a document created by an application that uses the Macintosh Script Management System to support more than one script system.

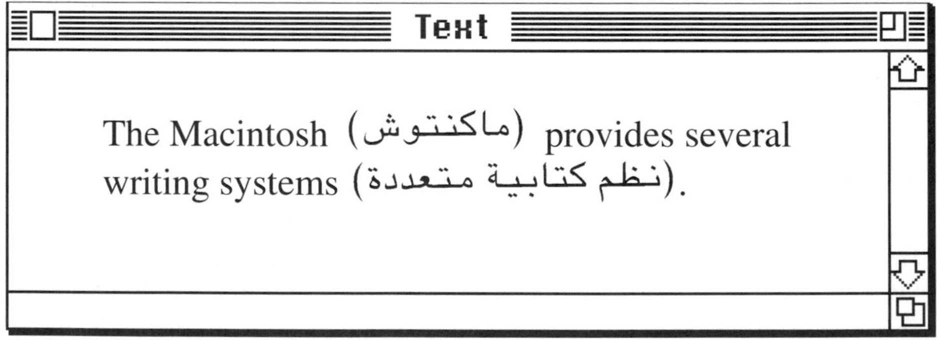

Figure 1-10. Using multiple scripts in a single document

See the Worldwide Software Overview chapter for an introduction to designing your application for worldwide markets, and see the User Interface Guidelines chapter for guidelines related to developing your application for use around the world. See the TextEdit chapter for information on using TextEdit when a non-Roman script system is in use. *Macintosh Worldwide Development: Guide to System Software* (available from APDA®) provides a complete description of all components of the worldwide system software, including routines in the Script Manager.

Communication Over a Network

The Macintosh Operating System provides many routines to support applications communicating and sharing data across a network. You can send events between applications located on different computers using the Event Manager or Apple Event Manager, and read and write low-level message blocks using the PPC Toolbox. You can send and retrieve information from a remote database or other data sources using the Data Access Manager. You can share data and files between applications on different computers using file sharing, the Edition Manager, and the Alias Manager.

In addition, you can use the network and communication services provided by the AppleTalk® Manager or Communications Toolbox. The AppleTalk Manager provides routines your application can use to send and receive information over an AppleTalk network.

The AppleTalk Manager in version 7.0 supports various link access protocols (for example, the LocalTalk® Link Access Protocol and the EtherTalk® Link Access Protocol) that can be used for AppleTalk communication. Your application can also use a new protocol, the AppleTalk Data Stream Protocol (ADSP), to exchange information between two equal entities. Either end of an ADSP connection can send data at any time. You can use ADSP to establish two-way communication between computers—for example, for use in office conferencing. See the AppleTalk Manager chapter for information on the device drivers and protocols associated with AppleTalk.

The Communications Toolbox provides your application with a standard interface for various communication services (such as data connections, file transfer, and terminal emulation) that are often used with a modem, other serial connections, or over an AppleTalk network. See *Macintosh Communications Toolbox Reference Guide* (available from APDA) for additional information on the routines provided by the Communications Toolbox.

Hardware Interfaces

The Macintosh family of computers supports many different types of hardware, including mouse devices, keyboards, display devices, hard disks, floppy disks, CD-ROM discs, and other devices. These devices are supported through various hardware interfaces, including SCSI (Small Computer System Interface), ADB (Apple Desktop Bus™), and SCC (Serial Communications Chip). In addition, a number of different devices can be supported through the expansion interfaces (the NuBus™ and processor-direct slots).

You can design expansion cards and drivers for the NuBus and processor-direct slots. For specific hardware information for the Macintosh family, see the *Guide to the Macintosh Family Hardware,* second edition. For information on writing a driver for the Macintosh family, see *Designing Cards and Drivers for the Macintosh Family,* second edition, and for system software information, see *Inside Macintosh,* Volumes I–VI.

Volume VI (this volume) contains information on the new Power Manager and additional information on the Slot Manager. The Power Manager is a new manager used with the Macintosh Portable. The Slot Manager in version 7.0 supports 32-bit addressing of NuBus cards. See the Power Manager chapter and Slot Manager chapter in this volume for specific information on these managers.

OVERVIEW OF CHAPTERS IN THIS VOLUME

The User Interface Guidelines chapter and Compatibility Guidelines chapter provide important information about designing your application to take advantage of the Macintosh user interface and to ensure compatibility across the Macintosh family of computers.

The rest of the chapters in this volume show how to use the new features of version 7.0 in your application. Each chapter gives detailed descriptions of each manager, including routines, parameters, and data structures.

Figure 1-11 shows where you can find a detailed description of how to use each feature of the system software version 7.0 environment.

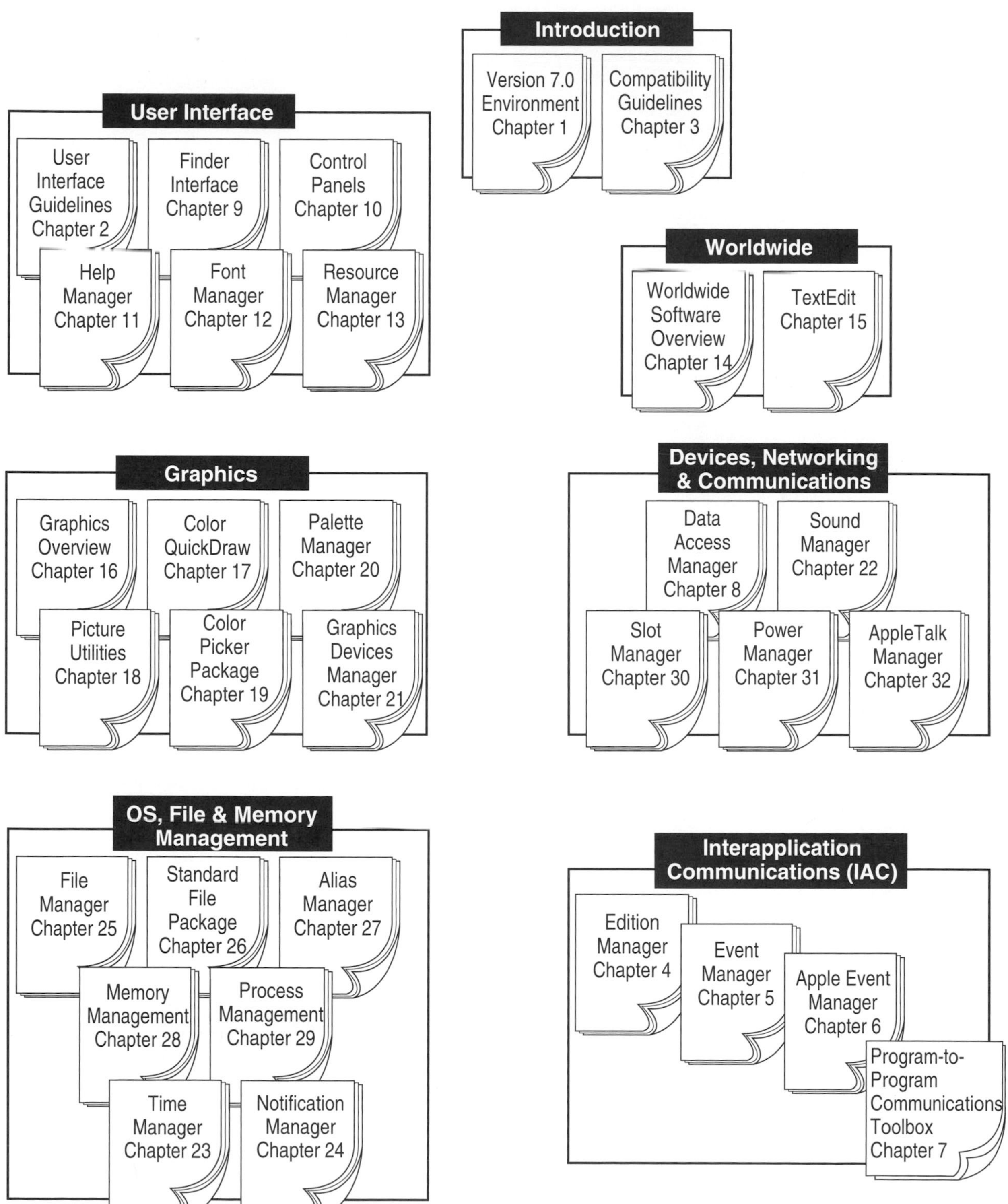

Figure 1-11. Overview of chapters in Volume VI

2 USER INTERFACE GUIDELINES

ABOUT THIS CHAPTER

This chapter provides recommendations about how to adapt your application's interface to the Apple® Desktop Interface provided with system software version 7.0. It describes new user interface guidelines and clarifies existing guidelines. It also introduces several user interface topics that you need to consider when you design or redesign an application. Throughout the chapter are references to places where you can find more information about technical implementation issues.

Your application should maintain the spirit of the Apple Desktop Interface and remain consistent with the guidelines presented earlier in *Inside Macintosh, Human Interface Notes,* and *Human Interface Guidelines: The Apple Desktop Interface*—which present a complete description of the Apple Desktop Interface.

USER INTERFACE DESIGN PRINCIPLES

This section describes the fundamental principles of the Apple Desktop Interface. It's a brief reminder of the basic premises that you should consider when you design your application for the Macintosh® computer.

- **Metaphors from the real world.** Concrete, simple metaphors provide people with a set of expectations to apply to computer environments. Whenever appropriate, audio and visual effects can support the metaphors.
- **Direct manipulation.** Each user action has a perceptible response and the Operating System provides feedback to verify the effect of the action. For example, icons move when users drag them. In the Macintosh interface, people don't have to trust that abstract commands entered in a text-based interface do what they promise. This means that when users choose the Bold command, a word changes immediately to boldface—in comparison to other operating systems in which users type in commands and wait to see the results when the document is printed.
- **See-and-point (not remember-and-type).** Users rely on recognition, not recall, so entities are visible when possible. People don't have to remember anything the computer already knows, such as which commands are available.
- **Consistency.** Effective applications are internally consistent *and* consistent with other applications.
- **WYSIWYG (what you see is what you get).** There is no significant difference between what users see on the screen and what eventually is printed.
- **User control.** Users, not the computer or the application, initiate and control all actions.
- **Feedback and dialog.** Users get feedback about all interactions with the computer, and it is immediate feedback when possible. This communication should be brief, direct, and expressed in the users' vocabulary rather than the programmer's.

- **Forgiveness.** As users explore the interface, their actions should generally be reversible so that people explore and learn by doing. Users should be able to identify in advance any actions that aren't reversible.
- **Perceived stability.** Users feel comfortable in a computer environment that remains understandable and familiar rather than one that changes randomly.
- **Aesthetic integrity.** Visually confusing or unattractive displays detract from the effectiveness of human-computer interactions. Therefore different things, like folders and documents, should look different on the screen. Also, users should be able to control the superficial appearance of their computer workplaces to display their own style and individuality. Messes are only acceptable if users make them. Applications aren't allowed this freedom.

For further explanation of these design principles, see *Human Interface Guidelines: The Apple Desktop Interface*.

WORLDWIDE SOFTWARE DEVELOPMENT

Macintosh worldwide system software is designed to address the complex problems you'll encounter when you design your applications to be compatible with regional, linguistic, and script differences around the globe. Worldwide system software consists of the Macintosh Script Management System (which is one or more script systems and the Script Manager) and related components that include the International Utilities Package, the international resources, and keyboard resources.

The Macintosh computer has always presented one of the most flexible architectures for developing worldwide software. Because of the enhanced support for script systems in version 7.0, it's easier for users to add one or more non-Roman script systems to their Macintosh computers. With version 7.0, software can be localized with greater ease. Now it's even more advantageous for you to create applications that can be used worldwide.

It's much easier to design software with worldwide support from the beginning of your development process. This may mean that you create your application so that it is easy to localize, or that you adapt it for use in a specific area. Localizing software involves translating an application's menus, dialog boxes, alert boxes, and content areas into a language or regional dialect.

You can also make your application Script Manager–compatible. The Script Manager routines and the International Utilities Package handle text issues for all script systems. If your application is not text-oriented but does simple text processing, using TextEdit provides adequate support.

If your application does moderate text processing, such as that accomplished by a simple word processor, you probably want to incorporate Script Manager capabilities. If it does intensive text processing, such as page layout, you can build in support beyond the Script Manager routines to handle text for a specific script system.

The following sections outline the major issues you need to consider when you develop software for local or worldwide use. For a complete description of the issues and a discussion of technical implementation, see the TextEdit and Worldwide Software Overview chapters later in this volume. These chapters discuss the routines that assist you in developing your application for worldwide use. See *Macintosh Worldwide Development: Guide to System Software* for a complete discussion of developing worldwide software. This book is available from APDA®.

Cultural Values

Whenever you design a user interface, consider that differences exist in the use of color, graphics, calendars, text, and the representation of time in various regions around the world. It's important that you be able to localize your user interface elements with ease. As an example, consider how different cultures assign different meanings to colors. The color white represents purity in one culture and death in another. Therefore you may want to localize elements of the user interface, such as the colors of text or graphics, in versions of your application designed for different regions.

Graphics have the potential to enhance your application, but they can also be offensive. In addition to colors, many cultures assign varying values and characteristics to living creatures, plants, and inanimate objects. In the United States the owl is a symbol of wisdom and knowledge, whereas in Central America the owl represents witchcraft and black magic. Some cultures forbid the depiction of uncovered bodies and body parts, while other cultures enhance marketing materials with pictures of scantily clad people. It's a good idea to avoid the use of seasons, holidays, or calendar events in software that you expect to distribute worldwide. Also avoid using graphics that represent holidays or seasons, such as Christmas trees, pumpkins, or snow—or be sure that the symbols can be localized. You can influence your audience in simple but profound ways by carefully selecting elements of your application's interface. Make sure that visible interface elements can be localized for other regions around the world.

Different calendars are used to mark time around the world. The United States and most of Europe observe time according to the Gregorian calendar. The traditional Arabic calendar, the Jewish calendar, and the Chinese calendar are lunar rather than solar. Often time is marked one way for business and government purposes while religious events are dated according to a different calendar. Therefore your application should be flexible in handling dates, and you may want to provide the user with a way to change the representation of time. Use the International Utilities Package to handle numbers, dates, and sorting.

Resources

It's essential to store region-dependent information in resources so that text the user sees can be translated (during localization) without modifying your application's code. When you create resources, consider text size, location, and direction. Remember that text size varies in different languages. Also, depending on the script system, the direction of text may change. Most Middle Eastern languages read from right to left instead of left to right, the direction of Roman script. Text location within a window should be easy to change.

Use the Macintosh Script Management System to handle these situations. See the Worldwide Software Overview, Compatibility Guidelines, and Resource Manager chapters in this volume for more information on using resources to store data the user sees. Also consult *Macintosh Worldwide Development: Guide to System Software* for more information.

Language Differences

Languages differ in grammar, structure, meaning, and nuance. Translating languages is a delicate task and often can cause confusion, so be wary of using colloquial phrases or nonstandard usage and syntax. Choose your words carefully for command names in menus and for messages in dialog boxes, alert boxes, and help balloons. When translated, text can become up to 50 percent larger than U.S. English text, so you can't rely on string length. Text needs room to grow up, down, and sideways.

Potential grammar problems may arise with error messages and the so-called user programming structure of languages like HyperTalk®. The word order of messages may be completely different in translation, thus rendering a message nonsense when translated. Simple concatenation of strings generally doesn't work when an application is translated. For example, word order in German usually places the verb at the end of a sentence. Suppose a German developer built an application that concatenated two strings to create an error message. When localized for the United States, the application might produce a sentence like "The file with the long name move." Instead of concatenating strings, use the ReplaceText function, which correctly assists with the syntactic ordering of elements. See the Worldwide Software Overview chapter for information on technical implementation.

Text Display and Text Editing

System software version 7.0 allows users to display different scripts at the same time. A script is a writing system for a human language. Scripts may differ in the direction in which their characters and lines run, the size of the character set used to represent the script, and context dependence. Whenever a user installs a non-Roman script system, at least two scripts are available, the Roman script that is present on all Macintosh computers and the non-Roman script. If you use the TextEdit and Dialog Manager routines, you can correctly handle most text in different scripts. For moderate text processing, the routines provided by the Script Manager can assist you in implementing these guidelines. The TextEdit and Worldwide Software Overview chapters in this volume discuss all of these issues thoroughly.

No matter what level of worldwide support you provide, it's important to avoid two common assumptions. Characters aren't necessarily 1 byte; they can be 2 bytes. You also shouldn't assume that text is always left-aligned and read from left to right.

Remember that the meaning of a character code depends on the font, and character codes may be 1 or 2 bytes long. The cursor should move between characters, not bytes, and the Delete key should erase characters, not bytes. Inserted characters should appear between other characters, not between bytes of a 2-byte character. Also be aware of the impact of 2-byte characters on data transmission.

Use the language-specific routines in the Macintosh Script Management System for breaking and wrapping words and for string comparison and sorting. Consider word boundaries and their impact on word wrapping, selection, search, and cut and paste.

Some scripts include multiple sets of numerals. For example, international business in Japan and the Middle East requires the use of Western digits as well as the digits from a Japanese script or an Arabic script. Applications that handle numbers should accept all the numerals in each set as valid. Use the International Utilities Package to handle numbers.

You need to provide metric and English measurements. Use numeric routines for international number formatting and interpretation.

Your application should appropriately position the cursor when the user clicks in text. The cursor, or caret, should appear where the next character will appear when typed. If this is ambiguous because of multidirectional text, use dual carets, as shown in Figure 2-1. For a detailed discussion of using dual carets, see the TextEdit chapter in this volume.

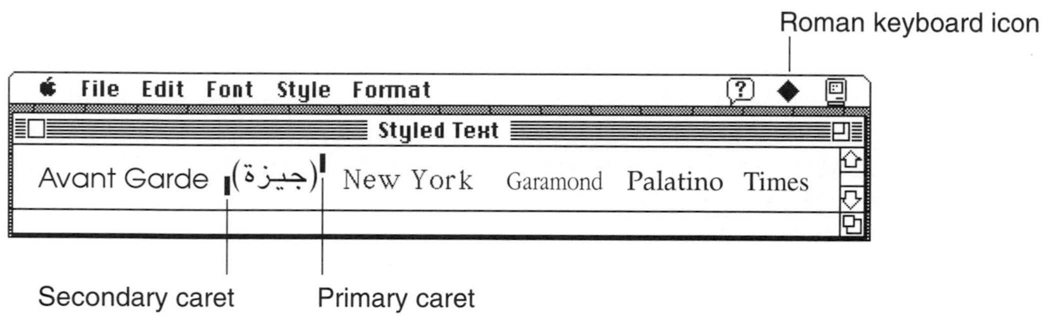

Figure 2-1. Dual carets in mixed-directional text

Highlighting should apply to a contiguous set of characters in memory, even though the glyphs may not appear contiguous on the screen. In other words, you should highlight characters in phonetic order (the order in which the user speaks, reads, or writes) rather than the order in which characters appear on screen. However, the arrow keys should move the cursor in the direction that the arrow points, regardless of text direction. This guideline applies across script boundaries when the user displays multiple scripts. In Figure 2-2 the multidirectional text appears correctly highlighted for editing; the words are highlighted in the order that the user reads, from right to left. The translation of the mixed-directional Hebrew and English sentence is in the window labeled "unidirectional highlighting." The corresponding English words, flowing from left to right, are highlighted for editing.

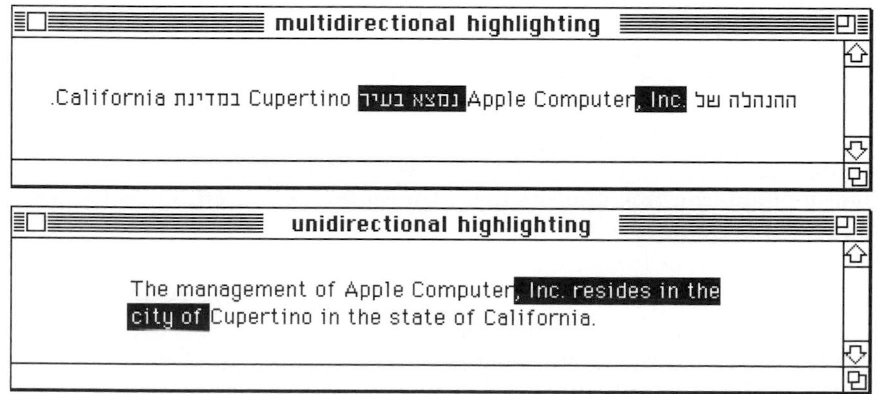

Figure 2-2. Multidirectional text correctly highlighted

Note: If your application uses TextEdit routines, most worldwide text issues are handled for you. If your application needs more sophisticated text handling, you should also consult the Worldwide Software Overview chapter in this volume.

Applications that work with tokens (abstractions that have multiple representations) or use characters that vary from script system to script system should work correctly in all scripts. For example, a token that represents the concept of "less than or equal to" might have two representations on a U.S. system, the 2-byte sequence <= or the 1-byte character ≤. If you use the IntlTokenize function to handle these details, your application doesn't have to be aware of the character codes.

Default Alignment of Interface Elements

When dialog boxes are localized for use with worldwide versions of system software, the text in the dialog box may become longer or shorter. Also, the alignment of controls in the dialog box may vary with localization. Arabic and Hebrew are written right to left, so the alignment of items in an Arabic or a Hebrew dialog box is generally right to left, just as dialog box items in English or Russian are generally left to right. The low-memory global variable TESysJust controls the alignment of interface elements.

When TESysJust is –1, the Control Manager reverses the alignment of check boxes and radio buttons, the Menu Manager reverses the alignment of menu items to be ordered and aligned on the right, and TextEdit aligns text by default on the right. Create your application so that it supports both left alignment and right alignment of controls and adjust the alignment as appropriate. Provide a way for the user to change the default line direction of text. Use the SetSysJust procedure to set the value of the global variable TESysJust.

When the alignment of items is reversed, it's important that the elements appear symmetrical. Therefore when you create dialog box items, try to make sure that their display rectangles are the same size. Figure 2-3 shows a typical dialog box and the same dialog box with the alignment of its elements reversed. You can see why it's important to create display rectangles of the same size.

Keyboards

As stated previously, in version 7.0 users can install multiple script systems. If the Operating System or an application determines that all conditions are met, it enables the script system, making it available to users. A script system can contain more than one keyboard layout that maps character codes to keys on a physical keyboard, and it can support more than one attached physical keyboard. All keyboards do not have the same set or number of keys and users may have more than one keyboard attached to their computer. See the Worldwide Software Overview chapter in this volume for information on installing and enabling script systems and keyboard resources.

Version 7.0 adds a new Keyboard menu when more than one script system is present or a localizable resource flag is set. This menu simplifies the user's access to scripts and keyboards. The icon for the Keyboard menu appears between the icons for the Help menu and the Application menu. A keyboard icon appears next to each keyboard name, and the icon of the active keyboard appears in the menu bar. As Figure 2-4 shows, the Keyboard menu displays a list of installed keyboard layouts for each enabled script system.

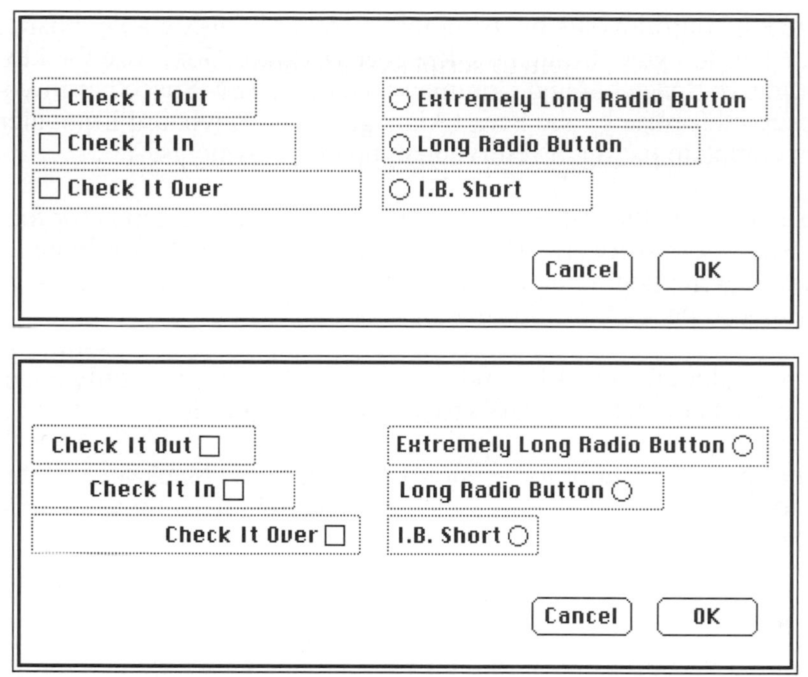

Figure 2-3. Reversing the alignment of dialog box items

The Keyboard menu groups the keyboard layouts by script system, which are separated by dotted or gray lines. In Figure 2-4, there are two Roman keyboard layouts (Spanish and United States); a single Hebrew keyboard layout; and two Japanese keyboard layouts. Only one keyboard layout and one physical keyboard are active at a time; the active condition is indicated by a checkmark in the menu.

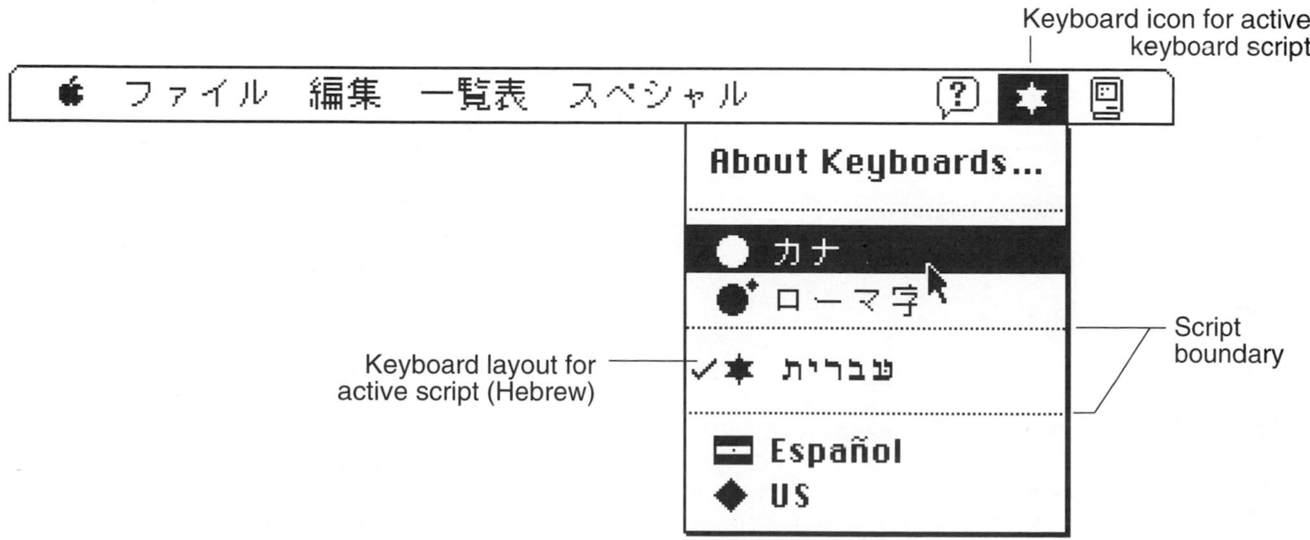

Figure 2-4. The Keyboard menu

Users can change keyboard layouts by using this menu or by using a keyboard equivalent, Command–Space bar, to cycle through the keyboard layouts. Don't use the keyboard equivalents Command–Space bar and Command–*modifier key*–Space bar in your application, since they are reserved for use by the Script Manager. See "Keyboard Equivalents" later in this chapter for a complete listing of reserved keyboard equivalents.

Table 2-1 shows some new black-and-white versions of keyboard icons for localized versions of Macintosh system software. They are shown in color on Color Plate I, "Examples of Keyboard Icons," at the beginning of this volume. A keyboard icon represents a localized keyboard layout. If you develop key-boards or keyboard resources, you must provide customized icons like these. You create a 16-by-16 pixel icon in 1-bit, 4-bit, and 8-bit color. If you use the same colors for the 4-bit and the 8-bit color icons, you only need to provide one 4-bit icon. This scheme takes up less space in the System file.

To represent your keyboard layout for version 7.0, replace the black-and-white symbol you previously used to represent a localized keyboard layout with an icon similar to those shown in Table 2-1 and Color Plate I.

If you are designing a new keyboard icon, use a solid symbol to represent a keyboard layout for a region that is larger or smaller than a country or province. For example, a diamond represents the Roman Script System, which is used in the United States, Central America, and most of Europe. Use the flag of a country or province if the keyboard layout is only used in that area. For example, the Union Jack represents the keyboard layout localized for use in

Table 2-1. Examples of keyboard icons

Icon	Name	Icon	Name
	Arabic		Netherlands, comma decimal separator
	Canada		Roman (U.S.)
	Cyrillic		Spain
	Cyrillic transliterated		Swiss French
	Denmark		Swiss German
	Faeroe Islands		Swiss Italian
	Germany		Turkey
	Hebrew		Turkish U.S. modified
	Japanese Romaji		United Kingdom (previously GB)
	Japanese Katakana		United States
	Korean		
	Netherlands, period decimal separator (previously NL.)		

the United Kingdom. Be sure to use the colors that appear on the nation's flag. You can also add a visual indicator to the flag to show some modification. Use a superscript diamond to indicate a QWERTY transliteration, which is a mapping of sounds from a language to the Roman keyboard layout. Use a subscript comma or period to indicate which decimal separator is used. See Table 2-1 for examples of icons with these symbols.

When you design the black-and-white version of a flag icon, use black and a 50 percent gray pattern. These choices provide the best contrast and legibility. To avoid confusion between flags of similar design, use the pattern substitutions for colors shown in Table 2-2. See Table 2-1 to see flags that use the correct pattern substitutions.

Table 2-2. Pattern substitutions for colors in keyboard icons

Pattern	Color
Black	Black or blue
50 percent gray	Red
25 percent gray	Light blue
Diagonal stripes	Green
White	White or yellow

When the user changes the keyboard layout, you should synchronize the font to that keyboard layout. You can use the FontScript function to periodically poll the Operating System to find out if the user has changed the keyboard layout. Choosing a font should set the keyboard layout to the script of that font. For example, if a user chooses a Japanese font such as Osaka, your application should change the keyboard script to Japanese. When a user clicks in text, your application should set the keyboard layout to correspond to the font of that text. For a well-designed application, the keyboard icon in the menu bar should always indicate the status of the font script. The TextEdit chapter in this volume provides an example of automatically synchronizing the font and the keyboard layout.

See the Worldwide Software Overview chapter in this volume for more information on the Keyboard menu.

Fonts

When you write software that supports non-Roman scripts, don't make assumptions about font sizes; let the user choose them. For example, system or application fonts may be preset to 12 or 18 points and a font with a resource ID of 0 is not always set to Chicago. Pay attention to the use of system and application fonts when the user cannot choose the font. If you must assign font sizes, use the Script Manager to find appropriate fonts and sizes. Use the proper font names as defined by worldwide system software. Whenever possible, display font names in the proper script and font in your Font menu.

Diacritical marks may extend beyond the ascent line. Some fonts, such as Japanese fonts, contain glyphs that extend to the boundaries of the enclosing rectangle of the font, or to *both* minimum-y and maximum-y lines. You should leave room for space between lines of text and between the top and bottom lines of any enclosing rectangle. See the Font Manager chapter in this volume for more information. Figure 2-5 shows some glyphs that demonstrate the boundaries you need to allow for lines of text.

Figure 2-5. The boundaries of a font

USER DOCUMENTATION

Documentation for users is an essential part of the user interface that you provide. It should be as well considered and developed as your application's user interface. Consider the audience that you address with your product and tailor the documentation to its needs. It's often useful to provide alternate types of documentation for the differing types of users who make up your audience. Beginners have different needs than expert users.

People have distinct learning styles. Some users learn by seeing, some learn by doing, some learn by hearing, and some learn through a combination of these styles. It's best to provide for the broadest possible range of learning styles. For example, including a written tutorial, a written reference manual, an on-line tutorial with visual and auditory feedback, and an on-line help system should meet the needs of nearly everyone who wants to learn to use your product. As an example of an on-line help system, you can look at Balloon Help™ in the Finder™ in version 7.0. For information on including your help system in the Help menu or implementing Balloon Help for you application, see the Help Manager chapter in this volume.

Develop task-oriented documentation that teaches users how to accomplish the tasks that you designed your application to perform. Avoid system-oriented documentation that describes everything that your application can do rather than teaching practical skills.

It's important to use standard terminology and nontechnical language in user documentation. Don't pass on technical jargon to users and expect them to understand or like it. When you must use technical terms, be sure to define them at first occurrence, and include a glossary if your document has many specialized terms. Be consistent in your use of terminology. Make sure that messages and terms that users see on the screen match what appears in the documentation.

Apple Computer, Inc., publishes the *Apple Publications Style Guide,* which codifies the way in which Apple documentation uses language. It's a guide to writing about the Apple Desktop Interface. You can obtain this publication through APDA.

It's very important to translate all user documentation, including tutorials, on-line help, and books, when you localize your software product. Making your documentation available in a user's native language greatly enhances the usability and marketability of your product.

TERMINOLOGY

Use regular language in your applications as well as your documentation. Don't use technical jargon or computer science terminology. The majority of users aren't programmers. It's especially important not to use programming terms in menus, dialog boxes, or user books.

In particular, don't use file type names to refer to Finder documents that users see. Call documents by the terms that appear in the Kind column in Finder windows. Use the terms in Table 2-3 in place of the four-letter type names.

Table 2-3. Translation chart for user documentation

Previously used term	Suggested terminology	Examples
cdev	control panel	Mouse control panel
RDEV	Chooser extension	LaserWriter® Chooser extension, AppleShare® Chooser extension
INIT	system extension (*not* startup document)	File Sharing Extension
adev	network extension	EtherTalk® network extension
ddev	database extension	Data Access Language (DAL) database extension
DA	desk accessory	Calculator desk accessory
FKEY	function key	⌘-Shift-3 screen-dump utility
standard file dialog box	directory dialog box	SFGetFile dialog box
MultiFinder® icon	active-application icon	TeachText application icon

In version 7.0 a cooperative multitasking operating environment is always available to users. Therefore it's no longer appropriate to use the term *MultiFinder* to distinguish this environment from the Finder environment. When you update or revise written material that relates to version 7.0, replace the term *MultiFinder* with the term *Finder*.

THE VERSION 7.0 ENVIRONMENT

This section briefly describes the general user interface recommendations that affect your application when it runs in the version 7.0 environment. The changes to system software and the operating environment are described in the Introduction to the System Software Version 7.0 Environment chapter and in the Compatibility Guidelines chapter in this volume.

In previous versions of system software, a cooperative multitasking environment was available to users with MultiFinder. Users could turn on MultiFinder so that they could open multiple applications at one time; however, most people didn't use MultiFinder regularly. In version 7.0 the cooperative multitasking environment is standard. Now all users can open as many applications and desk accessories as their computer's memory can support. The Macintosh computer manages applications in much the same way that each application handles its own windows.

As in previous versions of system software, only one application can be active at a time. The frontmost application, the one interacting with the user, is the active application. Its small icon represents the Application menu in the menu bar and appears next to the application's name in the Application menu. Your application should update the controls in the frontmost window whenever the user switches to your application. If you previously didn't update your application to be compatible with MultiFinder, you now need to modify your application's event loop to accommodate a cooperative environment. For more information on the operating environment in version 7.0, see the Compatibility Guidelines chapter.

User Feedback

When your application is the active application, you need to provide feedback to the user to indicate what's happening. A user learns to predict how long certain operations last. In the version 7.0 environment, multitasking, virtual memory, and network connectivity cause task length to become more variable. A user won't always be able to predict the length of time per task. Therefore it becomes more essential to display feedback about what is taking place. If you don't, the user may think that the Operating System stopped running and may attempt to correct a perceived error condition, perhaps by manually restarting the machine. At least use the spinning beach ball or animated watch cursor to indicate an operation in process. If you can approximately determine the amount of time a task will last, it's even better to use a progress indicator so that a user knows that the Operating System is still running and that an operation is occurring. Figure 2-6 shows an example of a progress indicator.

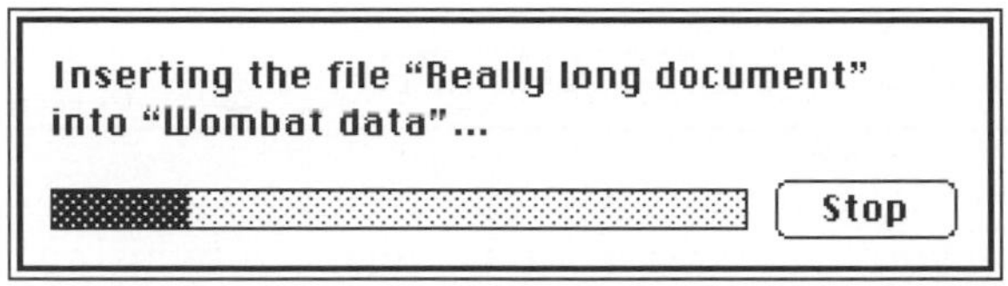

Figure 2-6. A progress indicator

Background Notification

When your application runs in the background, you may need to get the user's attention to respond to a task completion or a request for input. The Notification Manager provides several ways for your application to alert the user. When a background task is running and you need to notify the user, use the Notification Manager to alternate an icon in the menu bar with the icon for the Application menu or Apple menu as appropriate. In general, you should display an icon that corresponds to your application or system extension, so that the user gets a visual clue about which application is requesting attention. In addition, you should display a diamond-shaped mark next to your application's name in the Application menu. You can also play a sound. Figure 2-7 shows an example of a notification symbol.

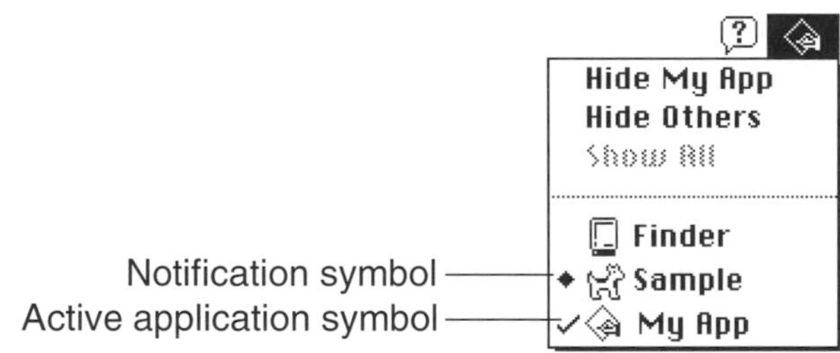

Figure 2-7. The Application menu with a notification symbol

Nothing more should happen until the user chooses to activate your application, at which time you can display a modal dialog box. Your dialog box or message must inform the user about what needs attention, why attention is needed, and what to do. For example, a dialog box might say "Transmission of the file My Phone List to 415-555-1212 could not be completed because the phone line went dead," and it might present the user with two buttons, Try Again and Cancel.

A background application should not take control from the user by placing an alert box on the screen when the user hasn't activated the application. If an immediate response is crucial and the user doesn't respond to the notification request, your application needs to handle the situation gracefully.

See the Notification Manager chapter in this volume for information about implementing these techniques.

COLOR DESIGN FOR VERSION 7.0

The appearance of system software version 7.0 is enhanced by using the color capabilities of the Macintosh. The use of color makes the interface more visually pleasing. The color also distinguishes the active window from other windows and enhances user controls on the window frame. It's important to recognize that color in the interface is applied to help users focus their attention on their work and not to draw attention to the interface itself. This section describes the use of color in the Macintosh interface and provides recommendations about how you can add color to your icons and applications. Color Plate II, "A Colorized Window," shown at the beginning of this volume, demonstrates the new appearance of colorized windows in version 7.0.

> **Note:** The figures that demonstrate the guidelines in this section appear on the color plates found at the beginning of this volume. The printed colors may vary slightly from the colors that you see on your screen.

The windows and dialog boxes in version 7.0 are designed for aesthetic consistency across all monitors from black-and-white displays to 8-bit color displays. For display on color monitors, color and shades of gray have been added to the frames of windows and to user controls. The window background remains white on all systems and the window contents remain black and white. For an example see Color Plate III, "A Colorized Movable Modal Dialog Box," which shows a colored frame, but black radio buttons and text. This updated design takes advantage of the color capabilities of the Macintosh but maintains the consistency of the Macintosh interface. On color screens, the racing stripes in the title bar and the scroll bars are gray. The user controls, close box, size box, zoom box, and scroll box are colored to make them more apparent. The borders of inactive windows are gray and recede into the background so that the active window's black frame emphasizes its position in front of the other windows.

For version 7.0 the standard window definition functions have been changed to display color windows and dialog boxes. Some control definition functions have been updated to display in color the window's scroll bars, scroll arrows, scroll box, close box, size box, and zoom box. If you use the standard window definition functions and standard control definition functions, your application's windows will match the appearance of version 7.0 system windows. If you create your own windows, be compatible with version 7.0 by using the standard window color table and the guidelines described in this section. Be aware that users can change the colors of windows and dialog boxes by using the Colors control panel. If you use the default window color table, you can be sure that the colors you use are consistent with any color that the user has access to with the Colors control panel. You can use the Palette Manager to associate a color palette with a window definition. See the Palette Manager chapter in this volume for more information.

General Color Design Guidelines

Always design for black and white first and then colorize that design. This method ensures that your design looks good on all Macintosh computers. One example of why this is important is the text selection mechanism. On a color monitor you might be tempted to change the color of text to indicate its selection; however, this technique wouldn't translate to a black-and-white monitor. In addition, a significant percentage of the population (up to 10 percent of the male population) has color deficiencies and wouldn't recognize the use of color to indicate selection. Therefore, you should never use color as the only means of communicating important information. Color should always be used redundantly. Color Plate IV, "Design for Black-and-White Monitors First," shows the correct process of designing for black-and-white monitors and then adding color to those designs. It demonstrates the consistency of the appearance of the icons and how the aesthetic integrity is maintained across the designs.

Keep black-and-white designs two-dimensional. It's important to maintain the visual consistency of the Macintosh interface across applications and computer systems. Don't cause unnecessary visual clutter by trying to mimic color effects, such as shadows, in black-and-white designs. Color Plate V, "Don't Mimic Color Effects in Black-and-White Designs," shows icons that were designed in color first and then adapted to a black-and-white design. It demonstrates the difficulty of trying to mimic color effects. This color plate shows how using only black pixels and white pixels limits your ability to re-create the appearance of color icons.

> **Note:** This guideline doesn't apply to keyboard icons discussed earlier in the "Worldwide Software Development" section. In that section, specific patterns represent colors for black-and-white versions of the keyboard icons.

Maintain a close visual relationship between a black-and-white design and its colorized version. Users should be able to easily recognize standard interface elements and icons across all monitor types. Users can have several monitors connected to a computer and several computers on which they use your applications. Your application should look consistent when a user changes the bit-depth of a monitor or when the user moves your icon or window from a color monitor to a monochrome monitor.

Use as few colors as possible in your designs. The fewer colors you use, the less flashing occurs when the screen's color table updates during screen redrawing. Using fewer colors also results in less visual clutter on the screen. If you use a graphics application to do design work, make sure that the colors you use are available in the default color tables. For more information about color palettes and color tables, see the Palette Manager chapter later in this volume.

Use light or subtle colors for large areas. Also use subtle colors to avoid visual clutter on the screen. To extend the range of light or subtle colors available, you can create colors that are lighter than those in the default color tables by using a 50 percent pattern of the color and white. Color Plate VI, "Use Light Colors for Large Areas," shows some icons that appropriately use colors. Color Plate VII, "Don't Use Bright Colors for Large Areas," shows how too many bright colors can be visually distracting.

Use bright colors sparingly and only in small areas. Bright colors attract the eye and can distract the user from the information that you're trying to convey. Bright colors can be effective in the contents of a window, such as in a chart. However, if bright colors appear all over the screen, it becomes difficult for the user to focus attention. You can use bright colors for small details. An example of this technique is the version 7.0 hardware icons (such as the hard disk icon) that use red and green pixels to represent the Apple logo. For an example of this guideline, see Color Plate VIII, "Use Bright Colors for Details."

For display on color screens in version 7.0 use true gray wherever you previously used a 50 percent gray pattern. Use true gray in menus for the dotted separator lines between groups of items and for dimmed menu items.

Use a consistent light source. On the Macintosh screen the light source always comes from the upper-left corner of the screen. Therefore windows and other elements have drop shadows on the lower-right side. Use the light source consistently, so that shading is consistent throughout the interface. Color Plate IX, "A Consistent Light Source," at the beginning of this volume, shows three desktop objects that have drop shadows consistent with a light source at the upper-left corner of the screen. Color Plate X, "Inconsistent Light Sources," shows three desktop objects that have different light sources and inconsistent drop shadows.

The Icon Family

In previous versions of system software, you provided a black-and-white 32-by-32 pixel icon for your application that was automatically reduced to 16-by-16 pixels when necessary. In system software version 7.0, you can provide multiple versions of an icon in black and white and in color. You can provide a family of icons that includes a 32-by-32 pixel and a 16-by-16 pixel icon, in 1-bit color (black and white), 4-bit color, and 8-bit color. The 32-by-32 pixel icons appear on the desktop and, if the user chooses by Icon from the View menu, these icons also appear in Finder windows. The 16-by-16 pixel icons appear in the menu as the Application menu's title when your application is active. They also appear next to your application's name in the Application menu and in Finder windows when the user chooses by Small Icon from the View menu. The user can also set the icon size to 16-by-16 pixels or 32-by-32 pixels in other views. For localized keyboards and keyboard layouts, you provide a 16-by-16 pixel icon only, in 1-bit, 4-bit, and 8-bit color. Figure 2-8, shown on this page in black and white, and Color Plate XI, "An Icon Family," show a family of icons for version 7.0.

Figure 2-8. An icon family

See the Finder Interface chapter in this volume for information about which icons you need to provide and how to create a bundle resource for your application.

The monitor displays the highest-quality icon that its screen allows. That is, if you provide an 8-bit color icon, a 4-bit color icon, and a black-and-white icon, the user sees the 8-bit color icon on the monitor that supports 8-bit color. If you provide an 8-bit icon but not a 4-bit icon, the black-and-white icon is displayed on the 4-bit monitor. If you provide a 4-bit icon but not an 8-bit icon, then the 4-bit icon is displayed on both 4-bit and 8-bit monitors. If you don't provide a color icon, then the Finder displays the black-and-white version of the 32-by-32 pixel icon on all types of monitors.

Black-and-White Icons

As stated previously, you should begin by designing a black-and-white icon. In general, you should use an outline of one black pixel to create the icon border. Use a minimal number of black pixels in the icon so that the icon's appearance is noticeably different when selected. Figure 2-9 shows an example of a well-designed icon that changes significantly during selection.

Figure 2-9. A well-designed icon and its selected version

If you use too much black or 50 percent gray in your icon, the icon doesn't appear significantly different when the pixels are reversed for selection. Figure 2-10 shows an example of an icon with too much black and 50 percent gray.

Figure 2-10. A poorly designed icon and its selected version

Small Icons

In version 7.0 you can provide a 16-by-16 pixel icon that you scale to size rather than relying on the Operating System to algorithmically reduce your 32-by-32 pixel icon. If you do not provide a small icon, the Finder reduces the larger icon based on an algorithmic formula that makes the icon look rough and creates less pleasing visual results.

You should provide a small version of your 32-by-32 pixel icon that you scale. Preserve as many graphical elements of the icon as possible. In essence you provide the same icon in a smaller scale. You can fine-tune the small icon by adding and removing pixels. Don't eliminate significant elements, or the smaller version of the icon may look different from the larger version. See Color Plate XII, "Consistently Designed Small Icons," which shows icons that a designer carefully scaled and tuned to preserve key elements of the icons' designs. Also see Color Plate XIII, "Inconsistently Designed Small Icons," to see small icons that don't match their corresponding 32-by-32 pixel versions. If you have difficulty distinguishing the consistency or inconsistency, it's a good idea to consult with a graphic designer to design or review your icons.

Color Icons

Version 7.0 ships with full-color icons that appear on color monitors. Your application can also provide color icons.

Don't design a color icon that's substantially different from your black-and-white icon. When you add color to an icon, it's best to leave the one-pixel black outline and fill the icon in with color. Coloring or graying the icon's outline makes the icon appear less distinct on the desktop. Remember that the user can change the background color of the desktop as well as its pattern, so your icon may not be displayed against the background on which you designed it. If you use ResEdit™ 2.1 to create your icons, it provides a way to look at your icon against different backgrounds to see whether your design is effective in various environments such as black-and-white displays or color displays of different bit depths. Color Plate XIV, "Icons With a Black Outline," and Color Plate XV, "Icons Without a Black Outline," demonstrate the importance of the black outline of an icon.

Color Plate XVI, "Apple Icon Colors," identifies the 34 colors used for icon design in version 7.0 in a palette with the standard 256 colors. If you use ResEdit 2.1 to design and create your icons, the Finder icon family editor provides easy access to these colors. Choose Apple Icon Colors from the Color menu. This command sets the palette in the editor (which is similar to the palette in most graphics applications) to contain the 34 colors used for Finder icons. See *ResEdit Reference* for information on using ResEdit 2.1.

If the default color table colors aren't available, the system software gracefully degrades to black and white, starting with comparable 8-bit colors, then using 4-bit colors if possible, and finally displaying the element in black and white if no other choice exists. The system software won't substitute colors that aren't visually close to colors that you assigned. If you choose colors other than the 34 marked in Color Plate XVI, use them for detail and not for essential parts of your windows or icons. The selection mechanism for color icons lowers the brightness of colors to indicate selection. This means that the colors appear darker when selected. On a color monitor, a black-and-white icon turns gray when selected. On a monochrome monitor, a black-and-white icon uses reverse video to show selection. In order for selected items to appear distinct from unselected ones, use light colors for large areas.

One technique for enhancing the appearance of your icons is to smooth angular or curved lines by coloring pixels on jagged edges. Designers refer to this technique as *anti-aliasing*. Change the pixel color where you can see a visual break in the outline of a black-and-white icon. Color Plate XVII, "Correct Anti-Aliasing," shows an icon in its normal state and then with anti-aliasing that changes the pixels on the outline of the icon. Color Plate XVIII, "Incorrect Anti-Aliasing," shows a different icon in its normal state and then with anti-aliasing that replaces internal pixels to improve the appearance of the icon. You can find these figures on the color plates at the beginning of this volume.

The Finder uses only one mask for each size in the icon family, so make sure that all your icons have the same outline shape. Don't add pixels or shadows to the outline shape of color icons. The Finder uses the icon mask for alignment and transformation effects, so make sure that the mask and all your icons are appropriate for each other.

Consistent Use of Icons

Use icons consistently throughout your designs. For example, if you reuse icon elements when you modify the generic document icon to represent your own application's files, make sure that they match. For example, the Macintosh computer inside the System Folder icon is the same as the Macintosh that appears as the Finder icon and as part of the Installer icon. The file server icon contains the same gray document icon and the same purple folder icon that appear on the desktop. Color Plate XIX, "Consistent Use of Icon Elements," and Color Plate XX, "Inconsistent Use of Icon Elements," at the beginning of this volume, demonstrate this guideline. Don't invent new icons to represent known entities such as folders and documents.

Customized Icons

You can provide the following customized icons if you support the associated features. You can customize these icons to represent your application, just as you can customize document icons.

- **Document icon.** This icon represents a document created with your application. You can customize this icon so that it relates to your application icon by adding graphics to it. Be sure to maintain the outline of the document. See the Finder Interface chapter in this volume for more information about displaying customized icons.

- **Stationery icon.** This icon represents a stationery pad that the user creates from a document. You can customize the stationery icon for each document icon by adding graphic elements to the stationery document page. See the Finder Interface chapter in this volume for more information about stationery.

- **Query document icon.** This icon represents a file that contains information that the Data Access Manager uses to transmit a query to a database. You can customize this icon by adding graphics to the document page. Be sure to maintain the outline of the icon and the volume symbol that represents the database. See the Data Access Manager chapter in this volume for more information on using the Data Access Manager.

- **Edition icon.** This icon represents an edition file that is created when a user chooses Create Publisher from the Edit menu. You can customize this icon by putting a different graphic inside the rectangle. Maintain the horizontal orientation and the double-dotted line of the icon that identify it as an edition icon. See the Edition Manager chapter in this volume for more information on implementing the Edition Manager.

- **Extension icon.** This icon represents a system extension. You can customize this icon by adding a graphic to the puzzle piece. You can display the puzzle piece in a horizontal or vertical orientation with the protruding part facing any direction. See the Finder Interface chapter in this volume for more information on displaying customized icons.

If you support these features but don't provide customized icons, the Finder displays default icons for these objects, depicted here in Figure 2-11 and in Color Plate XXI, "Default System Icon Families," at the beginning of this volume. See the Finder Interface chapter in this volume for information on how to use the bundle resource to associate these icons with your application.

Figure 2-11. Default system icons in black and white

If you develop control panels, you must provide an icon family for each control panel. The control panel icon is a square panel with an indicator on it to identify it. The indicator also appears on the Control Panels folder. You can add a graphic to the square to customize the icon. You can display the icon in either a horizontal or vertical orientation. Figure 2-12 shows some examples of control panel icons in both orientations. The examples are shown in color in Color Plate XXII, "Examples of Control Panel Icons," at the beginning of this volume.

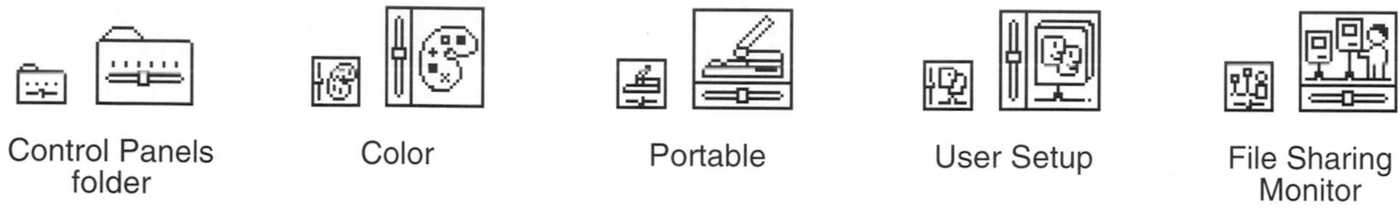

Figure 2-12. Examples of control panel icons

WINDOWS

This section provides information about window placement and behavior. It also presents general guidelines about windows and related dialog boxes and alert boxes.

Window Positions

To determine where to place a window, consider what kind of window your application is opening, what other windows are open and where, and the relationship between the content of a window and other windows or dialog boxes. Respect the user's control of the window and maintain the user's preferred size, state, and location for the window.

When your application opens a new document window, center it on the desktop. Open each additional window below and to the right of its predecessor. Before closing a window, check to see if the user has changed its size, state, or position. Save window positions, then reopen windows in the size, state, and location in which the user left them.

Before reopening a window, check to make sure that the size and state are reasonable for the user's current monitor or monitors, which may not be the same as the monitor on which the document was last open. For example, if a user is working on a word-processing document on a full-page display and then takes the document home and uses another computer to finish working, the second computer may have a 13-inch monitor. Then your application should open the document in a window sized appropriately for the smaller monitor and not necessarily in the saved size.

If the user hasn't changed a window's position, place windows in a position appropriate to the monitor type. If a user opens, moves, and closes a document window without making any changes, save the new window position but don't modify the date stamp.

When you open several windows on multiple screens, place the windows on the screen where the user is working. If a user drags a window from a Macintosh II monitor to a portrait display monitor, open subsequent windows on the portrait display monitor. The default position of a window must always be contained on a single screen.

Open dialog boxes and alert boxes on the screen where the user is working. For example, if a user has two monitors with a text document on the second monitor, open a find-and-replace dialog box on the screen where the related text document appears, not necessarily on the monitor where the menu bar is.

The Zoom Box and Window Behavior

A click in the zoom box toggles a window between two states, the user state and the standard state. The user state, as its name implies, is set by the user. In *Human Interface Guidelines: The Apple Desktop Interface,* a window's standard state definition is described as generally the full screen, or close to it, with the size and location that are best suited to working on the document.

But Macintosh monitors now come in all shapes, sizes, and configurations, so applications should never simply assume that the standard state should be as large as the screen. Frequently the monitor is larger, sometimes much larger, than the most useful size for a window. Screen real estate is valuable, so use screen-sized windows only when they make sense.

For example, a document for a word processor has a well-defined most-useful width (the width of a page) and a variable most-useful height (depending on the number of pages). Therefore the width of the standard state should be the width of a page or the width of the screen, whichever is smaller, and the height of the standard state should be the height of the document or the height of the screen, whichever is smaller.

When a user clicks the zoom box to change a window from the user state to the standard state, first determine the appropriate size of the standard state. If this size would fit completely on the screen without moving the upper-left corner of the window, keep this corner anchored. Otherwise, move the window to an appropriate default location.

Zooming behavior in multiscreen environments should not violate any of the guidelines described in this chapter, but it does introduce a single additional rule. The standard state should be on the monitor containing the largest portion of the window, not necessarily on the monitor with the menu bar. This means the standard state for a single window may be on different monitors at different times if the user moves the window around. In any case, the standard state for any window must always be fully contained on a single screen.

DIALOG BOXES

This section presents revised guidelines for design and layout of effective dialog boxes. The guidelines rely on the principles of feedback and dialog, forgiveness, and consistency as described in *Human Interface Guidelines: The Apple Desktop Interface*. These guidelines supersede previous guidelines about dialog boxes published in prior versions of *Inside Macintosh.*

Modal Dialog Box Behaviors

In version 7.0 the Dialog Manager has been updated to provide additional support for feedback mechanisms and menu bar access. When you display a modal dialog box, the Dialog Manager disables the Application menu, the About Balloon Help command in the Help menu, and the About Keyboards command in the Keyboard menu. It then checks to see if you are handling menus during a modal dialog box. These conditions are explained in detail in the Compatibility Guidelines chapter in this volume.

If the Dialog Manager determines that you are not handling your own menus, it disables the rest of the menu bar except for the Help menu. The Dialog Manager then determines whether the dialog box contains an active editable text box and if you have the standard keyboard equivalents for the Cut, Copy, and Paste commands. If both of these conditions are met, then the Dialog Manager enables the Edit menu and those commands in the Edit menu.

If the Dialog Manager detects that you are handling menus in your application, it only disables the Application menu. You must provide access to the Help and Edit menus. To support the Cut, Copy, and Paste commands you need to convert the Clipboard before and after you display a modal dialog box. You can also provide menu bar access in your application by enabling menus and commands in those menus that make sense in the context of the current task. See the Compatibility Guidelines chapter in this volume for information on enabling menus when you display a modal dialog box.

Movable Modal Dialog Boxes

Version 7.0 introduces a new window class, the movable modal dialog box. The user sometimes needs to see document contents that a modal dialog box obscures. To allow the user to move a dialog box in this case, you can use a movable modal dialog box rather than a modal dialog box. The movable modal dialog box has a title bar as part of its standard window so that the user can move the dialog box by dragging the title bar.

The design of the movable modal dialog box combines the standard modal window with a title bar with racing stripes, but no close box or zoom box. This design gives the user visual feedback that the dialog box is modal, and must be responded to before completing any other action in the active application, but the user can move it. Figure 2-13 shows a movable modal dialog box with attribute options that affect an area a user would want to see, such as the text that a border would surround.

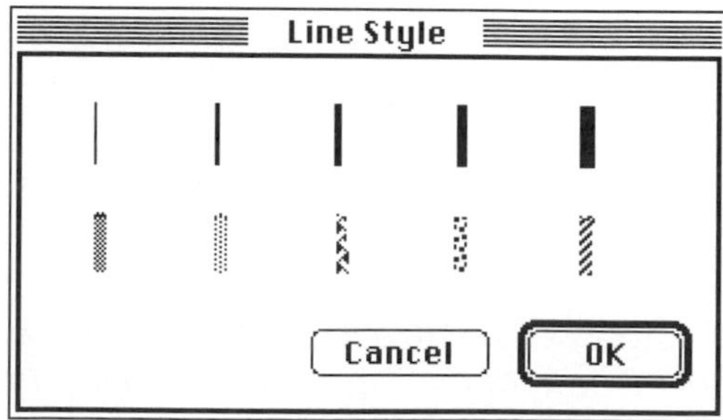

Figure 2-13. A movable modal dialog box

To create a movable modal dialog box, use the window definition ID of the movable modal dialog box in the standard resource type 'WDEF'. As with all movable windows, be sure to save the position of the movable modal dialog box window for the next time it's used. See "Creating Movable Modal Dialog Boxes" in the Compatibility Guidelines chapter in this volume for details on creating movable modal dialog boxes.

Movable modal dialog boxes should respond like modal dialog boxes in most ways. When you display a movable modal dialog box, however, there are some additional behaviors you need to support. You must make certain that the dialog box is modal within your application. That is, the user should not be able to switch to another of your application's windows while the dialog box is active. Allow your application to run in the background when you display a movable modal dialog box. For example, system software version 7.0 uses movable modal dialog boxes to show that an application is busy with a time-consuming operation, yet a user can still switch the application to the background. Figure 2-14 shows a movable modal dialog box displayed by the Finder when it is copying files.

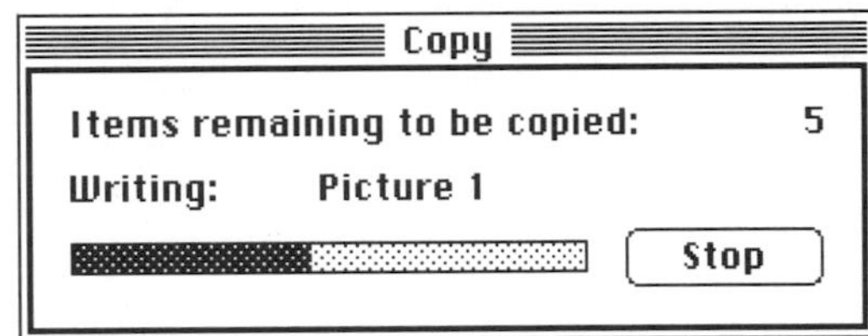

Figure 2-14. A Finder movable modal dialog box

You need to provide access to the menu bar when you display a movable modal dialog box. Provide access to the Help menu, the Edit menu, the Keyboard menu when appropriate, and any context-appropriate commands. Also enable the Application menu so the user can switch to another application.

It's important to consider whether you can use a modeless dialog box instead of a movable modal dialog box—to preserve the user's ability to perform any task in any order. See the Compatibility Guidelines chapter in this volume for information on implementing movable modal dialog boxes.

Keyboard Navigation in Dialog Boxes

In previous versions of system software you could select an item in the scrolling list in the standard file dialog box for opening files by using the keyboard. The ability to select an item from a set of items by typing the beginning character or characters of its name is called *type selection*. The user can also use the arrow keys to move the selection by one item in the direction of the arrow. Type selection has been extended to work in other lists, such as the list of files in a Finder window and the list of available devices in the Chooser.

Some dialog boxes have several elements, such as text boxes and scrolling lists, that can accept input from the keyboard. It's necessary to visually indicate which element is currently accepting input from the keyboard in order to let users know which of the possible elements is active. Each element has its own distinct indicator. As in the past, a text box displays a blinking insertion point or selected text range to indicate that it is accepting keyboard input.

When a scrolling list is the active element in a dialog box, its visual indicator is a rectangular border of two black pixels, which is separated from the list by one pixel of white space. Figure 2-15 shows the AppleTalk® Zones list in the Chooser as an active scrolling list area.

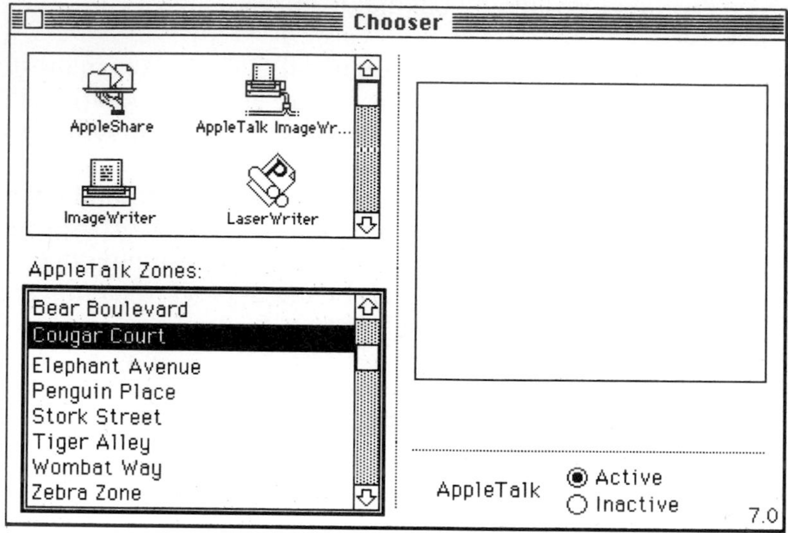

Figure 2-15. A selected scrolling list

When a user activates a scrolling list, using the following QuickDraw™ routines outlines the scrolling list in the standard way:

```
PenSize(2,2);
InsetRect(scrollRect,-3,-3);
FrameRect(scrollRect);
```

Since all typing goes to the active window, there should be only one active area and only one indicator at any time. If a dialog box has only one element that can accept keyboard input (and that element is a scrolling list), it's not necessary to outline a scrolling list. In the standard file dialog box the user can use type selection to identify the desired file in the list of files, but, since there's no other list or text box, the selected list doesn't have a border.

In a dialog box the user can move the active area to any interface element that accepts keyboard input, such as a text box, by clicking the desired element or by pressing the Tab key to cycle through the available elements.

Button Labels

Whenever possible, label a button with a verb that describes the action that it performs. Use book-title capitalization for button labels. In general, this means that you capitalize one-word titles and, in multiple-word titles, capitalize words of four or more letters. Usually you don't capitalize words like *in, an,* or *and.* The specific rules for this type of capitalization appear in detail in the *Apple Publications Style Guide.*

Provide a Cancel button whenever you can, and always map Command-period and the Esc (Escape) key to the Cancel button. Map the Return key and the Enter key to the default button, which is usually the button with the safest result or the most likely response. Don't display a default border around any button if you use the Return key in editable text boxes. Having two behaviors for one key confuses users and makes the interface less predictable.

In all dialog boxes, any buttons that are activated by key sequences must invert to give visual feedback that indicates which item has been chosen. A good rule of thumb is to invert the button for 8 ticks of the clock, which is long enough to be visible, but short enough that it's not annoying. All alert boxes and modal dialog boxes that use the ModalDialog procedure exhibit this behavior. If you implement your own dialog boxes or alert boxes, be sure to include this behavior. See the Compatibility Guidelines chapter in this volume for more information on the ModalDialog procedure.

A user typically reads the text in a dialog box until it becomes familiar and then relies on visual cues, such as button names or positions, to respond. Names such as Save, Quit, or Erase Disk allow users to identify and click the correct button quickly. These words are often more clear and precise than words like OK, Yes, and No. If the action can't be condensed into a word or two, OK and Cancel or Yes and No may serve the purpose. If you use these generic words, be sure to phrase the wording in the dialog box so that the action the button initiates is clear. Figure 2-16 shows a dialog box with appropriate OK and Cancel buttons.

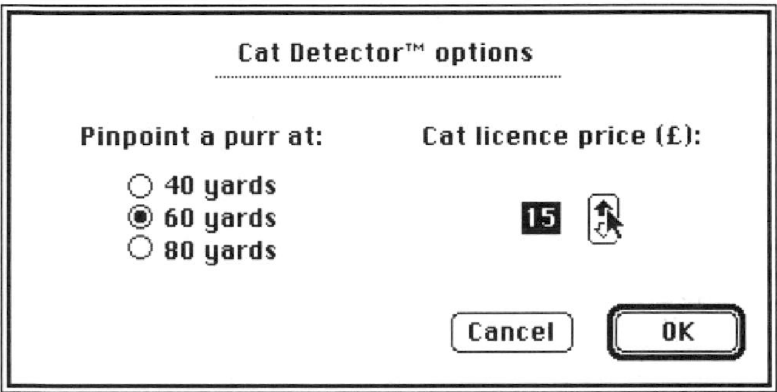

Figure 2-16. A dialog box with OK and Cancel buttons

Use Cancel for the button that closes the alert or dialog box and returns the computer to the state it was in before the alert or dialog box appeared. Cancel means "dismiss this operation, with no side effects." It does not mean "I've read this dialog box" or "stop what you're doing regardless."

When it is impossible to return to the state that existed before an operation began, don't use the word Cancel. You can use OK or Stop, which are useful in different situations. Use OK for the name of a button that closes the alert or dialog box and accepts any changes made while the dialog box was displayed. Figure 2-17 shows a dialog box that illustrates this guideline.

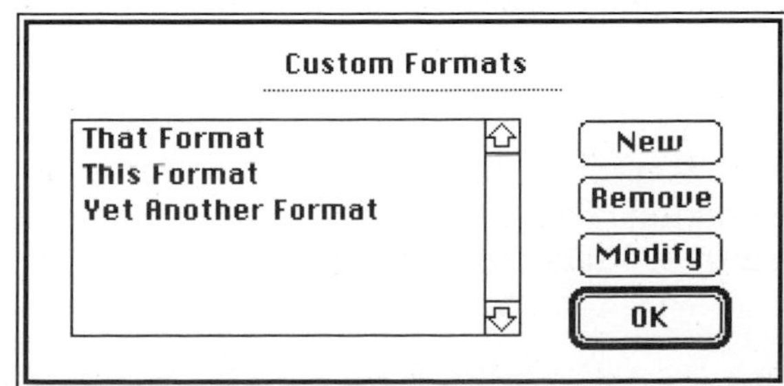

Figure 2-17. A dialog box with OK instead of a Cancel button

This dialog box uses OK because clicking the button maintains any changes that were made subsequent to the display of the dialog box. If the button were named Cancel, clicking it should remove any formats created, removed, or changed since the dialog box appeared, and it should return the computer to the state it was in before the dialog box appeared.

Use Stop for a button that halts an operation midstream while accepting the possible side effects. Stop may leave the results of a partially complete task intact, whereas Cancel always returns the computer to its previous state. It's appropriate to change the button name in the middle of the operation from Cancel to Stop if you can determine when it's no longer possible to cancel. Figure 2-18 shows a dialog box that illustrates this guideline.

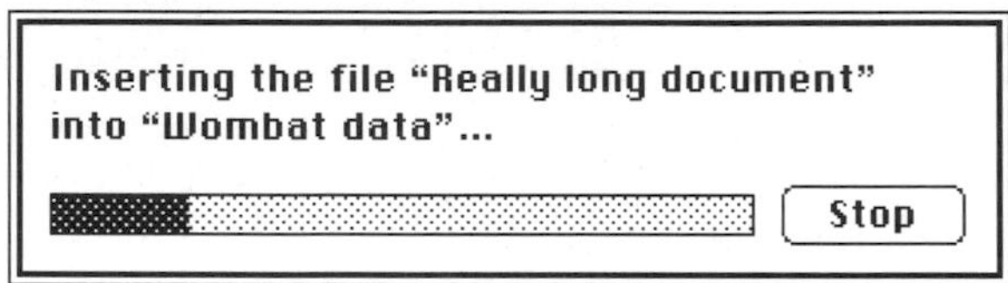

Figure 2-18. A progress indicator that uses a Stop button

The dialog box in Figure 2-18 uses Stop because clicking the button maintains the text that is already inserted while preventing completion of the insert operation.

In an alert box that requires confirmation, use a word that describes the result of accepting the message in the dialog box. For example, if a dialog box says "Revert to the last saved version of this document," label the button Revert rather than OK. Figure 2-19 shows a dialog box with appropriately labeled buttons.

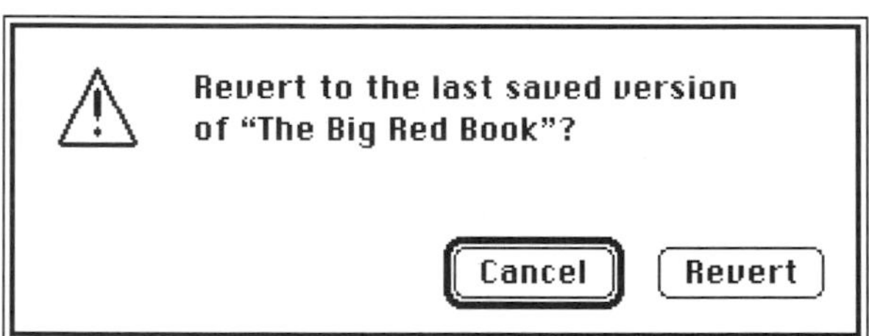

Figure 2-19. A confirmation alert box

If there is a most likely action, use a default button. This button usually completes the action that the user initiated to bring up the dialog box. The default button is outlined with an additional border of three black pixels, separated by a border of one white pixel, and its action is performed when the user clicks the button or presses the Return or Enter key.

Don't use a default button if the most likely action is dangerous—for example, if it causes a loss of user data. When there is no default button, pressing Return or Enter has no effect; the user must explicitly click a button. This guideline protects users from accidentally damaging their work by pressing Return or Enter out of habit. You can consider using a safe default button, such as Cancel.

A modal dialog box usually cuts the user off from the task. That is, he or she can't see the area of the document that changes when choices are made in the dialog box until dismissing the dialog box. Once the area becomes visible by dismissing the dialog box, the user sees whether the changes are the desired ones. If the changes aren't appropriate, then the user has to repeat the entire operation. To provide better feedback to the user, you need to provide a way for the user to see what the changes will be. Therefore, any selection made in a modal dialog box should immediately update the document contents, or you should provide a sample area in the dialog box that reflects the changes that the user's choices will make. In the case of immediate document updating, the OK button means "accept this change" and the Cancel button means "undo all changes done by this dialog box."

Some applications use an Apply button to approximate this behavior. This method confuses the meaning of OK and Cancel and is not recommended. If you must implement modal dialog boxes with an Apply button, you need to include a Cancel button and a Revert button in the dialog box. Otherwise the Cancel button becomes confusing to the user. When there is an Apply button, the Cancel button undoes the results of the Apply operation and dismisses the dialog box. The OK button dismisses the dialog box. The Revert button returns the document to the state it was in before the dialog box was displayed. The user must always be able to undo any actions caused by the dialog box.

Dialog Box Layout

In most simple dialog boxes, such as alert boxes, you should place buttons in functional and consistent locations, both within your application and across all applications that you develop. Place the action button in the lower-right corner with the Cancel button to its left. Figure 2-20 shows the recommended location for buttons and text. The default button can be any button; its assignment is secondary to the consistent placement of buttons. This rule keeps the action button and the Cancel button consistently placed. Otherwise, the buttons would keep changing location depending on the default choice for the dialog box.

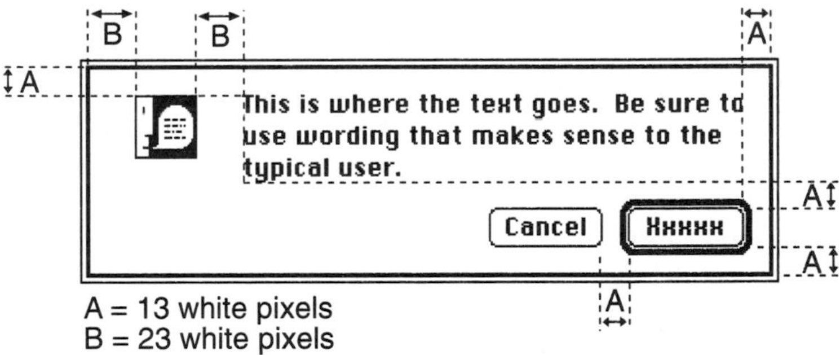

Figure 2-20. The recommended spacing of buttons and text in a dialog box

Use a consistent amount of white space between the border of the dialog box and its elements. This creates a balanced appearance in the dialog box. Otherwise the user might perceive a lopsidedness or other visual imbalance in your dialog box.

The Western reader's eye tends to move from the upper-left area of the dialog box to the lower-right area. Put the initial impression that you want to convey in the upper-left area (like the alert icon that appears in alert boxes), and place the buttons that a user clicks in the lower-right area. Following this guideline makes it easier for users to identify what's important in a dialog box.

When dialog boxes are localized for worldwide versions of system software, the text in the dialog box may become longer or shorter. The alignment of the items in the dialog box may vary with localization. Arabic and Hebrew are written right to left, so alignment of the items in an Arabic or Hebrew dialog box should be right to left. The Control Manager, Menu Manager, and TextEdit routines handle the alignment of dialog box components. For more information, see the chapters that describe those managers in this volume and previous volumes. Be sure to create dialog items of the same size, so that they align properly when a user has a script that reads from right to left. This guideline is discussed earlier in the "Worldwide Software Development" section of this chapter.

Dialog Box Messages

Write messages in dialog boxes and alert boxes that make sense to the user. Use simple, nontechnical language and don't provide system-oriented information that the user can't respond to. When possible, give the user information that helps explain how to correct the problem. Figure 2-21 shows an example of a well-written dialog box message that replaces the message users used to see, "The application is busy or missing."

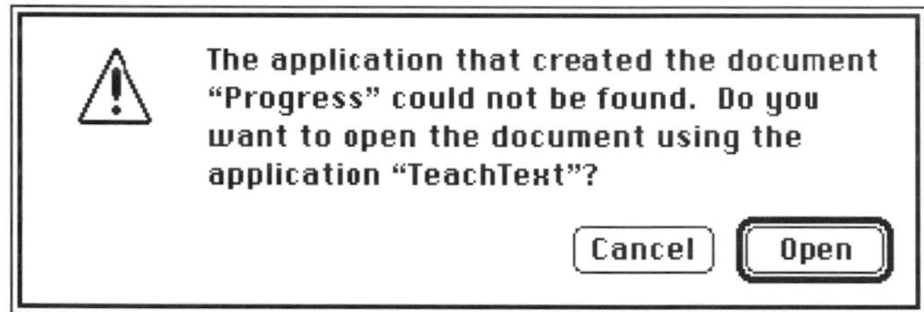

Figure 2-21. A well-written dialog box message

Use the name of the document or application in a dialog box when the text refers to it. For example, a dialog box that appears when a user chooses Shut Down after working on the company's annual report using the TeachText application should say "Save changes to the TeachText document "Annual Report" before quitting?" rather than simply "Save changes before quitting?" This kind of labeling helps users who are working with several documents or applications at once to make decisions about each one individually.

Standard File Dialog Boxes

The version 7.0 standard file dialog boxes present some new information to the user. They show a file's position in relation to the disk it's stored on. Instead of showing the root level of a hard disk as the highest level of the directory structure, the desktop now appears as the top level of the Hierarchical File System. The Drive button has been replaced with the Desktop button. A user can view and select disk drives from the standard file dialog box and can see other desktop entities such as the Trash folder. The dialog box that appears when the user chooses Save As includes a New Folder button that allows the user to create a folder in which to store the document. The pop-up menu in this dialog box now includes the downward-pointing triangle for additional visual feedback.

If you interact with the file system directly and use a dialog box similar to the standard file dialog boxes, you should replicate the organization and appearance of the standard file dialog boxes. Figure 2-22 shows an example of the new standard file dialog box for opening files. For more information, see the Standard File Package chapter in this volume.

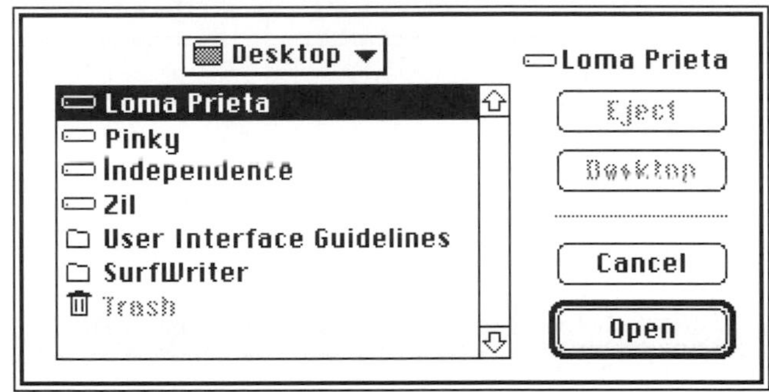

Figure 2-22. The new standard file dialog box for opening files

Save Changes Dialog Box

This section describes the new standard dialog box for saving all changes to a document before a user quits an application. The design presented in Volume IV of *Inside Macintosh* created some situations in which users, especially inexperienced users, could experience a loss of data. The new design addresses those concerns and standardizes the appearance of the dialog box so that users can quickly identify potentially dangerous actions.

Place the standard warning icon in the upper-left corner of the dialog box. This icon indicates to users that they need to carefully consider the dialog box message before clicking the default button or the Return key. The warning icon should always be in the same, predictable location so that users easily recognize it as a warning and respect its meaning.

Previously the buttons in the save changes dialog box were labeled Yes, No, and Cancel. The save changes dialog box changes the names of the buttons to correlate to the action users perform by pressing the button. The buttons should now read Save, Don't Save, and Cancel. Using these verbs reinforces the identity of each possible action to the user so that the experience is more intuitive. In other words, the Don't Save label provides much more context for the user than the word No does.

The new design provides a safeguard for the user by standardizing the location of buttons in a safe configuration. In order to prevent accidental clicks of the wrong button, you should always keep safe buttons apart from buttons that could cause data loss. Place the Save button in the lower-right corner with the Cancel button to its left. Place the Don't Save button on the left and left-aligned with the message text. This way, the user must explicitly move the pointer and click the button that could cause irretrievable loss of data. Figure 2-23 shows an example of a standard save changes dialog box.

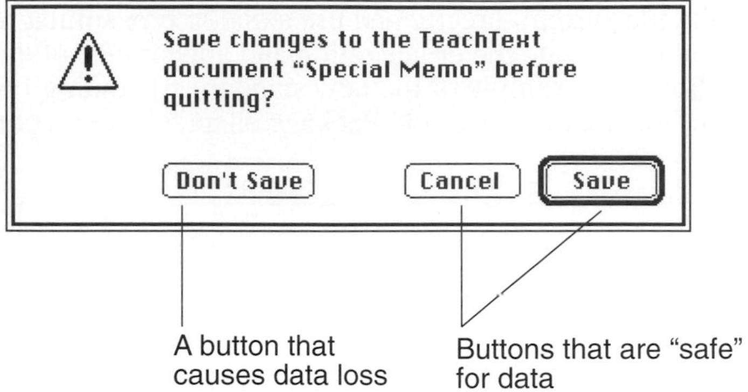

Figure 2-23. The save changes dialog box

Include the name of your application and the name of the document in the dialog box message, as shown in Figure 2-23. When a user shuts down the computer, several save changes dialog boxes may appear if there are several open documents on the desktop. This addition of information to the standard message helps the user by identifying to which application and document the message refers.

MENUS

This section describes changes to applications' menu style and contents in system software version 7.0. Applications can include several standard menu items that relate to new features of system software version 7.0. This section also presents the reserved list of keyboard equivalents for menu commands.

File Menu

Applications that support high-level database access, as described in the Data Access Manager chapter later in this volume, need to include the Open Query command in the File menu. This command opens a query document that establishes communication with a target database.

Edit Menu

If your application implements the capabilities of the Edition Manager, include its commands in the Edit menu, separated from the standard commands by a gray line. The commands are

- Create Publisher…
- Subscribe To…
- Publisher/Subscriber Options… (context-sensitive toggle command)
- Show/Hide Borders (optional context-sensitive toggle command)
- Stop All Editions (optional command)

Figure 2-24 shows a sample Edit menu that includes the required commands.

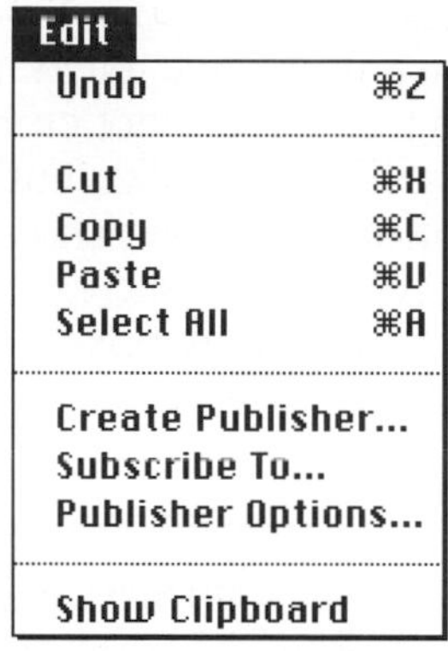

Figure 2-24. A sample Edit menu

If you find that you need all of the available space in the Edit menu for your application's commands, another way to accommodate the Edition Manager commands is by implementing a hierarchical menu. Include a Publishing command in the Edit menu as the title of the sub-menu. Use the standard indicator for a hierarchical menu, as shown in Figure 2-25, which also shows the submenu with the Edition Manager commands. Because hierarchical menus increase the complexity of your application, it's best to only use this approach when you have no other alternative.

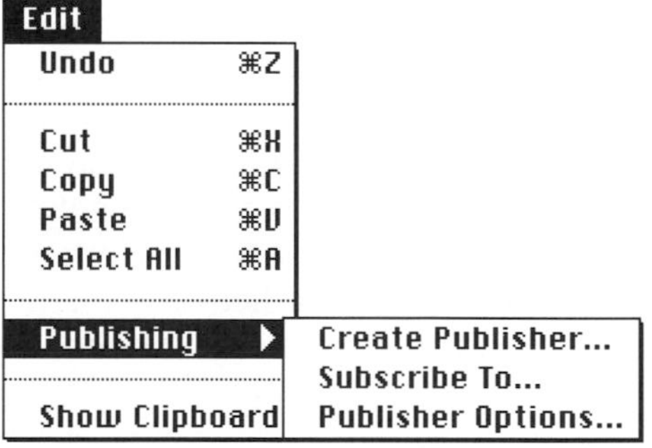

Figure 2-25. A sample hierarchical menu with Edition Manager commands

The user interface issues, as well as the technical implementation information related to the Edition Manager capabilities, are described in the Edition Manager chapter later in this volume.

Font Menu

System software version 7.0 includes TrueType™ fonts. If you decide to incorporate basic support for TrueType fonts into your application, remove the 127-point size limit for bitmapped fonts. Provide support for all font sizes in your application. Continue to outline font sizes in the menu for those sizes that appear in the user's System file. Use plain type for font sizes that aren't in the System file. If a TrueType font is present, outline all sizes of that font that you display in the menu. Provide a way for users to choose whatever font size they desire. When the user chooses a font size, place a checkmark next to the active font size.

One method that you can use to support TrueType fonts is to add an Other command to the end of the Size menu (or the end of the Font menu, if that's where your application allows users to choose font sizes). When the user chooses Other, display a dialog box that allows the user to choose any available font size. You can include a text box in which users can type the font size they want. If the user enters a font size that's not currently on the menu, add it to the list of choices. If the user is adding a TrueType font size, outline the size when you add it to the menu. If the user is working with a bitmapped font, show the new size in plain type. Provide a real-time display area to update the font size as the user changes it. Figure 2-26 displays a sample pull-down Size menu and font size dialog box. See the Font Manager chapter in this volume for more information on TrueType fonts.

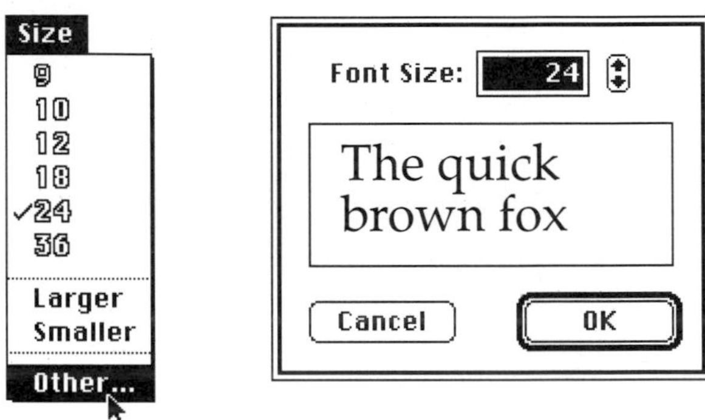

Figure 2-26. A sample pull-down Size menu and font size dialog box

Help Menu

System software version 7.0 includes on-line help for system software. The user can access Apple's Balloon Help from the Help menu. If you provide help information for your application, move the help commands that you provide to the Help menu. It's a good idea to include the name of your application next to your help command so that the user can easily distinguish the type of help to choose. For example, you might include a command called TeachText Help in the Help menu. Figure 2-27 shows the Help menu.

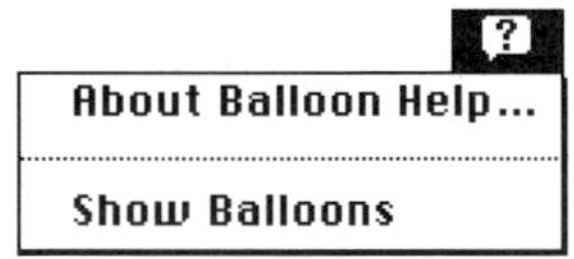

Figure 2-27. The Help menu

You can also use the Help Manager to implement Balloon Help for your application. See the Help Manager chapter for more information and implementation details.

Keyboard Equivalents

In the past, several keyboard equivalents were reserved by Apple for common commands. Table 2-4 and Table 2-5 show the standard Macintosh keyboard equivalents.

Table 2-4. Apple reserved keyboard equivalents for all systems

Menu	Keys	Command	Menu	Keys	Command
File	⌘-N	New	Edit	⌘-Z	Undo
File	⌘-O	Open…	Edit	⌘-X	Cut
File	⌘-W	Close	Edit	⌘-C	Copy
File	⌘-S	Save	Edit	⌘-V	Paste
File	⌘-P	Print…	Edit	⌘-A	Select All
File	⌘-Q	Quit			

Table 2-5 shows several keyboard equivalents that are reserved for use with worldwide versions of system software, localized keyboards, and keyboard layouts. These keyboard equivalents have actions that don't correspond directly to menu commands, so there is no menu column with command names in Table 2-5.

Table 2-5. Additional reserved keyboard equivalents for worldwide systems

Keys	Action
⌘–Space bar	Rotate through enabled script systems
⌘–Option–Space bar	Rotate through keyboard layouts within a script
⌘–*modifier key*–Space bar	Apple reserved

See the section on keyboard equivalents in the Worldwide Software Overview chapter in this volume for more discussion of handling keyboard equivalents in other script systems.

These key combinations are reserved across all applications. Even if your application doesn't support one of these menu commands, it shouldn't use these keyboard equivalents for another function. This guideline is for the user's benefit. Reserving these key combinations provides guaranteed, predictable behavior across all applications.

Creating a situation where Command-O means *open* 99 percent of the time and *ostracize* 1 percent of the time would do two things. First, users wouldn't consider using Command-O for the latter function because it is used by all other applications to mean *open*. Second, changing the meaning of Command-O in your application would weaken the user's perception of the consistency of the interface.

Some applications use other common keyboard equivalents, as shown in Table 2-6.

These keyboard equivalents are secondary to the standard keyboard equivalents listed in Table 2-4 and Table 2-5. If your product doesn't support one of these functions, then use these equivalents as you wish.

Table 2-6. Other common keyboard equivalents

Menu	Keys	Command	Menu	Keys	Command
File	⌘-F	Find	Style	⌘-B	Bold
File	⌘-G	Find Again	Style	⌘-I	Italic
Style	⌘-T	Plain Text	Style	⌘-U	Underline

You shouldn't assign keyboard equivalents for infrequently used menu commands. Doing so only burdens your users and constrains your application. Only add keyboard equivalents for the commands your users employ most frequently.

Pop-Up Menus

In previous versions of system software, pop-up menus did not look sufficiently different from other Macintosh interface elements. The 1-pixel drop shadow that differentiated pop-up menus from editable text boxes wasn't a strong visual cue that indicated a menu existed. This section presents the new standard appearance for pop-up menus that includes additional graphical feedback. It also describes how the new appearance enables some uses that were previously impossible.

Standard Pop-Up Menus

The new standard pop-up menu adds a downward-pointing triangle identical to the triangle used to indicate that a menu is too long to fit on the screen and must scroll. All pop-up menus should add this triangle. Figure 2-28 shows a simple pop-up menu in the new style.

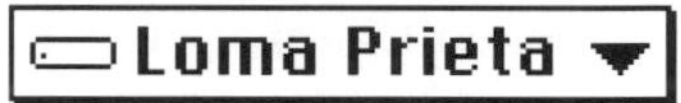

Figure 2-28. The appearance of a version 7.0 pop-up menu

When the user presses the mouse button while the pointer is over the pop-up menu or its label text, the triangle disappears. When the mouse button is released, the triangle reappears. Figure 2-29 shows this behavior.

Figure 2-29. An open version 7.0 pop-up menu

See the Compatibility Guidelines chapter in this volume for information on implementing the standard pop-up menu in your application.

Type-In Pop-Up Menus

Sometimes it is useful to display a list of choices but still allow the user to type in a choice that the application didn't know in advance. Keep in mind that users should be able to see and point; they should never have to remember and type. The type-in option should be an additional choice when appropriate, not a requirement. If the user types in an item that is already in the menu, place a checkmark next to the menu item. The menu always highlights the item that corresponds to the value in the text box. Your application also needs to highlight the value in the text box. This behavior prevents a quick click in the menu from accidentally wiping out the previous value. It also reinforces the idea that choosing a different value in the menu changes the value in the text box. You don't need to invert the menu's label in this situation. The new standard pop-up menu lends itself readily to this use, as shown in Figure 2-30.

Figure 2-30. A type-in pop-up menu

If the value typed into the text box does not match any of the items in the pop-up menu, the menu should add the type-in value as the first item and separate it from the rest of the standard values by a gray line, as shown in Figure 2-31. This appearance makes a clean distinction between common items that are always available and the typed-in value, which is only temporary.

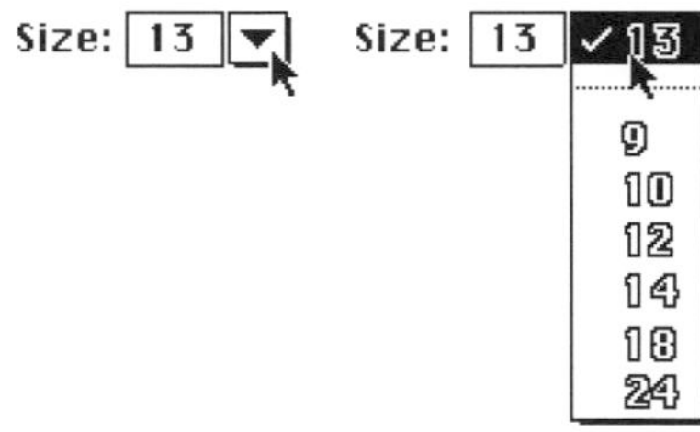

Figure 2-31. A type-in pop-up menu with user's choice added

See the Compatibility Guidelines chapter in this volume for more information about using the new standard pop-up menu in your application.

MORE USER INTERFACE INFORMATION

This chapter has presented the basic ideas you need to consider for supporting the new interface features of version 7.0. You'll find more interface information about using the new managers in the chapters that describe them. You can also get additional information from the following sources:

- *Human Interface Guidelines: The Apple Desktop Interface.* Reading, Mass.: Addison-Wesley, 1987.
- *Apple Publications Style Guide.* Apple Computer, Inc., 1990.
- *ResEdit Reference.* Reading, Mass.: Addison-Wesley, 1991.

- *Apple Direct*. This is a technical journal that presents various articles and a monthly column on human interface design.
- The AppleLink Developer Technical Services bulletin board. This bulletin board maintains a Human Interface Discussion folder that presents *Human Interface Notes* and provides answers for questions submitted by developers.

3 COMPATIBILITY GUIDELINES

ABOUT THIS CHAPTER

This chapter describes how you can write applications that have the greatest chance of operating on any Macintosh® computer, regardless of its hardware components or available system software, managers, and device drivers. It also addresses how you can take advantage of features that are new to system software version 7.0 in ways that are least likely to cause problems for users who are not running version 7.0. In a word, this chapter provides as much advice as possible to help you achieve maximum compatibility for your applications on all Macintosh computers, including those running version 7.0.

System software version 7.0 provides the most important test of software compatibility since the introduction of the Macintosh II, and you must understand how you may need to revise your current applications so that they operate correctly with this new system software. Fortunately, if you have followed the guidelines given in previous volumes of *Inside Macintosh,* your applications stand a very good chance of working correctly in version 7.0 without any modification whatsoever. However, version 7.0 introduces many new features and capabilities that you may wish to use in your applications. This chapter provides a number of additional guidelines to help you take advantage of those features while retaining compatibility with previous system software.

This chapter discusses several aspects of writing software that is compatible with all Macintosh computers:

- what can cause compatibility problems and how in general to avoid those problems
- how to update your application to take maximum advantage of new features of system software version 7.0
- how to write software that can be easily modified for use in other regions
- how to write applications that execute under A/UX®, Apple Computer, Inc.'s version of the UNIX® operating system
- how to determine what software and hardware features are available on a particular machine

The discussion of revising applications to take advantage of the new capabilities of system software version 7.0 also includes details about several new features of the Dialog and Menu Managers, including

- the new pop-up menu control definition
- the system menus
- movable modal dialog boxes
- new Dialog Manager routines to count and manipulate items in dialog boxes

This chapter also describes the Gestalt Manager, a set of three new Operating System functions that provide applications with a simple and efficient method for determining what software and hardware features are available on a given machine. You need to use the Gestalt Manager if your application takes advantage of particular hardware components (such as a floating-point unit) or software modules (such as Color QuickDraw™) that are not available on all Macintosh computers. Your software can also use the Gestalt Manager to inform the Operating System (and hence other applications) that it is present in the current environment.

The Gestalt Manager is available in system software versions 6.0.4 and later. Your development system may supply code that allows you to call Gestalt on earlier system software versions; check the documentation provided with your development system to see if this is possible. Of course, because you cannot use Gestalt to determine if the Gestalt Manager itself is present, you must do that in some other way; one such method is illustrated in "Determining Whether Gestalt Is Available" later in this chapter.

You need to read this chapter if you are interested in writing applications that execute on as many Macintosh computers as possible or under alternate operating systems such as A/UX. In particular, if you wish to enhance an existing product so that it supports new features of system software version 7.0 but also executes correctly in earlier versions of system software, or if you wish to write a new product that executes only in version 7.0, you should look at "Running in System Software Version 7.0" later in this chapter. Read the sections on the Gestalt Manager later in this chapter if you need to take advantage of specific software or hardware features that may not be present on all versions of the Macintosh, or if you wish to inform other applications of the presence of your application in the operating environment.

If you want your applications to run in system software versions earlier than 6.0.4 (where the Gestalt function is not available), you should be familiar with the Environs procedure, discussed in the Operating System Utilities chapters of Volumes II and IV, and the SysEnvirons function, discussed in the Compatibility Guidelines chapter of Volume V. Both Environs and SysEnvirons perform the kind of function that Gestalt performs—they allow you to determine what features are available on a specific machine. For reasons outlined later, however, you should not use either of these routines if the Gestalt function is available.

Unfortunately, no single chapter can provide all the information you need to achieve the greatest possible compatibility for your applications. Most of the subsequent chapters in this volume (and indeed all previous volumes of *Inside Macintosh*) contain numerous warnings and guidelines that you should heed if you wish to increase the likelihood that your applications will execute correctly on all members of the Macintosh family and under alternate operating systems such as A/UX. The Memory Management chapter in this volume, for example, contains a fuller account of 32-bit clean programming than is given here and is essential reading for all developers.

The Worldwide Software Overview chapter in this volume gives complete details on the Script Manager, which can help you write applications that are compatible worldwide. Similarly, the guidelines given in this chapter on writing A/UX-compatible Macintosh programs summarize and complement, but do not replace, the discussion in the separate publication *A/UX Toolbox: Macintosh ROM Interface*. So the complete story on Macintosh software compatibility does not end with this chapter, but it does begin here.

ABOUT COMPATIBILITY

Compatibility is the ability of a program to execute properly in different operating environments. Compatibility is important if you want to write software that runs, with little or no modification, on all members of the Macintosh family and in all system software versions. If you want to take advantage of particular software or hardware features that may not be present on all Macintosh computers, you need to know how to determine when those features are available.

To appreciate why compatibility is a real concern, imagine that from all the Macintosh computers currently in operation in the world, you were to choose two at random. You would quite likely find a number of differences in the hardware and software configurations of those two machines. You might find different CPUs, different memory management units (MMUs), different amounts of RAM, different shapes and sizes of monitors, and so forth. You are also likely to find different versions of system software, different ROM versions, different AppleTalk® drivers, different versions of managers, different printer interfaces, and so forth. Ideally, you want your product to run on both of those machines, regardless of the many significant differences between them. If you succeed in writing your application so that it does operate on both of those machines, you have succeeded in writing compatible software.

Fortunately, it is possible to write software that is compatible across the entire Macintosh line of computers. This section provides a number of guidelines that you should follow if you want your applications to run on the greatest number of Macintosh computers. Some of these guidelines are quite general and apply to all programs; some apply only if you are programming in assembly language.

One key to achieving compatibility is not to depend on things that may change. *Inside Macintosh* contains numerous warnings about which information is likely to change. As the Operating System and User Interface Toolbox evolve to accommodate the needs of developers and users, many of their elements will vary. Whenever possible, Apple strives to add features without altering existing interfaces. In general, you can assume that Operating System and Toolbox routines are less likely to change than data structures. Therefore, you should never directly manipulate data structures that are internal to a manager or system software routine, even if their structure is documented. Instead, you should manipulate those structures only indirectly, by calling Operating System and Toolbox routines that achieve the desired effect. In particular, you should never alter any portion of a data structure marked as unused or reserved.

Another key to writing compatible code is to code defensively. Do not assume that users perform actions in a particular order, and do not assume that function and procedure calls always succeed. You should always test the return values of routines for errors, as illustrated in most of the code samples presented in this volume.

Using Memory Wisely

A major cause of compatibility problems, especially in connection with applications running in the A/UX operating system, is misuse of the Memory Manager. Here are some important points to keep in mind:

- Do not set or clear bits in master pointers directly. Use Memory Manager traps (for example, HLock) instead.
- Always check the handle or pointer returned by a routine to make certain that it is not NIL. A NIL handle may indicate that a memory allocation failed or that a requested resource could not be found.
- Always check that a handle marked as purgeable has not been purged before using that handle. You can check for a purged handle like this:

  ```
  IF myHandle^ <> NIL THEN  {handle not purged}
  ```

- Do not create your own handles; instead, use the Memory Manager function NewHandle.
- Never make assumptions about the contents of Memory Manager data structures.

If you have followed all these guidelines, it is likely that your application is 32-bit clean; that is, it operates correctly in an environment where all 32 bits of handles and pointers are used to store memory addresses. When running with 32-bit addressing in system software version 7.0 and A/UX, your applications must be 32-bit clean or they may not operate correctly. See the Memory Management chapter in this volume for more information about these issues.

Using Assembly Language

In general, your software should not include 68000 instructions that require the processor to be in supervisor mode; these include instructions that modify the contents of the Status Register (SR). Do not modify the SR as a means of changing the Condition Code Register (CCR) half of the SR; instead, use an instruction that addresses the CCR directly. Do not use the User Stack Pointer or turn interrupts on and off.

If you wish to handle your own exceptions (thereby relying on the position of data in the exception's local stack frame), be aware that exception stack frames vary within the 68000 family.

In particular, don't use the TRAP instruction. Also, the Macintosh SE and Macintosh II hardware does not support the TAS instruction, which uses a special read-modify-write memory cycle.

Some Macintosh computers use memory protection and may prevent code from writing to addresses within code segments. Also, the 68020 and 68030 cache code as it is encountered. You should allocate data blocks on the stack or in heap blocks separate from the code, and your code should not modify itself.

Accessing Hardware

You should never address hardware directly; whenever possible, use the routines provided by the various device drivers and managers to send data to the available hardware. The addresses of memory-mapped hardware (like the VIA1, VIA2, SCC, and so forth) are always subject to change, as is the hardware itself. More important, direct access to such hardware is not possible in every operating environment. In multi-user systems like A/UX, for instance, the operating system manipulates all hardware; applications simply cannot write directly to hardware addresses.

You should also avoid writing directly to the screen. Use QuickDraw routines whenever possible to draw on the screen. If you absolutely must write directly to the screen, do not assume that the screen is a fixed size or that it is in a fixed location. The location, size, and bit depth of the screen differ in various machines. On machines without Color QuickDraw, you can use the QuickDraw global variables screenBits.bounds to determine the size of the main screen, screenBits.baseAddr to determine the start of the main screen, and screenBits.rowBytes to determine the offset between rows. On machines with Color QuickDraw, the device list (described in the Graphics Devices chapter in this volume) tells the location, size, and bit depth of each screen; screenBits contains the location and size of the main device; and the global variable GrayRgn contains a region describing the shape and size of the desktop.

Using Low-Memory Global Variables

Don't rely on low-memory global variables. Many of these variables have been previously documented in *Inside Macintosh,* but many have not. In particular, you must avoid undocumented low-memory global variables because they are most likely to change. But you should try to avoid even well-known global variables because they may not be available in all environments or in the future. In general, you can avoid using low-memory global variables by using available routines that return the same information. (For example, the TickCount function returns the same value that is contained in the low-memory global variable Ticks.)

Determining Whether a Trap Is Available

One important way that the Operating System and Toolbox have changed through successive versions of the ROM and system software is by the addition of numerous new traps. For example, the Time Manager released with system software version 7.0 includes a new trap, InsXTime, that provides certain improvements over the existing trap, InsTime. By using InsXTime instead of InsTime, your application can ensure that the periodic actions it requests execute at a fixed frequency that does not drift over time. Before using a trap that is not available on all machines, however, you need to determine whether it is available; if you call InsXTime on a machine that does not implement it, your program will crash.

There are several ways your application can check the availability of a particular trap. First, you can call the Gestalt function that is discussed later in this chapter to see if the appropriate version of the corresponding driver or manager is available. For example, the trap InsXTime is included in the extended Time Manager but not in earlier versions of the Time Manager. So you could use Gestalt to determine which version of the Time Manager is available in the current operating environment. If Gestalt reports that the extended Time Manager is present, you can safely call InsXTime to queue your request.

There are several cases, however, in which you cannot use Gestalt to determine whether a specific trap is implemented. You cannot, for instance, use Gestalt to determine whether the Gestalt trap itself is available. In addition, the trap whose existence you wish to test might not be included in any manager or, if it is, there might not be a Gestalt selector code for that manager. The WaitNextEvent trap is a good example of this: there is no way, using Gestalt, to determine whether WaitNextEvent is available.

A second way to determine the availability of a particular Operating System or Toolbox trap is by testing directly for the existence of the trap, using the technique illustrated in Listing 3-1. You should use this method to test whether Gestalt is available before calling Gestalt. You should also use it to test for the existence of traps not included in managers or drivers about which Gestalt can report. This listing illustrates how to test the availability of WaitNextEvent.

Listing 3-1. Determining whether a trap is available

```
FUNCTION NumToolboxTraps: Integer;
BEGIN
   IF NGetTrapAddress(_InitGraf, ToolTrap) =
            NGetTrapAddress($AA6E, ToolTrap) THEN
      NumToolboxTraps := $200
   ELSE
      NumToolboxTraps := $400;
END;

FUNCTION GetTrapType (theTrap: Integer) : TrapType;
CONST
   TrapMask = $0800;
BEGIN
   IF BAND(theTrap,TrapMask) > 0 THEN
      GetTrapType := ToolTrap
   ELSE
      GetTrapType := OSTrap;
END;

FUNCTION TrapAvailable (theTrap: Integer) : Boolean;
VAR
   tType: TrapType;
BEGIN
   tType := GetTrapType(theTrap);
   IF tType = ToolTrap THEN
   BEGIN
      theTrap := BAND(theTrap, $07FF);
      IF theTrap >= NumToolboxTraps THEN
         theTrap := _Unimplemented;
   END;
   TrapAvailable := NGetTrapAddress(theTrap, tType) <>
            NGetTrapAddress(_Unimplemented, ToolTrap);
END;

FUNCTION WNEAvailable: Boolean;
CONST
   _WaitNextEvent    =  $A860;    {trap number of WaitNextEvent}
BEGIN
   WNEAvailable :=  TrapAvailable(_WaitNextEvent);
END;
```

The NumToolboxTraps function relies on the fact that the InitGraf trap (trap number $A86E) is always implemented. If the trap dispatch table is large enough (that is, has more than $200 entries), then $AA6E always points to either Unimplemented or something else, but never to InitGraf. As a result, you can check the size of the trap dispatch table by checking to see if the address of trap $A86E is the same as $AA6E.

After receiving the information about the size of the dispatch table, the TrapAvailable function first checks to see if the trap to be tested has a trap number greater than the total number of traps available on the machine. If so, it sets the theTrap variable to Unimplemented before testing it against the Unimplemented trap.

> **Note:** The technique presented in Listing 3-1 for determining whether a particular trap is available differs from techniques formerly supported by Apple. The previous method determined the size of the trap dispatch table by checking the machine type. This type of check should not be used for any purposes other than simply displaying the information, as explained in "Using the Gestalt Manager" later in this chapter.

RUNNING IN SYSTEM SOFTWARE VERSION 7.0

The guidelines given in the previous sections apply to all Macintosh applications, regardless of the version of system software available. If you heed those guidelines, you are likely to produce applications that run reasonably well in all environments, including system software version 7.0. Those guidelines define a minimal level of conformance necessary for your applications to run in version 7.0. Applications that conform to the programming interfaces documented in *Inside Macintosh* and violate none of the guidelines presented earlier in this chapter are called **7.0-compatible** because they run in version 7.0 without problems.

An application can be 7.0-compatible, however, without taking advantage of the many new features available in system software version 7.0 and without exhibiting an awareness that other applications may be present and may wish to use processor time that would otherwise go unused. Among applications that do take advantage of new features, there are at least two levels of involvement with version 7.0.

An application is **7.0-friendly** if it takes advantage of some of the special features of version 7.0 when executing in that environment, but is still able to perform all its principal functions when executing in version 6.0. An application is **7.0-dependent** if it requires the existence of features that are available only in version 7.0; it might not even run in version 6.0. Even if 7.0-dependent applications do execute in version 6.0, they are virtually guaranteed to offer far fewer features there than in version 7.0.

The situation is similar to deciding whether your applications should use Color QuickDraw. If you revise existing black-and-white drawing programs to incorporate color, your applications operate either with or without Color QuickDraw. If you introduce new applications that require Color QuickDraw, they simply won't run on machines that don't support color.

The rest of this section gives guidelines on what you can do to existing applications to make them 7.0-friendly and not simply 7.0-compatible. The following pages describe in overview how to

- be aware that the user may have launched multiple applications
- support the required set of required Apple® events
- remove font size restrictions to support outline fonts
- make sure that your application operates correctly with virtual memory

Each of these items is discussed more completely elsewhere in this volume. For example, to learn what you need to do to support outline fonts in your application, see the Font Manager chapter. For information about cooperating with other open applications, see the Event Manager chapter and the Process Management chapter.

This section also discusses features of system software version 7.0 that simplify the creation and manipulation of several new or existing user-interface elements. These new capabilities allow you to

- get user menu selections while a modal dialog box is displayed
- coexist with system menus
- create movable modal dialog boxes
- create pop-up menus
- count and manipulate items in dialog boxes

Most of these features are not available on system software versions earlier than 7.0. The routines that allow you to count the number of items in a dialog item list and add or remove items from a dialog box have previously been available as part of the Communications Toolbox. You can determine whether those routines are available by using the Gestalt function to test for the Dialog Manager extensions. You can use the gestaltPopupAttr selector with Gestalt to determine if the new pop-up control definition function is available.

Note: The four Dialog Manager procedures CouldDialog, CouldAlert, FreeDialog, and FreeAlert are no longer supported.

Allowing Multiple Applications

System software version 7.0 continues the development of the Macintosh Operating System into a multitasking environment in which multiple applications can be active and must share the available system resources. The facilities provided with earlier versions of system software by the optional MultiFinder® package are now an integral part of system software version 7.0. This means that your application must display a certain awareness that other applications might be open at the same time and competing with it for processing time, memory, control of communications ports, and so forth.

Although most operating systems regulate the sharing of available resources by having the system parcel them out, the Macintosh Operating System relies on the willingness of foreground and background applications to share those resources among themselves. For example, you can indicate your application's memory requirements by specifying a minimum memory partition size (below which that application does not execute) and a preferred partition size (at which the application executes best). The Operating System itself has very little control over the partition size allotted to your application, other than by limiting that size to the available memory. Similarly, the Operating System has very little control over which applications receive processing time because the user ultimately decides when to bring a background application into the foreground. If your application holds onto the microprocessor for too long while being switched into the background, other applications may appear sluggish and unresponsive.

The lesson to be learned from all this is that in system software version 7.0 your application must be a good neighbor. You cannot expect the Operating System to force responsible behavior on your application; rather, you must ensure that your application can happily coexist with other open applications by following these guidelines:

- Include a 'SIZE' resource (with resource ID –1) that specifies reasonable minimum and preferred memory partition sizes; if you occasionally need larger amounts of memory, use the temporary memory routines described in the Memory Management chapter in this volume.
- Use the WaitNextEvent function instead of the GetNextEvent function in your main event loop to obtain events from the Toolbox Event Manager; this allows other applications to use processor time your application doesn't need and allows your application to perform operations while it is in the background.
- Modify your main event loop to process suspend and resume events; this reduces the time it takes to switch your application into the foreground or background.

For a more complete discussion of using WaitNextEvent and processing suspend and resume events, see the Event Manager chapter in this volume. That chapter also includes a description of the multitasking environment that is standard in system software version 7.0.

Supporting Required Apple Events

Possibly the most significant new feature in system software version 7.0 is interapplication communication (IAC), which will play an increasingly important role in future versions of the Macintosh Operating System. One central part of IAC is the addition of high-level events to those events that the Event Manager receives and conveys to applications. High-level events allow applications to communicate with one another by putting events in each other's event queues.

Apple Computer, Inc. has defined a protocol for high-level events called the Apple Event Interprocess Messaging Protocol. High-level events that adhere to this protocol are called Apple events. Some Apple events must be supported by an application that supports any Apple events; these are known as *required Apple events*. With a minimal amount of work, you can modify your main event loop so it supports the required Apple events. In doing so, you increase the level of compatibility of your application and ease the transition to the day when applications will expect other applications to support Apple events.

For information on how to support the required Apple events, see the Apple Event Manager chapter in this volume.

Removing Font Size Restrictions

System software version 7.0 introduces outline fonts, known as TrueType™ fonts. An outline font can be printed or displayed at any point size without the jagged appearance of some bitmapped fonts. A 7.0-friendly application should allow its users to take advantage of this improvement. Minimally, this means that users should be able to ask for any point size up to 32,768. Many applications now let users specify font sizes up to 127 points, but you should remove even this limitation when running in version 7.0. In addition, your application should allow users to increase or decrease the font size by 1 point.

You can use the IsOutline routine, documented in the Font Manager chapter in this volume, to see if a particular font is an outline font. If it is, you might wish to indicate that fact in your font size menu. For example, suppose that your Size menu for a particular bitmapped font looks like the one in Figure 3-1.

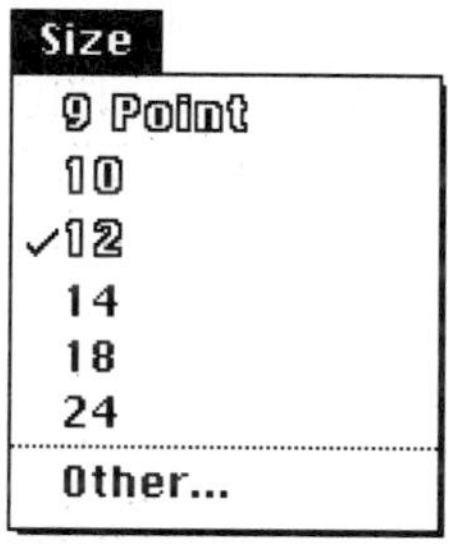

Figure 3-1. The size menu for a bitmapped font

To provide a visual indication that the selected font is an outline font that looks good at any size, you might change the menu to look like the one in Figure 3-2. One way to do this is by outlining all listed sizes, as well as the Other item.

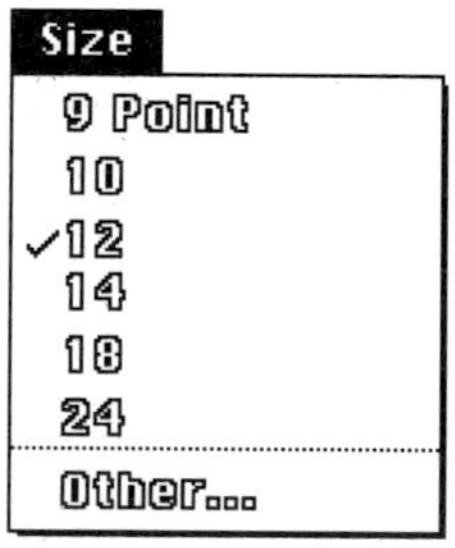

Figure 3-2. The size menu for an outline font

The User Interface Guidelines chapter in this volume contains additional suggestions on incorporating outline fonts into your application.

Operating With Virtual Memory

System software version 7.0 supports virtual memory, a memory management scheme that extends the logical address space of the machine by using part of the available secondary storage (usually, a hard disk) to store parts of memory that are not currently in use. When virtual memory is present, the perceived amount of RAM can extend up to 14 megabytes on systems with 24-bit ROMs and up to 4 gigabytes on systems with 32-bit clean ROMs. Because the Operating System has more addressable memory, your applications can ask for and receive larger blocks of memory than they would if virtual memory were not available.

Virtual memory is available only on machines equipped with a memory management unit (MMU). Currently, these machines include 68030-based machines (where the MMU is built into the CPU) as well as 68020-based machines that contain the 68851 Paged Memory Management Unit. You can use the Gestalt function to determine whether virtual memory is installed. If it is, you may need to exercise caution to ensure that the normally invisible operation of virtual memory does not adversely affect the execution of your application. Applications that might need to be concerned with virtual memory include those that have critical timing requirements, execute code at interrupt time, or perform debugging operations.

Note: The vast majority of applications do not need to know whether virtual memory is installed.

One type of application that might need to know if virtual memory is operating is a multimedia application that manages very large images or incorporates many sounds into its presentations. Imagine that such an application wants to display a large number of intricate color images in rapid succession, and that some of those images are as large as a megabyte each. If virtual memory is operating, it is very likely that parts of those images are on disk when they need to be displayed. This means that in the middle of drawing a picture, the system has to stop long enough to read those parts of the picture off the disk. The result is that a noticeable delay may occur, which may be unacceptable.

In a case like this, you can use routines that lock the appropriate data into RAM so that displaying the image requires no disk access. These routines are fully documented in the Memory Management chapter later in this volume. Other software that may need to know about those routines includes drivers, interrupt code, and debugging applications.

Enabling Menus During a Modal Dialog

The Dialog Manager in system software version 7.0 has been modified to make it easier for your application to allow access to the menu bar during a modal dialog. Sometimes it is useful (or even necessary) for users to be able to make menu selections while your application is displaying a modal dialog box. For example, a user might want to turn on Balloon Help during a modal dialog. Similarly, if the modal dialog box contains several editable text fields, the user might find it simpler to copy text from one text field and paste it into another.

In previous system software versions, user access to menus in the menu bar was prohibited during a modal dialog unless your application specifically allowed it. Moreover, keyboard equivalents of the standard Edit menu commands did not operate correctly in a modal dialog box unless your application provided a filter procedure to replace the standard filter procedure.

In system software version 7.0, the user can access selected menus in the menu bar during a modal dialog. When your application displays a modal dialog window (of type dBoxProc), these actions occur:

1. All menu items in the Help menu are disabled, except the Show Balloons (or Hide Balloons) command, which is enabled.

2. All menu items in the Application menu are disabled.

3. If the Keyboard menu appears in the menu bar (that is, if there is more than one script system installed in the system or if the smfShowIcon bit is set in the Script Manager flags long word), that menu is enabled, but the About Keyboards command is disabled.

In addition, if your application then calls the ModalDialog procedure, several other actions occur:

4. All your application's menus are disabled.

5. If the modal dialog box contains a visible and active editable text field and if the menu bar contains a menu having commands with the standard keyboard equivalents Command-X, Command-C, and Command-V, then those three commands are enabled. The user can then use either the menu commands or their keyboard equivalents to cut, copy, and paste text. (The menu item having keyboard equivalent Command-X must be one of the first five menu items.)

When the user dismisses the dialog box, all menus are restored to the state they were in prior to the appearance of the dialog box.

There are some cases in which actions 4 and 5 do not occur when you call ModalDialog. The enabling and disabling described in steps 4 and 5 does not occur if any of these conditions happen:

- Your application does not have an Apple menu.
- Your application has an Apple menu, but the menu is disabled when the dialog box is displayed.
- Your application has an Apple menu, but the first item in that menu is disabled when the dialog box is displayed.

Note: If your application already handles access to the menu bar during a modal dialog and you do not want the automatic menu enabling and disabling provided by system software version 7.0 to occur, you should ensure that one or more of those conditions is true when you display a modal dialog box.

Coexisting With the System Menus

In system software version 7.0, the menu bar may contain as many as four **system menus,** which are menus that provide access to system features such as application switching, Balloon Help, and keyboard scripts. The four system menus are the Apple menu, the Application menu, the Help menu, and the Keyboard menu. All four of these menus have icons as titles. The Apple menu icon is located in its usual location at the left side of the menu bar, but the three other menu icons are positioned at the right side of the menu bar.

The system menu icons are drawn automatically in the menu bar of any application that supports an Apple menu and that uses the default system menu bar definition procedure (that is, resource of type 'MBDF' having ID 0). The Application menu icon is always drawn. The Help menu icon is drawn if space is available, and the Keyboard menu icon is drawn if space is available and if more than one script system is available in the system.

Both the Help menu icon and the Keyboard menu icon disappear from the menu bar if your application installs a menu whose title has a right side that extends into the space occupied by one or both of those icons. This allows your application to reclaim any space in the menu bar that would have been occupied by one or both of those two menu icons, if necessary. However, the Application menu icon is always displayed in the menu bar. If your application installs a menu whose title is long enough to overlap space occupied by the Application menu icon, the overlapping portion of that title is placed behind the Application menu icon.

The system menus are installed into your application's menu list, so you should not make any assumptions about the last item (or items) in your menu list. Your application receives notice of mouse-down events in the menu bar, even when those events concern system menus. You can still call MenuSelect in response to a mouse-down event in the menu bar, however, because MenuSelect returns either 0 in the high word when the Apple, Application, or Keyboard menu is selected, or the HelpMgrID constant when the Help menu is selected.

Creating Movable Modal Dialog Boxes

The Window Manager in system software version 7.0 allows you to create a new type of window, called a movable modal dialog box, by specifying the following constant as the window definition ID when you call NewWindow:

```
CONST movableDBoxProc      = 5;    {movable modal dialog box}
```

The User Interface Guidelines chapter in this volume contains illustrations of movable modal dialog boxes and recommendations for their use. Note carefully that it is your application's responsibility to ensure that any movable modal dialog boxes you create display the behavior described there. In particular, you must provide the code that prevents the user from bringing another window in your application forward while a movable modal dialog box is displayed.

> **Note:** The term *movable modal dialog box* is likely to cause confusion because windows you create with the movableDBoxProc window definition ID cannot, in general, be manipulated like other (nonmovable) modal dialog boxes. For example, you should not call the ModalDialog procedure when the frontmost window is a movable modal dialog box.

Creating Pop-Up Menus

The Control Manager in system software version 7.0 makes it much easier for you to create pop-up menus. Pop-up menus provide the user with a simple way to select from among a list of choices without having to move up to the menu bar. They are particularly useful in a dialog box that requires the user to specify a number of settings or values. Figure 3-3 shows a pop-up menu in both its inactive and active states.

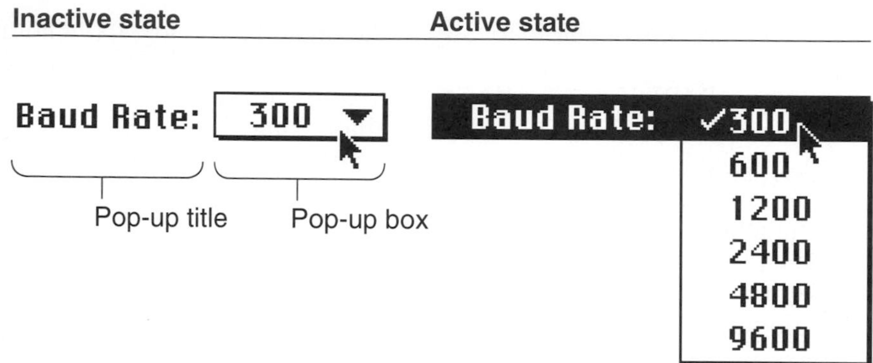

Figure 3-3. A pop-up menu in its inactive and active states

Prior to system software version 7.0 (or on earlier systems running without the Communications Toolbox installed), the easiest way to create pop-up menus was to create the pop-up title as a staticText item in a dialog item list and the pop-up box as a user item. Your application then needed to draw a box around that user item, draw the drop shadow, and insert text into the box. Then you could call the PopUpMenuSelect function to draw the pop-up menu and track the cursor within the menu, making sure to invert the pop-up title while the menu is active (to duplicate the behavior of menu titles in the menu bar).

The Control Manager in system software version 7.0 allows you to create a pop-up menu as a new type of control by using the following constant when you call NewControl:

```
CONST popupMenuCDEFProc    = 1008;      {pop-up menu}
```

If you specify popupMenuCDEFProc (plus any appropriate variation code) as the procID parameter in NewControl (or specify it as the procID of a control that you open with GetNewControl), the Control Manager creates a pop-up menu control, which includes the pop-up title and the pop-up box with a one-pixel drop shadow. The appearance of the pop-up title and the values in the menu are controlled by other parameters passed to NewControl (or stored in a resource), as described later in this chapter.

In system software version 7.0, the control definition function specified by the constant popupMenuCDEFProc also draws the downward-pointing triangle in the pop-up menu. Note that the triangle is not drawn automatically in earlier system software versions.

To create a pop-up menu, call NewControl and specify popupMenuCDEFProc (plus any appropriate variation code) as the procID parameter.

```
FUNCTION NewControl (theWindow: WindowPtr; boundsRect: Rect;
                     title: Str255; visible: Boolean; value: Integer;
                     min: Integer; max: Integer; procID: Integer;
                     refCon: LongInt) : ControlHandle;
```

The value, min, and max parameters behave differently with pop-up menus than with other controls created with NewControl. You can specify constants listed below to control the appearance and location of text in the control. If NewControl returns successfully (that is, if the returned ControlHandle is not NIL), the control minimum and maximum values contain information about the new pop-up menu, as described later in this section. In addition, NewControl may modify the boundsRect parameter to reflect the actual width of the pop-up menu box that is created.

When you call NewControl, the value parameter specifies the manner in which the title of the pop-up menu is to be aligned and drawn. The value parameter should be some combination of the following constants:

```
CONST   popupTitleLeftJust      =   $0000;   {left alignment}
        popupTitleCenterJust    =   $0001;   {center alignment}
        popupTitleRightJust     =   $00FF;   {right alignment}
        popupTitleBold          =   $0100;   {bold text}
        popupTitleItalic        =   $0200;   {italic text}
        popupTitleUnderline     =   $0400;   {underlined text}
        popupTitleOutline       =   $0800;   {outlined text}
        popupTitleShadow        =   $1000;   {shadow text}
        popupTitleCondense      =   $2000;   {condensed text}
        popupTitleExtend        =   $4000;   {extended text}
        popupTitleNoStyle       =   $8000;   {unstyled text}
```

Figure 3-4 illustrates the appearance of the pop-up control if you pass the popupTitleRightJust constant. Note that the position of the pop-up box and the pop-up title are reversed from their default (left-aligned) positions.

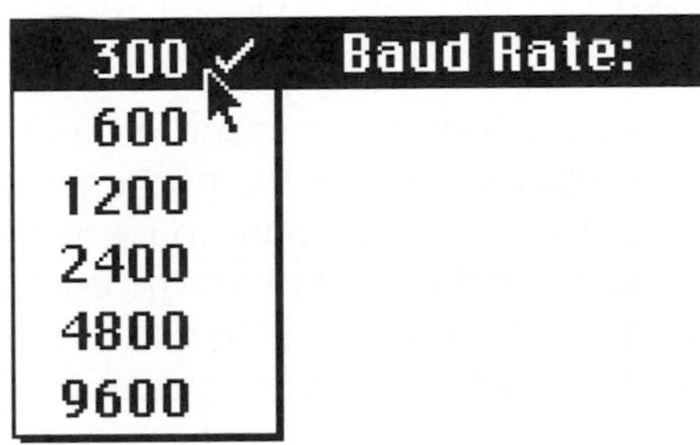

Figure 3-4. A pop-up control that is right-aligned

You can also pass a sum of constants in the value parameter to draw the pop-up title with more than one of these characteristics. If NewControl completes successfully, the value parameter contains the current minimum value of the menu. Your application can then use the value of the control to determine the currently selected item.

The min parameter specifies the resource ID of the menu in the pop-up control when the control is being created. After the control has been created, the pop-up menu control definition sets the minimum value of the control to 1.

The max parameter specifies the width of the pop-up title area when the control is being created. After the control has been created, the pop-up menu control definition sets the maximum value of the control to the number of items in the pop-up menu.

The procID parameter should contain the value popupMenuCDEFProc plus any desired variation code. Currently recognized variation codes are defined by constants:

```
CONST popupFixedWidth      = $0001;     {use fixed-width control}
      popupUseAddResMenu   = $0004;     {use resource for menu}
      popupUseWFont        = $0008;     {use window font}
```

Constant	**Description**
popupFixedWidth	Uses a constant control width. If your application specifies this value, the pop-up menu control definition function does not resize the control horizontally to fit long menu items. The width of the pop-up box is set to the width of the control, minus the width of the pop-up title your application specifies when it creates the control. If the contents of the pop-up box do not fit into the space provided, the text is truncated to fit and ellipses (...) are appended to its end. If you do not specify this variation code, the contents of the pop-up box are guaranteed to fit because the pop-up menu control definition function resizes the control horizontally (up to the size of the control's bounding rectangle).
popupUseAddResMenu	Gets menu items from a resource. If your application specifies this value, the pop-up menu control definition function interprets the refCon parameter passed to NewControl as a value of type ResType that specifies the resource type to load into the menu (using the AddResMenu procedure).
popupUseWFont	Uses the font of the specified window. If your application specifies this value, the pop-up menu control definition function draws the pop-up menu title using the font and size of the grafPort that owns the control. In addition, the pop-up menu, when active, is to use the font and size of that grafPort instead of the standard system font.

The refCon parameter is a long integer that is available for your application's use. However, if you specify popupUseAddResMenu as a variation code, the value in the refCon parameter is typecast to the type ResType and is used by AddResMenu to add items to the pop-up menu. For example, if the value in the refCon parameter is LongInt('FONT'), the pop-up menu control definition function appends a list of the fonts installed in the system to the menu associated with the pop-up menu control. After the control has been created, your application can use the control handle's refCon field for whatever use it requires. You can determine which menu item is currently selected by calling GetCtlValue.

Whenever the pop-up control is redrawn, the control definition function calls the CalcMenuSize procedure. This procedure recalculates the size of the menu associated with the control (to allow for the addition or deletion of items in the menu). The control definition function may also update the width of the pop-up menu control to the sum of the width of the pop-up title, the width of the longest item in the menu, the width of the downward arrow, and a small amount of white space. As previously described, your application can override this behavior by using the variation code popupFixedWidth.

You can obtain the menu handle and the menu ID of the menu associated with the pop-up control by dereferencing the contrlData field of the control record. The contrlData field is a handle to a block of private information. For pop-up menu controls, this field is a handle to a popupPrivateData structure:

```
TYPE popupPrivateData =
     RECORD
       mHandle:  MenuHandle;                    {handle to menu}
       mID:      Integer;                       {menu ID}
       mPrivate: ARRAY[0..0] OF SignedByte      {reserved}
     END;
```

The mHandle field contains a handle to the menu. The mID field is the ID of the menu. The mPrivate field is reserved.

Manipulating Dialog Item Lists

The Dialog Manager in system software version 7.0 includes several new routines that make it easier for you to manipulate dialog item lists. You can count the number of items in a dialog list by using the CountDITL function. You can add items to an item list by using the AppendDITL procedure and remove items from the end of an item list by calling the ShortenDITL procedure.

These Dialog Manager extensions are available in system software version 7.0 and also on any earlier system that has the Communications Toolbox installed. Before calling these routines, you should make sure that they are available by calling the Gestalt function with the gestaltDITLExtAttr selector.

Counting Items in a Dialog Item List

You can call the CountDITL function to count the items in a dialog item list.

```
FUNCTION CountDITL (theDialog: DialogPtr) : Integer;
```

CountDITL returns the number of items in the dialog item list associated with the dialog box pointed to by the parameter theDialog.

Appending Items to a Dialog Item List

You can call the AppendDITL procedure to append items to the end of a dialog item list.

```
PROCEDURE AppendDITL (theDialog: DialogPtr; theDITL: Handle; method:
                      DITLMethod);
```

The parameter theDialog specifies the dialog box to whose item list you want to append items. The parameter theDITL is a handle to the item list you want to append to that dialog box's existing item list. The method parameter specifies the manner in which you want the new item list to be appended. The available methods are defined by constants of type DITLMethod:

```
TYPE DITLMethod = Integer;

CONST overlayDITL          = 0;    {overlay existing items}
      appendDITLRight      = 1;    {append at right}
      appendDITLBottom     = 2;    {append at bottom}
```

Consider the initial dialog box and list of items to be appended that are illustrated in Figure 3-5.

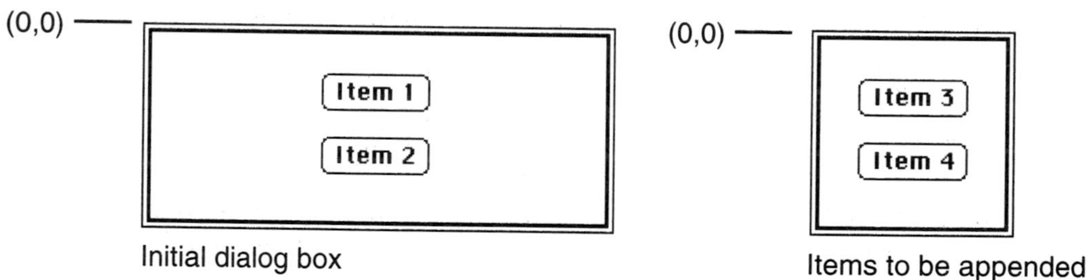

Figure 3-5. An initial dialog box and a list of items to append

If the method parameter is overlayDITL, the items to be appended are superimposed on any existing items in the dialog box. Figure 3-6 shows the result of overlaying new dialog items.

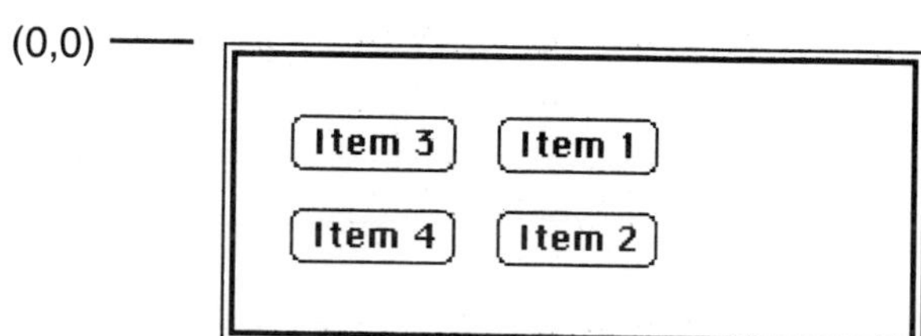

Figure 3-6. The dialog box after items are overlaid

The positions of the new items are determined by the coordinate system of the initial dialog box.

If the method parameter is appendDITLRight, the new items are appended to the right of the dialog box, as illustrated in Figure 3-7.

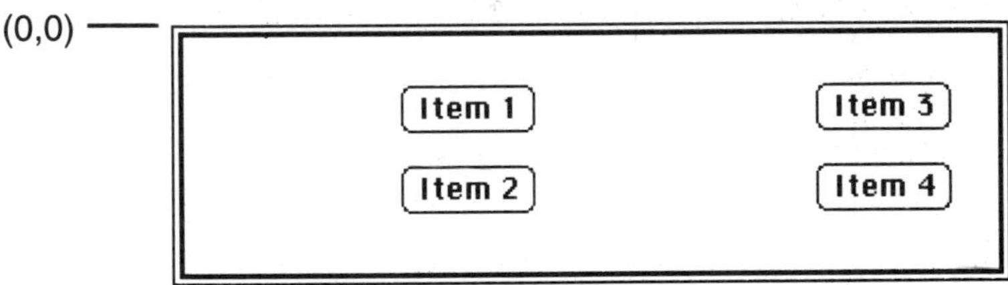

Figure 3-7. The dialog box after items are appended to the right

The positions of the new items are offset by the upper-right coordinate of the port rectangle of theDialog. AppendDITL automatically expands the dialog box to accommodate the new dialog items. If you know that your application will need to restore a dialog box to the size it was before you called AppendDITL, you should save the original size before calling AppendDITL.

If the method parameter is appendDITLBottom, the new items are appended to the bottom of the dialog box, as illustrated in Figure 3-8.

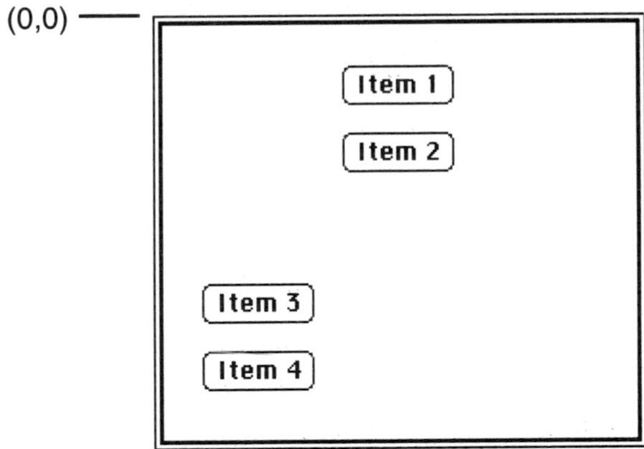

Figure 3-8. The dialog box after items are appended to the bottom

The positions of the new items are offset by the lower-left coordinate of the original dialog box. AppendDITL automatically expands the dialog box to accommodate the new dialog items. If you know that your application will need to restore a dialog box to the size it was before you called AppendDITL, you should save the original size before calling AppendDITL.

You can append a list of dialog items relative to existing items in the dialog box by passing a negative number in the method parameter. The absolute value of this number is interpreted as the item in the dialog box relative to which the new items are to be positioned. For example, if the method parameter is –2, the items to be appended are offset from the upper-left corner of item number 2, as illustrated in Figure 3-9.

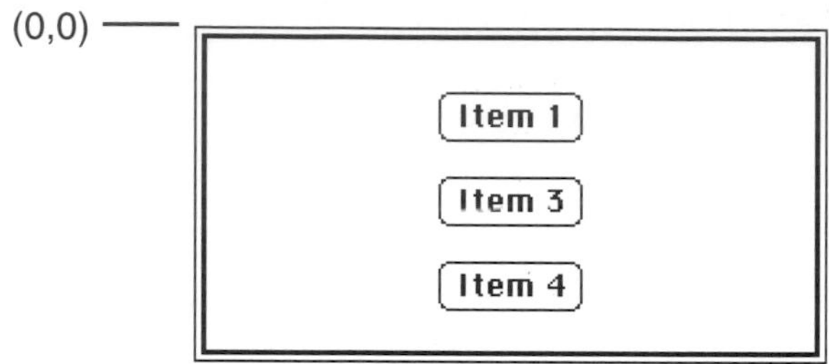

Figure 3-9. The dialog box after items are appended relative to Item 2

Because Item 3 was appended relative to the top-left corner of Item 2, it appears on top of Item 2.

Because AppendDITL modifies the contents of the parameter theDITL, your application must get rid of the dialog item list after calling AppendDITL. Here is a typical calling sequence:

```
myNewItems := GetResource('DITL', myID);
AppendDITL(myDialog, myNewItems, appendDITLBottom);
ReleaseResource(myNewItems);
```

Shortening a Dialog Item List

You can call the ShortenDITL procedure to remove items from the end of a dialog item list.

```
PROCEDURE ShortenDITL (theDialog: DialogPtr; numberItems: Integer);
```

The parameter theDialog specifies the dialog box from whose item list you want to remove items. The numberItems parameter specifies how many items to remove from the end of the item list. Note that ShortenDITL does not automatically resize the dialog box.

LOCALIZING MACINTOSH PROGRAMS

Localization is the process of adapting an application to a specific language, culture, and region. By planning ahead and making localization relatively painless, you'll ensure that your product is ready for international markets in the future. This section provides a brief overview of what you need to do to make it easy to localize your application. For the complete account of writing software that is compatible with Macintosh computers throughout the world, you should read the TextEdit chapter and the Worldwide Software Overview later in this volume. You should also consult the "Worldwide Software Development" section in the User Interface Guidelines chapter of this volume.

General Guidelines

The key to easy localization is to store region-dependent information used by your application as resources (rather than within the application's code). Text seen by the user can then be translated without modifying the code. In addition, storing such information in resources means that your application can be adapted for a different area of the world simply by substituting the appropriate resources. Make sure that at least the following kinds of information are stored in resources:

- all text, including special characters and delimiters
- menus and keyboard equivalents for menu commands (if available)
- character, word, phrase, and text translation tables
- address formats, including zip codes and telephone numbers

When you create resources for your applications, remember the following key points:

- text needs room to grow (up, down, and sideways)
  - translated text is often 50 percent larger than the U.S. English text
  - diacritical marks, widely used outside the United States, may extend up to the ascent line
  - some system fonts contain characters that extend to *both* the ascent and descent lines
- potential grammatical problems may arise from error messages, "natural" programming language structures, and so forth
- text location within a window should be easy to change

Localizing With the Toolbox

In addition to these general guidelines, you need to be aware of a host of other localization issues, such as differences in script systems and measurement systems. The User Interface Toolbox in system software version 7.0 contains updated versions of several packages and managers that you can use to facilitate localization of your applications—TextEdit, the International Utilities Package, and the Script Manager.

Perhaps the most important localization tool is the Script Manager, which contains routines that allow your application to function correctly with non-Roman scripts (writing systems). The Script Manager furnishes a standard interface that allows installation of different script systems, maintains global data structures, supports switching keyboards between different scripts, and provides a central dispatcher that gives your application access to script systems. It also contains utilities for text processing and parsing, which are useful for applications that do a lot of text manipulation. The Script Manager provides easy ways to translate your application into another writing system and to coordinate with the International Utilities Package.

The International Utilities Package provides routines for dealing with sorting, currency, measurement systems, and date and time formatting. These tend to vary in some degree from script to script, language to language, and region to region, and your application should take advantage of the Macintosh Operating System's ability to present this information in the correct format based on the current script. It is important that you use the routines in this package rather than the Operating System Utility routines such as UprString (documented in Volume II); the Operating System Utility routines do not handle diacritical marks and (because they are used by the File Manager) cannot be localized for different countries.

TextEdit provides routines that handle basic text formatting and editing capabilities, such as inserting new text or scrolling text within a window. The versions of TextEdit included in system software versions 6.0.4 and later contain new features that allow them to work with different scripts. For example, TextEdit takes advantage of the Script Manager's handling of double-byte characters to display scripts (such as Kanji) with improved accuracy and consistency.

For more information about the enhanced versions of TextEdit, see the TextEdit chapter in this volume. For complete information on both the International Utilities Package and the Script Manager, see the Worldwide Software Overview chapter.

RUNNING MACINTOSH PROGRAMS UNDER A/UX

A/UX is Apple's version of the UNIX operating system, which provides a multitasking and multi-user environment in which users can run applications. One of the most distinctive features of A/UX in comparison with other implementations of the UNIX operating system is its ability to run conforming Macintosh applications. Within limits described later in this section, applications developed for the Macintosh Operating System using the standard Macintosh User Interface Toolbox routines will execute under A/UX.

The ability to run Macintosh applications under A/UX is provided by enhancements to the A/UX kernel and by a library of functions known as the A/UX Toolbox. The **A/UX Toolbox** is a library of routines that enables a program running under A/UX to call Macintosh Toolbox routines and native Macintosh Operating System routines. The A/UX Toolbox provides a bridge between the Macintosh and A/UX environments, giving you two kinds of code compatibility:

- You can execute Macintosh binary code (applications compiled in the Macintosh environment) under A/UX, within the current limitations of the A/UX Toolbox.
- You can write common source code that can be separately built (that is, compiled and linked) into executable code for both environments.

The A/UX Toolbox operates transparently to the user and to applications. This means that (subject once again to qualifications detailed later) your applications developed for the Macintosh Operating System should execute under the A/UX operating system.

This section briefly explains how the A/UX Toolbox works and then provides details on writing Macintosh applications that execute under the A/UX operating system. A/UX provides such a high level of compatibility with Macintosh applications that your existing application may very well run under A/UX with no changes whatsoever. In general, if your application conforms to the interfaces documented in *Inside Macintosh,* is MultiFinder-aware, does not rely on low-memory global variables, and heeds the various guidelines presented in "About Compatibility" earlier in this chapter, it should operate under A/UX.

How the A/UX Toolbox Works

The primary function of the A/UX Toolbox is to make available to programs running under A/UX the standard Macintosh support code described in *Inside Macintosh*. Most of the support code consists of routines built into the Macintosh ROM.

The ROM routines fall into two categories, User Interface Toolbox routines and Macintosh Operating System routines. The A/UX Toolbox uses one of two strategies for supporting a call to a Macintosh ROM routine, depending on whether the call is to the User Interface Toolbox or to the native Macintosh Operating System.

When an A/UX Toolbox application calls one of the Macintosh User Interface Toolbox routines, the A/UX Toolbox intercepts the call and, if necessary, translates the parameters into a form usable by the ROM. After the A/UX Toolbox performs the translation, it invokes the ROM code that would be used in the native Macintosh environment.

When an A/UX Toolbox application calls one of the Macintosh Operating System routines, the A/UX Toolbox diverts the call to a substitute routine in its own library. The A/UX Toolbox Operating System routines call the standard A/UX libraries to perform the A/UX equivalents of the Macintosh Operating System functions. The Macintosh Operating System ROM code is never used under A/UX. Note that some of the built-in User Interface Toolbox routines generate calls to the Macintosh Operating System routines; these calls are also intercepted by the A/UX Toolbox and diverted to routines in its own library.

Figure 3-10 illustrates how the two elements of the A/UX Toolbox library interact with the application and the ROM code.

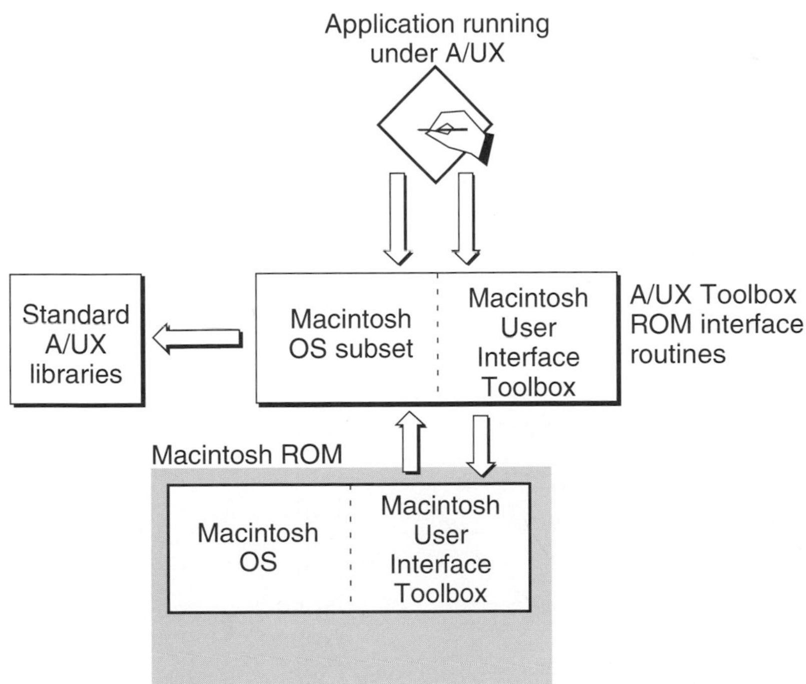

Figure 3-10. Interactions among an application, the A/UX Toolbox, and ROM code

Using the A/UX Toolbox

The primary limitation on Macintosh applications running under A/UX is that the A/UX Toolbox does not currently support all managers and drivers. Table 3-1 summarizes the status of various ROM libraries in A/UX Release 2.0. Note that "Full" support for a manager or driver means that the version of that manager released with system software 6.0.5 is available. In particular, there is currently no support under A/UX for any of the new features introduced in system software version 7.0.

Table 3-1. Status of User Interface Toolbox and Macintosh Operating System libraries in the A/UX Toolbox

ROM library	Implementation
Alias Manager	None
Apple Desktop Bus™	None
AppleTalk Manager	Full
Binary-Decimal Conversion Package	Full
Color Manager	Full
Color Picker Package	Full
Color QuickDraw	Full
Control Manager	Full
Data Access Manager	None
Deferred Task Manager	None
Desk Manager	Full
Device Manager	Full
Dialog Manager	Full
Disk Driver	Full
Disk Initialization Package	Full
Edition Manager	None
Event Manager, Operating System	Partial
Event Manager, Toolbox	Full*
File Manager	Full
Floating-Point Arithmetic and Transcendental Functions Packages	Full*
Font Manager	Full
Gestalt Manager	Full
Help Manager	None
International Utilities Package	Full
List Manager	Full
Memory Manager	Full
Menu Manager	Full
Notification Manager	Full
Package Manager	Full
Palette Manager	Full
Power Manager	None
PPC Toolbox	None
Printing Manager	Full
QuickDraw	Full
Resource Manager	Full
Scrap Manager	Full
Script Manager	Full
SCSI Manager	None

Table 3-1. Status of User Interface Toolbox and Macintosh Operating System libraries in the A/UX Toolbox (Continued)

ROM library	Implementation
Segment Loader	Partial
Serial Driver	Full
Shutdown Manager	Full*
Slot Manager	Full
Sound Manager	Full
Standard File Package	Full
Startup Manager	Full
System Error Handler	Full*
TextEdit	Full
Time Manager	Full*
Utilities, Operating System	Partial
Utilities, Toolbox	Full
Vertical Retrace Manager	Partial
Window Manager	Full

Note: When A/UX implements a particular manager or driver, the version of that manager or driver may not be the same as the version available in the Macintosh Operating System. This means that, whenever possible, you should use Gestalt to check for the existence of the particular features your application needs. In managers or drivers marked with an asterisk (*), all routines are implemented under A/UX, but the behavior is not identical to that in the Macintosh Operating System. See the publication *A/UX Toolbox: Macintosh ROM Interface* for complete details on the implementation of these managers and drivers.

A/UX Compatibility Guidelines

The A/UX Toolbox has been designed to allow as many Macintosh applications as possible to execute under the A/UX operating system. Because of profound differences between the two environments, however, it is possible that some applications may not execute correctly under A/UX. By following these guidelines, you can help ensure that your Macintosh applications run under A/UX.

- Make certain that your application is MultiFinder-friendly. MultiFinder is a standard part of A/UX, just as it is in system software version 7.0 (where the Finder™ and the Process Manager provide the cooperative multitasking environment). Your application should include a 'SIZE' resource and call the WaitNextEvent function in its main event loop. Note that the version of MultiFinder included with A/UX Release 2.0 is functionally equivalent to the version of MultiFinder released with system software version 6.0.5, but it has been customized for use under A/UX.

- Always use the available managers and drivers to manipulate hardware devices. In the Macintosh Operating System, individual processes and the various libraries can have much more control over the system than under A/UX, where the kernel manages all interaction between processes and the underlying hardware. In particular, do not attempt to read data from or write data to any of the memory-mapped hardware available on a Macintosh computer.

- Avoid relying on the low-memory global variables. Not all of them are available under A/UX.
- Make certain that your application is 32-bit clean (that is, it operates in an environment where all 32 bits of a handle or pointer are significant in determining memory addresses).
- Use the Gestalt Manager to determine which versions of managers and drivers are present in the current operating environment before relying on features that are not common to all released versions. Generally, the versions of managers available under A/UX Release 2.0 are the same as those versions included in Macintosh system software version 6.0.5.

Finally, your application should conform to the programming interfaces described in *Inside Macintosh* and should follow the basic compatibility guidelines presented in "About Compatibility" earlier in this chapter. For further details on running Macintosh applications under A/UX, see *A/UX Toolbox: Macintosh ROM Interface.*

ABOUT THE GESTALT MANAGER

The Macintosh family of computers includes many models of computers, and it is likely to grow in the future. Macintosh software runs on a number of different processors, some of which are accompanied by floating-point coprocessors or memory management units. In addition, the installed versions of the system software, drivers, and QuickDraw routines may vary from machine to machine. To ensure that your applications are maximally compatible with existing and future versions of the Macintosh, you should keep references to specific software and hardware features to a minimum.

In general, applications should communicate with the system software and hardware through the available managers and device drivers. If, however, it is necessary or useful for your applications to take advantage of software or hardware components that may not be present on all Macintosh computers, then you need some method of determining whether those components are available. The Gestalt Manager serves this need by allowing you to get information about the operating environment in a simple and efficient manner.

System software version 7.0 introduces several new managers and makes significant changes to many existing managers. To take advantage of new version 7.0 features, and to run on as many machines as possible, it is more important than ever before that your application determine the software and hardware components available in a particular operating environment. To help you develop software for the entire line of Macintosh computers, system software version 7.0 includes the Gestalt Manager. This manager includes the Gestalt function, which is a replacement for both the Environs procedure and the SysEnvirons function. The Gestalt function gives your application the ability to determine information about a large number of machine-dependent features. You can use the Gestalt function to find the following sorts of information about the hardware configuration and operating environment of the machine your application is executing on:

- the type of machine
- the version of the System file currently running

- the type of CPU
- the type of keyboard attached to the machine
- the type of floating-point processing unit (FPU), if any
- the type of MMU, if any
- the size of available RAM
- the amount of available virtual memory
- the versions of various drivers and managers
- the features of various drivers and managers
- the version of QuickDraw currently present
- whether the A/UX operating system is running or not

How your application uses the resulting information depends on what your application needs to accomplish. For example, in a case where critical hardware features are not available, your application might display an alert box to notify the user that the required hardware is missing and then terminate. Or if your application has determined that Color QuickDraw is available, it could execute alternate code to take advantage of the expanded capabilities of that software.

Associated with the Gestalt function are two other functions—one that allows an application to register new features with Gestalt and another that allows an application to change the function used by Gestalt to retrieve a particular piece of information. These two functions make it easy for your application to announce its presence to other applications, in case they wish to alter their actions in view of the presence of your application. For example, a macro utility that intercepts sequences of keyboard presses and translates them into other sequences can register itself with Gestalt at system initialization time; afterward, other applications can call Gestalt to determine if that utility is present. In this way, Gestalt can act as a central clearinghouse for information on the available hardware and software features of the operating environment, including any third-party applications that register themselves with Gestalt. Gestalt therefore provides a further means of cooperation and awareness among applications executing in the version 7.0 environment.

Although the Gestalt function can provide your application with most of the basic information it needs about particular software or hardware features, you may still need to call other routines to determine more specific features. For example, if you need to determine the resolution of the main Macintosh screen, you can use the Toolbox Utility procedure ScreenRes. (See the Toolbox Utilities chapter of *Inside Macintosh,* Volume I, for a description of this procedure.)

The Gestalt function replaces both the Environs procedure and the current implementation of the SysEnvirons function as the standard means of determining specific aspects of the operating environment. The Gestalt function is simpler to use and provides more information than either of those routines. Applications that use SysEnvirons still execute correctly in system software version 7.0 (the SysEnvirons function calls the Gestalt function).

Use of the Environs procedure is no longer recommended because it encourages you to think in terms of ROM versions, not in term of features that may be available. The Gestalt Manager can also provide information such as ROM version and size, but you should not write applications that infer the presence of particular software or hardware features on the basis of that information. When you need to know whether a particular feature is present, you should request information about it directly, using the appropriate Gestalt selector.

Although you can still call the SysEnvirons function, the Gestalt Manager is simpler and more efficient, and is the recommended way to get information about the operating environment. SysEnvirons returns a system environment record containing nine different pieces of information. Gestalt returns only the information requested by use of a specific selector code parameter. In most cases, your application really needs only a part of what is contained in the system environment record. With Gestalt, your application can request only the information it needs.

USING THE GESTALT MANAGER

The Gestalt Manager includes three functions—Gestalt, NewGestalt, and ReplaceGestalt. You can use the Gestalt function to obtain information about software or hardware components available on the current machine. You can use NewGestalt to register new software modules (such as drivers and patches) with the Operating System. Use ReplaceGestalt to replace the function associated with a particular selector code by some other function.

Note: Most applications do not need to use either NewGestalt or ReplaceGestalt.

Determining Features of the Operating Environment

When your application needs information about a specific software or hardware feature that can be provided by the Gestalt function, your application can pass Gestalt a **selector code** (or **selector**) as one of the parameters. The selector code is simply an indication of what information your application currently needs. There are two types of selector codes—predefined selector codes that are always recognized by Gestalt, and application-defined selector codes that applications may register with Gestalt by calling the NewGestalt function.

If Gestalt can determine the requested information, it returns that information in its second parameter, known as the response parameter. If Gestalt cannot obtain the desired information, it returns a result code indicating the cause of the error; in that case, the value of the response parameter is undefined. You should *always* check the result code returned by Gestalt to make sure that the response parameter contains meaningful information.

Note: When passed one of the predefined selector codes, Gestalt does not move or purge memory and therefore may be called at any time, even at interrupt time. However, selector functions associated with application-defined selector codes may move or purge memory, and applications can alter Gestalt's predefined selector functions. As a result, it is safest to assume that Gestalt might always move or purge memory. The NewGestalt function may move memory and should not be called at interrupt time.

There are two types of predefined selector codes: codes that return information that your application can use to guide its actions (known as **environmental selectors**), and codes that provide information only and should never be used as an indication of some feature's existence (known as **informational selectors**).

It is particularly important that you understand the difference between environmental and informational selectors. The response returned by Gestalt when it is passed an informational selector is for your (or the user's) edification only and should *never* be used by your application as a means of determining whether some specific software or hardware feature is available. For example, you can use Gestalt to test for the version of the ROM installed on a particular machine, but you should never use this information to guide any of your application's actions. Routines you expect to be in ROM may actually be in RAM; hence, you cannot determine that some routine usually found in ROM is not present simply by looking at the ROM version. Also, routines contained in ROM may have been patched by the system at startup time, in which case the system might not have the features that you think it has on the basis of the reported ROM version. Similar remarks apply to other informational selectors such as ROM size, machine type, and System file version.

You can use the following environmental selectors to determine information about the operating environment.

```
CONST
     gestaltAddressingModeAttr   = 'addr'; {addressing mode attributes}
     gestaltAliasMgrAttr         = 'alis'; {Alias Mgr attributes}
     gestaltAppleEventsAttr      = 'evnt'; {Apple events attributes}
     gestaltAppleTalkVersion     = 'atlk'; {AppleTalk version}
     gestaltAUXVersion           = 'a/ux'; {A/UX version if present}
     gestaltConnMgrAttr          = 'conn'; {Connection Mgr attributes}
     gestaltCRMAttr              = 'crm '; {Comm Resource Mgr attrs}
     gestaltCTBVersion           = 'ctbv'; {Comm Toolbox version}
     gestaltDBAccessMgrAttr      = 'dbac'; {Data Access Mgr attrs}
     gestaltDITLExtAttr          = 'ditl'; {Dialog Mgr extensions}
     gestaltEasyAccessAttr       = 'easy'; {Easy Access attributes}
     gestaltEditionMgrAttr       = 'edtn'; {Edition Mgr attributes}
     gestaltExtToolboxTable      = 'xttt'; {Ext Toolbox trap table base}
     gestaltFindFolderAttr       = 'fold'; {FindFolder attributes}
     gestaltFontMgrAttr          = 'font'; {Font Mgr attributes}
     gestaltFPUType              = 'fpu '; {FPU type}
     gestaltFSAttr               = 'fs  '; {file-system attributes}
     gestaltFXfrMgrAttr          = 'fxfr'; {File Transfer Mgr attrs}
     gestaltHardwareAttr         = 'hdwr'; {hardware attributes}
     gestaltHelpMgrAttr          = 'help'; {Help Mgr attributes}
     gestaltKeyboardType         = 'kbd '; {keyboard type}
     gestaltLogicalPageSize      = 'pgsz'; {logical page size}
     gestaltLogicalRAMSize       = 'lram'; {logical RAM size}
     gestaltLowMemorySize        = 'lmem'; {low-memory area size}
     gestaltMiscAttr             = 'misc'; {miscellaneous attributes}
     gestaltMMUType              = 'mmu '; {MMU type}
     gestaltNotificationMgrAttr  = 'nmgr'; {Notification Mgr attrs}
     gestaltNuBusConnectors      = 'sltc'; {NuBus connector bitmap}
     gestaltOSAttr               = 'os  '; {O/S attributes}
     gestaltOSTable              = 'ostt'; {O/S trap table base}
```

```
       gestaltParityAttr          = 'prty'; {parity attributes}
       gestaltPhysicalRAMSize     = 'ram '; {physical RAM size}
       gestaltPopupAttr           = 'pop!'; {pop-up CDEF attributes}
       gestaltPowerMgrAttr        = 'powr'; {Power Mgr attributes}
       gestaltPPCToolboxAttr      = 'ppc '; {PPC Toolbox attributes}
       gestaltProcessorType       = 'proc'; {processor type}
       gestaltQuickdrawVersion    = 'qd  '; {QuickDraw version}
       gestaltResourceMgrAttr     = 'rsrc'; {Resource Mgr attributes}
       gestaltScriptCount         = 'scr#'; {# of active script systems}
       gestaltScriptMgrVersion    = 'scri'; {Script Mgr version}
       gestaltSerialAttr          = 'ser '; {serial hardware attributes}
       gestaltSoundAttr           = 'snd '; {sound attributes}
       gestaltStandardFileAttr    = 'stdf'; {Standard File attributes}
       gestaltStdNBPAttr          = 'nlup'; {StandardNBP attributes}
       gestaltTermMgrAttr         = 'term'; {Terminal Mgr attributes}
       gestaltTextEditVersion     = 'te  '; {TextEdit version}
       gestaltTimeMgrVersion      = 'tmgr'; {Time Mgr version}
       gestaltToolboxTable        = 'tbtt'; {Toolbox trap table base}
       gestaltVersion             = 'vers'; {Gestalt version}
       gestaltVMAttr              = 'vm  '; {virtual memory attributes}
```

The following informational selectors are provided for informational purposes only. You can display the information returned when using these selectors, but you should never use this information as an indication of what software features or hardware may be available.

```
CONST gestaltMachineIcon         = 'micn'; {machine ICON/cicn res ID}
      gestaltMachineType         = 'mach'; {machine type}
      gestaltROMSize             = 'rom '; {ROM size}
      gestaltROMVersion          = 'romv'; {ROM version}
      gestaltSystemVersion       = 'sysv'; {System file version}
```

"Interpreting Gestalt Responses" later in this chapter explains the exact meaning of each of these selectors and of the values returned by Gestalt in each case.

Determining Whether Gestalt Is Available

Because the Gestalt Manager currently exists only in system software versions 6.0.4 and later (and in ROM on the Macintosh IIci, the Macintosh Portable, and later machines), you should make certain that it is actually available before attempting to call it. You can do this by using the TrapAvailable function defined previously in "Determining Whether a Trap Is Available." Listing 3-2 uses that function to determine whether the Gestalt Manager is available.

Listing 3-2. Determining whether Gestalt is available

```
FUNCTION GestaltAvailable: Boolean;
CONST
   _Gestalt    =  $A1AD;
BEGIN
   GestaltAvailable := TrapAvailable(_Gestalt);
END;
```

Note: If you are using the MPW® development system version 3.2 or later, then you do not need to perform this check because that version provides glue routines that allow you to call Gestalt even if it is not in ROM or in the System file. However, if you are programming in assembly language, this glue is not provided (and you still need to check that Gestalt is available before calling it).

If you need to know at several different places in your application whether Gestalt is available, it may be more efficient to define a global Boolean variable that you can test before calling Gestalt. Listing 3-3 illustrates how to do this. Once again, this code uses the TrapAvailable function defined earlier.

Listing 3-3. Using Gestalt to determine the Time Manager version

```
VAR
   gHasGestalt:    Boolean; {true if Gestalt is implemented}

gHasGestalt := TrapAvailable(_Gestalt);
   .
   .
   .
IF gHasGestalt THEN BEGIN
   myErr := Gestalt(gestaltTimeMgrVersion, myFeature);
   IF myErr <> noErr THEN
      DoError(myErr);
END;
```

This sample code returns (in the myFeature parameter) the version of the Time Manager available on the current machine. Before using that information, however, you should test the result code to make sure that Gestalt was able to determine the requested information.

Interpreting Gestalt Responses

When your application calls Gestalt to get information about the operating environment, the meaning of the value that Gestalt returns in the response parameter depends on the selector code with which it was called. For example, if you call Gestalt using the gestaltTimeMgrVersion selector, it returns a version code in the low-order byte of the response parameter. In this case, a returned value of 3 indicates that the extended Time Manager is available.

In almost all cases, the last few characters in the selector's symbolic name form a suffix that indicates what type of value you can expect Gestalt to return in the response parameter. For example, if the final characters in a Gestalt selector are Size, then Gestalt returns a size in the response parameter. The following list shows the meaningful suffixes.

Suffix	Meaning
Attr	The returned value is a range of 32 bits, the meaning of which must be determined by comparison with a list of constants. Note that bit 0 is the least significant bit of the long word.

Suffix	Meaning
Count	The returned value is a number indicating how many of the indicated type of item exist.
Size	The returned value is a size. Sizes reported by Gestalt are usually in bytes.
Table	The returned value is the base address of a table.
Type	The returned value is an index describing a particular type of feature.
Version	The returned value is a version number. Implied decimal points may separate digits of the returned value. For example, a value of $0605 returned in response to the gestaltSystemVersion selector indicates that system software version 6.0.5 is present.

Selectors that have the suffix Attr deserve special attention; they cause Gestalt to return a bit field that your application must interpret in order to determine whether a desired feature is present. For example, the gestaltOSAttr selector requests information about a number of Operating System features. To determine whether a particular Operating System feature is available, you need to read the appropriate bit in the response parameter, as Listing 3-4 illustrates.

Listing 3-4. Interpreting a bit field response

```
VAR
   myBit:       Integer;
   myFeature:   LongInt;
   myErr:       Integer;

IF ghasGestalt THEN BEGIN
   myErr := Gestalt(gestaltOSAttr, myFeature);
   IF myErr <> noErr THEN
      DoError(myErr)
   ELSE BEGIN
      myBit := gestaltTempMemSupport;
      IF BitTst(@myFeature, 31-myBit) = TRUE THEN
         WriteLn('temporary memory support available')
      ELSE
         WriteLn('temporary memory support not available');
   END;
END;
```

This code uses the Toolbox utility function BitTst to determine whether the appropriate bit in Gestalt's response is set to 1. Notice that because bit numbering with BitTst is the opposite of the usual MC680x0 numbering scheme used by Gestalt, the bit to be tested must be subtracted from 31. Also, the first parameter to BitTst is a pointer to a byte; hence the use of the @ operator. Your development system may have other ways of testing the appropriate bit. For example, if you are using MPW, you could write the test like this:

```
IF BTst(myFeature, myBit) = TRUE THEN
```

Interpreting Responses to Environmental Selectors

Gestalt returns one of the following responses when passed a predefined environmental selector.

Selector	Meaning

gestaltAddressingModeAttr	Returns information about the current addressing mode.
	`CONST gestalt32BitAddressing = 0;`
	`gestalt32BitSysZone = 1;`
	`gestalt32BitCapable = 2;`
	The gestalt32BitAddressing attribute indicates that the machine started up with 32-bit addressing. The gestalt32BitSysZone attribute indicates that the system heap has 32-bit clean block headers (regardless of the type of addressing the machine started up in). See the Memory Management chapter for more information about 32-bit addressing.

gestaltAliasMgrAttr	Returns information about the Alias Manager. `CONST gestaltAliasMgrPresent = 0;`
gestaltAppleEventsAttr	Returns information about Apple events. `CONST gestaltAppleEventsPresent = 0;`
gestaltAppleTalkVersion	Returns the version number of the AppleTalk driver currently installed. In particular, it returns the version number of the .MPP driver. The version number is placed into the low-order byte of the result, so you should ignore the three high-order bytes of the result. If an AppleTalk driver is not currently open, the response parameter is 0. The driver does not open until the user requests a network service (for example, by running the Chooser).
gestaltAUXVersion	Returns the version of A/UX if it is currently executing. The result is placed into the lower word of the response parameter. If A/UX is not executing, Gestalt returns gestaltUnknownErr.

gestaltConnMgrAttr	Returns information about the Connection Manager.
	`CONST gestaltConnMgrPresent = 0;`
	`gestaltConnMgrCMSearchFix = 1;`
	The gestaltConnMgrCMSearchFix bit flag indicates whether a fix is present that allows the CMAddSearch routine to work over the mAttn channel.

Selector	Meaning
gestaltCRMAttr	Returns information about the Communications Resource Manager. `CONST gestaltCRMPresent = 0;`
gestaltCTBVersion	Returns the version number of the Communications Toolbox.
gestaltDBAccessMgrAttr	Returns information about the Data Access Manager. `CONST gestaltDBAccessMgrPresent = 0;`
gestaltDITLExtAttr	Returns information about the Dialog Manager. `CONST gestaltDITLExtPresent = 0;` If this flag bit is TRUE, then the Dialog Manager extensions are available. See "Manipulating Dialog Item Lists" earlier in this chapter for details about the Dialog Manager extensions included in system software version 7.0.

gestaltEasyAccessAttr	Returns information about the status of Easy Access.
	`CONST gestaltEasyAccessOff = 0;`
	`gestaltEasyAccessOn = 1;`
	`gestaltEasyAccessSticky = 2;`
	`gestaltEasyAccessLocked = 3;`

gestaltEditionMgrAttr	Returns information about the Edition Manager. `CONST gestaltEditionMgrPresent = 0;`
gestaltExtToolboxTable	Returns the base address of the extended Toolbox trap table.
gestaltFindFolderAttr	Returns information about the FindFolder function. `CONST gestaltFindFolderPresent = 0;`
gestaltFontMgrAttr	Returns information about the Font Manager. `CONST gestaltOutlineFonts = 0;`

gestaltFPUType	Returns a value that indicates the type of floating-point coprocessor currently installed, if any.
	`CONST gestaltNoFPU = 0;`
	`gestalt68881 = 1;`
	`gestalt68882 = 2;`

gestaltFSAttr	Returns information about the file system.
	`CONST gestaltFullExtFSDispatching = 0;`
	`gestaltHasFSSpecCalls = 1;`
	The bit gestaltFullExtFSDispatch indicates that all the routines selected through the _HFSDispatch macro are avialable to external file systems.

Selector	Meaning
gestaltFXfrMgrAttr	Returns information about the File Transfer Manager. `CONST gestaltFXfrMgrPresent = 0;`

gestaltHardwareAttr	Returns information about the hardware configuration of the machine.
	`CONST gestaltHasVIA1 = 0;`
	`gestaltHasVIA2 = 1;`
	`gestaltHasASC = 3;`
	`gestaltHasSCC = 4;`
	`gestaltHasSCSI = 7;`

gestaltHelpMgrAttr	Returns information about the Help Manager. `CONST gestaltHelpMgrPresent = 0;`

gestaltKeyboardType	Returns a value that indicates the type of keyboard that is currently attached to the system.
	`CONST gestaltMacKbd = 1;`
	`gestaltMacAndPad = 2;`
	`gestaltMacPlusKbd = 3;`
	`gestaltExtADBKbd = 4;`
	`gestaltStdADBKbd = 5;`
	`gestaltPrtblADBKbd = 6;`
	`gestaltPrtblISOKbd = 7;`
	`gestaltStdISOADBKbd = 8;`
	`gestaltExtISOADBKbd = 9;`
	`gestaltADBKbdII = 10;`
	`gestaltADBISOKbdII = 11;`
	If the Apple Desktop Bus is in use, there may be multiple keyboards or other ADB devices attached to the machine. Gestalt returns the type of the keyboard on which the last keystroke occurred.

gestaltLogicalPageSize	Returns the logical page size. This value is an unknown on 68000-based machines because such machines do not have logical pages. On those machines, Gestalt returns an error.
gestaltLogicalRAMSize	Returns the amount of logical memory available. This value is the same as that returned by gestaltPhysicalRAMSize when virtual memory is not installed. On some machines, however, this value might be less than the value returned by gestaltPhysicalRAMSize because some RAM may be used by the video display and the Operating System.
gestaltLowMemorySize	Returns the size (in bytes) of the low-memory area. The low-memory area is used for vectors, global variables, and dispatch tables.

Selector	Meaning
gestaltMiscAttr	Returns information about miscellaneous pieces of the Operating System or hardware configuration. `CONST gestaltScrollingThrottle = 0; gestaltSquareMenuBar = 2;`
gestaltMMUType	Returns a value that indicates the type of MMU currently installed, if any. `CONST gestaltNoMMU = 0; gestaltAMU = 1; gestalt68851 = 2; gestalt68030MMU = 3;`
gestaltNotificationMgrAttr	Returns information about the Notification Manager. `CONST gestaltNotificationPresent = 0;`
gestaltNuBusConnectors	Returns information about the NuBus™ slot connector locations. The value returned is a bitmap. For example, the value returned on a Macintosh II would have bits 9 through E set, indicating that 6 NuBus slots are present (having locations 9 through E).
gestaltOSAttr	Returns general information about the Operating System, such as whether temporary memory handles are real handles. The low-order bits of the response parameter are interpreted as bit flags. A flag is set to 1 to indicate that the corresponding feature is available. Currently, the following bits are significant: `CONST gestaltSysZoneGrowable = 0; gestaltLaunchCanReturn = 1; gestaltLaunchFullFileSpec = 2; gestaltLaunchControl = 3; gestaltTempMemSupport = 4; gestaltRealTempMemory = 5; gestaltTempMemTracked = 6; gestaltIPCSupport = 7; gestaltSysDebuggerSupport = 8;` See the Memory Management chapter in this volume for a full explanation of the temporary memory features, and see the Process Management chapter for a full explanation of the launch control features.
gestaltOSTable	Returns the base address of the Operating System trap table.
gestaltParityAttr	Returns information about the parity-checking abilities of the machine. `CONST gestaltHasParityCapability = 0; gestaltParityEnabled = 1;` Note that parity is not considered to be enabled unless *all* installed memory is parity RAM.

Selector	Meaning
gestaltPhysicalRAMSize	Returns the number of bytes of physical RAM currently installed.
gestaltPopupAttr	Returns information about the pop-up control definition. `CONST gestaltPopupPresent = 0;` If the gestaltPopupPresent bit is set, the version 7.0 pop-up control definition procedure is present. See "Creating Pop-Up Menus" earlier in this chapter for details about creating pop-up menus.

gestaltPowerMgrAttr	Returns information about the Power Manager, if present.
	`CONST gestaltPMgrExists = 0;`
	`gestaltPMgrCPUIdle = 1;`
	`gestaltPMgrSCC = 2;`
	`gestaltPMgrSound = 3;`

gestaltPPCToolboxAttr	Returns information about the capabilities of the PPC Toolbox. `CONST gestaltPPCToolboxPresent = 0;`

gestaltProcessorType	Returns a value that indicates the type of processor that is currently running.
	`CONST gestalt68000 = 1;`
	`gestalt68010 = 2;`
	`gestalt68020 = 3;`
	`gestalt68030 = 4;`

gestaltQuickdrawVersion	Returns a 2-byte value indicating the version of QuickDraw currently present. The high-order byte of that number represents the major revision number, and the low-order byte represents the minor revision number. For example, the Macintosh IIci contains QuickDraw version 2.01 in ROM; on that machine, Gestalt returns the value $0201.
	`CONST gestaltOriginalQD = $000;`
	`gestaltOriginalQD1 = $001;`
	`gestalt8BitQD = $100;`
	`gestalt32BitQD = $200;`
	`gestalt32BitQD11 = $210;`
	`gestalt32BitQD12 = $220;`
	`gestalt32BitQD13 = $230;`
	Values having a major revision number of 1 or 2 indicate that Color QuickDraw is available, in either the 8-bit or 32-bit version. These results do not, however, indicate whether a color monitor is attached to the system. You need to use high-level QuickDraw routines to obtain that information.

Selector	**Meaning**
gestaltResourceMgrAttr	Returns information about the capabilities of the Resource Manager. `CONST gestaltPartialRsrcs = 0;`
gestaltScriptCount	Returns the number of script systems currently active.
gestaltScriptMgrVersion	Returns the version number of the Script Manager.

gestaltSerialAttr	Returns information about the serial hardware of the machine (such as whether or not the GPIa line is connected and can be used for external clocking).
	`CONST gestaltGPIaToDCDa = 0;`
	`gestaltGPIaToRTxCa = 1;`
	`gestaltGPIaToDCDb = 2;`

gestaltSoundAttr	Returns information about the sound capabilities of the machine.
	`CONST gestaltStereoCapability = 0;`
	`gestaltStereoMixing = 1;`
	`gestaltSoundIOMgrPresent = 3;`
	`gestaltBuiltInSoundInput = 4;`
	`gestaltHasSoundInputDevice = 5;`
	If the bit gestaltStereoCapability is TRUE, the available hardware can play stereo sounds. The bit gestaltStereoMixing indicates that the sound hardware of the machine mixes both left and right channels of stereo sound into a single audio signal for the internal speaker. The gestaltSoundIOMgrPresent bit indicates that the new sound input routines are available, and the gestaltBuiltInSoundInput bit indicates that a built-in sound input device is available. The gestaltHasSoundInputDevice bit indicates that some sound input device is available.

gestaltStandardFileAttr	Returns information about the Standard File Package. `CONST gestaltStandardFile58 = 0;` If this flag bit is set to 1, you can call the four new procedures StandardPutFile, StandardGetFile, CustomPutFile, and CustomGetFile. (The name of the constant reflects the enabling of selectors 5–8 on the trap macro that handles the Standard File Package.)
gestaltStdNBPAttr	Returns information about the call StandardNBP (Name-Binding Protocol). `CONST gestaltStdNBPPresent = 0;`
gestaltTermMgrAttr	Returns information about the Terminal Manager. `CONST gestaltTermMgrPresent = 0;`

Selector	Meaning
gestaltTextEditVersion	Returns a value that indicates which version of TextEdit is present.

```
CONST gestaltTE1 = 1;
      gestaltTE2 = 2;
      gestaltTE3 = 3;
      gestaltTE4 = 4;
      gestaltTE5 = 5;
```

See the TextEdit chapter in this volume for further information on the capabilities of the enhanced versions of TextEdit.

gestaltTimeMgrVersion	Returns a value that indicates the version of the Time Manager that is present.

```
CONST gestaltStandardTimeMgr = 1;
      gestaltRevisedTimeMgr  = 2;
      gestaltExtendedTimeMgr = 3;
```

See the Time Manager chapter in this volume for a complete explanation of the capabilities of each of these three versions.

gestaltToolboxTable	Returns the base address of the Toolbox trap table.
gestaltVersion	Returns the version of Gestalt. The current version is 1, corresponding to a returned value of $0001.
gestaltVMAttr	Returns information about virtual memory.

```
CONST gestaltVMPresent = 0;
```

Interpreting Responses to Informational Selectors

Gestalt returns the following responses when passed a predefined informational selector.

▲ **Warning:** Never infer the existence of certain hardware or software features from the responses that Gestalt returns to your application when you pass it these selectors. ▲

Selector	Meaning
gestaltMachineIcon	Returns an icon family resource ID for the current type of Macintosh.
gestaltMachineType	Returns one of the following values, indicating the type of machine on which the application is currently running.

```
CONST gestaltClassic    = 1;    {Macintosh 128K}
      gestaltMacXL      = 2;    {Macintosh XL}
      gestaltMac512KE   = 3;    {Macintosh 512KE}
      gestaltMacPlus    = 4;    {Macintosh Plus}
```

Selector	**Meaning**
gestaltMachineType *(continued)*	

```
gestaltMacSE       = 5;    {Macintosh SE}
gestaltMacII       = 6;    {Macintosh II}
gestaltMacIIx      = 7;    {Macintosh IIx}
gestaltMacIIcx     = 8;    {Macintosh IIcx}
gestaltMacSE030    = 9;    {Macintosh SE/30}
gestaltPortable    = 10;   {Macintosh Portable}
gestaltMacIIci     = 11;   {Macintosh IIci}
gestaltMacIIfx     = 13;   {Macintosh IIfx}
gestaltMacClassic  = 17;   {Macintosh Classic}
gestaltMacIIsi     = 18;   {Macintosh IIsi}
gestaltMacLC       = 19;   {Macintosh LC}
```

To obtain a string containing the machine's name, you can pass the returned value to GetIndString as an index into the resource of type 'STR#' in the System file having resource ID defined by the constant kMachineNameStrID.

```
CONST kMachineNameStrID = -16395;
```

gestaltROMSize	Returns the size of the installed ROM. The value is returned in a word.
gestaltROMVersion	Returns the version number of the installed ROM.
gestaltSystemVersion	Returns the version number of the currently active System file. This number is represented as two byte-long numbers. For example, if your application is running in version 6.0.4, then Gestalt returns the value $0604. You should ignore the high-order word of the returned value.

Adding Gestalt Selectors

You can add a new selector code to those already understood by Gestalt by calling the NewGestalt function. The NewGestalt function requires two parameters. The first parameter is the new selector to be registered. The second parameter is the address of a **selector function.** Gestalt executes the selector function when it needs to determine what value to pass back when it is called after the new selector code.

The selector code is a four-character sequence of type OSType. For example, Carl's Object-Oriented Linker might register itself using the selector code 'COOL'. If you have registered a creator string with Apple, you are strongly encouraged to use that sequence as your selector code.

Note: Apple reserves for its own use all four-character sequences consisting solely of lowercase letters and nonalphabetic ASCII characters.

The selector function whose address you specify when registering a new Gestalt selector code can be any function that resides in the system heap and whose calling syntax conforms to that defined in "Specifying Gestalt Selector Functions" later in this chapter. Listing 3-5 illustrates how to install a simple function into the system heap and pass its address to NewGestalt.

Listing 3-5. Installing a selector function into the system heap

```
PROGRAM NewGestaltSample;
USES
   Memtypes, OSIntf, ToolIntf,      {standard includes}
   PasLibIntf,                      {for standard I/O, etc.}
   GestaltEqu,                      {for Gestalt}
   Traps;                           {for trap numbers}
CONST
   mySelector        = 'COOL';      {Gestalt function selector}
   gstFuncRsrcType   = 'GDEF';      {Gestalt function resource type}
   gstFuncRsrcID     = 128;         {Gestalt function resource ID}
VAR
   gestaltErr:       OSErr;         {error returned by Gestalt}
   gstFuncHandle:    Handle;        {handle to Gestalt function}
   oldGestaltFunc:   ProcPtr;       {pointer to old function}
BEGIN
   {first make sure that Gestalt is available}
   IF NOT TrapAvailable(_Gestalt) THEN
      BEGIN
         WriteLn('Gestalt is not implemented.');
         IEexit(1)
      END;
   {load Gestalt function resource into system heap}
   gstFuncHandle := GetResource(gstFuncRsrcType, gstFuncRsrcID);
   IF gstFuncHandle = NIL THEN
      BEGIN
         WriteLn('Could not load Gestalt function resource.');
         IEexit(1)
      END;
   {detach it from the resource map so it stays around}
   DetachResource(gstFuncHandle);
   {add the new selector; first assume that it doesn't already exist}
   gestaltErr := NewGestalt(mySelector, ProcPtr(gstFuncHandle^));
   IF gestaltErr <> noErr THEN
      BEGIN
         WriteLn('Could not add as a new selector.');
         {try to replace existing selector}
         gestaltErr := ReplaceGestalt(mySelector,
            ProcPtr(gstFuncHandle^), oldGestaltFunc);
         IF gestaltErr <> noErr THEN
         BEGIN
            WriteLn('Could not replace selector either.');
            IEexit(1);
         END;
      END;
   WriteLn('Selector installed.');
   DisposHandle(gstFuncHandle);
END.
```

You can ensure that the new Gestalt selector function is installed into the system heap by defining it as a resource (in this case, of type 'GDEF') whose resource attributes are resSysHeap and resLocked (in other words, lock the resource into the system heap). The following linking instructions illustrate one way to accomplish this:

```
Link GestaltFunc.p.o -rn -ra =resSysHeap,resLocked -rt GDEF=128
            -o NewGestaltSample
```

If you are not using MPW, you can set the resource attributes by using ResEdit.

Listing 3-6 shows the actual function definition, contained in the file GestaltFunc.p.

Listing 3-6. Defining a new Gestalt function

```
UNIT GestaltFunc;
INTERFACE
   USES
      GestaltEqu;                         {for Gestalt}
   CONST
      myResult = $87654321;               {Gestalt function response}
   FUNCTION gestaltCool (gestaltSelector: OSType;
                         VAR gestaltResponse: LongInt) : OSErr;

IMPLEMENTATION
   FUNCTION gestaltCool;
      BEGIN
         gestaltResponse := myResult;     {return response}
         gestaltCool := noErr;            {return no error}
      END;
END.
```

Because the new selector function resides in the system heap, Gestalt recognizes and responds to the new selector until the machines restarts, even if your application terminates before that time. As a result, you might want your selector function to determine whether your application is still running before returning a value to Gestalt. If your application has terminated, the selector function should return an error.

Note that if you try to register a selector that has already been registered with Gestalt, an error results.

Modifying Gestalt Selectors

You can use the ReplaceGestalt function to modify the function that Gestalt executes when passed a particular selector code. As with the function whose address is passed to NewGestalt, the new function must reside in the system heap and have a calling syntax that conforms to that defined in the following section, "Specifying Gestalt Selector Functions." Listing 3-5 illustrates how to replace a Gestalt selector function.

To allow the new function to call the function previously associated with the selector in question, the ReplaceGestalt function returns the address of the previous function.

If you attempt to redefine a selector that is not yet defined, an error is returned; in that case, the address of the previous function is undefined. Accordingly, you should always test the result code of ReplaceGestalt before calling Gestalt with the selector in question.

> **Note:** If you modify the function associated with a predefined Gestalt selector, do not use any bits in the response parameter that are not documented in this chapter. Apple reserves all undocumented bits in the response parameter returned by predefined Gestalt selectors.

Specifying Gestalt Selector Functions

When you call the NewGestalt and ReplaceGestalt functions, you need to supply the address of a selector function that is called when some application passes the specified new or replacement selector to Gestalt. This selector function should have the following syntax and must reside in the system heap.

```
FUNCTION mySelectorFunction (selector: OSType; VAR response: LongInt) :
                             OSErr;
```

When you pass the new or replacement selector to Gestalt, Gestalt calls the specified selector function to determine the information that Gestalt should pass back to the calling software. Your function should place the result into the long integer pointed to by the response parameter and should return the result code that Gestalt will return. This function should be as simple as possible and cannot use global variables in the A5 world unless A5 is set up explicitly and then restored upon exit. (See the Memory Management chapter in this volume for an explanation of setting up and restoring the A5 world.)

Your selector function can, if necessary, call Gestalt and pass it other selector codes. Note that the response variable parameter is the address into which your function should place the information requested. You cannot depend on that address containing useful information when your selector function is called.

GESTALT MANAGER ROUTINES

This section describes the three functions in the Gestalt Manager—Gestalt, NewGestalt, and ReplaceGestalt. They allow you, respectively, to determine what hardware and software features are present in the operating environment, to add new selectors to those understood by the Gestalt function, and to replace the functions associated with known selectors.

Getting Information About the Operating Environment

Use the Gestalt function to obtain information about the operating environment. The information you need is indicated by the selector parameter, which Gestalt must already recognize.

```
FUNCTION Gestalt (selector: OSType; VAR response: LongInt) : OSErr;
```

Trap macro	_Gestalt
On entry	D0: selector code
On exit	A0: response
	D0: result code

Upon successful completion of the function, the response parameter contains the information requested. Note that Gestalt returns the response from all function selectors in a long integer, occupying 4 bytes. In some cases, not all 4 bytes are needed to hold the returned information, in which case Gestalt places the information in the low-order bytes of the response parameter.

Note: Although the response parameter is declared as a variable parameter, you cannot use it to pass information to Gestalt or to a Gestalt selector function. Gestalt interprets the response parameter as an address into which it is to place the result returned by the selector function specified by the selector parameter. Gestalt ignores any information already located at that address.

Result codes

noErr	0	No error
gestaltUnknownErr	–5550	Could not obtain the response
gestaltUndefSelectorErr	–5551	Undefined selector

Adding Selector Codes

Use the NewGestalt function to add selector codes to those already recognized by Gestalt.

```
FUNCTION NewGestalt (selector: OSType; selectorFunction: ProcPtr) :
                     OSErr;
```

Trap macro	_NewGestalt
On entry	A0: address of new selector function
	D0: selector code
On exit	D0: result code

NewGestalt takes as parameters the selector to be registered and the function that Gestalt calls when it receives this selector. The interface for the selectorFunction function is defined in "Specifying Gestalt Selector Functions" earlier in this chapter.

Result codes

noErr	0	No error
memFullErr	–108	Ran out of memory
gestaltDupSelectorErr	–5552	Selector already exists
gestaltLocationErr	–5553	Function not in system heap

Modifying Selector Codes

The ReplaceGestalt function allows an application to replace the function that is currently associated with a selector.

```
FUNCTION ReplaceGestalt (selector: OSType; selectorFunction: ProcPtr;
                         VAR oldGestaltFunction: ProcPtr) : OSErr;
```

Trap macro	_ReplaceGestalt
On entry	A0: address of new selector function
	D0: selector code
On exit	A0: address of old selector function
	D0: result code

The interface for the selectorFunction function is defined in "Specifying Gestalt Selector Functions" earlier in this chapter. The new function must reside in the system heap and may want to call the function previously associated with the named selector. It may do so by using the address returned in the parameter oldGestaltFunction. If ReplaceGestalt returns an error of any type, then the value of oldGestaltFunction is undefined.

Result codes

noErr	0	No error
gestaltUndefSelectorErr	–5551	Undefined selector
gestaltLocationErr	–5553	Function not in system heap

SUMMARY OF THE GESTALT MANAGER

Constants

```
CONST {environmental selector codes}
      gestaltAddressingModeAttr     = 'addr'; {addressing mode attributes}
      gestaltAliasMgrAttr           = 'alis'; {Alias Mgr attributes}
      gestaltAppleEventsAttr        = 'evnt'; {Apple events attributes}
      gestaltAppleTalkVersion       = 'atlk'; {AppleTalk version}
      gestaltAUXVersion             = 'a/ux'; {A/UX version if present}
      gestaltConnMgrAttr            = 'conn'; {Connection Mgr attributes}
      gestaltCRMAttr                = 'crm '; {Comm Resource Mgr attrs}
      gestaltCTBVersion             = 'ctbv'; {Comm Toolbox version}
      gestaltDBAccessMgrAttr        = 'dbac'; {Data Access Mgr attrs}
      gestaltDITLExtAttr            = 'ditl'; {Dialog Mgr extensions}
      gestaltEasyAccessAttr         = 'easy'; {Easy Access attributes}
      gestaltEditionMgrAttr         = 'edtn'; {Edition Mgr attributes}
      gestaltExtToolboxTable        = 'xttt'; {Ext Toolbox trap table base}
      gestaltFindFolderAttr         = 'fold'; {FindFolder attributes}
      gestaltFontMgrAttr            = 'font'; {Font Mgr attributes}
      gestaltFPUType                = 'fpu '; {FPU type}
      gestaltFSAttr                 = 'fs  '; {file-system attributes}
      gestaltFXfrMgrAttr            = 'fxfr'; {File Transfer Mgr attrs}
      gestaltHardwareAttr           = 'hdwr'; {hardware attributes}
      gestaltHelpMgrAttr            = 'help'; {Help Mgr attributes}
      gestaltKeyboardType           = 'kbd '; {keyboard type}
      gestaltLogicalPageSize        = 'pgsz'; {logical page size}
      gestaltLogicalRAMSize         = 'lram'; {logical RAM size}
      gestaltLowMemorySize          = 'lmem'; {low-memory area size}
      gestaltMiscAttr               = 'misc'; {miscellaneous attributes}
      gestaltMMUType                = 'mmu '; {MMU type}
      gestaltNotificationMgrAttr    = 'nmgr'; {Notification Mgr attrs}
      gestaltNuBusConnectors        = 'sltc'; {NuBus connector bitmap}
      gestaltOSAttr                 = 'os  '; {O/S attributes}
      gestaltOSTable                = 'ostt'; {O/S trap table base}
      gestaltParityAttr             = 'prty'; {parity attributes}
      gestaltPhysicalRAMSize        = 'ram '; {physical RAM size}
      gestaltPopupAttr              = 'pop!'; {popup CDEF attributes}
      gestaltPowerMgrAttr           = 'powr'; {Power Mgr attributes}
      gestaltPPCToolboxAttr         = 'ppc '; {PPC Toolbox attributes}
      gestaltProcessorType          = 'proc'; {processor type}
      gestaltQuickdrawVersion       = 'qd  '; {QuickDraw version}
      gestaltResourceMgrAttr        = 'rsrc'; {Resource Mgr attributes}
      gestaltScriptCount            = 'scr#'; {# of active script systems}
      gestaltScriptMgrVersion       = 'scri'; {Script Mgr version}
      gestaltSerialAttr             = 'ser '; {serial hardware attributes}
      gestaltSoundAttr              = 'snd '; {sound attributes}
      gestaltStandardFileAttr       = 'stdf'; {Standard File attributes}
      gestaltStdNBPAttr             = 'nlup'; {StandardNBP attributes}
```

```
gestaltTermMgrAttr          = 'term'; {Terminal Mgr attributes}
gestaltTextEditVersion      = 'te  '; {TextEdit version}
gestaltTimeMgrVersion       = 'tmgr'; {Time Mgr version}
gestaltToolboxTable         = 'tbtt'; {Toolbox trap table base}
gestaltVersion              = 'vers'; {Gestalt version}
gestaltVMAttr               = 'vm  '; {virtual memory attributes}

{informational selector codes}
gestaltMachineIcon     = 'micn';  {machine ICON/cicn res ID}
gestaltMachineType     = 'mach';  {machine type}
gestaltROMSize         = 'rom ';  {ROM size}
gestaltROMVersion      = 'romv';  {ROM version}
gestaltSystemVersion   = 'sysv';  {System file version}

{gestaltAddressingModeAttr response values}
gestalt32BitAddressing = 0;    {TRUE if booted in 32-bit mode}
gestalt32BitSysZone    = 1;    {32-bit compatible system zone}
gestalt32BitCapable    = 2;    {machine is 32-bit capable}

{gestaltAliasMgrAttr response values}
gestaltAliasMgrPresent = 0;    {TRUE if Alias Mgr is present}

{gestaltAppleEventsAttr response values}
gestaltAppleEventsPresent   = 0;    {TRUE if Apple events present}

{gestaltConnMgrAttr response values}
gestaltConnMgrPresent       = 0;    {TRUE if Connection Mgr present}
gestaltConnMgrCMSearchFix   = 1;    {TRUE if CMAddSearch fix present}

{gestaltCRMAttr response values}
gestaltCRMPresent    = 0;    {TRUE if Comm Resource Mgr present}

{gestaltDBAccessMgrAttr response values}
gestaltDBAccessMgrPresent   = 0;  {TRUE if Data Access Mgr present}

{gestaltDITLExtAttr response values}
gestaltDITLExtPresent   = 0; {TRUE if Dialog Mgr extensions present}

{gestaltEasyAccessAttr response values}
gestaltEasyAccessOff        = 0;  {Easy Access present but off}
gestaltEasyAccessOn         = 1;  {Easy Access on}
gestaltEasyAccessSticky     = 2;  {Easy Access sticky}
gestaltEasyAccessLocked     = 3;  {Easy Access locked}

{gestaltEditionMgrAttr response values}
gestaltEditionMgrPresent    = 0;  {TRUE if Edition Mgr present}
```

```
{gestaltFindFolderAttr response values}
gestaltFindFolderPresent = 0;  {TRUE if FindFolder present}

{gestaltFontMgrAttr response values}
gestaltOutlineFonts = 0;       {TRUE if outline fonts present}

{gestaltFPUType response values}
gestaltNoFPU     = 0;          {no FPU present}
gestalt68881     = 1;          {Motorola 68881 present}
gestalt68882     = 2;          {Motorola 68882 present}

{gestaltFSAttr response values}
gestaltFullExtFSDispatching = 0; {TRUE if new HFSDispatch present}
gestaltHasFSSpecCalls       = 1; {TRUE if FSSpec calls present}

{gestaltFXfrMgrAttr response values}
gestaltFXfrMgrPresent  = 0;    {TRUE if File Transfer Mgr present}

{gestaltHardwareAttr response values}
gestaltHasVIA1  = 0;           {has a VIA1}
gestaltHasVIA2  = 1;           {has a VIA2}
gestaltHasASC   = 3;           {has an ASC}
gestaltHasSCC   = 4;           {has an SCC}
gestaltHasSCSI  = 7;           {has SCSI}

{gestaltHelpMgrAttr response values}
gestaltHelpMgrPresent  = 0;    {true if Help Mgr present}

{gestaltKeyboardType response values}
gestaltMacKbd          = 1;    {Macintosh keyboard}
gestaltMacAndPad       = 2;    {Macintosh keyboard and keypad}
gestaltMacPlusKbd      = 3;    {Macintosh Plus keyboard}
gestaltExtADBKbd       = 4;    {Extended ADB keyboard}
gestaltStdADBKbd       = 5;    {Standard ADB keyboard}
gestaltPrtblADBKbd     = 6;    {Portable Std ADB keyboard}
gestaltPrtblISOKbd     = 7;    {Portable ISO ADB keyboard}
gestaltStdISOADBKbd    = 8;    {ISO Std ADB keyboard}
gestaltExtISOADBKbd    = 9;    {ISO Ext ADB keyboard}
gestaltADBKbdII        = 10;   {ADB Keyboard II}
gestaltADBISOKbdII     = 11;   {ISO ADB Keyboard II}

{gestaltMiscAttr response values}
gestaltScrollingThrottle = 0; {TRUE if scrolling throttle on}
gestaltSquareMenuBar     = 2; {TRUE if menu bar is square}

{gestaltMMUType response values}
gestaltNoMMU     = 0;          {no MMU present}
gestaltAMU       = 1;          {Mac II addr management unit}
```

```
gestalt68851      = 2;         {Motorola 68851 PMMU}
gestalt68030MMU   = 3;         {Motorola 68030 built-in MMU}

{gestaltNotificationMgrAttr response values}
gestaltNotificationPresent = 0; {Notification Mgr present}

{gestaltOSAttr response values}
gestaltSysZoneGrowable     = 0;  {system heap can grow}
gestaltLaunchCanReturn     = 1;  {can return from launch}
gestaltLaunchFullFileSpec = 2;  {LaunchApplication is available}
gestaltLaunchControl       = 3;  {Process Manager is available}
gestaltTempMemSupport      = 4;  {temp memory support present}
gestaltRealTempMemory      = 5;  {temp memory handles are real}
gestaltTempMemTracked      = 6;  {temp memory handles tracked}
gestaltIPCSupport          = 7;  {IPC support is present}
gestaltSysDebuggerSupport = 8;  {system debugger support}

{gestaltParityAttr response values}
gestaltHasParityCapability = 0; {machine can check parity}
gestaltParityEnabled       = 1; {parity RAM is installed}

{gestaltPopupAttr response values}
gestaltPopupPresent = 0;        {pop-up CDEF is present}

{gestaltPowerMgrAttr response values}
gestaltPMgrExists    = 0;       {Power Manager is present}
gestaltPMgrCPUIdle   = 1;       {CPU can idle}
gestaltPMgrSCC       = 2;       {can stop SCC clock}
gestaltPMgrSound     = 3;       {can turn off sound power}

{gestaltPPCToolboxAttr response values}
gestaltPPCToolboxPresent  = 0;  {TRUE if PPC Toolbox present}

{gestaltProcessorType response values}
gestalt68000  = 1;              {68000 processor}
gestalt68010  = 2;              {68010 processor}
gestalt68020  = 3;              {68020 processor}
gestalt68030  = 4;              {68030 processor}

{gestaltQuickdrawVersion response values}
gestaltOriginalQD  = $000;     {original QuickDraw}
gestaltOriginalQD1 = $001;     {original QuickDraw in System 7.0}
gestalt8BitQD      = $100;     {8-bit Color QuickDraw}
gestalt32BitQD     = $200;     {32-Bit Color QuickDraw}
gestalt32BitQD11   = $210;     {32-Bit Color QuickDraw vers. 1.1}
gestalt32BitQD12   = $220;     {32-Bit Color QuickDraw vers. 1.2}
gestalt32BitQD13   = $230;     {32-Bit Color QuickDraw vers. 1.3}
```

```
{gestaltResourceMgrAttr response values}
gestaltPartialRsrcs = 0;        {partial resource functions exist}

{gestaltSerialAttr response values}
gestaltGPIaToDCDa   = 0;        {GPI connected to DCD on port A}
gestaltGPIaToRTxCa  = 1;        {GPI connected to RTxC on port A}
gestaltGPIaToDCDb   = 2;        {GPI connected to DCD on port B}

{gestaltSoundAttr response values}
gestaltStereoCapability    = 0; {stereo capability present}
gestaltStereoMixing        = 1; {stereo mixing on internal speaker}
gestaltSoundIOMgrPresent   = 3; {sound input routines available}
gestaltBuiltInSoundInput   = 4; {built-in input device available}
gestaltHasSoundInputDevice = 5; {sound input device available}

{gestaltStandardFileAttr response values}
gestaltStandardFile58 = 0;      {new Std File routines available}

{gestaltStdNBPAttr response values}
gestaltStdNBPPresent  = 0;      {TRUE if StandardNBP present}

{gestaltTermMgrAttr response values}
gestaltTermMgrPresent = 0;      {TRUE if Terminal Mgr present}

{gestaltTextEditVersion response values}
gestaltTE1 = 1;     {in MacIIci ROM}
gestaltTE2 = 2;     {with 6.0.4 scripts on Mac IIci}
gestaltTE3 = 3;     {with 6.0.4 scripts on other machines}
gestaltTE4 = 4;     {in 6.0.5 and 7.0}
gestaltTE5 = 5;     {TextWidthHook available in TextEdit}

{gestaltTimeMgrVersion response values}
gestaltStandardTimeMgr = 1;     {standard Time Manager}
gestaltRevisedTimeMgr  = 2;     {revised Time Manager}
gestaltExtendedTimeMgr = 3;     {extended Time Manager}

{gestaltVMAttr response values}
gestaltVMPresent  = 0;          {virtual memory present}

{gestaltMachineType response values}
gestaltClassic      = 1;        {Macintosh 128K}
gestaltMacXL        = 2;        {Macintosh XL}
gestaltMac512KE     = 3;        {Macintosh 512K enhanced}
gestaltMacPlus      = 4;        {Macintosh Plus}
gestaltMacSE        = 5;        {Macintosh SE}
gestaltMacII        = 6;        {Macintosh II}
gestaltMacIIx       = 7;        {Macintosh IIx}
```

```
gestaltMacIIcx       = 8;         {Macintosh IIcx}
gestaltMacSE030      = 9;         {Macintosh SE/30}
gestaltPortable      = 10;        {Macintosh Portable}
gestaltMacIIci       = 11;        {Macintosh IIci}
gestaltMacIIfx       = 13;        {Macintosh IIfx}
gestaltMacClassic    = 17;        {Macintosh Classic}
gestaltMacIIsi       = 18;        {Macintosh IIsi}
gestaltMacLC         = 19;        {Macintosh LC}


kMachineNameStrID    = -16395;    {'STR#' resource that }
                                  { contains machine names}
```

Routines

```
FUNCTION Gestalt           (selector: OSType; VAR response: LongInt) :
                            OSErr;

FUNCTION NewGestalt        (selector: OSType; selectorFunction: ProcPtr)
                            : OSErr;

FUNCTION ReplaceGestalt    (selector: OSType; selectorFunction: ProcPtr;
                            VAR oldGestaltFunction: ProcPtr) : OSErr;
```

Application-Defined Routines

```
FUNCTION mySelectorFunction   (selector: OSType; VAR response: LongInt) :
                               OSErr;
```

Result Codes

noErr	0	No error
gestaltUnknownErr	–5550	Could not obtain the response
gestaltUndefSelectorErr	–5551	Undefined selector
gestaltDupSelectorErr	–5552	Selector already exists
gestaltLocationErr	–5553	Function not in system heap

SUMMARY OF THE WINDOW MANAGER

Constants

```
CONST {window definition ID}
      movableDBoxProc       = 5;      {movable modal dialog box}
```

SUMMARY OF THE CONTROL MANAGER

Constants

```
CONST {pop-up menu control definition}
      popupMenuCDEFProc     = 1008;  {pop-up menu}

      {pop-up menu title characteristics}
      popupTitleLeftJust    =         $0000;  {left alignment}
      popupTitleCenterJust  =         $0001;  {center alignment}
      popupTitleRightJust   =         $00FF;  {right alignment}
      popupTitleBold        =         $0100;  {bold text}
      popupTitleItalic      =         $0200;  {italic text}
      popupTitleUnderline   =         $0400;  {underlined text}
      popupTitleOutline     =         $0800;  {outlined text}
      popupTitleShadow      =         $1000;  {shadow text}
      popupTitleCondense    =         $2000;  {condensed text}
      popupTitleExtend      =         $4000;  {extended text}
      popupTitleNoStyle     =         $8000;  {unstyled text}

      {pop-up menu variation codes}
      popupFixedWidth       = $0001;  {use fixed-width control}
      popupUseAddResMenu    = $0004;  {use resource for menu}
      popupUseWFont         = $0008;  {use window font}
```

Data Type

```
TYPE popupPrivateData =
     RECORD
       mHandle:  MenuHandle;                  {handle to menu}
       mID:      Integer;                     {menu ID}
       mPrivate: ARRAY[0..0] OF SignedByte    {reserved}
     END;
```

SUMMARY OF THE DIALOG MANAGER

Constants

```
CONST {DITLMethod constants}
      overlayDITL          = 0;      {overlay existing items}
      appendDITLRight      = 1;      {append at right}
      appendDITLBottom     = 2;      {append at bottom}
```

Data Type

```
TYPE   DITLMethod = Integer;
```

Routines

```
FUNCTION CountDITL          (theDialog: DialogPtr) : Integer;
PROCEDURE AppendDITL        (theDialog: DialogPtr; theDITL: Handle;
                             method: DITLMethod);
PROCEDURE ShortenDITL       (theDialog: DialogPtr; numberItems: Integer);
```

4 THE EDITION MANAGER

ABOUT THIS CHAPTER

This chapter describes how you can use the Edition Manager to allow your users to share and automatically update data from numerous documents and applications.

The Edition Manager is available only in system software version 7.0. It can be used by many different applications located on a single disk or throughout a network of Macintosh® computers. To test for the existence of the Edition Manager, use the Gestalt function, described in the Compatibility Guidelines chapter of this volume.

Read the information in this chapter if you want your application's documents to share and automatically update data, or if you want to share and automatically update data with documents created by other applications that support the Edition Manager.

For example, a user might want to capture sales figures and totals from within a spreadsheet and then include this information in a word-processing document that summarizes sales for a given month. The Edition Manager establishes a connection between these two documents. When a user modifies the spreadsheet, the information in the word-processing document can be automatically updated to contain the latest changes. To accomplish this, both the spreadsheet application and the word-processing application must support the features of the Edition Manager.

To use this chapter, you should be familiar with sending and receiving high-level events, described in the Events Manager chapter of this volume. Your application must also support Apple® events to receive Apple events from the Edition Manager. See the Apple Event Manager chapter in this volume for detailed information.

ABOUT THE EDITION MANAGER

The Edition Manager provides you with the ability to

- capture data within a document and integrate it into another document
- modify information in a document and automatically update any document that shares its data
- share information between applications on the same computer or across a network of Macintosh computers

Building the capabilities of the Edition Manager into your program is similar to building cut-and-paste features into your program. Text, graphics, spreadsheet cells, database reports—any data that you can select, you can make accessible to other applications that support the Edition Manager.

This chapter first defines the main elements of the Edition Manager and then discusses how to save, open, read, and write a document that shares data. In addition, this chapter describes how to

- make data accessible to other applications
- integrate data into numerous documents
- set update options
- implement borders
- modify shared data
- customize dialog boxes

This chapter also describes an advanced feature that allows applications to share data directly from a file.

PUBLISHERS, SUBSCRIBERS, AND EDITIONS

A **section** is a portion of a document that shares its contents with other documents. The Edition Manager supports two types of sections: publishers and subscribers. A **publisher** is a section within a document that makes its data available to other documents or applications. A **subscriber** is a section within a document that obtains its data from other documents or applications.

Your application writes a copy of the data in each publisher to a separate file called an **edition container.** The actual data that is written to the edition container is referred to as the **edition.** Your application obtains the data for each subscriber by reading data from the edition container. Note that throughout this chapter, the term *edition* refers to the edition container and the data it contains.

You **publish** data when you want to make it available to other documents and applications. When data is published, it is stored in an edition container. You **subscribe** to data that a publisher makes available by reading an edition from its container.

> **Note:** *Section* and *edition container* are programmatic terms. You should not use them in your application or your documentation. Use *publishers, subscribers,* and *editions*. You should also refrain from using other terms such as *publication* or *subscription* to describe the dynamic sharing of information provided by the Edition Manager. Use the terms *publish* and *subscribe* to describe the Edition Manager features.

Each edition has an icon that is visible from the Finder. Figure 4-1 shows the default edition icon.

Figure 4-1. The default edition icon

The name that the user specifies for the edition is located beneath the edition icon. To create customized edition icons, see the Finder Interface chapter in this volume for detailed information. Figure 4-2 illustrates a document containing a single publisher, its corresponding edition, and a subscriber to the edition in another document.

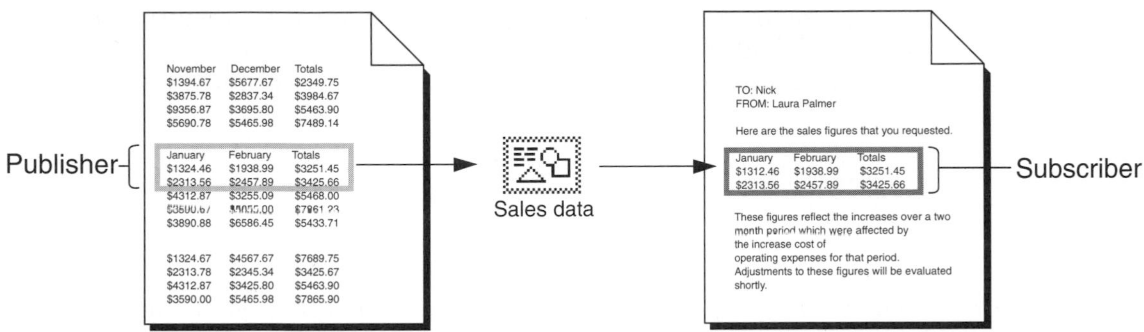

Figure 4-2. A publisher, an edition, and a subscriber

Note that the publisher and subscriber borders illustrated in Figure 4-2 may appear slightly different from the borders you see on screen. Figure 4-6 shows a screen-captured image of the publisher and subscriber borders that appear on screen.

Data always flows in one direction, from publisher to edition to subscriber. Documents that contain publishers and subscribers do not have to be open at the same time to share data. Whenever the user saves a document that contains a publisher, the edition changes to reflect the current data from the publisher. All subscribers update their contents from the edition. Any number of subscribers can subscribe to a single edition.

To create a publisher within a document, a user selects an area of the document to share and chooses Create Publisher from the Edit menu (illustrated later in this chapter). Figure 4-3 shows the dialog box that your application should display when the user chooses Create Publisher.

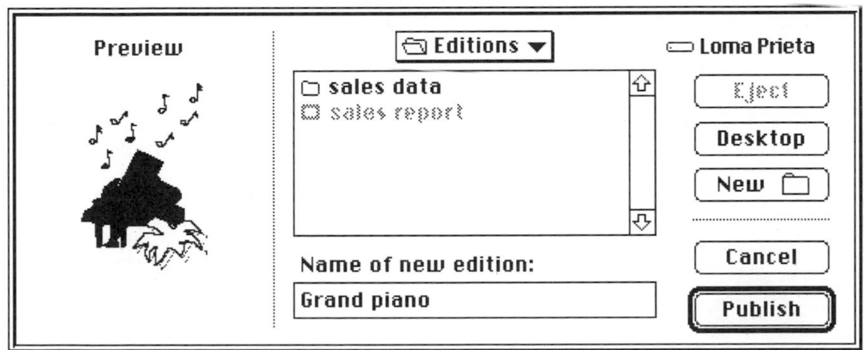

Figure 4-3. The publisher dialog box

Your application provides a thumbnail sketch of the edition data that the Edition Manager displays in the preview area of the publisher dialog box. Your preview of the edition in this dialog box should provide a visual cue about the type of information that the user has selected to publish.

A preview area also appears in the subscriber dialog box (see Figure 4-4). Your preview for an edition in this dialog box should provide a visual cue about the type of information the edition contains. For example, it should allow users to distinguish between text information and spreadsheet arrays.

The publisher dialog box uses the extended interface of the standard file dialog box that accompanies system software version 7.0. The user navigates through the contents of the disk using the mouse or keyboard.

A user can modify a publisher within a document just like any other portion of a document. As a default, each time a user saves a document containing a publisher, your application should automatically write the publisher's data to the edition. You also need to provide the user with the choice of sending new publisher data to an edition manually (that is, only at the user's specific request). You can provide these options by using the publisher options dialog box described later in "Using Publisher and Subscriber Options."

For example, one user may choose to automatically update an edition each time a document is saved. This update mode is useful for a user who creates a publisher within a spreadsheet application that records stock information. Each time the user updates the stock information and saves the spreadsheet, a new edition automatically becomes available to subscribers.

Another user may choose to update an edition only upon request. This update mode might be useful for a user who creates a publisher within a word-processing application for a quarterly sales report. The user incrementally updates the sales report throughout the entire quarter, but does not want this information to be available to subscribers until the end of the quarter. Only at the end of each quarter does the user specifically request to update the edition and make it available to any subscribers.

To create a subscriber within a document, the user places the insertion point and chooses Subscribe To from the Edit menu. Figure 4-4 shows the dialog box that your application should display when the user chooses Subscribe To.

Figure 4-4. The subscriber dialog box

The subscriber dialog box also uses the extended interface of the standard file dialog box introduced with system software version 7.0. Initially, the dialog box should highlight the name of the last edition published or subscribed to. This allows a user to create a publisher and immediately subscribe to its edition.

A subscriber receives its data from a single edition. By default, your application should automatically update a document containing a subscriber whenever a new edition is available. You also need to provide the user with the choice of receiving the latest edition manually (that is, only when the user specifically requests it). You can provide these options by using the subscriber options dialog box described later in "Using Publisher and Subscriber Options."

For example, one user may choose to automatically receive new editions as they become available. This update mode is useful for a user who subscribes to information from an edition that consists of daily sales figures. This user automatically acquires each version of the sales information as it becomes available.

Another user may choose to receive a new edition only upon request. This update mode is useful for a user who creates a subscriber to an edition that consists of graphics data (such as a company logo). The user may require only periodic versions of the logo and not need frequent updates. In this case, your application should only update the subscriber with a new edition when the user specifically requests it.

A user can select, cut, copy, or paste an entire subscriber. Although the contents of the subscriber as a whole can be modified, a user cannot edit portions of a subscriber. For example, a user can underline or italicize the entire subscriber text, but cannot delete a sentence or rotate a single graphical object. This restriction protects the user from losing changes to a subscriber when a new edition arrives. Remember that, as a default, new editions should automatically update a subscriber. Any changes that a user made to the subscriber text would have to be reapplied when the new edition arrives. See "Modifying a Subscriber" later in this chapter for further information.

A single document can contain any number or combination of publishers and subscribers. Figure 4-5 shows an example of a document that contains two publishers and one subscriber (and their corresponding editions). Remember that data always flows in one direction, from publisher to edition to subscriber. The "Concert flyer" document contains a publisher that is subscribed to by the "Benefit concert" document. The "Concert flyer" document also subscribes to a portion of the "Pianos & palm trees" document. In addition, the "Concert flyer" document as a whole is subscribed to by the "Sample flyer" document.

You should distinguish each selected publisher and subscriber within a document with a border. Display a publisher border as 3 pixels wide with 50 percent gray lines, and display a subscriber border as 3 pixels wide with 75 percent gray lines. A rectangle of one white pixel should separate the data from the border itself. Borders should be drawn *outside* the

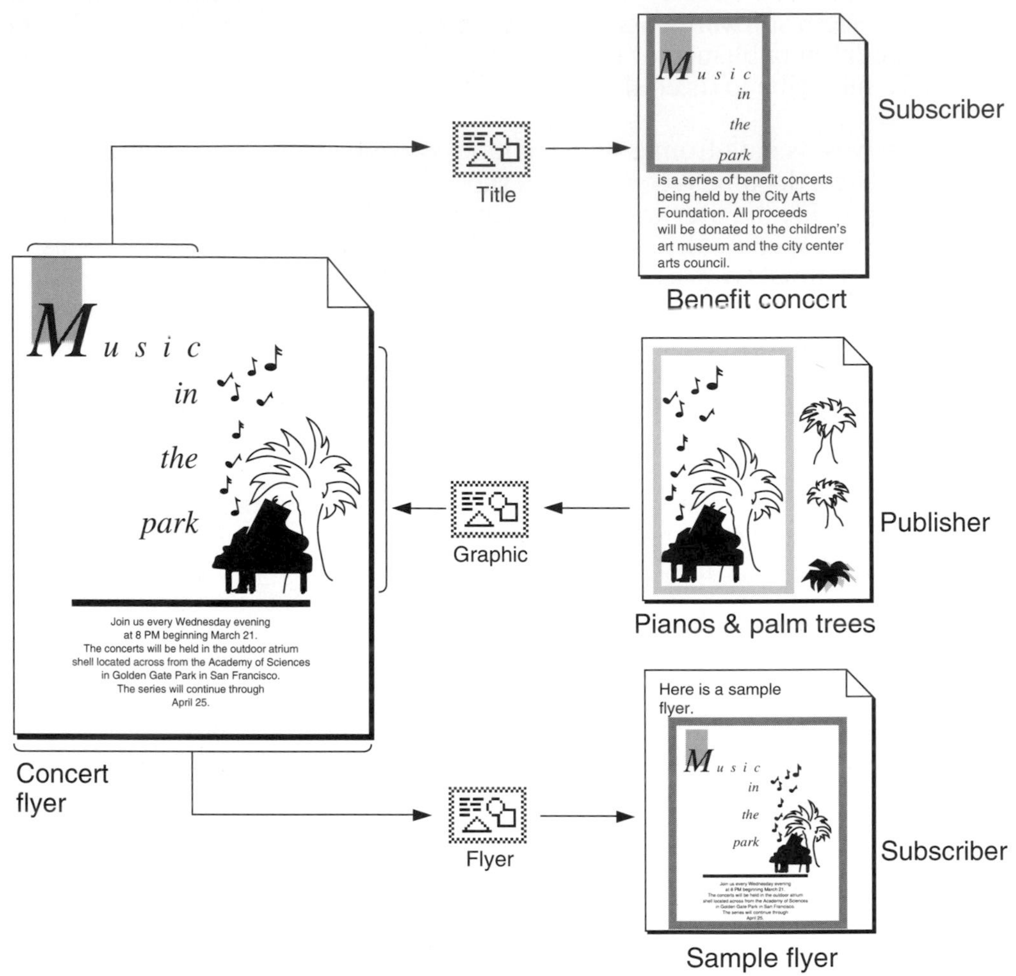

Figure 4-5. A document and its corresponding editions

contents of publishers and subscribers so that data is not obscured. See Figure 4-6 for an illustration of the borders as they appear on screen. See "Displaying Publisher and Subscriber Borders" later in this chapter for detailed information on how to implement borders for specific applications.

Figure 4-6 shows a document containing a publisher and a document containing a subscriber, with borders displayed for each.

Borders for publishers and subscribers should behave like the borders of 'PICT' graphics within a word-processing document. Your application should display a border whenever the

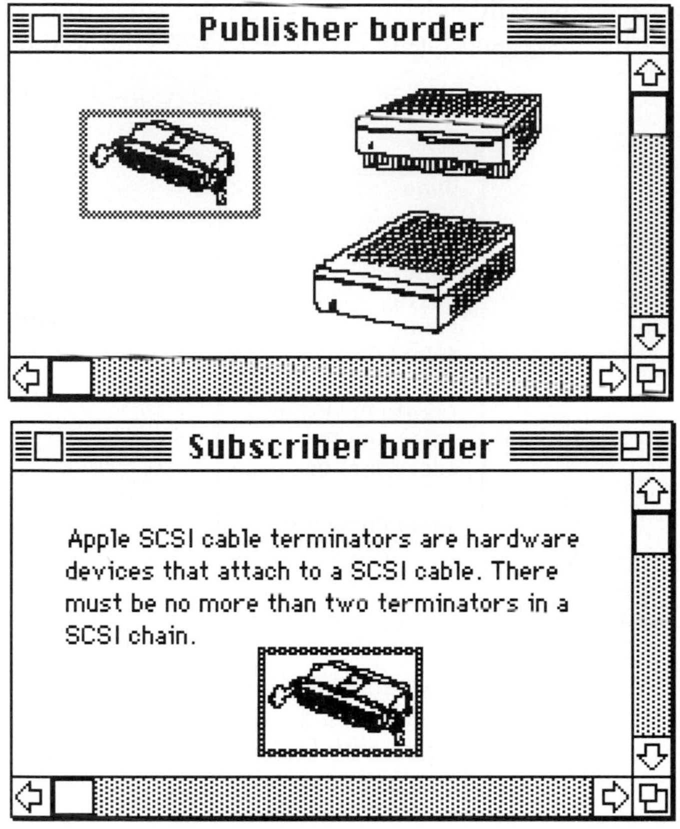

Figure 4-6. Publisher and subscriber borders

user clicks within the content area of a publisher or a subscriber. Your application should hide the border whenever the user clicks outside the content area. See "Displaying Publisher and Subscriber Borders" later in this chapter for detailed information on how to implement borders for specific applications.

You also need to support the standard Edition Manager menu commands in the Edit menu. These menu items include

- Create Publisher…
- Subscribe To…
- Publisher/Subscriber Options…
- Show/Hide Borders (optional)
- Stop All Editions (optional)

Use a dotted line to separate the Edition Manager menu commands from the standard Edit menu commands Cut, Copy, and Paste. Figure 4-7 shows the standard Edition Manager menu commands.

Figure 4-7. Edition Manager commands in the Edit menu

The Publisher Options menu command should toggle with Subscriber Options when a user selects either a publisher or a subscriber within a document. In addition, you may support a Show Borders menu command that toggles with Hide Borders to display or hide all publishers and subscriber borders within documents. You may also support a Stop All Editions menu command to provide a method for temporarily suspending all update activity in a document. When the user chooses this command, you should place a checkmark next to it. You should also stop all publishers from sending data to editions and all subscribers from receiving new editions. When the user chooses this command again, remove the checkmark and update any subscribers that are set up to receive new editions automatically.

If you find that you need all of the available space in the Edit menu for your application's commands, you may create a hierarchical menu for the Edition Manager menu commands. If you choose to implement this structure, you should allow users to access the Edition Manager menu commands through a Publishing menu command in the Edit menu. Because this menu structure is not as accessible to users, you should implement it only if you have no other alternative.

Figure 4-8 shows the Edition Manager menu commands in a hierarchical menu structure.

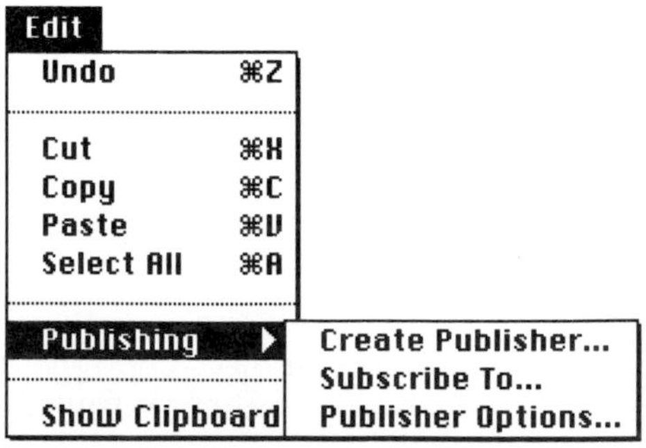

Figure 4-8. Edition Manager commands under the Publishing menu command

For each publisher or subscriber within an open document, you must have a section record and an alias record. The section record contains a time stamp that records the version of the data that resides in the section. The section record also identifies the section as either a publisher or subscriber, and it establishes a unique identity for each publisher or subscriber. The section record does *not* contain the data within the section. The alias record is a reference to the edition container from the document that contains the corresponding publisher or subscriber section.

There are special options associated with publishers and subscribers within documents. Your application can use the publisher and subscriber options dialog boxes provided by the Edition Manager to make these choices available to the user. For example, a user can select Open Publisher within the subscriber options dialog box to access the document containing the publisher. Your application can also allow a user to cancel subscribers or publishers within documents, specify when to update an edition from a publisher, or specify when to update a subscriber with a new edition. These options are described later in this chapter.

USING THE EDITION MANAGER

This section describes how your application can

- receive Apple events from the Edition Manager
- set up a section record and alias record for open documents containing sections
- save a document that contains sections
- open a document that contains sections
- read and write sections
- create a publisher within a document, create its edition container, and write data to it
- create a subscriber within a document and read its data from an edition

To begin, you must determine whether the Edition Manager is available on your system by using the Gestalt function. The Gestalt selector is gestaltEditionMgrAttr ('edtn'). If the response parameter returns 1 in the bit defined by the gestaltEditionMgrPresent constant (bit 0), the Edition Manager is present.

If the Edition Manager is present, load it into memory using the InitEditionPack function. This function determines whether your machine has enough space in the system heap for the Edition Manager to operate.

```
err := InitEditionPack;
```

If the InitEditionPack function returns noErr, you have enough space to load the package. If you do not have enough space, the application can either terminate itself or continue with the Edition Manager functionality disabled.

Receiving Apple Events From the Edition Manager

Applications that use the Edition Manager must support Apple events. This requires that your application support the required Open Documents event and Apple events sent by the Edition Manager. See the Apple Event Manager chapter in this volume for information on Apple events.

Apple events sent by the Edition Manager arrive as high-level events. The EventRecord data type defines the event record.

```
TYPE EventRecord =
     RECORD
        what:               Integer;       {kHighLevelEvent}
        message:            LongInt;       {'sect'}
        when:               LongInt;
        where:              Point;         {'read', 'writ', 'cncl', }
                                           { 'scrl'}
        modifiers:          Integer
     END;
```

The Edition Manager can send the following Apple events:

- Section Read events ('sect' 'read')
- Section Write events ('sect' 'writ')
- Section Cancel events ('sect' 'cncl')
- Section Scroll events ('sect' 'scrl')

Each time your application creates a publisher or a subscriber, the Edition Manager registers its section. When an edition is updated, the Edition Manager scans its list to locate registered subscribers. For each registered subscriber that is set up to receive updated editions automatically, your application receives a Section Read event.

If the Edition Manager discovers that an edition file is missing while registering a publisher, it creates a new edition file and sends the publisher a Section Write event.

When you receive a Section Cancel event, you need to cancel the specified section. Note that the current Edition Manager does not send you Section Cancel events, but you do need to provide a handler for future expansion.

If the user selects a subscriber within a document and then selects Open Publisher in the subscriber options dialog box, the publishing application receives the Open Documents event and opens the document containing the publisher. The publishing application also receives a Section Scroll event. Scroll to the location of the publisher, display this section on the user's screen, and turn on its border.

See "Opening and Closing a Document Containing Sections" later in this chapter for detailed information on registering and unregistering a section and writing data to an edition. See "Using Publisher and Subscriber Options" later in this chapter for information on publisher and subscriber options.

After receiving an Apple event sent by the Edition Manager, use the Apple Event Manager to extract the section handle. In addition, you must also call the IsRegisteredSection function to determine whether the section is registered. It is possible (due to a race condition) to receive an event for a section that you recently disposed of or unregistered. One way to ensure that an event corresponds to a valid section is to call the IsRegisteredSection function after you receive an event. The Apple Event Manager chapter in this volume provides detailed information on Apple Event Manager routines.

```
err := IsRegisteredSection (sectionH);
```

Listing 4-1 illustrates how to use the Apple Event Manager and install an event handler to handle Section Read events. You can write similar code for Section Write events, Section Scroll events, and Section Cancel events.

Listing 4-1. Accepting Section Read events and verifying if a section is registered

```
{The following goes in your initialization code.}
MyErr := AEInstallEventHandler(sectionEventMsgClass {'sect'},
                               sectionReadMsgID {'read'},
                               @MyHandleSectionReadEvent, 0, FALSE);

{This is the routine the Apple Event Manager calls when a Section Read }
{ event arrives.}

FUNCTION MyHandleSectionReadEvent(theAppleEvent, reply: AppleEvent;
                                  refCon: LongInt) : OSErr;
VAR
   getErr:      OSErr;
   sectionH:    SectionHandle;
BEGIN
   {Get section handle out of Apple event message buffer.}
   getErr := GetSectionHandleFromEvent(theAppleEvent, sectionH);

   IF getErr = noErr THEN
   BEGIN
      {Do nothing if section is not registered.}
      IF IsRegisteredSection(sectionH) = noErr
         THEN MyHandleSectionReadEvent := DoSectionRead(sectionH);
   END ELSE
   BEGIN
      MyHandleSectionReadEvent := getErr;
   END;
END; {MyHandleSectionReadEvent}

{The following routine should read in subscriber data and update its }
{ display.}
FUNCTION DoSectionRead(subscriber: SectionHandle) : OSErr;
BEGIN
     {Your code here.}
END; {DoSectionRead}
```

(Continued)

Listing 4-1. Accepting Section Read events and verifying if a section is registered (Continued)

```
{This is part of your Apple event-handling code.}
FUNCTION GetSectionHandleFromEvent(theAppleEvent: AppleEvent; VAR
                                   sectionH: SectionHandle) : OSErr;
VAR
   ignoreType: DescType;
   ignoreSize: Size;
BEGIN
   {Parse section handle out of message buffer.}
   GetSectionHandleFromEvent
      := AEGetParamPtr( theAppleEvent,     {event to parse}
                        keyDirectObject,   {Look for direct object.}
                        typeSectionH,      {Want a SectionHandle type.}
                        ignoreType,        {Ignore type it could get.}
                        @sectionH,         {Put SectionHandle here.}
                        SizeOf(sectionH),  {size of storage for }
                                           { SectionHandle}
                        ignoreSize);       {Ignore storage it used.}
END; {GetSectionHandleFromEvent}
```

Creating the Section Record and Alias Record

Your application is responsible for creating a section record and an alias record for each publisher and subscriber section within an open document.

The section record identifies each section as a publisher or subscriber and provides identification for each section. The section record does not contain the data within the section; it describes the attributes of the section. Your application must provide its own method for associating the data within a section with its section record. Your application is also responsible for saving the data in the section.

The alias field of the section record contains a handle to its alias record. The alias record is a reference to the edition container from the document which contains the publisher or subscriber section. You should be familiar with the Alias Manager's conventions for creating alias records and identifying files, folders, and volumes to locate files that have been moved, copied, or restored from backup.

When a user saves a document, your application should store all section records and alias records in the resource fork. Corresponding section records and alias records should have the same resource ID. This allows compatibility for future changes.

Figure 4-9 shows a document containing a publisher and subscriber, and the corresponding section records and alias records.

The SectionRecord data type defines the section record. A section record contains information to identify the data contained within a section as a publisher or a subscriber, a time stamp to record the last modification of the section, and unique identification for each section.

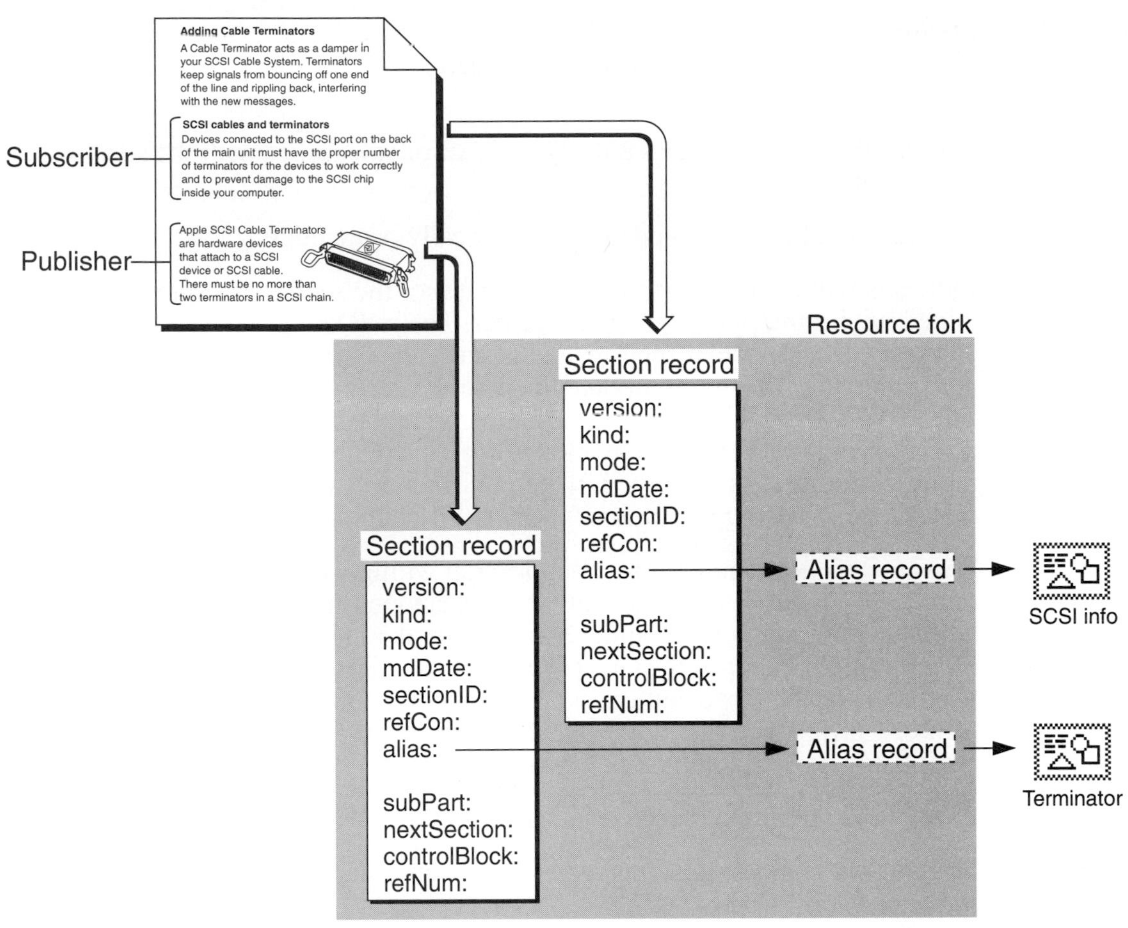

Figure 4-9. A document with a publisher and subscriber and its resource fork

```
TYPE SectionRecord =
     RECORD
        version:            SignedByte;      {always 1 in 7.0}
        kind:               SectionType;     {publisher or subscriber}
        mode:               UpdateMode;      {automatic or manual}
        mdDate:             TimeStamp;       {last change in document}
        sectionID:          LongInt;         {application-specific, }
                                             { unique per document}
        refCon:             LongInt;         {application-specific}
        alias:              AliasHandle;     {handle to alias record}

        {The following fields are private and are set up by the }
        { RegisterSection function described later within this }
        { chapter. Do not modify the private fields.}

        subPart:            LongInt;         {private}
        nextSection:        SectionHandle;   {private, do not use as a }
                                             { linked list}
        controlBlock:       Handle;          {may be used for comparison }
                                             { only}
        refNum:             EditionRefNum    {private}
     END;
```

Field descriptions

version	Indicates the version of the section record, currently $01.
kind	Defines the section type as either publisher or subscriber with the stPublisher or stSubscriber constant.
mode	Indicates if editions are updated automatically or manually.
mdDate	Indicates which version (modification date) of the section's contents is contained within the publisher or subscriber. The mdDate is set to 0 when you create a new subscriber section, and is set to the current time when you create a new publisher. Be sure to update this field each time publisher data is modified. The section's modification date is compared to the edition's modification date to determine whether the section and the edition contain the same data. The section modification date is displayed in the publisher and subscriber options dialog boxes. See "Closing an Edition" later in this chapter for detailed information.
sectionID	Provides a unique number for each section within a document. A simple way to implement this is to create a counter for each document that is saved to disk with the document. The counter should start at 1. The section ID is currently used as a tie breaker in the GoToPublisher function when there are multiple publishers to the same edition in a single document. The section ID should not be 0 or –1. See "Duplicating Publishers and Subscribers" later in this chapter for information on multiple publishers.
refCon	Available for application-specific use.
alias	Contains a handle to the alias record for a particular section within a document.

Whenever the user creates a publisher or subscriber, call the NewSection function to create the section record and the alias record.

```
err := NewSection (container, sectionDocument, kind, sectionID,
                   initialMode, sectionH);
```

The NewSection function creates a new section record (either publisher or subscriber), indicates whether editions are updated automatically or manually, sets the modification date, and creates an alias record from the document containing the section to the edition container.

The sectionDocument parameter can be NIL if your current document has never been saved. Use the AssociateSection function to update the alias record of a registered section when the user names or renames a document by choosing Save As from the File menu. If you are creating a subscriber with the initialMode parameter set to receive new editions automatically, your application receives a Section Read event each time a new edition becomes available for this subscriber.

If an error is encountered, the sectionH parameter is set to NIL. If not, sectionH contains the handle to the allocated section record.

Set the initialMode parameter to the update mode for each subscriber and publisher created. You can specify the update mode using these constants:

```
CONST sumAutomatic          = 0;        {subscriber receives new }
                                        { editions automatically}
      sumManual             = 1;        {subscriber receives new }
                                        { editions manually}
      pumOnSave             = 0;        {publisher sends new }
                                        { editions on save}
      pumManual             = 1;        {publisher does not send }
                                        { new editions until user }
                                        { request}
```

See "Using Publisher and Subscriber Options" later in this chapter for detailed information on update modes for publishers and subscribers.

Saving a Document Containing Sections

When saving a document that contains sections, you should write out each section record as a resource of type 'sect' and write out each alias record as a resource of type 'alis' with the same ID as the section record. See the Resource Manager chapters in Volume I and this volume for detailed information on resources.

If a user closes a document that contains newly created publishers without attempting to save its contents, you should display an alert box similar to the one shown in Figure 4-10.

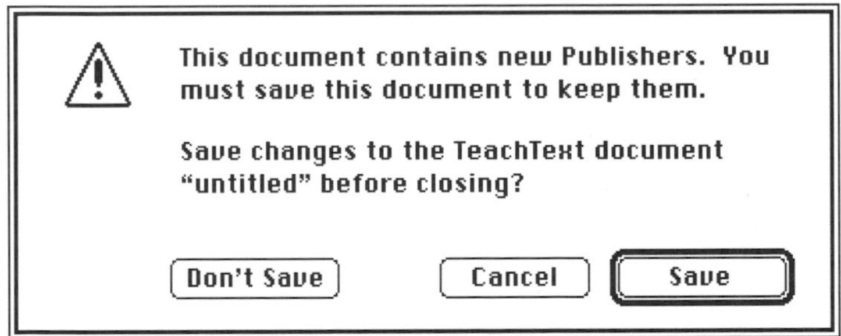

Figure 4-10. The new publisher alert box

If you keep the section records and alias records for each publisher and subscriber as resources, you can use the ChangedResource or WriteResource function. If you detach the section records and alias records from each section, you need to clone the handles and use the AddResource function. See the Resource Manager chapter in Volume V for detailed information on the ChangedResource, WriteResource, and AddResource functions.

Use the PBExchangeFiles function to ensure that each time you save a document that contains sections, the file ID remains the same. Saving a file typically involves creating a new file (with a temporary name), writing data to it, closing it, and then deleting the original file that you are replacing. You rename the temporary file with the original filename, which leads to a new file ID. The PBExchangeFiles function swaps the contents of the two files (even if they are open) by getting both catalog entries and swapping the allocation pointers. If the files are open, the file control block (FCB) is updated so that the reference numbers still access the same contents (under a new name). See the File Manager chapter in this volume for detailed information on the PBExchangeFiles function.

Listing 4-2 illustrates how to save a file that contains sections. As described earlier, you should write out the eligible section records and alias records as resources to allow for future compatibility. There are several different techniques for saving or adding resources; this listing illustrates one technique. The section handles are still valid after using the AddResource function because this listing illustrates just saving, not closing, the file.

Before you write out sections, you need to see if any publisher sections share the same control block. Publishers that share the same control block share the same edition.

If a user creates an identical copy of a file by choosing Save As from the File menu and does not make any changes to this new file, you simply use the AssociateSection function to indicate to the Edition Manager which document a section is located in.

Listing 4-2. Saving a document containing sections

```
PROCEDURE SaveDocument(thisDocument: MyDocumentInfoPtr;
                       numberOfSections: Integer);

VAR
   aSectionH:          SectionHandle;
   copiedSectionH:     Handle;
   copiedAliasH:       Handle;
   resID:              Integer;
   thisone:            Integer;

BEGIN
   {Write contents of publishers that need to be written during save. }
   { The GetSectionAliasPair function returns a handle and }
   { resID to a section. The CheckForDataChanged function }
   { returns TRUE if the data in the section has changed.}
   FOR thisone := 1 TO numberOfSections DO
   BEGIN
      aSectionH := GetSectionAliasPair(thisDocument, thisone, resID);
      IF (aSectionH^^.kind = stPublisher) &
         (aSectionH^^.mode = pumOnSave) &
         (CheckForDataChanged(aSectionH))
      THEN DoWriteEdition(aSectionH, thisDocument);
   END; {for}

   {Set the curResFile to be the resource fork of thisDocument.}
   UseResFile(thisDocument^.resForkRefNum);

   {Write all section and alias records to the document.}
   FOR thisone := 1 TO numberOfSections DO
   BEGIN
      {Given an index, get the next section handle and resID }
      { from your internal list of sections for this file.}
      aSectionH := GetSectionAliasPair(thisDocument, thisone, resID);
```

```
        {Check for duplication of control block values.}
        CheckForDupes(thisDocument, numberOfSections);

        {Save section record to disk.}
        copiedSectionH := Handle(aSectionH);
        HandToHand(copiedSectionH);
        AddResource(copiedSectionH, rSectionType, resID, '');

        {Save alias record to disk.}
        copiedAliasH := Handle(aSectionH^^.alias);
        HandToHand(copiedAliasH);
        AddResource(copiedSectionH, rAliasType, resID, '');
     END; {for}

       {Write rest of document to disk.}
END; {SaveDocument}
```

Opening and Closing a Document Containing Sections

When opening a document that contains sections, your application should use the GetResource function to get the section record and the alias record for each publisher and subscriber. Set the alias field of the section record to be the handle to the alias. See the Resource Manager chapter in Volume I for detailed information on the GetResource function.

You also need to register each section using the RegisterSection function. The RegisterSection function informs the Edition Manager that a section exists.

```
err := RegisterSection (sectionDocument, sectionH, aliasWasUpdated);
```

The RegisterSection function adds the section record to the Edition Manager's list of registered sections. This function assumes that the alias field of each section record is a handle to the alias record. The alias record is a reference to the edition container from the section's document. If the RegisterSection function successfully locates the edition container for a particular section, the section is registered through a shared control block. The control block is a private field in the section record.

If the RegisterSection function cannot find the edition container for a particular subscriber, RegisterSection returns the containerNotFoundWrn result code. If the RegisterSection function cannot find the edition container for a particular publisher, RegisterSection creates an empty edition container for the publisher in the last place the edition was located. The Edition Manager sends your application a Section Write event for that section.

When a user attempts to open a document that contains multiple publishers to the same edition, you should warn the user by displaying an alert box (see "Duplicating Publishers and Subscribers" later in this chapter).

When a user opens a document that contains a subscriber (with an update mode set to automatic), receives a new edition, and then closes the document without making any changes to the file, you should update the document and simply allow the user to close it. You do not need to prompt the user to save changes to the file.

When closing a document that contains sections, you must unregister each section (using the UnRegisterSection function) and dispose of each corresponding section record and alias record.

```
err := UnRegisterSection (sectionH);
```

The UnRegisterSection function removes the section record from the list of registered sections and unlinks itself from the shared control block.

Listing 4-3 illustrates how to open an existing file that contains sections. As described earlier, you should retrieve the section and alias resources, connect the pair through the alias field of the section record, and register the section with the Edition Manager. There are many different techniques for retrieving resources; this listing shows one technique. If an alias was out of date and was updated by the Alias Manager during the resolve, the Edition Manager sets the aliasWasUpdated parameter of the RegisterSection function to TRUE. This means that you should save the document. Additionally, your application must maintain its own list of registered sections for each open document that contains sections.

Listing 4-3. Opening a document containing sections

```
PROCEDURE OpenExistingDocument(thisDocument: MyDocumentInfoPtr);

VAR
   sectionH:          SectionHandle;
   aliasH:            AliasHandle;
   aliasWasUpdated:   Boolean;
   registerErr:       OSErr;
   resID:             Integer;
   thisone:           Integer;
   numberOfSections:  Integer;
   aName:             Str255;

BEGIN
   {Set the curResFile to be the resource fork of thisDocument.}
   UseResFile(thisDocument^.resForkRefNum);

   {Find out the number of section resources.}
   numberOfSections := Count1Resources(rSectionType);

   {In determining the number of section/alias resource pairs to }
   { get, this code only loops for as many sections it finds. }
   { It is unusual to have more section resources than alias }
   { resources. Your code may want to check this and handle it }
   { appropriately. You now have a count of the number of section/alias }
   { resource pairs to get. Loop to get them, connect them, and register }
   { the section.}
```

```
   FOR thisone := 1 TO numberOfSections DO
   BEGIN
      sectionH := SectionHandle(Get1IndResource(rSectionType,
                                thisone));
      {If sectionH is NIL, something could be wrong with the file. }
      { Be sure to check for this.}

      {Get the resource ID of the section and use this to get the }
      { alias with the same resource ID.}
      GetResInfo(Handle(sectionH), resID, rSectionType, aName);
      DetachResource(Handle(sectionH));
      {Detaching is not necessary, but it is convenient.}

      aliasH := AliasHandle(Get1Resource(rAliasType, resID));
      {If aliasH is NIL, then there could be something wrong }
      { with the file. Be sure to check for this.}

      DetachResource(Handle(aliasH));
      {Detaching is not necessary, but it is convenient.}

      {Connect section and alias together.}
      sectionH^^.alias := aliasH;

      {Register the section.}
      registerErr := RegisterSection(thisDocument^.fileSpec,
                                     sectionH, aliasWasUpdated);

      {The RegisterSection function may return an error if a section }
      { is not registered. This is not a fatal error. Continue looping }
      { to register remaining sections.}

      {Add this section/alias pair to your internal bookkeeping. }
      { The AddSectionAliasPair is a routine to accomplish this.}
      MyAddSectionAliasPair(thisDocument, sectionH, resID);

      {If the alias has changed, make note of this. It is }
      { important to know this when you save. AliasHasChanged is a }
      { routine that will do this.}
      IF aliasWasUpdated THEN AliasHasChanged(sectionH);
   END; {for}
END;  {OpenExistingDocument}
```

Reading and Writing a Section

Your application writes publisher data to an edition. New publisher data replaces the previous contents of the edition, making the previous edition information irretrievable. Your application reads data from an edition for each subscriber within a document.

The following sections describe how to

- use different formats to write to or read from an edition
- open an edition to initiate writing or reading
- set a format mark
- write to or read from an edition
- close an edition after successfully writing or reading data

Formats in an Edition

You can write data to an edition in several different formats. These formats are the same as Clipboard formats. Clipboard formats are indicated by a four-character tag.

Typically, when a user copies data, you identify the Clipboard formats and then write the data to scrap. With the Edition Manager, when a user decides to publish data, you identify the Clipboard formats and then write the data to an edition. You can write multiple formats of the same data.

For an edition, you should write your preferred formats first. In general, to write data to an edition, your application should use either 'TEXT' format or 'PICT' format. This allows your application to share data with most other applications. To subscribe to an edition, your application should be able to read both 'TEXT' and 'PICT' files. In addition, your application can write any other private formats that you want to support.

Clipboard formats are described in the Scrap Manager chapter in Volume I.

A few special formats are defined as constants.

```
CONST kPublisherDocAliasFormat    = 'alis';   {alias record from the }
                                              { edition to publisher}
      kPreviewFormat              = 'prvw';   {'PICT' thumbnail sketch}
      kFormatListFormat           = 'fmts';   {lists all available }
                                              { formats}
```

The kPublisherDocAliasFormat ('alis') format is written by the Edition Manager. It is an alias record from the edition to the publisher's document. Appended to the end of the alias is the section ID of the publisher, which the Edition Manager uses to distinguish between multiple publishers to a single edition. You should discourage users from making multiple copies of the same publisher. See "Duplicating Publishers and Subscribers" later in this chapter for detailed information.

The kPreviewFormat ('prvw') format should be written by any application that publishes large amounts of data that may be slow to draw a preview. This format holds a preview of the edition data that is displayed in the preview area of the subscriber dialog box. This format is actually a 'PICT' file that is generated by the publishing application and displays well in a rectangle of 120 by 120 pixels. You can also use this 'PICT' file to display subscriber data within a document (to save space).

To draw a preview in the 'prvw' format, the Edition Manager calls DrawPicture with a 120 by 120 rectangle. To draw a preview in the 'PICT' format, the Edition Manager examines the picture's bounding rectangle and calls DrawPicture with a rectangle that scales the picture proportionally and centers it in a 120 by 120 area.

The kFormatListFormat ('fmts') format is a virtual format that is read but never written. It is a list of all the formats and their lengths. Applications can use this format in place of the EditionHasFormat function (described in "Choosing Which Edition Format to Read" later in this chapter), which provides a procedural interface to determine which formats are available.

If your application can read two or more of the available formats, use 'fmts' to determine the priority of these formats for a particular edition. The order of 'fmts' reflects the order in which the formats were written.

The FormatsAvailable data type defines a record for the 'fmts' format.

```
TYPE FormatsAvailable = ARRAY[0..0] OF
     RECORD
         theType:            FormatType;     {format type for an edition}
         theLength:          LongInt         {length of edition format }
                                             { type}
     END;
```

For example, an edition container may have a format type 'TEXT' of length 100, and a format type 'styl' of length 32. A subscriber to this edition can open it and then read the format type 'fmts' to list all available formats. In this example, it returns 16 bytes: 'TEXT' $00000064 'styl' $00000020.

Opening an Edition

For a publisher, use the OpenNewEdition function to initiate the writing of data to an edition.

```
err := OpenNewEdition (publisherSectionH, fdCreator,
                       publisherSectionDocument, refNum);
```

The publisherSectionH parameter is the publisher section that you are writing to the edition. The fdCreator parameter is the Finder™ creator type of the new edition icon.

The publisherSectionDocument parameter is the document that contains the publisher. This parameter is used to create an alias from the edition to the publisher's document. If you pass NIL for publisherSectionDocument, an alias is not made in the edition file. The refNum parameter returns the reference number for the edition.

For a subscriber, use the OpenEdition function to initiate the reading of data from an edition.

```
err := OpenEdition (subscriberSectionH, refNum);
```

The subscriberSectionH parameter is a handle to the section record for a given section. The refNum parameter returns the reference number for the edition.

The user may rename or move the edition in the Finder. Before writing to or reading data from an edition, the Edition Manager verifies the name of the edition. This process is referred to as *synching* or synchronization. Synching ensures that the Edition Manager's existing edition names correspond to the Finder's existing edition names by updating the control block.

Format Marks

Each format has its own mark. The mark indicates the next position of a read or write operation. Initially, a mark automatically defaults to 0. After reading or writing data, the format mark is set past the last position written to or read from. The mark is similar to the File Manager's current read or write position marker for a data fork. Any time that an edition is open (after calling the OpenEdition or the OpenNewEdition function), any of the marks for each format can be queried or set.

To set the current mark for a section format to a new location, use the SetEditionFormatMark function.

```
err := SetEditionFormatMark (whichEdition, whichFormat,
                             setMarkTo);
```

To find where a current mark is for a format in an edition file, use the GetEditionFormatMark function.

```
err := GetEditionFormatMark (whichEdition, whichFormat,
                             currentMark);
```

Reading and Writing Edition Data

With the Edition Manager, you can read or write data a few bytes at a time instead of putting data into one block as the Scrap Manager does. This model is similar to the data fork of a Macintosh file. You can read sequentially by setting the mark to 0 and repeatedly calling read, or you can jump to a specific offset by setting the mark there. The Edition Manager also adds the capability to stream multiple formats by keeping a separate mark for each format. This allows you to write a few bytes of one format and then write a few bytes of another format, and so forth.

Once you have opened the edition container for a particular publisher, you can begin writing data to the edition. Use the WriteEdition function to write publisher data to an edition.

```
err := WriteEdition (whichEdition, whichFormat, buffPtr, buffLen);
```

The WriteEdition function writes the specified format (beginning at the current mark for that format type) from the buffer pointed to by the buffPtr parameter up to buffLen bytes.

After you open the edition container for a subscriber and determine which formats to read, use the ReadEdition function to read edition data.

```
err := ReadEdition (whichEdition, whichFormat, buffPtr, buffLen);
```

The ReadEdition function reads the data with the specified format (whichFormat) from the edition into the buffer. The ReadEdition function begins reading at the current mark for that format and continues to read up to buffLen bytes. The actual number of bytes read is returned in the buffLen parameter. Once the buffLen parameter returns a value smaller than the value you have specified, there is no additional data to read, and the ReadEdition function returns a noErr result code.

Closing an Edition

When you are done writing to or reading data from an edition, call the CloseEdition function.

```
err := CloseEdition (whichEdition, successful);
```

Each time a user edits a publisher within a document, you must update the modification date in the section record (even if the data is not yet written). When the update mode is set to Manually, the user can compare the modification dates for a publisher and its edition in the publisher options dialog box. One modification date indicates when the publisher last wrote data to the edition, and the other modification date indicates when the publisher section was last edited.

If the successful parameter for a publisher is TRUE, the CloseEdition function makes the newly written data available to subscribers and sets the modification date in the mdDate field of the edition to correspond to the modification date of the publisher's section record. If the two dates differ, the Edition Manager sends a Section Read event to all current subscribers.

If the successful parameter for a subscriber is TRUE, the CloseEdition function sets the modification date of the subscriber's section record to correspond to the modification date of the edition.

If you cannot successfully read from or write data to an edition, set the successful parameter to FALSE. For a publisher, data is not written to the edition, but it should still be saved with the document that contains the section. When the document is next saved, data can then be written to the edition. See "Closing an Edition After Reading or Writing" later in this chapter for additional information on the CloseEdition function.

Creating a Publisher

You need to support a Create Publisher menu command in the Edit menu. When a user selects a portion of a document and chooses Create Publisher from this menu, you should display the publisher dialog box on the user's screen. The Create Publisher menu command should remain dimmed until the user selects a portion of a document.

Use the NewPublisherDialog function to display the publisher dialog box on the user's screen. This function is similar to the CustomPutFile procedure described in the Standard File Package chapter in this volume.

```
err := NewPublisherDialog (reply);
```

The dialog box contains space for a preview (a thumbnail sketch) of the edition and a space for the user to type in the name of the edition in which to write the publisher data. Figure 4-11 illustrates a sample publisher dialog box.

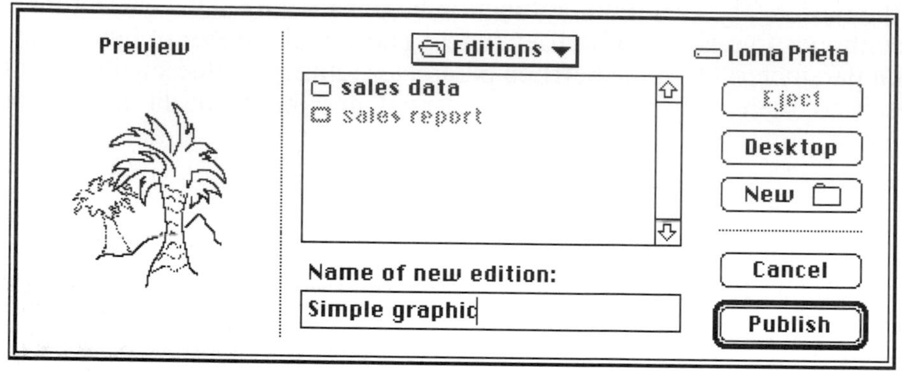

Figure 4-11. A sample publisher dialog box

The NewPublisherDialog function displays the preview (provided by your application), a text box with the default name of the edition (provided by your application), and handles all user input until the user clicks Publish or Cancel.

You pass a new publisher reply record as a parameter to the NewPublisherDialog function.

```
TYPE NewPublisherReply =
     RECORD
         canceled:            Boolean;        {user canceled dialog box}
         replacing:           Boolean;        {user chose existing }
                                              { filename for an edition}
         usePart:             Boolean;        {always FALSE in version 7.0}
         preview:             Handle;         {handle to 'prvw', 'PICT', }
                                              { 'TEXT', or 'snd' data}
         previewFormat:       FormatType;     {type of preview}
         container:           EditionContainerSpec      {edition chosen}
     END;
```

You fill in the usePart, preview, previewFormat, and container fields of the new publisher reply record.

Always set the usePart field to FALSE. The preview field contains either NIL or the data to display in the preview. The previewFormat field should contain 'PICT', 'TEXT', or 'prvw'.

Set the container field to be the default name and folder for the edition. The default name should reflect the data contained in the publisher. For example, if a user publishes a bar chart of sales information entitled “sales data,” then the default name for the edition could also be “sales data.” Otherwise, you should use the document name followed by a hyphen (-) and a number to establish uniqueness. For example, your default name could be “January Totals - 3.”

If the document has not been saved, the default name should be “untitled edition <*n*>” where *n* is a number to establish uniqueness. The default folder should be the same as the edition for the last publisher created in the same document. If this is the first publisher in the document, the default folder should be the same folder that the document is in.

The canceled field of the new publisher reply record indicates whether the user canceled from the dialog box. The replacing field indicates that the user chose to replace an existing edition file. If replacing returns FALSE, call the CreateEditionContainerFile function to create an edition file.

The container field is of data type EditionContainerSpec.

```
TYPE EditionContainerSpec =
     RECORD
        theFile:            FSSpec;         {file containing edition }
                                            { data}
        theFileScript:      ScriptCode;     {script code of filename}
        thePart:            LongInt;        {which part of file, }
                                            { always kPartsNotUsed}
        thePartName:        Str31;          {not used in version 7.0}
        thePartScript:      ScriptCode      {not used in version 7.0}
     END;
```

The field theFile is of type FSSpec. See the File Manager chapter in this volume for further information on file system specification records.

You identify the edition using a volume reference number, directory ID, and filename. When specifying an edition, follow the standard conventions described in the File Manager chapter of this volume.

After filling in the fields of the new publisher reply record, pass it as a parameter to the NewPublisherDialog function, which displays the publisher dialog box.

```
err := NewPublisherDialog (reply);
```

After displaying the publisher dialog box, use the CreateEditionContainerFile function to create the edition container, and then use NewSection function to create the section record and the alias record. See "Creating the Section Record and Alias Record" earlier in this chapter for detailed information.

In response to the user selecting the Create Publisher menu item, this code illustrates how your application might set up the preview for the edition, set the default name for the edition container, and call an application-defined function (DoNewPublisher function) to display the publisher dialog box on the user's screen. An application might call the DoNewPublisher function as a result of the user making a menu selection to create a publisher or in response to handling the Create Publisher event. See the Apple Event Manager chapter in this volume for an example handler that handles the Create Publisher event.

```
VAR
thisDocument:            MyDocumentInfoPtr;
promptForDialog:         Boolean;
preview:                 Handle;
previewFormat:           FormatType;
defaultLocation:         EditionContainerSpec;

BEGIN
   {Get a preview to show the user. The MyGetPreviewForSelection }
   { function returns a handle to the preview.}
   preview := MyGetPreviewForSelection(thisDocument);
   previewFormat := 'TEXT';
```

```
   defaultLocation := MyGetDefaultEditionSpec(thisDocument);
   promptForDialog := TRUE;
   myErr := DoNewPublisher(thisDocument, promptForDialog, preview,
                           previewFormat, defaultLocation);
END;
```

Creating the Edition Container

Use the CreateEditionContainerFile function to create an edition container to hold the publisher data.

```
err := CreateEditionContainerFile (editionFile, fdCreator,
                                   editionFileNameScript);
```

This function creates an edition container. The edition container is empty (that is, it does not contain any formats) at this time.

To create a customized icon for the edition container, put the creator signature of your application with the icon in your application's bundle. See the Finder Interface chapter in this volume for additional information. Depending on the contents of the edition, the file type will be 'edtp' (for graphics), 'edtt' (for text), or 'edts' (for sound).

After creating the edition container, use the NewSection function to create the section record and alias record for the section.

Listing 4-4 illustrates how to create a publisher. The DoNewPublisher function shown in the listing is a function provided by an application. Note that an application might call the DoNewPublisher function as a result of the user making a menu selection to create a publisher or in response to handling the Create Publisher event. See the Apple Event Manager chapter in this volume for an example handler that handles the Create Publisher event.

The parameters to the DoNewPublisher function include a pointer to information about the document, a Boolean value that indicates if the function should display the new publisher dialog box, the preview for the edition, the preview format, and an edition container.

The function displays the publisher dialog box if requested, letting the user accept or change the name of the edition and the location where the edition should reside. Use the CreateEditionContainerFile function to create the edition with the given name and location. Use the NewSection function to create a new section for the publisher.

After the section is created, you must write out the edition data. Be sure to add the newly created section to your list of sections for this document. There are several different techniques for creating publishers and unique IDs; this listing displays one technique.

Listing 4-4. Creating a publisher

```
FUNCTION DoNewPublisher(thisDocument: MyDocumentInfoPtr;
                        promptForDialog: Boolean; preview: Handle;
                        previewFormat: FormatType;
                        editionSpec: EditionContainerSpec) : OSErr;
VAR
   getLastErr, dialogErr:  OSErr;
   createErr, sectionErr:  OSErr;
```

```
      resID:                   Integer;
      thisSectionH:            SectionHandle;
      reply:                   NewPublisherReply;
   BEGIN
      {Set up info for new publisher reply record}
      reply.replacing := FALSE;
      reply.usePart := FALSE;
      reply.preview := preview;
      reply.previewFormat := previewFormat;
      reply.container := editionSpec;

      IF promptForDialog THEN
      BEGIN                            {user interaction is allowed}
                                 {Display dialog box and let user select.}
         dialogErr := NewPublisherDialog(reply);
         {Dispose of preview data handle.}
         DisposHandle(reply.preview);
         {There's usually no error returned here, but if there is, }
         { then it makes no sense to continue with this operation.}
         IF dialogErr <> noErr THEN MyErrHandler(dialogErr);
         {Do nothing if user canceled.}
         IF reply.canceled THEN
         BEGIN
            DoNewPublisher := userCanceledErr;
            EXIT(DoNewPublisher);
         END;
      END;
      {If user wants to replace an existing file, don't create one.}
      IF NOT reply.replacing THEN
      BEGIN
         createErr :=
               CreateEditionContainerFile(reply.container.theFile,
                                          kAppSignature,
                                          reply.container.theFileScript);
         {If the create failed, then this operation can't be completed}
         IF createErr <> noErr THEN
         BEGIN
            DoNewPublisher := errAEPermissionDenied;
            EXIT(DoNewPublisher);
         END;
      END;
      {Advance counter to make a new unique sectionID for this }
      { document. It is not required that you equate section IDs with }
      { resources.}
      thisDocument^.nextSectionID := thisDocument^.nextSectionID + 1;

      {Create a publisher section.}
      sectionErr := NewSection(reply.container,
                               thisDocument^.fileSpecPtr,
                               stPublisher, thisDocument^.nextSectionID,
                               pumOnSave, thisSectionH);
      IF (sectionErr <> noErr) & (sectionErr <> multiplePublisherWrn) &
         (sectionErr <> notThePublisherWrn) THEN
         {If a new section could not be created, don't continue with this }
         { operation.}
         MyErrHandler(sectionErr);

      resID := thisDocument^.nextSectionID;
```

(Continued)

Listing 4-4. Creating a publisher (Continued)

```
   {Add this section/alias pair to my internal bookkeeping. }
   { The AddSectionAliasPair is a routine to accomplish this.}
   AddSectionAliasPair(thisDocument, thisSectionH, resID);

   {Write out first edition.}
   DoWriteEdition(thisSectionH, thisDocument);

   {Remember that the section and alias records need to be }
   { saved as resources when the user saves the document.}

   {Set the function result appropriately}
   DoNewPublisher := MyGetLastError;

END; {DoNewPublisher}
```

Opening an Edition Container to Write Data

Several routines are required to write (publish) data from a publisher to an edition container. Before writing data to an edition, you must use the OpenNewEdition function. This function should be used only for a publisher within a document. Use this function to initiate the writing of data to an edition.

```
err := OpenNewEdition (publisherSectionH, fdCreator,
                       publisherSectionDocument, refNum);
```

A user may try to save a document containing a publisher that is unable to write its data to an edition—because another publisher (that shares the same edition) is writing, another subscriber (that shares the same edition) is reading, or a publisher located on another computer is registered to the section. In such a case, you may decide to refrain from writing to the edition so that the user does not have to wait. You should also refrain from displaying an error to the user. The contents of the publisher are saved to disk with the document. The next time that the user saves, you can write the publisher data to the edition. You should discourage users from making multiple copies of the same publisher and pasting them in the same or other documents by displaying an alert box (see "Duplicating Publishers and Subscribers" later in this chapter).

If a user clicks Send Edition Now within the publisher options dialog box (to write publisher data to an edition manually), and the publisher is unable to write its data to its edition (for any of the reasons outlined above), you should display an error message.

After you are finished writing data to an edition, use the CloseEdition function to close the edition.

Listing 4-5 illustrates how to write data to an edition. As described earlier, you must open the edition, write each format using the WriteEdition function, and close the edition using the CloseEdition function. This listing shows how to write text only. If the edition is written successfully, subscribers receive Section Read events.

Listing 4-5. Writing data to an edition

```
PROCEDURE DoWriteEdition(thePublisher: SectionHandle);

VAR
   eRefNum:        EditionRefNum;
   openErr:        OSErr;
```

```
   writeErr:        OSErr;
   closeErr:        OSErr;
   thisDocument:    MyDocumentInfoPtr;
   textHandle:      Handle;

BEGIN
   {Find out which document this section belongs to. }
   { The FindDocument function accomplishes this.}
   thisDocument := FindDocument(thePublisher);

   {Open edition for writing.}
   openErr := OpenNewEdition(thePublisher, kAppSignature,
                             thisDocument^.fileSpecPtr, eRefNum);
   IF openErr <> noErr THEN
   {If the open failed, then you can't write, }
   { so don't continue with this operation.}
   MyErrHandler(openErr);

   {Get the text data to write. The GetTextInSection }
   { function accomplishes this.}
   textHandle := GetTextInSection(thePublisher, thisDocument);

   {Write out text data.}
   HLock(textHandle);
   writeErr := WriteEdition(eRefNum, 'TEXT', textHandle^,
                            GetHandleSize(textHandle));
   HUnLock(textHandle);
   IF writeErr <> noErr THEN
   BEGIN
      {There were problems writing; simply close the edition. }
      { When successful = FALSE, the edition data <> section data. }
      { Note: this isn't fatal or bad; it just means that the }
      { data wasn't written and no Section Read events will be }
      { generated.}
      closeErr := CloseEdition(eRefNum, FALSE);
   END ELSE
   BEGIN
      {The write was successful; now close the edition. }
      { When successful = TRUE, the edition data = section data. }
      { This edition is now available to any subscibers. }
      { Section Read events will be sent to current subscribers.}
      closeErr := CloseEdition(eRefNum, TRUE);
   END;
END; {DoWriteEdition}
```

Creating a Subscriber

You need to create a Subscribe To menu command in the Edit menu. When a user chooses Subscribe To from this menu, your application should display the subscriber dialog box on the user's screen.

Use the NewSubscriberDialog function to display the subscriber dialog box on the user's screen. This function is similar to the CustomGetFile procedure described in the Standard File Package chapter in this volume.

To create a subscriber, you must get information from the user, such as the name of the edition being subscribed to. The dialog box displays a listing of all available editions and allows the user to see a preview (thumbnail sketch) of the edition selected. Figure 4-12 shows a sample subscriber dialog box.

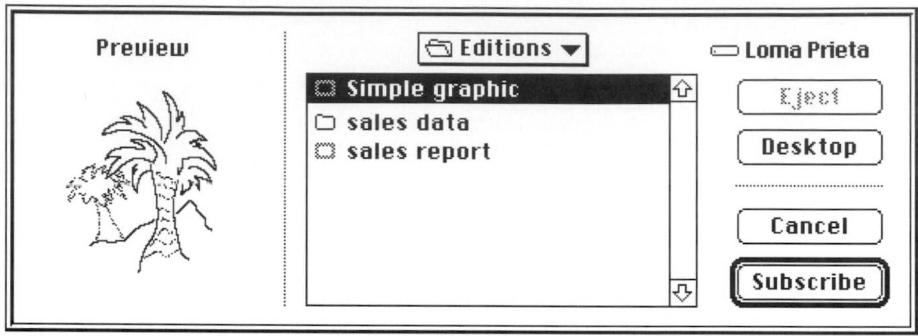

Figure 4-12. A sample subscriber dialog box

The subscriber dialog box allows the user to choose an edition to subscribe to. The NewSubscriberDialog function handles all user interaction until a user clicks Subscribe or Cancel. When a user selects an edition container, the Edition Manager accesses the preview for the edition container (if it is available) and displays it.

You pass a new subscriber reply record as a parameter to the NewSubscriberDialog function.

```
TYPE NewSubscriberReply =
     RECORD
        canceled:           Boolean;        {user canceled dialog box}
        formatsMask:        SignedByte;     {formats required}
        container:          EditionContainerSpec      {edition selected}
     END;
```

The canceled field returns a Boolean value of TRUE if the user clicked Cancel. To indicate which edition format types (text, graphics, or sound) your application can read, you set the formatsMask field to one or more of these constants:

```
CONST kPICTformatMask      = 1;         {Can subscribe to 'PICT', }
      kTEXTformatMask      = 2;         { 'TEXT', and }
      ksndFormatMask       = 4;         { 'snd '.}
```

To support a combination of formats, add the constants together. For example, a formatsMask of 3 displays both graphics and text edition format types in the subscriber dialog box.

The container field is of data type EditionContainerSpec. You must initialize the container field with the default edition volume reference number, directory ID, filename, and part. To do so, use the GetLastEditionContainerUsed function to obtain the name of the last edition displayed in the dialog box.

```
err := GetLastEditionContainerUsed (container);
```

This function returns the last edition container for which a new subscriber was created using the NewSection function. If there is no last edition, or if the edition was deleted,

GetLastEditionContainerUsed still returns the correct volume reference number and directory ID to use, but leaves the filename blank and returns the fnfErr result code.

The container field is of data type EditionContainerSpec.

```
TYPE EditionContainerSpec =
     RECORD
        theFile:            FSSpec;         {file containing edition }
                                            { data}
        theFileScript:      ScriptCode;     {script code of filename}
        thePart:            LongInt;        {which part of file, }
                                            { always kPartsNotUsed}
        thePartName:        Str31;          {not used in version 7.0}
        thePartScript:      ScriptCode      {not used in version 7.0}
     END;
```

The field theFile is of type FSSpec. See the File Manager chapter in this volume for further information on file system specification records.

After filling in the fields of the new subscriber reply record, pass it as a parameter to the NewSubscriberDialog function, which displays the subscriber dialog box.

```
err := NewSubscriberDialog (reply);
```

After displaying the subscriber dialog box, call the NewSection function to create the section record and the alias record. See "Creating the Section Record and Alias Record" earlier in this chapter for detailed information.

If the subscriber is set up to receive new editions automatically (not manually), the Edition Manager sends your application a Section Read event. Whenever your application receives a Section Read event, it should read the contents of the edition into the subscriber.

Listing 4-6 illustrates how to create a subscriber. As described earlier, you must set up and display the subscriber dialog box to allow the user to subscribe to all available editions. After your application creates a subscriber, your application receives a Section Read event to read in the data being subscribed to. Be sure to add the newly created section to your list of sections for this file. There are many different techniques for creating subscribers and unique IDs; this listing displays one technique.

Listing 4-6. Creating a subscriber

```
PROCEDURE DoNewSubscriber(thisDocument: MyDocumentInfoPtr);

VAR
   getLastErr:     OSErr;
   dialogErr:      OSErr;
   sectionErr:     OSErr;
   resID:          Integer;
   thisSectionH:   SectionHandle;
   reply:          NewSubscriberReply;
```

(Continued)

Listing 4-6. Creating a subscriber (Continued)

```
BEGIN
   {Put default edition name into reply record.}
   getLastErr := GetLastEditionContainerUsed(reply.container);

   {Can subscribe to pictures or text.}
   reply.formatsMask := kPICTformatsMask + kTEXTformatsMask;

   {Display dialog box and let user select.}
   dialogErr := NewSubscriberDialog(reply);
   {There's usually no error returned here, but if there is, }
   { then it makes no sense to continue with this operation. }
   { Pass control to MyErrHandler.}
   IF dialogErr <> noErr THEN MyErrHandler(dialogErr);

   {Do nothing if user canceled.}
   IF reply.canceled THEN EXIT(DoNewSubscriber);

   {Advance counter to make a new unique sectionID for this }
   { document. It is not necessary to equate section IDs with }
   { resources.}
   thisDocument^.nextSectionID := thisDocument^.nextSectionID + 1;

   {Create a subscriber section.}
   sectionErr := NewSection(reply.container,
                            thisDocument^.fileSpecPtr,
                            stSubscriber,
                            thisDocument^.nextSectionID,
                            sumAutomatic, thisSectionH);
   IF sectionErr <> noErr THEN
   {Same reasoning as above. If a new section could not be }
   { created, don't continue with this operation. Pass }
   { control to MyErrHandler.}
   MyErrHandler(sectionErr);

   resID := thisDocument^.nextSectionID;

   {Add this section/alias pair to your internal bookkeeping. }
   { AddSectionAliasPair is a routine to accomplish this.}
   AddSectionAliasPair(thisDocument, thisSectionH, resID);

   {Remember that you will receive a Section Read event to read }
   { in the edition that you just subscribed to because the initial }
   { mode is set to sumAutomatic.}

   {Remember that the section and alias records need to be saved }
   { as resources when the user saves the document.}

END; {DoNewSubscriber}
```

Opening an Edition Container to Read Data

Before reading data from an edition, you must use the OpenEdition function. Your application should only use this function for a subscriber. Use this function to initiate the reading of data from an edition.

```
err := OpenEdition (subscriberSectionH, refNum);
```

As a precaution, you should retain the old data until the user can no longer undo. This allows you to undo changes if the user requests it.

Your application can supply a procedure such as DoReadEdition to read in data from the edition to a subscriber. When your application opens a document containing a subscriber that is set up to receive new editions automatically, the Edition Manager sends you a Section Read event if the edition has been updated. The Section Read event supplies the handle to the section that requires updating. Listing 4-7 provides an example of reading data from an edition.

Choosing Which Edition Format to Read

After your application opens the edition container for a subscriber, it can look in the edition for formats that it understands. To accomplish this, use the EditionHasFormat function.

```
err := EditionHasFormat (whichEdition, whichFormat, formatSize);
```

The EditionHasFormat function returns the noTypeErr result code if a requested format is not available. If the requested format is available, this function returns the noErr result code, and the formatSize parameter contains the size of the data in the specified format or kFormatLengthUnknown (–1), which signifies that the size is unknown.

After your application opens the edition container and determines which formats it wants to read, call the ReadEdition function to read in the edition data. See "Reading and Writing Edition Data" earlier in this chapter for detailed information.

After you have completed writing the edition data into the subscriber section, call the CloseEdition function to close the edition. See "Closing an Edition" earlier in this chapter for detailed information.

Listing 4-7 illustrates how to read data from an edition. As described earlier, you must open the edition, determine which formats to read, use the ReadEdition function to read in data, and then use the CloseEdition function to close the edition. This listing shows how to read only text.

Listing 4-7. Reading in edition data

```
PROCEDURE DoReadEdition(theSubscriber: SectionHandle);

VAR
   eRefNum:       EditionRefNum;
   openErr:       OSErr;
   readErr:       OSErr;
   closeErr:      OSErr;
   thisDocument:  MyDocumentInfoPtr;
   textHandle:    Handle;
   formatLen:     Size;

BEGIN
   {Find out which document this section belongs to. }
   { The FindDocument function accomplishes this.}
   thisDocument := FindDocument(theSubscriber);

   {Open the edition for reading.}
   openErr := OpenEdition(theSubscriber, eRefNum);
   IF openErr <> noErr THEN
   {If the open failed, then most likely you can't read, }
   { so don't continue with this operation.}
      MyErrHandler(openErr);

   {Look for 'TEXT' format.}
   IF EditionHasFormat(eRefNum, 'TEXT', formatLen) = noErr THEN
   BEGIN
      {Get the handle of location to read to. }
      { The GetTextInSection function accomplishes this.}
      textHandle := GetTextInSection(theSubscriber, thisDocument);
      SetHandleSize(textHandle, formatLen);
      HLock(textHandle);
      readErr := ReadEdition(eRefNum, 'TEXT', textHandle^,
                             formatLen);
      HUnLock(textHandle);

      IF readErr = noErr THEN
      BEGIN
         {The read was successful; now close the edition. }
         { When successful = TRUE, the section data = edition data.}
         closeErr := CloseEdition(eRefNum, TRUE);
         EXIT(DoReadEdition);
      END;
   END;
   {'TEXT' format wasn't found or read error; just close }
   { the edition. FALSE tells the Edition Manager that your application }
   { did not get the latest edition.}
   closeErr := CloseEdition(eRefNum, FALSE);

END; {DoReadEdition}
```

Using Publisher and Subscriber Options

There are special options associated with publishers and subscribers within documents. Your application can use the publisher and subscriber options dialog boxes provided by the Edition Manager to make these choices available to the user. You should make these dialog boxes available to the user by creating a menu command in the Edit menu that toggles between Publisher Options (when the user has selected a publisher within a document) and Subscriber Options (when a user has selected a subscriber within a document).

When a user chooses these menu commands, you need to display the corresponding publisher or subscriber options dialog box. Use the SectionOptionsDialog function to display the appropriate dialog box on the user's screen.

```
err := SectionOptionsDialog (reply);
```

Each dialog box contains information regarding the section and its edition. Figure 4-13 shows the publisher options dialog box with the update mode set to On Save.

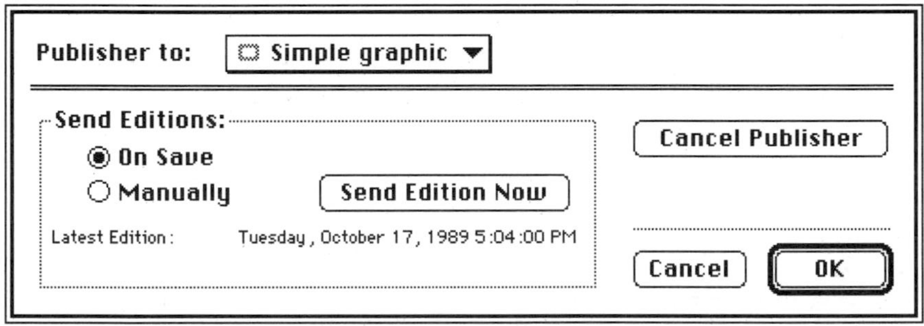

Figure 4-13. The publisher options dialog box with update mode set to On Save

Figure 4-14 shows the publisher options dialog box with the update mode set to Manually.

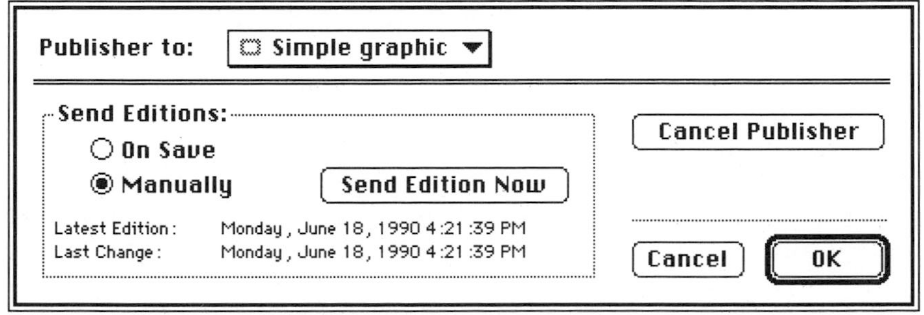

Figure 4-14. The publisher options dialog box with update mode set to Manually

As a shortcut for the user, you should display the publisher options dialog box when the user double-clicks on a publisher section within a document.

Figure 4-15 shows the subscriber options dialog box with the update mode set to Automatically.

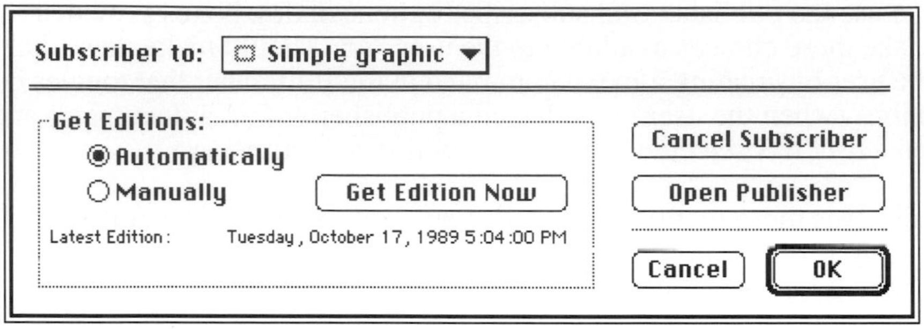

Figure 4-15. The subscriber options dialog box with update mode set to Automatically

Figure 4-16 shows the subscriber options dialog box with the update mode set to Manually.

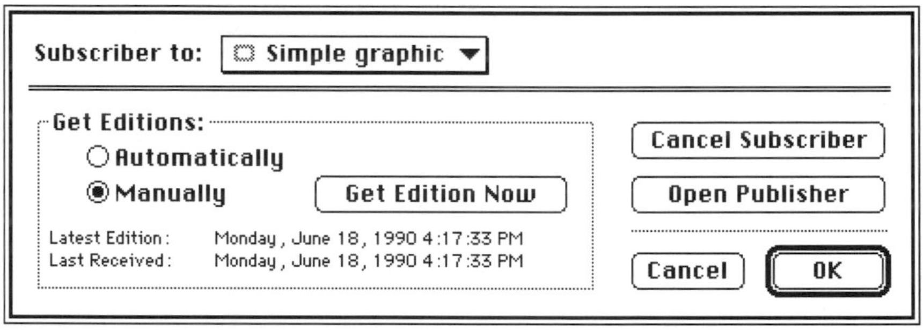

Figure 4-16. The subscriber options dialog box with update mode set to Manually

As a shortcut for the user, you should display the subscriber options dialog box when the user double-clicks on a subscriber section within a document.

You pass a section options reply record as a parameter to the SectionOptionsDialog function.

```
TYPE SectionOptionsReply =
     RECORD
         canceled:          Boolean;       {user canceled dialog box}
         changed:           Boolean;       {changed section record}
         sectionH:          SectionHandle; {handle to the specified }
                                           { section record}
         action:            ResType        {action codes}
     END;
```

Set the sectionH parameter to the handle to the section record for the section the user selected.

Upon return of the SectionOptionsDialog function, the canceled and changed fields are set. If the canceled parameter is set to TRUE, the user canceled the dialog box. Otherwise, this parameter is FALSE. If the changed parameter is TRUE, the section record is changed. For example, the user may have changed the update mode.

The action parameter contains the code for one of five user actions. All action codes dismiss the publisher and subscriber options dialog boxes when complete.

- action code is 'read' for user selection of the Get Edition Now button
- action code is 'writ' for user selection of the Send Edition Now button
- action code is 'goto' for user selection of the Open Publisher button
- action code is 'cncl' for user selection of the Cancel Publisher or Cancel Subscriber button
- action code is '   ' ($20202020) for user selection of the OK button

Listing 4-8 shows an example of how your application can respond to the action codes received from the section options reply record. There are several different techniques that your application can use to accomplish this—this listing shows one technique.

Listing 4-8. Responding to action codes

```
PROCEDURE DoOptionsDialog(theSection: SectionHandle);

VAR
   reply:            SectionOptionReply;
   theEditionInfo:   EditionInfoRecord;
   action:           ResType;
   sodErr:           OSErr;
   geiErr:           OSErr;
   gpiErr:           OSErr;

BEGIN
   reply.sectionH := theSection;
   sodErr := SectionOptionsDialog(reply);

   {Determine what the user did and handle appropriately.}
   IF reply.canceled THEN
      {The user changed his/her mind; simply return.}
      EXIT(DoOptionsDialog);

   IF reply.changed THEN
      {The section record has changed; make note of this. }
      { SectionHasChanged is a routine to accomplish this.}
      SectionHasChanged(theSection);
      {If you customize, you may want to do some post-processing now.}

   action := reply.action;     {Get the action code.}

   IF (action = 'read') THEN
   BEGIN {User selected Get Edition Now button.}
      DoReadEdition(theSection);
      EXIT(DoOptionsDialog);
   END;
```

(Continued)

Listing 4-8. Responding to action codes (Continued)

```
   IF (action = 'writ') THEN
   BEGIN {User selected Send Edition Now button.}
      DoWriteEdition(theSection);
      EXIT(DoOptionsDialog);
   END;

   IF (action = 'goto') THEN
   BEGIN {User selected Open Publisher button.}
      geiErr := GetEditionInfo(theSection, theEditionInfo);
      {There's usually no error returned here, but if }
      { there is, then don't continue with this operation.}
      IF geiErr <> noErr THEN MyErrHandler(geiErr);

      gpsErr := GotoPublisherSection(theEditionInfo.container);
      {Same comment as above. Pass control to MyErrHandler }
      { if there's an error.}
      IF gpsErr <> noErr THEN MyErrHandler(gpsErr);
      EXIT(DoOptionsDialog);
   END;

   IF (action = 'cncl') THEN
   BEGIN {User selected Cancel Publisher or Cancel Subscriber button.}
      {Call the UnRegisterSection function and dispose of the }
      { section record and the alias record.}
      EXIT(DoOptionsDialog);
   END;
END; {DoOptionsDialog}
```

The following sections describe the features of the publisher and subscriber options dialog boxes.

Publishing a New Edition While Saving or Manually

By default, your application should write publisher data to an edition each time the user saves the document and the contents of the publisher differ from the latest edition. In the publisher options dialog box, the user can choose to write new data to an edition each time the document is saved (by clicking On Save) or only when the user specifically requests it (by clicking Manually).

When the update mode is set to manual, a user must click the Send Edition Now button within the publisher options dialog box to write publisher data to an edition. When a user clicks Send Edition Now, the section options reply record contains the action code 'writ'. Write out the new edition beginning with the OpenNewEdition function. Writing to an edition manually is useful when a user tends to save a document numerous times while revising it.

Each time the user saves the document, check the update mode of the publisher section. If the publisher section sends its data to an edition on save, check to see whether the publisher data has changed since it was last written out to the edition. If so, write out the new edition.

In addition, you may also support a Stop All Editions menu command to provide a method for temporarily suspending all update activity. See "Publishers, Subscribers, and Editions" earlier in this chapter for additional information.

Subscribing to an Edition Automatically or Manually

By default, your application should subscribe to an edition each time new edition data becomes available. In the subscriber options dialog box, the user can choose to read new data from an edition as the data is available (by clicking Automatically) or only when the user specifically requests it (by clicking Manually).

When the update mode is set to manual, the user must click the Get Edition Now button within the subscriber options dialog box to receive new editions. When a user clicks this button, the section options reply record contains the action code 'read'. Read in the new edition beginning with the OpenEdition function. See "Opening an Edition Container to Read Data" earlier in this chapter for detailed information.

When the update mode is set to automatic, your application receives a Section Read event each time a new edition becomes available. In response, you should read the new edition data beginning with the OpenNewEdition function.

Your application does not receive Section Read events for subscribers that receive new editions manually.

You may also support a Stop All Editions menu command to provide a method for temporarily suspending all update activity. See "Publishers, Subscribers, and Editions" earlier in this chapter for additional information.

Canceling Sections Within Documents

The option of canceling publishers and subscribers is available to the user through the Cancel Publisher and Cancel Subscriber buttons in the corresponding options dialog boxes. When the user wants to cancel the publisher or cancel the subscriber within a document, the action code of the section options reply record is 'cncl'. See "Relocating an Edition" later in this chapter for additional information on canceling a section.

When a user cancels a section (either a publisher or subscriber) and then saves the document, or when a user closes an untitled document (which contains newly created sections) without saving, you must unregister each corresponding section record and alias record using the UnRegisterSection function. In addition, you should also delete the section record and alias record using the DisposHandle procedure. See the Memory Manager chapter in Volume I for additional information on the DisposHandle procedure.

When a user cancels a publisher section and then saves the document, or when a user closes an untitled document (which contains newly created publishers) without saving, you must also delete any corresponding edition containers (in addition to deleting section records and alias records).

Do not delete an edition container file, section record, or alias record until the user saves the document—the user may decide to undo changes before saving the document.

To locate the appropriate edition container to be deleted (before you use the UnRegisterSection function), use the GetEditionInfo function.

```
err := GetEditionInfo (sectionH, editionInfo);
```

The editionInfo parameter is a record of data type EditionInfoRecord.

```
TYPE EditionInfoRecord =
     RECORD
        crDate:              TimeStamp;      {date edition container }
                                             { was created}
        mdDate:              TimeStamp;      {date of last change}
        fdCreator:           OSType;         {file creator}
        fdType:              OSType;         {file type}
        container:           EditionContainerSpec      {the edition}
     END;
```

The GetEditionInfo function returns the edition container as part of the edition information.

The crDate field contains the creation date of the edition. The mdDate field contains the modification date of the edition.

The fdType and the fdCreator fields are the type and creator of the edition file. The container field includes a volume reference number, directory ID, filename, script, and part number for the edition.

To remove the edition container, use the DeleteEditionContainerFile function.

```
err := DeleteEditionContainerFile (editionFile);
```

Locating a Publisher Through a Subscriber

The user can locate a publisher from a subscriber within a document by clicking the Open Publisher button in the subscriber options dialog box. As a shortcut, Apple suggests that you also allow the user to locate a publisher when the user selects a subscriber within a document and presses Option–double-click.

When the action code of the SectionOptionsReply record is 'goto', use the GoToPublisherSection function.

```
err := GoToPublisherSection (container);
```

The GoToPublisherSection function locates the correct document by resolving the alias in the edition, and it launches the document's application if necessary (the Edition Manager sends an Open Documents event). The Edition Manager then sends the publishing application a Section Scroll event. If the document containing the requested publisher is located on the same computer as its subscriber, the document opens and scrolls to the location of the publisher. If the document containing the requested publisher is located on a shared volume (using file sharing), the document opens and scrolls to the location of the publisher only if the user has privileges to open the document from the Finder.

You need to provide the GoToPublisherSection function with the edition container. To accomplish this, use the GetEditionInfo function. See the previous section, "Canceling Sections Within Documents," for information on the GetEditionInfo function.

Renaming a Document Containing Sections

If a user renames a document that contains sections by choosing Save As from the File menu, or if a user pastes a portion of a document that contains a section into another document, use the AssociateSection function.

Use the AssociateSection function to update the alias record of a registered section.

```
err := AssociateSection (sectionH, newSectionDocument);
```

The AssociateSection function internally calls the UpdateAlias function. It is also possible to update the alias record using the Alias Manager (see the Alias Manager chapter in this volume for additional information).

Displaying Publisher and Subscriber Borders

Each publisher and subscriber within a document should have a border that appears when a user selects the contents of these sections. You should display a publisher border as 3 pixels wide with 50 percent gray lines and a subscriber border as 3 pixels wide with 75 percent gray lines. Separate the contents of the section from the border itself with one pixel of white space. To create your borders, you should use patterns—not colors. Depending on the user's monitor type, colors may not be distinguishable.

In general, borders for publishers and subscribers should behave like the borders of 'PICT' graphics within a word-processing document. A border should appear when the user clicks within the content area of a publisher or a subscriber and disappear when the user clicks outside the content area of a section. You can also make all publisher and subscriber borders appear or disappear by implementing an optional Show/Hide Borders menu command. Figure 4-17 displays the Edition Manager Show/Hide Borders menu command in the Edit menu.

Figure 4-17. Edit menu with Show/Hide Borders menu command

Depending on your application, you may choose to include resize handles or similar components in your borders. See “Object-Oriented Graphics Borders” later in this chapter for an example of resize handles.

Whenever a user selects a portion of a publisher or inserts a cursor into the publisher, you should display the border as 50 percent gray. A user can copy the contents of a publisher or subscriber without copying the section itself by selecting the data, copying, and then pasting the data in a new location. A user can cut and paste a selection that contains an *entire* publisher or subscriber, but you should discourage users from making multiple copies of a publisher. See “Duplicating Publishers and Subscribers” later in this chapter for detailed information.

When the user modifies a publisher, your application should grow or shrink its border to accommodate the new dimension of the section.

You should display only one publisher border within a document at a time. If a cursor is inserted within a publisher that is contained within a larger publisher, you should display only the smaller, internal publisher border. If it is absolutely necessary to display all section borders within a document at the same time, you can create a Show/Hide Borders menu item.

You do not need to provide support for publishers contained within other publishers. If you do not, you should dim the Create Publisher menu command (to indicate that it is not selectable) when a user attempts to create a publisher within an existing publisher.

Figure 4-18 shows the recommended border behavior for publishers when borders are shown, when a user selects the contents of a section, and when a user selects data within a document that includes a publisher section.

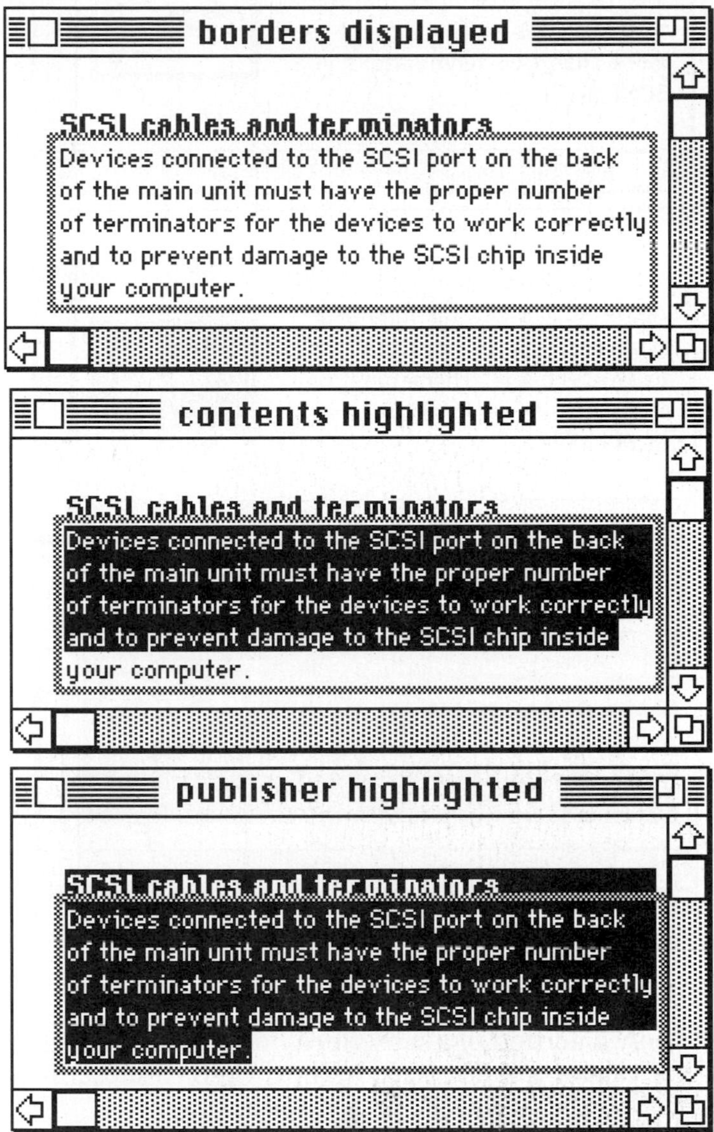

Figure 4-18. Publisher borders

Figure 4-19 shows the recommended border behavior for subscribers when borders are shown, when a user selects the contents of a section, and when a user selects data within a document that includes a subscriber section.

Figure 4-19. Subscriber borders

If a user tries to select only a portion of a subscriber, you should highlight the entire contents of the subscriber. A user cannot edit the data contained within a subscriber. See "Modifying a Subscriber" later in this chapter for detailed information.

If a user cancels a section using the publisher or subscriber options dialog box, your application should leave the contents of the section within the document, but you should be sure to remove the borders from this data, as it is no longer considered a section.

Generally, the appearance and function of publisher and subscriber borders should be the same across different applications. See the following sections entitled "Text Borders," "Spreadsheet Borders," "Object-Oriented Graphics Borders," and "Bitmapped Graphics Borders" for descriptions of specialized features for publisher and subscriber borders in word processing, spreadsheet, or graphics applications.

Text Borders

In word-processing documents, a publisher may contain other publishers. However, one publisher should not *overlap* another publisher. You should display only one publisher border at a time. If an insertion point is placed within a publisher that is encompassed by another larger publisher, you should display only the smaller internal publisher border.

In exceptional cases, it may be necessary to display more than one publisher or subscriber border at a time. For example, a publisher may consist of a paragraph that includes a marker for a footnote. The data contained within the footnote should also be considered part of the publisher. When a user selects the paragraph, you should simultaneously display a border around the footnote.

The border of a publisher that contains text should be located between characters within the text. The insertion point, when placed on such a boundary, should gravitate toward the publisher. That is, a click in front (to the left) of a publisher border should place the cursor inside the publisher, so that subsequent typing goes inside the publisher. Clicking at the end (to the right) of a publisher border should also place the cursor inside the publisher.

Whenever two separate borders are adjacent to one another (side by side), the boundary click should go in between them. This is also true for a border that is next to other nontextual aspects of a document, such as 'PICT' graphics or page breaks.

When a user removes information from a publisher that contains text data, the border should become smaller to accommodate the new text. When a user adds information to the publisher, the border should grow to show the enlarged area of the publisher. The insertion point should remain within the publisher.

If a user highlights the entire contents of a publisher and then chooses Cut from the Edit menu, you should not delete the publisher border within the document. The user may intend to delete the existing publisher data and replace it with new data, or the user may want to move the entire publisher and its data to a new location. Figure 4-20 shows this state.

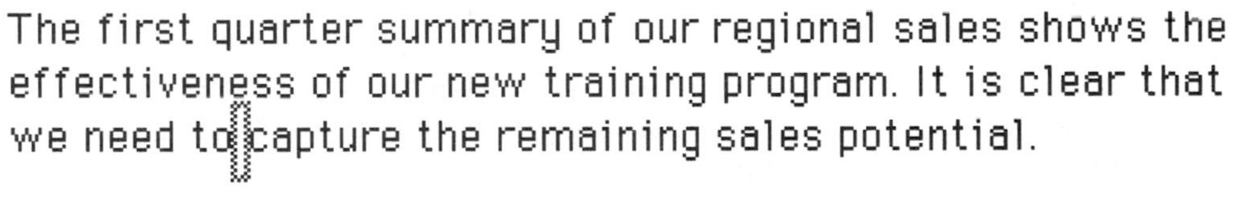

The first quarter summary of our regional sales shows the effectiveness of our new training program. It is clear that we need to capture the remaining sales potential.

Figure 4-20. A publisher with contents removed

You should leave the cursor inside the small publisher border for further typing. If the user inserts the cursor in a new location (instead of typing data inside the existing border), you need to remove the empty publisher border from the document to allow the user to move the publisher. This effectively deletes the publisher from the document. If the user pastes the publisher that is currently held in the Clipboard, you should recreate its border. If the user cuts or copies other data from the document before pasting the publisher from the Clipboard, the publisher should be removed from the Clipboard.

Spreadsheet Borders

Borders around spreadsheet data or other data in arrays should look and behave very much like text borders. Figure 4-21 shows a typical border within a spreadsheet document.

	A	B	C	D	E
1		January	February	March	
2	Cogs	14890	17849	274945	
3	Sprockets	16494	184384	304890	
4	Widgets	3780	5839	7900	
5					

Figure 4-21. A publisher border within a spreadsheet document

Note that the border goes below the column headers (A, B, C, D) and to the right of the row labels (1, 2, 3, 4)—it should not overlap these cell boundaries. The border at the bottom and the border on the right side can be placed within the adjacent cells (outside of the cells that constitute the publisher).

In contrast to word-processing applications, borders in spreadsheet documents (or other documents with array data) can overlap. That is, a user can select a row of cells to be a publisher and an overlapping column of those cells to be another publisher. You should never display more than one publisher border at a time. When a user selects a spreadsheet cell that is part of more than one publisher, you should display only the border of the publisher that was last edited. (This can be accomplished by comparing the modification dates of the publishers.)

If it is absolutely necessary to display all section borders within a document at the same time, you can create a Show/Hide Borders command in the Edit menu to toggle all borders on and off.

When data is added to or deleted from a publisher that consists of a spreadsheet cell or other array, its border should grow or shrink to accommodate the addition or deletion of data. A publisher should behave like a named range in a spreadsheet. For example, if a user cuts a row within a publisher that consists of a named range in a spreadsheet, you should shrink the publisher data and its border correspondingly.

When a user cuts a publisher and its entire contents within a spreadsheet document, the entire section should be held in the Clipboard. Do not leave an empty publisher border in a spreadsheet (as recommended for text borders). If a user attempts to paste a copy of an existing publisher, you should warn the user by displaying an alert box (see "Duplicating Publishers and Subscribers" later in this chapter).

Object-Oriented Graphics Borders

In an object-oriented drawing application, the publisher border should fit just around the selected objects.

You can provide resize handles that appear with all drawing objects to allow the user to resize the border of a publisher. Figure 4-22 shows a publisher border with resize handles.

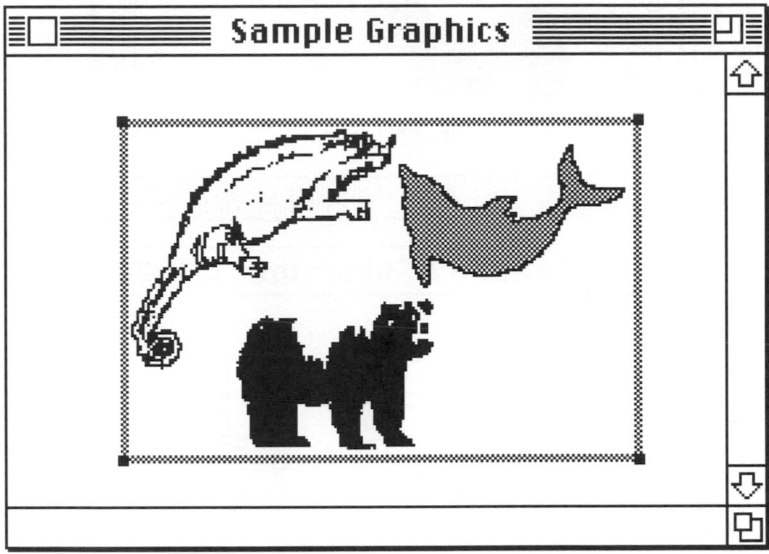

Figure 4-22. A publisher border with resize handles

A user can create freeform graphics within drawing applications that cause publisher borders to seemingly float over the area the user publishes. The border acts like a clipping rectangle—anything within the border becomes the publisher. Figure 4-23 shows a publisher that contains clipped graphics and its subscriber in another application.

A user can create publishers and subscribers that overlap each other. Thus, borders may overlap and it may no longer be possible to turn on a particular border when the user clicks within a publisher. Drawing applications should provide a menu command, Show Borders, that toggles to Hide Borders. This command should allow users to turn all publisher and subscriber borders on or off.

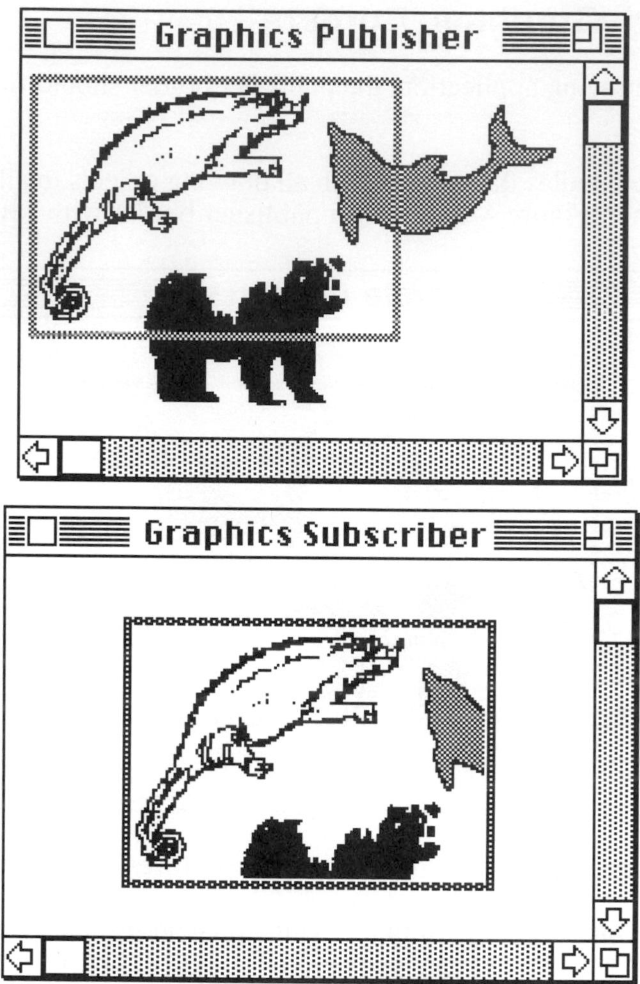

Figure 4-23. A publisher and subscriber with clipped graphics

Bitmapped Graphics Borders

Creating a border around bitmapped graphics in applications is similar to doing so in object-oriented drawing applications. The border appears around the selected area. The user can create overlapping publishers and subscribers in bitmapped graphics applications. You need to provide a Show/Hide Borders command to allow users to turn all borders on and off.

Duplicating Publishers and Subscribers

Whenever a user clicks a publisher or subscriber border, you should change the contents of the section to a selected state. You should discourage users from making multiple copies of a publisher and pasting them in the same or other documents, because the contents of the edition would be difficult or impossible to predict. Multiple copies of the same publisher also contain the same control block value. See "Creating and Registering a Section" later in this chapter for detailed information on control blocks.

When a user attempts to create a copy of a publisher that already exists, you should display an alert box such as the one shown in Figure 4-24.

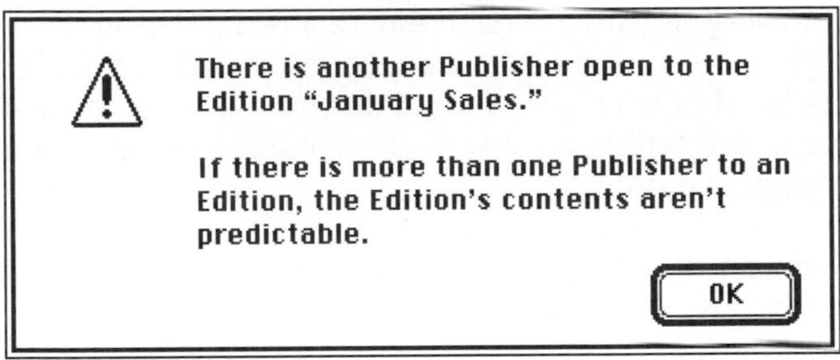

Figure 4-24. Creating multiple publishers alert box

When a user attempts to save a document that contains multiple copies of the same publisher, display an alert box such as the one shown in Figure 4-25.

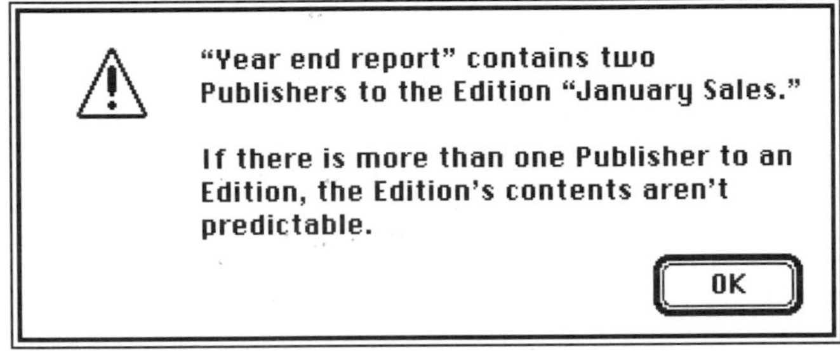

Figure 4-25. Saving multiple publishers alert box

If a user decides to ignore your alert box, your application should still save the document, but you should continue to display this error message *every time* the user saves this document.

A user can modify the contents of any duplicate publisher, but the contents of the edition will be whichever publisher was the last to write.

When a user chooses to copy and paste or duplicate a section, use the HandToHand function (described in the Operating System Utilities chapter in Volume II) to duplicate the section record and alias record. Put the alias field of the cloned section record with the handle to the cloned alias record and generate a unique section identification number for it. When exporting your Clipboard to the scrap, you should also place the section data, section record, and alias record in the scrap.

Use the RegisterSection function (described earlier in "Opening and Closing a Document Containing Sections") to register the cloned section's section record.

A user can select the *contents* of a publisher without selecting the border and copy just the data to a new location. In this case, the user has simply copied data (and not the publisher). Do not create a border for this data in the new location.

Modifying a Subscriber

When the user selects data or clicks in the data area of a subscriber, you should highlight the entire contents of the subscriber using reverse video. You can allow users to globally adorn subscribers. For example, a user might select a subscriber within a document and change all text from plain to bold. However, you should discourage users from modifying the individual elements contained within a subscriber—for example, by editing a sentence or rotating an individual graphical object.

Remember that each time a new edition arrives for a subscriber, any modifications that the user has introduced are overwritten. Global adornment of a subscriber is much easier for your application to regenerate.

If you do allow a user to edit a subscriber section, provide an enable/disable editing option within the subscriber options dialog box using the SectionOptionsExpDialog function, described later in "Customizing Dialog Boxes." When you allow a user to edit a subscriber, you should change the subscriber from a selected state to editable data.

In addition to global adornment, your application may also need to support partial selection of subscribers to enable spell checking and search operations.

Because a user can modify a publisher just like any other portion of a document, its subscriber may change in size as well as content. For example, a user may modify a publisher by adding two additional columns to a spreadsheet.

Relocating an Edition

In the Finder, users cannot move an edition across volumes. To relocate an edition, the user must first select its publisher and cancel the section (remember to remove the border). The user needs to republish and then select a new volume location for the edition. As a convenience for the user, you should retain the selection of all the publisher data after the user cancels the section to make it easy to republish the section.

Customizing Dialog Boxes

The expandable dialog box functions allow you to add items to the bottom of the dialog boxes, apply alternate mapping of events to item hits, apply alternate meanings to the item hits, and choose the location of the dialog boxes. See the Dialog Manager chapter in Volume I and the Standard File Package chapters in Volumes I and VI for additional information.

The expandable versions of these dialog boxes require five additional parameters. Use the NewPublisherExpDialog function to expand the publisher dialog box.

```
err := NewPublisherExpDialog (reply, where, expansionDITLresID,
                              dlgHook, filterProc, yourDataPtr);
```

Use the NewSubscriberExpDialog function to expand the subscriber dialog box.

```
err := NewSubscriberExpDialog (reply, where, expansionDITLresID,
                               dlgHook, filterProc, yourDataPtr);
```

Use the SectionOptionsExpDialog function to expand the publisher options and the subscriber options dialog boxes.

```
err := SectionOptionsExpDialog (reply, where, expansionDITLresID,
                                dlgHook, filterProc, yourDataPtr);
```

The reply parameter is a pointer to a NewPublisherReply, NewSubscriberReply, or SectionOptionsReply record, respectively.

You can automatically center the dialog box by passing (–1, –1) in the where parameter.

The expansionDITLresID parameter should be 0 or a valid dialog item list ('DITL') resource ID. This integer is the ID of a dialog item list whose items are appended to the end of the standard dialog item list. The dialog items keep their relative positions, but they are moved as a group to the bottom of the dialog box. See the Dialog Manager chapter in Volume I for additional information on dialog item lists.

The filterProc parameter should be a valid, expandable modal filter procedure pointer or NIL. This procedure is called by the ModalDialog function. The filterProc function enables you to map real events (such as a mouse-down event) to an item hit (such as clicking the Cancel button). For instance, you may want to map a keyboard equivalent to an item hit. See the Dialog Manager chapter in Volume I for information on the ModalDialog function.

The dlgHook parameter should be a valid, expandable dialog hook procedure pointer or NIL. This procedure is called after each call to the ModalDialog filter function. The dlgHook parameter takes the appropriate action, such as filling in a check box. The itemOffset parameter to the procedure is the number of items in the dialog item list before the expansion dialog items. You need to subtract the item offset from the item hit to get the relative item number in the expansion dialog item list. The return value from the dlgHook parameter is the absolute item number.

When the Edition Manager displays subsidiary dialog boxes in front of another dialog box on the user's screen, your dlgHook and filterProc parameters should check the refCon field in the WindowRecord data type (from the window field in the DialogRecord) to determine which window is currently in the foreground. The main dialog box for the NewPublisherExpDialog and the NewSubscriberExpDialog functions contains the following constant:

```
CONST sfMainDialogRefCon              = 'stdf';   {new publisher and }
                                                  { new subscriber}
```

The main dialog box for the SectionOptionsExpDialog function contains the following constant:

```
CONST emOptionsDialogRefCon              = 'optn';   {options dialog}
```

See "Summary of the Edition Manager" later in this chapter for additional constants.

The yourDataPtr parameter is reserved for your use. It is passed back to your hook and modal filter procedure. This parameter does not have to be of type Ptr—it can be any 32-bit quantity that you want. In Pascal, you can pass in register A6 for yourDataPtr, and make dlgHook and filterProc local functions without the last parameter. The stack frame is set up properly for these functions to access their parent local variables. See the Standard File Package chapter in this volume for detailed information.

For the NewPublisherExpDialog and NewSubscriberExpDialog functions, all the pseudo-items for the Standard File Package—such as sfHookFirstCall(–1), sfHookNullEvent(100), sfHookRebuildList(101), and sfHookLastCall(–2)—can be used, as well as emHookRedrawPreview(150).

For the SectionOptionsExpDialog function, the only valid pseudo-items are sfHookFirstCall(–1), sfHookNullEvent(100), sfHookLastCall(–2), emHookRedrawPreview(150), emHookCancelSection(160), emHookGoToPublisher(161), emHookGetEditionNow(162), emHookSendEditionNow(162), emHookManualUpdateMode(163), and emHookAutoUpdateMode(164). See the Standard File Package chapter in this volume for information on pseudo-items.

SUBSCRIBING TO NON-EDITION FILES

Using the Edition Manager, a subscriber can read data directly from another document, such as an entire 'PICT' file, instead of subscribing to an edition. This feature is for advanced applications that can set up bottleneck procedures for reading. Figure 4-26 shows a document that is subscribing directly to a 'PICT' file.

For each application, the Edition Manager keeps a pointer to a bottleneck function. The Edition Manager never opens or closes an edition container directly. Instead, the Edition Manager calls the current edition opener. The InitEditionPack function (described later in "Initializing the Edition Manager") sets up the current system opener function.

To override the standard opener function, create an opener function that contains the following parameters.

```
FUNCTION MyOpener (selector: EditionOpenerVerb;
                   VAR PB: EditionOpenerParamBlock) : OSErr;
```

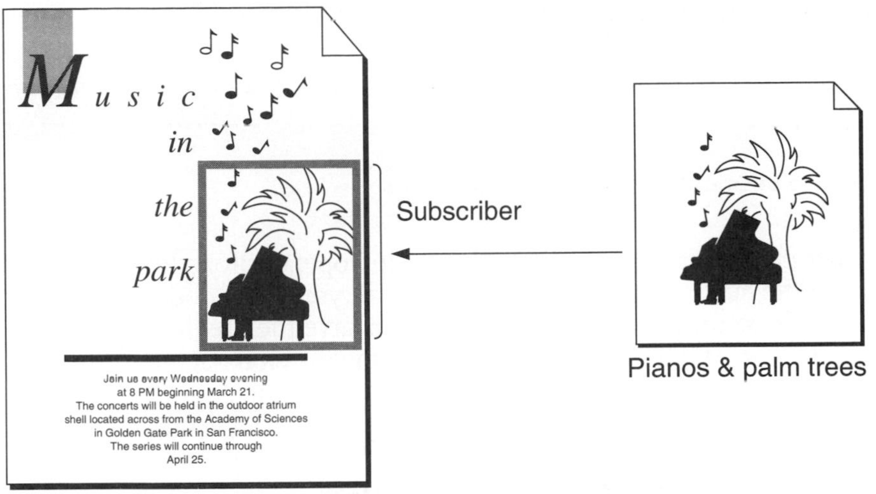

Figure 4-26. Subscribing directly to a 'PICT' file

Your opener needs to know which formats the file contains and how the data is supposed to be read or written.

The opener can allocate a handle or pointer to contain information such as file reference numbers. This value is passed as ioRefNum to the I/O procedures.

The eoOpen and eoOpenNew edition opener verbs (described later in "Calling an Edition Opener Procedure") return a pointer to a function to do the actual reading and writing.

The following sections describe

- how to get the current edition opener procedure
- how to set your own edition opener procedure
- how to call an edition opener procedure
- the edition opener parameters

Getting the Current Edition Opener

When you want to get the current edition opener procedure, use the GetEditionOpenerProc function.

```
err := GetEditionOpenerProc (opener);
```

The opener parameter returns the pointer to the current edition opener procedure. A different current opener is kept for each application. One application's opener is never called by another application.

Setting an Edition Opener

You can provide your own edition opener procedure. To do so, use the SetEditionOpenerProc function.

```
err := SetEditionOpenerProc (@MyOpener);
```

The @MyOpener parameter is a pointer to the edition opener procedure that you are providing. If you set the current opener to be a routine in your own code, be sure to call the GetEditionOpenerProc function first so that you can save the previous opener. If your opener is passed a selector that it does not understand, use the previous opener provided by the Edition Manager to handle it. See the next section for a list of selectors.

Calling an Edition Opener Procedure

You use the CallEditionOpenerProc function to call an edition opener procedure. Since the Edition Manager is a package that may move, a real pointer cannot be safely returned for the standard opener and I/O procedures. The system opener and the I/O routines are returned as a value that is not a valid address to a procedure. The CallEditionOpenerProc and CallFormatIOProc functions check for these values and call the system procedures.

You should never assume that a value for a system procedure is a fixed constant.

```
err := CallEditionOpenerProc (selector, PB, routine);
```

Set the selector parameter to one of the edition opener verbs. The edition opener verbs include

- eoCanSubscribe
- eoOpen
- eoClose
- eoOpenNew
- eoCloseNew

The PB parameter of the CallEditionOpenerProc function is an edition opener parameter block.

```
TYPE EditionOpenerParamBlock =
     RECORD
        info:            EditionInfoRecord;   {edition container to }
                                              { be subscribed to}
        sectionH:        SectionHandle;       {publisher or }
                                              { subscriber }
                                              { requesting open}
        document:        FSSpecPtr;           {document passed}
        fdCreator:       OSType;              {Finder creator type}
        ioRefNum:        LongInt;             {reference number}
```

```
        ioProc:             FormatIOProcPtr;     {routine to read }
                                                 { formats}
        success:            Boolean;             {reading or writing }
                                                 { was successful}
        formatsMask:        SignedByte           {formats required to }
                                                 { subscribe}
    END;
```

The routine parameter of the CallEditionOpenerProc function is a pointer to an edition opener procedure.

The following list shows which fields of the edition opener parameter block are used by the edition opener verbs.

Opener verb		Field	Description	Called by
eoCanSubscribe	→	info	Edition container to subscribe to.	NewSubscriberDialog function for a subscriber
	→	formatsMask	Formats required to subscribe.	
	←	Return value	A noErr code indicates that an edition container can be subscribed to. A noTypeErr code indicates that an edition container cannot be subscribed to.	
eoOpen	→	info	Edition container to open for reading.	OpenEdition and GetStandardFormats functions for a subscriber
	→	sectionH	Subscriber section requesting open or NIL.	
	←	ioRefNum	Reference number for use by I/O routine. Not the same as EditionRefNum.	
	←	ioProc	I/O routine to call to read formats.	
	←	Return value	A noErr code or appropriate error code.	
eoClose	→	info	Edition container to be closed for reading.	CloseEdition and GetStandardFormats functions for a subscriber
	→	sectionH	Subscriber section requesting close or NIL.	
	→	ioRefNum	Value returned by eoOpen.	
	→	ioProc	Value returned by eoOpen.	
	→	success	Success value passed to the CloseEdition function.	
	←	Return value	A noErr code or appropriate error code.	
eoOpenNew	→	info	Edition container to open for writing.	OpenNewEdition function for a publisher
	→	sectionH	Publisher section requesting open or NIL.	
	→	document	Document pointer passed into the OpenNewEdition function.	
	→	fdCreator	The fdCreator passed into the OpenNewEdition function.	
	←	ioRefNum	Reference number for use by I/O routine. Not the same as EditionRefNum.	
	←	ioProc	I/O routine to call to write formats.	
	←	Return value	A noErr code or appropriate error code.	

Opener verb		Field	Description	Called by
eoCloseNew	→	info	Edition container to be closed after writing.	CloseEdition function for a publisher
	→	sectionH	Publisher section requesting close or NIL.	
	→	ioRefNum	Value returned by eoOpenNew.	
	→	ioProc	Value returned by eoOpenNew.	
	→	success	Success value passed to the CloseEdition function.	
	←	Return value	A noErr code or appropriate error code.	

The sample code in Listing 4-9 demonstrates how to install your own edition opener function.

Listing 4-9. Using your own edition opener function

```
VAR
   gOriginalOpener: EditionOpenerProcPtr; {global variable}

{Install your edition opener by saving off current opener }
{ and then set the opener to point to your opener.}

PROCEDURE InstallMyOpener;
BEGIN
   FailOSErr(GetEditionOpenerProc(gOriginalOpener));
   FailOSErr(SetEditionOpenerProc(@MyEditionOpener));
END; {InstallMyOpener}

{This opener calls the original edition opener if it is passed }
{ a selector verb it does not understand.}

FUNCTION MyEditionOpener (selector: EditionOpenerVerb;
                          VAR PB: EditionOpenerParamBlock) : OSErr;
BEGIN
   WITH PB DO
   BEGIN
      CASE selector OF
         eoCanSubscribe:
            MyEditionOpener := MyCanSubscribe(PB);
         eoOpen:
            MyEditionOpener := MyEditionOpen(PB);
         eoClose:
            MyEditionOpener := MyEditionClose(PB);
         OTHERWISE
            MyEditionOpener := CallEditionOpenerProc
                     (selector, PB, gOriginalOpener);
      END; {case}
   END; {with}
END; {MyEditionOpener}
```

```
{This function returns noErr if it can subscribe to the request }
{ file. It is called by the Edition Manager to build the list of }
{ files in NewSubscriberDialog. Notice that it calls the original }
{ opener for files it does not understand.}

FUNCTION MyCanSubscribe (VAR PB: EditionOpenerParamBlock) : OSErr;
BEGIN
   {Check file type to see if it is a file you can emulate as an }
   { edition.}
   IF PB.info.fdType = {for example}'PICT'
      THEN MyCanSubscribe := noErr
      {Otherwise, let the saved off edition opener decide.}
      ELSE MyCanSubscribe := CallEditionOpenerProc(eoCanSubscribe,
                                               PB, gOriginalOpener);
END; {MyCanSubscribe}
```

Opening and Closing Editions

Each time the Edition Manager opens or closes an edition container, it calls the current edition opener procedure and passes it an opener verb and a parameter block.

Your opener must be careful when closing documents since a document may already have been opened by another application. Be sure to use the Open/Deny modes whenever possible. Do not close a document if it was already open when your application opened it.

Listing Files That Can Be Subscribed To

The NewSubscriberDialog function calls the eoCanSubscribe opener verb to build the list of files that can be subscribed to. The preview in the subscriber dialog box is generated by calling the GetStandardFormats function (described in "Edition Container Formats" later in this chapter), which calls the format I/O verbs eoOpen, ioHasFormat, ioRead, and then eoClose. See "Calling a Format I/O Procedure" later in this chapter for detailed information on format I/O verbs.

Reading From and Writing to Files

The I/O procedure is a routine that actually reads and writes the data. It too has an interface of a selector and a parameter block.

To override the standard reading and writing functions, create an I/O function. Note that you also need to provide your own opener function to call your I/O function. See "Calling an Edition Opener Procedure" earlier in this chapter.

```
FUNCTION MyIO (selector: FormatIOVerb; VAR PB: FormatIOParamBlock) :
               OSErr;
```

Calling a Format I/O Procedure

To indicate to the Edition Manager which format I/O procedure to use, use the CallFormatIOProc function.

```
err := CallFormatIOProc (selector, PB, routine);
```

Set the selector parameter to one of the format I/O verbs. The format I/O verbs include

- ioHasFormat
- ioReadFormat
- ioNewFormat
- ioWriteFormat

The PB parameter of the CallFormatIOProc function contains a format I/O parameter block.

```
TYPE FormatIOParamBlock =
     RECORD
        ioRefNum:         LongInt;      {reference number}
        format:           FormatType;   {edition format type}
        formatIndex:      LongInt;      {opener-specific enumeration }
                                        { of formats}
        offset:           LongInt;      {offset into format}
        buffPtr:          Ptr;          {data starts here}
        buffLen:          LongInt       {length of data}
     END;
```

The routine parameter of the CallFormatIOProc function is a pointer to a format I/O procedure.

The following list shows which fields of FormatIOParamBlock are used by the format I/O verbs.

Opener verb		Parameter	Description	Called by
ioHasFormat	→	ioRefNum	I/O reference number returned by opener.	EditionHasFormat, GetStandardFormats, and ReadEdition functions
	→	format	Check for this format.	
	←	formatIndex	An optional enumeration of the supplied format.	
	←	buffLen	If found, return the length size or –1 if size is unknown.	
	←	Return value	A noErr or noTypeErr code.	
ioReadFormat	→	ioRefNum	I/O reference number returned by opener.	ReadEdition and GetStandardFormats functions
	→	format	Get this format.	
	→	formatIndex	Value returned by ioHasFormat.	
	→	offset	Read format beginning from this offset.	

Opener verb		Parameter	Description	Called by
	→	buffPtr	Put data beginning here.	
	↔	buffLen	Specify buffer length to read, and return actual amount received.	
	←	Return value	A noErr code, or appropriate error code.	
ioNewFormat	→	ioRefNum	I/O reference number returned by opener.	SetEditionFormatMark and WriteEdition functions
	→	format	Create this format.	
	←	formatIndex	An optional enumeration of the supplied format.	
	←	Return value	A noErr code, or appropriate error code.	
ioWriteFormat	→	ioRefNum	I/O reference number returned by opener.	WriteEdition function
	→	format	Get this format.	
	→	formatIndex	Value returned by ioNewFormat.	
	→	offset	Write format beginning from this offset.	
	→	buffPtr	Get data beginning here.	
	↔	buffLen	Specify buffer length to write.	
	←	Return value	A noErr code or appropriate error code.	

The marks for each format are kept by the Edition Manager. The format I/O procedure only needs to be able to read or write, beginning at any offset. If you know that your application always reads an entire format sequentially, you can ignore the offset.

EDITION MANAGER ROUTINES

This section describes the routines for

- initializing the Edition Manager
- creating and registering a section
- creating and deleting an edition container
- setting and locating a format mark
- reading in edition data
- writing out edition data
- closing an edition after reading or writing
- displaying dialog boxes
- locating a publisher and edition from a subscriber
- reading edition container formats
- reading and writing non-edition files

Result codes appear at the end of each function where applicable. In addition to the specific result codes listed, you may receive errors generated by the Alias Manager, File Manager, and Memory Manager.

Initializing the Edition Manager

You use the InitEditionPack function to initialize the Edition Manager. Note that you should only call this function once. Before calling this function, be sure to determine whether the Edition Manager is available on your system by using the Gestalt function. The Gestalt selector is gestaltEditionMgrAttr ('edtn').

```
FUNCTION InitEditionPack : OSErr;
```

The InitEditionPack function returns an error if the package could not be loaded into the system heap and properly initialized. In addition, you may also receive resource errors.

Result codes

noErr	0	No error
memFullErr	–108	Could not load package

Creating and Registering a Section

You use the NewSection function to create a new section (either publisher or subscriber) and alias record (which is a reference to the edition container from the document containing the publisher or subscriber section). The NewSection function allocates two handles in the current zone: one handle for the section record and another handle for the alias record. Note that you are responsible for unregistering handles created by the Edition Manager.

```
FUNCTION NewSection (container: EditionContainerSpec; sectionDocument:
                     FSSpecPtr; kind: SectionType; sectionID:
                     LongInt; initialMode: UpdateMode; VAR sectionH:
                     SectionHandle) : OSErr;
```

The container parameter specifies the edition you want to publish or subscribe to. The sectionDocument parameter contains the volume reference number, directory ID, and filename of the document that contains a section. The sectionDocument parameter can be NIL if your current document has never been saved. If so, when the user finally saves the document, remember to call the AssociateSection function on each section to update its alias record.

The kind parameter designates the type of section (publisher or subscriber) being created.

A section ID is a unique number for a section within a document. The sectionID parameter initializes the sectionID field within the new section record. Do not use 0 or –1 for an ID number; these numbers are reserved. If your application copies a section, you need to specify a unique number for the copied section.

The initialMode parameter contains the update mode for the section. For publishers this is either the pumOnSave or pumManual constant, and for subscribers it is either sumAutomatic or sumManual. A subscriber created with sumAutomatic mode automatically receives a Section Read event. To prevent this initial Section Read event, you should set the initialMode parameter to sumManual and then, when NewSection returns, set the mode field of the section record to sumAutomatic.

If the NewSection function fails, the sectionH parameter is set to NIL. If the function is successful, sectionH contains the handle to the allocated section record.

Your application receives the multiplePublisherWrn result code if there is another registered publisher to the same edition. Your application receives the notThePublisherWrn result code if another publisher (to the same edition) was the last section to write to the edition. The multiplePublisherWrn result code takes priority over the notThePublisherWrn result code.

In addition, you may also receive memory and file opening errors.

Result codes

noErr	0	No error
editionMgrInitErr	–450	Manager not initialized
badSectionErr	–451	Not a valid section type
badSubPartErr	–454	Bad edition container spec
multiplePublisherWrn	–460	Already is a publisher
notThePublisherWrn	–463	Not the publisher

The NewSection function registers a section similar to the way that the RegisterSection function informs the Edition Manager about a section (except that the NewSection function does not resolve an alias to find the edition container).

```
FUNCTION RegisterSection (sectionDocument: FSSpec; sectionH:
                          SectionHandle; VAR aliasWasUpdated: Boolean) :
                          OSErr;
```

The sectionDocument parameter contains the volume reference number, directory ID, and filename of the document that contains a section. The sectionH parameter is a handle to the section record for a given section.

The aliasWasUpdated parameter returns TRUE if the alias for the edition container subscribed to was out of date and was updated. This may occur if the edition file was moved to a new location or was renamed.

The RegisterSection function adds the section record to the Edition Manager's list of registered sections and tries to allocate a control block. After calling the RegisterSection function, the controlBlock field of the section record is either NIL or a valid control block.

For a subscriber, the control block is NIL if the RegisterSection function could not locate the edition container being subscribed to. The RegisterSection function then returns either the containerNotFoundWrn or the userCanceledErr result code. For a publisher, if the RegisterSection function could not locate its corresponding edition container, the Edition

Manager creates an edition container in the last place the edition was located and creates a control block for it. If the RegisterSection function could not locate a publisher's corresponding edition container or its volume, the control block is NIL. You should never re-register a section that is already registered.

Note that you can compare control blocks for individual sections. If two sections contain the same control block value, these sections publish or subscribe to the same edition (unless the control block is NIL). The Edition Manager keeps track of how many sections are referencing a control block to know when it can be deallocated. The control block maintains a count of how many sections are referencing it. Each time you use the UnRegisterSection function, the control block subtracts one from the number of sections. When the number of sections reaches 0, the control block is deallocated.

Your application receives the multiplePublisherWrn result code if there is another registered publisher to the same edition. Your application receives the notThePublisherWrn result code if another publisher (to the same edition) was the last section to write to the edition. The multiplePublisherWrn result code takes priority over the notThePublisherWrn result code.

In addition, you may also receive memory and file opening errors.

Result codes

noErr	0	No error
userCanceledErr	–128	User chose Cancel from a mount server dialog box
editionMgrInitErr	–450	Manager not initialized
badSectionErr	–451	Not valid section type
multiplePublisherWrn	–460	Already is a publisher
containerNotFoundWrn	–461	Alias was not resolved
notThePublisherWrn	–463	Not the publisher

When a section needs to be disposed of because the document containing the section is closing, or the user has canceled the section, you need to call the UnRegisterSection function before disposing of the section.

```
FUNCTION UnRegisterSection (sectionH: SectionHandle) : OSErr;
```

The sectionH parameter is a handle to the section record for a given section.

The UnRegisterSection function removes the section from the Edition Manager's list of registered sections. You can then dispose of the section record and alias record with standard Memory and Resource Manager calls. Once unregistered, a section does not receive any events and cannot read or write any data. Depending on your Clipboard strategy, you may want to unregister sections that have been cut into the Clipboard.

Result codes

noErr	0	No error
fBsyErr	–47	Section doing I/O
editionMgrInitErr	–450	Manager not initialized
notRegisteredSectionErr	–452	Not registered

Using the IsRegisteredSection function, your application must verify that each event received is for a registered section. This is necessary because your application may have just called UnRegisterSection while the event was already being held in the event queue.

```
FUNCTION IsRegisteredSection (sectionH: SectionHandle) : OSErr;
```

The sectionH parameter is a handle to the section record for a given section. The IsRegisteredSection function does not return a Boolean—a noErr result code indicates that a section is registered.

Result codes

noErr	0	No error
notRegisteredSectionErr	–452	Not registered

If a user saves a document that contains sections under another name (using Save As) or pastes a portion of a document that contains a section into another document, use the AssociateSection function to update the section's alias record.

```
FUNCTION AssociateSection (sectionH: SectionHandle; newSectionDocument:
                          FSSpecPtr) : OSErr;
```

The sectionH parameter is a handle to the section record for a given section. The newSectionDocument parameter contains the volume reference number, directory ID, and filename of the new document. The AssociateSection function calls UpdateAlias on the section's alias record.

In addition, you may also receive update alias errors.

Result code

noErr	0	No error

Creating and Deleting an Edition Container

Each time a user creates a new publisher section within a document to an edition that does not already exist, you use the CreateEditionContainerFile function to create an empty edition container.

```
FUNCTION CreateEditionContainerFile (editionFile: FSSpec;
                                     fdCreator: OSType;
                                     editionFileNameScript: ScriptCode) :
                                     OSErr;
```

The editionFile parameter contains the volume reference number, directory ID, and filename for the edition container being created. The fdCreator parameter contains the creator type for the edition.

The editionFileNameScript parameter is the script of the filename. It is returned in the theFileScript field of the edition container specification record. (The new publisher reply record includes a container field for an edition container specification record.)

The CreateEditionContainerFile function creates an empty edition container file (it does not contain any formats). This function creates a file type 'edtu'. As soon as you write data to the edition, the type is updated (to 'edtp' for graphics, 'edtt' for text, or 'edts' for sound). If both text and pict are written, the type that was written first determines the file type. If your application has a bundle, you should designate an icon for the appropriate edition types that you can write.

In addition, you may also receive file creating errors.

Result codes

noErr	0	No error
editionMgrInitErr	–450	Manager not initialized

If a user cancels a publisher section within a document or closes a document containing a newly created publisher without saving, you need to remove the edition container.

To locate the appropriate edition container to be deleted, use the GetEditionInfo function. You use the UnRegisterSection function (only after using the GetEditionInfo function) to unregister the section record and alias record of the publisher being canceled. See “Locating a Publisher and Edition From a Subscriber” later in this chapter for detailed information on the GetEditionInfo function. See “Creating and Registering a Section” earlier in this chapter for detailed information on the UnRegisterSection function.

To remove the edition container, use the DeleteEditionContainerFile function.

```
FUNCTION DeleteEditionContainerFile (editionFile: FSSpec) : OSErr;
```

If the user cancels a publisher, do not call the DeleteEditionContainerFile function until the user saves the document. This allows the user to undo changes and revert to the last saved version of the document.

The DeleteEditionContainerFile function only deletes the edition container if there is no registered publisher. You need to unregister a publisher before you can delete its corresponding edition container.

The editionFile parameter contains the volume reference number, directory ID, and filename for the edition container being deleted.

You should use the DeleteEditionContainerFile function even if there are subscribers to the edition. When a subscriber section tries to read in data, it receives an error.

In addition, you may also receive file deleting errors.

Result codes

noErr	0	No error
editionMgrInitErr	–450	Manager not initialized

Setting and Locating a Format Mark

Use the SetEditionFormatMark function to set the current mark for a section format. The mark indicates the next position of a read or write operation. Initially, a mark defaults to 0. After reading or writing data, the format mark is set past the last position written to or read from.

```
FUNCTION SetEditionFormatMark (whichEdition: EditionRefNum; whichFormat:
                               FormatType; setMarkTo: LongInt) : OSErr;
```

The whichEdition parameter is the reference number for the edition. The whichFormat parameter indicates the format type for the edition, and the setMarkTo parameter is the offset for the next read or write for this format.

Result codes

noErr	0	No error
rfNumErr	–51	Bad edition reference number
noTypeErr	–102	Unknown format (subscriber only)
editionMgrInitErr	–450	Manager not initialized

Use the GetEditionFormatMark function to locate the current marker for a particular format.

```
FUNCTION GetEditionFormatMark (whichEdition: EditionRefNum; whichFormat:
                               FormatType; VAR currentMark: LongInt) :
                               OSErr;
```

The whichEdition parameter is the reference number for the edition. The whichFormat parameter indicates the format type for the edition, and the currentMark parameter is the mark for the format.

If the edition does not support the format specified in the whichFormat parameter, you receive a noTypeErr result code.

Result codes

noErr	0	No error
rfNumErr	–51	Bad edition reference number
noTypeErr	–102	Unknown format
editionMgrInitErr	–450	Manager not initialized

Reading in Edition Data

To initiate the reading of data from an edition (for a subscriber), use the OpenEdition function.

```
FUNCTION OpenEdition (subscriberSectionH: SectionHandle; VAR refNum:
                      EditionRefNum) : OSErr;
```

The subscriberSectionH parameter is a handle to the section record for a given section. The refNum parameter returns the reference number for the edition.

Multiple subscribers can each call the OpenEdition function simultaneously (each call returns a different reference number) and read data from a single edition. If a publisher (located on a different machine) is writing to an edition when you use the OpenEdition function, you receive an flLckedErr result code.

In addition, you may also receive memory, file opening, and file reading errors.

Result codes		
noErr	0	No error
flLckedErr	–45	Publisher writing to an edition
permErr	–54	Not a subscriber
editionMgrInitErr	–450	Manager not initialized

Use the EditionHasFormat function to learn in which formats the edition data is available.

```
FUNCTION EditionHasFormat (whichEdition: EditionRefNum; whichFormat:
                           FormatType; VAR formatSize: Size) : OSErr;
```

The whichEdition parameter is the reference number for the edition. The whichFormat parameter indicates the format type that you are requesting. For the whichFormat parameter, you should decide which formats to read in the same way that you do when using paste from the Scrap Manager. You can also get a list of all the available formats and their respective lengths by reading the kFormatListFormat ('fmts') format. The formatSize parameter specifies the format length.

If the requested format is available, this function returns noErr, and the formatSize parameter returns the size of the data in the specified format or kFormatLengthUnknown (–1), which signifies that the size is unknown. You should therefore continue to read the format until there is no more data.

Be aware that the EditionHasFormat function may return kFormatLengthUnknown for the length of the format.

Result codes		
noErr	0	No error
rfNumErr	–51	Bad edition reference number
noTypeErr	–102	Format not available
editionMgrInitErr	–450	Manager not initialized

Use the ReadEdition function to read data from an edition. This function reads from the current mark for the specified format.

```
FUNCTION ReadEdition (whichEdition: EditionRefNum; whichFormat:
                      FormatType; buffPtr: UNIV Ptr; VAR buffLen: Size) :
                      OSErr;
```

The whichEdition parameter is the reference number for the edition. The whichFormat parameter indicates the format type that you want to read.

The buffPtr parameter is a pointer to the buffer into which you want to read the data. The buffLen parameter is the number of bytes that you want to read into the buffer. The buffLen parameter is also a return value that returns the total number of bytes read into the buffer. If the buffLen parameter returns a value smaller than the value you have specified, there is no additional data to read, and the ReadEdition function returns a noErr result code. If you use the ReadEdition function after all data is read in, the ReadEdition function returns an eofErr result code.

You can read data from an edition while a publisher on the same machine is writing data to the same edition. The data that you are reading is the old edition (not the data that the publisher is writing). If the publisher finishes writing data before you are through reading the old edition data, the ReadEdition function returns an abortErr result code. If the ReadEdition function returns an abortErr result code, you should stop trying to read data and use the CloseEdition function with the successful parameter set to FALSE.

In addition, you may also receive file reading errors.

Result codes

noErr	0	No error
abortErr	–27	Publisher has written a new edition
eofErr	–39	No more data of that format
rfNumErr	–51	Bad edition reference number
noTypeErr	–102	Format not available
editionMgrInitErr	–450	Manager not initialized

Writing out Edition Data

To initiate the writing of data from a publisher to its edition container, use the OpenNewEdition function.

```
FUNCTION OpenNewEdition (publisherSectionH: SectionHandle; fdCreator:
                         OSType; publisherSectionDocument: FSSpecPtr; VAR
                         refNum: EditionRefNum) : OSErr;
```

The publisherSectionH parameter is the publisher section that is writing to the edition. The fdCreator parameter is the Finder creator type of the new edition icon.

The publisherSectionDocument parameter is the document that contains the publisher. This parameter is used to create an alias from the edition to the publisher's document. If you pass NIL for publisherSectionDocument, an alias is not made in the edition file.

The refNum parameter returns the reference number for the edition. This parameter is necessary for subsequent calls to WriteEdition, SetEditionFormatMark, and CloseEdition to specify which publisher is writing its data to an edition. If the edition cannot be opened for writing because there is another publisher writing to it, or because the file system does not allow writing, an error is returned and refNum is set to NIL.

The OpenNewEdition function returns an flLckdErr result code if there is a subscriber on another machine reading data from the same edition. The OpenNewEdition function returns a permErr result code if there is a registered publisher to that edition on another machine.

The Edition Manager allows two registered publishers that are located on the *same* machine to write to the same edition. Note that multiple publishers cannot write to the same edition simultaneously—only one publisher can write to an edition at a given time.

In addition, you may also receive file creating, file opening, file reading, resolve alias, and memory errors.

Result codes		
noErr	0	No error
flLckdErr	–45	Edition in use by another section
permErr	–54	Registered publisher on another machine
wrPermErr	–61	Not a publisher
editionMgrInitErr	–450	Manager not initialized

Use the WriteEdition function to write data to an edition. This function begins writing at the current mark for the specified format.

```
FUNCTION WriteEdition (whichEdition: EditionRefNum; whichFormat:
                       FormatType; buffPtr: UNIV Ptr; buffLen: Size) : OSErr;
```

The whichEdition parameter is the reference number for the edition. The whichFormat parameter indicates the format type that you want to write.

The buffPtr parameter is a pointer to the buffer that you are writing into the edition. The buffLen parameter is the number of bytes that you want to write. If the data cannot be entirely written to the edition, the WriteEdition function returns an error.

In addition, you may also receive file writing and memory errors.

Result codes		
noErr	0	No error
rfNumErr	–51	Bad edition reference number
editionMgrInitErr	–450	Manager not initialized

Closing an Edition After Reading or Writing

After finishing reading from or writing to an edition, use the CloseEdition function to close the edition.

```
FUNCTION CloseEdition (whichEdition: EditionRefNum; successful: Boolean)
                       : OSErr;
```

The whichEdition parameter is the reference number for the edition. The successful parameter indicates whether your application was successful in reading or writing data to the edition.

When a subscriber successfully finishes reading data from the edition, the CloseEdition function takes the modification date of the edition file that you have read and puts it in the mdDate field of the subscriber's section record. This indicates that the data contained in the edition and the subscriber section within the document are the same.

When a subscriber is unsuccessful in reading data from an edition (because there is not enough memory, or you didn't find a format that you can read), set the successful parameter to FALSE. The CloseEdition function then closes the edition, but does not set the mdDate field. This implies that the subscriber is not updated with the latest edition.

When a publisher successfully finishes writing data to an edition, the CloseEdition function makes the data that the publisher has written to the edition available to any subscribers and sets the corresponding edition file's modification date (ioFlMdDat) to the mdDate field of the publisher's section record. The Edition Manager then sends a Section Read event to all current subscribers set to automatic update mode. At this point, the file type of the edition file is set based on the first known format that the publisher wrote.

When a publisher is unsuccessful in writing data to an edition, the CloseEdition function discards what the publisher has written to the edition. The data contained in the edition prior to writing remains unchanged, and Section Read events are not sent to subscribers.

In addition, you may also receive file closing errors.

Result codes

noErr	0	No error
rfNumErr	–51	Bad edition reference number
editionMgrInitErr	–450	Manager not initialized

Displaying Dialog Boxes

Use the GetLastEditionContainerUsed function to get the default edition to display. This function allows a user to easily subscribe to the data recently published.

```
FUNCTION GetLastEditionContainerUsed (VAR container:
                                      EditionContainerSpec) : OSErr;
```

If the GetLastEditionContainer function locates the last edition for which a section was created, the container parameter contains its volume reference number, directory ID, filename, and part, and returns a noErr result code. (The last edition created is associated with the last time that your application or another application located on the same machine used the NewSection function.) If the last edition used is missing, the GetLastEditionContainerUsed function returns an fnfErr result code, but still returns the correct volume reference number and directory ID that you should use for the NewSubscriberDialog function.

Pass the information from the GetLastEditionContainerUsed function to the NewSubscriberDialog function.

Result codes

noErr	0	No error
fnfErr	–43	Edition container not found
editionMgrInitErr	–450	Manager not initialized

The Edition Manager supports three dialog boxes: publisher, subscriber, and options dialog boxes. Your application can display simple dialog boxes that appear centered on the user's screen, or you can customize your dialog boxes.

Unlike the Standard File routines, the NewPublisherDialog and the NewSubscriberDialog functions allow you to specify the initial volume reference number and directory ID so that there can be one default location for editions for all applications.

Use the NewSubscriberDialog function to display the subscriber dialog box on the user's screen.

```
FUNCTION NewSubscriberDialog (VAR reply: NewSubscriberReply) : OSErr;
```

The reply parameter contains the new subscriber reply record.

```
TYPE NewSubscriberReply =
      RECORD
         canceled:        Boolean;                   {user canceled }
                                                     { dialog box}
         formatsMask:     SignedByte;                {formats required}
         container:       EditionContainerSpec       {edition selected}
      END;
```

The NewSubscriberDialog function (which is based on the CustomGetFile procedure described in the Standard File Package chapter in this volume) switches to the volume reference number and directory ID and selects the filename of the edition container that you passed in. Use the GetLastEditionContainerUsed function to set the edition container to the last edition that was either published or subscribed to. This allows the user to publish and then easily subscribe.

The formatsMask field indicates which edition format type (text, graphics, and sound) to display within the subscriber dialog box. You can set the formatsMask field to the following constants: kTEXTformatMask (1), kPICTformatMask (2), or ksndFormatMask (4). To support a combination of formats, add the constants together. For example, a formatsMask of 3 displays both graphics and text edition format types in the subscriber dialog box.

Note that if an edition does not contain either 'PICT', 'TEXT', or 'snd ' data, it will not be seen by the NewSubscriberDialog function (unless you install an opener that adds it using eoCanSubscribe).

If the NewSubscriberDialog function returns with the canceled field set to TRUE, the user canceled the dialog box. Otherwise, this field is FALSE and the container field holds the edition container for the new subscriber.

Result codes

noErr	0	No error
editionMgrInitErr	–450	Package not initialized
badSubPartErr	–454	Bad edition container spec

Use the NewPublisherDialog function to display the publisher dialog box on the user's screen.

```
FUNCTION NewPublisherDialog (VAR reply: NewPublisherReply) : OSErr;
```

The reply parameter contains a new publisher reply record.

```
TYPE NewPublisherReply =
     RECORD
        canceled:      Boolean;             {user canceled dialog box}
        replacing:     Boolean;             {user chose existing }
                                            { filename for an edition}
        usePart:       Boolean;             {always false in version 7.0}
        preview:       Handle;              {handle to 'prvw', 'PICT', }
                                            { 'TEXT', or 'snd' data}
        previewFormat: FormatType;          {type of preview}
        container:     EditionContainerSpec {edition chosen}
     END;
```

The NewPublisherDialog function (which is based on the CustomPutFile procedure described in the Standard File Package chapter) switches to the volume reference number and directory ID and sets the text edit field to the filename of the edition container that you passed in. Set the fileName field of the file system specification record to be the default name of the edition file. (The new publisher reply record includes a container field for an edition container specification record, and the edition container specification record includes a field [theFile] for a file system specification record.) See "Creating a Publisher" earlier in this chapter for information on the default file specification.

The usePart field must be set to FALSE before calling the NewPublisherDialog function.

Set the preview field to be a handle to 'prvw', 'PICT', 'TEXT', or 'snd ' data. Set the previewFormat field to indicate which type of data the handle references.

Upon return of the NewPublisherDialog function, the canceled and replacing fields are set. If the canceled field is set to TRUE, the user canceled the dialog box. If the replacing field is TRUE, the user chose an existing filename from the list of available editions and confirmed this replacement. If the replacing field is TRUE, do not call the CreateEditionContainerFile function, which creates a new edition container. The container field contains the volume reference number, directory ID, and filename for the edition that the user selected.

You should deallocate the handle referenced by the preview field to free up memory.

Result codes

noErr	0	No error
editionMgrInitErr	–450	Package not initialized
badSubPartErr	–454	Bad edition container spec

Use the SectionOptionsDialog function to display the publisher options and subscriber options dialog boxes on the user's screen.

```
FUNCTION SectionOptionsDialog  (VAR reply: SectionOptionsReply) : OSErr;
```

The reply parameter contains a section options reply record.

```
TYPE SectionOptionsReply =
     RECORD
        canceled:       Boolean;        {user canceled dialog box}
        changed:        Boolean;        {changed the section record}
        sectionH:       SectionHandle;  {handle to the specified }
                                        { section record}
        action:         ResType         {action codes}
     END;
```

Set the sectionH parameter to the handle to the section record for the section the user selected.

Upon return of the SectionOptionsDialog function, the canceled and changed fields are set. If the canceled parameter is set to TRUE, the user canceled the dialog box. Otherwise, this parameter is FALSE. If the changed parameter is TRUE, the user changed the section record. For example, the update mode may have changed.

The action field contains the code for one of five user actions.

- action code is 'read' for user selection of the Get Edition Now button
- action code is 'writ' for user selection of the Send Edition Now button
- action code is 'goto' for user selection of the Open Publisher button
- action code is 'cncl' for user selection of the Cancel Publisher or Cancel Subscriber button
- action code is '   ' ($20202020) for user selection of the OK button

Note that you may receive memory errors.

The NewSubscriberExpDialog, NewPublisherExpDialog, and SectionOptionsExpDialog functions are the same as the simple dialog functions but have five additional parameters. These additional parameters allow you to add items to the bottom of the dialog boxes, apply alternate mapping of events to item hits, apply alternate meanings to the item hits, and choose the location of the dialog boxes.

```
FUNCTION NewSubscriberExpDialog (VAR reply: NewSubscriberReply; where:
                                 Point; expansionDITLresID: Integer;
                                 dlgHook: ExpDlgHookProcPtr; filterProc:
                                 ExpModalFilterProcPtr; yourDataPtr: UNIV
                                 Ptr) : OSErr;
```

```
FUNCTION NewPublisherExpDialog (VAR reply: NewPublisherReply; where:
                               Point; expansionDITLresID: Integer;
                               dlgHook: ExpDlgHookProcPtr; filterProc:
                               ExpModalFilterProcPtr; yourDataPtr: UNIV
                               Ptr) : OSErr;

FUNCTION SectionOptionsExpDialog (VAR reply: SectionOptionsReply; where:
                                 Point; expansionDITLresID: Integer;
                                 dlgHook: ExpDlgHookProcPtr;
                                 filterProc: ExpModalFilterProcPtr;
                                 yourDataPtr: UNIV Ptr) : OSErr;
```

The reply parameter contains a pointer from the new subscriber reply, new publisher reply, or the section options reply records.

You can automatically center the dialog box by passing (–1, –1) in the where parameter.

The expansionDITLresID parameter should be 0 or a valid dialog item list ('DITL') resource ID. This integer is the ID of a dialog item list whose items are appended to the end of the standard dialog item list. The dialog items keep their relative positions, but they are moved as a group to the bottom of the dialog box. See the Dialog Manager chapter in Volume I for additional information on dialog item lists.

The filterProc parameter should be a valid expandable modal filter procedure pointer or NIL. This procedure is called by the ModalDialog procedure. This function allows you to map real events (such as a mouse-down event) to an item hit (such as clicking a Cancel button). For instance, you may want to map a keyboard equivalent to an item hit.

The dlgHook parameter should be a valid expandable dialog hook procedure pointer or NIL. This procedure is called after each call to the ModalDialog procedure. The dialog hook procedure takes the appropriate action, such as filling in a check box. The itemOffset parameter to the procedure is the number of items in the dialog item list before your expansion dialog items. You need to subtract the item offset from the item hit to get the relative item number in the expansion dialog item list. The return value from the dialog hook procedure is the absolute item number.

The yourDataPtr parameter is reserved for your use. It is passed back to your hook and modal-dialog filter function. This parameter does not have to be of type Ptr—it can be any 32-bit quantity that you want. In Pascal, you can pass in register A6 for yourDataPtr, and make dialog hook and filter procedure local functions without the last parameter. The stack frame is set up properly for these functions to access their parent local variables. See the Standard File Package chapter in this volume for detailed information.

For the NewPublisherExpDialog and NewSubscriberExpDialog functions, all the pseudo-items for the Standard File Package such as hookFirstCall(–1), hookNullEvent(100), hookRebuildList(101), and hookLastCall(–2) can be used, as well as hookRedrawPreview(150).

For the SectionOptionsExpDialog function, the only valid pseudo-items are hookFirstCall(–1), hookNullEvent(100), hookLastCall(–2), emHookRedrawPreview(150), emHookCancelSection(160), emHookGoToPublisher(161), emHookGetEditionNow(162), emHookSendEditionNow(162), emHookManualUpdateMode(163), and emHookAutoUpdateMode(164).

If you have an expandable dialog hook function, it must contain the following parameters.

```
FUNCTION MyExpDlgHook (itemOffset: Integer; itemHit: Integer; theDialog:
                       DialogPtr; yourDataPtr: Ptr) : Integer;
```

If you have an expandable modal-dialog filter function, it must contain the following parameters.

```
FUNCTION MyExpModalFilter (theDialog: DialogPtr; VAR theEvent:
                           EventRecord; itemOffset: Integer; VAR itemHit:
                           Integer; yourDataPtr: Ptr) : Boolean;
```

Locating a Publisher and Edition From a Subscriber

The GetEditionInfo function returns information about a section's edition such as its location, last modification date, creator, and type.

```
FUNCTION GetEditionInfo (sectionH: SectionHandle; VAR editionInfo:
                         EditionInfoRecord) : OSErr;
```

The sectionH parameter is a handle to the section record for a given section. The editionInfo parameter contains an edition information record. The GetEditionInfo function returns the public information contained in the section's control block.

The Edition Manager synchronizes to ensure that the existing edition name corresponds to the Finder's existing edition name. If the control block field of the section record is NIL, or the edition cannot be located, the GetEditionInfo function returns an fnfErr result code.

```
TYPE EditionInfoRecord =
     RECORD
        crDate:      TimeStamp;             {date edition container }
                                            { was created}
        mdDate:      TimeStamp;             {date of last change}
        fdCreator:   OSType;                {file creator}
        fdType:      OSType;                {file type}
        container:   EditionContainerSpec   {the edition}
     END;
```

The crDate field contains the creation date of the edition. The mdDate field contains the modification date of the edition.

The fdCreator and fdType fields are the creator and type of the edition file. The container field includes a volume reference number, directory ID, filename, script, and part number for the edition.

Result codes

noErr	0	No error
fnfErr	–43	Not registered or file moved
editionMgrInitErr	–450	Manager not initialized

When the user wants to locate the publisher for a particular subscriber (by choosing Open Publisher in the subscriber options dialog box), the action code 'goto' is returned to you.

Use the GetEditionInfo function to find the edition container. You should next use the GoToPublisherSection function to open the document containing the publisher.

Use the GoToPublisherSection function to resolve the alias in the edition to find the document containing its publisher. In general, this function internally uses the GetStandardFormats function to get the alias to the publisher document and then resolves the alias. It next sends the Finder an Apple event to open the document (which launches its application if necessary) and, after the publisher is registered, sends a Section Scroll event to the publisher.

As an optimization, if there is a registered publisher, the GoToPublisherSection function simply sends a Section Scroll event to the publisher.

If the edition does not contain an alias and there are no registered publishers, then the GoToPublisherSection function sends an Open Documents event to open the edition to the creating application.

If the edition container is not an edition file (such as when you are using bottlenecks to subscribe to non-edition files), the GoToPublisherSection function sends the Finder an Apple event to open that file.

```
FUNCTION GoToPublisherSection (container: EditionContainerSpec) : OSErr;
```

The container parameter includes the edition volume reference number, directory ID, and filename. You obtain the edition container by calling the GetEditionInfo function.

In addition, you may also receive resolve alias errors.

Result codes

noErr	0	No error
editionMgrInitErr	–450	Manager not initialized
badSubPartErr	–454	Invalid edition container

Edition Container Formats

The Edition Manager calls the GetStandardFormats function to get the alias used in the GoToPublisherSection function and to get the preview shown in the subscriber dialog box. You probably do not need to call this function directly.

```
FUNCTION GetStandardFormats (container: EditionContainerSpec; VAR
                             previewFormat: FormatType; preview,
                             publisherAlias, formats: Handle)
                             : OSErr;
```

The container parameter is a pointer to the edition volume reference number, directory ID, filename, and part.

You should pass in valid handles for the formats that you want and NIL for the formats that you don't want. The handles are resized to the size of the data.

The preview parameter tries to find one of four formats: 'prvw', 'PICT', 'TEXT', or 'snd '. The publisherAlias parameter reads the format kPublisherDocAliasFormat ('alis'), and the formats parameter reads the virtual format kFormatListFormat ('fmts'). The first format that was written returns in the preview handle and the previewFormat parameter is set to its type. If one of the requested formats cannot be found, GetStandardFormats returns a noTypeErr result code.

Result codes

noErr	0	No error
noTypeErr	–102	Edition container not found
editionMgrInitErr	–450	Manager not initialized

Reading and Writing Non-Edition Files

The Edition Manager never opens or closes an edition container directly—it calls the current edition opener. See "Subscribing to Non-Edition Files" earlier in this chapter for additional information.

To override the standard opener function, you should create an opener function that contains the following parameters.

```
FUNCTION MyOpener (selector: EditionOpenerVerb; VAR PB:
                   EditionOpenerParamBlock) : OSErr;
```

When this function is called by the Edition Manager, the selector parameter is set to one of the edition opener verbs (eoOpen, eoClose, eoOpenNew, eoCloseNew, eoCanSubscribe). The PB parameter contains an edition opener parameter block record.

Use the GetEditionOpenerProc function to locate the current edition opener procedure.

```
FUNCTION GetEditionOpenerProc (VAR opener: EditionOpenerProcPtr) : OSErr;
```

The opener procedure returns the pointer to the current edition opener procedure.

Use the SetEditionOpenProc function to provide your own edition opener procedure.

```
FUNCTION SetEditionOpenerProc (opener: EditionOpenerProcPtr) : OSErr;
```

The opener parameter is a pointer to the edition opener procedure that you are providing.

Use the CallEditionOpenerProc function to call an edition opener procedure pointer.

```
FUNCTION CallEditionOpenerProc (selector: EditionOpenerVerb; VAR PB:
                                 EditionOpenerParamBlock; routine:
                                 EditionOpenerProcPtr) : OSErr;
```

When this function is called by the Edition Manager, the selector parameter is set to one of the edition opener verbs (eoOpen, eoClose, eoOpenNew, eoCloseNew, eoCanSubscribe). The PB parameter contains an edition opener parameter block record.

```
TYPE EditionOpenerParamBlock =
     RECORD
        info:             EditionInfoRecord;   {edition container to }
                                               { be subscribed to}
        sectionH:         SectionHandle;       {publisher or }
                                               { subscriber }
                                               { requesting open}
        document:         FSSpecPtr;           {document passed}
        fdCreator:        OSType;              {Finder creator type}
        ioRefNum:         LongInt;             {reference number}
        ioProc:           FormatIOProcPtr;     {routine to read }
                                               { formats}
        success:          Boolean;             {reading or writing }
                                               { was successful}
        formatsMask:      SignedByte           {formats required to }
                                               { subscribe}
     END;
```

The routine parameter is a pointer to an edition opener procedure.

To override the standard reading and writing functions, you should create an IO function that contains the following parameters.

```
FUNCTION MyIO (selector: FormatIOVerb; VAR PB: FormatIOParamBlock) :
               OSErr;
```

Set the selector parameter to one of the format I/O verbs (ioHasFormat, ioReadFormat, ioNewFormat, ioWriteFormat). The PB parameter contains a format I/O parameter block record.

4 Edition Manager

Use the CallFormatIOProc function to call a format IO procedure.

```
FUNCTION CallFormatIOProc (selector: FormatIOVerb; VAR PB:
                           FormatIOParamBlock; routine: FormatIOProcPtr)
                           : OSErr;
```

Set the selector parameter to one of the format I/O verbs (ioHasFormat, ioReadFormat, ioNewFormat, ioWriteFormat). The PB parameter contains a format I/O parameter block record.

```
TYPE FormatIOParamBlock =
     RECORD
         ioRefNum:        LongInt;     {reference number}
         format:          FormatType;  {edition format type}
         formatIndex:     LongInt;     {opener-specific enumeration }
                                       { of formats}
         offset:          LongInt;     {offset into format}
         buffPtr:         Ptr;         {data starts here}
         buffLen:         LongInt      {length of data}
     END;
```

The routine parameter is a pointer to a format I/O procedure.

SUMMARY OF THE EDITION MANAGER

Constants

```
CONST {resource types}
      rSectionType               = 'sect';     {resource type for a section}

      {section types}
      stSubscriber               = $01;        {subscriber section type}
      stPublisher                = $0A;        {publisher section type}

      {update modes}
      sumAutomatic               = 0;          {subscriber receives new }
                                               { editions automatically}
      sumManual                  = 1;          {subscriber receives new }
                                               { editions manually}
      pumOnSave                  = 0;          {publisher sends new }
                                               { editions on save}
      pumManual                  = 1;          {publisher does not send }
                                               { new editions until user }
                                               { request}

      {edition container subpart number}
      kPartsNotUsed              = 0;          {edition is the whole file}
      kPartNumberUnknown         = -1;         {not used in version 7.0}

      {preview size}
      kPreviewWidth              = 120;        {preview width}
      kPreviewHeight             = 120;        {preview height}

      {special formats}
      kPublisherDocAliasFormat = 'alis';       {alias record from the }
                                               { edition to publisher}
      kPreviewFormat             = 'prvw';     {'PICT' thumbnail sketch}
      kFormatListFormat          = 'fmts';     {list of all available }
                                               { formats and their sizes}

      {bits for formatMask}
      kPICTformatMask            = 1;          {graphics format}
      kTEXTformatMask            = 2;          {text format}
      ksndFormatMask             = 4;          {sound format}

      {Finder types for edition files}
      kPICTEditionFileType       = 'edtp';     {contains 'PICT', }
      kTEXTEditionFileType       = 'edtt';     { 'TEXT', and }
      ksndEditionFileType        = 'edts';     { 'snd ' file types}
      kUnknownEditionFileType    = 'edtu';     {unknown file type}
```

```
{miscellaneous}
kFormatLengthUnknown         = -1;       {length of format unknown}

{message IDs for Apple events sent by the Edition Manager}
sectionEventMsgClass         = 'sect';  {Apple events sent by the }
                                        { Edition Manager}
sectionReadMsgID             = 'read';  {Section Read events}
sectionWriteMsgID            = 'writ';  {Section Write events}
sectionScrollMsgID           = 'scrl';  {Section Scroll events}
sectionCancelMsgID           = 'cncl';  {Section Cancel events}

{refCon field when displaying stacked dialog boxes}
sfMainDialogRefCon           = 'stdf';  {new publisher and }
                                        { new subscriber}
sfNewFolderDialogRefCon      = 'nfdr';  {new folder}
sfReplaceDialogRefCon        = 'rplc';  {replace dialog}
sfStatWarnDialogRefCon       = 'stat';  {warning dialog}
sfErrorDialogRefCon          = 'err ';  {error dialog}
emOptionsDialogRefCon        = 'optn';  {options dialog}
emCancelSectionDialogRefCon  = 'cncl';  {cancel section}
emGotoPubErrDialogRefCon     = 'gerr';  {locate publisher}

{pseudo-item hits for dialogHooks}
emHookRedrawPreview          = 150;     {for NewPublisher or }
                                        { NewSubscriber dialogs}
emHookCancelSection          = 160;     {for SectionOptions dialog}
emHookGoToPublisher          = 161;     {for SectionOptions dialog}
emHookGetEditionNow          = 162;     {for SectionOptions dialog}
emHookSendEditionNow         = 162;     {for SectionOptions dialog}
emHookManualUpdateMode       = 163;     {for SectionOptions dialog}
emHookAutoUpdateMode         = 164;     {for SectionOptions dialog}
```

Data Types

```
TYPE TimeStamp              = LongInt;     {seconds since 1904}
     EditionRefNum          = Handle;      {for use in Edition I/O}
     UpdateMode             = Integer;     {sumAutomatic, }
                                           { sumManual, }
                                           { pumOnSave, pumManual}
     SectionType            = SignedByte;  {stSubscriber or stPublisher}
     FormatType             = PACKED ARRAY[1..4] OF CHAR;
                                           {similar to ResType used }
                                           { by the Scrap  Manager}

     SectionHandle          = ^SectionPtr;
     SectionPtr             = ^SectionRecord;
     SectionRecord =
     RECORD
        version:            SignedByte;    {always 1 in version 7.0}
```

```
    kind:             SectionType;    {publisher or subscriber}
    mode:             UpdateMode;     {automatic or manual}
    mdDate:           TimeStamp;      {last change to section}
    sectionID:        LongInt;        {application-specific, }
                                      { unique per document}
    refCon:           LongInt;        {application-specific}
    alias             AliasHandle;    {handle to alias record}

    {The following fields are private and are set up by the }
    { RegisterSection function.}

    subPart:          LongInt;        {private}
    nextSection:      SectionHandle;  {private}
    controlBlock:     Handle;         {private}
    refNum:           EditionRefNum   {private}
END;


EditionContainerSpecPtr =^EditionContainerSpec;
EditionContainerSpec    =
RECORD
    theFile:          FSSpec;         {file containing edition }
                                      { data}
    theFileScript:    ScriptCode;     {script code of filename}
    thePart:          LongInt;        {which part of file, }
                                      { always kPartsNotUsed}
    thePartName:      Str31;          {not used in version 7.0}
    thePartScript:    ScriptCode      {not used in version 7.0}
END;


FormatsAvailable = ARRAY[0..0] OF
RECORD
    theType:          FormatType;     {format type for an edition}
    theLength:        LongInt         {length of edition format }
                                      { type}
END;


EditionInfoRecord =
RECORD
    crDate:           TimeStamp;      {date edition container }
                                      { was created}
    mdDate:           TimeStamp;      {date of last change}
    fdCreator:        OSType;         {file creator}
    fdType:           OSType;         {file type}
    container:        EditionContainerSpec
                                      {the edition}
END;
```

4 Edition Manager

```
NewPublisherReply =
RECORD
    canceled:           Boolean;        {user canceled dialog box}
    replacing:          Boolean;        {user chose existing }
                                        { filename for an edition}
    usePart:            Boolean;        {always FALSE in version 7.0}
    preview:            Handle;         {handle to 'prvw', 'PICT', }
                                        { 'TEXT', or 'snd' data}
    previewFormat:      FormatType;     {type of preview}
    container:          EditionContainerSpec
                                        {edition chosen}
END;


NewSubscriberReply =
RECORD
    canceled:           Boolean;        {user canceled dialog box}
    formatsMask:        SignedByte;     {formats required}
    container:          EditionContainerSpec
                                        {edition selected}
END;


SectionOptionsReply =
RECORD
    canceled:           Boolean;        {user canceled dialog box}
    changed:            Boolean;        {changed the section record}
    sectionH:           SectionHandle;  {handle to the specified }
                                        { section record}
    action:             ResType         {action codes}
END;


EditionOpenerVerb       = (eoOpen, eoClose, eoOpenNew, eoCloseNew
                           eoCanSubscribe);
EditionOpenerParamBlock =
RECORD
    info:               EditionInfoRecord;
                                        {edition container to }
                                        { be subscribed to}
    sectionH:           SectionHandle;
                                        {publisher or  subscriber}
                                        { requesting open}
    document:           FSSpecPtr;      {document passed}
    fdCreator:          OSType;         {Finder creator type}
    ioRefNum:           LongInt;        {reference number}
    ioProc:             FormatIOProcPtr;
                                        {routine to read formats}
    success:            Boolean;        {reading or writing was }
                                        { successful}
    formatsMask:        SignedByte      {formats required to }
                                        { subscribe}
END;
```

```
FormatIOVerb            = (ioHasFormat, ioReadFormat, ioNewFormat,
                           ioWriteFormat);
FormatIOParamBlock =
RECORD
   ioRefNum:            LongInt;      {reference number}
   format:              FormatType;   {edition format type}
   formatIndex:         LongInt;      {opener-specific enumeration }
                                      { of formats}
   offset:              LongInt;      {offset into format}
   buffPtr:             Ptr;          {data starts here}
   buffLen:             LongInt       {length of data}
END;
```

Routines

Initializing the Edition Manager

```
FUNCTION InitEditionPack            : OSErr;
```

Creating and Registering a Section

```
FUNCTION NewSection                 (container: EditionContainerSpec;
                                     sectionDocument: FSSpecPtr; kind:
                                     SectionType; sectionID: LongInt;
                                     initialMode: UpdateMode; VAR sectionH:
                                     SectionHandle) : OSErr;

FUNCTION RegisterSection            (sectionDocument: FSSpec; sectionH:
                                     SectionHandle; VAR aliasWasUpdated:
                                     Boolean) : OSErr;

FUNCTION UnRegisterSection          (sectionH: SectionHandle) : OSErr;

FUNCTION IsRegisteredSection        (sectionH: SectionHandle) : OSErr;

FUNCTION AssociateSection           (sectionH: SectionHandle;
                                     newSectionDocument: FSSpecPtr) :
                                     OSErr;
```

Creating and Deleting an Edition Container

```
FUNCTION CreateEditionContainerFile (editionFile: FSSpec; fdCreator: OSType;
                                     editionFileNameScript: ScriptCode) :
                                     OSErr;

FUNCTION DeleteEditionContainerFile (editionFile: FSSpec) : OSErr;
```

4 Edition Manager

Setting and Locating a Format Mark

```
FUNCTION SetEditionFormatMark   (whichEdition: EditionRefNum; whichFormat:
                                 FormatType; setMarkTo: LongInt) : OSErr;

FUNCTION GetEditionFormatMark   (whichEdition: EditionRefNum; whichFormat:
                                 FormatType; VAR currentMark: LongInt) :
                                 OSErr;
```

Reading in Edition Data

```
FUNCTION OpenEdition         (subscriberSectionH: SectionHandle; VAR refNum:
                              EditionRefNum) : OSErr;

FUNCTION EditionHasFormat    (whichEdition: EditionRefNum; whichFormat:
                              FormatType; VAR formatSize: Size) : OSErr;

FUNCTION ReadEdition         (whichEdition: EditionRefNum; whichFormat:
                              FormatType; buffPtr: UNIV Ptr; VAR buffLen:
                              Size) : OSErr;
```

Writing out Edition Data

```
FUNCTION OpenNewEdition      (publisherSectionH: SectionHandle; fdCreator:
                              OSType; publisherSectionDocument: FSSpecPtr;
                              VAR refNum: EditionRefNum) : OSErr;

FUNCTION WriteEdition        (whichEdition: EditionRefNum; whichFormat:
                              FormatType; buffPtr: UNIV Ptr; buffLen: Size)
                              : OSErr;
```

Closing an Edition After Reading or Writing

```
FUNCTION CloseEdition        (whichEdition: EditionRefNum; successful:
                              Boolean) : OSErr;
```

Displaying Dialog Boxes

```
FUNCTION GetLastEditionContainerUsed (VAR container: EditionContainerSpec) :
                                      OSErr;

FUNCTION NewSubscriberDialog          (VAR reply: NewSubscriberReply) :
                                      OSErr;

FUNCTION NewPublisherDialog           (VAR reply: NewPublisherReply) :
                                      OSErr;
```

```
FUNCTION SectionOptionsDialog        (VAR reply: SectionOptionsReply) :
                                      OSErr;

FUNCTION NewSubscriberExpDialog      (VAR reply: NewSubscriberReply;
                                      where: Point; expansionDITLresID:
                                      Integer; dlgHook:
                                      ExpDlgHookProcPtr; filterProc:
                                      ExpModalFilterProcPtr; yourDataPtr:
                                      UNIV Ptr) : OSErr;

FUNCTION NewPublisherExpDialog       (VAR reply: NewPublisherReply;
                                      where: Point; expansionDITLresID:
                                      Integer; dlgHook:
                                      ExpDlgHookProcPtr; filterProc:
                                      ExpModalFilterProcPtr; yourDataPtr:
                                      UNIV Ptr) : OSErr;

FUNCTION SectionOptionsExpDialog     (VAR reply: SectionOptionsReply;
                                      where: Point; expansionDITLresID:
                                      Integer; dlgHook:
                                      ExpDlgHookProcPtr; filterProc:
                                      ExpModalFilterProcPtr; yourDataPtr:
                                      UNIV Ptr) : OSErr;
```

Locating a Publisher and Edition From a Subscriber

```
FUNCTION GetEditionInfo        (sectionH: SectionHandle; VAR editionInfo:
                                EditionInfoRecord) : OSErr;

FUNCTION GoToPublisherSection (container: EditionContainerSpec) : OSErr;
```

Edition Container Formats

```
FUNCTION GetStandardFormats    (container: EditionContainerSpec; VAR
                                previewFormat: FormatType; preview,
                                publisherAlias, formats: Handle) : OSErr;
```

Reading and Writing Non-Edition files

```
FUNCTION GetEditionOpenerProc   (VAR opener: EditionOpenerProcPtr) : OSErr;

FUNCTION SetEditionOpenerProc   (opener: EditionOpenerProcPtr) : OSErr;

FUNCTION CallEditionOpenerProc  (selector: EditionOpenerVerb; VAR PB:
                                 EditionOpenerParamBlock; routine:
                                 EditionOpenerProcPtr) : OSErr;

FUNCTION CallFormatIOProc       (selector: FormatIOVerb; VAR PB:
                                 FormatIOParamBlock; routine:
                                 FormatIOProcPtr) : OSErr;
```

Application-Defined Routines

```
FUNCTION MyExpDlgHook        (itemOffset: Integer; itemHit: Integer;
                              theDialog: DialogPtr; yourDataPtr: Ptr) :
                              Integer;

FUNCTION MyExpModalFilter    (theDialog: DialogPtr; VAR theEvent:
                              EventRecord; itemOffset: Integer; VAR
                              itemHit: Integer; yourDataPtr: Ptr) :
                              Boolean;

FUNCTION MyOpener            (selector: EditionOpenerVerb; VAR PB:
                              EditionOpenerParamBlock) : OSErr;

FUNCTION MyIO                (selector: FormatIOVerb; VAR PB:
                              FormatIOParamBlock) : OSErr;
```

Result Codes

noErr	0	No error
abortErr	–27	Publisher has written a new edition
eofErr	–39	No additional data in the format
fnfErr	–43	Edition container not found
flLckedErr	–45	Publisher writing to an edition
fBsyErr	–47	Section doing I/O
rfNumErr	–51	Bad edition reference number
permErr	–54	Not a subscriber
wrPermErr	–61	Not a publisher
noTypeErr	–102	Format not available
memFullErr	–108	Could not load package
userCanceledErr	–128	User chose Cancel from dialog box
editionMgrInitErr	–450	Manager not initialized or could not load package
badSectionErr	–451	Not a valid section type
notRegisteredSectionErr	–452	Not registered
badSubPartErr	–454	Bad edition container spec or invalid edition container
multiplePublisherWrn	–460	Already is a publisher
containerNotFoundWrn	–461	Alias was not resolved
notThePublisherWrn	–463	Not the publisher

5 THE EVENT MANAGER

ABOUT THIS CHAPTER

This chapter describes how your application can use the Toolbox Event Manager to send events to other applications and to receive events from other applications. The Toolbox Event Manager in system software version 7.0 provides routines for sending and receiving a new type of event, a high-level event. In addition, Apple Computer, Inc. has defined a protocol for high-level events called the Apple® Event Interprocess Messaging Protocol. High-level events that adhere to this protocol are called Apple events. Your application can also define other types of high-level events and send them to applications, either locally or across a network.

This chapter also describes the operation of the multitasking environment formerly known as MultiFinder®, which is now an integral part of the Macintosh® Operating System in system software version 7.0. In this environment, numerous applications can be open simultaneously, cooperatively sharing the available system resources. The Macintosh Operating System coordinates the execution of multiple applications by sending another type of event, an operating-system event, to applications whenever their execution status changes or whenever processor time is available for background processing. Your application takes advantage of this multitasking capability primarily by receiving operating-system events that guide its execution.

The Event Manager routines that let your application communicate with other applications depend on the services of the Program-to-Program Communications (PPC) Toolbox and are available in system software version 7.0. Before using any of the routines that handle high-level events, you should first use the Gestalt function to determine that the PPC Toolbox is present. You can also use Gestalt to determine which multitasking features of the Operating System are present. See the Compatibility Guidelines chapter in this volume for a full account of using Gestalt.

The ability to have multiple applications open at once is available when running system software version 7.0 or when running MultiFinder in system software versions 5.0 and 6.0. Any significant differences between the multitasking environment of version 7.0 and that provided by MultiFinder in earlier system versions are noted at the appropriate locations in this chapter. In system software earlier than version 7.0, there is no recommended way to determine whether MultiFinder is running or whether other applications are open if it is running. When running in system software version 7.0, applications that need to know what other applications are open (for example, to send high-level events to them) can get that information by calling one of three functions: the PPCBrowser function or the IPCListPorts function (both documented in the Program-to-Program Communications Toolbox chapter in this volume) or the GetNextProcess function (documented in the Process Management chapter in this volume).

The information in this chapter supplements the information in the Toolbox Event Manager chapter of *Inside Macintosh,* Volume I and Volume V. (In this chapter, the term *Event Manager* refers to the Toolbox Event Manager, not the Operating System Event Manager.) In addition, the sections on cooperative multitasking supersede the information in the *Programmer's Guide to MultiFinder.*

To use this chapter, you should be familiar with the way in which the Macintosh Operating System manages processes. See "About Process Management" in the Process Management chapter in this volume for a detailed description of how the Operating System schedules processes, performs context switches, and launches applications. If you want to communicate with applications across a network, then you should be familiar with the discussion of authentication in the Program-to-Program Communications Toolbox chapter in this volume.

ABOUT THE EVENT MANAGER

Most Macintosh programs are event-driven: they decide what to do from moment to moment by asking the Event Manager for events and responding to them one by one in whatever way is appropriate. The Event Manager is your application's primary link to the user, to other applications that are running at the same time as your application, to the various managers that are controlling operations in the Macintosh, and to the Operating System itself. Events sent to your application from these various sources can communicate important information to it and help ensure its smooth operation.

You can use the Event Manager to

- receive key presses and mouse clicks as input for your application
- receive indication that your application's windows need to be activated or updated
- allow other applications to use the available system resources when no events are pending for your application
- send events to other applications
- receive events from other applications
- respond to events received from other applications
- search for a specific event from another application

This chapter provides a brief introduction to events and then discusses a number of particular topics that are related to high-level events and the multitasking environment that is standard in system software version 7.0. It explains

- how to structure your main event loop to receive and process events
- how to create a 'SIZE' resource to specify your application's memory requirements and scheduling options
- how to receive and process high-level events
- how to send high-level events to other applications

This chapter also provides some information about Apple events, Apple's new protocol governing a class of high-level events. Additional information about Apple events, including descriptions of how to process the required Apple events, is provided in the Apple Event Manager chapter in this volume.

INTRODUCTION TO EVENTS

Events are of various types, distinguished according to their origin and meaning. On the most basic level, events are created every time a user presses a key on the keyboard, presses the mouse button, releases the mouse button, or inserts a disk.

Still other events can arise from changes in the processing status of an application. For example, if a user brings an application to the foreground, the Operating System sends a resume event to that application. Some of the work of reactivating the application is done automatically, both by the Operating System and by the Window Manager; the resume event is an indication for your application to take care of any further processing needed as a result of the application being reactivated.

In system software version 7.0, the Event Manager recognizes a new type of event—the high-level event—that allows communication and information transfer between cooperating applications. For example, a spreadsheet application may want to obtain some information from a database application. The spreadsheet can send a high-level event to the database requesting the information; the database can then reply with the requested information by sending another high-level event back to the spreadsheet.

Low-Level Events

Events that report actions by the user (such as pressing the mouse button, typing on the keyboard, or inserting a disk) and events that report that the Event Manager has no other events to report (null events) are called *low-level events* because they report very low-level hardware and software occurrences. Figure 5-1 depicts the relationships among the Operating System Event Manager, the Toolbox Event Manager, the Window Manager, and a single application.

The Operating System Event Manager detects and reports very low-level events such as changes in the attached hardware. Hardware-related events are mouse clicks, key presses, disk insertions, and so forth.

Other low-level events can arise from changes in windows on the screen. For example, if a user has several documents open while running an application, the user can switch from one document to another by clicking in the appropriate window. Before your application is sent such an event, the Window Manager does some work for you, such as highlighting the newly activated window and unhighlighting the deactivated window. As illustrated in Figure 5-1, activate and update events are not placed into the event queue but are sent directly to the Toolbox Event Manager.

Applications can generate events themselves and send them (using the PostEvent function) to the Operating System Event Manager for processing. These types of events are application-specific. In an environment where only one application can execute at a time, application-defined events allow your application to send events to itself. You should be careful not to post events that are not normally placed in the event queue (such as activate events).

> **Note:** In system software version 7.0, the work done by application-defined events must be accomplished using Apple events or other high-level events.

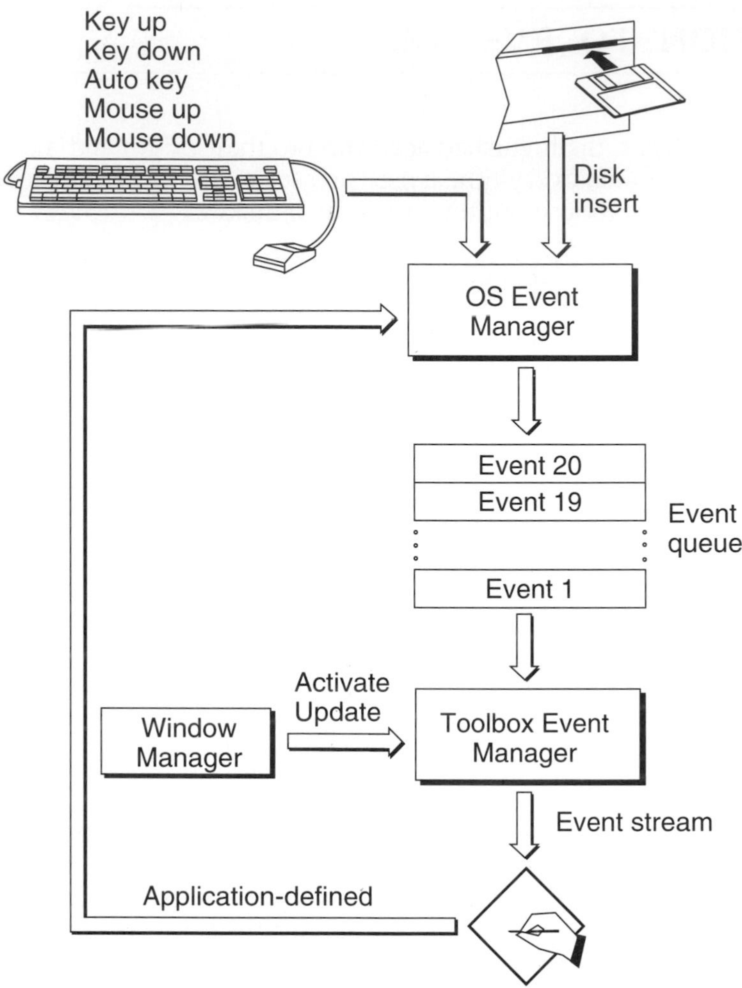

Figure 5-1. Events in a single application environment

Operating-System Events

The cooperative multitasking environment introduces a new type of event to allow the Operating System to communicate information to an application about changes in the operating status of that application. For example, when your application is switched into the background, the Operating System sends it a suspend event. Then, when your application is switched back into the foreground, it receives a resume event. These types of events are known as *operating-system events.*

Figure 5-2 illustrates how the Event Manager helps provide this cooperative multitasking environment. The main new source of events is the Macintosh Operating System itself, which sends suspend, resume, and mouse-moved events to applications through the Toolbox Event Manager. (In system software versions earlier than 7.0, these events are sent by MultiFinder.) In addition to the event queue created by the Operating System Event Manager, the Toolbox Event Manager maintains a separate event queue for each open application. The events in the Operating System Event Manager queue are always sent to the foreground application, but other events (for example, update events from the Window Manager) can be sent to background applications.

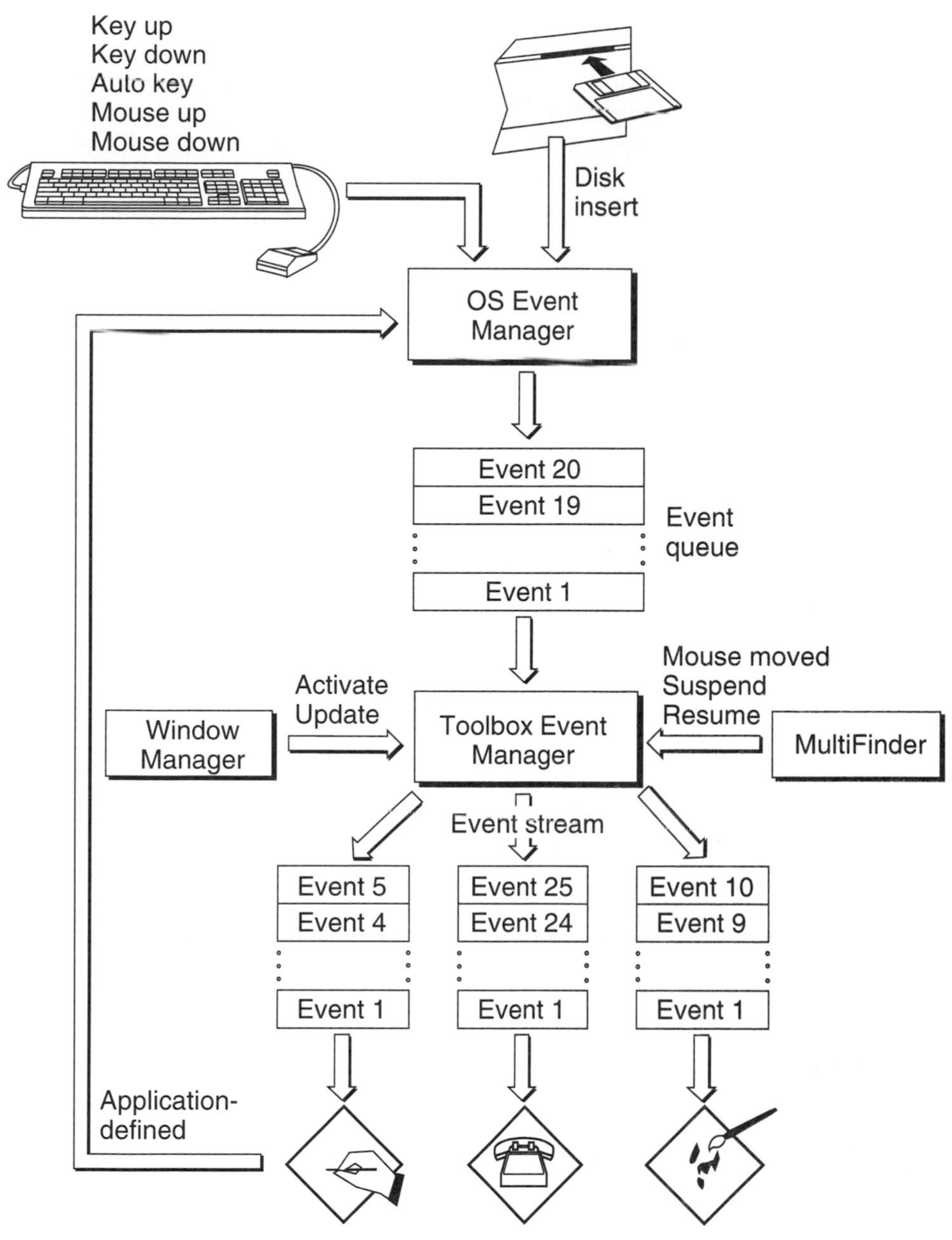

Figure 5-2. Events in a multi-application environment

Because your application might need to execute differently depending on whether it is running in the foreground or in the background, you can inspect the low bit of the message field of an operating-system event to determine whether the event is a suspend or a resume event. For example, if you need to notify the user of some special occurrence while your application is executing in the background, you cannot simply put up an alert box. Instead, you should use the Notification Manager to queue a notification request that will be presented to the user at the appropriate moment.

When your application receives a suspend event, it does not actually become inactive until it makes its next request to receive events from the Event Manager. At the time that it receives the suspend event, your application can inspect the convertClipboard flag in the message field of the event record to see whether it should convert any local scrap into the global scrap. Your application should also hide any floating windows, selections, and so on. Then you should call WaitNextEvent to relinquish the processor and allow the Operating System to schedule other processes for execution. It is important to minimize the processing you do in response to a suspend event because otherwise the machine may appear sluggish.

When control returns to your application, the first event it receives is a resume event. Your application may now convert the global scrap back to its private scrap, if necessary. As part of the resume or suspend event, the Operating System informs your application if the Clipboard has changed by setting bit 1 of the message field of the event record.

There are two other kinds of operating-system events, mouse-moved events and application-died events. A mouse-moved event is sent to an application to indicate that the user has moved the mouse outside of the region specified to the WaitNextEvent routine. The application-died event is sent whenever an application launched by your application terminates or crashes.

> **Note:** Some early versions of MultiFinder do not send application-died events, and your application should not depend on receiving them. These events are provided primarily for use by debuggers. In system software version 7.0, application-died events are now sent as Apple events.

High-Level Events

In system software version 7.0, the Event Manager introduces a new type of event, the high-level event, along with a number of new Event Manager routines that let applications communicate with each other by exchanging high-level events. A **high-level event** is an event that your application can send to another application to send it some information, to receive from it some information, or to have it perform some action. For example, your application can send an event to another application instructing that application to perform a specific action, such as adding a row to a spreadsheet or changing the font size of a paragraph. Your application can also send an event to another application requesting information from that application—for example, requesting a dictionary application to return the definition of a particular word. When you send a high-level event to another application, you can also include additional information or commands in an optional data buffer. For example, your application can use a high-level event to send a list of new words and definitions to a dictionary application.

Figure 5-3 shows the general event-handling mechanism in system software version 7.0. Three different applications are communicating with one another by sending and receiving high-level events. High-level events are placed in a separate event queue maintained by the Operating System. The Operating System maintains a high-level event queue for each application that has announced itself as capable of receiving high-level events. The high-level event queues are limited in size only by available memory.

> **Note:** Because high-level events are not stored in the Operating System event queue, you cannot flush high-level events by calling the FlushEvents procedure.

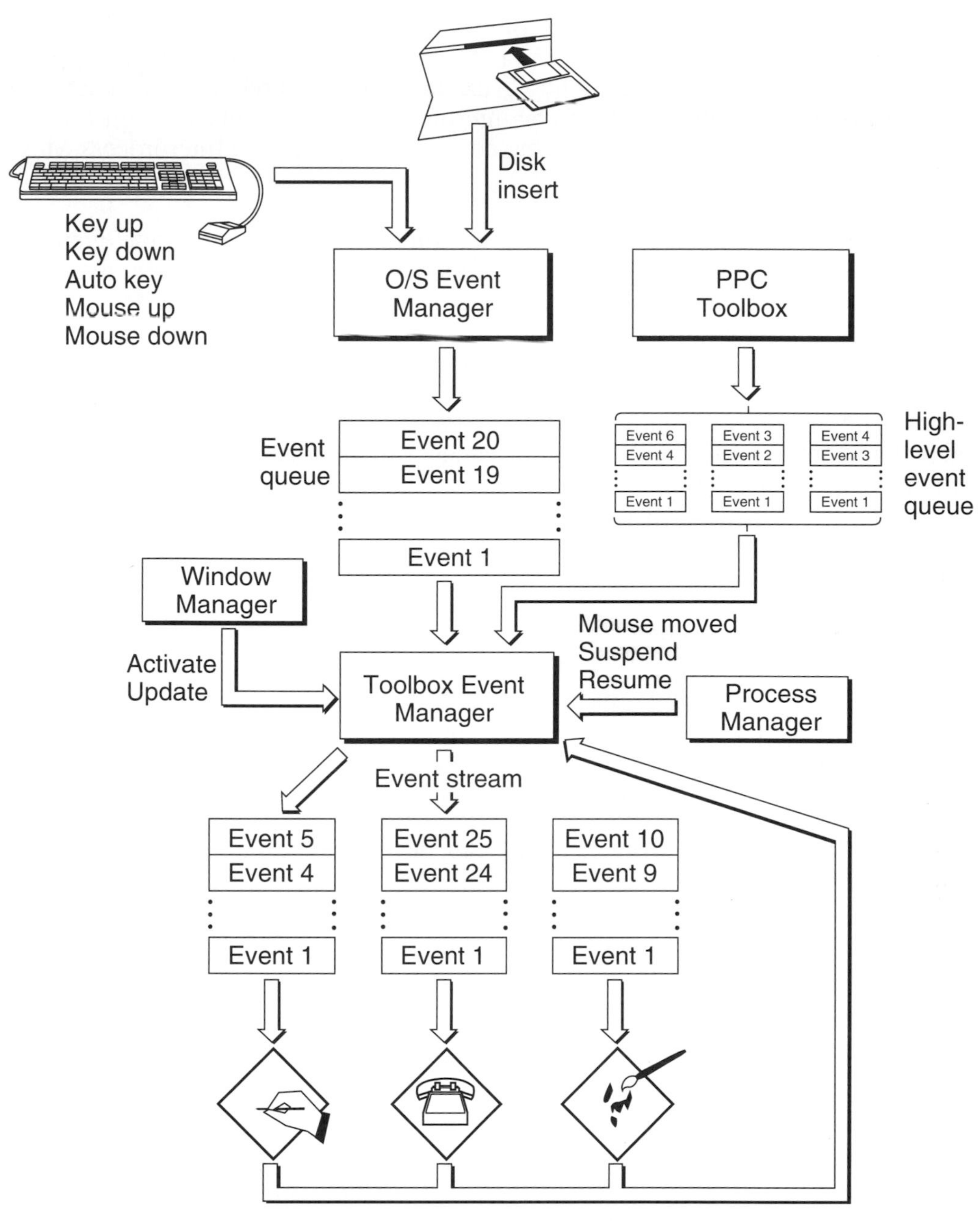

Figure 5-3. Events in system software version 7.0

For effective communication between applications, your application must define the set of high-level events it responds to and let other applications know the events it accepts. By implementing the capabilities to send events to and receive events from other applications, you allow other applications to interact with your application and provide enhanced capabilities to your users.

Generally, there is no restriction on the type of processing that one application can request from another by sending it a high-level event. For a high-level event sent by one application to be understood by another application, however, the sender and receiver must agree on a protocol, that is, on the way the event is to be interpreted. Apple events are high-level events whose structure and interpretation are determined by the Apple Event Interprocess Messaging Protocol.

To make your application 7.0-friendly, you should support the required Apple events, as described in the Apple Event Manager chapter in this volume. In addition, you may want your application to support other common Apple events. For example, the Edition Manager uses Apple events to communicate information about document sections among the various applications that may publish sections or subscribe to them. The Edition Manager sends the appropriate Apple events to applications that want to maintain up-to-date subscriber sections within their documents. If a user alters a section of a document that has previously been published and updates the edition, the Edition Manager might post an Apple event to the application indicating that a new edition is available. The application receiving the Apple event can then update the subscriber or ignore the information, as the user dictates. For complete information on responding to Apple events sent by the Edition Manager, see the Edition Manager chapter in this volume.

To ensure compatibility and smooth interaction with other Macintosh applications, you should use the Apple event protocol for high-level events whenever possible. You should define new protocols only if your application must communicate with applications on other computers that use different protocols or if your application has other special needs. For complete information about Apple events and on implementing the required set of Apple events, see the Apple Event Manager chapter in this volume.

> **Note:** All Macintosh system software that sends or receives high-level events uses the Apple events protocol.

EVENT PROCESSING

In system software version 7.0, the cooperative multitasking capabilities previously available through MultiFinder are an integral part of the Operating System. As a result, applications running under version 7.0 must process events and reserve memory in ways that contribute to the smooth operation of all applications that are open. In practice, this means that you should retrieve events from the Event Manager by using the WaitNextEvent function and that you should include a 'SIZE' resource that specifies a reasonable memory partition size. This section shows how to retrieve events from the Event Manager, how to mask out unwanted events, and how to specify memory and scheduling options for your application.

The Event Loop

In applications that are event-driven (that is, which decide what to do at any time by receiving and responding to events), you can obtain information about events that are pending by calling Event Manager routines. Since you call these routines repeatedly, the section of code in which you request events from the Event Manager usually takes the form of a loop; this section of code is the *event loop*.

A simple event loop might look something like the one given in Listing 5-1. It consists of an endless loop that retrieves an event and decides whether it is a null event. If the event is not a null event, the event loop calls DoEvent, an application-defined procedure, to process the event. Otherwise, the procedure calls an application-defined idling procedure, DoIdle.

Listing 5-1. A simple event loop

```
PROCEDURE EventLoop;
VAR
   cursorRgn:   RgnHandle;
   gotEvent:    Boolean;
   event:       EventRecord;
BEGIN
   cursorRgn := NewRgn; {pass an empty region the first time thru}
   REPEAT
      gotEvent := WaitNextEvent(everyEvent, event, GetSleep, cursorRgn);
      AdjustCursor(event.where, cursorRgn);
      IF gotEvent THEN
         DoEvent(event)
      ELSE
         DoIdle;
   UNTIL FALSE;      {loop forever}
END;
```

The DoEvent procedure must determine what kind of event the call to WaitNextEvent retrieved and act accordingly. Notice that the parameter passed to DoEvent is the event record received by WaitNextEvent. Essentially, the procedure is just a large conditional statement that branches according to the value of the what field of the event record. Listing 5-2 defines a simple DoEvent procedure.

Listing 5-2. Processing events

```
PROCEDURE DoEvent(event: EventRecord);
BEGIN
   CASE event.what OF
      mouseDown:
         DoMouseDown(event);
      mouseUp:
         DoMouseUp(event);
      keyDown, autoKey:
         DoKeyDown(event);
      activateEvt:
         DoActivate(event);
      updateEvt:
         DoUpdate(event);
      osEvt:
         DoOSEvent(event);
      kHighLevelEvent:
         DoHighLevelEvent(event);
   END;
END; {DoEvent}
```

The main addition to your application's event loop in system software version 7.0 is the recognition of high-level events (using the constant kHighLevelEvent) and the appropriate processing of those events. The procedure defined in Listing 5-2 calls DoHighLevelEvent, an application-defined routine, to interpret the high-level event further.

Event Masks

Several of the Event Manager routines can be restricted to operate on a specific event type or group of types. You do this by disabling (or "masking out") the events you are not interested in receiving. To specify which event types an Event Manager routine governs, supply a parameter known as an event mask. Masks for each individual event type are available as predefined constants:

```
CONST everyEvent          =   -1;        {every event}
      mDownMask           =   2;         {mouse-down}
      mUpMask             =   4;         {mouse-up}
      keyDownMask         =   8;         {key-down}
      keyUpMask           =   16;        {key-up}
      autoKeyMask         =   32;        {auto-key}
      updateMask          =   64;        {update}
      diskMask            =   128;       {disk-inserted}
      activMask           =   256;       {activate}
      highLevelEventMask  =   1024;      {high-level}
      osMask              =   -32768;    {operating-system}
```

You can form any particular mask you need by adding or subtracting mask constants. For example, to request the next available event that is not a mouse-up event, you can use the code

```
myErr := WaitNextEvent(everyEvent-mUpMask, myEvent, mySleep, myMRgnHnd);
```

Note that masking out types of events does not remove those events from the Operating System event queue. If a type of event is masked out, it is simply ignored by the Toolbox Event Manager when it reads the event queue. Note also that you cannot mask out null events. Even if every other kind of event is disabled, the Event Manager reports a null event.

In system software version 7.0, you can mask out high-level events by subtracting the constant highLevelEventMask from your event mask. (This constant has the same value as the defunct constant networkMask.)

Switching Contexts

Applications running in the background receive processing time when the front application makes an event call (that is, calls WaitNextEvent, GetNextEvent, or EventAvail) and there are no events pending for that front application. An application running in the background should relinquish the CPU regularly to ensure a timely return to the foreground application when necessary.

In system software version 7.0 (or under MultiFinder in earlier versions), the available processing time is distributed among multiple applications through a procedure known as *context switching* (or just *switching*). When a context switch occurs, the Process Manager allocates processing time to a process that is different from the one that had been receiving processing time. Two types of context switching may occur: major and minor. All switching occurs at a well-defined time, namely, when an application calls WaitNextEvent.

A *major switch* is a complete context switch: an application's windows are moved from the background to the foreground, or vice versa. In a major switch, two applications are involved, the one being switched to the foreground and the one being switched to the background. The A5 worlds of both applications are switched, as well as the relevant low-memory environment. If those applications receive suspend and resume events, they are so notified at the time that a major switch occurs.

Major switching does not occur when a modal dialog box is the frontmost window, although minor switching (discussed next) can still occur. To determine whether major switching can occur, the Operating System checks (among other things) to see if the window definition procedure of the frontmost window is dBoxProc because the type dBoxProc is specifically reserved for modal dialog boxes. (Major switching can still occur when a movable modal dialog box is the frontmost window.)

A *minor switch* occurs when an application is switched out to give time to background processes. A minor switch always involves two applications, a background application and the application yielding time to it (which may be some other background application). In a minor switch, the A5 worlds of those two applications are switched, as are the low-memory environments. However, the layers of windows are not switched, and neither application receives either suspend or resume events.

Note: Your application can also get switched out if it calls a Toolbox routine that makes an event call. For example, your application may get switched out when calling ModalDialog.

Specifying Memory Requirements and Scheduling Options

Every application executing under system software version 7.0, as well as every application executing under MultiFinder, should contain a 'SIZE' resource. One of the principal functions of the 'SIZE' resource is to inform the Operating System about the memory size requirements for the application (hence the name 'SIZE') so that the Operating System can set up an appropriately sized partition for the application. The 'SIZE' resource is also used to indicate certain scheduling options to the Operating System, such as whether the application can run in the background, whether it can accept suspend and resume events, and so forth. The 'SIZE' resource in system software version 7.0 contains additional information indicating whether the application is 32-bit clean, whether the application wishes to receive notification of the termination of any applications it has launched, and whether the application wishes to receive high-level events.

This section explains the structure of a 'SIZE' resource and the meaning of each of its fields. It also shows how to specify the Rez input for a 'SIZE' resource. You are responsible for creating the information in this resource.

The Structure of a 'SIZE' Resource

A 'SIZE' resource consists of a 16-bit flags field, followed by two 32-bit size fields. The flags field specifies operating characteristics of the application, and the size fields indicate the minimum and preferred partition sizes for the application. The **minimum partition size** is the actual limit below which your application will not run. The **preferred partition size** is the memory size at which your application can run most effectively and which the Operating System attempts to secure upon launch of the application. If that amount of memory is unavailable, the application is placed into the largest contiguous block available, provided that it is larger than the specified minimum size.

> **Note:** If the amount of available memory is between the minimum and the preferred sizes, the Finder™ displays a dialog box asking if the user wants to run the application using the amount of memory available. If your application does not have a 'SIZE' resource, it is assigned a default partition size of 512 KB.

When you define a 'SIZE' resource, you should give it a resource ID of –1. A user can modify the preferred size in the Finder's information window for your application. If the user does alter the partition size, the Operating System creates a new 'SIZE' resource having resource ID 0. At application launch time, the Launch function looks for a 'SIZE' resource with ID 0; if this resource is not found, it uses your original 'SIZE' resource with ID –1. This new 'SIZE' resource is also created when the user modifies any of the other settings in the resource.

Listing 5-3 shows the structure of the 'SIZE' resource.

Listing 5-3. A template for a 'SIZE' resource

```
type 'SIZE' {
   boolean  reserved;                      /*reserved*/
   boolean  ignoreSuspendResumeEvents,     /*ignores suspend-resume events*/
            acceptSuspendResumeEvents;     /*accepts suspend-resume events*/
   boolean  reserved;                      /*reserved*/
   boolean  cannotBackground,              /*does no background processing*/
            canBackground;                 /*can use background null events*/
   boolean  needsActivateOnFGSwitch,       /*needs activate event*/
            doesActivateOnFGSwitch;        /*needs no activate event*/
   boolean  backgroundAndForeground,       /*app has a user interface*/
            onlyBackground;                /*app has no user interface*/
   boolean  dontGetFrontClicks,            /*no mouse events on resume*/
            getFrontClicks;                /*get mouse events on resume*/
   boolean  ignoreAppDiedEvents,           /*applications use this*/
            acceptAppDiedEvents;           /*app launchers use this*/
   boolean  not32BitCompatible,            /*works with 24-bit addr*/
            is32BitCompatible;             /*works with 24- or 32-bit addr*/
   boolean  notHighLevelEventAware,        /*can't use high-level events*/
            isHighLevelEventAware;         /*can use high-level events*/
   boolean  onlyLocalHLEvents,             /*only local high-level events*/
            localAndRemoteHLEvents;        /*also remote high-level events*/
```

```
    boolean  notStationeryAware,        /*can't use stationery documents*/
             isStationeryAware;         /*can use stationery documents*/
    boolean  dontUseTextEditServices,   /*can't use inline services*/
             useTextEditServices;       /*can use inline services*/
    boolean  reserved;                  /*reserved*/
    boolean  reserved;                  /*reserved*/
    boolean  reserved;                  /*reserved*/
                                        /*memory sizes are in bytes*/
    unsigned longint;                   /*preferred memory size*/
    unsigned longint;                   /*minimum memory size*/
};
```

The nonreserved bits in the flags field have the following meanings.

Flag descriptions

acceptSuspendResumeEvents	When set, indicates that your application can process suspend and resume events (which the Operating System sends to your application before sending it into the back-ground or when bringing it into the foreground). In this way, your application knows when to process the global scrap.
canBackground	When set, indicates that your application wants to receive null event processing time while in the background. If your application has nothing to do in the background, you should not set this flag.
doesActivateOnFGSwitch	When set, indicates that your application takes responsibility for activating and deactivating any windows in response to a suspend or resume event. If the acceptSuspendResumeEvents flag is set, if the doesActivateOnFGSwitch flag is not set, and if the application is suspended, then the application receives an activate event. However, if you set the doesActivateOnFGSwitch flag, then your application won't receive activate events, and you must take care of activation and deactivation when it receives the corresponding suspend or resume event. This means that if the application's window is frontmost, the suspend event should be treated as though a deactivate event were received as well (assuming that both the doesActivateOnFGSwitch and acceptSuspendResumeEvents flags are set). For example, scroll bars should be deactivated, blinking insertion points should be hidden, and selected text should be deselected if your application moves to the back-ground. If you do not set this flag, then a window must be created to force the activate and deactivate events to occur.
onlyBackground	When set, indicates that your application runs only in the background. Usually this is because it does not have a user interface and cannot run in the foreground.

getFrontClicks	When set, indicates that your application is to receive the mouse-down and mouse-up events that are used to bring your application into the foreground when the user clicks in your application's frontmost window. Typically, the user simply wants to bring your application into the foreground, so it is usually not desirable to receive the mouse events (which would probably move the insertion point or start drawing immediately, depending on the application). The Finder is one application, however, that has the getFrontClicks flag set.
acceptAppDiedEvents	When set, indicates that your application is to be notified that an application launched by this application has terminated or crashed. See the Process Management chapter in this volume for more information about launching applications and receiving Application Died events.
is32BitCompatible	When set, indicates that your application can be run with the 32-bit Memory Manager. You should not set this flag unless you have thoroughly tested your application on a 32-bit system (such as a Macintosh IIci running system software version 7.0 in 32-bit mode, or under A/UX®).
isHighLevelEventAware	When set, indicates that your application can send and receive high-level events. If this flag is not set, the Event Manager does not give your application high-level events when you call WaitNextEvent. There is no way to mask out types of high-level events; if this flag is set, you will receive all types of high-level events sent to your application.
localAndRemoteHLEvents	When set, indicates that your application is to be visible to applications running on other computers on a network (in addition to applications running on the local machine). If this flag is not set, your application does not receive high-level events across a network.
isStationeryAware	When set, indicates that your application can recognize stationery documents. If this flag is not set and the user opens a stationery document, the Finder duplicates the document and prompts the user for a name for the duplicate document.
useTextEditServices	When set, indicates that your application can use the inline text services provided by TextEdit. See the TextEdit chapter in this volume for information about the inline input capabilities of TextEdit.

Note: If you set the acceptSuspendResumeEvents flag, you should also set the doesActivateOnFGSwitch flag.

The modifiers field in the event record now contains additional information about a mouse-down event. In system software version 7.0, the activeFlag modifier flag in the modifiers field of a mouse-down event record is set to indicate that the mouse-down event caused a foreground switch. Your application can use this flag to determine whether to process the mouse-down event (probably depending on whether the clicked item was visible before the foreground switch). This modifier is set for all mouse-down events that cause a foreground switch, regardless of whether your application's getFrontClicks flag is set or whether the mouse click was in your application's front window. In system software versions prior to 7.0, this flag is never set for mouse-down events, and your application cannot tell if the mouse click caused a foreground switch. As a result, your application should always process a mouse-down event if its getFrontClicks flag is set.

Listing 5-4 shows the input for a sample 'SIZE' resource.

Listing 5-4. The Rez input for a sample 'SIZE' resource

```
resource 'SIZE' (-1) {
   reserved,                    /*reserved*/
   acceptSuspendResumeEvents,  /*accepts suspend-resume events*/
   reserved,                    /*reserved*/
   canBackground,               /*can use background null events*/
   doesActivateOnFGSwitch,      /*needs no activate event*/
   backgroundAndForeground,     /*app has a user interface*/
   dontGetFrontClicks,          /*no mouse events on resume*/
   ignoreAppDiedEvents,         /*applications use this*/
   is32BitCompatible,           /*works with 24- or 32-bit addr*/
   isHighLevelEventAware,       /*can use high-level events*/
   localAndRemoteHLEvents,      /*also remote high-level events*/
   isStationeryAware,           /*can use stationery documents*/
   dontUseTextEditServices,     /*can't use inline input services*/
   reserved,                    /*reserved*/
   reserved,                    /*reserved*/
   reserved,                    /*reserved*/
   kPrefSize * 1024,            /*preferred memory size*/
   kMinSize * 1024              /*minimum memory size*/
};
```

This resource specification indicates, among other things, that the application is 32-bit clean, can handle stationery documents, and accepts both local and network high-level events. You are responsible for defining the constants kPrefSize and kMinSize; for example, if you set kPrefSize to 50, the preferred partition size will be 50 KB.

Creating a 'SIZE' Resource

When creating a 'SIZE' resource, you first need to determine the various operating characteristics of your application. For example, if your application has nothing useful to do when it is in the background, then you should not set the canBackground flag. Similarly, if you have not tested your application in an environment that uses all 32 bits of a handle or pointer for memory addresses, then you should not set the is32BitCompatible flag.

Next, you need to determine what your application's memory requirements are likely to be. There is no simple formula for determining the appropriate partition size requirements for all applications because so many factors affect memory requirements. An application's memory requirements depend on the static heap size, the dynamic heap, the A5 world, and the stack. The static heap size includes objects that are always present during the execution of the application—for example, code segments, Toolbox data structures for window records, and so on. Dynamic heap requirements come from various objects created on a per-document basis (which may vary in size proportionally with the document itself) and objects that are required for specific commands or functions. The size of the A5 world depends on the amount of global data and the number of intersegment jumps the application contains. Finally, the stack contains variables, return addresses, and temporary information. The application stack size varies among computers, so you should base your values for the stack size according to the stack size required on a Macintosh Plus (8 KB). The Process Manager automatically adjusts your requested amount of memory to compensate for the different stack sizes on different machines. For example, if you request 512 KB, more stack space (approximately 16 KB) will be allocated on machines with larger default stack sizes.

Unfortunately, it is simply impossible to forecast all of these conditions with any great degree of reliability. You should be able to determine reasonably accurate estimates for the stack size, static heap size, A5 world, and jump table. In addition, you can use tools such as MacsBug's heap-exploring commands to help you empirically determine your application's dynamic memory requirements.

USING THE EVENT MANAGER

You can use the Toolbox Event Manager to receive information about hardware-related events, about changes in the appearance of your application's windows, or about changes in the operating status of your application. You can also use the Event Manager to communicate directly with other applications. This communication can include sending events to other applications, receiving events from other applications, and searching for specific events from other applications.

The events that your application can send to and receive from other applications are called high-level events. Your application can both send and receive high-level events, but it generally only receives low-level events and should not send them. Your application receives both low-level and high-level events in the same way, which is by asking the Event Manager for the next available event. If the event your application receives is a high-level event, your application might need to use another Event Manager routine to retrieve an optional data buffer accompanying that event.

Receiving Low-Level Events

Applications receive events one at a time by asking the Event Manager for the next available event. You use Event Manager routines to receive (or in the case of EventAvail, simply to look at) the next available event that is pending for your application. The Event Manager returns to your application an event record, which includes the relevant information about that event.

Your application can use the WaitNextEvent, GetNextEvent, and EventAvail functions to retrieve events from the Event Manager. GetNextEvent returns the next available event of a specified type. Further, if the event returned is in the event queue, GetNextEvent removes it from the queue. EventAvail is just like GetNextEvent, except that if the event reported is in the event queue, it is left there. EventAvail thus allows your application to look at the next event in the event queue without actually processing the event.

You should use the WaitNextEvent function to retrieve an event from the Event Manager. WaitNextEvent requires four parameters: an event mask, an event record, a sleep value, and a mouse region. If WaitNextEvent returns successfully, the event record contains information about the retrieved event. The sleep parameter specifies the amount of time (in ticks) that your application agrees to relinquish the processor if no events are pending for it. When that time expires or when an event becomes available for your application, the Process Manager schedules your application for execution. In general, you should specify a value greater than 0 in the sleep parameter so that other applications can receive processing time if they need it. Your application should not sleep more than 15 ticks if you use TextEdit because the fastest cursor blink occurs every 15 ticks.

The mouseRgn parameter to WaitNextEvent specifies a screen region that lets you determine the conditions when your application is to receive notice of mouse-moved events. Your application receives mouse-moved events only when the mouse is outside of the specified region and your application is the foreground process. You can use the mouseRgn parameter as a convenient way to change the shape of the cursor—for example, when the mouse moves from the content area of a window to the scroll bar.

> **Note:** If your application calls WaitNextEvent, it should not call the SystemTask procedure.

For low-level events, the event record filled in by WaitNextEvent has the following structure:

```
TYPE EventRecord =
     RECORD
        what:               Integer;      {event code}
        message:            LongInt;      {event message}
        when:               LongInt;      {ticks since startup}
        where:              Point;        {mouse location}
        modifiers:          Integer       {modifier flags}
     END;
```

For high-level events, however, several of the fields of the event record have different meanings. See “Receiving High-Level Events” later in this chapter.

Responding to Operating-System Events

Operating-system events are of type osEvt and are assigned the event code previously assigned to app4Evts (type 4 application events).

```
CONST osEvt = 15;
```

If your application does not handle suspend and resume events (as indicated by a flag in its 'SIZE' resource), then the Operating System has to trick your application into performing scrap coercion to ensure that the contents of the Clipboard can be transferred from one application to another. This process adds to the time it takes to move the foreground application to the background and vice versa and thereby makes the user interface look cumbersome.

Your application should respond to a suspend event by moving its private scrap into the Clipboard and then returning to the main event loop. Also, your application can do anything else necessary to get ready for a major switch. When your application receives a resume event and if the Clipboard has been altered, your application should copy the contents of the Clipboard, convert them back to its private scrap, and do anything else required for a foreground switch. After processing the scrap in this way, your application resumes executing.

> **Note:** When switched into the background, an application should hide its Clipboard window. The contents of the Clipboard are not valid unless the application is frontmost.

In an osEvt event record, the message field contains information indicating whether the event is a mouse-moved, suspend, or resume event and whether Clipboard conversion is required when the application resumes execution. The message field has the following structure:

Bit	**Meaning**
0	0 if a suspend event 1 if a resume event
1	0 if Clipboard conversion not required 1 if Clipboard conversion required
2–23	Reserved
24–31	suspendResumeMessage if a suspend or resume event mouseMovedMessage if a mouse-moved event

Note that you need to examine the low byte of the message field to determine what kind of operating-system event you have received. The messages passed in bits 24–31 are defined by constants:

```
CONST suspendResumeMessage = $01;    {suspend or resume event}
      mouseMovedMessage    = $FA;    {mouse-moved event}
```

If the event is a suspend or resume event, you need to examine the first bit of the high byte to figure out whether that event is a suspend or resume event. Bits 0 and 1 are meaningful only if bits 24–31 indicate that the event is a suspend or resume event. You can use the constants resumeFlag and convertClipboardFlag to determine whether the event is a resume event, and whether Clipboard conversion is required:

```
CONST resumeFlag           = 1;      {resume event}
      convertClipboardFlag = 2;      {Clipboard conversion required}
```

Receiving High-Level Events

In system software version 7.0, your application can receive a high-level event when it retrieves an event from the Event Manager. As always, your application determines what kind of event it has received by looking at the what field of the event record returned by the Event Manager. The event code for high-level events is defined by a constant name.

```
CONST kHighLevelEvent       = 23;
```

For high-level events, two fields of the event record have special meanings. The message field and the where field of the event record together define the specific type of high-level event and are interpreted as type OSType, not LongInt or Point. The message field contains the event class of this high-level event. For example, Apple events sent by the Edition Manager have the event class 'sect'. You can define your own class of events that are specific to your application. If you have registered your application signature, then you can use your signature to define the class of events that belong to your application. Note, however, that Apple reserves all lowercase letters and nonalphabetic characters for the classes of events defined by Apple.

For high-level events, the where field in the event record contains a second message specifier, called the event ID. The event ID defines the particular type of event (or message) within the class of events defined by the event class. For example, the Section Read Apple event sent by the Edition Manager has event class 'sect' and event ID 'read'. The Open Documents Apple event sent by the Finder has event class 'aevt' and event ID 'odoc'. You can define your own set of event IDs, corresponding to your own event class. For example, if the message field contains 'biff' and the where field contains 'cmd1', then the high-level event indicates the type of event defined by 'cmd1' within the class of events defined by the application with the signature 'biff'.

Unlike low-level events and operating-system events, high-level events may not be completely determined by the event record returned to your application when it calls WaitNextEvent. For example, you might still need to know which other application sent you the high-level event or what additional data that application wants to send you. This further information about the high-level event is available to your application by calling the AcceptHighLevelEvent function. The additional information associated with a high-level event includes

- the identity of the sender of the event
- a unique number that identifies this particular event
- the address and length of a data buffer that can contain optional data

To obtain this additional information, your application must call AcceptHighLevelEvent before calling WaitNextEvent again. By convention, calling AcceptHighLevelEvent indicates that your application intends to process the high-level event.

Note: Because the where field of an event record for a high-level event is used to select a specific kind of event (within the class determined by the message field), high-level event records do not contain the mouse position at the time of the event. Moreover, it is dangerous to interpret the where field before interpreting the what field because different event classes can contain overlapping sets of event IDs.

The section "Responding to Events From Other Applications" later in this chapter describes how to use the AcceptHighLevelEvent function.

Identifying High-Level Event Senders and Receivers

When you receive a high-level event, part of the information returned by AcceptHighLevelEvent is the sender of the event. You can use that information to respond selectively to requests made by other applications or to know which application to send any replies to. The information about the sender is provided in the form of a target ID record, defined as follows:

```
TYPE TargetID =
     RECORD
        sessionID:    LongInt;             {session reference number}
        name:         PPCPortRec;          {sender's port name}
        location:     LocationNameRec;     {sender's port location}
        recvrName:    PPCPortRec           {reserved}
     END;
```

The sessionID field corresponds to the session reference number created by the PPC Toolbox. This is a 32-bit number that uniquely identifies a PPC Toolbox session (or connection) with another application. The name and location fields contain the sender's port name and port location (and have no meaning when posting an event). If the sending application is on the same machine as the receiving application, you can determine the sending application's process serial number by calling the GetProcessSerialNumberFromPortName function.

When you post a high-level event, you can specify its recipient in one of four ways:

- by port name and port location (specified in a target ID record)
- by a session ID
- by the application's creator signature
- by a process serial number

Note that to specify the recipient of a high-level event sent to an application across a network, you can use only its target ID or its session ID. You can use any of the four ways when sending high-level events to applications on the local machine.

When you are replying to a high-level event, it is easy to identify the recipient because you can use the target ID record that you receive from AcceptHighLevelEvent, the session ID contained in that target ID record, or the process serial number (if the receiving process is local). Note that replying by session ID is always the fastest way to respond to a high-level event.

When you are not replying to a previous event, you need to determine the identity of the target application yourself. You can use one of several methods to do this. If the target application is on the local machine, you can search for that application's creator signature or its process serial number by calling the GetProcessInformation function. See "Getting Information About Other Processes" in the Process Management chapter of this volume for a detailed explanation of GetProcessInformation and for examples of using it to generate a list of process serial numbers of all open processes on the local machine.

If the application to which you want to send a high-level event is located on a remote machine, you need to identify it either by its session ID or by its target ID. You can call the PPCBrowser function to let the user browse for a specific port. You can call the IPCListPorts function to obtain a list of all ports registered with the target PPC Toolbox. See the Program-to-Program Communications Toolbox chapter in this volume for an explanation of both of these functions.

Sending High-Level Events

You use the PostHighLevelEvent routine to send a high-level event to another application. When doing so, you need to provide six pieces of information:

- an event record with the event class and event ID assigned appropriately
- the identity of the recipient of the event
- a unique number that identifies this particular event
- a data buffer that can contain optional data
- the length of the data buffer
- options determining how the event is posted

Note: To send an Apple event, use the Apple Event Manager function AESend. The Apple Event Manager uses the Event Manager to post Apple events. For information on posting Apple events, see the Apple Event Manager chapter in this volume.

As indicated in the previous section, you can identify the recipient of the high-level event in one of four ways. Listing 5-5 illustrates how to send a high-level event to an application on the local machine. In this example, an application is sending an event to an application whose signature is 'boff'.

Listing 5-5. Posting a high-level event by application signature

```
PROCEDURE PostTest;
VAR
   myEvent:     EventRecord;     {an event record}
   myRecvID:    OSType;          {receiver ID}
   myOpts:      LongInt;         {posting options}
   myErr:       OSErr;
BEGIN
   myEvent.what := kHighLevelEvent;
   myEvent.message := LongInt('boff');
   myEvent.where := Point(LongInt('cmd1'));
   myOpts := receiverIDisSignature + nReturnReceipt;
   myRecvID := 'boff';
   myErr := PostHighLevelEvent(myEvent, @myRecvID, 0, NIL, 0, myOpts);
   IF myErr <> noErr THEN
      DoError(myErr);
END;
```

In this example, there is no additional data to transmit, so the sending application provides NIL as the pointer to the data buffer and sets the buffer length to 0. Note that the receiver is specified by its creator signature and that the sender requests a return receipt. The myOpts parameter specifies posting options, which are of two types: delivery options and options associated with the receiverID parameter. You can specify one or more delivery options to indicate if you want the other application to receive the event at the next opportunity and to indicate if you want acknowledgment that the other application received the event. You use the options associated with the receiverID parameter to indicate how you are specifying the recipient of the event. To set the various posting options, use constants.

```
CONST nAttnMsg              = $00000001;  {give this message priority}
      priorityMask          = $000000FF;
      nReturnReceipt        = $00000200;  {return receipt requested}
      systemOptionsMask     = $00000F00;
      receiverIDisTargetID  = $00005000;  {ID is target ID}
      receiverIDisSessionID = $00006000;  {ID is PPC session ID}
      receiverIDisSignature = $00007000;  {ID is creator signature}
      receiverIDisPSN       = $00008000;  {ID is process serial num}
      receiverIDMask        = $0000F000;
```

When you specify the receiving application in the receiverID parameter, you can use these constants to specify the receiver of the event by session ID, process serial number, signature, or target ID. Any of these specifications allows you to send an event to another application on the local machine. To send events to an application on a remote machine, you can specify the recipient only by the session ID or target ID.

When you specify the receiver of the event by target ID, use the constant receiverIDisTargetID in the postingOptions parameter and specify a pointer to a target ID record for the receiverID parameter.

```
TYPE TargetID =
     RECORD
        sessionID:        LongInt;
        name:             PPCPortRec;
        location:         LocationNameRec;
        recvrName:        PPCPortRec      {unused for posting}
     END;
```

When you pass a target ID record, you need to specify only the name and location fields. You can use the IPCListPorts function to list all of the existing port names along with information on whether the port will accept authenticated service on the machine specified by the port location name. For information on how to use the IPCListPorts function, see the PPC Toolbox chapter in this volume.

You can also use the PPCBrowser function to fill in a target ID record. Listing 5-6 illustrates how to use the PPCBrowser function to post a high-level event. In this example, the sending application wants to locate a dictionary application and have the dictionary return the definition of a word to it.

Listing 5-6. Using the PPCBrowser function to post a high-level event

```
FUNCTION PostWithPPCBrowser (aTextPtr: Ptr; textlength: LongInt ) : OSErr;
VAR
   myHLEvent:  EventRecord;
   myErr:      OSErr;
   myNumTries: Integer;
   myPortInfo: PortInfoRec;
   myTarget:   TargetID;
BEGIN
   {use PPCBrowser to get the target}
   myErr := PPCBrowser('Select an Application', 'Application', FALSE,
                       myTarget.location, myPortInfo, NIL, '');
   IF myErr = NoErr THEN
   BEGIN
      {copy portname into myTarget.name}
      myTarget.name := myPortInfo.name;

      myHLEvent.what := kHighLevelEvent;
      myHLEvent.message := LongInt('Dict');
      myHLEvent.where := Point(LongInt('Defn'));

      {if a connection is broken, then sessClosedErr is returned to }
      { PostHighLevelEvent; to reestablish the connection, just post }
      { the event one more time}
      myNumTries := 0;
      REPEAT
         myErr := PostHighLevelEvent(myHLEvent, @myTarget, 0, aTextPtr,
                                     textlength, receiverIDisTargetID);
         myNumTries := myNumTries + 1;
      UNTIL (myErr <> sessClosedErr) OR (myNumTries > 1);
   END;

   PostWithPPCBrowser := myErr;        {return any error}
END;
```

This example puts up a dialog box asking the user to select a dictionary. When one is selected, this code posts a high-level event to that dictionary application asking for the definition of the selected text. Note that the sending application and the receiving application must both agree that definition queries are to be of event class 'Dict' and event ID 'Defn'. It is necessary to define a private protocol only in cases where no suitable Apple event exists.

> **Note:** You should avoid passing handles to the receiving application in an attempt to share a block of data. It is better to put the relevant data into a buffer (as illustrated in Listing 5-6) and pass the address of the buffer. If you absolutely must share data by passing a handle, make sure that the block of data is located in the system heap.

If a high-level event is posted successfully, PostHighLevelEvent returns the result code noErr, which indicates only that the event was successfully passed to the PPC Toolbox. Your application needs to call another Event Manager routine (EventAvail, GetNextEvent, or WaitNextEvent) to give the other application an opportunity to receive the event.

The event you send may require the other application to return some information to your application by sending a high-level event back to your application. You can scan for the response by using GetSpecificHighLevelEvent. If your application must wait for this event, you might want to display a watch cursor or take other action as appropriate to your application. You also might want to implement a timeout mechanism in case your application never receives a response to the event.

Requesting Return Receipts

When you post a high-level event, you can request a return receipt by including the constant nReturnReceipt as one of the posting options. This requests that the Event Manager send your application a high-level event that tells you whether the other application accepted your event. Note that this does not necessarily mean that the other application performed any action you might have requested from it.

A *return receipt* is a high-level event having an event class and an event ID indicated by the two constants:

```
CONST HighLevelEventMsgClass        = 'jaym';
      rtrnReceiptMsgID              = 'rtrn';
```

Return receipts are posted by the Event Manager on the machine of the receiving application (and not by the receiving application itself). No data buffer is associated with a return receipt. However, the posting Event Manager sets the modifiers field of the high-level event record to one of the following values:

```
CONST msgWasNotAccepted             = 0;
      msgWasFullyAccepted           = 1;
      msgWasPartiallyAccepted       = 2;
```

The constant msgWasNotAccepted indicates that your event was not accepted by the receiving application. This means that the receiving application was notified of the arrival of your event (through WaitNextEvent) but did not call AcceptHighLevelEvent to accept the event. The constant msgWasFullyAccepted indicates that the receiving application did call AcceptHighLevelEvent and retrieved all the data in the optional data buffer. The constant msgWasPartiallyAccepted indicates that the receiving application called AcceptHighLevelEvent, but that the application's data buffer was too small to hold the data sent with your application and that the receiving application called WaitNextEvent before retrieving the rest of the buffer.

Note that a return receipt does not indicate the identity of the receiving application. To determine on whose behalf the Event Manager has sent you a particular return receipt, you need to call AcceptHighLevelEvent. When AcceptHighLevelEvent returns successfully, the sender parameter contains a target ID record with the fields filled in for the receiving application. With return receipts, the msgLen parameter is 0, the msgBuff parameter is NIL, and the msgRefCon field contains the unique number of the refCon parameter of the original high-level event sender (that is, your application).

Responding to Events From Other Applications

You can identify high-level events by the value in the what field of the event record. The message and where fields further classify the type of high-level event. Your application can choose to recognize as many events as are appropriate. Some high-level events may be fully specified by their event record only, while others may include additional information in an optional buffer. To get that additional information or to find the sender of the event, use the AcceptHighLevelEvent function.

Note: To respond to an Apple event, use the Apple Event Manager, as described in the Apple Event Manager chapter in this volume.

Listing 5-7 illustrates how to call AcceptHighLevelEvent. In general, you cannot know in advance how big the optional data buffer is, so you can allocate a zero-length buffer and then resize it if the call to AcceptHighLevelEvent returns the error bufferIsSmall.

Listing 5-7. Accepting a high-level event

```
VAR
   myTarg:      TargetID;          {target ID record}
   myRefCon:    LongInt;
   myBuff:      Ptr;
   myLen:       LongInt;
   myErr:       OSErr;

BEGIN
   myLen := 0;                     {start with a 0-byte buffer}
   myBuff := NIL;

   myErr := AcceptHighLevelEvent(myTarg, myRefCon, myBuff, myLen);

   IF myErr = bufferIsSmall THEN
   BEGIN
      myBuff := NewPtr(myLen);     {get new pointer}
      myErr := AcceptHighLevelEvent(myTarg, myRefCon, myBuff, myLen);
   END;

   IF myErr <> noErr THEN DoError(myErr);
END;
```

The ID of the sender of the event is returned in the first parameter, which is a target ID record. You can inspect the fields of that record to determine which application sent the event. That record also contains the session reference number that identifies this communication as well as the port name and port location of the sender. If the high-level event requires that you return information, you can use the value returned in the sender parameter to send an event back to the requesting application.

The buffer parameter points to any additional data associated with the event. Any data in the additional buffer is defined by the particular high-level event. On input, the length parameter contains the size of the buffer. If no error occurs, on output the length parameter contains the size of the message accepted. If the error bufferIsSmall occurs, the length parameter contains the size of the message yet to be received. The reference constant parameter is a unique number your application can use to identify communication associated with this event.

Searching for a Specific High-Level Event

Sometimes you do not want to accept the next available high-level event pending for your application. Instead, you might want to select one such event from among all the high-level events in your application's high-level event queue. For example, you might want to look for a return receipt for a high-level event you previously posted before processing other high-level events.

You can select a specific high-level event by calling the GetSpecificHighLevelEvent function. One of the parameters you pass to this function is a filter function that you provide. Your filter function should examine an event in your application's high-level event queue and determine if that message is the kind of event you wish to receive. If it is, your filter function returns TRUE. This indicates that your filter function does not want to inspect any more events. If the filter function finds an event of the desired type, it should call AcceptHighLevelEvent to retrieve it. When your function returns TRUE, the GetSpecificHighLevelEvent function itself returns TRUE.

If your filter function returns FALSE for an event in the high-level event queue, then GetSpecificHighLevelEvent looks at the next event in the high-level event queue and executes your filter function. If the filter function returns FALSE for all the high-level events in the queue, then GetSpecificHighLevelEvent itself returns FALSE to your application.

Here's how you declare the filter function whose address you pass to GetSpecificHighLevelEvent:

```
FUNCTION aFilter (yourDataPtr: Ptr; msgBuff: HighLevelEventMsgPtr;
                  sender: TargetID) : Boolean;
```

The yourDataPtr parameter indicates the criteria your function should use to search for a specific event. The msgBuff parameter contains a pointer to a high-level event message record that has this structure:

```
TYPE HighLevelEventMsg =
     RECORD
        HighLevelEventMsgHeaderLength:    Integer;
        version:                          Integer;
        reserved1:                        LongInt;
        theMsgEvent:                      EventRecord;
        userRefCon:                       LongInt;
        postingOptions:                   LongInt;
        msgLength:                        LongInt
     END;
```

When you call GetSpecificHighLevelEvent and it executes your filter function for a high-level event waiting in the high-level event queue, the fields of HighLevelEventMsg are filled in by the Event Manager. You can then compare the fields of this record to the information you pass in the yourDataPtr parameter to determine if that event suits your needs. For example, the yourDataPtr parameter might contain the signature of a return receipt. You can test its value against the event class contained in the theMsgEvent field of the high-level event message record.

EVENT MANAGER ROUTINES

In system software version 7.0, the Event Manager includes routines for receiving events, sending high-level events, receiving high-level events, and searching for specific high-level events.

Receiving Events

You can use the WaitNextEvent function to receive events one at a time from the Event Manager.

```
FUNCTION WaitNextEvent (eventMask: Integer; VAR theEvent: EventRecord;
                        sleep: LongInt; mouseRgn: RgnHandle) : Boolean;
```

The WaitNextEvent function returns in the theEvent parameter the next available event of a specified type or types and, if the event is in the event queue, removes it from the queue. If no events are pending for your application, WaitNextEvent waits for a specified amount of time for an event. (During this time, processing time may be allocated to background processes.) If an event occurs, it is returned as the value of the parameter theEvent. If no event occurs (and the queue is empty), WaitNextEvent returns a null event in theEvent. WaitNextEvent returns FALSE if the event being returned is a null event; otherwise, WaitNextEvent returns TRUE.

The eventMask parameter specifies which kinds of events are to be returned; this parameter is interpreted as a sum of event mask constants (listed earlier in "Event Masks"). If no event of any of the designated types is available, WaitNextEvent returns a null event.

The sleep parameter specifies the number of ticks (sixtieths of a second) that your application agrees to relinquish the processor if no events are pending for it.

The mouseRgn parameter specifies a region inside of which mouse movement does not cause mouse-moved events. In other words, your application receives mouse-moved events only when the cursor is outside of the specified region. The region is specified in global coordinates. If you pass an empty region or a NIL region handle, mouse-moved events are not generated. Note that your application should recalculate the mouseRgn parameter when it receives a mouse-moved event or it will continue to receive mouse-moved events as long as the cursor position is outside the original mouseRgn.

Some high-level events may be fully specified by their event record only, while others may include additional information in an optional buffer. To get any additional information and to find the sender of the event, use the AcceptHighLevelEvent function.

```
FUNCTION AcceptHighLevelEvent (VAR sender: TargetID; VAR msgRefcon:
                               LongInt; msgBuff: Ptr; VAR msgLen:
                               LongInt) : OSErr;
```

The sender of the event is specified in the sender parameter, which is a target ID record. The sender parameter contains the session reference number that identifies this communication and the port name and port location of the sender.

The msgRefcon parameter is a unique number that is used to identify this event. If you send a response to this event, you should specify the same value of msgRefcon so that the sender of the event can associate the reply with the original request.

The msgBuff parameter points to any additional data associated with the event. The msgLen parameter contains the size of the buffer. Your application is responsible for allocating the memory for the additional data pointed to by the msgBuff parameter. If the msgBuff parameter points to an area in memory that is not large enough to hold all the data associated with the event, AcceptHighLevelEvent returns the result code bufferIsSmall. If AcceptHighLevelEvent returns the result code bufferIsSmall, the msgLen parameter contains the number of bytes remaining. You can call AcceptHighLevelEvent again to receive the rest of the data.

Result codes

noErr	0	No error
bufferIsSmall	–607	Buffer is too small
noOutstandingHLE	–608	No outstanding high-level event

Sending Events

You can use the PostHighLevelEvent routine to send a high-level event to another application.

```
FUNCTION PostHighLevelEvent (theEvent: EventRecord; receiverID: Ptr {UNIV
                             LongInt}; msgRefcon: LongInt; msgBuff: Ptr;
                             msgLen: LongInt; postingOptions: LongInt) :
                             OSErr;
```

You specify the event to send in the parameter theEvent and include any additional data for the event by providing a pointer to a data buffer in the msgBuff parameter. The msgLen parameter specifies the size of the data buffer. The receiverID parameter specifies the recipient of the event. The msgRefcon parameter specifies a unique number associated with this event. Your application can set this field to any value it chooses.

You can specify the receiver of the event by session ID, process serial number, signature, or port name and port location. You can use any of these specifications to send an event to another application on the local machine. You can use only the session ID or port name and port location to send an event to an application on a remote machine.

You use the postingOptions parameter to specify delivery options and options associated with the receiverID parameter. You can specify one or more delivery options to indicate whether you want the other application to receive the event at the next opportunity and to indicate whether you want acknowledgment that the event was received by the other application. You use the options associated with the receiverID parameter to indicate how you are specifying the recipient of the event.

If the application to which you are sending a high-level event terminates, you will receive sessionClosedErr when you next call PostHighLevelEvent. If you do not care about any state information about that session, you can just resend your event. Otherwise, you must restart another session and resend your event.

If your application is running in the background and posts a high-level event that requires the network authentication dialog box to be displayed, your application will receive a noUserInteractionAllowed result code. This prevents a background application from displaying a modal dialog. Instead, you can use the Notification Manager to inform the user that your application needs attention. When the user brings your application to the foreground, you can repost the event. If the reposting is successful, your application can return to the background and continue to post high-level events without further user interaction. Note that the error noUserInteractionAllowed is returned only on the first posting of a high-level event to a remote target.

Result codes

noErr	0	No error
connectionInvalid	–609	Connection is invalid
noUserInteractionAllowed	–610	Cannot interact directly with user
sessionClosedErr	–917	Session closed

Receiving a Specific High-Level Event

You can use the GetSpecificHighLevelEvent function to select and optionally retrieve a specific high-level event from the high-level event queue.

```
FUNCTION GetSpecificHighLevelEvent (aFilter: GetSpecificFilterProcPtr;
                                    yourDataPtr: UNIV Ptr; VAR err:
                                    OSErr) : Boolean;
```

You specify your filter function in the aFilter parameter. GetSpecificHighLevelEvent calls your filter function once for each event in the high-level event queue until your filter function returns TRUE or the end of the queue is reached. You use the yourDataPtr parameter to specify the criteria your filter function should use to select a specific event. For example, you can specify the yourDataPtr parameter as a msgRefcon value to search for a particular event or as a pointer to a target ID record to search for a specific sender of an event. Or you can search for a specific class of event.

Result codes

noErr	0	No error
noOutstandingHLE	–608	No outstanding high-level event

Here's how you declare the filter function aFilter:

```
FUNCTION aFilter (yourDataPtr: Ptr; msgBuff: HighLevelEventMsgPtr;
                  sender: TargetID) : Boolean;
```

The yourDataPtr parameter indicates the criteria your filter function should use to search for a specific event. The msgBuff parameter contains a pointer to a record of type HighLevelEventMsg, which provides information about the event: the event record for the high-level event, the posting options of the event, and so forth. The sender parameter contains the target ID of the application that sent the event.

Your filter function can compare the contents of the yourDataPtr parameter with the contents of the msgBuff or senderID parameters. If your filter function finds a match, it should return TRUE. If your filter function does not find a match, it should return FALSE. Your filter procedure can call AcceptHighLevelEvent, if necessary.

Converting Process Serial Numbers and Port Names

The Event Manager provides two utility functions to convert between process serial numbers and port names. Both functions are intended to map serial numbers to port names (or vice versa) for applications open on the local machine. They do not return useful results for applications open on remote machines.

Use GetProcessSerialNumberFromPortName to get the serial number of the process registered at a specific port.

```
FUNCTION GetProcessSerialNumberFromPortName (portName: PPCPortRec; VAR
                                             PSN: ProcessSerialNumber) :
                                             OSErr;
```

The portName parameter specifies the port name registered to a process whose serial number you want. The process serial number is returned in the PSN parameter. You can use the returned process serial number to send a high-level event to that process. Do not interpret the value of the serial number.

Result codes

noErr	0	No error
noPortErr	–903	Invalid port name

Use GetPortNameFromProcessSerialNumber to get the port name registered to a process having a specific process serial number.

```
FUNCTION GetPortNameFromProcessSerialNumber (VAR portName: PPCPortRec;
                                             PSN: ProcessSerialNumber) :
                                             OSErr;
```

The PSN parameter specifies the process serial number that you want to map to a port name. The port name is returned in the portName parameter.

Result codes

noErr	0	No error
procNotFound	–600	No eligible process with specified process serial number

SUMMARY OF THE EVENT MANAGER

Constants

```
CONST {event masks}
      everyEvent              = -1;        {every event}
      mDownMask               =  2;        {mouse-down}
      mUpMask                 =  4;        {mouse-up}
      keyDownMask             =  8;        {key-down}
      keyUpMask               =  16;       {key-up}
      autoKeyMask             =  32;       {auto-key}
      updateMask              =  64;       {update}
      diskMask                =  128;      {disk-inserted}
      activMask               =  256;      {activate}
      highLevelEventMask      =  1024;     {high-level}
      osMask                  = -32768;    {operating-system}

      {flags for suspend and resume events}
      resumeFlag              = 1;         {resume event}
      convertClipboardFlag    = 2;         {Clipboard conversion required}

      {message codes for operating-system events}
      suspendResumeMessage    = $01;       {suspend or resume event}
      mouseMovedMessage       = $FA;       {mouse-moved event}

      {event codes for operating-system and high-level events}
      osEvt                   = 15;
      kHighLevelEvent         = 23;

      {high-level event posting options}
      nAttnMsg                = $00000001; {give this message priority}
      priorityMask            = $000000FF;
      nReturnReceipt          = $00000200; {return receipt requested}
      systemOptionsMask       = $00000F00;
      receiverIDisTargetID    = $00005000; {ID is target ID}
      receiverIDisSessionID   = $00006000; {ID is PPC session ID}
      receiverIDisSignature   = $00007000; {ID is creator signature}
      receiverIDisPSN         = $00008000; {ID is process serial num}
      receiverIDMask          = $0000F000;

      {class and ID values for return receipt}
      HighLevelEventMsgClass  = 'jaym';
      rtrnReceiptMsgID        = 'rtrn';

      {modifiers values in return receipt}
      msgWasNotAccepted       = 0;
      msgWasFullyAccepted     = 1;
      msgWasPartiallyAccepted = 2;
```

Data Types

```
TYPE TargetID =
     RECORD
        sessionID:          LongInt;           {session reference number}
        name:               PPCPortRec;        {sender's port name}
        location:           LocationNameRec;   {sender's port location}
        recvrName:          PPCPortRec         {reserved}
     END;

     TargetIDPtr            = ^TargetID;

     HighLevelEventMsg =
     RECORD
        HighLevelEventMsgHeaderLength:  Integer;
        version:                        Integer;
        reserved1:                      LongInt;
        theMsgEvent:                    EventRecord;
        userRefCon:                     LongInt;
        postingOptions:                 LongInt;
        msgLength:                      LongInt
     END;

     HighLevelEventMsgPtr = ^HighLevelEventMsg;

     GetSpecificFilterProcPtr = ProcPtr;
```

Routines

Receiving Events

```
FUNCTION WaitNextEvent          (eventMask: Integer; VAR theEvent:
                                 EventRecord; sleep: LongInt; mouseRgn:
                                 RgnHandle) : Boolean;

FUNCTION AcceptHighLevelEvent   (VAR sender: TargetID; VAR msgRefcon:
                                 LongInt; msgBuff: Ptr; VAR msgLen:
                                 LongInt) : OSErr;
```

Sending Events

```
FUNCTION PostHighLevelEvent     (theEvent: EventRecord; receiverID: Ptr
                                 {UNIV LongInt}; msgRefcon: LongInt;
                                 msgBuff: Ptr; msgLen: LongInt;
                                 postingOptions: LongInt) : OSErr;
```

Receiving a Specific High-Level Event

```
FUNCTION GetSpecificHighLevelEvent (aFilter: GetSpecificFilterProcPtr;
                                    yourDataPtr: UNIV Ptr; VAR err: OSErr)
                                    : Boolean;
```

Converting Process Serial Numbers and Port Names

```
FUNCTION GetProcessSerialNumberFromPortName  (portName: PPCPortRec; VAR PSN:
                                              ProcessSerialNumber) : OSErr;

FUNCTION GetPortNameFromProcessSerialNumber  (VAR portName: PPCPortRec; PSN:
                                              ProcessSerialNumber) : OSErr;
```

Application-Defined Routines

```
{filter function for GetSpecificHighLevelEvent}

FUNCTION aFilter                    (yourDataPtr: Ptr; msgBuff:
                                     HighLevelEventMsgPtr; sender:
                                     TargetID) : Boolean;
```

Result Codes

noErr	0	No error
procNotFound	–600	No eligible process with specified process serial number
bufferIsSmall	–607	Buffer is too small
noOutstandingHLE	–608	No outstanding high-level event
connectionInvalid	–609	Connection is invalid
noUserInteractionAllowed	–610	Cannot interact directly with user

6 THE APPLE EVENT MANAGER

ABOUT THIS CHAPTER

This chapter describes Apple® events and how your application can use the Apple Event Manager to receive and process the required set of Apple events sent by the Finder™. This chapter also describes how to use the Apple Event Manager to send Apple events to other applications and how to process Apple events received from other applications.

As explained in the Event Manager chapter in this volume, the Event Manager in system software version 7.0 introduces high-level events, along with a number of new Event Manager routines that let applications communicate with each other by sending high-level events. Using Event Manager routines, your application can create and process its own high-level events.

However, effective interapplication communication requires that applications agree on a standard set of conventions—a common vocabulary. To provide such a standard, Apple Computer, Inc., has defined a protocol called the **Apple Event Interprocess Messaging Protocol (AEIMP).** High-level events that adhere to this protocol are called **Apple events.** You can help ensure effective communication with other applications by using this protocol.

System software uses Apple events to communicate information to your application; you should support the required set of Apple events sent by the Finder to your application. In addition, you can support Apple events that are common to many applications. Using the routines of the Apple Event Manager, you can use Apple events to communicate with other applications in a standard way. Using Apple events to ensure better cooperation between your application and other applications helps users to get the most out of any one application or to use the best features from many applications—in effect, combining the features of many applications to achieve the desired result.

By following the standards specified by AEIMP, you can also define your own Apple events. You can choose to publish these so that other applications can use them, or you may choose to keep them unpublished for exclusive use by your own applications.

The Apple Event Manager is available only in system software version 7.0. To determine whether the Apple Event Manager is available, use the Gestalt function described in the Compatibility Guidelines chapter of this volume.

The interapplication communications architecture of system software version 7.0 consists of three main components: the Apple Event Manager, the Event Manager, and the Program-to-Program Communications (PPC) Toolbox. See the Introduction to the System Software Version 7.0 Environment chapter in this volume for an overview of the relationships among these components. If you intend to use high-level events that do not rely on AEIMP, read the Event Manager chapter of this volume. This chapter describes the information you need to know to support Apple events in your application. To allow your application to send Apple events to applications on remote computers, you may wish to use the PPCBrowser function, which is described in the Program-to-Program Communications Toolbox chapter of this volume.

While the Apple events used by the Edition Manager are discussed in this chapter, you must refer to the Edition Manager chapter of this volume for a full discussion of how to implement the Edition Manager's publish and subscribe features.

For descriptions of all publicly available Apple events, see the *Apple Event Registry,* available from Macintosh® Developer Technical Support.

ABOUT THE APPLE EVENT MANAGER

Apple events provide your application with a standard mechanism for communicating with other applications. You can use Apple events and the Apple Event Manager to

- respond to the required Apple events (Open Application, Open Documents, Print Documents, and Quit Application) that are sent by the Finder
- respond to the Apple events sent by the Edition Manager and allow users to share data among documents created by multiple applications
- provide services to other applications
- request services from other applications

By supporting the required Apple events, your application can take advantage of the more reliable launch and termination mechanisms built into system software version 7.0. You can also take advantage of the services provided by the Edition Manager by responding to the Apple events sent by the Edition Manager. These and additional core Apple events can be used by nearly all applications to communicate with system software or with other applications.

You can also support functional-area Apple events related to your application in order to provide services to other applications or to request services from other applications. Finally, if your application defines Apple events for all the actions that a user can perform, you can record user actions by generating the corresponding Apple event for each action, saving a copy of the Apple event, and then sending the Apple event to your own application for handling. Apple events that are recorded in this way can later be played back to automate tasks previously performed by the user.

To support Apple events in your application, you must

- decide which Apple events (in addition to the required ones) to support
- set bits in the 'SIZE' resource to indicate that your application supports high-level events
- create an Apple event dispatch table
- include code to handle high-level events in your main event loop
- handle the Apple events your application receives and wishes to support
- create the Apple events you wish your application to generate

This chapter begins with an introduction to Apple events and then describes

- the required Apple events that your application must support to be 7.0-friendly
- how to use the Apple Event Manager to send and process Apple events

INTRODUCTION TO APPLE EVENTS

Applications typically use Apple events to request services from and provide services to other applications. For example, the Open Documents event, sent by the Finder, requests that your application open specified documents. When your application supports this Apple event, it should respond by opening those documents in the manner that your application normally opens documents.

A transaction involving Apple events is initiated by a **client application,** which sends an Apple event to request a service (for example, printing a list of files, spell-checking a list of words, or performing a numerical calculation). The application providing the service is called a **server application.** These applications can reside on the same local computer or on remote computers connected to a network.

Figure 6-1 shows a common Apple event, the Open Documents event. You see that the Finder application is the client; it requests that the SurfWriter application open the documents named Dec. Invoice and Nov. Invoice. The SurfWriter application responds to the Finder's request by opening windows containing the specified documents.

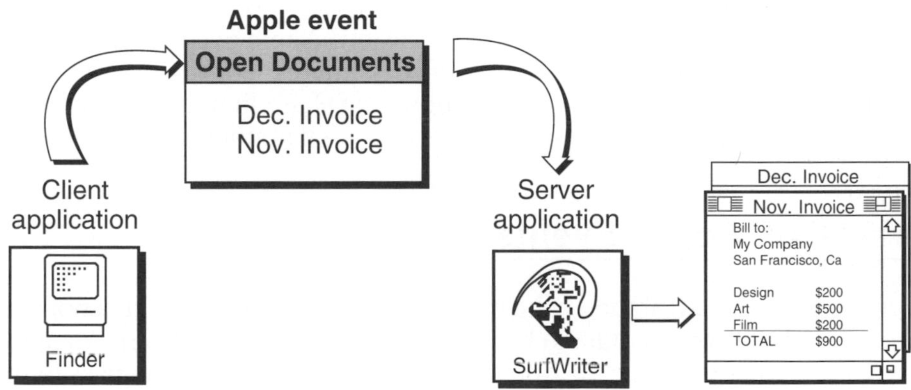

Figure 6-1. An Open Documents event

The Finder is also the source application of the Open Documents event. A **source application** is one that sends an Apple event to another application or to itself. In Figure 6-1, the SurfWriter application is the target application of the event. The **target application** is the one addressed to receive the Apple event. The terms *client application* and *source application* are not always synonymous, nor are the terms *server application* and *target application*. Typically, an Apple event client sends an Apple event requesting a service from an Apple event server; in this case, the server is the target application of the Apple event. The Apple event server may send back a different Apple event as a response—in which case, the client becomes the target of the responding Apple event.

Types of Apple Events

Apple events fall into one of several broad categories.

- **Required Apple events** consist of four core Apple events that the Finder sends to applications. These events are called Open Documents, Open Application, Print Documents, and Quit Application. They are a subset of the core Apple events and are described in detail later in this chapter.
- **Core Apple events** are used by nearly all applications to communicate. The suite of core Apple events is described in the *Apple Event Registry;* Apple recommends that all applications support the core Apple events.
- **Functional-area Apple events** are supported by applications with related features. Apple events related to text manipulation for word-processing applications and Apple events related to graphics manipulation for drawing applications are examples of functional-area Apple events. Functional-area Apple events are defined by Apple in consultation with interested developers and are published in the *Apple Event Registry.* Apple recommends that all developers support functional-area Apple events appropriate for their types of applications.
- **Custom Apple events** are defined by a developer for use by the developer's own applications. You should register all of your custom Apple events with Macintosh Developer Technical Support. You can choose to publish your Apple events in the *Apple Event Registry* so that other applications can share them, or you may choose to keep them unpublished for exclusive use by your own applications.

Components of Apple Events

An Apple event consists of attributes (which identify the Apple event and denote its task) and, often, parameters (which contain data to be used by the target application). An application uses the Apple Event Manager to create an Apple event. Using arguments you pass to the AECreateAppleEvent function and to other Apple Event Manager routines, the Apple Event Manager constructs the necessary data structures containing attributes and parameters and converts these structures into an Apple event. Applications must use the Apple Event Manager's AESend function to transmit the Apple event. After receiving an Apple event, applications must use Apple Event Manager routines to extract the attributes and parameters of the event.

Attributes are a fundamental component of Apple events. **Apple event attributes** are records that identify the event class, event ID, target application, and other characteristics of an Apple event. Taken together, the attributes of an Apple event denote the task to be performed on any data specified in the Apple event's parameters. You do not have any direct way to access the data stored in these records. You must use Apple Event Manager routines to extract or specify the attributes.

An **Apple event parameter** is a record containing data that the target application uses. Unlike Apple event attributes (which contain information that can be used by both the Apple Event Manager and the target application), Apple event parameters contain data used only by the target application. For example, an attribute like the event ID is used by the Apple Event

Manager to call a handler from the server application's dispatch table, and the server application must have a handler to process the event identified by that attribute. By comparison, the list of documents contained in a parameter to an Open Documents event is used only by the server application. As with attributes, you do not have any direct way to access the data structure of a parameter. You have to use Apple Event Manager functions to extract data from or put data into parameters.

Note that Apple event parameters are different from the parameters of Apple Event Manager functions. Apple event parameters are records private to the Apple Event Manager; function parameters are arguments you pass to the function or that the function returns to you. You typically specify the Apple event parameters (as well as the attributes) in parameters to Apple Event Manager functions. For example, the AEGetParamPtr function uses a buffer to return the data contained in an Apple event parameter. You specify which Apple event parameter in one of the parameters of the AEGetParamPtr function.

Apple events are identified by their event class and event ID attributes. The **event class** is the attribute that identifies a group of related Apple events. The event class appears in the message field of the event record for an Apple event. For example, the four required Apple events (in fact, all core Apple events) have the value 'aevt' in the message fields of their event records. The value 'aevt' can also be represented by the kCoreEventClass constant. Several event classes are shown here.

Event class	Value	Description
kCoreEventClass	'aevt'	A core Apple event
kAEFinderEvents	'FNDR'	An event that the Finder accepts
kSectionEventMsgClass	'sect'	An event sent by the Edition Manager

The **event ID** is the attribute that identifies the particular Apple event within its event class. In conjunction with the event class, the event ID uniquely identifies the Apple event and communicates what action the Apple event should perform. (The event IDs appear in the where field of the event record for an Apple event.) For example, the event ID of an Open Documents event has the value 'odoc' (which can also be represented by the kAEOpenDocuments constant). The kCoreEventClass constant in combination with the kAEOpenDocuments constant identifies the Open Documents event to the Apple Event Manager.

Shown here are the event IDs for the four required Apple events.

Event ID	Value	Description
kAEOpenApplication	'oapp'	Open your application
kAEOpenDocuments	'odoc'	Open documents
kAEPrintDocuments	'pdoc'	Print documents
kAEQuitApplication	'quit'	Quit your application

The target application's address is another required attribute. As previously described, the target application is the one addressed to receive the Apple event. Your application can send an Apple event to itself or to another application (on the same computer or on a remote computer connected to the network).

As with attributes, there are various types of Apple event parameters. A **direct parameter** contains the data to be acted upon by the server application. For example, a list of documents is contained in the direct parameter of the Print Documents event. Direct parameters are usually **required parameters**—parameters that the server application needs in order to carry out the task denoted by the Apple event. Some Apple events also take **additional parameters,** which the server application uses in addition to the data specified in the direct parameter. For example, an Apple event for arithmetic operations may include additional parameters that specify operands in an equation. Additional parameters may be required or optional.

An **optional parameter** is a supplemental parameter that also can be used to specify data to the server application. Optional parameters need not be included in an Apple event; default values for optional parameters are part of the event definition. The server application that handles the event must supply default values if the optional parameters are omitted.

Figure 6-2 shows in greater detail the components of the Open Documents event that was introduced in Figure 6-1.

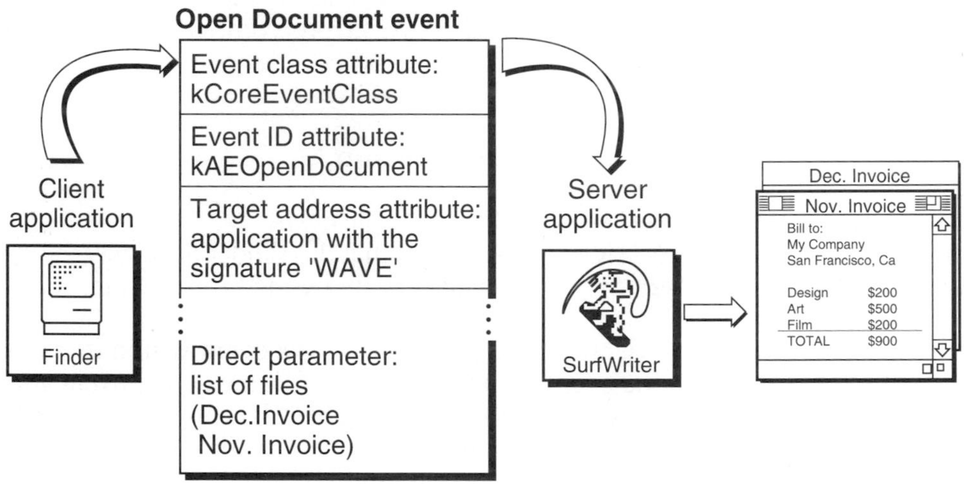

Figure 6-2. Major components of an Open Documents event

To process the information contained in the Open Documents event, the SurfWriter application uses the AEProcessAppleEvent function. The AEProcessAppleEvent function provides an easy way for your application to identify the event class and event ID of the Apple event and to direct the Apple Event Manager to call the code in your program that handles the Apple event.

Data Structures Within Apple Events

Applications must use Apple Event Manager functions to create and send an Apple event. The Apple Event Manager constructs its own internal data structures to contain the information in an Apple event. To gain access to this data, the target application also must use Apple Event Manager functions. Neither the sender nor the receiver of an Apple event can directly manipulate the data inside an Apple event; each must rely on Apple Event Manager functions to do so. This section describes the data structures that the Apple Event Manager uses to create and to process Apple events.

Descriptor records are the fundamental structures from which Apple events are constructed. A **descriptor record** is a data structure of type AEDesc; it consists of a handle to data and a descriptor type that identifies the type of the data referred to by the handle.

```
TYPE AEDesc =
     RECORD                                       {descriptor record}
        descriptorType:    DescType;              {type of data being passed}
        dataHandle:        Handle                 {handle to data being passed}
     END;
```

The data referred to by the dataHandle field in the descriptor record is private to the Apple Event Manager. You can supply or extract this data only by using Apple Event Manager routines.

The **descriptor type** is a structure of type DescType, which in turn is of data type ResType—that is, a four-character string. Constants are usually used in place of these four-character strings when referring to descriptor types. Descriptor types represent various data types. Here is a list of descriptor type constants, their values, and the types of data they represent.

Descriptor type	Value	Description
typeBoolean	'bool'	Boolean value
typeChar	'TEXT'	Unterminated string
typeSMInt	'shor'	16-bit integer
typeInteger	'long'	32-bit integer
typeSMFloat	'sing'	SANE® single
typeFloat	'doub'	SANE double
typeLongInteger	'long'	32-bit integer
typeShortInteger	'shor'	16-bit integer
typeLongFloat	'doub'	SANE double
typeShortFloat	'sing'	SANE single
typeExtended	'exte'	SANE extended
typeComp	'comp'	SANE comp
typeMagnitude	'magn'	Unsigned 32-bit integer
typeAEList	'list'	List of descriptor records
typeAERecord	'reco'	List of keyword-specified descriptor records
typeAppleEvent	'aevt'	Apple event record
typeTrue	'true'	TRUE Boolean value
typeFalse	'fals'	FALSE Boolean value
typeAlias	'alis'	Alias record
typeEnumerated	'enum'	Enumerated data
typeType	'type'	Four-character code for event class or event ID
typeAppParameters	'appa'	Process Manager launch parameters
typeProperty	'prop'	Apple event property
typeFSS	'fss '	File system specification
typeKeyword	'keyw'	Apple event keyword
typeSectionH	'sect'	Handle to a section record
typeWildCard	'****'	Matches any type
typeApplSignature	'sign'	Application signature
typeSessionID	'ssid'	Session ID
typeTargetID	'targ'	Target ID record
typeProcessSerialNumber	'psn '	Process serial number
typeNull	'null'	NULL or nonexistent data

Figure 6-3 illustrates a descriptor record with a descriptor type of typeType, which specifies that the data in the descriptor record must consist of a four-character code. The data in this particular descriptor record is specified by the constant kCoreEventClass, whose value is 'aevt'.

Data type AEDesc

Descriptor type:	typeType
Data:	Event class (kCoreEventClass)

Figure 6-3. A descriptor record with event class data

A descriptor record that contains the address of the target or source of an Apple event is called an **address descriptor record.**

```
TYPE AEAddressDesc = AEDesc;              {address descriptor record}
```

As you will see later, the address can be specified as an application signature, a process serial number, a session ID, a target ID record, or a data type that you define.

Data for attributes and parameters is contained in descriptor records. The attributes and parameters themselves are identified by **keywords.** The AEKeyword data type is defined as a four-character code.

```
TYPE AEKeyword = PACKED ARRAY[1..4] OF Char;
                                          {keyword for a descriptor }
                                          { record}
```

Constants are typically used for keywords. Shown here is a list of these keyword constants, their four-character codes, and the attributes and parameters they represent.

Attribute keyword	Value	Description
keyAddressAttr	'addr'	Address of target application
keyEventClassAttr	'evcl'	Event class of Apple event
keyEventIDAttr	'evid'	Event ID of Apple event
keyEventSourceAttr	'esrc'	Source of the Apple event
keyInteractLevelAttr	'inte'	Settings for allowing the Apple Event Manager to bring a server application to the foreground
keyMissedKeywordAttr	'miss'	First required parameter remaining in an Apple event
keyOptionalKeywordAttr	'optk'	List of optional parameters for the Apple event
keyReturnIDAttr	'rtid'	Return ID for reply Apple event
keyTimeoutAttr	'timo'	Length of time in ticks that the client will wait for a reply or a result from the server
keyTransactionIDAttr	'tran'	Transaction ID identifying a series of Apple events

Parameter keyword	Value	Description
keyDirectObject	'----'	Direct parameter
keyErrorNumber	'errn'	Error number parameter
keyErrorString	'errs'	Error string parameter
keyProcessSerialNumber	'psn '	Process serial number parameter

A data structure of type AEKeyDesc consists of a keyword and a descriptor record. This data structure, called a **keyword-specified descriptor record,** is used by the Apple Event Manager to fully identify and describe an attribute or a parameter of an Apple event.

```
TYPE AEKeyDesc =            {keyword-specified descriptor record}
     RECORD
        descKey:            AEKeyword;     {keyword}
        descContent:        AEDesc         {descriptor record}
     END;
```

Figure 6-4 illustrates a keyword-specified descriptor record for the event class attribute of an Open Documents event. The keyEventClassAttr keyword identifies its descriptor record as containing event class data. The data is of the typeType descriptor type, and the data identifies the event class as kCoreEventClass.

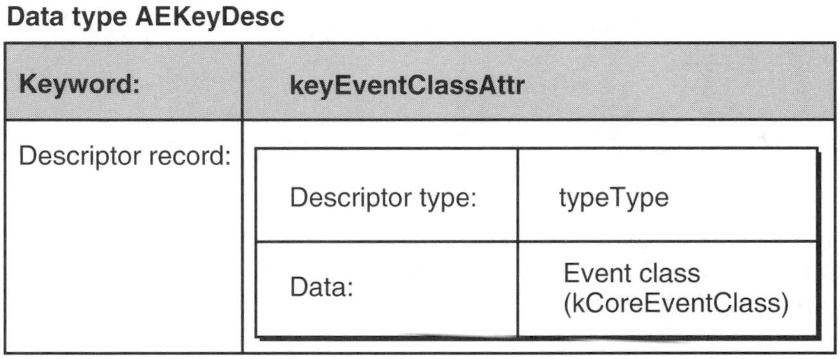

Data type AEKeyDesc

Keyword:	keyEventClassAttr	
Descriptor record:	Descriptor type:	typeType
	Data:	Event class (kCoreEventClass)

Figure 6-4. A keyword-specified descriptor record for the event class attribute of an Open Documents event

When extracting data from an Apple event, you use Apple Event Manager functions to return data in a buffer specified by a pointer, or to return descriptor records containing the data, or to return lists of descriptor records (called descriptor lists) containing the data. As previously noted, the descriptor record (of data type AEDesc) is the fundamental structure in Apple events, and it contains a handle to data. A **descriptor list** is a data structure of type AEDescList defined by the data type AEDesc—that is, a descriptor list is a descriptor record that contains a list of other descriptor records.

```
TYPE AEDescList = AEDesc;       {list of descriptor records}
```

An example of a descriptor list that you will be using is the direct parameter for the Open Documents event. As illustrated in Figure 6-5, this descriptor list is a list of descriptor records that contain alias records to filenames. (The Alias Manager chapter of this volume describes alias records in detail.)

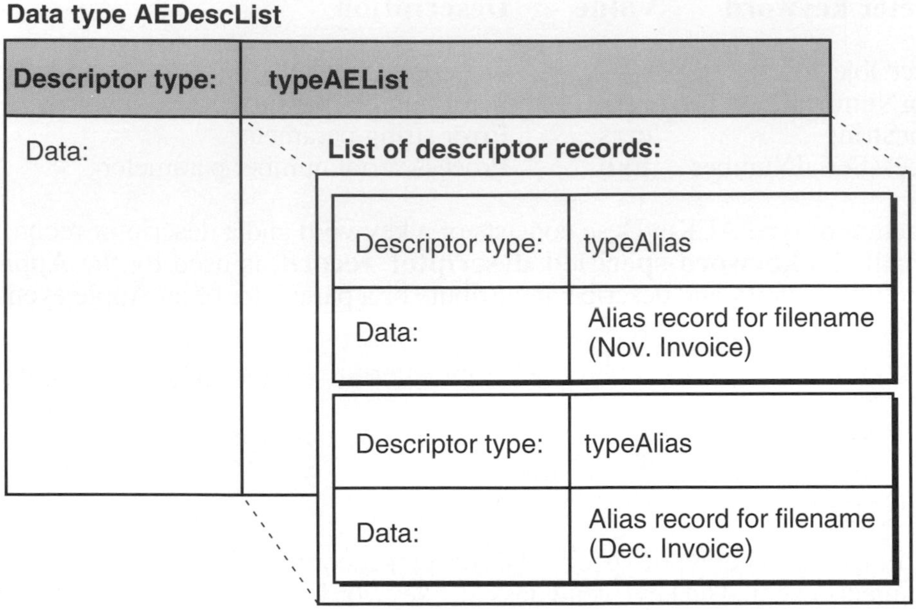

Figure 6-5. A descriptor list for a list of aliases

Closely related to a descriptor list is a structure of data type AERecord; in fact, it is defined by the data type AEDescList.

```
TYPE AERecord = AEDescList;      {list of keyword-specified }
                                 { descriptor records}
```

While a descriptor list is a descriptor record that contains a list of other descriptor records, an **AE record** of data type AERecord contains a list of keyword-specified descriptor records describing parameters. A descriptor list of data type AERecord contains no attributes, only parameters.

There is one final data structure to consider: the Apple event record. An **Apple event record** is a structure of data type AppleEvent defined as an AE record. It is used for describing a full-fledged Apple event.

```
TYPE AppleEvent = AERecord;      {list of attributes and parameters }
                                 { necessary for an Apple event}
```

An Apple event record is basically a descriptor record (of descriptor type typeAppleEvent) with a handle to a list of keyword-specified descriptor records. These descriptor records describe the attributes and parameters for an Apple event. When you use the AECreateAppleEvent function, the Apple Event Manager creates an Apple event record containing the attributes for an Apple event's event class, event ID, target address, return ID, and transaction ID. You then use Apple Event Manager functions such as AEPutParamDesc to add parameters to the Apple event. Figure 6-6 shows an example of an Apple event—a structure containing a list of keyword-specified descriptor records that name the attributes and parameters of an Open Documents event.

Data type AppleEvent

Descriptor type:	typeAppleEvent
Data:	List of attributes and parameters

Event class attribute

Keyword:	keyEventClassAttr
Descriptor record:	Descriptor type: typeType Data: Event class (kCoreEventClass)

Event ID attribute

Keyword:	keyEventIDAttr
Descriptor record:	Descriptor type: typeType Data: Event ID (kAEOpenDocuments)

Target application attribute

Keyword:	keyAddressAttr
Descriptor record:	Descriptor type: typeApplSignature Data: Target application's address ('WAVE')

Direct parameter

Keyword:	keyDirectObject
Descriptor record:	Descriptor type: typeAEList Data: List of descriptor records:

Descriptor type:	typeAlias
Data:	Alias record for filename (Nov. Invoice)

Descriptor type:	typeAlias
Data:	Alias record for filename (Dec. Invoice)

Figure 6-6. Data structures within an Open Documents event

The internal structure of an Apple event record is nearly identical to an AE record. They differ in the content referred to by the data handles that they contain: the former has a list of attributes and, possibly, parameters referred by its handle; the latter contains only parameters. However, you can pass an Apple event record to any Apple Event Manager function that expects an AE record. Since both are structures of data type AEDescList, which is derived from the data type AEDesc, you can pass Apple event records, AE records, descriptor lists, and descriptor records to any Apple Event Manager functions that expect records of data type AEDesc.

The data in Apple event records, AE records, and descriptor lists—all of which are descriptor records—is private to the Apple Event Manager. The Apple Event Manager maintains these different data structures because it stores different kinds of information in their handles. Although all the information you need is available by calling the appropriate Apple Event Manager functions, the Apple Event Manager needs a way to tell these different descriptor records apart. It does this by looking at their data types.

Responding to Apple Events

A client application uses the Apple Event Manager to create and send an Apple event requesting a service. A server application responds by using the Apple Event Manager to process the Apple event, to extract data from the attributes and parameters of the Apple event, and to return a result to the client application. The server provides its own routines for performing the action requested by the client's Apple event.

As its first step in supporting Apple events, your application must be able to respond to the required Apple events sent by the Finder. If you plan to implement publish and subscribe capabilities, your application must respond to the Apple events sent by the Edition Manager. You can also respond to Apple events sent by your own application or by other applications. This section provides a quick overview of the steps your application takes in responding to Apple events.

To respond to Apple events, your application must

- test for high-level events in its event loop
- use the AEProcessAppleEvent function to process Apple events
- provide handler routines for the Apple events it supports
- use Apple Event Manager functions to extract the parameters and attributes from Apple events
- use the AEInteractWithUser function—if your application requires input from the user when your application is responding to an Apple event—to bring your application to the foreground to interact with the user
- return a result for the client

Note that in order for your application to respond to Apple events sent from remote computers, the user of your application must allow network users to link to your application. The user does this by selecting your application from the Finder and choosing Sharing from the File menu and then clicking the Allow Remote Program Linking check box. If the user has not yet started program linking, the Sharing command offers to display the Sharing Setup control panel so that the user can start program linking. The user must also authorize remote users for program linking by using the Users and Groups control panel. Program linking and setting up authenticated sessions are described in the Program-to-Program Communications Toolbox chapter in this volume.

An Apple event (like all high-level events) is identified by a message class of kHighLevelEvent in the what field of the event record. You test the what field of the event record to determine whether an event is a high-level event. If the what field contains the kHighLevelEvent constant and your application defines any high-level events other than Apple events, test the message field of the event record to determine whether the high-level event is something other than an Apple event. If the high-level event is not one that you've defined for your application, assume that it is an Apple event. (Note that you are encouraged to use Apple events instead of defining your own high-level events whenever possible.)

After determining that an event is an Apple event, use the AEProcessAppleEvent function to let the Apple Event Manager identify the event. Figure 6-7 shows how the SurfWriter application accepts and begins to process an Apple event sent by the Finder.

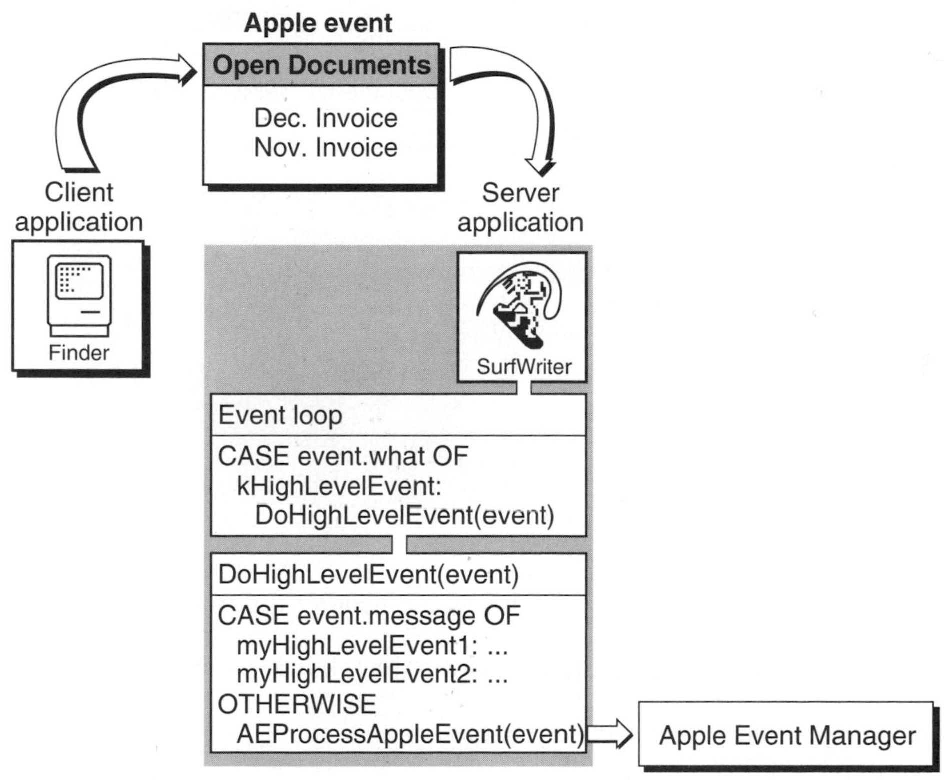

Figure 6-7. Accepting and processing an Open Documents event

The AEProcessAppleEvent function begins processing the Apple event. The AEProcessAppleEvent function identifies the Apple event by examining the data in the event class and event ID attributes. The AEProcessAppleEvent function in turn uses that data to call the Apple event handler that your application provides for that event. An **Apple event handler** is a function that extracts the pertinent data from the Apple event, performs the action requested by the Apple event, and returns a result. For example, if the event has an event class of kCoreEventClass and an event ID of kAEOpenDocuments, the AEProcessAppleEvent function calls your application's routine for handling the Open Documents event.

You install Apple event handlers by using the AEInstallEventHandler function. This function creates an **Apple event dispatch table** that the Apple Event Manager uses to map Apple events to handlers in your application. After being called by the AEProcessAppleEvent function to process an Apple event, the Apple Event Manager reads the Apple event dispatch table and, if your application has installed a handler for that Apple event, calls your handler to finish responding to the event. Figure 6-8 shows how the flow of control passes from your application to the Apple Event Manager and back to your application.

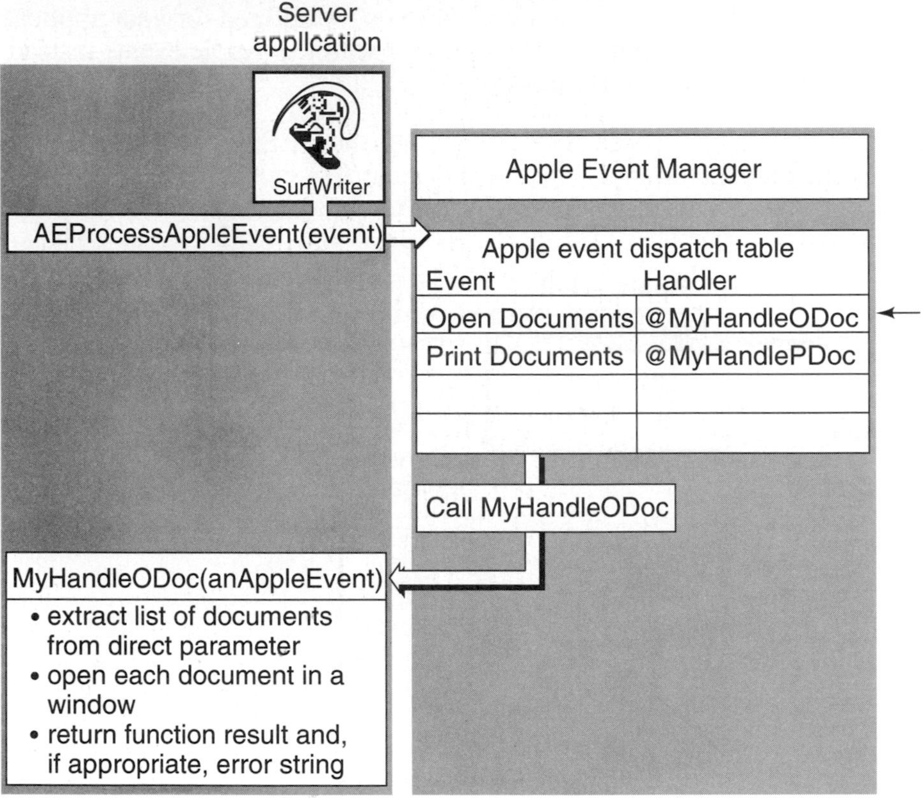

Figure 6-8. The Apple Event Manager calling the handler for an Open Documents event

Your Apple event handlers must generally perform the following tasks:

- extract the parameters and attributes for the Apple event
- check that all the required parameters have been extracted
- set user interaction level preferences if necessary and, if your application needs to interact with the user, use the AEInteractWithUser function to bring it to the foreground
- perform the action requested by the Apple event
- dispose of any copies of descriptor records that have been created
- return a result for the client

You must use Apple Event Manager functions to extract the data from Apple events. You can also use Apple Event Manager functions to get data out of descriptor records, descriptor lists, and AE records. Most of these routines are available in two forms: one that uses a buffer to return a copy of the desired data, and one that returns a copy of the descriptor record containing the data. The following list shows the main functions you can use to access the data of an Apple event.

Function	Description
AEGetParamPtr	Uses a buffer to return the data contained in a parameter; used, for example, to extract the result code from the keyErrorNumber parameter of a reply Apple event.
AEGetParamDesc	Returns the descriptor record or descriptor list for a parameter; used, for example, to extract the descriptor list for a list of alias records specified in the direct parameter of the Open Documents event.
AEGetAttributePtr	Uses a buffer to return the data contained in an attribute; used, for example, to determine the source of an Apple event by extracting the data from the keyEventSourceAttr attribute.
AEGetAttributeDesc	Returns the descriptor record for a parameter; used, for example, to make a copy of a descriptor record containing the address of an application.
AECountItems	Returns the number of descriptor records in a descriptor list; used, for example, to determine the number of alias records for documents specified in the direct parameter of the Open Documents event.
AEGetNthPtr	Uses a buffer to return the data for a descriptor record that is contained in a descriptor list; used, for example, to extract a document's alias record from the descriptor list specified in the direct parameter of the Open Documents event.
AEGetNthDesc	Returns a descriptor record from a descriptor list; used, for example, to get the descriptor record containing an alias record from the list specified in the direct parameter of the Open Documents event.

You can specify the descriptor type of the resulting data for these functions; if this is different from the descriptor type of the attribute or parameter, the Apple Event Manager attempts to coerce it to the specified type. In the direct parameter of the Open Documents event, for example, each descriptor record in the descriptor list is an alias record; each alias record specifies a document to be opened. As explained in the File Manager chapter of this volume, all your application usually needs is the file system specification (FSSpec) record of the document. When you extract the descriptor from the descriptor list, you can request that the Apple Event Manager return the data to your application as a file system specification record instead of as an alias record.

After extracting all known parameters, your handler should check that it retrieved all the required parameters by checking whether the keyMissedKeywordAttr attribute exists. If the attribute exists, then your handler has not retrieved all the required parameters, and it should return an error.

In some cases, the server may need to interact with the user when it handles an Apple event. For example, your handler for the Print Documents event may need to display a print options dialog box and get settings from the user before printing. Your handler should always use the AEInteractWithUser function before displaying a dialog box or alert box or otherwise interacting with the user. By specifying one of these flags to the AESetInteractionAllowed function, you can set your application's user interaction level preferences.

Flag	Description
kAEInteractWithSelf	User interaction with your server application in response to an Apple event may be allowed only when the client application is your own application—that is, only when your application is sending the Apple event to itself.
kAEInteractWithLocal	User interaction with your server application in response to an Apple event may be allowed only if the client application is on the same computer as your application; this is the default if the AESetInteractionAllowed function is not used.
kAEInteractWithAll	User interaction with your server application in response to an Apple event may be allowed for any client application on any computer.

For a server application to allow user interaction in response to the client's Apple event, two conditions must be met. First, the client application must request that your server application allow user interaction. Second, your server application must allow user interaction in response to the Apple event sent from that client application as described in the previous list. If these conditions are met and your application needs to interact with the user, the AEInteractWithUser function brings your application to the foreground if it isn't already in the foreground. Your application can then display its dialog box or alert box or otherwise interact with the user. AEInteractWithUser brings your server application to the front either directly or after the user responds to a notification request.

When your application acts on an Apple event, it should perform the standard action requested by that event. For example, if the Apple event is the Open Documents event, your application should open the specified documents in titled windows just as if the user had selected each document from the Finder and then chosen Open from the File menu. You should strive to create routines that can be called in response to both user events and Apple events. To do this, you need to isolate code for interacting with the user from the code that performs the requested action—such as opening a document. You then call the code that performs the requested action from your Apple event handler.

When you extract a descriptor record by using the AEGetParamDesc, AEGetAttributeDesc, AEGetNthDesc, or AEGetKeyDesc function, the Apple Event Manager creates a copy of the descriptor record for you to use. When your handler is finished using a copy of a descriptor record, you should dispose of it—and thereby deallocate the memory it uses—by calling the AEDisposeDesc function.

The required Apple events ask your application to perform tasks—open your application, open or print documents, or quit your application. Other Apple events may ask your application to return data. For example, if your application is a spelling checker, the client probably expects data in the form of a list of misspelled words to be returned from your application. If a reply is requested, the Apple Event Manager prepares a reply Apple event for the client by passing a default reply Apple event to your handler. The default reply Apple event has no parameters when it is passed to your handler. Your handler can add any parameters to the reply Apple event. If your application is a spelling checker, for example, you can return a list of misspelled words in a parameter.

Your handler routine should always set its function result either to noErr if it successfully handles the Apple event or to a nonzero result code if an error occurs. If an error occurs, the Apple Event Manager adds a keyErrorNumber parameter to the reply Apple event; this parameter contains the result code that your handler returns. The client should check whether the keyErrorNumber parameter exists to determine whether your handler performed the requested action. In addition to returning a result code, your handler can also return an error string in the keyErrorString parameter of the reply Apple event. The client can use this string in an error message to the user.

If the source requested a reply, the Apple Event Manager returns the reply Apple event to the source. The reply Apple event is identified by the event class kCoreEventClass and by the event ID kAEAnswer. When you have finished using the reply Apple event, you should dispose of it—and thereby deallocate the memory it uses—by calling the AEDisposeDesc function.

When your handler returns a result code to the Apple Event Manager, you have finished your response to the client's Apple event. Figure 6-9 shows the entire process of responding to an Apple event. The next section describes how to send an Apple event.

Requesting Services Through Apple Events

Your application can use Apple events to request services from other applications. By using Finder events, for example, your application can simulate the behavior of the Finder by requesting that the Finder perform such operations as launching an application on your behalf. By using functional-area Apple events, your application can request services from applications related to your own—for example, asking a spelling checker application to check the text in a document created by your application. All publicly available Apple events are defined and published in the *Apple Event Registry*. Consult the *Apple Event Registry* for the format and function of Apple events that your application may wish to send.

The previous section describes how a server application responds to a client application's request for services. This section briefly describes the steps your application must take to act as a client application and request such services. To request a service through an Apple event, your application must

- create an Apple event by calling the AECreateAppleEvent function
- use Apple Event Manager functions to add parameters and any other necessary attributes to the Apple event
- call the AESend function to send the Apple event
- dispose of any copies of descriptor records that you have created
- process the reply Apple event (optional)

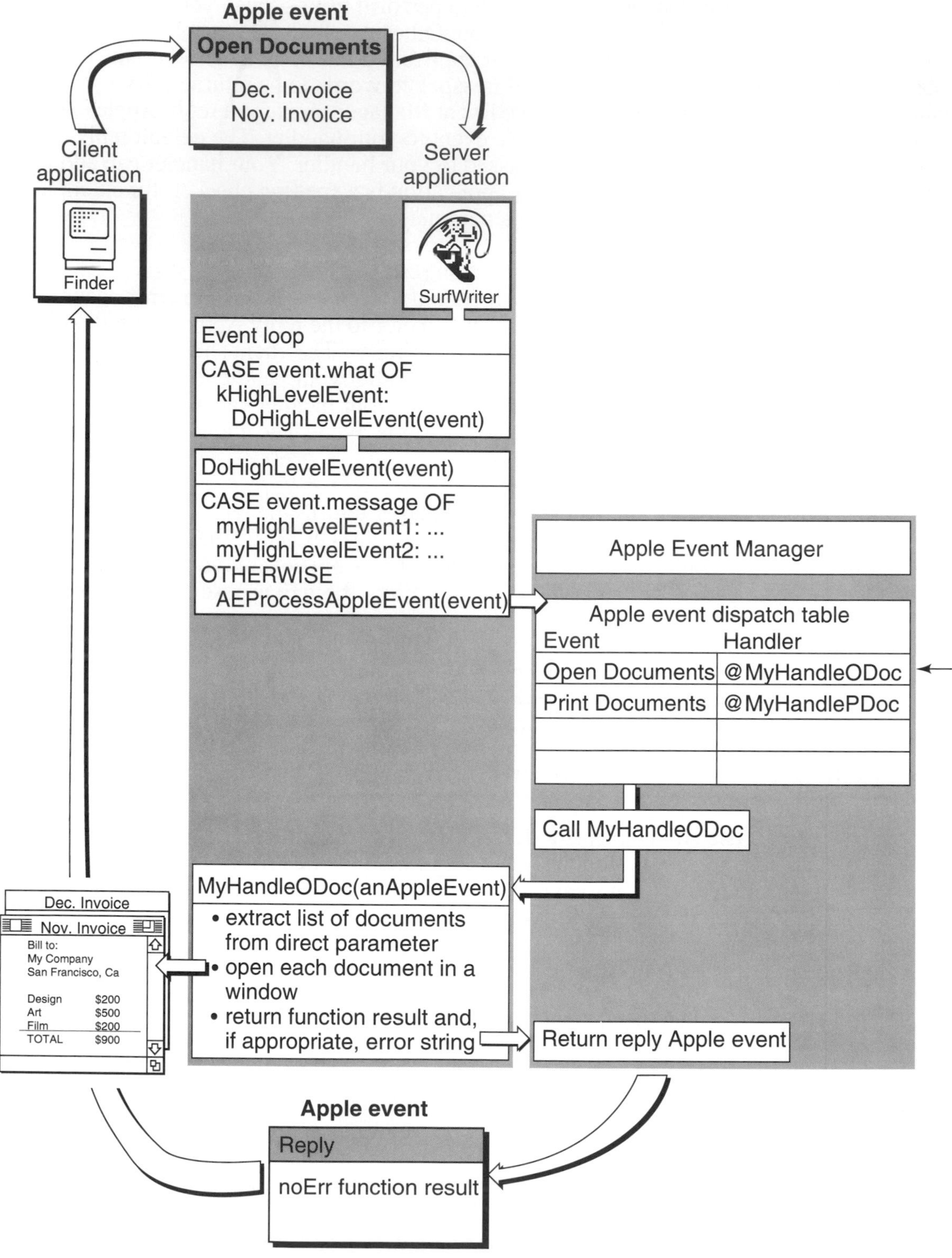

Figure 6-9. Responding to an Open Documents event

Use the AECreateAppleEvent function to create an Apple event record. Using the arguments you pass to the AECreateAppleEvent function, the Apple Event Manager constructs the data structures describing the event class, the event ID, and the target address attributes of an Apple event. The event class and event ID, of course, identify the particular event you wish to send. The target address identifies the application to which you wish to send the Apple event.

To act as a server application for your application, the target must support high-level events and must be open. The server can be your own application, another application running on the user's computer, or an application running on another user's computer connected to the network. Your application should offer some facility to launch a server application if it is not already running. It is recommended that you use the Open Selection event (identified by the event class kAEFinderEvents and the event ID kAEOpenSelection) to request that the Finder launch applications; however, the Process Manager also provides a means for your application to launch other applications. See the *Apple Event Registry* for information on Finder events, and see the Process Management chapter in this volume for information on using the Process Manager.

Your application should also offer a facility to allow the user to choose among the various applications available as servers. The PPCBrowser function allows users to select target applications on the user's computer as well as those available on computers connected to the network. The PPCBrowser function presents a standard user interface for choosing a target application, much as the Standard File Package provides a standard user interface for opening and saving files. See the Program-to-Program Communications Toolbox chapter of this volume for details on using the PPCBrowser function.

If the server application is on a remote computer on a network, the user of that computer must allow program linking to the server application. The user of the server application does this by selecting the application from the Finder and choosing Sharing from the File menu and then clicking the Allow Remote Program Linking check box. If the user has not yet started program linking, the Sharing command offers to display the Sharing Setup control panel so that the user can start program linking. The user must also authorize remote users for program linking by using the Users and Groups control panel. Program linking and setting up authenticated sessions are described in the Program-to-Program Communications Toolbox chapter in this volume.

There are two other attributes you specify in the AECreateAppleEvent function: the reply ID and the transaction ID. For the reply ID attribute, you'll usually specify the kAutoGenerateReturnID constant to the AECreateAppleEvent function. This constant ensures that the Apple Event Manager generates a unique return ID for the reply Apple event returned from the server. For the transaction ID attribute, you'll usually specify the kAnyTransactionID constant, which indicates that this Apple event is not one of a series of interdependent Apple events.

The Apple event record created with the AECreateAppleEvent function serves as a template for the Apple event you want to send. To add the remaining attributes and parameters necessary for your Apple event, you must use these additional Apple Event Manager functions.

Function	Description
AEPutParamPtr	Takes a keyword, descriptor type, and pointer to data, converts them into a parameter, and adds the parameter to or replaces it in an Apple event record; used, for example, to place numbers into the parameters of an Apple event requesting that the server perform a calculation.

Function	Description
AEPutParamDesc	Takes a keyword and a descriptor record, converts them into a parameter, and adds the parameter to or replaces it in an Apple event record; used, for example, to place a descriptor list containing alias records into the direct parameter of an Apple event that requests a server to manipulate files.
AEPutAttributePtr	Takes a keyword, descriptor type, and pointer to data, converts them into an attribute, and adds the attribute to or replaces it in an Apple event record; used, for example, to change the event ID of an Apple event record that is waiting to be sent.
AEPutAttributeDesc	Takes a keyword and a descriptor record, converts them into an attribute, and adds the attribute to or replaces it in an Apple event record; used, for example, to replace the descriptor record used for the target address attribute in an Apple event record waiting to be sent.

Descriptor records and descriptor lists are the basic components from which an Apple event record is constructed; these are passed to the AEPutParamDesc and AEPutAttributeDesc functions. Use the following functions to create descriptor records and descriptor lists.

Function	Description
AECreateDesc	Takes a descriptor type and a pointer to data and converts them into a descriptor record; used, for example, to create a descriptor record that is used as an attribute or a parameter in an Apple event record.
AEPutPtr	Takes a descriptor type and a pointer to data, converts them into a descriptor record, and adds the record to a descriptor list; used, for example, to place into a descriptor list a number that is used as the parameter of an Apple event requesting a calculation.
AEPutDesc	Adds a descriptor record to a descriptor list; used, for example, to add into the descriptor list an alias record that is used as the direct parameter of an Apple event requesting file manipulation.

After you add all the attributes and parameters required for the Apple event, use the AESend function to send the Apple event. The Apple Event Manager uses the Event Manager to transmit the Apple event to the server application.

The AESend function requires that you specify whether and how your application should wait for a reply from the server. When the server receives your Apple event, the Apple Event Manager prepares a reply Apple event for your application by passing a default reply Apple event to the server. The Apple Event Manager returns any nonzero result code from the server's handler in the keyErrorNumber parameter of the reply Apple event. If your application wants to return an error string, add it to the reply Apple event in the keyErrorString parameter. The server can also use this reply Apple event to return any data you requested—for example, the results of a numerical calculation or a list of misspelled words.

You specify how your application should wait for a reply by using one of these flags in the sendMode parameter of the AESend function.

Flag	Description
kAENoReply	Your application does not want a reply Apple event; the server processes your Apple event as soon as it has the opportunity.
kAEQueueReply	Your application wants a reply Apple event; the reply appears in your event queue as soon as the server has the opportunity to process and respond to your Apple event.
kAEWaitReply	Your application wants a reply Apple event and is willing to give up the processor while waiting for the reply; for example, if the server application is on the same computer as your application, your application yields the processor to allow the server to respond to your Apple event.

If you specify the kAEWaitReply flag, you may provide an idle function. This function should process any events that occur while your application is waiting for a reply. You supply a pointer to your idle function as a parameter to the AESend function. So that your application can process other Apple events while it is waiting for a reply, you can also specify an optional filter function to the AESend function that filters Apple events.

If your Apple event may require the user to interact with the server application (for example, to specify print or file options), you can communicate your user-interaction preferences to the server by specifying one of the following flags in the sendMode parameter of the AESend function.

Flag	Description
kAENeverInteract	The server application should never interact with the user in response to this Apple event. If this flag is set, AEInteractWithUser does not bring the server application to the foreground (this is the default when an Apple event is sent to a remote application).
kAECanInteract	The server application can interact with the user in response to this Apple event—by convention, if the user needs to supply information to the server. If this flag is set and the server allows interaction, AEInteractWithUser brings the server application to the foreground (this is the default when an Apple event is sent to a local application).
kAEAlwaysInteract	The server application can interact with the user in response to this Apple event—by convention, even if no information is needed from the user. If this flag is set and the server allows interaction, AEInteractWithUser brings the server application to the foreground. The Apple Event Manager does not distinguish between this flag and the kAECanInteract flag—distinguishing between them is the responsibility of the server application.

Flag	Description
kAECanSwitchLayer	If both the client and server allow interaction and this flag is set, AEInteractWithUser brings the server directly to the foreground if adherence to the principle of user control allows. If the action would be contrary to this principle, AEInteractWithUser uses the Notification Manager to request that the user bring the server application to the foreground. If both the client and server allow interaction and this flag is not set, AEInteractWithUser always uses the Notification Manager to request that the user bring the server application to the foreground.

The server can set its own interaction preferences. The interaction of your client's preferences and the server's is explained in "Interacting With the User" later in this chapter.

After you send an Apple event, your application is responsible for disposing of the Apple event record—and thereby deallocating the memory it uses—by calling the AEDisposeDesc function. If you create one descriptor record and add it to another, the Apple Event Manager creates a copy of the newly created one and adds that copy to the existing one. For example, you might use the AECreateDesc function to create a descriptor record that you wish to add to an Apple event. When you use the AEPutParamDesc function, it creates a copy of your newly created descriptor record and adds that copy as a parameter to an existing Apple event.

Your application should dispose of all the descriptor records that are created in order to add parameters and attributes to an Apple event. You normally dispose of your Apple event and its reply after you receive a result from the AESend function. You should dispose of these even if AESend returns an error result. If your application requests a reply Apple event, your application must also dispose of the reply Apple event when finished processing it.

Your application can request a reply Apple event. If you specify the kAEWaitReply flag, the reply Apple event is returned in a parameter you pass to the AESend function. If you specify the kAEQueueReply flag to the AESend function, the reply Apple event is returned in the event queue. In this case, the reply is identified by the event class kCoreEventClass and the event ID kAEAnswer; your application processes reply events that it receives in its event queue in the same manner that server applications process Apple events, as described earlier in "Responding to Apple Events."

Your application should check for the keyErrorNumber parameter of the reply Apple event to ensure that the server performed the requested action. Any error messages that the server returns for you to display to your user will appear in the keyErrorString parameter.

When your handler is finished using a copy of a descriptor record used in the reply Apple event, you should dispose of them both—and thereby deallocate the memory they use—by calling the AEDisposeDesc function.

The next section, "Using the Apple Event Manager," describes in greater detail the routines necessary for sending and responding to Apple events.

USING THE APPLE EVENT MANAGER

The following sections explain in more detail how to use the Apple Event Manager to receive, accept, and send Apple events. The first two sections describe how to accept and process Apple events and how to install entries into the Apple event dispatch table. The following section fully explains how your application should handle the required Apple events, and it provides code that shows sample handlers for the required Apple events.

Additional sections describe how to

- handle events that support publish and subscribe features
- get data out of an Apple event
- write handlers that perform the action requested by an Apple event
- reply to an Apple event
- dispose of Apple event data structures
- interact with the user when processing an Apple event
- create an Apple event
- send an Apple event
- write an idle function
- write a reply filter function
- write and install coercion handlers
- use the Application Died event to ascertain the termination of an application that has been launched by your application

The Apple Event Manager is available only in system software version 7.0. Use the Gestalt function with the gestaltAppleEventsAttr selector to determine whether the Apple Event Manager is available. In the response parameter, the bit defined by the constant gestaltAppleEventsPresent is set if the Apple Event Manager is available.

```
CONST gestaltAppleEventsAttr    = 'evnt'; {Gestalt selector}
      gestaltAppleEventsPresent = 0;      {if this bit is set, then }
                                          { Apple Event Mgr's available}
```

Accepting an Apple Event

To accept Apple events (or any other high-level events), you must set the appropriate flags in your application's 'SIZE' resource and include code to handle high-level events in your application's main event loop.

Two flags in the 'SIZE' resource determine whether an application receives high-level events:

- The isHighLevelEventAware flag must be set for your application to receive any high-level events.
- The localAndRemoteHLEvents flag must be set for your application to receive high-level events sent from another computer on the network.

Note that in order for your application to respond to Apple events sent from remote computers, the user of your application must also allow network users to link to your application. The user does this by selecting your application from the Finder and choosing Sharing from the File menu and then clicking the Allow Remote Program Linking check box. If the user has not yet started program linking, the Sharing command offers to display the Sharing Setup control panel so that the user can start program linking. The user must also authorize remote users for program linking by using the Users and Groups control panel. Program linking and setting up authenticated sessions are described in the Program-to-Program Communications Toolbox chapter in this volume.

For a complete description of the 'SIZE' resource, see the Event Manager chapter in this volume.

Apple events (and other high-level events) are identified by a message class of kHighLevelEvent in the what field of the event record. You can test the what field of the event record to determine whether the event is a high-level event.

Listing 6-1 is an example of a procedure called from an application's main event loop that handles events, including high-level events. The procedure determines the type of event received and then calls another routine to take the appropriate action.

Listing 6-1. A DoEvent procedure

```
PROCEDURE DoEvent (event: EventRecord);

BEGIN
   CASE event.what OF         {determine the type of event}
      mouseDown:
         DoMouseDown (event);
      .
      . {handle other kinds of events}
      .
      {handle high-level events, including Apple events}
      kHighLevelEvent:
         DoHighLevelEvent (event);
   END;
END;
```

Listing 6-2 is an example of a DoHighLevelEvent procedure that handles Apple events and also handles the high-level event identified by the event class mySpecialHLEventClass and the event ID mySpecialHLEventID. Note that, in most cases, you should use Apple events to communicate with other applications.

Listing 6-2. A DoHighLevelEvent procedure for handling Apple events and other high-level events

```
PROCEDURE DoHighLevelEvent (event: EventRecord);

VAR
   myErr: OSErr;
BEGIN
   IF (event.message = LongInt(mySpecialHLEventClass)) AND
      (LongInt(event.where) = LongInt(mySpecialHLEventID)) THEN
   BEGIN
   {it's a high-level event that doesn't use AEIMP}
      myErr := HandleMySpecialHLEvent(event);
      IF myErr <> noErr THEN
         DoError(myErr);   {perform the necessary error handling}
   END
   ELSE     {otherwise, assume that the event is an Apple event}
   BEGIN
      myErr := AEProcessAppleEvent(event);
      IF myErr <> noErr THEN
         DoError(myErr);
   END;
END;
```

If your application accepts high-level events that do not follow the Apple Event Interprocess Messaging Protocol (AEIMP), you must dispatch these high-level events before calling AEProcessAppleEvent. To dispatch a high-level event that does not follow AEIMP, for each event you should check the event class, the event ID, or both to see if the event is one that your application can handle.

After receiving a high-level event (and, if appropriate, checking whether it is a type of high-level event other than an Apple event), your application typically calls the AEProcessAppleEvent function. The AEProcessAppleEvent function determines the type of Apple event received, gets the event buffer that contains the parameters and attributes of the Apple event, and calls the corresponding Apple event handler routine in your application.

You should provide a handler routine for each Apple event that your application supports. Your handler routine for a particular Apple event is responsible for performing the action requested by the Apple event, and your handler can optionally return data in the reply Apple event.

After your handler finishes processing the Apple event and adds any parameters to the default reply, it should return a result code to AEProcessAppleEvent. If the client application is waiting for a reply, the Apple Event Manager returns the reply Apple event to the client.

Installing Entries Into the Apple Event Dispatch Tables

When your application receives an Apple event, use the AEProcessAppleEvent function to retrieve the data buffer of the event and to route the Apple event to the appropriate Apple event handler in your application. Your application supplies an Apple event dispatch table to provide a mapping between the Apple events your application supports and the Apple event handlers provided by your application.

To install entries into your application's Apple event dispatch table, use the AEInstallEventHandler function. You usually install entries for all of the Apple events that your application accepts into your application's Apple event dispatch table.

For each Apple event your application supports, you should install entries in your Apple event dispatch table that specify

- the event class of the Apple event
- the event ID of the Apple event
- the address of the Apple event handler for the Apple event
- a reference constant

You provide this information to the AEInstallEventHandler function. In addition, you indicate to the AEInstallEventHandler function whether the entry should be added to your application's Apple event dispatch table or the system Apple event dispatch table.

The **system Apple event dispatch table** is a table in the system heap that contains handlers that are available to all applications and processes running on the same computer. The handlers in your application's Apple event dispatch table are available only to your application. If AEProcessAppleEvent cannot find a handler for the Apple event in your application's Apple event dispatch table, it looks in the system Apple event dispatch table for a handler. If it doesn't find a handler there either, it returns the errAEEventNotHandled result code.

Listing 6-3 illustrates how to add entries for the required Apple events to your application's Apple event dispatch table.

Listing 6-3. Inserting entries for required Apple events into an application's Apple event dispatch table

```
myErr := AEInstallEventHandler (kCoreEventClass, kAEOpenApplication,
                                @MyHandleOAPP, 0, FALSE);
IF myErr <> noErr THEN DoError(myErr);
myErr := AEInstallEventHandler (kCoreEventClass, kAEOpenDocuments,
                                @MyHandleODOC, 0, FALSE);
IF myErr <> noErr THEN DoError(myErr);
myErr := AEInstallEventHandler (kCoreEventClass, kAEPrintDocuments,
                                @MyHandlePDOC, 0, FALSE);
IF myErr <> noErr THEN DoError(myErr);
myErr := AEInstallEventHandler (kCoreEventClass, kAEQuitApplication,
                                @MyHandleQUIT, 0, FALSE);
IF myErr <> noErr THEN DoError(myErr);
```

The code in Listing 6-3 creates an entry for all required Apple events in the Apple event dispatch table. The first entry creates an entry for the Open Application event. The entry indicates the event class and event ID of the Open Application event and the address of the handler for that event and specifies 0 as the reference constant. This entry is installed into the application's Apple event dispatch table.

The reference constant is passed to your handler by the Apple Event Manager each time your handler is called. Your application can use this reference constant for any purpose. If your application doesn't use the reference constant, use 0 as the value.

The last parameter to the AEInstallEventHandler function is a Boolean value that determines whether the entry is added to the system Apple event dispatch table or to your application's Apple event dispatch table. To add the entry to your application's dispatch table, use FALSE as the value of this parameter. If you specify TRUE, the entry is added to the system's Apple event dispatch table.

If you add a handler to the system Apple event dispatch table, the handler that you specify must reside in the system heap. If there was already an entry in the system Apple event dispatch table for the same event class and event ID, it is replaced. Therefore, if there is an entry in the system Apple event dispatch table for the same event class and event ID, you should chain it to your system handler as explained in "Creating and Managing the Apple Event Dispatch Tables" later in this chapter.

Note: When an application calls a system Apple event handler, the A5 register is set up for the calling application. For this reason, if you provide a system Apple event handler, it should never use A5 global variables or anything that depends on a particular context; otherwise, the application that calls the system handler may crash.

For any entry in your Apple event dispatch table, you can specify a wildcard value for the event class, event ID, or both. You specify a wildcard by supplying the typeWildCard constant when installing an entry into the Apple event dispatch table. A wildcard value matches all possible values.

For example, if you specify an entry with the typeWildCard event class and the kAEOpenDocuments event ID, the Apple Event Manager dispatches Apple events of any event class and an event ID of kAEOpenDocuments to the handler for that entry.

If you specify an entry with the kCoreEventClass event class and the typeWildCard event ID, the Apple Event Manager dispatches Apple events of the kCoreEventClass event class and any event ID to the handler for that entry.

If you specify an entry with the typeWildCard event class and the typeWildCard event ID, the Apple Event Manager dispatches all Apple events of any event class and any event ID to the handler for that entry.

If the AEProcessAppleEvent function cannot find a handler for an Apple event in either the application's Apple event dispatch table or the system Apple event dispatch table, it returns the result code errAEEventNotHandled to the Apple event server. If the client is waiting for a reply, AESend also returns this result code as its function result.

If your application supports the Edition Manager, you should also add entries to your application's Apple event dispatch table for the Apple events that your application receives from the Edition Manager. Listing 6-4 shows how to add entries for these Apple events to your application's Apple event dispatch table.

Listing 6-4. Inserting entries for Apple events sent by the Edition Manager into an application's Apple event dispatch table

```
myErr := AEInstallEventHandler(sectionEventMsgClass, sectionReadMsgID,
                               @MyHandleSectionReadEvent, 0, FALSE);
IF myErr <> noErr THEN DoError(myErr);
myErr := AEInstallEventHandler(sectionEventMsgClass,
                               sectionWriteMsgID,
                               @MyHandleSectionWriteEvent, 0, FALSE);
IF myErr <> noErr THEN DoError(myErr);
myErr := AEInstallEventHandler(sectionEventMsgClass,
                               sectionScrollMsgID,
                               @MyHandleSectionScrollEvent, 0, FALSE);
IF myErr <> noErr THEN DoError(myErr);
```

See "Handling Apple Events Sent by the Edition Manager" later in this chapter for the parameters associated with these events. See the Edition Manager chapter in this volume for information on how your application should respond to the Apple events sent by the Edition Manager.

Handling the Required Apple Events

This section describes the required Apple events—the Apple events your application must support to be 7.0-friendly—and the descriptor types for all parameters of the required Apple events. It also describes how to write the handlers for these events, and it provides sample code.

To support the required Apple events, you must set the necessary flags in the 'SIZE' resource of your application, install entries into your application's Apple event dispatch table, add code to the event loop of your application to recognize high-level events, and call the AEProcessAppleEvent function, as described in the preceding two sections. You must also write handlers to handle each Apple event; this section describes how to write these handlers.

Required Apple Events

When a user opens or prints a file from the Finder, the Finder sets up the information your application can use to determine which files to open or print. In version 7.0, if your application supports high-level events, the Finder communicates this information to your application through the required Apple events.

The Finder sends one of the required Apple events to your application to request that it open or print a list of documents, inform it that the Finder has just opened your application, or inform it that the Finder is about to terminate your application.

These are the required Apple events.

Apple event	Requested action
Open Application	Perform tasks associated with opening your application
Open Documents	Open the specified documents
Print Documents	Print the specified documents
Quit Application	Perform tasks—such as releasing memory, requesting the user to save documents, and so on—associated with quitting; when appropriate, the Finder sends this event to an application immediately after sending it a Print Documents event or if the user chooses Restart or Shut Down from the Finder's Special menu

The Finder uses the required Apple events as part of the new mechanisms in system software version 7.0 for launching and terminating applications. This new method of communicating Finder information to your application replaces the mechanisms used in earlier versions of system software.

Applications that do not support high-level events can still use the CountAppFiles, GetAppFiles, and ClrAppFiles procedures (or the GetAppParms procedure) to get the Finder information. See the Segment Loader chapter of Volume II for information on these routines. To make your application 7.0-friendly and compatible with earlier versions of system software, it must support both the old and new mechanisms.

Use the Gestalt function to determine whether the Apple Event Manager is present. If it is and the isHighLevelEventAware flag is set in your application's 'SIZE' resource, your application receives the Finder information through the required Apple events.

If your application accepts high-level events, the Finder sends it an Open Application, Open Documents, or Print Documents event immediately after launching your application. Upon receiving any of these events, your application should perform the action requested by the event.

> **Note:** This section describes the required Apple events as they are sent by the Finder. When sent by other applications or processes, these same Apple events—which are among the core Apple events described in the *Apple Event Registry*—can include optional parameters not listed here. To be 7.0-friendly, your application only needs to handle the required parameters that are described in this section.

Open Application—perform tasks associated with opening an application

Event class	kCoreEventClass
Event ID	kAEOpenApplication
Parameters	None
Requested action	Perform any tasks—such as opening an untitled document window—that you would normally perform when a user opens your application.

Open Documents—open the specified documents

Event class	kCoreEventClass
Event ID	kAEOpenDocuments
Required parameter	
Keyword:	keyDirectObject
Descriptor type:	typeAEList
Data:	A list of alias records for the documents to be opened
Requested action	Open the documents specified in the keyDirectObject parameter.

Print Documents—print the specified documents

Event class	kCoreEventClass
Event ID	kAEPrintDocuments
Required parameter	
Keyword:	keyDirectObject
Descriptor type:	typeAEList
Data:	A list of alias records for the documents to be printed
Requested action	Print the documents specified in the keyDirectObject parameter without opening windows for the documents.

Quit Application—perform tasks associated with quitting

Event class	kCoreEventClass
Event ID	kAEQuitApplication
Parameters	None
Requested action	Perform any tasks that your application would normally perform when the user chooses Quit. Such tasks typically include asking the user if he or she wants to save documents that have been changed. When appropriate, the Finder sends this event to an application immediately after sending it a Print Documents event or if the user chooses Restart or Shut Down from the Finder's Special menu.

Your application needs to recognize only two descriptor types to handle the required Apple events: descriptor lists and alias records. The Open Documents event and Print Documents event use descriptor lists to store a list of documents to open. Each document is specified as an alias record in the descriptor list.

You can retrieve the data that specifies the document to open as an alias record, or you can request that the Apple Event Manager coerce the alias record to a file system specification (FSSpec) record. The file system specification record provides a standard method of identifying files in version 7.0. See the File Manager chapter in this volume for a complete description of how to specify files using file system specification records.

Handling the Open Application Event

When the user opens your application, the Finder uses the Process Manager to launch your application. On startup, your application typically performs any needed initialization, and then begins to process events. If your application supports high-level events, your application receives the Open Application event.

To handle the Open Application event, your application should do just what the user expects it to do when your application is opened. For example, your application might open a new untitled window in response to an Open Application event.

Listing 6-5 shows a handler that processes the Open Application event. The Open Application event does not have any required parameters. This handler first calls an application-defined function called MyGotRequiredParams. This function checks to see if the Apple event contains any required parameters. By definition, the Open Application event should not contain any required parameters so, if the Apple event does contain any, the handler returns an error. Otherwise the handler opens a new document window.

Listing 6-5. A handler for the Open Application event

```
FUNCTION MyHandleOApp (theAppleEvent,reply: AppleEvent;
                       handlerRefcon: LongInt) : OSErr;
VAR
   myErr: OSErr;
BEGIN
   myErr := MyGotRequiredParams (theAppleEvent);
   IF myErr <> noErr THEN
      MyHandleOApp := myErr
   ELSE
   BEGIN
      DoNew;
      MyHandleOApp := noErr;
   END;
END;
```

The MyGotRequiredParams function checks that all required parameters have been extracted from the Apple event. See Listing 6-11 in "Writing Apple Event Handlers" later in this chapter for a description of the MyGotRequiredParams function.

Handling the Open Documents Event

To handle the Open Documents event, your application should open the documents specified in the Apple event. The Open Documents event contains a list of documents to open in its direct parameter. Your application extracts this information and then opens the specified documents.

Listing 6-6 shows a handler for the Open Documents event. The handler illustrates how to open the documents referred to in the direct parameter.

Listing 6-6. A handler for the Open Documents event

```
FUNCTION MyHandleODoc (theAppleEvent,reply: AppleEvent;
                       handlerRefcon: LongInt) : OSErr;
VAR
   myFSS:                 FSSpec;
   docList:               AEDescList;
   myErr:                 OSErr;
   index, itemsInList:    LongInt;
   actualSize:            Size;
   keywd:                 AEKeyword;
   returnedType:          DescType;
BEGIN
   {get the direct parameter--a descriptor list--and put it into docList}
   myErr := AEGetParamDesc(theAppleEvent, keyDirectObject, typeAEList,
                           docList);
   IF myErr <> noErr THEN DoError(myErr);
   {check for missing required parameters}
   myErr := MyGotRequiredParams(theAppleEvent);
   IF myErr <> noErr THEN     {an error occurred}
      BEGIN                   {do the necessary error handling}
         MyHandleODoc := myErr;
         Exit (MyHandleODoc);
      END;
   {count the number of descriptor records in the list}
   myErr := AECountItems (docList, itemsInList);
   {now get each descriptor record from the list, coerce the returned }
   { data to an FSSpec record, and open the associated file}
   FOR index := 1 TO itemsInList DO
      BEGIN
         myErr := AEGetNthPtr(docList, index, typeFSS, keywd,
                              returnedType, @myFSS, Sizeof(myFSS),
                              actualSize);
         IF myErr <> noErr THEN DoError(myErr);
         myErr := MyOpenFile(@myFSS);
         IF myErr <> noErr THEN DoError(myErr);
      END;
   myErr := AEDisposeDesc(docList);
   MyHandleODoc := noErr;
END;
```

The handler in Listing 6-6 first uses the AEGetParamDesc function to get the direct parameter (specified by the keyDirectObject keyword) out of the Apple event. The handler requests that AEGetParamDesc return a descriptor list in the docList variable. The handler then checks to make sure that it has retrieved all of the required parameters by calling the MyGotRequiredParams function (see Listing 6-11 for a description of this routine).

Once the handler has retrieved the descriptor list from the Apple event, it uses AECountItems to count the number of descriptors in the list. Using the returned number as an index, the handler can get the data of each descriptor record in the list. This handler requests that the AEGetNthPtr function coerce the data in the descriptor record to a file system specification record. The handler can then use the file system specification record as a parameter to its own routine for opening files.

For more information on the AEGetParamDesc function, see "Getting Data out of a Parameter" later in this chapter. Also see "Getting Data out of a Descriptor List" for further information on the AEGetNthPtr and AECountItems functions.

After extracting the file system specification record that describes the document to open, your application can use this record to open the file. For example, in Listing 6-6, the code passes the file system specification record to its routine for opening files, the MyOpenFile function.

The MyOpenFile function is designed so that it can be called both in response to the Open Documents event and to events generated by the user. For example, when the user chooses Open from the File menu, the code that handles the mouse-down event uses the StandardGetFile procedure to let the user choose a file; it then calls MyOpenFile, passing the file system specification record returned by StandardGetFile. By isolating code that performs a requested action from code that interacts with the user, you can easily adapt your application to handle Apple events that request the same action.

Note that your handler should use the AEDisposeDesc function to dispose of the descriptor list when your handler no longer requires the data in it. Your handler should also return a result code.

Handling the Print Documents Event

To handle the Print Documents event, your application should print the documents specified in the Apple event. The Print Documents event contains a list of documents to print in its direct parameter. Your application extracts this information and then prints the specified documents. Your application should not open any windows for the documents. Also note that your application should remain open after processing the Print Documents event; when appropriate, the Finder sends your application a Quit Application event immediately after sending it a Print Documents event.

Listing 6-7 shows a handler for the Print Documents event. This handler is similar to the handler for the Open Documents event. The code illustrates how to print the documents referred to in the direct parameter.

Listing 6-7. A handler for the Print Documents event

```
FUNCTION MyHandlePDoc (theAppleEvent,reply: AppleEvent;
                        handlerRefcon: LongInt) : OSErr;
VAR
   myFSS:                FSSpec;
   docList:              AEDescList;
   myErr:                OSErr;
   index, itemsInList:   LongInt;
   actualSize:           Size;
   keywd:                AEKeyword;
   returnedType:         DescType;
BEGIN
   {get the direct parameter--a descriptor list--and put it into docList}
   myErr := AEGetParamDesc(theAppleEvent, keyDirectObject, typeAEList,
                           docList);
   IF myErr <> noErr THEN DoError(myErr);
   {check for missing required parameters}
   myErr := MyGotRequiredParams(theAppleEvent);
   IF myErr <> noErr THEN {an error occurred}
      BEGIN
         {do the necessary error handling}
         MyHandlePDoc := myErr;
         Exit(MyHandlePDoc);
      END;
```

(Continued)

Listing 6-7. A handler for the Print Documents event (Continued)

```
   {count the number of descriptor records in the list}
   myErr := AECountItems (docList, itemsInList);
   {now get each descriptor record from the list, coerce the returned }
   { data to an FSSpec record, and print the associated file}
   FOR index := 1 TO itemsInList DO
      BEGIN
      myErr := AEGetNthPtr(docList, index, typeFSS, keywd, returnedType,
                           @myFSS, Sizeof(myFSS), actualSize);
      IF myErr <> noErr THEN DoError(myErr);
      myErr := MyPrintFile(@myFSS);
      IF myErr <> noErr THEN DoError(myErr);
      END;
   myErr := AEDisposeDesc(docList);
   MyHandlePDoc := noErr;
END;
```

Handling the Quit Application Event

To handle the Quit Application event, your application should take any actions that are necessary before it is terminated (such as saving any open documents). Listing 6-8 shows an example of a handler for the Quit Application event.

When appropriate, the Finder sends your application a Quit Application event immediately after a Print Documents event. The Finder also sends your application a Quit Application event if the user chooses Restart or Shut Down from the Finder's Special menu.

Listing 6-8. A handler for the Quit Application event

```
FUNCTION MyHandleQuit (theAppleEvent,reply: AppleEvent;
                          handlerRefcon: LongInt) : OSErr;
VAR
   userCanceled:  Boolean;
   myErr:         OSErr;
BEGIN
   {check for missing required parameters}
   myErr := MyGotRequiredParams(theAppleEvent);
   IF myErr <> noErr THEN {an error occurred}
      BEGIN
         {do the necessary error handling}
         MyHandleQuit := myErr;
         Exit (MyHandleQuit);
      END;
   userCanceled := MyPrepareToTerminate;
   IF userCanceled THEN
      MyHandleQuit := userCanceledErr
   ELSE
      MyHandleQuit := noErr;
END;
```

The handler in Listing 6-8 calls another function supplied by the application, the MyPrepareToTerminate function. This function saves the documents for any open windows and returns a Boolean value that indicates whether the Quit request was canceled by the user.

This is another example of isolating code for interacting with the user from the code that performs the requested action. Structuring your application in this way allows your application to use the same routine when responding to a user event (such as choosing the Quit command from the File menu) or to the corresponding Apple event. (For a description of the MyGotRequiredParams function, see "Writing Apple Event Handlers" later in this chapter.)

Note that your handler must not call the ExitToShell procedure. In Listing 6-8, the application calls the ExitToShell procedure only if the handler returns noErr as its function result.

Handling Apple Events Sent by the Edition Manager

If your application provides publish and subscribe capabilities, it should handle the Apple events sent by the Edition Manager in addition to the required Apple events. Your application should also handle the Create Publisher event. The Create Publisher event is described in the next section.

The Edition Manager sends your application Apple events to communicate information about the publishers and subscribers in your application's documents. Specifically, the Edition Manager uses Apple events to notify your application

- when the information in an edition is updated
- when your application needs to write the data from a publisher to an edition
- when your application should locate a particular publisher and scroll the document to that location

The Apple events sent by the Edition Manager to your application are the Section Read event, Section Write event, and Section Scroll event.

Section Read—read information into the specified section

Event class	SectionEventMsgClass
Event ID	SectionReadMsgID
Required parameter	
Keyword:	keyDirectObject
Descriptor type:	typeSectionH
Data:	A handle to the section record of the subscriber whose edition contains updated information
Requested action	Update the subscriber with the new information from the edition.

Section Write—write the specified section to an edition

Event class	SectionEventMsgClass
Event ID	SectionWriteMsgID
Required parameter	
Keyword:	keyDirectObject
Descriptor type:	typeSectionH
Data:	A handle to the section record of the publisher
Requested action	Write the publisher's data to its edition.

Section Scroll—scroll the document to the specified section

Event class	SectionEventMsgClass
Event ID	SectionScrollMsgID
Required parameter	
Keyword:	keyDirectObject
Descriptor type:	typeSectionH
Data:	A handle to the section record of the publisher to scroll to
Requested action	Scroll the document to the publisher identified by the specified section record.

See the Edition Manager chapter in this volume for details on how your application should respond to these events.

Handling the Create Publisher Event

If your application supports publish and subscribe capabilities, it should also handle the Create Publisher event.

Create Publisher—create a publisher

Event class	kAEMiscStdSuite
Event ID	kAECreatePublisher
Required parameter	None
Optional parameter	
Keyword:	keyDirectObject
Descriptor type:	typeObjectSpecifier
Data:	The part of the document to publish. If this parameter is omitted, publish the current selection.
Optional parameter	
Keyword:	keyAEEditionFileLoc
Descriptor type:	typeAlias
Data:	An alias record that contains the location of the edition container to create. If this parameter is omitted, use the default edition container.
Requested action	Create a publisher for the specified data using the specified location for the edition container. If the data isn't specified, publish the current selection. If the location of the edition isn't specified, use the default location.

When your application receives the Create Publisher event, it should create a publisher by writing the publisher's data to an edition. The data of the publisher, and the location and name of the edition, are defined by the Apple event. If the Create Publisher event includes a keyDirectObject parameter, then your application should publish the data contained in the parameter. If the keyDirectObject parameter is missing, then your application should publish the current selection. If the document doesn't have a current selection, your handler for the event should return a nonzero result code.

If the Create Publisher event includes a keyAEEditionFileLoc parameter, then your application should use the location and name contained in the parameter as the default location and name of the edition. If the keyAEEditionFileLoc parameter is missing, then your application should use the default location and name your application normally uses to specify the edition container.

Listing 6-9 shows a handler for the Create Publisher event. This handler checks for the keyDirectObject parameter and the keyAEEditionFileLoc parameter. If either of these is not specified, the handler uses default values. The handler uses the DoNewPublisher function, an application-defined function, to create the publisher and its edition, create a section record, and update other data structures associated with the document. See Listing 4-4 in the Edition Manager chapter for an example of the DoNewPublisher function.

Note that the handler uses the AEInteractWithUser function to determine whether user interaction is allowed. If user interaction is allowed, the handler sets the promptForDialog variable to TRUE, indicating that the DoNewPublisher function should display the publisher dialog box. If user interaction is not allowed, the handler sets the promptForDialog variable to FALSE, and the DoNewPublisher function does not prompt the user for the location or name of the edition.

Listing 6-9. A handler for the Create Publisher event

```
FUNCTION MyHandleCreatePublisherEvent(theAppleEvent,reply: AppleEvent;
                                      handlerRefcon: LongInt) : OSErr;
VAR
   myErr:                  OSErr;
   returnedType:           DescType;
   thePublisherDataDesc:   AEDesc;
   actualSize:             LongInt;
   promptForDialog:        Boolean;
   thisDocument:           MyDocumentInfoPtr;
   preview:                Handle;
   previewFormat:          FormatType;
   defaultLocation:        EditionContainerSpec;

BEGIN
   MyGetDocumentPtr(thisDocument);
   myErr := AEGetParamDesc(theAppleEvent, keyDirectObject,
                           typeObjectSpecifier, thePublisherDataDesc);
   CASE myErr OF
      errAEDescNotFound:
      BEGIN
         {use the current selection as the publisher and }
         { set up info for later when DoNewPublisher displays preview}
         preview := MyGetPreviewForSelection(thisDocument);
         previewFormat := 'TEXT';
      END;
      noErr:
         {use the data in keyDirectObject parameter as the publisher }
         { (which is returned in the thePublisherDataDesc variable), and}
         { set up info for later when DoNewPublisher displays preview}
```

(Continued)

Listing 6-9. A handler for the Create Publisher event (Continued)

```
         MySetInfoForPreview(thePublisherDataDesc, thisDocument,
                                  preview, previewFormat);
      OTHERWISE
         DoError(myErr);
   END;
   myErr := AEGetParamPtr(theAppleEvent, keyAEEditionFileLoc,
                          typeFSS, returnedType,
                          @defaultLocation.theFile,
                          SizeOf(FSSpec), actualSize);
   CASE myErr OF
      errAEDescNotFound:
         {use the default location as the edition container}
            myErr := MyGetDefaultEditionSpec(thisDocument,
                                             defaultLocation);
      noErr:
      BEGIN      {the keyAEEditionFileLoc parameter }
                 { contained a default location}
         defaultLocation.thePart := kPartsNotUsed;
         defaultLocation.theFileScript := smSystemScript;
      END;
      OTHERWISE
         DoError(myErr);
      END;
   myErr := MyGotRequiredParams(theAppleEvent);
   IF myErr <> noErr THEN
      BEGIN
      {handle the error appropriately}
      MyHandleCreatePublisherEvent := myErr;
      END;
   promptForDialog := (AEInteractWithUser(kAEDefaultTimeout, NIL,
                                          @MyIdleFunction) = noErr);
   myErr := DoNewPublisher(thisDocument, promptForDialog,
                          preview, previewFormat, defaultLocation);
   {add keyErrorNumber and keyErrorString parameters if desired}
   MyHandleCreatePublisherEvent := myErr;
END;
```

Getting Data out of an Apple Event

The Apple Event Manager stores the parameters and attributes of an Apple event in a format that is internal to the Apple Event Manager. You use Apple Event Manager functions to retrieve the data from an Apple event and return it to your application in a format your application can use.

The Apple Event Manager provides functions that retrieve data from parameters and attributes. Most of these functions are available in two forms: one that returns the desired data in a specified buffer and one that returns a descriptor record containing the same data. For example, the AEGetParamPtr function returns the data of a specified parameter, and the AEGetParamDesc function returns the descriptor record of a specified parameter.

You can also use Apple Event Manager functions to get data out of descriptor records, descriptor lists, and AE records. You use similar functions to put data into descriptor records, descriptor lists, and AE records.

When your handler receives an Apple event, you'll typically use the AEGetParamPtr, AEGetAttributePtr, AEGetParamDesc, or AEGetAttributeDesc function to get the data out of the Apple event.

Some Apple Event Manager functions let your application request that the data be returned using any descriptor type, even if it is different from the original descriptor type. If the original data is of a different descriptor type, the Apple Event Manager attempts to coerce the data to the requested descriptor type.

For example, the AEGetParamPtr function lets you specify the desired descriptor type of the resulting data.

```
VAR
   theAppleEvent: AppleEvent;
   returnedType:  DescType;
   multResult:    LongInt;
   actualSize:    Size;
   myErr:         OSErr;

myErr := AEGetParamPtr(theAppleEvent, keyMultResult, typeLongInteger,
                       returnedType, @multResult, SizeOf(multResult),
                       actualSize);
```

In this example, the desired type is specified in the third parameter by the typeLongInteger descriptor type. This requests that the Apple Event Manager coerce the data to the type defined by this descriptor type (a long integer) if it is not already of this type.

To ensure that no coercion is performed and that the descriptor type of the result is of the same type as the original, you can specify typeWildCard for the desired descriptor type.

The Apple Event Manager returns the descriptor type of the resulting data in the fourth parameter. This is useful information when you specify typeWildCard as the desired descriptor type; you can determine the descriptor type of the resulting data by examining the fourth parameter.

The Apple Event Manager can coerce many different types of data into another. For example, the Apple Event Manager can convert alias records to file system specification records, integers to Boolean data types, and characters to numeric data types, in addition to other data type conversions.

You can also provide your own coercion handlers to coerce other data types. See "Writing and Installing Coercion Handlers" later in this chapter for information on the coercion provided by the Apple Event Manager and how to provide your own coercion handlers.

Parameters are keyword-specified descriptor records. You can use AEGetParamDesc to get the descriptor record of a parameter, or you can use AEGetParamPtr to get the data out of the descriptor record of a parameter. Attributes are also keyword-specified descriptor records, and you can use similar routines to get the descriptor record of an attribute or to get the data out of an attribute.

The following sections show examples of how to use the AEGetParamPtr, AEGetAttributePtr, AEGetParamDesc, or AEGetAttributeDesc function to get the data out of an Apple event.

Getting Data out of a Parameter

You can use the AEGetParamPtr or AEGetParamDesc function to get the data out of a parameter. Use the AEGetParamPtr function to return the data contained in a parameter. Use the AEGetParamDesc function when you need to get the descriptor record of a parameter. You often use the AEGetParamDesc function to extract the descriptor list from a parameter.

You can also use the AEGetKeyPtr function to return the data contained in a parameter. The AEGetKeyPtr function provides an additional feature—you can use this function to get data out of an AE record. See "Getting Data and Keyword-Specified Descriptor Records From AE Records" later in this chapter for information on this function.

For example, you use an Apple Event Manager function to get the data out of a Section Read event. The Edition Manager sends your application a Section Read event to tell your application to read updated information from an edition into the specified subscriber. The direct parameter of the Apple event contains a handle to the section record of the subscriber. You can use the AEGetParamPtr function to get the data out of the Apple event.

You specify the Apple event that contains the desired parameter, the keyword of the desired parameter, the descriptor type the function should use to return the data, a buffer to store the data, and the size of this buffer as parameters to the AEGetParamPtr function. The AEGetParamPtr function returns the descriptor type of the resulting data and the actual size of the data, and it places the requested data in the specified buffer.

```
VAR
   sectionH:      SectionHandle;
   theAppleEvent: AppleEvent;
   returnedType:  DescType;
   actualSize:    Size;
   myErr:         OSErr;

myErr := AEGetParamPtr(theAppleEvent, keyDirectObject, typeSectionH,
                       returnedType, @sectionH, SizeOf(sectionH),
                       actualSize);
```

In this example, the keyDirectObject keyword specifies that the AEGetParamPtr function should extract information from the direct parameter; AEGetParamPtr returns the data in the buffer specified by the sectionH variable.

You can request that the Apple Event Manager return the data using the descriptor type of the original data or you can request that the Apple Event Manager coerce the data into a descriptor type that is different from the original. You can specify the desired descriptor type as typeWildCard if you don't want any coercion performed—in which case, the AEGetParamPtr function returns the original descriptor type of the parameter.

The typeSectionH descriptor type specifies that the returned data should be coerced to a handle to a section record. You can use the information returned in the sectionH variable to identify the subscriber and read in the information from the edition.

In this example, the AEGetParamPtr function returns in the returnedType variable the descriptor type of the resulting data. In most cases, the descriptor type of the resulting data matches the requested descriptor type, unless the Apple Event Manager wasn't able to coerce the data to the specified descriptor type. If the coercion fails, the Apple Event Manager returns the errAECoercionFail result code.

The AEGetParamPtr function returns the actual size of the data in the actualSize variable. If the value returned in the actualSize variable is greater than the amount your application allocated for the buffer to hold the returned data, your application can increase the size of its buffer to this amount, and get the data again. You can also choose to use the AEGetParamDesc function when your application doesn't know the size of the data.

You can use the AEGetParamDesc function to return the descriptor record of a parameter. This function is useful, for example, when extracting descriptor lists from a parameter.

You specify the Apple event that contains the desired parameter, the keyword of the desired parameter, the descriptor type the function should use to return the descriptor record, and a buffer to store the returned descriptor record as parameters to the AEGetParamDesc function. The AEGetParamDesc function returns the descriptor record using the specified descriptor type.

For example, the direct parameter of the Open Documents event contains a descriptor list that specifies the documents to open. You can use the AEGetParamDesc function to get the descriptor list out of the direct parameter.

```
VAR
   docList:        AEDescList;
   theAppleEvent:  AppleEvent;
   myErr:          OSErr;

myErr := AEGetParamDesc(theAppleEvent, keyDirectObject, typeAEList,
                        docList);
```

In this example, the Apple event specified by the variable theAppleEvent contains the desired parameter. The keyDirectObject keyword specifies that the AEGetParamDesc function should get the descriptor record of the direct parameter. The typeAEList descriptor type specifies that the descriptor record should be returned as a descriptor list. In this example, the AEGetParamDesc function returns a descriptor list in the docList variable.

The descriptor list contains a list of descriptor records. To get the descriptor records and their data out of a descriptor list, use the AECountItems function to find the number of descriptor records in the list, and then make repetitive calls to the AEGetNthPtr function to get the data out of each descriptor record. See "Getting Data out of a Descriptor List" later in this chapter for more information.

Note that the AEGetParamDesc function copies the descriptor record from the parameter. When you're done with a descriptor record that you obtained from AEGetParamDesc, you must dispose of it by calling the AEDisposeDesc function.

Getting Data out of an Attribute

You can use the AEGetAttributePtr or AEGetAttributeDesc function to get the data out of the attributes of an Apple event.

You can get the data out of an attribute using the AEGetAttributePtr function. You specify the Apple event that contains the desired attribute, the keyword of the desired attribute, the descriptor type the function should use to return the data, a buffer to store the data, and the size of this buffer as parameters to the AEGetAttributePtr function. The AEGetAttributePtr function returns the descriptor type of the returned data and the actual size of the data, and it places the requested data in the specified buffer.

For example, this code gets the data out of the keyEventSourceAttr attribute of an Apple event.

```
VAR
   theAppleEvent: AppleEvent;
   returnedType:  DescType;
   sourceOfAE:    Integer;
   actualSize:    Size;
   myErr:         OSErr;

myErr := AEGetAttributePtr(theAppleEvent, keyEventSourceAttr,
                           typeShortInteger, returnedType, @sourceOfAE,
                           SizeOf(sourceOfAE), actualSize);
```

The keyEventSourceAttr keyword specifies the attribute to get the data from. The typeShortInteger descriptor type specifies that the data should be returned as a short integer; the returnedType variable contains the actual descriptor type that is returned. You also must specify a buffer to hold the returned data and specify the size of this buffer. The AEGetAttributePtr function returns the actual size of the data returned in the actualSize variable. You can check this value to make sure you got all the data.

As with the AEGetParamPtr function, you can request that AEGetAttributePtr return the data using the descriptor type of the original data, or you can request that the Apple Event Manager coerce the data into a descriptor type that is different from the original.

In this example, the AEGetAttributePtr function returns the requested data in the sourceOfAE variable, and you can determine the source of the Apple event by examining this value.

The next example shows how to use the AEGetAttributePtr function to get data out of the keyMissedKeywordAttr attribute. After your handler extracts all known parameters from an Apple event, it should check whether the keyMissedKeywordAttr attribute exists. If it does, then your handler did not get all of the required parameters.

Note that if AEGetAttributePtr returns the errAEDescNotFound result code, then the keyMissedKeywordAttribute does not exist—which indicates that your application has extracted all of the required parameters. If AEGetAttributePtr returns noErr, then the keyMissedKeywordAttribute does exist—which indicates that your handler did not get all of the required parameters.

```
myErr := AEGetAttributePtr(theAppleEvent, keyMissedKeywordAttr,
                           typeWildCard, returnedType, NIL, 0,
                           actualSize);
```

The data in the keyMissedKeywordAttr attribute contains the first required parameter, if any, that your handler didn't retrieve. If you want this data returned, specify a buffer to hold the data and specify the size of the buffer. Otherwise, as in this example, specify NIL as the buffer and 0 as the size of the buffer.

Getting Data out of a Descriptor List

You can use the AECountItems function to count the number of items in a descriptor list, and you can use AEGetNthDesc or AEGetNthPtr to get a descriptor record or its data out of a descriptor list.

The Open Documents event contains a direct parameter that specifies the list of documents to open. The list of documents is contained in a descriptor list. After extracting the descriptor list from the parameter, you can determine the number of items in the list and then extract each descriptor record from the descriptor list. See Figure 6-6 in "Data Structures Within Apple Events" earlier in this chapter for a depiction of the Open Documents event.

For example, when your handler receives an Open Documents event, you can use the AEGetParamDesc function to return the direct parameter as a descriptor list. You can then use AECountItems to return the number of descriptor records in the list.

```
VAR
   theAppleEvent: AppleEvent;
   docList:       AEDescList;
   itemsInList:   LongInt;
   myErr:         OSErr;

myErr := AEGetParamDesc(theAppleEvent, keyDirectObject, typeAEList,
                        docList);
myErr := AECountItems(docList, itemsInList);
```

The AEGetParamDesc function returns in the docList variable the descriptor list from the direct parameter of the Open Documents event. You specify this list to the AECountItems function.

You specify the descriptor list whose items you want to count in the first parameter to AECountItems. The Apple Event Manager returns the number of items in the list in the second parameter. When extracting the descriptor records from a list, you often use the number of items as a loop index. Here's an example:

```
FOR index := 1 TO itemsInList DO
   BEGIN
   {for each descriptor record in the list, get its data}
   END;
```

The format of the descriptor records in a descriptor list is private to the Apple Event Manager. You must use the AEGetNthPtr or AEGetNthDesc function to extract descriptor records from a descriptor list.

You specify the descriptor list that contains the desired descriptor records and an index as parameters to the AEGetNthPtr function. The index represents a specific descriptor record in the descriptor list. AEGetNthPtr returns the data from the descriptor record represented by the specified index.

You also specify the descriptor type the function should use to return the data, a buffer to store the data, and the size of this buffer. The AEGetNthPtr function returns the keyword of the parameter, the descriptor type of the returned data, and the actual size of the data, and it places the requested data in the specified buffer.

Here's an example that uses the AEGetNthPtr function to extract an item from the descriptor list in the direct parameter of the Open Documents event.

```
myErr := AEGetNthPtr(docList, index, typeFSS, keywd, returnedType,
                     @myFSS, Sizeof(myFSS), actualSize);
```

The docList variable specifies the descriptor list from the direct parameter of the Open Documents event. The index variable specifies the index of the descriptor record to extract. You can use the typeFSS descriptor type, as in this example, to specify that the data be returned as a file system specification record. The Apple Event Manager automatically coerces the original data type of the descriptor record from an alias record to a file system specification record. The AEGetNthPtr function returns the keyword of the parameter in the keywd variable. The function returns in the returnedType variable the descriptor type of the resulting data.

You specify a buffer to hold the desired data and the size (in bytes) of the buffer as parameters to the AEGetNthPtr function. In this example, the myFSS variable specifies the buffer. The function returns the actual size of the data in the actualSize variable. If this size is larger than the size of the buffer you provided, you know that you didn't get all of the data for the descriptor record.

Listing 6-10 shows a more complete example of extracting the items from a descriptor list in the Open Documents event.

Listing 6-10. Extracting items from a descriptor list

```
VAR
   index:          LongInt;
   itemsInList:    LongInt;
   docList:        AEDescList;
   keywd:          AEKeyword;
   returnedType:   DescType;
   myFSS:          FSSpec;
   actualSize:     Size;
   myErr:          OSErr;

FOR index := 1 TO itemsInList DO
   BEGIN
      myErr := AEGetNthPtr(docList, index, typeFSS, keywd, returnedType ,
                           @myFSS, Sizeof(myFSS), actualSize);
```

```
      IF myErr <> noErr THEN DoError(myErr);
      myErr := MyOpenFile(@myFSS);
      IF myErr <> noErr THEN DoError(myErr);
   END;
   myErr := AEDisposeDesc(docList);
```

Writing Apple Event Handlers

For each Apple event your application supports, you must provide a function called an Apple event handler. The AEProcessAppleEvent function calls one of your Apple event handlers when it processes an Apple event. Your Apple event handlers should perform any action requested by the Apple event, add parameters to the reply Apple event if appropriate, and return a result code.

The Apple Event Manager uses dispatch tables to route Apple events to the appropriate Apple event handler. You must supply an Apple event handler for each entry in your application's Apple event dispatch table. Each handler must be a function that uses this syntax:

```
FUNCTION MyEventHandler (theAppleEvent: AppleEvent; reply: AppleEvent;
                         handlerRefcon: LongInt) : OSErr;
```

The parameter theAppleEvent is the Apple event to handle. Your handler uses Apple Event Manager functions to extract any parameters and attributes from the Apple event and then performs the necessary processing. The reply parameter is the default reply provided by the Apple Event Manager. ("Replying to an Apple Event" later in this chapter describes how to add parameters to the default reply.) The handlerRefcon parameter is the reference constant stored in the Apple event dispatch table entry for the Apple event. Your handler can ignore this parameter if your application does not use the reference constant.

After extracting all known parameters from the Apple event, every handler should determine whether the Apple event contains any further required parameters. Your handler can check that it retrieved all the required parameters by checking to see if the keyMissedKeywordAttr attribute exists. If the attribute exists, then your handler has not retrieved all the required parameters. If additional required parameters exist, then your handler should immediately return an error. If the attribute does not exist, then the Apple event does not contain any more required parameters.

Listing 6-11 shows a function that checks for a keyMissedKeywordAttr attribute. A handler calls this function after getting all the parameters it knows about from an Apple event.

Listing 6-11. A function that checks for a keyMissedKeywordAttr attribute

```
FUNCTION MyGotRequiredParams (theAppleEvent: AppleEvent) : OSErr;
VAR
   returnedType:  DescType;
   actualSize:    Size;
   myErr:         OSErr;
BEGIN
   myErr := AEGetAttributePtr (theAppleEvent, keyMissedKeywordAttr,
                               typeWildCard, returnedType, NIL, 0,
                               actualSize);
```

(Continued)

6 Apple Event Manager

Listing 6-11. A function that checks for a keyMissedKeywordAttr attribute (Continued)

```
IF myErr = errAEDescNotFound THEN     {you got all the required }
                                      { parameters}
   MyGotRequiredParams := noErr
ELSE IF myErr = noErr THEN            {you missed a required parameter}
   MyGotRequiredParams := errAEEventNotHandled
ELSE                                  {the call to AEGetAttributePtr }
                                      { failed}
   MyGotRequiredParams := myErr;
END;
```

The code in Listing 6-11 uses the AEGetAttributePtr function to get the keyMissedKeywordAttr attribute. This attribute contains the first required parameter, if any, that your handler didn't retrieve. If AEGetAttributePtr returns the errAEDescNotFound result code, the Apple event doesn't contain a keyMissedKeywordAttr attribute. If the Apple event doesn't contain this attribute, then your handler has extracted all of the required parameters.

If the AEGetAttributePtr function returns noErr as the result code, then the attribute does exist, meaning that your handler has not extracted all of the required parameters. In this case, your handler should return an error and not process the Apple event.

The first remaining required parameter is specified by the data of the keyMissedKeywordAttr attribute. If you want this data returned, specify a buffer to hold the data. Otherwise, specify NIL as the buffer and 0 as the size of the buffer. If you specify a buffer to hold the data, you can check the value of the actualSize parameter to see if the data is larger than the buffer you allocated.

Replying to an Apple Event

Your handler routine for a particular Apple event is responsible for performing the action requested by the Apple event, and can optionally return data in a reply Apple event. The Apple Event Manager passes a default reply Apple event to your handler. The default reply Apple event has no parameters when it is passed to your handler. Your handler can add parameters to the reply Apple event. If the client application requested a reply, the Apple Event Manager returns the reply Apple event to the client.

The reply Apple event is identified by the kCoreEventClass event class and by the kAEAnswer event ID.

When your handler finishes processing an Apple event, it returns a result code to AEProcessAppleEvent. The AEProcessAppleEvent function returns this result code as its function result. If your handler returns a nonzero result code, the Apple Event Manager also returns this result code to the client application by putting the result code into a keyErrorNumber parameter for the reply Apple event. The client can check for the existence of this parameter to determine whether the handler performed the requested action.

The client application specifies whether it wants a reply Apple event or not by specifying flags (represented by constants) in the sendMode parameter of the AESend function.

If the client specifies the kAEWaitReply flag in the sendMode parameter, the AESend function does not return until the timeout expires or the server returns a reply. When the server returns a reply, the reply parameter to AESend contains the reply Apple event that your handler returned to the AEProcessAppleEvent function.

If the client specified the kAEQueueReply flag, the client receives the reply event in its normal processing of other events.

If the client specified the kAENoReply flag, your handler may return a reply Apple event to AEProcessAppleEvent, but this reply is not returned to the client.

Your handler routine should always set its function result to noErr if it successfully handles the Apple event or to a nonzero result code if an error occurs. The Apple Event Manager automatically adds any nonzero result code that your handler returns to a keyErrorNumber parameter in the reply Apple event. In addition to returning a result code, your handler can also return an error string in the keyErrorString parameter of the reply Apple event. Your handler should provide meaningful text in the keyErrorString parameter, so that the client can display this string to the user if desired.

Listing 6-12 shows how to add the keyErrorString parameter to the reply Apple event. See "Adding Parameters to an Apple Event" later in this chapter for a description of the AEPutParamPtr function.

Listing 6-12. Adding the keyErrorString parameter to the reply Apple event

```
FUNCTION MyHandler (theAppleEvent: AppleEvent; reply: AppleEvent;
                    handlerRefcon: LongInt) : OSErr;
VAR
   myErr:   OSErr;
   errStr:  Str255;
BEGIN
   {if an error occurs when handling an Apple event, set the }
   { function result and error string accordingly}
   IF myErr <> noErr THEN
   BEGIN
   MyHandler := myErr;     {result code to be returned--the Apple Event }
                           { Manager adds this result code to the reply }
                           { Apple event as the keyErrorNumber parameter}
   {add error string parameter to the default reply}
   errStr := 'Reason why error occurred';
   myErr := AEPutParamPtr(reply, keyErrorString, typeChar,
                          @errStr[1], length(errStr));
   Exit(MyHandler);
   END;
END;
```

If your handler needs to return data to the client, it can add parameters to the reply Apple event. For example, Listing 6-13 shows how a handler for the Multiply event (an imaginary Apple event that asks the server to multiply two numbers) might return the results of the multiplication to the client.

Listing 6-13. Adding parameters to the reply Apple event

```
FUNCTION MyMultHandler (theAppleEvent: AppleEvent; reply: AppleEvent;
                        handlerRefcon: LongInt) : OSErr;
VAR
   myErr:               OSErr;
   number1,number2:     LongInt;
   replyResult:         LongInt;
   actualSize:          Size;
   returnedType:        DescType;
BEGIN
   {get the numbers to multiply from the parameters of the Apple event; }
   { put the numbers in the number1 and number2 variables and }
   { then perform the requested multiplication}
myErr := MyDoMultiply(theAppleEvent, number1, number2, replyResult);

{return the result of the multiplication in the reply Apple event}
IF myErr = noErr THEN
   BEGIN
   myErr := AEPutParamPtr(reply, keyDirectObject, typeLongInteger,
                          @replyResult, SizeOf(replyResult));
   MyMultHandler := myErr;
   END;
{if an error occurs, set the function result and error string }
{ accordingly, as shown in Listing 6-12}
END;
```

Disposing of Apple Event Data Structures

Whenever you use Apple Event Manager functions to create a descriptor record, descriptor list, or Apple event record, the Apple Event Manager allocates memory for these data structures. Likewise, when you extract a descriptor record by using Apple Event Manager functions, the Apple Event Manager creates a copy of the descriptor record for you to use.

Whenever you are done using a descriptor record or descriptor list that you have created or extracted from an Apple event, you must dispose of the descriptor record—and thereby deallocate the memory it uses—by calling the AEDisposeDesc function.

Also, when you are done using the Apple event specified in the AESend function and finished with the reply Apple event, you should dispose of their descriptor records using the AEDisposeDesc function. You should dispose of them even if AESend returns a nonzero result code.

Once you are done using them, you should dispose of any Apple event data structures created or returned by these functions:

AECoerceDesc	AEDuplicateDesc
AECoercePtr	AEGetAttributeDesc
AECreateAppleEvent	AEGetKeyDesc
AECreateDesc	AEGetNthDesc
AECreateList	AEGetParamDesc

Even if you add a descriptor record to an Apple event (for example, when you create a descriptor record by calling AECreateDesc and then put a copy of it into a parameter of an Apple event by calling AEPutParamDesc), you're still responsible for disposing of the original descriptor record.

In one case, the Apple Event Manager does take care of disposing of the Apple event data structures for you: when your handler returns to AEProcessAppleEvent, the Apple Event Manager disposes of the Apple event and the reply Apple event. Note that your handler is still responsible for disposing of any Apple event data structures created when extracting data from the Apple event. The Apple event and reply Apple event that your handler receives are only copies of the originals. The client application is responsible for disposing of the original data structures.

Interacting With the User

When your application receives an Apple event, it may need to interact with the user. For example, your application may need to display a dialog box asking for additional input or confirmation from the user. You must make sure that your application is in the foreground before interacting with the user. To do this, use the AEInteractWithUser function before actually interacting with the user. The AEInteractWithUser function checks the user interaction preferences set by the client application and the server application and, if user interaction is allowed, brings your application to the front (either directly or by posting a notification request) if it is not already in the front.

If both the client and server applications allow user interaction, AEInteractWithUser usually posts a notification request; AEInteractWithUser brings the server to the front after the user responds to the notification request. The AEInteractWithUser function can also bring the server application directly to the front—but only when doing so is in accordance with the principle of user control and if the client allows it.

Both the client and server specify their preferences for user interaction: the client specifies whether the server should be allowed to interact with the user, and the server specifies when it will allow user interaction while processing an Apple event.

An application that sends an Apple event indicates its preferences for how the server application should interact with the user by setting various flags in the sendMode parameter to AESend. The Apple Event Manager translates these flags into the corresponding flags in the keyInteractLevelAttr attribute of the Apple event, and sets them.

The server application sets its preferences by using the AESetInteractionAllowed function. This function lets your application specify whether it allows interaction with the user as a result of receiving an Apple event from itself; from itself and other processes on the local machine; or from itself, local processes, and processes from another computer on the network.

Your application calls the AEInteractWithUser function before interacting with the user. If AEInteractWithUser returns the noErr result code, then your application is currently in the front and your application is free to interact with the user. If AEInteractWithUser returns the errAENoUserInteraction result code, then the conditions didn't allow user interaction and your application should not interact with the user.

The client application sets user interaction preferences by setting flags in the sendMode parameter to the AESend function. The Apple Event Manager automatically adds the specified flags to the keyInteractLevelAttr attribute of the Apple event. These flags are represented by constants and are described here.

Flag	Description
kAENeverInteract	The server application should never interact with the user in response to this Apple event. If this flag is set, AEInteractWithUser does not bring the server application to the foreground (this is the default when an Apple event is sent to a remote application).
kAECanInteract	The server application can interact with the user in response to this Apple event—by convention, if the user needs to supply information to the server. If this flag is set and the server allows interaction, AEInteractWithUser brings the server application to the foreground (this is the default when an Apple event is sent to a local application).
kAEAlwaysInteract	The server application can interact with the user in response to this Apple event—by convention, even if no information is needed from the user. If this flag is set and the server allows interaction, AEInteractWithUser brings the server application to the foreground. The Apple Event Manager does not distinguish between this flag and the kAECanInteract flag—distinguishing between them is the responsibility of the server application.

If the client application doesn't specify any of the user interface flags, the Apple Event Manager sets either the kAENeverInteract or the kAECanInteract flag in the keyInteractLevelAttr attribute of the Apple event, depending on the location of the server application. If the server application is on a remote computer, the Apple Event Manager sets the kAENeverInteract flag as the default. If the server application is on the local computer, the Apple Event Manager sets the kAECanInteract flag as the default.

In addition, the client application can set another flag in the sendMode parameter to AESend to request that the Apple Event Manager immediately bring the server application to the front (instead of posting a notification request)—if user interaction is allowed and if the user interface guidelines permit.

Flag	Description
kAECanSwitchLayer	If both the client and server allow interaction and this flag is set, AEInteractWithUser brings the server directly to the foreground if adherence to the principle of user control allows. If the action would be contrary to this principle, AEInteractWithUser uses the Notification Manager to request that the user bring the server application to the foreground. If both the client and server allow interaction and this flag is not set, AEInteractWithUser always uses the Notification Manager to request that the user bring the server application to the foreground.

When a server application calls AEInteractWithUser, the function first checks to see if the kAENeverInteract flag in the keyInteractLevelAttr attribute of the Apple event is set. (The Apple Event Manager sets this attribute according to the flags specified in the sendMode parameter of AESend.) If the kAENeverInteract flag is set, AEInteractWithUser immediately returns the errAENoUserInteraction result code. If the client specified kAECanInteract or kAEAlwaysInteract, AEInteractWithUser checks the server's preferences for user interaction.

The server sets its user interaction preferences by using the AESetInteractionAllowed function. You use this function to tell the Apple Event Manager the processes for which your application is willing to interact with the user.

```
myErr := AESetInteractionAllowed(level);
```

The level parameter is of type AEInteractAllowed.

```
TYPE  AEInteractAllowed = (kAEInteractWithSelf, kAEInteractWithLocal,
                           kAEInteractWithAll);
```

You can specify one of these values for the interaction level.

Flag	Description
kAEInteractWithSelf	User interaction with your server application in response to an Apple event may be allowed only when the client application is your own application—that is, only when your application is sending the Apple event to itself.
kAEInteractWithLocal	User interaction with your server application in response to an Apple event may be allowed only if the client application is on the same computer as your application; this is the default if the AESetInteractionAllowed function is not used.
kAEInteractWithAll	User interaction with your server application in response to an Apple event may be allowed for any client application on any computer.

If the server application does not set the user interaction level, AEInteractWithUser uses kAEInteractWithLocal as the value.

If the application sent itself an Apple event (that is, the application is both the client and the server), AEInteractWithUser always allows user interaction. If the client application is a process on the local machine, and the server set the interaction level to the kAEInteractWithLocal or kAEInteractWithAll flag, then AEInteractWithUser allows user interaction. If the client is a process on a remote computer on the network, AEInteractWithUser allows user interaction only if the server specified the kAEInteractWithAll flag for the interaction level. In all other cases, AEInteractWithUser does not allow user interaction.

When AEInteractWithUser allows user interaction (based on the client's and server's preferences), AEInteractWithUser brings the server application to the front—either directly or after the user responds to a notification request—and then returns a noErr result code.

If AEInteractWithUser cannot bring the server application to the front within the specified timeout value, AEInteractWithUser returns the errAETimeout result code.

Your application may want to provide the user with a method of setting the interaction level. For example, some users may not want to be interrupted while background processing of an Apple event occurs, or they may not want to respond to dialog boxes when your application is handling Apple events sent from another computer.

Listing 6-14 illustrates the use of the AEInteractWithUser function. You call this function before your application displays a dialog box or otherwise interacts with the user when processing an Apple event. You specify a timeout value, a pointer to a Notification Manager record, and the address of an idle function as parameters to AEInteractWithUser.

Listing 6-14. Using the AEInteractWithUser function

```
myErr := AEInteractWithUser (kAEDefaultTimeOut, NIL, @MyIdleFunction);
IF myErr <> noErr THEN
   {the attempt to interact failed, do any error handling}
   DoError(myErr)
ELSE
   {interact with the user by displaying a dialog box }
   { or by interacting in any other way that is necessary}
   DisplayMyDialogBox;
```

You can set a timeout value, in ticks, in the first parameter to AEInteractWithUser. Use the kAEDefaultTimeout constant if you want the Apple Event Manager to use a default value for the timeout value. The Apple Event Manager uses a timeout value of about one minute if you specify this constant. You can also specify the kNoTimeOut constant if your application is willing to wait an indefinite amount of time for a response from the user. Usually you should provide a timeout value, so that your application can complete processing of the Apple event in a reasonable amount of time.

You can provide a pointer to a Notification Manager record in the second parameter, or you can specify NIL to use the default record provided by AEInteractWithUser. The AEInteractWithUser function only uses a Notification Manager record when user interaction is allowed and the kAECanSwitchLayer flag in the keyInteractLevelAttr attribute is not set.

The last parameter to AEInteractWithUser specifies an idle function provided by your application. Your idle function should handle any update events, null events, operating-system events, or activate events while your application is waiting to be brought to the front. See "Writing an Idle Function" later in this chapter for more information.

Creating an Apple Event

You create an Apple event by using the AECreateAppleEvent function. You specify the event class and event ID, the target address, the return ID, and the transaction ID to the function. The AECreateAppleEvent function creates and returns an Apple event with the attributes set as your application requested. You should not directly manipulate the contents of the Apple event; rather, use Apple Event Manager functions to add additional attributes or parameters to it.

This example creates a Multiply event using the AECreateAppleEvent function. You specify the event class, the event ID, the address of the server application, a return ID, a transaction ID, and a buffer to store the returned Apple event as parameters to AECreateAppleEvent.

```
myErr := AECreateAppleEvent(kArithmeticClass, kMultEventID,
                            targetAddress, kAutoGenerateReturnID,
                            kAnyTransactionID, theAppleEvent);
```

The event class here is identified by the kArithmeticClass constant and specifies that this event belongs to a specific class of Apple events for arithmetic operations. The event ID specifies the particular Apple event within the class—in this case, an Apple event to perform multiplication.

You specify the target of the Apple event in the third parameter to AECreateAppleEvent. The target address can identify an application on the local computer or another computer on the network. You can specify the address using a target ID record or session ID. For processes on the local computer, you can also use a process serial number or application signature to specify the address. See "Specifying a Target Address" later in this chapter for more information.

You specify the return ID of the Apple event in the fourth parameter. The return ID provides a way to associate this Apple event with the server's reply. The AECreateAppleEvent function assigns the specified return ID value to the keyReturnIDAttr attribute of the Apple event. If a server returns an Apple event in response to this event, the server should use the same return ID. When you receive an Apple event, you can check the keyReturnIDAttr attribute to determine whether the event is a response to an outstanding Apple event. You can use the kAutoGenerateReturnID constant to request that the Apple Event Manager generate a return ID that is unique to this session for the Apple event.

The fifth parameter specifies the transaction ID attribute of the Apple event. A **transaction** refers to a sequence of Apple events that are sent back and forth between the client and server applications, beginning with the client's initial request for a service. All Apple events that are part of one transaction must have the same transaction ID.

You can use a transaction ID to indicate that an Apple event is one of a sequence of Apple events related to a single transaction. The kAnyTransactionID constant indicates that the Apple event is not part of a transaction.

The AECreateAppleEvent function creates an Apple event with only the specified attributes and no parameters. To add parameters or additional attributes, use other Apple Event Manager functions.

Adding Parameters to an Apple Event

You can use the AEPutParamPtr or AEPutParamDesc function to add parameters to an Apple event. When you use either of these functions, the Apple Event Manager adds the specified parameter to the Apple event.

Use the AEPutParamPtr function when you want to add data specified in a buffer as the parameter of an Apple event. You specify the Apple event, the keyword of the parameter to add, the descriptor type, a buffer that contains the data, and the size of this buffer as parameters to the AEPutParamPtr function. The AEPutParamPtr function creates the descriptor record and adds the parameter to the Apple event.

For example, this code adds a parameter to the Multiply event using the AEPutParamPtr function.

```
CONST keyOperand1 = 'OPN1';
VAR
   number1:         LongInt;
   theAppleEvent:   AppleEvent;
   myErr:           OSErr;

number1 := 10;
myErr := AEPutParamPtr(theAppleEvent, keyOperand1, typeLongInteger,
                       @number1, SizeOf(number1));
```

In this example, the Apple Event Manager adds the parameter containing the first number to the specified Apple event.

Use the AEPutParamDesc function to add data specified in a descriptor record to an Apple event. The descriptor record you specify must have been previously created using the AECreateDesc or AEDuplicateDesc function.

You specify the descriptor type, a buffer that contains the data, and the size of this buffer as parameters to the AECreateDesc function. The AECreateDesc function returns the descriptor record that describes the data.

This example creates a descriptor record for the second parameter of the Multiply event:

```
VAR
   number2:          LongInt;
   multParam2Desc:   AEDesc;
   myErr:            OSErr;

number2 := 8;
myErr := AECreateDesc(typeLongInteger, @number2, SizeOf(number2),
                      multParam2Desc);
```

In this example, the AECreateDesc function creates a descriptor record with the typeLongInteger descriptor type and the data identified in the number2 variable.

Once you have created a descriptor record, you can use AEPutParamDesc to add the data to a parameter of an Apple event. You specify the Apple event to add the parameter to, the keyword of the parameter, and the descriptor record of the parameter as parameters to the AEPutParamDesc function.

This example adds a second parameter to the Multiply event using the AEPutParamDesc function.

```
CONST keyOperand2 = 'OPN2';

myErr := AEPutParamDesc(theAppleEvent, keyOperand2, multParam2Desc);
```

This example adds the keyOperand2 keyword and the descriptor record created in the previous example as the second parameter to the specified Apple event.

The previous examples showed how to add parameters to the imaginary Multiply event. After adding parameters to an Apple event, you can send the Apple event using the AESend function. See "Sending an Apple Event" later in this chapter for information on using this function.

Specifying a Target Address

When you create an Apple event, you must specify the address of the target. The **target address** identifies the particular application or process that you want to send the Apple event to. You can send Apple events to applications on the local machine or on remote computers on the network.

These are the descriptor types that identify the four methods of addressing an Apple event.

typeApplSignature	The application signature of the target
typeSessionID	The session ID of the target
typeTargetID	The target ID record of the target
typeProcessSerialNumber	The process serial number of the target

To address an Apple event to a target on a remote computer on the network, you must use either the typeSessionID or typeTargetID descriptor type.

If your application sends an Apple event to itself, it should address the Apple event using a process serial number. Use the kCurrentProcess constant to specify the process serial number of your application. This is the fastest way for your application to send an Apple event to itself.

You can use any of the four address types when sending an Apple event to another application on the local computer. To allow the user to choose the target of an Apple event, use the PPCBrowser function. The PPCBrowser function presents a standard user interface for choosing a target application, much as the Standard File Package provides a standard user interface for opening and saving files.

The PPCBrowser function returns information about the application the user chose in a target ID record. (Listing 6-16 later in this section shows how to use the PPCBrowser function to let the user choose a target.)

The Event Manager chapter in this volume describes all four types of addresses. Your application can also use another address type, if it also provides a coercion handler that coerces the address type into one of the four address types that the Apple Event Manager recognizes. See "Writing and Installing Coercion Handlers" later in this chapter for more information.

You specify the address using an address descriptor record (a descriptor record of data type AEAddressDesc). You must create a descriptor record of this type and then supply the address descriptor record as a parameter to the AECreateAppleEvent function.

You can use the AECreateDesc function to add any of the four target addresses to an address descriptor record. Listing 6-15 shows four possible ways to create an address, each using a different address type.

Listing 6-15. Creating a target address

```
PROCEDURE SetTargetAddresses(VAR targetAddress1, targetAddress2,
                             targetAddress3, targetAddress4:
                             AEAddressDesc; toTargetID: TargetID;
                             thePSN: ProcessSerialNumber;
                             theSignature: OSType;
                             theSessionID: PPCSessRefNum);
VAR
   myErr: OSErr;

BEGIN
   myErr := AECreateDesc(typeTargetID, @toTargetID, SizeOf(toTargetID),
                         targetAddress1);
   myErr := AECreateDesc(typeProcessSerialNumber, @thePSN, SizeOf(thePSN),
                         targetAddress2);
   myErr := AECreateDesc(typeApplSignature, @theSignature,
                         SizeOf(theSignature), targetAddress3);
   myErr := AECreateDesc(typeSessionID, @theSessionID, SizeOf(theSessionID),
                         targetAddress4);
END;
```

You specify the descriptor type for the address, a pointer to the buffer containing the address, and the size of the buffer to the AECreateDesc function to create an address descriptor record. The AECreateDesc function returns an address descriptor record with the specified characteristics.

After creating an address, you can specify the address in the AECreateAppleEvent function. See "Creating an Apple Event" earlier in this chapter for an example using the AECreateAppleEvent function.

When you specify an address to the AECreateAppleEvent function, the Apple Event Manager stores the address in the keyAddressAttr attribute of the Apple event.

You can use the PPCBrowser function to create a target ID record. Listing 6-16 shows how to use the information returned from the PPCBrowser function to create a target ID record. You can then use AECreateDesc to create the address descriptor record for an Apple event.

Listing 6-16. Specifying a target address in an Apple event

```
FUNCTION GetTargetAddress(myPrompt: Str255; myAppStr: Str255;
                          VAR myPortInfo: PortInfoRec;
                          VAR targetAddress: AEAddressDesc;
                          VAR toTargetID: targetID) : OSErr;

VAR
   myErr: OSErr;
BEGIN       {use PPCBrowser to let user choose the target}
   myErr := PPCBrowser(myPrompt, myAppStr, FALSE, toTargetID.location,
                       myPortInfo, NIL, '');
   IF myErr <> noErr THEN
      DoError(myErr)
   ELSE
   BEGIN
   toTargetID.name := myPortInfo.name;
```

```
            {create the descriptor record for the target address}
   myErr := AECreateDesc(typeTargetID, @toTargetID,
                         SizeOf(toTargetID), targetAddress);
   IF myErr <> noErr THEN
      DoError(myErr);
   END;
   GetTargetAddress := myErr;
END;
```

See the Program-to-Program Communications Toolbox chapter in this volume for more information on using the PPCBrowser function.

Sending an Apple Event

To send an Apple event, you first create an Apple event, add parameters and attributes to the Apple event, and then use the AESend function to send it.

When you send an Apple event, you specify various options to indicate how the server should handle the Apple event. You request a user interaction level from the server and specify whether the server can directly switch to the foreground if user interaction is needed, whether your application is willing to wait for a reply Apple event, whether reconnection is allowed, and whether your application wants a return receipt for the Apple event.

You specify these options in the sendMode parameter to AESend. Here are the constants that represent these options.

```
CONST kAENoReply          = $00000001;       {client doesn't want reply}
      kAEQueueReply       = $00000002;       {client wants server to }
                                             { reply in event queue}
      kAEWaitReply        = $00000003;       {client wants a reply and }
                                             { will give up processor}
      kAENeverInteract    = $00000010;       {server application should }
                                             { not interact with user }
                                             { for this Apple event}
      kAECanInteract      = $00000020;       {server may interact with }
                                             { user for this Apple event }
                                             { to supply information}
      kAEAlwaysInteract   = $00000030;       {server may interact with }
                                             { user for this Apple event }
                                             { even if no information }
                                             { is required}
      kAECanSwitchLayer   = $00000040;       {server should come directly }
                                             { to foreground when }
                                             { appropriate}
      kAEDontReconnect    = $00000080;       {don't reconnect if there }
                                             { is a PPC sessClosedErr}
      kAEWantReceipt      = nReturnReceipt;  {client wants return receipt}
```

If your application wants a reply Apple event, specify the kAEQueueReply or kAEWaitReply flag. If your application wants to receive the reply Apple event in its event queue, use kAEQueueReply. If your application wants to receive the reply Apple event in the reply parameter of AESend and is willing to give up the processor while waiting for the reply, use kAEWaitReply. If your application does not want a reply Apple event and does not need to wait for the server to handle the Apple event, specify kNoReply.

In most cases, your application should use kAEWaitReply or kAENoReply. You should not use kAEQueueReply if your application is sending an Apple event to itself.

If your application specifies kAENoReply or kAEQueueReply, the AESend function returns immediately after using the Event Manager to send the event. In this case, a noErr result code from AESend indicates that the Apple event was successfully sent by the Event Manager; it does not mean that the server accepted or handled the Apple event.

Also, the reply parameter to AESend does not contain valid data on return from AESend if your application specifies kAENoReply or kAEQueueReply. The kAENoReply flag indicates that the Apple Event Manager will not return the reply Apple event to your application. The kAEQueueReply flag indicates that your application wants to receive the reply in its event queue rather than through the reply parameter of AESend.

If your application specifies kAEWaitReply, the Apple Event Manager uses the Event Manager to send the event. The Apple Event Manager then calls the WaitNextEvent function on behalf of your application, causing your application to yield the processor. This gives the server application a chance to receive and handle the Apple event. Your application continues to yield the processor until the server handles the Apple event or the request times out.

You use one of the three flags—kAENeverInteract, kAECanInteract, and kAEAlwaysInteract—to specify whether the server should interact with the user when handling the Apple event. Specify kAENeverInteract if the server should not interact with the user when handling the Apple event. You might specify this constant if you don't want the user to be interrupted while the server is handling the Apple event.

Use the kAECanInteract flag if the server should interact with the user when necessary—for example, if the user needs to supply information to the server. Use the kAEAlwaysInteract flag if the server should interact with the user even when no information is needed from the user. Note that it is the responsibility of the server and client applications to agree on how to interpret the kAEAlwaysInteract flag.

If the client application does not set any one of the user interaction flags, the Apple Event Manager sets a default, depending on the location of the target of the Apple event. If the server application is on a remote computer, the Apple Event Manager sets the kAENeverInteract flag as the default. If the target of the Apple event is on the local computer, the Apple Event Manager sets the kAECanInteract flag as the default.

The server application should call AEInteractWithUser if it needs to interact with the user. If user interaction is allowed, the Apple Event Manager brings the server to the front if it is not already the foreground process. If the kAECanSwitchLayer flag is set and the principle of user control permits, the Apple Event Manager directly brings the server application to the front. If the action is contrary to the principle of user control, the Apple Event Manager posts a notification request to inform the user to bring the server application to the front.

You should specify the kAECanSwitchLayer flag only when the client and server applications reside on the same computer. In general, you should not set this flag if it would be confusing or inconvenient to the user for the server application to unexpectedly come to the front.

Specify the kAEDontReconnect flag if the Apple Event Manager should not reconnect if it receives a session closed error from the PPC Toolbox. If you don't set this flag, the Apple Event Manager automatically attempts to reconnect and reestablish the session.

Specify the kAEWantReceipt flag if your application wants notification that the server did not accept the Apple event. If you specify this flag, the AESend function returns the errAEEventNotHandled result code if the server did not accept the Apple event.

Listing 6-17 illustrates how to send a Multiply event (an imaginary Apple event for multiplying two long integers). It first creates an Apple event, adds parameters containing the numbers to multiply, then sends it, specifying various options. It also illustrates how to handle the reply Apple event that contains the result.

> **Note:** If you want to send Apple events, your application must also handle the required Apple events. See "Handling the Required Apple Events" earlier in this chapter for information on how to support the required Apple events.

Listing 6-17. Sending an Apple event

```
FUNCTION MySendMultiplyEvent (serverAddress: AEAddressDesc;
                              firstOperand: LongInt; secondOperand:
                              LongInt; replyResultLongInt: LongInt)
                              : OSErr;
CONST
   kArithmeticClass   =  'ARTH';   {event class for arithmetic Apple events}
   kMultiplyEventID   =  'MULT';   {event ID for Multiply event}
   keyMultOperand1    =  'OPN1';   {keyword for first parameter}
   keyMultOperand2    =  'OPN2';   {keyword for second parameter}

VAR
   theAppleEvent:     AppleEvent;
   reply:             AppleEvent;
   returnedType:      DescType;
   actualSize:        LongInt;
   myErr:             OSErr;
   errStr:            Str255;
   errNumber:         LongInt;
BEGIN
   myErr := AECreateAppleEvent(kArithmeticClass, kMultiplyEventID,
                               serverAddress, kAutoGenerateReturnID,
                               kAnyTransactionID, theAppleEvent);
   IF myErr <> noErr THEN
      DoError(myErr); {failed to create the event}
   {add the first operand}
   myErr := AEPutParamPtr(theAppleEvent, keyMultOperand1,
                          typeLongInteger, @firstOperand,
                          SizeOf(firstOperand));
   IF myErr <> noErr THEN
      DoError(myErr);   {failed to add first parameter--be sure to}
                        { dispose of the event before leaving routine}
   {add the second operand with the proper keyword}
   myErr := AEPutParamPtr(theAppleEvent, keyMultOperand2,
                          typeLongInteger, @secondOperand,
                          SizeOf(secondOperand));
   IF myErr <> noErr THEN
      DoError(myErr);   {be sure to dispose of the event and first }
                        { parameter before leaving routine}
   myErr := AESend(theAppleEvent, reply, kAEWaitReply + kAENeverInteract,
                   kAENormalPriority, 120, @myIdleFunction, NIL);
```

(Continued)

Listing 6-17. Sending an Apple event (Continued)

```
   IF myErr = noErr THEN {Apple event successfully sent}
   BEGIN       {check if it was successfully handled-- }
               { get result code returned by the server's handler}
      myErr := AEGetParamPtr(reply, keyErrorNumber, typeLongInteger,
                             returnedType, @errNumber,
                             Sizeof(errNumber), actualSize);
      IF (myErr = errAEDescNotFound) | (errNumber = noErr) THEN
         {if keyErrorNumber doesn't exist or server returned noErr }
      BEGIN          { then the Apple event was successfully handled-- }
                     { the reply Apple event contains the result in }
                     { the direct parameter}
         myErr := AEGetParamPtr(reply, keyDirectObject, typeInteger,
                                returnedType, @replyResultLongInt,
                                SizeOf(replyResultLongInt), actualSize);
         MySendMultiplyEvent := noErr;
         Exit(MySendMultiplyEvent);
      END
      ELSE
      BEGIN       {server returned an error, so get error string}
         myErr := AEGetParamPtr(reply, keyErrorString, typeChar,
                                returnedType, @errStr,
                                Sizeof(errStr), actualSize);
         IF myErr = noErr THEN
            MyDisplayError(errStr);
      END;
   END
   ELSE
   BEGIN
   {the Apple event wasn't successfully dispatched, }
   { the request timed out, the user canceled, or other error}
   END;
MySendMultiplyEvent := myErr;
END;
```

The code in Listing 6-17 first creates an Apple event with kArithmeticClass as the event class and kMultiplyEventID as the event ID. It also specifies the server of the Apple event. See "Specifying a Target Address" earlier in this chapter for information on various ways to specify a target address. See "Creating an Apple Event" earlier in this chapter for more information on how to create an Apple event.

The Multiply event shown in Listing 6-17 contains two parameters, each of which specifies a number to multiply. See "Adding Parameters to an Apple Event" earlier in this chapter for examples of how to specify the parameters for the AEPutParamPtr function.

After adding the parameters to the event, the code uses AESend to send the event. The first parameter to AESend specifies the Apple event to send—in this example, the Multiply event. The next parameter specifies the reply Apple event.

This example specifies kAEWaitReply in the third parameter, indicating that the client is willing to yield the processor for the specified timeout value (120 ticks, or 2 seconds). The kAENeverInteract flag indicates that the server should not interact with the user when processing the Apple event. The Multiply event is sent using normal priority, meaning it is placed at the end of the event queue. You can specify the kAEHighPriority flag to place the event in the front of the event queue.

The next to last parameter specifies the address of an idle function. If you specify kAEWaitReply you should provide an idle function. This function should process any update events, null events, operating-system events, or activate events that occur while your application is waiting for a reply. See "Writing an Idle Function" later in this chapter for sample code that shows an idle function.

The last parameter to AESend specifies a filter function. You can supply a filter function to filter high-level events that your application might receive while waiting for a reply Apple event. You can specify NIL for this parameter if you do not need to filter high-level events while waiting for a reply. See "Writing a Reply Filter Function" later in this chapter for more information.

If AESend returns a noErr result code and your application specified kAEWaitReply, you should first see whether a result code was returned from the handler routine by checking the reply Apple event for the existence of the parameter whose keyword is keyErrorNumber. If the keyErrorNumber parameter does not exist or contains the noErr result code, you can use AEGetParamPtr to get the parameter you're interested in from the reply Apple event.

The code in Listing 6-17 checks the function result of AESend. If AESend returns noErr, the code then checks the replyErrorNumber parameter of the reply Apple event to determine whether the server successfully handled the Apple event. If this parameter exists and indicates that an error occurred, then the code gets the error string out of the keyErrorString parameter. Otherwise, the server performed the request, and the reply Apple event contains the answer to the multiplication request.

When you are done using the Apple event specified in the AESend function and finished with the reply Apple event, you must dispose of their descriptor records using the AEDisposeDesc function.

Dealing With Timeouts

When your application calls AESend and chooses to wait for the server to handle the Apple event, it can also specify the maximum amount of time that it is willing to wait for a response. You can specify a timeout value in the timeOutInTicks parameter to AESend. You can either specify a particular length of time, in ticks, that your application is willing to wait, or you can specify the kNoTimeOut constant or the kAEDefaultTimeout constant.

Use the kNoTimeOut constant to indicate that your application is willing to wait forever for a response from the server. You should use this value only if your application is guaranteed that the server will respond in a reasonable amount of time. You should also implement a method of checking if the user wants to cancel. The idle function that you specify as a parameter to AESend should check the event queue for any instances of Command-period and immediately return TRUE as its function result if it finds a request to cancel in the event queue.

Use the kAEDefaultTimeout constant if you want the Apple Event Manager to use a default value for the timeout value. The Apple Event Manager uses a timeout value of about one minute if you specify this constant.

Note that if you set the kAEWaitReply flag and the server doesn't have a handler for the Apple event, AESend returns immediately with the errAEEventNotHandled result code.

If the server doesn't respond within the length of time specified by the timeout value, AESend returns the errAETimeout result code. This result code does not necessarily mean that the server failed to perform the requested action; it only means that the server did not complete processing within the specified time. The server might still be processing the Apple event, and it might still send a reply.

If the server finishes processing the Apple event sometime after the time specified in the timeout parameter has expired, it returns a reply Apple event to AEProcessAppleEvent. The Apple Event Manager then returns the reply to the client in the reply parameter that the client originally passed to the AESend function.

This means your application can continue to check the reply Apple event to see if the server has responded, even after the time expires. If the server has not yet sent the reply when the client attempts to extract data from the reply Apple event, the Apple Event Manager functions return the errAEReplyNotArrived result code. Once the reply Apple event returns from the server, the client can extract the data in the reply.

Additionally, the server can determine the timeout value specified by the client by examining the keyTimeoutAttr attribute in the Apple event. You can use the value of this attribute as a rough estimate of how much time your handler has to respond. You can assume that your handler has less time to respond than the timeout value, because transmitting the Apple event uses some of the available time, as does transmitting the reply Apple event back to the client.

If your handler needs more time than is specified in the keyTimeoutAttr attribute, you can reset the timer by using the AEResetTimer function. This function resets the timeout value of an Apple event to its starting value.

Writing an Idle Function

This section describes how to write an idle function when using the AESend or AEInteractWithUser function.

When your application sends an Apple event, you can wait for the server application to receive and finish handling the Apple event, or you can continue processing. If your application chooses to continue processing, the AESend function returns immediately after using the Event Manager to send the event. If your application chooses to wait for the server to handle the event, the AESend function does not return until either the server application finishes handling the Apple event or a specified amount of time expires.

Your application specifies its preferences by setting flags in the sendMode parameter to AESend. Your application can specify kAENoReply if it does not want to receive a reply, kAEQueueReply if it wants to receive the reply in its event queue, or kAEWaitReply if it wants the reply returned in the reply parameter of AESend and is willing to give up the processor while waiting for the reply.

If your application specifies the kAEWaitReply flag, the AESend function calls WaitNextEvent on behalf of your application. This yields the processor to other processes, so that the server has an opportunity to receive and process the Apple event sent by your application. While your application is waiting for a reply, it cannot receive events unless it provides an idle function.

If your application provides a pointer to an idle function as a parameter to the AESend function, AESend calls your idle function whenever an update event, null event, operating-system event, or activate event is received for your application. Your application can process high-level events that it receives while waiting for a reply by providing a reply filter function. See the next section, "Writing a Reply Filter Function," for more information.

In a similar manner, when your application calls the AEInteractWithUser function, your application can also yield the processor. If AEInteractWithUser needs to post a notification request to bring your application to the front, your application yields the processor until the user brings your application to the front. To receive events while waiting for the user to bring your application to the front, you must provide an idle function.

If your application provides a pointer to an idle function as a parameter to the AEInteractWithUser function, AEInteractWithUser calls your idle function whenever an update event, null event, operating-system event, or activate event is received for your application.

An idle function must use this syntax:

```
FUNCTION MyIdleFunction (VAR theEventRecord: EventRecord;
                         VAR sleepTime: LongInt;
                         VAR mouseRgn: RgnHandle) : Boolean;
```

The parameter theEventRecord is the event record of the event to process. The sleepTime parameter and mouseRgn parameter are values that your idle function sets the first time it is called; thereafter they contain the values your function set. Your idle function should return a Boolean value that indicates whether your application wishes to continue waiting. Set the function result to TRUE if your application is no longer willing to wait for a reply from the server or for the user to bring the application to the front. Set the function result to FALSE if your application is still willing to wait.

The first time your idle function is called, it receives a null event. At this time, you should set the values for the sleepTime and mouseRgn parameters. These parameters are used in the same way as the sleep and mouseRgn parameters of the WaitNextEvent function. Specify in the sleepTime parameter the amount of time (in ticks) during which your application agrees to relinquish the processor if no events are pending for it.

In the mouseRgn parameter, you specify a screen region that determines the conditions in which your application is to receive notice of mouse-moved events. Your idle function receives mouse-moved events only if your application is the front application and the mouse strays outside the region you specify.

Your idle function receives only update events, null events, operating-system events, and activate events. When your idle function receives a null event, it can use the idle time to update status reports, animate cursors, or perform similar tasks. If your idle function receives any of the other events, it should handle the event as it normally would if received in its event loop.

Listing 6-18 shows an example of an idle function that can be used as an idle function for AESend or AEInteractWithUser. The idle function processes update events, null events, operating-system events, and activate events. The first time the function is called it receives a null event. At this time, it sets the sleepTime and mouseRgn parameters. The function continues to process events until the server finishes handling the Apple event or the user brings the application to the front.

Your application should implement a method of checking to see if the user wants to cancel. The MyCancelInQueue function in Listing 6-18 checks the event queue for any instances of Command-period and immediately returns TRUE as its function result if it finds a request to cancel in the event queue.

Listing 6-18. An idle function

```
FUNCTION MyIdleFunction (VAR event: EventRecord;
                         VAR sleepTime: LongInt;
                         VAR mouseRgn: RgnHandle) : Boolean;
VAR
   hiByte: CHAR;
   myErr:  OSErr;
BEGIN
   MyIdleFunction := FALSE;
{the MyCancelInQueue function checks the event queue for Command-period}
   IF MyCancelInQueue THEN
      BEGIN
         MyIdleFunction := TRUE;
         Exit(MyIdleFunction);
      END;
   CASE event.what OF
      updateEvt,
      activateEvt,   {every idle function should handle these kinds }
      kOSEvent:      { of events}
         BEGIN
            AdjustCursor(event.where, gCursorRgn);
            DoEvent(event);
         END;
      nullEvent:
         BEGIN
            {set the sleepTime and mouseRgn parameters}
            mouseRgn := gCursorRgn;
            sleeptime := 10;  {use the correct value for your app}
            DoIdle;           {the application's idle handling}
         END
      END; {CASE}
END;
```

Writing a Reply Filter Function

If your application calls AESend and chooses to yield the processor to other processes while waiting for a reply, you can provide an idle function to process update, null, operating-system, and activate events and, additionally, you can provide a reply filter function to process high-level events. The previous section describes how an idle function processes events.

Your reply filter function can process any high-level events that it is willing to handle while waiting for a reply Apple event. For example, your application can choose to handle Apple events from other processes while waiting. Note, however, that your application must maintain any necessary state information. Your reply filter function must not accept any Apple events that can change the state of your application and make it impossible to return to its previous state.

A reply filter function must use this syntax:

```
FUNCTION MyWaitReplyFilter (VAR theEventRecord: EventRecord;
                           returnID: LongInt; transactionID: LongInt;
                           sender: AEAddressDesc) : Boolean;
```

The parameter theEventRecord is the event record for a high-level event. The next three parameters contain valid information only if the event is an Apple event. The transactionID parameter is the transaction ID for the Apple event. The returnID parameter is the return ID for the Apple event. The sender parameter contains the address of the application or process that sent the Apple event.

Your reply filter function should return TRUE as the function result if you want to accept the Apple event; otherwise it should return FALSE. If your filter function returns TRUE, the Apple Event Manager calls the AEProcessAppleEvent function on behalf of your application, and your handler routine is called to process the Apple event.

Writing and Installing Coercion Handlers

When your application extracts data from a parameter, it can request that the Apple Event Manager return the data using a descriptor type that is different from the original descriptor type. For example, when extracting data from the direct parameter of the Open Documents event, you can request that the alias records be returned as file system specification records. The Apple Event Manager can automatically coerce many different types of data from one to another. Table 6-1 later in this section shows descriptor types and the sorts of coercion that the Apple Event Manager can perform.

You can also provide your own routines, referred to as **coercion handlers,** to coerce other descriptor types. To install your own coercion handlers, use the AEInstallCoercionHandler function. You specify as parameters to this function

- the descriptor type of the data coerced by the handler
- the descriptor type of the resulting data
- the address of the coercion handler for this descriptor type
- a reference constant
- a Boolean value that indicates whether your coercion handler expects the data to be specified as a descriptor record or as a pointer to the actual data
- a Boolean value that indicates whether your coercion handler should be added to your application's coercion table or the system coercion table

The **system coercion table** is a table in the system heap that contains handlers that are available to all applications and processes running on the same computer. The handlers in your application's coercion table are available only to your application. When the Apple Event Manager is attempting to coerce data, it first looks for a coercion handler in your application's coercion table. If it cannot find a handler for the descriptor type, it looks in the system coercion table for a handler. If it doesn't find a handler there either, it returns the errAEHandlerNotFound result code.

If you add a handler to the system coercion table, the handler that you specify must reside in the system heap. If there was already an entry in the system coercion table for the same descriptor type, it is replaced. Therefore, if there is an entry in the system coercion table for the same descriptor type, you should chain it to your system handler as explained in "Creating and Managing the Coercion Handler Tables" later in this chapter.

> **Note:** When an application calls a system coercion handler, the A5 register is set up for the calling application. For this reason, if you provide a system coercion handler, it should never use A5 global variables or anything that depends on a particular context; otherwise, the application that calls the system coercion handler may crash.

You can provide a coercion handler that expects to receive the data in a descriptor record or a buffer referred to by a pointer. When you install your coercion handler, you specify how your handler wishes to receive the data. It's more efficient for the Apple Event Manager to provide your coercion handler with a pointer to the data so, whenever possible, you should write your coercion handler so that it can accept a pointer to the data.

A coercion handler that accepts a pointer to data must be a function with the following syntax:

```
FUNCTION MyCoercePtr (typeCode: DescType; dataPtr: Ptr; dataSize: Size;
                      toType: DescType; handlerRefcon: LongInt;
                      VAR result: AEDesc) : OSErr;
```

The typeCode parameter is the descriptor type of the original data. The dataPtr parameter is a pointer to the data to coerce; the dataSize parameter is the length, in bytes, of the data. The toType parameter is the desired descriptor type of the resulting data. The handlerRefcon parameter is a reference constant that is stored in the coercion table entry for the handler and passed to the handler by the Apple Event Manager whenever the handler is called. The result parameter is the resulting descriptor record returned by your coercion handler.

Your coercion handler should coerce the data to the desired descriptor type and return the resulting data in the descriptor record specified by the result parameter. Your handler should return the noErr result code if your handler successfully performs the coercion, and a nonzero result code otherwise.

A coercion handler that accepts a descriptor record must be a function with the following syntax:

```
FUNCTION MyCoerceDesc (theAEDesc: AEDesc; toType: DescType;
                       handlerRefcon: LongInt;
                       VAR result: AEDesc) : OSErr;
```

The parameter theAEDesc is the descriptor record that contains the data to be coerced. The toType parameter is the descriptor type of the resulting data. The handlerRefcon parameter is a reference constant that is stored in the coercion table entry for the handler and passed to the handler by the Apple Event Manager whenever the handler is called. The result parameter is the resulting descriptor record.

Your coercion handler should coerce the data in the descriptor record to the desired descriptor type and return the resulting data in the descriptor record specified by the result parameter. Your handler should return an appropriate result code.

Table 6-1 lists the descriptor types that the Apple Event Manager provides coercion for. The first column shows the descriptor type of the data to be coerced, and the second column shows the descriptor types that the Apple Event Manager can coerce it to.

Note: For many Apple Event Manager functions, the Apple Event Manager attempts to coerce data to the descriptor type you specify even if the result is no longer meaningful. To ensure that no coercion is performed and that the descriptor type of the result is of the same descriptor type as the original, specify typeWildCard for the desired type.

Table 6-1. Coercion handling provided by the Apple Event Manager

Original descriptor type	Desired descriptor type	Description
typeChar	typeInteger typeLongInteger typeSMInt typeSMFloat typeShortInteger typeLongFloat typeShortFloat typeExtended typeComp typeMagnitude	Any string that is a valid representation of a number can be coerced into an equivalent numeric value.
typeInteger typeLongInteger typeSMInt typeSMFloat typeShortInteger typeLongFloat typeShortFloat typeExtended typeComp typeMagnitude	typeChar	Any numeric descriptor type can be coerced into the equivalent text string.
typeInteger typeLongInteger typeSMInt typeSMFloat typeShortInteger typeLongFloat typeShortFloat typeExtended typeComp typeMagnitude	typeInteger typeLongInteger typeSMInt typeSMFloat typeShortInteger typeLongFloat typeShortFloat typeExtended typeComp typeMagnitude	Any numeric descriptor type can be coerced into any other numeric descriptor type.
typeTrue	typeBoolean	The result is the Boolean value TRUE.
typeFalse	typeBoolean	The result is the Boolean value FALSE.

(Continued)

Table 6-1. Coercion handling provided by the Apple Event Manager (Continued)

Original descriptor type	Desired descriptor type	Description
typeEnumerated	typeBoolean	The enumerated value 'true' becomes the Boolean value TRUE. The enumerated value 'fals' becomes the Boolean value FALSE.
typeBoolean	typeEnumerated	The Boolean value FALSE becomes the enumerated value 'fals'. The Boolean value TRUE becomes the enumerated value 'true'.
typeShortInteger	typeBoolean	A value of 1 becomes the Boolean value TRUE. A value of 0 becomes the Boolean value FALSE.
typeBoolean	typeShortInteger	A value of FALSE becomes 0. A value of TRUE becomes 1.
typeAlias	typeFSS	An alias record is coerced into a file system specification record.
typeAppleEvent	typeAppParameters	An Apple event is coerced into a list of application parameters for the LaunchParamBlockRec parameter block.
any descriptor type	typeAEList	A descriptor record is coerced into a descriptor list containing a single item.
typeAEList	*type of list item*	A descriptor list containing a single descriptor record is coerced into a descriptor record.

The Application Died Event

If an application launched by your application terminates, either normally or as the result of an error, the Process Manager can notify your application by sending it an Apple event—the Application Died event. To receive this notification, you must set the acceptAppDied flag in your application's 'SIZE' resource. (For a complete description of the 'SIZE' resource, see the Event Manager chapter in this volume.) See the Process Management chapter in this volume for information on how your application can launch other applications.

Application Died—inform that an application has terminated

Event class	kCoreEventClass
Event ID	kAEApplicationDied
Required parameters	
Keyword:	keyErrorNumber
Descriptor type:	typeLongInteger
Data:	A sign-extended OSErr value. A value of noErr indicates normal termination; any other value indicates that the application terminated due to an error.
Keyword:	keyProcessSerialNumber
Descriptor type:	typeProcessSerialNumber
Data:	The process serial number of the application that terminated.
Requested action	None. This Apple event is sent only to provide information.

The Process Manager gets the value of the keyErrorNumber parameter from the system global variable DSErrCode. This value can be set either by the application before it terminates or by the Operating System (which can occur as the result of a hardware exception or other problem).

APPLE EVENT MANAGER ROUTINES

This section describes the routines you use to manage Apple event dispatch tables, process Apple events, get parameters and attributes from Apple events, get data from Apple event data structures, create Apple event data structures, add parameters and attributes to Apple events, send Apple events, get information about and delete descriptor records, and coerce descriptor types. Result codes appear at the end of each function as applicable.

Creating and Managing the Apple Event Dispatch Tables

An Apple event dispatch table contains entries that specify the event class and event ID that refer to one or more Apple events, the address of the handler routine that handles those Apple events, and a reference constant. You use the AEInstallEventHandler function to add entries to the Apple event dispatch table. Using this function sets up the initial mapping between the handlers in your application and the Apple events that they handle.

If you need to remove any of your Apple event handlers after this mapping is established, you can use the AERemoveEventHandler function. To get the address of a handler currently in the Apple event dispatch table, use the AEGetEventHandler function.

You use the AEInstallEventHandler function to add an entry to either the application or the system Apple event dispatch table.

To create an entry in the Apple event dispatch table, supply the event class, event ID, and address of the handler routine that handles Apple events of the specified event class and event ID. You also specify a reference constant that the Apple Event Manager passes to your handler routine whenever your handler processes an Apple event.

```
FUNCTION AEInstallEventHandler (theAEEventClass: AEEventClass;
                                theAEEventID: AEEventID; handler:
                                EventHandlerProcPtr; handlerRefcon:
                                LongInt; isSysHandler: Boolean) : OSErr;
```

The parameters theAEEventClass and theAEEventID specify the event class and event ID of the Apple events to be handled by the handler for this dispatch table entry. For these parameters, you must provide one of the following combinations:

- the event class and event ID of a single Apple event to be dispatched to the handler for this dispatch table entry
- the typeWildCard constant for theAEEventClass and an event ID for theAEEventID, which indicates that Apple events from all event classes whose event IDs match theAEEventID should be dispatched to the handler for this dispatch table entry
- an event class for theAEEventClass and the typeWildCard constant for theAEEventID, which indicates that all events from the event class theAEEventClass should be dispatched to the handler for this dispatch table entry
- the typeWildCard constant for both the parameters theAEEventClass and theAEEventID, which specifies that all Apple events should be dispatched to the handler for this dispatch table entry

The handler parameter is a pointer to an Apple event handler for this dispatch table entry. Note that a handler in the system dispatch table must reside in the system heap; this means that if the value of the isSysHandler parameter is TRUE, the handler parameter should point to a location in the system heap. Otherwise, if you put your system handler code in your application heap, you must remove the handler when your application quits by using the AERemoveEventHandler function.

The handlerRefcon parameter is a reference constant that is passed by the Apple Event Manager to the handler each time the handler is called. If your handler doesn't use a reference constant, use 0 as the value of this parameter.

The isSysHandler parameter specifies the Apple event dispatch table to which you want to add the handler. If the value of isSysHandler is TRUE, the Apple Event Manager adds the handler to the system Apple event dispatch table. Entries in the system Apple event dispatch table are available to all applications. If the value of isSysHandler is FALSE, the Apple Event Manager adds the handler to your application's Apple event dispatch table. The application Apple event dispatch table is searched first; the system Apple event dispatch table is searched only if the necessary handler is not found in your application's Apple event dispatch table.

If there was already an entry in the specified event handler table for the same event class and event ID, it is replaced. Therefore, before installing a handler for a particular Apple event into the system dispatch table, use the AEGetEventHandler function to determine whether the table already contains a handler for that event. If an entry exists, AEGetEventHandler returns a reference constant and a pointer to that event handler. Chain these to your event handler by providing pointers to the previous handler and its reference constant in the handlerRefcon parameter of AEInstallEventHandler. When your handler is finished, use these pointers to call the previous handler. If you remove your system handler, be sure to reinstall the chained handlers.

Note: When an application calls a system Apple event handler, the A5 register is set up for the calling application. For this reason, if you provide a system Apple event handler, it should never use A5 global variables or anything that depends on a particular context; otherwise, the application that calls the system handler may crash.

Result codes

noErr	0	No error
paramErr	–50	Parameter error (handler pointer is NIL or odd)
memFullErr	–108	Not enough room in heap zone

The AEGetEventHandler function gets an entry from an Apple event dispatch table.

```
FUNCTION AEGetEventHandler (theAEEventClass: AEEventClass; theAEEventID:
                            AEEventID; VAR handler: EventHandlerProcPtr;
                            VAR handlerRefcon: LongInt; isSysHandler:
                            Boolean) : OSErr;
```

The parameter theAEEventClass is the value of the event class field of the dispatch table entry for the desired Apple event handler, and the parameter theAEEventID is the value of the event ID field of the dispatch table entry for the desired Apple event handler. You can use the typeWildCard constant for either or both of these parameters. (For an explanation of wildcard values, see the earlier description of the AEInstallEventHandler function.)

In the handler parameter, the AEGetEventHandler function returns a pointer to the Apple event handler.

In the handlerRefcon parameter, the AEGetEventHandler function returns the reference constant that is passed by the Apple Event Manager to the Apple event handler each time the handler is called.

The isSysHandler parameter specifies the Apple event dispatch table from which to get the handler. If isSysHandler is TRUE, the AEGetEventHandler function returns the handler from the system dispatch table. If isSysHandler is FALSE, AEGetEventHandler returns the handler from your application's dispatch table.

Result codes

noErr	0	No error
errAEHandlerNotFound	–1717	No handler found for an Apple event

The AERemoveEventHandler function removes an entry from an Apple event dispatch table.

```
FUNCTION AERemoveEventHandler (theAEEventClass: AEEventClass;
                               theAEEventID: AEEventID; handler:
                               EventHandlerProcPtr; isSysHandler:
                               Boolean) : OSErr;
```

The parameter theAEEventClass is the event class for the handler to be removed. The parameter theAEEventID is the event ID for the handler to be removed. You can use the typeWildCard constant for either or both of these parameters. (For an explanation of wildcard values, see the earlier description of the AEInstallEventHandler function.)

The handler parameter is a pointer to the Apple event handler to be removed. Although the parameters theAEEventClass and theAEEventID would be sufficient to identify the handler to be removed, providing the handler parameter is a safeguard that ensures that you're removing the correct handler.

The isSysHandler parameter specifies the Apple event dispatch table from which to remove the handler. If isSysHandler is TRUE, AERemoveEventHandler removes the handler from the system dispatch table. If isSysHandler is FALSE, AERemoveEventHandler removes the handler from your application's dispatch table.

Result codes

noErr	0	No error
errAEHandlerNotFound	–1717	No handler found for an Apple event

Dispatching Apple Events

After receiving a high-level event (and optionally checking whether it is a type of high-level event other than an Apple event that your application might support), your application typically calls the AEProcessAppleEvent function to determine the type of Apple event received and to call the corresponding handler routine.

The AEProcessAppleEvent function looks first in the application Apple event dispatch table and then in the system Apple event dispatch table for an entry that matches the event class and event ID of the specified Apple event. If AEProcessAppleEvent finds a matching entry, it calls the handler for that Apple event.

```
FUNCTION AEProcessAppleEvent (theEventRecord: EventRecord) : OSErr;
```

The parameter theEventRecord is the event record for the Apple event.

If the AEProcessAppleEvent function cannot find a handler for an Apple event in either the application or system Apple event dispatch table, the Apple Event Manager returns the result code errAEEventNotHandled to the server application (as the result of the AEProcessAppleEvent function). The Apple Event Manager also returns this result code to the client application if the client is waiting for a reply.

Result codes

noErr	0	No error
memFullErr	–108	Not enough room in heap zone
bufferIsSmall	–607	Buffer is too small
noOutstandingHLE	–608	No outstanding high-level event
errAECorruptData	–1702	Data in an Apple event could not be read
errAENewerVersion	–1706	Need a newer version of the Apple Event Manager
errAENotAppleEvent	–1707	Event is not an Apple event
errAEEventNotHandled	–1708	Event wasn't handled by an Apple event handler

Getting Parameters and Attributes From Apple Events

You use the AEGetParamPtr and AEGetParamDesc functions to gain access to the parameters of an Apple event. You use the AEGetAttributePtr and AEGetAttributeDesc functions to gain access to the attributes of an Apple event.

The AEGetParamPtr function uses a buffer to return the data contained in a specified parameter of an Apple event.

```
FUNCTION AEGetParamPtr (theAppleEvent: AppleEvent; theAEKeyword:
                         AEKeyword; desiredType: DescType; VAR typeCode:
                         DescType; dataPtr: Ptr; maximumSize: Size;
                         VAR actualSize: Size) : OSErr;
```

The parameter theAppleEvent is the Apple event containing the desired parameter.

The parameter theAEKeyword is the keyword that specifies the desired parameter.

The desiredType parameter specifies the descriptor type of the resulting data; if the desired parameter is not of this type, the Apple Event Manager attempts to coerce it into this type. If the value of desiredType is typeWildCard, no coercion is performed, and the descriptor type of the returned data is the same as the descriptor type of the parameter. The returned data's descriptor type is returned in the typeCode parameter.

The dataPtr parameter is a pointer to the buffer for storing the returned data.

The maximumSize parameter is the maximum length, in bytes, of the data to be returned. You must allocate at least this amount of storage for the buffer specified by the dataPtr parameter.

The AEGetParamPtr function returns in the actualSize parameter the actual length, in bytes, of the data for the Apple event parameter. If this value is larger than the value of maximumSize, not all of the data for the Apple event parameter was returned.

Result codes

noErr	0	No error
memFullErr	–108	Not enough room in heap zone
errAECoercionFail	–1700	Data could not be coerced to the requested descriptor type
errAEDescNotFound	–1701	Descriptor record was not found
errAEWrongDataType	–1703	Wrong descriptor type
errAENotAEDesc	–1704	Not a valid descriptor record
errAEReplyNotArrived	–1718	Reply has not yet arrived

The AEGetParamDesc function returns the descriptor record for an Apple event parameter.

```
FUNCTION AEGetParamDesc (theAppleEvent: AppleEvent; theAEKeyword:
                          AEKeyword; desiredType: DescType;
                          VAR result: AEDesc) : OSErr;
```

The parameter theAppleEvent is the Apple event containing the desired parameter.

The parameter theAEKeyword is the keyword that specifies the desired parameter.

The desiredType parameter specifies the descriptor type of the resulting descriptor record; if the parameter is not of this type, the Apple Event Manager attempts to coerce it into this type. If the value of desiredType is typeWildCard, no coercion is performed, and the descriptor type of the resulting descriptor record is the same as the descriptor type of the Apple event's parameter.

The AEGetParamDesc function returns in the result parameter the resulting descriptor record. This function creates a new descriptor record by copying the descriptor record from the parameter. Your application is responsible for using the AEDisposeDesc function to dispose of the resulting descriptor record once you are finished using it.

If the function returns a nonzero result code, a descriptor record with the typeNull descriptor type is returned. A descriptor record of this type does not contain any data.

Result codes

noErr	0	No error
memFullErr	–108	Not enough room in heap zone
errAECoercionFail	–1700	Data could not be coerced to the requested descriptor type
errAEDescNotFound	–1701	Descriptor type was not found
errAENotAEDesc	–1704	Not a valid descriptor record
errAEReplyNotArrived	–1718	Reply has not yet arrived

The AEGetAttributePtr function uses a buffer to return the data contained in an Apple event attribute.

```
FUNCTION AEGetAttributePtr (theAppleEvent: AppleEvent; theAEKeyword:
                            AEKeyword; desiredType: DescType;
                            VAR typeCode: DescType; dataPtr: Ptr;
                            maximumSize: Size; VAR actualSize:
                            Size) : OSErr;
```

The parameter theAppleEvent is the Apple event containing the desired attribute.

The parameter theAEKeyword is the keyword that specifies the desired attribute.

The desiredType parameter is the descriptor type of the data to be returned; if the desired attribute is not of this type, the Apple Event Manager attempts to coerce it into this type. If the value of desiredType is typeWildCard, no coercion is performed, and the descriptor type of the returned data is the same as the descriptor type of the attribute. The returned data's descriptor type is returned in the typeCode parameter.

The dataPtr parameter is a pointer to the buffer for storing the data that is returned.

The maximumSize parameter is the maximum length, in bytes, of the data to be returned.

The AEGetAttributePtr function returns in the actualSize parameter the actual length, in bytes, of the data for the attribute. If this value is larger than the value of maximumSize, not all of the data for the attribute was returned.

Result codes

noErr	0	No error
memFullErr	–108	Not enough room in heap zone
errAECoercionFail	–1700	Data could not be coerced to the requested descriptor type
errAEDescNotFound	–1701	Descriptor type was not found
errAENotAEDesc	–1704	Not a valid descriptor record
errAEReplyNotArrived	–1718	Reply has not yet arrived

The AEGetAttributeDesc function returns the descriptor record for an Apple event attribute.

```
FUNCTION AEGetAttributeDesc (theAppleEvent: AppleEvent; theAEKeyword:
                             AEKeyword; desiredType: DescType;
                             VAR result: AEDesc) : OSErr;
```

The parameter theAppleEvent is the Apple event containing the desired attribute.

The parameter theAEKeyword is the keyword that specifies the desired attribute.

The desiredType parameter is the descriptor type of the descriptor record to be returned; if the desired attribute is not of this type, the Apple Event Manager attempts to coerce it into this type. If the value of desiredType is typeWildCard, no coercion is performed, and the descriptor type of the resulting descriptor record is the same as the descriptor type of the attribute.

The AEGetAttributeDesc function returns in the result parameter the resulting descriptor record. This function creates a new descriptor record by copying the descriptor record from the parameter. Your application is responsible for using the AEDisposeDesc function to dispose of the resulting descriptor record once you are finished using it.

If the function returns a nonzero result code, a descriptor record with the typeNull descriptor type is returned. A descriptor record of this type does not contain any data.

Result codes

noErr	0	No error
memFullErr	–108	Not enough room in heap zone
errAECoercionFail	–1700	Data could not be coerced to the requested descriptor type
errAEDescNotFound	–1701	Descriptor record was not found
errAENotAEDesc	–1704	Not a valid descriptor record
errAEReplyNotArrived	–1718	Reply has not yet arrived

Counting the Items in Descriptor Lists

The AECountItems function counts the number of descriptor records in a descriptor list.

```
FUNCTION AECountItems (theAEDescList: AEDescList; VAR theCount:
                       LongInt) : OSErr;
```

The parameter theAEDescList is the descriptor list to be counted.

The AECountItems function returns the number of descriptor records in the list in the parameter theCount.

Result codes

noErr	0	No error
errAENotAEDesc	–1704	Not a valid descriptor record

Getting Items From Descriptor Lists

You can use the AEGetNthPtr and AEGetNthDesc functions to gain access to the data in a descriptor list. You can use the AEGetArray function to get data from an array contained in a descriptor list.

The AEGetNthPtr function uses a buffer to return the data for a descriptor record in a descriptor list.

```
FUNCTION AEGetNthPtr (theAEDescList: AEDescList; index: LongInt;
                      desiredType: DescType; VAR theAEKeyword:
                      AEKeyword; VAR typeCode: DescType; dataPtr:
                      Ptr; maximumSize: Size; VAR actualSize: Size) :
                      OSErr;
```

The parameter theAEDescList is the descriptor list containing the desired descriptor record.

The index parameter specifies the position of the desired descriptor record in the list (for example, 2 specifies the second descriptor record).

The desiredType parameter is the descriptor type of the resulting data; if the descriptor record is not of this type, the Apple Event Manager attempts to coerce it into this type. If the value of desiredType is typeWildCard, no coercion is performed, and the descriptor type of the resulting data is the same as the descriptor type of the original descriptor record.

If you are getting data from a list of keyword-specified descriptor records, the keyword of the specified descriptor record is returned in the parameter theAEKeyword; otherwise, the value typeWildCard is returned.

The returned data's descriptor type is returned in the typeCode parameter.

The dataPtr parameter is the pointer to the buffer for storing the data.

The maximumSize parameter is the maximum length, in bytes, of the data to be returned.

The AEGetNthPtr function returns in the actualSize parameter the actual length, in bytes, of the data for the descriptor record. If this value is larger than the value of maximumSize, not all of the data for the descriptor record was returned.

Result codes

noErr	0	No error
memFullErr	–108	Not enough room in heap zone
errAECoercionFail	–1700	Data could not be coerced to the requested descriptor type

errAEDescNotFound	–1701	Descriptor record was not found
errAEWrongDataType	–1703	Wrong descriptor type
errAENotAEDesc	–1704	Not a valid descriptor record
errAEReplyNotArrived	–1718	Reply has not yet arrived

The AEGetNthDesc function returns a descriptor record from a descriptor list.

```
FUNCTION AEGetNthDesc (theAEDescList: AEDescList; index: LongInt;
                       desiredType: DescType; VAR theAEKeyword:
                       AEKeyword; VAR result: AEDesc) : OSErr;
```

The parameter theAEDescList is the descriptor list from which to get the descriptor record.

The index parameter is the position of the descriptor record to get (for example, 2 specifies the second descriptor record in the list).

The desiredType parameter is the descriptor type of the resulting data; if the descriptor record is not of this type, the Apple Event Manager attempts to coerce it into this type. If the value of desiredType is typeWildCard, no coercion is performed, and the descriptor type of the resulting descriptor record is the same as the descriptor type of the original descriptor record.

If you are getting data from a list of keyword-specified descriptor records, the AEGetNthDesc function returns the keyword of the specified descriptor record in the parameter theAEKeyword; otherwise, AEGetNthDesc returns the typeWildCard constant.

The AEGetNthDesc function returns in the result parameter the resulting descriptor record. This function creates a new descriptor record by copying the descriptor record from the parameter. Your application is responsible for using the AEDisposeDesc function to dispose of the resulting descriptor record once you are finished using it.

If the function returns a nonzero result code, a descriptor record with the typeNull descriptor type is returned. A descriptor record of this type does not contain any data.

Result codes

noErr	0	No error
memFullErr	–108	Not enough room in heap zone
errAECoercionFail	–1700	Data could not be coerced to the requested descriptor type
errAEDescNotFound	–1701	Descriptor record was not found
errAENotAEDesc	–1704	Not a valid descriptor record
errAEReplyNotArrived	–1718	Reply has not yet arrived

The AEGetArray function converts an Apple event array (an array created with the AEPutArray function and stored in a descriptor list) into the corresponding Pascal or C array.

```
FUNCTION AEGetArray (theAEDescList: AEDescList; arrayType: AEArrayType;
                     arrayPtr: AEArrayDataPointer; maximumSize: Size;
                     VAR itemType: DescType; VAR itemSize: Size;
                     VAR itemCount: LongInt) : OSErr;
```

The parameter theAEDescList is the descriptor list from which to get the array.

The arrayType parameter is the Apple event array type to be converted. This is specified by one of the following constants: kAEDataArray, kAEPackedArray, kAEHandleArray, kAEDescArray, or kAEKeyDescArray.

The arrayPtr parameter is a pointer to the buffer for storing the array.

The maximumSize parameter is the maximum length, in bytes, of the data to be returned.

For packed, data, and handle arrays, the itemType parameter returns the descriptor type of the array elements that are returned.

For packed and data arrays, the itemSize parameter returns the size, in bytes, of the array elements that are returned.

The itemCount parameter returns the number of items in the resulting array.

Result codes

noErr	0	No error
memFullErr	–108	Not enough room in heap zone
errAEWrongDataType	–1703	Wrong descriptor type
errAENotAEDesc	–1704	Not a valid descriptor record
errAEReplyNotArrived	–1718	Reply has not yet arrived

Getting Data and Keyword-Specified Descriptor Records From AE Records

You can use the AEGetKeyPtr and AEGetKeyDesc functions to get data and keyword-specified descriptor records out of an AE record or an Apple event.

The AEGetKeyPtr function uses a buffer to return the data contained in a keyword-specified descriptor record. You can use this function to get data out of an AE record or an Apple event record.

```
FUNCTION AEGetKeyPtr (theAERecord: AERecord; theAEKeyword: AEKeyword;
                      desiredType: DescType; VAR typeCode: DescType;
                      dataPtr: Ptr; maximumSize: Size; VAR actualSize:
                      Size) : OSErr;
```

The parameter theAERecord is the AE record from which to get data.

The parameter theAEKeyword is the keyword that specifies the desired descriptor record.

The desiredType parameter specifies the descriptor type of the resulting data; if the desired data is not of this type, the Apple Event Manager attempts to coerce it into this type. If the value of desiredType is typeWildCard, no coercion is performed, and the descriptor type of resulting data is the same as the descriptor type of the original data. The returned data's descriptor type is returned in the typeCode parameter.

The dataPtr parameter is a pointer to the buffer for storing the data.

The maximumSize parameter is the maximum length, in bytes, of the data to be returned.

The AEGetKeyPtr function returns in the actualSize parameter the actual length, in bytes, of the data for the keyword-specified descriptor record. If this value is larger than the value of maximumSize, not all of the data for the keyword-specified descriptor record was returned.

Result codes

noErr	0	No error
memFullErr	–108	Not enough room in heap zone
errAECoercionFail	–1700	Data could not be coerced to the requested descriptor type
errAEDescNotFound	–1701	Descriptor record was not found
errAEWrongDataType	–1703	Wrong descriptor type
errAENotAEDesc	–1704	Not a valid descriptor record
errAEReplyNotArrived	–1718	Reply has not yet arrived

The AEGetKeyDesc function returns the descriptor record for a keyword-specified descriptor record. You can use this function to get a descriptor record out of an AE record or an Apple event.

```
FUNCTION AEGetKeyDesc (theAERecord: AERecord; theAEKeyword: AEKeyword;
                       desiredType: DescType; VAR result: AEDesc) :
                       OSErr;
```

The parameter theAERecord is the AE record from which to get the descriptor record.

The parameter theAEKeyword is the keyword that specifies the descriptor record to be returned.

The desiredType parameter specifies the descriptor type of the resulting descriptor record; if the original descriptor record is not of this type, the Apple Event Manager attempts to coerce it into this type. If the value of desiredType is typeWildCard, no coercion is performed, and the descriptor type of the resulting descriptor record is the same as the descriptor type of the original descriptor record.

The AEGetKeyDesc function returns in the result parameter the resulting descriptor record. This function creates a new descriptor record by copying the descriptor record from the AE record. Your application is responsible for using the AEDisposeDesc function to dispose of the resulting descriptor record once you are finished using it.

If the function returns a nonzero result code, a descriptor record with the typeNull descriptor type is returned. A descriptor record of this type does not contain any data.

Result codes

noErr	0	No error
memFullErr	–108	Not enough room in heap zone
errAECoercionFail	–1700	Data could not be coerced to the requested descriptor type
errAEDescNotFound	–1701	Descriptor record was not found
errAENotAEDesc	–1704	Not a valid descriptor record
errAEReplyNotArrived	–1718	Reply has not yet arrived

Requesting User Interaction

Your server application may need to interact with the user while processing an Apple event. Your application should use the AEInteractWithUser function before actually interacting with the user in response to an Apple event. Your application can also specify its user interaction preferences by using the AESetInteractionAllowed and AEGetInteractionAllowed functions.

A server application uses the AESetInteractionAllowed function to specify user interaction preferences for responding to Apple events.

```
FUNCTION AESetInteractionAllowed (level: AEInteractAllowed) : OSErr;
```

The level parameter must be one of three flags: kAEInteractWithSelf, kAEInteractWithLocal, or kAEInteractWithAll.

Specifying the kAEInteractWithSelf flag allows the server application to interact with the user in response to an Apple event only when the client application and server application are the same—that is, only when the application is sending the Apple event to itself.

Specifying the kAEInteractWithLocal flag allows the server application to interact with the user in response to an Apple event only if the client application is on the same computer as the server application; this is the default if the AESetInteractionAllowed function is not used.

Specifying the kAEInteractWithAll flag allows the server application to interact with the user in response to an Apple event sent from any client application on any computer.

Result code

noErr	0	No error

The AEGetInteractionAllowed function returns a value that indicates the user interaction preferences for responding to an Apple event. The value returned is the interaction level set by a previous call to AESetInteractionAllowed. The default value of kAEInteractWithLocal is returned if your application has not used AESetInteractionAllowed to explicitly set the interaction level.

```
FUNCTION AEGetInteractionAllowed (VAR level: AEInteractAllowed) :
                                           OSErr;
```

The level parameter returns one of the following flags: kAEInteractWithSelf, kAEInteractWithLocal, or kAEInteractWithAll.

The kAEInteractWithSelf flag indicates that the server application may interact with the user in response to an Apple event only when the client application and server application are the same—that is, only when the application is sending the Apple event to itself.

The kAEInteractWithLocal flag indicates that the server application may interact with the user in response to an Apple event only if the client application is on the same computer as the server application. This is the default if your application has not used the AESetInteractionAllowed function to explicitly set the interaction level.

The kAEInteractWithAll flag indicates that the server application may interact with the user in response to an Apple event sent from any client application on any computer.

Result code

noErr	0	No error

A server application calls the AEInteractWithUser function before displaying a dialog box or alert box or otherwise interacting with the user. If the user-interaction preference settings permit the application to come to the foreground, this function brings your application to the front, either directly or by posting a notification request.

```
FUNCTION AEInteractWithUser (timeOutInTicks: LongInt; nmReqPtr:
                             NMRecPtr; idleProc: IdleProcPtr) : OSErr;
```

The timeOutInTicks parameter is the amount of time (in ticks) that your handler is willing to wait for a response from the user.

The nmReqPtr parameter is a pointer to a Notification Manager record provided by your application. You can specify NIL for this parameter to get the default notification handling provided by the Apple Event Manager.

The idleProc parameter is a pointer to your application's idle function, which handles events while waiting for the Apple Event Manager to return control. For a description of how to write this function, see "Writing an Idle Function" earlier in this chapter.

The AEInteractWithUser function checks to see if the client application set the kAENeverInteract flag for the Apple event and, if so, returns an error. If not, then the AEInteractWithUser function checks the server application's preference set by the AESetInteractionAllowed function and compares it against the source of the Apple event—that is, whether it came from the same application, another application or process on the same computer, or an application or process running on another computer. AEInteractWithUser returns the errAENoUserInteraction result code if the user-interaction preferences don't allow user interaction. If user interaction is allowed, the Apple Event Manager brings your application to the front, either directly or by posting a notification request. If AEInteractWithUser returns the noErr result code, then your application is in the foreground and is free to interact with the user.

Result codes

noErr	0	No error
errAETimeout	–1712	Apple event timed out
errAENoUserInteraction	–1713	No user interaction allowed

Requesting More Time to Respond to Apple Events

The AEResetTimer function resets the timeout value for an Apple event to its starting value. A server application can call this function when it knows it cannot fulfill a client application's request (either by returning a result or by sending back a reply Apple event) before the client application is due to time out.

```
FUNCTION AEResetTimer (reply: AppleEvent) : OSErr;
```

The reply parameter is the default reply for an Apple event and is provided by the Apple Event Manager. When AEResetTimer is called, the Apple Event Manager uses the default reply to send a Reset Timer event to the client application; the Apple Event Manager for the client application intercepts this Apple event and resets the client application's timer for the Apple event. (The Reset Timer event is never dispatched to a handler, and the client application does not need a handler for it.)

Result codes

noErr	0	No error
errAEReplyNotValid	–1709	AEResetTimer was passed an invalid reply

Suspending and Resuming Apple Event Handling

The AESuspendTheCurrentEvent function suspends the processing of the Apple event that is currently being handled.

```
FUNCTION AESuspendTheCurrentEvent (theAppleEvent: AppleEvent) : OSErr;
```

The parameter theAppleEvent is the Apple event whose handling is to be suspended. Although the Apple Event Manager doesn't need the parameter theAppleEvent to identify the Apple event currently being handled, providing this parameter is a safeguard that ensures that you are suspending the correct Apple event.

After a server application makes a successful call to the AESuspendTheCurrentEvent function, it is no longer required to return a result or a reply for the Apple event that was being handled. It can, however, return a result if it later calls the AEResumeTheCurrentEvent function to resume event processing.

The Apple Event Manager does not automatically dispose of Apple events that have been suspended or of their default replies. (The Apple Event Manager does, however, automatically dispose of a previously suspended Apple event and its default reply if the server later resumes processing of the Apple event by calling the AEResumeTheCurrentEvent function.) If your server application does not resume processing of a suspended Apple event, it is responsible for using the AEDisposeDesc function to dispose of both the Apple event and its default reply when you are finished with them.

Result code

noErr	0	No error

The AEResumeTheCurrentEvent function informs the Apple Event Manager that your application wants to resume the handling of a previously suspended Apple event or that it has completed the handling of the Apple event.

```
FUNCTION AEResumeTheCurrentEvent (theAppleEvent, reply: AppleEvent;
                                  dispatcher: EventHandlerProcPtr;
                                  handlerRefcon: LongInt) : OSErr;
```

The parameter theAppleEvent is the Apple event whose processing is to be resumed.

The reply parameter is the default reply that is automatically provided by the Apple Event Manager for the Apple event.

The dispatcher parameter is one of the following:

- a pointer to a routine for handling the event
- the kAEUseStandardDispatch constant, which causes the Apple event to be dispatched in the way it was when it was first received
- the kAENoDispatch constant, which tells the Apple Event Manager that the processing of the Apple event is complete and that it does not need to be dispatched

If the value of the dispatcher parameter is not kAEUseStandardDispatch, the handlerRefcon parameter is a reference constant that is passed to the handler when the handler is called. If the value of the dispatcher parameter is kAEUseStandardDispatch, the Apple Event Manager ignores the handlerRefcon parameter and instead passes the reference constant that is stored in the Apple event dispatch table entry for the Apple event. (If you want to pass the same reference constant that is stored in the Apple event dispatch table, your application can obtain the reference constant by calling the AEGetEventHandler function.)

Result code

noErr	0	No error

The AESetTheCurrentEvent function specifies the Apple event to be handled. There is generally no reason for your application to use this function. Instead of calling this function, your application should let the Apple Event Manager go through the dispatch tables to set the current Apple event.

```
FUNCTION AESetTheCurrentEvent (theAppleEvent: AppleEvent) : OSErr;
```

The parameter theAppleEvent is the Apple event that is to be handled.

The AESetTheCurrentEvent function is used only to avoid going through the dispatch tables, and is used only in the following way:

1. An application suspends handling of an Apple event by calling the AESuspendTheCurrentEvent function.
2. The application calls the AESetTheCurrentEvent function to inform the Apple Event Manager that it is handling the Apple event that was previously suspended. It thereby makes the identity of the Apple event currently being handled available to routines that call the AEGetTheCurrentEvent function.
3. The application handles the Apple event. When it is finished, it calls the AEResumeTheCurrentEvent function with the value kAENoDispatch to tell the Apple Event Manager that the processing of the event is complete and that the Apple event does not need to be dispatched.

Result code

noErr	0	No error

The AEGetTheCurrentEvent function returns the Apple event that is currently being handled. In many applications, the handling of an Apple event involves one or more long chains of calls to routines within the application. The AEGetTheCurrentEvent function makes it unnecessary for these calls to include the current Apple event as a parameter; the routines can simply call AEGetTheCurrentEvent to get the current Apple event when it is needed.

```
FUNCTION AEGetTheCurrentEvent (VAR theAppleEvent: AppleEvent) :
                               OSErr;
```

This function returns the Apple event that is currently being handled in the parameter theAppleEvent.

Result code

noErr	0	No error

Creating Apple Events

The AECreateAppleEvent function creates an Apple event with several important attributes but no parameters.

```
FUNCTION AECreateAppleEvent (theAEEventClass: AEEventClass;
                             theAEEventID: AEEventID; target:
                             AEAddressDesc; returnID: Integer;
                             transactionID: LongInt;
                             VAR result: AppleEvent) : OSErr;
```

The parameter theAEEventClass is the event class of the Apple event to be created.

The parameter theAEEventID is the event ID of the Apple event to be created.

The target parameter is the address of the server application. See "Specifying a Target Address" earlier in this chapter for information on how to address an Apple event.

The returnID parameter is the return ID assigned to this Apple event; if the kAutoGenerateReturnID constant is used as the value, the Apple Event Manager assigns a return ID that is unique to the current session.

The transactionID parameter is the transaction ID for this Apple event. A transaction refers to a sequence of Apple events that are sent back and forth between the client and server applications, beginning with the client's initial request for a service. All Apple events that are part of a transaction must have the same transaction ID.

The AECreateAppleEvent function returns in the result parameter the resulting Apple event. Your application is responsible for using the AEDisposeDesc function to dispose of the resulting Apple event once you are finished using it.

If the function returns a nonzero result code, a descriptor record with the typeNull descriptor type is returned. A descriptor record of this type does not contain any data.

Result codes

noErr	0	No error
memFullErr	–108	Not enough room in heap zone

Creating and Duplicating Descriptor Records

The AECreateDesc function takes data and converts it into a descriptor record.

```
FUNCTION AECreateDesc (typeCode: DescType; dataPtr: Ptr; dataSize:
                       Size; VAR result: AEDesc) : OSErr;
```

The typeCode parameter is the descriptor type for the resulting descriptor record.

The dataPtr parameter is a pointer to the data for the descriptor record.

The dataSize parameter is the length, in bytes, of the data for the descriptor record.

The AECreateDesc function returns in the result parameter the resulting descriptor record. This function creates a new descriptor record by copying the descriptor record from the parameter. Your application is responsible for using the AEDisposeDesc function to dispose of the resulting descriptor record once you are finished using it. You normally do this after receiving a result from the AESend function.

If the function returns a nonzero result code, a descriptor record with the typeNull descriptor type is returned. A descriptor record of this type does not contain any data.

Result codes

noErr	0	No error
memFullErr	–108	Not enough room in heap zone

The AEDuplicateDesc function makes a copy of a descriptor record.

```
FUNCTION AEDuplicateDesc (theAEDesc: AEDesc; VAR result: AEDesc) :
                          OSErr;
```

The parameter theAEDesc is the descriptor record to be copied.

The AEDuplicateDesc function returns in the result parameter the resulting descriptor record. This function creates a new descriptor record by copying the descriptor record from the parameter. Your application is responsible for using the AEDisposeDesc function to dispose of the resulting descriptor record once you are finished using it. You normally do this after receiving a result from the AESend function.

If the function returns a nonzero result code, a descriptor record with the typeNull descriptor type is returned. A descriptor record of this type does not contain any data.

It's common for applications to send Apple events that have one or more attributes or parameters in common. For example, if you're sending a series of Apple events to the same application, the address attribute is the same. In these cases, the most efficient way to create the necessary Apple events is to make a template Apple event that you can then copy—by calling the AEDuplicateDesc function—as needed. You then fill in or change the remaining parameters and attributes of the copy, send the copy by calling AESend, and then dispose of the copy—by calling AEDisposeDesc—after AESend returns a result.

Result codes

noErr	0	No error
memFullErr	–108	Not enough room in heap zone

Creating Descriptor Lists and AE Records

The AECreateList function creates an empty descriptor list or AE record.

```
FUNCTION AECreateList (factoringPtr: Ptr; factoredSize: Size; isRecord:
                       Boolean; VAR resultList: AEDescList) : OSErr;
```

You can compress descriptor lists—thereby saving both space and, in some cases, transmission time—by isolating data at the beginning of each descriptor record that is the same for all descriptor records in the list. This common data is sent only once for all the descriptor records in the list. When an application gets descriptor records from a compressed descriptor list, the Apple Event Manager automatically decompresses them.

The factoringPtr parameter is a pointer to the data at the beginning of each descriptor that is the same for all descriptor records in the list. (The method for compressing descriptor lists is analogous to extracting the common factor from two or more numbers.) If there is no common data, or if you decide not to isolate the common data, provide NIL as the value of the factoringPtr parameter.

The factoredSize parameter is the size of the common data. If there is no common data, or if you decide not to isolate the common data, the value of factoredSize must be 0.

The isRecord parameter is a Boolean value that specifies the kind of list to create. If you set its value to TRUE, the Apple Event Manager creates an AE record. If you set its value to FALSE, the Apple Event Manager creates a descriptor list.

The AECreateList function returns in the resultList parameter the resulting descriptor list or AE record. This function creates a new descriptor record by copying the descriptor record from the parameter. Your application is responsible for using the AEDisposeDesc function to dispose of the resulting descriptor record once you are finished using it. You normally do this after receiving a result from the AESend function.

If the function returns a nonzero result code, a descriptor record with the typeNull descriptor type is returned. A descriptor record of this type does not contain any data.

Result codes

noErr	0	No error
paramErr	–50	Parameter error (handler pointer is NIL or odd)
memFullErr	–108	Not enough room in heap zone

Adding Items to Descriptor Lists

The AEPutPtr function takes data specified in a buffer and converts it to a descriptor record that it adds to a descriptor list.

```
FUNCTION AEPutPtr (theAEDescList: AEDescList; index: LongInt; typeCode:
                   DescType; dataPtr: Ptr; dataSize: Size) : OSErr;
```

The parameter theAEDescList is the descriptor list to which to add a descriptor record.

The index parameter is the position in the list for the descriptor record (for example, 2 specifies that it must be the second descriptor record). If there was already a descriptor record at that position, it is replaced. If the value of index is 0, the descriptor record is added at the end of the list.

The typeCode parameter is the descriptor type for the resulting descriptor record.

The dataPtr parameter is a pointer to the data for the descriptor record.

The dataSize parameter is the length, in bytes, of the data for the descriptor record.

Result codes

noErr	0	No error
memFullErr	–108	Not enough room in heap zone
errAEWrongDataType	–1703	Wrong descriptor type
errAENotAEDesc	–1704	Not a valid descriptor record
errAEBadListItem	–1705	Operation involving a list item failed
errAEIllegalIndex	–1719	Not a valid list index

The AEPutDesc function adds a descriptor record to a descriptor list.

```
FUNCTION AEPutDesc (theAEDescList: AEDescList; index: LongInt;
                    theAEDesc: AEDesc) : OSErr;
```

The parameter theAEDescList is the descriptor list to which you are adding a descriptor record.

The index parameter is the position in the list for the descriptor record (for example, 2 specifies that it must be the second descriptor record). If there was already a descriptor record at that position, it is replaced. If the value of index is 0, the descriptor record is added to the end of the list.

The parameter theAEDesc is the descriptor record to be added to the list.

Result codes

noErr	0	No error
memFullErr	–108	Not enough room in heap zone
errAEWrongDataType	–1703	Wrong descriptor type
errAENotAEDesc	–1704	Not a valid descriptor record
errAEBadListItem	–1705	Operation involving a list item failed
errAEIllegalIndex	–1719	Not a valid list index

The AEPutArray function puts the data for an Apple event array into a descriptor list.

```
FUNCTION AEPutArray (theAEDescList: AEDescList; arrayType: AEArrayType;
                     arrayPtr: AEArrayDataPointer; itemType: DescType;
                     itemSize: Size; itemCount: LongInt) : OSErr;
```

The parameter theAEDescList is the descriptor list into which to put the Apple event array. If there are any items already in the descriptor list, they are replaced.

The arrayType parameter is the Apple event array type to be created. This is specified by one of the following constants: kAEDataArray, kAEPackedArray, kAEHandleArray, kAEDescArray, or kAEKeyDescArray. The kAEDataArray constant refers to an array of integers; kAEPackedArray refers to an array of characters; kAEHandleArray refers to an array of handles; kAEDescArray refers to an array of descriptor records; and kAEKeyDescArray refers to an array of keyword-specified descriptor records.

If you are putting an array into a compressed descriptor list (see the description of the AECreateList function for information about compressing descriptor lists), the data for each array element must include the data that is common to all the descriptor records in the list. The Apple Event Manager automatically isolates the data you specified in the call to AECreateList that is common to all the elements of the array.

The arrayPtr parameter is a pointer to the buffer containing the array.

For packed, data, and handle arrays, the itemType parameter specifies the descriptor type of array items to be created.

For packed and data arrays, the itemSize parameter specifies the size, in bytes, of the array items to be created.

The itemCount parameter is the number of elements in the array.

Result codes

noErr	0	No error
memFullErr	–108	Not enough room in heap zone
errAEWrongDataType	–1703	Wrong descriptor type
errAENotAEDesc	–1704	Not a valid descriptor record

Adding Data and Keyword-Specified Descriptor Records to AE Records

The AEPutKeyPtr function takes a pointer to data, a descriptor type, and a keyword and converts them into a keyword-specified descriptor record that it adds to an AE record.

```
FUNCTION AEPutKeyPtr (theAERecord: AERecord; theAEKeyword: AEKeyword;
                      typeCode: DescType; dataPtr: Ptr; dataSize:
                      Size) : OSErr;
```

The parameter theAERecord is the AE record to which to add a keyword-specified descriptor record.

The parameter theAEKeyword is the keyword specifying the descriptor record. If there was already a descriptor record with this keyword, it is replaced.

The typeCode parameter is the descriptor type for the keyword-specified descriptor record.

The dataPtr parameter is a pointer to the data for the keyword-specified descriptor record.

The dataSize parameter is the length, in bytes, of the data for the keyword-specified descriptor record.

Result codes

noErr	0	No error
memFullErr	–108	Not enough room in heap zone
errAEWrongDataType	–1703	Wrong descriptor type
errAENotAEDesc	–1704	Not a valid descriptor record
errAEBadListItem	–1705	Operation involving a list item failed

The AEPutKeyDesc function takes a descriptor record and a keyword and converts them into a keyword-specified descriptor record that it adds to an AE record.

```
FUNCTION AEPutKeyDesc (theAERecord: AERecord; theAEKeyword: AEKeyword;
                       theAEDesc: AEDesc) : OSErr;
```

The parameter theAERecord is the AE record to which to add the keyword-specified descriptor record.

The parameter theAEKeyword is the keyword specifying the descriptor record. If there was already a keyword-specified descriptor record with this keyword, it is replaced.

The parameter theAEDesc is the descriptor record for the keyword-specified descriptor record.

Result codes

noErr	0	No error
memFullErr	–108	Not enough room in heap zone
errAEWrongDataType	–1703	Wrong descriptor type
errAENotAEDesc	–1704	Not a valid descriptor record
errAEBadListItem	–1705	Operation involving a list item failed

Adding Parameters and Attributes to Apple Events

The AEPutParamPtr function takes a pointer to data, a descriptor type, and a keyword and converts them into a parameter that it adds to an Apple event.

```
FUNCTION AEPutParamPtr (theAppleEvent: AppleEvent; theAEKeyword:
                        AEKeyword; typeCode: DescType; dataPtr: Ptr;
                        dataSize: Size) : OSErr;
```

The parameter theAppleEvent is the Apple event to which you are adding a parameter.

The parameter theAEKeyword is the keyword for the parameter. If there was already a parameter with this keyword in the Apple event, it is replaced.

The typeCode parameter is the descriptor type for the parameter.

The dataPtr parameter is a pointer to the data for the parameter.

The dataSize parameter is the length, in bytes, of the data for the parameter.

Result codes

noErr	0	No error
memFullErr	–108	Not enough room in heap zone
errAEWrongDataType	–1703	Wrong descriptor type
errAENotAEDesc	–1704	Not a valid descriptor record
errAEBadListItem	–1705	Operation involving a list item failed

The AEPutParamDesc function takes a descriptor record and a keyword and converts them into a parameter that it adds to an Apple event.

```
FUNCTION AEPutParamDesc (theAppleEvent: AppleEvent; theAEKeyword:
                         AEKeyword; theAEDesc: AEDesc) : OSErr;
```

The parameter theAppleEvent is the Apple event to which you are adding a parameter.

The parameter theAEKeyword is the keyword for the parameter. If there was already a parameter with this keyword in the Apple event, it is replaced.

The parameter theAEDesc is the descriptor record for the parameter.

Result codes

noErr	0	No error
memFullErr	–108	Not enough room in heap zone
errAEWrongDataType	–1703	Wrong descriptor type
errAENotAEDesc	–1704	Not a valid descriptor record
errAEBadListItem	–1705	Operation involving a list item failed

The AEPutAttributePtr function takes a pointer to data, a descriptor type, and a keyword and converts them into an attribute that it adds to an Apple event.

```
FUNCTION AEPutAttributePtr (theAppleEvent: AppleEvent; theAEKeyword:
                            AEKeyword; typeCode: DescType; dataPtr:
                            Ptr; dataSize: Size) : OSErr;
```

The parameter theAppleEvent is the Apple event to which you are adding an attribute.

The parameter theAEKeyword is the keyword of the attribute. If there was already an attribute with this keyword in the Apple event, it is replaced.

The typeCode parameter is the descriptor type for the attribute.

The dataPtr parameter is a pointer to the buffer containing the data to be assigned to the attribute.

The dataSize parameter is the length, in bytes, of the data to be assigned to the attribute.

Result codes

noErr	0	No error
memFullErr	–108	Not enough room in heap zone
errAECoercionFail	–1700	Data could not be coerced to the requested descriptor type
errAENotAEDesc	–1704	Not a valid descriptor record

The AEPutAttributeDesc function takes a descriptor record and a keyword and converts them into an attribute that it adds to an Apple event.

```
FUNCTION AEPutAttributeDesc (theAppleEvent: AppleEvent; theAEKeyword:
                            AEKeyword; theAEDesc: AEDesc) : OSErr;
```

The parameter theAppleEvent is the Apple event to which you are adding an attribute.

The parameter theAEKeyword is the keyword of the attribute. If there was already an attribute with this keyword in the Apple event, it is replaced.

The parameter theAEDesc is the descriptor record to be assigned to the attribute. The descriptor type of the specified descriptor record should match the defined descriptor type for that attribute. For example, the keyEventSourceAttr attribute has the typeShortInteger descriptor type.

If the descriptor type required for the attribute is different from the descriptor type of the descriptor record, the Apple Event Manager attempts to coerce the descriptor record into the required type, with one exception: the Apple Event Manager does not attempt to coerce the data for an address attribute, thereby allowing applications to use their own address types.

Result codes

noErr	0	No error
memFullErr	–108	Not enough room in heap zone
errAECoercionFail	–1700	Data could not be coerced to the requested descriptor type
errAENotAEDesc	–1704	Not a valid descriptor record

Sending Apple Events

The AESend function sends an Apple event.

```
FUNCTION AESend (theAppleEvent: AppleEvent; VAR reply: AppleEvent;
                sendMode: AESendMode; sendPriority: AESendPriority;
                timeOutInTicks: LongInt; idleProc: IdleProcPtr;
                filterProc: EventFilterProcPtr) : OSErr;
```

The parameter theAppleEvent specifies the Apple event to be sent.

The reply parameter specifies the reply Apple event that is returned if you specify the kAEWaitReply flag in the sendMode parameter. (If you specify the kAEQueueReply flag in the sendMode parameter, you receive the reply Apple event in your event queue.) If you specify either the kAEQueueReply flag or the kAENoReply flag, the data in the reply Apple event returned by this function is not valid. If this function returns a nonzero result, it also returns in the reply parameter a descriptor record whose descriptor type is typeNull—that is, one that does not contain data. If you specify kAEWaitReply, your application is responsible for using the AEDisposeDesc function to dispose of the resulting descriptor record.

The sendMode parameter allows you to specify the following: the reply mode for the Apple event (set with one of the constants kAENoReply, kAEQueueReply, or kAEWaitReply); the interaction mode (set with one of the constants kAENeverInteract, kAECanInteract, or kAEAlwaysInteract); the layer switch mode (set with the kAECanSwitchLayer constant); the reconnection mode (set with the kAEDontReconnect constant); and the return receipt mode (set with the kAEWantReceipt constant). You obtain the value for this parameter by adding the appropriate constants. These flags are stored in the interaction level attribute, whose keyword is keyInteractLevelAttr. The sendMode flags are described in a later part of this section.

In the sendPriority parameter, you specify flags that determine whether the Apple event is put at the back of the event queue (the kAENormalPriority flag) or at the front of the queue (the kAEHighPriority flag).

If the reply mode specified in the sendMode parameter is kAEWaitReply, or if a return receipt is requested, the timeOutInTicks parameter specifies the length of time (in ticks) that the client application is willing to wait for the reply or return receipt from the server application before timing out. Most applications should use the kAEDefaultTimeout constant, which tells the Apple Event Manager to provide an appropriate timeout duration. If the value of this parameter is kNoTimeOut, the Apple event never times out.

The idleProc parameter specifies a pointer to a function for any tasks (such as displaying a wristwatch or spinning beach ball cursor) that the application performs while waiting for a reply or a return receipt (see "Writing an Idle Function" earlier in this chapter).

The filterProc parameter specifies a pointer to a routine that accepts certain incoming Apple events that are received while the handler waits for a reply or a return receipt and filters out the rest (see "Writing a Reply Filter Function" earlier in this chapter).

You can use one of the following flags in the sendMode parameter to specify the reply mode for an Apple event. Only one of these flags may be set.

Flag	**Description**
kAENoReply	Your application does not want a reply Apple event; the server processes your Apple event as soon as it has the opportunity.
kAEQueueReply	Your application wants a reply Apple event; the reply appears in your event queue as soon as the server has the opportunity to process and respond to your Apple event.

Flag	Description
kAEWaitReply	Your application wants a reply Apple event and is willing to give up the processor while waiting for the reply; for example, if the server application is on the same computer as your application, your application yields the processor to allow the server to respond to your Apple event.

You can communicate your user-interaction preferences to the server by specifying one of these flags in the sendMode parameter of the AESend function. Only one of these flags may be set.

Flag	Description
kAENeverInteract	The server application should never interact with the user in response to this Apple event. If this flag is set, AEInteractWithUser does not bring the server application to the foreground (this is the default when an Apple event is sent to a remote application).
kAECanInteract	The server application can interact with the user in response to this Apple event—by convention, if the user needs to supply information to the server. If this flag is set and the server allows interaction, AEInteractWithUser brings the server application to the foreground (this is the default when an Apple event is sent to a local application).
kAEAlwaysInteract	The server application can interact with the user in response to this Apple event—by convention, even if no information is needed from the user. If this flag is set and the server allows interaction, AEInteractWithUser brings the server application to the foreground. The Apple Event Manager does not distinguish between this flag and the kAECanInteract flag—distinguishing between them is the responsibility of the server application.

The flags in the following list specify the layer switch mode, the reconnection mode, and the return receipt mode. Any of these flags may be set.

Flag	Description
kAECanSwitchLayer	If both the client and server allow interaction and this flag is set, AEInteractWithUser brings the server directly to the foreground if adherence to the principle of user control allows. If the action would be contrary to this principle, AEInteractWithUser uses the Notification Manager to request that the user bring the server application to the foreground. If both the client and server allow interaction and this flag is not set, AEInteractWithUser always uses the Notification Manager to request that the user bring the server application to the foreground.

Flag	**Description**
kAEDontReconnect	Specifies that the Apple Event Manager must not automatically try to reconnect if it receives a sessClosedErr result code from the PPC Toolbox.
kAEWantReceipt	The sender wants to receive a return receipt for this Apple event from the Event Manager. (Getting a return receipt means only that the receiving application accepted the Apple event; the Apple event may or may not be handled successfully after it is accepted.) If the receiving application does not send a return receipt before the request times out, AESend returns errAETimeout as its function result.

If the Apple Event Manager cannot find a handler for an Apple event in either the application or system Apple event dispatch table, it returns the result code errAEEventNotHandled to the server application (as the result of the AEProcessAppleEvent function). If the client is waiting for a reply, the Apple Event Manager also returns this result code to the client.

AESend returns noErr as the function result if the Apple event was successfully sent by the Event Manager. A noErr result from AESend does not indicate that the Apple event was handled successfully; it only indicates that the Apple event was successfully sent by the Event Manager. If a result code other than noErr is returned by the handler, and if the client is waiting for a reply, it is returned in the keyErrorNumber parameter of the reply Apple event.

Result codes

noErr	0	No error
memFullErr	–108	Not enough room in heap zone
connectionInvalid	–609	Connection is invalid
errAEEventNotHandled	–1708	Event wasn't handled by an Apple event handler
errAEUnknownSendMode	–1710	Invalid sending mode was passed
errAEWaitCanceled	–1711	User canceled out of wait loop for reply or receipt
errAETimeout	–1712	Apple event timed out
errAEUnknownAddressType	–1716	Unknown Apple event address type

Getting the Sizes and Descriptor Types of Descriptor Records

The AESizeOfNthItem function returns the size and descriptor type of a descriptor record in a descriptor list.

```
FUNCTION AESizeOfNthItem (theAEDescList: AEDescList; index: LongInt;
                          VAR typeCode: DescType; VAR dataSize: Size)
                          : OSErr;
```

The parameter theAEDescList is the descriptor list containing the descriptor record.

The index parameter is the position of the descriptor record in the list (for example, 2 specifies the second descriptor record).

The AESizeOfNthItem function returns the descriptor type of the descriptor record in the typeCode parameter.

This function returns the length, in bytes, of the data contained in the descriptor record in the dataSize parameter.

Result codes

noErr	0	No error
errAEDescNotFound	–1701	Descriptor record was not found
errAEReplyNotArrived	–1718	Reply has not yet arrived

The AESizeOfKeyDesc function returns the size and descriptor type of a keyword-specified descriptor record in an AE record.

```
FUNCTION AESizeOfKeyDesc (theAERecord: AERecord; theAEKeyword:
                          AEKeyword; VAR typeCode: DescType;
                          VAR dataSize: Size) : OSErr;
```

The parameter theAERecord is the AE record containing the desired keyword-specified descriptor record.

The parameter theAEKeyword is the keyword that specifies the desired descriptor record.

This function returns the descriptor type of the desired keyword-specified descriptor record in the typeCode parameter.

This function returns the length, in bytes, of the data contained in the keyword-specified descriptor record in the dataSize parameter.

Result codes

noErr	0	No error
errAEDescNotFound	–1701	Descriptor record was not found
errAENotAEDesc	–1704	Not a valid descriptor record
errAEReplyNotArrived	–1718	Reply has not yet arrived

The AESizeOfParam function returns the size and descriptor type of an Apple event parameter.

```
FUNCTION AESizeOfParam (theAppleEvent: AppleEvent; theAEKeyword:
                        AEKeyword; VAR typeCode: DescType;
                        VAR dataSize: Size) : OSErr;
```

The parameter theAppleEvent is the Apple event containing the parameter.

The parameter theAEKeyword is the keyword that specifies the desired parameter.

The function returns the descriptor type of the parameter in the typeCode parameter.

The function returns the length, in bytes, of the data contained in the desired parameter in the dataSize parameter.

Result codes

noErr	0	No error
errAEDescNotFound	–1701	Descriptor record was not found
errAENotAEDesc	–1704	Not a valid descriptor record
errAEReplyNotArrived	–1718	Reply has not yet arrived

The AESizeOfAttribute function returns the size and descriptor type of an Apple event attribute.

```
FUNCTION AESizeOfAttribute (theAppleEvent: AppleEvent; theAEKeyword:
                            AEKeyword; VAR typeCode: DescType;
                            VAR dataSize: Size) : OSErr;
```

The parameter theAppleEvent is the Apple event containing the attribute.

The parameter theAEKeyword is the keyword that specifies the attribute.

The function returns the descriptor type of the attribute in the typeCode parameter.

The function returns the length, in bytes, of the data contained in the attribute in the dataSize parameter.

Result codes

noErr	0	No error
errAEDescNotFound	–1701	Descriptor record was not found
errAENotAEDesc	–1704	Not a valid descriptor record
errAEReplyNotArrived	–1718	Reply has not yet arrived

Deleting Descriptor Records

The AEDeleteItem function deletes a descriptor record from a descriptor list.

```
FUNCTION AEDeleteItem (theAEDescList: AEDescList; index: LongInt) :
                       OSErr;
```

The parameter theAEDescList is the descriptor list containing the descriptor record to be deleted.

The index parameter is the position of the descriptor record to delete (for example, 2 specifies the second item).

Result codes

noErr	0	No error
errAEDescNotFound	–1701	Descriptor record was not found
errAENotAEDesc	–1704	Not a valid descriptor record
errAEBadListItem	–1705	Operation involving a list item failed

The AEDeleteKeyDesc function deletes a keyword-specified descriptor record from an AE record.

```
FUNCTION AEDeleteKeyDesc (theAERecord: AERecord; theAEKeyword:
                          AEKeyword) : OSErr;
```

The parameter theAERecord is the AE record containing the keyword-specified descriptor record to be deleted.

The parameter theAEKeyword is the keyword that specifies the descriptor record to be deleted.

Result codes

noErr	0	No error
errAEDescNotFound	–1701	Descriptor record was not found
errAENotAEDesc	–1704	Not a valid descriptor record
badListItem	–1705	Operation involving a list item failed

The AEDeleteParam function deletes an Apple event parameter.

```
FUNCTION AEDeleteParam (theAppleEvent: AppleEvent; theAEKeyword:
                        AEKeyword) : OSErr;
```

The parameter theAppleEvent is the Apple event containing the parameter to be deleted.

The parameter theAEKeyword is the keyword that specifies the parameter to be deleted.

Result codes

noErr	0	No error
errAEDescNotFound	–1701	Descriptor record was not found
errAENotAEDesc	–1704	Not a valid descriptor record
errAEBadListItem	–1705	Operation involving a list item failed

Deallocating Memory for Descriptor Records

The AEDisposeDesc function deallocates the memory used by a descriptor record. Because all Apple event structures (except for keyword-specified descriptor records) are descriptor records, you can use AEDisposeDesc for any of them.

```
FUNCTION AEDisposeDesc (VAR theAEDesc: AEDesc) : OSErr;
```

The parameter theAEDesc is the descriptor record to deallocate.

Result code

noErr	0	No error

Coercing Descriptor Types

The AECoercePtr function takes a pointer to data and a desired descriptor type and attempts to coerce the data into the desired descriptor type. If successful, it creates a descriptor record containing the newly coerced data.

```
FUNCTION AECoercePtr (typeCode: DescType; dataPtr: Ptr; dataSize: Size;
                      toType: DescType; VAR result: AEDesc) : OSErr;
```

The typeCode parameter is the descriptor type of the source data.

The dataPtr parameter is a pointer to the data to be coerced.

The dataSize parameter is the length, in bytes, of the data to be coerced.

The toType parameter is the desired descriptor type of the resulting descriptor record.

The AECoercePtr function returns in the result parameter the resulting descriptor record. This function creates a new descriptor record by copying the descriptor record from the parameter. Your application is responsible for using the AEDisposeDesc function to dispose of the resulting descriptor record once you are finished using it.

If the function returns a nonzero result code, a descriptor record with the typeNull descriptor type is returned. A descriptor record of this type does not contain any data.

> **Note:** To avoid infinite recursion, AECoercePtr must never be called by an application-supplied coercion routine.

Result codes

noErr	0	No error
memFullErr	–108	Not enough room in heap zone
errAECoercionFail	–1700	Data could not be coerced to the requested descriptor type

The AECoerceDesc function coerces the data in a descriptor record to another descriptor type.

```
FUNCTION AECoerceDesc (theAEDesc: AEDesc; toType: DescType; VAR result:
                       AEDesc) : OSErr;
```

The parameter theAEDesc is the descriptor record whose data is to be coerced.

The toType parameter is the desired descriptor type of the resulting descriptor record.

The AECoerceDesc function returns in the result parameter the resulting descriptor record. This function creates a new descriptor record by copying the descriptor record from the parameter. Your application is responsible for using the AEDisposeDesc function to dispose of the resulting descriptor record once you are finished using it.

If the function returns a nonzero result code, a descriptor record with the typeNull descriptor type is returned. A descriptor record of this type does not contain any data.

Note: To avoid infinite recursion, AECoerceDesc must never be called by an application-supplied coercion routine.

Result codes

noErr	0	No error
memFullErr	–108	Not enough room in heap zone
errAECoercionFail	–1700	Data could not be coerced to the requested descriptor type

Creating and Managing the Coercion Handler Tables

The AEInstallCoercionHandler function installs a coercion handler routine in either the application or system coercion table.

```
FUNCTION AEInstallCoercionHandler (fromType: DescType; toType: DescType;
                                   handler: ProcPtr; handlerRefcon:
                                   LongInt; fromTypeIsDesc: Boolean;
                                   isSysHandler: Boolean) : OSErr;
```

The fromType parameter is the descriptor type of the data coerced by the handler, and the toType parameter is the descriptor type of the resulting data. If there was already an entry in the specified coercion handler table for the same source descriptor type and result descriptor type, it is replaced.

Therefore, before installing a handler for a particular descriptor type into the system coercion table, use the AEGetCoercionHandler function to determine whether the table already contains a handler for that descriptor type. If an entry exists, AEGetCoercionHandler returns a reference constant and a pointer to that handler. Chain these to your coercion handler by providing pointers to the previous handler and its reference constant in the handlerRefcon parameter of AEInstallCoercionHandler. When your handler is finished, use these pointers to call the previous handler. If you remove your system handler, be sure to reinstall the chained handlers.

The handler parameter is a pointer to the coercion handler routine. Note that a handler in the system coercion table must reside in the system heap; this means that if the value of the isSysHandler parameter is TRUE, the handler parameter should point to a location in the system heap. Otherwise, if you put your system handler code in your application heap, you must remove the handler when your application quits by using the AERemoveCoercionHandler function.

The handlerRefcon parameter is a reference constant that is passed by the Apple Event Manager to the handler each time the handler is called. If your handler doesn't expect a reference constant, use 0 as the value of this parameter.

The fromTypeIsDesc parameter specifies the form of the data to be coerced. If its value is TRUE, the coercion handler expects the data to be passed as a descriptor record. If its value is FALSE, the coercion handler expects a pointer to the data to be coerced. Because it is more efficient for the Apple Event Manager to provide a pointer to data than to a descriptor record, all coercion routines should accept a pointer to data if possible.

The isSysHandler parameter specifies the coercion table to which to add the handler. If its value is TRUE, the handler is added to the system coercion table and made available to all applications. If its value is FALSE, the handler is added to the application coercion table. Note that a handler in the system coercion table must reside in the system heap; this means that if the value of the isSysHandler parameter is TRUE, the handler parameter must point to a location in the system heap.

> **Note:** When an application calls a system Apple event handler, the A5 register is set up for the calling application. For this reason, if you provide a system Apple event handler, it should never use A5 global variables or anything that depends on a particular context; otherwise, the application that calls the system handler may crash.

Result codes

noErr	0	No error
memFullErr	–108	Not enough room in heap zone

The AEGetCoercionHandler function returns the handler for a specified descriptor type coercion.

```
FUNCTION AEGetCoercionHandler (fromType: DescType; toType: DescType;
                               VAR handler: ProcPtr; VAR handlerRefcon:
                               LongInt; VAR fromTypeIsDesc: Boolean;
                               isSysHandler: Boolean) : OSErr;
```

The fromType parameter is the descriptor type of the data coerced by the handler, while the parameter toType is the descriptor type of the resulting data.

The function returns a pointer to the coercion handler routine in the handler parameter.

The function returns a reference constant in the handlerRefcon parameter. The Apple Event Manager passes this reference constant to the handler each time the handler is called.

If the function returns TRUE in the fromTypeIsDesc parameter, the coercion handler expects the data to be passed as a descriptor record. If the function returns FALSE, the coercion handler expects a pointer to the data.

The isSysHandler parameter specifies the coercion table from which to get the handler. If its value is TRUE, the handler is taken from the system coercion table. If its value is FALSE, the handler is taken from the application coercion table.

Result codes

noErr	0	No error
memFullErr	–108	Not enough room in heap zone
errAEHandlerNotFound	–1717	No coercion handler found

The AERemoveCoercionHandler function removes a coercion handler routine from either the application or system coercion table.

```
FUNCTION AERemoveCoercionHandler (fromType: DescType; toType: DescType;
                                  handler: ProcPtr; isSysHandler:
                                  Boolean) : OSErr;
```

The fromType parameter is the descriptor type of the data coerced by the handler.

The toType parameter is the descriptor type of the resulting data.

The handler parameter is a pointer to the coercion handler routine. Although the fromType and toType parameters would be sufficient to identify the handler to be removed, providing the handler parameter is a safeguard to ensure that you remove the correct handler.

The isSysHandler parameter specifies the coercion table from which to remove the handler. If its value is TRUE, the handler is removed from the system coercion table. If its value is FALSE, the handler is removed from the application coercion table.

Result codes

noErr	0	No error
memFullErr	–108	Not enough room in heap zone
errAEHandlerNotFound	–1717	No coercion handler found

Creating and Managing the Special Handler Tables

The AEInstallSpecialHandler function installs a handler in a special handler table.

```
FUNCTION AEInstallSpecialHandler (functionClass: AEKeyword; handler:
                                  ProcPtr; isSysHandler: Boolean) :
                                  OSErr;
```

The functionClass parameter is the keyword for the special handler that's installed. There is currently only one value allowed for this parameter: the keyPreDispatch constant, which identifies a handler routine that is called immediately before the Apple Event Manager dispatches an Apple event. If there was already an entry in the specified special handler table for the same value of functionClass, it is replaced.

The handler parameter is a pointer to the special handler. Note that a handler in the system handler table must reside in the system heap; this means that if the value of the isSysHandler parameter is TRUE, the handler parameter should point to a location in the system heap. Otherwise, if you put your system handler code in your application heap, you must remove the handler when your application quits by using the AERemoveSpecialHandler function.

The isSysHandler parameter specifies the special handler table to which to add the handler. If its value is TRUE, the handler is added to the system handler table and made available to all applications. If its value is FALSE, the handler is added to the application handler table.

Note: When an application calls a system Apple event handler, the A5 register is set up for the calling application. For this reason, if you provide a system Apple event handler, it should never use A5 global variables or anything that depends on a particular context; otherwise, the application that calls the system handler may crash.

Result codes

noErr	0	No error
paramErr	–50	Parameter error (handler pointer is NIL or odd)
memFullErr	–108	Not enough room in heap zone
errAENotASpecialFunction	–1714	Wrong keyword for a special function

The AEGetSpecialHandler function returns a specified special handler.

```
FUNCTION AEGetSpecialHandler (functionClass: AEKeyword; VAR handler:
                              ProcPtr; isSysHandler: Boolean) :
                              OSErr;
```

The functionClass parameter is the keyword that specifies the desired special handler. There is currently only one value allowed for this parameter: the keyPreDispatch constant, which identifies a handler routine that is called immediately before the Apple Event Manager dispatches an Apple event.

The function returns a pointer to the special handler in the handler parameter.

The isSysHandler parameter specifies the special handler table from which to get the handler. If its value is TRUE, the handler is taken from the system handler table. If its value is FALSE, the handler is taken from the application handler table.

Result codes

noErr	0	No error
memFullErr	–108	Not enough room in heap zone
errAENotASpecialFunction	–1714	Wrong keyword for a special function

The AERemoveSpecialHandler function removes a handler from a special handler table.

```
FUNCTION AERemoveSpecialHandler (functionClass: AEKeyword; handler: ProcPtr;
                                 isSysHandler: Boolean) : OSErr;
```

The functionClass parameter is the keyword for the special handler to be removed. There is currently only one value allowed for the functionClass parameter: the keyPreDispatch constant, which identifies a handler routine that is called immediately before the Apple Event Manager dispatches an Apple event.

The handler parameter is a pointer to the special handler to be removed. Although the functionClass parameter would be sufficient to identify the handler to be removed, providing the handler parameter is a safeguard to ensure that you remove the correct handler.

The isSysHandler parameter specifies the special handler table from which to remove the handler. If its value is TRUE, the handler is taken from the system handler table. If its value is FALSE, the handler is removed from the application handler table.

Result codes

noErr	0	No error
memFullErr	–108	Not enough room in heap zone
errAENotASpecialFunction	–1714	Wrong keyword for a special function

SUMMARY OF THE APPLE EVENT MANAGER

Constants

```
CONST gestaltAppleEventsAttr = 'evnt';      {selector for Apple events}
      gestaltAppleEventsPresent
                             = 0;           {if this bit set, then }
                                            { Apple Event Mgr's available}

      {Apple event descriptor types}
      typeBoolean            = 'bool';      {Boolean value}
      typeChar               = 'TEXT';      {unterminated string}
      typeSMInt              = 'shor';      {16-bit integer}
      typeInteger            = 'long';      {32-bit integer}
      typeSMFloat            = 'sing';      {SANE single}
      typeFloat              = 'doub';      {SANE double}
      typeLongInteger        = 'long';      {32-bit integer}
      typeShortInteger       = 'shor';      {16-bit integer}
      typeLongFloat          = 'doub';      {SANE double}
      typeShortFloat         = 'sing';      {SANE single}
      typeExtended           = 'exte';      {SANE extended}
      typeComp               = 'comp';      {SANE comp}
      typeMagnitude          = 'magn';      {unsigned 32-bit integer}
      typeAEList             = 'list';      {list of descriptor records}
      typeAERecord           = 'reco';      {list of keyword-specified }
                                            { descriptor records}
      typeAppleEvent         = 'aevt';      {Apple event record}
      typeTrue               = 'true';      {TRUE Boolean value}
      typeFalse              = 'fals';      {FALSE Boolean value}
      typeAlias              = 'alis';      {alias record}
      typeEnumerated         = 'enum';      {enumerated data}
      typeType               = 'type';      {Four-character code for }
                                            { event class or event ID}
      typeAppParameters      = 'appa';      {Process Manager launch }
                                            { parameters}
      typeProperty           = 'prop';      {Apple event property}
      typeFSS                = 'fss ';      {file system specification}
      typeKeyword            = 'keyw';      {Apple event keyword}
      typeSectionH           = 'sect';      {handle to a section record}
      typeWildCard           = '****';      {matches any type}
      typeApplSignature      = 'sign';      {application signature}
      typeSessionID          = 'ssid';      {session ID}
      typeTargetID           = 'targ';      {target ID record}
      typeProcessSerialNumber
                             = 'psn ';      {process serial number}
      typeNull               = 'null';      {NULL or nonexistent data}
```

```
{keywords for Apple event parameters}
keyDirectObject        = '----';     {direct parameter}
keyErrorNumber         = 'errn';     {error number parameter}
keyErrorString         = 'errs';     {error string parameter}
keyProcessSerialNumber = 'psn ';     {process serial number param}

{keywords for Apple event attributes}
keyTransactionIDAttr   = 'tran';     {transaction ID}
keyReturnIDAttr        = 'rtid';     {return ID}
keyEventClassAttr      = 'evcl';     {event class}
keyEventIDAttr         = 'evid';     {event ID}
keyAddressAttr         = 'addr';     {target application}
keyOptionalKeywordAttr = 'optk';     {list of optional }
                                     { parameters for the }
                                     { Apple event}
keyTimeoutAttr         = 'timo';     {number of ticks the client }
                                     { will wait}
keyInteractLevelAttr   = 'inte';     {settings to allow Apple }
                                     { Event Mgr to bring }
                                     { server to foreground}
keyEventSourceAttr     = 'esrc';     {source application}
keyMissedKeywordAttr   = 'miss';     {first required parameter }
                                     { remaining in an Apple }
                                     { event}

{keywords for special handlers}
keyPreDispatch         = 'phac';     {identifies a handler }
                                     { routine that is called }
                                     { immediately before the }
                                     { Apple Event Manager }
                                     { dispatches an Apple event}
keySelectProc          = 'selh';     {another selector}

{event class}
kCoreEventClass        = 'aevt';     {event class for core }
                                     { Apple events}

{event IDs}
kAEOpenApplication     = 'oapp';     {event ID for Open }
                                     { Application event}
kAEOpenDocuments       = 'odoc';     {event ID for Open }
                                     { Documents event}
kAEPrintDocuments      = 'pdoc';     {event ID for Print }
                                     { Documents event}
kAEQuitApplication     = 'quit';     {event ID for Quit }
                                     { Application event}
kAEAnswer              = 'ansr';     {event ID for Apple event }
                                     { replies}
kAEApplicationDied     = 'obit';     {event ID for Application }
                                     { Died event}
```

```
{constants for setting the sendMode parameter of AESend and for }
{ the keyInteractLevelAttr attribute}
kAENoReply              = $00000001;   {client doesn't want reply}
kAEQueueReply           = $00000002;   {client wants server to }
                                       { reply in event queue}
kAEWaitReply            = $00000003;   {client wants a reply and }
                                       { will give up processor}
kAENeverInteract        = $00000010;   {server application should }
                                       { not interact with user }
                                       { for this Apple event}
kAECanInteract          = $00000020;   {server may interact with }
                                       { user for this Apple event }
                                       { to supply information}
kAEAlwaysInteract       = $00000030;   {server may interact with }
                                       { user for this Apple event }
                                       { even if no information }
                                       { is required}
kAECanSwitchLayer       = $00000040;   {server should come }
                                       { directly to foreground }
                                       { when appropriate}
kAEDontReconnect        = $00000080;   {don't reconnect if there }
                                       { is a PPC sessClosedErr}
kAEWantReceipt          = nReturnReceipt;
                                       {client wants return receipt}

{constants for the sendPriority parameter of AESend}
kAENormalPriority       = $00000000;   {put event at the back of }
                                       { event queue}
kAEHighPriority         = nAttnMsg;    {put event at the front of }
                                       { the event queue}

{constant for the returnID parameter of AECreateAppleEvent}
kAutoGenerateReturnID  = -1;           {tells Apple Event Manager }
                                       { to generate a unique }
                                       { return ID}

{constant for transaction IDs}
kAnyTransactionID       = 0;           {the Apple event is not }
                                       { part of a transaction}

{constants for timeout durations}
kAEDefaultTimeout       = -1;          {use default timeout value}
kNoTimeOut              = -2;          {never time out}

{constants for the dispatcher parameter of AEResumeTheCurrentEvent}
kAENoDispatch           = 0;           {don't redispatch the }
                                       { Apple event}
kAEUseStandardDispatch = -1;           {redispatch the Apple event }
                                       { by using its entry in the }
                                       { Apple event dispatch table}
```

Data Types

```
TYPE
    AEEventClass =
        PACKED ARRAY[1..4] OF Char;          {event class for a }
                                             { high-level event}
    AEEventID =
        PACKED ARRAY[1..4] OF Char;          {event ID for a high-level }
                                             { event}
    AEKeyword =
        PACKED ARRAY[1..4] OF Char;          {keyword for a descriptor }
                                             { record}

    DescType                = ResType;       {descriptor type}

    AEDesc =
    RECORD                                   {descriptor record}
        descriptorType:     DescType;        {type of data being passed}
        dataHandle:         Handle           {handle to data being passed}
    END;

    AEKeyDesc =                              {keyword-specified }
                                             { descriptor record}
    RECORD
        descKey:            AEKeyword;       {keyword}
        descContent:        AEDesc           {descriptor record}
    END;

    AEAddressDesc           = AEDesc;        {address descriptor record}

    AEDescList              = AEDesc;        {list of descriptor records}

    AERecord                = AEDescList;    {list of keyword-specified }
                                             { descriptor records}

    AppleEvent              = AERecord;      {list of attributes and }
                                             { parameters necessary for }
                                             { an Apple event}

    AESendMode              = LongInt;       {flags that determine how }
                                             { an Apple event is sent}

    AESendPriority          = Integer;       {send priority of an Apple }
                                             { event}

    AEInteractAllowed = (kAEInteractWithSelf, kAEInteractWithLocal,
                         kAEInteractWithAll);
                                             {what processes may }
                                             { interact with the user}
```

```
AEEventSource = (kAEUnknownSource, kAEDirectCall, kAESameProcess,
                 kAELocalProcess, kAERemoteProcess);
                                          {the source of an Apple }
                                          { event}

AEArrayType = (kAEDataArray, kAEPackedArray, kAEHandleArray,
               kAEDescArray, kAEKeyDescArray);
                                          {type of an Apple event }
                                          { array}

AEArrayData =
RECORD                                    {data for an Apple event }
                                          { array}
   case AEArrayType OF
   kAEDataArray:
     (AEDataArray:      ARRAY[0..0] OF Integer);
   kAEPackedArray:
     (AEPackedArray:    PACKED ARRAY[0..0] OF Char);
   kAEHandleArray:
     (AEHandleArray:    ARRAY[0..0] OF Handle);
   kAEDescArray:
     (AEDescArray:      ARRAY[0..0] OF AEDesc);
   kAEKeyDescArray:
     (AEKeyDescArray:   ARRAY[0..0] OF AEKeyDesc);
END;

AEArrayDataPointer = ^AEArrayData;

EventHandlerProcPtr = ProcPtr;            {pointer to an Apple event }
                                          { handler routine}

IdleProcPtr = ProcPtr;                    {pointer to an app's }
                                          { idle function}

EventFilterProcPtr = ProcPtr;             {pointer to an app's filter }
                                          { procedure}
```

Routines

Creating and Managing the Apple Event Dispatch Tables

```
FUNCTION AEInstallEventHandler  (theAEEventClass: AEEventClass;
                                 theAEEventID: AEEventID; handler:
                                 EventHandlerProcPtr; handlerRefcon:
                                 LongInt; isSysHandler: Boolean) : OSErr;

FUNCTION AEGetEventHandler      (theAEEventClass: AEEventClass;
                                 theAEEventID: AEEventID; VAR handler:
                                 EventHandlerProcPtr; VAR handlerRefcon:
                                 LongInt; isSysHandler: Boolean) : OSErr;
```

6 Apple Event Manager

```
FUNCTION AERemoveEventHandler    (theAEEventClass: AEEventClass;
                                  theAEEventID: AEEventID; handler:
                                  EventHandlerProcPtr; isSysHandler:
                                  Boolean) : OSErr;
```

Dispatching Apple Events

```
FUNCTION AEProcessAppleEvent     (theEventRecord: EventRecord) : OSErr;
```

Getting Parameters and Attributes From Apple Events

```
FUNCTION AEGetParamPtr           (theAppleEvent: AppleEvent; theAEKeyword:
                                  AEKeyword; desiredType: DescType;
                                  VAR typeCode: DescType; dataPtr: Ptr;
                                  maximumSize: Size; VAR actualSize: Size)
                                  : OSErr;

FUNCTION AEGetParamDesc          (theAppleEvent: AppleEvent; theAEKeyword:
                                  AEKeyword; desiredType: DescType;
                                  VAR result: AEDesc) : OSErr;

FUNCTION AEGetAttributePtr       (theAppleEvent: AppleEvent; theAEKeyword:
                                  AEKeyword; desiredType: DescType;
                                  VAR typeCode: DescType; dataPtr: Ptr;
                                  maximumSize: Size; VAR actualSize: Size)
                                  : OSErr;

FUNCTION AEGetAttributeDesc      (theAppleEvent: AppleEvent; theAEKeyword:
                                  AEKeyword; desiredType: DescType;
                                  VAR result: AEDesc) : OSErr;
```

Counting the Items in Descriptor Lists

```
FUNCTION AECountItems        (theAEDescList: AEDescList; VAR theCount:
                              LongInt) : OSErr;
```

Getting Items From Descriptor Lists

```
FUNCTION AEGetNthPtr         (theAEDescList: AEDescList; index: LongInt;
                              desiredType: DescType; VAR theAEKeyword:
                              AEKeyword; VAR typeCode: DescType; dataPtr:
                              Ptr; maximumSize: Size; VAR actualSize: Size) :
                              OSErr;

FUNCTION AEGetNthDesc        (theAEDescList: AEDescList; index: LongInt;
                              desiredType: DescType; VAR theAEKeyword:
                              AEKeyword; VAR result: AEDesc) : OSErr;
```

```
FUNCTION AEGetArray          (theAEDescList: AEDescList; arrayType:
                              AEArrayType; arrayPtr: AEArrayDataPointer;
                              maximumSize: Size; VAR itemType: DescType;
                              VAR itemSize: Size; VAR itemCount: LongInt) :
                              OSErr;
```

Getting Data and Keyword-Specified Descriptor Records From AE Records

```
FUNCTION AEGetKeyPtr         (theAERecord: AERecord; theAEKeyword: AEKeyword;
                              desiredType: DescType; VAR typeCode: DescType;
                              dataPtr: Ptr; maximumSize: Size;
                              VAR actualSize: Size) : OSErr;

FUNCTION AEGetKeyDesc        (theAERecord: AERecord; theAEKeyword:
                              AEKeyword; desiredType: DescType; VAR result:
                              AEDesc) : OSErr;
```

Requesting User Interaction

```
FUNCTION AESetInteractionAllowed   (level: AEInteractAllowed) : OSErr;

FUNCTION AEGetInteractionAllowed   (VAR level: AEInteractAllowed) :
                                    OSErr;

FUNCTION AEInteractWithUser        (timeOutInTicks: LongInt; nmReqPtr:
                                    NMRecPtr; idleProc: IdleProcPtr) :
                                    OSErr;
```

Requesting More Time to Respond to Apple Events

```
FUNCTION AEResetTimer              (reply: AppleEvent) : OSErr;
```

Suspending and Resuming Apple Event Handling

```
FUNCTION AESuspendTheCurrentEvent  (theAppleEvent: AppleEvent) : OSErr;

FUNCTION AEResumeTheCurrentEvent   (theAppleEvent,reply: AppleEvent;
                                    dispatcher: EventHandlerProcPtr;
                                    handlerRefcon: LongInt) : OSErr;

FUNCTION AESetTheCurrentEvent      (theAppleEvent: AppleEvent) : OSErr;

FUNCTION AEGetTheCurrentEvent      (VAR theAppleEvent: AppleEvent) :
                                    OSErr;
```

Creating Apple Events

```
FUNCTION AECreateAppleEvent    (theAEEventClass: AEEventClass;
                                theAEEventID: AEEventID; target:
                                AEAddressDesc; returnID: Integer;
                                transactionID: LongInt; VAR result:
                                AppleEvent) : OSErr;
```

Creating and Duplicating Descriptor Records

```
FUNCTION AECreateDesc          (typeCode: DescType; dataPtr: Ptr; dataSize:
                                Size; VAR result: AEDesc) : OSErr;

FUNCTION AEDuplicateDesc       (theAEDesc: AEDesc; VAR result: AEDesc) :
                                OSErr;
```

Creating Descriptor Lists and AE Records

```
FUNCTION AECreateList          (factoringPtr: Ptr; factoredSize: Size;
                                isRecord: Boolean; VAR resultList: AEDescList)
                                : OSErr;
```

Adding Items to Descriptor Lists

```
FUNCTION AEPutPtr              (theAEDescList: AEDescList; index: LongInt;
                                typeCode: DescType; dataPtr: Ptr; dataSize:
                                Size) : OSErr;

FUNCTION AEPutDesc             (theAEDescList: AEDescList; index: LongInt;
                                theAEDesc: AEDesc) : OSErr;

FUNCTION AEPutArray            (theAEDescList: AEDescList; arrayType:
                                AEArrayType; arrayPtr: AEArrayDataPointer;
                                itemType: DescType; itemSize: Size;
                                itemCount: LongInt) : OSErr;
```

Adding Data and Keyword-Specified Descriptor Records to AE Records

```
FUNCTION AEPutKeyPtr           (theAERecord: AERecord; theAEKeyword: AEKeyword;
                                typeCode: DescType; dataPtr: Ptr; dataSize:
                                Size) : OSErr;

FUNCTION AEPutKeyDesc          (theAERecord: AERecord; theAEKeyword:
                                AEKeyword; theAEDesc: AEDesc) : OSErr;
```

Adding Parameters and Attributes to Apple Events

```
FUNCTION AEPutParamPtr       (theAppleEvent: AppleEvent; theAEKeyword:
                              AEKeyword; typeCode: DescType; dataPtr: Ptr;
                              dataSize: Size) : OSErr;
FUNCTION AEPutParamDesc      (theAppleEvent: AppleEvent; theAEKeyword:
                              AEKeyword; theAEDesc: AEDesc) : OSErr;
FUNCTION AEPutAttributePtr   (theAppleEvent: AppleEvent; theAEKeyword:
                              AEKeyword; typeCode: DescType; dataPtr: Ptr;
                              dataSize: Size) : OSErr;
FUNCTION AEPutAttributeDesc  (theAppleEvent: AppleEvent; theAEKeyword:
                              AEKeyword; theAEDesc: AEDesc) : OSErr;
```

Sending Apple Events

```
FUNCTION AESend             (theAppleEvent: AppleEvent; VAR reply:
                             AppleEvent; sendMode: AESendMode; sendPriority:
                             AESendPriority; timeOutInTicks: LongInt;
                             idleProc: IdleProcPtr; filterProc:
                             EventFilterProcPtr) : OSErr;
```

Getting the Sizes and Descriptor Types of Descriptor Records

```
FUNCTION AESizeOfNthItem    (theAEDescList: AEDescList; index: LongInt;
                             VAR typeCode: DescType; VAR dataSize: Size) :
                             OSErr;
FUNCTION AESizeOfKeyDesc    (theAERecord: AERecord; theAEKeyword:
                             AEKeyword; VAR typeCode: DescType;
                             VAR dataSize: Size) : OSErr;
FUNCTION AESizeOfParam      (theAppleEvent: AppleEvent; theAEKeyword:
                             AEKeyword; VAR typeCode: DescType;
                             VAR dataSize: Size) : OSErr;
FUNCTION AESizeOfAttribute  (theAppleEvent: AppleEvent; theAEKeyword:
                             AEKeyword; VAR typeCode: DescType;
                             VAR dataSize: Size) : OSErr;
```

Deleting Descriptor Records

```
FUNCTION AEDeleteItem       (theAEDescList: AEDescList; index: LongInt) :
                             OSErr;
FUNCTION AEDeleteKeyDesc    (theAERecord: AERecord; theAEKeyword:
                             AEKeyword) : OSErr;
FUNCTION AEDeleteParam      (theAppleEvent: AppleEvent; theAEKeyword:
                             AEKeyword) : OSErr;
```

Deallocating Memory for Descriptor Records

```
FUNCTION AEDisposeDesc      (VAR theAEDesc: AEDesc) : OSErr;
```

Coercing Descriptor Types

```
FUNCTION AECoercePtr        (typeCode: DescType; dataPtr: Ptr; dataSize:
                             Size; toType: DescType; VAR result: AEDesc) :
                             OSErr;

FUNCTION AECoerceDesc       (theAEDesc: AEDesc; toType: DescType; VAR
                             result: AEDesc) : OSErr;
```

Creating and Managing the Coercion Handler Tables

```
FUNCTION AEInstallCoercionHandler  (fromType: DescType; toType: DescType;
                                    handler: ProcPtr; handlerRefcon:
                                    LongInt; fromTypeIsDesc: Boolean;
                                    isSysHandler: Boolean) : OSErr;

FUNCTION AEGetCoercionHandler      (fromType: DescType; toType: DescType;
                                    VAR handler: ProcPtr;
                                    VAR handlerRefcon: LongInt;
                                    VAR fromTypeIsDesc: Boolean;
                                    isSysHandler: Boolean) : OSErr;

FUNCTION AERemoveCoercionHandler   (fromType: DescType; toType: DescType;
                                    handler: ProcPtr; isSysHandler:
                                    Boolean) : OSErr;
```

Creating and Managing the Special Handler Tables

```
FUNCTION AEInstallSpecialHandler   (functionClass: AEKeyword; handler:
                                    ProcPtr; isSysHandler: Boolean) :
                                    OSErr;

FUNCTION AEGetSpecialHandler       (functionClass: AEKeyword;
                                    VAR handler: ProcPtr; isSysHandler:
                                    Boolean) : OSErr;

FUNCTION AERemoveSpecialHandler    (functionClass: AEKeyword; handler:
                                    ProcPtr; isSysHandler: Boolean) :
                                    OSErr;
```

Application-Defined Routines

```
FUNCTION MyEventHandler      (theAppleEvent: AppleEvent; reply: AppleEvent;
                              handlerRefcon: LongInt) : OSErr;

FUNCTION MyIdleFunction      (VAR theEventRecord: EventRecord;
                              VAR sleepTime: LongInt; VAR mouseRgn:
                              RgnHandle) : Boolean;

FUNCTION MyWaitReplyFilter   (VAR theEventRecord: EventRecord;
                              returnID: LongInt; transactionID: LongInt;
                              sender: AEAddressDesc) : Boolean;

FUNCTION MyCoercePtr         (typeCode: DescType; dataPtr: Ptr; dataSize:
                              Size; toType: DescType; handlerRefcon:
                              LongInt; VAR result: AEDesc) : OSErr;

FUNCTION MyCoerceDesc        (theAEDesc: AEDesc; toType: DescType;
                              handlerRefcon: LongInt; VAR result: AEDesc) :
                              OSErr;
```

Result Codes

noErr	0	No error
paramErr	–50	Parameter error (handler pointer is NIL or odd)
memFullErr	–108	Not enough room in heap zone
bufferIsSmall	–607	Buffer is too small
noOutstandingHLE	–608	No outstanding high-level event
connectionInvalid	–609	Connection is invalid
errAECoercionFail	–1700	Data could not be coerced to the requested descriptor type
errAEDescNotFound	–1701	Descriptor record was not found
errAECorruptData	–1702	Data in an Apple event could not be read
errAEWrongDataType	–1703	Wrong descriptor type
errAENotAEDesc	–1704	Not a valid descriptor record
errAEBadListItem	–1705	Operation involving a list item failed
errAENewerVersion	–1706	Need a newer version of the Apple Event Manager
errAENotAppleEvent	–1707	Event is not an Apple event
errAEEventNotHandled	–1708	Event wasn't handled by an Apple event handler
errAEReplyNotValid	–1709	AEResetTimer was passed an invalid reply
errAEUnknownSendMode	–1710	Invalid sending mode was passed
errAEWaitCanceled	–1711	User canceled out of wait loop for reply or receipt
errAETimeout	–1712	Apple event timed out
errAENoUserInteraction	–1713	No user interaction allowed
errAENotASpecialFunction	–1714	Wrong keyword for a special function
errAEParamMissed	–1715	Handler did not get all required parameters
errAEUnknownAddressType	–1716	Unknown Apple event address type
errAEHandlerNotFound	–1717	No handler found for an Apple event or a coercion
errAEReplyNotArrived	–1718	Reply has not yet arrived
errAEIllegalIndex	–1719	Not a valid list index

Assembly-Language Information

Trap Macros Requiring Routine Selectors

_Pack8

Selector	Routine
$011E	AESetInteractionAllowed
$0204	AEDisposeDesc
$0219	AEResetTimer
$021A	AEGetTheCurrentEvent
$021B	AEProcessAppleEvent
$021D	AEGetInteractionAllowed
$022B	AESuspendTheCurrentEvent
$022C	AESetTheCurrentEvent
$0405	AEDuplicateDesc
$0407	AECountItems
$040E	AEDeleteItem
$0413	AEDeleteKeyDesc
$0413	AEDeleteParam
$0500	AEInstallSpecialHandler
$0501	AERemoveSpecialHandler
$052D	AEGetSpecialHandler
$0603	AECoerceDesc
$0609	AEPutDesc
$0610	AEPutKeyDesc
$0610	AEPutParamDesc
$061C	AEInteractWithUser
$0627	AEPutAttributeDesc
$0706	AECreateList
$0720	AERemoveEventHandler
$0723	AERemoveCoercionHandler
$0812	AEGetKeyDesc
$0812	AEGetParamDesc
$0818	AEResumeTheCurrentEvent
$0825	AECreateDesc
$0826	AEGetAttributeDesc
$0828	AESizeOfAttribute
$0829	AESizeOfKeyDesc
$0829	AESizeOfParam
$082A	AESizeOfNthItem
$091F	AEInstallEventHandler
$0921	AEGetEventHandler
$0A02	AECoercePtr
$0A08	AEPutPtr
$0A16	AEPutAttributePtr
$0A22	AEInstallCoercionHandler
$0A0B	AEGetNthDesc
$0A0F	AEPutKeyPtr
$0A0F	AEPutParamPtr
$0B0D	AEPutArray

Selector	Routine
$0B14	AECreateAppleEvent
$0B24	AEGetCoercionHandler
$0D0C	AEGetArray
$0D17	AESend
$0E11	AEGetKeyPtr
$0E11	AEGetParamPtr
$0E15	AEGetAttributePtr
$100A	AEGetNthPtr

7 THE PROGRAM-TO-PROGRAM COMMUNICATIONS TOOLBOX

ABOUT THIS CHAPTER

This chapter describes how you can use the Program-to-Program Communications (PPC) Toolbox to send and receive low-level message blocks between applications.

The PPC Toolbox can be used by different applications located on the same computer or across a network of Macintosh® computers. The PPC Toolbox is available only in system software version 7.0. To test for the existence of the PPC Toolbox, use the Gestalt function, described in the Compatibility Guidelines chapter of this volume.

Read this chapter if you want your application to transmit and receive data from other applications that support the PPC Toolbox. Applications that utilize the PPC Toolbox must be open and connected to each other to exchange data. The PPC Toolbox allows you to send large amounts of data to other applications; it is typically useful for code that is not event-based. The PPC Toolbox is called by the Macintosh Operating System and can also be called by applications, device drivers, desk accessories, or other programs.

The PPC Toolbox provides a method of communication that is particularly useful for applications that are specifically designed to work together and are dependent on each other for information. For example, suppose one user organizes large amounts of data using a database application and another user filters and plots the same data using a plotting application. If both applications use the PPC Toolbox, these two applications can directly transmit data to each other when both applications are open and connected to each other.

You can also use the PPC Toolbox if your application communicates with other applications using high-level events or Apple® events, and your application allows the user to choose another application to communicate with. You can use a PPC Toolbox routine that provides a standard user interface to display a dialog box on the user's screen that lists other applications that are available to exchange information. See "Browsing for Ports Using the Program Linking Dialog Box" later in this chapter for detailed information. Elsewhere in this volume, see the Events Manager chapter for information on high-level events, and see the Apple Event Manager chapter for information on Apple events.

The PPC Toolbox uses the AppleTalk® Data Stream Protocol (ADSP) and the Name-Binding Protocol (NBP). For detailed information on ADSP, see the AppleTalk Manager chapter in this volume. For further information on NBP, see the AppleTalk Manager chapters in Volume II, Volume V, and this volume.

> **Note:** The sample applications "store data," "display data," "send and receive," "make memo," and "spell quick" used in this chapter are not actual products of Apple Computer, Inc. They are used for illustrative purposes only.

ABOUT THE PPC TOOLBOX

The PPC Toolbox provides you with the ability to

- exchange data with other open applications on the same computer or across a network of Macintosh computers
- browse through a listing of applications that are available to exchange data
- verify user identities for communication across a network

To utilize the PPC Toolbox to exchange data between open applications, each application involved must support the PPC Toolbox.

This chapter first defines the main elements of the PPC Toolbox and then discusses how to

- set up your application for communication
- use security features prior to establishing communication
- locate other applications that can exchange data
- initiate communication between applications
- accept or reject incoming communications requests
- transmit and receive data between applications
- terminate communication between applications

PORTS, SESSIONS, AND MESSAGE BLOCKS

To initiate communication between applications, you must first open a port. A **port** is a portal through which your application can exchange information with another application. A port is designated by a port name and a location name.

A **port name** is a unique identifier for a particular application on a computer. The port name contains a name string, a type string, and a script code for localization. The **location name** identifies the location of the computer on the network. The location name contains an object string, a type string, and a zone. An application can specify an alias location name by modifying its type string.

Your application can open as many ports as it requires as long as each port name is unique within a particular computer. See "Specifying Port Names and Location Names" later in this chapter for detailed information on port names and location names.

Through its port, an open application can communicate with another open application during a **session.** One port can support any number of communication sessions. During a session, an application sends and receives data in the form of a **message block.** The PPC Toolbox treats each block of data as a byte stream and delivers it in the same sequence in which it was sent.

The words *port name, location name, session,* and *message block* are programmatic terms. You should not use them in the user interface of your application or in your user documentation. Instead, refer to a file that contains executable code as an *application program.* An application program that opens and uses PPC ports supports *program linking*. When you *link* two application programs together, you are forming a *program link.* A link allows two application programs to communicate with each other—you *unlink* two application programs when you break the link between them. You can compare the link between two application programs to the communication established using telephones. For example, a program link is similar to a telephone connection that enables various forms of communication such as human-to-human, modem-to-modem, and facsimile machine–to–facsimile machine.

Figure 7-1 shows a database application on one computer that has initiated a session with a spreadsheet application located on another computer on the network.

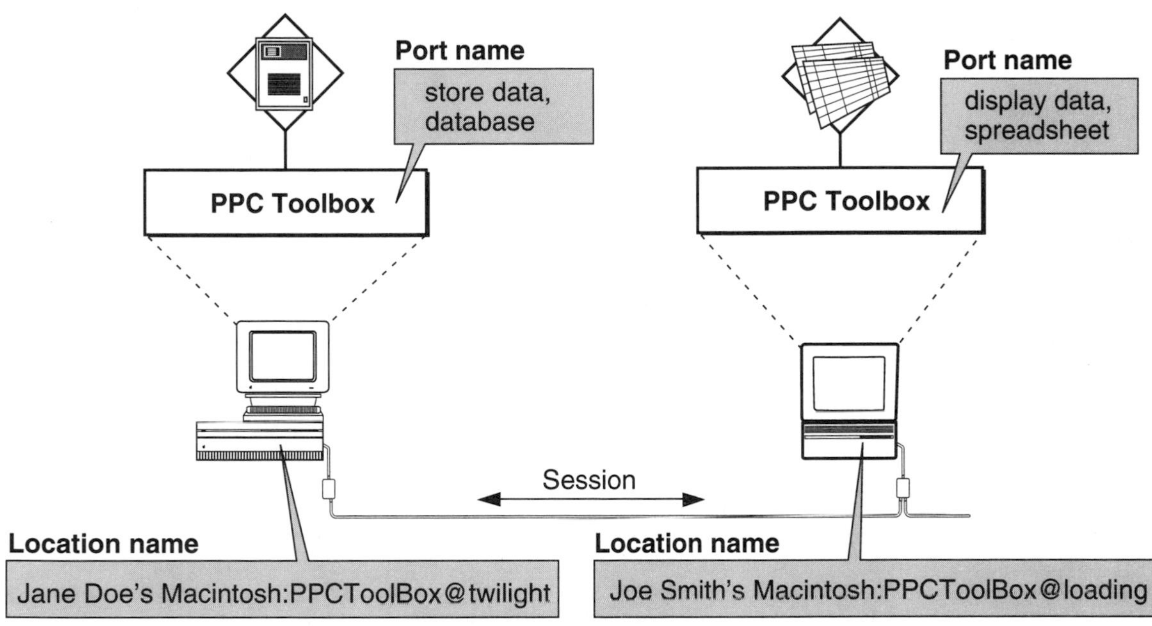

Figure 7-1. A PPC Toolbox session between two applications

The database application's port name consists of "store data" (the name string) and "database" (the type string). Its location name consists of "Jane Doe's Macintosh" (the object string), "PPCToolBox" (the type string), and "twilight" (the AppleTalk zone).

The spreadsheet application's port name consists of "display data" (the name string) and "spreadsheet" (the type string). Its location name consists of "Joe Smith's Macintosh" (the object string), "PPCToolBox" (the type string), and "loading" (the AppleTalk zone).

SETTING UP AUTHENTICATED SESSIONS

Network communication must be active to initiate sessions with other computers across a network. The user must activate AppleTalk in the Chooser and enable program linking using the Sharing Setup icon located in the Control Panels folder inside the System Folder. Figure 7-2 displays the Sharing Setup icon.

Figure 7-2. The Sharing Setup icon

Figure 7-3 shows the Sharing Setup control panel that the Finder™ displays when the user opens the Sharing Setup icon.

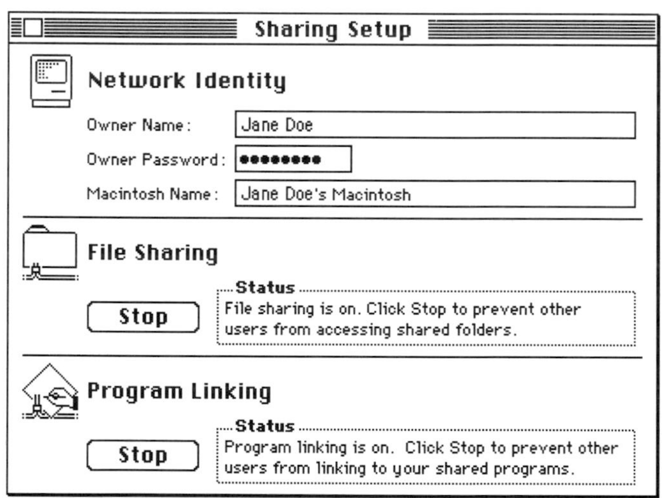

Figure 7-3. The Sharing Setup control panel

To permit other computers to initiate sessions with the owner's computer, the owner of the computer must click the Start button underneath Program Linking (Start toggles with Stop). The Sharing Setup control panel then indicates "Program linking is on. Click Stop to prevent other users from linking to your shared programs." To prevent other computers from initiating sessions, an owner simply clicks Stop underneath Program Linking. The Sharing Setup control panel then indicates "Program linking is off. Click Start to allow other users to link to your shared programs." Clicking the Start or Stop button also enables or disables the transmission of incoming Apple events across the network.

If a user clicks the Stop button while there are active incoming sessions (sessions initiated by other users), an alert box (shown in Figure 7-4) appears on the user's screen.

There are users currently linked to your programs, and the links will be immediately broken.

Cancel OK

Figure 7-4. The session termination alert box

If a user clicks OK, all active sessions initiated by other users are immediately terminated. Note that it is still possible for the owner of the computer to initiate sessions, even though other users may not initiate sessions with the owner's computer.

The PPC Toolbox establishes the identity of users through the process of **authentication.** The authentication mechanism of the PPC Toolbox identifies each user through an assigned name and password. Each session initiated with a port that is located on a remote computer requires authentication (unless guest access is enabled) before a session is permitted. Sessions between applications located on the same computer never require authentication.

A computer's owner can establish access for other users and guests by opening the users and groups icon located in the Control Panels folder. When an owner opens the users and groups icon, the Finder displays the users and groups control panel. The users and groups control panel allows an owner to specify the names and passwords of other users whose computers can initiate sessions with his or her ports across the network. When the computer's owner opens the users and groups control panel, the Guest icon appears. If the owner's name is specified in the Sharing Setup control panel, an icon with the owner's name also appears.

To specify a particular new user, the owner chooses New User from the File menu. The owner should type in the user's name. When the owner opens a user icon in the users and groups control panel, the Finder displays the users and groups dialog box on the owner's screen. Figure 7-5 shows the users and groups dialog box for a particular user.

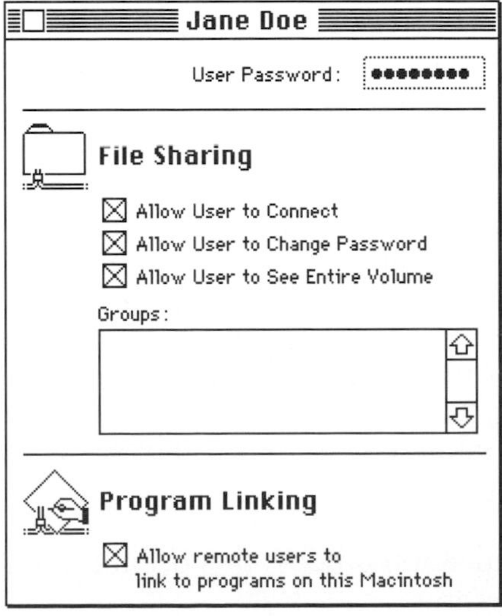

Figure 7-5. The users and groups dialog box

To permit authenticated session requests, the owner can specify a password for each user. The owner allows other users to utilize the PPC Toolbox by clicking the check box under Program Linking. If the owner clicks the check box again, all active sessions initiated by this particular user are immediately terminated. The user termination alert box (shown in Figure 7-6) is displayed as a warning.

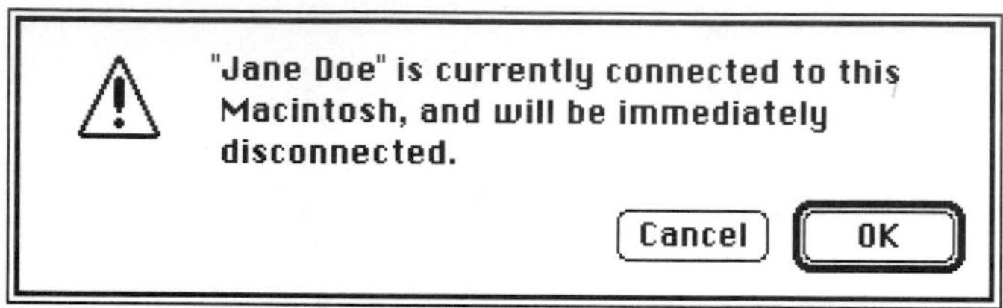

Figure 7-6. The user termination alert box

When the owner opens a Guest icon in the users and groups control panel, the Finder displays the guest dialog box on the owner's screen. Authentication is not required if the owner permits guest access. Figure 7-7 shows the guest dialog box.

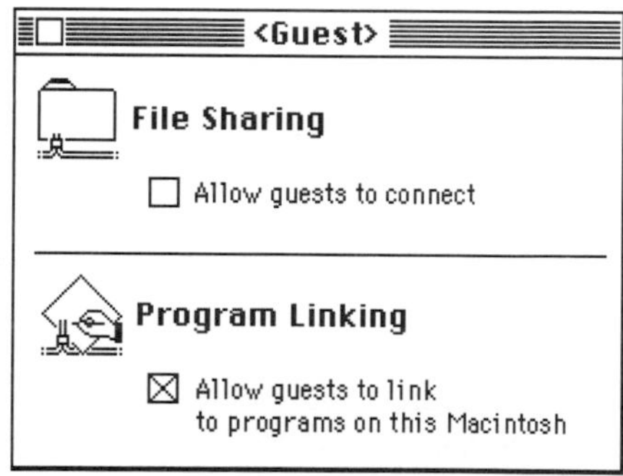

Figure 7-7. The guest dialog box

By clicking the check box under Program Linking, the owner permits guests to communicate using the PPC Toolbox or Apple events.

As an example of the authentication process, one user might decide to make a dictionary service available to other users. Another user may wish to employ this service in a word-processing program. Assuming both programs support the PPC Toolbox, the word-processing program attempts to gain access to the dictionary service that is open on the other user's computer by initiating a session. When the word-processing application requests a session, the PPC Toolbox attempts to authenticate the user by requesting a user name and a password (unless guest access is enabled). If the authentication process verifies the user's identity and the dictionary application accepts the request for a session, a session is established and the user can access the dictionary's data.

Figure 7-8 illustrates the authentication process that occurs when a user attempts to initiate a session.

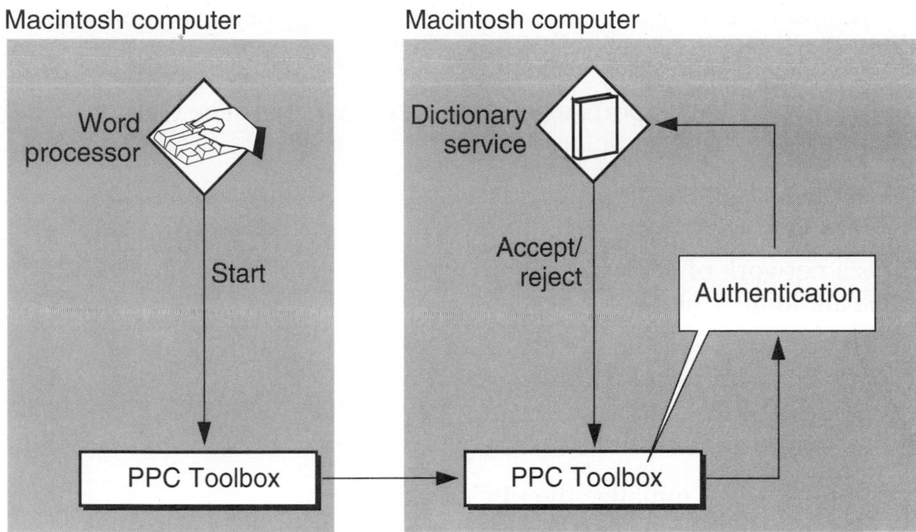

Figure 7-8. The PPC Toolbox authentication process

USING THE PPC TOOLBOX

This section describes

- PPC Toolbox calling conventions
- opening a port
- listing all available port locations on the network
- indicating that a port is available to accept session requests
- initiating a session
- accepting and rejecting session requests
- reading and writing data during a session
- ending a session after data is transmitted and received
- closing a port when it is no longer needed to transmit or receive data
- invalidating users

To begin, you must determine whether the PPC Toolbox is available on the user's computer system by using the Gestalt function. The Gestalt selector is gestaltPPCToolboxAttr. A noErr result code indicates that the PPC Toolbox is present.

The Gestalt function returns a combination of the following constants: gestaltPPCToolboxPresent, gestaltPPCSupportsRealTime, gestaltPPCSupportsOutGoing, and gestaltPPCSupportsIncoming.

The PPC Toolbox currently supports only sessions in real time. The Gestalt function returns gestaltPPCSupportsRealTime by default. If this bit is not set, you need to initialize the PPC Toolbox.

The Gestalt function returns gestaltPPCSupportsOutGoing to indicate support of outgoing sessions across a network of Macintosh computers. If this bit is not set, the user hasn't enabled AppleTalk in the Chooser.

The Gestalt function returns gestaltPPCSupportsIncoming if the user has enabled program linking in the Sharing Setup control panel. If this bit is not set, the user either hasn't enabled AppleTalk in the Chooser or hasn't enabled program linking in the Sharing Setup control panel.

Use the PPCInit function to initialize the PPC Toolbox.

```
err := PPCInit;
```

Listing 7-1 illustrates how you use the PPCInit function to initialize the PPC Toolbox.

Listing 7-1. Initializing the PPC Toolbox using the PPCInit function

```
FUNCTION MyPPCInit : OSErr;

VAR
   PPCAttributes: LongInt;
   err:           OSErr;

BEGIN {myPPCInit}
   err := Gestalt(gestaltPPCToolboxAttr, PPCAttributes);
   IF err = noErr
      THEN {PPC Toolbox is present}
         BEGIN
            IF BAND(PPCAttributes, gestaltPPCSupportsRealTime) = 0
               THEN {PPC Toolbox needs initialization}
                  BEGIN
                     {initialize the PPC Toolbox and set function result}
                     err := PPCInit;
                     {test the attributes for the PPC Toolbox}
                     err := Gestalt(gestaltPPCToolboxAttr,
                                    PPCAttributes);
                  END;

            IF BAND(PPCAttributes, gestaltPPCSupportsOutGoing) <> 0
               THEN
                  {ports can be opened to the outside world}
               ELSE;
                  {it's likely that AppleTalk is disabled, so you may }
                  { want to tell the user to activate AppleTalk from }
                  { the Chooser}
```

```
            IF BAND(PPCAttributes, gestaltPPCSupportsIncoming) <> 0
               THEN
                  {ports can be opened with location names that the }
                  { outside world can see}
               ELSE;
                  {it's likely that program linking is disabled, so you }
                  { may want to tell the user to start program linking }
                  { from the Sharing Setup control panel}
         END;
   MyPPCInit := err;
END;  {MyPPCInit}
```

Figure 7-9 illustrates a database application (on the left) that has initiated a session with a spreadsheet application (on the right) to exchange data using the PPC Toolbox. This figure includes an example of the sequence of PPC Toolbox routines executed by these applications. Detailed descriptions of the functions appear in the sections that follow.

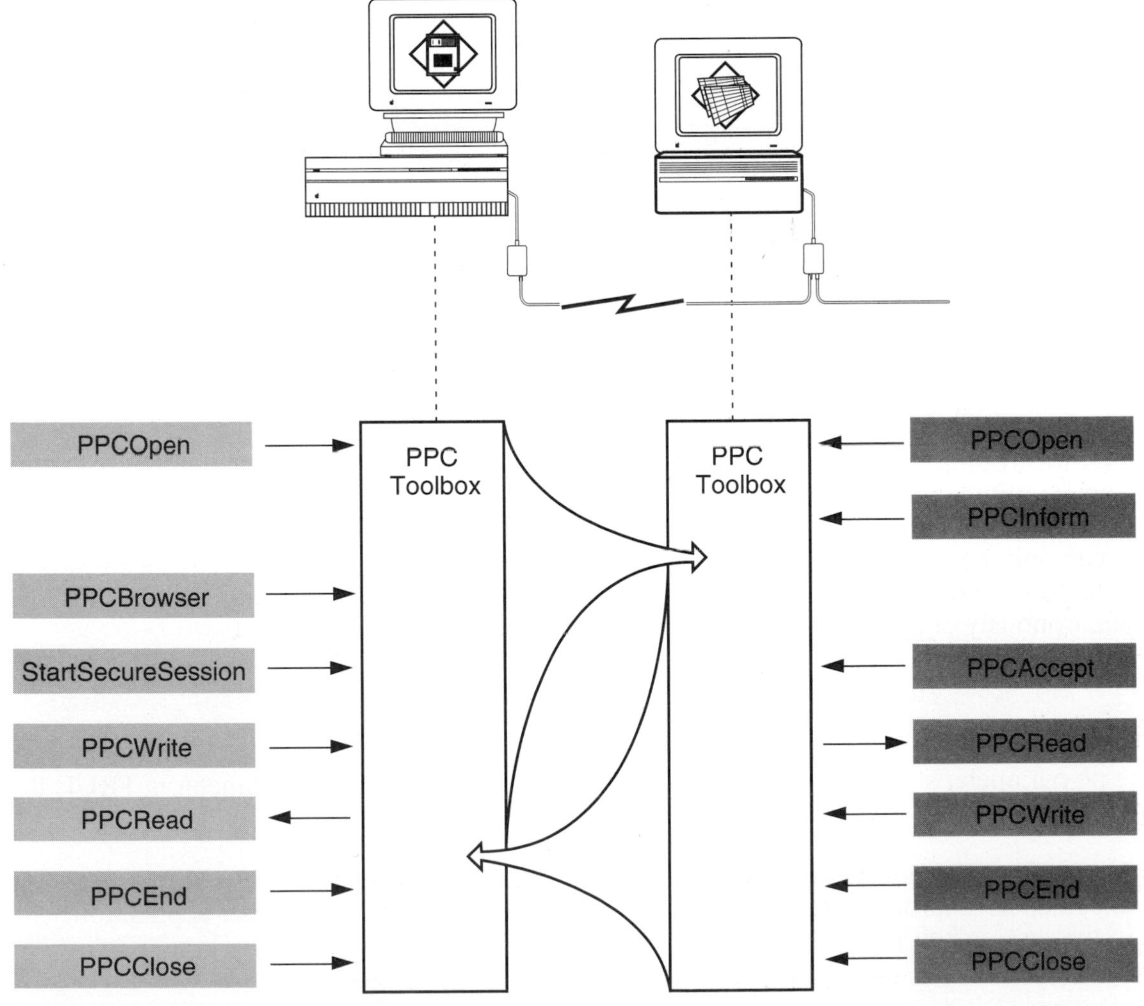

Figure 7-9. Database and spreadsheet applications using the PPC Toolbox

To establish a session, each application must first open a port using the PPCOpen function. The spreadsheet application prepares to receive session requests by calling the PPCInform function.

Before initiating a session or opening a port, the database application can let the user browse through the list of available ports (using the PPCBrowser function). If the user decides to communicate with the spreadsheet application, the database application initiates a session with the spreadsheet application's port using the StartSecureSession function. After the PPC Toolbox authenticates the user name and password of the initiating port, the spreadsheet application accepts the session request (using the PPCAccept function).

Once the session is established, the applications exchange information in the form of message blocks (using the PPCRead and PPCWrite functions). During a session, an application can both read from and write message blocks to another application. After the information exchange is done, each application ends the session (PPCEnd) and then closes its port (PPCClose) when it quits.

The PPCOpen function returns a port reference number. The port reference number is a reference number for the port through which you are requesting a session. The database application uses the port reference number in subsequent calls to the StartSecureSession and PPCClose functions. The StartSecureSession function returns a session reference number. The session reference number is used to identify the session during the exchange of data. It is used in subsequent calls to the PPCWrite, PPCRead, and PPCEnd functions.

The PPCOpen function returns a port reference number that the spreadsheet uses in subsequent calls to the PPCInform and PPCClose functions. The PPCInform function returns a session reference number that is used in subsequent calls to the PPCAccept, PPCRead, PPCWrite, and PPCEnd functions.

PPC Toolbox Calling Conventions

Most PPC Toolbox functions can execute synchronously (meaning that the application cannot continue until the function completes execution) or asynchronously (meaning that the application is free to perform other tasks while the function is executing). The PPC Toolbox functions that can only be executed synchronously include PPCInit, PPCBrowser, StartSecureSession, DeleteUserIdentity, and GetDefaultUser. All other PPC Toolbox functions can execute asynchronously or synchronously. Here's an example:

```
FUNCTION MyPPCFunction (pb: PPCParamBlockPtr; async: Boolean) : OSErr;
```

The pb parameter should point to a PPC parameter block. The async parameter is TRUE if the function is to be executed asynchronously.

> **Note:** The PPCInform, PPCRead, and PPCWrite functions should always be executed asynchronously, because they require interaction from the other application in the session before they complete execution.

The PPCParamBlockRec data type defines the PPC parameter block.

```
TYPE PPCParamBlockRec =
     RECORD
        CASE Integer OF
        0: (openParam:         PPCOpenPBRec);          {PPCOpen params}
        1: (informParam:       PPCInformPBRec);        {PPCInform params}
        2: (startParam:        PPCStartPBRec);         {PPCStart params}
        3: (acceptParam:       PPCAcceptPBRec);        {PPCAccept params}
        4: (rejectParam:       PPCRejectPBRec);        {PPCReject params}
        5: (writeParam:        PPCWritePBRec);         {PPCWrite params}
        6: (readParam:         PPCReadPBRec);          {PPCRead params}
        7: (endParam:          PPCEndPBRec);           {PPCEnd params}
        8: (closeParam:        PPCClosePBRec);         {PPCClose params}
        9: (listPortsParam:    IPCListPortsPBRec)      {IPCListPorts }
                                                       { params}
     END;
```

Your application transfers ownership of the PPC parameter block (and any buffers or records pointed to by the PPC parameter block) to the PPC Toolbox until a PPC function completes execution. Once the function completes, ownership of the parameter block (and any buffers or records it points to) is transferred back to your application. If a PPC Toolbox function is executed asynchronously, your program cannot alter memory that might be used by the PPC Toolbox until that function completes.

A PPC Toolbox function that is excuted asynchronously must specify NIL or the address of a completion routine in the ioCompletion field of the PPC parameter block. You should use the ioResult field to determine the actual result code when an asynchronously executed PPC Toolbox function completes.

If you specify NIL in the ioCompletion field, you should poll the ioResult field of the PPC parameter block after the function is called in order to determine whether the PPC function has completed the requested operation. You should poll the ioResult field within the event loop of your application. If the ioResult field contains a value other than 1, the function has completed execution. Note that you must not poll the ioResult field at interrupt time to determine whether the function has completed execution.

If you specify a completion routine in the ioCompletion field, it is called at interrupt time when the PPC Toolbox function completes execution.

> ▲ **Warning:** Completion routines execute at the interrupt level and must preserve all registers other than A0, A1, and D0–D2. (Note that MPW® C and MPW Pascal do this automatically.) Your completion routine must not make any calls to the Memory Manager directly or indirectly, and it can't depend on the validity of handles to unlocked blocks. The PPC Toolbox preserves the application global register A5. ▲

You can write completion routines in C, Pascal, or assembly language. A completion routine declared in Pascal has this format:

```
PROCEDURE MyCompletionRoutine (pb: PPCParamBlockPtr);
```

The pb parameter points to the PPC parameter block passed to the PPC Toolbox function.

You may call another PPC Toolbox function from within a completion routine, but the function called must be executed asynchronously. It is recommended that you allocate parameter blocks of data type PPCParamBlockRec so that you may reuse the pb parameter to call another PPC Toolbox function from within a completion routine. For example, you should call either the PPCAccept function or the PPCReject function asynchronously from within a PPCInform completion routine to accept or reject the session request.

If your application is executing PPC Toolbox functions asynchronously, you may want to define your own record type to hold all data associated with a session. You can attach the data to the end of the parameter block. Here's an example:

```
TYPE
   SessRecHndl = ^SessRecPtr;
   SessRecPtr = ^SessRec;
   SessRec =
   RECORD
      pb:                    PPCParamBlockRec;
                             {must be first item in record}
      thePPCPortRec:         PPCPortRec;
      theLocationNameRec:    LocationNameRec;
      theUserName:           Str32
   END;
```

The additional data elements in your record can be accessed during execution of a completion routine by coercing the pb parameter to a pointer to your record type.

Specifying Port Names and Location Names

Before initiating a session, you must open a port to communicate with other programs. A port name and location name identify each port. An application can open as many ports as it requires as long as each port name is unique within a particular computer. You specify both the port name and the location name in the PPC parameter block.

Figure 7-10 illustrates a single Macintosh computer with two applications, and their corresponding port names and location names.

To open a port, you need to specify a port name. A port name consists of a name string, a type string, and a script code for localization. For example, you can designate "make memo" as the application's name string, "word processor" as its type string, and "smRoman" as its script code.

A port name is defined by a PPC port record. The PPC port record contains a script code, name string, port kind selector, and type string. The script code is an integer script identifier used for localization. The name string consists of a 32-byte character string that designates the application name. You should keep both the script code and the name string in a resource. The port kind selector is an integer that selects the kind of type string. You should make it consistent internationally. The type string can be either a 32-byte character string or a 4-character creator and a 4-character application type. See the Finder Interface chapter for information on creators and file types. See the Worldwide Software Overview chapter for information on script codes and localization.

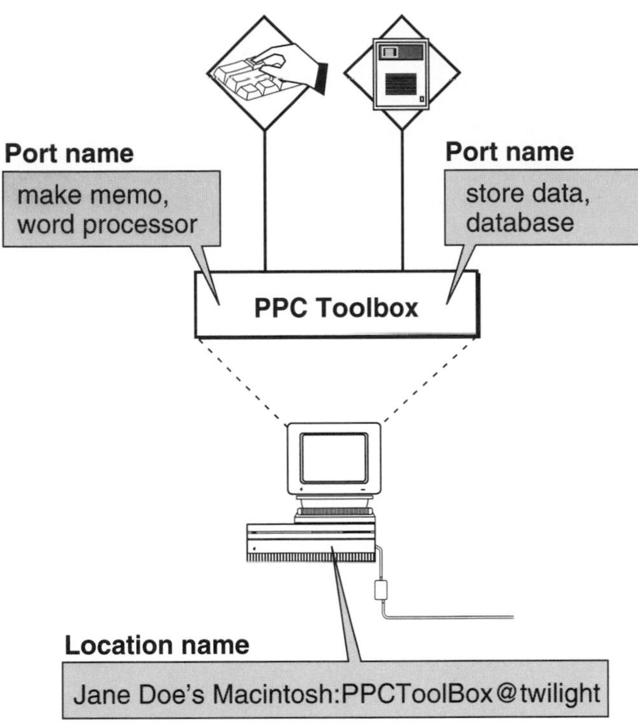

Figure 7-10. Two Macintosh applications and their corresponding ports

The PPCPortRec data type defines the PPC port record.

```
TYPE PPCPortRec =
     RECORD
        nameScript:          ScriptCode;   {script identifier}
        name:                Str32;        {port name in program }
                                           { linking dialog box}
        portKindSelector:    PPCPortKinds; {general category of }
                                           { application}
        CASE PPCPortKinds OF
                             ppcByString:
                                           (portTypeStr: Str32);
                             ppcByCreatorAndType:
                                           (portCreator: OSType;
                                            portType: OSType)
     END;
```

The location name identifies the location of the computer on the network. The PPC Toolbox provides the location name when the user starts up the computer. The location name is specified in the standard Name-Binding Protocol (NBP) form, <*object string*>:PPCToolBox @<*AppleTalk zone*>. The object string is the name provided in the Sharing Setup control panel in the Control Panels folder. By default, the type string is "PPCToolBox". The AppleTalk zone is the zone to which the particular Macintosh computer belongs. For example, "Jane Doe's Macintosh:PPCToolBox@twilight" specifies the object string, type string, and AppleTalk zone for a particular computer.

The LocationNameRec data type defines the location name record. The locationKindSelector field can be set to ppcNoLocation, ppcNBPLocation, or ppcNBPTypeLocation.

```
TYPE LocationNameRec =
     RECORD
        locationKindSelector: PPCLocationKind;        {which variant}
        CASE PPCLocationKind OF
                    {ppcNoLocation: storage not used by this value}
                    ppcNBPLocation:     (nbpEntity: EntityName);
                                        {NBP name entity}
                    ppcNBPTypeLocation: (nbpType: Str32);
                                        {just the NBP type string }
                                        { for the PPCOpen function}
     END;
```

The ppcNoLocation constant is used when the location received from or passed to a PPC Toolbox function is the location of the local machine.

The ppcNBPLocation constant is used when a full NBP entity name is received from or passed to a PPC Toolbox function.

> **Note:** You should assign an NBP value directly—do not pack it using nbpSetEntity.

The ppcNBPTypeLocation constant is used only by the PPCOpen function when an alias location name is needed.

The NBP type to be used for the alias location name is passed in the location name record's nbpType field. Alias location names allow you to filter the NBP objects (Macintosh computers) displayed by the program linking dialog box (shown in Figure 7-12) using the PPCBrowser function. See "Browsing for Ports Using the Program Linking Dialog Box" later in this chapter for information on the PPCBrowser function.

An alias location name could be used to advertise a service (such as a dictionary service) that is available to any application located on the network. For example, "Joe Smith's Macintosh: dictionary@ozone" specifies the object string, type string, and AppleTalk zone for a particular dictionary service.

To search for all dictionary services available within a zone, you use the PPCBrowser function and a filter. Figure 7-11 illustrates a Macintosh dictionary service application, its corresponding port name, and its alias location name.

Opening a Port

To open a port and associate a name with it, use the PPCOpen function. Listing 7-2 illustrates how you use the PPCOpen function to open a port. In this listing, the name is "Inside Macintosh" and the port type string is "Example". The location name is <*object string*>:PPC Example@<*AppleTalk zone*>.

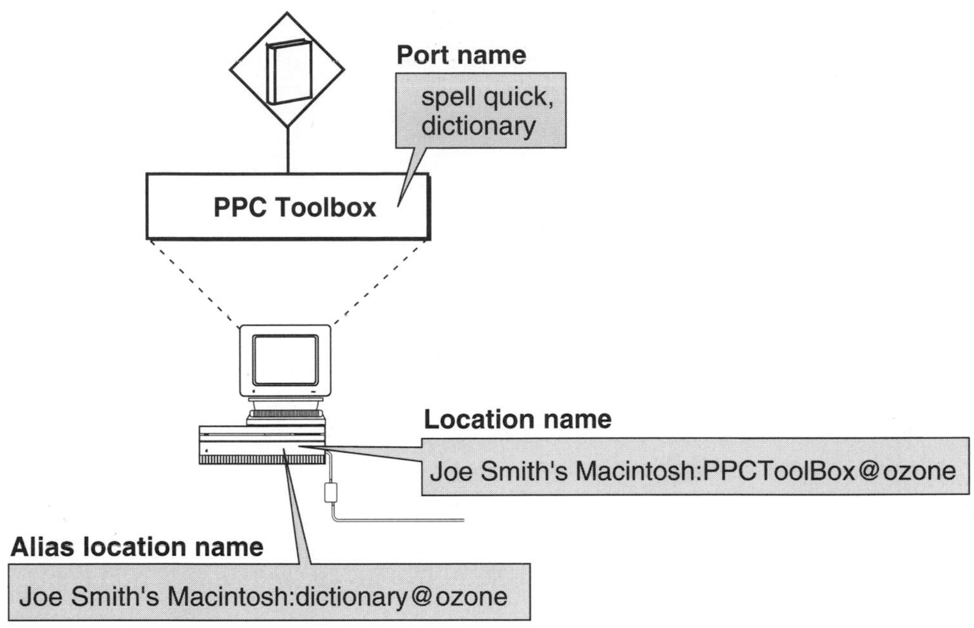

Figure 7-11. The PPC Toolbox and a dictionary service application

Listing 7-2. Opening a PPC port

```
FUNCTION MyPPCOpen(VAR thePortRefNum: PPCPortRefNum;
                   VAR nbpRegisteredFlag: Boolean) : OSErr;

VAR
   thePPCOpenPBRec:      PPCOpenPBRec;
   thePPCPortRec:        PPCPortRec;
   theLocationNameRec:   LocationNameRec;

BEGIN
   WITH thePPCPortRec DO
      BEGIN
         {nameScript and name should be resources to allow easy }
         { localization}
         nameScript := smRoman;  {Roman script}
         name := 'Inside Macintosh';
         {the port type should always be hard-coded to allow the }
         { application to find ports of a particular type even after }
         { the name is localized}
         portKindSelector := ppcByString;
         portTypeStr := 'Example';
      END;
   WITH theLocationNameRec DO
      BEGIN
         locationKindSelector := ppcNBPTypeLocation;
         nbpType := 'PPC Example';
      END;
```

(Continued)

Listing 7-2. Opening a PPC port (Continued)

```
   WITH thePPCOpenPBRec DO
      BEGIN
         serviceType := ppcServiceRealTime;
         resFlag := 0;                        {must be 0 for 7.0}
         portName := @thePPCPortRec;
         locationName := @theLocationNameRec;
         networkVisible := TRUE;              {make this a visible }
                                              { entity on the network}
      END;
   MyPPCOpen := PPCOpen(@thePPCOpenPBRec, FALSE);  {synchronous}
   thePortRefNum := thePPCOpenPBRec.portRefNum;
   nbpRegisteredFlag := thePPCOpenPBRec.nbpRegistered;
END;
```

The PPCOpen function opens a port with the port name and location name specified in the name and location fields of the parameter block. When the PPCOpen function completes execution, the portRefNum field returns the port reference number. You can use the port reference number in the PPCInform, PPCStart, StartSecureSession, and PPCClose functions to refer to the port you have opened.

Browsing for Ports Using the Program Linking Dialog Box

Before initiating a session, you can use either the PPCBrowser function or the IPCListPorts function to locate a port to communicate with.

Use the PPCBrowser function to display the program linking dialog box (shown in Figure 7-12) on the user's screen.

Note: Because this function displays a dialog box on the user's screen, you must not call the PPCBrowser function from an application that is running in the background.

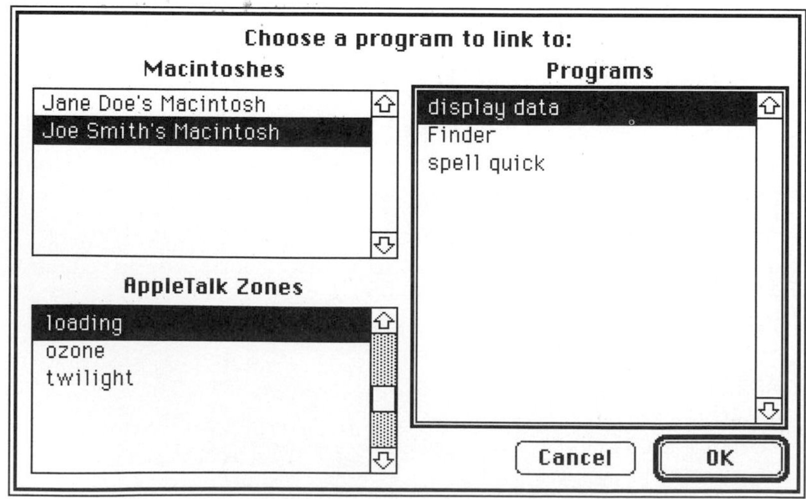

Figure 7-12. The program linking dialog box

In the program linking dialog box, the user chooses the computer, zone, and application. The zone list is not displayed if there is no network connection. Figure 7-13 shows the dialog box without the zone list.

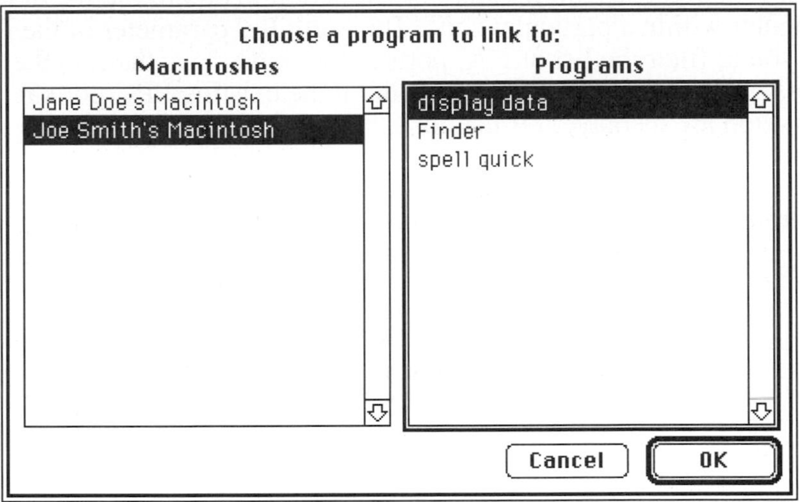

Figure 7-13. The program linking dialog box without a zone list

As shortcuts for the user, the program linking dialog box supports standard keyboard equivalents. Pressing Command-period or the Esc (Escape) key selects Cancel—pressing Enter or Return selects the OK button.

Each list is sorted in alphabetical order. As in the Chooser, the current list is indicated by a thick outline around its border. The program linking dialog box supports keyboard navigation and use of the arrow keys to select items from the current list. Pressing Tab or clicking the rectangle of another list switches the current list. Pressing Shift-Tab reverses the order in which the lists are selected. In addition, double-clicking an application name in the Programs list of the program linking dialog box is equivalent to clicking the OK button.

The PPCBrowser function allows users to browse for PPC ports.

```
err := PPCBrowser (prompt, applListLabel, defaultSpecified, theLocation,
                   thePortInfo, portFilter, theLocNBPType);
```

If the defaultSpecified parameter is TRUE, the PPCBrowser function tries to select the PPC port specified by the parameters theLocation and thePortInfo when the program linking dialog box first appears. If the default cannot be found, the PPCBrowser selects the first PPC port in the list.

An application can open multiple ports as long as each port name is unique within a particular computer. Unique ports can have duplicate name fields but different types. For example, you can designate “make memo” as the application’s name string and “word processor” as its type string. You can also designate a separate port as “make memo” (the application’s name string) and “text only” (its type string).

In such a case, the PPCBrowser function does a secondary sort based on the port type. Ports with a type selector of ppcByCreatorAndType are displayed before ppcByString ports, and types are sorted alphabetically within each type selector.

The PPCBrowser function uses the IPCListPorts function to obtain the list of existing ports on a particular computer within a particular zone. The portFilter parameter of the PPCBrowser function allows you to filter the list of PPC ports before it displays them in the program linking dialog box. If this parameter is NIL, the names of all the existing PPC ports returned by the IPCListPorts function are displayed. If the portFilter field is not NIL, it must contain a pointer to a port filter function that you create.

Listing 7-3 illustrates how you use a sample port filter function. In this listing, the MyBrowserPortFilter function returns TRUE for ports with the port type string "Example".

Listing 7-3. Using a port filter function

```
FUNCTION MyBrowserPortFilter(theLocationNameRec: LocationNameRec;
                             thePortInfoRec: PortInfoRec) : Boolean;

BEGIN
   IF thePortInfoRec.name.portKindSelector = ppcByString
      THEN
         IF thePortInfoRec.name.portTypeStr = 'Example'
            THEN MyBrowserPortFilter := TRUE
            ELSE MyBrowserPortFilter := FALSE
      ELSE MyBrowserPortFilter := FALSE;
END;
```

The PPCBrowser function calls your filter function once for each port on the selected computer. Your function should return TRUE for each port you want to display in the program linking dialog box, and FALSE for each port that you do not want to display. Do not modify the data in the filter function parameters theLocationNameRec and thePortInfoRec.

The PPCBrowser function returns the selected port name in the parameter thePortInfo. The IPCListPorts function returns the port names in the area of memory pointed to by the bufferPtr field of the IPCListPorts parameter block. Both functions specify each port name in a port information record.

```
TYPE PortInfoRec =
     RECORD
        filler1:           SignedByte;    {space holder}
        authRequired:      Boolean;       {authentication required}
        name:              PPCPortRec     {port name}
     END;
```

If the authRequired field is TRUE, the port requires authentication before a session can begin. You should use the StartSecureSession function to initiate a session with this port. If this field returns FALSE, you can use either the PPCStart function or the StartSecureSession function to initiate a session. See "Initiating a PPC Session" later in this chapter for detailed information. The name field of the port information record specifies an available port name.

Listing 7-4 illustrates how you use the PPCBrowser function to display the program linking dialog box in order to obtain the location and name of a port chosen by the user. In this listing, the PPCBrowser function builds lists of zones (shown in the AppleTalk Zones list of the program linking dialog box), objects (shown in the Macintoshes list), and ports (shown in the Programs list). In this example, the PPCBrowser function next tries to default to object "Moof™" in the "Twilight" zone. If it matches the object and zone, it also tries to default to the port "Inside Macintosh" with the port type "Example".

Note that the data in the records LocationNameRec and PortInfoRec is used to match the names in the program linking dialog box. The data has nothing to do with the NBP type used by NBPLookup or the filtered PPC ports that show up in the program linking dialog box. NBPLookup uses the NBP type supplied in theLocNBPType. The PPC port names are filtered using the MyBrowserPortFilter function shown in the previous listing.

Listing 7-4. Browsing through dictionary service ports

```
FUNCTION MyPPCBrowser(VAR theLocationNameRec: LocationNameRec;
                      VAR thePortInfoRec: PortInfoRec) : OSErr;

VAR
   prompt:            Str255;
   applListLabel:     Str255;
   defaultSpecified: Boolean;
   theLocNBPType:     Str32;

BEGIN
   prompt := 'Choose an example to link to:';
   applListLabel := 'Examples';
   defaultSpecified := TRUE;

   WITH theLocationNameRec DO
      BEGIN
         locationKindSelector := ppcNBPLocation;
         WITH nbpEntity DO
            BEGIN
               objStr := 'Moof™';
               {typeStr is ignored}
               zoneStr := 'Twilight';
            END;
      END;

   WITH thePortInfoRec.name DO
      BEGIN
         {nameScript and name should be resources to allow easy }
         { localization}
         nameScript := smRoman;  {Roman script}
         name := 'Inside Macintosh';
         {the port type should always be hard-coded to allow the }
         { application to find ports of a particular type even after }
         { the name is localized}
         portKindSelector := ppcByString;
         portTypeStr := 'Example';
      END;
```

(Continued)

Listing 7-4. Browsing through dictionary service ports (Continued)

```
        {when building the list of objects (Macintoshes), show only }
        { those with the NBP type "PPC Example"}

   theLocNBPType := 'PPC Example';  {match this NBP type}
   MyPPCBrowser := PPCBrowser(prompt, applListLabel, defaultSpecified,
                              theLocationNameRec, thePortInfoRec,
                              @myBrowserPortFilter, theLocNBPType);
END;
```

Obtaining a List of Available Ports

To generate a list of ports without displaying dialog boxes, you can use the IPCListPorts function. The IPCListPorts function allows you to obtain a list of ports on a particular computer within a particular zone. To obtain a list of ports, several steps are required. First, use the GetZoneList function to obtain a list of zones. Next, you must use the PLookupName function to obtain a list of computers with ports. After establishing the zone and the computer, you can use the IPCListPorts function to obtain the list of available ports. See the AppleTalk Manager chapter in this volume for information on the GetZoneList function. See the AppleTalk Manager chapters in Volume II and Volume V for information on the PLookupName function.

Listing 7-5 illustrates how you use the IPCListPorts function to obtain a list of ports on a particular computer. This function returns a list of port information records in the buffer pointed to by the parameter thePortInfoBufferPtr. The actual number of port information records is returned in the parameter theActualCount.

Listing 7-5. Using the IPCListPorts function to obtain a list of ports

```
FUNCTION MyIPCListPorts(theStartIndex: Integer; theRequestCount: Integer;
                        VAR theActualCount: Integer; theObjStr: Str32;
                        theZoneStr: Str32; thePortInfoBufferPtr:
                        PortInfoArrayPtr) : OSErr;
VAR
   theIPCListPortsPBRec:   IPCListPortsPBRec;
   thePPCPortRec:          PPCPortRec;
   theLocationNameRec:     LocationNameRec;
BEGIN
   {list all PPC ports at the specified location}
   WITH thePPCPortRec DO
      BEGIN
         nameScript := csRoman;
         name := '=';                {match all names}
         portKindSelector := ppcByString;
         portTypeStr := '=';         {match all types}
      END;
   {The application must choose and supply the NBP zone string from }
   { the list returned by GetZoneList. Then, the application must }
```

```
    { choose and supply the NBP object string from the list returned by }
    { NBPLookup. This example looks for NBP type "PPC Example". If you }
    { don't supply your own NBP type, you should use "PPCToolBox" for }
    { the NBP type string.}

    WITH theLocationNameRec DO
       BEGIN
          locationKindSelector := ppcNBPLocation;
          WITH nbpEntity DO
             BEGIN
                objStr := theObjStr;
                typeStr := 'PPC Example';
                zoneStr := theZoneStr;
             END;
       END;
    WITH theIPCListPortsPBRec DO
       BEGIN
          startIndex := theStartIndex;
          requestCount := theRequestCount;
          portName := @thePPCPortRec;
          locationName := @theLocationNameRec;
          bufferPtr := thePortInfoBufferPtr;
       END;
    MyIPCListPorts := IPCListPorts(@theIPCListPortsPBRec, FALSE);
    theActualCount := theIPCListPortsPBRec.actualCount;
END;
```

The IPCListPorts function returns information about ports that are on the computer specified in the locationName field of the list ports parameter block. If the locationName field is NIL or if the locationKindSelector field in the location name record is ppcNoLocation, the IPCListPorts function returns only the port names for the local computer.

The bufferPtr field points to an area of memory that contains the requested port names. You are responsible for allocating enough memory to hold the requested port names. The buffer length must be equal to

```
sizeof(PortInfoRec) * requestCount
```

Preparing for a Session

To communicate, you can open a port for your application and make it available to receive session requests, to initiate sessions, or both. Applications that are able to receive session requests can choose to accept or reject incoming session requests.

Before an application can accept and establish a session with another application, the PPC Toolbox authenticates the initiating user (unless guest access is enabled or the applications are located on the same computer). Once a session begins, the two applications can exchange data with each other.

Initiating a PPC Session

Once you have established the name and the location of the port that you want to communicate with, you can initiate a session. You can use either the StartSecureSession function or the PPCStart function to initiate a session. The StartSecureSession function displays several dialog boxes on the user's screen to identify each user who requests a session. You may prefer to use the PPCStart function for low-level code such as that used for drivers, which typically do not provide a user interface. You may also prefer to use PPCStart when the application you are initiating a session with does not require authentication. The IPCListPorts and PPCBrowser functions return information about whether a particular port requires authentication.

> **Note:** Do not call the StartSecureSession function from an application that is running in the background, since it requires that several dialog boxes appear on the user's screen.

The StartSecureSession function provides authentication services to identify each user who requests a session. This function combines the processes of prompting for user name and password and initiating a session into one synchronous procedure call. If authentication fails, the PPC Toolbox rejects the incoming session request.

```
err := StartSecureSession (pb, userName, useDefault, allowGuest,
                           guestSelected, prompt);
```

Set the useDefault parameter to TRUE if you want the StartSecureSession function to use the default user identity (described later in this section). If the default user identity cannot be authenticated, the StartSecureSession function displays a dialog box to allow a user to log on. Figure 7-14 shows the user identity dialog box.

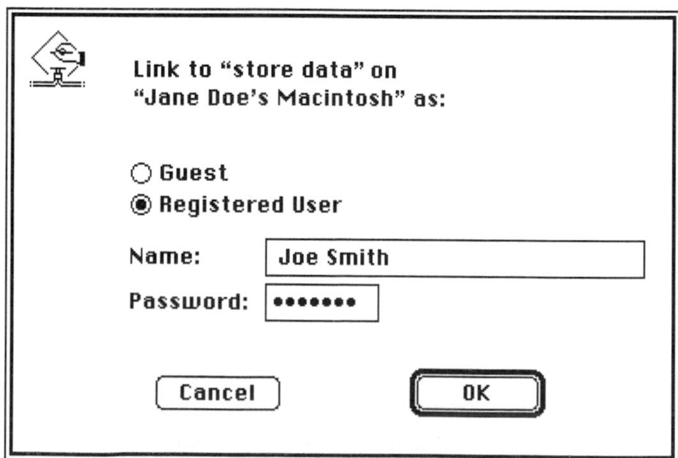

Figure 7-14. The user identity dialog box

The prompt parameter of the StartSecureSession function allows you to specify a line of text that the dialog box can display. The allowGuest parameter specifies whether to enable the Guest radio button. If a port requires authentication, you should set this parameter to FALSE.

The userName parameter specifies the name of the user who is attempting to initiate a session. If the user name is not specified, the user identity dialog box appears on the user's screen with the owner name provided from the Sharing Setup control panel.

If the user enters an invalid password, the StartSecureSession function displays the dialog box shown in Figure 7-15.

Figure 7-15. The incorrect password dialog box

After the user clicks OK, the user identity dialog box reappears in the foreground so that the user can enter the password again.

If the user's name is invalid, the StartSecureSession function displays the dialog box shown in Figure 7-16.

Figure 7-16. The invalid user name dialog box

After the user clicks OK, the user identity dialog box reappears so that the user can enter a new user name.

The StartSecureSession function remains in this loop until a secure session is initiated or the user clicks Cancel in the user identity dialog box. If a secure session is initiated, StartSecureSession returns the user reference number in the corresponding field in the PPCStart parameter block. The user reference number represents the user name and password. A user reference number of 0 indicates that a session has been initiated with guest access. See "Setting Up Authenticated Sessions" earlier in this chapter for detailed information.

Before your application quits, you need to invalidate all user reference numbers obtained with the StartSecureSession function except for the default user reference number and the guest reference number (0). See "Invalidating Users" later in this chapter for detailed information.

Listing 7-6 illustrates how to use the StartSecureSession function to establish an authenticated session. This listing shows only one session, although your application may conduct multiple sessions at one time.

Listing 7-6. Using the StartSecureSession function to establish a session

```
FUNCTION MyStartSecureSession(thePortInfoPtr: PortInfoPtr;
                              theLocationNamePtr: LocationNamePtr;
                              thePortRefNum: PPCPortRefNum;
                              VAR theSessRefNum: PPCSessRefNum;
                              VAR theUserRefNum: LongInt;
                              VAR theRejectInfo: LongInt;
                              VAR userName: Str32;
                              VAR guestSelected: Boolean) : OSErr;
VAR
   thePPCStartPBRec: PPCStartPBRec;
   useDefault:       Boolean;
   allowGuest:       Boolean;
   err:              OSErr;
BEGIN
   WITH thePPCStartPBRec DO
      BEGIN
         ioCompletion := NIL;
         portRefNum := thePortRefNum;        {from the PPCOpen function}
         serviceType := ppcServiceRealTime;
         resFlag := 0;
         portName := @thePortInfoPtr^.name;  {from the PPCBrowser }
                                             { function}
         locationName := theLocationNamePtr; {from the PPCBrowser }
                                             { function}
         userData := 0;                      {application-specific }
                                             { data that the PPCInform }
                                             { function sees}
      END;
   {try to connect with default user identity}
   useDefault := TRUE;
   {highlight the Guest button appropriately}
   allowGuest := NOT thePortInfoPtr^.authRequired;

   err := StartSecureSession(@thePPCStartPBRec, userName, useDefault,
                             allowGuest, guestSelected, stringPtr(NIL)^);
   IF err = noErr THEN
         BEGIN
            theSessRefNum := thePPCStartPBRec.sessRefNum;
            theUserRefNum := thePPCStartPBRec.userRefNum;
         END
      ELSE
         IF err = userRejectErr
            THEN     {return rejectInfo from the PPCReject function}
               theRejectInfo := thePPCStartPBRec.rejectInfo;
   MyStartSecureSession := err;
END;
```

For low-level code such as that used for drivers (which typically do not provide a user interface), you can use the PPCStart function instead of the StartSecureSession function to initiate a session. You can also use the IPCListPorts function (instead of displaying the program linking dialog box) to obtain a list of ports.

If the authRequired field of the port information record contains FALSE, the port allows guest access. If the authRequired field of the port information record contains TRUE, use the PPCStart function and the user reference number obtained previously from the StartSecureSession function to reestablish an authenticated session.

You can also attempt to log on as the default user using the GetDefaultUser function to obtain the default user reference number and the default user name. The default user name is established after the owner starts up the computer.

```
err := GetDefaultUser (userRef, userName);
```

The userRef parameter is a reference number that represents the user name and password of the default user. The userName parameter contains the owner name that is specified in the Sharing Setup control panel.

The GetDefaultUser function returns an error when the default user identity does not exist (no name is specified in the Sharing Setup control panel) or the user is not currently logged on.

Listing 7-7 illustrates how you use the PPCStart function to initiate a session. The PPCStart function uses the port information record and the location name record to attempt to open a session with the selected PPC port.

Listing 7-7. Initiating a session using the PPCStart function

```
FUNCTION MyPPCStart(thePortInfoPtr: PortInfoPtr; theLocationNamePtr:
                    LocationNamePtr; thePortRefNum: PPCPortRefNum;
                    VAR theSessRefNum: PPCSessRefNum; VAR theUserRefNum:
                    LongInt; VAR theRejectInfo: LongInt) : OSErr;
VAR
   thePPCStartPBRec: PPCStartPBRec;
   userName:         Str32;
   err:              OSErr;

BEGIN
   WITH thePPCStartPBRec DO
      BEGIN
         ioCompletion := NIL;
         portRefNum := thePortRefNum;         {from the PPCOpen function}
         serviceType := ppcServiceRealTime;
         resFlag := 0;
         portName := @thePortInfoPtr^.name;   {destination port}
         locationName := theLocationNamePtr;  {destination location}
         userData := 0;                       {application-specific }
                                              { data for PPCInform}
      END;
```

(Continued)

Listing 7-7. Initiating a session using the PPCStart function (Continued)

```
   err := GetDefaultUser(thePPCStartPBRec.userRefNum, userName);
   IF err <> noErr
      THEN
         thePPCStartPBRec.userRefNum := 0;

   IF thePortInfoPtr^.authRequired AND (thePPCStartPBRec.userRefNum = 0)
      THEN  {port selected does not allow guests and you do not have }
            { a default user reference number, so you cannot log on to }
            { this port}
         err := authFailErr
      ELSE  {attempt to log on}
         err := PPCStart(@thePPCStartPBRec, FALSE);

   IF err = noErr
      THEN
         BEGIN
            theSessRefNum := thePPCStartPBRec.sessRefNum;
            theUserRefNum := thePPCStartPBRec.userRefNum;
         END
      ELSE
         IF err = userRejectErr
            THEN  {return rejectInfo from the PPCReject function}
               theRejectInfo := thePPCStartPBRec.rejectInfo;
   MyPPCStart := err;
END;
```

The port to which you wish to connect must have an outstanding PPCInform function to successfully start a session. You cannot initiate a session with a port that is not able to receive session requests.

If the port is open, has an outstanding PPCInform posted, and accepts your session request, the PPCStart function returns a noErr result code and a valid session reference number. This session reference number is used to identify the session during the exchange of data.

Receiving Session Requests

Your application can open as many ports as it requires as long as each port name is unique within a particular computer. A single port can support a number of communication sessions. To allow a port to receive session requests, use the PPCInform function. (Note that you must open a port to obtain a port reference number before calling the PPCInform function.) A port may have any number of outstanding PPCInform requests.

Listing 7-8 illustrates how you use the PPCInform function to allow a port to receive session requests. In this listing, the parameter thePPCParamBlockPtr points to a PPC parameter block record allocated by the application. The portRefNum, autoAccept, portName, locationName, userName, and ioCompletion parameters of the PPC parameter block record must be supplied. If you want to automatically accept all incoming session requests, you can set the autoAccept field in the PPCInform parameter block.

Listing 7-8. Using the PPCInform function to enable a port to receive sessions

```
FUNCTION MyPPCInform(thePPCParamBlockPtr: PPCParamBlockPtr;
                     thePPCPortPtr: PPCPortPtr; theLocationNamePtr:
                     LocationNamePtr; theUserNamePtr: stringPtr;
                     thePortRefNum: PPCPortRefNum) : OSErr;
BEGIN
   WITH thePPCParamBlockPtr^.informParam DO
      BEGIN
         ioCompletion := @MyInformCompProc;
         portRefNum := thePortRefNum;        {from the PPCOpen function}
         autoAccept := FALSE;                {the completion routine }
                                             { handles accepting or }
                                             { rejecting requests}
         portName := thePPCPortPtr;
         locationName := theLocationNamePtr;
         userName := theUserNamePtr;
      END;

   MyPPCInform := PPCInform(PPCInformPBPtr(thePPCParamBlockPtr),
                            TRUE);           {asynchronous}
END;
```

A PPC parameter block record is used instead of a PPCInform parameter block record so that the same parameter block can be reused to make other PPC Toolbox calls from the PPCInform completion routine. The parameter block and the records it points to cannot be deallocated until all calls that use the parameter block and records have completed.

You should make the call to PPCInform asynchronously. For each function that you use asynchronously, you should provide a completion routine. This procedure gets called at interrupt time when the PPCInform function completes. If there are no errors, it sets the global variable gSessionOpen to TRUE. The global variable gPBInUse is set to FALSE to inform the application that the parameter block and the records it points to are no longer in use.

Listing 7-9 illustrates a completion routine for a PPCInform function. You can use the data passed into your PPCInform completion routine (user name, user data, port name, and location name) to determine whether to accept or reject the session request.

Listing 7-9. Completion routine for a PPCInform function

```
PROCEDURE MyInformCompProc(pb: PPCParamBlockPtr);

BEGIN
   IF pb^.informParam.ioResult = noErr
      THEN
         BEGIN
            {decide if this session should be accepted or rejected }
            { by looking at data supplied by the session requester}
            IF pb^.informParam.userData <> -1
               THEN
                  DoPPCAccept(pb)
               ELSE
                  DoPPCReject(pb);
         END
```

(Continued)

Listing 7-9. Completion routine for a PPCInform function (Continued)

```
      ELSE
         {use a global to tell the application that PPCParamBlockRec }
         { and the records it points to can be deallocated}
         gPBInUse := FALSE;
END;
```

Accepting or Rejecting Session Requests

Use the PPCAccept function or the PPCReject function to accept or reject an incoming session request.

▲ **Warning:** If the PPCInform function (with the autoAccept parameter set to FALSE) returns a noErr result code, you must call either the PPCAccept function or the PPCReject function. The computer trying to initiate a session (using the StartSecureSession function or the PPCStart function) waits (hangs) until the session attempt is either accepted or rejected, or until an error occurs. ▲

Listing 7-10 illustrates how you use the PPCAccept function to accept a session request. This listing reuses the parameter block used in the PPCInform function, so the sessRefNum field already contains the session reference number needed by the PPCAccept function.

Listing 7-10. Accepting a session request using the PPCAccept function

```
PROCEDURE DoPPCAccept(pb: PPCParamBlockPtr);

VAR
   err:  OSErr;

BEGIN {accept the session}
   pb^.acceptParam.ioCompletion := @MyAcceptCompProc;
   {the sessRefNum field is set by the PPCInform function}
   err := PPCAccept(@pb^.acceptParam, TRUE); {asynchronous}
END;
```

For each function that you use asynchronously, you should provide a completion routine. Listing 7-11 illustrates a completion routine for a PPCAccept function. This procedure gets called at interrupt time when the PPCAccept function completes. If there are no errors, it sets the global variable gSessionOpen to TRUE. The global variable gPBInUse is set to FALSE to inform the application that the parameter block and the records it points to are no longer in use.

You can use the session reference number in subsequent PPCWrite, PPCRead, and PPCEnd functions once a session is accepted.

Listing 7-11. Completion routine for a PPCAccept function

```
PROCEDURE MyAcceptCompProc(pb: PPCParamBlockPtr);

BEGIN
   IF pb^.acceptParam.ioResult = noErr
      THEN {accept completed so the session is completely open}
         gSessionOpen := TRUE;
   {use a global to tell the application that PPCParamBlockRec }
   { and the records it points to can be deallocated}
   gPBInUse := FALSE;
END;
```

Use the PPCReject function to reject an incoming session request. Listing 7-12 illustrates how you use the PPCReject function to reject a session request.

This listing reuses the parameter block used in the PPCInform function, so the sessRefNum field already contains the session reference number needed by the PPCReject function.

Listing 7-12. Rejecting a session request using the PPCReject function

```
PROCEDURE DoPPCReject(pb: PPCParamBlockPtr);

VAR
   err:  OSErr;

BEGIN {reject the session}
   WITH pb^.rejectParam DO
      BEGIN
         ioCompletion := @MyRejectCompProc;
         {the sessRefNum field is set by the PPCInform function}
         rejectInfo := -1;
      END;
   err := PPCReject(@pb^.rejectParam, TRUE); {asynchronous}
END;
```

Listing 7-13 illustrates a completion routine for a PPCReject function. This procedure gets called at interrupt time when the PPCReject function completes. In this example, the global variable gPBInUse is set to FALSE to inform the application that the parameter block and the records it points to are no longer in use.

Listing 7-13. Completion routine for a PPCReject function

```
PROCEDURE MyRejectCompProc(pb: PPCParamBlockPtr);

BEGIN
   {use a global to tell the application that PPCParamBlockRec and }
   { the records it points to can be deallocated}
   gPBInUse := FALSE;
END;
```

Exchanging Data During a PPC Session

After a session begins, each application can send data to and receive data from the other using a sequence of message blocks. The PPC Toolbox treats each message block as a byte stream and does not interpret the contents of the message block. The size of a message block can be between 0 and (2^{32}–1) bytes. The PPC Toolbox treats the buffer size as an unsigned long integer.

The PPC Toolbox delivers the message blocks in the same sequence as they are sent and without duplicates. In Figure 7-17, an application transmits message blocks during a session.

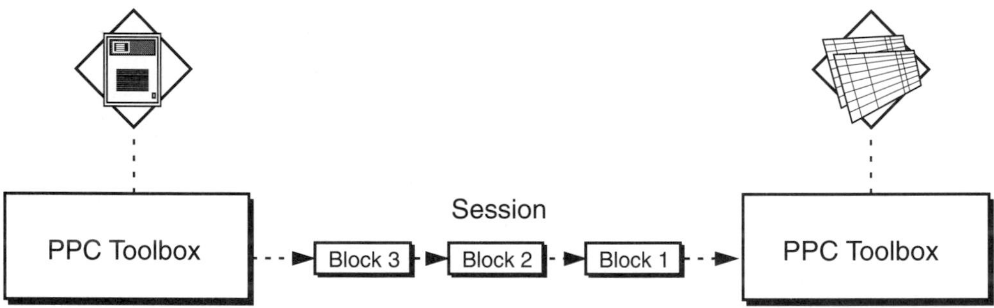

Figure 7-17. Transmitting message blocks

For each message block, you specify a block creator, block type, and user data. The first PPCWrite function that you use to create a new message block sets the attributes for the block. The PPCRead function returns the block creator, block type, and user data attributes for the current message block when the call completes.

Although the PPC Toolbox does not interpret these attributes, they can give the receiving application information about how to process the contents of the message block. For example, a database application may specify a counter to indicate the block number (block number 20 of 30 total blocks) in the block creator field. This application could also specify a code, such as 'DREC', in the block type field to indicate that the information it contains is a database record. In addition, this application could specify the length of the message block in the user data field.

Reading Data From an Application

An application can both read from and write data to another application during a session. Use the PPCRead function during a session to read incoming blocks of data from another application.

Once a session is initiated, you should have a PPCRead function pending. You can issue a PPCRead function from inside a completion routine. This provides you with immediate notification if an error condition arises or the session closes.

The blockCreator, blockType, and userData fields are returned for the block you are reading. (These fields are set by the PPCWrite function.) To determine whether there is additional data to be read, check the more field. This field is FALSE to indicate the end of a message block.

Listing 7-14 illustrates how you use the PPCRead function to read data during a session.

Listing 7-14. Using the PPCRead function to read data during a session

```
FUNCTION MyPPCRead(thePPCReadPBPtr: PPCReadPBPtr; theSessRefNum:
                   PPCSessRefNum; theBufferLength: Size; theBufferPtr:
                   Ptr) : OSErr;
BEGIN
   WITH thePPCReadPBPtr^ DO
      BEGIN
         ioCompletion := NIL;
         sessRefNum := theSessRefNum;  {from the PPCStart function }
                                       { or the PPCInform function}
         bufferLength := theBufferLength;
         bufferPtr := theBufferPtr;
      END;
   MyPPCRead := PPCRead(thePPCReadPBPtr, TRUE); {asynchronous}
END;
```

You should make any calls to PPCRead asynchronously. You can provide a completion routine that will be called when the PPCRead function has completed, or you can poll the ioResult field of the PPC parameter block to determine whether the PPCRead function has completed. A PPCRead completion routine can issue another asynchronous PPC Toolbox call or set global variables. If another PPC Toolbox call is made from a completion routine, then the PPCRead function must use a record of data type PPCParamBlockRec instead of type PPCReadPBRec.

Listing 7-15 illustrates a function that can be used to poll the ioResult field of a record of data type PPCReadPBRec. The function returns TRUE when the PPCRead function associated with PPCReadPBRec has completed.

Listing 7-15. Polling the ioResult field to determine if a PPCRead function has completed

```
FUNCTION MyReadComplete(thePPCReadPBPtr: PPCReadPBPtr; VAR err: OSErr) :
                        Boolean;
BEGIN
   err := thePPCReadPBPtr^.ioResult;
   MyReadComplete := err <> 1;
END;
```

Sending Data to an Application

Use the PPCWrite function to send a message block during a session specified by the session reference number.

You should call the PPCWrite function asynchronously. You can provide a completion routine that will be called when the PPCWrite function has completed, or you can poll the ioResult field of the PPC parameter block to detemine whether the PPCWrite function has completed. A PPCWrite completion routine can issue another PPC Toolbox call or set global variables. If another PPC Toolbox call is made from a completion routine, then the PPCWrite function must use a record of data type PPCParamBlockRec instead of type PPCWritePBRec. Note that message blocks are sent in the order in which they are written.

Listing 7-16 illustrates how you use the PPCWrite function to write data during a session.

Listing 7-16. Using the PPCWrite function to write data during a session

```
FUNCTION MyPPCWrite(thePPCWritePBPtr: PPCWritePBPtr; theSessRefNum:
                    PPCSessRefNum; theBufferLength: Size; theBufferPtr:
                    Ptr) : OSErr;
BEGIN
   WITH thePPCWritePBPtr^ DO
      BEGIN
         ioCompletion := NIL;
         sessRefNum := theSessRefNum;   {from the PPCStart function or }
                                        { the PPCInform function}
         bufferLength := theBufferLength;
         bufferPtr := theBufferPtr;
         more := FALSE;                 {no more data to read}
         userData := 0;                 {application-specific data}
         blockCreator := '????';        {application-specific data}
         blockType := '????';           {application-specific data}
      END;
   MyPPCWrite := PPCWrite(thePPCWritePBPtr, TRUE); {asynchronous}
END;
```

The first PPCWrite function that you use to create a new message block sets the block creator, block type, and user data attributes for the block. These attributes are returned to the application when it reads from the message block. Set the more field to FALSE to indicate the end of the message block or set this field to TRUE if you want to append additional data to a message block.

Listing 7-17 illustrates a function that can be used to poll the ioResult field of a record of data type PPCWritePBRec. The function returns TRUE when the PPCWrite function associated with PPCWritePBRec has completed.

Listing 7-17. Polling the ioResult field to determine if a PPCWrite function has completed

```
FUNCTION MyWriteComplete(thePPCWritePBPtr: PPCWritePBPtr;
                         VAR err: OSErr) : Boolean;
BEGIN
   err := thePPCWritePBPtr^.ioResult;
   MyWriteComplete := err <> 1;
END;
```

Ending a Session and Closing a Port

After data is written and read in, use the PPCEnd function to end the session (identified by the session reference number). You may receive an error if you use the PPCEnd function to end a session that has already been terminated.

Listing 7-18 illustrates how you use the PPCEnd function to end a session.

Listing 7-18. Ending a PPC session using the PPCEnd function

```
FUNCTION MyPPCEnd(theSessRefNum: PPCSessRefNum) : OSErr;

VAR
   thePPCEndPBRec:    PPCEndPBRec;

BEGIN
   thePPCEndPBRec.sessRefNum := theSessRefNum;
   MyPPCEnd := PPCEnd(@thePPCEndPBRec, FALSE);   {synchronous}
END;
```

The PPCEnd function causes all calls to the PPCRead and PPCWrite functions to complete (with a sessClosedErr result code) and invalidates the session reference number. The PPCEnd function also releases any PPC Toolbox resources so that they can be reused.

Use the PPCClose function to close the port specified by the port reference number. When you close a port, all sessions associated with a port are ended. Any active asynchronous calls associated with a session then call their completion routines (if they have one).

Listing 7-19 illustrates how you use the PPCClose function to close a port.

Listing 7-19. Closing a PPC port using the PPCClose function

```
FUNCTION MyPPCClose(thePortRefNum: PPCPortRefNum) : OSErr;

VAR
   theClosePBRec: PPCClosePBRec;

BEGIN
   theClosePBRec.portRefNum := thePortRefNum;       {from the }
                                                    { PPCOpen function}
   MyPPCClose := PPCClose(@theClosePBRec, FALSE);   {synchronous}
END;
```

In this example, the call to PPCClose is made synchronously.

Invalidating Users

It is your responsibility to invalidate all user reference numbers obtained with the StartSecureSession function before your application quits. However, while your application remains open, you may want to keep track of a user reference number to start a session with a port, end it, and then later start another session with the same port.

Use the DeleteUserIdentity function to invalidate the user reference number for a particular user.

```
err := DeleteUserIdentity (userRef);
```

The DeleteUserIdentity function removes a user by invalidating the specified user reference number. Note that you cannot invalidate the guest reference number (0) and, in most cases, you should not dispose of the default user reference number.

Listing 7-20 illustrates how you use the DeleteUserIdentity function to invalidate a user reference number obtained from a StartSecureSession function. The sample code does not invalidate the user reference number if it is either the default user reference number or the guest reference number (0).

Listing 7-20. Using the DeleteUserIdentity function to invalidate a user identity

```
FUNCTION DeleteNewUserRefNum(newUserRef: LongInt) : OSErr;

VAR
   err:           OSErr;
   defUserRef:    LongInt;
   defUserName:   Str32;

BEGIN
   IF newUserRef <> 0 THEN
      {user reference number passed was not the guest}
      BEGIN
         err := GetDefaultUser(defUserRef, defUserName);
         IF err = noErr
            THEN     {there is a default user}
               BEGIN
                  IF newUserRef <> defUserRef
                     THEN  {it's not the default, so delete it}
                        err := DeleteUserIdentity(newUserRef);
               END
            ELSE  {there is no default, so delete it}
               err := DeleteUserIdentity(newUserRef);
         DeleteNewUserRefNum := err;
      END
   ELSE {user reference number passed was the guest}
      DeleteNewUserRefNum := noErr;
END;
```

PPC TOOLBOX ROUTINES

This section describes the routines for

- initializing the PPC Toolbox
- listing available ports
- opening and closing a port
- starting and ending a session

- accepting and rejecting a session
- reading and writing data
- obtaining the default user reference number and name
- invalidating a user reference number

Also included in this section is the PPC parameter block. Result codes appear after each function where applicable.

The PPC Toolbox Parameter Block and Completion Routine

PPC Toolbox functions require a pointer to a PPC parameter block. You must fill out any fields of the parameter block that the specific PPC Toolbox function requires.

```
TYPE PPCParamBlockRec =
     RECORD
        CASE Integer OF
        0: (openParam:         PPCOpenPBRec);          {PPCOpen params}
        1: (informParam:       PPCInformPBRec);        {PPCInform params}
        2: (startParam:        PPCStartPBRec);         {PPCStart params}
        3: (acceptParam:       PPCAcceptPBRec);        {PPCAccept params}
        4: (rejectParam:       PPCRejectPBRec);        {PPCReject params}
        5: (writeParam:        PPCWritePBRec);         {PPCWrite params}
        6: (readParam:         PPCReadPBRec);          {PPCRead params}
        7: (endParam:          PPCEndPBRec);           {PPCEnd params}
        8: (closeParam:        PPCClosePBRec);         {PPCClose params}
        9: (listPortsParam:    IPCListPortsPBRec)      {IPCListPorts }
                                                       { params}
     END;
```

The qLink, csCode, intUse, intUsePtr, and reserved fields are used internally by the PPC Toolbox. Your application should not rely on the PPC Toolbox to preserve these fields across calls.

Figure 7-18 shows the PPC Toolbox parameter blocks. Note that the reserved fields are not included in the illustration.

Your application transfers ownership of the PPC Toolbox parameter block (and any buffers or records pointed to by the PPC Toolbox parameter block) to the PPC Toolbox until a PPC function is complete. Once the function completes, ownership of the parameter block (and any buffers or records it points to) is transferred back to your application. If a PPC Toolbox function is executed asynchronously, your program cannot alter memory that might be used by the PPC Toolbox until that function completes.

A PPC Toolbox function that is executed asynchronously must specify NIL or the address of a completion routine in the ioCompletion field of the PPC parameter block. The ioResult field should be used to determine the actual result code when an asynchronously executed PPC Toolbox function completes.

Offset	PPCOpenPBRec	PPCClosePBRec	PPCInformPBRec	PPCStartPBRec	PPCEndPBRec	PPCAcceptPBRec	PPCRejectPBRec	PPCWritePBRec	PPCReadPBRec	IPCListPortsPBRec
38	portRefNum	portRefNum	portRefNum	portRefNum	filler1	filler1	filler1	filler1	filler1	filler1
40	filler1		sessRefNum	sessRefNum	sessRefNum	sessRefNum	sessRefNum	sessRefNum	sessRefNum	startIndex
42							filler2			requestCount
44	serviceType		serviceType	serviceType			filler3	bufferLength	bufferLength	actual Count
45	resFlag		autoAccept	resFlag						
46	portName		portName	portName						portName
48							filler4	actualLength	actualLength	
50	locationName		locationName	locationName						locationName
52							rejectInfo	bufferPtr	bufferPtr	
54	networkVisible		userName	rejectInfo						bufferPtr
55	nbpRegistered									
56								more	more	
57								filler2	filler2	
58			userData	userData				userData	userData	
62			requestType	userRefNum				blockCreator	blockCreator	
66								blockType	blockType	

Figure 7-18. The PPC Toolbox parameter blocks

If you specify a completion routine in the ioCompletion field, it is called at interrupt time when the PPC Toolbox function completes execution.

▲ **Warning:** Completion routines execute at the interrupt level and must preserve all registers other than A0, A1, and D0–D2. (Note that MPW C and MPW Pascal do this automatically.) Your completion routine must not make any calls to the Memory Manager, directly or indirectly, and it can't depend on the validity of handles to unlocked blocks. The PPC Toolbox preserves the application global register A5. ▲

You can write completion routines in C, Pascal, or assembly language. A completion routine declared in Pascal is

```
PROCEDURE MyCompletionRoutine (pb: PPCParamBlockPtr);
```

The pb parameter points to the PPC parameter block passed to the PPC Toolbox function.

Initializing the PPC Toolbox

Use the PPCInit function to initialize the PPC Toolbox.

```
FUNCTION PPCInit : OSErr;
```

On entry	D0: 0
On exit	D0: result code

After initialization, most PPC Toolbox routines can execute either synchronously or asynchronously.

Result codes

noErr	0	No error
noGlobalsErr	–904	System unable to allocate memory, critical error

Note that a noGlobalsErr result code indicates that the PPC Toolbox is not loaded properly.

Using the Program Linking Dialog Box

You can use either the PPCBrowser function or the IPCListPorts function to locate a port to communicate with.

Use the PPCBrowser function to display the program linking dialog box, which allows a user to select a port to communicate with.

```
FUNCTION PPCBrowser (prompt: Str255; applListLabel: Str255;
                     defaultSpecified: Boolean; VAR theLocation:
                     LocationNameRec; VAR thePortInfo: PortInfoRec;
                     portFilter: PPCFilterProcPtr; theLocNBPType: Str32)
                     : OSErr;
```

The prompt parameter is a line of text that the PPCBrowser function displays as a prompt in the program linking dialog box. If you specify NIL or an empty string is passed, the default prompt "Choose a program to link to:" is used.

The applListLabel parameter specifies the title of the list of PPC ports. If you specify NIL or an empty string is passed, the default title "Programs" is used.

If the defaultSpecified parameter is TRUE, the PPCBrowser function tries to select the PPC port specified by the parameters theLocation and thePortInfo when the program linking dialog box first appears. The locationKindSelector field in the location name record must be set to the ppcNoLocation constant (which specifies the local computer) or the ppcNBPLocation constant (which specifies the NBP object and NBP zone). The ppcNBPTypeLocation constant is not supported for matching. When matching the location, only the object string and the zone string of the entity name are used—the type string is ignored. When matching the port, the entire PPC port record (script, name, and port type) is used in the port information record. The location name record and the port information record can be left uninitialized if the defaultSpecified parameter is FALSE. The authRequired field of the port information record is ignored.

The portFilter parameter determines how the list of PPC ports is filtered. If this parameter is NIL, the names of all existing PPC ports are displayed. If this parameter isn't NIL, it must be a pointer to a port filter function.

A sample declaration for a port filter function named MyPortFilter follows.

```
FUNCTION MyPortFilter (theLoc: LocationNamePtr; thePortInfo:
                       PortInfoPtr) : Boolean;
```

The PPCBrowser function calls your port filter function once for each port before it adds that port to the dialog list. This function should return TRUE for each port that should be displayed in the program linking dialog box, and FALSE for each port that shouldn't be displayed.

The parameter theLocNBPType of the PPCBrowser function specifies the NBP type passed to NBPLookup to generate the list of computers. If you specify NIL or an empty string is passed, the default, "PPCToolBox", is used. Note that the current computer is always included in the list of computers (even if a location with the specified type does not exist for it). If the parameter theLocNBPType contains either of the NBP wildcard characters (= or ≈), the PPCBrowser function returns a paramErr result code.

If the PPCBrowser function returns noErr, the parameters theLocation and thePortInfo specify the port chosen by the user. If the PPCBrowser returns a userCanceledErr result code, the user clicked the Cancel button, and no port was selected. If the function returns a memFullErr result code, there was not enough memory to load the PPCBrowser package, and the dialog box did not appear.

Note: You must not call the PPCBrowser function from an application that is running in the background, since this function displays a dialog box on the user's screen.

Result codes

noErr	0	No error
memFullErr	–108	Not enough memory to load PPCBrowser package
userCanceledErr	–128	User decided not to conduct a session

Obtaining a List of Ports

Use the IPCListPorts function to generate a list of existing ports without displaying a dialog box. The IPCListPortsPBRec data type defines the parameter block used by the IPCListPorts function.

```
FUNCTION IPCListPorts (pb: IPCListPortsPBPtr; async: Boolean) : OSErr;
```

On entry	A0: pointer to a parameter block D0: selector (10)
On exit	D0: result code

Parameter block

→	12	ioCompletion	long	address of a completion routine
←	16	ioResult	word	result code
→	40	startIndex	word	index to the port entry list
→	42	requestCount	word	number of port names requested
←	44	actualCount	word	number of port names returned
→	46	portName	long	pointer to PPCPortRec
→	50	locationName	long	pointer to LocationNameRec
→	54	bufferPtr	long	pointer to array of PortInfoRec

If your application calls this function asynchronously, you must specify in the ioCompletion field either the address of a completion routine or NIL. If ioCompletion is NIL, you should poll the ioResult field of the PPC parameter block (from your application's main event loop) to determine whether the PPC Toolbox has completed the requested operation. A value in the ioResult field other than 1 indicates that the call is complete. Note that it is unsafe to poll the ioResult field at interrupt time since the PPC Toolbox may be in the process of completing a call. See "PPC Toolbox Calling Conventions" earlier in this chapter for detailed information.

If you call the IPCListPorts function asynchronously, you must not change any of the fields in the parameter block until the call completes. The port name, location name, and buffer pointed to by IPCListPortsPBRec are owned by the PPC Toolbox until the call completes. These objects must not be deallocated or moved in memory while the call is in progress.

The startIndex field specifies the index to the list of ports on the remote machine from which the PPC Toolbox begins to get the list. In most cases, you'll want to start at the beginning, so set the startIndex field to 0. The requestCount field specifies the maximum number of port information records that can fit into your buffer.

The actualCount field returns the actual number of entries returned. Your program can use the IPCListPorts function repeatedly to obtain the entire list of ports. Ports that are not visible to the network are not included in the ports listing on a remote machine. (If you specify FALSE for the networkVisible field in the PPCOpen function, the port is not included in the listing of available ports across a network.)

The portName field must contain a pointer to a PPC port record that specifies which PPC ports to list. You can specify particular values in the PPC port record or you can use an equal sign (=) in the name or the portTypeStr fields as a wildcard to match all port names or port types.

The locationName field should contain a pointer to a location name record that designates the computer that contains the PPC ports you want returned. If the locationKindSelector field in the location name record is ppcNoLocation or if the locationName pointer is NIL, then the location is the local machine. If the locationKindSelector field in the location name record is ppcNBPLocation, then the location is a remote machine designated by the location name record's nbpEntity field.

The IPCListPorts function returns an array (list) of port information records in the area of memory pointed to by bufferPtr. Make sure that the buffer pointed to by the bufferPtr field is at least sizeof(PortInfoRec) * requestCount.

Result codes

noErr	0	No error
notInitErr	–900	PPC Toolbox has not been initialized yet
nameTypeErr	–902	Invalid or inappropriate locationKindSelector in location name
noGlobalsErr	–904	System unable to allocate memory, critical error
localOnlyErr	–905	Network activity is currently disabled
sessTableErr	–907	PPC Toolbox is unable to create a session
noResponseErr	–915	Unable to contact application
badPortNameErr	–919	PPC port record is invalid
networkErr	–925	An error has occurred in the network
badLocNameErr	–931	Location name is invalid

Opening and Closing a Port

You open a port using the PPCOpen function and close a port using the PPCClose function.

```
FUNCTION PPCOpen (pb: PPCOpenPBPtr; async: Boolean) : OSErr;
```

On entry	A0: pointer to a parameter block D0: selector (1)
On exit	D0: result code

Parameter block

→	12	ioCompletion	long	address of a completion routine
←	16	ioResult	word	result code
←	38	portRefNum	word	port reference number of port opened
→	44	serviceType	byte	service type requested—must be ppcServiceRealTime
→	45	resFlag	byte	reserved field—must be 0
→	46	portName	long	pointer to PPCPortRec
→	50	locationName	long	pointer to LocationNameRec
→	54	networkVisible	byte	make this port network visible
←	55	nbpRegistered	byte	port location was registered on the network

If your application calls this function asynchronously, you must specify in the ioCompletion field either the address of a completion routine or NIL. If ioCompletion is NIL, you should poll the ioResult field of the PPC parameter block (from your application's main event loop) to determine whether the PPC Toolbox has completed the requested operation. A value in the ioResult field other than 1 indicates that the call is complete. Note that it is unsafe to poll the ioResult field at interrupt time since the PPC Toolbox may be in the process of completing a call. See "PPC Toolbox Calling Conventions" earlier in this chapter for detailed information.

If you call the PPCOpen function asynchronously, you must not change any of the fields in the parameter block until the call completes. The port name and location name pointed to by the PPCOpen parameter block record are owned by the PPC Toolbox until the call completes. These objects must not be deallocated or moved in memory while the call is in progress.

The portRefNum field returns the PPC port identifier. Use this port reference number to initiate a session for this particular port. Set the serviceType field to indicate that this port accepts sessions in real time. For system software version 7.0, this field must always be set to the ppcServiceRealTime constant. You must set the resFlag field to 0.

The portName field must contain a pointer to a PPC port record that specifies the name of the PPC port to be opened.

The locationName field should contain a pointer to a location name record that designates the location of the PPC port to be opened. If the locationName pointer is NIL, then the default name PPC Toolbox is used. If a location name record is used, then the locationKindSelector field in the location name record must be ppcNBPTypeLocation, and an alias location name specified by the location name record's nbpType field is used.

The networkVisible field indicates whether the port should be made visible (for browsing as well as incoming network requests). If you specify FALSE, this port is not visible in the listing of available ports across a network (although it is still included within the local machine's listing of available ports).

The nbpRegistered field returns TRUE if the location name specified was registered on the network.

Result codes

noErr	0	No error
notInitErr	–900	PPC Toolbox has not been initialized yet
nameTypeErr	–902	Invalid or inappropriate locationKindSelector in location name
noPortErr	–903	Unable to open port
noGlobalsErr	–904	System unable to allocate memory, critical error
badReqErr	–909	Bad parameter or invalid state for this operation
portNameExistsErr	–910	Another port is already open with this name
badPortNameErr	–919	PPC port record is invalid
badServiceMethodErr	–930	Service method is other than ppcServiceRealTime
badLocNameErr	–931	Location name is invalid
nbpDuplicateName	–1027	Location name represents a duplicate on this computer

You use the PPCClose function to close the port specified by the port reference number.

```
FUNCTION PPCClose (pb: PPCClosePBPtr; async: Boolean) : OSErr;
```

On entry	A0: pointer to a parameter block D0: selector (9)
On exit	D0: result code

Parameter block

→	12	ioCompletion	long	address of a completion routine
←	16	ioResult	word	result code
→	38	portRefNum	word	port reference number of port to close

If your application calls this function asynchronously, you must specify in the ioCompletion field either the address of a completion routine or NIL. If ioCompletion is NIL, you should poll the ioResult field of the PPC parameter block (from your application's main event loop) to determine whether the PPC Toolbox has completed the requested operation. A value in the ioResult field other than 1 indicates that the call is complete. Note that it is unsafe to poll the ioResult field at interrupt time since the PPC Toolbox may be in the process of completing a call. See "PPC Toolbox Calling Conventions" earlier in this chapter for detailed information.

The portRefNum field specifies the PPC port identifier of the port to close. The port reference number must be a valid port reference number returned from a previous call to the PPCOpen function.

Result codes

noErr	0	No error
notInitErr	–900	PPC Toolbox has not been initialized yet
noPortErr	–903	Bad port reference number
noGlobalsErr	–904	System unable to allocate memory, critical error

Starting and Ending a Session

You use the PPCStart or StartSecureSession function to initiate a session with another port, and you use the PPCEnd function to end a session. The PPCStart function initiates a session with the destination port specified in the name and location fields.

```
FUNCTION PPCStart (pb: PPCStartPBPtr; async: Boolean) : OSErr;
```

On entry	A0: pointer to a parameter block D0: selector (2)
On exit	D0: result code

Parameter block

→	12	ioCompletion	long	address of a completion routine
←	16	ioResult	word	result code
→	38	portRefNum	word	port reference number of this session
←	40	sessRefNum	long	session reference number of this session
→	44	serviceType	byte	service type requested—must be ppcServiceRealTime
→	45	resFlag	byte	reserved field—must be 0
→	46	portName	long	pointer to PPCPortRec
→	50	locationName	long	pointer to LocationNameRec
←	54	rejectInfo	long	value from PPCReject if session was rejected
→	58	userData	long	application-specific data
→	62	userRefNum	long	user reference number

If your application calls this function asynchronously, you must specify in the ioCompletion field either the address of a completion routine or NIL. If ioCompletion is NIL, you should poll the ioResult field of the PPC parameter block (from your application's main event loop) to determine whether the PPC Toolbox has completed the requested operation. A value in the ioResult field other than 1 indicates that the call is complete. Note that it is unsafe to poll the ioResult field at interrupt time, since the PPC Toolbox may be in the process of completing a call. See "PPC Toolbox Calling Conventions" earlier in this chapter for detailed information.

If you call the PPCStart function asynchronously, you must not change any of the fields in the parameter block until the call completes. The port name and location name pointed to by the PPCStart parameter block record are owned by the PPC Toolbox until the call completes. These objects must not be deallocated or moved in memory while the call is in progress.

You specify the PPC port identifier in the portRefNum field. The port reference number is a reference number for the port through which you are requesting a session. The value you specify must correspond to the port reference number returned from the PPCOpen function.

The sessRefNum field returns a session identifier. This number, which is provided by the PPC Toolbox, is used while data is being exchanged to identify a particular session. You must set the serviceType field to indicate that the session is to be connected in real time. For system software version 7.0, this field must always be set to the ppcServiceRealTime constant. You must set the resFlag field to 0.

The portName field must contain a pointer to a PPC port record. The locationName field should contain a pointer to a location name record or NIL. The PPC port record and the location name record specify the name and location of the PPC port to initiate a session with, and they are usually obtained from the PPCBrowser function. If the locationKindSelector field in the location name record is ppcNoLocation or if the locationName pointer is NIL, then the location is the local machine. If the locationKindSelector field in the location name record is ppcNBPLocation, then the location is a remote machine designated by the location name record's nbpEntity field.

If the ioResult field of the PPC parameter block returns a userRejectErr result code, the rejectInfo field contains the same value as the rejectInfo field in the PPCReject parameter block. The rejectInfo field is defined by your application.

The initiating port can specify any information in the userData field. The PPCInform function reports this data to the responding port upon its completion.

The userRefNum field specifies an authenticated user. The authentication mechanism of the PPC Toolbox identifies each user through an assigned name and a password. A user reference number of 0 indicates that you want to specify a guest.

Result codes

noErr	0	No error
notInitErr	–900	PPC Toolbox has not been initialized yet
nameTypeErr	–902	locationKindSelector is not ppcNBPLocation or ppcNoLocation
noPortErr	–903	Bad port reference number
noGlobalsErr	–904	System unable to allocate memory, critical error
localOnlyErr	–905	Network activity is currently disabled
destPortErr	–906	Port does not exist at destination

sessTableErr	–907	PPC Toolbox is unable to create a session
noUserNameErr	–911	User name unknown on destination machine
userRejectErr	–912	Destination rejected the session request
noResponseErr	–915	Unable to contact application
portClosedErr	–916	The port was closed
badPortNameErr	–919	PPC port record is invalid
networkErr	–925	An error has occurred in the network
noInformErr	–926	PPCStart failed because target application did not have an inform pending
authFailErr	–927	User's password is wrong
noUserRecErr	–928	Invalid user reference number
badServiceMethodErr	–930	Service method is other than ppcServiceRealTime
guestNotAllowedErr	–932	Destination port requires authentication

The StartSecureSession function prompts for user name and password and calls PPCStart—all in one synchronous procedure call. Use the StartSecureSession function whenever a port destination requires authentication.

```
FUNCTION StartSecureSession (pb: PPCStartPBPtr; VAR userName: Str32;
                             useDefault: Boolean; allowGuest: Boolean;
                             VAR guestSelected: Boolean; prompt: Str255)
                             : OSErr;
```

On entry	A0: pointer to a StartSecureParams record D0: selector (14)
On exit	D0: result code

Your program fills out a parameter block just as though it were calling the PPCStart function. You specify all input fields in the parameter block except for the userRefNum field. The userRefNum field is returned when the StartSecureSession function successfully completes.

The pb parameter is a pointer to the PPCStart parameter block.

The userName parameter is a pointer to a 32-byte character string to be displayed as the user's name. If the Pascal string length is 0, the default user name is used. The default user name is the name specified in the Sharing Setup control panel. The default user name is returned in the userName buffer.

Set the useDefault parameter to TRUE if you want the StartSecureSession function to use the default user identity (and possibly prevent the user identity dialog box from appearing). The allowGuest parameter specifies whether the Guest radio button in the user identity dialog box is active. It is usually set to the inverse of the authRequired field in the port information record. For example, if authRequired is TRUE, then allowGuest should be set to FALSE.

The guestSelected parameter returns TRUE if the user has logged on as a guest. The prompt parameter of the StartSecureSession function allows you to specify a line of text that the dialog box can display. Specify NIL or an empty string for the prompt parameter to enable the PPC Toolbox to use the default prompt. The PPC Toolbox uses the default string "Link to <*port name*> on <*object string*> as:". The port name is obtained from the name string of the port name, and the object string is obtained from the object string of the location name.

Note: Do not call the StartSecureSession function from an application that is running in the background, since this function requires that several dialog boxes appear on the user's screen.

Result codes

noErr	0	No error
userCanceledErr	–128	User decided not to conduct a session
notInitErr	–900	PPC Toolbox has not been initialized yet
nameTypeErr	–902	locationKindSelector is not ppcNBPLocation or ppcNoLocation
noPortErr	–903	Bad port reference number
noGlobalsErr	–904	System unable to allocate memory, critical error
localOnlyErr	–905	Network activity is currently disabled
destPortErr	–906	Port does not exist at destination
sessTableErr	–907	PPC Toolbox is unable to create a session
noResponseErr	–915	Unable to contact application
portClosedErr	–916	The port was closed
badPortNameErr	–919	PPC port record is invalid
noUserRefErr	–924	Unable to create a new user reference number
networkErr	–925	An error has occurred in the network
noInformErr	–926	PPCStart failed because application did not have an inform pending
badServiceMethodErr	–930	Service method is other than ppcServiceRealTime
guestNotAllowedErr	–932	Destination port requires authentication

Use the PPCEnd function to end a session. This function completes all outstanding asynchronous calls associated with the session reference number.

```
FUNCTION PPCEnd (pb: PPCEndPBPtr; async: Boolean) : OSErr;
```

On entry	A0: pointer to a parameter block D0: selector (8)
On exit	D0: result code

Parameter block

→	12	ioCompletion	long	address of a completion routine
←	16	ioResult	word	result code
→	40	sessRefNum	long	session reference number of session to end

If your application calls this function asynchronously, you must specify in the ioCompletion field either the address of a completion routine or NIL. If ioCompletion is NIL, you should poll the ioResult field of the PPC parameter block (from your application's main event loop) to determine whether the PPC Toolbox has completed the requested operation. A value in the ioResult field other than 1 indicates that the call is complete. Note that it is unsafe to poll the ioResult field at interrupt time since the PPC Toolbox may be in the process of completing a call. See "PPC Toolbox Calling Conventions" earlier in this chapter for detailed information.

You provide a session identifier in the sessRefNum field to identify the session that you are terminating. The PPCStart, StartSecureSession, or PPCInform function returns the session reference number.

Result codes

noErr	0	No error
notInitErr	–900	PPC Toolbox has not been initialized yet
noGlobalsErr	–904	System unable to allocate memory, critical error
noSessionErr	–908	Invalid session reference number

Receiving, Accepting, and Rejecting a Session

You use the PPCInform function to receive session requests. After the PPCInform function completes (with the autoAccept field set to FALSE), you must accept or reject the session request using the PPCAccept and PPCReject functions.

As long as a port has been opened, you can call the PPCInform function at any time. You can have any number of outstanding PPCInform functions.

```
FUNCTION PPCInform (pb: PPCInformPBPtr; async: Boolean) : OSErr;
```

On entry	A0: pointer to a parameter block D0: selector (3)
On exit	D0: result code

Parameter block

→	12	ioCompletion	long	address of a completion routine
←	16	ioResult	word	result code
→	38	portRefNum	word	port reference number of this session
←	40	sessRefNum	long	session reference number of this session
←	44	serviceType	byte	service type of this session
→	45	autoAccept	byte	if TRUE, session is accepted automatically

(Continued)

→	46	portName	long	pointer to PPCPortRec, may be NIL
→	50	locationName	long	pointer to LocationNameRec, may be NIL
→	54	userName	long	pointer to Str32, may be NIL
←	58	userData	long	application-specific data
←	62	requestType	byte	network or local request

If your application calls this function asynchronously, you must specify in the ioCompletion field either the address of a completion routine or NIL. If ioCompletion is NIL, you should poll the ioResult field of the PPC parameter block (from your application's main event loop) to determine whether the PPC Toolbox has completed the requested operation. A value in the ioResult field other than 1 indicates that the call is complete. Note that it is unsafe to poll the ioResult field at interrupt time since the PPC Toolbox may be in the process of completing a call. See "PPC Toolbox Calling Conventions" earlier in this chapter for detailed information.

If you call the PPCInform function asynchronously, you must not change any of the fields in the parameter block until the call completes. The port name, location name, user name, and buffer pointed to by the record of type PPCInformPBRec are owned by the PPC Toolbox until the call completes. These objects must not be deallocated or moved in memory while the call is in progress.

You provide the PPC port identifier in the portRefNum field. A PPCOpen function returns the port identifier. The sessRefNum field returns a session identifier.

The serviceType field indicates the service type. For system software version 7.0, this field always returns the ppcServiceRealTime constant.

If you set the autoAccept field to TRUE, session requests are automatically accepted as they are received. When the PPCInform function completes execution with a noErr result code and you set the autoAccept field to FALSE, you need to accept or reject the session.

> ▲ **Warning:** If the PPCInform function (with the autoAccept parameter set to FALSE) returns a noErr result code, you must call either the PPCAccept function or the PPCReject function. The computer trying to initiate a session using the StartSecureSession function or the PPCStart function waits (hangs) until the session attempt is either accepted or rejected, or until an error occurs. ▲

The portName field must contain NIL or a pointer to a PPC port record. If the portName field contains NIL, then the name of the PPC port that initiated the session is not returned. If the portName field points to a PPC port record, then the PPC port record is filled with the name of the PPC port that initiated the session when the PPCInform function completes.

The locationName field must contain NIL or a pointer to a location name record. If the locationName field contains NIL, then the location of the PPC port that initiated the session is not returned. If the locationName field points to a location name record, then the location name record is filled with the location of the PPC port that initiated the session when the PPCInform function completes. If the locationKindSelector field of the location name record returned is ppcNoLocation, then the location is the local machine. If the locationKindSelector field of the location name record returned is ppcNBPLocation, then the location is a remote machine designated by the location name record's nbpEntity field.

The userName field must contain NIL or a pointer to a 32-byte character string. If the userName field contains NIL, then the user name string is not returned. If the userName field points to a 32-byte character string, then the 32-byte character string is filled with the name of the user making the session request (if authenticated) when the PPCInform function completes.

When the PPCInform function completes, the userData field contains the user data provided by the application making the session request. This field is transparent to the PPC Toolbox. The application can send any data in this field.

When the PPCInform function completes, the requestType field contains either ppcRemoteOrigin or ppcLocalOrigin, depending on whether the session request is initiated by a computer across the network or by a port on the same computer.

You should execute the PPCInform function asynchronously.

Result codes

noErr	0	No error
notInitErr	–900	PPC Toolbox has not been initialized yet
noPortErr	–903	Unable to open port or bad port reference number
noGlobalsErr	–904	System unable to allocate memory, critical error
portClosedErr	–916	The port was closed

Use the PPCAccept function to indicate that an application is willing to accept an incoming session request after a PPCInform function completes.

```
FUNCTION PPCAccept (pb: PPCAcceptPBPtr; async: Boolean) : OSErr;
```

On entry	A0: pointer to a parameter block D0: selector (4)
On exit	D0: result code

Parameter block

→	12	ioCompletion	long	address of a completion routine
←	16	ioResult	word	result code
→	40	sessRefNum	long	session reference number of session to accept

If your application calls this function asynchronously, you must specify in the ioCompletion field either the address of a completion routine or NIL. If ioCompletion is NIL, you should poll the ioResult field of the PPC parameter block (from your application's main event loop) to determine whether the PPC Toolbox has completed the requested operation. A value in the ioResult field other than 1 indicates that the call is complete. Note that it is unsafe to poll the ioResult field at interrupt time since the PPC Toolbox may be in the process of completing a call. See "PPC Toolbox Calling Conventions" earlier in this chapter for detailed information.

The sessRefNum field specifies a session identifier. Use the session reference number returned from the completed PPCInform parameter block to accept the session request.

Result codes

noErr	0	No error
notInitErr	–900	PPC Toolbox has not been initialized yet
noGlobalsErr	–904	System unable to allocate memory, critical error
noSessionErr	–908	Invalid session reference number
badReqErr	–909	Invalid state for this operation

Use the PPCReject function to reject a session request after a PPCInform function completes.

```
FUNCTION PPCReject (pb: PPCRejectPBPtr; async: Boolean) : OSErr;
```

On entry	A0: pointer to a parameter block D0: selector (5)
On exit	D0: result code

Parameter block

→	12	ioCompletion	long	address of a completion routine
←	16	ioResult	word	result code
→	40	sessRefNum	long	session reference number of session to reject
→	54	rejectInfo	long	value to return if session is rejected

If your application calls this function asynchronously, you must specify in the ioCompletion field either the address of a completion routine or NIL. If ioCompletion is NIL, you should poll the ioResult field of the PPC parameter block (from your application's main event loop) to determine whether the PPC Toolbox has completed the requested operation. A value in the ioResult field other than 1 indicates that the call is complete. Note that it is unsafe to poll the ioResult field at interrupt time since the PPC Toolbox may be in the process of completing a call. See "PPC Toolbox Calling Conventions" earlier in this chapter for detailed information.

The sessRefNum field specifies a session to be rejected. This must be a valid session reference number returned from a previous PPCInform function. The rejectInfo field is an optional field. The application receiving a session request may specify any data in this field. The initiating application receives this information in the PPCStart parameter block.

Result codes

noErr	0	No error
notInitErr	–900	PPC Toolbox has not been initialized yet
noGlobalsErr	–904	System unable to allocate memory, critical error
noSessionErr	–908	Invalid session reference number
badReqErr	–909	Invalid state for this operation

Reading and Writing Data

The PPCRead function reads incoming data from an application, and the PPCWrite function writes data to an application during a session.

Use the PPCRead function to read message blocks during a session.

```
FUNCTION PPCRead (pb: PPCReadPBPtr; async: Boolean) : OSErr;
```

On entry	A0: pointer to a parameter block D0: selector (7)
On exit	D0: result code

Parameter block

→	12	ioCompletion	long	address of a completion routine
←	16	ioResult	word	result code
→	40	sessRefNum	long	session reference number
→	44	bufferLength	long	length of data buffer
←	48	actualLength	long	actual length of data read
→	52	bufferPtr	long	pointer to data buffer
←	56	more	byte	TRUE if more data in this block to be read
←	58	userData	long	application-specific data
←	62	blockCreator	long	creator of block read
←	66	blockType	long	type of block read

If your application calls this function asynchronously, you must specify in the ioCompletion field either the address of a completion routine or NIL. If ioCompletion is NIL, you should poll the ioResult field of the PPC parameter block (from your application's main event loop) to determine whether the PPC Toolbox has completed the requested operation. A value in the ioResult field other than 1 indicates that the call is complete. Note that it is unsafe to poll the ioResult field at interrupt time since the PPC Toolbox may be in the process of completing a call. See "PPC Toolbox Calling Conventions" earlier in this chapter for detailed information.

If you call the PPCRead function asynchronously, you must not change any of the fields in the parameter block until the call completes. The buffer pointed to by the record of data type PPCReadPBRec is owned by the PPC Toolbox until the call completes. These objects must not be deallocated or moved in memory while the call is in progress.

The sessRefNum field specifies a session to read data from. This must be a valid session reference number returned from a previous PPCStart, StartSecureSession, or PPCInform function. The bufferLength and bufferPtr fields specify the length and location of a buffer the message block will be read into. Your application must allocate the storage for the buffer. The actualLength field returns the actual size of the data read into your data buffer.

The more field is TRUE if the provided buffer cannot hold the remainder of the message block. Your application may read a message block in several pieces. It is not necessary to have a buffer large enough to read in the entire message block, so a message block can span multiple calls to the PPCRead function.

Upon completion of the PPCRead function, the userData, blockCreator, and blockType fields contain information regarding the contents of the message block. You specify these fields using the PPCWrite function. See "Exchanging Data During a PPC Session" earlier in this chapter for additional information.

You should execute the PPCRead function asynchronously.

Result codes

noErr	0	No error
notInitErr	–900	PPC Toolbox has not been initialized yet
noGlobalsErr	–904	System unable to allocate memory, critical error
noSessionErr	–908	Invalid session reference number
badReqErr	–909	Invalid state for this operation
sessClosedErr	–917	The session has closed

Use the PPCWrite function to write message blocks during a session.

```
FUNCTION PPCWrite (pb: PPCWritePBPtr; async: Boolean) : OSErr;
```

On entry	A0: pointer to a parameter block D0: selector (6)
On exit	D0: result code

Parameter block

→	12	ioCompletion	long	address of a completion routine
←	16	ioResult	word	result code
→	40	sessRefNum	long	session reference number
→	44	bufferLength	long	length of data buffer
←	48	actualLength	long	actual length of data written

→	52	bufferPtr	long	pointer to data buffer
→	56	more	byte	TRUE if more data in this block to be written
→	58	userData	long	application-specific data
→	62	blockCreator	long	creator of block written
→	66	blockType	long	type of block written

If your application calls this function asynchronously, you must specify in the ioCompletion field either the address of a completion routine or NIL. If ioCompletion is NIL, you should poll the ioResult field of the PPC parameter block (from your application's main event loop) to determine whether the PPC Toolbox has completed the requested operation. A value in the ioResult field other than 1 indicates that the call is complete. Note that it is unsafe to poll the ioResult field at interrupt time since the PPC Toolbox may be in the process of completing a call. See "PPC Toolbox Calling Conventions" earlier in this chapter for detailed information.

If you call the PPCWrite function asynchronously, you must not change any of the fields in the parameter block until the call completes. The buffer pointed to by the record of data type PPCWritePBRec is owned by the PPC Toolbox until the call completes. These objects must not be deallocated or moved in memory while the call is in progress.

The sessRefNum field specifies a session identifier. This must be a valid session reference number returned from a previous PPCStart, StartSecureSession, or PPCInform function.

The bufferLength and bufferPtr fields specify the length and location of a buffer the message block is sent to. If the PPCWrite function returns a noErr result code, the actualLength field returns the actual size of the message block that was written.

Set the more field to TRUE to indicate that you will be using another PPCWrite function to append data to this message block. Set the more field to FALSE to indicate that this is the end of the data in this message block.

The initiating port can specify any information in the userData field. The PPCRead function reports this data to the responding port upon its completion.

Set the userData, blockCreator, and blockType fields for each message block that you create. These fields can give the receiving application information about how to process the contents of the message block. They are ignored when you append information to a message block. Set the more field to TRUE to append additional data to a message block; otherwise, set this field to FALSE. See "Exchanging Data During a PPC Session" earlier in this chapter for additional information.

You should execute the PPCWrite function asynchronously.

Result codes

noErr	0	No error
notInitErr	–900	PPC Toolbox has not been initialized yet
noGlobalsErr	–904	System unable to allocate memory, critical error
noSessionErr	–908	Invalid session reference number
badReqErr	–909	Invalid state for this operation
sessClosedErr	–917	The session has closed

Locating a Default User and Invalidating a User

The GetDefaultUser function returns the user reference number and the name of the default user. The default user is specified in the Sharing Setup control panel. This function is useful if your application uses the PPCStart function to initiate a session with an application that does not support guest access.

```
FUNCTION GetDefaultUser (VAR userRef: LongInt; VAR userName: Str32) :
                         OSErr;
```

On entry	A0: pointer to a GetDefaultUserParams record D0: selector (13)
On exit	D0: result code

If the GetDefaultUser function completes with no errors, then the userRef parameter returns the user reference number that represents the user name and password of the default user. The userName parameter must contain NIL or a 32-byte character string. If the userName parameter contains NIL, then the user name string is not returned. If the userName parameter is a 32-byte character string, the 32-byte character string contains the user name that is specified in the Sharing Setup control panel when the GetDefaultUser function completes (with no errors).

▲ **Warning:** If you are using Pascal, you cannot pass NIL for the userName parameter. For example, you cannot pass StringPtr(NIL)^ due to Pascal range checking of string bounds. ▲

Result codes

noErr	0	No error
noDefaultUserErr	–922	User has not specified owner name in Sharing Setup control panel
noLoggedInErr	–923	Default user reference number does not yet exist

To invalidate a particular user name and corresponding password, use the DeleteUserIdentity function.

```
FUNCTION DeleteUserIdentity (userRef: LongInt) : OSErr;
```

Trap macro	_DeleteUser
On entry	A0: pointer to a DeleteUserParams record D0: selector (12)
On exit	D0: result code

You specify the reference number representing the user name and password to be deleted.

Result codes

noErr	0	No error
noUserRecErr	–928	Invalid user reference number

SUMMARY OF THE PPC TOOLBOX

Constants

```
CONST {service type}
      ppcServiceRealTime          = 1;       {real time only in system }
                                             { software version 7.0}

      {gestalt selectors}
      gestaltPPCToolboxAttr       = 'ppc ';  {PPC Toolbox attributes}
      gestaltPPCToolboxPresent    = $0000;   {PPC Toolbox is present}
      gestaltPPCSupportsRealTime  = $1000;   {real time only in system }
                                             { software version 7.0}
      gestaltPPCSupportsOutGoing  = $0002;   {support of outgoing }
                                             { sessions across a network}
      gestaltPPCSupportsIncoming  = $0001;   {user enabled program }
                                             { linking in Sharing Setup }
                                             { control panel}

      {look-up type}
      ppcNoLocation               = 0;       {there is no PPCLocName use}
      ppcNBPLocation              = 1;       { AppleTalk NBP}
      ppcNBPTypeLocation          = 2;       {use just the NBP type, fill}
                                             { in the rest with default}

      {port type}
      ppcByCreatorAndType         = 1;       {port type is specified as }
                                             { standard Mac creator and }
                                             { type}
      ppcByString                 = 2;       {port type is in Pascal }
                                             { string format}

      {session request type returned in the PPCInform function}
      ppcLocalOrigin              = 1;       {session initiated on }
                                             { local computer}
      ppcRemoteOrigin             = 2;       {session initiated on }
                                             { remote computer}
```

Data Types

```
TYPE
     PPCServiceType          = SignedByte;  {service type}
     PPCLocationKind         = Integer;     {look-up type}
     PPCPortKinds            = Integer;     {port type}
     PPCSessionOrigin        = SignedByte;  {local or remote}
     PPCPortRefNum           = Integer;     {port reference number}
     PPCSessRefNum           = LongInt;     {session reference number}
```

```
LocationNamePtr = ^LocationNameRec;
LocationNameRec =
RECORD
   locationKindSelector : PPCLocationKind;
                          {which variant}
   CASE PPCLocationKind OF              {ppcNoLocation: storage not }
                                        { used by this value}
     ppcNBPLocation:    (nbpEntity: EntityName);
                                        {NBP name entity}
     ppcNBPTypeLocation:(nbpType: Str32)
                                        {just the NBP type string }
                                        { for the PPCOpen function}
END;

PortInfoPtr = ^PortInfoRec;
PortInfoRec =
RECORD
   filler1:             SignedByte;    {space holder}
   authRequired:        Boolean;       {authentication required}
   name:                PPCPortRec     {port name}
END;

PPCPortPtr = ^PPCPortRec;
PPCPortRec =
RECORD
   nameScript:          ScriptCode;    {script identifier}
   name:                Str32;         {port name shown in program }
                                       { linking dialog box}
   portKindSelector:    PPCPortKinds;  {general category of }
                                       { application}
   CASE PPCPortKinds OF
     ppcByString:       (portTypeStr: Str32);
                                       {32 characters}
     ppcByCreatorAndType:
                        (portCreator: OSType; portType: OSType)
                                       {4-character creator and }
                                       { type}
END;

PPCParamBlockPtr = ^PPCParamBlockRec;
PPCParamBlockRec =
RECORD
   CASE Integer OF
   0: (openParam:       PPCOpenPBRec);         {PPCOPen params}
   1: (informParam:     PPCInformPBRec);       {PPCInform params}
   2: (startParam:      PPCStartPBRec);        {PPCStart params}
   3: (acceptParam:     PPCAcceptPBRec);       {PPCAccept params}
   4: (rejectParam:     PPCRejectPBRec);       {PPCReject params}
   5: (writeParam:      PPCWritePBRec);        {PPCWrite params}
   6: (readParam:       PPCReadPBRec);         {PPCRead params}
   7: (endParam:        PPCEndPBRec);          {PPCEnd params}
   8: (closeParam:      PPCClosePBRec);        {PPCClose params}
   9: (listPortsParam:  IPCListPortsPBRec)     {IPCListPorts params}
END;
```

```
PortInfoArrayPtr = ^PortInfoArray;
PortInfoArray    = ARRAY[0..0] OF PortInfoRec;

PPCOpenPBPtr = ^PPCOpenPBRec;
PPCOpenPBRec =
RECORD
   qLink:          Ptr;                {private}
   csCode:         Integer;            {private}
   intUse:         Integer;            {private}
   intUsePtr:      Ptr;                {private}
   ioCompletion:   PPCCompProcPtr;     {address of a completion }
                                       { routine}
   ioResult:       OSErr;              {completion of operation}
   reserved:       ARRAY[1..5] OF LongInt;
                                       {private}
   portRefNum:     PPCPortRefNum;      {PPC port identifier}
   filler1:        LongInt;            {space holder}
   serviceType:    PPCServiceType;     {real time only}
   resFlag:        SignedByte;         {reserved field}
   portName:       PPCPortPtr;         {name of port to be opened }
   locationName:   LocationNamePtr;    {location of port to be }
                                       { opened}
   networkVisible: Boolean;            {port is visible for }
                                       { browsing}
   nbpRegistered:  Boolean             {location name registered }
                                       { on network}
END;

PPCInformPBPtr = ^PPCInformPBRec;
PPCInformPBRec =
RECORD
   qLink:          Ptr;                {private}
   csCode:         Integer;            {private}
   intUse:         Integer;            {private}
   intUsePtr:      Ptr;                {private}
   ioCompletion:   PPCCompProcPtr;     {address of a completion }
                                       { routine}
   ioResult:       OSErr;              {completion of operation}
   reserved:       ARRAY[1..5] OF LongInt;
                                       {private}
   portRefNum:     PPCPortRefNum;      {port identifier}
   sessRefNum:     PPCSessRefNum;      {session identifier}
   serviceType:    PPCServiceType;     {real time only}
   autoAccept:     Boolean;            {automatic session }
                                       { acceptance}
   portName:       PPCPortPtr;         {name of port that }
                                       { initiated a session}
   locationName:   LocationNamePtr;    {location of port that }
                                       { initiated a session}
   userName:       StringPtr;          {name of user that }
                                       { initiated a session}
   userData:       LongInt;            {application-defined}
   requestType:    PPCSessionOrigin    {local or remote}
END;
```

```
PPCStartPBPtr = ^PPCStartPBRec;
PPCStartPBRec =
RECORD
   qLink:          Ptr;               {private}
   csCode:         Integer;           {private}
   intUse:         Integer;           {private}
   intUsePtr:      Ptr;               {private}
   ioCompletion:   PPCCompProcPtr;    {address of a completion }
                                      { routine}
   ioResult:       OSErr;             {completion of operation}
   reserved:       ARRAY[1..5] OF LongInt;
                                      {private}
   portRefNum:     PPCPortRefNum;     {identifier for requested }
                                      { port}
   sessRefNum:     PPCSessRefNum;     {session identifier}
   serviceType:    PPCServiceType;    {real time only}
   resFlag:        Signed Byte;       {reserved field}
   portName:       PPCPortPtr;        {name of port to be opened}
   locationName:   LocationNamePtr;   {location of port to be }
                                      { opened}
   rejectInfo:     LongInt;           {rejection of session}
   userData:       LongInt;           {application-specific}
   userRefNum:     LongInt            {specifies an authenticated }
                                      { user}
END;

PPCAcceptPBPtr = ^PPCAcceptPBRec;
PPCAcceptPBRec =
RECORD
   qLink:          Ptr;               {private}
   csCode:         Integer;           {private}
   intUse:         Integer;           {private}
   intUsePtr:      Ptr;               {private}
   ioCompletion:   PPCCompProcPtr;    {address of a completion }
                                      { routine}
   ioResult:       OSErr;             {completion of operation}
   reserved:       ARRAY[1..5] OF LongInt;
                                      {private}
   filler1:        Integer;           {space holder}
   sessRefNum:     PPCSessRefNum      {session identifier}
END;

PPCRejectPBPtr = ^PPCRejectPBRec;
PPCRejectPBRec =
RECORD
   qLink:          Ptr;               {private}
   csCode:         Integer;           {private}
   intUse:         Integer;           {private}
   intUsePtr:      Ptr;               {private}
   ioCompletion:   PPCCompProcPtr;    {address of a completion }
                                      { routine}
   ioResult:       OSErr;             {completion of operation}
```

```
      reserved:         ARRAY[1..5] OF LongInt;
                                             {private}
      filler1:          Integer;             {space holder}
      sessRefNum:       PPCSessRefNum;       {session identifier}
      filler2:          Integer;             {space holder}
      filler3:          LongInt;             {space holder}
      filler4:          LongInt;             {space holder}
      rejectInfo:       LongInt              {rejection of session}
   END;

   PPCWritePBPtr = ^PPCWritePBRec;
   PPCWritePBRec =
   RECORD
      qLink:            Ptr;                 {private}
      csCode:           Integer;             {private}
      intUse:           Integer;             {private}
      intUsePtr:        Ptr;                 {private}
      ioCompletion:     PPCCompProcPtr;      {address of a completion }
                                             { routine}
      ioResult:         OSErr;               {completion of operation}
      reserved:         ARRAY[1..5] OF LongInt;
                                             {private}
      filler1:          Integer;             {space holder}
      sessRefNum:       PPCSessRefNum;       {session identifier}
      bufferLength:     Size;                {length of buffer to be }
                                             { written}
      actualLength:     Size;                {actual size of data written}
      bufferPtr:        Ptr;                 {location of buffer to be }
                                             { written}
      more:             Boolean;             {additional data to be }
                                             { written}
      filler2:          SignedByte;          {space holder}
      userData:         LongInt;             {application-specific}
      blockCreator:     OSType;              {creator of block to be }
                                             { written}
      blockType:        OSType               {type of block to be written}
   END;

   PPCReadPBPtr = ^PPCReadPBRec;
   PPCReadPBRec =
   RECORD
      qLink:            Ptr;                 {private}
      csCode:           Integer;             {private}
      intUse:           Integer;             {private}
      intUsePtr:        Ptr;                 {private}
      ioCompletion:     PPCCompProcPtr;      {address of a completion }
                                             { routine}
      ioResult:         OSErr;               {completion of operation}
      reserved:         ARRAY[1..5] OF LongInt;
                                             {private}
      filler1:          Integer;             {space holder}
      sessRefNum:       PPCSessRefNum;       {session identifier}
      bufferLength:     Size;                {length of buffer to be read}
```

```
      actualLength:    Size;                   {actual size of the data }
                                               { read}
      bufferPtr:       Ptr;                    {location of buffer to be }
                                               { read}
      more:            Boolean;                {additional data to be read}
      filler2:         SignedByte;             {space holder}
      userData:        LongInt;                {application-specific}
      blockCreator:    OSType;                 {creator of block to be read}
      blockType:       OSType                  {type of block to be read}
   END;

   PPCEndPBPtr = ^PPCEndPBRec;
   PPCEndPBRec =
   RECORD
      qLink:           Ptr;                    {private}
      csCode:          Integer;                {private}
      intUse:          Integer;                {private}
      intUsePtr:       Ptr;                    {private}
      ioCompletion:    PPCCompProcPtr;         {address of a completion }
                                               { routine}
      ioResult:        OSErr;                  {completion of operation}
      reserved:        ARRAY[1..5] OF LongInt;
                                               {private}
      filler1:         Integer;                {space holder}
      sessRefNum:      PPCSessRefNum           {identifier of session to }
                                               { be terminated}
   END;

   PPCClosePBPtr = ^PPCClosePBRec;
   PPCClosePBRec =
   RECORD
      qLink:           Ptr;                    {private}
      csCode:          Integer;                {private}
      intUse:          Integer;                {private}
      intUsePtr:       Ptr;                    {private}
      ioCompletion:    PPCCompProcPtr;         {address of a completion }
                                               { routine}
      ioResult:        OSErr;                  {completion of operation}
      reserved:        ARRAY[1..5] OF LongInt;
                                               {private}
      portRefNum:      PPCPortRefNum           {identifier of port to }
                                               { be closed}
   END;

   IPCListPortsPBPtr = ^IPCListPortsPBRec;
   IPCListPortsPBRec =
   RECORD
      qLink:           Ptr;                    {private}
      csCode:          Integer;                {private}
      intUse:          Integer;                {private}
      intUsePtr:       Ptr;                    {private}
      ioCompletion:    PPCCompProcPtr;         {address of a completion }
                                               { routine}
```

```
ioResult:           OSErr;               {completion of operation}
   reserved:        ARRAY[1..5] OF LongInt;
                                         {private}
   filler1:         Integer;             {space holder}
   startIndex:      Integer;             {index to the port entry }
                                         { list}
   requestCount:    Integer;             {number of entries to }
                                         { be returned}
   actualCount:     Integer;             {actual number of port names}
   portName:        PPCPortPtr;          {list of port names}
   locationName:    LocationNamePtr;     {location of port names}
   bufferPtr:       PortInfoArrayPtr     {pointer to a buffer}
END;
```

Routines

Initializing the PPC Toolbox

```
FUNCTION PPCInit : OSErr;
```

Using the Program Linking Dialog Box

```
FUNCTION PPCBrowser        (prompt: Str255; applListLabel: Str255;
                            defaultSpecified: Boolean; VAR theLocation:
                            LocationNameRec; VAR thePortInfo: PortInfoRec;
                            portFilter: PPCFilterProcPtr; theLocNBPType:
                            Str32) : OSErr;
```

Obtaining a List of Ports

```
FUNCTION IPCListPorts      (pb: IPCListPortsPBPtr; async: Boolean) : OSErr;
```

Opening and Closing a Port

```
FUNCTION PPCOpen           (pb: PPCOpenPBPtr; async: Boolean) : OSErr;

FUNCTION PPCClose          (pb: PPCClosePBPtr; async: Boolean) : OSErr;
```

Starting and Ending a Session

```
FUNCTION PPCStart             (pb: PPCStartPBPtr; async: Boolean) : OSErr;
FUNCTION StartSecureSession   (pb: PPCStartPBPtr; VAR userName: Str32;
                               useDefault: Boolean; allowGuest: Boolean;
                               VAR guestSelected: Boolean; prompt: Str255)
                               : OSErr;
FUNCTION PPCEnd               (pb: PPCEndPBPtr; async: Boolean) : OSErr;
```

Receiving, Accepting, and Rejecting a Session

```
FUNCTION PPCInform           (pb: PPCInformPBPtr; async: Boolean) : OSErr;
FUNCTION PPCAccept           (pb: PPCAcceptPBPtr; async: Boolean) : OSErr;
FUNCTION PPCReject           (pb: PPCRejectPBPtr; async: Boolean) : OSErr;
```

Reading and Writing Data

```
FUNCTION PPCRead             (pb: PPCReadPBPtr; async: Boolean) : OSErr;
FUNCTION PPCWrite            (pb: PPCWritePBPtr; async: Boolean) : OSErr;
```

Locating a Default User and Invalidating a User

```
FUNCTION GetDefaultUser       (VAR userRef: LongInt; VAR userName: Str32) :
                               OSErr;
FUNCTION DeleteUserIdentity  (userRef: LongInt) : OSErr;
```

Application-Defined Routines

```
PROCEDURE MyCompletionRoutine (pb: PPCParamBlockPtr);
FUNCTION MyPortFilter          (locationName: LocationNameRec;
                                thePortInfo: PortInfoRec) : Boolean;
```

Result Codes

noErr	0	No error
paramErr	–50	Illegal parameter
memFullErr	–108	Not enough memory to load PPCBrowser package
userCanceledErr	–128	User decided not to conduct a session
notInitErr	–900	PPC Toolbox has not been initialized yet
nameTypeErr	–902	Invalid or inappropriate locationKindSelector in location name
noPortErr	–903	Unable to open port or bad port reference number
noGlobalsErr	–904	System unable to allocate memory, critical error
localOnlyErr	–905	Network activity is currently disabled
destPortErr	–906	Port does not exist at destination
sessTableErr	–907	PPC Toolbox is unable to create a session
noSessionErr	–908	Invalid session reference number
badReqErr	–909	Bad parameter or invalid state for this operation
portNameExistsErr	–910	Another port is already open with this name
noUserNameErr	–911	User name unknown on destination machine
userRejectErr	–912	Destination rejected the session request
noResponseErr	–915	Unable to contact application
portClosedErr	–916	The port was closed
sessClosedErr	–917	The session has closed
badPortNameErr	–919	PPC port record is invalid
noDefaultUserErr	–922	User has not specified owner name in Sharing Setup control panel
notLoggedInErr	–923	Default user reference number does not yet exist
noUserRefErr	–924	Unable to create a new user reference number
networkErr	–925	An error has occurred in the network
noInformErr	–926	PPCStart failed because target application did not have an inform pending
authFailErr	–927	User's password is wrong
noUserRecErr	–928	Invalid user reference number
badServiceMethodErr	–930	Service method is other than ppcServiceRealTime
badLocNameErr	–931	Location name is invalid
guestNotAllowedErr	–932	Destination port requires authentication
nbpDuplicate	–1027	Location name represents a duplicate on this computer

Assembly-Language Information

Trap Macros Requiring Routine Selectors

$A0DD

Selector	Routine
$0100	InitEditionPack
$0206	UnRegisterSection
$0208	IsRegisteredSection
$0210	DeleteEditionContainerFile
$0224	GoToPublisherSection
$0226	GetLastEditionContainerUsed
$022A	GetEditionOpenerProc
$022C	SetEditionOpenerProc
$0232	NewSubscriberDialog
$0236	NewPublisherDialog
$023A	SectionOptionsDialog
$0316	CloseEdition
$040C	AssociateSection
$0412	OpenEdition
$0422	GetEditionInfo
$050E	CreateEditionContainerFile
$052E	CallEditionOpenerProc
$0530	CallFormatIOProc
$0604	RegisterSection
$0618	EditionHasFormat
$061E	GetEditionFormatMark
$0620	SetEditionFormatMark
$0814	OpenNewEdition
$081A	ReadEdition
$081C	WriteEdition
$0A02	NewSection
$0A28	GetStandardFormats
$0B34	NewSubscriberExpDialog
$0B38	NewPublisherExpDialog
$0B3C	SectionOptionsExpDialog

8 THE DATA ACCESS MANAGER

ABOUT THIS CHAPTER

This chapter describes how your application can use the Data Access Manager to gain access to data in another application. It also tells you how to provide templates to be used for data transactions.

The Data Access Manager is available with system software version 7.0. Use the Gestalt function described in the Compatibility Guidelines chapter of this volume to determine whether the Data Access Manager is present.

The Data Access Manager allows your application to communicate with a database or other data source even if you do not know anything about databases in general or the specific data source with which the users of your software will be communicating. All your application needs is a few high-level Data Access Manager functions and access to a file called a **query document.** The query document, provided by another application, contains commands and data in the format appropriate for the database or other data source. The string of commands and data sent to the data source are referred to as a **query.** Note that a query does not necessarily extract data from a data source; it might only send data or commands to a database or other application.

The Data Access Manager makes it easy for your application to communicate with data sources. You need only add a menu item that opens a query document, using a few standard Data Access Manager functions to implement the menu selection. Users of your application can then gain access to a database or other data source whenever they have the appropriate query documents. A user of a word-processing program might use this feature, for example, to obtain access to archived material, dictionaries in a variety of languages, or a database of famous quotations. A user of a spreadsheet program might use a query document to obtain tax records, actuarial tables, or other data. A user of an art or CAD program might download archived illustrations or designs. And for the user of a database application for the Macintosh® computer, the Data Access Manager can provide the resources and power of a mainframe database.

The Data Access Manager also provides a low-level interface for use by applications that are capable of creating their own queries and that therefore do not have to use query documents.

If your application uses only the high-level interface and relies on query documents created by other programs, then all the routines you need to know are described in this chapter. However, if you want to create a query document or an application that uses the low-level interface, then you must also be familiar with the command language used by the data server.

You need the information in this chapter if you want your application to be able to gain access to data in other applications or if you want to write a query document.

> **Note:** The Data Access Manager makes it easy for your application to communicate with a database running on a remote computer, and this chapter generally assumes that you are using it for that purpose. However, there is no reason why the database could not be local—that is, running on the same computer as your application. To implement such a system, you would have to have a database that runs on a Macintosh computer and that has a command-language interface, plus a database extension that can use that command language. In most cases, it would be much simpler to run the database as a separate application and use the Clipboard to transfer data into and out of the database.

Note also that the program containing the data need not be a database. With the appropriate database extension, your application could read data from a spreadsheet, for example, or any other program that stores data.

Apple Computer, Inc. provides a database extension that uses Data Access Language (DAL). A **database extension** provides an interface between the Data Access Manager and the database or other program that contains the data. If you want to write an application that uses the low-level interface to communicate with a Data Access Language server, or if you want to create a query document that uses Data Access Language, you must be familiar with that language. *Data Access Language Programmer's Reference,* available from APDA®, fully describes this language.

ABOUT THE DATA ACCESS MANAGER

The Data Access Manager constitutes a standard interface that allows Macintosh applications to communicate with any number of databases or other data sources through a variety of data servers. As used in this chapter, a **data server** is the application that acts as an interface between the database extension on the Macintosh computer and the data source, which can be on the Macintosh computer or on a remote host computer. A data server can be a database server program, such as a Data Access Language server, which can provide an interface to a variety of different databases, or it can be the data source itself, such as a Macintosh application.

The Data Access Manager has two application interfaces: the high-level interface and the low-level interface. If the proper database extension and query documents are available in the user's system, you can use the high-level interface to communicate with a data source without having any knowledge of the command language that the data server uses. Even if you use the low-level interface, your application can isolate the user from any specific knowledge of the data source or the data server's command language.

This section presents an overview and description of the Data Access Manager, including diagrams and conceptual descriptions of the components and processes involved in using the high-level and low-level interfaces. Next, "Using the Data Access Manager" includes descriptions, flowcharts, and program fragments that provide a step-by-step guide to the use of the high-level and low-level interfaces. "Creating a Query Document" describes the contents and function of a query document. You do not have to read this section unless you are writing an application that creates query documents, although if you are using the high-level interface you might be interested to know just how a query document works.

Figure 8-1 illustrates connections between Macintosh applications and a database on a remote computer. The arrows in Figure 8-1 show the flow of information, not the paths of commands or control signals. See Figures 8-2 and 8-3 for the sequences involved in sending and retrieving data.

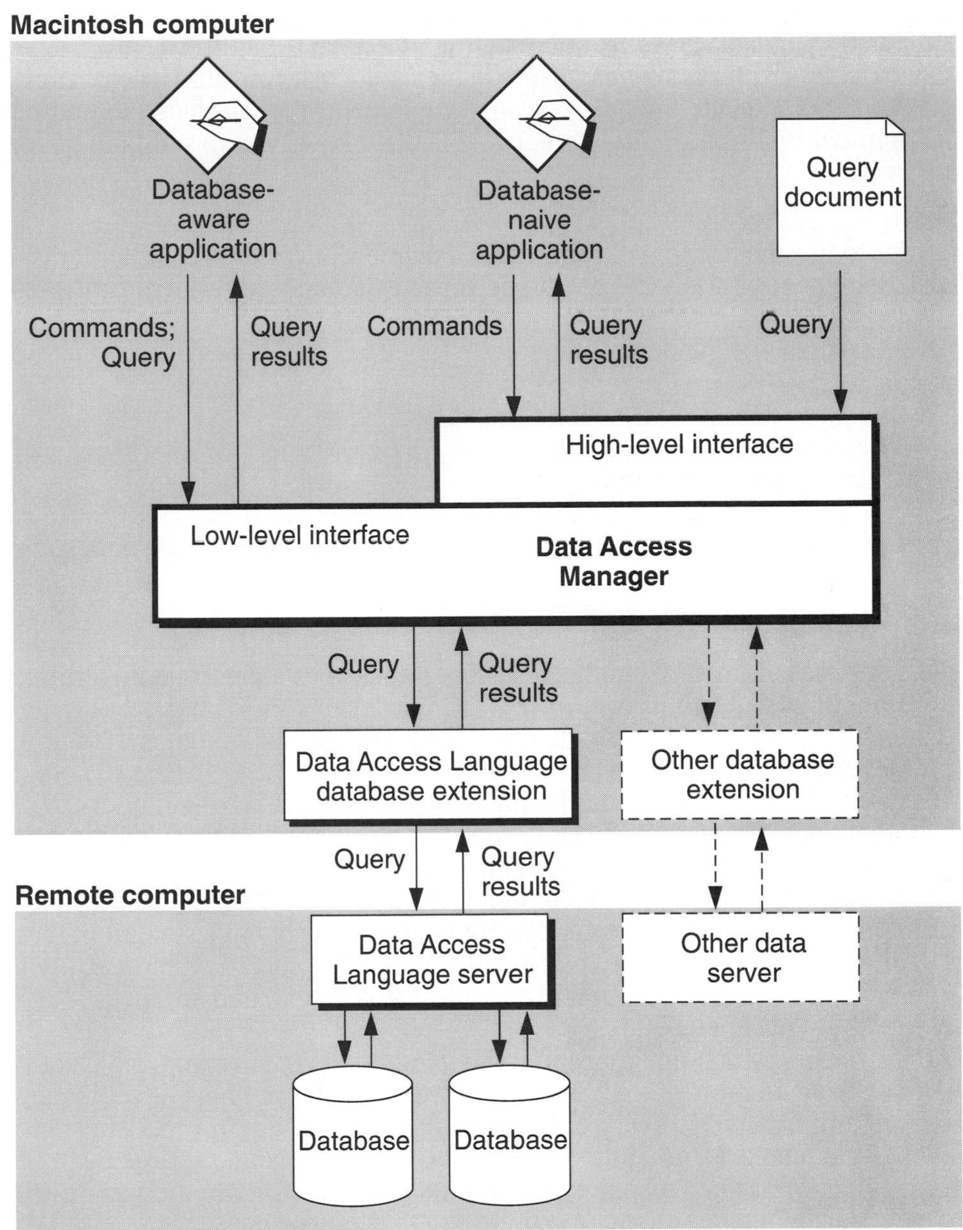

Figure 8-1. A connection with a database

The High-Level Interface

As Figure 8-1 shows, a database-naive application—that is, one that cannot prepare a query for a specific data server—uses the Data Access Manager's high-level routines to communicate with a data server. Because the application cannot prepare a query, it must use a query document to provide one. A query document can contain code, called a **query definition function,** that prompts the user for information and modifies the query before the Data Access Manager sends it to the data server. The exact format of a query definition function is described in "Writing a Query Definition Function" later in this chapter.

> **Note:** The term *query* refers to any string of commands (and associated data) that can be executed by a data server. A query can send data to a data source, retrieve data from a data source, or reorganize the data in a data source. The Data Access Manager does not interpret or execute the query; it only implements the interface (sometimes called the *application program interface,* or API) that allows you to send the query to the data server.

When you want to use the high-level routines to execute a query on a data server, you first select a query document or allow the user to select one. You use high-level routines to

- get the query from the query document
- execute the query definition function to modify the query
- send the query to the data server
- retrieve the results from any query that asks for information from the data source
- convert to text the results returned by a query

For example, suppose a company that makes rubber ducks has a database on a minicomputer that contains a mailing list of all its customers. The database has a Data Access Language interface and the company's marketing manager has a Macintosh computer with an application that uses high-level Data Access Manager routines to communicate with the remote database server. As Figure 8-2 illustrates, the marketing manager must also have a query document, created by another application, that she can use to get an address from the mailing list on the remote minicomputer. The query document can be as complex or as simple as its creator cares to make it; in this example, the query document is designed specifically to obtain addresses from the rubber duck mailing list. The marketing manager might have several other query documents available as well: one to extract a mailing list for a specific zip code, one to list all of the customers who have made a purchase within the last year, and so on.

Notice that once the query document has sent the query to the data server, the Data Access Manager handles the data retrieval. Although query documents and high-level Data Access Manager routines make it very easy for you to *request* data from a data source, there is no way for a query document to verify that data *sent* to a data source has been successfully received. For that reason, it is recommended that you use the low-level interface to send data to a data source or update data in a data source.

Sending a Query Through the High-Level Interface

To obtain a list of addresses from the mailing list, the marketing manager chooses the Open Query menu command from the File menu in her application. From the list of query documents displayed, she chooses one named Rubber Duck Address List.

The application calls the Data Access Manager function DBGetNewQuery. This function opens the Rubber Duck Address List query document and creates a partial query from the information in the query document. The partial query specifies the type of data (character strings) and the columns from which the data items should come (the name and address columns). The partial query lacks some specific data (the rows that should be searched) that is needed to complete the search criteria.

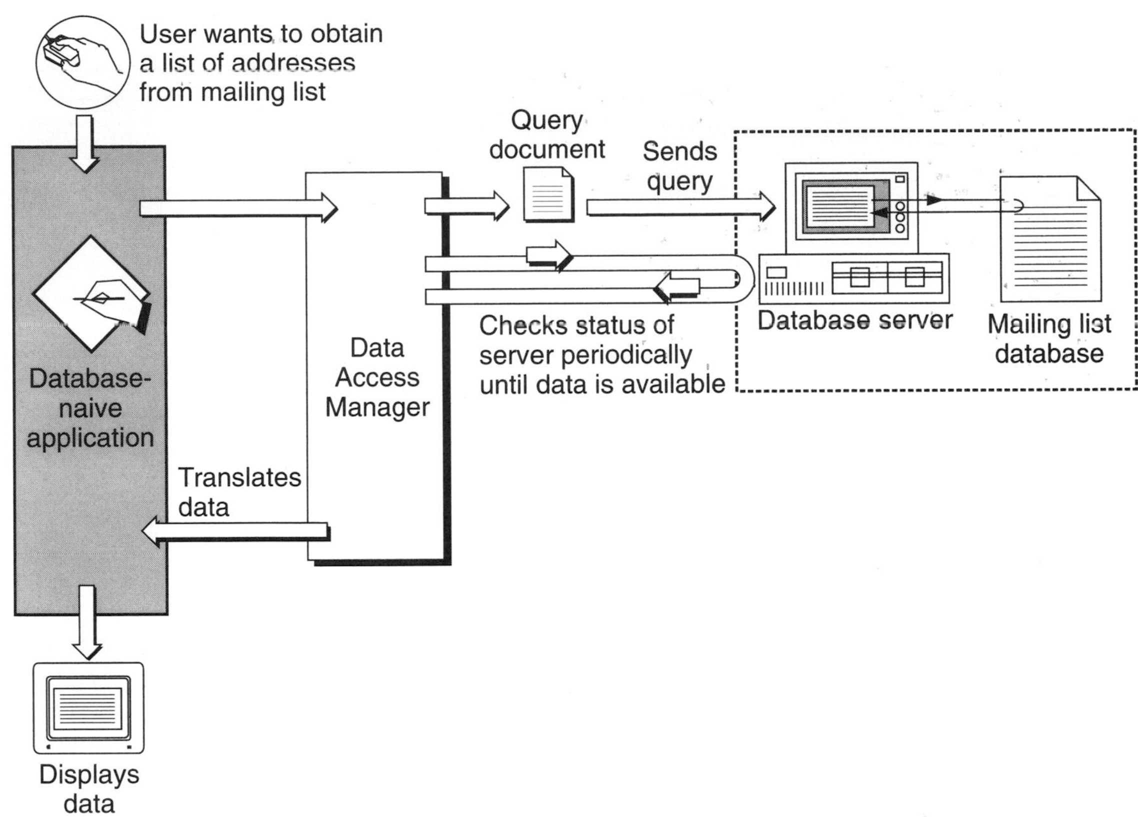

Figure 8-2. Using high-level Data Access Manager routines

Next, the application calls the DBStartQuery function, which in turn calls the query definition function in the query document. The query definition function displays a dialog box that asks for the purchase dates to search. When the marketing manager types in the requested information and clicks OK, the query definition function adds the data to the partial query in memory. The query is now ready to be executed.

Next, the DBStartQuery function sends the query to the Data Access Language database extension, and the database extension sends the query over a communications network to the remote Data Access Language server. Finally, the DBStartQuery function commands the Data Access Language server to execute the query.

Retrieving Data Through the High-Level Interface

When the application is ready to retrieve the data that it requested from the database, the application calls the DBGetQueryResults function. This function determines when the data is available, retrieves it from the data server, and places the data in a record in memory. The application can then call the DBResultsToText function, which uses routines called **result handlers** to convert each data item to a character string. The DBResultsToText function passes to the application a handle to the converted data. The application then displays the list of customers for the marketing manager.

Data items and result handlers are described in "Processing Query Results" later in this chapter.

The Low-Level Interface

A database-aware application communicates through the low-level interface of the Data Access Manager. You can use the low-level interface to

- initiate communication with the data server, sending the user name, password, and other information to the data server
- send a query to the data server
- execute the query that you have sent to the data server
- halt execution of the query
- return status and errors from the data server
- send data to the data source
- retrieve data from the data source

For example, suppose once again that a company that makes rubber ducks has a mailing list of all of its customers in a database on a minicomputer, and the database has a Data Access Language interface. This time, suppose the Macintosh application the marketing manager is using calls low-level Data Access Manager routines to communicate with the remote database server. Figure 8-3 illustrates the use of the low-level interface. Notice that if you use the high-level interface (Figure 8-2), the query document and the Data Access Manager prepare the query, send the query, retrieve the query results, and translate the data for you. If you use the low-level interface, however, you must perform these functions yourself.

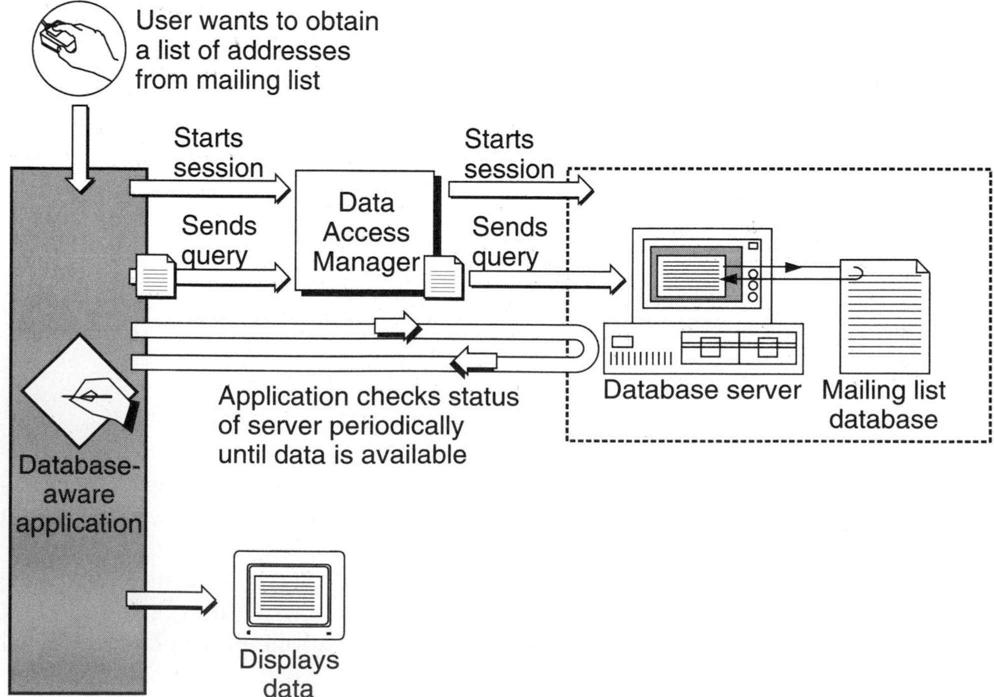

Figure 8-3. Using low-level Data Access Manager routines

Sending a Query Through the Low-Level Interface

To update the mailing list with a new address for customer Marvin M., the marketing manager enters the new address into her application. The application prepares a Data Access Language statement (a query) that specifies the type of data (a character string), the column into which the data item should go (the address column), the row to be modified (the Marvin M. row), plus the actual data the application wishes to send (Marvin M.'s address). The application then passes this query to the Data Access Manager using the low-level interface. (The application can send the query in several pieces or all at once.) The Data Access Manager sends the query to the Data Access Language database extension in the Macintosh computer, and the database extension sends the query to the remote Data Access Language server.

Retrieving Data Through the Low-Level Interface

Once the query begins executing, the application can periodically check with the data server to determine whether the data is ready (Figure 8-3). When the data is available, the application must retrieve it one data item at a time. An application that uses the low-level interface must determine the data type of each data item, convert the data into a format that is meaningful to the user, and store the data in memory allocated by the application. Data types are described in "Getting Query Results" later in this chapter.

Note that neither the Data Access Manager nor the DAL database extension reads, modifies, or acts on the query that an application sends to the data server. The data server does execute the query, causing the data source to accept new data or prepare data for the application. To use the low-level interface to communicate with a data server, your application must be capable of preparing a query that can be executed by the data server.

Comparison of the High-Level and Low-Level Interfaces

An application that uses the low-level interface to send a query to the data server must prepare the query, initiate communication with the data server, send the query to the data server, and execute the query. If it requested data to be returned, the application must determine when the data is ready, and retrieve the data one item at a time. Each step in this process requires calling one or more low-level routines.

The high-level interface between the Data Access Manager and the application, in contrast, consists of only a few routines, each of which might call several low-level routines to accomplish its tasks. For example, a single high-level function can call the query definition function, initiate communication with the data server, send the query to the data server, and execute the query.

Because the high-level interface is very easy to use and requires no specific knowledge of the data source or database server, you can add high-level data access to your application very easily. Then, whenever someone provides a query document for use with a specific data server, the user can take advantage of the data access capability included in your application. However, because there is no way for a query document to verify that data *sent* to a data source has been successfully received, it is recommended that you use the low-level interface to send data to a data source or update data in a data source.

Although in concept the low-level routines and high-level routines serve separate purposes, there is nothing to prevent you from using calls to both in a single application. For example, you might use low-level routines to send a query to a data server and high-level routines to read the results and convert them to text.

USING THE DATA ACCESS MANAGER

There are at least three different ways in which you can use the Data Access Manager to communicate with a data source.

- You can use low-level interface routines to send queries and retrieve data from the data source. In this case, your application must be capable of preparing a query in a language appropriate for the data server.
- You can use high-level interface routines to send queries and retrieve data from the data source. In this case, you must have one or more query documents provided by another application.
- You can create your own query documents and use high-level interface routines to send queries and retrieve data from the data source. In this case, your application must be capable of preparing a query, but it can use the same query repeatedly once it has been prepared.

This section describes how to use the high-level and low-level interfaces to the Data Access Manager to send queries to a data server. This section also describes how to call Data Access Manager functions asynchronously; how to determine the status of the high-level functions at various points in their execution (and cancel execution if you so desire); how to obtain information about Data Access Manager sessions that are in progress; and how to retrieve query results and convert them to text.

Executing Routines Asynchronously

All of the Data Access Manager low-level routines and some of the high-level routines can execute asynchronously—that is, the routine returns control to your application before the routine has completed execution. Your application must call the WaitNextEvent function periodically to allow an asynchronous routine to complete execution.

> **Note:** The database extension is responsible for implementing asynchronous execution of Data Access Manager routines. For example, if you call the DBSend function to send a query to a data server, and the database extension calls a device driver, the database extension can return control to your application as soon as the device driver has placed its routine in the driver I/O queue. If you attempt to execute a routine asynchronously and the database extension that the user has selected does not support asynchronous execution, the routine returns a result code of rcDBAsyncNotSupp and terminates execution.

All Data Access Manager routines that can execute asynchronously take as a parameter a pointer to a parameter block known as the *asynchronous parameter block.* If this pointer is NIL, the function is executed synchronously—that is, the routine does not return control to your application until execution is complete.

General Guidelines for the User Interface

When you use the Data Access Manager to provide data access, you should keep two important principles in mind: keep the user in control, and provide feedback to the user.

Keep the User in Control

When designing a data access feature or application, keep in mind that the user should have as much access to the Macintosh computer's abilities as possible. Design your application so that most of the data access process happens in the background. Call the Data Access Manager asynchronously whenever the database extension you are using supports asynchronous calls. Because data retrieval queries can take minutes or even hours to complete, they should always run in the background.

After issuing a query, return control of the computer to users so that they may work on other tasks or switch to other applications while the query runs. Whenever a background task requires the user's attention, follow the suggestions in the User Interface Guidelines chapter of this volume regarding user notification. A background task should never take control from the user by posting an alert box in front of the active application's windows. Any message that you post should identify the query that requires attention. For example, an alert box might display the message "The query Get Employee Information was canceled because the connection was unexpectedly broken."

If your application allows more than one simultaneous connection to data sources, or allows more than one query document to run, provide a modeless window that lists the open connections and queries, displays the status of each, and allows the user to cancel them if necessary.

Allow the user to limit the amount of disk space that must remain free after any transaction. For example, a user may wish to specify that 1 MB of space always be free. Cancel any transaction that would exceed the user's limit and notify the user.

Provide Feedback to the User

Keep the user informed about status, progress, and error conditions, and allow the user to cancel an interaction whenever possible. Inform the user before the application becomes modal and the computer becomes unavailable. Use the spinning beach ball cursor or the animated wristwatch cursor to indicate a process that takes several seconds to complete. Use a dialog box to indicate any process that lasts longer than a few seconds. For example, connecting to a remote database could take a couple of minutes. In this case include a Cancel button in the dialog box so that the user can cancel the operation. When possible, display a progress indicator to show how long a process lasts. Warn the user before doing anything potentially dangerous or irreversible, such as deleting all of a user's data files to replace them with data retrieved from a data source.

When a data retrieval query terminates prematurely, make the data that was retrieved available to the user with a warning that it is incomplete. This allows the user to evaluate the partial data before deciding whether to run the query again.

Using the High-Level Interface

Use the high-level interface to the Data Access Manager if you want to use a query document to do the work of communicating with a data source. You can use the high-level interface to open a query document, execute the query definition function in the query document, establish communication (initiate a session) with a data server, send the query to the data server, execute the query, retrieve any data requested by the query, and convert the retrieved data to text. Although two or three high-level routines accomplish most of these tasks, you may need to call a few low-level routines as well to control a session with a data server.

Applications that implement this type of data access must provide user control and feedback as described earlier in "General Guidelines for the User Interface." In addition, you should include an Open Query command in the File menu. The Open Query command is equivalent to the Open (file) command in meaning. When the user chooses this command, display an open file dialog box filtered to show only query documents (file type 'qery'). The user can then choose the desired query document. The query document sends the query to the data source. Depending on the type of query, the data source could receive information, send back information, report the status of the data source, or perform some other task.

Figure 8-4 is a flowchart of a typical session using the high-level interface.

As Figure 8-4 illustrates, you must follow this procedure to use the high-level interface:

1. Call the InitDBPack function to initialize the Data Access Manager.

2. Select the query document that you want to use and determine the resource ID of the 'qrsc' resource in that query document. You can use any method you like to select the query document. One possibility is to use the StandardGetFile procedure to let the user select the query document. A query document should contain only one 'qrsc' resource; you can then use the Resource Manager to determine the resource ID of the 'qrsc' resource in the document that the user selected. The StandardGetFile procedure is described in the Standard File Manager chapter of this volume, and the Resource Manager is described in Volume I.

3. Call the DBGetNewQuery function. The DBGetNewQuery function creates in memory a data structure called a *query record* from the 'qrsc' resource that you specify.

4. Call the DBStartQuery function specifying the handle to the query record that you created with the DBGetNewQuery function (step 3).

   You should also provide the DBStartQuery function with a handle to your status routine. A **status routine** is a routine that you provide that can update windows, check the results of the low-level calls made by the DBStartQuery and DBGetQueryResults functions, and cancel execution of these functions when you consider it appropriate to do so.

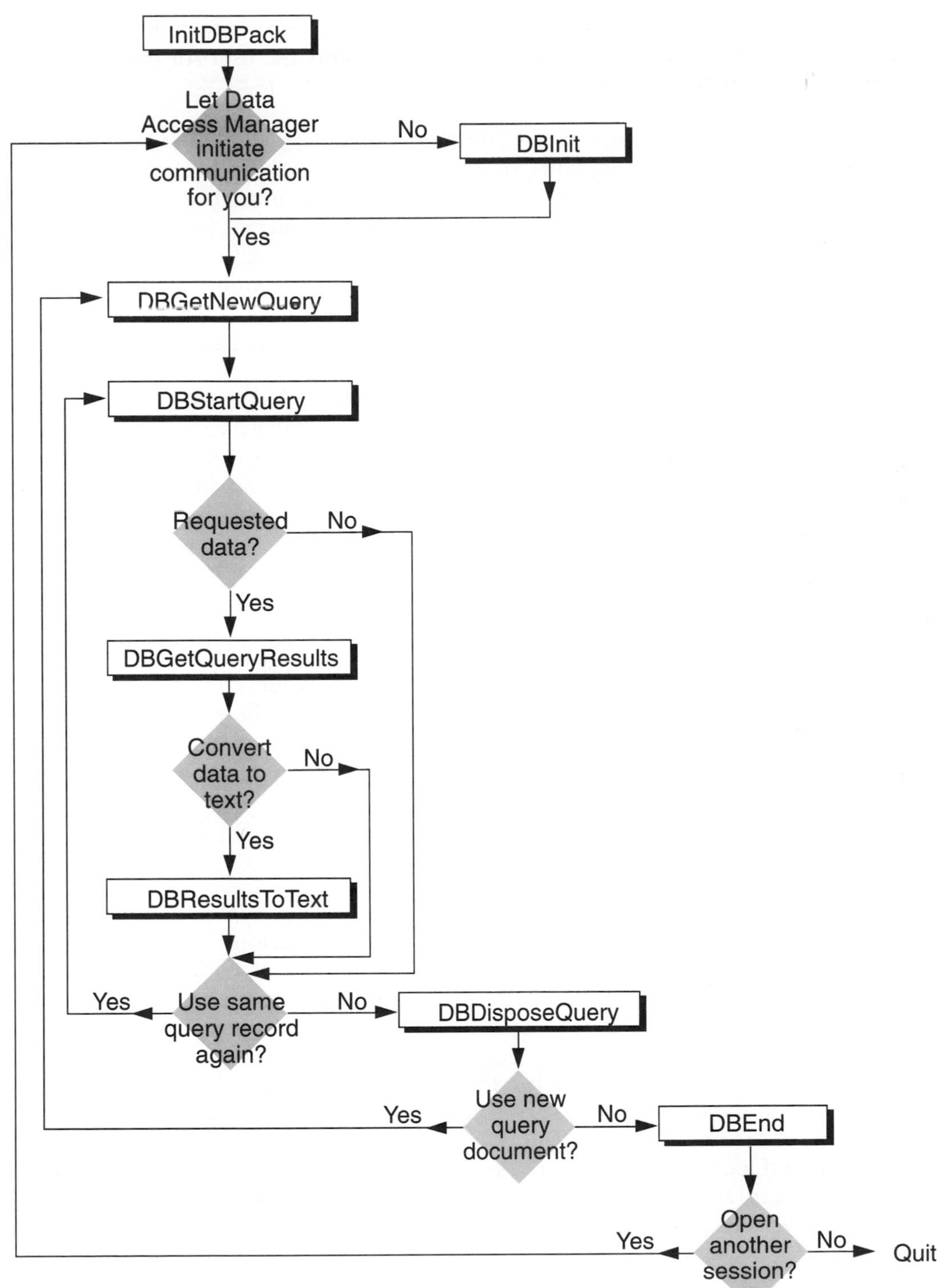

Figure 8-4. A flowchart of a session using the high-level interface

The DBStartQuery function calls the query definition function referred to by the query record (if any). The query definition function can prompt the user for information and modify the query record.

After the query definition function has completed execution, the DBStartQuery function calls your status routine so that you can update your windows if necessary. The DBStartQuery function then checks to see if communication has been established with the data server. If not, it calls your status routine so that you can put up a status dialog box, and then calls the DBInit function to establish communication (initiate a session) with the data server. The DBStartQuery function obtains the values it needs for the DBInit function parameters from the query record. When the DBInit function completes execution, the DBStartQuery function calls your status routine again.

The DBInit function returns an identification number, called a **session ID.** This session ID is unique; no other current session, for any database extension, has the same session ID. You must specify the session ID any time you want to send data to or retrieve data from this session. If you prefer, you can use the DBInit function to establish communication before you call the DBStartQuery function. In that case, you must specify the session ID as an input parameter to the DBStartQuery function. See "Using the Low-Level Interface" later in this chapter for more information on using the DBInit function.

Once communication has been established, the DBStartQuery function calls the DBSend function to send the query specified by the query record to the data server, and, when the DBSend function has completed execution, calls your status routine. Finally, the DBStartQuery function uses the DBExec function to execute the query. The DBStartQuery function calls your status routine after the DBExec function has completed execution (that is, the query has started executing and the DBExec function has returned control to the DBStartQuery function) and again just before the DBStartQuery function completes execution.

5. If you requested data and want to know when the data is available, but do not want to retrieve the data immediately, you can call the DBState function. This function tells you when the data server has finished executing the query, but it does not retrieve the data. If you requested data and want to retrieve it as soon as it is available, you do not have to call the DBState function; go on to step 6 instead.

   If you did not request data, you can use the DBState function to determine the status of the query. When the data server has finished executing the query, skip to step 8.

6. Call the DBGetQueryResults function. If the query has not finished executing, this function returns the rcDBExec result code. If the query has finished executing, the DBGetQueryResults function calls the DBGetItem function repeatedly until the data server has returned all of the data available.

   The DBGetQueryResults function puts the returned data into a record that contains handles to arrays that contain the data, the type of data in each column, and the length of each data item. The Data Access Manager allocates the memory for this data in the application heap.

   The DBGetQueryResults function calls your status routine after it retrieves each data item. You can use this opportunity to display the data item for the user and to give the user the opportunity to cancel execution of the function. The DBGetQueryResults function also calls your status routine just before completing execution, so that you can dispose of any memory allocated by the status routine, remove any dialog box that you displayed, and update your windows if necessary.

To convert the returned data to text, go on to the next step. If you do not want to convert the returned data to text, skip to step 9.

7. Call the DBResultsToText function. This function calls a result handler function for each data type. The result handler converts the data to text, places it in a buffer, and returns a handle to the buffer. Some result handlers are provided with the Data Access Manager; you can provide as many with your application as you wish. Result handlers are discussed in "Converting Query Results to Text" later in this chapter.

8. If you are finished using the query record, call the DBDisposeQuery function to dispose of the query record and free all the memory associated with the query record. If you want to reuse the same query, return to step 5. You should close the query document when you are finished using it.

   If you want to use a new query document, return to step 3.

9. When you are finished using the data source, you must use the DBEnd function to terminate the session. You must call the DBEnd function after the DBInit function has returned a nonzero session ID, even if it also returned an error.

Listing 8-1 illustrates the use of the high-level interface. This code sample initiates a session with a remote database, lets the user select a query document to execute, opens the selected file, finds a 'qsrc' resource, and creates a query record. Next, it executes the query, checks the status of the remote database server, retrieves the data when it's available, and converts this data to text. When the query has finished executing, the code disposes the query record, ends the session, and closes the user-selected query document. In general, there's no reason why there can't be multiple sessions open at once. You can identify each session by its session ID. Listing 8-1 shows just one session.

Listing 8-1 assumes that you are using a database extension that supports asynchronous execution of Data Access Manager routines. This listing shows just one possible approach to sending a query and retrieving data asynchronously.

Listing 8-1. Using the high-level interface

```
PROCEDURE MyHiLevel(VAR rr: ResultsRecord; MyTextHdl: Handle;
                    VAR thisSession: LongInt; VAR sessErr: OSErr);


TYPE
   {Define a record to include space for the current value in }
   { A5 so a completion routine can find it.}
   CRRec = RECORD
      QPB: DBAsyncParamBlockRec;        {the parameter block}
      appsA5: LongInt                   {append A5 to the parameter block}
   END;
   CRRecPtr = ^CRRec;
```

(Continued)

Listing 8-1. Using the high-level interface (Continued)

```
VAR
   StartPB, GetQRPB:                         CRRec;
   SFR:                                      StandardFileReply;
   packErr, startQErr, getQErr, disposeQErr: OSErr;
   getnewQErr, gStartQErr, gGetQRErr:        OSErr;
   endErr, fsopenErr, fscloseErr, resultsErr:OSErr;
   gStart, gQueryResults:                    Boolean;
   qrscHandle:                               Handle;
   rsrcId:                                   Integer;
   rsrcType:                                 ResType;
   rsrcName:                                 Str255;
   MyQHandle:                                QueryHandle;
   SavedResFile:                             Integer;
   TypeList:                                 SFTypeList;
   fsRefNum:                                 Integer;

FUNCTION GetQPB: CRRecPtr;
   INLINE $2E88;             {MOVE.L  A0,(SP)}

BEGIN
   gStart := FALSE;
   gQueryResults := FALSE;
   sessErr := noErr;                   {assume everything went fine}
   packErr := InitDBPack;              {initialize the Data Access Mgr}

   {Display a dialog box to let the user pick a query document.}
   TypeList[0] := 'qery';
   StandardGetFile(NIL, 1, TypeList, SFR);
   IF SFR.sfGood = FALSE THEN
   BEGIN
      EXIT(MyHiLevel);
   END;
   fsopenErr := FSpOpenRF(SFR.sfFile, fsCurPerm, fsRefNum);

   IF fsopenErr <> noErr THEN
   BEGIN
      sessErr := fsopenErr;
      EXIT(MyHiLevel);
   END;
   SavedResFile := CurResFile;         {save current resource file}
   UseResFile(fsRefNum);               {get query info from here}

   {A query document should have only one 'qrsc' resource.}

   qrscHandle := Get1IndResource('qrsc',1);

   {There shouldn't be an error unless there really isn't a }
   { 'qrsc' resource in the file the user selected.}
   IF ResError <> noErr THEN
   BEGIN
      sessErr := ResError;
      EXIT(MyHiLevel);
   END;
```

```
{Get the resource ID of the 'qrsc' resource}
GetResInfo(qrscHandle, rsrcID, rsrcType, rsrcName);

{Create a query record using the resource ID.}
getnewQErr := DBGetNewQuery(rsrcID, MyQHandle);
IF getnewQErr <> noErr THEN
BEGIN
   sessErr := getnewQErr ;
   endErr := DBEnd(thisSession, NIL);
   EXIT(MyHiLevel);
END;

StartPB.QPB.completionProc := @MyStartCompRoutine;
StartPB.appsA5 := SetCurrentA5;      {save this for the }
                                     { completion routine}

{MyStartStatus is a status routine that handles messages sent }
{ by the DBStartQuery function when it calls a low-level function.}

startQErr := DBStartQuery(thisSession, MyQHandle,
                          @MyStartStatus, @StartPB);
IF startQErr <> noErr THEN
BEGIN
   sessErr := startQErr;
   IF thisSession <> 0 THEN endErr := DBEnd(thisSession, NIL);
   EXIT(MyHiLevel);
END;

WHILE NOT gStart DO
{While waiting for gStart to go TRUE, the routine GoDoSomething }
{ calls WaitNextEvent to give other routines a chance to run.}
BEGIN
   GoDoSomething;
END;  {while}

{The DBStartQuery call has completed.}
IF gStartQErr <> noErr THEN
BEGIN
   sessErr := gStartQErr;
   IF thisSession <> 0 THEN endErr := DBEnd(thisSession, NIL);
   EXIT(MyHiLevel);
END;

GetQRPB.QPB.completionProc := @MyGetQRCompRoutine;
GetQRPB.appsA5 := SetCurrentA5;      {save this for the }
                                     { completion routine}
```

(Continued)

Listing 8-1. Using the high-level interface (Continued)

```
    {MyGetQRStatus is a status routine that handles messages sent }
    { by the DBGetQueryResults function when it calls a low-level }
    { function.}

    getQErr := DBGetQueryResults(thisSession, rr, kDBWaitForever,
                                 @MyGetQRStatus, @GetQRPB);
    IF getQErr <> noErr THEN
    BEGIN
       sessErr := getQErr;
       endErr := DBEnd(thisSession, NIL);
       EXIT(MyHiLevel);
    END;

    WHILE NOT gQueryResults DO
    BEGIN
       GoDoSomething;
    END; {while}

    {The DBGetQueryResults call has completed. Assuming the call }
    { completed successfully, you may want to convert the retrieved }
    { data to text, return memory you have borrowed, and end the session.}

    IF gGetQRErr <> noErr THEN
    BEGIN
       sessErr := gGetQRErr;
       endErr := DBEnd(thisSession, NIL);
       EXIT(MyHiLevel);
    END;

    {The data has been retrieved; convert it to text.}
    resultsErr := DBResultsToText(rr, MyTextHdl);

    {The current query is finished.  You can elect to execute }
    { the next 'qrsc' resource of the file, or select another }
    { query document.  This example just returns to the caller.}

    disposeQErr := DBDisposeQuery(MyQHandle);
    UseResFile(SavedResFile);           {restore current resource file}

    fscloseErr := FSClose(fsRefNum);    {close the query document}
    IF fscloseErr <> noErr THEN DoError(fscloseErr);

    endErr := DBEnd(thisSession, NIL);
    IF endErr <> noErr THEN DoError(endErr);

END;
```

```
{The following two routines illustrate one way to implement a }
{ completion routine.}

PROCEDURE MyStartCompRoutine(aCRRecPtr: CRRecPtr);

VAR
   curA5:          LongInt;

BEGIN
   aCRRecPtr := GetQPB;                 {get the param block}
   curA5 := SetA5(aCRRecPtr^.appsA5);   {set A5 to the app's A5}

   gStart := TRUE;                      {query has been started}
   gStartQErr := aCRRecPtr^.QPB.result; {send back the result code}

{Do whatever else you want to do.}

   curA5 := SetA5(curA5);               {restore original A5}
END;  {MyStartCompRoutine}

PROCEDURE MyGetQRCompRoutine(aCRRecPtr: CRRecPtr);

VAR
   curA5:          LongInt;

BEGIN
   aCRRecPtr := GetQPB;                 {get the param block}
   curA5 := SetA5(aCRRecPtr^.appsA5);   {set A5 to the app's A5}

   gQueryResults := TRUE;               {query results are complete}
   gGetQRErr := aCRRecPtr^.QPB.result;  {send back the result code}

{Do whatever else you want to do.}

   curA5 := SetA5(curA5);               {restore original A5}
END;  {MyGetQRCompRoutine}
```

Writing a Status Routine for High-Level Functions

Both of the two main high-level functions, DBStartQuery and DBGetQueryResults, call low-level functions repeatedly. After each time they call a low-level function, these high-level functions call a routine that you provide, called a *status routine*. Your status routine can check the result code returned by the low-level function, and can cancel execution of the high-level function before it calls the next low-level function. Your status routine can also update your application's windows after the DBStartQuery function has displayed a dialog box.

You provide a pointer to your status routine in the statusProc parameter to the DBStartQuery and DBGetQueryResults functions.

Here is a function declaration for a status routine.

```
FUNCTION MyStatusFunc (message: Integer; result: OSErr; dataLen,
                       dataPlaces,dataFlags: Integer; dataType: DBType;
                       dataPtr: Ptr) : Boolean;
```

Your status routine should return a value of TRUE if you want the DBStartQuery or DBGetQueryResults function to continue execution, or FALSE to cancel execution of the function. In the latter case, the high-level function returns the userCanceledErr result code.

> **Note:** If you call the DBStartQuery or DBGetQueryResults function asynchronously, you cannot depend on the A5 register containing a pointer to your application's global variables when the Data Access Manager calls your status routine.

The message parameter tells your status routine the current status of the high-level function that called it. The possible values for the message parameter depend on which function called your routine.

The value of the result parameter depends on the value of the message parameter, as summarized in the following list.

Message	Result
kDBUpdateWind	0
kDBAboutToInit	0
kDBInitComplete	Result of DBInit
kDBSendComplete	Result of DBSend
kDBExecComplete	Result of DBExec
kDBStartQueryComplete	Result of DBStartQuery
kDBGetItemComplete	Result of DBGetItem
kDBGetQueryResultsComplete	Result of DBGetQueryResults

The dataLen, dataPlaces, dataFlags, dataType, and dataPtr parameters are returned only by the DBGetQueryResults function, and only when the message parameter equals kDBGetItemComplete. When the DBGetQueryResults function calls your status routine with this message, the dataLen, dataPlaces, and dataType parameters contain the length, decimal places, and type of the data item retrieved, and the dataPtr parameter contains a pointer to the data item.

The least significant bit of the dataFlags parameter is set to 1 if the data item is in the last column of the row. The third bit of the dataFlags parameter is 1 if the data item is NULL.

You can use this information, for example, to check the data to see if it meets some criteria of interest to the user, or to display each data item as the DBGetItem function receives it. You can use the constants kDBLastColFlag and kDBNullFlag to test for these flag bits.

The DBGetQueryResults function returns a results record, which contains a handle to the retrieved data. The address in the dataPtr parameter points inside the array specified by this handle. Because the dataPtr parameter is not a pointer to a block of memory allocated by the Memory Manager, but just a pointer to a location inside such a block, you cannot use this pointer in any Memory Manager routines (such as the GetPtrSize function). Note also that you cannot rely on this pointer remaining valid after you return control to the DBGetQueryResults function.

The following constants can be sent to your status routine in the message parameter by the DBStartQuery function:

```
CONST {DBStartQuery status messages}
      kDBUpdateWind          = 0; {update windows}
      kDBAboutToInit         = 1; {about to call DBInit}
      kDBInitComplete        = 2; {DBInit has completed}
      kDBSendComplete        = 3; {DBSend has completed}
      kDBExecComplete        = 4; {DBExec has completed}
      kDBStartQueryComplete  = 5; {DBStartQuery is about to complete}
```

DBStartQuery message constant	**Meaning**
kDBUpdateWind	The DBStartQuery function has just called a query definition function. Your status routine should process any update events that your application has received for its windows.
kDBAboutToInit	The DBStartQuery function is about to call the DBInit function to initiate a session with a data server. Because initiating the session might involve establishing communication over a network, and because in some circumstances the execution of a query can tie up the user's computer for some length of time, you might want to display a dialog box giving the user the option of canceling execution at this time.
kDBInitComplete	The DBInit function has completed execution. When the DBStartQuery function calls your status routine with this message, the result parameter contains the result code returned by the DBInit function. If the DBInit function returns the noErr result code, the DBStartQuery function calls the DBSend function next. If the DBInit function returns any other result code, you can display a dialog box informing the user of the problem before returning control to the DBStartQuery function. The DBStartQuery function then returns an error code and stops execution.

DBStartQuery message constant	Meaning
kDBSendComplete	The DBSend function has completed execution. When the DBStartQuery function calls your status routine with this message, the result parameter contains the result code returned by the DBSend function. If the DBSend function returns the noErr result code, the DBStartQuery function calls the DBExec function next. If the DBSend function returns any other result code, you can display a dialog box informing the user of the problem before returning control to the DBStartQuery function. The DBStartQuery function then returns an error code and stops execution.
kDBExecComplete	The DBExec function has completed execution. When the DBStartQuery function calls your status routine with this message, the result parameter contains the result code returned by the DBExec function. If the DBExec function returns the noErr result code, the DBStartQuery function returns control to your application next. If the DBExec function returns any other result code, you can display a dialog box informing the user of the problem before returning control to the DBStartQuery function. The DBStartQuery function then returns an error code and stops execution.
kDBStartQueryComplete	The DBStartQuery function has completed execution and is about to return control to your application. The function result is in the result parameter passed to your status routine. Your status routine can use this opportunity to peform any final tasks, such as disposing of memory that it allocated or removing from the screen any dialog box that it displayed.

The following constants can be sent to your status routine in the message parameter by the DBGetQueryResults function:

```
CONST {DBGetQueryResults status messages}
      kDBGetItemComplete          = 6;    {DBGetItem has completed}
      kDBGetQueryResultsComplete  = 7;    {DBGetQueryResults has }
                                          { completed}
```

DBGetQueryResults message constant	Meaning
kDBGetItemComplete	The DBGetItem function has completed execution. When the DBGetQueryResults function calls your status routine with this message, the result parameter contains the result code returned by the DBGetItem function. The DBGetQueryResults function also returns values for the dataLen, dataPlaces, dataType, dataFlags, and dataPtr parameters, as discussed earlier in this section.

DBGetQueryResults message constant	Meaning
	For each data item that it retrieves, the DBGetQueryResults function calls the DBGetItem function twice: once to obtain information about the next data item and once to retrieve the data item. The DBGetQueryResults function calls your status routine only after calling the DBGetItem function to retrieve a data item. If your status routine returns a function result of FALSE in response to the kDBGetItemComplete message, the results record returned by the DBGetQueryResults function to your application contains data through the last full row retrieved. Data types and results records are described in "Getting Query Results" later in this chapter.
kDBGetQueryResultsComplete	The DBGetQueryResults function has completed execution and is about to return control to your application. The function result is in the result parameter passed to your status routine. Your status routine can use this opportunity to peform any final tasks, such as disposing of memory that it allocated or removing from the screen any dialog box that it displayed.

Listing 8-2 shows a status routine for the DBStartQuery function. This routine updates the application's windows in response to the kDBUpdateWind message, displays a dialog box giving the user the option of canceling before the data access is initiated, and checks the results of calls to the DBInit, DBSend, and DBExec functions. If one of these functions returns an error, the status routine displays a dialog box describing the error.

Listing 8-2. A sample status routine

```
FUNCTION MyStartStatus(message: Integer; result: OSErr;
                       dataLen,dataPlaces,dataFlags: Integer;
                       dataType: DBType; dataPtr: Ptr) : Boolean;

VAR
   myString:       Str255;
   continue:       Boolean;

BEGIN
   continue := TRUE;        {assume user wants to continue with the query}
   CASE message OF
      kDBUpdateWind:
      BEGIN
         {A qdef function has just been called.  Find your }
         { activate and update events and handle accordingly.}

         MyDoActivate;      {find and handle activate events}
         MyDoUpdate;        {find and handle update events}
      END;  {kDBUpdateWind}
```

(Continued)

Listing 8-2. A sample status routine (Continued)

```
kDBAboutToInit:
BEGIN
   {about to initiate a session}

   {MyDisplayDialog is a routine that displays a dialog box. }
   { It takes as input a string you want to display }
   { and returns a Boolean telling DBStartQuery }
   { whether to continue.}

   myString := 'The Data Access Manager is about to open a
               session.  This could take a while.  Do you
               want to continue?';
   MyDisplayDialog(@myString, continue);
END;  {kDBAboutToInit}
kDBInitComplete:
BEGIN
   {The DBInit function has completed execution.  If there's an }
   { error, let the user know what it is.}
   IF result <> noErr THEN
   BEGIN
      CASE result OF
         rcDBError:
         BEGIN
            myString := 'The Data Access Manager was unable to
                        open the session.  Please check your
                        connections and try again later.';
            {DisplayString displays a dialog box containing }
            { the string you want to display.}
            DisplayString(@myString);
         END;
         rcDBBadDDev:
         BEGIN
            myString := 'The Data Access Manager cannot find
                        the database extension file it needs
                        in order to open a session.  Please check
                        with your system administrator to obtain
                        a copy of this file.';
            DisplayString(@myString);
         END;
         ELSE
         BEGIN
            myString := 'The Data Access Manager was unable to
                        open the session.  The error code returned
                        was'
            {DisplayError displays a dialog box containing }
            { the string you want to display plus an error code.}
            DisplayError(@myString, result);
         END;
      END;  {CASE result}
   END;
END; {kDBInitComplete}
```

```
kDBSendComplete:
BEGIN
   {The DBSend function has completed execution.  If there's an }
   { error, let the user know what it is.}
   IF result <> noErr THEN
   BEGIN
      IF result = rcDBError THEN
         BEGIN
            myString := 'An error occurred while the
                        Data Access Manager was trying to
                        send the query.  Please
                        try again later.';
            DisplayString(@myString);
         END;
      ELSE
         BEGIN
            myString := 'An error occurred while the
                        Data Access Manager was trying to
                        send the query.  The error code returned
                        was'
            DisplayError(@myString, result);
         END;
   END;
END;  {kDBSendComplete}
kDBExecComplete:
BEGIN
   {The DBExec function has completed execution.  If there's an }
   { error, let the user know what it is.}
   IF result <> noErr THEN
   BEGIN
      IF result = rcDBError THEN
         BEGIN
            myString := 'The Data Access Manager was
                        unable to execute the query.
                        There may be a problem with the query
                        document or with the database.  Check
                        with your system administrator.';
            DisplayString(@myString);
         END;
      ELSE
         BEGIN
            myString := 'An error occurred while the
                        Data Access Manager was trying to
                        execute the query.  The error code
                        returned was'
            DisplayError(@myString, result);
         END;
   END;
END;  {kDBExecComplete}
```

(Continued)

Listing 8-2. A sample status routine (Continued)

```
      kDBStartQueryComplete:
      BEGIN
         {The DBStartQuery function is about to return control }
         { to your application.  You can clean up memory }
         { and any dialog boxes you left on the screen. }
         { MyCleanUpWindows is a routine that does that.}
         MyCleanUpWindows;
      END;  {kDBStartQueryComplete}
   END; {CASE message}
   MyStartStatus := continue;
END;
```

Using the Low-Level Interface

You can use the low-level interface to establish communication (initiate a session) with a data server, send a query to the data server, execute the query, and retrieve any data requested by the query. You call one or more low-level routines to accomplish each of these tasks.

Applications that implement this type of data access must provide user control and feedback, as described in "General Guidelines for the User Interface" earlier in this chapter. When the data source is ready to return data, you can retrieve it all and then display it to the user, or you can display the data as it arrives. If the data arrives slowly, it's best to display it one record at a time as it arrives. This way the user can preview the data, decide if it's the desired information, and cancel the query if not.

Figure 8-5 is a flowchart of a typical session using the low-level interface.

As Figure 8-5 illustrates, you must follow this procedure to use the low-level interface:

1. Call the InitDBPack function to initialize the Data Access Manager.

2. Call the DBInit function to establish communication with the data server. The DBInit function returns an identification number, called a *session ID.* This session ID is unique; no other current session, for any database extension, has the same session ID. You must specify the session ID any time you want to send data to or retrieve data from this session.

   The DBInit function requires as input parameters the name of the database extension and character strings for the host system, user name, password, and connection string. All of these parameters depend on the user and the user's computer system, including the specific database extension, host computer, data server, and database management software in use. You will not know the user name and password when you are writing an application, and you might not know the values of any of these parameters. Therefore, you must display a dialog box that prompts the user for the necessary information.

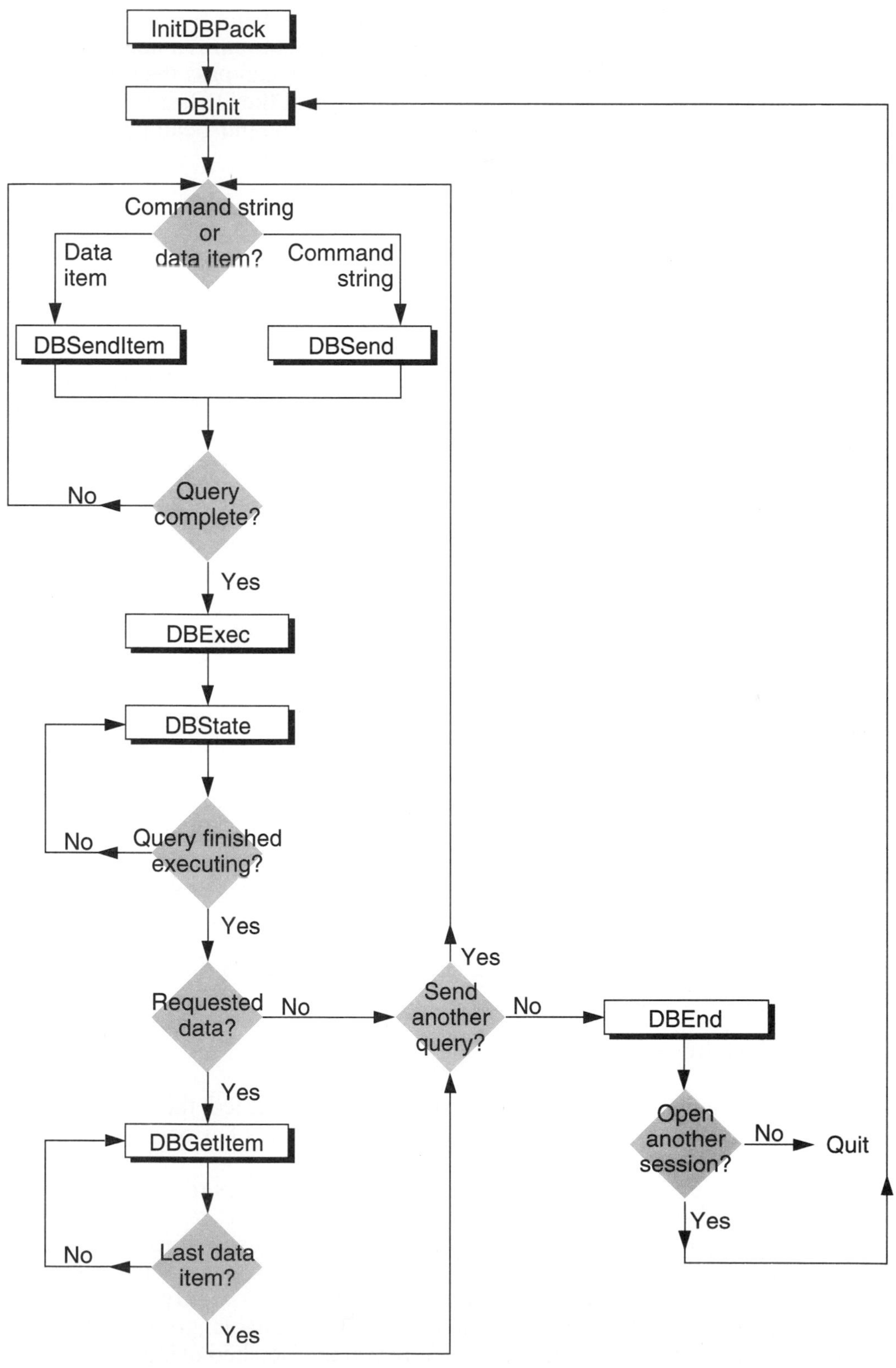

Figure 8-5. A flowchart of a session using the low-level interface

Depending on the database extension you are using, the DBInit function might return a session ID of zero if it fails to initiate a session, or it might return a nonzero session ID and a result code other than noErr. In the latter case, you can pass the session ID to the DBGetErr function to determine the cause of the error. If the DBInit function returns a nonzero session ID and a result code other than noErr, you must call the DBEnd function before making another attempt to open the session.

3. Prepare a query, and send it to the data server by calling the DBSend and DBSendItem functions one or more times.

   An application that uses the low-level interface must be capable of creating a query for the data server in the language and format required by that data server.

   The DBSend function sends a query or a portion of a query to the data server. The data server appends this portion of the query to any portion you sent previously. Because the Data Access Manager and data server do not modify the string you send in any way, they do not insert any delimiter between fragments of queries that you send to the data server. If you want a blank or a semicolon to be included between query fragments, or if you want to use return characters to divide the query into lines of text, you must include them in the character string that you send with the DBSend function. The data string that you send with the DBSend function can be any length up to 64 KB.

   The DBSendItem function sends a single data item to the data server. Use the DBSendItem function to send data items to the data source in the same format as they are retrieved from the data source by the DBGetItem function. You must specify the data type as an input parameter and, for any data type that does not have an implied length, you must specify the length as well. The database extension or the data server (depending on how the system is implemented) converts the data item to a character string and appends it to the query, just as a query program fragment is appended to the query by the DBSend function.

   You can call the DBSend and DBSendItem functions as many times as you wish to send your query to the data server.

   Listing 8-3 sends the Data Access Language query fragment "print 451+222;" to the Data Access Language server.

4. Use the DBExec function to initiate execution of the query.

   Depending on the way the system you are using is implemented, the DBExec function might return control to your application as soon as the query has begun execution.

5. Use the DBState function to determine the status of the data source.

   The DBState function tells you when the data server has finished executing the query you just sent. If you have requested data, the data server stores the data you requested but does not send it to your application until you request it explicitly. The DBState function tells you when the data is available; if data is available, go on to step 6. If you wish to send another query, return to step 3. If you are finished using the data source, skip to step 7.

Listing 8-3. Sending a query fragment

```
VAR
   value1:      LongInt;
   value2:      LongInt;
   text1:       Str15;
   text2:       Str15;
   text3:       Str15;
   rc:          OSErr;

BEGIN
   text1 := 'print ';
   value1 := 451;
   text2 := '+';
   value2 := 222;
   text3 := ';';

   rc := DBSend (sessID, P2CStr(StringPtr(ORD(@text1))),
                 LENGTH(text1), NIL);

   IF rc = noErr THEN
      rc := DBSendItem (sessID, typeInteger, 0, 0, 0,
                        Ptr(ORD(@value1)), NIL);

   IF rc = noErr THEN
      rc := DBSend (sessID, P2CStr(StringPtr(ORD(@text2))),
                    LENGTH(text2), NIL);

   IF rc = noErr THEN
      rc := DBSendItem (sessID, typeInteger, 0, 0, 0,
                        Ptr(ORD(@value2)), NIL);

   IF rc = noErr THEN
      rc := DBSend (sessID, P2CStr(StringPtr(ORD(@text3))),
                    LENGTH(text3), NIL);

   MySendFragment := rc;

END;
```

6. Call the DBGetItem function repeatedly to retrieve the data.

   The DBGetItem function retrieves the next data item from the data server. You can also use this function to obtain information about the next data item without retrieving the data. When you use the DBGetItem function to retrieve a data item, you must specify the location and size of the buffer into which the function is to place that item. If you know beforehand what kind of data to expect, you can allocate a buffer of the exact size you need. If you do not know what type of data to expect, you can first call the DBGetItem function with a NIL pointer to the data buffer. The DBGetItem function then returns information about the next data item without actually retrieving it. You can then allocate the appropriate buffer and call DBGetItem again.

Alternatively, to avoid calling DBGetItem twice for each data item, you can allocate a buffer that you expect to be of sufficient size for any data item and call the DBGetItem function. If the buffer is not large enough for the data item, the DBGetItem function returns the rcDBError result code, but still returns information about the data item. You can then allocate the necessary buffer, call the DBUnGetItem function to go back one data item, and call the DBGetItem function again to retrieve the data item a second time.

The DBGetItem function includes a timeout parameter that you can use to specify the maximum amount of time that the database extension should wait to receive results from the data server before canceling the command. If the database extension you are using does not support asynchronous execution of routines, you can use the timeout parameter to return control to your application while a query is executing. To use the timeout parameter in this way, call the DBGetItem function periodically with a short value set for the timeout parameter. Your application can then retrieve the next data item as soon as execution of the query is complete without having to call the DBState function to determine when data is available. The DBGetItem function ignores the timeout parameter if you make an asynchronous call to this function.

7. When you are finished using the data source, you must use the DBEnd function to terminate the session. You must call the DBEnd function after the DBInit function has returned a nonzero session ID, even if it also returned an error.

Listing 8-4 uses the low-level interface to send a Data Access Language routine to the Data Access Language server on a remote computer, and retrieves the results. The code initiates a session with a remote database and calls the MySendFragment routine (Listing 8-3) to send a query. Next, it executes the query, checks the status of the remote database server, and retrieves the data when it's available. This example retrieves only one data item. To retrieve more than one data item, put the data-retrieval code in a loop.

Listing 8-4 assumes that the database extension does not support asynchronous execution of Data Access Manager routines. For an example of asynchronous execution of routines, see Listing 8-1.

Listing 8-4. Using the low-level interface

```
PROCEDURE MyLoLevel(VAR thisSession: LongInt; VAR sessErr: OSErr);

VAR
   theDDevName:                         Str63;
   theHost, theUser:                    Str255;
   thePasswd, theConnStr:               Str255;

   packErr, initErr, sendErr, execErr: OSErr;
   stateErr, getErr, endErr:            OSErr;

   myTimeout:                           LongInt;
   myType:                              DBType;
   len, places, flags:                  Integer;
   myBuffer:                            Ptr;
   myDataInfo:                          Boolean;
   myDataReturned:                      Boolean;
```

```
BEGIN
   sessErr := noErr;          {assume everything went finc}
   packErr := InitDBPack;  {init the Data Access Mgr}

   {Set up values for theDDevName, theHost, theUser, thePasswd, }
   { and theConnStr. You can display a dialog box prompting }
   { the user to supply some of these parameters.}

   theDDevName := 'DAL';
   theHost := 'The Host System Name';
   theUser := 'Joe User';
   thePasswd := 'secret';
   theConnStr := 'extra stuff as needed';

   initErr := DBInit(thisSession, theDDevName, theHost, theUser,
                     thePasswd, theConnStr, NIL);

   IF initErr <> noErr THEN
   BEGIN
      sessErr := initErr;
      IF thisSession <> 0 THEN endErr := DBEnd(thisSession, NIL);
      EXIT(MyLoLevel);
   END;

   {Send a query or query fragment to the remote data server. }
   { MySendFragment is such a routine.}

   sendErr := MySendFragment(thisSession);

   {If there's an error, then probably something went wrong with }
   { DBSend or DBSendItem.  Don't forget to end the session.}
   IF sendErr <> noErr THEN
   BEGIN
      sessErr := sendErr;
      endErr := DBEnd(thisSession, NIL);
      EXIT(MyLoLevel);
   END;

   {The query has been sent.  This example assumes that }
   { the query will return data.}

   execErr := DBExec(thisSession, NIL);
   IF execErr = noErr THEN
   BEGIN
      {While waiting for stateErr <> rcDBExec you can }
      { let other apps run by calling WaitNextEvent. }
      { GoDoSomething does that.}

      stateErr := rcDBExec;
      WHILE (stateErr = rcDBExec) DO
      BEGIN
         GoDoSomething;
         stateErr := DBState(thisSession, NIL);
      END;
```

(Continued)

Listing 8-4. Using the low-level interface (Continued)

```
{DBState returned a result code other than rcDBExec. }
{ If it's rcDBValue, there are results to retrieve. }
{ Otherwise, it's probably an error.}

IF stateErr = rcDBValue THEN
BEGIN
   {Call DBGetItem once to get info on }
   { the data item and call DBGetItem a second time }
   { to actually get the data item.}

   myTimeout := 2*60;          {2*60 ticks = 2 secs}
   myType := typeAnyType;
   myDataInfo := FALSE;
   WHILE NOT myDataInfo DO
   BEGIN
      getErr := DBGetItem(thisSession, myTimeout, myType,
                          len, places, flags, NIL, NIL);

      {If you timed out, then give up control.  When }
      { control returns, continue getting the info.}
      IF getErr = rcDBBreak THEN GoDoSomething
      ELSE IF getErr = noErr OR
         getErr = rcDBValue THEN myDataInfo := TRUE
      ELSE
      BEGIN
         sessErr := getErr;
         endErr := DBEnd(thisSession, NIL);
         EXIT(MyLoLevel);
      END;
   END; {while}

   {At this point, you may want to examine the info }
   { about the data item before calling DBGetItem a }
   { second time to actually retrieve it.}

   {GimmeMySpace returns a pointer to where you want }
   { the data item to go.}
   myBuffer := GimmeMySpace(len);

   myDataReturned := FALSE;
   WHILE NOT myDataReturned DO
   BEGIN
      getErr := DBGetItem(thisSession, myTimeout, myType,
                          len, places, flags, myBuffer, NIL);
      {If you timed out, then give up control.  When }
      { control returns, continue getting the data.}
      IF getErr = rcDBBreak THEN GoDoSomething
      ELSE IF getErr = noErr OR
         getErr = rcDBValue THEN myDataReturned := TRUE
      ELSE
```

```
            BEGIN
               sessErr := getErr;
               endErr := DBEnd(thisSession, NIL);
               EXIT(MyLoLevel);
            END;
         END; {while}
      END
      ELSE sessErr := stateErr;
   END
   ELSE sessErr := execErr;

   endErr := DBEnd(thisSession, NIL);
END;
```

Note that, even if you are using the low-level interface to send queries to the data server, you might want to use the high-level functions to retrieve data and convert it to text.

Getting Information About Sessions in Progress

If your application is only one of several on a single Macintosh computer connected to data servers, you can use the DBGetConnInfo and DBGetSessionNum functions to obtain information about the sessions in progress. If you know the session ID (which is returned by the DBInit function when you open a session), you can use the DBGetConnInfo function to determine the database extension being used, the name of the host system on which the session is running, the user name and connection string that were used to initiate the session, the time at which the session started, and the status of the session. The status of the session specifies whether the data server is executing a query or waiting for another query fragment, whether there is output data available, and whether execution of a query ended in an error.

If you do not know the session ID, or if you want to get information about all open sessions, you can specify a database extension and a session number when you call the DBGetConnInfo function. Although there can be only one active session with a given session ID, session numbers are unique only for a specific database extension. Because the database extension assigns session numbers sequentially, starting with 1, you can call the DBGetConnInfo function repeatedly for a given database extension, incrementing the session number each time, to obtain information about all sessions open for that database extension. Your application need not have initiated the session to obtain information about it in this fashion.

The DBGetSessionNum function returns the session number when you specify the session ID. You can use this function to determine the session numbers for the sessions opened by your own application. You might want this information, for example, so you can distinguish your own sessions from those opened by other applications when you use the DBGetConnInfo function to get information about all open sessions.

Processing Query Results

You can use the low-level function DBGetItem to retrieve a single data item returned by a query, or you can use the high-level function DBGetQueryResults to retrieve all of the query results at once. If you use the DBGetQueryResults function, you can then use the DBResultsToText function to convert the results to ASCII text. The DBResultsToText function calls routines called *result handlers,* which are installed in memory by applications or by system extensions (files containing 'INIT' resources). This section discusses the use of the DBGetItem and DBGetQueryResults functions and describes how to write and install a result handler.

Getting Query Results

The DBGetItem function retrieves a single data item that was returned by a data source in response to a query. When you call the DBGetItem function, you specify the data type to be retrieved. If you do not know what data type to expect, you can specify the typeAnyType constant for the dataType parameter, and the data server returns the next data item regardless of data type. It also returns information about the data item, including data type and length.

If you do not know the length of the next data item, you can specify NIL for the buffer parameter in the DBGetItem function, and the data server returns the data type, length, and number of decimal places without retrieving the data item. The next time you call the DBGetItem function with a nonzero value for the buffer parameter, the function retrieves the data item.

If you want to skip a data item, specify the typeDiscard constant for the dataType parameter. Then the next time you call the DBGetItem function, it retrieves the following data item.

You should use the DBGetItem function if you want complete control over the retrieval of each item of data. If you want the Data Access Manager to retrieve the data for you, use the DBGetQueryResults function instead.

Table 8-1 shows the data types recognized by the Data Access Manager. You use a constant to specify each data type, as follows:

```
CONST {data types}
      typeAnyType       = 0;          {can be any data type}
      typeNone          = 'none';     {no more data expected}
      typeBoolean       = 'bool';     {Boolean}
      typeSMInt         = 'shor';     {short integer}
      typeInteger       = 'long';     {integer}
      typeSMFloat       = 'sing';     {short floating point}
      typeFloat         = 'doub';     {floating point}
      typeDate          = 'date';     {date}
      typeTime          = 'time';     {time}
      typeTimeStamp     = 'tims';     {date and time}
      typeChar          = 'TEXT';     {character}
      typeDecimal       = 'deci';     {decimal number}
      typeMoney         = 'mone';     {money value}
      typeVChar         = 'vcha';     {variable character}
      typeVBin          = 'vbin';     {variable binary}
```

```
typeLChar        = 'lcha';    {long character}
typeLBin         = 'lbin';    {long binary}
typeDiscard      = 'disc';    {discard next data item}
typeUnknown      = 'unkn';    {result handler for unknown }
                              { data type}
typeColBreak     = 'colb';    {result handler for column break}
typeRowBreak     = 'rowb';    {result handler for end of line}
```

The writer of a database extension can define other data types to support specific data sources or data servers.

Each data type has a standard definition, shown in Table 8-1. For example, if the DBGetItem function returns the typeInteger constant for the dataType parameter, you know that the data item represents an integer value and that a 4-byte buffer is necessary to hold it. Similarly, if you are using the DBSendItem function to send to the data server a data item that you identify as typeFloat, the data server expects to receive an 8-byte floating-point value.

Notice that some of these data types are defined to have a specific length (referred to as an *implied length*), and some do not. The len parameter of the DBSendItem and DBGetItem functions indicates the length of an individual data item. The DBGetQueryResults function returns a handle to an array of lengths, decimal places, and flags in the colInfo field of the results record. The typeAnyType, typeColBreak, and typeRowBreak constants do not refer to specific data types, and therefore the length specification is not applicable for these constants.

Table 8-1. Data types defined by the Data Access Manager

Constant	Length	Definition
typeAnyType	NA	Any data type (used as an input parameter to the DBGetItem function only; never returned by the function).
typeNone	0	Empty.
typeBoolean	1 byte	TRUE (1) or FALSE (0).
typeSMInt	2 bytes	Signed integer value.
typeInteger	4 bytes	Signed long integer value.
typeSMFloat	4 bytes	Signed floating-point value.
typeFloat	8 bytes	Signed floating-point value.
typeDate	4 bytes	Date; a long integer value consisting of a year (most significant 16 bits), month (8 bits), and day (least significant 8 bits).
typeTime	4 bytes	Time; a long integer value consisting of an hour (0–23; most significant 8 bits), minute (8 bits), second (8 bits), and hundredths of a second (least significant 8 bits).

(Continued)

Table 8-1. Data types defined by the Data Access Manager (Continued)

<table>
<tr><th>Constant</th><th>Length</th><th>Definition</th></tr>
<tr><td>typeTimeStamp</td><td>8 bytes</td><td>Date and time. A long integer date value followed by a long integer time value.</td></tr>
<tr><td>typeChar</td><td>Any</td><td>Fixed-length character string, not NULL terminated. The length of the string is defined by the specific data source.</td></tr>
<tr><td>typeDecimal</td><td>Any</td><td>Packed decimal string. A contiguous string of 4-bit nibbles, each of which contains a decimal number, except for the low nibble of the highest-addressed byte (that is, the last nibble in the string), which contains a sign. The value of the sign nibble can be 10, 12, 14, or 15 for a positive number or 11 or 13 for a negative number; 12 is recommended for a positive number and 13 for a negative number. The most significant digit is the high-order nibble of the lowest-addressed byte (that is, the first nibble to appear in the string).

The total number of nibbles (including the sign nibble) must be even; therefore, the high nibble of the highest-addressed byte of a number with an even number of digits must be 0.

For example, the number +123 is represented as $123C

<table>
<tr><td> 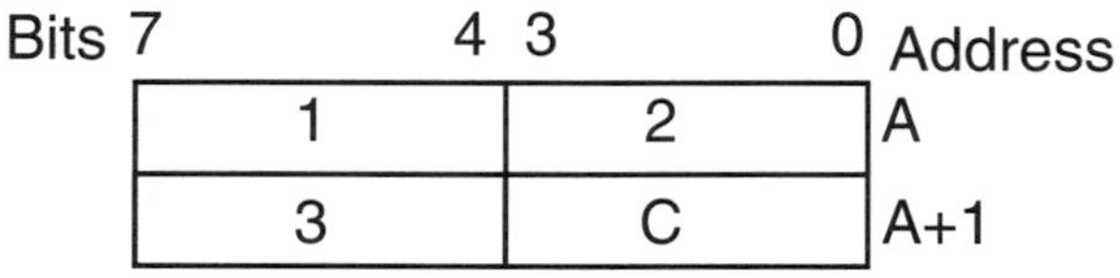Bits 7 … 4</td><td>3 … 0</td><td>Address</td></tr>
<tr><td>1</td><td>2</td><td>A</td></tr>
<tr><td>3</td><td>C</td><td>A+1</td></tr>
</table>

and the number –1234 is represented as $01234D.

<table>
<tr><td>Bits 7 … 4</td><td>3 … 0</td><td>Address</td></tr>
<tr><td>0</td><td>1</td><td>A</td></tr>
<tr><td>2</td><td>3</td><td>A+1</td></tr>
<tr><td>4</td><td>D</td><td>A+2</td></tr>
</table>

The length of a packed decimal string is defined as the number of bytes, including any extra leading 0 and the sign nibble. A packed decimal string can have from 0 to 31 digits, not including the sign nibble.

In addition to the length of a packed decimal string, each data item has an associated value that indicates the number of digits that follow the decimal place. The places parameter in the DBGetItem and DBSendItem functions indicates the number of decimal places in an individual data item. The DBGetQueryResults function returns the number of decimal places.</td></tr>
<tr><td>typeMoney</td><td>Any</td><td>Same as typeDecimal, but always has two decimal places.</td></tr>
<tr><td>typeVChar</td><td>Any</td><td>Variable-length character string, NULL terminated.</td></tr>
</table>

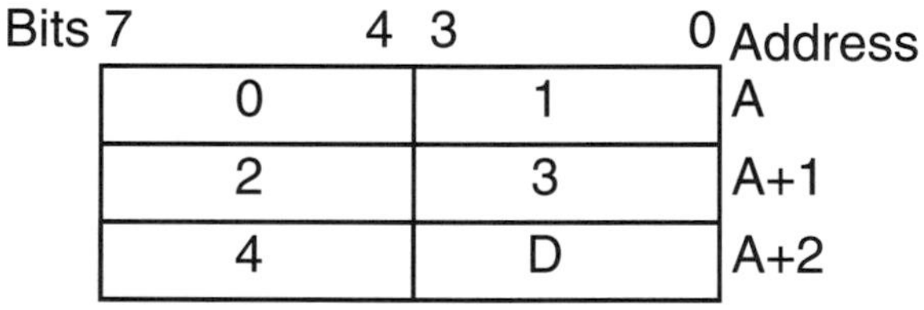

Table 8-1. Data types defined by the Data Access Manager (Continued)

Constant	Length	Definition
typeVBin	Any	Not defined. Reserved for future use.
typeLChar	Any	Not defined. Reserved for future use.
typeLBin	Any	Not defined. Reserved for future use.
typeDiscard	NA	Do not retrieve the next data item (used as an input parameter to the DBGetItem function only; never returned by the function).
typeUnknown	NA	A dummy data type for the result handler that processes any data type for which no other result handler is available (used as an input parameter to the DBInstallResultHandler, DBRemoveResultHandler, and DBGetResultHandler functions only; never returned by the DBGetItem function).
typeColBreak	NA	A dummy data type for the result handler that the DBGetQueryResults function calls after each item that is not the last item in a row (used as an input parameter to the DBInstallResultHandler, DBRemoveResultHandler, and DBGetResultHandler functions only; never returned by the DBGetItem function).
typeRowBreak	NA	A dummy data type for the result handler that the DBGetQueryResults function calls at the end of each row (used as an input parameter to the DBInstallResultHandler, DBRemoveResultHandler, and DBGetResultHandler functions only; never returned by the DBGetItem function).

The DBGetQueryResults function retrieves all of the data that was returned by a data source in response to a query, unless insufficient memory is available to hold the data, in which case it retrieves as many complete rows of data as possible. The DBGetQueryResults function stores the data in a structure called a *results record.* You must allocate the results record data structure and pass this record to the DBGetQueryResults function. The Data Access Manager allocates the handles inside the results record. When your application is finished using the results record, you must deallocate both the results record and the handles inside the results record.

The results record is defined by the ResultsRecord data type.

```
TYPE ResultsRecord =
     RECORD
        numRows:       Integer;           {number of rows retrieved}
        numCols:       Integer;           {number of columns per row}
        colTypes:      ColTypesHandle;    {type of data in each column}
        colData:       Handle;            {array of data items}
        colInfo:       ColInfoHandle      {info about each data item}
     END;
```

The numRows field in the results record indicates the total number of rows retrieved. If the DBGetQueryResults function returns a result code other than rcDBValue, then not all of the data actually returned by the data source was retrieved. This could happen, for instance, if the user's computer does not have sufficient memory space to hold all the data. In this case, your application can make more space available (by writing the data in the data record to disk, for example) and then call the DBGetQueryResults function again to complete retrieval of the data.

Note: The DBGetQueryResults function retrieves whole rows only; if it runs out of space in the middle of a row, it stores the partial row in a private buffer so that the data in the results record ends with the last complete row. Because the last partial row is no longer available from the data server, you cannot start to retrieve data with the DBGetQueryResults function and then switch to the DBGetItem function to complete the data retrieval.

The numCols field indicates the number of columns in each row of data.

The colTypes field is a handle to an array of data types, specifying the type of data in each column. The number of elements in the array is equal to the value in the numCols parameter. Table 8-1 shows the standard data types.

The colData field is a handle to the data retrieved by the DBGetQueryResults function.

The colInfo field is a handle to an array of records of type DBColInfoRecord, each of which specifies the length, places, and flags for a data item. There are as many records in the array as there are data items retrieved by the DBGetQueryResults function. Here is the DBColInfoRecord type definition:

```
TYPE DBColInfoRecord =
     RECORD
        len:                 Integer;         {length of data item}
        places:              Integer;         {places for decimal and }
                                              { money data items}
        flags:               Integer          {flags for data item}
     END;
```

The len field indicates the length of the data item. The DBGetQueryResults function returns a value in this field only for those data types that do not have implied lengths; see Table 8-1.

The places field indicates the number of decimal places in data items of types typeMoney and typeDecimal. For all other data types, the places field returns 0.

The least significant bit of the flags field is set to 1 if the data item is in the last column of the row. The third bit of the flags field is 1 if the data item is NULL. You can use the constants kDBLastColFlag and kDBNullFlag to test for these flag bits.

Converting Query Results to Text

The DBResultsToText function provided by the high-level interface converts the data retrieved by the DBGetQueryResults function into strings of ASCII text. This function makes it easier for you to display retrieved data for the user.

For the DBResultsToText function to convert data of a specific type to text, either the application or the system software must have a routine called a *result handler.* With system software version 7.0, Apple Computer, Inc. is providing system result handlers for the data types listed here. (These data types are described in Table 8-1.)

Data type	Constant	Data type	Constant
Boolean	typeBoolean	Time	typeTime
Short integer	typeSMInt	Date and time	typeTimeStamp
Integer	typeInteger	Character	typeChar
Short floating point	typeSMFloat	Decimal number	typeDecimal
Floating point	typeFloat	Money value	typeMoney
Date	typeDate	Variable character	typeVChar

Note: Apple's system result handler for the variable character (typeVChar) data type strips trailing spaces from the character string.

In addition to the result handlers for these standard data types, Apple is providing the following three system result handlers that do not correspond to any specific data type:

Data type	Constant
Unknown	typeUnknown
Column break	typeColBreak
End of line	typeRowBreak

The typeUnknown result handler processes any data type for which no other result handler is available. The DBResultsToText function calls the typeColBreak result handler after each item that is not the last item in a row. This result handler does not correspond to any data type, but adds a delimiter character to separate columns of text. The default typeColBreak result handler inserts a tab character. Similarly, the DBResultsToText function calls the typeRowBreak result handler at the end of each row of data to add a character that separates the rows of text. The default typeRowBreak result handler inserts a return character. Your application can install your own typeColBreak and typeRowBreak result handlers to insert whatever characters you wish—or to insert no character at all, if you prefer.

You can install result handlers for any data types you know about. When you call the DBInstallResultHandler function, you can specify whether the result handler you are installing is a system result handler. A **system result handler** is available to all applications that use the system. All other result handlers (called **application result handlers**) are associated with a particular application. The DBResultsToText function always uses a result handler for the current application in preference to a system result handler for the same data type. When you install a system result handler for the same data type as an already installed system result handler, the new result handler replaces the old one. Similarly, when you install an application result handler for the same data type as a result handler already installed for the same application, the new result handler replaces the old one for that application.

Result handlers are stored in memory. The Data Access Manager installs its system result handlers the first time the Macintosh Operating System loads the Data Access Manager into memory. You must reinstall your own application result handlers each time your application starts up. You can also install your own system result handlers each time your application starts up, or you can provide a system extension (that is, a file with an 'INIT' resource) that installs system result handlers each time the user starts up the system.

Here is a function declaration for a result handler function.

```
FUNCTION MyResultHandler (dataType: DBType; theLen,thePlaces,theFlags:
                          Integer; theData: Ptr; theText: Handle) :
                          OSErr;
```

The dataType parameter specifies the data type of the data item that the DBResultsToText function is passing to the result handler. Table 8-1 describes the standard data types.

The parameters theLen and thePlaces specify the length and number of decimal places of the data item that the DBResultsToText function wants the result handler to convert to text.

The parameter theFlags is the value returned for the flags parameter by the DBGetItem function. If the least significant bit of this parameter is set to 1, the data item is in the last column of the row. If the third bit of this parameter is set to 1, the data item is NULL. You can use the constants kDBLastColFlag and kDBNullFlag to test for these flag bits.

The parameter theData is a pointer to the data that the result handler is to convert to text.

The parameter theText is a handle to the buffer that is to hold the text version of the data. The result handler should use the SetHandleSize function to increase the size of the buffer as necessary to hold the new text, and append the new text to the end of the text already in the buffer. The SetHandleSize function is described in the Memory Manager chapter of Volume II.

If the result handler successfully converts the data to text, it should return a result code of 0 (noErr).

You can use the DBInstallResultHandler function to install a result handler and the DBRemoveResultHandler function to remove an application result handler. You can install and replace system result handlers, but you cannot remove them.

The following line of code installs an application result handler. The first parameter (typeInteger) specifies the data type that this result handler processes. The second parameter (MyTypeIntegerHandler) is a pointer to the result handler routine. The last parameter (FALSE) is a Boolean specifying that this routine is not a system result handler.

```
err := DBInstallResultHandler (typeInteger,MyTypeIntegerHandler,FALSE);
```

Listing 8-5 shows a result handler that converts the integer data type to text.

Listing 8-5. A result handler

```
FUNCTION MyTypeIntegerHandler(datatype: DBType; theLen: Integer;
                              theData: Ptr; theText: Handle) : OSErr;

VAR   theInt:      LongInt;
      theTextLen: LongInt;
      temp:        Str255;
      atemp1:      Ptr;
      atemp2:      LongInt;
      atemp3:      LongInt;

BEGIN
   BlockMove(theData, @theInt, sizeof(theInt));
   NumToString(theInt, temp);               {convert to text}
   theTextLen := GetHandleSize(theText)     {get current size of theText}
   SetHandleSize(theText, theTextLen + LongInt(LENGTH(temp));
                                            {grow text handle}

   IF (MemError <> noErr) THEN TypeIntegerHandler := MemError
   ELSE
   BEGIN
      atemp1 := Ptr(ORD(@temp));
      atemp2 := LongInt(theText^) + theTextLen;
      atemp3 := LongInt(LENGTH(temp));
      {use BlockMove to append text}
      BlockMove(P2CStr(atemp1), Ptr(atemp2), atemp3);
      TypeIntegerHandler := MemError;
   END;
END;
```

CREATING A QUERY DOCUMENT

A query document is a file of type 'qery' that contains a 'qrsc' resource and one or more 'wstr' resources, and may contain a 'qdef' resource plus other resources. Query documents make it possible for you to write applications that can communicate with data servers without requiring familiarity with the command language used by the data server. Because a query document is most useful if it can be used by many different applications, no query document should depend on the presence of a particular application in order to function.

An application can call the DBGetNewQuery function to convert a 'qrsc' resource into a **query record** in memory. The query record points to a 'wstr' resource that contains either a complete query or a template for a query. If the 'wstr' resource is a template, it contains the commands and data necessary to create a query, without any information that the user must add just before the query is sent. The 'qdef' resource contains a query definition function, which can modify the query record and, if necessary, fill in the query template to create a complete query. The DBStartQuery function sends the query pointed to by a query record to a data server. The following sections describe the contents of a query document, describe query records, and define the 'qrsc', 'wstr', and 'qdef' resources.

User Interface Guidelines for Query Documents

All query documents should behave in fundamentally the same way. They should be self-explanatory and should never execute a query without an explicit command from the user. When your application opens a query document, the query document should display a dialog box with enough information about the query so that the user can decide if it's the right query. The dialog box should describe the purpose of the query, what kind of data it transfers and in which direction, the type of data source it accesses, and any warnings or instructions. The dialog box can describe how the user interprets the data, such as the name of each field in a record. Figure 8-6 shows an example of a query document dialog box.

This dialog box should allow the user to cancel the request for data. In addition, it may be useful to allow the user to set parameters with text boxes, check boxes, or radio buttons. For example, a query to a database of financial information could provide a list of these options: a trial balance, profit-and-loss statements, or net worth reports. Save the last set of user-specified parameters with the query document. This way the user can review the parameters used to generate the data or use the same parameters the next time.

Once a query starts running, it must be able to complete its task without user intervention. If a query must run modally (that is, it must run to completion before returning control to the user), display a dialog box that shows the query's progress and be sure to return control to the user as soon as possible. The philosophy of this process is similar to that of receiving electronic mail—that is, inform the user when the information arrives, but let the user decide when to read it.

Whenever possible, query documents should check data before it is transmitted to a data source to be sure it's compatible. Establish a connection with a data source only after you have checked the data.

Contents of a Query Document

The query document must contain

- one 'qrsc' resource, as defined in the next section, "Query Records and Query Resources"
- an 'STR#' resource that contains the name of the database extension to be used, plus any host, user name, password, and connection string needed for the DBInit function
- one or more 'wstr' resources containing queries—that is, strings of commands and data that the DBSend function sends to the data server and that the DBExec function executes

A 'wstr' resource consists of a 2-byte length field followed by a character string. (The *w* in 'wstr' refers to the length word as opposed to the length byte used in an 'STR ' resource.) Each 'wstr' resource contains one query (or one query template, to be modified by the query definition function before it is sent to the data server). The 'qrsc' resource includes an array that lists the resource ID numbers of all of the 'wstr' resources in the query document and an index into the array that specifies which one of the 'wstr' resources should be sent to the data server.

In addition, the query document may contain

- a 'qdef' resource that contains a query definition function
- any resources needed by the query definition function, such as 'DLOG' and 'DITL' resources (which support dialog boxes)

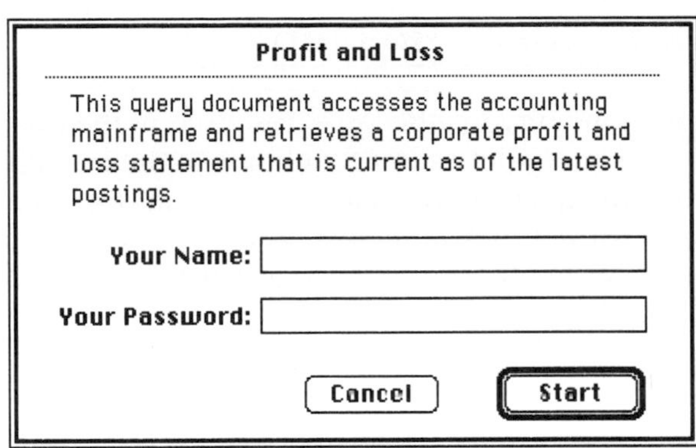

Figure 8-6. A query document dialog box

- resources to support a customized icon (to replace the default icon that the Finder™ uses for files of type 'qery'); see the Finder Interface chapter in this volume for more information on icon resources and the User Interface Guidelines chapter for guidelines for customized icons.

Figure 8-7 illustrates the relationship between a query document, the query record, and the query definition function. The following sections describe 'qrsc' resources, query records, and 'qdef' resources in detail.

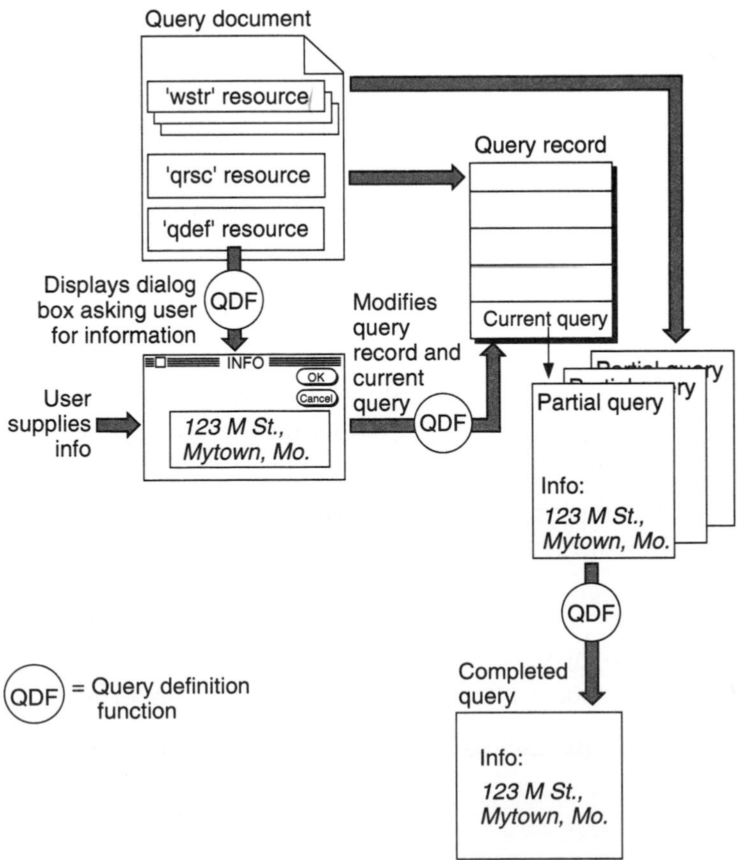

Figure 8-7. Function of a query document

Query Records and Query Resources

The DBGetNewQuery function converts the 'qrsc' resource in the query document into a query record in memory. The query definition function can then modify the query record before the application sends the query to the data server. This section describes a query record, and then defines the format of a 'qrsc' resource. A later section, "Writing a Query Definition Function," describes 'qdef' resources and query definition functions.

Query Records

The QueryRecord data type defines a query record.

```
TYPE QueryRecord =
     RECORD
        version:        Integer;         {query record format version}
        id:             Integer;         {resource ID of 'qrsc'}
        queryProc:      Handle;          {handle to qdef}
        ddevName:       Str63;           {name of database extension}
        host:           Str255;          {name of host computer}
        user:           Str255;          {name of user}
        password:       Str255;          {user's password}
        connStr:        Str255;          {connection string}
        currQuery:      Integer;         {current query}
        numQueries:     Integer;         {number of queries}
        queryList:      QueryListHandle; {handles to queries}
        numRes:         Integer;         {number of resources}
        resList:        ResListHandle;   {list of resources}
        dataHandle:     Handle;          {handle to memory for qdef}
        refCon:         LongInt          {reserved for use by app}
     END;
```

Field descriptions

version	The version number of the query record format. For the Data Access Manager released with system software version 7.0, the version number is 0.
id	The resource ID of the 'qrsc' resource from which the Data Access Manager created this query record.
queryProc	A handle to the query definition function that the DBStartQuery function calls. This handle is NIL if there is no query definition function—that is, if the DBStartQuery function should send the query specified by this query record to the data server without modifications.
ddevName	The database extension name used as a parameter to the DBInit function.

host — The name of the host computer system used as a parameter to the DBInit function.

user — The name of the user, used as a parameter to the DBInit function.

password — The user's password, used as a parameter to the DBInit function.

connStr — The connection string used as a parameter to the DBInit function.

currQuery — An index value from 1 through numQueries, indicating which element in the array of query handles represents the current query. The current query is the one actually sent to the data server. If the query document contains more than one 'wstr' resource, the query definition function can prompt the user to select a new current query and modify this field in the query record appropriately.

numQueries — The number of queries referred to by the queryList field.

queryList — A handle to an array of handles. Each handle in this array refers to a query. Each query is created from a 'wstr' resource in the query document and is stored in memory as a 2-byte length field followed by ASCII text. (The length does not include the 2 bytes of the length field.) The query definition function can create a new query. To add a new handle to the array of handles, use the Memory Manager's SetHandleSize function to increase the size of the array. Don't forget to change the value of the numQueries field as well.

numRes — The number of resources referred to by the resList field.

resList — A handle to an array of records of type ResListElem. Each record in the array contains the type and ID of a resource that is needed by the query definition function.

```
TYPE ResListElem =
     RECORD
        theType:       ResType;        {resource type}
        id:            Integer         {resource ID}
     END;
```

dataHandle — A handle to memory for use by the query definition function. When the Data Access Manager first creates the query record, this field is NIL. The query definition function can allocate memory and place a handle to it in this field. The query definition function should dispose of any memory it allocates before it returns control to the Data Access Manager.

refCon — The query record's reference value. The application can use this field for any purpose.

Query Resources

Each query document should contain a single 'qrsc' resource. Here is the structure of the 'qrsc' resource, in the format used by the Rez resource compiler supplied with MPW®.

```
type 'qrsc' {
     Integer;                 /* version */
     Integer;                 /* ID of 'qdef' resource */
     Integer;                 /* ID of 'STR#' resource that contains
                                 ddevName, host, user, password,
                                 connection string */
     Integer;                 /* current query */

     /* array of IDs of 'wstr' resources that contain queries */

     Integer = $$CountOf(QueryArray);     /* array size */
     wide array QueryArray{
         Integer;                         /* ID of 'wstr' resource */
     };

     /* array of resource types and IDs for other resources
        in the query document */

     Integer = $$CountOf(ResArray);       /* array size */
     wide array ResArray{
         literal LongInt;                 /* resource type */
         Integer;                         /* resource ID */
     };
     };
```

The first field in the 'qrsc' resource is the version number of the 'qrsc' format. For the Data Access Manager released with system software version 7.0, the version number is 0.

The second field is the resource ID of the 'qdef' resource containing the query definition function that the Data Access Manager is to call when it opens this 'qrsc' resource. Use an ID of 0 if there is no query definition function for this resource—that is, if the Data Access Manager should send the query in this resource to the data server without modifications.

The third field is the ID of an 'STR#' resource that contains five Pascal strings corresponding to some of the parameters used by the DBInit function. If the query definition function is going to prompt the user for the values of these parameters before entering them in the query record, they should be zero-length strings in the 'STR#' resource.

The sixth field in the 'qrsc' resource is an array of ID numbers of the 'wstr' resources in the query document. The fifth field is the size of the array of 'wstr' IDs, and the fourth field is an index value indicating which element in the array of 'wstr' IDs represents the current query. (The array elements are numbered starting with 1.) The current query is the one actually sent to the data server. If the query document contains more than one 'wstr' resource, the query definition function can prompt the user to select the query to use and modify the current query field in the query record appropriately.

The eighth field in the 'qrsc' resource is an array listing the resource types and IDs of all the resources in the query document other than the standard resources included in all query documents. The seventh field is the size of this array. The resources listed in this final array are those used by the query definition function. This list should include resources embedded in other resources, such as a 'PICT' resource that is included in a 'DITL' resource.

Writing a Query Definition Function

When the Data Access Manager creates a query record, it calls the query definition function specified by the queryProc field in the query record. The purpose of the query definition function is to modify the query and the query record before the query is sent to the data server. The query definition function can use dialog boxes to request information from the user. Because a query document is most useful if it can be used by many different applications, no query definition function should depend on the presence of a particular application.

If you want to include a query definition function, you must make it the first piece of code in a resource of type 'qdef' in the query document.

Here is a function declaration for a query definition function.

```
FUNCTION MyQDef (VAR sessID: LongInt; query: QueryHandle) : OSErr;
```

If the application has already initiated a session with the data server, the DBStartQuery function passes the session ID for that session in the sessID parameter to the query definition function. If the query definition function receives a 0 in this parameter, then the Data Access Manager has not initiated a session. In this case, the query definition function can return a 0 in the sessID parameter, or it can call the DBInit function to initiate a session and then return the session ID in this parameter.

If the query definition function returns a 0 in the sessID parameter, the DBStartQuery function calls the DBInit function and then calls the DBSend function to send a query to the data server. If the query definition function returns a session ID in this parameter, the DBStartQuery function calls the DBSend function immediately.

The query parameter to the query definition function specifies a handle to the query record. The query definition function can modify any of the fields in the query record, including the currQuery field that specifies which query is to be sent to the data server. In addition, the query definition function can modify an existing query or create a new query, adding the handle to the new query to the query list. Note that, because a query in memory consists only of a 2-byte length value followed by a character string, the query definition function has to know the exact contents and structure of a query in order to modify it.

The query definition function must return the noErr result code as the function result if the function executed successfully. If it returns any other value, the DBStartQuery function does not call the DBSend function. The query definition function can return any result code, including noErr, userCanceledErr, or rcDBError.

When the DBStartQuery function calls the query definition function, the current resource file is the file that contains the 'qrsc' resource from which the Data Access Manager created the query record. When the query definition function returns control to the Data Access Manager, the current resource file must be unchanged.

The query definition function can allocate memory and use the dataHandle field in the query record to store a handle to it. The query definition function must free any memory it allocates before terminating.

Listing 8-6 shows a query definition function that uses a dialog box to prompt the user for a user name and password and then modifies the query record accordingly.

Listing 8-6. A query definition function

```
FUNCTION MyQDef(VAR sessID: LongInt; query: QueryHandle) : OSErr;

CONST
   myNameItem =       7;
   myPassWordItem =   8;

VAR
   myNumRes:          Integer;
   myResList:         ResListHandle;
   myResLPtr:         ResListPtr;
   myIndex:           Integer;
   myDialog:          DialogPtr;
   myDlogID:          Integer;
   itemType:          Integer;
   itemHName:         Handle;
   itemHPasswd:       Handle;
   itemBox:           Rect;
   mySTR:             Array[1..2] OF Str255;
   itemHit:           Integer;
   myQErr:            OsErr;

BEGIN
   {If sessID = 0, no session has been }
   { initiated.  Your qdef may optionally initiate a }
   { session, or it can let the DBStartQuery routine take }
   { care of this.  In this example, the qdef doesn't }
   { check the sessID parameter.}

   HLock(Handle(query));
   myNumRes := query^^.numRes;
   myResList := query^^.resList;
   HLock(Handle(myResList));
   myResLPtr := myResList^;
   myIndex := 0;

   {look for a 'DLOG' resource}
   WHILE (myIndex < myNumRes) AND
         (myResLPtr^[myIndex].theType <> 'DLOG') DO
   BEGIN
      myIndex := myIndex + 1;
   END;
```

```
   {Was a 'DLOG' resource found, or did the index run out?}
   IF (myIndex < myNumRes) THEN
      myDlogID := myResLPtr^[myIndex].id
      {We found the 'DLOG' resource.}
   ELSE
   BEGIN
      {The 'DLOG' wasn't found; exit with no error.  This }
      { is probably okay; it just means that the query }
      { and the query record don't get modified.}
      MyQDEF := noErr;
      HUnlock(Handle(query));
      HUnlock(Handle(myResList));
      EXIT(MyQDef);
   END;

   {Found the 'DLOG' and its ID; now put up the dialog box.}
   myDialog := GetNewDialog(myDlogID, Ptr(NIL), WindowPtr(-1));
   SetPort(GrafPtr(myDialog));

   {Now you can change the query record or the query itself. }
   { What you change is entirely up to you. In this example, }
   { the qdef changes only the user and password fields }
   { of the query record.}

   GetDItem(myDialog, myNameItem, itemType, itemHName, itemBox);
   GetItext(itemHName, mySTR[1]);
   GetDItem(myDialog, myPassWordItem, itemType, itemHPasswd, itemBox);
   GetItext(itemHPasswd, mySTR[2]);

   {Make available to the filter routine the strings }
   { we want the user to edit.}
   WindowPeek(myDialog)^.refCon := LongInt(@mySTR);

   {myNamePasswdFltrFunc is a routine that allows the user to edit }
   { the name and password fields in the dialog box.}

   ModalDialog(myNamePasswdFltrFunc, itemHit);
   IF itemHit = ok THEN
   BEGIN
      {The user clicked the OK button. Update the user and password }
      { fields of the query record.}
      query^^.user := mySTR[1];
      query^^.password := mySTR[2];
      MyQDef := noErr;
   END
   ELSE MyQDef := userCanceledErr;
   HUnlock(Handle(query));
   HUnlock(Handle(myResList));
   DisposDialog(myDialog);

END;
```

DATA ACCESS MANAGER ROUTINES

The Data Access Manager has high-level routines, low-level routines, and routines that manipulate result handlers. This section describes all of the Data Access Manager routines.

All of the low-level routines and some of the high-level routines have as a parameter a pointer to an asynchronous parameter block. If you specify a nonzero value for this parameter, the database extension executes the function asynchronously—that is, it returns control to the Data Access Manager before the routine has completed execution, and the Data Access Manager returns control to your application. If you specify NIL for the pointer to the asynchronous parameter block, the database extension does not return control to your application until the routine has finished execution.Your application must call the WaitNextEvent function periodically to allow an asynchronous routine to complete execution. The WaitNextEvent function is described in the Event Manager chapter of this volume.

You can tell when an asynchronous routine has completed execution and check the result code by looking at values in the asynchronous parameter block. The asynchronous parameter block is described in the next section, "Asynchronous Execution of Routines."

Note: A noErr result code returned by a routine that has been called asynchronously indicates only that the routine *began* execution successfully. You must check the result field of the asynchronous parameter block for the final result of the routine.

Assembly-language note: You can invoke each of the Data Access Manager routines with a macro that has the same name as the routine, but preceded with an underscore; for example, the macro for the DBInit function is named _DBInit. Each of these macros places a routine selector in the D0 register and calls the trap _Pack13. The routine selectors are listed in "Summary of the Data Access Manager" at the end of this chapter.

Asynchronous Execution of Routines

Each Data Access Manager routine that can be called asynchronously (that is, that can return control to your application before it has completed execution) takes as a parameter a pointer to a parameter block known as the *asynchronous parameter block.* If this pointer is NIL, the routine does not return control to your application until it has completed execution.

Note: The asynchronous parameter block is passed on to the database extension, which is responsible for implementing the asynchronous routine. If the database extension does not support asynchronous routines, the Data Access Manager returns the rcDBAsyncNotSupp result code and terminates execution of the routine.

The DBAsyncParamBlockRec data type defines the asynchronous parameter block.

```
TYPE DBAsyncParamBlockRec =
     RECORD
        completionProc: ProcPtr;  {pointer to completion routine}
        result:         OSErr;    {result of call}
        userRef:        LongInt;  {reserved for use by application}
        ddevRef:        LongInt;  {reserved for use by database }
                                  { extension}
        reserved:       LongInt   {reserved for use by Data Access Mgr}
     END;

     DBAsyncParmBlkPtr = ^DBAsyncParamBlockRec;
```

The completionProc field is a pointer to a completion routine that the database extension calls when it has completed executing the asynchronous function. Before calling the completion routine, the Data Access Manager places a pointer to the asynchronous parameter block in the A0 register. If you do not want to use a completion routine, set this parameter to NIL.

The database extension sets the result field to 1 while the routine is executing, and places the result code in it when the routine completes. Your application can poll this field to determine when an asynchronous routine has completed execution.

The userRef field is reserved for the application's use. Because the Data Access Manager passes a pointer to the parameter block to the completion routine, you can use this field to pass information to the completion routine.

The ddevRef field is reserved for use by the database extension, and the reserved field is reserved for use by the Data Access Manager.

You can use the DBKill function to cancel an asynchronous routine.

Initializing the Data Access Manager

You must initialize the Data Access Manager before you can use it.

```
FUNCTION InitDBPack : OSErr;
```

The InitDBPack function initializes the Data Access Manager. You must call the InitDBPack function before you call any other Data Access Manager routines. If the Data Access Manager has already been initialized, the InitDBPack function returns the noErr result code but does nothing else.

The interface routine that implements the InitDBPack function includes a version number for the Data Access Manager. If the Data Access Manager is a different version from that specified by the interface routine, then the InitDBPack function returns the rcDBWrongVersion result code.

Result codes

noErr	0	No error
rcDBWrongVersion	–812	Wrong version number

High-Level Interface

The high-level interface to the Data Access Manager allows applications to manipulate query documents and to get the results of the query provided by a query document. The use and contents of query documents are discussed in "Creating a Query Document" earlier in this chapter.

Handling Query Documents

The routines described in this section open query documents, create query records, dispose of query records, and use query documents to establish communication with and send queries to a data server.

```
FUNCTION DBGetNewQuery (queryID: Integer; VAR query: QueryHandle) :
                        OSErr;
```

The DBGetNewQuery function creates a query record from the 'qrsc' resource with the resource ID you specify in the queryID parameter. The query parameter returns a handle to the query record. The resource file that contains the 'qrsc' resource must remain open until after the DBStartQuery function has completed execution. If you do not already know the resource ID of the 'qrsc' resource (for example, if you call the StandardGetFile procedure to let the user select the query document), you can use Resource Manager routines to determine the resource ID. The StandardGetFile procedure is described in the Standard File Package chapter of this volume, and the Resource Manager is described in Volume I.

Result codes

noErr	0	Query record built successfully
rcDBPackNotInited	–813	The InitDBPack function has not yet been called

```
FUNCTION DBDisposeQuery (query: QueryHandle) : OSErr;
```

The DBDisposeQuery function disposes of a query record and frees all the memory that the Data Access Manager allocated when it created the query record. You should call this function after you are finished using a query record.

The query parameter is a handle to the query record.

Result codes

noErr	0	Query record disposed of successfully
rcDBPackNotInited	–813	The InitDBPack function has not yet been called

```
FUNCTION DBStartQuery (VAR sessID: LongInt; query: QueryHandle;
                        statusProc: ProcPtr; asyncPB: DBAsyncParmBlkPtr) :
                        OSErr;
```

The DBStartQuery function performs the following tasks, in the order specified:

1. It calls the query definition function (if any) pointed to by the query record. The query definition function modifies the query record and the query, usually by asking the user for input. The query definition function can display a dialog box that gives the user the option of canceling the query; if the user does cancel the query, the DBStartQuery function returns the userCanceledErr result code.

2. If you specify a nonzero value for the statusProc parameter, the DBStartQuery function calls your status routine with the kDBUpdateWind constant in the message parameter so that your application can update its windows.

3. If you specify a nonzero value for the statusProc parameter, the DBStartQuery function calls your status routine with the kDBAboutToInit constant in the message parameter so that your application can display a dialog box informing the user that a session is about to be initiated with a data server, and giving the user the option of canceling execution of the function.

4. If the sessID parameter is 0, the DBStartQuery function calls the DBInit function to initiate a session, and returns a session ID.

5. If you specify a nonzero value for the statusProc parameter and the DBStartQuery function calls the DBInit function, the DBStartQuery function calls your status routine with the kDBInitComplete constant in the message parameter and the result of the DBInit function in the function result.

6. The DBStartQuery function calls the DBSend function to send the query to the data server.

7. If you specify a nonzero value for the statusProc parameter, the DBStartQuery function calls your status routine with the kDBSendComplete constant in the message parameter and the result of the DBSend function in the result parameter.

8. The DBStartQuery function calls the DBExec function to execute the query.

9. If you specify a nonzero value for the statusProc parameter, the DBStartQuery function calls your status routine with the kDBExecComplete constant in the message parameter and the result of the DBExec function in the result parameter.

10. If you specify a nonzero value for the statusProc parameter, the DBStartQuery function calls your status routine with the kDBStartQueryComplete constant in the message parameter and the result of the DBStartQuery function in the result parameter.

You can use the sessID parameter to specify a session ID if your application or another application has already initiated a session with the data server. If you specify NIL for this parameter, then the DBStartQuery function initiates a session and returns the session ID in the sessID parameter.

You use the query parameter to specify a handle to a query record.

You can use the statusProc parameter to specify a pointer to a status routine that your application can use to update its windows after the query definition function has completed execution. (The DBStartQuery function does not attempt to update your application's windows.) The DBStartQuery function also calls your status routine before it initiates a session with a data server, after it calls the DBInit function, after it calls the DBSend function, and after it calls the DBExec function. Status routines are discussed in "Writing a Status Routine for High-Level Functions" earlier in this chapter.

If you specify a pointer to an asynchronous parameter block in the asyncPB parameter, the DBStartQuery function calls the DBInit, DBSend, and DBExec functions asynchronously. As soon as the DBInit function has started execution, it returns control to your application. Your application must then call the WaitNextEvent function periodically to allow these asynchronous routines to run, and it must check the result field of the asynchronous parameter block to determine when each routine has completed execution.

Result codes

noErr	0	No error
userCanceledErr	–128	User canceled the query
rcDBError	–802	Error initiating session, sending text, or executing query
rcDBBadSessID	–806	Session ID is invalid
rcDBBadDDev	–808	Couldn't find the specified database extension, or error occurred in opening database extension
rcDBAsyncNotSupp	–809	The database extension does not support asynchronous calls
rcDBPackNotInited	–813	The InitDBPack function has not yet been called

Handling Query Results

The routines in this section retrieve query results and convert them to text.

```
FUNCTION DBGetQueryResults (sessID: LongInt; VAR results: ResultsRecord;
                            timeout: LongInt; statusProc: ProcPtr;
                            asyncPB: DBAsyncParmBlkPtr) : OSErr;
```

The DBGetQueryResults function retrieves the results returned by a query and places them in memory. If there is sufficient memory available, this function retrieves all of the results at once. If the DBGetQueryResults function runs out of memory, it places as much data as possible in memory, up to the last whole row. You can then make more memory available and call the DBGetQueryResults function again to retrieve more data.

The DBGetQueryResults function can be used to retrieve the results of any query, not only queries sent and executed by the DBStartQuery function.

The sessID parameter specifies the ID of the session from which you wish to retrieve results.

The results parameter is the results record, which contains handles to the retrieved data. Results records are described in "Getting Query Results" earlier in this chapter. You must allocate the results record data structure and pass this record to the DBGetQueryResults function. The Data Access Manager allocates the handles inside the results record. When your application is finished using the results record, you must deallocate both the results record and the handles inside the results record.

The timeout parameter specifies the value that the DBGetQueryResults function uses for the timeout parameter each time it calls the DBGetItem function. The timeout parameter specifies the maximum amount of time that the database extension should wait to receive results from the data server before canceling the DBGetItem function. Specify the timeout parameter in sixtieths of a second. To disable the timeout feature, set the timeout parameter to the kDBWaitForever constant. Some database extensions ignore the timeout parameter when you specify a nonzero value for the asyncPB parameter.

You can use the statusProc parameter to specify a pointer to a status routine that you provide. The DBGetQueryResults function calls your status routine after it calls the DBGetItem function to retrieve a data item. When it calls the status routine, the DBGetQueryResults function provides the result of the DBGetItem function, the data type, data length, number of decimal places, and flags associated with the data item, and a pointer to the data item. Status routines are discussed in "Writing a Status Routine for High-Level Functions" earlier in this chapter.

If you specify a pointer to an asynchronous parameter block in the asyncPB parameter, the DBGetQueryResults function calls the DBGetItem function asynchronously for each data item. As soon as the DBGetItem function has started execution, it returns control to your application. Your application must then call the WaitNextEvent function periodically to allow this asynchronous routine to run, and it must check the result field of the asynchronous parameter block to determine when the routine has completed execution.

Result codes

noErr	0	Query execution successful; no results returned
userCanceledErr	–128	Function canceled by status routine
rcDBValue	–801	Data available
rcDBError	–802	Query execution ended in an error
rcDBBreak	–804	Function timed out
rcDBExec	–805	Query currently executing
rcDBBadSessID	–806	Session ID is invalid
rcDBAsyncNotSupp	–809	The database extension does not support asynchronous calls
rcDBPackNotInited	–813	The InitDBPack function has not yet been called

```
FUNCTION DBResultsToText (results: ResultsRecord; VAR theText:
                          Handle) : OSErr;
```

The DBResultsToText function calls result handlers to convert to text the data retrieved by the DBGetQueryResults function. Result handlers are described in "Converting Query Results to Text" earlier in this chapter.

The results parameter is the results record returned by the DBGetQueryResults function. The parameter theText contains a handle to the converted text. This handle is allocated by the Data Access Manager.

Result codes

noErr	0	No error
rcDBPackNotInited	–813	The InitDBPack function has not yet been called

Low-Level Interface

The low-level interface to the Data Access Manager allows applications to open and close sessions with a data server, send and execute queries, retrieve query results, and obtain information about any current session.

Controlling the Session

The functions in this section initiate and close sessions, obtain information about sessions, and cancel functions that were called asynchronously.

```
FUNCTION DBInit (VAR sessID: LongInt; ddevName: Str63; host,user,
                 password,connStr: Str255; asyncPB: DBAsyncParmBlkPtr) :
                 OSErr;
```

The DBInit function initiates a session with a data server. You must initiate a session before you call any Data Access Manager function that requires a session ID as an input parameter. If the DBInit function returns a nonzero session ID, you must call the DBEnd function to terminate the session, even if the DBInit function also returns a result code other than noErr.

Because the high-level function DBStartQuery can call the DBInit function, you do not have to call the DBInit function if you have called the DBStartQuery function.

The DBInit function returns the session ID in the sessID parameter. This session ID is unique; no other current session, for any database extension, has the same session ID. You must specify the session ID any time you want to send data to or retrieve data from this session. Depending on the database extension you are using, the DBInit function might return a session ID of zero if it fails to initiate a session, or it might return a nonzero session ID and a result code other than noErr. In the latter case, you can pass the session ID to the DBGetErr function to determine the cause of the error.

The ddevName parameter is a string of no more than 63 characters that specifies the name of the database extension. The name of the database extension is contained in the database extension file in a resource of type 'STR ' with an ID of 128. For the Data Access Language database extension provided by Apple, for example, this string is “DAL”.

The host parameter specifies the name of the host system on which the data server is located. This name depends on the manner in which the database extension initiates communication with the data server and how the system administrator has set up the computer system.

The user parameter specifies the name of the user, and the password parameter specifies the password associated with the user name.

The connStr parameter is a string that is passed to the data server, which might pass it on to the database management software on the host computer. This string is necessary in some systems to complete log-on procedures.

The asyncPB parameter is a pointer to the asynchronous parameter block. If you do not want to call the function asynchronously, set this parameter to NIL.

Result codes

noErr	0	No error
rcDBError	–802	Error initiating session
rcDBBadDDev	–808	Couldn't find the specified database extension, or error occurred in opening database extension
rcDBAsyncNotSupp	–809	The database extension does not support asynchronous calls
rcDBPackNotInited	–813	The InitDBPack function has not yet been called

```
FUNCTION DBEnd (sessID: LongInt; asyncPB: DBAsyncParmBlkPtr) : OSErr;
```

The DBEnd function terminates a session with a data server and terminates the network connection between the application and the host computer. You must call the DBEnd function to terminate a session.

The sessID parameter is the session ID that was returned by the DBInit function.

The asyncPB parameter is a pointer to the asynchronous parameter block. If you do not want to call the function asynchronously, set this parameter to NIL.

Result codes

noErr	0	No error
rcDBError	–802	Error ending session
rcDBBadSessID	–806	Session ID is invalid
rcDBAsyncNotSupp	–809	The database extension does not support asynchronous calls
rcDBPackNotInited	–813	The InitDBPack function has not yet been called

```
FUNCTION DBGetConnInfo (sessID: LongInt; sessNum: Integer; VAR
                         returnedID,version: LongInt; VAR ddevName:
                         Str63; VAR host,user,network,connStr: Str255;
                         VAR start: LongInt; VAR state: OSErr; asyncPB:
                         DBAsyncParmBlkPtr) : OSErr;
```

The DBGetConnInfo function returns information about the specified session, including

- the version of the database extension
- the name of the host system on which the session is running

- the user name
- the connection string that was used to initiate communication
- the name of the network
- the time at which the session started, in ticks
- the status of the session

In addition, if you include a nonzero value for the sessID parameter when you call the DBGetConnInfo function, the function returns the name of the database extension. If you use 0 for the sessID parameter and specify the database extension and session number instead, the function returns the session ID.

You can use this function to get information about a particular session, or you can call the function repeatedly, incrementing the session number each time, to get information about all of the sessions associated with a particular database extension.

The sessID parameter is the session ID that was returned by the DBInit function. The sessNum parameter is the session number of the session about which you want information. You can specify either the session ID or the session number when you call the DBInit function. If you specify the sessID parameter, use 0 for the sessNum parameter. If you specify the sessNum parameter, then use 0 for the sessID parameter. If you specify the sessNum parameter, you must specify a value for the ddevName parameter as well. If you specify the session number and the database extension, then the DBGetConnInfo function returns the session ID in the returnedID parameter.

The version parameter returns the version number of the database extension that is currently in use.

The ddevName parameter is a string of no more than 63 characters that specifies the name of the database extension. If you specify 0 for the session ID, you must include the name of the database extension as well as a session number. If you specify a valid session ID, then the DBGetConnInfo function returns the name of the database extension in the ddevName parameter. The name of the database extension is contained in the database extension file in a resource of type 'STR ' with an ID of 128. For the Data Access Language database extension provided by Apple, for example, this string is “DAL”.

The host, user, and connStr parameters are the host, user, and connection strings that were used to initiate communication with the data server.

The network parameter is the name of the network through which the database extension is communicating with the data server. This parameter is an empty string if you are not communicating through a network.

The start parameter is the time, in ticks, at which this session was initiated.

The state parameter returns one of the following values to provide information about the status of the session:

```
CONST noErr       =    0;   {no error; ready for more text}
      rcDBValue   = -801;   {output data available}
      rcDBError   = -802;   {execution ended in an error}
      rcDBExec    = -805;   {busy; currently executing query}
```

The asyncPB parameter is a pointer to the asynchronous parameter block. If you do not want to call the function asynchronously, set this parameter to NIL.

Result codes

noErr	0	No error
rcDBBadSessID	–806	Session ID is invalid or database extension name is invalid
rcDBBadSessNum	–807	Invalid session number
rcDBBadDDev	–808	Couldn't find the specified database extension, or error occurred in opening database extension
rcDBAsyncNotSupp	–809	The database extension does not support asynchronous calls
rcDBPackNotInited	–813	The InitDBPack function has not yet been called

```
FUNCTION DBGetSessionNum (sessID: LongInt; VAR sessNum: Integer;
                           asyncPB: DBAsyncParmBlkPtr) : OSErr;
```

The DBGetSessionNum function returns the session number of the session you specify with the sessID parameter. The session number is unique for a particular database extension, but the same session number might be in use for different database extensions at the same time.

The asyncPB parameter is a pointer to the asynchronous parameter block. If you do not want to call the function asynchronously, set this parameter to NIL.

Result codes

noErr	0	No error
rcDBBadSessID	–806	Session ID is invalid
rcDBAsyncNotSupp	–809	The database extension does not support asynchronous calls
rcDBPackNotInited	–813	The InitDBPack function has not yet been called

```
FUNCTION DBKill (asyncPB: DBAsyncParmBlkPtr) : OSErr;
```

The DBKill function cancels the execution of the asynchronous call specified by the asyncPB parameter.

The asyncPB parameter is a pointer to the asynchronous parameter block.

Result codes

noErr	0	Asynchronous routine canceled successfully
rcDBError	–802	Error canceling routine
rcDBBadAsynchPB	–810	Invalid parameter block specified
rcDBPackNotInited	–813	The InitDBPack function has not yet been called

Sending and Executing Queries

The functions in this section send queries or portions of queries to the data server, execute a query that has been sent, return information about queries that have been sent, and halt execution of queries that are executing.

```
FUNCTION DBSend (sessID: LongInt; text: Ptr; len: Integer;
                 asyncPB: DBAsyncParmBlkPtr) : OSErr;
```

The DBSend function sends a query or a portion of a query to the data server. The data server appends this portion of the query to any portion you sent previously. Because the Data Access Manager does not modify the string you send in any way, it does not insert any delimiter between fragments of queries that you send to the data server. If you want a blank or a semicolon to be included between query fragments, or if you want to use return characters to divide the query into lines of text, you must include them in the character string that you send with this function.

The data server does not execute the query until you call the DBExec function.

The sessID parameter is the session ID that was returned by the DBInit function.

The text parameter is a pointer to the query or query fragment that you want to send to the data server. The query or query fragment must be a character string. The len parameter specifies the length of the character string. If the len parameter has a value of –1, then the character string is assumed to be NULL terminated (that is, the string ends with a NULL byte); otherwise, the len parameter specifies the number of bytes in the string.

The asyncPB parameter is a pointer to the asynchronous parameter block. If you do not want to call the function asynchronously, set this parameter to NIL.

Result codes

noErr	0	No error
rcDBError	–802	Error trying to send text
rcDBBadSessID	–806	Session ID is invalid
rcDBAsyncNotSupp	–809	The database extension does not support asynchronous calls
rcDBPackNotInited	–813	The InitDBPack function has not yet been called

```
FUNCTION DBSendItem (sessID: LongInt; dataType: DBType; len,places,
                     flags: Integer; buffer: Ptr; asyncPB:
                     DBAsyncParmBlkPtr) : OSErr;
```

The DBSendItem function sends a single data item to the data server. You can use this function to send to the data server the data that you wish to include in a query. The database extension or the data server (depending on how the system is implemented) converts the data item to a character string and appends it to the query, just as the DBSend function appends a query program fragment to the query. The query is not executed until you call the DBExec function.

The sessID parameter is the session ID that was returned by the DBInit function.

The dataType, len, and places parameters specify the data type, length, and number of decimal places for the data item that you are sending to the data server. The database extension and data server ignore the len parameter if the data type has an implied length. The database extension and data server ignore the places parameter for all values of the dataType parameter except typeDecimal and typeMoney. Data types are discussed in "Getting Query Results" earlier in this chapter.

The buffer parameter is a pointer to the memory location of the data item that you want to send. When you use the DBSendItem function to send an item of data to a data server, the database extension and data server format the data according to the data type, length, and decimal places you specify, convert it to a character string, and append the data to the query.

Set the flags parameter to 0. There are no flags currently defined for the DBSendItem function.

The asyncPB parameter is a pointer to the asynchronous parameter block. If you do not want to call the function asynchronously, set this parameter to NIL.

Result codes

noErr	0	No error
rcDBError	–802	Error trying to send item
rcDBBadSessID	–806	Session ID is invalid
rcDBAsyncNotSupp	–809	The database extension does not support asynchronous calls
rcDBPackNotInited	–813	The InitDBPack function has not yet been called

```
FUNCTION DBExec (sessID: LongInt; asyncPB: DBAsyncParmBlkPtr) : OSErr;
```

The DBExec function initiates execution of a query that you have sent to the data server. Use the DBSend and DBSendItem functions to send a query to the data server. Use the DBState function to determine the status of a query after you have initiated execution.

The sessID parameter is the session ID that was returned by the DBInit function.

The asyncPB parameter is a pointer to the asynchronous parameter block. If you do not want to call the function asynchronously, set this parameter to NIL.

Result codes

noErr	0	Execution has begun
rcDBError	–802	Error trying to begin execution
rcDBBadSessID	–806	Session ID is invalid
rcDBAsyncNotSupp	–809	The database extension does not support asynchronous calls
rcDBPackNotInited	–813	The InitDBPack function has not yet been called

```
FUNCTION DBState (sessID: LongInt; asyncPB: DBAsyncParmBlkPtr) : OSErr;
```

The result code returned by the DBState function indicates the status of the data server. You can use this function to determine whether the data server has successfully executed a query and whether it has data available for you to retrieve.

The sessID parameter is the session ID that was returned by the DBInit function.

The asyncPB parameter is a pointer to the asynchronous parameter block. If you do not want to call the function asynchronously, set this parameter to NIL.

Result codes

noErr	0	No error; ready for more text
rcDBValue	–801	Output data available
rcDBError	–802	Error executing function
rcDBExec	–805	Query currently executing
rcDBBadSessID	–806	Session ID is invalid
rcDBAsyncNotSupp	–809	The database extension does not support asynchronous calls
rcDBPackNotInited	–813	The InitDBPack function has not yet been called

```
FUNCTION DBGetErr (sessID: LongInt; VAR err1,err2: LongInt; VAR item1,
                   item2,errorMsg: Str255; asyncPB: DBAsyncParmBlkPtr) :
                   OSErr;
```

The DBGetErr function retrieves error codes and error messages from a data server. You can use this function to obtain information when a low-level function returns the result code rcDBError. If the DBState function returns the rcDBError result code, indicating that execution of a query ended in an error, the error information can help you debug the query. The meaning of each error code and error message returned by this function depends on the data server with which you are communicating; see the documentation for that data server for more information.

The sessID parameter is the session ID that was returned by the DBInit function.

The err1 and err2 parameters return the primary and secondary error codes. The item1 and item2 parameters return strings that describe the objects of the error message. The errorMsg parameter returns the error message.

The asyncPB parameter is a pointer to the asynchronous parameter block. If you do not want to call the function asynchronously, set this parameter to NIL.

Result codes

noErr	0	No error
rcDBError	–802	Error retrieving error information
rcDBBadSessID	–806	Session ID is invalid
rcDBAsyncNotSupp	–809	The database extension does not support asynchronous calls
rcDBPackNotInited	–813	The InitDBPack function has not yet been called

```
FUNCTION DBBreak (sessID: LongInt; abort: Boolean; asyncPB:
                  DBAsyncParmBlkPtr) : OSErr;
```

The DBBreak function can halt execution of a query and reinitialize the data server, or it can unconditionally terminate a session with a data server. You can use this function to cancel a query if you determine that it is taking too long to complete execution, for example.

The sessID parameter is the session ID that was returned by the DBInit function.

If the abort parameter is TRUE (nonzero), the data server halts any query that is executing and terminates the current session. If the abort parameter is FALSE (0), the data server halts any query that is executing and reinitializes itself.

The asyncPB parameter is a pointer to the asynchronous parameter block. If you do not want to call the function asynchronously, set this parameter to NIL.

Result codes

noErr	0	Execution has begun
rcDBError	–802	Break or abort attempt was unsuccessful
rcDBBadSessID	–806	Session ID is invalid
rcDBAsyncNotSupp	–809	The database extension does not support asynchronous calls
rcDBPackNotInited	–813	The InitDBPack function has not yet been called

Retrieving Results

The functions in this section allow you to retrieve a data item from the data server, to obtain information about the next data item, and to retrieve the same data item more than once.

```
FUNCTION DBGetItem (sessID: LongInt; timeout: LongInt; VAR dataType:
                    DBType; VAR len,places,flags: Integer; buffer: Ptr;
                    asyncPB: DBAsyncParmBlkPtr) : OSErr;
```

The DBGetItem function retrieves the next data item from the data server. You can also use this function to obtain information about the next data item without retrieving the data. You can use the DBGetItem function after you have executed a query and the DBState function has returned the rcDBValue result code, indicating that data is available. You can repeat the DBGetItem function as many times as is necessary to retrieve all of the data returned by the data source in response to a query.

The sessID parameter is the session ID that was returned by the DBInit function.

You can use the timeout parameter to specify the maximum amount of time that the database extension should wait to receive results from the data server before canceling the function. Specify the timeout parameter in sixtieths of a second. To disable the timeout feature, set the timeout parameter to the kDBWaitForever constant. If the timeout period expires, the DBGetItem function returns the rcDBBreak result code. The DBGetItem function ignores the timeout parameter if you call the function asynchronously.

One use for the timeout parameter is to call the DBGetItem function periodically with a short value set for this parameter in order to return control to your application while a query is executing. Your application can then retrieve the next data item as soon as execution of the query is complete without having to call the DBState function to determine when data is available.

You can set the dataType parameter to specify the data type that you expect the next data item to be. If the item is not of the expected data type, the database extension returns the rcDBBadType result code. If you want to retrieve the next data item regardless of type, set the dataType parameter to the typeAnyType constant. To skip the next data item, set the dataType parameter to the typeDiscard constant. The data server sets the dataType parameter to the actual type of the data item when it retrieves the data item or returns information about the data item. Data types are discussed in "Getting Query Results" earlier in this chapter.

Set the len parameter to the length of the data buffer pointed to by the buffer parameter. If you use the DBGetItem function to obtain information only (by setting the buffer parameter to NIL), then the data server ignores the len parameter. The data server sets the len parameter to the actual length of the data item when it retrieves the data item or returns information about the data item.

The data server returns in the places parameter the number of decimal places in data items of types typeMoney and typeDecimal. For all other data types, the data server returns 0 for the places parameter.

The buffer parameter is a pointer to the location where you want the retrieved data item to be stored. You must ensure that the location you specify contains enough space for the data item that will be returned. To determine the data type, length, and number of decimal places of the next data item without retrieving it, specify NIL for the buffer parameter.

If the least significant bit of the flags parameter is set to 1, the data item is in the last column of the row. If the third bit of this parameter is set to 1, the data item is NULL. You can use the constants kDBLastColFlag and kDBNullFlag to test for these flag bits.

The asyncPB parameter is a pointer to the asynchronous parameter block. If you do not want to call the function asynchronously, set this parameter to NIL.

Result codes

noErr	0	No error; no next data item
rcDBNull	–800	The data item was NULL
rcDBValue	–801	A nonzero data item was successfully retrieved
rcDBError	–802	Execution ended in an error
rcDBBadType	–803	Next data item not of requested data type
rcDBBreak	–804	Function timed out
rcDBBadSessID	–806	Session ID is invalid
rcDBAsyncNotSupp	–809	The database extension does not support asynchronous calls
rcDBPackNotInited	–813	The InitDBPack function has not yet been called

```
FUNCTION DBUnGetItem (sessID: LongInt; asyncPB: DBAsyncParmBlkPtr) :
                       OSErr;
```

The DBUnGetItem function reverses the effect of the last call to the DBGetItem function, in the sense that the next time you call the DBGetItem function it retrieves the same item a second time. It does not remove the just-retrieved data item from the input buffer. The DBUnGetItem function can reverse the effect of only one call to the DBGetItem function; you cannot use it to step back through several previously retrieved data items.

The sessID parameter is the session ID that was returned by the DBInit function.

The asyncPB parameter is a pointer to the asynchronous parameter block. If you do not want to call the function asynchronously, set this parameter to NIL.

Result codes

noErr	0	No error
rcDBError	–802	Error executing function
rcDBBadSessID	–806	Session ID is invalid
rcDBAsyncNotSupp	–809	The database extension does not support asynchronous calls
rcDBPackNotInited	–813	The InitDBPack function has not yet been called

Installing and Removing Result Handlers

The functions in this section install, remove, and return pointers to result handlers. Result handlers are discussed in "Converting Query Results to Text" earlier in this chapter.

```
FUNCTION DBInstallResultHandler (dataType: DBType; theHandler: ProcPtr;
                                 isSysHandler: Boolean) : OSErr;
```

The DBInstallResultHandler function installs a result handler for the data type specified by the dataType parameter. The result handler is then used by the DBResultsToText function to convert data of the specified type into a character string.

The parameter theHandler is a pointer to the result handler. The isSysHandler parameter specifies whether the result handler is an application result handler—to be used only when the DBResultsToText function is called by the application that installed the result handler—or a system result handler—to be used by every application running on the system. If the isSysHandler parameter is TRUE, the result handler is a system result handler.

When you install an application result handler, it replaces any result handler with the same name previously installed by that application. Similarly, when you install a system result handler, it replaces any existing system result handler with the same name. Before you temporarily replace an existing result handler, use the DBGetResultHandler function to obtain a pointer to the present handler, and save the present result handler in your application's private storage. Then you can reinstall the original result handler when you are finished using the temporary one.

Because an application result handler is used in preference to a system result handler if both are available, you can temporarily replace a system result handler for purposes of your application by installing an application result handler for the same data type. You can then use the DBRemoveResultHandler function to remove the application result handler and return to using the system result handler whenever you wish.

Result codes

noErr	0	No error
rcDBPackNotInited	–813	The InitDBPack function has not yet been called

```
FUNCTION DBGetResultHandler (dataType: DBType; VAR theHandler: ProcPtr;
                              getSysHandler: Boolean) : OSErr;
```

The DBGetResultHandler function returns a pointer to a result handler for the data type specified with the dataType parameter. The pointer is returned in the parameter theHandler.

If you set the getSysHandler parameter to FALSE (0), the function returns a pointer to the current application result handler for the specified data type, or it returns NIL if there is no application result handler for that data type. If you set the getSysHandler parameter to TRUE (nonzero), the function returns a pointer to the current system result handler for the specified data type, or it returns NIL if there is no system result handler for that data type.

You can use this function to obtain a pointer to a result handler so that you can use it to convert to text an individual data item retrieved by the DBGetItem function. The DBGetQueryResults function automatically converts to text all of the data pointed to by the results record.

Result codes

noErr	0	No error
rcDBNoHandler	–811	There is no handler for this data type installed for the current application
rcDBPackNotInited	–813	The InitDBPack function has not yet been called

```
FUNCTION DBRemoveResultHandler (dataType: DBType) : OSErr;
```

The DBRemoveResultHandler function removes from memory the application result handler for the data type that you specify with the dataType parameter. This function cannot remove a system result handler.

Result codes

noErr	0	No error
rcDBNoHandler	–811	There is no handler for this data type installed for the current application
rcDBPackNotInited	–813	The InitDBPack function has not yet been called

SUMMARY OF THE DATA ACCESS MANAGER

Constants

```
CONST {DBStartQuery status messages}
      kDBUpdateWind          = 0;   {update windows}
      kDBAboutToInit         = 1;   {about to call DBInit}
      kDBInitComplete        = 2;   {DBInit has completed}
      kDBSendComplete        = 3;   {DBSend has completed}
      kDBExecComplete        = 4;   {DBExec has completed}
      kDBStartQueryComplete  = 5;   {DBStartQuery is about to complete}

      {DBGetQueryResults status messages}
      kDBGetItemComplete          = 6; {DBGetItem has completed}
      kDBGetQueryResultsComplete = 7; {DBGetQueryResults has completed}

      {data types}
      typeAnyType       = 0;        {can be any data type}
      typeNone          = 'none';   {no more data expected}
      typeBoolean       = 'bool';   {Boolean}
      typeSMInt         = 'shor';   {short integer}
      typeInteger       = 'long';   {integer}
      typeSMFloat       = 'sing';   {short floating point}
      typeFloat         = 'doub';   {floating point}
      typeDate          = 'date';   {date}
      typeTime          = 'time';   {time}
      typeTimeStamp     = 'tims';   {date and time}
      typeChar          = 'TEXT';   {character}
      typeDecimal       = 'deci';   {decimal number}
      typeMoney         = 'mone';   {money value}
      typeVChar         = 'vcha';   {variable character}
      typeVBin          = 'vbin';   {variable binary}
      typeLChar         = 'lcha';   {long character}
      typeLBin          = 'lbin';   {long binary}
      typeDiscard       = 'disc';   {discard next data item}
      typeUnknown       = 'unkn';   {result handler for unknown data type}
      typeColBreak      = 'colb';   {result handler for column break}
      typeRowBreak      = 'rowb';   {result handler for end of line}

      kDBWaitForever    = -1;       {infinite timeout value for DBGetItem}
      kDBLastColFlag    = $0001;    {data item is last column of the row}
      kDBNullFlag       = $0004;    {data item is NULL}

      noErr             =    0;     {no error; ready for more text}
      rcDBValue         = -801;     {output data available}
      rcDBError         = -802;     {execution ended in an error}
      rcDBExec          = -805;     {busy; currently executing query}
```

Data Types

```
TYPE DBType =            OSType;   {data type}

     DBAsyncParamBlockRec =
     RECORD
        completionProc: ProcPtr;  {pointer to completion routine}
        result:         OSErr;    {result of call}
        userRef:        LongInt;  {reserved for use by application}
        ddevRef:        LongInt;  {reserved for use by database extension}
        reserved:       LongInt   {reserved for use by Data Access Mgr}
     END;

     DBAsyncParmBlkPtr = ^DBAsyncParamBlockRec;

     QueryArray = ARRAY[0..255] OF Handle;
     QueryListPtr = ^QueryArray;
     QueryListHandle = ^QueryListPtr;

     ResListElem =
     RECORD
        theType:        ResType;          {resource type}
        id:             Integer           {resource ID}
     END;

     ResListArray = ARRAY[0..255] OF ResListElem;
     ResListPtr = ^ResListArray;
     ResListHandle = ^ResListPtr;

     QueryPtr = ^QueryRecord;
     QueryHandle = ^QueryPtr;

     QueryRecord =
     RECORD
        version:        Integer;          {query record format version}
        id:             Integer;          {resource ID of 'qrsc'}
        queryProc:      Handle;           {handle to qdef}
        ddevName:       Str63;            {name of database extension}
        host:           Str255;           {name of host computer}
        user:           Str255;           {name of user}
        password:       Str255;           {user's password}
        connStr:        Str255;           {connection string}
        currQuery:      Integer;          {current query}
        numQueries:     Integer;          {number of queries}
        queryList:      QueryListHandle;  {handles to queries}
        numRes:         Integer;          {number of resources}
        resList:        ResListHandle;    {list of resources}
        dataHandle:     Handle;           {handle to memory for qdef}
        refCon:         LongInt           {reserved for use by app}
     END;
```

```
ResultsRecord =
RECORD
   numRows:        Integer;          {number of rows retrieved}
   numCols:        Integer;          {number of columns per row}
   colTypes:       ColTypesHandle;   {type of data in each column}
   colData:        Handle;           {array of data items}
   colInfo:        ColInfoHandle     {info about each data item}
END;

ColTypesPtr = ^ColTypesArray;
ColTypesHandle = ^ColTypesPtr;
ColTypesArray = ARRAY[0..255] OF DBType;


DBColInfoRecord =
RECORD
   len:            Integer;          {length of data item}
   places:         Integer;          {places for decimal and money }
                                     { data items}
   flags:          Integer           {flags for data item}
END;
ColInfoPtr = ^ColInfoArray;
ColInfoHandle = ^ColInfoPtr;
ColInfoArray = ARRAY[0..255] OF DBColInfoRecord;
```

Routines

Initializing the Data Access Manager

```
FUNCTION InitDBPack          : OSErr;
```

High-Level Interface: Handling Query Documents

```
FUNCTION DBGetNewQuery      (queryID: Integer; VAR query: QueryHandle) :
                             OSErr;

FUNCTION DBDisposeQuery     (query: QueryHandle) : OSErr;

FUNCTION DBStartQuery       (VAR sessID: LongInt; query: QueryHandle;
                             statusProc: ProcPtr; asyncPB:
                             DBAsyncParmBlkPtr) : OSErr;
```

High-Level Interface: Handling Query Results

```
FUNCTION DBGetQueryResults (sessID: LongInt; VAR results: ResultsRecord;
                            timeout: LongInt; statusProc: ProcPtr; asyncPB:
                            DBAsyncParmBlkPtr) : OSErr;

FUNCTION DBResultsToText   (results: ResultsRecord; VAR theText: Handle)
                            : OSErr;
```

Low-Level Interface: Controlling the Session

```
FUNCTION DBInit            (VAR sessID: LongInt; ddevName: Str63; host,
                            user,password,connStr: Str255; asyncPB:
                            DBAsyncParmBlkPtr) : OSErr;

FUNCTION DBEnd             (sessID: LongInt; asyncPB: DBAsyncParmBlkPtr)
                            : OSErr;

FUNCTION DBGetConnInfo     (sessID: LongInt; sessNum: Integer; VAR
                            returnedID,version: LongInt; VAR ddevName:
                            Str63; VAR host,user,network,connStr: Str255;
                            VAR start: LongInt; VAR state: OSErr;
                            asyncPB: DBAsyncParmBlkPtr) : OSErr;

FUNCTION DBGetSessionNum   (sessID: LongInt; VAR sessNum: Integer;
                            asyncPB: DBAsyncParmBlkPtr) : OSErr;

FUNCTION DBKill            (asyncPB: DBAsyncParmBlkPtr) : OSErr;
```

Low-Level Interface: Sending and Executing Queries

```
FUNCTION DBSend            (sessID: LongInt; text: Ptr; len: Integer;
                            asyncPB: DBAsyncParmBlkPtr) : OSErr;

FUNCTION DBSendItem        (sessID: LongInt; dataType: DBType; len,
                            places,flags: Integer; buffer: Ptr; asyncPB:
                            DBAsyncParmBlkPtr) : OSErr;

FUNCTION DBExec            (sessID: LongInt; asyncPB: DBAsyncParmBlkPtr)
                            : OSErr;

FUNCTION DBState           (sessID: LongInt; asyncPB: DBAsyncParmBlkPtr)
                            : OSErr;

FUNCTION DBGetErr          (sessID: LongInt; VAR err1,err2: LongInt; VAR
                            item1,item2,errorMsg: Str255; asyncPB:
                            DBAsyncParmBlkPtr) : OSErr;

FUNCTION DBBreak           (sessID: LongInt; abort: Boolean; asyncPB:
                            DBAsyncParmBlkPtr) : OSErr;
```

Low-Level Interface: Retrieving Results

```
FUNCTION DBGetItem          (sessID: LongInt; timeout: LongInt; VAR
                             dataType: DBType; VAR len,places,flags:
                             Integer; buffer: Ptr; asyncPB:
                             DBAsyncParmBlkPtr) : OSErr;

FUNCTION DBUnGetItem        (sessID: LongInt; asyncPB: DBAsyncParmBlkPtr)
                             : OSErr;
```

Installing and Removing Result Handlers

```
FUNCTION DBInstallResultHandler (dataType: DBType; theHandler: ProcPtr;
                                 isSysHandler: Boolean) : OSErr;

FUNCTION DBGetResultHandler     (dataType: DBType; VAR theHandler: ProcPtr;
                                 getSysHandler: Boolean) : OSErr;

FUNCTION DBRemoveResultHandler  (dataType: DBType) : OSErr;
```

Application-Defined Routines

```
FUNCTION MyStatusFunc       (message: Integer; result: OSErr;
                             dataLen,dataPlaces,dataFlags: Integer;
                             dataType: DBType; dataPtr: Ptr) : Boolean;

FUNCTION MyResultHandler    (dataType: DBType; theLen,thePlaces,theFlags:
                             Integer; theData: Ptr; theText: Handle) :
                             OSErr;

FUNCTION MyQDef             (VAR sessID: LongInt; query: QueryHandle) :
                             OSErr;
```

Result Codes

noErr	0	No error
userCanceledErr	–128	User canceled the query
rcDBNull	–800	The data item was NULL
rcDBValue	–801	Data available or successfully retrieved
rcDBError	–802	Error executing function
rcDBBadType	–803	Next data item not of requested data type
rcDBBreak	–804	Function timed out
rcDBExec	–805	Query currently executing
rcDBBadSessID	–806	Session ID is invalid
rcDBBadSessNum	–807	Invalid session number
rcDBBadDDev	–808	Couldn't find the specified database extension, or error occurred in opening database extension

rcDBAsyncNotSupp	–809	The database extension does not support asynchronous calls
rcDBBadAsynchPB	–810	Invalid parameter block specified
rcDBNoHandler	–811	There is no handler for this data type installed for the current application
rcDBWrongVersion	–812	Wrong version number
rcDBPackNotInited	–813	The InitDBPack function has not yet been called

Assembly-Language Information

Asynchronous Parameter Block Data Structure

completionProc	long	pointer to completion routine
result	word	result of call
userRef	long	for application's use
ddevRef	long	for database extension's use
reserved	long	for internal use

Data Structure for Resource List in Query Record

theType	long	resource type
id	word	resource ID

Query Record Data Structure

version	word	version
id	word	ID of 'qrsc' this came from
queryProc	long	handle to query def proc
ddevName	64 bytes	database extension name
host	256 bytes	host
user	256 bytes	user
password	256 bytes	other connection info
currQuery	word	current query
numQueries	word	number of queries in query list
queryList	long	handle to list of queries
numRes	word	number of resources in resource list
resList	long	handle to list of other resources
dataHandle	long	data used by query def proc
refCon	long	query's reference value

Results Record Data Structure

numRows	word	number of rows in result
numCols	word	number of columns per row
colTypes	long	data type array
colData	long	actual results
colLens	long	length array

Trap Macros Requiring Routine Selectors

_Pack13

Selector	Routine
$0100	InitDBPack
$020E	DBKill
$0210	DBDisposeQuery
$0215	DBRemoveResultHandler
$030F	DBGetNewQuery
$0403	DBEnd
$0408	DBExec
$0409	DBState
$040D	DBUnGetItem
$0413	DBResultsToText
$050B	DBBreak
$0514	DBInstallResultHandler
$0516	DBGetResultHandler
$0605	DBGetSessionNum
$0706	DBSend
$0811	DBStartQuery
$0A12	DBGetQueryResults
$0B07	DBSendItem
$0E02	DBInit
$0E0A	DBGetErr
$100C	DBGetItem
$1704	DBGetConnInfo

9 THE FINDER INTERFACE

ABOUT THIS CHAPTER

The Finder™ is an application that works with the system software to manage the user's desktop display. This chapter describes how your application interacts with the Finder. This chapter replaces the Finder Interface chapters in Volumes III and IV.

Read this chapter to learn how to

- set up the resources the Finder needs to display and start up your application
- make your application compatible with the new interface features of the Finder
- use the new organization of the System Folder and its related directories
- check or change Finder-related information stored in a volume's catalog
- read a volume's database of icons, applications, and comments

To use this chapter, you should already be familiar with resources. Resources are collections of data—such as menus, icons, and dialog box messages—and the code used by an application or by the system software. The Resource Manager chapter in Volume I introduces resources, and the Resource Manager chapters in Volumes IV, V, and VI describe updates to the Resource Manager.

This chapter does not explain how to use Apple® events to communicate with the Finder. When a user opens or prints a file from the Finder, the Finder sends your application information so that your application can open or print the file. In system software version 7.0, applications that support high-level events receive this information through the required Apple events.

Refer to the Apple Event Manager chapter in this volume for instructions on how your application should respond to the required Apple events: Open Application, Open Documents, Print Documents, and Quit Application. By supporting these Apple events, your application can take advantage of the more reliable launch and termination mechanisms built into system software version 7.0. In addition, your application can use another set of Apple events—called Finder events—to request services from the Finder. For example, your application can ask the Finder to perform such operations as launching another application on your behalf. See the *Apple Event Registry* for the definitions of Finder events that your application may wish to support.

ABOUT THE FINDER INTERFACE

The Finder is an application that manages the user's desktop interface. It displays icons representing your application and the documents it creates, and it tracks user activity on the desktop. When appropriate, the Finder starts up your application and tells it what documents to open or print. To perform these tasks, the Finder relies on information you provide through resources. When the user creates or installs a file, the File Manager initially stores some of this information in the volume catalog; the Finder extracts this information from the catalog and builds a desktop database for quick access to your resource information. This chapter describes how to create the resources the Finder needs to build its desktop database, and how to gain access to relevant data in the catalog and the desktop database. This chapter also discusses other Finder-related information that could be of interest to you.

Like the rest of the Macintosh® computer's system software, the Finder has become both more powerful and more complicated since it was first released. The Finder includes a number of new user interface features that have a small impact on applications.

The original desktop display was designed for a black-and-white monitor. In system software version 7.0, you can provide the Finder with color versions of your icons. You can also define what the small versions of your icons should look like. (Before version 7.0, the Finder scaled icons to half size.)

If your application supports the new stationery pad, Edition Manager, or Data Access Manager features, you can create icons that distinguish the stationery pads, editions, or query documents that users create with your application. You might also like your application to take advantage of customized document icons. If, instead of producing an application, you produce and distribute information documents (such as database files, stationery pads, query documents, clip art libraries, or dictionaries) to be used by other applications, you can also provide icons that distinguish your documents.

To take advantage of the new stationery pad feature when opening a document from the Standard File Package, your application should check a Finder flag for the document to determine if the document is stationery.

If your application bypasses the Finder or the Standard File Package when opening files of any type, it should use the ResolveAliasFile function to open the correct file.

Users of system software version 7.0 no longer utilize the Font/DA Mover for installing fonts, desk accessories, or other system resources. If you're thinking about producing desk accessories, you should probably create small applications instead because there will be little distinction to users between desk accessories and applications. If you plan to produce fonts, sounds, keyboard layouts, or script system resource collections, you need to provide them to users as movable resource files; users of version 7.0 can install them by dragging their icons to the System Folder icon instead of using the Font/DA Mover.

Users of system software version 7.0 have access to on-line assistance in the form of help balloons. You can customize the help balloon that system software displays for your application icon.

In version 7.0, the System Folder contains a set of folders for storing related files. If your application needs to store a file in the System Folder, put it in one of the new directories described in this chapter. The Toolbox provides a new function, FindFolder, to help your application utilize this new organization.

For each volume, the system software has always maintained a central database of information used by the Finder. In version 7.0, that database is available to your application through a set of Desktop Manager routines.

An important function of the Finder is to start up your application whenever the user opens it from the Finder and whenever the user asks to open or print a document that has been created by your application. "Messages When the Finder Can't Find Your Application" later in this chapter describes what happens when the Finder can't find your application.

Macintosh system software originally ran only one application at a time. System software version 7.0 lets users run multiple applications simultaneously. (In previous versions of system software, the MultiFinder® option provided this feature.) Your application is now expected to provide the Finder with the information it needs to manage your application in a shared-memory environment, as explained in the Compatibility Guidelines and Event Manager chapters of this volume.

To help you make the best use of the Finder, this chapter

- describes the resources that the Finder uses to extract information about your application and documents (Generally, all applications should provide these resources for their files.)
- introduces the new Finder features that might affect your application (Generally, most applications should take advantage of some or all of these new features.)
- details the Finder information structure stored in a volume's catalog (Generally, most applications need to determine—and many might wish to set—information in the catalog.)
- describes the new directories typically located in the System Folder and tells you how to access them (Generally, many applications will want to access these new folders.)
- explains how to gain access to a volume's database of icons, applications, and comments (Generally, very few applications need to access this information because the Finder maintains and displays it.)

FINDER-RELATED RESOURCES

The Finder needs quick access to some key information about your application, including its signature and the icons to display for it and for the documents it creates. You supply most of this information in the resource fork of your application file.

The Finder extracts this information and uses it to maintain its own central database of the resources it needs. The Finder records the location of your application on disk in this database so that it can find your application quickly when the user opens one of your documents.

For compatibility with the Finder, your application should have

- a signature resource, so that the Finder can identify and start up your application when a user double-clicks documents created by your application
- a set of icon resources, to visually represent for the user your application and any documents it creates
- a set of file reference resources, to link icons with the files types they represent and to allow users to launch your application by dragging document icons to your application icon
- a bundle resource, to group together your application's signature, icon, and file reference resources

- a size resource, to tell the Finder how much memory to allocate for your application when it starts up and whether your application supports various system software features
- either a name string resource in your application's documents (to display the name of your application if the user tries to open or print a document created by your application when your application is missing) or a message string resource in your application's documents (to explain why the user can't open or print a document used by your application)

Note: Supply a name string resource for documents that you intend for users to open with your application; supply a message string resource for documents (such as a preferences file) that your application uses but which users shouldn't open. You supply only one of these resources in a document—never both.

Your application can also make use of these resources:

- version resources, so that users can easily find out the version of your application and, if applicable, the version of your application's superset of files
- a help resource, which the Finder uses to display your customized Balloon Help™ message for your application, control panel, system extension, or desk accessory icon

If you sell or distribute data in the form of a document to be used by other applications, you can assist users by providing

- an appropriate file type to allow users to open your document from the Finder by dragging its icon to an application icon or by choosing the Open command from the File menu within an application
- a family of icon resources to represent your document to the user
- a name string resource or message string resource, so the Finder can assist users who try to open or print your documents from the Finder
- version resources, so that users can easily find out the version of your application and, if your application file is one of a larger collection of files, the version of the entire superset of files

These resources are described in the following sections.

Creators, File Types, and the Signature Resource

The Finder identifies your application through its **signature,** a unique, four-character sequence. The signature must not conflict with the signature of any other application. To ensure uniqueness, you must register your application's signature with Apple Computer, Inc. at Macintosh Developer Technical Support.

Note: There is no need to register your own resource types because they're usually used in your own applications or documents only.

You must include in your resource file a special resource that has the application's signature as its resource type. By convention, the signature resource has a resource ID of 0. The signature resource typically contains a string that specifies the name, version number, and release date of your application. If you do not provide specific version information through a 'vers' resource (described in "Version Resources" later in this chapter), the Finder displays the string stored in the signature resource when the user selects your application and chooses Get Info from the File menu.

The following sample code illustrates a signature resource in Rez input format. (Rez is the resource compiler provided with Apple's Macintosh Programming Workshop [MPW®], available from APDA®.)

```
type 'WAVE' as 'STR ';                  /* WAVE is the signature */
resource 'WAVE' (0, purgeable) {        /* resource ID is 0 */
   "MyApplication 2.0 © 1991"           /* default Get Info string */
};
```

Note: The signature resource alone is not sufficient to fully establish your application's signature. You must also supply a bundle resource, described in "The Bundle Resource" later in this chapter.

Whenever your application creates a document, it assigns the document a creator and a file type. Typically, as described in "Finder Information in the Volume Catalog" later in this chapter, your application sets its signature as the document's creator. When a user double-clicks a document or selects it and chooses Open or Print from the Finder's File menu, the Finder reads the creator field of that file to find the document's creator. The Finder then searches for an application with a signature by that name. When it finds that application, the Finder launches that application.

If the document's creator is your application's signature, for example, the Finder calls the Process Manager to start your application. The Finder sets up the information your application needs to open or print the document. In version 7.0, applications that support high-level events (that is, have the isHighLevelEventAware flag set in the 'SIZE' resource) receive the Finder information through Apple events. The Apple Event Manager chapter in this volume describes how your application processes Apple events to open or print files.

Applications that do not support high-level events can use the CountAppFiles, GetAppFiles, and ClrAppFiles procedures or the GetAppParms procedure to get the Finder information. See the Segment Loader chapter of Volume II for information on these routines.

As described in "Finder Information in the Volume Catalog" later in this chapter, your application typically assigns a file type to a document when it creates one. The file type can be a type especially defined for your application, or it can be one of the existing general types, such as those listed here.

File type	Description
'APPL'	Launchable application
'DFIL'	File for storing desk accessories
'DRVR'	Driver

File type	Description
'FFIL'	File for storing fonts
'INIT'	System extension
'PICT'	QuickDraw™ picture
'PRER'	Printer driver
'RDEV'	Chooser extension
'TEXT'	Stream of ASCII characters
'adev'	Network extension (like EtherTalk® 2.0)
'appe'	Background-only application
'cdev'	Control panel
'edtp'	Edition for sharing graphics-oriented data
'edts'	Edition for sharing sound-oriented data
'edtt'	Edition for sharing text-oriented data
'ffil'	Font
'ifil'	Script system resource collection
'kfil'	Keyboard layout
'pref'	Preferences file
'qery'	Query document for database access
'scri'	System extension for script systems
'sfil'	Sound
'tfil'	TrueType™ font
'ttro'	TeachText read-only file
'zsys'	A system file (such as the System file itself)

Note: Apple reserves the use of all signatures and file types whose names contain only lowercase and nonalphabetic characters. Your signature and the file types created especially for your application must contain at least one uppercase character. Since the system software never displays signatures and file types to users, signatures and file types can consist of character combinations that are incomprehensible to anyone but you.

Like signatures, file types must be registered with Apple. Your application must have a file type of 'APPL'. The creator field of your application file should contain its own signature. Most programming environments provide a simple tool for setting the creator field of your application file.

Your application can create documents of any type, and it can specify any application as the creator. You could write a utility application, for example, that creates a new document by opening one text file and appending onto it another text file. The application would give the new document the same creator as the first original text file so that the Finder can call on that application when the user wants to open or print the new document.

Assign the standard file type 'TEXT' to files that consist only of text—that is, a stream of characters with return characters at the ends of paragraphs. Most word processors allow the user to create text-only files. A document of file type 'TEXT' can be opened or printed by any application that accepts such file types. Your application can still assign its own signature as the file's creator so that the Finder can call on it to open or print the file when appropriate.

Users can also open a document created by your application—as well as a document of a file type supported by your application—by selecting its icon and dragging it to your application's icon. Because the document's file type is stored in the catalog and the Finder stores a list of your application's supported file types in the desktop database, the Finder can determine whether to launch your application. If the document's file type is supported by your application, the Finder launches your application and passes it the name of the document. (These topics are detailed in subsequent sections of this chapter.)

For example, if your application is a page layout program, it might create documents of its own file type while also supporting documents of 'TEXT' and 'PICT' file types. A user can launch your application by dragging a document of any of these file types to your application icon.

Your application also relies on file types to determine which files to let the user open when your application is running. When your application calls the Standard File Package to open a file, your application supplies either a list of the file types that your application can open or a filter function for those types. The open file dialog box then displays only files of the specified types. (See the Standard File Package chapter in this volume for details.)

Icon Resources

The Finder represents your files as icons. To distinguish your product on the desktop, you can design your own icons for all the files associated with your application, including

- your application file itself
- standard documents created by your application
- stationery pads that users create from your application's documents
- data-sharing editions that users create from your application's documents
- other special documents, such as read-only, graphics, and query documents, which are either created by your Macintosh application or provided by you for use by other Macintosh applications

For most effective display, you should create an icon family for each of your files. An **icon family** is the set of icons that represent a single object, such as an application or document, on the desktop. An entire icon family consists of

- a large (32-by-32 pixel) black-and-white icon and mask (resource type 'ICN#')
- a small (16-by-16 pixel) black-and-white icon and mask (resource type 'ics#')
- a large (32-by-32 pixel) color icon with 4 bits of color data per pixel (resource type 'icl4')
- a small (16-by-16 pixel) color icon with 4 bits of color data per pixel (resource type 'ics4')
- a large (32-by-32 pixel) color icon with 8 bits of color data per pixel (resource type 'icl8')
- a small (16-by-16 pixel) color icon with 8 bits of color data per pixel (resource type 'ics8')

If you do not design your own icons, the Finder uses a set of its own default application and document icons for display. Figure 9-1 shows the Finder's default large black-and-white icons. Note that the Finder in system software version 7.0 also displays desk accessories with icons.

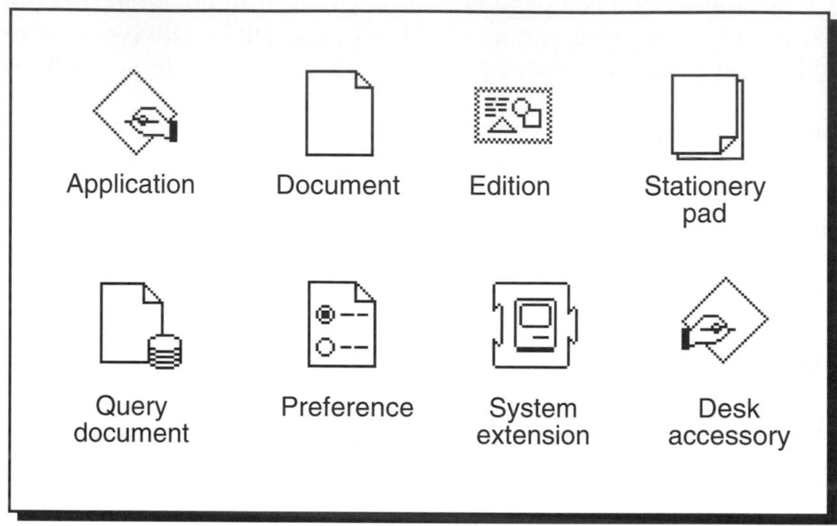

Figure 9-1. Default large black-and-white icons

If you don't want the Finder to display the default icons for your application, desk accessory, or documents, you must at least define an 'ICN#' resource (called an *icon list*) for each icon. The two icons defined in the 'ICN#' resource are a 32-by-32 pixel, black-and-white icon and its mask. You can also define color and 16-by-16 pixel icons in other resources described in this section. (If you don't define color icons, the Finder displays the black-and-white icon defined in your 'ICN#' resource on all displays, and if you don't define 16-by-16 pixel icons, the Finder algorithmically reduces the 32-by-32 pixel icon to half size when needed.)

An 'ICN#' resource defines one desktop icon. It contains two icon descriptions: the actual icon for display on the desktop and an all-black mask that shows the area covered by the icon. The Finder uses the mask to crop the icon's outline into whatever background color or pattern is on the desktop. The Finder then draws the icon into this shape. Therefore, it's important that the mask be exactly the same shape as the icon. The mask also defines the area that users need to click to select the icon. Therefore, it's best not to have any holes in the mask; otherwise, users may have trouble selecting your icon. Figure 9-2 shows an application icon and its mask.

Figure 9-2. An application icon and its mask

An 'ICN#' resource is defined to be an array of String[128]. Typically, you use a high-level tool like the ResEdit™ application, which is available through APDA, to create your 'ICN#' resources. Figure 9-3 shows how the 'ICN#' resource for the icon and mask in Figure 9-2 was created using the ResEdit icon editor.

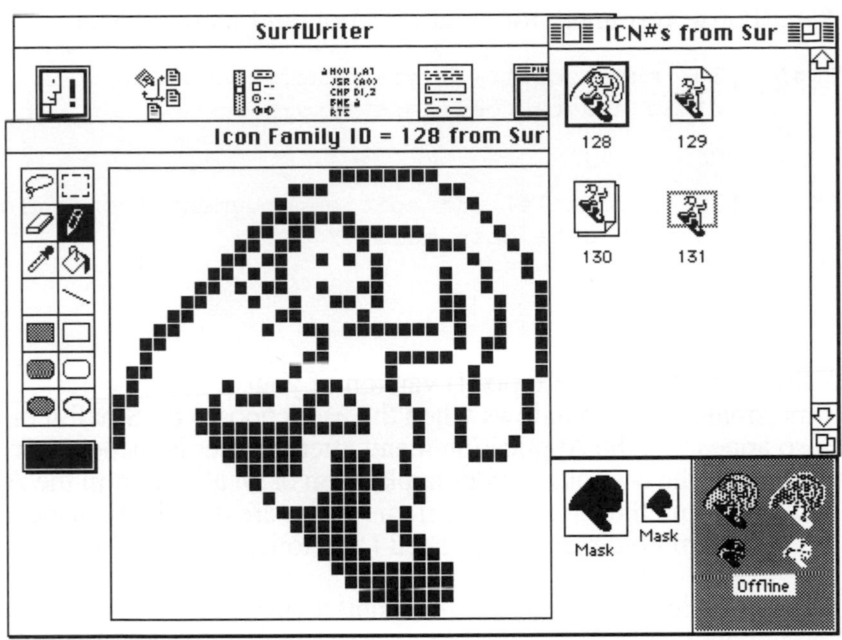

Figure 9-3. The ResEdit view of an icon and its mask

When you are satisfied with the appearance of your icons, you typically use the DeRez decompiler to convert your 'ICN#' resources into Rez input. Listing 9-1 is a partial listing of the Rez input for the 'ICN#' resources shown in Figure 9-3. This listing and those that follow in this chapter use Rez format to help you understand the format of the resources and see how they work together.

Listing 9-1. 'ICN#' resources for an application and its documents

```
resource 'ICN#' (128, purgeable) {   /* application icon and mask */
   {                       /* array: 2 elements */
                           /* first element: the application icon */
      $"00 11 E2 00"       /* each line holds 4 bytes (32 bits) */
      .                    /* 32 lines total for icon */
      .
      .
      $"00 00 0F 00"       /* 32nd line of icon */
      ,                    /* second element: the mask */
      $"00 00 FF 00
      .                    /* 32 lines total for icon */
      .
      .
      $"00 00 0F 00"       /* 32nd line of mask */
   }
};
resource 'ICN#' (129, purgeable) {   /* text document icon and mask */
   {               /* icon data goes here */
   }
};
```

(Continued)

Listing 9-1. 'ICN#' resources for an application and its documents (Continued)

```
resource 'ICN#' (130, purgeable) {/* stationery document icon and mask */
   {              /* icon data goes here */
   }
};
resource 'ICN#' (131, purgeable) {/* edition document icon and mask */
   {              /* icon data goes here */
   }
};
```

You can also define a small (16-by-16 pixel) version of your icon in the 'ics#' resource. The Finder displays the small icon in windows when the user chooses by Small Icon from the View menu. It also appears in the Application menu after the user launches your application and in the Apple menu if the user places your application or an alias to it in the Apple Menu Items folder. (Alias files and the Apple Menu Items folder are described, respectively, in "Aliases" and "The System Folder and Its Related Directories" later in this chapter.)

You can define color versions of both large and small icons by using several resource types. The resource for each icon variation has the same resource ID as the 'ICN#' resource that defines the large black-and-white icon. For example, if the resource ID of your application icon's 'ICN#' resource is 128, its small black-and-white icon resource, 'ics#', should have a resource ID of 128; and the 'icl4', 'ics4', 'icl8', and 'ics8' resources should also have resource IDs of 128.

Don't define masks for your color icon resources. The 'icl4' and 'icl8' resources use the black-and-white icon mask defined in their companion 'ICN#' resource, and the 'ics4' and 'ics8' resources use the black-and-white icon mask defined in their companion 'ics#' resource. Because of this, the outline shapes of your color icons should exactly match those defined in your 'ICN#' and 'ics#' resources.

ResEdit 2.1 includes an icon family editor to help you easily manage the creation of these related resources. See the *ResEdit Reference* for details.

See the User Interface Guidelines chapter in this volume for information about the most effective use of color and shape for your icons. Choose your colors from the 36 recommended icon colors in the system palette. (If you use ResEdit 2.1, these colors appear in a palette when you choose Apple Icon Colors from the Color menu.) Note that you cannot specify your own color table for these as you can with the 'cicn' resources described in the Color QuickDraw chapter of Volume V.

For more information about color palettes, see the Graphics Overview, Color QuickDraw, and Palette Manager chapters later in this volume. While the Palette Manager allows you to define a palette for the system to use when it needs to define the color environment, you should rely on the system palette colors for your icon family. Remember that users may often use the Finder when your application is not running and that the user can switch to another application when your application is running. Relying on the system palette gives your icons a more consistent look in the Finder regardless of what the active application is. And because users can change the desktop color and pattern, your application also gives users more control over their work environment if your icons rely on the system palette. Users can always alter your color definitions by selecting an icon and choosing a color from the Label menu. The Finder then blends the chosen color into those of the selected icon. To restore the original colors, users must choose None from the Label menu.

If your application creates documents, it should also define at least two additional icon families: one to be displayed for documents created by your application, and another to be displayed when the user creates a stationery pad from one of your application's documents. (See "Stationery Pads" later in this chapter for a description of stationery pads.)

Your application might also define icons for other types of documents. If your application supports data sharing through the Edition Manager, your application should also define an icon family for editions. (For a description of edition file types, see "Edition Icons" later in this chapter and the Edition Manager chapter of this volume.) If your Macintosh application is a database program or serves as a source for data (as a spreadsheet program often does), you might wish to create query documents so that other Macintosh applications can gain access to that data through the Data Access Manager; in this case, your application should also define an icon family for its query documents. (See the Data Access Manager chapter in this volume for information on sharing data in this manner.)

If your application creates other variations of its documents, you can assist your users by providing different icons for the different documents. For example, TeachText has separate icon families to distinguish its read-only and graphics documents.

Figure 9-4 shows the large black-and-white icons for the various documents that the sample SurfWriter application creates: text, stationery pad, and edition.

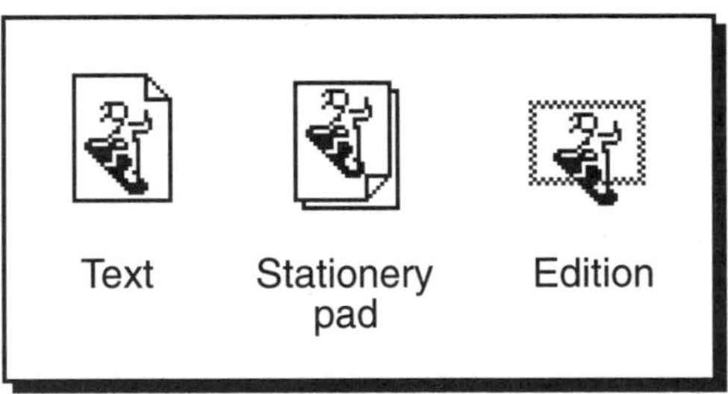

Figure 9-4. Examples of document icons

Defining icon resources is not enough to display your icons. In addition, you must follow one of two sets of procedures:

- If you are an application developer, you must define file reference resources and a bundle resource for your application as described in the next two sections.
- If you are an information provider or database developer—that is, you provide documents that are used by other applications—you don't need to create file reference resources or a bundle resource to provide document icons on Macintosh computers running system software version 7.0. You can instead create customized icons for your documents as described in "Customized Icons" later in this chapter. (However, if you want your document to appear with its own icons on earlier versions of system software, you must create a file reference resource and a bundle resource as described in the next two sections.)

Note: In system software version 7.0, the Finder no longer uses the PlotIcon and PlotCIcon procedures (described, respectively, in Volumes I and V) to draw icons. If you use these procedures, note that they draw only those icons defined by 'ICN#' and 'cicn' resources. These procedures will not draw any icons that are defined by the icon resources new to system software version 7.0—namely, the 'ics#', 'icl4', 'ics4', 'icl8', and 'ics8' resources.

File Reference Resources

File reference ('FREF') resources perform two main functions. First, they associate icons you define with file types used by your application. Second, they allow users to drag document icons to your application icon in order to open them from your application.

Create an 'FREF' resource for your application file itself and create separate 'FREF' resources for each file type that your application can open. Listing 9-2 shows, in Rez input format, the file reference resources for the SurfWriter application file, text documents, stationery pads, and editions, and for TeachText read-only documents.

Listing 9-2. Using file reference resources

```
resource 'FREF' (208, purgeable) {   /* SurfWriter application */
   'APPL', 0,   /* type 'APPL', maps to 'ICN#' w/ local ID 0 in 'BNDL' */
   ""           /* leave empty string for name: not implemented */
};

resource 'FREF' (209, purgeable) {   /* SurfWriter document */
   'TEXT', 1,   /* type 'TEXT', maps to 'ICN#' w/ local ID 1 in 'BNDL' */
   ""
};

resource 'FREF' (210, purgeable) {   /* SurfWriter stationery pad */
   'sEXT', 2,   /* type 'sEXT', maps to 'ICN#' w/ local ID 2 in 'BNDL' */
   ""
};

resource 'FREF' (211, purgeable) {   /* SurfWriter edition */
   'edtt', 3,   /* type 'edtt',  maps to 'ICN#' w/ local ID 3 in 'BNDL' */
   ""
};

resource 'FREF' (212, purgeable) {   /* TeachText read-only files */
   'ttro', 4,   /* These documents have TeachText as their creator. */
   ""           /* Finder uses TeachText's 'ICN#' for these documents. */
                /* included here so users can drag these docs to  */
                /*  SurfWriter's app icon */
};
```

Each 'FREF' resource specifies a file type and a local ID. The file type can be defined for files created by your application only, for files created by other applications that your application supports, or for files of the existing general types, such as 'TEXT' or 'PICT'.

As described in the next section, "The Bundle Resource," the local ID maps the file type to an 'ICN#' resource that is assigned the same local ID in the bundle. If you wanted two file types to share the same icon, for example, you could create two separate 'FREF' resources that share the same local ID, which the bundle would map to the same 'ICN#' resource. (Creating two file types that share the same icon is not recommended, however, because a shared icon would make it very difficult for the user to distinguish between the different file types on the desktop.)

If you provide your own icon for the stationery pads that users create from your application's documents, create an 'FREF' resource for your stationery pads. Assign this 'FREF' resource a file type in the following manner: use the file type of the document upon which the stationery pad is based, but replace the first letter of the original document's file type with a lowercase *s*. As with other 'FREF' resources, you map this to an 'ICN#' resource in the bundle. (This convention necessitates that you make the names of your documents' file types unique in their last three letters.) For example, in Listing 9-2, the 'sEXT' file type assigned within the 'FREF' resource is used for stationery pads created from documents of the 'TEXT' file type. In this case, when the isStationery bit (described in "Finder Information in the Volume Catalog" later in this chapter) is set on a document of file type 'TEXT', the Finder looks in the SurfWriter application's 'BNDL' resource to determine what icon is mapped to documents of type 'sEXT'. The Finder then displays the document using the stationery pad icon shown in Figure 9-4.

When the user drags a document icon to your application icon, the Finder checks a list of your 'FREF' resources. If the document's file type appears in the 'FREF' resource list, the Finder launches your application with a request to open that document.

If your application supports file types for which it doesn't provide icons, you can still define 'FREF' resources for them, and then users can launch your application by dragging these document icons to your application icon. For example, the 'FREF' resource with resource ID 212 in Listing 9-2 is created so that the Finder launches the SurfWriter application when users drag TeachText read-only documents to the SurfWriter application icon. Since these documents have TeachText as their creator, the Finder displays the icon that the TeachText application defines for them in its own bundle.

If your application supports the Open Documents event, you can also specify disks, folders, and a wildcard file type for all possible files in your 'FREF' resources so that users can launch your application by dragging their icons to your application icon. As explained in the Apple Event Manager chapter, the Open Documents event is one of the four required Apple events. After the Finder uses the Process Manager to launch an application that supports high-level events, the Finder sends the application an Open Documents event, which includes a list of alias records for desktop objects that the application should open.

Since alias records can specify volumes and directories as well as files, an Open Documents event gives you the opportunity to handle cases where users drag disk or folder icons to your application. Create an 'FREF' resource and specify 'disk' as the file type to allow users to drag hard disk and floppy disk icons to your application icon. Create an 'FREF' resource and specify 'fold' to allow users to drag folder icons to your application icon. Create an 'FREF' resource that specifies '****' as the file type to allow users to drag all file types—including applications, system extensions, documents, and so on, but not including disks or folders—to your application icon. If you create three 'FREF' resources that specify 'disk', 'fold', and '****' as their file types and if your application supports the Open Documents event, you effectively allow users to launch your application by dragging any desktop icon to your application icon. It is up to your application to open disks, folders, or all possible file types in a manner appropriate to the needs of the user.

The Bundle Resource

A bundle is a resource that associates all of the resources used by the Finder for your application; in particular, it associates your application and its documents with their icons. The bundle resource ('BNDL') contains

- the application's signature and the resource ID of its signature resource (which should always be 0)
- the assignment of local IDs to the resource IDs of all 'ICN#' resources defined for the application
- the assignment, for compatibility reasons, of local IDs to 'FREF' resource IDs (For consistency, these can be the same local IDs that are assigned inside the 'FREF' resources, but they don't have to be—they only need to be unique for every 'FREF' resource.)

When the Finder first displays your application on the user's desktop, it checks the catalog (as described in "Finder Information in the Volume Catalog" later in this chapter) to see if your application has a bundle. If it doesn't, the Finder displays the default icons shown in Figure 9-1. If your application has a bundle, the Finder installs the information from the 'BNDL' resource and all its bundled resources into either the desktop database for a hard disk or into the Desktop file for a floppy disk and uses this information to display icons for the file types associated with your application.

You must assign local IDs to your 'ICN#' resources within your 'BNDL' resource. Make sure that for all your file types with icons, these local IDs match the local IDs you assigned inside their corresponding 'FREF' resources. In the Desktop file on floppy disks (and on hard disks running earlier versions of system software), the Finder renumbers the resource IDs that you've assigned to your resources to avoid conflicts with the resources of other applications. Therefore, the bundle has to rely on these local IDs to map icon list resources to their file reference resources; that is, the 'BNDL' resource uses the local ID you assign to an 'ICN#' resource to map it to the 'FREF' resource that has the same local ID assigned inside itself.

For example, the 'FREF' resource with resource ID 208 in Listing 9-2 shows that the file type 'APPL' (the SurfWriter application file) is assigned a local ID of 0. In the 'BNDL' resource shown in Listing 9-3, you see that local ID 0 is assigned to the 'ICN#' resource with resource ID 128. This maps the icon defined by this resource (see Figure 9-3) to the SurfWriter application file. Listing 9-3 shows the bundle resource for the icons and 'FREF' resources defined in Listings 9-1 and 9-2.

Listing 9-3. Using a bundle resource

```
resource 'BNDL' (128, purgeable) {  /* SurfWriter bundle resource ID */
   'WAVE',          /* SurfWriter signature */
   0,               /* resource ID of signature resource: should be 0 */
   {
      'ICN#',       /* mapping local IDs in 'FREF's to 'ICN#' IDs */
      {
         0, 128,    /* 'FREF' with local ID 0 maps to 'ICN#' res ID 128 */
         1, 129,    /* 'FREF' with local ID 1 maps to 'ICN#' res ID 129 */
```

```
        2, 130,   /* 'FREF' with local ID 2 maps to 'ICN#' res ID 130 */
        3, 131    /* 'FREF' with local ID 3 maps to 'ICN#' res ID 131 */
                  /*  no 'FREF' with local ID 4 in this list: */
                  /*  TeachText's icons used for 'ttro' file type */
     },
     'FREF',      /* local resource IDs for 'FREF's: no duplicates */
     {
        10, 208,  /* local ID 10 assigned to 'FREF' res ID 208 */
        11, 209,  /* local ID 11 assigned to 'FREF' res ID 209 */
        12, 210,  /* local ID 12 assigned to 'FREF' res ID 210 */
        13, 211,  /* local ID 13 assigned to 'FREF' res ID 211 */
        14, 212   /* local ID 14 assigned to 'FREF' res ID 212 */
     }
  }
};
```

In Listing 9-3, notice that you also assign local IDs to 'FREF' resources inside the 'BNDL' resource. This assignment is superfluous because the Finder doesn't map these local IDs to any other resources. The local ID assignment for 'FREF' resources inside the bundle was implemented for the earliest versions of Macintosh system software, and it remains this way today to maintain backward compatibility. For compatibility with the format of the 'BNDL' resource, assign local IDs to 'FREF' resource IDs. You may number them any way you like, except that each local ID in this particular list must be unique.

Of all the icon resource types that make up an icon family, you need to list only the 'ICN#' resource in the 'BNDL' resource. The Finder automatically recognizes and loads all the other members of the icon family.

If the user drags documents created by other applications to your application icon, and if you have created 'FREF' resources for these documents' file types, the Finder launches your application and passes it the names of the documents. You should create 'FREF' resources for all file types that your application supports. Do not provide icon resources for file types created by other applications because the Finder won't use them, but will instead use the icon resources defined by the documents' creators. Though the local IDs of such an 'FREF' resource are superfluous in the 'FREF' resource and at the bottom of the 'BNDL' resource, the resource formats require that you provide local IDs in both.

For example, notice in Listing 9-2 that the 'FREF' resource with resource ID 212 is assigned a local ID of 4, but that no 'ICN#' resource is assigned to local ID 4 in the 'BNDL' resource in Listing 9-3. This 'FREF' resource, which specifies a file type of 'ttro', was created in Listing 9-2 to make the Finder launch the SurfWriter application when users drag TeachText read-only documents to the SurfWriter application icon. No icon mapping is made for this file type in the SurfWriter application's bundle because the Finder displays the icons defined for it by the TeachText application. The 'FREF' resource with resource ID 212 is assigned to local ID 14 in the 'BNDL' resource in Listing 9-3 because the format of the resource requires a local ID for all 'FREF' associated resources.

You alert the Finder that your application has a bundle resource by setting a bit in the file's Finder flags field. (Most development environments provide a simple tool for setting the bundle bit. "Finder Information in the Volume Catalog" later in this chapter describes Finder flags.)

Figure 9-5 illustrates how the bundle resource created in Listing 9-3 uses local IDs to map icon list resources to file reference resources.

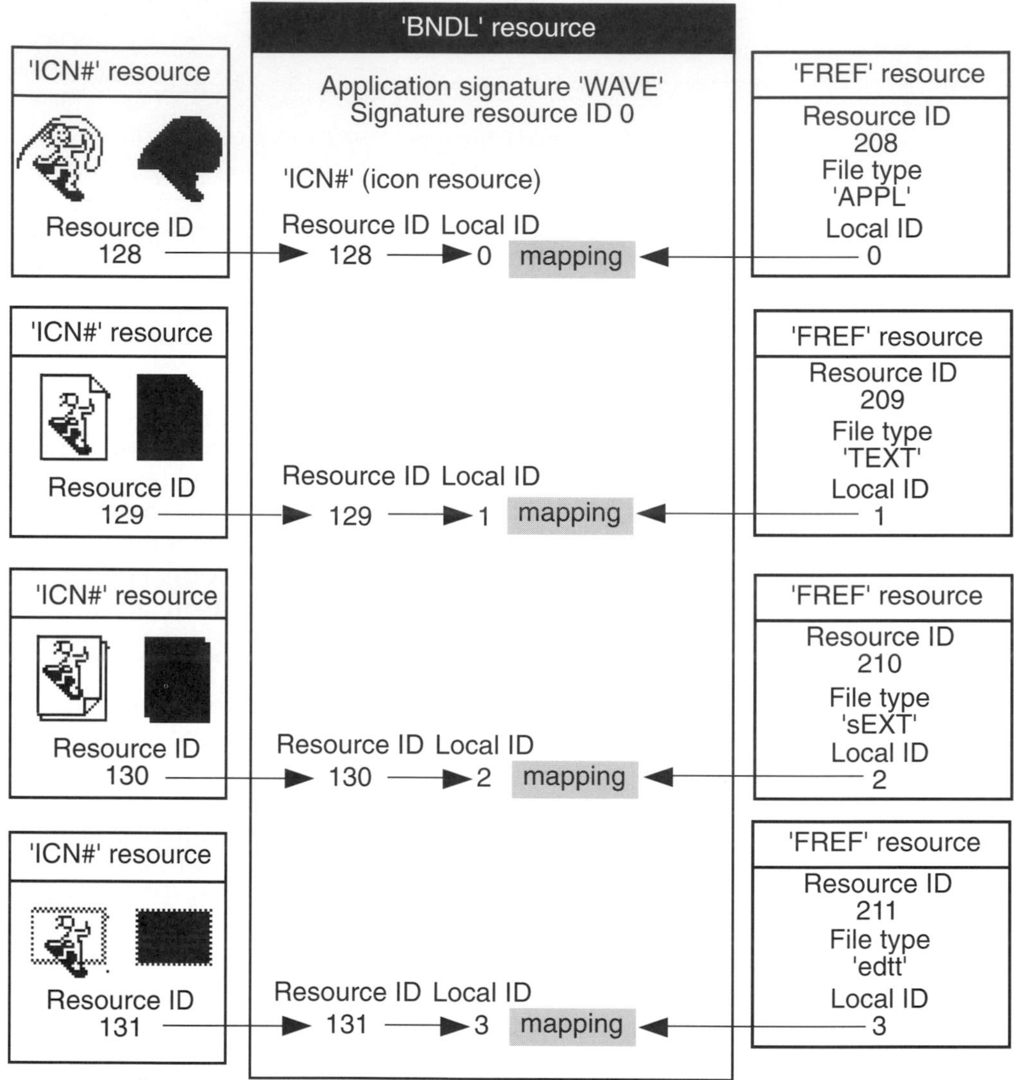

Figure 9-5. Linking 'ICN#' and 'FREF' resources in a 'BNDL' resource

Figure 9-5 illustrates two main concepts: first, that one bundle ties together all the icon resources and file reference resources for your application and all of its documents; and second, that the icon resources and their associated file reference resources are mapped together by local IDs. In Figure 9-5, the application file's 'ICN#' resource has resource ID 128 while its 'FREF' resource has resource ID 208. For maintainability, you should probably assign the same resource ID to a file's 'FREF' resource that you assigned to its 'ICN#' resource. However, because the Finder renumbers these whenever it adds them to a Desktop file, you must map them by using local IDs. In Figure 9-5, the application file's 'ICN#' resource is assigned local ID 0. This maps the icon to the file type described by the 'FREF' resource with local ID 0—in this case, the 'FREF' resource with resource ID 208.

Figure 9-5 also illustrates the general steps you must take to provide icons for applications and documents. These steps are enumerated here in more detail and assume that you are using a tool, such as ResEdit, that allows you to open and edit several resources simultaneously. (Remember that these resources must have resource IDs of 128 or greater.)

To provide your application with icon families for itself and for its documents, follow these steps:

1. Create an icon list ('ICN#') resource for your application file.
2. Create the other members of the icon family of the application file—resources of types 'ics#', 'icl8', 'icl4', 'ics8', and 'ics4'—and give each of these the same resource ID as the 'ICN#' resource.
3. Create a bundle ('BNDL') resource.
4. Within the bundle resource, list the resource ID of the application file's 'ICN#' resource and assign it a local ID of 0.
5. Create an 'FREF' resource for the application file.
6. Within the 'FREF' resource, assign the application a file type of 'APPL' and assign it a local ID of 0.
7. Within the bundle resource, list the resource ID of the 'FREF' resource for the application file and assign it a unique local ID—for example, 0 to maintain consistency with the local ID assigned in the 'FREF' resource.
8. Create another icon family—consisting of resources of types 'ICN#,' 'ics#', 'icl8', 'icl4', 'ics8', and 'ics4'—to represent one type of document that your application creates.
9. Within the application's bundle resource, list the resource ID of the document's 'ICN#' resource and assign it a local ID of 1.
10. Create an 'FREF' resource for the document.
11. Within the 'FREF' resource for the document, assign it a file type (for example, 'TEXT' or 'edtt') and assign it a local ID of 1.
12. Within the bundle resource, list the resource ID of the 'FREF' resource for the document and assign it a unique local ID—for example, 1 to maintain consistency with the local ID assigned in the 'FREF' resource.
13. Assigning unique local IDs for every type of document your application creates, repeat steps 8 through 12.
14. If your application supports file types of other applications, define 'FREF' resources for them, but do not create icon resources for them.
15. Create a signature resource (as previously described in "Creators, File Types, and the Signature Resource") with resource ID 0; in it, set the creator to your signature.
16. Set the file's hasBundle bit, and clear its hasBeenInited bit in the file's Finder flags. (Finder flags are described in "Finder Information in the Volume Catalog" later in this chapter.)
17. Save and close all of the resources. (When your restart your Macintosh, the application should appear with its own icon. If you later alter any of your icons, clear the hasBeenInited bit and rebuild your desktop database by pressing the Command-Option keys when restarting.)

The Size Resource

The 'SIZE' resource tells the Finder and the Process Manager which features your application supports and how much memory to allocate when it starts up your application. The following sample code illustrates a 'SIZE' resource.

```
resource 'SIZE' (-1, purgeable)  {
reserved,
acceptSuspendResumeEvents,
reserved,
canBackground,
doesActivateOnFGSwitch,
backgroundAndForeground,
dontGetFrontClicks,
ignoreAppDiedEvents,
is32BitCompatible,
isHighLevelEventAware,
localAndRemoteHLEvents,
isStationeryAware,
dontUseTextEditServices,
reserved,
reserved,
reserved,
kPrefSize * 1024,
kMinSize * 1024
};
```

Set up your application's 'SIZE' resource with a resource ID of –1. The user can change the preferred memory size requested for your application. If the user does change the memory size, the Finder stores the new size in a 'SIZE' resource with a resource ID of 0. When it launches your application, the Finder looks first for a 'SIZE' resource with an ID of 0. If it finds none, it uses the 'SIZE' resource with an ID of –1.

Notice that the tenth field, isHighLevelEventAware, tells the Finder that this application supports high-level events. The application must then be able to process the four required Apple events—Open Application, Open Documents, Print Documents, and Quit Application—that the Finder sends in response to actions that the user performs from the desktop. See the Apple Event Manager and Event Manager chapters of this volume for more information about handling high-level events.

Notice that the twelfth field, isStationeryAware, tells the Finder that this application supports stationery pads, which are described in "Stationery Pads" later in this chapter.

For a complete description of the 'SIZE' resource and its fields, see the Event Manager chapter in this volume.

Messages When the Finder Can't Find Your Application

When the user double-clicks a file or selects it and chooses either the Open or the Print command from the Finder's File menu, the Finder looks for the application whose signature is stored in the file's creator field. The Finder starts up that application and tells it which documents the user wants to open or print. If the Finder cannot find the creator application, it displays an alert box.

If the document is of either file type 'TEXT' or 'PICT' and if the TeachText application is available, an alert box asks the user whether the TeachText application should be used to open the document. For documents of any other file type, or if the TeachText application is not present, the Finder displays an alert box like the one shown in Figure 9-6.

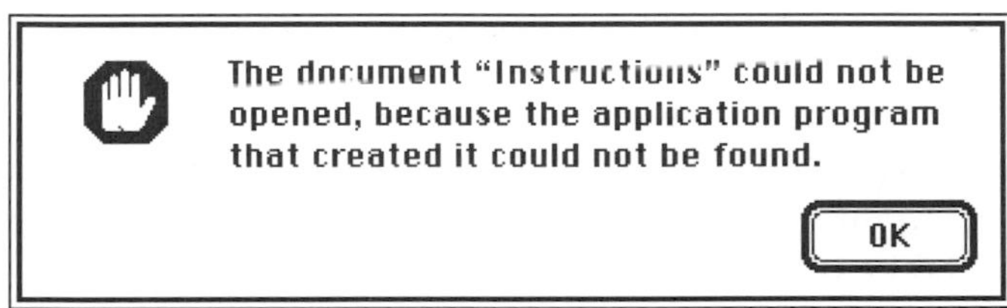

Figure 9-6. The default application-unavailable alert box

Your application should store one of two string resources in its documents to make the alert box message more useful than the default shown in Figure 9-6.

Before displaying the default message shown in Figure 9-6, the Finder looks in the document for one of two special 'STR ' resources: a message string or a name string. If the Finder can't find the document's creator on any mounted volume, it looks first for the message string resource. Provide a message string resource if you do not intend for users to open the file. The message should explain why the file can't be opened. If the Finder does not find a message string resource, it looks for the name string resource. Provide a name string resource if you intend for users to open the file. The name string should be your application's name; the Finder displays it in an alert box to inform the user that your application is needed.

You supply either the message string resource or the name string resource; don't supply both. Supply a message string resource for documents (such as a preferences file) that your application uses but that users should not open; supply a name string resource for documents that you intend for users to open with your application.

Your name string resource (an 'STR ' resource with a resource ID of –16396) should contain the name of your application. For example, an application named SurfWriter has a name string resource that looks like this:

```
resource 'STR ' (-16396, purgeable) {   /* the application name */
   "SurfWriter"
};
```

Use the AddResource and WriteResource procedures (described in the Resource Manager chapter of Volume I) to store this resource in the documents created by your application. Then, if the user tries to open or print one of your application's documents when your application is not present, the Finder can specify your application's name in the alert box, as illustrated in Figure 9-7.

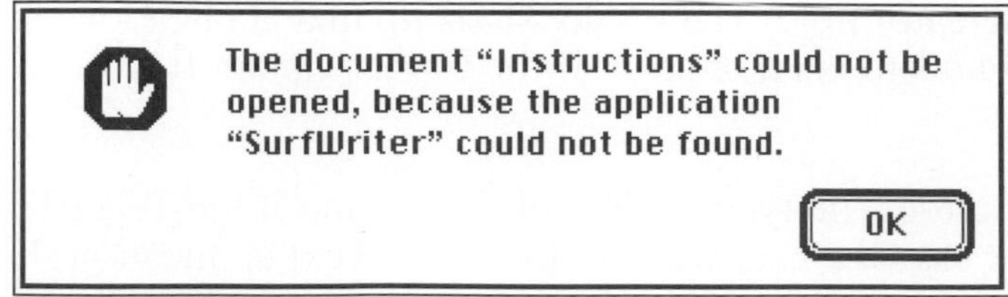

Figure 9-7. The application-unavailable alert box specifying an application's name

Your message string resource (an 'STR ' resource with a resource ID of –16397) should explain why the user cannot open or print a document. Use this resource for files—such as your application's preferences file—that are not intended to be opened or printed by the user. Register a signature (as explained in "Creators, File Types, and the Signature Resource" earlier in this chapter) that is different from the signature of your application, and set this signature as the creator of files that you don't want your users to open. This ensures that the Finder displays your message instead of launching your application when the user double-clicks these documents.

The following resource illustrates a customized message explaining why the user cannot open a preferences file:

```
resource 'STR ' (-16397, purgeable) {   /* the message */
   "This document describes user preferences for the application "
"SurfWriter. You cannot open or print this document. To be effective, "
"this document must be stored in the Preferences folder in the System "
"Folder."
};
```

Figure 9-8 shows the alert box generated by this resource.

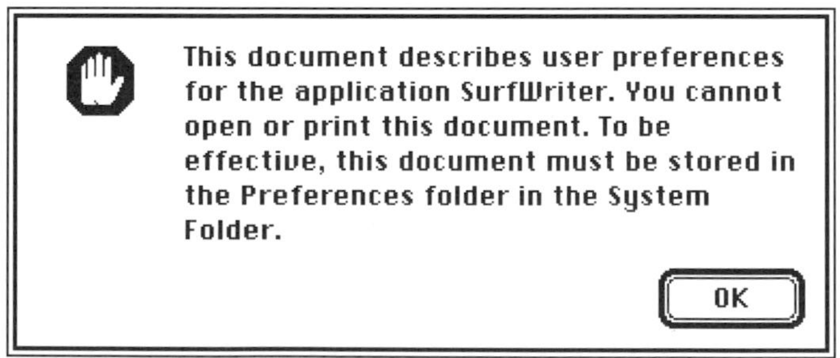

Figure 9-8. The application-unavailable alert box with a customized message

Note that if your application creates documents of file types 'TEXT' or 'PICT', if the TeachText application is available, and if your application is missing when the user tries to open them from the Finder, the Finder always displays the alert box shown in Figure 9-9. For these file types, the Finder displays this alert box even if you provide name or message string resources.

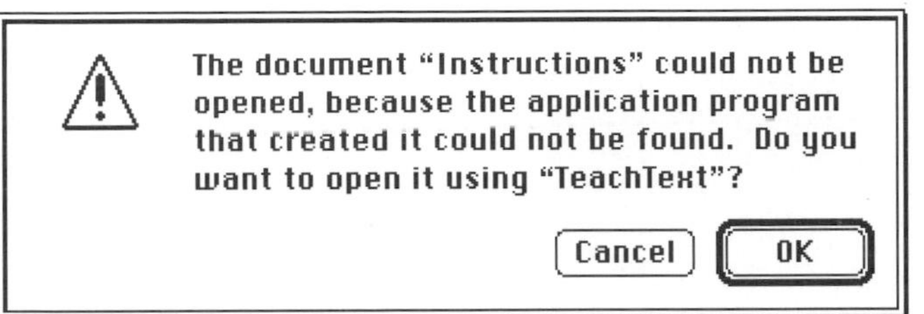

Figure 9-9. The application-unavailable alert box for 'TEXT' and 'PICT' documents

Version Resources

You can use 'vers' resources to record version information for your application. If the user opens the Views control panel, clicks the Show Version box, and then chooses any command from the View menu other than by Icon or by Small Icon, filenames and their version numbers from the 'vers' resource appear in the active Finder window. The Finder also displays version information when the user selects your application and chooses Get Info from the File menu.

The 'vers' resource allows you to store a version number, a version message, and a region code. (Because the Get Info command's information window already displays the name of your application, the version message should not include the name of your application.) Each 'vers' resource uses this Rez template:

```
type 'vers' {
   byte;     /* first part of version number in BCD */
   byte;     /* second and third parts of version number */
   byte;     /* development=0x20, alpha=0x40, beta=0x60, release=0x80 */
   byte;     /* stage of prerelease version */
   integer;  /* region code, as in International Utilities */
   pstring;  /* version number */
   pstring;  /* version message */
}
```

You can use 'vers' resources to assign version information to an individual file and, if it is a part of a larger collection of files, to the entire superset of files. The 'vers' resource with a resource ID of 1 specifies the version of the file; the 'vers' resource with a resource ID of 2 specifies the version of the set of files.

The following sample code illustrates the 'vers' resources, in Rez input format, for a spelling checker application and for the word-processing system of which it is a part. Notice that the spelling checker is version 1.1 while the set of files that compose the entire word-processing system is version 2.0.

```
resource 'vers' (1, purgeable) {
   0x01, 0x01, release, 0x00, verUS,
   "1.1",
   "1.1 (US), © My Company, Inc. 1991"
};
```

```
resource 'vers' (2, purgeable) {
   0x02, 0x00, release, 0x00, verUS,
   "2.0",
   "(for SurfWriter 2.0)"
};
```

Figure 9-10 illustrates how these resources are displayed in the information window.

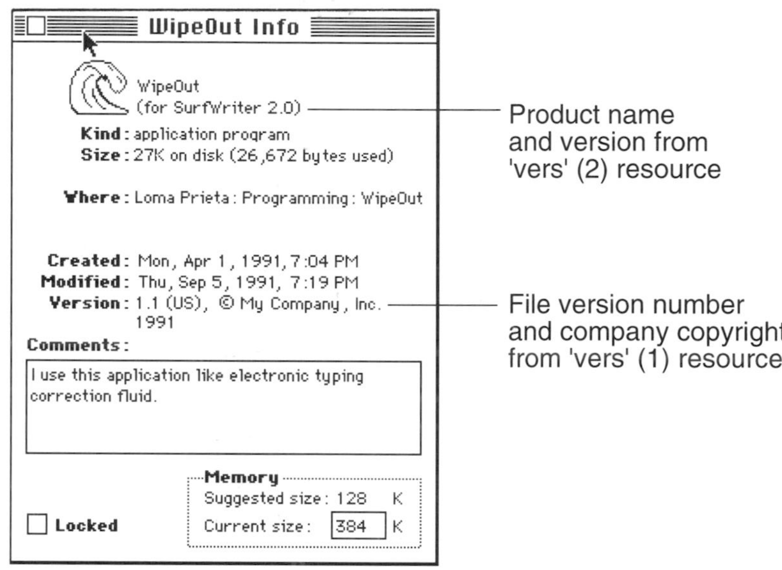

Figure 9-10. The version data in the information window

You can store version resources in any kind of file, not just an application. If your application does not contain a 'vers' resource with a resource ID of 1, the Finder displays the string from your signature resource as the version information in the information window for your application.

How and When the Finder Launches Your Application

The previous sections in this chapter explain the resources that the Finder uses to display and launch your application. This section provides a brief summary of how the Finder—using the previously described resources—starts up your application whenever the user requests the Finder to launch your application or to open or print a document supported by your application.

The simplest scenarios under which the Finder launches your application occur when the user double-clicks your application icon or selects it and chooses Open from the Finder's File menu. In these cases, the Finder calls the Process Manager to start your application. The Process Manager creates a partition of memory for your application, loads your code into this partition, and sets up the stack, heap, and A5 world for your application. The Process Manager returns control to the Finder, which then relinquishes control to your application. (See the Process Management chapter in this volume for more information.) Your application then performs the tasks necessary to open itself—such as opening an untitled document window, for example.

When the user requests the Finder to open or print a document supported by your application, the Finder calls the Process Manager and launches your application in the same way, except that the Finder also sets up the information your application needs to open or print the document and passes this information to your application. This information includes a list of files to open or print. Applications that do not support high-level events use the CountAppFiles, GetAppFiles, and ClrAppFiles procedures or the GetAppParms procedure to get this information. In system software version 7.0, applications that support high-level events receive this information through Apple events. The Apple Event Manager chapter in this volume describes how your application processes Apple events to open or print files.

The user can request the Finder to open documents created by your application by double-clicking one of their icons, and the user can request the Finder to open or print documents by selecting one or more icons and choosing Open or Print from the Finder's File menu. The Finder reads the creator field of each selected file to find the document's creator. Typically (as described in "Finder Information in the Volume Catalog" later in this chapter), your application sets the four-character string specified in its signature resource as the creator of its documents. The Finder searches for the application whose signature matches each document's creator. If the document's creator matches your application's signature, the Finder calls the Process Manager, launches your application, and then passes your application the name of the selected document or selected multiple documents. Your application should then open the documents in titled windows or print them, as appropriate.

If the user tries to open documents created by your application and your application is missing, the Finder displays an alert box telling the user that your application is missing. The Finder displays the name of your application in this alert box if you provide your documents with a string resource (of resource ID –16396) containing your application's name.

Sometimes when your application is already running, the user might double-click a document created by your application. If your application supports high-level events, the Finder sends your application the Open Documents event. If your application does not support high-level events, the Process Manager accommodates the user by simulating a mouse-down event that calls your application's menu command for opening files. The Process Manager accomplishes this by first looking for a File menu with an item named Open. Since some applications do not have a File menu and since others use a command with a different name, the Process Manager then looks in the application's resource fork for 'mstr' and 'mst#' resources with resource IDs 102 and 103. An 'mstr' resource has the same format as an 'STR ' resource. An 'mstr' resource with resource ID 102 should contain the name of the menu containing the Open command. An 'mstr' resource with resource ID 103 should contain the name of the menu item containing the Open command. An 'mst#' resource has the same format as an 'STR#' resource. An 'mst#' resource with resource ID 102 should contain the name or names of the menu or menus containing the Open command. An 'mst#' resource with resource ID 103 should contain the name or names of the menu item or items containing the Open command.

The user can also request the Finder to launch your application by dragging one icon or several icons to your application's icon. The Finder determines whether to launch your application by comparing the document's file type (which is stored in the volume catalog) against the list of your application's supported file types. The Finder compiles this list from the 'FREF' resources you create for your application; the Finder stores this list in the desktop database. If the document's file type appears in the 'FREF' list for your application, the Finder calls the Process Manager, launches your application, and passes it the name of the selected document or selected multiple documents. Your application should then open the documents in titled windows.

If your application supports the Open Documents event, you can also specify disks, folders, and a wildcard file type for all other files in your 'FREF' resources so that users can launch your application by dragging their icons to your application icon. After the Finder uses the Process Manager to launch an application that supports high-level events, the Finder sends the application an Open Documents event, which includes a list of alias records for desktop objects that the application should open. It is up to your application to open disks, folders, or all possible file types in a manner appropriate to the needs of the user.

To support stationery, your application should specify the isStationeryAware constant in its 'SIZE' resource and always check the isStationery bit of a document passed to it by the Finder. If the isStationery bit is set for a file that the user wants to open, your application should copy the stationery pad's contents into a new document and open the document in an untitled window. (Stationery is described in the next section.)

System software version 7.0 allows users to create aliases, which are desktop objects that represent other files, directories, or volumes. If the user opens an alias that represents a document created by your application, the Finder resolves the alias for you; that is, it passes your application the name and location of the document itself, not the alias. (Aliases are described in the next section.)

FINDER-RELATED CHANGES TO THE USER INTERFACE

The Finder in system software version 7.0 offers a number of new interface features, most of which have no effect on applications. This section summarizes the new features that might affect your application.

Stationery Pads

System software version 7.0 supports **stationery pads,** which are special documents used as templates. Opening a stationery pad should not open the document itself; instead, it should open a new document with the same contents as the stationery pad. To turn any document into a stationery pad, the user selects it, chooses Get Info from the File menu, and clicks the Stationery pad check box in the information window. The Finder tags a document as being a stationery pad by setting the isStationery bit in the file's Finder flags field (see "Finder Information in the Volume Catalog" later in this chapter for a description of Finder flags).

When the user opens a stationery pad from the Finder, the Finder first checks your application's 'SIZE' resource to see if your application supports stationery (see "The Size Resource" earlier in this chapter). If the isStationeryAware bit is not set, the Finder creates a new document from the template and prompts the user for a name. The Finder then starts up your application as usual, passing it the name of the new document.

If the isStationeryAware bit is set, the Finder informs your application that the user has opened a document and passes your application the name of the stationery pad. To support stationery, your application should

- specify the isStationeryAware constant in its 'SIZE' resource
- always check the isStationery bit of a document passed to it by either the Finder or the Standard File Package

The isStationery bit alone identifies whether a document is stationery. If the isStationery bit is set for a file that the user wants to open, your application should copy the template's contents into a new document and open the document in an untitled window.

As described in the Standard File Package chapter in this volume, your application can check the sfFlags field of the standard file reply record to determine whether the isStationery bit is set. Unlike the Finder, the Standard File Package always passes your application the stationery pad itself, not a copy of it, regardless of the setting of the isStationery bit. When the user opens a stationery pad from within your application, the Standard File Package checks your application's 'SIZE' resource. If your application does not support stationery, the Standard File Package displays an alert box warning the user that the stationery pad itself, not a copy of it, is being opened. As you can see, the user can still easily change the template and mistakenly write over it by choosing Save without assigning a new name. You can prevent this unnecessary user frustration by making your application stationery-aware.

You can supply the icon to be displayed for stationery pads created from your application's documents by using the resources described in "Finder-Related Resources" earlier in this chapter.

If you do not supply your own stationery pad icon, the Finder uses the default stationery pad icon illustrated in Figure 9-1.

In your documentation, tell users to choose the Get Info command to make stationery pads. You may also want to give examples of useful stationery pads created with your application. For example, if your application supports text and graphics, you may provide samples of stationery pads for business letterheads or billing statements.

Edition Icons

New to system software version 7.0 is the Edition Manager, which enables users to share and automatically update data from numerous documents and applications. For example, a user might want to capture sales figures and totals from within a spreadsheet and then include this information in a word-processing document that summarizes sales for a given month. If both the spreadsheet and word-processing applications support the Edition Manager, the user begins by selecting data within the spreadsheet document and creating a publisher. The spreadsheet application then writes a copy of that data to a separate file, called an *edition*. The edition is represented by an icon; by default, it appears as the icon shown in Figure 9-1. If the user opens a word-processing document and creates a subscriber to the spreadsheet document's edition, the word-processing application then incorporates the desired sales figures and totals from the spreadsheet document's edition into the document.

If you want your application to publish or subscribe to data among its own documents or among documents created by other applications that support the Edition Manager, see the Edition Manager chapter in this volume. If your application creates editions, consider creating an icon that uniquely identifies your editions and that associates them with your application's documents. See "Icon Resources" earlier in this chapter for information about creating icon resources. The file type for your edition containers should be 'edtt' (for text-oriented data), 'edtp' (for graphics-oriented data), or 'edts' (for sound-oriented data); and the creator, of course, should be the signature of your application.

Customized Icons

You can create customized icons for your documents. Users can also create customized icons. Customized icons are stored with resource ID –16455 in the resource fork of the file. (Compare this to the method described in "Finder-Related Resources" earlier in this chapter whereby icons are defined through a bundle resource and its associated icon list and file reference resources.)

In system software version 7.0, the user can customize individual icons. By selecting a file and choosing Get Info from the File menu, the user sees the information window for that file. The user can then select the icon displayed in the upper-left corner of the information window and use the Paste command in the Edit menu to replace it with a picture from the Clipboard. The Finder creates a family of icons based on the user's customized icon, assigns a resource ID of –16455 to each icon resource in the family, stores these resources in the resource fork of the file that the icon represents, and sets the hasCustomIcon bit in the file's Finder flags field.

Your application can use the same strategy to provide customized icons to the documents that it creates. For example, a drawing application might create miniature versions of the illustrations contained within its documents and use those for the documents' icons.

If you are a database developer who creates and distributes query documents that support the Data Access Manager, you can also use this strategy to create icons that identify your database's query documents. Similarly, if instead of producing an application you produce and distribute information (such as database files, stationery pads, clip art libraries, or dictionaries) to be used by other applications, you might want to provide icons that distinguish your documents.

To make the version 7.0 Finder display customized icons for a document, you must create—at least—an 'ICN#' resource with resource ID –16455 and store it in the document's resource fork. (To create this while your application is running, your application can call the AddResource procedure, described in the Resource Manager chapter in Volume I.) You can use the following constant in place of the ID number.

```
CONST   kCustomIconResource = -16455;     {res ID for custom icon}
```

If you provide only an 'ICN#' resource, the Finder uses a black-and-white icon on all screen displays and automatically reduces it when a small version of the icon is required. To create color versions and to define a small version of the icon, create an entire icon family as described in "Icon Resources" earlier in this chapter.

After creating icon resources with the kCustomIconResource constant as their IDs, you must set the hasCustomIcon bit in the file's Finder flags field. To prevent users from changing these icons, set the nameLocked bit in the file's Finder flags field. (Most development environments for version 7.0 provide tools for setting these bits. "Finder Information in the Volume Catalog" later in this chapter describes Finder flags.)

> **Note:** If you want your document to appear with its own icons on earlier versions of system software, you must create a file reference resource and a bundle resource for it as described in "File Reference Resources" and "The Bundle Resource" earlier in this chapter.

Aliases

The Finder for system software version 7.0 allows the user to create multiple desktop icons to represent a single document or other desktop object (such as a disk, a folder, or the Trash). One of the icons represents the actual file; the others are aliases that point to the file. An **alias** is an object on the desktop that represents some other file, directory, or volume. An alias looks like the icon of its target, but its name is displayed in a different style. The style depends on the system script; for Roman and most other scripts, alias names are displayed in italic.

To the user, the icons of the actual file and its aliases are functionally identical. Aliases give the user more flexibility in organizing the desktop and offer a convenient way to store a local copy of a large or dynamic file that resides on a file server.

As a desktop object, the alias depicts a file called the **alias file,** which contains a record that points to the file, directory, or volume represented by the icon. Alias files are created and managed by the user through the Finder.

Although your application shouldn't create alias files or change users' desktop aliases, your application can create and use its own alias records for storing identifying information about files or directories. An **alias record** is a data structure that identifies a file, folder, or volume. Whenever your application needs to store file or directory information, you can record the location and other identifying information in an alias record. The next time your application needs the file or directory, you can use the Alias Manager to locate it, even if the user has renamed it, copied it, restored it from backup, or moved it. You can also use alias records to identify objects on other volumes, including AppleShare® volumes. See the Alias Manager chapter of this volume for details about creating and managing information in alias records.

Ordinarily, when the user wants to open or print files, your application does not need to be concerned with whether they are aliases because both the Finder and the Standard File Package resolve aliases before passing them to your application. If the user opens an alias that represents a document created by your application, the Finder passes your application the name and location of the document itself, not the alias. Similarly, when the user opens an alias from within your application, the Standard File Package passes your application the name of the target document.

If your application bypasses the Finder or the Standard File Package when manipulating documents, it should check for and resolve aliases itself by using the ResolveAliasFile function.

Resolving Alias Files

The ResolveAliasFile function is part of the Alias Manager and is available only in system software version 7.0. Use the Gestalt function with the Gestalt selector gestaltAliasMgrAttr to determine whether you can use the ResolveAliasFile function.

An alias file contains an alias record, stored as a resource of type 'alis', that points to the target of the alias (see the Alias Manager chapter of this volume for a description of alias records).The alias file might also contain the target object's icon descriptions. The Finder identifies an alias file by setting the isAlias bit in the file's Finder flags field (see "Finder Information in the Volume Catalog" later in this chapter for a description of Finder flags).

An alias file that represents a document typically has the same type and creator as the file it represents. However, many desktop objects—such as disks, folders, and the Trash—do not have file types. Instead, alias files for these objects are assigned special file types, called *alias types.* Here are the alias types for those desktop objects for which users can provide aliases:

Desktop object	**Alias type**	**Constant**
Apple Menu Items folder	'faam'	kAppleMenuFolderAliasType
AppleShare drop folder	'fadr'	kDropFolderAliasType
Application	'adrp'	kApplicationAliasType
Control Panels folder	'fact'	kControlPanelFolderAliasType
Exported AppleShare folder	'faet'	kExportedFolderAliasType
Extensions folder	'faex'	kExtensionFolderAliasType
File server	'srvr'	kContainerServerAliasType
Floppy disk	'flpy'	kContainerFloppyAliasType
Folder	'fdrp'	kContainerFolderAliasType
Hard disk	'hdsk'	kContainerHardDiskAliasType
Mounted AppleShare folder	'famn'	kMountedFolderAliasType
Other objects that can contain files	'drop'	kContainerAliasType
Preferences folder	'fapf'	kPreferencesFolderAliasType
PrintMonitor Documents folder	'fapn'	kPrintMonitorDocsFolderAliasType
Shared AppleShare folder	'fash'	kSharedFolderAliasType
Startup Items folder	'fast'	kStartupFolderAliasType
System Folder	'fasy'	kSystemFolderAliasType
Trash	'trsh'	kContainerTrashAliasType

(The Extensions, Preferences, Apple Menu Items, Control Panels, Startup Items, and PrintMonitor Documents folders are described in "The System Folder and Its Related Directories" later in this chapter.)

Since users of system software version 7.0 can replace files with aliases, if your application opens a file or a directory without going through the Finder or the Standard File Package (if, for example, it uses preference files or dictionary files), it should always call the ResolveAliasFile function just before opening the file.

```
FUNCTION ResolveAliasFile (VAR theSpec: FSSpec; resolveAliasChains:
                           Boolean; VAR targetIsFolder: Boolean; VAR
                           wasAliased: Boolean) : OSErr;
```

ResolveAliasFile, like all other Alias Manager routines, accepts and returns file specifications only in the form of file system specification records defined by the FSSpec data type, described in the File Manager chapter of this volume. The file system specification record represents a simple and complete description of a file system object. It contains a volume reference number, a parent directory ID, and a name. Use the new File Manager function MakeFSSpec to convert other forms of file identification, such as full pathnames, into file system specifications.

You specify the file or directory you plan to open by passing a file system specification record in the parameter theSpec. ResolveAliasFile returns the name and location of the target file in theSpec.

ResolveAliasFile can follow a chain of aliases, up to a reasonable maximum defined for the system, to the ultimate target. Set the resolveAliasChains parameter to TRUE if you want ResolveAliasFile to resolve all aliases in a chain, stopping only when it reaches the target file. Set it to FALSE if you want to resolve only one alias file, even if the target is another alias file.

The parameters targetIsFolder and wasAliased are return parameters only. ResolveAliasFile always initializes these parameters to FALSE. It sets targetIsFolder to TRUE if the parameter theSpec points to a directory or a volume. It sets wasAliased to TRUE if the file originally passed in the parameter theSpec points to an alias file.

ResolveAliasFile first checks the catalog entry for the file or directory specified in theSpec to determine whether it is an alias and whether it is a file or a directory. If the object is not an alias, ResolveAliasFile leaves theSpec unchanged, sets the targetIsFolder parameter to TRUE for a directory or volume and FALSE for a file, sets wasAliased to FALSE, and returns noErr. If the object is an alias, ResolveAliasFile resolves it, places the target in the parameter theSpec, and sets the wasAliased flag to TRUE.

When ResolveAliasFile finds the specified volume and parent directory but fails to find the target file or directory in that location, ResolveAliasFile returns a result code of fnfErr and fills in the parameter theSpec with a complete file system specification record describing the target (that is, the volume reference number, parent directory ID, and filename or folder name). The file system specification record is valid, although the object it describes does not exist. This information is intended as a "hint" that lets you explore possible solutions to the resolution failure. You can, for example, use the file system specification record to create a replacement for a missing file with the File Manager function FSpCreate.

If ResolveAliasFile receives an error code while resolving an alias, it leaves the input parameters as they are and exits, returning the error code. In addition to any of these result codes, ResolveAliasFile can also return any Resource Manager or File Manager errors.

Result codes

nsvErr	–35	Volume not found
fnfErr	–43	Target not found, but volume and parent directory found, and theSpec parameter contains a valid file system specification record
dirNFErr	–120	Parent directory not found

When opening a file without going through the Finder or the Standard File Package, you call ResolveAliasFile immediately before opening the file. In Listing 9-4, the customized open function, MyOpen, ensures that the file to be opened is the target file, and then opens the data fork with the FSpOpenDF function.

Listing 9-4. Using the ResolveAliasFile function to open a file

```
FUNCTION MyOpen(VAR theSpec: FSSpec; perm: SignedByte;
                VAR fRefNum: Integer) : OSErr;

VAR
   myErr:           OSErr;
   targetIsFolder:  Boolean;
   wasAliased:      Boolean;
```

(Continued)

Listing 9-4. Using the ResolveAliasFile function to open a file (Continued)

```
BEGIN
   fRefNum := -1;                      {initialize fRefNum}

   myErr := ResolveAliasFile(theSpec, TRUE, targetIsFolder, wasAliased);

   IF targetIsFolder THEN
      myErr := paramErr                {cannot open a folder}
   ELSE IF (myErr <> noErr ) THEN      {try to open it}
      myErr := FSpOpenDF(theSpec, perm, fRefNum);
   MyOpen := myErr;
END;
```

Desk Accessories

System software version 7.0 no longer employs the Font/DA Mover. Desk accessories are now represented by icons, and users install desk accessories by dragging their icons to the System Folder icon. The Finder then moves them to the Apple Menu Items folder. ("The System Folder and Its Related Directories" later in this chapter describes the new organization of the System Folder.) From the user's point of view, there is little or no distinction between desk accessories and applications in version 7.0.

Desk accessories now behave more like applications. When a desk accessory is open, its name appears in the Application menu. A desk accessory can have its own About command in the Apple menu, and it can be brought to the foreground and sent to background independently of other desk accessories.

As described in "Icon Resources" earlier in this chapter, you can design a family of icons for your desk accessory and include all the icons used by applications: large, small, black-and-white, 4-bit color, and 8-bit color icons. If you don't provide icon resources, the Finder displays your desk accessory icon by using a mirror image of the default application icon, as shown in Figure 9-1.

Users don't even need to store desk accessories in the Apple Menu Items folder. Instead, users can store them as they store applications—that is, anywhere in the file system. Users can open desk accessories from the Finder in the same way they open applications: by double-clicking their icons or by selecting them and choosing Open from the File menu.

In previous versions of system software, the File menu for desk accessories included two commands, Close and Quit. The user chose Close to close and quit the active desk accessory. The user chose Quit to quit all desk accessories. In system software version 7.0, the Close command closes the active window and the desk accessory remains open. The Quit command now terminates the active desk accessory only. Close and Quit have keyboard equivalents of Command-W and Command-Q, respectively.

Users of previous versions of system software are accustomed to opening their desk accessories from the Apple menu. Users of version 7.0 can use this convenient method to open any of their applications. Any application or alias to an application that users drag to the Apple Menu Items folder appears in the Apple menu. Choosing a name from the Apple menu, of course, opens the application.

These similarities in installation, user access, and capability make desk accessories and applications more consistent in their appearance and behavior. There are no compelling reasons to create desk accessories for system software version 7.0. Instead, if you wish to develop a desk accessory–like tool, it's a better idea to write a small application, because desk accessories are generally more difficult to write and less powerful than applications.

You may decide to upgrade your existing desk accessory instead of rewriting it as an application, or you may wish to write a desk accessory because you want it to run in previous versions of system software where MultiFinder is optional. If you create a desk accessory, in your documentation you should instruct users of system software version 7.0 that if they want the desk accessory to appear in the Apple menu, they should install it by dragging its icon to the System Folder icon. A dialog box appears asking the user to verify that the desk accessory should be installed in the Apple Menu Items folder. The user clicks OK to accept this installation. The user also has the option to click Cancel to prevent the installation.

> **Note:** If users drag a desk accessory icon to the open System Folder window instead of to the System Folder icon, the Finder copies or moves the desk accessory into the System Folder directory instead of installing it in the Apple Menu Items directory.

You can also provide a message for your desk accessory that appears in an alert box when the user chooses the About command from the Apple menu in system software version 7.0. To provide this message, create a resource called 'dast' as an owned resource with a sub ID of 0. For example, the 'dast' resource with a sub ID of 0 for a desk accessory with a 'DRVR' ID of 12 (also called the owner ID in ResEdit) gets a resource ID of –16000. (See the Resource Manager chapter in Volume I for a discussion of owned resources.) Your 'dast' resource must contain a Pascal string only. When the user chooses the About command for your desk accessory, this string appears in an alert box along with the icon you provide for your desk accessory.

As described in "Balloon Help for Icons" later in this chapter, you can also provide a custom help balloon message for your desk accessory icon that overrides the Finder's default help balloon for desk accessory icons.

Fonts, Sounds, and Other Movable Resources

As described in the previous section, the Finder for system software version 7.0 provides the services previously performed by the Font/DA Mover. You can now distribute fonts, sounds, keyboard layouts, and script system resource collections in individual, movable resource files.

Like desk accessories, movable resources such as fonts, keyboard layouts, and sounds are represented on the screen by icons. To install these resources, the user drags their icons to the System Folder icon, and the Finder puts them in the System file. By double-clicking the System Folder to open it and then double-clicking the System file so that it opens like a folder, the user can see which movable resources are installed. (For a description of the new organization of the System Folder, see "The System Folder and Its Related Directories" later in this chapter.)

To make one of these resources visible on the screen, assign it one of the special file types defined by the Finder for movable resources. The following list shows the resources that can be moved, their assigned file types, and their icons.

Resource	File type	Large black-and-white icon
Font	'ffil'	
TrueType font	'tfil'	
Sound	'sfil'	
Keyboard layout	'kfil'	
Script system resource collection	'ifil'	

Note: You can't provide your own icons for these file types. Even if you define icons in a movable resource's bundle, the Finder displays the file using one of the icons shown above. You or your users can give customized icons to these file types (as described in "Customized Icons" earlier in this chapter) as long as the files are not moved into the System file; but as soon as users install them into the System file, the Finder displays them using the icons shown in the previous list.

The user can still store fonts and desk accessories in files that have suitcase icons, which is how they were previously distributed for installation or saved by the user using the Font/DA Mover. A suitcase file that holds desk accessories is of type 'DFIL', and a suitcase file that holds fonts is of type 'FFIL'. All suitcase files have a creator of 'DMOV'.

In your documentation, tell users to install fonts, sounds, or script system resource collections by dragging their icons to the System Folder icon. A dialog box appears asking the user to verify that the resource should be installed in the System file. The user clicks OK to accept the installation. The user also has the option to click Cancel to prevent the installation.

Note: If users drag icons to the open System Folder window instead of to the System Folder icon, the Finder copies or moves the files into the System Folder directory instead of installing them into the System file.

Balloon Help for Icons

The Finder offers Balloon Help on-line assistance for users. After the user chooses Show Balloons from the Help menu, descriptive help balloons appear when the user moves the cursor to an area of the screen (such as a menu, a window control, or a dialog box) that has a help resource associated with it.

The Finder provides default help balloons for application, control panel, system extension, and desk accessory icons. You can provide a customized help balloon for your application, control panel, system extension, or desk accessory icon by adding an 'hfdr' resource with resource ID –5696 to the resource fork of your application. Figure 9-11 compares the default help balloon with a customized help balloon for the SurfWriter application icon.

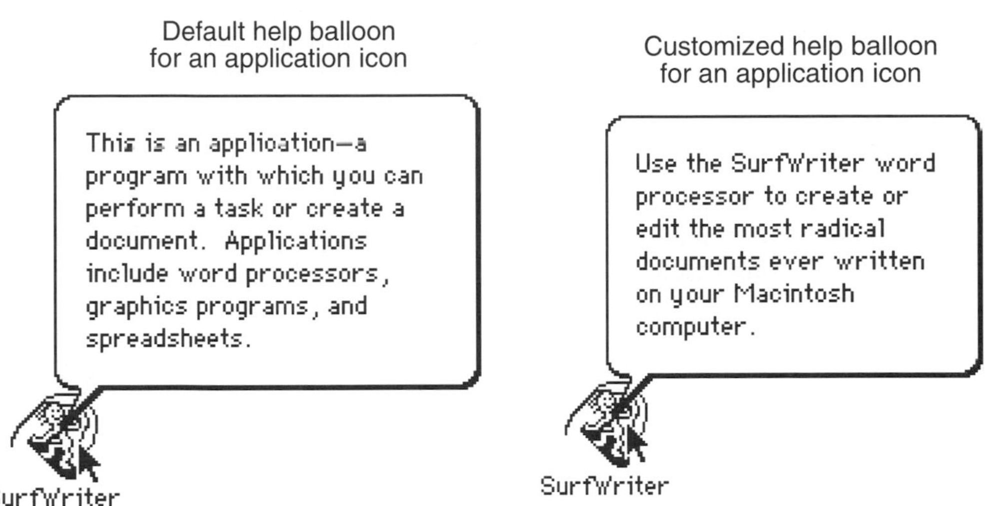
Default help balloon for an application icon
This is an application—a program with which you can perform a task or create a document. Applications include word processors, graphics programs, and spreadsheets.
SurfWriter
Customized help balloon for an application icon
Use the SurfWriter word processor to create or edit the most radical documents ever written on your Macintosh computer.
SurfWriter

Figure 9-11. Default and customized help balloons for application icons

Listing 9-5 shows the Finder help override resource and its associated 'STR ' resource that are used for the customized help balloon in Figure 9-11.

Listing 9-5. Creating a help balloon resource for an application icon

```
resource 'hfdr' (-5696, purgeable) {    /* help for SurfWriter app icon */
   HelpMgrVersion, hmDefaultOptions, 0, 0,   /* header information */
   {
   HMSTRResItem { /* use 'STR ' resource 1001 */
      1001
      }
   }
};

resource 'STR ' (1001, purgeable) { /* help message for app icon */
   "Use the SurfWriter word processor to create or edit the most "
   "radical documents ever written on your Macintosh computer."
};
```

Note: You cannot override the default help balloon that the Finder uses for document icons.

The Help Manager chapter of this volume describes in detail how to provide Balloon Help for your application icon and for other elements of your application.

FINDER INFORMATION IN THE VOLUME CATALOG

A catalog exists on every volume to maintain relationships between the files and directories on that volume. (A volume is any storage medium formatted to contain files.) Although it's used mostly by the File Manager, the catalog also contains information used by the Finder. The information for files is listed in data structures defined by the FInfo and FXInfo data types; the information for directories is listed in data structures defined by the DInfo and DXInfo data types.

Normally, your application sets the file type and the creator information in fields of the file's FInfo record when your application creates a new file. (For a discussion of the recommended new functions available for creating files, see the File Manager chapter in this volume.) The Finder manipulates the other fields in the FInfo record.

```
TYPE FInfo =
     RECORD
        fdType:           OSType;        {file type}
        fdCreator:        OSType;        {file creator}
        fdFlags:          Integer;       {Finder flags}
        fdLocation:       Point;         {file's location in }
                                         { directory}
        fdFldr:           Integer        {directory that contains }
                                         { file}
     END;
```

You typically set a file's type and creator when you create the file; for example, the FSpCreate function takes a creator and a file type as parameters. After you have created a file, you can use the GetFInfo function to return the FInfo record, then change the fdType and fdCreator fields by using the SetFInfo function.

You can always check the information in this record by calling the GetFInfo or GetCatInfo function. (See the File Manager chapter in Volume IV for information about these functions.) In particular, you may want to check the file type or creator for a file, or you may want to check or set one of your document's Finder flags, which are listed here.

Flag name	Bit number	Description
isAlias	15	The file is an alias file. Reserved for directories—in which case, set to 0.
isInvisible	14	The file or directory is invisible from the Finder and from the Standard File Package dialog boxes.
hasBundle	13	The file contains a bundle resource. Reserved for directories—in which case, set to 0.
nameLocked	12	The file or directory can't be renamed from the Finder, and the icon cannot be changed.
isStationery	11	The file is a stationery pad. Reserved for directories—in which case, set to 0.

Flag name	Bit number	Description
hasCustomIcon	10	The file or directory contains a customized icon.
Reserved	9	Reserved; set to 0.
hasBeenInited	8	The Finder has recorded information from the file's bundle resource into the desktop database and given the file or folder a position on the desktop.
hasNoINITS	7	The file contains no 'INIT' resources; set to 0. Reserved for directories; set to 0.
isShared	6	The application is available to multiple users. Defined only for applications; otherwise, set to 0.
requiresSwitchLaunch	5	Unused and reserved in version 7.0; set to 0.
colorReserved	4	Unused and reserved in version 7.0; set to 0.
color	1–3	Three bits of color coding.
isOnDesk	0	Unused and reserved in version 7.0; set to 0.

Masks for two of these bits are available as predefined constants:

```
CONST fHasBundle =        8192;          {set if file has a bundle}
      fInvisible =        16384;         {set if icon is invisible}
```

Of these Finder flags, the only ones that you might ever want to set are these:

- **isInvisible.** This flag specifies that a file is invisible from the Finder and from the Standard File Package dialog boxes. Making a file invisible is generally not recommended. Not even temporary files need to be invisible because the Temporary Items folder into which they should be written is invisible.

- **hasBundle.** This flag specifies that a file has a 'BNDL' resource that associates the file with your own icons. When the Finder displays or manipulates a file, it checks the file's hasBundle bit (also called the **bundle bit**). If that bit is not set, the Finder displays a default icon for that file type. If the hasBundle bit is set, the Finder checks the hasBeenInited bit. If the hasBeenInited bit is set, the Finder uses the information in the desktop database to display that file's icon. If the hasBeenInited bit is not set, the Finder installs the information from the bundle resource in the desktop database and sets the hasBeenInited bit. Most development environments provide a simple tool for setting the bundle bit when you create your application.

- **nameLocked.** This flag specifies that a file cannot be renamed from the Finder and that the file cannot have customized icons assigned to it by users.

- **isStationery.** This flag specifies that a file is a stationery pad. To support stationery pads, your application should check this bit for every document passed to it by either the Finder or the Standard File Package. (As described in the Standard File Package chapter in this volume, StandardGetFile and CustomGetFile return this flag in the sfType field of the standard file reply record.) If the isStationery bit is set for a file that a user wants to open, your application should copy the template's contents into a new document and open the document in an untitled window. ("Stationery Pads" earlier in this chapter discusses stationery pads.)

- **hasCustomIcon.** This flag specifies that a file has a customized icon. "Customized Icons" earlier in this chapter explains how users or your application can use customized icons.

The Finder manipulates the fields in the FXInfo, DInfo, and DXInfo records; your application shouldn't have to directly check or set any of these fields. The FXInfo and DXInfo records have been changed slightly with system software version 7.0. To update the information presented in Volume V, the new definitions are shown here.

```
TYPE FXInfo =
     RECORD
         fdIconID:          Integer;          {icon ID}
         fdUnused:          ARRAY[1..3] OF Integer;
                                              {unused but reserved 6 bytes}
         fdScript:          SignedByte;       {script flag and code}
         fdXFlags:          SignedByte;       {reserved}
         fdComment:         Integer;          {comment ID}
         fdPutAway:         LongInt           {home dir ID}
     END;

TYPE DXInfo =
     RECORD
         frScroll:          Point;            {scroll position}
         frOpenChain:       LongInt;          {directory ID chain of open }
                                              { folders}
         frScript:          SignedByte;       {script flag and code}
         frXFlags:          SignedByte;       {reserved}
         frComment:         Integer;          {comment}
         frPutAway:         LongInt           {home dir ID}
     END;
```

Previously reserved or unused fields in these two records are now partly used by the byte-length fdScript and frScript fields. These new fields are available for future enhancements of the script display capability of the Finder.

Ordinarily, the Finder displays the names of all desktop objects in the current system script, which depends on the region-specific configuration of the system. The high bit of the bytes in the fdScript and frScript fields is set by default to 0, which causes the Finder to display the filename or directory name in the current system script. If the high bit is set to 1, the Finder and the Standard File Package display the filename and directory name in the script whose code is recorded in the remaining 7 bits. However, in system software version 7.0, the Window Manager and Dialog Manager have not been enhanced to support multiple simultaneous scripts, so the system script is used for displaying filenames and directory names in dialog boxes, window titles, and other user interface elements used by the Finder. Therefore, until the system software's script capability is fully implemented, you should still treat these fields as reserved.

THE SYSTEM FOLDER AND ITS RELATED DIRECTORIES

The System Folder is a directory that stores essential system software such as the System file, the Finder, and printer drivers. Since this directory has appeared on all Macintosh computers, it's also been a dependable place to store and locate files—some that Apple software has installed, some that applications have installed, and some that users have installed. But for users of earlier versions of system software, this led to cluttered System Folders whose contents were often difficult to decipher or maintain.

System software version 7.0 introduces a new organization for the System Folder, which contains a set of new subdirectories to hold related files. The Finder uses these subdirectories to facilitate file management for the user. For example, by sorting and storing such files as desk accessories, control panels, fonts, preferences files, system extensions, and temporary files into separate folders for the user, the Finder keeps the top level of the System Folder from being cluttered with dozens, or even hundreds, of files.

The user can easily install and remove fonts, sounds, keyboard layouts, control panels, and system extensions by dragging their icons to the System Folder icon. The Finder then moves them into the proper subdirectory. When a control panel icon is dragged to the System Folder icon, for example, the Finder presents a dialog box that asks the user, "Place this control panel into the 'Control Panels' folder?" The user accepts by clicking OK or declines by clicking Cancel.

> **Note:** If users drag icons to the open System Folder window instead of to the System Folder icon, the Finder copies or moves the files into the System Folder directory instead of copying or moving them to the proper subdirectory.

Figure 9-12 shows a user's view of the new directory organization typically found within the System Folder.

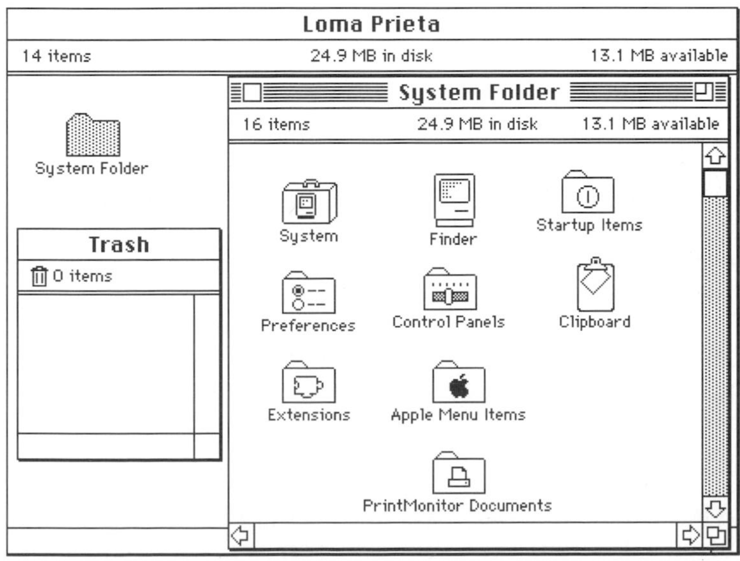

Figure 9-12. The System Folder and related folders

Additional related directories are located at the root directory. Notice the Trash window. It shows the contents of the Trash directory, which is represented to the user by the Trash icon. The Trash directory exists at the root level of the volume. In system software version 7.0, a Macintosh sharing files among users in a network environment maintains separate Trash subdirectories within a shared, network Trash directory. That is, for every user who opens a volume located on a Macintosh server and drags an object to the Trash icon, the server creates a separate, uniquely named Trash subdirectory for that user. All Trash subdirectories within a shared, network Trash directory are invisible to users. On the desktop, the user sees only the Trash icon of his or her local Macintosh computer. When the user double-clicks the Trash icon, a window reveals the names of only those files that he or she has thrown away; no distinction is made to the user as to which computers any of these files originated from.

At the root level of the volume, the Finder also maintains a Temporary Items folder and a Desktop Folder, both of which are invisible to the user and so don't appear in Figure 9-12.

Figure 9-12 illustrates the folder organization typically found on single-user systems. Of all these related directories, your application is likely to use only the Preferences folder and the Temporary Items folder. However, you cannot be certain of the location of these or any of the other system-related directories. In the future, these system-related directories may not be located in the System Folder or in the root directory. Therefore, you should always use the new FindFolder function to help you locate these directories. The FindFolder function is available only in system software version 7.0. Use the Gestalt function to determine if FindFolder is available to your application.

Folder Organization

Your application may freely use these two directories for storing and locating important files:

- **Preferences,** located in the System Folder, holds preferences files to record local configuration settings. Your application can store its preferences file in this directory. The active Finder Preferences file is always stored in the Preferences folder. Do not use the Preferences folder to hold information that is to be shared by users on more than one Macintosh computer on a network. Ensure that your application can always operate even if its preferences file has been deleted.

- **Temporary Items,** located at the root level of the volume, holds temporary files created by applications. The Temporary Items folder is invisible to the user. Your application can place its temporary files in this directory. A temporary file should exist only as long as your application needs to keep it open. As soon as your application closes the file, your application should remove the temporary file. You should also ensure that you are assigning a unique name to your temporary file so that you don't write over another application's file.

It's important to bear in mind a few rules about storing your application's files. First, don't store any files at the top level of the System Folder. Use the Preferences directory or one of the other directories described in the following list.

Second, use the FindFolder function described in the next section, "Finding Directories," to locate or put files in the right place. Don't assume files are on the same volume as your application; they could be on a different local volume, or on a remote volume on the network.

Third, don't store any files that multiple users may need to access, such as dictionaries and format converters, in the Preferences directory or in any of the directories located in the

System Folder. Remember that the files in the System Folder are generally accessible only to the person who starts up from the System file in that System Folder.

In system software version 7.0, there are other new directories that either the user or the Finder uses for storing and locating important files; these directories are described here. Generally, your application should not store files in these directories.

- **Apple Menu Items,** located in the System Folder, holds the standard desk accessories plus any other desk accessories, applications, files, folders, or aliases that the user wants to display in the Apple menu. System software version 7.0 treats desk accessories like applications, not like system resources. Desk accessories are no longer stored in a volume's System file. (For more detail, see "Desk Accessories" earlier in this chapter.) Only the user and the Installer should put things into the Apple Menu Items folder.
- **Control Panels,** located in the System Folder, holds control panels. The Apple Menu Items folder holds an alias to the Control Panels folder so that the user can also reach the control panels through the Apple menu. Only the user and the Installer should put things into the Control Panels folder.
- **Desktop Folder,** which is invisible to users of system software version 7.0, is located at the root level of the volume. The Desktop Folder stores information about the icons that appear on the desktop area of the screen. The user controls the contents of the Desktop Folder by arranging icons on the screen. What appears on the screen to the user is the union of the contents of Desktop Folders for all mounted volumes.
- **Extensions,** located in the System Folder, holds extensions—that is, code that is not part of the basic system software but that provides system-level services, such as printer drivers and system extensions. Files of type 'INIT', previously called startup documents, and of type 'appe', also known as background-only applications, are routed by the Finder to this folder. Files of type 'scri' (system extensions for script systems) are also routed to this folder. Only the user and the Installer should put things into the Extensions folder.
- **PrintMonitor Documents,** located in the System Folder, holds spooled documents waiting to be printed. Only the printing software uses the PrintMonitor Documents folder.
- **Rescued Items from *volume name*,** located in the Trash directory, is a directory created by the Finder at system boot, restart, or shutdown only when the Finder finds items in the Temporary Items folder. Since applications should remove their temporary files when they close them, the existence of a file in a Temporary Items folder indicates a system crash. When the Finder discovers a file in the Temporary Items folder, the Finder creates a Rescued Items from *volume name* directory that is named for the volume on which the Temporary Items folder exists. For example, the Finder creates a directory called Rescued Items from Loma Prieta when a file is discovered in the Temporary Items folder on a volume named Loma Prieta. The Finder then moves the temporary file to that directory so that users can examine the file in case they want to recreate their work up to the time of the system crash. When a user empties the Trash, all Rescued Items folders disappear. Only the Finder should put anything into Rescued Items directories.
- **Startup Items,** located in the System Folder, holds applications and desk accessories (or their aliases) that the user wants started up every time the Finder starts up. Only the user should put things into the Startup Items folder. Note that there is a distinction between startup applications that users put in the Startup Items folder and system extensions of file type 'INIT' (previously called startup documents), which are typically installed in the Extensions folder.

- **System file,** located in the System Folder, contains the basic system software plus some system resources, such as font and sound resources. In version 7.0, the System file behaves as a folder in this regard: although it looks like a suitcase icon, double-clicking it opens a window that reveals movable resource files (such as fonts, sounds, keyboard layouts, and script system resource collections) stored in the System file. ("Fonts, Sounds, and Other Movable Resources" earlier in this chapter describes the resources that can be moved into the System file.) Only the user and the Installer should put resources into the System file.
- **Trash,** located at the root level of a volume, holds items that the user moves to the Trash icon. After opening the Trash icon, the user sees the collection of all items that the user has moved to the Trash icon—that is, the union of all appropriate Trash directories from all mounted volumes. A Macintosh set up to share files among users in a network environment maintains separate Trash subdirectories for remote users within its shared, network Trash directory. That is, for every remote user who opens a volume located on a Macintosh file server and drags an object to the Trash icon, the server creates a separate, uniquely named Trash subdirectory for that user. All Trash subdirectories and the shared, network Trash directory are invisible to users. The Finder for system software version 7.0 empties a Trash directory (or, in the case of a file server, a Trash subdirectory) only when the user of that directory chooses the Empty Trash command.

Although the names of the visible system-related folders vary on different international systems, the invisible directories Temporary Items and Desktop Folder keep these names on all systems. System software assigns unique names for invisible Trash subdirectories.

Generally, you should store application-specific files in the folder with your application, not in any of these system-related directories. Your application may want to provide users with a mechanism to specify a directory in which to look for auxiliary files. For example, you could design a customized version of the open file dialog box that allows users to specify a path to locations where files are stored. This technique may be useful for finding files that are shared by several applications. It's also possible to track the location of files by using the Alias Manager. For details, see the Alias Manager chapter in this volume.

When you design your application, it's important to consider the user's view of the tools that you provide. In most cases you'll want to build your application so that the user deals with one icon that represents the entire set of abilities your application provides. This scheme simplifies the user's world by restricting the complexity of installing and maintaining your product. If you provide optional tools—such as a dictionary and thesaurus—that have their own icons, it's a good idea to allow these tools to work from any location in the file system rather than relying on their storage somewhere in the System Folder.

Finding Directories

You can use the FindFolder function to get the path information you need to gain access to the directories described in the previous section. Those you're most likely to want to access are Preferences, Temporary Items, and Trash. For example, you might wish to check for the existence of a user's configuration file in Preferences, create a temporary file in Temporary Items, or—if your application runs out of storage when trying to save a file—check how much storage is taken by items in the Trash directory and report this to the user.

The FindFolder function is available only in system software version 7.0. Use the Gestalt function with the Gestalt selector gestaltFindFolderAttr. Test the bit field indicated by the gestaltFindFolderPresent constant in the response parameter. If the bit is set, then the FindFolder function is present.

```
CONST gestaltFindFolderPresent = 0;        {if this bit is set, }
                                           { FindFolder is present}
```

Your application passes the FindFolder function a target volume and a constant that tells it which directory you're interested in. FindFolder returns a volume reference number and a directory ID. If the specified directory does not exist, FindFolder can create it and return the new directory ID.

Don't assume files are on the same volume as your application; they could be on a different local volume or on a remote volume on a network.

The system-related directories in system software version 7.0, the folder types of these directories, and the constants that represent them are listed here.

Directory	Folder type	Constant
Apple Menu Items	'amnu'	kAppleMenuFolderType
Control Panels	'ctrl'	kControlPanelFolderType
Desktop Folder	'desk'	kDesktopFolderType
Extensions	'extn'	kExtensionFolderType
Preferences	'pref'	kPreferencesFolderType
PrintMonitor Documents	'prnt'	kPrintMonitorDocsFolderType
Shared, network Trash directory	'empt'	kWhereToEmptyTrashFolderType
Single-user Trash directory	'trsh'	kTrashFolderType
Startup Items	'strt'	kStartupFolderType
System Folder	'macs'	kSystemFolderType
Temporary Items	'temp'	kTemporaryFolderType

Note: The Finder identifies the subdirectories of the System Folder, and their folder types, in a resource of type 'fld#' located in the System file. Do not modify or rely on the contents of the 'fld#' resource in the System file; use only the FindFolder function and these constants to find the appropriate directories.

Use the kTrashFolderType constant to locate the current user's Trash directory for a given volume—even one located on a file server. On a file server, you can use the kWhereToEmptyTrashFolderType constant to locate the parent directory of all logged-on users' Trash subdirectories.

In calls to FindFolder, you can also use these three constants:

```
CONST kOnSystemDisk       = $8000;  {use vRefNum for the boot disk}
      kCreateFolder       = TRUE;   {create folder if it doesn't exist}
      kDontCreateFolder   = FALSE;  {don't create folder}
```

Call the FindFolder function to get a volume reference number and directory ID for any of these directories.

```
FUNCTION FindFolder (vRefNum: Integer; folderType: OSType; createFolder:
                     Boolean; VAR foundVRefNum: Integer; VAR foundDirID:
                     LongInt) : OSErr;
```

The FindFolder function returns the volume reference number and directory ID of a specified folder type for a specified volume.You specify a volume reference number (or the constant kOnSystemDisk for the boot disk) in the vRefNum parameter. In the folderType parameter, specify a constant from the previous list. Use the constant kCreateFolder in the createFolder parameter to tell FindFolder to create a directory if it does not already exist; otherwise, use the constant kDontCreateFolder. FindFolder puts the results in foundVRefNum and foundDirID.

Remember that the specified folder used for a given volume might be located on a different volume in the future; therefore, do not assume the volume that you specify in vRefNum and the volume returned in foundVRefNum will be the same.

> **Note:** Directories inside the System Folder are created only if the System Folder directory exists. FindFolder will not create a System Folder directory even if the kCreateFolder constant is specified.

The FindFolder function returns a nonzero result code if the folder isn't found, and it can also return other file system errors reported by the File Manager or Memory Manager.

Result codes

noErr	0	No error
fnfErr	–43	Type not found in 'fld#' resource, or disk doesn't have System Folder support or System Folder in volume header, or disk does not have desktop database support for Desktop Folder—in all cases, folder not found
dupFNErr	–48	File found instead of folder

THE DESKTOP DATABASE

For quick access to the resources it needs, the Finder maintains a central **desktop database** of information about the files and directories on a volume. The Finder updates the database when applications are added, moved, renamed, or deleted.

Normally, your application won't need to use the information in the desktop database or to use Desktop Manager routines to manipulate it. Instead, your application should let the Finder manipulate the desktop database and handle such Desktop Manager tasks as launching applications when users double-click icons, maintaining user comments associated with files, and managing the icons used by applications.

Although there may be instances where you would like to gain access to the desktop database by using Desktop Manager routines, you should never change, add to, or remove any of this information. Manipulating the desktop database is likely to wreak havoc on your users' systems.

In case you should discover some important need to retrieve information from the desktop database or even to change the desktop database from within your application, Desktop Manager routines are provided for you to do so. While your application probably won't ever need to use them, for the sake of completeness they are described in this section.

Much of the information in the desktop database comes from the bundle resources for applications and other files on the volume. (See "Finder Information in the Volume Catalog" earlier in this chapter for a discussion on setting the bundle bit of an application so that its bundled resources get stored in the desktop database.) The desktop database contains all icon definitions and their associated file types. It lists all the file types that each application can open and all copies or versions of the application that's listed as the creator of a file. The desktop database also lists the location of each application on the disk and any comments that the user has added to the information windows for desktop objects. The Desktop Manager provides a new set of routines that lets your application retrieve this information from the desktop database. These are described in "Desktop Manager Routines" later in this chapter.

The Finder maintains a desktop database for each volume with a capacity greater than 2 MB. For most volumes, such as hard disks, the database is stored on the volume itself. For read-only volumes—such as some compact discs—that don't contain their own desktop database, the Desktop Manager creates it and stores it in the System Folder of the boot drive.

> **Note:** If you distribute read-only media, it is generally a good idea to store on each volume both a desktop database (for users running system software version 7.0) and a Desktop file (for users running older versions of system software). Create a desktop database on your master volume by pressing Command-Option when booting your system with system software version 7.0. Then create a Desktop file by pressing Command-Option and restarting your system with version 6.0.

For compatibility with older versions of system software, the Finder keeps the information for ejectable volumes with a capacity smaller than 2 MB in a resource file instead of a database.

Although the Desktop Manager provides tools for both reading and changing the desktop database, your application should not ordinarily change anything in the database. You can read the database to retrieve information, such as the icons defined by other applications.

> **Note:** The desktop database doesn't store customized icons (that is, those with resource IDs of –16455 described in "Customized Icons" earlier in this chapter), so your application can't retrieve them by using Desktop Manager routines.

History of the Desktop Database

In earlier versions of system software, Finder information for each volume was stored in the volume's Desktop file, a resource file created and used by the Finder and invisible to the user. This strategy meets the needs of a single-user system with reasonably small volumes. The Desktop file is still used on ejectable volumes with a capacity less than 2 MB so that these floppy disks can be shared with Macintosh computers running earlier versions of system software. (Note, however, that resources can't be shared. Since the Finder is always running in system software version 7.0, it keeps each floppy disk's Desktop file open, so your application can't read or write it.)

Because resources can't be shared, a different strategy has been used for AppleShare volumes, which are available to multiple users over a network. The Desktop Manager in system software version 7.0 uses the strategy for large local volumes that AppleShare file servers have previously used for shared volumes. When a volume is first mounted, the Finder collects the bundle information from all applications on the disk and builds the desktop database. Whenever an application is added to or removed from the disk, the Finder updates the desktop database. Through Desktop Manager routines, the database is also accessible to any other application running on the system.

Using the Desktop Database

You can manipulate the desktop database with a set of low-level routines that follow the parameter-block conventions used by the File Manager. (For a description of parameter blocks, see the File Manager chapter of Volume IV.)

The desktop database functions use this parameter block:

```
TYPE DTPBRec =
     RECORD
        qLink:              QElemPtr;       {next queue entry}
        qType:              Integer;        {queue type}
        ioTrap:             Integer;        {routine trap}
        ioCmdAddr:          Ptr;            {routine address}
        ioCompletion:       ProcPtr;        {completion routine}
        ioResult:           OSErr;          {result code}
        ioNamePtr:          StringPtr;      {file, directory, or }
                                            { volume name}
        ioVRefNum:          Integer;        {volume reference number}
        ioDTRefNum:         Integer;        {desktop database reference }
                                            { number}
        ioIndex:            Integer;        {index into icon list}
        ioTagInfo:          LongInt;        {tag information}
        ioDTBuffer:         Ptr;            {data buffer}
        ioDTReqCount:       LongInt;        {requested length of data}
        ioDTActCount:       LongInt;        {actual length of data}
        filler1:            SignedByte;     {unused}
        ioIconType:         SignedByte;     {icon type}
        filler2:            Integer;        {unused}
        ioDirID:            LongInt;        {parent directory ID}
        ioFileCreator:      OSType;         {file creator}
        ioFileType:         OSType;         {file type}
        ioFiller3:          LongInt;        {unused}
        ioDTLgLen:          LongInt;        {logical length of desktop }
                                            { database}
        ioDTPyLen:          LongInt;        {physical length of desktop }
                                            { database}
        ioFiller4:          ARRAY[1..14] OF Integer;
                                            {unused}
        ioAPPLParID:        LongInt         {parent directory ID of }
                                            { application}
     END;
```

Because you cannot use the Desktop Manager functions on a disk that does not have a desktop database, call PBHGetVolParms to verify that the target disk has a desktop database before calling any of the Desktop Manager functions. (For a description of the PBHGetVolParms function and the bHasDesktopMgr bit that you should check, see the File Manager chapter in this volume.)

Because the Finder uses the desktop database, the database is almost always open. When the Desktop Manager opens the database, it assigns the database a reference number that represents the access path. Use the PBDTGetPath function to get the reference number, which you must specify when calling most other Desktop Manager functions (see the following section, "Desktop Manager Routines"). If the desktop database is not open, PBDTGetPath opens it.

If you are manipulating the database in the absence of the Finder, you can open the database with PBDTOpenInform, which performs the same functions as PBDTGetPath and also sets a flag to tell your application whether the desktop database was empty when it was opened. Your application should never close the database.

The Desktop Manager provides different functions for manipulating different kinds of information in the database. Not all manipulations are possible with all kinds of data.

You can retrieve five kinds of information from the database:

- icon definitions
- file types and icon types supported by a known creator
- name and location of applications with a known creator
- user comments for a file or a directory
- size and parent directory of the desktop database

To retrieve an icon definition, call PBDTGetIcon. You must specify a file creator, file type, and icon type. The database recognizes both large and small icons, with 1, 4, or 8 bits of color encoding. (See the earlier description of icons in "Finder-Related Resources" for details.)

To step through a list of all the icon types supported by an application, make repeated calls to PBDTGetIconInfo. Each time you call PBDTGetIconInfo, you specify a creator and an index value. Set the index to 1 on the first call, and increment it on each subsequent call until PBDTGetIconInfo returns the result code afpItemNotFound. For each entry in the icon list, PBDTGetIconInfo reports the icon type, the file type it is associated with, and the size of its icon data.

To identify the application that can open a file with a given creator, call PBDTGetAPPL. In each call to PBDTGetAPPL, you specify a creator (which is the application's signature) and an index value. An index value of 0 retrieves the "first choice" application—that is, the one with the most recent creation date. By setting the index to 1 on the first call and incrementing it on each subsequent call until PBDTGetAPPL returns the result code afpItemNotFound, you can make multiple calls to PBDTGetAPPL to find all copies or versions of the application with this signature on the disk. PBDTGetAPPL returns them all in arbitrary order. PBDTGetAPPL returns the name, parent directory ID, and creation date of each application in the desktop database.

To retrieve the user comments for a file or directory, call PBDTGetComment. The user can change comments at any time by typing in the comment box of the information window for any desktop object.

Your application should not ordinarily call the functions for adding and removing data to and from the database. If your application does need to write to or delete information from the desktop database, it must call PBDTFlush to update the copy stored on the volume.

The following list summarizes the data manipulation functions.

Kind of data	**Read**	**Write**	**Remove**
Icon definitions	PBDTGetIcon	PBDTAddIcon	—
Icon types supported by an application	PBDTGetIconInfo	—	—
Applications with a given creator	PBDTGetAPPL	PBDTAddAPPL	PBDTRemoveAPPL
User comments	PBDTGetComment	PBDTSetComment	PBDTRemoveComment
Entire desktop database	PBDTGetInfo (returns the size and parent directory of the database)	PBDTFlush (updates the copy stored on the volume)	PBDTDelete and PBDTReset (neither should be called by your application)

Desktop Manager Routines

This section describes the low-level routines for using the desktop database.

All low-level routines exchange parameters with your application through a parameter block. When calling a low-level routine, you pass a pointer to the parameter block. See the introduction to low-level routines in the File Manager chapter of Volume IV for a description of the standard parameters in a low-level routine.

Three Desktop Manager functions—namely, PBDTGetPath, PBDTOpenInform, and PBDTCloseDown—run synchronously only. All other Desktop Manager routines can run either asynchronously or synchronously. There are three versions of each of these routines. The first version takes two parameters: a pointer to the parameter block, and a Boolean value that determines whether the routine is run asynchronously (TRUE) or synchronously (FALSE). Here, for example, is the first version of a routine that retrieves the user's comment stored for a file or a directory:

```
FUNCTION PBDTGetComment (paramBlock: DTPBPtr; async: Boolean) : OSErr;
```

The second version does not take a second parameter; instead, it adds the suffix "Async" to the name of the routine.

```
FUNCTION PBDTGetCommentAsync (paramBlock: DTPBPtr) : OSErr;
```

Similarly, the third version of the routine does not take a second parameter; instead, it adds the suffix "Sync" to the name of the routine.

```
FUNCTION PBDTGetCommentSync (paramBlock: DTPBPtr) : OSErr;
```

All routines in this section are documented using the first version only. Note, however, that the second and third versions of these routines do not use the glue code that the first versions use and are therefore more efficient.

Assembly-language note: You can invoke each of the Desktop Manager routines with a macro that has the same name as the routine preceded by an underscore. These macros, however, aren't really trap macros. Instead, they expand to invoke the trap macro _HFSDispatch. The File Manager determines which routine to execute from the routine selector, an integer placed in register D0. The routine selectors appear in the assembly-language information in the chapter summary.

Locating and Opening the Desktop Database

To get the access path to a database or to create a database if one doesn't exist, use the PBDTGetPath or PBDTOpenInform function. These routines run synchronously only.

```
FUNCTION PBDTGetPath (paramBlock: DTPBPtr) : OSErr;
```

Parameter block

←	16	ioResult	word	result code
→	18	ioNamcPtr	long	volume name or full pathname
→	22	ioVRefNum	word	volume reference number
←	24	ioDTRefNum	word	desktop database reference number

PBDTGetPath returns the desktop database reference number in the ioDTRefNum field, which represents the access path to the database. You specify the volume by passing a pointer to its name in the ioNamePtr field or a volume reference number in the ioVRefNum field. If the desktop database is not already open, PBDTGetPath opens it and then returns the reference number. If the desktop database doesn't exist, PBDTGetPath creates it. If PBDTGetPath fails, it sets the ioDTRefNum field to 0.

Note: You cannot use the desktop reference number as a file reference number in any File Manager calls.

▲ **Warning:** Do not call PBDTGetPath at interrupt time—it allocates memory in the system heap. ▲

Result codes

noErr	0	No error
ioErr	–36	I/O error
extFSErr	–58	External file system—file system identifier is nonzero
desktopDamagedErr	–1305	The desktop database has become corrupted—the Finder will fix this, but if your application is not running with the Finder, use PBDTReset or PBDTDelete

PBDTOpenInform performs the same function as PBDTGetPath, but it also reports whether the desktop database was empty when it was opened.

```
FUNCTION PBDTOpenInform (paramBlock: DTPBPtr) : OSErr;
```

Parameter block

←	16	ioResult	word	result code
→	18	ioNamePtr	long	volume name or full pathname
→	22	ioVRefNum	word	volume reference number
←	24	ioDTRefNum	word	desktop database reference number
←	28	ioTagInfo	long	return flag (in low bit)

If the desktop database was just created in response to PBDTOpenInform (and is therefore empty), PBDTOpenInform sets the low bit in the ioTagInfo field to 0. If the desktop database had been created before you called PBDTOpenInform, PBDTOpenInform sets the low bit in the ioTagInfo field to 1.

Result codes

noErr	0	No error
ioErr	–36	I/O error
paramErr	–50	Parameter error; use PBDTGetPath
extFSErr	–58	External file system—file-system identifier is nonzero
desktopDamagedErr	–1305	The desktop database has become corrupted—the Finder will fix this, but if your application is not running with the Finder, use DTReset or DTDelete

The PBDTCloseDown function is used by system software to close the desktop database, though your application should never do this itself. PBDTCloseDown runs synchronously only, and though it will not close down the desktop databases of remote volumes, it will invalidate all local DTRefNum values for remote desktop databases.

```
FUNCTION PBDTCloseDown (paramBlock: DTPBPtr;) : OSErr;
```

Parameter block

←	16	ioResult	word	result code
→	24	ioDTRefNum	word	desktop database reference number

PBDTCloseDown closes the database specified in ioDTRefNum and frees all resources allocated by PBDTOpenInform or PBDTGetPath.

▲ **Warning:** Applications should not call PBDTCloseDown. The system software closes the database when the volume is unmounted. ▲

Result codes

noEff	0	No error
ioErr	–36	I/O error
rfNumErr	–51	Reference number invalid
extFSErr	–58	External file system—file system identifier is nonzero

Reading the Desktop Database

To retrieve an icon definition, use the PBDTGetIcon function.

```
FUNCTION PBDTGetIcon (paramBlock: DTPBPtr; async: Boolean) : OSErr;
```

Parameter block

→	12	ioCompletion	long	completion routine
←	16	ioResult	word	result code
→	24	ioDTRefNum	word	database reference number
←	28	ioTagInfo	long	reserved; must be initialized to 0
→	32	ioDTBuffer	long	pointer to icon data
→	36	ioDTReqCount	long	requested size of icon bitmap
←	40	ioDTActCount	long	actual size of icon bitmap
→	45	ioIconType	byte	icon type
→	52	ioFileCreator	long	icon's file creator
→	56	ioFileType	long	icon's file type

PBDTGetIcon returns the bitmap for an icon that represents a file of a given type and creator. You pass a pointer to the buffer for the icon bitmap in the ioDTBuffer field. The bitmap is returned in the buffer pointed to by ioDTBuffer. You specify the desktop database in ioDTRefNum, the file creator in ioFileCreator, and the file type in ioFileType. For the icon type in ioIconType, specify a constant from the following list.

Constant	Value	Corresponding resource type	Description
kLargeIcon	1	'ICN#'	Large black-and-white icon with mask
kLarge4BitIcon	2	'icl4'	Large 4-bit color icon
kLarge8BitIcon	3	'icl8'	Large 8-bit color icon
kSmallIcon	4	'ics#'	Small black-and-white icon with mask
kSmall4BitIcon	5	'ics4'	Small 4-bit color icon
kSmall8BitIcon	6	'ics8'	Small 8-bit color icon

The value you supply in ioDTReqCount is the size in bytes of the buffer that you've allocated for the icon's bitmap pointed to by ioDTBuffer; this value depends on the icon type. Be sure to allocate enough storage for the icon data; 1024 bytes is the largest amount required for any icon under system software version 7.0. You can use a constant from the following list.

Constant	Value (bytes in bitmap)	Corresponding resource type	Description
kLargeIconSize	256	'ICN#'	Large black-and-white icon with mask
kLarge4BitIconSize	512	'icl4'	Large 4-bit color icon
kLarge8BitIconSize	1024	'icl8'	Large 8-bit color icon
kSmallIconSize	64	'ics#'	Small black-and-white icon with mask
kSmall4BitIconSize	128	'ics4'	Small 4-bit color icon
kSmall8BitIconSize	256	'ics8'	Small 8-bit color icon

The value in ioDTActCount reflects the size of the bitmap actually retrieved. If ioDTActCount is larger than ioDTReqCount, only the amount of data allowed by ioDTReqCount is valid.

Result codes

noErr	0	No error
ioErr	–36	I/O error
rfNumErr	–51	Reference number invalid
extFSErr	–58	External file system—file system identifier is nonzero
afpItemNotFound	–5012	Information not found

To retrieve the icon type and associated file type, use the PBDTGetIconInfo function.

```
FUNCTION PBDTGetIconInfo (paramBlock: DTPBPtr; async: Boolean) :
                         OSErr;
```

Parameter block

→	12	ioCompletion	long	completion routine
←	16	ioResult	word	result code
→	24	ioDTRefNum	word	database reference number
→	26	ioIndex	word	index into icon list
←	28	ioTagInfo	long	reserved; must be initialized to 0
←	40	ioDTActCount	long	size of icon bitmap
←	45	ioIconType	byte	icon type
→	52	ioFileCreator	long	icon's file creator
←	56	ioFileType	long	icon's file type

PBDTGetIconInfo retrieves the icon type and the associated file type of an icon in the database. You use it to identify the set of icons associated with a given creator. You specify the creator by placing its signature in ioFileCreator, and you specify the database by placing the desktop database reference number in the ioDTRefNum field. PBDTGetIconInfo returns the size of the bitmap in ioDTActCount, the file type in ioFileType, and the icon size and color depth in ioIconType.

See the previous description of the PBDTGetIcon function for a list of values and their constants returned by PBDTGetIconInfo in the ioIconType field. Ignore any values that may be returned in ioIconType and that are not listed there; they represent special icons used only by the Finder.

To step through a list of the icon types supported by an application, make repeated calls to PBDTGetIconInfo, specifying a creator and an index value for ioIndex each call. Set the index to 1 on the first call, and increment it on each subsequent call until ioResult returns afpItemNotFound.

Result codes

noErr	0	No error
ioErr	–36	I/O error
rfNumErr	–51	Reference number invalid
extFSErr	–58	External file system—file system identifier is nonzero
afpItemNotFound	–5012	Information not found

To identify the application that can open a file with a given creator, use the PBDTGetAPPL function.

```
FUNCTION PBDTGetAPPL (paramBlock: DTPBPtr; async: Boolean) : OSErr;
```

Parameter block

→	12	ioCompletion	long	completion routine
←	16	ioResult	word	result code
→	18	ioNamePtr	long	pointer to application's name
→	24	ioDTRefNum	word	database reference number
→	26	ioIndex	word	index into application list
←	28	ioTagInfo	long	application's creation date
→	52	ioFileCreator	long	application's signature
←	100	ioAPPLParID	long	application's parent directory

For an application in the database specified in ioDTRefNum with the signature specified in ioFileCreator, PBDTGetAPPL returns the filename in ioNamePtr, the parent directory ID in ioAPPLParID, and the creation date in ioTagInfo. A single call, with ioIndex set to 0, finds the application file with the most recent creation date. If you want to retrieve all copies of the application with the given signature, start with ioIndex set to 1 and increment until ioResult returns afpItemNotFound; when called multiple times in this fashion, PBDTGetAPPL returns the application's copies, including the file with the most recent creation date, in arbitrary order.

Result codes

noErr	0	No error
ioErr	–36	I/O error
rfNumErr	–51	Reference number invalid
extFSErr	–58	External file system—file system identifier is nonzero
afpItemNotFound	–5012	Information not found

To retrieve the user comments for a file or directory, use the PBDTGetComment function.

```
FUNCTION PBDTGetComment (paramBlock: DTPBPtr; async: Boolean) : OSErr;
```

Parameter block

→	12	ioCompletion	long	completion routine
←	16	ioResult	word	result code
→	18	ioNamePtr	long	pointer to file or directory name
→	24	ioDTRefNum	word	desktop database reference number
→	32	ioDTBuffer	long	pointer to comment text (200 bytes)
←	40	ioDTActCount	long	comment size
→	48	ioDirID	long	parent directory of file or directory

PBDTGetComment retrieves the comment stored for a file or directory in the database specified in ioDTRefNum. You specify the filename or directory name and its parent directory ID through ioNamePtr and ioDirID. You allocate a buffer big enough to hold the largest comment, 200 bytes, and put a pointer to it in the ioDTBuffer field. PBDTGetComment places the comment in the buffer as a plain text string and places the length of the comment in ioDTActCount.

Result codes

noErr	0	No error
ioErr	–36	I/O error
fnfErr	–43	File or directory doesn't exist
rfNumErr	–51	Reference number invalid
extFSErr	–58	External file system—file system identifier is nonzero
afpItemNotFound	–5012	Information not found

Adding to the Desktop Database

Your application should not ordinarily call the functions for adding data to the database. If your application does need to write to or delete information from the desktop database, it must call PBDTFlush to update the copy stored on the volume.

To add an icon definition to the desktop database, use the PBDTAddIcon function.

```
FUNCTION PBDTAddIcon (paramBlock: DTPBPtr; async: Boolean) : OSErr;
```

Parameter block

→	12	ioCompletion	long	completion routine
←	16	ioResult	word	result code
→	24	ioDTRefNum	word	desktop database reference number
→	28	ioTagInfo	long	reserved; must be initialized to 0
→	32	ioDTBuffer	long	pointer to icon data

→	36	ioDTReqCount	long	size of icon bitmap
→	45	ioIconType	byte	icon type
→	52	ioFileCreator	long	icon's file creator
→	56	ioFileType	long	icon's file type

PBDTAddIcon adds an icon definition to the desktop database specified in ioDTRefNum. You specify the creator and file type that the icon is associated with in the ioFileCreator and ioFileType fields. For the icon type in ioIconType, specify either a constant or a value from the following list.

Constant	Value	Corresponding resource type	Description
kLargeIcon	1	'ICN#'	Large black-and-white icon with mask
kLarge4BitIcon	2	'icl4'	Large 4-bit color icon
kLarge8BitIcon	3	'icl8'	Large 8-bit color icon
kSmallIcon	4	'ics#'	Small black-and-white icon with mask
kSmall4BitIcon	5	'ics4'	Small 4-bit color icon
kSmall8BitIcon	6	'ics8'	Small 8-bit color icon

The value you supply in ioDTReqCount is the size in bytes of the buffer that you've allocated for the icon's bitmap pointed to by ioDTBuffer; this value depends on the icon type. Be sure to allocate enough storage for the icon data; 1024 bytes is the largest amount required for any icon under system software version 7.0. You can use a constant from the following list.

Constant	Value (bytes in bitmap)	Corresponding resource type	Description
kLargeIconSize	256	'ICN#'	Large black-and-white icon with mask
kLarge4BitIconSize	512	'icl4'	Large 4-bit color icon
kLarge8BitIconSize	1024	'icl8'	Large 8-bit color icon
kSmallIconSize	64	'ics#'	Small black-and-white icon with mask
kSmall4BitIconSize	128	'ics4'	Small 4-bit color icon
kSmall8BitIconSize	256	'ics8'	Small 8-bit color icon

You pass a pointer to the icon bitmap in the ioDTBuffer field. You must initialize the ioTagInfo field to 0.

If the database already contains an icon definition for an icon of that type, file type, and file creator, the new definition replaces the old.

Result codes

noErr	0	No error
ioErr	–36	I/O error
wPrErr	–44	Volume is locked through hardware
vLckdErr	–46	Volume is locked through software
rfNumErr	–51	Reference number invalid
extFSErr	–58	External file system—file system identifier is nonzero
afpIconTypeError	–5030	Sizes of new icon and one it replaces don't match

To add an application to the desktop database, use the PBDTAddAPPL function.

```
FUNCTION PBDTAddAPPL (paramBlock: DTPBPtr; async: Boolean) : OSErr;
```

Parameter block

→	12	ioCompletion	long	completion routine
←	16	ioResult	word	result code
→	18	ioNamePtr	long	pointer to application's name
→	24	ioDTRefNum	word	desktop database reference number
→	28	ioTagInfo	long	reserved; must be set to 0
→	48	ioDirID	long	application's parent directory
→	52	ioFileCreator	long	application's signature

PBDTAddAPPL adds an entry in the desktop database specified in ioDTRefNum for an application with the specified signature. You pass the application's signature in ioFileCreator, a pointer to the application's filename in ioNamePtr, and the application's parent directory ID in ioDirID. Initialize ioTagInfo to 0.

Result codes

noErr	0	No error
ioErr	–36	I/O error
fnfErr	–43	Application not present on volume
wPrErr	–44	Volume is locked through hardware
vLckdErr	–46	Volume is locked through software
rfNumErr	–51	Reference number invalid
extFSErr	–58	External file system—file system identifier is nonzero

To add a user comment for a file or a directory to the desktop database, use the PBDTSetComment function.

```
FUNCTION PBDTSetComment (paramBlock: DTPBPtr; async: Boolean) : OSErr;
```

Parameter block

→	12	ioCompletion	long	completion routine
←	16	ioResult	word	result code
→	18	ioNamePtr	long	pointer to file or directory name
→	24	ioDTRefNum	word	desktop database reference number
→	32	ioDTBuffer	long	pointer to comment text
→	36	ioDTReqCount	long	comment length
→	48	ioDirID	long	parent directory of file or directory

PBDTSetComment establishes the user comment associated with a file or directory in the database specified in ioDTRefNum. You specify the object name through ioNamePtr and the parent directory ID in ioDirID. You put the comment as a plain text string in a buffer pointed to by ioDTBuffer, and you specify the length of the buffer (in bytes) in ioDTReqCount. The maximum length of a comment is 200 bytes; longer comments are clipped. Since the comment is a plain text string and not a Pascal string, the Desktop Manager relies on the value in ioDTReqCount for determining the length of the buffer.

If the specified object already has a comment in the database, the new comment replaces the old.

Result codes

noErr	0	No error
ioErr	–36	I/O error
fnfErr	–43	File or directory doesn't exist
wPrErr	–44	Volume is locked through hardware
vLckdErr	–46	Volume is locked through software
rfNumErr	–51	Reference number invalid
extFSErr	–58	External file system—file system identifier is nonzero

Deleting Entries From the Desktop Database

Your application should not ordinarily call the functions for adding and removing data to and from the database. If your application does need to write to or delete information from the desktop database, it must call PBDTFlush to update the copy stored on the volume.

To remove an application from the desktop database, call the PBDTRemoveAPPL function.

```
FUNCTION PBDTRemoveAPPL (paramBlock: DTPBPtr; async: Boolean) : OSErr;
```

Parameter block

→	12	ioCompletion	long	completion routine
←	16	ioResult	word	result code
→	18	ioNamePtr	long	pointer to application's name
→	24	ioDTRefNum	word	desktop database reference number
→	48	ioDirID	long	application's parent directory
→	52	ioFileCreator	long	application's signature

PBDTRemoveAPPL removes the mapping information for an application from the database specified in ioDTRefNum. You specify the application's name through ioNamePtr, its parent directory ID in ioDirID, and its signature in ioFileCreator.

You can call PBDTRemoveAPPL even if the application is not present on the volume.

Result codes

noErr	0	No error
ioErr	–36	I/O error
wPrErr	–44	Volume is locked through hardware
vLckdErr	–46	Volume is locked through software
rfNumErr	–51	Reference number invalid
extFSErr	–58	External file system—file system identifier is nonzero
afpItemNotFound	–5012	Application not found

To remove a user comment from the desktop database, call the PBDTRemoveComment function.

```
FUNCTION PBDTRemoveComment (paramBlock: DTPBPtr; async: Boolean) :
                            OSErr;
```

Parameter block

→	12	ioCompletion	long	completion routine
←	16	ioResult	word	result code
→	18	ioNamePtr	long	pointer to filename or directory name
→	24	ioDTRefNum	word	database reference number
→	48	ioDirID	long	parent directory of file or directory

PBDTRemoveComment removes the comment associated with a file or directory from the database specified in ioDTRefNum. You specify the file or directory name through ioNamePtr and the parent directory ID in ioDirID. You cannot remove a comment if the file or directory is not present on the volume. If no comment was stored for the file, PBDTRemoveComment returns an error.

Result codes

noErr	0	No error
ioErr	–36	I/O error
fnfErr	–43	File or directory doesn't exist
wPrErr	–44	Volume is locked through hardware
vLckdErr	–46	Volume is locked through software
rfNumErr	–51	Reference number invalid
extFSErr	–58	External file system—file system identifier is nonzero
afpItemNotFound	–5012	Comment not found

Manipulating the Desktop Database Itself

To save your changes to the desktop database, use the PBDTFlush function.

```
FUNCTION PBDTFlush (paramBlock: DTPBPtr; async: Boolean) : OSErr;
```

Parameter block

→	12	ioCompletion	long	completion routine
←	16	ioResult	word	result code
→	24	ioDTRefNum	word	database reference number

PBDTFlush writes the contents of the desktop database specified in ioDTRefNum to the volume.

Note: If your application has manipulated information in the database using any of the routines described earlier in "Desktop Manager Routines," you must call PBDTFlush to update the copy stored on the volume.

Result codes

noErr	0	No error
ioErr	–36	I/O error
wPrErr	–44	Volume is locked through hardware
vLckdErr	–46	Volume is locked through software
rfNumErr	–51	Reference number invalid
extFSErr	–58	External file system—file system identifier is nonzero

To determine the parent directory and the amount of space used by the desktop database on a particular volume, use the PBDTGetInfo function.

```
FUNCTION PBDTGetInfo (paramBlock: DTPBPtr; async: Boolean) : OSErr;
```

Parameter block

→	12	ioCompletion	long	completion routine
←	16	ioResult	word	result code
↔	24	ioDTRefNum	word	desktop database reference number
→	26	ioIndex	word	number of files in desktop database
←	48	ioDirID	long	parent directory of desktop database
←	64	ioDTLgLen	long	logical length of database files
←	68	ioDTPyLen	long	physical length of database files

Specify the volume of the desktop database in ioDTRefNum. The parent directory of the desktop database for the volume is returned in ioDirID. The sum of the logical lengths of the files that constitute the desktop database for a given volume is returned in ioDTLgLen; the sum of the physical lengths of the files that constitute the desktop database for a given volume is returned in ioDTPyLen. The number of files maintained by the Desktop Manager is returned in ioIndex. The volume containing the file is returned in ioDTRefNum.

Result codes

noErr	0	No err
ioErr	–36	I/O error
rfNumErr	–51	Reference number invalid
extFSErr	–58	External file system—file system identifier is nonzero

The PBDTReset and PBDTDelete functions remove information from the desktop database. Unless you are manipulating the desktop database in the absence of the Finder, you should never use these functions.

```
FUNCTION PBDTReset (paramBlock: DTPBPtr; async: Boolean) : OSErr;
```

Parameter block

→	12	ioCompletion	long	completion routine
←	16	ioResult	word	result code
→	24	ioDTRefNum	word	database reference number
→	26	ioIndex	word	must be 0

Note: Your application should never call PBDTReset.

PBDTReset removes all icons, application mappings, and comments from the desktop database specified in ioDTRefNum. You can call PBDTReset only when the database is open. It remains open after the data is cleared.

Result codes

noErr	0	No error
ioErr	–36	I/O error
wPrErr	–44	Volume is locked through hardware
vLckdErr	–46	Volume is locked through software
rfNumErr	–51	Reference number invalid
extFSErr	–58	External file system—file system identifier is nonzero

```
FUNCTION PBDTDelete (paramBlock: DTPBPtr; async: Boolean) : OSErr;
```

Parameter block

→	12	ioCompletion	long	completion routine
←	16	ioResult	word	result code
→	22	ioVRefNum	word	volume reference number
→	26	ioIndex	word	must be 0

Note: Your application should never call PBDTDelete.

PBDTDelete removes the desktop database from a local volume. You specify the volume by passing a volume reference number in ioVRefNum. You can call PBDTDelete only when the database is closed.

Result codes

noErr	0	No error
ioErr	–36	I/O error
wPrErr	–44	Volume is locked through hardware
vLckdErr	–46	Volume is locked through software
rfNumErr	–51	Reference number invalid
extFSErr	–58	External file system—file system identifier is nonzero

SUMMARY OF THE FINDER INTERFACE

Constants

```
CONST {Gestalt selectors}
      gestaltFindFolderAttr        = 'fold';    {selector for FindFolder}

      {interpreting Gestalt selector responses}
      gestaltFindFolderPresent     = 0;         {if this bit is set, }
                                                { FindFolder is present}

      {for custom icons}
      kCustomIconResource          = -16455;    {resource ID for }
                                                { custom icon}

      {for mapping icons to ioIconType in the desktop database}
      kLargeIcon                   = 1;         {'ICN#'}
      kLarge4BitIcon               = 2;         {'icl4'}
      kLarge8BitIcon               = 3;         {'icl8'}
      kSmallIcon                   = 4;         {'ics#'}
      kSmall4BitIcon               = 5;         {'ics4'}
      kSmall8BitIcon               = 6;         {'ics8'}

      {for allocating storage for icon data in the desktop database}
      kLargeIconSize               = 256;       {'ICN#'}
      kLarge4BitIconSize           = 512;       {'icl4'}
      kLarge8BitIconSize           = 1024;      {'icl8'}
      kSmallIconSize               = 64;        {'ics#'}
      kSmall4BitIconSize           = 128;       {'ics4'}
      kSmall8BitIconSize           = 256;       {'ics8'}

      {for Finder flags}
      fHasBundle                   = 8192;      {set if file has a bundle}
      fInvisible                   = 16384;     {set if icon is invisible}

      {for FindFolder}
      kOnSystemDisk                = $8000;     {use vRefNum for the }
                                                { boot disk}
      kCreateFolder                = TRUE;      {create folder if it }
                                                { doesn't exist}
      kDontCreateFolder            = FALSE;     {don't create folder}

      {for special folder types}
      kSystemFolderType            = 'macs';    {System Folder}
      kDesktopFolderType           = 'desk';    {Desktop Folder}
      kTrashFolderType             = 'trsh';    {single-user Trash dir}
      kWhereToEmptyTrashFolderType = 'empt';    {shared, network Trash}
      kPrintMonitorDocsFolderType  = 'prnt';    {PrintMonitor Documents }
                                                { folder}
```

```
kStartupFolderType            = 'strt';   {Startup Items folder}
kAppleMenuFolderType          = 'amnu';   {Apple Menu Items folder}
kControlPanelFolderType       = 'ctrl';   {Control Panels folder}
kExtensionFolderType          = 'extn';   {Extensions folder}
kPreferencesFolderType        = 'pref';   {Preferences folder}
kTemporaryFolderType          = 'temp';   {Temporary Items folder}

{for alias types}
kContainerFolderAliasType     = 'fdrp';   {'file' type for folder }
                                          { aliases}
kContainerTrashAliasType      = 'trsh';   {'file' type for Trash }
                                          { folder aliases}
kContainerHardDiskAliasType   = 'hdsk';   {'file' type for hard }
                                          { disk aliases}
kContainerFloppyAliasType     = 'flpy';   {'file' type for floppy }
                                          { disk aliases}
kContainerServerAliasType     = 'srvr';   {'file' type for server }
                                          { aliases}
kApplicationAliasType         = 'adrp';   {'file' type for }
                                          { application aliases}
kContainerAliasType           = 'drop';   {'file' type for all }
                                          { other containers}
kSystemFolderAliasType        = 'fasy';   {'file' type for System }
                                          { Folder alias}
kAppleMenuFolderAliasType     = 'faam';   {'file' type for Apple }
                                          { Menu Items folder alias}
kStartupFolderAliasType       = 'fast';   {'file' type for Startup }
                                          { Items folder alias}
kPrintMonitorDocsFolderAliasType
                              = 'fapn';   {'file' type for Print- }
                                          { Monitor Doc alias}
kPreferencesFolderAliasType   = 'fapf';   {'file' type for Prefer- }
                                          { ences folder alias}
kControlPanelFolderAliasType = 'fact';    {'file' type for Control }
                                          { Panels folder alias}
kExtensionFolderAliasType     = 'faex';   {'file' type for Exten- }
                                          { sion folder alias}
kExportedFolderAliasType      = 'faet';   {'file' type for export }
                                          { folder alias}
kDropFolderAliasType          = 'fadr';   {'file' type for drop }
                                          { folder alias}
kSharedFolderAliasType        = 'fash';   {'file' type for shared }
                                          { folder alias}
kMountedFolderAliasType       = 'famn';   {'file' type for mounted }
                                          { folder alias}
```

Data Types

```
TYPE DTPBPtr = ^DTPBRec;
     DTPBRec =              {parameter block for desktop database}
     RECORD
        qLink:          QElemPtr;       {next queue entry}
        qType:          Integer;        {queue type}
        ioTrap:         Integer;        {routine trap}
        ioCmdAddr:      Ptr;            {routine address}
        ioCompletion:   ProcPtr;        {completion routine}
        ioResult:       OSErr;          {result code}
        ioNamePtr:      StringPtr;      {file, directory, or volume name}
        ioVRefNum:      Integer;        {volume reference number}
        ioDTRefNum:     Integer;        {desktop database reference number}
        ioIndex:        Integer;        {index into icon list}
        ioTagInfo:      LongInt;        {tag information}
        ioDTBuffer:     Ptr;            {data buffer}
        ioDTReqCount:   LongInt;        {requested length of data}
        ioDTActCount:   LongInt;        {actual length of data}
        filler1:        SignedByte;     {unused}
        ioIconType:     SignedByte;     {icon type}
        filler2:        Integer;        {unused}
        ioDirID:        LongInt;        {parent directory ID}
        ioFileCreator: OSType;          {file creator}
        ioFileType:     OSType;         {file type}
        ioFiller3:      LongInt;        {unused}
        ioDTLgLen:      LongInt;        {logical length of desktop }
                                        { database}
        ioDTPyLen:      LongInt;        {physical length of desktop }
                                        { database}
        ioFiller4:      ARRAY[1..14] OF Integer;
                                        {unused}
        ioAPPLParID:    LongInt         {parent directory ID of }
                                        { application}
     END;

     VersRecPtr  = ^VersRec;
     VersRecHndl = ^VersRecPtr;
     versRec =
     RECORD                  {numeric version part of 'vers' resource}
        numericVersion: NumVersion;   {encoded version number}
        countryCode:    Integer;      {region code from int'l utils}
        shortVersion:   Str255;       {version number string, worst case}
        reserved:       Str255        {longMessage string packed after }
                                      { shortVersion}
        END;
```

```
{Finder information records in the volume catalog}
FInfo =
RECORD
   fdType:        OSType;        {file type}
   fdCreator:     OSType;        {file creator}
   fdFlags:       Integer;       {Finder flags}
   fdLocation:    Point;         {file's location in directory}
   fdFldr:        Integer        {directory that contains file}
END;

FXInfo =
RECORD
   fdIconID:      Integer;       {icon ID}
   fdUnused:      ARRAY[1..3] OF Integer;
                                 {unused but reserved 6 bytes}
   fdScript:      SignedByte;    {script flag and code}
   fdXFlags:      SignedByte;    {reserved}
   fdComment:     Integer;       {comment ID}
   fdPutAway:     LongInt        {home dir ID}
END;

DXInfo =
RECORD
   frScroll:      Point;         {scroll position}
   frOpenChain:   LongInt;       {dir ID chain of open folders}
   frScript:      SignedByte;    {script flag and code}
   frXFlags:      SignedByte;    {reserved}
   frComment:     Integer;       {comment}
   frPutAway:     LongInt        {dir ID}
END;
```

Routines

Resolving Alias Files

```
FUNCTION ResolveAliasFile    (VAR theSpec: FSSpec; resolveAliasChains:
                              Boolean; VAR targetIsFolder: Boolean; VAR
                              wasAliased: Boolean) : OSErr;
```

Finding Directories

```
FUNCTION FindFolder          (vRefNum: Integer; folderType: OSType;
                              createFolder: Boolean; VAR foundVRefNum:
                              Integer; VAR foundDirID: LongInt) : OSErr;
```

Locating and Opening the Desktop Database

```
FUNCTION PBDTGetPath         (paramBlock: DTPBPtr) : OSErr;

FUNCTION PBDTOpenInform      (paramBlock: DTPBPtr) : OSErr;

FUNCTION PBDTCloseDown       (paramBlock: DTPBPtr) : OSErr;
```

Reading the Desktop Database

```
FUNCTION PBDTGetIcon            (paramBlock: DTPBPtr; async: Boolean) :
                                 OSErr;
FUNCTION PBDTGetIconAsync       (paramBlock: DTPBPtr) : OSErr;
FUNCTION PBDTGetIconSync        (paramBlock: DTPBPtr) : OSErr;
FUNCTION PBDTGetIconInfo        (paramBlock: DTPBPtr; async: Boolean) :
                                 OSErr;
FUNCTION PBDTGetIconInfoAsync   (paramBlock: DTPBPtr) : OSErr;
FUNCTION PBDTGetIconInfoSync    (paramBlock: DTPBPtr) : OSErr;
FUNCTION PBDTGetAPPL            (paramBlock: DTPBPtr; async: Boolean) :
                                 OSErr;
FUNCTION PBDTGetAPPLAsync       (paramBlock: DTPBPtr) : OSErr;
FUNCTION PBDTGetAPPLSync        (paramBlock: DTPBPtr) : OSErr;
FUNCTION PBDTGetComment         (paramBlock: DTPBPtr; async: Boolean) :
                                 OSErr;
FUNCTION PBDTGetCommentAsync    (paramBlock: DTPBPtr) : OSErr;
FUNCTION PBDTGetCommentSync     (paramBlock: DTPBPtr) : OSErr;
```

Adding to the Desktop Database

```
FUNCTION PBDTAddIcon            (paramBlock: DTPBPtr; async: Boolean) :
                                 OSErr;
FUNCTION PBDTAddIconAsync       (paramBlock: DTPBPtr) : OSErr;
FUNCTION PBDTAddIconSync        (paramBlock: DTPBPtr) : OSErr;
FUNCTION PBDTAddAPPL            (paramBlock: DTPBPtr; async: Boolean) :
                                 OSErr;
FUNCTION PBDTAddAPPLAsync       (paramBlock: DTPBPtr) : OSErr;
FUNCTION PBDTAddAPPLSync        (paramBlock: DTPBPtr) : OSErr;
FUNCTION PBDTSetComment         (paramBlock: DTPBPtr; async: Boolean) :
                                 OSErr;
FUNCTION PBDTSetCommentAsync    (paramBlock: DTPBPtr) : OSErr;
FUNCTION PBDTSetCommentSync     (paramBlock: DTPBPtr) : OSErr;
```

Deleting Entries From the Desktop Database

```
FUNCTION PBDTRemoveAPPL          (paramBlock: DTPBPtr; async: Boolean) :
                                  OSErr;
FUNCTION PBDTRemoveAPPLAsync     (paramBlock: DTPBPtr) : OSErr;
FUNCTION PBDTRemoveAPPLSync      (paramBlock: DTPBPtr) : OSErr;
FUNCTION PBDTRemoveComment       (paramBlock: DTPBPtr; async: Boolean) :
                                  OSErr;
FUNCTION PBDTRemoveCommentAsync (paramBlock: DTPBPtr) : OSErr;
FUNCTION PBDTRemoveCommentSync   (paramBlock: DTPBPtr) : OSErr;
```

Manipulating the Desktop Database Itself

```
FUNCTION PBDTFlush          (paramBlock: DTPBPtr; async: Boolean) : OSErr;
FUNCTION PBDTFlushAsync     (paramBlock: DTPBPtr) : OSErr;
FUNCTION PBDTFlushSync      (paramBlock: DTPBPtr) : OSErr;
FUNCTION PBDTGetInfo        (paramBlock: DTPBPtr; async: Boolean) : OSErr;
FUNCTION PBDTGetInfoAsync   (paramBlock: DTPBPtr) : OSErr;
FUNCTION PBDTGetInfoSync    (paramBlock: DTPBPtr) : OSErr;
FUNCTION PBDTReset          (paramBlock: DTPBPtr; async: Boolean) : OSErr;
FUNCTION PBDTResetAsync     (paramBlock: DTPBPtr) : OSErr;
FUNCTION PBDTResetSync      (paramBlock: DTPBPtr) : OSErr;
FUNCTION PBDTDelete         (paramBlock: DTPBPtr; async: Boolean) : OSErr;
FUNCTION PBDTDeleteAsync    (paramBlock: DTPBPtr) : OSErr;
FUNCTION PBDTDeleteSync     (paramBlock: DTPBPtr) : OSErr;
```

Result Codes

noErr	0	No error
nsrErr	–35	Volume not found
ioErr	–36	I/O error
fnfErr	–43	For FindFolder: type not found in 'fld#' resource, or disk doesn't have System Folder support or System Folder in volume header, or disk does not have desktop database support for Desktop Folder—in all cases, folder not found For ResolveAliasFile: Target not found, but volume and parent directory found and theSpec parameter contains a valid file system specification record For Desktop Manager calls: file or directory doesn't exist

wPrErr	–44	Volume is locked through hardware
vLckdErr	–46	Volume is locked through software
dupFNErr	–48	File found instead of folder
paramErr	–50	Parameter error; use PBDTGetPath
rfNumErr	–51	Reference number invalid
extFSErr	–58	External file system—file system identifier is nonzero
dirNFErr	–120	Parent directory not found
desktopDamagedErr	–1305	The desktop database has become corrupted—the Finder will fix this, but if your application is not running with the Finder, use PBDTReset or PBDTDelete
afpItemNotFound	–5012	Information not found
afpIconTypeError	–5030	Sizes of new icon and one it replaces don't match

Assembly-Language Information

Desktop Manager Parameter Block

→	12	ioCompletion	long	completion routine
←	16	ioResult	word	result code
→	18	ioNamePtr	long	pointer to file, directory, or volume name
→	22	ioVRefNum	word	volume reference number
↔	24	ioDTRefNum	word	desktop database reference number
→	26	ioIndex	word	index into icon list; or no. of files in database
↔	28	ioTagInfo	long	tag information
→	32	ioDTBuffer	long	pointer to icon data
→	36	ioDTReqCount	long	requested size of icon data buffer
←	40	ioDTActCount	long	actual size of icon definition
↔	45	ioIconType	byte	icon's type
↔	48	ioDirID	long	parent directory
→	52	ioFileCreator	long	file creator
↔	56	ioFileType	long	file type
←	64	ioDTLgLen	long	logical length of database files
←	68	ioDTPyLen	long	physical length of database files
←	100	ioAPPLParID	long	application's parent directory

Trap Macros Requiring Routine Selectors

_HFSDispatch

Selector	Routine
$0020	PBDTGetPath
$0021	PBDTCloseDown
$0022	PBDTAddIcon
$0023	PBDTGetIcon
$0024	PBDTGetIconInfo
$0025	PBDTAddAPPL
$0026	PBDTRemoveAPPL
$0027	PBDTGetAPPL
$0028	PBDTSetComment
$0029	PBDTRemoveComment
$002A	PBDTGetComment
$002B	PBDTFlush
$002C	PBDTReset
$002D	PBDTGetInfo
$002E	PBDTOpenInform
$002F	PBDTDelete

10 CONTROL PANELS

ABOUT THIS CHAPTER

All versions of the Macintosh® Operating System previous to system software version 7.0 provide a desk accessory called the *Control Panel*. The Control Panel allows users to control certain system features, such as speaker volume, date and time, and desktop pattern. With the release of System file version 4.1, documented in Volume V, the Control Panel became extensible by the addition of control panel files (of file type 'cdev') to the System Folder. The contents and operation of control panel files are described in the Control Panel chapter of Volume V.

In system software version 7.0, the Control Panel, as a discrete desk accessory, has been eliminated. Instead, the Finder™ can now open each file of file type 'cdev'. Each control panel file is now displayed as an independent dialog box rather than as a panel in the Control Panel desk accessory.

This chapter describes how to write a control panel file that is compatible with both the earlier Control Panel and version 7.0, and how to write an extension for the Monitors control panel file.

In this chapter, the dialog box defined by a file of file type 'cdev' is referred to as **control panel** (as opposed to *the* Control Panel), and the file itself is referred to as a **control panel file.**

Only the manufacturer of a video device should write an extension to the Monitors control panel for that device. Therefore, if you are not developing a video card for the Macintosh computer, you do not need the information in this chapter on the Monitors control panel.

ABOUT CONTROL PANELS

In system software version 7.0, the Control Panel desk accessory no longer exists as one entity. Each of the individual control panels now appears as a modeless dialog box. Users can open control panels in the same way as any other document, and several control panels can be open at one time. The main reason to create a control panel file rather than an application is to maintain compatibility with the Control Panel for users who are using earlier operating systems. Any control panel file that follows the rules and suggestions given in the Control Panel chapter of Volume V will continue to work without problems in version 7.0.

A control panel can open in a window of any size. However, you may want to constrain any new panels that you develop to fit in the space provided by the previous Control Panel desk accessory. Doing so guarantees that the control panel can be opened either by the Control Panel desk accessory in earlier versions of system software or by the Finder in version 7.0.

The user can store control panels in the Control Panels folder or the Apple® Menu Items folder (both in the System Folder), or at any other location in the file system.

You should refer to a file of type 'cdev' as a *control panel file* in any user documentation that you provide. Don't pass on the file type name of this file or any other file to users.

The next section, "Writing Control Panel Files," provides more information about developing control panels that work in all versions of system software.

WRITING CONTROL PANEL FILES

You should keep the following points in mind if you are writing or modifying a control panel file:

- A control panel file displays a modeless dialog box with no menu bar. You can use the editing functions in the Finder's menu bar if necessary, but you cannot add any menu choices. The Finder passes messages to your cdev function for the following standard selections from the Edit menu: Undo, Cut, Copy, Paste, and Clear. Your cdev function can respond to these messages when it is appropriate to do so; for example, if your control panel has an editable text box, you can respond to these editing functions when the insertion point is within this field. See the Control Panel chapter in Volume V for a description of the cdev function.

- The rectangles defined by the 'nrct' resource are no longer restricted to the size of the Control Panel; however, to maintain compatibility with previous operating systems, the rectangles' coordinates should not exceed (–1,87,255,322).

- There is no longer a guarantee that the resources provided by the Control Panel are available when your control panel file is running. If your control panel file uses any Control Panel resources, it might not run in version 7.0. If your control panel file strictly follows the specifications in the Control Panel chapter of Volume V, however, it should run with no difficulty in version 7.0.

- Your control panel file can continue to use the CPDialog parameter passed to the cdev function to obtain the dialog item list and the numItems parameter to determine the number of items in the dialog item list. If you use these parameters in your control panel file to gain access to the items in your dialog item list, your control panel file will operate correctly with both the Control Panel and the Finder. If you assume some value for the numItems parameter, however, your control panel file will not operate correctly in both situations. Dialog item lists are described in the Dialog Manager chapter of Volume I.

- If the 'mach' resource in your control panel file indicates that the cdev function cannot run, the Finder displays an error message for the user and does not open the control panel file. In contrast, the Control Panel does not display the icon for a control panel file if the 'mach' resource indicates the cdev function cannot run. If your control panel file can run on all Macintosh computers, set the 'mach' resource to $FFFF 0000. If your control panel file can run only when certain hardware or software is present, set the 'mach' resource to $0000 FFFF. In the latter case, the Finder calls your cdev function with the message parameter set to the constant macDev (8). Your cdev function should then call the Gestalt function to determine the software and hardware configuration of the machine. If your control panel file cannot run, return a result code of 0; if your control panel file can run, return a result code of 1. The Gestalt function is described in the Compatibility Guidelines chapter in this volume.

- The Finder now handles the result codes returned by your cdev function. Whereas the Control Panel dims the icon for a control panel file in response to certain result codes, the Finder displays an error message but does not dim the control panel file icon.

ABOUT THE MONITORS CONTROL PANEL

The Monitors control panel that is provided with system software version 7.0 is extensible. If you are the developer of a video card, you can add items to the Monitors control panel that allow users to control features of the video device.

The Monitors control panel allows a user to

- select which one of the monitors connected to the computer system should display the menu bar
- select which monitor to use as a startup screen
- inform the Operating System about the relative locations of the monitors
- control some features of the monitors, such as whether a color monitor displays in color or in black and white, or the number of colors or gray-scale values to display

Figure 10-1 shows an example of the Monitors control panel.

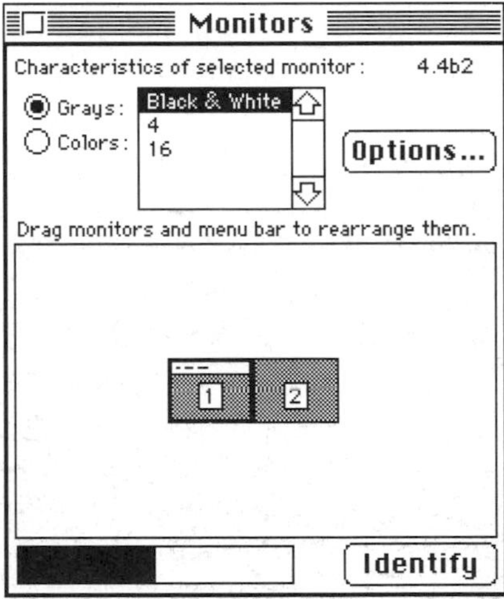

Figure 10-1. The Monitors control panel

As Figure 10-1 illustrates, the Monitors control panel now includes a button labeled *Options;* when the user clicks this button, another dialog box appears with additional controls. When you add an extension to the Monitors control panel, the controls you add appear in this dialog box. In this chapter, the dialog box that appears when the user clicks the Options button in the Monitors control panel is referred to as the *Options dialog box*. Figure 10-2 shows an example of an Options dialog box. The OK and Cancel buttons are standard for all Options dialog boxes. The screen-saver control ("Minutes before sleep") is added by the Monitors extension. If there is more than one video card installed in the computer, the Monitors control panel shows all of the connected monitors. In this case, the user selects one monitor and the Monitors control panel displays the Options dialog box for that monitor (monitor 1 in Figure 10-1).

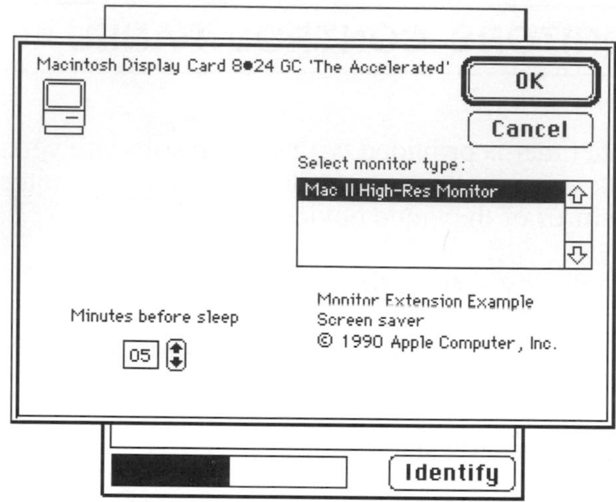

Figure 10-2. An Options dialog box for a Monitors control panel

You should provide an extension to the Monitors control panel whenever you want to provide users with a simple way to control your video device. However, if you require a more complex interface—such as your own menu items or several levels of nested dialog boxes—you should provide a small application rather than an extension to the Monitors control panel. If you do provide a small application, you might want to instruct the user to place it in the Control Panels folder within the System Folder.

DESIGNING AN EXTENSION FOR THE MONITORS CONTROL PANEL

If you develop a video card, you can provide a file of type 'cdev' that adds controls to the Options dialog box of the Monitors control panel. An extension to the Monitors control panel should control features of the video card only; a Monitors extension should not control system-wide features. For example, a Monitors control panel extension might allow the user to set the virtual screen size for a single monitor, but not to set the size of the menu bar, which can appear on any monitor.

It is not advisable to add a button to the Options dialog box that puts up yet another dialog box. If the features that you want to implement require an extensive or complex set of controls, it would be better to write a small application rather than an extension to the Monitors control panel file.

> ▲ **Warning:** Only the manufacturer of the video card should write an extension to the Monitors control panel file. There can be only one extension to the Monitors control panel file for each video card. Apple Computer, Inc., reserves the right to supply control panel files for its own video cards. ▲

The extension file for the Monitors control panel must be a file of type 'cdev' containing at least the following resources:

- 'card' (ID can be any number from –4080 through –4065)
- 'mntr' (ID = –4096)
- 'RECT' (ID = –4096)
- 'DITL' (ID = –4096)

Your Monitors extension file can also include any of the following resources:

- 'ICON' (ID = –4096)
- 'cicn' (ID = –4096)
- 'vers' (ID = 1)
- 'vers' (ID = 2)
- 'STR#' (ID = –4096)
- 'gama' (ID can be any number from –4080 through –4065)
- 'FREF'
- 'BNDL'
- icon family resources 'ICN#', 'ics#', 'icl8', 'icl4', 'ics8', and 'ics4'
- 'INIT'
- signature resource

The following sections describe these resources. You can use resource ID numbers of –4080 through –4065 for any private resources in your Monitors extension.

The 'card' Resource

The 'card' resource contains a Pascal string (that is, a length byte followed by an ASCII string) identical to the name of a video card. (The name of a video card is located in the Board sResource data structure in the ROM of the card, as described in *Designing Cards and Drivers for the Macintosh Family,* second edition.) The extension file can contain as many 'card' resources as you wish, so that one extension file can handle several versions of one video card. The Options dialog box displays the name in the 'card' resource unless you also include an 'STR#' resource in the extension file, as described in "The 'STR#' Resource" later in this chapter. The Slot Manager chapter in Volume V describes the SGetCString function. For a description of video cards, see *Designing Cards and Drivers for the Macintosh Family,* second edition.

The 'mntr' Resource

The 'mntr' resource contains the code that carries out the functions of your Monitors extension. This resource must begin with a function that you provide, referred to in this chapter as the *monitor function.* The parameters passed to the monitor function by the Monitors control panel allow your code to determine what action to perform. You can use the function result to keep a handle to local storage or to return an error code. These options are described in the parameter descriptions in the next section.

An 'mntr' resource is a code resource. In MPW®, you can set the code resource type to 'mntr' when you link the program.

The Monitor Function

The 'mntr' resource must contain a function that responds to the various events that can occur while the Options dialog box is on the screen. The declaration for a monitor function named MyMntr is as follows:

```
FUNCTION MyMntr (message,item,numItems: Integer; monitorValue: LongInt;
                mDialog: DialogPtr; theEvent: EventRecord;
                screenNum: Integer; VAR screens: ScrnRsrcHandle;
                VAR scrnChanged: Boolean) : LongInt;
```

Parameter descriptions

message — A message number, from the list defined in the following section, that your monitor function can use to determine what action to take.

item — The dialog-item-list number of the item that the user clicked. To calculate the dialog-item-list number in your 'DITL' resource, subtract the number passed in the numItems parameter from the number in the item parameter.

When the message parameter equals StartupMsg, the item parameter indicates whether the user is a superuser—that is, whether the user can be assumed to be very knowledgeable. If the user is a superuser, the item parameter is 1; if not, it is 0.

numItems — The dialog-item-list number of the last standard item in the Options dialog box. You number the items in your 'DITL' resource starting with 1; the Monitors control panel adds the value of the numItems parameter to each number in the 'DITL' resource and uses the result for the dialog-item-list number.

monitorValue — The result returned by your monitor function the last time it was called. Because control panel routines cannot have global variables, you might want to use the function result to return a handle to the storage of your local data. This handle is then available in the monitorValue parameter the next time the monitor function is called. The monitorValue parameter is 0 the first time the Monitors control panel calls your monitor function (that is, when the message parameter equals startupMsg).

If your monitor function returns a function result in the range 1 through 255, the Monitors control panel interprets this result as an error and closes your Options dialog box. Therefore, your monitor function cannot receive a value in this range in the monitorValue parameter.

mDialog — The dialog pointer for the Options dialog box. See the Dialog Manager chapter of Volume I for a description of dialog pointers.

theEvent — The event record for an event that caused a hitMsg, nulMsg, or keyEvtMsg message. See the Event Manager chapter of this volume for a discussion of event records.

screenNum — The number of the screen device (that is, the monitor) that the user has selected. The Monitors control panel numbers monitors consecutively, in the same order as the slots in which the cards are installed, starting with 1.

screens — A handle to the 'scrn' resource. The 'scrn' resource is described in the Graphics Devices Manager chapter of this volume.

scrnChanged — A Boolean value that you can use to indicate whether you have modified the 'scrn' resource. Set this parameter to TRUE if you have modified the 'scrn' resource. When the scrnChanged parameter is TRUE, the Monitors control panel checks the 'scrn' resource to make sure that the values in it are still valid; if there is a problem, the Monitors control panel tries to correct it.

This parameter makes it easier to implement a control that changes the apparent area displayed on the screen. For example, your monitor might be able to display either two pages of a document or a magnified view of a single page. If the user changes the area displayed on one screen in a system with multiple screens, the displays on adjacent screens could overlap or show gaps. When you change the 'scrn' resource to implement this change, the coordinates of the global rectangles for adjacent screens are no longer contiguous. In this case, if you have set the scrnChanged parameter to TRUE, the Monitors control panel shifts the virtual locations of the screens to eliminate the gaps or overlaps.

Your monitor function can return either an error code or a value that you want to have available the next time the Monitors extension is called. Each time the extension is called, the monitorValue parameter contains the value that your monitor function returned the last time it was called.

If an error occurs, your monitor function should display an error dialog box and then return a value between 1 and 255. If your code returns a value in this range, the Monitors control panel closes the Options dialog box immediately and no more calls are made to your code. If your code returns an error in response to the initMsg or startupMsg message, the Monitors control panel does not display the Options dialog box. You can display an alert box describing the error before returning control to the Monitors control panel.

Messages to the Monitor Function

The message passed as a parameter to the monitor function can have any of the values defined by these constants:

```
CONST initMsg          = 1;    {initialization}
      okMsg            = 2;    {user clicked OK button}
      cancelMsg        = 3;    {user clicked Cancel button}
      hitMsg           = 4;    {user clicked control in Options dialog }
                               { box}
      nulMsg           = 5;    {periodic event}
      updateMsg        = 6;    {update event}
      activateMsg      = 7;    {not used}
      deactivateMsg    = 8;    {not used}
      keyEvtMsg        = 9;    {keyboard event}
      superMsg         = 10;   {show superuser controls}
      normalMsg        = 11;   {show only normal controls}
      startupMsg       = 12;   {code has been loaded}
```

Constant	**Meaning**
initMsg	Sent before the Options dialog box is displayed, after the Monitors control panel has located any resources (such as 'gama' resources) referred to by your monitor function. When you receive this message you should execute initialization code. You can use initialization code to set default values for controls and allocate memory for local storage, for example. If you do allocate storage, be sure to pass a handle to the storage as the function result. The next time your extension is called, this value will be available in the monitorValue parameter. This message is preceded by the startup message and followed by either the super message or the normal message.
okMsg	Indicates the user has clicked the OK button. The OK button is a standard control put in the Options dialog box by the Monitors control panel. You should not make any changes irreversible until you receive this message. When the user clicks the OK button, the Monitors control panel hides the Options dialog box and calls your monitor function with this message. This is your last chance to check the values of dialog items that the user might have changed. You should release any private memory allocated by your extension file before returning control to the Monitors control panel.
cancelMsg	Indicates the user has clicked the Cancel button. The Cancel button is a standard control put in the Options dialog box by the Monitors control panel. Return the computer system to the condition it was in before the user clicked the Options button, release any private memory allocated by your extension file, and return control to the Monitors control panel.

Constant	Meaning
hitMsg	Indicates the user has clicked an enabled control in the Options dialog box. The dialog-item-list number of the control is passed in the item parameter to the monitor function; see the preceding section for a discussion of this parameter.
nulMsg	Sent periodically to allow you to perform tasks that have to be done repeatedly, such as blinking an insertion point. Do not assume any particular timing for this message.
updateMsg	Sent on every update event.
activateMsg	Sent on every activate event for which the Options dialog box becomes active. Currently, this message is not used, because the Options dialog box is modal. However, you should handle this message as you would any activate event, because in future versions of the Operating System this dialog box might be modeless.
deactivateMsg	Sent on every activate event for which the Options dialog box becomes inactive. Currently, this message is not used, because the Options dialog box is modal. However, you should handle this message as you would any activate event because in future versions of the Operating System, this dialog box might be modeless.
keyEvtMsg	Sent on every keyboard event.
superMsg	Indicates the user is a superuser—that is, the user can be assumed to be very knowledgeable. This message is sent when the user holds down the Option key while clicking the Options button, and it could be sent by other mechanisms in the future. You should display any controls that you have reserved for such users. This message or the normal message is sent immediately following the initialization message.
normalMsg	Indicates you should not display controls reserved for superusers. This message or the super message is sent immediately following the initialization message.
startupMsg	Sent as soon as the code in your 'mntr' resource has been loaded, before the Monitors control panel finds any resources referred to by your monitor function. You can then load and modify any resources that must allow for the capabilities of the computer system or for superusers. You can use this opportunity, for example, to modify your 'DITL' resource to display special controls for superusers. You can call the Gestalt function to determine the capabilities of the user's computer system, and you can check the value of the item parameter to determine whether the user is a superuser. If the user is a superuser, the Monitors control panel sets the item parameter to 1 when it sends the startup message. This message is the first message sent.

The 'RECT' Resource

You use the 'RECT' resource to describe the size and shape of the area taken up by your controls. In assigning coordinates to your controls, assume that the origin (that is, the upper-left corner) of the local coordinate system for your dialog items is at (0,0). (In this coordinate system, the Options dialog items displayed by the Monitors control panel would have a right edge at 319 and a negative top coordinate.) The Monitors control panel expands the Options dialog box, placing the rectangle defined by your 'RECT' resource so that its upper edge starts immediately below the standard controls put in the Options dialog box by the Monitors control panel. In Figure 10-2, for example, the OK and Cancel buttons and the Select monitor type box are standard controls, and the screen-saver control has been added by a Monitors extension.

Because the Monitors control panel transforms the coordinates of your controls to the coordinate system that it uses for the Options dialog box, you must use the GetDItem procedure (described in the Dialog Manager chapter of Volume I) to get the true locations of your dialog items.

The 'DITL' Resource

The 'DITL' resource is a standard dialog item list, as described in the Dialog Manager chapters of Volumes I and V. For an example of this resource, see "A Sample of an Extension to the Monitors Control Panel" later in this chapter.

You can start your controls immediately below the standard controls put in the Options dialog box by the Monitors control panel, as shown in Figure 10-2. If you add additional controls for superusers, you should separate the superuser controls from the other controls with a horizontal dividing line, as illustrated in Figure 10-3.

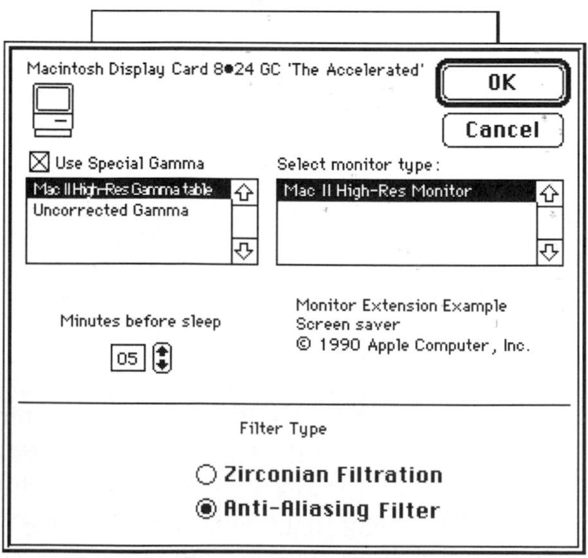

Figure 10-3. An Options dialog box with superuser controls

To draw a dividing line, make it a separate dialog item of type userItem. The procedure for the dialog item should consist of a FrameRect procedure that draws a 1-pixel-high rectangle. The coordinates for the dividing line are in the coordinate system used by your 'RECT' resource. If you wish, you can use a gray pattern for this line in a manner similar to that used for divider lines in menus. Dialog items are discussed in the Dialog Manager chapter of Volume I, and the FrameRect procedure is described in the QuickDraw™ chapter of Volume I. Listing 10-1 later in this chapter includes code to draw a dividing line.

The 'ICON' and 'cicn' Resources

The 'ICON' resource defines a black-and-white icon. The 'cicn' resource, described in the Color QuickDraw chapter of Volume V, defines a color icon. If you include either of these resources in the Monitors extension file, the icon is displayed in the Options dialog box of the Monitors control panel (Figures 10-2 and 10-3).

The 'vers' Resources

You can include 'vers' resources to provide version information for your Monitors extension file. The 'vers' resource with a resource ID of 1 specifies the version of your Monitors extension file. The 'vers' resource with a resource ID of 2 specifies the version of the group to which your file belongs—for example, the version number of the video card that your extension file supports. See the Finder Interface chapter in this volume for more information on 'vers' resources.

The 'STR#' Resource

If the name for the video card that you want to display in the Options dialog box is different from the name in the declaration ROM of the video card, you can include an 'STR#' resource. This resource must contain pairs of Pascal strings. The first string in each pair must be identical to the name of the video card as returned by the Slot Manager's SReadDrvrName function (minus the period that the Slot Manager prefixes to the name). The second string in each pair is the name that you want to display in the Options dialog box. You can have as many pairs of names in one 'STR#' resource as you wish; the Monitors control panel uses the first match it finds.

The 'gama' Resources

When the user presses the Option key while clicking the Options button in the Monitors control panel, a list of gamma tables is displayed (Figure 10-3). The software driver for a video card uses a **gamma table** to correct for the fact that the intensity of each color on a video display is not linearly proportional to the intensity of the electron beam; in other words, the gamma table helps the video driver to provide the most accurate colors possible for a video display. Because the user might prefer a nonstandard color correction, many developers of video cards provide more than one gamma table for a given card.

To include one or more gamma tables for a video card, include in the Monitors extension file a named resource of type 'gama' for each gamma table. The user can select which gamma table to use with the monitor by clicking the name of that table, or the user can select the default gamma table for that monitor by clicking the box that appears above the gamma table. The default gamma table for a monitor is the one listed in the 'scrn' resource. Gamma tables are discussed in *Designing Cards and Drivers for the Macintosh Family,* second edition. The 'scrn' resource is described in the Graphics Devices Manager chapter of this volume.

The 'FREF', 'BNDL', Icon Family, and Signature Resources

The 'FREF', 'BNDL', icon family, and signature resources work together to give your file a distinctive appearance on the desktop. These resource types are described in the Finder Interface chapter of this volume, and examples of these resources are given in Listing 10-2 later in this chapter.

The 'INIT' Resource

A file that contains an extension to the Monitors control panel can contain an 'INIT' resource. If this file is in the Control Panels folder, the Extensions folder, or the base level of the System Folder, then the Operating System executes the 'INIT' resource when the machine is switched on or reset. (Before system software version 7.0, all 'INIT' resource files had to be located in the base level of the System Folder.) 'INIT' resources are discussed in the System Resource File chapter of Volume IV and in the Start Manager chapter of Volume V. The 'INIT' resource acts independently of other resources in the file; it need not be related to the Monitors extension in any way.

A Sample of an Extension to the Monitors Control Panel

Listing 10-1 shows code that defines an extension to the Monitors control panel. Listing 10-2 shows the resources for this extension in Rez format.

In response to the startup message, the Monitors extension shown in Listing 10-1 checks the value of the item parameter to determine whether the user is a superuser. If the user is not a superuser, the Monitors extension uses the default values for the 'RECT' resource shown in Listing 10-2. This rectangle ends just before the dividing line, so that the superuser controls are not displayed. If the user is a superuser, the SetUpData function in Listing 10-1 extends the rectangle in the 'RECT' resource so that the rectangle includes all of the controls in the 'DITL' resource.

The code for the startup message allocates memory for the use of the Monitors extension and returns a handle to this memory as the function result. For all subsequent messages, the Monitors control panel passes the previous function result to the extension in the monitorValue parameter. In order to preserve the handle to this memory, Listing 10-1 sets the monitor function equal to the monitorValue parameter for all messages that the function does not process.

The Monitors control panel extension shown in Listings 10-1 and 10-2 is illustrated in Figures 10-2 and 10-3.

Listing 10-1. Sample of an extension to the Monitors control panel

```
{Pascal source code}

CONST
   textItem       = 1;     {StaticText item in cdev}
   lineItem       = 2;     {separation line}
   downItem       = 3;     {Down Arrow user item}
   upItem         = 4;     {Up Arrow user item}
   countItem      = 6;     {frame for count}
   brightItem     = 9;     {radio button "filter"}
   lessItem       = 10;    {radio button "aliasing"}
   slotCount      = 6;     {a reasonable value}
   initMsg        = 1;     {initialization}
   okMsg          = 2;     {user clicked OK button}
   cancelMsg      = 3;     {user clicked Cancel button}
   hitMsg         = 4;     {user clicked control in Options }
                           { dialog  box}
   nulMsg         = 5;     {periodic event}
   updateMsg      = 6;     {update event}
   activateMsg    = 7;     {not used}
   deactivateMsg  = 8;     {not used}
   keyEvtMsg      = 9;     {keyboard event}
   superMsg       = 10;    {show superuser controls}
   normalMsg      = 11;    {show only normal controls}
   startupMsg     = 12;    {code has been loaded}
   {resource IDs}
   MemErrAlert    = 130;   {alert to tell user you ran out of memory}
   deepAlert      = 131;   {all other errors}
   dataRes        = -4080; {store data}

TYPE ScrnRecord =
     RECORD                        {'scrn' info for each screen}
      srDrvrHW:       Integer; {spDrvrHW from Slot Manager}
      srSlot:         Integer; {slot number for the screen's video card}
      srDCtlDevBase: LongInt; {base address of card's memory}
      srMode:         Integer; {sRsrcID for desired mode}
      srFlagMask:     Integer; {$77FE}
      srFlags:        Integer; {active, main screen, B/W or color}
      srColorTable:   Integer; {resource ID of desired 'clut'}
      srGammaTable:   Integer; {resource ID of desired 'gama'}
      srRect:         Rect;    {device's rectangle, global }
                               { coordinates}
      srCtlCount:     Integer  {number of control calls}
     END;
     ScrnRecordPtr = ^ScrnRecord;
     ScrnRecordHandle = ^ScrnRecordPtr;

     ScrnRsrc =
     RECORD                        {complete 'scrn' resource}
         count:       Integer; {number of screens configured here}
         scrnRecs:    ARRAY[1..slotCount] OF ScrnRecord
                               {config for each one}
     END;
```

(Continued)

Listing 10-1. Sample of an extension to the Monitors control panel (Continued)

```
   ScrnRsrcPtr = ^ScrnRsrc;
   ScrnRsrcHandle = ^ScrnRsrcPtr;

   MonitorData =
   RECORD                             {local data for the extension}
      isSuperUser:       Boolean; {is the user a superuser?}
      filteringSetting: Integer; {new filter setting}
      oldFiltering:      Integer; {previous filter setting}
      sleepTime:         Integer; {new sleep time}
      oldSleep:          Integer  {previous sleep time}
   END;

MonitorDataPtr = ^MonitorData;
MonitorDataHandle = ^MonitorDataPtr;

RectPtr = ^Rect;
RectHandle = ^RectPtr;

IntPtr = ^Integer;
IntHandle = ^IntPtr;

PROCEDURE DrawMyRect(theWindow: WindowPtr; itemNo: Integer);
   FORWARD;
FUNCTION SetUpData(superUser: Integer; storage: MonitorDataHandle) : OSErr;
   FORWARD;
PROCEDURE HandleHits(mDialog: DialogPtr; whichItem,numItems: Integer;
                     dataHand: MonitorDataHandle);
   FORWARD;
PROCEDURE SaveNewValues(dataRecHand: MonitorDataHandle);
   FORWARD;
PROCEDURE SetParamText(sleep: Integer);
   FORWARD;

FUNCTION MonExtend (message,item,numItems: Integer;
                    monitorValue: LongInt; mDialog: DialogPtr;
                    theEvent: EventRecord; ScreenNum: Integer;
                    VAR screens: ScrnRsrcHandle;
                    VAR scrnChanged: Boolean) : LongInt;

VAR
   ItemType: Integer;
   dItem: Handle;
   box: Rect;
   dataRecHand: MonitorDataHandle;
   result: OSErr;
   i: Integer;

BEGIN
   dataRecHand := MonitorDataHandle (monitorValue);
                                   {set up handle to local data}
   CASE message OF
   startupMsg:                     {time to check for superusers}
```

```
BEGIN
{first allocate memory to hold your local data}
   dataRecHand :=
   MonitorDataHandle(NewHandle(sizeof(MonitorData)));
   IF dataRecHand <> NIL THEN
   BEGIN
      result := SetUpData(item, dataRecHand);
                              {initialize all fields}
      IF result = noErr THEN
      BEGIN
         MonExtend := LongInt(dataRecHand);
                              {this comes back in monitorValue}
      END
      ELSE
      BEGIN
         MonExtend := result; {error should stop any further action}
      END
   END
   ELSE
   BEGIN {display error message}
      i := StopAlert(MemErrAlert,NIL);
      MonExtend := 255;
   END;
   Exit(MonExtend);
END;

initMsg:                      {initialize cdev}
BEGIN
{set controls to their initial values and set the proc that }
{ draws user items}
   GetDItem(mDialog,numItems+lineItem,itemType,dItem,box);
   IF itemType = userItem THEN
      SetDItem(mDialog,numItems+lineItem,itemType,@DrawMyRect,box);
   GetDItem(mDialog,numItems+countItem,itemType,dItem,box);
   IF itemType = userItem THEN
      SetDItem(mDialog,numItems+countItem,itemType,@DrawMyRect,box);
   SetParamText(dataRecHand^^.sleepTime);
   IF dataRecHand^^.isSuperUser THEN
   BEGIN
      IF dataRecHand^^.oldFiltering = 0 THEN
         GetDItem(mDialog,numItems+lessItem,itemType, dItem, box);
      IF itemType = radCtrl + ctrlItem THEN
         SetCtlValue(ControlHandle(dItem),1)
      ELSE
         GetDItem(mDialog,numItems+brightItem,itemType,dItem,box);
      IF itemType = radCtrl + ctrlItem THEN
         SetCtlValue(ControlHandle(dItem),1);
   END;
END;

hitMsg:
BEGIN
   HandleHits(mDialog, item, numItems,dataRecHand);
END;
```

(Continued)

Listing 10-1. Sample of an extension to the Monitors control panel (Continued)

```
   okMsg:                     {user wants to implement changes}
      BEGIN
         {execute any hardware changes here}
         SaveNewValues(dataRecHand);
         DisposeHandle(dataRecHand) {release memory}
      END;

   cancelMSG:                 {user does not want to save changes}
      BEGIN
         {make sure no changes are made permanent}
         DisposeHandle(dataRecHand) {release memory}
      END;
   END;

   MonExtend := monitorValue; {return handle to local data}
END; {MonExtend}

{The following procedure is used both to frame the minutes-to-sleep box }
{ and to draw the line separating the superuser controls from the }
{ other controls.}
PROCEDURE DrawMyRect(theWindow: WindowPtr; itemNo: Integer);
VAR
   ItemType: Integer;
   dItem: Handle;
   box: Rect;

BEGIN
   GetDItem(theWindow,itemNo,itemType, dItem, box);
   FrameRect(box);
END;

FUNCTION SetUpData(superUser: Integer; storage: MonitorDataHandle) :
                   OSErr;

VAR
   filterType, sleepyTime: Handle;
   i: Integer;
   result: OSErr;
   rHandle: Handle;

BEGIN
   result := noErr;
   HLock(Handle(storage));
   WITH storage^^ DO
   BEGIN
      sleepyTime := GetResource('SLEP',dataRes);
      IF sleepyTime <> NIL THEN
      BEGIN
         oldSleep := IntHandle(sleepyTime)^^;    {get old value}
         sleepTime := oldSleep;
         ReleaseResource(sleepyTime);            {get rid of the resource}
         IF superUser = 1 THEN
```

```
         BEGIN
            isSuperUser := TRUE;
            filterType := GetResource('INTE',dataRes);
            IF filterType <> NIL THEN
            BEGIN
               oldFiltering := IntHandle(filterType)^^;
                                                 {get old value}
               filteringSetting := oldFiltering;
               ReleaseResource(filterType);  {get rid of the resource}
{if the user is a superuser, change the RECT to display more controls}
               rHandle := GetResource('RECT',-4096);
               IF rHandle <> NIL THEN
                  RectHandle(rHandle)^^.top := -160
               ELSE
                  result := 255
            END
            ELSE
            result := 255;
         END
      END
      ELSE
         result := 255;          {flag error}
      IF result = 255 THEN
      BEGIN
         DisposHandle(Handle(storage));
         i := StopAlert(deepAlert,NIL);
                                 {tell the user there's a problem}
      END
   END;
   HUnlock(Handle(storage));
   SetUpData := result;          {nonzero result should stop any }
                                 { further action}
END;

PROCEDURE SaveNewValues(dataRecHand: MonitorDataHandle);
{save the current settings in resources}

VAR
   resHandle: Handle;

BEGIN
   WITH dataRecHand^^ DO
   BEGIN
      IF sleepTime <> oldSleep THEN
      BEGIN
         resHandle := GetResource('SLEP',dataRes);
         IF resHandle <> NIL THEN
         BEGIN                   {set sleep time}
            IntHandle(resHandle)^^ := sleepTime;
            ChangedResource(resHandle);
            WriteResource(resHandle);
         END
      END;
```

(Continued)

Listing 10-1. Sample of an extension to the Monitors control panel (Continued)

```
      IF isSuperUser THEN        {settings only for superusers}
         IF filteringSetting <> oldFiltering THEN
         BEGIN
            resHandle := GetResource('INTE',dataRes);
            IF resHandle  <> NIL THEN
            BEGIN                {set superuser controls}
               IntHandle(resHandle)^^ := filteringSetting;
               ChangedResource(resHandle);
               WriteResource(resHandle);
            END
         END
   END
END;

PROCEDURE HandleHits(mDialog: DialogPtr; whichItem,numItems: Integer;
                     dataHand: MonitorDataHandle);

VAR
   ItemType: Integer;
   dItem: Handle;
   box: Rect;

BEGIN
   HLock(Handle(dataHand));
   WITH dataHand^^ DO
   BEGIN
      CASE whichItem - numItems OF
      upItem:
      BEGIN
         GetDItem(mDialog,numItems+countItem,itemType, dItem, box);
                                  {get the text box}
         sleepTime := (sleepTime + 1) MOD 26;
         SetParamText(sleepTime);
         InvalRect(box);
      END;
      downItem:
      BEGIN
         GetDItem(mDialog,numItems+countItem,itemType, dItem, box);
         sleepTime := sleepTime - 1;
         IF sleepTime < 0 THEN
            sleepTime := 25;
         SetParamText(sleepTime);
         InvalRect(box);
         END;
```

```
            brightItem:
            BEGIN
               GetDItem(mDialog,whichItem ,itemType, dItem, box);
               IF itemType = radCtrl + ctrlItem THEN
                  SetCtlValue(ControlHandle(dItem),1);
               GetDItem(mDialog,numItems+lessItem,itemType, dItem, box);
               IF itemType = radCtrl + ctrlItem THEN
                  SetCtlValue(ControlHandle(dItem),0);
               filteringSetting := 1;
            END;
            lessItem:
            BEGIN
               GetDItem(mDialog,numItems+brightItem ,itemType, dItem, box);
               IF itemType = radCtrl + ctrlItem THEN
                  SetCtlValue(ControlHandle(dItem),0);
               GetDItem(mDialog,whichItem,itemType, dItem, box);
               IF itemType = radCtrl + ctrlItem THEN
                  SetCtlValue(ControlHandle(dItem),1);
               filteringSetting := 0;
            END;
         END; {CASE}
      END;
      HUnlock(Handle(dataHand));
END;

PROCEDURE SetParamText (Sleep: Integer);

VAR
   countStr:   Str255;

BEGIN
   NumToString(Sleep, countStr);
   IF (Sleep < 10 ) THEN
   BEGIN
      countStr[0] := Char(Integer(countStr[0]) + 1);
      countStr[2] := countStr[1];
      countStr[1] := '0'
   END;
   ParamText(countStr,'','','');
END;

END
```

Listing 10-2 shows, in Rez format, the resources that are used by the Monitors control panel extension shown in Listing 10-1.

Listing 10-2. Resources for a file that extends the Monitors control panel

```
#include "Types.r"
#include "Pict.r"
#include "SysTypes.r"

type 'kcah' as 'STR ';

type 'card' as 'STR ';

type 'sysz' { unsigned hex longint; };

type 'RECT'
{
   rect;
};

/* used to keep track of filter type */
type 'INTE'
{
   integer;
};

/* used to maintain setting of sleep interval */
type 'SLEP'
{
   integer;
};

resource 'sysz' (0, purgeable) {
   $1000    /* about 64 KB needed in system heap */
};


resource 'vers' (1) {
   0x01, 0x00, release, 0x00,
   verUS,
   "1.00",
   "1.00, Copyright © 1990 Apple Computer, Inc."
};

resource 'kcah' (0, purgeable) {
   "Monitors Extension Sample"
};

resource 'BNDL' (128, purgeable) {
   'kcah',
   0,
   {
   'ICN#', {0, 128},
   'FREF', {0, 128}
   }
};
```

```
resource 'ICN#' (128, purgeable) {
   {  /* array: 2 elements */
      /* [1] */
      $"0000 0000 07FF FFE0 0800 0010 09FF FF90"
      $"0A00 0050 0A00 0050 0AF3 CE50 0A8A 2950"
      $"0A8A 2950 0AF3 CE50 0A82 4950 0A82 2950"
      $"0A82 2E50 0A00 0050 0A00 0050 0A00 0050"
      $"09FF FF90 0800 0010 0FFF FFF0 0800 0010"
      $"0800 0010 0800 0010 0800 7F10 0800 0010"
      $"0800 0010 0800 0010 0800 0010 07FF FFE0"
      $"0400 0020 0400 0020 0400 0020 07FF FFE0",
      /*[2] */
      $"0000 0000 07FF FFE0 0FFF FFF0 0FFF FFF0"
      $"0FFF FFF0 0FFF FFF0 0FFF FFF0 0FFF FFF0"
      $"0FFF FFF0 0FFF FFF0 0FFF FFF0 0FFF FFF0"
      $"0FFF FFF0 0FFF FFF0 0FFF FFF0 0FFF FFF0"
      $"0FFF FFF0 0FFF FFF0 0FFF FFF0 0FFF FFF0"
      $"0FFF FFF0 0FFF FFF0 0FFF FFF0 0FFF FFF0"
      $"0FFF FFF0 0FFF FFF0 0FFF FFF0 07FF FFE0"
      $"07FF FFE0 07FF FFE0 07FF FFE0 07FF FFE0"
   }
};

data 'ICON' (-4096, purgeable) {
   $"0000 0000 07FF FFE0 0800 0010 09FF FF90"
   $"0A00 0050 0A00 0050 0AF3 CE50 0A8A 2950"
   $"0A8A 2950 0AF3 CE50 0A82 4950 0A82 2950"
   $"0A82 2E50 0A00 0050 0A00 0050 0A00 0050"
   $"09FF FF90 0800 0010 0FFF FFF0 0800 0010"
   $"0800 0010 0800 0010 0800 7F10 0800 0010"
   $"0800 0010 0800 0010 0800 0010 07FF FFE0"
   $"0400 0020 0400 0020 0400 0020 07FF FFE0"
   $"0000 0000 07FF FFE0 0FFF FFF0 0FFF FFF0"
   $"0FFF FFF0 0FFF FFF0 0FFF FFF0 0FFF FFF0"
   $"0FFF FFF0 0FFF FFF0 0FFF FFF0 0FFF FFF0"
   $"0FFF FFF0 0FFF FFF0 0FFF FFF0 0FFF FFF0"
   $"0FFF FFF0 0FFF FFF0 0FFF FFF0 0FFF FFF0"
   $"0FFF FFF0 0FFF FFF0 0FFF FFF0 0FFF FFF0"
   $"0FFF FFF0 0FFF FFF0 0FFF FFF0 07FF FFE0"
   $"07FF FFE0 07FF FFE0 07FF FFE0 07FF FFE0"
};

resource 'DITL' (-4096, purgeable) {
   {  /* array DITLarray: 10 elements */
      /* [1] */
      {10, 161, 73, 301},
      StaticText {
         disabled,
         "Monitor Extension Example \n Screen saver"
         "\n© 1990 Apple Computer, Inc."
```

(Continued)

Listing 10-2. Resources for a file that extends the Monitors control panel (Continued)

```
/* [2] */
{80, 1, 81, 319},
UserItem {
   enabled
},
/* [3] */
{50, 79, 59, 88},
UserItem {
   enabled
},
/* [4] */
{39, 79, 49, 88},
UserItem {
   enabled
},
/* [5] */
{43, 58, 58, 78},
StaticText {
   enabled,
   "^0"
},
/* [6] */
{41, 55, 57, 75},
UserItem {
   enabled
},
/* [7] */
{89, 128, 106, 236},
StaticText {
   enabled,
   "Filter Type"
},
/* [8] */
{21, 25, 38, 162},
StaticText {
   enabled,
   "Minutes before sleep"
},
/* [9] */
{112, 102, 131, 249},
RadioButton {
   enabled,
   "Zirconian Filtration"
},
/* [10] */
{132, 102, 151, 244},
RadioButton {
   enabled,
   "Anti-Aliasing Filter"
},
```

```
        /* [11] */
        {40, 79, 58, 90},
        Picture {
            enabled,
            -4080
        }
    }
};

resource 'FREF' (128, purgeable) {
    'cdev',
    0,
    ""
};

resource 'RECT' (-4096, purgeable)
{
    {-80,0,0,320}
};

/* The 'card' resources ensure that this cdev is
    called when Options is pressed and the following
    cards are being used:

    Macintosh Display Card
    Macintosh Display Card 8•24 GC
*/

resource 'card' (-4080, purgeable)
{
    "Macintosh Display Card"
};
resource 'card' (-4079, purgeable)
{
    "Macintosh Display Card 8•24 GC"
};

/* The 'STR#' resource is used if for some reason you want to display
    a name for the card that is different from the one in the
    sResource of the board.
*/
resource 'STR#' (-4096, purgeable)
{
    {   "Macintosh Display Card";
        "Macintosh Display Card 8•24";
        "Macintosh Display Card 8•24 GC";
        "Macintosh Display Card 8•24 GC 'The Accelerated'"};
};
```

(Continued)

Listing 10-2. Resources for a file that extends the Monitors control panel (Continued)

```
resource 'ALRT' (130, purgeable) {
   {50, 30, 190, 400},
   130,
   {  /* array: 4 elements */
      /* [1] */
      OK, visible, sound1,
      /* [2] */
      OK, visible, sound1,
      /* [3] */
      OK, visible, sound1,
      /* [4] */
      OK, visible, sound1
   }
};

resource 'ALRT' (131, purgeable) {
   {50, 30, 190, 400},
   131,
   {  /* array: 4 elements */
      /* [1] */
      OK, visible, sound1,
      /* [2] */
      OK, visible, sound1,
      /* [3] */
      OK, visible, sound1,
      /* [4] */
      OK, visible, sound1
   }
};

resource 'DITL' (130, purgeable) {
   {  /* array DITLarray: 2 elements */
      /* [1] */
      {90, 267, 110, 337},
      Button {
         enabled,
         "OK"
      },
      /* [2] */
      {10, 60, 70, 350},
      StaticText {
         disabled,
         "There is not enough memory"
      }
   }
};

resource 'DITL' (131, purgeable) {
   {  /* array DITLarray: 2 elements */
      /* [1] */
      {90, 267, 110, 337},
```

```
        Button {
            enabled,
            "OK"
        },
        /* [2] */
        {10, 60, 70, 350},
        StaticText {
            disabled,
            "An error occurred. \nI cannot display"
            " the options. "
        }
    }
};

/* used to keep the setting of the filter type controls */
resource 'INTE' (-4080, purgeable) {
  5
};

/* used to keep the setting of the time to sleep */
resource 'SLEP' (-4080, purgeable) {
  5
};

/* PICT used to display the arrows to increase/decrease the sleep time */
resource 'PICT' (-4080) {
    {134, 272, 152, 283},
    VersionOne {
        {   /* array OpCodes: 2 elements */
            /* [1] */
            clipRgn {
                {-30000, -30000, 30000, 30000},
                $""
            },
            /* [2] */
            bitsRect {
                2,
                {254, 352, 272, 368},
                {254, 352, 272, 363},
                {134, 272, 152, 283},
                srcCopy,
                $"3F80 4040 8420 8E20 9F20 BFA0 8E20 8E20"
                $"8020 8020 8E20 8E20 BFA0 9F20 8E20 8420"
                $"4040 3F80"
            }
        }
    }
};
```

INCLUDING ANOTHER CONTROL PANEL DEFINITION IN A MONITORS EXTENSION FILE

A control panel file that contains an extension to the Monitors control panel can also contain a definition for another, separate control panel. You might want to include both an extension to the Monitors control panel and a new control panel definition in the same file, for example, if each controlled some features of the same video card. Any control panel definition must include a 'cdev' resource and the other resources described in the Control Panel chapter of Volume V.

Because the control panel resources and the Monitors extension resources in the file have different resource ID numbers, the Finder handles them separately. If the user opens a control panel file containing both a control panel definition and an extension to the Monitors control panel, the control panel defined in that file appears on the screen and the Finder ignores the Monitors extension in that file. If the user opens the Monitors control panel file, then the Monitors cdev function searches the other control panel files in the same folder for extensions and ignores any 'cdev' resources it finds in those files. The user cannot open a control panel file that contains only an extension to the Monitors control panel; such a file can be opened only by the Monitors cdev function.

SUMMARY OF THE EXTENSION FILE FOR THE MONITORS CONTROL PANEL

Constants

```
CONST initMsg        = 1;    {initialization}
      okMsg          = 2;    {user clicked OK button}
      cancelMsg      = 3;    {user clicked Cancel button}
      hitMsg         = 4;    {user clicked control in Options dialog box}
      nulMsg         = 5;    {periodic event}
      updateMsg      = 6;    {update event}
      activateMsg    = 7;    {not used}
      deactivateMsg  = 8;    {not used}
      keyEvtMsg      = 9;    {keyboard event}
      superMsg       = 10;   {show superuser controls}
      normalMsg      = 11;   {show only normal controls}
      startupMsg     = 12;   {code has been loaded}
```

Application-Defined Routine

```
FUNCTION MyMntr           (message,item,numItems: Integer; monitorValue:
                           LongInt; mDialog: DialogPtr; theEvent:
                           EventRecord; screenNum: Integer; VAR screens:
                           ScrnRsrcHandle; VAR scrnChanged: Boolean) :
                           LongInt;
```

11 THE HELP MANAGER

ABOUT THIS CHAPTER

This chapter describes how you can use the Help Manager to provide your users with Balloon Help™ on-line assistance—information that describes the actions, behaviors, or properties of elements of your application. When the user turns on Balloon Help assistance, the Help Manager displays small **help balloons** as the user moves the cursor over areas such as scroll bars, buttons, menus, or rectangular areas in your windows. Help balloons are rounded-rectangle windows that contain explanatory information for the user. (With tips pointing at the objects they annotate, help balloons look like the balloons used for dialog in comic strips.) You provide the content for these help balloons in the form of descriptive text or pictures. The information should be short and pertinent to the object or element that the cursor is over.

For example, when a user moves the cursor to a menu command, a help balloon pointing to that command explains its function. The help balloon is displayed until the user moves the cursor away.

The user turns on Balloon Help on-line assistance for all applications by choosing the Show Balloons command from the Help menu. All normally available features of your application are still active when Balloon Help is enabled. The help balloons only provide information; the actions that the user performs by pressing the mouse button still take effect as they normally would.

The Help Manager is available only in system software version 7.0. Use the Gestalt function to determine whether the Help Manager is present.

Read this chapter if you want to provide descriptive information for the menus, windows, dialog boxes, or alert boxes used by your application, desk accessory, control panel, Chooser extension, or other software that interacts with the user. If you presently offer another help facility for your users, you should now let users gain access to your information through the Help menu. This chapter explains how you can add your own menu items to the Help menu to provide one convenient and consistent place for the user to look for help information.

You can provide help for the menus, dialog boxes, and alert boxes of your existing applications, desk accessories, or control panels by simply adding resources to your resource fork. In addition, you can provide help for the content area of windows by using either resources or Help Manager routines.

To use this chapter, you should be familiar with the Resource Manager. You provide help for your application by storing the information regarding help balloons in resources. To provide help for menus, windows, dialog boxes, or alert boxes, you should also be familiar with the Menu Manager, Window Manager, Dialog Manager, and Control Manager as described in previous volumes of *Inside Macintosh.*

ABOUT THE HELP MANAGER

You can use the Help Manager to provide help for these elements of your application:

- menu titles and menu items
- dialog boxes and alert boxes
- windows, including any object in the frame or content area
- other application-defined areas

Providing help balloons for menus, dialog boxes, or alert boxes is quite simple: you need only create resources containing the help information that you want to relay to the user. The Help Manager automatically sizes, positions, and draws the help balloon and its content for you. It is equally simple to provide help balloons for a window whose elements don't change location within its content area.

It takes a little more work to provide help balloons for windows in your application that contain objects that are dynamic or that change their position within the content area of the window. You provide Balloon Help assistance for these objects by tracking the cursor yourself and using Help Manager routines to display help balloons. You can let the Help Manager remove the help balloon, or your application can determine when to remove the help balloon.

The user turns on Balloon Help on-line assistance by choosing Show Balloons from the Help menu. As shown in Figure 11-1, the Help menu is identified by an icon consisting of a question mark enclosed in a small help balloon. It appears to the left of the Application menu (and to the left of the Keyboard menu, if a non-Roman script system is installed) and to the right of all other menus. Users can turn on Balloon Help assistance even when your application presents a modal dialog box, because the Help menu is always enabled.

Figure 11-1. The Help menu for the Finder

When Balloon Help assistance is turned on, the Help Manager displays any help balloons for the current application whenever the user moves the cursor over a rectangular area that has a help balloon associated with it.

The Help Manager provides a default help balloon for inactive windows and displays default help balloons for the title bar and other parts of the active window. The Help Manager also displays default help balloons for other standard elements of an application's user interface. A later section, "Default Help Balloons for Menus, Windows, and Icons," describes the default help balloons. (Though you probably won't want or need to change the messages in these default balloons, you have the ability to do so, as described later in "Overriding Other Default Help Balloons.") The Help Manager displays the default help balloons for your application whenever Balloon Help assistance is enabled, even if your application does not explicitly use or create help balloons.

All normal features of your application are available when Balloon Help assistance is on. The Help Manager can display a balloon when the mouse button is pressed as well as when the mouse button is up. Help balloons do not interfere with your application. The user can still click and double-click as normal when Balloon Help assistance is enabled.

The display of help balloons is driven mainly by the action of the user. For those balloons defined as standard help resource types, the Help Manager automatically tracks the cursor and generates the shape and calculates the position for the help balloon. The Help Manager displays each help balloon as the user moves the cursor to the area associated with it. The Help Manager removes the help balloon when the cursor is no longer over the associated area.

Once the user chooses Show Balloons, help is enabled for all applications. When the user chooses Hide Balloons from the Help menu, the Help Manager removes any visible help balloon and stops displaying help balloons until Balloon Help assistance is turned on again.

This chapter provides a brief description of how the Help Manager displays help balloons, gives information on the default help balloons, and then discusses how to

- create the text or picture content for help balloons
- create resources for help balloons for menus, dialog boxes, and alert boxes
- create resources for help balloons for windows
- add your own menu items to the Help menu
- override the default help balloons provided by system software
- write your own balloon definition function

Help Balloon Display

The Help Manager performs most of the work involved with rendering help balloons for your application. This section gives an overview of the facilities that the Help Manager uses to display balloons and how you employ them in your application.

The Help Manager uses the Window Manager to create a special type of window for the help balloon and then draws the content of the help balloon in the port rectangle of the window. The Help Manager is responsible for

- calculating the size of the help balloon (based on the content of the user help information you provide)
- determining line breaks for text in a help balloon
- calculating where to display the help balloon so that it appears on screen
- drawing the help balloon and its content on screen

A **balloon definition function,** which is an implementation of a window definition function, defines the general appearance of the help balloon. A standard balloon definition function is provided for you, and it's responsible for

- calculating the content region and structure region of the help balloon (based on the rectangle calculated by the Help Manager)
- drawing the frame of the help balloon

The standard balloon definition function is the window definition function (a 'WDEF' resource) with resource ID 126. Figure 11-2 shows the general shape of a help balloon drawn with this standard balloon definition function.

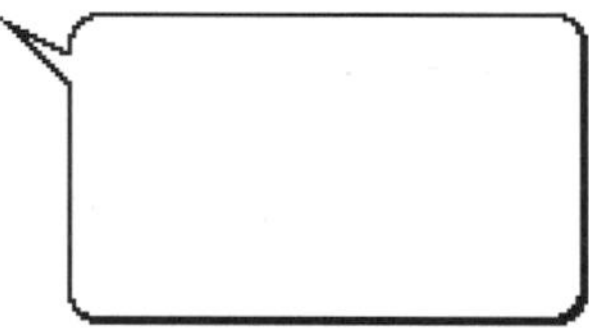

Figure 11-2. A help balloon drawn with the standard balloon definition function

Every help balloon is further defined by its tip, a hot rectangle, and a variation code.

A small pointer extends from a corner of every help balloon; this element indicates what object or area is explained in the help balloon. The **tip** is the point at the end of that element. Figure 11-3 shows an example of a help balloon for a control. The balloon tip is at coordinates (38,158) of the window.

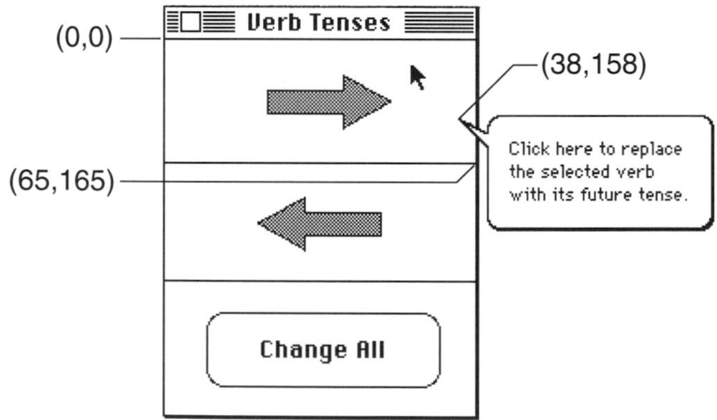

Figure 11-3. The tip and hot rectangle for a help balloon

The **hot rectangle** encloses the area for which you want to provide Balloon Help on-line assistance. If the cursor is over a hot rectangle, the Help Manager displays its help balloon. The Help Manager removes the help balloon when the cursor is moved away. The user must pause with the cursor at the same location for a brief amount of time (around one-tenth of a second) before the Help Manager displays the help balloon. This prevents excessive flashing of help balloons. The length of time that a user must pause before a help balloon appears is set by the system software and cannot be changed.

In Figure 11-3, the help balloon is displayed for a hot rectangle defined by local coordinates (0,0,65,165). The Help Manager displays and removes the help balloon as the cursor moves in and out of the area defined by the hot rectangle.

A **variation code** specifies the preferred position of the help balloon relative to the hot rectangle. The balloon definition function draws the frame of the help balloon based on that variation code.

As shown in Figure 11-4, the standard balloon definition function provides eight different positions, which you can specify with a variation code from 0 to 7. The figure also shows the boundary rectangle for each shape. Note that the tip of the help balloon always aligns with an edge of the boundary rectangle. If you write your own balloon definition function, you should support the tip locations defined by the standard variation codes.

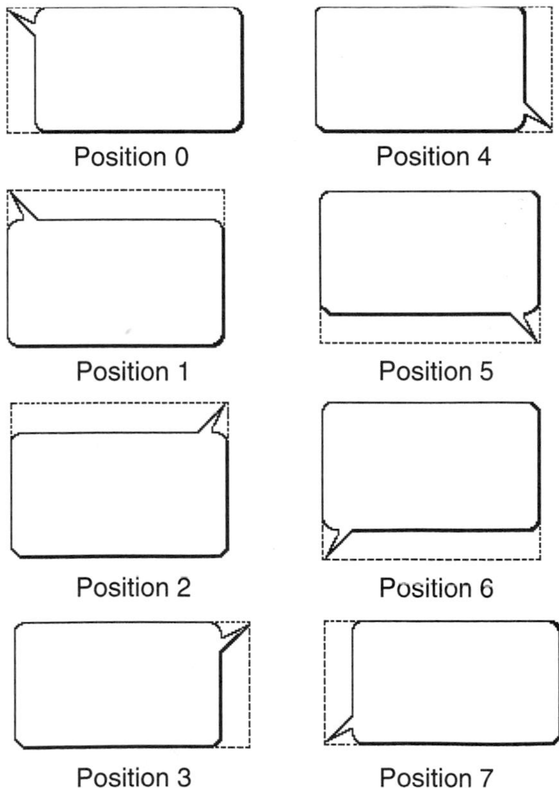

Figure 11-4. Standard balloon positions and their variation codes

For most of the help balloons it displays, the Finder™ uses variation code 6. A balloon with variation code 6 has its tip in the lower-left corner and projects up slightly and to the right.

If a help balloon is on screen and not in the menu bar, the Help Manager uses the specified variation code to display the help balloon. If a help balloon is offscreen or in the menu bar, the Help Manager attempts to display the help balloon by using a combination of different variation codes and different tip locations.

Usually, the Help Manager moves the tip by transposing it across the horizontal and vertical planes of the hot rectangle. However, when you use dialog item help ('hdlg') resources or the HMShowBalloon and HMShowMenuBalloon functions, the Help Manager allows you to specify **alternate rectangles** for transposing balloon tips. Alternate rectangles give you additional flexibility in positioning your help balloons on screen. If you make your alternate rectangle smaller than your hot rectangle, for example, you have greater assurance that the Help Manager will be able to fit the help balloon on screen; if you specify an alternate rectangle that is larger than your hot rectangle, you have greater assurance that the help balloon will not obscure some element explained by the balloon.

Figure 11-5 shows the Help Manager making three attempts to fit a help balloon on screen by moving the tip to three different sides of the hot rectangle and using an appropriate variation code for each tip.

When positioning a help balloon on screen, the Help Manager first checks whether the screen has enough horizontal space and then enough vertical space to display the balloon using the specified variation code and tip. If the help balloon is either too wide or too long to fit on

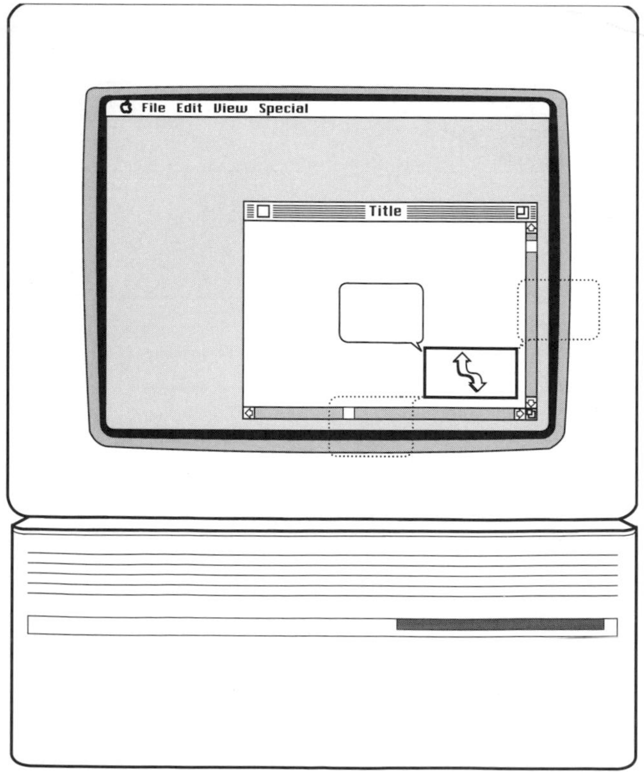

Figure 11-5. Alternate positions of a help balloon

screen at this position, the Help Manager tries a different variation code. If the help balloon lies within the hot rectangle (or, if appropriate, within the alternate rectangle), the Help Manager—using the new variation code—keeps the specified tip and again tests whether the help balloon fits. If, as in Figure 11-5, the help balloon lies outside of the hot rectangle (or the alternate rectangle), the Help Manager—using the new variation code—moves the tip to a different side of the rectangle and again tests whether the help balloon fits. If, after exhausting all possible positions, the Help Manager still cannot fit the entire help balloon on screen, the Help Manager displays a help balloon at the position that best fits on screen and clips the content of the balloon to fit at this position.

You create help resources that describe the content, the balloon definition function, the variation code, and, when necessary, the tip and the hot rectangle or alternate rectangle for the Help Manager to use in drawing a help balloon. These help resources are

- the menu help ('hmnu') resource to provide help balloons for menus and menu items
- the dialog item help ('hdlg') resource to provide help balloons for items in dialog boxes or alert boxes
- the rectangle help ('hrct') resource to associate a help balloon with a hot rectangle in a static window
- the window help ('hwin') resource to map an 'hrct' or 'hdlg' resource to a hot rectangle in a window or to a dialog item in a dialog box or alert box
- the Finder help override ('hfdr') resource to provide a customized help balloon for your application icon
- the default help override ('hovr') resource to override the content of default help balloons provided in system software

To put help balloons in your application, you are responsible for

- Creating any necessary help resources for your application.
- Providing the user help information that forms the content of the help balloons. Although you can store this information in the help resources themselves or in data structures, localizing your help content is much easier if you store it in other resources—such as 'PICT', 'STR#', 'STR ', 'TEXT', and 'styl' resources—that are easier to edit.
- Specifying in your help resources a balloon definition function for your help balloons. Typically, you should use the standard balloon definition function that draws shapes similar to that shown in Figure 11-2. This helps maintain a consistent look across all help balloons used by the Finder and other applications. However, if you feel absolutely compelled to change the shape of help balloons in your application, you can write your own balloon definition function as described in "Writing Your Own Balloon Definition Function" later in this chapter. Be aware that a different help balloon shape may initially confuse your users.
- Specifying in your help resources a variation code. The variation code positions your balloons on screen according to the general shape described by their balloon definition function. If you use the standard balloon definition function, you'll use variation codes 0 to 7 to display the help balloons shown in Figure 11-4. The preferred variation code is 0. If you are unsure of which variation code to use, specify 0; the Help Manager will use a different variant if another is more appropriate. If you write your own balloon definition function, you must define your own variation codes.

For objects other than menu items, you are also responsible for

- Specifying in your help resources the tip location for the help balloon. For menu items, the Help Manager automatically places the tip just inside the right edge of the menu item.
- Specifying rectangles in your help resources. The rectangles around menu items and dialog items define their hot rectangles for you. For 'hdlg' resources, you specify alternate rectangles for moving the help balloon. For 'hrct' resources, you specify hot rectangles, which define the areas on screen for association of help balloons.
- Tracking the cursor in dynamic windows, and, when the cursor moves over a hot rectangle in your window, calling Help Manager routines (such as HMShowBalloon) to display your help balloons. You can let your application or the Help Manager remove the help balloon when the user moves the cursor off the hot rectangle.

In summary then, the Help Manager automatically displays help balloons in the following manner. The user turns Balloon Help assistance on, then moves the cursor to an area described by a hot rectangle. The Help Manager calculates the size of the help balloon based on its content. For text or strings, the Help Manager uses TextEdit to determine the word and line breaks of text in the help balloon. The Help Manager then determines the size of the help balloon and uses the Window Manager to create a new help balloon. The Window Manager calls the balloon definition function to determine the help balloon's general shape and position. (If the variation code places the help balloon offscreen or in the menu bar, the Help Manager tries a different variation code or moves the tip of the help balloon to another side of the hot rectangle or the alternate rectangle.) The window definition function draws the window frame, and the Help Manager draws the content of the help balloon.

For most interface elements that you want to provide help for, you create the content of the help balloon (preferably in a separate, easily edited resource) and, in the help resources themselves, you specify the standard balloon definition function, one of the eight variation codes, the tip location, and a hot rectangle.

The Help Manager does not automatically display help balloons for dynamic windows or for menus using customized menu definitions. To provide help balloons for these elements or in other circumstances where you want more control over help balloons, you must identify hot rectangles, create your own data structures to store their locations, track the cursor yourself, and call HMShowBalloon when the cursor moves to your hot rectangles. If you wish to, you can also write your own balloon definition function and tip function.

Default Help Balloons for Menus, Windows, and Icons

The Help Manager displays many default help balloons for an application when help is enabled and the user moves the cursor to certain standard areas of the user interface. These areas include the standard window frame and the menu titles and menu items in the Apple® menu, Help menu, Keyboard menu, and Application menu. You don't need to create any resources or use any Help Manager routines to take advantage of the default help balloons. The following list summarizes the items that have default help balloons.

Interface item	Description
Application icon in Finder	Default help also for desk accessories, system extensions, control panels; can be customized
Document icon in Finder	Cannot be customized
Standard file dialog boxes	You add balloons for extra dialog items
Window title bar	In standard and customized WDEFs
Window close box	In standard and customized WDEFs
Window zoom box	In standard and customized WDEFs
Inactive window	Can be customized
Apple menu title	Standard menu definition procedure only
Apple menu items	Default balloons are provided for items in the Apple Menu Items folder, but there is no default balloon for the About command or other items that your application adds
Help menu title	Standard menu definition procedure only
Help menu items	Default balloons are provided only for the About Balloon Help and Hide/Show Balloons items
Application menu title and items	Standard menu definition procedure only
Keyboard menu title and items	Standard menu definition procedure only

System software version 7.0 uses the Help Manager to display help balloons for most dialog boxes and alert boxes. For example, the Standard File Package provides help balloons for its standard file dialog boxes. If your application uses a system software routine (such as the StandardPutFile procedure) that provides help balloons, and the user has turned on Balloon Help assistance, the Help Manager displays each help balloon as the user moves the cursor to each hot rectangle. If you've added your own buttons, check boxes, or controls to such a dialog box or alert box, you can also provide these elements with help balloons.

The Help Manager displays help balloons for the standard window frame and other standard elements described in the 'hovr' resource. You can override any of the default help balloons defined in the 'hovr' resource by providing your own resource of type 'hovr'. See "Overriding Other Default Help Balloons" later in this chapter for more information.

The Help Manager uses the window definition function of a window to determine whether the cursor is in the window frame and, if so, which part of the window frame (title, close box, or zoom box) the cursor is over. If the cursor is in any of these areas, the Help Manager displays the associated help balloon. Figure 11-6 shows the default help balloons for the active window of an application that uses the standard window definition function. If you use a customized window definition function, the Help Manager also displays these default help balloons for the corresponding elements in your windows.

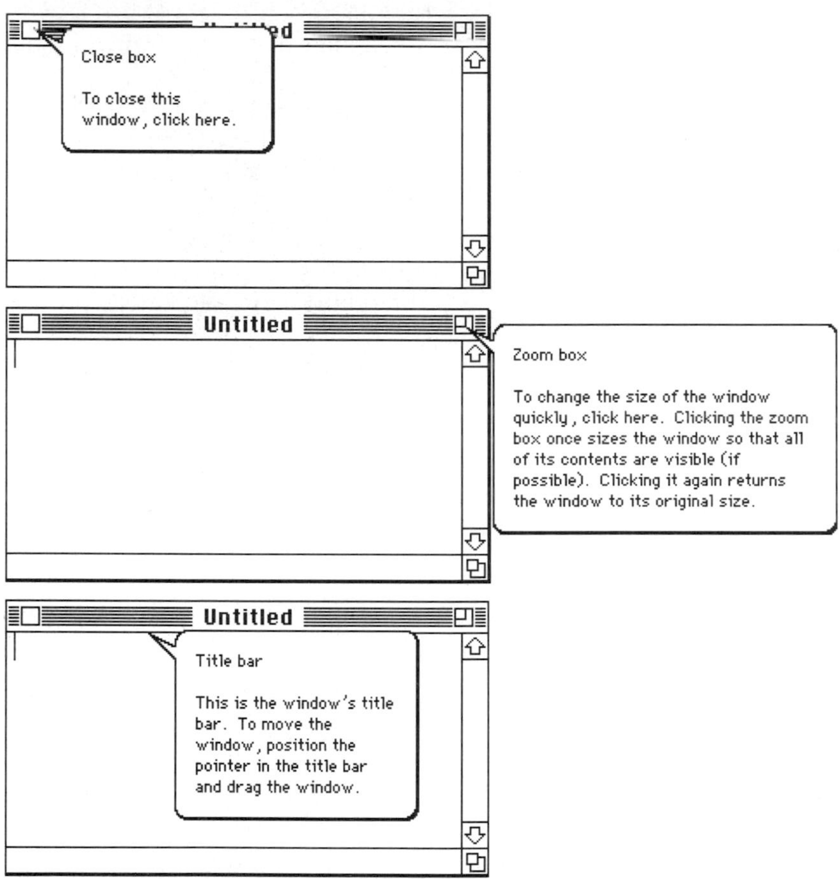

Figure 11-6. Default help balloons for the window frame

The Finder also uses these help balloons for its window titles and its close and zoom boxes. The Finder provides additional help for other elements of its windows—for example, the scroll bar and size box—although this help is not provided for the windows in your application.

The Help Manager displays default help balloons for the Apple menu, Help menu, and Application menu. The Menu Manager uses the Help Manager to display help balloons for these menus regardless of whether you supply help balloons for the rest of your menus. The Help Manager also provides default help balloons for the Keyboard menu when a non-Roman script system is installed. Figure 11-7 shows the default help balloons for the Apple menu and Help menu titles.

Note: The Help Manager displays default help balloons only for applications that use the standard menu definition procedure. If you use your own menu definition procedure, your application must track the cursor and use Help Manager routines to display and remove help balloons, as described later in "Using Your Own Menu Definition Procedure."

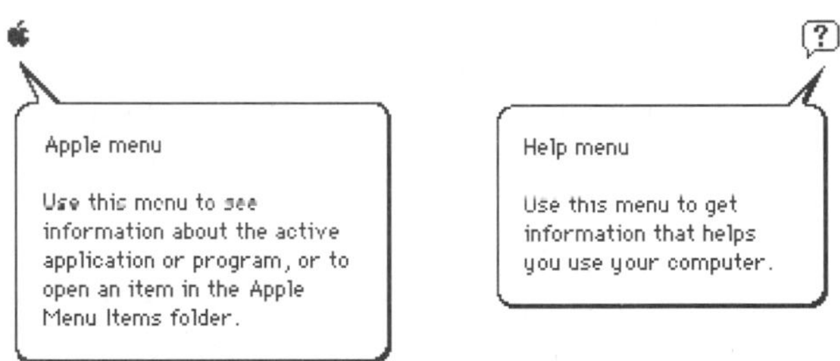

Figure 11-7. Default help balloons for the Apple and Help menus

The Help Manager does not provide default help balloons for items you put at the top of your application's Apple menu or items you add to the Help menu. You typically put one item at the top of the Apple menu: the About command for your application. If you have additional user help facilities, list them in the Help menu—not in the Apple menu. You have control only over those items that you add to these menus; system software handles help balloons for the rest of the items.

The Finder provides default help balloons for your application icon and any documents created by your application. Figure 11-8 shows the default help balloon for the SurfWriter application and a document created by this application. You can customize the help balloon for your application icon by providing an 'hfdr' resource; however, you can't customize the default help balloon for the documents created by your application.

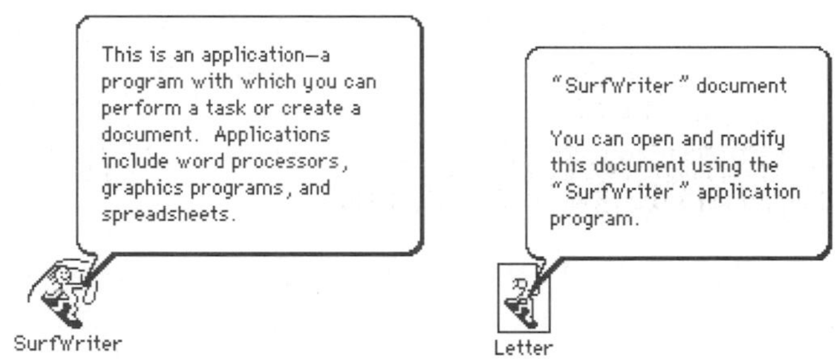

Figure 11-8. Default help balloons for application and document icons

USING THE HELP MANAGER

You can use the Help Manager to provide information to the user that describes the action, behavior, or properties of elements of your application. For example, you can create a help balloon for each menu command to describe what it does.

The Help Manager is available only in system software version 7.0. Use the Gestalt function with the Gestalt selector gestaltHelpMgrAttr. Test the bit field indicated by the gestaltHelpMgrPresent constant in the response parameter. If the bit is set, then the Help Manager is present.

```
CONST gestaltHelpMgrPresent = 0;   {if this bit is set, then }
                                   { Help Manager is present}
```

The Help Manager is initialized at startup time. The user controls whether help is enabled by choosing the Show Balloons or Hide Balloons command from the Help menu.

The Help menu is specific to each application, just as the File and Edit menus are specific to each application. The Help menu items that are defined by the Help Manager are common to all applications, but you can add your own menu items for help-related information.

When your application calls the InsertMenu procedure, the Menu Manager automatically appends the Help menu to your menus. The Help menu is automatically appended to the right of all your menus and to the left of the Application menu (and to the left of the Keyboard menu if a non-Roman script system is installed).

You can create help balloons for the menus, dialog boxes, alert boxes, or content area of windows belonging to your application. You can also override some of the default help balloons—such as the default help balloon for the title bar of a window.

You can specify the content of a help balloon using text strings, styled text, or pictures. Although you should always strive for brevity in your help messages, text strings can contain up to 255 characters. You can use up to 32 KB with styled text. The Help Manager determines the actual size of the help balloon and, for text strings, uses TextEdit to determine the word and line breaks of text.

The Help Manager automatically tracks the cursor and generates help balloons defined in standard help resources. Your application can also track the cursor and use Help Manager routines to display and remove help balloons.

Providing Text or Pictures for Help Balloons

Use help balloons to provide the user with information that describes or explains elements of your application. The information you supply in help balloons should follow a few general guidelines in order to provide the most useful information to the user. This section describes these guidelines.

For examples of how your application should use help balloons, observe the help balloons provided by the Finder, the TeachText application, and system software.

Defining the Help Balloon Content

Use help balloons to explain parts of the interface of your application that might confuse a new user or elements that could help a user become an expert user. The information you provide in help balloons should identify interface elements in your application or describe how to use them. Each help balloon should answer at least one of these questions:

- **What is this?** For example, when the user moves the cursor to the item count in the upper-right corner of a Finder window, the Finder displays a help balloon that reads "This is the number of files or folders in this window."
- **What does this do?** For example, when the user moves the cursor to the Find command in the Finder's File menu, the Finder displays a help balloon that reads "Finds and selects files and folders with the characteristics you specify."
- **What happens when I click this?** For example, when the user moves the cursor to the close box of a window, the Window Manager displays a help balloon that first defines the element ("Close box") and then explains "To close this window, click here."

The content of help balloons should be short and easy to understand. You should not include lengthy instructions or numbered steps in help balloons. Use help balloons to clarify the meaning of objects in your application—for example, tool symbols in palettes.

Use simple, clear language in the information you provide. Include definitions in help balloons when appropriate.

You can use graphics or styled text in help balloons to illustrate the effects of a command. For example, to demonstrate the Bold command in a word-processing application, you might use styled text to show a word in boldface.

You can provide separate help balloons for each state of a menu item or dialog item. The help balloon that you provide for an enabled menu item should explain the effect of choosing the item. The help balloon that you provide for a dimmed menu item should explain why it isn't currently available, or, if more appropriate, how to make it available.

Complicated dialog boxes can often benefit from help balloons that explain what's essential about the dialog box. You can use help balloons to describe groups of controls rather than individual controls. For example, if a dialog box has several distinct regions that contain radio buttons or check boxes, you could provide a help balloon for each set of radio buttons, rather than providing a separate balloon for each button.

If you use a function to customize standard dialog boxes, use as many of the existing help balloons as possible. For example, if your application uses any of the standard file dialog boxes and provides an extra button, you can create a help balloon for the extra button, and the Help Manager continues to use the default help balloons for other elements of the dialog box.

To make localization easier, you should store the content of your help balloons in resources separate from the help resources. See the Worldwide Software Overview and User Interface Guidelines chapters in this volume for extensive information about developing software for a worldwide market.

Using Clear, Concise Phrases

You can provide up to 255 characters of information using text strings in help balloons. (You can use up to 32 KB if you use styled text.) However, you should include only the most relevant information in the help balloon. To determine what to provide, decide what information would be most useful to a user. This information doesn't usually give the object's name, which normally doesn't matter to the user, but instead tells what the object is for and what the object does. This information does matter to the user.

You might eventually translate your help content into other languages, so try to keep the information as short as possible. When translated, your help messages may require more words or longer words—and therefore larger balloons and more screen space. (Translated text is often 50 percent longer than the equivalent U.S. English text.) Also avoid language or phrasing that might be colloquial, offensive, or likely to lose its meaning when translated into another language.

If an item already has a commonly used name, or if it's a special case of a larger category of objects, name it in the balloon. The Finder, for example, displays the message "Drag the title bar to move the window," since title bars and windows are commonly used names. However, you don't need to name everything in your application just so that you can refer to it in a help balloon. The tip of the help balloon points to the subject of the help balloon. You can easily say "To apply the style, click here," rather than "The Apply button activates the Styles command. Click the button to activate the command."

For balloons that describe menu items, you can use sentence fragments. The subject can be omitted because it is obvious from the context. Using sentence fragments lets users assimilate the content of the balloon more quickly because they have fewer words to read. For example, the help balloon for the Open command could read "Opens the selected file" rather than "This command opens the selected file."

Using Active Constructions

Try to use short, active phrases in help balloons. Avoid passive constructions. An active construction is more forceful because it communicates how a subject (usually the user in this context) performs an action. In the sentence "To turn the page, click here," the implied "you" (that is, the user) is the subject, and "click" is the action that the subject performs. Passive constructions show subjects being acted upon rather than performing the action. For example, both "page" and "button" are acted upon in their respective clauses in the sentence "The page will be turned when this button is clicked."

Research suggests that in instructional materials it's better to present the goal clause before the action clause to help readers quickly recognize how the information meets their needs. Users are then able to determine whether the content is relevant to what they want to do. A goal might be "To turn the page," "To calculate the result," or "To apply the style." For example, the message "To turn the page, click here" starts with a goal statement and then describes the action necessary to fulfill it; users find this more helpful than a purely descriptive message like "This button turns the page."

Using Parallel Structure

Use similar syntax for help balloons that describe similar objects. For example, all help balloons that describe buttons should have the same structure. In a style dialog box, you might provide these messages for the buttons: "To see the style, click Apply," "To implement the style, click OK," and "To do nothing to change the previous style, click Cancel."

Users see help balloons provided by many different applications, so a consistent approach within your application helps them to quickly identify types of balloons and to develop realistic expectations about their content.

Using Consistent Terminology

You should employ consistent terminology in all your help balloons. Use language that users understand. Avoid introducing technical jargon or computer terminology into help balloons. Follow the style and usage standardized by Apple Computer, Inc., in the *Apple Publications Style Guide* (available through APDA®) to make the most effective use of the information and vocabulary with which users are already familiar.

Defining the Help Balloon Position

When you provide a help balloon, you specify its content, the tip of the help balloon, and the variation code for its preferred position. The tip of the help balloon should point to the object the help balloon describes. You should specify the tip location and the variation code so that the help balloon doesn't obscure the object you're providing help for. In most cases, the tip of the help balloon should point to an edge of the object you're providing help for.

You should also consider how the Help Manager repositions the balloon if the variation code places it offscreen. "Help Balloon Display" earlier in this chapter describes how the Help Manager repositions the help balloon if necessary.

Specifying the Format for Help Balloon Content

You specify the format for the content of your help balloons as text strings within the help resource, as text strings within 'STR ' resources, as lists of text strings within 'STR#' resources, as styled text using 'TEXT' and 'styl' resources, or as pictures within 'PICT' resources.

You can easily add Balloon Help on-line assistance to your existing application without changing its code by adding the help resources described in the following subsections of "Using the Help Manager." When you use help resources, the Help Manager tracks the cursor and displays and removes help balloons for you. With the routines described later in "Help Manager Routines," you can also provide Balloon Help on-line assistance without using the help resources. However, this requires that your application track the cursor and display and remove balloons.

Later sections in this chapter describe all the help resources in detail. Common to all the help resources are the following identifiers, by which you identify the format of your user help information:

Identifier	Help content format
HMStringItem	Pascal string within the help resource
HMPictItem	'PICT' resource
HMStringResItem	'STR#' resource
HMTEResItem	'TEXT' and 'styl' resources
HMSTRResItem	'STR ' resource
HMSkipItem	No content—skip this item

You can use the HMStringItem identifier to store Pascal strings directly in a help resource. However, you can make it much easier to localize your product by storing your user help content in separate resources—namely, in 'STR#', 'PICT', 'STR ', and 'TEXT' resources—that can be modified by nonprogrammers using tools like the ResEdit™ resource editor.

To display a diagram or illustration in 'PICT' format, use the HMPictItem identifier. You provide help content by specifying the resource ID of the 'PICT' resource that contains the diagram or illustration, and the Help Manager displays the picture in a help balloon.

To display a string stored in a string list ('STR#') resource, use the HMStringResItem identifier. As illustrated later in "Providing Help Balloons for Menus," you provide help content by specifying two items in your help resource: the resource ID of an 'STR#' resource, and the index to the particular string that you want displayed from within that list.

To display styled text, use the HMTEResItem identifier. You provide help content by specifying a resource ID that is common to both a style scrap ('styl') resource and a 'TEXT' resource, and the Help Manager employs TextEdit routines to display your text with your prescribed styles. For example, you might create a 'TEXT' resource with resource ID 1000 that contains the words "Displays your text in boldface print" and a 'styl' resource with resource ID 1000 that applies boldface style to the message. (See the TextEdit chapter in Volume V for a description of the style scrap.)

To display text from a simple text string ('STR ') resource, use the HMSTRResItem identifier. You provide help content by specifying the resource ID of an 'STR ' resource, and the Help Manager displays the text from that resource in a help balloon. With 'STR ' resources, each text string must be stored in a separate resource. It is usually more convenient to group related help messages in a single 'STR#' resource and use the HMStringResItem identifier as previously described.

You can use the HMSkipItem identifier for items or rectangles for which you don't want to provide a help balloon. For example, you specify HMSkipItem for the dashed lines that appear in menus. (Dashed lines cannot have help balloons.)

Specifying Options in Help Resources

Each help resource contains a field in its header that allows you to specify certain options. Notice the options field in the following header component for a menu help resource.

```
resource 'hmnu' (130, "Edit", purgeable) {
   HelpMgrVersion,    /* version of Help Manager */
   hmDefaultOptions, /* options */
   0,                 /* balloon definition function */
   0,                 /* variation code */
```

You should normally use the hmDefaultOptions constant, as shown in the preceding example, to get the standard behavior for help balloons. However, you can also use the constants listed here for the options field. (Note that not all options are available for every help resource.)

```
CONST hmDefaultOptions     = 0;     {use defaults}
      hmUseSubID           = 1;     {use subrange resource IDs }
                                    { for owned resources}
      hmAbsoluteCoords     = 2;     {ignore coords of window }
                                    { origin and treat upper left }
                                    { corner of window as 0,0}
      hmSaveBitsNoWindow   = 4;     {don't create window; save }
                                    { bits; no update event}
      hmSaveBitsWindow     = 8;     {save bits behind window }
                                    { and generate update event}
      hmMatchInTitle       = 16;    {match window by string }
                                    { anywhere in title string}
```

If you're providing help balloons for a desk accessory or a driver that uses owned resources, use the hmUseSubID constant in the options field. Otherwise, the Help Manager treats the resource IDs specified in the rest of your help resource as standard resource IDs. (See the Resource Manager chapter in Volume I for a discussion of owned resources and their resource IDs.)

As described later in this chapter, you often specify tip and rectangle coordinates in your help resources. You might want to use the hmAbsoluteCoords constant when providing help for elements in a scrolling window or whenever the window origin is offset from the origin of the port rectangle. If you specify the hmAbsoluteCoords constant, the Help Manager ignores the local coordinates of the port rectangle when tracking the cursor, and instead tracks the mouse position relative to the window origin. When you specify the hmAbsoluteCoords constant as an option in a help resource, the Help Manager subtracts the coordinates of the window origin from the coordinates of the mouse position, and the Help Manager uses these results for the current mouse position, as shown here:

```
mousepoint.h := mousepoint.h - portRect.left;
mousepoint.v := mousepoint.v - portRect.top;
```

With the hmAbsoluteCoords option specified, the Help Manager always assigns coordinates (0,0) to the point in the upper-left corner of the window. So, for example, if the cursor is positioned at point (4,5) in a port rectangle and the window origin is at (3,4), the Help Manager calculates the cursor to be at (1,1). If this option is not specified, the Help Manager uses the port rectangle's local coordinates when tracking the cursor—for example, when using the GetMouse procedure.

The Help Manager draws and removes help balloons on screen in three different ways. For all help resources except 'hmnu' resources, the Help Manager by default draws and removes help balloons as if they were windows. That is, when drawing a balloon, the Help Manager does not save bits behind the balloon and, when removing the balloon, the Help Manager generates an update event. By specifying the hmDefaultOptions constant in your help resources, you always get the standard behavior of help balloons. However, you can often specify two options that change the way balloons are drawn and removed from the screen.

If you specify the hmSaveBitsNoWindow constant in the options field, the Help Manager does not create a window for displaying the balloon. Instead, the Help Manager creates a help balloon that is more like a menu than a window. The Help Manager saves the bits behind the balloon when it creates the balloon. When it removes the balloon, the Help Manager restores the bits without generating an update event. You should only use this option in a modal environment where the bits behind the balloon cannot change from the time the balloon is drawn to the time it is removed. For example, you might choose the hmSaveBitsNoWindow option in a modal environment when providing help balloons that overlay complex graphics, which might take a long time to redraw with an update event. Note that the Help Manager always uses this behavior when drawing and removing help balloons specified in your 'hmnu' resources. That is, when you specify the hmDefaultOptions constant in an 'hmnu' resource, the Help Manager provides this sort of balloon instead of drawing a window for a balloon. (In an 'hmnu' resource, you cannot even specify options for drawing a window for a balloon.)

If you specify the hmSaveBitsWindow constant, the Help Manager treats the help balloon as a hybrid having properties of both a menu and a window. That is, the Help Manager saves the bits behind the balloon when it creates the balloon and, when it removes the balloon, it both restores the bits and generates an update event. You'll rarely need this option. It is necessary only in a modal environment that might immediately change to a nonmodal environment—that is, where the bits behind the help balloon are static when the balloon is drawn, but can possibly change before the help balloon is removed. For example, if you use an 'hmnu' resource to provide help balloons for menu titles and menu items, you'll notice that the Help Manager automatically provides this sort of behavior (even when you don't specify the hmSaveBitsWindow option) when creating help balloons for menu titles.

In the preceding list of constants, the values for the constants represent bit positions that are set to 1. To override more than one default, add the values of the bit positions for the desired options and specify this sum, instead of a constant, in the options field. For example, to use subrange IDs, ignore the window port origin coordinates, and save bits behind the help balloon without generating an update event, you should add the values of the bit positions of these options (1, 2, and 4) and specify their sum (7) in the options field.

If you supply the hmDefaultOptions constant, the Help Manager treats the resource IDs in this resource as regular resource IDs and not as subrange IDs; it uses the port rectangle's local coordinates when tracking the cursor; it creates windows when drawing balloons and it generates update events without saving or restoring bits when removing balloons.

The hmMatchInTitle constant is used only in window help ('hwin') resources to match windows containing a specified number of characters in their titles. This constant is explained later in more detail in "Help Balloons in Static Windows."

The next sections describe how to create help resources that provide help balloons for the standard user interface elements of your application.

Providing Help Balloons for Menus

If your application uses the standard menu definition procedure, you'll find that it's easier to provide help balloons for menus than for any of your other interface elements. This section is relatively lengthy compared to the sections describing dialog boxes, alert boxes, and windows only because it explains in greater detail much of the work you'll also perform while providing help balloons for those elements.

This section assumes that your application uses the standard menu definition procedure. If your application uses its own menu definition procedure, you must use Help Manager routines to display and remove help balloons. These are described in "Displaying and Removing Help Balloons" later in this chapter. Even if you use these routines, you should read this section so that your balloons emulate the behavior that the Help Manager provides for standard menus.

To create help balloons for a menu—pull-down, pop-up, or hierarchical—that uses the standard menu definition procedure, create a resource of type 'hmnu'. You can provide help balloons for the menu title and for each individual menu item.

The Help Manager can display different help balloons for the various states of a menu item. Each menu item can have up to four help balloons associated with it, one for each state:

- enabled
- disabled (that is, dimmed for the user)
- enabled and checked
- enabled and marked (that is, marked by a symbol other than a checkmark—for example, a bullet or a diamond)

For example, you can define a help balloon that the Help Manager displays when the Cut command is enabled and another help balloon for display when the Cut command is dimmed. Remember that the help balloon that you provide for a dimmed menu item should explain why it isn't currently available or, if more appropriate, how to make it available.

> **Note:** Although *enabled* and *disabled* are the commands you use in a resource file to display or to dim menus and menu items, you shouldn't use these terms in your help balloons or user guides. Rather, use the terms *menus, menu commands,* or *menu items* for those that are enabled, and use the terms *not available* or *dimmed* to distinguish those that have been disabled.

When your application calls the MenuSelect or MenuKey function, the Menu Manager tracks the cursor, highlights enabled menu items, and pulls down any additional hierarchical or pop-up menus as the user moves the mouse. As the user drags the cursor across or through a menu, the Menu Manager uses the Help Manager to display any help balloons associated with the current state of the menu title or menu item.

Figure 11-9 shows different help balloons for two instances of a menu, one with the Cut command dimmed, the other with the Cut command enabled.

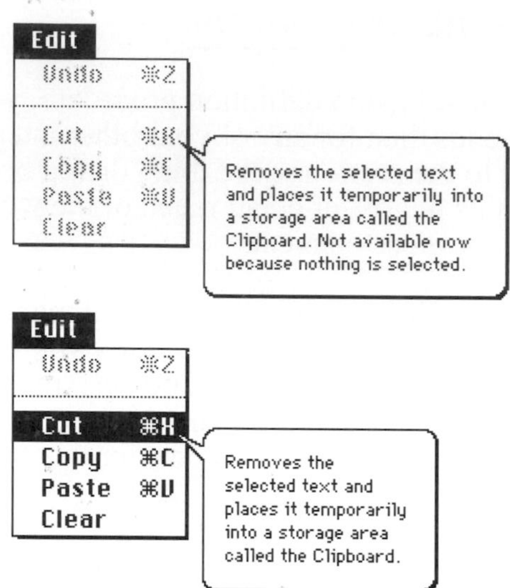

Figure 11-9. Help balloons for different states of the Cut command

You don't specify hot rectangles or tip locations for menus. The rectangles defined by the Menu Manager for menu titles and menu items are used for the hot rectangles. The Help Manager initially tries to draw a help balloon for a menu item using variation code 0 (shown in Figure 11-4) with the tip placed eight pixels inside the right edge and halfway between the top and bottom edges of the menu item's rectangle. If the balloon's initial position lies wholly or partially offscreen, the Help Manager tries to redraw the balloon by moving its tip to the left edge of the item rectangle and using variation code 3. The Help Manager uses variation codes 1 and 2 in its attempts to draw help balloons for menu titles. The Help Manager never moves the tip for menu titles; instead, the tip is always located just below the bottom of the menu bar at the midpoint of the menu title's text.

The resource ID of each 'hmnu' resource should match the corresponding menu ID. For example, to provide help balloons for a menu with ID 130, create an 'hmnu' resource with resource ID 130.

The 'hmnu' resource contains four distinct components: the header, the help balloon content for any menu items missing from or unspecified in the rest of the 'hmnu' resource, the help balloon content for the menu title, and the help balloon content for a variable number of menu items.

Here is the general format of an 'hmnu' resource.

Component	Menu help resource element
Header	Help Manager version Options Balloon definition function Variation code

Component	**Menu help resource element**
Missing items	Identifier for help balloon content Balloon content for missing enabled items Balloon content for missing dimmed items Balloon content for missing enabled-and-checked items Balloon content for missing enabled-and-marked items
Menu title	Identifier for help balloon content Balloon content for enabled state of menu title Balloon content for dimmed state of menu title Balloon content when the menu title is dimmed by presence of a modal dialog box Balloon content for all menu items dimmed by presence of a modal dialog box
First menu item	Identifier for help balloon content Balloon content for enabled item Balloon content for dimmed item Balloon content for enabled-and-checked item Balloon content for enabled-and-marked item
Next menu item	(Same as for first menu item) . . .

Listing 11-1 shows an example of part of a simplified menu help resource for an Edit menu.

Listing 11-1. A partial menu help resource

```
resource 'hmnu' (130, "Edit", purgeable) {
   /* header information */
   HelpMgrVersion,
   hmDefaultOptions, /* options */
   0,                /* balloon definition function */
   0,                /* variation code */
   /* missing items information */
   HMSkipItem {
      /* no missing items, so skip to menu title information */
      },
      { /* Edit menu title's help balloon content */
         HMStringItem { /* use following pstrings */
               /* use string below when menu is enabled */
            "Use this menu to manipulate text.",
               /* use string below when menu is dimmed */
            "Not available now because this file cannot be changed.",
               /* use string below if modal dialog box is present */
            "This menu's not available; respond to the dialog box.",
               /* use string below if modal dialog box is present */
            "This command's not available; respond to the dialog box.",
         },
```

(Continued)

Listing 11-1. A partial menu help resource (Continued)

```
      /* Undo command's help balloon content */
         HMStringItem { /* use following pstrings */
               /* use string below when command is enabled */
            "Undoes your last edit.",
               /* use string below when menu is dimmed */
            "Not available now; only editing changes can be undone.",
               /* can't be checked, so empty string goes below */
            "",
               /* can't be marked, so empty string goes below */
            "",
         },
      /* dashed line between Undo and Cut commands */
         HMSkipItem { /* no help balloons for dashed lines */
         },
      /* Cut command's help balloon content */
         HMStringItem { /* use following pstrings */
               /* use string below when command is enabled */
            "Cuts the selected text to the Clipboard.",
               /* use string below when command is dimmed */
            "Not available now because no text is selected.",
               /* can't be checked, so empty string goes below */
            "",
               /* can't be marked, so empty string goes below */
            "",
         }
      /* Copy, Paste, and Clear commands' help balloons go here */
      }
};
```

The header component comprises these fields:

- Help Manager version
- options
- balloon definition function
- variation code

In the header component, always specify the HelpMgrVersion constant in the first field.

In the options field, specify a constant (normally, hmDefaultOptions) or the sum of several constants' values from this list. ("Specifying Options in Help Resources" earlier in this chapter describes these options.)

```
CONST hmDefaultOptions     = 0;    {use defaults}
      hmUseSubID           = 1;    {use subrange resource IDs }
                                   { for owned resources}
      hmAbsoluteCoords     = 2;    {ignore coords of window }
                                   { origin and treat upper-left }
                                   { corner of window as 0,0}
```

Note that the Help Manager never creates a window for a help balloon specified in an 'hmnu' resource. The Help Manager saves the bits behind the balloon when it creates the balloon. When it removes the balloon, the Help Manager restores the bits without generating an update event. You cannot specify options for drawing a window for a balloon in an 'hmnu' resource.

The balloon definition function field in the header specifies the resource ID of the window definition function that is used to draw the frame of the help balloon. To use the standard balloon definition function, specify a 0 for this field; this is the suggested default. If you use your own balloon definition function (as described in "Writing Your Own Balloon Definition Function" later in this chapter), specify its resource ID in this field.

The variation code field in the header specifies the preferred position of the help balloon. For example, the standard balloon definition function displays help balloons according to eight different positions. If you specified the standard balloon definition in the preceding field, supply a variation code from 0 to 7 to display the balloon according to one of the eight positions shown in Figure 11-4. The preferred variation code is 0. If you are unsure of which variation code to use, specify 0; the Help Manager will use different variant if another is more appropriate. If you use your own balloon definition function, you specify its variation code in this field in the header.

After the header, you specify the format and content for help balloons for missing items, the menu title, and menu items.

Use the missing items component of this resource to specify how the Help Manager should handle menu items that are not described in the 'hmnu' resource. The missing field is also used for menu items that are described in the 'hmnu' resource but which lack help content for any states.

The missing items component of this resource is useful when you have menu items with similar characteristics or when the number of menu items is variable. For example, if the help information for a dimmed item applies to all dimmed menu items, you can specify the help information in the dimmed field of the missing items component instead of in the dimmed fields of the components for individual menu items.

For missing items (as in the rest of the items listed in an 'hmnu' resource), you store the help balloon content in text strings within this resource, or in separate 'STR ', 'STR#', 'PICT', or 'TEXT' and 'styl' resources. As described earlier in "Specifying the Format for Help Balloon Content," you'll use these identifiers in the resource.

Identifier	**Help content format**
HMStringItem	Pascal string within the help resource
HMPictItem	'PICT' resource
HMStringResItem	'STR#' resource
HMTEResItem	'TEXT' and 'styl' resources
HMSTRResItem	'STR ' resource
HMSkipItem	No content—skip this item

Specify an identifier from the preceding list to describe the format of the help balloon content. Then, depending on the identifier you specified, in the next four fields supply either text strings for the balloon content or resource IDs of resources that contain the help balloon content.

The next four fields correspond to the following states of missing menu items:

- the balloon's content when a menu item is enabled, and either its content is not specified in the help resource (though the menu item is specified in the help resource) or the menu item itself is not specified in the help resource
- the balloon's content when a menu item is dimmed, and either it is missing from this resource or its help content is specified with either an empty string ("") or a resource ID of 0
- the balloon's content when a menu item is enabled and checked, and either it is missing from this resource or its help content is unspecified
- the balloon's content when a menu item is enabled and marked (with a character other than a checkmark), and either it is missing from this resource or its help content is unspecified

The content you supply is displayed in a help balloon for any menu item that appears at the end of the menu but is not described in this resource, and for any menu item in this resource whose content is specified as either "" (empty) for strings or 0 for resource IDs.

There are two additional identifiers that you can specify for menu items in 'hmnu' resources. These are explained later in this section.

Identifier	**Purpose**
HMCompareItem	Provide help only when string matches current menu item
HMNamedResourceItem	Get help content from the resource that has the same name as the current menu item

Listing 11-2 illustrates the help resource for a menu titled Colors. Notice in the missing items component that the field describing dimmed states for menu items has the message "Not available; either you have not selected text to color, or your monitor does not support color." Because this resource doesn't specify a message for any command's dimmed state, this message appears in help balloons for the Blue, Red, and Green commands whenever they're dimmed.

After the missing items component, you specify the help balloon content for the menu title and the menu items, in the same order in which they appear in the 'MENU' resource.

You can use the HMSkipItem identifier for items that appear in your menu but for which you don't provide a help balloon. For example, you can specify HMSkipItem for dashed lines that appear in menus. (Dashed lines cannot have help balloons.) If you specify HMSkipItem, the Help Manager does not display help balloons for that menu item, even if the missing items component provides help information.

Listing 11-2. The missing items component in a menu help resource

```
resource 'hmnu' (132, "Colors", purgeable) {
   /* header information */
   HelpMgrVersion, hmDefaultOptions, 0, 0,
   /* missing items information */
   HMStringItem {
      "",    /* no missing enabled items */
            /* balloon content for all dimmed items below */
      "Not available; either you have not selected text to color, "
         "or your monitor does not support color.",
      "",    /* no missing enabled-and-checked items */
      "",    /* no missing enabled-and-marked items */
      },
   { /* Help for menu title and items */
      /* Colors menu title's help balloon content */
      HMStringItem { /* use following Pascal strings content */
            /* use string below when menu is enabled */
         "Use this menu to display text in color.",
            /* use string below when menu is dimmed */
         "Not available because this monitor does not support color.",
            /* use string below when modal dialog box is present */
         "Use this menu to display text in color. Not available until "
            "you respond to the alert or dialog box.",
            /* use string below when modal dialog box is present */
         "Colors your selected text. Not available until you "
            "respond to the alert or dialog box.",
      },
      /* Blue command's help balloon content */
      HMStringItem { /* use following Pascal strings for content */
            /* use string below when command is enabled */
         "Displays the selected text in blue.",
         "",    /* use missing items content when menu is dimmed */
         "",    /* command can't be checked, so use empty string here */
         "",    /* command can't be marked, so use empty string here */
      },
      /* Green command's help balloon content */
      HMStringItem { /* use following Pascal strings for content */
            /* use string below when command is enabled */
         "Displays the selected text in green.",
         "",    /* use missing items content when menu is dimmed */
         "",    /* command can't be checked, so use empty string here */
         "",    /* command can't be marked, so use empty string here */
      },
      /* Red command's help balloon content */
      HMStringItem { /* use following Pascal strings for content */
            /* use string below when command is enabled */
         "Displays the selected text in red.",
         "",    /* use missing items content when menu is dimmed */
         "",    /* command can't be checked, so use empty string here */
         "",    /* command can't be marked, so use empty string here */
      }
   }
};
```

For the menu title component, as for the missing items component, you begin by specifying the identifier that describes the format for the help content. Depending on the identifier you specify, in the next four fields you supply either text strings for the balloon content or the resource IDs of resources that contain the help balloon content. These four fields correspond to these states of the menu title:

- the balloon content when the menu title is enabled
- the balloon content when the menu title is dimmed
- the balloon content for the dimmed title when a modal dialog box appears
- the balloon content for all dimmed menu items when a modal dialog box appears

The third and fourth fields of the menu title component specify help information for menus that are dimmed when an alert box or modal dialog box is the frontmost window. Users of system software version 7.0 can access selected menus in the menu bar while displaying an alert box or a modal dialog box. For example, the Show Balloons (or Hide Balloons) command is always available from the Help menu so that users can see your help balloons for the modal dialog box or alert box. While some menus are accessible, others may not be. The Compatibility Guidelines chapter in this volume describes the circumstances under which menus are enabled or not when a modal dialog box is displayed.

With users having access to your menus whenever a modal dialog box or alert box is present, it is important to provide help that explains to users why your menus and items are dimmed by the dialog or alert box. Use the third field in the menu title component of an 'hmnu' resource to specify the help balloon content that the Help Manager displays for that menu title when it is dimmed by the presence of a modal dialog box. For example, the Colors menu help resource shown in Listing 11-2 displays this message to the user when a modal dialog box is present: "Use this menu to display text in color. Not available until you respond to the alert or dialog box."

Use the fourth field to specify the help balloon content for all menu items that become dimmed when a modal dialog box appears. For example, in the Colors menu example, this message is displayed to the user who selects the Blue, Green, or Red command when a modal dialog box is present: "Colors your selected text. Not available until you respond to the alert or dialog box."

After you provide the header, missing items, and menu title information, you specify the help content for each menu item. Each item in this resource must appear in the order that it appears in the corresponding menu. For each menu item, begin by specifying one of the previously listed identifiers to describe the format for the item's help balloons. Then, depending on the identifier you specify, supply either a text string for the balloon content or the resource ID of a resource that contains the help balloon content.

Each field for a menu item corresponds to one of the following states:

- the balloon's content when this menu item is enabled
- the balloon's content when this menu item is dimmed
- the balloon's content when this menu item is enabled and checked
- the balloon's content when this menu item is enabled and marked with a character other than a checkmark

Note that, for any item in the resource, you can specify only one format for the content of the states specified in the component. For example, if you specify the HMSTRResItem identifier for the Undo command, you must store the help content for all the states of the command in 'STR ' resources. (However, if you specify a resource ID of 0 or an empty string as the content of any items in order to use the content from the missing items component of the resource, the content will follow the format specified in the missing items component.)

You do not have to provide help balloon content for every state of the menu item. If you do not provide help content for a particular state, the Help Manager uses the help information defined in the missing items component. If the missing items component does not provide help information for that menu state, then the Help Manager does not display a help balloon for that state of the item.

Listing 11-3 shows a sample 'hmnu' resource for another Edit menu. (Although Listings 11-1 and 11-2 illustrate menu help resources that contain their help balloon content in the form of Pascal strings within their own resources, you should keep your help balloon content in separate, more easily localized resources.) The 'hmnu' resource in Listing 11-3 stores its help balloon content in a separate 'STR#' resource (which is given a corresponding resource ID of 130 for easier maintenance).

Listing 11-3. Corresponding 'hmnu' and 'STR#' resources

```
resource 'hmnu' (130, "Edit menu help", purgeable) {
   HelpMgrVersion, 0, 0, 0,   /* standard header information */
   HMSkipItem {    /* missing items information */
      /* no missing items, so skip to menu title information */
      },
   {  /* menu title and items below */
      /* Edit menu title's help balloon content */
      HMStringResItem { /* use an 'STR#' resource for content */
         130,1,    /* 'STR#' res ID, index when menu is enabled */
         130,2,    /* 'STR#' res ID, index when menu is dimmed */
         130,3,    /* 'STR#', index for title with modal dialog box */
         130,4     /* 'STR#', index for items with modal dialog box */
      },
         /* Undo command's help balloon content */
      HMStringResItem { /* use an 'STR#' resource for content */
         130,5,    /* 'STR#' res ID, index when command is enabled */
         130,6,    /* 'STR#' res ID, index when command is dimmed */
         0,0,      /* command can't be checked */
         0,0       /* command can't be marked */
      },
         /* dashed item */
      HMSkipItem {    /* no balloon help for dashed items */
      },
         /* Cut command's help balloon content */
      HMStringResItem { /* use an 'STR#' resource for content */
         130,7,    /* 'STR#' res ID, index when command is enabled */
         130,8,    /* 'STR#' res ID, index when command is dimmed */
         0,0,      /* command can't be checked */
         0,0       /* command can't be marked */
      },
         /* content for Copy command's help balloons goes here */
   }
};
```

(Continued)

Listing 11-3. Corresponding 'hmnu' and 'STR#' resources (Continued)

```
resource 'STR#' (130, "Edit menu help strings") { /* Edit help text */
   { /* array StringArray: 17 elements */
   /* [1] help text for enabled Edit menu title */
   "Use this menu to undo your last action, to manipulate text, to "
      "select the entire content of a document, and to show what's "
      "on the Clipboard.";
   /* [2] help text for dimmed Edit menu title */
   "Use this menu to undo your last action, to manipulate text, to "
      "select the entire content of a document, and to show what's "
      "on the Clipboard. This menu is unavailable now.";
   /* [3] help for dimmed Edit menu title with modal dialog present */
   "Use this menu to undo your last action, to manipulate text, to "
      "select the entire content of a document, and to show what's "
      "on the Clipboard. This menu is unavailable until you respond to "
      "the alert box or dialog box.";
   /* [4] help for dimmed Edit menu items with modal dialog present */
   "This command is unavailable until you respond to the alert or "
      "dialog box.";
   /* [5] help text for enabled Undo command */
   "Undoes your last action; use this command to replace material "
      "you have cut or pasted, or to remove material you have pasted "
      "or typed.";
   /* [6] help text for dimmed Undo command */
   "Undoes your last action; use this command to replace material "
      "you have cut or cleared, or to remove material you have pasted "
      "or typed. Not available now because your last action did not "
      "involve cutting, clearing, pasting, or typing.";
   /* help text for all other commands goes here */
   }
};
```

The 'hmnu' resource in Listing 11-3 specifies the standard balloon definition function and variation code in the third and fourth fields of the header. The missing items component is specified using the HMSkipItem identifier, meaning that this 'hmnu' resource does not provide any help balloons for menu items that are missing from this resource or that do not have help content specified for any states.

Following the menu title, each menu item is listed in the order in which it appears in the menu. For items that do not specify information for a particular state, the Help Manager normally uses the information from the missing item. However, this 'hmnu' resource does not provide help content in the missing item component. Instead, all help content is specified with each menu item in this resource. Because there are no enabled-and-checked or enabled-and-marked states for the Undo and Copy commands, these states are specified with resource IDs of 0.

If you have a menu item that changes names, you can use the HMCompareItem identifier to compare a string against the current menu item in that position. If the string specified after the HMCompareItem identifier matches the name of the current menu item, the Help Manager displays the help balloon content specified in the next four fields of the help menu resource. Because of performance considerations, the HMCompareItem identifier shouldn't be used unless necessary.

Here is the general format for specifying help within an 'hmnu' resource for a changing menu item.

Component	Menu help resource element
Changing menu item	HMCompareItem identifier String to compare against current menu item Identifier for help balloon content Balloon content for enabled item Balloon content for dimmed item Balloon content for enabled-and-checked item Balloon content for enabled-and-marked item

In the 'hmnu' resource, create components that use the HMCompareItem identifier for every name that can appear in that menu position. For example, Listing 11-4 shows an 'hmnu' resource for a menu command that toggles between Show Colors and Hide Colors.

Listing 11-4. Using HMCompareItem for a changing menu item

```
resource 'hmnu' (132, "Colors menu help", purgeable) {
   /* see Listing 11-2 for missing items example */
   /* see Listing 11-2 for Colors menu title's help example */
      HMCompareItem { /* help content if first command is Show Colors */
         "Show Colors",
         HMStringResItem {
            132, 1,              /* enabled */
            0, 0,             /* use missing items */
            0, 0,             /* item can't be checked */
            0, 0              /* no marked state */
         },
      },
      HMCompareItem { /* help if the first command is Hide Colors */
         "Hide Colors",
         HMStringResItem {
            132, 2,           /* enabled */
            0, 0,             /* use missing items */
            0, 0,             /* item can't be checked */
            0, 0              /* no marked state */
         },
      },
      /* Blue command's help balloon content */
      HMStringItem { /* use following Pascal strings for content */
            /* use string below when command is enabled */
         "Displays the selected text in blue.",
         "",    /* use missing items content when menu is dimmed */
         "",    /* command can't be checked, so use empty string here */
         "",    /* command can't be marked, so use empty string here */
      },
      /* see Listing 11-2 for other commands' examples */
   }
};
```

(Continued)

Listing 11-4. Using HMCompareItem for a changing menu item (Continued)

```
resource 'STR#' (132, "Hide & Show Colors commands help text") {
      {
      /* [1] help text for enabled Show command */
      "Show text in previously selected colors.";
      /* [2] help text for enabled Hide command */
      "Show text in black and white only.";
      }
};
```

As illustrated in Figure 11-10, when the menu command is Show Colors, the Help Manager displays the help balloon content described by the first HMCompareItem component. When the menu command is Hide Colors, the Help Manager displays the help balloon content described by the second HMCompareItem identifier.

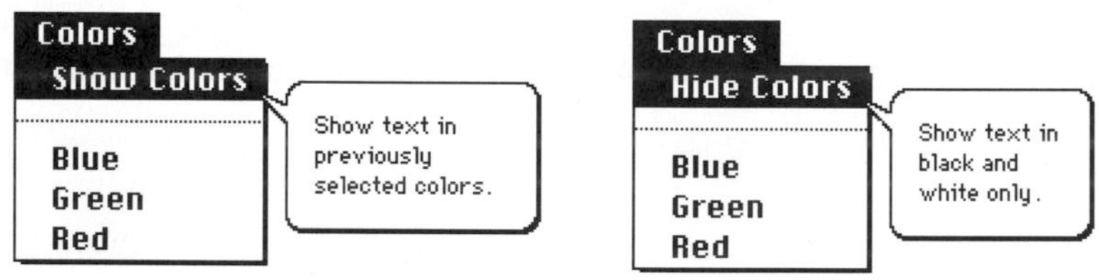

Figure 11-10. Help balloons for a changing menu item

You can also specify the content of a help balloon with the HMNamedResourceItem identifier, which causes the Help Manager to use a resource whose name matches the current name and state of the menu item. After the HMNamedResourceItem identifier, you specify the resource type ('STR ', 'STR#', 'PICT', or, for text, 'TEXT'), and the Help Manager uses the GetNamedResource function to find the resource with same name as the current menu item. (If you specify 'TEXT', you also get style information for the 'TEXT' resource by creating a 'styl' resource with the same name.)

If the menu item is dimmed, the Help Manager appends an exclamation mark to the menu item string and searches for a resource by that name. If the menu item is enabled and marked with a checkmark or other mark, the Help Manager appends the mark to the menu item string and looks for a resource with that name.

For example, this 'hmnu' resource specifies that the Help Manager extracts help content from a resource named Red of type 'STR ' when displaying a help balloon for an enabled menu command named Red. If the menu item is dimmed, the Help Manager gets the 'STR ' resource with the name Red! and uses its text string for the balloon content. If the Red command could be marked with an asterisk (*), the Help Manager would search for the resource with the name Red* of type 'STR '.

```
resource 'hmnu' (132, "Colors menu help", purgeable) {
        /* see Listing 11-2 for header info, missing items help, menu */
        /* title help, other menu items help */
     HMNamedResourceItem {  /* Red command's help balloon content */
        'STR '/* use the 'STR ' resource named "Red" */
     }
   }
};
resource 'STR ' (333, "Red") {   /* help text for enabled Red command */
     "Displays the selected text in red."
};
resource 'STR ' (334, "Red!") {  /* help text for dimmed Red command */
     "Not available; either you have not selected text to color, "
        "or your monitor does not support color.",
};
```

If there is sufficient memory, the standard menu definition procedure saves the bits behind the help balloon and restores these bits for quick updating of the screen. If there isn't sufficient memory to save the bits behind the help balloon, then—as with menus—the procedure generates appropriate update events.

Providing Help Balloons for Items in Dialog Boxes and Alert Boxes

For dialog boxes and alert boxes created with a dialog item list ('DITL'), you can provide help balloons for individual items in the dialog box or alert box by supplying a resource of type 'hdlg' (dialog item help). When the user moves the cursor over an item that has a help balloon associated with it, the Help Manager automatically displays and removes the help balloon as the cursor moves into and out of the item's rectangle. The Help Manager can display different help balloons for various states of a dialog item—by control value if the dialog item is a control, and by enabled and disabled states for dialog items that are not controls.

You can also provide help balloons for other areas of a dialog box or alert box using the 'hwin' (window help) resource as described in "Help Balloons in Static Windows" later in this chapter.

To create help balloons for items in dialog boxes or alert boxes, create an 'hdlg' resource that corresponds to a 'DITL' resource. You associate the help information defined in the 'hdlg' resource in one of three ways:

- by adding an item of type helpItem to the 'DITL' resource
- by supplying a resource of type 'hwin'
- by calling the HMScanTemplateItems function from your application

The 'hdlg' resource describes the tip, the alternate rectangle, and help information for dialog items in a dialog box or alert box. The 'DITL' resource describes the dialog items, and if it includes an item of type helpItem, it can contain the resource ID of a corresponding 'hdlg' resource. The Help Manager uses the item rectangles defined in the 'DITL' resource as the hot rectangles for the items. The Help Manager uses the alternate rectangles specified in the 'hdlg' resource for transposing help balloons' tips when trying to fit the balloons on screen.

If the dialog or alert box has an item of type helpItem in its 'DITL', help is enabled, and your application calls the ModalDialog procedure or the IsDialogEvent function, the Help Manager automatically tracks the cursor and displays help balloons as the user moves the cursor over items designated in the 'hdlg' resource.

If the cursor passes over any active windows, including dialog or alert boxes, the Help Manager searches the current resource file for resources of type 'hwin' (described in "Help Balloons in Static Windows" later in this chapter). The Help Manager attempts to match either the title of the window or the windowKind value in its window record with the title or windowKind value specified in an 'hwin' resource. The matched 'hwin' resource, in turn, specifies the resource ID of an 'hdlg' or 'hrct' (rectangle help) resource that contains the relevant help balloon content. (The 'hrct' resource is described in "Help Balloons in Static Windows" later in this chapter.) As described later in "Providing Help Balloons for Window Content," the 'hwin' resource can provide help for various elements across the entire window as well as for items in a dialog box or an alert box.

If you prefer, you can track and display help balloons for modal dialog boxes and alert boxes yourself by using a filter function and calling the HMScanTemplateItems function. Whereas adding a helpItem item to a 'DITL' or adding an 'hwin' requires only that you add resources, using HMScanTemplateItems requires you to modify your code. HMScanTemplateItems is described in "Getting and Setting Information for Help Resources" later in this chapter.

As shown here, the 'hdlg' resource contains header information, missing items information, and the help information for individual dialog items.

Component	**Dialog item help resource element**
Header	Help Manager version Index number of starting dialog item (first item is number 0) Options Balloon definition function Variation code
Missing items	Tip location Alternate rectangle Identifier for help balloon content Balloon content for missing highlighted controls, or for missing enabled items that are not controls Balloon content for missing dimmed controls, or for missing disabled items that are not controls Balloon content for missing active controls that are checked Balloon content for missing multipart controls

Component	Dialog item help resource element
First dialog item	Tip location Alternate rectangle Identifier for help balloon content Balloon content for a highlighted control, or for an enabled item that is not a control Balloon content for a dimmed control, or for a disabled item that is not a control Balloon content for an active control item that is checked Balloon content for a multipart control
Next dialog item	(Same as for first dialog item) . . .

The state of a dialog item depends on whether the dialog item is a control, such as a check box or radio button, or something else, such as a static text field or an icon.

The header specifies the Help Manager version number, the starting index, options, the balloon definition function, and the variation code. As in the other help resources, specify the HelpMgrVersion constant in the first field of the header component of the 'hdlg' resource.

You can use the starting index field to start the help information with any dialog item and then continue sequentially. To derive a dialog item number to start from, the Help Manager adds the index number you specify in this field to the number of the first item in the dialog item list ('DITL') resource. So index number 0 starts with the item number 1 in the 'DITL' resource (because 0 plus 1 equals 1). For example, to describe help information for only the fifth through seventh dialog items, specify 4 as the starting index in the header and, because 4 plus 1 equals 5, provide help content starting with the fifth and proceeding through the sixth and seventh dialog items.

In the options field, specify a constant (normally, hmDefaultOptions) or the sum of several constants' values from this list. ("Specifying Options in Help Resources" earlier in this chapter describes these options.)

```
CONST hmDefaultOptions      = 0;    {use defaults}
      hmUseSubID            = 1;    {use subrange resource IDs }
                                    { for owned resources}
      hmAbsoluteCoords      = 2;    {ignore coords of window }
                                    { origin and treat upper-left }
                                    { corner of window as 0,0}
      hmSaveBitsNoWindow    = 4;    {don't create window; save }
                                    { bits; no update event}
      hmSaveBitsWindow      = 8;    {save bits behind window }
                                    { and generate update event}
```

Specify the balloon definition function and variation code (both typically 0) in the fourth and fifth fields of the header. (These are described in detail earlier in "Providing Help Balloons for Menus.")

Following the header, you can specify the help content for dialog items that are missing from the 'hdlg' resource or that are present but have no help content defined for a particular state. (The missing items component is explained in detail earlier in "Providing Help Balloons for Menus.") In the missing items component, you specify a single tip location and a single alternate rectangle for all help balloons described in this component.

The tip location is always relative to the item's position in the dialog window. If you specify the point (0,0) as a default tip, then it is placed 10 pixels from the right and 10 pixels from the bottom of the item's rectangle (as specified in the 'DITL' resource) for all missing items. To move the missing item's tip relative to this default location, you can specify positive or negative integers in place of the coordinates (0,0).

For the missing item's alternate rectangle, you specify offsets from the dialog items' rectangles if you want alternate rectangles that are either larger or smaller than the items' rectangles. (The alternate rectangle, you'll remember, is used by the Help Manager for transposing the tip if a help balloon does not fit on screen.) The Help Manager adds the top, left, bottom, and right offsets that you specify to the coordinates of the items' rectangles. For example, if you specify (0,0,0,0) as the missing item's alternate rectangle offsets, the Help Manager uses the items' rectangles as alternate rectangles for all missing items. You can specify positive or negative integers for these parameters to move alternate rectangles' coordinates relative to the item rectangles' coordinates.

You also specify an identifier from the following list that describes the format of the help balloon content, and then, for each state of a missing dialog item, either a text string for the balloon content or the resource ID of a resource that contains the help balloon content.

Identifier	**Help content format**
HMStringItem	Pascal string within the help resource
HMPictItem	'PICT' resource
HMStringResItem	'STR#' resource
HMTEResItem	'TEXT' and 'styl' resources
HMSTRResItem	'STR ' resource
HMSkipItem	No content—skip this item

When displaying help balloons for a control, the Help Manager examines the highlight state in the contrlHilite field of the control record. An active—that is, highlighted—control has a contrlHilite value of 1. Specify the help balloon content for a highlighted control in the first field of the missing items component or the dialog item components of the 'hdlg' resource. An inactive—that is, dimmed—control has a contrlHilite value of 0. Specify the help balloon content for a dimmed control in the second field of the missing items component or the dialog item components of the 'hdlg' resource. If, as with check boxes and radio buttons, the user can turn on an off/on control, you provide help balloon content for a highlighted, "on" control in the third fields. A multipart control, such as a dial, has a contrlHilite value greater than 1. Specify the help balloon content for a multipart control in the fourth field of the missing items component or the dialog item components of the 'hdlg' resource. (See the Control Manager chapter in Volume I for information about controls.)

When displaying help for dialog items that are not controls, the Help Manager examines only whether the item is enabled or disabled, as specified in the dialog item list ('DITL') resource. When an item is enabled, the Dialog Manager informs your application about events involving this item. For an enabled item other than a control, you specify help balloon content in the first field of its component in the 'hdlg' resource. When an item is disabled, the Dialog Manager does not inform your application about events involving this item. You specify its help balloon content in the second field. The third and fourth fields do not apply to items that are not controls. Though the Help Manager never uses these states, you should supply their fields with either empty strings or resource IDs of 0, depending on the format you specify from the previous list of identifiers.

After the missing items component, you provide the help content for the dialog items, starting with the dialog item number indexed in the header and continuing in the same order in which they appear in the 'DITL' resource.

Specify the tip and an alternate rectangle for each dialog item. Use coordinates local to the dialog item's display rectangle (which is specified in the 'DITL' resource) to specify the tip. You can specify (0,0) to place the tip 10 pixels from the right and 10 pixels from the bottom of the dialog item's rectangle.

The Help Manager uses the item rectangles specified in the 'DITL' resource as the hot rectangles for displaying help balloons. You cannot specify different hot rectangles in an 'hdlg' resource. (If you must specify hot rectangles that are different from the items' rectangles, use the 'hrct' resource as described later in "Help Balloons in Static Windows.") You can, however, specify alternate rectangles in 'hdlg' resources that are different from the item rectangles defined in the 'DITL' resource. Alternate rectangles give you additional flexibility in positioning your help balloons on screen. If you make your alternate rectangle smaller than the item rectangle, for example, you have greater assurance that the Help Manager will be able to fit the help balloon on screen; if you specify an alternate rectangle that is larger than the item rectangle, you have greater assurance that the help balloon will not obscure some important element within the item rectangle.

Specify offsets from the dialog item's rectangle if you want an alternate rectangle that is different from the item rectangle. The Help Manager adds the top, left, bottom, and right offsets that you specify to the coordinates of the item rectangle. For example, if you specify (0,0,0,0) as the alternate rectangle's offsets, the Help Manager uses the item rectangle as its alternate rectangle. You can specify positive or negative integers for these parameters to move the alternate rectangle's coordinates relative to the item rectangle's coordinates.

Specify the format for the help content using one of the previously listed identifiers. Note that for any dialog item in the resource, you can specify only one format for the content of all its states.

Each dialog item in the 'hdlg' resource has four fields that can contain descriptive information. As previously described for missing dialog items, the Help Manager interprets these states differently according to whether the dialog item is or is not a control. In each field of a dialog item component, supply either a text string for the balloon content or the resource ID of a resource that contains the help balloon content.

You do not have to provide help balloon content for every state of a dialog item. If you do not provide help content for a particular state, the Help Manager uses the help information defined in the missing items component. If the missing items component does not provide help information for that state, then the Help Manager does not display a help balloon for that state.

You can use the HMSkipItem identifier for dialog items for which you do not want to provide help. If you specify HMSkipItem, the Help Manager does not display help balloons for that dialog item, even if the missing item provides help information.

Listing 11-5 shows a sample dialog item help resource along with its associated dialog item list ('DITL') and string list resources.

Listing 11-5. A dialog item list and its help resource

```
resource 'DITL' (145, "Spelling options", purgeable) {
   {  {124, 194, 144, 254},
      Button {
         enabled,
         "OK"
      },
      {48, 23, 67, 202},
      CheckBox {
         enabled,
         "Ignore Words in All Caps"
      },
      {83, 23, 101, 196},
      CheckBox {
         enabled,
         "Ignore Valley Girl Slang"
      },
      {13, 23, 33, 254},
      StaticText {
         disabled,
         "WipeOut typing correction options:"
      },
      /* item for Cancel button goes here */
      {0,0,0,0},  /* for help balloon: scan 'hdlg' with res ID 145 */
      HelpItem {
         disabled,
         HMScanhdlg  /* scan resource type 'hdlg' */
         {145}       /* get the resource with ID 145 */
      }
   }
};

resource 'hdlg' (145, "Spell options help", purgeable) {
   HelpMgrVersion, /* version of Help Manager */
   0,              /* start help with first item in 'DITL' */
   hmDefaultOptions, /* options */
   0,              /* balloon definition ID */
   3,              /* variation code: hang left of items */
   HMSkipItem {    /* no missing items help information */
      },
   {               /* help information for dialog items */
      HMStringResItem { /* store help for OK button in 'STR#' 145 */
         {0, 0},      /* default tip: middle right edge of item rect */
         {0,0,0,0},   /* default alternate rectangle: use item rect */
         145, 1,      /* enabled OK button */
```

```
            0, 0,         /* OK button is never dimmed */
            0, 0,         /* no enabled-and-checked state for button */
            0, 0          /* no other marked states for button */
        },
        HMStringResItem { /* store help for ALL CAPS option in 'STR#' */
            {6, 6},       /* place tip in check box */
            {0,0,0,0},    /* default alternate rectangle: use item rect */
            145, 2,       /* highlighted state of check box */
            145, 3,       /* dimmed state of check box */
            145, 4,       /* check box is checked */
            0, 0          /* not applicable to this control */
        },
        HMStringResItem { /* store help for slang option in 'STR#' 145 */
            {6, 6},       /* place tip in check box */
            {0,0,0,0},    /* default alternate rectangle: use item rect */
            145, 5,       /* highlighted state of check box */
            145, 6,       /* dimmed state of check box */
            145, 7,       /* check box is checked */
            0, 0          /* not applicable to this control */
        }
        /* help for Cancel button goes here */
    }
};

resource 'STR#' (145, "Spell options help text") {
    {
    /* [1] */
    "Click here to accept the checked options.";
    /* [2] */
    "Click this option to prevent the spelling checker from tagging "
        "words--such as acronyms--that consist entirely of "
        "capital letters.";
    /* [3] */
    "Not available until you install the main dictionary.";
    /* [4] */
    "Click this option to tag words that consist entirely of capital "
        "letters--such as acronyms--during your next spelling check.";
    /* [5] */
    "Click this option to prevent the spelling checker from tagging "
        "words considered to be part of Valley girl slang.";
    /* [6] */
    "Not available until you install the dictionary of Valley "
    "girl slang.";
    /* [7] */
    "Click this option to tag words that are considered to be "
        "Valley girl slang during your next spelling check.";
        /* help strings for Cancel button go here */
    }
};
```

The 'hdlg' resource in Listing 11-5 defines help information for the first three dialog items in the dialog item list. Figure 11-11 shows the Help Manager displaying a help balloon for the second item.

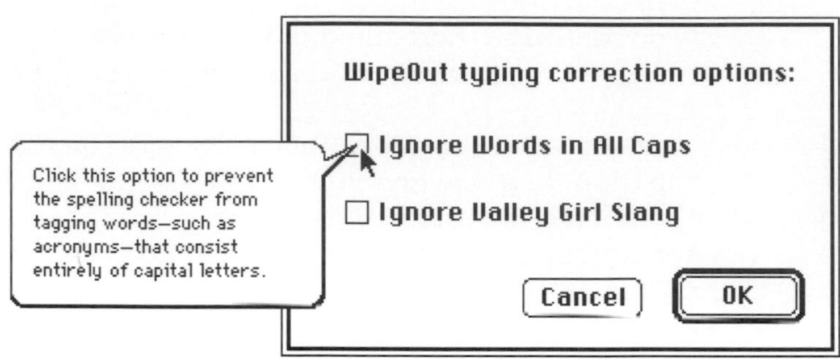

Figure 11-11. A help balloon in a modal dialog box

You may notice in Listing 11-5 that the Dialog Manager for system software version 7.0 supports a new item type for help—called helpItem. The help item isn't visible to the user; it's provided so that the Help Manager can find the corresponding help resource.

Specify an empty rectangle—that is, one with coordinates (0,0,0,0)—for the display rectangle of a helpItem item. Specify disabled for its state. Describe whether the help resource is of type 'hdlg' or 'hrct' by specifying either HMScanhdlg or HMScanhrct in the next field of the resource. (The 'hrct' resource is described in "Help Balloons in Static Windows" later in this chapter.) Then specify the ID of the resource that provides the help information for these dialog items.

Adding an item of type helpItem to a 'DITL' is the simplest method of associating the help balloons defined in your 'hdlg' resource with the dialog items defined in the 'DITL'. A slightly more involved method requires you to create an 'hwin' (window help) resource. The tradeoffs between the two methods are listed here.

The advantages of adding an item for help to the 'DITL' are that

- it's simple (you only have to create one resource, the 'hdlg' resource)
- it works for dialog boxes or alert boxes that have no titles and for those whose windowKind values do not adequately differentiate them from other windows (the windowKind field of window records is descibed in the Window Manager chapter in Volume I)

The disadvantages of adding an item for help to the 'DITL' are that

- it allows you to associate help balloons *only* with items listed in the 'DITL'
- it can't provide help balloons for alert boxes that have no dialog items

The advantages of using 'hwin' (window help) resources are that

- you can provide help balloons for alert boxes that have no dialog items
- you can provide a single help balloon for a group of related dialog items (rather than having separate help balloons for all the dialog items)
- you can provide help balloons for elements other than dialog items

The disadvantages of using 'hwin' resources are that

- it's slightly more complex (you must create additional resources)
- it only works for dialog boxes and alert boxes that have titles or windowKind values that differentiate them from other windows

Using the 'hwin' resource requires treating the dialog box or alert box as a static window. When the cursor passes over an active window, the Help Manager attempts to match either the title of the window or the windowKind value (from its window record) with a title or windowKind value you specify in an 'hwin' resource. The section "Help Balloons for Static Windows" later in this chapter describes how to use 'hwin' resources for dialog boxes, alert boxes, and other kinds of static windows you may wish to define.

Providing Help Balloons for Window Content

You can create help balloons for objects within the content area of your windows. How you choose to provide help balloons for the content area of your windows depends mainly on whether your windows are static or dynamic.

A **static window** doesn't change its title or reposition any of the objects within its content area. A **dynamic window** may reposition any of its objects within the content area and its title may change.

For example, any window that scrolls past areas of interest to the user is a dynamic window, because the objects with associated help balloons can change location as the user scrolls. A window that only displays a picture that cannot be resized or scrolled is an example of a static window. Figure 11-12 shows examples of static and dynamic windows. The next two sections describe how to provide help balloons for these types of windows.

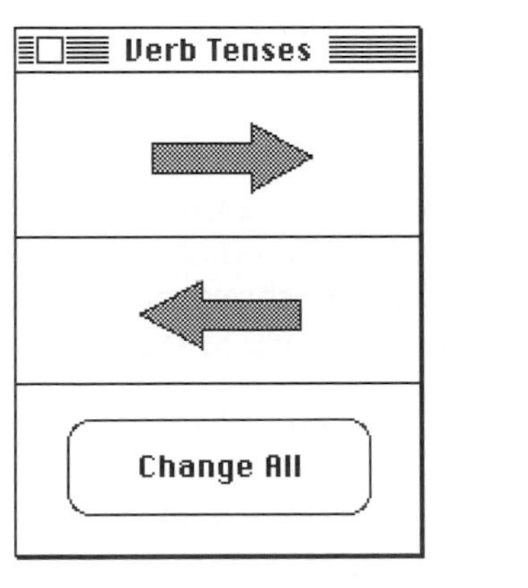

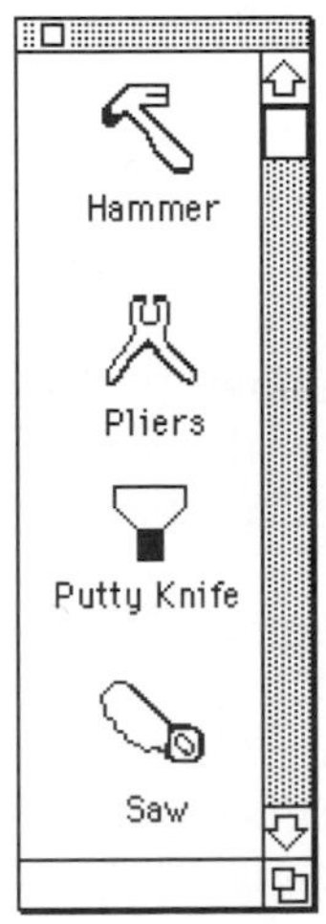

Figure 11-12. Static and dynamic windows

Help Balloons in Static Windows

To provide help balloons for the static windows of your application without modifying its code, create a resource of type 'hwin' (window help) and additional resources of type 'hrct' (rectangle help) or 'hdlg' (dialog item help). If your static windows provide help balloons with these resources, the Help Manager automatically tracks the cursor and displays and removes help balloons as the cursor moves into and out of the hot rectangles associated with these resources.

The 'hwin' resource allows you to associate 'hrct' and 'hdlg' resources with your static windows. You use the 'hrct' and 'hdlg' resources to define help balloons for the individual elements within your windows. While the Help Manager uses the item rectangles defined in the 'DITL' resource as the hot rectangles for 'hdlg' resources, you can specify your own hot rectangles for dialog boxes and other static windows when using 'hrct ' resources.

An 'hrct' resource specifies tip locations, hot rectangles, balloon definition functions, variation codes, and help content for areas within a static window.

As explained in the earlier section "Providing Help Balloons for Items in Dialog Boxes and Alert Boxes," the 'hdlg' resource describes the tip, alternate rectangle, and help information for dialog items in a dialog box. That section also describes how to associate the 'hdlg' resource with a dialog box by adding an item of type helpItem to the dialog box's 'DITL' resource. This section describes how you can instead treat your dialog boxes or alert boxes as static windows and use an 'hwin' resource instead of helpItem items to associate them with 'hdlg' resources.

The 'hwin' resource identifies windows by their titles or by their windowKind values. You can list all of your windows within one 'hwin' resource, or you can create separate 'hwin' resources for your separate windows. (You'll probably find that it is easier to maintain your window help if you create only one 'hwin' resource, but, as described later in this section, you must create separate 'hwin' resources for windows that require different options—for example, one window matched to its 'hwin' resource by a string anywhere in the window's title and another window matched to its 'hwin' resource only by the exact string of the window's title.) An 'hwin' resource contains the resource ID (or IDs) of one or more 'hrct' and 'hdlg' resources. An 'hwin' resource can use 'hrct' and 'hdlg' resources for various parts of the same window.

To use an 'hwin' resource, the window must have either a title or a windowKind value in its window record that adequately distinguishes it from other windows. Within an 'hwin' resource, you could identify the Verb Tenses window shown in Figure 11-12 by its title, and you could identify the scrolling palette window in Figure 11-12 by its windowKind value.

The Window Manager chapter in Volume I describes the windowKind field of the window record. Note that windowKind values of 0, 1, and 3 through 7 are reserved by the Operating System and that dialog boxes or alert boxes must have a value of 2. Because your dialog boxes and alert boxes must have a windowKind value of 2, you can use this value to define only one 'hwin' resource for all untitled dialog boxes and alert boxes. You may find it difficult—using help resources alone—to provide help balloons for untitled dialog and alert boxes. However, you can use an 'hwin' resource to associate generic help for the common elements of all your untitled dialog boxes and alert boxes, and you can use the HMSetDialogResID function to provide help for the unique elements among them. "Getting and Setting Information for Help Resources" later in this chapter explains the HMSetDialogResID function.

You describe the tip, a rectangle, and help information for each object in static windows using either 'hrct' or 'hdlg' resources. Shown here is the general format of an 'hrct' resource. ("Providing Help Balloons for Items in Dialog Boxes and Alert Boxes" earlier in this chapter describes 'hdlg' resources.)

Component	**Rectangle help resource element**
Header	Help Manager version Options Balloon definition function Variation code
First hot rectangle	Identifier for help balloon content Tip location Hot rectangle coordinates Balloon content for hot rectangle
Next hot rectangle	(Same as for first hot rectangle) . . .

The 'hrct' resource contains a header and information that describes the hot rectangles within the window and the help balloons associated with each hot rectangle.

As with the other help resources, specify the HelpMgrVersion constant in the first field of the header component of the 'hrct' resource. In the options field, specify a constant (normally, hmDefaultOptions) or the sum of several constants' values from this list. ("Specifying Options in Help Resources" earlier in this chapter describes these options.)

```
CONST hmDefaultOptions      = 0;    {use defaults}
      hmUseSubID            = 1;    {use subrange resource IDs }
                                    { for owned resources}
      hmAbsoluteCoords      = 2;    {ignore coords of window }
                                    { origin and treat upper-left }
                                    { corner of window as 0,0}
      hmSaveBitsNoWindow    = 4;    {don't create window; save }
                                    { bits; no update event}
      hmSaveBitsWindow      = 8;    {save bits behind window }
                                    { and generate update event}
```

Specify the balloon definition function and variation code (both typically 0) in the third and fourth fields of the header. (These are described in detail earlier in "Providing Help Balloons for Menus.")

Following the header, you specify tip locations, hot rectangles, and associated help content for all the areas in the window that would benefit by having help balloons.

For each hot rectangle, specify the format that the help content takes. As with the other help resources, specify the format using one of these identifiers:

Identifier	Help content format
HMStringItem	Pascal string within the help resource
HMPictItem	'PICT' resource
HMStringResItem	'STR#' resource
HMTEResItem	'TEXT' and 'styl' resources
HMSTRResItem	'STR ' resource
HMSkipItem	No content—skip this item

After specifying the format of the help content, give the points of the tip locations and the hot rectangles in local coordinates. Then provide your help content for that rectangle, as either a text string or a resource ID.

Specify the format, tip, hot rectangle, and help content for every applicable area in the window. You'll create an 'hwin' resource that contains the resource ID of this 'hrct' resource and that associates this resource with a titled window. The Help Manager automatically tracks the cursor and displays and removes help balloons as the user moves the cursor into and out of the hot rectangles defined in this resource.

If you need to supply a help balloon for an area within another area that needs a different help balloon, create 'hrct' resources for both the inner and outer areas and specify their areas as hot rectangles. In the resource fork of your file, list the 'hrct' resource for the inner area ahead of the 'hrct' resource for the outer area. Then, with the cursor within the inner hot rectangle, the Help Manager scans its 'hrct' resource first and displays its help balloon instead of the help balloon for the outer hot rectangle. When the cursor moves from the inner hot rectangle to the outer, the Help Manager removes the inner area's help balloon and instead displays the balloon for the outer hot rectangle.

As previously explained, you can create an 'hdlg' resource to specify the tips, alternate rectangles, balloon definitions, variation codes, and help content for dialog items and use an 'hwin' resource to associate that 'hdlg' with a dialog box or alert box. When help is enabled and your application calls ModalDialog or IsDialogEvent, the Help Manager automatically tracks the cursor and displays and removes help balloons for items specified in the 'hdlg' resource.

To associate 'hrct' and 'hdlg' resources with windows, create an 'hwin' resource. Shown here is the general format of an 'hwin' resource.

Component	Window help resource element
Header	Help Manager version Options
First window	Resource ID of associated 'hrct' or 'hdlg' resource Resource type ('hdlg' or 'hrct') Length used to compare title strings—or, if flagged by a minus sign (–), the windowKind value of an untitled window Window title string—or empty string if untitled

Component	Window help resource element
Next window	(Same as for first window)
	.
	.
	.

The 'hwin' resource maps windows to 'hrct' resources and 'hdlg' resources. Within the 'hwin', you identify 'hrct' resources and 'hdlg' resources by their resource IDs and by their types. As shown in the preceding list, the first two fields of a window component contain the resource ID and type. You identify windows in one of these two ways:

- by specifying the number of characters used for matching a window title in the third field, and by specifying a string containing this number of sequential characters from the window's title in the next field
- by flagging the third field of the component with a minus sign (–) and specifying the windowKind value from the window's window record in this field; leave an empty string in the next field

When an active window has a title or windowKind value that matches an 'hwin' resource, the Help Manager provides help balloons for the hot rectangles associated with the specified 'hrct' or 'hdlg' resources.

The 'hwin' resource specifies the Help Manager version and options in the header. Specify the HelpMgrVersion constant in the first field of the header. In the options field, specify a constant (normally, hmDefaultOptions) or the sum of several constants' values from this list. Notice that compared to the other resources related to the Help Manager, options regarding local coordinates and bits behind the balloon are not applicable to the 'hwin' resource, but the 'hwin' resource has a unique option—hmMatchInTitle.

```
CONST hmDefaultOptions     = 0      {use help resource defaults}
      hmUseSubID           = 1;     {use subrange resource IDs }
                                    { for owned resources}
      hmMatchInTitle       = 16;    {match window by string }
                                    { anywhere in title string}
```

If you're providing help balloons for a desk accessory or a driver that owns other resources, use the hmUseSubID constant in the options field. (See the Resource Manager chapter in Volume I for a discussion of owned resources and their resource IDs.)

You can specify the hmMatchInTitle constant to match windows containing a specified number of sequential characters starting with any character position in the window title. If you do not specify the hmMatchInTitle constant in the options field, the Help Manager matches characters starting with the first character of the window title.

For example, if the 'hwin' resource specifies the hmMatchInTitle constant, 4 as the number of characters to match, and "Test" as the window title, the Help Manager uses this 'hwin' resource when the cursor is located in any active window that is titled Test, Window Test, or Test Case or is given a title with any other string that contains the characters "Test."

If you supply the hmDefaultOptions constant, the Help Manager treats the resource IDs in this resource as regular resource IDs and not as subrange IDs, and it begins matching characters at the first character of the window string. As long as they all use the same options, you can list help for all your windows in a single 'hwin' resource. You must create separate 'hwin' resources for windows that require different options.

Following the header, multiple 'hdlg' or 'hrct' resources can be specified. You specify the window title and the resource ID for each 'hdlg' or 'hrct' resource. You also specify how many characters of the window title the Help Manager should use when matching the window with the 'hdlg' resource.

For dialog boxes and alert boxes, you can use 'hrct' resources to define hot rectangles in addition to or other than those associated with the dialog items. For example, you might want to use an 'hwin' and an 'hrct' resource in a dialog box to associate a single help balloon with a group of related dialog items rather than provide separate help balloons for all the individual dialog items. (To provide help balloons for individual dialog items by using 'hdlg' resources alone, see "Providing Help Balloons for Items in Dialog Boxes and Alert Boxes" earlier in this chapter.)

Figure 11-13 shows a sample palette an application might use and the help balloon displayed for the hammer tool.

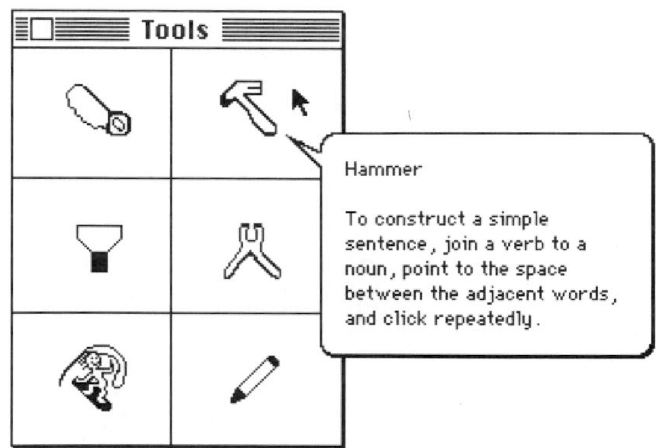

Figure 11-13. A tool palette with a help balloon

Listing 11-6 shows the window help resource and the hot rectangle help resource for the palette in Figure 11-13.

Listing 11-6. Corresponding 'hwin' and 'hrct' resources for a tool palette

```
resource 'hwin' (128, "Window help resource", purgeable) {
   HelpMgrVersion,
   hmDefaultOptions,
   {
      128,      /* resource ID of type specified on next line */
      'hrct',   /* resource type for defining help */
      5,        /* length to use when comparing strings */
      "Tools"   /* window's title string */
   }
};
```

```
resource 'hrct' (128, "Tools palette help") {
   HelpMgrVersion,
   hmDefaultOptions,
   0,                  /* balloon definition function */
   0,                  /* variation code */
   {
   /* definition for saw tool goes here */
   HMStringResItem { /* definition for hammer tool */
      {50, 127},       /* tip */
      {22,99,54,131},/* hot rectangle */
      147,2            /* 'STR#' resource ID and index */
      }
   /* definitions for other tools go here */
   }
};

resource 'STR#' (147, "Tools palette help text") {
   {
   /* [1] saw tool */
   /* help text for saw tool goes here */
   /* [2] hammer tool */
   "Hammer \n\nTo construct a simple sentence, join "
      "a verb to a noun, point to the space between the adjacent words, "
      "and click repeatedly.";
   /* help for other tools goes here */
   }
};
```

You can also use the 'hwin' resource to associate help for dialog items in a window. Figure 11-14 shows the Help Manager displaying a help balloon for an item in the dialog box titled Verb Tenses.

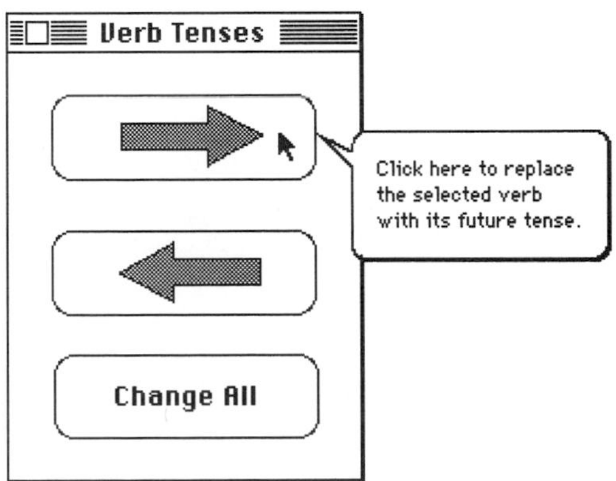

Figure 11-14. A help balloon for a dialog box with a title

Listing 11-7 shows how the 'hwin' resource associates an 'hdlg' resource with the dialog box illustrated in Figure 11-14. This 'hwin' resource associates help for three different windows: the first is the window titled Tools, the second is an untitled window with a windowKind value of 10, and the third is the dialog box titled Verb Tenses.

Listing 11-7. Specifying help for titled and untitled windows with an 'hwin' resource

```
resource 'hwin' (128, "Window help resource", purgeable) {
   HelpMgrVersion,
   hmDefaultOptions,
   {
      128,       /* help resource ID for Tools window */
      'hrct',    /* resource type for defining help */
      5,         /* length to use when comparing strings */
      "Tools",   /* window's title string */

      129,       /* help res ID for untitled window  */
      'hdlg',    /* resource type for defining help */
      -10,       /* match on windowKind values of 10 */
      "",        /* matching on windowKind, so empty string goes here */

      130,       /* help res ID for Verb Tenses window */
      'hdlg',    /* resource type for defining help */
      11,        /* length to use when comparing strings */
      "Verb Tenses", /* dialog box's title string */
   }
};

resource 'hdlg' (130, "Help for Verb Tense control", purgeable) {
   HelpMgrVersion,    /* version of Help Manager */
   0,                 /* start with first dialog item in 'DITL' */
   hmDefaultOptions,  /* options */
   0,                 /* balloon definition ID */
   0,                 /* variation code */
   HMSkipItem {       /* no missing dialog item help information */
      },
   {                  /* help information for dialog items */
      HMStringResItem {
         {20, 130},   /* tip (local to item rect) */
         {0,0,0,0},   /* default alternate rectangle: use item rect */
         131, 1,      /* highlighted control for future tense */
         131, 2,      /* dimmed control for future tense */
         0, 0,        /* no checked state for control */
         0, 0         /* no other states for control */
      },
      HMStringResItem {
         {20, 130},   /* tip (local to item rect) */
         {0,0,0,0},   /* default alternate rectangle: use item rect */
         131, 3,      /* highlighted control for past tense */
         131, 4,      /* dimmed control for past tense */
         0, 0,        /* no enabled and checked control */
         0, 0         /* no other marks for control */
      },
```

```
      HMStringResItem {
         {20, 130},   /* tip (local to item rect) */
         {0,0,0,0},   /* default alternate rectangle: use item rect */
         131, 5,      /* Change All button */
         0, 0,        /* no dimmed Change All button */
         0, 0,        /* no checked state Change All button */
         0, 0         /* no other states for Change All button */
      }
   }
};

resource 'STR#' (131, "Verb tense help strings") {
   {
   /* [1] highlighted control for future tense: help text */
   "Click here to replace the selected verb with its future tense.";
   /* [2] dimmed control for future tense: help text */
   "Click here to replace a verb with its future tense. "
      "Not available now because you have not selected a verb.";
   /* [3] /* highlighted control for past tense: help text */
   "Click here to replace the selected verb with its past tense.";
   /* [4] dimmed control for past tense: help text */
   "Click here to replace a verb with its past tense. "
      "Not available now because you have not selected a verb.";
   /* [5] Change All button's help text */
   "Click here to repeat your last change for all verbs within "
         "your document.";
   }
};
```


Help Balloons in Dynamic Windows

To create help balloons for objects whose location in the content area of windows may vary, your application needs to use Help Manager routines to display and remove balloons as the user moves the cursor.

You should display or remove help balloons for dynamic windows at the same time that you normally check the mouse position to display or change the cursor. For example, if you provide your own DoIdle procedure, you can also check the mouse position and, if the cursor is over a hot rectangle, you should display the associated help balloon.

To create help balloons for the content area of a dynamic window, you need to

- identify the hot rectangles for each area or object
- create data structures to store the locations of the hot rectangles
- determine how to calculate their changing locations
- track and update the hot rectangles
- when the cursor is over a hot rectangle, display its help balloon by using the HMShowBalloon function

After defining all the hot rectangles within your content region, create separate 'STR ', 'STR#', 'PICT', or 'TEXT' and 'styl' resources for the help balloons' content. You don't have to store the content in these resources when using HMShowBalloon, but doing so makes your application easier to localize.

When you use the HMShowBalloon function, your application is responsible for tracking the cursor and determining when to display the help balloon. If you use the HMShowBalloon function, you can let the Help Manager track the cursor and determine when to remove the help balloon, or your application can remove the balloon when necessary by calling the HMRemoveBalloon function. If you display your own help balloons using the HMShowBalloon function, you should use the HMGetBalloons function to determine whether help is enabled before displaying a help balloon. If help is not enabled, you don't need to call any Help Manager routines that display balloons, since they won't do anything unless HMGetBalloons returns TRUE.

The HMShowBalloon function is useful for

- windows whose content changes
- windows that can be resized
- windows that contain hot rectangles with variable locations
- situations in which your application wants more control over the display and removal of the help balloon

For example, windows with scrolling file icons (such as Finder windows) or scrolling tool symbols (such as those shown in Figure 11-12) require you to use HMShowBalloon to display help balloons for the icons or symbols. Likewise, if you have tools—such as rulers that users configure for tab stops in a word-processing document—that scroll with a document, you'll need to use HMShowBalloon to display help balloons for the scrolling tools.

The Help Manager provides default help balloons for certain areas of the window frame. "Overriding Other Default Help Balloons" later in this chapter describes how to override these default help balloons.

When using HMShowBalloon, you specify the help content, a tip location, a rectangle to use if the Help Manager needs to change the tip location, an optional pointer to a function that can modify the tip and rectangle coordinates, the balloon definition function, and the variation code. In the final parameter to the HMShowBalloon function, you should also provide a constant that tells the Help Manager whether it should save the bits behind the balloon.

```
myErr := HMShowBalloon(aHelpMsg, tip, alternateRect, tipProc, theProc,
                       variant, method);
```

Specify the help content in the aHelpMsg parameter to the HMShowBalloon function. You can specify the help information for each hot rectangle using text strings, 'STR ' resource types, 'STR#' resource types, styled text resources, 'PICT' resource types, handles to styled text records, or handles to pictures.

The HMMessageRecord data type defines the help message record.

```
TYPE HMMessageRecord =
     RECORD
        hmmHelpType:       Integer;           {type of next field}
        CASE Integer OF
         khmmString:       (hmmString: Str255);         {Pascal string}
         khmmPict:         (hmmPict: Integer);          {'PICT' resource ID}
         khmmStringRes:    (hmmStringRes: HMStringResType); {'STR#' res }
                                                        { ID and index}
         khmmTEHandle:     (hmmTEHandle: TEHandle);     {TextEdit handle}
         khmmPictHandle:   (hmmPictHandle: PicHandle); {picture handle}
         khmmTERes:        (hmmTERes: Integer);         {'styl'/'TEXT' }
                                                        { resource ID}
         khmmSTRRes:       (hmmSTRRes: Integer)         {'STR' resource ID}
     END;
```

The hmmHelpType field is a constant that specifies the data type of the next field of the help message record. The field following the hmmHelpType field can be one of a number of different data types. You specify the content of the help balloon in this field.

You can specify the help content using a text string, a text string stored in a resource of type 'STR ', or a text string stored as a an 'STR#' resource. You can also provide the information using styled text resources, or you can provide a handle to a styled text record. If you want to provide the help content as a picture, you can use a resource of type 'PICT' or provide a handle to a picture.

You specify one of these constants for the hmmHelpType field.

```
CONST khmmString          = 1;     {Pascal string}
      khmmPict            = 2;     {'PICT' resource ID}
      khmmStringRes       = 3;     {'STR#' res ID and index}
      khmmTEHandle        = 4;     {styled text handle}
      khmmPictHandle      = 5;     {handle to a picture}
      khmmTERes           = 6;     {'TEXT' & 'styl' res ID}
      khmmSTRRes          = 7;     {'STR ' resource ID}
```

You can use the khmmString constant to specify a Pascal string. Here's an example of how to use the khmmString constant in the help message record. (Although you can specify a string from within your code, storing the strings in resources and then accessing them through the Resource Manager makes localization easier.)

```
VAR
   aHelpMsg:      HMMessageRecord;
   tip:           Point;
   alternateRect: RectPtr;

BEGIN
   aHelpMsg.hmmHelpType := khmmString;
   aHelpMsg.hmmString := 'To turn the page, click here.';
   {be sure to initialize tip and alternateRect here}
   err := HMShowBalloon(aHelpMsg,tip,alternateRect,
                        NIL,0,0,kHMRegularWindow);
END;
```

To use a picture you can either store the picture as a 'PICT' resource or create the 'PICT' graphic from within your application and provide a handle to it. Because the Help Manager uses the resource itself or the actual handle that you pass to HMShowBalloon, your 'PICT' resource should be purgeable, or, when using a handle to a 'PICT' resource, you should release the handle or dispose of it when you are finished with it.

Here's an example that specifies a 'PICT' resource ID.

```
VAR
   aHelpMsg:      HMMessageRecord;
   tip:           Point;
   alternateRect: RectPtr;

BEGIN
   aHelpMsg.hmmHelpType := khmmPict;
   aHelpMsg.hmmPict := 128;           {resource ID of 'PICT' resource}
   {be sure to initialize tip and alternateRect here}
   err := HMShowBalloon(aHelpMsg,tip,alternateRect,
                        NIL,0,0,kHMRegularWindow);
END;
```

Here's an example of providing a handle to a 'PICT' resource.

```
VAR
   pict:          PicHandle;
   aHelpMsg:      HMMessageRecord;
   tip:           Point;
   pictFrame:     Rect;
   alternateRect: RectPtr;

BEGIN
   {be sure to initialize pictFrame here}
   pict := OpenPicture(pictFrame);
   DrawString('Test Balloon');
   ClosePicture;
   aHelpMsg.hmmHelpType := khmmPictHandle;
   aHelpMsg.hmmPictHandle := pict;
   {be sure to initialize tip and alternateRect here}
   err := HMShowBalloon(aHelpMsg,tip,alternateRect,
                        NIL,0,0,kHMRegularWindow);
   KillPicture(pict);
END;
```

The HMStringResType data type defines a Help Manager string list record.

```
TYPE HMStringResType =
     RECORD
        hmmResID:      Integer;     {res ID of 'STR#' resource}
        hmmIndex:      Integer      {index of string}
     END;
```

The hmmResID field specifies the resource ID of the 'STR#' resource, and the hmmIndex field specifies the index of the string within that resource to use for the help information.

To use a string stored in an 'STR#' resource, use the khmmStringRes constant in the hmmHelpType field and use a record of data type HMStringResType in the next field.

```
VAR
   aHelpMsg:       HMMessageRecord;
   tip:            Point;
   alternateRect:  RectPtr;
   khmmStringRes:  HMStringResType;

BEGIN
   aHelpMsg.hmmHelpType := khmmStringRes;
   GetIndString(aHelpMsg.hmmStringRes,1000,1);
   {be sure to initialize tip and alternateRect here}
   err := HMShowBalloon(aHelpMsg,tip,alternateRect,
                        NIL,0,0,kHMRegularWindow);
END;
```


To use styled text resources, use the khmmTERes constant in the hmmHelpType field. In the next field, supply a resource ID that is common to both a style scrap ('styl') resource and a 'TEXT' resource. For example, you might create a 'TEXT' resource with resource ID 1000 that contains the words “Displays your text in boldface print.” You would also create an 'styl' resource with resource ID 1000 that applies boldface style to the word “boldface.” When you specify the HMTEResItem constant and resource ID 1000 for a help balloon, the Help Manager employs TextEdit routines to display your text with your prescribed styles. (See the TextEdit chapter in Volume V for a description of the style scrap.)

To use a handle to a styled text record, supply the khmmTEHandle constant in the hmmHelpType field.

```
VAR
   aHelpMsg:       HMMessageRecord;
   tip:            Point;
   alternateRect:  RectPtr;
   hTE:            TEHandle;

BEGIN
   hTE := TEStyleNew(destRect,viewRect); {or, use TENew}
   {be sure to fill in data in handle here}
   aHelpMsg.hmmHelpType := khmmTEHandle;
   aHelpMsg.hmmTEHandle := hTE;
   {be sure to initialize tip and alternateRect here}
   err := HMShowBalloon(aHelpMsg,tip,alternateRect,
                        NIL,0,0,kHMRegularWindow);
END;
```

You specify the tip and the rectangle pointed to by alternateRect in global coordinates. The Help Manager calculates the location and size of the help balloon. If the help balloon fits on screen, the Help Manager displays the help balloon using the specified tip.

If you use the previously described help resources to define help balloons, the Help Manager uses the hot rectangles you specify in the help resources for two purposes: first, to associate areas of the screen with help balloons and, second, to move the tip if the help balloon doesn't fit on screen.

If you use the HMShowBalloon function to display help balloons, you must identify hot rectangles, create your own data structures to store their locations, track the cursor yourself, and call HMShowBalloon when the cursor moves to your hot rectangles. The Help Manager does not know the locations of your hot rectangles, so it cannot use them for moving the tip if the help balloon is placed offscreen. Instead, the Help Manager uses the alternate rectangle that you point to with the alternateRect parameter. Often, you specify the same coordinates for the alternate rectangle that you specify for your hot rectangle. However, you may choose to make your alternate rectangle smaller or larger than your hot rectangle. If you make your alternate rectangle smaller than your hot rectangle, you have greater assurance that the Help Manager will be able to fit the help balloon on screen; if you specify an alternate rectangle that is larger than your hot rectangle, you have greater assurance that the help balloon will not obscure some element explained by the balloon.

If you specify a rectangle in the alternateRect parameter, the Help Manager automatically calls HMRemoveBalloon to remove the balloon when the cursor leaves the area bounded by the rectangle.

If you specify NIL for the alternateRect parameter, your application is responsible for tracking the cursor and determining when to remove the help balloon. The Help Manager also does not attempt to calculate a new tip position if the help balloon is offscreen.

When you call the HMShowBalloon function, the Help Manager does not display the help balloon or attempt to modify the tip location under either of these conditions:

- the help balloon's tip is offscreen or in the menu bar and you don't specify an alternate rectangle
- both the help balloon's tip and the alternate rectangle are offscreen

The final parameter in HMShowBalloon specifies how the Help Manager should draw and remove the balloon. Use the following constants for the parameter.

```
CONST kHMRegularWindow      = 0;    {don't save bits; just update}
      kHMSaveBitsNoWindow   = 1;    {save bits; don't do update}
      kHMSaveBitsWindow     = 2;    {save bits; do update event}
```

If you specify kHMRegularWindow, the Help Manager draws and removes the help balloon as if it were a window. That is, when drawing the balloon the Help Manager does not save bits behind the balloon, and when removing the balloon the Help Manager generates an update event. This is the standard behavior of help balloons—and the behavior you should normally use.

If you specify kHMSaveBitsNoWindow in the method parameter, the Help Manager does not create a window for displaying the balloon. Instead, the Help Manager creates a help balloon that is more like a menu than a window. The Help Manager saves the bits behind the balloon when it creates the balloon. When it removes the balloon, the Help Manager restores the bits without generating an update event. You should only use this in a modal environment where the bits behind the balloon cannot change from the time the balloon is drawn to the time it is removed. For example, you might specify the kHMSaveBitsNoWindow constant when providing help balloons for pop-up menus that overlay complex graphics, which might take a long time to redraw with an update event.

If you specify kHMSaveBitsWindow, the Help Manager treats the help balloon as a hybrid having properties of both a menu and a window. That is, the Help Manager saves the bits behind the balloon when it creates the balloon and, when it removes the balloon, it both restores the bits and generates an update event. You'll rarely need this option. It is necessary only in a modal environment that might immediately change to a nonmodal environment—that is, where the bits behind the help balloon are static when the balloon is drawn, but can possibly change before the help balloon is removed.

Listing 11-8 shows a sample routine that displays help balloons for hot rectangles within the content area of a window.

Listing 11-8. Using HMShowBalloon to display help balloons

```
PROCEDURE FindAndShowBalloon(window: WindowPtr);
VAR
   i:           Integer;
   mouse:       Point;
   savePort:    GrafPtr;
   helpMsg:     HMMessageRecord;
   result:      OSErr;
   inRect:      Boolean;

BEGIN
   IF (window = FrontWindow) THEN      {only do frontmost windows }
   BEGIN
      GetPort(savePort);    {save the old port for later}
      SetPort(window);      {set the port to the front window}
      GetMouse(mouse);      {get the mouse in local coords}
      inRect:= FALSE;       {clear flag saying mouse wasn't in any Rect}

      IF PtInRect(mouse,window^.portRect) THEN
         {if the cursor is in the window }
         FOR i:= 1 TO 10 DO {check all 10 predefined rects in the window}
            IF PtInRect(mouse,MyPredefinedRects[i]) THEN
            BEGIN {cursor in rect}
               IF (i <> gLastBalloon) THEN
               {cursor wasn't same as last time}
               BEGIN
                  hotRect  := MyPredefinedRects[i];
                  LocalToGlobal(hotRect.topLeft);
                  {converting rect to global}
                  LocalToGlobal(hotRect.botRight);
```

(Continued)

Listing 11-8. Using HMShowBalloon to display help balloons (Continued)

```
                  WITH hotRect DO   {put the tip in the middle}
                     SetPt(mouse,(right-left) div 2, (bottom-top) div 2);
                  helpMsg.hmmHelpType := khmmStringRes;
                  {want 'STR#' resource}
                  helpMsg.hmmStringRes.hmmResID := OurHelpMsgsID;
                  {this resID}
                  helpMsg.hmmStringRes.hmmIndex := i; {this index}

                  result := HMShowBalloon(helpMsg,
                                          {use just-made help msg}
                            mouse,        {pointing to this tip}
                            @MyPredefinedRects[i], {this rectangle}
                            NIL,          {no special tip proc}
                            0,0,          {using default balloon}
                            FALSE);       {don't save bits behind}

                  IF (result = noErr) THEN {then remember balloon}
                     gLastBalloon := i;
               END;
               inRect := TRUE; {remember when the cursor is in any rect}
            END;
      IF not inRect THEN
         gLastBalloon := -1;  {clear last balloon global for no hit}
      SetPort(savePort);      {restore the port}
   END;
END;
```

The FindAndShowBalloon procedure in Listing 11-8 tracks the cursor, and, if the cursor is over a predefined hot rectangle, it displays a help balloon for that rectangle. In this example there are 10 predefined rectangles (in the MyPredefinedRects array) and 10 corresponding help messages in an 'STR#' resource (of ID OurHelpMsgsID)—one message for each hot rectangle. Other supporting routines can update the coordinates of the hot rectangles as their locations change.

You can also use the HMShowBalloon function from the filter function of a modal dialog box or alert box. See "Displaying a Help Balloon" and "Removing a Help Balloon" later in this chapter for more information on the HMShowBalloon and HMRemoveBalloon functions.

Overriding Help Balloons for Application Icons

The Finder displays a default help balloon for application icons. By specifying an 'hfdr' resource in your application's resource fork, you can provide your own help balloon for the Finder to display when the user moves the cursor over your application icon.

> **Note:** You cannot override the default help balloon that the Finder uses for document icons.

Shown here is the general format of an 'hfdr' resource.

Component	Finder icon help resource element
Header	Help Manager version Options Balloon definition function Variation code
Icon help	Identifier for help balloon content Balloon content for application icon

Use resource ID –5696 for your 'hfdr' resource. If an 'hfdr' resource with that ID exists for an application, the Help Manager uses it instead of the default help balloon provided by the Finder.

As with the other help resources, specify the HelpMgrVersion constant in the first field of the header component of the 'hfdr' resource. In the options field, specify a constant (normally, hmDefaultOptions) or the sum of several constants' values from this list. ("Specifying Options in Help Resources" earlier in this chapter describes these options.)

```
CONST hmDefaultOptions      = 0;    {use defaults}
      hmUseSubID            = 1;    {use subrange resource IDs }
                                    { for owned resources}
      hmAbsoluteCoords      = 2;    {ignore coords of window }
                                    { origin and treat upper-left }
                                    { corner of window as 0,0}
      hmSaveBitsNoWindow    = 4;    {don't create window; save }
                                    { bits; no update event}
      hmSaveBitsWindow      = 8;    {save bits behind window }
                                    { and generate update event}
```

Specify the balloon definition function and variation code (both typically 0) in the third and fourth fields of the header. (These are described in detail earlier in "Providing Help Balloons for Menus.")

In the icon help component of this resource, specify the format that the help content takes. As with the other help resources, specify the format using one of these identifiers:

Identifier	Help content format
HMStringItem	Pascal string within the help resource
HMPictItem	'PICT' resource
HMStringResItem	'STR#' resource
HMTEResItem	'TEXT' and 'styl' resources
HMSTRResItem	'STR ' resource
HMSkipItem	No content—skip this item

If you specify HMSkipItem, no help balloon appears.

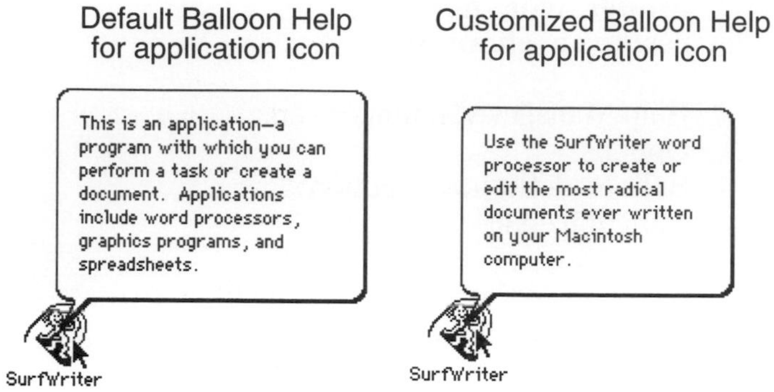

Default Balloon Help
for application icon
This is an application—a program with which you can perform a task or create a document. Applications include word processors, graphics programs, and spreadsheets.
SurfWriter
Customized Balloon Help
for application icon
Use the SurfWriter word processor to create or edit the most radical documents ever written on your Macintosh computer.
SurfWriter

Figure 11-15. Default and customized help balloons for an application icon

The default help balloon for application icons is shown on the left in Figure 11-15. A customized help balloon for the same icon appears on the right in Figure 11-15. The customized help balloon is supplied with the resources shown in Listing 11-9.

Listing 11-9. Creating a help balloon resource for an application icon

```
resource 'hfdr' (-5696) {   /* help balloon for SurfWriter app icon */
   HelpMgrVersion, hmDefaultOptions, 0, 0,    /* header information */
   {
   HMSTRResItem { /* use 'STR ' resource 1001 */
      1001
      }
   }
};

resource 'STR ' (1001) {    /* help message for SurfWriter app icon */
   "Use the SurfWriter word processor to create or edit the most "
   "radical documents ever written on your Macintosh computer."
};
```

Overriding Other Default Help Balloons

In addition to help balloons for application and document icons, the Help Manager provides default help balloons for the title bar and the close and zoom boxes of an active window. It also provides default help balloons for windows of inactive applications, inactive windows of an active application, and the area outside of a modal dialog box.

Apple has researched and tested these help messages to ensure that they are as effective as possible for users. Normally, you shouldn't need to override them. However, you can override one or more of these defaults if you feel you absolutely must by creating a resource of type 'hovr'. Shown here is the format for the 'hovr' resource.

Using an 'hovr' resource sets the default help balloons for your application only. It does not affect the default help balloons used by other applications.

Component	Default help override resource element
Header	Help Manager version (use HelpMgrVersion constant) Options Balloon definition function Variation code
Missing items help	Identifier for help balloon content Balloon content for items missing from this resource or lacking balloon content
Title bar help	Identifier for help balloon content Balloon content for title bar of active window
Reserved	Always use HMSkipItem identifier here Reserved; skip this item
Close box help	Identifier for help balloon content Balloon content for close box of active window
Zoom box help	Identifier for help balloon content Balloon content for zoom box of active window
Help for active application's inactive windows	Identifier for help balloon content Balloon content for inactive window of active application
Help for inactive application's windows	Identifier for help balloon content Balloon content for window of inactive application
Help for area outside of a modal dialog box or alert box	Identifier for help balloon content Balloon content for area outside of a modal dialog box

As with the other help resources, specify the HelpMgrVersion constant in the first field of the header component of the 'hrct' resource. In the options field, specify a constant (normally, hmDefaultOptions) or the sum of several constants' values from this list. ("Specifying Options in Help Resources" earlier in this chapter describes these options.)

```
CONST hmDefaultOptions     = 0;    {use defaults}
      hmUseSubID           = 1;    {use subrange resource IDs }
                                   { for owned resources}
      hmAbsoluteCoords     = 2;    {ignore coords of window }
                                   { origin and treat upper-left }
                                   { corner of window as 0,0}
      hmSaveBitsNoWindow   = 4;    {don't create window; save }
                                   { bits; no update event}
      hmSaveBitsWindow     = 8;    {save bits behind window }
                                   { and generate update event}
```

Specify the balloon definition function and variation code (both typically 0) in the third and fourth fields of the header. (These are described in detail earlier in "Providing Help Balloons for Menus.")

For each element, specify the format that the help content takes. As with the other help resources, specify the format using one of these identifiers:

Identifier	Help content format
HMStringItem	Pascal string within the help resource
HMPictItem	'PICT' resource
HMStringResItem	'STR#' resource
HMTEResItem	'TEXT' and 'styl' resources
HMSTRResItem	'STR ' resource
HMSkipItem	No content—skip this item

Supply an identifier and help balloon content for the missing items component. The Help Manager expects the components of an 'hovr' resource to be listed in the order previously shown. To use any of the default help balloons, specify HMSkipItem in the corresponding field of the 'hovr' resource. The Help Manager supplies help balloons with the missing items' balloon content for components you leave off the bottom of this list. The Help Manager also uses the missing items' balloon content if you provide an identifier for a component but specify an empty string or a resource ID of 0 for that item's balloon content.

Listing 11-10 shows a resource of type 'hovr' that overrides all of the default help balloons.

Listing 11-10. Overriding default help balloons

```
resource 'hovr' (1000) {
   HelpMgrVersion,
   hmDefaultOptions, /* options */
   0,       /* the balloon definition ID */
   0,       /* variation code */
   HMStringItem { /* missing items in case this res is short items */
      "Missing override message"
         },
      {
      HMSkipItem {   /*  title bar help */
         /* HMSkipItem means use default help balloon for this element */
      },
      HMSkipItem {   /* reserved; always specify HMSkipItem here */
      },
      HMStringItem { /* close box help */
         ""          /* empty string means use missing items help */
      },
      HMStringItem { /* zoom box help */
         "Get this message if in Zoom In or Zoom Out box."
      },
      HMStringItem { /* help for active app's inactive window */
         "Get this message if in inactive window of active application."
      },
      HMStringItem {/* help for inactive app's window */
         "Get this message if in window of inactive application."
      },
```

```
      HMStringItem { /* outside of modal dialog help */
         "Get this message if outside modal dialog box."
      }
   }
};
```

Adding Your Own Menu Items to the Help Menu

The Help menu is specific to each application, just as the File and Edit menus are. The Help menu items defined by the Help Manager should be common to all applications, but you can add your own menu items for help-related information.

If you currently provide your users with help information when they choose the About command from the Apple menu, you should instead append a command for your own help to the Help menu. This gives users one consistent place to obtain help information.

When adding your own items to the Help menu, include the name of your application in the command so that users can easily determine which application the help relates to. For example, Figure 11-16 shows the Help menu with two items appended to it by related components of the same application.

Figure 11-16. The Help menu with two appended menu items

You add items to the Help menu by using the HMGetHelpMenuHandle function and by providing an 'hmnu' resource and specifying the kHMHelpMenuID constant as the resource ID.

The HMGetHelpMenuHandle function returns a copy of the handle to the Help menu. Do not use the GetMHandle function to get a handle to the Help menu, because GetMHandle returns a handle to the global Help menu, not the Help menu that is specific to your application. Once you have a handle to the Help menu that is specific to your application, you can add items to it using the AppendMenu procedure or other Menu Manager routines. For example, this code adds the two menu items displayed in Figure 11-16.

```
VAR
   mh: MenuHandle;

BEGIN
   err := HMGetHelpMenuHandle(mh);
   IF err = NoErr THEN
      IF mh <> NIL THEN
```

```
         BEGIN
            AppendMenu(mh,'SurfWriter help');
            AppendMenu(mh,'WipeOut help');
         END;
   DrawMenuBar;
END;
```

Be sure to use an 'hmnu' resource to provide help balloons for items you've added to the Help menu. Use the kHMHelpMenuID constant (–16490) to specify the 'hmnu' resource ID. After the header component of the 'hmnu' resource, provide a missing items component and then the components for your appended items. You don't provide a menu title component here; instead, the Help Manager automatically creates the help balloons for the Help menu title and the standard Help menu items. The Help Manager automatically adds a dashed line between the end of the standard Help menu items and your appended items.

Listing 11-11 shows an 'hmnu' resource for the appended menu items shown in Figure 11-16.

Listing 11-11. A sample menu help resource for items in the Help menu

```
resource 'hmnu' (kHMHelpMenuID, "Help", purgeable) {
   HelpMgrVersion, 0, 0, 0,    /* header information */
   HMSkipItem {    /* missing items information */
      /* no missing items, so skip to appended menu items */
      /*  information */
      },
   {      /* SurfWriter help command's help balloon content */
      HMStringResItem { /* use an 'STR#' resource for content */
      146,1,    /* 'STR#' res ID, index when command's enabled */
      146,2,    /* 'STR#' res ID, index when dimmed */
      146,3,    /* 'STR#' res ID, index when command's checked */
      0,0       /* command can't be marked */
      },
         /* WipeOut help command's help balloon content */
      HMStringResItem { /* use an 'STR#' resource for content */
      146,4,    /* 'STR#' res ID, index when command's enabled */
      146,5,    /* 'STR#' res ID, index when dimmed */
      146,6,    /* 'STR#' res ID, index when command's checked */
      0,0       /* command can't be marked */
      },
   }
};
resource 'STR#' (146, "My help menu items' strings") {
   { /* array StringArray: 6 elements */
   /* [1] enabled "SurfWriter help" command help text */
   "Displays tutorial help for SurfWriter word processor.";
   /* [2] dimmed "SurfWriter help" command help text */
   "Displays tutorial help for SurfWriter word processor. "
      "Not available until you open a SurfWriter document.";
   /* [3] checked "SurfWriter help" command help text */
   "Closes tutorial help for SurfWriter word processor.";
```

```
   /* [4]  enabled "WipeOut help" command help text */
   "Displays tutorial help for WipeOut typing corrector.";
   /* [5] dimmed "WipeOut help" command help text */
   "Displays tutorial help for WipeOut typing corrector. "
      "Not available until you open a SurfWriter document.";
   /* [6] checked "WipeOut help" command help text */
   "Closes tutorial help for WipeOut typing corrector.";
   }
};
```

The menu help resource that you create allows you to specify help balloons for four states of a menu item: enabled, dimmed, enabled and checked, and enabled and marked with a symbol other than a check. You cannot specify a help balloon for a Help menu item when a modal dialog box disables it, because you don't have access to the missing items component of the Help menu. When a modal dialog box appears, the Help Manager displays a default help balloon for all dimmed Help menu items.

The Help Manager automatically processes the event when a user chooses any of the standard menu items in the Help menu. The Help Manager automatically enables and disables help when the user chooses Show Balloons or Hide Balloons from the Help menu. The setting of help is global and affects all applications.

The MenuSelect and MenuKey functions return a result with the menu ID in the high word and the menu item in the low word of the function result. Both functions return the kHMHelpMenuID constant (–16490) in the high word when the user chooses an appended item from the Help menu. The menu item number of the appended item is returned in the low word of the function result. The MyMenuClick procedure shown here handles mouse clicks for those items defined by the application to appear in the Help menu.

```
PROCEDURE MyMenuClick(menuCode: LongInt);
VAR   menu:     Integer;
      item:     Integer;
      window:   WindowPtr;
BEGIN
   window := FrontWindow;
   menu := HiWord(menuCode);
   item := LoWord(menuCode);
   CASE menu OF
      mApple:        {handle About box and other items}
      mFile:         FileClick(window,item);
      mEdit:         EditClick(window,item);
      mFonts:        FontClick(window,item);
      kHMHelpMenuID: HelpClick(window,item);
   END;
   HiliteMenu(0);
END;
```

In the future, Apple may choose to add other items to the Help menu. To determine the number of items in the Help menu, call the CountMItems function, which is descibed in the Menu Manager chapter in Volume I.

Writing Your Own Balloon Definition Function

The Help Manager takes care of positioning, sizing, and drawing your help balloons, and the standard balloon definition function provides a consistent, attractive general shape to balloons across all applications.

Though it takes extra work on your part and your balloons will not share the consistent appearance of help balloons used by the Finder and by other applications, you can create your own balloon definition function. The balloon definition function defines the appearance of the help balloon. A help balloon is a special type of window. You implement a balloon definition function by writing a window definition function that performs the tasks described in this section. The standard balloon definition function is of type 'WDEF' with resource ID 126.

A balloon definition function is responsible for calculating the content region and structure region of the help balloon window and drawing the frame of the help balloon. The content region is the area inside the balloon frame; it contains the user help information. The structure region is the boundary region of the entire balloon, including the content area and the pointer that extends from one of the help balloon's corners. (Figure 11-4 illustrates the structure regions of the eight standard help balloons.)

The Help Manager first calculates the size of the rectangle that can enclose the help information and determines where to display the help balloon. The Help Manager uses TextEdit to determine any word and line breaks in the help information. The Help Manager determines where to display the help balloon based on the tip location and alternate rectangle.

The Help Manager then adds a system-defined distance to the size of the rectangle. This distance allows for the tip of the help balloon. Note that the tip must always align with an edge of the boundary rectangle. The Help Manager uses the resulting rectangle as the boundary rectangle for the help balloon window.

The Help Manager uses the NewWindow function to create the help balloon. The Help Manager specifies the calculated rectangle and the window definition ID as parameters to the NewWindow function.

The NewWindow function calls the balloon definition function in the same manner as a window definition function. See the Window Manager chapter in Volume I for more information on writing a window definition function.

The Window Manager calls your balloon definition function with four parameters: the variation code that specifies the shape and relative tip position of the help balloon, a pointer to the window, the action to perform, and a parameter that has variable contents depending on the action to perform.

Here's an example that shows the declaration for a balloon definition function called MyBalloonDef.

```
FUNCTION MyBalloonDef (variant: Integer; theBalloon: WindowPtr; message:
                        Integer; param: LongInt) : LongInt;
```

The variant parameter is the variation code used to specify the shape and position of the help balloon. You should use the same relative position for the tip of the help balloon that the standard variation codes 0 through 7 specify (see Figure 11-4). This ensures that the tip of the help balloon points to the object that the help balloon describes.

The parameter theBalloon is a pointer to the window of the help balloon.

The message parameter identifies the action your balloon definition function should perform. Your balloon definition function can be sent the same messages as a window definition function, but the only ones your balloon definition function needs to process are the wDraw and wCalcRgns messages, which are described in the Window Manager chapter of Volume I.

When your balloon definition function receives the wCalcRgns message, your function should calculate the content region and structure region of the help balloon.

When your balloon definition function receives the wDraw message, your function should draw the frame of the help balloon.

If you want to process other messages in your balloon definition function (for example, performing any additional initialization), you can also process the other standard 'WDEF' messages.

The value of the param parameter depends on the value of the message parameter. The wCalcRgns and wDraw messages do not use this parameter.

If you want the Help Manager to use your balloon definition function, you specify its resource ID and the desired variation code either in the HMShowBalloon function or in the appropriate fields of the 'hmnu', 'hdlg', or 'hrct' resources. The Help Manager derives your balloon's window definition ID from its resource ID.

HELP MANAGER ROUTINES

This section describes the routines you use to display help balloons for the windows of your application. It also describes how to determine whether help is enabled; how to get the name and size of the text font in help balloons; how to set or override the help resources used with a menu, dialog box, or window; how to get information about the window the help balloon is displayed in; and how to display help balloons when using your own menu definition procedure.

If you only want to provide help balloons for the menus, alert boxes, and dialog boxes of your application, you only need to create the resources containing the descriptive information. "Using the Help Manager" and its subsections earlier in this chapter give details on how to create these resources.

If help is not enabled, most Help Manager routines do nothing and return the hmHelpDisabled result code.

Determining Whether Help Is Enabled

The user turns Balloon Help assistance on by choosing Show Balloons from the Help menu. You can use the HMGetBalloons function to determine whether help is currently enabled. If you display your own help balloons using the HMShowBalloon function, you should use the HMGetBalloons function to determine whether help is enabled before displaying a help balloon. If help is not enabled, you cannot display any help balloons.

```
FUNCTION HMGetBalloons : Boolean;
```

The HMGetBalloons function returns TRUE if help is currently enabled and FALSE if help is currently not enabled. Because this function does not load the Help Manager package into memory, it is a very fast way to determine whether help is enabled.

You can enable or disable help using the HMSetBalloons function. If you enable or disable help, you do so for all applications. The setting of Balloon Help on-line assistance should be under the user's control. In most cases, you should not modify the setting chosen by the user. If you must modify this setting, return it to its previous state as soon as possible.

```
FUNCTION HMSetBalloons (flag: Boolean) : OSErr;
```

The flag parameter specifies whether help should be enabled or disabled for all applications and the system software. If the flag parameter is TRUE, help is enabled. If the flag parameter is FALSE, help is disabled and, if a help balloon is showing, you must first remove it using the HMRemoveBalloon function.

When help is disabled, the Help Manager does not display help balloons for any applications. When help is disabled, the HMShowBalloon and HMShowMenuBalloon functions do not display help balloons and return a nonzero result code.

Result codes

noErr	0	No error
paramErr	–50	Error in parameter list
memFullErr	–108	Not enough room in heap zone
resNotFound	–192	Unable to read resource

Determining Whether a Help Balloon Is Showing

You can use the HMIsBalloon function to determine whether a help balloon is currently displayed on the screen.

```
FUNCTION HMIsBalloon : Boolean;
```

The HMIsBalloon function returns TRUE if a help balloon is currently displayed on the screen and FALSE if a help balloon is not currently displayed. This function is useful for checking whether a balloon is showing before you perform an action that redraws the screen. For example, you might want to determine whether a balloon is displayed so that you can remove it before opening or closing a window.

Displaying and Removing Help Balloons

When help is enabled, the Help Manager automatically tracks the cursor and displays and removes help balloons as the user moves the cursor over hot rectangles specified in 'hrct' resources or over item rectangles associated with menu items and dialog items that are specified in 'hmnu' and 'hdlg' resources. If you want to provide help balloons for areas not defined in these resources, then your application is responsible for tracking the cursor and determining when to display and remove help balloons for these application-defined areas.

Use the HMShowBalloon function to display a help balloon. You specify the descriptive help information for the help balloon using the help message record. The help message record lets you specify the help information in a number of formats. If your application uses your own menu definition procedure, you can use the HMShowMenuBalloon function to display help balloons for the menus that your menu definition procedure manages. The next sections describe how to use Help Manager routines to display and remove help balloons.

Displaying a Help Balloon

The HMShowBalloon function lets you display a help balloon for the content area of any window of your application. You need provide only the descriptive help information, the location of the tip the Help Manager should use to display the help balloon, and a constant specifying what method to use for displaying and removing the balloon. You can also provide an alternate rectangle that the Help Manager uses for moving the help balloon's tip when it tries to fit the help balloon on screen. You can specify your own balloon definition function and variation code, and you can provide a pointer to a tip function that lets your application test and adjust the balloon before displaying it.


```
FUNCTION HMShowBalloon (aHelpMsg: HMMessageRecord; tip: Point;
                         alternateRect: RectPtr; tipProc: Ptr; theProc,
                         variant: Integer; method: Integer) : OSErr;
```

If help is enabled, the HMShowBalloon function displays a help balloon with the descriptive help information specified in the aHelpMsg parameter. You specify the help information in the aHelpMsg parameter using the help message record. "Help Balloons in Dynamic Windows" earlier in this chapter shows how to specify this information.

You specify the tip and the rectangle pointed to by the alternateRect parameter in global coordinates. The Help Manager calculates the location and size of the help balloon. If it fits on screen, the Help Manager displays the help balloon using the specified tip location.

If you use the previously described help resources to define help balloons, the Help Manager uses the hot rectangles you specify in the help resources for two purposes: first, to associate areas of the screen with help balloons and, second, to move the tip if the help balloon doesn't fit on screen.

If you use the HMShowBalloon function to display help balloons, you must identify hot rectangles, create your own data structures to store their locations, track the cursor yourself, and call HMShowBalloon when the cursor moves to your hot rectangles. The Help Manager does not know the locations of your hot rectangles, so it cannot use them for moving the tip if the help balloon is placed offscreen. Instead, the Help Manager uses the alternate rectangle that you point to with the alternateRect parameter. Often, you specify the same coordinates for the alternate rectangle that you specify for your hot rectangle. However, you may choose to make your alternate rectangle smaller or larger than your hot rectangle. If you make your alternate rectangle smaller than your hot rectangle, you have greater assurance that the Help Manager will be able to fit the help balloon on screen; if you specify an alternate rectangle that is larger than your hot rectangle, you have greater assurance that the help balloon will not obscure some element explained by the balloon.

If you specify a rectangle in the alternateRect parameter, the Help Manager automatically calls HMRemoveBalloon to remove the balloon when the cursor leaves the area bounded by the rectangle.

If the balloon's first position is partly offscreen or it intersects the menu bar, the Help Manager tries a combination of different balloon variation codes and different tip positions along the sides of the alternate rectangle to make the balloon fit. Figure 11-5 shows what happens when the balloon's first two positions are located offscreen. If, after exhausting all possible positions, the Help Manager cannot fit the entire help balloon on screen, the Help Manager displays a help balloon at the position that best fits on screen and clips the content of the balloon to fit at this position. If the coordinates specified by both the original tip and the alternateRect parameter are offscreen, the Help Manager does not display the help balloon at all.

If you specify NIL for the alternateRect parameter, your application is responsible for tracking the cursor and determining when to remove the help balloon. The Help Manager also does not attempt to calculate a new tip location if the help balloon is offscreen.

Once the Help Manager determines the location and size of the help balloon, the Help Manager calls the function pointed to by the tipProc parameter before displaying the balloon. Specify NIL in the tipProc parameter to use the Help Manager's default tip function.

You can supply your own tip function (as described later in "Using Your Own Tip Function") and point to it in the tipProc parameter. The Help Manager calls the tip function after calculating the location of the help balloon and before displaying it. In the parameters of your tip function, the Help Manager returns the tip, the region boundary of the entire balloon, the region boundary for the content area within the balloon frame, and the variation code to be used for the help balloon. This allows you to examine and possibly adjust the balloon before it is displayed.

The parameter theProc in the HMShowBalloon function specifies the balloon definition function to use. To use your own balloon definition function, specify the resource ID of its 'WDEF' resource in the parameter theProc. The Help Manager reads the balloon definition function specified by the parameter theProc into memory if it isn't already in memory. If the balloon definition function can't be read into memory, the help balloon is not displayed and the HMShowBalloon function returns the resNotFound result code.

Specify 0 in the parameter theProc to use the standard balloon definition function. The variant parameter is the variation code for the balloon definition function. Specify 0 in the variant parameter to use the default help balloon shape, or specify a code from 1 to 7 to use one of the other positions provided by the standard balloon definition function (see Figure 11-4). If you write your own balloon definition function, you should support the tip locations defined by the standard variation codes.

The method parameter specifies whether the Help Manager should save the bits behind the balloon and whether to do an update event. Use the following constants for the parameter.

```
CONST kHMRegularWindow      = 0;    {don't save bits; just update}
      kHMSaveBitsNoWindow   = 1;    {save bits; don't do update}
      kHMSaveBitsWindow     = 2;    {save bits; do update event}
```

If you specify kHMRegularWindow, the Help Manager draws and removes the help balloon as if it were a window. That is, when drawing the balloon the Help Manager does not save bits behind the balloon, and when removing the balloon the Help Manager generates an update event. This is the standard behavior of help balloons—and the behavior you should normally use.

If you specify kHMSaveBitsNoWindow in the method parameter, the Help Manager does not create a window for displaying the balloon. Instead, the Help Manager creates a help balloon that is more like a menu than a window. The Help Manager saves the bits behind the balloon when it creates the balloon. When it removes the balloon, the Help Manager restores the bits without generating an update event. You should only use this in a modal environment where the bits behind the balloon cannot change from the time the balloon is drawn to the time it is removed. For example, you might specify the kHMSaveBitsNoWindow constant when providing help balloons for pop-up menus that overlay complex graphics, which might take a long time to redraw with an update event.

If you specify kHMSaveBitsWindow, the Help Manager treats the help balloon as a hybrid having properties of both a menu and a window. That is, the Help Manager saves the bits behind the balloon when it creates the balloon and, when it removes the balloon, it both restores the bits and generates an update event. You'll rarely need this option. It is necessary only in a modal environment that might immediately change to a nonmodal environment—that is, where the bits behind the help balloon are static when the balloon is drawn, but can possibly change before the help balloon is removed.

HMShowBalloon returns the noErr result code if the help balloon was successfully displayed.

Result codes

noErr	0	No error; the help balloon was displayed
paramErr	–50	Error in parameter list
memFullErr	–108	Not enough room in heap zone
resNotFound	–192	Unable to read resource
hmHelpDisabled	–850	Help balloons are not enabled
hmBalloonAborted	–853	Because of constant cursor movement, the help balloon wasn't displayed
hmOperationUnsupported	–861	Invalid value passed in the method parameter

Using Your Own Menu Definition Procedure

The Help Manager displays help balloons for applications that provide 'hmnu' resources and use the standard menu definition procedure. If your application uses your own menu definition procedure, you can still use the Help Manager to display help balloons for the menus that your menu definition procedure manages. The HMShowMenuBalloon function described in this section uses the standard balloon definition function to display the help balloon. If you want to use your own balloon definition function from within your menu definition procedure, call the HMShowBalloon function (described in the previous section) and specify the kHMSaveBitsNoWindow constant for the method parameter. You must also use the HMShowBalloon function if you don't provide an 'hmnu' resource for your menu.

After your menu definition procedure determines that the cursor is over a menu item, you can use the HMShowMenuBalloon function to display any help balloons associated with that item. You must then use the HMRemoveBalloon function to remove the balloon when the cursor moves away from the menu item.

```
FUNCTION HMShowMenuBalloon (itemNum: Integer; itemMenuID: Integer;
                            itemFlags: LongInt; itemReserved: LongInt;
                            tip: Point; alternateRect: RectPtr; tipProc:
                            Ptr; theProc: Integer; variant: Integer) :
                            OSErr;
```

The itemNum parameter is the menu item number of the item that the cursor is currently over. Use a positive number in the itemNum parameter to specify a menu item, use –1 if the cursor is over a dashed line, or use 0 if the cursor is over the menu title.

The itemMenuID parameter is the menu ID of the menu the cursor is currently in.

The itemFlags parameter is a long integer from the menu flags, which tells whether a menu item is enabled or dimmed, and whether the menu itself is enabled or dimmed. The Help Manager uses this value to determine which balloon to display from the 'hmnu' resource.

The itemReserved parameter is reserved for future use by Apple. Specify 0 in this parameter.

The tip parameter specifies the tip for the help balloon. The standard menu definition procedure places the tip eight pixels from either the right or left edge of the menu item. For menu titles, the standard menu definition procedure centers the tip at the bottom of the menu bar. Note that you should not specify a tip with coordinates in the menu bar for any menu titles.

The Help Manager uses the tip you specify unless it places the help balloon offscreen or in the menu bar. If the tip is offscreen, the Help Manager uses the rectangle specified in the alternateRect parameter to calculate a new tip location.

If you use the HMShowMenuBalloon function to display help balloons, you must identify hot rectangles, create your own data structures to store their locations, track the cursor yourself, and call HMShowMenuBalloon when the cursor moves to your hot rectangles. The Help Manager does not know the locations of your hot rectangles, so it cannot use them for moving the tip if the help balloon is placed offscreen. Instead, the Help Manager uses the alternate rectangle that you point to with the alternateRect parameter.

The alternateRect parameter is the rectangle the Help Manager uses to calculate a new tip location. (The standard menu definition procedure specifies the alternate rectangle as the rectangle that encloses the menu title or menu item.) If the balloon's first position is offscreen or in the menu bar, the Help Manager tries a different balloon variation code or calculates a new tip by transposing it to an opposite side of the alternate rectangle. If you specify NIL for the alternateRect parameter, the Help Manager does not attempt to calculate a new tip position if the help balloon is offscreen.

Note that, unlike the way the alternateRect parameter works in the HMShowBalloon function, specifying an alternate rectangle to HMShowMenuBalloon does not cause the Help Manager to track the cursor and remove the balloon for you. You must still track the cursor and use the HMRemoveBalloon function to remove the balloon when the cursor moves out of the area specified by the hot rectangle.

Specify NIL in the tipProc parameter to use the tip function values calculated by the Help Manager. If you supply your own tip function (as described later in "Using Your Own Tip Function") and specify it in the tipProc parameter, the Help Manager returns the tip, the region boundary of the entire balloon, the region boundary for the content area within the balloon frame, and the variation code to be used for the help balloon before displaying it. This allows you to examine and possibly adjust the balloon before it is displayed.

The parameter theProc is reserved for use by Apple. Specify 0 in this parameter.

You can specify the variation code for the standard balloon definition function using the variant parameter. Specify 0 to use the default balloon position or a code between 1 and 7 to use one of the other standard positions shown in Figure 11-4.

The HMShowMenuBalloon function saves the bits behind the help balloon before displaying the help balloon. When the help balloon is removed, the Help Manager restores the bits that were previously behind the help balloon.

Result codes

noErr	0	No error; the help balloon was displayed
memFullErr	–108	Not enough room in heap zone
hmHelpDisabled	–850	Help balloons are not enabled
hmBalloonAborted	–853	Because of constant cursor movement, the help balloon wasn't displayed
hmSameAsLastBalloon	–854	Menu and item are same as last menu and item

Removing a Help Balloon

The Help Manager automatically tracks the cursor and removes the help balloon (when the user moves the cursor outside of the hot rectangle) for balloons defined in 'hmnu', 'hdlg', and 'hrct' resources. Your application does not need to remove help balloons created by these resources.

If you use the HMShowBalloon function to display help balloons, you can either let the Help Manager track the cursor and remove the help balloon when the cursor moves out of the hot rectangle, or your application can track the cursor and determine when to remove the balloon. To let the Help Manager track the cursor and remove the help balloon when using the HMShowBalloon function, specify a rectangle in the alternateRect parameter. If you want your application to track the cursor and remove the help balloon when using the HMShowBalloon function, specify NIL in the alternateRect parameter. You must then use the HMRemoveBalloon function to remove the balloon when the user moves the cursor outside of the rectangle.

If you use the HMShowMenuBalloon function to display help balloons, you must always track the cursor and use the HMRemoveBalloon function to remove the help balloon when the cursor moves out of the hot rectangle.

▲ **Warning:** The HMRemoveBalloon function removes any help balloon that is currently visible, regardless of the application that displayed it. You should only call HMRemoveBalloon when the cursor is in the content area of your application window but not in a hot rectangle, and you should never call it when your application is in the background. ▲

```
FUNCTION HMRemoveBalloon : OSErr;
```

The HMRemoveBalloon function removes any balloon that is currently visible—unless the user is using Close View and is pressing the Shift key. This action keeps the help balloon on screen even while the user moves away from the hot rectangle under Close View. The HMRemoveBalloon function returns a result code of hmCloseViewActive in this case.

If you use your own menu bar definition procedure, you should call HMRemoveBalloon when your procedure receives the Save bits and Restore bits messages before you save or restore any bits. (The Save and Restore bits messages are described in the Menu Manager chapter in Volume V.)

Result codes

noErr	0	No error or the help balloon was removed
hmHelpDisabled	–850	Help balloons are not enabled
hmNoBalloonUp	–862	No balloon showing
hmCloseViewActive	–863	User using Close View won't let you remove balloon

Using Your Own Tip Function

When you use the HMShowBalloon and HMShowMenuBalloon functions to display help balloons, you pass a pointer to a tip function in the tipProc parameter. Normally, you supply NIL in this parameter to use the Help Manager's default tip function. However, you can also supply your own tip function. The Help Manager calls your tip function after calculating the size and the location of a help balloon and before displaying it. This allows you to examine and, if necessary, adjust the balloon before it is displayed. For example, if you determine that the help balloon would obscure an object that requires extensive redrawing, you might use a different variation code to move the balloon.

Here's how to declare a tip function called MyTip.

```
FUNCTION MyTip (tip: Point; structure: RgnHandle; VAR r: Rect;
                VAR variant: Integer) : OSErr;
```

The Help Manager returns the balloon tip in the tip parameter, a handle to its region structure in the structure parameter, the content region in the r parameter, and the variation code to be used for the help balloon in the variant parameter. The content region is the area inside the balloon frame; it contains the user help information. The structure region is the boundary region of the entire balloon, including the content area and the pointer that extends from one of the help balloon's corners. (Figure 11-4 illustrates the structure regions of the eight standard help balloons.)

If the help balloon that HMShowBalloon or HMShowMenuBalloon initially calculates is not appropriate for your current screen display, you can make minor adjustments to it by specifying a different rectangle in the r parameter (the Help Manager automatically adjusts the structure parameter so that the entire balloon is larger or smaller as necessary) or by specifying a different variation code in the variant parameter. (Figure 11-4 shows the different balloon positions assigned to the standard variation codes.)

If you need to make a major adjustment to the help balloon, return the hmBalloonAborted result code and call HMShowBalloon or HMShowMenuBalloon with appropriate new parameter values. To use the values returned in your tip function's parameters, return the noErr result code.

Here's an example of using a tip function to refrain from displaying a balloon if it obscures an area of the screen that requires extensive drawing.

```
VAR
   temprect:          Rect;
   DontObscureRect:   Rect;
   tip:               Point;
   structure:         RgnHandle;
   aHelpMsg:          HMMessageRecord;
```

```
BEGIN
   {be sure to determine DontObscureRect and fill in aHelpMsg}
   IF HMShowBalloon(aHelpMsg,tip,NIL,@MyTip,0,0,kHMRegularwindow) = noErr
   THEN
      {test whether balloon obscures complex graphic in DontObscureRect}
      IF SectRect(structure^^.rgnBBox,DontObscureRect,temprect) THEN
         {don't show this balloon but call HMShowBalloon later}
         MyTip := hmBalloonAborted
      ELSE  {use the balloon as calculated by the Help Manager}
         MyTip := noErr;
END;
```

Adding Items to the Help Menu

The Help Manager automatically appends the Help menu when your application calls InsertMenu and then DrawMenuBar. The Help menu is automatically appended to the right of all your menus and to the left of the Application menu (and to the left of the Keyboard menu if a non-Roman script system is installed).

The Help menu is specific to each application. The Help menu items defined by the Help Manager should be common to all applications, but you can append your own menu items for help-related information.

You can append items to the Help menu using the HMGetHelpMenuHandle function. Do not use the GetMHandle function to get a handle to the Help menu, because GetMHandle returns a handle to the global Help menu, not the Help menu that is specific to your application. Once you have a handle to the Help menu that is specific to your application, you can add items to it using the AppendMenu procedure or other Menu Manager routines.

```
FUNCTION HMGetHelpMenuHandle (VAR mh: MenuHandle) : OSErr;
```

The HMGetHelpMenuHandle function returns a copy of a handle to the Help menu in the mh parameter. Once you have a handle to the Help menu that is specific to your application, you can append items to it using the AppendMenu routine or related Menu Manager routines. The Help Manager automatically adds the dashed line that separates your items from the rest of the menu.

Be sure to define help balloons for your items in the Help menu by creating an 'hmnu' resource and specifying the kHMHelpMenuID constant as its resource ID. (See "Adding Your Own Menu Items to the Help Menu" earlier in this chapter for more details.)

The MenuSelect and MenuKey functions return a result with the menu ID in the high word and the menu item in the low word of the function result. Both functions return the HelpMgrID constant in the high word when the user chooses an appended item from the Help menu.

The menu item number of the appended menu item is returned in the low word of the function result. In the future, Apple may choose to add other items to the Help menu. To determine the number of items in the Help menu, call the CountMItems function.

Result codes

noErr	0	No error
paramErr	–50	Error in parameter list
memFullErr	–108	Not enough room in heap zone
resNotFound	–192	Unable to read resource
hmHelpManagerNotInited	–855	Help menu not set up

Getting and Setting the Font Name and Size

You can get information about the font name and size currently used for text strings displayed in help balloons, and you can change the font name and size.

▲ **Warning:** If your application changes the font name or size, the change affects all applications and software that display help balloons. ▲

You can use the HMGetFont function to get information about the font that is currently used to display text (that is, Pascal strings and strings from 'STR#' and 'STR ' resources) in help balloons. This does not apply to text in 'PICT' or styled text resources, or to text in handles to either of these resources.

```
FUNCTION HMGetFont (VAR font: Integer) : OSErr;
```

The HMGetFont function returns the global font number used to display text in help balloons in the font parameter.

Result codes

noErr	0	No error
memFullErr	–108	Not enough room in heap zone

You can use the HMGetFontSize function to get information about the font size that is currently used to display text in help balloons.

```
FUNCTION HMGetFontSize (VAR fontSize: Integer) : OSErr;
```

The HMGetFontSize function returns the global font size used to display text in help balloons in the fontSize parameter.

Result codes

noErr	0	No error
memFullErr	–108	Not enough room in heap zone

The HMSetFont function sets the font used to display text in help balloons.

```
FUNCTION HMSetFont (font: Integer) : OSErr;
```

The font parameter specifies the global font number for the Help Manager to use to display text in help balloons. This sets the font for help balloons in all applications and software that display help balloons. Use this function with extreme restraint; the default font provides a consistent look across applications.

Result codes

noErr	0	No error
memFullErr	–108	Not enough room in heap zone

The HMSetFontSize function sets the font used to display text in help balloons.

```
FUNCTION HMSetFontSize (fontSize: Integer) : OSErr;
```

The font parameter specifies the global font size for the Help Manager to use to display text in help balloons. This sets the font size for help balloons in all applications and software that display help balloons. Use this function only with extreme caution; the choice of font size should always be under the user's control.

Result codes

noErr	0	No error
memFullErr	–108	Not enough room in heap zone

Getting and Setting Information for Help Resources

Using the HMSetMenuResID or HMScanTemplateItems function, you can set help resources for menus, dialog boxes, or windows of your application that do not currently have help resources associated with them. You can also supplement the 'hmnu' and 'hdlg' resources currently associated with the menus and dialog boxes of your application by using the HMSetMenuResID or HMSetDialogResID function.

You can supplement whatever 'hdlg' resources may be specified in 'DITL' resources by using the HMSetDialogResID function. The resource you specify in the HMSetDialogResID function adds to any help that already exists in the form of an 'hdlg' resource for the next dialog box or alert box to be displayed. If you create dialog boxes or alert boxes on the fly, you can use an 'hdlg' resource (described earlier in “Providing Help Balloons for Items in Dialog Boxes and Alert Boxes”) to provide help balloons for items in a template, and you can use the HMSetDialogResID function to provide help balloons for items that you add to your dialog box template.

You can use the HMGetDialogResID function to get the resource ID of the 'hdlg' resource that will be used by the next dialog box as a result of a previous call to the HMSetDialogResID function. If the 'hdlg' resource currently in use has not been overridden by a call to HMSetDialogResID, the HMGetDialogResID function returns a result code of resNotFound.

You can use the HMGetDialogResID and HMSetDialogResID functions when displaying nested dialog boxes. For example, you can save the 'hdlg' resource of the current dialog box, set a new 'hdlg' resource, display the new dialog box, and then restore the setting of the previous 'hdlg' resource when you close the second dialog box.

You can set the resource ID for the 'hdlg' template used to display the next dialog box using the HMSetDialogResID function.

```
FUNCTION HMSetDialogResID (resID: Integer) : OSErr;
```

The resID parameter specifies the resource ID of the 'hdlg' resource to use when displaying the next dialog box or alert box. This supplements whatever 'hdlg' resource might already be associated with that dialog box or alert box by a helpItem item in its 'DITL'.

Specify –1 in the resID parameter to reset or clear a previous call to the HMSetDialogResID function.

Result codes

noErr	0	No error
memFullErr	–108	Not enough room in heap zone

You can use the HMGetDialogResID function to get the resource ID of the 'hdlg' resource that will be used by the next dialog box as a result of a previous call to the HMSetDialogResID function.

```
FUNCTION HMGetDialogResID (VAR resID: Integer) : OSErr;
```

The HMGetDialogResID function returns in the resID parameter the resource ID of the last 'hdlg' resource that was previously set by calling the HMSetDialogResID function. If the 'hdlg' resource currently in use was not set by calling the HMSetDialogResID function, the HMGetDialogResID function returns a result code of resNotFound.

Result codes

noErr	0	No error
memFullErr	–108	Not enough room in heap zone
resNotFound	–192	Unable to read resource

You can use the HMSetMenuResID function to set the 'hmnu' resource for a menu that did not previously have one or to supplement the existing 'hmnu' resource for a menu.

```
FUNCTION HMSetMenuResID (menuID,resID: Integer) : OSErr;
```

The menuID parameter specifies the menu to associate with the 'hmnu' resource. The resID parameter specifies the resource ID of the 'hmnu' resource to use for the menu specified by the menuID parameter. The menu identified by the menuID parameter should correspond to an existing menu in your menu list. The Help Manager maintains a list of the menus whose 'hmnu' resources you map (set or override) using the HMSetMenuResID function.

Specify –1 in the resID parameter to unmap the pairing of a particular menu and 'hmnu' resource that you previously mapped using the HMSetMenuResID function. You should unmap any resource IDs before your application quits.

Result codes

noErr	0	No error
memFullErr	–108	Not enough room in heap zone

You can use the HMGetMenuResID function to get information about the menus you have mapped with the HMSetMenuResID function.

```
FUNCTION HMGetMenuResID (menuID: Integer; VAR resID: Integer) : OSErr;
```

The menuID parameter specifies the menu for which you want the mapped resource ID. The value specified in the menuID parameter must have been previously mapped using the HMSetMenuResID function.

The HMGetMenuResID function returns in the resID parameter the resource ID of the mapped 'hmnu' resource associated with the menu specified by the menuID parameter. If the menu does not have an 'hmnu' resource that was previously mapped by calling HMSetMenuResID, the HMGetMenuResID function returns –1 in the resID parameter and a nonzero result code.

Result codes

noErr	0	No error
resNotFound	–192	Unable to read resource

You can use the HMScanTemplateItems function to search for a particular resource of type 'hdlg' or 'hrct' and, if the resource is found, use it for the active window. (If you want this capability without modifying your code, you can add a helpItem item to your 'DITL' resources or add an 'hwin' resource—as described previously in "Providing Help Balloons for Items in Dialog Boxes and Alert Boxes" and "Providing Help Balloons for Window Content.")

```
FUNCTION HMScanTemplateItems (whichID,whichResFile: Integer; whichType:
                              ResType) : OSErr;
```

The whichID parameter specifies the resource ID to search for. The whichResFile parameter specifies the file reference number of the resource file to search. The resource file must already be open. Specify –1 in the whichResFile parameter to search the current resource file.

The whichType parameter specifies the type of help resource to search for—either 'hdlg' or 'hrct'. If the specified resource is found, the Help Manager applies the help information specified in the resource to the frontmost window.

Result codes

noErr	0	No error
fnOpnErr	–38	File not open
memFullErr	–108	Not enough room in heap zone
resNotFound	–192	Unable to read resource

Getting the Dimensions of a Help Balloon

The Help Manager provides three functions that allow you to get information about a help balloon before or during display. You probably won't need to call these functions. If your application does extensive drawing, however, these functions could be helpful for determining the location of your help balloons before displaying them. Then you could ensure that your help balloons don't obscure an area that requires an inordinate amount of time to update.

To get information about a help balloon before the Help Manager displays it, use the HMBalloonRect or HMBalloonPict function. To get a pointer to the window record of the currently displayed help balloon, use the HMGetBalloonWindow function.

You can specify the help information for a help balloon and then use the HMBalloonRect function to get the coordinates of the rectangle that the Help Manager would use to display the help balloon.

```
FUNCTION HMBalloonRect (aHelpMsg: HMMessageRecord; VAR coolRect: Rect)
                        : OSErr;
```

You specify the help information for a help balloon in the aHelpMsg parameter. The aHelpMsg parameter is of data type HMMessageRecord. "Help Balloons in Dynamic Windows" earlier in this chapter describes the fields of this record.

The HMBalloonRect function calculates the coordinates that the Help Manager will use if you show this help balloon. The HMBalloonRect function returns the rectangle coordinates in the coolRect parameter. The coordinates of the returned rectangle are zero-based, with (0,0) the coordinates of the upper-left corner of the rectangle. The coolRect parameter gives the coordinates of the rectangle that encloses the user help information.

You can use the HMBalloonRect function to find out the size (not the position) of the rectangle for a help balloon message.

Note that the HMBalloonRect function does not display the help balloon; it returns the rectangle that the Help Manager will use if you choose to display a help balloon with the specified user help information.

Result codes

noErr	0	No error
paramErr	–50	Error in parameter list
memFullErr	–108	Not enough room in heap zone

You can specify the help information for a help balloon and then use the HMBalloonPict function to get a handle to the picture that the Help Manager will generate if you later choose to display the help balloon.

```
FUNCTION HMBalloonPict (aHelpMsg: HMMessageRecord; VAR coolPict:
                        PicHandle) : OSErr;
```

The aHelpMsg parameter specifies the help information for a help balloon. The aHelpMsg parameter is of data type HMMessageRecord. "Help Balloons in Dynamic Windows" earlier in this chapter describes the fields of this record.

The HMBalloonPict function calculates the picture handle the Help Manager will use if you later choose to display this help balloon. The HMBalloonPict function returns a handle to the picture in the coolPict parameter.

The HMBalloonPict function does not display the help balloon; it returns a handle to the picture that the Help Manager will use if you later choose to display a help balloon with the specified information.

The pictFrame field of the picture handle in the coolPict parameter contains the same rectangle as the rectangle obtained from the HMBalloonRect function. The rectangle specifies the display rectangle that surrounds the picture.

Result codes

noErr	0	No error
paramErr	–50	Error in parameter list
memFullErr	–108	Not enough room in heap zone

The Help Manager displays help balloons in special windows. You can get a pointer to the window record of the currently displayed help balloon using the HMGetBalloonWindow function.

```
FUNCTION HMGetBalloonWindow (VAR window: WindowPtr) : OSErr;
```

The HMGetBalloonWindow function returns a pointer to the window record of the currently displayed help balloon in the window parameter. If a help balloon is not currently displayed, the HMGetBalloonWindow function returns NIL in the window parameter. The HMGetBalloonWindow function also returns NIL for balloons created with the HMShowMenuBalloon function because no windows are created; likewise, NIL is returned for balloons created with the HMShowBalloon function when the kHMSaveBitsNoWindow constant is specified as the method parameter.

Result codes

noErr	0	No error
memFullErr	–108	Not enough room in heap zone

Getting the Content of a Help Balloon

Using the HMExtractHelpMsg and HMGetIndHelpMsg functions, you can extract information from existing help resources.

You can use HMExtractHelpMsg to extract the help balloon content specified in existing help resources. You might find this useful if you have duplicate commands and you want to store help messages in only one resource. For example, if you have a dialog box that replicates portions of a pull-down menu, you could specify help information in the 'hmnu' resource for the pull-down menu, and use HMExtractHelpMsg to extract those help messages to use with related dialog items in the dialog box's 'hdlg' resource.

```
FUNCTION HMExtractHelpMsg      (whichType: ResType; whichResID,whichMsg,
                                whichState: Integer; VAR aHelpMsg:
                                HMMessageRecord) : OSErr;
```

The whichType parameter specifies the format of the help message. Supply one of these constants.

```
CONST kHMMenuResType        = 'hmnu';   {menu help resource type}
      kHMDialogResType      = 'hdlg';   {dialog help resource type}
      kHMRectListResType    = 'hrct';   {rect help resource type}
      kHMOverrideResType    = 'hovr';   {help override resource type}
      kHMFinderApplResType = 'hfdr';   {app icon help resource type}
```

Note: If HMCompareItem appears as a component of an 'hmnu' resource that you're examining, neither this function nor HMGetIndHelpMsg performs a comparison against the current name of any menu item. Instead, these functions return the messages listed in your HMCompareItem components in the order in which they appear in the 'hmnu' resource.

Supply the whichResID parameter with the resource ID of the help resource whose content you wish to extract. Specify the index of the component you wish to extract in the whichMsg parameter. (Don't count the header information as a component to index.) After the header information, for example, the first component in a menu help resource defines help for missing items; the second item defines help for the menu title.

For menu items and dialog items, the whichState parameter specifies the state of the item whose message you wish to extract. Use one of the following constants for the whichState parameter.

```
CONST kHMEnabledItem        = 0; {enabled state for menu items; }
                                 { contrlHilite value of 1 for controls}
      kHMDisabledItem       = 1; {disabled state for menu items; }
                                 { contrlHilite value of 0 for controls}
      kHMCheckedItem        = 2; {enabled-and-checked state for menu }
                                 { items; contrlHilite value of 1 for }
                                 { controls that are "on"}
      kHMOtherItem          = 3; {enabled-and-marked state for menu }
                                 { items; contrlHilite value greater than }
                                 { 1 for controls}
```

For the kHMRectListResType, kHMOverrideResType, and kHMFinderApplResType resource types—which don't have states—supply the kHMEnabledItem constant for the whichState parameter.

HMExtractHelpMsg returns a help message record in the aHelpMsg parameter. The aHelpMsg parameter is of data type HMMessageRecord. "Help Balloons in Dynamic Windows" earlier in this chapter describes the fields of this record.

In the following example, a menu help resource has a resource ID of 128. A 2 is supplied as the whichMsg parameter to retrieve information about the resource's second component (the second component after the header, that is), which is the menu title. The menu title has four possible states; to retrieve the help message for the menu title in its dimmed state, the constant kHMDisabledItem is used for the whichState parameter. The help message record returned in aHelpMsg is then passed to HMShowBalloon, which displays the message in a balloon with its tip located at the point specified in the tip parameter.

```
VAR
   aHelpMsg:       HMMessageRecord;
   tip:            Point;
   alternateRect: Rect;
   err:            OSErr;

BEGIN
   err := HMExtractHelpMsg(HMMenuListResType,128,2,kDisabledItem,aHelpMsg);
   IF err = noErr THEN
      {be sure to assign a tip and rectangle coordinates here}
      err := HMShowBalloon(aHelpMsg,tip,alternateRect,
                           NIL,0,0,kHMRegularWindow);
END;
```


To retrieve all of the help balloon messages for a given resource, set whichMsg to 1 and make repeated calls to HMExtractHelpMsg, incrementing whichMsg by 1 on each subsequent call until it returns the hmSkipBalloon result code.

Result codes

noErr	0	No error
paramErr	–50	Error in parameter list
memFullErr	–108	Not enough room in heap zone
resNotFound	–192	Unable to read resource
hmSkipBalloon	–857	No balloon content to fill in
hmWrongVersion	–858	Wrong version of Help Manager resource
hmUnknownHelpType	–859	Help message record contained a bad type

In addition to extracting the help balloon content specified in existing help resources as HMExtractHelpMsg does, HMGetIndHelpMsg returns additional information regarding the help resource, such as its variation code, tip location, and so on.

```
FUNCTION HMGetIndHelpMsg (whichType: ResType; whichResID,whichMsg,
                          whichState: Integer; VAR options: LongInt;
                          VAR tip: Point; VAR altRect: Rect; VAR theProc:
                          Integer; VAR variant: Integer; VAR aHelpMsg:
                          HMMessageRecord; VAR count: Integer) : OSErr;
```

The information you supply to the HMGetIndHelpMsg function is similar to what you supply to the HMExtractHelpMsg function. (See the description of the HMExtractHelpMsg function above for information about the whichType, whichResID, whichMsg, and whichState parameters.)

HMGetIndHelpMsg returns the following information about the specified help resource: the value of the options field in the options parameter; the coordinates of the tip location in the tip parameter; the coordinates of the alternate rectangle in the altRect parameter; the resource ID of its 'WDEF' resource in the theProc parameter; the balloon definition function's variation code in the variant parameter; the help message record in the aHelpMsg parameter; and, in the count parameter, the number of components defined in the resource (not counting the header information).

To retrieve all of the help balloon messages and related information for a given resource, set whichMsg to 1 and make repeated calls to HMGetIndHelpMsg, incrementing whichMsg by 1 on each subsequent call until it returns the hmSkipBalloon result code.

Result codes

noErr	0	No error
paramErr	–50	Error in parameter list
mcmFullErr	–108	Not enough room in heap zone
resNotFound	–192	Unable to read resource
hmSkipBalloon	–857	No balloon content to fill in
hmWrongVersion	–858	Wrong version of Help Manager resource
hmUnknownHelpType	–859	Help message record contained a bad type

SUMMARY OF THE HELP MANAGER

Constants

```
CONST gestaltHelpMgrAttr     = 'help';    {Gestalt selector}
      gestaltHelpMgrPresent  = 0;         {if this bit is set, then }
                                          { Help Manager is present}
      hmBalloonHelpVersion   = $0002;     {Help Manager version}

      {Help menu constants}
      kHMHelpMenuID          = -16490;    {Help menu res and menu ID}
      kHMAboutHelpItem       = 1;         {About Balloon Help menu item}
      kHMShowBalloonsItem    = 3;         {Show/Hide Balloons menu item}

      kHMHelpID              = -5696;     {ID of various Help Manager }
                                          { package resources (in }
                                          { Pack14 range); also used }
                                          { for res ID for 'hfdr'/icon }
                                          { help}
      kBalloonWDEFID         = 126;       {res ID of standard balloon }
                                          { 'WDEF' function}

      {dialog item template type constant}
      HelpItem               = 1;         {key value in 'DITL' template }
                                          { that corresponds to help }
                                          { item}

      {option bits for help resources}
      hmDefaultOptions       = 0;         {use help resource defaults}
      hmUseSubID             = 1;         {use subrange resource IDs }
                                          { for owned resources}
      hmAbsoluteCoords       = 2;         {ignore coords of window }
                                          { origin and treat upper-left }
                                          { corner of window as 0,0}
      hmSaveBitsNoWindow     = 4;         {don't create window; save }
                                          { bits; no update event}
      hmSaveBitsWindow       = 8;         {save bits behind window and }
                                          { generate update event}
      hmMatchInTitle         = 16;        {match window by string }
                                          { anywhere in title string}

      {constants for hmmHelpType field of HMMessageRecord}
      khmmString             = 1;         {Pascal string}
      khmmPict               = 2;         {'PICT' resource ID}
      khmmStringRes          = 3;         {'STR#' res ID and index}
      khmmTEHandle           = 4;         {styled text handle}
      khmmPictHandle         = 5;         {picture handle}
      khmmTERes              = 6;         {'styl' and 'TEXT' res ID}
      khmmSTRRes             = 7;         {'STR' resource ID}
```

```
{resource types for styled TE handles in resources}
kHMTETextResType       = 'TEXT';   {'TEXT' resource type}
kHMTEStyleResType      = 'styl';   {'styl' resource type}

{generic defines for whichState parameter when extracting help }
{ message records from 'hmnu' & 'hdlg' resources}
kHMEnabledItem         = 0;        {enabled state for menu items; }
                                   { contrlHilite value of 1 for }
                                   { controls}
kHMDisabledItem        = 1;        {disabled state for menu items; }
                                   { contrlHilite value of 0 for }
                                   { controls}
kHMCheckedItem         = 2;        {enabled-and-checked state for }
                                   { menu items; contrlHilite value }
                                   { of 1 for controls that are "on"}
kHMOtherItem           = 3;        {enabled-and-marked state for }
                                   { menu items; contrlHilite value }
                                   { greater than  1 for controls}

{resource types for whichType parameter used when extracting }
{ help message content}
kHMMenuResType         = 'hmnu';   {menu help resource type}
kHMDialogResType       = 'hdlg';   {dialog help resource type}
kHMWindListResType     = 'hwin';   {window help resource type}
kHMRectListResType     = 'hrct';   {rectangle help resource type}
kHMOverrideResType     = 'hovr';   {help override resource type
kHMFinderApplResType   = 'hfdr';   {app icon help resource type}

{constants for method parameter in HMShowBalloon}
kHMRegularWindow       = 0;        {don't save bits; just update}
kHMSaveBitsNoWindow    = 1;        {save bits; don't do update}
kHMSaveBitsWindow      = 2;        {save bits; do update event}

{constants for help types in 'hmnu', 'hdlg', 'hrct', 'hovr', & }
{ 'hfdr' resources--useful only for walking these resources}
kHMStringItem          = 1;        {Pascal string}
kHMPictItem            = 2;        {'PICT' resource ID}
kHMStringResItem       = 3;        {'STR#' resource ID & index}
kHMTEResItem           = 6;        {'TEXT' & 'styl' resource ID}
kHMSTRResItem          = 7;        {'STR ' resource ID}
kHMSkipItem            = 256;      {don't display a balloon}
kHMCompareItem         = 512;      {for hmnu, use help content }
                                   { if menu item matches string}
kHMNamedResourceItem   = 1024;     {for hmnu, use menu item as }
                                   { a call to get resource}
kHMTrackCntlItem       = 2048;     {reserved}
```

Data Types

```
TYPE HMMessageRecPtr = ^HMMessageRecord;

     HMMessageRecord =
     RECORD
        hmmHelpType:       Integer;
        CASE Integer OF
           khmmString:     (hmmString: STR255);       {Pascal string}
           khmmPict:       (hmmPict: Integer);        {'PICT' resource ID}
           khmmStringRes:  (hmmStringRes: HMStringResType); {'STR#' res }
                                                      { ID and index}
           khmmTEHandle:   (hmmTEHandle: TEHandle);   {TextEdit handle}
           khmmPictHandle: (hmmPictHandle: PicHandle); {picture handle}
           khmmTERes:      (hmmTERes: Integer);       {'styl'/'TEXT' }
                                                      { resource ID}
           khmmSTRRes:     (hmmSTRRes: Integer)       {'STR' resource ID}
     END;

     HMStringResType  =
     RECORD
        hmmResID: Integer;     {res ID of 'STR#' resource}
        hmmIndex: Integer      {index of string}
     END;
```

Routines

Determining Whether Help Is Enabled

```
FUNCTION HMGetBalloons         : Boolean;

FUNCTION HMSetBalloons         (flag: Boolean) : OSErr;
```

Determining Whether a Help Balloon Is Showing

```
FUNCTION HMIsBalloon           : Boolean;
```

Displaying and Removing Help Balloons

```
FUNCTION HMShowBalloon         (aHelpMsg: HMMessageRecord; tip: Point;
                                alternateRect: RectPtr; tipProc: Ptr;
                                theProc, variant: Integer; method: Integer) :
                                OSErr;
```

11 Help Manager

```
FUNCTION HMShowMenuBalloon    (itemNum: Integer; itemMenuID: Integer;
                               itemFlags: LongInt; itemReserved: LongInt;
                               tip: Point; alternateRect: RectPtr; tipProc:
                               Ptr; theProc: Integer; variant: Integer) :
                               OSErr;

FUNCTION HMRemoveBalloon      : OSErr;
```

Adding Items to the Help Menu

```
FUNCTION HMGetHelpMenuHandle (VAR mh: MenuHandle) : OSErr;
```

Getting and Setting the Font Name and Size

```
FUNCTION HMGetFont            (VAR font: Integer) : OSErr;

FUNCTION HMGetFontSize        (VAR fontSize: Integer) : OSErr;

FUNCTION HMSetFont            (font: Integer) : OSErr;

FUNCTION HMSetFontSize        (fontSize: Integer) : OSErr;
```

Getting and Setting Information for Help Resources

```
FUNCTION HMSetDialogResID     (resID: Integer) : OSErr;

FUNCTION HMGetDialogResID     (VAR resID: Integer) : OSErr;

FUNCTION HMSetMenuResID       (menuID,resID: Integer) : OSErr;

FUNCTION HMGetMenuResID       (menuID: Integer; VAR resID: Integer) :
                               OSErr;

FUNCTION HMScanTemplateItems (whichID,whichResFile: Integer; whichType:
                               ResType) : OSErr;
```

Getting the Dimensions of a Help Balloon

```
FUNCTION HMBalloonRect        (aHelpMsg: HMMessageRecord; VAR coolRect:
                               Rect) : OSErr;

FUNCTION HMBalloonPict        (aHelpMsg: HMMessageRecord; VAR coolPict:
                               PicHandle) : OSErr;

FUNCTION HMGetBalloonWindow  (VAR window: WindowPtr) : OSErr;
```

Getting the Content of a Help Balloon

```
FUNCTION HMExtractHelpMsg     (whichType: ResType; whichResID,whichMsg,
                               whichState: Integer; VAR aHelpMsg:
                               HMMessageRecord) : OSErr;

FUNCTION HMGetIndHelpMsg      (whichType: ResType; whichResID,whichMsg,
                               whichState: Integer; VAR options: LongInt;
                               VAR tip: Point; VAR altRect: Rect; VAR
                               theProc: Integer; VAR variant: Integer; VAR
                               aHelpMsg: HMMessageRecord; VAR count:
                               Integer) : OSErr;
```


Application-Defined Routines

```
FUNCTION MyBalloonDef         (variant: Integer; theBalloon: WindowPtr;
                               message: Integer; param: LongInt) : LongInt;

FUNCTION MyTip                (tip: Point; structure: RgnHandle; VAR r:
                               Rect; VAR variant: Integer) : OSErr;
```

Result Codes

noErr	0	No error
fnOpnErr	–38	File not open
paramErr	–50	Error in parameter list
memFullErr	–108	Not enough room in heap zone
resNotFound	–192	Unable to read resource
hmHelpDisabled	–850	Help balloons are not enabled
hmBalloonAborted	–853	Because of constant cursor movement, the help balloon wasn't displayed
hmSameAsLastBalloon	–854	Menu and item are same as previous menu and item
hmHelpManagerNotInited	–855	Help menu not set up
hmSkippedBalloon	–857	No balloon content to fill in
hmWrongVersion	–858	Wrong version of Help Manager resource
hmUnknownHelpType	–859	Help message record contained a bad type
hmOperationUnsupported	–861	Invalid value passed in the method parameter
hmNoBalloonUp	–862	No balloon showing
hmCloseViewActive	–863	User using Close View won't let you remove balloon

Assembly-Language Information

Trap Macros Requiring Routine Selectors

_Pack14

Selector	Routine
$0002	HMRemoveBalloon
$0003	HMGetBalloons
$0007	HMIsBalloon
$0104	HMSetBalloons
$0108	HMSetFont
$0109	HMSetFontSize
$010C	HMSetDialogResID
$0200	HMGetHelpMenuHandle
$020A	HMGetFont
$020B	HMGetFontSize
$020D	HMSetMenuResID
$0213	HMGetDialogResID
$0215	HMGetBalloonWindow
$0314	HMGetMenuResID
$040E	HMBalloonRect
$040F	HMBalloonPict
$0410	HMScanTemplateItems
$0711	HMExtractHelpMsg
$0B01	HMShowBalloon
$0E05	HMShowMenuBalloon
$1306	HMGetIndHelpMsg

12 THE FONT MANAGER

ABOUT THIS CHAPTER

System software version 7.0 introduces Apple's new outline fonts, called TrueType™ fonts. This chapter describes what outline fonts are and how you can use them in your application.

You need to read this chapter if you want to know what TrueType fonts are, how they differ from bitmapped fonts, and how to take advantage of both in your application. To test for the availability of outline fonts, use the Gestalt function, described in the Compatibility Guidelines chapter in this volume.

This chapter does not contain information about the format of the new 'sfnt' resource that defines an outline font, nor does it explain how to build TrueType fonts or create font editors. If you want to create your own TrueType fonts or font editors, consult the *TrueType Font Format Specification* book, available from APDA®.

You may want to read the Font Manager chapters in Volume I, Volume IV, and Volume V. Volume I contains definitions you may need to understand some concepts in this chapter, and it describes the relationship between the Font Manager and QuickDraw™. Volume IV describes the 'NFNT' and 'FOND' resources and fractional character widths. Volume V describes how to build color bitmapped fonts and provides further information about fractional character widths. You may also want to read the QuickDraw chapter in Volume I, which describes how QuickDraw draws text.

ABOUT THE FONT MANAGER

The Macintosh® Operating System uses two types of fonts: TrueType (outline) and bit-mapped fonts. Both types of fonts produce text; they differ in the form in which they are stored and the flexibility with which they change size and shape.

This section explains the terms used to refer to elements of both TrueType and bitmapped fonts and the way in which the Font Manager measures fonts of either type. This section also describes how the Font Manager changes both types of fonts from one point size to another through a process called *scaling*. Lastly, it explains how the Font Manager renders TrueType fonts in any point size.

Font Terminology

The smallest element in any type of font is a **character,** which is a symbol that represents the concept of, for example, a lowercase "b", the number "2", or the arithmetic operator "+". You cannot show a generic lowercase "b" on a display device; no matter how you might decide to show the character, certain features of representation distinguish your lowercase "b" from someone else's lowercase "b". What you actually see on a display device is a **glyph,** the distinct visual representation of the character. One glyph can represent one character, such as a lowercase "b"; more than one character, such as the "fi" ligature, which is two characters but only one glyph; or a nonprinting character, such as the space character.

Because there are two types of fonts, there are two types of glyphs. A **bitmapped glyph** is a bitmap designed at a fixed point size for a particular display device, such as a monitor or a printer. A font designer, having decided that a glyph should be so many pixels tall and so many pixels wide, carefully chooses the pixels that create the finished glyph image or **bitmap.** (A **pixel** is the smallest dot the screen can display. The resolution of a screen or printer is measured in dots per inch or **dpi.**) The font stores the bitmapped glyph as a picture for the display device.

An **outline glyph** is a model of how a glyph should look. A font designer uses lines and curves, not pixels, to draw the glyph. The **outline,** a mathematical description of an outline glyph, has no designated point size or display device characteristic (such as the size of a pixel) attached to it. The Font Manager uses the outline as a pattern to create bitmaps at any size for any display device.

Remember that a glyph is a representation of a character, and every glyph has some characteristics that distinguish it from the other glyphs that represent the same character: for example, the shape of the oval, the design of the stem, whether or not the glyph has a serif. If all the glyphs for a particular character set share the same characteristics, they form a **typeface,** which is a distinctly designed collection of glyphs. Each typeface has its own name, such as New York, Geneva, or Symbol. The same typeface can be used with different hardware, such as a typesetting machine, monitor, or laser printer.

Certain stylized changes can be made to the look of a glyph. **Font styles** (in previous volumes of *Inside Macintosh* called *character styles*) are variations in the appearance of a typeface. Styles available on the Macintosh computer include plain, bold, italic, underline, outline, shadow, condensed, and extended. QuickDraw can add stylistic variations such as bold or italic to bitmaps, or a font designer can design a font in a specific style (for instance, Courier Bold).

In previous volumes of *Inside Macintosh,* **font** refers to a complete set of glyphs in a particular typeface, size, and style. Courier plain 10-point, Courier bold 10-point, and Courier plain 12-point, for example, are considered three different fonts. This definition still works well for **bitmapped fonts** (of resource type 'FONT' or 'NFNT'). Manufacturers of bitmapped fonts design an individual bitmap for each glyph in each size and style. If the user requests a font that is not available in a particular size, QuickDraw can alter a bitmapped font at a different size to create the required glyphs. However, this generated bitmap often appears to be slightly irregular in some way.

An **outline font** (of resource type 'sfnt') is a collection of outline glyphs in a particular typeface and style with no size restriction. The Font Manager can generate thousands of point sizes from the same TrueType font: a single outline Courier font can produce Courier 10-point, Courier 12-point, and Courier 200-point. Handles to font records, found in data structures such as the global width table or the FMOutput record, point to fonts named by the 'sfnt' resource, as well as to fonts named by the 'FONT' and 'NFNT' resources.

When there are two or more fonts of the same typeface (whether of different styles, point sizes, or type—bitmapped or outline), the Font Manager groups them into **font families** (of resource type 'FOND'). An outline plain font for Geneva and two bitmapped fonts for Geneva plain 12-point and Geneva italic 12-point might make up one font family, to which a user could subsequently add other sizes or styles.

When you want to print or display a particular glyph, you need to refer directly to the character that the glyph represents. The Font Manager accesses an individual character by a **character code**—a hexadecimal number from $00 through $FF—and displays the glyph for that character in the font of the current grafPort record.

Figure 12-1 shows the standard Roman character set. Characters that are highlighted in gray are represented by the missing character glyph or are specific to the system font Chicago (⌘,✓,◇, and). (A complete list of characters, character codes, and their PostScript® names can be found in Appendix E.) The Font Manager uses the missing character glyph if a font manufacturer does not include a particular character in a font. It is commonly represented on the Macintosh computer by an empty rectangle, such as ▯. A font manufacturer must include the missing character glyph for a font. The Font Manager does not use the missing character glyph for nonprinting characters, such as the space character, that are included in the 'FONT', 'NFNT', or 'sfnt' resource.

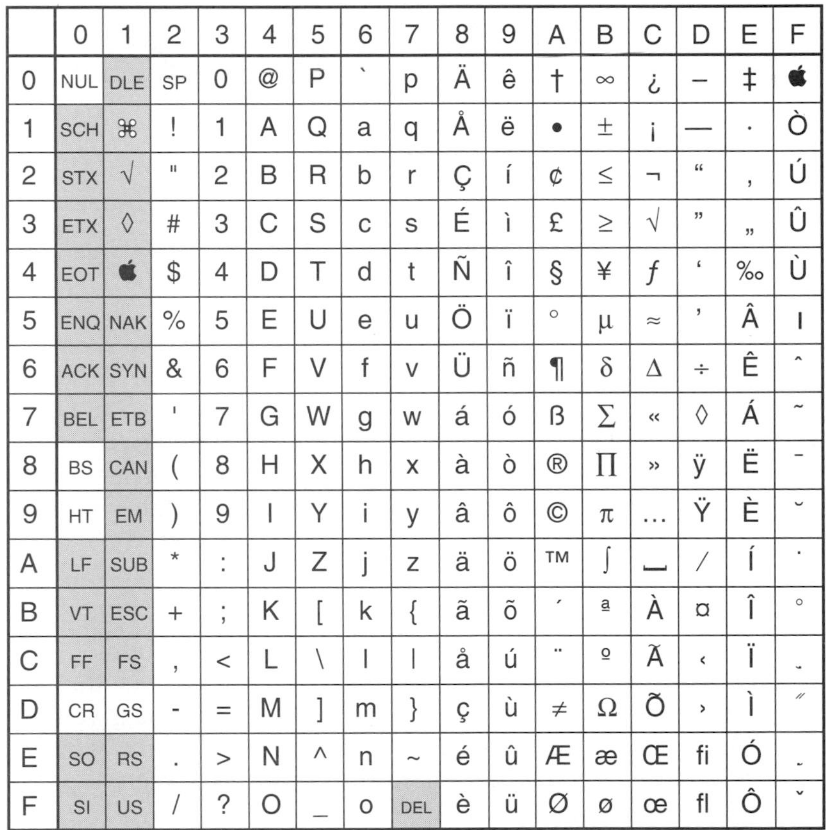

	0	1	2	3	4	5	6	7	8	9	A	B	C	D	E	F
0	NUL	DLE	SP	0	@	P	`	p	Ä	ê	†	∞	¿	–	‡	
1	SCH	⌘	!	1	A	Q	a	q	Å	ë	•	±	¡	—	·	Ò
2	STX	√	"	2	B	R	b	r	Ç	í	¢	≤	¬	“	‚	Ú
3	ETX	◊	#	3	C	S	c	s	É	ì	£	≥	√	”	„	Û
4	EOT		$	4	D	T	d	t	Ñ	î	§	¥	ƒ	‘	‰	Ù
5	ENQ	NAK	%	5	E	U	e	u	Ö	ï	°	µ	≈	’	Â	ı
6	ACK	SYN	&	6	F	V	f	v	Ü	ñ	¶	δ	∆	÷	Ê	ˆ
7	BEL	ETB	'	7	G	W	g	w	á	ó	ß	∑	«	◊	Á	˜
8	BS	CAN	(	8	H	X	h	x	à	ò	®	∏	»	ÿ	Ë	¯
9	HT	EM	)	9	I	Y	i	y	â	ô	©	π	…	Ÿ	È	˘
A	LF	SUB	*	:	J	Z	j	z	ä	ö	™	∫	⎵	/	Í	˙
B	VT	ESC	+	;	K	[	k	{	ã	õ	´	ª	À	¤	Î	˚
C	FF	FS	,	<	L	\	l	|	å	ú	¨	º	Ã	‹	Ï	¸
D	CR	GS	-	=	M	]	m	}	ç	ù	≠	Ω	Õ	›	Ì	˝
E	SO	RS	.	>	N	^	n	~	é	û	Æ	æ	Œ	ﬁ	Ó	˛
F	SI	US	/	?	O	_	o	DEL	è	ü	Ø	ø	œ	ﬂ	Ô	ˇ

Figure 12-1. The standard Roman character set

Font Measurements

Font designers have specific terms to describe parts of a glyph and parts of a font, whether outline or bitmapped. Figure 12-2 labels some of these measurements.

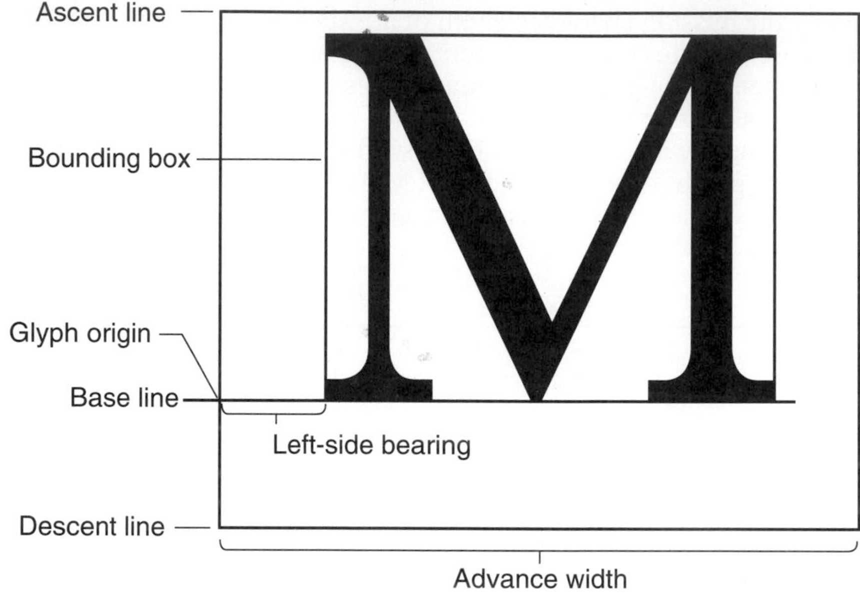

Figure 12-2. Terms for font measurements

> **Note:** Fonts for script systems around the world use some of these measurements, but the definitions given here are based on the characteristics of the Roman script system, which uses fonts meant to be read left to right and is associated with most European languages. There are different definitions for most of these terms for Asian, Arabic, or other script systems.

Some of the measurements shown in Figure 12-2 apply to a single glyph. The **bounding box** is the smallest rectangle that entirely encloses the pixels of the bitmap. The **glyph origin** is where QuickDraw begins drawing the glyph. You may notice that there is some white space between the glyph origin and the recognizable start of the glyph. The white space that precedes the glyph is the **left-side bearing.** The **advance width** is the full horizontal measurement of the glyph as measured from the glyph origin to wherever the glyph stops, including the white space on both sides.

Some measurements apply to many glyphs. To begin with, most glyphs in a font appear to sit on the **base line,** an imaginary horizontal line. The **ascent line** is an imaginary horizontal line chosen by the font's designer that corresponds approximately with the tops of the uppercase letters in the font, because these are generally the tallest commonly used glyphs in a font. The ascent line is the same distance from the base line for all glyphs in the font. The **descent line** is an imaginary horizontal line that usually corresponds with the bottoms of descenders (the tails on glyphs like "p" or "g"), and it's the same distance from the base line in every glyph of the font. The ascent and descent lines are part of the font designer's recommendations about line spacing as measured from base line to base line. (All of these lines are horizontal because Roman text is read left to right, in a straight horizontal line. In some script systems, these lines are vertical.)

For bitmapped fonts, the ascent line marks the maximum y-value and the descent line marks the minimum y-value. For outline fonts, a font designer can create individual glyphs that extend above the ascent line or below the descent line. The integral in Figure 12-3, for example, is much taller than the uppercase "M". In this case, the maximum y-value is more important than the ascent line for determining the proper line spacing for a line containing both of these glyphs. You can have the Font Manager reduce such oversized glyphs so that they fit between the ascent and descent lines. See "Preserving the Glyph's Shape" later in this chapter for details.

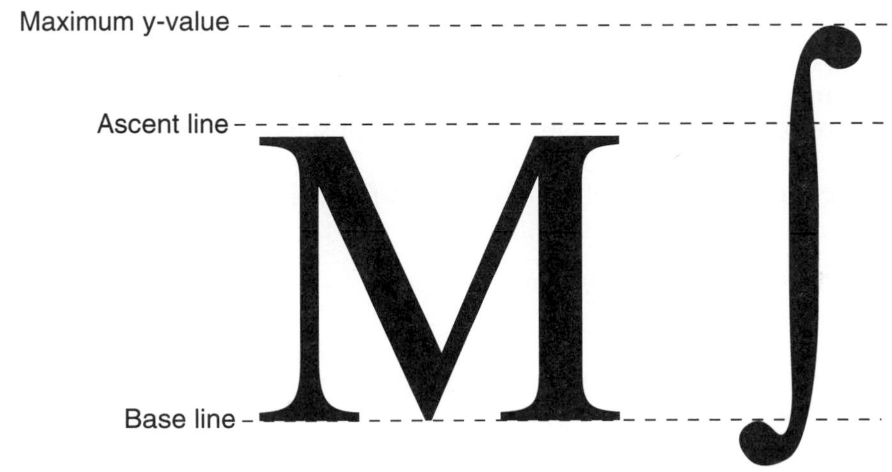

Figure 12-3. The ascent line and maximum y-value

Font size indicates the size of a font's glyphs as measured from the base line of one line of text to the base line of the next line of single-spaced text. In the United States, font size is traditionally measured in **points,** and there are 72.27 points per inch. However, QuickDraw and the PostScript language define 1 point to be 1⁄72 of an inch, so there are exactly 72 points per inch. Previously, the Font Manager required fonts to be less than or equal to 127 points in size, but this restriction no longer applies to any type of font. All bitmaps must fit on the QuickDraw coordinate plane; on a 72 dpi display device, fonts have an upper size limit of 32,767 points. Point size is one of the characteristics inherent in a bitmapped font, because the font's designer must create the font at a fixed point size as well as in a specific typeface.

Leading is the amount of blank vertical space between the descent line of one line of text in a font and the ascent line of the next line of single-spaced text in the same font. The Font Manager returns this number, which is in pixels, in the FontMetrics or GetFontInfo procedure for both TrueType and bitmapped fonts. You'll note that this measurement is not in Figure 12-2, because, although the font's manufacturer has a recommended amount of leading for a font, you can always change the amount if you need more or less space between lines of text in your application. The **line spacing** for a font can be calculated by adding the value of the leading and the distance from the ascent line to the descent line.

Font Scaling

Font scaling is the process of changing a glyph from one size or shape to another. The Font Manager can scale bitmapped and TrueType fonts in three ways: changing a glyph's point size on the same display device, modifying the glyph but keeping the point size constant when using a different display device, and altering the shape of the glyph.

The simplest form of scaling occurs when the Font Manager changes a glyph from one point size to another on the same display device. If the glyph is bitmapped and the requested font size is not available, there are certain rules the Font Manager follows to create a new bitmapped glyph from an existing one; these rules are discussed in the Font Manager chapter of Volume I. If the glyph is an outline glyph, the Font Manager uses the original outline for that glyph to create a new bitmap at a different size. In Figure 12-4, the Font Manager scales a TrueType font and a bitmapped font from 9 points to 40 points for screen display. The bitmaps available to the Font Manager to create all 32 point sizes were 9, 10, 12, 14, 18, and 24 points. A single TrueType outline produces a smoother bitmap in all point sizes.

TrueType screen font scaled from 9 points to 40 points

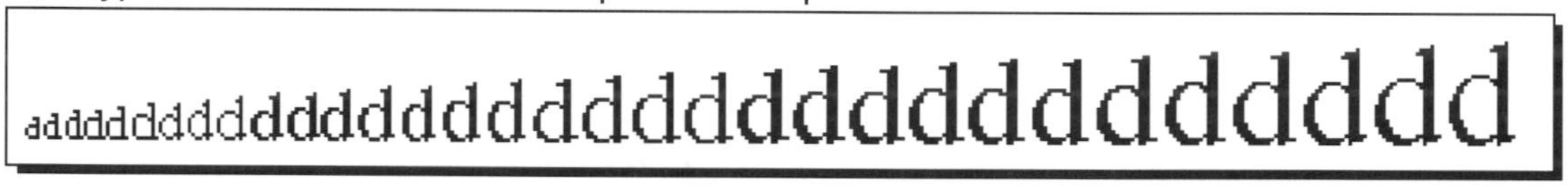

Bitmapped screen font scaled from 9 points to 40 points

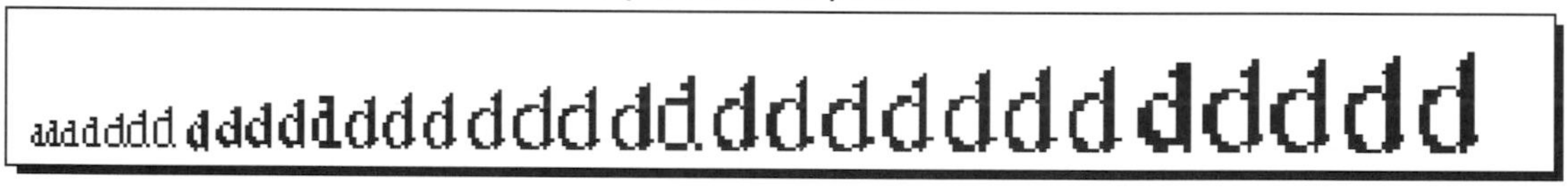

Figure 12-4. A comparison of scaled TrueType and bitmapped fonts

The Font Manager also scales a glyph when moving it from one device to another device with a different resolution: for instance, from the screen to a printer. A bitmap that is 72 pixels high on a 72 dpi screen measures one inch, but on a 144 dpi printer it measures a half inch. In order to produce a figure the same size as the original screen bitmap, the Font Manager needs a bitmap twice the size of the original. If there are no bitmaps available in twice the point size of the bitmap that appears on the screen, QuickDraw scales the original bitmap to twice its original size in order to print it on the printer.

Your application can scale a glyph by stretching or shrinking it, which changes the glyph from a familiar point size to something a little stranger—for example, a glyph that is 12 points high but as wide as a whole page of text. Your application tells the Font Manager how to scale a glyph using font scaling factors, which are represented as proportions or fractions that indicate how the Font Manager should scale the glyph in the vertical and horizontal directions. The ratio given by the font scaling factors determines whether the glyph grows or shrinks; if the ratio is greater than one, the glyph increases in size, and if it is less than one, the glyph decreases in size. If the font scaling factors are 1-to-1 (1/1) for both horizontal and vertical scaling, the glyph does not change size.

In Figure 12-5, the font scaling factors are 2/1 in the horizontal direction and 1/1 in the vertical direction. The glyph stays the same height, but grows twice as large in width.

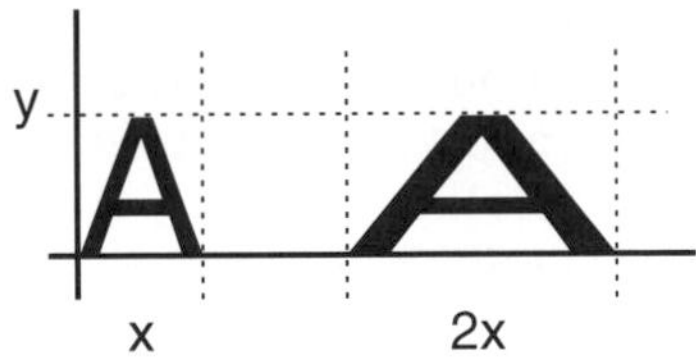

Figure 12-5. A glyph stretched horizontally

In Figure 12-6, the font scaling factors are 2/1 in the vertical direction and 1/1 in the horizontal direction. The glyph stays the same width, but grows to twice its original height.

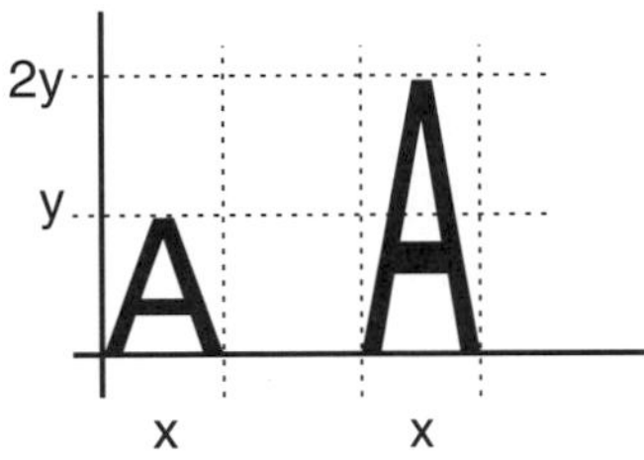

Figure 12-6. A glyph stretched vertically

In Figure 12-7, the font scaling factors are 1/1 in the vertical direction and 1/2 in the horizontal direction. The glyph stays the same height but retains only half its width.

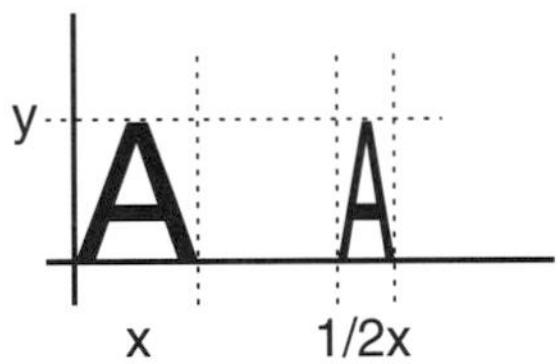

Figure 12-7. A glyph condensed horizontally

If the font scaling factors are 2/2 in both directions, QuickDraw draws the glyph at a point size twice that of the original. In the case of bitmapped fonts, QuickDraw first looks for a bitmap at twice the size of the original before redrawing the glyph at the new point size.

The Font Manager produces better results by scaling TrueType glyphs, because it changes the font's original outline to the new size or shape, and then makes the bitmap. Outlines give better results than bitmaps when scaled, because the outlines are intended for use at all point sizes, whereas the bitmaps are not.

How the Font Manager Renders TrueType Fonts

TrueType fonts are stored as a collection of **outline points.** (Don't confuse these outline points with the points that determine point size, or the Point data type, which specifies a place on the QuickDraw coordinate plane.) The Font Manager draws lines and curves between the points, sets the bits that make the bitmap, and then displays the bitmap on the screen.

There are two types of outline points: on-curve points define the endpoints of lines, and off-curve points determine the curve of the line between the on-curve points. Two consecutive on-curve points define a straight line. If you want to draw a curve, you need a third point that is off the curve and between the two on-curve points.

The Font Manager uses this parametric Bézier equation to draw the curves of the outline glyph:

$$F(t) = (1 - t)^2 * A + 2t (1 - t) * B + t^2 * C$$

where t ranges between 0 and 1 as the curve moves from point A to point C. A and C are on-curve points; B is an off-curve point.

Figure 12-8 shows two **Bézier curves.** The positions of on-curve points A and C remain constant, while off-curve point B shifts. The curve changes in relation to the position of point B.

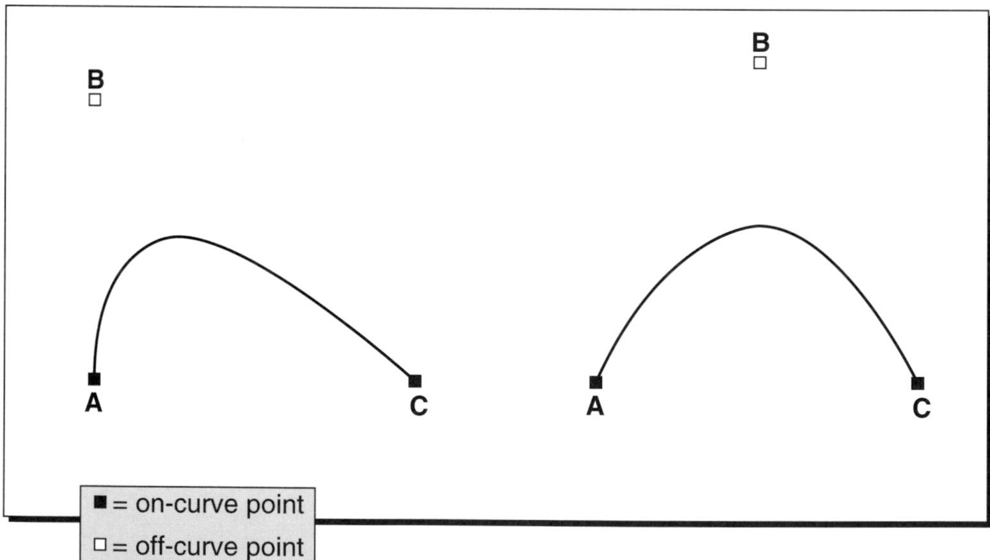

Figure 12-8. The effect of an off-curve point on two Bézier curves

A font designer can use any quantity of outline points to create a TrueType outline. These points must be numbered in a logical order, because the Font Manager draws lines and curves sequentially. This process produces a glyph such as the lowercase "b" in Figure 12-9.

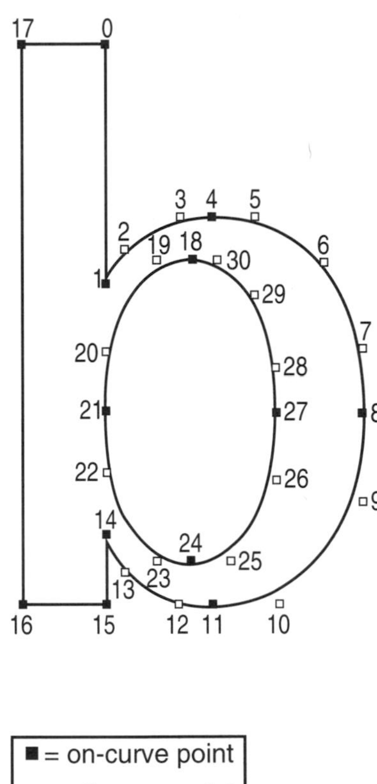

Figure 12-9. An outline with points on and off the curve

There are several groups of points in Figure 12-9 that include two consecutive off-curve points. For instance, points 2 and 3 are both off-curve. In this case, the Font Manager places an on-curve point midway between the two off-curve points, thereby defining two Bézier curves, as shown in Figure 12-10. Note that this additional on-curve point is for creation of the outline glyph only; the Font Manager does not alter the 'sfnt' resource's list of points.

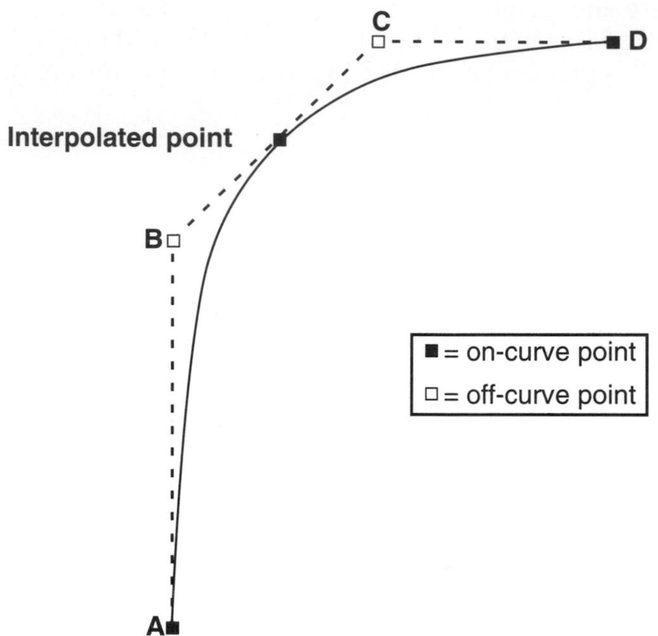

Figure 12-10. A curve with consecutive off-curve points

When the Font Manager has completed drawing a closed loop, it has completed one **contour** of the outline. The font designer groups the points in the 'sfnt' resource into contours. In Figure 12-9, the Font Manager draws the first contour in the outline glyph from point 0 to point 17, and the second contour from point 18 to the end, creating the glyph in Figure 12-11.

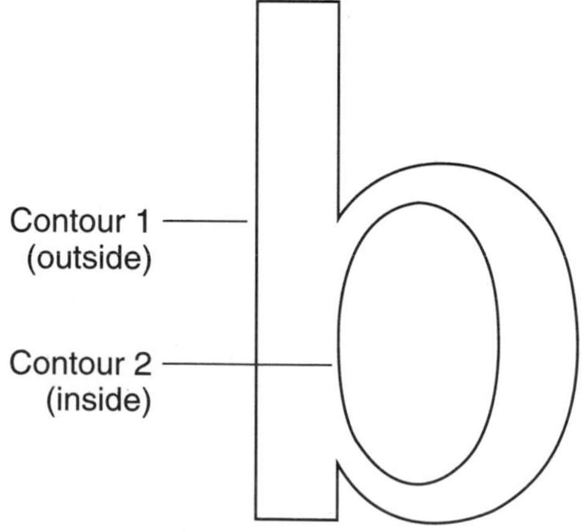

Figure 12-11. An outline glyph

At this stage, the outline glyph does not have a fixed point size. Remember that point size is measured as the distance from the base line of one line of text to the base line of the next line of single-spaced text. Because the Font Manager has the measurements relative to the base line and ascent line for the outline and the intended point size, it can correlate the two and calculate how large the outline should be for that point size.

The Macintosh computer's display screen is a grid made of pixels. The Font Manager fits the outline glyph, scaled for the correct size, to this grid. If the center of one section of this grid—comparable to a pixel or a printer dot—falls on a contour or within two contours, the Font Manager sets this bit for the bitmap.

The Font Manager uses the contours as the boundaries for deciding which bits make up the bitmap for this outline glyph when it is displayed. Because there are two contours for the glyph in Figure 12-11, the Font Manager begins with pixels at the boundary marked by contour 1 and stops when it gets to contour 2. Some glyphs need only one contour, such as the uppercase "I" in some fonts. Others have three or more contours, such as the ✍ glyph from ITC Zapf Dingbats®.

If the pixels are tiny in proportion to the outline (when resolution is high or the point size of the glyph is large), they fill out the outline smoothly, and any pixels that jut out from the contours are not noticeable. If the display device has a lower resolution or the point size is small, the pixels are large in relation to the outline. You can see in Figure 12-12 that the outline has produced an unattractive bitmap because the centers of some pixels fall on the wrong side of the contours, producing gaps and blocky areas that would not be found in the high-resolution versions of the same glyph.

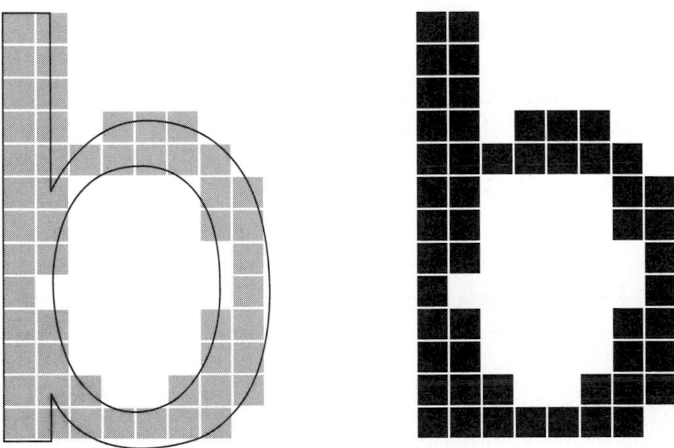

Figure 12-12. An unmodified outline glyph at a small point size

The pixels of the display device cannot change, so the outline should adapt in order to produce a better bitmap. A font manufacturer must include **instructions** in the 'sfnt' resource that indicate how to change the shape of the outline under various conditions, such as low resolution or small point size. The lowercase "b" outline in Figure 12-13 is the same one depicted in Figure 12-12, except that the Font Manager has applied the instructions to the figure and produced a better bitmapped glyph. (These instructions are to the effect of "move these points here" or "change the angle formed by these points." General-purpose applications do not need to use instructions; however, if you want to know more about them, order the *TrueType Font Format Specification* book from APDA.)

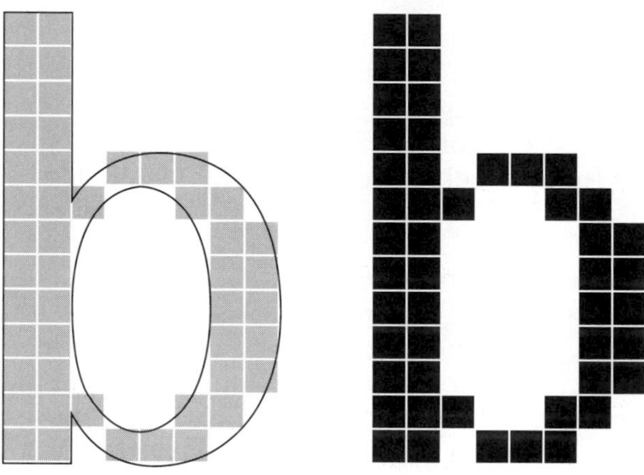

Figure 12-13. An instructed outline glyph

Once the Font Manager has produced the outline according to the design and instructions, it turns on the pixels and draws the bitmap on the screen. It then saves the bitmapped glyph in memory and uses it whenever the user requests this glyph in this font at this point size.

USING THE FONT MANAGER

This section describes how you can use fonts in general and TrueType fonts specifically. There are certain guidelines you should consider when integrating fonts into your application—for instance, how to show which point size is currently selected and how to make sure that the font used in a document is the same on different computer systems. If you want to take best advantage of TrueType fonts, your application should be aware of how TrueType glyphs may behave differently than bitmapped glyphs.

To determine whether your application can use TrueType fonts on a user's computer system, call the Gestalt function with the selector gestaltFontMgrAttr. If the Gestalt function returns noErr and bit 0 of the response (gestaltOutlineFonts) is 1, outline fonts are present in the system software. (See the Compatibility Guidelines chapter in this volume for more information on the Gestalt function.)

Adding Font Sizes and Names to the Menu

Here are some things you should do to accommodate the new font sizes:

- Support all font sizes. The 127-point size limit no longer exists for outline or bitmapped fonts and should be removed from your application. The maximum point size on the QuickDraw coordinate plane is 32,767 points.
- Provide a small list of the most useful point sizes. For the menu where your application displays font sizes, you shouldn't predefine a static list of sizes available to the user or allow the default to be every possible font size, because outline fonts can produce thousands of sizes.
- Provide a method of increasing or decreasing the point size by one point at a time. You can add a Larger or Smaller command, which makes choosing slightly different sizes for outline fonts easier for the user. Also, the user should be able to choose any possible point size at any time in a simple manner.
- Place a check next to the active size. This is how most applications now indicate the active size.
- Display available font sizes in outline style. With bitmapped fonts, the RealFont function returns TRUE if the font is available in that point size and FALSE if the font is not. However, be careful with outline fonts. The font's designer may decide that there is a lower limit to the point sizes at which the font looks acceptable. The RealFont function returns FALSE for an outline font if the size requested is smaller than this lower value.

Figure 12-14 shows one possible method of doing these things.

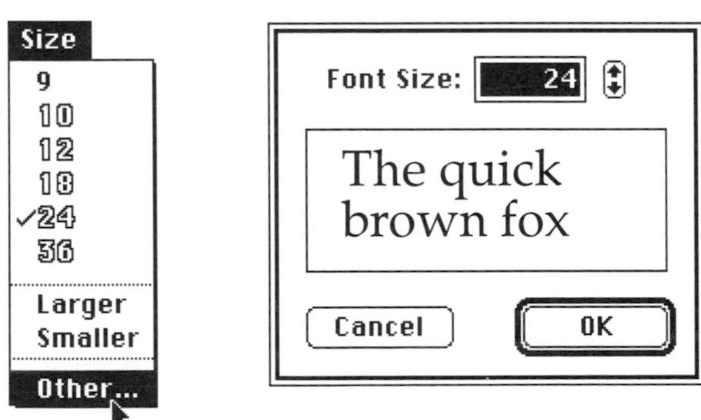

Figure 12-14. A sample Size menu and font size dialog box

Use the AddResMenu procedure to create a menu that displays font names. The AddResMenu procedure ensures that any changes to the Font Manager do not affect your application and the menu that displays font names is not dependent on how fonts are stored in your system software. The AddResMenu procedure is documented in the Menu Manager chapter of Volume I.

Storing a Font Name in a Document

One problem with identifying fonts by font family ID rather than by name is the plethora of font families for the Macintosh. Many share the same font family ID, and even though the font the user wants is present in the System file, another font with the same ID may appear in a font menu. Another problem is that one font family may have different IDs on different computer systems, so that when the application opens the document using this font family on a different computer system, it can't find the proper font, even though it is there, and substitutes another.

If you've stored the name of the font in the document, you can find its font family ID by calling GetFNum (documented in the Font Manager chapter of Volume I). However, if the font isn't present in the system software where the user opens the document, GetFNum returns 0 for the ID. Zero is also, you may remember, the system font ID. In this case you need to double-check the name of the font from the document against the name of the system font, as illustrated in Listing 12-1.

Listing 12-1. Checking a font family ID against the font name

```
FUNCTION GetFontNumber(fontName: Str255; VAR fontNum: Integer) : Boolean;
{GetFontNumber returns in the fontNum parameter the number for the font }
{ with the given font name. If there's no such font, it returns FALSE.}

VAR
   systemFontName: Str255;

BEGIN
   GetFNum(fontName, fontNum);
   IF fontNum = 0 THEN
   BEGIN
      {Either the font was not found, or it is the system font.}
      GetFontName(0, systemFontName);
      GetFontNumber := EqualString(fontName, systemFontName, FALSE,
                                   FALSE);
   END ELSE
      {If theNum was not 0, the font is available.}
      GetFontNumber := TRUE;
END;
```

Storing a font's name rather than its font family ID is a more reliable method of finding a font, because the name, unlike the font family ID, does not change from one computer system to another. You may also want to store the checksum of a font with its name, to be sure that the version of the font is the same on different computer systems.

Using TrueType Fonts in Preference to Bitmapped Fonts

If a document uses a font that is available as both a TrueType font and a bitmapped font, the default behavior of the Font Manager is to use the bitmapped font when your application opens the document. This default avoids problems with documents that were created on a computer system on which TrueType fonts were not available.

You can use the SetOutlinePreferred procedure to choose which type of font the Font Manager should use in a document. If you call SetOutlinePreferred with TRUE as the value of the outlinePreferred parameter, the Font Manager chooses TrueType fonts over bitmapped fonts. The GetOutlinePreferred function returns the setting that indicates whether the Font Manager prefers TrueType fonts, and you should save the setting with the current document. When the user opens the document, call SetOutlinePreferred with this value so that your application chooses the proper fonts.

If only one type of font is available, the Font Manager chooses that type of font to use in the document, no matter which type of font is preferred.

Preserving the Glyph's Shape

Most glyphs in an alphabetic font fit between the ascent line and the descent line, which roughly mark (respectively) the tops of the uppercase letters and the bottoms of the descenders. One aim of outline fonts is to provide glyphs that are more accurate renditions of the original typeface design, and there are glyphs in some typefaces that exceed the ascent or descent line (or both). An example of this type of glyph is an uppercase letter with an accent on it: "N" with a tilde produces "Ñ". Your application should preserve the original shape of a glyph, because many languages use glyphs that extend beyond the ascent line or descent line.

However, these glyphs may disturb the line spacing in a line or a paragraph. The glyph that exceeds the ascent line on one line may cross the descent line of the line above it, where it may overwrite a glyph that has a descender. You can determine if there are outline glyphs that exceed the ascent and descent lines by using the OutlineMetrics function. OutlineMetrics returns the maximum and minimum y-values for whatever glyphs you choose. You can get the values of the ascent and descent lines using the GetFontInfo function or FontMetrics function. If a glyph's maximum or minimum y-values are greater than, respectively, the ascent or descent lines, you can opt for one of two paths of action: you can change the height of the glyph, or you can change the line spacing to accommodate the glyph.

The Font Manager's default behavior is to change the height of the glyph, so as to provide compatibility with bitmapped fonts, which are scaled between the ascent and descent lines. Figure 12-15 shows the difference between an "Ñ" scaled to fit in the same amount of space as an "N" and another, well-formed "Ñ". The tilde on the preserved "Ñ" clearly exceeds the ascent line.

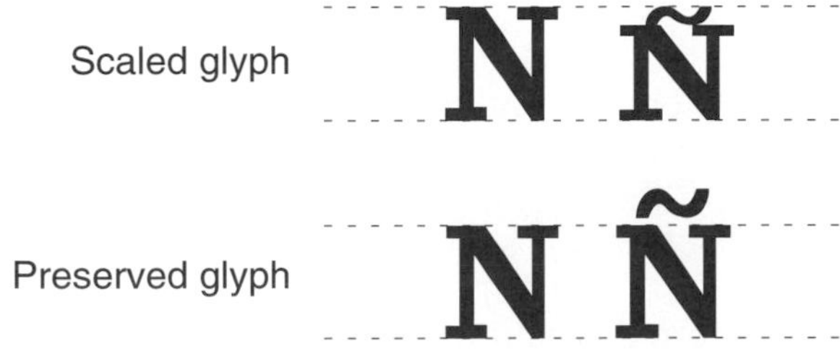

Figure 12-15. The difference between a scaled glyph and a preserved glyph

You can use the SetPreserveGlyph procedure to preserve the original shape of the glyph. If you call SetPreserveGlyph with TRUE as the value of the preserveGlyph parameter, the Font Manager keeps the shape of the glyph intended by the font's designer. The GetPreserveGlyph function returns a setting that indicates whether the Font Manager maintains the form of TrueType glyphs, and you should save the setting with the current document. When the user opens the document, call SetPreserveGlyph with this value so that the Font Manager scales the glyphs appropriately.

FONT MANAGER ROUTINES

The Font Manager has routines that deal specifically with TrueType fonts. You can use these routines to choose TrueType fonts over bitmapped fonts, or to determine which type of font the current grafPort record uses. You can find out the exact measurements of a TrueType glyph. If the size of a TrueType glyph interferes with the line spacing in a document, you can use the Font Manager to scale the glyph to the same size as other glyphs on the line. If your application is a font editor or otherwise needs to manipulate the 'sfnt' resource, you may need a routine to erase the Font Manager's memory caches.

Choosing TrueType Fonts Over Bitmapped Fonts

You can use the SetOutlinePreferred, GetOutlinePreferred, and IsOutline routines to use TrueType fonts instead of bitmapped fonts when both are available or to determine which type of font is being used in a document.

You can use the SetOutlinePreferred procedure to cause the Font Manager to prefer TrueType fonts over bitmapped fonts.

```
PROCEDURE SetOutlinePreferred (outlinePreferred: Boolean);
```

If a TrueType font and a bitmapped font are available for a font request, the default behavior for the Font Manager is to choose the bitmapped font, in order to maintain compatibility with documents that were created on computer systems on which TrueType fonts were not available. The SetOutlinePreferred procedure sets the preference of which type of font to use in this situation.

If you want the Font Manager to choose outline fonts over any bitmapped font counterparts, set the outlinePreferred parameter to TRUE. If only outline fonts are available and outlinePreferred is set to FALSE, the outline font is chosen regardless. If only bitmapped fonts are available and outlinePreferred is set to TRUE, the bitmapped font is still chosen.

You can use the GetOutlinePreferred function to determine whether or not TrueType fonts are preferred over bitmapped fonts.

```
FUNCTION GetOutlinePreferred : Boolean;
```

If both types of fonts are available for a particular font request, the GetOutlinePreferred function returns a Boolean value indicating whether the Font Manager chooses TrueType fonts over bitmapped fonts. By default, the Font Manager prefers to use bitmapped fonts, for which the GetOutlinePreferred function returns FALSE; you can also set the behavior of the Font Manager with the SetOutlinePreferred procedure.

You can use the IsOutline function to find out whether the current grafPort uses a TrueType font.

```
FUNCTION IsOutline (numer: Point; denom: Point) : Boolean;
```

The IsOutline function returns TRUE if the Font Manager, after applying the font scaling factors in the numer and denom parameters to the font named by the current grafPort, would choose an outline font for the grafPort. The current setting of whether TrueType or bitmapped fonts are preferred may also affect what IsOutline returns. Use the GetOutlinePreferred function to find out what the current setting is.

The numer and denom parameters are of type Point, and each contains two integers—the first is the numerator or denominator of the ratio for vertical scaling; the second is the numerator or denominator of the ratio for horizontal scaling. The Font Manager applies the font scaling factors to the font used in the current grafPort in order to calculate the measurements for the glyphs in the block of text.

Scaling Fonts

You can use the OutlineMetrics function to determine the measurements, such as heights or advance widths, of the glyphs in any line of text you choose. On the basis of these measurements, you can decide whether to use SetPreserveGlyph to keep the original sizes of the glyphs. The GetPreserveGlyph function tells you whether the glyphs in the current grafPort record are scaled.

```
FUNCTION OutlineMetrics (byteCount: Integer; textPtr: Ptr; numer: Point;
                          denom: Point; VAR yMax: Integer; VAR yMin:
                          Integer; awArray: FixedPtr; lsbArray: FixedPtr;
                          boundsArray: RectPtr) : OSErr;
```

The OutlineMetrics function takes a block of text you provide and returns the maximum y-value, minimum y-value, advance widths, left-side bearings, and bounding boxes for this text only in the current font, point size, and font style. (For definitions of these terms, see "Font Measurements" earlier in this chapter.) You can use these measurements when laying out text. You may need to adjust line spacing to accommodate exceptionally large glyphs. OutlineMetrics works on TrueType fonts only.

Parameter descriptions

byteCount	The number of bytes on which you want the OutlineMetrics function to work.
textPtr	The pointer to the block of text you are providing to OutlineMetrics.

numer — The numerators of the vertical and horizontal scaling factors. The numer parameter is of type Point, and contains two integers—the first is the numerator of the ratio for vertical scaling; the second is the numerator of the ratio for horizontal scaling. The Font Manager applies the font scaling factors to the font used in the current grafPort in order to calculate the measurements for the glyphs in the block of text.

denom — Thc dcnominators of the vertical and horizontal scaling factors. The denom parameter is of type Point, and contains two integers—the first is the denominator of the ratio for vertical scaling; the second is the denominator of the ratio for horizontal scaling. The Font Manager applies the font scaling factors to the font used in the current grafPort in order to calculate the measurements for the glyphs in the block of text.

yMax — The maximum y-value for the text. Pass NULL in this parameter if you don't want this value returned.

yMin — The minimum y-value for the text. Pass NULL in this parameter if you don't want this value returned.

awArray — A pointer to an array of the advance width measurements for the glyphs being considered. These measurements are in pixels, based on the point size and font scaling factors of the font used by the current grafPort record. The number of entries in the array is given by the byteCount parameter.

The awArray parameter is of type FixedPtr. The FixedPtr data type is a pointer to an array, and each entry in the array is of type Fixed, which is 4 bytes in length. Multiply byteCount by 4 to calculate the memory you need in bytes. Allocate the memory needed for the array and pass a pointer to the array in the awArray parameter.

If the FractEnable global variable has been set to TRUE using the SetFractEnable procedure, the values in awArray have fractional character widths. If FractEnable has been set to FALSE, the Font Manager returns integers for the advance widths, with 0 in the decimal part of the values. The SetFractEnable procedure is discussed in the Font Manager chapter of Volume IV.

Pass a NIL in this parameter if you don't want the advance width values returned.

lsbArray — A pointer to an array of the left-side bearing measurements for the glyphs being considered. The measurements are in pixels, based on the point size of the font used by the current grafPort record. The number of entries in the array is given by the byteCount parameter.

The lsbArray parameter is of type FixedPtr. The FixedPtr data type is a pointer to an array, and each entry in the array is of type Fixed, which is 4 bytes in length. Multiply byteCount by 4 to calculate the memory you need in bytes. Allocate the memory needed for the array and pass a pointer to the array in the lsbArray parameter. The left-side bearing values are never rounded.

Pass a NIL in this parameter if you don't want the left-side bearing values returned.

boundsArray — A pointer to the array of bounding boxes for the glyphs being considered. Bounding boxes are the smallest rectangles that fit around the pixels of the glyph. The bounding box measurements returned by OutlineMetrics may be slightly larger than the those for the actual glyph. The number of entries in the array is given by the byteCount parameter.

The boundsArray parameter is of type RectPtr. The RectPtr data type is a pointer to QuickDraw's Rect data type, which is 8 bytes in length. Multiply byteCount by 8 to calculate the memory you need in bytes. Allocate the memory needed for the array and pass a pointer to the array in the boundsArray parameter.

Pass a NIL in this parameter if you don't want the bounding box values returned.

The SetPreserveGlyph procedure tells the Font Manager whether to preserve the original shape of an outline glyph, which in some cases may exceed the ascent or descent lines.

```
PROCEDURE SetPreserveGlyph (preserveGlyph: Boolean);
```

The default behavior for the Font Manager is to scale a glyph so that it fits between the ascent and descent lines; however, this alters the look of the glyph. If you set the preserveGlyph parameter in the SetPreserveGlyph procedure to TRUE, the measurements of all glyphs are preserved, and your application may have to alter the leading between lines in a document if some of these glyphs extend beyond the ascent or descent lines. If you set preserveGlyph to FALSE, all glyphs are scaled to fit between the ascent and descent lines.

Save the setting of whether glyphs are preserved or not and call SetPreserveGlyph with this value as the parameter every time the user opens the application.

The GetPreserveGlyph function returns a Boolean value indicating whether the Font Manager preserves the shape of TrueType glyphs, which by default is FALSE. Your application can set the behavior of the Font Manager using the SetPreserveGlyph procedure.

```
FUNCTION GetPreserveGlyph : Boolean;
```

Erasing the Font Manager's Memory Caches

You can use the FlushFonts function to clear the Font Manager's memory.

```
FUNCTION FlushFonts : OSErr;
```

The FlushFonts function erases all of the Font Manager's memory caches. Your application doesn't need this function unless it directly manipulates data in the 'sfnt' resource. Font Manager caches include the width tables, the bitmaps created from the outlines of the 'sfnt' resource, the outlines, and a small cache of 'FOND' resources that have been read into memory.

SUMMARY OF THE FONT MANAGER

Constants

```
CONST gestaltFontMgrAttr      = 'font';       {Gestalt selector}
      gestaltOutlineFonts     = 0;            {TRUE if outline fonts are }
                                              { present}
```

Routines

Choosing TrueType Fonts Over Bitmapped Fonts

```
PROCEDURE SetOutlinePreferred (outlinePreferred: Boolean);

FUNCTION GetOutlinePreferred  : Boolean;

FUNCTION IsOutline             (numer: Point; denom: Point) : Boolean;
```

Scaling Fonts

```
FUNCTION OutlineMetrics      (byteCount: Integer; textPtr: Ptr;
                              numer: Point; denom: Point; VAR yMax:
                              Integer; VAR yMin: Integer; awArray:
                              FixedPtr; lsbArray: FixedPtr; boundsArray:
                              RectPtr) : OSErr;

PROCEDURE SetPreserveGlyph   (preserveGlyph: Boolean);

FUNCTION GetPreserveGlyph    : Boolean;
```

Erasing the Font Manager's Memory Caches

```
FUNCTION FlushFonts         : OSErr;
```

13 THE RESOURCE MANAGER

ABOUT THIS CHAPTER

This chapter describes changes to the Resource Manager, the resource types that are available for your application's use, and the new technique for reading or writing part of a resource instead of an entire resource. This chapter also lists the standard resource types found in the System file in system software version 7.0.

The ability to use partial resources is available only in version 7.0. To check for the existence of the new partial resource routines, use the Gestalt function.

You need the information in this chapter if you want your application to take advantage of partial resources or to create or open resource files. This chapter also provides resource ID ranges for definition procedures, font families, and scripts, and it lists the system icons and packages that are available in system software version 7.0.

The information in this chapter supplements chapters on the Resource Manager in Volumes I, IV, and V.

RESOURCES

A resource consists of data or code stored in a resource file. A resource fork is the part of a file that contains data used by an application, such as menus, fonts, and icons. An executable file's code is also stored in the resource fork. The Resource Manager distinguishes resources by their resource types and resource IDs. The resource type is always a sequence of four alphanumeric characters (including the space character). For instance, 'MENU' is the resource type for a menu. A resource ID is a number that, together with the resource type, uniquely identifies a particular resource. Resources can be created from textual descriptions by resource compilers, such as the Rez compiler in the Macintosh Programmer's Workshop (MPW®).

> **Note:** Your application should not depend on any specific resource being in ROM or in the System file. The resource types available in ROM vary. A resource that *is* in ROM may not be available because the System file may override any resource in ROM, making it unavailable or replacing it with a resource from the System file.

Resource Types

A resource type can be any sequence of four alphanumeric characters, including the space character. You can create resource types for your applications, provided the type names you choose consist of all uppercase letters and do not conflict with the resource types already created. Apple Computer, Inc., reserves any other combination. (The standard Roman character set can be found in the Font Manager chapter of this volume.)

The System file contains system resources, the standard resources for the Macintosh® computer that are shared by all applications. Table 13-1 lists all the resource types in the System file that your application can use. Uppercase resource types are listed first.

Table 13-1. Resource types available for your application's use

Resource type	Description
'ADBS'	Apple Desktop Bus™ service routine
'ALRT'	Alert box template
'BNDL'	Bundle
'CDEF'	Control definition function
'CNTL'	Control template
'CODE'	Application code segment
'CURS'	Cursor
'DITL'	Item list in a dialog or alert box
'DLOG'	Dialog box template
'DRVR'	Desk accessory or other device driver
'FKEY'	Command-Shift-number combination
'FOND'	Font family record
'FONT'	Bitmapped font
'FREF'	File reference
'ICN#'	List of 32-by-32 pixel (large) black-and-white icons, with mask
'ICON'	Icon
'INIT'	System extension
'KCAP'	Physical keyboard description (used by Key Caps desk accessory)
'KCHR'	Keyboard layout (software); maps virtual keycodes to character codes
'LDEF'	List definition procedure
'MBAR'	Menu bar
'MDEF'	Menu definition procedure
'MENU'	Menu
'NFNT'	Bitmapped font
'PACK'	Package
'PAT '	Pattern
'PAT#'	Pattern list
'PICT'	QuickDraw™ picture
'POST'	PostScript® resource
'PREC'	Print record
'SICN'	16-by-16 pixel (small) icon and mask
'SIZE'	Size of application's partition and other information
'STR '	String
'STR#'	String list
'WDEF'	Window definition function
'WIND'	Window template
'actb'	Alert box color table
'alis'	Alias record
'card'	Video card name
'cctb'	Control color table
'cicn'	Color icon
'clut'	Color look-up table
'crsr'	Color cursor
'dctb'	Dialog box color table

Table 13-1. Resource types available for your application's use (Continued)

Resource type	Description
'ddev'	Database extension
'eadr'	Ethernet hardware address
'fctb'	Font color table
'hdlg'	Help for dialog box or alert box items
'hfdr'	Help for application icons
'hmnu'	Help for application menus
'hovr'	Help that overrides Finder™ help
'hrct'	Help for areas in windows
'hwin'	Association of 'hrct' and 'hdlg' resources to specific windows
'icl4'	Large icon, 4-bit color
'icl8'	Large icon, 8-bit color
'ics#'	List of 16-by-16 pixel (small) black-and-white icons, with mask
'ics4'	Small icon, 4-bit color
'ics8'	Small icon, 8-bit color
'ictb'	Color table dialog item
'itl0'	Date and time formats
'itl1'	Names of days and months
'itl2'	International Utilities Package sort hooks
'itl4'	Localizable tables and code
'itlk'	Remappings of certain key combinations before KeyTrans function is called for the corresponding 'KCHR' resource
'kcs#'	List of small black-and-white icons, with mask, for a corresponding 'KCHR' resource
'kcs4'	Small icon, 4-bit color, for a corresponding 'KCHR' resource
'kcs8'	Small icon, 8-bit color, for a corresponding 'KCHR' resource
'mctb'	Menu color information table
'mntr'	Monitors control pancl
'pltt'	Color palette
'ppat'	Pixel pattern
'qdef'	Query definition function
'qrsc'	Query resource
'sect'	Section record
'sfnt'	Outline font
'snd '	Sound
'snth'	Synthesizer or modifier
'sysz'	System heap space required by a system extension
'vers'	Version number of the system software
'wctb'	Window color table
'wstr'	String (uses word for length byte)

Table 13-2 lists resource types that are reserved for the Operating System's use only. These resource types consist entirely of uppercase letters or combinations of uppercase and lowercase letters and the number sign (#). Other resource types specific to the Operating System that consist entirely of lowercase letters or other characters are not included in Table 13-2. This list is provided for your information; you should not use these resource types in your application.

Table 13-2. Resource types reserved for the Operating System's use

Resource type	Description
'CACH'	RAM cache code
'DSAT'	System startup alert table
'FCMT'	"Get Info" comments
'FMTR'	3.5-inch disk formatting code
'FOBJ'	Folder information for an MFS volume
'FRSV'	IDs of system fonts
'INTL'	International resource (obsolete)
'KMAP'	Keyboard mapping (hardware); maps raw keycodes to virtual keycodes
'KSWP'	Defines special key combinations for Script Manager operations
'MBDF'	Default menu definition procedure
'MMAP'	Mouse-tracking code
'NBPC'	AppleTalk® bundle
'PDEF'	Printing code
'PTCH'	ROM patch code
'ROv#'	List of ROM resources to override
'ROvr'	Code for overriding ROM resources
'SERD'	RAM Serial Driver

Resource IDs

To prevent conflicts, the IDs for resources used by the Operating System and those used by applications are assigned from separate ranges. If you use these ranges correctly, your application's resources are guaranteed not to conflict with system resources and to be compatible with future system resources.

System resources use IDs in the range –32768 through 127, and application resource IDs must fall between 128 and 32767. Some categories of resources, such as definition procedures and font families, have different ID ranges available or are broken down into structured ranges. This list shows a breakdown of the ID ranges used for most resources.

Range	Description
–32768 through –16385	Reserved; do not use. Any application resource whose ID is in this range will not work properly in current versions of system software.
–16384 through –4065	Used for system resources owned by other system resources.
–4064 through –4033	Reserved for use by control panels. (See the Control Panels chapter in Volume V.)
–4032 through –1	Used for system resources owned by other system resources. The exception is the 'SIZE' resource, whose ID is always –1.

Range	Description
0 through 127	Used for system resources and any definition procedures in the system software. Applications should not use these resource IDs.
128 through 32767	Available for your use. Your application's definition procedures should use IDs in the range 128 through 4095, although other resources may use these IDs as well. Font families and scripts have additional restrictions defined in "Font Families and Scripts" later in this chapter.

Definition Procedures

Definition procedures (which are usually contained in resources such as the 'WDEF' or 'CDEF' resources) have an ID range limited to 12 bits (0 through 4095). The system software's own definition procedures, which are located in the System file, have resource IDs from 0 through 127. Your definition procedures should have IDs in the range 128 through 4095.

Font Families and Scripts

A **font family** is a set of fonts in one typeface design, including different font styles and sizes in that typeface. For example, the Geneva font family may include an outline font in plain style and bitmapped fonts in various point sizes and in italic, bold, shadow, or other styles. (For more information about outline and bitmapped fonts, see the Font Manager chapter in this volume.)

At present a font family is exclusively identified by the 'FOND' resource. This resource groups fonts using a font association table, which contains a word to hold each font's point size, a word for its style, and a word for its associated 'FONT', 'NFNT', or 'sfnt' resource ID. (If the size entry in the table is 0, the resource ID is for an 'sfnt' resource. System software version 7.0 does not recognize a 'FONT' or 'NFNT' resource with its size set to 0, and your application should not depend on finding these resources.) For font family resources, Apple reserves resource IDs 0 through 1023 and 16000 through 16383. (The font association table is described in the Font Manager chapter of Volume IV.)

> **Note:** When the Macintosh computer was first introduced, prior to the introduction of the 'FOND' resource, fonts were grouped into font families by storing the family ID in bits 7 through 14 of the font's resource ID. (The font's point size was stored in bits 0 through 6.) The font family was named by including a 'FONT' resource with a point size of 0. Since the font family ID had to fit into 8 bits, the range of numbers available was only 0 through 255; 0 through 127 were reserved for Apple, and 128 through 255 were available for third-party developers. Font families identified using this method are still recognized by the Operating System, but you should not use these IDs or this method of identification.

Scripts are writing systems (such as Roman, Japanese, and Arabic) that are used to represent human languages. Script systems include character sets, fonts, keyboards, and resources that determine text collation and word breaks. Scripts may differ in terms of the direction in which their characters and lines run, the size of the character set used to represent the script, and the context sensitivity of the script.

The Roman script system (used by English and many European languages) has the largest number of font families available. It uses font family IDs between 2 and 16383. The following list shows the defined ID ranges for the font families associated with Roman script systems. (The other resources associated with a script, such as 'itl0', 'itl1', 'itl2', 'itl4', 'KCHR', 'itlk', 'kcs#', 'kcs4', and 'kcs8' resources, have resource IDs in the same range as the 'FOND' IDs for that script. For more information on script systems, resources such as 'itl0' or 'KCHR', and developing software for worldwide markets, see the Worldwide Software Overview chapter in this volume. Note that the 'INTL' resource is obsolete and you should use the most appropriate currently valid resource, such as 'itl0', 'itl1', or 'itl2'.)

Range	Description
0	System font. This is reserved in any script system. The Operating System may map any font family from any script system to this ID.
1	Application font. This is reserved in any script system. The Operating System may map any font family from any script system to this ID.
2 through 255	Font families for the Roman script system that were named using the method described in the Font Manager chapter of Volume I. Do not continue to use these IDs. Note that Apple's system fonts (Chicago, Geneva, New York, and so on) always retain their old font family IDs.
256 through 1023	Reserved numbers. These numbers should be thought of as reserved space that the Operating System can use to resolve past and future font family ID conflicts. Numbers in this range should not be used as a font family's original resource ID.
1024 through 3071	Noncommercial and public domain font families.
3072 through 15999	Commercial font manufacturers' font families.
16000 through 16383	Reserved.

The next list shows the script code and the range of font family IDs assigned to each script system on the Macintosh computer. Non-Roman scripts use font family IDs in the range 16384 through 32767 and in the range –28672 through –24577, and each non-Roman script has a total of 512 font family IDs available. Script codes 33 through 40 are invalid and should not be used.

Script system	Script code	Font family IDs
[System reserved]	Any	0 through 1
Roman	0	2 through 16383
Japanese	1	16384 through 16895
Traditional Chinese	2	16896 through 17407

Script system	Script code	Font family IDs
Korean	3	17408 through 17919
Arabic	4	17920 through 18431
Hebrew	5	18432 through 18943
Greek	6	18944 through 19455
Cyrillic	7	19456 through 19967
Uninterpreted right-to-left symbols	8	19968 through 20479
Devanagari	9	20480 through 20991
Gurmukhi	10	20992 through 21503
Gujarati	11	21504 through 22015
Oriya	12	22016 through 22527
Bengali	13	22528 through 23039
Tamil	14	23040 through 23551
Telugu	15	23552 through 24063
Kannada	16	24064 through 24575
Malayalam	17	24576 through 25087
Sinhalese	18	25088 through 25599
Burmese	19	25600 through 26111
Cambodian	20	26112 through 26623
Thai	21	26624 through 27135
Laotian	22	27136 through 27647
Georgian	23	27648 through 28159
Armenian	24	28160 through 28671
Simplified Chinese	25	28672 through 29183
Tibetan	26	29184 through 29695
Mongolian	27	29696 through 30207
Ethiopian	28	30208 through 30719
Extended Roman for Slavic/Baltic	29	30720 through 31231
Vietnamese	30	31232 through 31743
Extended Arabic (for Sindhi, etc.)	31	31744 through 32255
Uninterpreted left-to-right symbols	32	32256 through 32767
Reserved	41	–28672 through –28161
Reserved	42	–28160 through –27649
Reserved	43	–27648 through –27137
Reserved	44	–27136 through –26625
Reserved	45	–26624 through –26113
Reserved	46	–26112 through –25601
Reserved	47	–25600 through –25089
Reserved	48	–25088 through –24577

For every script, the Operating System always maps the correct system font to ID 0 and the correct application font to ID 1. (In a Roman script system, Chicago is the system font and Geneva is the application font. This is not the case in any non-Roman script system.)

Apple has created a pseudo-script at script code 32, called smUninterp, which provides a range of IDs (32256 through 32767) that you can use to identify fonts that are used as tools in your application. (For example, the MacPaint® drawing program uses a special font for its palette symbols.) If the glyphs in such a font should be handled as right-to-left glyphs instead of left-to-right glyphs, use the pseudo-script smRSymbol instead. This pseudo-script, at script code 8, has a font family ID range of 19928 through 20479.

RESOURCES IN THE SYSTEM FILE

The System file contains resources that are shared by all applications and used by the User Interface Toolbox and Operating System as well.

▲ **Warning:** Your application should not directly add resources to, delete resources from, or modify resources in the System file. ▲

If your application needs to install drivers, you should ship it with the Installer and an Installer script for drivers. In order to distribute the Installer, you need to license the Apple® system software, which includes the Installer.

In system software version 7.0, resources such as fonts, scripts, keyboards, and sounds are added to the System file when the user drags their icons to the System Folder. Desk accessories and resources such as system extensions are now stored in the subdirectories of the System Folder, not in the System file. (See the Finder Interface chapter in this volume for details.) These resources and others, such as the folders found in the System Folder, are represented by system icons. You can use these system icons in your application.

The System file also contains resources that convey information specific to the current computer on which your application is running, such as the user's name, the computer's name, or the current printer. You call the Gestalt function to obtain this information.

Some routines in the system software are located in packages inside the System file. A complete list of packages is provided. The change in behavior of a particular function key resource is also discussed.

System Icons

The Operating System uses system icons to represent documents, applications, folders, disks, and other elements of the Macintosh interface. These are commonly known as "Finder icons," but they are stored in the System file. You can design your own icons for many of these icons, but if you do not include a customized icon, your application can display the appropriate system icon by calling the GetResource function. It is recommended that you refer to the system icons by their constant names and not by resource ID. The GetResource function is documented in the Resource Manager chapter of Volume I.

Most icons are available in at least two sizes: large (32-by-32 pixels) and small (16-by-16 pixels). They are also available in three bit depths: 8-bit color, 4-bit color, and black and white. An icon family consists of the large and small icons for an object, each with a mask, and each available in the three different color depths. See the User Interface Guidelines chapter in this volume for more information on the proper design of system icons. See the Finder Interface chapter in this volume for information on how to create your own icons for your application.

Many of the system icons are also available in a tiny (12-by-12 pixels) size, represented by the 'SICN' resource, used primarily by the standard file dialog boxes. Tiny icons are also used in windows in the Finder that display the contents of disks or folders by name, date, size, or kind. The Views control panel in version 7.0 allows the user to choose large, small, or tiny icons for these windows. (The standard file dialog boxes use only the tiny icons.) You cannot design customized icons in the tiny size.

Document and Application Icons

These icons represent documents, including special classes of documents such as stationery, and applications and desk accessories. You can include customized versions of the icons in this section with your documents and applications. There are icon families and 'SICN' resources for all of these icons, unless otherwise noted.

Constant name and icon	Resource ID	Description
genericQueryDocumentIconResource	–16506	The default query document icon. This is the document used by the Data Access Manager for database queries. There is no tiny size for this icon.
genericExtensionIconResource	–16415	The default extension icon. The Finder displays this icon for any extension that does not have a customized icon. Extension files appear in the Extensions folder, which is located inside the System Folder.
genericDocumentIconResource	–4000	The default document icon. The Finder displays this icon if your application does not have a customized document icon.
genericApplicationIconResource	–3996	The default application icon. The Finder displays this icon for any application that does not have a customized icon.
genericDeskAccessoryIconResource	–3991	The default desk accessory icon. In version 7.0 desk accessories are represented on the desktop like applications, each with its own icon. The Finder displays this icon for any desk accessory that does not have a customized icon.
genericEditionFileIconResource	–3989	The default edition file icon. This is the intermediary file used by the Edition Manager. (See the Edition Manager chapter in this volume.)
genericStationeryIconResource	–3985	The default stationery file icon. Applications can use this file as stationery. (See the Finder Interface chapter in this volume.)
genericPreferencesIconResource	–3971	The default preference file icon. Preference files appear in the Preferences folder, which is located inside the System Folder. There is no tiny size for this icon.

Folder Icons

These icons represent the different types of folders found on the desktop. There are icon families and 'SICN' resources for all of these icons, unless otherwise noted.

Constant name and icon	Resource ID	Description
genericFolderIconResource 	–3999	The default folder icon. This is the folder seen on the desktop.
privateFolderIconResource 	–3994	The icon for a folder to which the user does not have access. It is dimmed and has a distinctly marked border. The Finder displays an alert box when a user without privileges attempts to open this folder.
ownedFolderIconResource 	–3980	The icon for a folder that is owned by a particular user, usually on a shared volume like a file server. There is no tiny size for this icon.
dropFolderIconResource 	–3979	The icon for a folder in which any user may store documents, applications, and so on, but from which only a specified group of users can retrieve the contents. There is no tiny size for this icon.
sharedFolderIconResource 	–3978	The icon for a folder that the owner has made available for file sharing. There is no tiny size for this icon.
mountedFolderIconResource 	–3977	The icon for a folder that a guest has mounted on a remote volume. This icon appears only for the guest. There is no tiny size for this icon.

System Folder Icons

These icons represent the different types of folders found in the System Folder. You should not alter the appearance of these icons. There are icon families only for these icons, unless otherwise noted.

Constant name and icon	Resource ID	Description
systemFolderIconResource 	–3983	The System Folder icon. This folder contains the System file and other system-related folders.

Constant name and icon	Resource ID	Description
appleMenuFolderIconResource	–3982	The Apple Menu Items folder icon. This folder contains items found in the Apple menu.
startupFolderIconResource	–3981	The Startup Items folder icon. This folder contains documents, aliases, applications, and other objects that open when the computer starts up.
controlPanelFolderIconResource	–3976	The Control Panels folder icon. This folder contains control panels.
printMonitorFolderIconResource	–3975	The PrintMonitor Documents folder icon. This folder contains documents that are in the queue to be printed.
preferencesFolderIconResource	–3974	The Preferences folder icon. This folder contains preference files for the Finder and other software that needs to remember user preferences.
extensionsFolderIconResource	–3973	The Extensions folder icon. This folder contains extensions to the System file, the Chooser, a network, a database, and so on. (See "Terminology" in the User Interface Guidelines chapter in this volume for examples of extensions.)

Desktop Icons

These icons appear on the desktop. The standard file dialog boxes use these icons in tiny size. There are icon families and 'SICN' resources for these icons, unless otherwise noted.

Constant Name and icon	Resource ID	Description
floppyIconResource	–3998	The default icon for a 3.5-inch disk.
trashIconResource	–3993	The default empty Trash icon. The Standard File Package also uses this icon to represent the Trash.
fullTrashIconResource	–3984	The default full Trash icon, with bulging midsection. This represents the Trash when full. There is no tiny size for this icon.

Standard File Package Icons

These icons are used only by the Standard File Package and appear only in the tiny icon size, unless noted otherwise. You can't design customized icons in the tiny size. The pop-up menu in the standard file dialog box indicates where the list of files shown in the dialog box is located (whether on the desktop, at the top level of a volume, or inside a series of folders on a volume).

Constant name and icon	Resource ID	Description
openFolderIconResource	–3997	The open folder icon, which appears in a pop-up menu only. The standard file dialog boxes display this icon to indicate which folder is currently open.
genericHardDiskIconResource	–3995	The hard disk icon, which appears in a pop-up menu only. The same icon is used to represent internal and external disks. A different icon may appear on the desktop, because the manufacturer of the hard disk can design a special icon for a particular volume.
desktopIconResource	–3992	The desktop icon, which appears in a pop-up menu only. The standard file dialog boxes display this icon to indicate which files and folders are available on the desktop. In addition to the 'SICN' resource, there is also an icon family without an 'ICN#' resource for this icon.
genericFileServerIconResource	–3972	The file server volume icon. This represents any servers open on the desktop. A different icon may appear on the desktop, because the manufacturer can design a special icon for a particular server.
genericSuitcaseIconResource	–3970	The suitcase icon. This represents any suitcase, such as font suitcases or desk accessory suitcases. There are different icons for these suitcases in larger sizes, depending on the contents.
genericMoverObjectIconResource	–3969	The icon for any object that you can move into the System file. These objects include fonts, scripts, keyboards, sounds, and so on.

User Information Resources

There are resources in the System file that detail the user's name, the computer's name, the model of computer, the icon for that particular computer, and the current printer the computer uses.

Information	**Description**
User name	The name of the person who "owns" the machine or is the current user. This is stored in the System file as a 'STR ' resource with resource ID –16096. Use the GetString function to return the user name.
Computer name	The name of the computer, which is now distinct from the user name. It is also distinct from any internal hard disks that may be present. The computer name is stored in the System file as a 'STR ' resource with resource ID –16413. The default name of the computer is "*User name*'s Macintosh." Use the GetString function to return the computer name.
Computer model	The model of the computer, such as Macintosh SE/30 or Macintosh IIci. The computer model is stored in the System file as a 'STR#' resource with resource ID –16395. The Gestalt selector for the computer model is gestaltMachineModel, and the Gestalt function returns a response value for this selector. Use this value as an index into the 'STR#' resource, using the GetIndString procedure. You should never use the model of computer as an indication of what software features or hardware may be available.
Computer icon	The icon for the computer model, such as the Macintosh II or Macintosh IIci. The icons for computers are stored in icon families. The Gestalt selector for the computer icon is gestaltMachineIcon. Use the response value for this selector as the resource ID of the icon resource you want. (For more information about icon families, see the Finder Interface chapter in this volume.)
Printer type	The type of printer to which the computer sends documents, such as a LaserWriter® printer. There is no method for retrieving the name of the printer. The printer type is stored in the System file as a 'STR ' resource with resource ID –8192. Use the GetString function to return the type of printer.

The GetString function and GetIndString procedure are documented in the Toolbox Utilities chapter of Volume I. The Gestalt function is documented in the Compatibility Guidelines chapter of this volume.

Packages

A package is a set of routines and data types that forms a part of the Toolbox or Operating System and is stored as a resource. On the original Macintosh computer, all packages were disk-based and brought into memory only when needed; some packages are now in ROM.

The System file contains the standard Macintosh packages and the resources they use or own.

Package name	Resource ID
List Manager Package	0
Disk Initialization Package	2
Standard File Package	3
Floating-Point Arithmetic Package	4
Transcendental Functions Package	5
International Utilities Package	6
Binary-Decimal Conversion Package	7
Apple Event Manager	8
PPC Browser	9
Edition Manager	11
Color Picker Package	12
Data Access Manager	13
Help Manager	14
Picture Utilities Package	15

Function Key Resources

Function key resources (of the 'FKEY' resource type) are Command-Shift-number key combinations that are captured and processed by the WaitNextEvent function. The screen utility resource 'FKEY' 3 now produces a screen shot, contained in a 'PICT' file, when the user presses Command-Shift-3. 'FKEY' resource IDs 0 through 2 and 4 through 9 are reserved for future use by Apple. The WaitNextEvent function is described in the Event Manager chapter of this volume.

USING THE RESOURCE MANAGER

The Resource Manager in version 7.0 allows you to read a portion of a resource into memory or write a block of data to a resource stored on disk, even if the size of the memory you have to work in is smaller than the entire resource. You can also change the size of a resource on disk.

Using Partial Resources

Some resources, such as the 'snd ' and 'sfnt' resources, can be quite large—larger, in fact, than the memory available. The partial resource routines in version 7.0 allow you to read a portion of the resource into memory or alter a section of the resource while it is still on disk. You can also enlarge or reduce the size of a resource on disk. The ReadPartialResource procedure reads a portion of a resource from disk into memory, and the WritePartialResource procedure writes a portion of data to a resource on disk. You can also change the size of the resource on disk to any desired size, using the SetResourceSize procedure. When you use the partial resource routines, you specify how far into the resource you want to begin reading or writing and how many bytes you actually want to read or write at that spot, so you must be sure of the location of the data.

▲ **Warning:** Be aware that having a copy of a resource in memory when you are using the partial resource routines may cause problems. If you have modified the copy in memory and then access the resource on disk using either the ReadPartialResource or WritePartialResource procedure, you will lose changes made to the copy in memory. ▲

To read or write any part of a resource, call the SetResLoad procedure specifying FALSE for its load parameter, and then use the GetResource function to get an empty handle to the resource. (Because of the call to the SetResLoad procedure, the GetResource function does not load the entire resource into memory.) Use the ResError function to check for errors. (The SetResLoad procedure, the GetResource function, and the ResError function are described in the Resource Manager chapter in Volume I.)

To check for the existence of the new partial resource routines, use the Gestalt function with the gestaltResourceMgrAttr selector. (See the Compatibility Guidelines chapter in this volume for information on Gestalt.) This selector returns a range of bits, the meaning of which must be determined by comparison with a list of constants. If the bit defined by the constant gestaltPartialRsrcs is set, the partial resource routines are available.

Listing 13-1 illustrates one way to deal with partial resources. This procedure begins with a call to the SetResLoad procedure. A handle to the resource from which you want to read is put into the myResHdl variable. If there is no error on the call to the GetResource function, a call is made to the ReadPartialResource routine with the handle to the resource. If there are no errors with this call, you exit the procedure. DoError is the name of your routine that handles and processes errors.

Listing 13-1. Using partial resource calls

```
PROCEDURE ReadAPartial(start: LongInt; count: LongInt;
                       VAR PutItHere: Ptr);
VAR
   myRsrcType: ResType;
   myRsrcID:   Integer;
   myResHdl:   Handle;
   resErr:     OSErr;
   RPRErr:     OSErr;

BEGIN
   SetResLoad(FALSE);         {don't load resource}
   {Set up myRsrcType and myRsrcID to your liking.}
   myResHdl := GetResource(myRsrcType, myRsrcID);
   resErr := ResError;
   SetResLoad(TRUE);          {reset to always load}
   IF resErr = NoErr THEN
   BEGIN
      ReadPartialResource(myResHdl, start, PutItHere, count);
      RPRErr := ResError;
      {Check and report error.}
      IF RPRErr <> noErr THEN DoError(RPRErr);
   END
   ELSE  {there's an error from GetResource}
      DoError(resErr);
END;  {ReadAPartial}
```

Creating and Opening Resource Files

Version 7.0 introduces a simple, standard format for identifying a file or directory, the file system specification (FSSpec) record. This record contains the volume reference number of the volume on which a file or directory resides, the directory ID of the parent directory, and the name of the file or directory. (For a complete introduction to and description of the MFS and HFS file systems and file system specification records, see the File Manager chapter in this volume.)

```
TYPE FSSpecPtr =      ^FSSpec;
     FSSpec    =
     RECORD
        vRefNum:      Integer;      {volume reference number}
        parID:        LongInt;      {directory ID of parent}
                                    {directory}
        name:         Str63         {filename or directory name}
     END;
```

The FSpOpenResFile function and FSpCreateResFile procedure open and create resource files for files or directories named by the file system specification record.

If you want to open or create resource files under the Hierarchical File System (HFS) but are not using the file system specification record in your application, you can use the HOpenResFile function and HCreateResFile procedure.

Storing Fonts in a Resource Fork

Storing a font in an application's resource fork can create serious problems for a user who tries to print a document in that font when background printing is on. Never store fonts in a document's resource fork, since this can cause heap corruption. If you feel that a document needs to have a particular font available, you should license it for distribution and let users install it in their System files.

If you use a font as a way to store symbols that your application uses in a palette or for some other special purpose, use a font family ID in the range assigned for uninterpreted symbols. (For more information about font family ID ranges, see "Font Families and Scripts" earlier in this chapter. For more information about scripts and script systems, see the Worldwide Software Overview chapter in this volume.)

RESOURCE MANAGER ROUTINES

The first group of routines described here deals with modified routines for opening or creating resource files. These routines are compatible with new file specification conventions for version 7.0 and the Hierarchical File System (HFS). Version 7.0 introduces a simple, standard format for identifying a file or directory, the file system specification (FSSpec) record. For a discussion of HFS and file system specification records, see the File Manager chapter in this volume.

The other new Resource Manager routines pertain to reading and writing partial resources. If you are working with a very large resource, you can alter a part of the resource instead of having to read it into memory, which may be impossible. You can also change the size of a resource on disk. Note that if you increase the size of the resource, the new portion of the resource will be uninitialized, and if you decrease the size, you may lose valuable data in the resource.

Creating Resource Files

The FSpCreateResFile and HCreateResFile procedures are alternate ways of creating resource files in HFS. These routines are based on the CreateResFile procedure, which is documented in the Resource Manager chapter of Volume I. HCreateResFile is a simple function designed for HFS; FSpCreateResFile uses file system specification records.

```
PROCEDURE FSpCreateResFile (spec: FSSpec; creator,fileType: OSType;
                            scriptTag: ScriptCode);
```

The FSpCreateResFile procedure opens the file named in the spec parameter. The creator parameter contains the signature of the application that created the file, and the fileType parameter indicates what type of file it is. The value of the scriptTag parameter should be the script code of the script system in which the Finder and the standard file dialog boxes display the name of the file. If you specify NIL, the FSpCreateResFile function defaults to the Roman script system. If you use Standard File Package routines, note that the StandardPutFile procedure returns a standard file reply record that contains information about the file. Call the ResError function to check for errors.

The file system specification record is described in the File Manager chapter in this volume. The StandardPutFile procedure and the standard file reply record are described in the Standard File Package chapter of this volume. The result codes for the FSpCreateResFile procedure are the same as those for the HCreateResFile function.

```
PROCEDURE HCreateResFile (vRefNum: Integer; dirID: LongInt; fileName:
                          Str255);
```

The HCreateResFile procedure creates a resource file in the directory specified by the values of vRefNum and dirID. The vRefNum parameter contains the volume reference number of the volume on which the file is located. The dirID parameter contains the directory ID of the directory where the file is located. The string passed in the fileName parameter is the name of the resource file. Call the ResError function to check for errors.

Result codes

dirFulErr	–33	Directory full
dskFulErr	–34	Disk full
nsvErr	–35	No such volume
ioErr	–36	I/O error
bdNamErr	–37	There may be no bad names in the final system
tmfoErr	–42	Too many files open
wPrErr	–44	Disk is write-protected
fLckdErr	–45	File is locked

vLckdErr	–46	Volume is locked
dupFNErr	–48	Duplicate filename (rename)
opWrErr	–49	File already open with write permission
extFSErr	–58	Volume belongs to an external file system
dirNFErr	–120	Directory not found

Opening Resource Files

The FSpOpenResFile and HOpenResFile functions are alternate ways of opening resource files using HFS. These functions are based on the OpenResFile function, which is documented in Volume I. HOpenResFile is a simple function designed for HFS; FSpOpenResFile uses file system specification records.

```
FUNCTION FSpOpenResFile (spec: FSSpec; permission: SignedByte) :
                        Integer;
```

The FSpOpenResFile function opens the file named in the spec parameter. The FSpOpenResFile function lets you open a resource file without creating a working directory. The permission parameter can contain any one of the following constants:

```
CONST
      fsCurPerm    = 0; {whatever is currently allowed}
      fsRdPerm     = 1; {request for read permission only}
      fsWrPerm     = 2; {request for write permission}
      fsRdWrPerm   = 3; {request for exclusive read/write permission}
      fsRdWrShPerm = 4; {request for shared read/write permission}
```

More information about these constants can be found in the "Low-Level File Manager Routines" section of the File Manager chapter of Volume IV.

Call the ResError function to check for errors. If the FSpOpenResFile function failed to open the resource file, the reference number returned is –1. The result codes for the FSpOpenResFile function are the same as those for the HOpenResFile function.

```
FUNCTION HOpenResFile (vRefNum: Integer; dirID: LongInt; fileName:
                      Str255; permission: SignedByte) : Integer;
```

The HOpenResFile function opens the resource file with the name given by the fileName parameter. This function also lets you open a resource file without creating a working directory. Call the ResError function to check for errors. If HOpenResFile failed to open the resource file, the reference number returned is –1.

The vRefNum parameter contains the volume reference number of the volume on which the file is located. The dirID parameter contains the directory ID of the directory where the file is located. The constants used for the permission parameter are the same as those listed for the FSpOpenResFile function.

Result codes

nsvErr	–35	No such volume
ioErr	–36	I/O error
bdNamErr	–37	There may be no bad names in the final system
eofErr	–39	End of file
tmfoErr	–42	Too many files open
fnfErr	–43	File not found
opWrErr	–49	File already open with write permission
permErr	–54	Permissions error (on file open)
extFSErr	–58	Volume belongs to an external file system
memFullErr	–108	Not enough room in heap zone
dirNFErr	–120	Directory not found
mapReadErr	–199	Map inconsistent with operation

Reading and Writing Partial Resources

You can use the ReadPartialResource and WritePartialResource procedures to manipulate a subsection of a large, unwieldy resource that may not otherwise fit in memory. You can use the SetResourceSize procedure to change the size of a resource on disk to a size that you specify.

Be aware that having a copy of a resource in memory when you are using the partial resource routines may cause problems. If you have modified the copy in memory and then access the resource on disk using either the ReadPartialResource or WritePartialResource procedure, you will lose changes made to the copy in memory.

Assembly-language note: You can invoke each of the partial resource routines with the _ResourceDispatch macro. The routine selectors are listed in the "Summary of the Resource Manager" at the end of this chapter.

```
PROCEDURE ReadPartialResource (theResource: Handle; offset: LongInt;
                               buffer: UNIV Ptr; count: LongInt);
```

The ReadPartialResource procedure reads part of a resource in from disk, which allows you to work with small portions of large resources. This procedure reads into memory a section of the resource, which is specified by the parameter theResource. The value of the offset parameter marks the beginning of the subsection as measured in bytes from the start of the resource. The length of the section is given by the value of the count parameter. The ReadPartialResource procedure reads the partial resource into the buffer you indicate with the buffer parameter. You are responsible for the memory management of this buffer. You cannot use the ReleaseResource procedure (documented in the Resource Manager chapter of Volume I) to release the memory occupied by this buffer. Call the ResError function to check for errors.

The ReadPartialResource procedure always tries to read resources from the disk. If a resource is already in memory, the Resource Manager still reads it from the disk and ResError returns the resourceInMemory result code. If you have loaded the resource into memory and modified it, you will lose any changes to the resource once you call the ReadPartialResource procedure. If you try to read past the end of a resource or your offset is out of bounds, ResError returns the inputOutOfBounds error. If the handle named by the parameter theResource is not in any open resource files, ResError returns the resNotFound result code.

When using partial resource routines, you should call the SetResLoad procedure specifying FALSE for its load parameter before you call the GetResource function. SetResLoad prevents the Resource Manager from reading the entire resource into memory. Be sure to restore the normal state of the SetResLoad procedure after you call the GetResource function. (The SetResLoad procedure and the GetResource function are described in the Resource Manager chapter of Volume I.)

> **Note:** If the resource is in memory and you want part of its data, you should use the BlockMove procedure instead of the ReadPartialResource procedure, because BlockMove is faster. The BlockMove procedure is documented in the Memory Manager chapter of Volume II.

Result codes

resourceInMemory	–188	Resource already in memory
inputOutOfBounds	–190	Offset or count out of bounds
resNotFound	–192	Resource not found

```
PROCEDURE WritePartialResource (theResource: Handle; offset: LongInt;
                                buffer: UNIV Ptr; count: LongInt);
```

The WritePartialResource procedure writes part of a resource to disk, which allows you to work with small portions of large resources. The resource is specified by the parameter theResource from the offset parameter, which is in bytes, through the number of bytes given by the value of the count parameter. The Resource Manager writes to the resource from the buffer you indicate with the buffer parameter. You are responsible for the memory management of this buffer. Call the ResError function to check for errors.

If the disk or the file is locked, the ResError function returns the appropriate file system error. If you try to write past the end of a resource, the Resource Manager attempts to enlarge the resource. ResError returns the writingPastEnd result code if the attempt is successful. If it cannot enlarge the resource, ResError returns the appropriate file system error. If you pass an invalid value in the offset parameter, ResError returns the inputOutOfBounds result code.

If the resource is in memory when you call the WritePartialResource procedure, the Resource Manager tries to write the resource. If the attempt is successful, ResError returns resourceInMemory and does not update the copy in memory. You should be aware that in this situation, the copy in memory is different from the resource on disk. If the attempt to write the resource to disk is not successful, ResError returns the appropriate error.

When using partial resource routines, you should call the SetResLoad procedure specifying FALSE for its load parameter before you call the GetResource function. The SetResLoad procedure prevents the Resource Manager from reading the entire resource into memory. Be sure to restore the normal state of the SetResLoad procedure after you call the GetResource function. (The SetResLoad procedure and the GetResource function are described in the Resource Manager chapter of Volume I.)

Result codes

dskFulErr	–34	Disk full
resourceInMemory	–188	Resource already in memory
writingPastEnd	–189	Writing past end of file
inputOutOfBounds	–190	Offset or count out of bounds

```
PROCEDURE SetResourceSize (theResource: Handle; size: LongInt);
```

The SetResourceSize procedure sets the size of a resource without writing data. You can change the size of any resource, regardless of the amount of memory you have available. Note that if you make the resource smaller, you lose any data at the end of that resource.

The parameter theResource is a handle that specifies the resource on disk. The value of the size parameter is the size you want the resource to occupy on disk, in bytes. If you set the size smaller than it was, you lose any data at the end of the resource. If the size is set larger, all data is preserved, but the enlarged area is uninitialized. Call ResError to check for errors.

If the disk is locked or full, or the file is locked, ResError returns the appropriate file system error. If the resource is in memory, the Resource Manager tries to set the size of the resource on disk. If the attempt is successful, ResError returns the resourceInMemory result code and does not update the copy in memory. If it is not successful, ResError returns the appropriate file system error.

Result codes

resourceInMemory	–188	Resource already in memory
writingPastEnd	–189	Writing past end of file

SUMMARY OF THE RESOURCE MANAGER

Constants

```
CONST {system icon definition IDs}
      genericQueryDocumentIconResource = -16506; {default query document }
                                                 { icon}
      genericDocumentIconResource      = -4000;  {default document icon}
      genericFolderIconResource        = -3999;  {default folder icon}
      floppyIconResource               = -3998;  {default 3.5-in. disk icon}
      openFolderIconResource           = -3997;  {open folder icon}
      genericApplicationIconResource   = -3996;  {default application icon}
      genericHardDiskIconResource      = -3995;  {hard disk icon}
      privateFolderIconResource        = -3994;  {folder without privileges }
                                                 { for this user icon}
      trashIconResource                = -3993;  {default empty Trash icon}
      desktopIconResource              = -3992;  {desktop icon}
      genericDeskAccessoryIconResource = -3991;  {default desk accessory }
                                                 { icon}
      genericEditionFileIconResource   = -3989;  {default edition icon}
      genericStationeryIconResource    = -3985;  {default stationery icon}
      fullTrashIconResource            = -3984;  {default full Trash icon}
      systemFolderIconResource         = -3983;  {System Folder icon}
      appleMenuFolderIconResource      = -3982;  {Apple Menu Items folder }
                                                 { icon}
      startupFolderIconResource        = -3981;  {Startup Items folder icon}
      ownedFolderIconResource          = -3980;  {owned folder icon}
      dropFolderIconResource           = -3979;  {drop folder icon}
      sharedFolderIconResource         = -3978;  {shared folder icon}
      mountedFolderIconResource        = -3977;  {mounted folder icon}
      controlPanelFolderIconResource   = -3976;  {Control Panels folder }
                                                 { icon}
      spoolFolderIconResource          = -3975;  {PrintMonitor Documents }
                                                 { folder icon}
      preferencesFolderIconResource    = -3974;  {Preferences folder icon}
      extensionsFolderIconResource     = -3973;  {Extensions folder icon}
      genericFileServerIconResource    = -3972;  {file server icon}
      genericPreferencesIconResource   = -3971;  {default preference file }
                                                 { icon}
      genericSuitcaseIconResource      = -3970;  {suitcase icon}
      genericMoverObjectIconResource   = -3969;  {System file object icon}

      {Gestalt codes for the Resource Manager}
      gestaltResourceMgrAttr           = 'rsrc'; {Gestalt selector};
      gestaltPartialRsrcs              = 0;      {partial resources exist}
```

Routines

Creating Resource Files

```
PROCEDURE FSpCreateResFile  (spec: FSSpec; creator,fileType: OSType;
                             scriptTag: ScriptCode);

PROCEDURE HCreateResFile    (vRefNum: Integer; dirID: LongInt; fileName:
                             Str255);
```

Opening Resource Files

```
FUNCTION FSpOpenResFile    (spec: FSSpec; permission: SignedByte)
                            : Integer;

FUNCTION HOpenResFile      (vRefNum: Integer; dirID: LongInt;
                            fileName: Str255; permission: SignedByte)
                            : Integer;
```

Reading and Writing Partial Resources

```
PROCEDURE ReadPartialResource  (theResource: Handle; offset: LongInt;
                                buffer: UNIV Ptr; count: LongInt);

PROCEDURE WritePartialResource (theResource: Handle; offset: LongInt;
                                buffer: UNIV Ptr; count: LongInt);

PROCEDURE SetResourceSize      (theResource: Handle; size: LongInt);
```

Result Codes

dirFulErr	–33	Directory full
dskFulErr	–34	Disk full
nsvErr	–35	No such volume
ioErr	–36	I/O error
bdNamErr	–37	There may be no bad names in the final system
eofErr	–39	End of file
tmfoErr	–42	Too many files open
fnfErr	–43	File not found
wPrErr	–44	Disk is write-protected
fLckdErr	–45	File is locked
vLckdErr	–46	Volume is locked
dupFNErr	–48	Duplicate filename (rename)
opWrErr	–49	File already open with write permission
permErr	–54	Permissions error (on file open)
extFSErr	–58	Volume belongs to an external file system
memFullErr	–108	Not enough room in heap zone

dirNFErr	–120	Directory not found
resourceInMemory	–188	Resource already in memory
writingPastEnd	–189	Writing past end of file
inputOutOfBounds	–190	Offset or count out of bounds
resNotFound	–192	Resource not found
mapReadErr	–199	Map inconsistent with operation

Assembly-Language Information

Trap Macros Requiring Routine Selectors

_ResourceDispatch

Selector	Routine
$0001	ReadPartialResource
$0002	WritePartialResource
$0003	SetResourceSize

14 WORLDWIDE SOFTWARE OVERVIEW

ABOUT THIS CHAPTER

Read this chapter if you wish to create applications that are adapted to regions other than your own or that work with any non-Roman script system. The information in this chapter is essential if you would like to plan and provide for such development in future versions of your applications. Furthermore, you may want to take advantage of several other text-handling capabilities described in this chapter and not available elsewhere in the Macintosh® Toolbox.

This chapter provides the essential background to developing Macintosh software for worldwide markets. It introduces you to the use of the Macintosh worldwide software, whose specific features are provided by the Script Manager, the International Utilities Package, the international and keyboard resources, and script systems. You can use worldwide software to make your applications compatible in the global market.

This chapter provides an overview of the Script Manager routines and data structures that let you represent scripts on the Macintosh. (**Scripts,** in this context, are writing systems such as Roman, Japanese, and Arabic that are used to represent human languages.) The Script Manager allows you to deal with script-related issues such as character representation, text direction, contextual forms, diacritical marks, uppercase and lowercase characters, character reordering, word demarcation, and text alignment.

This chapter provides an overview of the International Utilities Package routines and data structures that permit you to sort strings and to format dates, times, currency, and numbers according to the conventions of the script, language, or region of the software market you address. Throughout this chapter, **language** refers to the whole body of written words and of methods of combining words used by a particular group of people, and **region** denotes a linguistic or cultural entity that may or may not correspond to a geographic area.

This chapter gives details on the international and keyboard resources that help you specify information that pertains to a particular script, language, or region. Such information includes fonts, long and short date formats, keyboard layouts, preferred sorting order, and relationships between scripts, languages, and regions. Other pertinent data is delineated in resource tables for character type, case conversion, and word breaks. The resources also allow you to specify tokens, character set encodings, and keyboard mapping information that includes hardware-specific modifications to keyboard layouts.

This chapter introduces the Macintosh **script systems**—collections of software facilities that work with the Script Manager to provide for basic differences between writing systems, such as character sets, fonts, keyboards, text collation, and word breaks. Examples of script systems are Roman, Japanese, Arabic, Traditional Chinese, Simplified Chinese, Hebrew, Cyrillic, Thai, and Korean.

Finally, the chapter furnishes an extensive set of guidelines for adapting your applications to other languages and regions and for writing software for other scripts.

The information in this chapter, particularly, on the Macintosh Script Management System and the concepts underlying the Macintosh script systems, provides you with the understanding you need to make your applications run on Macintosh computers with multiple script systems installed. To make your applications work in a region other than your own, you will find especially valuable the information on the International Utilities Package, the international resources, the keyboard resources, and the concepts underlying the localization process.

This chapter also supplements the information in Volumes I and V. In addition to describing the enhancements available with system software version 7.0, the chapter provides brief descriptions of system software that has not been previously documented in *Inside Macintosh*. Included are brief descriptions of the Script Manager version 2.0 routines, two routines in the International Utilities Package, two international resources ('itlk' and 'itl4'), and several enhancements to the international resources available with system software versions 6.0.4, 6.0.5, and 6.0.7.

The essential technical reference on the features in worldwide software prior to system software version 7.0 is the beta draft of *Macintosh Worldwide Development: Guide to System Software*. This manual, currently available through APDA®, supplements this chapter. It covers in depth the Script Manager routines and data structures and the international and keyboard resources. Together with this overview chapter, *Macintosh Worldwide Development: Guide to System Software* tells you what you need to know about making your software compatible worldwide.

You should also be familiar with the User Interface Guidelines chapter in this volume and with *Human Interface Guidelines: The Apple Desktop Interface,* available through Addison-Wesley Publishing Company, Inc., and with the following information found in this volume and in earlier volumes of *Inside Macintosh:*

- text manipulation functions in QuickDraw™
- the Font Manager's support for QuickDraw
- the Binary-Decimal Conversion Package

The TextEdit chapter, later in this volume, provides some examples of how to use the Script Manager.

ABOUT WORLDWIDE SOFTWARE

The Macintosh **worldwide system software** helps you address the issues you'll encounter when you design your applications to be compatible with regional, linguistic, and script differences around the globe. It enables you to create applications that run in other regions or work with different scripts. Worldwide system software consists of the **Macintosh Script Management System** (the Script Manager and one or more script systems) and related components, including the International Utilities Package, international resources, keyboard resources, and certain keyboard-handling routines.

As you enter the process of developing applications for worldwide markets, it is important to consider variations that are specific to script, language, and region. Scripts may differ in the direction in which their characters and lines run, the size of the character set used to represent the script, and context sensitivity. Examples of script-specific features include text display, text rendering, text editing, fonts, input methods, and character set encoding. Examples of language-specific features include sorting order and word boundaries. Region-specific features include date and time format, number format, and case conversion. All of these possible differences are discussed later in this chapter.

> **Note:** Read "An Introduction to Scripts" later in this chapter to acquaint yourself with the concepts you must understand if you want to create software for writing systems other than your own.

The Graphic Representation of Languages

The worldwide system software described in this chapter—especially the Macintosh Script Management System—deals primarily with the graphic representation of language, not with spoken language. This has implications for the treatment of languages, including the numeric codes assigned to represent each language. A spoken language that may be written in more than one script is treated on the Macintosh as several languages: one for each script in which the language is written. In some cases, this distinction is already present in the names of spoken languages. For example, Romanian and Moldavian are essentially the same spoken language; however, in Romania this language is written in Roman script, whereas in the adjacent Soviet province of Moldavia, this language is written in Cyrillic script. In other cases, this distinction is not present: the official language of Malaysia may be written in either Roman or Arabic script, but the spoken language is called Malay in either case. The Macintosh Script Management System distinguishes the written versions with **language codes** (numbers used to indicate particular languages on the Macintosh) such as langMalayRoman and langMalayArabic.

Localized Versions of the Macintosh System Software

Localization is the process of adapting software to a particular region and language. This can include translating text to another language, using the region's date, time, and number formats, adapting icons and other graphic elements to the cultural conventions of the target region, and so on. Although localization often requires language capability in the system software and may require script capability, it is not synonymous with adding script or language capability to a system. Localization is an operation that can potentially affect every part of the system software. For example, the Japanese Script System might be localized for France so that the text in the Japanese Script System control panels would appear in French.

The Macintosh Script Management System accommodates worldwide differences with the concept of regions, which provide a finer and more complex level of granularity than script and language. For example, the French language is used in France, in parts of Belgium, Switzerland, and Canada, and in other countries such as Luxembourg, Haiti, Mali, Zaïre, Tahiti, and Vanuatu. Each of these areas may have different conventions for time, date, and number formats. Some differences may also occur in the behavior of the written language. For example, in France, accents on most characters are generally omitted if the character is written in uppercase; in Quebec, the accents are usually preserved. A **region code** is a number that may designate a region that is conceptually smaller or larger than a country (for example, "French Swiss" or "Arabic"), as long as the region shares the characteristics described above.

Localized versions of the Macintosh system software (including the Roman Script System, the Macintosh Operating System, the Toolbox, and so forth) combine information specific to scripts, languages, and regions.

> **Note:** Currently the following localized versions of the Macintosh system software are available: Arabic, Australian, British, Croatian, Danish, Dutch, Farsi, Finnish, French, French Belgian and Luxembourgian, French Canadian, French Swiss, German, German Swiss, Greek, Hebrew, Hindi (India), Icelandic, Irish, Italian, Japanese, Korean, Maltese, Norwegian, Portuguese, Simplified Chinese, Spanish, Swedish, Thai, Traditional Chinese, Turkish, and U.S. Codes for these appear in "Summary of the International Utilities Package" near the end of this chapter.

For more on the process of localization in worldwide software, see the beta draft of *Guide to Software Localization,* currently available through APDA.

Multiple Script Systems and Multiple Languages on the Macintosh Computer

At least two script systems are always present when a non-Roman script system is installed. For example, the Japanese system software is the combination of the U.S. system software (which includes the Roman Script System, the Macintosh Operating System, the Toolbox, and so forth) and KanjiTalk™ (the Japanese Script System), all of which are localized for Japan. Localized versions of the Macintosh system software with more than one script system installed—such as the Japanese system—have been adapted to particular regions, languages, or countries. However, systems such as the French and Turkish versions are simply localized variations of the U.S. system software, which do not include a second script system. With system software version 7.0, script systems may be installed either as a **secondary script** (also called auxiliary script), which just provides script capability, or as the primary script (also called **system script**), which affects system defaults and is the script used for dialog boxes, menus, and alerts.

The Script Manager has always supported the simultaneous use of more than one non-Roman script. System software version 7.0 makes it easier for users to install multiple script systems, and in version 7.0, script systems function properly even if they are not the system script. These enhancements provide increased opportunity for your applications to take advantage of the Script Manager's handling of multiple scripts.

You may decide to support multiple languages in your applications. Word processors, for example, might tag a text run with a language attribute in a manner similar to style attributes; this language tag could then govern the behavior of spelling checkers, hyphenators, and so on. In addition, you can let users choose a presentation language for your application, that is, the language for menus, dialog boxes, and alerts.

Identifying Scripts, Languages, and Regions

Scripts, languages, and regions are organized into a strict hierarchy. The Macintosh Script Management System distinguishes languages at a finer level than usual. If a language in the traditional sense can be written in more than one script, each language and script combination is called a separate language in this context.

Three basic principles underlie the hierarchy of script, language, and region:

- Every different character set encoding has a different **script code.** (For historical reasons, this is not strictly true for some localized versions of the Roman Script System.)
- Languages always belong to a particular script.
- Region codes always belong to a particular language (a localized version of the system software is for a particular language in a particular country or other region). Several regions may be associated with a particular language.

Figure 14-1 illustrates the script, language, and region hierarchy.

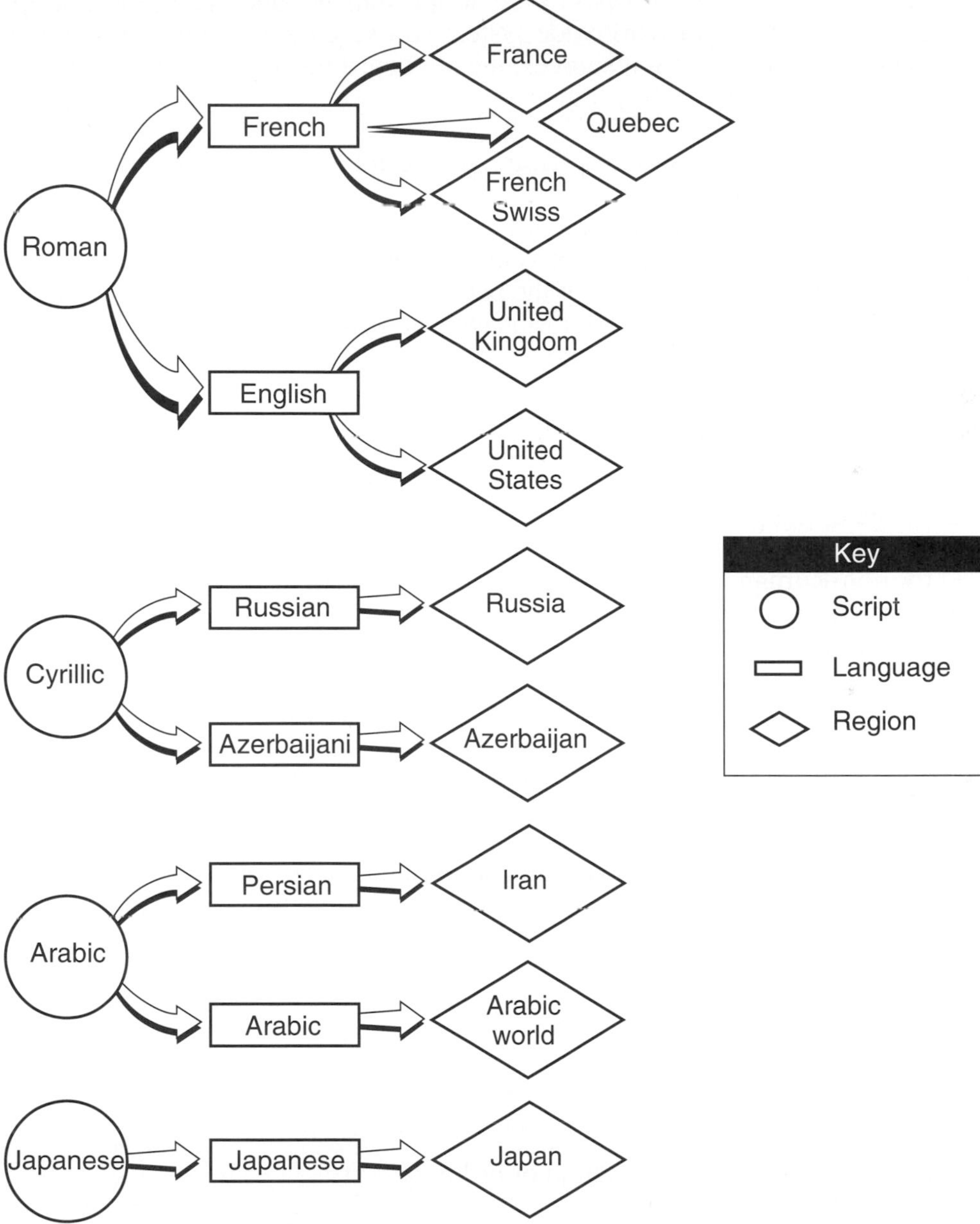

Figure 14-1. The script, language, and region hierarchy

With system software version 7.0 several changes and additions have been made to the script, language, and region codes used by the Script Management System. Most of the changes are backward-compatible. See the "Summary of the Script Manager" near the end of this chapter for a complete list of these codes, including changes to the constant code names for scripts, languages, and versions.

About the Script Management System

The Script Management System consists of the Script Manager and one or more script systems. Related components of worldwide system software include the International Utilities Package, the international resources, the keyboard resources, and keyboard-handling routines.

At the center of the worldwide system software, the Script Manager allows different script systems to be installed, maintains global data structures, supports switching keyboards between different scripts, supplies several utility routines itself, and provides a standard interface for programmatic access to script systems. The Script Manager routines allow you to write your application independently of the particular script in use. Since the Roman Script System is always installed with the Script Manager, you can use these routines with the Roman Script System for text manipulation.

The Script Manager provides basic capability in each of the scripts and languages that it supports. Although TextEdit provides text-handling support when rudimentary text-handling support is adequate, you will find the Script Manager useful when your applications have no special knowledge of the particular script or language with which they are dealing. Applications requiring a medium level of text-handling support should use the Script Manager if they are targeted for non-Roman scripts and multiple countries. Sophisticated text-intensive applications targeted to a particular language or script may need to go beyond the capabilities of the Script Manager.

Currently, script systems are available for the Roman, Japanese, Arabic, Traditional Chinese, Simplified Chinese, Hebrew, Cyrillic, Thai, and Korean scripts as well as for most scripts of India and Bangladesh, including Devanagari, Bengali, Gurmukhi, Gujarati, and others. These script systems supply fonts, ways to represent various keyboards, text collation, word breaks, and the formatting of dates, times, and numbers. Some of these script systems include special routines for handling exceedingly large character sets, which have comprehensive procedures for character input, and for handling bidirectional or contextual text. See "Representing Scripts on the Macintosh" later in this chapter for more information.

About the Script Manager

The Script Manager provides

- standard routines for the manipulation of ordinary text
- a means to make your application work with many writing systems
- access to and coordination with the International Utilities Package to provide localizable date, time, and number conversion

New Script Manager features available with system software version 7.0 allow you to

- retrieve font and style information in each script's local variables
- determine if a double-byte script system is installed
- obtain a pointer to the current 'KCHR' resource

- determine the current region code
- obtain improved information on word boundaries for word selection and line breaking (using information that individual script systems supply with appropriate tables in the 'itl2' resource)
- perform more sophisticated and faster word selection and word wrap
- truncate text in a way that improves its adaptation to different scripts and languages
- substitute text in a way that improves its adaptation to different scripts and languages
- perform uppercase and lowercase conversion more easily
- strip diacritical marks
- handle fully justified text with intercharacter spacing and multiple style runs on a line, using special scaling if desired
- create simple script systems that use the Roman Script System
- use the Keyboard menu to select keyboard layouts
- install and remove multiple scripts, keyboards, and fonts
- use new KeyScript verbs to select the next available keyboard within a script, to restrict the available keyboards temporarily

The features that let you set and retrieve font and style information, determine if a double-byte script system is installed, determine the current region code, and obtain a pointer to the current 'KCHR' resource are described in "Checking and Modifying Global and Local Variables" later in this chapter.

Descriptions of the routines that are new with system software version 7.0 are included in "Script Manager Routines" later in this chapter.

The following sections supply some background on how the Script Manager

- uses local and global variables to set up an environment in which users can install multiple script systems
- allows your application to organize text into runs to accommodate more than one script on a line and in a document
- parses text into tokens so your application can recognize meaningful symbols without making script-specific assumptions
- lets you localize dates, locations, and times
- allows your applications to localize the display of formatted numbers

Local and Global Variables

The Script Manager maintains a number of global variables that your application can read with the GetEnvirons function. These variables can be set by the corresponding SetEnvirons function. In addition, each script system maintains variables of its own, called *local variables*. You can read and set the local variables using GetScript and SetScript.

The Script Manager uses the global variables to set up and maintain the environment. For example, the global variable smgrDoubleByte, new with system software version 7.0, indicates if a double-byte script system is installed. Some local variables provide information on how scripts work; others control how they operate. For example, the local variable scriptMonoFondSize, new with system software version 7.0, specifies the default mono-spaced font and its size.

See the descriptions of the GetEnvirons and SetEnvirons functions in *Macintosh Worldwide Development: Guide to System Software* for detailed discussions of variables available prior to system software version 7.0.

Style Runs and Higher-Level Text Organization

All Script Manager text-handling routines are based on the concept of **runs** (that is, consecutive text with the same attributes) including style runs, script runs, and direction runs. The Script Manager organizes text into a hierarchy beginning with style (or format) runs. A **style run** is a sequence of text all in the same font, size, style, color, and script. A **script run** is a sequence of text all in the same script. A **direction run** is a sequence of text with characters having the same direction. See Figure 15-4, "Different Levels of Runs in a Line of Text," in the TextEdit chapter in this volume for an illustration of the ordering of style, script, and direction runs.

Tokens

Programs that parse text (for example, compilers and assemblers) usually assign sequences of characters to abstract categories called **tokens**—such as variable names, meaningful symbols, and quoted literals. The IntlTokenize function allows your application to recognize tokens without making assumptions that depend on a particular script. For example, a single token for less than or equal to might have two representations in the U.S. system software: the two-character sequence <= or the single-byte character ≤. The latter is not available in the Japanese system software, which instead uses a 2-byte coding for the single character ≤. The IntlTokenize function handles these details so your application need not be aware of the differences. The tokenizer identifies the different elements in an arbitrary string of text by using localized information from the 'itl4' resource. (The 'itl4' resource contains the localized code and resources for the tokenizer. See "The 'itl4' Resource" later in this chapter for details.)

Certain symbols in the standard Roman character set were not supported in earlier versions of the system software and had no corresponding token types. With system software version 6.0.4, the Script Manager added five new token types for some of these characters. See "Summary of the Script Manager" near the end of this chapter for details.

With system software version 7.0, two new token types have been added: tokenEllipsis and tokenCenterDot. The tokenEllipsis type is used for the character that indicates truncation. The TruncText and TruncString functions obtain the corresponding default canonical character from the untoken table in the 'itl4' resource. The tokenCenterDot type is used for the various forms of the centered dot, such as the one used by AppleShare® for echoing passwords. The corresponding default or canonical character can be obtained from the untoken table in the 'itl4' resource. For the values of tokenEllipsis and tokenCenterDot, see "Summary of the Script Manager" near the end of this chapter.

Date Conversion

The Macintosh extended date routines can handle a range of roughly 35,000 years. If your application needs a large range of dates, you can use system routines rather than produce your own, which may not be compatible worldwide. Date and time conversion may depend upon geographic information. For details, see "Date and Time Utilities" later in this chapter.

Geographic Information

You can also access the stored location (latitude and longitude) and time zone of the Macintosh from parameter RAM. The Map control panel gives users the ability to change and reference these values. For details, see "Worldwide Control Panels and Desk Accessory" and "Reading and Storing Locations" later in this chapter.

Number Conversion

The Script Manager number routines supplement the Standard Apple Numerics Environment (SANE®) and allow applications to display formatted numbers and to read both formatted and simple numbers. The formatting strings allow display and entry of numbers and editing of format strings, even though the numbers and the format strings may have been entered using different localized system software. For brief descriptions of the number routines, see "Number Utilities" later in this chapter. For a thorough treatment of number conversion, see *Macintosh Worldwide Development: Guide to System Software*.

About the International Utilities Package

The International Utilities Package provides sorting routines that support primary and secondary orderings of characters and other features. The package also handles formats for the presentation of dates, time, currency, and numbers in regions around the world. These formats may vary from script to script, language to language, and region to region.

With system software version 7.0, the International Utilities Package includes new routines that make it easier for an application to supply 'itl2' or 'itl4' resources, call sorting routines with explicit specification of an 'itl2' resource handle, provide ways to sort strings that may be in different scripts or languages, and obtain tables from an 'itl2' or 'itl4' resource. See "Using the International Utilities Package Routines" later in this chapter for details.

About the International and Keyboard Resources

The international resources and several of the keyboard resources contain information specific to language or region, such as date and time formats. You can use multiple formats for different languages or regions with the same script system by adding multiple versions of **international resources.** Each installed script has an 'itlb' resource and one or more 'itl0', 'itl1', 'itl2', 'itl4', and optional 'itl5' resources, and the resource IDs are generally in the range used for the script's 'FOND' resources (except for the 'itlb' resource). The **keyboard resources** include some localizable information such as keyboard layouts ('KCHR' resources) as well as hardware-specific information (for example, the 'KMAP' and 'KCAP' resources). The section "Using the International and Keyboard Resources" later in this chapter includes details on the following resources and on version 7.0 enhancements.

- The 'itlc' resource is the configuration resource that specifies the system script code, the size of the keyboard cache, the states of the font force flags, the international keyboard flag (used for the Macintosh Plus), the general bit flags for the Script Manager, and the region code (new with system software version 7.0) that identifies a regional version.

- The 'itlm' resource (new with system software version 7.0) is the configuration resource that specifies the preferred sorting order for script codes, language codes, and region codes, and specifies the default language for each script, the parent script for each language, and the parent language for each region.

- Each 'itlb' resource functions partially as the bundle for a particular script: it specifies the resource IDs for the script's resources. In addition, it contains the script bit flags, the default language code, and the number and date representation codes for the script. With system software version 7.0, the 'itlb' resource also specifies font information, script initialization data, valid styles for the script, and the style to use for designating aliases.

- Each 'itl0' resource contains short date and time formats and formats for currency and numbers and the preferred unit of measurement. It also contains the region code for this particular 'itl0'.

- Each 'itl1' resource specifies the long date format for a particular region, including the names of days and months. Each 'itl1' resource also contains the region code for this particular 'itl1'. With system software version 7.0, 'itl1' has an optional extension for additional month and day names as well as abbreviated month and day names.

- Each 'itl2' resource contains the International Utilities Package sorting hooks and routines and tables for character type, case conversion, and word breaks. With system software version 7.0, 'itl2' includes length information for the code and tables it contains.

- Each 'itl4' resource contains localizable tables and code for the IntlTokenize function and localizable number parts tables for the formatted number routines. With system software version 7.0, 'itl4' has length information for the code and tables it contains, and it includes a table of white space characters for the script.

- Each 'itl5' resource specifies the character set encoding and rendering behavior in a script-specific format. This optional resource is new with system software version 7.0.

- The 'KCHR' resource specifies a logical keyboard layout, that is, the mapping of virtual key codes to character codes. (It is important to note that changes for different localized versions of system software occur in the 'KCHR'—not the 'KMAP' resource.) With system software version 7.0, the U.S. keyboard layout resource, 'KCHR' (0) has improved consistency with changes in the Command–Caps Lock, Command–dead key, and Command–Option–Caps Lock key combinations. Also new with version 7.0, the Script Manager only loads the 'KCHR' resource from the System file. See "The 'KCHR' Resource" later in this chapter for details.

- The 'kcs#', 'kcs4', and 'kcs8' resources specify **keyboard icons** for screens of different bit depths. These resources are new with system software version 7.0 and replace the 'SICN' resource associated with keyboard layouts in earlier versions of system software. These icons are used in the new Keyboard menu and in the Keyboard control panel. See "Using the Keyboard Menu" and "Selecting Keyboard Layouts" later in the chapter for details. For guidelines for designing your own keyboard icons, see the User Interface Guidelines chapter earlier in this volume.

- The 'KCAP' resource specifies the physical arrangement of keyboards and is used by the Key Caps desk accessory. See "Key Caps and the 'KCAP' Resource" later in this chapter for details.

- The 'KSWP' resource specifies modifier-plus-key combinations that can be used to change the keyboard script and the current keyboard layout. New with system software version 7.0, the 'KSWP' resource can be used to change the keyboard layout within a script.

- The optional 'itlk' resource provides hardware-specific modifications to keyboard layout by indicating how to remap certain key combinations. Beginning with system software version 7.0, the Script Manager only loads this resource from the System file.

About the Macintosh Script Systems

In many cases, the versatility provided by script systems allows applications to be localized for other scripts, languages, and regions with no change to their program code. (Script systems are typically localized for a language and region that belong to the script; this affects the formatting of dates, times, numbers, and so on.) Multiple script systems can be installed at one time on a Macintosh computer allowing the user to switch back and forth between different scripts. With system software version 7.0, users can change the active keyboard script by using the Keyboard menu. The menu is present whenever multiple scripts are installed or when a localizer sets a flag in the script's 'itlc' resource. When the Keyboard menu is present, an icon indicating the presence of the menu and the active keyboard (and hence the active script) appears near the right end of the menu bar to the left of the Application menu icon. See "Using the Keyboard Menu" later in this chapter for details.

Figure 14-2 shows the types of script systems currently available. The Roman and Cyrillic Script Systems are relatively straightforward. These **simple script systems** represent writing systems with small character sets that require only single-byte characters, have a text direction of left to right, and are not context-dependent. Such script systems provide for basic differences between scripts and related languages, such as character sets, fonts, keyboards, text collation, and word breaking. The Roman Script System is standard on all Macintosh computers, and the standard Roman character set includes characters for a number of European languages.

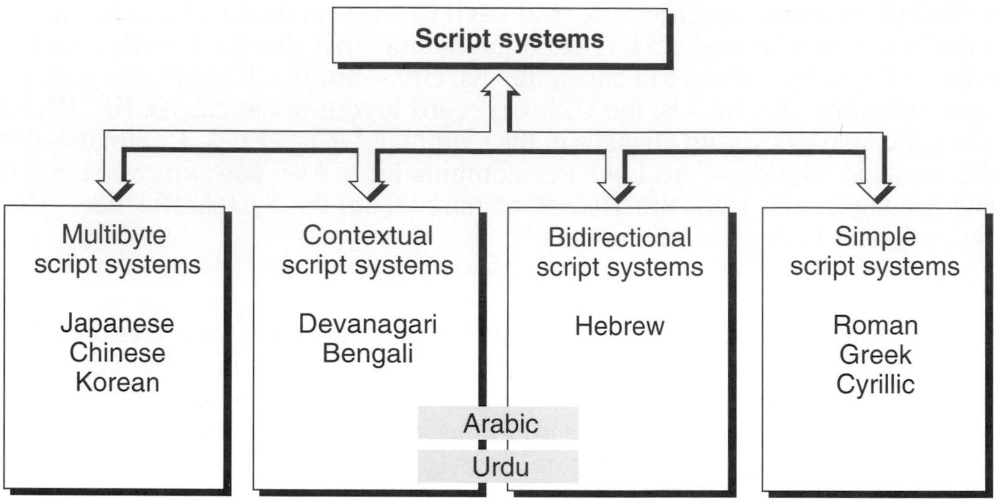

Figure 14-2. Types of script systems

The other script systems represent some of the most complex modern writing systems and go far beyond basic script support. Japanese, Chinese, and Korean have exceedingly large character sets, and these script systems have comprehensive procedures for character input. These **multibyte script systems** have character sets that are too large to be represented with single bytes (the character set includes both single-byte and double-byte character codes) and require an independent font mechanism for display and printing.

Arabic and Hebrew are **bidirectional script systems,** where text is generally flush right and is written from right to left, but also includes characters that are written left to right.

Contextual script systems are scripts where the displayed form of a character depends on the adjacent characters. Arabic and Urdu are examples of contextual script systems.

Each script system determines the components for the script: character encoding; fonts; input methods; sorting; date, time, and number formats; and script-specific access routines. For example, each script's composition rules support all of the necessary features of the script: direction, conjunct characters, accent placement, and so forth. For further details on Macintosh script systems, see *Macintosh Worldwide Development: Guide to System Software*.

Many script systems also have a control panel or a desk accessory to allow the user to configure the individual characteristics of the script system at any time. (Simple script systems do not generally have such a control panel.)

The Script Management System and Related Worldwide Components

Figure 14-3 illustrates all the related worldwide system software components, including the Macintosh Script Management System, which consists of the Script Manager and one or more script systems. Each script system contains its own script system routines (including special font-mapping routines, if necessary), fonts, international resources ('itlb', 'itl0', 'itl1', 'itl2', 'itl4', and optional 'itl5'), keyboard resources ('KCHR', 'kcs#', 'kcs4', 'kcs8',

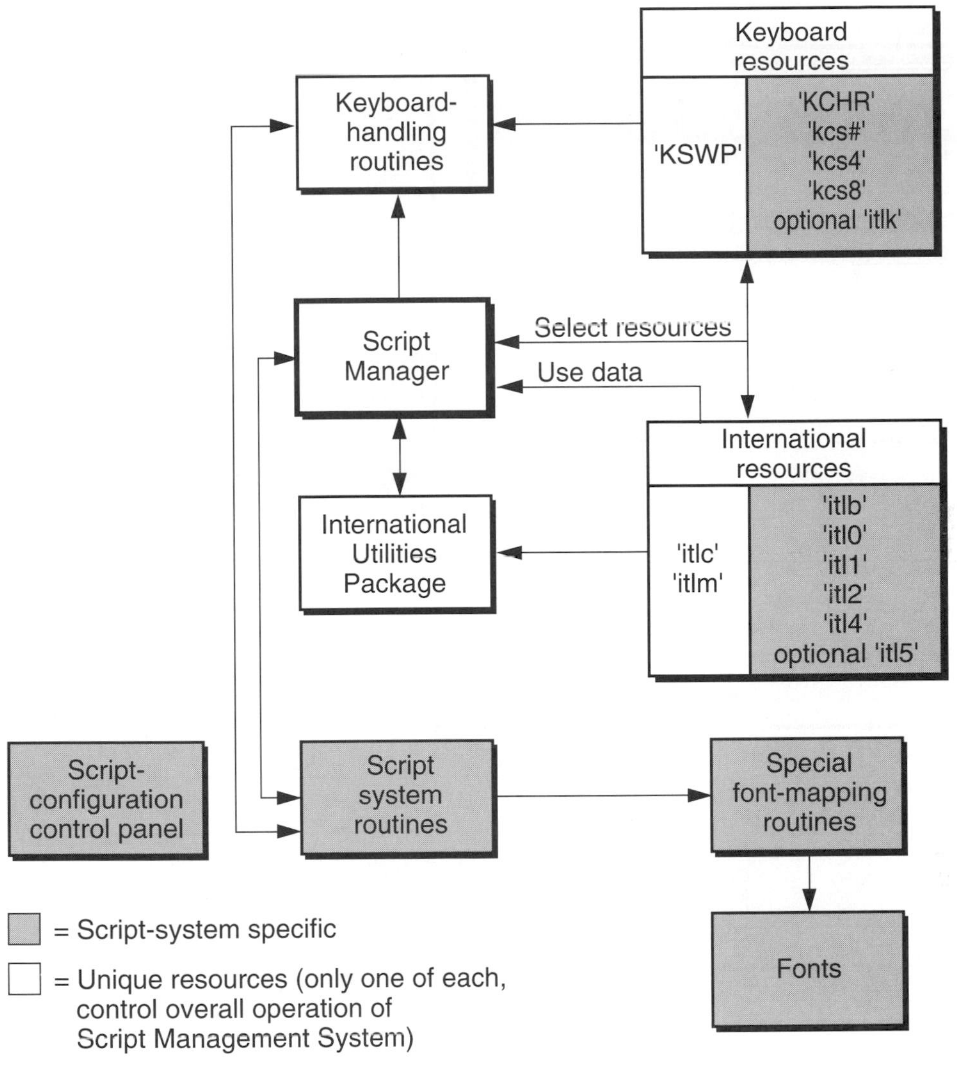

Figure 14-3. The components of the Macintosh Script Management System

and optional 'itlk'), and one or more optional script-configuration control panels. In addition, each script system may replace one or more of the unique system resources 'KSWP', 'itlc', and 'itlm'. The arrows between the components in the figure illustrate the flow of action and information between the Script Manager and other worldwide components.

Here are some examples of the interaction of these components.

- The Script Manager frequently calls routines in the International Utilities Package, such as the IUGetIntl function, to take advantage of information stored in the international resources. For instance, the Script Manager's LowerText procedure uses data in the 'itl2' resource for case conversion.

- The International Utilities Package also uses the international resources. For example, the IUTimeString procedure utilizes the 'itl0' resource for its time information, and the IUCompString function applies information from the 'itl2' resource in its string comparison.

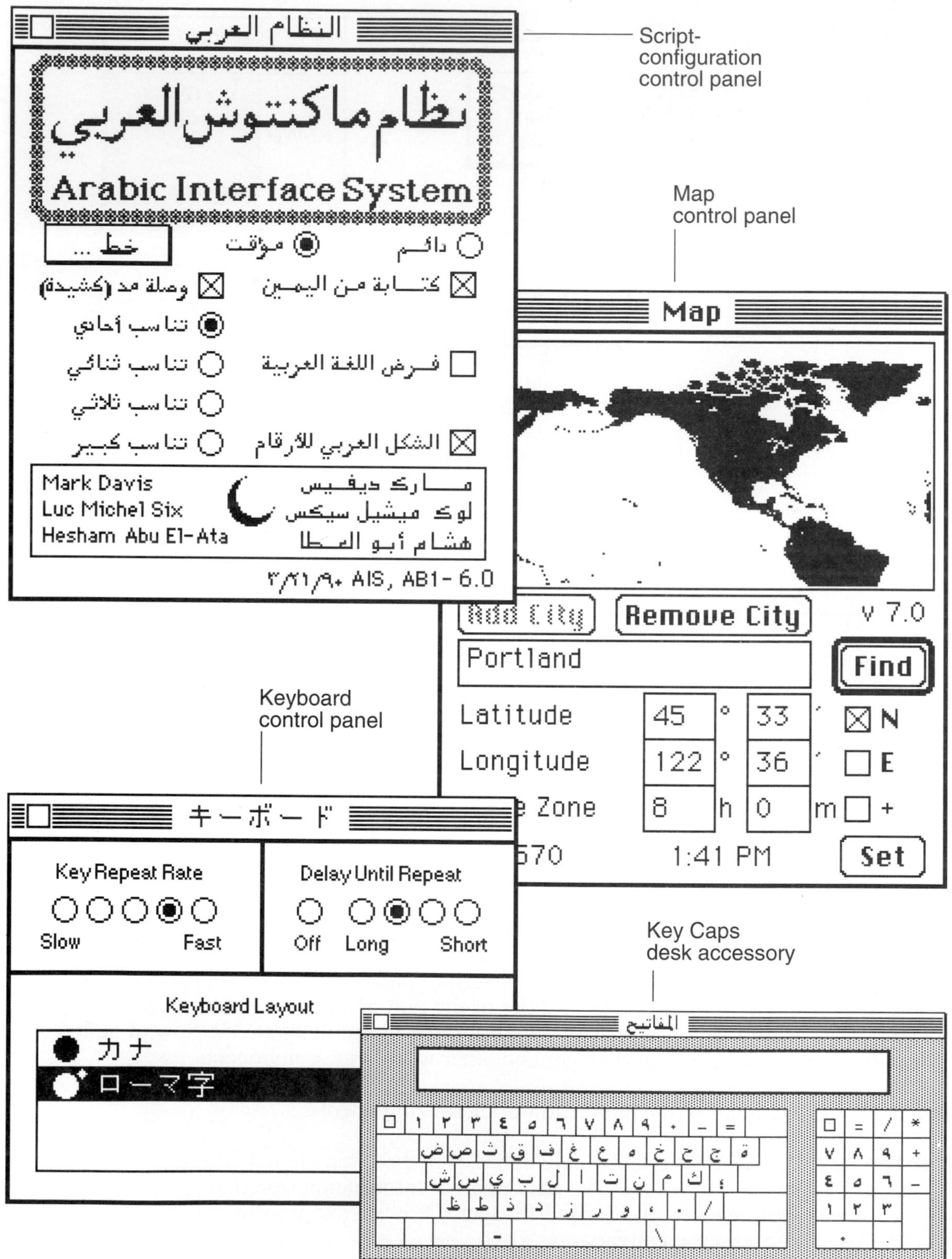

Figure 14-4. Worldwide control panels and desk accessory

- When the user changes the keyboard script, the Script Manager alters information in the keyboard driver data structures and loads the selected 'KCHR' and possibly an 'itlk' resource for use by the KeyTrans function. The Script Manager also updates the Keyboard menu data structures.

Worldwide Control Panels and Desk Accessory

Figure 14-4 shows examples of worldwide control panels and the Key Caps desk accessory, including a script-configuration control panel.

- A script-configuration control panel lets users specify different features in a script system. The Arabic Script System control panels shown in Figure 14-4 let the user specify alignment, the font for Roman text, and the type of calendar to be used. Another example of a configuration control panel (not shown) is the Japanese Script System control panel that allows users to specify input methods for Japanese characters.
- The Keyboard control panel allows users to specify a particular keyboard layout and to control the way keyboards operate.
- The Map control panel lets users indicate the location of their Macintosh computer.
- The Key Caps desk accessory shows the active keyboard layout in a particular script using a specified font. See "Key Caps and the 'KCAP' Resource" later in this chapter for details about version 7.0 enhancements, including dead-key feedback and additional key shapes.

Installing and Removing Script Systems, Keyboards, and Fonts

With system software version 7.0, the user installs each non-Roman script system with an Installer that permits users to install the script as a primary or secondary script. Also, the Finder™ allows users to add or remove secondary script systems. The Finder permits users to move a collection of script resources into the System file. Also, if a script system has not been enabled, users can take the script system's resources out of the System file. When the Finder moves a collection of script resources, it transfers the resources specified by the script's 'itlb' resource: the 'itl0', 'itl1', 'itl2', 'itl4', optional 'itl5', 'KCHR', 'kcs#', 'kcs4', and 'kcs8' resources. When the System file is opened, any scripts that can be moved out of the System file are displayed. Figure 14-5 shows the icon representations for various scripts, keyboards, and fonts.

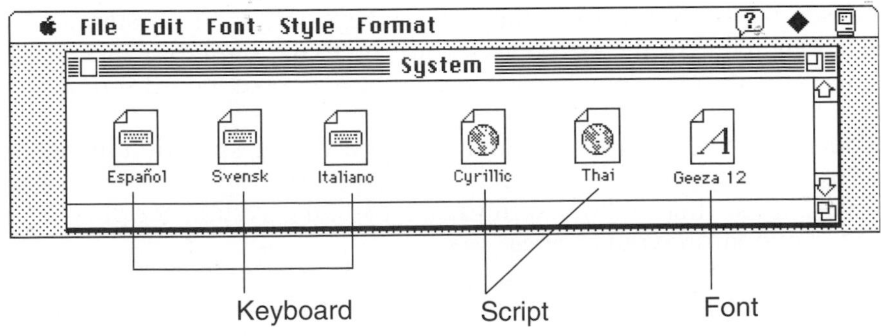

Figure 14-5. Default icons for keyboards, fonts, and scripts

The user can also move keyboards (that are not part of a script resource collection) and fonts into and out of the System file. When the System file is opened, any fonts and keyboards that can be moved out are listed, also as shown in Figure 14-5. See the Finder Interface chapter in this volume for details about the file types of fonts and about moving fonts.

Users can install a script system with the Finder and move a script resource collection, any additional keyboards, and fonts into the System file. Some script systems may also require a file of type 'scri' containing 'INIT' resources; this must be put into the Extensions folder inside the System Folder.

Using the Keyboard Menu

With system software version 7.0, a new menu, the Keyboard menu, displays a list of all the keyboard layouts available in the system. (See Figure 14-6 for an example of the Keyboard menu.)

> **Note:** The Keyboard menu displays the keyboard layouts that belong to any script systems that have been installed and enabled. If you place a 'KCHR' resource in your system that does not belong with any of the script systems you have installed, the Keyboard menu does not display that 'KCHR'.
>
> For example, if you install German, French, Japanese, and U.S. 'KCHR' resources in a system that only contains the Roman Script System (that is, any generic U.S. system) and set the appropriate bit in the 'itlc' resource, only the German, French, and U.S. keyboards are displayed in the menu.

The Keyboard menu groups the keyboard layouts by script. The script groups are delineated by gray lines. In Figure 14-6, the Roman script includes two keyboard layouts (Spanish and U.S.); the Hebrew script contains a single keyboard layout; and the Japanese script includes two keyboard layouts (Kana and Romaji).

The Keyboard menu appears if there are multiple script systems installed in the system or if the smfShowIcon bit in the Script Manager flags long word is set when system menus are initialized during system startup. The Script Manager initializes the smfShowIcon bit from the flags byte in the 'itlc' resource earlier in the system startup process. If the menu is available at startup, the keyboard icon for the system script's default keyboard appears in the menu bar to the left of the Application menu icon.

Each menu item includes a keyboard icon and the name of the keyboard layout (which may be in a non-Roman script). In Figure 14-6, the Hebrew keyboard icon—a star of David—is to the left of the Hebrew name of the keyboard layout and to the right of a checkmark that indicates that this is the current default keyboard in the active keyboard script.

The list of keyboard layouts corresponds to the script ordering specified in the 'itlm' resource. Within each script, the keyboards are listed in the script's sorting order. The system script's keyboards always appear first in the list. In Figure 14-6, the system script is Roman, so the Spanish and U.S. keyboard layouts appear first.

The keyboard icons that appear in each menu item are defined by the new keyboard color icon family: 'kcs#', 'kcs4', and 'kcs8'. If a keyboard layout does not include a keyboard icon when it's installed in the system, a default keyboard icon is used.

For each script there is a current default keyboard. The default keyboard for the active keyboard script is the active keyboard and is indicated by a checkmark. In Figure 14-6, the active keyboard layout is Hebrew.

Figure 14-6 shows the Japanese Kana keyboard layout being selected. When the mouse button is released, the Kana keyboard icon will appear in the menu bar. When the About Keyboards item at the top of the Keyboard menu is selected, a dialog box appears with additional information about the menu and changing keyboards. Balloon Help™ is also available for the Keyboard menu.

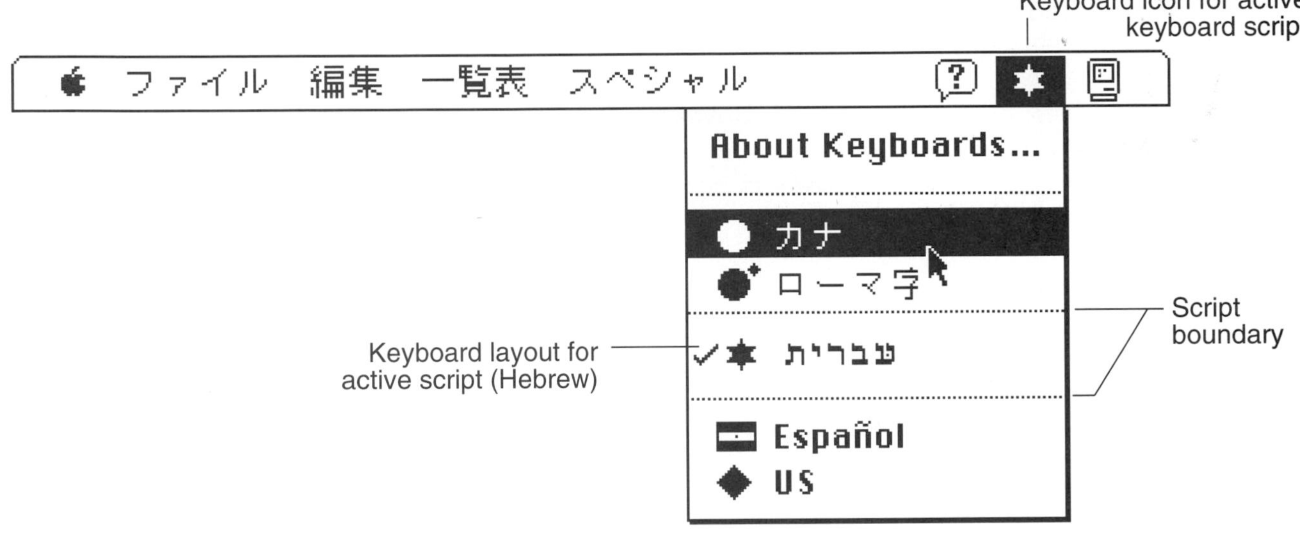

Figure 14-6. The Keyboard menu

Selecting Keyboard Layouts

Several ways are available to select different keyboard layouts:

- Selecting the desired layout from the Keyboard menu.
- Using keyboard equivalents such as Command–Space bar to switch to the next available script and the current default keyboard for that script.
- Using the Keyboard control panel to select the keyboard for the active keyboard script. If the Keyboard menu appears and the user selects a new keyboard layout, the Keyboard menu data structures are updated so the Keyboard menu reflects the new selection.

Distinguishing Scripts

Each script is distinguished by a unique script code. The script codes currently defined are in the range 0–32, although the Script Manager can support 64 scripts at the same time. The resource ID number for a script's 'itlb' resource is the same as the script code. The resource ID numbers for the other resources associated with a script are in a range specific to that script. For Roman, this range is 0–16383. Scripts with script codes in the range 1–32 have a range of 512 resource ID numbers beginning at 16384 + 512 * (script code – 1). Scripts with script codes in the range 33–64 have a range of 512 resource ID numbers beginning at –32768 + 512 * (script code –33). For example, the script code for Korean is 3, so Korean resources have resource IDs in the range 17408–17919. Figure 14-7 illustrates the font ranges for the Roman, Japanese, and Devanagari scripts. A full table of resource ID ranges is provided in the Resource Manager chapter in this volume.

> **Note:** Some script codes above 32 are not usable because they correspond to resource ID ranges that are reserved for other purposes. Script codes 33 through 40 are invalid; furthermore, script codes above 48 are currently unavailable and may become invalid.

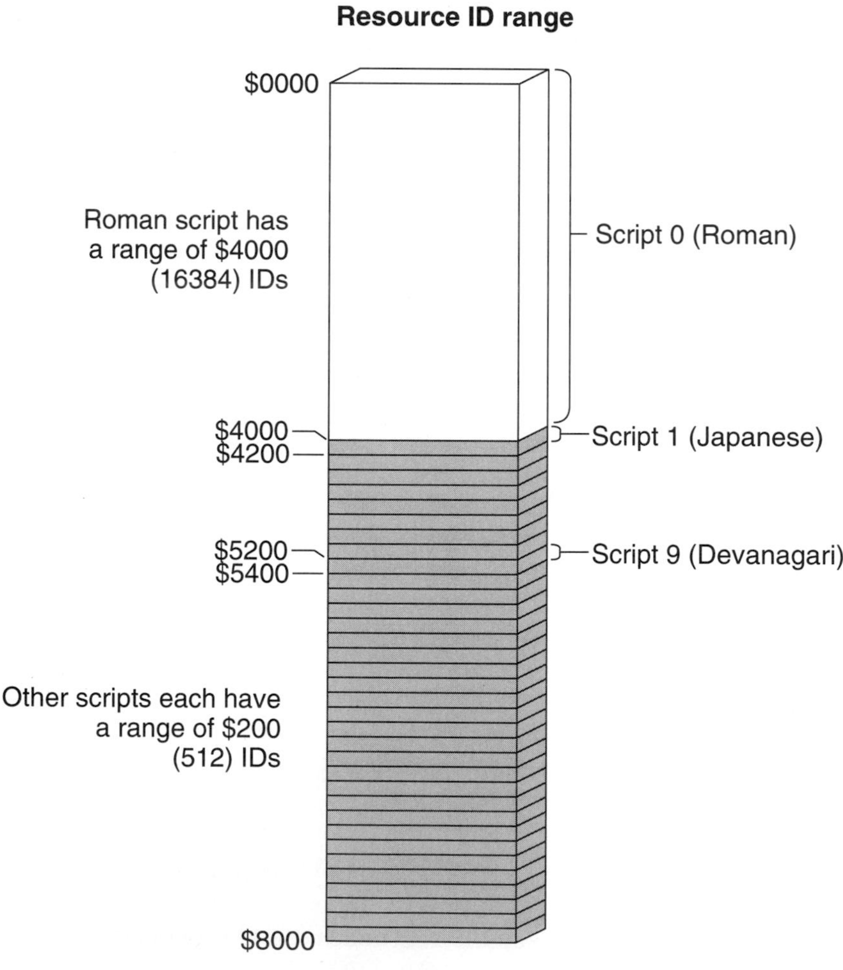

Figure 14-7. Distinguishing scripts with resource ID ranges for script codes 0–32

The font used for text indicates the script for that text. A text string in a font with a 'FOND' resource ID of 200 is interpreted as Roman text, while the same text string in a font whose 'FOND' ID is 18432 is interpreted as Hebrew text and displayed accordingly. The meaning of each character code depends on the font. In an Arabic font, the code $CC represents the character ج (jiim), while in a Roman font, the code $CC represents the character Ã. However, character codes $00 through $7F are always interpreted the same way—except when they are the second byte of a double-byte character (codes $00 through $1F are never the second byte of a double-byte character). For historical reasons within the Chinese and Roman Script Systems, even within a given script, the meaning of character codes may depend on the font: the Symbol font is in the Roman script range, but character codes in the Symbol font have a different meaning from the same character codes in the Geneva font. This situation now only occurs in the Roman Script System. The Traditional Chinese and Simplified Chinese Script Systems are different script systems and use different character set encodings, but until recently they shared the same script code.

There is an additional consideration for 'FOND' resource IDs. The special 'FOND' resource IDs 0 and 1 specify the Macintosh system font and the default application font and do not necessarily indicate a Roman font and the Roman Script System. On Roman script systems, the Chicago font is the system font, and it has a 'FOND' ID of 0. On non-Roman script systems, Chicago has a different 'FOND' ID (usually 16383), and 'FOND' ID 0 is mapped to the system font for the appropriate non-Roman system. On the Japanese Script System, for example, 'FOND' ID 0 is mapped to the Osaka font, which has a 'FOND' ID of 16384.

The script can be determined by just the 'FOND' ID. Therefore, even when an entire font family is missing, the Font Manager can still substitute a font of the same script.

▲ **Warning:** If a non-Roman font has a 'FOND' ID with an ID in the Roman range, it will not be handled correctly. ▲

Keyboards

The Macintosh keyboard routines handle the keyboard properly for script systems. Except for purely hardware-specific characteristics, the function of the keyboard is completely determined by keyboard character tables in the keyboard layouts. These are resources of type 'KCHR' with an optional associated resource of type 'itlk'. Each table specifies the character produced by each key in combination with each modifier key (Command, Shift, Caps Lock, Control, and Option). In addition, the 'KCHR' resource also handles dead keys by means of additional subtables. **Dead keys** are the modifier-plus-key combinations that usually produce no immediate effect but instead affect the character or characters produced by the next key—called the *completer key*—that is pressed. For example, pressing Option-E produces nothing (no event is posted), but subsequently typing E produces *é*.

Note that you can edit the 'KCHR' resources by using ResEdit™. For details on all the keyboard resources, see the relevant sections under "Using the International and Keyboard Resources" later in this chapter.

Figure 14-8 illustrates the process of keyboard translation. Keyboards produce raw key codes. The hardware-dependent 'KMAP' resource is then used to map these key codes to hardware-independent virtual key codes and to set bits indicating the state of the modifier keys. (If you do not have access to the MPW® file SysTypes.r, which contains a Rez type definition of the 'KMAP' resource, consult Macintosh Developer Technical Support for details.)

The 'KCHR' resource specifies how to map a modifier state and a virtual key code to a character code. It includes information on how to process dead keys.

The optional 'itlk' resource specifies how to remap certain key combinations on certain keyboards before the 'KCHR' mapping is used. The 'itlk' resource transforms this information based on which keyboard is in use and reintroduces hardware dependence because certain scripts, languages, and regions need subtle differences in layout for specific keyboards. Generally, the 'itlk' resource only affects a few keys.

The 'KCHR' and 'itlk' resources are used by the KeyTrans function.

Note: Do not change the 'KMAP' resource because everything you need is in the 'KCHR' and 'itlk' resources. You only need to work with 'KMAP' if you are making your own keyboard.

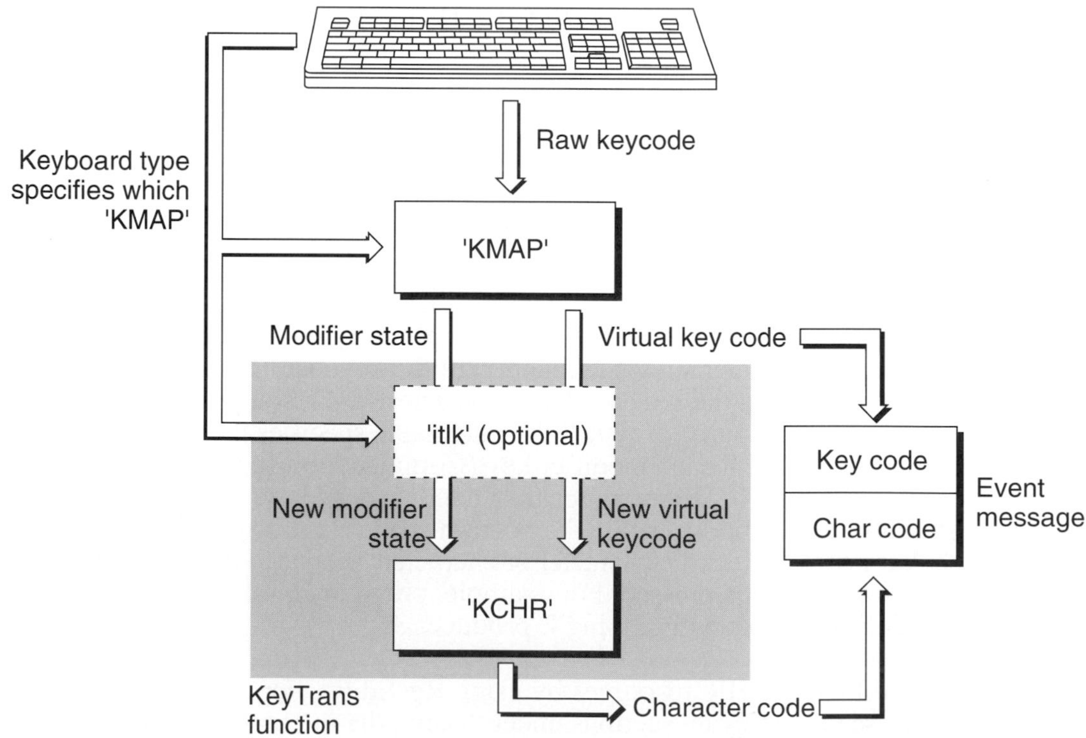

Figure 14-8. Keyboard translation

The net result of the process of keyboard translation illustrated in Figure 14-8 is a virtual keycode and a character code. See "The 'KCHR' Resource" later in this chapter for details about the internal structure and the function of the 'KCHR' resource.

The 'KSWP' resource specifies which modifier-plus-key combinations you can use to change scripts and keyboard layouts within scripts. For example, the standard 'KSWP' resource specifies that pressing Command–Space bar changes the keyboard to the default keyboard for the next script. For details on these keyboard resources and other keyboard issues, see "Using the International and Keyboard Resources" later in this chapter and *Macintosh Worldwide Development: Guide to System Software*.

Fonts

Fonts share the following attributes across all script systems:

- Single fonts, although belonging to a single script, may contain characters from multiple scripts (typically Roman plus the font's native script). A script system may substitute a Roman font for some of the character encodings, typically the 128 ASCII low-order codes. In this case, the font routines that return information, such as the ascent or descent, have been modified to return the proper information, usually the maximum of the corresponding values for the two fonts.

- Fonts may have zero-width characters. These are usually overlapping diacritical marks, which typically follow the base character in memory (also called backing-store order). With double-byte characters, all but the first (high-order, low-address) byte are measured as zero width (for example, with the MeasureText procedure).

- Since the script systems are built on top of the Toolbox graphics routines, all of the normal QuickDraw font features are usually available on the screen and when printing, including styles (bold, italic, and so on), variable sizes (12 point, 18 point, and so on), and multiple font families. Certain styles may be disabled in some scripts.

LOCALIZATION

Localization involves the adaptation of an application to a specific region or language. To create software that is easy to localize, it is first important to understand certain concepts regarding sorting and the formatting of dates, times, currency, measurement, and numbers, described in the sections that follow. See "Localizing to Other Languages and Regions" later in this chapter for specific guidelines on the use of text, fonts, sorting, and date and time display.

The process of localization includes the specification of the system script. The **system script** is the script that determines the system font used for menus and dialog boxes and the default application font for documents, among other things. It also determines the default line direction.

Sorting

String sorting is used in a number of places in the Macintosh Operating System (for example, in a standard file dialog box) and in applications (for instance, spreadsheets). When performing such sorting, it is important to order strings in the manner expected by the user—that is, according to the rules of the language and region for which the system is localized. The International Utilities Package provides several routines that compare two strings and indicate whether the first should be sorted before, after, or at the same place as the second string. For details, see "Using the International Utilities Package Routines" later in this chapter.

Sorting or comparing strings can be an extremely intricate operation. Subtle issues like expansion, contraction, ignorable characters, and exceptional words may be taken into account. Sorting cannot be done properly by a simple table look-up, even for such straightforward cases as English. Sorting depends not just on the script, but on the individual language. While broad similarities in sorting exist between languages that share the same script, definite variations between languages must be taken into account.

The Script Manager, the International Utilities Package, and international resource 'itl2' have long provided for many sorting issues, including primary or secondary order, expansion, contraction, and ignorable characters. With system software version 7.0, several new sorting capabilities provide support for systems with multiple installed scripts and language capabilities.

- You can sort strings in different scripts and languages. See "Determining Interscript Sorting Order" later in this chapter for details.
- A new international resource, 'itlm', indicates the preferred sorting order for scripts, languages, and region codes, and indicates how to map region codes to languages and language codes to scripts. See "The 'itlm' Resource" later in this chapter for details.
- You can explicitly specify the handle of the resource to be used for sorting. This is helpful for multilingual systems. See "Specifying Resource Handles Explicitly" later in this chapter for details.
- The 'itl2' and 'itl4' resource handles for all active scripts are cached by the Script Manager. You can call a routine to clear the cache so application-supplied resources can be used. See "Manipulating the 'itl2' and 'itl4' Resources" later in this chapter for details.

Primary or Secondary Order

Sorting order is determined by a ranking of the entire standard Roman character set. This ranking can be thought of as a two-dimensional table. Each row is a class of characters—for example, all of the forms of uppercase and lowercase *A* with and without various diacritical marks. The characters are ordered within the row, but that ordering is secondary to the primary ordering of the rows themselves. For example, all of the forms of *A* precede all of the forms of *B*, as follows:

A < Å < a < å

B < b

Primary sorting characteristics denote a strong ranking; if any primary differences are present, all secondary differences are ignored. For instance, only primary sorting is needed to determine that *abc* precedes *bc*. Secondary sorting characteristics indicate that if certain differences are present, a second pass is made that introduces a weak ordering. Here's an example:

abc < åbc.

Expansion

A single character may be sorted as if it were a sequence of characters. First, the single character is expanded; then the primary sorting occurs based on this expansion. In the secondary sorting, the characters are recombined. For instance, *ä* in German may be sorted as if it were the two characters *ae,* as in this example:

bäk < baek < bäks

Contraction

A sequence of characters may be sorted as a single character. For instance, *ch* in Spanish may be sorted as if it were one character that sorts after *c,* as in this example:

czar < char< dar

Ignorable Characters

Certain characters should be ignored unless the strings are otherwise equal. In other words, they have no effect on primary sorting, but they do influence secondary sorting. Examples of ignorable characters in English are hyphens, apostrophes, and spaces. Here is an example of how a hyphen influences secondary sorting:

blackbird < black-bird < blackbirds

Exceptional Words

Sometimes the sorting order changes drastically for special cases. For instance, when words are understood to be abbreviations, the strings are sorted as if they were spelled out.

McDonald < Mary	{McDonald is treated as MacDonald} {Thus, MacDonald < Mary}
St. James < Smith	{St. is an abbreviation for Saint} {Saint James < Smith}
Easy Step < Easy St.	{St. is an abbreviation for Street} {Easy Step < Easy Street}

Such cases require a direct dictionary look-up and are not handled by the Macintosh Script Management System. Note that abbreviations are context-dependent; for example, *St.* may denote *Saint* or *Street,* depending on the meaning of the adjacent text.

Formats

The following sections discuss the enormous differences in the forms of dates, times, and numbers. These differences should all be considered and accounted for when using worldwide system software, particularly the Macintosh Script Management System.

Date and Time

Formatting dates and times for a particular script and region requires the specification of the elements in the date or time, the number of digits used for each numeric element (for example, 3/01/90 or 3/1/90), the names of the months and the days of the week, and other characteristics such as the order of the elements and the use of A.M. and P.M. instead of a 24-hour clock.

Each 'itl0' resource contains short date and time formats. Each 'itl1' resource contains long date formats. With system software version 7.0, the 'itl1' resource can be optionally extended to contain a list of extra day names for calendars with more than 7 days, a list of extra month names for calendars with more than 12 months, a list of abbreviated day names, a list of abbreviated month names, and a list of additional date separators. See “The 'itl0' Resource” and “The 'itl1' Resource” later in this chapter for details.

Currency and Measurement

Currency formats include the specification of the currency indicator (for example, $, £, or DM) and whether it precedes or follows the value. Units of measurement can be specified as metric or imperial (inches and miles). Each 'itl0' resource contains formats for currency and indicates the preferred measurement unit. See “The 'itl0' Resource” later in this chapter for details.

Calendars

Although it is very accurate and on the whole conforms to natural phenomena, the standard **Gregorian calendar** used in Europe and the Americas is not universally accepted. For example, different calendar systems are often used in Japan and the Arabic world.

For instance, the **Arabic calendar** is lunar rather than solar. The months are alternately 29 and 30 days long, so the Arabic calendar year is about 11 days shorter than the Gregorian year. The months have no fixed relation to the sun, so they slowly rotate through all of the seasons of the year (that is, every three years the months shift forward one month). The Arabic calendar is used extensively throughout the Middle East. Examples of other calendars include Chinese, Coptic, Japanese, and Jewish.

The Macintosh represents dates in memory as the absolute number of seconds since January 1, 1904. For more on this topic, see the discussion “Working With Date Formats and Calendar Conversion” in *Macintosh Worldwide Development: Guide to System Software*.

With system software version 7.0, the 'itl1' resource has been extended to contain an optional calendar code. Multiple calendars may be available on some systems, and it is necessary to identify the particular calendar for use with the 'itl1' resource. Constants for the various calendars are listed in “Summary of the Script Manager” near the end of this chapter.

Numbers

Scripts differ in many aspects of the representation of numbers, so you need to make allowances for different formats of numbers. The Japanese script, for instance, uses the standard ASCII Western digits, double-byte encodings of the same Western digits, and native Japanese number characters, which occur in both a standard and a nonforgeable form—that is, a form that cannot be converted into another digit by the addition of strokes (used for financial instruments and so forth). Each 'itl0' resource contains formats for numbers.

AN INTRODUCTION TO SCRIPTS

A script, as used in this chapter, is a writing system for a human language. There are about 30 living scripts that are used to represent the official languages of one or more regions and countries. Examples of writing systems are Roman, Chinese, Japanese, Hebrew, and Arabic. They all have distinct attributes. Simple scripts, such as Roman, Greek, and Cyrillic, usually have fewer than 256 characters; the Japanese script theoretically contains more than 40,000. The characters of printed Roman are relatively independent of each other; Arabic characters change shape depending on the characters that surround them.

Scripts may vary in other attributes: the direction in which their characters and lines run, the size of the character set used to represent the script, and the context sensitivity of the script. Some scripts, such as Japanese, actually include multiple subscripts. (A **subscript** is a distinguishable subset of characters that is included within a script. Subscripts in the Japanese script include Hiragana, Kanji, Katakana, and Romaji.) Each of these attributes significantly affects the script's representation on the computer, and each is discussed in the following sections. Figure 14-9 shows notations for the names of various scripts, languages, and regions in the appropriate script.

Figure 14-9. Scripts

Character Representation

Scripts differ in the kind and number of characters they require to represent words. Some scripts are basically **alphabetic:** the characters in the script symbolize, more or less, the discrete phonemic elements in the languages represented by the script. Other scripts, such as Japanese Hiragana and Katakana, are **syllabic:** the characters stand for syllables in the language. The languages that syllabic scripts represent tend to have relatively simple syllables.

Other scripts—namely, Japanese Kanji, Chinese Hanzi, and Korean Hanja—include **ideographic** characters. These do not represent pronunciation alone, but are also related to the component meanings of words. A typical character set for ideographic scripts is quite large, ranging from 7,000 to 30,000 characters. Obviously, a standard single-byte encoding (limited to 256 distinct values) cannot be used to represent these characters, nor can a keyboard be used to enter so many characters directly.

Figure 14-10 shows examples of alphabetic, syllabic, and ideographic **character representations.**

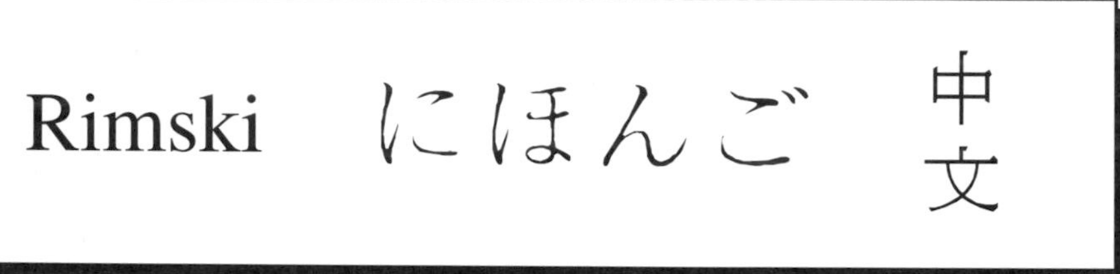

Figure 14-10. Alphabetic, syllabic, and ideographic representations of characters

Text Direction

Scripts also vary in the direction in which characters are written. In Roman scripts, characters are inscribed from left to right, with horizontal lines of characters written from top to bottom. However, scripts like Arabic and Hebrew have most characters written from right to left, although the horizontal lines of text are still written from top to bottom. In Japanese and Chinese, characters are traditionally written from top to bottom, with vertical lines (columns) of characters written from right to left. Figure 14-11 shows three text directions. These three script types (that is, left-right top-bottom, right-left top-bottom, and top-bottom right-left) are the most common of the eight possible combinations of character and line directions.

Different scripts can occur in the same line on a screen. Thus a line of text containing both Arabic and English is actually bidirectional: some characters go from left to right, and some from right to left.

The Macintosh script systems, accessed through the Script Manager, provide the capability to write from right to left, as required by Arabic, Hebrew, and other bidirectional scripts, to mix right-to-left and left-to-right directional text within lines and blocks of text, and to use ideographic text. Your application can add the capability to handle vertical text, if desired.

Figure 14-11. Three text directions

Contextual Forms

The displayed form, or **glyph,** that represents a character in printed English does not usually depend on bordering characters. This is not the case for many scripts. Even in cursive English, for example, when one letter is joined to the preceding letter, the connecting line varies according to which letters are being joined. Characters may also have considerably different shapes depending on where they occur within a word, for example, at the beginning (initial form) or elsewhere in the word (noninitial form). Figure 14-12 illustrates two of these variations in cursive English, which are called *contextual forms.*

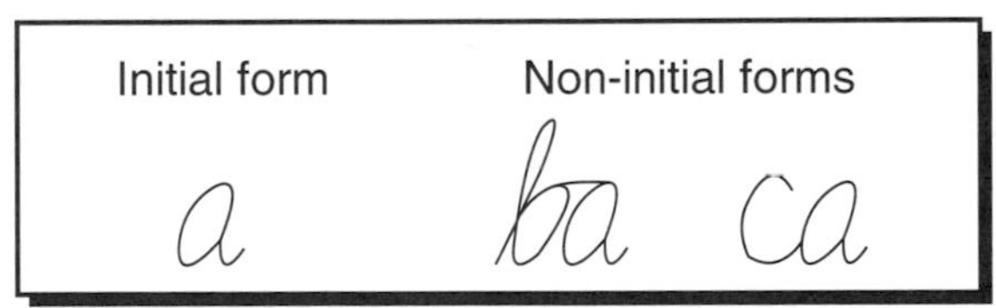

Figure 14-12. Contextual forms in cursive English

The ability to represent contextual forms is required for the proper display of Arabic text. Figure 14-13 shows stand-alone and contextual forms in Arabic.

Figure 14-13. Stand-alone and contextual forms in Arabic

Furthermore, certain character forms may be combined into a new form when they occur together. Figure 14-14 provides an example of how characters combine to form *ligatures* or *conjunct characters* in Roman text.

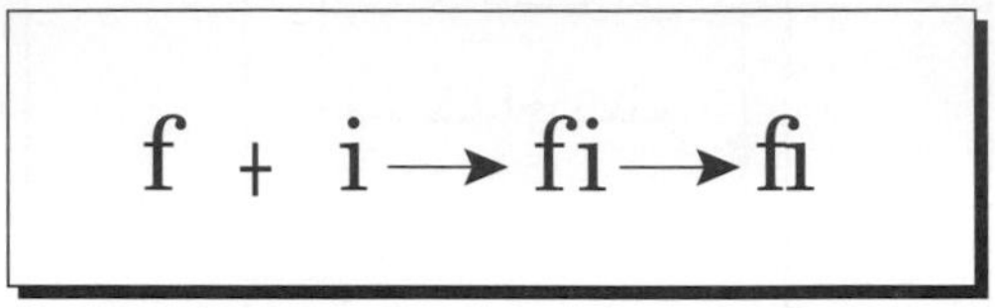

f + i → fi → ﬁ

Figure 14-14. A ligature in Roman text

The use of ligatures can be highly developed in Arabic text, and some ligatures are required for the proper display of Arabic text. Figure 14-15 provides examples of ligatures in Arabic text.

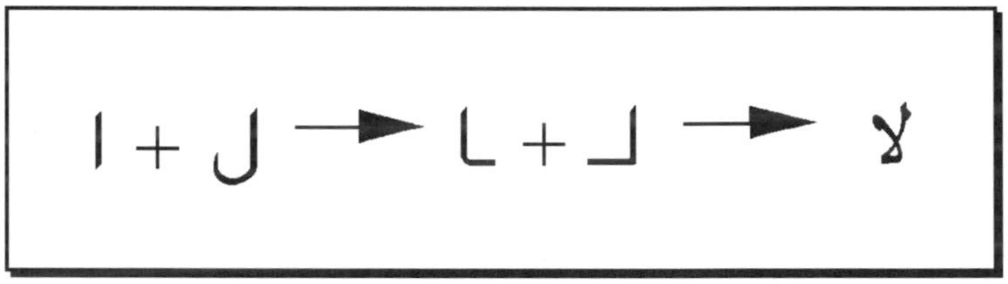

Figure 14-15. Ligatures in Arabic text

In script systems, **context dependence** means that character forms may be modified by the values of preceding and following characters in the input stream. In Arabic, the displayed form of many characters changes depending on other characters nearby. Context analysis is usually handled by the script system under the control of the Script Manager.

Diacritical Marks

Many scripts use **diacritical marks,** that is, signs that modify the implicit sound or value of the characters with which they are associated. Some diacritical marks are often referred to as accents in Roman scripts: the acute accent in *é,* for instance. Others, such as certain Vietnamese diacritical marks, may indicate pitch, while certain Arabic diacritical marks, such as shadda, specify the doubling of consonants. See *Macintosh Worldwide Development: Guide to System Software* for details on diacritical marks available in the standard Roman character set. With system software version 7.0, routines are provided that strip diacritical marks. See “Converting Case and Stripping Diacritical Marks” later in this chapter for details.

Uppercase and Lowercase Characters

English speakers are familiar with uppercase and lowercase characters in Roman script; however, the majority of the world’s scripts do not have separate uppercase and lowercase forms. The implications for computer applications are primarily in the areas of searching, sorting, and proofreading (for example, spell-checking). With system software version 7.0, routines are provided that perform uppercase and lowercase conversion. See “Converting Case and Stripping Diacritical Marks” later in this chapter for details.

Note: In the Roman script, different languages (and even different regions or countries that use the same language) have different conventions for the treatment of accents and diacritical marks on uppercase characters.

Character Reordering

Principles of text ordering differ according to the type of script under consideration. With Roman and simple scripts (such as Greek and Cyrillic) as well as bidirectional scripts (such as Arabic and Hebrew), phonetic and writing order are synonymous except for vowel signs and other marks. With certain Southeast Asian scripts, there may be significant differences between phonetic and writing order.

Figure 14-16 shows an example of the reordering of vowels for the word *hindi* in the Devanagari script. The box on the left illustrates the phonetic order of the characters, whereas the box on the right depicts their writing order. The consonants in this example take a default vowel (a). To modify the vowel, you add a vowel marker. Some vowel markers are written to the right of the consonant they modify; others are written to the left, above, or below.

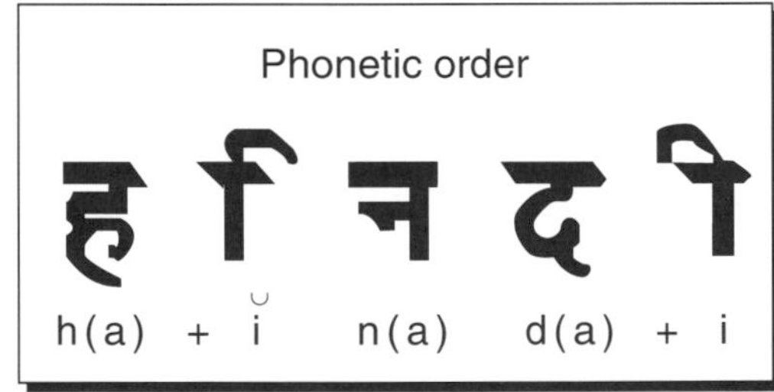

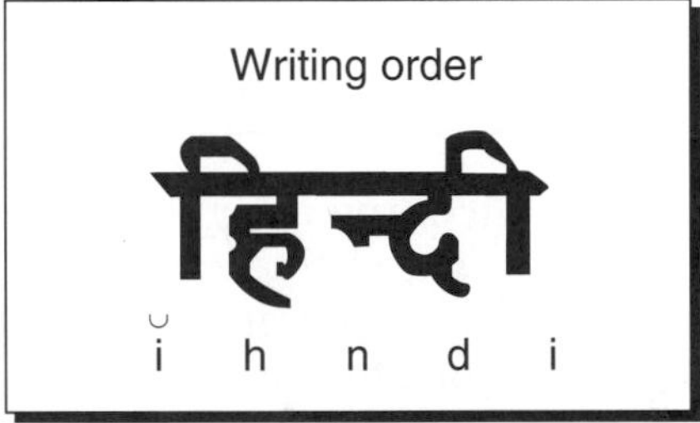

Figure 14-16. Character reordering in Devanagari script (for the word *hindi*)

Word Demarcation

Words in Roman scripts are generally delimited by spaces and punctuation marks. In contrast, many Asian scripts (for example, Japanese and Thai) typically have no word delimiters, so the Script Manager provides a more sophisticated method of finding word boundaries. (For details, see *Macintosh Worldwide Development: Guide to System Software*.) System software version 7.0 generalizes and speeds up the Script Manager FindWord procedure that supplies the word demarcation mechanism. See "Localizing Word Selection and Line Break Tables" later in this chapter for details.

Alignment and Justification of Text

Alignment is the horizontal placement of lines of text with respect to the left and right edges of the destination rectangle. Alignment can be flush left, flush right, centered, or justified (that is, flush on both left and right edges of the destination rectangle). TextEdit supports text alignment that is flush left, centered, flush right, and flush according to the line direction of the script. TextEdit does not support fully justified alignment. The Script Manager supplies routines you can use to provide support for fully justified text in your applications.

Justification (or fully justified alignment) is the spreading or compressing of printed text to fit a given line width. It is usually performed in Roman text primarily by altering the size of the interword spaces. Arabic, however, inserts extension bar characters between joined characters and widens blank characters to fill any remaining gaps. Scripts that don't use interword spaces must modify the intercharacter spacing. The Script Manager provides routines that take these justification methods into account when drawing, measuring, or selecting text. The justification is done by the script systems themselves. See "Handling Justified Text" later in this chapter for details.

REPRESENTING SCRIPTS ON THE MACINTOSH

Worldwide system software makes it possible to represent many scripts and languages on the Macintosh. The Macintosh Script Management System extends the Macintosh computer's text-manipulation capabilities beyond Roman scripts. Character representation and the keyboard are the first components to be considered when attempting to represent any script on a Macintosh computer.

Character Set Encoding

Character set encoding refers to the numeric codes that represent the characters of a script in memory. The character set encoding for a script determines the behavior of many of the features of the script, including sorting and composition rules for drawing and measuring. Therefore, the character set encoding is fixed; it cannot be changed without significant consequences. For example, features such as sorting depend on the fact that the coding does not change.

Most scripts fit within the limits set by the size of a byte, with up to 256 distinct characters. Scripts with ideographic characters, such as Chinese, Japanese, and Korean, need more than 256 distinct characters.

A variety of solutions have been implemented for scripts that require 2-byte codes for computer storage in addition to or in place of the 1-byte codes that are sufficient for Roman scripts. Proper use of the Script Manager routines permits your application to run without knowing whether 1-byte or 2-byte codes are being used, as long as it has been written to allow the possibility of 2-byte codes.

▲ **Warning:** Typically, ideographic scripts use a mixture of single-byte and double-byte encodings to represent characters; therefore, you cannot use the terms *byte* and *character* interchangeably. ▲

Note: Currently, every different character set encoding does not have a different script code. For example, the Symbol font is in the Roman range but has a different character assignment. Before system software version 7.0, the traditional and simplified Chinese systems used different character codings, but had the same script code (2). With system software version 6.0.5, these systems have been assigned separate script codes: smTradChinese (2) and smSimpChinese (25).

Character Input

Character input is often more complicated than simply providing a keyboard layout. Ideographic scripts such as Japanese cannot simply use a larger keyboard or multiple dead keys for effective input. The sheer number of characters demands a more complex solution, such as providing ways to transcribe phonetic text into ideographic text. Most ideographic script systems provide for the complex parsing of phonetic sequences and character clusters.

Composition Rules

Each script system contains composition rules that determine the behavior (that is, the visual appearance) of text when it is drawn, measured, or edited. These intricate rules also provide for other features of the script, such as determining when a sequence of characters forms a word or whether a byte is a single character or part of a double-byte character.

Text Manipulation

With a flexible operating system, most script features are implemented transparently. Usually, your application does not need to know that its dialog boxes can accept Japanese text. However, if your application depends more heavily on features of the language, you need access to information that varies with the script.

For example, to perform word selection and **word wrap** (the automatic continuation of text from the end of one line to the beginning of the next without breaking in the middle of a word), your application may need routines to determine the boundaries of words in the script. In Roman scripts, you can determine word boundaries fairly easily: spaces delimit words that are not otherwise delimited (for example, by punctuation). Other scripts, such as Japanese and Thai, do not use characters such as spaces to delimit words. Word boundaries are not well defined, and native writers of the language may not agree on where particular word boundaries occur.

Because of differences in the treatment of uppercase and lowercase characters and diacritical marks, your application may need routines and tables to perform case conversion and, when sorting is to be done, to strip diacritical marks. The Macintosh Script Management System supplies such routines; they are described briefly in "Modifying Text" and "Converting Case and Stripping Diacritical Marks" later in this chapter and in *Macintosh Worldwide Development: Guide to System Software*.

In addition, your application may require routines to determine whether a byte represents a single character or is part of a double-byte character, or to highlight bidirectional text (for example, Arabic mixed with English). To allow applications to function independently of scripts, the Macintosh Script Management System provides such routines; they are described briefly in "Drawing and Editing Text" later in this chapter and in *Macintosh Worldwide Development: Guide to System Software*.

Text Rendering

The process of displaying characters that are stored in memory is called **text rendering.** **Backing-store order** refers to the order in which character codes are stored in memory. In general, characters for a given script are stored in writing order, that is, the order in which someone would set the characters down on paper. This may be different from the **display order,** that is, the left-to-right order in which characters are *drawn* on a device by QuickDraw. The Script Manager then handles differences between backing-store order and QuickDraw display order. For example, Hebrew characters appear on the screen so that the glyph corresponding to the first character in the string actually appears on the right of the string (see Figure 14-17). In another example, when diacritical marks are stored as separate overlapping characters, they are typically stored *after* the base character. Writing order is very similar to **phonetic order,** that is, the order in which the characters are pronounced, but the two differ in certain circumstances. In some cases, the phonetic order is not well defined, as with diacritical characters.

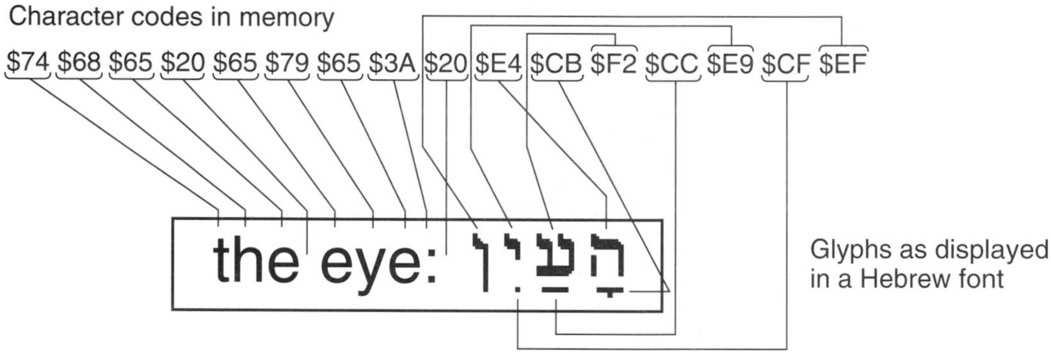

Figure 14-17. Backing-store and display order

USING THE SCRIPT MANAGER

This section describes how to find out the current version number of the Script Manager, determine the number of active script systems, initialize the Script Manager, create simple script systems, and call the Script Manager.

Determining the Features of the Script Manager

Use the Gestalt function to determine the current version of the Script Manager and the number of active script systems. These can also be determined by calling the Script Manager GetEnvirons function. For details on the Gestalt function, see the Compatibility Guidelines chapter in this volume.

Use Gestalt with the gestaltScriptMgrVersion selector to obtain a result in the response parameter that identifies the version number of the Script Manager. This is the same value returned by GetEnvirons(smVersion).

Use the Gestalt selector gestaltScriptCount to obtain a result in the response parameter that gives the number of active script systems. This is the same value returned by GetEnvirons(smEnabled).

Initializing the Script Manager

The Script Manager is initialized at startup. After the Script Manager is initialized, each script system present is installed. When initializing itself, the script system first checks to make sure that there is enough memory to enable itself and then checks to see that all the appropriate resources are present in the System file (for example, its system font and script bundle). If these resources are not available, the script system remains disabled and the other script systems enabled. So even though script systems can install themselves, only those with the proper resources available in the System file are enabled (that is, available for use by the Script Manager and applications).

Creating Simple Script Systems

You can create simple script systems—that is, script systems that contain small character sets and are noncontextual and left to right (for example, Greek or Cyrillic). You are only required to supply the appropriate fonts and the following international, keyboard, and font resources: 'itlb' (with the smsfAutoInit bit on, as described below), 'itl0', 'itl1', 'itl2', 'itl4', 'KCHR', and the keyboard color icon family ('kcs#', 'kcs4', and 'kcs8'). You must also supply 'FOND' and 'NFNT' or 'sfnt' resources.

Such simple script systems can use the Roman Script System routines; however, to operate as a script system, they need their own local variables.

> **Note:** The capability to create simple script systems is available beginning with system software version 6.0.7.

If the flag word in a script's 'itlb' resource in the System file has the smsfAutoInit bit set, the Script Manager initializes the local variables for that script and fills in the font and style information from fields in 'itlb'.

To provide built-in support for all simple script systems, the Roman FindScriptRun function has been modified to use an optional table in the 'itl2' resource that specifies the location of Roman characters in a non-Roman font. See "The 'itl2' Resource" later in this chapter for details.

Calling the Script Manager

The Script Manager implements several routines itself, but for many other routines it acts as a dispatcher to the appropriate script system. For example, each script system provides a CharType function. When a program calls CharType, the Script Manager uses the current **font script** (that is, the script that corresponds to the font of the current grafPort) to dispatch the call to the correct script system. Your application does not need to know whether a particular routine is implemented by the Script Manager or by a script system.

Assembly-language note: All Script Manager routines except the LowerText, UpperText, StripText, and StripUpperText procedures are called via the _ScriptUtil trap.

▲ **Warning:** You should always have the grafPort and A5 world set appropriately before you call any Script Manager or International Utilities Package routine. A5 must point to the QuickDraw global variables, and thePort^.txFont must be set correctly. ▲

Figure 14-18 shows how the Script Manager calls a script system when an application calls a Script Manager routine that is implemented by each script system (for example, the Pixel2Char function). When your application calls Pixel2Char, the Script Manager uses the font script to determine which script system to call. In the example in Figure 14-18, the assumption is that a Japanese font is the font of the current grafPort, so the Script Manager dispatches to the Japanese Script System. The Pixel2Char function in the Japanese Script System is used, and it returns the result directly to the application that called Pixel2Char.

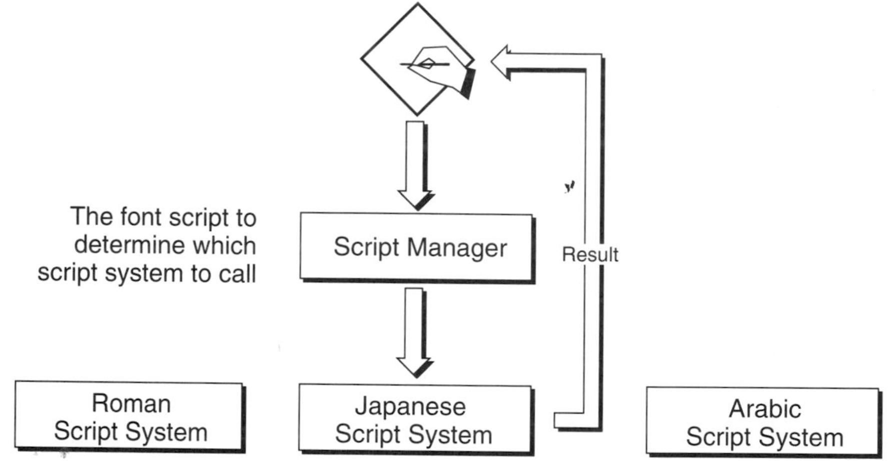

Figure 14-18. Calling the Script Manager routines implemented by a script system

When an application calls a Script Manager routine that is implemented directly by the Script Manager itself (for example, the FontScript function), the flow of control is as shown in Figure 14-19.

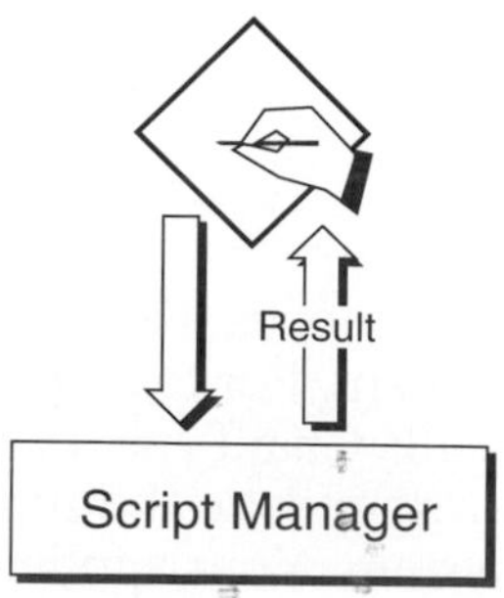

Figure 14-19. Calling the Script Manager routines

OVERVIEW OF THE SCRIPT MANAGER ROUTINES

The Script Manager routines are described briefly in this section. The Script Manager 2.0 routines have not previously been documented in *Inside Macintosh*. They are included in this section, and their interfaces appear in "Summary of the Script Manager" near the end of this chapter. The new routines available with system software version 7.0 are identified by an asterisk (*). The section "Script Manager Routines" later in this chapter describes the routines new with version 7.0 that let you localize word selection and line break tables, truncate text, substitute text, convert case and strip diacritical marks, and handle justified text. For comprehensive discussions of the Script Manager routines available prior to system software version 7.0, see *Macintosh Worldwide Development: Guide to System Software*.

You can use the Script Manager routines to

- check and modify the Script Manager's global and local variables
- check and set system variables
- set or restrict the current keyboard
- obtain script information
- obtain character information
- manipulate text
- interpret different scripts and languages lexically by converting text into a series of text-independent tokens
- manipulate dates and times
- manipulate formatted numbers

Assembly-language note: You can invoke each of the Script Manager routines that uses the _ScriptUtil trap with a macro that has the same name as the routine preceded by an underscore. See "Summary of the Script Manager" near the end of this chapter for a list of the routines that use the _ScriptUtil trap.

Checking and Modifying Global and Local Variables

The GetScript, SetScript, GetEnvirons, and SetEnvirons functions provide ways to inspect and change global and local variables. (Global variables are for the Script Manager, and local variables are for the script systems.)

With system software version 7.0, the GetScript and SetScript functions now accept implicit script codes listed in the next section, "Accepting Implicit Script Codes."

Version 7.0 also includes new verbs for all four functions. A **verb** is an integer constant that controls the function of a multipurpose routine; in this case, the Script Manager uses verbs to figure out which variable you want to read or set. The new verbs let you set and retrieve font and style information, determine if a double-byte script system is installed, determine the current region code, and obtain a pointer to the current 'KCHR' resource. The verbs are listed in Tables 14-1 and 14-2.

GetScript	Retrieves the local variables and routine vectors maintained for the specified script
SetScript	Sets the local variables and routine vectors maintained for the specified script
GetEnvirons	Retrieves the global variables maintained for all scripts
SetEnvirons	Sets the global variables maintained for all scripts

Accepting Implicit Script Codes

In addition to accepting explicit script code constants (for example, smRoman, smThai, and so forth), the script parameter for the GetScript and SetScript functions now accepts implicit script codes, which are special negative values as follows:

Implicit script code	Value	Meaning
smSystemScript	–1	System script
smCurrentScript	–2	Font script

Verbs for GetScript and SetScript

Every Apple®-supplied Macintosh script system supports the verbs listed in Table 14-1 for the GetScript and SetScript functions. If you provide or create a script system, you should also support these verbs.

With version 7.0, each script system's local variables contain fields that supply the following information pertaining to that script: default monospaced font and its size, user-preferred font and size, default small font and size, system font and size, application font and size, and Balloon Help font and size. The 'FOND' ID is stored in the high word, and the size is stored in the low word. Sizes are important; for example, a 9-point font may be too small in Chinese. Table 14-1 lists the new GetScript and SetScript verbs for retrieving font information.

With version 7.0, each script system's local variables contain fields that specify relevant style information for the script. When GetScript is called with the smScriptValidStyles verb, the low-order byte of the returned value is a style mask that includes all of the valid styles for the script. The bit corresponding to each QuickDraw style is set if that style is valid for the specified script. When GetScript is called with the smScriptAliasStyle verb, the low-order byte of the returned value is the style that should be used in that script for indicating alias names (for example, in the Roman script, alias names are indicated in italic). Table 14-1 lists the new SetScript and GetScript verbs for retrieving style information.

Table 14-1. GetScript and SetScript verbs

Verb	Value	Local variable size (in bytes)	Meaning
smScriptVersion	0	2	Script system version number
smScriptMunged	2	2	Local variables modification count
smScriptEnabled	4	1	Script-enabled flag
smScriptRight	6	1	Right-to-left flag
smScriptJust	8	1	Script alignment flag
smScriptRedraw	10	1	Word redraw flag
smScriptSysFond	12	2	Preferred system 'FOND'
smScriptAppFond	14	2	Preferred application 'FOND'
smScriptBundle	16		Beginning of verbs for 'itlb' section
smScriptNumber	16	2	Script 'itl0' ID from 'itlb'
smScriptDate	18	2	Script 'itl1' ID from 'itlb'
smScriptSort	20	2	Script 'itl2' ID from 'itlb'
smScriptFlags	22	2	Script flags from 'itlb'
smScriptToken	24	2	Script 'itl4' ID from 'itlb'
smScriptEncoding	26	2	Optional script 'itl5' ID from 'itlb' resource
smScriptLang	28	2	Current language for script from 'itlb' resource
smScriptNumDate	30	2	Number (high) and date (low) format bytes from 'itlb' resource
smScriptKeys	32	2	Script default 'KCHR' ID from 'itlb'
smScriptIcon	34	2	Script default 'kcs#', 'kcs4', and 'kcs8' IDs from 'itlb' resource
smScriptPrint	36	4	Script printer action routine
smScriptTrap	38	4	Trap entry pointer
smScriptCreator	40	4	Script file creator
smScriptFile	42	4	Script filename
smScriptName	44	4	Script name
smScriptMonoFondSize*	78	4	Default 'FOND' and size for monospaced text
smScriptPrefFondSize*	80	4	User's preferred 'FOND' and size
smScriptSmallFondSize*	82	4	Default 'FOND' and size for small text
smScriptSysFondSize*	84	4	Default system 'FOND' and size
smScriptAppFondSize*	86	4	Default application 'FOND' and size
smScriptHelpFondSize*	88	4	Default 'FOND' and size for Balloon Help
smScriptValidStyles*	90	1	Set of all valid styles for script
smScriptAliasStyle*	92	1	Style to use for indicating aliases

* New with system software version 7.0

Verbs for GetEnvirons and SetEnvirons

When you call GetEnvirons or SetEnvirons, you use a verb to describe the variable that interests you. The names, values, sizes, and meanings of the GetEnvirons and SetEnvirons verbs are listed in Table 14-2.

With version 7.0, the Script Manager global variables include a variable that indicates if a double-byte script system (that is, one containing double-byte character codes) is installed. The Boolean variable is accessible with the smDoubleByte verb. (Examples of double-byte script systems include KanjiTalk and Zhong-WenTalk™.)

With version 7.0, the Script Manager global variables also contain a pointer to the cache that stores the current 'KCHR' resource data. The pointer is accessible with the smKCHRCache verb.

Finally, with version 7.0, an integer, accessible with the smRegionCode verb, has been added to the Script Manager global variables. This integer contains the current region code obtained from the 'itlc' resource.

Table 14-2. Verbs for GetEnvirons and SetEnvirons

Verb	Value	Global size (in bytes)	Meaning
smVersion	0	2	Script Manager version number
smMunged	2	2	Global modification count
smEnabled	4	1	Script count; 0 if Script Manager not enabled
smBidirect	6	1	Bidirectional script flag; TRUE if bidirectional script installed
smFontForce	8	1	fontForce flag
smIntlForce	10	1	intlForce flag
smForced	12	1	TRUE if current script forced to system script
smDefault	14	1	TRUE if current script defaulted to Roman Script System
smPrint	16	4	Print action vector
smSysScript	18	2	Preferred system script
smLastScript	20	2	Last keyboard script
smKeyScript	22	2	Keyboard script
smSysRef	24	2	System Folder (volume reference number)
smKeyCache	26		Keyboard cache (obsolete)
smKeySwap	28	4	Keyboard swapping resource handle
smGenFlags	30	4	General flags
smOverride	32	4	Script override flags
smCharPortion†	34	2	Proportion of intercharacter versus white space, 4.12 fixed-point format
smDoubleByte*	36	1	Flag; TRUE if double-byte script system installed
smKCHRCache*	38	4	Pointer to cache containing current 'KCHR' resource
smRegionCode*	40	2	Integer with current region code

*New with system software version 7.0

†The variable specified by the smCharPortion verb is used for text justification. It denotes the weight allocated to intercharacter space versus white space (10 percent by default for Roman). The 4.12 fixed-point format specifies 4 bits of integer and 12 bits of fraction.

Note: To identify a localized non-U.S. script system, look at the smRegionCode verb.

Checking and Setting System Variables

The GetDefFontSize, GetSysFont, GetAppFont, GetMBarHeight, and GetSysJust routines return the most recent values of given (low-memory) global variables. SetSysJust sets the global variable that represents the default line direction for the system.

GetDefFontSize	Returns the size of the current default font
GetSysFont	Returns the identification number of the current system font
GetAppFont	Returns the identification number of the current application font
GetMBarHeight	Returns the height of the menu bar required to hold menu titles in the current system font. This routine is useful for calculating window size or dragLimit rect
GetSysJust	Returns the value of TESysJust, the global variable that represents the default line direction (left to right or right to left) for text in the system script
SetSysJust	Sets the value of TESysJust (see the description of GetSysJust for a description of TESysJust)

Setting the Active Keyboard Script

The main purpose of the KeyScript procedure is to update the keyboard layout (by using the 'KCHR' and 'itlk' resources) and the keyboard script based on the verb with which it is called. If the Keyboard menu is displayed, KeyScript also updates the Keyboard menu.

Verbs can explicitly specify a script, implicitly specify a script (for example, the next script), or implicitly specify a keyboard (for example, the next keyboard in the active script). If the verb specifies a script, then the active default keyboard layout for that script becomes the active keyboard. You can call KeyScript with an argument that is either an explicit script code or a negative verb with a special meaning. The KeyScript verbs are listed in Table 14-3.

> **Note:** Beginning with system software version 7.0, KeyScript only loads 'KCHR' and 'itlk' resources if they are present in the System file.

The smKeyNextScript, smKeySysScript, and smKeySwapScript verbs existed in system software version 6.0, but were not documented. They all set the active keyboard script. New with system software version 7.0, the smKeyNextKybd verb switches to the next keyboard within the active keyboard script. (See Table 14-3.)

When the user is typing the name of an HFS object—for example, in the Finder or a standard file dialog box—the keyboard script must be restricted to scripts that display correctly in the Finder, dialog boxes, menus, and alerts. KeyScript is called with the smKeyDisableKybds verb to disable keyboard input temporarily in any script except Roman or the system script. Keyboards in other scripts will appear disabled in the Keyboard menu. When entry of the name has been completed, KeyScript is called with smKeyEnableKybds to reenable keyboard input in all enabled scripts.

Table 14-3. Verbs for the KeyScript procedure

Verb	Value	Meaning
(any script code)	0..64	Switch to specified script
smKeyNextScript	–1	Switch to next available script
smKeySysScript	–2	Switch to system script
smKeySwapScript	–3	Switch to previously used script
smKeyNextKybd	–4	Switch to next keyboard in active script
smKeySwapKybd*	–5	Switch to previously used keyboard in active script
smKeyDisableKybds	–6	Disable keyboards not in script system or Roman Script System
smKeyEnableKybds	–7	Enable keyboards for all enabled scripts
smKeyToggleInline†	–8	Toggle inline input for current script
smKeyToggleDirection†	–9	Toggle default line direction
smKeyNextInputMethod†	–10	Switch to next input method in current script
smKeySwapInputMethod†	–11	Switch to previously used input method in current script
smKeyDisableKybdSwitch	–12	Disable switching from the current keyboard

*Not implemented in system software version 7.0

†Not implemented in U.S. system software, but may be implemented by appropriate script systems

When keyboard layouts and scripts are being moved into or out of the System file, it is imperative that no user action changes the active keyboard or active script system. To ensure the integrity of both the current (active) script system and the other enabled script systems, a new KeyScript verb has been provided to remove the possibility of a user corrupting the system. To prevent all keyboard switching and to disable all the Keyboard menu items, KeyScript is called with the verb smKeyDisableKybdSwitch. When the move has been completed, KeyScript is called with smKeyEnableKybds to reenable keyboard switching.

Obtaining Script Information

The FontScript, Font2Script, and IntlScript functions give you ways to determine the script code based on the font of the current grafPort that is subject to two control flags, FontForce and IntlForce. These flags can be set and tested with SetEnvirons and GetEnvirons.

FontScript — Returns the script code for the font of the current grafPort, unless the FontForce flag is on. (For details on the FontForce flag, see *Macintosh Worldwide Development: Guide to System Software.*)

Font2Script — Translates a font identification number into a script code.

IntlScript — Returns the code of the script whose resources will be used by the International Utilities Package routines IUDateString and IUTimeString and depends on the font of the current grafPort. If the IntlForce flag is TRUE, IntlScript returns the system script; otherwise, it returns the font script. (For details on the IntlForce flag, see "Using the International and Keyboard Resources" later in this chapter.)

Note: With system software version 7.0, if the font of the current grafPort corresponds to a script that is not installed and enabled, these routines default to the system script. Before system software version 7.0, the routines defaulted to the Roman Script System.

Obtaining Character Information

The CharByte, CharType, and ParseTable functions allow you to get data pertaining to specific characters.

CharByte	Identifies a specified byte in a text buffer as a single-byte character or as the first or second byte of a double-byte character
CharType	Returns more information about the specified character
ParseTable	Returns a 256-byte table that indicates for each byte value, when it appears as the first byte of a character, whether there is an additional byte in the character (in the script of thePort^.txFont)

Manipulating Text

The Script Manager supplies a variety of routines that help you draw, edit, format, and modify text. New routines available with system software version 7.0, identified by an asterisk (*), allow you to justify, substitute, and truncate text, perform case conversion, and strip diacritical marks.

Drawing and Editing Text

The Char2Pixel, DrawJust, FindWord, HiliteText, MeasureJust, and Pixel2Char routines help you draw and edit text. With system software version 7.0, the Char2Pixel, DrawJust, MeasureJust, and Pixel2Char routines handle intercharacter spacing in all scripts, if appropriate. In addition, there are new NChar2Pixel, NDrawJust, NMeasureJust, NPixel2Char, and NPortionText routines that also allow you to specify additional parameters to improve the handling of fully justified text. Also new with system version 7.0, the NFindWord procedure is a more powerful version of FindWord that lets you specify word boundaries for more than one script.

Char2Pixel	Finds the screen position of carets and selection points given a text buffer, an offset, and a slop value
NChar2Pixel*	Supplies a more powerful version of Char2Pixel that works with intercharacter spacing, lets you indicate the position of a style run within a line for lines with multiple style runs, and accepts scaling parameters
DrawJust	Draws the given text at the current pen location in the current font, style, and size, taking into account the slop value

NDrawJust*	Supplies a more powerful version of DrawJust that works with intercharacter spacing, lets you indicate the position of a style run within a line for lines with multiple style runs, and accepts scaling parameters
FindWord	Returns two offsets in the array defined by the OffsetTable data type that specify the boundaries of the word defined by the offset parameter and the leadingEdge flag (for details on the OffsetTable data type, see "Summary of the Script Manager" near the end of this chapter)
NFindWord*	Supplies a faster and more powerful version of FindWord that can replace script-dependent versions of FindWord so that script systems must only supply appropriate tables (in the 'itl2' resource)
HiliteText	Finds the characters that should be highlighted between two offsets
MeasureJust	Given a slop value, a pointer to an array of characters, an integer indicating the number of characters in that text, and a pointer to an array of integers, fills each element in the array of integers with the width from the beginning of the string to the corresponding character in the array of characters (the supplied widths take the slop value into account—that is, they will be the widths necessary to justify the text)
NMeasureJust*	Supplies a more powerful version of MeasureJust that works with intercharacter spacing, lets you indicate the position of a style run within a line for lines with multiple style runs, and accepts scaling parameters
Pixel2Char	Finds the nearest character offset within a text buffer corresponding to a given pixel width, taking into account the slop value
NPixel2Char*	Supplies a more powerful version of Pixel2Char that works with intercharacter spacing, lets you indicate the position of a style run within a line for lines with multiple style runs, and accepts scaling parameters

Formatting Text

The FindScriptRun, PortionText, GetFormatOrder, StyledLineBreak, and VisibleLength routines allow you to format text. The NPortionText function, available with system software version 7.0, provides a more powerful version of PortionText that lets you work with scaling and indicate the position of a style run within a line.

FindScriptRun	Finds the next block of Roman or native text within a script run; within scripts that contain subscripts, blocks of native text are limited to a subscript
PortionText	Indicates the correct proportion of justification to be allocated to given text when compared to other text; used to determine how to distribute the slop of a line among the style runs on the line
NPortionText *	Supplies a new version of PortionText that lets you indicate the position of a style run within a line for lines with multiple style runs and accepts scaling parameters
GetFormatOrder	Tells in what order format runs should be drawn based on line direction for a particular line of text

StyledLineBreak	Breaks a line on a word boundary
VisibleLength	Returns the length of text, excluding trailing white space and accounting for the script of the text

Modifying Text

The LowerText, Transliterate, and UpperText routines let you localize text into a base form and convert text from lowercase into uppercase, providing for the localizable stripping of diacritical marks. The StripText and StripUpperText procedures, available with system software version 7.0, provide localizable stripping of diacritical characters and conversion of the characters into uppercase. LowerText and UpperText, also new with version 7.0, are faster and easier to use than Transliterate, but less powerful.

LowerText*	Provides localizable lowercasing of text up to 32 KB in length (LwrText is a synonym for LowerText)
StripText *	Provides localizable stripping of diacritical characters for text up to 32 KB in length
StripUpperText *	Provides localizable stripping of diacritical characters for text up to 32 KB in length and converts them to uppercase characters
Transliterate	Converts characters from a set of scripts or subscripts to the closest possible approximation in a different script or subscript, and performs localizable uppercasing and lowercasing
UpperText*	Provides localizable uppercasing for text up to 32 KB in length

Note: UpperText is different from UprText, which provides nonlocalizable uppercasing using the _UprString trap.

Substituting Text

The ReplaceText function, new with system software version 7.0, allows you to substitute text correctly for all scripts. It provides a global way for you to do parameter text replacement in your applications. ReplaceText searches specified text for instances of a string specified by the key parameter and replaces each instance with the replacement text supplied.

Truncating Text

The TruncString and TruncText functions, new with system software version 7.0, let you truncate text at the end or in the middle in order to fit it into a specified pixel width.

TruncString*	Ensures that a string supplied as Str255 fits into the specified pixel width by truncating the string, if necessary, in a manner dependent on the script associated with the font of the active grafPort
TruncText*	Is similar to TruncString except that the string is defined by a pointer and a length

Lexically Interpreting Different Scripts

The IntlTokenize function takes arbitrary text and breaks it into tokens like the lexical analyzer of a compiler. IntlTokenize allows a program to recognize tokens such as variables, symbols, and quoted literals without making assumptions that depend on a particular script.

Date and Time Utilities

The Script Manager contains four categories of routines that help with worldwide date and time conversion. The routines convert among various formats for dates and times, change long dates, modify and verify date and time records, and read and store geographic locations. For details on related time and date data structures, see "Summary of the Script Manager" near the end of this chapter and *Macintosh Worldwide Development: Guide to System Software*.

Converting Worldwide Dates and Times

The InitDateCache, String2Date, and String2Time functions let you convert worldwide dates and times.

InitDateCache	Formats the date cache record (defined by the DateCacheRecord data type) for use by the String2Date and String2Time routines
String2Date	Expects the date at beginning of text and parses text for use in the date-time record (defined by the LongDateRec data type)
String2Time	Expects the time at beginning of text and parses text for use in the date-time record

Converting Long Dates

The LongDate2Secs and LongSecs2Date procedures allow you to convert dates between the LongDateRec format (an explicit year, month, day, and so forth) and the LongDateTime format (an 8-byte signed value, seconds since January 1, 1904).

LongDate2Secs	Converts the time specified in a long date record to a LongDateTime format
LongSecs2Date	Converts the date specified in a LongDateTime format to a long date record

Modifying and Verifying Date and Time Records

The ToggleDate and ValidDate functions allow you to change date and time records and check the validity of the resulting data structures.

ToggleDate	Modifies a LongDateTime parameter by toggling one of the corresponding fields of the long date record up or down or by setting it explicitly (for a list of error code constants for ToggleDate, see "Summary of the Script Manager" near the end of this chapter)
ValidDate	Checks the validity of a long date record

Reading and Storing Locations

The ReadLocation and WriteLocation procedures let you access, manipulate, and store the geographic location of the Macintosh and related time zone information.

ReadLocation	Accesses the stored geographic location of the Macintosh and the time zone information from the parameter RAM
WriteLocation	Stores the geographic location of the Macintosh and the time zone information in parameter RAM

Number Utilities

The Script Manager number utilities let you change the ways numbers are represented so they can be displayed in various international formats. A **canonical number format** is a private, internal format that specifies the number format in a way that is independent of region, language, and other multicultural considerations.

Converting to and From Canonical Number Formats

The Str2Format and Format2Str functions change format strings typed by users into a private, internal format and let applications change private, internal formats into localized format strings.

Str2Format	Converts a format string typed by users into a canonical number format
Format2Str	Allows programs to convert previously entered canonical number formats to a format string that depends on the localized version of the system software

Working With Formatted Numbers

The FormatX2Str and FormatStr2X functions change an internal floating-point representation of a number into a localized formatted numeric string and vice versa.

FormatX2Str	Converts an internal floating-point (SANE) representation of a number into a localized formatted numeric string

Note: If you compile your application to use the 881 option, you need to convert 96-bit numbers to 80-bit numbers before they can be passed to FormatX2Str.

FormatStr2X	Converts a localized formatted numeric string into an internal floating-point representation of a number

Note: FormatStr2X returns an 80-bit, not a 96-bit, representation.

SCRIPT MANAGER ROUTINES

This section describes new Script Manager routines available with system software version 7.0. The routines allow you to localize word selection and line break tables, truncate text, substitute text, perform case conversion, and strip diacritical marks.

Localizing Word Selection and Line Break Tables

Until system software version 7.0, each script system provided its own version of the FindWord procedure, which locates word boundaries for word selection and line breaking by examining a block of text to determine the boundaries of the word that includes a specified character in the block. The NFindWord procedure is a new, state-table-driven version of FindWord that is faster and more powerful. It can replace the script-dependent versions of FindWord so that script systems need only supply the appropriate tables in their 'itl2' resource. The break tables used by NFindWord are in a new format, which is documented in the next section, "Defining Word Boundaries and Line Breaks."

When FindWord is called, the Script Manager examines the breaks parameter to determine if the call can be routed to the NFindWord procedure. If breaks is an explicit pointer to a break table and the table is in the new format, the call is routed to NFindWord. Also, if breaks is 0 or –1 to specify one of the default break tables and if the script's 'itl2' resource contains tables in the new format, the call is routed to NFindWord. Otherwise, the call is routed to the script's FindWord procedure so that old-format break tables continue to work. The Script Manager assumes tables are in the new format if the high-order bit of the first byte is 1.

You can also call NFindWord directly, as follows:

```
PROCEDURE NFindWord (textPtr: Ptr; textLength: Integer; offset: Integer;
                     leadingEdge: Boolean; nbreaks: NBreakTablePtr;
                     VAR offsets: OffsetTable);
```

The NFindWord interface is identical to that of the FindWord routine except that the nbreaks parameter must be an explicit pointer to a new-format break table; the values 0 and –1 may not be used to indicate default break tables.

To specify the text block, you pass two parameters: the textPtr parameter, a pointer to the beginning of the text to be examined, and the textLength parameter, the length of the text to be examined. Since the offset parameter specifies a position between two characters, additional information is required to determine which character should be used as a basis for finding the word boundaries. This is supplied by the leadingEdge parameter. If leadingEdge is TRUE, the offset corresponds to the character whose leading edge borders the offset. (The leadingEdge parameter corresponds to the left side in a left-to-right script such as Roman.) If leadingEdge is FALSE, the offset is on the trailing edge of the specified character. To specify word definitions, you pass the nbreaks parameter, which is a pointer to a word break table, a table that determines where word breaks occur.

NFindWord returns information about word boundaries in the offsets array. This is an array of three offset pairs. The first integer in the first pair contains the offset before the leading edge of the first character of the word; the second integer in the first pair contains the offset after the trailing edge of the last character of the word. The remaining values in the offsets array are set to 0.

FindWord and NFindWord are often used in conjunction with the Pixel2Char and HiliteText routines, and the interfaces to FindWord and NFindWord have been designed for smooth integration with these routines.

Defining Word Boundaries and Line Breaks

This section describes how the NFindWord procedure uses state machines and associated tables to determine word boundaries and line breaks. For more details on the NFindWord procedure, see the previous section, "Localizing Word Selection and Line Break Tables."

The NFindWord procedure examines a block of text to determine the boundaries of the word that includes a specified character in the block. Usually, NFindWord uses different state tables to define words for word selection and words for word wrap (line breaking).

> **Note:** NFindWord considers offsets within a block of text to be positions between characters—for example, an offset of 1 in Roman text is between the first and second characters (or on the trailing edge of the first and on the leading edge of the second).

NFindWord uses a state machine to determine word boundaries. The state machine must start at a point at or before the beginning of the word that includes the specified character. This can be accomplished in two ways. First, if the specified character is sufficiently close to the beginning of the text buffer, the state machine simply starts from the beginning of the buffer. This is determined by the doBackupMin parameter in the tables: if the offset parameter is less than doBackupMin, the state machine starts from the beginning. Otherwise, NFindWord uses a second state table, BackwardTable, for backward processing. With BackwardTable, NFindWord starts at the specified character, moving backward as necessary until it encounters a word break.

Once determined, this starting point is saved as an initial word break location. From this point, the NFindWord state machine moves forward using ForwardTable until it encounters another word break. If that word break is still before the specified character, its location is saved as the starting point, and the state machine is restarted from that location. This process repeats until the state machine finds a word break that is after the specified character. At that point, NFindWord returns the last saved word break location and the current word break location as the offset pair defining the word boundaries.

The state machine operates in a similar manner whether moving backward or forward; any differences in behavior are determined by the tables. The machine begins in the start state (state 1). It then cycles one character at a time until it finds a word break and exits. Each cycle proceeds as follows: the current character is mapped to a class number. The character class and the current state are used as indices into a two-dimensional array of byte-length action codes. Each action code specifies the following:

- whether to mark the current offset
- the next state, which may be the exit state (state 0)

When the state machine exits, it has encountered a word break. The location of the word break is the last character offset that was marked. In general, the state machine marks a character offset when it determines that the word that began at its starting point extends at least to the marked offset.

Figure 14-20 gives two examples of the forward operation of the state machine for word selection. In each case, the state at a given offset and the class of the character following the offset determine (1) whether to mark that offset, (2) whether to exit at that point, and, if not exiting, (3) what the state at the next offset will be. When the state machine exits, the first and last marked offsets are returned as the word boundaries.

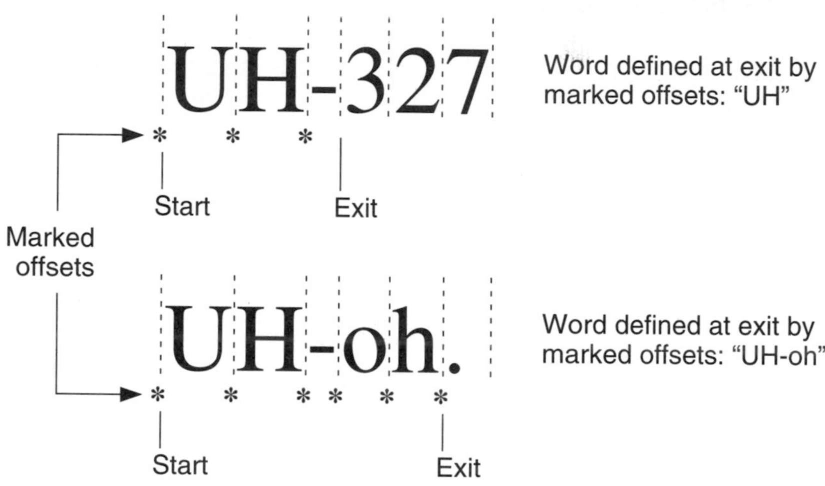

Figure 14-20. Forward operation of the state machine for word selection

Mapping characters to classes is simple for single-byte characters, but the process gets a little more involved for double-byte character codes. The byte value at the current character offset is used as an offset into the ClassTable array, an array of 256 signed bytes. If the value in ClassTable is positive, it signifies that the byte at the current character offset is a single-byte character, and the value in ClassTable is the class number for the character. If the value in ClassTable is negative, it signifies that the byte at the current character offset is the first byte of a double-byte character code, and AuxClassTable must be used to determine the character class.

The AuxClassTable class table begins with a variable-length word array. The first word contains a default class number for double-byte character codes. The following words are offsets to RowTables, which have the same format as ClassTable, but are used by NFindWord for mapping the second byte of a double-byte character code to a class number. If the value in ClassTable was –1 (or any odd, negative number), the double-byte character code is assigned the default class from the first word of AuxClassTable. For other double-byte characters, the value in ClassTable is an even negative number; NFindWord negates this value to provide an offset from the beginning of AuxClassTable to the appropriate RowTable offset. The RowTable table specified by this offset in this way is used to map the second byte of the character to a class number.

> **Note:** There is a maximum of 128 classes and 128 states (including the start and exit states).

Figures 14-21 provides a description of the new break table. Note that the high bit of the first word is set to indicate that this table is in the new format; otherwise, FindWord assumes that the tables are in the old format. The new break table begins with an 8-word header, followed by the class and state tables.

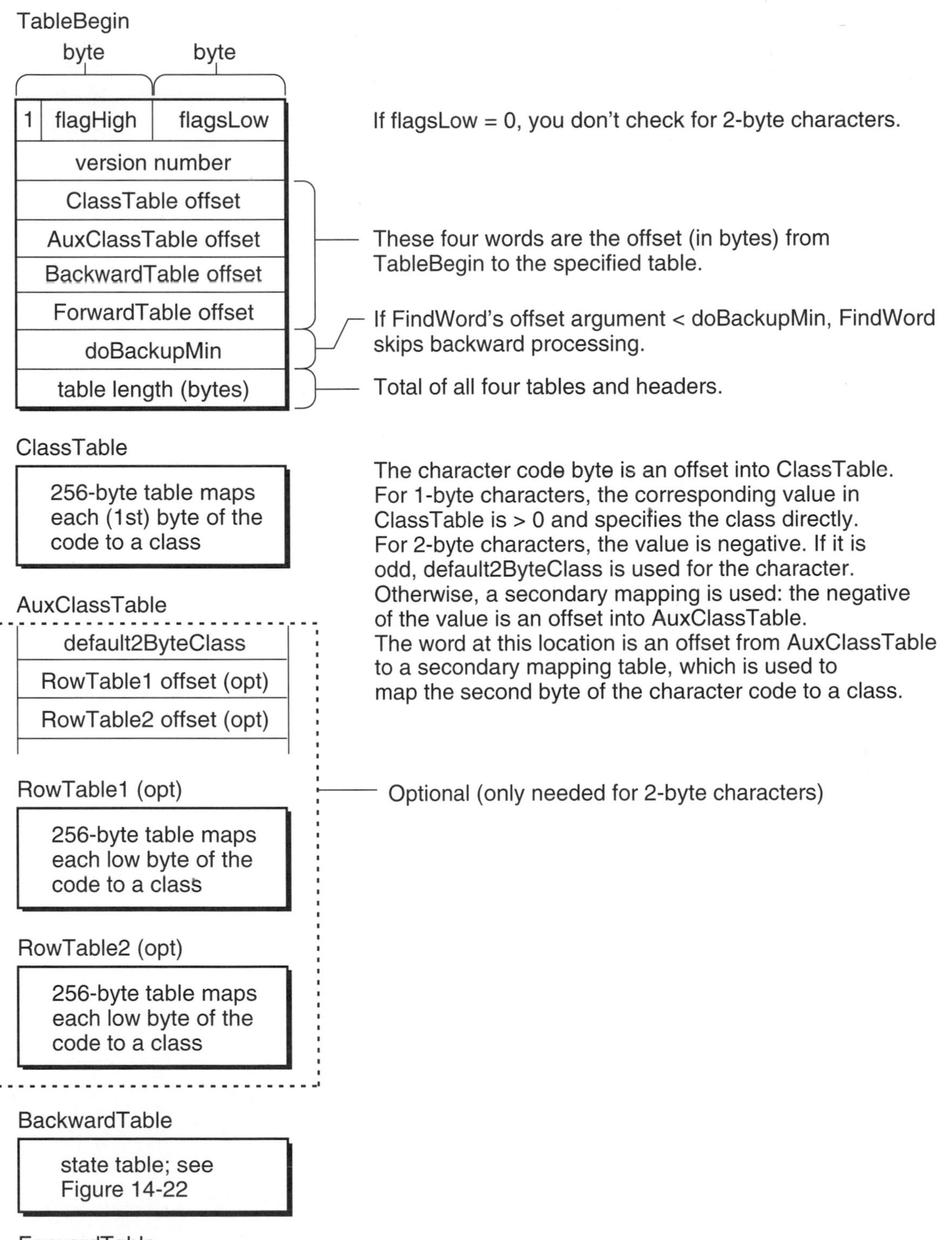
TableBegin
byte
byte
1
flagHigh
flagsLow
If flagsLow = 0, you don't check for 2-byte characters.
version number
ClassTable offset
AuxClassTable offset
BackwardTable offset
ForwardTable offset
These four words are the offset (in bytes) from TableBegin to the specified table.
doBackupMin
If FindWord's offset argument < doBackupMin, FindWord skips backward processing.
table length (bytes)
Total of all four tables and headers.
ClassTable
256-byte table maps each (1st) byte of the code to a class
The character code byte is an offset into ClassTable. For 1-byte characters, the corresponding value in ClassTable is > 0 and specifies the class directly. For 2-byte characters, the value is negative. If it is odd, default2ByteClass is used for the character. Otherwise, a secondary mapping is used: the negative of the value is an offset into AuxClassTable. The word at this location is an offset from AuxClassTable to a secondary mapping table, which is used to map the second byte of the character code to a class.
AuxClassTable
default2ByteClass
RowTable1 offset (opt)
RowTable2 offset (opt)
RowTable1 (opt)
256-byte table maps each low byte of the code to a class
Optional (only needed for 2-byte characters)
RowTable2 (opt)
256-byte table maps each low byte of the code to a class
BackwardTable
state table; see Figure 14-22
ForwardTable
state table; see Figure 14-22

Figure 14-21. NFindWord header and class tables

Figure 14-22 shows the NFindWord state table. It begins with a list of words containing byte offsets from the beginning of the state table to the rows of the state table; this is followed by a C-by-S byte array, where C is the number of classes and S is the number of states. The bytes in this array are stored with the column index varying most rapidly; that is, the bytes for the State 1 row precede the bytes for the State 2 row. Each byte in this array is an action code whose format is defined in Figure 14-23.

Reserved (must be 0)
Offset to State 1 row
Offset to State 2 row
Offset to State 3 row
Offset to State 4 row
Offset to State 5 row

	Class 0	Class 1	Class 2	Class 3	Class 4
State 1 row	action	action	action	action	action
State 2 row	action	action	action	action	action
State 3 row	action	action	action	action	action
State 4 row	action	action	action	action	action
State 5 row	action	action	action	action	action

Figure 14-22. NFindWord state table

Figure 14-23 shows the format of an action code.

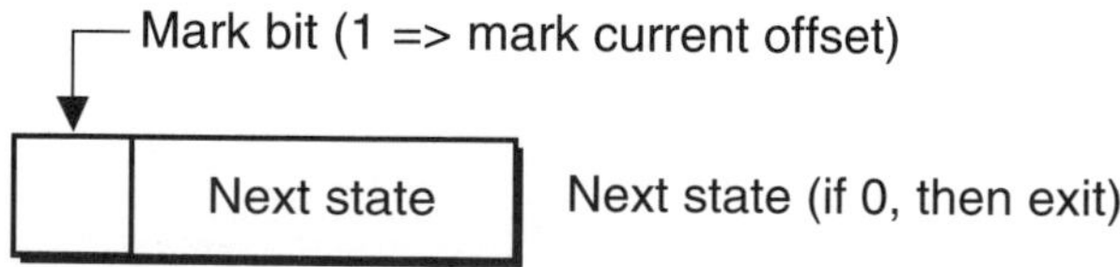

Figure 14-23. Format of NFindWord action code

Determining Word Selection: An Example

This section provides an example of how a script system determines word selection.

Note: The definition of a word in the Roman Script System may vary slightly with localization.

Table 14-4 provides the class numbers, character classes, and explanations of the class names for the U.S. word selection algorithm.

Table 14-4. U.S. word selection algorithm

Class number	Class name	Used for
0	break	Everything not included below
1	nonBreak	Nonbreaking spaces
2	letter	Letters, ligatures, and accents
3	number	Digits
4	midLetter	Hyphen
5	midLetNum	Apostrophe (vertical or right single quote)
6	preNum	$ £ ¥ ¤
7	postNum	% ‰ ¢
8	midNum	, /
9	preMidNum	.
10	blank	Space, tab, null
11	cr	Return

The NFindWord table in the U.S. 'itl2' resource defines words as any of the following configurations of the classes listed in Table 14-4:

- A sequence of letters, possibly separated by a hyphen, apostrophe, or period and possibly followed by a sequence of numbers (defined next). Some examples are *ultra-cool*, *Bob's*, and *record.field.*
- A sequence of numbers, possibly separated by a comma, fraction sign, apostrophe, or period; possibly preceded by a decimal point or currency sign; and possibly followed by a percentage sign or by a sequence of letters (defined previously). Some examples are *1.234*, *$23.14*, *.70*, and *12ea–b.*
- A sequence of spaces, tabs, or nulls, possibly followed by a *cr*.
- Characters that are words by themselves and not included as part of the above definitions.

Note: With system software version 7.0, the treatment of a sequence of one or more nonbreaking spaces has changed. If there is a non-whitespace character (that is, a character that is neither *blank* nor *cr*) on either side of the sequence, the sequence becomes part of the word that includes the non-whitespace character. Thus, if the sequence is between non-whitespace characters, it joins the words of which they are a part. Otherwise, the nonbreaking spaces are treated as blanks.

Table 14-5 shows where word breaks occur in various character sequences. In the table, *other* denotes any character that is not *blank, cr,* or *nonBreak.*

Table 14-5. Occurrence of word breaks in various character sequences

Character	Word break	Character	Word break	Character
blank	no	*nonBreak*	no	*blank*
blank	no	*nonBreak*	no	*cr*
blank	yes	*nonBreak*	no	*other*
cr	yes	*nonBreak*	no	*blank*
cr	yes	*nonBreak*	no	*cr*
cr	yes	*nonBreak*	no	*other*
other	no	*nonBreak*	yes	*blank*
other	no	*nonBreak*	yes	*cr*
other	no	*nonBreak*	no	*other*

Table 14-6 describes the meaning of each state number shown in Figure 14-24.

Table 14-6. Significance of the state numbers in the Roman word selection algorithm

State number	Meaning
1	Start, or has detected initial *nonBreak* sequence
2	Has detected a *letter*
3	Has detected a *number*
4	Has detected a non-whitespace character that should stand alone; now anything but *nonBreak* generates an exit
5	Has detected *preMidNum* or *preNum;* now anything but *number* or *nonBreak* generates an exit
6	Has detected a *blank*
7	Has detected a *letter* followed by *midLetter, midLetNum,* or *preMidNum;* now anything but *letter* generates an exit
8	Has detected a non-whitespace character followed by *nonBreak* (the *nonBreak* should be treated as non-whitespace)
9	Has detected a *number* followed by *midNum, midLetNum,* or *preMidNum;* now anything but *number* generates an exit
10	Marks current offset (include one more character), then exits
11	Has detected *blank* followed by *nonBreak* (the *nonBreak* should be treated as *blank*)

Figure 14-24 illustrates the process of determining whether a sequence of characters is to be selected as a word. It shows the possible paths through the states of the Roman word selection algorithm defined in Table 14-7.

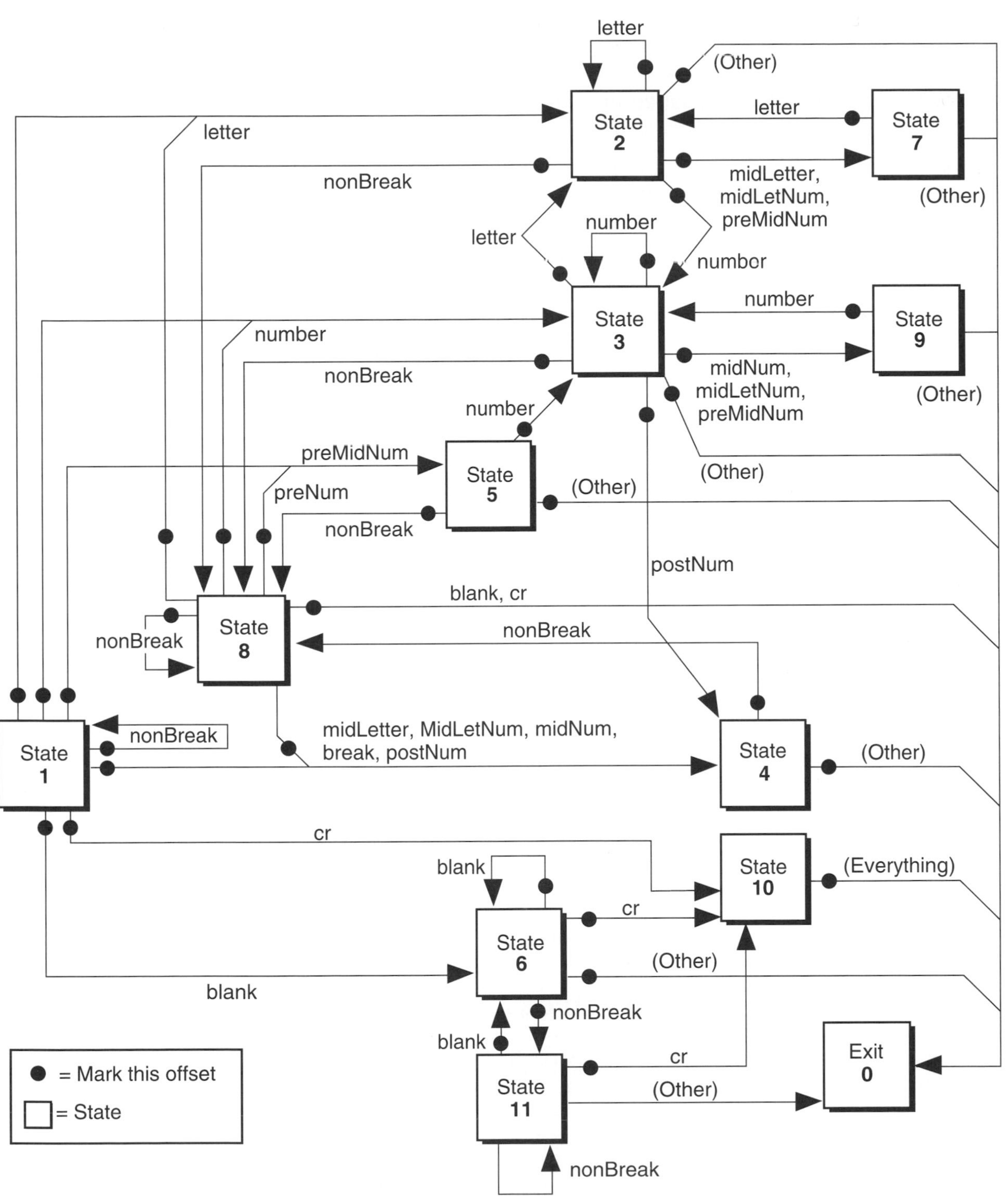

Figure 14-24. Roman word selection state transitions

Table 14-7 shows the U.S. word selection transition table for forward processing. Each column shows the action codes for a current state.

Note: In this table, the first column must be all nonzero values with '*'.

Table 14-7. U.S. word select transition table for forward processing

Class number	Class name	State number 1	2	3	4	5	6	7	8	9	10	11
0	break	*4	*0	*0	*0	*0	*0	0	*4	0	*0	0
1	nonBreak	*8	*8	*8	*8	*8	*0	0	*8	0	*0	11
2	letter	*2	*2	*2	*0	*0	*0	*2	*2	0	*0	0
3	number	*3	*3	*3	*0	*3	*0	0	*3	*3	*0	0
4	midLetter	*4	*7	*0	*0	*0	*0	0	*4	0	*0	0
5	midLetNum	*4	*7	*9	*0	*0	*0	0	*4	0	*0	0
6	preNum	*5	*0	*0	*0	*0	*0	0	*5	0	*0	0
7	postNum	*4	*0	*4	*0	*0	*0	0	*4	0	*0	0
8	midNum	*4	*0	*9	*0	*0	*0	0	*4	0	*0	0
9	preMidNum	*5	*7	*9	*0	*0	*0	0	*5	0	*0	0
10	blank	*6	*0	*0	*0	*0	*6	0	*0	0	*0	*6
11	cr	*10	*0	*0	*0	*0	*10	0	*0	0	*0	*10

* Means "mark the offset before this character"

Optimized Word Break Tables

Listing 14-1 shows how to obtain a copy of the word selection table from the default 'itl2' resource. You may want to do this so that you can pass the word selection table directly to NFindWord or FindWord in a loop. This example assumes that inside the loop you are trying to find word boundaries. Outside the loop, you set up for this task by getting a copy of the table needed for the word break routine. See "Manipulating the 'itl2' and 'itl4' Resources" later in this chapter for more on the IUGetItlTable procedure and "Localizing Word Selection and Line Break Tables" earlier in this chapter for details on the NFindWord procedure.

Listing 14-1. Obtaining optimized word break tables

```
FUNCTION GetWordSelect: Ptr;
VAR
   itlHandle:     Handle;
   tableOffset:   LongInt;
   tableLength:   LongInt;
   wordBreakPtr:  Ptr;
   tempPtr:       Ptr;
BEGIN
   GetWordSelect := NIL;                    {assume failure}
   IUGetItlTable(iuSystemScript,iuWordSelectTable,itlHandle,tableOffset,
                 tableLength);
   {If script is incorrect or the table is not available, the handle }
   { will return as NIL.}
   IF (itlHandle <> NIL) THEN
   BEGIN
      wordBreakPtr := NewPtr(tablelength);
      IF (wordBreakPtr <> NIL) THEN
      BEGIN
         tempPtr := Ptr(LongInt(itlHandle^)+tableOffset);
         BlockMove(tempPtr,wordBreakPtr,tablelength);
         GetWordSelect := wordBreakPtr;     {return a valid ptr}
      END;
   END;
   END;
```

Truncating Text

The TruncString and TruncText functions truncate text in a localizable way.

The TruncString function ensures that a string supplied as Str255 fits into the specified pixel width, by truncating the string, if necessary, in a manner dependent on the font script.

```
FUNCTION TruncString (width: Integer; VAR theString: Str255;
                      truncWhere: TruncCode) : Integer;
```

The TruncText function ensures that a string defined by a pointer and a byte length fits into the specified pixel width, by truncating the string as described above.

```
FUNCTION TruncText (width: Integer; textPtr: Ptr; VAR length: Integer;
                    truncWhere: TruncCode) : Integer;
```

The text truncation functions ensure that a text string fits into the pixel width specified by the width parameter and then truncates the string, when necessary. These functions use the font script to determine how to perform truncation. If truncation occurs, they also insert a truncation indicator (such as an ellipsis in English).

The truncWhere parameter specifies whether truncation occurs at the end of the string or in the middle (the latter is useful for pathnames, for example). Specify the constant smTruncEnd to truncate the string at the end. Specify the constant smTruncMiddle to truncate the string in the middle. In the TruncString function, the string is supplied as Str255. The TruncText function defines the string by a pointer and byte length. If truncation occurs, the string length is updated to reflect the new length. If general errors occur, the result code is smTruncErr and the length is set to 0. In any case, the length never increases.

With system software version 7.0, a new token type, tokenEllipsis, has been defined; the TruncString and TruncText functions obtain the corresponding character from the untoken table in the 'itl4' resource. See "Summary of the Script Manager" near the end of this chapter and *Macintosh Worldwide Development: Guide to System Software* for more information on the 'itl4' tables and related data structures.

The TruncString and TruncText functions are implemented by the Script Manager itself, not by script systems. Both text truncation functions may move memory.

Result codes

smNotTruncated	0	No truncation necessary
smTruncated	1	Truncation performed
smTruncErr	–1	General error (At present, this only occurs if truncation is necessary, but the truncation indicator alone is wider than the specified width. If this error occurs, the length is set to 0.)
resNotFound	–192	Cannot get the correct 'itl4' resource or resource is not in current format

See Listing 14-2 in "Substituting and Truncating Text" for an example of how to use the TruncText function.

Substituting Text

The ReplaceText function, new with system software version 7.0, allows you to substitute text.

```
FUNCTION ReplaceText (baseText: Handle; substitutionText: Handle;
                      key: Str15) : Integer;
```

ReplaceText searches the text specified by the baseText parameter for instances of the key string and replaces each instance with the text indicated by the substitutionText parameter. The key parameter contains a string to be used as the substitution marker. Although the substitution text may contain the key string, the text is inserted verbatim into the base text, and no recursive substitution occurs.

ReplaceText returns a positive value indicating the number of substitutions performed or a negative value indicating an error. The constant noErr is returned if there is no error or no substitutions performed.

The following are general Memory Manager errors. When ReplaceText returns these errors by using the following constants, they have these specific meanings:

Result codes
(special meanings of Memory Manager errors returned by ReplaceText)

memFullErr	108	SetHandleSize fails on baseText
nilHandleErr	109	GetHandleSize fails on baseText or substitutionText
memWZErr	–111	GetHandleSize fails on baseText or substitutionText

Note: ReplaceText may move memory.

See the next section, "Substituting and Truncating Text," for an example of how to use the ReplaceText function.

Substituting and Truncating Text

Listing 14-2 uses the ReplaceText and TruncText functions and assumes that you have Str255 strings containing base text and substitution text and that you want the result to fit in a specified number of pixels.

Listing 14-2. Substituting and truncating text

```
CONST
   maxInt    =  32767;

VAR
   baseString: Str255;
   subsString: Str255;
   baseHandle: Handle;
   subsHandle: Handle;
   keyStr:     Str15;
   sizeL:      LongInt;
   myWidth:    Integer;
   length:     Integer;
   result:     Integer;
   myErr:      OSErr;
BEGIN
   baseString := 'abcdefghijklmnopqrstuvwxyzabcdefghijklmnopqrstuvwxyz';

   subsString := 'KILROY WAS HERE';        {insert into baseString...}
   keyStr := 'mnop';                       {...in place of this sequence}
   myWidth := 500;                         {...and truncate with this width}

   sizeL := ord(baseString[0]);
   myErr := PtrToHand(@baseString[1], baseHandle, sizeL);
   IF myErr <> noErr THEN DoError(myErr);
   sizeL := ord(subsString[0]);
   myErr := PtrToHand(@subsString[1], subsHandle, sizeL);
```

(Continued)

Listing 14-2. Substituting and truncating text (Continued)

```
   IF myErr <> noErr THEN DoError(myErr);
   result := ReplaceText(baseHandle, subsHandle, keyStr);
   IF result < 0 THEN DoError(result);
   sizeL := GetHandleSize(baseHandle);
   IF MemError <> noErr THEN DoError(MemError);
   length := sizeL;
   HLock(baseHandle);
   IF MemError <> noErr THEN DoError(MemError); {oops, a Mem Mgr error}

   result := TruncText(myWidth, baseHandle^, length, smTruncEnd);
   IF result < 0 THEN DoError(result);

   DrawText(baseHandle^, 0, length);
   HUnlock(baseHandle);

   IF MemError <> noErr THEN DoError(myErr);     {oops, a Mem Mgr error}

END;
```

Converting Case and Stripping Diacritical Marks

The LwrText procedure was available with Script Manager 2.0 as a high-level interface to the _LwrString trap. Beginning with system software version 6.0.4, LwrText was localizable by using tables in the 'itl2' resource. The UprText procedure was also available in Script Manager 2.0 as a high-level interface to the _UprString trap but was generally not localized.

In system software version 7.0, a new set of routines is available from both assembly and high-level languages to provide localizable lowercasing, uppercasing, and stripping of diacritical marks. All of these routines—LowerText, UpperText, StripText, and StripUpperText—use trap $A056 (formerly called LwrString), but they set the operating-system trap flags to indicate which function is desired. UpperText provides a localizable version of UprText. The name LwrString can still be used; however, you are encouraged to use the new names that have been defined for the various functions of the LwrString trap.

> **Note:** The LowerText, UpperText, StripText, and StripUpperText procedures may move memory.

```
PROCEDURE LowerText (textPtr: Ptr; len: Integer);
```

Trap macro	_LowerText
On entry	A0: pointer to first character of string D0: length of string in bytes (word); must be less than 32 KB
On exit	D0: result code

The LowerText procedure provides localizable lowercase conversion of text up to 32 KB in length.

Note: The LwrText interface is still available and is identical to LowerText.

```
PROCEDURE UpperText (textPtr: Ptr; len: Integer);
```

Trap macro	_UpperText
On entry	A0: pointer to first character of string
	D0: length of string in bytes (word); must be less than 32 KB
On exit	D0: result code

The UpperText procedure provides localizable uppercase conversion of text up to 32 KB in length.

```
PROCEDURE StripText (textPtr: Ptr; len: Integer);
```

Trap macro	_StripText
On entry	A0: pointer to first character of string
	D0: length of string in bytes (word); must be less than 32 KB
On exit	D0: result code

The StripText procedure provides localizable stripping of diacritical characters for text up to 32 KB in length.

```
PROCEDURE StripUpperText (textPtr: Ptr; len: Integer);
```

Trap macro	_StripUpperText
On entry	A0: pointer to first character of string
	D0: length of string in bytes (word); must be less than 32 KB
On exit	D0: result code

The StripUpperText procedure provides localizable stripping of diacritical characters for text up to 32 KB in length and converts them to uppercase characters.

The following result codes apply to all four text truncation trap macros:

Result codes

noErr	0	No error
resNotFound	–192	Can't get correct 'itl2' resource or resource is not in current format (the string will not be modified)

Handling Justified Text

With system software version 7.0, the Script Manager provides several changes that are needed for handling fully justified text in the following list of Script Manager routines. These routines assume that a **slop value** for the line—the difference between the desired width and the actual width before justification—is to be distributed among the style runs on a line and among the words and characters within a style run. The actual width before justification is the sum of values returned by the TextWidth function for each style run on the line.

Here is a summary of how the justification routines available prior to system software version 7.0 work. (For details on these routines, see *Macintosh Worldwide Development: Guide to System Software*.)

- PortionText lets you determine how to distribute the slop value for the line among the style runs on the line.
- DrawJust allows you to draw a style run on a line and to provide a slop value for the style run.
- MeasureJust fills an array that specifies, for each character in a style run, the width from the beginning of the style run through that character.
- Char2Pixel converts a character offset in a style run to a pixel width in the style run.
- Pixel2Char converts a pixel width in a style run to a character offset in the style run.

The Roman Script System versions of the original justification routines did not handle intercharacter spacing and did not provide enough information for these routines to supply proper intercharacter spacing between style runs when there are multiple style runs (that is, more than one font, size, or QuickDraw style) on a line.

In system software version 7.0, all of these routines handle intercharacter spacing properly in all scripts and on all ports. When relevant, the amount of intercharacter spacing can be controlled using the Script Manager's smgrCharPortion global variable, which can be set with the SetEnvirons function.

Version 7.0 also provides a second interface for each of the existing routines. Each new interface name begins with *N* (for example, NPortionText), and each interface contains additional parameters that specify the visual position of the style run in the line and the desired scaling factors. The scaling factors are supplied as numerator and denominator parameters in a manner identical to the QuickDraw StdText procedure. The slop argument in these routines is a signed value that specifies the number of screen pixels by which the style run should be extended (or shrunk, if the value is negative) after the numerator-denominator scaling has been applied.

Other improvements in the new routines for handling justified text include the following:

- For future use, parameters that specify a character position or length change from integer to long integer; parameters that specify a pixel width change from integer to fixed. However, some routines currently only use the integer part of a LongInt parameter.
- NPixel2Char includes a VAR parameter (widthRemaining: Fixed). If the pixelWidth parameter that is passed into NPixel2Char is greater than the width of the text specified

by the textBuf and textLen parameters, the amount of excess width is returned in the widthRemaining parameter; otherwise, widthRemaining is set to –1.

- A new picture opcode saves the line layout information needed for these routines. See the Color QuickDraw chapter in this volume for a discussion of the new picture opcode.

Providing for Spacing Between Multiple Style Runs

To handle the spacing between multiple style runs on a line correctly, the new justification routines take a styleRunPosition parameter that specifies the position of the style run on a line.

The values for styleRunPosition are as follows:

Constant	Value	Meaning
smOnlyStyleRun	0	This style run is the only one on the line.
smLeftStyleRun	1	Multiple style runs are on the line, and this is the leftmost.
smRightStyleRun	2	Multiple style runs are on the line, and this is the rightmost.
smMiddleStyleRun	3	Multiple style runs are on the line, and this is neither the leftmost nor the rightmost.

If styleRunPosition has the value smOnlyStyleRun, the justification routines behave exactly like their earlier versions. For other values of styleRunPosition, the behavior may depend on the script. The behavior for the Roman script is described in "Justifying Text on the Roman Script System" later in this chapter.

```
FUNCTION NPortionText (textPtr: Ptr; textLen: LongInt;
                       styleRunPosition: JustStyleCode; numer: Point;
                       denom: Point) : Fixed;
```

The NPortionText function allows you to find out how to distribute the slop value for a line among the style runs on the line. The textPtr parameter is a pointer to the text while textLength is a long integer that indicates the length of the text. The function returns a fixed "magic number" that is based on the number of spaces, number of characters, font, size, style, styleRunPosition value, and the scaling parameters.

You should call NPortionText for all of the style runs on a line, and the slop value for the line should be allocated among the style runs in the same ratio as their NPortionText return values. To allocate spacing among multiple style runs, you can specify the position of a style run within the line by using the styleRunPosition parameter of type JustStyleCode. See the beginning of this section for a list of the values and meanings for these constants.

For example, suppose that there are three style runs on a line: A, B, and C. The line needs to be widened by 11 pixels for justification. Calling PortionText on these format runs yields the first row in Table 14-8.

Table 14-8. Proportions of slop value to be distributed

	A	B	C	Total
PortionText	5.4	7.3	8.2	20.9
Normalized	.258	.349	remainder	1.00
Pixels (p)	2.84	3.84	remainder	11.0
Rounded (r)	3	4	remainder	11

You can use these values to compute weighted spacing. The proportion of the justification to be allotted to A is 25.8 percent, so it receives 3 pixels out of 11. In general, to prevent rounding errors, $r_n = \text{round}(\Sigma_{1..n}\, p) - \Sigma_{1..n-1}\, r$ (which can be computed iteratively); for example, r_B is round(3.84+2.84) – 3, and r_C is round(11.0) – 7.

Listing 14-3 provides a code sample that illustrates the action of the NPortionText function. The CalcJustAmount routine in Listing 14-3 expects an array of the following type of records.

```
RunRecord    =  RECORD
   tPtr:               Ptr;          {ptr to the text}
   tLength:            LongInt;      {length of run}
   tFace:              style;        {txFace of run}
   tFont:              Integer;      {font family number for run's font}
   tSize:              Integer;      {pt size}
   tPlaceOnLine:       JustStyleCode;
   tnumer,tdenom:      Point;        {scaling factors}
   tJustAmount:        Fixed         {this value calculated here}
END;
RunArray = ARRAY[1..MaxRuns] OF RunRecord;
```

The CalcJustAmount routine also takes as a parameter a count of the total number of records that the array contains. Finally, the extra pixel width to be distributed is passed in as the TotalPixelSlop parameter. The routine calculates the amount of slop that should be allocated to each run, and assigns that value to the field tJustAmount.

Listing 14-3. Distributing slop value among style runs

```
PROCEDURE CalcJustAmount(rArray: RunArray; NRuns: Integer;
                         TotalPixelSlop: Integer);
VAR
   I:                    Integer;
   TotalSlopProportion: Fixed;
BEGIN
{First find the proportion for each run, temporarily remembering it }
{ in the tJustAmount field of the record, and summing the }
{ returned values in TotalSlopProportion.}
   TotalSlopProportion := 0;
   FOR I := 1 TO NRuns DO
   WITH rArray[I] DO BEGIN
   {set the grafPort's font settings to correspond to this run}
   TextFace(tFace);
   TextFont(tFont);
   TextSize(tSize);
```

```
   tJustAmount := NPortionText(tPtr,tLength,tPlaceOnLine,
                              tnumer,tdenom);
   TotalSlopProportion := TotalSlopProportion + tJustAmount;
   END;
{Having found the portion of slop to be allocated to each run, }
{ normalize it ( runportion / totalportion), and then convert }
{ that value to }
{ UnRounded Pixels ( (runportion / totalportion) * TotalPixelSlop ).}
   FOR I := 1 TO NRuns DO
   WITH rArray[I] DO
{Note you can round the value calculated here by using }
{ the FixRound routine.}
   tJustAmount :=
   FixMul(FixDiv(tJustAmount,TotalSlopProportion),TotalPixelSlop);
END;
```

You can draw text at the current pen location with NDrawJust.

```
PROCEDURE NDrawJust (textPtr: Ptr; textLen: LongInt; slop: Fixed;
                     styleRunPosition: JustStyleCode; numer: Point;
                     denom: Point);
```

The NDrawJust procedure draws the given text at the current pen location in the current font, style, and size. The slop parameter indicates how many extra pixels are to be added to the width of the text after it has been scaled according to the numer and denom parameters. This routine is useful for justifying text. For correct spacing between multiple style runs, you can specify the position of a style run within the line by using the styleRunPosition parameter of type JustStyleCode. See the beginning of this section for a list of the values and meanings for these constants.

> **Note:** In the NMeasureJust, NChar2Pixel, and NPixel2Char routines, described in the following sections, the text length should equal the entire visible part of the style run on a line and should include trailing spaces if and only if they are displayed. (They may not be displayed for the last style run in the line, for example.) Otherwise, the results for the last character on the line may be invalid.

```
PROCEDURE NMeasureJust (textPtr: Ptr; textLen: LongInt; slop: Fixed;
                        charLocs: Ptr; styleRunPosition: JustStyleCode;
                        numer: Point; denom: Point);
```

The NMeasureJust procedure measures text that may be justified. The charLocs parameter points to an array of textLen+1 integers where textLen is the number of bytes. The slop parameter indicates how many extra pixels are to be added to the width of the text after it has been scaled according to the numer and denom parameters. NMeasureJust computes the width from the beginning of the string to the trailing edge of each character, taking into account slop, scaling, and style run position. On return, the first charLocs entry contains 0; remaining entries contain the widths to the corresponding offsets in the string. For correct spacing between multiple style runs, you can specify the position of a style run within the line by using the styleRunPosition parameter of type JustStyleCode. See the beginning of this section for a list of the values and meanings for these constants.

```
FUNCTION NChar2Pixel (textBuf: Ptr; textLen: LongInt; slop: Fixed;
                       offset: LongInt; direction: Integer;
                       styleRunPosition: JustStyleCode; numer: Point;
                       denom: Point) : Integer;
```

The NChar2Pixel function finds the screen position of carets and selection points, given the text buffer and an offset. NChar2Pixel is the inverse of NPixel2Char. For left-to-right scripts (including Kanji), this function works the same way as the QuickDraw TextWidth function. For correct spacing between multiple style runs, you can specify the position of a style run within the line by using the styleRunPosition parameter of type JustStyleCode. See the beginning of this section for a list of the values and meanings for these constants.

```
FUNCTION NPixel2Char (textBuf: Ptr; textLen: LongInt; slop: Fixed;
                       pixelWidth: Fixed; VAR leadingEdge: Boolean;
                       VAR widthRemaining: Fixed; styleRunPosition:
                       JustStyleCode; numer: Point; denom: Point) :
                       Integer;
```

The NPixel2Char function helps you find the nearest character offset within a text buffer corresponding to a given pixel width. It returns an integer that is the offset of the character closest to pixelWidth. It is the inverse of the NChar2Pixel function. The most common application of NPixel2Char is identifying the character where a mouse-down event occurs in text and whether it is on the leading or trailing edge of the character. For correct spacing between multiple style runs, you can specify the position of a style run within the line by using the styleRunPosition parameter of type JustStyleCode. See the beginning of this section for a list of the values and meanings for these constants.

Justifying Text on the Roman Script System

This section describes several important points about the way text is justified in the Roman Script System:

- The weight for allocating extra space to each nonspace character is in the form of a percentage. This percentage is given by the Script Manager's smgrCharPortion global variable as a 4.12 fixed-point number, which can be read with GetEnvirons and set with SetEnvirons by using the smCharPortion verb. There is no threshold for initiating intercharacter spacing, so this is not a highly sophisticated model.
- Every space in a style run is allocated the same amount of extra width and thus is the same size, whether or not it is at the beginning or end of the line or the style run.
- For characters that are neither at the beginning nor at the end of the line, half of the charExtra width is allocated on each side of the character. Characters that are at the beginning or end of the line are only allocated half of the charExtra width, which appears on the side of the character toward the center of the line.
- The Script Manager text justification routines do not automatically strip trailing spaces. To strip trailing spaces in the last style run on the line, call the VisibleLength function for the last style run and pass its return value to these routines as the length of the last run.

Figure 14-25 illustrates this model for the justification of text.

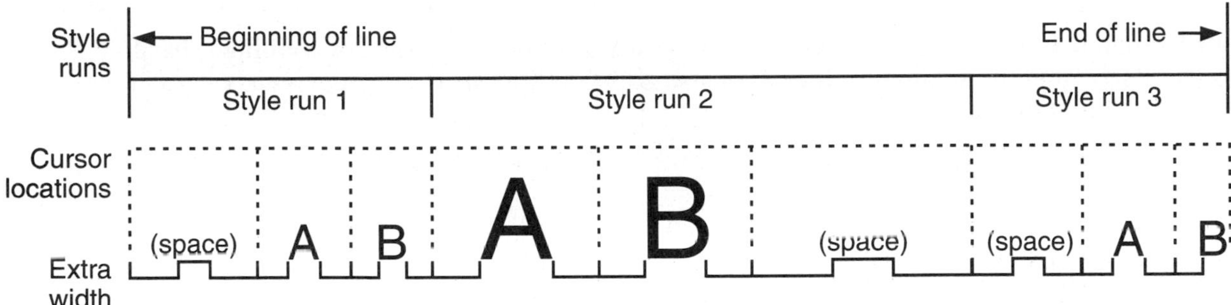

Figure 14-25. Justification in Roman text

Here's how the Script Manager computes the spacing factors for Roman text.

At the beginning of the line layout process, the Script Manager bases its values on information obtained by examining the text and a global variable that contains the ratio used to allocate space among intercharacter spacing and interword spacing.

> **Note:** The elements in the equations used subsequently in this discussion are defined here.

Value	Meaning
NumChars	The number of nonspace characters in the style run.
NumSpaces	The number of space characters in the style run.
CharPortion	The weight for allocating slop to intercharacter spacing versus interword spacing.
SpacePortion	1.0 – CharPortion; the weight for allocating slop to interword spacing.

The number of intercharacter spaces in a given style run is not necessarily the same as NumChars because characters at the beginning or end of the line are only allocated half an intercharacter space. The styleRunPosition parameter for the style run must be used to determine NumInterCharSpaces for the style run.

NumInterCharSpaces equals

- NumChars – 1.0, if styleRunPosition = smOnlyStyleRun
- NumChars – 0.5, if styleRunPosition = smLeftStyleRun
- NumChars – 0.5, if styleRunPosition = smRightStyleRun
- NumChars, if styleRunPosition = smMiddleStyleRun

A total weighted spacing for the style run can then be computed, as follows:

TotWeightedSpace = (NumInterCharSpaces * CharPortion) + (NumSpaces * SpacePortion)

For Roman text, the NPortionText function returns a value based on TotWeightedSpace, the font size, and the scaling factors. It is also adjusted by a factor of 32 for backward compatibility with PortionText results.

NPortionText = TotWeightedSpace * fontSize * (numer.h/denom.h) / 32.0

By calling NPortionText for each style run on a line, the slop value for the line can be allocated among each of the style runs on the line to obtain StyleRunSlop for each style run.

StyleRunSlop equals the amount of slop value allocated to this style run—that is, the number of pixels by which the style run should be increased or decreased in width *after* numerator-denominator scaling has been applied.

Finally, using TotWeightedSpace and StyleRunSlop, the values MoreSpaceExtra and MoreCharExtra for the style run can be determined—that is, the extra width for each space character and nonspace character *after* numerator-denominator scaling has been applied.

MoreSpaceExtra = (SpacePortion * StyleRunSlop / TotWeightedSpace)

MoreCharExtra = (CharPortion * StyleRunSlop / TotWeightedSpace)

Figure 14-26 demonstrates the capabilities of the Roman justification routines, DrawJust and NDrawJust, compared to the QuickDraw routines, DrawText and StdText.

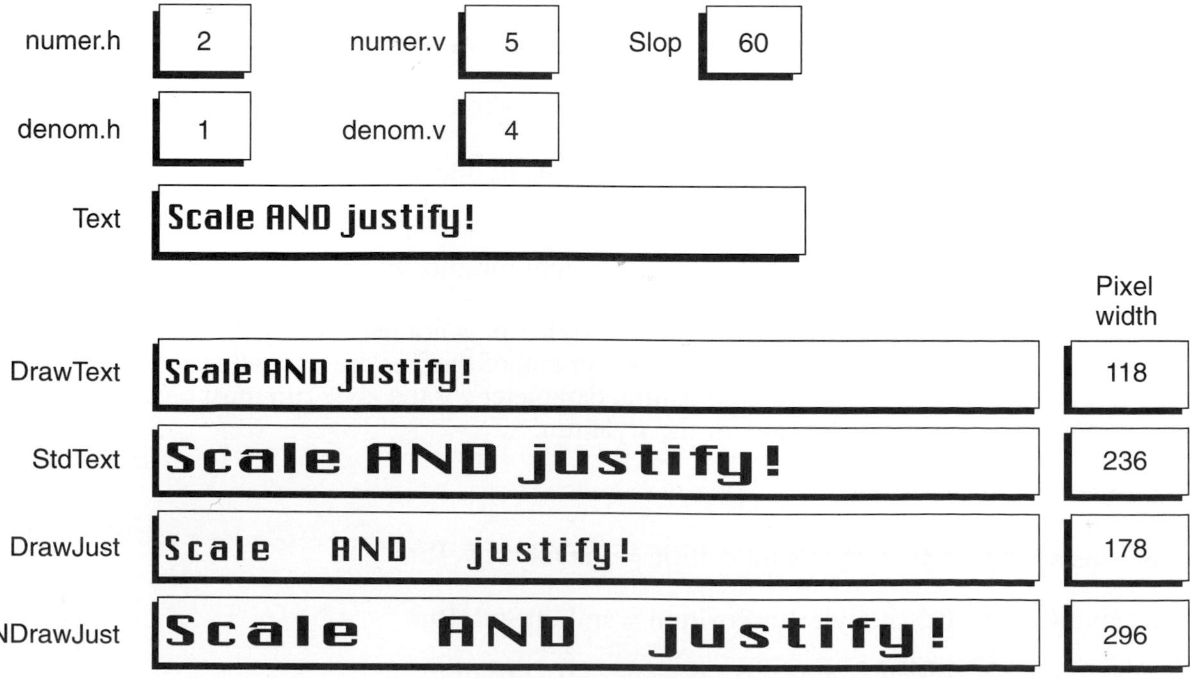

Figure 14-26. The effects of the Roman justification routines

USING THE INTERNATIONAL UTILITIES PACKAGE ROUTINES

The International Utilities Package is part of the System file. It has the resource type 'PACK' and resource ID 6. This package contains code that uses the information in the international resources to handle string comparison and the presentation of time, currency, and numbers around the world. These vary from script to script, language to language, and region to region, and your application should take advantage of the Macintosh Operating System's ability to present this information in the correct format.

The International Utilities Package works in conjunction with the Script Manager. Formatting options provide flexibility in specifying exactly how dates and times are to be displayed. The string comparison capabilities handle non-Roman writing systems, such as Arabic and Japanese.

For more information about packages in general, see the Package Manager chapters in Volumes I and V.

You need to use the International Utilities Package to enable your application to run in regions other than your own. For details on the International Utilities Package routines and data structures available prior to system software version 7.0, see Volumes I and V.

The following enhancements are available in the International Utilities Package with system software version 7.0. You can now

- obtain tables from the 'itl2' and 'itl4' resources
- use application-supplied 'itl2' and 'itl4' resources more easily
- specify resource handles explicitly for additional routines
- determine the interscript sorting order
- use special script and language codes with the new routines

Brief descriptions of the routines and features appear in the next section, "Overview of the International Utilities Package Routines."

With system software version 7.0, the new IUScriptOrder, IULangOrder, IUStringOrder, IUTextOrder, and IUGetItlTable routines (described in "Facilitating Interscript Sorting Order" and "Manipulating the 'itl2' and 'itl4' Resources" later in this chapter) accept special script or language codes. These script and language codes facilitate the process of sorting text between scripts and languages. For these routines, system software version 7.0 has defined these new types: ScriptCode and LangCode. A valid ScriptCode type can be an integer in the range 0–64 that explicitly indicates a particular script, or it can be a negative value with a special meaning. A valid LangCode type can be a nonnegative integer that explicitly indicates a particular language, or it can be a negative value with a special meaning. See "Summary of the International Utilities Package" near the end of this chapter for the list of these codes.

OVERVIEW OF THE INTERNATIONAL UTILITIES PACKAGE ROUTINES

All the International Utilities Package routines are described briefly in this section. The routines IULDateString and IULTimeString, previously undocumented in *Inside Macintosh,* are also summarized, and their interfaces appear in "Summary of the International Utilities Package" near the end of this chapter. The new routines available with system software version 7.0 are identified by an asterisk (*).

Comparing Strings

The International Utilities Package includes a number of routines to compare strings and give their exact sorting relationship or determine whether or not they are equal. System software version 7.0 includes parallel forms for the sorting functions IUCompString, IUMagString, IUEqualString, and IUMagIDString to permit explicit specification of an 'itl2' resource handle. These parallel forms, whose names end with PString, are in the following list. If this handle is NIL, the routines behave just like the previous routines that don't permit explicit specification of the handle.

IUCompString	Compares two Pascal strings for primary and secondary ordering and determines whether one is greater than, less than, or equal to another
IUCompPString*	Compares two Pascal strings for primary and secondary ordering and determines whether one is greater than, less than, or equal to another and permits explicit specification of the 'itl2' resource to be used for string comparison
IUMagString	Compares two strings defined by a pointer and character length for primary and secondary ordering and determines whether one is greater than, less than, or equal to another
IUMagPString*	Compares two strings defined by a pointer and character length for primary and secondary ordering and determines whether one is greater than, less than, or equal to another and permits explicit specification of the 'itl2' resource to be used for string comparison
IUEqualString	Compares two Pascal strings for equality in primary ordering only
IUEqualPString*	Compares two Pascal strings for equality in primary ordering only and permits explicit specification of the 'itl2' resource to be used for string comparison
IUMagIDString	Compares two strings defined by a pointer and character length for equality in primary ordering only
IUMagIDPString*	Compares two strings defined by a pointer and character length for equality in primary ordering only and permits explicit specification of the 'itl2' resource to be used for string comparison

Modifying the Standard String Comparison

To modify the standard string comparison, you need to construct your own 'itl2' resource. You may want to modify the standard string comparison if the one provided by the International Utilities Package doesn't meet your needs or if the string comparison for the language that concerns you is not available. If you supply an 'itl2' resource in an application, you will need to call the IUClearCache procedure or call one of the new *PString* comparison routines that allow you to pass in a handle to an 'itl2' resource. (See "Accessing the International Resources," "Manipulating the 'itl2' and 'itl4' Resources," and "Specifying Resource Handles Explicitly" later in this chapter.)

For details on modifying the standard string comparison, consult Macintosh Developer Technical Support.

Assembly-language note: See "Summary of the International Utilities Package" near the end of this chapter for a corrected version of the stack frame, IUSortFrame, used for the 'itl2' sorting routines before system software version 7.0 and for the stack frame, IUNSortFrame, used beginning with version 7.0. Consult Macintosh Developer Technical Support for more information on using these sorting frames and for the source code for the U.S. 'itl2' resource, which you may use as a basis for creating your own 'itl2' resource.

Facilitating Interscript Sorting Order

With system software version 7.0, the IUScriptOrder, IULangOrder, IUStringOrder, and IUTextOrder functions make it easier to sort text between different scripts. The functions use the special script and language codes described in "Script and Language Codes" later in this chapter.

IUScriptOrder*	Given a pair of script codes, indicates in what order the text in the two scripts should be sorted
IULangOrder*	Given a pair of language codes, indicates in what order the text in the two languages should be sorted
IUStringOrder*	Given a pair of strings with a script and language code for each, indicates the proper sorting order of the strings
IUTextOrder*	Given a pair of strings defined by a pointer and character length (with a script and language code for each), indicates the proper sorting order of the strings

The ordering of script and language codes is based on information in the 'itlm' resource. However, the system script is always sorted first, and scripts that are not enabled and installed are sorted last.

Accessing the International Resources

With system software version 7.0, three improvements have been made to the caching of handles for the 'itl2' and 'itl4' resources.

- System and application caches are separate. The application cache is part of the context that is handled by the Process Manager. The system cache is initialized during system startup with handles to the 'itl2' and 'itl4' resources in the System file. When an application is launched, the application cache is initialized from the system cache.
- Although any application can call the SetScript function to change the default ID for a particular script's 'itl2' or 'itl4' resource, this alone no longer affects any cached handles. An application must call the IUClearCache procedure in order for its cache to be reloaded. When the cache is reloaded, the current default IDs for each script are used. Consequently, applications that provide their own 'itl2' and 'itl4' resources do not affect the use of these resources in other applications, nor do they affect system behavior that depends on these resources.
- To provide increased efficiency in a multiscript environment, each cache has an entry for the 'itl2' and 'itl4' handles for every installed script.

New with system software version 7.0, the IUGetItlTable and IUClearCache procedures allow you to obtain specific tables from the 'itl2' and 'itl4' resources and make it easier for you to supply your own 'itl2' and 'itl4' resources. The supported table codes for the IUGetItlTable procedure appear in "Manipulating the 'itl2' and 'itl4' Resources" and "Summary of the International Utilities Package" later in this chapter.

IUGetIntl	Given the type of international resource ('itl0', 'itl1', 'itl2', or 'itl4'), returns a handle to the correct resource based on the current font script, the system script, and the IntlForce flag
IUSetIntl	Only sets fields in the obsolete 'INTL' 0 and 'INTL' 1 resources, which have been superseded by the 'itl0' and 'itl1' resources (It has been retained for backward compatibility.)
IUClearCache*	Clears the application cache containing the 'itl2' and 'itl4' handles, which is useful if applications want to supply an 'itl2' or 'itl4' resource
IUGetItlTable*	Given a script code and a table code, returns a handle to the 'itl2' or 'itl4' resource that contains the table, the offset of the specified table from the beginning of the resource, and the length of the resource

Localizing Dates, Times, and Metric Information

You can obtain a string corresponding to a date or time by passing the long integer you get from the operating-system GetDateTime procedure to the IUDateString or IUTimeString procedure. These procedures get the localized information to format the data from the 'itl0' resource or 'itl1' resource. The IULDateString and IULTimeString routines take a date specified as a LongDateTime type and return formatted strings. These two routines have not been previously documented in *Inside Macintosh*. For interfaces to IULDateString and IULTimeString, see "Summary of the International Utilities Package" near the end of this chapter. See *Macintosh Worldwide Development: Guide to System Software* for comprehensive details on the IULDateString and IULTimeString routines.

With the IUDatePString, IUTimePString, IULDateString, and IULTimeString routines, you explicitly specify the handle of an international resource that contains the format information. The IUMetric function lets you find out whether the metric system is to be used.

IUDateString	Fills out a string representing a short, abbreviated, or long form of the date corresponding to the long integer date returned by GetDateTime
IUDatePString	Fills out a string representing a date corresponding to the long integer date returned by GetDateTime by using format information from the specified resource
IULDateString	Takes a date specified in a LongDateTime format and returns a short date, abbreviated date, or long date as a string formatted according to the specified international resource
IUTimeString	Takes a long integer time returned by GetDateTime and returns a formatted string
IUTimePString	Takes a long integer time returned by GetDateTime and returns a string formatted according to the specified international resource
IULTimeString	Takes a time specified in a LongDateTime format and returns a string formatted according to the specified international resource
IUMetric	Indicates whether or not the metric system is to be used

INTERNATIONAL UTILITIES PACKAGE ROUTINES

With system software version 7.0, the International Utilities Package supplies a number of routines and data types that make it easier for you to use multiple scripts and languages in your applications.

Script and Language Codes

The International Utilities Package provides the IUScriptOrder, IULangOrder, IUStringOrder, IUTextOrder, and IUGetItlTable routines that accept script or language codes. For these routines, the data types ScriptCode and LangCode are defined as follows:

```
TYPE ScriptCode = Integer;
     LangCode   = Integer;
```

Valid values for a parameter of type ScriptCode are integers in the range 0–64 that explicitly indicate a particular script, or one of the following negative values:

Constant	**Value**	**Meaning**
iuSystemScript	–1	System script
iuCurrentScript	–2	Current script (as returned by FontScript)

A valid value for a parameter of type LangCode is a nonnegative integer that explicitly indicates a particular language, or is one of the following negative values:

Constant	Value	Meaning
iuSystemCurLang	–2	Current language for system script (from script global variables)
iuSystemDefLang	–3	Default language for system script (from 'itlm' resource)
iuCurrentCurLang	–4	Current language for current script (from script global variables)
iuCurrentDefLang	–5	Default language for current script (from 'itlm' resource)
iuScriptCurLang*	–6	Current language for specified script (from script global variables)
iuScriptDefLang	–7	Default language for specified script (from 'itlm' resource)

*If the script system is not installed, the International Utilities Package can't determine the current language, so it uses the default language.

Not all of the routines that have ScriptCode or LangCode parameters support all of the special negative values; the exceptions are noted in relevant routine descriptions in "Manipulating the 'itl2' and 'itl4' Resources" and "Determining Interscript Sorting Order" later in this chapter.

Manipulating the 'itl2' and 'itl4' Resources

With system software version 7.0, the IUGetItlTable and IUClearCache procedures let you get specific tables from the 'itl2' and 'itl4' resources and facilitate the process of supplying your own 'itl2' and 'itl4' resources.

```
PROCEDURE IUClearCache;
```

The IUClearCache procedure clears the application cache containing the 'itl2' and 'itl4' resource handles for the current script. Applications that provide their own 'itl2' or 'itl4' resource and want them to be used as the default for the corresponding script should call IUClearCache at entry to ensure that the supplied 'itl2' or 'itl4' resource is used instead of the system's 'itl2' and 'itl4' resources.

Note: The current default ID numbers for the script's 'itl2' and 'itl4' resources are stored in the script's local variables. These values may be read with the GetScript and SetScript functions using the verbs smScriptSort (for the 'itl2' resource) and smScriptToken (for the 'itl4' resource). Before calling IUClearCache, you should set the script's default ID number to the ID of the resource that you are supplying.

If the IntlForce flag is TRUE, the ID must be in the system script range. Otherwise, the ID must be in the appropriate range of the font script. See the discussion of the IntlForce flag in "Using the International and Keyboard Resources" later in this chapter for details.

▲ **Warning:** If you use the SetScript function to change the value of the 'itl2' resource ID, you should restore the original resource ID before your application quits. This minimizes the effects on other applications. ▲

```
PROCEDURE IUGetItlTable (script: ScriptCode; tableCode: Integer;
                         VAR itlHandle: Handle; VAR offset: LongInt;
                         VAR length: LongInt);
```

Given a script code and a table code, IUGetItlTable returns a handle to the 'itl2' or 'itl4' resource containing the table, the offset of the specified table from the beginning of the resource, and the length of the resource. At present, the supported table codes are as follows:

Table code symbol	Value	Retrieves
iuWordSelectTable	0	Word selection break table ('itl2')
iuWordWrapTable	1	Word wrap break table ('itl2')
iuNumberPartsTable	2	Default number parts table ('itl4')
iuUnTokenTable	3	Untoken table ('itl4')
iuWhiteSpaceList	4	White space list table ('itl4')

IUGetItlTable only checks the default 'itl2' or 'itl4' resource for the script—that is, the 'itl2' or 'itl4' resource whose ID is specified in the script's local variables. The itlHandle parameter is set to 0 for any of the following error conditions: the script or the table code is invalid; the script is not installed or not enabled; or the required resource can't be found or is not in the current format. For details on the word selection break table and word wrap break table, see "Localizing Word Selection and Line Break Tables" earlier in this chapter. For details on the white space list table, see "The 'itl4' Resource" later in this chapter. For details on the default number parts table and the untoken table, consult Macintosh Developer Technical Support.

Specifying Resource Handles Explicitly

Currently, the IUDateString and IUTimeString procedures have the parallel forms IUDatePString and IUTimePString, which permit the caller to specify a resource handle explicitly. System software version 7.0 includes similar parallel forms for the sorting functions—IUCompPString, IUMagPString, IUEqualPString, and IUMagIDPString—that permit explicit specification of an 'itl2' resource handle in the itl2Handle parameter. If this handle is NIL, the routines behave just like the forms that don't permit explicit specification of the handle. See the International Utilities Package chapter in Volume I for more information on the IUCompString, IUMagString, IUEqualString, and IUMagIDString functions.

```
FUNCTION IUCompPString (aStr,bStr: Str255; itl2Handle: Handle) :
                        Integer;
```

```
FUNCTION IUMagPString (aPtr,bPtr: Ptr; aLen,bLen: Integer;
                       itl2Handle: Handle) : Integer;
```

```
FUNCTION IUEqualPString (aStr,bStr: Str255; itl2Handle: Handle) :
                        Integer;
```

```
FUNCTION IUMagIDPString (aPtr,bPtr: Ptr; aLen,bLen: Integer;
                        itl2Handle: Handle) : Integer;
```

Note: The IUCompPString and IUEqualPString functions are available for high-level languages only.

Determining Interscript Sorting Order

The IUScriptOrder, IULangOrder, IUStringOrder, and IUTextOrder functions provide for interscript and interlanguage sorting.

```
FUNCTION IUScriptOrder (script1,script2: ScriptCode) : Integer;
```

The IUScriptOrder function takes a pair of script codes and returns –1, 1, or 0, depending on whether text in the first script should be sorted before, after, or in the same place as text in the second script. The system script is always sorted first.

```
FUNCTION IULangOrder (language1,language2: LangCode) : Integer;
```

The IULangOrder function takes a pair of language codes and returns –1, 1, or 0, depending on whether text in the first language should be sorted before, after, or in the same place as text in the second language. The language codes iuScriptCurLang and iuScriptDefLang are not valid for IULangOrder because no script is specified. Languages that belong to different scripts are sorted in the same order as the scripts to which they belong.

```
FUNCTION IUStringOrder (aStr,bStr: Str255; aScript,
                       bScript: ScriptCode;
                       aLang,bLang: LangCode) : Integer;
```

```
FUNCTION IUTextOrder (aPtr,bPtr: Ptr; aLen,bLen: Integer;
                     aScript,bScript: ScriptCode;
                     aLang,bLang: LangCode) : Integer;
```

The IUStringOrder and IUTextOrder functions are similar to the IUCompString and IUMagString functions, except that they take a script and language code for each string. IUStringOrder and IUTextOrder use IUScriptOrder, IULangOrder, and IUMagPString to return –1, 0, or 1, indicating the proper ordering of strings that may be in different scripts or languages. If the result of IUScriptOrder(aScript,bScript) is not 0, then it is returned as the result of IUStringOrder or IUTextOrder. If the result is 0, aLang and bLang are checked; if these are different, then they determine the function result. If they are not different, the strings are in the same script and language and are compared using the sorting for that script and language. If that script is not installed and enabled, the sorting is performed using the script specified by IntlScript.

The IUStringOrder and IUTextOrder functions are primarily used to insert strings in a sorted list; for sorting, it may be faster to sort first by script and language by using the IUScriptOrder and IULangOrder functions, and then to call IUCompPString to sort strings within a script or language group.

Note: The IUStringOrder function is for high-level languages only.

For all of these sorting functions, invalid script or language codes are sorted after valid ones. Note that these functions can move memory.

USING THE INTERNATIONAL AND KEYBOARD RESOURCES

This section gives an overview of the international resources, including the keyboard resources. The 'itlm', optional 'itl5', 'kcs#', 'kcs4', and 'kcs8' resources described here are new with system software version 7.0. The 'itl4' and the optional 'itlk' resources described here are not new with system software version 7.0; however, they have not been previously documented in *Inside Macintosh*.

The international resources are stored in the System file as types 'itl0', 'itl1', 'itl2', 'itl4', 'itl5', 'itlb', 'itlc', 'itlk', and 'itlm'. The 'itl0' and 'itl1' resources contain date, time, and number formats, and basically correspond to the obsolete 'INTL' (0) and (1) resources. The formats are similar, but the Script Manager allows multiple 'itl0' and 'itl1' resources (not possible with the old 'INTL' (0) and (1) designations). With system software version 7.0, the 'itl1' resource permits additional date format information.

The 'itl2' resource contains procedures for sorting and, beginning with system software version 6.0.4, contains tables used by the LwrText procedure and by the Roman Script System's CharType, Transliterate, and FindWord routines. In version 7.0, these tables are also used by the LowerText, UpperText, StripText, and StripUpperText procedures.

The 'itl4' resource contains localizable tables, code for the tokenizer, and number parts for use by the Script Manager's number parsing and formatting routines. The optional 'itl5' resource provides information on character set encoding and text rendering behavior. The 'itlb' resource contains bundle and configuration information for each script. The 'itlc' resource contains international configuration information for the system as a whole. The 'itlm' resource specifies preferred sorting order of script codes, language codes, and region codes and specifies the hierarchical arrangement of these codes.

Each installed script has an associated list of international resource numbers, generally in the range used for its fonts. For example, the Arabic script has the resources 'itl0', 'itl1', 'itl2', and 'itl4' with numbers in the range $4600 to $47FF; the Roman script has the resources 'itl0', 'itl1', 'itl2', and 'itl4' with numbers in the range $0 to $3FFF. The only international resources without an ID in the font range are the 'itlb' resource, whose ID is its script number, and the 'itlc' and 'itlm' resources, whose IDs are always 0.

If the IntlForce flag is TRUE, the resources used by the International Utilities Package are determined by the system script. However, you can force them to be determined by the font script by clearing the IntlForce flag. You can set and clear the IntlForce flag by using the SetEnvirons function, described in detail in *Macintosh Worldwide Development: Guide to System Software*. The selected resources are then used internally by the International Utilities Package.

Table 14-9 shows which international and keyboard resources are included in the U.S. system software and whether script systems or localized versions of the system software add them to or replace them in the System file.

Versions of the 'itl0', 'itl1', 'itl2', 'itl4', 'KCHR', 'kcs#', 'kcs4', and 'kcs8' resources are available for all localized versions of the system software. Some localized versions also provide the 'itlk' resource. Some non-Roman systems may use an 'itl5' resource.

Table 14-9. The international and keyboard resources

Resource type	U.S. system software including Roman Script System	Localized versions of system software or other script systems
'itlc'	Roman 'itlc'	May replace 'itlc'
'itlm'*	Default 'itlm'	May replace 'itlm'
'itlb'	Roman 'itlb'	May add non-Roman 'itlb'
'itl0'	U.S. 'itl0'	Adds non-U.S. 'itl0'
'itl1'	U.S. 'itl1'	Adds non-U.S. 'itl1'
'itl2'	U.S. 'itl2'	Adds non-U.S. 'itl2'
'itl4'	U.S. 'itl4'	Adds non-U.S. 'itl4'
'itl5'*	None	May add non-Roman 'itl5'
'itlk'	None	May add an 'itlk'†
'KCHR'	U.S. 'KCHR'	Adds non-U.S. 'KCHR'
'KSWP'	Standard 'KSWP'	May replace 'KSWP'
'KMAP'	Includes all necessary 'KMAP's	None
'kcs#'*	U.S. 'kcs#'	Adds non-U.S. 'kcs#'†
'kcs4'*	U.S. 'kcs4'	Adds non-U.S. 'kcs4'†
'kcs8'*	U.S. 'kcs8'	Adds non-U.S. 'kcs8'†

*New with system software version 7.0

†ID corresponds to 'KCHR'

Enhancements to International Resources

System software version 7.0 provides several enhancements to the international resources, including the following:

- The 'itlc' resource specifies a region code that identifies a particular localized version of the Macintosh system software.
- The 'itlm' resource (new with system software version 7.0) specifies the ordering of script codes, language codes, and region codes and the hierarchical arrangement of these codes.
- The 'itlb' resource specifies font and style information for the script as well as other script initialization data.

- The 'itl1' resource can be optionally extended to include additional day and month names, abbreviated day and month names, additional date separators, and a calendar code.
- The 'itl2' resource includes length information so that tables (specifically the FindWord tables and the optional FindScriptRun table) and code blocks now have a length as well as an offset.
- The optional 'itl5' resource (new with system software version 7.0) supplies character set encoding data and information on text rendering behavior.

With the exception of the optional 'itl5' resource, these enhancements are described in the sections that follow.

The 'itlc' Resource

The 'itlc' resource is a configuration resource. Only one 'itlc' is provided per system. The 'itlc' resource specifies

- system script code
- keyboard cache size
- font force flags
- international keyboard flag (for the Macintosh Plus)
- general bit flags for the Script Manager that indicate
  - a Boolean that indicates whether to always show a keyboard icon (before version 7.0) or Keyboard menu (beginning with version 7.0)
  - a Boolean that indicates whether to use a dual caret for a bidirectional script
- keyboard icon location (beginning with system software version 6.0.4; not used in system software version 7.0)
- preferred region code (beginning with system software version 7.0)

The preferred region code is located in a new field replacing part of the reserved space at the end of 'itlc'. The field is an integer that contains the system's preferred region code. The available values are given by constants whose names begin with the prefix *ver* (for example, verFrance). At startup, this integer is copied into a Script Manager global variable that can be accessed with the GetEnvirons function using the verb smRegionCode. The 'itlc' type definition has been updated, and a corresponding itlcRegionCode field has been added to the ItlcRecord data structure. There is no change in the size of the 'itlc' resource or the ItlcRecord data structure. See "Summary of the International Utilities Package" at the end of this chapter for a list of these region code values.

```
TYPE ItlcRecord =
     RECORD
         itlcSystem:         Integer;        {default system script}
         itlcReserved:       Integer;        {reserved}
         itlcFontForce:      SignedByte;     {default font force flag}
         itlcIntlForce:      SignedByte;     {default intl force flag}
         itlcOldKybd:        SignedByte;     {old keyboard}
         itlcFlags:          SignedByte;     {general flags}
         itlcIconOffset:     Integer;        {keyboard icon offset; }
                                             { beginning with version }
                                             { 7.0, not used}
         itlcIconSide:       SignedByte;     {icon side}
         itlcIconRsvd:       SignedByte;     {rsvd for other icon info}
         itlcRegionCode:     Integer;        {preferred verXxx code}
         itlcReserved3:      ARRAY[0..33] OF SignedByte
                                             {for future use}
     END;
```

If you do not have access to the MPW file SysTypes.r, which contains the Rez type definition of the 'itlc' resource, consult with Macintosh Developer Technical Support for details.

The 'itlm' Resource

New with system software version 7.0, the 'itlm' resource specifies the preferred sorting order for script codes, language codes, and region codes. It also indicates the default language for each script, the parent script for each language, and the parent language for each region.

The resource contains a header and three tables. The header includes the version number, format code, and offsets to the three tables.

- The first table, scriptData, contains a list of script codes in their preferred sorting order. Each script is paired with the default language code for that script. The max script code specifies the highest script code that will be handled by the internal Script Manager structures derived from this table. For example, a max script code of smUninterp(32) would cover the scripts with codes 0 through 32.

- The second table, langData, consists of a list of language codes in their preferred sorting order. Each language code is paired with the code for its parent script. The max language code specifies the highest language code that will be handled by the internal Script Manager structures derived from this table. For example, a max language code of langRussian(32) would cover the languages with codes 0 through 32.

- The third table, regionData, is a list of region codes in their preferred sorting order. Each region code is paired with the code for its parent language. The max region code specifies the highest region code that will be handled by the internal Script Manager structures derived from this table. For example, a max region code of verPakistan(34) would cover the regions with codes 0 through 34.

Listing 14-4 shows the Rez format for the 'itlm' resource.

Listing 14-4. Multiscript mapping and sorting

```
type 'itlm' {
   unsigned hex integer;                   /*version number*/
   unsigned hex integer;                   /*format code*/
   unsigned integer = 3;                   /*number of offset/length pairs*/
   unsigned longint = scriptData >> 3; /*offset to scriptData table*/
   unsigned longint = (endScriptData - scriptData) >> 3;
                                           /*length of it*/
   unsigned longint = langData >> 3;   /*offset to langData table*/
   unsigned longint = (endLangData - langData) >> 3;
                                           /*length of it*/
   unsigned longint = regionData >> 3; /*offset to regionData table*/
   unsigned longint = (endRegionData - regionData) >> 3;
                                           /*length of it*/

scriptData:
   integer Script;                   /*max script code for script->lang mapping*/
   integer Language;                 /*default lang code for scripts not */
                                     /* in table*/
   integer = $$CountOf(scriptArray);/*number of entries in table*/
   array scriptArray {               /*entries are ordered by script sort order*/
      integer Script;                /*script code*/
      integer Language;              /*default lang code for script*/
   };
endScriptData:

langData:
   integer Language;                 /*max lang code for lang->script mapping*/
   integer Script;                   /*default script code for langs not */
                                     /* in table*/
   integer = $$CountOf(langArray);/*number of entries in table*/
   array langArray {                 /*entries are ordered by lang sort order*/
      integer Language;              /*language code*/
      integer Script;                /*parent script code for language*/
   };
endLangData:

regionData:
   integer Region;                   /*max region code for region->lang mapping*/
   integer Language;                 /*default lang code for regions not */
                                     /* in table*/
   integer = $$CountOf(regionArray);/*number of entries in table*/
   array regionArray {               /*entries are ordered by region sort order*/
      integer Region;                /*region code*/
      integer Language;              /*parent language code for region*/
   };
endRegionData:
};
```

Table 14-10 lists a sample hierarchy of script, language, and region codes reflected in the 'itlm' resource. Region codes do not currently exist for all language codes. See "Summary of the Script Manager" and "Summary of the International Utilities Package" near the end of this chapter for details.

Table 14-10. Script, language, and region codes

Script code	Language code	Region code
smRoman	langEnglish	verUS
		verBritain
		verAustralia
	langFrench	verFrance
		verFrCanada
		verFrSwiss
	langGerman	verGermany
		verGrSwiss
	langItalian	verItaly
	langDutch	verNetherlands
	langSwedish	verSweden
	langSpanish	verSpain
	langDanish	verDenmark
	langPortuguese	verPortugal
	langNorwegian	verNorway
	langFinnish	verFinland
	langIcelandic	verIceland
	langMaltese	verMalta
	langTurkish	verTurkey
	langLithuanian	verLithuania
	langEstonian	verEstonia
	langLettish	verLatvia
	langLappish	verLapland
	langFaeroese	verFaeroeIsl
	langCroatian	verYugoCroatian
smEastEurRoman	langPolish	verPoland
	langHungarian	verHungary
smGreek	langGreek	verGreece
smCyrillic	langRussia	verRussia
smArabic	langArabic	verArabic
	langUrdu	verPakistan
	langFarsi	verIran
smHebrew	langHebrew	verIsrael
smDevanagari	langHindi	verIndiaHindi
smThai	langThai	verThailand
smJapanese	langJapanese	verJapan
smTradChinese	langTradChinese	verTaiwan
smSimpChinese	langSimpChinese	verChina
smKorean	langKorea	verKorea

The 'itlb' Resource

An 'itlb' resource functions as a bundle for the corresponding script. Each installed script has one 'itlb' resource. The resource ID number for each 'itlb' resource is its corresponding script code. The 'itlb' resource specifies

- resource IDs for the script's default resources: 'itl0', 'itl1', 'itl2', 'itl4', optional 'itl5', 'KCHR', 'kcs#', 'kcs4', and 'kcs8' (or 'SICN' in system software version 6.0)
- script bit flags (Beginning with system software version 7.0, the bit flags include a new flag that instructs the Script Manager to initialize a script automatically.)
- language code
- number and date representation codes
- font information (beginning with system software version 7.0)
- style information (beginning with system software version 7.0)
- script system initialization data (beginning with system software version 7.0)

The 'itlb' type has been updated in version 7.0. A formerly reserved field in the 'itlb' resource is now used to store the ID of the optional 'itl5' resource. This field, itlbEncoding, is 0 if the resource is not present. (The 'itl5' resource is not used in the standard U.S. system.) However, the size of the ItlbRecord data type has not changed because other structures depend on it remaining a fixed size. Instead, a new data structure, the extended 'itlb' record, defined by the data type ItlbExtRecord, includes the ItlbRecord data type and adds extensions.

Several new fields in the extended 'itlb' record specify the default 'FOND' ID and font size for the following: system and application fonts, small font (such as Geneva 9), monospaced font, user's preferred font, and the font for Balloon Help. Additional fields specify the set of valid styles for the script and the set of styles to mark aliases.

The updated data structures defined by the ItlbRecord and ItlbExtRecord data types are as follows:

```
TYPE  ItlbRecord =
      RECORD
         itlbNumber:       Integer;       {'itl0' ID number}
         itlbDate:         Integer;       {'itl1' ID number}
         itlbSort:         Integer;       {'itl2' ID number}
         itlbFlags:        Integer;       {script flags}
         itlbToken:        Integer;       {'itl4' ID number}
         itlbEncoding:     Integer;       {'itl5' ID number (optional }
                                          { character encoding)}
         itlbLang:         Integer;       {current language for script}
         itlbNumRep:       SignedByte;    {number representation code}
         itlbDateRep:      SignedByte;    {date representation code}
         itlbKeys:         Integer;       {'KCHR' ID number}
         itlbIcon:         Integer        {ID number of 'SICN' or 'kcs#', }
                                          { 'kcs4', 'kcs8' family}
      END;
```

```
ItlbExtRecord =
RECORD
      base:              ItlbRecord;    {unextended ItlbRecord}
      itlbLocalSize:     LongInt;       {size of script's local record}
      itlbMonoFond:      Integer;       {default monospaced 'FOND' ID}
      itlbMonoSize:      Integer;       {default monospaced font size}
      itlbPrefFond:      Integer;       {preferred 'FOND' ID}
      itlbPrefSize:      Integer;       {preferred font size}
      itlbSmallFond:     Integer;       {default small 'FOND' ID}
      itlbSmallSize:     Integer;       {default small font size}
      itlbSysFond:       Integer;       {default system 'FOND' ID}
      itlbSysSize:       Integer;       {default system font size}
      itlbAppFond:       Integer;       {default application 'FOND' ID}
      itlbAppSize:       Integer;       {default application font size}
      itlbHelpFond:      Integer;       {default Help Mgr 'FOND' ID}
      itlbHelpSize:      Integer;       {default Help Mgr font size}
      itlbValidStyles:   Style;         {set of valid styles for script}
      itlbAliasStyle:    Style          {set of styles to mark aliases}
   END;
```

The new bit flag, defined for the script flags word, is located in the itlbFlags field in the 'itlb' record data structure. Set the smsfAutoInit bit in a script's 'itlb' to instruct the Script Manager to initialize the script system automatically. (See "Creating Simple Script Systems" earlier in this chapter for details.)

If you do not have access to the MPW file SysTypes.r, which contains the Rez type for the 'itlb' resource, consult Macintosh Developer Technical Support for details.

The 'itl0' Resource

Documented in the International Utilities Package chapter in Volume V as a replacement for the 'INTL' (0) resource, the 'itl0' resource contains short date, time, number, and currency formats as well as the region code for this particular 'itl0' resource. Each installed script has one or more 'itl0' resources. The resource ID for each 'itl0' resource is in the script's resource number range. The default 'itl0' resource for a script is specified by the script's 'itlb' resource. Each 'itl0' resource specifies

- number format (decimal separator, thousands separator, and list separator)
- currency format (including currency symbol and position, leading or trailing zeros, and how to show negatives)
- short date format
- time format
- region code for this particular 'itl0' resource

If you do not have access to the MPW file SysTypes.r, which contains a Rez definition of type 'itl0', consult Macintosh Developer Technical Support for details.

Note: The 'INTL' (0) resource is obsolete and will not be supported in future versions of the system software.

The 'itl1' Resource

Documented in the International Utilities Package in Volume V as a replacement for the 'INTL' (1) resource, the basic 'itl1' resource provides information on long date formats: the order of the date elements, which elements to include, the names of days and months, and how to abbreviate the names. Each installed script has one or more 'itl1' resources. The resource ID for each 'itl1' resource is in the script's resource number range. The default 'itl1' resource for a script is specified by the script's 'itlb' resource. The basic 'itl1' resource specifies

- long date format (including month and day names)
- region code for this particular 'itl1' resource

However, this basic format presents several limitations. First, it assumes that 7 day names and 12 month names are sufficient,which is not true for some calendars. For example, the traditional Jewish calendar can have 13 months. Second, it assumes that day and month names can be abbreviated by simply truncating them to a fixed length, but this not true in many languages.

With system software version 7.0, the 'itl1' resource may be optionally extended to provide additional information that solves these problems. As indicated in the discussion in Volume V about future extensions to this resource, the fields present in the old format have not been moved. The International Utilities Package routines that generate date strings use information in the 'itl1' extension if it is present.

> **Note:** The 'INTL' (1) resource is obsolete and will not be supported in future versions of the system software.

The old 'itl1' format was identical to the 'INTL' (1) format, which ended with a variable-length field intended to be used for code that altered the standard sorting behavior. This “local routine” field has been ignored since the introduction of the 'itl0', 'itl1', and 'itl2' resources because the code for changing the sorting behavior was moved to the 'itl2' resource. Consequently, in most existing 'itl1' resources, the local routine field merely contains a single RTS instruction (hexadecimal $4E75). The extended format is now indicated by the presence of the hexadecimal value $A89F as the first word in the local routine field; this is the unimplemented trap instruction, which could not have been the first word of any valid local routine. The new Rez template for the 'itl1' type can be used to perform a DeRez operation on old-format 'itl1' resources with $4E75 in this field as well as extended-format 'itl1' resources in which the extended data begins with the value $A89F.

The extended data provides the following additional information, which you can see as part of the Rez type definition for the 'itl1' resource in Listing 14-5, which follows this list:

- A version number. The byte-length version number in the old part of the 'itl1' resource has been used for various special purposes over the years, so this field provides a *real* version number.
- A separate format code. This code is distinct from the version number. The current extended format has a format code of 0.
- A calendar code. Multiple calendars may be available on some systems, and it is necessary to identify the particular calendar for use with this 'itl1' resource. Constants for the various calendars are provided in the “Summary of the Script Manager” near the end of this chapter.

- A list of extra day names (extraDays). This format is for those calendars with more than 7 days.
- A list of extra month names (extraMonths). This format is for those calendars with more than 12 months.
- A list of abbreviated day names (abbrevDays).
- A list of abbreviated month names (abbrevMonths).
- A list of additional date separators (extraSeparators). When parsing date strings, the String2Date function permits the separators in this list to be used in addition to the date separators specified elsewhere in the 'itl0' and 'itl1' resources.

Listing 14-5 shows the new Rez type for the 'itl1' resource.

Listing 14-5. International date and time information

```
type 'itl1' {
                                                /*day names*/
   array [7] {
      pstring[15];                              /*Sunday, Monday...*/
   };

                                                /*month names*/
   array [12] {
      pstring[15];                              /*January, February...*/
   };

   byte  dayName, none=255;                     /*suppressDay*/
   byte  dayMonYear, monDayYear = 255;          /*longDate format*/
   byte  noDayLeadZero, dayLeadZero = 255;      /*dayLeading0*/
   byte;                                        /*abbrLen*/
   string[4];                                   /*st0*/
   string[4];                                   /*st1*/
   string[4];                                   /*st2*/
   string[4];                                   /*st3*/
   string[4];                                   /*st4*/
   byte     Region;                             /*region code*/
   byte;                                        /*version*/
   switch   {
      case oldFormat:
         key hex integer = $4E75;               /*old-format key*/
      case extFormat:
         key hex integer = $A89F;               /*extended-format key*/
         hex integer;                           /*version*/
         hex integer;                           /*format*/
         integer;                               /*calendar code*/

         /*offset to & length of extraDays table*/
         unsigned longint = extraDays >> 3;
         unsigned longint = (endExtraDays - extraDays) >> 3;
```

```
        /*offset to & length of extraMonths table*/
        unsigned longint = extraMonths >> 3;
        unsigned longint = (endExtraMonths - extraMonths) >> 3;

        /*offset to & length of abbrevDays table*/
        unsigned longint = abbrevDays >> 3;
        unsigned longint = (endAbbrevDays - abbrevDays) >> 3;

        /*offset to & length of abbrevMonths table*/
        unsigned longint = abbrevMonths >> 3;
        unsigned longint = (endAbbrevMonths - abbrevMonths) >> 3;

        /*offset to & length of extraSeparators table*/
        unsigned longint = extraSeparators >> 3;
        unsigned longint = (endExtraSeparators - extraSeparators) >> 3;

extraDays:                          /*count and list of extra day names*/
        integer = $$CountOf(extraDaysArray);
        array extraDaysArray {
           pstring;
        };
endExtraDays:

extraMonths:                  /*count and list of extra month names*/
        integer = $$CountOf(extraMonthArray);
        array extraMonthArray {
           pstring;
        };
endExtraMonths:

abbrevDays:                      /*count and list of abbreviated day names*/
        integer = $$CountOf(abbrevDaysArray);
        array abbrevDaysArray {
           pstring;
        };
endAbbrevDays:

abbrevMonths:                 /*count and list of abbreviated month names*/
        integer = $$CountOf(abbrevMonthArray);
        array abbrevMonthArray {
           pstring;
        };
endAbbrevMonths:

extraSeparators:        /*count and list of extra date separator names*/
        integer = $$CountOf(extraSeparatorsArray);
        array extraSeparatorsArray {
           pstring;
        };
endExtraSeparators:
      };
};
```

The 'itl2' Resource

The 'itl2' resource contains the International Utilities Package's sorting hooks and tables for character type, case conversion, and word breaks. Each installed script has one or more 'itl2' resources. The resource ID for each 'itl2' resource is in the script's resource number range. The default 'itl2' resource for a script is specified by the script's 'itlb' resource. Each 'itl2' resource contains

- a header with offsets and lengths (beginning with system software version 7.0) of all the code blocks and tables in the 'itl2' resource
- routines and tables for modifying standard string comparison
- optional character type tables for use by a script system's CharType function (beginning with system software version 6.0.4)
- optional tables for case conversion and stripping diacritical marks, for use by a script system's Transliterate function, by the LwrText procedure (beginning with system software version 6.0.4), and by the LowerText, UpperText, StripText, and StripUpperText procedures (beginning with system software version 7.0)

  These tables only need to be present for single-byte script systems.
- word break tables for the FindWord procedure

  Beginning with system software version 6.0.4, the word break tables used by the Roman FindWord procedure are included in the 'itl2' resource. Beginning with system software version 7.0, the word break tables for all scripts are located in each script's 'itl2' resource.
- an optional new table that provides information on the location of Roman characters in a non-Roman font to be used by the Roman version of the FindScriptRun function (beginning with system software version 7.0)

Note: In addition to these changes, the U.S. 'itl2' resource available with system software version 7.0 includes word break tables that use the new state table format for the NFindWord procedure and that support cedilla, double-acute accent, ogonek, and hacek as letter characters.

If you do not have access to the MPW file SysTypes.r, which contains the new 'itl2' template, consult Macintosh Developer Technical Support for details.

The Script Manager's CharType, Transliterate, and (before system software version 7.0) FindWord routines are implemented by each script system, and the implementation details may be different in each case. Before system software version 6.0.4, the Roman versions of CharType, Transliterate, and FindWord used tables that were built into the code; consequently, these tables could not be localized to reflect language-specific or region-specific differences in uppercase conventions and word boundaries. The old LwrText and LwrString routines used the case conversion tables from the Roman version of Transliterate.

With system software version 6.0.4, the tables used by LwrText and LwrString and by the Roman Script System versions of CharType, Transliterate, and FindWord were removed from the code and added to the 'itl2' resource, and the Roman versions of these routines have been modified to get their tables from the 'itl2' resource (using the IUGetIntl function).

The advantages of the relocation of these tables include increased localizability of character type assignments, word break definitions, and case conversion (primarily for accented Roman characters). For example, the handling of accents when lowercase characters are converted to uppercase characters depends on language and region, but these tables were not previously localizable on a region-by-region basis.

▲ **Warning:** Since system software version 6.0.4, LwrString and some script versions of CharType, Transliterate, and FindWord have gained access to the 'itl2' resource by using the IUGetIntl function. The relocation of the tables used by these routines may cause the following problems:

- If IUGetIntl needs to load 'itl2', it may cause memory to move. As a result, some of these routines that previously had no effect on memory may now cause memory to move. (The CharType function is the only one of these that was specified as a routine that would not move memory.)
- To get the correct tables, the Script Manager examines the current font of the current grafPort. As a result, LwrString now depends on the A5 register specifying the current grafPort and the font being set correctly, whereas previously it never depended on A5. ▲

Note: Before system software version 7.0, LwrText was the high-level interface to the LwrString trap. Although this name is still available in version 7.0, the recommended name is now LowerText for both high-level and assembly-language users.

The 'itl2' Resource Header

The 'itl2' resource header allows you to index localized character type and conversion tables in the Roman Script System. Figure 14-27 shows the structure of the 'itl2' resource header. All fields in this header are 16-bit words. Each field designated as an offset is the signed offset, in bytes, from the beginning of the 'itl2' resource to the specified code block or table. The header is followed by the actual code chunks and tables, which may be in any order. The position of each is specified by the corresponding offset in the header.

With system software version 7.0, the 'itl2' header has been extended to include two new sections: section 3, containing fields for the lengths of all of the code blocks and tables for which there are offsets in sections 1 and 2 in the 'itl2' resource header, and section 4, containing offset and length pairs for tables that are new with system software version 6.0.7 and for future tables.

Section 1 of the header contains a format flag and five offsets to code chunks that can be used to modify the default sorting behavior. Before system software version 6.0.4, the rsvdHook offset was an unused sorting hook offset. It now is a format flag: a value of –1 indicates that the 'itl2' resource is in the system software version 6.0.4 (or newer) format.

Section 2 contains offsets to tables for character type (typeList offset, classArray offset), character conversion (upperList offset, lowerList offset, upperNoMarkList offset, and noMarkList offset), and word break (wordTable offset and wrapTable offset). These offsets to tables are used by the LowerText, UpperText, StripText, and StripUpperText procedures and by the Script Manager's CharType, Transliterate, and FindWord routines. They are only used in system software version 6.0.4 and later, and may not be present on earlier systems. It also contains a version number and a format code that are used by DeRez.

The wordTable offset and wrapTable offset are also offsets to tables used by the Roman FindWord routines in system software version 6.0.4 and by the general FindWord routine in system software version 7.0.

The remainder of the fields in the resource header, in Section 3 and Section 4, are only required in system software version 7.0 and later, and may not be present in earlier versions.

Section 3 contains fields for the lengths of all of the code blocks and tables for which there are offsets in sections 1 and 2 of the 'itl2' resource header. Lengths in this section need only be supplied for tables that may be returned by the GetItlTable procedure.

Section 4 contains offset and length pairs for tables to be added in the future. The first offset/length pair in this section is reserved for the FindScriptTable data type, which defines an optional table that associates every character code in a single-byte script's character set with either the Roman or native script. If this table is not present, the offset and length should be 0.

The data structure defined by the FindScriptTable type consists of a series of byte pairs with the format <character code, script code>. The character code is the last character code in a range of characters that belongs to the script specified by the script code. The first character code in the range is assumed to be the last character code in the previous range plus 1, or 0 for the first range. The last pair must have character code $FF. For example, if the character set encoding for script smSample were defined such that $00–7F and $A0 were Roman characters and the remaining characters were native characters in smSample, the table would appear as follows:

```
dc.b   $7F,smRoman
dc.b   $9F,smSample
dc.b   $A0,smRoman
dc.b   $FF,smSample
```

Figure 14-27 describes the new 'itl2' header format.

The 'itl4' Resource

Each installed script has one or more 'itl4' resources. The resource ID for each 'itl4' resource is in the script's resource number range. The default 'itl4' resource for a script is specified by the script's 'itlb' resource. Each 'itl4' resource contains

- a header containing offsets to all of the code blocks and tables in the 'itl4' resource and (beginning with system software version 7.0) the size of each code block and table
- localizable tables and code for the IntlTokenize function

Offset	Field	Section
0	initHook offset	Section 1: offsets to sorting hooks
2	fetchHook offset	
4	vernierHook offset	
6	projectHook offset	
8	rsvdHook offset/fmt flag	
10	exitHook offset	
12	typeList offset	Section 2: offsets to character type, conversion, and word break tables
14	classArray offset	
16	upperList offset	
18	lowerList offset	
20	upperNoMarkList offset	
22	wordTable offset	
24	wrapTable offset	
26	noMarkList offset	
28	versionNumber	
30	format code	
32	initHook length	Section 3: sizes of the code blocks and tables
34	fetchHook length	
36	vernierHook length	
38	projectHook length	
40	reserved	
42	exitHook length	
44	typeList length	
46	classArray length	
48	upperList length	
50	lowerList length	
52	upperNoMarkList length	
54	wordTable length	
56	wrapTable length	
58	noMarkList length	
60	FindScriptTable offset	Section 4: offset and length pairs for additional tables
62	FindScriptTable length	

Figure 14-27. The 'itl2' resource header

- localizable number parts tables used by the Str2Format, Format2Str, FormatX2Str, and FormatStr2X functions
- a table of all the white space characters in the script (new with system software version 7.0)

As with the 'itl2' resource, lengths need only be supplied for tables that may be returned by the GetItlTable procedure. A new 'itl4' record defined by the NItl4Rec data type reflects these changes.

```
TYPE NItl4Handle = ^NItl4Ptr;

     NItl4Rec =
     RECORD
        flags:              Integer;     {reserved}
        resourceType:       LongInt;     {contains 'itl4'}
        resourceNum:        Integer;     {resource ID}
        version:            Integer;     {version number}
        format:             Integer;     {format code}
        resHeader:          Integer;     {reserved}
        resHeader2:         LongInt;     {reserved}
        numTables:          Integer;     {number of tables, one-based}
     {The following are offsets from the beginning of the resource to }
     { tables & code chunks.}
        mapOffset:          LongInt;     {offset to table that maps }
                                         { byte to token}
        strOffset:          LongInt;     {offset to routine that }
                                         { copies canonical string}
        fetchOffset:        LongInt;     {offset to routine that gets }
                                         { next byte of character}
        unTokenOffset:      LongInt;     {offset to untoken table, maps }
                                         { token to canonical string}
        defPartsOffset:     LongInt;     {offset to default number }
                                         { parts table}
        whtSpListOffset:    LongInt;     {offset to white space code list}
        resOffset7:         LongInt;     {reserved}
        resOffset8:         LongInt;     {reserved}
        resLength1:         Integer;     {reserved}
        resLength2:         Integer;     {reserved}
        resLength3:         Integer;     {reserved}
        unTokenLength:      Integer;     {length of untoken table}
        defPartsLength:     Integer;     {length of default number }
                                         { parts table}
        whtSpListLength:    Integer;     {length of white space code list}
        resLength7:         Integer;     {reserved}
        resLength8:         Integer      {reserved}
     END;
```

A new section of the 'itl4' resource contains a table of white space characters in the script. A formerly reserved field in the header specifies the offset to this whiteSpaceList table, and a new field specifies its length. The format of the table defined by whiteSpaceList is similar to the format of the untoken table:

```
dc.w   (length of whiteSpaceList in bytes)
dc.w   (number of entries)
dc.w   (offset from beginning of whiteSpaceList to first entry)
dc.w   (offset from beginning of whiteSpaceList to second entry)
 :
```

Each entry is a Pascal string specifying a single white space character (which may be 1 or 2 bytes). (If you do not have access to the MPW file SysTypes.r, which contains the Rez type definition for the 'itl4' resource, consult Macintosh Developer Technical Support.)

Keyboard Types and Modifier Bits

Table 14-11 furnishes a list of the keyboard types. These are used in some of the keyboard resources: 'KCAP', 'KSWP', and 'itlk'. The 'KCHR', 'KSWP', and 'itlk' resources are described in the following sections. The 'KCAP' resource is discussed in "Key Caps and the 'KCAP' Resource" later in this chapter.

Table 14-11. The keyboard types

Keyboard type*	Keyboard
1	Apple Keyboard (Domestic layout)
2	Apple Extended Keyboard and Apple Extended Keyboard II (Domestic layout)
3	Macintosh 512K Keyboard (Domestic layout)
4	Apple Keyboard (ISO layout)
5	Apple Extended Keyboard II (ISO layout)
6	Apple Macintosh Portable Keyboard (Domestic layout)
7	Apple Macintosh Portable Keyboard (ISO layout)
8	Apple Macintosh Keyboard II (Domestic layout)
9	Apple Macintosh Keyboard II (ISO layout)
259	Macintosh 512K Keyboard (ISO layout)

*This is also the resource ID of the corresponding 'KCAP' resource. The KbdType low-memory global variable contains the low byte of this value for the last keyboard used.

Table 14-12 supplies meanings of the keyboard modifier bits in the high byte of the modifiers field of an event record (defined by the EventRecord data type). The byte consisting of these bits is used to control the selection of tables in the 'KCHR' resource.

Table 14-12. The keyboard modifier bits

Bit	Key
7	(Right Control if used)
6	(Right Option if used)
5	(Right Shift if used)
4	Control (Left Control if different from Right Control)
3	Option (Left Option if different from Right Option)
2	Caps Lock
1	Shift (Left Shift if different from Right Shift)
0	Command

The 'KCHR' Resource

The 'KCHR' resource specifies the mapping of virtual key codes to character codes (for example, ASCII). Each installed script system has one or more 'KCHR' resources; there may be one or more for each language or region to suit the preference of the user. The resource ID for each 'KCHR' resource is in the script's resource number range. The default 'KCHR' resource for a script is specified by the script's 'itlb' resource. For more on virtual key codes, see the Toolbox Event Manager chapter in Volume V. If you do not have access to the MPW file SysTypes.r, which contains the Rez type definition for the 'KCHR' resource, consult Macintosh Developer Technical Support.

> **Note:** Prior to system software version 7.0, an application could force a script system to load a 'KCHR' resource that only existed inside its resource fork. Since 'KCHR' resources are used across the system (that is, are not application-specific), this was an extremely undesirable situation. If an application failed to restore the appropriate script system variables properly when it terminated or was switched into the background, the Script Manager attempted to find a 'KCHR' resource that was no longer available.
>
> With version 7.0, the Script Manager has been revised to load only 'KCHR' resources that are installed in the System file. However, if your application needs to modify the keyboard layout temporarily without forcing users to install a new keyboard, you should load a 'KCHR' resource from your resource fork and pass a pointer to that 'KCHR' resource directly to the _KeyTrans trap.

Figure 14-28 shows the parts of the 'KCHR' resource and how they are used. First, the modifier state information—8 bits, each indicating the state of one modifier key—is treated as a byte that is mapped through a 256-byte table-selection table to a table code. The table code specifies which of several 128-byte mapping tables is used to map the virtual key code to a character-code byte. If the mapping table has a nonzero entry for a particular virtual key code, that entry is the desired character code. If the entry is 0, the dead-key tables are searched for a match with the virtual key code. If there is a match, dead-key state information is set that affects how the next virtual key code is processed, but no event is posted.

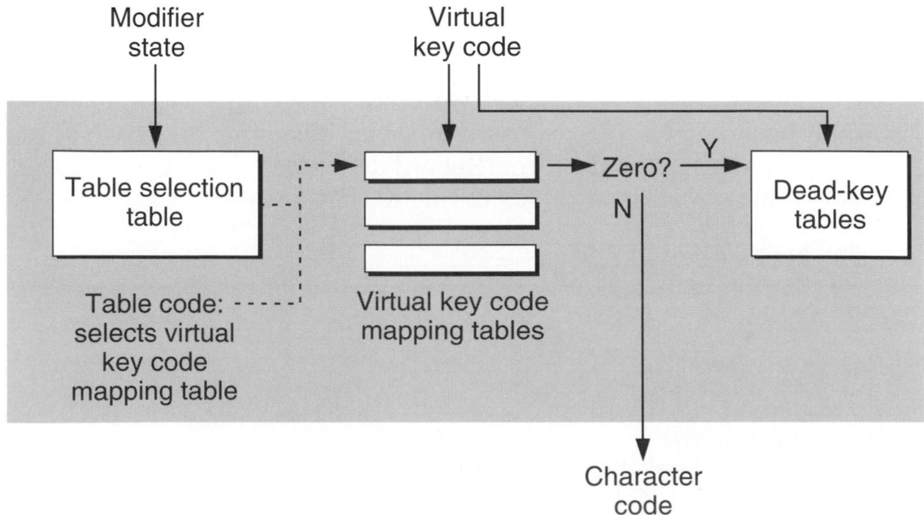

Figure 14-28. Inside the 'KCHR' resource

With system software version 7.0, the following changes in the U.S. 'KCHR' resource (0) have been introduced for greater consistency:

- Since the Shift key is ignored if the Command key is pressed, the 'KCHR' resource has been changed so the Caps Lock key is also ignored if the Command key is pressed.
- Table 14-13 lists the changes in the handling of Option-Shift-key and Option–Caps Lock–key combinations. These changes are based on the following principles:
  - If either the Option-key or the Option-Shift-key combination produces a letter, then the Option–Caps Lock–key combination should produce the same character as the Option-key, not the Option-Shift-key, combination.
  - If the Option-key combination is a dead key for a particular accent, then the Option-Shift-key combination produces the accent directly.
- System software version 7.0 also includes some changes in default dead-key completers, so that the completer is a "real" accent character instead of a low-ASCII approximation. The default completer is used when a dead key is entered, but the following key is either a space or a key for a character that cannot take the accent corresponding to the dead key. Table 14-14 summarizes these changes.

Table 14-13. Changes in handling 'KCHR' (0) key combinations

Key combination	Old character	New character	Reason
Option–Caps Lock–E	‰	´	Acute accent for dead-key Option-E
Option–Caps Lock–G	Ì	©	Be like Option-G, not Option-Shift-G
Option–Caps Lock–I	È	ˆ	Circumflex accent for dead-key Option-I
Option–Caps Lock–K	($F0)	˚	Be like Option-K, not Option-Shift-K
Option–Caps Lock–M	˜	Â	
Option–Caps Lock–N	ˆ	˜	Tilde accent for dead-key Option-N
Option–Caps Lock–R	Â	®	Be like Option-R, not Option-Shift-R
Option–Caps Lock–T	Ê	†	Be like Option-T, not Option-Shift-T
Option–Caps Lock–U	Ë	¨	Umlaut for dead-key Option-U
Option–Caps Lock–V	◊	√	Be like Option-V, not Option-Shift-V
Option–Caps Lock–W	„ ($E3)	∑	Be like Option-W, not Option-Shift-W
Option–Caps Lock–X	Ù	≈	Be like Option-X, not Option-Shift-X
Option–Caps Lock–Z	Û	Ω	Be like Option-Z, not Option-Shift-Z
Option-Shift-E	‰ ($E4)	´	Acute accent for dead-key Option-E
Option-Shift-G	Ì	˝ ($FD)	Make ˝ (double-acute accent) available for keyboard
Option-Shift-I	È	ˆ ($F6)	Circumflex accent for dead-key Option-I
Option-Shift-M	˜ ($F7)	Â	
Option-Shift-N	ˆ ($F6)	˜ ($F7)	Tilde accent for dead-key Option-N
Option-Shift-R	Â	‰	Moved ‰ from Option-Shift-E
Option-Shift-T	Ê	ˇ ($FF)	Make ˇ (hacek) available from keyboard
Option-Shift-U	Ë	¨	Umlaut for dead-key Option-U
Option-Shift-X	Ù	˛ ($FE)	Make ˛ (ogonek) available for keyboard
Option-Shift-Z	Û	¸ ($FC)	Make ¸ (cedilla) available for keyboard
Option-Shift-\`	Ÿ	\`	Grave accent for dead key Option-\`

14 Worldwide Software

Table 14-14. Changes in 'KCHR' dead-key completers

Dead key	Old default completer	New default completer
Option-N	~ ($7E)	˜ ($F7)
Option-U	^ ($5E)	ˆ ($F6)

The 'kcs#', 'kcs4', and 'kcs8' Resources

With system software version 7.0, a keyboard color icon family is available to specify the small icon that corresponds to each 'KCHR' resource. This color icon family replaces the 'SICN' resource associated with each 'KCHR' resource. See the User Interface Guidelines chapter earlier in this volume for details on color icon families.

> **Note:** If the 4-bit and 8-bit icons in your application are the same (resources 'kcs4' and 'kcs8'), then you only need to provide a 4-bit icon.

Some differences exist between the color icon family for keyboards and the color icon families used elsewhere in the Macintosh Operating System. First, only small icons (16-by-16 pixels) are supplied; there are no large keyboard icons (32-by-32 pixels). Second, the resource type for keyboard small color icons is different from the resource type used elsewhere for small color icons. This is to avoid resource ID conflicts because the keyboard color icons—like the 'KCHR' resources—may have IDs anywhere in the range $0–$BFFF (that is, 0 to 32767 and –32768 to –16385). The keyboard color icon types and the equivalent standard color icon types are shown in Table 14-15.

Table 14-15. Keyboard color icon types and standard icon equivalents

Keyboard icon type	Standard icon equivalent	Bit depth
'kcs#'	'ics#'	1
'kcs4'	'ics4'	4
'kcs8'	'ics8'	8

These keyboard icons are used in the Keyboard control panel and in the Keyboard menu when it is displayed on some localized versions of the system software. For details on the Keyboard menu, see "Using the Keyboard Menu" earlier in this chapter. The resource ID for each 'kcs#', 'kcs4', or 'kcs8' resource is the same as that of the 'KCHR' resource to which it corresponds.

The 'KSWP' Resource

The 'KSWP' resource consists of a series of entries, each of which specifies modifier-plus-key combinations that can be used to change keyboards and scripts—for example, the Command–Space bar combination that users press to rotate to the next keyboard script on most script systems.

Figure 14-29 shows the format of each entry. For the meanings of the special negative codes, see Table 14-3, "Verbs for the KeyScript Procedure," earlier in this chapter.

Script code or special negative code (integer)	Virtual key code (byte)	Modifier state (byte)

Figure 14-29. Format of entries in the 'KSWP' resource

If you do not have access to the MPW file SysTypes.r, which contains the Rez type definition of the 'KSWP' resource, consult Macintosh Developer Technical Support for details.

The 'itlk' Resource

The 'itlk' resource is used to make the various international keyboard layouts work on all of the keyboard models. It specifies how to remap certain key combinations before the KeyTrans function is called.

> **Note:** Starting with system software version 7.0, the Script Manager only loads the 'itlk' resource from the System file.

Figure 14-30 shows the 'itlk' resource. It consists of an integer count of entries succeeded by a set of 8-byte entries.

Current keyboard type (integer)	Current modifiers (byte)	Current key code (byte)	Character modifiers (byte)	Character code (byte)	New modifiers (byte)	New key code (byte)

Figure 14-30. The 'itlk' resource entries

Before KeyTrans begins processing with the 'KCHR' resource, the current keyboard type, key code, and modifiers are compared against each entry. If there is a match, it substitutes the new modifiers and key code before calling KeyTrans. Each pair of character modifiers and character codes is defined to produce a number of new modifiers and new key codes. Here is how the 'itlk' resource can produce multiple modifiers:

1. An AND operation is performed on the new modifiers and key code with the character modifiers and character code from the entry.

2. An AND operation is performed on the current modifiers and key code with the complement of the character modifiers and character code from the entry.

3. The logical OR of these two products is the final result. This allows for a more compact table when several characters on one key are mapped together to a different key.

If you do not have access to the MPW file SysTypes.r, which contains the Rez type definition for the 'itlk' resource, consult Macintosh Developer Technical Support for details.

KEY CAPS AND THE 'KCAP' RESOURCE

This section discusses some enhancements to the Key Caps desk accessory and describes its related resource, 'KCAP', which specifies the physical layout of keyboards. With system software version 7.0, Key Caps supplies additional feedback on using dead keys to produce accented characters. The 'KCAP' resource is used by the Key Caps desk accessory.

> **Note:** The Keyboard Layout file formerly associated with Key Caps no longer exists. The 'KCAP' resources that were formerly located in this file now reside in the System file.

Dead-Key Feedback

The Key Caps desk accessory provides feedback on using dead keys to produce accented characters. It indicates dead keys with dotted borders, as shown in the Key Caps window in Figure 14-31, which shows the U.S. keyboard layout with the Option key pressed.

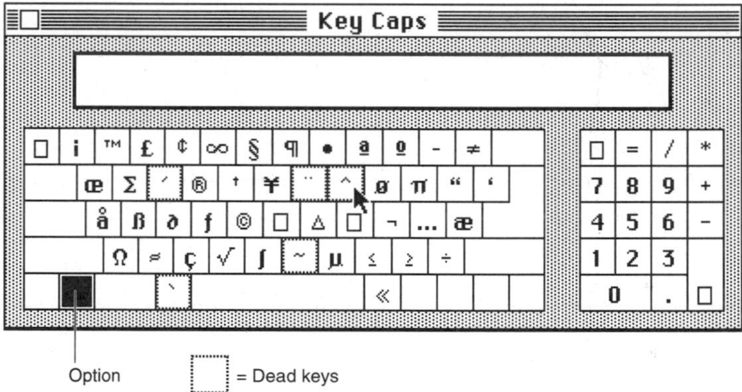

Figure 14-31. Key Caps display of dead keys with Option key pressed

If a dead key is entered, such as the circumflex dead-key combination (Option-I), the display changes to highlight the completer keys for this dead key that users can press to generate valid accented character combinations, as shown in the Key Caps window in Figure 14-32. If your application displays keyboards, you should use a similar method of indicating dead keys and completers.

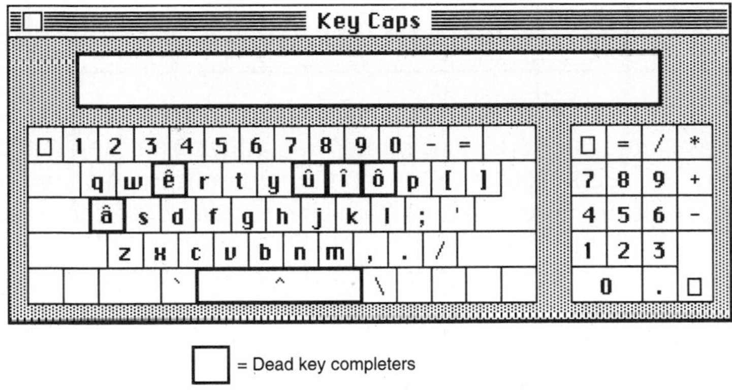

Figure 14-32. Key Caps display of completer keys after circumflex dead key has been pressed

The 'KCAP' Resource

The 'KCAP' resource specifies the physical layout of keyboards and is used by the Key Caps desk accessory. Prior to system software version 7.0, 'KCAP' was located in the Key Layout file. With version 7.0, it is located in the System file.

See Table 14-11 earlier in this chapter for a list of the current 'KCAP' identification numbers (which are also their resource IDs) and the keyboards they represent.

Listing 14-6 shows the Rez format for the 'KCAP' resource.

Listing 14-6. Physical layout of keyboards

```
type 'KCAP' {
   rect;                      /*boundsRect*/
   rect;                      /*textRect*/
   integer = $$CountOf(MainArray);
   array MainArray {
      integer = $$CountOf(ShapeArray) - 1;
      wide array ShapeArray {
         point;               /*shapePoint*/
      };
      integer = $$CountOf(KeyArray) - 1;
      wide array KeyArray {
         byte;                /*mask*/
         boolean or, and;
         bitstring[7];        /*keyCode*/
         integer;             /*dv*/
         integer;             /*dh*/
      };
   };
};
```

LOCALIZING TO OTHER LANGUAGES AND REGIONS

You can use existing resources or create new ones to localize your applications to other languages or regions. The sections that follow contain guidelines and tips for localizing your applications successfully. See *Guide to Software Localization* for details on the localization process.

Using Resources

Be certain that you place the following information in an appropriate resource:

- all user-visible text
- lengths of string and text
- dialog box formats
- menus and command keys
- character, word, phrase, and text translation tables
- font family numbers, names, sizes, styles, and widths of numeric fields
- special characters and delimiters

Note: Other information may vary from locale to locale such as address formats, including zip codes and telephone numbers.

Text and Dialog Translation Tips

Follow these guidelines for translating visible text in your applications to other languages:

- Do not place in the program code any text that the user will see.
- Do not assume that all languages or regions have the same rules or conventions for punctuation, word order, and alphabetizing.
- Be aware that grammar problems may arise from error messages, natural programming language structures, and so forth.
- Text needs room to grow—up, down, and sideways! (This is especially true for numbers.) For example, translated text data can be 50 percent larger than the U.S. English text data; therefore, do not rely on strings having a particular length.
- Text location within a window should be easy to change.

- Note that the arrangement of dialog-box items may vary with localization. The low-memory global variable TESysJust indicates the system line direction. On Arabic and Hebrew systems, the line direction usually defaults to right to left, so text in dialog boxes should generally be right to left. When creating a column of check boxes or radio buttons, make sure the text boxes are the same sizes. Then when the line direction is reversed, the check boxes or radio buttons align correctly.

Note: Natural programming language structures refer to programming languages that attempt to use human-like command structures. For example, it is unreasonable to write a command in one language and expect it to survive the process of translation without making accommodations for word order at the very least. An English command like "Put It Into Field 7" could translate into Japanese word order as "It (as-for) Field 7 Into Put."

Adapting Text Operations

Follow these recommendations for adapting text operations to other languages and regions:

- Use the Script Manager routines for displaying and measuring text and testing for mouse-down events in text, or use TextEdit, which now uses the Script Manager for these operations.

- Use language-specific string comparison and sorting. For example, be sure that names are sorted using the correct sorting order for the system on which your application is running. To do this, use IUCompString or a similar function.

- Use language-specific word-break and word-wrap routines. Consider word boundaries and their impact on word wrap, selection, search, and cut and paste. Use the FindWord or NFindWord procedure to specify word breaks.

- Use language-specific character type information. Consider character boundaries and their impact on search, replace, sort, word wrap, backspace, delete, and cut and paste. Use the CharType function and its associated constants to obtain more information about character type. See "Summary of the Script Manager" near the end of this chapter for details on the CharType constants.

- Use language-specific case conversion. Use the UpperText and LowerText procedures for localizable uppercase and lowercase conversion of characters.

- Keep in mind that the length of text may vary from language to language.

- Avoid assumptions about the number of letters in the alphabet. For example, if your program relies on properties of the ASCII code table or uses data compression codes, remember that not all alphabets have the same number of characters.

- Don't break text into arbitrary blocks for drawing, measuring, and so forth. As a minimum, always group text on the same line into style runs for drawing and measuring.

Using Fonts

Here are some hints for planning for font-related issues in your applications:

- Diacritical marks, used in many languages, extend up to the ascent line.
- Some system fonts contain characters that extend to both the ascent and descent lines.

Avoiding Special Character Codes as Delimiters

Your application may need to use a character code or range of codes to represent noncharacter data (such as field delimiters). Character codes below $20 are never affected by the script system. Some of these can be used safely for special purposes. Note, however, that most characters in this range are already assigned special meanings by parts of the Macintosh Toolbox, such as TextEdit, or certain programming languages like C.

The low ASCII characters (with hexadecimal representations) that you should avoid as delimiters are as follows:

Character or key	Code	Character or key	Code
Null	$00	Page Up	$0B
Home	$01	Page Down	$0C
Enter	$03	Carriage return	$0D
End	$04	F1 through F15	$10
Help	$05	System characters	$11, $12, $13, $14
Backspace	$08	Clear	$1B
Tab	$09	Arrow keys	$1C, $1D, $1E, $1F
Line feed	$0A		

Using the Standard Roman Character Set

Be aware that the "traditional" Macintosh character set (that is, the original set described in Volume I as the Macintosh character set) stops at code $D8 and contains a limited set of European accented forms. The standard Roman character set now includes the remaining character codes ($D9–$FF); it supplies uppercase versions of all of the lowercase accented forms in the traditional set, new symbols, and other forms. These characters are available in most LaserWriter® and TrueType™ fonts, but not in the Apple bitmap versions of Chicago, Geneva, or Monaco. See the Font Manager chapter in this volume for an illustration of the standard Roman character set. See *Macintosh Worldwide Development: Guide to System Software* for further information on the standard Roman character set (there referred to as the extended Roman character set).

Since system software version 6.0.4, there has been full support for the standard Roman character set. This version has supplied more completeness and consistency in the handling of accented forms in the fonts that contain these forms.

Also with system software version 6.0.4, the U.S. keyboard resource 'KCHR' (0) has been modified to make it possible to enter the accented forms with dead keys. Users can enter all the accented forms in the original Macintosh character set with dead keys.

> **Note:** With system software version 7.0, the keyboard entry of the following four characters is now possible using the U.S. 'KCHR' resources: cedilla (¸), double-acute accent (˝), ogonek (˛), and hacek (ˇ). These characters are represented by codes $FC–FF.

The tables used by the Script Manager's CharType, Transliterate, and FindWord routines (in 'itl2'), by the IntlTokenize function (in 'itl4'), and by the International Utilities Package (in Pack6) have been modified in the U.S. system for proper treatment of the character-set extensions as well as the traditional characters ß, ø, and Ø.

Adapting Keyboard Equivalents

Applications that make extensive use of keyboard equivalents face numerous challenges on the worldwide market. When multiple script systems are installed on a system, the challenges increase. When the Command key is pressed, some characters, such as the period (.), cannot be produced on certain keyboard layouts. This is mainly a problem if symbols are used as keyboard equivalents. To make Command-key handling work in these cases, it may be necessary to determine which character would have been produced if the Command key were not pressed. The code in Listing 14-7 illustrates one approach.

Listing 14-7. Making keyboard equivalents work with multiple scripts

```
CONST
   menuIdMask = $FFFF0000;     {mask for menu ID in MenuKey result}

   newModifierMask = $FC00;    {high byte of modifiers, without }
                               { cmdKey bit}
   Ascii1Mask = $00FF0000;     {ASCII 1 in Key Trans result}
   Ascii2Mask = $000000FF;     {ASCII 2 in Key Trans result}
VAR
   myEvent:           EventRecord;
   myChar:            Char;
   menuResult:        LongInt;
   myNewModifiers:    Integer;
   myVirtualCode:     Integer;
   myKeyCode:         Integer;
   myKCHRPtr:         Ptr;
   myDeadState:       LongInt;
   myNewChars:        LongInt;
   myNewChar:         Char;
```

(Continued)

Listing 14-7. Making keyboard equivalents work with multiple scripts (Continued)

```
BEGIN
   {Assume that here is a key-down or auto-key event.}
   myChar := CHAR(BAnd(myEvent.message, charCodeMask));
   IF BAnd(myEvent.modifiers, cmdKey) <> 0 THEN
      {Command key is down.}
      IF myEvent.what = keyDown THEN
      BEGIN
         menuResult := MenuKey(myChar);
         IF BAnd(menuResult, menuIdMask) = 0 THEN
         BEGIN
            {Didn't match, so see if there is a match with }
            { the character that would have been produced if }
            { Command were not down.}

            {First, make keyCode parameter for KeyTrans, }
            { but turn off the Command key bit.}
            myNewModifiers := BAnd(myEvent.modifiers, newModifierMask);
            myVirtualCode := BSR(BAnd(myEvent.message, keyCodeMask), 8);
            myKeyCode := BOr(myNewModifiers, myVirtualCode);
            {Now, get current 'KCHR' pointer. This requires version 7.0.}
            myKCHRPtr := Ptr(GetEnvirons(smKCHRCache));
            {Now set dead state to 0 and call KeyTrans.}
            myDeadState := 0;
            myNewChars := KeyTrans(myKCHRPtr, myKeyCode, myDeadState);
            {If there is a nonzero result in the high word, try it; }
            { else if there is a nonzero result in the low word, }
            { try it.}
            myNewChar := CHAR(BSR(BAnd(myNewChars, Ascii1Mask), 16));
            IF myNewChar = CHAR(0) THEN
               myNewChar := CHAR(BAnd(myNewChars, Ascii2Mask));
            IF myNewChar <> CHAR(0) THEN
               menuResult := MenuKey(myNewChar);
            {Note that the menu ID field of menuResult may still be 0.}

         END;
         {Now do menu handling based on menuResult.}
      END
   ELSE BEGIN
      {Not a Command key; do other handling.}
   END;
END;
```

Many applications extend the set of standard Macintosh interface modifier-plus-key combinations for specific purposes. Be sure to supply alternative methods of gaining access to functions. Avoid keyboard equivalents that use the Space bar in combination with the Command key and other modifier keys. The Script Manager and various script systems reserve and may use these combinations.

Note: The Script Manager removes from the event queue any Command key combinations involving the Space bar if that Command key combination indicates a useful function on the current system. For example, if multiple script systems are installed, the Script Manager strips the Command–Space bar combination (which indicates changing scripts) from the event queue. If multiple script systems are not installed, this event is not removed, so users can use it in Command key macros. Applications, however, should never depend on Command key combinations involving the Space bar.

Modifying the Representation of Dates, Times, and Numbers

Be sure to allow for variations in the representation of dates, times, and numbers in all the localized versions of your application.

- Dates, times, and numbers should be displayed in local format as specified by the system script's 'itl0' and 'itl1' resources.
- Parsing of dates, times, and numbers should work for local formats (the Script Manager provides routines to do this). See "Date and Time Utilities" and "Number Utilities" earlier in this chapter for details.
- Units of measure should be localized. For example, lines per inch is meaningless in the metric world. The International Utilities Package provides routines for determining the appropriate units of measurement.

WRITING SOFTWARE FOR OTHER SCRIPTS

To ensure that your applications are compatible with other scripts, particularly non-Roman scripts, follow the guidelines presented here as well as those provided in the previous section.

Working With Fonts

- Don't hard-code font IDs or sizes. System and application fonts have different font IDs and sizes on various script systems. If you must, use a font size of 0; otherwise, let the user choose. 'FOND' IDs 0 and 1 always map to system and application fonts for the system script. Font size 0 always maps to the default system font size. If the user cannot select fonts and sizes, use the default values listed above.
- On non-Roman systems, the Chicago font does not have ID 0.
- Don't make assumptions about font sizes. System or application fonts may be 12 or 18 point, or other sizes.
- Don't make assumptions about menu bar height; call GetMBarHeight to get the correct value.

- Special script codes (smUninterp and smRSymbol) are defined for fonts that contain characters that should not be treated as normal text, such as menu and palette symbols. These script codes have their own ranges for defining 'FOND' IDs.
- The non-Roman fonts have always included Roman characters for compatibility. However, in word processors, you'll find that your text-processing operations are greatly simplified if you extract the Roman characters and reassign them to a Roman font.

  The Script Manager's FindScriptRun function allows you to extract blocks of Roman text in a non-Roman font to deal with them properly in higher-level runs. Word processors should call FindScriptRun to decompose text so that it fits in the format run framework. For an example of extracting blocks of Roman text, see Figure 14-33.

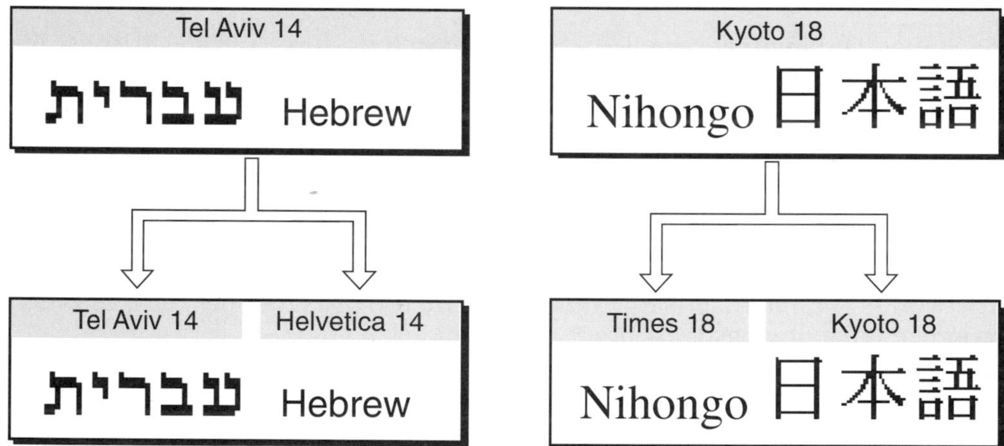

Figure 14-33. Extracting blocks of Roman text

- Display font names in the proper script and proper font. In the Fonts menu in word processors, for example, font names should appear in their own font (and script). First, this lets users know the appearance of the font. Second, some fonts—like Arabic, Hebrew, and Japanese fonts—have non-ASCII names that only display correctly in their own script.

Working With Character Codes

In addition to remembering that the meaning of a character code depends on the font, keep the following principles in mind:

- The character codes may be 1 or 2 bytes.
- The caret (insertion point) should sit between characters, not bytes (that is, it should not be inserted between bytes of a 2-byte character).
- The Delete key should delete entire characters, not bytes.
- Two-byte characters may affect data transmission and reception.

- The arrow keys should move over characters, not bytes.
- A character code should ideally have a unique meaning in a particular script, although this is not always the case. For example, the Symbol font is in the Roman range but uses a different character assignment from the standard Roman character set.

Working With Text Direction

When working with scripts that display mixed-directional text, remember the following guidelines:

- Convert mouse-down events to text offsets correctly, regardless of text direction. See the description of Pixel2Char in *Macintosh Worldwide Development: Guide to System Software* for comprehensive details.
- Right or left alignment of dialog box text and menu items should depend on TESysJust, a low-memory global variable set by the script system. Word processors should allow users to set the default line direction on a paragraph-by-paragraph basis.
- The caret (insertion point) should be displayed where the next entered character will appear. If the position occurs at a direction-run boundary, use a **dual caret.** The high caret, called the **primary caret,** should indicate where the next character in the primary line direction will appear, and the low caret, called the **secondary caret,** should indicate where the next character in the opposing line direction will appear. See the TextEdit chapter in this volume for more information on dual carets.
- Highlighting should apply to a contiguous set of characters in memory, which may not be visually contiguous. See the TextEdit chapter in this volume for more information on highlighting with mixed-directional text.
- The arrow keys should move the caret in the direction the arrow points, regardless of the text direction, even across direction-run boundaries.

Synchronizing Keyboards and Fonts

Three rules govern the synchronization of keyboards and fonts in non-Roman scripts:

- Clicking in text should set the keyboard script to the script of the text.
- Typing a character from the current keyboard should select an appropriate font.
- Selecting a font should set the keyboard to the script of the font.

Handling Numbers

Some scripts include multiple sets of digits. Applications that handle numbers should accept these as valid digits (the Script Manager number utilities routines help you do this). For details, see "Number Utilities" earlier in this chapter for brief descriptions, and see *Macintosh Worldwide Development: Guide to System Software* for details on the routines.

Identifying Keywords and Tokens

Keyword and token identification should work correctly in all scripts. For details, see *Macintosh Worldwide Development: Guide to System Software.*

Possible Printing Problems

If you use the wrong LaserWriter driver for a script system, characters map incorrectly because the drivers are localized and have different encodings. For instance, a Turkish system with a U.S. LaserWriter driver might print unexpected forms instead of the substituted characters in the Turkish font.

State information you need may not be saved in picture comments—for example, modified width tables are not saved. With system software version 7.0, parameters for justified text are now saved.

Scripts such as Japanese or Arabic modify the normal QuickDraw text handling in order to represent text properly. On the screen, this is done by trapping StdText and StdTxtMeasure and by transforming the text before printing. Hebrew or Arabic text might be reversed because text normally goes from right to left in those scripts.

Printer drivers require slightly different handling, for two reasons:

- A printer driver might not call the standard QuickDraw procedures. For example, the LaserWriter writes directly in PostScript®.
- A printer driver might need to format the text for accurate line layout. In this case, the text needs to be transformed before the driver performs line layout. If the driver is spooling the text and will replay the text a second time, the text cannot be transformed a second time because that would ruin the appearance.

For example, the ImageWriter® driver calls QuickDraw procedures twice, once to spool and once to unwind the spool. The text must be transformed when spooling so that line layout can be done, but during unwinding, the transformation must be turned off completely.

Note that some drivers, such as the LaserWriter, use QuickDraw reentrantly. The application program calls a QuickDraw routine, which is directed to the driver's grafProcs, which in turn call QuickDraw internally to put up status messages on the screen. (The PrintAction procedure allows the script system to install the proper QuickDraw hooks, which then handle printing properly.)

The Script Manager PrintAction procedure allows the printer driver to be independent of the particular scripts being used. The printer driver should call this routine whenever it changes the grafProcs in the printing grafPort. The PrintAction routine then substitutes grafProcs of its own in the grafProcs record and saves the original routine addresses.

The PrintAction procedure actually calls a PrintAction routine for each script system that is currently enabled. Each PrintAction procedure does the tasks appropriate for its script system. For more information, see "Working With Print Drivers" in *Macintosh Worldwide Development: Guide to System Software.*

SUMMARY OF THE SCRIPT MANAGER

Constants

```
CONST {script codes}
      smSystemScript       = -1;      {system script}
      smCurrentScript      = -2;      {current font script}
      smRoman              = 0;
      smJapanese           = 1;
      smTradChinese        = 2;       {Traditional Chinese}
      smKorean             = 3;
      smArabic             = 4;
      smHebrew             = 5;
      smGreek              = 6;
      smCyrillic           = 7;
      smRSymbol            = 8;       {right-left symbols}
      smDevanagari         = 9;
      smGurmukhi           = 10;
      smGujarati           = 11;
      smOriya              = 12;
      smBengali            = 13;
      smTamil              = 14;
      smTelugu             = 15;
      smKannada            = 16;      {Kannada/Kanarese}
      smMalayalam          = 17;
      smSinhalese          = 18;
      smBurmese            = 19;
      smKhmer              = 20;
      smThai               = 21;
      smLaotian            = 22;
      smGeorgian           = 23;
      smArmenian           = 24;
      smSimpChinese        = 25;      {Simplified Chinese}
      smTibetan            = 26;
      smMongolian          = 27;
      smGeez               = 28;      {Geez/Ethiopic}
      smEthiopic           = 28;      {synonym for smGeez}
      smEastEurRoman       = 29;      {extended Roman for Slavic }
                                      { and Baltic languages}
      smVietnamese         = 30;      {extended Roman for Vietnamese}
      smExtArabic          = 31;      {extended Arabic for Sindhi }
                                      { and so forth}
      smUninterp           = 32;      {uninterpreted symbols}

      {obsolete script system names (kept for backward compatibility)}
      smChinese            = 2;       {use smTradChinese or }
                                      { smSimpChinese}
      smRussian            = 7;       {old name for smCyrillic}
      smMaldivian          = 25;      {with version 7.0, no more }
                                      { smMaldivian}
```

```
smAmharic             = 28;     {old name for smGeez, kept for }
                                { compatibility}
smSlavic              = 29;     {old name for smEastEurRoman}
smSindhi              = 31;     {old name for smExtArabic}

{language codes (moved to Language.p)}
langEnglish           = 0;      {smRoman script}
langFrench            = 1;      {smRoman script}
langGerman            = 2;      {smRoman script}
langItalian           = 3;      {smRoman script}
langDutch             = 4;      {smRoman script}
langSwedish           = 5;      {smRoman script}
langSpanish           = 6;      {smRoman script}
langDanish            = 7;      {smRoman script}
langPortuguese        = 8;      {smRoman script}
langNorwegian         = 9;      {smRoman script}
langHebrew            = 10;     {smHebrew script}
langJapanese          = 11;     {smJapanese script}
langArabic            = 12;     {smArabic script}
langFinnish           = 13;     {smRoman script}
langGreek             = 14;     {smGreek script}
langIcelandic         = 15;     {smRoman script}
langMaltese           = 16;     {smRoman script}
langTurkish           = 17;     {Turkish in smRoman script}
langCroatian          = 18;     {Serbo-Croatian in smRoman script}
langTradChinese       = 19;     {Chinese in traditional characters}
langUrdu              = 20;     {smArabic script}
langHindi             = 21;     {smDevanagari script}
langThai              = 22;     {smThai script}
langKorean            = 23;     {smKorean script}
langLithuanian        = 24;     {smEastEurRoman script}
langPolish            = 25;     {smEastEurRoman script}
langHungarian         = 26;     {smEastEurRoman script}
langEstonian          = 27;     {smEastEurRoman script}
langLettish           = 28;     {smEastEurRoman script}
langLatvian           = 28;     {synonym for langLettish}
langLapponian         = 29;     {synonym for langLapppish}
langLappish           = 29;     {synonym for langLapponian}
langFaeroese          = 30;     {smRoman script}
langFarsi             = 31;     {smArabic script}
langPersian           = 31;     {synonym for langFarsi}
langRussian           = 32;     {smCyrillic script}
langSimpChinese       = 33;     {Chinese in simplified characters}
langFlemish           = 34;     {smRoman script}
langIrish             = 35;     {smRoman script}
langAlbanian          = 36;     {smRoman script}
langRomanian          = 37;     {smEastEurRoman script}
langCzech             = 38;     {smEastEurRoman script}
langSlovak            = 39;     {smEastEurRoman script}
langSlovenian         = 40;     {smEastEurRoman script}
langYiddish           = 41;     {smHebrew script}
langSerbian           = 42;     {smCyrillic script}
langMacedonian        = 43;     {smCyrillic script}
```

```
langBulgarian       = 44;    {smCyrillic script}
langUkrainian       = 45;    {smCyrillic script}
langByelorussian    = 46;    {smCyrillic script}
langUzbek           = 47;    {smCyrillic script}
langKazakh          = 48;    {smCyrillic script}
langAzerbaijani     = 49;    {Azerbaijani in smCyrillic }
                             { script (USSR)}
langAzerbaijanAr    = 50;    {Azerbaijani in smArabic script }
                             { (Iran)}
langArmenian        = 51;    {smArmenian script}
langGeorgian        = 52;    {smGeorgian script}
langMoldavian       = 53;    {smCyrillic script}
langKirghiz         = 54;    {smCyrillic script}
langTajiki          = 55;    {smCyrillic script}
langTurkmen         = 56;    {smCyrillic script}
langMongolian       = 57;    {smMongolian script}
langMongolianCyr    = 58;    {smCyrillic script}
langPashto          = 59;    {smArabic script}
langKurdish         = 60;    {smArabic script}
langKashmiri        = 61;    {smArabic script}
langSindhi          = 62;    {smExtArabic script}
langTibetan         = 63;    {smTibetan script}
langNepali          = 64;    {smDevanagari script}
langSanskrit        = 65;    {smDevanagari script}
langMarathi         = 66;    {smDevanagari script}
langBengali         = 67;    {smBengali script}
langAssamese        = 68;    {smBengali script}
langGujarati        = 69;    {smGujarati script}
langPunjabi         = 70;    {smGurmukhi script}
langOriya           = 71;    {smOriya script}
langMalayalam       = 72;    {smMalayalam script}
langKannada         = 73;    {smKannada script}
langTamil           = 74;    {smTamil script}
langTelugu          = 75;    {smTelugu script}
langSinhalese       = 76;    {smSinhalese script}
langBurmese         = 77;    {smBurmese script}
langKhmer           = 78;    {smKhmer script}
langLao             = 79;    {smLaotian script}
langVietnamese      = 80;    {smVietnamese script}
langIndonesian      = 81;    {smRoman script}
langTagalog         = 82;    {smRoman script}
langMalayRoman      = 83;    {smRoman script}
langMalayArabic     = 84;    {smArabic script}
langAmharic         = 85;    {smEthiopic script}
langTigrinya        = 86;    {smEthiopic script}
langGalla           = 87;    {smEthiopic script}
langOromo           = 87;    {synonym for langGalla}
langSomali          = 88;    {smRoman script}
langSwahili         = 89;    {smRoman script}
langRuanda          = 90;    {smRoman script}
langRundi           = 91;    {smRoman script}
langChewa           = 92;    {smRoman script}
langMalagasy        = 93;    {smRoman script}
langEsperanto       = 94;    {modified Roman script}
```

```
langWelsh           = 128;    {smRoman script}
langBasque          = 129;    {smRoman script}
langCatalan         = 130;    {smRoman script}
langLatin           = 131;    {smRoman script}
langQuechua         = 132;    {smRoman script}
langGuarani         = 133;    {smRoman script}
langAymara          = 134;    {smRoman script}
langTatar           = 135;    {smCyrillic script}
langUighur          = 136;    {smArabic script}
langDzongkha        = 137;    {language of Bhutan, smTibetan script}
langJavaneseRom     = 138;    {smRoman script}
langSundaneseRom    = 139;    {smRoman script}

{obsolete language names}
langPortugese       = 8;      {old misspelled version, kept }
                              { for compatibility}
langMalta           = 16;     {old misspelled version, kept }
                              { for compatibility}
langYugoslavian     = 18;     {use langCroatian, langSerbian, }
                              { and so forth}
langChinese         = 19;     {use langTradChinese or }
                              { langSimpChinese}

{calendar (date representation codes} used in the }
{ date representation fields of the 'itlb' resource}
{returned in the low byte when you call Get Script }
{ with smScriptNumDate verb}
calGregorian        = 0;      {Gregorian calendar}
calArabicCivil      = 1;      {Arabic civil calendar}
calArabicLunar      = 2;      {Arabic lunar calendar}
calJapanese         = 3;      {Japanese calendar}
calJewish           = 4;      {Jewish calendar}
calCoptic           = 5;      {Coptic calendar}
calPersian          = 6;      {Persian calendar}

{integer format (number representation) codes used in the }
{ number representation fields of the 'itlb' resource}
{returned in the high byte when you call Get Script }
{ with smScriptNumDate verb}
intWestern          = 0;
intArabic           = 1;
intRoman            = 2;
intJapanese         = 3;
intEuropean         = 4;
intOutputMask       = $8000;

{CharByte function byte types}
smSingleByte        = 0;      {single byte character}
smFirstByte         = -1;     {high (most significant) byte with }
                              { the lower address (comes first }
                              { in memory)}
smLastByte          = 1;      {low byte with the higher }
                              { address (in memory)}
smMiddleByte        = 2;      {reserved for future extensions}
```

```
{CharType function field masks}
smcTypeMask             = $000F;
smcReserved             = $00F0;
smcClassMask            = $0F00;
smcOrientationMask      = $1000;    {Far Eastern script systems }
                                    { glyph orientation}
smcRightMask            = $2000;
smcUpperMask            = $4000;
smcDoubleMask           = $8000;

{basic CharType character types}
smCharPunct             = $0000;    {punctuation character type}
smCharAscii             = $0001;    {ASCII letter}
smCharEuro              = $0007;    {old name for smCharExtAscii}
smCharExtAscii          = $0007;    {extended ASCII letter}

{additional CharType character types for script systems}
smCharKatakana          = $0002;    {Japanese Katakana}
smCharHiragana          = $0003;    {Japanese Hiragana}
smCharIdeographic       = $0004;    {Hanzi, Kanji, Hanja}
smCharTwoByteGreek      = $0005;    {2-byte Greek in Far }
                                    { Eastern script systems}
smCharTwoByteRussian    = $0006;    {2-byte Cyrillic in Far }
                                    { Eastern script systems}
smCharBidirect          = $0008;    {Arabic/Hebrew}
smCharHangul            = $000C;    {Korean Hangul}
smCharJamo              = $000D;    {Korean Jamo}

{CharType Jamo classes for Korean systems}
smJamoJaeum             = $0000;    {simple consonant char}
smJamoBogJaeum          = $0100;    {complex consonant char}
smJamoMoeum             = $0200;    {simple vowel char}
smJamoBogMoeum          = $0300;    {complex vowel char}

{CharType classes for punctuation (smCharPunct)}
smPunctNormal           = $0000;
smPunctNumber           = $0100;
smPunctSymbol           = $0200;
smPunctBlank            = $0300;

{additional CharType classes for punctuation in 2-byte }
{ script systems}
smPunctRepeat           = $0400;    {repeat marker}
smPunctGraphic          = $0500;    {line graphics}

{CharType ideographic classes for 2-byte script systems}
smIdeographicLevel1     = $0000;    {level 1 char}
smIdeographicLevel2     = $0100;    {level 2 char}
smIdeographicUser       = $0200;    {user char}

{CharType Katakana & Hiragana classes for 2-byte script systems}
smKanaSmall             = $0100;    {small kana character}
smKanaHardOK            = $0200;    {can have dakuten}
smKanaSoftOK            = $0300;    {can have dakuten or }
                                    { han-dakuten}
```

```
{Transliterate function target types for Roman script}
smTransAscii            = 0;        {convert to ASCII}
smTransNative           = 1;        {convert to native script }
                                    { (that is, the script of }
                                    { the current font)}
smTransCase             = $FE;      {convert case for all text}
smTransSystem           = $FF;      {convert to system script; }
                                    { not available in MPW 3.0}

{Transliterate target types for 2-byte script systems}
smTransAscii1           = 2;        {1-byte Roman}
smTransAscii2           = 3;        {2-byte Roman}
smTransKana1            = 4;        {1-byte Japanese Katakana}
smTransKana2            = 5;        {2-byte Japanese Katakana}
smTransGana2            = 7;        {2-byte Japanese Hiragana }
                                    { (no 1-byte Hiragana)}
smTransHangul2          = 8;        {2-byte Korean Hangul}
smTransJamo2            = 9;        {2-byte Korean Jamo}
smTransBopomofo2        = 10;       {2-byte Chinese Bopomofo}

{Transliterate target modifiers (not available in MPW 3.0)}
smTransLower            = $4000;    {target becomes lowercase}
smTransUpper            = $8000;    {target becomes uppercase}

{Transliterate source mask - general}
smMaskAll               = $FFFFFFFF;   {convert all text}

{Transliterate source masks for Roman Script System}
smMaskAscii             = $00000001;
smMaskNative            = $00000002;

{Transliterate source masks for 2-byte script systems}
smMaskAscii1            = $00000004;   {2^smTransAscii1}
smMaskAscii2            = $00000008;   {2^smTransAscii2}
smMaskKana1             = $00000010;   {2^smTransKana1}
smMaskKana2             = $00000020;   {2^smTransKana2}
smMaskGana2             = $00000080;   {2^smTransGana2}
smMaskHangul2           = $00000100;   {2^smTransHangul2}
smMaskJamo2             = $00000200;   {2^smTransJamo2}
smMaskBopomofo2         = $00000400;   {2^smTransBopomofo2}

{results returned by GetEnvirons, SetEnvirons, GetScript, & }
{ SetScript functions}
smNotInstalled          =  0;       {routine not available in script}
smBadVerb               = -1;       {invalid verb passed to a routine}
smBadScript             = -2;       {invalid script code passed to a }
                                    { routine}

{byte values for script redraw flag (smScriptRedraw) that describes }
{ how much of a line should be redrawn when text is being entered}
smRedrawChar            = 0;        {redraw character only}
smRedrawWord            = 1;        {redraw entire word }
                                    { (2-byte systems)}
```

```
smRedrawLine            = -1;       {redraw entire line }
                                    { (bidirectional systems)}

{bits in the script flags word (smScriptFlags) }
{ (bits above 7 are nonstatic)}
smsfIntellCP     = 0;    {script has intelligent cut and paste}
smsfSingByte     = 1;    {script has only single bytes}
smsfNatCase      = 2;    {native characters have uppercase and lowercase}
smsfContext      = 3;    {contextual script, for example, based on }
                         { Arabic Script System}
smsfNoForceFont  = 4;    {will not force characters}
smsfB0Digits     = 5;    {has alternate digits at B0-B9}
smsfAutoInit     = 6;    {initialize script automatically}
smsfForms        = 13;   {uses contextual forms for letters}
smsfLigatures    = 14;   {uses contextual ligatures}
smsfReverse      = 15;   {reverses native text right to left}

{TokenType values}
tokenIntl               = 4;    {designates which international }
                                { resource could be used for the }
                                { tokenizer}
tokenEmpty              = -1;   {used internally as an empty flag}
tokenUnknown            = 0;    {used for characters that do not }
                                { correspond to any of existing }
                                { token types}
tokenWhite              = 1;    {white space}
tokenLeftLit            = 2;    {literal begin ("left }
                                { literal marker")}
tokenRightLit           = 3;    {literal end ("right }
                                { literal marker")}
tokenAlpha              = 4;    {alphabetic}
tokenNumeric            = 5;    {numeric}
tokenNewLine            = 6;    {new line}
tokenLeftComment        = 7;    {open comment ("left comment")}
tokenRightComment       = 8;    {close comment ("right comment")}
tokenLiteral            = 9;    {literal}
tokenEscape             = 10;   {character escape (for example, '\' }
                                { in "\n", "\t")}
tokenAltNum             = 11;   {alternate number }
                                { (for example, $B0-B9)}
tokenRealNum            = 12;   {real number}
tokenAltReal            = 13;   {alternate real number}
tokenReserve1           = 14;   {reserved1}
tokenReserve2           = 15;   {reserved2}
tokenLeftParen          = 16;   {open parenthesis }
                                { ("left parenthesis")}
tokenRightParen         = 17;   {close parenthesis }
                                { ("right parenthesis")}
tokenLeftBracket        = 18;   {open square bracket }
                                { ("left bracket")}
tokenRightBracket       = 19;   {close square bracket }
                                { ("right bracket")}
```

```
tokenLeftCurly          = 20;  {open curly bracket }
                               { ("left curly bracket")}
tokenRightCurly         = 21;  {close curly bracket }
                               { ("right curly bracket")}
tokenLeftEnclose        = 22;  {open guillemet ("left }
                               { European double quote")}
tokenRightEnclose       = 23;  {close guillemet ("right }
                               { European double quote")}
tokenPlus               = 24;  {plus}
tokenMinus              = 25;  {minus}
tokenAsterisk           = 26;  {times/multiply}
tokenDivide             = 27;  {divide}
tokenPlusMinus          = 28;  {plus/minus}
tokenSlash              = 29;  {slash}
tokenBackSlash          = 30;  {backslash}
tokenLess               = 31;  {less than}
tokenGreat              = 32;  {greater than}
tokenEqual              = 33;  {equal}
tokenLessEqual2         = 34;  {less than or equal to (2 symbols)}
tokenLessEqual1         = 35;  {less than or equal to }
                               { (single symbol)}
tokenGreatEqual2        = 36;  {greater than or equal to }
                               { (2 symbols)}
tokenGreatEqual1        = 37;  {greater than or equal to }
                               { (single symbol)}
token2Equal             = 38;  {double equal}
tokenColonEqual         = 39;  {colon equal}
tokenNotEqual           = 40;  {not equal}
tokenLessGreat          = 41;  {less/greater (not equal }
                               { in Pascal)}
tokenExclamEqual        = 42;  {exclamation equal (not equal in C)}
tokenExclam             = 43;  {exclamation point}
tokenTilde              = 44;  {centered tilde (as opposed to }
                               { real tilde at $F7)}
tokenComma              = 45;  {comma}
tokenPeriod             = 46;  {period}
tokenLeft2Quote         = 47;  {open double quote }
                               { ("left double quote")}
tokenRight2Quote        = 48;  {close double quote }
                               { ("right double quote")}
tokenLeft1Quote         = 49;  {open single quote }
                               { ("left single quote")}
tokenRight1Quote        = 50;  {close single quote }
                               { ("right single quote")}
token2Quote             = 51;  {double quote}
token1Quote             = 52;  {single quote}
tokenSemicolon          = 53;  {semicolon}
tokenPercent            = 54;  {percent}
tokenCaret              = 55;  {caret}
tokenUnderline          = 56;  {underline}
tokenAmpersand          = 57;  {ampersand}
tokenAtSign             = 58;  {at sign}
tokenBar                = 59;  {vertical bar}
tokenQuestion           = 60;  {question mark}
```

```
tokenPi                   = 61;  {pi}
tokenRoot                 = 62;  {square root}
tokenSigma                = 63;  {capital sigma}
tokenIntegral             = 64;  {integral}
tokenMicro                = 65;  {micro}
tokenCapPi                = 66;  {capital pi}
tokenInfinity             = 67;  {infinity}
tokenColon                = 68;  {colon}
tokenHash                 = 69;  {pound sign (U.S.)}
tokenDollar               = 70;  {dollar sign}
tokenNoBreakSpace         = 71;  {nonbreaking space}
tokenFraction             = 72;  {fraction}
tokenIntlCurrency         = 73;  {intl currency}
tokenLeftSingGuillemet    = 74;  {open single guillemet }
                                 { ("left single guillemet")}
tokenRightSingGuillemet   = 75;  {close single guillemet }
                                 { ("right single guillemet")}
tokenPerThousand          = 76;  {per thousands}
tokenEllipsis             = 77;  {ellipsis}
tokenCenterDot            = 78;  {center dot}
tokenNil                  = 127; {nil}
delimPad                  = -2;  {delimiter pad}

{the number parts record indexes}
tokLeftQuote              = 1;
tokRightQuote             = 2;
tokLeadPlacer             = 3;
tokLeader                 = 4;
tokNonLeader              = 5;
tokZeroLead               = 6;
tokPercent                = 7;
tokPlusSign               = 8;
tokMinusSign              = 9;
tokThousands              = 10;
{11 is a reserved field}
tokSeparator              = 12;
tokEscape                 = 13;
tokDecPoint               = 14;
tokEPlus                  = 15;
tokEMinus                 = 16;
tokMaxSymbols             = 31;

curNumberPartsVersion     = 1;   {current version of number }
                                 { parts record}
fVNumber                  = 0;   {first version of number format string}

{verbs for GetEnvirons and SetEnvirons}
smGenFlags                = 30;  {general flags}
smOverride                = 32;  {script override flags}
smCharPortion             = 34;  {intercharacter space versus white }
                                 { space proportion}
smDoubleByte              = 36;  {indicates if a double-byte }
                                 { script system is installed}
```

```
smKCHRCache              = 38;   {pointer to cache containing }
                                 { the current 'KCHR'}
smRegionCode             = 40;   {integer containing the }
                                 { current region code}

{verbs for GetScript and SetScript (note that verbs private to }
{ script systems are negative, while those general across }
{ script systems are non-negative)}
smScriptEncoding         = 26;   {optional script 'itl5' ID }
                                 { from 'itlb' resource}
smScriptLang             = 28;   {current language for script }
                                 { from 'itlb' resource}
smScriptNumDate          = 30;   {number and date format bytes }
                                 { from 'itlb' resource}
smScriptKeys             = 32;   {script default 'KCHR' ID }
                                 { from 'itlb' resource}
smScriptIcon             = 34;   {script default 'kcs#', 'kcs4', & }
                                 { 'kcs8' ID from 'itlb' resource}
smScriptPrint            = 36;   {script printer action routine}
smScriptTrap             = 38;   {trap entry pointer}
smScriptCreator          = 40;   {script file creator}
smScriptFile             = 42;   {script filename}
smScriptName             = 44;   {script name}
smScriptMonoFondSize     = 78;   {default 'FOND' (high word) }
                                 { & size for monospaced text }
                                 { (low word)}
smScriptPrefFondSize     = 80;   {user's preferred 'FOND' (high word) }
                                 { & size (low word)}
smScriptSmallFondSize    = 82;   {default 'FOND' (high word) & size }
                                 { for small text (low word)}
smScriptSysFondSize      = 84;   {default system 'FOND' (high word) }
                                 { & size (low word)}
smScriptAppFondSize      = 86;   {default application 'FOND' (high }
                                 { word) & size (low word)}
smScriptHelpFondSize     = 88;   {default 'FOND' (high word) & }
                                 { size (low word) for Balloon Help}
smScriptValidStyles      = 90;   {set of all valid styles for }
                                 { script}
smScriptAliasStyle       = 92;   {style to use for indicating aliases}

{verbs for KeyScript}
{any script code         = 0…64; switch to specified script}
smKeyNextScript          = -1;   {switch to next available script}
smKeySysScript           = -2;   {switch to the system script}
smKeySwapScript          = -3;   {switch to previously used script}
smKeyNextKybd            = -4;   {switch to next keyboard }
                                 { in current script}
smKeySwapKybd            = -5;   {switch to previously used }
                                 { keyboard in current script}
smKeyDisableKybds        = -6;   {disable keyboards not in }
                                 { system or Roman script}
smKeyEnableKybds         = -7;   {enable keyboards for all }
                                 { enabled scripts}
```

```
smKeyToggleInline        = -8;  {toggle inline input for }
                                { current script}
smKeyToggleDirection     = -9;  {toggle default line direction}
smKeyNextInputMethod     = -10; {switch to next input method }
                                { in current script}
smKeySwapInputMethod     = -11; {switch to previously used }
                                { input method in current script}
smKeyDisableKybdSwitch   = -12; {disable switching from }
                                { the current keyboard}

{bits in the smScriptFlags word; bits above 7 are nonstatic; }
{ scripts flag word is initialized from 'itlb' resource}
smsfIntellCP         = 0;   {script has intelligent cut and paste}
smsfSingByte         = 1;   {script has only single bytes}
smsfNatCase          = 2;   {native characters have upper- and lowercase}
smsfContext          = 3;   {script is contextual}
smsfNoForceFont      = 4;   {script will not force characters}
smsfB0Digits         = 5;   {script has alternate digits at $B0-$B9}
smsfAutoInit         = 6;   {automatically initialize the script}
smsfForms            = 13;  {script uses contextual forms for letters}
smsfLigatures        = 14;  {script uses contextual ligatures}
smsfReverse          = 15;  {script reverses native text, right to left}

{bits in Script Manager general flags (smGenFlags) long word; first }
{ (high-order) byte is set from 'itlc' flags byte}
smfNameTagEnab       = 29;  {reserved for internal use}
smfDualCaret         = 30;  {use dual caret for mixed-directional text}
smfShowIcon          = 31;  {show icon even if only one script}

{Script Manager font equates}
smFondStart          = $4000;  {start from 16 KB}
smFondEnd            = $C000;  {past end of range at 48 KB}

{miscellaneous font equates}
smUprHalfCharSet     = $80;    {first character code in top half }
                               { of standard Roman character set}

{character set extensions}
diaeresisUprY        = $D9;
fraction             = $DA;
intlCurrency         = $DB;
leftSingGuillemet    = $DC;
rightSingGuillemet   = $DD;
fiLigature           = $DE;
flLigature           = $DF;
dblDagger            = $E0;
centeredDot          = $E1;
baseSingQuote        = $E2;
baseDblQuote         = $E3;
perThousand          = $E4;
circumflexUprA       = $E5;
circumflexUprE       = $E6;
acuteUprA            = $E7;
diaeresisUprE        = $E8;
```

```
graveUprE            = $E9;
acuteUprI            = $EA;
circumflexUprI       = $EB;
diaeresisUprI        = $EC;
graveUprI            = $ED;
acuteUprO            = $EE;
circumflexUprO       = $EF;
appleLogo            = $F0;
graveUprO            = $F1;
acuteUprU            = $F2;
circumflexUprU       = $F3;
graveUprU            = $F4;
dotlessLwrI          = $F5;
circumflex           = $F6;
tilde                = $F7;
macron               = $F8;
breveMark            = $F9;
overDot              = $FA;
ringMark             = $FB;
cedilla              = $FC;
doubleAcute          = $FD;
ogonek               = $FE;
hachek               = $FF;

{String2Date status values (masks for result bits in the }
{ String2DateStatus word returned by String2Date and String2Time)}
fatalDateTime        = $8000;  {a fatal error}
longDateFound        = 1;      {long date found}
leftOverChars        = 2;      {leftover characters}
sepNotIntlSep        = 4;      {nonstandard separators}
fieldOrderNotIntl    = 8;      {nonstandard field order}
extraneousStrings    = 16;     {unparsable strings in text}
tooManySeps          = 32;     {too many separators}
sepNotConsistent     = 64;     {inconsistent separators}
tokenErr             = $8100;  {IntlTokenize error}
cantReadUtilities    = $8200;  {can't load intl resources}
dateTimeNotFound     = $8400;  {date or time not found}
dateTimeInvalid      = $8800;  {date or time invalid}

{date equates}
validDateFields       = -1;
maxDateField          = 10;
genCdevRangeBit       = 27;    {restrict date/time to range used by }
                               { general control panel}
togDelta12HourBit     = 28;    {If toggling hour up and down, restrict }
                               { to 12-hour range (A.M./P.M.).}
togCharZCycleBit      = 29;    {modifies togChar12HourBit to use }
                               { 0-11 hour range}
togChar12HourBit      = 30;    {If toggling hour by character, hour }
                               { field is modified as if displayed in }
                               { 12-hour time (1-12 hour range).}
smallDateBit          = 31;    {restrict valid date/time to range of }
                               { Time global}
```

```
{long date record field masks}
{The following masks specify the long date record fields for ValidDate }
{ to check (that is, for ValidDate flags parameter, and the ToggleDate }
{ TogglePB.togFlags value).}
eraMask             = $0001;
yearMask            = $0002;
monthMask           = $0004;
dayMask             = $0008;
hourMask            = $0010;
minuteMask          = $0020;
secondMask          = $0040;
dayOfWeekMask       = $0080;
dayOfYearMask       = $0100;
weekOfYearMask      = $0200;
pmMask              = $0400;
dateStdMask         = $007F; {default value for ValidDate flags }
                             { and TogglePB.togFlags}

{results that ToggleDate function can return}
toggleUndefined     = 0;
toggleOK            = 1;
toggleBadField      = 2;
toggleBadDelta      = 3;
toggleBadChar       = 4;
toggleUnknown       = 5;
toggleBadNum        = 6;
toggleOutOfRange    = 7;     {synonym for toggleErr3}
toggleErr3          = 7;
toggleErr4          = 8;
toggleErr5          = 9;


{codes for styleRunPosition argument in NPortionText, }
{ NDrawJust, NMeasureJust, NChar2Pixel, and NPixel2Char routines}
smOnlyStyleRun      = 0;     {only style run on the line}
smLeftStyleRun      = 1;     {multiple style runs on }
                             { line; this is leftmost}
smRightStyleRun     = 2;     {multiple style runs on }
                             { line; this is rightmost}
smMiddleStyleRun    = 3;     {multiple style runs on }
                             { line; this is neither leftmost }
                             { nor rightmost}

{constants for truncWhere argument in TruncString and TruncText}
smTruncEnd          = 0;     {truncate at end}
smTruncMiddle       = $4000; {truncate in middle}

{constants for TruncText and TruncString results}
smNotTruncated      =  0;    {no truncation was necessary}
smTruncated         =  1;    {truncation performed}
smTruncErr          =  -1;   {general error}
```

Data Types

```
TYPE TruncCode = Integer;      {new type for system software version 7.0}

     JustStyleCode = Integer;  {new type for system software version 7.0}

     TokenResults = (tokenOK, tokenOverflow,stringOverflow, badDelim,
                    badEnding,crash);


     LongDateField = (eraField, yearField, monthField, dayField,
                     hourField, minuteField, secondField,
                     dayOfWeekField, dayOfYearField, weekOfYearField,
                     pmField, res1Field, res2Field, res3Field);



     CharByteTable =
     PACKED ARRAY[0..255] OF SignedByte;

     FormatOrderPtr = ^FormatOrder;
     FormatOrder =
     ARRAY[0..0] OF Integer;

     FormatClass = (fPositive,fNegative,fZero);
     FormatStatus = Integer;


     WideChar =
     RECORD
        CASE Boolean OF
          TRUE:
            (a: PACKED ARRAY[0..1] OF CHAR); {0 is the high-order character}
          FALSE:
            (b: Integer)
     END;


     WideCharArr =
        RECORD
          size: Integer;
          data: PACKED ARRAY[0..9] OF WideChar
     END;


     NumFormatString =
     PACKED RECORD
        fLength: Byte;
        fVersion: Byte;
        data: PACKED ARRAY[0..253] OF SignedByte       {private data}
     END;
```

```
FormatResultType = (fFormatOK, fBestGuess, fOutOfSynch,
                    fSpuriousChars, fMissingDelimiter,
                    fExtraDecimal, fMissingLiteral, fExtraExp,
                    fFormatOverflow, fFormStrIsNAN, fBadPartsTable,
                    fExtraPercent, fExtraSeparator,
                    fEmptyFormatString);


ScriptRunStatus =
RECORD
   script:        SignedByte;
   variant:       SignedByte
END;


ToggleResults = Integer;


LongDateTime = Comp;
LongDateCvt =
RECORD
CASE Integer OF
   0:
     (c: Comp);
   1:
     (lHigh: LongInt;
      lLow: LongInt)
END;


LongDateRec =
RECORD
   CASE Integer OF
     0:
         (era:        Integer;
          year:       Integer;
          month:      Integer;
          day:        Integer;
          hour:       Integer;
          minute:     Integer;
          second:     Integer;
          dayOfWeek:  Integer;
          dayOfYear:  Integer;
          weekOfYear: Integer;
          pm:         Integer;
          res1:       Integer;
          res2:       Integer;
          res3:       Integer);
     1:
         (list: ARRAY[0..13] OF Integer); {index by LongDateField}
     2:
         (eraAlt: Integer;
          oldDate: DateTimeRec)
END;
```

```
DateDelta = SignedByte;

MachineLocation=
RECORD
   latitude:      Fract;
   longitude:     Fract;
   CASE Integer OF
     0:
       (dlsDelta:     SignedByte);  {signed byte; daylight savings delta}
     1:
       (gmtDelta:     LongInt)      {must mask—see "Macintosh }
                                    { Worldwide Development: }
                                    { Guide to System Software"}
END;

String2DateStatus = Integer;

DateCachePtr = ^DateCacheRecord;
DateCacheRecord =
PACKED RECORD
   hidden:                ARRAY[0..255] OF Integer
                          {only for temporary use}
END;

BreakTablePtr = ^BreakTable;
BreakTable =
RECORD
   charTypes: ARRAY[0..255] OF SignedByte;
   tripleLength: Integer;
   triples: ARRAY[0..0] OF Integer
END;

{new for system software version 7.0}
NBreakTablePtr = ^NBreakTable;
NBreakTable =
RECORD
   flags1:          SignedByte;
   flags2:          SignedByte;
   version:         Integer;
   classTableOff:   Integer;
   auxCTableOff:    Integer;
   backwdTableOff:  Integer;
   forwdTableOff:   Integer;
   doBackup:        Integer;
   reserved:        Integer;
   charTypes:       ARRAY[0..255] OF SignedByte;
   tables:          ARRAY[0..0] OF Integer
END;

OffPair =
RECORD
```

```
   offFirst: Integer;
   offSecond: Integer
END;

OffsetTable = ARRAY[0..2] OF OffPair;

NumberPartsPtr = ^NumberParts;
NumberParts =
RECORD
   version:     Integer;
   data:        ARRAY[1..31] OF WideChar;
                {index by[tokLeftQuote..tokMaxSymbols]}
   pePlus:      WideCharArr;
   peMinus:     WideCharArr;
   peMinusPlus: WideCharArr;
   altNumTable: WideCharArr;
   reserved:    PACKED ARRAY[0..19] OF Char      {must be zeroed}
END;

FVector =
RECORD
   start:                Integer;
   length:               Integer
END;

TripleInt =
ARRAY[0..2] OF FVector; {index by [fPositive..fZero]}

StyledLineBreakCode = (smBreakWord,smBreakChar,smBreakOverflow);

TogglePB =
RECORD
   togFlags:   LongInt;   {caller normally sets low word }
                          { to dateStdMask = $7F}
   amChars:    ResType;   {from 'itl0' resource}
   pmChars:    ResType;   {from 'itl0' resource}
   reserved:   ARRAY[0..3] OF LongInt
END;

TokenBlockPtr = ^TokenBlock;
TokenBlock =
RECORD
   source:           Ptr;        {pointer to stream of characters}
   sourceLength:     LongInt;    {length of source stream}
   tokenList:        Ptr;        {pointer to array of tokens}
   tokenLength:      LongInt;    {maximum length of TokenList}
   tokenCount:       LongInt;    {number of tokens generated }
                                 { by tokenizer}
   stringList:       Ptr;        {pointer to stream of identifiers}
   stringLength:     LongInt;    {length of string list}
   stringCount:      LongInt;    {number of bytes currently used}
```

```
    doString:          Boolean;    {make strings and put }
                                   { into StringList}
    doAppend:          Boolean;    {append to TokenList rather }
                                   { than replace}
    doAlphanumeric:    Boolean;    {identifiers may include numeric}
    doNest:            Boolean;    {do comments nest?}
    leftDelims:        ARRAY[0..1] OF TokenType;
    rightDelims:       ARRAY[0..1] OF TokenType;
    leftComment:       ARRAY[0..3] OF TokenType;
    rightComment:      ARRAY[0..3] OF TokenType;
    escapeCode:        TokenType;  {escape symbol code}
    decimalCode:       TokenType;
    itlResource:       Handle;     {handle to an 'itl4' resource}
    reserved:          ARRAY[0..7] OF LongInt
                                   {must be zero}
END;


TokenType = Integer;        {see TokenType values in this summary}


DelimType = ARRAY[0..1] OF TokenType;


CommentType = ARRAY[0..3] OF TokenType;


TokenRecPtr = ^TokenRec;
TokenRec =
RECORD
    theToken:           TokenType;
    position:           Ptr;         {ptr into original source}
    length:             LongInt;     {length of text in original source}
    stringPosition:     StringPtr    {Pascal/C string copy of }
                                     { identifier}
END;


UntokenTablePtr = ^UntokenTable;
UntokenTableHandle = ^UntokenTablePtr;
UntokenTable =
RECORD
    len:                  Integer;
    lastToken:            Integer;
    index:                ARRAY[0..255] OF Integer
                          {index table; last = lastToken}
END;
```

Routines

Localizing Word Selection and Line Break Tables

```
PROCEDURE NFindWord         (textPtr: Ptr; textLength: Integer;
                             offset: Integer; leadingEdge: Boolean; nbreaks:
                             NBreakTablePtr; VAR offsets: OffsetTable);
```

Truncating Text

```
FUNCTION TruncString        (width: Integer; VAR theString: Str255;
                             truncWhere: TruncCode) : Integer;

FUNCTION TruncText          (width: Integer; textPtr: Ptr;
                             VAR length: Integer;
                             truncWhere: TruncCode) : Integer;
```

Substituting Text

```
FUNCTION ReplaceText        (baseText: Handle; substitutionText: Handle;
                             key: Str15) : Integer;
```

Converting Case and Stripping Diacritical Marks

```
PROCEDURE UprText           (textPtr: Ptr; len: Integer);

PROCEDURE LwrText           (textPtr: Ptr; len: Integer);

{new with system software version 7.0}

PROCEDURE LowerText         (textPtr: Ptr; len: Integer);

PROCEDURE UpperText         (textPtr: Ptr; len: Integer);

PROCEDURE StripText         (textPtr: Ptr; len: Integer);

PROCEDURE StripUpperText    (textPtr: Ptr; len: Integer);
```

Providing for Spacing Between Multiple Style Runs

```
{new with system software version 7.0}

FUNCTION NPortionText       (textPtr: Ptr; textLen: LongInt;
                             styleRunPosition: JustStyleCode;
                             numer: Point; denom: Point) : Fixed;
```

```
PROCEDURE NDrawJust        (textPtr: Ptr; textLen: LongInt;
                            slop: Fixed; styleRunPosition:
                            JustStyleCode; numer: Point; denom: Point);
PROCEDURE NMeasureJust     (textPtr: Ptr; textLen: LongInt;
                            slop: Fixed; charLocs: Ptr;
                            styleRunPosition: JustStyleCode;
                            numer: Point; denom: Point);
FUNCTION NChar2Pixel       (textBuf: Ptr; textLen: LongInt;
                            slop: Fixed; offset: LongInt;
                            direction: Integer;
                            styleRunPosition: JustStyleCode;
                            numer: Point; denom: Point) : Integer;
FUNCTION NPixel2Char       (textBuf: Ptr; textLen: LongInt;
                            slop: Fixed; pixelWidth: Fixed;
                            VAR leadingEdge: Boolean;
                            VAR widthRemaining: Fixed;
                            styleRunPosition: JustStyleCode;
                            numer: Point; denom: Point) : Integer;
```

Obtaining Character Information

```
FUNCTION ParseTable        (VAR table: CharByteTable) : Boolean;
```

Drawing and Editing Text

```
PROCEDURE HiliteText       (textPtr: Ptr; textLength: Integer;
                            firstOffset: Integer; secondOffset: Integer;
                            VAR offsets: OffsetTable);
```

Formatting Text

```
FUNCTION FindScriptRun     (textPtr: Ptr; textLen: LongInt;
                            VAR lenUsed: LongInt) : ScriptRunStatus;
FUNCTION PortionText       (textPtr: Ptr; textLen: LongInt) : Fixed;
PROCEDURE GetFormatOrder   (ordering: FormatOrderPtr;
                            firstFormat: Integer; lastFormat: Integer;
                            lineRight: Boolean; rlDirProc: Ptr;
                            dirParam: Ptr);
FUNCTION StyledLineBreak   (textPtr: Ptr; textLen: LongInt;
                            textStart: LongInt; textEnd: LongInt;
                            flags: LongInt; VAR textWidth: Fixed;
                            VAR textOffset: LongInt) :
                            StyledLineBreakCode;
```

```
FUNCTION VisibleLength      (textPtr: Ptr; textLen: LongInt) : LongInt;
```

Lexically Interpreting Different Scripts

```
FUNCTION IntlTokenize       (tokenParam: TokenBlockPtr) : TokenResults;
```

Date and Time Utilities

```
FUNCTION InitDateCache      (theCache: DateCachePtr) : OSErr;
FUNCTION String2Date        (textPtr: Ptr; textLen: LongInt; theCache:
                             DateCachePtr; VAR lengthUsed: LongInt;
                             VAR dateTime: LongDateRec) :
                             String2DateStatus;
FUNCTION String2Time        (textPtr: Ptr; textLen: LongInt;
                             theCache: DateCachePtr;
                             VAR lengthUsed: LongInt;
                             VAR dateTime: LongDateRec) :
                             String2DateStatus;
PROCEDURE LongDate2Secs     (lDate: LongDateRec; VAR lSecs: LongDateTime);
PROCEDURE LongSecs2Date     (VAR lSecs: LongDateTime; VAR lDate:
                             LongDateRec);
FUNCTION ToggleDate         (VAR lSecs: LongDateTime;
                             field: LongDateField; delta: DateDelta;
                             ch: Integer; params: TogglePB) :
                             ToggleResults;
FUNCTION ValidDate          (VAR vDate: LongDateRec; flags: LongInt;
                             VAR newSecs: LongDateTime) : Integer;
```

Reading and Storing Locations

```
PROCEDURE ReadLocation      (VAR loc: MachineLocation);
PROCEDURE WriteLocation     (loc: MachineLocation);
```

Number Utilities

```
FUNCTION Str2Format         (inString: Str255; partsTable: NumberParts;
                             VAR outString: NumFormatString) : FormatStatus;
FUNCTION Format2Str         (myCanonical: NumFormatString;
                             partsTable: NumberParts;
                             VAR outString: Str255;
                             VAR positions: TripleInt) : FormatStatus;
```

```
FUNCTION FormatX2Str        (x: Extended; myCanonical: NumFormatString;
                             partsTable: NumberParts; VAR outString: Str255) :
                             FormatStatus;

FUNCTION FormatStr2X        (source: Str255;
                             myCanonical: NumFormatString;
                             partsTable: NumberParts;
                             VAR x: Extended) : FormatStatus;
```

Assembly-Language Information

Trap Macros Requiring Routine Selectors

_ScriptUtil $A8B5

Selector	Routine	
$8008FFF0	LongSecs2Date	
$8008FFF2	LongDate2Secs	
$800E001C	HiliteText	
$8012FFE2	NFindWord	
$8012FFFC	GetFormatOrder	
$80160032	NDrawJust	
$801A0034	NMeasureJust	
$8202002A	IsSpecialFont	; 2-byte script systems only
$82040022	ParseTable	
$8204FFF8	InitDateCache	
$8204FFFA	IntlTokenize	
$8208FFE0	TruncString	
$820C0026	FindScriptRun	
$820CFFDC	ReplaceText	
$820CFFDE	TruncText	
$820CFFE4	ValidDate	
$820CFFEC	Str2Format	
$820EFFEE	ToggleDate	
$8210FFE6	FormatStr2X	
$8210FFE8	FormatX2Str	
$8210FFEA	Format2Str	
$8214FFF4	String2Time	
$8214FFF6	String2Date	
$8216002C	RawPrinterValues	; 2-byte script systems only
$821C0030	NChar2Pixel	
$821CFFFE	StyledLineBreak	
$8222002E	NPixel2Char	
$84080024	PortionText	
$84080028	VisibleLength	
$84120036	NPortionText	

SUMMARY OF THE INTERNATIONAL UTILITIES PACKAGE

Constants

```
CONST {special script code values for International Utilities Package}
      iuSystemScript         = -1;       {system script}
      iuCurrentScript        = -2;       {current script for font of }
                                         { grafPort (as returned by }
                                         { FontScript)}

      {special language code values for International Utilities Package}
      iuSystemCurLang        = -2;       {current ('itlb') language for }
                                         { system script (from script }
                                         { globals)}
      iuSystemDefLang        = -3;       {default language for system }
                                         { script (from 'itlm' resource)}
      iuCurrentCurLang       = -4;       {current ('itlb') language for }
                                         { current script (from script }
                                         { globals)}
      iuCurrentDefLang       = -5;       {default language for current }
                                         { script (from 'itlm' resource)}
      iuScriptCurLang        = -6;       {current ('itlb') language for }
                                         { specified script }
                                         { (from script globals)}
      iuScriptDefLang        = -7;       {default language for specified }
                                         { script (from 'itlm' resource)}

      {table selectors for GetItlTable}
      iuWordSelectTable      = 0;        {word select break table }
                                         { from the 'itl2' resource}
      iuWordWrapTable        = 1;        {word wrap break table }
                                         { (from 'itl2')}
      iuNumberPartsTable     = 2;        {default number parts table }
                                         { from the 'itl4' resource}
      iuUnTokenTable         = 3;        {untoken table }
                                         { from the 'itl4' resource}
      iuWhiteSpaceList       = 4;        {white space list table }
                                         { from the 'itl4' resource}

      {regional versions}
      verUS                  = 0;
      verFrance              = 1;
      verBritain             = 2;
      verGermany             = 3;
      verItaly               = 4;
      verNetherlands         = 5;
      verFrBelgiumLux        = 6;        {French for Belgium & Luxembourg}
      verSweden              = 7;
      verSpain               = 8;
      verDenmark             = 9;
      verPortugal            = 10;
```

```
verFrCanada          = 11;
verNorway            = 12;
verIsrael            = 13;
verJapan             = 14;
verAustralia         = 15;
verArabic            = 16;      {verArabia synonym}
verFinland           = 17;
verFrSwiss           = 18;      {French Switzerland}
verGrSwiss           = 19;      {German Switzerland}
verGreece            = 20;
verIceland           = 21;
verMalta             = 22;
verCyprus            = 23;
verTurkey            = 24;
verYugoCroatian      = 25;      {Croatian version for Yugoslavia; }
                                { new synonym}
verIndiaHindi        = 33;      {Hindi version for India; }
                                { new synonym}
verPakistan          = 34;      {Urdu version}
verLithuania         = 41;
verPoland            = 42;
verHungary           = 43;
verEstonia           = 44;
verLatvia            = 45;
verLapland           = 46;
verFaeroeIsl         = 47;
verIran              = 48;
verRussia            = 49;
verIreland           = 50;      {English language version for Ireland}
verKorea             = 51;
verChina             = 52;
verTaiwan            = 53;
verThailand          = 54;
minCountry           = verUS;
maxCountry           = verThailand;

{obsolete regional version names}
verBelgiumLux        = 6;       {use verFrBelgiumLux instead, }
                                { less ambiguous}
verArabia            = 16;
verYugoslavia        = 25;      {use verYugoCroatian instead, }
                                { less ambiguous}
verIndia             = 33;      {use verIndiaHindi instead, }
                                { less ambiguous}
```

Data Types

```
TYPE ScriptCode = Integer;
     LangCode   = Integer;
```

Routines

Manipulating the 'itl2' and 'itl4' Resources

```
PROCEDURE IUClearCache;

PROCEDURE IUGetItlTable     (script: ScriptCode; tableCode: Integer;
                             VAR itlHandle: Handle; VAR offset: LongInt;
                             VAR length: LongInt);
```

Specifying Resource Handles Explicitly

```
FUNCTION IUCompPString      (aStr,bStr: Str255;
                             itl2Handle: Handle) : Integer;

FUNCTION IUMagPString       (aPtr,bPtr: Ptr; aLen,bLen: Integer;
                             itl2Handle: Handle) : Integer;

FUNCTION IUEqualPString     (aStr,bStr: Str255; itl2Handle: Handle) :
                             Integer;

FUNCTION IUMagIDPString     (aPtr,bPtr: Ptr; aLen,bLen: Integer;
                             itl2Handle: Handle) : Integer;
```

Determining Interscript Sorting Order

```
FUNCTION IUScriptOrder      (script1,script2: ScriptCode) : Integer;

FUNCTION IULangOrder        (language1,language2: LangCode) : Integer;

FUNCTION IUStringOrder      (aStr,bStr: Str255;
                             aScript,bScript: ScriptCode;
                             aLang,bLang: LangCode) : Integer;

FUNCTION IUTextOrder        (aPtr,bPtr: Ptr; aLen,bLen: Integer;
                             aScript,bScript: ScriptCode; aLang,bLang:
                             LangCode) : Integer;
```

Localizing Dates, Times, and Metric Information

```
PROCEDURE IULDateString     (VAR dateTime: LongDateTime; longFlag: DateForm;
                             VAR Result: Str255; intlParam: Handle);

PROCEDURE IULTimeString     (VAR dateTime: LongDateTime;
                             wantSeconds: Boolean; VAR Result: Str255;
                             intlParam: Handle);
```

Assembly-Language Information

Trap Macro Requiring Routine Selectors

_Pack6	$A9ED

Selector	Routine
$0014	IULDateString
$0016	IULTimeString
$0018	IUClearCache
$001A	IUMagPString
$001C	IUMagIDPString
$001E	IUScriptOrder
$0020	IULangOrder
$0022	IUTextOrder
$0024	IUGetItlTable

```
;stack frame for 'itl2' sorting routines

IUSortFrame record      {oldA6},decrement
result      ds.w  1
aStrText    ds.l  1
bStrText    ds.l  1
aStrLen     ds.w  1
bStrLen     ds.w  1
return      ds.l  1
oldA6       ds.l  1
aInfo       ds    IUStrData
bInfo       ds    IUStrData
wantMag     ds.b  1     ;0 to use primary differences only; else 1
weakEq      ds.b  1     ;signals at most weak equality
msLock      ds.b  1     ;(obsolete, not used)
weakMag     ds.b  1     ;-1 to force magnitude result (-1, 0, 1); else 0
supStorage  ds.b  18    ;extra storage
weakAPtr    ds.l  1     ;sup. pointer
weakBPtr    ds.l  1     ;sup. pointer
lkSize      equ   *     ;frame size
paramBytes  equ   aStrText-return
                  endr
```

```
;New stack frame for 'itl2' sorting routines in version 7.0
;adds itl2Handle field.

IUNSortFrame record     {oldA6},decrement
result       ds.w  1
aStrText     ds.l  1
bStrText     ds.l  1
aStrLen      ds.w  1
bStrLen      ds.w  1
return       ds.l  1
oldA6        ds.l  1
aInfo        ds    IUStrData
bInfo        ds    IUStrData
wantMag      ds.b  1      ;0 to use primary differences only; else 1
weakEq       ds.b  1      ;signals at most weak equality
msLock       ds.b  1      ;(obsolete, not used)
weakMag      ds.b  1      ;-1 to force magnitude result (-1, 0, 1); else 0
supStorage   ds.b  18     ;extra storage
weakAPtr     ds.l  1      ;sup. pointer
weakBPtr     ds.l  1      ;sup. pointer
itl2Handle   ds.l  1      ;itl2 handle, if supplied
lkSize       equ   *      ;frame size
paramBytes   equ   aStrText-return
                   endr
```

SUMMARY OF THE INTERNATIONAL RESOURCES

Data Types

```
TYPE Itl4Ptr = ^Itl4Rec;
     Itl4Handle = ^Itl4Ptr;
     Itl4Rec =
     RECORD
        flags:                Integer;      {reserved}
        resourceType:         LongInt;      {contains 'itl4'}
        resourceNum:          Integer;      {resource ID}
        version:              Integer;      {version number}
        resHeader1:           LongInt;
        resHeader2:           LongInt;
        numTables:            Integer;      {one-based}
        mapOffset:            LongInt;      {offsets are from record start}
        strOffset:            LongInt;
        fetchOffset:          LongInt;
        unTokenOffset:        LongInt;
        defPartsOffset:       LongInt;
        resOffset6:           LongInt;
        resOffset7:           LongInt;
        resOffset8:           LongInt
     END;

     {new for system software version 7.0}
     NItl4Ptr = ^NItl4Rec;
     NItl4Handle = ^NItl4Ptr;
     NItl4Rec =
     RECORD
        flags:                Integer;      {reserved}
        resourceType:         LongInt;      {contains 'itl4'}
        resourceNum:          Integer;      {contains resource ID}
        version:              Integer;      {version number}
        format:               Integer;      {format code}
        resHeader:            Integer;      {reserved}
        resHeader2:           LongInt;      {reserved}
        numTables:            Integer;      {number of tables, }
                                            { one-based}
{The following are offsets from beginning of resource to tables & code chunks.}
        mapOffset:            LongInt;      {offset to table that maps byte }
                                            { to token}
        strOffset:            LongInt;      {offset to routine that copies }
                                            { canonical string}
        fetchOffset:          LongInt;      {offset to routine that gets next }
                                            { byte of character}
```

```
      unTokenOffset:        LongInt;        {offset to untoken table, }
                                            { maps token to canonical string}
      defPartsOffset:       LongInt;        {offset to default number parts }
                                            { table}
      whtSpListOffset:      LongInt;        {offset to white space code list}
      resOffset7:           LongInt;        {reserved}
      resOffset8:           LongInt;        {reserved}
      resLength1:           Integer;        {reserved}
      resLength2:           Integer;        {reserved}
      resLength3:           Integer;        {reserved}
      unTokenLength:        Integer;        {length of untoken table}
      defPartsLength:       Integer;        {length of default }
                                            { number parts table}
      whtSpListLength:      Integer;        {length of white space code list}
      resLength7:           Integer;        {reserved}
      resLength8:           Integer         {reserved}
   END;


   ItlbRecord =
   RECORD
      itlbNumber:           Integer;        {'itl0' ID number}
      itlbDate:             Integer;        {'itl1' ID number}
      itlbSort:             Integer;        {'itl2' ID number}
      itlbFlags:            Integer;        {script flags}
      itlbToken:            Integer;        {'itl4' ID number}
      itlbEncoding:         Integer;        {'itl5' ID number (optional }
                                            { character encoding)}
      itlbLang:             Integer;        {current language for script}
      itlbNumRep:           SignedByte;     {number representation code}
      itlbDateRep:          SignedByte;     {date representation code}
      itlbKeys:             Integer;        {'KCHR' ID number}
      itlbIcon:             Integer         {ID number of 'SICN' }
                                            { or 'kcs#', 'kcs4', }
                                            { 'kcs8' family}

   END;


   ItlbExtRecord =
   RECORD
      base:                 ItlbRecord;     {unextended ItlbRecord}
      itlbLocalSize:        LongInt;        {size of script's local record}
      itlbMonoFond:         Integer;        {default monospaced 'FOND' ID}
      itlbMonoSize:         Integer;        {default monospaced font size}
      itlbPrefFond:         Integer;        {preferred 'FOND' ID}
      itlbPrefSize:         Integer;        {preferred font size}
      itlbSmallFond:        Integer;        {default small 'FOND' ID}
      itlbSmallSize:        Integer;        {default small font size}
      itlbSysFond:          Integer;        {default system 'FOND' ID}
      itlbSysSize:          Integer;        {default system font size}
      itlbAppFond:          Integer;        {default application 'FOND' ID}
      itlbAppSize:          Integer;        {default application font size}
      itlbHelpFond:         Integer;        {default Help Mgr 'FOND' ID}
      itlbHelpSize:         Integer;        {default Help Mgr font size}
```

```
   itlbValidStyles:     Style;          {set of valid styles for script}
   itlbAliasStyle:      Style           {style (set) to mark aliases}
END;


ItlcRecord =
RECORD
   itlcSystem:          Integer;        {default system script}
   itlcReserved:        Integer;        {reserved}
   itlcFontForce:       SignedByte;     {default font force flag}
   itlcIntlForce:       SignedByte;     {default intl force flag}
   itlcOldKybd:         SignedByte;     {old keyboard}
   itlcFlags:           SignedByte;     {general flags}
   itlcIconOffset:      Integer;        {keyboard icon offset; beginning }
                                        { with version 7.0, not used}
   itlcIconSide:        SignedByte;     {icon side}
   itlcIconRsvd:        SignedByte;     {rsvd for other icon info}
   itlcRegionCode:      Integer;        {preferred verXxx code}
   itlcReserved3:       ARRAY[0..33] OF SignedByte
                                        {for future use}
END;
```

15 TEXTEDIT

ABOUT THIS CHAPTER

This chapter describes the features that TextEdit provides for working with different scripts. You can use TextEdit to provide the basic text-editing and formatting capabilities needed in your application. TextEdit uses the Script Manager routines just as any application would to work across all scripts. This chapter describes some routines, not previously documented in *Inside Macintosh,* that are not specific to working with script systems. It also clarifies several previously documented routines and includes an overview of all TextEdit data structures.

Read this chapter if you are interested in using TextEdit to write applications that exhibit the correct behavior for editing and displaying text in multiple styles and different scripts. Most new features of TextEdit are only apparent for non-Roman script systems.

To use this chapter, you should be familiar with the basic concepts and structures behind QuickDraw™, the Toolbox Event Manager, the Window Manager, the Font Manager, the Script Manager, and the Gestalt function.

For more information on QuickDraw, the Toolbox, the Window Manager, and the Font Manager, see the corresponding chapters in this volume and in Volumes I, IV, and V. For information on the Gestalt function, see the Compatibility Guidelines chapter in this volume.

The information in this chapter supplements the material in the TextEdit chapters in Volumes I, IV, and V. See these volumes for details on TextEdit routines and data structures provided prior to system software version 7.0.

For an introduction to the Macintosh® Script Management System, see the Worldwide Software Overview chapter earlier in this volume.

In this chapter, the version of TextEdit referred to is included with system software version 6.0.5 and later unless otherwise stated.

ABOUT TEXTEDIT

In addition to all the text-handling features of earlier versions, TextEdit now allows you to take advantage of the Script Manager's treatment of system software with more than one script system installed. TextEdit uses the Script Manager to support such systems. TextEdit exhibits the correct behavior for editing and displaying text in multiple styles and different scripts. Multiple scripts can even exist on a single line due to styled TextEdit's use of the Script Manager.

This chapter describes the situations in which TextEdit uses the Script Manager and the visual results. It describes how TextEdit

- handles mixed-directional text
- synchronizes fonts and keyboards

- handles double-byte characters
- determines word boundaries and line breaks

This chapter also tells how you can use TextEdit in your applications to

- provide outline highlighting for inactive text
- buffer text for performance improvements
- allow inline input in a double-byte script system
- permit left alignment in right-to-left directional scripts
- customize word breaking
- customize measuring

Throughout this chapter, **script** is used to mean a writing system such as Roman, Japanese, or Arabic. **Script system** is used to denote a specific collection of software components for handling text in a particular script. Examples of script systems are the Roman Script System, the Japanese Script System (KanjiTalk™), as well as the Traditional Chinese Script System and the Simplified Chinese Script System (both referred to as Zhong-WenTalk™).

At least two script systems are always present when a non-Roman script system is installed. For example, Japanese system software is the combination of the U.S. system software (which includes the Roman Script System, the Macintosh Operating System, the Toolbox, and so forth) and the Japanese Script System, all of which are localized for Japan.

Localized system software—such as the Japanese system software—has been adapted to a particular region or language. The French and Turkish versions of the Macintosh system software are simply examples of localized variations of the U.S. system software that do not include a second script system.

MIXED-DIRECTIONAL TEXT

TextEdit now handles text with more than one script and direction. The following sections explore how TextEdit treats **mixed-directional text**—the combination of scripts with left-to-right and right-to-left directional text—within a single line.

Figure 15-1 shows a line of Arabic text that contains some English text. In this case, the primary line direction is right to left. The **primary line direction** is the dominant line direction of the current script system and is specified by the value of the system alignment global variable, TESysJust. (TESysJust was referred to in previous volumes as the system *justification* global variable.) The value of TESysJust is –1 for a right-to-left primary line direction and 0 for a left-to-right line direction. The default value of this global variable is normally based on the system script. Your application can use the SetSysJust procedure to change this value while drawing, but should restore it afterward. See *Macintosh Worldwide Development: Guide to System Software* for details.

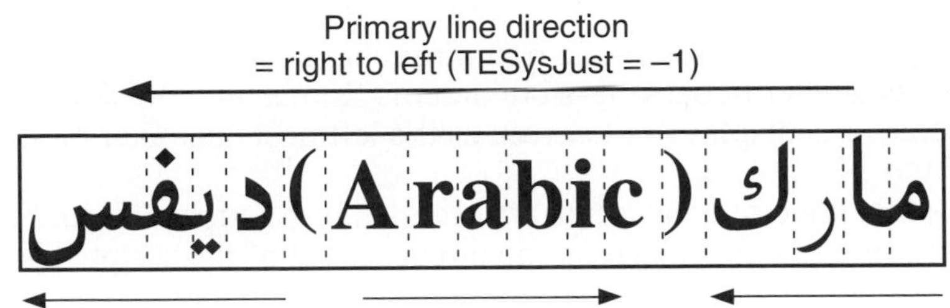

Figure 15-1. A right-to-left primary line direction

TextEdit organizes text logically into a hierarchy of **runs** (consecutive characters in memory with the same attributes) including style runs, script runs, and direction runs. A **style run** is a sequence of text all in the same font, style, size, and script. A **script run** is a sequence of text all in the same script. A **direction run** is a sequence of text all in the same direction. Figure 15-1 also shows three direction runs in the line.

Style runs (also called *format runs*) are displayed in display order rather than backing-store order for a right-to-left directional script. **Display order** refers to the directional order in which the glyphs are displayed on the device, which may be different from the way in which the characters they represent are stored in the text buffer. **Backing-store order** is the sequence in which characters are stored in memory.

Do not assume that display and backing-store orders are the same in any script. For example, in left-to-right scripts, display and backing-store orders are usually the same for most characters, whereas when right-to-left scripts are present, the orders are often different. So for the characters that appear in Figure 15-1, the display order is as shown in Figure 15-2.

مارك(Arabic)ديفس

Figure 15-2. The display order

The backing-store order of the characters in Figure 15-1 is as shown in Figure 15-3.

> **Note:** The visual appearance of some of the Arabic characters in Figures 15-2 and 15-3 is different. To show characters correctly in backing-store order, the independent forms of the characters are used, but the display order of these same characters in Figure 15-2 shows the normal Arabic contextual forms. See the Worldwide Software Overview chapter in this volume for more about contextual forms in scripts.

Figure 15-3. The backing-store order

If the first character in backing-store order is Arabic and the line direction is right to left, then this character is displayed on screen as the rightmost character on the line. The converse is also true: if the first character in backing-store order is Roman and the line direction is left to right, then this character is displayed on screen as the leftmost character on the line.

Figure 15-4 shows that style runs on a line are grouped into script runs, and the order of both style runs and script runs is determined by the direction run of the script. Therefore, whenever your application calls any TextEdit routine that requires line adjustment or redrawing, testing for mouse-down events, or measuring of mixed-directional text (for example, TEDelete, TEInsert, or TEDoText), TextEdit arranges the style runs so that they can be displayed in display order—not in backing-store order. It uses the Script Manager procedure GetFormatOrder to order the style runs for a line.

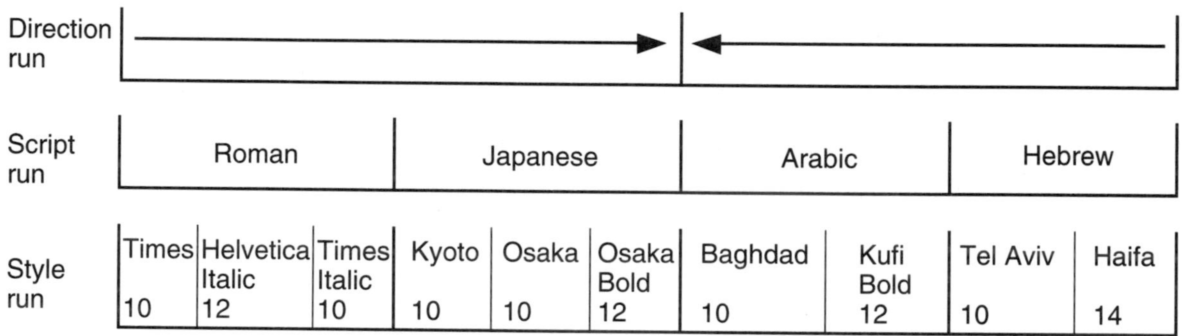

Figure 15-4. Different levels of runs in a line of text

Read the following sections to find out how TextEdit

- highlights characters in mixed-directional text
- defines mouse-down event regions in mixed-directional text
- displays dual carets to mark insertion points at direction boundaries
- provides cursor movement across direction boundaries

Highlighting

TextEdit highlights a group of characters that is contiguous in memory (backing-store order). However, the highlighted text may appear discontinuous on the display line if the selection contains mixed-directional text, as shown in Figure 15-5. This is because TextEdit draws characters in display order, which may be different from backing-store order. The caret positions are also determined similarly. The display order is determined by the ordering of the characters within a direction run and the ordering of direction runs in the primary line direction.

Character offsets are byte offsets of the characters in the text buffer, and the values of character offsets correspond to the backing-store order of characters. A **caret position** is a

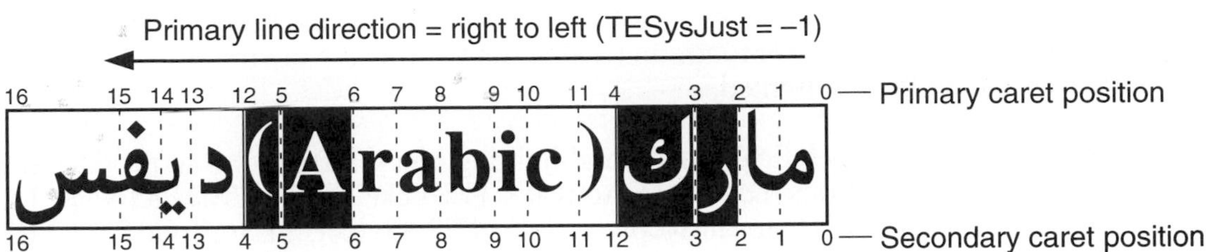

Figure 15-5. Discontinuous highlighting display

location on the screen corresponding to a leading or trailing edge of a displayed character. In mixed-directional text, one character offset may correspond to two caret positions, and one caret position may correspond to two character offsets.

These ambiguous cases occur at direction boundaries because the character offset is associated with two different characters—the one before and the one after the offset. When these characters are not adjacent in the display, two caret positions result. The **primary caret position** is the screen location associated with the character that has the same direction as the primary line direction. The **secondary caret position** is the screen location associated with the character that has a different direction from the primary line direction. TextEdit uses only the primary caret positions in determining which characters are highlighted.

In Figures 15-5 and 15-6, you can see how the primary and secondary caret positions differ at direction boundaries 4 and 12. In Figure 15-6, you can see the relationship between the character offsets and the primary and secondary caret positions. Figure 15-6 illustrates how TextEdit uses primary caret positions to define highlighting boundaries for the highlighting of characters 2, 3, 4, and 5. The shaded regions indicate the highlighted characters. To highlight characters 2 and 3, TextEdit inverts the entire area between primary caret positions 2 and 4. To highlight characters 4 and 5, it inverts the entire area between primary caret positions 12 and 6.

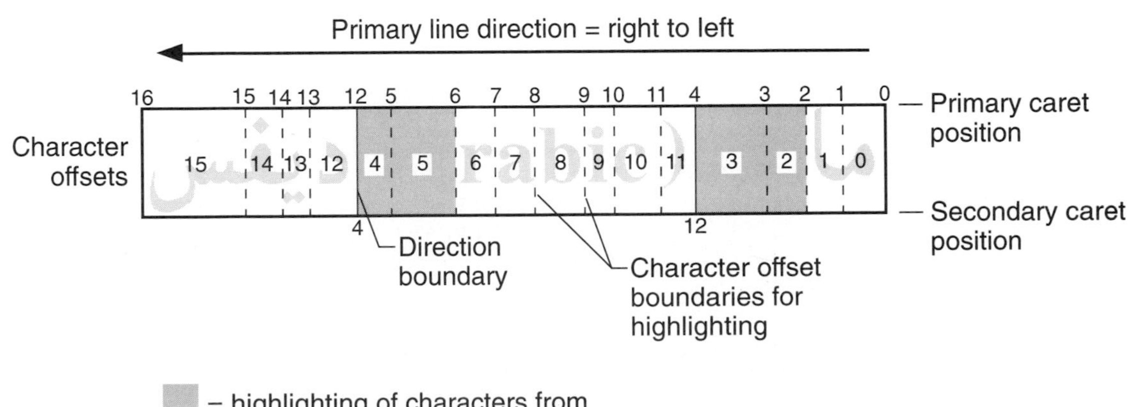

Figure 15-6. Highlighting mixed-directional text

When a non-Roman script system is installed, TextEdit calls the Script Manager's HiliteText procedure and the Char2Pixel function (with a direction value of smHilite) to ascertain which characters should be highlighted.

TextEdit routines that specifically need highlighting of a selection or that produce highlighting as a result of their functions include TEActivate, TEClick, TECut, TEDeactivate, TEDelete, TEDoText, TEInsert, TEPaste, TEReplaceStyle, TESetSelect, TESetStyle, and TEStylInsert.

Mouse-Down Regions

As noted in the preceding section, a single caret position can correspond to two character offsets. However, a mouse-down event occurs either to the left or the right of a caret position. (Consistent with QuickDraw, a screen position is an infinitely thin line; hence, a mouse-down event cannot occur exactly on a caret position.) The region between the caret position and the middle of an adjacent character maps unambiguously to a single character offset. This region is called a **mouse-down region.**

Figure 15-7 shows how TextEdit determines mouse-down regions and in so doing decides which character offset the mouse-down event belongs to. In the figure, direction boundaries (that is, the borders between left-to-right and right-to-left text) are denoted by solid vertical lines and occur at primary caret positions 12 and 4. (These caret positions are also secondary caret positions 4 and 12, respectively.)

In the figure, character offset boundaries (the boundaries of mouse-down regions) are shown by dotted lines. The shaded regions indicate where a mouse-down region does not span a primary caret position. For example, if a mouse click occurs to the left of the direction boundary at primary caret position 12, the mouse-down region is defined as within the leading edge of character 12. However, if a mouse click occurs to the right of primary caret position 12, the mouse-down region is defined as within the leading edge of character 4.

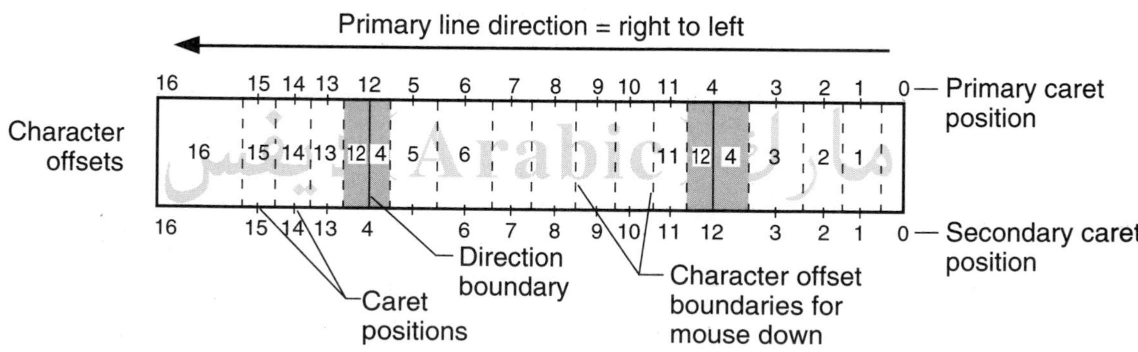

Figure 15-7. Mouse-down region specifics

Dual Carets

As noted in "Highlighting" earlier in this chapter, a single character offset can correspond to two caret positions. In this case, TextEdit draws **dual carets,** a high caret and a low caret, each measuring half the line's height. The high caret is displayed at the primary caret position for the character offset. The low caret is displayed at the secondary caret position. When the caret position is unambiguous (for example, not on a direction boundary), the **primary** (high) and **secondary** (low) **carets** are at the same position, so the user sees one caret. (The appearance of dual carets may change in the future.)

Figure 15-8 shows the dual caret bordering the Arabic text where the overall line direction is left to right but the Arabic script run is right to left. In this case, the primary caret is associated with the English text and the secondary caret is associated with the Arabic text.

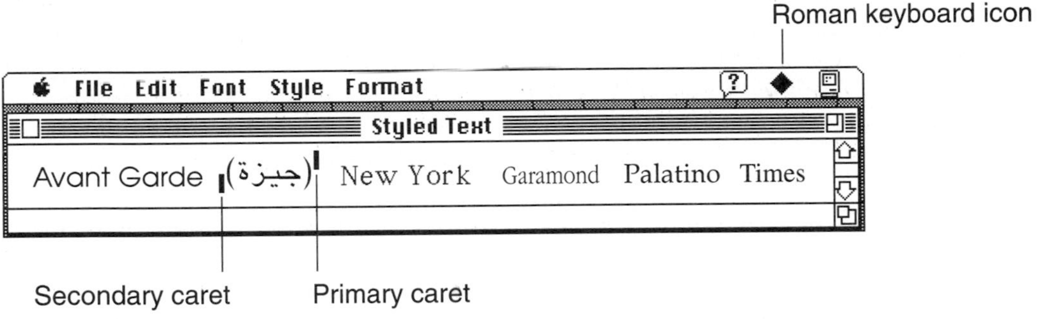

Figure 15-8. Dual carets in mixed-directional text

When TextEdit pastes multiple styles and script runs into a record, the caret is positioned after the newly pasted text, and the keyboard script reflects the font of the last character of the newly pasted text. In Figure 15-9, the **keyboard script** (that is, the script for keyboard input) is Roman to reflect the font of the last character of the newly pasted text.

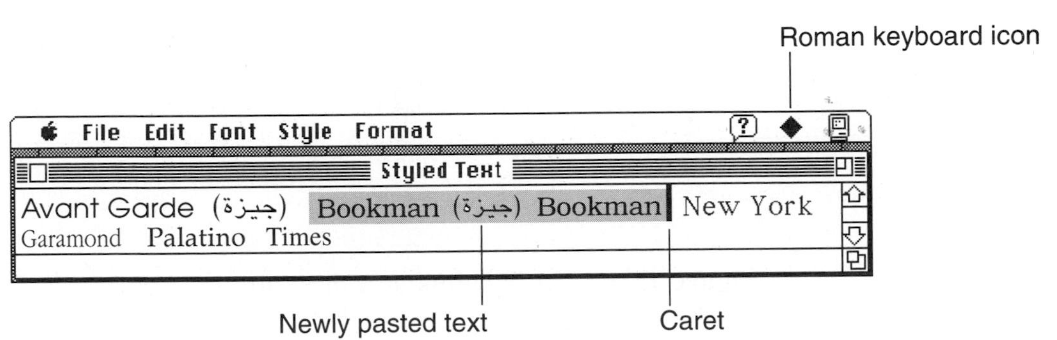

Figure 15-9. Pasting styled text

In Figure 15-10, drawing A illustrates that when a mouse click occurs to the left of primary caret position 12, TextEdit places a primary caret at primary caret position 12 and a secondary caret at secondary caret position 4. However, when a mouse click occurs to the right of primary caret position 12, TextEdit places a primary caret in primary caret position 4 and a secondary caret in secondary caret position 12, as shown in drawing B in Figure 15-10.

> **Note:** There is a relationship between the keyboard icon and the dual caret. The setting of the keyboard script is reflected by the keyboard icon. In this case, the primary linc direction is right to left, so if the Roman keyboard icon is displayed, text is entered at the secondary caret position. If an Arabic keyboard icon is displayed, text is entered at the primary caret position.

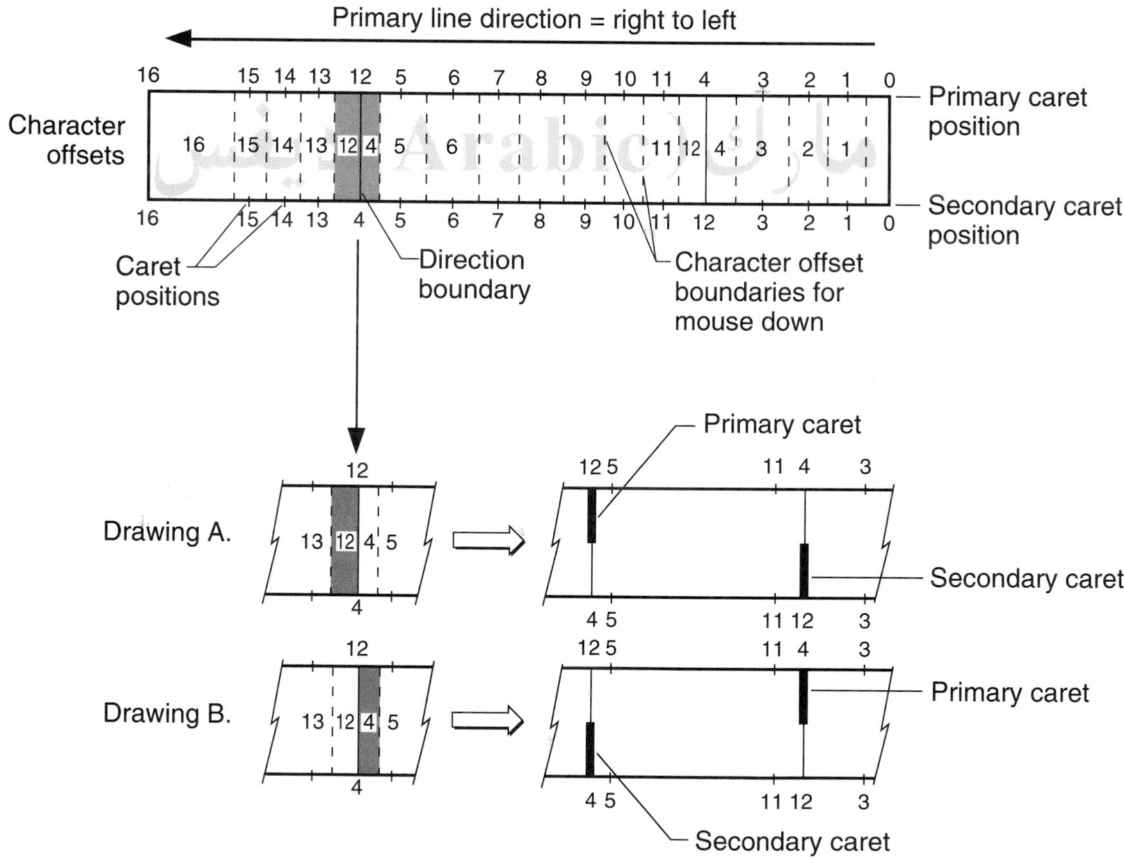

Figure 15-10. Dual carets at a direction boundary

Caret Movement Across Direction Boundaries

When a user presses the arrow keys to move the caret left or right across characters on a line, TextEdit moves the caret uniformly in the direction of the arrow. This sequence is unambiguous when a user moves the caret in the middle of a style run. However, on direction boundaries, only the primary caret moves uniformly in the direction of the arrows.

Figure 15-11 shows a sequence of two Right Arrow key presses and their impact on caret display and movement in a mixed-directional line. If the original caret position is 13 and the Right Arrow key is pressed, TextEdit displays a dual caret at primary caret position 12 and secondary caret position 4, with the primary caret moving to the next position in the direction of the arrow. If the Right Arrow key is pressed again, the new caret position is at primary caret position 5.

> **Note:** TextEdit currently deviates from this model for caret movement in unstyled left-to-right text (displayed in a non-Roman font) on any right-to-left script system. On the Arabic Script System, for example, it is possible to display Roman characters from an Arabic font. If a user presses the arrow keys to move through these characters, the caret moves in the opposite direction of the arrow. Because of keyboard and font synchronization, this situation is not common.

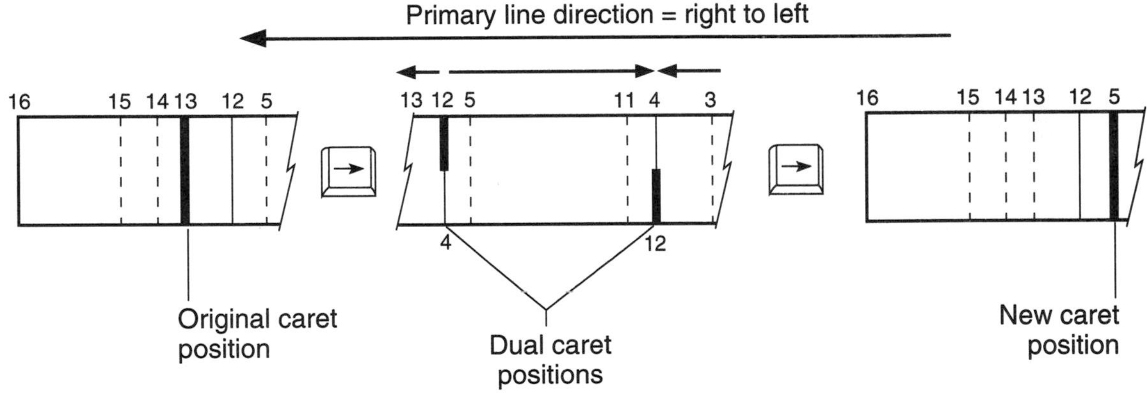

Figure 15-11. Caret movement across a direction boundary

FONT AND KEYBOARD SYNCHRONIZATION

It is important to distinguish between two kinds of scripts: the font script and the keyboard script. The **font script** is the script that corresponds to the font of the active grafPort (also, the font used for displaying characters). The keyboard script is the script for keyboard input. It determines the character input method and the keyboard mapping—that is, what character codes are produced when a sequence of keys is pressed. The upper half of Figure 15-12 shows an example of font and keyboard synchronization with the user entering the characters for *keisanki* when the font script corresponds to the keyboard script, which is Japanese. The lower half of Figure 15-12 provides an example of the characters that are displayed when the user enters the same characters when the font script does not map to the keyboard script.

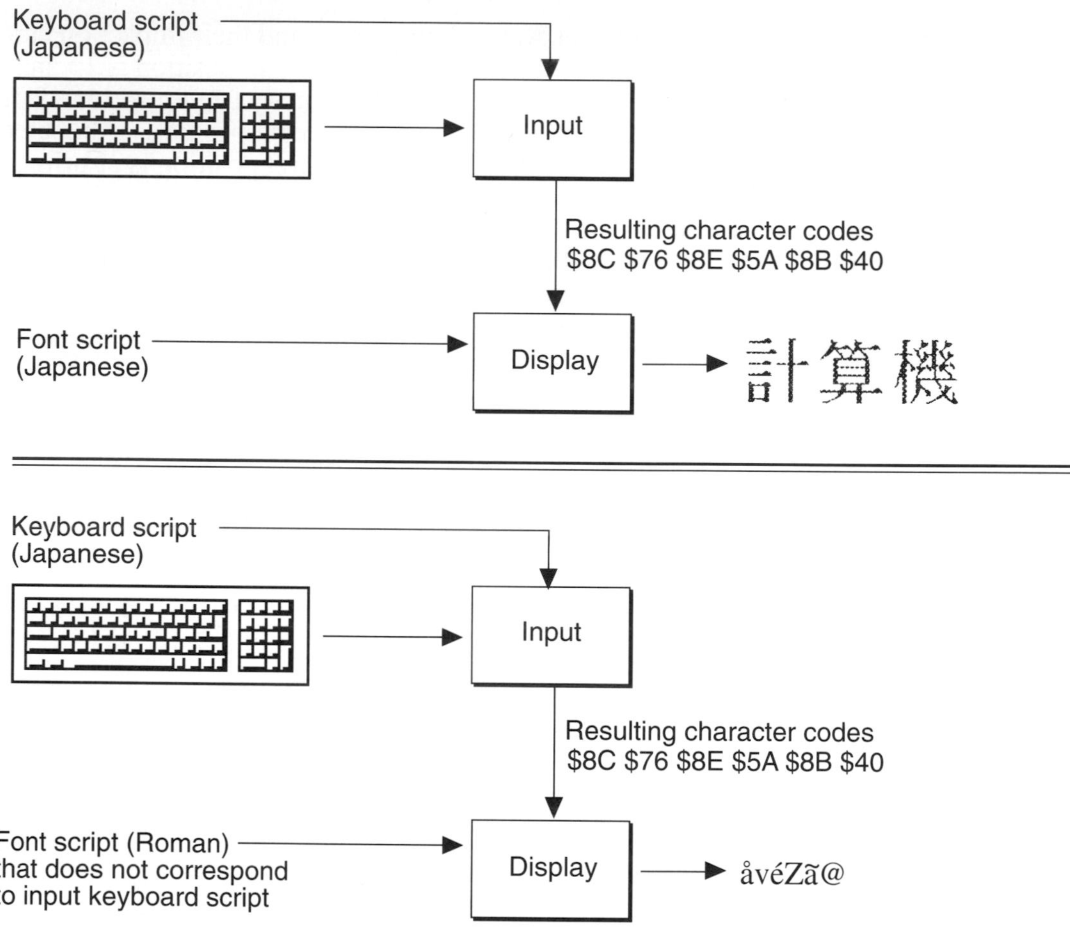

Figure 15-12. Font and keyboard script synchronization

TextEdit incorporates the following concepts for styled text:

- If your application calls TEClick, TESetSelect, or TESetStyle to change the font style or to process a mouse-down event in text as either an insertion point or a selection, TextEdit alters the keyboard script to correspond to the font script. This means, for example, that if users type Arabic text followed by Roman text and click in the Arabic text, the keyboard changes to Arabic without their changing the keyboard manually. Similarly, if users click in the Roman text, the keyboard changes to Roman without their altering the keyboard.

- If the selection point is not empty (that is, the value of the selStart field of the edit record, defined by the TERec data type, does not equal the value of the selEnd field), then TextEdit uses the font corresponding to the selStart field to alter the keyboard script. When a selection point falls on a script boundary, the keyboard is synchronized to the font of the character preceding the boundary (in backing-store order).
- If your application calls TEKey to input a character and if the keyboard script is different from the font script at the selection point, the font script changes to correspond to the keyboard script. If a font was selected and never used, thus remaining in TextEdit's style scrap record (defined by the StScrpRec data type), and if the font script coincides with the keyboard script, then this font is used. Otherwise, TextEdit searches through the preceding fonts in the style run table until it locates a font that corresponds to the keyboard. If one does not exist, then it uses the application font.
- If the font script at the selection point is the same as the keyboard script, then this font is used.

Note: There is one exception to this behavior: when the insertion point has been placed in Roman characters from a non-Roman font, the keyboard script is Roman, and the font and the keyboard remain unsynchronized to allow the user to enter more Roman characters in the non-Roman font.

If your application uses styled TextEdit and allows users to select fonts, TextEdit displays text correctly in all scripts. Otherwise, your application should use the application font as the best default for TextEdit.

DOUBLE-BYTE CHARACTERS

TextEdit takes advantage of the Script Manager's handling of double-byte characters so that they can be displayed with improved accuracy and consistency. If a double-byte character, such as a Kanji character, is typed, the first byte is buffered by TextEdit until the second byte is processed, at which time the character is displayed.

The internal buffer used for a double-byte character is unique to each edit record. Therefore, if TextEdit buffers the first byte of a double-byte character in a record and then the TEKey procedure is called on another record, the byte remains in the original buffer until TEKey processes another byte for that edit record.

When the TEKey procedure is called by a Right Arrow, Left Arrow, or Backspace keyboard event at a double-byte character, then the selection range is updated beyond the second byte in order for the caret to move once over the entire character. TextEdit also depends on the Script Manager routines to handle double-byte characters correctly with mouse-down events, caret display, highlighting, and other text-processing functions.

VERTICAL MOVEMENT OF THE CARET

When TEKey is called for an Up Arrow keyboard event, the caret moves up by one line each time the user presses the Up Arrow key, even in lines of text containing fonts of different sizes. Prior to this version of TextEdit, the caret occasionally skipped a line because it moved up by the height of the largest font on the current line.

If the line height of the current line is greater than the line height of the succeeding line and if the caret is positioned at the end of the line, a Down Arrow event places the caret on the next line. In system software earlier than this version of TextEdit, the caret remained on the current line.

If the current line corresponds to the first line in the edit record and if TEKey processes an Up Arrow event, the new caret position is at the beginning of the text on the first line, at primary caret position 0. This position corresponds to the visible right end of a line when the primary line direction is right to left and to the left end of a line when the primary line direction is left to right.

ARROW KEY ACTIONS FOR SELECTED TEXT

If a region of text is selected (that is, the selStart field of the edit record does not equal the selEnd field) and a user presses either the Up Arrow or Down Arrow key, the caret moves from the beginning of the selected region (or the selStart position). If the user presses the Right Arrow key, the caret appears one character to the right from the end of the highlighted region, and if the user presses the Left Arrow key, the caret appears one character to the left from the beginning of the selected text.

CARET POSITION AT LINE ENDS

Prior to this version of TextEdit, if spaces at the end of a line extended beyond the edge of the view rectangle, TextEdit drew the caret outside the view rectangle. This effect depended on the combination of line direction (TESysJust) and line alignment (teJust).

TextEdit no longer draws the caret outside the view rectangle. The caret is always drawn at the line end (that is, at the edge of the view rectangle) even when spaces extend beyond the edge of the view rectangle.

When TextEdit determines that a new position for the caret is at the start or end of a line, the line where the caret is displayed depends on the current caret position and the value in the clikStuff field in the edit record. TextEdit sets this field to reflect whether the most recent mouse-down event occurred on the leading or trailing edge of a character. If the last mouse-down event was on the leading edge of a character, the new caret position is at the line end that corresponds to the leading edge of the new character offset. For example, in Figure 15-13, if the new caret position is at character offset 3, then the caret appears at the end of the first line if the last mouse-down event was on the *trailing* edge of a character. This corresponds to a leading edge (clikStuff) value of FALSE. Otherwise, the caret appears at the beginning of the second line.

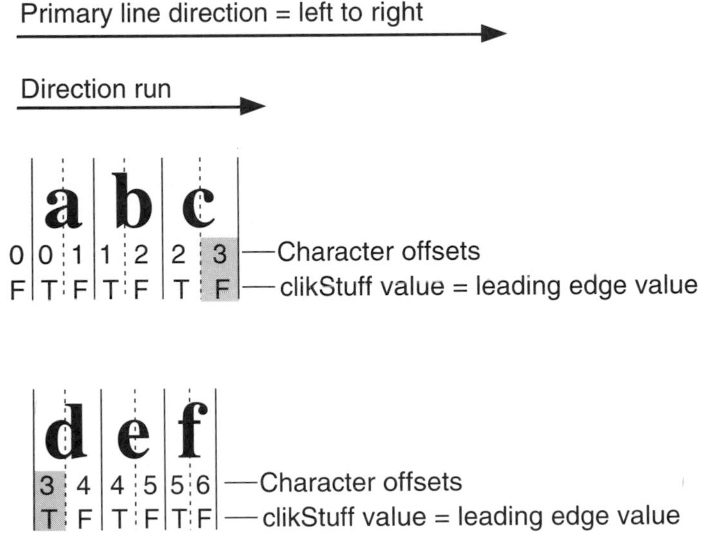

Figure 15-13. The caret position at line end

WORD SELECTION AND LINE BREAKS

Because TextEdit depends on the Script Manager's FindWord procedure, TextEdit's definition of a **word** has been extended. Prior to this version, TextEdit used its own FindWord procedure to determine word selection and line breaks. It now relies on the Script Manager's FindWord procedure for word selection on all systems and also relies on the Script Manager's FindWord and StyledLineBreak routines for line breaking on systems with more than one script system installed.

The way TextEdit uses FindWord to calculate word breaks has a significant impact on word selection. For example, on a Roman-only system that is localized for the United States, parentheses and other punctuation marks are no longer included as part of a word selection. However, this behavior may vary on other localized versions of a Roman system due to the localizability of the Script Manager's FindWord procedure. Furthermore, when a user double-clicks a series of spaces, that series of spaces is selected as a word. (Prior to this version of TextEdit, single spaces were selected as a word.)

Figure 15-14 illustrates how double-clicking the word *Apple* selects only the word *Apple,* and not the enclosing parentheses. In the figure, the arrows point to the word breaks.

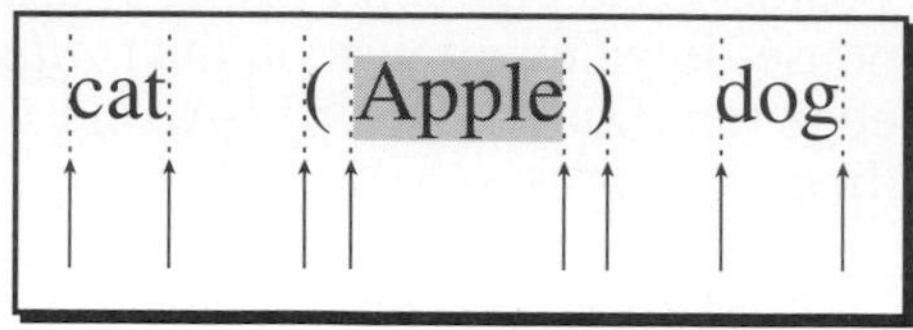

Figure 15-14. Word breaks for word selection

For backward compatibility, system software with only the Roman Script System installed still breaks lines at spaces. On systems with another script system installed, TextEdit calls the Script Manager's FindWord and StyledLineBreak routines for line breaking. Lines then break correctly when a hyphenated word is at the end of a line, as shown in Figure 15-15. This change is noticeable if you compare a line break on a computer using system software with only the Roman Script System installed to the same line on a computer with more than one script system installed.

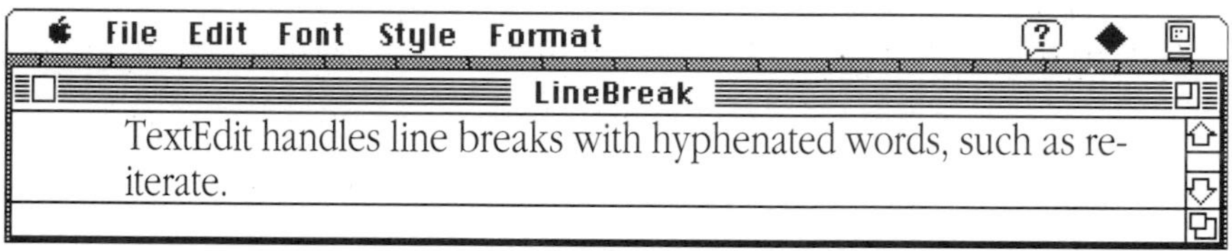

Figure 15-15. A line break with multiple scripts installed

ACCURATE LINE MEASUREMENT

TextEdit measures a line accurately by removing any trailing white space from the end of the line and taking the line direction into account. It uses the Script Manager's VisibleLength function to exclude trailing white space that occurs on the right side of the display line for a script system with a left-to-right line direction (TESysJust = 0) and with flush-right alignment (teJust = teJustRight or teFlushRight). It also uses VisibleLength if the text alignment is flush left (teJust = teForceLeft or teFlushLeft) regardless of the line direction.

Note: An anomaly exists in the way TextEdit draws at line ends. When the primary line direction of a script system is right to left (for instance, on an Arabic system), when the alignment is teFlushLeft or teCenter, and when spaces are being entered in a right-to-left font, TextEdit measures spaces at the end of the line and thus may draw the text beyond the right edge of the view rectangle. The caret, however, remains in view and is pinned to the left edge of the view rectangle.

This anomaly also exists when the primary line direction of a script system is left to right and the alignment is teCenter. In this instance,TextEdit measures spaces at the end of the line. As more spaces are added (and, thus measured), the visible text in the line is drawn out of view beyond the left edge of the view rectangle. The caret, however, remains in view and is pinned to the right edge of the view rectangle.

TEXTEDIT AND TRUETYPE FONTS

If your application is using a TrueType™ font, the default behavior of the Font Manager is to ensure that glyphs fit within the font's ascent and descent. Glyphs that extend beyond the ascent or descent, such as certain accented fonts, are scaled down to fit. If your application has set the preserveGlyph parameter of the SetPreserveGlyph procedure to TRUE to preserve the original unscaled shape of the glyph, TextEdit sets it to FALSE before it calls DRAWHook to perform any drawing. This is to guarantee that the glyphs whose bounding boxes exceed the font's ascent or descent are scaled down to prevent them from colliding with other glyphs on the lines above or below. TextEdit then restores the preserveGlyph parameter to its previous value before proceeding. See "Preserving the Glyph's Shape" in the Font Manager chapter for further discussion of glyph preservation. See "Replacing the Drawing Routine" later in this chapter for details on DRAWHook.

USING TEXTEDIT

This section provides a variety of information on using this version of TextEdit. It discusses how to determine the version of TextEdit that you are using and describes three new hooks that provide a way to replace TextEdit's dependency on the Script Manager for word breaking and measuring. This section also discusses several additional TextEdit features available through a new function, TEFeatureFlag. Finally, it updates and clarifies the use of several previously documented TextEdit routines and their effects.

Determining the Version of TextEdit

You can determine the version of TextEdit using the Gestalt selector gestaltTextEditVersion. When you call Gestalt with this selector, the result returned in the response parameter identifies the current version of TextEdit. If the Gestalt function returns the gestaltUndefSelectorErr result code, an earlier version of TextEdit without Script Manager compatibility is installed.

```
CONST {constants for Gestalt function}
      gestaltTE1 = 1;    {U.S. system software version 6.0.4 containing }
                         { TextEdit on a Macintosh IIci}
      gestaltTE2 = 2;    {version 6.0.4 non-Roman script system containing }
                         { a Script Manager-compatible version of }
                         { TextEdit including the new measuring hook }
                         { nWIDTHHook for the Macintosh IIci}
      gestaltTE3 = 3;    {version 6.0.4 non-Roman script system containing }
                         { a Script Manager-compatible version of }
                         { TextEdit including the new measuring hook }
                         { nWIDTHHook for Macintosh Plus, }
                         { Macintosh SE, Macintosh SE/30, }
                         { Macintosh II, Macintosh Portable, }
                         { Macintosh IIx, or Macintosh IIcx}
```

15 TextEdit

```
gestaltTE4 = 4;   {system software versions 6.0.5 and later, }
                  { which contain a Script Manager-compatible }
                  { version of TextEdit including the new measuring }
                  { hook nWIDTHHook & the outline-highlighting & }
                  { text-buffering features, on any Macintosh}
gestaltTE5 = 5;   {system software version 7.0, which contains a }
                  { Script Manager-compatible version of TextEdit }
                  { including two new measuring hooks, nWIDTHHook }
                  { & TextWidthHook, outline highlighting, text }
                  { buffering, new features for inline input, & }
                  { capability to disable inline input}
```

TextEdit is Script Manager–compatible if the returned value is gestaltTE2 or greater.

TextEdit contains the new measuring hook nWIDTHHook if the returned value is gestaltTE2 or greater.

The outline-highlighting and text-buffering features of TextEdit, included with the new function TEFeatureFlag, are available if the returned value is gestaltTE4 or greater. Outline highlighting, text buffering, new features for inline input, and the capability to disable inline input, included with the new function TEFeatureFlag, are available if the returned value is gestaltTE5 or greater.

The new measuring hook TextWidthHook is available if the returned value is gestaltTE5 or greater.

For more on the TEFeatureFlag function, see "Outline Highlighting, Text Buffering, and Inline Input" later in this chapter. For more on TextEdit's width measuring hooks, see "Replacing the Measuring Routines" later in this chapter.

Customizing TextEdit's Features

To customize TextEdit's capabilities to the specifications of your own application, you can replace some of TextEdit's routines with routines of your own that accomplish the same function. To allow you to do this, TextEdit supplies hooks, fields in which you can store the address to a routine if you require different behavior from that provided by TextEdit. Normally, you use TextEdit's standard or default routines whose addresses are contained in these fields in the edit record. To override these routines, you can place the address of your hook routine in the appropriate field by using the TECustomHook procedure. See "Customizing TextEdit" later in this chapter for details.

▲ **Warning:** If you use any of the TextEdit hooks to override default TextEdit behavior, the results may no longer be Script Manager–compatible. You must determine whether more than one script system is installed before replacing TextEdit's routines with an alternate routine.

Also, before placing the address of your routine in the TextEdit dispatch record (defined by the TEDispatchRec data type), you should strip the addresses using the Operating System Utilities StripAddress function to guarantee that your application is 32-bit clean. ▲

Measuring the Width of Components of a Line

Earlier versions of TextEdit used the hook WIDTHHook any time the width of various components of a line was measured. TextEdit now uses three hooks—nWIDTHHook, TextWidthHook, and WIDTHHook—to measure the width of various components of a line. The hook nWIDTHHook lets you replace TextEdit's new measuring routine for non-Roman script systems. TextWidthHook allows you to replace all the new calls to the QuickDraw TextWidth function in TextEdit with your own measuring routine. WIDTHHook retains its original measuring function to provide backward compatibility for your applications. See "Replacing the Measuring Routines" later in this chapter for details.

Defining Word Boundaries

TextEdit provides a higher-level hook, TEFindWord, that allows you to customize word breaking. TextEdit now disregards the wordBreak hook on non-Roman script systems and only uses it on system software with only the Roman Script System installed if an application has supplied an alternate routine in the hook. See "Replacing the Word Breaking Routine" later in this chapter for details.

Controlling Outline Highlighting, Text Buffering, and Inline Input

TextEdit provides outline highlighting for inactive text. This highlighting is similar to the behavior of MPW® selections. TextEdit also supplies text buffering for performance improve-ments. Finally, support for inline input for double-byte script systems is provided with TextEdit. This support includes several new features for inline input and the capability to disable inline input. All these features are controlled with the TEFeatureFlag function. See "Outline Highlighting, Text Buffering, and Inline Input" later in this chapter for details.

Setting Left Alignment for Right-to-Left Directional Scripts

Prior to this version of TextEdit, the TESetJust procedure provided three possible choices for alignment in its just parameter: the constants teJustLeft (0), teJustCenter (1), and teJustRight (–1). These choices are appropriate for script systems that are read from left to right. However, in script systems that are read from right to left, text is incorrectly displayed as left aligned in dialog boxes and in other areas of applications where users cannot explicitly set the alignment.

An additional constant for the just parameter to the TESetJust procedure allows you to specify left alignment if the primary line direction is right to left (that is, TESysJust = –1). This value for the just parameter is teForceLeft (–2).

The behavior of the constant teJustLeft makes alignment occur in the primary line direction specified by TESysJust. Therefore, if you use teJustLeft when the line direction is right to left, right alignment takes place as it does when you use the value teJustRight.

If your application does not allow the user to change the alignment, then it should use teJustLeft; if it does allow the user to change the alignment, then it should use teForceLeft for left alignment.

Note: TextEdit does not support fully justified alignment. The Script Manager supplies routines you can use to provide support for justified text in your applications. See the Worldwide Software Overview chapter earlier in this volume for details.

Because of the conflict between the names of the just parameter's constants and their effects within TextEdit, new names have been provided as shown in Table 15-1.

Table 15-1. Constants for the just parameter of TESetJust

New constant	Old constant	Value	Description
teFlushRight	teJustRight	–1	Flush right for all scripts
teFlushLeft	teForceLeft	–2	Flush left for all scripts
teCenter	teJustCenter	1	Centered for all scripts
teFlushDefault	teJustLeft	0	Flush according to line direction

Using WordRedraw for Line Calculations

WordRedraw is a low-memory global variable used in TextEdit for line calculations after the user types in a character. TextEdit sets the correct value for WordRedraw in TEInit based upon the installed script systems. If a double-byte script is installed, TEInit performs an OR operation on WordRedraw with a 1; if a right-to-left script is installed, TEInit performs an OR operation on WordRedraw with an $FF. The size of this global is 1 byte.

TextEdit interprets the final value of WordRedraw as follows:

Value	Description
0	Redraws the character before the entered character.
1	Redraws the word before the entered character.
$FF	Redraws the whole line.

Using the lineStarts Array to Determine Line Length

The lineStarts array is a field in the edit record that contains the offset position of the first character of each line. This array has the following boundary conditions:

- The first entry has index 0 and value 0.
- The last entry in the array has index nLines and value teLength (hence, there are nLines + 1 entries).

- The beginning of the first line is given by lineStarts[0], and the beginning of the second line is given by lineStarts[1]; hence, the length of the first line is given by lineStarts[1] – lineStarts[0].
- The maximum number of entries is 16,000.

To determine the length of a line, you can use the information contained in the lineStarts array and the nLines field. For example, if you want to determine the length of the line *n* (where *n* = 0 for the first line), subtract its start location (contained in the array entry with index n) from its end location (contained in the array with index *n* + 1):

```
lengthOfLineN := myTE^^.lineStarts[n+1] - myTE^^.lineStarts[n];
```

The terminating condition for this measurement is when *n* is equal to nLines plus 1.

It is important not to change the information contained in the lineStarts array.

Using TextEdit's Default Click Procedure

TextEdit's default click procedure for automatic scrolling (which can be replaced using the clikLoop hook) depends on the value in the clickTime field in the edit record. When TextEdit's click procedure, TEClick, is called, clickTime contains the time when the TEClick procedure was last called. TextEdit now adjusts the value in clickTime within its default click procedure to allow slower scrolling to occur.

If you modify this value inside your own click procedure, be aware that TextEdit resets it to the current tick count upon exit from the TEClick procedure and uses the new value at reentry when TEClick is subsequently called.

TEXTEDIT ROUTINES

This section describes in detail the new function TEFeatureFlag and four other routines new with system software version 6.0: TECustomHook, TEContinuousStyle, SetStylScrap, and TENumStyles. Three new hooks are described: nWIDTHHook and TextWidthHook, accessed through the TECustomHook procedure, and the low-memory TEFindWord hook. Finally, this section includes updated information on several existing TextEdit routines, including TEKey, TEGetPoint, and TESetStyle.

Assembly-language note: The TextEdit routines TEContinuousStyle, TESetStylScrap, TENumStyles, TECustomHook, and the new TextEdit function TEFeatureFlag, which are described in this section, are called by using the TEDispatch trap macro. See "Summary of TextEdit" at the end of this chapter for a list of the decimal selectors for these routines.

Outline Highlighting, Text Buffering, and Inline Input

The TEFeatureFlag function allows you to enable outline highlighting and text buffering in your application. You can also use this function to disable inline input in a particular edit record and to enable several new features that have been provided so that inline input works correctly with TextEdit.

> **Note:** To test for the availability of these features, you can call the Gestalt function with the gestaltTextEditVersion selector. A result of gestaltTE4 or greater returned in the response parameter indicates that outline highlighting and text buffering are available. A result of gestaltTE5 or greater returned in the response parameter indicates that the two inline input features are available. (For details, see "Determining the Version of TextEdit" earlier in this chapter.)
>
> The inline input features are also available on version 6.0.7 systems with non-Roman script systems installed. However, there is no Gestalt constant that indicates this availability.

```
FUNCTION TEFeatureFlag (feature: Integer; action: Integer;
                        hTE: TEHandle) : Integer;
```

The feature parameter allows you to disable inline input in a particular edit record or to specify the features you want to enable—outline highlighting, text buffering, and features provided for inline input in TextEdit. The action parameter lets you enable and disable these features by using the TEBitSet and TEBitClear constants and lets you test the settings of these feature bits by using the TEBitTest constant. The hTE parameter is a handle to the edit record.

The TEFeatureFlag function returns the previous setting of the feature's bit, either TEBitSet or TEBitClear.

```
CONST {constants for feature parameter values}
      teFTextBuffering    =  1;        {text buffering}
      teFOutlineHilite    =  2;        {outline highlighting}
      teFInlineInput      =  3;        {inline input features}
      teFUseTextServices  =  4;        {use inline input service}

      {constants for action parameter values}
      TEBitClear          =  0;        {clear TEFeatureFlag features}
      TEBitSet            =  1;        {set TEFeatureFlag features}
      TEBitTest           = -1;        {test TEFeatureFlag features}
```

Outline Highlighting

Use the teFOutlineHilite constant in the feature parameter of TEFeatureFlag to enable outline highlighting. If a highlighted region exists in an edit record in an inactive window, then the highlighted region is outlined (or framed) when the window is in the background, a behavior similar to MPW selections. If the caret is in the window and the window is no longer active, the caret is then drawn in a gray pattern so that it appears dimmed. To do the framing and caret dimming, TextEdit temporarily replaces the current address in the highHook and caretHook fields of the edit record, redraws the caret or highlighted region, and then immediately restores the hooks to their previous addresses.

Text Buffering

Use the teFTextBuffering constant in the feature parameter of TEFeatureFlag to perform text buffering. Text buffering can be enabled for performance improvements, especially with double-byte scripts. TextEdit buffers each TEKey input of a graphic character. The entire buffer will then be inserted at one time if any TextEdit routine is called other than TEKey for another graphic character. This includes any routines that handle a mouse-down event, a style change, font and keyboard synchronization, the input of a nongraphic character, or a call to the TEIdle procedure. The buffer is dumped before this routine is handled.

▲ **Warning:** This buffer is a global buffer (and differs from TEKey's internal double-byte buffer) and is used across all active edit records. These records may be in a single application or in multiple applications. Exercise care when you enable TEFeatureFlag's text-buffering capability in more than one active record; otherwise, the bytes that are buffered from one edit record may appear in another edit record. You also need to be sure that buffering is not turned off in the middle of processing a double-byte character.

To guarantee the integrity of your record, it is important that you wait for an idle event before you disable buffering or enable buffering in a second edit record. ▲

If text buffering is enabled on a non-Roman script system and the keyboard has changed, TextEdit flushes the text of the current script from the buffer before buffering characters in the new script.

Note: If the text-buffering feature teFTextBuffering is enabled, your application must ensure that TEIdle is called before any pause of more than a few ticks—for example, before WaitNextEvent. A possibility of a long delay before characters appear on the screen exists—especially in non-Roman systems. If you do not call TEIdle, the characters may end up in the edit record of another application.

Inline Input

If your application follows the guidelines for inline input available from Macintosh Developer Technical Support, then you should set the new flag useTextEditServices in the 'SIZE' resource in your application. (For details on the 'SIZE' resource, see the Event Manager chapter in this volume.) This allows inline input to work with your application. **Inline input** is a keyboard input method (often used for double-byte script systems) in which conversion from a phonetic to an ideographic representation of a character takes place at the current line position where the text is intended to appear. This allows the user to type text directly in the line as opposed to a special conversion window. If inline input is installed and the useTextEditServices flag in the 'SIZE' resource is set, inline input sets TextEdit's teFUseTextServices feature bit whenever an edit record is created. This bit is not used by TextEdit.

Inline input checks the teFUseTextServices bit during text editing to determine if an inline session should begin. If you want to disable inline input for a particular edit record, your application can clear this bit after the edit record is created. You can also clear this bit to disable inline input temporarily and then restore it, but the edit record should always be deactivated before the state of the bit is changed.

In the future, other text services may use this same mechanism. If you follow the guidelines specified here, your application should also work with future text services.

> **Note:** You *must* deactivate an edit record before changing the state of the feature bits or any fields in the edit record.

When an inline edit session begins, inline input also sets the teFInlineInput bit to provide the following features so that inline input will work correctly with TextEdit:

- disabling font and keyboard synchronization
- forcing a multiple-line selection to be highlighted line by line using a separate rectangle for each line rather than using a minimum number of rectangles for optimization
- highlighting a line only to the edge of the text rather than beyond the text to the edge of the view rectangle

The teFInlineInput bit is cleared by inline input when an inline session ends. Use the teFInlineInput constant in the feature parameter of TEFeatureFlag to include these features in your application even when inline input is not installed. Be careful about changing the state of this bit if the teFUseTextServices bit is set. Again, the edit record should always be deactivated before the state of the teFInlineInput bit is changed.

> ▲ **Warning:** If you clear the teFUseTextServices bit and you set the teFInlineInput bit, inline input is disabled, but your application retains the features listed above. ▲

Customizing TextEdit

The TECustomHook procedure lets your application customize the features of TextEdit by setting the TextEdit hooks.

```
PROCEDURE TECustomHook (which: TEIntHook; VAR addr: ProcPtr;
                        hTE: TEHandle);
```

The which parameter specifies which hook to replace. The values for the which parameter are

```
CONST intEOLHook          = 0;        {end-of-line hook}
      intDrawHook         = 1;        {drawing hook}
      intWidthHook        = 2;        {width measurement hook}
      intHitTestHook      = 3;        {hit test hook}
      intNWidthHook       = 6;        {new width measurement hook }
                                      { nWIDTHHook}
      intTextWidthHook    = 7;        {new width measurement hook }
                                      { TextWidthHook}
```

You specify your customized hook in the addr parameter. When TECustomHook returns, the addr parameter contains the address of the previous hook specified by the which parameter. This address is returned so that hooks can be daisy-chained. The two new hooks, nWIDTHHook and TextWidthHook, specified by the intNWidthHook and intTextWidthHook constants, are described in "Replacing the Measuring Routines" later in this chapter.

Two integer fields of the edit record, not used for their original purposes but still named recalBack and recalLines, combine to hold a handle to the TextEdit dispatch record, which contains a list of TextEdit hooks. (See Figure 15-20 for an illustration of the edit record, the dispatch record, and all the TextEdit data structures.) Each edit record has its own set of such routines to provide for maximum flexibility. You should always use the TECustomHook procedure to change these hooks instead of modifying the edit record directly.

▲ **Warning:** Do not simply copy the recalBack and recalLines fields to another edit record. If you do, a duplicate handle to the initial TextEdit dispatch record is stored in recalBack and recalLines in your copy of the record. When one of the edit records is disposed, the handle stored in the copy becomes invalid, and TextEdit can crash if the copy is used. ▲

EOLHook, WIDTHHook, nWIDTHHook, TextWidthHook, DRAWHook, and HITTESTHook are fields into the TextEdit dispatch record and are described in the next sections.

Note: When you replace these hooks, note that all registers except those specified as containing return values must be preserved. Registers A3 and A4 contain a pointer and a handle, respectively, to the edit record. You can obtain line start positions from the lineStarts array in the edit record. A5 is always valid.

Note: The TextBox procedure only uses these hooks when it needs to allocate an edit record.

Replacing the End-of-Line Routine

The EOLHook field contains the address of a routine that tests a given character to determine whether it is an end-of-line character and returns with the appropriate status flags set in the status register. The default action is to merely compare the character with $0D (a carriage return) and return.

Assembly-language note: For EOLHook, the registers are set at entry as specified, and TextEdit depends on the registers being set at exit as specified:

On entry	D0:	character to compare (byte)
	A3:	pointer to the edit record (long)
	A4:	locked handle to the edit record (long)
On exit	Z flag in the status register clear if end-of-line character; set otherwise	

Replacing the Measuring Routines

TextEdit's width hooks are called each the time the width of various components of a line is calculated. This section describes two new hooks, nWIDTHHook and TextWidthHook, and their relationships with the original WIDTHHook hook. The new hook nWIDTHHook allows you access to TextEdit's measuring routine for non-Roman script systems and provides a way for you to replace this routine with your own script-compatible measuring routine. TextWidthHook provides a way for you to replace the new calls to the TextWidth function in TextEdit with your own measuring routine.

Note: To test for the availability of the new width-measuring hooks, you can call the Gestalt function with the gestaltTextEditVersion selector. A result of gestaltTE2 or greater returned in the response parameter indicates that the new width measurement hook nWIDTHHook is available. A result of gestaltTE5 or greater returned in the response parameter indicates that the new text width measurement hook TextWidthHook is available. (For details, see "Determining the Version of TextEdit" earlier in this chapter.)

TextWidthHook is available for version 6.0.7 systems with non-Roman script systems installed. However, there is no Gestalt constant that indicates this availability.

The original WIDTHHook hook is available to provide backward compatibility for your applications. TextEdit still uses WIDTHHook; however, it now performs additional checks to determine whether to use WIDTHHook or nWIDTHHook. TextEdit first determines whether a non-Roman script system is installed. If it is, TextEdit uses the new nWIDTHHook routine even if an application has overridden WIDTHHook with a different measuring routine. If

TextEdit finds that only the Roman Script System is installed, it checks to see if WIDTHHook contains the address of TextEdit's default routinc for mcasuring. If it does, TextEdit uses the nWIDTHHook routine. Otherwise, an application has provided a different measuring routine to be used for system software with only the Roman Script System installed, so TextEdit uses this routine instead of its own default routine.

It is possible for you to provide alternate routines for both of these hooks to guarantee that your routine is always used. However, unless the routine measures correctly for non-Roman scripts, you should only replace WIDTHHook and TextWidthHook.

The appropriate font, face, and size characteristics have already been set into the current port by the time any of these routines is called.

The default action for WIDTHHook is to call the QuickDraw TextWidth function and return.

Assembly-language note: For WIDTHHook, the registers are set at entry as specified, and TextEdit depends on the registers being set as specified:

On entry	D0:	length (in bytes) of text to measure (word)
	D1:	first byte of text to measure (word)
	A0:	pointer to text buffer (long)
	A3:	pointer to the edit record (long)
	A4:	locked handle to the edit record (long)
On exit	D1:	pixel width of measured text (word)

The default action for nWIDTHHook is to call the Script Manager's Char2Pixel function or TextWidth to measure accurately for non-Roman scripts. For more information on Char2Pixel, see the Worldwide Software Overview chapter in this volume. For comprehensive details, refer to *Macintosh Worldwide Development: Guide to System Software*.

Assembly-language note: For nWIDTHHook, the registers are set at entry as specified, and TextEdit depends on the registers being set at exit as specified:

On entry	D0:	overall style run length, bounded by the line end (word)
	D1:	offset position within style run on the current line (word)
	D2:	slop (low word); direction flag (high word) (long)
	A0:	pointer to text buffer (long)
	A2:	pointer to current line start (from TextEdit's lineStarts array) (long)
	A3:	pointer to the edit record (long)
	A4:	locked handle to the edit record (long)
On exit	D1:	pixel width of measured text (word)

For a discussion of the slop value, see the Worldwide Software Overview chapter in this volume.

TextEdit also includes the new TextWidthHook routine that provides a way for you to replace the new TextWidth calls in TextEdit with your own measuring routine. You must use TextWidthHook in addition to WIDTHHook and nWIDTHHook to replace TextEdit's measuring routines completely.

> **Note:** There is a TextWidth call in the TextBox procedure that does not use this hook because no edit record is allocated.

The default action for TextWidthHook is to always call the QuickDraw TextWidth function (the same default action as for the original WIDTHHook routine).

Assembly-language note: For TextWidthHook, the registers are set at entry as specified. TextEdit depends on the registers being set at exit as specified:

On entry	D0:	length (in bytes) of text to be measured (word)
	D1:	offset in text of first byte to measure (word)
	A0:	pointer to text to measure (long)
	A3:	pointer to the edit record (long)
	A4:	locked handle to the edit record (long)
On exit	D1:	pixel width of measured text (word)

Replacing the Drawing Routine

TextEdit calls DRAWHook any time the various components of a line are drawn. The appropriate font, face, and size characteristics have already been set into the current port by the time this routine is called. If your application is using TrueType fonts, TextEdit has also set the preserveGlyph parameter of the Font Manager's SetPreserveGlyph procedure to FALSE, so your hook may need to reset this parameter if your application depends on it. The default action of this hook is to call the QuickDraw DrawText procedure and return.

Assembly-language note: For DRAWHook, the registers are set at entry as specified:

On entry	D0:	offset into text (word)
	D1:	length of text to draw (word)
	A0:	pointer to text to draw (long)
	A3:	pointer to the edit record (long)
	A4:	locked handle to the edit record (long)

Replacing the Hit Test Routine

TextEdit calls HITTESTHook to determine the character position in a line, given the pixel width from the left edge of the view rectangle. The default action is to call the TextWidth function to determine if the pixel width of the measured text is greater than the input width. If it is, then HITTESTHook calls the Script Manager's Pixel2Char function and returns. For more information on Pixel2Char, refer to the Worldwide Software Overview chapter in this volume. For comprehensive details, see *Macintosh Worldwide Development: Guide to System Software*.

Assembly-language note: For HITTESTHook, the registers are set at entry as specified, and TextEdit depends on the registers being set at exit as specified:

On entry	D0:	length of text block (style run) to measure (word)
	D1:	pixel width from start of text block (word)
	D2*:	slop (should equal 0) (word)
	A0:	pointer to start of text block (long)
	A3:	pointer to the edit record (long)
	A4:	locked handle to the edit record (long)
On exit	D0:	pixel width to character offset in text block (low word); Boolean = TRUE if a character offset corresponding to the given pixel width was found (high word)
	D1:	character offset (word)
	D2:	Boolean = TRUE if the pixel width falls within the leading edge of the character (word)

*In earlier versions of TextEdit, the value in this register was not always used. If you daisy-chain in a routine and then call HITTESTHook, D2 must be 0.

Replacing the Word Breaking Routine

The wordBreak hook (the wordBreak field in the edit record) exists to replace TextEdit's word breaking routine. However, unless you include explicit tests for scripts, the algorithms you provide may be incorrect for non-Roman scripts. To provide better compatibility for your application, TextEdit

- disregards the wordBreak hook on non-Roman script systems
- supplies a higher-level hook, TEFindWord, which allows you to customize TextEdit's word breaking

The TEFindWord hook is at a higher level than the wordBreak hook and replaces TextEdit's word breaking routine. This gives your application more control over the breaking process and allows you to write more efficient routines. However, unless your routine correctly determines breaks for all scripts, you must be sure to check for non-Roman scripts before replacing TextEdit's routine, which calls the Script Manager's FindWord procedure.

Here's how the default TEFindWord routine works:

- TextEdit initially determines whether a non-Roman script system is installed. If one is installed, TextEdit always uses the Script Manager's FindWord procedure for line breaking and word selection.

- If TextEdit determines that only the Roman Script System is installed and TEFindWord is being called for line breaking, it calls the wordBreak hook.

- If TEFindWord is called for word selection for system software with only the Roman Script System installed, TextEdit checks to see if your application has placed the address of a different word breaking routine in the wordBreak field of the edit record. If so, TextEdit calls your word breaking routine. Otherwise, if the wordBreak field contains the address of TextEdit's internal word breaking routine, TextEdit uses the Script Manager's FindWord procedure to determine word breaks.

The hook TEFindWord is global and supersedes this default behavior. If you prefer to customize TextEdit, remember to check for non-Roman scripts if you desire to replace the word breaking code only on the Roman Script System with no other scripts installed. To check if non-Roman scripts are enabled, use the GetEnvirons function with the smEnabled verb. See the Worldwide Software Overview chapter for details on GetEnvirons.

If you replace TEFindWord, be careful to set the correct values in the appropriate registers on exit.

Assembly-language note: For TEFindWord, the registers are set at entry as specified, and TextEdit depends on the registers being set at exit as specified:

On entry	D0:	current position (the value of selStart field in edit record) (word)			
	D2:	identifier of routine that called FindWord (word)			
		teWordSelect	EQU	4	called for word selection
		teWordDrag	EQU	8	called for extending word selection
		teFromFind	EQU	12	called for determining new line breaks
		teFromRecal	EQU	16	called for word breaking in line recalculation
	A3:	pointer to the edit record (long)			
	A4:	locked handle to the edit record (long)			
On exit	D0:	word start (word)			
	D1:	word end (word)			

When TextEdit calls the Script Manager's FindWord procedure, it uses information in the edit record to provide the necessary parameters. TextEdit determines the current script boundaries for the Script Manager's FindWord routine by using the font-run information in the style record (defined by the TEStyleRec data type). TextEdit also determines the length of the script run and the offset within the script run from which to begin searching for a word boundary. TextEdit uses the value in the clikStuff field of the edit record to determine the leadingEdge flag for the Script Manager's FindWord procedure. You must use similar information to replace TEFindWord correctly for non-Roman scripts. For more information, see the Worldwide Software Overview chapter in this volume and *Macintosh Worldwide Development: Guide to System Software*.

Backspacing to the Beginning of a Style

The TEKey procedure replaces the selection range in the specified text with a given character and leaves an insertion point just past the inserted character.

The TEKey procedure was modified in system software version 6.0 so that it no longer deletes a style if the user backspaces to the beginning of a style. Instead, TEKey saves the style in the nullScrap field of the null style record (defined by the NullStRec data type) to be applied to subsequent typed characters. As soon as the user backspaces past the beginning of the style or clicks in another area of the text, TEKey removes the style.

```
PROCEDURE TEKey (key: Char; hTE: TEHandle);
```

The hTE parameter is a handle to the edit record. The key parameter indicates the character with which you wish to replace the selection range specified by hTE. For complete details on the TEKey procedure, see the TextEdit chapter in Volume I.

Determining the Position of an Ambiguous Offset

The TEGetPoint function returns the point corresponding to the given offset into the specified text. This point indicates the bottom left of the character at the specified offset.

```
FUNCTION TEGetPoint (offset: Integer; hTE: TEHandle) : Point;
```

The hTE parameter is a handle to the edit record. The offset parameter indicates a position in the text that is specified by hTE.

With this version of TextEdit, the TEGetPoint function returns a valid result even when no text is in the edit record. The point returned is based on the values in the record's destination rectangle. The line height, taken either from the lineHeight field for an unstyled edit record or from the line-height element array for a styled edit record, is also used to determine the vertical component. Both the line and system alignments (teJust and TESysJust) are used to determine the horizontal component.

In the case of the offset equal to a line end (which is also the line start of the next line), TEGetPoint returns a point corresponding to the line start of the next line. For example, as shown in Figure 15-16, if the offset 3 is passed to TEGetPoint, the point returned corresponds to the offset 3 before the character *d* on the second line. In the case of a mixed-directional line, the primary caret position (the one corresponding to the line direction) is returned. See "Mixed-Directional Text" earlier in this chapter for details on primary caret positions in a line containing mixed-directional text.

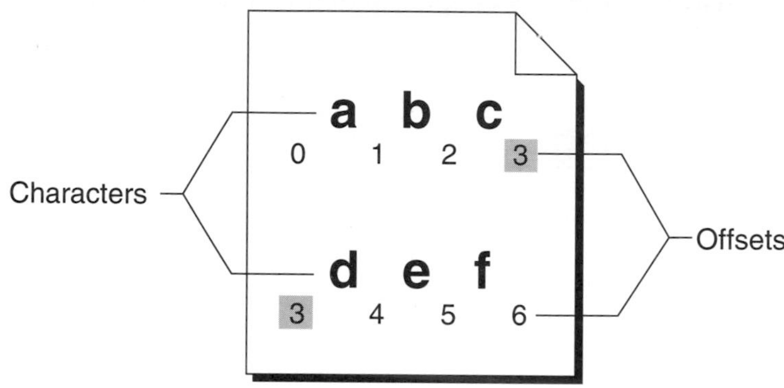

Figure 15-16. A character offset at a line break

Toggling a Style

The TESetStyle procedure lets you set a new style for the current selection specified by the edit record. For details on TESetStyle, see the TextEdit chapter in Volume V.

```
PROCEDURE TESetStyle (mode: Integer; newStyle: TextStyle;
                      redraw: Boolean; hTE: TEHandle);
```

You specify the new style with the newStyle parameter. The hTE parameter is a handle to a styled edit record.The mode parameter allows you to control which style attributes to set. The style attributes may be any additive combination of the TESetStyle mode constants. (See the "Summary of TextEdit" at the end of this chapter for a list of the TESetStyle mode constants.) The redraw parameter indicates whether to redraw the current selection in its new style.

The TESetStyle procedure was enhanced in system software version 6.0 to accept an additional mode, doToggle (= 32). If doToggle is specified along with doFace and if a style specified in the given newStyle parameter exists across the entire selected range, then TESetStyle removes (turns off) that style. Otherwise, if the style doesn't exist across the entire selection range, all of the selected text is set to include that style. When a particular style is set for an entire selection range, that style is said to be continuous over the selection.

For example, in the selected text in Figure 15-17, the bold style is continuous over the selection range and the italic style is not.

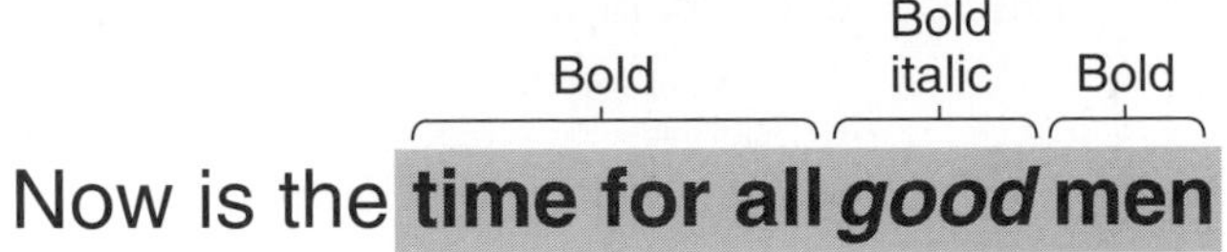

Figure 15-17. An initial selection before TESetStyle is called

If you call TESetStyle with a mode of doFace + doToggle and a newStyle parameter with a tsFace field of bold, the resulting selection is as shown in Figure 15-18. (The text style record is defined by the TextStyle data type.)

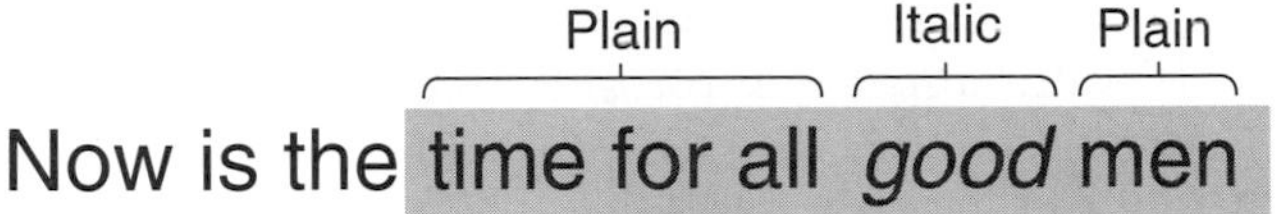

Figure 15-18. The result of calling TESetStyle to toggle with a bold style

On the other hand, if you call TESetStyle with a mode of doFace + doToggle and a newStyle parameter with a tsFace field of italic, the resulting selection is shown in Figure 15-19.

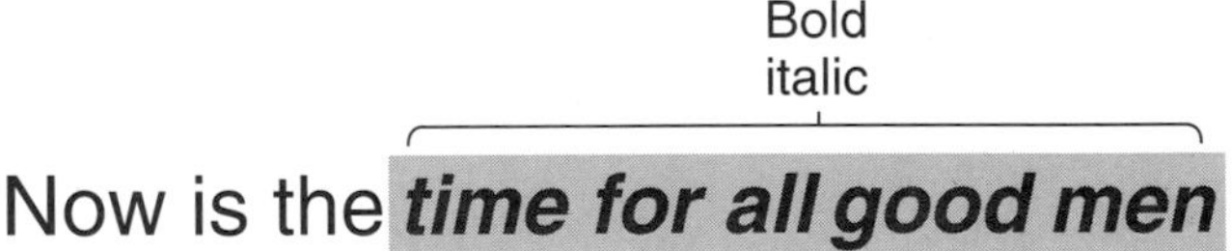

Figure 15-19. The result of calling TESetStyle to toggle with an italic style

If the redraw parameter is set to TRUE, TextEdit redraws the current selection in the new style, recalculating line breaks, line heights, and line ascents. If the redraw parameter is FALSE, TextEdit does not recalculate line breaks, line heights, and line ascents. Therefore, when a routine is called that uses any of this information, such as TEGetHeight (which returns a total height between two specified lines), it does not reflect the new style information set with TESetStyle. Instead, the routine uses the information set before TESetStyle was called. To update this information, you must call the TECalText procedure. A simpler way to be certain that current information is always reflected when drawing is to call the TESetStyle procedure with the redraw parameter set to TRUE.

> **Note:** TEReplaceStyle also has a redraw parameter with the same behavior specified above.

Determining Styles Across a Selection

The TEContinuousStyle function, new with system software version 6.0, gives you information about the attributes of the current selection.

```
FUNCTION TEContinuousStyle (VAR mode: Integer; VAR aStyle: TextStyle;
                            hTE: TEHandle) : Boolean;
```

The mode parameter, which takes the same values as in TESetStyle, specifies which attributes should be checked. When TEContinuousStyle returns, the mode parameter indicates which of the checked attributes is continuous over the selection range, and the aStyle parameter reflects the continuous attributes. For details on TESetStyle, refer to the TextEdit chapter in Volume V.

TEContinuousStyle returns TRUE if all of the attributes to be checked are continuous and returns FALSE if they are not. In other words, if the mode parameter is the same before and after the call, then TEContinuousStyle returns TRUE.

Listing 15-1 illustrates how TEContinuousStyle is useful for marking the Style menu items so they correspond to the current selection.

Listing 15-1. Marking the Style menu items so they correspond to the current selection

```
VAR
   mode:        Integer;
   aStyle:      TextStyle;
   myTE:        TEHandle;
   styleMenu:   MenuHandle;
BEGIN
   mode := doFace;
   IF TEContinuousStyle(mode, aStyle, myTE) THEN
   BEGIN
      {There is at least one face that is continuous over }
      { the selection. Note that it might be plain, which is }
      { actually the absence of all styles.}
      CheckItem(styleMenu, plainItem, aStyle.tsFace = []);
      CheckItem(styleMenu, boldItem, bold IN aStyle.tsFace);
      CheckItem(styleMenu, italicItem, italic IN aStyle.tsFace);
      {Set other menu items appropriately.}
   END
   ELSE
   BEGIN
      {No text face is common to the entire selection.}
      CheckItem(styleMenu, plainItem, FALSE);
      CheckItem(styleMenu, boldItem, FALSE);
      CheckItem(styleMenu, italicItem, FALSE);
      {Set other menu items appropriately.}
   END;
END;
```

You can also use TEContinuousStyle to determine the actual values for those attributes that are continuous for the selection. Note that a field in the text style record is only valid if the corresponding bit is set in the mode variable; otherwise, the field contains invalid information. Listing 15-2 illustrates how you might use TEContinuousStyle to determine the font, face, size, and color of the current selection.

Listing 15-2. Determining the font, face, size, and color of the current selection

```
VAR
   mode:        Integer;
   continuous: Boolean;
   aStyle:      TextStyle;
   myTE:        TEHandle;
BEGIN
   mode := doFont + doFace + doSize + doColor;
   continuous := TEContinuousStyle(mode, aStyle, myTE);
   IF BitAnd(mode, doFont) <> 0 THEN
      {font for selection = aStyle.tsFont}
   ELSE
      {more than one font in selection};

   IF BitAnd(mode, doFace) <> 0 THEN
      {aStyle.tsFace contains the text faces (or plain) that }
      { are common to the selection.}
   ELSE
      {No text face is common to the entire selection.};

   IF BitAnd(mode, doSize) <> 0 THEN
      {size for selection = aStyle.tsSize}
   ELSE
      {more than one size in selection};

   IF BitAnd(mode, doColor) <> 0 THEN
      {color for selection = aStyle.tsColor}
   ELSE
      {more than one color in selection};

END;
```

When TEContinuousStyle returns a mode that contains doFace and returns an aStyle parameter with a tsFace field of [bold, italic], it means that the selected text is all bold and all italic, but may contain other text faces as well. None of the other faces applies to all of the selected text, or it would have been included in the tsFace field. But if the tsFace field is the empty set, then all of the selected text is plain.

If the current selection range is an insertion point, TEContinuousStyle returns the style information for the next character to be typed. TEContinuousStyle always returns TRUE in this case, and each field of the text style record is set if the corresponding bit in the mode parameter was set. If hTE is a handle to an unstyled edit record, TEContinuousStyle returns the simple style information of the entire record.

Setting Styles in TextEdit's Scrap Record

The SetStylScrap procedure, new with system software version 6.0, performs the opposite function of the GetStylScrap function.

```
PROCEDURE SetStylScrap (rangeStart: LongInt; rangeEnd: LongInt;
                        newStyles: StScrpHandle; redraw: Boolean;
                        hTE: TEHandle);
```

The SetStylScrap procedure uses the newStyles parameter (a handle to a style scrap record) and sets its style information into the style scrap record for a range of text specified by rangeStart and rangeEnd. If newStyles is NIL or hTE is a handle to an unstyled edit record, SetStylScrap does nothing.

If the redraw parameter is TRUE, the text is redrawn to reflect this new style information; and line breaks, line heights, and line ascents are recalculated. Otherwise, this new information is not reflected in the view rectangle until the TEUpdate procedure is called. Regardless of whether the text is redrawn, the current selection range is not changed. So if characters are highlighted before SetStylScrap is called, they remain highlighted after it is called. They also reflect the new style information if redraw was TRUE and if they were within the range of the specified text.

Each element in the style scrap record contains a scrpStartChar field that is the offset to the start of the element's style. As with the style run array, the scrpStartChar field defines the boundaries for the scrap's style runs. SetStylScrap applies the first element's style to the characters from rangeStart up to the scrpStartChar field of the next element.

SetStylScrap terminates without error if it prematurely reaches the end of the range or if there are not enough scrap style elements to cover the whole range. In the latter case, SetStylScrap applies the last style in the style scrap record to the remainder of the range.

Determining the Number of Styles

The TENumStyles function returns the number of style changes contained in the given range, counting one for the start of the range. Note that this number does not necessarily represent the number of unique styles for the range because some styles may be repeated. For unstyled edit records, TENumStyles always returns 1.

```
FUNCTION TENumStyles (rangeStart: LongInt; rangeEnd: LongInt;
                      hTE: TEHandle) : LongInt;
```

The rangeStart and rangeEnd parameters indicate the range. The text containing the range is specified by the hTE parameter, a handle to the edit record.

You can use TENumStyles to calculate the amount of memory that would be required if TECut or TECopy were called. Since the style scrap record is linear in nature, with one element for each style change, you can multiply the result that TENumStyles returns by SizeOf(ScrpSTElement) and add 2 to get the amount of memory needed.

TEXTEDIT DATA STRUCTURES

This section supplies a brief overview of the contents of the various TextEdit data structures and their relationships. Figure 15-20 shows how the TextEdit data structures create an environment for the editing of unstyled or styled text through the use of an edit record and a style record. It also portrays a number of supporting data structures, including a style run table, a line-height table, a null style record, a style scrap record, and a dispatch record.

> **Note:** Use the information in this diagram and in the explanations that follow only for debugging so you understand the organization of the TextEdit data structures. For reading or writing of these data structures, use the TextEdit routines. This practice will ensure future compatibility.

Refer to the TextEdit chapters in Volumes I and V for more in-depth discussions of the TextEdit data structures.

Here is a list of the functions and relationships of the TextEdit data structures:

- The edit record, defined by the TERec data type, stores the display and editing information for TextEdit.
- The style record, defined by the TEStyleRec data type, stores the style information for the text of the edit record. If an edit record has associated style information, its txFont and txFace fields combine to hold a style handle, TEStyleHandle, to its style record.
- The style run table, defined by the StyleRun data type, is an array that contains the boundaries of each style run and an index to its style information in the style element array.
- The style element array, defined by the TEStyleTable data type, contains one entry for each distinct style used in the text of the edit record. Each style entry is defined by the STElement data type. The styleTab field of the style record contains a handle, STHandle, to this style element array. The styleIndex field in the style run array is an index into this data structure.
- The line-height table, defined by the LHTable data type, provides an array of line heights to hold the vertical spacing information for a given edit record. It also contains line ascent information. TextEdit uses this table only if the lineHeight field in the edit record is negative. The lhTab field of the style record contains a handle to this line-height table. A line number is a direct index into this array.
- The null style record, defined by the NullStRec data type, contains the style information for a null selection. The nullStyle field of the style record contains a handle to this null style record.
- The style scrap record, defined by the StScrpRec data type, is a place to store style information in the desk scrap. The scrap style table array within this record, defined by the ScrpStyleTab data type, contains a separate data structure for style records in the scrap. The nullScrap field of the null style record contains a handle, STScrpHandle, to the scrap style table.

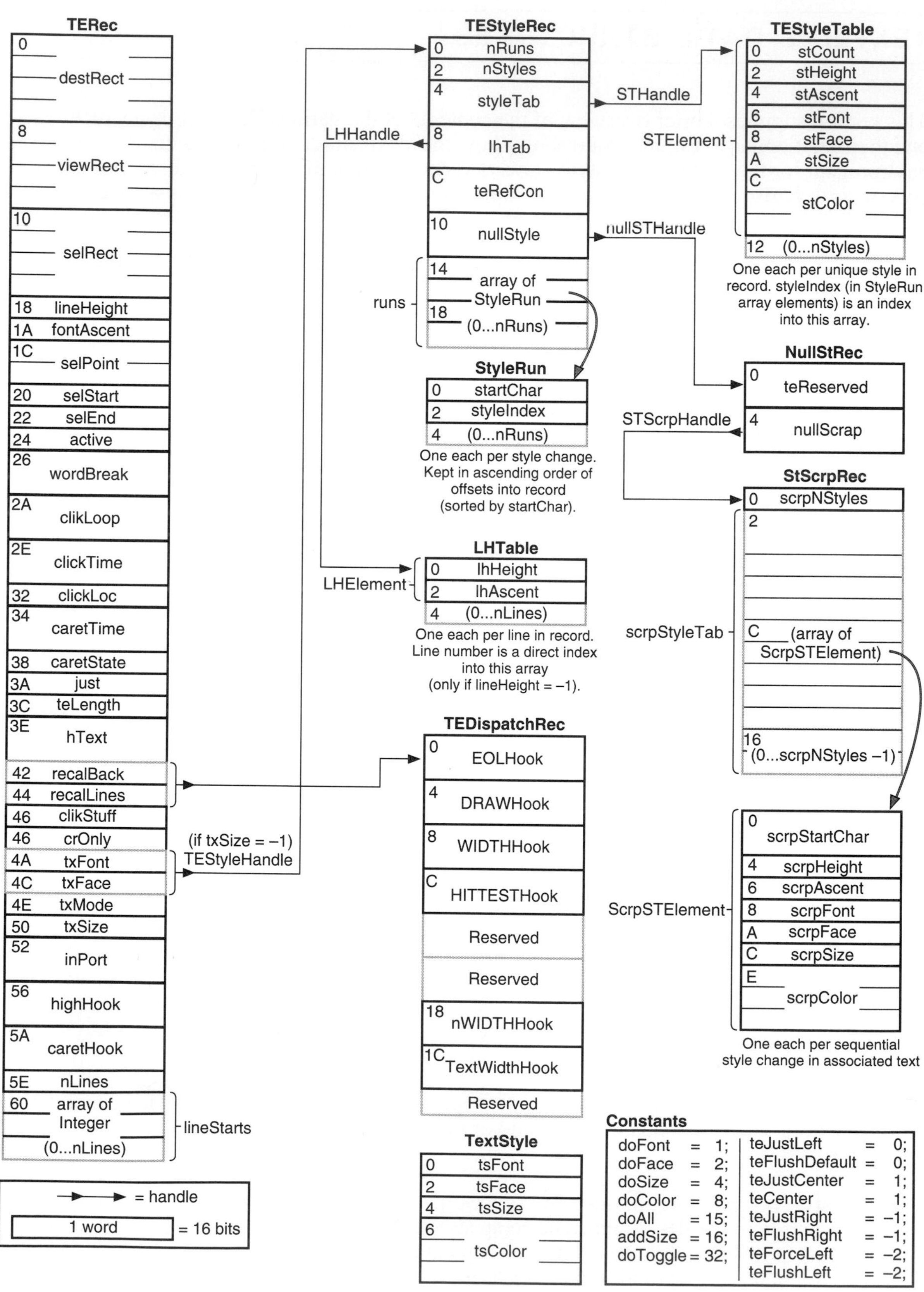

Figure 15-20. The TextEdit data structures

- The scrap style table, defined by the ScrpStyleTab data type, is contained in the style scrap record. The elements of this table are style records defined by the scrap style element record.

- The scrap style element record, defined by the ScrpSTElement data type, contains the style information for an element in the scrap style table and is similar to the style element array. One scrap style element record exists for each sequential style change in the scrap style table.

- The TextEdit dispatch record, defined by the TEDispatchRec data type, contains the internal addresses of the TextEdit routines for EOLHook, DRAWHook, WIDTHHook, HITTESTHook, nWIDTHHook, and TextWidthHook unless you replace them with the addresses of your own customized versions of these routines. TextEdit combines the recalBack and recalLines fields of the edit record to store a handle to the TextEdit dispatch record.

- The text style record, defined by the TextStyle data type, furnishes a record of text styles for communicating information between your application and the TextEdit routines.

▲ **Warning:** The space beyond the hooks in the TextEdit dispatch record is reserved for internal use. If you attempt to use this private area, you will corrupt TextEdit data. ▲

SUMMARY OF TEXTEDIT

Constants

```
CONST {constants for Gestalt function}
      gestaltTE1 = 1;     {U.S. system software version 6.0.4 containing }
                          { TextEdit on a Macintosh IIci}
      gestaltTE2 = 2;     {version 6.0.4 non-Roman script system containing }
                          { a Script Manager-compatible version of }
                          { TextEdit including the new measuring hook }
                          { nWIDTHHook for the Macintosh IIci}
      gestaltTE3 = 3;     {version 6.0.4 non-Roman script system containing }
                          { a Script Manager-compatible version of }
                          { TextEdit including the new measuring hook }
                          { nWIDTHHook for Macintosh Plus, }
                          { Macintosh SE, Macintosh SE/30, }
                          { Macintosh II, Macintosh Portable, }
                          { Macintosh IIx, or Macintosh IIcx}
      gestaltTE4 = 4;     {system software versions 6.0.5 and later, }
                          { which contain a Script Manager-compatible }
                          { version of TextEdit, including the new measuring}
                          { hook nWIDTHHook & the outline-highlighting & }
                          { text-buffering features, on any Macintosh}
      gestaltTE5 = 5;     {system software version 7.0, which contains a }
                          { Script Manager-compatible version of TextEdit }
                          { including the new measuring hooks, nWIDTHHook }
                          { & TextWidthHook, outline highlighting, text }
                          { buffering, features for inline input, & }
                          { capability to disable inline input}

      {new constant names for the just parameter of TESetJust procedure}
      teFlushRight        = -1;      {flush right for all scripts }
                                     { — corresponds to teJustRight}
      teFlushLeft         = -2;      {flush left for all scripts }
                                     { — corresponds to teForceLeft}
      teCenter            =  1;      {centered for all scripts }
                                     { — corresponds to teJustCenter}
      teFlushDefault      =  0;      {flush according to line direction }
                                     { — corresponds to teJustLeft}

      {constants for TEFeatureFlag feature parameter values}
      teFTextBuffering   = 1;        {text buffering}
      teFOutlineHilite   = 2;        {outline highlighting}
      teFInlineInput     = 3;        {inline input features}
      teFUseTextServices = 4;        {use inline input service}
```

```
{constants for TEFeatureFlag action parameter values}
TEBitClear          = 0;        {clear TEFeatureFlag features}
TEBitSet            = 1;        {set TEFeatureFlag features}
TEBitTest           = -1;       {test TEFeatureFlag features}

{selectors for TECustomHook}
intEOLHook          = 0;        {end-of-line hook}
intDrawHook         = 1;        {drawing hook}
intWidthHook        = 2;        {width measurement hook}
intHitTestHook      = 3;        {hit text hook}
intNWidthHook       = 6;        {new width measurement hook }
                                { nWIDTHHook}
intTextWidthHook    = 7;        {new width measurement hook }
                                { TextWidthHook}

{constants for identifying the routine that called FindWord }
teWordSelect        = 4;        {called for determining new }
                                { line breaks}
teWordDrag          = 8;        {called for extending word selection}
teFromFind          = 12;       {called for word selection}
teFromRecal         = 16;       {called for word breaking in line }
                                { recalculation}

{values for TESetStyle/TEContinuousStyle modes}
doFont              = 1;        {set font (family) number}
doFace              = 2;        {set character style}
doSize              = 4;        {set type size}
doColor             = 8;        {set color}
doAll               = 15;       {set all attributes}
addSize             = 16;       {adjust type size}
doToggle            = 32;       {toggle mode for TESetStyle }
                                { and TEContinuousStyle}

{offsets into TEDispatchRec}
EOLHook             = 0;        {[ProcPtr] TEEOLHook}
DRAWHook            = 4;        {[ProcPtr] TEWidthHook}
WIDTHHook           = 8;        {[ProcPtr] TEDrawHook}
HITTESTHook         = 12;       {[ProcPtr] TEHitTestHook}
nWIDTHHook          = 24;       {[ProcPtr] nTEWidthHook}
TextWidthHook       = 28;       {[ProcPtr] TETextWidthHook}
```

Data Type

```
TYPE  TEIntHook = Integer;
```

Routines

Outline Highlighting, Text Buffering, and Inline Input

```
FUNCTION TEFeatureFlag      (feature: Integer; action: Integer;
                             hTE: TEHandle) : Integer;
```

Customizing TextEdit

```
PROCEDURE TECustomHook      (which: TEIntHook; VAR addr: ProcPtr;
                             hTE: TEHandle);
```

Backspacing to the Beginning of a Style

```
PROCEDURE TEKey             (key: Char; hTE: TEHandle);
```

Determining the Position of an Ambiguous Offset

```
FUNCTION TEGetPoint         (offset: Integer; hTE: TEHandle) : Point;
```

Toggling a Style

```
PROCEDURE TESetStyle        (mode: Integer; newStyle: TextStyle;
                             redraw: Boolean; hTE: TEHandle);
```

Determining Styles Across a Selection

```
FUNCTION TEContinuousStyle  (VAR mode: Integer; VAR aStyle: TextStyle; hTE:
                             TEHandle) : Boolean;
```

Setting Styles in TextEdit's Scrap Record

```
PROCEDURE SetStylScrap      (rangeStart: LongInt; rangeEnd: LongInt;
                             newStyles: StScrpHandle; redraw: Boolean;
                             hTE: TEHandle);
```

Determining the Number of Styles

```
FUNCTION TENumStyles        (rangeStart: LongInt; rangeEnd: LongInt;
                             hTE: TEHandle) : LongInt;
```

Global Variables

WordRedraw	$BA5	Used for line calculations to determine how much of a line must be redrawn after a character is entered.
TEFindWord	$7F8	The low-memory address for TextEdit's word breaking routine.
TESysJust	$BAC	The system alignment whose default value is set by the last installed script.

Assembly-Language Information

Trap Macros Requiring Routine Selectors

_TEDispatch

Selector	Routine
$0001	TESetStyle
$0008	TEGetPoint
$000A	TEContinuousStyle
$000B	SetStylScrap
$000C	TECustomHook
$000D	TeNumStyles
$000E	TEFeatureFlag

16 GRAPHICS OVERVIEW

ABOUT THIS CHAPTER

This chapter presents an overview of Macintosh® graphics. It surveys the components and processes of Color QuickDraw™, the other graphics managers with which it interacts, and how colors flow from your application to the screen.

Read the information in this chapter if your application uses color or gray scales. To use this chapter, you should have a basic understanding of the original QuickDraw described in Volume I, but need not have read any other graphics chapters in this or other volumes of *Inside Macintosh*. Figure 16-1 charts your path into the world of Macintosh graphics.

ABOUT MACINTOSH GRAPHICS

Macintosh graphics begin with QuickDraw and end with glowing phosphor. The early Macintosh systems, with their built-in screens and integral graphics hardware, made well-defined and comparatively limited demands on your understanding of graphics: if you learned QuickDraw, you were set.

The Macintosh II computer introduced two features that greatly increased graphics capabilities: slots and color. **Slots** allow the addition of specialized hardware to the system. (In the original Macintosh II, the graphics hardware was always added in NuBus™ standard slots. Current systems allow a number of hardware expansion modes in addition to NuBus slots.)

With slots, the characteristics of the output device can vary from machine to machine. With color, the extent of variation can be very great: screens not only can vary in horizontal and vertical dimensions, but they can also vary in depth. To the single-bit-per-pixel depth of the original Macintosh systems, the Macintosh II added pixel depths of 2, 4, and 8 bits. Output devices range from black-and-white systems to cards and screens capable of presenting hundreds of colors from palettes of millions. Furthermore, users can combine screens: a user may move your application's window so that it overlaps screens of very different characteristics.

To remove the burden of worrying about output devices (for most applications), Color QuickDraw is device-independent. Applications using color can work in an abstract color space defined by three axes of red, green, and blue (RGB). Your application can specify a color as an RGB value, in which each component is defined as a 16-bit integer. Color QuickDraw compares such a 48-bit value with the colors actually available on the hardware at execution time and chooses the closest match. Precolor applications and those not concerned with color or gray-scale graphics need not change, and those concerned only with straightforward color usage can ignore the problems of output devices.

When the Macintosh II was introduced, the maximum pixel value was limited to a single byte. Each pixel's byte can specify one of 256 (2^8) different values, and, rather than simply truncating the least significant bits of each component to get a color, Color QuickDraw treats such pixel values as indexes into a color table. If your application asks for a 48-bit RGB color, the Color Manager examines the colors available in the card. If the video device

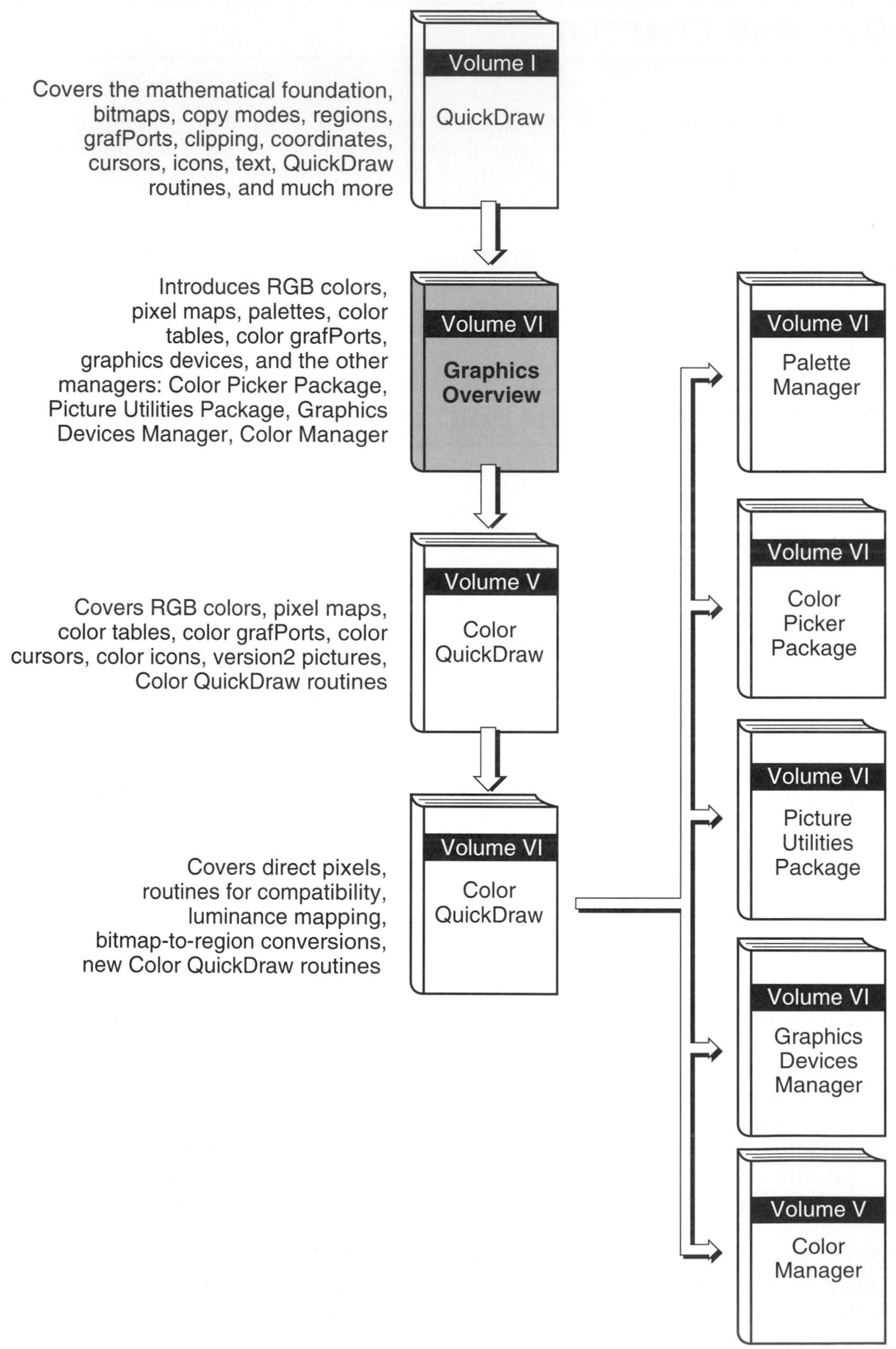

Figure 16-1. Macintosh graphics chapters

supports 8 bits per pixel, the card contains a color look-up table (CLUT) with 256 entries, each entry an RGB value. The Color Manager determines which RGB value is closest to the requested color and tells Color QuickDraw what the index for that color is.

Storage and movement of such indexed color values require a maximum of 8 bits, rather than 48, saving space and time. (The RAM needed to hold a 640-by-480 pixel screen at 8 bits per pixel is about 300,000 bytes.) And because the table is variable—it can be loaded with different colors—applications can display up to 16 million colors, although only 256 different colors can appear at once.

With the addition of direct pixel values, first made available with system software version 6.0.5, the 256 simultaneous color limit has been removed. Color QuickDraw can now also process **direct pixel** values, which use 16 or 32 bits to directly represent a color. Using direct color not only removes much of the complexity of the color table mechanism, but it also allows the display of thousands or millions of colors simultaneously, resulting in near-photographic realism.

The device-independence of Color QuickDraw is such that on a three-screen system—for example, with displays for gray-scale indexed pixels, color indexed pixels, and direct pixels—the user can move your window to span all three devices and each will show its best representation of your image.

This overview introduces Color QuickDraw and the related graphics managers with which it works.

- Color QuickDraw calls upon the Color Manager to map color requests to the actual colors available. Most applications never need to call the Color Manager directly.
- The Palette Manager allows your application to specify the set of colors that it needs on a window-by-window basis, and makes the colors available (within application-determined ranges) in a graceful manner.
- The Color Picker Package allows your application to solicit a color choice from the user in a standard way.
- The Picture Utilities Package provides routines with which your application can extract information, such as pixel depth and colors used, from pixel maps and pictures.
- The Graphics Devices Manager offers routines for preparing images offscreen, and it manages the data structures that track the characteristics of the graphics hardware of a particular system.
- The Slot Manager controls communication with expansion boards of all types, including video cards.

The rest of this chapter

- introduces the basic graphics components and further defines the differences between indexed and direct pixel images
- presents overviews of the important color graphics data structures: the color tables and palettes that hold colors, the pixel maps that hold information about images, the color grafPorts that hold information about windows, and the graphics device records that describe the capabilities of a particular screen

- describes the startup process as it applies to graphics, to show how the data structures are created and initialized
- traces the path of a user's request for a color through the graphics system and onto a screen, in both the indexed and direct pixel systems
- tells you how to determine which version of QuickDraw is actually running

THE COMPONENTS OF MACINTOSH GRAPHICS

Broadly speaking, a Macintosh graphics system has three parts: QuickDraw, the video card and screen that constitute the display device, and the interface between them.

QuickDraw

QuickDraw comes in three varieties: the original version offered with systems equipped with a 68000 microprocessor; the original Color QuickDraw, which appeared with the Macintosh II; and the current Color QuickDraw, which was introduced as 32-Bit QuickDraw and is now part of system software version 7.0.

In general, applications that use the original QuickDraw routines are compatible with all Macintosh systems. Applications using the original Color QuickDraw work even better under the new Color QuickDraw. But applications that use Color QuickDraw routines cannot execute under the original QuickDraw, nor can applications using direct pixel images run on the original Color QuickDraw.

Note that the original QuickDraw contains a simple eight-color system that is compatible with all machines (although the colors cannot be displayed on early black-and-white systems), so if your application needs eight colors or fewer, you can maximize compatibility by using that system, which is described in the QuickDraw chapter of Volume I.

Whenever possible, earlier versions of QuickDraw have been upgraded with later features. For example, later versions of the original QuickDraw can process pictures that include color information. Although such QuickDraw versions cannot display color, they display the best black-and-white approximation possible.

The Interface

Figure 16-2 shows how QuickDraw, the other graphics managers, and the graphics hardware interrelate.

The Monitors control panel lets users arrange their screens in relation to each other in space (above or below, side by side) and select how many colors, if any, a device is to display.

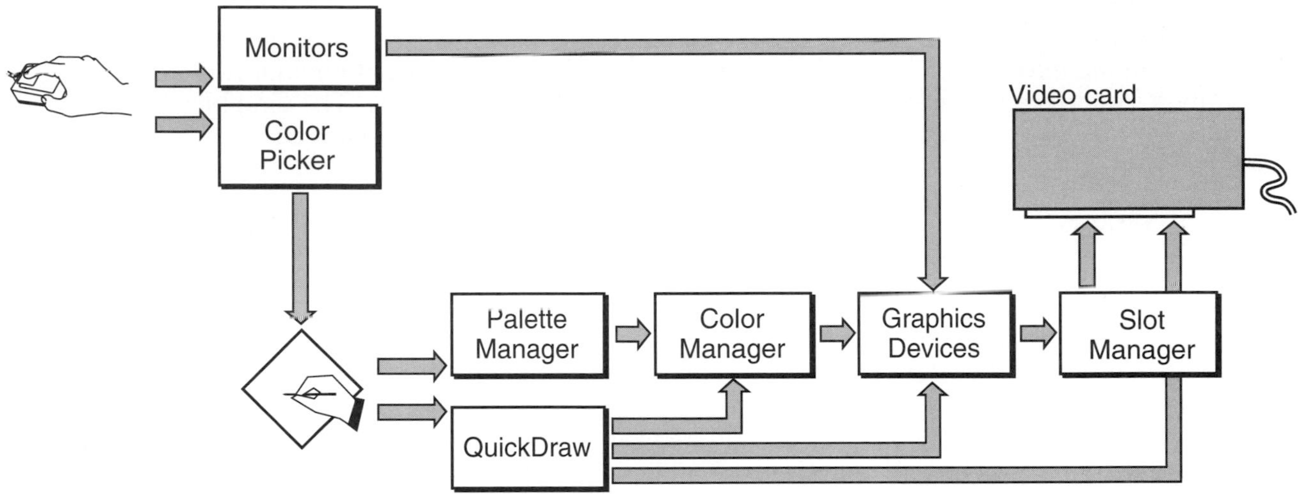

Figure 16-2. QuickDraw and the graphics managers

The Color Picker Package offers you a standard way to present the user with a color-selection dialog box. The Color Picker's wheel and slide controls let the user preview and select any color the hardware can produce. (The Color control panel, for example, uses the Color Picker to let the user choose a highlight color to be used on the desktop.)

The Monitors control panel and the Color Picker are user interface modules that demonstrate an important axiom: *the user is in charge.* The user can select any one of trillions of colors through the Color Picker, and that same user may set the color device to show only black and white pixels.

The Palette Manager provides a set of routines with which you can create and control the set of colors needed by your application window. Palettes are especially important with indexed screen devices, which support only displays that show a maximum of 256 colors at once. Since all or parts of several applications and the desktop may be visible on the screen, and they may all have different color schemes, contention can arise for those 256 table places. The Palette Manager can arbitrate among the contenders and automatically see that the color requirements of the frontmost, or active, window are met first.

And no matter how wild a neon-blacklit-backlit effect you create, the Palette Manager restores graphics order when your application terminates.

The Palette Manager and Color QuickDraw both use the low-level graphics abilities of the Color Manager to find the best color available when all color table indexes are taken and another color is needed on the screen. The Color Manager examines the available colors and determines which of them is closest to the requested color. If your application needs to paint a race car British racing green, for example, you can ask for it by using a Color QuickDraw routine, and hope that whatever the Color Manager finds available is a close enough match to look good. Or you can ask the Palette Manager for the color and specify how close the match has to be. If no color comes as close as you like, the Palette Manager loads the exact color you requested into the color table for the device.

The Graphics Devices Manager and the Slot Manager are the final links to the video driver and its card. The Slot Manager examines every installed card when the system starts up, and from the information the cards supply, the Slot Manager supplies QuickDraw and the graphics interface managers with the information they need to operate. The Graphics Devices Manager manages the record that describes the capabilities of the graphics card.

The Video Card and Screen

Your application can declare colors in RGB space, but what the user finally sees depends on the characteristics of the actual video card and screen. Screens may display color or black and white, and have indexed pixels of 2-bit, 4-bit, or 8-bit bit depths, or direct pixels of 16-bit or 32-bit depths.

Preparing an image for display in the original QuickDraw means preparing a bitmap, which specifies the memory arrangement of the bits that describe whether each pixel on a screen is to be on or off. Specifying on or off takes just 1 bit. You can describe the state of 8 pixels in a single byte. Entire black-and-white screen images can be stored in what is now considered a modest amount of memory.

Preparing a color or gray-scale image requires a pixel map, where more than one bit may be assigned to determine the color of each screen pixel. Two bits per pixel provide indexes into a table of four colors, but if two colors are black and white, only two other hues can be shown. A four-index color table might contain the following entries.

Index	**Color**
00	White (turn all three RGB phosphors full on)
01	Gray (turn all three on halfway)
10	Pale blue for highlighting (turn all three on, but use more blue)
11	Black (turn all of them off)

If a 2-bit memory space representing a pixel had a value of 00, the resulting screen pixel would be white. The sequence 10 10 10 10 would use the third entry in the table to generate a series of pale blue pixels on the screen.

Four bits can provide indexes into a table of 16 colors, a number sufficient for many straightforward graphics purposes, such as charts, presentations, or displaying flags of the nations.

Using a byte (8 bits) for each pixel, 256 colors can be displayed, which for many images is enough to produce near-photographic quality. The problem is that the colors good for one near-photographic image may not be good for another. Rembrandt's browns and umbers don't do much for a still from *The Wizard of Oz.* To solve this problem, the Macintosh II video card uses a variable color table (rather than a fixed one). You can display Rembrandt with one set of 256 colors, then reload the table for another image.

The main reason for using variable color tables is that a relatively small index value is sufficient to specify any one color out of a palette of millions. You need less RAM to store an image and less time to move it around than if you use large RGB values directly. An extra benefit is color table animation, by which your application can change colors on the screen without actually reassigning pixel values. (By changing the colors of the 256 entries of an 8-bit table, you change all the screen's colors—without any changes in screen memory.) Drawbacks are that since only 256 colors can appear on the screen at once, windows must compete for colors, and pairing an RGB request to the closest actual color in the table requires the complex inverse-table matching scheme implemented by the Color Manager.

Video boards that implement direct pixels, in which the pixel value specifies an RGB color rather than an index into a table of colors, eliminate the competition for limited table spaces and remove the need for color table matching. The direct pixel system is simpler. The cost is larger amounts of RAM needed to hold the larger pixel values; the benefit—thousands and even millions of colors on the screen at once—is worth the cost for many applications, some of which would not exist without such a capability.

THE MAJOR DATA STRUCTURES

Understanding Macintosh graphics is easier with some knowledge of the data structures that hold the information and define the graphics environment. QuickDraw supplies routines for querying and altering the fields of these data structures; you should not alter them directly. (If you have existing programs that change fields directly, see the Color QuickDraw chapter in this volume for a description of routines that you can use to notify QuickDraw of such changes.)

The smallest place to begin is the RGB color record, which holds a single color.

The RGB Color Record

The RGB color record consists of three 16-bit values, one each for red, green, and blue.

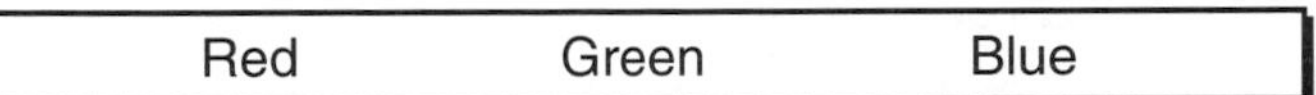

Your application can specify RGB colors, and the graphics system will find the closest matching color on the target hardware. To draw a yellow line, for example, you might set the foreground pen to an RGB color in which the red and green values are high and the blue value is low, such as (to take the brightest example) $FFFF FFFF 0000.

If the red, green, and blue values are equal, the resulting color is black (if they are 0), white (if they are at or close to $FFFF), or gray (if they are in between).

Color Collections

RGB color records are included in two forms of collective color sets: the color table and the palette. Each associates additional information with the RGB color record.

A **color table** consists of a header containing flags and information such as the size of the table, and a number of RGB color records, each record preceded by a value. The RGB color plus a value is defined as a color specification record. (See "Summary of Graphics Data Types" at the end of this chapter for Pascal definitions of these data structures.) The value has one of two uses, depending on a header flag. If the color table belongs to a pixel map, the value is the color's index.

There are five RGB colors in this table			
Value	Red	Green	Blue
Value	Red	Green	Blue
Value	Red	Green	Blue
Value	Red	Green	Blue
Value	Red	Green	Blue

The other form in which colors are usefully gathered is the **palette,** a color collection of colors that can be used by a window. A palette comprises a header and a collection of color information records, which contain RGB colors with information about how the colors are to be used and how closely the graphics system must match them.

There are four entries in this palette				
Red	Green	Blue	Usage	Tolerance
Red	Green	Blue	Usage	Tolerance
Red	Green	Blue	Usage	Tolerance
Red	Green	Blue	Usage	Tolerance

The Palette Manager manipulates both color tables and palettes, and it has routines for converting one into the other. By using the Palette Manager, your application can exercise exquisite control of color allocation. For example, you can specify the usage information in a palette such that a selected set of colors appears if the window is displayed on an 8-bit-deep screen, and another set of colors appears if the window is displayed on a 4-bit-deep screen. The Palette Manager has sets of default colors for different pixel depths, so that a screen will return to a well-balanced state after gaudy applications terminate. See the Palette Manager chapter in this volume for more information on creating and manipulating palettes.

The Pixel Map Record

The **pixel map** is the modern successor to the bitmap: to that original image-mapping record, the pixel map record adds information about the depth of the pixels that make up an image. In black-and-white systems, such as the original Macintosh computers, only 1 bit was needed per pixel, since black and white can be indicated by 0 and 1. Color QuickDraw now recognizes pixel depths of 1, 2, 4, 8, 16, and 32 bits. The pixel map not only describes the pixel depth; it also specifies how each pixel's information is organized: either as indexes to color tables or as direct color specifications.

The pixel map record is defined in the Color QuickDraw chapter of Volume V. The Color QuickDraw chapter in this volume explains how some fields can have additional values, although the format of the pixel map record is unchanged.

Field	Description
baseAddr	Pointer to the image data
rowBytes	Flags, and bytes in a row
bounds	Boundary rectangle
pmVersion	Pixel map version number
packType	Packing format
packSize	Size of data in packed state
hRes	Horizontal resolution in dots per inch
vRes	Vertical resolution in dots per inch
pixelType	Format of pixel image
pixelSize	Physical bits per pixel
cmpCount	Number of components in each pixel
cmpSize	Number of bits in each component
planeBytes	Offset to next plane
pmTable	Handle to a color table for this image

As in a bitmap record, the baseAddr, rowBytes, and bounds fields describe where in memory the image information begins, how many bytes are used for each row of the image, and its boundary rectangle.

The hRes and vRes fields describe the horizontal and vertical resolution of the image. For example, images destined for display on a screen might be set to 72 dots per inch (dpi) in each direction; those prepared for printing on a LaserWriter® might be set to 300 dpi.

The pixelType field indicates whether the pixel values for the image are to be treated as indexes to a color table or taken as the real color.

The pixelSize field shows the size of each pixel value in memory: 1, 2, 4, or 8 bits for indexed pixel values, and 16 or 32 bits for direct pixel values.

Indexed pixels have one component, the index value. Direct pixels have three components, one each for red, green, and blue. The cmpCount field contains either 1 or 3, accordingly.

The cmpSize field lists the component sizes: 1, 2, 4, or 8 bits for the single component of an indexed pixel, and 5 or 8 bits for each component in a direct pixel. (The three direct pixel components are the same size, either 5-5-5 or 8-8-8 for the red, green, and blue values.)

The pmTable field contains a handle to the color table for this image. Since indexed pixel values are just that, indexes, a color table needs to be bundled with each pixel map to show what color each index value indicates. (Pixel map records for direct pixel values don't need tables, since the image memory contains the actual colors, but the pmTable field references a dummy table for compatibility.)

Pixel map records are key elements of the last two data structures discussed in this chapter: color grafPort records, which describes graphics ports, such as windows, and the graphics device records, which describe output devices, such as screens.

Port Characteristics: The Color GrafPort Record

The **color grafPort** contains the information Color QuickDraw needs to maintain a color drawing environment for a window. Most or all of the color grafPort records you need are created for you by the Window Manager.

The color grafPort record is fully described in the Color QuickDraw chapter of Volume V.

A color grafPort contains much more information than its immediate ancestor, the grafPort, but for compatibility it has maintained the same size by using pointers to other information. Like the grafPort, it contains such essential information as where the pen is currently positioned and how big it is, what font to draw with, and what parts of a window are currently visible.

The portPixMap field, located in the same relative position as the grafPort's portBits field, contains a handle to the pixel map record that defines the image for the port. Since a pixel map record contains a reference to a color table, a color grafPort has its own set of colors.

The last field in the color grafPort record is a pointer to the low-level Color QuickDraw drawing routines, which some graphics applications intercept, usually to add a preprocessing or postprocessing flourish. Some applications intercept the routines while examining a version 2 picture file (the format used to store pictures) so that they can watch the picture's drawing commands and intercept those of special interest.

Although most color grafPort records are created and maintained by the Window Manager, which includes a color grafPort record within a color window record, you can also create grafPorts that aren't attached to any window. By using an offscreen grafPort you can prepare an image offscreen and then pop it into view when it's complete. This tactic may make updates

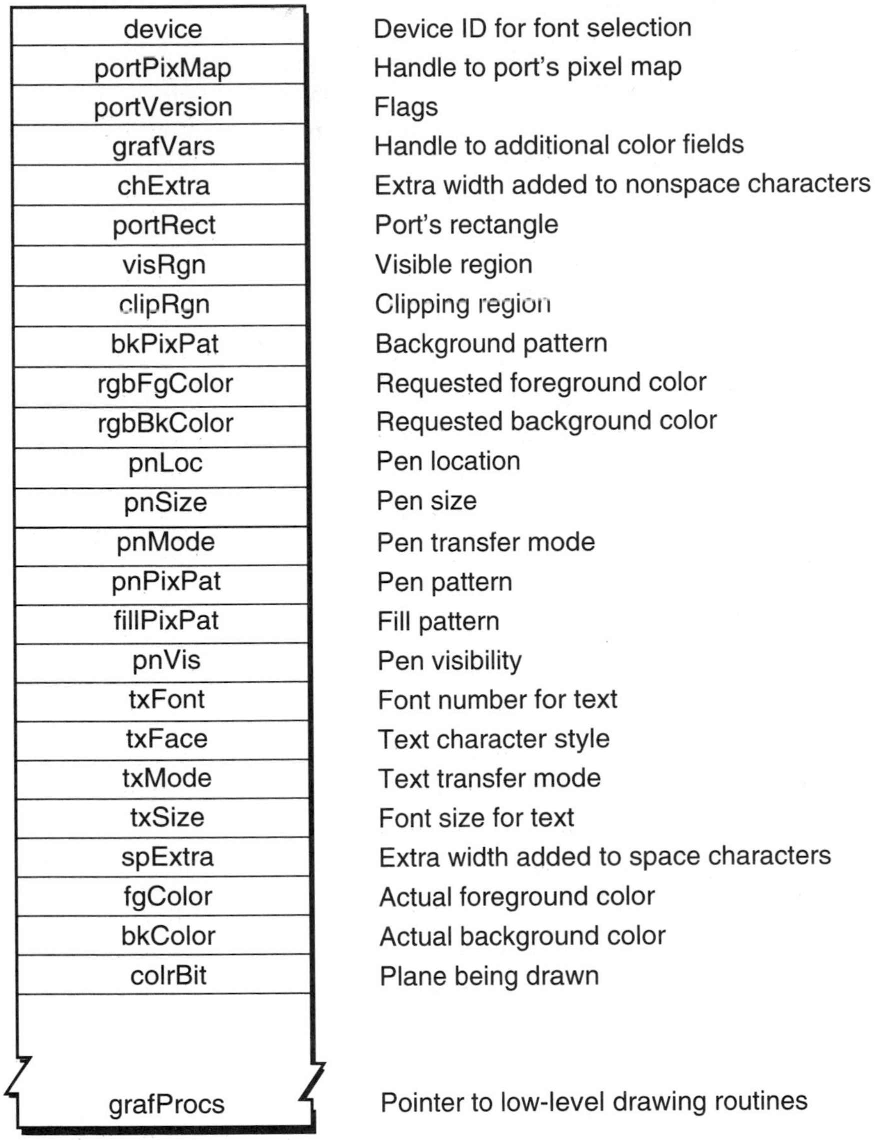

Field	Description
device	Device ID for font selection
portPixMap	Handle to port's pixel map
portVersion	Flags
grafVars	Handle to additional color fields
chExtra	Extra width added to nonspace characters
portRect	Port's rectangle
visRgn	Visible region
clipRgn	Clipping region
bkPixPat	Background pattern
rgbFgColor	Requested foreground color
rgbBkColor	Requested background color
pnLoc	Pen location
pnSize	Pen size
pnMode	Pen transfer mode
pnPixPat	Pen pattern
fillPixPat	Fill pattern
pnVis	Pen visibility
txFont	Font number for text
txFace	Text character style
txMode	Text transfer mode
txSize	Font size for text
spExtra	Extra width added to space characters
fgColor	Actual foreground color
bkColor	Actual background color
colrBit	Plane being drawn
grafProcs	Pointer to low-level drawing routines

faster in situations where recreating the contents of the screen is time consuming. The process is greatly simplified with the offscreen graphics routines, described in the Graphics Devices Manager chapter of this volume.

Device Characteristics: The Graphics Device Record

The color grafPort record contains information about a window, but there can be many windows on a screen, and even many screens. The **graphics device record** is the data structure that holds information about the physical characteristics of a drawing environment.

Like the grafPort, the graphics device record is created automatically for you: the Graphics Devices Manager uses information supplied by the Slot Manager to create a graphics device record for each device found in a slot card during startup.

Color QuickDraw needs ready access to a number of characteristics of the display devices. It collects this vital information in the graphics device record, whose contents can be manipulated by a set of routines described in the Graphics Devices Manager chapter in this volume. These routines issue standard device control calls to the card's device-specific driver, which set and query characteristics such as pixel depth. The Graphics Devices Manager routines are also responsible for updating the graphics device records.

Much of the information in a graphics device record is too esoteric for an overview, and the new offscreen graphics routines (described in the Graphics Devices Manager chapter in this volume) provide a procedural interface to its fields. But a look at this last link is important in the conceptual chain.

Field	Description
gdRefNum	Reference number of driver
gdID	Client ID for search procedure
gdType	Type of device (indexed, direct)
gdITable	Handle to inverse table for Color Manager
gdResPref	Preferred resolution
gdSearchProc	Handle to list of search functions
gdCompProc	Handle to list of complement functions
gdFlags	Graphics device flags
gdPMap	Handle to pixel map for displayed image
gdRefCon	Reference value
gdNextGD	Handle to next graphics device record
gdRect	Device's global bounds
gdMode	Device's current mode

The gdITable field points to an inverse table, which the Color Manager creates and maintains, and uses to quickly find the nearest match for a requested color. (The technique is described in the Color Manager chapter of Volume V.) The process is very fast once the table is built, but if a color is changed in the device's CLUT, the Color Manager must rebuild the inverse table the next time it has to find a color. Using high tolerance values in the palettes associated with your windows, rather than always demanding exact matches to your colors, lessens the recalculations required. (For an explanation of tolerance values, see the Palette Manager chapter in this volume.)

The gdPMap field contains a handle to the pixel map that reflects the imaging capabilities of the device. The pixel map's type, size, and component fields indicate whether the device is direct or indexed and what pixel depth it displays. The pixel map's color table is synchronized with the CLUT on the device.

The gdRect field describes the device's bounds in global coordinates.

If you want to work with offscreen graphics that have characteristics different from those of the actual devices on the system, you can use the offscreen graphics world routines to create and maintain offscreen port and device records. (See the Graphics Devices Manager chapter in this volume.)

GRAPHICS INITIALIZATION

In the initialization process, illustrated in Figure 16-3, the firmware in a video card's ROM supplies information about what sort of graphics device it is (indexed or direct), how much card RAM is available, and so on. Some of this information is stored in the graphics device record for that card, where it is available to the entire graphics system.

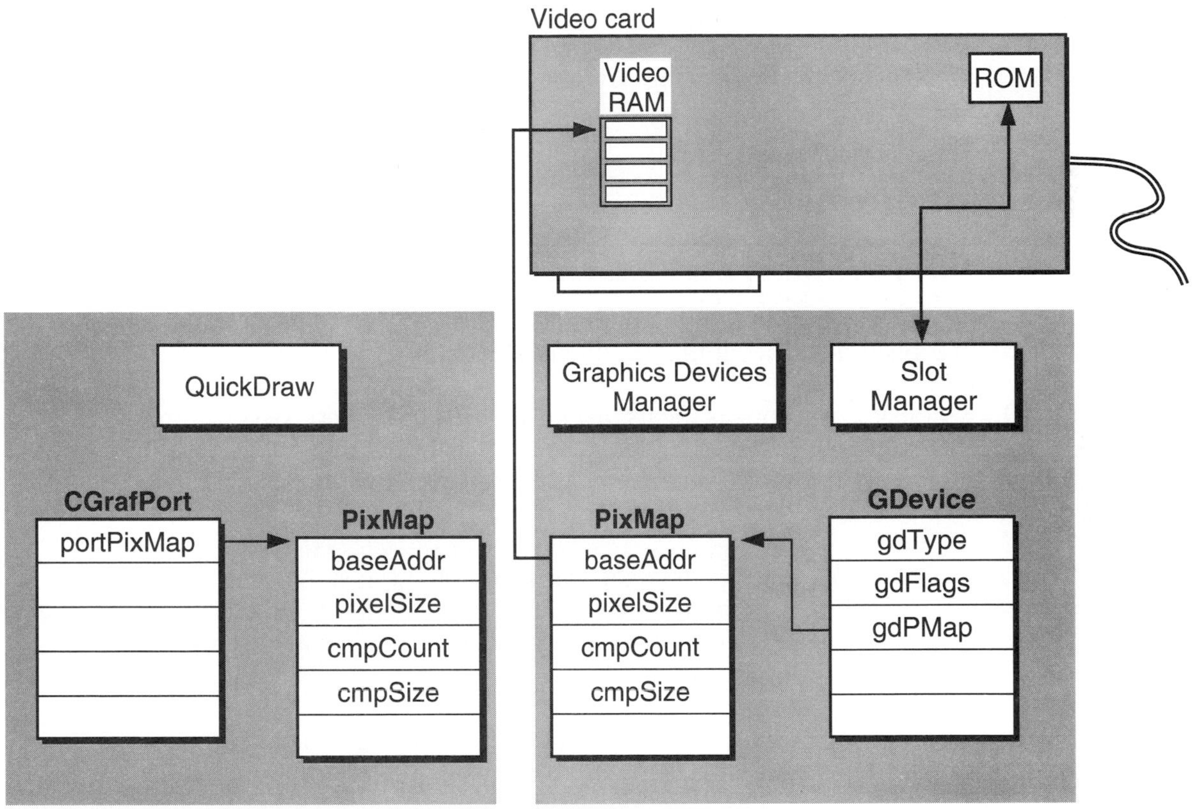

Figure 16-3. Initializing Macintosh graphics

When you open a window, the color grafPort record contains a handle to a pixel map record that was cloned from the pixel map record in the main screen's graphics device record. The pixel map record for your window thereby contains the correct pixel specifications for the screen on which it is displayed.

The situation is more complex when a window is displayed in a multiscreen environment, but QuickDraw does the housekeeping for you. When a multiscreen system starts up, one of the screens is determined to be the startup screen, the screen on which the "happy Macintosh" appears. (If the user has specified a startup screen in the Monitors control panel, then that screen is used.) By default, the menu bar appears on the startup screen. The screen with the menu bar is called the **main screen.** Global coordinates are anchored to the main screen, whose upper-left corner is at (0,0).

Each screen has its own graphics device record created from information in the video card's ROM. Thus, there is a graphics destination for each screen, but QuickDraw lets you draw to the window's grafPort as if it were all on one screen. Color QuickDraw internally calculates the changes required for drawing to the other screens.

During the startup of a multiscreen environment, the InitWindows procedure is called to create a region that is the union of all the active screen devices (minus the menu bar and the rounded corners on the outermost screens). It saves this region as the global variable GrayRgn. The **gray region** describes and defines the desktop, the area on which windows can be dragged.

Windows can be dragged anywhere within the gray region, from one screen to another or spanning screen boundaries. QuickDraw calculates the global coordinates of the rectangle into which it must draw and issues the drawing command to each device the rectangle intersects.

THE GRAPHICS PATH

Tracing the path from data in memory to a dot on a screen traverses the major parts of the Macintosh graphics system and recapitulates much of the discussion in this chapter.

Color QuickDraw considers colors as ideals: an RGB color record consists of three 16-bit values, one each for red, green, and blue. The resulting 48-bit record is sufficient to specify far more colors than the human eye can discern. Color QuickDraw and the graphics environment determine how this ideal becomes real.

The largest pixel value usable with system software version 7.0 is a 32-bit direct pixel, of which the red, green, and blue components have 8 bits each, and 8 bits are currently unused. RGB values of 24 bits can specify 16 million colors, which the human eye can just barely distinguish.

Advances in technology don't always mean increases in complexity. The color table system devised for Color QuickDraw was an expedient, to allow a smaller amount of RAM to display nearly full-color images. Direct pixel specification is inherently simpler—at the cost of additional RAM to hold the greater information needed to specify an image, and additional machine cycles to move it around.

The following two sections trace the steps from a user selecting a color to sending signals to a video screen. Of necessity, these explanations are simplified to provide an overview of the process.

How Indexed Pixels Work

Indexed devices expect that the pixel maps pointed to by color grafPort and graphics device records are based on an indexed pixel system, in which the stored image values are indexes to a table, not the RGB values themselves.

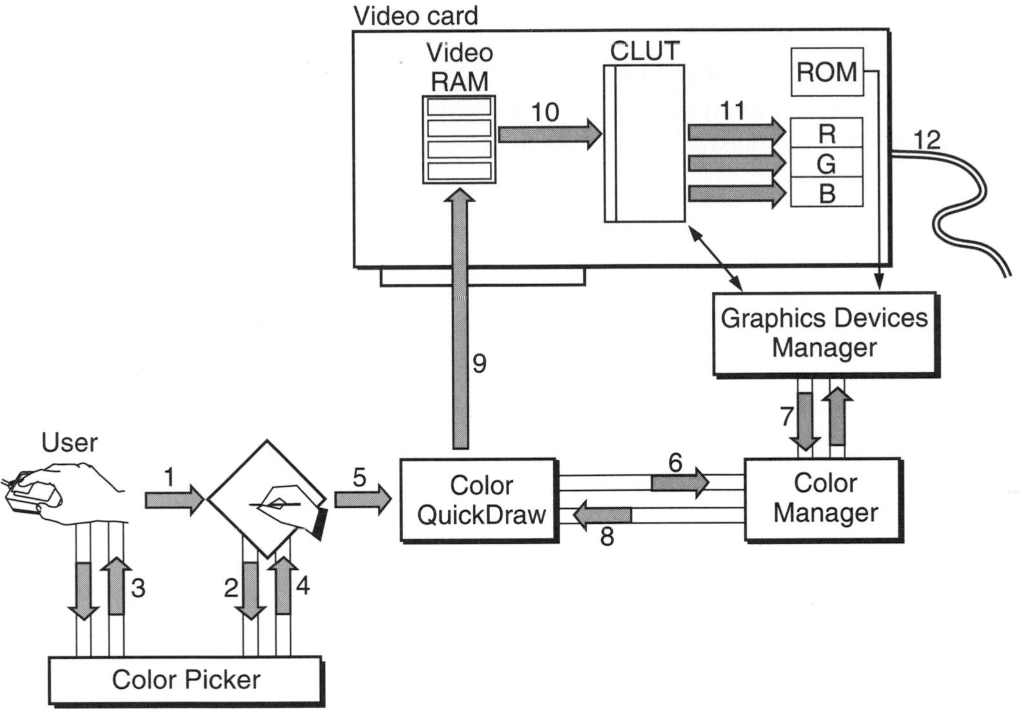

Figure 16-4. The indexed pixel path

As illustrated in Figure 16-4, the user tells the application to choose a color for some object (1). The application calls the Color Picker (2), which offers its color wheel dialog box to the user (3), who selects a color. The Color Picker returns that color to the application as a full 48-bit RGB value (4). The application tells Color QuickDraw to draw the object in that color (5). Color QuickDraw asks the Color Manager to determine what color in the card's color table comes closest to the color requested (6).

At startup, the video card's declaration ROM supplied information for the creation of a graphics device record for the card, describing its characteristics. The resulting graphics device record contains a color table that is kept synchronized with the card's CLUT. The Color Manager need only look into the current graphics device record's inverse table to find what RGB colors are currently available (7) and decide which comes closest in RGB space to the color requested by the application. (The inverse table is described in the Color Manager chapter of Volume V.) The Color Manager gets the index value for the best match in the table and returns that value to Color QuickDraw (8), which puts the index value into those places in video RAM that store the object (9).

The card continuously displays video RAM by taking the index values, converting them to RGB colors according to the CLUT entry at that index (10), and sending them to digital-to-analog converters (11) that produce a signal for the screen (12).

How Direct Pixels Work

When pixels are directly specified, the Color Manager's inverse table look-up isn't needed. The color value is derived from the most significant 5 or 8 bits of each component. The first few steps are the same as the steps for indexed devices.

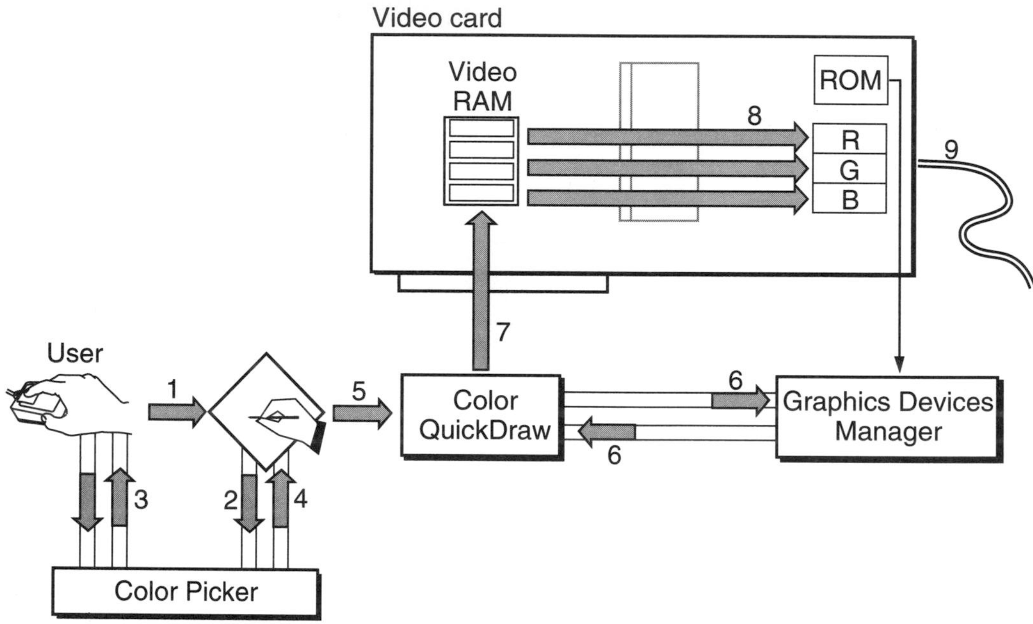

Figure 16-5. The direct pixel path

As illustrated in Figure 16-5, the user tells the application to choose a color for some object (1). The application calls the Color Picker (2), which offers its color wheel dialog box to the user (3), who selects a color. The Color Picker returns that color to the application as a full 48-bit RGB value (4). The application tells Color QuickDraw to draw the object in that color (5). Color QuickDraw knows from the graphics device record (6) that the screen is a direct device in which pixels are 32 bits deep, which means that 8 bits are used for each of the red, green, and blue components (8 are unused). Color QuickDraw passes the high 8 bits from each 16-bit component of its 48-bit RGB value to the card (7), which stores that 24-bit value in video RAM for each location of the object. The card continuously displays video RAM by sending the three 8-bit red, green, and blue values to digital-to-analog converters (8) that produce a signal for the screen (9).

DETERMINING THE QUICKDRAW VERSION

Remember that the three varieties of QuickDraw are upwardly compatible: programs you write for the original QuickDraw run on all varieties of QuickDraw, and indexed-pixel Color QuickDraw programs run under direct-pixel systems (although colors may look different— they'll be closer to what you request). The reverse is not true; Color QuickDraw uses hardware features of the 68020 microprocessor and above, which means it cannot execute on 68000-based machines; in addition, the original Color QuickDraw does not have the ability to handle direct pixel values.

By checking at run time to see which version of QuickDraw is available, you can adapt your program to make best use of the hardware, or at least inform the user that your program has graphics needs that aren't being met. (Remember also that this information doesn't matter to many programs; they use no color, use the original QuickDraw color system, or, if they use Color QuickDraw, specify only RGB colors.)

In system software versions 6.0.5 and later you can use the Gestalt environment selector gestaltQuickDrawVersion to determine which of the QuickDraw versions is available. Gestalt returns a 4-byte value in the response parameter; the low-order word contains QuickDraw version data. In that low-order word, the high-order byte represents the major revision number and the low-order byte represents the minor revision. The major revisions currently defined are the original QuickDraw, the original Color QuickDraw, and Color QuickDraw with direct pixel capability (which Gestalt calls QD32). See the Compatibility Guidelines chapter in this volume for information on the use of Gestalt.

WHAT ELSE TO READ

The two introductory chapters on Macintosh graphics are the QuickDraw chapter in Volume I and this overview. Proceed from here according to your inclination. If your application never uses color or gray scales, you may have all the information you need. If you use color at all, read the Color QuickDraw chapter in Volume V and the Color QuickDraw and Palette Manager chapters in this volume. If your application creates offscreen bitmaps or pixel maps, you should read the Graphics Devices Manager chapter in this volume.

If your application needs to offer the user a means of selecting a color, read the Color Picker Package chapter in this volume.

If your application manipulates pixel maps or pictures and needs a means of determining their contents—for example, what fonts a picture contains, or how many colors are in a pixel map, read the Picture Utilities Package chapter in this volume.

The Color Manager chapter in Volume V describes the Color Manager and other low-level information that most applications seldom need to use. Read that chapter if you need to modify the color-matching system used with indexed devices.

If you write graphics drivers or firmware for cards, read the Slot Manager chapter in this volume and *Designing Cards and Drivers for the Macintosh Family,* second edition.

SUMMARY OF GRAPHICS DATA TYPES

Data Types

```
TYPE RGBColor =
     RECORD
        red:             Integer;     {red component}
        green:           Integer;     {green component}
        blue:            Integer      {blue component}
     END;

     CTabHandle = ^CTabPtr;
     CTabPtr    = ^ColorTable;

     ColorTable =
     RECORD
        ctSeed:          LongInt;     (unique identifier from table}
        ctFlags:         Integer;     {high bit: 1 = device, 0 = PixMap}
        ctSize:          Integer;     {number of ctTable entries - 1}
        ctTable:         CSpecArray   {array of color specification entries}
     END;

     CSpecArray:         ARRAY[0..0] OF ColorSpec;

     ColorSpec =
     RECORD
        value:           Integer;     {index or other value}
        rgb:             RGBColor     {true color}
     END;

     PalettePtr = ^Palette;
     PaletteHandle = ^PalettePtr;

     Palette =
     RECORD
        pmEntries:       Integer;     {entries in pmTable}
        pmDataFields:    ARRAY[0..6] OF Integer;
                                      {private fields}
        pmInfo:          ARRAY[0..0] OF ColorInfo
                                      {color information}
     END;
```

```
ColorInfo =
RECORD
   ciRGB:            RGBColor;      {absolute RGB values}
   ciUsage:          Integer;       {color usage information}
   ciTolerance:      Integer;       {tolerance value}
   ciDataFields:     ARRAY[0..2] OF Integer;
                                    {private fields}
END;


PixMapHandle  = ^PixMapPtr;
PixMapPtr     = ^PixMap;

PixMap =
RECORD
   baseAddr:         Ptr;           {pointer to image data}
   rowBytes:         Integer;       {flags and bytes in a row}
   bounds:           Rect;          {boundary rectangle}
   pmVersion:        Integer;       {pixel map version number}
   packType:         Integer;       {packing format}
   packSize:         LongInt;       {size of data in packed state}
   hRes:             Fixed;         {horizontal resolution}
   vRes:             Fixed;         {vertical resolution}
   pixelType:        Integer;       {format of pixel image}
   pixelSize:        Integer;       {physical bits per pixel}
   cmpCount:         Integer;       {logical components per pixel}
   cmpSize:          Integer;       {logical bits per component}
   planeBytes:       LongInt;       {offset to next plane}
   pmTable:          CTabHandle;    {pointer to color table for }
                                    { this image}
   pmReserved:       LongInt        {reserved for future expansion}
END;


CGrafPtr  = ^CGrafPort;

CGrafPort =
RECORD
   device:           Integer;       {device ID for font selection}
   portPixMap:       PixMapHandle;  {handle to port's pixel map}
   portVersion:      Integer;       {flags; highest 2 bits always set}
   grafVars:         Handle;        {handle to additional color fields}
   chExtra:          Integer;       {extra width added to nonspace }
                                    { characters}
   pnLocHFrac:       Integer;       {pen fraction}
   portRect:         Rect;          {port rectangle}
   visRgn:           RgnHandle;     {visible region}
   clipRgn:          RgnHandle;     {clipping region}
   bkPixPat:         PixPatHandle;  {background pattern}
   rgbFgColor:       RGBColor;      {requested foreground color}
   rgbBkColor:       RGBColor;      {requested background color}
   pnLoc:            Point;         {pen location}
   pnSize:           Point;         {pen size}
   pnMode:           Integer;       {pen transfer mode}
```

```
    pnPixPat:         PixPatHandle; {pen pattern}
    fillPixPat:       PixPatHandle; {fill pattern}
    pnVis:            Integer;      {pen visibility}
    txFont:           Integer;      {font number for text}
    txFace:           Style;        {text's character style}
    txMode:           Integer;      {text's transfer mode}
    txSize:           Integer;      {font size for text}
    spExtra:          Fixed;        {extra width added to space }
                                    { characters}
    fgColor:          LongInt;      {actual foreground color}
    bkColor:          LongInt;      {actual background color}
    colrBit:          Integer;      {plane being drawn}
    patStretch:       Integer;      {used internally}
    picSave:          Handle;       {picture being saved}
    rgnSave:          Handle;       {region being saved}
    polySave:         Handle;       {polygon being saved}
    grafProcs:        CQDProcsPtr   {pointer to low-level drawing }
                                    { routines}
END;


GDHandle    = ^GDPtr;
GDPtr       = ^GDevice;

GDevice     =
RECORD
    gdRefNum:         Integer;      {reference number of driver}
    gdID:             Integer;      {client ID for search procedure}
    gdType:           Integer;      {type of device (indexed, direct)}
    gdITable:         ITabHandle;   {inverse table for Color Manager}
    gdResPref:        Integer;      {preferred resolution}
    gdSearchProc:     SProcHndl;    {list of search functions}
    gdCompProc:       CProcHndl;    {list of complement functions}
    gdFlags:          Integer;      {graphics device flags}
    gdPMap:           PixMapHandle; {pixel map for displayed image}
    gdRefCon:         LongInt;      {reference value}
    gdNextGD:         GDHandle;     {handle to next graphics device}
    gdRect:           Rect;         {device's global bounds}
    gdMode:           LongInt;      {device's current mode}
    gdCCBytes:        Integer;      {width of expanded cursor data}
    gdCCDepth:        Integer;      {depth of expanded cursor data}
    gdCCXData:        Handle;       {handle to cursor's expanded data}
    gdCCXMask:        Handle;       {handle to cursor's expanded mask}
    gdReserved:       LongInt       {reserved for future use. Must be 0}
END;
```

17 COLOR QUICKDRAW

ABOUT THIS CHAPTER

This chapter describes extensions to the color facilities of Color QuickDraw™. It discusses other new features, notably luminance mapping techniques, new routines for copying pixel maps, extensions to the version 2 picture format, and routines by which existing applications can signal QuickDraw that a data structure has been modified directly.

To use this chapter, you should be familiar with the Graphics Overview chapter in this volume and with the Color QuickDraw chapter in Volume V. If you develop graphics cards and drivers, you should also be familiar with the Slot Manager, Graphics Devices Manager, and Control Panels chapters in this volume, and with the description of the Slot Manager in *Designing Cards and Drivers for the Macintosh Family,* second edition.

If you use offscreen graphics to prepare images before copying them to the screen, read the Graphics Devices Manager chapter in this volume for a description of new routines that considerably reduce the complexity of that task.

ABOUT COLOR QUICKDRAW

Color QuickDraw in system software version 7.0 supports images that use direct, as well as indexed, specification of pixels.

Although an application specifies a color in terms of RGB space, the actual value Color QuickDraw sends to the graphics card frame buffer (video RAM) is an index value, which is used as input to the color look-up table (CLUT). An 8-bit index can specify 256 different entries ($2^8 = 256$). On CLUT devices, the relationship between the index value and the color generated depends on the colors and their current locations in the table.

At the cost of larger RAM requirements and, in some situations, slower performance, direct pixel specification eliminates the need for color table look-ups and inverse tables, and it lets your application directly specify over 16 million colors. (For a comparison of the differences between indexed and direct pixels, see the Graphics Overview chapter in this volume.)

In addition to direct pixel specification, Color QuickDraw now provides

- new facilities for copying pixel map records
- support for a true gray-scale display, providing better image fidelity on gray-scale devices
- a routine that converts a bitmap record to a region, allowing you, in effect, to use region-manipulating routines on bitmap or 1-bit pixel map records
- a routine that creates pictures with variable dots-per-inch (dpi) resolution
- four routines that allow you to signal Color QuickDraw when your application directly modifies a device's color table, pixel pattern, grafPort, or graphics device record (direct modification is still discouraged)

The rest of this chapter

- describes the changes to the pixel map record that support direct pixel values, and presents examples of converting between various pixel depths
- explains the compatibility implications of manipulating QuickDraw data structures directly, rather than using the routines provided for that purpose, and describes routines that warn QuickDraw when such a direct change has taken place
- describes new techniques for copying and displaying pixel maps
- describes new routines for converting a bitmap to a region and determining when drawing to a port has completed
- presents extensions to the version 2 picture format that support direct pixels and store font and line justification information

DIRECT PIXELS

Color QuickDraw now supports pixel maps with direct pixel specification as well as the indexed method supported by the original release of Color QuickDraw. Since QuickDraw has always striven to be device-independent, many applications need make no changes. If your application specifies RGB colors, the system determines the best matching colors for indexed devices and passes your RGB colors to direct devices.

Changes to the Color QuickDraw interface to implement direct pixels affect only these two color-specification data structures:

- the pixel map record that describes an image
- the version 2 picture format in which images and graphics drawing operations are stored

The new version 2 picture opcodes are described in "Extensions to the Version 2 Picture Format" later in this chapter; extensions to the pixel map record are described next.

Pixel Map Record Extensions

Color QuickDraw supports two new pixel formats corresponding to 16-bit and 32-bit pixel depths. In both cases, the pixel's displayed color is directly specified by the pixel value; the pixel value is not an index into a color table.

Note that the format of a pixel map record is not changed from that introduced with the Macintosh® II computer, but six pixel map fields can have new values. This chapter describes only those fields. For a complete description of the pixel map record, see the Color QuickDraw chapter in Volume V.

```
TYPE PixMap =
    RECORD
        baseAddr:     Ptr;            {pointer to image data}
        rowBytes:     Integer;        {flags, and bytes in a row}
        bounds:       Rect;           {boundary rectangle}
        pmVersion:    Integer;        {pixel map version number}
        packType:     Integer;        {packing format}
        packSize:     LongInt;        {size of data in packed state}
        hRes:         Fixed;          {horizontal resolution}
        vRes:         Fixed;          {vertical resolution}
        pixelType:    Integer;        {format of pixel image}
        pixelSize:    Integer;        {physical bits per pixel}
        cmpCount:     Integer;        {logical components per pixel}
        cmpSize:      Integer;        {logical bits per component}
        planeBytes:   LongInt;        {offset to next plane}
        pmTable:      CTabHandle;     {pointer to color table for }
                                      { this image}
        pmReserved:   LongInt         {reserved for future expansion}
    END;
```

Field descriptions

rowBytes — The restriction that the value of rowBytes be less than $2000 has been relaxed: rowBytes must be less than $4000. The value must be even, and for best performance it should be a multiple of 4.

pmVersion — The value of pmVersion is normally 0. If pmVersion is 4, Color QuickDraw treats the pixel map's baseAddr field as being 32-bit clean. (All other flags are private.) Most applications never need to set pmVersion.

pixelType — Direct pixel values are specified by a pixelType field value of RGBDirect, or 16. In a pixel map of the graphics device record for a direct device, the pixelType field is set to the constant RGBDirect when the screen depth is set.

pixelSize — Pixel sizes must be powers of 2. The original Color QuickDraw supported pixel sizes of 1, 2, 4, and 8 bits; with direct pixels, pixel sizes may also be 16 and 32 bits.

cmpCount — With indexed pixels, each pixel is a single value representing an index in a color table, and therefore the cmpCount field of a pixel map record is 1—the index is the single component. With direct pixels, each pixel contains three components, one integer each for the intensities of red, green, and blue, so cmpCount is 3. Other values are undefined.

cmpSize — For an indexed pixel value, which has only one component, the value of cmpSize is the same as the value of pixelSize: 1, 2, 4, or 8. A 32-bit pixel consists of three components (red, green, and blue values) of 8 bits each. Since cmpCount * cmpSize (3 * 8 = 24) is less than the value of pixelSize, 8 bits in the pixel are not part of any component. These bits are unused: Color QuickDraw sets them to 0 in any image it creates. If presented with a 32-bit image—for example, in the CopyBits procedure—it passes whatever bits are there. (Generally, therefore, your application should clear image memory to 0 before creating a 32-bit image.)

A 16-bit pixel consists of three components of 5 bits each. This leaves an unused high-order bit, which Color QuickDraw sets to 0.

Color QuickDraw expects that the sizes of all components are the same, and that cmpCount * cmpSize is less than or equal to pixelSize.

In each direct pixel, the pixel value is the concatenation of the red, green, and blue components, where red is in the most significant bits and blue is in the least significant bits. The entire direct pixel is right aligned; unused bits occupy the highest-order bits.

Direct Pixel Values

This section presents some examples of direct pixel values and the results of converting between direct and indexed pixels. Figure 17-1 shows a 32-bit direct pixel value in which the pixel and component fields have been set up as

```
pixelType   =  16;   {RGBDirect}
pixelSize   =  32;   {must be a power of 2}
cmpCount    =  3;    {red, green, and blue values}
cmpSize     =  8;    {8 bits for each component}
```

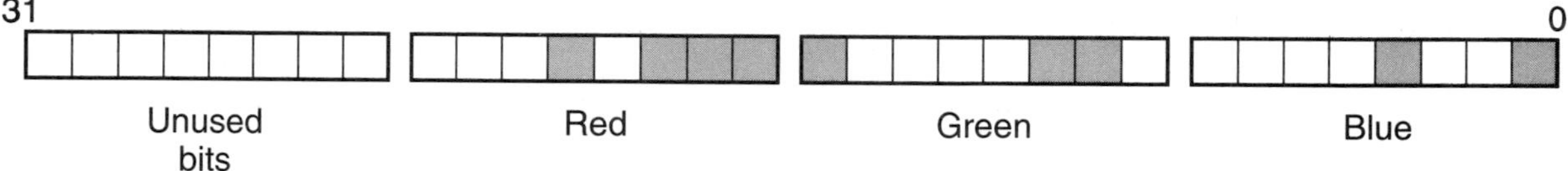

Figure 17-1. A 32-bit direct pixel

In this example, the pixel value (hexadecimal) is $00178609, which deconstructs into component values of $17 red, $86 green, and $09 blue, resulting in a medium green. Figure 17-2 approximates the same color as the one in Figure 17-1 using a 16-bit pixel specified as follows:

```
pixelType   =  16;   {RGBDirect}
pixelSize   =  16;   {must be a power of 2}
cmpCount    =  3;    {red, green, and blue values}
cmpSize     =  5;    {5 bits for each component}
```

15 0

Red Green Blue

Figure 17-2. A 16-bit direct pixel

Here the pixel value is $0A01, with component values of $02, $10, and $01 for red, green, and blue.

When converting a 32-bit pixel value to 16 bits, the 3 least significant bits are dropped for each component. When converting a 16-bit pixel value to 32 bits, the most significant 3 bits of each component are replicated and added to constitute the least significant 3 bits of each 8-bit component, as illustrated in Figure 17-3.

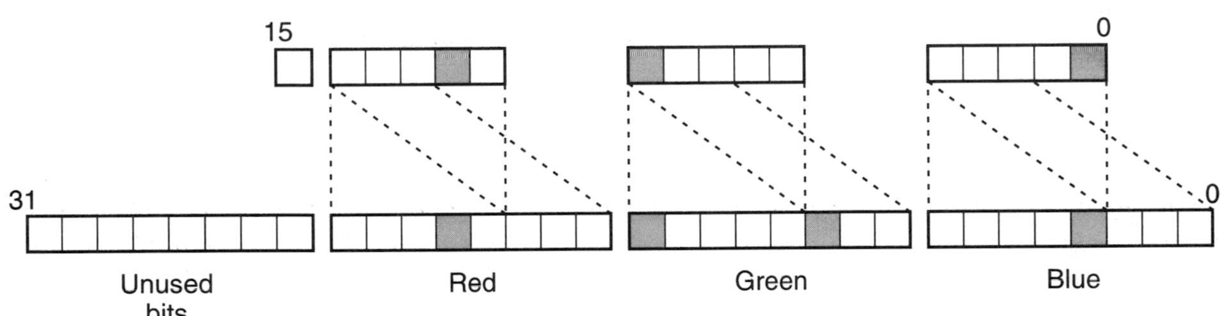

Figure 17-3. Converting a 16-bit direct pixel to a 32-bit direct pixel

In this way, white remains white, black remains black, and other values are spread evenly.

Figures 17-4 to 17-9 show first how Color QuickDraw converts a full 48-bit RGB color to 32-bit, 16-bit, and 8-bit values (the latter indexed) and then the reverse process of converting those values back to 48 bits.

A 32-bit direct pixel uses the most significant 8 bits of each component, with 8 unused bits in the high byte, as shown in Figure 17-4.

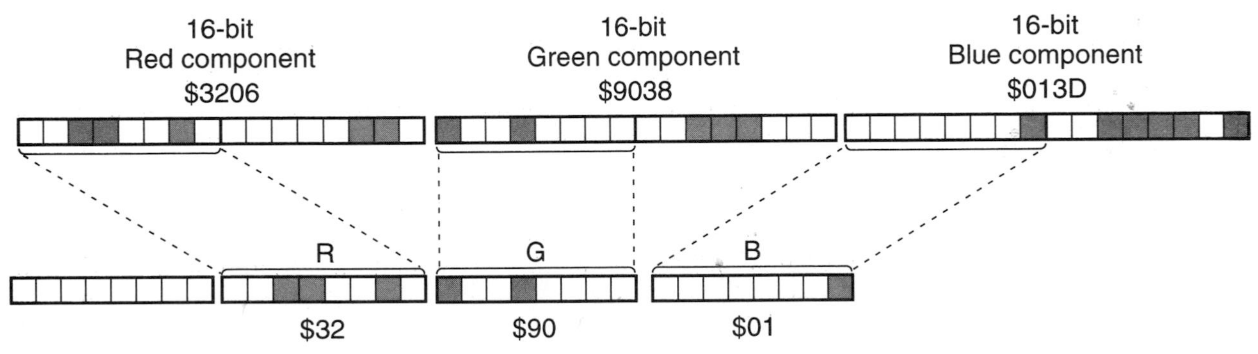

Figure 17-4. Converting a 48-bit RGB color to a 32-bit direct pixel

A 16-bit direct pixel uses the most significant 5 bits of each component and has an unused high bit, as shown in Figure 17-5.

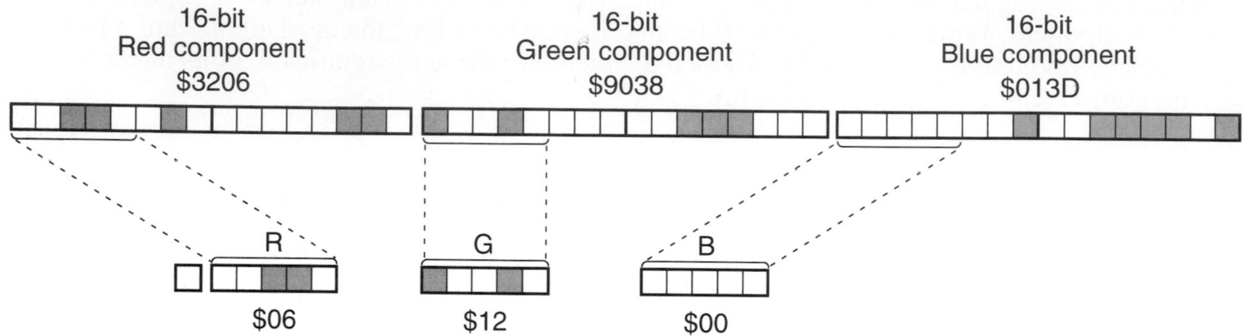

Figure 17-5. Converting a 48-bit RGB color to a 16-bit direct pixel

To obtain an 8-bit indexed pixel value from a 48-bit RGB color, the Color Manager determines the closest RGB value in the CLUT; its index value is stored in the 8-bit pixel. In the standard 8-bit color table, the 'CLUT' resource whose ID is 8, the nearest value to the original RGB value of Figure 17-4 is in table entry 161, as shown in Figure 17-6. Note that with indexed pixels, the pixel value has no direct relation to the original RGB value.

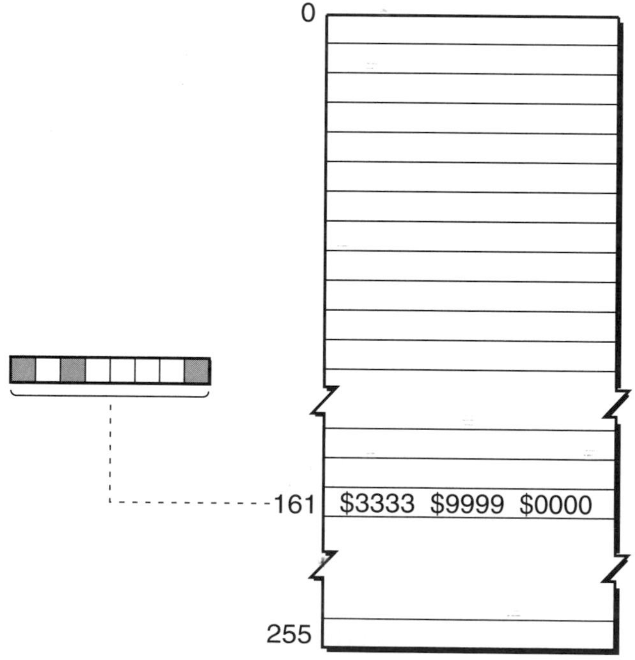

Figure 17-6. Converting a 48-bit RGB color to an 8-bit indexed pixel

Figure 17-7 shows how Color QuickDraw expands a 32-bit pixel to a 48-bit value by dropping the unused high byte and doubling each 8-bit component. Note that the resulting 48-bit value differs (in the least significant 8 bits of each component) from the original value in Figure 17-4.

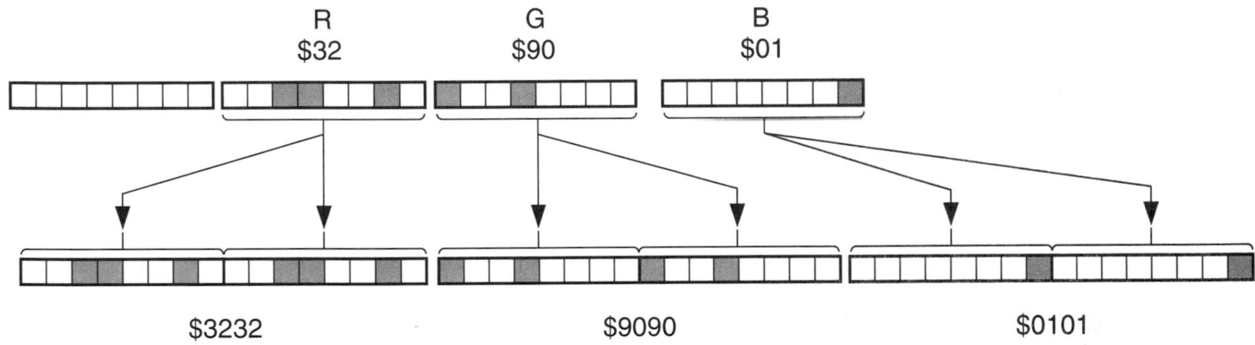

Figure 17-7. Converting a 32-bit pixel to a 48-bit RGB color

Color QuickDraw expands a 16-bit pixel to a 48-bit RGB color by dropping the unused high bit and inserting three copies of each 5-bit component and a copy of the most significant bit into each 16-bit component of the destination value. Note that the result differs (in the least significant 11 bits of each component) from the original value.

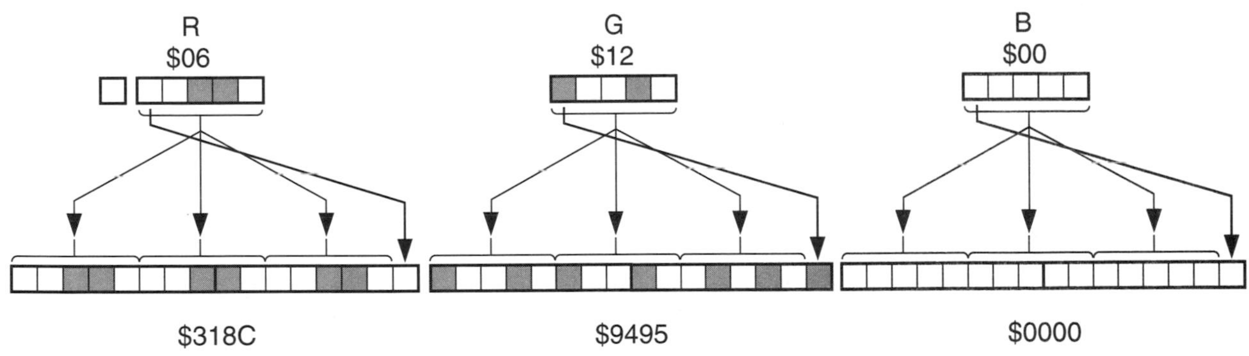

Figure 17-8. Converting a 16-bit pixel to a 48-bit RGB color

Color QuickDraw expands an 8-bit indexed pixel to a 48-bit RGB color by taking the 48-bit value pointed to in the CLUT, as shown in Figure 17-9. The difference between this value and the original 48-bit value varies, depending on the CLUT values.

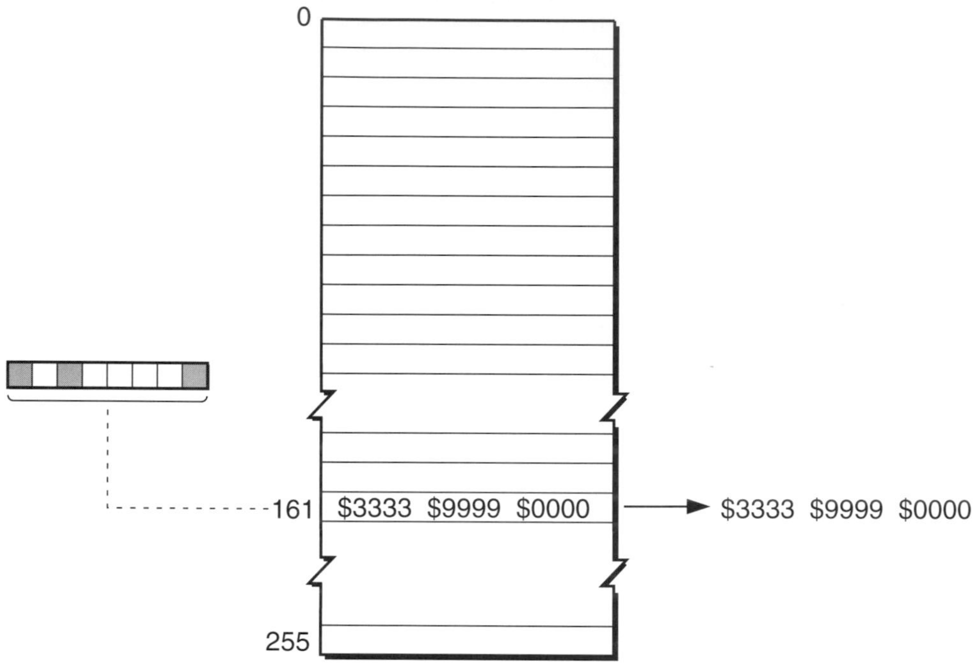

Figure 17-9. Converting an 8-bit indexed pixel to a 48-bit RGB color

WRITING COMPATIBLE GRAPHICS APPLICATIONS

Over the years, some developers have written applications that modify the QuickDraw data structures directly, rather than using the routines provided for that purpose. Then, when engineers at Apple Computer, Inc., improve QuickDraw, the applications break. As QuickDraw, graphics applications, and cards such as graphics accelerators grow more complex, the problem becomes acute. This section points to new routines you can use to signal QuickDraw when your application modifies certain data structures directly so that QuickDraw can take note and act accordingly.

Applications should not directly change fields in graphics data structures, but should use the following routines instead:

AddComp	ColorBit	HidePen
AddSearch	CopyPixPat	HiliteColor
BackColor	DelComp	MakeRGBPat
BackPat	DelSearch	Move
BackPixPat	ForeColor	MovePortTo
CharExtra	GrafDevice	MoveTo
ClipRect	HideCursor	ObscureCursor

OpColor
PenMode
PenNormal
PenPat
PenPixPat
PenSize
PortSize
RGBBackColor
RGBForeColor
SetCCursor
SetClientID
SetClip
SetCursor
SetDeviceAttribute
SetGDevice
SetOrigin
SetPenState
SetPort
SetPortBits
SetPortPix
ShowCursor
ShowPen
SpaceExtra
TextFace
TextFont
TextMode
TextSize

Using these routines rather than directly modifying the data structures ensures that your application will fully benefit from any future improvements to QuickDraw. In particular, the off-screen graphics world routines described in the Graphics Devices Manager chapter of this volume remove much of the need for directly modifying graphics data structures.

Apple Computer, Inc., strongly recommends that new applications follow these guidelines; asynchronously operating graphics cards especially need close cooperation with QuickDraw.

It is possible to make existing applications more compatible by calling one of the following procedures after directly changing a QuickDraw data structure and before calling any other QuickDraw routine:

CTabChanged
PixPatChanged
PortChanged
GDeviceChanged

These procedures inform QuickDraw that a direct modification has occurred so it can update its tracking of the graphics environment. They are described in "Reporting Data Structure Changes" later in this chapter.

USING COLOR QUICKDRAW

If your application uses color in straightforward ways, it will probably execute without change in a direct pixel environment.

For most other applications, the main concern is in the creation and use of special-purpose pixel map and graphics device records. By using the offscreen graphics world routines described in the Graphics Devices Manager chapter in this volume, you will find such tasks far easier than before.

If you must work with color grafPort, pixel map, and graphics device records in ways beyond the scope of the offscreen graphics world routines, the following guidelines may aid you in adapting to Color QuickDraw's direct pixel environment:

- Don't draw directly to the screen. Create your own offscreen graphics world, as described in the Graphics Devices Manager chapter in this volume, and use the CopyBits, CopyMask, or CopyDeepMask routine.

- Don't directly change the fgColor or bkColor field of a grafPort and expect them to be used as the pixel values. Color QuickDraw recalculates these values for each device. If you really want to draw in an index instead of a color, use a palette with explicit colors, as described in the Palette Manager chapter in this volume. For device-independent colors, use the RGBForeColor and RGBBackColor procedures.

- Fill out all the fields in a new pixel map record. The NewPixMap function returns a pixel map record that is cloned from the pixel map record pointed to by theGDevice. If you don't want a copy of the main screen's pixel map record—for example, you want one that is a different depth—then you must fill out more fields than just pixelSize: you must fill out the pixelType, cmpCount, and cmpSize fields. Set pmVersion to 0 when initializing your own pixel map record. For future compatibility you should also set packType, packSize, planeBytes, and pmReserved to 0.

- Don't clone a graphics device record's pixel map record. Instead, use the NewPixMap function or the CopyPixMap procedure. If you must create or manually clone a pixel map record, make sure to set the pmVersion field and other unused fields to 0 for future compatibility.

- Fill out all the fields of a new graphics device record. When creating an offscreen graphics device record by calling NewGDevice with the mode parameter set to –1, you must fill out the fields of the graphics device record (for instance, gdType) yourself. If you want a copy of an existing graphics device record, then copy the gdType field from it. If you explicitly want an indexed device, then set gdType to 0.

- Don't assume a pixel map record has a color table. A direct pixel map record need not have a color table. For compatibility, a direct pixel map record should have a dummy pmTable handle that points to a color table header with a seed value equal to cmpSize * cmpCount, and the color table's ctSize field should be set to 0.

Again, all these problems are simplified if you use the offscreen graphics world routines.

Manipulating Pixel Map Images

QuickDraw's facilities for copying pixel maps continues to evolve. With system software version 7.0, the CopyMask procedure has been expanded, and a new routine, CopyDeepMask, combines the functions of CopyBits and CopyMask. In addition, colorizing (copying a black-and-white image with the foreground or background set to a color) now is done in RGB space, and the classic transfer modes OR, BIC, and XOR work correctly with colored images.

Copying With Masks

One step in the evolution of QuickDraw's copying facilities came with the introduction of Color QuickDraw, when the original CopyBits procedure, which copied a bitmap using a transfer mode and a region mask, was modified so that a pixel map could be copied by the same method, as shown in Figure 17-10.

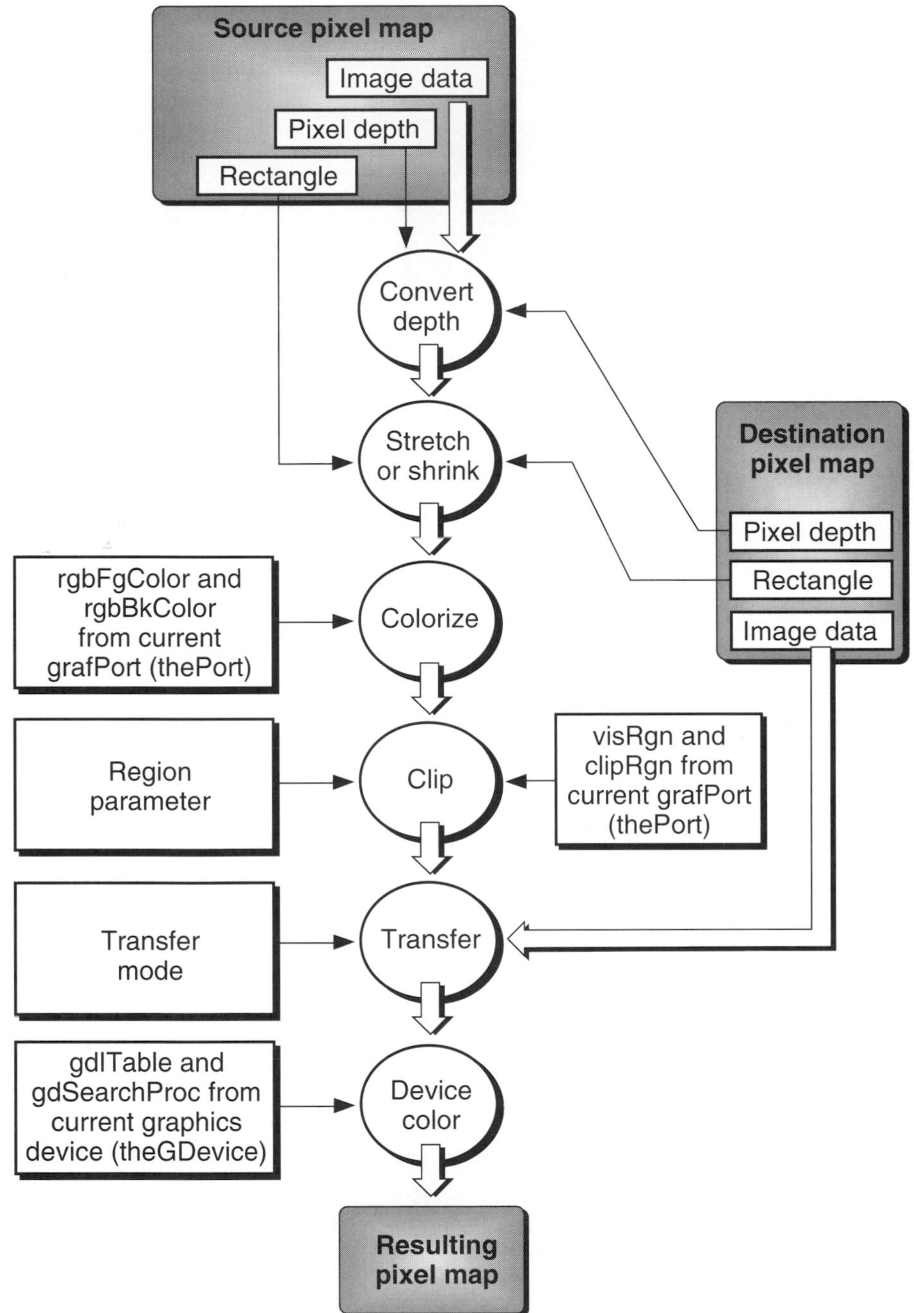

Figure 17-10. Copying pixel maps with CopyBits

The CopyMask procedure, introduced with the Macintosh Plus computer, allowed a bitmap to act as a mask when copying bitmaps. With system software version 7.0, the

CopyMask procedure has been expanded to allow a pixel map to be the mask, as shown in Figure 17-11 and Color Plate XXIII, "Copying With a Pixel Map as a Mask".

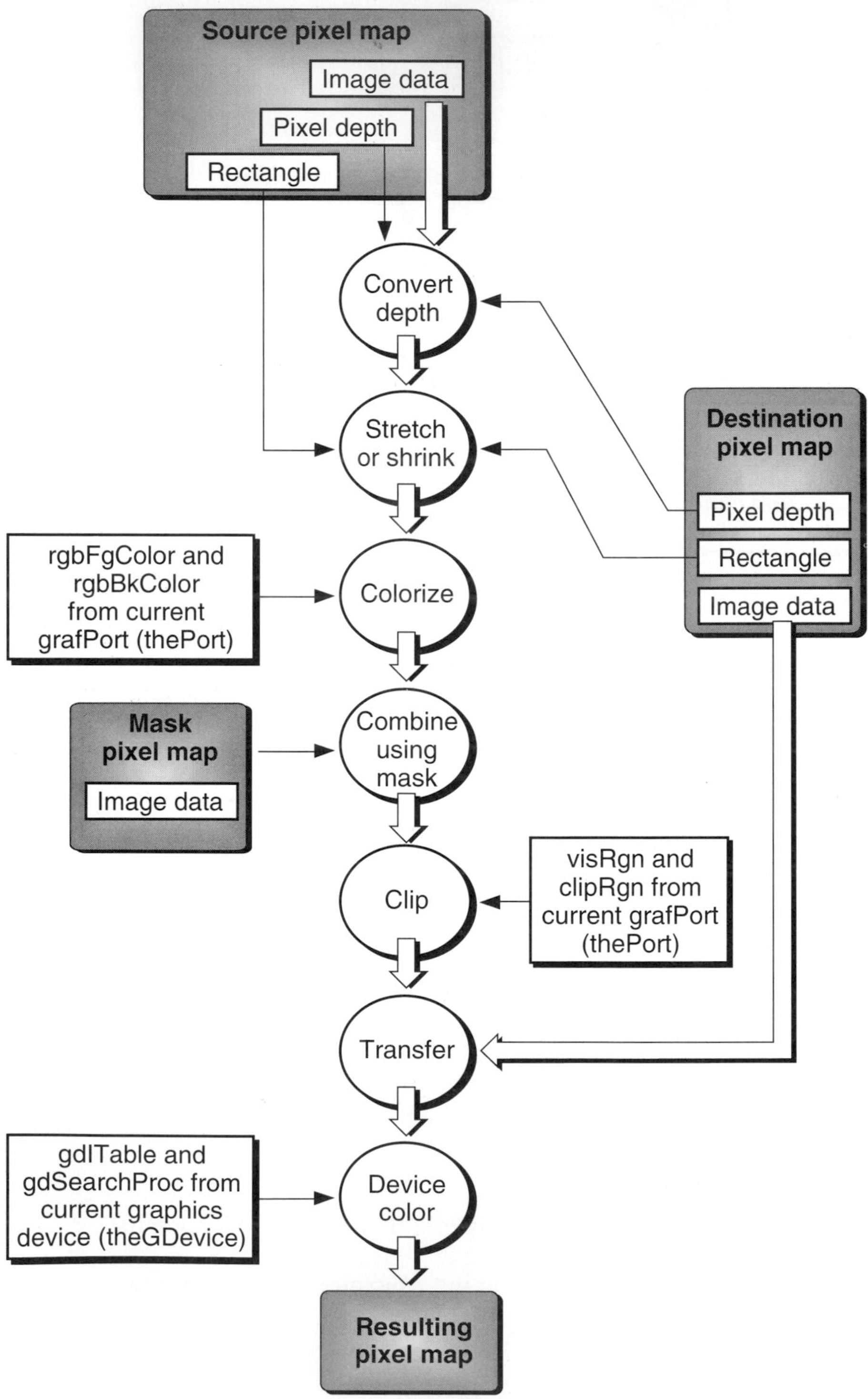

Figure 17-11. Copying pixel maps with CopyMask

A new procedure, CopyDeepMask, combines the functions of CopyBits and CopyMask. With CopyDeepMask you can supply a pixel map mask as well as copy modes and a mask region, as shown in Figure 17-12.

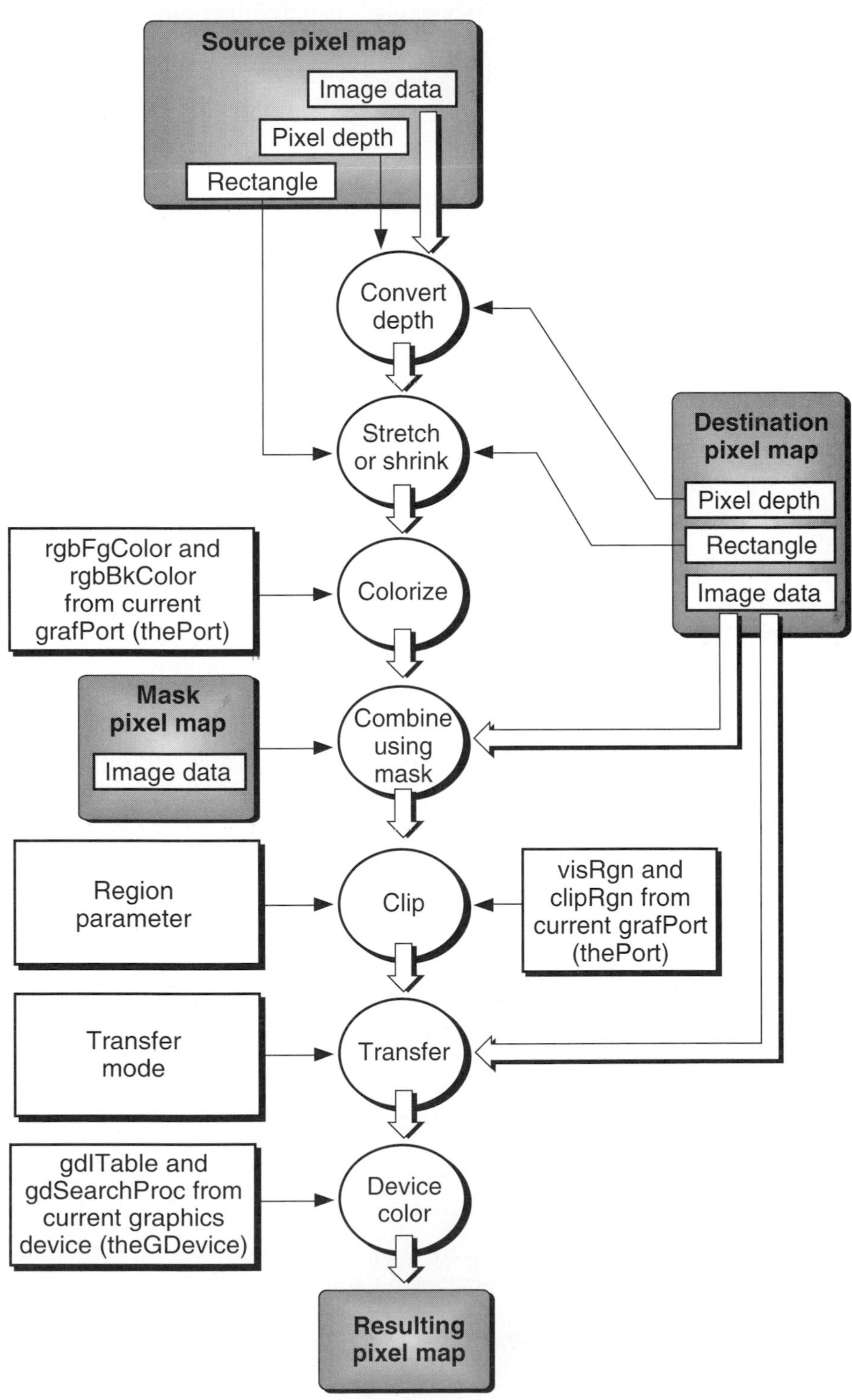

Figure 17-12. Copying pixel maps with CopyDeepMask

> **Note:** Pixel map records are always copied using the color table of the source pixel map for source information, and the color table of the current graphics device record for destination color information. (The color table attached to the destination pixel map is ignored.) If you need to copy to an offscreen pixel map with characteristics differing from those of the current graphics device (usually the main screen), you should create an appropriate offscreen graphics device record and set it as the current graphics device before the copy operation. (See the Graphics Devices Manager chapter in this volume for information about offscreen graphics.)

When the pixel map mask is 1 bit deep, it has the same effect as a bitmap mask: a black mask bit means that the pixel is to take the source value; a white mask bit means that the pixel is to take the destination value. Intermediate values in deeper pixel map masks specify that a weighted average is to be taken between the source and destination pixel maps. Within each pixel, the calculation is done in RGB space, on a color component basis. A gray pixel map mask, for example, works like blend mode in a CopyBits procedure. A red mask (high values for the red component in all pixels) filters out red values coming from the source pixel map.

Colorizing

Setting either the foreground or background (or both) to colors other than black and white before executing a CopyBits procedure results in **colorizing** effects. Before system software version 7.0, the colorizing was done by indexes, yielding arbitrary results unless the color table had been arranged carefully. Now your application can colorize pixels in RGB space (where $FFFF represents the full intensity of a component), so that setting the foreground to blue and the background to red, for example, turns a gray-scale image into appropriate shades of blue and red. See Color Plate XXIV, "Colorizing."

You can decide what to do with source pixels on a color component basis. Your application can

- pass a pixel's component, unchanged, by setting the foreground for that component to $0000 and the background to $FFFF
- invert them by setting the foreground for that component to $FFFF and the background to $0000
- zero them by setting both foreground and background for that component to $0000
- force them to 1 by setting both the foreground and background for that component to $FFFF

Note that arithmetic transfer modes have no colorizing effect.

Transfer Modes

The classic transfer modes OR, BIC, and XOR, which previously were problematic with color images, now work as you would expect:

- Using the OR mode when you copy an image you are transferring to a white background always results in the source image, regardless of the destination depth.
- Using the BIC mode when you copy an image causes black in the source image to erase, resulting in white in the destination image.

- The XOR mode inverts black in the source image but not white, at all destination depths, including 16-bit and 32-bit direct pixels.

When you work with color pixels, transfer modes produce different results on indexed and direct devices.

You can use a new text drawing mode, grayishTextOr, to draw dimmed text on the screen. If the destination device is color, it draws with a blend of the foreground and background colors. If the destination device is black and white, the grayishTextOr mode dithers black and white. Note that grayishTextOr is not a standard transfer mode in that currently it is not stored in pictures and printing with it is undefined. (It does pass through the bottleneck procedures.) The primary use for grayishTextOr is to display disabled user interface items.

Dithering

The CopyBits and CopyDeepMask procedures can now use **dithering,** a technique of mixing existing colors to create the effect of additional colors.

```
CONST ditherCopy = 64;      {dithering flag for CopyBits}
```

If you copy using dithering, then the CopyBits and CopyDeepMask procedures do their best to provide error diffusion during the copy operation. As with arithmetic transfer modes, dithering ignores hidden colors. Therefore, when you copy to an indexed device, color matching is limited by the resolution of the inverse table for the destination graphics device. (See the section "Inverse Tables" in the Color Manager chapter of Volume V.) Dithering provides good results for most images—for example, it allows you to shrink images more efficiently. However, dithering does have drawbacks: it is slower, and because of error diffusion, a clipped dithering operation does not provide pixel-for-pixel equivalence to the same unclipped dithering operation. Clipped XOR dithered copies, for example, do not perform as erase operations.

Currently, if a color search procedure is present, CopyBits and CopyDeepMask use plain copy mode instead of dithering. (This may change in future versions.)

Using plain copy mode (without dithering), your application does color mapping on a pixel-by-pixel basis—no errors are accumulated, and hidden colors are ignored. If the source pixel map is indexed and a color search procedure is present, Color QuickDraw calls the procedure once for each color in the color table. If the source is a direct pixel map and a search procedure is present, the procedure is called once for each color in the source pixel map. (With a source pixel map of many colors, this can take a long time.)

Color QuickDraw never uses dithering if you copy to a direct pixel map, but you can always use dithering when copying to an indexed pixel map.

Resizing Images

When copying from direct pixel maps, if the destination rectangle is smaller than the source rectangle, Color QuickDraw uses an averaging technique to produce the destination pixels, maintaining high-quality images when shrinking them.

Color QuickDraw also averages pixels when shrinking indexed images using dithering. Shrinking 1-bit images using dithering can produce much better representations of the original images than without using dithering.

Luminance Mapping

When Color QuickDraw displays a color on a gray-scale device, it computes the **luminance,** or intensity of light, of the desired color and uses that value to determine the appropriate gray value to draw. A gray-scale device can be a color device that the user sets to gray-scale mode; for such a device, Color QuickDraw places an evenly spaced set of grays, forming a linear ramp from white to black, in the device's CLUT. A gray-scale device can also be a device whose color table consists only of grays if the animated entries are not counted.

To facilitate the creation of gray-scale devices, the GetCTable function has been enhanced to recognize additional standard color table IDs. As described in the Color QuickDraw chapter of Volume V, the GetCTable function looks like this:

```
FUNCTION GetCTable (ctID: Integer) : CTabHandle;
```

You can obtain the default gray-scale color table for a given pixel depth by calling GetCTable with a ctID value of pixelSize + 32 (decimal), as shown in Table 17-1.

Table 17-1. The default color tables for gray-scale devices

pixelSize	ctID	Color table composition
1	33	Black, white
2	34	Black, 33% gray, 66% gray, white
4	36	Black, 14 shades of gray, white
8	40	Black, 254 shades of gray, white

You can obtain the equivalent default color tables by adding 64 to the pixel depth, as shown in Table 17-2. (For more information, see the Palette Manager chapter in this volume.)

Table 17-2. The default color tables for color devices

pixelSize	ctID	Color table composition
2	66	Black, 50% gray, highlight color, white
4	68	Black, 14 colors including a highlight color, white
8	72	Black, 254 colors including a highlight color, white

Image Resolution

Color QuickDraw supports pixel maps of resolutions other than 72 dpi. In the past, applications have accepted pixel maps of a certain number of rows and columns and assumed that they were generated on a 72-dpi device. Such pixel maps were usually copied and printed at a 72-dpi resolution, lending the impression that QuickDraw could not handle pixel maps of higher density.

With the advent of frame grabbers and scanners, many pixel maps have dpi resolutions of 150, 200, 300, or greater. A user expects pixel maps to display an approximation of the information on a 72-dpi display but to print on a higher resolution device to the best of the device's ability.

Displaying Variable-Resolution Pixel Maps and Pictures

The resolution of a pixel map record, measured in dpi, is contained in its hRes and vRes fields. These values are expressed as fixed-point integers.

When importing a picture, your application should check the picture type to see if it was created with the OpenCPicture function, which stores the hRes and vRes values in the picture header. See the Picture Utilities Package chapter in this volume for information on determining a picture's characteristics.

An alternative is to replace the StdBits bottleneck procedure (from the grafProcs field in the color grafPort record) during playback. When QuickDraw calls your StdBits procedure, you should

1. make sure the source is a pixel map record by checking that the high bit of the rowBytes field is set

2. read the hRes and vRes information from the source pixel map record (At this point, the source rectangle field indicates the size of the source in pixels at the resolution specified by the hRes and vRes fields.)

To display a picture at another resolution, your application should compute the destination rectangle field value appropriately. For example, if the source resolution is 300 dpi and you want to display it at 75 dpi, then your application should compute the destination rectangle width and height as $^1/_4$ of that of the source rectangle.

Exporting Pixel Map Records

When exporting pixel map records, your application should ensure that the hRes and vRes fields accurately reflect the image data. During picture recording, the destination rectangle of the CopyBits procedure should be appropriate for display at 72 dpi. If you want an entire picture to be a different resolution, use the OpenCPicture function.

Converting a Bitmap to a Region

A new function, BitMapToRegion, converts a bitmap to a region, allowing your application to use Color QuickDraw's region manipulation routines on the converted bitmap. If you use the PaintRgn procedure on the converted region, the resulting region is the same as the bitmap.

The BitMapToRegion procedure may be useful if you want to test for mouse clicks on the black pixels in a bitmap, or drag the outline of a bitmap using DragGrayRegion, described in the Window Manager chapter of Volume V.

Determining Whether Drawing Is Complete

A new function, QDDone, checks to see whether QuickDraw drawing operations have finished in a grafPort. This function is useful if your application is executing in an environment with a graphics accelerator, where drawing operations may proceed asynchronously.

EXTENSIONS TO THE VERSION 2 PICTURE FORMAT

The version 2 picture format presented in the Color QuickDraw chapter of Volume V has been extended: four opcodes previously listed as reserved have been defined, and one defined opcode has been redefined.

- Opcode $002C signals font name information.
- Opcode $002D signals line justification spacing information.
- Opcodes $009A and $009B now define direct pixel pictures, with pixel maps containing three components that directly specify RGB values.
- Opcode $0C00 still signifies a header record, and it is still 24 bytes in size, but its contents have changed.

This section describes the new version 2 picture opcodes and presents a sample version 2 picture file. The five changed opcodes are shown in Table 17-3.

Table 17-3. The new version 2 picture opcodes

Opcode	Name	Description	Data size (in bytes)
$002C	fontName	Data length (word), old font ID (word), name length (byte), font name	5 + name length
$002D	lineJustify	Opcode + operand data length (word), intercharacter spacing (fixed), total extra space for justification (fixed)	10
$009A	DirectBitsRect	pixMap, srcRect, dstRect, mode (word), pixData	[variable]
$009B	DirectBitsRgn	pixMap, srcRect, dstRect, mode (word), maskRgn, pixData	[variable]
$0C00	HeaderOp	Version (word), reserved (word), hRes, vRes (Fixed), srcRect (Rect), reserved (long)	24

Font Name

The font name information begins with a word containing the field's data length, followed by a word containing the old font ID, a byte containing the length of the font name, and then the font name itself.

You can extract font names, IDs, and other information from a picture by using the Picture Utilities Package, described in this volume.

Line Justification

The line justification information contains the line-layout state of the Script Manager so that it can be restored when the picture is played back. It begins with a word containing the field's data length, which should always be 8 bytes. The operands are two fixed-point values, describing the Script Manager's extra character width value and the total extra width that was added to the style run (each StdText call) to perform justification.

For example, if the intercharacter spacing were 1 pixel and the total extra width added were 10 pixels, the following hexadecimal bytes would be generated for the picture:

```
2D 00 08 00 01 00 00 00 0A 00 00
```

In this example, the $002D opcode is followed by the length word, 00 08, and then the integer part of the intercharacter spacing, 00 01, its fractional part, 00 00, and then the integer part of the total extra spacing, 00 0A, and its fractional part, 00 00.

Direct Pixel Images

The version 2 picture format defined for the original Color QuickDraw only supports images consisting of color table indexes. In system software version 7.0, the version 2 picture format can also record images with pixels that directly specify a given color. To the current imaging opcodes BitsRect, BitsRgn, PackBitsRect, and PackBitsRgn, Color QuickDraw adds DirectBitsRect and DirectBitsRgn. These opcodes allow your application to cut, paste, and store images with up to 32 bits of color information per pixel.

Unlike previous opcodes, DirectBitsRect and DirectBitsRgn store the baseAddr field of the pixel map structure in a version 2 picture. For compatibility with existing systems, the baseAddr field is set to $000000FF. Monochrome machines can display pixel maps that are in pictures. On systems without direct pixel support, opcodes $009A and $009B read a word from the picture and then skip a word of data. The next opcode retrieved from the picture is $00FF, which terminates picture playback. (Note that if you play back a picture on a machine without direct pixel support, it terminates picture parsing.)

The DirectBitsRect opcode is followed by this structure:

```
pixMap:                   {described later}
srcRect:    Rect;         {source rectangle}
dstRect:    Rect;         {destination rectangle}
mode:       Mode;         {transfer mode}
pixData:                  {described later}
```

The DirectBitsRgn opcode is followed by this structure:

```
pixMap:                 {described later}
srcRect:    Rect;       {source rectangle}
dstRect:    Rect;       {destination rectangle}
mode:       Mode;       {transfer mode}
maskRgn:    Region;     {region for masking}
pixData:                {described later}
```

In a picture, the packType field of a pixel map specifies the manner in which the pixel data was compressed. To facilitate banding of images when memory is short, all data compression is done on a scan-line basis. The following pseudocode describes the pixel data.

```
pixData:
If packType = 1 (unpacked) or rowbytes < 8 then data is unpacked, and
      data size = rowBytes * (bounds.bottom - bounds.top);

If packType = 2 (drop pad byte) then the high-order pad byte of a
      32-bit direct pixel is dropped, and
      data size = (3/4) * rowBytes * (bounds.bottom - bounds.top);

If packType > 2 (packed) then
      Image contains (bounds.bottom - bounds.top) packed scan lines
      Each scan line consists of [byteCount] [data].
      If rowBytes > 250 then byteCount is a word, else it is a byte.
```

Here are the currently defined packing types.

Packing type	Meaning
0	Use default packing
1	Use no packing
2	Remove pad byte—supported only for 32-bit pixels (24-bit data)
3	Run length encoding by pixelSize chunks, one scan line at a time—supported only for 16-bit pixels
4	Run length encoding one component at a time, one scan line at a time, red component first—supported only for 32-bit pixels (24-bit data)

For future compatibility, other packType values skip scan-line data and draw nothing. Since Color QuickDraw assumes that pixel map data in memory is unpacked regardless of the packType field value, you can use packType to tell the picture-recording mechanism what packing technique to use on that data. A packType value of 0 in memory indicates that the default packing scheme should be used. (Using the default packing scheme is recommended.) Currently, the default packType value for a pixelSize value of 16 is type 3; for a pixelSize of 32, it is type 4. Regardless of the setting of packType at the time of picture recording, the packType value actually used to save the image is recorded in the picture.

Since each scan line of packed data is preceded by a byte count, packSize is not used and must be 0 for future compatibility.

When the pixel type is direct chunky, cmpCount * cmpSize is less than or equal to pixelSize. For storing 24-bit data in a 32-bit pixel, set cmpSize to 8 and cmpCount to 3. If you set cmpCount to 4, then the high byte is compressed by packing scheme 4 and stored in the picture.

A new routine, the OpenCPicture function, lets your application create a version 2 format picture and include rectangle and resolution information, which is stored in the version 2 picture header. This provides a simple mechanism for creating images with spatial resolution other than 72 dpi. The OpenCPicture function is described in "Creating an Extended Version 2 Picture" later in this chapter.

The HeaderOp information is passed to the OpenCPicture function as an OpenCPicParams record, which has this structure:

```
TYPE OpenCPicParams =
     RECORD
        srcRect:       Rect;        {source rectangle for best display }
                                    { at hRes, vRes resolution}
        hRes:          Fixed;       {best horizontal resolution}
        vRes:          Fixed;       {best vertical resolution}
        version:       Integer;     {set to -2}
        reserved1:     Integer;     {reserved for future use}
        reserved2:     LongInt      {reserved for future use}
     END;
```

Note that in the header to a version 2 picture the information is reordered, and appears in this format:

```
TYPE PictureHeader =
     RECORD
        version:       Integer;     {set to -2}
        reserved1:     Integer;     {reserved for future use}
        hRes:          Fixed;       {best horizontal resolution}
        vRes:          Fixed;       {best vertical resolution}
        srcRect:       Rect;        {source rectangle for best }
                                    { display at hRes, vRes resolution}
        reserved2:     LongInt      {reserved for future use}
     END;
```

Sample Extended Version 2 Picture

An example of an extended version 2 picture that can display a single direct pixel image is shown in Table 17-4.

Table 17-4. Version 2 picture example

Opcode size (in bytes)	Name	Description
2	picSize	Low word of picture size
8	picFrame	Rectangular bounding box of picture, at 72 dpi
Picture Definition Data:		
2	versionOp	Version opcode = $0011
2	version	Version number = $02FF
2	HeaderOp	Header opcode = $0C00
2	version	Set to –2 for extended version 2 picture file
2	reserved	Reserved for future Apple use
4	hRes	Native horizontal resolution
4	vRes	Native vertical resolution
8	srcRect	Native source rectangle
4	reserved	Reserved for future Apple use
2	opBitsRect	Bitmap opcode = $009A for direct pixels
4	baseAddr	For direct pixels must be $000000FF (see "Direct Pixels" earlier in this chapter)
2	rowBytes	Integer, must have high bit set to signal pixel map
8	bounds	Rectangle, boundary rectangle at source resolution
2	pmVersion	Integer, pixel map version number = 0
2	packType	Integer, defines packing format
4	packSize	Long integer, length of pixel data = 0
4	hRes	Fixed, horizontal resolution (dpi) of source data, normally $00480000 (72 dpi)
4	vRes	Fixed, vertical resolution (dpi) of source data, normally $00480000 (72 dpi)
2	pixelType	Integer, defines pixel type; 16 for direct pixels
2	pixelSize	Integer, number of bits in pixel; 16 or 32 for direct pixels
2	cmpCount	Integer, number of components in pixel; 3 for direct pixels
2	cmpSize	Integer, number of bits per component; 5 or 8 for direct pixels
4	planeBytes	Long integer, offset to next plane = 0
	pmTable	Color table = 0
	pmReserved	Reserved = 0
4	ctSeed	Long integer, color table seed
2	ctFlags	Integer, flags for color table
2	ctSize	Integer, number of entries in ctTable – 1
8 * (ctSize + 1)	ctTable	Color table data
8	srcRect	Rectangle, source rectangle at source resolution
8	dstRect	Rectangle, destination rectangle at 72-dpi resolution
2	mode	Integer, transfer mode
–	pixData	Pixel data (see "Direct Pixels" earlier in this chapter)
2	endPICTop	End-of-picture opcode = $00FF

COLOR QUICKDRAW ROUTINES

Since recognizing direct pixel values only requires internal Color QuickDraw changes, no new routines are defined for direct pixel specification.

Creating an Extended Version 2 Picture

OpenCPicture performs the same functions as OpenPicture, except that it creates an extended version 2 format picture, with pixel resolution and the best imaging rectangle stored in the header. OpenCPicture works on all Macintosh computers running system software version 7.0, including machines without Color QuickDraw.

```
FUNCTION OpenCPicture (newHeader: OpenCPicParams) : PicHandle;
```

Use the newHeader parameter to describe the rectangle that encloses the drawing information you supply for the picture and to describe the best horizontal and vertical resolutions for displaying the picture in the rectangle. See "Direct Pixel Images" earlier in this chapter for a description of the OpenCPicParams data type.

As with OpenPicture, you close the picture using ClosePicture, and draw it using DrawPicture.

Creating Regions From Bitmaps

You can convert bitmaps or pixel maps to regions using the BitMapToRegion function.

```
FUNCTION BitMapToRegion (region: RgnHandle; bMap: BitMap) : OSErr;
```

The region parameter must be a valid region handle created with a NewRgn function. The old region contents are lost.

The bMap parameter may either be a bitmap or pixel map record. If you pass a pixel map record, its pixel size (bits per pixel) must be 1.

Result codes

pixmapTooDeepErr	–148	Pixel map record is deeper than 1 bit per pixel
rgnTooBigErr	–500	Bitmap would convert to a region greater than 64 KB

Copying Pixel Map Images

The CopyDeepMask procedure combines the effects of the CopyBits and CopyMask procedures.

```
PROCEDURE CopyDeepMask    (srcBits: BitMap; maskBits: BitMap; dstBits:
                           BitMap; srcRect: Rect; maskRect: Rect; dstRect:
                           Rect; mode: Integer; maskRgn: RgnHandle);
```

The CopyDeepMask procedure copies the source bitmap or pixel map to a destination bitmap or pixel map, using a bitmap or pixel map as a mask. The transfer can be performed in any of the copy modes described in the QuickDraw chapters of Volume I and Volume V of *Inside Macintosh,* with or without ditherCopy set, as described earlier in this chapter.

The result is clipped to the mask region and the boundary rectangle of the destination. The source and mask rectangles should be the same size. The mask rectangle selects the portion of the mask pixel map to use as the mask. If you don't want to clip to a mask region, pass NIL for the maskRgn parameter. The dstRect and maskRgn coordinates are in the destination coordinate system; the srcRect coordinates are in the source coordinate system; the maskRect coordinates are in the mask coordinate system.

All three pixel maps may range from 1 to 32 in pixel depth. The pixel values of the mask pixel map are applied as a filter between the source and destination pixel maps. A black mask pixel value means that the copy operation is to take the source pixel; a white value means that the copy operation is to take the destination pixel. Intermediate values specify a weighted average, which is calculated on a color component basis. For each pixel's color component the calculation is

$$(1 - mask) * source + (mask) * destination$$

Thus high mask values for a pixel's color component reduce that component's contribution from the source pixel map.

As with the CopyMask procedure, CopyDeepMask calls are not recorded in pictures, and do not print. The mask pixel map cannot come from the screen.

Determining Whether QuickDraw Has Finished Drawing

You can use the QDDone function to ensure that all drawing is done and avoid the possibility that new drawing operations might be overlaid by previously issued but unexecuted operations. This function is especially useful if a graphics accelerator is present and operating asynchronously.

```
FUNCTION QDDone (port: GrafPtr) : Boolean;
```

The QDDone function returns TRUE if drawing operations have finished in the designated graphics port, FALSE if any remain to be executed. If you pass NIL as the port parameter, then QDDone returns TRUE only if drawing operations have completed in all ports. (If a port has a clock or other continuously operating process, QDDone may never return TRUE.)

Reporting Data Structure Changes

You can use the following routines to mitigate possible side effects of directly changing a color table, pixel pattern, grafPort, or graphics device record.

```
PROCEDURE CTabChanged (ctab: CTabHandle);
```

Call CTabChanged after modifying the content of the color table specified by the ctab parameter. CTabChanged calls GetCTSeed to get a new seed (a unique identifier) for the color table and notifies QuickDraw of the change.

```
PROCEDURE PixPatChanged (ppat: PixPatHandle);
```

Call PixPatChanged after modifying either the pixel pattern record specified by the ppat parameter or any of its substructures (pattern map or pattern data records). PixPatChanged sets the patXValid flag to –1 and notifies QuickDraw of the change.

If your application changes the pmTable *field* of the pattern map's pixel pattern, it should call PixPatChanged. However, if your application changes the *content* of the color table referenced by the pixel map's pmTable field, it should call CTabChanged as well.

```
PROCEDURE PortChanged (port: GrafPtr);
```

Call PortChanged after modifying the content of a grafPort or any of its substructures. PortChanged notifies QuickDraw of the change.

You should not directly change any of the pixel pattern records pointed to by a color grafPort record. Instead, use the PenPixPat and BackPixPat procedures. However, if your application changes the content of one of the pixel pattern records, it should call PixPatChanged.

If your application changes the pmTable *field* of the port's pixel map, it should call PortChanged. However, if your application changes the *content* of the color table referenced by pmTable, it should call CTabChanged as well.

```
PROCEDURE GDeviceChanged (gdh: GDHandle);
```

Call GDeviceChanged after modifying the graphics device record specified by the gdh parameter or any of its substructures. GDeviceChanged notifies QuickDraw of the change.

If your application changes the pmTable *field* of the graphics device's pixel map, it should call GDeviceChanged. However, if your application changes the *content* of the color table referenced by gdPMap, it should call CTabChanged as well.

Obtaining Intermediate Colors

The GetGray function provides your application with the best intermediate color in RGB space that is available for a given device.

```
FUNCTION GetGray (device: GDHandle; backGround: RGBColor;
                  VAR foreGround: RGBColor) : Boolean;
```

In the device parameter you supply a handle to the device; in the backGround and foreGround parameters you supply the two colors for which you want the best intermediate RGB color. One use for GetGray is to return the best gray, as when dimming a menu item: supply black and white as the two colors, and GetGray returns the best available gray that lies between them.

If no gray is available (or, if you supplied two colors, no distinguishable third color is available), the foreGround parameter is unchanged, and the function returns FALSE. If at least one gray or intermediate color is available, it or the best one is stored in the foreGround parameter, and the function returns TRUE.

Interpreting New QDError Result Codes

The QDError function, introduced with Color QuickDraw in Volume V, returns the error result from the last Color QuickDraw or Color Manager call. It has a number of new result codes, and it has also been modified so that it does not fail on a black-and-white system (where it always returns FALSE). Its format is the same:

```
FUNCTION QDError : Integer;
```

QuickDraw uses stack space for work buffers. For complex operations such as depth conversion, dithering, and image resizing, stack space may not be sufficient. Color QuickDraw now attempts to get temporary memory from other parts of the system. If that is still not enough, QDError returns this code:

mfStackErr	–149	Insufficient stack

If your application receives this result code, divide the operation—for example, divide the image into left and right halves—and try again.

When you record drawing operations in an open region, the resulting region description may overflow the 64 KB limit. Should this happen, QDError returns –147.

regionTooBigError	–147	Region too big or complex

Since the resulting region is potentially corrupt, the closeRgn procedure returns an empty region if it detects QDError has been set to –147. A similar error can occur during conversion of a bitmap to a region.

rgnTooBigErr	–500	Bitmap would convert to a region greater than 64 KB

The BitMapToRegion function can also generate an error if a pixel map is supplied that is greater than 1 bit per pixel.

pixmapTooDeepErr	–148	Pixel map record is deeper than 1 bit per pixel

You may be able to recover from this problem by imaging your too-deep pixel map into a 1-bit pixel map and calling BitMapToRegion again.

Using a Custom Color Search Function

The interface to the custom color search mechanism, described in the Color Manager chapter of Volume V, omitted a VAR tag for the rgb parameter. The Color Manager's SearchProc function description looks like this:

```
FUNCTION SearchProc (VAR rgb: RGBColor; VAR position: LongInt) : Boolean;
```

This means that your custom search procedure can manipulate a color in some way, darkening it, for example, then return it. Setting the function result to FALSE causes the Color Manager to ignore the position parameter and perform its standard look-up on the altered color.

SUMMARY OF COLOR QUICKDRAW

Constants

```
CONST {new constants for Color QuickDraw}
      ditherCopy      = 64;   {dither mode for CopyBits}
      RGBDirect       = 16;   {16 & 32 bits/pixel pixelType value}
      grayishTextOr   = 49;   {draw with grayed text}
```

Data Types

```
  TYPE PixMapHandle = ^PixMapPtr;
       PixMapPtr    = ^PixMap;

       PixMap =
       RECORD
          baseAddr:       Ptr;         {pointer to image data}
          rowBytes:       Integer;     {flags, and bytes in a row}
          bounds:         Rect;        {boundary rectangle}
          pmVersion:      Integer;     {pixel map version number}
          packType:       Integer;     {packing format}
          packSize:       LongInt;     {size of data in packed state}
          hRes:           Fixed;       {horizontal resolution}
          vRes:           Fixed;       {vertical resolution}
          pixelType:      Integer;     {format of pixel image}
          pixelSize:      Integer;     {physical bits per pixel}
          cmpCount:       Integer;     {logical components per pixel}
          cmpSize:        Integer;     {logical bits per component}
          planeBytes:     LongInt;     {offset to next plane}
          pmTable:        CTabHandle;  {pointer to color table for }
                                       { this image}
          pmReserved:     LongInt      {reserved for future expansion}
       END;

       OpenCPicParams =
       RECORD
          srcRect:        Rect;        {source rectangle for best display }
                                       { at hRes, vRes resolution}
          hRes:           Fixed;       {best horizontal resolution}
          vRes:           Fixed;       {best vertical resolution}
          version:        Integer;     {set to -2}
          reserved1:      Integer;     {reserved for future use}
          reserved2:      LongInt      {reserved for future use}
       END;
```

```
PictureHeader =
RECORD
   version:       Integer;    {set to -2}
   reserved1:     Integer;    {reserved for future use}
   hRes:          Fixed;      {best horizontal resolution}
   vRes:          Fixed;      {best vertical resolution}
   srcRect:       Rect;       {source rectangle for best }
                              { display at hRes, vRes resolution}
   reserved2:     LongInt     {reserved for future use}
END;
```

Routines

Creating an Extended Version 2 Picture

```
FUNCTION OpenCPicture      (newHeader: OpenCPicParams) : PicHandle;
```

Creating Regions From Bitmaps

```
FUNCTION BitMapToRegion    (region: RgnHandle; bMap: BitMap) : OSErr;
```

Copying Pixel Map Images

```
PROCEDURE CopyDeepMask     (srcBits: BitMap; maskBits: BitMap; dstBits:
                            BitMap; srcRect: Rect; maskRect: Rect; dstRect:
                            Rect; mode: Integer; maskRgn: RgnHandle);
```

Determining Whether QuickDraw Has Finished Drawing

```
FUNCTION QDDone            (port: GrafPtr) : Boolean;
```

Reporting Data Structure Changes

```
PROCEDURE CTabChanged      (ctab: CTabHandle);

PROCEDURE PixPatChanged    (ppat: PixPatHandle);

PROCEDURE PortChanged      (port: GrafPtr);

PROCEDURE GDeviceChanged   (gdh: GDHandle);
```

Obtaining Intermediate Colors

```
FUNCTION GetGray           (device: GDHandle; backGround: RGBColor; VAR
                            foreGround: RGBColor) : Boolean;
```

Interpreting New QDError Result Codes

```
FUNCTION QDError : Integer;
```

Using a Custom Color Search Function

```
FUNCTION SearchProc          (VAR rgb: RGBColor; VAR position: LongInt) :
                              Boolean;
```

Result Codes

regionTooBigError	–147	Region too big or complex
pixmapTooDeepErr	–148	Pixel map record is deeper than 1 bit per pixel
mfStackErr	–149	Insufficient stack
rgnTooBigErr	–500	Bitmap would convert to a region greater than 64 KB

18 THE PICTURE UTILITIES PACKAGE

ABOUT THIS CHAPTER

This chapter describes the Picture Utilities Package, a set of routines with which you can obtain qualitative and quantitative information about pictures and pixel maps. You might want to find out about the text in a picture, for example, to see if the fonts it uses are available in the system. You can determine the number of colors a picture uses and obtain an optimal color table or palette for displaying it.

To use this chapter, you should have read the Graphics Overview and Color QuickDraw™ chapters of this volume and the Color QuickDraw chapter in Volume V.

The Picture Utilities Package is available with system software versions 7.0 and later. With system 7.0, the picture utilities work using the original QuickDraw, but with the limitation that any palette handles returned are NIL.

ABOUT THE PICTURE UTILITIES PACKAGE

The two most common forms of storing image information are pixel maps and pictures. The Picture Utilities Package consists of a number of routines for extracting information from a picture, or from a pixel map record and its associated image.

Unless they contain specialized code for parsing pictures, many applications deal with pictures as black boxes, perhaps imaging them into a pixel map and then dealing with the picture as pixel map data. The Picture Utilities Package provides a way to open that black box and deal with its contents intelligently.

The OpenCPicture routine described in the Color QuickDraw chapter of this volume stores resolution information in the picture header. The Picture Utilities Package returns this information for pictures created with OpenCPicture, and returns the standard screen resolution (72 dots per inch) for all other pictures.

USING THE PICTURE UTILITIES PACKAGE

You can use Picture Utilities Package routines and data structures to gather information about a single pixel map or picture, or you can survey a number of them. To get information about a single picture or pixel map, use either the GetPictInfo or GetPixMapInfo function, and all the information will be returned in a picture information record.

To collect information about a number of pictures and pixel maps, you need to make at least four calls: the NewPictInfo function creates an identifier for the collection. RecordPictInfo and RecordPixMapInfo collect information from pictures and pixel maps, respectively. RetrievePictInfo returns the collected information, and DisposPictInfo disposes of the data structures private to the collection. Information about the collection of pictures and pixel maps is returned in a picture information record.

An entire picture need not be read into memory; pictures can be spooled to the GetPictInfo or RecordPictInfo function, following the spooling procedure described in the Color QuickDraw chapter of Volume V.

Getting Color Information

If you want information about the colors of a picture or pixel map, you indicate how many colors you want to know about, what sort of color sampling you want done, and whether you want colors returned in a palette or color table.

Currently the Picture Utilities Package has two color-sampling methods: one that gives you the most frequently used colors and one that gives you the widest range of colors. Each has advantages in different situations. For example, suppose a forest image has 400 colors, of which 300 are greens, 80 are browns, and the rest are a scattering of gold sunlight effects. If you ask for the 250 most popular colors, you might, in early summer, get all greens. If you ask for a range of 250 colors, you will receive an assortment stretching from the greens and golds at one locus of RGB space to the browns at the other, including colors in between that might not actually appear in the image. If you need to use less than the image's full color set, you now have some information that may help you make the selection.

You can specify that the Picture Utilities Package chooses which color-sampling method to use (with the constant systemMethod), or you can specify one of the two color-sampling methods. By letting the Picture Utilities Package decide, you assure that when new methods are made available they will be chosen when appropriate.

```
CONST systemMethod  =   0;       {method chosen by picture utilites}
      popularMethod =   1;       {most frequently used colors}
      medianMethod  =   2;       {range of colors}
```

You can also supply a color-sampling algorithm of your own, as described in "Creating Custom Color-Sampling Methods" later in this chapter. In that case, you pass the resource ID of your color-sampling method.

▲ **Warning:** When you ask for color information about a picture, the Picture Utilities Package only takes into account the version 2 picture opcodes RGBFgCol, RGBBkCol, BkPixPat, PnPixPat, FillPixPat, and HiliteColor (as well as pixel map or bitmap data). Each occurrence of these opcodes is treated as 1 pixel, regardless of the number and sizes of the objects drawn with that color. If you need an accurate set of colors from a complex picture, create an image of the picture in an offscreen pixel map, and then call GetPixMapInfo to obtain color information about that pixel map. ▲

You can request that colors be returned in a color table, a palette, or both, and that black and white not be returned in palettes or color tables. You can also ask for information about comments and fonts encountered in the picture.

```
CONST returnColorTable       =  1;   {returns colors in a color table}
      returnPalette          =  2;   {returns colors in a palette}
      recordComments         =  4;   {creates a handle to comments}
      recordFontInfo         =  8;   {creates a handle to fonts}
      suppressBlackAndWhite  = 16;   {suppresses black and white from }
                                     { color tables and palettes}
```

When you use the returnColorTable, returnPalette, recordComments, and recordFontInfo values, you create handles to the additional information they provide. It is your responsibility to dispose of these handles. If you run version 7.0 with the original QuickDraw, the Picture Utilities Package always returns NIL for the palette.

Collecting Information From Multiple Pixel Maps or Pictures

You can survey a number of pixel maps or pictures and accumulate information about them in the picture information record. You can perform a number of such surveys simultaneously; they are identified by a unique identifier created when you call the NewPictInfo function to begin a survey.

You indicate which pixel maps or pictures to survey by making repeated calls to the RecordPixMapInfo or RecordPictInfo function. When you want to check the accumulated statistics, use the RetrievePictInfo function, and the picture information record will be filled with the latest information.

When you have finished a survey, call the DisposPictInfo function to dispose of the data structures associated with the identifier for that survey. Note that DisposPictInfo does not dispose of the handles returned in the picture information record.

Storing Information: The Picture Information Record

The PictInfo data type defines the record that stores pixel map and picture information, as gathered from a single image or from surveying a number of them. When you collect pixel map information, the first seven fields of the picture information record are of primary interest; the count fields contain 0, except for bitMapCount and pixMapCount, which contain the number of bitmaps and pixel maps encountered.

```
TYPE PictInfo =
     RECORD
        version:          Integer;         {Picture Utilities version}
        uniqueColors:     LongInt;         {total colors in pixel map }
                                           { or picture}
        thePalette:       PaletteHandle;   {handle to returned palette}
        theColorTable:    CTabHandle;      {handle to returned color }
                                           { table}
        hRes:             Fixed;           {horizontal resolution (dpi)}
        vRes:             Fixed;           {vertical resolution (dpi)}
```

```
        depth:            Integer;            {pixel depth of pixel map}
        sourceRect:       Rect;               {best rectangle for imaging}
        textCount:        LongInt;            {number of text objects}
        lineCount:        LongInt;            {number of lines}
        rectCount:        LongInt;            {number of rectangles}
        rRectCount:       LongInt;            {number of round rectangles}
        ovalCount:        LongInt;            {number of ovals}
        arcCount:         LongInt;            {number of arcs}
        polyCount:        LongInt;            {number of polygons}
        regionCount:      LongInt;            {number of regions}
        bitMapCount:      LongInt;            {number of bitmaps}
        pixMapCount:      LongInt;            {number of pixel maps}
        commentCount:     LongInt;            {total number of comments}
        uniqueComments:   LongInt;            {number of unique comments }
                                              { (by ID)}
        commentHandle:    CommentSpecHandle;  {handle to comment data}
        uniqueFonts:      LongInt;            {number of fonts}
        fontHandle:       FontSpecHandle;     {handle to font data}
        fontNamesHandle:  Handle;             {handle to list of font }
                                              { names}
        reserved1:        LongInt;
        reserved2:        LongInt
    END;
```

Field descriptions

version — The version number of the Picture Utilities Package, currently set to 0.

uniqueColors — The number of colors in the collected pictures or pixel maps.

thePalette — A handle to the resulting palette if you requested that colors be returned in a palette. That palette contains either the number of colors you requested to see, or, if there aren't that many, the number found. On systems running the original QuickDraw, this field is always returned as NIL.

theColorTable — A handle to the resulting color table if you requested that colors be returned in a color table. If there are fewer colors found than you requested, the remaining places in your color table are filled with black.

If a picture has more than 256 colors or has direct pixel maps (16- or 32-bit pixel values), then the colors returned in the color table are truncated internally to 16-bit direct RGB values. In such a case the returned colors have a slight loss of resolution, and the uniqueColors field reflects the number of colors distinguishable at that resolution.

hRes — The horizontal resolution of the last pixel map or picture encountered. See the description of the sourceRect field.

vRes — The vertical resolution of the last pixel map or picture encountered. See the description of the sourceRect field. Note that, although hRes and vRes are usually the same, they don't have to be.

depth — The deepest pixel depth of all pixel map records encountered.

sourceRect	The sourceRect value from the version 2 picture header for the last picture encountered. It contains the picture's rectangle size at the resolution indicated by hRes and vRes. The top-left corner of the rectangle is always (0,0). Pictures created with the OpenCPicture function have the hRes, vRes, and sourceRect fields built into their headers. Since pictures following the older version 2 picture format created by OpenPicture don't have this information, the hRes and vRes fields are set to 72 pixels per inch, and the source rectangle is calculated using the picture's picFrame field.
textCount	The total number of text objects in all the pictures.
lineCount	The total number of lines in all the pictures.
rectCount	The total number of rectangles in all the pictures.
rRectCount	The total number of round rectangles in all the pictures.
ovalCount	The total number of ovals in all the pictures.
arcCount	The total number of arcs in all the pictures.
polyCount	The total number of polygons in all the pictures.
regionCount	The total number of regions in all the pictures.
bitMapCount	The total number of bitmaps in all the pictures.
pixMapCount	The total number of pixel maps in all the pictures.
commentCount	The total number of comments in all the pictures.
uniqueComments	The number of comments (both long and short form) encountered that have different IDs. This field is valid only if you requested comment information.
commentHandle	A handle to a list of comment specification records if you asked for comment information.
uniqueFonts	The number of different fonts encountered in the picture. This field is valid only if you requested font information.
fontHandle	A handle to a list of font specification records if you requested font information.
fontNamesHandle	A handle to a list of the names of the fonts in the picture. The offset to a particular name is stored in the nameOffset field of the font specification record for that font. This field is valid only if you requested font information.

When you have examined multiple pixel maps, the hRes and vRes fields of the picture information record contain the last resolution encountered, the depth field contains the deepest pixel depth encountered, the uniqueColors field contains the total number of different colors encountered (up to the accuracy of the Picture Utility Package's storage bank for colors), and the color table or palette contains the most popular or widest range of colors across all the pixel map records and object colors examined.

If you requested a count of the comments in your GetPictInfo function, the picture information record contains a handle to an array of comment specification records. The uniqueComments field value indicates the number of comment specification records listed.

```
TYPE CommentSpec =
     RECORD
        count:          Integer;  {number of times this comment occurs}
        ID:             Integer   {ID assigned to this comment}
     END;
```

If you requested that font information be collected in your GetPictInfo function, the picture information record contains a handle to an array of font specification records.

```
TYPE FontSpec =
     RECORD
        pictFontID:     Integer;  {ID of the font as stored in the picture}
        sysFontID:      Integer;  {ID of the font as found in this system}
        size:           ARRAY[0..3] of LongInt;
                                  {font sizes used}
        style:          Integer;  {font styles used}
        nameOffset:     LongInt   {offset to font name in fontNamesHandle}
     END;
```

Field descriptions

pictFontID — The pictFontID field contains the ID number of the font as it is stored in the picture.

sysFontID — The sysFontID field contains the ID number of the font as it is stored in the current System file.

size — The size field contains 128 bits, in which a bit is set for each point size encountered, from 1 to 127 points. Bit 0 is set if a size larger than 127 is found.

style — The style field indicates the text styles (such as bold or italic) that were encountered for this font at any of its sizes. The style field is defined by the StyleItem data type, described in the QuickDraw chapter of Volume I.

nameOffset — The nameOffset field contains the offset into the list of font names (pointed to by the fontNamesHandle field of the picture information record) at which this font name is stored.

You must dispose of the handles that the picture information record gives you (thePalette, theColorTable, commentHandle, fontHandle, and fontNamesHandle) when you are through with them.

PICTURE UTILITIES PACKAGE ROUTINES

This section describes Picture Utilities Package routines, which examine pixel maps and pictures. All of these routines can potentially move and purge memory.

Assembly-language note: The trap macro for the Picture Utilities Package is _Pack15. You can call a specific routine by placing a 4-byte value (which includes the routine selector) in the register D0. These values are listed in "Assembly Language Information" at the end of this chapter.

Collecting Information From a Single Image

The GetPixMapInfo function examines a single pixel map, returning information in the picture information record. You must supply a handle to the pixel map record to be examined and a pointer to the picture information record that will hold the information.

```
FUNCTION GetPixMapInfo (thePixMapHandle: PixMapHandle; VAR thePictInfo:
                        PictInfo; verb: Integer; colorsRequested:
                        Integer; colorPickMethod: Integer; version:
                        Integer) : OSErr;
```

In the verb parameter you indicate whether you want colors from the image returned as a palette or a color table by setting the returnPalette or returnColorTable bit of the verb. You may set both bits, in which case you will get both a color table and a palette. You can also specify suppressBlackAndWhite in the verb parameter to request that black and white not be counted when surveying colors. (Since the Palette Manager adds black and white when creating a palette, this technique can be useful when you are sampling colors destined for a palette or the screen: ask for the number of colors you want minus 2, and suppress black and white.)

In the colorsRequested parameter you specify the number of colors you want returned in the palette or color table; it may be from 1 to 256.

Use the colorPickMethod parameter to indicate what colors to return. If you specify popularMethod, GetPixMapInfo returns the colors used most frequently. If you specify medianMethod, GetPixMapInfo returns a weighted distribution of colors. If you specify systemMethod, the Picture Utilities Package chooses the more appropriate. You can also create your own color-sampling method, as described in "Creating Custom Color-Sampling Methods" later in this chapter. To use your own method, specify its resource ID in the colorPickMethod parameter. The ID must be in the range from 128 to 32768. The resource type is 'cpmt'.

Set the version parameter to 0.

Result codes

pictInfoVersionErr	–11000	Version number not 0
pictInfoVerbErr	–11002	Invalid verb combination specified
cantLoadPickMethodErr	–11003	Custom pick method not in resource chain
colorsRequestedErr	–11004	Number out of range or greater than passed to NewPictInfo

```
FUNCTION GetPictInfo (thePictHandle: PicHandle; VAR thePictInfo:
                      PictInfo; verb: Integer; colorsRequested:
                      Integer; colorPickMethod: Integer; version:
                      Integer) : OSErr;
```

The GetPictInfo function examines a single picture, returning information in the picture information record. You must supply a handle to the picture to be examined in the thePictHandle parameter, and a pointer to the picture information record that will hold the information in the parameter thePictInfo.

As explained in the description of the GetPixMapInfo function, the verb parameter indicates whether colors are to be returned in a color table or palette, or both, and whether to suppress black and white. With the GetPictInfo function, you can also use the verb parameter to request comment or font information, which you specify by recordComments or recordFontInfo.

The colorsRequested parameter must contain the number of colors you want returned in the palette or color table.

Use the colorPickMethod parameter to indicate the color-sampling method. Its value can be systemMethod, popularMethod, medianMethod, or the resource ID of your own method.

Set the version parameter to 0.

Result codes

pictInfoVersionErr	–11000	Version number not 0
pictInfoVerbErr	–11002	Invalid verb combination specified
cantLoadPickMethodErr	–11003	Custom pick method not in resource chain
colorsRequestedErr	–11004	Number out of range or greater than passed to NewPictInfo
pictureDataErr	–11005	Invalid picture data

Collecting Information From Multiple Images

To survey a number of pixel maps or pictures, you first create an identifier, called the picture information ID, which associates a series of requests and allocates data structures to contain the gathered information.

```
FUNCTION NewPictInfo (VAR thePictInfoID: PictInfoID; verb: Integer;
                      colorsRequested: Integer; colorPickMethod: Integer;
                      version: Integer) : OSErr;
```

The NewPictInfo function sets the parameter thePictInfoID to a unique value. The verb parameter selects what information (palettes or color tables, comments or fonts) is to be returned by subsequent calls to RetrievePictInfo. For surveying pixel map records, valid choices are returnPalette, returnColorTable, and suppressBlackAndWhite, which are explained in the description of the GetPixMapInfo function earlier in this chapter.

For pictures, you can also use the verb parameter to request the collection of comment and font information by specifying recordComments and recordFontInfo.

The colorsRequested parameter must contain the number of colors you want returned in the palette or color table.

In the colorPickMethod parameter you specify whether you want to retrieve colors using the sampling method systemMethod, popularMethod, medianMethod, or the resource ID of your own method.

Set the version parameter to 0.

Result codes

pictInfoVersionErr	–11000	Version number not 0
pictInfoVerbErr	–11002	Invalid verb combination specified
cantLoadPickMethodErr	–11003	Custom pick method not in resource chain
colorsRequestedErr	–11004	Number out of range or greater than passed to NewPictInfo

```
FUNCTION RecordPixMapInfo (thePictInfoID: PictInfoID; thePixMapHandle:
                           PixMapHandle) : OSErr;

FUNCTION RecordPictInfo (thePictInfoID: PictInfoID; thePictHandle:
                         PicHandle) : OSErr;
```

These routines have parallel functions, one surveying pixel maps, the other pictures. In the parameter thePictInfoID you must pass the value returned from the NewPictInfo function, in thePixMapHandle you pass a handle to a pixel map record, and in thePictHandle you pass a handle to a picture. You can call these routines repeatedly to accumulate information about a number of pixel maps or pictures.

Result codes

pictInfoIDErr	–11001	Invalid picture information ID
pictureDataErr	–11005	Invalid picture data

```
FUNCTION RetrievePictInfo (thePictInfoID: PictInfoID; VAR thePictInfo:
                           PictInfo; colorsRequested: Integer) : OSErr;
```

The RetrievePictInfo function returns the information requested by the verb parameter passed to the associated NewPictInfo function specified by thePictInfoID. You supply a pointer to the picture information record in thePictInfo. If you requested a palette or color table, specify the number of colors you want in the colorsRequested parameter.

You can call this function repeatedly, gathering new information after additional calls to RecordPixMapInfo or RecordPictInfo. Remember to dispose of the handles returned to you (thePalette, theColorTable, commentHandle, fontHandle, and fontNamesHandle) when you finish with them.

Result codes

pictInfoIDErr	–11001	Invalid picture information ID
colorsRequestedErr	–11004	Number out of range or greater than passed to NewPictInfo

```
FUNCTION DisposPictInfo (thePictInfoID: PictInfoID) : OSErr;
```

The DisposPictInfo function disposes of all data structures private to the parameter thePictInfoID. It does not dispose of any of the handles returned to you by a call to RetrievePictInfo.

Result code

pictInfoIDErr	–11001	Invalid picture information ID

You can dispose of palettes by using the DisposePalette procedure, dispose of color tables by using the DisposeCTable procedure, and dispose of other allocations with the DisposHandle procedure.

Creating Custom Color-Sampling Methods

Assembly-language programmers can create a custom method for sampling colors. You specify its use by placing the resource ID of your function in the colorPickMethod parameters of the GetPixMapInfo, GetPictInfo, and NewPictInfo functions. Your custom function should be in a resource of type 'cpmt'.

Your function is called with a routine selector in register D0.

D0 value	Subroutine to call
D0 = 0	MyInitPickMethod
D0 = 1	MyRecordColors
D0 = 2	MyCalcColorTable
D0 = 3	MyDisposeColorPickMethod

The MyInitPickMethod function is called first; it should allocate storage or perform any other initialization required by your function. The MyRecordColors function is called to record colors if you create your own custom color bank. The MyCalcColorTable function is called if there are more colors in the picture being examined than your application requested to see or if you are recording your own colors. The MyDisposeColorPickMethod function is called when the application is done with the color sampling method. It should release memory requested by the MyInitPickMethod function.

If your routines return an error, that error is passed back to the application.

```
FUNCTION MyInitPickMethod (colorsRequested: Integer; VAR dataRef: LongInt;
                           VAR colorBankType: Integer) : OSErr;
```

Your MyInitPickMethod function must allocate whatever data you need and store a handle to your data in the location pointed to by the dataRef parameter. It should also return the type of color bank your function uses for color storage in colorBankType.

There are three valid color bank types:

```
CONST colorBankIsCustom       = -1;  {records colors you specify}
      colorBankIsExactAnd555  =  0;  {records exact colors}
      colorBankIs555          =  1;  {records colors in a 5-5-5 }
                                     { histogram}
```

Return colorBankIsCustom if you want to record your own colors; this is the only case in which your RecordColors routine is called. Your CalcColorTable function will also be called.

Return colorBankIs555 if you want the colors stored in a 5-5-5 histogram. The Picture Utilities Package calls the CalcColorTable routine with a pointer to the color bank (the 5-5-5 histogram) when the application retrieves color information. The Picture Utilities Package does not call your MyRecordColors function.

ColorBankIsExactAnd555 tells the Picture Utilities Package to return exact colors. The MyCalcColorTable function should only be called if there are more colors in the picture or pixel map than the application requests. (This is the same as ColorBankIs555 except that the Picture Utilities Package returns the exact colors whenever possible.)

The format of the 5-5-5 histogram is like a reversed color table. It is an array of 32,768 integers, where the *index* into the array is the color: 5 bits of red, followed by 5 bits of green, followed by 5 bits of blue. Each *entry* in the array is the number of colors in the picture that are approximated by the color that indexes this entry.

For example, suppose there were three instances of the following color in the pixel map:

red = %1101101010101110
green = %0111101010110001
blue = %0101101101101010

This color would be represented by index % 0 11011 01111 01011 (in hex $6DEB) and the value in the histogram at this index would be 3 (because there were three instances of this color).

```
FUNCTION MyRecordColors (dataRef: LongInt; colorsArray: RGBColorArray;
                         colorCount: LongInt; VAR uniqueColors: LongInt)
                         : OSErr;
```

The Picture Utilities Package calls your MyRecordColors function only if your InitPickMethod function returned colorBankIsCustom. MyRecordColors is called repeatedly for all the colors in the picture or pixel map. MyRecordColors should store the color information for the array of 48-bit colors that it was passed. The RGB color array is defined as

```
  TYPE RGBColorArray  =  ARRAY[0..0] of RGBColor;
```

The colorCount parameter indicates how many colors there are in the array colorsArray.

Your function must also calculate the number of unique colors (to the resolution of the color bank) that were added by this call to your MyCalcColorTable function. It should add this delta amount to the uniqueColors parameter that is passed to it.

```
FUNCTION MyCalcColorTable (dataRef: LongInt; colorsRequested: Integer;
                           colorBankPtr: Ptr; VAR resultPtr: CSpecArray)
                           : OSErr;
```

Your MyCalcColorTable function should look either at your own internal color bank or at the 5-5-5 histogram passed in the colorBankPtr parameter, and it should fill the array of color specification records pointed to by resultPtr with as many colors as were requested. If more colors are requested than you can return, fill the remaining entries with black (0000 0000 0000). If your MyInitPickMethod function returned colorBankIsCustom, the colorBankPtr value will not be valid, since your color-sampling method is responsible for keeping a record of the colors.

The colorBankPtr parameter is of type Ptr because the data stored in the color bank is of the type specified by the MyInitPickMethod function. Thus, if you specified colorBankIs555 in the colorBankType parameter, the color bank would be an array of integers (see the description of MyInitPickMethod). However, if the Picture Utilities Package supports other data types in the future, the colorBankPtr parameter could point to completely different objects. For now, you should always coerce colorBankPtr to a pointer to an integer. In the future you may need to coerce colorBankPtr to a pointer of the type you specify in MyInitPickMethod.

```
FUNCTION MyDisposeColorPickMethod (dataRef: LongInt) : OSErr;
```

Your MyDisposeColorPickMethod function should release any memory that you allocated in your MyInitColorMethod function.

SUMMARY OF THE PICTURE UTILITIES PACKAGE

Constants

```
CONST {color-sampling methods}
      systemMethod            = 0;  {method chosen by picture utilites}
      popularMethod           = 1;  {most frequently used colors}
      medianMethod            = 2;  {range of colors}

      {form and content of picture information}
      returnColorTable        = 1;  {returns colors in a color table}
      returnPalette           = 2;  {returns colors in a palette}
      recordComments          = 4;  {creates a handle to comments}
      recordFontInfo          = 8;  {creates a handle to fonts}
      suppressBlackAndWhite   =16;  {suppresses black and white from }
                                    { color tables and palettes}

      {color bank types}
      colorBankIsCustom       =-1;  {records colors you specify}
      colorBankIsExactAnd555  = 0;  {records exact colors}
      colorBankIs555          = 1;  {records colors in a 5-5-5 }
                                    { histogram}
```

Data Types

```
TYPE PictInfoID = LongInt;

     RGBColorArray  =  ARRAY[0..0] of RGBColor;

     PictInfoHandle = ^PictInfoPtr;
     PictInfoPtr = ^PictInfo;
     PictInfo =
     RECORD
        version:          Integer;        {Pict Utilities version}
        uniqueColors:     LongInt;        {total colors in pixel map }
                                          { or picture}
        thePalette:       PaletteHandle;  {handle to returned palette}
        theColorTable:    CTabHandle;     {handle to returned color }
                                          { table}
        hRes:             Fixed;          {horizontal resolution (dpi)}
        vRes:             Fixed;          {vertical resolution (dpi)}
        depth:            Integer;        {pixel depth of pixel map}
        sourceRect:       Rect;           {best rectangle for imaging}
        textCount:        LongInt;        {number of text objects}
        lineCount:        LongInt;        {number of lines}
```

```
   rectCount:        LongInt;         {number of rectangles}
   rRectCount:       LongInt;         {number of round rectangles}
   ovalCount:        LongInt;         {number of ovals}
   arcCount:         LongInt;         {number of arcs}
   polyCount:        LongInt;         {number of polygons}
   regionCount:      LongInt;         {number of regions}
   bitMapCount:      LongInt;         {number of bitmaps}
   pixMapCount:      LongInt;         {number of pixel maps}
   commentCount:     LongInt;         {total number of comments}
   uniqueComments:   LongInt;         {number of unique comments }
                                      { (by ID)}
   commentHandle:    CommentSpecHandle;
                                      {handle to comment data}
   uniqueFonts:      LongInt;         {number of fonts}
   fontHandle:       FontSpecHandle;  {handle to font data}
   fontNamesHandle:  Handle;          {handle to list of font names}
   reserved1:        LongInt;
   reserved2:        LongInt
END;

CommentSpecHandle = ^CommentSpecPtr;
CommentSpecPtr = ^CommentSpec;
CommentSpec =
RECORD
   count:            Integer;         {number of times this comment occurs}
   ID:               Integer          {ID assigned to this comment}
END;

FontSpecHandle = ^FontSpecPtr;
FontSpecPtr = ^FontSpec;
FontSpec =
RECORD
   pictFontID:       Integer;         {ID of the font as stored in the }
                                      { picture}
   sysFontID:        Integer;         {ID of the font as found in this }
                                      { system}
   size:             ARRAY[0..3] of LongInt;
                                      {font sizes used}
   style:            Integer;         {font styles used}
   nameOffset:       LongInt          {offset to font name in }
                                      { fontNamesHandle}
END;
```

Routines

Collecting Information From a Single Image

```
FUNCTION GetPixMapInfo      (thePixMapHandle: PixMapHandle; VAR thePictInfo:
                             PictInfo; verb: Integer; colorsRequested:
                             Integer; colorPickMethod: Integer; version:
                             Integer) : OSErr;

FUNCTION GetPictInfo        (thePictHandle: PicHandle; VAR thePictInfo:
                             PictInfo; verb: Integer; colorsRequested:
                             Integer; colorPickMethod: Integer; version:
                             Integer) : OSErr;
```

Collecting Information From Multiple Images

```
FUNCTION NewPictInfo        (VAR thePictInfoID: PictInfoID; verb: Integer;
                             colorsRequested: Integer; colorPickMethod:
                             Integer; version: Integer) : OSErr;

FUNCTION RecordPixMapInfo   (thePictInfoID: PictInfoID; thePixMapHandle:
                             PixMapHandle) : OSErr;

FUNCTION RecordPictInfo     (thePictInfoID: PictInfoID; thePictHandle:
                             PicHandle) : OSErr;

FUNCTION RetrievePictInfo   (thePictInfoID: PictInfoID; VAR thePictInfo:
                             PictInfo; colorsRequested: Integer) : OSErr;

FUNCTION DisposPictInfo     (thePictInfoID: PictInfoID) : OSErr;
```

Application-Defined Routines

```
FUNCTION MyInitPickMethod          (colorsRequested: Integer; VAR dataRef:
                                    LongInt; VAR colorBankType: Integer) :
                                    OSErr;

FUNCTION MyRecordColors            (dataRef: LongInt; colorsArray:
                                    RGBColorArray; colorCount: LongInt; VAR
                                    uniqueColors: LongInt) : OSErr;

FUNCTION MyCalcColorTable          (dataRef: LongInt; colorsRequested:
                                    Integer; colorBankPtr: Ptr; VAR
                                    resultPtr: CSpecArray) : OSErr;

FUNCTION MyDisposeColorPickMethod (dataRef: LongInt) : OSErr;
```

Result Codes

pictInfoVersionErr	–11000	Version number not 0
pictInfoIDErr	–11001	Invalid picture information ID
pictInfoVerbErr	–11002	Invalid verb combination specified
cantLoadPickMethodErr	–11003	Custom pick method not in resource chain
colorsRequestedErr	–11004	Number out of range or greater than passed to NewPictInfo
pictureDataErr	–11005	Invalid picture data

Assembly-Language Information

Trap Macro Requiring Routine Selectors

_Pack15

Selector	Routine
$0206	DisposPictInfo
$0403	RecordPictInfo
$0404	RecordPixMapInfo
$0505	RetrievePictInfo
$0602	NewPictInfo
$0800	GetPictInfo
$0801	GetPixMapInfo

19 THE COLOR PICKER PACKAGE

ABOUT THIS CHAPTER

This chapter describes how you can use the Color Picker Package to offer users a standard dialog box for choosing a color. The Color Picker Package also provides routines for converting color specifications from one color model to another.

You should be familiar with the material in the Graphics Overview chapter in this volume, especially the discussion of direct and indexed screen devices. Effective use of the Color Picker also requires familiarity with Color QuickDraw™, described in Volume V of *Inside Macintosh* and in this volume.

This chapter supersedes the description of the Color Picker in Volume V. The Color Picker Package is available in system software versions 4.1 and later. With system software version 7.0 the Color Picker's dialog box can be displayed on black-and-white devices.

You need to read this chapter if your application uses the color system introduced with Color QuickDraw (rather than the eight-color system available with the original QuickDraw) and you need to solicit color choices from users. If your application limits user selection to a specific list of colors, you may need to construct your own dialog box for color selection using Palette Manager routines, because the Color Picker allows users to choose colors from the entire range of 48-bit RGB values available with Color QuickDraw.

ABOUT THE COLOR PICKER PACKAGE

The Color Picker Package provides you with a standard way of soliciting a color choice from the user. When your application calls the Color Picker's GetColor function, the Color Picker presents its dialog box to the user, as shown in Figure 19-1.When the user is satisfied with a chosen color and clicks the OK button, GetColor returns that color to your application as an RGB value.

The Color Picker Package also has utility routines for converting between RGB values and several other color models, and for converting between the fixed integers Color QuickDraw uses for RGB colors and the SmallFract values the Color Picker Package uses with alternate color models.

This chapter begins by describing the color models the Color Picker Package works with. It then explains how to set up and present the Color Picker dialog box to users and how to use the Color Picker's conversion facilities.

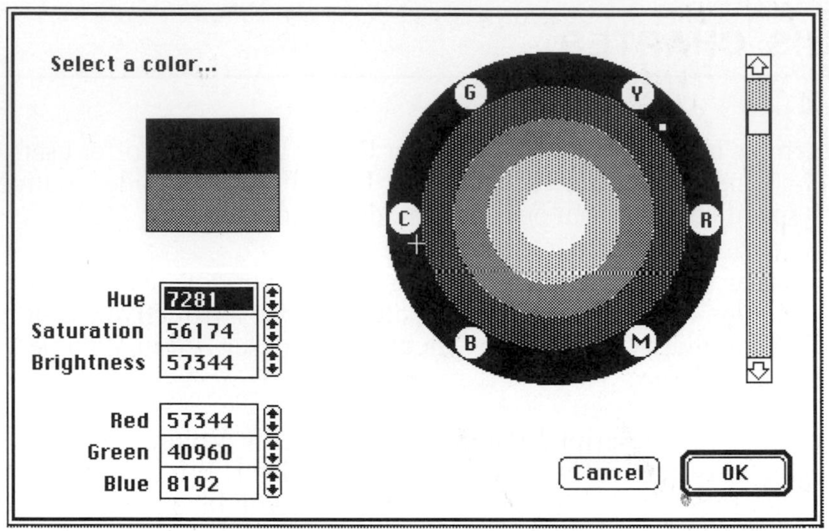

Figure 19-1. The Color Picker dialog box

COLOR MODELS

Both Color QuickDraw and standard screen devices work with an RGB (red, green, blue) color model, but graphic arts and design use other color models, such as HLS (hue, lightness, saturation) or HSV (hue, saturation, value), and in printing, the CMYK (cyan, magenta, yellow, black) model predominates. Great books have been written about color; this section presents a quick survey of the models with which the Color Picker Package works.

The RGB Model

In the RGB model, the three colors are additive. The more of each color you add, the closer the resulting color is to white. This is the way light-produced colors work; turning on the red, green, and blue phosphors of a television screen produces white, as does shining lights of red, green, and blue upon a stage.

The RGB color record is the Color QuickDraw data structure for the RGB color model.

```
TYPE RGBColor =
     RECORD
        red:        Integer;     {red component}
        green:      Integer;     {green component}
        blue:       Integer      {blue component}
     END;
```

The frontispiece of Volume V of *Inside Macintosh* shows a color cube that represents the values possible in an RGB system. Figure 19-2 is a black-and-white representation of that cube.

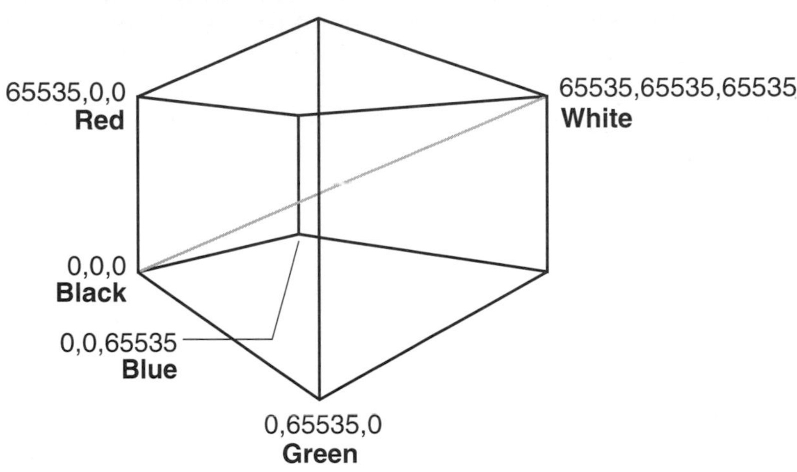

Figure 19-2. The RGB color cube

Starting at one corner, with 0 values for each color, is black. Increasing any one of the values produces shades of that color, increasing its saturation. Increasing all three values equally generates a diagonal line across the cube toward full value (65,535) for each, which is white. Values on that diagonal are shades of gray; values off the line in any direction are colors. For example, pink in the RGB model would be full red with some equal amount of green and blue, in effect moving from the black corner of the color cube up along the edge to full red, then traversing a diagonal across the top face from red toward white, as illustrated in Figure 19-3.

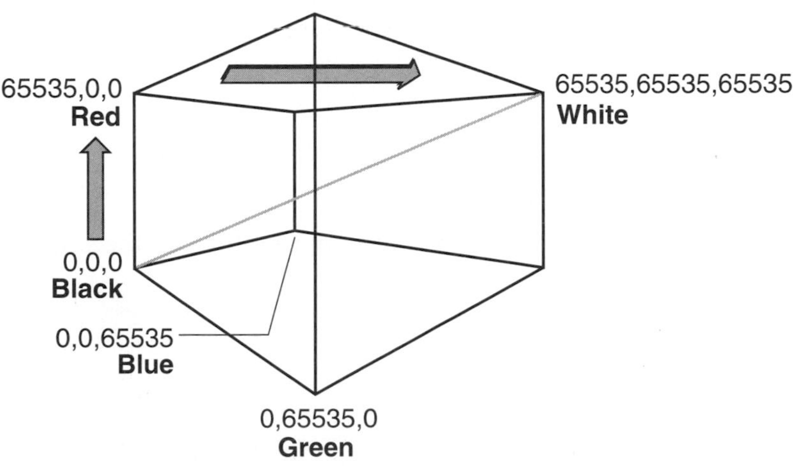

Figure 19-3. Getting to pink

The CMYK Model

In the CMYK model, which is used by printers, the three colors and black are subtractive: Increasing values moves the result closer to black. This model is intuitive for printing, which is usually done on white paper—to get white, don't print anything. In theory, black could be achieved by mixing full values of cyan, magenta, and yellow, but purity in chemicals is more problematic than purity in light, and four-color print processes use black as well. The Color Picker's CMYColor data type defines only the three colors. It uses SmallFract values, which are the fractional parts of fixed values, as described in the section "Using Conversion Facilities" later in this chapter.

```
TYPE CMYColor =
     RECORD                              {CMY and RGB are complements}
        cyan:          SmallFract;       {cyan component}
        magenta:       SmallFract;       {magenta component}
        yellow:        SmallFract        {yellow component}
     END;
```

Note in Figure 19-4 that cyan, magenta, and yellow are complements of red, green, and blue.

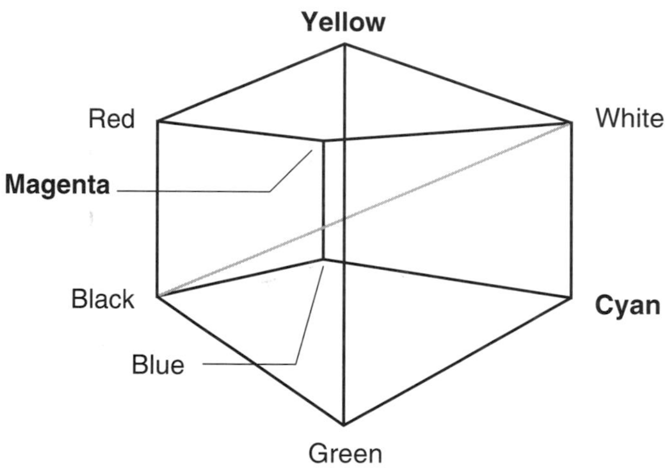

Figure 19-4. Cyan, magenta, and yellow on the color cube

The HLS and HSV Models

The components of the HLS and HSV models are not three diverse colors, as in the RGB and CMYK models. The HLS and HSV models separate color, or hue, from brightness and saturation.

Brightness is a measure of the amount of black in a color (the less black, the brighter the color); **saturation** is a measure of how much white it contains (the less white, the more saturated the color). **Hue** is indicated by an arbitrary assignment of numbers to colors. The amount of that hue is indicated by a saturation value, and the brightness of the color is a third value. The best representation for such a system is an inverted cone, as shown in Figure 19-5, in which hues vary around the perimeter, where they are most highly saturated, and brightness increases from the tip of thc cone to the disk. The gray line from black to white begins at the tip and runs up through the cone to the center of the disk.

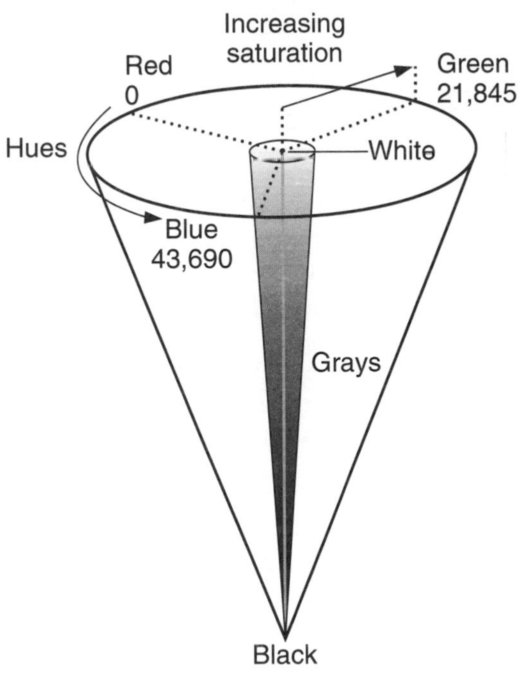

Figure 19-5. The HLS/HSV color cone

This is the model portrayed in the Color Picker's dialog box. The disk is shown full face, the hues are at their most saturated around the rim, and the brightness line down the cone is controlled by the scroll bar at the right of the dialog box.

In the Color Picker's color wheel the value for pure red is 0, pure green is 21,845, and pure blue is 43,690. The amount of black is set by the value for brightness (corresponding to *lightness* in HLS, *value* in HSV), and the amount of color in the mix is set by saturation. Pink in the HLS or HSV system would be obtained by setting hue to red, saturation to some amount less than full, and brightness to full.

The HLS and HSV systems are sufficiently similar that the Color Picker can treat them as one by a simple expedient: the Color Picker treats the HLS model as if its components were ordered HSL; this puts hue and saturation in the same relative positions in the data structures of both models.

```
TYPE HSLColor =
     RECORD
        hue:           SmallFract;    {fraction of circle, red at 0}
        saturation:    SmallFract;    {0-1, 0 is gray, 1 is pure color}
        lightness:     SmallFract     {0-1, 0 is black, 1 is white}
     END;
```

```
TYPE HSVColor =
     RECORD
        hue:            SmallFract;     {fraction of circle, red at 0}
        saturation:     SmallFract;     {0-1, 0 is gray, 1 is pure color}
        value:          SmallFract      {0-1, 0 is black, 1 is max intensity}
     END;
```

Color Models in the Dialog Box

The controls in the dialog box are designed for use in the HLS and HSV models: the user chooses hue by moving the cursor around the color wheel, saturation by moving the cursor into or out from the center, and brightness (value or lightness) by using the scroll bar at the right. The way the RGB values vary in response to the dialog controls is not intuitive, but their responses help to show how the models relate.

The dialog box cannot exactly match printing's subtractive effect, and it does not offer CMYK controls, but the Color Picker Package does include routines for converting between RGB and CMY (cyan, magenta, yellow, without a black component).

USING THE COLOR PICKER PACKAGE

Most applications only use the Color Picker Package to display the Color Picker's dialog box. A few applications may need to use the color model and SmallFract conversion routines.

Presenting the Color Picker Dialog Box

Your application can present a user with the Color Picker dialog box, shown in Figure 19-1, by using the Color Picker's GetColor function.

When called by your application, GetColor displays the dialog box, including prompt text, which appears in the upper-left corner, and the starting color, which appears in the lower of the two rectangles below the prompt. The color that the user is selecting, displayed in the upper rectangle, ranges over the entire color space in response to the controls in the rest of the dialog box. Your application can supply the prompt text, the starting color, and the location of the upper-left corner of the dialog box, and it can specify whether the dialog box should appear on the main screen (the screen with the menu bar) or the screen with the greatest pixel depth.

The two groups of numeric fields (Hue, Saturation, Brightness; Red, Green, Blue) show the parameters of the color being picked in the two color models. The user can increase or decrease the values using the arrow controls or can enter values directly into any of the six fields.

The range for each of the component values is 0 to 65,535. Larger values are truncated to 65,535 after the user exits the field. The hue value for pure red is 0; pure green is 21,845; pure blue is 43,690. Hue values wrap around from 0 to 65,535, so the user can circumnavigate the wheel with arrow controls just as with the cursor. The user can select a single RGB value from Color QuickDraw's entire range of 2^{48} color values.

On black-and-white hardware (or in less than 4-bit mode), the display appears in black and white; the Color Picker returns the RGB value selected, but it does not call any color routines in the course of responding to user actions.

On a device with a variable color look-up table (CLUT), the Color Picker temporarily borrows a CLUT entry to display the exact color in the rectangle that shows the color currently being picked. (If you let the Color Manager approximate the user's value when your application subsequently displays the chosen color, the result will probably differ somewhat from the one picked.) The Color Picker restores the color environment when it is done.

Using Conversion Facilities

In addition to the GetColor function that displays the Color Picker dialog box, the Color Picker Package provides six procedures for converting between an RGB color record and a CMY, HLS, or HSV color record, and it provides two functions that convert between SmallFract and fixed numbers. Most applications are likely to use only the GetColor function.

The Color Picker Package defines the CMY color, HSL color, and HSV color records with SmallFract values rather than integer values (as used in the RGB color record). A SmallFract value is the fractional part—that is, the low-order word—of a fixed number.

```
TYPE SmallFract = Integer;    {unsigned fraction between 0 and 1}
```

The integer values in the RGB color record are actually used as unsigned integer-sized values; by using SmallFract values, the Color Picker Package avoids sign extension problems in the conversion math.

The Color Picker Package provides two functions for converting between SmallFract and fixed numbers. Most applications do not need to use these facilities.

COLOR PICKER PACKAGE ROUTINES

The Color Picker Package comprises nine routines: the GetColor function that displays the Color Picker's dialog box, six procedures for converting between color record types, and two functions for converting between SmallFract and fixed values. Most applications are likely to use only the GetColor function.

Assembly-language note: To gain access to the Color Picker Package routines, use the trap macro _Pack12.

Displaying the Color Picker Dialog Box

The GetColor function displays the Color Picker dialog box on a screen.

```
FUNCTION GetColor (where: Point; prompt: Str255; inColor: RGBColor; VAR
                  outColor: RGBColor) : Boolean;
```

The dialog box appears with its upper-left corner located at the point you designate with the where parameter. The GetColor function can display the dialog box and accept color selection on any screen, not just the main screen. If you set where to (0,0), the dialog box is positioned neatly on the main screen—centered horizontally, with one-third of the empty space above the box and two-thirds below, regardless of the screen size. If you set the where parameter to (–1,–1), the GetColor function displays the dialog box on what the Color Picker determines to be the best screen, optimizing depth and color.

The prompt string is displayed in the upper-left corner of the dialog box. The inColor parameter is the starting color, which the user may want for comparison; it is displayed immediately below the current output color (the one the user is picking). The outColor parameter is set to the last color value the user picks before clicking OK. On entry, the outColor parameter is treated as undefined, so the output color sample initially matches the input. Although the color being picked may vary widely, the input color sample remains fixed, and clicking the input sample resets the output color sample to match it.

GetColor returns TRUE if the user exits by clicking the OK button, FALSE if the user exits by clicking the Cancel button.

Converting Between Color Models

These six procedures offer conversions between the RGB color model and each of the CMY, HLS, and HSV models.

```
PROCEDURE CMY2RGB (cColor: CMYColor; VAR rColor: RGBColor);
```

The CMY2RGB procedure converts a CMY color record to its equivalent RGB color record.

```
PROCEDURE HSL2RGB (hColor: HSLColor; VAR rColor: RGBColor);
```

The HSL2RGB procedure converts an HSL color record to its equivalent RGB color record.

```
PROCEDURE HSV2RGB (hColor: HSVColor; VAR rColor: RGBColor);
```

The HSV2RGB procedure converts an HSV color record to its equivalent RGB color record.

```
PROCEDURE RGB2CMY (rColor: RGBColor; VAR cColor: CMYColor);
```

The RGB2CMY procedure converts an RGB color record to its equivalent CMY color record.

```
PROCEDURE RGB2HSL (rColor: RGBColor; VAR hColor: HSLColor);
```

The RGB2HSL procedure converts an RGB color record to its equivalent HSL color record.

```
PROCEDURE RGB2HSV (rColor: RGBColor; VAR hColor: HSVColor);
```

The RGB2HSV procedure converts an RGB color record to its equivalent HSV color record.

Converting Between SmallFract and Fixed Values

A SmallFract value can represent a value between 0 and 65,535. The Color Picker Package uses SmallFract values in its CMY color, HSL color, and HSV color records. You can use these functions if you need to convert SmallFract values to or from fixed values. (They can be assigned directly to and from integers.)

```
FUNCTION SmallFract2Fix (s: SmallFract) : Fixed;
```

The SmallFract2Fix function converts a SmallFract value to a fixed integer.

```
FUNCTION Fix2SmallFract (f: Fixed) : SmallFract;
```

The Fix2SmallFract function converts a fixed integer to a SmallFract value.

SUMMARY OF THE COLOR PICKER PACKAGE

Constants

```
CONST
      MaxSmallFract   =  $0000FFFF;   {maximum SmallFract value, as LongInt}
```

Data Types

```
TYPE CMYColor =
     RECORD                                  {CMY and RGB are complements}
        cyan:           SmallFract;          {cyan component}
        magenta:        SmallFract;          {magenta component}
        yellow:         SmallFract           {yellow component}
     END;

     HSLColor =
     RECORD
        hue:            SmallFract;          {fraction of circle, red at 0}
        saturation:     SmallFract;          {0-1, 0 is gray, 1 is pure color}
        lightness:      SmallFract           {0-1, 0 is black, 1 is white}
     END;

     HSVColor =
     RECORD
        hue:            SmallFract;          {fraction of circle, red at 0}
        saturation:     SmallFract;          {0-1, 0 is gray, 1 is pure color}
        value:          SmallFract           {0-1, 0 is black, 1 is max intensity}
     END;

     SmallFract = Integer;                   {unsigned fraction between 0 and 1}
```

Routines

Displaying the Color Picker Dialog Box

```
FUNCTION GetColor           (where: Point; prompt: Str255; inColor:
                             RGBColor; VAR outColor: RGBColor) : Boolean;
```

Converting Between Color Models

```
PROCEDURE  CMY2RGB     (cColor: CMYColor; VAR rColor: RGBColor);
PROCEDURE  HSL2RGB     (hColor: HSLColor; VAR rColor: RGBColor);
PROCEDURE  HSV2RGB     (hColor: HSVColor; VAR rColor: RGBColor);
PROCEDURE  RGB2CMY     (rColor: RGBColor; VAR cColor: CMYColor);
PROCEDURE  RGB2HSL     (rColor: RGBColor; VAR hColor: HSLColor);
PROCEDURE  RGB2HSV     (rColor: RGBColor; VAR hColor: HSVColor);
```

Converting Between SmallFract and Fixed Values

```
FUNCTION SmallFract2Fix    (s: SmallFract) : Fixed;
FUNCTION Fix2SmallFract    (f: Fixed) : SmallFract;
```

Assembly-Language Information

Trap Macro Requiring Routine Selectors

_Pack12

Selector	Routine
$0001	Fix2SmallFract
$0002	SmallFract2Fix
$0003	CMY2RGB
$0004	RGB2CMY
$0005	HSL2RGB
$0006	RGB2HSL
$0007	HSV2RGB
$0008	RGB2HSV
$0009	GetColor

20 THE PALETTE MANAGER

ABOUT THIS CHAPTER

The Palette Manager monitors the color needs of the graphics environment. The Palette Manager can track the combined color and gray-scale requirements of the Operating System, your application, and other applications, and it can do so across multiple screens. This chapter describes how you can use the Palette Manager to ensure that a set of colors is available whenever one of your application's windows is active.

System software versions 6.0.5 and later, or those using the 32-Bit QuickDraw™ system extension, incorporate the revised and expanded Palette Manager. This chapter presents a complete description of the new Palette Manager. It replaces the Palette Manager chapter in Volume V.

You need to read this chapter if your application uses Color QuickDraw's color system, rather than the eight-color system supplied with the original QuickDraw, or no color at all.

You should be familiar with the Graphics Overview and Color QuickDraw chapters in this volume, and with the original Color QuickDraw chapter in Volume V.

ABOUT THE PALETTE MANAGER

Your application should use Palette Manager routines if it needs to

- set up and maintain collections of colors or grays
- manage shared color resources
- provide exact colors for displaying images
- initiate color table animation

Your application can specify a color as an RGB value, and Color QuickDraw and the Color Manager determine the closest match available on the hardware at the time the color is needed. On direct hardware, the match is virtually exact; on indexed hardware, the match depends both on the capabilities of the video device and on the color needs of the Operating System and other applications. By creating a palette of colors for your application, you ensure that appropriate colors are available when its window becomes frontmost.

The Palette Manager acts as intermediary between the palettes you create for your application's windows and the color look-up tables (CLUTs) that contain the colors an indexed device can display. When your window is opened or brought to the front, the Palette Manager checks your palette's colors against those in the color tables of all devices the window touches. The Palette Manager then loads colors into the color tables as needed, taking into account the sizes of the color tables and the importance you have placed on various colors in your palette.

You create palettes as resources of type 'pltt'. In the palette resource you specify the RGB colors your application needs. You can also indicate whether each color needs to be matched exactly and, if not, how close a match is required. You can tailor your palettes to different possible video devices—indicating, for example, that certain colors in the palette should be used with 4-bit pixel depths, that a different set should be used with 8-bit pixel depths, and that neither set should be used with gray-scale devices. Palettes can also be created from color tables.

The Palette Manager can handle different screen depths across multiple devices. If the user moves your application window so that it overlaps one gray-scale, one indexed-pixel, and one direct-pixel screen, the Palette Manager chooses appropriate grays and colors for all three.

The Palette Manager has access to all palettes used by all windows throughout the system. A set of default color tables for devices of various depths ensures that the Palette Manager always returns to a known set of colors when an application terminates, and, when your application begins executing, it executes in an environment equipped with as broad a range of colors or grays as the hardware allows.

The rest of this chapter describes

- palettes, and the usage categories to which colors in palettes are assigned
- how the Palette Manager changes the environment by allocating new colors when, for example, a window is brought to the front
- how the Palette Manager restores the environment when your application finishes executing
- how you can use the Palette Manager's color categories
- how to create palettes from resources from within your application, and from color tables

PALETTES

A **palette** is a data structure that contains a header and a collection of color records, one for each color in the palette. The header contains the number of color records in the palette and the private fields used by the Palette Manager.

```
TYPE PaletteHandle          = ^PalettePtr;
     PalettePtr             = ^Palette;

     Palette =
     RECORD
        pmEntries:          Integer;        {entries in pmInfo}
        pmDataFields:       ARRAY[0..6] OF Integer;
                                            {private fields}
        pmInfo:             ARRAY[0..0] OF ColorInfo
                                            {color information}
     END;
```

Each color is listed as a color information record, which comprises an RGB color value, information describing how the color is to be used, a tolerance value for colors that need only be approximated, and private fields. You should not create and modify the public fields directly; instead, use the Palette Manager routines.


```
TYPE ColorInfo =
     RECORD
        ciRGB:              RGBColor;        {absolute RGB values}
        ciUsage:            Integer;         {color usage information}
        ciTolerance:        Integer;         {tolerance value}
        ciDataFields:       ARRAY[0..2] OF Integer
                                             {private fields}
     END;
```

You can create palettes as resources of type 'pltt', or by using Palette Manager routines from within your application.

Your application can create a default palette for the Palette Manager to use when one of your application's windows doesn't have a palette specified. (This may be especially useful to color applications that use old-style, black-and-white dialog and alert boxes.)

Color Usage Categories

When the user activates a window, the Palette Manager examines the window's palette, if it has one, to determine whether colors need to be loaded into the current device's color look-up tables. If your window requires 180 shades of green, for example, chances are the current CLUTs lack the necessary colors. Whether the Palette Manager must change a color table depends on what colors are in it already, what colors you ask for, and the categories into which your colors fall.

The Palette Manager tracks colors in six **usage categories,** which you specify to control the way the Palette Manager allocates colors. You assign usage categories to colors when you create your palette, and you can change the categories using Palette Manager routines.

- A **courteous color** accepts whatever value the Color Manager determines to be the closest match currently available in the color table. On indexed devices, the Palette Manager lets the Color Manager select appropriate pixel values from those already in the CLUT. On direct devices, courteous colors always display as specified. Courteous colors have no special properties, but their use offers you a convenient holding place for collecting colors.

- A **tolerant color** also accepts the Color Manager's choices on an indexed device, but, unlike a courteous color, a tolerant color specifies an acceptable range for color matching. If no color in the device's color table falls within that range, the Palette Manager loads the color required. On direct devices, the Palette Manager matches tolerant colors as closely as the hardware allows.

- An **animated color** is used for special color animation effects, as described in "Animated Colors" later in this chapter. Animated colors are reserved by a palette until its window is closed, and until then their spaces are unavailable to (and can't be used to match) any other request for color. The effects of color animation depend on the existence of a device color table, and, since a direct device doesn't have one, color animation has no effect on a direct device's display. If your window spans two devices, one indexed and one direct, the Palette Manager is dexterous enough to animate the portion on the indexed device's screen.

- An **explicit color** specifies an index value, and always generates the corresponding entry from the device's color table. Explicit colors are useful if you wish to display the contents of a color table—for example, to display to a user some or all of the colors actually available.
- An **inhibited color** is prevented from appearing on color and gray-scale devices of specified pixel depths. Inhibited colors are always combined with other usage categories. You can create a large palette—for example, with two different sets of color ranges, one optimized for a 4-bit device, the other optimized for an 8-bit device—and then inhibit colors on the devices for which they are not intended.
- **PmWhite and pmBlack colors** are assigned to white or black on 1-bit devices. If your application is working with red and dark blue, for example, both might get mapped to black on a 1-bit device. By assigning pmWhite to one and pmBlack to the other, you assure that they will be distinct. These categories may be combined with other usage categories, but combining them with each other is undefined.

Several color usage categories can be combined. You can specify that a color is both tolerant and explicit, for example, which means that your RGB color, or a tolerably close match, is placed in the color table at the index corresponding to that palette entry (as opposed to merely being available somewhere in the table), on all devices that touch the window.

When you specify colors for a palette within a 'pltt' resource, you usually assign the same usage value to each color in the palette. However, if you must use a particular color differently than the others, you can assign it a different usage value, either when creating the resource file, or within the application by means of the SetEntryUsage procedure.

CHANGING THE COLOR ENVIRONMENT

The colors available in any particular hardware environment depend on the color or black-and-white settings and the pixel depths that the attached cards and screens can support, and on what they are set to by the system or by the user.

Since your palette may define more colors than the available hardware can display, the Palette Manager allocates your requests according to their priority. To make the best use of the Palette Manager, you should understand the allocation process. Prioritization is important only when the ActivatePalette procedure is called, which occurs automatically when your window becomes the frontmost window. (You may also call ActivatePalette yourself after changing one or more of the palette's colors or usage categories.)

The Palette Manager first allocates animated colors that are also marked for explicit usage. Colors that are marked as tolerant and explicit are allocated next.

The Palette Manager allocates animated colors next. Starting with the first entry in your window's palette (entry 0), the Palette Manager checks to see if it is an animated entry. It checks each animated entry to see that the entry has a reserved index for each appro-priate device, selecting and reserving an index if it doesn't. This process continues until all animated colors have been satisfied or until the available indexes are exhausted.

The Palette Manager handles tolerant colors next. It assigns each tolerant color an index until all tolerant colors have been satisfied. The Palette Manager then calculates for each entry the difference between the desired color and the color associated with the selected index. If the difference exceeds the tolerance you have specified, the Palette Manager marks the selected device entry to be changed to the desired color.

Since explicit colors designate index values, not the colors at those index locations, and since courteous colors are amenable to being assigned any RGB value, neither is considered during prioritization.

When the Palette Manager has matched as many animated and tolerant entries as possible, it checks to see if the current CLUT is adequate. If modifications are needed, the Palette Manager overrides any calls made to the Color Manager outside the Palette Manager and then calls the Color Manager to change the device's color environment accordingly (with the SetEntries procedure).

Finally, if the color environment on a given device has changed, the Palette Manager checks to see if this change has affected any other window in the system. If another window is affected, the Palette Manager checks that window to see if it specifies an update in the case of such changes. Applications can use the SetPalette, NSetPalette, or SetPaletteUpdates procedure to specify whether a window should be updated when its environment has been changed because of actions by another window. (If so, the InvalRect procedure, described in the Window Manager chapter of Volume I, updates the window, using the boundary rectangle of the device that has been changed.)

RESTORING THE COLOR ENVIRONMENT

When a window closes, the Palette Manager resets each display device to its default color table, except for those indexes still reserved by another application. Eventually, the application that owns those indexes will terminate or voluntarily release the indexes. You can run a long sequence of color-stealing, wildly animated programs, quit them all, return to the Finder™, and find every screen in the system fully restocked with default system color tables. (But if an application calls the Color Manager procedure ProtectEntries to lock a device index, the Palette Manager cannot restore the default color tables.)

The Palette Manager restores an animated entry to a default color state when the index is no longer needed.

The Palette Manager provides default color tables for differing screen devices.

Screen device	**Default color table**
Any device in black-and-white mode or 1 bit deep	A gray-scale ramp, that is, an evenly spaced range from white in index 0 to black in the last index.
A color device in 2-bit mode	Indexes 0 to 3 contain white, 50 percent gray, the highlight color, and black, respectively.
A color device in 4-bit mode	The resource 'clut' with a resource ID of 4. If the color closest to the highlight color differs from it by more than $3000 in any component, the color is averaged with the highlight color.
A color device in 8-bit mode	The resource 'clut' with resource ID 8.

The 'clut' resource IDs 1, 2, 4, and 8 are the standard color tables for those bit depths; they are shown in Color Plate XXV, "Default Color Tables." The 'clut' resource IDs 34, 36, and 40—the bit depth plus 32—are gray-scale ramps for those bit depths. The default color tables with the highlight color added are 'clut' resource IDs 66, 68, and 72—that is, the bit depth plus 64. To get these color tables, use the GetCTable function (not GetResource), as described in the Color QuickDraw chapter in this volume.

USING THE PALETTE MANAGER

The Palette Manager is extremely versatile, and your application can use it to obtain an additional level of color control. The Palette Manager can selectively apply QuickDraw, Color Manager, and Graphics Devices Manager routines, thereby giving you color control across windows and devices.

Working With Color Usage Categories

You define the usage category for each color in a palette, using these constants:

```
CONST pmCourteous    = $0000;      {courteous color}
      pmTolerant     = $0002;      {tolerant color}
      pmAnimated     = $0004;      {animated color}
      pmExplicit     = $0008;      {explicit color}
      pmWhite        = $0010;      {use on 1-bit device}
      pmBlack        = $0020;      {use on 1-bit device}
      pmInhibitG2    = $0100;      {inhibit on 2-bit gray-scale device}
      pmInhibitC2    = $0200;      {inhibit on 2-bit color device}
      pmInhibitG4    = $0400;      {inhibit on 4-bit gray-scale device}
      pmInhibitC4    = $0800;      {inhibit on 4-bit color device}
      pmInhibitG8    = $1000;      {inhibit on 8-bit gray-scale device}
      pmInhibitC8    = $2000;      {inhibit on 8-bit color device}
```

Effective use of the Palette Manager requires a considered assignment of usage categories for the colors of your palette.

Courteous Colors

Courteous colors may seem so polite as to be useless, but they can serve as convenient placeholders. If your application uses a small number of colors, you can place them in a palette, ordered according to your preference and designated as courteous.

Suppose you have an open window named myColorWindow that has a palette resource consisting of a set of eight colors: white, black, red, orange, yellow, green, blue, and violet, in that order, each with a usage category specified as courteous, as shown in Figure 20-1.

	RGB value	Usage	Tolerance
0	White	c	-
1	Black	c	-
2	Red	c	-
3	Orange	c	-
4	Yellow	c	-
5	Green	c	-
6	Blue	c	-
7	Violet	c	-

Figure 20-1. A courteous palette

The following example paints the rectangle myRect in yellow (palette entry 4, where white is 0).

```
SetPort (myColorWindow);
PmForeColor (4);
PaintRect (myRect);
```

This is exactly analogous to the following sequence of Color QuickDraw routines, where yellowRGB is of type ColorSpec:

```
yellowRGB.red := $FFFF;
yellowRGB.green := $FFFF;
yellowRGB.blue := $0000;

SetPort (myColorWindow);
RGBForeColor (yellowRGB);
PaintRect (myRect);
```

Colors with specified usage categories that can't be satisfied by the Palette Manager default to courteous colors. This occurs, for example, when drawing to a direct device or one with a fixed CLUT.

Tolerant Colors

Tolerant colors allow you to change the current color environment if the available colors are not sufficiently close to those your application needs. When your window becomes the frontmost window on a device, its palette's colors are given preference. Each tolerant color is compared to the best match available in the current color environment. (In a multi-screen environment this comparison is done for each device on which the window is drawn.) When the difference between your color and the best available match is greater than the tolerance you specify, the Palette Manager loads an exact match into the CLUT.

The Palette Manager compares the tolerance value associated with each palette entry to a measure of the difference between two RGB color values. This difference is an approximation of the distance between the two points as measured in a Cartesian coordinate system where the axes are the unsigned red, green, and blue values. The distance formula used is

Δ RGB = maximum of (abs(Red1 – Red2), abs(Green1 – Green2), abs(Blue1 – Blue2))

A tolerance value of $0000 means that only an exact match is acceptable. (Any value of $0*xxx* other than $0000 is reserved and should not be used in applications.) A value of $5000 is generally sufficient to allow matching without updates in well-balanced color environments, such as those provided by the default palettes.

If your palette requires more colors than the number of unreserved table indexes, the Palette Manager checks to see if some other palette has reserved indexes for animation. If so, it cancels their reservation and makes their indexes available for your palette.

If you ask for more colors than are available on a device, the Palette Manager cannot honor your request. Color requests that can't be met default to courteous colors, and the Color Manager selects the best color available. (That selection will of necessity match one of the colors elsewhere in your palette, since the Palette Manager runs out of colors only after it has given your palette all that are available. This procedure works as well as possible for a given device, but, of course, works better if your window is moved to a deeper device where the request can be met.)

Note that two tolerant entries may match to the same index even if space isn't the problem. For instance, when all indexes are initially assigned to black, activating a palette with 256 shades of gray with tolerance $2000 uses up four indexes, that being sufficient to match all 256 shades within a tolerance of $2000. If the tolerance were decreased to $1000, then eight indexes would be altered.

On direct devices, tolerant entries always match exactly.

Animated Colors

Animated colors allow you to reserve device indexes for color table animation.

One way to change the color of an object on the screen is to change the pixel values in the object's part of the pixel map—you draw it again in a different color. In certain situations, you can get the same effect at less cost in processing and memory by changing the colors in the video device's color table instead. All pixel values corresponding to the altered indexes suddenly appear on the display device in a new color. By careful selection of index values and the corresponding colors, you can achieve a number of special animation effects.

To use an animated color, you must first draw with it using the PmForeColor or PmBackColor procedure. To create color table animation, you then change that entry's RGB color by using the AnimateEntry procedure. You can animate a contiguous set of colors by supplying RGB colors from a color table, using the AnimatePalette procedure.

The way the Palette Manager reserves indexes for animated colors creates some side effects. The Palette Manager first checks each animated color to see if it already has a reserved index for the target device. If it does not, the Palette Manager checks all windows and reserves the least frequently used indexes for your palette. (This reservation process is analogous to that used by the Color Manager procedure ReserveEntry.) The device's index and its corresponding color value are removed from the matching scheme used by Color QuickDraw; you cannot draw with the color by calling RGBForeColor. (However, when you call PmForeColor, the Palette Manager locates the reserved index and configures your window's port to draw with it.) On a multiscreen system the index reserved is likely to be different for each device, but this process is invisible to your application.

After reserving one or more device indexes for each animated color it detects, the Palette Manager changes the color environment to match the RGB values specified in the palette.

The Palette Manager returns the indexes used by your animated entries to each screen device in any of these situations:

- a window owning those animated entries moves off of that screen
- your application changes the usage of an animated color
- your application disposes of the palette owning those entries (merely hiding a window does not release its entries)

The Palette Manager replaces previously animated indexes with the corresponding colors from the default color table for that device.

The Palette Manager receives notice when the screen depth changes, so that it can take appropriate action at that time, such as setting color tables to their defaults.

Displaying Animated Colors on Direct Devices

Color table animation doesn't work on a direct device—it has no color table. To present the best appearance, for example, on a window that spans an indexed device and a direct device, the Palette Manager records two colors in the ciRGB field of the color information record: the last color the entry was set to by SetEntryColor, and the last color the entry was set to by AnimateEntry or AnimatePalette. In the palette record, the high bytes of the components in the ciRGB field reflect the animated color, and the low bytes contain the color set by SetEntryColor. (GetEntryColor returns the last color the entry was animated to.) When you draw with an animated color on a direct device (or on any device on which the animated color was not allocated and reserved), then the color set by SetEntryColor is used. This allows successive updates of an animated image on a direct device to match correctly. A side effect is that GetEntryColor does not necessarily return an exact match of the color originally set (only the top 8 bits are an exact match).

▲ **Warning:** This internal usage of the color information fields may change. For maximum safety, use the procedures SetEntryColor, SetEntryUsage, GetEntryColor, and GetEntryUsage. ▲

Explicit Colors

Use explicit entries when your primary concern is the index value rather than the color stored at that index.

Explicit colors cause no change in the color environment. For indexed devices, the Palette Manager ignores the RGB value in a palette if a color is an explicit color. When you draw with an explicit color, you get the color that is currently at the CLUT entry whose index corresponds to the explicit color's position in the palette. When you call PmForeColor with a parameter of 12, it places a value of 12 into the foreground color field of your window's color grafPort. (Since the value wraps around the table, the value placed into the foreground field would be

12 modulo (*maxIndex* + 1)

where *maxIndex* is the maximum available index for each device under consideration.)

On direct devices an explicit entry produces the color for that entry in the palette.

You can use explicit colors to monitor the color environment on an indexed screen device. For example, you could draw a 16-by-16 grid of 256 explicit colors in a small window. Whatever colors appear are exactly those in the device's color table. If color table animation is taking place simultaneously, the corresponding colors in the small window animate as well. If you display such a window on a 4-bit device, the first 16 colors match the 16 colors available in the device, and each row thereafter is a copy of the first row.

Inhibited Colors

The Palette Manager recognizes six inhibited usage categories that give you control of which palette entries can and cannot appear on depths of 2, 4, and 8 bits per pixel, on color or gray-scale devices. The categories are specified using these constants:

```
CONST   pmInhibitG2 = $0100;  {inhibit on 2-bit gray-scale device}
        pmInhibitC2 = $0200;  {inhibit on 2-bit color device}
        pmInhibitG4 = $0400;  {inhibit on 4-bit gray-scale device}
        pmInhibitC4 = $0800;  {inhibit on 4-bit color device}
        pmInhibitG8 = $1000;  {inhibit on 8-bit gray-scale device}
        pmInhibitC8 = $2000;  {inhibit on 8-bit color device}
```

Here is an example of how these categories can be combined.

```
myColor8Usage :=
   SetEntryUsage  (myPalHandle,300,pmAnimated+pmExplicit+pmInhibitG2+
                   pmInhibitC2 +pmInhibitG4+pmInhibitC4+pmInhibitG8,0);
```

This sets the usage of entry 300 of the palette specified by myPalHandle to the combined usages of animated and explicit, to be allocated only on color 8-bit devices. (Since 300 is greater than 255, the highest index on an 8-bit device, the index associated with that entry wraps around to 44.)

You should always inhibit tolerant colors on gray-scale devices. Color QuickDraw now allows luminance mapping on gray-scale devices. The default CLUT on a gray-scale device is an evenly spaced gray ramp from black to white. Since this is usually the best possible spread on a gray-scale device, you could specify all three inhibited gray-scale categories.

As another example, on a 4-bit device you might want to allocate 14 tolerant colors, while on an 8-bit device there are sufficient indexes that you can also use a number of animated colors. By inhibiting the animated entries on 4-bit devices, you ensure that your 14 tolerant colors are allocated. Merely sequencing the palette doesn't solve this problem, because the animated colors always take precedence over the tolerant colors. (For more information about sequencing, see "Assigning Colors to a Palette" later in this chapter.)

Combined Usage Categories

The inhibited usage category is always combined with some other usage category. In addition, the explicit usage category can be combined with the tolerant and animated categories.

The main purpose for using explicit colors is to provide a convenient interface to color table indexes. You can select any of these colors for drawing by setting your window's palette to contain as many explicit colors as are in the target device with the greatest number of indexes. PmForeColor configures the color grafPort to draw with the index of your choice. So that you can easily create effective explicit palettes, two color usage categories can be combined: pmTolerant + pmExplicit and pmAnimated + pmExplicit.

The pmTolerant + pmExplicit combined usage means that you get the color you want at the index you want, across all devices that the window touches. As with pmTolerant, other windows may use those colors in their displays.

The pmAnimated + pmExplicit combined usage means that you get the color you want at the index you want, across all devices that intersect the window, but windows that don't share the palette can't use that index. The entry can be animated by a call to the AnimateEntry procedure.

Since the value of an explicit entry is treated as the entry modulo the bit depth, index collisions can occur between entries of the same usage within a palette. In this case, the lower-numbered entry gets the index. For example, if palette entries 1 and 17 were both pmAnimated + pmExplicit, then on a 4-bit screen, entry 1 would get index 1, and entry 17, although it wraps around to 1, would get nothing.

Unallocated pmTolerant + pmExplicit colors revert to pmTolerant. Unallocated pmAnimated + pmExplicit colors revert to pmCourteous.

Creating Palettes

Typically, you create a palette from the colors in a resource of type 'pltt' using the GetNewPalette function. You can also create a palette from the colors in a color table by using the NewPalette function.

Assigning Colors to a Palette

The inhibited usage categories are the best way to be sure that the right colors are available for screens of different depths, but in many situations you can achieve the same effect with a single set of colors if you sequence the colors in the palette, or arrange them according to the screen depth of the device that uses them, from least to greatest depth.

Color QuickDraw, to support standard QuickDraw features, puts white and black at the beginning and end, respectively, of each device's color table, and the Palette Manager never changes them. Thus the maximum number of indexes available for animated or tolerant colors is really the maximum number of indexes minus 2.

After white and black, you should assign the next two colors to the two you wish to have if the device is a 2-bit device. Likewise, the first 16 colors should be the optimal palette entries for a 4-bit device, and the first 256 colors should be the optimal palette entries for an 8-bit device.You should inhibit colors for gray-scale devices.

Creating a Palette in a Resource File

The format of a palette resource (type 'pltt') is an image of the palette structure itself. The private fields in both the header and in each color information record are reserved for future use. Listing 20-1 shows a palette resource with 16 entries as it would appear within a resource file. Each entry has a tolerance value of 0, meaning that the color should be matched exactly.

Listing 20-1. A palette ('pltt') resource

```
#define zeroTolerance 0

resource 'pltt' (128, "Simple Palette") {
  {       /* array ColorInfo: 16 elements */
    /* [1]  white */
    65535,  65535,  65535, pmTolerant, zeroTolerance,
    /* [2]  black */
    0,      0,  0,         pmTolerant, zeroTolerance,
    /* [3]  yellow, for bit depths >= 2 */
    64512,  62333,  1327,  pmTolerant, zeroTolerance,
    /* [4]  orange */
    65535,  25738,  652,   pmTolerant, zeroTolerance,
    /* [5]  blue-green used in bit depths >= 4 */
    881,    50943,  40649, pmTolerant, zeroTolerance,
    /* [6]  green */
    0,      22015,  0,     pmTolerant, zeroTolerance,
    /* [7]  blue */
    22015,  0,  0,         pmTolerant, zeroTolerance
    /* [8]  red */
    56683,  2242,   1698,  pmTolerant, zeroTolerance,
```

```
    /* [9]  light gray */
    49152,  49152,  49152, pmTolerant, zeroTolerance,
    /* [10] medium gray */
    32768,  32768,  32768, pmTolerant, zeroTolerance,
    /* [11] beige */
    65535,  50140,  33120, pmTolerant, zeroTolerance,
    /* [12] brown */
    37887,  10266,  4812,  pmTolerant, zeroTolerance,
    /* [13] olive green */
    25892,  49919,  0,     pmTolerant, zeroTolerance,
    /* [14] bright green */
    0,      65535,  1265,  pmTolerant, zeroTolerance,
    /* [15] sky blue */
    0,      0,  65535,     pmTolerant, zeroTolerance,
    /* [16] violet */
    32768,  0,  65535,     pmTolerant, zeroTolerance
  }
};
```

Use GetNewPalette to obtain a 'pltt' resource; it initializes private fields in the palette data structure. (Don't use GetResource.)

Listing 20-2 shows a palette with a variety of usage categories. The first two entries, for white and black, are the same as in the palette in Listing 20-1. The next three entries are animated and explicit, and inhibited on gray-scale devices. Entries 6 through 14 are tolerant with zero tolerance and inhibited on gray-scale devices. The last two entries in the palette are inhibited on color devices as well if they can only display 16 colors.

Listing 20-2. A multi-use palette

```
#define zeroTolerance 0

#define pmInhibitG2 0x0100
#define pmInhibitC2 0x0200
#define pmInhibitG4 0x0400
#define pmInhibitC4 0x0800
#define pmInhibitG8 0x1000
#define pmInhibitC8 0x2000
/* inhibit in all gray-scale devices */
#define grayDevInhibit (pmInhibitG2  +  pmInhibitG4  +  pmInhibitG8)


#define pmTolerant   2
#define pmAnimated   4
#define pmExplicit   8

#define pmAnimDevInhibit (pmAnimated  +  grayDevInhibit)

/* QD does the best job at displaying colors in gray-scale devices
   so it is a good idea to inhibit colors in all gray-scale devices. */
```

(Continued)

Listing 20-2. A multi-use palette (Continued)

```
resource 'pltt' (129, "Inhibiting Palette") {
  { /* array ColorInfo: 16 elements */
    /* [1] */
    65535,  65535,  65535, pmTolerant, zeroTolerance,
    /* [2] */
    0,      0,      0,      pmTolerant, zeroTolerance,
    /* request animated entries to go in known 'clut' slots */
    /* [3] */
    64512,  62333,  1327,   (pmAnimDevInhibit + pmExplicit), zeroTolerance,
    /* [4] */
    65535,  25738,  652,    (pmAnimDevInhibit + pmExplicit), zeroTolerance,
    /* [5] */
    881,    50943,  40649, (pmAnimDevInhibit + pmExplicit), zeroTolerance,
    /* now let the Palette Manager put the next colors where it wants */
    /* [6] */
    0,     22015,   22015, (pmTolerant + grayDevInhibit), zeroTolerance,
    /* [7] */
    22015,  0,      0,      (pmTolerant + grayDevInhibit), zeroTolerance,
    /* [8] */
    56683,  2242,   1698,   (pmTolerant + grayDevInhibit), zeroTolerance,
    /* [9] */
    49152,  49152,  49152, (pmTolerant + grayDevInhibit), zeroTolerance,
    /* [10] */
    32768,  32768,  32768, (pmTolerant + grayDevInhibit), zeroTolerance,
    /* [11] */
    65535,  50140,  33120, (pmTolerant + grayDevInhibit), zeroTolerance,
    /* [12] */
    37887,  10266,  4812,   (pmTolerant + grayDevInhibit), zeroTolerance,
    /* [13] */
    25892,  49919,  0,      (pmTolerant + grayDevInhibit), zeroTolerance,
    /* [14] */
    0,      65535,  1265,   (pmTolerant + grayDevInhibit), zeroTolerance,
    /* inhibit the last two entries in 4-bit deep devices */
    /* [15] */
    0,      65535,  0, (pmTolerant + grayDevInhibit + pmInhibitC4), zeroTolerance,
    /* [16] */
    32768,  0, 65535,   (pmTolerant + grayDevInhibit + pmInhibitC4), zeroTolerance
  }
};
```

Assigning a Default Palette to an Application

Your application can define a palette for the Operating System to use when it needs to define the color environment. Defining a default palette for your color application is useful if all your windows use the same palette, or if you use old-style dialog and alert boxes: without an application palette, the system uses its own default palette to define the color environment.

You set a palette as the application default by assigning it a resource ID of 0. If the system needs a palette to define a color environment, it looks in the resource fork of the application for the 'pltt' resource with an ID equal to 0 and uses the palette that it contains. If the system cannot find this resource in the application's resource fork, it uses its own default palette (resource 'pltt' ID = 0 in the System file). If the system has no default palette, it uses the Palette Manager's built-in palette.

Once your application has set its color environment (by calling InitMenus, or InitPalettes in unusual instances when there are no menus), you can find the default palette for your application by using the GetPalette function.

```
myPaletteHndl := GetPalette (WindowPtr (-1));
```

You can change the default palette by specifying a palette in the SetPalette procedure.

```
SetPalette (WindowPtr (-1),newDefPlttHndl,TRUE);
```

Linking a Color Table to a Palette

Suppose your application displays an image drawn with 64 gray levels in a window and uses a control to adjust the brightness or contrast. If you draw your image with animated palette entries, you can then use AnimatePalette to change the particular shades rapidly. But you have to call PmForeColor with the index of the upper-left pixel, paint a 1-by-1 rectangle, call PmForeColor for the next pixel, paint a rectangle, and so on.

Color QuickDraw now supports a method by which a color table can refer to palette indexes instead of RGB values. Setting bit 14 (using OR with $4000) in the ctFlags field of the color table record causes the fields in a source pixel map's color table to be interpreted as follows:

Field descriptions

ctSeed	A unique value.
ctFlags	Flags, with bit 14 set, as described in the previous paragraph.
ctSize	The size of the color table, less 1.
ctTable	An array [0..ctSize] of colorSpec values (each an index value and an RGB value).
ctTable[*x*].value	The palette entry to use when drawing pixels with value *x*. (Note that this is different from previous uses, where the value field specified which pixel number the entry applied to.)
ctTable[*x*].rgb	The color used if there is no available palette or if the palette is too small to contain the specified entry.

For example, to draw a 64-level image in animated colors (as described in "Animated Colors" earlier in this chapter), you put the palette entry number you want for pixel value 0 into the first value field of the source color table's color specification record, the palette entry corresponding to pixel value 1 in the next value field, and so on. If your palette is arranged in the same order as the pixel values, the value fields simply count from 0 to 63. By calling the AnimatePalette procedure for each of those entries, you can produce color table animation on all screens that have reserved an animated entry, are crossed by the window, and are able to display such an image.

Since 16-bit and 32-bit direct devices do not have CLUTs, you may wish to post an update to display an image of those areas that intersect a direct device.

In the case of an animated picture adjustment, like a contrast or brightness control, it is better to animate while the user is moving the indicator and update when the user releases it.

Associating One Palette With Many Ports

The SetPalette and NSetPalette procedures allow you to associate one palette with many color grafPort and color window records, thus simplifying the use of a single palette with multiple ports and windows.

One important implication of this feature is that the DisposeWindow procedure does not dispose of the associated palette automatically, since it may be allocated to other ports or windows. The only exception to this behavior is when an application has used GetNewCWindow to create the window, there is a 'pltt' resource with the same ID as the window, and the application has not called GetPalette for the window.

PALETTE MANAGER ROUTINES

The Palette Manager has a number of routines for establishing and maintaining palettes and for interacting with the Window Manager. It also has two procedures for actual drawing, PmForeColor and PmBackColor. In Palette Manager usage, those procedures replace Color QuickDraw's RGBForeColor and RGBBackColor procedures.

The procedures SaveFore, RestoreFore, SaveBack, RestoreBack, ResizePalette, and RestoreDeviceClut are available only with system software versions 6.0.5 and later, and with the 32-Bit QuickDraw system extension.

Initializing the Palette Manager

The Palette Manager is initialized during the first InitWindows call after system startup, and it continues to run as needed whenever windows are moved. The InitWindows procedure calls InitPalettes, which initializes the Palette Manager, if necessary, and searches the device list to find all active CLUT devices.

```
PROCEDURE InitPalettes;
```

InitPalettes initializes the Palette Manager. It searches for devices that support a CLUT and initializes an internal data structure for each one. This procedure is called by InitWindows and does not have to be called by your application.

```
FUNCTION PMgrVersion : Integer;
```

The PMgrVersion function returns an integer specifying the version number of the currently executing Palette Manager. Returned values may be as follows.

Value	Description
$0202	System software version 7.0
$0201	System software version 6.0.5
$0200	Original 32-Bit QuickDraw system extension

Initializing and Allocating Palettes

Normally, you create a new palette from a 'pltt' resource using the GetNewPalette function. To create a palette from within your application, use the NewPalette function. Regardless of how you create the palette, you can then use the SetPalette procedure to render the palette on the screen. The DisposePalette procedure disposes of the entire palette.

```
FUNCTION GetNewPalette (paletteID: Integer) : PaletteHandle;
```

GetNewPalette creates a palette from information supplied by the palette specified in the paletteID parameter; it then initializes the new palette and attaches it to the current window.

If you open a new color window with GetNewCWindow, the Window Manager calls GetNewPalette automatically with paletteID equal to the window's resource ID. A palette resource is identified by type 'pltt'. A palette ID of 0 is reserved for the application's palette resource, which is used as the default palette for a window (either color or black and white) without an assigned palette. If there is no assigned palette or application default palette, GetNewPalette uses the system palette whose resource ID is 0, if present.

```
FUNCTION NewPalette (entries: Integer; srcColors: CTabHandle; srcUsage,
                     srcTolerance: Integer) : PaletteHandle;
```

NewPalette allocates a new palette from colors in the color table specified by srcColors, with enough room for the number of colors specified by the entries parameter. NewPalette fills the palette with as many RGB values from the color table as it has or as it can fit. NewPalette sets the usage field of each color to the value in the srcUsage parameter and the tolerance value of each color to the value in the srcTolerance parameter. If no color table is provided (srcColors = NIL), then all colors in the palette are set to black (red, green, and blue equal to $0000).

```
PROCEDURE DisposePalette (srcPalette: PaletteHandle);
```

DisposePalette disposes of the palette specified in the srcPalette parameter. If the palette has any entries allocated for animation on any screen device, these entries are relinquished before the palette's memory is released.

Interacting With the Window Manager

The ActivatePalette procedure adjusts the color environment whenever your window's status changes. Your application can also use ActivatePalette after making changes to a palette. You can use GetPalette to return a handle to the palette currently associated with a specified window.

```
PROCEDURE ActivatePalette (srcWindow: WindowPtr);
```

The Window Manager calls ActivatePalette when your window's status changes—for example, when your window opens, closes, moves, or becomes frontmost. Call ActivatePalette after making changes to a palette with Palette Manager routines such as SetEntryColor. Such changes do not take effect until the next call to ActivatePalette, thereby allowing you to make a series of palette changes without any immediate change in the color environment.

If the window specified in the srcWindow parameter is frontmost, ActivatePalette examines the information stored in the window's palette and attempts to provide the color environment described therein. It determines a list of devices on which to render the palette by intersecting the port rectangle of the window with each device. If the intersection is not empty, and if the device has a CLUT, then ActivatePalette checks to see if the color environment is sufficient. If a change is required, ActivatePalette calls the Color Manager to reserve or modify the device's color entries as needed. It then generates update events for all windows that need color updates.

Calling ActivatePalette with an offscreen port has no effect.

```
FUNCTION GetPalette (srcWindow: WindowPtr) : PaletteHandle;
```

GetPalette returns a handle to the palette associated with the window specified in the srcWindow parameter. If the window has no associated palette, or if the window is not a color window, GetPalette returns NIL.

```
PROCEDURE SetPalette (dstWindow: WindowPtr; srcPalette: PaletteHandle;
                      cUpdates: Boolean);
```

SetPalette changes the palette associated with the window specified in the dstWindow parameter to the palette specified in the srcPalette parameter. It also records whether the window is to receive updates as a result of changes to its color environment. If you want the window to be updated whenever its color environment changes, set the cUpdates parameter to TRUE.

```
PROCEDURE NSetPalette (dstWindow: WindowPtr; srcPalette: PaletteHandle;
                       nCUpdates: Integer);
```

NSetPalette is identical to SetPalette, except that the nCUpdates parameter is an integer rather than a Boolean value. NSetPalette changes the palette associated with the window specified in the dstWindow parameter to the palette specified by srcPalette. NSetPalette also records whether the window is to receive updates as a result of changes to its color environment. If you want the window to be updated whenever its color environment changes, set nCUpdates to the constant pmAllUpdates. If you are interested in updates only when the window is the active window, set nCUpdates to the constant pmFgUpdates. If you are interested in updates only when the window is *not* the active window, set nCUpdates to the constant pmBkUpdates.

```
CONST pmNoUpdates     = $8000;     {no updates}
      pmBkUpdates     = $A000;     {background updates only}
      pmFgUpdates     = $C000;     {foreground updates only}
      pmAllUpdates    = $E000;     {all updates}
```


NSetPalette is available in system software versions 6.0.2 and later.

```
PROCEDURE SetPaletteUpdates (p: PaletteHandle; updates: Integer);
```

The SetPaletteUpdates procedure sets the update attribute of a palette. In the p parameter you supply a handle to the palette, and in the updates parameter you supply one of the update attributes described for the NSetPalette procedure.

```
FUNCTION GetPaletteUpdates (p: PaletteHandle) : Integer;
```

The GetPaletteUpdates function returns the update attribute of a palette. In the p parameter you supply a handle to the palette, and the function returns one of the update attributes described for the NSetPalette procedure.

Drawing With Color Palettes

The PmForeColor and PmBackColor procedures allow applications to specify foreground and background drawing colors with the assistance of the Palette Manager. Substitute these procedures for the Color QuickDraw procedures RGBForeColor and RGBBackColor when you wish to use a color from a palette. You can still use RGBForeColor and RGBBackColor whenever you wish to specify drawing colors—for example, when you wish to use a color that is not contained in your palette.

You can save and restore the current foreground and background colors by using the SaveFore, RestoreFore, SaveBack, and RestoreBack procedures.

```
PROCEDURE PmForeColor (dstEntry: Integer);
```

PmForeColor sets the current color grafPort's RGB and index foreground color fields to match the palette entry of the window record's current color grafPort corresponding to the value in the dstEntry parameter.

For courteous and tolerant entries, PmForeColor calls the RGBForeColor procedure using the RGB color of the palette entry. For animated colors, PmForeColor selects the recorded device index previously reserved for animation (if still present) and installs it in the color grafPort. The RGB foreground color field is set to the value from the palette entry. For explicit colors, PmForeColor places the value

dstEntry modulo (*maxIndex* +1)

into the color grafPort, where *maxIndex* is the largest index available in a device's CLUT. When multiple devices with different depths are present, the value of *maxIndex* varies appropriately for each device.

```
PROCEDURE PmBackColor (dstEntry: Integer);
```

PmBackColor sets the current color grafPort's RGB and index background color fields to match the palette entry of the window record's current color grafPort corresponding to the value in the dstEntry parameter.

For courteous and tolerant entries, PmBackColor calls the RGBBackColor procedure using the RGB color of the palette entry. For animated colors, PmBackColor selects the recorded device index previously reserved for animation (if still present) and installs it in the color grafPort. The rgbBgColor field is set to the value from the palette entry. For explicit colors, PmBackColor places the value

dstEntry modulo (*maxIndex* +1)

into the color grafPort, where *maxIndex* is the largest index available in a device's CLUT. When multiple devices with different depths are present, *maxIndex* varies appropriately for each device.

```
PROCEDURE SaveFore (VAR c: ColorSpec);
```

The SaveFore procedure returns the current foreground color in the c parameter. A value of 0 in the value field of the color specification record specifies an RGB color (obtained from the rgbFgColor field of the color grafPort record); a value of 1 in the value field specifies a palette entry (obtained from the pmFgColor field of the GrafVars record).

```
PROCEDURE RestoreFore (c: ColorSpec);
```

The RestoreFore procedure stores the RGB color of the color specification record specified by the c parameter as the current foreground color. If you specify 0 in the value field of the color specification record, the RestoreFore procedure stores the RGB value in the rgbFgColor field of the current color grafPort record. If you specify 1 in the value field of the color specification record, the RestoreFore procedure stores the RGB value in the pmFgColor field of the GrafVars record.

```
PROCEDURE SaveBack (VAR c: ColorSpec);
```

The SaveBack procedure returns the current background color in the c parameter. A value of 0 in the value field of the color specification record specifies an RGB color (obtained from the rgbBkColor field of the color grafPort record); a value of 1 in the value field specifies a palette entry (obtained from the pmBkColor field of the GrafVars record).

```
PROCEDURE RestoreBack (c: ColorSpec);
```

The RestoreBack procedure stores the RGB color of the color specification record specified by the c parameter as the current foreground color. If you specify 0 in the value field of the color specification record, the RestoreBack procedure stores the RGB value in the rgbFgColor field of the current color grafPort record. If you specify 1 in the value field of the color specification record, the RestoreBack procedure stores the RGB value in the pmBkColor field of the GrafVars record.

Animating Color Tables

To use color table animation, you can change the colors in a palette and on corresponding devices with the AnimateEntry and AnimatePalette procedures.

```
PROCEDURE AnimateEntry (dstWindow: WindowPtr; dstEntry: Integer; srcRGB:
                        RGBColor);
```

AnimateEntry changes the RGB value of a window's palette entry. The window is specified in the dstWindow parameter; the palette entry is specified in the dstEntry parameter; the new RGB value is specified in the srcRGB parameter. Each device for which an index has been reserved is immediately modified to contain the new value. This is not considered to be a change to the device's color environment, because no other windows should be using the animated entry.

If the palette entry is not an animated color, or if the associated indexes are no longer reserved, no animation occurs.

If you have blocked color updates in a window by using SetPalette with cUpdates set to FALSE, you may observe unintentional animation. This occurs when ActivatePalette reserves for animation device indexes that are already used in the window. Redrawing the window, which normally is the result of a color update event, removes any animated colors that do not belong to the window.

```
PROCEDURE AnimatePalette (dstWindow: WindowPtr; srcCTab: CTabHandle;
                          srcIndex,dstEntry,dstLength: Integer);
```

AnimatePalette is similar to AnimateEntry, but it acts upon a range of palette entries. Beginning at the index specified by the srcIndex parameter (which has a minimum value of 0), the number of entries specified in dstLength are copied from the source color table to the destination window's palette, beginning at the entry specified in the dstEntry parameter. If the source color table specified in srcCTab is not sufficiently large to accommodate the request, AnimatePalette modifies as many entries as possible and leaves the remaining entries unchanged.

Manipulating Palettes and Color Tables

You can use the CopyPalette procedure to copy palettes from other palettes and from color tables, and you can use the ResizePalette procedure to resize palettes. The RestoreDeviceClut procedure restores the CLUT of a device to its default set of colors. CTab2Palette copies the specified color table into a palette, and its opposite, Palette2CTab, copies a palette into a color table. Each procedure resizes the target object as needed.

```
PROCEDURE CopyPalette (srcPalette,dstPalette: PaletteHandle;
                       srcEntry,dstEntry,dstLength: Integer);
```

CopyPalette copies entries from the source palette into the destination palette. The copy operation begins at the values specified by the srcEntry and dstEntry parameters, copying into as many entries as are specified by the dstLength parameter. CopyPalette resizes the destination palette when the number of entries after the copy operation is greater than it was before the copy operation.

CopyPalette does not call ActivatePalette, so your application is free to change the palette a number of times without causing a series of intermediate changes to the color environment. Your application should call ActivatePalette after completing all palette changes.

If either of the palette handles is NIL, CopyPalette does nothing.

```
PROCEDURE ResizePalette (srcPalette: PaletteHandle; size: Integer);
```

ResizePalette sets the palette specified in srcPalette to the number of entries indicated in the size parameter. If ResizePalette adds entries at the end of the palette, it sets them to pmCourteous, with the RGB values set to (0,0,0)—that is, black. If ResizePalette deletes entries from the end of the palette, it safely disposes of them.

```
PROCEDURE RestoreDeviceClut (gdh: GDHandle);
```

RestoreDeviceClut changes the CLUT of the device specified by the gdh parameter to its default state. If this process changes any entries, color updates are posted to windows intersecting the device. Passing NIL in gdh causes all screens to be restored. Do not call this procedure frivolously, but you can use it to update screens after the highlight color has changed.

```
PROCEDURE CTab2Palette (srcCTab: CTabHandle; dstPalette: PaletteHandle;
                        srcUsage,srcTolerance: Integer);
```

CTab2Palette is a convenience procedure that copies the fields from an existing color table record into an existing palette record. If the records are not the same size, then CTab2Palette resizes the palette record to match the number of entries in the color table record. If the palette in dstPalette has any entries allocated for animation on any screen device, they are relinquished before the new colors are copied. The srcUsage and srcTolerance parameters are the value that you assign to the new colors.

If you want to use color table animation, you can use AnimateEntry and AnimatePalette to change the colors in a palette and on corresponding devices. Changes made to a palette by CTab2Palette don't take effect until the next ActivatePalette procedure is performed. If either the color table handle or the palette handle is NIL, CTab2Palette does nothing.

```
PROCEDURE Palette2CTab (srcPalette: PaletteHandle; dstCTab: CTabHandle);
```

Palette2CTab is a convenience procedure that copies all of the colors from an existing palette record into an existing color table record. If the records are not the same size, then Palette2CTab resizes the color table record to match the number of entries in the palette record. If either the palette handle or the color table handle is NIL, Palette2CTab does nothing.

Manipulating Palette Entries

GetEntryColor, GetEntryUsage, SetEntryColor, and SetEntryUsage allow your application to retrieve and modify the fields of a palette. Entry2Index returns an index for a palette entry.

```
PROCEDURE GetEntryColor (srcPalette: PaletteHandle; srcEntry: Integer;
                         VAR dstRGB: RGBColor);
```

GetEntryColor gives your application access to the color of a palette entry. It takes the RGB color of the entry specified by the srcEntry parameter and stores it in the destination RGB color record. You can modify the color using the SetEntryColor procedure.


```
PROCEDURE GetEntryUsage (srcPalette: PaletteHandle; srcEntry: Integer;
                         VAR dstUsage,dstTolerance: Integer);
```

GetEntryUsage gives your application access to the usage and tolerance fields of a palette entry. It takes the usage and tolerance values of the entry specified by the srcEntry parameter and stores them in the dstUsage and dstTolerance parameters. You can modify these values by using the SetEntryUsage procedure.

```
PROCEDURE SetEntryColor (dstPalette: PaletteHandle; dstEntry: Integer;
                         srcRGB: RGBColor);
```

SetEntryColor provides a convenient way for your application to modify the color of a single palette entry. It stores the RGB color of the srcRGB parameter in the palette entry specified by the dstEntry parameter. SetEntryColor marks the entry as having changed, but it does not change the color environment. The change occurs upon the next call to ActivatePalette. SetEntryColor marks modified entries such that the palette is updated, even though no update is required by a change in the color environment.

```
PROCEDURE SetEntryUsage (dstPalette: PaletteHandle; dstEntry: Integer;
                         srcUsage,srcTolerance: Integer);
```

SetEntryUsage provides a convenient way for your application to modify the usage category of a single palette entry. The usage and tolerance values specified by the srcUsage and srcTolerance parameters are stored in the palette entry specified by the dstEntry parameter. SetEntryUsage marks the entry as having changed, but it does not change the color environment. The change occurs upon the next call to ActivatePalette. Modified entries are marked such that the palette is updated even though no update is required by a change in the color environment. If either srcUsage or srcTolerance is set to $FFFF (–1), the entries are not changed.

This procedure allows you to easily modify a palette created with NewPalette or modified by CTab2Palette. For such palettes the ciUsage and ciTolerance fields of the color information record are the same, because you can designate only one value for each. You typically call SetEntryUsage after NewPalette or CTab2Palette to adjust and customize your palette.

```
FUNCTION Entry2Index (entry: Integer) : LongInt;
```

Given an entry number, this function returns the index for that entry in the current grafPort's palette on the current device.

SUMMARY OF THE PALETTE MANAGER

Constants

```
CONST {usage constants}
      pmCourteous    = $0000; {courteous color}
      pmTolerant     = $0002; {tolerant color}
      pmAnimated     = $0004; {animated color}
      pmExplicit     = $0008; {explicit color}
      pmWhite        = $0010; {use on 1-bit device}
      pmBlack        = $0020; {use on 1-bit device}
      pmInhibitG2    = $0100; {inhibit on 2-bit gray-scale device}
      pmInhibitC2    = $0200; {inhibit on 2-bit color device}
      pmInhibitG4    = $0400; {inhibit on 4-bit gray-scale device}
      pmInhibitC4    = $0800; {inhibit on 4-bit color device}
      pmInhibitG8    = $1000; {inhibit on 8-bit gray-scale device}
      pmInhibitC8    = $2000; {inhibit on 8-bit color device}

      {NSetPalette update constants}
      pmNoUpdates    = $8000; {no updates}
      pmBkUpdates    = $A000; {background updates only}
      pmFgUpdates    = $C000; {foreground updates only}
      pmAllUpdates   = $E000; {all updates}
```

Data Types

```
TYPE PaletteHandle          = ^PalettePtr;
     PalettePtr             = ^Palette;

     Palette =
     RECORD
        pmEntries:          Integer;        {entries in pmInfo}
        pmDataFields:       ARRAY[0..6] OF Integer;
                                            {private fields}
        pmInfo:             ARRAY[0..0] OF ColorInfo
                                            {color information}
     END;


     ColorInfo =
     RECORD
        ciRGB:              RGBColor;       {absolute RGB values}
        ciUsage:            Integer;        {color usage information}
        ciTolerance:        Integer;        {tolerance value}
        ciDataFields:       ARRAY[0..2] OF Integer
                                            {private fields}
     END;
```

Routines

Initializing the Palette Manager

```
PROCEDURE InitPalettes;
FUNCTION PMgrVersion          : Integer;
```

Initializing and Allocating Palettes

```
FUNCTION GetNewPalette        (paletteID: Integer) : PaletteHandle;
FUNCTION NewPalette           (entries: Integer; srcColors: CTabHandle;
                               srcUsage,srcTolerance: Integer) :
                               PaletteHandle;
PROCEDURE DisposePalette      (srcPalette: PaletteHandle);
```

Interacting With the Window Manager

```
PROCEDURE ActivatePalette     (srcWindow: WindowPtr);
FUNCTION GetPalette           (srcWindow: WindowPtr) : PaletteHandle;
PROCEDURE SetPalette          (dstWindow: WindowPtr; srcPalette:
                               PaletteHandle; cUpdates: Boolean);
PROCEDURE NSetPalette         (dstWindow: WindowPtr; srcPalette:
                               PaletteHandle; nCUpdates: Integer);
PROCEDURE SetPaletteUpdates   (p: PaletteHandle; updates: Integer);
FUNCTION GetPaletteUpdates    (p: PaletteHandle) : Integer;
```

Drawing With Color Palettes

```
PROCEDURE PmForeColor         (dstEntry: Integer);
PROCEDURE PmBackColor         (dstEntry: Integer);
PROCEDURE SaveFore            (VAR c: ColorSpec);
PROCEDURE RestoreFore         (c: ColorSpec);
PROCEDURE SaveBack            (VAR c: ColorSpec);
PROCEDURE RestoreBack         (c: ColorSpec);
```

Animating Color Tables

```
PROCEDURE AnimateEntry        (dstWindow: WindowPtr; dstEntry: Integer;
                               srcRGB: RGBColor);

PROCEDURE AnimatePalette      (dstWindow: WindowPtr; srcCTab: CTabHandle;
                               srcIndex,dstEntry,dstLength: Integer);
```

Manipulating Palettes and Color Tables

```
PROCEDURE CopyPalette         (srcPalette,dstPalette: PaletteHandle;
                               srcEntry,dstEntry,dstLength: Integer);

PROCEDURE ResizePalette       (srcPalette: PaletteHandle; size: Integer);

PROCEDURE RestoreDeviceClut   (gdh: GDHandle);

PROCEDURE CTab2Palette        (srcCTab: CTabHandle; dstPalette:
                               PaletteHandle; srcUsage,srcTolerance:
                               Integer);

PROCEDURE Palette2CTab        (srcPalette: PaletteHandle; dstCTab:
                               CTabHandle);
```

Manipulating Palette Entries

```
PROCEDURE GetEntryColor       (srcPalette: PaletteHandle; srcEntry: Integer;
                               VAR dstRGB: RGBColor);

PROCEDURE GetEntryUsage       (srcPalette: PaletteHandle; srcEntry:
                               Integer; VAR dstUsage,dstTolerance:
                               Integer);

PROCEDURE SetEntryColor       (dstPalette: PaletteHandle; dstEntry:
                               Integer; srcRGB: RGBColor);

PROCEDURE SetEntryUsage       (dstPalette: PaletteHandle; dstEntry:
                               Integer; srcUsage,srcTolerance: Integer);

FUNCTION Entry2Index          (entry: Integer) : LongInt;
```

21 THE GRAPHICS DEVICES MANAGER

ABOUT THIS CHAPTER

This chapter describes how you can use the Graphics Devices Manager to manage offscreen graphics. You can use offscreen graphics to prepare images offscreen and then move them quickly into view with a single routine. This technique prevents the choppiness that can occur when you build object-oriented graphics directly on the screen. By building a picture in an environment you create and control, you can be sure that no other application or desk accessory changes the characteristics of the picture's environment.

The Graphics Devices Manager also contains routines and data structures used by QuickDraw™, the Palette Manager, and the Color Manager to communicate with the graphics devices attached to a particular system. Such devices may include printers as well as screens. Most of these routines are used only by the Operating System; some may be used by graphics-intensive applications.

Before reading this chapter, you should read the Graphics Overview and Color QuickDraw chapters in this volume and the Color QuickDraw chapter in Volume V. If your application uses color, you should also be familiar with the Palette Manager, as described in this volume.

This chapter replaces the Graphics Devices chapter in Volume V.

ABOUT THE GRAPHICS DEVICES MANAGER

The Graphics Devices Manager works with an application's graphics environment. The **graphics environment** is defined by grafPorts, which contain information about windows, and graphics device records, which contain information about graphics devices such as screens that are attached to the system. Since these records are created automatically by the Operating System, many applications won't have to work directly with the Graphics Devices Manager.

If you are developing a graphics-intensive application, you may need to create additional color grafPort and graphics device records, in which case the Graphics Devices Manager's high-level routines probably provide all the features you need. With these routines you can create an **offscreen graphics world:** a graphics environment in which you control specifications such as pixel depth and whether the pixel values are indexed or direct. Using these routines minimizes the possibility of compatibility problems, because these routines and data structures, collectively called the offscreen graphics world interface, will be maintained as Macintosh® graphics systems evolve. With system software version 7.0, the offscreen graphics world routines are available on black-and-white machines (lacking Color QuickDraw), but they create an extended grafPort record, not a true color grafPort record.

A few applications may need exacting control of the graphics environment. Routines that work directly with the graphics device record are described in "Low-Level Routines" later in this chapter.

The rest of this chapter

- describes offscreen graphics, which is the most common use of the Graphics Devices Manager
- introduces the offscreen graphics world routines
- delineates the graphics world flags, by which you set and obtain offscreen graphics attributes
- covers several advanced topics that most developers do not need to study: the graphics device record, the 'scrn' resource, and the proper way to set the screen depth from within an application

OFFSCREEN GRAPHICS

The most common reasons for drawing offscreen are speed and visual smoothness. For example, suppose your application draws individual graphics objects, and it needs to redraw part of a window that has been covered by another window or a menu. Your application may be able to put an offscreen bitmap onto the screen faster than it could re-create the drawing steps, and at the same time avoid the choppy effect that can arise from drawing a large number of separate objects.

In a multitasking situation you may want to create an image offscreen to avoid having some other application or desk accessory change the graphics environment in the midst of your processing. An offscreen graphics environment that you create cannot be modified by any other application.

Most important, today's Macintosh computer systems may have several screens, of different sizes, pixel depths, and color capabilities, and the user may decide to put your application's window on (or even across) any of them. By preparing the image offscreen in a graphics world that you create, you can control the image's characteristics. When the image is ready for display, you can check the graphics environment and react accordingly, such as by calling CopyBits if everything is as you expect, or by adjusting the image to match the pixel depth of the deepest screen your window touches. If the environment is not suitable—for example, if the user has moved the window for your multicolor display of the Bayeux tapestry to a 9-inch black-and-white monitor—you can display the best image possible and issue a gentle remonstrance.

An offscreen graphics world is an extension of the color grafPort record described in the Color QuickDraw chapter of Volume V. It contains a color grafPort describing the offscreen port, a reference to the offscreen device associated with the offscreen graphics world, and other state information. The actual data structure is kept private to allow for future extensions.

The pointer type of the offscreen graphics world is defined as follows:

```
TYPE GWorldPtr = CGrafPtr;
```

On black-and-white machines lacking Color QuickDraw, the graphics world pointer points to an extension of the original QuickDraw grafPort record.

USING THE GRAPHICS DEVICES MANAGER

Your use of the Graphics Devices Manager routines depends on the degree to which you need to control the characteristics of your images. If your only concern is to avoid flicker by presenting a completed image, you can choose to create an offscreen color grafPort record but not a new graphics device record. Your offscreen grafPort is then linked to the current graphics device, from which it takes characteristics such as pixel depth. If you need to control the pixel depth or create a new color table, you must create a new graphics device record.

You create an offscreen graphics world with the NewGWorld function. You can specify that a new graphics device record is to be created, or you can specify that an existing graphics device record be used, such as the graphics device record of the main screen (the screen with the menu bar) or of the deepest screen touched. In either case, the Graphics Devices Manager uses that graphics device record's characteristics to create the pixel map for your image. If you use a screen's graphics device record, then before doing any drawing you should check to be sure that the device's depth or color/black-and-white settings haven't been changed by the user. If they have, call the UpdateGWorld function.

To address the pixel map record created for an offscreen graphics world, use the GetGWorldPixMap function. (Don't dereference the graphics world pointer to get to the pixel map.)

Before actually drawing to or from the offscreen graphics world, call LockPixels to lock the offscreen buffer in memory. As soon as the drawing is completed, always call UnlockPixels.

When the user resizes or moves a window, changes the pixel depth of screens a window intersects, or modifies a color table, you should call the UpdateGWorld function; your application may be able to reflect those changes in the offscreen graphics world without having to re-create it and redraw its content. Calling UpdateGWorld when the window moves can ensure a maximum refresh speed when using CopyBits to move the offscreen image on screen.

When you no longer need your offscreen graphics world, dispose of it by calling DisposeGWorld.

Offscreen Graphics World Flags

The GWorldFlags type is used by various routines to retrieve and set the characteristics of offscreen graphics worlds.

```
TYPE GWorldFlags =
     SET OF (
         pixPurge,           {used by NewGWorld to make offscreen buffer }
                             { purgeable}
         noNewDevice,        {used by NewGWorld to not create an offscreen }
                             { device}
```

```
        useTempMem,        {used by NewGWorld to allocate pixels in }
                           { temporary memory}
        keepLocal,         {used to keep data structures in main memory}
        gWorldFlag4,       {reserved}
        gWorldFlag5,       {reserved}
        pixelsPurgeable,   {used by Get/SetPixelsState for purgeable }
                           { pixels}
        pixelsLocked,      {used by Get/SetPixelsState for locked pixels}
        gWorldFlag8,       {reserved}
        gWorldFlag9,       {reserved}
        gWorldFlag10,      {reserved}
        gWorldFlag11,      {reserved}
        gWorldFlag12,      {reserved}
        gWorldFlag13,      {reserved}
        gWorldFlag14,      {reserved}
        gWorldFlag15,      {reserved}
        mapPix,            {set by UpdateGWorld if color mapping occurred}
        newDepth,          {set by UpdateGWorld if pixels were scaled to }
                           { a different depth}
        alignPix,          {set by UpdateGWorld if pixels were realigned }
                           { to screen alignment}
        newRowBytes,       {set by UpdateGWorld if pixel map was }
                           { reconfigured in a new rowBytes}
        reallocPix,        {set by UpdateGWorld if offscreen buffer had }
                           { to be reallocated}
        gWorldFlag21,      {reserved}
        gWorldFlag22,      {reserved}
        gWorldFlag23,      {reserved}
        gWorldFlag24,      {reserved}
        gWorldFlag25,      {reserved}
        gWorldFlag26,      {reserved}
        gWorldFlag27,      {reserved}
        clipPix,           {used by UpdateGWorld to clip pixels}
        stretchPix,        {used by UpdateGWorld to stretch or shrink }
                           { pixels}
        ditherPix,         {used by UpdateGWorld to dither pixels}
        gwFlagErr,         {set by UpdateGWorld if it failed}
    );
```

Example of Offscreen Graphics Code

The code sample in Listing 21-1 creates an offscreen graphics world. The GetGWorld procedure saves the settings of the graphics port and device so that the current environment can be restored. The NewGWorld function returns a pointer (in the variable parameter fDrawingPort) to the newly created offscreen graphics world, which is initialized to a pixel depth of 8, a boundary rectangle specified by sizeOfDoc, and a color table specified by gOurColors. The SetGWorld procedure sets the offscreen world to be the current graphics environment. The LockPixels function locks the image memory before any drawing operations, in this case an EraseRect procedure, after which memory is unlocked and the original environment restored.

Listing 21-1. Sample offscreen graphics world

```
PROCEDURE BuildOffWorld (sizeOfDoc: Rect);
VAR   oldPerm:     Boolean;
      fi:          FailInfo;
      currDevice:  GDHandle;
      currPort:    GrafPtr;
      erry:        OSErr;

   PROCEDURE BadBuildOff (error: OSErr; message: LongInt);
      BEGIN
         oldPerm := PermAllocation (oldPerm);   {Set memory back to previous.}
         SetGDevice (currDevice);               {Set device back to main, }
                                                { just in case.}
         SetPort (currPort)
      END;
BEGIN
   GetGWorld (currPort,currDev);
   CatchFailures (fi,BadBuildOff);
   erry := NewGWorld (fDrawingPort,8,sizeOfDoc,gOurColors,NIL,GWorldFlags(0));
   FailOSErr (erry);

   SetGWorld (fDrawingPort,NIL);
   IF (NOT LockPixels (fDrawingPort^.portPixMap)) THEN FailOSErr (QDError);
   EraseRect (fDrawingPort^.portRect);
   UnlockPixels (fDrawingPort^.portPixMap);
   SetGWorld (currPort,currDev)
END;  {BuildOffWorld}
```

ADVANCED FEATURES OF THE GRAPHICS DEVICES MANAGER

The offscreen graphics world routines provide facilities for the needs of most graphics applications. Some graphics-intensive applications may need to work more directly with the graphics device record, which is described next. The 'scrn' resource, used at startup to determine initial screen settings, is likely to concern only applications involved in device management, such as drivers.

The Graphics Device Record

All information that is needed to communicate with a graphics device is stored in a graphics device record. This information may describe many types of devices, including screens, printers, and offscreen drawing environments. Most applications will not need to work directly with a graphics device record.

When the system starts up, one handle to a graphics device record is allocated and initialized for each video card the system finds. These graphics device records are linked together in a list, called the device list. (A handle to the first element in the device list is kept in the global variable DeviceList.) By default, the graphics device record corresponding to the first video card found is marked as an active device (a device your program can use for drawing); all other devices in the list are initially marked as inactive.

When your application draws on a device, that device becomes the active device, which the Graphics Devices Manager stores in the global variable TheGDevice.

Graphics device records that correspond to screens have drivers associated with them. These drivers can be used to change the mode of the device from black and white to color, or to change the pixel depth. The set of routines supported by a video driver is defined and described in *Designing Cards and Drivers for the Macintosh Family,* second edition. Graphics device records that your application creates usually won't require drivers.

```
TYPE GDHandle              = ^GDPtr;
     GDPtr                 = ^GDevice;

     GDevice =
     RECORD
         gdRefNum:         Integer;      {reference number of driver}
         gdID:             Integer;      {client ID for search procedure}
         gdType:           Integer;      {type of device (indexed, direct)}
         gdITable:         ITabHandle;   {inverse table for Color Manager}
         gdResPref:        Integer;      {preferred resolution}
         gdSearchProc:     SProcHndl;    {list of search functions}
         gdCompProc:       CProcHndl;    {list of complement functions}
         gdFlags:          Integer;      {graphics device flags}
         gdPMap:           PixMapHandle; {pixel map for displayed image}
         gdRefCon:         LongInt;      {reference value}
         gdNextGD:         GDHandle;     {handle to next graphics device}
         gdRect:           Rect;         {device's global bounds}
         gdMode:           LongInt;      {device's current mode}
         gdCCBytes:        Integer;      {width of expanded cursor data}
         gdCCDepth:        Integer;      {depth of expanded cursor data}
         gdCCXData:        Handle;       {handle to cursor's expanded data}
         gdCCXMask:        Handle;       {handle to cursor's expanded mask}
         gdReserved:       LongInt       {reserved for future use; }
                                         { must be 0}
     END;
```

Field descriptions

gdRefNum — The gdRefNum field contains the reference number of the driver for the screen associated with the card. For most screen devices, this information is set at system startup time.

gdID — The gdID field contains an ID number your application can set to identify the current client of the port. It is also used for search and complement procedures.

gdType — The gdType field specifies the general type of device. Values include

0 = CLUT device (mapped colors with look-up table)
1 = fixed colors (no color look-up table)
2 = direct RGB

These device types are described in the Color Manager chapter of Volume V.

gdITable — The gdITable field contains a handle to the inverse table for color mapping.

gdResPref — The gdResPref field contains the preferred resolution for inverse tables.

gdSearchProc — The gdSearchProc field is a pointer to the list of search functions; its value is NIL for a default procedure.

gdCompProc — The gdCompProc field is a pointer to a list of complement functions; its value is NIL for a default procedure.

gdFlags — The gdFlags field contains the graphics device record's attributes. Do not set these flags directly; always use the procedures described in this chapter.

gdPMap — The gdPMap field is a handle to a pixel map giving the dimension of the image buffer, along with the characteristics of the device (resolution, storage format, color depth, color table). For graphics device records, the high bit of the global variable TheGDevice^^.gdPMap^^.pmTable^^.ctFlags is always set.

gdRefCon — The gdRefCon field is used to pass device-related parameters. Since a device is shared, you shouldn't store data here.

gdNextGD — The gdNextGD field contains a handle to the next device in the device list. If this is the last device in the device list, this is set to 0.

gdRect — The gdRect field contains the boundary rectangle of the graphics device record. The main screen has the top-left corner of the rectangle set to (0,0). All other devices are relative to it.

gdMode — The gdMode field specifies the current setting for the device mode. This is the value passed to the driver to set its pixel depth and to specify color or black and white.

gdCCBytes — The gdCCBytes field contains the rowBytes value of the expanded cursor. Applications should not change this field.

gdCCDepth — The gdCCDepth field contains the depth of the expanded cursor. Applications should not change this field.

gdCCXData — The gdCCXData field contains a handle to the cursor's expanded data. Applications should not change this field.

gdCCXMask — The gdCCXMask field contains a handle to the cursor's expanded mask. Applications should not change this field.

gdReserved — The gdReserved field is reserved for future expansion; it must be set to 0 for future compatibility.

To set the attribute bits in the gdFlags field, use the SetDeviceAttribute procedure. You can set the following attributes:

```
CONST {bit assignments for gdFlags}
      gdDevType     = 0;   {set if device supports color}
      burstDevice   = 7;   {set if device supports block transfer}
      ext32Device   = 8;   {set if device must be accessed in 32-bit }
                           { mode}
      ramInit       = 10;  {set if device has been initialized from RAM}
      mainScreen    = 11;  {set if device is main screen}
      allInit       = 12;  {set if devices were initialized from }
                           { 'scrn' resource}
      screenDevice  = 13;  {set if device is a screen device}
      noDriver      = 14;  {set if device has no driver}
      screenActive  = 15;  {set if device is active}
```

The 'scrn' Resource

The user can use the Monitors control panel to set the desired depth of each screen, whether it displays color or black and white, and its position relative to the main screen. All of this information is stored in a resource of type 'scrn' in the System file.

The 'scrn' resource contains all the screen configuration information for a multiscreen system. Only the 'scrn' resource whose ID is 0 is used by the system. Normally your application won't have to alter or examine this resource. It's created by the Monitors control panel and used by InitGraf. When InitGraf initializes QuickDraw, it checks the System file for the 'scrn' resource. If the 'scrn' resource is found and it matches the hardware, InitGraf organizes the screens according to the contents of this resource; if not, then only the startup screen is used.

The 'scrn' resource consists of a sequence of records, each describing one screen device. The first word in an 'scrn' resource is the number of devices in the resource. Following that is information about each screen device. For each screen device, the resource contains the following fields:

Name	Size	Description
spDrvrHw	word	Slot Manager hardware ID
slot	word	Slot number
dCtlDevBase	long	dCtlDevBase from Device Control Entry (DCE)
mode	word	Slot Manager ID for screen's mode
flagMask	word	Has the value $77FE
flags	word	Indicates device state bit 0 = 0 if black and white; 1 if color bit 11 = 1 if device is main screen bit 15 = 1 if device is active

Name	Size	Description
colorTable	word	Resource ID of desired 'clut'
gammaTable	word	Resource ID of desired 'gama'
globalRect	rect	Device's global rectangle
ctlCount	word	Number of control calls

For each control call of the screen device, the resource contains the following fields:

Name	Size	Description
csCode	word	Control code for this call
length	word	Number of bytes in parameter block
param blk	[variable]	Data to be passed in control call

The records in the 'scrn' resource must be in the same order as the video cards in the slots (starting with the lowest slot). InitGraf scans through the video cards in the slots and compares them with the descriptors in the 'scrn' resource. If the spDrvrHw, slot, and dCtlDevBase fields all match for every screen device in the system, InitGraf uses the 'scrn' resource to initialize the screens. Otherwise it ignores the 'scrn' resource. Thus if you move, add, or remove a video card, the 'scrn' resource becomes invalid until the next time the system starts up.

The spDrvrHw field is a Slot Manager field that identifies the type of hardware on the card. (The spDrvrSw field on the card must identify it as an Apple®-compatible video driver.) The slot field is the number of the slot containing the card. The dCtlDevBase field is the beginning of the device's address space, taken from the device's DCE structure.

If all screen devices match, the rest of the information in the 'scrn' resource is used to configure the screens. The mode field is actually the Slot Manager ID designating the descriptor for that mode. This same mode number is passed to the video driver to tell it which mode to use.

The flags bits in the 'scrn' resource determine whether the device is active (that is, whether it will be used), whether it's color or black and white, and whether it's the main screen. The flagMask field tells which bits in the flags word are used.

To use the default color table for a device, set the colorTable field to –1. To use the default gamma table for a device, set the gammaTable field to –1. (Gamma correction is a technique used to select the appropriate intensities of the colors sent to a screen device.)

The globalRect field specifies the coordinates of the device relative to other devices. The main device must have the top-left corner of the rectangle set to (0,0). The coordinates of all other devices are specified relative to this device. Devices may not overlap, and must share at least part of an edge with another device.

The union of all active screens (minus the menu bar and the rounded corners of the outermost screens) is a region that is stored in the global variable GrayRgn. It defines the area on which windows can be dragged.

Setting a Device's Pixel Depth

The Monitors control panel is the user interface for changing the depth, color capabilities, and positions of graphic devices. Since the user can control the device's capabilities, applications are always encouraged to be flexible: although your application may have a preferred screen depth, it should do its best to accommodate less-than-ideal conditions.

Use the new Graphics Devices Manager function SetDepth, with which your application can change the pixel depth of a graphics device, only in consultation with the user. With it you can offer a convenience: if your application must have a specific pixel depth, display a dialog box that offers the user a choice between going to that depth or quitting your application. This saves the user from having to go to the Monitors control panel and return to your application. (You can use a companion function, HasDepth, before offering the dialog box, to be sure that the available hardware can support the depth you require.)

GRAPHICS DEVICES MANAGER ROUTINES

Graphics Devices Manager routines fall into two classes: high-level routines, which are used for creating and maintaining offscreen graphics worlds, and low-level routines, which are used by the Operating System and specialized applications to directly manage graphics device records.

High-Level Routines

The Graphics Devices Manager's high-level routines allow you to create an offscreen graphics world, establish it as the current port and device, manage its pixel map, update it when necessary, and dispose of it all when done.

Creating a Graphics World

The NewGWorld function creates a graphics world: it allocates an offscreen port and pixel map and its associated offscreen memory. It also allocates a new offscreen graphics device record unless you specify that an existing graphics device record be used—either one you supply or the one having the deepest pixel depth in the rectangle defined by the boundsRect parameter.

```
FUNCTION NewGWorld (VAR offscreenGWorld: GWorldPtr; pixelDepth:
                    Integer; boundsRect: Rect; cTable: CTabHandle;
                    aGDevice: GDHandle; flags: GWorldFlags) : QDErr;
```

NewGWorld sets the pixel depth, boundary rectangle, color table, and graphics world flags. It returns a pointer to the offscreen graphics world in the offscreenGWorld parameter.

Applications typically use the NewGWorld function to create an offscreen world optimized for an image's characteristics—for example, its best pixel depth.

However, NewGWorld has an alternate use: it can create an offscreen graphics world optimized for speed in copying onto the attached graphics devices. To use NewGWorld in this way, set the pixelDepth parameter to 0. This setting requests that the deepest device intersecting your boundsRect value in screen space be used for the offscreen graphics device record. Set the port's portRect field to the same size as boundsRect with the top-left coordinates set to (0,0). The pixel map's bounds and the device's gdRect value are computed so that CopyBits operations between the offscreen pixel map and the screen are optimized. (Typically, the pixel map's bounds are a few pixels wider than those indicated by portRect.)

Parameter implications of this alternate use of the NewGWorld function are noted in each parameter description.

Parameter descriptions

pixelDepth — The pixelDepth parameter determines the pixel resolution of the offscreen world. Possible depths are 0, 1, 2, 4, 8, 16, and 32 bits per pixel.

If you set pixelDepth to 0, the NewGWorld function uses the deepest device intersecting the rectangle specified by your boundsRect parameter to create the offscreen graphics device record.

boundsRect — The boundsRect parameter determines the offscreen pixel map's size and coordinate system, and it becomes the offscreen port's portRect value, the offscreen pixel map's bounds, and the offscreen device's gdRect value. It is used to determine the pixel map's rowBytes value and the size necessary for allocating the offscreen buffer.

If you set pixelDepth to 0, NewGWorld takes the boundsRect parameter in global coordinates to find the deepest device that intersects the boundsRect rectangle.

cTable — The cTable parameter is a handle to the color table to be used. NewGWorld makes a copy of that color table and puts its reference in the offscreen pixel map. It is your application's responsibility to make sure that cTable specifies a valid color table for the pixel depth. If cTable is NIL, the default color table for the pixel depth is used.

If you set pixelDepth to 0, the color table of the deepest device intersecting the boundsRect rectangle is used, and the cTable parameter is ignored.

aGDevice — NewGWorld uses the graphics device record specified in the aGDevice parameter to create the offscreen graphics world when the noNewDevice flag is set.

If you set pixelDepth to 0 (or if you do not set noNewDevice), the aGDevice parameter is ignored, so you should set it to NIL.

flags — The flags parameter provides some options to the application. It can be a combination of the flags pixPurge, noNewDevice, keepLocal, and useTempMem, all members of the GWorldFlags set.

If you set the pixPurge flag, NewGWorld makes the offscreen buffer a purgeable block. Before drawing to or from the offscreen graphics world, your application should call the LockPixels function and ensure that it returns TRUE. If LockPixels returns FALSE, the offscreen buffer has been purged, and your application should either call UpdateGWorld to reallocate it or draw directly in the window it represents. Never draw to a purged offscreen buffer.

If you set noNewDevice, NewGWorld does not create a new offscreen device, and the depth and color table of the aGDevice parameter are used to create the offscreen graphics world. (If you set pixelDepth to 0, the deepest device intersecting the boundsRect rectangle is used.)

NewGWorld keeps a reference to whichever device it uses in the offscreen graphics world data structure, and the SetGWorld procedure uses that device to set the current device.

Note that, to use a custom color table in an offscreen graphics world, you need to create the associated offscreen device, because Color QuickDraw needs the device's inverse table to draw.

If you set the keepLocal flag, your offscreen graphics environment is kept in Macintosh main memory and is not cached to a graphics accelerator card. Use this flag carefully, as it gives up the advantages of a graphics acceleration card, if present.

If you set the useTempMem flag, NewGWorld allocates pixels in temporary memory. You should use temporary memory only for fleeting purposes, and only in conjunction with the AllowPurgePixels procedure so that other applications can launch.

NewGWorld initializes the offscreen port by calling OpenCPort (described in the QuickDraw chapter of Volume V). It sets the port's visRgn field to a rectangular region coincident with its port rectangle. NewGWorld initializes the offscreen device according to pixelDepth, boundsRect, cTable, and default values. NewGWorld generates an inverse table with the Color Manager procedure MakeITable, unless one of the screen devices has the same color table as the offscreen device, in which case it copies the inverse table from that device.

You can compute the size of the offscreen memory buffer using this formula:

rowBytes * (boundsRect.bottom – boundsRect.top)

The actual address of the offscreen buffer is not directly accessible from the pixel map. If you need access to the pixels without going through QuickDraw, call GetPixBaseAddr to get a pointer to the pixels.

Result codes

noErr	0	No error
paramErr	–50	Illegal parameter
cDepthErr	–157	Invalid pixel resolution

Working With a Graphics World's Pixel Map

The Graphics Devices Manager routines that work with pixel maps use handles of type PixMapHandle, which you can obtain with the GetGWorldPixMap function. The routines assume that the pixel maps were created by offscreen graphics world routines. You can use the GetPixBaseAddr and PixMap32Bit functions on pixel map records that are not part of your offscreen graphics world; the other routines won't fail, but they don't return useful information.

```
FUNCTION LockPixels (pm: PixMapHandle) : Boolean;
```

You must call LockPixels before drawing to or from an offscreen graphics world. In the pm parameter pass the pixel map handle returned from a GetGWorldPixMap function. LockPixels locks the offscreen buffer in memory for the duration of the drawing.

If the offscreen buffer is purgeable and has indeed been purged, LockPixels returns FALSE to signal that no drawing can be made to the buffer memory. At that point, the application should either call UpdateGWorld to reallocate the buffer or draw directly in the window it represents.

If the offscreen buffer hasn't been purged or is not purgeable, LockPixels returns TRUE.

As soon as the drawing is completed, you should call UnlockPixels.

```
PROCEDURE UnlockPixels (pm: PixMapHandle);
```

UnlockPixels unlocks the offscreen buffer. Call UnlockPixels as soon as the application finishes drawing to or from the offscreen pixel map. You don't need to call UnlockPixels if LockPixels returned FALSE, because LockPixels doesn't lock purged pixels. (However, calling UnlockPixels on purged pixels does no harm.)

```
PROCEDURE AllowPurgePixels (pm: PixMapHandle);
```

AllowPurgePixels marks the pixel map's offscreen buffer as purgeable.

```
PROCEDURE NoPurgePixels (pm: PixMapHandle);
```

NoPurgePixels marks the pixel map's offscreen buffer as unpurgeable.

```
FUNCTION GetPixelsState (pm: PixMapHandle) : GWorldFlags;
```

GetPixelsState returns the state of the pixel map's offscreen buffer. The state can be a combination of the flags pixelsPurgeable, pixelsLocked, and keepLocal, which are members of the GWorldFlags set. Use GetPixelsState in conjunction with SetPixelsState to save and restore the state of these flags. You can save the flags, change any of them using one of the preceding routines, and then restore their original state by passing the result of GetPixelsState back to the SetPixelsState procedure.

```
PROCEDURE SetPixelsState (pm: PixMapHandle; state: GWorldFlags);
```

The SetPixelsState procedure sets the lock and purge states of the pixel map's offscreen buffer to the given flags by calling LockPixels or UnlockPixels and AllowPurgePixels or NoPurgePixels. Pass the pixel map handle returned from a GetGWorldPixMap function, and a setting of 0 or 1 for the GWorldFlags pixelsPurgeable and pixelsLocked.

You can also use SetPixelsState to set the keepLocal flag: pass keepLocal as a state parameter to specify that the offscreen graphics world stays in main memory rather than being cached on an accelerator card. A graphics world that has already been cached will be brought back to main memory. Clearing the flag will again allow caching. Use this setting carefully, as keeping a graphics world local surrenders the benefits of graphics accelerators.

```
FUNCTION GetPixBaseAddr (pm: PixMapHandle) : Ptr;
```

GetPixBaseAddr returns a 32-bit pointer to the beginning of the pixel map's pixels. Your application should always call GetPixBaseAddr before accessing the pixels of an offscreen pixel map directly. Then your application should switch to 32-bit mode, access the pixels, and switch back to 24-bit mode (if that's the mode you want to use). Your application should never access the baseAddr field of the pixel map directly.

If the offscreen buffer has been purged, GetPixBaseAddr returns NIL.

If QuickDraw is called after GetPixBaseAddr, the contents of the offscreen buffer are not guaranteed to be accurate.

```
FUNCTION PixMap32Bit (pmHandle: PixMapHandle) : Boolean;
```

PixMap32Bit returns TRUE if the specified pixel map requires 32-bit addressing mode for access to its pixels.

Updating the Graphics World

The UpdateGWorld function is similar in form to the NewGWorld function; your application can use it to change one or more of the offscreen world's attributes.

```
FUNCTION UpdateGWorld (VAR offscreenGWorld: GWorldPtr; pixelDepth:
                       Integer; boundsRect: Rect; cTable: CTabHandle;
                       aGDevice: GDHandle; flags: GWorldFlags) :
                       GWorldFlags;
```

UpdateGWorld updates the offscreen graphics world described by offscreenGWorld to the new pixelDepth, boundsRect, and cTable values. The pixelDepth, boundsRect, and cTable parameters have the same meaning and work generally in the same way as in NewGWorld.

If pixelDepth is set to 0, the device list is rescanned to find the new deepest device intersecting with the new boundary rectangle in global screen space.

If the offscreen buffer has been purged, UpdateGWorld reallocates it.

If aGDevice is not NIL, the depth and color table of the graphics device record specified by aGDevice are used instead of those specified by pixelDepth and cTable.

With the flags parameter you can set the keepLocal flag, which keeps the graphics world data structures in Macintosh main memory (or returns them if they were previously cached), or you can clear it if it was previously set, allowing the graphics world to be cached on a graphics accelerator card, if present. The flags can also include a combination of the flags clipPix, ditherPix, and stretchPix. Some combinations are illegal; the legal uses of these flags are as follows:

[ ] (no flags)
clipPix
stretchPix
clipPix, ditherPix
stretchPix, ditherPix

If none of the flags is set, the pixels are not updated.

If clipPix is set, the pixels are updated, and they are clipped if the boundsRect value has changed.

If stretchPix is set, the pixels are updated, with stretching or shrinking if the boundsRect value has changed. If boundsRect hasn't changed, stretchPix is equivalent to clipPix.

If ditherPix is set, the pixels are first updated according to the state of clipPix or stretchPix. Then they are dithered if necessary.

UpdateGWorld returns a pointer to the new offscreen graphics world in the offscreenGWorld parameter. If offscreenGWorld was the current graphics world and UpdateGWorld changed it, the current graphics world is set to the updated offscreen graphics world.

The result of UpdateGWorld is a combination of the flags mapPix, newDepth, alignPix, newRowBytes, reallocPix, clipPix, stretchPix, ditherPix, and gwFlagErr, which are members of the GWorldFlags set. If gwFlagErr is set, UpdateGWorld was unsuccessful and offscreenGWorld is left unchanged. The result of UpdateGWorld must be coerced to a long integer and contain one of the following result codes:

Result codes

paramErr	–50	Illegal parameter
cDepthErr	–157	Invalid pixel resolution

If UpdateGWorld is successful, the other flags must be interpreted as follows:

Flag	**Meaning**
mapPix	Color table mapping occurred.
newDepth	Pixels were scaled to a different depth.
alignPix	Pixels were realigned to the screen alignment.
newRowBytes	The pixel map was reconfigured with a new rowBytes value.
reallocPix	The offscreen buffer had to be reallocated; your image was discarded.
clipPix	Pixels were clipped.
stretchPix	Pixels were stretched or shrunk.
ditherPix	Pixels were dithered.

UpdateGWorld uses the following algorithm for pixel preservation.

1. If cTable is new, the pixels are mapped to the new color table.
2. If pixelDepth is new, the pixels are scaled to the new pixel depth.
3. If boundsRect is new but has the same size, the pixel map is just realigned for optimum CopyBits performance.
4. If boundsRect is smaller and clipPix is set, the pixels in the bottom and right edges are clipped.
5. If boundsRect is bigger and clipPix is set, the bottom and right edges are undefined.
6. If boundsRect is smaller and stretchPix is set, the pixel map is reduced to the new size.
7. If boundsRect is bigger and stretchPix is set, the pixel map is stretched to the new size.
8. If the offscreen buffer was purged, it is reallocated, but the pixels are lost.

Setting and Retrieving the Graphics World

With these routines you can set and retrieve the current port and graphics device records, which can be useful for saving and restoring an environment. You can also retrieve the graphics device and pixel map of a graphics world.

```
PROCEDURE SetGWorld (port: CGrafPtr; gdh: GDHandle);
```

SetGWorld sets the current graphics world. SetGWorld can be used with a port parameter of type GrafPtr, CGrafPtr, or GWorldPtr (with proper type coercion).

If the port parameter is of type GrafPtr or CGrafPtr, the current port is set to the port specified by the port parameter, and the current device is set to the device specified by the gdh parameter.

If the port parameter is of type GWorldPtr, the current port is set to the port specified by the port parameter, and the current device is set to the device attached to the given graphics world. The gdh parameter is ignored.

```
PROCEDURE GetGWorld (VAR port: CGrafPtr; VAR gdh: GDHandle);
```

GetGWorld returns the current graphics world in the port and gdh parameters. The port parameter is set to the current port, which can be of type GrafPtr, CGrafPtr, or GWorldPtr. The gdh parameter is set to the current device.

```
FUNCTION GetGWorldDevice (offscreenGWorld: GWorldPtr) : GDHandle;
```

GetGWorldDevice returns a handle to the device attached to the offscreen world specified by the offscreenGWorld parameter. This device is generally the offscreen device created by

NewGWorld. If offscreenGWorld was created with the noNewDevice flag set, the attached device is one of the screen devices or the device passed to NewGWorld or UpdateGWorld.

If offscreenGWorld points to a regular grafPort or color GrafPort, GetGWorldDevice returns the current device.

```
FUNCTION GetGWorldPixMap (offscreenGWorld: GWorldPtr) : PixMapHandle;
```

GetGWorldPixMap returns a handle to the pixel map record created for an offscreen graphics world. Use GetGWorldPixMap whenever you need to address the pixel map record created for an offscreen graphics world, rather than dereferencing the GWorld pointer, to ensure compatibility on systems that have the offscreen graphics world routines but are running the original QuickDraw (not Color QuickDraw).

For example, you should use this function before calling CopyBits when copying from the pixel map of an offscreen graphics world:

```
pixBase := GetGWorldPixMap (myWorld);
CopyBits (pixBase^,myWindow^.portBits,aRect,otherR,srcCopy,NIL);
```

Use the GetGWorldPixMap function with offscreen graphics world routines, such as LockPixels, AllowPurgePixels, and GetPixelsState, that use a handle to a pixel map.

```
UnlockPixels (GetGWorldPixMap (myGWorld));
```

GetGWorldPixMap is not available prior to system software version 7.0.

Disposing of a Graphics World

DisposeGWorld disposes of all the memory allocated for the offscreen port data structure and substructures, offscreen pixel map and color table, and offscreen buffer.

```
PROCEDURE DisposeGWorld (offscreenGWorld: GWorldPtr);
```

If an offscreen graphics device was created, DisposeGWorld disposes of its GDevice structure and substructures.

Call DisposeGWorld only when the application no longer needs the offscreen buffer. If the current device was the offscreen device attached to offscreenGWorld, the current device is reset to the device stored in the global variable MainDevice.

Low-Level Routines

A few low-level routines are called by the higher-level offscreen graphics world routines; the majority are called by the graphics system to manage the graphics device record and the device list. Normally you won't need to call any of them yourself.

Supporting the Offscreen Graphics World

The Graphics Devices Manager calls these routines as it manages the offscreen graphics worlds.

```
FUNCTION NewScreenBuffer (globalRect: Rect; purgeable: Boolean; VAR gdh:
                          GDHandle; VAR offscreenPixMap: PixMapHandle) :
                          QDErr;
```

NewScreenBuffer allocates an offscreen pixel map and an offscreen buffer, using the depth and color table of the deepest device intersecting with the global rectangle in screen space. A handle to that device is returned in gdh, and a handle to the offscreen pixel map is returned in offscreenPixMap. If purgeable is TRUE, the offscreen buffer is made purgeable.

Result codes

noErr	0	No error
paramErr	–50	Illegal parameter
cNoMemErr	–152	Failed to allocate memory for structures

The routines LockPixels, UnlockPixels, AllowPurgePixels, NoPurgePixels, GetPixelsState, SetPixelsState, and GetPixBaseAddr can all be called with offscreenPixMap as a parameter.

```
FUNCTION NewTempScreenBuffer (globalRect: Rect; purgeable: Boolean; VAR
                              gdh: GDHandle; VAR offscreenPixMap:
                              PixMapHandle) : QDErr;
```

NewTempScreenBuffer performs the same functions as NewScreenBuffer except that it allocates pixels in temporary memory.

```
PROCEDURE DisposeScreenBuffer (offscreenPixMap: PixMapHandle);
```

DisposeScreenBuffer is called by DisposeGWorld. It disposes of the memory allocated for the offscreen buffer, the offscreen pixel map, and the color table.

Managing the Graphics Device Record

These routines enable your application to create, initialize, and dispose of graphics device records, and to obtain handles to particular graphics device records, such as those for the main and deepest devices. A new procedure, DeviceLoop, simplifies the steps your application must take in order to check screen characteristics before drawing.

```
FUNCTION NewGDevice (refNum: Integer; mode: LongInt) : GDHandle;
```

The NewGDevice function allocates a new graphics device data structure and all of its handles, then calls InitGDevice to initialize it for the device specified by the refNum parameter in the specified mode. If the request is unsuccessful, NewGDevice returns a NIL handle. The new graphics device record and all of its handles are allocated in the system heap. All attributes in the gdFlags field are set to FALSE.

If your application creates a graphics device record without a driver, it should set the mode parameter to –1. In this case, InitGDevice is not called to initialize the graphics device record. Your application must perform all initialization.

A graphics device's default mode is defined as 128, as described in *Designing Cards and Drivers for the Macintosh Family,* second edition; this is assumed to be a black-and-white mode. If the mode parameter is not the default mode, the device's gdDevType attribute bit is set to TRUE, to indicate that the device is capable of displaying color (see the description of the SetDeviceAttribute procedure later in this chapter).

NewGDevice doesn't automatically insert the graphics device record into the device list. In general, your application shouldn't add devices that it creates to the device list.


```
PROCEDURE InitGDevice (gdRefNum: Integer; mode: LongInt; gdh: GDHandle);
```

The InitGDevice procedure sets the screen device whose driver has the reference number specified in gdRefNum to the specified mode. It then fills out the graphics device record structure specified by the gdh parameter to contain all information describing that mode. The graphics device handle should have been allocated by a call to NewGDevice.

The mode parameter determines the configuration of the device; possible modes for a device can be determined by interrogating the video card's ROM via calls to the Slot Manager (refer to the Slot Manager chapter in this volume and *Designing Cards and Drivers for the Macintosh Family,* second edition). See the Device Manager chapter in Volume V for more details about the interaction of devices and their drivers.

The information describing the new mode is primarily contained in the video card's ROM. If the device has a fixed color table, then that table is read directly from the ROM. If the device has a variable color table, then the default color table for that depth is used (the 'clut' resource with ID equal to the depth).

In general, your application should never need to call InitGDevice. All screens are initialized at start time and users change their modes through the Monitors control panel. If your program initializes a device without a driver, this procedure will do nothing; your application must initialize all fields of the graphics device record. After your program initializes the color table for the device, it needs to call MakeITable to build the inverse table for the device.

```
FUNCTION GetGDevice : GDHandle;
```

The GetGDevice function returns a handle to the current graphics device record. This is useful for determining the characteristics of the current output device (for instance, its pixel size or color table). Note that since a window can span screen boundaries, this function does not return the device that describes a port.

A handle to the currently active device is kept in the global variable TheGDevice.

```
FUNCTION GetDeviceList : GDHandle;
```

The GetDeviceList function returns a handle to the first device in the global variable DeviceList.

```
FUNCTION GetMainDevice : GDHandle;
```

The GetMainDevice function returns a handle to the graphics device record that corresponds to the main screen. Your application can examine this graphics device record to determine the size or depth of the main screen.

A handle to the current main device is kept in the global variable MainDevice.

```
FUNCTION GetMaxDevice (globalRect: Rect) : GDHandle;
```

The GetMaxDevice function returns a handle to the deepest device that intersects the specified global rectangle. Your application might use this function to allocate offscreen pixel maps.

```
FUNCTION GetNextDevice (curDevice: GDHandle) : GDHandle;
```

The GetNextDevice function returns a handle to the next graphics device record in the device list. If there are no more devices in the list, it returns NIL.

```
PROCEDURE SetGDevice (gdh: GDHandle);
```

The SetGDevice procedure sets the specified graphics device record as the current device. Your application won't generally need to use this procedure except to draw to offscreen graphics devices.

```
PROCEDURE SetDeviceAttribute (gdh: GDHandle; attribute: Integer; value:
                              Boolean);
```

The SetDeviceAttribute procedure can be used to set a device's attribute bits. SetDeviceAttribute allows you to indicate whether the device is a screen device, is the main screen, supports color, and so forth. For more information on the attributes you can set, see "The Graphics Device Record" earlier in this chapter.

```
FUNCTION TestDeviceAttribute (gdh: GDHandle; attribute: Integer) :
                              Boolean;
```

The TestDeviceAttribute function tests a single attribute to see if its value is TRUE. If your application is scanning through the device list, it typically uses this function to determine whether a device is a screen device, and, if so, to determine whether it's active. Then your application can draw to any active screen devices.

```
PROCEDURE DisposGDevice (gdh: GDHandle);
```

The DisposGDevice procedure disposes of the current graphics device record, releases the space allocated for it, and disposes of all data structures allocated by NewGDevice.

```
FUNCTION HasDepth (aDevice: GDHandle; depth: Integer; whichFlags:
                   Integer; flags: Integer) : Integer;
```

The HasDepth function checks to see whether the device you specify in the aDevice parameter supports the pixel depth you specify in the depth parameter. In the whichFlags parameter you specify which of the gdFlags set to check; in the flags parameter you specify the value to check for. The function returns 0 if the device does not support the mode you inquire after; if the device does support the mode, the function returns the mode ID. (See the Slot Manager chapter in this volume and *Designing Cards and Drivers for the Macintosh Family,* second edition, for information about device modes.)

You should always test a device for a particular depth before setting the device's depth.

```
FUNCTION SetDepth (aDevice: GDHandle; depth: Integer; whichFlags:
                   Integer; flags: Integer) : OSErr;
```

The SetDepth function sets the mode of the specified device to the pixel depth you specify in the depth parameter. It does not change the 'scrn' resource; when the system is rebooted, the original depth is restored.

> **Note:** This function is a convenience for applications that need to run on devices of a particular depth and are unable to adapt to any other depth. Your application should use it *only* after asking the user's permission.

In the whichFlags parameter you specify which of the gdFlags set to modify; in the flags parameter you specify the value. (Currently, the first flag, gdDevType, is the only one that can be set with a SetDepth call.) For example, if you wanted to switch a device to black and white, you would specify a whichFlags value of 0001 and a flags value of 0000.

Call the HasDepth function before calling SetDepth to verify that the device in question can be set to the depth desired.

```
PROCEDURE DeviceLoop (drawingRgn: RgnHandle; drawingProc:
                      DeviceLoopDrawingProcPtr; userData: LongInt;
                      flags: DeviceLoopFlags);
```

The DeviceLoop procedure searches all active screen devices, calling your drawing procedure whenever it encounters a screen that intersects your drawing region. You supply a handle to the region in which you wish to draw and a pointer to your drawing procedure. The drawing region is in local coordinates, and is the same as a window port's visRgn value, for example, after a BeginUpdate call. In the userData parameter, you pass a long integer of data that is forwarded to your drawing procedure.

If the DeviceLoop procedure encounters similar devices—having the same pixel depth, black-and-white/color setting, and matching color table seeds—it makes only one call to your drawing procedure, pointing to the first such device encountered. You can modify this behavior by supplying a flags parameter with one of the following values.

Flag	Meaning
singleDevices	If you set the singleDevices flag, then similar devices are not grouped together when the drawing procedure is called. If this flag is not set, DeviceLoop only calls your drawing procedure once for each set of similar devices, and the first one found is passed as the target device. (It is assumed to be representative of all the similar devices.)
dontMatchSeeds	If you set the dontMatchSeeds flag, then DeviceLoop doesn't consider color table seeds when comparing devices for similarity. DeviceLoop ignores this flag if the singleDevices flag is set.
allDevices	If you set the allDevices flag, the drawingRgn parameter is ignored, and DeviceLoop calls your drawing procedure for all active screens. The current port's visRgn value is not affected when this flag is set.

Each time your drawing procedure is called, the current port's visRgn field will have been set to the intersection of the original port's visRgn and the intersecting portion of the target device.

Your drawing procedure should be declared as follows:

```
PROCEDURE MyDrawingProc (depth: Integer; deviceFlags: Integer;
                         targetDevice: GDHandle; userData: LongInt);
```

The depth parameter contains the pixel size of the target device, the deviceFlags parameter contains the gdFlags values from the target device's graphics device record, and the targetDevice parameter is a handle to the target device.

The long integer of user data passed to DeviceLoop is passed on to your drawing procedure.

When called from a computer without Color QuickDraw, the targetDevice parameter is set to NIL.

SUMMARY OF THE GRAPHICS DEVICES MANAGER

Constants

```
CONST {values for gdType}
      clutType      = 0;    {0 if look-up table}
      fixedType     = 1;    {1 if fixed table}
      directType    = 2;    {2 if direct pixel values}

      {bit assignments for gdFlags}
      gdDevType     = 0;    {set if device supports color}
      burstDevice   = 7;    {set if device supports block transfer}
      ext32Device   = 8;    {set if device must be accessed in 32-bit mode}
      ramInit       = 10;   {set if device has been initialized from RAM}
      mainScreen    = 11;   {set if device is main screen}
      allInit       = 12;   {set if devices were initialized from 'scrn' }
                            { resource}
      screenDevice  = 13;   {set if device is a screen device}
      noDriver      = 14;   {set if device has no driver}
      screenActive  = 15;   {set if device is active}
```


Data Types

```
TYPE GWorldPtr = CGrafPtr;

       GWorldFlags =
       SET OF (
          pixPurge,          {used by NewGWorld to make offscreen buffer }
                             { purgeable}
          noNewDevice,       {used by NewGWorld to not create an offscreen }
                             { device}
          useTempMem,        {used by NewGWorld to allocate pixels in }
                             { temporary memory}
          keepLocal,         {used to keep data structures in main memory}
          gWorldFlag4,       {reserved}
          gWorldFlag5,       {reserved}
          pixelsPurgeable,   {used by Get/SetPixelsState for purgeable }
                             { pixels}
          pixelsLocked,      {used by Get/SetPixelsState for locked pixels}
          gWorldFlag8,       {reserved}
          gWorldFlag9,       {reserved}
          gWorldFlag10,      {reserved}
          gWorldFlag11,      {reserved}
          gWorldFlag12,      {reserved}
          gWorldFlag13,      {reserved}
```

```
      gWorldFlag14,      {reserved}
      gWorldFlag15,      {reserved}
      mapPix,            {set by UpdateGWorld if color mapping occurred}
      newDepth,          {set by UpdateGWorld if pixels were scaled }
                         { to a different depth}
      alignPix,          {set by UpdateGWorld if pixels were realigned }
                         { to screen alignment}
      newRowBytes,       {set by UpdateGWorld if pixel map was }
                         { reconfigured in a new rowBytes}
      reallocPix,        {set by UpdateGWorld if offscreen buffer had }
                         { to be reallocated}
      gWorldFlag21,      {reserved}
      gWorldFlag22,      {reserved}
      gWorldFlag23,      {reserved}
      gWorldFlag24,      {reserved}
      gWorldFlag25,      {reserved}
      gWorldFlag26,      {reserved}
      gWorldFlag27,      {reserved}
      clipPix,           {used by UpdateGWorld to clip pixels}
      stretchPix,        {used by UpdateGWorld to stretch or shrink }
                         { pixels}
      ditherPix,         {used by UpdateGWorld to dither pixels}
      gwFlagErr,         {set by UpdateGWorld if it failed}
   );

GDHandle               = ^GDPtr;
GDPtr                  = ^GDevice;

GDevice =
RECORD
   gdRefNum:           Integer;       {reference number of driver}
   gdID:               Integer;       {client ID for search procedure}
   gdType:             Integer;       {type of device (indexed, direct)}
   gdITable:           ITabHandle;    {inverse table for Color Manager}
   gdResPref:          Integer;       {preferred resolution}
   gdSearchProc:       SProcHndl;     {list of search functions}
   gdCompProc:         CProcHndl;     {list of complement functions}
   gdFlags:            Integer;       {graphics device flags}
   gdPMap:             PixMapHandle;  {pixel map for displayed image}
   gdRefCon:           LongInt;       {reference value}
   gdNextGD:           GDHandle;      {handle to next graphics device}
   gdRect:             Rect;          {device's global bounds}
   gdMode:             LongInt;       {device's current mode}
   gdCCBytes:          Integer;       {width of expanded cursor data}
   gdCCDepth:          Integer;       {depth of expanded cursor data}
   gdCCXData:          Handle;        {handle to cursor's expanded data}
   gdCCXMask:          Handle;        {handle to cursor's expanded mask}
   gdReserved:         LongInt        {reserved for future use; }
                                      { must be 0}
END;
```

Routines

Creating a Graphics World

```
FUNCTION NewGWorld            (VAR offscreenGWorld: GWorldPtr; pixelDepth:
                               Integer; boundsRect: Rect; cTable:
                               CTabHandle; aGDevice: GDHandle; flags:
                               GWorldFlags) : QDErr;
```

Working with a Graphics World's Pixel Map

```
FUNCTION LockPixels           (pm: PixMapHandle) : Boolean;
PROCEDURE UnlockPixels        (pm: PixMapHandle);
PROCEDURE AllowPurgePixels    (pm: PixMapHandle);
PROCEDURE NoPurgePixels       (pm: PixMapHandle);
FUNCTION GetPixelsState       (pm: PixMapHandle) : GWorldFlags;
PROCEDURE SetPixelsState      (pm: PixMapHandle; state: GWorldFlags);
FUNCTION GetPixBaseAddr       (pm: PixMapHandle) : Ptr;
FUNCTION PixMap32Bit          (pmHandle: PixMapHandle) : Boolean;
```

Updating the Graphics World

```
FUNCTION UpdateGWorld         (VAR offscreenGWorld: GWorldPtr; pixelDepth:
                               Integer; boundsRect: Rect; cTable:
                               CTabHandle; aGDevice: GDHandle; flags:
                               GWorldFlags) : GWorldFlags;
```

Setting and Retrieving the Graphics World

```
PROCEDURE SetGWorld           (port: CGrafPtr; gdh: GDHandle);
PROCEDURE GetGWorld           (VAR port: CGrafPtr; VAR gdh: GDHandle);
FUNCTION GetGWorldDevice      (offscreenGWorld: GWorldPtr) : GDHandle;
FUNCTION GetGWorldPixMap      (offscreenGWorld: GWorldPtr) : PixMapHandle;
```

Disposing of a Graphics World

```
PROCEDURE DisposeGWorld       (offscreenGWorld: GWorldPtr);
```

Supporting the Offscreen Graphics World

```
FUNCTION NewScreenBuffer         (globalRect: Rect; purgeable: Boolean; VAR
                                  gdh: GDHandle; VAR offscreenPixMap:
                                  PixMapHandle) : QDErr;

FUNCTION NewTempScreenBuffer     (globalRect: Rect; purgeable: Boolean; VAR
                                  gdh: GDHandle; VAR offscreenPixMap:
                                  PixMapHandle) : QDErr;

PROCEDURE DisposeScreenBuffer    (offscreenPixMap: PixMapHandle);
```

Managing the Graphics Device Record

```
FUNCTION NewGDevice              (refNum: Integer; mode: LongInt) : GDHandle;

PROCEDURE InitGDevice            (gdRefNum: Integer; mode: LongInt; gdh:
                                  GDHandle);

FUNCTION GetGDevice              : GDHandle;

FUNCTION GetDeviceList           : GDHandle;

FUNCTION GetMainDevice           : GDHandle;

FUNCTION GetMaxDevice            (globalRect: Rect) : GDHandle;

FUNCTION GetNextDevice           (curDevice: GDHandle) : GDHandle;

PROCEDURE SetGDevice             (gdh: GDHandle);

PROCEDURE SetDeviceAttribute     (gdh: GDHandle; attribute: Integer; value:
                                  Boolean);

FUNCTION TestDeviceAttribute     (gdh: GDHandle; attribute: Integer) :
                                  Boolean;

PROCEDURE DisposGDevice          (gdh: GDHandle);

FUNCTION HasDepth                (gd: GDHandle; depth: Integer; whichFlags:
                                  Integer: flags: Integer) : Integer;

FUNCTION SetDepth                (gd: GDHandle; depth: Integer; whichFlags:
                                  Integer; flags: Integer) : OSErr;

PROCEDURE DeviceLoop             (drawingRgn: RgnHandle; drawingProc:
                                  DeviceLoopDrawingProcPtr; userData: LongInt;
                                  flags: DeviceLoopFlags);
```

Application-Defined Routine

```
PROCEDURE MyDrawingProc          (depth: Integer; deviceFlags: Integer;
                                  targetDevice: GDHandle; userData: LongInt);
```

Global Variables

DeviceList	A handle to the first element in the device list.
GrayRgn	Contains the size and shape of current desktop.
TheGDevice	A handle to the current active device.
MainDevice	A handle to the current main device.

Result Codes

noErr	0	No error
paramErr	–50	Illegal parameter
cNoMemErr	–152	Failed to allocate memory for structures
cDepthErr	–157	Invalid pixel resolution

Assembly-Language Information

GDevice Data Structure

gdRefNum	word	reference number of driver
gdID	word	client ID for search procedure
gdType	word	type of device (indexed, direct)
gdITable	long	inverse table for Color Manager
gdResPref	word	preferred resolution
gdSearchProc	long	list of search functions
gdCompProc	long	list of complement functions
gdFlags	word	graphics device flags
gdPMap	long	pixel map for displayed image
gdRefCon	long	reference value
gdNextGD	long	handle to next graphics device
gdRect	2 longs	device's global bounds
gdMode	long	device's current mode
gdCCBytes	word	width of expanded cursor data
gdCCDepth	word	depth of expanded cursor data
gdCCXData	long	handle to cursor's expanded data
gdCCXMask	long	handle to cursor's expanded mask
gdReserved	long	reserved for future use; must be 0
gdRec	[variable]	size of graphics device record

22 THE SOUND MANAGER

ABOUT THIS CHAPTER

This chapter describes how your application can use the Sound Manager to create, modify, and play sounds. The information in this chapter supersedes the information in the Sound Manager chapter of *Inside Macintosh,* Volume V. The Sound Manager is a replacement for the older Sound Driver, which is documented in *Inside Macintosh,* Volume II. The Sound Driver is obsolete, and you should use the Sound Manager for all sound-related activity.

The Sound Manager was first released for all Macintosh® computers as part of system software version 6.0 and has been significantly enhanced in later system software versions. System software versions 6.0.7 and later include an enhanced Sound Manager that provides routines for sound input, continuous play from disk, sound-channel mixing, and audio compression and expansion. There are no specific hardware requirements for running this enhanced version of the Sound Manager, except that the continuous play-from-disk routines and the ability to produce concurrent multiple channels of sampled sound are currently available only on machines equipped with the Apple® Sound Chip (ASC). Also, you can use the sound input routines to record sounds only on machines equipped with a sound input device. Use the Gestalt function (described in the Compatibility Guidelines chapter in this volume) to determine whether the capabilities you need are present before attempting to use them.

You should read this chapter if you want your application to create or manipulate sounds. For example, your application might be specifically concerned with creating and storing sounds. Such applications include those that synthesize sound or speech, record and play back sampled sounds, and synchronize multimedia presentations. Other applications that use sound include those that provide voice mail and voice annotation capabilities for documents. For compatibility reasons, you should use the services provided by the Sound Manager rather than access the available audio hardware directly. This increases the likelihood that your application will run unmodified on future hardware or on alternate operating systems (such as A/UX®). Moreover, by using the Sound Manager, your application can monitor and control the amount of processing time consumed by its sound-related activity, and hence coexist cooperatively with other open applications.

Even if your application is not specifically concerned with creating or playing sounds, you can often improve your application at very little programming expense by using the Sound Manager to integrate sound into its user interface. For example, you can play appropriate sounds to signal that some operation has completed or to alert the user that something exceptional (perhaps unexpected) has happened. If you use sound in this way, you should be aware that there may be cultural biases or preferences associated with certain sounds. Unless they are very large, therefore, you should store all application-specific sounds as resources, which can be easily modified for local regions. You should also make this sort of sound optional because there might be users who object to it or environments where it is inappropriate.

You should note in particular that the SysBeep procedure, documented in *Inside Macintosh,* Volume II, as one of the Operating System Utilities, is now a Sound Manager routine. Hence, even if you are developing an application that does not employ any sound other than an occasional system alert sound, you need to be aware of certain situations that may prevent the sound from being heard by the user. If your applications use the SysBeep procedure, you should look at the discussion in "Producing an Alert Sound"; some sections of the "Introduction to Sound" may be helpful to you as well.

If you wish to create files containing sampled sounds (such as recorded speech or special effects), you may need to refer to the information on the Audio Interchange File Format (AIFF) and the Audio Interchange File Format extension for Compression (AIFF-C). You can find a partial specification of both of these file formats in "Sound Files" later in this chapter. A more complete description of the AIFF file format is available from APDA®.

ABOUT THE SOUND MANAGER

The Sound Manager is a collection of routines that your application can use to create sounds without a knowledge of or dependence on the actual sound-producing hardware available on any particular Macintosh computer. You can use the Sound Manager to

- play simple sequences of frequencies
- play sounds described by complex waveforms
- play digitally recorded or computed sampled sounds
- record sampled sounds
- mix and synchronize multiple channels of sound
- play a sound continuously from disk while other processing continues
- produce a sound to alert the user
- compress sound data to maximize the available disk storage space
- expand compressed sound data for playback in real time
- obtain information about existing sound channels
- monitor and limit the amount of CPU time consumed by sound-related activity

If you use the Sound Manager for all sound-related activity instead of accessing the sound-producing hardware directly, you can maximize the likelihood that your applications will run without modification on all current and future hardware configurations.

This chapter provides a brief introduction to sound on Macintosh computers and then discusses

- sound synthesizers
- sound commands
- sound channels

A thorough understanding of these topics is essential to efficient use of the Sound Manager in your applications. Thereafter, this chapter provides a preliminary discussion of the major features that are new to the enhanced Sound Manager provided with system software versions 6.0.7 and later, including

- mixing multiple channels of sampled sound
- compressing and expanding sound data
- playing sounds stored on disk while other applications execute
- recording sounds on Macintosh computers having appropriate sound input hardware
- obtaining status information about sound channels

This chapter also describes sound resources and sound files, the two sound storage formats supported by the Sound Manager. Most applications do not need to know the details of these storage formats because the Sound Manager provides routines that allow you to read and create both sound resources and sound files. In most cases, your application should use those routines rather than create or parse sound resources or files directly.

Most applications are likely to need only a few of the many capabilities of the enhanced Sound Manager. If your application's use of sound falls into one or more of the following categories, you can proceed right to the indicated sections in this chapter to find the information you need.

- **Controlling the system alert sound.** Your application can use the Sound Manager to play, disable, or enable the **system alert sound** selected by the user in the Sound control panel. The system alert sound is played whenever an application issues the SysBeep procedure. For more information about controlling the system alert sound, see "Producing an Alert Sound" later in this chapter.

- **Playing prerecorded sounds.** Your application can play back prerecorded sampled sounds by calling the SndPlay function. The sampled sound can contain speech, sound effects, or other sounds needed by your application. For more information on playing back prerecorded sounds, see "Playing 'snd ' Resources" later in this chapter. If the sound you want to play back is too large to fit into RAM, you can play it by calling SndStartFilePlay. This routine should be used only with very large sounds because it consumes more processing time than SndPlay. For more information on playing sampled sounds from disk, see "Continuous Play From Disk" later in this chapter.

- **Compressing and expanding sounds.** If your application uses lots of sounds, you might want to compress those sounds to reduce the size of the data shipped with your application. The Sound Manager provides several routines to handle this compression of audio data. The real-time expansion and playback are handled automatically by the Sound Manager when you issue a request to play the sampled sound data. For more information on compressing and expanding sounds, see "Sound Compression and Expansion" later in this chapter.

- **Recording sounds.** Any Macintosh computer equipped with sound input hardware and an associated driver is able to record sounds (several Macintosh computers include these items as standard features). By using one of several recording routines, your application can record sounds to provide capabilities such as voice mail, voice annotation, speech recognition, and even overdubbing. For more information on sound input, see "Sound Recording" later in this chapter.

- **Mixing multiple channels of sound.** On Macintosh computers with sufficient processing capability, multiple channels of sampled sound can be played simultaneously. This means that your application can play several sampled sounds simultaneously, or that your application can play sampled sounds while other applications do so also. For more information on mixing multiple channels of sampled sound, see "Multiple Channels of Sound" later in this chapter. Mixing can also include more than just simultaneous playback of sampled sounds. Certain audio characteristics can be altered in real time while a sound is playing. See "Manipulating a Sound That Is Playing" later in this chapter for more details.

- **Designing sound.** The Sound Manager has facilities for designing and controlling complex sounds. Your application can play a series of frequencies at specified durations in a manner that will be familiar to users. You can use custom waveforms to change the timbre of these sounds, and you can play them on multiple channels concurrently. Sounds can be speeded up or slowed down, made louder or less loud, or panned left, right, or center in real time. To understand the full power of the Sound Manager, start by reading "Sound Synthesizers" later in this chapter and then look over the table of contents for specific areas of interest.

INTRODUCTION TO SOUND

Sound is created on a Macintosh computer when the Sound Manager (or an application) sends data to whatever audio hardware is available on the machine. The audio hardware is a digital-to-analog converter (DAC) that translates digital audio data into analog audio signals; those signals are then sent to the internal speaker or to a sound output connector (to which the user can connect headphones, external speakers, or sound amplification equipment). The DAC in all current Macintosh computers is a Sony sound chip. The Macintosh II family of computers and more recent models (such as the Macintosh SE/30 and Macintosh Portable) contain two Sony sound chips (to provide stereo output capability) as well as an Apple Sound Chip, a customized chip that provides enhanced audio output characteristics as well as emulation capabilities for the earlier sound hardware. There are also NuBus™ expansion boards available from third-party developers that provide other audio DAC hardware.

To maximize compatibility across the entire family of Macintosh computers, your application should never address any built-in audio hardware directly. Instead, you should always create sound by sending the appropriate instructions to the Sound Manager. The Sound Manager is responsible for managing all communication between your application and the available audio hardware, as illustrated in Figure 22-1.

Your application creates sound by sending sound commands to the Sound Manager, which interprets those commands and places them into a sound channel. A sound channel is a first-in, first-out (FIFO) queue. Queued commands are sent to the sound hardware through a **sound synthesizer,** which is like a device driver insofar as it is responsible for managing the last stage of communication with the audio hardware. Every sound channel is linked to one of three available synthesizers, depending on the type of sound to be produced.

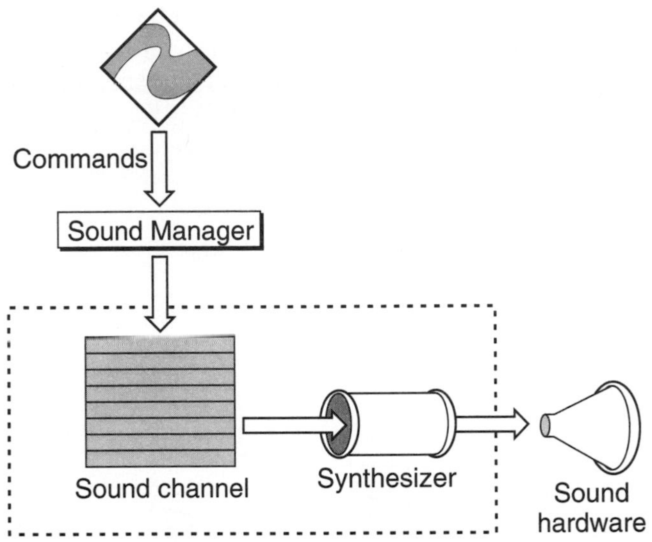

Figure 22-1. The position of the Sound Manager

Sometimes it is necessary to bypass the queue of sound commands altogether. If you want to stop all sound production on a particular channel immediately, for example, it would be counterproductive to send a command to the sound channel because that command remains queued until it becomes the next command processed by the synthesizer. Instead, you can send commands directly to the synthesizer, as illustrated in Figure 22-2.

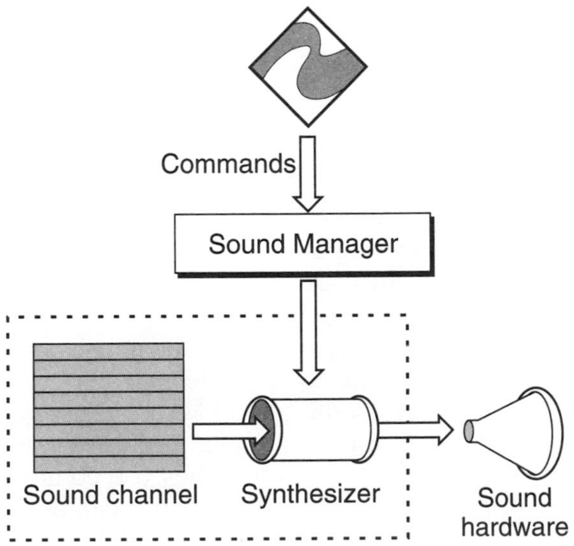

Figure 22-2. Bypassing the command queue

When you bypass the sound channel in this way, any commands that are already queued but not yet sent to the synthesizer remain queued. You can, however, flush the channel at any time by sending the Sound Manager the appropriate command.

With the enhanced Sound Manager, you can have multiple channels of sampled sound open and multiple commands sent to the sampled sound synthesizer concurrently. For example, two different applications can each open a sound channel and send commands to it. Figure 22-3 illustrates such a situation.

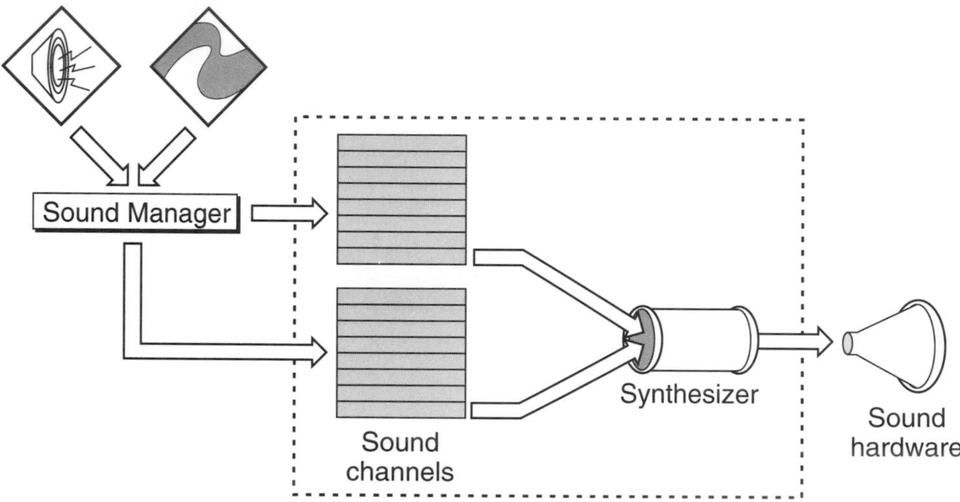

Figure 22-3. Mixing multiple channels of sampled sound

In this illustration, two applications are sending sound commands to the sampled sound synthesizer. The Sound Manager maintains a separate queue of commands for each application but mixes the audio data before sending it to the sampled sound synthesizer. The result is a single audio signal that is sent to the available audio hardware.

Sound Synthesizers

A **synthesizer** is the code responsible for interpreting sound commands and using the available hardware to produce sounds. The Sound Manager insulates an application from the underlying hardware primarily by selecting the sound hardware drivers (or synthesizers) that are best suited to the available audio hardware.

Synthesizers that drive the built-in audio hardware on Macintosh computers are provided by Apple Computer, Inc. and are stored in the System file as resources of type 'snth'. Depending on the type of sound you wish to produce, the Sound Manager uses either the square-wave synthesizer, the wave-table synthesizer, or the sampled sound synthesizer to interpret commands and data sent to it by your application. Sometimes you do not need to specify which synthesizer you wish to use because some sound commands can be interpreted by all three.

The Square-Wave Synthesizer

The **square-wave synthesizer** is the simplest of the playback synthesizers supplied with the Sound Manager. You can use it to generate a sound based on a square wave, and it is functionally equivalent to the square-wave synthesizer contained in the old Sound Driver. Your application can use the square-wave synthesizer to play a simple sequence of sounds in which each sound is described completely by three factors: its frequency or pitch, its amplitude (or volume), and its duration.

The square-wave synthesizer can play only one frequency at a time through a sound channel, and it cannot play back a waveform sound description or a recorded sound. The square-wave synthesizer requires very little CPU time, however, and it is very easy for your application to use.

The Wave-Table Synthesizer

To produce more complex sounds than are possible using the square-wave synthesizer, your applications can use the **wave-table synthesizer.** As the name indicates, the wave-table synthesizer can produce sounds that are based on a description of a single wave cycle. This cycle is called a *wave table* and is represented as an array of bytes that describe the timbre (or tone) of a sound at any point in the cycle.

Your application can use any number of bytes to represent the wave, but 512 is the recommended number because the Sound Manager resizes a wave table to 512 bytes if the table is not exactly that long. Your application can compute the wave table at run time or load it from a resource. You can open multiple wave-table channels (up to a maximum of four).

A **wave table** is a sequence of wave amplitudes measured at fixed intervals. For instance, a sine wave can be converted into a wave table by taking the value of the wave's amplitude at every 1/512 interval of the wave (see Figure 22-4).

22 Sound Manager

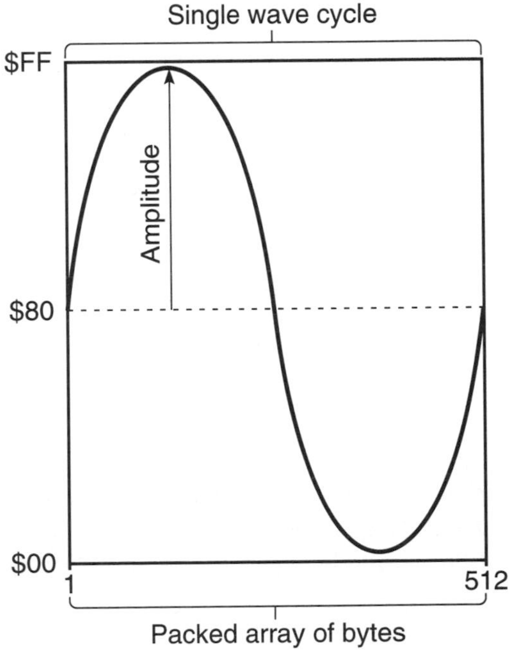

Figure 22-4. A graph of a wave table

A wave table is represented as a packed array of bytes. Each byte contains a value in the range $00–$FF. These values are interpreted as offset values, where $80 represents an amplitude of 0. The largest negative amplitude is $00 and the largest positive amplitude is $FF. When playing a wave-table description of a sound, the wave-table synthesizer loops through the wave table for the duration of the sound.

The Sampled Sound Synthesizer

You can use the **sampled sound synthesizer** to play back sounds that have been digitally recorded (that is, sampled) as well as sounds that are computed, possibly at run time. The sampled sound synthesizer is the most widely used of all the available synthesizers, primarily because it is relatively easy to generate a sampled sound and because such samples can contain a wide variety of sounds. The sampled sound synthesizer is typically used to play back prerecorded sounds such as speech or special sound effects.

You can use the Sound Manager to store sounds in one of two ways, either as resources of type 'snd ' or as AIFF or AIFF-C format files. The structure of resources of type 'snd ' is given in "Sound Resources" later in this chapter, and the structure of AIFF and AIFF-C files is given in "Sound Files" later in this chapter. If you simply want to play short prerecorded sampled sounds, you should probably include the sound data in an 'snd ' resource. If you want to allow the user to transfer recorded sound data from one application to another (or from one operating system to another), you should probably store the sound data in an AIFF or AIFF-C file. In certain cases, you need to store sampled sounds in files and not in resources. For example, some sampled sounds might be too large to store as resources; in those cases, you should store the sounds in an AIFF or AIFF-C file.

Regardless of how you store a sampled sound, you can use Sound Manager routines to play that sound using the sampled sound synthesizer. If you choose to store sampled sounds in files of type AIFF or AIFF-C, you can play those sounds by calling the SndStartFilePlay function. If you store sampled sounds in resources, your application can play those sounds by passing the Sound Manager function SndPlay a handle to a resource of type 'snd ' that contains a sampled sound header. (The SndStartFilePlay function can also play 'snd ' resources directly from disk.) There are three types of sampled sound headers: the standard sound header (used for monophonic sampled sounds), the extended sound header (used for stereo samples), and the compressed sound header (used for compressed samples, whether monophonic or stereo). The sampled sound header contains information about the sample (such as the original sampling rate, the length of the sample, and so forth), together with an indication of where the sample data is to be found. The data can be stored in a buffer separate from the sound resource or as part of the sound resource at the end of the sound header.

> **Note:** The terminology *sampled sound header* can be confusing because in most cases the sound header (and hence the 'snd ' resource) contains the sound data as well as information describing the data.

You can play a sampled sound at its original rate or play it at some other rate to change its pitch. Thus, once you install a sampled sound header into a channel, it can be played at varying rates to provide a number of pitches and hence can be used as a voice to play a series of sounds.

Sound Commands

The Sound Manager provides routines that allow you to create and dispose of sound channels and send control information directly to synthesizers. These routines allow you to manipulate sound channels and synthesizers, but (except for the SndPlay and SndStartFilePlay functions) they do not directly produce any sounds. To actually produce sounds, you need to issue sound commands. A **sound command** is an instruction to a synthesizer to produce sound, modify sound, or otherwise assist in the overall process of sound production.

You can issue sound commands in several ways. You can send sound commands one at a time into a sound channel by repeatedly calling the SndDoCommand function. Or you can bypass a sound channel altogether and send commands directly to a playback synthesizer by calling the SndDoImmediate function. You can also issue sound commands by calling the function SndPlay and specifying a sound resource of type 'snd ' that contains the sound commands you want to issue. A sound resource can contain any number of sound commands and can be used to send commands and data to any of the available sound synthesizers. As a result, you may be able to accomplish all sound-related activity simply by creating sound resources and calling SndPlay in your application. See "Sound Resources" later in this chapter for details on the format of an 'snd ' resource.

Generally speaking, no matter how they are issued, all sound commands are eventually sent to the playback synthesizer, which interprets the commands and plays the sound on the available audio hardware. All synthesizers are designed to accept the most general set of sound commands, although some commands are specific to a particular synthesizer. Here is the structure of a generic sound command:

```
TYPE SndCommand =
     PACKED RECORD
        cmd:          Integer;       {command number}
        param1:       Integer;       {first parameter}
        param2:       LongInt        {second parameter}
     END;
```

Commands are always 8 bytes in length. The first 2 bytes are the command number, and the next 6 make up the command's options. The format of the last 6 bytes depends on the command in use, although typically those 6 bytes are interpreted as an integer followed by a long integer. For example, an application can install a wave table into a sound channel by using SndDoCommand with a sound command whose cmd field is the waveTableCmd constant. In that case, the param1 field specifies the length of the wave table, and the param2 field is a pointer to the wave-table data itself. Other sound commands may interpret the 6 parameter bytes differently or may not use them at all.

The sound commands available to your application are defined by constants.

```
CONST nullCmd          = 0;  {do nothing}
      quietCmd         = 3;  {stop a sound that is playing}
      flushCmd         = 4;  {flush a sound channel}
      reInitCmd        = 5;  {reinitialize a sound channel}
      waitCmd          = 10; {suspend processing in a channel}
      pauseCmd         = 11; {pause processing in a channel}
      resumeCmd        = 12; {resume processing in a channel}
      callBackCmd      = 13; {execute a callback procedure}
      syncCmd          = 14; {synchronize channels}
      availableCmd     = 24; {see if initialization option available}
      versionCmd       = 25; {determine synthesizer version}
      totalLoadCmd     = 26; {report total CPU load}
      loadCmd          = 27; {report CPU load for a new channel}
      freqDurationCmd  = 40; {play a frequency for specified duration}
      restCmd          = 41; {rest a channel for specified duration}
      freqCmd          = 42; {change the pitch of a sound}
```

```
ampCmd              = 43; {change the amplitude of a sound}
timbreCmd           = 44; {change the timbre of a sound}
getAmpCmd           = 45; {get the amplitude of a sound}
waveTableCmd        = 60; {install a wave table as a voice}
soundCmd            = 80; {install a sampled sound as a voice}
bufferCmd           = 81; {play a sampled sound}
rateCmd             = 82; {set the pitch of a sampled sound}
getRateCmd          = 85; {get the pitch of a sampled sound}
```

For details on each sound command, see the relevant sections in "Using the Sound Manager" later in this chapter. Also see Table 22-6 for a complete summary of the available sound commands, their parameters, and their uses.

Sound Channels

A **sound channel** is a queue of sound commands that is managed by the Sound Manager. The commands placed into the channel might originate from an application or from the Sound Manager itself (in response to instructions from a playback synthesizer). The commands in the queue are passed one by one, in a first-in, first-out (FIFO) manner, to the playback synthesizer.

The Sound Manager uses the SndChannel data type to define a sound channel.

```
TYPE SndChannel =
     PACKED RECORD
         nextChan:        SndChannelPtr;      {pointer to next channel}
         firstMod:        Ptr;                {used internally}
         callBack:        ProcPtr;            {pointer to callback proc}
         userInfo:        LongInt;            {free for application's use}
         wait:            Time;               {used internally}
         cmdInProgress:   SndCommand;         {used internally}
         flags:           Integer;            {used internally}
         qLength:         Integer;            {used internally}
         qHead:           Integer;            {used internally}
         qTail:           Integer;            {used internally}
         queue:           ARRAY[0..stdQLength-1] OF SndCommand
     END;
```

Most applications do not need to worry about creating or disposing of sound channels because the high-level Sound Manager routines take care of these automatically. If you are using low-level Sound Manager routines, you can create your own sound channels (with the SndNewChannel function).

Multiple Channels of Sound

One of the most useful enhancements made to the Sound Manager is the ability to have multiple channels of sampled sound produce output on the Macintosh audio hardware concurrently. Previous versions of the Sound Manager could play only a single channel of sampled sound at a time. One consequence of this was that if a system alert sound was called while a sampled sound was playing, the alert sound would not be heard (although, if you were lucky, the menu bar might flash). A more important consequence was that it was impossible to provide the layering of sound that can bring a touch of reality to a simulation or presentation. Furthermore, the limitation to one sampled sound at a time made it very difficult for an application to incorporate Macintosh-synthesized voice output with any other kind of Macintosh-generated sound.

Using the enhanced Sound Manager, your application can open several channels of sampled sound for concurrent output on the available audio hardware. Similarly, multiple applications can each open channels of sampled sound. The number and quality of concurrent channels of sound are limited only by the abilities of the machine, particularly by the speed of the CPU. Different Macintosh computers have different CPU clock speeds and execute instructions at quite different rates. This means that some machines can manage more channels of sound and produce higher-quality sound than other machines. For example, a Macintosh II may be able to support several channels of high-quality stereo sound without significant impact on other processing, whereas a Macintosh Plus is able to support only a single channel before other processing slows significantly. The enhanced Sound Manager provides the capability to balance CPU loads for sound-related activity, thereby further insulating the application from the underlying hardware.

The Sound Manager currently supports multiple channels of sampled sound only on machines equipped with an Apple Sound Chip. To maintain maximum compatibility between machines for your applications, you should always check the operating environment (using the Gestalt function documented in the Compatibility Guidelines chapter in this volume) to make sure that the ability to play multiple channels of sampled sound is present before attempting to do so.

Sound Compression and Expansion

One minute of single-channel sound recorded with the fidelity you would expect from a commercial compact disc occupies about 5.3 MB of disk space. One minute of sound digitized by the current low-fidelity digitizing peripherals for the Macintosh occupies more than 1 MB of disk space. Even one minute of telephone-quality speech takes up more than half of a megabyte on a disk. Despite the increased capacities of mass-storage devices, disk space can be a problem if your application incorporates sound. The space problem is particularly acute for multimedia applications. Because a large portion of the space occupied by a multimedia application is likely to be taken up by sound data, the complexity and richness of the application's sound component are limited.

To help remedy this problem, the enhanced Sound Manager includes a set of new routines known collectively as **Macintosh Audio Compression and Expansion (MACE).** MACE enables you to provide more audio information in a given amount of storage space by allowing you to compress sound data and then expand it for playback. These enhancements are based entirely in software and require no specialized hardware.

The new audio compression and expansion features allow you to enhance your applications by including more audio data. MACE also relieves some distribution problems by reducing the number of disks required for shipping an application that relies heavily on sound. MACE may make some new kinds of applications feasible as well, such as talking dictionaries and language-instruction software.

MACE adds three main kinds of capabilities to those already present in the Sound Manager—audio data compression, real-time expansion and playback of compressed audio data, and buffered expansion and playback of compressed audio data.

- **Compression.** The Sound Manager can compress a buffer of digital audio data either in the original buffer or in a separate buffer. If a segment of audio data is too large to fit into a single buffer, then your application can make repeated calls to the compression routine.

- **Real-time expansion playback.** The Sound Manager can expand compressed audio data contained in a small internal buffer and play it back at the same time. Since the audio data expansion and playback occur at the same time, there is greater CPU loading when using this method of sound expansion rather than buffered expansion.

- **Buffered expansion.** The Sound Manager can expand a specified buffer of compressed audio data and store the result in a separate buffer. The expanded buffer can then be played back using other Sound Manager routines with minimal processor overhead during playback. Applications that require screen updates or user interaction during playback (such as animation or multimedia applications) should use buffered expansion.

MACE provides audio data compression and expansion capabilities in ratios of either 3:1 or 6:1 for all currently supported Macintosh models, from the Macintosh Plus forward. The principal trade off when using MACE is that the expanded audio data suffers a loss of fidelity in comparison to the original data. A small amount of noise is introduced into a 3:1 compressed sound when it is expanded and played back, and a greater amount of noise for the 6:1 ratio. The 3:1 buffer-to-buffer compression and expansion option is well suited for high-fidelity sounds. The 6:1 buffer-to-buffer compression and expansion option provides greater compression at the expense of lower-fidelity results and is recommended for voice data only. This technique reduces the frequency bandwidth of the audio signal by a factor of two to achieve the higher compression ratio.

Table 22-1 provides a summary of the available compression and expansion options.

Table 22-1. Audio compression and expansion options

Computer	3:1 and 6:1 compression	3:1 and 6:1 expansion and playback	Stereo expansion and playback	Sample-rate conversion
Macintosh Plus	Real-time	Real-time	No	No
Macintosh SE	Real-time	Real-time	No	No
Macintosh Portable	Real-time	Real-time	Yes	Yes
Macintosh II and successors	Real-time	Real-time	Yes	Yes

Note: Macintosh Plus, Macintosh SE, and Macintosh Portable computers play only the right channel of stereo 'snd ' data through the internal speaker. Certain Macintosh II models may play only a single channel through the internal speaker.

Existing applications that use the Sound Manager's SndPlay function to play digitized audio signals can play compressed audio signals without modification or recompilation.

The MACE routines assume that each sample consists of 8 contiguous bits of data. The compression techniques do not, however, depend on a particular sample rate. The compression techniques produce their best quality output when the sample rate is the same as the output rate of the sound hardware of the machine playing the audio data. The output rate used in current Macintosh computers is 22.254 kilohertz (hereafter referred to as the 22 kHz rate). Because of speed limitations, the Macintosh Plus and Macintosh SE cannot perform sample-rate conversion during expansion playback. On those machines, all sounds are played back at a 22 kHz rate. To provide consistent quality in sounds that may be played on different machines, you should record all sounds at a 22 kHz sample rate.

The MACE algorithms are optimized to provide the best sound quality possible through the internal speaker in real time. However, the user who employs high-quality speakers may notice a high-frequency hiss for some sounds compressed at the 3:1 ratio. This hiss results from a design trade off between maintaining real-time operation on the Macintosh Plus and preserving as much frequency bandwidth of the signal as possible. If you think that your output may be played on high-quality speakers, you may want to filter out the hiss before compression by passing the audio output through an equalizer that removes frequencies above 10 kHz. When you use the 6:1 compression and expansion ratio, your frequency response is cut in half. For example, when you use the 22 kHz sample rate, the highest frequency possible would normally be 11 kHz; however, after compressing and expanding the data at the 6:1 ratio, the highest frequency you could get would be only 5.5 kHz.

Continuous Play From Disk

The enhanced Sound Manager provides the ability to play a sampled sound continuously from disk while other tasks execute. You might think of the **play-from-disk** routines as providing you with the ability to install a "tape player" in a sound channel. Once the sound begins to play, it continues uninterrupted unless an application pauses or stops it.

A new function, SndStartFilePlay, allows you to play sounds stored in AIFF format or AIFF-C format, as well as 'snd ' resources, continuously from disk. SndStartFilePlay works like SndPlay but does not require that the entire sound be in RAM at one time. Hence, SndStartFilePlay is ideal for playing very large sounds. The continuous play-from-disk routines use a buffer area that is smaller than the sampled sound, and they update the buffer from disk by using a double-buffering scheme. This technique minimizes RAM usage at the expense of additional disk overhead. The disk overhead is relatively light, however, and most mass-storage devices currently available for Macintosh computers have response times good enough that SndStartFilePlay can retrieve audio data from disk and play the sound without gaps.

There are no limits on the number of concurrent disk-based sampled sound playbacks other than those imposed by processor speed. On machines with sufficient CPU resources, several continuous playbacks may occur at once. Disk fragmentation can also affect the performance of playing sampled sound files from disk. It is recommended that no more than one file per hard disk be played at any time.

When multiple disk-based sampled sounds are playing, the Sound Manager automatically mixes the playbacks for output on the available sound hardware. Note, however, that the

Sound Manager supports continuous play from disk only on machines equipped with an Apple Sound Chip. Also, if a sound channel is being used for continuous play from disk, then no other sound commands can be sent to that channel.

Sound Recording

The Sound Manager provides your application with the ability to record and digitally store sounds in a device-independent manner. Your applications can create a resource or a file containing a recorded sound simply by calling SndRecord or SndRecordToFile. In cases where you need very fine control over the recording process, you can call various low-level sound input routines. You can then use the recorded sound in any way appropriate to your application.

The sound input and storage routines can be used with any available sound input hardware for which there is an appropriate device driver. To allow the user to select from among multiple possible input devices, the Sound control panel lists the available sound input devices, as illustrated in Figure 22-5.

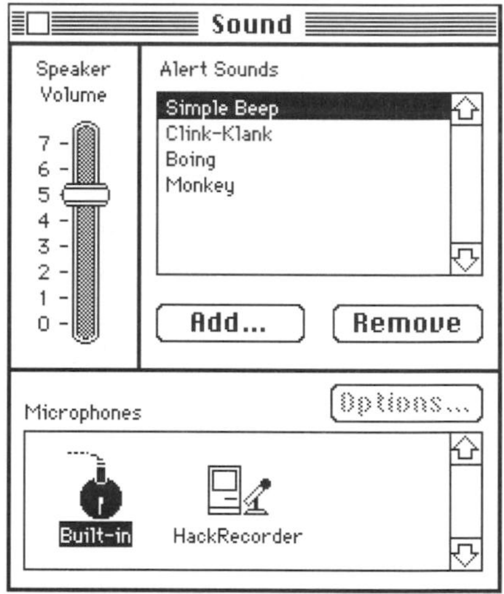

Figure 22-5. The Sound control panel

Devices are listed if their drivers have previously registered themselves with the Sound Manager and provided a name and device icon. In Figure 22-5, two sound input devices are available, a device named Built-in and a device named HackRecorder. The user has selected Built-in. The selected device is the current sound input device.

The new Sound control panel also includes three new buttons, Add, Remove, and Options. These buttons allow the user to add sounds to and remove sounds from the list of available system alert sounds and to set any device-specific recording options. The Add button is used to record a new alert sound and add it to the list. Clicking the Add button causes the Sound Manager to put up a sound recording dialog box (explained in the next section). Clicking the Remove button causes the Sound Manager to remove the selected alert sound from the list. The user can achieve the same effect by selecting a sound and then choosing the Clear command in the Edit menu. If no sound input drivers are installed in the system, then these three buttons do not appear.

If the sound recording dialog box was called up by clicking the Add button of the Sound control panel, then the recorded sound is saved as a resource of type 'snd ' in the System file. That sound then appears in the list of available alert sounds. Note that the standard Edit menu commands can be used on sounds stored in the System file. The Cut command copies the selected sound to the Clipboard and removes it from the list of system alert sounds. The Copy command just copies the selected sound to the Clipboard. The Paste command copies a sound from the Clipboard and places it in the list of available alert sounds. However, the Undo command does not work with sound-related editing operations.

The Sound Manager provides two high-level routines that allow your application to record sounds from the user and store them in memory or in a file. When you call either SndRecord or SndRecordToFile, the Sound Manager presents a sound recording dialog box to the user, illustrated in Figure 22-6.

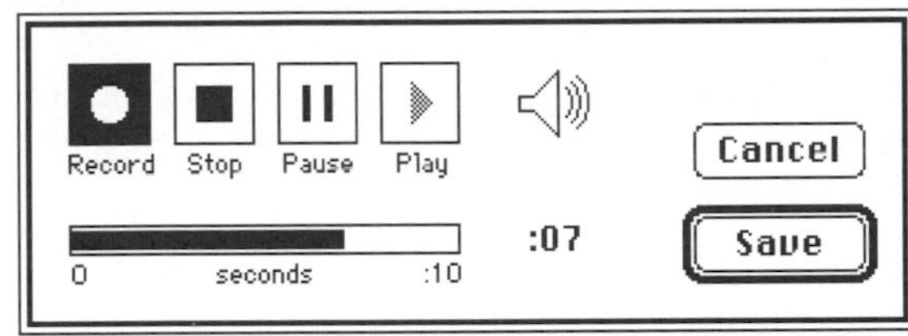

Figure 22-6. The sound recording dialog box

Using the controls in this dialog box, the user can start, pause, resume, and stop recording on the currently selected sound input device. The user can also play back the recorded sound. The time indicator bar provides an indication of the current length of the recorded sound. When the user clicks the Save button, another dialog box appears asking the user to give the sound a name. Unless the user cancels the save operation at that point, the recorded sound is saved into a file (if SndRecordToFile was called) or into RAM (if SndRecord was called).

The Sound Manager also provides a set of low-level routines that are of interest to you only if your application needs to intervene in the normal sound-recording process or if you are writing a driver to support a sound input device. If you simply want a resource (or a file) that contains a recorded sound, you can get that most easily by calling SndRecord (or SndRecordToFile). If you need to modify the features or operation of the sound recording dialog box, you can usually do so by defining a custom filter procedure.

In instances where you need to gain greater control over the recording process, you can use a set of routines that manipulate the incoming sound data by using sound parameter blocks. The parameter blocks contain information about the current recording device, the length recorded, a routine to call on completion of the recording, and so forth. You can call SPBRecord (or SPBRecordToFile) to begin a recording. Then you can use the functions SPBPauseRecording, SPBResumeRecording, and SPBStopRecording to control the recording. Note that you need to open a device (using SPBOpenDevice) before you can record from it. On completion of the recording, you should close the device (using SPBCloseDevice).

There are also several routines intended for use by sound input device drivers. Sound input drivers need to register with the Sound Manager by calling SPBSignInDevice. This makes that device visible in the Sound control panel for possible selection as the current input device. You can remove a device from that panel by calling SPBSignOutDevice.

Two functions—SPBGetDeviceInfo and SPBSetDeviceInfo—allow you to examine and change certain settings in a sound input device. For example, you can set the recording quality by passing the appropriate selector code and setting to SPBSetDeviceInfo.

SOUND STORAGE FORMATS

The Sound Manager can create and play back sounds stored as sound resources (of format 1 'snd ' resources) and as sound files (of type 'AIFF' or 'AIFC'). In general, your application should use the available Sound Manager routines to create or play back sounds stored in one or both of these two ways. The information in this section is important only if you want to read or write sound data directly (without the assistance of the Sound Manager).

Sound Resources

The Sound Manager uses two types of resources to help it interpret and play sounds: 'snd ' resources (also called **sound resources**) and 'snth' resources (also called sound synthesizers). The 'snth' resources are code resources that interpret Sound Manager commands and data destined for a particular synthesizer. Apple provides 'snth' resources for all three supported synthesizers, which are contained in the System file. Applications generally do not need to know anything about 'snth' resources.

Resources of type 'snd ' can contain both sound commands and sound data, and are widely used by sound-producing applications. These resources provide a simple and portable way for you to incorporate sounds into your applications. For example, the sounds that a user can select in the Sound control panel as the system alert sound are stored in the System file as 'snd ' resources. Unless you use the new sound-recording routines provided by the enhanced Sound Manager, creating 'snd ' resources requires an understanding of sound synthesis to build a sampled sound header, wave-table data, or sound commands. You can also use the SetupSndHeader function to help you create an 'snd ' resource (format 1).

There are two types of 'snd ' resources, known as format 1 and format 2. Figure 22-7 illustrates the structures of both kinds of 'snd ' resources.

> **Note:** Resource IDs for 'snd ' resources in the range 0 to 8191 are reserved for use by Apple Computer, Inc. The 'snd ' resources numbered 1 through 4 are defined to be the standard system alert sounds.

The format 1 'snd ' resource is the most general kind of sound resource. A format 1 'snd ' resource may contain a specification of the intended output synthesizer, along with a sequence of Sound Manager commands and associated sound data (such as a sampled sound header or a wave table). In this case, your application can produce sounds simply by passing a handle to that resource to the SndPlay function, which loads the specified synthesizer into memory, opens a sound channel, and sends the commands and data contained in the resource into the channel. Alternatively, a format 1 'snd ' may contain a sequence of commands that describe a sound, without specifying a synthesizer and without providing any other sound data. In this case, your application can use the SndPlay function to play the sound on any channel. Accordingly, you can use a format 1 'snd ' with any one of the available synthesizers.

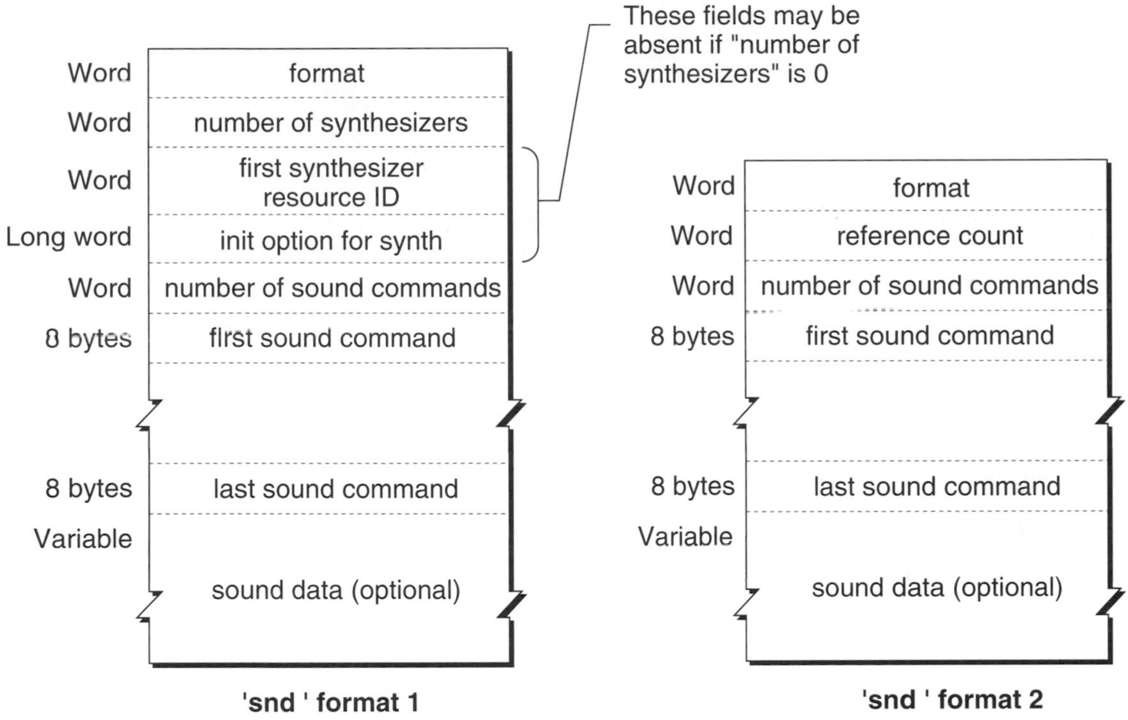

Figure 22-7. The structure of 'snd ' resources

The format 2 'snd ' resource is obsolete and your applications should use format 1 'snd ' resources. The format 2 'snd ' resource was designed for use by HyperCard® and can be used with the sampled sound synthesizer only. A format 2 'snd ' resource simply contains a sound command that points to a sampled sound header.

When a sound command contained in an 'snd ' resource has associated sound data, the high bit of the command is set. This changes the param2 field of the command to an offset value that specifies the distance in bytes from the resource's beginning to the location of the associated sound data. Figure 22-8 illustrates the location of this data offset bit.

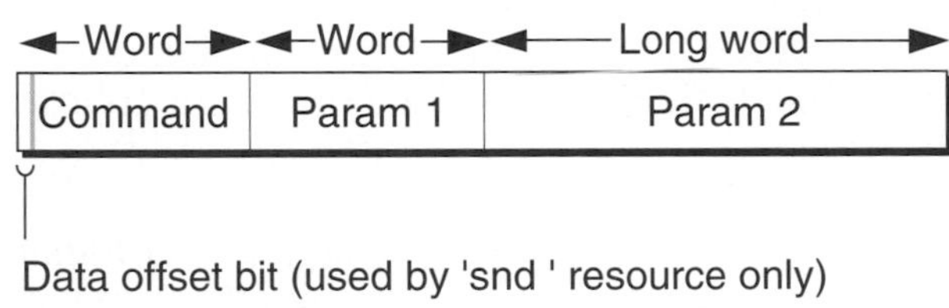

Figure 22-8. The location of the data offset bit

The offset bit is used only by sound commands that are stored in sound resources of type 'snd ' and that have associated sound data (that is, sampled sound or wave-table data). If the high bit of the command is set, then param2 is interpreted as an offset in bytes from the beginning of the sound resource to the associated data.

You can use a constant to set that flag.

```
CONST dataOffsetFlag  = $8000;     {sound command data offset bit}
```

If the offset bit is not set, param2 is interpreted instead as a pointer to the location in memory (outside the sound resource) where the data is located.

To calculate the offset for a format 1 'snd ' resource, use the following formula:

offset = 6 + (number of synthesizers * size of synthesizer information) + (number of commands * size of command)

For example, if a format 1 'snd ' resource specifies that a sound channel is to be linked to a synthesizer and if that resource contains a single sound command (perhaps bufferCmd), then the offset from the beginning of the resource to the associated sound data is as follows:

offset = 6 + (1 * 6) + (1 * 8) = 20 bytes

To calculate this offset for a format 2 'snd ' resource, use this formula:

offset = 6 + (number of commands * 8)

The first few bytes of the resource contain 'snd ' header information and are a different size for each format. A synthesizer specified in a format 1 'snd ' requires 6 bytes. The number of synthesizers multiplied by 6 is added to this offset. The number of commands multiplied by 8 bytes, the size of a sound command, is added to the offset.

The Format 1 'snd ' Resource

Figure 22-7 shows the fields of a format 1 'snd ' resource. A format 1 'snd ' resource contains information about the format of the resource (namely, 1), the intended output synthesizer, and the initialization options for that synthesizer. A format 1 'snd ' resource may also contain the actual sound data for the wave-table synthesizer or the sampled sound synthesizer.

If an 'snd ' resource specifies a synthesizer, it can supply an initialization option in the field immediately following the resource ID. You specify the number of commands in the resource in the number of sound commands field. The sound commands follow in the order in which they should be sent to the channel.

The format 1 'snd ' resource might contain only a sequence of commands describing a sound that can be played by any synthesizer. In this case, the number of synthesizers should be 0, and there should be no synthesizer resource ID or initialization option in the 'snd ' resource. This allows the 'snd ' to be used on any channel.

Listing 22-1 shows the output of the MPW® tool DeRez when applied to the 'snd ' resource with resource ID 1 contained in the System file.

Listing 22-1. A format 1 'snd ' resource

```
data 'snd ' (1, "Simple Beep", purgeable) {
   $"00 01 00 01 00 01 00 00 00 00 00 1B 00 2C 00 5A"
   $"00 00 00 00 00 2B 00 E0 00 00 00 00 00 2A 00 00"
   $"00 00 00 45 00 0A 00 28 00 00 00 00 00 2B 00 C8"
   $"00 00 00 00 00 0A 00 28 00 00 00 00 00 2B 00 C0"
   $"00 00 00 00 00 0A 00 28 00 00 00 00 00 2B 00 B8"
   $"00 00 00 00 00 0A 00 28 00 00 00 00 00 2B 00 B0"
   $"00 00 00 00 00 0A 00 28 00 00 00 00 00 2B 00 A8"
   $"00 00 00 00 00 0A 00 28 00 00 00 00 00 2B 00 A0"
   $"00 00 00 00 00 0A 00 28 00 00 00 00 00 2B 00 90"
   $"00 00 00 00 00 0A 00 28 00 00 00 00 00 2B 00 80"
   $"00 00 00 00 00 0A 00 28 00 00 00 00 00 2B 00 60"
   $"00 00 00 00 00 0A 00 28 00 00 00 00 00 2B 00 40"
   $"00 00 00 00 00 0A 00 28 00 00 00 00 00 2B 00 20"
   $"00 00 00 00 00 0A 00 28 00 00 00 00 00 2B 00 00"
   $"00 00 00 00"
};
```

In Listing 22-1, DeRez simply lists the raw data contained in that resource. To make sense of this data, see Listing 22-2, which shows the same data restructured and commented.

Listing 22-2. A restructured format 1 'snd ' resource

```
data 'snd ' (1, "Simple Beep", purgeable) {
   $"0001"      /*format type*/
   $"0001"      /*number of synthesizers*/
   $"0001"      /*resource ID of square-wave synthesizer*/
   $"00000000"  /*initialization option*/
   $"001B"      /*number of sound commands that follow (27)*/
   $"002C"      /*command 1--timbreCmd 090 000*/
   $"005A00000000"
   $"002B"      /*command 2--ampCmd  224 000*/
   $"00E000000000"
   $"002A"      /*command 3--freqCmd 000 069*/
   $"000000000045"
   $"000A"      /*command 4--waitCmd 040 000*/
   $"002800000000"
   $"002B"      /*command 5--ampCmd  200 000*/
   $"00C800000000"
   /*commands 6 through 26 are omitted; they are alternating pairs */
   /* of waitCmd and ampCmd commands, where the first parameter of */
   /* ampCmd has the values */
   /* 192, 184, 176, 168, 160, 144, 128, 96, 64, and 32*/
   $"002B"      /*command 27--ampCmd  000 000*/
   $"000000000000"
};
```

As you can see, the Simple Beep is actually a rather sophisticated sound, where the loudness (or amplitude) of the beep gradually decreases from an initial value of 224 to 0.

Notice that the sound described in the previous two listings is played by the square-wave synthesizer and is completely determined by a sequence of specific commands. ("Play an A at loudness 224, wait 20 milliseconds, play it at loudness 200....") Often an 'snd ' resource consists only of a single sound command (usually the bufferCmd command) together with data that describes a sampled sound to be played. Listing 22-3 illustrates an example like this; once again, the output of DeRez has been restructured and commented to improve readability.

Listing 22-3. A format 1 'snd ' resource containing sampled sound data

```
data 'snd ' (19068, "hello daddy", purgeable) {
   $"0001"          /*format type*/
   $"0001"          /*number of synthesizers*/
   $"0005"          /*resource ID of first synthesizer*/
   $"00000080"      /*initialization option: initMono*/
   $"0001"          /*number of sound commands that follow (1)*/
   $"8051"          /*command 1--bufferCmd*/
   $"0000"          /*param1 = 0*/
   $"00000014"      /*param2 = offset to sound header (20 bytes)*/
   $"00000000"      /*pointer to data (it follows immediately)*/
   $"00000BB8"      /*number of bytes in sample (3000 bytes)*/
   $"56EE8BA3"      /*sampling rate of this sound (22 kHz)*/
   $"000007D0"      /*starting of the sample's loop point*/
   $"00000898"      /*ending of the sample's loop point*/
   $"00"            /*standard sample encoding*/
   $"3C"            /*baseFrequency at which sample was taken*/
   /*the sampled sound data*/
   $"80 80 81 81 81 81 81 81 80 80 80 80 80 81 82 82"
   $"82 83 82 82 81 80 80 7F 7F 7F 7E 7D 7D 7D 7C 7C"
   $"7C 7C 7D 7D 7D 7D 7E 7F 80 80 81 81 82 82 83 83"
   $"83 83 82 81 81 80 80 81 81 81 81 81 82 81 81 80"
   $"80 80 81 81 81 83 83 83 82 81 81 80 7F 7E 7D 7D"
   $"7F 7F 7F 7F 7E 7F 7F 7F 7F 7F 7F 7F 7F 7F 7F 80"
   /*rest of data omitted in this example*/
};
```

This 'snd ' resource specifies the sampled sound synthesizer and includes a call to a single sound command, the bufferCmd command. The offset bit of the command number is set to indicate that the sound data is contained in the resource itself. Following that command and its two parameters is the sampled sound header, the first part of which contains important information about the sample. The second parameter to the bufferCmd command indicates the offset from the beginning of the resource to the sampled sound header, in this case 20 bytes.

It is not always necessary to specify 'snd ' resources by listing the raw data stream contained in them; indeed, for certain types of format 1 'snd ' resources, it can be easier to supply a resource specification like the one given in Listing 22-4.

Listing 22-4. A resource specification

```
resource 'snd ' (9000, "New Beep", purgeable) {
   FormatOne {
      {  /*array Synthesizers: 1 element*/
      /*[1]*/
      squareWaveSynth, 0
      }
   },
```

```
   {      /*array SoundCmnds: 3 elements*/
   /*[1]*/ noData, timbreCmd {90},
   /*[2]*/ noData, freqDurationCmd {480, $00000045},
   /*[3]*/ noData, quietCmd {},
      },
   {      /*array DataTables: 0 elements*/
   };
};
```

When you pass a handle to this resource to the SndPlay function, three commands are executed by the square-wave synthesizer: a timbreCmd command, a freqDurationCmd command, and a quietCmd command. The sound specified in Listing 22-4 is just like the Simple Beep, except that there is no gradual reduction in the loudness. To duplicate the Simple Beep exactly, you could use the resource specification given in Listing 22-5.

Listing 22-5. Resource specification for the Simple Beep

```
resource 'snd ' (9001, "Copy of Simple Beep", purgeable) {
   FormatOne {
      {  /*array Synthesizers: 1 element*/
         /*[1]*/
         squareWaveSynth, 0
      }
   },
   {  /*array SoundCmnds: 27 elements*/
      /*[1]*/  noData, timbreCmd {90},
      /*[2]*/  noData, ampCmd {224},
      /*[3]*/  noData, freqCmd {69},
      /*[4]*/  noData, waitCmd {40},
      /*[5]*/  noData, ampCmd {200},
      /*[6]*/  noData, waitCmd {40},
      /*[7]*/  noData, ampCmd {192},
      /*[8]*/  noData, waitCmd {40},
      /*[9]*/  noData, ampCmd {184},
      /*[10]*/ noData, waitCmd {40},
      /*[11]*/ noData, ampCmd {176},
      /*[12]*/ noData, waitCmd {40},
      /*[13]*/ noData, ampCmd {168},
      /*[14]*/ noData, waitCmd {40},
      /*[15]*/ noData, ampCmd {160},
      /*[16]*/ noData, waitCmd {40},
      /*[17]*/ noData, ampCmd {144},
      /*[18]*/ noData, waitCmd {40},
      /*[19]*/ noData, ampCmd {128},
      /*[20]*/ noData, waitCmd {40},
      /*[21]*/ noData, ampCmd {96},
      /*[22]*/ noData, waitCmd {40},
      /*[23]*/ noData, ampCmd {64},
      /*[24]*/ noData, waitCmd {40},
      /*[25]*/ noData, ampCmd {32},
      /*[26]*/ noData, waitCmd {40},
      /*[27]*/ noData, ampCmd {0}
   },
   {  /*array DataTables: 0 elements*/
   }
};
```

The Format 2 'snd ' Resource

The SndPlay function can also play format 2 'snd ' resources, which are designed for use only with the sampled sound synthesizer. The SndPlay function supports this format by automatically opening a channel to the sampled sound synthesizer and using the bufferCmd command to send the data contained in the resource to that synthesizer.

Figure 22-7 illustrates the fields of a format 2 'snd ' resource. The reference count field is for your application's use and is not used by the Sound Manager. The number of sound commands field and the sound command fields are the same as described in a format 1 resource. The last field of this resource contains the sampled sound. The first command should be either a soundCmd command or bufferCmd command with the data offset bit set in the command to specify the location of this sampled sound header.

Listing 22-6 shows a resource specification that illustrates the structure of a format 2 'snd ' resource; it contains the information necessary to create a sound with SndPlay and the sampled sound synthesizer.

Listing 22-6. A format 2 'snd ' resource

```
data 'snd ' (9003, "Pig Squeal", purgeable) {
   $"0002"          /*format type*/
   $"0000"          /*reference count for application's use*/
   $"0001"          /*number of sound commands that follow (1)*/
   $"8051"          /*command 1--bufferCmd*/
   $"0000"          /*param1 = 0*/
   $"0000000E"      /*param2 = offset to sound header (14 bytes)*/
   $"00000000"      /*pointer to data (it follows immediately)*/
   $"00000BB8"      /*number of bytes in sample (3000 bytes)*/
   $"56EE8BA3"      /*sampling rate of this sound (22 kHz)*/
   $"000007D0"      /*starting of the sample's loop point*/
   $"00000898"      /*ending of the sample's loop point*/
   $"00"            /*standard sample encoding*/
   $"3C"            /*baseFrequency at which sample was taken*/
   $"80 80 81 82 84 87 93 84" /*the sampled sound data*/
   $"6F 68 6D 65 72 7B 82 88"
   $"91 8E 8D 8F 86 7E 7C 79"
   $"6F 6D 71 70 70 79 7F 81"
   $"89 8F 8D 8B" /*rest of data omitted in this example*/
};
```

For a complete explanation of the fields following the sampling rate field, see the description of the sampled sound header in “Playing Sampled Sounds.” To play the sounds described by these resources, see the instructions given in “Playing 'snd ' Resources.” Both sections occur later in this chapter.

Sound Files

Although most sampled sounds that you want your application to produce can be stored as resources of type 'snd ', there are times when it is preferable to store sounds in **sound files,** not in resources. For example, it is usually easier for different applications to share files than it is to share resources. So if you want your application to play sampled sounds created by other applications (or if you want other applications to be able to play sampled sounds created by your application), it might be better to store the sampled sound data in a file, not in a resource. Similarly, if you are developing versions of your application that are intended to run on other operating systems, you might need a method of storing sounds that is independent of the Macintosh Operating System and its reliance on resources to store data. Generally, it is easier to transfer data stored in files from one operating system to another than it is to transfer data stored in resources.

There are other reasons you might want to store some sampled sounds in files and not in resources. If you have a very large sampled sound, it may be impossible to create a resource large enough to hold all the audio data. Resources are limited in size by the structure of resource files (and in particular because offsets to resource data are stored as 24-bit quantities). Sound files, however, can be much larger because the only size limitations are those imposed by the file system on all files. If the sampled data for some sound occupies more than about a half megabyte of space, you should probably store the sound as a file.

To address these various needs, Apple and several third-party developers have defined two sampled sound file formats, known as the **Audio Interchange File Format (AIFF)** and the Audio Interchange File Format extension for Compression (AIFF-C). The names emphasize that the formats are designed primarily as data interchange formats. However, you should find both AIFF and AIFF-C flexible enough to use as data storage formats as well. Even if you choose to use a different storage format, your application should be able to convert to and from AIFF and AIFF-C if you want to facilitate sharing of sound data among applications.

The main difference between the AIFF and AIFF-C formats is that AIFF-C allows you to store both compressed and noncompressed audio data, whereas AIFF allows you to store noncompressed audio data only. The AIFF-C format is more general than the AIFF format and is easier to modify. The AIFF-C format can be extended to handle new compression types and application-specific data. As a result, you should revise any application that currently supports only AIFF files to also support AIFF-C files. An application that currently reads AIFF files should also be able to read AIFF-C files. An application that currently writes AIFF files should also be able to write AIFF-C files. It is recommended that the default write format be AIFF-C. Table 22-2 summarizes the capabilities of the AIFF and AIFF-C file formats.

Table 22-2. AIFF and AIFF-C capabilities

File type	Read sampled	Read compressed	Write sampled	Write compressed
AIFF	Yes	No	Yes	No
AIFF-C	Yes	Yes	Yes	Yes

The enhanced Sound Manager includes support for reading and writing both AIFF and AIFF-C files. You can play from disk a sampled sound stored in a file of type AIFF or type AIFF-C by opening that file and passing its file reference number to the SndStartFilePlay function. (If the file is of type AIFF-C and if the data is compressed, the data is automatically expanded during playback.) You can create files of type AIFF or AIFF-C by calling the SndRecordToFile and SPBRecordToFile functions. SndRecordToFile creates an AIFF or AIFF-C file, complete with compressed sound data and all the needed chunks. SPBRecordToFile, however, simply records audio data (compressing it if necessary) and saves that data into a specified file. SPBRecordToFile does not create any AIFF or AIFF-C chunks. You can, however, use the SetupAIFFHeader function to create the appropriate headers before you call SPBRecordToFile.

Note: Both SndRecordToFile and SPBRecordToFile automatically compress the recorded audio data if instructed to do so. Neither function does any expansion.

The following six sections describe in detail the structure of AIFF and AIFF-C files. Both of these types of sound files are collections of "chunks" that define characteristics of the sampled sound or other relevant data about the sound. Currently, the AIFF and AIFF-C specifications include the following chunk types.

Chunk types

Form Chunk	Contains all the other chunks of an AIFF or AIFF-C file
Format Version Chunk	Contains an indication of the version of the AIFF-C specification according to which this file is structured (AIFF-C only)
Common Chunk	Contains information about the sampled sound, such as the sampling rate and sample size
Sound Data Chunk	Contains the sample frames that comprise the sampled sound
Marker Chunk	Contains markers that point to positions in the sound data
Comments Chunk	Contains comments about markers in the file
Sound Accelerator Chunk	Contains information intended to allow applications to accelerate the decompression of compressed audio data
Instrument Chunk	Defines basic parameters that an instrument (such as a sampling keyboard) can use to play back the sound data
MIDI Data Chunk	Contains MIDI data
Audio Recording Chunk	Contains information pertaining to audio recording devices
Application Specific Chunk	Contains application-specific information
Name Chunk	Contains the name of the sampled sound
Author Chunk	Contains one or more names of the authors (or creators) of the sampled sound
Copyright Chunk	Contains a copyright notice for the sampled sound
Annotation Chunk	Contains a comment

The following sections document only four of the kinds of chunks that can occur in AIFF and AIFF-C files. A more complete specification of AIFF files is available from APDA.

Chunk Organization and Data Types

An AIFF or AIFF-C file is a file that is organized as a collection of "chunks" of data. For example, there is a Common Chunk that specifies important parameters of the sampled sound, such as its size and sample rate. There is also a Sound Data Chunk that contains the actual audio samples. A chunk consists of some header information followed by some data. The header information consists of a chunk ID number and a number that indicates the size of the chunk data. In general, therefore, a chunk has the structure illustrated in Figure 22-9.

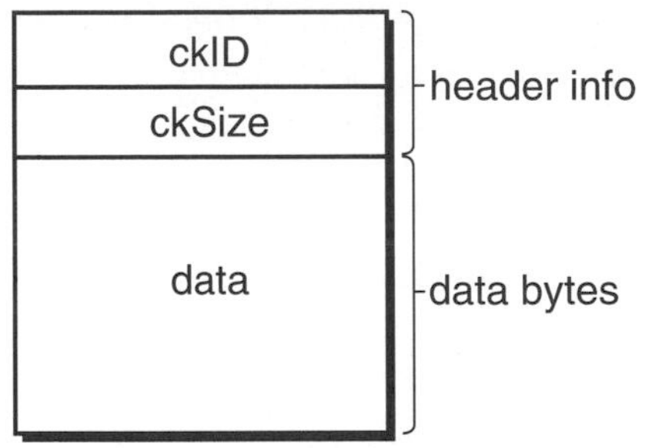

Figure 22-9. The general structure of a chunk

The header information of a chunk has this structure:

```
TYPE ChunkHeader =
     RECORD
        ckID:          ID;                 {chunk type ID}
        ckSize:        LongInt             {number of bytes of data}
     END;
```

The ckID field specifies the chunk type. An ID is a 32-bit concatenation of any four printable ASCII characters in the range ' ' (space character, ASCII value $20) through '~' (ASCII value $7E). Spaces cannot precede printing characters, but trailing spaces are allowed. Control characters are not allowed. You can specify values for the four types of chunks described later by using these constants:

```
CONST FormID            = 'FORM'; {chunk ID for Form Chunk}
      FormatVersionID = 'FVER'; {chunk ID for Format Version Chunk}
      CommonID          = 'COMM'; {chunk ID for Common Chunk}
      SoundDataID       = 'SSND'; {chunk ID for Sound Data Chunk}
```

The ckSize field specifies the size of the data portion of a chunk and does not include the length of the chunk header information.

The Form Chunk

The chunks that define the characteristics of a sampled sound and that contain the actual sound data are grouped together into a container chunk, known as the Form Chunk. The Form Chunk defines the type and size of the file and holds all remaining chunks in the file. The chunk ID for this container chunk is 'FORM'.

A chunk of type 'FORM' has this structure:

```
TYPE ContainerChunk =
     RECORD
         ckID:        ID;                 {'FORM'}
         ckSize:      LongInt;            {number of bytes of data}
         formType:    ID                  {type of file}
     END;
```

The fields of this chunk have the following meanings:

Field descriptions

ckID — The ID of this chunk. For a Form Chunk, this ID is 'FORM'.

ckSize — The size of the data portion of this chunk. Note that the data portion of a Form Chunk is divided into two parts, formType and the chunks that follow the formType field. These chunks are called *local chunks* because their chunk IDs are local to the Form Chunk.

formType — The type of audio file. For AIFF files, formType is 'AIFF'. For AIFF-C files, formType is 'AIFC'.

The local chunks can occur in any order in a sound file. As a result, your application should be designed to get a local chunk, identify it, and then process it without making any assumptions about what kind of chunk it is based on its order in the Form Chunk.

The Format Version Chunk

One difference between the AIFF and AIFF-C file formats is that files of type AIFF-C contain a Format Version Chunk and files of type AIFF do not. The Format Version Chunk contains a timestamp field that indicates when the format version of this AIFF-C file was defined. This in turn indicates what format rules this file conforms to and allows you to ensure that your application can handle a particular AIFF-C file. Every AIFF-C file must contain one and only one Format Version Chunk.

In AIFF files, there is no Format Version Chunk.

In AIFF-C files, a Format Version Chunk has this structure:

```
TYPE FormatVersionChunk =
     RECORD
         ckID:        ID;                 {'FVER'}
         ckSize:      LongInt;            {4}
         timestamp:   LongInt             {date of format version}
     END;
```

The fields of this chunk have the following meanings:

Field descriptions

ckID — The ID of this chunk. For a Format Version Chunk, this ID is 'FVER'.

ckSize — The size of the data portion of this chunk. This value is always 4 in a Format Version Chunk because the timestamp field is 4 bytes long (the 8 bytes used by ckID and ckSize fields are not included).

timestamp — An indication of when the format version for this kind of file was created. The value indicates the number of seconds since January 1, 1904, following the normal time conventions used by the Macintosh Operating System. (See the Operating System Utilities chapter of Volume II for several routines that allow you to manipulate timestamps.)

You should not confuse the format version timestamp with the creation date of the file. The format version timestamp indicates the time of creation of the version of the format according to which this file is structured. Because Apple defines the formats of AIFF-C files, only Apple can change this value. The current version is defined by a constant:

```
CONST AIFCVersion1   = $A2805140;         {2726318400 in decimal}
```


The Common Chunk

Every AIFF and AIFF-C file must contain a Common Chunk that defines some fundamental characteristics of the sampled sound contained in the file. Note that the format of the Common Chunk is different for AIFF and AIFF-C files. As a result, you need to determine the type of file format (by inspecting the formType field of the Form Chunk) before reading the Common Chunk.

For AIFF files, the Common Chunk has this structure:

```
TYPE CommonChunk =
     RECORD
        ckID:            ID;          {'COMM'}
        ckSize:          LongInt;     {size of chunk data}
        numChannels:     Integer;     {number of channels}
        numSampleFrames: LongInt;     {number of sample frames}
        sampleSize:      Integer;     {number of bits per sample}
        sampleRate:      Extended     {number of frames per second}
     END;
```

For AIFF-C files, the Common Chunk has this structure:

```
TYPE ExtCommonChunk =
     RECORD
        ckID:            ID;          {'COMM'}
        ckSize:          LongInt;     {size of chunk data}
```

```
        numChannels:      Integer;       {number of channels}
        numSampleFrames: LongInt;       {number of sample frames}
        sampleSize:       Integer;       {number of bits per sample}
        sampleRate:       Extended;      {number of frames per second}
        compressionType: ID;            {compression type ID}
        compressionName: PACKED ARRAY[0..0] OF Byte
                                         {compression type name}
    END;
```

The fields that exist in both types of Common Chunk have the following meanings:

Field descriptions

ckID	The ID of this chunk. For a Common Chunk, this ID is 'COMM'.
ckSize	The size of the data portion of this chunk. In AIFF files, this field is always 18 in the Common Chunk because the 8 bytes used by the ckID and ckSize fields are not included. In AIFF-C files, this size is 22 plus the number of bytes in the compressionName string.
numChannels	The number of audio channels contained in the sampled sound. A value of 1 indicates monophonic sound; a value of 2 indicates stereo sound; a value of 4 indicates four-channel sound, and so forth. Any number of audio channels may be specified. The actual sound data is stored elsewhere, in the Sound Data Chunk.
numSampleFrames	The number of sample frames in the Sound Data Chunk. Note that this field contains the number of sample frames, not the number of bytes of data and not the number of sample points. For noncompressed sound data, the total number of sample points in the file is numChannels * numSampleFrames. (See the discussion of the Sound Data Chunk in the following section for a definition of a sample frame.)
sampleSize	The number of bits in each sample point of noncompressed sound data. The sampleSize field can contain any integer from 1 to 32. For compressed sound data, this field indicates the number of bits per sample in the original sound data, before compression.
sampleRate	The sample rate at which the sound is to be played back, in sample frames per second.

An AIFF-C Common Chunk includes two fields that describe the type of compression (if any) used on the audio data:

Field descriptions

compressionType	The ID of the compression algorithm, if any, used on the sound data.
compressionName	A human-readable name for the compression algorithm ID specified in the compressionType field. This string is useful when putting up alert boxes (perhaps because a necessary decompression routine is missing).

Remember to pad the end of this array with a byte having the value 0 if the length of this array is not an even number (but do not include the pad byte in the count).

Here are the currently available compression IDs and their associated compression names:

compressionType	compressionName	Description
'NONE'	'not compressed'	Noncompressed samples
'ACE2'	'ACE 2-to-1'	IIGS® 2-to-1 compressed
'ACE8'	'ACE 8-to-3'	IIGS 8-to-3 compressed
'MAC3'	'MACE 3-to-1'	Macintosh 3-to-1 compressed
'MAC6'	'MACE 6-to-1'	Macintosh 6-to-1 compressed

You can define your own compression types, but you should register them with Apple.

The Sound Data Chunk

The Sound Data Chunk contains the actual sample frames that make up the sampled sound. The Sound Data Chunk has this structure:

```
TYPE SoundDataChunk =
     RECORD
        ckID:          ID;             {'SSND'}
        ckSize:        LongInt;        {size of chunk data}
        offset:        LongInt;        {offset to sound data}
        blockSize:     LongInt         {size of alignment blocks}
     END;
```

The fields in a Sound Data Chunk have the following meanings:

Field descriptions

ckID — The ID of this chunk. For a Sound Data Chunk, this ID is 'SSND'.

ckSize — The size of the data portion of this chunk. This size does not include the 8 bytes occupied by the values in the ckID and the ckSize fields. If the data following the blockSize field contains an odd number of bytes, a pad byte with a value of 0 is added at the end to preserve an even length for this chunk. If there is a pad byte, it is not included in the ckSize field.

offset — An offset (in bytes) to the beginning of the first sample frame in the chunk data. Most applications do not need to use the offset field and should set it to 0.

blockSize — The size (in bytes) of the blocks to which the sound data is aligned. This field is used in conjunction with the offset field for aligning sound data to blocks. As with the offset field, most applications do not need to use the blockSize field and should set it to 0.

The format of the sound data following the blockSize field depends on whether the data is compressed or noncompressed, which you can determine by inspecting the compressionType field in the Common Chunk. If the compression type is 'NONE', then each sample point in a sample frame is a linear, two's complement value. Sample points are from 1 to 32 bits wide, as determined by the sampleSize parameter in the Common Chunk. Each sample point is stored in an integral number of contiguous bytes. Sample points that are from 1 to 8 bits wide are stored in 1 byte; sample points that are from 9 to 16 bits wide are stored in 2 bytes, and so forth. When the width of a sample point is less than a multiple of 8 bits, the sample point data is left aligned (using a shift-left instruction), and the low-order bits at the right end are set to 0.

For multichannel sounds, a sample frame is an interleaved set of sample points. (For monophonic sounds, a sample frame is just a single sample point.) The sample points within a sample frame are interleaved by channel number. For example, the sound data for a stereo, noncompressed sound is illustrated in Figure 22-10.

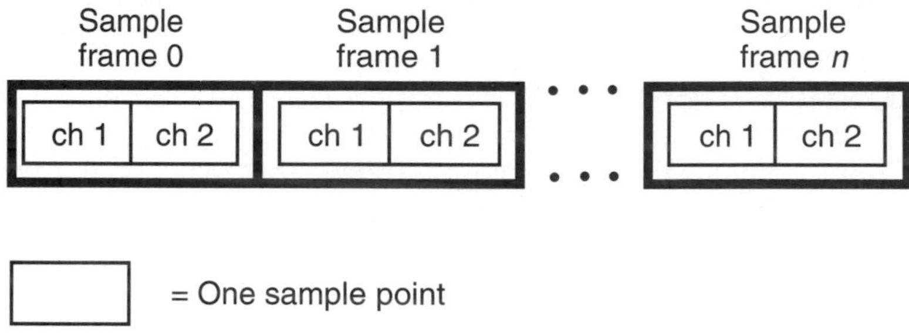

Figure 22-10. Interleaving stereo sample points

Sample frames are stored contiguously in order of increasing time. There are no pad bytes between samples or between sample frames.

> **Note:** The Sound Data Chunk is required unless the numSampleFrames field in the Common Chunk is 0. A maximum of one Sound Data Chunk can appear in an AIFF or AIFF-C file.

Reading and Writing Sound Files

Figure 22-11 illustrates an AIFF-C format file that contains approximately 4.476 seconds of 8-bit monophonic sound data sampled at 22 kHz. The sound data is not compressed. Note that the number of sample frames in this example is odd, forcing a pad byte to be inserted after the sound data. This pad byte is not reflected in the ckSize field of the Sound Data Chunk, which means that special processing is required to correctly determine the actual chunk size.

On a Macintosh computer, the Form Chunk (and hence all the other chunks in an AIFF or AIFF-C file) is stored in the data fork of the file. The file type of an AIFF format file is 'AIFF' and the file type of an AIFF-C format file is 'AIFC'. Macintosh applications should not store any information in the resource fork of an AIFF or AIFF-C file because that information might not be preserved by other applications that edit sound files.

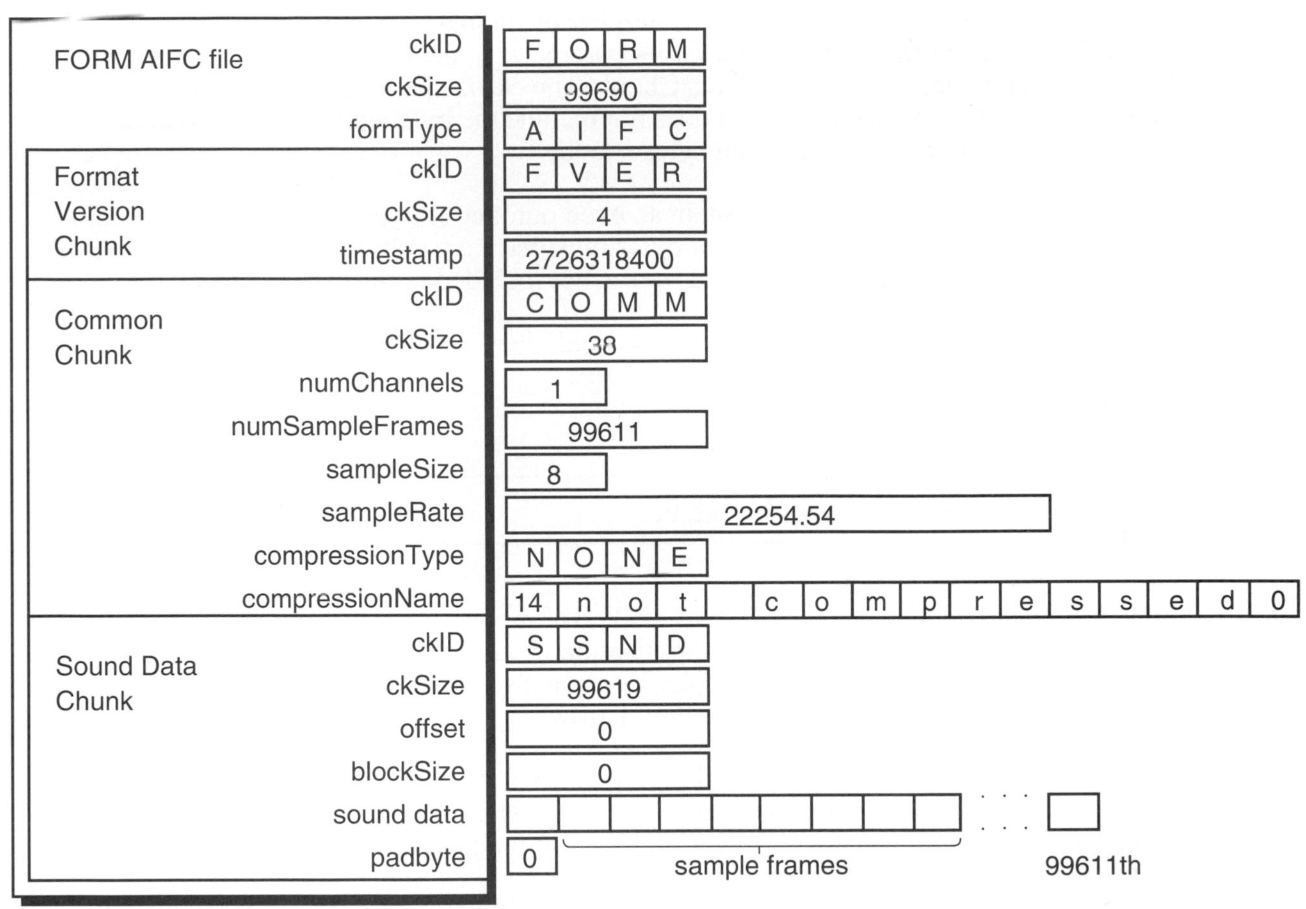

Figure 22-11. A sample AIFF-C file

Every Form Chunk must contain a Common Chunk and every AIFF-C file must contain a Format Version Chunk. In addition, if the sampled sound has a length greater than 0, there must be a Sound Data Chunk in the Form Chunk. All other chunk types are optional. Your application should be able to read all the required chunks if it uses AIFF or AIFF-C files, but it can choose to ignore any of the optional chunks.

When reading or writing AIFF or AIFF-C files, you should keep the following points in mind:

- Remember that the local chunks in an AIFF or AIFF-C file can occur in any order. An application that reads these types of files should be designed to get a chunk, identify it, and then process it without making any assumptions about what kind of chunk it is based on its order in the Form Chunk.

- If your application allows modification of a chunk, then it must also update other chunks that may be based on the modified chunk. However, if there are chunks in the file that your application does not recognize, you must discard those unrecognized chunks. Of course, if your application is simply copying the AIFF or AIFF-C file without any modification, you should copy the unrecognized chunks, too.

- You can get the clearest indication of the number of sample frames contained in an AIFF or AIFF-C file from the numSampleFrames parameter in the Common Chunk, not from the ckSize parameter in the Sound Data Chunk. The ckSize parameter is padded to include the fields that follow it, but it does not include the byte with a value of 0 at the end if the total number of sound data bytes is odd.
- Remember that each chunk must contain an even number of bytes. Chunks whose total contents would yield an odd number of bytes must have a pad byte with a value of 0 added at the end of the chunk. This pad byte is not included in the ckSize parameter.
- Remember that the ckSize parameter of any chunk does not include the first 8 bytes of the chunk (which specify the chunk type).

USING THE SOUND MANAGER

The Sound Manager provides a wide range of methods for creating sound and manipulating audio data on the Macintosh. Usually, your application needs to use only a few of the many routines or sound commands that are available. You can also use Sound Manager routines to record sounds through any available sound input hardware.

The Sound Manager routines can be divided into high-level routines and low-level routines. The high-level routines (like SndRecord, SndPlay, and SysBeep) give you the ability to produce very complex audio output at very little programming expense. The next section shows how your application can produce sounds simply by obtaining a handle to an existing 'snd ' resource and passing that handle to the SndPlay function. Moreover, if the data in the 'snd ' resource is stored in a compressed format, SndPlay automatically expands it for play-back in real time without further intervention from your application.

Although the high-level Sound Manager routines are sufficient for many applications, low-level Sound Manager routines are available to provide your application with much greater control over sound recording and production than is provided by the high-level routines. Using these low-level routines, your application can record directly from sound input devices, allocate and release sound channels, queue sound commands to a channel or bypass a sound queue altogether, perform modifications on sound data and commands sent into a channel, create and mix multiple channels of sound, compress and expand audio data, disable and enable the system alert sound, obtain information about current sound activity, and play sounds continuously from disk.

Some of these operations are carried out by specialized low-level routines, but most of them are accomplished by passing appropriate sound commands to the SndDoCommand, SndDoImmediate, and SndControl functions. For example, your application can alter the pitch of a sampled sound that is currently playing by calling SndDoImmediate with the rateCmd command as one of its parameters.

Some of the Sound Manager routines and commands cannot be called at interrupt time because they attempt to allocate or release memory. In particular, the routines SndNewChannel, SndDisposeChannel, SndAddModifier, SysBeep, SndPlay, SndStartFilePlay, SndRecord, and SndRecordToFile cannot be called at interrupt time. In addition, callback procedures, specified in calls to SndNewChannel and SndStartFilePlay, and doubleback routines, specified in calls to SndPlayDoubleBuffer, are executed at interrupt time and therefore must not allocate, release, or move memory. You can safely call all other Sound Manager routines at interrupt time.

Playing 'snd ' Resources

Perhaps the simplest Sound Manager routine is SndPlay, which requires nothing more than a handle to an existing 'snd ' resource. An 'snd ' resource contains the information necessary for the Sound Manager to create a channel linked to the required synthesizer, together with the sound commands that are to be sent to that synthesizer to play the desired sound. The 'snd ' resource may or may not contain sound data. If it does, as in the case of a sampled sound, that data can be either compressed or uncompressed. As long as the resource is created correctly, SndPlay will play it. Listing 22-7 illustrates how to play back an 'snd ' resource.

Listing 22-7. Playing an 'snd ' resource with SndPlay

```
PROCEDURE CallSndPlay;
CONST
   kAsync = TRUE;                   {play is asynchronous}
   mySndID = 9000;                  {resource ID of an 'snd '}
VAR
   mySndHandle:    Handle;          {handle to an 'snd ' resource}
   mySndChan:      SndChannelPtr;   {pointer to a sound channel}
   myErr:          OSErr;
BEGIN
   mySndChan := NIL;
   mySndHandle := GetResource ('snd ', mySndID);
   IF mySndHandle <> NIL THEN       {check for a NIL handle}
   BEGIN
      myErr := SndPlay (mySndChan, mySndHandle, kAsync);
      IF myErr <> noErr THEN DoError(myErr);
   END;
END;
```

When your application uses SndPlay and passes NIL as the pointer to a sound channel, it does not need to concern itself with any memory allocation or deallocation. The Sound Manager automatically opens a sound channel (in the application's heap) and then closes it when the sound is completed.

For more complete control of the sound channel, your application can open a sound channel by using SndNewChannel. The application then sends commands to that channel with SndDoCommand or SndDoImmediate. When the sound is completed, your application closes the channel with SndDisposeChannel. Listing 22-8 shows how your application can use low-level Sound Manager routines in the simple case of calling the sampled sound synthesizer to play back a buffer of sampled sound. The buffer can be either compressed or uncompressed. This example assumes that the sampled sound is uncompressed and that the sound header whose address is passed as an argument has already been filled out correctly.

Listing 22-8. Using low-level Sound Manager routines

```
PROCEDURE DoBufferCmd(mySHPtr: SoundHeaderPtr);
VAR
   mySndChan:   SndChannelPtr;         {pointer to a sound channel}
   mySndCmd:    SndCommand;            {a sound command}
   myErr:       OSErr;
BEGIN
   mySndChan := NIL;                   {Sound Mgr allocates channel}
   mySndCmd.cmd := bufferCmd;          {the command is bufferCmd}
   mySndCmd.param1 := 0;               {not used here}
   mySndCmd.param2 := ORD4(mySHPtr);   {pointer to SoundHeader}

   {allocate a sound channel}
   myErr := SndNewChannel(mySndChan, sampledSynth, initMono, NIL);
   IF myErr <> noErr THEN DoError(myErr);

   {queue bufferCmd in the sound channel}
   myErr := SndDoCommand(mySndChan, mySndCmd, FALSE);
   IF myErr <> noErr THEN DoError(myErr);

   {dispose of the channel when finished}
   myErr := SndDisposeChannel(mySndChan, FALSE);
   IF myErr <> noErr THEN DoError(myErr);
END;
```

The Sound Manager functions used in Listing 22-8 (SndNewChannel, SndDoCommand, and SndDisposeChannel) are explained in detail in the following sections. Note that the procedure does not do proper error handling; it is intended primarily to illustrate the proper order in which you should call the low-level Sound Manager routines.

Allocating Sound Channels

To use most of the low-level Sound Manager routines, you must specify a sound channel that maintains a queue of commands destined for a particular synthesizer. Generally you do not need to worry about allocating memory for sound channels because the SndNewChannel function automatically allocates a sound-channel record in the application's heap if passed a pointer to a NIL sound channel. For example, the following lines of code request that the Sound Manager open a new sound channel and link it to the sampled sound synthesizer:

```
mySndChan := NIL;
myErr := SndNewChannel(mySndChan, sampledSynth, 0, NIL);
```

If you are concerned with memory management, you can allocate your own channel memory and pass the address of that memory as the first parameter to SndNewChannel. Listing 22-9 illustrates one way to do this.

Listing 22-9. Creating a sound channel

```
FUNCTION CreateSndChannel : SndChannelPtr;
VAR
   mySndChan:   SndChannelPtr;            {pointer to a sound channel}
   myErr:       OSErr;
BEGIN
   {allocate a sound channel}
   mySndChan := SndChannelPtr(NewPtrClear(Sizeof(SndChannel)));
   IF mySndChan <> NIL THEN
   BEGIN
      mySndChan^.qLength := stdQLength;   {128 sound commands}
      myErr := SndNewChannel(mySndChan, sampledSynth, initMono, NIL);
   END;
   CreateSndChannel := mySndChan;         {return SndChannelPtr}
END;
```

Note that if you allocate your own channel memory, you must set the size of the sound channel (the number of sound commands that the channel can store). You should set the size by assigning a value to the qLength field of the sound channel you allocate. You can use the constant stdQLength, as illustrated in Listing 22-9, or provide a value of your own.

```
CONST stdQLength       = 128;  {default size of standard sound channel}
```

Note: The number of sound commands in a channel should be an integer greater than 0. If you open a channel with a 0-length queue, most of the Sound Manager routines will return a badChannel result code.

The second parameter in the SndNewChannel function is the resource ID of the playback synthesizer that is to be linked to the new sound channel. Currently recognized playback synthesizer values are

```
CONST squareWaveSynth  = 1;     {square-wave synthesizer}
      waveTableSynth   = 3;     {wave-table synthesizer}
      sampledSynth     = 5;     {sampled sound synthesizer}
```

The third parameter in the SndNewChannel function specifies the initialization parameters to be associated with the new channel. These are discussed in the following section. The fourth parameter in the SndNewChannel function is a pointer to a callback procedure. If your application produces sounds asynchronously or needs to be alerted when a command has completed, you can specify a callback procedure by passing the address of that procedure in the fourth parameter. If you pass NIL as the fourth parameter, then no callback routine executes. See "Specifying Callback Routines" later in this chapter for more information on setting up and using callback procedures.

Initializing Sound Channels

When you first create a sound channel with SndNewChannel, you can request that the channel have certain characteristics as specified by a **sound-channel initialization parameter.** For example, to indicate that you want to allocate a channel capable of producing stereo sound, you might use the following code:

```
myErr := SndNewChannel(mySndChan, sampledSynth, initStereo, NIL);
```

These are the currently recognized constants for the sound-channel initialization parameter.

```
CONST initChanLeft      = $0002;  {left channel--sampledSynth only}
      initChanRight     = $0003;  {right channel--sampledSynth only}
      initChan0         = $0004;  {channel 1--wave table only}
      initChan1         = $0005;  {channel 2--wave table only}
      initChan2         = $0006;  {channel 3--wave table only}
      initChan3         = $0007;  {channel 4--wave table only}
      initMono          = $0080;  {mono channel--sampledSynth only}
      initStereo        = $00C0;  {stereo channel--sampledSynth only}
      initMACE3         = $0300;  {3:1 compression--sampledSynth only}
      initMACE6         = $0400;  {6:1 compression--sampledSynth only}
      initNoInterp      = $0004;  {no linear interpolation}
      initNoDrop        = $0008;  {no drop-sample conversion}
```

Constant	**Description**
initChanLeft	Play sounds through the left channel of the Macintosh audio jack.
initChanRight	Play sounds through the right channel of the Macintosh audio jack.
initChan0	Play sounds through the first channel of the wave-table synthesizer.
initChan1	Play sounds through the second channel of the wave-table synthesizer.
initChan2	Play sounds through the third channel of the wave-table synthesizer.
initChan3	Play sounds through the fourth channel of the wave-table synthesizer.
initMono	Play sounds through both channels of the Macintosh audio jack and the internal speaker. This is the default channel mode.
initStereo	Play sounds through both channels of the Macintosh audio jack and the internal speaker. A stereo sound contains left and right samples that are interleaved (that is, left, right, left, right, and so forth). Note that some machines cannot play stereo sounds.
initMACE3	Assume that the sounds to be played through the channel are MACE 3:1 compressed. The loadCmd command and the SndNewChannel function calculate CPU loading based on MACE 3:1 overhead. A noncompressed sound plays normally, even through a channel that has been initialized for MACE.

initMACE6 — Assume that the sounds to be played through the channel are MACE 6:1 compressed. The loadCmd command and the SndNewChannel function calculate CPU loading based on MACE 6:1 overhead. A noncompressed sound plays normally, even through a channel that has been initialized for MACE.

initNoInterp — Do not use linear interpolation when playing a sound back at a different frequency from the sound's recorded frequency. Using the initNoInterp initialization parameter decreases the CPU load for this channel. Sounds most affected by the absence of linear interpolation are sinusoidal sounds. Sounds least affected are noisy sound effects like explosions and screams.

initNoDrop — Do not use drop-sample conversion when playing a sound back.

Note: Most Macintosh computers play *only* the left channel of stereo sounds out the internal speaker. Some machines (for example, the Macintosh SE/30 and Macintosh IIsi) mix both channels together before sending a signal to the internal speaker. You can use the Gestalt function to determine if a particular machine mixes both left and right channels to the internal speaker. All models of the Macintosh, however, play stereo signals out the headphone jack.

Because MACE is extremely CPU-intensive, using the initMACE3 and initMACE6 options reserves considerably more time for a channel than does using the other options. If you can determine whether MACE sounds will be used for a given channel, then the CPU loading values will be much more accurate.

The initialization parameters are additive. To initialize a channel for stereo sound with no linear interpolation, simply pass an initialization parameter that is the sum of the desired characteristics, as follows:

```
myErr := SndNewChannel(mySndChan, sampledSynth, initStereo+initNoInterp,
                       NIL);
```

Note that the call to SndNewChannel is really only a request that the Sound Manager open a channel having the desired characteristics. It is possible that the parameters requested cannot be provided without consuming too much CPU time. See "Managing the CPU Load" later in this chapter for a method of determining when a call to SndNewChannel succeeds. In general, you should initialize a sound channel for the most processor-intensive case (that is, monophonic sound with linear interpolation and MACE 3:1 compression) unless you know exactly what kind of sound is to be played.

When the Sound Manager does succeed in opening a new sound channel with the requested characteristics, it links that channel to the desired playback synthesizer. The synthesizer reacts to that command by allocating any private memory it needs and performing other necessary initialization procedures.

You can alter certain initialization parameters, even while a channel is actively playing a sound, by issuing the reInitCmd sound command. For example, you can change the output channel from left to right, as follows:

```
mySndCmd.cmd := reInitCmd;
mySndCmd.param1 := 0;              {unused}
mySndCmd.param2 := initChanRight;  {new init parameter}
```

```
myErr := SndDoImmediate(mySndChan, mySndCmd);
IF myErr <> noErr THEN DoError(myErr);
```

The reInitCmd command accepts the initNoInterp constant to toggle linear interpolation on and off; it should be used with uncompressed sounds only. If an uncompressed sound is playing when you send a reInitCmd command with this constant, linear interpolation begins immediately. You can also pass initMono, initChanLeft, or initChanRight to pan to both channels, to the left channel, or to the right channel. This affects only monophonic sounds. Note that the Sound Manager remembers the settings you pass and applies them to all further sounds played on that channel.

Releasing Sound Channels

To release a sound channel that you have allocated with SndNewChannel, use SndDisposeChannel. SndDisposeChannel requires two parameters, a pointer to the channel that is to be disposed and a Boolean value that indicates whether the channel should be flushed before disposal. Here's an example:

```
myErr := SndDisposeChannel (mySndChan, TRUE);
```

Because the second parameter is TRUE, the Sound Manager sends both a flushCmd command and a quietCmd command to the sound channel (using SndDoImmediate). This removes all commands from the sound channel and stops any sound already in progress. Then the Sound Manager disposes of the channel.

If the second parameter is FALSE, the Sound Manager simply queues a quietCmd command (using SndDoCommand) and waits until quietCmd is received by the synthesizer before disposing of the channel. In this case, the call to SndDisposeChannel is synchronous.

Note: It is important to remember that sound channels are for temporary use and that you should create them just before playing sounds. Once the sound is completed, you should dispose of the channel. One reason for this is that only one playback synthesizer can be active at any time. If your application is switched into the background and does not release a sound channel, then other applications are unable to open channels linked to other synthesizers. In particular, the system alert sound may not be heard and the user may not be notified of important system occurrences.

Determining Features of Synthesizers

You can determine certain information about the capabilities of a synthesizer by using the SndControl function. For example, you can determine whether a particular synthesizer supports a particular initialization option (some synthesizers do not support all initialization options). This can be most useful if you want your application to run under the enhanced Sound Manager as well as under earlier versions where the playback synthesizers do not have the same output characteristics. By first determining whether the intended synthesizer supports the desired output characteristics, you can avoid requesting characteristics that are not available. Because you generally need to know about the capabilities of a synthesizer before you actually create a sound channel, you can call SndControl even if no channel has been created for the synthesizer.

To determine whether an initialization option is supported by a particular synthesizer, call the SndControl function and pass it the availableCmd command. Listing 22-10 illustrates how to determine if the sampled sound synthesizer supports stereo sound output.

Listing 22-10. Using the availableCmd command

```
mySndCmd.cmd := availableCmd;
mySndCmd.param1 := 0;           {unused on input}
mySndCmd.param2 := initStereo;  {test for stereo}

myErr := SndControl(sampledSynth, mySndCmd);
IF myErr <> noErr THEN DoError(myErr);

StereoAvailable := (mySndCmd.param1 <> 0);
```

The SndControl function requires two parameters. The first parameter indicates the resource ID of the synthesizer whose characteristics are to be determined. The second parameter is a sound command. In the case illustrated, the cmd field of that sound command is set to availableCmd. The param2 field of the sound command contains the initialization parameter in question. (The initialization parameters are discussed in the preceding section, "Initializing Sound Channels.") The param1 field of the sound command is unused on input. If SndControl returns successfully, then param1 contains 1 if the synthesizer has the requested characteristics and 0 otherwise.

To determine which version of a synthesizer is available, call the SndControl function with the versionCmd command. Neither param1 nor param2 of the sound command passed to SndControl is used on input. If the function returns successfully, the version is returned in param2 of the sound command. For example, version 2.0 of a synthesizer would be returned as $00020000. Listing 22-11 illustrates how to use the versionCmd command.

Listing 22-11. Using the versionCmd command

```
mySndCmd.cmd := versionCmd;
mySndCmd.param1 := 0;           {unused on input}
mySndCmd.param2 := 0;           {unused on input}

{determine version of sampled sound synthesizer}
myErr := SndControl(sampledSynth, mySndCmd);
IF myErr <> noErr THEN
   DoError(myErr)
ELSE
   version := mySndCmd.param2;
```

Playing Frequencies

You can play frequencies one at a time by using the SndDoCommand or SndDoImmediate function to issue freqDurationCmd sound commands. A sound plays for a specified duration at a specified frequency. You can use any of the three available playback synthesizers to play the sound. If you use the wave-table synthesizer or sampled sound synthesizer, then a voice must previously have been installed in the channel. (See "Installing Voices Into Channels" later in this chapter for instructions on installing wave tables and sampled sounds as voices.)

You can also play frequencies by issuing the freqCmd command, which is identical to the freqDurationCmd command, except that no duration is specified when you issue freqCmd.

> **Note:** A freqDurationCmd command continues playing until another command is available in the sound channel. Therefore, to play a single frequency for a specified duration, you should issue freqDurationCmd followed immediately by quietCmd. See "Manipulating a Sound That Is Playing" later in this chapter for further details on quietCmd.

When you use the freqDurationCmd command and are using a sampled sound as the voice, freqDurationCmd starts at the beginning of a sampled sound. The freqDurationCmd command plays the sound between the loop points specified in the sampled sound header to extend the sound to the specified duration. There must be an ending-point for the loop specified in the header in order for freqDurationCmd to work properly.

The structure of a freqDurationCmd command is slightly different from that of most other sound commands. The param1 field contains the duration of the sound, specified in half-milliseconds. (A duration of 2000 represents a duration of 1 second. The maximum duration is a duration of 32,767, or about 16 seconds.) The param2 field specifies the frequency of the sound. The frequency is specified as a MIDI value. Listing 22-12 demon-strates the use of the freqDurationCmd command.

Listing 22-12. Using the freqDurationCmd command

```
VAR
   mySndChan:   SndChannelPtr; {pointer to a sound channel}
   mySndCmd:    SndCommand;    {a sound command}
   myErr:       OSErr;
BEGIN
   mySndCmd.cmd := freqDurationCmd;
   mySndCmd.param1 := 2000;    {duration in half-milliseconds}
   mySndCmd.param2 := 60;

   {play the sound}
   {assume that mySndChan points to a valid sound channel}
   myErr := SndDoCommand(mySndChan, mySndCmd, false);
   IF myErr <> noErr THEN DoError(myErr);
END;
```

Table 22-3 shows the decimal values that can be sent with a freqDurationCmd or freqCmd command. Middle C is represented by a value of 60. These values correspond to MIDI values.

To calculate a duration, use the following formula:

duration = (2000/(repetitions per minute/60)) * repetitions per sound

You can rest a channel for a specified duration by issuing a restCmd command. The duration, specified in half-milliseconds, is passed in the param1 field of the sound command.

Table 22-3. MIDI values

	A	A#	B	C	C#	D	D#	E	F	F#	G	G#
Interval 1					1	2	3	4	5	6	7	8
Interval 2	9	10	11	12	13	14	15	16	17	18	19	20
Interval 3	21	22	23	24	25	26	27	28	29	30	31	32
Interval 4	33	34	35	36	37	38	39	40	41	42	43	44
Interval 5	45	46	47	48	49	50	51	52	53	54	55	56
Interval 6	57	58	59	60	61	62	63	64	65	66	67	68
Interval 7	69	70	71	72	73	74	75	76	77	78	79	80
Interval 8	81	82	83	84	85	86	87	88	89	90	91	92
Interval 9	93	94	95	96	97	98	99	100	101	102	103	104
Interval 10	105	106	107	108	109	110	111	112	113	114	115	116
Interval 11	117	118	119	120	121	122	123	124	125	126	127	

Playing Sampled Sounds

You can play a sampled sound by calling the SndPlay function and passing it a handle to an 'snd ' resource that contains a sampled sound header. To gain greater control over the sound output, you can use a number of sound commands, including bufferCmd, soundCmd, rateCmd, and getRateCmd. Both bufferCmd and soundCmd specify a pointer to a sampled sound header that is locked into memory. The soundCmd command is used to install a sampled sound into a channel as a voice and is discussed in the next section, "Installing Voices Into Channels."

To play a sampled sound in one-shot mode (without any looping), use the bufferCmd command. The pointer in the param2 field of the sound command is the location of a sampled sound header. A bufferCmd command is queued in the channel until the preceding commands have been processed. If the bufferCmd command is contained within an 'snd ' resource, the high bit of the command must be set. If the sound was loaded in from an 'snd ' resource, your application is expected to unlock this resource and allow it to be purged after using it.

You can use the bufferCmd command to handle compressed sound samples in addition to sounds that are not compressed. To expand and play back a buffer of compressed samples, you pass the sampled sound synthesizer a bufferCmd command where param2 points to a compressed sound header.

> **Note:** Using the bufferCmd command to play several consecutive compressed samples on the Macintosh Plus and the Macintosh SE is not guaranteed to work without an audible pause or click.

To play sampled sounds that are not compressed, pass bufferCmd a standard or extended sound header. The extended sound header is used for stereo sampled sounds. The standard sampled sound header is used for all other noncompressed sampled sounds.

You can divide large sampled sounds into multiple buffers and then issue successive bufferCmd commands to play that sound. In this case, each buffer must contain a sampled sound header. Except as noted just above, the sound will play smoothly, without audible gaps. It is usually much easier, however, to play large sampled sounds from disk by using the play-from-disk routines or the SndPlayDoubleBuffer function. See "Playing Sampled Sounds From Files" and "Managing Double Buffers" later in this chapter for complete details.

Note: If a sound is playing and you send a bufferCmd command by using SndDoImmediate, the sound specified in the bufferCmd command will not play. You should send all bufferCmd commands by using SndDoCommand, or else you should first stop the sound that is playing by sending a quietCmd command with SndDoImmediate. Alternatively, you can call the SndChannelStatus function repeatedly until the scChannelBusy flag of the sound-channel status record turns FALSE.

This is the structure of the standard sampled sound header used by the sampled sound synthesizer:

```
TYPE SoundHeader =
     PACKED RECORD
        samplePtr:       Ptr;      {if NIL, samples in sampleArea}
        length:          LongInt;  {number of samples in array}
        sampleRate:      Fixed;    {sample rate}
        loopStart:       LongInt;  {loop point beginning}
        loopEnd:         LongInt;  {loop point ending}
        encode:          Byte;     {sample's encoding option}
        baseFrequency:   Byte;     {base frequency of sample}
        sampleArea:      PACKED ARRAY[0..0] OF Byte
     END;
```

Field descriptions

samplePtr — A pointer to the sampled sound data. If the sampled sound is located in memory immediately after the baseFrequency field, then this field should be set to NIL. Otherwise, this field is a pointer to the memory location of the sampled sound data.

length — The number of bytes in the sampled sound data.

sampleRate — The rate at which the sample was originally recorded. The approximate sample rates are shown in Table 22-4. Note that the sample rate is declared as a Fixed data type, but the most significant bit is not treated as a sign bit; instead, that bit is interpreted as having the value 32,768.

loopStart — The starting point of the portion of the sampled sound header that is to be used by the Sound Manager when determining the duration of freqDurationCmd. These loop points specify the byte numbers in the sampled data to be used as the beginning and end points to cycle through when playing the sound.

loopEnd — The end point of the portion of the sampled sound header that is to be used by the Sound Manager when determining the duration of freqDurationCmd. If no looping is desired, set both loopStart and loopEnd to 0.

encode — The method of encoding used to generate the sampled sound data. The current encoding option values are

```
CONST stdSH      = $00;   {standard sound header}
      extSH      = $FF;   {extended sound header}
      cmpSH      = $FE;   {compressed sound header}
```

For a standard sound header, you should specify the constant stdSH. Encode option values in the ranges 0 through 63 and 128 to 255 are reserved for use by Apple. You are free to use numbers in the range 64 through 127 for your own encode options.

baseFrequency — The pitch at which the original sample was taken. This value must be in the range 1 through 127. Table 22-3 lists the possible baseFrequency values. The baseFrequency value allows the Sound Manager to calculate the proper playback rate of the sample when an application uses the freqDurationCmd command. Applications should not alter the baseFrequency field of a sampled sound; to play the sample at different pitches, use freqDurationCmd or freqCmd.

sampleArea — An array of bytes, each of which contains a value similar to the values in a wave-table description. These values are interpreted as offset values, where $80 represents an amplitude of 0. The value $00 is the most negative amplitude and $FF is the largest positive amplitude. The samples are numbered 1 through the value in the length parameter.

The Sound Manager can play sounds sampled at any rate up to 64 kHz. Table 22-4 lists approximate values for the most common sample rates. When you specify a value in the sampleRate field of a sound header, you should use the values in the third column of Table 22-4.

Table 22-4. Sample rates

Rate (kHz)	Rate (Hz)	sampleRate value (Fixed)
5 kHz	5563.6363	$15BBA2E8
7 kHz	7418.1818	$1CFA2E8B
11 kHz	11127.2727	$2B7745D1
22 kHz	22254.5454	$56EE8BA3
44 kHz	44100.0000	$AC440000

Here is the structure of the extended sampled sound header used by the sampled sound synthesizer:

```
TYPE ExtSoundHeader =
     PACKED RECORD
         samplePtr:            Ptr;         {if NIL, samples in sampleArea}
         numChannels:          LongInt;     {number of channels in sample}
         sampleRate:           Fixed;       {rate of original sample}
         loopStart:            LongInt;     {loop point beginning}
         loopEnd:              LongInt;     {loop point ending}
         encode:               Byte;        {sample's encoding option}
         baseFrequency:        Byte;        {base freq. of original sample}
         numFrames:            LongInt;     {total number of frames}
         AIFFSampleRate:       Extended;    {rate of original sample}
         markerChunk:          Ptr;         {pointer to marker info}
         instrumentChunks:     Ptr;         {pointer to instrument info}
         AESRecording:         Ptr;         {pointer to audio info}
         sampleSize:           Integer;     {number of bits per sample}
```

```
      futureUse1:          Integer;    {reserved}
      futureUse2:          LongInt;    {reserved}
      futureUse3:          LongInt;    {reserved}
      futureUse4:          LongInt;    {reserved}
      sampleArea:          PACKED ARRAY[0..0] OF Byte
   END;
```

Field descriptions

samplePtr	A pointer to the sampled sound data. If the sampled sound is located in memory immediately after the futureUse4 field, then this field should be set to NIL. Otherwise, this field is a pointer to the memory location of the sampled sound data.
numChannels	The number of channels in the sampled sound data.
sampleRate	The rate at which the sample was originally recorded. The approximate sample rates are shown in Table 22-4. Note that the sample rate is declared as a Fixed data type, but the most significant bit is not treated as a sign bit; instead, that bit is interpreted as having the value 32,768.
loopStart	The starting point of the portion of the extended sampled sound header that is to be used by the Sound Manager when determining the duration of freqDurationCmd. These loop points specify the byte numbers in the sampled data to be used as the beginning and end points to cycle through when playing the sound.
loopEnd	The end point of the portion of the extended sampled sound header that is to be used by the Sound Manager when determining the duration of freqDurationCmd.
encode	The method of encoding used to generate the sampled sound data. For an extended sound header, you should specify the constant extSH. Encode option values in the ranges 0 through 63 and 128 to 255 are reserved for use by Apple. You are free to use numbers in the range 64 through 127 for your own encode options.
baseFrequency	The pitch at which the original sample was taken. This value must be in the range 1 through 127. Table 22-3 lists the possible baseFrequency values. The baseFrequency value allows the Sound Manager to calculate the proper playback rate of the sample when an application uses the freqDurationCmd command. Applications should not alter the baseFrequency field of a sampled sound; to play the sample at different pitches, use freqDurationCmd or freqCmd.
numFrames	The number of frames in the sampled sound data.
AIFFSampleRate	The sample rate at which the frames were sampled before compression, as expressed in an extended data type representation.
markerChunk	Synchronization information. The markerChunk field is not presently used and should be set to NIL.
instrumentChunks	Instrument information.
AESRecording	Audio information.
sampleSize	The number of bits in each sample frame.

futureUse1	Reserved.
futureUse2	Reserved.
futureUse3	Reserved.
futureUse4	The four futureUse fields are reserved for use by Apple. To maintain compatibility with future releases of system software, you should always set these fields to 0.
sampleArea	An array of bytes, each of which contains a value similar to the values in a wave-table description. These values are interpreted as offset values, where $80 represents an amplitude of 0. The value $00 is the largest negative amplitude and $FF is the largest positive amplitude.

To store and operate on compressed audio data, you use a compressed sound header, a record of type CmpSoundHeader that is a logical extension of the sound header. The compressed sound header is defined like this:

```
TYPE  CmpSoundHeader =
   PACKED RECORD
      samplePtr:        Ptr;                {if NIL, samples in sampleArea}
      numChannels:      LongInt;            {number of channels in sample}
      sampleRate:       Fixed;              {rate of original sample}
      loopStart:        LongInt;            {loop point beginning}
      loopEnd:          LongInt;            {loop point ending}
      encode:           Byte;               {sample's encoding option}
      baseFrequency:    Byte;               {base freq. of original sample}
      numFrames:        LongInt;            {length of sample in frames}
      AIFFSampleRate:   Extended;           {rate of original sample}
      markerChunk:      Ptr;                {unused}
      futureUse1:       Ptr;                {reserved}
      futureUse2:       Ptr;                {reserved}
      stateVars:        StateBlockPtr;      {pointer to StateBlock}
      leftOverSamples:  LeftOverBlockPtr;   {pointer to LeftOverBlock}
      compressionID:    Integer;            {ID of compression algorithm}
      packetSize:       Integer;            {number of bits per packet}
      snthID:           Integer;            {ID of compression synth}
      sampleSize:       Integer;            {bits in each sample point}
      sampleArea:       PACKED ARRAY[0..0] OF Byte
   END;
```

Field descriptions

samplePtr	Indicates the location of the compressed sound frames. If samplePtr is NIL, then the frames are located in the sampleArea field of the compressed sound header. Otherwise, samplePtr points to a buffer that contains the frames.
numChannels	Indicates how many channels are in the sample.
sampleRate	Indicates the sample rate at which the frames were sampled before compression. The approximate sample rates are shown in Table 22-4. Note that the sample rate is declared as a Fixed data type, but the most significant bit is not treated as a sign bit; instead, that bit is interpreted as having the value 32,768.

loopStart	Indicates the beginning of the loop points of the sound before compression.
loopEnd	Indicates the end of the loop points of the sound before compression.
encode	Indicates the method of encoding (if any) used to generate the sampled sound data. For a compressed sound header, you should specify the constant cmpSH. Encode option values in the ranges 0 through 63 and 128 to 255 are reserved for use by Apple. You are free to use numbers in the range 64 through 127 for your own encode options.
baseFrequency	Indicates the pitch of the original sampled sound. It is not used by bufferCmd. If you wish to make use of baseFrequency with a compressed sound, you must first expand it and then play it with soundCmd and freqDurationCmd.
numFrames	Indicates the number of frames contained in the compressed sound header. When you store multiple channels of uncompressed sound, store them as interleaved sample frames (as in AIFF). When you store multiple channels of compressed sounds, store them as interleaved packet frames.
AIFFSampleRate	Indicates the sample rate at which the frames were sampled before compression, as expressed in an extended data type representation.
markerChunk	Specifies synchronization information. The markerChunk field is not presently used and should be set to NIL.
futureUse1 futureUse2	Reserved. The two futureUse fields are reserved for use by Apple. To maintain compatibility with future releases of system software, you should always set these fields to 0.
stateVars	Points to a state block record. The stateVars field is used to store the state variables for a given algorithm across consecutive calls.
leftOverSamples	Points to a left over block record. You can use this block to store samples that will be truncated across algorithm invocations.
compressionID	Identifies the compression algorithm used on the samples in the compressed sound header. You can use a constant to define the compression algorithm.

```
CONST notCompressed    = 0;  {noncompressed samples}
      threeToOne       = 3;  {3:1 compressed samples}
      sixToOne         = 4;  {6:1 compressed samples}
```

Apple reserves the right to use compression IDs in the range 0 through 511.

packetSize	Indicates the size, specified in bits, of the smallest element that a given expansion algorithm can work with. You can use a constant to define the packet size.

```
CONST sixToOnePacketSize    = 8;    {size for 6:1}
      threeToOnePacketSize  = 16;   {size for 3:1}
```

snthID — Indicates the resource ID number of the 'snth' resource that was used to compress the packets contained in the compressed sound header. A 3:1 'snd ' resource would have a snthID of 11, and a 6:1 'snd ' would have a snthID of 13. If a compressed sound header contains samples that aren't compressed, you should set the snthID field to 0.

sampleSize — Indicates the size of the sample before it was compressed. Currently, the Sound Manager works only with 8-bit samples. The samples should be in offset binary format; applications that read their data from AIFF files must convert the samples from two's complement format to the binary format. The samples passed in the compressed sound header should always be byte-aligned, and any padding done to achieve byte alignment should be done from the left with zeros.

sampleArea — Contains the sample frames, but only when the samplePtr field is NIL. Otherwise, the sample frames are in the location indicated by samplePtr.

Listing 22-13 illustrates the structure of an 'snd ' resource that contains compressed sound data.

Listing 22-13. An 'snd ' resource containing compressed sound data

```
data 'snd ' (9004, "Sample 1", purgeable) {
   $"0001"      /*format type*/
   $"0001"      /*number of synthesizers*/
   $"0005"      /*resource ID of first synthesizer*/
   $"00000380" /*initialization option: initMACE3 + initMono*/
   $"0001"      /*number of sound commands that follow (1)*/
   $"8051"      /*cmd: bufferCmd*/
   $"0000"      /*param1: unused*/
   $"00000014" /*param2: offset to sound header (20 bytes)*/
                /*compressed sound header follows:*/
   $"00000000" /*pointer to data (it follows immediately)*/
   $"00000001" /*number of channels in sample*/
   $"56EE8BA3" /*sampling rate of this sound (22 kHz)*/
   $"00000000" /*starting of the sample's loop point; not used*/
   $"00000000" /*ending of the sample's loop point; not used*/
   $"FE"        /*compressed sample encoding*/
   $"00"        /*baseFrequency; not used*/
   $"00006590" /*number of frames in sample (26,000)*/
   $"400DADDD1745D145826B" /*AIFFSampleRate (22 kHz in extended type)*/
   $"00000000" /*markerChunk; NIL for 'snd ' resource*/
   $"00000000" /*futureUse1; NIL for 'snd ' resource*/
   $"00000000" /*futureUse2; NIL for 'snd ' resource*/
   $"00000000" /*stateVars; NIL for 'snd ' resource*/
   $"00000000" /*leftOverBlockPtr; not used here*/
   $"0003"      /*compressionID, 3 means 3:1*/
   $"0010"      /*packetSize, packetSize for 3:1 is 16 bits*/
   $"000B"      /*snthID is 11*/
   $"0008"      /*sampleSize, sound was 8-bit before processing*/
   $"2F 85 81 32 64 87 33 86" /*the compressed sound data*/
   $"6F 48 6D 65 72 6B 82 88"
   $"91 FE 8D 8E 86 4E 7C E9"
   $"6F 6D 71 70 7E 79 4F 83"
   $"59 8F 8F 65" /*rest of data omitted in this example*/
};
```

This resource has the same general structure as the 'snd ' resource illustrated in "The Format 1 'snd ' Resource" earlier in this chapter. The principal difference is that the standard sound header is replaced by the compressed sound header. This example resource specifies a monophonic sound compressed by using the 3:1 compression algorithm.

Installing Voices Into Channels

You can play frequencies through any of the three available playback synthesizers. By playing a frequency through the wave-table or sampled sound synthesizer, you can achieve a different sound than by playing that same frequency through the square-wave synthesizer. To do that, however, you need to install a voice into the sound channel to which you want to send freqDurationCmd commands.

You can install a wave table into a channel as a voice by issuing the waveTableCmd command. The param1 field of the sound command specifies the length of the wave table and the param2 field is a pointer to the wave-table data itself. Note that the Sound Manager will resample the wave table so that it is exactly 512 bytes long.

You can install a sampled sound into a channel as a voice by issuing the soundCmd command. You can either issue this command from your application or put it into an 'snd ' resource. If your application sends this command, param2 is a pointer to the sampled sound locked in memory. If soundCmd is contained within an 'snd ' resource, the high bit of the command must be set. To use a sampled sound 'snd ' as a voice, first obtain a pointer to the sampled sound header locked in memory. Then pass this pointer in param2 of a soundCmd command. After using the sound, your application is expected to unlock this resource and allow it to be purged.

Manipulating a Sound That Is Playing

The Sound Manager provides a number of sound commands that allow you to manipulate sounds currently in progress. You can also pause or stop a sound currently in progress. See "Pausing and Restarting Sound Channels" later in this chapter for information on how to pause the processing of a sound channel.

You can use the getRateCmd command to determine the rate at which a sampled sound is currently playing. If SndDoImmediate returns noErr when you pass it getRateCmd, the current rate of the channel is returned as a Fixed value in param2 of the sound command. (As usual, the high bit of the value returned is not interpreted as a sign bit.)

To modify the pitch of the sampled sound currently playing, use the rateCmd command. The current pitch is set to the rate specified in the param2 field of the sound command. Listing 22-14 illustrates how to halve the frequency of a sampled sound.

You can also use rateCmd and getRateCmd to pause a sampled sound that is currently playing. To do this, read the rate at which it is playing, issue a rateCmd command with a rate of 0, and then issue a rateCmd command with the previous rate when you want the sound to resume playing.

Listing 22-14. Halving the frequency of a sampled sound

```
PROCEDURE HalveFreq (mySndChan: SndChannelPtr);
VAR
   myRate:      LongInt;
   mySndCmd:    SndCommand;
BEGIN
   mySndCmd.cmd := getRateCmd;
   mySndCmd.param1 := 0;            {unused}
   mySndCmd.param2 := @myRate;
   myErr := SndDoImmediate(mySndChan, mySndCmd);
   IF myErr = noErr THEN
   BEGIN
      mySndCmd.cmd := rateCmd;
      mySndCmd.param1 := 0;         {unused}
      mySndCmd.param2 := FixDiv(myRate, $0002000);
      myErr := SndDoImmediate(mySndChan, mySndCmd);
   END;
   IF myErr <> noErr THEN DoError(myErr);
END;
```


You can use the getAmpCmd command to determine the current amplitude of a sound in progress. The getAmpCmd command is similar to getRateCmd, except that the value returned is an integer. The value returned is in the range 0–255. Here's an example:

```
VAR
   myAmp:       Integer;
BEGIN
   mySndCmd.cmd := getAmpCmd;
   mySndCmd.param1 := 0;            {unused}
   mySndCmd.param2 := @myAmp;
   myErr := SndDoImmediate(mySndChan, mySndCmd);
END;
```

To change the amplitude of the sound in progress, issue the ampCmd command. If no sound is currently playing, ampCmd sets the amplitude of the next sound. The desired new amplitude is passed in the param1 field of the sound command and should be a value in the range 0 to 255.

To modify the timbre of a sound being played by the square-wave synthesizer, use the timbreCmd command. A sine wave is specified as 0 in param1 and produces a very clear sound. A value of 255 in param1 represents a modified square wave and produces a buzzing sound. You should change the square-wave synthesizer's timbre before playing the sound. Only a Macintosh with the Apple Sound Chip allows this command to be sent while a sound is in progress.

To cause a synthesizer to stop playing the sound in progress, send the quietCmd sound command. Here's an example:

```
mySndCmd.cmd := quietCmd;  {the command is quietCmd}
mySndCmd.param1 := 0;      {unused}
mySndCmd.param2 := 0;      {unused}

{stop the sound now playing}
myErr := SndDoImmediate(mySndChan, mySndCmd, FALSE);
```

To stop a sound that is currently playing on the specified sound channel, send a quietCmd command. To bypass the command queue, you should issue quietCmd by using SndDoImmediate. Any sound commands that are already in the sound channel remain there, however, and further sound commands can be queued in that channel.

Flushing Sound Channels

If you wish to flush a sound channel without disturbing any sounds already in progress, issue the flushCmd command. Here's an example:

```
mySndCmd.cmd := flushCmd;    {the command is flushCmd}
mySndCmd.param1 := 0;        {unused}
mySndCmd.param2 := 0;        {unused}

{flush the channel}
myErr := SndDoImmediate(mySndChan, mySndCmd, FALSE);
```

If you want to stop all sound production by a particular sound channel immediately, you should issue a flushCmd command and then a quietCmd command. If you issue only a flushCmd command, the sound currently playing is not stopped. If you issue only a quietCmd command, the synthesizer stops playing the current sound but continues with any other queued commands. (By calling flushCmd before quietCmd command, you ensure that there are no other queued commands to process.)

> **Note:** The Sound Manager sends a quietCmd command when your application calls the SndDisposeChannel function. The quietCmd command is preceded by a flushCmd command if the quietNow parameter is TRUE.

Pausing and Restarting Sound Channels

If you want to pause command processing in a particular channel, you can use either of two sound commands, waitCmd or pauseCmd. The waitCmd command suspends all processing in a channel for a specified number of half-milliseconds. Here's an example:

```
mySndCmd.cmd := waitCmd;     {the command is waitCmd}
mySndCmd.param1 := 2000;     {1 second wait duration}
mySndCmd.param2 := 0;        {unused}

{pause the channel}
myErr := SndDoImmediate(mySndChan, mySndCmd, FALSE);
```

To pause the processing of commands in a sound channel for an unspecified duration, use the pauseCmd command. Unlike waitCmd, pauseCmd suspends processing for an undetermined amount of time. Processing does not resume until the Sound Manager receives a resumeCmd command for the specified channel.

To issue waitCmd or pauseCmd, you can use either SndDoImmediate or SndDoCommand, depending on whether you want the suspension of sound-channel processing to begin immediately or when the synthesizer reaches that command in the normal course of reading commands from a sound channel. The resumeCmd command, which is simply the opposite of pauseCmd, should be issued by using SndDoImmediate. Neither waitCmd nor pauseCmd stops any sound that is currently playing; these commands simply stop further processing of commands queued in the sound channel.

Note: Synthesizers expect to receive additional commands after a resumeCmd command. If no other commands are pending in the sound channel, the Sound Manager sends an emptyCmd command. The emptyCmd command is sent only by the Sound Manager and should not be issued by your application.

Synchronizing Sound Channels

You can synchronize several different sound channels by issuing syncCmd commands. The param1 field of the sound command contains a count, and the param2 field contains an arbitrary identifier. Every syncCmd command is held in the channel, suspending any further processing until its count equals 0. The Sound Manager first decrements the count and then waits for another syncCmd command having the same identifier to be received on another channel.

For example, to synchronize four wave-table channels, send a syncCmd command to the first channel with a count equal to 4, to the second channel with a count equal to 3, and so on, giving each command the same identifier. The Sound Manager decrements the count for each channel having a given identifier each time it receives a syncCmd command. As a result, after you send the fourth channel a count equal to 1, all four channels will have their count set to 0 and will resume processing their queued commands.

Note: The syncCmd command is intended to make it easy to synchronize channels linked either to the wave-table synthesizer or to the square-wave synthesizer. Applications needing to synchronize and control the execution of multiple channels of sampled sound should probably use the Time Manager.

Managing the CPU Load

When you want to open multiple channels of sound, or even when you want to open a single channel of sound that requires intensive processing to provide a high-quality sound (for example, real-time expansion of compressed sampled sound with stereo output and linear interpolation), you may want to pay close attention to the amount of processing power consumed by your sound-related activity. The new Sound Manager allows you to monitor and limit the load placed on the CPU by sound activity.

You need to be able to monitor the sound processing done by your application because every Macintosh computer has some absolute limit to its processing power, which is determined largely by the speed of the CPU. Other factors also affect how much sound-related activity a given computer can support, such as processing necessary to track mouse movements, processing done by the Operating System, processing done by interrupt routines, and so on. When no sound channels are open, the Sound Manager considers the computer to be completely available for sound tasks. In that case, the current load value is 0 percent. As sound channels are opened, the current CPU loading value increases from 0 percent to the maximum value, 100 percent. The amount of increase due to a new sound channel depends on the initialization parameters specified in the call to SndNewChannel that created that channel.

> **Note:** The CPU load values provided by the Sound Manager do not account for any nonsound processing, such as networking software or other interrupt code.

In the enhanced Sound Manager, the loadCmd command returns (in param1) the percentage of CPU load that would be reserved by calling SndNewChannel with the initialization parameters passed into param2 of the loadCmd command. On a Macintosh II, the value returned in param1 might be 15 percent, indicating that a stereo sound channel would need 15 percent of the available processor power to play sound.

The totalLoadCmd command returns a potentially more useful number. The totalLoadCmd command is identical to the loadCmd command except that instead of returning just the percentage of processor power for the specified initialization parameters, it adds the current CPU loading value to that number. The value returned in param1 is the total processor power that would be used by the Sound Manager if those initialization parameters were actually used to allocate a sound channel. If the number returned is greater than 100 percent, allocating that channel would not be advisable.

Producing an Alert Sound

You can produce a **system alert sound** to catch the user's attention by calling the SysBeep procedure. The SysBeep procedure is a Sound Manager routine that plays the system alert sound, selected by the user in the Sound control panel. Here's an example of calling SysBeep:

```
IF myErr <> noErr THEN SysBeep(30);
```

You must supply a parameter when you call the SysBeep procedure, even though the Sound Manager ignores that parameter in most cases. All system alert sounds are stored as format 1 'snd ' resources in the System file and are played by the Sound Manager. There is, however, one exception to this rule: if the user has selected the Simple Beep as the system alert sound on a Macintosh Plus or Macintosh SE, then the beep is generated by code stored in ROM rather than by the Sound Manager, and the duration parameter is interpreted in ticks.

If an application has an open sound channel, your call to the SysBeep procedure may not generate any sound because only one synthesizer can be active at any time. For example, if an application is using the square-wave synthesizer to play sounds, SysBeep may fail to generate the system alert sound because that sound uses the sampled sound synthesizer. Even if the user has selected the Simple Beep as the system alert sound (which uses the square-wave synthesizer), the alert sound will not be heard if some application already has an open channel linked to the square-wave synthesizer. This is because only one channel at a time can be linked to the square-wave synthesizer.

In cases like these where the system alert sound cannot be created, the Operating System flashes the menu bar. Applications using any of the sound synthesizers should dispose of their channels as soon as they have finished making a sound so that the system alert sound can be played. Once again, Macintosh computers without the Apple Sound Chip (that is, the Macintosh Plus and Macintosh SE) operate differently: when the Simple Beep is selected, the beep is heard because the Operating System bypasses the Sound Manager to make the sound.

The SysBeep procedure cannot be called at interrupt time because doing so may cause the Sound Manager to attempt to allocate memory and load a resource.

Note: If your primary use of the SysBeep procedure is to alert the user of important or abnormal occurrences, it may be better to use the Notification Manager. See the Notification Manager chapter in this volume for complete details on alerting the user.

The new Sound Manager includes two functions—SndGetSysBeepState and SndSetSysBeepState—that allow you to determine and alter the status of the system alert sound. Currently, two states are defined:

```
CONST sysBeepDisable        = $0000;        {system alert sound disabled}
      sysBeepEnable         = $0001;        {system alert sound enabled}
```

When the system alert sound is disabled, the Sound Manager effectively ignores all calls to SysBeep. No sound is created and the menu bar will not flash. Also, no resources are loaded into memory. Even when the system alert sound is enabled, it is possible that the system alert sound will not be played; for example, the speaker volume may be set to 0, or playing the requested system alert sound might require too much CPU time. In these cases, the menu bar will flash. By default, the system alert sound is enabled.

Compressing and Expanding Sounds

Some of the capabilities provided by MACE are transparently available to your application. For example, if you pass the SndPlay function a handle to an 'snd ' resource that contains a compressed sampled sound, the sampled sound synthesizer automatically expands the sound data for playback in real time. Your application does not need to know whether the 'snd ' resource contains compressed or noncompressed samples when it calls SndPlay. This is because sufficient information is in the resource itself to allow the synthesizer to determine whether it should expand the data samples.

However, aside from expansion playback, all of the MACE capabilities need to be specifically requested by your application. For example, you can use the procedures Comp3to1 or Comp6to1 if you want to compress a sampled sound (for example, to create an 'snd ' resource containing compressed audio data). And you can use the procedures Exp1to3 and Exp1to6 to expand compressed audio data.

All of these procedures require you to specify both an input and an output buffer, from and to which the sampled sound data to be converted is read and written. Your application must allocate the appropriate amount of storage for each buffer. For example, if you want to expand a buffer of compressed sampled sound data by using Exp1to6, the output buffer must be at least six times the size of the input buffer.

When calling these routines, you must also specify addresses of two small buffers (128 bytes each) that the Sound Manager uses to maintain state information about the compression or expansion process. When you first call a MACE routine, the state buffers should be filled with zeros to initialize the state information. You can pass NIL for both buffers if you do not want to save state information across calls to the MACE routines. Listing 22-15 illustrates the use of the Comp3to1 procedure.

Because the numChannels and the whichChannel parameters are both set to 1, CompressBy3 compresses monophonic audio data.

Listing 22-15. Compressing audio data

```
PROCEDURE CompressBy3 (inBuf: Ptr; outBuf: Ptr; numSamp: LongInt);
VAR
   myInState:  Ptr;  {input state buffer}
   myOutState: Ptr;  {output state buffer}
BEGIN
   myInState :=   NewPtrClear(128);
   myOutState :=  NewPtrClear(128);
   IF (myInState <> NIL) AND (myOutState <> NIL) THEN
      Comp3to1(inBuf, outBuf, numSamp, myInState, myOutState, 1, 1);
END;
```

Playing Sampled Sounds From Files

There are three functions that you can use to initiate and control a continuous playback of sampled sounds stored in files—SndStartFilePlay, SndPauseFilePlay, and SndStopFilePlay. You use SndStartFilePlay to initiate the playing of the sound. You use SndPauseFilePlay to temporarily suspend a sound from playing. If a sound is playing and you call SndPauseFilePlay, then the sound is paused. If the sound is paused and you call SndPauseFilePlay again, then the sound resumes playing. Hence, the SndPauseFilePlay routine acts like a pause button on a tape player, which toggles the tape between playing and pausing. (You can determine the current state of a play from disk by using the SndChannelStatus function. See "Obtaining Information About a Single Sound Channel" later in this chapter for complete details.) Finally, you can use SndStopFilePlay to stop the file from playing.

SndStartFilePlay can play sampled sounds stored in 'snd ' resources (either format 1 or format 2) or in files that conform to the AIFF or AIFF-C format. In addition, you can specify whether the play from disk should be asynchronous or synchronous. The SndStartFilePlay function is a high-level Sound Manager routine, like SndPlay. If you specify NIL as the sound channel, then SndStartFilePlay allocates memory for a channel internally. However, since you must specify a sound-channel pointer when calling either SndPauseFilePlay or SndStopFilePlay, you must allocate a sound channel yourself and call SndStartFilePlay asynchronously if you want to be able to pause or stop the sound prior to its natural ending point.

Playing an 'snd ' Resource From Disk

To play a sampled sound that is contained in an 'snd ' resource, you need to pass SndStartFilePlay the resource ID number of the resource to play. Listing 22-16 illustrates how to play an 'snd ' resource synchronously from disk.

Notice that the second parameter passed to SndStartFilePlay here is set to 0. That parameter is used only when playing files from disk.

Listing 22-16. Playing an 'snd ' resource from disk

```
PROCEDURE SyncStartFilePlay (myResNum: Integer);
CONST
   kTotalSize  = 16*1024;
   kAsync      = TRUE;      {play sound asynchronously?}
   kQuietNow   = TRUE;      {quiet channel now?}
VAR
   myErr:      OSErr;
   mySndChan:  SndChannelPtr;
BEGIN
   {allocate a sound channel}
   mySndChan := NIL;
   myErr := SndNewChannel (mySndChan, sampledSynth, initMono, NIL);
   IF myErr <> noErr THEN DoError(myErr);

   {play the 'snd ' resource}
   myErr := SndStartFilePlay(mySndChan, 0, myResNum, kTotalSize, NIL,
                             NIL, NIL, NOT kAsync);
   IF myErr <> noErr THEN DoError(myErr);

   {dispose of the channel}
   IF mySndChan <> NIL THEN
      myErr := SndDisposeChannel(mySndChan, NOT kQuietNow);
   IF myErr <> noErr THEN DoError(myErr);
END;
```


Playing a File From Disk

To play a sampled sound that is contained in a file, you need to pass SndStartFilePlay the file reference number of the file to play. The sample should be stored in either AIFF or AIFF-C format. If the sample is compressed, then it will be automatically expanded during playback.

For example, to play a sampled sound that is found in a file whose file reference number is stored in the variable myfRefNum, you could write

```
myErr := SndStartFilePlay (mySndChan, myfRefNum, 0, kTotalSize, NIL, NIL,
                           NIL, FALSE);
```

Notice that the third parameter passed to SndStartFilePlay here is set to 0. That parameter is used only when playing resources from disk.

Playing Selections

The sixth parameter passed to SndStartFilePlay is a pointer to an audio selection record, which allows you to specify that only part of the sound be played. If that parameter has a value different from NIL, then SndStartFilePlay plays only a specified selection of the entire sound. You indicate which part of the entire sound to play by giving two offsets from the beginning of the sound, a time at which to start the selection and a time at which to end the selection. Currently, both time offsets must be specified in seconds.

Here is the structure of an audio selection record:

```
TYPE AudioSelection =
     PACKED RECORD
        unitType:     LongInt;       {type of time unit}
        selStart:     Fixed;         {starting point of selection}
        selEnd:       Fixed          {ending point of selection}
     END;
```

Field descriptions

unitType — The type of unit of time used in the start and end fields. You should set this to seconds by specifying the constant unitTypeSeconds.

selStart — The starting point in seconds of the sound to play.

selEnd — The ending point in seconds of the sound to play.

Use a constant to specify the unit type.

```
CONST unitTypeSeconds      = $0000;  {seconds}
      unitTypeNoSelection  = $FFFF;  {no selection}
```

Recording Sounds Through the Sound Input Dialog Box

You can record sounds from the current input device by using the SndRecord or SndRecordToFile function. You can use the SndRecord function to present a standard user interface for recording sounds. When calling SndRecord, you need to provide a handle to a block of memory where the incoming data should be stored. If you pass the address of a NIL handle, however, the Sound Manager allocates a large block of space and resizes it when the recording stops. Listing 22-17 illustrates how to call SndRecord.

Listing 22-17. Recording through the sound input dialog box

```
PROCEDURE RecordThruDialog (VAR mySndH: Handle);
VAR
   myErr:       OSErr;
   myCorner:    Point;
BEGIN
   SetPt(myCorner, 50, 50);

   mySndH := NIL;
   myErr := SndRecord(NIL, myCorner, siBetterQuality, mySndH);
END;
```

If you pass a sound handle that is not NIL, the time of recording is derived from the amount of space reserved by that handle. The handle is resized on completion of the recording.

The first parameter in the call to SndRecord is the address of a filter procedure that determines how user actions in the dialog box are filtered. In Listing 22-17, no filter procedure is desired, so the parameter is specified as NIL. The third parameter specifies the quality of the recording. Currently three values are supported:

```
CONST siBestQuality        = 'best';       {the best quality available}
      siBetterQuality      = 'betr';       {a quality better than good}
      siGoodQuality        = 'good';       {a good quality}
```

The precise meanings of these constants are driver-specific. The constant siBestQuality indicates that you want the highest quality recorded sound, usually at the expense of increased storage space (probably because no compression is performed on the sound data). The constant siGoodQuality indicates that you are willing to sacrifice audio quality if necessary to minimize the amount of storage space required (typically this means that MACE 6:1 compression is performed on the sound data). For most voice recording, you should specify siGoodQuality. The constant siBetterQuality defines a quality and storage space combination that is between those provided by the other two constants.

After the procedure in Listing 22-17 has executed successfully, you could play the recorded sound by calling SndPlay and passing it mySndH. Note that mySndH is a handle to some data in memory that has the structure of an 'snd ' resource, not a handle to an existing resource. To save the recorded data as a resource, you can call AddResource.

To record a sound directly into a file, you can call SndRecordToFile. The SndRecordToFile function works exactly like SndRecord, except that you must pass it the file reference number of an open file instead of a handle to some memory. When SndRecordToFile exits successfully, that file contains the recorded audio data in AIFF or AIFF-C format. You can then play the recorded sound by passing that file reference number to the SndStartFilePlay function.

Recording Sounds Directly From a Device

There are a number of routines that are intended for use by applications that need more control over the recording process (such as the ability to intercept sound input data at interrupt time). You can open a sound input device and read data from it by calling these low-level Sound Manager routines. Several of these routines access information through a sound input parameter block:

```
TYPE SPB =
     RECORD
        inRefNum:          LongInt;  {reference number of input device}
        count:             LongInt;  {number of bytes to record}
        milliseconds:      LongInt;  {number of milliseconds to record}
        bufferLength:      LongInt;  {length of buffer to record into}
        bufferPtr:         Ptr;      {pointer to buffer to record into}
        completionRoutine: ProcPtr;  {pointer to a completion routine}
        interruptRoutine:  ProcPtr;  {pointer to an interrupt routine}
        userLong:          LongInt;  {for application's use}
        error:             OSErr;    {error returned after recording}
        unused1:           LongInt   {reserved}
     END;
```

Field descriptions

inRefNum	The reference number of the sound input device (as received from SPBOpenDevice) from which the recording is to occur.
count	On input, the number of bytes to record. On output, the number of bytes actually recorded. If this field specifies a longer recording time than the milliseconds field, then the milliseconds field is ignored on input.
milliseconds	On input, the number of milliseconds to record. On output, the number of milliseconds actually recorded. If this field specifies a longer recording time than the count field, then the count field is ignored on input.
bufferLength	The length of the buffer into which recorded sound data is placed. The recording time specified by the count or milliseconds field is truncated to fit into this length, if necessary.
bufferPtr	A pointer to the buffer into which recorded data is placed. If this field is NIL, then the count, milliseconds, and bufferLength fields are ignored and the recording will continue indefinitely until SPBStopRecording is called. However, the data is not stored anywhere, so setting this field to NIL is useful only if you want to do something in your interrupt routine but do not want to save the recorded sound.
completionRoutine	A pointer to a completion routine that is called when the recording terminates as a result of your calling SPBStopRecording or when the limit specified by the count or milliseconds field is reached. The completion routine executes only if SPBRecord is called asynchronously and therefore is called at interrupt time.
interruptRoutine	A pointer to a routine that is called by asynchronous recording devices when their internal buffers are full.
userLong	A long integer available for the application's own use. You can use this field, for instance, to pass a handle to an application-defined structure to the completion routine or to the interrupt routine.
error	A code describing any errors that occur during the recording. If the recording terminates without an error, this field contains noErr. If any error occurs during the recording, this field contains a value of type OSErr. If the recording is terminated by a call to SPBStopRecording, this field contains the value abortErr. You can poll this field while recording asynchronously to determine if any errors have occurred.
unused1	Reserved for use by Apple. You should always initialize this field to 0.

Listing 22-18 shows how to set up an SPB structure and record synchronously using the SPBRecord function. This procedure takes one parameter, a handle where the recorded sound data is to be stored. It is assumed that the handle is large enough to hold the sound to be recorded.

Listing 22-18. Recording directly from a sound input device

```
PROCEDURE RecordSnd (mySndH: Handle);
CONST
   kAsynch = TRUE;
VAR
   mySPB:       SPB;                          {a sound input parameter block}
   myErr:       OSErr;
   myInRefNum:  LongInt;                      {device reference number}
   myBuffSize:  LongInt;                      {size of buffer to record into}
   myHeadrLen:  Integer;                      {length of sound header}
   myNumChans:  Integer;                      {number of channels}
   mySampSize:  Integer;                      {size of a sample}
   mySampRate:  Fixed;                        {sample rate}
   myCompType:  OSType;                       {compression type}
BEGIN
   {open the default input device for reading and writing}
   myErr := SPBOpenDevice('', siWritePermission, myInRefNum);

   IF myErr = noErr THEN
   BEGIN
      {get current settings of sound input device }
      { using an application-defined routine}
      GetDeviceSettings(myInRefNum, myNumChans, mySampRate, mySampSize,
                        myCompType);

      {set up handle to contain the proper 'snd ' resource header}
      myErr := SetupSndHeader(mySndH, myNumChans, mySampRate, mySampSize,
                              myCompType, 60, 0, myHeadrLen);

      {leave room in buffer for the sound header}
      myBuffSize := GetHandleSize(mySndH) - myHeadrLen;

      {lock down the sound handle until the recording is over}
      HLock(mySndH);

      {set up the sound input parameter block}
      WITH mySPB do
      BEGIN
         inRefNum := myInRefNum;         {input device reference number}
         count := myBuffSize;            {number of bytes to record}
         milliseconds := 0;              {no milliseconds}
         bufferLength := myBuffSize;     {length of buffer}
         bufferPtr := Ptr(ORD4(mySndH^) + myHeadrLen);
                                         {put data after 'snd ' header}
         completionRoutine := NIL;       {no completion routine}
         interruptRoutine := NIL;        {no interrupt routine}
         userLong := 0;                  {no user data}
         error := noErr;                 {clear error field}
         unused1 := 0;                   {clear reserved field}
      END;
```

(Continued)

Listing 22-18. Recording directly from a sound input device (Continued)

```
      {record synchronously through the open sound input device}
      myErr := SPBRecord(@mySPB, not kAsynch);

      {recording is done, so unlock the sound handle}
      HUnlock(mySndH);

      {now fill in the number of bytes actually recorded}
      myErr := SetupSndHeader(mySndH, myNumChans, mySampRate, mySampSize,
                              myCompType, 60, mySPB.count, myHeadrLen);

      {close the input device}
      myErr := SPBCloseDevice(myInRefNum);
   END;
END;
```

The RecordSnd procedure defined in Listing 22-18 opens the default sound input device by using the SPBOpenDevice function. You can specify one of two values for the permissions parameter of SPBOpenDevice:

```
CONST siReadPermission      = 0;     {open device for reading}
      siWritePermission     = 1;     {open device for reading/writing}
```

If SPBOpenDevice successfully opens the specified device for reading and writing, RecordSnd calls the GetDeviceSettings procedure (defined in Listing 22-20). That procedure calls the Sound Manager function SPBGetDeviceInfo (explained in "Getting and Setting Sound Input Device Information" later in this chapter) to determine the current number of channels, sample rate, sample size, and compression type in use by the device.

This information is then passed to the SetupSndHeader function, which loads the initial segment of the handle with a sound header describing the current device settings. After doing this, RecordSnd sets up a sound input parameter block and calls SPBRecord to record a sound. Note that the handle must be locked during the recording because the parameter block contains a pointer to the input buffer. After the recording is done, RecordSnd calls SetupSndHeader once again to fill in the actual number of bytes recorded.

Once the procedure defined in Listing 22-18 executes successfully, the handle mySndH points to a resource of type 'snd '. Your application can then play the recorded sound, for example, by executing the following lines of code:

```
RecordSnd(mySndH);                  {procedure shown in Listing 22-18}
myErr := SndPlay(NIL, mySndH, FALSE);
```

Defining a Sound Input Completion Routine

The completionRoutine field of the SPB structure contains the address of a completion routine that executes when the recording terminates normally either by reaching its prescribed time or size limits, or by the application calling SPBStopRecording. A completion routine should have the following format:

```
PROCEDURE MyRecordCompletionRoutine (inParamPtr: SPBPtr);
```

The completion routine is passed the address of the sound input parameter block that was passed to SPBRecord. You can gain access to other data structures in your application by passing an address in the userLong field of the parameter block. After the completion routine executes, your application should check the error field of the sound input parameter block to see if an error code was returned.

Defining an Interrupt Routine

The interruptRoutine field of the sound input parameter block contains the address of a routine that executes when the internal buffers of an asynchronous recording device are filled. The internal buffers contain raw samples taken directly from the input device. The interrupt routine can modify the samples in the buffer in any way it requires. The processed samples are then written to the application buffer. If compression is enabled, then the modified data is compressed after your interrupt routine operates on the samples and before the samples are written to the application buffer. You can determine the size of the sample buffer by calling SPBGetDeviceInfo with the 'dbin' selector.

Assembly-language note: Interrupt routines are typically written in assembly language to maximize real-time performance in recording sound. On entry, registers are set up as follows:

A0:	Address of the sound parameter block passed to SPBRecord
A1:	Address of the start of the sample buffer
D0:	Peak amplitude for sample buffer if metering is on
D1:	Size of the sample buffer in bytes

Your interrupt routine is always called at interrupt time, so it should not call routines that might move or compact memory.

Getting and Setting Sound Input Device Information

You can get information about a specific sound input device and alter that information by calling the functions SPBGetDeviceInfo and SPBSetDeviceInfo. These functions accept selectors that determine which information you need or want to change. The currently defined selectors are defined by constants of type OSType:

```
CONST
   siActiveChannels        = 'chac';  {channels active}
   siActiveLevels          = 'lmac';  {levels active}
   siAGCOnOff              = 'agc ';  {automatic gain control state}
   siAsync                 = 'asyn';  {asynchronous capability}
   siNumberChannels        = 'chan';  {current number of channels}
   siChannelAvailable      = 'chav';  {number of channels available}
   siCompressionAvailable  = 'cmav';  {compression types available}
   siCompressionFactor     = 'cmfa';  {current compression factor}
   siCompressionHeader     = 'cmhd';  {return compression header}
   siCompressionType       = 'comp';  {current compression type}
```

```
      siContinuous              = 'cont';  {continuous recording}
      siDeviceBufferInfo        = 'dbin';  {size of interrupt buffer}
      siDeviceConnected         = 'dcon';  {input device connection status}
      siDeviceIcon              = 'icon';  {input device icon}
      siLevelMeterOnOff         = 'lmet';  {level meter state}
      siDeviceName              = 'name';  {input device name}
      siOptionsDialog           = 'optd';  {display options dialog box}
      siPlayThruOnOff           = 'plth';  {play-through state}
      siRecordingQuality        = 'qual';  {recording quality}
      siSampleRate              = 'srat';  {current sample rate}
      siSampleRateAvailable     = 'srav';  {sample rates available}
      siSampleSizeAvailable     = 'ssav';  {sample sizes available}
      siSampleSize              = 'ssiz';  {current sample size}
      siTwosComplementOnOff     = 'twos';  {two's complement state}
      siVoxRecordInfo           = 'voxr';  {VOX record parameters}
      siVoxStopInfo             = 'voxs';  {VOX stop parameters}
```

The format of the relevant data (either returned by the Sound Manager or provided by you) depends on the selector you provide. For example, if you want to determine the name of some sound input device, you can pass the siDeviceName selector and a pointer to a 256-byte buffer to the SPBGetDeviceInfo function. If SPBGetDeviceInfo can get the information, it fills that buffer with the name of the specified sound input device. Listing 22-19 illustrates one way you can determine the name of a particular sound input device.

Listing 22-19. Determining the name of a sound input device

```
FUNCTION DeviceName (myInRefNum: LongInt; VAR dName: Str255) : OSErr;
VAR
   myErr:   OSErr;
BEGIN
   myErr := SPBGetDeviceInfo(myInRefNum, siDeviceName, Ptr(dName));
   DeviceName := myErr;
END;
```

Some selectors cause SPBGetDeviceInfo to return data of other types. Listing 22-20 illustrates how to determine the number of channels, the sample rate, the sample size, and the compression type currently in use by a given sound input device. The procedure defined in Listing 22-20 is called in the procedure defined in Listing 22-18.

Listing 22-20. Determining some sound input device settings

```
PROCEDURE GetDeviceSettings (myInRefNum: LongInt; VAR numChannels:
                              Integer; VAR sampleRate: Fixed; VAR
                              sampleSize: Integer; VAR compressionType:
                              OSType);
VAR
   myErr:   OSErr;
BEGIN
   {get number of active channels}
   myErr := SPBGetDeviceInfo(myInRefNum, siNumberChannels,
                              Ptr(@numChannels));
```

```
    {get sample rate}
    myErr := SPBGetDeviceInfo(myInRefNum, siSampleRate,
                              Ptr(@sampleRate));
    {get sample size}
    myErr := SPBGetDeviceInfo(myInRefNum, siSampleSize,
                              Ptr(@sampleSize));
    {get compression type}
    myErr := SPBGetDeviceInfo(myInRefNum, siCompressionType,
                              Ptr(@compressionType));
END;
```

Some other selectors return a list of items, which your application must interpret. Table 22-5 lists the available selectors together with the size and meaning of the associated information whose address is passed or returned in the infoData parameter. Note that all of the selectors returning a handle will allocate the memory for that handle in the current heap zone; you are responsible for disposing of that handle when you are done with it.

Table 22-5. Sound input device information selectors

Selector	Description		
'agc '	Gets or sets the current state of the automatic gain control feature.		
	infoData	Integer	0 if off, 1 if on
'asyn'	Determines if driver supports asynchronous recording functions. Some sound input drivers might support synchronous recording only.		
	infoData	Integer	0 if synchronous calls only, 1 otherwise
'chac'	Gets or sets the channels to record from. When setting the active channels, the data passed in is a long integer that is interpreted as a bitmap describing the channels to record from. For example, if bit 0 is set, then the first channel is made active. The samples for each active channel are stored one after another in the application's buffer. When reading the active channels, the data returned is a bitmap of the active channels.		
	infoData	LongInt	bitmap of active channels
'chan'	Gets or sets the number of channels this device is to record.		
	infoData	Integer	number of channels
'chav'	Gets the maximum number of channels this device can record.		
	infoData	Integer	number of available channels
'cmav'	Gets the number and list of compression types this device can produce.		
	infoData	Integer	number of compression types supported
		Handle	list of compression types (each is OSType, 4 bytes)
'cmfa'	Gets the number of samples per byte at the current compression setting.		
	infoData	Integer	compression factor
'cmhd'	Gets a compression header for the current recording settings. Your application passes in a pointer to a compressed sound header and the driver fills it in. Before calling SPBGetDeviceInfo with this selector, you should set the numFrames field of the compressed sound header to the number of bytes in the sound. When SPBGetDeviceInfo returns successfully, that field contains the number		

(Continued)

Table 22-5. Sound input device information selectors (Continued)

Selector	Description
'cmhd' *(continued)*	of sample frames in the sound. This selector is needed only by drivers that use compression types that are not directly supported by Apple. If you call this selector after recording a sound, your application can get enough information about the sound to play it or save it in a file. infoData Pointer pointer to a compressed sound header
'comp'	Gets or sets the compression type. Some devices allow the incoming samples to be compressed before being placed in your application's input buffer. infoData OSType compression type
'cont'	Gets or sets the state of continuous recording from this device. If continuous recording is being turned on, the driver records samples into an internal buffer between calls to SPBRecord. This allows a subsequent recording to begin where the previous one stopped. If continuous recording is being turned off, the driver stops recording samples to its internal buffer. infoData Integer state of continuous recording (0 is off, 1 is on)
'dbin'	Gets the size of the device's internal buffer. This information can be useful when you want to modify sound input data at interrupt time. infoData LongInt size of device's internal buffer

'dcon'	Gets the state of the device connection.
	infoData Integer one of the following values:
	`CONST`
	`siDeviceIsConnected = 1; {device is connected and ready}`
	`siDeviceNotConnected = 0; {device is not connected}`
	`siDontKnowIfConnected = -1; {can't tell if device connected}`

'icon'	Gets the device's icon and icon mask. infoData Handle icon and icon mask
'lmac'	Gets the current signal level for each active channel. Each value returned is an integer, and the number of values returned depends on the number of active channels. You can determine how many channels are active by calling SPBGetDeviceInfo with the 'chan' selector. infoData Integer level meter setting
'lmet'	Gets or sets the current state of the level meter. Once the level meter has been turned on, calling SPBGetDeviceInfo returns a value in the level meter setting that ranges from 0 (no volume) to 255 (full volume). infoData Integer state of level meter (0 is off, 1 is on) Integer level meter setting
'name'	Gets the name of the sound input device. Your application must pass a pointer to a buffer that will be filled in with the device's name. The buffer needs to be large enough to hold a Str255 data type. infoData Pointer pointer to buffer for name of device

Table 22-5. Sound input device information selectors (Continued)

Selector	Description
'optd'	Gets or sets the Options dialog box feature. The Options dialog box is designed to allow the user to configure device-specific features of the sound input hardware. Note that no argument should be supplied when you pass this selector to SPBSetDeviceInfo. infoData Integer 1 if device supports options, 0 otherwise
'plth'	Gets or sets the current play-through volume. infoData Integer volume (0 is off, 1–7 otherwise)
'qual'	Gets or sets the current quality of recorded sound. Currently three qualities are supported: 'good', 'betr', and 'best'. infoData OSType recording quality
'srat'	Gets or sets the sample rate to be produced by this device. The sample rate must be in the range 0 to 65535.99998 Hz. Note that the sample rate is declared as a Fixed data type, but the most significant bit is not treated as a sign bit; instead, that bit is interpreted as having the value 32,768. infoData Fixed sample rate
'srav'	Gets the range of sample rates this device can produce. The first 2 bytes of the information returned specify how many different sample rates the device supports. If that number is 0, then the next two sample rates define a continuous range of sample rates. Otherwise, a list is returned that contains the sample rates supported. Each sample rate is of type Fixed and occupies 4 bytes. Note that the sample rates are declared as Fixed data types, but their most significant bit is not treated as a sign bit; instead, that bit is interpreted as having the value 32,768. infoData Integer number of sample rates Handle list of sample rates
'ssav'	Gets the range of sample sizes supported by this device. The first 2 bytes of the information returned specify how many different sample sizes the device supports. A list is returned that contains the sample sizes supported. Each sample size is an integer and occupies 2 bytes. infoData Integer number of sample sizes Handle list of sample sizes
'ssiz'	Gets or sets the sample size to be produced by this device. Because some compression formats require specific sample sizes, this selector may return an error when compression is used. infoData Integer sample size
'twos'	Gets or sets the current state of the two's complement feature. infoData Integer 1 if two's complement output desired, 0 otherwise
'voxr'	Gets or sets the current VOX record parameters. The first 2 bytes of the infoData parameter indicate whether VOX recording is on or off. The next 2 bytes contain the VOX record trigger value. Trigger values range from 0 to 255 (0 is trigger immediately, 255 is trigger only on full volume). infoData Integer 0 if off, 1 if on Integer record trigger value

(Continued)

Table 22-5. Sound input device information selectors (Continued)

Selector	Description
'voxs'	Gets or sets the current VOX stop parameters. The first 2 bytes of the infoData parameter indicate whether VOX stopping is on or off. The next 2 bytes contain the VOX stop trigger value. Trigger values range from 0 to 255 (255 is stop immediately, 0 is stop only on total silence). The final 2 bytes indicate how many milliseconds the trigger value must be continuously valid for recording to be stopped. Delay values range from 0 to 65,535. infoData Integer 0 if off, 1 if on Integer record trigger value Integer delay value

Obtaining Information About Sound Features

Developments in the sound hardware available on Macintosh computers and in the Sound Manager routines that allow you to drive that hardware have made it imperative that your application pays close attention to the sound-related features of the operating environment. For example, the routines that provide continuous play from disk operate only on machines that are equipped with an Apple Sound Chip that have the enhanced Sound Manager. So before issuing any play-from-disk calls, you should check to make sure that the target machine provides the features you need.

Similarly, the ability to have multiple channels of sound open simultaneously makes it important that you monitor the load placed on the CPU by those channels. The enhanced Sound Manager provides several new routines that you can use to determine information about open sound channels and the amount of CPU loading they create.

To make appropriate decisions about the sound you want to produce, you may need to know some or all of the following types of information:

- whether the machine can produce stereophonic sounds
- whether the internal speaker mixes both right and left channels of sound
- whether the sound input routines and hardware are available
- whether multiple channels of sound are supported
- how much CPU load is produced by a single channel of sound or by all channels of sound
- whether the system beep has been disabled
- how much of the available processing power a new channel of sound would consume
- whether a sound playing from disk is active or paused
- how many channels of sound are currently open

To determine how much of the available processing power a new channel of sound would consume, you can use the loadCmd sound command, described earlier in "Managing the CPU Load." The following sections describe how to use the Gestalt function and new Sound Manager routines to determine these other types of information.

Obtaining Information About Available Sound Features

You can use the Gestalt function with the gestaltSoundAttr selector to determine whether various new Sound Manager capabilities are present (for example, whether the machine can produce stereophonic sounds and whether it can mix both left and right channels of sound on the external speaker). Currently, Gestalt returns a bit field that may have some or all of the following bits set:

```
CONST
   gestaltStereoCapability     = 0;  {stereo capability present}
   gestaltStereoMixing         = 1;  {stereo mixing on internal speaker}
   gestaltSoundIOMgrPresent    = 3;  {sound input routines available}
   gestaltBuiltInSoundInput    = 4;  {built-in input device available}
   gestaltHasSoundInputDevice  = 5;  {sound input device available}
```


If the bit gestaltStereoCapability is TRUE, the available hardware can play stereo sounds. The bit gestaltStereoMixing indicates that the sound hardware of the machine mixes both left and right channels of stereo sound into a single audio signal for the internal speaker. The gestaltSoundIOMgrPresent bit indicates that the new sound input routines are available, and the gestaltBuiltInSoundInput bit indicates that a built-in sound input device is available. The gestaltHasSoundInputDevice bit indicates that some sound input device is available.

Obtaining Version Information

The Sound Manager provides functions that allow you to determine the version numbers of the Sound Manager itself and of two distinct subsets of the Sound Manager routines, the MACE compression and expansion routines and the sound input routines. Generally, you should avoid trying to determine which features or routines are present by reading a version number. Usually, the Gestalt function discussed in the previous section provides a better way to find out if some set of features, such as sound input capability, is available. In some cases, however, you can use these version routines to overcome current limitations of the information returned by Gestalt.

All three of these functions return a value of type NumVersion that contains the same information as the first 4 bytes of a resource of type 'vers'. The first and second bytes contain the major and minor version numbers, respectively; the third and fourth bytes contain the release level and the stage of the release level. For most purposes, the major and minor release version numbers are sufficient to identify the version. (See the Finder Interface chapter in this volume for a complete discussion of the format of 'vers' resources.)

You can use the SndSoundManagerVersion function to determine which version of the Sound Manager is present. The Sound Manager provided with system software version 6.0.7 and later contains the routines supporting multichannel sound, play from disk, and channel status inquiries.

You can use the MACEVersion function to determine the version number of the available MACE routines (for example, Comp3to1).

You can use the SPBVersion function to determine the version number of the available sound input routines (for example, SndRecord). If SPBVersion returns a value that is greater than 0, then the sound input routines are available.

Obtaining Information About a Single Sound Channel

You can use the SndChannelStatus function to obtain information about a single sound channel and about the status of a disk-based playback on that channel, if one exists. For example, you can use SndChannelStatus to determine if a channel is being used for play from disk, how many seconds of the sound have been played, and how many seconds remain to be played.

One of the parameters required by the SndChannelStatus function is a pointer to a sound-channel status record, which you must allocate before calling SndChannelStatus. A sound-channel status record has this structure:

```
TYPE SCStatus =
   RECORD
      scStartTime:          Fixed;   {starting time for play from disk}
      scEndTime:            Fixed;   {ending time for play from disk}
      scCurrentTime:        Fixed;   {current time for play from disk}
      scChannelBusy:        Boolean; {TRUE if channel is making sound}
      scChannelDisposed:    Boolean; {reserved}
      scChannelPaused:      Boolean; {TRUE if channel is paused}
      scUnused:             Boolean; {unused}
      scChannelAttributes:  LongInt; {attributes of this channel}
      scCPULoad:            LongInt  {CPU load for this channel}
   END;
```

Field descriptions

scStartTime	If scChannelBusy is TRUE, then scStartTime is the starting time in seconds for a play from disk on the specified channel. If scChannelBusy is FALSE, then scStartTime is 0.
scEndTime	If scChannelBusy is TRUE, then scEndTime is the ending time in seconds for a play from disk on the specified channel. If scChannelBusy is FALSE, then scEndTime is 0.
scCurrentTime	If scChannelBusy is TRUE, then scCurrentTime is the current time in seconds for a play from disk on the specified channel. If scChannelBusy is FALSE, then scCurrentTime is 0.
scChannelBusy	If the specified channel is currently making sound, then scChannelBusy is TRUE; otherwise, scChannelBusy is FALSE.
scChannelDisposed	Reserved for use by Apple.
scChannelPaused	If the specified channel is paused, then scChannelPaused is TRUE; otherwise, scChannelPaused is FALSE.

scUnused — Reserved for use by Apple.

scChannelAttributes — The current attributes of the specified channel. These attributes are in the channel initialization parameters format.

scCPULoad — The CPU load for the specified channel.

You can mask out certain values in the scChannelAttributes field to how a channel has been initialized.

```
CONST initPanMask      = $0003;     {mask for right/left pan values}
      initSRateMask    = $0030;     {mask for sample rate values}
      initStereoMask   = $00C0;     {mask for mono/stereo values}
      initCompMask     = $FF00;     {mask for compression IDs}
```

Listing 22-21 illustrates the use of the SndChannelStatus function. It defines a function that takes a sound-channel pointer as a parameter and determines whether a disk-based playback on that channel is paused.

Listing 22-21. Determining whether a sound channel is paused

```
FUNCTION ChannelIsPaused (chan: SndChannelPtr) : Boolean;
VAR
   myErr:      OSErr;
   mySCStatus: SCStatus;
BEGIN
   ChannelIsPaused := FALSE;
   myErr := SndChannelStatus (chan, Sizeof(SCStatus), @mySCStatus);
   IF myErr = noErr THEN
      ChannelIsPaused := mySCStatus.scChannelPaused;
END;
```

The function defined here simply reads the scChannelPaused field to see if the playback is currently paused.

Obtaining Information About All Sound Channels

You can use the SndManagerStatus function to determine information about all the sound channels that are currently allocated by all applications. For example, you can use this function to determine how many channels are currently allocated.

One of the parameters required by the SndManagerStatus function is a pointer to a Sound Manager status record, which you must allocate before calling SndManagerStatus. A Sound Manager status record has this structure:

```
TYPE SMStatus =
     PACKED RECORD
        smMaxCPULoad:    Integer;    {maximum load on all channels}
        smNumChannels:   Integer;    {number of allocated channels}
        smCurCPULoad:    Integer     {current load on all channels}
     END;
```

Field descriptions

smMaxCPULoad — The maximum load that the Sound Manager will not exceed when allocating channels. The smMaxCPULoad field is set to a default value of 100 when the system starts up.

smNumChannels — The number of sound channels that are currently allocated by all applications. This does not mean that the channels allocated are being used, only that they have been allocated and that CPU loading is being reserved for these channels.

smCurCPULoad — The CPU load that is being taken up by currently allocated channels.

Listing 22-22 illustrates the use of SndManagerStatus. It defines a function that returns the number of sound channels currently allocated by all applications.

Listing 22-22. Determining the number of allocated sound channels

```
FUNCTION NumChannelsAllocated : Integer;
VAR
   myErr:       OSErr;
   mySMStatus: SMStatus;
BEGIN
   NumChannelsAllocated := 0;
   myErr := SndManagerStatus (Sizeof(SMStatus), @mySMStatus);
   IF myErr = noErr THEN
      NumChannelsAllocated := mySMStatus.smNumChannels;
END;
```

Using Double Buffers

The play-from-disk routines make extensive use of the SndPlayDoubleBuffer function. You can use this function in your application if you wish to bypass the normal play-from-disk routines. You might want to do this if you wish to maximize the efficiency of your application while maintaining compatibility with the Sound Manager. By using SndPlayDoubleBuffer instead of the normal play-from-disk routines, you can specify your own doubleback procedure (that is, the algorithm used to switch back and forth between buffers) and customize several other buffering parameters.

> **Note:** SndPlayDoubleBuffer is a very low-level routine and is not intended for general use. You should use SndPlayDoubleBuffer only if you require very fine control over double buffering.

You call SndPlayDoubleBuffer by passing it a pointer to a sound channel (into which the double-buffered data is to be written) and a pointer to a sound double-buffer header. Here's an example:

```
myErr := SndPlayDoubleBuffer (mySndChan, @myDoubleHeader);
```

A SndDoubleBufferHeader record has the following structure:

```
TYPE SndDoubleBufferHeader =
     PACKED RECORD
         dbhNumChannels:     Integer;    {number of sound channels}
         dbhSampleSize:      Integer;    {sample size, if uncompressed}
         dbhCompressionID:   Integer;    {ID of compression algorithm}
         dbhPacketSize:      Integer;    {number of bits per packet}
         dbhSampleRate:      Fixed;      {sample rate}
         dbhBufferPtr:       ARRAY[0..1] OF SndDoubleBufferPtr;
                                         {pointers to SndDoubleBuffer}
         dbhDoubleBack:      ProcPtr     {pointer to doubleback procedure}
     END;
```

Field descriptions

dbhNumChannels — Indicates the number of channels for the sound (1 for monophonic sound, 2 for stereo).

dbhSampleSize — Indicates the sample size for the sound if the sound is not compressed. If the sound is compressed, dbhSampleSize should be set to 0. Samples that are 1–8 bits have a dbhSampleSize value of 8; samples that are 9–16 bits have a dbhSampleSize value of 16. Currently, only 8-bit samples are supported. For further information on sample sizes, refer to the AIFF specification.

dbhCompressionID — Indicates the compression identification number of the compression algorithm, if the sound is compressed. If the sound is not compressed, dbhCompressionID should be set to 0.

dbhPacketSize — Indicates the packet size for the compression algorithm specified by dbhCompressionID, if the sound is compressed.

dbhSampleRate — Indicates the sample rate for the sound. Note that the sample rate is declared as a Fixed data type, but the most significant bit is not treated as a sign bit; instead, that bit is interpreted as having the value 32,768.

dbhBufferPtr — Indicates an array of two pointers, each of which should point to a valid SndDoubleBuffer record.

dbhDoubleBack — Points to the application-defined routine that is called when the double buffers are switched and the exhausted buffer needs to be refilled.

The values for the dbhCompressionID, dbhNumChannels, and dbhPacketSize fields are the same as those for the compressionID, numChannels, and packetSize fields of the compressed sound header, respectively.

The dbhBufferPtr array contains pointers to two records of type SndDoubleBuffer. These are the two buffers between which the Sound Manager switches until all the sound data has been sent into the sound channel. When the call to SndPlayDoubleBuffer is made, the two buffers should both already contain a nonzero number of frames of data.

Here is the structure of a sound double buffer:

```
TYPE SndDoubleBuffer =
     PACKED RECORD
       dbNumFrames: LongInt;                    {number of frames in buffer}
       dbFlags:     LongInt;                    {buffer status flags}
       dbUserInfo:  ARRAY[0..1] OF LongInt;     {for application's use}
       dbSoundData: PACKED ARRAY[0..0] OF Byte
                                                {array of data}
     END;
```

Field descriptions

dbNumFrames	The number of frames in the dbSoundData array.
dbFlags	Buffer status flags.
dbUserInfo	Two long words into which you can place information that you need to access in your doubleback procedure.
dbSoundData	A variable-length array. You write samples into this array, and the synthesizer reads samples out of this array.

The buffer status flags field for each of the two buffers may contain either of these values:

```
CONST dbBufferReady          = $00000001;
      dbLastBuffer           = $00000004;
```

All other bits in the dbFlags field are reserved by Apple, and your application should not modify them.

The following two sections illustrate how to fill out these data structures, create your two buffers, and define a doubleback procedure to refill the buffers when they become empty.

Setting Up Double Buffers

Before you can call SndPlayDoubleBuffer, you need to allocate two buffers (of type SndDoubleBuffer), fill them both with data, set the flags for the two buffers to dbBufferReady, and then fill out a record of type SndDoubleBufferHeader with the appropriate information. Listing 22-23 illustrates how you might accomplish these tasks.

Listing 22-23. Setting up double buffers

```
CONST
   kDoubleBufferSize = 4096;         {size of each buffer (in bytes)}

TYPE
   LocalVarsPtr = ^LocalVars;
```

```
   LocalVars =                           {variables used by doubleback proc}
   RECORD
      bytesTotal:    LongInt;            {total number of samples}
      bytesCopied:   LongInt;            {number of samples copied to buffers}
      dataPtr:       Ptr                 {pointer to sample to copy}
   END;

{This function uses SndPlayDoubleBuffer to play the sound specified.}
FUNCTION DBSndPlay (chan: SndChannelPtr; sndHeader: SoundHeaderPtr) :
                    OSErr;
VAR
   myVars:         LocalVars;
   doubleHeader:   SndDoubleBufferHeader;
   doubleBuffer:   SndDoubleBufferPtr;
   status:         SCStatus;
   i:              Integer;
   err:            OSErr;
BEGIN
   {set up myVars with initial information}
   myVars.bytesTotal := sndHeader^.length;
   myVars.bytesCopied := 0;                      {no samples copied yet}
   myVars.dataPtr := Ptr(@sndHeader^.sampleArea[0]);
                                                 {pointer to first sample}
   {set up SndDoubleBufferHeader}
   doubleHeader.dbhNumChannels := 1;             {one channel}
   doubleHeader.dbhSampleSize := 8;              {8-bit samples}
   doubleHeader.dbhCompressionID := 0;           {no compression}
   doubleHeader.dbhPacketSize := 0;              {no compression}
   doubleHeader.dbhSampleRate := sndHeader^.sampleRate;
   doubleHeader.dbhDoubleBack := @MyDoubleBackProc;

   FOR i := 0 TO 1 DO                            {initialize both buffers}
   BEGIN
      {get memory for double buffer}
      doubleBuffer := SndDoubleBufferPtr(NewPtr(Sizeof(SndDoubleBuffer) +
                                         kDoubleBufferSize));
      IF doubleBuffer = NIL THEN
         BEGIN
            DBSndPlay := MemError;
            DoError;
         END;

      doubleBuffer^.dbNumFrames := 0;            {no frames yet}
      doubleBuffer^.dbFlags := 0;                {buffer is empty}
      doubleBuffer^.dbUserInfo[0] := LongInt(@myVars);

      {fill buffer with samples}
      MyDoubleBackProc(sndChan, doubleBuffer);

      {store buffer pointer in header}
      doubleHeader.dbhBufferPtr[i] := doubleBuffer;
   END;
```

(Continued)

Listing 22-23. Setting up double buffers (Continued)

```
    {start the sound playing}
    err := SndPlayDoubleBuffer(sndChan, @doubleHeader);
    IF err <> noErr THEN
       BEGIN
          DBSndPlay := err;
          DoError;
       END;

    {wait for the sound to complete by watching the channel status}
    REPEAT
       err := SndChannelStatus(chan, sizeof(status), @status);
    UNTIL NOT status.scChannelBusy;

    {dispose double-buffer memory}
    FOR i := 0 TO 1 DO
       DisposPtr(Ptr(doubleHeader.dbhBufferPtr[i]));

    DBSndPlay := noErr;
END;
```

The function DBSndPlay takes two parameters, a pointer to a sound channel and a pointer to a sound header. It reads the sound header to determine the characteristics of the sound to be played (for example, how many samples are to be sent into the sound channel). Then DBSndPlay fills in the fields of the double-buffer header, creates two buffers, and starts the sound playing. The doubleback procedure MyDoubleBackProc is defined in the next section.

Writing a Doubleback Procedure

The dbhDoubleBack field of a double-buffer header specifies the address of a doubleback procedure, an application-defined procedure that is called when the double buffers are switched and the exhausted buffer needs to be refilled. The doubleback procedure should have this format:

```
PROCEDURE MyDoubleBackProc (chan: SndChannelPtr; exhaustedBuffer:
                            SndDoubleBufferPtr);
```

The primary responsibility of the doubleback procedure is to refill an exhausted buffer of samples and to mark the newly filled buffer as ready for processing. Listing 22-24 illustrates how to define a doubleback procedure. Note that the sound-channel pointer passed to the doubleback procedure is not used in this procedure.

This doubleback procedure extracts the address of its local variables from the dbUserInfo field of the double-buffer record passed to it. These variables are used to keep track of how many total bytes need to be copied and how many bytes have been copied so far. Then the procedure copies at most a buffer-full of bytes into the empty buffer and updates several fields in the double-buffer record and in the structure containing the local variables. Finally, if all the bytes to be copied have been copied, the buffer is marked as the last buffer.

Note: Because the doubleback procedure is called at interrupt time, it cannot make any calls that move memory either directly or indirectly. (Despite its name, the BlockMove procedure does not cause blocks of memory to move or be purged, so you can safely call it in your doubleback procedure, as illustrated in Listing 22-24.)

Listing 22-24. Defining a doubleback procedure

```
PROCEDURE MyDoubleBackProc (chan: SndChannelPtr; doubleBuffer:
                            SndDoubleBufferPtr);
VAR
   myVarsPtr:      LocalVarsPtr;
   bytesToCopy:    LongInt;
BEGIN
   {get pointer to my local variables}
   myVarsPtr := LocalVarsPtr(doubleBuffer^.dbUserInfo[0]);

   {get number of bytes left to copy}
   bytesToCopy := myVarsPtr^.bytesTotal - myVarsPtr^.bytesCopied;

   {If the amount left is greater than double-buffer size, }
   { then limit the number of bytes to copy to the size of the buffer.}
   IF bytesToCopy > kDoubleBufferSize THEN
      bytesToCopy := kDoubleBufferSize;

   {copy samples to double buffer}
   BlockMove(myVarsPtr^.dataPtr, @doubleBuffer^.dbSoundData[0],
             bytesToCopy);

   {store number of samples in buffer and mark buffer as ready}
   doubleBuffer^.dbNumFrames := bytesToCopy;
   doubleBuffer^.dbFlags := BOR(doubleBuffer^.dbFlags, dbBufferReady);

   {update data pointer and number of bytes copied}
   myVarsPtr^.dataPtr := Ptr(ORD4(myVarsPtr^.dataPtr) + bytesToCopy);
   myVarsPtr^.bytesCopied := myVarsPtr^.bytesCopied + bytesToCopy;

   {If all samples have been copied, then this is the last buffer.}
   IF myVarsPtr^.bytesCopied = myVarsPtr^.bytesTotal THEN
      doubleBuffer^.dbFlags := BOR(doubleBuffer^.dbFlags, dbLastBuffer);
END;
```

Specifying Callback Routines

The SndNewChannel function allows you to associate a completion routine or callback procedure with a sound channel. This procedure is called whenever a callBackCmd command is received by the synthesizer linked to that channel, and the procedure can be used for various purposes. Generally, your application uses a callback procedure to determine that the channel has completed its commands and to arrange for disposal of the channel. The callback procedure cannot itself dispose of the channel because it may execute at interrupt time. A callback procedure can also be used to signal that a channel has reached a certain point in the queue. Your application may wish to perform particular actions based on how far along the sequence of commands a channel has processed. This allows you, for example, to synchronize sound output with other actions in the computer.

A callback procedure has the following syntax:

```
PROCEDURE MyCallBack (chan: SndChannelPtr; cmd: SndCommand);
```

When called, the procedure is passed two parameters—a pointer to the sound channel that received the callBackCmd command and the sound command that caused the callback procedure to be called. Applications can use param1 or param2 of the sound command as flags to pass information or instructions to the callback procedure. If a callback procedure is to use an application's global data storage, it must first reset A5 to the application's A5 and then restore it on exit. For example, Listing 22-25 illustrates how to set up a callBackCmd command that contains the required A5 information. The InstallCallBack function defined there must be called at a time when the application's A5 world is known to be valid.

Listing 22-25. Issuing a callback command

```
FUNCTION InstallCallBack (mySndChan: SndChannelPtr) : OSErr;
CONST
   kWaitIfFull =  TRUE;                {wait for room in queue}
VAR
   mySndCmd:    SndCommand;
BEGIN
   mySndCmd.cmd := callBackCmd;        {install the callback command}
   mySndCmd.param1 := kSoundComplete;  {last command for this channel}
   mySndCmd.param2 := SetCurrentA5;    {pass the callback the A5}
   InstallCallBack := SndDoCommand (mySndChan, mySndCmd, kWaitIfFull);
END;
```

In this function, kSoundComplete is an application-defined global constant that indicates that the requested sound has finished playing. You could define it like this:

```
CONST kSoundComplete =  1;                  {sound is done playing}
```

Because param2 of a sound command is a long integer, you can use it to pass the application's A5 to the callback procedure. That allows the callback procedure to gain access to the application's A5 world. The sample callback procedure defined in Listing 22-26 can set A5 to access the application's global variables when the synthesizer receives this command.

Here, the callback procedure simply sets a global variable that indicates that the callback procedure has been called. The application can then read that variable to determine that it can safely dispose of the corresponding sound channel. The functions SetCurrentA5 and SetA5 are documented in the Memory Management chapter in this volume.

> **Note:** These callback routines are called at interrupt time and therefore must not attempt to allocate, move, or dispose of memory, dereference an unlocked handle, or call other routines that do so.

Listing 22-26. Defining a callback procedure

```
PROCEDURE SampleCallBack (theChan: SndChannelPtr; theCmd: SndCommand);
VAR
   myA5: LongInt;
BEGIN
   IF (theCmd.param1 = kSoundComplete) THEN
      BEGIN
         myA5 := SetA5(theCmd.param2); {set my A5}
         gCallBackPerformed := TRUE;   {set a global flag}
         myA5 := SetA5(myA5);          {restore the current A5}
      END;
END;
```

Assembly-language note: A callback procedure is a Pascal procedure and must preserve all registers other than A0–A1 and D0–D2.

SOUND MANAGER ROUTINES

This section describes the routines you use to play 'snd ' resources, allocate new sound channels and dispose of old ones, send sound commands to a synthesizer, play sounds directly from disk, balance CPU loading during sound production, determine the status of sound channels, and manage the reading and writing of sound double buffers.

This section also describes the routines you can use to record sound on machines equipped with some sound input hardware. The Sound Manager provides two general classes of sound input routines, a set of high-level routines for recording and storing sound input from the user, and a set of low-level routines. Most applications should be able to accomplish all sound input by using just the high-level routines. The low-level routines are provided primarily for applications that need more control over the recording process or that need to intercept sound input data at interrupt time. There are also low-level routines that are intended for use by sound input drivers.

Playing Sound Resources

You can use the SndPlay function to play the sounds that are stored in an 'snd ' resource, either format 1 or format 2. You can use the SysBeep procedure to play the system alert sound. Alert sounds are stored in the System file as format 1 'snd ' resources. The user selects an alert sound in the Sound control panel. The default alert sound is a simple beep.

SndPlay and SysBeep are the highest-level sound routines and are generally used separately from the other Sound Manager routines. Depending on the needs of your application, you may be able to accomplish all desired sound-related activity simply by using SysBeep to produce the system alert sound or by using SndPlay to play other sounds that are stored as 'snd ' resources.

```
FUNCTION SndPlay (chan: SndChannelPtr; sndHdl: Handle; async: Boolean) :
                  OSErr;
```

SndPlay attempts to play the sound located at sndHdl, which is expected to have the structure of a format 1 or format 2 'snd ' resource. If the sound handle is in format 1 and specifies a synthesizer, then the appropriate 'snth' resource is loaded into memory and linked to the channel. All commands and data contained in the sound handle are then sent to the channel. Note that you can pass SndPlay a handle to some data created by calling SndRecord as well as a handle to an actual 'snd ' resource that you have loaded into memory.

The chan parameter is a pointer to a sound channel. If your application passes NIL as the channel pointer, the Sound Manager creates a channel in your application's heap. The Sound Manager releases this memory after the sound has completed. If your application passes NIL as the sound-channel pointer, the async parameter is ignored and the sound plays synchronously.

If, however, your application does supply a sound-channel pointer in the chan parameter, then the sound can be produced asynchronously. When a sound is played asynchronously, a completion routine can be called when the last command has finished processing. This procedure is the callback procedure supplied to SndNewChannel.

If a format 1 'snd ' resource does not specify which synthesizer is to be used, SndPlay defaults to the square-wave synthesizer. SndPlay also supports format 2 'snd ' resources using the sampled sound synthesizer and a bufferCmd command. Note that to use SndPlay and the sampled sound synthesizer with a format 1 'snd ' resource, you must include a bufferCmd command in the resource.

Result codes

noErr	0	No error
resProblem	–204	Problem loading the resource
badChannel	–205	Channel is corrupt or unusable
badFormat	–206	Resource is corrupt or unusable

```
PROCEDURE SysBeep (duration: Integer);
```

The SysBeep procedure causes the Sound Manager to play the system alert sound selected in the Sound control panel. The duration parameter specifies the duration (in ticks) of the resulting sound and is used only on a Macintosh Plus, Macintosh SE, or Macintosh Classic when the system alert sound is the Simple Beep. In all other cases, the duration parameter is ignored, but you must specify it when you call this procedure.

The volume of the sound produced depends on the setting of the current speaker volume, which the user can adjust in the Sound control panel. If the speaker volume has been set to 0 (silent) and the system alert sound is enabled, SysBeep causes the menu bar to blink once.

```
PROCEDURE SndGetSysBeepState (VAR sysBeepState: Integer);
```

SndGetSysBeepState is used to determine whether SysBeep is enabled. It returns one of two states in the sysBeepState parameter, either the sysBeepDisable or the sysBeepEnable constant.

```
FUNCTION SndSetSysBeepState (sysBeepState: Integer) : OSErr;
```

You can use SndSetSysBeepState to set the state of the system alert sound. The sysBeepState parameter should be set to either sysBeepDisable or sysBeepEnable.

Result codes

noErr	0	No error
paramErr	–50	A parameter is incorrect

Allocating and Releasing Sound Channels

You can allocate a new sound channel by using the SndNewChannel function.

```
FUNCTION SndNewChannel (VAR chan: SndChannelPtr; synth: Integer;
                        init: LongInt; userRoutine: ProcPtr) : OSErr;
```

If you pass a pointer to NIL as the chan parameter, SndNewChannel allocates a sound-channel record in your application's heap and returns a pointer to that record. Applications that allocate their own channel memory can pass a pointer to a sound-channel record in the chan parameter. Each channel holds 128 commands as a default size. Your application can allocate a channel that is larger or smaller than the default size by creating its own channel in memory.

The synth parameter specifies which playback synthesizer is to be used. You specify a synthesizer by its resource ID, and this 'snth' resource is loaded into memory and linked to the channel. To create a channel without linking it to a synthesizer, pass 0 as the synth parameter. In general, however, you should specify a nonzero value in the synth parameter to ensure that CPU load tests are performed and hence that you can actually produce sound in the new channel.

The init parameter specifies an initialization option that should be sent to the synthesizer when you open the channel. For example, to open the third wave-table channel, use initChan2 as the init parameter. Only the wave-table synthesizer and sampled sound synthesizer currently use the init options. To determine if a particular option is understood by the synthesizer, use the availableCmd command with the SndControl function.

If your application produces sounds asynchronously or needs to be alerted when a command has completed, define a callback procedure and pass a pointer to that procedure in the userRoutine parameter. This routine is called once the synthesizer has received the callBackCmd command. If you pass NIL as the userRoutine parameter, then any callBackCmd commands are ignored.

Result codes

noErr	0	No error
resProblem	–204	Problem loading the resource
badChannel	–205	Channel is corrupt or unusable

To release the memory previously allocated to a sound channel that is no longer needed, call SndDisposeChannel.

```
FUNCTION SndDisposeChannel (chan: SndChannelPtr; quietNow: Boolean) :
                            OSErr;
```

The SndDisposeChannel function disposes of the channel specified in the chan parameter and releases all memory allocated by the Sound Manager for that channel. If your application created its own sound-channel record in memory or installed a sound as a voice, the Sound Manager does not dispose of that memory.

SndDisposeChannel can dispose of a channel immediately or wait until the queued commands are processed. If quietNow is set to TRUE, a flushCmd command and then a quietCmd command are sent to the channel. This removes all commands, stops any sound in progress, and closes the channel. If quietNow is set to FALSE, then the Sound Manager issues a quietCmd command only and waits until the quietCmd command is received by the synthesizer before disposing of the channel.

Result codes

noErr	0	No error
badChannel	–205	Channel is corrupt or unusable

Linking Synthesizers to Sound Channels

The Sound Manager uses the SndAddModifier function to link synthesizers to sound channels.

```
FUNCTION SndAddModifier (chan: SndChannelPtr; modifier: ProcPtr; id:
                         Integer; init: LongInt) : OSErr;
```

SndAddModifier installs a synthesizer into an open channel specified in the chan parameter. The modifier parameter should be NIL, and the id parameter is the resource ID of the synthesizer. SndAddModifier causes the Sound Manager to load the 'snth' resource, lock it in memory, and link it to the channel specified.

Note: SndAddModifier is for internal Sound Manager use only. You should not call it in your application.

Result codes

noErr	0	No error
resProblem	–204	Problem loading the resource
badChannel	–205	Channel is corrupt or unusable

Sending Commands to a Sound Channel

Once a sound channel is opened and linked to a particular synthesizer, you can send commands to that synthesizer by issuing requests with the SndDoCommand and SndDoImmediate functions.

```
FUNCTION SndDoCommand (chan: SndChannelPtr; cmd: SndCommand; noWait:
                       Boolean) : OSErr;
```

The SndDoCommand function sends the sound command specified in the cmd parameter to the command queue of the channel specified in the chan parameter. If the noWait parameter is set to FALSE and the queue is full, the Sound Manager waits until there is space to add the command. If noWait is set to TRUE and the channel is full, the Sound Manager does not send the command and returns the queueFull result code.

Result codes

noErr	0	No error
queueFull	–203	No room in the queue
badChannel	–205	Channel is corrupt or unusable

The SndDoImmediate function operates much like SndDoCommand, except that it bypasses the existing command queue of the sound channel and sends the specified command directly to the synthesizer. This routine also overrides any waitCmd, pauseCmd, or syncCmd commands that may have already been received by the synthesizer.

```
FUNCTION SndDoImmediate (chan: SndChannelPtr; cmd: SndCommand) : OSErr;
```

The chan parameter is a pointer to a sound channel. The requested command is specified in the cmd parameter. Unlike SndDoCommand, SndDoImmediate loops indefinitely when you pass it a freqDurationCmd command. To cause the sound to play for the specified duration, send a quietCmd command into the channel.

Result codes

noErr	0	No error
badChannel	–205	Channel is corrupt or unusable

Table 22-6 lists the sound commands that you can send using SndDoCommand, SndDoImmediate, or (in several cases) SndControl.

Table 22-6. Sound commands

Command	**Description**
ampCmd	Changes the amplitude (or loudness) of a sound. If no sound is currently playing, then ampCmd sets the amplitude of the next sound to be played. The amplitude is sent in param1 and should be an integer in the range 0 to 255. You can send ampCmd to any of the available synthesizers. param1 desired amplitude param2 0 (ignored on input and output)
availableCmd	Determines if the initialization parameters passed in param2 are supported by the synthesizer to which this command is sent. The result is returned in param1; the result is 1 if the synthesizer supports the desired characteristics and 0 if it does not. You can send availableCmd to any of the available synthesizers, but you must send it by using SndControl. param1 0 on input; result of command on output param2 initialization parameters

(Continued)

Table 22-6. Sound commands (Continued)

Command	Description
bufferCmd	Plays a buffer of sampled sound data. If the high bit of the command is set, param2 is interpreted as an offset from the beginning of the 'snd ' resource containing the command to the sound data. If the high bit is not set, param2 is interpreted as a pointer to the sound data. You can send bufferCmd only to the sampled sound synthesizer. param1 0 (ignored on input and output) param2 offset or pointer to sound data
callBackCmd	Executes the callback procedure specified as a parameter to SndNewChannel. Both param1 and param2 are application-specific; you can use these two parameters to send data to your callback routine. You can send callBackCmd to any of the available synthesizers. param1 application-defined param2 application-defined
flushCmd	Removes all commands currently queued in the specified sound channel. A flushCmd command does not affect any sound that is currently in progress. You can send flushCmd to any of the available synthesizers, but you should send it by using SndDoImmediate. param1 0 (ignored on input and output) param2 0 (ignored on input and output)
freqCmd	Changes the frequency (or pitch) of a sound. If no sound is currently playing, then freqCmd causes the synthesizer linked to the specified channel to begin playing indefinitely at the frequency specified in param2. If, however, the channel is linked to the wave-table or sampled sound synthesizer and no instrument is installed in the channel, no sound is produced. The param2 parameter must contain a value in the range 0 to 127. The freqCmd command is identical to the freqDurationCmd command, except that no duration is specified to a freqCmd command. You can send freqCmd to any of the available synthesizers. param1 0 (ignored on input and output) param2 desired frequency
freqDurationCmd	Plays the frequency specified in param2 for the duration specified in param1. The param2 parameter must contain a value in the range 0 to 127. You can send freqDurationCmd to any of the available synthesizers. param1 duration in half-milliseconds (0 to 32,767) param2 desired frequency
getAmpCmd	Determines the current amplitude (or loudness) of a sound. The amplitude is returned in an integer variable whose address you pass in param2 and is in the range 0 to 255. You can send getAmpCmd to any of the available synthesizers. param1 0 (ignored on input and output) param2 pointer to amplitude variable
getRateCmd	Determines the sample rate of the sampled sound currently playing. The current rate of the channel is returned in a Fixed variable whose address you pass in param2 of the sound command. You can send getRateCmd

Table 22-6. Sound commands (Continued)

Command	Description
	only to the sampled sound synthesizer, but you should send it by using SndDoImmediate. param1 0 (ignored on input and output) param2 pointer to rate variable
loadCmd	Determines the CPU load factor that would be incurred by a new channel of sound having the initialization parameters specified in param2. The load factor returned in param1 is the percentage of CPU processing power that the specified sound channel would require. You can send loadCmd to any of the available synthesizers. You should send loadCmd using SndControl. param1 0 on input, load factor on output param2 initialization options
nullCmd	Does nothing. You can send nullCmd to any of the available synthesizers. param1 0 (ignored on input and output) param2 0 (ignored on input and output)
pauseCmd	Pauses any further command processing in a channel until resumeCmd is received. You can send pauseCmd to any of the available synthesizers. param1 0 (ignored on input and output) param2 0 (ignored on input and output)
quietCmd	Stops the sound that is currently playing. You can send quietCmd to any of the available synthesizers, but you should send it by using SndDoImmediate. param1 0 (ignored on input and output) param2 0 (ignored on input and output)
rateCmd	Sets the rate (or pitch) of a sampled sound that is currently playing. The new pitch is set to the value specified in param2. You can send rateCmd only to the sampled sound synthesizer. param1 0 (ignored on input and output) param2 desired rate of sound
reInitCmd	Resets the initialization parameters specified in param2 for the specified channel. You can send reInitCmd to any of the available synthesizers. param1 0 (ignored on input and output) param2 initialization options
restCmd	Rests a channel for a specified duration. The duration is specified in half-milliseconds in param1. You can send restCmd to any of the available synthesizers. param1 duration in half-milliseconds (0 to 32,767) param2 0 (ignored on input and output)
resumeCmd	Resumes command processing in a channel that was previously paused by pauseCmd. You can send resumeCmd to any of the available synthesizers. param1 0 (ignored on input and output) param2 0 (ignored on input and output)

(Continued)

Table 22-6. Sound commands (Continued)

Command	Description
soundCmd	Installs a sampled sound as a voice in a channel. If the high bit of the command is set, param2 is interpreted as an offset from the beginning of the 'snd ' resource containing the command to the sound data. If the high bit is not set, param2 is interpreted as a pointer to the sound data. You can send soundCmd only to the sampled sound synthesizer. param1 0 (ignored on input and output) param2 offset or pointer to sound data
syncCmd	Synchronizes multiple channels of sound. A syncCmd command is held in the specified channel, suspending all further command processing. The param2 parameter contains an identifier that is arbitrary. Each time the Sound Manager receives syncCmd, it decrements the count parameter for each channel having that identifier. When the count for a specific channel reaches 0, command processing in that channel resumes. You can send syncCmd to any of the available synthesizers. param1 count param2 identifier
timbreCmd	Changes the timbre (or tone) of the sound currently being played by the square-wave synthesizer. You can send timbreCmd only to the square-wave synthesizer. param1 desired timbre (0 to 255) param2 0 (ignored on input and output)
totalLoadCmd	Determines the total CPU load factor for all existing sound activity and for a new sound channel having the initialization options specified in param2. You can send totalLoadCmd to any of the available synthesizers. You should send totalLoadCmd using SndControl. param1 0 on input, load factor on output param2 initialization options
versionCmd	Determines which version of the specified synthesizer is available. The result is returned in param2. The high word of the result indicates the major revision number, and the low word indicates the minor revision number. For example, version 2.0 of a synthesizer would be returned as $00020000. You can send versionCmd to any of the available synthesizers, but you must send it by using SndControl. param1 0 (ignored on input and output) param2 0 on input; version of synthesizer on output
waitCmd	Suspends further command processing in a channel until the specified duration has elapsed. You can send waitCmd to any of the available synthesizers. param1 duration in half-milliseconds (0 to 65,535) param2 0 (ignored on input and output)
waveTableCmd	Installs a wave table as a voice in the specified channel. The param1 parameter specifies the length of the wave table, and the param2 parameter is a pointer to the wave-table data itself. You can send waveTableCmd only to the wave-table synthesizer. param1 length of wave table param2 pointer to wave-table data

Obtaining Information

You can obtain information about a sound channel and about the Sound Manager itself by calling the SndControl, SndChannelStatus, and SndManagerStatus functions. You can obtain the version numbers of the Sound Manager, the MACE tools, and the sound input routines by calling the SndSoundManagerVersion, MACEVersion, and SPBVersion functions, respectively.

> **Note:** You can call all of the functions documented in this section at interrupt time except SndControl (because it may need to load a resource into memory).

```
FUNCTION SndControl (id: Integer; VAR cmd: SndCommand) : OSErr;
```

The SndControl function sends control commands directly to a synthesizer specified by its resource ID. This can be called even if no channel has been created for the synthesizer. This control function is used with availableCmd or versionCmd to request information about a synthesizer. You can also use the totalLoadCmd and loadCmd commands with SndControl to determine the sound-related CPU load factor. The requested information is returned in the cmd parameter.

Result code

noErr	0	No error

You can use SndChannelStatus to determine the status of a Sound Manager sound channel.

```
FUNCTION SndChannelStatus (chan: SndChannelPtr; theLength: Integer;
                           theStatus: SCStatusPtr) : OSErr;
```

The chan parameter should be a pointer to a valid sound channel. The parameter theLength should be the size in bytes of the status structure that theStatus points to. The parameter theStatus should be a pointer to an SCStatus structure. On successful completion of the call, the fields of that structure contain the information about the specified sound channel.

Result codes

noErr	0	No error
paramErr	–50	A parameter is incorrect
badChannel	–205	Channel is corrupt or unusable

You can use SndManagerStatus to determine information about the Sound Manager.

```
FUNCTION SndManagerStatus (theLength: Integer; theStatus: SMStatusPtr) :
                           OSErr;
```

The parameter theLength should be the size in bytes of the SMStatus structure. The parameter theStatus is a pointer to an SMStatus structure, which is filled out with the status information.

Result code

noErr	0	No error

You can use SndSoundManagerVersion to determine the version of the Sound Manager tools available on a machine.

```
FUNCTION SndSoundManagerVersion : NumVersion;
```

SndSoundManagerVersion returns a version number that contains the same information as in the first 4 bytes of a 'vers' resource.

You can use MACEVersion to determine the version of the MACE tools available on a machine.

```
FUNCTION MACEVersion : NumVersion;
```

MACEVersion returns a version number that contains the same information as in the first 4 bytes of a 'vers' resource.

You can use SPBVersion to determine the version of the sound input tools available on a machine.

```
FUNCTION SPBVersion : NumVersion;
```

SPBVersion returns a version number that contains the same information as in the first 4 bytes of a 'vers' resource.

Playing From Disk

Use the SndStartFilePlay, SndPauseFilePlay, and SndStopFilePlay functions to manage a continuous play from disk.

```
FUNCTION SndStartFilePlay (chan: SndChannelPtr; fRefNum: Integer;
                            resNum: Integer; bufferSize: LongInt;
                            theBuffer: Ptr; theSelection:
                            AudioSelectionPtr; theCompletion: ProcPtr;
                            async: Boolean) : OSErr;
```

SndStartFilePlay is used to initiate continuous play from disk on a sound channel. The chan parameter is a pointer to a sound channel. If chan is not NIL, it is used as a valid channel. If chan is NIL, an internally allocated sound channel is used for play from disk. This internally allocated sound channel is not passed back to you. Since the other two play-from-disk routines require a sound-channel pointer, you must allocate your own channel if you wish to use those routines.

The sounds you wish to play can be stored either in a file or in an 'snd ' resource. If you are playing a file, then fRefNum should be the file reference number of the file to be played, and the parameter resNum should be set to 0.

If you are playing an 'snd ' resource, then fRefNum should be set to 0, and resNum should be the resource ID number (not the file reference number) of the resource to play. Both format 1 and format 2 'snd ' resources are supported.

The bufferSize parameter contains the number of bytes of memory that the Sound Manager is to use for input buffering while reading in sound data. If theBuffer is a NIL pointer, then the Sound Manager internally allocates two relocatable blocks, each of which is half the size of bufferSize; otherwise, theBuffer should be a pointer to a nonrelocatable block of size bufferSize.

If theSelection is a NIL pointer, then the entire sound is played; otherwise, theSelection should point to an audio selection record. You use that record to specify the segment of the sound to be played.

The theCompletion parameter is a pointer to a routine that is called when the sound is finished playing. Set theCompletion to NIL if you do not wish to specify a completion routine. The completion routine should be declared like this:

```
PROCEDURE MyFilePlayCompletionRoutine (chan: SndChannelPtr);
```

This routine is called at interrupt time and must preserve all registers other than D0–D2 and A0–A1. In addition, it must not make any calls to the Memory Manager, either directly or indirectly. If your completion routine needs to access your application's global variables, you must ensure that register A5 contains your application's A5. (You can use the userInfo field of the sound channel pointed to by the chan parameter to pass that value to your completion routine.)

If the async parameter is TRUE, then the call is made asynchronously; otherwise, the call is synchronous.

Result codes

noErr	0	No error
notEnoughHardwareErr	–201	Insufficient hardware available
queueFull	–203	No room in the queue
badChannel	–205	Channel is corrupt or unusable
badFormat	–206	Resource is corrupt or unusable
notEnoughBufferSpace	–207	Insufficient memory available
badFileFormat	–208	File is corrupt or unusable
channelBusy	–209	Channel is busy
buffersTooSmall	–210	Buffer is too small
siInvalidCompression	–223	Invalid compression type

Note: SndStartFilePlay allocates memory so it cannot be called at interrupt level.

You can use SndPauseFilePlay alternately to suspend and resume asynchronous play from disk.

```
FUNCTION SndPauseFilePlay (chan: SndChannelPtr) : OSErr;
```

SndPauseFilePlay is used in conjunction with SndStopFilePlay to control play from disk on a sound channel. Note that this call can be made only if your application has already called SndStartFilePlay with a valid sound channel. This function cannot be used with a synchronous SndStartFilePlay because, by definition, program control does not return to the caller until after the sound has completely finished playing.

The chan parameter should be a pointer to a valid sound channel. If the channel is not being used for play from disk, then SndPauseFilePlay returns the result code channelNotBusy. If the channel is busy and paused, then play from disk is resumed. If the channel is busy and the channel is not paused, then play from disk is suspended.

Result codes

noErr	0	No error
queueFull	–203	No room in the queue
badChannel	–205	Channel is corrupt or unusable
channelNotBusy	–211	Channel not currently used

Note: You can call SndPauseFilePlay at interrupt time.

You can use SndStopFilePlay to stop an asynchronous play from disk.

```
FUNCTION SndStopFilePlay (chan: SndChannelPtr; async: Boolean) : OSErr;
```

The chan parameter should be a pointer to a valid sound channel. If the async parameter is TRUE, then the play from disk stops as soon as possible, and program control returns to your application. All asynchronous file I/O calls will have completed, and any internally allocated memory will have been released. If async is FALSE, then SndStopFilePlay lets the sound complete normally and returns only after the sound has completed, all asynchronous file I/O calls have completed, and any internal allocated memory has been released.

Note: You can call SndStopFilePlay at interrupt time.

Result codes

noErr	0	No error
badChannel	–205	Channel is corrupt or unusable

Managing Double Buffers

SndPlayDoubleBuffer is a low-level routine that gives you maximum efficiency and control over double buffering while still maintaining compatibility with the Sound Manager.

```
FUNCTION SndPlayDoubleBuffer (chan: SndChannelPtr; theParams:
                              SndDoubleBufferHeaderPtr) : OSErr;
```

The chan parameter is a pointer to a valid sound channel. The parameter theParams is a pointer to a SndDoubleBufferHeader record.

Result codes

noErr	0	No error
badChannel	–205	Channel is corrupt or unusable

Compressing and Expanding Audio Data

You can use the procedures Comp3to1 and Comp6to1 to compress sounds, and you can use the procedures Exp1to3 and Exp1to6 to expand compressed audio data. The procedures Comp3to1 and Comp6to1 compress a sound at ratios of 3:1 and 6:1, respectively.

```
PROCEDURE Comp3to1   (inBuffer: Ptr; outBuffer: Ptr; cnt: LongInt;
                      inState: Ptr; outState: Ptr; numChannels: LongInt;
                      whichChannel: LongInt);

PROCEDURE Comp6to1   (inBuffer: Ptr; outBuffer: Ptr; cnt: LongInt;
                      inState: Ptr; outState: Ptr; numChannels: LongInt;
                      whichChannel: LongInt);
```

The inBuffer parameter is a pointer to a buffer of samples to be compressed. The samples must be in 8-bit offset binary format. The outBuffer parameter is a pointer to a buffer where the samples are to be written. This buffer must be greater than or equal to cnt/6 bytes for 6:1 compression and cnt/3 bytes for 3:1 compression. The cnt parameter is the number of samples to compress.

The inState parameter is a pointer to a buffer from which the input state of the algorithm is read. To initialize the algorithm, this buffer should be filled with zeros. The size of the buffer should be 128 bytes for both algorithms.

The outState parameter is a pointer to a buffer to which the output state of the algorithm is written. The size of the buffer should be 128 bytes for both algorithms. The inState and outState parameters may point to the same buffer.

The numChannels parameter is the number of channels in the buffer pointed to by the inBuffer parameter. It is assumed that if numChannels is greater than 1, then the uncompressed sound is stored in interleaved format on a sample basis.

The whichChannel parameter is used to specify which channel to expand when numChannels is greater than 1. When numChannels is set to 1, whichChannel is unused. Acceptable values of the whichChannel parameter range from 1 to numChannels.

> **Note:** The output stream that is produced by these two compression routines is always monophonic, regardless of the value you pass in the numChannels parameter.

The procedures Exp1to3 and Exp1to6 expand a sound that was previously compressed at ratios of 3:1 and 6:1, respectively.

```
PROCEDURE Exp1to3    (inBuffer: Ptr; outBuffer: Ptr; cnt: LongInt;
                      inState: Ptr; outState: Ptr; numChannels: LongInt;
                      whichChannel: LongInt);

PROCEDURE Exp1to6    (inBuffer: Ptr; outBuffer: Ptr; cnt: LongInt;
                      inState: Ptr; outState: Ptr; numChannels: LongInt;
                      whichChannel: LongInt);
```

The inBuffer parameter is a pointer to a buffer of packets to be expanded. The samples must be in 8-bit offset binary format. The outBuffer parameter is a pointer to a buffer where the expanded samples will be written. This buffer must be at least cnt * 6 bytes in size for both 3:1 and 6:1 expansion.

The cnt parameter is the number of packets to expand. The packet size for 3:1 is 2 bytes; therefore one packet of 3:1 expands into 6 bytes. The packet size for 6:1 is 1 byte; therefore, one packet of 6:1 expands into 6 bytes.

The inState parameter is a pointer to a buffer from which the input state of the algorithm is read. To initialize the algorithm, this buffer should be filled with zeros. The size of the buffer should be 128 bytes for both algorithms.

The outState parameter is a pointer to a buffer to which the output state of the algorithm is written. The size of the buffer should be 128 bytes for both algorithms. The inState and outState parameters may point to the same buffer.

The numChannels parameter is the number of channels in the buffer pointed to by the inBuffer parameter. It is assumed that if numChannels is greater than 1, then the compressed sound is stored in interleaved format on a packet basis.

The whichChannel parameter is used to specify which channel to expand when numChannels is greater than 1. When numChannels is set to 1, whichChannel is unused. Acceptable values of the whichChannel parameter range from 1 to numChannels.

> **Note:** The output stream that is produced by these expansion routines is always monophonic, regardless of the value you pass in the numChannels parameter.

Recording Sounds

The Sound Manager provides two high-level sound input routines, SndRecord and SndRecordToFile, for recording sound. These input routines are analogous to the two output routines SndPlay and SndStartFilePlay. By using these high-level routines, you can be assured that your application will present a user interface that is consistent with that displayed by other applications doing sound input. Both SndRecord and SndRecordToFile attempt to record sound data from the sound input hardware currently selected in the Sound control panel.

The SndRecord function records sound into memory. The recorded data has the structure of a format 1 'snd ' resource and can later be played using SndPlay or can be stored as a resource.

```
FUNCTION SndRecord (filterProc: ProcPtr; corner: Point; quality: OSType;
                    VAR sndHandle: Handle) : OSErr;
```

SndRecord displays a sound input dialog box and is always called synchronously. Controls in the dialog box allow the user to start, stop, pause, and resume sound recording, as well as to play back the recorded sound. The dialog box also lists the amount of time remaining to record and the current microphone sound level.

The filterProc parameter determines how user actions in the dialog box are filtered (and hence is similar to the filterProc parameter specified in a call to ModalDialog). By specifying your own filter procedure, you can override or add to the default actions of the items in the dialog box. If filterProc isn't NIL, SndRecord filters events by calling the procedure that filterProc points to.

The corner parameter gives the horizontal and vertical coordinates of the upper-left corner of the dialog box (in global coordinates).

The quality parameter defines the desired quality of the recorded sound. Currently, three values are recognized for the quality parameter: 'good', 'betr', and 'best'. The precise meanings of these parameters are dependent on the sound input driver. For Apple-supplied drivers, this parameter determines whether the recorded sound is to be compressed, and if so, whether at a 6:1 or a 3:1 ratio. A quality of 'best' does not compress the sound and provides the best quality output, but at the expense of memory. The quality 'betr' is suitable for most nonvoice recording, and 'good' is suitable for voice recording.

The sndHandle parameter is a handle to some storage space. You must pass in either a valid handle or NIL. If sndHandle is NIL, the Sound Manager allocates the largest amount of space in the application's heap that it can and then resizes the handle when the user clicks the Save button in the sound input dialog box. If the sndHandle parameter passed to SndRecord is not NIL, the recording time is derived from the amount of memory reserved by the handle.

Result codes

noErr	0	No error
userCanceledErr	–128	User canceled the operation
siBadSoundInDevice	–221	Invalid sound input device
siUnknownQuality	–232	Unknown quality

You can use SndRecordToFile to record sound data into a file. SndRecordToFile operates exactly like SndRecord except that it stores the sound input data into a file. The resulting file is in either AIFF or AIFF-C format and contains the information necessary to play the file by using SndStartFilePlay. SndRecordToFile is always called synchronously.

```
FUNCTION SndRecordToFile (filterProc: ProcPtr; corner: Point; quality:
                          OSType; fRefNum: Integer) : OSErr;
```

The filterProc, corner, and quality parameters are identical to those provided to SndRecord. The fRefNum parameter indicates the file reference number of an open file to save the audio data in. (In other words, your application must first open the file with write access, pass the returned file reference number to SndRecordToFile, and eventually close the file.) If the audio data to be recorded into a file is uncompressed, then SndRecordToFile writes a file of type AIFF. If the data is compressed, SndRecordToFile writes a file of type AIFF-C.

Result codes

noErr	0	No error
userCanceledErr	–128	User canceled the operation
siBadSoundInDevice	–221	Invalid sound input device
siUnknownQuality	–232	Unknown quality

Manipulating Sound Input Devices

The Sound Manager provides a number of routines for use by sound input drivers or by applications that need more control over the recording process (such as the ability to intercept sound input data at interrupt time). These routines allow low-level recording to memory or to a file, configuration of recording parameters, and monitoring of the recording status.

Opening and Closing Sound Input Devices

You can open and close sound input devices by calling SPBOpenDevice and SPBCloseDevice. You must open a device before you can record from it by using SPBRecord.

```
FUNCTION SPBOpenDevice (deviceName: Str255; permission: Integer; VAR
                        inRefNum: LongInt) : OSErr;
```

The SPBOpenDevice function attempts to open a sound input device having name deviceName. If the call succeeds, it returns a device reference number in inRefNum. The permission parameter indicates whether subsequent operations with that device are to be read/write or read-only. If the device is not already in use, read/write permission is granted; otherwise, only read-only operations are allowed. To make any recording calls or to call SPBSetDeviceInfo, read/write permission must be available.

You can request that the current default sound input device be opened by passing either a zero-length string or a NIL string as the deviceName parameter. If only one sound input device is installed, that device is used. Generally you should open the default device unless you specifically want to use some other device. You can get a list of the available devices by calling SPBGetIndexedDevice.

Result codes

noErr	0	No error
permErr	–54	Attempt to open locked file for writing
siBadDeviceName	–228	Invalid device name

```
FUNCTION SPBCloseDevice (inRefNum: LongInt) : OSErr;
```

The SPBCloseDevice function closes a device that was previously opened by SPBOpenDevice.

Result codes

noErr	0	No error
siBadRefNum	–229	Invalid reference number

Recording Sounds Directly From Sound Input Devices

The Sound Manager provides a number of routines that allow you to begin, pause, resume, and stop recording directly from a sound input device. (These low-level routines do not present the sound input dialog box to the user.)

You can use the SPBRecord function to record audio data into memory, either synchronously or asynchronously.

```
FUNCTION SPBRecord (inParamPtr: SPBPtr; asynchFlag: Boolean) : OSErr;
```

Parameter block

→	0	inRefNum	long	input device reference number
↔	4	count	long	number of bytes to record
↔	8	milliseconds	long	number of milliseconds to record
→	12	bufferLength	long	length of buffer
→	16	bufferPtr	long	address of buffer
→	20	completionRoutine	long	pointer to completion routine
→	24	interruptRoutine	long	pointer to interrupt routine
→	28	userLong	long	for application's use
←	32	error	word	error returned after recording
→	36	unused1	long	reserved

The SPBRecord function starts recording into memory from a specified device. The sound data recorded is simply stored in the buffer indicated, so it is up to your application to insert whatever headers are needed to play the sound with the Sound Manager. The asynchFlag parameter specifies whether the recording occurs asynchronously.

SPBRecord accepts a sound input parameter block to control the recording process. The inRefNum field of the parameter block should contain the reference number of the device to record from. The count field contains the number of bytes to record and the milliseconds field contains the number of milliseconds to record. If one of these fields specifies a longer recording time than the other, then the longer time is used and both fields are updated to reflect the actual amount recorded.

The bufferPtr field points to the buffer to record into, and the bufferLength field gives the length (in bytes) of that buffer. The recording times given in the count and milliseconds fields are always truncated to the size of this buffer, if necessary. If the bufferPtr field contains NIL, then the count, milliseconds, and bufferLength fields are ignored, and the recording continues indefinitely until you call SPBStopRecording. If bufferPtr is NIL, the audio data is not saved anywhere; this feature is useful only if you want to do something in your interrupt routine and do not want to save the audio data. If the recording is synchronous and bufferPtr is NIL, SPBRecord returns the result code siNoBufferSpecified.

The completion routine specified in the completionRoutine field is called when the recording terminates (either when you call SPBStopRecording or when the prescribed limit is reached). The completion routine is called only for asynchronous recording.

The interrupt routine specified in the interruptRoutine field is called by asynchronous recording devices when their internal buffers are full.

You can set the userLong field to any value. The error field contains a value greater than 0 while recording occurs. When recording terminates without an error, the error field is set to 0. If an error occurs during the recording, the error field will contain a value that is less than 0 and is of type OSErr.

Note: If more than one channel is being recorded, the samples are interleaved into the buffer.

Result codes

noErr	0	No error
siNoSoundInHardware	–220	No sound input hardware available
siBadSoundInDevice	–221	Invalid sound input device
siNoBufferSpecified	–222	No buffer specified
siDeviceBusyErr	–227	Sound input device is busy

You can use the SPBRecordToFile function to record audio data into a file, either synchronously or asynchronously.

```
FUNCTION SPBRecordToFile (fRefNum: Integer; inParamPtr: SPBPtr;
                          asynchFlag: Boolean) : OSErr;
```

Parameter block

→	0	inRefNum	long	input device reference number
↔	4	count	long	number of bytes to record
↔	8	milliseconds	long	number of milliseconds to record
→	20	completionRoutine	long	pointer to completion routine
→	24	interruptRoutine	long	pointer to interrupt routine
→	28	userLong	long	for application's use
←	32	error	word	error returned after recording
→	36	unused1	long	reserved

The SPBRecordToFile function starts recording from a specified device into a file. The sound data recorded is simply stored in the file, so it is up to your application to insert whatever headers are needed to play the sound with the Sound Manager. The fRefNum parameter must contain a valid reference number for an open file. (In other words, your application must first open the file with write access, pass the returned file reference number to SPBRecordToFile, and eventually close the file.) The asynchFlag parameter specifies whether the recording occurs asynchronously. The fields in the parameter block specified by the inParamPtr parameter are identical to the fields in the parameter block passed to SPBRecord, except that the bufferLength and bufferPtr fields are not used. The interruptRoutine field is ignored by SPBRecordToFile, but you should initialize it to NIL.

SPBRecordToFile writes samples to disk in the same format that they are read in from the sound input device. If compression is enabled, then the samples written to the file are compressed.

If any errors occur during file writes, recording is suspended. All File Manager errors are returned through the function's return value if the routine is called synchronously. If the routine is called asynchronously and the completion routine is not NIL, the completion routine is called and is passed a single parameter on the stack that points to the sound input parameter block; any errors are returned in the error field of the sound input parameter block. The error field in the sound input parameter block is 1 while input is active, 0 when input is complete, and less than 0 if an error occurs.

Result codes

noErr	0	No error
permErr	–54	Attempt to open locked file for writing
siNoSoundInHardware	–220	No sound input hardware available
siBadSoundInDevice	–221	Invalid sound input device
siHardDriveTooSlow	–224	Hard drive too slow to record

```
FUNCTION SPBPauseRecording (inRefNum: LongInt) : OSErr;
```

The SPBPauseRecording function pauses recording from the device specified by the inRefNum parameter. The recording must be asynchronous for this call to have any effect.

Result codes

noErr	0	No error
siBadSoundInDevice	–221	Invalid sound input device

```
FUNCTION SPBResumeRecording (inRefNum: LongInt) : OSErr;
```

The SPBResumeRecording function resumes recording from the device specified by the inRefNum parameter. The recording must be asynchronous for this call to have any effect.

Result codes

noErr	0	No error
siBadSoundInDevice	–221	Invalid sound input device

```
FUNCTION SPBStopRecording (inRefNum: LongInt) : OSErr;
```

The SPBStopRecording function stops recording from the device specified by the inRefNum parameter. The recording must be asynchronous for this call to have any effect. When you call SPBStopRecording, the completion routine specified in the completionRoutine field of the sound input parameter block is called and the error field of that parameter block is set to abortErr.

Result codes

noErr	0	No error
siBadSoundInDevice	–221	Invalid sound input device

You can use SPBGetRecordingStatus to obtain recording status information about a sound input device.

```
FUNCTION SPBGetRecordingStatus (inRefNum: LongInt;
                                VAR recordingStatus: Integer;
                                VAR meterLevel: Integer;
                                VAR totalSamplesToRecord: LongInt;
                                VAR numberOfSamplesRecorded: LongInt;
                                VAR totalMsecsToRecord: LongInt;
                                VAR numberOfMsecsRecorded: LongInt) :
                                OSErr;
```

The inRefNum parameter contains the reference number of a sound input device. While the input device is recording, recordingStatus is greater than 0. When the recording terminates without an error, recordingStatus is equal to 0. If any error occurs during the recording, recordingStatus is less than 0 and contains an error code. If the recording is terminated by calling SPBStopRecording, then recordingStatus contains the abortErr result code.

The meterLevel parameter gives the current input signal level. Values returned are in the range 0 to 255.

The totalSamplesToRecord and numberOfSamplesRecorded parameters give an indication of how many samples have been recorded out of the total to record. The totalMsecsToRecord and numberOfMsecsRecorded parameters likewise give an indication of how much time has been recorded out of the total to record.

Result codes

noErr	0	No error
siBadSoundInDevice	–221	Invalid sound input device

Manipulating Device Settings

You can use the two functions SPBGetDeviceInfo and SPBSetDeviceInfo to read and change the settings of a sound input device.

```
FUNCTION SPBGetDeviceInfo (inRefNum: LongInt; infoType: OSType;
                           infoData: Ptr) : OSErr;
```

The SPBGetDeviceInfo function returns information about the sound input device specified by the inRefNum parameter. The type of information you desire is specified in the infoType parameter. The information is copied into infoData as an address to the appropriate data.

Result codes

noErr	0	No error
siBadSoundInDevice	–221	Invalid sound input device
siUnknownInfoType	–231	Unknown type of information

```
FUNCTION SPBSetDeviceInfo (inRefNum: LongInt; infoType: OSType;
                           infoData: Ptr) : OSErr;
```

The SPBSetDeviceInfo function sets information in the device specified in the inRefNum parameter. The infoType parameter is a selector that specifies the type of information you want to set, and infoData provides a pointer to the data. A number of selectors are defined by Apple (listed in “Getting and Setting Sound Input Device Information” earlier in this chapter). Third-party devices can support additional selectors to allow applications to control special features available on that hardware.

Result codes

noErr	0	No error
permErr	–54	Attempt to open locked file for writing
siBadSoundInDevice	–221	Invalid sound input device
siDeviceBusyErr	–227	Sound input device is busy
siUnknownInfoType	–231	Unknown type of information

Constructing Sound Resource and File Headers

The Sound Manager provides two functions, SetupSndHeader and SetupAIFFHeader, to help you set up headers for 'snd ' resources and AIFF files.

```
FUNCTION SetupSndHeader (sndHandle: Handle; numChannels: Integer;
                         sampleRate: Fixed; sampleSize: Integer;
                         compressionType: OSType; baseFrequency: Integer;
                         numBytes: LongInt; VAR headerLen: Integer) :
                         OSErr;
```


You can use SetupSndHeader to construct a sampled sound header that can be passed to SndPlay or stored as an 'snd ' resource. SetupSndHeader creates a format 1 'snd ' resource header for a sampled sound only, containing one synthesizer field (the sampled synthesizer) and one sound command (a bufferCmd command to play the accompanying data). A sampled sound header is stored immediately following the sound command and is in one of three formats depending on several of the parameters passed. Table 22-7 shows how SetupSndHeader determines what kind of sound header to create.

Table 22-7. The sound header format used by SetupSndHeader

compressionType	numChannels	sampleSize	Sound header format
'NONE'	1	8	SoundHeader
'NONE'	1	more than 8	ExtSoundHeader
'NONE'	2 or more	8 or more	ExtSoundHeader
not 'NONE'	any	any	CmpSoundHeader

The sndHandle parameter is a handle that is at least large enough to store the 'snd ' header information. The handle is not resized in any way upon successful completion of SetupSndHeader. SetupSndHeader simply fills the beginning of the handle with the header information needed for a format 1 'snd ' resource. It is your application's responsibility to append the desired sampled sound data.

The numChannels parameter specifies the number of channels for the sound. The sampleRate parameter specifies the sampling rate for the sound (that is, samples per second). Note that the most significant bit of this value is interpreted as having the value 32,768 (not as a sign bit). The sampleSize parameter specifies the sample size for the sound (that is, bits per sample). The compressionType parameter specifies the compression type for the sound ('NONE', 'MAC3', 'MAC6', or other third-party types). The baseFrequency parameter specifies the base frequency for the sound.

The numBytes parameter specifies the number of bytes of audio data that are to be stored in the handle. (This value is not necessarily the same as the number of samples in the sound.)

The headerLen parameter returns the size of the 'snd ' resource header that is created, in bytes. This allows you to put the audio data right after the header in the handle. The value returned depends on the type of sound header created.

A good way to use this function is to create a handle that you want to store a sampled sound in, then call SetupSndHeader with the numBytes parameter set to 0 to see how much room the header for that sound will occupy and hence where to append the audio data. Then record the data into the handle and call SetupSndHeader again with numBytes set to the correct amount of sound data recorded. The handle filled out in this way can be passed to SndPlay to play the sound.

Result codes

noErr	0	No error
siInvalidCompression	–223	Invalid compression type

You can use the SetupAIFFHeader function to set up a file that can be played by SndStartFilePlay.

```
FUNCTION SetupAIFFHeader (fRefNum: Integer; numChannels: Integer;
                          sampleRate: Fixed; sampleSize: Integer;
                          compressionType: OSType; numBytes: LongInt;
                          numFrames: LongInt) : OSErr;
```

Depending on the parameters passed, SetupAIFFHeader creates an AIFF or AIFF-C file header:

- Uncompressed sounds of any type are stored in AIFF format (that is, compressionType is 'NONE').
- Compressed sounds of any type are stored in AIFF-C format (that is, compressionType is different from 'NONE').

The fRefNum parameter contains a file reference number for a file that is open for writing. The AIFF header information is written starting at the current file position, and the file position is left at the end of the header upon completion.

The numChannels parameter, the sampleRate parameter, the sampleSize parameter, and the compressionType parameter have the same meanings as with the SetupSndHeader function.

The numBytes parameter specifies the number of bytes of audio data that are to be stored in the Common Chunk of the AIFF or AIFF-C file. This data should be stored right after the sound header in the file. (This value is not necessarily the same as the number of samples in the sound.)

The numFrames parameter specifies the number of sample frames for the sound. A value needs to be passed here only for third-party compression types. If you are using 'NONE', 'MAC3', or 'MAC6' compression types, you can pass a 0 in this field, and SetupAIFFHeader will calculate the number of sample frames and store it in the header.

A good way to use this routine is to create a file that you want to store a sound in, then call SetupAIFFHeader with numBytes set to 0 to see how much room the header will take up and hence to position the file to be ready to write the audio data. Then record the data to the file, set the file position to the beginning of the file, and call SetupAIFFHeader again with numBytes set to the correct amount of sound data recorded. The file created in this way can be passed to SndStartFilePlay to play the sound.

Registering Sound Input Devices

Drivers for sound input devices must call SPBSignInDevice to register with the Sound Manager before they can use its sound input services. You might call this routine at system startup time from within a resource of type 'INIT' to install a sound input driver. You can get information about registered devices by calling SPBGetIndexedDevice. You can unregister your driver by calling SPBSignOutDevice.

```
FUNCTION SPBSignInDevice (deviceRefNum: Integer; deviceName: Str255) :
                          OSErr;
```

The SPBSignInDevice function registers with the Sound Manager the device whose driver reference number is deviceRefNum. The deviceName parameter specifies this device's name as it is to appear to the user in the Sound control panel (which is not the name of the driver itself). Accordingly, the name should be as descriptive as possible. You should call SPBSignInDevice after you have already opened your driver by calling normal Device Manager routines.

Result codes

noErr	0	No error
siBadSoundInDevice	–221	Invalid sound input device

```
FUNCTION SPBSignOutDevice (deviceRefNum: Integer) : OSErr;
```

The SPBSignOutDevice function unregisters the device whose driver reference number is deviceRefNum; the device is unregistered from the Sound Manager's list of available drivers.

Result codes

noErr	0	No error
siBadSoundInDevice	–221	Invalid sound input device
siDeviceBusyErr	–227	Sound input device is busy

```
FUNCTION SPBGetIndexedDevice (count: Integer; VAR deviceName: Str255;
                              VAR deviceIconHandle: Handle) : OSErr;
```

The SPBGetIndexedDevice function returns the name and icon of the device whose index is specified in the count parameter. Your application can create a list of sound input devices by calling this function with a count starting at 1 and incrementing until the function returns siBadSoundInDevice. On completion, the deviceName parameter contains a string that is the name of the device, and the deviceIconHandle parameter is a handle to a block of memory in your application's heap containing the device's icon. The SPBGetIndexedDevice function allocates this memory for you, but it is your responsibility to dispose of that handle when you are finished with it.

Note: You cannot call SPBGetIndexedDevice at interrupt time.

Result codes

noErr	0	No error
siBadSoundInDevice	–221	Invalid sound input device

Converting Between Milliseconds and Bytes

The Sound Manager provides two routines that allow you to convert between millisecond and byte values.

```
FUNCTION SPBMilliSecondsToBytes (inRefNum: LongInt; VAR milliseconds:
                                 LongInt) : OSErr;
```

The SPBMilliSecondsToBytes function reports how many bytes are required to hold a recording of duration milliseconds, given the input device's current sample rate, sample size, number of channels, and compression factor. The inRefNum parameter indicates the input device to use, and the milliseconds parameter points to a millisecond value to convert. On return, the number of bytes is returned in the milliseconds parameter.

Result codes

noErr	0	No error
siBadSoundInDevice	–221	Invalid sound input device

```
FUNCTION SPBBytesToMilliSeconds (inRefNum: LongInt; VAR byteCount:
                                 LongInt) : OSErr;
```

The SPBBytesToMilliSeconds function reports how many milliseconds of audio data can be recorded in a buffer that is byteCount bytes long, given the input device's current sample rate, sample size, number of channels, and compression factor. The inRefNum parameter indicates the input device to use, and the byteCount parameter points to a byte value to convert. On return, the number of milliseconds is returned in the byteCount parameter.

Result codes

noErr	0	No error
siBadSoundInDevice	–221	Invalid sound input device

SUMMARY OF THE SOUND MANAGER

Constants

```
CONST {Gestalt response bit flags}
      gestaltStereoCapability    = 0;  {stereo capability present}
      gestaltStereoMixing        = 1;  {stereo mixing on internal speaker}
      gestaltSoundIOMgrPresent   = 3;  {sound input routines available}
      gestaltBuiltInSoundInput   = 4;  {built-in input device available}
      gestaltHasSoundInputDevice = 5;  {sound input device available}

      {channel initialization parameters}
      initChanLeft          = $0002;   {left channel--sampledSynth only}
      initChanRight         = $0003;   {right channel--sampledSynth only}
      initChan0             = $0004;   {channel 1--wave table only}
      initChan1             = $0005;   {channel 2--wave table only}
      initChan2             = $0006;   {channel 3--wave table only}
      initChan3             = $0007;   {channel 4--wave table only}
      initMono              = $0080;   {mono channel--sampledSynth only}
      initStereo            = $00C0;   {stereo channel--sampledSynth only}
      initMACE3             = $0300;   {3:1 compression--sampledSynth only}
      initMACE6             = $0400;   {6:1 compression--sampledSynth only}
      initNoInterp          = $0004;   {no linear interpolation}
      initNoDrop            = $0008;   {no drop-sample conversion}

      initPanMask           = $0003;   {mask for right/left pan values}
      initSRateMask         = $0030;   {mask for sample rate values}
      initStereoMask        = $00C0;   {mask for mono/stereo values}
      initCompMask          = $FF00;   {mask for compression IDs}

      {sound command numbers}
      nullCmd               = 0;     {do nothing}
      quietCmd              = 3;     {stop a sound that is playing}
      flushCmd              = 4;     {flush a sound channel}
      reInitCmd             = 5;     {reinitialize a sound channel}
      waitCmd               = 10;    {suspend processing in a channel}
      pauseCmd              = 11;    {pause processing in a channel}
      resumeCmd             = 12;    {resume processing in a channel}
      callBackCmd           = 13;    {execute a callback procedure}
      syncCmd               = 14;    {synchronize channels}
      availableCmd          = 24;    {see if initialization option }
                                     { available}
      versionCmd            = 25;    {determine synthesizer version}
      totalLoadCmd          = 26;    {report total CPU load}
      loadCmd               = 27;    {report CPU load for a new channel}
      freqDurationCmd       = 40;    {play a frequency for a specified }
                                     { duration}
      restCmd               = 41;    {rest a channel for specified duration}
      freqCmd               = 42;    {change the pitch of a sound}
```

```
ampCmd                   = 43;      {change the amplitude of a sound}
timbreCmd                = 44;      {change the timbre of a sound}
getAmpCmd                = 45;      {get the amplitude of a sound}
waveTableCmd             = 60;      {install a wave table as a voice}
soundCmd                 = 80;      {install a sampled sound as a
voice}
bufferCmd                = 81;      {play a sampled sound}
rateCmd                  = 82;      {set the pitch of a sampled sound}
getRateCmd               = 85;      {get the pitch of a sampled sound}

{sampled sound header encoding options}
stdSH                    = $00;     {standard sound header}
extSH                    = $FF;     {extended sound header}
cmpSH                    = $FE;     {compressed sound header}

{size of data structures}
stdQLength               = 128;     {default size of standard sound }
                                    { channel}

{sound command mask}
dataOffsetFlag           = $8000;   {sound command data offset bit}

{synthesizer resource IDs}
squareWaveSynth          = 1;       {square-wave synthesizer}
waveTableSynth           = 3;       {wave-table synthesizer}
sampledSynth             = 5;       {sampled sound synthesizer}

{system beep states}
sysBeepDisable           = $0000;   {system alert sound disabled}
sysBeepEnable            = $0001;   {system alert sound enabled}

{values for the unitType field in AudioSelection}
unitTypeSeconds          = $0000;   {seconds}
unitTypeNoSelection      = $FFFF;   {no selection}

{double-buffer status flags}
dbBufferReady            = $00000001;
dbLastBuffer             = $00000004;

{values for the compressionID field of CmpSoundHeader}
notCompressed            = 0;       {noncompressed samples}
threeToOne               = 3;       {3:1 compressed samples}
sixToOne                 = 4;       {6:1 compressed samples}

{values for the packetSize field of CmpSoundHeader}
sixToOnePacketSize       = 8;       {packet size for 6:1}
threeToOnePacketSize     = 16;      {packet size for 3:1}

{information selectors for sound input drivers}
siActiveChannels         = 'chac';  {channels active}
siActiveLevels           = 'lmac';  {levels active}
```

```
siAGCOnOff              = 'agc ';  {automatic gain control state}
siAsync                 = 'asyn';  {asynchronous capability}
siChannelAvailable      = 'chav';  {number of channels available}
siCompressionAvailable  = 'cmav';  {compression types available}
siCompressionFactor     = 'cmfa';  {current compression factor}
siCompressionHeader     = 'cmhd';  {return compression header}
siCompressionType       = 'comp';  {current compression type}
siContinuous            = 'cont';  {continuous recording}
siDeviceBufferInfo      = 'dbin';  {size of interrupt buffer}
siDeviceConnected       = 'dcon';  {input device connection status}
siDeviceIcon            = 'icon';  {input device icon}
siDeviceName            = 'name';  {input device name}
siLevelMeterOnOff       = 'lmet';  {level meter state}
siNumberChannels        = 'chan';  {current number of channels}
siOptionsDialog         = 'optd';  {display options dialog box}
siPlayThruOnOff         = 'plth';  {play-through state}
siRecordingQuality      = 'qual';  {recording quality}
siSampleRate            = 'srat';  {current sample rate}
siSampleRateAvailable   = 'srav';  {sample rates available}
siSampleSize            = 'ssiz';  {current sample size}
siSampleSizeAvailable   = 'ssav';  {sample sizes available}
siTwosComplementOnOff   = 'twos';  {two's complement state}
siVoxRecordInfo         = 'voxr';  {VOX record parameters}
siVoxStopInfo           = 'voxs';  {VOX stop parameters}

{sound-recording qualities}
siBestQuality           = 'best';  {the best quality available}
siBetterQuality         = 'betr';  {a quality better than good}
siGoodQuality           = 'good';  {a good quality}

{sound input device permissions}
siReadPermission        = 0;       {open device for reading}
siWritePermission       = 1;       {open device for reading/writing}

{device-connection states}
siDeviceIsConnected     = 1;       {device is connected and ready}
siDeviceNotConnected    = 0;       {device is not connected}
siDontKnowIfConnected   = -1;      {can't tell if device is connected}

{IDs for AIFF and AIFF-C file chunks}
FormID                  = 'FORM';  {chunk ID for Form Chunk}
FormatVersionID         = 'FVER';  {chunk ID for Format Version Chunk}
CommonID                = 'COMM';  {chunk ID for Common Chunk}
SoundDataID             = 'SSND';  {chunk ID for Sound Data Chunk}

{version of AIFC format specification}
AIFCVersion1        = $A2805140;   {2726318400 in decimal}
```

Data Types

```
TYPE Time = LongInt;            {in half-milliseconds}


SndCommand =                 {generic sound command}
     PACKED RECORD
        cmd:                 Integer;        {command number}
        param1:              Integer;        {first parameter}
        param2:              LongInt         {second parameter}
     END;


SndChannelPtr = ^SndChannel;
SndChannel =                 {sound channel}
     PACKED RECORD
        nextChan:            SndChannelPtr;  {pointer to next channel}
        firstMod:            Ptr;            {used internally}
        callBack:            ProcPtr;        {pointer to callback proc}
        userInfo:            LongInt;        {free for application's use}
        wait:                Time;           {used internally}
        cmdInProgress:       SndCommand;     {used internally}
        flags:               Integer;        {used internally}
        qLength:             Integer;        {used internally}
        qHead:               Integer;        {used internally}
        qTail:               Integer;        {used internally}
        queue:               ARRAY[0..stdQLength-1] OF SndCommand
     END;

SoundHeaderPtr = ^SoundHeader;
SoundHeader =                {standard sampled sound header}
     PACKED RECORD
        samplePtr:           Ptr;            {if NIL, samples in sampleArea}
        length:              LongInt;        {number of samples in array}
        sampleRate:          Fixed;          {sample rate}
        loopStart:           LongInt;        {loop point beginning}
        loopEnd:             LongInt;        {loop point ending}
        encode:              Byte;           {sample's encoding option}
        baseFrequency:       Byte;           {base frequency of sample}
        sampleArea:          PACKED ARRAY[0..0] OF Byte
     END;

ExtSoundHeaderPtr = ^ExtSoundHeader;
ExtSoundHeader =                {extended sampled sound header}
     PACKED RECORD
        samplePtr:              Ptr;         {if NIL, samples in sampleArea}
        numChannels:            LongInt;     {number of channels in sample}
        sampleRate:             Fixed;       {rate of original sample}
        loopStart:              LongInt;     {loop point beginning}
        loopEnd:                LongInt;     {loop point ending}
        encode:                 Byte;        {sample's encoding option}
        baseFrequency:          Byte;        {base frequency of original sample}
```

```
      numFrames:          LongInt;     {total number of frames}
      AIFFSampleRate:     Extended;    {rate of original sample}
      markerChunk:        Ptr;         {pointer to marker info}
      instrumentChunks:   Ptr;         {pointer to instrument info}
      AESRecording:       Ptr;         {pointer to audio info}
      sampleSize:         Integer;     {number of bits per sample}
      futureUse1:         Integer;     {reserved}
      futureUse2:         LongInt;     {reserved}
      futureUse3:         LongInt;     {reserved}
      futureUse4:         LongInt;     {reserved}
      sampleArea:         PACKED ARRAY[0..0] OF Byte
   END;

CmpSoundHeaderPtr = ^CmpSoundHeader;
CmpSoundHeader =           {compressed sampled sound header}
   PACKED RECORD
      samplePtr:         Ptr;                {if NIL, samples in sampleArea}
      numChannels:       LongInt;            {number of channels in sample}
      sampleRate:        Fixed;              {rate of original sample}
      loopStart:         LongInt;            {loop point beginning}
      loopEnd:           LongInt;            {loop point ending}
      encode:            Byte;               {sample's encoding option}
      baseFrequency:     Byte;               {base freq. of original sample}
      numFrames:         LongInt;            {length of sample in frames}
      AIFFSampleRate:    Extended;           {rate of original sample}
      markerChunk:       Ptr;                {unused}
      futureUse1:        Ptr;                {reserved}
      futureUse2:        Ptr;                {reserved}
      stateVars:         StateBlockPtr;      {pointer to StateBlock}
      leftOverSamples:   LeftOverBlockPtr;   {pointer to LeftOverBlock}
      compressionID:     Integer;            {ID of compression algorithm}
      packetSize:        Integer;            {number of bits per packet}
      snthID:            Integer;            {ID of compression synth}
      sampleSize:        Integer;            {bits in each sample point}
      sampleArea:        PACKED ARRAY[0..0] OF Byte
   END;

SCStatusPtr = ^SCStatus;
SCStatus =                          {sound-channel status record}
   RECORD
      scStartTime:            Fixed;    {starting time for play from disk}
      scEndTime:              Fixed;    {ending time for play from disk}
      scCurrentTime:          Fixed;    {current time for play from disk}
      scChannelBusy:          Boolean;  {TRUE if channel is making sound}
      scChannelDisposed:      Boolean;  {reserved}
      scChannelPaused:        Boolean;  {TRUE if channel is paused}
      scUnused:               Boolean;  {unused}
      scChannelAttributes:    LongInt;  {attributes of this channel}
      scCPULoad:              LongInt   {CPU load for this channel}
   END;
```

```
SMStatusPtr = ^SMStatus;
SMStatus =                {Sound Manager status record}
     PACKED RECORD
        smMaxCPULoad:     Integer;    {maximum load on all channels}
        smNumChannels:    Integer;    {number of allocated channels}
        smCurCPULoad:     Integer     {current load on all channels}
     END;

AudioSelectionPtr = ^AudioSelection;
AudioSelection =          {audio selection}
     PACKED RECORD
        unitType:         LongInt;    {type of time unit}
        selStart:         Fixed;      {starting point of selection}
        selEnd:           Fixed       {ending point of selection}
     END;

SndDoubleBufferPtr = ^SndDoubleBuffer;
SndDoubleBuffer =    {double buffer for play from disk}
     PACKED RECORD
       dbNumFrames: LongInt;                  {number of frames in buffer}
       dbFlags:     LongInt;                  {buffer status flags}
       dbUserInfo:  ARRAY[0..1] OF LongInt;   {for application's use}
       dbSoundData: PACKED ARRAY[0..0] OF Byte
                                              {array of data}
     END;

SndDoubleBufferHeaderPtr = ^SndDoubleBufferHeader;
SndDoubleBufferHeader =    {double-buffer header for play from disk}
     PACKED RECORD
        dbhNumChannels:   Integer;    {number of sound channels}
        dbhSampleSize:    Integer;    {sample size, if uncompressed}
        dbhCompressionID: Integer;    {ID of compression algorithm}
        dbhPacketSize:    Integer;    {number of bits per packet}
        dbhSampleRate:    Fixed;      {sample rate}
        dbhBufferPtr:     ARRAY[0..1] OF SndDoubleBufferPtr;
                                      {pointers to SndDoubleBuffer}
        dbhDoubleBack:    ProcPtr     {pointer to doubleback procedure}
     END;

SPBPtr = ^SPB;
SPB =    {sound input parameter block}
     RECORD
        inRefNum:           LongInt;    {reference number of input device}
        count:              LongInt;    {number of bytes to record}
        milliseconds:       LongInt;    {number of milliseconds to record}
        bufferLength:       LongInt;    {length of buffer to record into}
        bufferPtr:          Ptr;        {pointer to buffer to record into}
        completionRoutine:  ProcPtr;    {pointer to a completion routine}
        interruptRoutine:   ProcPtr;    {pointer to an interrupt routine}
        userLong:           LongInt;    {for application's use}
        error:              OSErr;      {error returned after recording}
        unused1:            LongInt     {reserved}
     END;
```

```
TYPE ID = LongInt;              {chunk ID type}

ChunkHeader =                   {AIFF and AIFF-C file chunk header}
      RECORD
         ckID:                  ID;           {chunk type ID}
         ckSize:                LongInt       {number of bytes of data}
      END;

ContainerChunk =                {Container Chunk}
      RECORD
         ckID:                  ID;           {'FORM'}
         ckSize:                LongInt;      {number of bytes of data}
         formType:              ID            {type of file}
      END;

FormatVersionChunk =            {Format Version Chunk}
      RECORD
         ckID:                  ID;           {'FVER'}
         ckSize:                LongInt;      {4}
         timestamp:             LongInt       {date of format version}
      END;

CommonChunk =                   {AIFF Common Chunk}
      RECORD
         ckID:                  ID;           {'COMM'}
         ckSize:                LongInt;      {size of chunk data}
         numChannels:           Integer;      {number of channels}
         numSampleFrames:       LongInt;      {number of sample frames}
         sampleSize:            Integer;      {number of bits per sample}
         sampleRate:            Extended      {number of frames per second}
      END;

ExtCommonChunk =                {AIFF-C Common Chunk}
      RECORD
         ckID:                  ID;           {'COMM'}
         ckSize:                LongInt;      {size of chunk data}
         numChannels:           Integer;      {number of channels}
         numSampleFrames:       LongInt;      {number of sample frames}
         sampleSize:            Integer;      {number of bits per sample}
         sampleRate:            Extended;     {number of frames per second}
         compressionType:       ID;           {compression type ID}
         compressionName:       PACKED ARRAY[0..0] OF Byte
                                              {compression type name}
      END;

SoundDataChunk =                {Sound Data Chunk}
      RECORD
         ckID:                  ID;           {'SSND'}
         ckSize:                LongInt;      {size of chunk data}
         offset:                LongInt;      {offset to sound data}
         blockSize:             LongInt       {size of alignment blocks}
      END;
```

Routines

Playing Sound Resources

```
FUNCTION SndPlay              (chan: SndChannelPtr; sndHdl: Handle; async:
                               Boolean) : OSErr;
PROCEDURE SysBeep             (duration: Integer);
PROCEDURE SndGetSysBeepState (VAR sysBeepState: Integer);
FUNCTION SndSetSysBeepState  (sysBeepState: Integer) : OSErr;
```

Allocating and Releasing Sound Channels

```
FUNCTION SndNewChannel       (VAR chan: SndChannelPtr; synth: Integer; init:
                              LongInt; userRoutine: ProcPtr) : OSErr;
FUNCTION SndDisposeChannel   (chan: SndChannelPtr; quietNow: Boolean) :
                              OSErr;
```

Linking Synthesizers to Sound Channels

```
FUNCTION SndAddModifier      (chan: SndChannelPtr; modifier: ProcPtr; id:
                              Integer; init: LongInt) : OSErr;
```

Sending Commands to a Sound Channel

```
FUNCTION SndDoCommand        (chan: SndChannelPtr; cmd: SndCommand; noWait:
                              Boolean) : OSErr;
FUNCTION SndDoImmediate      (chan: SndChannelPtr; cmd: SndCommand) :
                              OSErr;
```

Obtaining Information

```
FUNCTION SndControl              (id: Integer; VAR cmd: SndCommand) : OSErr;
FUNCTION SndChannelStatus        (chan: SndChannelPtr; theLength: Integer;
                                  theStatus: SCStatusPtr) : OSErr;
FUNCTION SndManagerStatus        (theLength: Integer; theStatus:
                                  SMStatusPtr) : OSErr;
FUNCTION SndSoundManagerVersion : NumVersion;
FUNCTION MACEVersion             : NumVersion;
FUNCTION SPBVersion              : NumVersion;
```

Playing From Disk

```
FUNCTION SndStartFilePlay    (chan: SndChannelPtr; fRefNum: Integer;
                              resNum: Integer; bufferSize: LongInt;
                              theBuffer: Ptr; theSelection:
                              AudioSelectionPtr; theCompletion: ProcPtr;
                              async: Boolean) : OSErr;

FUNCTION SndPauseFilePlay    (chan: SndChannelPtr) : OSErr;

FUNCTION SndStopFilePlay     (chan: SndChannelPtr; async: Boolean) :
                              OSErr;
```

Managing Double Buffers

```
FUNCTION SndPlayDoubleBuffer (chan: SndChannelPtr; theParams:
                              SndDoubleBufferHeaderPtr) : OSErr;
```

Compressing and Expanding Audio Data

```
PROCEDURE Comp3to1         (inBuffer: Ptr; outBuffer: Ptr; cnt:
                            LongInt; inState: Ptr; outState: Ptr;
                            numChannels: LongInt; whichChannel: LongInt);

PROCEDURE Comp6to1         (inBuffer: Ptr; outBuffer: Ptr; cnt: LongInt;
                            inState: Ptr; outState: Ptr; numChannels:
                            LongInt; whichChannel: LongInt);

PROCEDURE Exp1to3          (inBuffer: Ptr; outBuffer: Ptr; cnt: LongInt;
                            inState: Ptr; outState: Ptr; numChannels:
                            LongInt; whichChannel: LongInt);

PROCEDURE Exp1to6          (inBuffer: Ptr; outBuffer: Ptr; cnt: LongInt;
                            inState: Ptr; outState: Ptr; numChannels:
                            LongInt; whichChannel: LongInt);
```

Recording Sounds

```
FUNCTION SndRecord         (filterProc: ProcPtr; corner: Point; quality:
                            OSType; VAR sndHandle: Handle) : OSErr;

FUNCTION SndRecordToFile   (filterProc: ProcPtr; corner: Point; quality:
                            OSType; fRefNum: Integer) : OSErr;
```

Opening and Closing Sound Input Devices

```
FUNCTION SPBOpenDevice     (deviceName: Str255; permission: Integer; VAR
                            inRefNum: LongInt) : OSErr;

FUNCTION SPBCloseDevice    (inRefNum: LongInt) : OSErr;
```

Recording Sounds Directly From Sound Input Devices

```
FUNCTION SPBRecord              (inParamPtr: SPBPtr; asynchFlag: Boolean) :
                                 OSErr;
FUNCTION SPBRecordToFile        (fRefNum: Integer; inParamPtr: SPBPtr;
                                 asynchFlag: Boolean) : OSErr;
FUNCTION SPBPauseRecording      (inRefNum: LongInt) : OSErr;
FUNCTION SPBResumeRecording     (inRefNum: LongInt) : OSErr;
FUNCTION SPBStopRecording       (inRefNum: LongInt) : OSErr;
FUNCTION SPBGetRecordingStatus (inRefNum: LongInt; VAR recordingStatus:
                                 Integer; VAR meterLevel: Integer; VAR
                                 totalSamplesToRecord: LongInt; VAR
                                 numberOfSamplesRecorded: LongInt; VAR
                                 totalMsecsToRecord: LongInt; VAR
                                 numberOfMsecsRecorded: LongInt) : OSErr;
```

Manipulating Device Settings

```
FUNCTION SPBGetDeviceInfo   (inRefNum: LongInt; infoType: OSType; infoData:
                             Ptr) : OSErr;
FUNCTION SPBSetDeviceInfo   (inRefNum: LongInt; infoType: OSType;
                             infoData: Ptr) : OSErr;
```

Constructing Sound Resource and File Headers

```
FUNCTION SetupSndHeader     (sndHandle: Handle; numChannels: Integer;
                             sampleRate: Fixed; sampleSize: Integer;
                             compressionType: OSType; baseFrequency:
                             Integer; numBytes: LongInt; VAR headerLen:
                             Integer) : OSErr;
FUNCTION SetupAIFFHeader    (fRefNum: Integer; numChannels: Integer;
                             sampleRate: Fixed; sampleSize: Integer;
                             compressionType: OSType; numBytes: LongInt;
                             numFrames: LongInt) : OSErr;
```

Registering Sound Input Devices

```
FUNCTION SPBSignInDevice     (deviceRefNum: Integer; deviceName: Str255) :
                              OSErr;
FUNCTION SPBSignOutDevice    (deviceRefNum: Integer) : OSErr;
FUNCTION SPBGetIndexedDevice (count: Integer; VAR deviceName: Str255; VAR
                              deviceIconHandle: Handle) : OSErr;
```

Converting Between Milliseconds and Bytes

```
FUNCTION SPBMilliSecondsToBytes (inRefNum: LongInt; VAR milliseconds:
                                LongInt) : OSErr;

FUNCTION SPBBytesToMilliSeconds (inRefNum: LongInt; VAR byteCount:
                                LongInt) : OSErr;
```

Application-Defined Routines

```
PROCEDURE MyRecordCompletionRoutine   (inParamPtr: SPBPtr);

PROCEDURE MyDoubleBackProc            (chan: SndChannelPtr;
                                       exhaustedBuffer:
                                       SndDoubleBufferPtr);

PROCEDURE MyCallBack                  (chan: SndChannelPtr; cmd:
                                       SndCommand);

PROCEDURE MyFilePlayCompletionRoutine (chan: SndChannelPtr);
```

Result Codes

noErr	0	No error
noHardwareErr	–200	Required sound hardware not available
notEnoughHardwareErr	–201	Insufficient hardware available
queueFull	–203	No room in the queue
resProblem	–204	Problem loading the resource
badChannel	–205	Channel is corrupt or unusable
badFormat	–206	Resource is corrupt or unusable
notEnoughBufferSpace	–207	Insufficient memory available
badFileFormat	–208	File is corrupt or unusable, or not AIFF or AIFF-C
channelBusy	–209	Channel is busy
buffersTooSmall	–210	Buffer is too small
channelNotBusy	–211	Channel not currently used
noMoreRealTime	–212	Not enough CPU time available
siNoSoundInHardware	–220	No sound input hardware available
siBadSoundInDevice	–221	Invalid sound input device
siNoBufferSpecified	–222	No buffer specified
siInvalidCompression	–223	Invalid compression type
siHardDriveTooSlow	–224	Hard drive too slow to record
siInvalidSampleRate	–225	Invalid sample rate
siInvalidSampleSize	–226	Invalid sample size
siDeviceBusyErr	–227	Sound input device is busy
siBadDeviceName	–228	Invalid device name
siBadRefNum	–229	Invalid reference number
siInputDeviceErr	–230	Input device hardware failure
siUnknownInfoType	–231	Unknown type of information
siUnknownQuality	–232	Unknown quality

Assembly-Language Information

Sound Input Parameter Block Data Structure

→	0	inRefNum	long	input device reference number
↔	4	count	long	number of bytes to record
↔	8	milliseconds	long	number of milliseconds to record
→	12	bufferLength	long	length of buffer
→	16	bufferPtr	long	address of buffer
→	20	completionRoutine	long	pointer to completion routine
→	24	interruptRoutine	long	pointer to interrupt routine
→	28	userLong	long	for application's use
←	32	error	word	error returned after recording
→	36	unused1	long	reserved

23 THE TIME MANAGER

ABOUT THIS CHAPTER

This chapter describes how you can use the Time Manager to schedule execution of a routine after a specified amount of time has elapsed. This chapter replaces the Time Manager chapter in Volume IV. It includes all the information about the original Time Manager, as well as additional information about the revised Time Manager included with system software version 6.0.3 (and later) and about the extended Time Manager included with system software version 7.0.

Because different versions of the Time Manager are available under different system software versions, your application may need to determine which version is available in its current operating environment. To do so, you can use the Gestalt function explained in the Compatibility Guidelines chapter of this volume.

To use this chapter, you should already be familiar with

- operating-system queues, as described in the Operating System Utilities chapter of Volume II
- the Vertical Retrace Manager, as described in the Vertical Retrace Manager chapter in Volume II and Volume V

You need to know about operating-system queues because all Time Manager routines involve inserting entries into a queue and then activating or removing queued entries. You should be acquainted with the Vertical Retrace Manager because it provides an alternative (and sometimes preferable) method for scheduling routines for future or periodic execution.

ABOUT THE TIME MANAGER

The primary service that the Time Manager provides to applications is a method for scheduling routines to execute at a later time. By suitably defining the task that later executes, you can use the Time Manager to accomplish a wide range of time-related activities. For example, because one of the actions a routine can perform is to reschedule itself for later execution, the Time Manager provides your application with a means to perform periodic or repeated actions. You can use the Time Manager to

- schedule routines to execute after a specified delay
- set up tasks that run periodically
- compute the time a routine takes to execute
- coordinate and synchronize actions in the Macintosh® computer

The Time Manager provides a hardware-independent method of performing these and other time-related tasks. You should use the Time Manager instead of cycle-counting timing loops, which can vary in duration because they are dependent upon clock speed and interrupt-handling speed. Furthermore, on machines with 68020 or 68030 microprocessors, it is almost impossible to rely on cycle-counting loops because instructions may be both cached and pipelined. In such cases, it is very difficult to tell what part of the instruction cycle the machine is currently in.

To use the Time Manager, you must first issue a request by passing the Time Manager the address of a task record, one of whose fields contains the address of the routine that is to execute. Then you need to activate that request by specifying the delay until the routine is to execute. The Time Manager maintains requests that you issue in a queue, whose structure is similar to that of standard Macintosh operating-system queues. Any number of outstanding requests can be in the Time Manager queue, and each application can add any number of entries to the queue. If several requests happen to schedule routines for execution at exactly the same time, those routines will execute as close to the scheduled time as possible, in the order in which they entered the Time Manager queue.

The routine you place in the queue can perform any desired action so long as it does not call the Memory Manager, either directly or indirectly. You cannot call the Memory Manager because Time Manager tasks execute at interrupt time.

Time Manager Versions

The Time Manager included in system software version 7.0 is the third version released. The three versions are all upwardly compatible—that is, each succeeding Time Manager version is a functional superset of the previous one, and code written for a version of the Time Manager executes on any later version. The reverse, however, is not true, and code written for the extended Time Manager may not execute properly on either the original or revised version. As a result, it is sometimes important to know which Time Manager version is available on a specific machine. You can use the Gestalt function to determine which version is present.

The Original Time Manager

The Time Manager was first introduced with the Macintosh Plus ROMs (which are also contained in the Macintosh 512K enhanced) and was intended for use internally by the Operating System. Volume IV of *Inside Macintosh* documented the routines in the original Time Manager, and thereafter some applications used them to schedule tasks to be executed at later times. The original Time Manager allows delays as small as 1 millisecond, resulting in a maximum range of about 24 days.

To schedule a task for later execution, you place an entry into the Time Manager queue and then activate it. All Time Manager routines manipulate elements of the Time Manager queue, which are stored in a Time Manager task record. The task record for the original Time Manager looks like this:

```
TYPE TMTask =          {original and revised Time Manager task record}
     RECORD
        qLink:         QElemPtr;            {next queue entry}
        qType:         Integer;             {queue type}
        tmAddr:        ProcPtr;             {pointer to task}
        tmCount:       LongInt              {reserved}
     END;
```

Of the four fields in this record, your application needs to supply only the tmAddr field, which contains a pointer to the routine that is to be executed at some time in the future. The remaining fields are used internally by the Time Manager or are reserved by Apple Computer, Inc. Your application should set these remaining fields to 0 when you set up a task record.

The original Time Manager includes three routines:

- The InsTime procedure installs a task record into the Time Manager queue.
- The PrimeTime procedure schedules a previously queued task record for future execution.
- The RmvTime procedure removes a task record from the Time Manager queue.

Note that installing a request into the Time Manager queue (using the InsTime procedure) does not by itself schedule the specified routine for future execution. After you queue a request, you still need to activate (or *prime*) the request by specifying the desired delay until execution (using the PrimeTime procedure). Note also that the task record is not automatically removed from the Time Manager queue after the routine executes. As a result, the task may be reactivated when you subsequently call PrimeTime; you do not have to reinstall the task record. To remove a task record from the queue, you must call the RmvTime procedure. RmvTime removes a task record from the Time Manager queue whether or not that task was ever activated and whether or not its specified time delay has expired.

The Revised Time Manager

System software version 6.0.3 contains a revised version of the Time Manager. This version provides better time resolution and the ability to perform measurements of elapsed time with much greater accuracy. You can represent time delays in the revised Time Manager as microseconds as well as milliseconds, with a maximum resolution of 20 microseconds. The external programming interface did not change from the original to the revised Time Manager, although the revised version provides a means to distinguish microsecond delays from millisecond delays. The revised Time Manager interprets negative time values (which were not formerly allowed) as negated microseconds. For example, a value of –50 is interpreted as a delay of 50 microseconds. Positive time values continue to represent milliseconds. When you specify delays as microseconds, the maximum delay is about 35 minutes. When you specify delays as milliseconds in the revised Time Manager, the maximum delay is about 1 day. The delay specified to PrimeTime is converted to an internal form, so it makes no difference which unit you use if the delay falls within the ranges of both.

The revised Time Manager provides additional Time Manager features. The principal change concerns the tmCount field of the Time Manager task record (previously reserved for use by Apple). When you remove an active task from the revised Time Manager's queue, any time remaining until the scheduled execution time is returned in the tmCount field. This change allows you to use the Time Manager to compute elapsed times (as explained in "Computing Elapsed Time" later in this chapter). In addition, the high-order bit of the qType field of the task record is now a flag to indicate whether the task timer is active. The InsTime procedure initially clears this bit, PrimeTime sets it, and it is cleared when the time expires or when your application calls RmvTime.

Although the revised Time Manager supports delay times specified in microseconds, you should use this feature primarily for the more accurate measurement of elapsed times. Applications that specify very small delay times in order to execute a routine at a high frequency may use a considerable amount of processor time. The amount of processor time consumed by such timing services varies, depending largely on the performance of the CPU. With low-performance CPUs, little or no time may be left for other processing on the system (for instance, moving the mouse or running the application).

The Extended Time Manager

The extended Time Manager (available with system software version 7.0) contains all the features of earlier Time Managers, with several extensions intended primarily to provide drift-free, fixed-frequency timing services. These services ensure that a routine executes promptly after a specified delay and are important for sound and multimedia applications that require precise timing and real-time synchronization among different events.

In the original and revised Time Managers, the delay time passed to PrimeTime indicates a delay that is relative to the current time (that is, the time at which you execute PrimeTime). This presents problems when you need a fixed-frequency timing service and attempt to implement it by having the task reissue a PrimeTime call. The problem is that the time consumed by the Time Manager and by any interrupt latency (which is not predictable) causes the task to be called at a slightly slower and unpredictable frequency, which drifts over time. In Figure 23-1, a fixed frequency of 1000 microseconds is desired but cannot be achieved because the Time Manager overhead and interrupt latency cause a small and unpredictable delay each time the task is reactivated.

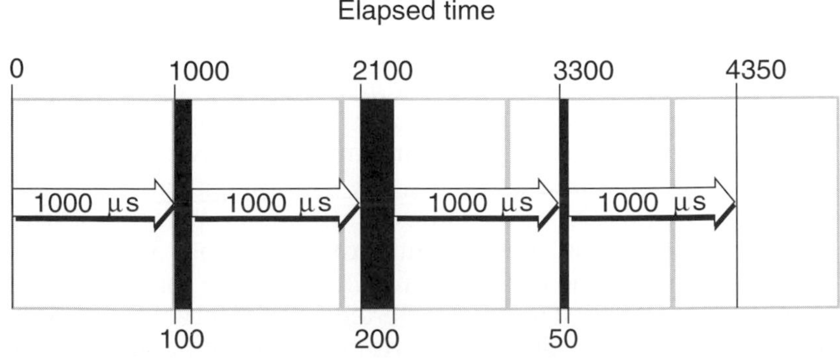

Figure 23-1. Original and revised Time Managers (drifting, unpredictable frequency)

The extended Time Manager solves this problem by allowing you to reinstall a task with an execution time that is relative to the time when the task last expired—not relative to the time when the task is reinstalled. The extended Time Manager compensates for the delay between the time when the task last expired and the time at which it was reinstalled, thereby providing a truly drift-free, fixed-frequency timing service.

For example, if an application needs to execute a routine periodically at 1-millisecond intervals, it can reactivate the existing Time Manager queue element by calling PrimeTime in the task with a specified delay of 1 millisecond. When the Time Manager receives this new execution request, it determines how long ago the previous PrimeTime task expired and then decrements the specified delay by that amount. For instance, if the previous task expired 100 microseconds ago, then the Time Manager installs the new task with a delay of 900 microseconds. This is illustrated in Figure 23-2.

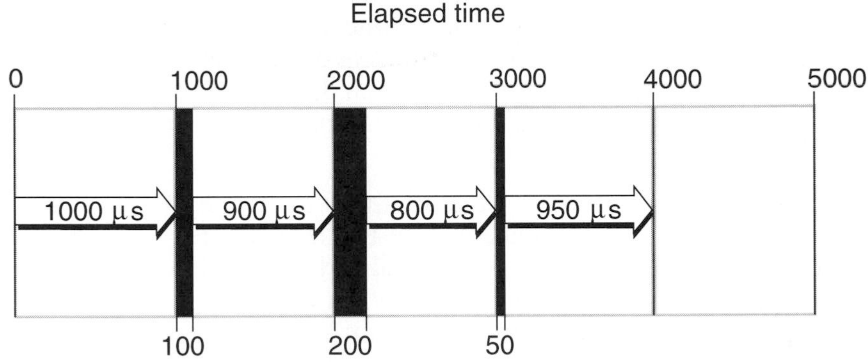

Figure 23-2. The extended Time Manager (drift-free, fixed frequency)

The extended Time Manager implements these features by recognizing an expanded task record and providing a new procedure, InsXTime. The Time Manager task record for the extended Time Manager looks like this:

```
TYPE TMTask =                  {extended Time Manager task record}
     RECORD
        qLink:                 QElemPtr;       {next queue entry}
        qType:                 Integer;        {queue type}
        tmAddr:                ProcPtr;        {pointer to task}
        tmCount:               LongInt;        {unused time}
        tmWakeUp:              LongInt;        {wakeup time}
        tmReserved:            LongInt         {reserved for future use}
     END;
```

Once again, your application provides the tmAddr field. You should set tmWakeUp and tmReserved to 0 when you first install an extended Time Manager task. The remaining fields are used internally by the Time Manager. As in the revised Time Manager, the tmCount field holds the time remaining until the scheduled execution of the task (this field is set by RmvTime).

The tmWakeUp field contains the time at which the Time Manager task specified by tmAddr last executed or contains 0 if it has not yet executed. Its principal intended use is to provide drift-free, fixed-frequency timing services, which are available only when you use the extended Time Manager and only when you install Time Manager tasks using the new InsXTime procedure. When your application installs an extended Time Manager task (using the InsXTime procedure), the behavior of the PrimeTime procedure changes slightly, as described earlier in this section. If the tmWakeUp field is zero when PrimeTime is called, the delay parameter to PrimeTime is interpreted as relative to the current time (just as in the original Time Manager), but the Time Manager sets the tmWakeUp field to a nonzero value that indicates when the delay time should expire. When your application calls PrimeTime on a Time Manager task that has a nonzero value in the tmWakeUp field, the Time Manager interprets the specified delay as relative to the time that the last call to PrimeTime on this task was supposed to expire.

> **Note:** Nonzero values in tmWakeUp are in a format that is used internally by the Time Manager and is subject to change. Your application should never use the value stored in this field and should either set it to 0 or leave it unchanged. When you first create an extended task record, you must ensure that the tmWakeUp field is 0; otherwise, the Time Manager may interpret it as a prior execution time.

The extended Time Manager allows for a situation that was previously impossible and that may lead to undesirable results. It is possible to call PrimeTime with an execution time that is in the past instead of in the future. (With the original and revised Time Managers, only future execution times are possible.) This situation arises when the time in the tmWakeUp field is sometime in the past (which is most common in the tmAddr service routine) and you issue a new PrimeTime request with a delay value that is not large enough to cause the execution time to be in the future. This may occur when fixed, high-frequency execution is required and the time needed to process each execution, including the Time Manager overhead, is greater than the delay time between requests.

When your application issues a PrimeTime request with a tmWakeUp value that would result in a negative delay, the actual delay time is set to 0. The Time Manager updates the tmWakeUp field to indicate the time when the task should have awakened (in the past). Because the actual delay time is set to 0, the task executes immediately. If your application continually issues PrimeTime requests for times in the past, the Time Manager and the tmAddr tasks consume all of the processor cycles. As a result, no time is left for the application to run. This situation is a function of processor speed, so you should test applications that use extended Time Manager features on the slowest processors to ensure compatibility. Another solution to this problem is to vary the wakeup frequency according to the processing power of the machine.

Other Time-Related Facilities

The Operating System and Toolbox include several other time-related facilities that complement the services provided by the Time Manager. There are three principal facilities: the TickCount function, the Delay function, and the Vertical Retrace Manager. One or more of these services may be more appropriate for your particular timing needs than the Time Manager.

The TickCount Function

The Toolbox Event Manager includes the TickCount function, which returns the total number of ticks (sixtieths of a second) that have elapsed since the system last started up. The tick count (maintained in the Ticks global variable) is incremented during the vertical retrace interrupt. Because this interrupt can sometimes be disabled, the value TickCount returns may not be exact.

Using the TickCount function, you can write code that mimics some of the capabilities of the Time Manager. For example, your application can cause a routine to be executed at some time in the future by simply waiting until the appropriate time and then executing the desired routine. Your application can delay its own operation by repeatedly calling TickCount until Ticks exceeds a specified threshold value. Similarly, your application can obtain elapsed-time information by reading the current tick count at the beginning and at the end of the routine that you want to time.

The Delay Function

There is a better way for your application to delay its own operation than repeatedly calling the TickCount function—namely, by executing Delay, an operating-system routine that causes the system to wait a specified number of ticks before resuming execution of your application. When Delay exits, the Operating System returns the current value of the Ticks global variable to the calling application. Delay is used primarily to suspend an application for a particular amount of time and to execute a routine at a later time—after Delay has exited. But this provides much less control over a routine's future execution than that provided by the scheduling services of the Time Manager. With the Delay function, you cannot return to your application's code during the delay. Once you queue and activate a Time Manager task, however, control immediately returns to your application.

Furthermore, the Time Manager provides far greater accuracy than the Delay function. Using the TickCount and Delay functions may provide sufficiently accurate timing control, but you need to use the Time Manager routines in cases where very high resolutions are required, as in performance measurements based on elapsed-time information.

The Vertical Retrace Manager

Originally, the Vertical Retrace Manager handled the queuing and execution of tasks scheduled to run during VBL interrupts, which occurred each time the electron beam in the video screen returned from the lower-right to the upper-left corner of the built-in screen. The VBL interrupts occurred at a known frequency (once every sixtieth of a second), and an application could use the VInstall function to schedule execution of a task once or continually after some specified number of VBL interrupts. In this way, your application could schedule periodic tasks even before the Time Manager existed.

Once it became possible to use external monitors with certain Macintosh computers, the Vertical Retrace Manager was changed to support different refresh rates and multiple queues. New slot-based VBL interrupts were added—one for each attached video device, with a rate determined by that video device. The older once-a-tick VBL interrupts were retained, however, for compatibility reasons. So an application can still schedule routines for execution during a slot-generated VBL interrupt (using the slotVInstall function) or during a system-generated VBL interrupt (using the original VInstall). In either case, the indicated routine runs at the future time specified in the call.

You can use either the Time Manager or the Vertical Retrace Manager to schedule future or periodic tasks. The main difference between the two scheduling methods is the precision with which those tasks can be scheduled. You can call system-generated VBL tasks with a minimum period of 1 tick (one-sixtieth of a second), which is approximately 16 milliseconds. You can call slot-generated VBL tasks with a minimum period that depends on the refresh rate of the particular video device associated with that slot, which is usually close to 1 tick. The extended Time Manager routines provide much finer resolution, up to 20 microseconds. Hence, the resolution of the Time Manager is about 1000 times greater than that of the Vertical Retrace Manager. So in cases where very high resolution is important, you should use the Time Manager routines instead of the Vertical Retrace Manager routines.

Unlike the Time Manager, the Vertical Retrace Manager is not an absolute time mechanism. Its operations are always relative to the VBL interrupt, which may be disabled (for instance, during disk access). As a result, you should use the Time Manager in cases where absolute time delays are important. Use the Vertical Retrace Manager, however, in cases where the scheduled actions need simply to be synchronized with other VBL tasks, such as cursor movement or screen refresh. Applications that do animation on the screen (for example, some games or multimedia applications) are the kinds of programs that should probably use VBL tasks instead of Time Manager tasks to perform periodic actions.

USING THE TIME MANAGER

The Time Manager is automatically initialized when the system starts up. At that time, the queue of Time Manager task records is empty. The Operating System and applications may place records into the queue. Because the delay time for a given task can be as small as 20 microseconds, you need to install an element into the Time Manager queue before actually issuing a request to execute it at some future time. You place elements into the queue by calling the InsTime procedure or (if you need the fixed-frequency services of the extended Time Manager) the InsXTime procedure. To activate the request, call PrimeTime. The Time Manager then marks the specified task record as active by setting the high-order bit in the qType field of that record.

The tmAddr field of the Time Manager task record contains the address of a task that the Time Manager calls when the time delay specified by a previous call to PrimeTime has elapsed. The task can perform any desired actions, so long as those actions do not call the Memory Manager (either directly or indirectly) and do not depend on the validity of handles to unlocked blocks. Time Manager tasks must also preserve all registers other than A0–A3 and D0–D3.

If the routine specified in the Time Manager task record is loaded into the application's heap, then the application must still be active when the specified delay elapses, or the application should call RmvTime before it terminates. Otherwise, the Time Manager will not know that the address of that routine is not valid when the routine is called. The Time Manager will then attempt to call the task, but with a stale pointer. If you want to let the application terminate after it has installed and activated a Time Manager task record, you should load the routine into the system heap. Generally, however, you should avoid loading routines into the system heap.

Assembly-language note: In the revised and extended Time Managers, when a Time Manager task is called, register A1 contains a pointer to the Time Manager task record associated with that routine.

There are two ways in which an active queue element can become inactive. First, the specified time delay can elapse, in which case the routine pointed to by the tmAddr field is called. Second, your application can call the RmvTime procedure, in which case the amount of time remaining before the delay would have elapsed (the unused time) is reported in the tmCount field of the task record. This feature allows you to use the Time Manager to compute elapsed times (see "Computing Elapsed Time" later in this chapter), which is useful for obtaining performance measurements. Calling RmvTime removes an element from the queue whether or not that task is active at the time RmvTime is called.

To use the Time Manager to perform actions periodically, you simply need to have the routine pointed to by tmAddr call PrimeTime again. This technique is illustrated in "Performing Periodic Tasks" later in this chapter. Similarly, you can set up a Time Manager task to execute a specific number of times by keeping a count of the number of times the task has been called. In cases where the task needs access to your application's global variables (such as a count variable), you need to ensure that the A5 register points to your application's global variables when the task executes and that A5 contains its original value when your task exits. A technique for doing this is illustrated in "Using Application Global Variables in Tasks" later in this chapter.

Installing and Activating Task Records

Listing 23-1 shows how to install and activate a Time Manager task. It assumes that the procedure MyTask has already been defined; see Listings 23-3 and 23-4 for examples of simple task definitions.

Listing 23-1. Installing and activating a Time Manager task

```
PROCEDURE InstallTMTask;
VAR
   myTMTask:    TMTask;                     {an extended task record}
   myDelay:     LongInt;                    {delay value}
BEGIN
   myDelay := 2000;                         {no. of milliseconds to delay}
   myTMTask.tmAddr := @MyTask;              {get address of task}
   myTMTask.tmWakeUp := 0;                  {initialize tmWakeUp}
   myTMTask.tmReserved := 0;                {initialize tmReserved}
   InsXTime(@myTMTask);                     {install the task record}
   PrimeTime(@myTMTask, myDelay);           {activate the task record}
END;
```

In this example, InstallTMTask installs an extended task record into the Time Manager queue and then activates the task. After the specified delay has elapsed (in this case, 2000 milliseconds, or 2 seconds), the procedure MyTask executes.

In cases where no task is to run after the specified time delay has elapsed, you should set the tmAddr field to NIL. To determine if the time has expired, you can check the task-active bit in the qType field.

Calling PrimeTime on a Time Manager task record that has not yet expired yields unpredictable results and should therefore be avoided. If a prior unexpired request exists in the Time Manager queue that you wish to reactivate for some different delay, you should call RmvTime to cancel the prior request, then call InsTime to reinstall the timer task, and finally call PrimeTime to reschedule the task. Note, however, that it is possible and sometimes desirable to call PrimeTime in a Time Manager task that you want to reactivate, because the timer will have expired before the task is called.

Using Application Global Variables in Tasks

When a Time Manager task executes, the A5 world of the application that installed the corresponding task record into the Time Manager queue might not be valid (for example, the task might execute at interrupt time when that application is not the current application). If so, an attempt to read the application's global variables would return erroneous results because the A5 register would point to the application global variables of some other application. When a Time Manager task uses an application's global variables, it must therefore ensure that register A5 contains the address of the boundary between the application global variables and the application parameters of the application that launched it. The task must also restore register A5 to its original value before exiting.

It is relatively straightforward to read the current value of the A5 register when a Time Manager task begins to execute (using the SetCurrentA5 function) and to restore it before exiting (using the SetA5 function). It is more complicated, however, to pass to a Time Manager task the value to which it should set A5 before accessing its application's global variables. The reason for this is quite simple: neither the original nor the extended Time Manager task record contains an unused field in which the application could pass this information to the task. The situation here is unlike the situation with Notification Manager tasks or Sound Manager callback routines (both of which provide an easy way to pass the address of the application's A5 world to the task), but it is similar to the situation with VBL tasks.

One way to gain access to the global variables of the application that launched a Time Manager task from within that task is to pass to InsTime (or InsXTime) and PrimeTime the address of a structure, the first segment of which is simply the corresponding Time Manager task record and the remaining segment of which contains the address of the application's A5 world. For example, you can define a new data structure, a Time Manager information record, as follows:

```
TYPE TMInfo =                          {Time Manager information record}
     RECORD
         atmTask:      TMTask;         {original and revised TM task record}
         tmWakeUp:     LongInt;        {tmWakeUp in extended task record}
         tmReserved:   LongInt;        {tmReserved in extended task record}
         tmRefCon:     LongInt         {space to pass address of A5 world}
     END;

TMInfoPtr = ^TMInfo;
```

Then you can install and activate your Time Manager task as illustrated in Listing 23-2.

Listing 23-2. Passing the address of the application's A5 world to a Time Manager task

```
PROCEDURE InstallTMTask;
VAR
   myTMInfo:    TMInfo;                    {a TM information record}
   myDelay:     LongInt;                   {delay value}
BEGIN
   myDelay := 2000;                        {no. of milliseconds to delay}
   myTMInfo.atmTask.tmAddr := @MyTask;     {get address of task}
   myTMInfo.tmWakeUp := 0;                 {initialize tmWakeUp}
   myTMInfo.tmReserved := 0;               {initialize tmReserved}
   myTMInfo.tmRefCon := SetCurrentA5;      {store address of your A5 world}
   InsTime(@myTMInfo);                     {install the info record}
   PrimeTime(@myTMInfo, myDelay);          {activate the info record}
END;
```

With the revised and extended Time Managers, the task is called with register A1 containing the address passed to InsTime (or InsXTime) and PrimeTime. So the Time Manager task simply needs to retrieve the TMInfo record and extract the appropriate value of the application's A5 world. Listing 23-3 illustrates a sample task definition that does this.

Listing 23-3. Defining a Time Manager task that can manipulate global variables

```
FUNCTION GetTMInfo: TMInfoPtr;
   INLINE $2E89;                           {MOVE.L A1,(SP)}

PROCEDURE MyTask;                          {for revised and extended TMs}
VAR
   oldA5:    LongInt;                      {A5 when task is called}
   recPtr:   TMInfoPtr;
BEGIN
   recPtr := GetTMInfo;                    {first get your record}
   oldA5 := SetA5(recPtr^.tmRefCon);       {set A5 to app's A5 world}

   {do something with the application's globals in here}

   oldA5 := SetA5(oldA5);                  {restore original A5 }
                                           { and ignore result}
END;
```

The main reason that this technique works is that the revised and extended Time Managers do not care if the record whose address is passed to InsTime (or InsXTime) and PrimeTime is bigger than what they are expecting. If you use this technique, however, you should take care to retrieve the address of the task record from register A1 as soon as you enter the Time Manager task (because some compilers generate code that uses registers A0 and A1 to dereference structures).

Note: The technique illustrated in Listing 23-3 cannot be used with the original Time Manager because that version of the Time Manager does not pass the address of the task record in register A1. To gain access to your application's global variables when using the original Time Manager, you would need to store your application's A5 in one of the application's code segments (in particular, in the code segment that contains the Time Manager task). This technique involves the use of self-modifying code segments and is not recommended. Applications that attempt to modify their own 'CODE' resources may crash in operating environments that restrict an application's access to its own code segments (as, for example, in A/UX®).

Performing Periodic Tasks

One way to install a periodic Time Manager task is to have the task reactivate itself. Because the task record is already inserted into the Time Manager task queue, the task can simply call PrimeTime to do this. To call PrimeTime, however, the task needs to know the address of the corresponding task record. In the revised and extended Time Managers, the task record's address is placed into register A1 when the task is called. Listing 23-4 illustrates how the task can reactivate itself by retrieving the address in register A1 and passing that address to PrimeTime.

Listing 23-4. Defining a periodic Time Manager task

```
FUNCTION GetTMInfo: TMInfoPtr;
   INLINE $2E89;                {MOVE.L A1,(SP)}

PROCEDURE MyTask;               {for revised and extended TMs}
VAR
   recPtr:  TMInfoPtr;
   myDelay: LongInt;            {delay value}
BEGIN
   recPtr := GetTMInfo;         {first get your own address}
   myDelay := 2000;             {no. of milliseconds to delay}

   {do something in here}

   PrimeTime(QElemPtr(recPtr), myDelay);
END;
```

Note: The technique illustrated in Listing 23-4 cannot be used with the original Time Manager because that version of the Time Manager does not pass the address of the task record in register A1.

Computing Elapsed Time

The RmvTime procedure in the revised and extended Time Managers returns any unused time in the tmCount field of the task record. This feature makes the Time Manager extremely useful for computing elapsed times, which can, in turn, provide performance measurements.

To compute the amount of time that a routine takes to execute, call PrimeTime at the beginning of the interval to be measured and specify a delay greater than the expected elapsed time. Then call RmvTime at the end of the interval and subtract the unused time returned in tmCount from the original delay passed to PrimeTime. To obtain the most accurate results, you should do all timing in microseconds (in which case the tmCount field of the task record has a range of about 35 minutes). To get an exact measurement, you should compute the overhead associated with calling the Time Manager and subtract it from the preliminary result. Listing 23-5 illustrates a technique for doing this.

Listing 23-5. Computing elapsed time

```
;allocate and clear a TMTask record on the stack
;setting tmAddr := 0 means no task
        moveq.l  #(tmQSize/2)-1,d0 ;set up loop counter
                                   ; to clear TMTask
@clear  clr.w    -(sp)             ;allocate and clear TMTask record
        dbra     d0,@clear         ;clear it a word at a time
        move.l   #60*1000*1000,d7  ;D7 := delay in microseconds
                                   ; (1 minute)
        movea.l  sp,a0             ;A0 points to TMTask
        _InsTime                   ;install the task
        move.l   d7,d6             ;D6 := copy of initial delay
        move.l   d7,d0             ;D0 := delay time
        neg.l    d0                ;negate it for microseconds
        _PrimeTime                 ;start the timer
        _RmvTime                   ;immediately stop it
;unused time will be returned in negated microseconds,
; so adding is really subtracting
        add.l    tmCount(a0),d7    ;D7 := initial delay -
                                   ; time remaining
;D7 now contains the overhead in microseconds of _PrimeTime and _RmvTime
        movea.l  sp,a0             ;A0 points to TMTask record
        _InsTime                   ;install the task
        move.l   d6,d0             ;D0 := delay time
        neg.l    d0                ;negate it for microseconds
        _PrimeTime                 ;start the timer
;beginning of code to be timed
; (in this example, a TimeDBRA loop)
        move.w   TimeDBRA,d0       ;number of DBRAs per millisecond
@dbraLoop   dbra     d0,@dbraLoop  ;waste a millisecond
;end of code to be timed
        _RmvTime                   ;stop the timer
        add.l    tmCount(a0),d6    ;D6 := time used in microseconds
        sub.l    d7,d6             ;subtract the Time Mgr overhead
        adda.w   #tmQSize,sp       ;deallocate TMTask record
;register D6 now contains the number of microseconds
; used by the timed code
```

If you run this code, you might notice that on some models of the Macintosh, register D6 is not very close to 1000 (one millisecond). This is *not* due to a problem in the Time Manager. Rather, this occurs because TimeDBRA is the number of DBRA instructions per millisecond when executing out of ROM, and RAM accesses have different timing on some models.

Note: You should not run this sample code on a Macintosh Plus because that computer's ROM does not support the TimeDBRA variable.

TIME MANAGER ROUTINES

You can insert a task record into the Time Manager's queue by calling InsTime or InsXTime. Use InsXTime only if you wish to use the drift-free, fixed-frequency timing services of the extended Time Manager; use InsTime in all other cases. After you have queued a task record, you can activate it by calling PrimeTime. You can remove a task record from the queue by calling RmvTime.

```
PROCEDURE InsTime (tmTaskPtr: QElemPtr);
```

Trap macro	_InsTime
On entry	A0: address of TMTask record
On exit	D0: result code

InsTime adds the Time Manager task record specified by tmTaskPtr to the Time Manager queue. Your application should fill in the tmAddr field of the task record and should set the remaining fields to 0. The tmTaskPtr parameter must point to an original Time Manager task record.

With the revised and extended Time Managers, you can set tmAddr to NIL if you do not want a task to execute when the delay passed to PrimeTime expires. Also, calling InsTime with the revised Time Manager causes the high-order bit of the qType field to be reset to 0.

Use the InsXTime procedure if you want to take advantage of the drift-free, fixed-frequency timing services of the extended Time Manager.

```
PROCEDURE InsXTime (tmTaskPtr: QElemPtr);
```

Trap macro	_InsXTime
On entry	A0: address of TMTask record
On exit	D0: result code

InsXTime adds the Time Manager task record specified by tmTaskPtr to the Time Manager queue. The tmTaskPtr parameter must point to an extended Time Manager task record. Your application must fill in the tmAddr field of that task. You should set the tmWakeUp and tmReserved fields to 0 the first time you call InsXTime.

With the extended Time Manager, you can set tmAddr to NIL if you do not want a task to execute when the delay passed to PrimeTime expires. Also, InsXTime resets the high-order bit of the qType field to 0.

The PrimeTime procedure schedules the routine specified by the tmAddr field of tmTaskPtr for execution after the delay specified by the count parameter has elapsed.

```
PROCEDURE PrimeTime (tmTaskPtr: QElemPtr; count: LongInt);
```

Trap macro	_PrimeTime
On entry	A0: address of TMTask record
	D0: specified delay time (long)
On exit	D0: result code

If the count parameter is a positive value, it is interpreted in milliseconds. If count is a negative value, it is interpreted in negated microseconds. (Microsecond delays are allowable only in the revised and extended Time Managers.) The task record specified by tmTaskPtr must already be inserted into the queue (by a previous call to InsTime or InsXTime) before your application calls the PrimeTime procedure. The PrimeTime procedure returns immediately, and the specified routine is executed after the specified delay has elapsed. If you call PrimeTime with a time delay of 0, the procedure runs as soon as interrupts are enabled.

In the revised and extended Time Managers, PrimeTime sets the high-order bit of the qType field to 1. In addition, any value of the count parameter that exceeds the maximum millisecond delay is reduced to the maximum. If you pause an unexpired task (with RmvTime) and then reinstall it (with InsXTime), you can continue the previous delay by calling PrimeTime with the count parameter set to 0.


```
PROCEDURE RmvTime (tmTaskPtr: QElemPtr);
```

Trap macro	_RmvTime
On entry	A0: address of TMTask record
On exit	D0: result code

The RmvTime procedure removes the Time Manager task record specified by tmTaskPtr from the Time Manager queue. In both the revised and extended Time Managers, if the specified task record is active (that is, it has been activated but the specified time has not yet elapsed), the tmCount field of the task record returns the amount of time remaining. To provide the greatest accuracy, the unused time is reported as negated microseconds if that value is small enough to fit into the tmCount field (even if the delay was originally specified in milliseconds); otherwise, the unused time is reported in positive milliseconds. If the time has already expired, tmCount contains 0.

In the revised and extended Time Managers, PrimeTime sets the high-order bit of the qType field to 0.

SUMMARY OF THE TIME MANAGER

Data Types

```
TMTaskPtr = ^TMTask;

TYPE TMTask =           {original and revised Time Manager task record}
     RECORD
        qLink:          QElemPtr;        {next queue entry}
        qType:          Integer;         {queue type}
        tmAddr:         ProcPtr;         {pointer to task}
        tmCount:        LongInt          {reserved}
     END;

TYPE TMTask             {extended Time Manager task record}
     RECORD
        qLink:          QElemPtr;        {next queue entry}
        qType:          Integer;         {queue type}
        tmAddr:         ProcPtr;         {pointer to task}
        tmCount:        LongInt;         {unused time}
        tmWakeUp:       LongInt;         {wakeup time}
        tmReserved:     LongInt          {reserved for future use}
     END;
```

Routines

```
PROCEDURE InsTime          (tmTaskPtr: QElemPtr);

PROCEDURE InsXTime         (tmTaskPtr: QElemPtr);

PROCEDURE PrimeTime        (tmTaskPtr: QElemPtr; count: LongInt);

PROCEDURE RmvTime          (tmTaskPtr: QElemPtr);
```

Assembly-Language Information

Structure of Original and Revised Time Manager Queue Entry

qLink	long	pointer to next queue entry
qType	word	queue type
tmAddr	long	pointer to task
tmCount	long	unused time; returned to caller

Structure of Extended Time Manager Queue Entry

qLink	long	pointer to next queue entry
qType	word	queue type
tmAddr	long	pointer to task
tmCount	long	unused time; returned to caller
tmWakeUp	long	wakeup time; used internally by the Time Manager
tmReserved	long	reserved for future use

24 THE NOTIFICATION MANAGER

ABOUT THIS CHAPTER

This chapter describes how you can use the Notification Manager to inform users of significant occurrences in applications that are running in the background or in software that is largely invisible to the user. This software includes device drivers, vertical blanking (VBL) tasks, Time Manager tasks, completion routines, and desk accessories that operate behind the scenes. It also includes code that executes during the system startup sequence, such as code contained in 'INIT' resources.

The Notification Manager is available in system software versions 6.0 and later. You can use the Gestalt function to determine whether the Notification Manager is present. See the Compatibility Guidelines chapter in this volume for complete details on using Gestalt.

The information in this chapter supersedes the information that was previously published in Appendix D of the *Programmer's Guide to MultiFinder*. You need to read this chapter if your application, desk accessory, or device driver might need to notify the user of some occurrence while it is running in the background or is otherwise invisible to the user. You also need to read this chapter if you want to write 'INIT' resources that might need to inform the user of important occurrences during their execution at system startup time.

ABOUT THE NOTIFICATION MANAGER

The Notification Manager provides an asynchronous notification service. It allows software running in the background (or otherwise unseen by the user) to communicate information to the user. For example, applications that manage lengthy background tasks (such as printing many documents or transferring large amounts of data to other machines) might need to inform the user that the operation is complete. These applications cannot use the standard methods of communicating with the user, such as alert or dialog boxes, because such windows might easily be obscured by the windows of other applications. Moreover, even if those windows are visible, the background application cannot be certain that the user is aware of the change. So some more reliable method must be used to manage the communication between a background application and the user, who might be awaiting the completion of the background task while running other applications in the foreground.

In the same way, relatively invisible operations such as Time Manager tasks, VBL tasks, or device drivers might need to inform the user that some previously started routine is complete or perhaps that some error has rendered further execution undesirable or impossible.

In all these cases, the communication generally needs to occur in one direction only, from the background application (or task, or driver) to the user. The Notification Manager, included in system software versions 6.0 and later, allows you to post to the user a **notification,** which is an audible or visible indication that your application (or other piece of software) requires the user's attention. You post a notification by issuing a **notification request** to the Notification Manager, which places your request into a queue. When your request reaches the top of the queue, the Notification Manager posts a notification to the user.

You can request three types of notification:

- **Polite notification.** A small icon appears to flash by periodically alternating with the Apple® menu icon (which is the Apple symbol) or the Application menu icon in the menu bar.
- **Audible notification.** The Sound Manager plays the system alert sound or a sound contained in an 'snd ' resource.
- **Alert notification.** An alert box containing a short message appears on the screen. The user must dismiss the alert box (by clicking the OK button) before foreground processing can continue.

These types of notification are not mutually exclusive; for example, an application can request both audible and alert notifications. Moreover, if the requesting software is listed in the Application menu (and hence represents a process that is loaded into memory), you can instruct the Notification Manager to place a diamond-shaped mark next to the name of the requesting process. The mark is usually intended to prompt the user to switch the marked application into the foreground. Finally, you can request that the Notification Manager execute a **notification response procedure,** which is a procedure that is executed as the final step in a notification.

In short, a notification consists of one or more of five possible actions. If you request more than one action, they occur in the following order:

1. A diamond-shaped mark appears next to the name of your application in the Application menu, as illustrated in Figure 24-1. Note that the diamond is present only when your application is in the background (because the diamond is replaced by a checkmark if your application is the active application). In Figure 24-1, the Other App application is the active application.

2. A small icon alternates with the Apple menu icon or the Application menu icon in the menu bar. Typically, the small icon is your application's small icon. Note that several applications might post notifications, so there might be a series of small icons alternating in the menu bar. The location of each flashing icon follows that of the posting application's mark (if any). If your application is marked with a diamond (or a checkmark) in the Application menu, the icon flashes above the Application menu; otherwise, the icon flashes above the Apple menu.

3. The Sound Manager plays a sound. Your application can supply its own sound (by passing the Notification Manager a handle to an 'snd ' resource loaded into memory) or request that the Sound Manager use the user's system alert sound.

Figure 24-1. A notification in the Application menu

4. An alert box appears, and the user dismisses it. Your application specifies the text in the alert box; the box looks like the alert box shown in Figure 24-2.

5. A response procedure executes. You can use the response procedure to remove the notification request from the queue or perform other processing.

The mark in the Application menu and the alternating small icon remain until the requesting application removes the notification request from the queue. However, the sound and the alert box are presented only once, if at all.

Any applications, desk accessories, tasks, routines, or drivers can use the Notification Manager, whether they are running in the background or not. It is especially useful for background applications, such as the PrintMonitor application. (The system alarm, which is called by the Alarm Clock desk accessory, also uses the Notification Manager.) Foreground applications can, however, use the services of the Notification Manager to achieve effects (such as the alternating small icon) that are otherwise more difficult to create. For the same reasons, the Notification Manager can be useful even to applications that might be executing in a Finder™-only environment under system software version 6.0.

The Notification Manager provides applications with a standard user interface for notifying the user of significant events. It is suggested that your application adopt the following three-level notification strategy for communicating with the user:

1. Display a diamond next to the name of the application in the Application menu.

2. Insert a small icon into the list of icons that alternate with the Apple menu icon or the Application menu icon in the menu bar, and display a diamond next to the name of your application in the Application menu.

3. Display a diamond, insert a small icon, and put up an alert box to notify the user that something needs to be done.

Ideally, the user should be allowed to set the desired level of notification. The suggested default level of notification is level 2. In levels 2 and 3, you might also play a sound, but the user should have the ability to turn the sound off. In addition, a user should have the ability to turn off background notification altogether, except in cases where damage might occur or data would be lost.

Note: This suggested notification strategy may not be appropriate for your application. Notifications posted by system software do not follow these guidelines.

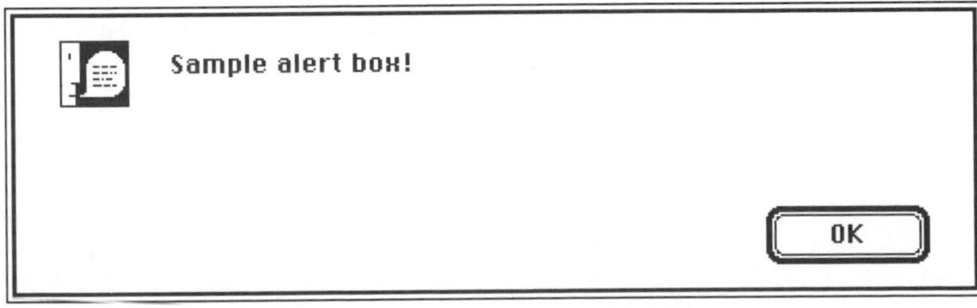

Figure 24-2. A sample alert box

Each application, desk accessory, and device driver can issue any number of notification requests. Each requested notification is presented separately to the user. For this reason, you should try to avoid posting multiple notification requests for the same occurrence. Depending on the method of notification you specify, multiple requests might result in an annoying number of notification sounds or a large number of alert boxes that the user must dismiss before continuing.

Note that the Notification Manager provides a one-way communications path from an application to the user. There is no provision for carrying information back from the user to the requesting application, although it is possible for the requesting application to determine if the notification was received. If you require this secondary communications link, do not use the Notification Manager. Instead, you should wait until the user switches your application into the foreground and then use standard means (for example, a dialog box) to obtain the required information.

USING THE NOTIFICATION MANAGER

To issue a notification to the user, you need to create a notification request and install it into the notification queue. The Notification Manager interprets the request and presents the notification to the user at the earliest possible time. After you have notified the user in the desired manner (that is, placed a diamond mark in the Application menu, added a small icon to the list of icons that alternate in the menu bar, played a sound, or presented the user with an alert box), you might want the Notification Manager to call a response procedure. The response procedure is useful for determining that the user has indeed seen the notification or for reacting to the successful posting of the notification. Eventually, you will need to remove the notification request from the notification queue; you can do this in the response procedure or when your application returns to the foreground.

The Notification Manager is automatically initialized at system startup time. It includes two functions, one that allows you to install a request into the notification queue and one that allows you to remove a request from that queue.

Creating a Notification Request

Information describing each notification request is contained in the **notification queue,** which is a standard Macintosh® queue, as described in the Operating System Utilities chapter of Volume II. When installing a request into the notification queue, your application must supply a pointer to a notification record that indicates the type of notification you desire. Each entry in the notification queue is a **notification record**—a static and nonrelocatable record of type NMRec.

```
TYPE NMRec =
     RECORD
        qLink:          QElemPtr;     {next queue entry}
        qType:          Integer;      {queue type: ORD(nmType) = 8}
        nmFlags:        Integer;      {reserved}
        nmPrivate:      LongInt;      {reserved}
        nmReserved:     Integer;      {reserved}
        nmMark:         Integer;      {item to mark in menu}
```

```
        nmIcon:          Handle;         {handle to icon}
        nmSound:         Handle;         {handle to sound resource}
        nmStr:           StringPtr;      {string to appear in alert box}
        nmResp:          ProcPtr;        {pointer to response procedure}
        nmRefCon:        LongInt         {for application's use}
    END;
```

To set up a notification request, you need to fill in the fields qType, nmMark, nmIcon, nmSound, nmStr, nmResp, and nmRefCon. The remaining fields of this record are used internally by the Notification Manager or are reserved for use by Apple Computer, Inc.

Note: In system software version 6.0, the field nmIcon is named nmSIcon and should contain a handle to a small icon (a 16-by-16 bitmap, often stored as an 'SICN' resource).

Field descriptions

qLink — Points to the next element in the queue. This field is used internally by the Notification Manager.

qType — Indicates the type of operating-system queue. You should set this field to the value ORD(nmType), which is 8.

nmFlags — Reserved for use by Apple.

nmPrivate — Reserved for use by Apple.

nmReserved — Reserved for use by Apple.

nmMark — Indicates whether to place a diamond-shaped mark next to the name of the application in the Application menu. If nmMark is 0, no such mark appears. If nmMark is 1, the mark appears next to the name of the calling application. If nmMark is neither 0 nor 1, it is interpreted as the reference number of a desk accessory. An application should pass 1, a desk accessory should pass its own reference number, and a driver or a detached background task (such as a VBL task or Time Manager task) should pass 0.

nmIcon — Contains a handle to a small icon or to an icon family containing a small color icon that is to alternate periodically in the menu bar. If nmIcon is NIL, no icon appears in the menu bar. If nmIcon is not NIL, then the Notification Manager determines whether it is a handle to a small icon or to an icon family containing a small color icon. This handle must be valid at the time that the notification occurs; it does not need to be locked, but must be nonpurgeable.

nmSound — Contains a handle to a sound resource to be played with SndPlay. If nmSound is NIL, no sound is produced. If nmSound is –1, then the system alert sound plays. This handle does not need to be locked, but it must be nonpurgeable.

nmStr — Points to a string that appears in the alert box. If nmStr is NIL, no alert box appears. Note that the Notification Manager does not make a copy of this string, so your application should not dispose of this storage until it removes the notification request.

nmResp — Points to a response procedure. If nmResp is NIL, no response procedure executes when the notification is posted. If nmResp is –1, then a predefined procedure removes the notification request immediately after it has completed.

nmRefCon — A long integer available for your application's own use.

Listing 24-1 illustrates how to set up a notification record.

Listing 24-1. Setting up a notification record

```
VAR
   myNotification:   NMRec;       {a notification record}
   myResNum:         Integer;     {resource ID of small icon resource}
   myResHand:        Handle;      {handle to small icon resource}
   myText:           Str255;      {string to print in alert box}
BEGIN
   myResNum := 1234;              {resource ID in resource fork}
   myResHand := GetResource('SICN', myResNum);
                                  {get small icon from resource fork}
   myText := 'Sample Alert Box'; {set message for alert box}

   WITH myNotification DO
   BEGIN
      qType := ORD(nmType);       {set queue type}
      nmMark := 1;                {put mark in Application menu}
      nmIcon := myResHand;        {alternating icon}
      nmSound := Handle(-1);      {play system alert sound}
      nmStr := @myText;           {display alert box}
      nmResp := NIL;              {no response procedure}
      nmRefCon := NIL;            {not needed}
   END;
END;
```

This notification record requests all three types of notification—polite (alternating small icon), audible (system alert sound), and alert (alert box). In addition, the diamond appears in front of the application's name in the Application menu. In this case, the small icon has resource ID 1234 of type 'SICN' in the application's resource fork.

Defining a Response Procedure

The nmResp field of the notification record contains the address of a response procedure that executes as the final stage of a notification. If you do not need to do any processing in response to the notification, then you can supply the value NIL in that field. If you supply the address of your own response procedure in the nmResp field, the Notification Manager passes it one parameter, a pointer to your notification record. For example, this is how you would declare a response procedure having the name MyResponse:

```
PROCEDURE MyResponse (nmReqPtr: NMRecPtr);
```

When the Notification Manager calls this response procedure, it does not set up A5 or low-memory global variables for you. If you need to access your application's global variables, you should save its A5 in the nmRefCon field. See the Memory Management chapter in this volume for more information on saving and restoring the A5 world.

Response procedures should never draw on the screen or otherwise affect the human interface. Rather, you should use them simply to remove notification requests from the notification queue and free any memory. If you specify the special nmResp value of –1, the Notification Manager removes the queue element from the queue automatically, so you don't have to do it yourself. You have to pass your own response routine, however, if you need to do anything else in the response procedure, such as free the memory block containing the queue element or set an application global variable that indicates that the notification was received.

If you choose to use audible or alert notifications, you should probably use an nmResp value of –1 so that the notification record is removed from the queue as soon as the sound has finished or the user has dismissed the alert box. However, if either nmMark or nmIcon is nonzero, you should not use an nmResp value of –1 because the Notification Manager would remove the diamond mark or the small icon before the user could see it. Note that an nmResp value of –1 does not free the memory block containing the queue element; it merely removes that element from the notification queue.

Since the response procedure executes as the last step in the notification process, your application can determine that the notification was posted by examining a global variable that you set in the response procedure. In addition, to determine that the user has actually received the notification, you need to request an alert notification. This is because the response procedure executes only after the user has clicked the OK button in the alert box.

Installing a Notification Request

To add a notification request to the notification queue, call NMInstall. For example, you can install the notification request defined in Listing 24-1 with the following line of code:

```
myErr := NMInstall (@myNotification);  {install notification request}
```

Before calling NMInstall, you should check to make sure that your application is running in the background. If your application is in the foreground, you do not need to use the Notification Manager to notify the user; instead, you can simply use standard methods for playing sounds or putting up alert boxes.

> **Note:** VBL tasks, Time Manager tasks, and device drivers that want to install notification requests do not need to make this check because they are never in the foreground. Generally, however, a VBL task or a Time Manager task can avoid issuing notification requests by setting a global flag that informs the application that installed it that a notification needs to be requested. When that application receives some processing time, it can alert the user in the appropriate manner (that is, by putting up an alert box or by issuing a notification request). This method allows you to keep interrupt-time tasks, such as VBL and Time Manager tasks, small and quick.

If the call to NMInstall returns an error, then you cannot install the notification request in the notification queue. In that case, your application must wait for the user to switch it into the foreground before doing further processing. While waiting for a resume event, your application should take care of other events, such as updates. Note, however, that the only reason that NMInstall might fail is if it is passed invalid information, namely, the wrong value for qType.

You can install notification requests at any time, even when the system is executing 'INIT' resources as part of the system startup sequence. If you need to notify the user of some important occurrence during the execution of your 'INIT' resource, you should use the Notification Manager to install a request in the notification queue. The system notifies the user after the startup process completes, that is, when the normal event mechanism begins. This saves you from having to interrupt the system startup sequence with dialog or alert boxes and results in a cleaner and more uniform startup appearance.

Removing a Notification Request

To remove a notification request from the notification queue, call NMRemove. For example, you can remove a notification request with this code:

```
myErr := NMRemove (@myNotification);    {remove notification request}
```

You can remove requests at any time, either before or after the notification actually occurs. Note that requests that have already been issued by the Notification Manager are not automatically removed from the queue.

NOTIFICATION MANAGER ROUTINES

The Notification Manager includes two functions, one to install a notification request and one to remove a notification request. To install a notification request, use the function NMInstall.

```
FUNCTION NMInstall (nmReqPtr: NMRecPtr) : OSErr;
```

Trap macro	_NMInstall
On entry	A0: address of NMRec record
On exit	D0: result code

NMInstall has a single parameter, nmRecPtr, which is a pointer to a notification record. It adds the notification request specified by that record to the notification queue and returns a result code.

Result codes

noErr	0	No error
nmTypErr	–299	Invalid qType (must be ORD(nmType))

Note: NMInstall does not move or purge memory, so you can call it from completion routines or interrupt handlers as well as from the main body of an application and from the response procedure of a notification request.

NMRemove removes the notification request identified by nmReqPtr from the notification queue and returns a result code.

```
FUNCTION NMRemove (nmReqPtr: NMRecPtr) : OSErr;
```

Trap macro	_NMRemove
On entry	A0: address of NMRec record
On exit	D0: result code

Result codes

noErr	0	No error
qErr	–1	Not in queue
nmTypErr	–299	Invalid qType (must be ORD(nmType))

Note: NMRemove does not move or purge memory, so you can call it from completion routines or interrupt handlers as well as from the main body of an application and from the response procedure of a notification request.

SUMMARY OF THE NOTIFICATION MANAGER

Constant

```
CONST nmType        = 8;
```

Data Types

```
TYPE NMRec =
     RECORD
        qLink:          QElemPtr;       {next queue entry}
        qType:          Integer;        {queue type: ORD(nmType) = 8}
        nmFlags:        Integer;        {reserved}
        nmPrivate:      LongInt;        {reserved}
        nmReserved:     Integer;        {reserved}
        nmMark:         Integer;        {item to mark in menu}
        nmIcon:         Handle;         {handle to icon}
        nmSound:        Handle;         {handle to sound resource}
        nmStr:          StringPtr;      {string to appear in alert box}
        nmResp:         ProcPtr;        {pointer to response procedure}
        nmRefCon:       LongInt         {for application's use}
     END;

     NMRecPtr = ^NMRec;
```

Routines

```
FUNCTION NMInstall          (nmReqPtr: NMRecPtr) : OSErr;

FUNCTION NMRemove           (nmReqPtr: NMRecPtr) : OSErr;
```

Application-Defined Routines

```
PROCEDURE MyResponse        (nmReqPtr: NMRecPtr);
```

Result Codes

noErr	0	No error
qErr	–1	Not in queue
nmTypErr	–299	Invalid qType (must be ORD(nmType))

25 THE FILE MANAGER

ABOUT THIS CHAPTER

This chapter describes how your application can use the File Manager features introduced in system software version 7.0 to manipulate files. This chapter supplements the File Manager information in Volumes IV and V.

Read this chapter if your application creates, saves, or opens files.

Most of the features described in this chapter are available only in system software version 7.0 or later. To determine which features are available in a specific operating environment, use the Gestalt function, described in the Compatibility Guidelines chapter of this volume. The availability of some features depends on the characteristics of the volume rather than on the system software. To determine which features a volume supports, use the PBHGetVolParms function, described in this chapter. A complete description of how you check for various new features appears at the beginning of "Using the File Manager" in this chapter.

To use this chapter you must be familiar with the file system documentation in Volume IV.

ABOUT THE FILE MANAGER

The File Manager is the part of the Operating System that gives your application access to data storage devices such as disk drives. You use the File Manager to create, write, and read files.

To fully exploit system software version 7.0, your application should adopt two new File Manager features:

- the file system specification record, a new convention for identifying files and directories (see "Identifying Files, Directories, and Volumes" later in this chapter)
- the strategy of updating a stored file by changing the catalog entries (see "A Simpler Safe-Save Strategy" later in this chapter)

The File Manager in version 7.0 also introduces a number of special-purpose functions that you can use to

- search an entire volume quickly, matching entries in almost any of the catalog information fields, such as file creation date or file length
- track files by assigning and resolving file identification numbers
- mount volumes
- manipulate access-control privileges in foreign file systems

Version 7.0 supplies high-level versions of some functions previously available only as low-level functions. These functions have been available historically in some development environments but have not been documented before in *Inside Macintosh.*

The PBHGetVolParms function, which reports volume information, has been expanded and updated to reflect features in version 7.0. Some File Manager routines have been modified to accommodate file identification numbers.

System software version 7.0 includes a local version of Apple's file-server application, AppleShare®. This feature allows the user to make some or all of the files on a local volume available over a network, increasing the chance that your application may be used in a shared environment. As long as you follow the standard guidelines for Macintosh® programming, your application should work in a shared environment. If you want to exploit the full power of a shared environment, follow the guidelines in the File Manager Extensions in a Shared Environment chapter of Volume V.

To help you understand and use the version 7.0 File Manager, the first few sections of this chapter introduce the new features you should use: the new convention for identifying files and directories and the new strategy for updating stored files safely. The "New Special-Purpose Features" section later in this chapter introduces an assortment of other powerful but more specialized features.

The "Using the File Manager" section later in this chapter contains instructions for using the new features of the File Manager to

- recognize and use a standard file identification convention
- update a stored file safely
- search a volume for one or more files or directories
- assign and resolve file ID numbers
- manipulate the permission information that controls access to files on volumes controlled by different operating systems, such as A/UX®

IDENTIFYING FILES, DIRECTORIES, AND VOLUMES

Your application typically specifies a filename and location when it calls the File Manager to open or delete a file. It typically receives filenames and locations from the Standard File Package and the Finder™, which handle the user interface for creating, saving, opening, and removing files.

File System Specifications

Conventions for identifying files, directories, and volumes have evolved as the File Manager has matured. Version 7.0 introduces a simple, standard form for identifying a file or directory, called a file system specification. You can use a file system specification whenever you must identify a file or directory for the File Manager.

The file system specification contains

- the volume reference number of the volume on which the file or directory resides
- the directory ID of the parent directory
- the name of the file or directory

For a complete description of the new data structure, the file system specification (FSSpec) record, see "Using FSSpec Records" later in this chapter.

The Standard File Package in system software version 7.0 uses FSSpec records to identify files to be saved or opened. The File Manager provides a new set of high-level routines that accept FSSpec records as input, so that your application can pass the data directly from the Standard File Package to the File Manager. The Alias Manager and the Edition Manager accept file specifications only in the form of FSSpec records.

The Finder in version 7.0 uses alias records, which are resolved into FSSpec records, to identify files to be opened or printed. (The description of required Apple® events in the Apple Event Manager chapter of this volume explains how the Finder passes file information to your application and how your application retrieves it.)

Version 7.0 also introduces the FSMakeFSSpec function, which creates an FSSpec record for a file or directory. For a complete description of FSMakeFSSpec, see "Using FSSpec Records" and "Making FSSpec Records" later in this chapter.

The Evolution of File Specification Strategies

The original Macintosh File System (MFS) is a "flat" file system—that is, a system in which all files are stored at the same level on a volume (the volume is not subdivided into directories). To uniquely identify a file, you need to specify only a volume and a filename. In high-level MFS functions, you pass the specification in parameters called vRefNum and fileName. (For a complete description of MFS, see the File Manager chapter in Volume II or IV.)

In MFS, you can specify a file in either of two ways:

- a full pathname, which contains the names of both the volume and the file, in the fileName parameter
- filename by name in the fileName parameter and volume by volume reference number, a unique number assigned when the volume is mounted, in the vRefNum parameter

Figure 25-1 illustrates the two ways to identify a file in MFS.

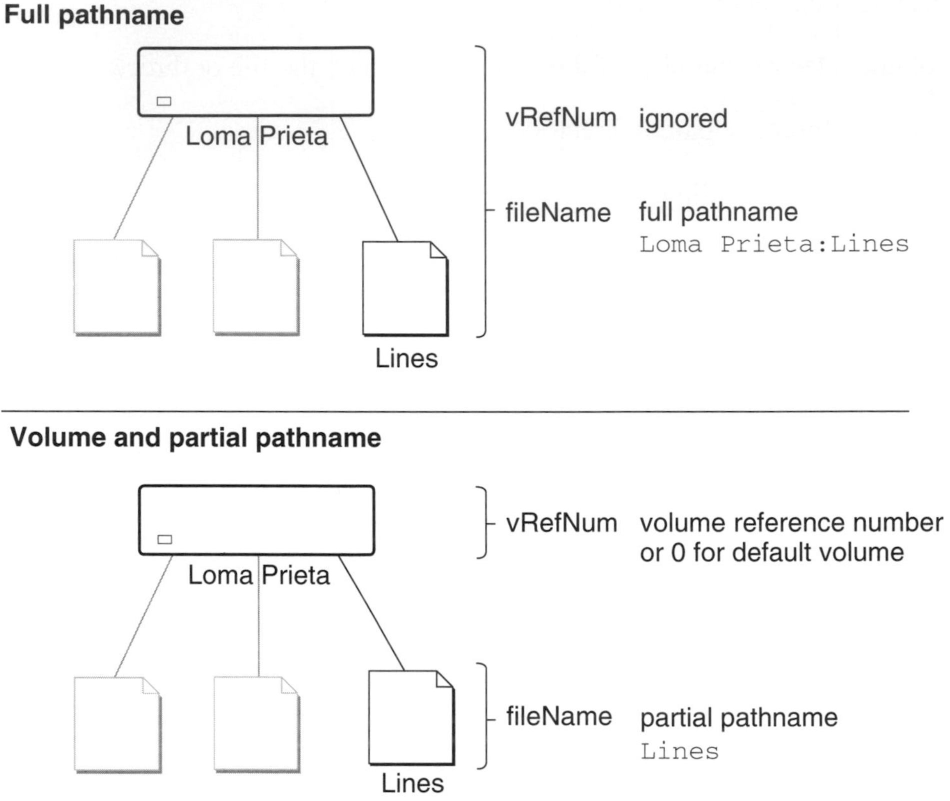

Figure 25-1. Identifying a file in MFS

To improve performance, especially with larger volumes, Apple Computer, Inc., introduced the Hierarchical File System (HFS) on the Macintosh Plus computer and later models. In HFS, a volume can be divided into smaller units known as **directories,** which can themselves contain files or other directories. Each file on an HFS volume is stored in a directory. To identify a file in HFS, you must specify its volume, its parent directory, and its name. The File Manager assigns each directory a directory ID, and the user or the system software assigns each directory a name. The HFS File Manager routines include an additional parameter, the dirID parameter, to handle the directory specification. (For a complete description of HFS, see the File Manager chapter in Volume IV.)

In HFS, each folder created by the user is a directory. The folders represent a true hierarchy in the file system. In MFS, folders are an illusion maintained for the user by the system software. The first-level directory on a volume, the one that contains all of the other directories, is known as the root directory.

For compatibility between HFS and MFS, Apple introduced the concept of **working directories.** A working directory is a combined directory and volume specification. To make a directory into a working directory, the File Manager establishes a control block that contains both the volume and the directory ID of the target directory. The File Manager then returns a unique working directory reference number, which you can use to identify the directory. You can use the working directory reference number in place of a volume specification in all of the MFS functions.

> **Note:** Working directories were introduced solely for compatibility between HFS and MFS. If you are writing an application to run in system software version 7.0, you do not need to use working directories.

In summary, HFS recognizes three kinds of file system objects: files, directories, and volumes. You can identify them using these labels:

File filename

Directory directory name
directory ID
working directory reference number, which also implies a volume

Volume volume name
volume reference number
working directory reference number, which also implies a directory

In HFS, you can pass a complete file specification in any of four ways:

- full pathname
- volume reference number and partial pathname
- working directory reference number and partial pathname
- volume reference number, directory ID, and partial pathname

A full pathname consists of the name of the volume, the names of all directories between the root directory and the target, and the name of the target. A full pathname starts with a character other than a colon and contains at least one colon. If the first character is a colon, or if the pathname contains no colons, it is a partial pathname. If a partial pathname starts with the name of a parent directory, the first character in the pathname must be a colon. If a partial pathname contains only the name of the target file or directory, the leading colon is optional.

You can identify a volume in the vRefNum parameter by volume reference number or drive number, but volume reference number is preferred. A value of 0 represents the default volume. A volume name in the pathname overrides any other volume specification. Unlike a volume name, a volume reference number is guaranteed to be unique. It changes, however, each time a volume is mounted.

> **Note:** The system software that accompanied the release of HFS introduced the PBHSetVol function for setting the default volume on a hierarchical disk. Do not use the PBHSetVol function or the high-level version, HSetVol, which is available in some development environments. If you need to set the default volume, use SetVol or PBSetVol, described in the File Manager chapter of Volume IV.

A working directory reference number represents both the directory ID and the volume reference number. If you specify any value other than 0 for the dirID parameter, that value overrides the directory ID implied by a working directory reference number in the volume parameter. The volume specification remains valid.

Figure 25-2 illustrates the four ways to identify a file in HFS.

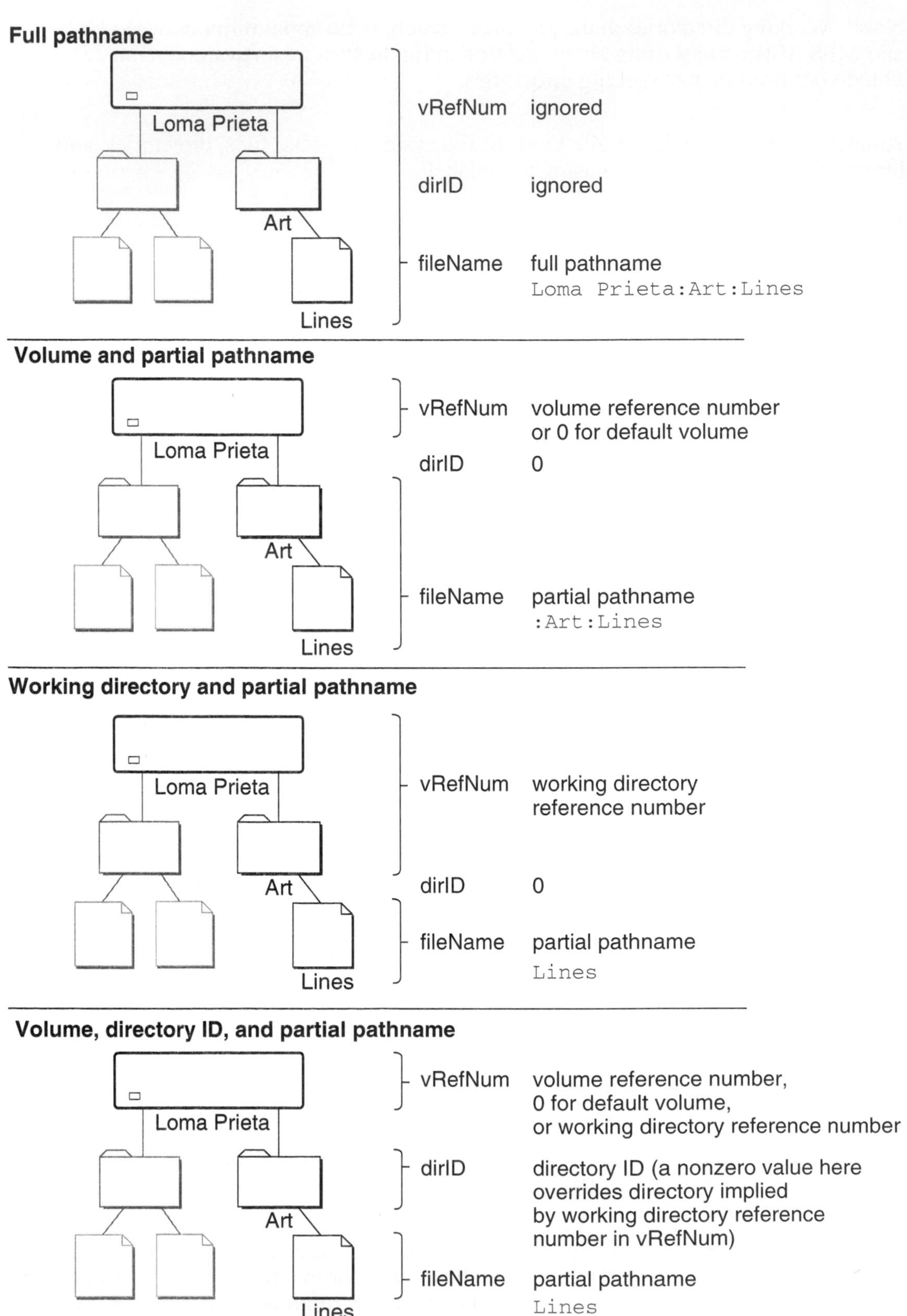

Figure 25-2. Identifying a file in HFS

The FSSpec record described in the previous section, "File System Specifications," replaces both the MFS and the HFS conventions for identifying files and directories in most cases. In system software version 7.0, you use the historical forms primarily when calling low-level File Manager functions.

LIMITATIONS ON MFS DISKS

System software version 7.0 still supports MFS disks, insofar as your application can still read and write files on MFS disks. There are, however, limitations on MFS disks in version 7.0.

- MFS disks cannot be renamed.
- MFS disks cannot have comments; however, files located within MFS disks can have comments.
- The Finder in system software version 7.0 ignores folders created on an MFS disk by older versions of the Finder. The folders are not displayed. A file in such a folder appears in the root level of the disk but has the same relative position in the window that it has in the MFS folder.
- The Finder does not use or save window position or size information about files located on an MFS disk.
- You cannot create an alias for an MFS volume. More generally, Alias Manager functions and the FSMakeFSSpec function do not work if their target is an MFS volume. You can, however, create aliases for files on an MFS volume. Similarly, you can use the new File Manager functions that use FSSpec records on files on an MFS volume.
- You should not call the File Manager function PBGetFCBInfo on MFS volumes.
- The Process Manager's GetProcessInformation function may not return correct results about the location of the application file if the application file resides on an MFS volume.
- If the user renames an edition located on an MFS volume, the Edition Manager may not be able to find that edition for any document that publishes to or subscribes to it. Also, if the user opens an edition in the Finder that is located on an MFS volume and updates that edition, the Findcr window closes.

A SIMPLER SAFE-SAVE STRATEGY

When the user saves a changed version of a document, most applications perform a "safe save"—a sequence of updating, renaming, saving, and deleting files that preserves the contents of the old file until the new version is safely recorded. Typically, an application saves the new version of the file under a temporary name, renames both files, and then discards the original.

Version 7.0 introduces the FSpExchangeFiles and PBExchangeFiles functions, which simplify a safe save. Both functions exchange the contents of two files by altering the catalog entries for the files. To save a new version of a file using file exchange, you save the copy, exchange the contents of the two files, and discard the newly saved file, which now holds the original version of the file. See "Updating Files" later in this chapter for a description of how to update files with FSpExchangeFiles.

Updating a file with FSpExchangeFiles preserves the file's ID, which is used by the Alias Manager. (See "File IDs" later in this chapter for a description of file IDs; see the Finder Interface chapter of this volume for a description of Finder aliases and the Alias Manager chapter of this volume for a description of the underlying software.) Although the Alias Manager is usually able to resolve an alias with an obsolete file ID, you can improve the reliability of aliases by preserving file IDs on all saves.

NEW SPECIAL-PURPOSE FEATURES

Version 7.0 contains a number of specialized functions that give you more control over various kinds of file manipulation. You can use these functions to examine the information in a volume's catalog, to track files on a volume, and to manipulate access privileges on non-Macintosh file systems.

A Quick, Thorough Catalog Search

Version 7.0 introduces the PBCatSearch function, a new function for examining a volume's **catalog,** which contains descriptions of all the files and directories on the volume.

A single call to the PBCatSearch function can replace a series of indexed calls to the PBGetFInfo, PBHGetFInfo, or PBGetCatInfo function, which all return a collection of catalog information about an individual file or directory. In MFS, you could examine all catalog entries on a volume by calling PBGetFInfo repeatedly, using an index to step through the catalog. On an HFS volume, indexed calls to the equivalent function, PBHGetFInfo, examine the files and directories in only one directory. To examine the catalog information for all files on an HFS volume with PBHGetFInfo, or all the files and directories with PBGetCatInfo, you have to perform a recursive search through the hierarchy. Especially on a large hierarchical volume, searching the catalog with a series of individual calls can be time-consuming.

The PBCatSearch function lets you search the entire catalog with a single procedure call. It compares each catalog entry with a set of specifications you provide, and it gives you a list of all entries that meet your search criteria. For a detailed description of how to use the PBCatSearch function, see "Searching a Volume" later in this chapter.

File IDs

Version 7.0 introduces the **file ID,** a tool for identifying a file that your application may need to find again later. The file ID lets you reference a file through its file number in the volume catalog.

A file number is a unique number assigned to a file when it's created. The File Manager can set up an internal record in the volume's catalog that records the filename and parent directory ID of the file with a given file number, establishing the file number as the file's ID and enabling you to reference the file by that number. (For more information about the volume's catalog, see the File Manager chapter of Volume IV.)

Note: The file ID is a low-level tool and is unique only on one HFS volume. In most cases, your application should track files using the Alias Manager, described in the Alias Manager chapter of this volume. The Alias Manager can track files across volumes. It creates a detailed record describing a file that you want to track, and, when you need to resolve the record later, it performs a sophisticated search. The Alias Manager uses file IDs internally.

A file ID is analogous to a directory ID. A file ID is unique only within a volume. A file ID remains constant even when the file is moved or renamed. When a file is copied or restored from backup, however, the file ID changes. Like file numbers, file IDs are unique over time—that is, once a number has been assigned to a file, that number is not reused even after the file has been deleted.

The file ID represents a permanent reference for a file, a reference that a user cannot change. Your application can store a file ID so that it can locate a specific file quickly and automatically, even if the user has moved or renamed it on the same volume.

File IDs are intended only as a tool for tracking files, not as a new element in file specification conventions. Neither high-level nor low-level File Manager functions accept file IDs as parameters. If you want to use file IDs, you must use the new functions for manipulating them, described in "Tracking Files With File IDs" and "Functions for Manipulating File IDs" later in this chapter.

Shared Environments

AppleShare, Apple's file-server application, allows users to share data, applications, and disk storage over a network. System software version 7.0 introduces a local version of AppleShare that allows users to make some or all of the files on a volume available over the network.

Most applications do not have to accommodate shared environments explicitly. As long as you follow the programming guidelines recommended in *Inside Macintosh,* your application should work in a shared environment. If your application directly manipulates files across a network, however, it should use the File Manager extensions described in Volume V.

This section introduces two new File Manager features for use in shared environments: volume mounting and manipulating privilege information in foreign file systems.

Remote Mounting

The user mounts remote shared volumes through the Chooser. The version 7.0 File Manager provides a set of calls that you can use to collect the mounting information from a mounted volume and then use that information to mount the volume again later, without going through the Chooser.

Privilege Information in Foreign File Systems

Virtually every file system has its own **privilege model,** that is, conventions for controlling access to stored files. A number of non-Macintosh file systems support access from a Macintosh computer by mapping their native privilege models onto the model defined by the AppleTalk Filing Protocol (AFP). Most applications that manipulate files in foreign file systems can rely on the intervening software to translate AFP privileges into whatever is required by the remote system.

The correlation is not always simple, however, and some applications require more control over the files stored on the foreign system. The A/UX privilege model, for example, recognizes four kinds of access: read, write, execute, and search. The AFP model recognizes only read and read-and-write access. (See the File Manager chapter of Volume V for a description of the AFP model.) If a shell program running on the Macintosh Operating System wants to allow the user to set native A/UX privileges on a remote file, it has to communicate with the A/UX file system using the A/UX privilege model.

System software version 7.0 provides two new functions, PBGetForeignPrivs and PBSetForeignPrivs, for manipulating privileges in a non-Macintosh file system. These functions do not relieve a foreign file system of the need to map its own privilege model onto the AFP calls.

USING THE FILE MANAGER

This section provides specific techniques for using the new features of the File Manager.

- You can pass FSSpec records received from the Standard File Package and the Finder directly to a set of high-level File Manager functions.
- You can exchange the contents of two files when updating a stored file, using the FSpExchangeFiles function.
- You can search a volume's catalog quickly, looking for files or directories that meet the criteria you specify, using the PBCatSearch function.
- You can track files within a volume by file number, using the set of functions that create and manipulate file ID references.
- You can mount a remote volume programmatically, without going through the Chooser, using the remote mounting functions.
- You can read and change privilege information in foreign file systems using the PBGetForeignPrivs and PBSetForeignPrivs functions.

Some of the new File Manager features depend on the system software; others depend on the characteristics of the volume. Before using any of the new File Manager features, check for availability by calling either the Gestalt function or the PBHGetVolParms function, depending on whether the feature's presence depends on the system software or the characteristics of the volume.

You can use Gestalt to determine whether or not you can call the functions that accept and support FSSpec records. Call Gestalt with the gestaltFSAttr selector to check for File Manager features. The response parameter has two relevant bits.

Constant	Meaning
gestaltFullExtFSDispatching	All of the routines selected through the _HFSDispatch trap macro are available to external file systems.
gestaltHasFSSpecCalls	The operating environment provides the file system specification versions of the basic file manipulation functions, plus the FSMakeFSSpec function.

For a complete description of the Gestalt function, see the Compatibility Guidelines chapter of this volume.

To test for the availability of the features that depend on the volume, you call the low-level function PBHGetVolParms, documented later in "Reading Volume Information." PBHGetVolParms returns the volume description in an attributes buffer, defined in system software version 7.0 as the GetVolParmsInfoBuffer record.

```
TYPE GetVolParmsInfoBuffer =
     RECORD
        vMVersion:          Integer;        {version number}
        vMAttrib:           LongInt;        {bit vector of attributes; }
                                            { see vMAttrib constants}
        vMLocalHand:        Handle;         {handle to private data}
        vMServerAdr:        LongInt;        {network server address}
        vMVolumeGrade:      LongInt;        {relative speed rating}
        vMForeignPrivID:    Integer         {access privilege model}
     END;
```

The first four fields are the same as those in the original PBHGetVolParms attributes buffer, introduced with the network software described in the File Manager Extensions in a Shared Environment chapter of Volume V. The last two fields are new in system software version 7.0.

Offset	Field	Size	Meaning
14	vMVolumeGrade	long	Relative speed rating of volume. This scale is currently uncalibrated. Generally, lower values represent faster speeds. A value of 0 means the volume is unrated.
18	vMForeignPrivID	word	Code for the privilege model supported by the volume. This field now has two possible values: 0 represents a standard HFS volume, which might or might not support the AFP privilege model; fsUnixPriv represents an A/UX volume.

To determine whether the functions for manipulating privilege information in foreign file systems are available on a volume, check the vMForeignPrivID field in the attributes buffer. If this field contains a nonzero value, the functions are available.

PBHGetVolParms returns the bulk of its volume description in the vMAttrib field of the attributes buffer. Version 7.0 has defined additional bits in the vMAttrib field to signal whether the following features are present.

Feature	Constant
Volume supports PBCatSearch	bHasCatSearch
Volume supports the file ID functions, including PBExchangeFiles	bHasFileIDs
Volume supports inherited access privileges for folders	bHasBlankAccessPrivileges
Volume supports the Desktop Manager functions, described in the Finder Interface chapter of this volume	bHasDesktopMgr
Volume supports a shorter name, for compatibility with other file systems	bHasShortName
Local file sharing is enabled	bHasPersonalAccessPrivileges
Volume supports the Users and Groups file and thus the AFP privilege functions, documented in the File Manager chapter of Volume V	bHasUserGroupList

The description of PBHGetVolParms in "Reading Volume Information" lists all of the bits in the vMAttrib field and their meanings.

Listing 25-1 illustrates how you can determine whether the PBCatSearch function is available before using it to search a volume's catalog.

Listing 25-1. Testing for PBCatSearch

```
FUNCTION SupportsCatSearch (yourVRef: Integer) : Boolean;

VAR
   myHPBRec:    HParamBlockRec;
   myHPBPtr:    HParmBlkPtr;
   VParmsBuf:   GetVolParmsInfoBuffer;
   myErr:       OSErr;

BEGIN
   myHPBPtr := @myHPBRec;

   WITH myHPBRec DO
   BEGIN
      ioCompletion := NIL; {no completion routine}
      ioVRefNum := yourVRef;
      ioBuffer := @VParmsBuf;
      ioReqCount := SIZEOF(GetVolParmsInfoBuffer);
   END;
```

```
   myErr := PBHGetVolParms(myHPBPtr, FALSE);
   IF myErr <> NoErr THEN DoError(myErr);     {process the error}
   IF BAND(VParmsBuf.vMAttrib, BSL(1,bHasCatSearch)) <> 0
      THEN SupportsCatSearch := TRUE
   ELSE SupportsCatSearch := FALSE
END;
```

To determine whether the remote mounting functions are available, you must attempt to call one of them. If they are not available, the functions return a result code of paramErr.

Using FSSpec Records

The system software now recognizes the **file system specification (FSSpec) record,** which provides a simple, standard way to specify the name and location of a file or directory.

```
TYPE FSSpec         =
     RECORD
          vRefNum:  Integer;         {volume reference number}
          parID:    LongInt;         {directory ID of parent directory}
          name:     Str63            {filename or directory name}
     END;

FSSpecPtr           =     ^FSSpec;
FSSpecHandle        =     ^FSSpecPtr;
```

The FSSpec record can describe only a file or a directory, not a volume. A volume can be identified by its root directory, although the system software never uses an FSSpec record to describe a volume. (The directory ID of the root's parent directory is fsRtParID, defined in the interface files. The name of the root directory is the same as the name of the volume.)

Some of the system software uses arrays of FSSpec records.

```
TYPE FSSpecArray          =       ARRAY[0..0] OF FSSpec;
     FSSpecArrayPtr       =       ^FSSpecArray;
     FSSpecArrayHandle    =       ^FSSpecArrayPtr;
```

Your application typically receives FSSpec records from the Standard File Package or the Finder and passes them on to the File Manager. For example, the sample code fragments in Listing 25-2 illustrate how your application might call first the Standard File Package and then the File Manager when the user chooses Open from the File menu.

Listing 25-2. Opening a document using the FSSpec record

```
VAR
   mySFR:       StandardFileReply;   {reply record}
   myTypeList:  SFTypeList;          {list of types to display}
   fsopenErr:   OSErr;               {error returned by open function}
   fsRefNum:    Integer;             {path reference number}
```

(Continued)

Listing 25-2. Opening a document using the FSSpec record (Continued)

```
BEGIN
   myTypeList[0] := 'TEXT';          {set up list of types}
   myTypeList[1] := 'RAYS';
   StandardGetFile(NIL, 2, myTypeList, mySFR);
   IF mySFR.sfGood = TRUE THEN
      BEGIN
         fsopenErr := FSpOpenDF(mySFR.sfFile, fsCurPerm, fsRefNum);
         myErrCheck(fsopenErr);  {check for errors}
         {display document, or whatever else your application does}
      END
   ELSE
      BEGIN
         {if the user cancels the open, do whatever cleanup is necessary}
      END;
END;
```

If you need to convert a file specification into an FSSpec record, call the new FSMakeFSSpec function. Do not fill in the fields of an FSSpec record yourself.

Three of the parameters to FSMakeFSSpec represent the volume, directory, and file specifications of the target object. You can provide this information in any of the four combinations described earlier in "The Evolution of File Specification Strategies." Table 25-1 details the ways your application can identify the name and location of a file or directory in a call to FSMakeFSSpec.

Table 25-1. How FSMakeFSSpec interprets file specifications

vRefNum	dirID	fileName	Interpretation
Ignored	Ignored	Full pathname	Full pathname overrides any other information
Volume reference number or drive number	Directory ID	Partial pathname	Partial pathname starts in the directory whose parent is specified in the dirID parameter
Working directory reference number	Directory ID	Partial pathname	Directory specification in dirID overrides the directory implied by the working directory reference number Partial pathname starts in the directory whose parent is specified in dirID
Volume reference number or drive number	0	Partial pathname	Partial pathname starts in the root directory of the volume specified in vRefNum
Working directory reference number	0	Partial pathname	Partial pathname starts in the directory specified by the working directory reference number

Table 25-1. How FSMakeFSSpec interprets file specifications (Continued)

vRefNum	dirID	fileName	Interpretation
Volume reference number or drive number	Directory ID	Empty string or NIL	The target object is the directory specified by the directory ID in dirID
Working directory reference number	0	Empty string or NIL	The target object is the directory specified by the working directory reference number in vRefNum
Volume reference number or drive number	0	Empty string or NIL	The target object is the root directory of the volume specified in vRefNum

The fourth parameter to FSMakeFSSpec is a pointer to the FSSpec record.

For a detailed description of FSMakeFSSpec, see "Making FSSpec Records" later in this chapter.

Updating Files

You can update an existing file simply and safely with the new FSpExchangeFiles function.

FSpExchangeFiles exchanges the contents of two files on a volume. You can use it to update a file without writing over the old version until the new version is stored safely. To update a file with FSpExchangeFiles, you first save a copy of the new data, and then call FSpExchangeFiles to put the new data in the original file. The file that you created to hold the new data now holds the original (obsolete) data. Updating files with the FSpExchangeFiles function preserves a file's Finder information and file ID.

FSpExchangeFiles does not move the data on the volume; it merely changes the information in the volume's catalog and, if the files are open, in the file control blocks (FCBs). The catalog entry for a file contains

- fields that describe the physical data, such as the first allocation block, physical end, and logical end of both the resource and data forks
- fields that describe the file within the file system, such as file number and parent directory ID

Fields that describe the data remain with the data; fields that describe the file remain with the file. The creation date remains with the file; the modification date remains with the data.

Table 25-2 illustrates the effects of FSpExchangeFiles on a set of sample catalog information.

Table 25-2. The effect of FSpExchangeFiles on a catalog entry

Before FSpExchangeFiles			**After FSpExchangeFiles**	
First catalog entry	**Second catalog entry**	**Catalog information**	**First catalog entry**	**Second catalog entry**
		File description		
File A	File B	Filename	File A	File B
30	100	Parent directory	30	100
3000	100	File number	3000	100
Jan 1990	June 2000	Creation date	Jan 1990	June 2000
		Data description		
300	1000	First allocation block	1000	300
1024	7680	Physical end of data fork	7680	1024
998	7649	Logical end of data fork	7649	998
April 1990	July 2000	Last modification date	July 2000	April 1990

If one or both files are open, FSpExchangeFiles also updates the file control block, which describes the access path to data identified by a path reference number. Like the catalog entry, the file control block contains both physical information about the data and file system information about the file. Table 25-3 illustrates the effects of FSpExchangeFiles on the file control block.

Table 25-3. The effect of FSpExchangeFiles on a file control block

Before FSpExchangeFiles			**After FSpExchangeFiles**	
Path reference number 4	**Path reference number 10**	**FCB information**	**Path reference number 4**	**Path reference number 10**
		File description		
File A	File B	Filename	File B	File A
30	100	Parent directory	100	30
		Data description		
300	1000	First allocation block	300	1000
1024	7680	Physical end-of-file	1024	7680
998	7649	Logical end-of-file	998	7649

Listing 25-3 illustrates the safe-save strategy using FSpExchangeFiles for an application that uses a memory-based editing system.

For complete descriptions of FSpExchangeFiles and PBExchangeFiles, see “Exchanging the Data in Two Files” and “Swapping Data Between Two Files” later in this chapter.

Listing 25-3. Updating a file with FSpExchangeFiles

```
VAR
   reply:           StandardFileReply;
   error:           OSErr;
   seconds:         LongInt;
   tempFileName:    Str255;
   tempVRefNum:     Integer;
   tempDirID:       LongInt;
   tempFSSpec:      FSSpec;
   fileRefNum:      Integer;
   buffer:          Ptr;
   count:           LongInt;

BEGIN
   StandardPutFile('Safe Save', 'filename', reply);
   IF reply.sfGood THEN    {user saves file}
      BEGIN
         IF reply.sfReplacing THEN
            BEGIN
            GetDateTime(seconds);       {make up a temporary filename}
            NumToString(seconds, tempFileName);
            error := FindFolder(reply.sfFile.vRefNum,
                                kTemporaryFolderType, kCreateFolder,
                                tempVRefNum, tempDirID);
                                       {find the temporary folder; }
                                       { create it if necessary}
            {check for error}
            error := FSMakeFSSpec(tempVRefNum, tempDirID,
                                  tempFileName, tempFSSpec);
                                       {make an FSSpec for the }
                                       { temporary filename}
            {check for error}
            error := FSpCreate(tempFSSpec, 'trsh', 'trsh',
                               reply.sfScript);
                                       {create a temporary file}
            error := FSpOpenDF(tempFSSpec, fsRdWrPerm, fileRefNum);
                                       {open the newly created file}
            {check for error}
            GetMyDataSizeLoc(count, buffer);
                                       {get the data's size and location}
            error := FSWrite(fileRefNum, count, buffer);
                                       {write to the file}
            {check for error}
            error := FSClose(fileRefNum);
                                       {close the temporary file}
            {check for error}
            error := FSpExchangeFiles(tempFSSpec, reply.sfFile);
                                       {exchange the contents of the }
                                       { two files}
            {check for error}
            error := FSpDelete(tempFSSpec);
                                       {delete the temporary file}
            {check for error}
            END;
      END;
END;
```

Searching a Volume

You can search a volume's catalog efficiently using the new PBCatSearch function. PBCatSearch looks at all entries in all directories on the volume, and it returns a list of all files or directories that match the criteria you specify. You can ask PBCatSearch to match for names or partial names; file and directory attributes; Finder information; physical and logical file length; creation, modification, and backup dates; and parent directory ID.

Like all low-level File Manager functions, PBCatSearch exchanges information with your application through a parameter block. The PBCatSearch function uses a new parameter block variant, CSParam, which contains these fields:

```
CSParam:
     (ioMatchPtr:      FSSpecArrayPtr; {pointer to list of matches}
     ioReqMatchCount: LongInt;        {maximum number of matches to return}
     ioActMatchCount: LongInt;        {actual number of matches}
     ioSearchBits:    LongInt;        {enable bits for matching rules}
     ioSearchInfo1:   CInfoPBPtr;     {pointer to values and lower bounds}
     ioSearchInfo2:   CInfoPBPtr;     {pointer to masks and upper bounds}
     ioSearchTime:    LongInt;        {maximum time to search, in }
                                      { Time Manager form}
     ioCatPosition:   CatPositionRec; {current catalog position}
     ioOptBuffer:     Ptr;            {pointer to optional read buffer}
     ioOptBufSize:    LongInt);       {length of optional read buffer}
```

For a description of all fields in the parameter block and how they are used, see the description of PBCatSearch in "Searching a Catalog" later in this chapter.

PBCatSearch manipulates file and directory data in a catalog information (CInfoPBRec) record. (This record, also used by the PBGetCatInfo function, is described fully in the File Manager chapter of Volume IV.) You specify the limits of the search criteria to PBCatSearch in two catalog information records, called ioSearchInfo1 and ioSearchInfo2.

Some fields in the catalog information records apply only to files, some only to directories, and some to both. Some of the fields that apply to both have different names, depending on whether the target of the record is a file or a directory. PBCatSearch uses only some fields in the catalog information record. Table 25-4 lists the fields used for files, and Table 25-5 lists the fields used for directories.

The fields in ioSearchInfo1 and ioSearchInfo2 have different uses:

- The name field in ioSearchInfo1 holds a pointer to the target string; the name field in ioSearchInfo2 must be NIL. (If you're not searching for the name, the name field in ioSearchInfo1 must also be NIL.)
- The date and length fields in ioSearchInfo1 hold the lowest values in the target range; the date and length fields in ioSearchInfo2 hold the highest values in the target range. PBCatSearch looks for values greater than or equal to the field values in ioSearchInfo1 and less than or equal to the values in ioSearchInfo2.
- The attributes and Finder information fields in ioSearchInfo1 hold the target values; the same fields in ioSearchInfo2 hold masks that specify which bits are relevant. (File attributes are described in the File Manager chapter of Volume IV, and the Finder information is described in the Finder Interface chapter of this volume.)

Table 25-4. Fields in ioSearchInfo1 and ioSearchInfo2 used for a file

Offset	Field	Size	Meaning
18	ioNamePtr	Long	Filename
30	ioFlAttrib	Byte	File attributes
32	ioFlFndrInfo	16 bytes	Finder information (FInfo record, described in the Finder Interface chapter of this volume)
54	ioFlLgLen	Long	Data fork logical length
58	ioFlPyLen	Long	Data fork physical length
64	ioFlRLgLen	Long	Resource fork logical length
68	ioFlRPyLen	Long	Resource fork physical length
72	ioFlCrDat	Long	File creation date
76	ioFlMDat	Long	File modification date
80	ioFlBakDat	Long	File backup date
84	ioFlXFndrInfo	16 bytes	Extended Finder information (FXInfo record, described in the Finder Interface chapter of this volume)
100	ioFlParID	Long	File's parent directory ID

Table 25-5. Fields in ioSearchInfo1 and ioSearchInfo2 used for a directory

Offset	Field	Size	Meaning
18	ioNamePtr	Long	Directory name
30	ioFlAttrib	Byte	Directory attributes
32	ioDrUsrWds	16 bytes	Finder information (DInfo record, described in the Finder Interface chapter of this volume)
52	ioDrNmFls	Word	Number of files in the directory
72	ioDrCrDat	Long	Directory creation date
76	ioDrMdDat	Long	Directory modification date
80	ioDrBakDat	Long	Directory backup date
84	ioDrFndrInfo	16 bytes	Extended Finder information (DXInfo record, described in the Finder Interface chapter of this volume)
100	ioDrParID	Long	Directory's parent directory ID

In a pair of records that describe a file, for example, the variable fields have these meanings:

Field	ioSearchInfo1	ioSearchInfo2
ioNamePtr	Target string	Reserved (must be NIL)
ioFlAttrib	Desired attributes	Mask specifying which attributes are used in search
ioFlFndrInfo	Desired Finder profile	Mask specifying which Finder information is used in search
ioFlLgLen	Smallest desired size	Largest desired size
ioFlPyLen	Smallest desired size	Largest desired size
ioFlRLgLen	Smallest desired size	Largest desired size
ioFlCrDat	Earliest desired date	Latest desired date

Field	**ioSearchInfo1**	**ioSearchInfo2**
ioFlMDat	Earliest desired date	Latest desired date
ioFlBakDat	Earliest desired date	Latest desired date
ioFlXFndrInfo	Desired extended Finder profile	Mask specifying which extended Finder information is used in search

PBCatSearch searches only on bits 0 and 4 in the file attributes field (ioFlAttrib).

Attributes bit	**Meaning**
0	File or directory is locked
4	Entry is a directory

To fully describe the search criteria to PBCatSearch, you pass it a pair of catalog information records that determine the limits of the search and a mask that identifies the relevant fields within the catalog information records. You pass the mask in the ioSearchBits field in the PBCatSearch parameter block. To determine the value of ioSearchBits, add together the appropriate constants.

```
CONST fsSBPartialName   =     1;    {substring of name}
      fsSBFullName      =     2;    {full name}
      fsSBFlAttrib      =     4;    {directory flag; software lock flag}
      fsSBNegate        = 16384;    {reverse match status}

      {for files only}
      fsSBFlFndrInfo    =     8;    {Finder file info}
      fsSBFlLgLen       =    32;    {data fork logical length}
      fsSBFlPyLen       =    64;    {data fork physical length}
      fsSBFlRLgLen      =   128;    {resource fork logical length}
      fsSBFlRPyLen      =   256;    {resource fork physical length}
      fsSBFlCrDat       =   512;    {file creation date}
      fsSBFlMdDat       =  1024;    {file modification date}
      fsSBFlBkDat       =  2048;    {file backup date}
      fsSBFlXFndrInfo   =  4096;    {more Finder file info}
      fsSBFlParID       =  8192;    {file's parent ID}

      {for directories only}
      fsSBDrUsrWds      =     8;    {Finder directory info}
      fsSBDrNmFls       =    16;    {number of files in directory}
      fsSBDrCrDat       =   512;    {directory creation date}
      fsSBDrMdDat       =  1024;    {directory modification date}
      fsSBDrBkDat       =  2048;    {directory backup date}
      fsSBDrFndrInfo    =  4096;    {more Finder directory info}
      fsSBDrParID       =  8192;    {directory's parent ID}
```

Figure 25-3 illustrates how the value in ioSearchBits determines which fields are used in ioSearchInfo1 and ioSearchInfo2.

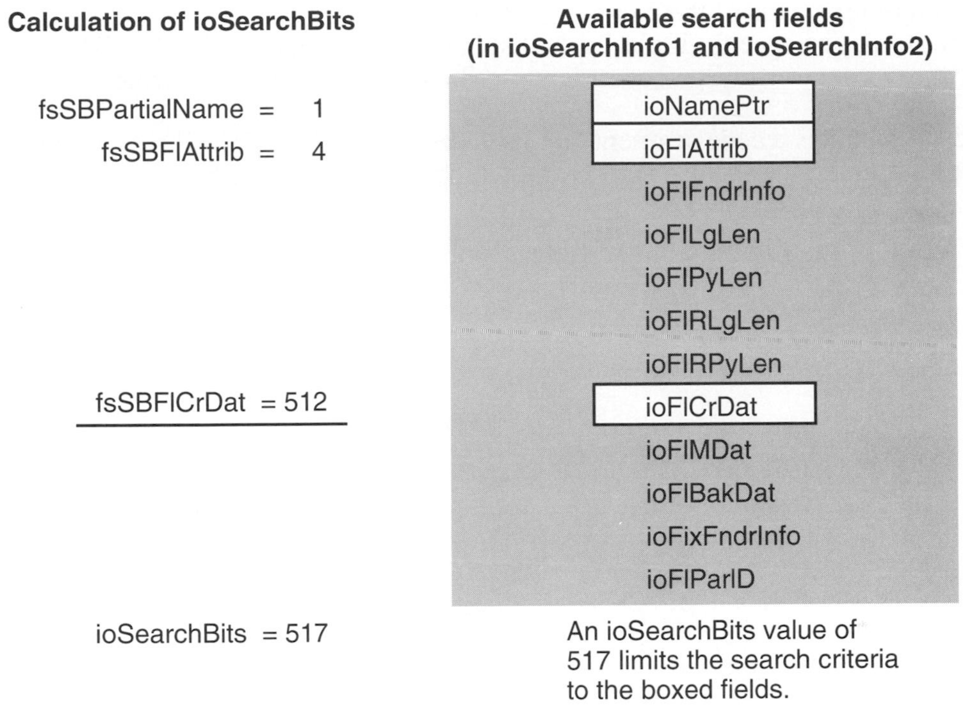

Figure 25-3. The effect of ioSearchBits on interpretation of ioSearchInfo1 and ioSearchInfo2

A catalog entry must meet all of the specified criteria to be placed in the list of matches. After PBCatSearch has completed its scan of each entry, it checks the fsSBNegate bit. If that bit is set, PBCatSearch reverses the entry's match status (that is, if the entry is a match but the fsSBNegate bit is set, the entry is not put in the list of matches; if it is not a match, it is put in the list).

Although the use of PBCatSearch is significantly more efficient than searching the directories recursively, searching a large volume can take long enough to affect user response time. You can break a search into several shorter searches by specifying a maximum length of time in the ioSearchTime field and keeping an index in the ioCatPosition field. PBCatSearch stores its directory-location index in a catalog position record.

```
TYPE CatPositionRec =                          {catalog position record}
  RECORD
     initialize:   LongInt;                    {starting point}
     priv:         ARRAY[1..6] OF Integer      {private data}
END;
```

To start a search at the beginning of the catalog, set the initialization field to 0. When it exits because of a timeout, PBCatSearch updates the record so that it describes the next entry to be searched. When you call PBCatSearch to resume the search after a timeout, pass the entire record that was returned by the last call.

PBCatSearch returns a list of the names and parent directories of all files and directories that match the criteria you specify. It places the list in an array pointed to by the FSSpecArrayPtr field. The array contains FSSpec records, described earlier in "Using FSSpec Records."

Listing 25-4 illustrates a code segment that uses PBCatSearch to find all files (not directories) whose names contain the string "Temp" and which were created within the past two days.

Listing 25-4. Searching a volume with PBCatSearch

```
CONST
   kMaxMatches        = 30;           {find up to 30 matches in one pass}
   kOptBufferSize     = 16384;        {use a 16K search cache for speed}

VAR
   err:               OSErr;
   loopy:             Integer;        {loop control variable}
   fileName:          Str255;         {name of string to look for}
   vRefNum:           Integer;        {volume on which to search}
   dirID:             LongInt;        {ignored dir ID for HGetVol}
   currentDateTime:   LongInt;        {current date in seconds}
   twoDaysAgo:        LongInt;        {date two days ago in seconds}
   pb:                HParamBlockRec;
                                      {parameter block for PBCatSearch}
   theResults:        PACKED ARRAY[1..kMaxMatches] OF FSSpec;
                                      {put matches here}
   spec1:             CInfoPBRec;     {search criteria, part 1}
   spec2:             CInfoPBRec;     {search criteria, part 2}
   buffer:            PACKED ARRAY[1..kOptBufferSize] OF Char;
                                      {search cache}
   done:              Boolean;        {set to TRUE when all matches found}

PROCEDURE SetupForFirstTime;
BEGIN
   err := HGetVol(NIL, vRefNum, dirID);
                                      {search on default volume}
   fileName := 'Temp';                {search for "Temp"}
   GetDateTime(currentDateTime);      {get current time in seconds}
   twoDaysAgo := currentDateTime - (2 * 24 * 60 * 60);
   WITH pb DO
      BEGIN
         ioCompletion := NIL;         {no completion routine}
         ioNamePtr := NIL;            {no volume name; use vRefNum}
         ioVRefNum := vRefNum;        {volume to search}
         ioMatchPtr := FSSpecArrayPtr(@theResults);
                                      {points to results buffer}
         ioReqMatchCount := kMaxMatches;
                                      {number of matches}
         ioSearchBits := fsSBPartialName
                                      {search on partial name}
           + fsSBFlAttrib             {search on file attributes}
           + fsSBFlCrDat;             {search on creation date}
         ioSearchInfo1 := @spec1;     {points to first criteria set}
         ioSearchInfo2 := @spec2;     {points to second criteria set}
```

```
            ioSearchTime := -1;         {don't time out on searches}
            ioCatPosition.initialize := 0;
                                        {set hint to 0}
            ioOptBuffer := @buffer;     {point to search cache}
            ioOptBufSize := kOptBufferSize;
                                        {size of search cache}
         END;
      WITH spec1 DO
         BEGIN
            ioNamePtr := @fileName;     {point to string to find}
            ioFlAttrib := $00;          {clear bit 4 to ask for files}
            ioFlCrDat := twoDaysAgo;    {lower bound of creation date}
         END;
      WITH spec2 DO
         BEGIN
            ioNamePtr := NIL;           {set to NIL}
            ioFlAttrib := $10;          {set mask for bit 4}
            ioFlCrDat := currentDateTime;
                                        {upper bound of creation date}
         END;
   END;

   BEGIN
      SetupForFirstTime;                {initialize data records}
      REPEAT
         err := PBCatSearchSync(@pb); {get some files}
         done := (err = eofErr);       {eofErr returned when all done}
         IF ((err = noErr) | done) & (pb.ioActMatchCount > 0) THEN
            FOR loopy := 1 TO pb.ioActMatchCount DO
                                        {report all matches found}
               Writeln(theResults[loopy].name);
      UNTIL done;
   END.
```

Tracking Files With File IDs

The File Manager provides a set of three low-level functions for creating, resolving, and deleting file ID references. These functions were developed for use by the Alias Manager, which uses them to track files that have been moved or renamed. In most cases, your application should track files with the Alias Manager, described in the Alias Manager chapter of this volume, not with file IDs.

You establish a file ID reference when you need to identify a file by file number (see "File IDs" earlier in this chapter). You create a file ID reference with the PBCreateFileIDRef function. Because the File Manager assigns file numbers independently on each volume, a file ID is not guaranteed to be unique across volumes.

You can resolve a file ID reference by calling the PBResolveFileIDRef function, which determines the name and parent directory ID of the file with a given ID. With this information and a volume specification, you can uniquely identify any file in the file system.

If you no longer need a file ID, remove its record from the directory by calling the PBDeleteFileIDRef function. Removing a file ID is seldom appropriate, but the function is provided for completeness.

To preserve a file's ID when you are saving a new version of it, you should use the new safe-save strategy described earlier in "Updating Files."

Mounting Volumes Programmatically

Your application can mount remote volumes, without requiring the user to go through the Chooser, using a set of three new functions: PBGetVolMountInfoSize, PBGetVolMountInfo, and PBVolumeMount.

Ordinarily, before you can mount a volume programmatically, you must record its mounting information while it's mounted. Because the size of the mounting information can vary, you first call the PBGetVolMountInfoSize function, which returns the size of the record you'll need to allocate to hold the mounting information. You then allocate the record and call PBGetVolMountInfo, passing a pointer to the record. When you want to mount the volume later, you can pass the record directly to the PBVolumeMount function.

> **Note:** The functions for mounting volumes programmatically are low-level functions designed for specialized applications. Even if your application needs to track and access volumes automatically, it can ordinarily use the Alias Manager, described in the Alias Manager chapter of this volume. The Alias Manager can record mounting information and later remount most volumes, even those that do not support the programmatic mounting functions.

The programmatic mounting functions can now be used to mount AppleShare volumes. The functions have been designed so that they can eventually be used to mount local Macintosh volumes, such as partitions on devices that support partitioning, and local or remote volumes managed by non-Macintosh file systems.

The programmatic mounting functions use the ioParam variant of the ParamBlockRec record, described in the File Manager chapter of Volume IV. They store the mounting information in a variable-sized structure called the VolMountInfoHeader record.

```
TYPE VolMountInfoHeader =
     RECORD
        length:   Integer;       {length of mounting information, }
                                 { including standard header and }
                                 { variable-length data}
        media:    VolumeType;    {type of volume}
        {volume-specific, variable-length location data}
     END;
```

The size and contents of the record can vary, depending on the external file system that's handling the particular volume.

The length field contains the length of the structure (that is, the total length of the structure header described here plus the variable-length location data). The length of the record is flexible so that non-Macintosh file systems can store whatever information they need for volume mounting.

The media field identifies the volume type of the remote volume. The value AppleShareMediaType (a constant that translates to 'afpm') represents an AppleShare volume. If you are adding support for the programmatic mounting functions to a non-Macintosh file system, you should register a four-character identifier for your volumes with Macintosh Developer Technical Support at Apple Computer, Inc.

The only volumes that currently support the programmatic mounting functions are AppleShare servers, which use this volume mounting record.

```
TYPE AFPVolMountInfo =
     RECORD
        length:              Integer;     {length of mounting }
                                          { information, including }
                                          { standard header and }
                                          { variable-length data}
        media:               VolumeType;  {type of volume}
        flags:               Integer;     {reserved; must be set to 0}
        nbpInterval:         SignedByte;  {NBP retry interval}
        nbpCount:            SignedByte;  {NBP retry count}
        uamType:             Integer;     {user authentication method}
        zoneNameOffset:      Integer;     {offset from start of record }
                                          { to zone name}
        serverNameOffset:    Integer;     {offset from start of record }
                                          { to server name}
        volNameOffset:       Integer;     {offset from start of record }
                                          { to volume name}
        userNameOffset:      Integer;     {offset from start of record }
                                          { to user name}
        userPassWordOffset:  Integer;     {offset from start of record }
                                          { to user password}
        volPassWordOffset:   Integer;     {offset from start of record }
                                          { to volume password}
        AFPData:             PACKED ARRAY[1..144] OF Char;
                                          {standard AFP mounting info}
        {optional volume-specific, variable-length data}
     END;
```

The length and media fields in the AFP volume mounting record are the same as the length and media fields in the generic volume mounting record.

The nbpInterval and nbpCount fields are used by the AppleTalk® Name-Binding Protocol (NBP). Their functions are described in the AppleTalk Manager chapter of Volume II.

The uamType field specifies the access-control method used by the remote volume. AppleShare uses four methods:

```
CONST kNoUserAuthentication   = 1;  {guest status; no password needed}
      kPassword               = 2;  {8-byte password}
      kEncryptPassword        = 3;  {encrypted 8-byte password}
      kTwoWayEncryptPassword  = 6;  {two-way random encryption; }
                                    { authenticate both user and server}
```

The six offset fields contain the offsets from the beginning of the record, in bytes, to the entries in the data field of the volume's AppleShare zone and server name, the volume name, the name of the user, the user's password, and the volume password.

PBGetVolMountInfo does not return the user and volume passwords; they're returned as blank. Typically, your application asks the user for any necessary passwords and fills in those fields just before calling PBVolumeMount. No passwords are required for mounting a volume with guest status.

If you have enough information about the volume, you can fill in the mounting record yourself and call PBVolumeMount, even if you did not save the mounting information while the volume was mounted. To mount an AFP volume, you must fill in the record with at least the zone name, server name, user name, user password, and volume password. You can lay out the fields in any order within the data field, as long as you specify the correct offsets.

Manipulating Privilege Information in Foreign File Systems

Version 7.0 includes two low-level functions that support interaction with foreign file systems: PBGetForeignPrivs and PBSetForeignPrivs. These functions let you manipulate privilege information on a file system with a non-Macintosh privilege model.

The access-control functions were designed for use by shell programs, such as the Finder, that need to use the native privilege model of the foreign file system. Most applications can rely on using AFP functions, which are recognized by file systems that support the Macintosh privilege model. The new access-control functions do not relieve a foreign file system of the need to map its own privilege model onto the AFP functions.

Like all other low-level File Manager functions, the access-control functions exchange information with your application through parameter blocks. The meanings of some fields depend on what the foreign file system is. These fields are currently defined for A/UX, and you can define them for other file systems. If you are defining a new privilege model, register it with Macintosh Developer Technical Support.

You can identify the foreign file system through the PBHGetVolParms function, described later in "Reading Volume Information." Version 7.0 defines a new attributes buffer for the PBHGetVolParms function, with a field for the foreign privilege model, vMForeignPrivID.

> **Note:** The value of vMForeignPrivID is unrelated to whether the remote volume supports the AFP access-control functions, described in the File Manager chapter of Volume V. You can determine whether the volume supports the AFP access-control functions by checking the bHasAccessCntl bit in the vMAttrib field. See the description of PBHGetVolParms in "Reading Volume Information" later in this chapter.

A value of 0 for vMForeignPrivID signifies an HFS volume that supports no foreign privilege models. The field currently has one other defined value.

```
CONST fsUnixPriv = 1;       {A/UX privilege model}
```

For an updated list of supported models and their constants and fields, contact Macintosh Developer Technical Support.

A volume can support no more than one foreign privilege model.

The access-control functions store information in a new parameter block type, ForeignPrivParam, described in "Accessing Privilege Information in Foreign File Systems" later in this chapter.

The parameter block can store access-control information in one or both of

- a buffer of any length, whose location and size are stored in the parameter block
- four long words of data stored in the parameter block itself

The meanings of the fields in the parameter block depend on the definitions established by the foreign file system.

HIGH-LEVEL FILE MANAGER ROUTINES

Version 7.0 introduces three kinds of high-level File Manager routines:

- functions that identify files with the new FSSpec record, introduced in version 7.0, including a new function that exchanges the data in two files
- a new set of three functions for opening only the data fork of a file, to be used instead of the earlier function FSOpen
- functions that identify files using the three parameters vRefNum, dirID, and fileName, introduced with the Hierarchical File System

Most of the new functions in version 7.0 are adaptations of functions introduced either in the original Macintosh File System or with the Hierarchical File System. Modified functions bear the same root name as the original functions. The prefix FSp identifies functions modified to accommodate FSSpec records; the prefix H identifies functions modified to accommodate directory IDs for compatibility with HFS.

Routines That Use FSSpec Records

Version 7.0 of the system software introduces the FSSpec record, a simple, standard way to specify the name and location of a file or directory. Other parts of the Macintosh system software now identify files and directories with FSSpec records. The File Manager supports FSSpec records by providing

- a function for converting other file specifications to FSSpec records
- a set of File Manager functions that accept and return FSSpec records instead of the parameters vRefNum, dirID, and fileName

The new FSpExchangeFiles function, which exchanges the data in two files, accepts file specifications in a pair of FSSpec records.

Making FSSpec Records

You use the FSMakeFSSpec function to convert a conventional file or directory specification into an FSSpec record.

```
FUNCTION FSMakeFSSpec (vRefNum: Integer; dirID: LongInt;
                       fileName: Str255; VAR spec: FSSpec) : OSErr;
```

FSMakeFSSpec places the specification in the spec parameter. (See "Using FSSpec Records" earlier in this chapter for a description of the FSSpec record.) Call FSMakeFSSpec whenever you want to create an FSSpec record.

The vRefNum parameter is the volume reference number, a working directory reference number, a drive number, or 0 for the default volume.

The dirID parameter is usually the parent directory ID of the target object. If the directory is sufficiently specified by either vRefNum or fileName, dirID can be 0. If you explicitly specify dirID (that is, if it is any value other than 0), and if vRefNum is a working directory reference number, dirID overrides the directory ID included in vRefNum. If the fileName parameter is an empty string, FSMakeFSSpec creates an FSSpec record for a directory specified by either the dirID or vRefNum parameter.

The fileName parameter is a full or partial pathname. If it is a full pathname, FSMakeFSSpec ignores vRefNum and dirID. A partial pathname might identify only the final target, or it might include one or more parent directory names. If fileName is a partial pathname, vRefNum, dirID, or both must be valid.

The spec parameter is an FSSpec record, which FSMakeFSSpec fills in.

You can pass the input to FSMakeFSSpec in any of the four ways described in "The Evolution of File Specification Strategies" earlier in this chapter. See Table 25-1 in "Using FSSpec Records" earlier in this chapter for details of how FSMakeFSSpec interprets input.

If the specified volume is mounted and the specified parent directory exists, but the target file or directory doesn't exist in that location, FSMakeFSSpec fills in the record and then returns fnfErr instead of noErr. The record is valid, but it describes a target that doesn't exist. You can use the record for other operations, such as creating a file with the FSpCreate function.

In addition to the result codes listed here, FSMakeFSSpec can return a number of different File Manager error codes. If you receive any result code other than noErr or fnfErr, FSMakeFSSpec returns a NIL FSSpec record.

Result codes

noErr	0	No error
fnfErr	–43	File or directory does not exist (FSSpec is still valid)

Exchanging the Data in Two Files

You use the FSpExchangeFiles function to exchange the data between two files on a volume.

```
FUNCTION FSpExchangeFiles (source: FSSpec; dest: FSSpec) : OSErr;
```

FSpExchangeFiles swaps the files' data by changing the information in the volume's catalog and, if the files are open, in the file control blocks. Tables 25-2 and 25-3 in "Updating Files" earlier in this chapter illustrate how FSpExchangeFiles alters the catalog entries and file control blocks.

You should use FSpExchangeFiles when updating an existing file, so that if the file is being tracked through its file ID, the ID remains valid. Typically, you use PBExchangeFiles after creating a new file during a safe save (see "Updating Files" earlier in this chapter). You identify the two files to be exchanged in the source and dest parameters. FSpExchangeFiles changes the fields in the catalog entries that record the location of the data and the modification dates. It swaps both the data forks and the resource forks.

FSpExchangeFiles works on either open or closed files. If either file is open, FSpExchangeFiles updates any file control blocks associated with the file. Exchanging the contents of two files requires essentially the same access as opening both files for writing.

FSpExchangeFiles does not require that file IDs exist for the files being exchanged.

Result codes

noErr	0	No error
nsvErr	–35	Volume not found
ioErr	–36	I/O error
fnfErr	–43	File not found
fLckdErr	–45	File locked
volOfflinErr	–53	Volume is off line
extFSErr	–58	External file system
wrgVolTypeErr	–123	Not an HFS volume
notAFileErr	–1302	Specified file is a directory
diffVolErr	–1303	Files on different volumes

Functions Modified to Accept FSSpec Records

The File Manager contains modified versions of the basic functions for manipulating files so that you can use FSSpec records for tasks such as creating, opening, and deleting files. This section specifies the syntax of the new functions. For descriptions of how the functions work, see the entries for the equivalent functions in the File Manager chapter of Volume IV.

```
FUNCTION FSpOpenDF (spec: FSSpec; permission: SignedByte;
                    VAR refNum: Integer) : OSErr;
```

The FSpOpenDF function creates an access path to the data fork of a file. It is the FSSpec version of the new function HOpenDF, which replaces the functions FSOpen and HOpen. The difference is that HOpenDF opens only the data fork of a file; FSOpen and HOpen can open either a driver or the data fork of a file. Using FSpOpenDF eliminates the ambiguity and ensures that you can open even a file whose name begins with a period (.). You specify the file to be opened with an FSSpec record in the spec parameter. FSpOpenDF opens the data fork and places the path reference number in the refNum parameter.

FSpOpenDF takes a permission parameter not available in FSOpen. Set this parameter to request the kind of access path permission you want.

```
CONST fsCurPerm     = 0;   {exclusive read/write permission if it is }
                           { available; otherwise, exclusive read, if }
                           { that is available}
      fsRdPerm      = 1;   {exclusive read permission}
      fsWrPerm      = 2;   {exclusive write permission}
      fsRdWrPerm    = 3;   {exclusive read/write permission}
      fsRdWrShPerm  = 4;   {shared read/write permission}
```

In most cases, you can simply set the permission parameter to fsCurPerm. Some applications request fsRdWrPerm, to ensure that they can both read and write to a file. For more information about permissions, see the description of the ioParam variants of the parameter block records (ParamBlockRec and HParamBlockRec) in the File Manager chapter of Volume IV. In shared environments, permission requests are translated into the “deny-mode” permissions defined by AppleShare and described in the File Manager chapter of Volume V.

For more information, see the entry for FSOpen in the File Manager chapter of Volume IV.

```
FUNCTION FSpOpenRF (spec: FSSpec; permission: SignedByte;
                    VAR refNum: Integer) : OSErr;
```

The FSpOpenRF function creates an access path to the resource fork of a file. It is the high-level, FSSpec version of the PBHOpenRF function, documented in the File Manager chapter of Volume IV.

```
FUNCTION FSpCreate (spec: FSSpec; creator: OSType; fileType: OSType;
                    scriptTag: ScriptCode) : OSErr;
```

The FSpCreate function creates a new file and sets the type and creator. It is the high-level, FSSpec version of the PBHCreate function, documented in the File Manager chapter of Volume IV. The scriptTag parameter specifies the code of the script system in which the docu-ment name is to be displayed. If you have established the name and location of the new file through either the StandardPutFile or CustomPutFile procedure, specify the script code returned in the reply record. (See the Standard File Package chapter of this volume for a description of StandardPutFile and CustomPutFile.) Otherwise, specify the system script by setting the scriptTag parameter to smSystemScript. See the Worldwide Software Overview chapter of this volumc for more information on script systems.

```
FUNCTION FSpDirCreate (spec: FSSpec; scriptTag: ScriptCode;
                       VAR createdDirID: LongInt) : OSErr;
```

The FSpDirCreate function creates a new directory. It is a high-level, FSSpec version of PBDirCreate, documented in the File Manager chapter of Volume IV.

```
FUNCTION FSpDelete (spec: FSSpec) : OSErr;
```

The FSpDelete function removes a closed file. It is the high-level, FSSpec version of the PBHDelete function, which is documented in the File Manager chapter of Volume IV.

```
FUNCTION FSpGetFInfo (spec: FSSpec; VAR fndrInfo: FInfo) : OSErr;
```

The FSpGetFInfo function returns the Finder information from the volume catalog entry for the specified file or directory. It provides only the original Finder information—the FInfo and DInfo records, not FXInfo and DXInfo. (See the Finder Interface chapter of this volume for a discussion of Finder information.) It is the high-level, FSSpec version of the PBHGetFInfo function, documented in the File Manager chapter of Volume IV.

```
FUNCTION FSpSetFInfo (spec: FSSpec; fndrInfo: FInfo) : OSErr;
```

The FSpSetFInfo function sets the Finder information in the volume catalog entry for the specified file or directory. It affects only the original Finder information—the FInfo and DInfo records, not FXInfo and DXInfo. (See the Finder Interface chapter of this volume for a discussion of Finder information.) It is the high-level, FSSpec version of the PBHSetFInfo function, documented in the File Manager chapter of Volume IV.

```
FUNCTION FSpSetFLock (spec: FSSpec) : OSErr;
```

The FSpSetFLock function locks a file. It is the high-level, FSSpec version of the PBHSetFLock function, documented in the File Manager chapter of Volume IV.

```
FUNCTION FSpRstFLock (spec: FSSpec) : OSErr;
```

The FSpRstFLock function unlocks a file. It is the high-level, FSSpec version of the PBHRstFLock function, documented in the File Manager chapter of Volume IV.

```
FUNCTION FSpRename (spec: FSSpec; newName: Str255) : OSErr;
```

The FSpRename function changes the name of a file or directory. It is the high-level, FSSpec version of the PBHRename function, documented in the File Manager chapter of Volume IV.

```
FUNCTION FSpCatMove (source: FSSpec; dest: FSSpec) : OSErr;
```

The FSpCatMove function moves the file or directory specified by the source parameter to the destination specified by the dest parameter. It is the high-level, FSSpec version of the low-level function PBCatMove, documented in the File Manager chapter of Volume IV. The source and dest parameters specify the name and location of the file or directory before and after the move.

Opening a Data Fork

The File Manager contains three new functions for opening only the data fork of a file. FSpOpenDF, the function that accepts an FSSpec record, is documented earlier in "Functions Modified to Accept FSSpec Records." The other two functions accept file specifications in the traditional MFS and HFS forms.

```
FUNCTION HOpenDF (vRefNum: Integer; dirID: LongInt; fileName: Str255;
                  permission: SignedByte; VAR refNum: Integer) : OSErr;
```

The HOpenDF function creates an access path to the data fork of a file. It is an HFS version of OpenDF. The vRefNum parameter can hold a volume reference number or a working directory reference number. The dirID parameter holds a directory ID.

```
FUNCTION OpenDF (fileName: Str255; vRefNum: Integer; VAR refNum: Integer)
                : OSErr;
```

The OpenDF function creates an access path to the data fork of a file. It is almost identical to FSOpen, which is documented in the File Manager chapter of Volume IV. The difference is that FSOpen can open both files and devices, but OpenDF can open only files. Using OpenDF instead of FSOpen when your application is opening a file prevents naming conflicts or ambiguities and ensures that your application can open files whose names start with a period (.).

Managing HFS

When HFS was first introduced, it was accompanied by a set of low-level functions with no high-level equivalents. Some of these functions were designed for handling hierarchical volumes; some were simply modifications of MFS routines, adapted to accommodate directory information. This section documents the high-level versions of the low-level functions introduced with HFS. For more information, see the entries for the equivalent low-level functions in the File Manager chapter of Volume IV.

Functions New With HFS

This section documents the high-level versions of the functions for handling hierarchical volumes.

```
FUNCTION AllocContig (refNum: Integer; VAR count: LongInt) : OSErr;
```

The AllocContig function is a high-level function that calls PBAllocContig, which is documented in the File Manager chapter of Volume IV.

```
FUNCTION DirCreate (vRefNum: Integer; parentDirID: LongInt;
                    directoryName: Str255; VAR createdDirID: LongInt) :
                    OSErr;
```

The DirCreate function is a high-level function that calls PBDirCreate, which is documented in the File Manager chapter of Volume IV.

```
FUNCTION CatMove (vRefNum: Integer; dirID: LongInt; oldName: Str255;
                  newDirID: LongInt; newName: Str255) : OSErr;
```

The CatMove function is a high-level function that calls PBCatMove, which is documented in the File Manager chapter of Volume IV.

```
FUNCTION OpenWD (vRefNum: Integer; dirID: LongInt; procID: LongInt;
                 VAR wdRefNum: Integer) : OSErr;
```

The OpenWD function is a high-level function that calls PBOpenWD, which is documented in the File Manager chapter of Volume IV.

```
FUNCTION CloseWD (wdRefNum: Integer) : OSErr;
```

The CloseWD function is a high-level function that calls PBCloseWD, which is documented in the File Manager chapter of Volume IV.

```
FUNCTION GetWDInfo (wdRefNum: Integer; VAR vRefNum: Integer;
                    VAR dirID: LongInt; VAR procID: LongInt) : OSErr;
```

The GetWDInfo function is a high-level function that calls PBGetWDInfo, which is documented in the File Manager chapter of Volume IV.

MFS Functions Modified to Accommodate Directory IDs

This section documents the high-level versions of the basic file manipulation functions introduced with HFS. These functions are all adaptations of MFS functions, modified to accept a directory ID parameter. Some of these functions have been superseded by the new functions that accept FSSpec records, documented earlier in "Functions Modified to Accept FSSpec Records."

```
FUNCTION HCreate (vRefNum: Integer; dirID: LongInt; fileName: Str255;
                  creator: OSType; fileType: OSType) : OSErr;
```

The HCreate function creates a new file and sets the type and creator. It is a high-level function that calls PBHCreate, documented in the File Manager chapter of Volume IV.

```
FUNCTION HOpen (vRefNum: Integer; dirID: LongInt; fileName: Str255;
                permission: SignedByte; VAR refNum: Integer) : OSErr;
```

The HOpen function creates an access path to the data fork of a file. It is a high-level function that calls PBHOpen, documented in the File Manager chapter of Volume IV.

```
FUNCTION HOpenRF (vRefNum: Integer; dirID: LongInt; fileName: Str255;
                  permission: SignedByte; VAR refNum: Integer) : OSErr;
```

The HOpenRF function creates an access path to the resource fork of a file. It is a high-level function that calls PBHOpenRF, documented in the File Manager chapter of Volume IV.

```
FUNCTION HDelete (vRefNum: Integer; dirID: LongInt; fileName: Str255) :
                  OSErr;
```

The HDelete function removes a closed file. It is a high-level function that calls PBHDelete, documented in the File Manager chapter of Volume IV.

```
FUNCTION HSetFLock (vRefNum: Integer; dirID: LongInt; fileName: Str255) :
                    OSErr;
```

The HSetFLock function locks a file. It is a high-level function that calls PBHSetFLock, documented in the File Manager chapter of Volume IV.

```
FUNCTION HRstFLock (vRefNum: Integer; dirID: LongInt; fileName: Str255) :
                    OSErr;
```

The HRstFLock function unlocks a file. It is a high-level function that calls PBHRstFLock, documented in the File Manager chapter of Volume IV.

```
FUNCTION HRename (vRefNum: Integer; dirID: LongInt; oldName: Str255;
                  newName: Str255) : OSErr;
```

The HRename function changes the name of a file or directory. It is a high-level function that calls PBHRename, documented in the File Manager chapter of Volume IV.

```
FUNCTION HGetFInfo (vRefNum: Integer; dirID: LongInt; fileName: Str255;
                    VAR fndrInfo: FInfo) : OSErr;
```

The HGetFInfo function returns the Finder information stored in the volume's catalog for a file. It is a high-level function that calls PBHGetFInfo, documented in the File Manager chapter of Volume IV.

```
FUNCTION HSetFInfo (vRefNum: Integer; dirID: LongInt; fileName: Str255;
                    fndrInfo: FInfo) : OSErr;
```

The HSetFInfo function changes the Finder information stored in the volume's catalog for a file. It is a high-level function that calls PBHSetFInfo, documented in the File Manager chapter of Volume IV.

```
FUNCTION HGetVol (volName: StringPtr; VAR vRefNum: Integer;
                  VAR dirID: LongInt) : OSErr;
```

The HGetVol function returns the volume reference number of the default volume. It is a high-level function that calls PBHGetVol, documented in the File Manager chapter of Volume IV.

LOW-LEVEL FILE MANAGER ROUTINES

This section describes the low-level File Manager routines new in version 7.0.

All low-level routines exchange parameters with your application in a parameter block, which is a data structure in the heap or stack. When calling low-level routines, you usually pass a pointer to the parameter block and a Boolean value that determines whether the routine is run synchronously (FALSE) or asynchronously (TRUE). The new routines for mounting volumes take only a pointer to the parameter block. These functions are always run synchronously. See the introduction to low-level routines in the File Manager chapter of Volume IV for a description of the standard parameters in a low-level function.

You cannot assume that a series of asynchronous calls will be executed in the order in which they are issued, especially in a shared environment. When the order and timing of functions are important (if, for example, you are first reading and then writing data), you can either call the functions synchronously or check the completion routines of functions called asynchronously before acting on the result.

Reading Volume Information

The PBHGetVolParms function describes the characteristics of a volume. You specify a volume (by either name or volume reference number) and a buffer size, and PBHGetVolParms fills in the volume-attributes buffer, as described in this section.

```
FUNCTION PBHGetVolParms (paramBlock: HParmBlkPtr; async: Boolean) :
                         OSErr;
```

Parameter block

→	12	ioCompletion	long	pointer to completion routine
←	16	ioResult	word	error result code
→	22	ioVRefNum	word	volume specification
→	32	ioBuffer	long	pointer to GetVolParmsInfo record
→	36	ioReqCount	long	size of buffer area
←	40	ioActCount	long	length of attributes data

A volume's characteristics can change when the user enables and disables file sharing. You might have to make repeated calls to PBHGetVolParms to ensure that you have the current status of a volume.

The ioCompletion field holds an optional pointer to a completion routine, which executes after PBHGetVolParms completes if you call the function asynchronously. Set this field to NIL when you call the function synchronously.

PBHGetVolParms puts the result code in the ioResult field.

Specify the volume to be described with a volume reference number, drive number, or working directory reference number in the ioVRefNum field.

You must allocate memory to hold the returned attributes and put a pointer to the buffer in the ioBuffer field. Specify the size of the buffer in the ioReqCount field.

PBHGetVolParms places the attributes information in the buffer pointed to by the ioBuffer field and specifies the actual length of the data in the ioActCount field.

The new version of PBHGetVolParms uses a new format for the GetVolParmsInfo attributes buffer.

Offset	**Field**	**Size**	**Meaning**
0	vMVersion	word	Version number (02 in system software version 7.0)
2	vMAttrib	long	Attributes
6	vMLocalHand	long	Reserved
10	vMServerAdr	long	AppleTalk server address (0 if not supported)
14	vMVolumeGrade	long	Relative speed rating of volume
18	vMForeignPrivID	word	Foreign privilege model supported (two values are currently defined: 0 for an HFS volume; fsUnixPriv for an A/UX volume)

The vMVersion field specifies the version of the attributes buffer.

The vMAttrib field contains 32 bits that describe the volume. When set, the bits in vMAttrib have these meanings:

Bit	**Name**	**Meaning**
31	bLimitFCBs	Limit the number of file control blocks used during copying to 8 instead of 16.
30	bLocalWList	Use the returned shared volume handle for the Finder's local window list.
29	bNoMiniFndr	Disable Mini Finder menu item.
28	bNoVNEdit	Lock volume name against editing.
27	bNoLclSync	Do not let Finder change the modification date.
26	bTrshOffLine	Zoom volume when it is unmounted.
25	bNoSwitchTo	Do not switch launch to any application on the volume.

Bit	Name	Meaning
24–21		Reserved.
20	bNoDeskItems	Do not place objects on the Finder desktop.
19	bNoBootBlks	Not a startup volume. Startup menu item disabled. Boot blocks not copied.
18	bAccessCntl	Volume supports AppleTalk AFP access-control interfaces. The GetLoginInfo, GetDirAccess, SetDirAccess, MapID, and MapName functions are supported. Special folder icons are used. The Access Privileges menu command is enabled for disk and folder items. The privileges field of GetCatInfo calls is assumed to be valid.
17	bNoSysDir	Volume doesn't support a system directory. Do not switch launch to this volume.
16	bHasExtFSVol	Volume is an external file system volume. Disk initialization package is not called. Erase Disk menu command is disabled.
15	bHasOpenDeny	Volume supports _OpenDeny and OpenRFDeny. For copy operations, source files are opened with reading enabled and writing denied; destination files are opened with writing enabled and reading and writing disabled.
14	bHasCopyFile	Volume supports _CopyFile. _CopyFile is used in copy and duplicate operations if both source and destination volumes have the same server address.
13	bHasMoveRename	Volume supports _MoveRename.
12	bHasDesktopMgr	Volume supports all of the new desktop functions (described in the Finder Interface chapter of this volume).
11	bHasShortName	Volume supports a name that fits the shorter length requirements of another file system.
10	bHasFolderLock	Folder is locked.
9	bHasPersonalAccessPrivileges	Local file sharing is enabled.
8	bHasUserGroupList	Volume supports the Users and Groups file and thus the AFP privilege functions.
7	bHasCatSearch	Volume supports PBCatSearch.
6	bHasFileIDs	Volume supports file ID functions, including PBExchangeFiles.
5	bHasBtreeMgr	Reserved for internal use.
4	bHasBlankAccessPrivileges	Volume supports inherited access privileges for folders.
3–0		Reserved.

The vMLocalHand field is reserved.

The vMServerAdr field specifies the internet address of the server that manages an AppleTalk server volume. This value is 0 if the volume does not have a server.

The vMVolumeGrade field specifies the relative speed rating of the volume. This scale is currently uncalibrated. Generally, lower values represent faster speeds, but a value of 0 means that the volume is unrated.

The vMForeignPrivID field specifies an operating system with which the volume can communicate access-control information. For more information about access-control privileges, see "Manipulating Privilege Information in Foreign File Systems" earlier in this chapter and "Accessing Privilege Information in Foreign File Systems" later in this chapter. A value of 0 means that the volume cannot share privilege information with any other file system; a value of fsUnixPriv means it can share privilege information with the A/UX file system.

Result codes

noErr	0	No error
nsvErr	–35	Volume not found
paramErr	–50	Volume doesn't support the function

Searching a Catalog

The PBCatSearch function searches a volume's catalog, using a set of search criteria that you specify. It builds a list of all files or directories that meet your specifications.

```
FUNCTION PBCatSearch (paramBlock: HParmBlkPtr; async: Boolean) : OSErr;
```

Parameter block

→	12	ioCompletion	long	pointer to completion routine
←	16	ioResult	word	result code
→	18	ioNamePtr	long	pointer to volume name
→	22	ioVRefNum	word	volume specification
→	24	ioMatchPtr	long	pointer to array of matches
→	28	ioReqMatchCount	long	maximum match count
←	32	ioActMatchCount	long	actual match count
→	36	ioSearchBits	long	enable bits for fields in criteria records
→	40	ioSearchInfo1	long	values and lower bounds
→	44	ioSearchInfo2	long	masks and upper bounds
→	48	ioSearchTime	long	maximum elapsed search time
→	52	ioCatPosition	16 bytes	current catalog position
→	68	ioOptBuffer	long	pointer to optional read buffer
→	72	ioOptBufSize	long	length of optional read buffer

PBCatSearch searches the volume you specify for files or directories that match two coordinated sets of selection criteria. PBCatSearch returns a pointer to an array of FSSpec records identifying the files and directories that match the criteria.

Field descriptions

ioCompletion A pointer to the completion routine.

ioResult Result code.

ioNamePtr	A pointer to the name of the volume to be searched.
ioVRefNum	The volume specification (volume reference number, working directory reference number, drive number, or 0 for default volume).
ioMatchPtr	A pointer to an array where the file and directory names that match the selection criteria are returned. The array must be large enough to hold the largest possible number of FSSpec records, as determined by the ioReqMatchCount field.
ioReqMatchCount	The maximum number of matches to return. This number should be the number of FSSpec records that will fit in the memory pointed to by ioMatchPtr. Use this field to avoid a possible excess of matches for criteria that prove to be too general.
ioActMatchCount	The number of actual matches found.
ioSearchBits	The fields of the parameter blocks ioSearchInfo1 and ioSearchInfo2 that are relevant to the search. See "Searching a Volume" earlier in this chapter for the values of ioSearchBits.
ioSearchInfo1	A pointer to a CInfoPBRec parameter block that contains values and the lower bounds of ranges for the fields selected by ioSearchBits.
ioSearchInfo2	A pointer to a second CInfoPBRec parameter block that contains masks and upper bounds of ranges for the fields selected by ioSearchBits.
ioSearchTime	A time limit on a search, in Time Manager format. Use this field to limit the run time of a single call to PBCatSearch. A value of 0 imposes no time limit.
ioCatPosition	A position in the catalog where searching should begin. Use this field to keep an index into the catalog when breaking PBCatSearch down into a number of smaller searches. This field is valid whenever PBCatSearch exits because it either spends the maximum time allowed by ioSearchTime or finds the maximum number of matches allowed by ioReqMatchCount. To start at the beginning of the catalog, set the initialize field of ioCatPosition to 0. Before exiting after an interrupted search, PBCatSearch sets that field to the next catalog entry to be searched. To resume where the previous call stopped, pass the entire CatPosition record returned by the previous call as input to the next.
ioOptBuffer	A pointer to an optional read buffer. The ioOptBuffer and ioOptBufSize fields let you specify a part of memory as a read buffer, increasing search speed.
ioOptBufSize	The length of the buffer pointed to by ioOptBuffer. Buffer effectiveness varies with models and configurations, but a 16 KB buffer is likely to be optimal. Even a 1 KB buffer provides some performance improvement.

See the earlier section "Searching a Volume" for a description of how to use PBCatSearch.

If the catalog changes between two timed calls to PBCatSearch (when you are using ioSearchTime and ioCatPosition to search a volume in segments and the catalog changes between searches), PBCatSearch returns a result code of catalogChangedErr. Depending on what has changed on the volume, ioCatPosition might be invalid, most likely by a few entries in one direction or another. You can continue the search, but you risk either skipping some entries or reading some twice.

When PBCatSearch has searched the entire catalog, it returns eofErr. If it exits because it either spends the maximum time allowed by ioSearchTime or finds the maximum number of matches allowed by ioReqMatchCount, it returns noErr.

Result codes

noErr	0	No error (entire catalog has not been searched)
nsvErr	–35	Volume not found
ioErr	–36	I/O error
eofErr	–39	Logical end-of-file reached
paramErr	–50	Parameters don't specify an existing volume
extFSErr	–58	External file system
catalogChangedErr	–1304	Catalog has changed and catalog position record may be invalid

Creating FSSpec Records

Use the PBMakeFSSpec function to make an FSSpec record that identifies a file or directory.

```
FUNCTION PBMakeFSSpec (paramBlock: HParmBlkPtr; async: Boolean) : OSErr;
```

Parameter block

→	12	ioCompletion	long	pointer to completion routine
←	16	ioResult	word	result code
→	18	ioNamePtr	long	pointer to file or directory name
→	22	ioVRefNum	word	volume specification
→	28	ioMisc	long	pointer to FSSpec record
→	48	ioDirID	long	parent directory ID

Given a complete specification for a file or directory, PBMakeFSSpec fills in an FSSpec record that identifies the file or directory. (See Table 25-1 in "Using FSSpec Records" for a detailed description of valid file specifications.)

Field descriptions

ioCompletion	A pointer to the completion routine.
ioResult	Result code.
ioNamePtr	A pointer to the file or directory name.

ioVRefNum	The volume specification (volume reference number, working directory reference number, drive number, or 0 for default volume).
ioMisc	A pointer to the FSSpec record.
ioDirID	The directory or parent directory specification.

If the specified volume is mounted and the specified parent directory exists, but the target file or directory doesn't exist in that location, PBMakeFSSpec fills in the record and returns fnfErr instead of noErr. The record is valid, but it describes a target that doesn't exist. You can use the record for another operation, such as creating a file to replace one that is missing.

In addition to the result codes listed here, PBMakeFSSpec can return a number of different File Manager error codes. When PBMakeFSSpec returns any result other than noErr or fnfErr, all fields of the resulting FSSpec record are set to 0.

Result codes

noErr	0	No error
fnfErr	–43	File or directory does not exist (FSSpec is still valid)

Swapping Data Between Two Files

Use the PBExchangeFiles function to swap the data stored in two files on the same volume.

```
FUNCTION PBExchangeFiles (paramBlock: HParmBlkPtr; async: Boolean) : OSErr;
```

Parameter block

→	12	ioCompletion	long	pointer to completion routine
←	16	ioResult	word	result code
→	18	ioNamePtr	long	pointer to first filename
→	22	ioVRefNum	word	volume specification (volume reference number, working directory reference number, drive number, or 0 for default volume)
→	28	ioDestNamePtr	long	pointer to second filename
→	36	ioDestDirID	long	second parent directory ID
→	48	ioSrcDirID	long	first parent directory ID

PBExchangeFiles swaps the data in two files by changing the information in the volume catalog and, if the files are open, in the file control blocks. See Tables 25-2 and 25-3 in the earlier section "Updating Files" for an illustration of how PBExchangeFiles changes the catalog entries and file control blocks. PBExchangeFiles uses the file ID parameter block, described in "Creating and Using File IDs" later in this chapter.

You should use PBExchangeFiles or FSpExchangeFiles to preserve the file ID when updating an existing file, in case the file is being tracked through its file ID.

Typically, you use PBExchangeFiles after creating a new file during a safe save. You identify the names and parent directory IDs of the two files to be exchanged in the fields ioNamePtr, ioDestNamePtr, ioSrcDirID, and ioDestDirID. PBExchangeFiles changes the fields in the catalog entries that record the location of the data and the modification dates. It swaps both the data forks and the resource forks.

PBExchangeFiles works on either open or closed files. If either file is open, PBExchangeFiles updates any file control blocks associated with the file. Exchanging the contents of two files requires essentially the same access as opening both files for writing.

PBExchangeFiles does not require that file IDs exist for the files being exchanged.

Result codes

noErr	0	No error
nsvErr	–35	Volume not found
ioErr	–36	I/O error
fnfErr	–43	File not found
fLckdErr	–45	File locked
volOfflinErr	–53	Volume is off line
extFSErr	–58	External file system
wrgVolTypeErr	–123	Not an HFS volume
diffVolErr	–1303	Files on different volumes

Creating and Using File IDs

This section describes the new functions for tracking files with file IDs and lists the previously released functions that have been affected by file IDs.

The functions for manipulating file IDs use a new parameter block variant, FIDParam.

```
CASE ParamBlockType OF
     FIDParam:
         (filler14:       LongInt;     {filler}
         ioDestNamePtr:   StringPtr;   {pointer to destination filename}
         filler15:        LongInt;     {filler}
         ioDestDirID:     LongInt;     {destination parent directory ID}
         filler16:        LongInt;     {filler}
         filler17:        LongInt;     {filler}
         ioSrcDirID:      LongInt;     {source parent directory ID}
         filler18:        Integer;     {filler}
         ioFileID:        LongInt);    {file ID}
```

The ioDestNamePtr and ioDestDirID fields are used only with the PBExchangeFiles function, described in the preceding section.

The fields common to all low-level functions and the other parameter block types are described in the File Manager chapter of Volume IV.

Functions for Manipulating File IDs

Use the PBCreateFileIDRef function to establish a file ID reference for a file.

```
FUNCTION PBCreateFileIDRef (paramBlock: HParmBlkPtr; async: Boolean) :
                            OSErr;
```

Parameter block

→	12	ioCompletion	long	pointer to completion routine
←	16	ioResult	word	result code
→	18	ioNamePtr	long	pointer to filename
→	22	ioVRefNum	word	volume specification
→	48	ioSrcDirID	long	parent directory ID
←	54	ioFileID	long	file ID

Given a volume reference number, filename, and parent directory ID, PBCreateFileIDRef creates a record to hold the name and parent directory ID of the specified file. PBCreateFileIDRef places the file ID in the ioFileID field. If a file ID reference already exists for the file, PBCreateFileIDRef supplies the file ID but returns fidExists.

Result codes

noErr	0	No error
nsvErr	–35	Volume not found
ioErr	–36	I/O error
fnfErr	–43	File not found
wPrErr	–44	Hardware volume lock
vLckdErr	–46	Software volume lock
volOfflinErr	–53	Volume is off line
extFSErr	–58	External file system
wrgVolTypeErr	–123	Not an HFS volume
fidExists	–1301	File ID already exists
notAFileErr	–1302	Specified file is a directory

Use the PBDeleteFileIDRef function to delete a file ID reference.

```
FUNCTION PBDeleteFileIDRef (paramBlock: HParmBlkPtr; async: Boolean) :
                           OSErr;
```

Parameter block

→	12	ioCompletion	long	pointer to completion routine
←	16	ioResult	word	result code
→	18	ioNamePtr	long	pointer to filename
→	22	ioVRefNum	word	volume specification
→	54	ioFileID	long	file ID

PBDeleteFileIDRef invalidates the specified file ID on the volume specified by ioVRefNum or ioNamePtr. After it has invalidated a file ID, the File Manager can no longer resolve that ID to a filename and parent directory ID.

Result codes

noErr	0	No error
nsvErr	–35	Volume not found
ioErr	–36	I/O error
wPrErr	–44	Hardware volume lock
vLckdErr	–46	Software volume lock
volOfflinErr	–53	Volume is off line
extFSErr	–58	External file system
fidNotFoundErr	–1300	File ID not found

Use the PBResolveFileIDRef function to retrieve the filename and parent directory ID of the file with a specified file ID.

```
FUNCTION PBResolveFileIDRef (paramBlock: HParmBlkPtr; async: Boolean) :
                            OSErr;
```

Parameter block

→	12	ioCompletion	long	pointer to completion routine
←	16	ioResult	word	result code
↔	18	ioNamePtr	long	pointer to filename
→	22	ioVRefNum	word	volume specification
←	48	ioSrcDirID	long	parent directory ID
→	54	ioFileID	long	file ID

PBResolveFileIDRef returns the filename and parent directory ID of the file referred to by file ID in the ioFileID field. It places the filename in the string pointed to by the ioNamePtr field and the parent directory ID in the ioSrcDirID field. If the name string is NIL, PBResolveFileIDRef returns only the parent directory ID. If the name string is not NIL but is only a volume name, PBResolveFileIDRef ignores the value in the ioVRefNum field, uses the volume name instead, and overwrites the name string with the filename. A return code of fidNotFoundErr means that the specified file ID has become invalid, either because the file was deleted or because the file ID was destroyed by PBDeleteFileIDRef.

Result codes

noErr	0	No error
nsvErr	–35	Volume not found
ioErr	–36	I/O error
fnfErr	–43	File not found
volOfflinErr	–53	Volume is off line
extFSErr	–58	External file system
wrgVolTypeErr	–123	Not an HFS volume
fidNotFoundErr	–1300	File ID not found
notAFileErr	–1302	Specified file is a directory

Functions Changed to Accommodate File IDs

Some existing HFS functions now support file IDs as appropriate. Support for file IDs requires some change in function, but no changes in the program interface. This section lists the affected functions and describes how they accommodate file IDs.

```
FUNCTION PBHDelete (paramBlock: HParmBlkPtr; async: Boolean) : OSErr;
```

If a file ID reference exists for the file being deleted, the file ID reference is also deleted.

```
FUNCTION PBHRename (paramBlock: HParmBlkPtr; async: Boolean) : OSErr;
```

If a file ID exists for the file being renamed, the file ID remains with the file.

```
FUNCTION PBCatMove (paramBlock: CMovePBPtr; async: Boolean) : OSErr;
```

If a file ID exists for the file being moved, the file ID remains with the file.

```
FUNCTION PBGetCatInfo (paramBlock: CInfoPBPtr; async: Boolean) : OSErr;
```

You can use the PBGetCatInfo function to determine whether a file has a file ID. The value of the file ID is returned in the ioDirID field. Because that parameter could also represent a directory ID, call PBResolveFileIDRef to see if the value is a real file ID. If you want to both determine whether a file ID exists for a file and create one if it doesn't, use PBCreateFileIDRef, which either creates a file ID or returns fidExists.

Mounting Volumes

A set of three functions allows your application to record the mounting information for a volume and then to mount the volume later.

The programmatic mounting functions store the mounting information in a structure called the AFPVolMountInfo record, described earlier in "Mounting Volumes Programmatically."

The programmatic mounting functions use the ioParam variant of the ParamBlockRec record, described in the File Manager chapter of Volume IV.

You use the PBGetVolMountInfoSize function to determine how much space to allocate for the volume-mounting record.

```
FUNCTION PBGetVolMountInfoSize (paramBlock: ParmBlkPtr) : OSErr;
```

Parameter block

→	12	ioCompletion	long	pointer to completion routine
←	16	ioResult	word	result code
→	22	ioVRefNum	word	volume specification
→	32	ioBuffer	long	pointer to storage for size (4 bytes of storage)

For a specified volume, the PBGetVolMountInfoSize function provides the size of the record needed to hold the volume's mounting information.

Result codes

noErr	0	No error
nsvErr	–35	Volume not found
paramErr	–50	Parameter error
extFSErr	–58	External file system error; typically, function is not available for that volume

After ascertaining the size of the record needed and allocating storage, you call the PBGetVolMountInfo function to retrieve a record containing all the information needed to mount the volume, except for passwords. You can later pass this record to the PBVolumeMount function to mount the volume.

```
FUNCTION PBGetVolMountInfo (paramBlock: ParmBlkPtr) : OSErr;
```

Parameter block

→	12	ioCompletion	long	pointer to completion routine
←	16	ioResult	word	result code
→	22	ioVRefNum	word	volume specification
→	32	ioBuffer	long	pointer to mounting information

PBGetVolMountInfo places the mounting information for a specified volume into the buffer pointed to by the ioBuffer field. The mounting information for an AppleShare volume is stored as an AFP mounting record, described earlier in “Mounting Volumes Programmatically.” The length of the buffer is specified by the value pointed to by the ioBuffer field in a previous call to PBGetVolMountInfoSize.

PBGetVolMountInfo does not return the user password or volume password in the AFPVolMountInfo record. Your application solicits these passwords from the user and fills in the record before attempting to mount the remote volume.

Result codes

noErr	0	No error
nsvErr	–35	Volume not found
paramErr	–50	Parameter error
extFSErr	–58	External file system error; typically, function is not available for that volume

You use the PBVolumeMount function to mount a volume, using either the information returned by the PBGetVolMountInfo function or a structure you filled in yourself.

```
FUNCTION PBVolumeMount (paramBlock: ParmBlkPtr) : OSErr;
```

Parameter block

→	12	ioCompletion	long	pointer to completion routine
←	16	ioResult	word	result code
←	22	ioVRefNum	word	volume reference number
→	32	ioBuffer	long	pointer to mounting information

The PBVolumeMount function mounts a volume and returns its volume reference number. If you’re mounting an AppleShare volume, place the volume’s AFP mounting record in the buffer pointed to by the ioBuffer field. Because the password fields are not included in an AFP mounting record returned by PBGetVolMountInfo, you must set these fields before calling PBVolumeMount.

Result codes

noErr	0	No error
notOpenErr	–28	AppleTalk is not open
nsvErr	–35	Volume not found
paramErr	–50	Parameter error; typically, zone, server, and volume name combination is not valid or not complete, or the user name is not recognized
extFSErr	–58	External file system error; typically, file system signature was not recognized, or function is not available for that volume
memFullErr	–108	Not enough memory to create a new volume control block for mounting the volume
afpBadUAM	–5002	User authentication method is unknown

afpBadVersNum	–5003	Workstation is using an AFP version that the server doesn't recognize
afpNoServer	–5016	Server is not responding
afpUserNotAuth	–5023	User authentication failed (usually, password is not correct)
afpPwdExpired	–5042	Password has expired on server
afpBadDirIDType	–5060	Not a fixed directory ID volume
afpCantMountMoreSrvrs	–5061	Maximum number of volumes has been mounted
afpAlreadyMounted	–5062	Volume already mounted
afpSameNodeErr	–5063	Attempt to log on to a server running on the same machine

Accessing Privilege Information in Foreign File Systems

The File Manager provides two functions that an application or shell program can use to communicate with a foreign file system about its native access-control system. The functions retrieve and set access permissions on the foreign file system. The access-control functions use a new parameter block variant, ForeignPrivParam.

```
CASE ParamBlockType OF
     ForeignPrivParam:
         (filler21:                LongInt;  {filler}
         filler22:                 LongInt;  {filler}
         ioForeignPrivBuffer:      Ptr;      {privileges data}
         ioForeignPrivReqCount:    LongInt;  {size of buffer}
         ioForeignPrivActCount:    LongInt;  {amount of buffer used}
         filler23:                 LongInt;  {filler}
         ioForeignPrivDirID:       LongInt;  {parent directory ID of }
                                             { foreign file or directory}
         ioForeignPrivInfo1:       LongInt;  {privileges data}
         ioForeignPrivInfo2:       LongInt;  {privileges data}
         ioForeignPrivInfo3:       LongInt;  {privileges data}
         ioForeignPrivInfo4:       LongInt); {privileges data}
```

Use the PBGetForeignPrivs function to determine the native access-control information for a file or directory stored on a volume managed by a foreign file system.

```
FUNCTION PBGetForeignPrivs (paramBlock: HParmBlkPtr; async: Boolean) :
                            OSErr;
```

Parameter block

→	12	ioCompletion	long	pointer to completion routine
←	16	ioResult	word	result code
→	18	ioNamePtr	long	pointer to file or directory name
→	22	ioVRefNum	word	volume specification
→	32	ioForeignPrivBuffer	long	pointer to privilege info buffer

→	36	ioForeignPrivReqCount	long	size allocated for buffer
←	40	ioForeignPrivActCount	long	amount of buffer used
→	48	ioForeignPrivDirID	word	parent directory ID
←	52	ioForeignPrivInfo1	long	information specific to privilege model
←	56	ioForeignPrivInfo2	long	information specific to privilege model
←	60	ioForeignPrivInfo3	long	information specific to privilege model
←	64	ioForeignPrivInfo4	long	information specific to privilege model

PBGetForeignPrivs retrieves access information for a file or directory on a volume managed by a file system that uses a privilege model different from the AFP model. See "Manipulating Privilege Information in Foreign File Systems" earlier in this chapter for a fuller explanation of access-control privileges. See the File Manager chapter of Volume V for a description of the AFP privilege model.

Result codes

noErr	0	No error
nsvErr	–35	Volume not found
paramErr	–50	Volume is HFS or MFS (that is, it has no foreign privilege model), or foreign volume does not support these calls

Use the PBSetForeignPrivs function to change the native access-control information for a file or directory stored on a volume managed by a foreign file system.

```
FUNCTION PBSetForeignPrivs (paramBlock: HParmBlkPtr; async: Boolean) :
                            OSErr;
```

Parameter block

→	12	ioCompletion	long	pointer to completion routine
←	16	ioResult	word	result code
→	18	ioNamePtr	long	pointer to file or directory name
→	22	ioVRefNum	word	volume specification
→	32	ioForeignPrivBuffer	long	pointer to privilege info buffer
→	36	ioForeignPrivReqCount	long	size allocated for buffer
→	40	ioForeignPrivActCount	long	amount of buffer used
→	48	ioForeignPrivDirID	word	parent directory ID
→	52	ioForeignPrivInfo1	long	information specific to privilege model
→	56	ioForeignPrivInfo2	long	information specific to privilege model
→	60	ioForeignPrivInfo3	long	information specific to privilege model
→	64	ioForeignPrivInfo4	long	information specific to privilege model

PBSetForeignPrivs modifies access information for a file or directory on a volume managed by a file system that uses a privilege model different from the AFP model.

Result codes

noErr	0	No error
nsvErr	–35	Volume not found
paramErr	–50	Volume is HFS or MFS (that is, it has no foreign privilege model), or volume doesn't support these functions

Opening Data Forks

Use the PBOpenDF function to open the data fork of a file. PBOpenDF replaces PBOpen, which can open either a driver or the data fork of a file.

```
FUNCTION PBOpenDF (paramBlock: ParmBlkPtr; async: Boolean) : OSErr;
```

Parameter block

→	12	ioCompletion	long	pointer to completion routine
←	16	ioResult	word	result code
→	18	ioNamePtr	long	pointer to file or directory name
→	22	ioVRefNum	word	volume specification
←	24	ioRefNum	word	access path number
→	27	ioPermssn	byte	permission

PBOpenDF creates an access path to the data fork of a file. It is almost identical to PBOpen, which is documented in the File Manager chapter of Volume IV. The difference is that PBOpen can open both files and drivers, but PBOpenDF can open only files. Using OpenDF instead of FSOpen when your application is opening a file prevents naming conflicts or ambiguities and ensures that your application can open files whose names begin with a period (.).

Result codes

noErr	0	No error
nsvErr	–35	Volume not found
ioErr	–36	I/O error
bdNamErr	–37	Bad filename
tmfoErr	–42	Too many files open
fnfErr	–43	File not found
opWrErr	–49	File already open for writing
extFSErr	–58	External file system

Use the PBHOpenDF function to open the data fork of a file on a hierarchical volume. PBHOpenDF replaces PBHOpen, which can open either a driver or the data fork of a file.

```
FUNCTION PBHOpenDF (paramBlock: HParmBlkPtr; async: Boolean) : OSErr;
```

Parameter block

→	12	ioCompletion	long	pointer to completion routine
←	16	ioResult	word	result code
→	18	ioNamePtr	long	pointer to file or directory name
→	22	ioVRefNum	word	volume specification
←	24	ioRefNum	word	access path number
→	27	ioPermssn	byte	permission
→	48	ioDirID	long	parent directory ID

PBHOpenDF creates an access path to the data fork of a file. It is almost identical to PBHOpen, which is documented in the File Manager chapter of Volume IV. The difference is that PBHOpen can open both files and drivers, but PBHOpenDF can open only files. Using PBHOpenDF instead of PBHOpen when your application is opening a file prevents naming conflicts or ambiguities and ensures that your application can open files whose names begin with a period (.).

Result codes

noErr	0	No error
nsvErr	–35	Volume not found
ioErr	–36	I/O error
bdNamErr	–37	Bad filename
tmfoErr	–42	Too many files open
fnfErr	–43	File not found
opWrErr	–49	File already open for writing
extFSErr	–58	External file system
dirNFErr	–120	Directory not found

SUMMARY OF THE FILE MANAGER

Constants

```
CONST {Gestalt constants}
      gestaltFSAttr      ='fs  ';    {file system attributes selector}
      gestaltFullExtFSDispatching
                         =      0;   {exports HFSDispatch traps}
      gestaltHasFSSpecCalls
                         =      1;   {supports FSSpec records}

      {values for ioSearchBits in PBCatSearch param block}
      fsSBPartialName    =      1;   {substring of name}
      fsSBFullName       =      2;   {full name}
      fsSBFlAttrib       =      4;   {directory flag; software lock flag}
      fsSBNegate         = 16384;    {reverse match status}

      {for files only}
      fsSBFlFndrInfo     =      8;   {Finder file info}
      fsSBFlLgLen        =     32;   {data fork logical length}
      fsSBFlPyLen        =     64;   {data fork physical length}
      fsSBFlRLgLen       =    128;   {resource fork logical length}
      fsSBFlRPyLen       =    256;   {resource fork physical length}
      fsSBFlCrDat        =    512;   {file creation date}
      fsSBFlMdDat        =   1024;   {file modification date}
      fsSBFlBkDat        =   2048;   {file backup date}
      fsSBFlXFndrInfo    =   4096;   {more Finder file info}
      fsSBFlParID        =   8192;   {file's parent ID}

      {for directories only}
      fsSBDrUsrWds       =      8;   {Finder directory info}
      fsSBDrNmFls        =     16;   {number of files in directory}
      fsSBDrCrDat        =    512;   {directory creation date}
      fsSBDrMdDat        =   1024;   {directory modification date}
      fsSBDrBkDat        =   2048;   {directory backup date}
      fsSBDrFndrInfo     =   4096;   {more Finder directory info}
      fsSBDrParID        =   8192;   {directory's parent ID}

      {permissions for opening files}
      fsCurPerm          =      0;   {exclusive read/write permission if it }
                                     { is available; otherwise, exclusive }
                                     { read, if that is available}
      fsRdPern           =      1;   {exclusive read permission}
      fsWrPerm           =      2;   {exclusive write permission}
      fsRdWrPerm         =      3;   {exclusive read/write permission}
      fsRdWrShPerm       =      4;   {shared read/write permission}

      {value of vMForeignPrivID in file attributes buffer}
      fsUnixPriv         =      1;   {A/UX privilege model}
```

```
{vMAttribut bit position constants}
bLimitFCBs          =    31;   {limit file control blocks}
bLocalWList         =    30;   {use shared volume handle for }
                               { window list}
bNoMiniFndr         =    29;   {disable Mini Finder menu item}
bNoVNEdit           =    28;   {lock volume name}
bNoLclSync          =    27;   {do not let Finder change }
                               { modification date}
bTrshOffLine        =    26;   {zoom volume when it is unmounted}
bNoSwitchTo         =    25;   {do not switch launch to applications}
bNoDeskItems        =    20;   {do not place objects on the }
                               { Finder desktop}
bNoBootBlks         =    19;   {not a startup volume}
bAccessCntl         =    18;   {volume supports AFP access control}
bNoSysDir           =    17;   {no system directory}
bHasExtFSVol        =    16;   {external file system volume}
bHasOpenDeny        =    15;   {volume support shared access modes}
bHasCopyFile        =    14;   {volume supports _CopyFile}
bHasMoveRename      =    13;   {volume supports _MoveRename}
bHasDesktopMgr      =    12;   {volume supports Desktop Manager}
bHasShortName       =    11;   {volume supports shorter name}
bHasFolderLock      =    10;   {folder is locked}
bHasPersonalAccessPrivileges
                    =     9;   {local file sharing is enabled}
bHasUserGroupList   =     8;   {volume supports AFP privileges}
bHasCatSearch       =     7;   {volume supports PBCatSearch}
bHasFileIDs         =     6;   {volume supports fileID functions}
bHasBtreeMgr        =     5;   {reserved}
bHasBlankAccessPrivileges
                    =     4;   {volume supports inherited access }
                               { privileges for folders}

{media type in remote mounting information}
AppleShareMediaType = 'afpm'; {an AppleShare volume}

{user authentication methods in AFP remote mounting information}
kNoUserAuthentication     =  1;  {guest status; no password needed}
kPassword                 =  2;  {8-byte password}
kEncryptPassword          =  3;  {encrypted 8-byte password}
kTwoWayEncryptPassword    =  6;  {two-way random encryption; }
                                 { authenticate both user and server}
```

Data Types

```
TYPE FSSpec =
        RECORD
          vRefNum:     Integer;     {volume reference number}
          parID:       LongInt;     {directory ID of parent directory}
          name:        Str63        {filename or directory name}
        END;

     FSSpecPtr          =           ^FSSpec;
     FSSpecHandle       =           ^FSSpecPtr;

     FSSpecArray        =           ARRAY[0..0] OF FSSpec;
     FSSpecArrayPtr     =           ^FSSpecArray;
     FSSpecArrayHandle
                        =           ^FSSpecArrayPtr;


     CatPositionRec =                     {catalog position record}
        RECORD
          initialize:       LongInt;      {starting point}
          priv:             ARRAY[1..6] OF Integer
                                          {private data}
        END;


     GetVolParmsInfoBuffer =
     RECORD
        vMVersion:            Integer;    {version number}
        vMAttrib:             LongInt;    {bit vector of attributes; }
                                          { see vMAttrib constants}
        vMLocalHand:          Handle;     {handle to private data}
        vMServerAdr:          LongInt;    {network server address}
        vMVolumeGrade:        LongInt;    {relative speed rating}
        vMForeignPrivID:      Integer     {access privilege model}
     END;


     VolumeType = OSType;
     VolMountInfoHeader =                 {template volume mounting }
                                          { information}
     RECORD
        length:     Integer;              {length of mounting information, }
                                          { including standard header and }
                                          { variable-length data}
        media:      VolumeType;           {type of volume}
        {volume-specific, variable-length private data}
     END;
     VolMountInfoPtr = ^VolMountInfoHeader;
```

```
AFPVolMountInfo =                        {AFP volume mounting information}
RECORD
   length:              Integer;         {length of mounting information, }
                                         { including standard header and }
                                         { variable-length data}
   media:               VolumeType;      {type of volume}
   flags:               Integer;         {reserved; must be set to 0}
   nbpInterval:         SignedByte;      {NBP retry interval}
   nbpCount:            SignedByte;      {NBP retry count}
   uamType:             Integer;         {user authentication method}
   zoneNameOffset:      Integer;         {offset from start of record }
                                         { to zone name}
   serverNameOffset:    Integer;         {offset from start of record }
                                         { to server name}
   volNameOffset:       Integer;         {offset from start of record }
                                         { to volume name}
   userNameOffset:      Integer;         {offset from start of record }
                                         { to user name}
   userPassWordOffset:  Integer;         {offset from start of record }
                                         { to user password}
   volPassWordOffset:   Integer;         {offset from start of record }
                                         { to volume password}
   AFPData:             PACKED ARRAY[1..144] OF Char;
                                         {standard AFP mounting info}
   {optional volume-specific, variable-length data}
END;
AFPVolMountInfoPtr = ^AFPVolMountInfo;


HParmBlkPtr        = ^HParamBlockRec;
HParamBlockRec =
RECORD
   qLink:          QElemPtr;          {next queue entry}
   qType:          Integer;           {queue type}
   ioTrap:         Integer;           {routine trap}
   ioCmdAddr:      Ptr;               {routine address}
   ioCompletion:   ProcPtr;           {completion routine}
   ioResult:       OSErr;             {result code}
   ioNamePtr:      StringPtr;         {pointer to pathname}
   ioVRefNum:      Integer;           {volume reference number, drive }
                                      { number, or working directory }
                                      { reference number}

 CASE ParamBlkType OF
 {other types described in Volume IV}


 FIDParam:                     {file ID functions and PBExchangeFiles}
    (filler14:       LongInt;         {filler}
    ioDestNamePtr:   StringPtr;       {pointer to destination filenames}
    filler15:        LongInt;         {filler}
    ioDestDirID:     LongInt;         {destination parent directory ID}
    filler16:        LongInt;         {filler}
    filler17:        LongInt;         {filler}
```

```
    ioSrcDirID:       LongInt;          {source parent directory ID)
    filler18:         Integer;          {filler}
    ioFileID:         LongInt);         {file ID}

CSParam:                                {PBCatSearch}
   (ioMatchPtr:       FSSpecArrayPtr;   {pointer to array of matches}
    ioReqMatchCount:  LongInt;          {maximum number of matches }
                                        { to return}
    ioActMatchCount:  LongInt;          {actual number of matches}
    ioSearchBits:     LongInt;          {enable bits for matching rules}
    ioSearchInfo1:    CInfoPBPtr;       {pointer to values and lower }
                                        { bounds}
    ioSearchInfo2:    CInfoPBPtr;       {pointer to masks and upper }
                                        { bounds}
    ioSearchTime:     LongInt;          {maximum time to search, }
                                        { in Time Manager form}
    ioCatPosition:    CatPositionRec;   {current catalog position}
    ioOptBuffer:      Ptr;              {pointer to optional read }
                                        { buffer}
    ioOptBufSize:     LongInt);         {length of optional read buffer}

ForeignPrivParam:
   (filler21:                LongInt;   {filler}
    filler22:                LongInt;   {filler}
    ioForeignPrivBuffer:     Ptr;       {privileges data}
    ioForeignPrivReqCount:   LongInt;   {size of buffer}
    ioForeignPrivActCount:   LongInt;   {amount of buffer used}
    filler23:                LongInt;   {filler}
    ioForeignPrivDirID:      LongInt;   {parent directory ID of }
                                        { foreign file or directory}
    ioForeignPrivInfo1:      LongInt;   {privileges data}
    ioForeignPrivInfo2:      LongInt;   {privileges data}
    ioForeignPrivInfo3:      LongInt;   {privileges data}
    ioForeignPrivInfo4:      LongInt);  {privileges data}

ioParam:
   (ioRefNum:       Integer;            {path reference number}
    ioVersNum:      SignedByte;         {version number}
    ioPermssn:      SignedByte;         {read/write permission}
    ioMisc:         Ptr;                {miscellaneous}
    ioBuffer:       Ptr;                {data buffer}
    ioReqCount:     LongInt;            {requested number of bytes}
    ioActCount:     LongInt;            {actual number of bytes}
    ioPosMode:      Integer;            {positioning mode and newline}
    ioPosOffset:    LongInt)            {positioning offset}
END;
```

Routines

Making FSSpec Records

```
FUNCTION FSMakeFSSpec       (vRefNum: Integer; dirID: LongInt;
                             fileName: Str255; VAR spec: FSSpec) : OSErr;
```

Exchanging the Data in Two Files

```
FUNCTION FSpExchangeFiles   (source: FSSpec; dest: FSSpec) : OSErr;
```

Functions Modified to Accept FSSpec Records

```
FUNCTION FSpOpenDF          (spec: FSSpec; permission: SignedByte;
                             VAR refNum: Integer) : OSErr;

FUNCTION FSpOpenRF          (spec: FSSpec; permission: SignedByte; VAR
                             refNum: Integer) : OSErr;

FUNCTION FSpCreate          (spec: FSSpec; creator: OSType;
                             fileType: OSType; scriptTag: ScriptCode) :
                             OSErr;

FUNCTION FSpDirCreate       (spec: FSSpec; scriptTag: ScriptCode;
                             VAR createdDirID: LongInt) : OSErr;

FUNCTION FSpDelete          (spec: FSSpec) : OSErr;

FUNCTION FSpGetFInfo        (spec: FSSpec; VAR fndrInfo: FInfo) : OSErr;

FUNCTION FSpSetFInfo        (spec: FSSpec; fndrInfo: FInfo) : OSErr;

FUNCTION FSpSetFLock        (spec: FSSpec) : OSErr;

FUNCTION FSpRstFLock        (spec: FSSpec) : OSErr;

FUNCTION FSpRename          (spec: FSSpec; newName: Str255) : OSErr;

FUNCTION FSpCatMove         (source: FSSpec; dest: FSSpec) : OSErr;
```

Opening a Data Fork

```
FUNCTION HOpenDF            (vRefNum: Integer; dirID: LongInt;
                             fileName: Str255; permission: SignedByte;
                             VAR refNum: Integer) : OSErr;

FUNCTION OpenDF             (fileName: Str255; vRefNum: Integer;
                             VAR refNum: Integer) : OSErr;
```

Functions New With HFS

```
FUNCTION AllocContig      (refNum: Integer; VAR count: LongInt) : OSErr;
FUNCTION DirCreate        (vRefNum: Integer; parentDirID: LongInt;
                           directoryName: Str255;
                           VAR createdDirID: LongInt) : OSErr;
FUNCTION CatMove          (vRefNum: Integer; dirID: LongInt; oldName:
                           Str255; newDirID: LongInt; newName: Str255) :
                           OSErr;
FUNCTION OpenWD           (vRefNum: Integer; dirID: LongInt;
                           procID: LongInt; VAR wdRefNum: Integer) :
                           OSErr;
FUNCTION CloseWD          (wdRefNum: Integer) : OSErr;
FUNCTION GetWDInfo        (wdRefNum: Integer; VAR vRefNum: Integer; VAR
                           dirID: LongInt; VAR procID: LongInt) : OSErr;
```

MFS Functions Modified to Accommodate Directory IDs

```
FUNCTION HCreate          (vRefNum: Integer; dirID: LongInt; fileName:
                           Str255; creator: OSType; fileType: OSType) :
                           OSErr;
FUNCTION HOpen            (vRefNum: Integer; dirID: LongInt; fileName:
                           Str255; permission: SignedByte; VAR refNum:
                           Integer) : OSErr;
FUNCTION HOpenRF          (vRefNum: Integer; dirID: LongInt; fileName:
                           Str255; permission: SignedByte; VAR refNum:
                           Integer) : OSErr;
FUNCTION HDelete          (vRefNum: Integer; dirID: LongInt; fileName:
                           Str255) : OSErr;
FUNCTION HSetFLock        (vRefNum: Integer; dirID: LongInt; fileName:
                           Str255) : OSErr;
FUNCTION HRstFLock        (vRefNum: Integer; dirID: LongInt; fileName:
                           Str255) : OSErr;
FUNCTION HRename          (vRefNum: Integer; dirID: LongInt; oldName:
                           Str255; newName: Str255) : OSErr;
FUNCTION HGetFInfo        (vRefNum: Integer; dirID: LongInt; fileName:
                           Str255; VAR fndrInfo: FInfo) : OSErr;
FUNCTION HSetFInfo        (vRefNum: Integer; dirID: LongInt; fileName:
                           Str255; fndrInfo: FInfo) : OSErr;
FUNCTION HGetVol          (volName: StringPtr; VAR vRefNum: Integer; VAR
                           dirID: LongInt) : OSErr;
```

Reading Volume Information

```
FUNCTION PBHGetVolParms     (paramBlock: HParmBlkPtr; async: Boolean) :
                             OSErr;
```

Searching a Catalog

```
FUNCTION PBCatSearch        (paramBlock: HParmBlkPtr; async: Boolean) :
                             OSErr;
```

Creating FSSpec Records

```
FUNCTION PBMakeFSSpec       (paramBlock: HParmBlkPtr; async: Boolean) :
                             OSErr;
```

Swapping Data Between Two Files

```
FUNCTION PBExchangeFiles    (paramBlock: HParmBlkPtr; async: Boolean) :
                             OSErr;
```

Functions for Manipulating File IDs

```
FUNCTION PBCreateFileIDRef  (paramBlock: HParmBlkPtr; async: Boolean) :
                             OSErr;

FUNCTION PBDeleteFileIDRef  (paramBlock: HParmBlkPtr; async: Boolean) :
                             OSErr;

FUNCTION PBResolveFileIDRef (paramBlock: HParmBlkPtr; async: Boolean) :
                             OSErr;
```

Functions Changed to Accommodate File IDs

```
FUNCTION PBHDelete          (paramBlock: HParmBlkPtr; async: Boolean) :
                             OSErr;

FUNCTION PBHRename          (paramBlock: HParmBlkPtr; async: Boolean) :
                             OSErr;

FUNCTION PBCatMove          (paramBlock: CMovePBPtr; async: Boolean) :
                             OSErr;

FUNCTION PBGetCatInfo       (paramBlock: CInfoPBPtr; async: Boolean) :
                             OSErr;
```

Mounting Volumes

```
FUNCTION PBGetVolMountInfoSize  (paramBlock: ParmBlkPtr) : OSErr;
FUNCTION PBGetVolMountInfo      (paramBlock: ParmBlkPtr) : OSErr;
FUNCTION PBVolumeMount          (paramBlock: ParmBlkPtr) : OSErr;
```

Accessing Privilege Information in Foreign File Systems

```
FUNCTION PBGetForeignPrivs (paramBlock: HParmBlkPtr; async: Boolean) :
                            OSErr;
FUNCTION PBSetForeignPrivs (paramBlock: HParmBlkPtr; async: Boolean) :
                            OSErr;
```

Opening Data Forks

```
FUNCTION PBOpenDF          (paramBlock: ParmBlkPtr; async: Boolean) :
                            OSErr;
FUNCTION PBHOpenDF         (paramBlock: HParmBlkPtr; async: Boolean) :
                            OSErr;
```

Result Codes

noErr	0	No error
notOpenErr	–28	AppleTalk is not open
nsvErr	–35	Volume not found
ioErr	–36	I/O error
bdNamErr	–37	Bad filename
eofErr	–39	Logical end-of-file reached
tmfoErr	–42	Too many files open
fnfErr	–43	File not found
wPrErr	–44	Hardware volume lock
fLckdErr	–45	File locked
vLckdErr	–46	Software volume lock
opWrErr	–49	File already open for writing
paramErr	–50	Parameter error
volOfflinErr	–53	Volume is off line
extFSErr	–58	External file system
memFullErr	–108	Insufficient memory available
dirNFErr	–120	Directory not found
wrgVolTypeErr	–123	Not an HFS volume
fidNotFoundErr	–1300	File ID not found
fidExists	–1301	File ID already exists
notAFileErr	–1302	Specified file is a directory
diffVolErr	–1303	Files on different volumes

catalogChangedErr	–1304	Catalog has changed and catalog position record may be invalid
afpBadUAM	–5002	User authentication method is unknown
afpBadVersNum	–5003	Workstation is using an AFP version that the server doesn't recognize
afpNoServer	–5016	Server is not responding
afpUserNotAuth	–5023	User authentication failed (usually, password is not correct)
afpPwdExpired	–5042	Password has expired on server
afpBadDirIDType	–5060	Not a fixed directory ID volume
afpCantMountMoreSrvrs	–5061	Maximum number of volumes has been mounted
afpAlreadyMounted	–5062	Volume already mounted
afpSameNodeErr	–5063	Attempt to log on to a server running on the same machine

Assembly-Language Information

FSSpec Data Structure

vRefNum	2 bytes	volume reference number
parID	4 bytes	directory ID
name	64 bytes	filename

Catalog Position Data Structure

initialize	4 bytes	starting place for next search
priv	12 bytes	private data

Volume Mounting Information Data Structure

length	2 bytes	length of record
media	4 bytes	type of volume
variable-length private data		

AFP Mounting Information Data Structure

length	2 bytes	length of record
media	4 bytes	type of volume
flags	2 bytes	reserved
nbpInterval	byte	NBP retry interval
nbpCount	byte	NBP retry count
uamType	2 bytes	user authentication method
zoneNameOffset	2 bytes	offset to zone name
serverNameOffset	2 bytes	offset to server name
volNameOffset	2 bytes	offset to volume name
userNameOffset	2 bytes	offset to user name
userPassWordOffset	2 bytes	offset to user password
volPassWordOffset	2 bytes	offset to volume password
AFPData	144 bytes	mounting data
variable-length private data		

Catalog Search Parameter Block

24	long	ioMatchPtr	pointer to match array
28	long	ioReqMatchCount	maximum match count
32	long	ioActMatchCount	actual match count
36	long	ioSearchBits	search criteria selector
40	long	ioSearchInfo1	pointer to search values and lower bounds
44	long	ioSearchInfo2	pointer to search values and upper bounds
48	long	ioSearchTime	time limit on search
52	16 bytes	ioCatPosition	catalog position record
68	long	ioOptBuffer	pointer to optional read buffer
72	long	ioOptBufSize	length of optional read buffer

File ID Parameter Block

24	long	filler14	filler
28	long	ioDestNamePtr	pointer to destination filename
32	long	filler15	filler
36	long	ioDestDirID	destination parent directory ID
40	long	filler16	filler
44	long	filler17	filler
48	long	ioSrcDirID	parent directory ID
52	2 bytes	filler18	filler
54	long	ioFileID	file ID

Foreign Privileges Parameter Block

24	long	filler21	filler
28	long	filler22	filler
32	long	ioForeignPrivBuffer	pointer to privileges data buffer
36	long	ioForeignPrivReqCount	size allocated for buffer
40	long	ioForeignPrivActCount	amount of buffer used
44	long	filler23	filler
48	long	ioForeignPrivDirID	parent directory ID of target
52	long	ioForeignPrivInfo1	privileges data
56	long	ioForeignPrivInfo2	privileges data
60	long	ioForeignPrivInfo3	privileges data
64	long	ioForeignPrivInfo4	privileges data

Trap Macros Requiring Routine Selectors

_HFSDispatch

Selector	Routine
$0014	PBCreateFileIDRef
$0015	PBDeleteFileIDRef
$0016	PBResolveFileIDRef
$0017	PBExchangeFiles
$0018	PBCatSearch
$0030	PBHGetVolParms
$003F	PBGetVolMountInfoSize
$0040	PBGetVolMountInfo
$0041	PBVolumeMount
$0060	PBGetForeignPrivs
$0061	PBSetForeignPrivs

_HighLevelFSDispatch

Selector	Routine
$0001	FSMakeFSSpec
$0002	FSpOpenDF
$0003	FSpOpenRF
$0004	FSpCreate
$0005	FSpDirCreate
$0006	FSpDelete
$0007	FSpGetFInfo
$0008	FSpSetFInfo
$0009	FSpSetFLock
$000A	FSpRstFLock
$000B	FSpRename
$000C	FSpCatMove
$000D	FSpOpenResFile
$000E	FSpCreateResFile
$000F	FSpExchangeFiles

26 THE STANDARD FILE PACKAGE

26 Standard File

ABOUT THIS CHAPTER

This chapter describes how your application can use the Standard File Package in system software version 7.0 to present a standard user interface for naming and identifying files. The Standard File Package displays the dialog boxes that let the user specify the names and locations of files to be saved or opened, and it reports the user's choices to your application. The new procedures introduced in version 7.0 allow your application to either streamline its interaction with the Standard File Package or exercise more control over the user interface. This chapter supplements the Standard File Package chapters in Volumes I and IV.

Read this chapter if your application lets the user save and open files.

The features described in this chapter are available only in system software version 7.0 or later. Call the Gestalt function, described in the Compatibility Guidelines chapter of this volume, to determine whether the new features are present.

To use this chapter you must be familiar with earlier versions of the Standard File Package, described in Volumes I and IV; the Dialog Manager, described in Volume I; the file system specification (FSSpec) record, described in the File Manager chapter of this volume; and the new features of the version 7.0 Finder™, described in the Finder Interface chapter of this volume.

ABOUT THE STANDARD FILE PACKAGE

The Standard File Package handles the interface between the user and your application when the user saves or opens a document. It displays dialog boxes through which the user specifies the name and location of the document to be saved or opened. It allows your application to customize the dialog boxes and, through callback routines, to handle user actions during the dialogs. The Standard File Package procedures describe the user's choices through a reply record.

The Standard File Package in version 7.0 introduces

- a pair of simplified procedures that you call to display and handle the standard Open and Save dialog boxes
- a pair of customizable procedures that you call when you need more control over the interaction
- a new reply record (StandardFileReply) that identifies files and folders with a file system specification record and that accommodates the new Finder features
- a new layout for the default dialog boxes

USING THE STANDARD FILE PACKAGE

You use the Standard File Package to handle the user interface when the user must specify a file to be saved or opened. You typically call the Standard File Package after the user chooses Save, Save As, or Open from the File menu.

When saving a document, you call one of the "PutFile" procedures; when opening a document, you call one of the "GetFile" procedures. The Standard File Package in version 7.0 introduces two new pairs of procedures:

- StandardPutFile and StandardGetFile, for presenting the standard interface
- CustomPutFile and CustomGetFile, for presenting a customized interface

The next section illustrates the standard file dialog boxes.

Before calling any of the new Standard File Package procedures, verify that they are available by calling the Gestalt function with a selector of gestaltStandardFileAttr. If Gestalt sets the gestaltStandardFile58 bit in the reply, the four new procedures are available. For a complete description of the Gestalt function, see the Compatibility Guidelines chapter of this volume.

All the new procedures return the results of the dialog boxes in a new reply record, StandardFileReply.

```
TYPE StandardFileReply =
     RECORD
        sfGood:        Boolean;       {user did not cancel}
        sfReplacing:   Boolean;       {replace file with same name}
        sfType:        OSType;        {file type}
        sfFile:        FSSpec;        {selected file, folder, or volume}
        sfScript:      ScriptCode;    {script of file, folder, or }
                                      { volume name}
        sfFlags:       Integer;       {Finder flags}
        sfIsFolder:    Boolean;       {selected item is a folder}
        sfIsVolume:    Boolean;       {selected item is a volume}
        sfReserved1:   LongInt;       {reserved}
        sfReserved2:   Integer        {reserved}
     END;
```

The reply record identifies selected files with a file system specification (FSSpec) record. You can pass the FSSpec record directly to a set of new File Manager functions provided with version 7.0. The reply record also contains additional fields that support the Finder features introduced in system software version 7.0.

The sfGood field reports whether the reply record is valid. The value is TRUE after the user clicks Save or Open, FALSE after the user clicks Cancel. When the user has completed the dialog box, the other fields in the reply record are valid only if sfGood is TRUE.

The sfReplacing field reports whether a file to be saved replaces an existing file of the same name. This field is valid only after a call to the StandardPutFile or CustomPutFile procedure. When the user assigns a name that duplicates that of an existing file, the Standard File Package asks for verification by displaying a subsidiary dialog box (illustrated in Figure 26-4). If the user verifies the name, the Standard File Package sets the sfReplacing field to TRUE and returns to your application; if the user cancels the overwriting of the file, the Standard File Package returns to the main dialog box. If the name does not conflict with an existing name, the Standard File Package sets the field to FALSE and returns. Your application can rely on the value of this field instead of checking for and handling name conflicts itself.

The sfType field contains the file type of the selected file. (File types are described in the Finder Interface chapter of this volume.) Only StandardGetFile and CustomGetFile return a file type in this field.

The sfFile field describes the selected file, folder, or volume with a file system specification record, which contains a volume reference number, parent directory ID, and name. (See the File Manager chapter of this volume for a complete description of the file system specification record.) If the selected item is an alias for another item, the Standard File Package resolves the alias and places the file system specification record for the target in the sfFile field when the user completes the dialog. If the selected file is a stationery pad, the reply record describes the file itself, not a copy of the file.

The sfScript field identifies the script in which the name of the document is to be displayed. (This information is used by the Finder and by the Standard File Package. See the Script Manager section of the Worldwide Software Overview chapter in this volume for a list of defined script codes.) A script code of smSystemScript (–1) represents the default system script.

The sfFlags field contains the Finder flags from the Finder information record in the catalog entry for the selected file. (See the Finder Interface chapter in this volume for a description of the Finder flags.) This field is returned only by StandardGetFile and CustomGetFile. If your application supports stationery, it should check the stationery bit in the Finder flags to determine whether to treat the selected file as stationery. Unlike the Finder, the Standard File Package does not automatically create a document from a stationery pad and pass your application the new document. If the user opens a stationery document from within an application that does not support stationery, the Standard File Package displays a dialog box warning the user that the master copy is being opened.

The sfIsFolder field reports whether the selected item is a folder (TRUE) or a file or volume (FALSE).

The sfIsVolume field reports whether the selected item is a volume (TRUE) or a file or folder (FALSE).

Presenting the Default Interface

If your application has no special interface requirements, you can use the StandardGetFile and StandardPutFile procedures to display the default dialog boxes for opening and saving documents.

The version 7.0 Standard File Package introduces a number of user interface enhancements, most of which have no effect on your application. Most noticeably, the version 7.0 standard file dialog boxes use a slightly different point of view. Instead of displaying only one volume at a time and showing the root of that volume at the top of the hierarchy, the file list now displays all mounted volumes and shows the desktop as the top level of the hierarchy. The Drive button, which previously allowed users to move among all mounted volumes, is now the Desktop button, which returns the display to the top of the hierarchy.

You use the StandardGetFile procedure when you want to let the user choose a file to be opened. Figure 26-1 illustrates a sample dialog box displayed by StandardGetFile.

Figure 26-1. The default Open dialog box

When you call StandardGetFile, you can supply a list of the file types that your application can open. StandardGetFile then displays only files of the specified types. You can also supply your own filter function to determine which files are displayed. (See "Opening Files" later in this chapter for details.)

When the user is opening a document, StandardGetFile interprets keystrokes as selectors in the displayed list. Pressing A, for example, selects the first item in the list that starts with the letter *a* (or, if no items in the list start with the letter *a,* the item that starts with the letter closest to *a*). The Standard File Package sets a timer on keystrokes: keystrokes in rapid succession form a string; keystrokes spaced in time are processed separately.

When the user is saving a document, StandardPutFile can direct keystrokes to either of two targets: the filename field or the displayed list. When the dialog box first appears, keystrokes are directed to the filename field. If the user presses the Tab key or clicks to select an item in the displayed list, subsequent keystrokes are interpreted as selectors in the displayed list. Each time the user presses the Tab key, keyboard input shifts between the two targets. (The list at the end of this section describes all keystrokes that affect the standard file dialog boxes.)

When the user is saving a file, the new Save dialog box offers the option of creating a new folder, as illustrated in Figure 26-2.

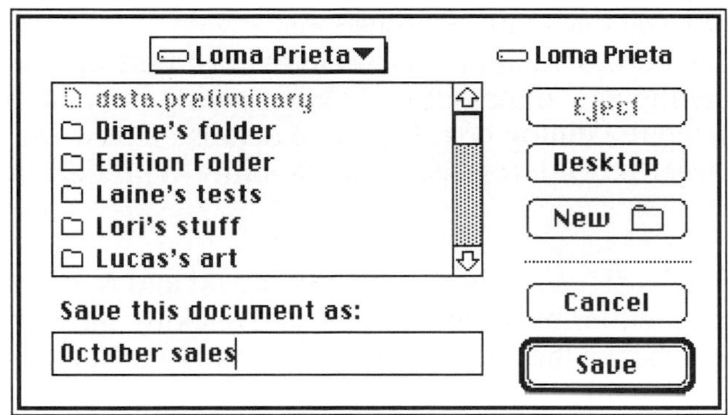

Figure 26-2. The default Save dialog box

When the user clicks the New Folder button, the Standard File Package presents a subsidiary dialog box like the example in Figure 26-3.

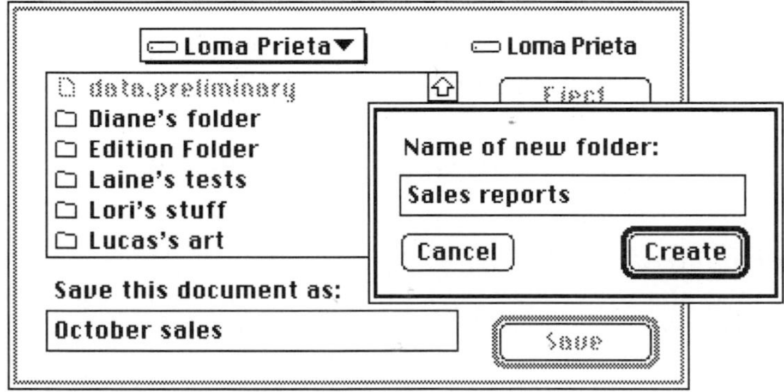

Figure 26-3. The New Folder dialog box

If the user asks to save a file with a name that already exists at the specified location, the Standard File Package displays a subsidiary dialog box to verify that the new file should replace the existing file, as illustrated in Figure 26-4.

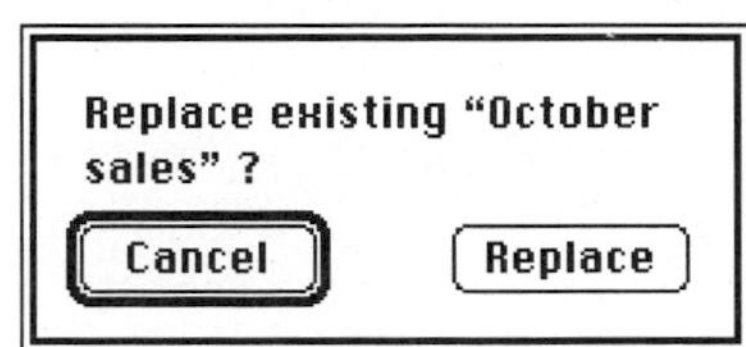

Figure 26-4. The name conflict dialog box

The StandardGetFile and StandardPutFile procedures always display the new dialog boxes. The procedures available before version 7.0 (SFGetFile, SFPutFile, SFPGetFile, and SFPPutFile) also display the new dialog boxes when running in version 7.0, unless the application has customized the dialog box. For more details on how the version 7.0 Standard File Package handles earlier procedures, see "Compatibility With Earlier Procedures" later in this chapter.

StandardGetFile and StandardPutFile fill in the reply record and return when the user completes the dialog box—either by selecting a file and clicking Save or Open, or by clicking Cancel. Your application checks the values in the reply record to see what action to take, if any. If the selected item is an alias for another item, the reply record describes the target of the alias. (See the Finder Interface chapter of this volume for a description of aliases.)

You can pass file descriptions directly from the Standard File Package to the File Manager. The new reply record identifies files with file system specification records, which are recognized by a new set of high-level File Manager functions. (See the File Manager chapter of this volume for a description of the new File Manager functions that use file system specification records.)

Listing 26-1 illustrates how an application calls first the Standard File Package and then the File Manager after the user chooses Open from the File menu.

Listing 26-1. Opening a document

```
VAR
   mySFR:       StandardFileReply;   {reply record}
   myTypeList:  SFTypeList;          {list of types to display}
   fsOpenErr:   OSErr;               {error returned by open function}
   fsRefNum:    Integer;             {path reference number, to be set }
                                     { by open function}

BEGIN
   myTypeList[0] := 'MDOC';          {set up type list}
   myTypeList[1] := 'YDOC';

   StandardGetFile(NIL, 2, myTypeList, mySFR);
                                     {display dialog box}
   IF mySFR.sfGood = TRUE THEN       {user clicks Open}
   BEGIN
      fsOpenErr := FSpOpenDF(mySFR.sfFile, fsCurPerm, fsRefNum);
                                     {open the file}
      LetMeCheck(fsopenErr);         {routine to check errors}
      {open document through reference number returned by FSpOpenDF}
   END;
END;
```

The Standard File Package now recognizes a longer list of keyboard equivalents during dialogs.

Keystrokes	**Action**
Up Arrow	Scroll up (backward) through displayed list
Down Arrow	Scroll down (forward) through displayed list
Command–Up Arrow	Display contents of parent
Command–Down Arrow	Display contents of selected directory or volume
Command–Left Arrow	Display contents of previous volume
Command–Right Arrow	Display contents of next volume
Command–Shift–Up Arrow	Display contents of desktop
Command-Shift-1	Eject disk in drive 1
Command-Shift-2	Eject disk in drive 2
Tab	Move to next keyboard target
Return *or* Enter	Invoke the default option for the dialog box (Open or Save)
Escape *or* Command-.	Cancel
Command-O	Open the selected item
Command-D	Display contents of desktop
Command-N	Create a new folder
Option-Command-O *or* Option-[click Open]	Select the target of the selected alias item instead of opening it

When the user selects a button in the dialog box using a keyboard equivalent, the button flashes.

Customizing Your Interface

If your application requires it, you can customize the user interface for identifying files.

Note: Alter the dialog boxes only if necessary. Apple Computer, Inc., does not guarantee future compatibility if you use a customized dialog box.

To customize a dialog box, you should

- design your display and create the resources that describe it
- write callback routines, if necessary, to process user actions in the dialog box
- call the Standard File Package using the CustomPutFile and CustomGetFile procedures, passing the resource IDs of the customized dialog boxes and pointers to the callback routines

Whether or not you change the dialog box display, you can write your own dialog hook callback function to handle user actions in the dialog box.

Customized Dialog Boxes

To describe a dialog box, you must supply a 'DLOG' resource that defines the box itself and a 'DITL' resource that defines the items in the dialog box.

Listing 26-2 shows the resource definition of the default Open dialog box, in Rez input format. (Rez is the resource compiler provided with Apple's Macintosh Programmer's Workshop [MPW®]. For a description of Rez format, see the manual that accompanies the MPW software, *MPW: Macintosh Programmer's Development Environment.*)

Listing 26-2. The definition of the default Open dialog box

```
resource 'DLOG' (-6042, purgeable)
   {
      {0, 0, 166, 344}, dBoxProc, invisible, noGoAway, 0,
       -6042, "", noAutoCenter
   };
```

Listing 26-3 shows the resource definition of the default Save dialog box, in Rez input format.

Listing 26-3. The definition of the default Save dialog box

```
resource 'DLOG' (-6043, purgeable)
   {
      {0, 0, 188, 344}, dBoxProc, invisible, noGoAway, 0,
       -6043, "", noAutoCenter
   };
```

The default Standard File Package dialog boxes now support color. The System file contains 'dctb' resources with the same resource IDs as the default dialog boxes, so that the Dialog Manager uses color grafPorts for the default dialog boxes. (See the Dialog Manager chapter of Volume V for a description of the 'dctb' resource.) If you create your own dialog boxes, include 'dctb' resources.

You must provide an item list (in a 'DITL' resource with the ID specified in the 'DLOG' resource) for each dialog box you define. Add new items to the end of the default lists. CustomGetFile expects the first nine items in a customized dialog box to have the same functions as the corresponding items in the StandardGetFile dialog box; CustomPutFile expects the first twelve items to have the same functions as the corresponding items in the StandardPutFile dialog box. If you want to eliminate one of the standard items from the display, leave it in the item list but place its coordinates outside the bounds of the dialog box rectangle.

Listing 26-4 shows the dialog item list for the default Open dialog box, in Rez input format. The constant statements in the next section, "Callback Routines," list which elements the items represent in the dialog boxes.

Listing 26-5 shows the dialog item list for the default Save dialog box, in Rez input format.

Listing 26-4. The item list for the default Open dialog box

```
resource 'DITL'(-6042)
  { {
    {135, 252, 155, 332}, Button { enabled, "Open" },
    {104, 252, 124, 332}, Button { enabled, "Cancel" },
    {0, 0, 0, 0}, HelpItem { disabled, HMScanhdlg {-6042}},
    {8, 235, 24, 337}, UserItem { enabled },
    {32, 252, 52, 332}, Button { enabled, "Eject" },
    {60, 252, 80, 332}, Button { enabled, "Desktop" },
    {29, 12, 159, 230}, UserItem { enabled },
    {6, 12, 25, 230}, UserItem { enabled },
    {91, 251, 92, 333}, Picture  { disabled, 11 },
  } };
```

Listing 26-5. The item list for the default Save dialog box

```
resource 'DITL'(-6043)
  { {
    {161, 252, 181, 332}, Button { enabled, "Save" },
    {130, 252, 150, 332}, Button { enabled, "Cancel" },
    {0, 0, 0, 0}, HelpItem { disabled, HMScanhdlg {-6043}},
    {8, 235, 24, 337}, UserItem { enabled },
    {32, 252, 52, 332}, Button { enabled, "Eject" },
    {60, 252, 80, 332}, Button { enabled, "Desktop" },
    {29, 12, 127, 230}, UserItem { enabled },
    {6, 12, 25, 230}, UserItem { enabled },
    {119, 250, 120, 334}, Picture { disabled, 11 },
    {157, 15, 173, 227}, EditText { enabled, "" },
    {136, 15, 152, 227}, StaticText { disabled, "Save as:" },
    {88, 252, 108, 332}, UserItem { disabled },
  } };
```

The third item in each list (HelpItem) supplies Apple's Balloon Help™ for items in the dialog box. HelpItem specifies the resource ID of the 'hdlg' resource that contains the help strings for the standard dialog items. To provide Balloon Help for your own items, supply a second 'hdlg' resource and reference it with another help item at the end of the list. For more information about Balloon Help, see the Help Manager chapter of this volume.

Callback Routines

You can supply callback routines that control these elements of the user interface:

- determining which files the user can open
- handling user actions in the dialog boxes
- handling user events received from the Event Manager
- highlighting the display when keyboard input is directed at a customized field defined by your application

You can also supply data of your own to be passed into the callback routines through a new parameter, yourDataPtr, that you can pass to CustomGetFile and CustomPutFile.

A **file filter function** determines which files appear in the display list when the user is opening a file. Both StandardGetFile and CustomGetFile recognize file filter functions, which are described in the Standard File Package chapter in Volume I.

When the Standard File Package is displaying the contents of a volume or folder, it checks the file type of each file and filters out files whose types do not match your application's specifications. (Your application can specify which file types are to be displayed through the typeList parameter to either StandardGetFile or CustomGetFile, as described in "Opening Files" later in this chapter.) If your application also supplies a file filter function, the Standard File Package calls that function each time it identifies a file of an acceptable type. The file filter function receives a pointer to the file's catalog information record (described in the File Manager chapter of Volume IV). It evaluates the catalog entry and returns a Boolean value that determines whether the file is filtered (that is, a value of TRUE suppresses display of the filename, and a value of FALSE allows the display). If you do not supply a file filter function, the Standard File Package displays all files of the specified types.

A file filter function to be called by StandardGetFile must use this syntax:

```
FUNCTION MyStandardFileFilter (pb: CInfoPBPtr) : Boolean;
```

When your file filter function is called by CustomGetFile, it can also receive a pointer to any data that you passed in through the call to CustomGetFile. A file filter function to be called by CustomGetFile must use this syntax:

```
FUNCTION MyCustomFileFilter (pb: CInfoPBPtr; myDataPtr: Ptr) : Boolean;
```

A **dialog hook function** handles item hits in the dialog box. It receives a dialog record and an item number from the ModalDialog procedure via the Standard File Package each time the user causes a hit on one of the dialog items. Your dialog hook function checks the item number of each item hit, and then either handles the hit or passes it back to the Standard File Package. (The dialog hook function is described in the Standard File Package chapters in Volumes I and IV.)

If you provide a dialog hook function, CustomPutFile and CustomGetFile call your function immediately after calling ModalDialog. They pass your function the item number returned by ModalDialog, a pointer to the dialog record, and a pointer to the data received from your application, if any. The dialog hook function must use this syntax:

```
FUNCTION MyDlgHook (item: Integer; theDialog: DialogPtr; myDataPtr: Ptr)
                    : Integer;
```

Your dialog hook function returns an item number or the sfHookNullItem constant as its function result. If it returns one of the item numbers in the following list of constants, the Standard File Package handles the item hit as described. If your dialog hook function does not handle an item hit, it should pass the item number back to the Standard File Package for processing by setting its return value equal to the item number.

```
MyDlgHook := item;
```

When your application handles the item hit, it should return the sfHookNullEvent constant. When the Standard File Package receives either sfHookNullEvent or an item number that it doesn't recognize from a dialog hook function, it does nothing.

The Standard File Package recognizes these item numbers:

```
CONST {default items in dialog boxes}
      sfItemOpenButton       =     1;  {Save or Open button}
      sfItemCancelButton     =     2;  {Cancel button}
      sfItemBalloonHelp      =     3;  {Balloon Help}
      sfItemVolumeUser       =     4;  {volume icon and name}
      sfItemEjectButton      =     5;  {Eject button}
      sfItemDesktopButton    =     6;  {Desktop button}
      sfItemFileListUser     =     7;  {display list}
      sfItemPopUpMenuUser    =     8;  {directory pop-up menu}
      sfItemDividerLinePict  =     9;  {dividing line between buttons}

      {items that appear in Save dialog boxes only}
      sfItemFileNameTextEdit =    10;  {filename field}
      sfItemPromptStaticText =    11;  {filename prompt text area}
      sfItemNewFolderUser    =    12;  {New Folder button}

      {pseudo-items available prior to version 7.0}
      sfHookFirstCall        =    -1;  {initialize display}
      sfHookCharOffset       = $1000;  {offset for character input}
      sfHookNullEvent        =   100;  {null event}
      sfHookRebuildList      =   101;  {redisplay list}
      sfHookFolderPopUp      =   102;  {display parent-directory menu}
      sfHookOpenFolder       =   103;  {display contents of selected }
                                       { folder or volume}

      {additional pseudo-items available with version 7.0}
      sfHookLastCall         =    -2;  {clean up after display}
      sfHookOpenAlias        =   104;  {resolve alias}
      sfHookGoToDesktop      =   105;  {display contents of desktop}
      sfHookGoToAliasTarget  =   106;  {select target of alias}
      sfHookGoToParent       =   107;  {display contents of parent}
      sfHookGoToNextDrive    =   108;  {display contents of next drive}
      sfHookGoToPrevDrive    =   109;  {display contents of }
                                       { previous drive}
      sfHookChangeSelection  =   110;  {select target of reply record}
      sfHookSetActiveOffset  =   200;  {switch active item}
```

You must write your own dialog hook function to handle any items you have added to the dialog box.

The Standard File Package uses a set of modal-dialog filter functions (described later in this section) to map user actions during the dialog onto the defined item numbers. Some of the mapping is indirect. A click on the Open button, for example, is mapped to sfItemOpenButton only if a file is selected in the display list. If a folder or volume is selected, the Standard File Package maps the hit onto the pseudo-item sfHookOpenFolder.

The lists that follow summarize when various items are generated and how they are handled. The lists describe the simplest mouse action that generates each item; many of the items can also be generated by keyboard actions, as described earlier in "Presenting the Default Interface."

The first twelve defined constants represent the items in the Save and Open dialog boxes. The constants that represent disabled items (sfItemBalloonHelp, sfItemDividerLinePict, and sfItemPromptStaticText) have no effect, but they are defined in the header files for the sake of completeness. Except under extraordinary circumstances, your dialog hook function always passes any of the first twelve item numbers back to the Standard File Package for processing.

Constant	Cause	Effect
sfItemOpenButton	The user clicks Open or Save while a filename is selected.	The Standard File Package fills in the reply record (setting sfGood to TRUE), removes the dialog box, and returns.
sfItemCancelButton	The user clicks Cancel.	The Standard File Package sets sfGood to FALSE, removes the dialog box, and returns.
sfItemVolumeUser	The user clicks the volume icon or its name.	The Standard File Package rebuilds the display list to show the contents of the folder that is one level up the hierarchy (that is, the parent directory of the current parent directory).
sfItemEjectButton	The user clicks Eject.	The Standard File Package ejects the volume that is currently selected.
sfItemDesktopButton	The user clicks the Drive button in a customized dialog box defined by one of the earlier procedures. You never receive this item number with the new procedures; when the user clicks the Desktop button, the action is mapped to the item sfHookGoToDesktop, described in a list later in this section.	The Standard File Package displays the contents of the next drive.

Constant	Cause	Effect
sfItemFileListUser	The user clicks an item in the display list. The Standard File Package updates the selection and generates this item for your information.	No action.
sfItemPopUpMenuUser	Never generated. The Standard File Package's modal-dialog filter function maps clicks on the directory pop-up menu to sfHookFolderPopUp, described in a list later in this section.	No action.
sfItemFileNameTextEdit	The user clicks in the filename field. TextEdit and the Standard File Package process mouse clicks in the filename field, but the item number is generated for your information.	No action.
sfItemNewFolderUser	The user clicks New Folder.	The Standard File Package displays the New Folder dialog box.

The pseudo-items are messages that allow your application and the Standard File Package to communicate and support various features added since the original design of the Standard File Package.

The Standard File Package generates three pseudo-items that give your application the chance to control a customized display.

Constant	Cause	Response
sfHookFirstCall	The Standard File Package generates this item as a signal to your dialog hook function that it is about to display a dialog box.	If you want to initialize the display, do it when you receive this item. You can specify where in the file system the dialog box should open either by returning sfHookGoToDesktop or by changing the reply record and returning sfHookChangeSelection.
sfHookLastCall	The Standard File Package generates this item number as a signal to your dialog hook function that it is about to remove a dialog box.	If you created any structures when the dialog box was first displayed, remove them when you receive this item.

Constant	Cause	Response
sfHookNullEvent	The Standard File Package issues this null item periodically if no user action has taken place.	Your application can use this event to perform any updating or periodic processing that might be necessary.

Your application can generate three pseudo-items to request services from the Standard File Package.

Constant	Cause	Effect
sfHookRebuildList	Your dialog hook function returns this item to the Standard File Package when it needs to redisplay the file list. Your application might need to redisplay the list if, for example, it allows the user to change the file types to be displayed.	The Standard File Package rebuilds and displays the list of files that can be opened.
sfHookChangeSelection	Your application returns this value to the Standard File Package after changing the reply record so that it describes a different file or folder.	The Standard File Package rebuilds the display list to show the contents of the folder or volume containing the object described in the reply record. It selects the item described in the reply record.
sfHookSetActiveOffset	Your application adds this constant to an item number and sends the result to the Standard File Package.	The Standard File Package activates that item in the dialog box, making it the target of keyboard input. This constant allows your application to activate a specific field in the dialog box without explicit input from the user.

The Standard File Package's own modal-dialog filter functions generate a number of pseudo-items that allow its dialog hook functions to support various features introduced since the original design of the standard file dialog boxes. Except under extraordinary circumstances, your dialog hook function always passes any of these item numbers back to the Standard File Package for processing.

Constant	Cause	Effect
sfHookCharOffset	The Standard File Package adds this constant to the value of an ASCII character when it's using keyboard input for item selection.	The Standard File Package uses the decoded ASCII character to select an entry in the display list.
sfHookFolderPopUp	The user clicks the directory pop-up menu.	The Standard File Package displays the pop up menu showing all parent directories.
sfHookOpenFolder	The user clicks the Open button while a folder or volume is selected in the display list.	The Standard File Package rebuilds the display list to show the contents of the folder or volume.
sfHookOpenAlias	The Standard File Package generates this item number as a signal that the selected item is an alias for another file, folder, or volume.	If the selected item is an alias for a file, the Standard File Package resolves the alias, places the file system specification record of the target in the reply record, and returns. If the selected item is an alias for a folder or volume, the Standard File Package resolves the alias and rebuilds the display list to show the contents of the alias target.
sfHookGoToDesktop	The user clicks the Desktop button.	The Standard File Package displays the contents of the desktop in the display list.
sfHookGoToAliasTarget	The user presses the Option key while opening an item that is an alias.	The Standard File Package rebuilds the display list to display the volume or folder containing the alias target and selects the target.
sfHookGoToParent	The user presses Command–Up Arrow.	The Standard File Package rebuilds the display list to show the contents of the folder that is one level up the hierarchy (that is, the parent directory of the current parent directory).

Constant	Cause	Effect
sfHookGoToNextDrive	The user presses Command–Right Arrow.	The Standard File Package displays the contents of the next volume.
sfHookGoToPrevDrive	The user presses Command–Left Arrow.	The Standard File Package displays the contents of the previous volume.

The CustomGetFile and CustomPutFile procedures call your dialog hook function for item hits in both the main dialog box and any subsidiary dialog boxes (such as the dialog box for naming a new folder while saving a document through CustomPutFile). To determine whether the dialog record describes the main dialog box or a subsidiary dialog box, check the value of the refCon field in the window record in the dialog record.

> **Note:** Prior to system software version 7.0, the Standard File Package did not call your dialog hook function during subsidiary dialog boxes. Dialog hook functions for the new CustomGetFile and CustomPutFile procedures must check the refCon field to determine the target of the dialog record.

The defined values for the refCon field represent the standard file dialog boxes.

Constant	Value	Dialog box
sfMainDialogRefCon	'stdf'	Main dialog box, either Open or Save
sfNewFolderDialogRefCon	'nfdr'	New Folder dialog box
sfReplaceDialogRefCon	'rplc'	Verification for replacing a file of the same name
sfStatWarnDialogRefCon	'stat'	Warning that the user is opening the master copy of a stationery pad, not a piece of stationery
sfErrorDialogRefCon	'err '	Report of a general error
sfLockWarnDialogRefCon	'lock'	Warning that the user is opening a locked file and won't be able to save any changes

A **modal-dialog filter function** controls events closer to their source by filtering the events received from the Event Manager. The modal-dialog filter function is described in the Dialog Manager chapter of Volume I. The Standard File Package itself contains a modal-dialog filter function that maps keypresses and other user input onto the equivalent dialog box item hits. If you want to process events yourself, you can supply your own filter function.

Your modal-dialog filter function determines how the Dialog Manager procedure ModalDialog filters events when called by the CustomGetFile and CustomPutFile procedures. (Those procedures retrieve item hits by calling ModalDialog.) ModalDialog retrieves events by calling the Event Manager function GetNextEvent. If you provide a modal-dialog filter function, ModalDialog calls your filter function before processing an event and passes it a pointer to the dialog record, a pointer to the event record, the item number, and a pointer to the data received from your application, if any.

```
FUNCTION MyModalFilter (theDialog: DialogPtr; VAR theEvent: EventRecord;
                        VAR itemHit: Integer; myDataPtr: Ptr) : Boolean;
```

Your modal-dialog filter function returns a Boolean value that reports whether it handled the event. If your function returns a value of FALSE, ModalDialog processes the event through its own filters. If your function returns a value of TRUE, ModalDialog returns with no further action.

This function is the same as the modal-dialog filter function passed directly to ModalDialog (described in the Dialog Manager chapter of Volume I), with the addition of the optional pointer to your own data.

The CustomGetFile and CustomPutFile procedures call your filter function to process events in both the main dialog box and any subsidiary dialog boxes (such as the dialog box for naming a new folder while saving a document through CustomPutFile). To determine whether the dialog record describes the main dialog box or a subsidiary dialog box, check the value of the refCon field in the window record in the dialog record, as described earlier in the description of dialog hook functions.

The **activation procedure** controls the highlighting of dialog items that are defined by your application and can receive keyboard input. Ordinarily, you need to supply an activation procedure only if your application builds a list from which the user can select entries. The Standard File Package supplies the activation procedure for the file display list and for all TextEdit fields. You can also use the activation procedure to keep track of which field is receiving keyboard input, if your application needs that information.

The target of keyboard input is called the **active field.** The two standard keyboard-input fields are the filename field (present only in Save dialog boxes) and the display list. Unless you override it through your own dialog hook function, the Standard File Package handles the highlighting of its own items and TextEdit fields. When the user changes the keyboard target by pressing the mouse button or the Tab key, the Standard File Package calls your activation procedure twice: the first call specifies which field is being deactivated, and the second specifies which field is being activated. Your application is responsible for removing the highlighting when one of its fields becomes inactive and for adding the highlighting when one of its fields becomes active. The Standard File Package can handle the highlighting of all TextEdit fields, even those defined by your application.

The activation procedure receives four parameters: a dialog pointer, a dialog item number, a Boolean that specifies whether the field is being activated (TRUE) or deactivated (FALSE), and a pointer to your own data.

```
PROCEDURE MyActivateProc (theDialog: DialogPtr; itemNo: Integer;
                          activating: Boolean; myDataPtr: Ptr);
```

Compatibility With Earlier Procedures

The Standard File Package still recognizes all procedures available before version 7.0 (SFGetFile, SFPutFile, SFPGetFile, and SFPPutFile). It displays the new interface for all applications that use the default dialog boxes (that is, applications that specify both the dialog hook and the modal-dialog filter pointers as NIL and that specify no alternative dialog ID).

When the Standard File Package can't use the new interface because an application customized thc dialog box with the earlier procedures, it nevertheless makes some changes to the display:

- It changes the label of the Drive button to Desktop and makes the desktop the root of the display.
- It moves the volume icon slightly to the right, to make room for selection highlighting around the display list field.

If, however, a customized dialog box has suppressed the file display list (by specifying co-ordinates outside of the dialog box), the Standard File Package uses the earlier interface, on the assumption that the dialog box is designed for volume selection.

STANDARD FILE PACKAGE ROUTINES

This section describes the new routines in version 7.0 of the Standard File Package. The StandardPutFile and StandardGetFile procedures are simplified versions of the original procedures for handling the user interface when storing and retrieving files. The CustomPutFile and CustomGetFile procedures are customizable versions of the same procedures.

The callback routines in the new custom procedures all take an additional parameter not available in earlier versions of the Standard File Package. The new parameter is an optional pointer to data set up by your application and passed into the calling procedure in the yourDataPtr parameter.

Saving Files

Use the StandardPutFile procedure to display the default Save dialog box when the user is saving a file.

```
PROCEDURE StandardPutFile (prompt: Str255; defaultName: Str255;
                           VAR reply: StandardFileReply);
```

StandardPutFile presents a dialog box through which the user specifies the name and location of a file to be written to. During the dialog, StandardPutFile gets and handles events until the user completes the interaction, either by selecting a name and authorizing the save or by canceling the save. StandardPutFile returns the user's input in a standard file reply record, described earlier in "Using the Standard File Package."

The prompt parameter specifies the prompt message to be displayed over the text field.

The defaultName parameter contains the initial name of the file, if any.

The reply parameter is the reply record, which StandardPutFile fills in before returning.

Use the CustomPutFile procedure when your application requires more control over the Save dialog box.

```
PROCEDURE CustomPutFile (prompt: Str255; defaultName: Str255;
                         VAR reply: StandardFileReply; dlgID: Integer;
                         where: Point; dlgHook: DlgHookYDProcPtr;
                         filterProc: ModalFilterYDProcPtr;
                         activeList: Ptr;
                         activateProc: ActivateYDProcPtr;
                         yourDataPtr: UNIV Ptr);
```

CustomPutFile is an alternative to StandardPutFile when you want to display a customized Save dialog box or handle the default dialog box in a customized way.

The first three parameters are identical to the parameters of StandardPutFile. The prompt parameter specifies the prompt message to be displayed over the text field. The defaultName parameter contains the initial name of the file, if any. The reply parameter is the reply record, which StandardPutFile fills in before returning.

The dlgID parameter is the resource ID of a customized dialog template. To use the standard template, set this parameter to 0.

The where parameter specifies the upper-left corner of the dialog box in global coordinates. If you specify the point (–1,–1), CustomPutFile automatically centers the dialog box on the screen.

The dlgHook parameter points to your dialog hook function, which handles item hits received from the Dialog Manager. Specify a value of NIL if you have not added any items to the dialog box and want the standard items handled in the standard ways. See "Callback Routines" earlier in this chapter for a description of the dialog hook function, which uses this syntax:

```
FUNCTION MyDlgHook (item: Integer; theDialog: DialogPtr;
                    myDataPtr: Ptr) : Integer;
```

The filterProc parameter points to your modal-dialog filter function, which determines how the ModalDialog procedure filters events when called by the CustomPutFile procedure. Specify a value of NIL if you are not supplying your own function. See "Callback Routines" earlier in this chapter for a description of the modal-dialog filter function, which uses this syntax:

```
FUNCTION MyModalFilter (theDialog: DialogPtr;
                        VAR theEvent: EventRecord;
                        VAR itemHit: Integer; myDataPtr: Ptr) :
                        Boolean;
```

The activeList parameter points to a list of all items in the dialog box that can be activated—that is, can be the target of keyboard input. If you supply an activeList parameter of NIL, CustomPutFile uses the default targets (the filename field and the list of files and folders that can be opened). If you have added any fields that can accept keyboard input, you must modify the list. The list is stored as an array of 16-bit integers. The first integer is the number of items in the list. The remaining integers are the item numbers of all possible keyboard targets, in the order that they are activated by the Tab key.

The activateProc parameter points to your activation procedure, which controls the highlighting of dialog items that are defined by your application and that can receive keyboard input. See "Callback Routines" earlier in this chapter for a description of the activation procedure, which uses this syntax:

```
PROCEDURE MyActivateProc (theDialog: DialogPtr; itemNo: Integer;
                           activating: Boolean; myDataPtr: Ptr);
```

The yourDataPtr parameter points to optional data supplied by your application. When CustomPutFile calls any of your callback routines, it pushes this parameter on the stack, making the data available to your callback routines. If you are not supplying any data of your own, you can specify a value of NIL.

Opening Files

Use the StandardGetFile procedure to display the default Open dialog box when the user is opening a file.

```
PROCEDURE StandardGetFile (fileFilter: FileFilterProcPtr;
                            numTypes: Integer; typeList: SFTypeList;
                            VAR reply: StandardFileReply);
```

StandardGetFile presents a dialog box through which the user specifies the name and location of a file to be opened. During the dialog, StandardGetFile gets and handles events until the user completes the interaction, either by selecting a file to open or by canceling the operation. StandardGetFile returns the user's input in a standard file reply record, described earlier in "Using the Standard File Package."

The fileFilter, numTypes, and typeList parameters together determine which files appear in the display list. (These three parameters are still used as described in the Standard File Package chapter of Volume I. The rules are summarized here for your convenience.) The first filtering is by file type, which you specify in the numTypes and typeList parameters.

- The numTypes parameter specifies the number of file types to be displayed. You can specify one or more types. If you specify a numTypes value of –1, the first filtering passes files of all types. A numTypes value of 0 filters out all files.

- The typeList parameter is the list of types to be displayed.

The fileFilter parameter points to an optional file filter function, provided by your application, through which StandardGetFile passes files of the specified types. See "Callback Routines" earlier in this chapter for a description of the file filter function, which uses this syntax:

```
FUNCTION MyStandardFileFilter (pb: CInfoPBPtr) : Boolean;
```

The reply parameter is the reply record, which StandardPutFile fills in before returning.

Call the CustomGetFile procedure when your application requires more control over the Open dialog box.

```
PROCEDURE CustomGetFile (fileFilter: FileFilterYDProcPtr;
                         numTypes: Integer; typeList: SFTypeList;
                         VAR reply: StandardFileReply; dlgID: Integer;
                         where: Point; dlgHook: DlgHookYDProcPtr;
                         filterProc: ModalFilterYDProcPtr;
                         activeList: Ptr;
                         activateProc: ActivateYDProcPtr;
                         yourDataPtr: UNIV Ptr);
```

CustomGetFile is an alternative to StandardGetFile when you want to use a customized dialog box or handle the default Open dialog box in a customized way.

The first four parameters are similar to the same parameters in StandardGetFile. The fileFilter, numTypes, and typeList parameters determine which files appear in the list of choices. If you specify a value of –1 in the numTypes parameter, CustomGetFile displays or passes to your file filter function all files and folders at the current level of the display hierarchy, not just the files. If you provide a filter function, CustomGetFile passes it both the pointer to the catalog entry for each file to be processed and also a pointer to the optional data passed by your application in its call to CustomGetFile.

```
FUNCTION MyCustomFileFilter (pb: CInfoPBPtr; myDataPtr: Ptr) :
                             Boolean;
```

The reply parameter is the reply record, which CustomGetFile fills in before returning.

The dlgID parameter is the resource ID of a customized dialog template. To use the standard template, set this parameter to 0.

The where parameter specifies the upper-left corner of the dialog box in global coordinates. If you specify the point (–1,–1), CustomGetFile automatically centers the dialog box on the screen.

The dlgHook parameter points to your dialog hook function, which handles item hits received from the Dialog Manager. Specify a value of NIL if you have not added any items to the dialog box and want the standard items handled in the standard ways. See “Callback Routines” earlier in this chapter for a description of the dialog hook function, which uses this syntax:

```
FUNCTION MyDlgHook (item: Integer; theDialog: DialogPtr;
                    myDataPtr: Ptr) : Integer;
```

26 Standard File

The filterProc parameter points to your modal-dialog filter function, which determines how ModalDialog filters events when called by CustomGetFile. Specify a value of NIL if you are not supplying your own function. See "Callback Routines" earlier in this chapter for a description of the modal-dialog filter function, which uses this syntax:

```
FUNCTION MyModalFilter (theDialog: DialogPtr;
                        VAR theEvent: EventRecord;
                        VAR itemHit: Integer; myDataPtr: Ptr) :
                        Boolean;
```

The activeList parameter points to a list of all items in the dialog box that can be activated—that is, made the target of keyboard input. The list is stored as an array of 16-bit integers. The first integer is the number of items in the list. The remaining integers are the item numbers of all possible keyboard targets, in the order that they are activated by the Tab key. If you supply an activeList parameter of NIL, CustomGetFile directs all keyboard input to the displayed list.

The activateProc parameter points to your activation procedure, which controls the highlighting of dialog items that are defined by your application and that can receive keyboard input. See "Callback Routines" earlier in this chapter for a description of the activation procedure, which uses this syntax:

```
PROCEDURE MyActivateProc (theDialog: DialogPtr; itemNo: Integer;
                          activating: Boolean; myDataPtr: Ptr);
```

The yourDataPtr parameter points to optional data supplied by your application.When CustomGetFile calls any of your callback routines, it pushes this parameter on the stack, making the data available to your callback routines. If you are not supplying any data of your own, specify a value of NIL.

SUMMARY OF THE STANDARD FILE PACKAGE

Constants

```
CONST {Gestalt selector and reply}
      gestaltStandardFileAttr = 'stdf';
      gestaltStandardFile58   =      0;

      {standard dialog resource IDs}
      sfPutDialogID         = -6043;    {Save dialog box}
      sfGetDialogID         = -6042;    {Open dialog box}

      {default items in dialog boxes}
      sfItemOpenButton         =  1;    {Save or Open button}
      sfItemCancelButton       =  2;    {Cancel button}
      sfItemBalloonHelp        =  3;    {Balloon Help}
      sfItemVolumeUser         =  4;    {volume icon and name}
      sfItemEjectButton        =  5;    {Eject button}
      sfItemDesktopButton      =  6;    {Desktop button}
      sfItemFileListUser       =  7;    {display list}
      sfItemPopUpMenuUser      =  8;    {directory pop-up menu}
      sfItemDividerLinePict    =  9;    {dividing line between buttons}

      {items that appear in Save dialog boxes only}
      sfItemFileNameTextEdit   = 10;    {filename field}
      sfItemPromptStaticText   = 11;    {filename prompt text area}
      sfItemNewFolderUser      = 12;    {New Folder button}

      {pseudo-items available prior to version 7.0}
      sfHookFirstCall       =    -1;    {initialize display}
      sfHookCharOffset      = $1000;    {offset for character input}
      sfHookNullEvent       =   100;    {null event}
      sfHookRebuildList     =   101;    {redisplay list}
      sfHookFolderPopUp     =   102;    {display parent-directory menu}
      sfHookOpenFolder      =   103;    {display contents of selected }
                                        { folder or volume}

      {additional pseudo-items available with version 7.0}
      sfHookLastCall          =  -2;    {clean up after display}
      sfHookOpenAlias         = 104;    {resolve alias}
      sfHookGoToDesktop       = 105;    {display contents of desktop}
      sfHookGoToAliasTarget   = 106;    {select target of alias}
      sfHookGoToParent        = 107;    {display contents of parent}
      sfHookGoToNextDrive     = 108;    {display contents of next drive}
      sfHookGoToPrevDrive     = 109;    {display contents of previous }
                                        { drive}
      sfHookChangeSelection   = 110;    {select target of reply record}
      sfHookSetActiveOffset   = 200;    {switch active item}
```

```
{refCon field in the window record in the dialog record}
sfMainDialogRefCon        = 'stdf';    {main dialog box}
sfNewFolderDialogRefCon   = 'nfdr';    {New Folder dialog box}
sfReplaceDialogRefCon     = 'rplc';    {name conflict dialog box}
sfStatWarnDialogRefCon    = 'stat';    {stationery warning}
sfErrorDialogRefCon       = 'err ';    {general error report}
sfLockWarnDialogRefCon    = 'lock';    {software lock warning}
```

Data Types

```
TYPE StandardFileReply  =
     RECORD
        sfGood:          Boolean;         {user did not cancel}
        sfReplacing:     Boolean;         {replace file with same name}
        sfType:          OSType;          {file type}
        sfFile:          FSSpec;          {selected file, folder, or volume}
        sfScript:        ScriptCode;      {script of file, folder, or }
                                          { volume name}
        sfFlags:         Integer;         {Finder flags of selected item}
        sfIsFolder:      Boolean;         {selected item is a folder}
        sfIsVolume:      Boolean;         {selected item is a volume}
        sfReserved1:     LongInt;         {reserved}
        sfReserved2:     Integer          {reserved}
     END;

     SFTypeList = ARRAY[0..3] OF OSType;

     FileFilterYDProcPtr  =  ProcPtr;  {see sample file filter function}
     DlgHookYDProcPtr     =  ProcPtr;  {see sample dialog hook function}
     ModalFilterYDProcPtr =  ProcPtr;  {see sample modal-dialog filter }
                                       { function}
     ActivateYDProcPtr    =  ProcPtr;  {see sample activation procedure}
```

Routines

Saving Files

```
PROCEDURE StandardPutFile    (prompt: Str255; defaultName: Str255;
                              VAR reply: StandardFileReply);

PROCEDURE CustomPutFile      (prompt: Str255; defaultName: Str255;
                              VAR reply: StandardFileReply;
                              dlgID: Integer; where: Point;
                              dlgHook: DlgHookYDProcPtr;
                              filterProc: ModalFilterYDProcPtr;
                              activeList: Ptr;
                              activateProc: ActivateYDProcPtr;
                              yourDataPtr: UNIV Ptr);
```

Opening Files

```
PROCEDURE StandardGetFile   (fileFilter: FileFilterProcPtr;
                             numTypes: Integer; typeList: SFTypeList;
                             VAR reply: StandardFileReply);

PROCEDURE CustomGetFile     (fileFilter: FileFilterYDProcPtr;
                             numTypes: Integer; typeList: SFTypeList;
                             VAR reply: StandardFileReply;
                             dlgID: Integer; where: Point;
                             dlgHook: DlgHookYDProcPtr;
                             filterProc: ModalFilterYDProcPtr;
                             activeList: Ptr;
                             activateProc: ActivateYDProcPtr;
                             yourDataPtr: UNIV Ptr);
```

Application-Defined Routines

```
FUNCTION MyStandardFileFilter   (pb: CInfoPBPtr) : Boolean;

FUNCTION MyCustomFileFilter     (pb: CInfoPBPtr; myDataPtr: Ptr) :
                                 Boolean;

FUNCTION MyDlgHook              (item: Integer; theDialog: DialogPtr;
                                 myDataPtr: Ptr) : Integer;

FUNCTION MyModalFilter          (theDialog: DialogPtr;
                                 VAR theEvent: EventRecord;
                                 VAR itemHit: Integer; myDataPtr: Ptr) :
                                 Boolean;

PROCEDURE MyActivateProc        (theDialog: DialogPtr; itemNo: Integer;
                                 activating: Boolean; myDataPtr: Ptr);
```

Assembly-Language Information

Standard File Reply Record

sfGood	byte	command-valid flag
sfReplacing	byte	replace existing file flag
sfType	4 bytes	file type
sfFile	70 bytes	selected item
sfScript	2 bytes	display script
sfFlags	2 bytes	Finder flags from catalog
sfIsFolder	byte	folder flag
sfIsVolume	byte	volume flag
sfReserved1	4 bytes	reserved
sfReserved2	2 bytes	reserved

Trap Macro Requiring Routine Selector

_Pack3

Selector	Routine
$0001	SFPutFile
$0002	SFGetFile
$0003	SFPPutFile
$0004	SFPGetFile
$0005	StandardPutFile
$0006	StandardGetFile
$0007	CustomPutFile
$0008	CustomGetFile

27 THE ALIAS MANAGER

ABOUT THIS CHAPTER

This chapter describes how your application can use the Alias Manager to establish and resolve **alias records,** which are data structures that describe file system objects (that is, files, directories, and volumes).

You create an alias record to take a fingerprint of a file system object, usually a file, that you might need to locate again later. You can store the alias record, instead of a standard file specification, and then let the Alias Manager find the file again when it's needed. The Alias Manager contains algorithms for locating files that have been moved, renamed, copied, or restored from backup.

> **Note:** The Alias Manager lets you exploit alias records. It does not directly manipulate Finder™ aliases, which are created and managed by the user through the Finder. The Finder Interface chapter in this volume describes Finder aliases and how your application can accommodate them.

The Alias Manager is available only in system software version 7.0 or later. Call the Gestalt function, described in the Compatibility Guidelines chapter of this volume, to determine whether the Alias Manager is present.

Read this chapter if you want your application to create and resolve alias records. You might store an alias record, for example, to identify a customized dictionary from within a word-processing document. When the user runs a spelling checker on the document, your application can ask the Alias Manager to resolve the record to find the correct dictionary.

To use this chapter, you should be familiar with the File Manager's conventions for identifying files, directories, and volumes, as described in the File Manager chapter in this volume.

ABOUT THE ALIAS MANAGER

The Alias Manager creates and resolves alias records. The next section, "About Alias Records," describes how you can use alias records.

In general, you should use the Alias Manager to create an alias record whenever you find yourself storing a specific file description, such as filename and parent directory ID. The Alias Manager stores this information and more in the alias record, and it also provides a set of search strategies for resolving the record later. The search strategies are described later in this chapter in "Resolving Alias Records."

You can use the Alias Manager to

- create alias records
- resolve alias records
- update alias records
- get information about alias records

The Alias Manager can track files and directories across volumes. If the target of an alias record is on an unmounted AppleShare® volume, the Alias Manager automatically mounts the volume when it resolves the alias. If the target object is on an unmounted ejectable volume, the Alias Manager prompts the user to insert the volume.

When the Alias Manager creates an alias record, it allocates the storage, fills in the record, and returns a handle to it. Your application is responsible for storing the record and retrieving it when needed. Your application must also supply strategies for handling various alias-resolution problems, described in "Resolving Alias Records" later in this chapter.

To help you understand and use the Alias Manager, this chapter provides

- an overview of alias records
- a description of how the Alias Manager resolves alias records
- specific techniques for using the Alias Manager in your application

ABOUT ALIAS RECORDS

An alias record is a data structure that describes a file, directory, or volume. The record contains

- location information, such as name and parent directory ID
- verification information, such as creation date, file type, and creator
- volume mounting information (that is, server and zone), if applicable

By storing alias records, you can allow your users to create a robust connection to a file—that is, a connection that can survive the moving or renaming of the target file. The Finder in system software version 7.0, for example, stores alias records in aliases created by the user to represent other files or folders. The Edition Manager uses alias records to support data sharing among separate documents. (The Finder Interface and Edition Manager chapters in this volume describe those features in detail.)

An alias record is a reliable way to identify a file system object when your application is communicating with a process that might be running on a different machine.

The creation of an alias record has no effect on the target of the record, except to establish a file ID if one did not previously exist for the target file. (See the File Manager chapter of this volume for a description of file IDs.)

The alias record contains only two fields of public information available to your application. The bulk of the record is managed privately by the Alias Manager.

```
TYPE AliasRecord =
    RECORD
        userType:       OSType;       {application's signature}
        aliasSize:      Integer       {size of record when created}
        {variable-length private data}
    END;
```

Your application can use the userType field to store its own signature or any other data that fits into 4 bytes. When the Alias Manager creates an alias record, it stores 0 in that field.

The Alias Manager stores the size of the record when it was created in the aliasSize field. Knowing the starting size allows you to store and retrieve data of your own at the end of the record (see "Customizing Alias Records" later in this chapter). An alias record is typically 200 to 300 bytes long.

The private Alias Manager data includes all of the location, verification, and mounting information needed to resolve the alias record with the various search strategies described in this chapter.

When you create an alias record, you have the option of recording a **relative path,** that is, a path to the **target** from another file or directory on the same volume. (Relative paths don't work across volumes.) The beginning point of a relative path is called the fromFile. To record a relative path, the Alias Manager saves the distances from the target and the fromFile to their **common parent,** that is, the lowest-level directory that appears in the pathnames of both. The Alias Manager can later use those distances in conjunction with the full pathname to conduct a relative search.

Suppose, for example, that you are writing a word-processing application that allows the user to build a customized, supplemental dictionary for each document. You create the dictionary as a separate document in the same directory as the document it serves, as Figure 27-1 shows.

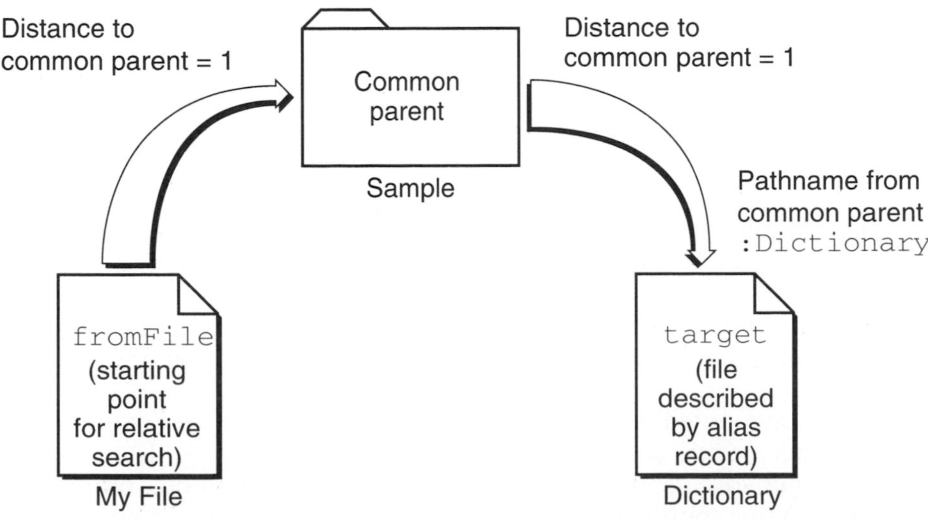

Figure 27-1. Resolving a relative path

When resolving the alias record by using a relative path, the Alias Manager starts at the directory that is the specified distance above the fromFile, the directory named Sample in the example in Figure 27-1. The Alias Manager then constructs a partial pathname by extracting one field of the absolute pathname for each step from the target to the common parent. In this example, the distance is one, so the pathname contains only the name of the target document, Dictionary.

In some circumstances, a relative search identifies the correct target when a direct search cannot. For example, suppose the user of your word-processing application creates a working copy of a document and dictionary by copying the entire folder Sample to another disk. The user later updates the original document and dictionary by copying the folder from the working disk. All of the underlying file and directory identifications change, but the filenames and relative path remain the same. When the user later runs the spelling checker on the document, a relative-path search finds the correct target dictionary.

The Alias Manager accepts and returns file specifications in the form of file system specification records (FSSpec records), described in the File Manager chapter of this volume. The FSSpec record represents a standard, complete description of a file system object. It contains a volume reference number, a parent directory ID, and a name.

SEARCH STRATEGIES FOR RESOLVING ALIAS RECORDS

One of the key features of the Alias Manager is the search strategies built into the alias-resolution functions. The search strategies are designed to find the original target of an alias record, even if the target has been moved, renamed, copied, or restored from backup.

The Alias Manager provides two basic alias-resolution algorithms: a fast search and an exhaustive search. This section describes the search algorithms. For descriptions of the functions that perform the searches, see "Resolving Alias Records" and "Resolving and Reading Alias Records" later in this chapter.

The first step in any nonrelative search is to identify the volume on which the target resides. The volume search considers the volume's name, creation date (which acts almost as a unique identifier for a volume), and type (for example, a hard disk, a 3.5-inch floppy disk, or an AppleShare volume).

The Alias Manager first looks for a volume that matches all three criteria: name, creation date, and type. The search succeeds if the volume is mounted and if its name and creation date have not changed since the record was created. If the search fails, the Alias Manager attempts to match by creation date and type only. This step locates volumes that have been renamed. Finally, the Alias Manager attempts to match by volume name and type only.

If the target is on an unmounted AppleShare volume, the Alias Manager attempts to mount the volume. It presents a name and password dialog box if appropriate. If the target is on an unmounted ejectable volume, the Alias Manager displays a dialog box prompting the user to insert the volume. Your application can suppress the automatic mounting, as explained in the description of the MatchAlias function in "Resolving and Reading Alias Records" later in this chapter.

Fast Search

The fast-search algorithm is designed to find the target of an alias record quickly.

Depending on how you invoke it, the fast-search algorithm starts with either a relative search (described earlier in "About Alias Records") or a direct search (described in this section). Fast search can perform a relative search whether or not it has identified the target volume, but it must identify the volume before it can perform a direct search.

In a direct search, the fast-search algorithm first looks for the target by file ID (if the target is a file) or directory ID (if the target is a directory). (File IDs and directory IDs are described in the File Manager chapter of this volume.) Even if a file has been renamed or moved on a volume, the Alias Manager can find it quickly through its file ID.

If the search by file ID or directory ID fails, fast search looks for the target by name in the original parent directory. This search locates the target if its file or directory ID has changed but it still exists by the same name in the parent directory (for example, if the target was restored from backup). Fast search compares file numbers on files found by name in the correct parent directory. If the file numbers do not match, the file is treated as a possible match—that is, it is put on the list of candidates and the search continues. If the target is not found by name in the parent directory, fast search looks for a file by file number in the parent directory. A file with the same file number but a different name replaces a file with the same name but a different file number in the list of matches.

If the search by file ID or directory ID fails and if fast search cannot find the original parent directory, it searches for the target by full pathname. This search finds the target if it resides in the same location on the volume but the directory ID of its parent directory has changed (for example, if the entire parent directory was restored from backup).

If the search by full pathname fails, fast search attempts to find the file by tracing partial pathnames up through all parent directories, using parent directory IDs instead of directory names. For example, consider this full pathname:

Loma Prieta:MyReports:October:Sales Report

If the search by full pathname fails, fast search first looks for the partial pathname :Sales Report in the directory with the ID that the directory Loma Prieta:MyReports:October had when the alias record was created. If that search fails, it looks for :October:Sales Report in the directory with the ID that Loma Prieta:MyReports had, and so on.

If you do not ask for a search by relative path first but do provide a starting point for a relative search, and if the alias record contains relative path information, fast search performs a relative search after the direct search. The relative search succeeds if the relative path is the same as when the record was created and if the names of the target and its intervening parent directories have not changed.

Exhaustive Search

The exhaustive-search algorithm scans an entire volume to look for possible matches.

The Alias Manager typically performs an exhaustive search by calling the File Manager function PBCatSearch, searching for files or directories with a matching creation date, creator, and type. (See the File Manager chapter of this volume for a description of PBCatSearch.)

PBCatSearch is available only on HFS volumes, not on MFS volumes. (See the File Manager chapter of this volume for a description of the two file systems.) PBCatSearch is also available only on systems running version 7.0 and later. When PBCatSearch is not available, exhaustive search performs a search of the entire volume by making a series of indexed File Manager calls, searching for objects with matching creation date, type, creator, or file number.

USING THE ALIAS MANAGER

You use the Alias Manager primarily to create and resolve alias records. You can also use it to get information about and update alias records.

The Alias Manager creates an alias record in memory and provides you with a handle to the record. When you no longer need a record in memory, free the memory by calling the DisposHandle procedure, described in the Memory Manager chapter of Volume II. You can store and retrieve alias records as resources of type 'alis'.

Alias Manager functions accept and return file specifications in the form of FSSpec records, which contain a volume reference number, a parent directory ID, and a target name. See the File Manager chapter in this volume for a description of file identification conventions.

Before calling any of the Alias Manager functions, verify that the Alias Manager is available by calling the Gestalt function with a selector of gestaltAliasMgrAttr. If Gestalt sets the gestaltAliasMgrPresent bit in the response parameter, the Alias Manager is present. For a complete description of the Gestalt function, see the Compatibility Guidelines chapter of this volume.

For more detailed descriptions of the functions described in this section, see “Alias Manager Routines” later in this chapter.

Creating Alias Records

You create a new alias record by calling one of three functions: NewAlias, NewAliasMinimal, or NewAliasMinimalFromFullpath. The NewAlias function creates a complete alias record that can make full use of the alias-resolution algorithms. The other two functions are streamlined variations designed for circumstances when speed is more important than robust resolution services. All three functions allocate the memory for the record, fill it in, and provide a handle to it.

NewAlias always records the name and the file or directory ID of the target, its creation date, the parent directory name and ID, and the volume name and creation date. It also records the full pathname of the target and a collection of other information. You can request that NewAlias store relative path information as well by supplying a starting point for a relative path (see "About Alias Records" earlier in this chapter for a description of relative path).

Call NewAlias when you want to create an alias record to store for later use. For example, suppose you are writing a word-processing application that allows the user to customize a dictionary for use with a single text file. Your application stores the custom data in a separate dictionary file in the same directory as the document. As soon as you create the dictionary file, you call NewAlias to create an alias record for that file, including path information relative to the user's text file:

```
VAR
   textFile:    FSSpecPtr;
   target:      FSSpec;
   myAliasHdl: AliasHandle;
myErr := NewAlias(textFile, target, myAliasHdl);
```

The textFile parameter is a pointer to a file system specification record that identifies the starting point for the relative search, in this case the user's text file. If you do not want relative path information recorded, pass a value of NIL in the first parameter.

The target parameter is a file system specification record that identifies the target file, in this example the dictionary file.

The myAliasHdl parameter is a variable in which the Alias Manager returns the handle to the alias record that describes the target.

The two variations on the NewAlias function, NewAliasMinimal and NewAliasMinimalFromFullpath, record only a minimum of information about the target. NewAliasMinimal records only the target's name, parent directory ID, volume name and creation date, and volume mounting information. NewAliasMinimalFromFullpath records only the full pathname of the target, including the volume name.

Use NewAliasMinimal or NewAliasMinimalFromFullpath when you are willing to give up robust alias-resolution service in return for speed. The Finder, for example, stores minimal aliases in the Apple® events that tell your application to open or print a document. Because the alias record is resolved almost immediately, the description is likely to remain valid, and the shorter record is probably safe.

You can use NewAliasMinimalFromFullpath to create an alias record for a target that doesn't exist or that resides on an unmounted volume.

Resolving Alias Records

The Alias Manager provides two alias-resolution functions:

- the high-level function ResolveAlias, which performs a fast search and identifies only one target
- the low-level function MatchAlias, which can perform a fast search, an exhaustive search, or both, and which can return a list of target candidates

In general, when you want to identify only the single most likely target of an alias record, you call ResolveAlias. You call MatchAlias when you want your program to control the search.

This section describes the alias-resolution functions. The section "Search Strategies for Resolving Alias Records" earlier in this chapter describes the underlying fast and exhaustive searches.

ResolveAlias

Typically, you call the ResolveAlias function to resolve an alias record. ResolveAlias performs a fast search (described earlier in "Fast Search") and exits after it identifies one target.

By calling low-level functions, ResolveAlias compares some key information about the identified target with the information stored in the alias record. If any of the information is different, ResolveAlias automatically updates the record.

> **Note:** As with all other Alias Manager functions, ResolveAlias updates the record only in memory. Your application is responsible for updating alias records stored on disk when appropriate.

In the dictionary example illustrated in Figure 27-1 earlier in this chapter, the application calls ResolveAlias with a relative path specification when the user runs the spelling checker on a document with a customized dictionary.

```
myErr := ResolveAlias(textFile, myAliasHdl, target, wasChanged);
```

The textFile parameter is a pointer to a file system specification record that identifies the starting point for the relative search, in this case the user's text file. If you do not want relative path information used in the search, pass a value of NIL in the first parameter. If you provide a relative starting point, ResolveAlias performs the relative search first.

The myAliasHdl parameter is a handle to the alias record to be resolved. In this example, the alias record describes the dictionary file.

The target parameter is the file system specification record where the Alias Manager places the results of its search. After ResolveAlias completes, target contains the specification for the dictionary file.

The ResolveAlias function uses the wasChanged parameter to report whether it updated the alias record. After ResolveAlias completes, wasChanged is TRUE if the record was updated and FALSE if it was not. If you are storing the alias record, check the value of wasChanged (as well as the function's result code) to see whether to update the stored record after resolving an alias.

If ResolveAlias can't resolve the alias record, it returns a nonzero result code. A result code of fnfErr signals that ResolveAlias has found the correct volume and parent directory but not the target file or folder. In this case, ResolveAlias constructs a valid FSSpec record that describes the target. You can use this record to explore possible solutions to the resolution failure. You can, for example, use the FSSpec record to create a replacement for a missing file with the File Manager function FSpCreate.

MatchAlias

The MatchAlias function is a low-level routine that gives your application control over the searching algorithm.

You can control

- whether to attempt an automatic mounting of unmounted volumes
- whether to search on more than one volume
- whether to perform a fast search, an exhaustive search, or both
- the order of the direct and relative searches in a fast search
- whether to pursue search strategies that require interaction with the user (such as asking for a password while mounting an AppleShare volume)

You can also specify a maximum number of candidates that MatchAlias can identify.

See "Resolving and Reading Alias Records" later in this chapter for details about controlling a search with the MatchAlias function.

You can supply an optional filter function that MatchAlias calls

- each time it identifies a possible match
- when three seconds have elapsed without a match

The filter function determines whether each candidate is added to the list of possible targets. It can also terminate the search. See "Filtering Possible Targets" later in this chapter for a description of the filter function.

MatchAlias returns all candidates that it identifies in an array of file system specification records.

Maintaining Alias Records

You can store alias records as resources of type 'alis'.

```
CONST rAliasType = 'alis';     {resource type for saved alias records}
```

To store and retrieve resources, use the standard Resource Manager functions (AddResource, GetResource, and GetNamedResource) described in the Resource Manager chapter of Volume I.

To update an alias record, use the UpdateAlias function. You typically call UpdateAlias any time you know that the target of an alias record has been renamed or otherwise changed.

You are most likely to call UpdateAlias after a call to the MatchAlias function. If MatchAlias identifies a single target, it sets a flag telling you whether or not the key information about the target file matches the information in the alias record. It is the responsibility of your application to update the record.

The ResolveAlias function automatically updates an alias record if any of the the key information about the identified target does not match the information in the record.

Getting Information About Alias Records

To retrieve information from an alias record without actually resolving the record, call the GetAliasInfo function. You can use GetAliasInfo to retrieve the name of the target, the names of the target's parent directories, the name of the target's volume, or, in the case of an AppleShare volume, its zone or server name.

Customizing Alias Records

An alias record contains two kinds of information: public information available to your application and private information available only to the Alias Manager. Your application can use the first field, userType, to store its own signature or any other data that fits into 4 bytes. Your application can use the second field, aliasSize, to customize the alias record for storing additional data.

The Alias Manager stores the size of the record when it is created or updated in the aliasSize field. To customize an alias record, you first increase the size of the record with the SetHandleSize procedure, described in the Memory Manager chapter of Volume II. You can then find the starting address of your own data in the record by adding the record's starting address to the length recorded in the aliasSize field. If you expand the record through the Memory Manager, the Alias Manager preserves your data, even if it changes the size of its own data when updating the record.

In general, you should customize only alias records that you have created.

ALIAS MANAGER ROUTINES

This section describes the routines you use to create, update, resolve, and read alias records.

Alias Manager routines use file system specification records (FSSpec records) to identify files, directories, and volumes. To create an FSSpec record, call the function MakeFSSpec, described in the File Manager chapter of this volume.

The Alias Manager routines can return the result codes listed in this section or any other applicable file system or memory management result codes.

Creating and Updating Alias Records

You use the NewAlias function to create a complete alias record.

```
FUNCTION NewAlias (fromFile: FSSpecPtr; target: FSSpec;
                   VAR alias: AliasHandle) : OSErr;
```

NewAlias creates an alias record that describes the specified target. It allocates the storage, fills in the record, and puts a record handle in the alias parameter. NewAlias always records the name and file or directory ID of the target, its creation date, the parent directory name and ID, and the volume name and creation date. It also records the full pathname of the target and a collection of other information relevant to locating the target, verifying the target, and mounting the target's volume, if necessary. You can request that it store relative path information as well by supplying a starting point for a relative path (see "About Alias Records" earlier in this chapter for a description of relative path).

The fromFile parameter represents the starting point for a relative path, to be used later in a relative search. If you do not need relative path information in the record, pass a fromFile value of NIL. If you want NewAlias to record relative path information, pass a pointer to a valid FSSpec record in this parameter. The two files or directories, fromFile and target, must reside on the same volume.

The target parameter is an FSSpec record for the target of the alias record.

NewAlias puts a handle to the newly created alias record in the alias parameter. If the function fails to create an alias record, it sets alias to NIL.

Result code

noErr	0	No error

You use the NewAliasMinimal function to create a short alias record quickly.

```
FUNCTION NewAliasMinimal (target: FSSpec; VAR alias: AliasHandle) :
                          OSErr;
```

NewAliasMinimal creates an alias record that contains only the minimum information necessary to describe the target: the target name, the parent directory ID, the volume name and creation date, and the volume mounting information. NewAliasMinimal uses the standard alias record data structure, but fills in only parts of the record.

The target parameter points to an FSSpec record for the target of the alias record.

NewAliasMinimal puts a handle to the newly created alias record in the alias parameter. If the function fails to create an alias record, it sets alias to NIL.

The ResolveAlias function, described in "Resolving and Reading Alias Records" later in this chapter, never updates a minimal alias record.

Result code

noErr	0	No error

You use the function NewAliasMinimalFromFullpath to quickly create an alias record that contains only the full pathname of the target.

```
FUNCTION NewAliasMinimalFromFullpath (fullpathLength: Integer;
                                      fullpath: Ptr; zoneName: Str32;
                                      serverName: Str31;
                                      VAR alias: AliasHandle) : OSErr;
```

NewAliasMinimalFromFullpath creates an alias record that identifies the target by full pathname. You can call NewAliasMinimalFromFullpath to create an alias record for a file that doesn't exist or that resides on an unmounted volume. NewAliasMinimalFromFullpath uses the standard alias record data structure, but it fills in only the information provided in the input parameters. You can therefore use NewAliasMinimalFromFullpath to create alias records for targets on unmounted volumes.

The fullpathLength parameter identifies the number of characters in the full pathname.

The fullpath parameter is a pointer to a buffer that contains the full pathname of the target. The full pathname starts with the name of the volume, includes all of the directory names in the path to the target, and ends with the target name. (For a description of pathnames, see the File Manager chapter in this volume.)

The parameters zoneName and serverName are strings that identify the AppleTalk® zone and server name of the AppleShare volume on which the target resides. Set these parameters to null strings if you do not need them.

NewAliasMinimalFromFullpath puts a handle to the newly created alias record in the alias parameter. If the function fails to create an alias record, it sets alias to NIL.

Result code

noErr	0	No error

You use the UpdateAlias function to update an alias record.

```
FUNCTION UpdateAlias (fromFile: FSSpecPtr; target: FSSpec;
                      alias: AliasHandle; VAR wasChanged: Boolean) :
                      OSErr;
```

UpdateAlias updates the alias record pointed to by the alias parameter so that it describes the target specified by the target parameter. UpdateAlias rebuilds the entire alias record, and fills it in as the NewAlias function would.

The fromFile parameter represents the starting point for a relative path, to be used later in a relative search. If you do not need relative path information in the record, pass a fromFile value of NIL. If you want UpdateAlias to record relative path information, pass a pointer to a valid FSSpec record in this parameter. The two files or directories, fromFile and target, must reside on the same volume.

The target parameter is the target of the alias record. This parameter must be a valid FSSpec record.

The alias parameter is a handle to the alias record to be updated.

If the newly constructed alias record is exactly the same as the old one, UpdateAlias sets the wasChanged parameter to FALSE. Otherwise, it sets it to TRUE. Check this parameter to determine whether you need to save an updated record.

UpdateAlias always creates a complete alias record. When you update a minimal alias record with UpdateAlias, you convert the minimal record to a complete record.

Result codes

noErr	0	No error
paramErr	–50	Target, alias, or both are NIL, or the alias record is corrupt

Resolving and Reading Alias Records

You use the ResolveAlias function to identify the single most likely target of an alias record.

```
FUNCTION ResolveAlias (fromFile: FSSpecPtr; alias: AliasHandle;
                       VAR target: FSSpec; VAR wasChanged: Boolean) :
                       OSErr;
```

ResolveAlias performs a fast search for the target of the alias, as described earlier in "Fast Search." If the resolution is successful, ResolveAlias returns the FSSpec record for the target file system object through the target parameter, updates the alias record if necessary, and reports whether the record was updated through the wasChanged parameter. If the target is on an unmounted AppleShare volume, ResolveAlias automatically mounts the volume. If the target is on an unmounted ejectable volume, ResolveAlias asks the user to insert the volume. ResolveAlias exits after it finds one acceptable target.

The fromFile parameter represents the starting point for a relative search. If you pass a fromFile parameter of NIL, ResolveAlias performs only a direct search. If you pass a pointer to a valid FSSpec record in the fromFile parameter, ResolveAlias performs a relative search for the target, followed by a direct search only if the relative search fails. If you want to perform a direct search followed by a relative search, you must use the MatchAlias function.

The alias parameter is a handle to the alias record to be resolved and, if necessary, updated.

The target parameter receives the FSSpec record of the target file system object.

After it identifies a target, ResolveAlias compares some key information about the target with the information in the alias record. (The description of the MatchAlias function that follows lists the key information.) If the information differs, ResolveAlias updates the record to match the target. If it updates the alias record, ResolveAlias sets the wasChanged parameter to TRUE. Otherwise, it sets it to FALSE. (Because ResolveAlias never updates a minimal alias, it never sets wasChanged to TRUE when resolving a minimal alias.)

When it finds the specified volume and parent directory but fails to find the target file or directory in that location, ResolveAlias returns a result code of fnfErr and fills in the target parameter with a complete FSSpec record describing the target (that is, the volume reference number, parent directory ID, and filename or folder name). The FSSpec record is valid, although the object it describes does not exist. This information is intended as a "hint" that lets you explore possible solutions to the resolution failure. You can, for example, use the FSSpec record to create a replacement for a missing file with the File Manager function FSpCreate.

ResolveAlias displays the standard dialog boxes when it needs input from the user, such as a name and password for mounting a remote volume. The user can cancel the resolution through these dialog boxes.

Result codes

noErr	0	No error
nsvErr	–35	The volume is not mounted
fnfErr	–43	Target not found, but volume and parent directory found; if aliasCount is 1, target parameter contains a valid FSSpec record
paramErr	–50	Target, alias, or both are NIL, or the alias record is corrupt
dirNFErr	–120	Parent directory not found
usrCanceledErr	–128	The user canceled the operation

You use the MatchAlias function to identify a list of possible matches and pass the list through an optional selection filter. The filter can pass more than one possible match.

```
FUNCTION MatchAlias (fromFile: FSSpecPtr; rulesMask: LongInt;
                     alias: AliasHandle; VAR aliasCount: Integer;
                     aliasList: FSSpecArrayPtr; VAR needsUpdate: Boolean;
                     aliasFilter: AliasFilterProcPtr; yourDataPtr: UNIV
                     Ptr) : OSErr;
```

MatchAlias resolves the alias record specified by the alias parameter, following the rules specified by the rulesMask parameter, and returns a list of possible candidates in the structure specified by the aliasList parameter. MatchAlias places the number of candidates identified in the aliasCount parameter.

The fromFile parameter represents the starting point for a relative search. If you do not want MatchAlias to perform a relative search, set fromFile to NIL. If you want MatchAlias to perform a relative search, pass a pointer to a file system specification record that describes the starting point for the search.

The rulesMask parameter specifies a set of rules to guide the resolution. Pass the sum of all of the rules you want to invoke.

Constant	**Description**
kARMSearch	Perform a fast search for the alias target. If kARMSearchRelFirst is not set, perform a direct search first, followed by a relative search only if the fromFile parameter is not NIL and the list of matches is not full.

Constant	**Description**
kARMSearchMore	Perform an exhaustive search for the alias target. On HFS volumes, the exhaustive search uses the File Manager function PBCatSearch to identify candidates with matching creation date, type, and creator. PBCatSearch is available only on HFS volumes and only on systems running version 7.0 or later. On MFS volumes or HFS volumes that do not support PBCatSearch the exhaustive search makes a series of indexed calls to File Manager functions, using the same search criteria. If you set kARMSearchMore and one or both of kARMSearch and kARMSearchRelFirst, MatchAlias performs the fast search first.
kARMSearchRelFirst	If kARMSearch is also set, perform a relative search before the direct search. (If kARMSearch is also set and the target is found through the direct search, MatchAlias sets the needsUpdate flag to TRUE.) If neither kARMSearch nor kARMSearchMore is set, perform only a relative search. If kARMSearch is not set but kARMSearchMore is set, perform a relative search followed by an exhaustive search.
kARMMountVol	Automatically try to mount the target's volume if it is not mounted.
kARMMultVols	Search all mounted volumes. The search begins with the volume on which the target resided when the record was created. When you specify a fast search of all mounted volumes, MatchAlias performs a formal fast search only on the volume described in the alias record. On all other volumes, it looks for the target by ID or by name in the directory with the specified parent directory ID. When you specify an exhaustive search of multiple volumes, MatchAlias performs the same search on all volumes. When resolving an alias record created by NewAliasMinimalFromFullpath, MatchAlias ignores this flag.
kARMNoUI	Stop if a search requires user interaction, such as a password dialog box when mounting a remote volume. If user interaction is needed and kARMNoUI is in effect, the search fails.

You must specify at least one of the first three parameters: kARMSearch, kARMSearchMore, and kARMSearchRelFirst.

The alias parameter is a handle to the alias record to be resolved.

Your application can specify a maximum number of possible matches by setting the aliasCount parameter. MatchAlias changes the aliasCount parameter to the actual number of candidates identified. If MatchAlias finds the parent directory on the correct volume but does not find the target, it sets the aliasCount parameter to 1, puts the file system specification record for the target in the results list, and returns fnfErr. The FSSpec record is valid, although the object it describes does not exist. This information is intended as a "hint" that lets you explore possible solutions to the resolution failure. You can, for example, use the FSSpec record to create a replacement for a missing file with the File Manager function FSpCreate.

The aliasList parameter points to the array that holds the results of the search.

The needsUpdate flag is a signal to your application that the record might need to be updated. After it identifies a target, MatchAlias compares some key information about the target with the same information in the record. If the information does not match, MatchAlias sets the needsUpdate flag to TRUE. The key information is

- the name of the target
- the directory ID of the target's parent
- the file ID or directory ID of the target
- the name and creation date of the volume on which the target resides

MatchAlias also sets the needsUpdate flag to TRUE if it identifies a list of possible matches rather than a single match or if kARMsearchRelFirst is set but the target is identified through either a direct search or an exhaustive search. Otherwise, MatchAlias sets the needsUpdate flag to FALSE. MatchAlias always sets the needsUpdate flag to FALSE when resolving an alias created by NewAliasMinimal. If you want to update the alias record to reflect the final results of the resolution, call UpdateAlias.

The aliasFilter parameter points to a filter function supplied by your application. The Alias Manager executes this function each time it identifies a possible match and after the search has continued for three seconds without a match. Your filter function returns a Boolean value that determines whether the possible match is discarded (TRUE) or added to the list of possible targets (FALSE). It can also terminate the search by setting the variable parameter quitFlag. See "Filtering Possible Targets" later in the chapter for a description of the filter function, which follows this syntax:

```
FUNCTION MyMatchAliasFilter (cpbPtr: CInfoPBPtr;
                             VAR quitFlag: Boolean;
                             myDataPtr: Ptr) : Boolean;
```

The yourDataPtr parameter can point to any data that your application might need in the filter function. Use the myDataPtr parameter to pass global or local data to your filter function.

Result codes

noErr	0	No error
nsvErr	–35	The volume is not mounted
fnfErr	–43	Target not found, but volume and parent directory found; if aliasCount is 1, target parameter contains a valid FSSpec record
paramErr	–50	Target, alias, or both are NIL, or the alias record is corrupt
usrCanceledErr	–128	The user canceled the operation

You use the GetAliasInfo function to get information from an alias record without actually resolving the record.

```
FUNCTION GetAliasInfo (alias: AliasHandle; index: AliasInfoType;
                        VAR theString: Str63) : OSErr;
```

GetAliasInfo retrieves the information specified by the index parameter from the record pointed to by the alias parameter and places it in the parameter theString.

The alias parameter is a handle to the alias record to be read.

The index parameter specifies the kind of information to be retrieved. If index is a positive integer, GetAliasInfo retrieves the parent directory that has the same hierarchical level above the target as the index parameter (for example, an index value of 2 returns the name of the parent directory of the target's parent directory). You can therefore assemble the names of the target and all of its parent directories by making repeated calls to GetAliasInfo with incrementing index values, starting with a value of 0. When index is greater than the number of levels between the target and the root, GetAliasInfo returns an empty string. You can also set the index parameter to one of the following five values.

Constant	Value	Description
asiZoneName	–3	If the record represents a target on an AppleShare volume, retrieve the server's zone name. Otherwise, return an empty string.
asiServerName	–2	If the record represents a target on an AppleShare volume, retrieve the server name. Otherwise, return an empty string.
asiVolumeName	–1	Return the name of the volume on which the target resides.
asiAliasName	0	Return the name of the target.
asiParentName	1	Return the name of the parent directory of the target of the record. If the target is a volume, return the volume name.

GetAliasInfo places the requested information in the parameter theString.

GetAliasInfo returns the information stored in the alias record, which might not be current. To ensure that the information is current, you can resolve and update the alias record before calling GetAliasInfo.

GetAliasInfo cannot provide all kinds of information on a minimal alias.

Result codes

noErr	0	No error
paramErr	–50	Alias, theString, or both are NIL; the index is less than asiZoneName; or the alias record is corrupt

Filtering Possible Targets

You can write your own filter function to examine possible targets identified by the MatchAlias function. MatchAlias calls your filter function each time it identifies a possible match and when three seconds have elapsed without a match.

The filter function takes three parameters and returns a Boolean value:

```
FUNCTION MyMatchAliasFilter (cpbPtr: CInfoPBPtr; VAR quitFlag: Boolean;
                             myDataPtr: Ptr) : Boolean;
```

The cpbPtr parameter points to the catalog information parameter block record (as returned by the File Manager function PBGetCatInfo) of the possible match. MatchAlias sets this parameter to NIL if it is calling your function to give it the periodic chance to terminate the search. (Do not use this pointer without checking for NIL.)

Your filter function sets the quitFlag parameter to terminate the search.

The myDataPtr parameter points to any customized data that your application passed when it called MatchAlias. This parameter allows your filter function to access any data that your application has set up on its own.

The Boolean return value determines whether the possible match is discarded (TRUE) or added to the list of possible targets (FALSE).

SUMMARY OF THE ALIAS MANAGER

Constants

```
CONST gestaltAliasMgrAttr    = 'alis';
      gestaltAliasMgrPresent = 0;

      rAliasType           = 'alis';      {alias record resource type}

      {rulesMask for MatchAlias}
      kARMMountVol         = $00000001;  {mount the volume automatically}
      kARMNoUI             = $00000002;  {suppress user interface}
      kARMMultVols         = $00000008;  {search on multiple volumes}
      kARMSearch           = $00000100;  {perform a fast search}
      kARMSearchMore       = $00000200;  {perform an exhaustive search}
      kARMSearchRelFirst   = $00000400;  {perform a relative search first}

      {index values for GetAliasInfo}
      asiZoneName          = -3;          {get zone name}
      asiServerName        = -2;          {get server name}
      asiVolumeName        = -1;          {get volume name}
      asiAliasName         =  0;          {get target name}
      asiParentName        =  1;          {get parent directory name}
```

Data Types

```
TYPE AliasHandle     =          ^AliasPtr;
     AliasPtr        =          ^AliasRecord;

     AliasRecord     =
     RECORD
        userType:   OSType;     {application's signature}
        aliasSize:  Integer     {size of record when created}
        {variable-length private data}
     END;

     AliasInfoType        =    Integer;  {alias record information type}

     AliasFilterProcPtr   =    ProcPtr;  {application-defined routine; }
                                         { see sample }
                                         { FUNCTION MyMatchAliasFilter}
```

Routines

Creating and Updating Alias Records

```
FUNCTION NewAlias                          (fromFile: FSSpecPtr; target: FSSpec;
                                            VAR alias: AliasHandle) : OSErr;

FUNCTION NewAliasMinimal                   (target: FSSpec;
                                            VAR alias: AliasHandle) : OSErr;

FUNCTION NewAliasMinimalFromFullpath       (fullpathLength: Integer;
                                            fullpath: Ptr; zoneName: Str32;
                                            serverName: Str31;
                                            VAR alias: AliasHandle) : OSErr;

FUNCTION UpdateAlias                       (fromFile: FSSpecPtr; target: FSSpec;
                                            alias: AliasHandle;
                                            VAR wasChanged: Boolean) : OSErr;
```

Resolving and Reading Alias Records

```
FUNCTION ResolveAlias        (fromFile: FSSpecPtr; alias: AliasHandle;
                              VAR target: FSSpec;
                              VAR wasChanged: Boolean) : OSErr;

FUNCTION MatchAlias          (fromFile: FSSpecPtr; rulesMask: LongInt;
                              alias: AliasHandle; VAR aliasCount: Integer;
                              aliasList: FSSpecArrayPtr;
                              VAR needsUpdate: Boolean; aliasFilter:
                              AliasFilterProcPtr; yourDataPtr: UNIV Ptr) :
                              OSErr;

FUNCTION GetAliasInfo        (alias: AliasHandle; index: AliasInfoType;
                              VAR theString: Str63) : OSErr;
```

Application-Defined Routine

```
FUNCTION MyMatchAliasFilter (cpbPtr: CInfoPBPtr; VAR quitFlag: Boolean;
                             myDataPtr: Ptr) : Boolean;
```

Result Codes

nsvErr	–35	The volume is not mounted
fnfErr	–43	Target not found, but volume and parent directory found; if aliasCount is 1, target parameter contains a valid FSSpec record
paramErr	–50	Target, alias, or both are NIL, or the alias record is corrupt
dirNFErr	–120	Parent directory not found
usrCanceledErr	–128	The user canceled the operation

Assembly-Language Information

Alias Record Data Structure

userType	4 bytes	file type of target file
aliasSize	2 bytes	size of record in bytes

{variable-length private data}

28 MEMORY MANAGEMENT

ABOUT THIS CHAPTER

This chapter describes several new features of memory management on Macintosh® computers introduced in system software version 7.0, including changes to the Memory Manager—the part of the Operating System that controls the dynamic allocation of space in the application heap and the system heap. Two important additions to memory management in version 7.0 are support for 32-bit addressing and virtual memory. This chapter also describes changes to the temporary memory routines that were already available under MultiFinder® starting with system software version 6.0.

The information in this chapter supplements the chapters on the Memory Manager found in *Inside Macintosh*, Volumes I, II, and IV, and it supersedes the discussion of temporary memory routines contained in Chapter 3 of the *Programmer's Guide to MultiFinder*. To use this chapter, you should already be familiar with the material presented in those chapters of *Inside Macintosh.*

The changes and additions to memory management on Macintosh computers described here are available only in system software version 7.0. Support for 32-bit addressing is available only on machines with 32-bit clean ROMs (for example, the Macintosh IIci and the Macintosh IIfx). You can use the Gestalt function documented in the Compatibility Guidelines chapter of this volume to determine whether a machine was started up with 32-bit addressing and whether the enhanced temporary memory routines are available. Virtual memory is available only on machines equipped with a memory management unit (MMU). Currently, these machines include 68030-based machines (where the MMU is built into the CPU) as well as 68020-based machines that contain the 68851 Paged Memory Management Unit (PMMU). You can use the Gestalt function to determine whether virtual memory is installed. Most applications, however, do not need to know whether virtual memory is installed.

You need to read this chapter if your application

- uses any of the temporary memory routines available under MultiFinder in system software version 6.0 and built into the Operating System in version 7.0
- has critical timing requirements, executes code at interrupt time, or performs debugging operations, any of which might be affected by the presence of virtual memory
- is not 32-bit clean (that is, does not operate correctly in an environment that uses the full 32 bits of a pointer or handle for memory addresses)
- uses customized window definitions (resources of type 'WDEF') or customized control definitions (resources of type 'CDEF')
- uses the StripAddress function documented in the Operating System Utilities chapter of Volume V
- installs routines (such as Time Manager tasks, VBL tasks, Notification Manager tasks, I/O completion routines, and so forth) that execute at interrupt time or at times when your application is not the active application

This chapter begins with an overview of memory management on Macintosh computers and explains the connections between cooperative multitasking, the Memory Manager, virtual memory, and your application's use of its own private memory. This overview also describes how the user controls various aspects of memory management through the Memory control panel. The subsequent sections provide greater detail about 32-bit addressing, virtual memory, and temporary memory.

ABOUT MEMORY MANAGEMENT

The Macintosh Operating System manages the loading of applications, desk accessories, resources, and other code into and out of memory. Prior to the introduction of MultiFinder in system software version 5.0, only one application could execute at a time. As a result, the organization of the available physical memory was relatively simple, as shown below in Figure 28-1. The available RAM was divided into two broad zones, a system zone and an application zone. The system zone, which resides at the bottom of memory, contains room for system global variables and a system heap. The system global variables maintain information about the operation of the Operating System itself (for example, the amount of time elapsed since the system was started up). The system heap contains the executable code for the Operating System, as well as some of the data structures used by the system software.

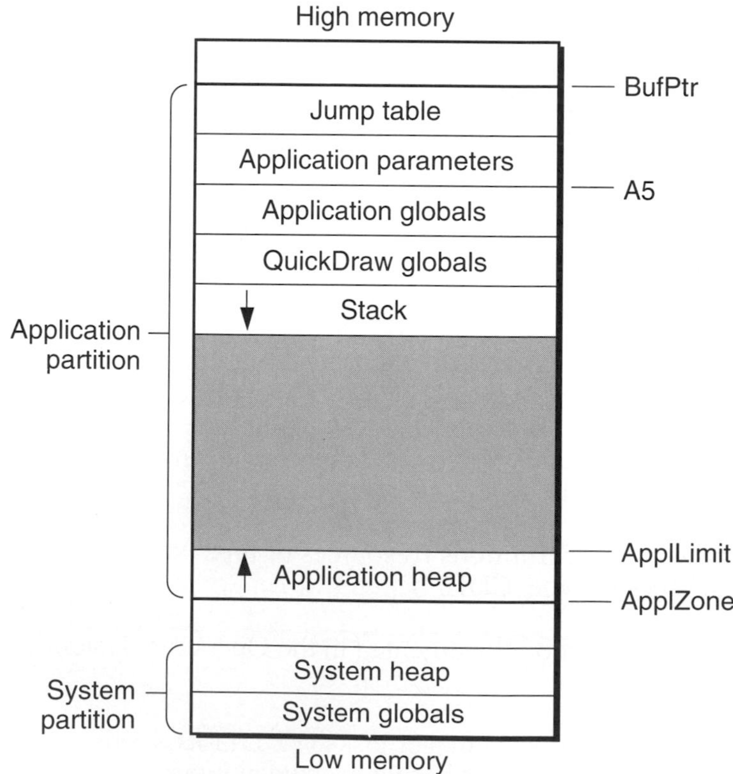

Figure 28-1. The memory organization in a single-application environment

When your application is launched, it is allocated a partition or heap of memory called the *application partition*. That partition must contain required segments of the application code as well as any other data associated with the application. You allocate space within your application's partition by making calls to the Memory Manager, either directly (for instance, using the NewHandle function) or indirectly (for instance, using a routine like NewWindow that calls Memory Manager routines). The Memory Manager controls the dynamic allocation of space in your application's heap.

The application partition is divided into three main parts: an application heap (which holds the executable code of the application and perhaps some of the application's resources), a stack, and a set of parameters and global variables that are private to the application. This set includes the application's QuickDraw™ global variables, the application's own global variables and parameters, and a jump table. The divisions of the application partition are illustrated in Figure 28-2.

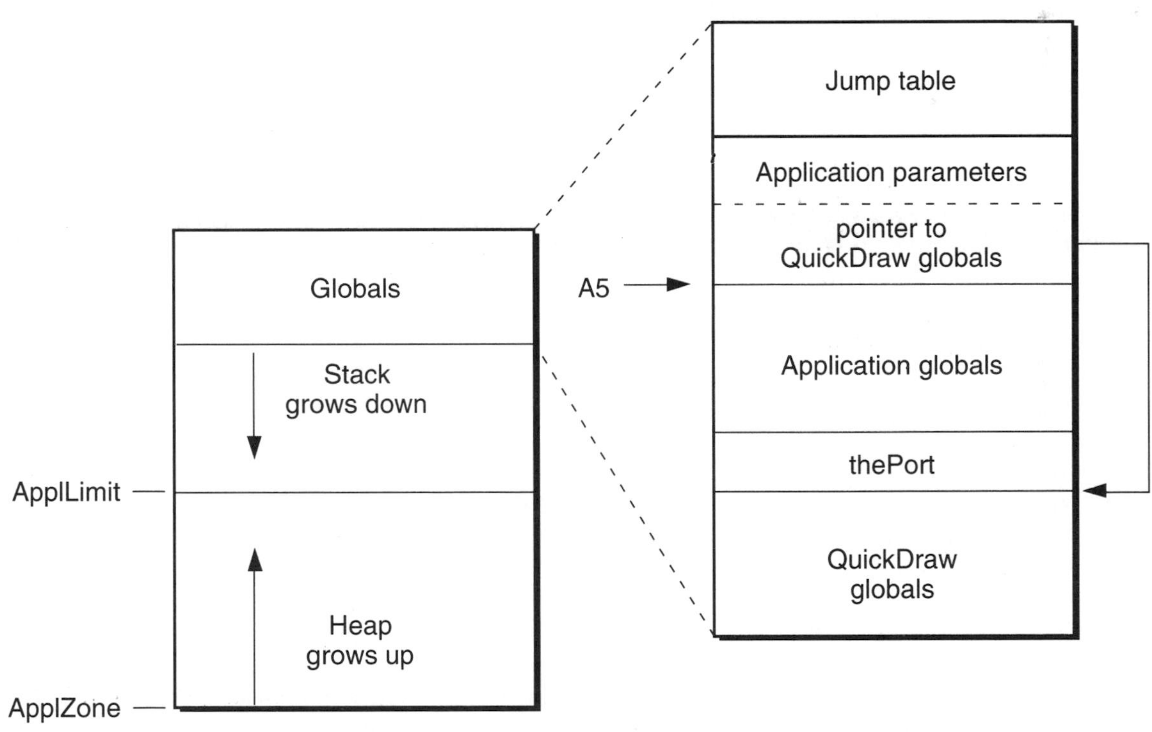

Figure 28-2. The organization of the application partition

The Operating System keeps track of information in the application partition by storing various addresses in system global variables. For instance, the beginning of the application heap is stored in the global variable ApplZone. Similarly, the system global variable CurrentA5 points to the application parameters, the first long word of which is a pointer to the application's QuickDraw global variables.

Note that CurrentA5 points to a boundary between the application's parameters and its global variables, so the application's own global variables are found as negative offsets from the value of CurrentA5. This particular boundary is important because the Operating System uses it as a way of accessing your application's QuickDraw globals and application globals as well as the application parameters and the jump table, both of which are fixed distances from that boundary. This information is known collectively as the **A5 world** because the Operating System uses the microprocessor's A5 register to point to that boundary.

> **Note:** An application's global variables may appear either above or below the QuickDraw global variables because the relative locations of these items are linker-dependent.

Dividing Memory Among Multiple Applications

In system software version 7.0 (or when running MultiFinder in system software versions 5.0 and 6.0), the user can have multiple applications open at once. The Operating System organizes the available memory in a slightly different manner, as shown in Figure 28-3. Here two applications are open, sharing the available memory.

When multiple applications are open, there are multiple application partitions, each with its own copy of QuickDraw global variables, application global variables, and so forth. Each application allocates and frees space within its own application zone by using Memory Manager routines. Even though multiple applications are open, only one application at a time can have control of the CPU. When your application is brought into the foreground or when it receives processing time in the background, the Operating System ensures that certain low-memory global variables have appropriate values and that the A5 register contains the address of the boundary between your application's parameters and global variables.

It sometimes happens, however, that your routines execute at times when the low-memory global variables and the A5 register are not set up for your application. For instance, the application in partition 2 (in Figure 28-3) might have installed a Time Manager task to run periodically. That task can execute even though that application is not in control of the processor because the Time Manager task executes at interrupt time. Problems may occur if that task tries to access any information in its A5 world, for register A5 might not be pointing to its A5 world when the task is called. Accessing this information includes reading or writing the values of the application's global variables and QuickDraw global variables, as well as calling subroutines that are in different segments (because different segments are accessed through the jump table, which is part of the A5 world).

In a task or completion routine that may run even when the application that created it is not the active process, you need to save and restore the value of the A5 register whenever you access information in the application's A5 world. These tasks include all routines that execute at interrupt time, such as Time Manager tasks, VBL tasks, Sound Manager completion routines, I/O completion routines, device drivers, and so forth. You can use the two functions SetCurrentA5 and SetA5 to save and restore the value of the A5 register. See "Setting and Restoring the A5 Register" later in this chapter for a detailed discussion of these functions.

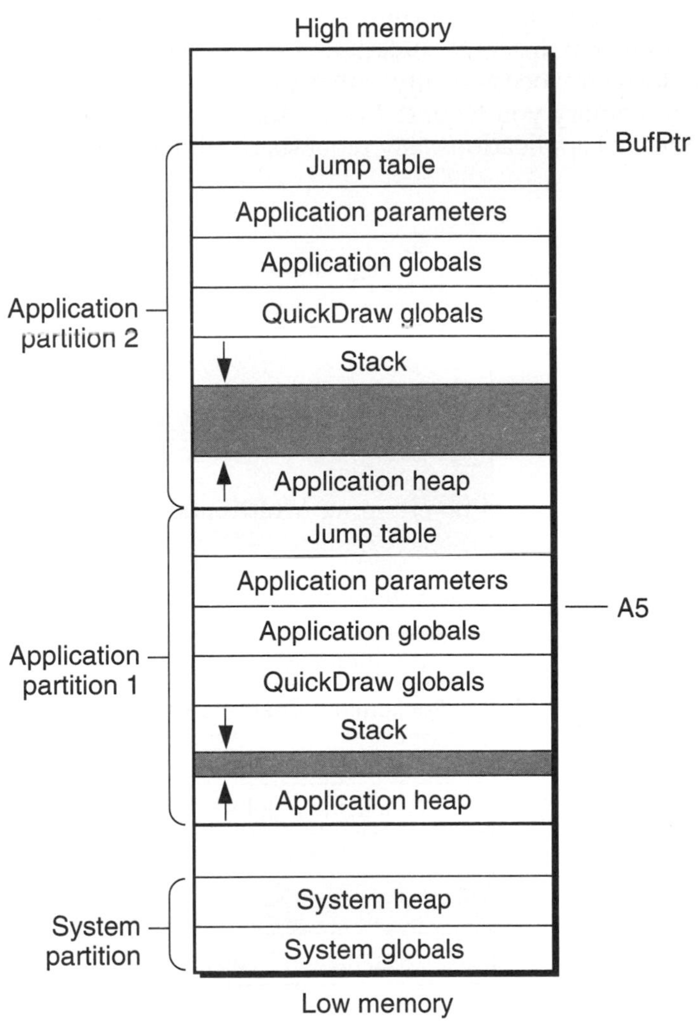

Figure 28-3. The memory organization in a multiple application environment

Extending an Application's Available Memory

In the Macintosh multitasking environment, each application is limited to a particular memory partition (the size of which is determined by information in the 'SIZE' resource of that application). The size of your application's memory partition places certain limits on how big your application heap can become and hence on how large the buffers and other data structures that your application uses can be. If for some purpose you need more memory than is currently available in your application heap, you can ask the Operating System to let you use any available memory that is not yet allocated to any other application. This memory is known as **temporary memory** and is allocated from the available unused RAM; in general, that memory is not contiguous with the memory in the requesting application's zone. Figure 28-4 shows an application using some temporary memory.

Your application should use temporary memory only for occasional short-term purposes that could be accomplished in less space, though perhaps less efficiently. One good reason for using temporary memory only occasionally is that you cannot assume that you will always receive the temporary memory you request. For example, in Figure 28-3, all the available memory is used by the two applications; any requests by either one for some temporary memory would fail.

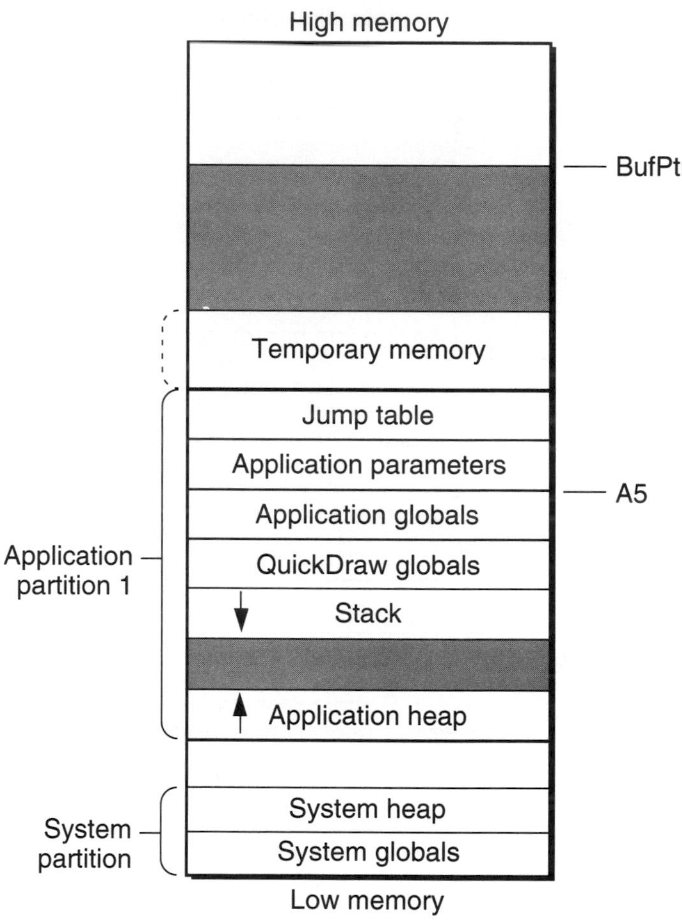

Figure 28-4. Using temporary memory

Note that temporary memory is provided by the Operating System and not by the Memory Manager (because the Memory Manager can allocate space only within your application heap or the system heap). In system software version 7.0, however, you can free temporary memory by using normal Memory Manager routines. In system software version 6.0, you need to use special operating-system routines to allocate temporary memory. There are also special routines to lock, unlock, and free temporary memory.

Extending the Operating System's Available Memory

In system software version 7.0, suitably equipped Macintosh computers can take advantage of an operating-system feature known as **virtual memory,** by which the machines have a logical address space that extends beyond the limits of the available physical memory. This means that a user can load more programs and data into the logical address space than if limited to the actual physical RAM installed in the machine. The Operating System extends the address space by using part of the available secondary storage (that is, part of a hard disk) to hold portions of programs and data that are not currently needed in RAM. When some of those portions of memory are needed, the Operating System swaps other parts of programs or data that are not needed out to the secondary storage, thereby making room for the parts that are needed.

It is important to realize that virtual memory operates transparently to most applications. You allocate and release memory in your application heap exactly as you always have, by calling Memory Manager routines. You can also request temporary memory by using special Operating System routines. But unless your application has time-critical needs that might be adversely affected by the operation of virtual memory, you do not need to know whether virtual memory is operating.

Controlling the System Memory Settings

A user can alter several of the system memory configuration settings by changing controls in the Memory control panel. This panel contains controls governing the operation of the disk cache, virtual memory, and the addressing used by the Memory Manager. Figure 28-5 shows the Memory control panel.

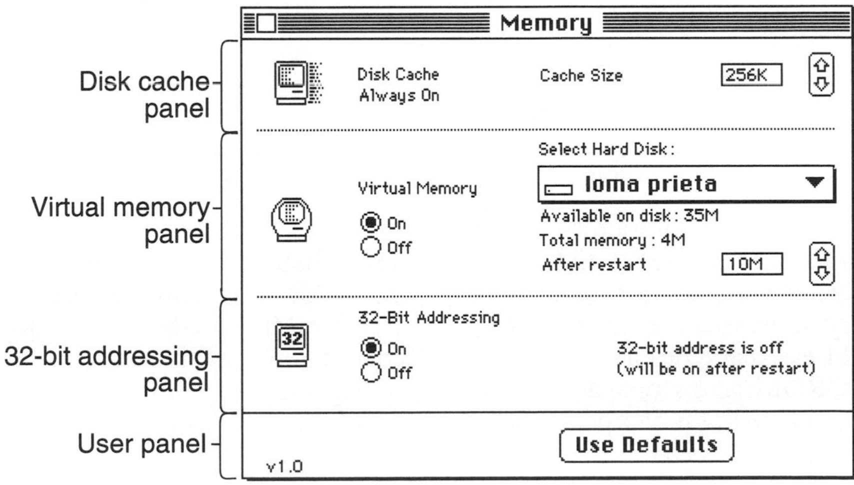

Figure 28-5. The Memory control panel

The Disk Cache panel is a replacement for the HFS RAM Cache panel found in earlier system software versions in the General control panel. The controls allow the user to configure the size of the disk cache used by the Operating System during file access operations. In system software version 7.0, unlike earlier versions, the user cannot turn off disk caching.

A **disk cache** is a part of RAM that acts as an intermediate buffer when data is read from and written to file systems on secondary storage devices. Data is saved there in case it is needed again in the very near future. If it is, then the Operating System reads the data from the disk cache and not from the secondary storage device (which would take considerably longer). By increasing the cache size, the user can increase the likelihood that data recently read from or written to the file system is still in the cache. The minimum cache size is 32 KB. The default size is 32 KB per megabyte of installed RAM (so a machine with 4 MB of RAM would have a default disk cache size of 128 KB). The maximum disk cache size is 128 KB per megabyte of installed RAM (so a machine with 4 MB of RAM would have a maximum disk cache size of 512 KB).

The Virtual Memory controls allow a user to set various features of virtual memory, including whether virtual memory is turned on and, if so, how much virtual memory is available. The user can also specify the volume of the **backing-store file,** the file used by the Operating System to store unused portions of code and data. The user must restart the machine for any changes to the virtual memory configuration to take effect. Note that the Virtual Memory panel appears only on machines capable of supporting virtual memory.

The 32-Bit Addressing controls determine the size of the address space to use in the machine. The size of the address space is determined by the number of bits used to store memory addresses, as explained in the next section. The 32-Bit Addressing panel appears only on machines capable of running with 32-bit addressing. The user can use these controls to turn 32-bit addressing off and on. Any changes made to the addressing will not take place until the machine is restarted.

ABOUT THE MEMORY MANAGER

On suitably equipped Macintosh computers, system software version 7.0 supports **32-bit addressing,** that is, the ability to use all 32 bits of a pointer or handle in determining memory addresses. Earlier versions of system software use 24-bit addressing, where the upper 8 bits of memory addresses are ignored or used as flag bits. In a 24-bit addressing scheme, the logical address space has a size of 16 MB. Because 8 MB of this total are reserved for I/O space, ROM, and slot space, the largest contiguous program address space is 8 MB. When 32-bit addressing is in operation in system software version 7.0, the maximum program address space is 1 GB.

The ability to operate with 32-bit addressing is available only on certain models of the Macintosh, namely those with ROMs that contain a 32-bit Memory Manager. (For compatibility reasons, these ROMs also contain a 24-bit Memory Manager.) In order for your application to work when the machine is using 32-bit addressing, it must be **32-bit clean,** that is, able to run in an environment where all 32 bits of a memory address are significant. Fortunately, writing applications that are 32-bit clean is relatively easy if you follow the guidelines given in *Inside Macintosh.* The major reason that some applications are not 32-bit clean is that their developers have violated warnings not to manipulate data structures directly. In particular, the single most common reason that some applications are not 32-bit clean is that they manipulate bits in master pointers directly (for instance, to mark the associated memory blocks as locked or purgeable) instead of using Memory Manager routines that achieve the desired result.

> ▲ **Warning:** You should never make assumptions about the contents of Memory Manager data structures, including master pointers and zone headers. These structures have changed in the past and they are likely to change again in the future. ▲

The following four sections provide more explanation of how to make sure that your application is 32-bit clean, with detailed discussion of several additional issues, including customized window and control definition functions, and the StripAddress trap.

Using Master Pointers

The Memory Manager on the original Macintosh computers used a 24-bit addressing system. To the underlying hardware, only the lower 24 bits of a 32-bit address were significant. The upper 8 bits were always ignored in an address reference, a circumstance that led both system software developers and third-party software developers to put those 8 bits to some other use. For example, the Memory Manager itself took advantage of the upper 8 bits of an address in a master pointer to maintain information about heap blocks. (Master pointers are pointers to blocks of memory in the heap.) In the original Macintosh computers, the master pointers had a structure illustrated in Figure 28-6.

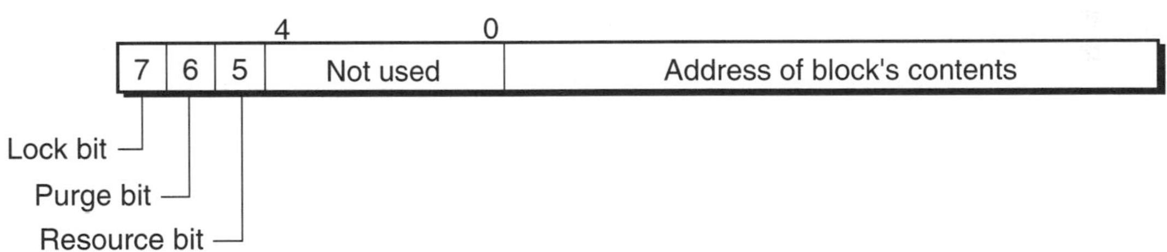

Figure 28-6. A master pointer structure in the 24-bit Memory Manager

Both A/UX® and system software version 7.0 support 32-bit addressing, where all 32 bits of a memory address are significant. In this case, the flag bits in a master pointer must be stored elsewhere. Applications do not need to know where or how those flags are now stored if they use routines provided by the Memory Manager for setting and clearing those flags. (For example, to set or clear the Lock flag, you should use the procedures HLock and HUnlock.) If your application bypasses these routines and takes advantage of knowledge about the structure of master pointers to set and clear the flag bits directly, then it will not execute correctly in an environment where all 32 bits of the master pointer are significant. On such systems, setting or clearing the upper 3 bits of a master pointer directly does not change the flags but changes the address itself.

> **Note:** The issue of being 32-bit clean is not limited to direct manipulation of a master pointer's flag bits. Rather, *every* memory address must contain a full 32 bits. If, under systems using 24-bit addressing, you have used any of the upper 8 bits of pointers or handles for anything other than part of an address, then you must find an alternate representation for that information.

Using Window and Control Definition Functions

Two other times that you need to avoid 32-bit address violations are when using customized window definition functions (stored in resources of type 'WDEF') and when using customized control definition functions (stored in resources of type 'CDEF'). In earlier versions of system software, the Window Manager stored the window variant code number (which defines how the window looks) in the upper 8 bits of the handle to the window definition procedure. Under version 7.0, this is no longer true. As a result, if you need to retrieve the window variant code, use the GetWVariant function.

Similarly, the Control Manager used to store a variant code in the high bits of the control definition procedure handle. This also has changed under system software version 7.0, so you should use the GetCVariant function to retrieve the variant control value for a control.

A further problem arises if you define your own controls. To define a customized control, you need to provide a control definition function that interprets messages indicating what action your function is to perform. A customized control definition function is a function having the following declaration:

```
FUNCTION MyControl (varCode: Integer; theControl: ControlHandle; message:
                    Integer; param: LongInt) : LongInt;
```

Previously, when passed the calcCRgns message, your control definition needed to test the high-order bit of the param parameter to determine whether to return a handle to the region of the control indicator or to the region of the entire control. In addition, your function had to clear the high bit of that parameter before passing back a handle to the calculated region. As a result, it was impossible to write a 32-bit clean control definition. The Control Manager in system software version 7.0 has a new mechanism for instructing your control definition to calculate control regions. In particular, two new messages have been defined:

```
CONST calcCntlRgn       = 10;    {calculate control's region}
      calcThumbRgn      = 11;    {calculate indicator's region}
```

When the 32-bit Memory Manager is in operation, the Control Manager uses one of these two new messages in cases where it would previously have used calcCRgns. When the 24-bit Memory Manager is in operation, the Control Manager still uses calcCRgns. If your application uses customized control definitions, you should update it to support the new messages as soon as possible. Because many users will still be running your application on machines with 24-bit addressing, you should also continue to support calcCRgns.

Manipulating 24-Bit and 32-Bit Memory Addresses

In environments where the machine might be executing with a 24-bit Memory Manager, it is sometimes necessary to strip off the flag bits of a memory address before you use that address. The Memory Manager provides the StripAddress function to allow you to do this.

```
FUNCTION StripAddress (address: UNIV Ptr) : Ptr;
```

The StripAddress function takes an address as a parameter and returns the value of the low-order 3 bytes if the 24-bit Memory Manager is operating. Otherwise, StripAddress returns the full 32-bit address unchanged.

> **Note:** This discussion replaces the information about the StripAddress function in the Operating System Utilities chapter of Volume V.

To appreciate the need for StripAddress, you need to distinguish between the addressing state of the Memory Manager and the addressing state of the underlying hardware. Macintosh II hardware, for example, is fully capable of handling all 32 bits of a memory address. For consistency with earlier Macintoshes, the Macintosh II CPU spends most of its time in 24-bit mode and ignores the high-order byte of all memory addresses. (The information encoded there is of significance only to the Memory Manager, not to the CPU.) However, a driver might temporarily switch the CPU to 32-bit mode to access a hardware address on a NuBus™ card. Suppose that this driver has an address in the heap (which is under the control of the Memory Manager) to which it wants to transfer data. If a 24-bit Memory Manager is in operation, the driver must call StripAddress on the heap address before using that address; otherwise, the CPU would interpret the high byte of that heap address as part of the address and (probably) transfer the data to the wrong address.

Even if you are not writing Macintosh drivers, you might still find it useful to call StripAddress. Occasionally, you need to compare two memory addresses (for example, two master pointers). If you're using the 24-bit Memory Manager and you compare those addresses without first stripping off the flag bits, you might end up with invalid results. You should call StripAddress to convert those addresses to the correct format.

As you can see, the operation of StripAddress is not dependent on the 24-bit or 32-bit state of the hardware, but on the 24-bit or 32-bit state of the Memory Manager. Calling StripAddress is necessary only when a 24-bit Memory Manager is operating. When a 32-bit Memory Manager is operating, StripAddress does nothing to addresses passed to it because those addresses are already valid 32-bit addresses.

Sometimes drivers or other code must run in 32-bit mode to perform special hardware manipulations. You can use the Translate24To32 function to translate 24-bit addresses into 32-bit addresses.

USING THE MEMORY MANAGER

In system software version 7.0, you can continue to use any memory management routines documented in Volumes I, II, and IV, with two notable exceptions. The SetupA5 procedure and the RestoreA5 procedure documented in the Operating System Utilities chapter of Volume II do not work properly when used with some optimizing compilers. The MPW® Version 3.0 (and later) development system provides two new functions, SetCurrentA5 and SetA5, that perform the same operations without the problems of the earlier procedures. See "Setting and Restoring the A5 Register" for examples of using these two new functions. If you are using a development system other than MPW, you can include inline function definitions for these functions, as explained in "Manipulating A5 Without MPW," later in this chapter.

Several Memory Manager routines have changed to support operations on temporary memory as well as memory allocated from your application's heap. For example, you can now dispose of temporary memory by calling DisposHandle. Changes to the Memory Manager connected to temporary memory are discussed in "Using Temporary Memory," later in this chapter. The behavior of Memory Manager routines on blocks in your application's heap remains unchanged.

Setting and Restoring the A5 Register

Suppose you want to alert the user about something important that happens when your application is running in the background. To do so, you can use the Notification Manager to install a notification request. You request a notification by passing the Notification Manager the address of a notification record, which contains information about the ways in which the Notification Manager should alert the user. One of the fields in the notification record (nmRefCon) is a reference constant that is reserved for your application's use. When you set up a notification request, you can use that field to hold the value in the A5 register. Listing 28-1 illustrates how to save the current value in the A5 register and pass that value to a response procedure.

Listing 28-1. Passing A5 to a notification response procedure

```
VAR
   myNotif: NMRec;                {a notification record}
BEGIN
   WITH myNotif DO
   BEGIN
      qType := nmType;            {set queue type}
      nmMark := 1;                {put mark in Application menu}
      nmIcon := NIL;              {no alternating icon}
      nmSound := Handle(-1);      {play system alert sound}
      nmStr := NIL;               {no alert box}
      nmResp := @SampleResponse;  {set response procedure}
      nmRefCon := SetCurrentA5;   {pass A5 to notification task}
   END;
END;
```

The key step is to save the value of the CurrentA5 global variable in a location where the response procedure can find it—in this case, in the nmRefCon field. You must call SetCurrentA5 at non-interrupt time (or else you cannot be certain that it is returning you the correct value).

When the notification's response procedure executes, the first thing it should do is set register A5 to the application's value of CurrentA5. The response procedure needs to set up the application's A5 because it may execute at a time when that application is not the active application. Listing 28-2 shows a simple response procedure that sets up A5, modifies a global variable, and then restores A5.

You can use similar techniques with other routines that may execute when your application is not in control of the CPU. However, not every manager provides such facilities for passing the value of an application's CurrentA5 to a task or completion routine. For example, the Time Manager task record does not contain a field that you can use to store this value. As a result, you need to use other techniques to pass that value to a Time Manager task. See "Using Application Global Variables in Tasks" in the Time Manager chapter in this volume for an example of one technique for doing this.

Listing 28-2. Setting up and restoring A5

```
PROCEDURE SampleResponse (nmReqPtr: NMRecPtr);
VAR
   oldA5:   LongInt;                   {A5 when procedure is called}
BEGIN
   oldA5 := SetA5(nmReqPtr^.nmRefCon); {set A5 to the app's A5}
   g_NotifReceived := TRUE;            {set an application global }
                                       { to show alert was received}
   oldA5 := SetA5(oldA5);              {restore A5 to original value}
END;
```

> **Note:** Many optimizing compilers (including MPW) may put the address of a global variable into a register before the call to SetA5, thereby possibly generating incorrect references to global data. To avoid this problem, you can divide your completion routine into two separate routines, one to set up and restore A5 and one to do the actual completion work. Check the documentation for your development environment to see if this division is necessary, or contact Macintosh Developer Technical Support.

Manipulating A5 Without MPW

> **Note:** If you are using MPW Version 3.0 or later, you do not need to be concerned with the information in this section.

If you are not using the MPW Version 3.0 (or later) development system, you can achieve the same results as SetCurrentA5 and SetA5 by including the following inline definitions:

```
FUNCTION SetCurrentA5 : LongInt;
      INLINE $2E8D, $2A78, $0904;

FUNCTION SetA5 (newA5 : LongInt) : LongInt;
      INLINE $2F4D, $0004, $2A5F;
```

If you are programming in assembly language or are using a compiler that is not able to handle multiple inline functions, you can use the following definitions:

```
SetCurrentA5    move.l   A5,4(A7)      ;store old A5 as function result
                move.l   currentA5,A5  ;set A5 to low-memory global
                rts

SetA5           move.l   (A7)+,A0      ;save return address
                move.l   A5,4(A7)      ;store old A5 as function result
                move.l   (A7)+,A5      ;set A5 to passed value
                jmp      (A0)
```

MEMORY MANAGER ROUTINES

You can use several utility routines to set and restore the A5 world and to manipulate memory addresses. The routines documented in this section supplement the Memory Manager routines documented in Volumes I, II, and IV.

Setting and Restoring the A5 World

You can use the functions SetCurrentA5 and SetA5 to save and restore your application's A5 world. Use SetCurrentA5 to get the current value of the system global variable CurrentA5.

```
FUNCTION SetCurrentA5 : LongInt;
```

The SetCurrentA5 function does two things: First, it gets your application's A5 and returns it to your application. Second, SetCurrentA5 sets register A5 to the value of the application's low-memory global variable CurrentA5.

Use the SetA5 function to set the A5 register to the application's A5.

```
FUNCTION SetA5 (newA5: LongInt) : LongInt;
```

Calling SetA5 performs two tasks: It sets the A5 register to the address specified as newA5, and it returns the actual address that is in register A5 before the function is called.

Manipulating Memory Addresses

The Memory Manager includes several routines that allow you to manipulate memory addresses. The StripAddress function allows you to mask out the high-order byte of a 24-bit address to obtain an address that is meaningful to the 32-bit Memory Manager.

```
FUNCTION StripAddress (address: UNIV Ptr) : Ptr;
```

You can use the Translate24To32 function to translate 24-bit addresses into the 32-bit address space.

```
FUNCTION Translate24To32 (addr24: UNIV Ptr) : Ptr;
```

Unlike the StripAddress function, this function does not necessarily return an address that is meaningful to the 24-bit Memory Manager.

ABOUT VIRTUAL MEMORY

Virtual memory is the part of system software version 7.0 that allows any Macintosh computer equipped with an MMU to extend the available amount of memory beyond the limits of physical RAM. Virtual memory extends the logical address space by using part of the available secondary storage (such as a hard disk) to hold portions of programs and data that are not currently in use. When an application needs to operate on portions of memory that have been transferred to disk, the Operating System loads those portions back into physical memory by making them trade places with other, unused segments of memory. This process of shuttling portions (or **pages**) of memory between physical RAM and the hard disk is called **paging.**

For the most part, virtual memory operates invisibly to applications and to the user. Most applications do not need to know whether virtual memory is installed unless they have critical timing requirements, execute code at interrupt time, or perform debugging operations. The only time that users need to know about virtual memory is when they configure it in the Memory control panel. One visible cost of this extra memory is the use of an equivalent amount of storage on a backing device, such as a SCSI hard disk. Another cost of using virtual memory is a possible loss of speed as paged-out segments of memory are pulled back into physical memory. Performance degradation when using virtual memory ranges from unnoticeable to severe, depending on the ratio of virtual to physical RAM and the behavior of the actual applications running.

The principal benefit of using virtual memory is that users can run more applications at once and work with larger amounts of data than would be possible if the logical address space were limited to the available RAM. Instead of equipping a machine with amounts of RAM large enough to handle all possible needs, a user can install only enough RAM to meet average needs. Then, when more memory is occasionally needed for large tasks or many applications, virtual memory can provide the extra amount of memory required. When virtual memory is present, the perceived amount of RAM can be extended to as much as 14 MB on systems with 24-bit addressing and as much as 1 GB on systems with 32-bit addressing.

There are two main requirements for running virtual memory. First, the Macintosh must be running system software version 7.0. Second, the Macintosh must be equipped with an MMU or PMMU. Apple's 68030-based machines have an MMU built into the CPU and are ready to run virtual memory with only a software upgrade to version 7.0; no additional hardware is needed. A Macintosh II (68020-based) can take advantage of virtual memory if it has the 68851 PMMU coprocessor on its main logic board in place of the standard address management unit. (The PMMU is the same coprocessor needed to run A/UX.) Apple's 68000-based machines cannot take advantage of the virtual memory capability of version 7.0, even though they can run version 7.0 if they have at least 2 MB of RAM.

Users control and configure virtual memory through the Memory control panel. Controls in this panel allow the user to turn virtual memory on or off, set the size of virtual memory, and set the volume on which resides the invisible backing-store file (the file that the Operating System uses to store the contents of non-resident portions of memory). Other memory-related user controls are combined in this control panel. These include settings for the disk cache and for 24-bit or 32-bit Memory Manager addressing. If users change the virtual memory, addressing, or disk cache settings, they must restart the machine in order for the changes to take effect.

Note that the amount of virtual memory that users select in the control panel is the *total* amount of memory that is to be available to the system (and not simply the amount of memory to be added to available RAM). Also, the backing-store file is as large as the amount of virtual memory. This backing-store file might be located on any HFS volume that allows block-level access. (This volume is known as the **paging device** or **backing volume.**) Because the paging device must support block-level access, users cannot select as the paging device a volume that they mount using AppleShare®. Also, users cannot select removable disks, including floppy disks, as paging devices.

USING VIRTUAL MEMORY

The routines described in this section allow drivers and applications with critical timing needs to intervene in the otherwise automatic workings of the virtual memory paging mechanism.

> **Note:** The vast majority of applications do not need to use these routines. They are used primarily by drivers, debuggers, and other interrupt-servicing code.

If necessary, your software can request that a range of memory be held in physical memory. *Holding* means that the specified memory range cannot be paged out to disk, although it might be moved around within physical RAM. As a result, no page faults can result from reading or writing memory addresses of pages that are held in memory.

Similarly, a page or range of pages can be locked into physical memory. *Locking* means that the specified memory cannot be paged out to disk and that the memory cannot change its real (physical) RAM location. (Locking, therefore, is a superset of holding.) You can also request that a range of pages be locked into contiguous physical memory, although contiguity is not guaranteed. Locking pages into contiguous physical memory is used primarily when external hardware transfers data directly into physical RAM. This might be useful for keeping a contiguous range of memory stationary during operations of an external CPU (on a NuBus card, for example) that cannot support a DMA action.

Most applications do not need to hold or lock pages into physical RAM because the operation of virtual memory is usually fast enough that your application is not affected by any delay that might result from paging. Software that does need to hold or lock pages, such as drivers or sound and animation applications with critical timing requirements, normally needs only to hold memory, not lock it. Here are some general rules regarding when to hold or lock memory:

- Avoid executing tasks that could cause page faults at interrupt time. The less work done at interrupt time, the better things are for all applications running.
- You cannot hold or lock memory (or call any other Memory Manager routine) at interrupt time.
- Don't lock or hold everything in RAM. Sometimes either holding or locking pages in RAM is essential, but if you are ever in doubt, then probably neither one is needed.
- Whatever is held or locked must be explicitly unheld or unlocked by the application. If for some reason an area of RAM gets held and locked, or held twice, then it must be unheld and unlocked, or unheld twice.

This last directive is especially important. Your application is responsible for undoing any of the effects it causes by locking or holding ranges of memory. In particular, virtual memory does not automatically unlock pages that have been locked down. If you do not undo these effects in a timely fashion, you are likely to cause poor performance. In the worst case, you could cause the system to run out of physical memory.

Holding and Releasing Memory

You can use the HoldMemory function to make a portion of the address space resident in physical memory and ineligible for paging. This function is intended primarily for use by drivers that access user data buffers at interrupt level, whether transferring data to or from them. Calling HoldMemory on the appropriate memory ranges thus prevents them from causing page faults at interrupt level. The contents of the specified range of virtual addresses can move in physical memory, but they are guaranteed always to be in physical memory when accessed.

> **Note:** If you use the device-level Read and Write functions when doing data transfers, the Operating System automatically ensures that the data buffers are held down before the transfer of data.

The following sample code instructs the Operating System to hold in RAM the range of memory that starts at address $32500 and that is 8192 bytes long.

```
myAddress := $32500;
myLength := 8192;
myErr := HoldMemory (myAddress, myLength);
```

Note that holding is applied to whole pages of the virtual address space, regardless of the starting address and length parameters you supply. If the starting address parameter supplied to the HoldMemory function is not on a page boundary, then it is rounded down to the nearest page boundary. Similarly, if the specified range does not end on a page boundary, the length parameter is rounded up so that the entire range of memory is held. This rounding might result in the holding of several pages of physical memory, even if the specified range is less than a page.

To release memory that was held down using HoldMemory, you must use the UnholdMemory function, which simply reverses the effects of the HoldMemory function. For example, the pages held in memory in the previous example can be released as follows:

```
myErr := UnholdMemory (myAddress, myLength);
```

As with holding, letting go is applied to whole pages of the virtual address space. Similar rounding of the address and length parameters is performed as required to keep the range on page boundaries.

> **Note:** The system heap is always held in memory and is never paged out.

Locking and Unlocking Memory

You can use the LockMemory function to make a portion of the address space immovable in physical memory and ineligible for paging. The Operating System may move the contents of the specified range of logical addresses to a more convenient location in physical memory during the locking operation, but on completion, the contents of the specified range of logical addresses are resident and do not move in physical memory.

LockMemory is used by drivers and other code when hardware other than the Macintosh CPU is transferring data to or from user buffers, such as any NuBus master peripheral card or DMA hardware. This function prevents both paging and physical relocation of a specified memory area and enables the physical addresses of a memory area to be exported to the non-CPU hardware. Typically, you would use this service for the duration of a single I/O request. However, you could use this service to lock data structures that are permanently shared between driver or other code and a NuBus master.

> **Note:** Do not confuse locking addresses in RAM (using LockMemory) with locking a handle (using HLock). A locked handle can still be paged out.

The main reason to disable movement of pages in physical memory is to translate virtual addresses to physical addresses. This translation is needed by bus masters, which must write to memory in the physical address space. To avoid stale data, the memory locked in RAM is marked noncacheable in the CPU cache.

You can lock a range of memory into contiguous physical memory by using the LockMemoryContiguous function. This function is used by driver and NuBus master or driver and DMA hardware combinations when a non-CPU device accessing memory is unable to handle physically discontiguous data transfers. You can also use this service when it is possible to handle physically discontiguous data transfers, but doing so causes performance degradation. However, the call to LockMemoryContiguous may be expensive because entire pages might need to be copied in order to make a range contiguous.

> **Note:** It might not be possible to make a range physically contiguous if any of the pages contained in the range are already locked. Because a call to LockMemoryContiguous is not guaranteed to return the desired results, all code that uses LockMemoryContiguous must have an alternate method for locking the necessary ranges of memory.

To unlock a range of previously locked pages, use the UnlockMemory function. This function reverses the effects of LockMemory or LockMemoryContiguous. Unlocked pages are marked as cacheable.

Locking, contiguous locking, and unlocking operations are applied to ranges of the logical address space. If necessary to force the ranges onto page boundaries, the Operating System performs rounding of addresses and sizes, as described in the previous section, “Holding and Releasing Memory.”

Obtaining Information About Virtual Memory

If your application or driver needs to use the virtual memory routines described so far, you might also need to obtain information about the operation of virtual memory. You can get two kinds of information: information about the system memory configuration and information about the page-mapping employed by virtual memory. Use the Gestalt function for the first sort of information, and use the GetPhysical function for the second sort.

Information About the System Memory Configuration

To obtain information regarding the system memory configuration, use the Gestalt function, which is documented in the Compatibility Guidelines chapter of this volume. Gestalt can provide information about the amount of physical memory installed in a machine, the amount of logical memory available in a machine, the version of virtual memory installed (if any), and the size of a logical page. By obtaining this information from Gestalt, you can help insulate your applications or drivers from possible future changes in the details of the virtual memory implementation.

You should always determine whether virtual memory is installed before attempting to use the services it provides. To do this, pass Gestalt the gestaltVMAttr selector. Gestalt's response indicates the version of virtual memory, if any, installed. If bit 0 of the response is set to 1, then the system software version 7.0 implementation of virtual memory is installed.

Information About Page Mapping

To obtain information about page mapping between logical and physical addresses, use the GetPhysical function. GetPhysical translates logical addresses into their corresponding physical addresses. It provides drivers with actual physical memory addresses of pages in a specified logical address range. This information is needed to permit non-CPU devices to access memory mapped by the CPU. Mapping information is needed to enable data transfers by non-CPU devices to physically discontiguous memory by means of external software or hardware mapping mechanisms.

The GetPhysical routine takes as one of its parameters a parameter block with a table to store pairs of physical addresses and counts.

```
TYPE MemoryBlock =
     RECORD
        address:             Ptr;          {start of block}
        count:               LongInt       {size of block}
     END;
```

The translation table is an array of ordered pairs of addresses and counts. GetPhysical translates up to the size of the table or until the translation is completed, whichever comes first.

If you call GetPhysical with a table size of 0, it returns the number of table entries necessary to translate the entire address range. On exit, the virtual information is updated to indicate the next virtual address and the number of bytes left to translate. If the translation is incomplete, the same translation table can again be passed to GetPhysical to continue the translation of the remaining addresses. The return value from the routine indicates the number of pairs of physical addresses and counts actually placed in the translation table.

The translation parameter block consists of two elements, the virtual information and the physical translation table, and is defined as follows:

```
TYPE LogicalToPhysicalTable =
     RECORD
        logical:     MemoryBlock;         {logical block}
        physical:    ARRAY[0..defaultPhysicalEntryCount-1] OF
                                          MemoryBlock
                                          {equivalent physical blocks}
     END;
```

The information is stored as an ordered pair of address and count. The physical translation table is an array of address and count pairs that define sections of physical memory representing the virtual address range input parameter. On exit, the virtual information is updated to reflect the address range that was not translated. The virtual address field contains the next virtual address to be translated, and the virtual count field has the number of bytes left to be translated. The parameter count is used to indicate the size of the translation table array. The actual count value is the number of physical ordered pairs that can be returned in the translation table. Passing in the size of the table allows the calling software to adjust the table size to fit its application. Calling software can then make the necessary trade-offs between memory and complexity versus the overhead for multiple calls.

When GetPhysical returns, the physicalEntryCount parameter contains the number of address and count pairs that were filled into the translation table. In addition, if physicalEntryCount contained 0, the total number of entries required to map the entire logical space is returned (and the contents of the table are unchanged). Listing 28-3 provides an example of using GetPhysical.

Listing 28-3. Translating logical to physical addresses

```
VAR
   table:               LogicalToPhysicalTable;
   myErr:               OSErr;
   numPhysicalBlocks:   Integer;
BEGIN
   table.logical.address := bufferAddress;      {virtual address}
   table.logical.count   := bufferSize;         {bytes in buffer}

   WHILE table.logical.count <> 0 DO
   BEGIN
      numPhysicalBlocks := SIZEOF(table) DIV SIZEOF(MemoryBlock) - 1;
      myErr := GetPhysical(table, numPhysicalBlocks);
      IF myErr <> noErr THEN DoError(myErr);
      aRoutine(table, numPhysicalBlocks);       {your routine to }
                                                { process results}
   END;
END;
```

Note: The address range passed to GetPhysical must be locked (using LockMemory). This is necessary to guarantee that the translation data returned are accurate (that is, that paging activity has not invalidated the translation data). An error is returned if you call GetPhysical on an address range that is not locked.

Deferring User Interrupt Handling

During the time that the Macintosh is handling a page fault, it is critical that no other page faults occur. Since no other work is explicitly done by the system while it is handling a page fault, the only code that can cause this to occur is code that runs as a result of an interrupt. Consequently, the HoldMemory function must be called on buffers or code that are to be referenced by any interrupt service routine. You must call this function at non-interrupt level because the MemoryDispatch calls may cause movement of memory and possible I/O.

The use of procedure pointers (ProcPtrs) in specifying I/O completion routines, socket listeners, and so forth makes it impossible for drivers to know the exact location and size of all code or buffers that might be referenced when invoking these routines. However, these routines must still be called only at a safe time, when paging is not currently in progress. Because the locations of all needed pages cannot be known, an alternate strategy is used to prevent a fatal double page-fault condition.

The DeferUserFn routine is provided to allow interrupt service routines to defer, until a safe time, code that might cause page faults. DeferUserFn determines whether the call can be made immediately and, if it is safe, makes the call. If a page fault is in progress, the address of the service routine and its parameter are saved, and the routine is deferred until page faults are again permitted.

Debugger Support Under Virtual Memory

Note: You need the information in this section only if you are writing a debugger that is to operate under virtual memory.

Debuggers running under virtual memory can use any of the virtual memory routines discussed in the previous sections. For example, if a debugger is in a situation where page faulting would be fatal, it can use DeferUserFn to defer the debugging until paging is safe. However, debuggers running under virtual memory might require a few routines that differ from those available to all applications. In addition, debuggers might depend on some specific features of virtual memory that other applications should not.

For example, because debugger code might be entered at a time when paging would be unsafe, you should lock (and not just hold) the debugger and all of its data and buffer space in memory. Normally, the locking operation is used to allow NuBus masters or other DMA devices to transfer data directly into physical memory. This requires that data caching be disabled on the locked page. You might, however, want your debugger to benefit from the performance of the data cache on pages belonging solely to the debugger. The DebuggerLockMemory function does exactly what LockMemory does, except that it leaves data caching enabled on the affected pages. The DebuggerUnlockMemory function reverses the effects of DebuggerLockMemory.

Other special debugger support functions determine whether paging is safe, allow the debugger to enter supervisor mode, enter and exit the debugging state, obtain keyboard input while in the debugging state, and determine the state of a page of logical memory. All of these functions are implemented as extensions of the DebugUtil trap, a new trap intended for use by debuggers to allow greater machine independence. This trap is not present in the Macintosh II, Macintosh IIx, Macintosh IIcx, or Macintosh SE/30, but it is present in all later ROMs. Virtual memory implements this trap for all machines that it supports, so a debugger can use DebugUtil (and functions defined in terms of DebugUtil) if Gestalt reports that virtual memory is present.

When the virtual memory extensions to DebugUtil are not present (that is, the machine supports virtual memory but is *not* a Macintosh II, Macintosh IIx, Macintosh IIcx, or Macintosh SE/30), DebugUtil provides functions that can determine the highest DebugUtil function supported, enter the debugging state, poll the keyboard for input, and exit the debugging state.

You can call DebugUtil to determine how many of the debugger functions or extensions are present. The DebuggerGetMax function returns the highest function number supported by the DebugUtil trap. The numbers correspond to the following functions:

Selector	Routine
$0000	DebuggerGetMax
$0001	DebuggerEnter
$0002	DebuggerExit
$0003	DebuggerPoll
$0004	GetPageState
$0005	PageFaultFatal
$0006	DebuggerLockMemory
$0007	DebuggerUnlockMemory
$0008	EnterSupervisorMode

Bus Error Vectors

When a page of memory is read in from disk, it is triggered by a bus error (this kind of bus error is called a *page fault*). The Operating System needs to intercept these page faults and do the necessary paging. In addition, various applications and pieces of system software need to handle other kinds of bus errors. Virtual memory takes care of the complications of bus error handling by having two bus error vectors. The vector that applications and other system software see is the one in low memory (at address $8). The vector that virtual memory uses (the one actually used by the processor) is in virtual memory's private storage and is pointed to by the vector base register (VBR). Virtual memory's bus error handler handles page faults and passes other bus errors to the vector in low memory at address $8.

When a debugger wants the contents of a page to be loaded into memory, it can read a byte from that page. The Operating System detects the page fault and loads the appropriate page (perhaps swapping another page to disk).

Note that a debugger will probably temporarily replace one or both of the bus error vectors while it is executing. A debugger that wants virtual memory to continue paging while the debugger runs can put a handler only in the low-memory bus error vector. A debugger that displays memory without allowing virtual memory to continue paging can put a handler in the virtual memory's bus error vector (at VBR+$8).

Because the current version of virtual memory is not reentrant, there are times when trying to load a page into memory would be fatal. To allow for this, you can use the PageFaultFatal function to determine whether a page fault would be fatal at that time. If this function returns TRUE, the debugger should not allow the virtual memory's bus error handler to detect any page faults. This means that the virtual memory's bus error vector should always be replaced if the PageFaultFatal function returns TRUE.

Special Nonmaskable Interrupt Needs

Since a debugger can be triggered with a nonmaskable interrupt (level 7, triggered by the interrupt switch), it has special needs that other code in the system does not. For example, because a nonmaskable interrupt might occur while virtual memory is moving pages around (to make them contiguous, for example), debugger code must be locked down (instead of held, like most other code that must run at a time when page faults would be fatal). Unfortunately, the LockMemory function is intended for use by device drivers and automatically disables data caching for the locked pages. Because this is not desirable for the debugger, the debugger support functions DebuggerLockMemory and DebuggerUnlockMemory lock pages without inhibiting the caching of those pages. Note that both the stack, code, and other storage used by the debugger might need to be locked in this way.

Supervisor Mode

Because a debugger is typically activated through one of the processor vectors, it normally executes in supervisor mode, allowing it access to all of memory and all processor registers. When the debugger is entered in another way—for example, through the Debugger or DebugStr trap or when it is first loaded—it is necessary to enter supervisor mode. You can accomplish this with the following assembly-language instructions:

```
MOVEQ EnterSupervisorMode,D0
_DebugUtil                      ;OS trap to DebugUtils
                                ;on exit, D0 holds old SR
```

This code switches the caller into supervisor mode. The previous status register is returned in register D0 so that when the debugger returns to the interrupted code, the previous interrupt level, condition codes, and so forth, can be restored. When the debugger is ready to return to user mode, it simply loads the status register with the result returned in D0.

The Debugging State

When activated by an exception, Debug or DebugStr trap, or any other means, the debugger should call DebuggerEnter to notify DebugUtil that the debugger is entering the debugging state. Then DebugUtil can place hardware in a quiescent state and prepare for subsequent DebugUtil calls.

Before returning to the interrupted application code, the debugger must call DebuggerExit to allow DebugUtil to return hardware affected by DebuggerEnter to its previous state.

Keyboard Input

A debugger can obtain the user's keyboard input by using the DebuggerPoll procedure. This routine can obtain keyboard input even with interrupts disabled. After you call this service, you must then obtain keyboard events through the normal event queue mechanism.

Page States

Debuggers need a way to display the contents of memory without paging or to display the contents of pages that are currently on disk. The GetPageState function returns the state of a page containing a virtual address. GetPageState returns one of these values:

```
TYPE PageState = Integer;

CONST kPageInMemory         = 0;          {page is in RAM}
      kPageOnDisk           = 1;          {page is on disk}
      kNotPaged             = 2;          {address is not paged}
```

A debugger can use this information to determine whether certain memory addresses should be referenced. Note that ROM and I/O space are not pageable and therefore are considered not paged.

VIRTUAL MEMORY ROUTINES

This section describes the routines you can use to hold logical pages in physical memory and let go of them, lock and unlock pages in physical memory, obtain information about page-mapping, and handle interrupts. It also describes the routines that pertain primarily to debuggers; you can use those routines to determine the state of a page, determine whether a page fault would be fatal, enter the supervisor mode, enter and exit the debugging state, and obtain keyboard input while in the debugging state. You can also use special debugger versions of the routines that lock and unlock pages in memory.

Holding and Releasing Pages

The HoldMemory function makes a portion of the address space resident in physical memory and ineligible for paging.

```
FUNCTION HoldMemory (address: UNIV Ptr; count: LongInt) : OSErr;
```

Trap macro	_MemoryDispatch
On entry	D0: selector code
	A0: address
	A1: count
On exit	D0: result code

The address parameter is the start address of the range of memory that is to be held in RAM, and count is the size in bytes of that range. If the starting address parameter supplied to the HoldMemory function is not on a page boundary, then it is rounded down to the nearest page boundary. Similarly, if the specified range does not end on a page boundary, the count parameter is rounded up so that the entire range of memory is held.

Result codes

noErr	0	No error
paramErr	–50	Error in parameter list
notEnoughMemoryErr	–620	Insufficient physical memory
interruptsMaskedErr	–624	Called with interrupts masked

The UnholdMemory function makes eligible for paging again a portion of the address space that is currently held. This function reverses the effects of HoldMemory.

```
FUNCTION UnholdMemory (address: UNIV Ptr; count: LongInt) : OSErr;
```

Trap macro	_MemoryDispatch
On entry	D0: selector code
	A0: address
	A1: count
On exit	D0: result code

The address parameter is the start address of the range that is to be let go, and count is the size in bytes of that range. If the starting address parameter supplied to the UnholdMemory function is not on a page boundary, then it is rounded down to the nearest page boundary. Similarly, if the specified range does not end on a page boundary, the count parameter is rounded up so that the entire range of memory is let go.

Result codes

noErr	0	No error
paramErr	–50	Error in parameter list
notHeldErr	–621	Specified range of memory is not held
interruptsMaskedErr	–624	Called with interrupts masked

Locking and Unlocking Pages

The LockMemory function makes a portion of the address space immovable in physical memory and ineligible for paging.

```
FUNCTION LockMemory (address: UNIV Ptr; count: LongInt) : OSErr;
```

Trap macro	_MemoryDispatch
On entry	D0: selector code
	A0: address
	A1: count
On exit	D0: result code

The address parameter is the start address of the range that is to be locked in RAM, and count is the size in bytes of that range. If the starting address parameter supplied to the LockMemory function is not on a page boundary, then it is rounded down to the nearest page boundary. Similarly, if the specified range does not end on a page boundary, the count parameter is rounded up so that the entire range of memory is locked. Locked pages are marked noncacheable by the CPU.

Result codes

noErr	0	No error
paramErr	–50	Error in parameter list
notEnoughMemoryErr	–620	Insufficient physical memory
interruptsMaskedErr	–624	Called with interrupts masked

The LockMemoryContiguous function is exactly like the LockMemory function, except that it attempts to obtain a contiguous block of physical memory associated with the logical address range specified.

```
FUNCTION LockMemoryContiguous (address: UNIV Ptr; count: LongInt) : OSErr;
```

Trap macro	_MemoryDispatch
On entry	D0: selector code
	A0: address
	A1: count
On exit	D0: result code

The address parameter is the start address of the range that is to be locked in RAM, and count is the size in bytes of that range. If the specified address is not on a page boundary, it is rounded down to the nearest page boundary. Similarly, if the specified range does not end on a page boundary, the count parameter is rounded up so that the entire range of contiguous memory is locked. Locked pages are marked noncacheable by the CPU.

Result codes

noErr	0	No error
paramErr	–50	Error in parameter list
notEnoughMemoryErr	–620	Insufficient physical memory
cannotMakeContiguousErr	–622	Cannot make specified range contiguous
interruptsMaskedErr	–624	Called with interrupts masked

The UnlockMemory function makes a portion of the address space movable in real memory and eligible for paging again. It undoes the effects of both LockMemory and LockMemoryContiguous.

```
FUNCTION UnlockMemory (address: UNIV Ptr; count: LongInt) : OSErr;
```

Trap macro	_MemoryDispatch
On entry	D0: selector code
	A0: address
	A1: count
On exit	D0: result code

The address parameter is the start address of the range that is to be unlocked, and count is the size in bytes of that range. If the specified address is not on a page boundary, it is rounded down to the nearest page boundary. Similarly, if the specified range does not end on a page boundary, the length parameter is rounded up so that the entire range of memory is unlocked.

Result codes

noErr	0	No error
paramErr	–50	Error in parameter list
notLockedErr	–623	Specified range of memory is not locked
interruptsMaskedErr	–624	Called with interrupts masked

Obtaining Page-Mapping Information

The GetPhysical function translates logical addresses into their corresponding physical addresses.

```
FUNCTION GetPhysical (VAR addresses: LogicalToPhysicalTable;
                      VAR physicalEntryCount: LongInt) : OSErr;
```

Trap macro	_MemoryDispatchA0Result
On entry	D0: selector code
	A0: addresses
	A1: physicalEntryCount in table
On exit	A0: physicalEntryCount translated
	D0: result code

The addresses parameter is a translation table, that is, an array of ordered pairs (address and count). The physicalEntryCount parameter specifies the number of physical entries to translate. GetPhysical translates up to the size of the table or until the translation is completed, whichever comes first. If GetPhysical is called with a table size of 0, the number of table entries needed to translate the entire address range is returned. On exit from this function, the virtual information is updated to indicate the next virtual address and the number of bytes left to translate. The logical address range must be locked to ensure validity of the translation data.

Result codes

noErr	0	No error
paramErr	–50	Error in parameter list
notLockedErr	–623	Specified range of memory is not locked
interruptsMaskedErr	–624	Called with interrupts masked

Deferring User Interrupt Handling

You can use the DeferUserFn function to determine whether code that might cause page faults can safely be called immediately. If the code can be called safely, then it is called. If a page fault is in progress, however, the routine address and its parameter are saved, and the routine is deferred until page faults are again permitted.

```
FUNCTION DeferUserFn (userFunction: ProcPtr; argument: UNIV Ptr) : OSErr;
```

Trap macro	_DeferUserFn
On entry	D0: argument
	A0: function
On exit	D0: result code

You pass DeferUserFn the address of the routine that you want to run and a pointer to the argument to pass to the specified routine. The specified routine is called with register A0 containing the value of the argument parameter to the DeferUserFn call. Note that the routine can be called immediately (before returning to the caller of DeferUserFn). Deferred functions must follow the register conventions used by interrupt handlers: they may use registers A0–A3 and D0–D3, and must restore all other registers used.

Result codes

noErr	0	No error
cannotDeferErr	–625	Unable to defer additional user functions

Determining Which Debugger Functions Are Present

The DebuggerGetMax function returns a long integer indicating the highest function number supported by the DebugUtil trap.

```
FUNCTION DebuggerGetMax: LongInt;
```

Trap macro	_DebugUtil
On entry	D0: selector
On exit	D0: highest available selector

The returned value is the highest selector number of the debugger functions that are defined in terms of the DebugUtil trap. See "Debugger Support Under Virtual Memory" earlier in this chapter for a complete list of these numbers.

Determining Whether Paging Is Safe

A debugger can use the PageFaultFatal function to determine whether it should capture all bus errors or whether it is safe to allow them to flow through to virtual memory. When paging is safe, the debugger can allow virtual memory to continue to service page faults, thus allowing the user to view all of memory.

```
FUNCTION PageFaultFatal: Boolean;
```

Trap macro	_DebugUtil
On entry	D0: selector
On exit	D0: returned value

If this function returns TRUE, then the debugger should not allow the virtual memory's bus error handler to detect any page faults.

Locking and Unlocking Memory With Caching Enabled

The DebuggerLockMemory function performs the same operations as LockMemory, except that it leaves data caching enabled on the affected pages.

```
FUNCTION DebuggerLockMemory (address: UNIV Ptr; count: LongInt) : OSErr;
```

Trap macro	_DebugUtil
On entry	D0: selector code A0: address A1: count
On exit	D0: result code

The address parameter is the start address of the range that is to be locked in RAM, and count is the size in bytes of that range. If the starting address parameter supplied to the DebuggerLockMemory function is not on a page boundary, then it is rounded down to the nearest page boundary. Similarly, if the specified range does not end on a page boundary, the length parameter is rounded up so that the entire range of memory is locked.

Result codes		
noErr	0	No error
paramErr	–50	Error in parameter list
notEnoughMemoryErr	–620	Insufficient physical memory

The DebuggerUnlockMemory function reverses the effects of DebuggerLockMemory.

```
FUNCTION DebuggerUnlockMemory (address: UNIV Ptr; count: LongInt) :
                               OSErr;
```

Trap macro	_DebugUtil
On entry	D0: selector code A0: address A1: count
On exit	D0: result code

DebuggerUnlockMemory makes the portion of the address space starting with address and continuing for count bytes movable in physical memory and eligible for paging again. Unlocking is applied to whole pages of the virtual address space. Unlocked pages are marked as cacheable.

Result codes		
noErr	0	No error
paramErr	–50	Error in parameter list
notLockedErr	–623	Specified range of memory is not locked

Entering and Exiting the Debugging State

The two procedures DebuggerEnter and DebuggerExit allow you to enter and exit the debugger state. These calls allow the DebugUtil trap to make preparations for subsequent debugging calls and to clean up after all debugging calls are completed.

```
PROCEDURE DebuggerEnter;

PROCEDURE DebuggerExit;
```

Trap macro	_DebugUtil
On entry	D0: selector code

Obtaining Keyboard Input

A debugger can use the DebuggerPoll procedure to poll for keyboard input.

```
PROCEDURE DebuggerPoll;
```

Trap macro	_DebugUtil
On entry	D0: selector code
On exit	D0: result code

The DebuggerPoll procedure can be used even if interrupts are disabled.

Determining Page State

The GetPageState function returns the state of a page of logical memory.

```
FUNCTION GetPageState (address: UNIV Ptr) : PageState;
```

Trap macro	_DebugUtil
On entry	D0: selector code
	A0: address
On exit	D0: page state

The address parameter specifies an address in the page whose state you want to determine. The returned value is one of these constants:

```
CONST
        kPageInMemory        = 0;        {page is in RAM}
        kPageOnDisk          = 1;        {page is on disk}
        kNotPaged            = 2;        {address is not paged}
```

ABOUT TEMPORARY MEMORY

To operate efficiently with other applications in the system software version 7.0 environment, your application should contain a 'SIZE' resource that specifies both a minimum and a preferred memory partition size. The actual partition size allocated to your application upon launch is set to the preferred size if that much contiguous memory is available, or to some smaller size if that much contiguous memory is not available. Note that once the application is launched, its partition cannot change in size, so the application's heap must always remain within some predetermined limit.

Rather than specify a preferred partition size that is large enough to contain the largest possible application heap, you should specify a smaller but adequate partition size. When you need more memory for temporary use, you can use a set of temporary memory allocation services provided by the Operating System. The memory allocated using these services is known as *temporary memory.*

By using the temporary memory allocation routines, your application can request some additional memory for occasional short-term needs. For example, the Finder™ uses these temporary memory routines to secure buffer space to be used during file copy operations. Any available memory (that is, memory currently unallocated to any application's partition) is dedicated to this purpose. The Finder releases this memory as soon as the copy is completed, thus making the memory available to other applications or to the Operating System for launching new applications.

Because the requested amount of memory might not be available, you should not rely on always getting the memory you need when you issue a temporary memory request. You should make sure that your applications still work even if no temporary memory is available when you request it. For example, if the Finder cannot allocate a large temporary copy buffer, it performs the copying using a reserved small copy buffer from within its own heap zone. While the copying might take longer, it is nonetheless performed.

In system software version 6.0, any memory you allocated using the temporary memory routines had to be released before your next call to GetNextEvent or WaitNextEvent. In addition, you had to perform all operations on that temporary memory by using specialized MultiFinder routines rather than the usual Memory Manager routines. In version 7.0, both of these restrictions have been relaxed (though not completely removed). The memory you allocate using the temporary memory routines can now be used for longer intervals and does not need to be released before the next call to WaitNextEvent. In version 7.0, you can think of temporary memory simply as an extension of your application's heap. You should still use temporary memory for as short a time as possible, and you must release that memory before your application terminates.

Because temporary memory is taken from RAM that is reserved for (but not yet used by) other applications, you might prevent the user from being able to launch other applications by using too much temporary memory or by holding temporary memory for long periods of time. You can hold temporary memory indefinitely, however, in certain circumstances. For example, if the temporary memory is used for open files and the user can free that memory simply by closing those files, it is safe to hold onto that memory as long as necessary. But you should make sure not to lock temporary memory across event calls.

Temporary memory is tracked (or monitored) for each application, so you must use it only for code that is running on an application's behalf. Moreover, because the Operating System frees all temporary memory allocated to an application when it quits or crashes, you should not use temporary memory for procedures such as VBL tasks or Time Manager tasks that you want to continue running after the application quits. Similarly, it is wise not to use temporary memory for interprocess buffers (that is, a buffer whose address is passed to another application in a high-level event) because the originating application could crash, thereby causing the temporary memory to be released before (or even while) the receiving application uses that memory.

Another main difference between temporary memory routines under version 6.0 and version 7.0 is that although you must still allocate temporary memory by using special routines, you can release and otherwise manipulate it by using normal Memory Manager routines. Even though you don't know where the additional memory comes from, you are encouraged to operate on that memory in the same way that you manipulate memory allocated from the application or system heaps. In short, temporary memory *allocation* remains specialized, but operations on *existing* temporary blocks can be performed by using Memory Manager routines.

Under system software version 7.0, the following Memory Manager routines work even if the handle or pointer is allocated by one of the temporary memory routines.

DisposHandle	HPurge
EmptyHandle	HSetRBit
GetHandleSize	HSetState
HandleZone	HUnlock
HClrRBit	ReallocHandle
HGetState	RecoverHandle
HLock	SetHandleSize
HNoPurge	

Prior to system software version 7.0, you need to use these seven routines on temporary memory:

TempFreeMem	TempHUnlock
TempMaxMem	TempNewHandle
TempDisposeHandle	TempTopMem
TempHLock	

Note: In system software version 6.0, these routines have the following names: MFFreeMem, MFMaxMem, MFTempDisposHandle, MFTempHLock, MFTempHUnlock, MFTempNewHandle, MFTopMem. For compatibility, you can continue to use these names.

Note that TempDisposeHandle, TempHLock, TempHUnlock, and TempTopMem are now obsolete, although they still work (for the sake of compatibility).

▲ **Warning:** Although you can determine the zone from which the temporary memory is generated (using HandleZone), do not use this information to make new blocks or perform heap operations on your own. ▲

Some of these routines rely on the current zone if the handle has been purged. They have been made to work correctly in this case, even if the current zone is the application or system zone and the handle is from a temporary block.

The Gestalt function includes several selectors that return information about the temporary memory routines. See "Determining Features of Temporary Memory" later in this chapter for examples of using Gestalt in this manner.

USING TEMPORARY MEMORY

You can use temporary memory routines to determine how much memory is available for temporary allocation, to allocate blocks of memory for temporary use, to lock and unlock relocatable blocks of temporary memory, and to release memory previously allocated for temporary use.

As indicated in "About Temporary Memory," you do not need to use the special temporary memory routines to lock, unlock, or release temporary memory blocks if your application is executing under system software version 7.0. Instead, you can employ the usual Memory Manager routines to accomplish those tasks. You can use temporary memory longer under version 7.0 than under version 6.0. Before taking advantage of these two new features, however, you should make sure that they are present. Methods for doing this are presented in "Determining Features of Temporary Memory," later in this chapter.

Allocating Temporary Memory

You can request a block of memory for temporary use by calling the TempNewHandle function. This function attempts to allocate a new relocatable block of the specified size for temporary use. For example, to request a block that is one-quarter megabyte in size, you might issue these commands:

```
mySize := $40000; {one-quarter megabyte}
myHandle := TempNewHandle(mySize, myErr);
```

If the routine succeeds, it returns a handle to the block of memory. The block of memory returned by a successful call to TempNewHandle is unlocked. If an error occurs and the routine fails, it returns a NIL handle. You should always check for NIL handles before using any temporary memory. If you detect a NIL handle, the second parameter (in this example, myErr) contains the result code from the function.

Instead of asking for a specific amount of memory and then checking the returned handle to see if you actually got it, you might prefer to determine beforehand how much temporary memory is available. There are two functions that return information on the amount of free memory available for allocation using the temporary memory routines. First, you can use the TempFreeMem function, as follows:

```
memFree: LongInt;     {amount of free temporary memory}
memFree := TempFreeMem;
```

The result is a long integer containing the amount of free memory, in bytes, available for temporary allocation. It usually isn't possible to allocate a block of this same size because of fragmentation due to nonrelocatable or locked blocks. Consequently, you'll probably want to use the function TempMaxMem to determine what is the largest contiguous block of space available. To allocate that block, you can write:

```
mySize := TempMaxMem(myGrow);
myHandle := TempNewHandle(mySize, myErr);
```

TempMaxMem compacts the heap zone and returns the size in bytes of the largest contiguous free block available for temporary allocation. (TempMaxMem is therefore analogous to MaxMem; see the discussion of MaxMem in the Memory Manager chapter of Volume II for full details on MaxMem.) The myGrow parameter is a variable parameter of type Size; after the function is called, it always contains 0 because the temporary memory does not come from the application's heap. Even when you use TempMaxMem to size that available memory, you should check the handle returned to make sure that is it not NIL.

The temporary memory routines include the TempTopMem function, originally designed to help you determine how much memory is available in the current executing environment. TempTopMem returns a pointer to the top of the addressable RAM space. Note that the return value indicates the total amount of usable machine memory, not the amount of memory available to your application, so you should not use TempTopMem to calculate the size of your application's memory partition. Because you can determine the amount of available memory by using the Gestalt function (using the gestaltLogicalRAMSize selector), you should consider the TempTopMem function to be obsolete.

Locking Temporary Memory

Under system software version 7.0, you can lock a relocatable block of temporary memory by calling the Memory Manager procedure HLock, thereby preventing that block from being moved within the heap zone. In system software version 6.0, you can do this by using the TempHLock procedure.

Unlocking Temporary Memory

To unlock a specified relocatable block of temporary memory, you can use the HUnlock procedure. Once again, you can accomplish the same result in system software version 6.0 by calling the TempHUnlock procedure.

Releasing Temporary Memory

When you finish using a block of memory that you allocated using TempNewHandle, you can release it by calling the DisposHandle routine.

In system software version 6.0, you can free temporary memory blocks by calling the TempDisposeHandle procedure.

Determining Features of Temporary Memory

Because the temporary memory routines are present only on systems that are running MultiFinder (or on systems in which the functionality of MultiFinder is a standard part of the Operating System) and because the features of those routines have changed in system software version 7.0, you should always check that those routines are available and that they have the features you require before calling them. This is easy to do if the Gestalt function is available because Gestalt includes a selector to determine whether those routines are present in the operating environment and, if they are, whether the temporary memory handles are real (that is, whether you can use the normal Memory Manager routines to manipulate them) and whether those handles are tracked. It is also possible to determine whether the routines are available even if the Gestalt function is not available.

You can determine whether the temporary memory routines are implemented by checking the return value of the TempMemCallsAvailable function that is defined in Listing 28-4.

Listing 28-4. Determining whether temporary memory routines are available

```
FUNCTION TempMemCallsAvailable: Boolean;
CONST
   _OSDispatch = $A88F;      {trap number of temp memory routines}
VAR
   myErr:    OSErr;          {result code returned by Gestalt}
   myRsp:    LongInt;        {response returned by Gestalt}
BEGIN
   TempMemCallsAvailable := FALSE;
   IF gHasGestalt THEN       {gHasGestalt is set by other code}
   BEGIN
      myErr := Gestalt(gestaltOSAttr, myRsp);
      IF myErr <> noErr THEN
         DoError(myErr)
      ELSE
         TempMemCallsAvailable := BitTst(myRsp, gestaltTempMemSupport);
   END
   ELSE                      {Gestalt is not available}
      TempMemCallsAvailable := TrapAvailable(_OSDispatch);
END;
```

The TrapAvailable function is defined in the Compatibility Guidelines chapter of this volume. You can use similar code to determine whether temporary memory handles are real and whether the temporary memory is tracked (that is, you can hold temporary memory until your application terminates).

TEMPORARY MEMORY ROUTINES

This section describes the routines you can use to allocate temporary memory, lock temporary memory blocks into RAM, unlock locked blocks, free temporary memory, and obtain information about the amount of temporary memory available. Remember that most of these routines can be replaced in system software version 7.0 by their normal Memory Manager counterparts.

Requesting Temporary Memory

To find out how much memory is available for temporary use, you can use either TempFreeMem or TempMaxMem.

```
FUNCTION TempFreeMem : LongInt;
```

TempFreeMem returns the total amount of free memory available for temporary allocation using TempNewHandle. The returned value is a long integer that indicates the total number of bytes free.

TempMaxMem compacts the heap zone and returns the size of the largest contiguous block available for temporary allocation.

```
FUNCTION TempMaxMem (VAR grow: Size) : Size;
```

The grow parameter always contains 0 after the function call because the temporary memory does not come from the application's heap.

You use TempNewHandle to allocate a new relocatable block of temporary memory.

```
FUNCTION TempNewHandle (logicalSize: Size; VAR resultCode: OSErr) :
                        Handle;
```

TempNewHandle returns a handle to a block of size Size. The first parameter indicates how many bytes you wish the block to contain. The second parameter contains the result code from the function call.

Result codes

noErr	0	No error
memFullErr	–108	Not enough memory

Locking and Unlocking Temporary Memory

You can use TempHLock to lock a specified relocatable block of temporary memory, thereby preventing it from being moved within the heap zone.

```
PROCEDURE TempHLock (h: Handle; VAR resultCode: OSErr);
```

The first parameter is a handle to the block to be locked, which you must have obtained by a call to TempNewHandle. TempHLock returns a result code in its second parameter.

Result codes

noErr	0	No error
nilHandleErr	–109	NIL master pointer
memWZErr	–111	Attempt to operate on a free block

In system software version 7.0, you can use the Memory Manager routine HLock to lock temporary memory blocks.

You can use TempHUnlock to unlock a block of temporary memory. Once it is unlocked, that block is allowed to move memory locations as needed to compact the heap.

```
PROCEDURE TempHUnlock (h: Handle; VAR resultCode: OSErr);
```

The first parameter is a handle to the block to be unlocked, which must have been obtained by a call to TempNewHandle. TempHUnlock returns a result code in its second parameter.

Result codes

noErr	0	No error
nilHandleErr	–109	NIL master pointer
memWZErr	–111	Attempt to operate on a free block

Under system software version 7.0, you can use the Memory Manager routine HUnlock to unlock temporary memory blocks.

Freeing Temporary Memory

You can use TempDisposeHandle to release the memory occupied by a relocatable temporary memory block.

```
PROCEDURE TempDisposeHandle (h: Handle; VAR resultCode: OSErr);
```

The first parameter is a handle to the block to be freed, which you must have obtained by a call to TempNewHandle. TempDisposeHandle returns a result code in its second parameter.

Result codes

noErr	0	No error
memWZErr	–111	Attempt to operate on a free block

In system software version 7.0, you can use the Memory Manager routine DisposHandle to free temporary memory blocks.

SUMMARY OF MEMORY MANAGEMENT

Constants

```
CONST gestaltAddressingModeAttr = 'addr'; {addressing mode attributes}
      gestalt32BitAddressing    = 0;      {booted in 32-bit mode}
      gestalt32BitSysZone       = 1;      {32-bit compatible sys. zone}
      gestalt32BitCapable       = 2;      {machine is 32-bit capable}

      gestaltOSAttr             = 'os  '; {O/S attributes}
      gestaltTempMemSupport     = 4;      {temp memory support present}
      gestaltRealTempMemory     = 5;      {temp memory handles are real}
      gestaltTempMemTracked     = 6;      {temp memory handles tracked}

      gestaltVMAttr             = 'vm  '; {virtual memory attributes}
      gestaltVMPresent          = 0;      {virtual memory present}

      {default number of physical blocks in table}
      defaultPhysicalEntryCount = 8;

      {page states}
      kPageInMemory             = 0;      {page is in RAM}
      kPageOnDisk               = 1;      {page is on disk}
      kNotPaged                 = 2;      {address is not paged}

      calcCntlRgn               = 10;     {calculate control's region}
      calcThumbRgn              = 11;     {calculate indicator's region}
```

Data Types

```
TYPE PageState              = Integer;

     MemoryBlock =
     RECORD
        address:            Ptr;           {start of block}
        count:              LongInt        {size of block}
     END;

     LogicalToPhysicalTable =
     RECORD
        logical:   MemoryBlock;            {logical block}
        physical:  ARRAY[0..defaultPhysicalEntryCount-1] OF MemoryBlock
                                           {equivalent physical blocks}
     END;
```

Memory Manager Routines

Setting and Restoring the A5 World

```
FUNCTION SetCurrentA5       : LongInt;
FUNCTION SetA5              (newA5: LongInt) : LongInt;
```

Manipulating Memory Addresses

```
FUNCTION StripAddress       (address: UNIV Ptr) : Ptr;
FUNCTION Translate24To32    (addr24: UNIV Ptr) : Ptr;
```

Virtual Memory Routines

Holding and Releasing Pages

```
FUNCTION HoldMemory         (address: UNIV Ptr; count: LongInt) : OSErr;
FUNCTION UnholdMemory       (address: UNIV Ptr; count: LongInt) : OSErr;
```

Locking and Unlocking Pages

```
FUNCTION LockMemory             (address: UNIV Ptr; count: LongInt) : OSErr;
FUNCTION LockMemoryContiguous   (address: UNIV Ptr; count: LongInt) : OSErr;
FUNCTION UnlockMemory           (address: UNIV Ptr; count: LongInt) : OSErr;
```

Obtaining Page-Mapping Information

```
FUNCTION GetPhysical        (VAR addresses: LogicalToPhysicalTable; VAR
                             physicalEntryCount: LongInt) : OSErr;
```

Deferring User Interrupt Handling

```
FUNCTION DeferUserFn        (userFunction: ProcPtr; argument: UNIV Ptr) :
                             OSErr;
```

Determining Which Debugger Functions Are Present

```
FUNCTION DebuggerGetMax     : LongInt;
```

Determining Whether Paging Is Safe

```
FUNCTION PageFaultFatal     : Boolean;
```

Locking and Unlocking Memory With Caching Enabled

```
FUNCTION DebuggerLockMemory   (address: UNIV Ptr; count: LongInt) : OSErr;
FUNCTION DebuggerUnlockMemory (address: UNIV Ptr; count: LongInt) : OSErr;
```

Entering and Exiting the Debugging State

```
PROCEDURE DebuggerEnter;
PROCEDURE DebuggerExit;
```

Obtaining Keyboard Input

```
PROCEDURE DebuggerPoll;
```

Determining Page State

```
FUNCTION GetPageState       (address: UNIV Ptr) : PageState;
```

Temporary Memory Routines

Requesting Temporary Memory

```
FUNCTION TempFreeMem        : LongInt;
FUNCTION TempMaxMem         (VAR grow: Size) : Size;
FUNCTION TempNewHandle      (logicalSize: Size; VAR resultCode: OSErr) :
                             Handle;
```

Locking and Unlocking Temporary Memory

```
PROCEDURE TempHLock        (h: Handle; VAR resultCode: OSErr);
PROCEDURE TempHUnlock      (h: Handle; VAR resultCode: OSErr);
```

Freeing Temporary Memory

```
PROCEDURE TempDisposeHandle  (h: Handle; VAR resultCode: OSErr);
```

Result Codes

noErr	0	No error
memFullErr	–108	Not enough memory
nilHandleErr	–109	NIL master pointer
memWZErr	–111	Attempt to operate on a free block
notEnoughMemoryErr	–620	Insufficient physical memory
notHeldErr	–621	Specified range of memory is not held
cannotMakeContiguousErr	–622	Cannot make specified range contiguous
notLockedErr	–623	Specified range of memory is not locked
interruptsMaskedErr	–624	Called with interrupts masked
cannotDeferErr	–625	Unable to defer additional user functions

Assembly-Language Information

Trap Macros Requiring Routine Selectors

_MemoryDispatch

Selector	Routine
$0000	HoldMemory
$0001	UnholdMemory
$0002	LockMemory
$0003	UnlockMemory
$0004	LockMemoryContiguous

_MemoryDispatchA0Result

Selector	Routine
$0005	GetPhysical

_DebugUtil

Selector	Routine
$0000	DebuggerGetMax
$0001	DebuggerEnter
$0002	DebuggerExit
$0003	DebuggerPoll
$0004	GetPageState
$0005	PageFaultFatal
$0006	DebuggerLockMemory
$0007	DebuggerUnlockMemory
$0008	EnterSupervisorMode

_OSDispatch

Selector	Routine
$0015	TempMaxMem
$0016	TempTopMem
$0018	TempFreeMem
$001D	TempNewHandle
$001E	TempHLock
$001F	TempHUnlock
$0020	TempDisposeHandle

29 PROCESS MANAGEMENT

ABOUT THIS CHAPTER

This chapter describes how process management in version 7.0 provides a cooperative multitasking environment. The Process Manager manages access to shared resources and the scheduling and execution of applications. The Finder™ uses the Process Manager to launch your application in response to the user opening either your application or a document created by your application. This chapter discusses how your application can control its execution and get information about itself or any other open application, such as the number of free bytes in the application's heap.

Read this chapter for an overview of how the Process Manager schedules applications and loads applications into memory. If your application needs to launch other applications, read this chapter for information on the new high-level function that lets your application launch other applications.

Although earlier versions of system software provide process management, the Process Manager is available to your application only in system software version 7.0. The Process Manager provides a cooperative multitasking environment, similar to the features provided by the MultiFinder® option in earlier versions of system software. Use the Gestalt function to find out if the Process Manager routines are available and to see which features of the launch routine are available.

The information in this chapter about the Finder information supplements the description in the Segment Loader chapters of *Inside Macintosh,* Volume II and Volume IV.

The information in this chapter about launching applications replaces the corresponding discussion in the *Programmer's Guide to MultiFinder.*

You should be familiar with how your application uses memory, as described in the Memory Management chapter of this volume, and with how your application receives events, as discussed in the Event Manager chapter of this volume.

This chapter provides an introduction to process management and then describes how you can

- control the execution of your application
- get information about your application
- launch other applications or desk accessories
- get information about applications launched by your application
- generate a list of all open applications and information about each one

ABOUT PROCESS MANAGEMENT

The Process Manager schedules the processing of all applications and desk accessories, and allows multiple applications to share the CPU and other resources. Applications share the available memory and access to the CPU. Several applications can be open (loaded into memory) at once, but only one uses the CPU at any one time.

The Process Manager manages the scheduling of processes. A **process** is an open application or, in some cases, an open desk accessory. (Desk accessories that are opened in the context of an application are not considered processes.) In version 7.0, the number of processes is limited only by available memory.

The Process Manager maintains information about each process—for example, the current state of the process, the address and size of its partition, its type, its creator, a copy of its low-memory globals, information about its 'SIZE' resource, and a process serial number. This process information is referred to as the **context** of a process. The Process Manager assigns a **process serial number** to identify each process. A process serial number identifies a particular instance of an application; this number is unique during a single boot of the local machine.

The **foreground process** is the one currently interacting with the user; it appears to the user as the active application. The foreground process displays its menu bar, and its windows are in front of the windows of all other applications.

A **background process** is a process that isn't currently interacting with the user. At any given time a process is either in the foreground or the background; a process can switch between the two states at well-defined times.

The foreground process has first priority for accessing the CPU. Other processes can access the CPU only when the foreground process yields time to them. There is only one foreground process at any one time. However, multiple processes can exist in the background.

An application that is in the background can get CPU time but can't interact with the user while it is in the background. (However, the user can choose to bring the application to the foreground—for example, by clicking in one of the application's windows.) Any application that has the canBackground flag set in its 'SIZE' resource is eligible to obtain access to the CPU when it is in the background.

Applications can be designed without a user interface. A **background-only application** is an application that does not have a user interface. A background-only application does not call the InitWindows routine and is identified by having the onlyBackground flag set in its 'SIZE' resource. Background-only applications do not display windows or a menu bar and are not listed in the Application menu.

Background-only applications and applications that can run in the background should be designed to relinquish the CPU often enough so that the foreground process can perform its work and respond to the user.

Once an application is executing, in either the foreground or the background, the CPU is available only to that application. The application can be interrupted only by hardware interrupts, which are transparent to the scheduling of the application. However, to give processing time to background applications and to allow the user to interact with the foreground application or switch to another application, you must periodically relinquish the CPU using the WaitNextEvent or EventAvail functions. (You can also use the GetNextEvent function; however, you should use WaitNextEvent to provide greater support for multitasking.) Use these Event Manager functions to let the user interact with your application and also with other applications.

How the Process Manager Creates Processes

When a user first opens your application, the Process Manager creates a partition for it. A **partition** is a contiguous block of memory that the Process Manager allocates for the application's use. The partition is divided into specific areas: application heap, A5 world, and stack. The **application heap** contains the application's 'CODE' segment 1, data structures, resources, and other code segments as needed. The **A5 world** refers to the QuickDraw™ globals, application global variables, and its jump table, all of which are accessed through the A5 register. The application **jump table** contains one entry for every externally referenced routine in every code segment of your application. The application **stack** is used to store temporary variables. See the Memory Management chapter of this volume for illustrations of these areas of your application's partition.

When you create an application, you specify in the 'SIZE' resource how much memory you want the Process Manager to allocate for your application's partition. You specify two values: the preferred amount of memory to allocate, and the minimum amount of memory to allocate. When a user opens your application from the Finder, the Process Manager first attempts to allocate a partition of the preferred size. If your application cannot be launched in the preferred amount of memory, the Finder displays a dialog box giving the user the option of opening the application using less than the preferred size. The Finder will not launch your application if the minimum amount of memory specified for your application is not available.

After the Process Manager creates a partition for your application, the Process Manager loads your code into memory and sets up the stack, heap, and A5 world (including the jump table) for your application. If the user selected one or more files to open or print, the Finder sets up information your application can use to determine which files to open or print.

The Process Manager assigns the application a process serial number, records its context, and returns control to the launching application (usually the Finder). The Process Manager transfers control to the new application after the launching application makes a subsequent call to WaitNextEvent or EventAvail.

The next section describes how your application can allow other applications to receive CPU time and how the Process Manager schedules CPU time among processes.

How the Process Manager Schedules Processes

Your application achieves control of how it receives processing time by using the Event Manager functions WaitNextEvent or EventAvail. By calling these Event Manager functions, your application agrees to yield the CPU. (Only at this well-defined time can your application be switched out.) Whenever your application calls one of these functions, the Process Manager checks the status of your process and takes the opportunity to schedule other processes.

> **Note:** Your application can also yield processing time to other processes as a result of calling other Toolbox routines that internally call WaitNextEvent or EventAvail. For example, your application can yield the CPU to other processes as a result of calling either of the Apple Event Manager functions AESend or AEInteractWithUser. See the Apple Event Manager chapter for information on using these two functions.

In general, if any events are pending for your application, it continues to receive processing time. When your application is the foreground process, it yields time to other processes in these situations: when the user wants to switch to another application or when no events are pending for your application. Your application can also choose to yield processing time to other processes when it is performing a lengthy operation.

A **major switch** occurs when the Process Manager switches the context of the foreground process with the context of a background process (including the A5 worlds and low-memory globals) and brings the background process to the front, sending the previous foreground process to the background.

When your application is the foreground process and the user chooses to work with another application (by clicking in a window of another application, for example), the Process Manager sends your application a suspend event. When your application receives a suspend event, it should prepare to suspend foreground processing, allowing the user to switch to the other application. For example, in response to the suspend event, your application should remove the highlighting from the controls of its frontmost window and take any other necessary actions. Your application is actually suspended the next time your application calls WaitNextEvent or EventAvail.

After your application receives the suspend event and calls WaitNextEvent or EventAvail, the Process Manager saves the context of your process, restores the context of the process to which the user is switching, and sends a resume event to that process.

In response to a resume event, your application should resume processing and start interacting with the user. For example, your application should highlight the controls of its frontmost window.

A major switch also occurs when the user hides the active application (by using the Application menu). In general, a major switch cannot occur when a modal dialog box is the frontmost window. However, a major switch can occur when a movable modal dialog box is the frontmost window.

A **minor switch** occurs when the Process Manager switches the context of a process to give time to a background process without bringing the background process to the front.

For example, a minor switch occurs when no events are pending in the event queue of the foreground process. In this situation, processes running in the background have an opportunity to execute when the foreground process calls WaitNextEvent or EventAvail. (If the foreground process has one or more events pending in the event queue, then the next event is returned and the foreground process again has sole access to the CPU.)

When an application is switched out in this way, the Process Manager saves the context of the current process, restores the context of the next background process scheduled to run, and sends the background process an event. At this time, the background process can receive either update, null, or high-level events.

A background process should not perform any task that would significantly limit the ability of the foreground process to respond quickly to the user. A background process should call WaitNextEvent often enough to let the foreground process be responsive to the user. Upon receiving an update event, the background process should update only the content of its windows. Upon receiving a null event, the background process can use the CPU to perform tasks that do not require significant amounts of processing time.

The next time the background process calls WaitNextEvent or EventAvail, the Process Manager saves the context of the background process and restores the context of the foreground process (if the foreground process is not waiting for a specified amount of time to expire before being scheduled again). The foreground process is then scheduled to execute. If no events are pending for the foreground process and it is waiting for a specified amount of time to expire, the Process Manager schedules the next background process to run. The Process Manager continues to manage the scheduling of processes in this manner.

In version 7.0, drivers and VBL tasks in the system heap are scheduled regardless of which application is currently executing. Drivers installed in an application's heap are not scheduled to run when the application is not executing.

See the Compatibility Guidelines chapter and the Event Manager chapter in this volume for specific information on how your application can handle suspend and resume events and how your application can take advantage of the cooperative multitasking environment.

How Your Application Specifies Scheduling Options

Whenever your application calls WaitNextEvent or EventAvail, the Process Manager checks the status of your process and takes the opportunity to schedule other processes. Using the WaitNextEvent function, you can control when your process is eligible to be switched out.

The sleep parameter to WaitNextEvent specifies a length of time, in ticks, during which the application relinquishes the CPU if no events are pending. For example, if you specify 15 ticks in the sleep parameter and no events are pending in your application's event queue when you call WaitNextEvent, the Process Manager saves the context of your process and schedules other processes until an event becomes available or the time expires. Once the specified time expires or an event becomes available for your application, your process becomes eligible to run and the Process Manager schedules your process to run at the next available chance. You can also use the WakeUpProcess function to make a process eligible to run before the time in the sleep parameter expires.

In general, you should specify a value greater than 0 in the sleep parameter so that those applications that need processing time can get it. If your application performs any periodic task, then the frequency of the task usually determines what value you specify in the sleep parameter. The less frequent the task, the higher the value of the sleep parameter.

USING THE PROCESS MANAGER

The Process Manager manages the scheduling of all processes. You can use the Process Manager routines to

- control the execution of your application
- use the information provided by the Finder to open or print documents
- get information about processes
- launch other applications
- launch desk accessories

The Process Manager assigns a process serial number to each open application (or desk accessory, if it is not opened in the context of an application). The process serial number is unique to each process on the local machine and is valid for a single boot of the machine. You can use the process serial number to specify a particular process for most Process Manager routines. You can use the process serial number returned from the GetCurrentProcess, GetNextProcess, GetFrontProcess, and LaunchApplication functions in other Process Manager routines.

Opening or Printing Files Based on Finder Information

When a user opens or prints a file from the Finder, the Finder uses the Process Manager to launch the application that created the file. The Finder sets up the information your application can use to determine which files to open or print. The Finder information includes a list of files to open or print.

In version 7.0, applications that support high-level events (that is, that have the isHighLevelEventAware flag set in the 'SIZE' resource) receive the Finder information through Apple events. The Apple Event Manager chapter in this volume describes how your application processes Apple events to open or print files.

Applications that do not support high-level events can use the CountAppFiles, GetAppFiles, and ClrAppFiles routines or the GetAppParms routine to get the Finder information. See the Segment Loader chapter of Volume II for information on these routines.

Getting Information About Other Processes

You can use the GetNextProcess, GetFrontProcess, or GetCurrentProcess functions to get the process serial number of a process. The GetCurrentProcess function returns the process serial number of the process that is currently executing. The **current process** is the process whose A5 world is currently valid; this process can be in the background or foreground. The GetFrontProcess function returns the process serial number of the foreground process. For example, if your process is running in the background, you can use GetFrontProcess to determine which process is in the foreground.

The Process Manager maintains a list of all open processes. You can specify the process serial number of a process currently in the list and use GetNextProcess to get the process serial number of the next process in the list. The interpretation of the value of a process serial number and the order of the list of processes is internal to the Process Manager.

When specifying a particular process, use only a process serial number returned by a high-level event, Process Manager routine, or constants defined by the Process Manager. You can use these constants to specify special processes.

```
CONST   kNoProcess        = 0;          {process doesn't exist}
        kSystemProcess    = 1;          {process belongs to OS}
        kCurrentProcess   = 2;          {the current process}
```

In all Process Manager routines, the constant kNoProcess refers to a process that doesn't exist, the constant kSystemProcess refers to a process belonging to the Operating System, and the constant kCurrentProcess refers to the current process.

To begin enumerating a list of processes, use the GetNextProcess function and specify the constant kNoProcess as the parameter to return the process serial number of the first process in the list. You can use the returned process serial number to get the process serial number of the next process in the list. The GetNextProcess function returns the constant kNoProcess and the result code procNotFound at the end of the list.

You can also use a process serial number to specify a target application when your application sends a high-level event. See the Event Manager chapter for information on how to use a process serial number when your application sends a high-level event.

You can use the GetProcessInformation function to obtain information about any process, including your own. For example, for a specified process, you can find the application's name as it appears in the Application menu, the type and signature of the application, the number of bytes in the application partition, the number of free bytes in the application heap, the application that launched the application, and other information.

The GetProcessInformation function returns information about the requested process in a process information record. The process information record is defined by the ProcessInfoRec data type.

```
TYPE ProcessInfoRec =
     RECORD
        processInfoLength: LongInt;             {length of record}
        processName:       StringPtr;           {name of process}
        processNumber:     ProcessSerialNumber; {psn of the process}
        processType:       LongInt;             {file type of app file}
        processSignature:  OSType;              {signature of app file}
        processMode:       LongInt;             {'SIZE' resource flags}
        processLocation:   Ptr;                 {address of partition}
        processSize:       LongInt;             {partition size}
        processFreeMem:    LongInt;             {free bytes in heap}
        processLauncher:   ProcessSerialNumber; {process that launched}
        processLaunchDate: LongInt;             {time when launched}
        processActiveTime: LongInt;             {accumulated CPU time}
        processAppSpec:    FSSpecPtr            {location of the file}
     END;
```

You specify the values for three fields of the process information record: processInfoLength, processName and processAppSpec. You must either set the processName and processAppSpec fields to NIL or set these fields to point to storage that you have allocated for them. The GetProcessInformation function returns information in all other fields of the process information record.

The processInfoLength field is the number of bytes in the process information record. For compatibility, you should specify the length of the record in this field.

The name returned in the processName field is the name of the application or desk accessory. For applications, this field contains the name of the application as designated by the user at the time the application was opened. For example, for foreground applications, the processName field is the name as it appears in the Application menu. For desk accessories, the processName field contains the name of the 'DRVR' resource. You must specify NIL in the processName field if you do not want the application name or the desk accessory name returned. Otherwise, you should allocate at least 32 bytes of storage for the string pointed to by the processName field. Note that the processName field specifies the name of either the application or the 'DRVR' resource, whereas the processAppSpec field specifies the location of the file.

The processNumber field specifies the process serial number. The process serial number is a 64-bit number; the meaning of these bits is internal to the Process Manager. You should not interpret the value of the process serial number.

The processType field indicates the file type of the application, generally 'APPL' for applica-tions, and 'appe' for background-only applications launched at startup. If the process is a desk accessory, the processType field is the type of the file containing the 'DRVR' resource.

The processSignature field indicates the signature of the file containing the application or the 'DRVR' resource (for example, the signature of the TeachText application is 'ttxt').

The processMode field indicates whether the process is an application or desk accessory. For applications, this field also returns information specified in the application's 'SIZE' resource. This information is returned as flags.You can refer to these flags by using these constants.

```
CONST modeDeskAccessory                = $00020000;
      modeMultiLaunch                  = $00010000;
      modeNeedSuspendResume            = $00004000;
      modeCanBackground                = $00001000;
      modeDoesActivateOnFGSwitch       = $00000800;
      modeOnlyBackground               = $00000400;
      modeGetFrontClicks               = $00000200;
      modeGetAppDiedMsg                = $00000100;
      mode32BitCompatible              = $00000080;
      modeHighLevelEventAware          = $00000040;
      modeLocalAndRemoteHLEvents       = $00000020;
      modeStationeryAware              = $00000010;
      modeUseTextEditServices          = $00000008;
```

The processLocation field is the beginning address of the application partition.

The processSize field is the number of bytes in the application's partition (including the heap, stack, and A5 world).

The processFreeMem field is the number of free bytes in the application's heap.

The processLauncher field is the process serial number of the process that launched the application or desk accessory. If the original launcher of the process is no longer open, this field contains the constant kNoProcess.

The processLaunchDate field contains the value of the Ticks global variable at the time that the process was launched.

The processActiveTime field represents the accumulated time, in ticks, during which the process has used the CPU, including both foreground and background processing time.

The processAppSpec field specifies the address of a file specification record that stores the location of the file containing the application or 'DRVR' resource. You should specify NIL in the processAppSpec field if you do not want the FSSpec record of the file returned.

Listing 29-1 shows how you can use the GetNextProcess function with the GetProcessInformation function to search the process list for a specific process.

Listing 29-1. Searching for a specific process

```
FUNCTION FindAProcess(signature: OSType; VAR process:
                      ProcessSerialNumber; VAR InfoRec: ProcessInfoRec;
                      aFSSpecPtr: FSSpecPtr) : Boolean;
BEGIN
   FindAProcess := FALSE;                   {assume FALSE to begin with}
   process.highLongOfPSN := 0;
   process.lowLongOfPSN := kNoProcess;      {start from the beginning}

   InfoRec.processInfoLength := sizeof(ProcessInfoRec);
   InfoRec.processName := StringPtr(NewPtr(32));
   InfoRec.processAppSpec := aFSSpecPtr;

   WHILE (GetNextProcess(process) = noErr) DO
   BEGIN
      IF GetProcessInformation(process, InfoRec) = noErr THEN
      BEGIN
         IF (InfoRec.processType = LongInt('APPL')) AND
            (InfoRec.processSignature = signature) THEN
         BEGIN                              {found the process}
            FindAProcess := TRUE;
            Exit(FindAProcess);
         END;
      END;
   END; {while}
END;
```

The code in Listing 29-1 searches the process list for the application with the specified signature. For example, you might want to find a specific process in order to send a high-level event to it.

Launching Other Applications

You can launch other applications using the high-level LaunchApplication function. The LaunchApplication function lets your application control various options associated with launching an application. For example, you can

- allow the application to be launched in a partition smaller than the preferred size but greater than the minimum size, or allow it to be launched only in a partition of the preferred size
- launch an application without terminating your own application, bring the launched application to the front, and get information about the launched application
- request that your application be notified if any application that it has launched terminates

Earlier versions of system software used a shorter parameter block as a parameter to the _Launch trap macro. The _Launch trap macro still supports the use of this parameter block. Applications using the LaunchApplication function should use the new launch parameter block (LaunchParamBlockRec). Use the Gestalt function and specify the selector gestaltOSAttr to determine which launch features are available. See the Compatibility Guidelines chapter for information on how to use the Gestalt function.

Most applications don't need to launch other applications. However, if your application includes a desk accessory or another application, you might use either the high-level LaunchApplication function to launch an application or the LaunchDeskAccessory function to launch a desk accessory. For example, if you have implemented a spelling checker as a separate application, you might use the LaunchApplication function to open the spelling checker when the user chooses Check Spelling from one of your application's menus.

You specify a launch parameter block as a parameter to the LaunchApplication function. You use the launch parameter block to specify the filename of the application to launch, to specify whether to allocate the preferred size for the application's heap or to allow a partition size less than the preferred size, and to set various other options—for example, whether your application should continue or terminate after it launches the specified application.

The LaunchApplication function launches the application from the specified file and returns the process serial number, preferred partition size, and minimum partition size if the application is successfully launched.

Note that if you launch another application without terminating your application, the launched application does not actually begin executing until you make a subsequent call to WaitNextEvent or EventAvail.

The launch parameter block is defined by the LaunchParamBlockRec data type.

```
TYPE LaunchParamBlockRec =
     RECORD
        reserved1:          LongInt;            {reserved}
        reserved2:          Integer;            {reserved}
        launchBlockID:      Integer;            {extended block}
        launchEPBLength:    LongInt;            {length of block}
        launchFileFlags:    Integer;            {Finder flags of }
                                                { application}
```

```
        launchControlFlags:   LaunchFlags;           {launch options}
        launchAppSpec:        FSSpecPtr;             {location of }
                                                     { application file}
        launchProcessSN:      ProcessSerialNumber;   {returned psn}
        launchPreferredSize:  LongInt;               {returned pref size}
        launchMinimumSize:    LongInt;               {returned min size}
        launchAvailableSize:  LongInt;               {returned available }
                                                     { size}
        launchAppParameters:  AppParametersPtr       {high-level event}
    END;
```

Specify the constant extendedBlock in the launchBlockID field to identify the parameter block and to indicate that you are using the fields following it in the launch parameter block.

In the launchEPBLength field, specify the constant extendedBlockLen to indicate the length of the remaining fields in the launch parameter block. For compatibility, you should always specify the length value in this field.

The launchFileFlags field contains the Finder flags for the application file. (See the Finder Interface chapter in this volume for a description of the Finder flags.) The LaunchApplication function sets this field for you if you set the bit defined by the launchNoFileFlags constant in the launchControlFlags field. Otherwise, you must get the Finder flags from the application file and set this field yourself (by using GetFInfo, for example).

In the launchControlFlags field, you specify various options that control how the specified application is launched. See the next section, "Specifying Launch Options," for information on the launch control flags.

You specify the application to launch using the launchAppSpec field of the launch parameter block. You specify a pointer to a file system specification record (FSSpec) in this field. See the File Manager chapter in this volume for a complete description of the file system specification record.

LaunchApplication sets the initial default volume of the application to the parent directory of the application file.

If LaunchApplication successfully launched the application, LaunchApplication returns in the launchProcessSN field a process serial number that you can use in Process Manager routines to refer to this application.

The launchPreferredSize and launchMinimumSize fields of the launch parameter block are returned by LaunchApplication and are based on their corresponding values in the 'SIZE' resource. These values may be greater than those specified in the application's 'SIZE' resource because the returned sizes include any adjustments to the size of the application's stack. See the Event Manager chapter in this volume for information on how the size of the application stack is adjusted. LaunchApplication always returns values for these fields whether or not the launch was successful. These values are 0 if an error occurred—for example, if the application file could not be found.

The launchAvailableSize field is returned by LaunchApplication only when the memFullErr result code is returned. This value indicates the largest partition size currently available for allocation.

The launchAppParameters field specifies the first high-level event sent to an application. If you set this field to NIL, the LaunchApplication function automatically creates and sends an Open Application event to the launched application. (See the Apple Event Manager chapter for a description of this event.) To send a particular high-level event to the launched application, you can specify a pointer to an application parameters record. The application parameters record is defined by the data type AppParameters.

```
TYPE AppParameters =
     RECORD
         theMsgEvent:         EventRecord;           {event (high-level)}
         eventRefCon:         LongInt;               {reference constant}
         messageLength:       LongInt;               {length of buffer}
         messageBuffer:       ARRAY [0..0] OF SignedByte
     END;
```

You specify the high-level event in the fields theMsgEvent, eventRefCon, messageLength, and messageBuffer. The Event Manager chapter in this volume describes how to use high-level events.

Listing 29-2 shows an example of using the LaunchApplication function.

Listing 29-2. Launching an application

```
PROCEDURE LaunchAnApplication (mySFReply: StandardFileReply);
VAR
   myLaunchParams:        LaunchParamBlockRec;
   launchedProcessSN:     ProcessSerialNumber;
   launchErr:             OSErr;
   prefSize:              LongInt;
   minSize:               LongInt;
   availSize:             LongInt;

BEGIN
   WITH myLaunchParams DO
   BEGIN
      launchBlockID := extendedBlock;
      launchEPBLength := extendedBlockLen;
      launchFileFlags:= 0;
      launchControlFlags:= launchContinue + launchNoFileFlags;
      launchAppSpec:= @mySFReply.sfFile;
      launchAppParameters := NIL;
   END;
   launchErr := LaunchApplication(@myLaunchParams);

   prefsize := myLaunchParams.launchPreferredSize;
   minsize := myLaunchParams.launchMinimumSize;
   IF launchErr = noErr THEN
      launchedProcessSN := myLaunchParams.launchProcessSN
   ELSE IF launchErr = memFullErr THEN
      availSize := myLaunchParams.launchAvailableSize
   ELSE
      DoError(launchErr);
END;
```

In Listing 29-2, the application file to launch is specified by using a file system specification record returned by the StandardGetFile routine and specifying a pointer to this record in the launchAppSpec field. The launchControlFlags field indicates that LaunchApplication should extract the Finder flags from the application file, launch the application in the preferred size, bring the launched application to the front, and that LaunchApplication should not terminate the current process.

Specifying Launch Options

When you use the LaunchApplication function, you specify the launch options in the launchControlFlags field of the launch parameter block. These are the constants you can specify in the launchControlFlags field.

```
CONST launchContinue        = $4000;
      launchNoFileFlags     = $0800;
      launchUseMinimum      = $0400;
      launchDontSwitch      = $0200;
      launchInhibitDaemon   = $0080;
```

Set the launchContinue flag if you want your application to continue after the specified application is launched. If you do not set this flag, LaunchApplication terminates your application after launching the specified application, even if the launch fails.

Set the launchNoFileFlags flag if you want the LaunchApplication function to ignore any value specified in the launchFileFlags field. If you set the launchNoFileFlags flag, the LaunchApplication function extracts the Finder flags from the application file for you. If you want to extract the file flags, clear the launchNoFileFlags flag and specify the Finder flags in the launchFileFlags field of the launch parameter block.

Clear the launchUseMinimum flag if you want the LaunchApplication function to attempt to launch the application in the preferred size (as specified in the application's 'SIZE' resource). If you set the launchUseMinimum flag, the LaunchApplication function attempts to launch the application using the largest available size greater than or equal to the minimum size but less than the preferred size. If the LaunchApplication function returns the result code memFullErr or memFragErr, the application cannot be launched given the current memory conditions.

Set the launchDontSwitch flag if you do not want the launched application brought to the front. If you set this flag, the launched application runs in the background until the user brings the application to the front—for example, by clicking in one of the application's windows. Note that most applications expect to be launched in the foreground. If you clear the launchDontSwitch flag, the launched application is brought to the front, and your application is sent to the background.

Set the launchInhibitDaemon flag if you do not want LaunchApplication to launch a background-only application. (A background-only application has the onlyBackground flag set in its 'SIZE' resource.)

Controlling Launched Applications

When your application launches another application using LaunchApplication, the launched application is automatically brought to the front, sending the foreground application to the background. If you don't want to bring the application to the front when it is first launched, set the launchDontSwitch flag in the launchControlFlags field of the launch parameter block.

In addition, if you want your application to continue to run after it launches another application, you must set the launchContinue flag in the launchControlFlags field of the launch parameter block.

You can control the scheduling of the launched application in a limited way by using the Process Manager routines SetFrontProcess and WakeUpProcess.

If you want your application to be notified when an application it has launched terminates, set the acceptAppDiedEvents flag in your 'SIZE' resource. If you set this flag and an application launched by your application terminates, your application receives an Application Died event ('aevt' 'obit'). See the Apple Event Manager chapter for information on receiving the Application Died event and other Apple events.

Launching Desk Accessories

In version 7.0, when a desk accessory is opened, the Process Manager launches the desk accessory in its own partition. The Process Manager gives it a process serial number and an entry in the process list. The Process Manager puts the name of the desk accessory in the list of open applications in the Application menu and also gives the active desk accessory its own About menu item in the Apple menu that contains the name of the desk accessory. This makes desk accessories more consistent with the user interface of small applications.

Your application can launch desk accessories using the LaunchDeskAccessory function. However, you should use this function only when your application needs to launch a desk accessory for some reason other than in response to the user choosing a desk accessory from the Apple menu. In version 7.0, the Apple menu can contain any Finder object that the user chooses to add to the menu. When the user chooses any item from the Apple menu that you didn't add specifically for your application, use the OpenDeskAcc function.

PROCESS MANAGER ROUTINES

You can use the Process Manager to get information about any currently open applications, to launch other applications, and to control the scheduling of applications.

Use the Gestalt function with the selector gestaltOSAttr to see if the Process Manager is available and to find out which features of the launch routine are available. These constants are names for the bit numbers returned in the response parameter to the Gestalt function.

```
CONST gestaltLaunchCanReturn       = 1; {can return from launch}
      gestaltLaunchFullFileSpec    = 2; {LaunchApplication available}
      gestaltLaunchControl         = 3; {Process Manager is available}
```

The bit defined by the constant gestaltLaunchCanReturn is set if the _Launch trap macro can return to the caller. The _Launch trap macro in version 7.0 (and in earlier versions of system software running MultiFinder) provides an application with the option to continue running after launching another application. The _Launch trap macro forces the launching application to quit in earlier versions of system software not running MultiFinder.

The bit defined by the constant gestaltLaunchFullFileSpec is set if the launchControlFlags field supports control flags in addition to the launchContinue flag, and if the parameters to the _Launch trap macro include the launchAppSpec, launchProcessSN, launchPreferredSize, launchMinimumSize, launchAvailableSize, and launchAppParameters fields in the launch parameter block.

The bit defined by the constant gestaltLaunchControl is set if the Process Manager is available.

Getting Process Information

You can use the Process Manager to get the process serial number of a particular process, to get information about processes, or to change the scheduling status of a process.

```
FUNCTION GetCurrentProcess(VAR PSN: ProcessSerialNumber): OSErr;
```

The GetCurrentProcess function returns in the PSN parameter the process serial number of the process that is currently executing. The currently executing process is the one currently accessing the CPU; this is the application associated with the CurrentA5 global variable. This application can be running in either the foreground or the background.

Applications can use this function to find their own process serial number. Drivers can use this function to find the process serial number of the current process. You can use the returned process serial number in other Process Manager routines.

Result code

noErr	0	No error

```
FUNCTION GetNextProcess(VAR PSN: ProcessSerialNumber): OSErr;
```

The Process Manager maintains a list of all open processes. You can derive this list by using repetitive calls to GetNextProcess. Begin generating the list by calling GetNextProcess and by specifying the constant kNoProcess in the PSN parameter. You can then use the returned process serial number to get the process serial number of the next process. Note that the order of the list of processes is internal to the Process Manager. GetNextProcess returns the constant kNoProcess in the PSN parameter and the result code procNotFound when the end of the list is reached.

The process serial number you specify in the PSN parameter should be a valid process serial number returned from LaunchApplication, GetNextProcess, GetFrontProcess, or GetCurrentProcess, or the defined constant kNoProcess.

You can use the returned process serial number in other Process Manager routines. You can also use this process serial number to specify a target application when your application sends a high-level event.

Result codes

noErr	0	No error
paramErr	–50	Process serial number is invalid
procNotFound	–600	No process in the process list following the specified process

```
FUNCTION GetProcessInformation(PSN: ProcessSerialNumber; VAR info:
                               ProcessInfoRec): OSErr;
```

The GetProcessInformation function returns information about the specified process in a process information record. The information returned in the info parameter includes the application's name as it appears in the Application menu, the type and signature of the application, the address of the application partition, the number of bytes in the application partition, the number of free bytes in the application heap, the application that launched the application, the time at which the application was launched, and the location of the application file. The section "Getting Information About Other Processes," earlier in this chapter, shows the structure of the process information record.

The GetProcessInformation function also returns information about the application's 'SIZE' resource and indicates whether the process is an application or a desk accessory.

You need to specify values for the processInfoLength, processName, and processAppSpec fields of the process information record. Specify the length of the process information record in the processInfoLength field. If you do not want information returned in the processName and processAppSpec fields, specify NIL for these fields. Otherwise, allocate at least 32 bytes of storage for the string pointed to by the processName field and specify a pointer to an FSSpec record in the processAppSpec field.

The process serial number you specify in the PSN parameter should be a valid process serial number returned from LaunchApplication, GetNextProcess, GetFrontProcess, GetCurrentProcess, or a high-level event. You can use the constant kCurrentProcess to get information about the current process.

Note: Do not call GetProcessInformation from a routine that executes at interrupt time.

Result codes

noErr	0	No error
paramErr	–50	Process serial number is invalid

```
FUNCTION SameProcess(PSN1,PSN2: ProcessSerialNumber; VAR result:
                     Boolean): OSErr;
```

The SameProcess function compares two process serial numbers and determines whether they refer to the same process. If the process serial numbers specified in the PSN1 and PSN2 parameters refer to the same process, the SameProcess function returns TRUE in the result parameter; otherwise, it returns FALSE in the result parameter.

When you compare two process serial numbers, use the SameProcess function rather than any other means, because the interpretation of the bits in a process serial number is internal to the Process Manager.

The process serial numbers you use should be valid process serial numbers returned from LaunchApplication, GetNextProcess, GetFrontProcess, GetCurrentProcess, or a high-level event. You can also use the constant kCurrentProcess to refer to the current process.

Result codes

noErr	0	No error
paramErr	–50	Process serial number is invalid

```
FUNCTION GetFrontProcess(VAR PSN: ProcessSerialNumber): OSErr;
```

The GetFrontProcess function returns in the PSN parameter the process serial number of the process running in the foreground. You can use this function to determine if your process or some other process is in the foreground. You can use the process serial number returned in the PSN parameter in other Process Manager routines.

If no process is running in the foreground, GetFrontProcess returns the result code procNotFound.

Result codes

noErr	0	No error
paramErr	–50	Process serial number is invalid
procNotFound	–600	No process in the foreground

```
FUNCTION SetFrontProcess(PSN: ProcessSerialNumber): OSErr;
```

The SetFrontProcess function schedules the specified process to become the foreground process. The specified process becomes the foreground process after the current foreground process makes a subsequent call to WaitNextEvent or EventAvail.

The process serial number in the PSN parameter should be a valid process serial number returned from LaunchApplication, GetNextProcess, GetFrontProcess, GetCurrentProcess, or a high-level event. You can also use the constant kCurrentProcess to refer to the current process.

If the specified process serial number is invalid or if the specified process is a background-only application, SetFrontProcess returns a nonzero result code and does not change the current foreground process.

If a modal dialog box is the frontmost window, the specified process does not become the foreground process until after the user dismisses the modal dialog box.

Note: Do not call SetFrontProcess from a routine that executes at interrupt time.

Result codes

noErr	0	No error
procNotFound	–600	Process with specified process serial number doesn't exist or process is suspended by high-level debugger
appIsDaemon	–606	Specified process is background-only

```
FUNCTION WakeUpProcess(PSN: ProcessSerialNumber): OSErr;
```

The WakeUpProcess function makes a process suspended by WaitNextEvent eligible to receive CPU time. When a process specifies a nonzero value for the sleep parameter in the WaitNextEvent function, and there are no events for that process pending in the event queue, the process is suspended. This process remains suspended until the time specified in the sleep parameter expires or an event becomes available for that process. You can use WakeUpProcess to make the process eligible for execution before the time specified in the sleep parameter expires.

The WakeUpProcess function does not change the order of the processes scheduled for execution; it only makes the specified process eligible for execution.

The process serial number specified in the PSN parameter should be a valid process serial number returned from LaunchApplication, GetNextProcess, GetFrontProcess, GetCurrentProcess, or a high-level event.

Result codes

noErr	0	No error
procNotFound	–600	Suspended process with specified process serial number doesn't exist

Launching Applications and Desk Accessories

Your application can use the LaunchApplication function to launch other applications and the LaunchDeskAccessory function to launch desk accessories.

The LaunchApplication function launches the application from the specified file and returns the process serial number, preferred partition size, and minimum partition size if the application is successfully launched.

Note that if you launch another application without terminating your application, the launched application is not actually executed until you make a subsequent call to WaitNextEvent or EventAvail.

Set the launchContinue flag in the launchControlFlags field of the launch parameter block if you want your application to continue after the specified application is launched. If you do not set this flag, LaunchApplication terminates your application after launching the specified application, even if the launch fails.

```
FUNCTION LaunchApplication(LaunchParams: LaunchPBPtr): OSErr;
```

Trap macro	_Launch
On entry	A0: Launch parameter block pointer
On exit	A0: Launch parameter block pointer D0: Result code

Parameter block

→	6	launchBlockID	word	extended block
→	8	launchEPBLength	long	length of following fields
→	12	launchFileFlags	word	Finder flags for the application file
→	14	launchControlFlags	word	flags for launch options
→	16	launchAppSpec	long	location of application file to launch
←	20	launchProcessSN	2 longs	process serial number
←	28	launchPreferredSize	long	preferred application partition size
←	32	launchMinimumSize	long	minimum application partition size
←	36	launchAvailableSize	long	maximum available partition size
→	40	launchAppParameters	long	high-level event for launched app

Field descriptions

launchBlockID — A value that indicates whether you are using the fields following it in the launch parameter block. Specify the constant extendedBlock if you use the fields that follow it.

launchEPBLength — The length of the fields following this field in the launch parameter block. Use the constant extendedBlockLen to specify this value.

launchFileFlags — The Finder flags for the application file. Set the launchNoFileFlags constant in the launchControlFlags field if you want the LaunchApplication function to extract the Finder flags from the application file and to set the launchFileFlags field for you.

launchControlFlags
: The launch options that determine how the application is launched. You can specify these constant values to set various options:

```
CONST
launchContinue          = $4000;
launchNoFileFlags       = $0800;
launchUseMinimum        = $0400;
launchDontSwitch        = $0200;
launchInhibitDaemon     = $0080;
```

See "Specifying Launch Options" earlier in this chapter for a complete description of these flags.

launchAppSpec
: A pointer to a file specification record that gives the location of the application file to launch.

launchProcessSN
: The process serial number returned to your application if the launch is successful. You can use this process serial number in other Process Manager routines to refer to the launched application.

launchPreferredSize
: The preferred partition size for the launched application as specified in the launched application's 'SIZE' resource. LaunchApplication sets this field to 0 if an error occurred or if the application is already open.

launchMinimumSize
: The minimum partition size for the launched application as specified in the launched application's 'SIZE' resource. LaunchApplication sets this field to 0 if an error occurred or if the application is already open.

launchAvailableSize
: The maximum partition size that is available for allocation. This value is returned to your application only if the memFullErr result code is returned. If the application launch fails (because there isn't enough memory), you can use this value to determine if there is enough memory available to launch in the minimum size.

launchAppParameters
: The first high-level event to send to the launched application. If you specify NIL for this field, LaunchApplication creates and sends the Open Application event to the launched application.

Result codes

noErr	0	No error
memFullErr	–108	Not enough memory to allocate the partition size specified in the 'SIZE' resource
memFragErr	–601	Not enough room to launch application with special requirements
appModeErr	–602	Memory mode is 32-bit, but application is not 32-bit clean
appMemFullErr	–605	More memory for the partition size is required than the amount specified in the 'SIZE' resource
appIsDaemon	–606	Application is background-only, and launch flags don't allow this

Your application can launch desk accessories using the LaunchDeskAccessory function. Use this function only when your application needs to launch a desk accessory for some reason other than in response to the user choosing a desk accessory from the Apple menu. (When the user chooses any item from the Apple menu that you didn't add specifically for your application, use the OpenDeskAcc function.)

```
FUNCTION LaunchDeskAccessory(pFileSpec: FSSpecPtr; pDAName: StringPtr):
                                OSErr;
```

LaunchDeskAccessory searches the resource fork of the file specified by the pFileSpec parameter for the desk accessory with the 'DRVR' resource name specified in the pDAName parameter. If the 'DRVR' resource name is found, LaunchDeskAccessory launches the desk accessory. If the desk accessory is already open, it is brought to the front.

Specify the file to search using the pFileSpec parameter. Specify NIL for pFileSpec if you want to search the current resource file and the resource files opened before it. Otherwise, specify the file using a pointer to an FSSpec record.

In the pDAName parameter, specify the 'DRVR' resource name of the desk accessory to launch. Specify NIL in pDAName if you want to launch the first 'DRVR' resource found in the file as returned by the Resource Manager. Because the LaunchDeskAccessory function opens the specified resource file for exclusive access, you cannot launch more than one desk accessory from the same resource file.

If the 'DRVR' resource is in a resource file that is already open by the current process or if the driver is in the System file and the Option key is down, LaunchDeskAccessory launches the desk accessory in the application's heap. Otherwise, the desk accessory is given its own partition and launched in the system heap.

Result codes

noErr	0	No error
resNotFound	–192	Resource not found

SUMMARY OF PROCESS MANAGER ROUTINES

Constants

```
CONST kNoProcess                  = 0;          {process doesn't exist}
      kSystemProcess              = 1;          {process belongs to OS}
      kCurrentProcess             = 2;          {the current process}

      {launch control flags}
      launchContinue              = $4000;      {continue after launch}
      launchNoFileFlags           = $0800;      {ignore launchFileFlags}
      launchUseMinimum            = $0400;      {use minimum or greater }
                                                { size}
      launchDontSwitch            = $0200;      {launch application in }
                                                { background}
      launchAllow24Bit            = $0100;      {reserved}
      launchInhibitDaemon         = $0080;      {don't launch }
                                                { background application}

      {launch parameter block length}
      extendedBlockLen            = sizeof(LaunchParamBlockRec) - 12;
      extendedBlock               = $4C43;      {extended block}

      {flags in processMode field}
      modeDeskAccessory           = $00020000;  {process is desk acc}
      modeMultiLaunch             = $00010000;  {from app file's flags}
      modeNeedSuspendResume       = $00004000;  {from 'SIZE' resource}
      modeCanBackground           = $00001000;  {from 'SIZE' resource}
      modeDoesActivateOnFGSwitch  = $00000800;  {from 'SIZE' resource}
      modeOnlyBackground          = $00000400;  {from 'SIZE' resource}
      modeGetFrontClicks          = $00000200;  {from 'SIZE' resource}
      modeGetAppDiedMsg           = $00000100;  {from 'SIZE' resource}
      mode32BitCompatible         = $00000080;  {from 'SIZE' resource}
      modeHighLevelEventAware     = $00000040;  {from 'SIZE' resource}
      modeLocalAndRemoteHLEvents  = $00000020;  {from 'SIZE' resource}
      modeStationeryAware         = $00000010;  {from 'SIZE' resource}
      modeUseTextEditServices     = $00000008;  {from 'SIZE' resource}
      gestaltOSAttr               = 'os  ';     {OS gestalt selector}

      {Process Mgr attributes}
      gestaltLaunchCanReturn      = 1;          {can return from launch}
      gestaltLaunchFullFileSpec   = 2;          {LaunchApplication is }
                                                { available}
      gestaltLaunchControl        = 3;          {Process Manager }
                                                { is available}
```

Data Types

```
TYPE ProcessSerialNumberPtr   = ^ProcessSerialNumber;
     ProcessSerialNumber =
     RECORD
        highLongOfPSN:        LongInt;              {process serial }
        lowLongOfPSN:         LongInt               { number}
     END;

     ProcessInfoRecPtr = ^ProcessInfoRec;
     ProcessInfoRec =
     RECORD
        processInfoLength:    LongInt;              {length of record}
        processName:          StringPtr;            {name of process}
        processNumber:        ProcessSerialNumber;  {psn of the process}
        processType:          LongInt;              {file type of app file}
        processSignature:     OSType;               {signature of app file}
        processMode:          LongInt;              {'SIZE' resource flags}
        processLocation:      Ptr;                  {address of partition}
        processSize:          LongInt;              {partition size}
        processFreeMem:       LongInt;              {free bytes in heap}
        processLauncher:      ProcessSerialNumber;  {process that launched}
        processLaunchDate:    LongInt;              {time when launched}
        processActiveTime:    LongInt;              {accumulated CPU time}
        processAppSpec:       FSSpecPtr             {location of the file}
     END;


     AppParametersPtr =       ^AppParameters;
     AppParameters =
     RECORD
        theMsgEvent:          EventRecord;          {event (high-level)}
        eventRefCon:          LongInt;              {reference constant}
        messageLength:        LongInt;              {length of buffer}
        messageBuffer:        ARRAY [0..0] OF SignedByte
     END;


     LaunchFlags =             Integer;
     LaunchPBPtr =             ^LaunchParamBlockRec;
     LaunchParamBlockRec =
     RECORD
        reserved1:             LongInt;             {reserved}
        reserved2:             Integer;             {reserved}
        launchBlockID:         Integer;             {extended block}
        launchEPBLength:       LongInt;             {length of block}
        launchFileFlags:       Integer;             {Finder flags of }
                                                    { application}
        launchControlFlags:    LaunchFlags;         {launch options}
        launchAppSpec:         FSSpecPtr;           {location of }
                                                    { application file}
        launchProcessSN:       ProcessSerialNumber; {returned psn}
```

```
      launchPreferredSize:  LongInt;           {returned pref size}
      launchMinimumSize:    LongInt;           {returned min size}
      launchAvailableSize:  LongInt;           {returned avail size}
      launchAppParameters:  AppParametersPtr   {high-level event}
   END;
```

Routines

Getting Process Information

```
FUNCTION GetCurrentProcess       (VAR PSN: ProcessSerialNumber): OSErr;

FUNCTION GetNextProcess          (VAR PSN: ProcessSerialNumber): OSErr;

FUNCTION GetProcessInformation   (PSN: ProcessSerialNumber; VAR info:
                                  ProcessInfoRec): OSErr;

FUNCTION SameProcess             (PSN1,PSN2: ProcessSerialNumber; VAR
                                  result: Boolean): OSErr;

FUNCTION GetFrontProcess         (VAR PSN: ProcessSerialNumber): OSErr;

FUNCTION SetFrontProcess         (PSN: ProcessSerialNumber): OSErr;

FUNCTION WakeUpProcess           (PSN: ProcessSerialNumber): OSErr;
```

Launching Applications and Desk Accessories

```
FUNCTION LaunchApplication       (LaunchParams: LaunchPBPtr): OSErr;

FUNCTION LaunchDeskAccessory     (pFileSpec: FSSpecPtr; pDAName:
                                  StringPtr): OSErr;
```

Result Codes

noErr	0	No error
paramErr	–50	Process serial number is invalid
memFullErr	–108	Not enough memory to allocate the partition size specified in the 'SIZE' resource
resNotFound	–192	Resource not found
procNotFound	–600	No eligible process with specified process serial number
memFragErr	–601	Not enough room to launch application with special requirements
appModeErr	–602	Memory mode is 32-bit, but application is not 32-bit clean
appMemFullErr	–605	Partition size specified in 'SIZE' resource is not big enough for launch
appIsDaemon	–606	Application is background-only

Assembly-Language Information

Process Information Record Data Structure

processInfoLength	long	length of this record
processName	long	name of process
processNumber	2 longs	process serial number
processType	long	type of application file
processSignature	long	signature of application file
processMode	long	flags from 'SIZE' resource
processLocation	long	address of process partition
processSize	long	partition size (in bytes)
processFreeMem	long	amount of free memory
processLauncher	2 longs	launcher of process
processLaunchDate	long	value of TICKS at time of launch
processActiveTime	long	total time spent using the CPU
processAppSpec	long	location of the file

Launch Parameter Block

	0	reserved1	long	reserved
	4	reserved2	word	reserved
→	6	launchBlockID	word	specifies whether block is extended
→	8	launchEPBLength	long	length (in bytes) of rest of parameter block
→	12	launchFileFlags	word	the Finder flags for the application file
→	14	launchControlFlags	word	flags that specify launch options
→	16	launchAppSpec	long	address of FSSpec that specifies the application file to launch
←	20	launchProcessSN	2 longs	process serial number
←	28	launchPreferredSize	long	application's preferred partition size
←	32	launchMinimumSize	long	application's minimum partition size
←	36	launchAvailableSize	long	maximum partition size available
→	40	launchAppParameters	long	high-level event for launched application

30 THE SLOT MANAGER

ABOUT THIS CHAPTER

This chapter describes the enhancements and new routines that have been added to the Slot Manager with system software version 7.0. The information in this chapter supplements the information in the Slot Manager chapter inVolume V.

You need to use Slot Manager routines only if you are writing an application or device driver that must address a NuBus™ card directly. For example, you need to use the Slot Manager if you are writing a driver for a video card, but not if you only want to display information on a screen for which a device driver already exists. If you *do* have to use the Slot Manager, read this chapter to see if any of the functions added to the Slot Manager by system software version 7.0 are of use to you.

There are two variations of the system software version 7.0 Slot Manager: version 1 and version 2. Version 1 of the Slot Manager is supplied with the version 7.0 System file on disk for use with Macintosh® II–family computers that were designed and built before system software version 7.0 was available. Version 2 is included in the ROM of newer Macintosh II–family computers.

The Slot Manager polls the NuBus cards in the system and initializes the cards before patches to the Operating System are loaded from disk. Version 1 of the 7.0 Slot Manager polls all NuBus cards again in case any cards that must be addressed in 32-bit mode were not recognized by the older Slot Manager. It is not necessary for version 2 of the Slot Manager to poll the NuBus cards a second time. Both versions of the Slot Manager reinitialize all NuBus cards after RAM patches have been loaded, in case any card requires RAM patches to be available before the card is used. Other than this difference in initialization sequence, the two versions of the Slot Manager are identical.

You can use the SVersion function, described in this chapter, to determine whether the system software version 7.0 Slot Manager is available and, if it is available, whether it is version 1 or version 2. You cannot use the other routines described in this chapter if the system software version 7.0 Slot Manager is not available.

Once the system software version 7.0 Slot Manager has been loaded into memory, the Slot Manager no longer executes the InitSDeclMgr, SInitSRsrcTable, SInitPRAMRecs, and SPrimaryInit functions. Because these functions are used for card initialization and all initialization is handled by the Operating System, the availability of these functions should not affect your program. See "Card Initialization" later in this chapter for more information about the initialization of NuBus cards by the Slot Manager.

If you are writing a device driver, you need the book *Designing Cards and Drivers for the Macintosh Family,* second edition. You will also find useful information in the chapters on the Device Manager in Volumes II, IV, and V of *Inside Macintosh.*

ABOUT THE SLOT MANAGER

The Slot Manager provided with system software version 7.0 addresses NuBus cards in 32-bit mode to ensure that the Operating System recognizes all NuBus cards. It also performs card initialization in a fashion different from that used by older versions of the Slot Manager to ensure that all NuBus cards—including those that must be addressed in 32-bit mode—are initialized correctly.

Several new routines have been added to the Slot Manager. You can use the new Slot Manager routines to

- determine which version of the Slot Manager is available
- determine what sResource data structures are available
- get information about an sResource data structure, whether or not the sResource data structure is enabled
- get information about all sResource data structures that match the type of a specific sResource data structure
- enable and disable sResource data structures
- restore an sResource data structure that has been deleted from the Slot Resource Table

Note: An sResource data structure is sometimes referred to as a *slot resource.* Note, however, that a slot resource is a data structure in the firmware of a NuBus card and not a type of Macintosh resource. The structure and content of an sResource data structure are described in detail in *Designing Cards and Drivers for the Macintosh Family,* second edition.

All of the Slot Manager routines use a data structure called the Slot Manager parameter block to exchange information with the Slot Manager. The Slot Manager parameter block has been modified to add a flag field that is used by two new Slot Manager routines: SGetSRsrc and SGetTypeSRsrc. These routines search for sResource data structures.

CARD INITIALIZATION

When the user starts up a Macintosh II–family computer, the Slot Manager in ROM searches each slot for a declaration ROM. It identifies all of the sResource data structures in each declaration ROM and creates a table—the **Slot Resource Table**—that lists all of the sResource data structures currently available to the system. The Slot Manager then initializes the parameter RAM bytes reserved for each slot and executes the initialization code in the PrimaryInit record in the declaration ROM of each NuBus card.

The Slot Manager in the ROM of early Macintosh II computers (revision A of the ROM) can address NuBus cards only in 24-bit mode and can search for declaration ROMs only in the 1-megabyte (MB) slot space for each slot—that is, in addresses $Fsxx xxxx, where s is the slot number. Because some NuBus cards have a declaration ROM that must be addressed with 32-bit addresses, not all NuBus cards can be addressed or even located by the Slot Manager in ROM revision A. The Slot Manager released with system software version 7.0 remedies this problem.

There are two versions of the Slot Manager that address NuBus cards in 32-bit mode: version 1 and version 2 (see "Determining the Version of the Slot Manager" later in this chapter). When version 1 of the Slot Manager is loaded into memory, it conducts a second search for declaration ROMs, this time addressing all of the slots in 32-bit mode. If it finds any new NuBus cards, the Slot Manager adds their sResource data structures to the Slot Resource Table and executes the code in the PrimaryInit records on those cards. Version 2 of the Slot Manager conducts only one search for declaration ROMs—before RAM patches are loaded into memory—and it executes PrimaryInit records at that time.

After RAM patches to the Operating System have been loaded from disk, either variant of the system software version 7.0 Slot Manager executes the code in any SecondaryInit records it finds in any of the declaration ROMs. It does *not*

- reexecute any PrimaryInit records that were executed by the ROM-based Slot Manager
- reinitialize the parameter RAM values that were initialized by the ROM-based Slot Manager
- restore any sResource data structures that were loaded by the ROM-based Slot Manager and subsequently deleted by the PrimaryInit code

The Slot Manager executes the code in PrimaryInit records with interrupts disabled before Operating System patches have been loaded into RAM, but it executes SecondaryInit records with interrupts enabled after system patches have been loaded.

A SecondaryInit record has the same format as a PrimaryInit record. To include a SecondaryInit record in your declaration ROM, you must include a SecondaryInit field—a field with an identification (ID) number of 38—in the Board sResource data structure. (The Board sResource data structure is a type of sResource data structure that must be present in the firmware of every NuBus card that communicates with the computer. The format of a PrimaryInit record and the Board sResource data structure are described in *Designing Cards and Drivers for the Macintosh Family,* second edition.)

The system software version 7.0 Slot Manager allows you to disable a card temporarily until the SecondaryInit record is executed. The SecondaryInit record can then enable the card and complete initialization. You can use this feature, for example, to ensure that a card that requires Color QuickDraw™ is not used until after Color QuickDraw has been loaded into memory.

USING THE SLOT MANAGER

The Slot Manager released with system software version 7.0 allows you to do four things you couldn't do before:

- You can temporarily disable and then reenable a NuBus card.
- You can enable and disable sResource data structures.
- You can search for disabled sResource data structures.
- You can restore an sResource data structure that was deleted from the Slot Resource Table.

This section describes how to do each of these things and provides some sample code to illustrate how to do them.

Enabling and Disabling NuBus Cards

If your NuBus card must be addressed in 32-bit mode or requires that RAM-based system software patches be loaded into memory before the card is initialized, you can use the code in the PrimaryInit record to disable the card temporarily and the code in the SecondaryInit record to reenable it. To determine whether the system software version 7.0 (or later) Slot Manager is present and, if present, whether it is the RAM-based version (version 1) or the ROM-based version (version 2), use the SVersion function described in "Determining the Version of the Slot Manager" later in this chapter. If version 2 of the Slot Manager is present, you can assume that the Slot Manager operates in 32-bit mode. However, if you want to be sure that all RAM patches to the Operating System have been loaded before your card is used, you can still use the method described here to disable your NuBus card temporarily.

To disable a NuBus card temporarily, the initialization routine in your PrimaryInit record should return in the seStatus field of the SEBlock data structure an error code with a value in the range svTempDisable ($8000) through svDisabled ($8080). The Slot Manager places this error code in the siInitStatusV field of the sInfo record that the Slot Manager maintains for that slot, and it places the fatal error smInitStatVErr (–315) in the siInitStatusA field of the sInfo record. The card and its sResource data structures are then unavailable for use by the Operating System.

After the Operating System loads RAM patches, the system software version 7.0 Slot Manager checks the value of the siInitStatusA field. If this value is greater than or equal to 0, indicating no error, the Slot Manager executes the SecondaryInit code in the declaration ROM of the NuBus card. If the value in the siInitStatusA field is smInitStatVErr, the Slot Manager checks the siInitStatusV field. If the value of the siInitStatusV field is in the range svTempDisable through svDisabled, the Slot Manager clears the siInitStatusA field to 0 and runs the SecondaryInit code. In other words, the version 7.0 Slot Manager runs the SecondaryInit code if the PrimaryInit code returns no error or returns an error in the range svTempDisable through svDisabled. If the PrimaryInit code returns any other result code less than 0 (that is, any other fatal error), the NuBus card remains disabled and the Slot Manager does not run the SecondaryInit code. The sExec parameter block and the sInfo record are described in the Slot Manager chapter in Volume V.

For examples of PrimaryInit and SecondaryInit records that test for the presence of the version 7.0 Slot Manager and act accordingly, see *Designing Cards and Drivers for the Macintosh Family,* second edition.

Enabling and Disabling SResource Data Structures

Under certain circumstances, you might want to disable an sResource data structure while it remains listed in the Slot Resource Table. For example, a NuBus card might provide several modes of operation, only one of which can be active at a given time. Your application might want to disable the sResource data structures associated with all but the active mode, but still list all available modes in a menu. When the user selects a new mode, your application can then disable the currently active sResource data structure and enable the one the user selected.

You use the SetSRsrcState function to enable or disable an sResource data structure. Listing 30-1 disables the sResource data structure in slot $0A with an ID of 128 and enables the sResource data structure in the same slot with an ID of 131.

Listing 30-1. Disabling and enabling sResource data structures

```
VAR
   mySpBlk: SpBlock;
   myErr:   OSErr;

BEGIN
{Set required values in parameter block.}
   WITH mySpBlk DO
   BECIN
      spParamData := 1;                {disable}
      spSlot := $0A;                   {slot number}
      spID := 128;                     {sResource ID}
      spExtDev := 0;                {ID of the external device}
   END;
   myErr := SetSRsrcState(@mySpBlk);
   IF myErr <> noErr THEN DoError(myErr);

   WITH mySpBlk DO
   BEGIN
      spParamData := 0;                {enable}
      spSlot := $0a;                   {slot number}
      spID := 131;                     {sResource ID}
      spExtDev := 0;                {ID of the external device}
   END;
   myErr := SetSRsrcState(@mySpBlk);
   IF myErr <> noErr THEN DoError(myErr);
END;
```

Searching for Disabled SResource Data Structures

Whereas the Slot Manager routines described in Volume V act only on enabled sResource data structures, you can use system software version 7.0 Slot Manager routines to search for both enabled and disabled sResource data structures. The system software version 7.0 Slot Manager also allows you to specify whether the search should be for the specified sResource data structure or the next sResource data structure and whether the search should include only the specified slot or should include the specified slot plus all slots with higher numbers. In addition, you can specify the type of the sResource data structure for which you want to search; then the Slot Manager ignores all sResource data structures that do not match the specified type.

Table 30-1 summarizes the Slot Manager search routines and the options available for each.

Table 30-1. Slot Manager search routines

Function	State of sResources it searches for	Slots it searches	Which sResource it searches for	Type of sResource it searches for
SNextSRsrc	Enabled only	Specified slot and higher slots	Next sResource only	Any type
SGetSRsrc*	Your choice of enabled only or both enabled and disabled	Your choice of one slot only or specified slot and higher slots	Your choice of specified sResource or next sResource	Any type
SNextTypeSRsrc	Enabled only	Specified slot and higher slots	Next sResource only	Specified type only
SGetTypeSRsrc*	Your choice of enabled only or both enabled and disabled	Your choice of one slot only or specified slot and higher slots	Next sResource only	Specified type only

* Available only with system software version 7.0 Slot Manager

Listing 30-2 shows how to search all slots for all sResource data structures with a specific value in the Category and cType fields, whether enabled or disabled. The Slot Manager ignores the DrvrSW and DrvrHW fields of the resource type.

Restoring Deleted SResource Data Structures

Some NuBus cards have sResource data structures to support a variety of combinations of system configurations or modes. The Slot Manager loads all of the sResource data structures during system initialization, and then the PrimaryInit code in the declaration ROM deletes from the Slot Resource Table any sResource data structures that are not appropriate for the

Listing 30-2. Searching for sResource data structures

```
VAR
   mySpBlk: SpBlock;
   myErr:   OSErr;

BEGIN
{Set required values in parameter block.}
   WITH mySpBlk DO
   BEGIN
      spParamData := 1;           {fAll flag set to 1 to include }
                                  { disabled resources; fOneslot }
                                  { flag set to 0 to search specified }
                                  { slot plus higher-numbered slots}
      spCategory := catDisplay;   {Category field of sRsrcType }
                                  { entry in sResource}
      spCType := typeVideo;       {cType field of sRsrcType entry in }
                                  { sResource}
      spDrvrSW := 0;              {DrvrSW field of sRsrcType entry in }
                                  { sResource; this field is not }
                                  { being matched}
      spDrvrHW := 0;              {DrvrHW field of sRsrcType entry in }
                                  { sResource; this field is not }
                                  { being matched}
      spTBMask := 3;              {match only spCategory and spcType }
                                  { fields}
      spSlot := 0;                {start search from here}
      spID := 128;                {start search from here}
      spExtDev := 0;          {ID of the external device}
   END;
   myErr := 0;

   WHILE myErr = noErr DO         {loop to search sResources}
   BEGIN
      myErr := SGetTypeSRsrc(@mySpBlk);
      MysRsrcProc(mySpBlk);       {your routine to process results}
   END;
   IF myErr <> smNoMoresRsrcs THEN DoError(myErr);
END;
```

system as configured. The system software version 7.0 Slot Manager gives you the option of reinstalling a deleted sResource data structure if, for example, the user changes the system configuration or selects a different mode of operation. The SDeleteSRTRec function, described in the Slot Manager chapter in Volume V, deletes sResource data structures; the InsertSRTRec function reinstalls them.

Because none of the Slot Manager functions can search for sResource data structures that have been deleted from the Slot Resource Table, you must keep a record of all sResource data structures that you have deleted so that you will have the appropriate parameter values available if you want to reinstall one.

When you reinstall an sResource data structure, you can also update the dCtlDevBase field in the device driver's Device Control Entry (DCE) data structure. The dCtlDevBase field holds the address of the sResource data structure that is used by that device driver. For a video driver, for example, the dCtlDevBase field might contain the address of the frame buffer. Use the InsertSRTRec function to update the dCtlDevBase field. See the Device Manager chapters of Volumes II and V for a definition of the DCE data structure.

SLOT MANAGER ROUTINES

This section describes the new Slot Manager routines. All Slot Manager routines take one parameter: a pointer to a Slot Manager parameter block. Each routine description includes a list of the fields affected by that routine. Each field in the list is preceded by an arrow that indicates how the field is used.

Arrow	**Meaning**
→	You provide the value of the parameter as input to the Slot Manager.
←	The Slot Manager returns the value of the parameter after the function has completed execution.
↔	You provide a value for the parameter, and the Slot Manager returns another value.

For a general description of the parameter block, see the following section, "The Slot Manager Parameter Block."

You can use the sVersion function, described in "Determining the Version of the Slot Manager" to determine the version of the Slot Manager available to your program. The routines described in "Getting Information About SResource Data Structures" replace or supplement three of the Slot Manager routines described in the Slot Manager chapter in Volume V. These routines can be used by applications as well as by device drivers. You can use the routines described in "Enabling, Disabling, or Restoring SResource Data Structures," to enable or disable sResource data structures, or to restore sResource data structures deleted from the Slot Resource Table. These routines are intended primarily for use by device drivers.

Assembly-language note: You can use an assembly-language macro to call each of the Slot Manager routines. The assembly-language macro for a routine has the same name as the Pascal routine, except that the name is preceded by an underscore. However, these macros do not directly invoke the trap mechanism. Instead, each of these macros places a routine selector in the D0 register and calls the trap macro _SlotManager. The routine selectors for the new Slot Manager routines are shown in "Assembly-Language Information" in the summary at the end of this chapter.

Place a pointer to the Slot Manager parameter block in the A0 register when you call each Slot Manager routine in assembly language. Each routine returns with the status result in the low-order word of the D0 register.

The Slot Manager Parameter Block

The spParamData field replaces the spStackPtr field in the parameter block used by all Slot Manager routines. (The spStackPtr field was not used by any Slot Manager routines.) For your convenience, the entire parameter block is listed here, with a brief description of each field. Each Slot Manager routine uses only a subset of these fields. See the routine descriptions for a list of the fields used with each routine.


```
TYPE SpBlock =
     PACKED RECORD
        spResult:       LongInt;      {result}
        spsPointer:     Ptr;          {structure pointer}
        spSize:         LongInt;      {size of structure}
        spOffsetData:   LongInt;      {offset/data field returned }
                                      { by SOffsetData function}
        spIOFileName:   Ptr;          {reserved for Slot Manager}
        spsExecPBlk:    Ptr;          {pointer to SEBlock data structure}
        spParamData:    LongInt;      {flags}
        spMisc:         LongInt;      {reserved for Slot Manager}
        spReserved:     LongInt;      {reserved}
        spIOReserved:   Integer;      {reserved for Slot Manager}
        spRefNum:       Integer;      {Slot Resource Table ref number}
        spCategory:     Integer;      {sRsrc_Type: Category field}
        spCType:        Integer;      {sRsrc_Type: cType field}
        spDrvrSW:       Integer;      {sRsrc_Type: DrvrSW field}
        spDrvrHW:       Integer;      {sRsrc_Type: DrvrHW field}
        spTBMask:       SignedByte;   {type bit mask}
        spSlot:         SignedByte;   {slot number}
        spID:           SignedByte;   {ID of the sResource}
        spExtDev:       SignedByte;   {ID of the external device}
        spHwDev:        SignedByte;   {ID of the hardware device}
        spByteLanes:    SignedByte;   {byte lanes from card ROM }
                                      { format block}
        spFlags:        SignedByte;   {reserved for Slot Manager}
        spKey:          SignedByte    {reserved for Slot Manager}
     END;
```

Field descriptions

spResult — A general-purpose field used to contain the results returned by several different routines.

spsPointer — A pointer to a data structure. This field can point to an sResource data structure, a data block, or the declaration ROM of a NuBus card, depending on the routine being executed.

spSize — The size of a data block.

spOffsetData — The contents of the offset/data portion of a field in an sResource data structure. This parameter is returned by the SOffsetData function.

spIOFileName — Reserved for use by Apple Computer, Inc.

spsExecPBlk — A pointer to an SEBlock data structure. This field is used only by the SExec function.

spParamData — A long word that indicates whether an sResource data structure is enabled or disabled (if 0, the sResource data structure is enabled; if 1, it is disabled) or that sets the values of one or more of the following flags:

Bit	Flag	Meaning
0	fAll	If 1, include disabled sResource data structures in the search; if 0, ignore disabled sResource data structures.
1	fOneslot	If 1, restrict search to the slot specified in the spSlot field of the parameter block; if 0, search the specified slot plus all slots with higher numbers than the specified slot.
2	fNext	If 1, search for the sResource data structure that *follows* the one specified by the spSlot, spID, and spExtDev fields of the parameter block; if 0, search for the sResource data structure specified by these fields.
3–31	Reserved	Reserved for future use. These bits must be cleared to 0.

spMisc — Reserved for use by the Slot Manager.

spReserved — Reserved for future use.

spIOReserved — Reserved for use by the Slot Manager.

spRefNum — Device-driver reference number assigned by the Device Manager.

spCategory — Same as the Category field of the sRsrcType entry in the sResource data structure you specify.

spCType — Same as the cType field of the sRsrcType entry in the sResource data structure you specify.

spDrvrSW — Same as the DrvrSW field of the sRsrcType entry in the sResource data structure you specify.

spDrvrHW — Same as the DrvrHW field of the sRsrcType entry in the sResource data structure you specify.

spTBMask — A byte that allows you to specify which fields of the sRsrcType entry in the sResource data structure should not be used by the SNextTypeSRsrc or SGetTypeSRsrc function. Set a bit to 1 to mask a field.

Bit	Field masked
0	DrvrHW
1	DrvrSW
2	cType
3	Category

spSlot	The number of the slot containing the NuBus card you wish to address.
spID	The sResource identification number from the sResource directory.
spExtDev	An external-device identification number. If a NuBus card contains more than one device, the card can use this number to distinguish between the devices.
spHwDev	The hardware-device identification number from the sRsrc_HWDevId field of the sResource data structure.
spByteLanes	The NuBus byte lanes the Slot Manager is to use when communicating with the NuBus card's declaration ROM. You can read the byte-lane setting for a NuBus card from the card's format block. The SReadFHeader function returns a card's format block.
spFlags	Reserved for use by the Slot Manager.
spKey	Reserved for use by Apple.

Determining the Version of the Slot Manager

You can use the SVersion function to determine which version of the Slot Manager is in use by the Operating System.

```
FUNCTION SVersion (spBlkPtr: SpBlockPtr) : OSErr;
```

Parameter block

←	00	spResult	long	Slot Manager version number
←	04	spsPointer	long	pointer to additional information

The SVersion function returns the version number of the Slot Manager in the spResult field. The system software version 7.0 Slot Manager returns version number 1 for a RAM-based Slot Manager and version number 2 for a ROM-based Slot Manager. Older versions of the Slot Manager do not recognize the SVersion function and return the nonfatal error smSelOOBErr. The SVersion function returns a pointer to additional information, if any, in the spsPointer field.

Result codes

noErr	0	No error
smSelOOBErr	–338	Selector out of bounds; function not implemented

Getting Information About SResource Data Structures

The Slot Manager routines described in the Slot Manager chapter of Volume V ignore any disabled sResource data structures. However, there are times when you might want to know what sResource data structures are available even if they are disabled and cannot be used. The routines in this section perform the same tasks as routines described in Volume V, except that the new routines give you the option of including disabled sResource data structures.

```
FUNCTION SGetSRsrc (spBlkPtr: SpBlockPtr) : OSErr;
```

Parameter block

←	04	spsPointer	long	pointer to the sResource
↔	24	spParamData	long	input: fAll, fOneslot, fNext flags output: sResource enabled or disabled
←	38	spRefNum	word	Slot Resource Table reference number
←	40	spCategory	word	Category field of sRsrcType entry in sResource
←	42	spCType	word	cType field of sRsrcType entry in sResource
←	44	spDrvrSW	word	DrvrSW field of sRsrcType entry in sResource
←	46	spDrvrHW	word	DrvrHW field of sRsrcType entry in sResource
↔	49	spSlot	byte	slot number
↔	50	spID	byte	ID of the sResource
↔	51	spExtDev	byte	ID of the external device
←	52	spHwDev	byte	ID of the hardware device

When you specify an sResource data structure, the SGetSRsrc function returns information about that sResource data structure, the next sResource data structure in the same slot, or the next sResource data structure in any higher-numbered slot. It performs the same function as the SNextSRsrc function described in the Slot Manager chapter of Volume V, except that for the SGetSRsrc function, you set the fAll, fOneslot, and fNext flags to specify which type of search the function is to perform.

You specify an sResource data structure with the spSlot, spID, and spExtDev fields. You must also set bits 0, 1, and 2 of the spParamData field as follows:

- Set the fAll flag (bit 0) to search both enabled and disabled sResource data structures.
- Clear the fAll flag to search only enabled sResource data structures.
- Set the fOneslot flag (bit 1) to search only the specified slot.
- Clear the fOneslot flag to search all slots.
- Set the fNext flag (bit 2) to search for the sResource data structure that follows the specified sResource data structure.
- Clear the fNext flag to return data about the sResource data structure that you specified.

The SGetSRsrc function returns new values in the spSlot, spID, and spExtDev fields specifying the sResource data structure that it found, and it returns in the spsPointer field a pointer to the sResource data structure. If you cleared the fNext flag to 0, then the spSlot, spID, and spExtDev fields return the same values that you specified when you called the function. The SGetSRsrc function also returns information about the sResource data structure in the spRefNum, spCategory, spCType, spDrvrSW, spDrvrHW, and spHwDev fields. In addition, the function returns 0 in the spParamData field if the sResource data structure is enabled or 1 if it is disabled.

Result codes

noErr	0	No error
smNoMoresRsrcs	–344	Specified sResource data structure not found

```
FUNCTION SGetTypeSRsrc (spBlkPtr: SpBlockPtr) : OSErr;
```

Parameter block

←	04	spsPointer	long	pointer to the sResource
↔	24	spParamData	long	input: fAll, fOneslot flags output: sResource enabled or disabled
←	38	spRefNum	word	Slot Resource Table reference number
↔	40	spCategory	word	Category field of sRsrcType entry in sResource
↔	42	spCType	word	cType field of sRsrcType entry in sResource
↔	44	spDrvrSW	word	DrvrSW field of sRsrcType entry in sResource
↔	46	spDrvrHW	word	DrvrHW field of sRsrcType entry in sResource
→	48	spTBMask	byte	type bit mask
↔	49	spSlot	byte	slot number
↔	50	spID	byte	ID of the sResource
↔	51	spExtDev	byte	ID of the external device
←	52	spHwDev	byte	ID of the hardware device

When you specify an sResource data structure and specify which resource-type fields to match, the SGetTypeSRsrc function returns information either about the next sResource data structure of the matching type it finds in the same slot or about the next sResource data structure of the matching type it finds in any higher-numbered slot. It performs the same function as the SNextTypeSRsrc function described in Volume V, except that for the SGetTypeSRsrc function, you set the fAll and fOneslot flags to specify which type of search the function is to perform.

You specify an sResource data structure with the spSlot, spID, and spExtDev fields. You must also use the spTBMask field to specify which fields of the sRsrcType entry in the sResource data structure should not be included in the search, as follows:

- Set bit 0 to ignore the DrvrHW field.
- Set bit 1 to ignore the DrvrSW field.
- Set bit 2 to ignore the cType field.
- Set bit 3 to ignore the Category field.

In addition, you must clear the fAll flag of the spParamData field (bit 0) to 0 to search only enabled sResource data structures or set the fAll flag to 1 to search both enabled and disabled sResource data structures. Set the fOneslot flag (bit 1) to 1 to search only the specified slot or clear it to 0 to search all slots.

The SGetTypeSRsrc function returns new values in the spSlot, spID, and spExtDev fields specifying the sResource data structure that it found, and it returns in the spsPointer field a pointer to the sResource data structure. The SGetTypeSRsrc function also returns information about the sResource data structure in the spRefNum, spCategory, spCType, spDrvrSW, spDrvrHW, and spHwDev fields. In addition, the function returns 0 in the spParamData field if the sResource data structure is enabled or 1 if it is disabled.

Result codes

noErr	0	No error
smNoMoresRsrcs	–344	Specified sResource data structure not found

Enabling, Disabling, or Restoring SResource Data Structures

The routines in this section are primarily for use by device drivers. The first routine enables and disables sResource data structures. The second routine restores sResource data structures that have been deleted from the Slot Resource Table.

```
FUNCTION SetSRsrcState (spBlkPtr: SpBlockPtr) : OSErr;
```

Parameter block

→	24	spParamData	long	enable or disable the sResource
→	49	spSlot	byte	slot number
→	50	spID	byte	ID of the sResource
→	51	spExtDev	byte	ID of the external device

The SetSRsrcState function enables or disables an sResource data structure. An enabled sResource data structure can be used by the Operating System and is recognized by all Slot Manager routines. A disabled sResource data structure is recognized only by the SGetSRsrc and SGetTypeSRsrc functions, and then only if you set the fAll flag of the spParamData field.

You specify an sResource data structure with the spSlot, spID, and spExtDev fields and use the spParamData field to specify whether the sResource data structure should be enabled or disabled. Set spParamData to 0 to enable the sResource data structure or to 1 to disable the sResource data structure.

Result codes

noErr	0	No error
smNoMoresRsrcs	–344	Specified sResource data structure not found

```
FUNCTION InsertSRTRec (spBlkPtr: SpBlockPtr) : OSErr;
```

Parameter block

→	04	spsPointer	long	NIL
→	24	spParamData	long	flags
→	38	spRefNum	word	Slot Resource Table reference number
→	49	spSlot	byte	slot number
→	50	spID	byte	ID of the sResource
→	51	spExtDev	byte	ID of the external device

The InsertSRTRec function adds an sResource data structure to the Slot Resource Table. You can use the function to restore an sResource data structure that was deleted from the Slot Resource Table with the SDeleteSRTRec function, described in Volume V. For example, if the user makes a selection in the Monitors control panel that requires your video card to switch to a new sResource data structure that was deleted by the PrimaryInit code, you can use the InsertSRTRec function to restore that sResource data structure.

You specify an sResource data structure with the spSlot, spID, and spExtDev fields. You must set the spsPointer to all zeros. Set the spParamData field to 1 to disable the restored sResource data structure or to 0 to enable it.

If you place a valid device-driver reference number in the spRefNum field, then the Slot Manager updates the dCtlDevBase field in that device driver's DCE data structure (that is, in the DCE that has that device-driver reference number in the dCtlRefNum field). The dCtlDevBase field contains the base address of the memory buffer for data provided by the sResource data structure that is used by that device driver. The Slot Manager calculates this address by using bit 2 (the f32BitMode flag) of the sRsrc_Flags field of the sResource data structure and the MinorBaseOS or MajorBaseOS field of the sResource data structure. Table 30-2 shows how the Slot Manager determines what format to use for this address.

The DCE data structure is described in the Device Manager chapters of Volumes II and V. The sResource data structure is described in *Designing Cards and Drivers for the Macintosh Family,* second edition.

Result codes

noErr	0	No error
memFullErr	–108	Not enough room in heap
smUnExBusErr	–308	Unexpected bus error
smBadRefId	–330	Reference ID not found in list
smBadsList	–331	Bad sResource structure: Id1 < Id2 < Id3 ... format is not followed
smReservedErr	–332	Reserved field not 0
smSlotOOBErr	–337	Slot number out of bounds
smNoMoresRsrcs	–344	Specified sResource data structure not found
smBadsPtrErr	–346	Bad pointer was passed to sCalcSPointer function
smByteLanesErr	–347	ByteLanes field in card's format block was determined to be 0

Table 30-2. How the Slot Manager determines the base address used by an sResource data structure

sRsrc_Flags	MinorBaseOS	MajorBaseOS	Address format	Address type
Field missing	$xxxxx	Any or none	$Fssx xxxx	1 MB address space; can be used in either 24-bit or 32-bit mode
Field missing	None	$xxxxxx	$sxxx xxxx	Superslot space
Bit 2 is 0	$xxxxx	Any or none	$Fssx xxxx	1 MB slot space
Bit 2 is 0	None	$xxxxxx	$sxxx xxxx	Superslot space
Bit 2 is 1	$xxxxxx	Any or none	$Fsxx xxxx	Standard slot space (32-bit minor base address)
Bit 2 is 1	None	$xxxxxxx	$sxxx xxxx	Superslot space (32-bit major base address)

Note: In a hexadecimal number in this table, x is any value and s is a slot number.

SUMMARY OF THE SLOT MANAGER

Constants

```
CONST svDisabled      = $8080;   {top of range of error codes to disable }
                                 { a NuBus card}
      svTempDisable   = $8000;   {start of range of error codes to }
                                 { disable a NuBus card}
```

Data Types

```
TYPE SpBlock =
     PACKED RECORD
        spResult:       LongInt;      {result}
        spsPointer:     Ptr;          {structure pointer}
        spSize:         LongInt;      {size of structure}
        spOffsetData:   LongInt;      {offset/data field returned }
                                      { by SOffsetData function}
        spIOFileName:   Ptr;          {reserved for Slot Manager}
        spsExecPBlk:    Ptr;          {pointer to SEBlock data structure}
        spParamData:    LongInt;      {flags}
        spMisc:         LongInt;      {reserved for Slot Manager}
        spReserved:     LongInt;      {reserved}
        spIOReserved:   Integer;      {reserved for Slot Manager}
        spRefNum:       Integer;      {Slot Resource Table ref number}
        spCategory:     Integer;      {sRsrc_Type: Category field}
        spCType:        Integer;      {sRsrc_Type: cType field}
        spDrvrSW:       Integer;      {sRsrc_Type: DrvrSW field}
        spDrvrHW:       Integer;      {sRsrc_Type: DrvrHW field}
        spTBMask:       SignedByte;   {type bit mask}
        spSlot:         SignedByte;   {slot number}
        spID:           SignedByte;   {ID of the sResource}
        spExtDev:       SignedByte;   {ID of the external device}
        spHwDev:        SignedByte;   {ID of the hardware device}
        spByteLanes:    SignedByte;   {byte lanes from card ROM }
                                      { format block}
        spFlags:        SignedByte;   {reserved for Slot Manager}
        spKey:          SignedByte    {reserved for Slot Manager}
     END;

     SpBlockPtr = ^SpBlock;
```

Routines

Determining the Version of the Slot Manager

```
FUNCTION SVersion          (spBlkPtr: SpBlockPtr) : OSErr;
```

Getting Information About SResource Data Structures

```
FUNCTION SGetSRsrc         (spBlkPtr: SpBlockPtr) : OSErr;
FUNCTION SGetTypeSRsrc     (spBlkPtr: SpBlockPtr) : OSErr;
```

Enabling, Disabling, or Restoring SResource Data Structures

```
FUNCTION SetSRsrcState     (spBlkPtr: SpBlockPtr) : OSErr;
FUNCTION InsertSRTRec      (spBlkPtr: SpBlockPtr) : OSErr;
```

Result Codes

noErr	0	No error
memFullErr	–108	Not enough room in heap
smUnExBusErr	–308	Unexpected bus error
smBadRefId	–330	Reference ID not found in list
smBadsList	–331	Bad sResource structure: Id1 < Id2 < Id3 ... format is not followed
smReservedErr	–332	Reserved field not 0
smSlotOOBErr	–337	Slot number out of bounds
smSelOOBErr	–338	Selector out of bounds; function not implemented
smNoMoresRsrcs	–344	Specified sResource data structure not found
smBadsPtrErr	–346	Bad pointer was passed to sCalcSPointer function
smByteLanesErr	–347	ByteLanes field in card's format block was determined to be 0

Assembly-Language Information

Slot Manager Parameter Block

00	spResult	long	result
04	spsPointer	long	address of structure
08	spSize	long	size of structure
12	spOffsetData	long	offset/data field
16	spIOFileName	long	reserved for Slot Manager
20	spsExecPBlk	long	address of SEBlock data structure
24	spParamData	long	flags
28	spMisc	long	reserved for Slot Manager
32	spReserved	long	reserved for future expansion
36	spIOReserved	word	reserved for Slot Manager
38	spRefNum	word	Slot Resource Table reference number
40	spCategory	word	Category field of sRsrcType entry in sResource
42	spCType	word	cType field of sRsrcType entry in sResource
44	spDrvrSW	word	DrvrSW field of sRsrcType entry in sResource
46	spDrvrHW	word	DrvrHW field of sRsrcType entry in sResource
48	spTBMask	byte	type bit mask
49	spSlot	byte	slot number
50	spID	byte	ID of the sResource
51	spExtDev	byte	ID of the external device
52	spHwDev	byte	ID of the hardware device
53	spByteLanes	byte	byte lanes from card ROM format block
54	spFlags	byte	reserved for Slot Manager
55	spKey	byte	reserved for Slot Manager

Trap Macros Requiring Routine Selectors

_SlotManager

Selector	Routine
$08	sVersion
$09	sSetsRsrcState
$0A	sInsertSRTRec
$0B	sGetsRsrc
$0C	sGetTypesRsrc

31 THE POWER MANAGER

ABOUT THIS CHAPTER

The **Power Manager,** provided only in the firmware of the Macintosh® Portable computer, controls power to the internal hardware devices of the Macintosh Portable in order to conserve power whenever the computer is not in use. The Macintosh Portable operates only with system software version 6.0.4 and later versions.

The Macintosh Portable computer operates from a built-in battery that can be charged from a voltage converter plugged into an electric socket. The Macintosh Portable has no power switch; instead, it contains firmware and hardware that can put the computer into two low–power-consumption states, the idle state and the sleep state.

In the **idle state,** the Power Manager firmware slows the computer from its normal 16-megahertz (MHz) clock speed to a 1 MHz clock speed. The Power Manager puts the Macintosh Portable in the idle state when the system has been inactive for 15 seconds. When the Macintosh Portable has been inactive for an additional period of time (the user can set the length of this period), the Power Manager and the various device drivers shut off power or remove clocks from the computer's various subsystems, including the CPU, RAM, ROM, and I/O ports. This condition is known as the **sleep state.**

No data is lost from RAM when the Macintosh Portable is in the sleep state. Most applications can be interrupted by the idle and sleep states without any adverse effects. When the user resumes use of the computer (by pressing a key, for example), most of the applications that were running before the Macintosh Portable entered the sleep state are still loaded in memory and resume running as if nothing had happened. If your application cannot tolerate the sleep state, you can add an entry to an operating-system queue called the *sleep queue.* The Power Manager calls every sleep queue routine before the computer goes into the sleep state.

The user can also use the Battery desk accessory or either of two Finder™ menu items to cause the Macintosh Portable to go into the sleep state immediately. If the user chooses Sleep from the Battery desk accessory or from the Special menu in the Finder, the Power Manager checks to see if any network communications will be interrupted by going into the sleep state. If network communications will be affected, a built-in sleep queue routine displays a dialog box giving the user the option of canceling the Sleep command. If the user chooses Shut Down from the Special menu in the Finder, the Power Manager puts the Macintosh Portable in the sleep state regardless of whether any network communication routines are running at the time.

The Power Manager described in this chapter is the firmware that provides an interface to the 50753 microprocessor (the Power Manager Integrated Circuit or **Power Manager IC**) in the Macintosh Portable computer. The Power Manager firmware also provides some services unique to the Macintosh Portable—such as reading the current clock speed—that are not directly related to power control. The power management circuits and the microcode in the on-chip ROM of the Power Manager IC are described in the *Guide to the Macintosh Family Hardware,* second edition. The Power Manager provides routines that your program can use to enable and disable the idle state, to control power to some of the subsystems of the Macintosh Portable computer, and to ensure that your program is not adversely affected when the Power Manager puts the Macintosh Portable into the sleep state.

This chapter describes the idle and sleep states and explains how your program can use Power Manager routines. You need the information in this chapter only if you are writing a program—such as a device driver—that must control power to a subsystem of the Macintosh Portable computer, or if you are writing a program that might be affected by the idle or sleep state.

Because the Power Manager saves the contents of all of the CPU's registers, including the stack pointer, before putting the Macintosh Portable in the sleep state, and because the contents of RAM are preserved while the Macintosh Portable is in the sleep state, most applications are not adversely affected by the sleep state. Because the Macintosh Portable does not enter the idle state when almost any sort of activity is going on or even when the watch cursor is being displayed, few programs are adversely affected by the idle state. Therefore, it is probable that your application will not have to make calls to the Power Manager.

This chapter first describes the relationships among the power management hardware, microcode, and firmware in the Macintosh Portable computer. It then discusses the idle and sleep states and the sleep queue in some detail. The section "Using the Power Manager" describes how to use Power Manager routines to control the idle and sleep states and how to use the sleep queue.

ABOUT THE POWER MANAGER

The power management circuits in the Macintosh Portable computer include a battery-voltage monitor, a voltage regulator and battery-charging circuit, and the Power Manager IC. The Power Manager IC controls the clocks and power lines to the various internal components and external ports of the Macintosh Portable computer. The microcode in the Power Manager IC implements many of the Macintosh Portable computer's power management features, such as power and clock control and the wakeup timer. A user or an application can set the **wakeup timer** to return the computer from the sleep state to the operating state at a specific time.

Figure 31-1 illustrates the relationships among your application, the Power Manager firmware, the Power Manager IC, the power management circuits, and the other subsystems of the Macintosh Portable computer. The Power Manager firmware in the ROM of the Macintosh Portable provides an interface that allows your application to control some of the functions of the Power Manager IC. Under control of the microcode in the Power Manager IC, the power management hardware charges the battery, provides the voltages needed by the system, and automatically shuts down all power and clocks to the system if the battery voltage falls below 5.65 volts. The automatic shutdown function helps to prevent possible damage to the battery resulting from low voltage.

You can use the routines described in this chapter to

- enable, disable, or delay the idle feature
- read the current clock speed
- set or disable the wakeup timer and read its current setting
- place an entry in the sleep queue so that the Power Manager calls your routine before putting the Macintosh Portable into the sleep state or returning it to the operating state

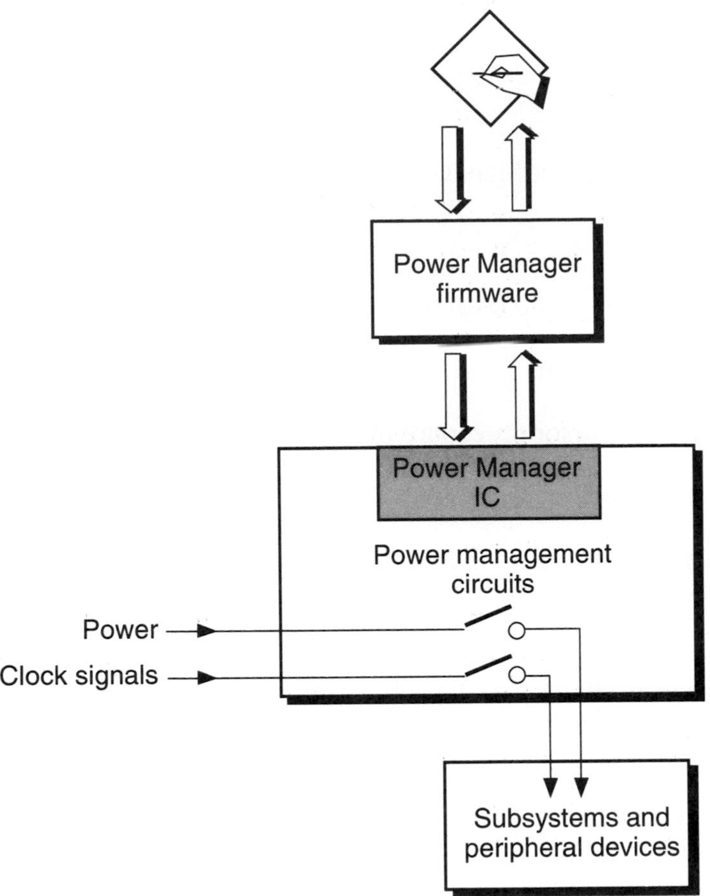

Figure 31-1. Relationship of an application to the Power Manager

- remove an entry from the sleep queue
- control power to the internal modem and serial ports
- read the status of the internal modem
- read the state of the battery charge and the status of the battery charger

THE IDLE STATE

When the Macintosh Portable computer is inactive for 15 seconds, the Power Manager firmware causes the CPU to insert 64 wait states into each RAM or ROM access, effectively changing the clock speed from 16 MHz to 1 MHz. This condition is referred to as the *idle state.*

> **Note:** The inactivity timeout interval, clock speed, and hardware implementation of the idle state are subject to change in future portable Macintosh computers.

For the purposes of the idle state, inactivity is defined as the absence of any of the following:

- any execution of the PBRead or PBWrite function by the File Manager or Device Manager
- a call to the Operating System Event Manager's PostEvent function
- any events in the event queue
- any access of the Apple® Sound Chip (ASC)
- completion of an Apple Desktop Bus™ (ADB) transaction
- a call to the QuickDraw™ SetCursor procedure that changes the cursor
- the cursor displayed as the watch cursor

Whenever the Power Manager detects one of these forms of activity, it resets a timer called the *activity timer* to 15 seconds and, if the Macintosh Portable is in the idle state, returns the computer to the operating state.

Neither the user nor your program can change the activity timer to use a period other than 15 seconds. However, the user can disable the activity timer through the Portable control panel, and your application can reset, disable, and enable the activity timer by using the IdleUpdate, EnableIdle, and DisableIdle routines. Your application can also use the GetCPUSpeed function to determine whether the Macintosh Portable is currently in the idle state. "Enabling or Disabling the Idle State" later in this chapter discusses these routines.

THE SLEEP STATE

The Operating System sends a sleep command to the Power Manager IC when the user requests it (through the Battery desk accessory or the Finder), when the battery voltage falls below a preset level, or when the system has remained inactive for an amount of time that the user sets through the Portable control panel.

The Operating System uses the Power Manager IC to shut down power to the CPU, the ROM, and some of the control logic. Sufficient power is maintained to the RAM so that no data is lost. Before the Operating System sends the sleep command to the Power Manager IC, it performs the following tasks:

- It pushes the contents of all of the CPU's internal registers onto the stack.
- It calls all routines listed in the sleep queue to inform them that the system is about to be put into the sleep state. These routines include the device drivers for the serial ports and floppy disk drives. Each device driver must call the Power Manager IC to stop power or clocks to the peripheral device controlled by that driver. If the device contains any internal registers, the device driver must save their contents before turning off power to the device. The sleep queue is described in the following section, "The Sleep Queue."

- It pushes onto the stack the Reset vector, the contents of the versatile interface adapter (VIA) chip, and the contents of the Apple Sound Chip (ASC) control registers.
- It saves the stack pointer in memory.

While the Macintosh Portable computer is in the sleep state, the clock to the Power Manager IC is off so that the chip does no processing. On each rising edge of the 60 Hz clock signal (from one of the Macintosh Portable computer's logic chips), a hardware circuit restores the clock signal to the Power Manager IC. The Power Manager IC updates the time in the real-time clock and checks the status of the system to determine whether to return the Macintosh Portable to its operating state. The Power Manager IC checks for the existence of the following conditions:

- A key on the keyboard has been pressed.
- The wakeup timer is enabled and the time to which the wakeup timer is set equals the time in the real-time clock.
- An internal modem is installed, the user has activated the ring-detect feature, and the modem has detected a ring (that is, someone has called the modem).

Note that use of the mouse or trackball cannot be detected by the Power Manager IC.

If the Power Manager IC does not detect any of these conditions, it deactivates its own clock until the next rising edge of the 60 Hz clock signal. If the Power Manager IC does detect one of these conditions, it restores power to the CPU, ROM, and any other hardware that was running when the computer entered the sleep state. Then the Power Manager's wakeup procedure reverses the procedure that put the Macintosh Portable into the sleep state, including calling each routine listed in the sleep queue to allow it to restore power to any subsystems it controls.

THE SLEEP QUEUE

The Power Manager maintains an operating-system queue called the **sleep queue.** The sleep queue contains pointers to all of the routines that the Power Manager must call before it puts the Macintosh Portable into the sleep state or returns it to the operating state. Each device driver, for example, must place in the sleep queue a pointer to a routine that controls power to the subsystem that the driver controls. When the Power Manager is ready to put the Macintosh Portable into the sleep state, it calls each of the routines listed in the sleep queue. Each routine performs whatever tasks are necessary to prepare for the sleep state, including calling Power Manager routines, and then returns control to the Power Manager. Similarly, the Power Manager calls each routine in the sleep queue when it is returning the Macintosh Portable to the operating state.

If you are writing a device driver or if you want your program to be informed before the Macintosh Portable enters the sleep state, you must place an entry for your routine in the sleep queue. If you do place an entry in the sleep queue, remember to remove it before your device driver or application terminates. You use the SleepQInstall and SleepQRemove procedures to install and remove sleep queue entries, as described in "Placing a Routine in the Sleep Queue" later in this chapter.

The Power Manager can call the routines listed in the sleep queue with a sleep request, a sleep demand, a wakeup demand, or a sleep-request revocation, as discussed in the following sections.

Sleep Requests

A **sleep request** informs a routine that the Power Manager would like to put the Macintosh Portable computer into the sleep state. The routine then has the option of denying the sleep request. If any routine in the sleep queue denies the sleep request, the Power Manager sends a sleep-request revocation to each routine that it has already called with a sleep request, and the Macintosh Portable does not enter the sleep state. If every routine in the sleep queue accepts the sleep request, then the Power Manager sends a sleep demand to each routine in the sleep queue. After every routine has processed the sleep demand, the Power Manager IC puts the Macintosh Portable into the sleep state.

Figure 31-2 illustrates the sequence of events that occurs when the Power Manager issues a sleep request.

Before calling any of the routines in the sleep queue with a sleep request, the Power Manager calls a built-in sleep queue entry that checks the status of certain network services, as summarized in Table 31-1. Only if all of the network services permit sleep does the Power Manager continue to send sleep requests to the routines in the sleep queue. The network services in Table 31-1 are described in the AppleTalk Manager chapter of this volume.

The Power Manager issues a sleep request when a sleep timeout occurs (that is, when the period of inactivity set by the user in the Portable control panel has expired).

Table 31-1. Response of network services to sleep requests and demands

Network service in use	Response to sleep request	Response to conditional sleep demand	Response to unconditional sleep demand
.MPP low-level protocol (DDP, NBP, RTMP, AEP)	Close driver if Macintosh Portable is on battery; else deny request	Close driver if user gives okay; else deny request	Close driver
.XPP extended protocol (ASP, AFP); no server volume mounted	Close driver if Macintosh Portable is on battery; else deny request	Close driver if user gives okay; else deny request	Close driver
.XPP; server volume mounted	Deny request	Close server sessions and close driver if user gives okay; else deny request	Close server sessions and close driver
An application is currently using AppleTalk®	Deny request	Close server sessions and close driver if user gives okay; else deny request	Close server sessions and close driver

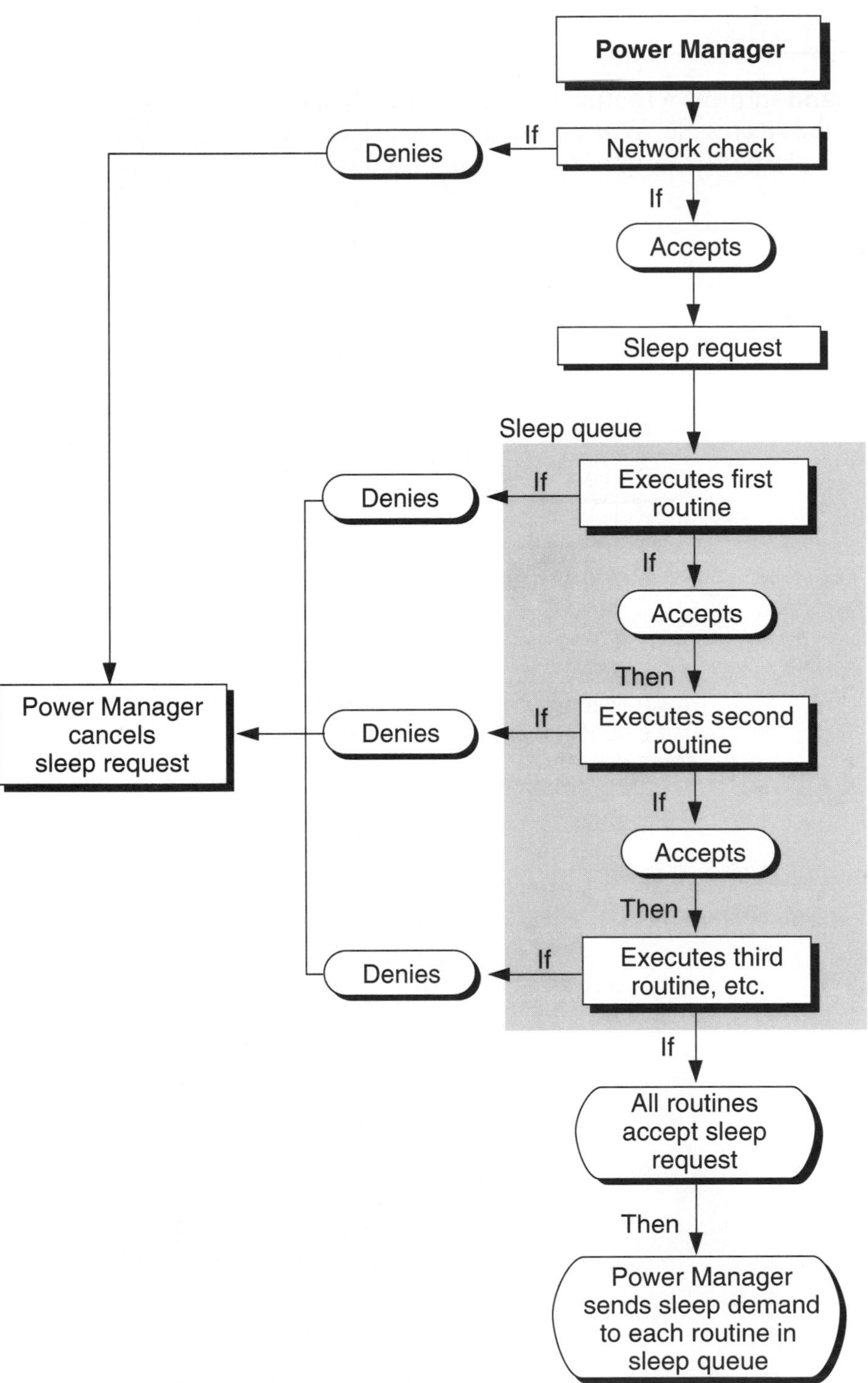

Figure 31-2. How the sleep queue handles a sleep request

Sleep Demands

A **sleep demand** informs a routine that the Power Manager is about to put the Macintosh Portable into the sleep state. When a routine in the sleep queue receives a sleep demand, it must prepare for the sleep state as quickly as possible and return control to the Power Manager.

Figure 31-3 illustrates the sequence of events that occurs when the Power Manager issues a sleep demand.

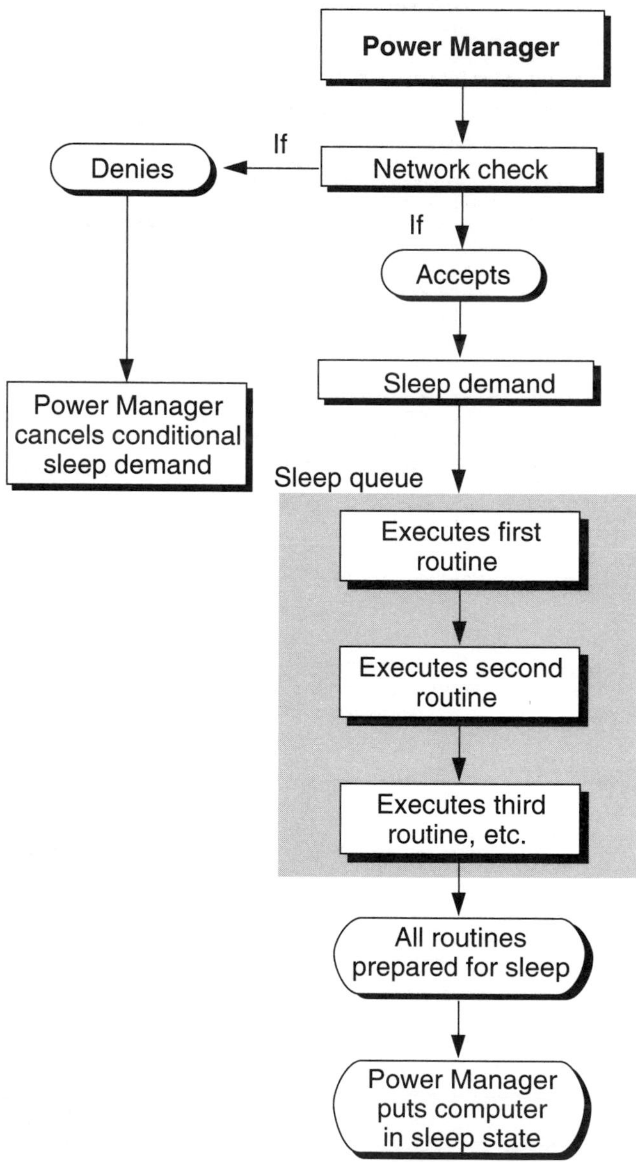

Figure 31-3. How the sleep queue handles a sleep demand

From the point of view of the Power Manager, there are two types of sleep demands—conditional and unconditional. The Power Manager might cancel a conditional sleep demand if certain network services are in use; an unconditional sleep demand cannot be canceled. When your sleep queue routine receives a sleep demand, however, your routine has no way to determine whether it originated as a conditional sleep demand or an unconditional sleep demand. Your device driver or application must prepare for the sleep state and return control promptly to the Power Manager when it receives a sleep demand.

The Power Manager processes a conditional sleep demand when the user chooses Sleep from the Battery desk accessory or from the Special menu in the Finder. When the Power Manager processes a conditional sleep demand, it first sends a sleep request to the network driver's sleep queue routine (see Table 31-1). Whenever one of the network services is in use, the sleep queue routine displays a dialog box requesting the user's permission to put the Macintosh Portable into the sleep state. The wording of the message in the dialog box depends on the nature of the network service in use. For example, if an .XPP driver protocol is in use, has opened a server, and has mounted a volume, then the message warns the user that the volume will be closed when the Macintosh Portable is put into the sleep state.

If the user denies permission to close the driver, the Power Manager does not send sleep demands to the routines in the sleep queue. If the user does give permission to close the driver, the Power Manager sends a sleep demand to the network driver's sleep queue routine and then to every other routine in the sleep queue.

The Power Manager issues an unconditional sleep demand when the battery voltage falls below a preset level or when the user chooses Shut Down from the Special menu in the Finder. In this case, the Power Manager sends a sleep demand to the network driver's sleep queue entry, which closes all network drivers. Then the Power Manager sends a sleep demand to every other routine in the sleep queue. As always for a sleep demand, each routine must prepare for the sleep state and return control to the Power Manager as quickly as possible. In this case, the Power Manager does not display any warnings or dialog boxes; neither the network services, the user, nor any application can deny the sleep demand.

Wakeup Demands

After restoring full power to the CPU, RAM, and ROM, the Power Manager's wakeup procedure calls each routine in the sleep queue with a wakeup demand. A **wakeup demand** informs your routine that it must reverse whatever steps it followed when it prepared for the sleep state. For example, a database application might reestablish communications with a remote database.

Sleep-Request Revocations

If any routine in the sleep queue denies a sleep request, the Power Manager sends a **sleep-request revocation** to every routine that it has already called with a sleep request. Your routine must reverse whatever steps it followed when it prepared to receive a sleep demand. A communications application that prevents users from opening new sessions while it is waiting to receive a sleep demand, for example, might once again allow users to open new sessions.

USING THE POWER MANAGER

If you are writing an application that is sensitive to the clock speed of the computer, you can use the Power Manager to disable the idle state when necessary.

> **Note:** Do not disable the idle state except when executing a routine that must run at full speed. Disabling the idle state shortens the amount of time the user can operate the Macintosh Portable computer from a battery.

If you want to ensure that the Macintosh Portable is in the operating state at a particular time in the future, you can use the SetWUTime function to set the wakeup timer. You can use the wakeup timer in conjunction with the Time Manager, for example, when you want to use the Macintosh Portable to perform tasks that must be done at a specific time, like printing a large file in the middle of the night.

If you are writing an application that might be affected by the sleep state of the computer, you can place in the sleep queue a routine that handles whatever preparations are necessary to protect your program when the Macintosh Portable enters the sleep state. "Placing a Routine in the Sleep Queue" and "Responding When the Sleep Queue Calls Your Routine" later in this chapter describe the sleep queue.

If you are writing a device driver for the Macintosh Portable computer, you might need to use the Power Manager to control power to the subsystem that your driver controls. See "Switching Serial Power On and Off" later in this chapter, for a discussion of power control for the serial communications subsystem. For power control for other devices, consult Apple Developer Technical Support. The Power Manager cannot control power to external peripheral devices such as hard disks and CD-ROM drives because such devices have their own power supplies.

You can also use Power Manager functions to read the status of the internal modem and to read the state of charge of the battery and the status of the battery charger.

Determining Whether the Power Manager Is Present

You can use the Gestalt function with the gestaltPowerMgrAttr selector to determine whether the Power Manager is available and whether certain other devices in the computer can be put into the sleep state. The Gestalt function returns a 32-bit field that may have some or all of the following bits set:

```
CONST gestaltPMgrExists    = 0;          {Power Manager is present}
      gestaltPMgrCPUIdle   = 1;          {CPU can idle}
      gestaltPMgrSCC       = 2;          {can stop SCC clock}
      gestaltPMgrSound     = 3;          {can shut off sound circuits}
```

If the gestaltPMgrExists bit is set, the Power Manager is present. If the gestaltPMgrCPUIdle bit is set, the CPU is capable of going into a low–power-consumption state. If the gestaltPMgrSCC bit is set, it is possible to stop the SCC clock, thus effectively turning off the serial ports. If the gestaltPMgrSound bit is set, it is possible to turn off power to the sound circuits.

Enabling or Disabling the Idle State

You can reset the activity timer to 15 seconds, disable and enable the idle state, and read the current CPU clock speed by using Power Manager routines.

Keep in mind that it is almost always better to design your code so that it is not affected by the idle state; then the Macintosh Portable can conserve power whenever possible. Note also that disabling the idle state does not disable the sleep state. To prevent your program from being adversely affected by the sleep state, place a routine in the sleep queue, as described in "Placing a Routine in the Sleep Queue" later in this chapter.

To reset the activity timer to count down another 15 seconds before the Power Manager puts the Macintosh Portable in the idle state, use the IdleUpdate function. The IdleUpdate function takes no parameters; it returns the value in the Ticks global variable at the time the function was called.

If you want to disable the idle state—that is, prevent the Macintosh Portable from entering the idle state—for more than 15 seconds, use the DisableIdle procedure. If your application cannot tolerate the idle state at all, you can call the DisableIdle procedure when your application starts up and then call the EnableIdle procedure when your application terminates.

Assembly-language note: Although MPW® provides assembly-language macros to execute the EnableIdle, DisableIdle, and GetCPUSpeed routines, each of these macros calls the _IdleState trap. To call the _IdleState trap directly, you must first put a longword routine selector in D0, as follows:

D0 < 0	GetCPUSpeed; speed returned as a single byte in D0
D0 = 0	EnableIdle
D0 > 0	DisableIdle

The EnableIdle procedure cancels the last call to the DisableIdle procedure. Note that canceling the last call to the DisableIdle procedure is not the same thing as enabling the idle state. For example, if the user has used the Portable control panel to disable the idle state, then a call to the EnableIdle procedure does not enable the idle state. Similarly, if your routine called the DisableIdle procedure more than once or if another routine has called the DisableIdle procedure, then a call to the EnableIdle procedure cancels only the last call to the DisableIdle procedure; it does not enable the idle state.

The Power Manager does not actually reenable the idle state until every call to the DisableIdle procedure has been matched by a call to the EnableIdle procedure, and then only if the user has not disabled the idle state through the Portable control panel. For this reason, you must be very careful to match each call to the DisableIdle procedure with a single call to the EnableIdle procedure. Be careful to avoid making extra calls to the EnableIdle procedure so that you do not inadvertently reenable the idle state while another routine needs it to remain disabled.

Calls to the EnableIdle procedure are not cumulative; that is, after you make several calls to the EnableIdle procedure, a single call to the DisableIdle procedure still disables the idle state. Disabling the idle state always takes precedence over enabling the idle state. A call to the DisableIdle procedure disables the idle state no matter how many times the EnableIdle procedure has been called and whether or not the user has enabled the idle state through the Portable control panel.

The following examples might help to clarify these concepts:

- If the application calls the EnableIdle routine but the user disables or has disabled the idle state, the idle state is disabled.
- If the application calls the DisableIdle routine and the user enables or has enabled the idle state, the idle state is disabled.
- If the application calls the DisableIdle routine twice in a row and then calls the EnableIdle routine once, the idle state is disabled.
- If the application calls the EnableIdle routine twice in a row and then calls the DisableIdle routine once, the idle state is disabled.
- If the idle state is initially enabled and if the application calls the DisableIdle routine twice in a row and then calls the EnableIdle routine twice, the Power Manager first disables and then reenables the idle state.

To determine whether the Macintosh Portable is currently in the idle state, read the current clock speed with the GetCPUSpeed function. The only values returned by the GetCPUSpeed function are 1 and 16, indicating the effective clock speed in megahertz.

Setting, Disabling, and Reading the Wakeup Timer

When the Macintosh Portable computer is in the sleep state, the Power Manager IC updates the real-time clock and compares it to the wakeup timer once each second. When the real-time clock and the wakeup timer have the same setting, the power management circuits return the Macintosh Portable to the operating state. The Power Manager provides functions that set the wakeup timer, disable the wakeup timer, and read the wakeup timer's current setting.

Use the SetWUTime function to set the wakeup timer. You pass one parameter to the SetWUTime function: an unsigned long word specifying the number of seconds since midnight, January 1, 1904. Setting the wakeup timer automatically enables it.

To disable the wakeup timer, you can set the wakeup timer to any time earlier than the current setting of the real-time clock (that is, to some time in the past), or you can use the DisableWUTime function. To reenable the wakeup timer, you must use the SetWUTime function to set the timer to a new time in the future.

To get the current setting of the wakeup timer, use the GetWUTime function. This function returns two parameters: the time to which the wakeup timer is set (in seconds since midnight, January 1, 1904) and a flag indicating whether the wakeup timer is enabled.

If the Macintosh Portable is already in the operating state when the real-time clock reaches the setting in the wakeup timer, nothing happens.

The power management circuits do not return the Macintosh Portable to the operating state while battery voltage is low, even if the wakeup timer and real-time clock settings coincide.

Placing a Routine in the Sleep Queue

If you want your routine to be notified before the Power Manager puts the Macintosh Portable into the sleep state or returns it to the operating state, you must put an entry in the sleep queue. If you do place an entry in the sleep queue, remember to remove it before your device driver or application terminates.

The sleep queue is a standard operating-system queue, as described in the Operating System Utilities chapter in Volume II. The SleepQRec data type defines a sleep queue record as follows:

```
TYPE SleepQRec =
     RECORD
        sleepQLink:   SleepQRecPtr; {pointer to next queue element}
        sleepQType:   Integer;      {queue type = 16}
        sleepQProc:   ProcPtr;      {pointer to your sleep routine}
        sleepQFlags:  Integer       {reserved}
     END;
```


The sleepQLink field contains a pointer to the next element in the queue. This pointer is maintained by the Power Manager; your application should not modify this field.

The sleepQType field indicates the type of the queue, which must be the constant slpQType (16).

The sleepQProc field contains a pointer to the routine that you provide. The sleepQFlags field is reserved for use by Apple Computer, Inc.

To add an entry to the sleep queue, fill in the sleepQType and sleepQProc fields of a sleep queue record and then execute the SleepQInstall procedure. The SleepQInstall procedure takes one parameter, a pointer to your sleep queue record. Listing 31-1 adds an entry to the sleep queue.

Listing 31-1. Adding an entry to the sleep queue

```
VAR
   MyRec:    SleepQRec;

BEGIN
   {set up the record before installing onto the sleep queue}
   WITH MyRec DO
   BEGIN
      sleepQLink := 0;
      sleepQType := slpQType;     {sleep queue type, 16}
      sleepQProc := @MySleepRtn; {address of some sleep routine}
      sleepQFlags := 0;           {reserved field}
   END;
   SleepQInstall(@MyRec);         {install}
END
```

To remove your routine from the sleep queue, use the SleepQRemove procedure. This procedure also takes as its one parameter a pointer to your sleep queue record.

Responding When the Sleep Queue Calls Your Routine

When you add an entry to the sleep queue, the Power Manager calls your routine when the Power Manager issues a sleep request, a sleep demand, a wakeup demand, or a sleep-request revocation. Whenever the Power Manager calls your routine, the A0 register contains a pointer to your sleep queue record and the D0 register has a code indicating the reason your routine is being called, as follows:

Value in D0	Meaning
1	Sleep request
2	Sleep demand
3	Wakeup demand
4	Sleep-request revocation

When your routine receives a sleep request, it must either allow or deny the request and place its response in the D0 register. To allow the sleep request, clear the D0 register to 0 before returning control to the Power Manager. To deny the sleep request, return a nonzero value in the D0 register. (Note that you cannot deny a sleep demand.)

If your routine or any other routine in the sleep queue denies the sleep request, the Power Manager sends a sleep-request revocation to each routine that it has already called with a sleep request. If none of the routines denies sleep, then the Power Manager sends a sleep demand to each routine in the sleep queue. Because your routine will be called a second time in any case, it is not necessary to prepare for sleep in response to a sleep request; your routine need only allow or deny the sleep request and return the result in the D0 register.

When your routine receives a sleep demand, it must prepare for the sleep state and return control to the Power Manager as quickly as possible. Because sleep demands are never sent by an interrupt handler, your routine can perform whatever tasks are necessary to prepare for sleep, including making calls to the Memory Manager. You can, for example, display an alert box to inform the user of potential problems, or you can even display a dialog box that requires the user to specify the action to be performed. However, if several applications display alert or dialog boxes, the user might become confused or alarmed. More important, if the user is not present to answer the alert box or dialog box, control is never returned to the Power Manager, and the Macintosh Portable does not go to sleep.

▲ **Warning:** If your sleep routine displays an alert box or modal dialog box, the Macintosh Portable does not enter the sleep state until the user responds. If the Macintosh Portable remains in the operating state until the battery voltage drops below a preset value, the Power Manager IC automatically shuts off all power to the system, without preserving the state of open applications or data that has not been saved to disk. To prevent this from happening, you should automatically remove your dialog box after several minutes have elapsed. ▲

When your routine receives a wakeup demand, it must prepare for the operating state and return control to the Power Manager as quickly as possible.

When your routine receives a sleep-request revocation, it must reverse any changes it made in response to the sleep request that preceded it, and return control to the Power Manager.

Listing 31-2 checks the contents of the D0 register to determine whether your sleep queue routine is being called with a sleep request, a sleep demand, or a wakeup demand. If the D0 register contains a value of 1, indicating a sleep request, the routine clears the register to 0 to allow sleep. If the D0 register contains a 2, 3, or 4, the routine executes its sleep, wakeup, or request-cancelation procedures and terminates. If the D0 register contains any other value, the procedure just returns to the caller. Because Listing 31-2 reads from and writes to the D0 register, the main routine is written in assembly language rather than Pascal.

Listing 31-2. A sleep queue routine

```
MySlpQProc   PROC

StackFrame   RECORD   {A6Link},DECR    ;build a stack frame record
ParamBegin   EQU      *                ;start parameters after this point
ParamSize    EQU      ParamBegin-*     ;size of all the passed parameters
RetAddr      DS.L     1                ;placeholder for return address
A6Link       DS.L     1                ;placeholder for A6 link
LocalSize    EQU      *                ;size of all the local variables
             ENDR

             WITH     StackFrame       ;cover our local stack frame
             LINK     A6,#LocalSize    ;allocate our local stack frame

             CMPI.L   #1,D0            ;is it a sleep request?
             BNE      @1               ;no
             JSR      RequestSleep     ;function to get answer to
                                       ; sleep request
                                       ;SleepRequest puts answer on stack
             MOVE.l   (SP)+,D0         ;place answer in D0
             BRA      Exit

@1           CMPI.L   #2,D0            ;is it a sleep demand?
             BNE      @2               ;no
             JSR      SleepDemand      ;routine to prepare for sleep
             BRA      Exit

@2           CMPI.L   #3,D0            ;is it a wakeup demand?
             BNE      @3               ;no
             JSR      WakeupDemand     ;routine to prepare for wakeup
             BRA      Exit

@3           CMPI.L   #4,D0            ;is it a sleep-request revocation?
             BNE      Exit             ;no, it's undefined, just exit
             JSR      RevokeRequest    ;routine to reverse changes
                                       ; made for sleep request

Exit         UNLK     A6               ;undo the link
             MOVEA.L  (SP)+,A0         ;pull off the return address
             ADDA.L   #ParamSize,SP    ;strip all of the caller's parameters
             JMP      (A0)             ;return to caller

             ENDP
```

(Continued)

Listing 31-2. A sleep queue routine (Continued)

```
FUNCTION RequestSleep : LongInt;

BEGIN
   {return a 1 to deny sleep or return a 0 to permit sleep}
END;

PROCEDURE SleepDemand;

BEGIN
   {prepare for sleep}
END;

PROCEDURE WakeupDemand;

BEGIN
   {prepare to return to operating state}
END;

PROCEDURE RevokeRequest;

BEGIN
   {reverse any changes made in response to sleep request}
END;
```

Switching Serial Power On and Off

The serial I/O subsystem of the Macintosh Portable computer includes the following components:

- the Serial Communications Controller (SCC) chip
- the serial driver chips
- the –5 volt supply
- the internal modem (if installed)

Because serial drivers always use these components in certain combinations, the Power Manager provides five serial power procedures that perform the following tasks:

- The AOn procedure switches on power to serial port A and switches on power to the internal modem if it is installed.
- The AOnIgnoreModem procedure switches on power to serial port A (the modem port) but does not switch on power to the internal modem.
- The BOn procedure switches on power to serial port B.
- The AOff procedure switches off power to serial port A and to the internal modem if it is in use.
- The BOff procedure switches off power to serial port B.

Assembly-language note: Although MPW provides assembly-language macros to execute these routines, each of these macros calls the _SerialPower trap macro. To call the _SerialPower trap macro directly, you must first put a routine selector in the D0 register, setting the bits as follows:

Bit	**Use**
0	Set to 0 to use internal modem; set to 1 to ignore modem.
2	Set to 0 for port B; set to 1 for port A.
7	Set to 0 to switch on power; set to 1 to switch off power.

If no internal modem is installed, then calling any of the power-on routines switches on power to the SCC, the serial driver chips, and the –5 volt supply.

To switch power on for port B whether or not there is an internal modem installed, use the BOn procedure. This procedure switches on power to the SCC, the serial driver chips, and the –5 volt supply.

If the internal modem is installed, then you can use the AOn procedure to switch on the modem. In this case, this procedure switches on power to the SCC, the –5 volt supply, and the modem; the internal modem does not use the serial driver chips.

If the internal modem is installed but you do not want to use it (whether or not the user has used the Portable control panel to disconnect the modem), then use the AOnIgnoreModem procedure to switch on power to the SCC, the serial driver chips, and the –5 volt supply.

POWER MANAGER ROUTINES

This section describes the routines you can use to enable, disable, and read the idle state, control and read the wakeup timer, add and remove elements from the sleep queue, control power to the serial ports, read the status of the internal modem, and read the status of the battery and battery charger.

All Power Manager routines return the same result codes, listed in "Result Codes" in the summary at the end of this chapter.

Controlling the Idle State

You can use the IdleUpdate function to reset the activity timer, you can use the EnableIdle and DisableIdle procedures to enable and disable the idle state, and you can use the GetCPUSpeed function to read the current CPU clock speed.

```
FUNCTION IdleUpdate : LongInt;
```

The IdleUpdate function takes no parameters. It returns the value in the Ticks global variable at the time the function was called.

```
PROCEDURE EnableIdle;
```

The EnableIdle procedure cancels the effect of a call to the DisableIdle procedure. A call to the EnableIdle procedure enables the idle state only if the user has not used the Portable control panel to disable the idle state and if every call to the DisableIdle procedure has been balanced by a call to the EnableIdle procedure.

```
PROCEDURE DisableIdle;
```

The DisableIdle procedure disables the idle state, even if the user has used the Portable control panel to enable the idle state. Every call to the DisableIdle procedure must be balanced by a call to the EnableIdle procedure before the idle state is reenabled.

```
FUNCTION GetCPUSpeed : LongInt;
```

Trap macro	_GetCPUSpeed
On exit	D0: the CPU clock speed; $1 or $10

The GetCPUSpeed function returns the current effective clock speed of the CPU. The only values that are returned by this function are 1 and 16, indicating the clock speed in megahertz.

Controlling and Reading the Wakeup Timer

The Power Manager provides one function to set the wakeup timer, one to disable the wake-up timer, and one to read the current setting of the wakeup timer.

```
FUNCTION SetWUTime (WUTime: LongInt) : OSErr;
```

The SetWUTime function sets and enables the wakeup timer. When the Macintosh Portable computer is in the sleep state, the Power Manager IC updates the real-time clock and compares it to the wakeup timer once each second. When the real-time clock and the wakeup timer have the same setting, the Power Manager IC returns the Macintosh Portable to the operating state.

The WUTime parameter specifies the time at which the Power Manager IC will return the Macintosh Portable to the operating state. You specify the time as the number of seconds since midnight, January 1, 1904.

If the Macintosh Portable is not in the sleep state when the wakeup timer and the real-time clock settings coincide, nothing happens. If you set the wakeup timer to a time earlier than the current setting of the real-time clock, you effectively disable the wakeup timer.

```
FUNCTION DisableWUTime : OSErr;
```

The DisableWUTime function disables the wakeup timer. You must set a new wakeup time to reenable the wakeup timer.

```
FUNCTION GetWUTime (VAR WUTime: LongInt; VAR WUFlag: Byte) : OSErr;
```

The GetWUTime function returns the current setting of the wakeup timer and indicates whether the wakeup timer is enabled.

The value returned by the WUTime parameter is the current setting of the wakeup timer specified as the number of seconds since midnight, January 1, 1904. If the low-order bit (bit 0) of the WUFlag parameter is set to 1, the wakeup timer is enabled. The other bits in the WUFlag parameter are reserved.

Controlling the Sleep Queue

You can use the SleepQInstall procedure to add an entry to the sleep queue, and you can use the SleepQRemove procedure to remove an entry from the sleep queue.

```
PROCEDURE SleepQInstall (qRecPtr: SleepQRecPtr);
```

The qRecPtr parameter is a pointer to a sleep queue record that you must provide. The structure of a sleep queue record is shown in "Placing a Routine in the Sleep Queue" earlier in this chapter.

```
PROCEDURE SleepQRemove (qRecPtr: SleepQRecPtr);
```

The qRecPtr parameter is a pointer to the sleep queue record that you provided when you added your routine to the sleep queue.

Controlling Serial Power

The five procedures in this section control power to the serial ports and internal modem.

```
PROCEDURE AOn;
```

The AOn procedure always switches on power to the SCC and the –5 volt supply. If the internal modem is installed and is connected to port A, this procedure also switches on power to the modem. If either of these conditions is not met, the AOn procedure switches on power to the serial driver chips.

```
PROCEDURE AOnIgnoreModem;
```

The AOnIgnoreModem procedure switches on power to the SCC, the –5 volt supply, and the serial driver chips. This procedure does not switch on power to the internal modem, even if the user has used the Portable control panel to select the modem.

```
PROCEDURE BOn;
```

The BOn procedure always switches on power to the SCC, the –5 volt supply, and the serial driver chips.

```
PROCEDURE AOff;
```

The AOff procedure always switches off power to the SCC and the –5 volt supply if serial port B is not in use. If the internal modem is installed, connected to port A, and switched on, this procedure switches off power to the modem. If any of these conditions are not met, it switches off power to the serial driver chips, unless they are being used by port B.

```
PROCEDURE BOff;
```

The BOff procedure switches off power to the SCC and the –5 volt supply if serial port A is not in use. If the internal modem is installed, connected to port B, and switched on, this procedure switches off power to the modem. Otherwise, the BOff procedure switches off power to the serial driver chips, unless they are being used by port A.

Reading the Status of the Internal Modem

The Power Manager application interface provides a function that allows you to determine the status of the internal modem.

```
FUNCTION ModemStatus (VAR Status: Byte) : OSErr;
```

The ModemStatus function returns information about the internal modem in the Macintosh Portable computer.

The bits in the Status parameter are defined as follows:

Bit	Meaning
7	Reserved.
6	Reserved.
5	The modem is on or off hook. If 1, the modem is off hook.
4	The ring-detect state. If 1, the modem has detected an incoming call.
3	The modem is or is not installed. If 1, an internal modem is installed.
2	The state of the ring-wakeup feature. If 1, the ring-wakeup feature is enabled.
1	Reserved; must always be set to 1.
0	The modem's power is on or off. If 1, the modem is switched on.

You can use the constants shown in the summary section of this chapter to check the values of these bits.

The user can use the Portable control panel to enable or disable the ring-wakeup feature. When the ring-wakeup feature is enabled and the Macintosh Portable is in the sleep state, the Power Manager returns the computer to the operating state when the modem receives an incoming call.

You can use the serial power control functions described in "Switching Serial Power On and Off" earlier in this chapter to control power to the modem.

The modem indicates that it is off hook whenever it is busy sending or receiving data or processing commands. The modem cannot receive an incoming call when it is off hook.

Reading the Status of the Battery and of the Battery Charger

The Power Manager monitors the voltage level of the internal battery and warns the user when the voltage drops below a threshold value stored in parameter RAM. If the voltage continues to drop and falls below another, lower value stored in parameter RAM, the Power Manager puts the computer into the sleep state. The Power Manager provides a function that allows you to read the state of charge of the battery and the status of the battery charger.

```
FUNCTION BatteryStatus (VAR Status: Byte; VAR Power: Byte) : OSErr;
```

The BatteryStatus function returns the status of the battery charger and the voltage level of the battery. The bits in the Status parameter are defined as follows:

Bit	Meaning
7	Reserved.
6	Reserved.
5	The charger connection has or has not changed state. If 1, the charger has been recently connected or disconnected.
4	The battery warning. If 1, the battery voltage is low.
3	The dead battery indicator. This bit is always 0.
2	The hicharge counter overflow. If 1, the hicharge counter has overflowed.
1	The charge rate. If 1, the battery is charging at the hicharge rate.
0	The charger is or is not connected. If 1, the charger is connected.

You can use the constants shown in the summary section of this chapter to check the values of these bits.

Use the following formula to calculate the battery voltage, where *Power* is the value of the Power parameter returned by this function:

voltage = ((Power/100) + 5.12) volts

Due to the nature of lead-acid batteries, the battery power remaining is difficult to measure accurately. Temperature, load, and other factors can alter the measured voltage by 30 percent or more. The Power Manager takes as many of these factors into account as possible, but the voltage measurement can still be in error by up to 10 percent. The measurement is most accurate when the Macintosh Portable has been in the sleep state for at least 30 minutes.

When the battery charger is connected to a Macintosh Portable computer with a low battery, the battery is charged at the hicharge rate (1.5 amps) until battery voltage reaches 7.2 volts. The Power Manager has a counter (the **hicharge counter**) that measures the time required to raise the battery voltage to this level.

After the 7.2 volt level is reached, the power management circuits maintain the hicharge connection until the hicharge counter counts down to 0. This ensures that the battery is fully charged. At the end of that time, the power management circuits supply the battery with just enough current to replace the voltage lost through self-discharge. When the hicharge counter has overflowed, it indicates that the charging circuit is having trouble charging the battery.

Bit 5 is set when the charger connection is changed—either connected or disconnected. When this bit is set, the Power Manager IC sends an interrupt to the CPU.

The battery warning bit (bit 4) is set whenever battery voltage drops below the value set in parameter RAM. The Power Manager IC sends an interrupt to the CPU once every second when battery voltage is low.

If bit 3 were set, it would indicate a dead battery; however, the Power Manager automatically shuts the system down when the battery voltage drops below a preset level, so this bit is always 0.

SUMMARY OF THE POWER MANAGER

Constants

```
CONST slpQType              = 16;    {sleep queue type}

      {Bit positions for ModemByte}
      modemOnBit            =  0;    {1 if modem is on}
      ringWakeUpBit         =  2;    {1 if ring wakeup is enabled}
      modemInstalledBit     =  3;    {1 if internal modem is installed}
      ringDetectBit         =  4;    {1 if incoming call is detected}
      modemOnHookBit        =  5;    {1 if modem is off hook}

      {masks for ModemByte}
      modemOnMask           = $1;    {modem on}
      ringWakeUpMask        = $4;    {ring wakeup enabled}
      modemInstalledMask    = $8;    {internal modem installed}
      ringDetectMask        =$10;    {incoming call detected}
      modemOnHookMask       =$20;    {modem off hook}

      {bit positions for BatteryByte}
      chargerConnBit        =  0;    {1 if charger is connected}
      hiChargeBit           =  1;    {1 if charging at hicharge rate}
      chargeOverFlowBit     =  2;    {1 if hicharge counter has overflowed}
      batteryDeadBit        =  3;    {always 0}
      batteryLowBit         =  4;    {1 if battery is low}
      connChangedBit        =  5;    {1 if charger connection has changed}

      {masks for BatteryByte}
      chargerConnMask       = $1;    {charger is connected}
      hiChargeMask          = $2;    {charging at hicharge rate}
      chargeOverFlowMask    = $4;    {hicharge counter has overflowed}
      batteryDeadMask       = $8;    {battery is dead}
      batteryLowMask        =$10;    {battery is low}
      connChangedMask       =$20;    {connection has changed}

      {commands to SleepQRec sleepQProc}
      sleepRequest          =  1;    {sleep request}
      sleepDemand           =  2;    {sleep demand}
      sleepWakeUp           =  3;    {wakeup demand}
      sleepRevoke           =  4;    {sleep request revocation}
```

Data Types

```
TYPE SleepQRec =
     RECORD
        sleepQLink:   SleepQRecPtr; {pointer to next queue element}
        sleepQType:   Integer;      {queue type = 16}
        sleepQProc:   ProcPtr;      {pointer to your sleep routine]
        sleepQFlags:  Integer       {reserved}
     END;

     SleepQRecPtr = ^SleepQRec;
```

Routines

Controlling the Idle State

```
FUNCTION IdleUpdate :         LongInt;

PROCEDURE EnableIdle;

PROCEDURE DisableIdle;

FUNCTION GetCPUSpeed :        LongInt;
```

Controlling and Reading the Wakeup Timer

```
FUNCTION SetWUTime            (WUTime: LongInt) : OSErr;

FUNCTION DisableWUTime        : OSErr;

FUNCTION GetWUTime            (VAR WUTime: LongInt; VAR WUFlag: Byte) :
                               OSErr;
```

Controlling the Sleep Queue

```
PROCEDURE SleepQInstall       (qRecPtr: SleepQRecPtr);

PROCEDURE SleepQRemove        (qRecPtr: SleepQRecPtr);
```

Controlling Serial Power

```
PROCEDURE AOn;

PROCEDURE AOnIgnoreModem;

PROCEDURE BOn;

PROCEDURE AOff;

PROCEDURE BOff;
```

Reading the Status of the Internal Modem

```
FUNCTION ModemStatus        (VAR Status: Byte) : OSErr;
```

Reading the Status of the Battery and of the Battery Charger

```
FUNCTION BatteryStatus      (VAR Status: Byte; VAR Power: Byte) : OSErr;
```


Result Codes

noErr	0	No error
pmBusyErr	–13000	Power Manager IC stuck busy
pmReplyTOErr	–13001	Timed out waiting to begin reply handshake
pmSendStartErr	–13002	Power Manager IC did not start handshake
pmSendEndErr	–13003	During send, Power Manager did not finish handshake
pmRecvStartErr	–13004	During receive, Power Manager did not start handshake
pmRecvEndErr	–13005	During receive, Power Manager did not finish handshake

Sleep Queue Data Structure

sleepQLink	long	pointer to next element in the queue
sleepQType	word	queue type = 16
sleepQProc	long	pointer to your sleep routine
sleepQFlags	word	reserved

Trap Macros Requiring Routine Selectors

_IdleState

Selector	**Routine**
0	EnableIdle
Any positive number	DisableIdle
Any negative number	GetCPUSpeed

_SerialPower

Selector	**Routine**
$04	AOn
$05	AOnIgnoreModem
$00	BOn
$84	AOff
$80	BOff

32 THE APPLETALK MANAGER

ABOUT THIS CHAPTER

AppleTalk® is a communications network system including personal computer workstations, computers acting as file servers and print servers, printers, and a variety of types of communications hardware and software. The AppleTalk Manager provides an interface to this communications network system for applications running on Macintosh® computers. This chapter describes changes to the AppleTalk Manager introduced since the publication of *Inside Macintosh,* Volume V, and included with system software version 7.0. This chapter supplements the information in the AppleTalk Manager chapters of *Inside Macintosh,* Volumes II and V.

This chapter describes

- new routines for the .MPP, .ATP, and .XPP device drivers
- a new wildcard character for use with the Name-Binding Protocol
- a new operating-system queue, called the AppleTalk Transition Queue
- a new set of operating-system utilities, collectively called the LAP Manager
- the application interface routines provided by a new AppleTalk protocol, the AppleTalk Data Stream Protocol (ADSP)
- the .ENET driver and the routines your application can use to control this driver

Together with the AppleTalk Manager chapters of Volumes II and V, this chapter describes the routines that your application can use to send and receive information within an AppleTalk network system. Because the AppleTalk network system includes both hardware and software—and because the software includes not only the AppleTalk Manager but also file servers, print servers, internet routers, drivers for circuit cards, and so forth—the information in *Inside Macintosh* constitutes only a small part of the body of literature documenting AppleTalk.

For a detailed description of AppleTalk protocols, see *Inside AppleTalk,* second edition. For a complete description of the LAP Manager, EtherTalk®, and alternate AppleTalk connections, see the *Macintosh AppleTalk Connections Programmer's Guide.* To learn how to install and operate an AppleTalk internet, see the *AppleTalk Internet Router Administrator's Guide* and the *AppleTalk Phase 2 Introduction and Upgrade Guide.* For an introduction to the hardware and software of an entire AppleTalk network, see *Understanding Computer Networks* and the *AppleTalk Network System Overview.* For information on designing circuit cards and device drivers for Macintosh computers, see *Designing Cards and Drivers for the Macintosh Family,* second edition.

The changes to AppleTalk other than ADSP and the LAP Manager are collectively referred to as **AppleTalk Phase 2.** (When necessary for purposes of differentiation, the previous version of AppleTalk is referred to in this chapter as AppleTalk Phase 1.) The Phase 2 versions of the AppleTalk drivers are included as part of system software version 7.0 and can be installed on any Macintosh computer other than the Macintosh 128K, Macintosh 512K, Macintosh 512K enhanced, and Macintosh XL computers. If you want to provide AppleTalk Phase 2 drivers with your product, you must obtain a license from Apple® Software Licensing.

ABOUT THE APPLETALK MANAGER

The AppleTalk Manager includes a number of protocols that are implemented in various device drivers. The AppleTalk Manager also includes the LAP Manager (which interfaces the AppleTalk link access protocols to the higher-level AppleTalk protocols) and hardware device drivers for specific data links. Software that supports AppleTalk data links is contained in files of type 'adev', referred to as *AppleTalk connection files*. This section lists the new features of AppleTalk, describes the organization of the AppleTalk Manager, and briefly discusses what each component of the AppleTalk Manager does.

Changes to the AppleTalk Manager

The AppleTalk features that are new or improved include

- a new .MPP driver function that returns information about the .MPP driver (see "Getting Information About the .MPP Driver" later in this chapter)
- a new Name-Binding Protocol (NBP) wildcard character that can substitute for one or more characters in AppleTalk names (see "A New NBP Wildcard Character")
- the LAP Manager, a set of operating-system utilities that provide a standard interface between the AppleTalk protocols and the **data links** used by AppleTalk, such as LocalTalk®, EtherTalk, and TokenTalk® (see "The LAP Manager")
- the AppleTalk Transition Queue, an operating-system queue that can notify your application each time an AppleTalk driver is opened or closed or each time certain other transitions occur (see "The AppleTalk Transition Queue")
- an implementation of parts of the IEEE 802.2 protocol, which allows you to attach and detach your own protocol handlers for EtherTalk data packets (see "The LAP Manager 802.2 Protocol")
- new .ATP driver functions that allow you to set a value for the .ATP release timer and to cancel all pending asynchronous calls to the ATPGetRequest function for a specific socket (see "The .ATP Driver")
- new .XPP driver functions that provide information from ZIP about zones (see "The .XPP Driver")
- improvements to the AppleTalk protocols that allow a single network, other than LocalTalk, to contain more than one zone (see "Using the .XPP Driver to Obtain Information About Zones")
- the AppleTalk Data Stream Protocol (ADSP), which provides full-duplex data stream communications for use by applications (see "AppleTalk Data Stream Protocol (ADSP)")
- the .ENET driver, an Ethernet driver for the EtherTalk NB card that is manufactured by Apple Computer, Inc. (see "The .ENET Driver")

AppleTalk Protocols

The AppleTalk Manager includes the following protocols:

- LocalTalk Link Access Protocol (LLAP)
- EtherTalk Link Access Protocol (ELAP)
- TokenTalk Link Access Protocol (TLAP)
- Datagram Delivery Protocol (DDP)
- Routing Table Maintenance Protocol (RTMP)
- AppleTalk Transaction Protocol (ATP)
- Name-Binding Protocol (NBP)
- AppleTalk Echo Protocol (AEP)
- Zone Information Protocol (ZIP)
- AppleTalk Session Protocol (ASP)
- AppleTalk Data Stream Protocol (ADSP)
- AppleTalk Filing Protocol (AFP)

The LocalTalk Link Access Protocol, EtherTalk Link Access Protocol, TokenTalk Link Access Protocol, and other link access protocols provide interfaces between the AppleTalk Manager and the different types of data link hardware used by AppleTalk.

Note: The LocalTalk Link Access Protocol (LLAP) was originally called the AppleTalk Link Access Protocol (ALAP). With the addition of the EtherTalk Link Access Protocol (ELAP) and other link access protocols, this protocol was renamed to indicate the specific data link it supports.

Figure 32-1 shows the relationships among the various AppleTalk protocols. A connection between one protocol and another above or below it in the figure indicates that the upper protocol is a **client** of the lower protocol; that is, the upper protocol uses services provided by the lower protocol in order to carry out some functions.

Note: The various AppleTalk protocols are sets of rules, not computer programs, and so can be implemented in many different ways on many different systems. All of the AppleTalk protocol functions that you can address or control from a Macintosh application are implemented as Macintosh device drivers or managers. Many other features of these protocols are implemented in software located only on internet routers that are not used to run general applications. Some parts of protocols are implemented by server software such as file servers and print servers. Therefore, when this chapter refers to a protocol as "doing" or "controlling" something, you should understand the statement to mean that some program that implements the protocol actually carries out the operation.

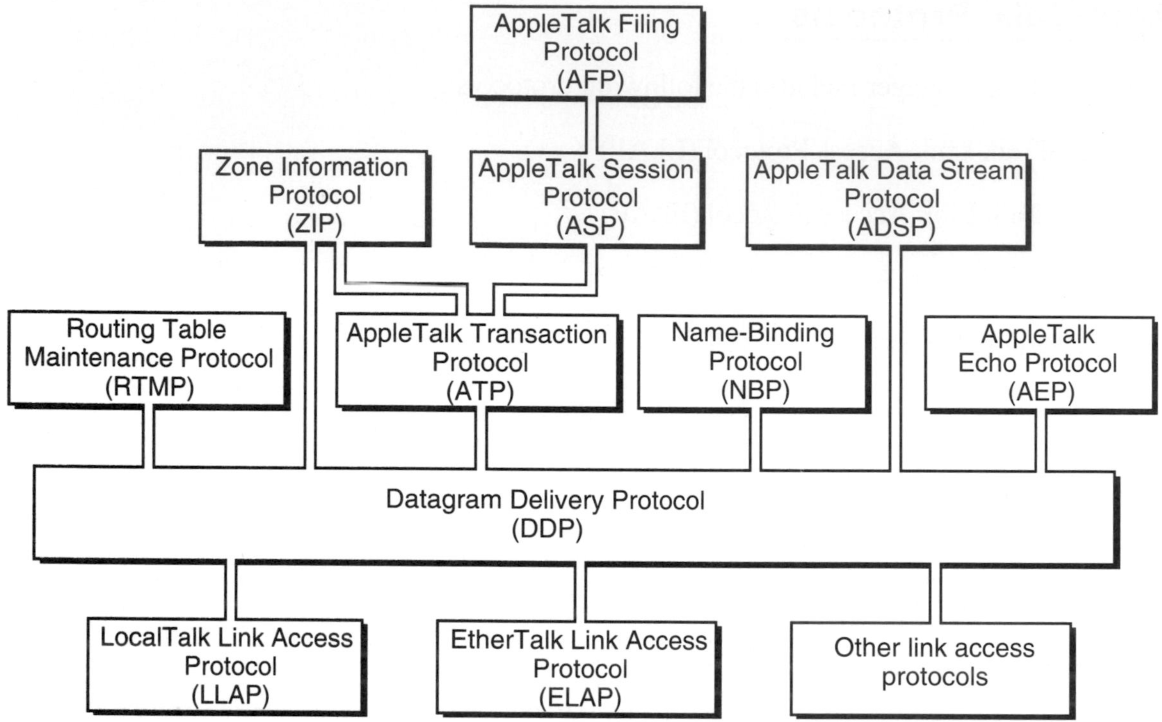

Figure 32-1. AppleTalk protocols

As shown in Figure 32-1, a **link access protocol** controls the access of the node to the network hardware and makes it possible for many nodes to share the same communications hardware. Each link access protocol assigns a node ID to the node and decodes the node addresses of messages it receives. A link access protocol provides node-to-node delivery of data packets. Examples of link access protocols include the LocalTalk Link Access Protocol, the EtherTalk Link Access Protocol, and the TokenTalk Link Access Protocol.

Whereas earlier implementations of AppleTalk were restricted to one 16-bit network number per network (that is, one network number for all nodes connected with no intervening routers) and 254 nodes per network number, AppleTalk Phase 2 allows more than one network number for each network (other than LocalTalk, which is still limited to one network number per network). A network of a type that allows more than one network number is known as an **extended network.** Each node in an extended network must now be specified by both its 16-bit network number and its 8-bit node ID. In principle, each network (other than LocalTalk) can now have over 16 million (2^{24}) nodes. In any specific implementation, the hardware or software might limit the network to fewer nodes.

The **Datagram Delivery Protocol (DDP)** provides socket-to-socket delivery of data packets within an AppleTalk internet. The address of a DDP packet includes the socket number, node ID, and network number. Application interface routines for DDP are described in "Datagram Delivery Protocol" in the AppleTalk Manager chapter of Volume II.

The **Routing Table Maintenance Protocol (RTMP)** is used by routers on an AppleTalk internet to determine how to forward a data packet to the network number to which it is addressed. The RTMP implementation on a router maintains a table, called a **routing table,** that specifies the shortest path to each possible destination network number. The AppleTalk protocol software in a workstation (that is, a node other than a router) contains only a small part of RTMP, called the **RTMP stub,** that DDP uses to determine the network number (or range of network numbers) of the network cable to which the node is conncted and to determine the network number and node ID of one router on that network cable. There is no application interface to the RTMP stub.

The **AppleTalk Transaction Protocol (ATP)** provides reliable delivery of data by retransmitting any data packets that are lost. ATP also ensures that data packets are delivered in the correct sequence. ATP is a **transaction-based protocol,** meaning that one socket client transmits a request for some action and the other socket client carries out the action and transmits a response. Although—as you can see from Figure 32-1—the AppleTalk Manager provides high-level protocols that are clients of ATP, many applications use ATP directly to transmit data over an AppleTalk internet. The application interface to ATP is described in the AppleTalk Manager chapter of Volume II. There are some enhancements to ATP in AppleTalk Phase 2, described in "The .ATP Driver" later in this chapter.

The **Name-Binding Protocol (NBP)** maintains a table that contains the internet address and name of each entity in the node that is visible to other entities on the internet (that is, each entity that has registered a name with NBP). The **internet address** includes the socket number, node ID, and network number. The **name** consists of three fields: the object, type, and zone. The **object** and **type** are assigned by the entity itself and can be anything the user or application assigns. A **zone** is a logical grouping of a subset of the nodes on the internet. The zone field of the name is the zone in which the node resides.

NBP also allows its clients to obtain the internet address of any network-visible entity in the internet by providing its name. NBP maps this name to an internet address, thus providing the link between the user-supplied name for an entity and the internet address that is used by DDP to send and receive data packets. The application interface to NBP is described in the AppleTalk Manager chapter of Volume II. There is one enhancement to NBP in AppleTalk Phase 2, described in "A New NBP Wildcard Character" later in this chapter.

The **AppleTalk Echo Protocol (AEP)** listens for special packets sent by other nodes and, when it receives such a packet, echoes it back to the sender. AEP is used by some clients of DDP to determine whether another node (known to have AEP) can be accessed over the internet, and to determine how long it takes a packet to reach another node. There is no application interface to AEP.

The **Zone Information Protocol (ZIP)** maintains a table in each router, called the *zone information table,* that lists the relationships between zone names and networks. In AppleTalk Phase 2, a single network number can be associated with more than one zone name, or a single zone name can be associated with more than one network. You can use .XPP driver routines to obtain information from ZIP. These routines are discussed in "Using the .XPP Driver to Obtain Information About Zones" later in this chapter.

The **AppleTalk Session Protocol (ASP)** sets up and maintains sessions between a workstation and a server. A **session** consists of a logical (as opposed to physical) connection between two entities on the internet. ASP is a nonsymmetrical protocol; that is, only one of the two entities involved in the session (the workstation) can send commands. The other entity (the server) is restricted to responding to the commands. ASP is used by the AppleTalk Filing Protocol, for example, to allow a user to manipulate files on a file server. As long as the session is open, the workstation can request directory information, change filenames, and so forth. The file server must respond to the workstation's commands and cannot initiate any actions on its own. ASP is discussed in the AppleTalk Manager chapter of Volume V.

The **AppleTalk Data Stream Protocol (ADSP)** appears to its clients to maintain an open pipeline between two entities on the internet. Either entity can write a stream of bytes to the pipeline or read data bytes from the pipeline. ADSP is a **symmetrical protocol;** that is, the two clients at either end of the connection are equal and can perform exactly the same operations. ADSP is especially useful for exchanging information between two equal entities, as in a telephone communications network, or as required by a terminal emulation program for sending or receiving a continuous stream of data. Because ADSP, like all other high-level AppleTalk protocols, is a client of DDP, the data is actually sent as data packets. This allows ADSP to correct transmission errors in a way that would not be possible for a true data stream connection. Thus, ADSP retains many of the advantages of a transaction-based protocol while providing to its clients a full-duplex data stream. ADSP is discussed in the sections "Using ADSP" and ".DSP Driver Routines" later in this chapter.

The **AppleTalk Filing Protocol (AFP)** provides an interface between an application and a file server. AFP is a client of ASP and is used to access AppleShare® file servers on Macintosh computer workstations. When the user opens a session with an AppleShare file server over an internet, it appears to any application running on the workstation that uses File Manager routines as if the files on the file server were located on a disk drive connected to the workstation. The application interface to AFP is described in the AppleTalk Manager chapter of Volume V.

AppleTalk Device Drivers, AppleTalk Connection Files, and the LAP Manager

A protocol is only a set of rules, not a computer program. The various AppleTalk protocols are implemented as Macintosh device drivers, including

- the .MPP driver, which implements LLAP, DDP, the RTMP stub, NBP, and AEP
- the .ATP driver, which implements ATP
- the .XPP driver, which implements ASP and the workstation portions of ZIP and AFP
- the .DSP driver, which implements ADSP
- the .ENET driver, which implements an interface to the Ethernet data link

A Macintosh computer on an AppleTalk network can also include one or more AppleTalk connection files. An **AppleTalk connection file** has file type 'adev' and contains a link access protocol implementation for a data link (ELAP for EtherTalk, for example). The LAP Manager makes it possible for the user to select among AppleTalk connection files by using the Network control panel to specify which network is to be used for the node's AppleTalk connection. The AppleTalk connection file and LAP Manager work together with the Network control panel (Network 'cdev') file. When the user selects a connection from the Network control panel, the LAP Manager routes AppleTalk communications through the selected link access protocol and hence through the selected hardware.

The AppleTalk device drivers, LAP Manager, and AppleTalk connection files are shown in Figure 32-2. As you can see from the figure, each device driver implements one or more AppleTalk protocols.

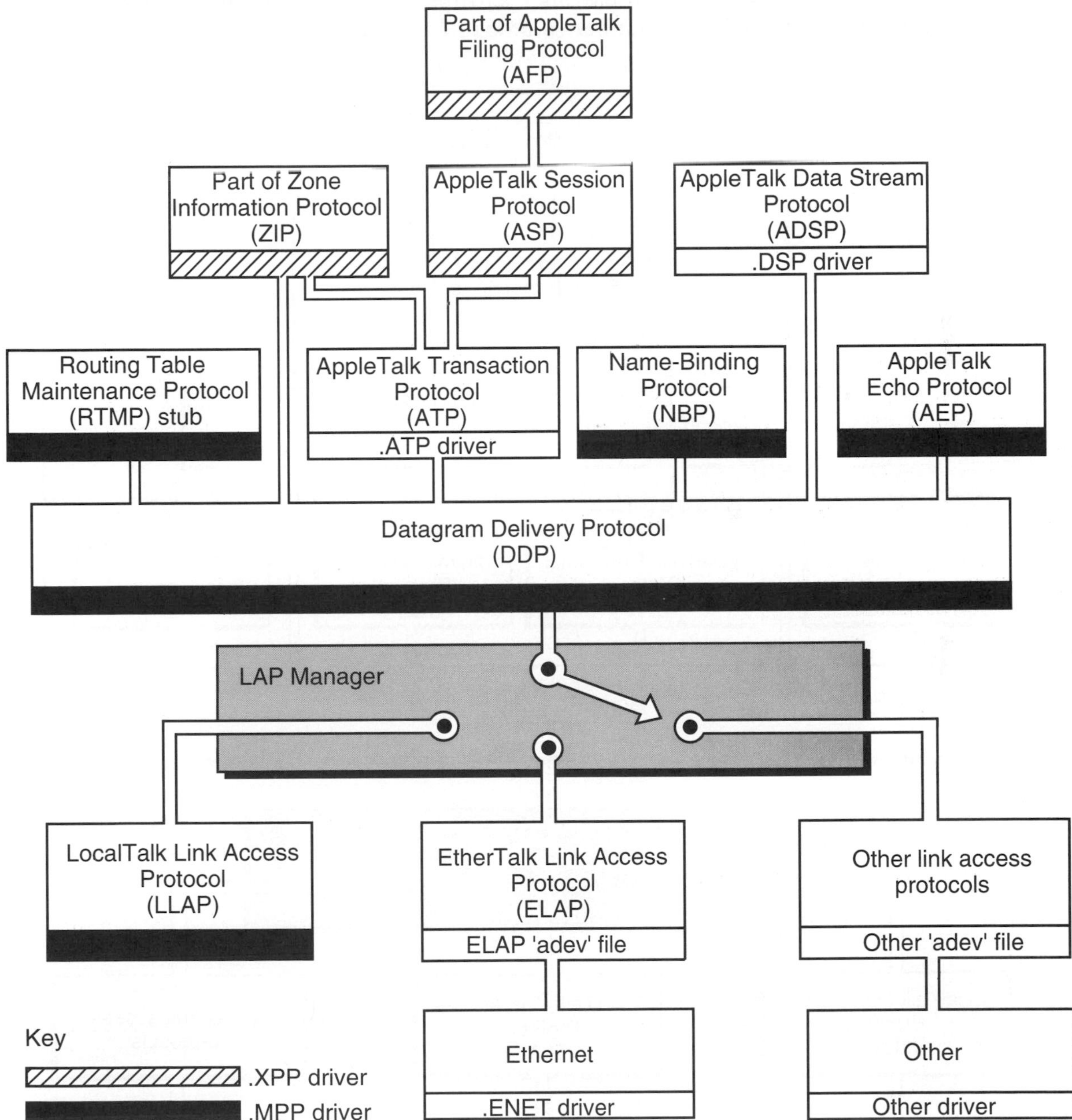

Figure 32-2. AppleTalk device drivers

Figure 32-3 shows the interfaces between a general application on a Macintosh computer being used as an AppleTalk workstation and the AppleTalk protocols, the LAP Manager, and the Ethernet hardware device driver. The lines connecting the application to the various components of AppleTalk indicate which components have application interfaces. As discussed in the preceding section, "AppleTalk Protocols," each application interface is described, at least in part, in this or another volume of *Inside Macintosh.*

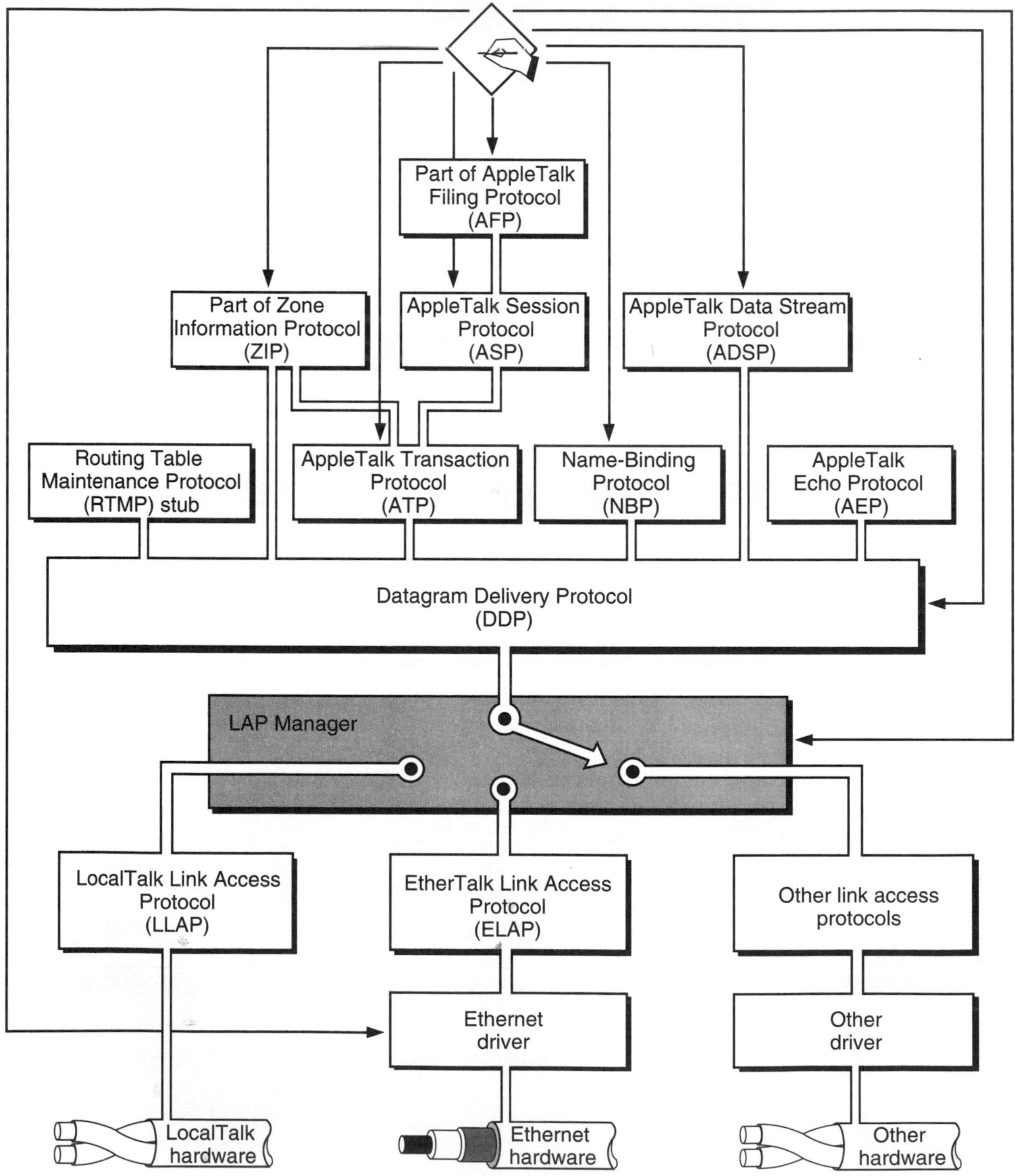

Figure 32-3. AppleTalk application interfaces

USING THE APPLETALK MANAGER

This section describes how to determine whether AppleTalk Phase 2 drivers are present and gives some advice on how to select the AppleTalk protocol that best serves your purposes. This section also describes how to use the features added to AppleTalk with Phase 2 and provides programming examples of the use of the .DSP driver and several other new AppleTalk features.

Determining Whether AppleTalk Phase 2 Drivers Are Present

Once the .MPP driver has been loaded into memory, you can use the Gestalt function with the gestaltAppleTalkVersion selector to check the version of AppleTalk. The Gestalt function returns the version of the .MPP driver. If the version is equal to or greater than 53, then the .MPP driver supports AppleTalk Phase 2, and you can assume the other Phase 2 drivers are present.

Alternatively, you can call the SysEnvirons function as described in the Compatibility Guidelines chapter of Volume V. If the atDrvrVersNum field of the SysEnvRec data structure returned by this function is equal to or greater than 53, then the .MPP driver supports AppleTalk Phase 2.

The ExtendedBit flag returned by the PGetAppleTalkInfo function is TRUE if the node is connected to an extended AppleTalk network. (The ExtendedBit flag is bit 15 of the configuration parameter returned by this function.) Note that the presence of the AppleTalk Phase 2 drivers does not of itself indicate that the node is connected to an extended network.

Deciding Which AppleTalk Protocol to Use

AppleTalk offers a variety of communications protocols at a variety of levels. Your choice of protocol or protocols to use depends primarily on your needs and can be influenced by your familiarity with network communications in general.

You can write your own protocol handlers and call the low-level AppleTalk device drivers directly. However, if you are not a communications expert and have no desire to design your own network protocols, you should probably use one of three AppleTalk protocols for sending and receiving data over the AppleTalk internet: the AppleTalk Transaction Protocol (ATP), the AppleTalk Session Protocol (ASP), or the AppleTalk Data Stream Protocol (ADSP).

ATP is a lower-level protocol than ASP or ADSP. You cannot use ATP to establish a session and keep it open; rather, you request data from another socket client or send a response (up to eight packets of data) from your socket to another socket client that has requested data. You should use ATP if you want only to send a small amount of data and do not need the overhead required to maintain an open connection. ATP is described in the AppleTalk Manager chapters of Volume II and Volume V.

ASP is designed to support a session between a server and one or more workstations. It is an asymmetrical protocol: all exchanges are initiated by a workstation and responded to by a server. The server cannot initiate an exchange of data except to send to a workstation an attention message that directs the workstation to request data from the server. An application running on a workstation must make calls to ASP to communicate with any server that uses ASP. If you want to develop a new type of asymmetrical, transaction-oriented server, you should consider using ASP to implement it. ASP is described in the AppleTalk Manager chapter of Volume V.

ADSP is a symmetrical protocol that you can use to establish and maintain a connection between two equal entities (a peer-to-peer connection). Either end of an ADSP connection can send data at any time. Although ADSP is a client of DDP and therefore sends and receives data in packets (as do ATP and ASP), to an application using ADSP the data appears to be sent and received as a continuous stream. In addition to the duplex data stream maintained by an ADSP session, ADSP allows either end of a connection to send an attention message to the other end. You can use ADSP to establish two-way communication between computers, such as an interoffice party line or a terminal emulation program. If you want to develop an application that requires two-way communication, you should consider using ADSP to implement it. ADSP is described in "Using ADSP" later in this chapter.

THE .MPP DRIVER

Within the AppleTalk Manager, the .MPP driver implements the LocalTalk Link Access Protocol (LLAP), the Datagram Delivery Protocol (DDP), the Routing Table Maintenance Protocol (RTMP) stub, the Name-Binding Protocol (NBP), and the AppleTalk Echo Protocol (AEP). The AppleTalk Phase 2 version of the .MPP driver includes a new function that returns information about the .MPP driver, functions that send messages to routines in the AppleTalk Transition Queue, and a new wildcard character for NBP.

Getting Information About the .MPP Driver

You can use the PGetAppleTalkInfo function to obtain information about the .MPP driver. The PGetAppleTalkInfo function returns

- a pointer to the .MPP global variables
- a pointer to the .MPP driver's device control entry (DCE) data structure
- configuration flags that indicate the status of certain conditions that are set at startup
- a value (the selfSend flag) that indicates whether the node can send packets to itself
- the range of network numbers for the network to which the node is attached
- the 8-bit node ID and 16-bit network number of the node
- the 8-bit node ID and 16-bit network number of the last router from which the node has heard
- the maximum capacities of the .MPP driver, such as the maximum number of protocol handlers and the maximum number of static sockets allowed by this driver

- a pointer to the registered names queue
- the address of the node on the underlying data link (for example, the Ethernet hardware address)
- the node's zone name

The data link address (for example, the Ethernet hardware address) and the zone name are returned only for extended networks—that is, network types that allow more than one network number per network. You must allocate memory for and provide pointers to the data buffers into which the PGetAppleTalkInfo function returns the data link address and zone name. You use the laLength parameter to specify the length of the data link address you want returned; the function returns the actual length of the data in the laLength parameter and returns the data in the buffer you provide.

> **Note:** Always use the PGetAppleTalkInfo function to obtain information about the .MPP driver. You can no longer rely on the validity of the global variables described in the AppleTalk Manager chapter of Volume II.


```
FUNCTION PGetAppleTalkInfo (thePBptr: MPPPBPtr; async: Boolean) : OSErr;
```

Parameter block

←	16	ioResult	word	result code
→	26	csCode	word	always PGetAppleTalkInfo
→	28	version	word	version of function
←	30	varsPtr	long	pointer to .MPP globals
←	34	dcePtr	long	pointer to DCE for .MPP
←	38	portID	word	port number
←	40	configuration	long	configuration flags
←	44	selfSend	word	nonzero if self-send is enabled
←	46	netLo	word	low value of the network range
←	48	netHi	word	high value of the network range
←	50	ourAddr	long	local 24-bit AppleTalk address
←	54	routerAddr	long	24-bit address of router
←	58	numOfPHs	word	max number of protocol handlers
←	60	numOfSkts	word	max number of static sockets
←	62	numNBPEs	word	max concurrent NBP requests
←	64	ntQueue	long	pointer to registered names table
↔	68	laLength	word	length in bytes of data link address (extended networks only)
→	70	linkAddr	long	pointer to data link address buffer (extended networks only)
→	74	zoneName	long	pointer to zone name buffer

The PGetAppleTalkInfo function returns information about the .MPP driver. If the node on which your program is running happens also to be running AppleTalk Internet Router software in the background, more than one set of .MPP global variables may be in RAM. To make sure you are obtaining information about the .MPP driver that handles application software, always use the PGetAppleTalkInfo function rather than the Device Manager's PBControl function. If you are using assembly language or want to use the PBControl function, you must use a device driver reference number of –10 for the .MPP driver.

Field descriptions

ioResult — The result of the function. When you execute the function asynchronously, the function sets this parameter to 1 and returns a function result of noErr as soon as the function begins execution. When the function completes execution, it sets the ioResult parameter to the actual result code.

csCode — Routine selector, automatically set by the MPW® interface. Always equal to PGetAppleTalkInfo for this function.

version — The version number of the PGetAppleTalkInfo function you are calling. For version number 53 of the .MPP driver, this number is always 1.

varsPtr — A pointer to the .MPP global variables. This parameter is reserved for the use of Apple Computer, Inc.; you cannot rely on the validity of the variables pointed to by this parameter.

dcePtr — A pointer to the device control entry (DCE) data structure for the .MPP driver. The DCE is described in the Device Manager chapters of Volumes II and V.

portID — The port number for the .MPP driver. The port number is always 0 unless you are requesting information for an .MPP driver being used by a router.

configuration — A 32-bit long word of configuration flags. The following flags are currently defined:

Bit	Flag	Description
31	SrvAdrBit	TRUE (1) if the routine that opened the .MPP driver requested a server node number. Server node numbers are described in the AppleTalk Manager chapter of Volume V. This flag indicates only that the server node number was requested, not that it was returned. Some AppleTalk data links, such as EtherTalk, do not honor a request for a server node number.
30	RouterBit	TRUE (1) if an AppleTalk Internet Router was loaded at system startup (that is, there's a router operating on the same node as your application). A router can be loaded and not active.

Bit	Flag	Description
15	ExtendedBit	TRUE (1) if the node is on an extended network. Testing this bit is the only way to determine whether you are on an extended network.
7	BadZoneHintBit	TRUE (1) if the zone name of the node you are on was not the same as the zone name stored in parameter RAM (sometimes referred to as the *zone name hint*) when the .MPP driver was opened. If the zone name hint is invalid, then the AppleTalk Manager uses the default zone for the network. The default zone is defined by the network administrator.
6	OneZoneBit	TRUE (1) if only one zone is assigned to your extended network or if you are not on an extended network. Use the ExtendedBit flag to determine whether you are on an extended network.

selfSend — The ability of a node to send packets to itself. This feature is enabled when this parameter is nonzero. Use the PSetSelfSend function, described in the AppleTalk Manager chapter of Volume V, to enable or disable this feature.

netLo — The low value of the range of network numbers on the local cable. Only extended networks can have a range of network numbers. For a nonextended network, this parameter returns the network number.

netHi — The high value of the range of network numbers on the local cable. Only extended networks can have a range of network numbers. For a nonextended network, this parameter returns the network number.

ourAddr — The 24-bit AppleTalk network address of the node you are on. The least significant byte of the long word is the node ID. The middle 16 bits are the network number. The most significant byte of the long word is reserved for use by Apple Computer, Inc.

routerAddr — The 24-bit AppleTalk network address of the last router from which your node heard traffic. The least significant byte of the long word is the node ID. The middle 16 bits are the network number. The most significant byte of the long word is reserved for use by Apple Computer, Inc. You should always use this address when you want to communicate with a router.

numOfPHs — The maximum number of protocol handlers that this .MPP driver allows.

numOfSkts — The maximum number of statically assigned sockets that this .MPP driver allows. Statically assigned sockets are described in *Inside AppleTalk,* second edition.

numNBPEs — The maximum number of concurrent requests to NBP that this .MPP driver allows.

ntQueue — A pointer to the first entry in the names table for the local node. You can use NBP routines to look up and register names in the names table. The names table is described in "Name-Binding Protocol" in the AppleTalk Manager chapter of Volume II.

laLength — The number of bytes of the data link address that the function should place in the buffer pointed to by the LinkAddr parameter. You use this parameter when you call the PGetAppleTalkInfo function on a node on an extended network. If you request more bytes than the total number of bytes in the address, then the function returns in the laLength parameter the actual number of bytes it placed in the buffer. If the address is longer than the size of the buffer, then the PGetAppleTalkInfo function fills the buffer and returns in the laLength parameter the actual length of the address, not the number of bytes returned. The function does *not* return an error when the buffer is too large or too small for the address. A value of 6 bytes for laLength is sufficient for most purposes.

linkAddr — A pointer to a buffer for the data link address returned for extended networks only. You use the laLength parameter to specify the number of bytes of the address that you want placed in this buffer. You must allocate a buffer large enough to hold the number of bytes you specify. Specify NIL for this parameter if you do not want the function to provide a data link address.

zoneName — A pointer to a buffer into which the PGetAppleTalkInfo function places the local node's zone name. You must allocate a buffer of at least 33 bytes to hold this data, or you must specify NIL for the zoneName parameter if you do not want to obtain the zone name. This field is returned only if the node is on an extended network.

Result codes

noErr	0	No error
paramErr	–50	Version number is too high

A New NBP Wildcard Character

The Name-Binding Protocol (NBP) allows the use of certain wildcard characters in AppleTalk names when you call the PLookupName function. NBP now supports the following wildcard characters:

NBP wildcard characters

= All possible values. The equal sign (=) can be used alone instead of a name in the object or type field.

* This zone. The asterisk (*) can be used in place of the name of the zone to which this node belongs.

≈ Any or no characters in this position. The double tilde (≈) can be used to obtain matches for object or type fields. For example, pa≈l matches pal, paul, paper ball, and so forth. You can use only one double tilde in any string. Press Option-x to type the double tilde character on a Macintosh keyboard. If you use the double tilde alone, it has the same meaning as the equal sign (=). Note that any node not running AppleTalk Phase 2 drivers will not recognize this character.

THE LAP MANAGER

The **LAP Manager** is a set of operating-system utilities that provide a standard interface between the AppleTalk protocols and the various link access protocols, such as LocalTalk (LLAP), EtherTalk (ELAP), and TokenTalk (TLAP). Because the LAP Manager is running even when the .MPP driver is not open, the LAP Manager also maintains the AppleTalk Transition Queue. In addition, the LAP Manager contains protocol handlers for certain types of 802.2 packets.

This section describes the AppleTalk Transition Queue and the LAP Manager 802.2 protocol handler, tells you how to add or remove an AppleTalk Transition Queue entry, and describes how to attach or detach your own 802.2 protocol handler. In addition to the LAP Manager features described here, you can use the LAP Manager to interface new data links to AppleTalk. For more information about the LAP Manager, see the *Macintosh AppleTalk Connections Programmer's Guide*.

The AppleTalk Transition Queue

At any given time there might be two or more applications running that use AppleTalk. If one of these applications opens the AppleTalk drivers, the other AppleTalk applications are affected. If the Operating System closes the AppleTalk drivers, all AppleTalk applications are affected. To ensure that your application is not adversely affected by such an event, your application can place an entry in the **AppleTalk Transition Queue.** The LAP Manager sends a message to each entry in the AppleTalk Transition Queue each time the Operating System or any routine

- opens the .MPP driver
- closes the .MPP driver
- indicates that it intends to close the .MPP driver
- cancels its intention to close the .MPP driver
- defines its own AppleTalk event and calls the AppleTalk Transition Queue to inform it that such an event occurred

Each of these events is referred to as an **AppleTalk transition.**

Because the .MPP driver is not necessarily open when the AppleTalk Transition Queue must be called, the LAP Manager maintains the queue. Each entry in the AppleTalk Transition Queue is defined by the ATQentry data type.

```
TYPE ATQEntry =
     RECORD
        qLink:         ATQEntryPtr;       {next queue entry}
        qType:         Integer;           {reserved}
        CallAddr:      ProcPtr            {pointer to your routine}
     END;
```

When you want to add an entry to the AppleTalk Transition Queue, you must create an ATQentry data structure and give the LAP Manager a pointer to it. The qLink field is a pointer to the next queue entry. You should set this field to NIL; the LAP Manager fills it in when an application adds another entry to the queue. The qType field is reserved to maintain consistency with other operating-system queues. The CallAddr field is a pointer to a routine that you provide, as described in "How the AppleTalk Manager Calls Your AppleTalk Transition Queue Entry" later in this chapter.

Because you provide the memory for the AppleTalk Transition Queue entry, you can add as many fields to the end of the entry as you wish for your own purposes. Whenever your routine is called, the caller provides you with a pointer to the queue entry so that you can have access to the information you stored at the end of your queue entry.

There are four LAP Manager functions you can use that are related to the AppleTalk Transition Queue:

- The LAPAddATQ function adds an entry to the AppleTalk Transition Queue. This function is described in the following section, "Adding and Removing AppleTalk Transition Queue Entries."
- The LAPRmvATQ function removes an entry from the AppleTalk Transition Queue. This function is described in the following section, "Adding and Removing AppleTalk Transition Queue Entries."
- The ATEvent procedure calls all the entries in the AppleTalk Transition Queue with an AppleTalk transition event of your own definition. This function is described in the section "Defining Your Own AppleTalk Transition" later in this chapter.
- The ATPreFlightEvent function calls all the entries in the AppleTalk Transition Queue with an AppleTalk transition event of your own definition and gives each entry the opportunity to respond. This function is described in the section "Defining Your Own AppleTalk Transition" later in this chapter.

Adding and Removing AppleTalk Transition Queue Entries

You can use LAP Manager routines to add an entry to or remove an entry from the AppleTalk Transition Queue.

```
FUNCTION LAPAddATQ (theATQEntry: ATQEntryPtr) : OSErr;
```

On entry	D0: 23
	A0: pointer to AppleTalk Transition Queue entry
On exit	D0: result code

The LAPAddATQ function adds an entry to the AppleTalk Transition Queue. The parameter theATQEntry is a pointer to an ATQentry data structure. The CallAddr field of the data structure holds a pointer to the routine that AppleTalk calls for any AppleTalk transition event. The ATQentry data structure is described in the preceding section, "The AppleTalk Transition Queue."

Result code

noErr	0	No error

Assembly-language note: From assembly language, you add and remove AppleTalk Transition Queue entries by placing a routine selector in the D0 register, placing a pointer to your AppleTalk Transition Queue entry in the A0 register, and executing a JSR instruction to an offset past the start of the LAP Manager. The start of the LAP Manager is contained in the global variable LAPMgrPtr ($B18). The offset to the LAP Manager routines is given by the constant LAPMgrCall (2).

Here is assembly-language code that adds or removes AppleTalk Tranisition Queue entries:

```
LAPMgrPtr    EQU      $B18            ;entry point for LAP Manager
LAPMgrCall   EQU      2               ;offset to LAP Manager routines
ATQEntry     EQU      *               ;pointer to ATQ entry

             MOVEQ    #RSel,D0        ;place routine selector
                                      ; in D0 (23 to add an entry, 24
                                      ; to remove one)
             MOVE.L   LAPMgrPtr,An    ;put pointer to LAP Mgr in An
             MOVE.L   ATQEntry,A0     ;put ATQ entry in A0
             JSR      LAPMgrCall(An)  ;jump to start of LAP Mgr
                                      ; routines
```

```
FUNCTION LAPRmvATQ (theATQEntry: ATQEntryPtr) : OSErr;
```

On entry	D0: 24 A0: pointer to AppleTalk Transition Queue entry
On exit	D0: result code

The LAPRmvATQ function removes an entry from the AppleTalk Transition Queue. The parameter theATQEntry is a pointer to an ATQentry data structure.

Note: You must not call the LAPRmvATQ function at interrupt time or through a callback routine. This restriction is to prevent any routine from removing an entry from the AppleTalk Transition Queue while another routine is in the process of adding or removing an entry.

Result codes

noErr	0	No error
qErr	–1	Queue element not found

Sending Messages to the AppleTalk Transition Queue

Whereas it is unlikely that opening the .MPP driver will adversely affect another program, an application should never close the .MPP driver, because another program might be using it. Under certain circumstances, however, the system might close the .MPP driver. The system uses the .MPP driver's PATalkClosePrep function to send a permission-to-close transition to each routine in the AppleTalk Transition Queue. This transition indicates that the system intends to close the .MPP driver so that each routine in the queue has the opportunity to deny permission to do so.

When the system calls the PATalkClosePrep function, any routine in the AppleTalk Transition Queue that wishes to deny permission to close the .MPP driver may return a pointer to a Pascal string. The Pascal string should be the name of the application that placed the entry in the queue. If any routine in the AppleTalk Transition Queue denies permission to close the .MPP driver, the PATalkClosePrep function returns the result code closeErr.

If any routine denies permission to close the .MPP driver, the AppleTalk Manager sends a cancel-close transition to every routine in the AppleTalk Transition Queue that previously received the permission-to-close transition. The caller of the PATalkClosePrep function may display a dialog box informing the user that another application is using the .MPP driver and showing the name (if any) returned by the AppleTalk Transition Queue routine. The dialog box gives the user the option of canceling the request to close AppleTalk or of closing AppleTalk anyway.

If the user chooses to close AppleTalk despite the fact that an application is using it, the system calls the MPPClose function. AppleTalk then calls each application in the AppleTalk Transition Queue, this time informing each one that AppleTalk is about to close. In this case, your AppleTalk Transition Queue routine must prepare for the imminent closing of AppleTalk; it cannot deny permission to the MPPClose function.

```
FUNCTION PATalkClosePrep (thePBptr: MPPPBPtr; async: Boolean) : OSErr;
```

Parameter block

→	26	csCode	word	always PATalkClosePrep
←	28	appName	long	pointer to name of application that denies request

The PATalkClosePrep function calls each routine listed in the AppleTalk Transition Queue to request permission to close the .MPP driver.

If a routine in the AppleTalk Transition Queue denies permission to close the .MPP driver, that routine can return a pointer to a Pascal string. The Pascal string should contain the name of the application that placed the entry in the AppleTalk Transition Queue. The PATalkClosePrep function returns that pointer in the appName field. The function also returns the result code closeErr, indicating that the calling routine has been denied permission to close the .MPP driver. The routine that called PATalkClosePrep can then display a dialog box telling the user the name of the application that is currently using AppleTalk and asking whether to close AppleTalk anyway.

The csCode parameter is a routine selector; it is always equal to PATalkClosePrep for this function.

Result codes

noErr	0	No error
closeErr	–24	Permission to close .MPP driver was denied

How the AppleTalk Manager Calls Your AppleTalk Transition Queue Entry

When you have used the LAPAddATQ function to add an entry to the AppleTalk Transition Queue, the AppleTalk Manager calls your entry when any of the following events occurs:

- A routine opens the .MPP driver.
- A routine closes the .MPP driver.
- A routine calls the PATalkClosePrep function.
- One of the routines in the AppleTalk Transition Queue denies permission for the routine that called the PATalkClosePrep function to close AppleTalk.
- An application calls the ATEvent or ATPreFlightEvent routine to send its own AppleTalk transition event to the entries in the AppleTalk Transition Queue.

When the AppleTalk Manager calls your AppleTalk Transition Queue routine, the stack looks like this:

SP →	Return address (4 bytes)
	Routine selector
	Pointer to AppleTalk Transition Queue entry (4 bytes)
	Routine-dependent parameter (4 bytes)
	Previous contents

The first item on the stack (after the return address) is a routine selector. There is one routine selector for each type of transition. The open, prepare-to-close, permission-to-close, and cancel-close transitions each have a single-digit routine selector; all other routine selectors for AppleTalk transition events are 4-character codes. Codes starting with an uppercase letter (A through Z) are reserved for use by developers. All other codes are reserved for use by Apple Computer, Inc.

Routine selector	**Transition**
$00 00 00 00	.MPP driver opened
$00 00 00 02	.MPP driver about to close
$00 00 00 03	PATalkClosePrep function has been called
$00 00 00 04	Closing of .MPP driver has been canceled
$41 *xx xx xx* –$5A *xx xx xx*	Reserved for use by developers
all others	Reserved for use by Apple Computer

You can use the following constants for the standard AppleTalk transitions:

```
CONST ATTransOpen        = 0;  {open transition}
      ATTransClose       = 2;  {prepare-to-close transition}
      ATTransClosePrep   = 3;  {permission-to-close transition}
      ATTransCancelClose = 4;  {cancel-close transition}
```

The second item passed to your routine on the stack is a pointer to your routine's entry in the AppleTalk Transition Queue. You can use this pointer to get access to any fields at the end of the queue entry that you allocated for your own use. The last item passed to your routine on the stack is a parameter whose meaning depends on the type of transition.

The interface between the AppleTalk Transition Queue and your routine follows these conventions: your routine must preserve all registers except D0, D1, D2, A0, and A1; all parameters are passed on the stack as long words. Because your routine might be called at interrupt time, your routine must not make any direct or indirect calls to the Memory Manager and can't depend on handles to unlocked blocks being valid. If you want to use any of your application's global variables, you must save the contents of the A5 register before using the variables, and you must restore the A5 register before your routine terminates. These restrictions do not apply to the open transition or the prepare-to-close transition.

> **Note:** It is important that you return a 0 in the D0 register whenever you receive a transition event routine selector that you do not recognize or do not choose to handle. Returning a nonzero value in the D0 register might cause the system to cancel an attempt to close AppleTalk, for example, or might be misinterpreted in some other way.

Open Transition

When an application calls the MPPOpen function, the AppleTalk Manager first attempts to open the .MPP driver. If the .MPP driver is already open, the AppleTalk Manager does not call the AppleTalk Transition Queue. If the AppleTalk Manager successfully opens the .MPP driver, it then calls every routine listed in the AppleTalk Transition Queue with an open transition.

The third item on the stack for an open transition is a pointer to the start of the Device Manager extended parameter block used by the routine that opened the .MPP driver. This pointer is provided for your information only; you must not change any of the fields in this parameter block.

Your AppleTalk Transition Queue routine can perform any tasks you wish in response to the notification that the .MPP driver has been opened, such as using the Name-Binding Protocol (NBP) to register a name on the internet. Return 0 in the D0 register to indicate that your routine executed with no error.

Prepare-to-Close Transition

When any routine calls the MPPClose function to close the .MPP driver, the AppleTalk Manager calls every routine listed in the AppleTalk Transition Queue before the .MPP driver closes. If the .MPP driver is already closed when a routine calls the MPPClose function, the AppleTalk Manager does not call the routines in the AppleTalk Transition Queue.

When the AppleTalk Manager calls your routine for a prepare-to-close transition, the third item on the stack is a NIL pointer.

Your routine can perform any tasks you wish to prepare for the imminent closing of AppleTalk, such as ending a session with a remote terminal and informing the user that the connection is being closed. You must return control to the AppleTalk Manager as quickly as possible. Return 0 in the D0 register to indicate that your routine executed with no error.

> **Note:** When the AppleTalk Manager calls your routine with a prepare-to-close transition (that is, a routine selector of ATTransClose), you cannot prevent the .MPP driver from closing.

Permission-to-Close Transition

When a routine calls the PATalkClosePrep function to inform the AppleTalk Manager that it wants to close the .MPP driver, the AppleTalk Manager calls every routine listed in the AppleTalk Transition Queue to request permission to close the .MPP driver.

When the AppleTalk Manager calls your routine to request permission to close the .MPP driver, the third parameter on the stack is a pointer to a 4-byte buffer. If you intend to deny the request to close AppleTalk, you should place in the buffer a pointer to a Pascal string containing the name of your application. The PATalkClosePrep function returns this pointer. The routine that called the PATalkClosePrep function can then display a dialog box telling the user the name of the application that is currently using AppleTalk.

Your routine can return either a function result of 0 in the D0 register, indicating that it accepts the request to close, or a 1 in the D0 register, indicating that it denies the request to close. Note that the Operating System might elect to close AppleTalk anyway; for example, if the user grants permission to close in response to a dialog box.

Because the AppleTalk Manager calls your routine again (with the routine selector set to ATTransClose) before the .MPP driver actually closes, it is not necessary for your routine to do anything other than grant or deny permission in response to being called for a permission-to-close transition. However, you might want to prohibit the users from opening new sessions or establishing new connections while you are waiting for the .MPP driver to close.

Cancel-Close Transition

When any routine in the AppleTalk Transition Queue denies permission for the .MPP driver to close, the AppleTalk Manager calls each routine listed in the AppleTalk Transition Queue that has already received the permission-to-close transition to inform it that the request to close the .MPP driver has been canceled.

When the AppleTalk Manager calls your AppleTalk Transition Queue routine for a cancel-close transition, the third item on the stack is a NIL pointer.

If your routine performed any tasks to prepare for the closing of AppleTalk, it should reverse their effects when it is called with the routine selector set to ATTransCancelClose. Return 0 in the D0 register to indicate that your routine executed with no error.

Developer-Defined Transitions

Any AppleTalk transition event code that begins with an uppercase letter (that is, any value in the range $41 00 00 00 through $5A FF FF FF) indicates a developer-defined event. You can use such events to send messages to your own entries in the AppleTalk Transition Queue, or you can define events and make them public for others to use. Because you cannot tell how the originator of such an event might interpret a nonzero function result, you must always return 0 in the D0 register for any AppleTalk transition event code that you do not recognize.

When you return a nonzero result code for certain developer-defined transitions, the AppleTalk Manager may call your AppleTalk Transition Queue routine a second time with a cancel transition analogous to the cancel-close transition.

Defining Your Own AppleTalk Transition

You can define your own AppleTalk transition to have any meaning you choose. For example, you might want to call every routine in the AppleTalk Transition Queue each time you open an AppleTalk Data Stream Protocol (ADSP) connection.

You can use either the ATEvent procedure or the ATPreFlightEvent function to notify all of the routines in the AppleTalk Transition Queue that your AppleTalk transition has occurred. Whereas the ATEvent procedure only calls the routines in the queue with a transition event, the ATPreFlightEvent function also allows each routine in the AppleTalk Transition Queue to return a result code and other information to your calling routine.

> **Note:** You can call the ATEvent and ATPreFlightEvent routines only at virtual-memory safe time. See the Memory Management chapter in this volume for information on virtual memory.

```
PROCEDURE ATEvent (event: LongInt; infoPtr: Ptr);
```

The ATEvent procedure calls all of the routines in the AppleTalk Transition Queue with the AppleTalk transition event code you specify in the event parameter. The AppleTalk transition event code can be any 4-character string that starts with an uppercase letter—that is, any value in the range $41 00 00 00 through $5A FF FF FF. You can use the infoPtr parameter to point to any information that you want to make available to the AppleTalk Transition Queue routines; for an ADSP-open transition, for example, you might pass a pointer to the parameter block used by the dspOpen routine. If you do not want to pass any information to the AppleTalk Transition Queue routines, set the infoPtr parameter to NIL.

```
FUNCTION ATPreFlightEvent (event,cancel: LongInt; infoPtr: Ptr) : OSErr;
```

The ATPreFlightEvent function calls all of the routines in the AppleTalk Transition Queue with the AppleTalk transition event code you specify in the event parameter. If any routine in the AppleTalk Transition Queue returns a nonzero function result, the ATPreFlightEvent function calls each of the routines that it has already called, this time with the AppleTalk transition event code you specify in the cancel parameter. The AppleTalk transition event codes can be any 4-character strings that start with an uppercase letter—that is, any values in the range $41 00 00 00 through $5A FF FF FF. You can use the infoPtr parameter to point to any information that you want to make available to the AppleTalk Transition Queue routines. If you do not want to pass any information to the AppleTalk Transition Queue routines, set the infoPtr parameter to NIL.

Result code

noErr	0	No error, or unrecognized event code

Note: AppleTalk transitions defined by developers might return other result codes.

The LAP Manager 802.2 Protocol

The Institute of Electrical and Electronics Engineers (IEEE) has defined a series of communications protocols for use on a variety of networks. At the physical level, these protocols include the 802.3 CSMA/CD protocol, the 802.4 token bus protocol, and the 802.5 token ring protocol. At the data link level, you access these protocols through another IEEE protocol, the 802.2 protocol. The AppleTalk LAP Manager includes two routines that allow you to attach and detach protocol handlers for 802.2 Type 1 data packets: the L802Attach and L802Detach routines. You can write an application that reads 802.2 Type 1 data packets and use the L802Attach routine to install your application as a client of the LAP Manager. The ANSI/IEEE standards for the 802 protocols are published by the IEEE.

The first 14 bytes of a packet sent or received by the .ENET driver constitute the header. The first 12 bytes consist of the destination and source data-link addresses, such as the Ethernet hardware addresses. If the value of the last 2 bytes in the header is greater than 1500, then the .ENET driver treats that field as an Ethernet protocol type discriminator. See "The .ENET Driver" later in this chapter for more information on Ethernet protocols. If the value of the last 2 bytes in the header is less than or equal to 1500, then the packet is an 802.3 protocol packet and this field indicates the length of the 802.3 data. The .ENET driver passes all 802.3 packets to the LAP Manager.

The LAP Manager receives the entire 802.3 packet from the .ENET driver. The first 3 bytes of the 802.3 data constitute the header for the 802.2 protocol. The first byte of the 802.2 header is known as the destination service access point (DSAP). If the DSAP field is equal to $AA, then the first 5 bytes of the 802.2 data constitute a protocol discriminator known as the subnetwork access protocol (SNAP) type. If the SNAP type field is $00000080F3, indicating the AppleTalk Address Resolution Protocol (AARP), then the next 4 bytes of the 802.2 data constitute a third type field, the AARP packet type. AARP is discussed in *Inside AppleTalk,* second edition.

The first packet header in Figure 32-4, for example, indicates an Ethernet packet containing AppleTalk Phase 1 data. The .ENET driver would deliver this packet to the AppleTalk Phase 1 protocol handler.

By contrast, the second data packet header in the figure indicates an 802.3 packet containing AppleTalk Phase 2 data. The .ENET driver would deliver this packet to the Phase 2 LAP Manager.

Similarly, the third data packet header in Figure 32-4 indicates an 802.3 packet to be delivered to the Phase 2 EtherTalk AARP handler.

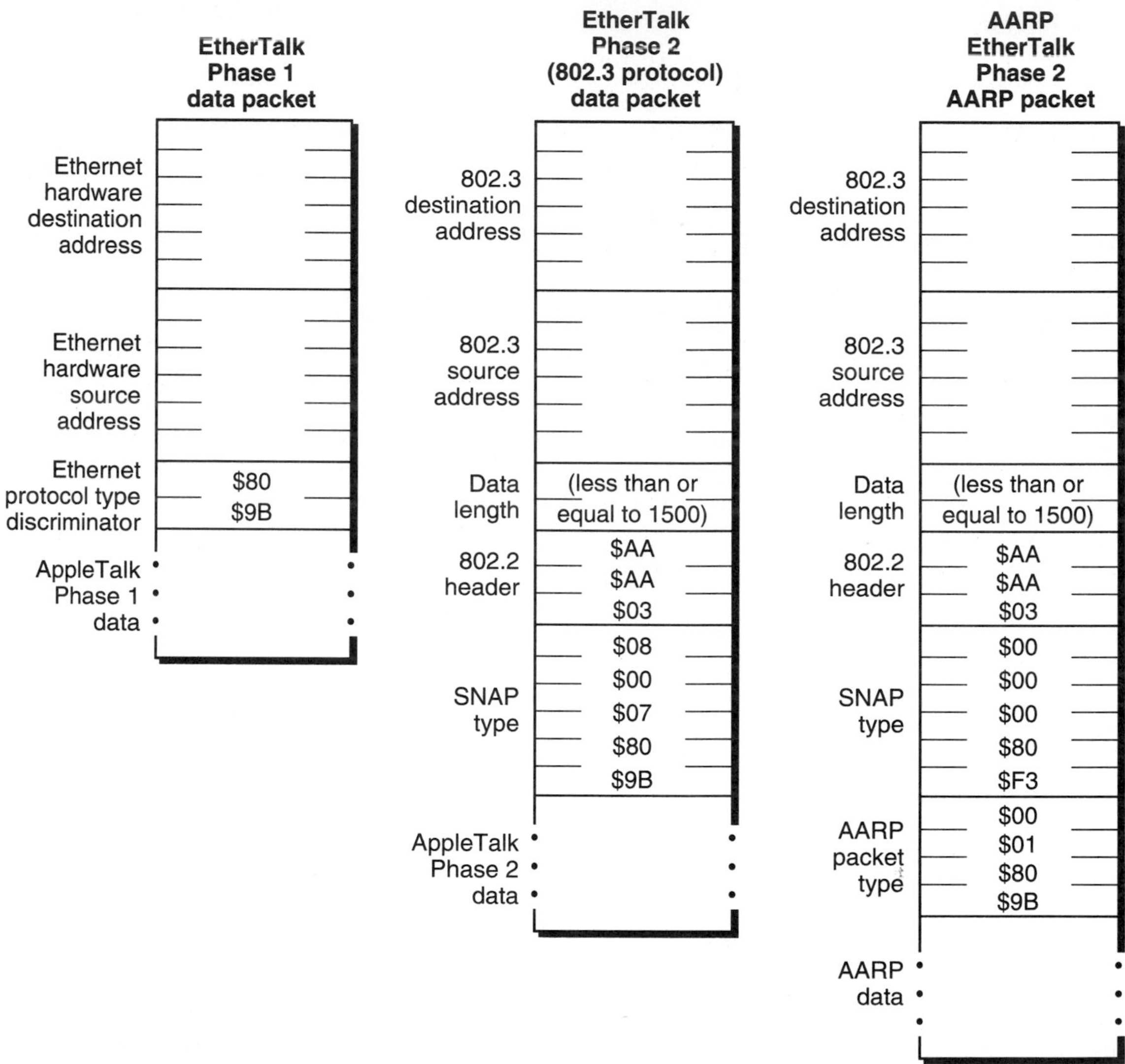

Figure 32-4. AppleTalk Ethernet packet formats

When you call the L802Attach routine, you provide a pointer to your protocol handler, the reference number of the .ENET driver, and a pointer to a string containing one or more type fields. The type fields indicate the DSAP value and any other protocol type fields (such as the SNAP type and the AARP type). The LAP Manager delivers to your protocol handler any 802.2 data packets that have the protocol type you specify.

Attaching and Detaching 802.2 Protocol Handlers

You can attach to the LAP Manager your own protocol handler for 802.2 protocols. The LAP Manager has permanent handlers for certain types of EtherTalk packets. You cannot replace or override the permanent LAP Manager protocol handlers.

There are no high-level interfaces for the LAP Manager 802.2 protocol routines. You call these routines from assembly language by placing a routine selector in the D0 register and executing a JSR instruction to an offset 2 bytes past the start of the LAP Manager. The start of the LAP Manager is contained in the global variable LAPMgrPtr ($B18).

Before you call these routines, you must place the reference number of the .ENET driver in the D2 register and a pointer to the protocol type specification in the A1 register. Before you call the L802Attach routine, you must also place a pointer to your protocol handler in the A0 register. Both routines return a nonzero value in the D0 register if there is an error.

Listing 32-1 shows how to call a LAP Manager L802.2 routine from assembly language.

Listing 32-1. Calling a LAP Manager L802.2 routine from assembly language

```
LAPMgrPtr    EQU      $B18            ;entry point for LAP Manager
LAPMgrCall   EQU      2               ;offset to LAP Manager routines
L802Entry    EQU      *               ;L802 routine entry

             MOVEQ    #RSel,D0        ;place routine selector
                                      ; in D0
             MOVEQ    #refNum,D2      ;place driver reference number
                                      ; in D2
             MOVE.L   PHndlrPtr,A0    ;put pointer to protocol
                                      ; handler in A0 (L802Attach
                                      ; only)
             MOVE.L   PSpecPtr,A1     ;put pointer to protocol
                                      ; specification in A1)
             MOVE.L   LAPMgrPtr,An    ;put pointer to LAP Mgr in An
             JSR      LAPMgrCall(An)  ;jump to start of LAP Mgr
                                      ; routines
```

L802Attach

The L802Attach routine attaches to the LAP Manager a protocol handler for a specific IEEE 802.2 protocol type.

On entry	D0: 21 D2: reference number of .ENET driver A0: pointer to your protocol handler A1: pointer to protocol specification
On exit	D0: nonzero if error

Before calling this routine, you must put the value 21 in the D0 register and the reference number of the .ENET driver in the D2 register. The .ENET driver reference number is returned by the OpenSlot function. If you are not using the .ENET driver or a driver that uses the same interface as the .ENET driver, you cannot use the L802Attach routine.

You must put a pointer to your protocol handler in the A0 register and a pointer to the protocol-type specification for this protocol handler in the A1 register. The protocol-type specification consists of one or more protocol-type fields, each preceded by a length byte. The LAP Manager reads the protocol-type fields in the 802.2 data packet header to determine to which protocol handler (if any) to deliver the packet. The first type field in your protocol specification is the 1-byte DSAP. If the DSAP type field is equal to $AA, then the protocol-type specification must contain a second type field, the 5-byte SNAP type. If the SNAP type field is $00000080F3, indicating the AppleTalk Address Resolution Protocol (AARP), then the protocol-type specification must contain a third type field, the 4-byte AARP protocol type. Terminate the list of protocol-type fields with a byte of zeros.

The following protocol-type specification, for example, is for the permanent LAP Manager protocol handler for an 802.3 packet containing AppleTalk data. The .ENET driver would deliver this packet to the AppleTalk Phase 2 LAP Manager. The first byte, $01, is the length byte for the first protocol-type field (the DSAP type field), $AA. The third byte, $05, is the length byte for the next protocol-type field, the SNAP. The final byte ($00) terminates the type specification.

```
01 AA 05 08 00 07 80 9B 00
```

The following protocol-type specification is for the permanent LAP Manager protocol handler for an 802.3 packet to be delivered to the EtherTalk AARP handler. Notice that the SNAP field is followed by an additional type field, the AARP protocol type.

```
01 AA 05 00 00 00 80 F3 04 00 01 80 9B 00
```

Note: The DSAP value of $AA is reserved for use with protocol-type specifications that include a SNAP field. The SNAP value of $08 00 07 80 9B is reserved for AppleTalk data. The SNAP value of $00 00 00 80 F3 is reserved for AARP data. The AARP protocol type value of $00 01 80 9B is reserved for EtherTalk AARP packets.

See the ANSI/IEEE standard 802.2 for more information about 802.2 protocols, and see *Inside AppleTalk,* second edition, for more information about AARP.

L802Detach

The L802Detach routine detaches from the LAP Manager a protocol handler for a specific IEEE 802.2 protocol type.

On entry	D0: 22 D2: reference number of .ENET driver A1: pointer to protocol specification
On exit	D0: nonzero if error

Before calling this routine, you must put the value 22 in the D0 register and the reference number of the .ENET driver in the D2 register. The .ENET driver reference number is returned by the OpenSlot function. If you are not using the .ENET driver or a driver that uses the same interface as the .ENET driver, you cannot use the L802Detach routine.

You must put a pointer to the protocol-type specification for this protocol handler in the A1 register. You must specify exactly the same protocol type as you specified for the L802Attach routine when you attached the protocol handler.

THE .ATP DRIVER

AppleTalk Phase 2 includes two changes to the .ATP driver: you can now cancel all calls to the ATPGetRequest function that are pending execution, and you can now set the release timer for AppleTalk Transaction Protocol (ATP) exactly-once (XO) service to one of five different values.

Canceling All Calls to the ATPGetRequest Function

The ATPGetRequest function sets a socket to receive a request sent by another socket. If you call the ATPGetRequest function asynchronously, you can have several calls to the function simultaneously pending execution. The ATPKillAllGetReq function cancels all calls to the ATPGetRequest function pending for a specific socket without closing the socket.

```
FUNCTION ATPKillAllGetReq (thePBptr: ATPPBPtr; async: Boolean) : OSErr;
```

Parameter block

→	26	csCode	word	always ATPKillAllGetReq
→	28	atpSocket	byte	socket for which to cancel all calls to ATPGetRequest

The ATPKillAllGetReq function cancels all pending asynchronous calls to the ATPGetRequest function for the socket you specify with the atpSocket parameter. The ATPKillAllGetReq function also calls the completion routine for each call to the ATPGetRequest function with the value reqAborted (–1105) in the D0 register.

Unlike the ATPCloseSocket function, the ATPKillAllGetReq function does not close the socket. You should call the ATPKillAllGetReq function before closing a socket. The csCode parameter is a routine selector, automatically set by the MPW interface. It is always equal to ATPKillAllGetReq for this function.

Result codes

noErr	0	No error
cbNotFound	–1102	Control block not found; no pending asynchronous calls

Setting the Timeout Value for the ATP Release Timer

The .ATP driver maintains a timer, called the *release timer,* for each call to the PSendResponse function that is part of an exactly-once (XO) transaction. If the timer expires before the transaction is complete (that is, before the socket receives the transaction release packet), the driver completes the PSendResponse function. Before AppleTalk Phase 2, the release timer was always set to 30 seconds. To set the other connection end's release timer to another value, set bit 2 of the atpFlags field in the parameter block for the PSendRequest or the PNSendRequest function and add a new byte field to the parameter block at offset 50—the TRelTime field. (The PSendRequest and PNSendRequest functions use the SendRequestParm variant of the ATP parameter block.) Here is the ATP parameter block for the PSendRequest and PNSendRequest functions:

```
TYPE ATPParamBlock =
     PACKED RECORD                            {extended parameter block }
                                              { for PSendRequest and }
                                              { PNSendRequest}
        qLink:          QElemPtr;             {next queue entry}
        qType:          Integer;              {queue type}
        ioTrap:         Integer;              {routine trap}
        ioCmdAddr:      Ptr;                  {routine address}
        ioCompletion:   ProcPtr;              {completion routine}
        ioResult:       OSErr;                {result code}
        userData:       LongInt;              {ATP user bytes}
        reqTID:         Integer;              {request transaction ID}
        ioRefNum:       Integer;              {driver reference number}
        csCode:         Integer;              {primary command code}
        atpSocket:      Byte;                 {currBitMap or socket number}
        atpFlags:       Byte;                 {control information - set bit 2 }
                                              { for extended parameter block}
        addrBlock:      AddrBlock;            {source socket address}
        reqLength:      Integer;              {request size in bytes}
        reqPointer:     Ptr;                  {pointer to request data}
        bdsPointer:     Ptr;                  {pointer to response buffer }
                                              { data structure}
        numOfBuffs:     Byte;                 {number of responses expected}
        timeOutVal:     Byte;                 {timeout interval}
        numOfResps:     Byte;                 {number of responses }
                                              { actually received}
        retryCount:     Byte;                 {number of retries}
        intBuff:        Integer;              {used internally for PNSendRequest}
        TRelTime:       Byte                  {release timer setting}

     END;
```

The lower three bits of the TRelTime field indicate the time to which the release timer is to be set, as follows:

TRelTime field	Setting of release timer
000	30 seconds
001	1 minute

TRelTime field	Setting of release timer
010	2 minutes
011	4 minutes
100	8 minutes

Note: The nodes at both ends of the ATP connection must be running AppleTalk Phase 2 drivers for this feature to work.

XO service, the release timer, and the SendRequest function are described in the AppleTalk Manager chapter of Volume II. The ATP parameter block and the PNSendRequest function are described in the AppleTalk Manager chapter of Volume V.

THE .XPP DRIVER

The .XPP driver provides these functions that return information about zones:

- The GetMyZone function returns the AppleTalk zone name of the node on which your application is running. This function works for both extended and nonextended networks.
- The GetLocalZones function returns a list of zone names on the network that includes the node on which your application is running. This function works for extended networks only.
- The GetZoneList function returns a complete list of zones on the internet.

Note: Before the AppleTalk Phase 2 version of the .XPP driver, you had to use the AppleTalk Transaction Protocol (ATP) to obtain zone information and request it directly from a router. The Zone Information Protocol (ZIP) functions provided by the new version of the .XPP driver make it much easier for you to obtain this information. To ensure compatibility with future versions of AppleTalk, you should always use the functions described in this section to obtain zone information.

For the GetMyZone, GetLocalZones, and GetZoneList functions, the .XPP driver uses the xCallParam variant to the XPP parameter block.

```
TYPE XPPParamBlock =
     PACKED RECORD
        qLink:            QElemPtr;      {next queue entry}
        qType:            Integer;       {queue type}
        ioTrap:           Integer;       {routine trap}
        ioCmdAddr:        Ptr;           {routine address}
        ioCompletion:     ProcPtr;       {completion routine}
        ioResult:         OSErr;         {result code}
        cmdResult:        LongInt;       {command result}
        ioVRefNum:        Integer;       {volume reference number}
        ioRefNum:         Integer;       {driver reference number}
```

```
    csCode:              Integer;        {primary command code}
    CASE XPPPrmBlkType OF
       xCallParam
          xppSubCode:    Integer;        {secondary command code}
          xppTimeOut:    Byte;           {timeout period for .XPP}
          xppRetry:      Byte;           {retry count}
          filler1:       Integer;        {reserved}
          zipBuffPtr:    Ptr;            {returned zone names}
          zipNumZones:   Integer;        {number of zones returned}
          zipLastFlag:   Byte;           {nonzero when all zone }
                                         { names have been returned}
          filler2:       Byte;           {reserved}
          zipInfoField:  PACKED ARRAY[1..70] OF Byte
                                         {reserved for use by .XPP}
END;
XPPParmBlkPtr = ^XPPParamBlock;
```

As for all other AppleTalk Manager preferred interface functions, the MPW interface calls the Device Manager PBControl function to implement these ZIP protocol functions. The qLink, qType, ioTrap, ioCmdAddr, and ioVRefNum fields are filled in by the Device Manager; your application should not have to set or read these fields. The ioResult field returns the result of the function. If you call the function asynchronously, the Device Manager sets this field to 1 as soon as you call the function, and it changes the field to the actual result code when the function completes execution. The ioCompletion field is a pointer to a completion routine that you can provide; the Device Manager calls your completion routine when it completes execution of the PBControl function. If you are not providing a completion routine, specify NIL for this field.

The value of the ioRefNum field is returned by the OpenDriver function; you must provide this value in each call to an .XPP driver routine. The csCode and xppSubCode fields specify the command to be executed; the MPW Pascal interface fills in these fields for you.The .XPP zone information functions do not use the cmdResult field.

Using the .XPP Driver to Obtain Information About Zones

The Zone Information Protocol (ZIP) obtains the zone information by using the AppleTalk Transaction Protocol (ATP) to send an information request to a router. The xppTimeOut field specifies the amount of time, in seconds, that the .ATP driver should wait between attempts to obtain the data. The xppRetry field specifies the number of times the .ATP driver should attempt to obtain the data before returning the reqFailed (request failed) result code.

The zipBuffPtr field is a pointer to a data buffer that you must allocate. This buffer must be 578 bytes for the GetZoneList and GetLocalZones functions and 33 bytes for the GetMyZone function. ZIP returns the zone names (as a packed array of packed Pascal strings) into this buffer. The zipNumZones field returns the actual number of zone names that ZIP placed in the buffer. You must set the zipLastFlag field to 0 (FALSE) before you execute the GetZoneList or GetLocalZones function. If the zipLastFlag parameter is still 0 when the command has completed execution, then ZIP is waiting to return more zone names. In this case you must empty the buffer (or allocate a new one) and call the GetZoneList or GetLocalZones function again immediately. When there are no more zone names to return, ZIP sets the zipLastFlag field to a nonzero (TRUE) value.

The zipInfoField field is a 70-byte data buffer that you must allocate for use by the .XPP driver. The first time you call any of these functions, you must set the first word of this field to 0. You must not change any values in this field subsequently.

Listing 32-2 illustrates the use of the GetZoneList function. The GetLocalZones function operates in exactly the same fashion.

Listing 32-2. Using the GetZoneList function

```
PROCEDURE doGetZoneList;

VAR
   myXPPPB: XPPParamBlock;          {.XPP parameter block}
   myErr:   OSErr;

BEGIN
   WITH myXPPPB DO
   BEGIN
      xppTimeOut := 3;              {timeout period for .XPP}
      xppRetry := 4;                {retry count}
      zipBuffPtr := NewPtr(578);    {zone names returned here}
      zipLastFlag := 0;             {set to 0 the first time through}
      zipInfoField[1] := 0;
      zipInfoField[2] := 0;         {first word is 0 the first }
                                    { time through}
   END;
   myErr := noErr;

{Check the zipNumZones field to determine how many zone names }
{ have been returned in the buffer.  Append the zone names to the }
{ end of your own buffer before returning to read more zone names.}

   {loop to get all of the zone names}
   WHILE (myXPPPB.zipLastFlag = 0) & (myErr = noErr) DO
   BEGIN
      myErr := GetZoneList(@myXPPPB, FALSE);
      EmptyDataBuf(@myXPPPB);       {your routine to empty }
                                    { data buffer}
   END;
   YourZIPProc(@myXPPPB);           {your routine to process names}
   IF myErr <> noErr THEN DoError(myErr);
                                    {there's an error}
   DisposPtr(myXPPPB.zipBuffPtr);   {give space back}
END;
```

Listing 32-3 illustrates the use of the GetMyZone function.

Listing 32-3. Using the GetMyZone function

```
PROCEDURE doGetMyZone;

VAR
   myXPPPB:     XPPParamBlock;     {.XPP parameter block}
   myZoneName: ARRAY[1..33] OF CHAR;
   myErr:       OSErr;

BEGIN
   WITH myXPPPB DO
   BEGIN
      xppTimeOut := 3;            {timeout period for .XPP}
      xppRetry := 4;              {retry count}
      zipBuffPtr := @myZoneName; {zone name returned here}
      zipInfoField[1] := 0;
      zipInfoField[2] := 0;       {first word is 0 the first }
                                  { time through}
   END;
   myErr := GetMyZone(@myXPPPB, FALSE);
   IF myErr <> noErr THEN DoError(myErr);
                                  {there's an error}
END;
```

Obtaining Zone Information

The .XPP driver provides three functions that obtain information about zones. All three functions use the Zone Information Protocol (ZIP) to return the names of zones.

Assembly-language note: The .XPP driver functions all use the same value (xCall, which is equal to 246) for the csCode parameter to the XPP parameter block. The xCall routine uses the value of the xppSubCode parameter to distinguish between the functions, as follows:

Function	xppSubCode	Value
GetMyZone	zipGetMyZone	7
GetLocalZones	zipGetLocalZones	5
GetZoneList	zipGetZoneList	6

```
FUNCTION GetMyZone (thePBptr: XPPParmBlkPtr; async: Boolean) : OSErr;
```

Parameter block

←	16	ioResult	word	result code
→	26	csCode	word	routine selector; always xCall

→	28	xppSubCode	word	routine selector; zipGetMyZone
→	30	xppTimeOut	byte	retry interval in seconds
→	31	xppRetry	byte	retry count
→	34	zipBuffPtr	long	pointer to data buffer
→	42	zipInfoField	70 bytes	for use by ZIP; first word set to 0

The GetMyZone function returns only the AppleTalk zone name of the node on which your application is running.

The ioResult field returns the result of the function. If you call the function asynchronously, the function sets this field to 1 as soon as it begins execution, and it changes the field to the actual result code when it completes execution. The csCode and xppSubCode fields are routine selectors and are automatically set by the MPW interface to xCall and zipGetMyZone for this function. The xppTimeOut field specifies the amount of time, in seconds, that the .ATP driver should wait between attempts to obtain the data. A value of 3 or 4 for the xppTimeOut field generally gives good results. The xppRetry field specifies the number of times the .ATP driver should attempt to obtain the data before returning the reqFailed (request failed) result code. A value of 3 or 4 for the xppRetry field usually works well.

The zipBuffPtr field is a pointer to a 33-byte data buffer that you must allocate. ZIP returns the zone name into this buffer as a Pascal string. The zipInfoField field is a 70-byte data buffer that you must allocate for use by ZIP. You must set the first word of this buffer to 0 before you call the GetMyZone function.

Result codes

noErr	0	No error
noBridgeErr	–93	No router is available
reqFailed	–1096	Request to contact router failed; retry count exceeded
tooManyReqs	–1097	Too many concurrent requests
noDataArea	–1104	Too many outstanding ATP calls

```
FUNCTION GetLocalZones (thePBptr: XPPParmBlkPtr; async: Boolean) : OSErr;
```

Parameter block

←	16	ioResult	word	result code
→	26	csCode	word	routine selector; always xCall
→	28	xppSubCode	word	routine selector; zipGetLocalZones
→	30	xppTimeOut	byte	retry interval in seconds
→	31	xppRetry	byte	retry count
→	34	zipBuffPtr	long	pointer to data buffer
←	38	zipNumZones	word	number of names returned
←	40	zipLastFlag	byte	nonzero if no more names
→	42	zipInfoField	70 bytes	for use by ZIP; first word set to 0

The GetLocalZones function returns a list of all the zone names on the local network—that is, the network that includes the node on which your application is running.

The ioResult field returns the result of the function. If you call the function asynchronously, the function sets this field to 1 as soon as it begins execution, and it changes the field to the actual result code when it completes execution. The csCode and xppSubCode fields are routine selectors and are automatically set by the MPW interface to xCall and zipGetLocalZones for this function. The xppTimeOut field specifies the amount of time, in seconds, that the .ATP driver should wait between attempts to obtain the data. A value of 3 or 4 for the xppTimeOut field generally gives good results. The xppRetry field specifies the number of times the .ATP driver should attempt to obtain the data before returning the reqFailed (request failed) result code. A value of 3 or 4 for the xppRetry field usually works well.

The zipBuffPtr field is a pointer to a 578-byte data buffer that you must allocate. ZIP returns the zone names into this buffer as a packed array of Pascal strings. The zipNumZones parameter returns the number of zone names that ZIP placed in the data buffer.

The .XPP driver sets the zipLastFlag field to 1 if there are no more zone names for your network. If the zipLastFlag field is still 0 when the GetLocalZones function has completed execution, you must empty the data buffer pointed to by the zipBuffPtr parameter and immediately call the GetLocalZones function again without changing the value in the zipInfoField parameter. The zipInfoField parameter is a 70-byte data buffer that you must allocate for use by ZIP. You must set the first word of this buffer to 0 before you call the GetLocalZones function the first time, and you must not change the contents of this field thereafter.

Result codes

noErr	0	No error
noBridgeErr	–93	No router is available
reqFailed	–1096	Request to contact router failed; retry count exceeded
tooManyReqs	–1097	Too many concurrent requests
noDataArea	–1104	Too many outstanding ATP calls

```
FUNCTION GetZoneList (thePBptr: XPPParmBlkPtr; async: Boolean) : OSErr;
```

Parameter block

←	16	ioResult	word	result code
→	26	csCode	word	routine selector; always xCall
→	28	xppSubCode	word	routine selector; zipGetZoneList
→	30	xppTimeOut	byte	retry interval in seconds
→	31	xppRetry	byte	retry count
→	34	zipBuffPtr	long	pointer to data buffer
←	38	zipNumZones	word	number of names returned
←	40	zipLastFlag	byte	nonzero if no more names
→	42	zipInfoField	70 bytes	for use by ZIP; first word set to 0

The GetZoneList function returns a complete list of all the zone names on the internet. To obtain a list of only the zone names on the local network, use the GetLocalZones function instead.

The ioResult field returns the result of the function. If you call the function asynchronously, the function sets this field to 1 as soon as it begins execution, and it changes the field to the actual result code when it completes execution. The csCode and xppSubCode fields are routine selectors and are automatically set by the MPW interface to xCall and zipGetZoneList for this function. The xppTimeOut field specifies the amount of time, in seconds, that the .ATP driver should wait between attempts to obtain the data. A value of 3 or 4 for the xppTimeOut field generally gives good results. The xppRetry field specifies the number of times the .ATP driver should attempt to obtain the data before returning the reqFailed (request failed) result code. A value of 3 or 4 for the xppRetry field usually works well.

The zipBuffPtr field is a pointer to a 578-byte data buffer that you must allocate. ZIP returns the zone names into this buffer as Pascal strings. The zipNumZones parameter returns the number of zone names that ZIP placed in the data buffer.

The .XPP driver sets the zipLastFlag field to 1 if there are no more zone names for the internet. If the zipLastFlag field is still 0 when the GetZoneList function has completed execution, you must empty the data buffer pointed to by the zipBuffPtr parameter and immediately call the GetZoneList function again without changing the value in the zipInfoField parameter. The zipInfoField parameter is a 70-byte data buffer that you must allocate for use by ZIP. You must set the first word of this buffer to 0 before you call the GetZoneList function the first time, and not change the contents of this field thereafter.

If you use the GetZoneList function on a nonextended network, it returns the reqFailed result code.

Result codes

noErr	0	No error
noBridgeErr	–93	No router is available
reqFailed	–1096	Request to contact router failed; retry count exceeded
tooManyReqs	–1097	Too many concurrent requests
noDataArea	–1104	Too many outstanding ATP calls

APPLETALK DATA STREAM PROTOCOL (ADSP)

One of the significant new features of AppleTalk included as part of system software version 7.0 is the AppleTalk Data Stream Protocol (ADSP), which provides a full-duplex data stream connection between two nodes in an AppleTalk internet. Like the AppleTalk Session Protocol, Printer Access Protocol, and AppleTalk Transaction Protocol, ADSP uses the Datagram Delivery Protocol (DDP) to send its data over the internet. Therefore, even though ADSP appears to its clients to handle data as a stream of bytes, the data is actually transmitted and received by DDP in packets. ADSP takes advantage of this fact by including control and status information in the DDP packet header. You can use the .DSP driver routines described in ".DSP Driver Routines" later in this chapter to control an ADSP connection. The .DSP driver takes care of the implementation of ADSP for you.

Every ADSP connection is between two sockets in an AppleTalk internet. Each socket can maintain concurrent ADSP connections with several other sockets, but there can be only one ADSP connection between any two sockets at one time. When a pair of sockets establishes an ADSP connection, each socket client initializes and maintains a certain amount of control and state information that it uses for synchronizing communication with the other socket client and for error checking.

The combination of a socket and the ADSP information maintained by the socket client is referred to as a **connection end.** When two connection ends establish communication, the connection is considered an **open connection.** When both connection ends terminate the link and dispose of the connection information each maintains, the connection is considered a **closed connection.** If one connection end is established but the other connection end is unreachable or has disposed of its connection information, the connection is considered a **half-open connection.** No communication can occur over a half-open or closed connection. To prevent a half-open connection from tying up resources, ADSP automatically closes any half-open connection that cannot reestablish communication within 2 minutes.

Using ADSP

You can use ADSP to implement a data stream connection between any two sockets on an internet. (Note that although there can be only one ADSP connection between any two sockets, a single socket can maintain connections with several other sockets.) This section describes how to open, maintain, and close a connection between two sockets on an internet. It also describes how to establish and use a **connection listener**—that is, a connection end that waits passively to receive a connection request and then passes the connection request on to its client, the connection server. Finally, this section describes how to write a routine (referred to as a *user routine*) that ADSP calls when your connection end receives an unsolicited connection event.

The ADSP Connection Control Block

When you establish an ADSP connection end, you must allocate a nonrelocatable block of memory for, and provide a pointer to, a **connection control block (CCB)** data structure, which is used by ADSP to store state information about the connection end. You may read the fields in the CCB to obtain information about the connection end, but you are not allowed to write to any of the fields except one, the userFlags field. The CCB requires 242 bytes and is defined by the TRCCB data type.

```
TYPE TRCCB =
     PACKED RECORD
        ccbLink:            TPCCB;          {link to next CCB}
        refNum:             Integer;        {reference number}
        state:              Integer;        {state of the connection end}
        userFlags:          Byte;           {user flags for connection}
        localSocket:        Byte;           {local socket number}
        remoteAddress:      AddrBlock;      {remote end internet address}
        attnCode:           Integer;        {attention code received}
        attnSize:           Integer;        {size of attention data}
        attnPtr:            Ptr;            {pointer to attention data}
        reserved:           PACKED ARRAY[1..220] OF Byte
                                            {reserved for use by ADSP}
     END;
```

The internet address of the remote connection end is defined in the CCB by the AddrBlock data type:

```
TYPE AddrBlock =
     PACKED RECORD
        aNet:              Integer;       {network number}
        aNode:             Byte;          {node ID}
        aSocket:           Byte           {socket number}
     END;
```

Field descriptions

ccbLink — A pointer to the next CCB. This field is for use by ADSP only.

refNum — The reference number of the CCB. This number is assigned by ADSP when you establish the connection end.

state — The state of the connection end, as follows:

State	Value	Meaning
sListening	1	The socket is a **connection listening socket**—that is, a socket that accepts ADSP requests to open connections and passes them on to a socket client. This state is ordinarily used only by connection servers.
sPassive	2	The socket client is inactive but capable of accepting an ADSP request to open a connection. Unlike a connection listening socket, which passes the open-connection request on to a routine that can establish the connection on any socket, a socket client in the sPassive state can accept an open-connection request only to establish itself as a connection end.
sOpening	3	The socket client has sent an open-connection request and is waiting for acknowledgment.
sOpen	4	The connection is open.
sClosing	5	The socket client has requested that ADSP close the connection, and ADSP is sending data or waiting for acknowledgment of data it has sent before closing the connection.
sClosed	6	The connection.is closed.

userFlags — Flags that indicate an unsolicited connection event has occurred. An **unsolicited connection event** is an event initiated by ADSP or the remote connection end that is not in response to any .DSP routine that you executed.

userFlags *(continued)* Each time an unsolicited connection event occurs, ADSP sets a flag in the userFlags field of the CCB and calls the routine you specified in the userRoutine parameter to the dspInit routine (if any). The user routine must read the userFlags field and then clear the flag to 0. ADSP cannot notify your routine of future events unless you clear the flag after each event.

ADSP recognizes four types of unsolicited connection events, one corresponding to each of the flags in this field. The events and flags are defined as follows, where bit 7 is the most significant bit:

Event	Flag bit	Meaning
eClosed	7	ADSP has been informed by the remote connection end that the remote connection end has closed the connection.
eTearDown	6	ADSP has determined that the remote connection end is not responding and so has closed the connection.
eAttention	5	ADSP has received an attention message from the remote connection end.
eFwdReset	4	ADSP has received a forward reset command from the remote connection end, has discarded all ADSP data not yet delivered—including the data in the local client end's receive queue—and has resynchronized the connection.
none	3–0	Reserved.

localSocket — The socket number through which DDP transmits and receives the ADSP packets.

remoteAddress — The internet address of the socket used by the remote connection end.

attnCode — The attention code received by ADSP when the remote connection end sends an attention message.

attnSize — The size of the attention message received by ADSP when the remote connection end sends an attention message.

attnPtr — A pointer to a buffer containing the attention message received by ADSP from the remote connection end.

reserved — A data buffer reserved for use by ADSP.

The .DSP Parameter Block

You execute the .DSP routines by calling the Device Manager's PBControl function. Each time you call a .DSP routine, you provide a pointer to a parameter block that includes all of the parameters needed by that command.

The .DSP parameter block, defined by the DSPParamBlock data type, is a variant parameter block for the PBControl function.

```
TYPE DSPParamBlock =
     PACKED RECORD
        qLink:             QElemPtr;        {next queue entry}
        qType:             Integer;         {queue type}
        ioTrap:            Integer;         {routine trap}
        ioCmdAddr:         Ptr;             {routine address}
        ioCompletion:      ProcPtr;         {completion routine}
        ioResult:          OSErr;           {result code}
        ioNamePtr:         StringPtr;       {used only for dspOpen}
        ioVRefNum:         Integer;         {volume reference number}
        ioCRefNum:         Integer;         {driver reference number}
        csCode:            Integer;         {primary command code}
        qStatus:           LongInt;         {reserved for ADSP}
        ccbRefNum:         Integer;         {CCB reference number}

        CASE Integer OF
        dspInit,
        dspCLInit:
        (
           ccbPtr:         TPCCB;           {pointer to CCB}
           userRoutine:    ProcPtr;         {pointer to user routine}
           sendQSize:      Integer;         {size of send queue}
           sendQueue:      Ptr;             {pointer to send queue}
           recvQSize:      Integer;         {size of receive queue}
           recvQueue:      Ptr;             {pointer to receive queue}
           attnPtr:        Ptr;             {pointer to attention- }
                                            { message buffer}
           localSocket:    Byte;            {local socket number}
           filler1:        Byte             {filler for proper alignment}
        );

        dspOpen,
        dspCLListen,
        dspCLDeny:
        (
           localCID:       Integer;         {local connection ID}
           remoteCID:      Integer;         {remote connection ID}
           remoteAddress:  AddrBlock;       {remote internet address}
           filterAddress:  AddrBlock;       {address filter}
           sendSeq:        LongInt;         {send sequence number}
           sendWindow:     Integer;         {size of remote buffer}
           recvSeq:        LongInt;         {receive sequence number}
           attnSendSeq:    LongInt;         {attention send seq number}
           attnRecvSeq:    LongInt;         {attention receive seq num}
           ocMode:         Byte;            {connection-opening mode}
           ocInterval:     Byte;            {interval bet open requests}
           ocMaximum:      Byte;            {retries of open-conn req}
           filler2:        Byte             {filler for proper alignment}
        );
```

```
   dspClose,
   dspRemove:
   (
      abort:          Byte;         {abort send requests}
      filler3:        Byte          {filler for proper alignment}
   );

   dspStatus:
   (
      statusCCB:      TPCCB;        {pointer to CCB}
      sendQPending:   Integer;      {bytes waiting in send queue}
      sendQFree:      Integer;      {available send-queue buffer}
      recvQPending:   Integer;      {bytes in receive queue}
      recvQFree:      Integer       {avail receive-queue buffer}
   );

   dspRead,
   dspWrite:
   (
      reqCount:       Integer;      {requested number of bytes}
      actCount:       Integer;      {actual number of bytes}
      dataPtr:        Ptr;          {pointer to data buffer}
      eom:            Byte;         {1 if end of message}
      flush:          Byte          {1 to send data now}
   );

   dspAttention:
   (
      attnCode:       Integer;      {client attention code}
      attnSize:       Integer;      {size of attention data}
      attnData:       Ptr;          {pointer to attention data}
      attnInterval:   Byte;         {reserved}
      filler4:        Byte          {filler for proper alignment}
   );

   dspOptions:
   (
      sendBlocking:   Integer;      {send-blocking threshold}
      sendTimer:      Byte;         {reserved}
      rtmtTimer:      Byte;         {reserved}
      badSeqMax:      Byte;         {retransmit advice threshold}
      useCheckSum:    Byte          {DDP checksum for packets}
   );

   dspNewCID:
   (
      newCID:         Integer       {new connection ID}
   )
END;
```

The qLink, qType, ioTrap, ioCmdAddr, ioNamePtr, and ioVRefNum fields are filled in by the Device Manager; your application should not have to set or read these fields. The ioResult field returns the result of the function. If you call the routine asynchronously, the Device Manager sets this field to 1 as soon as you call the routine, and it changes the field to the actual result code when the routine completes execution. The ioCompletion field is a pointer to a completion routine that you can provide; the Device Manager calls your completion routine when it completes execution of the PBControl function. If you are not providing a completion routine, specify NIL for this field.

The ioCRefNum field is returned by the OpenDriver function. You must specify this number every time you call the .DSP driver.

The csCode field specifies the command to be executed. You must fill in this field before calling the PBControl function. You can use the following constants as values for the csCode field:

```
CONST {ADSP routine selectors}
      dspInit       = 255;  {create a new connection end}
      dspRemove     = 254;  {remove a connection end}
      dspOpen       = 253;  {open a connection}
      dspClose      = 252;  {close a connection}
      dspCLInit     = 251;  {create a connection listener}
      dspCLRemove   = 250;  {remove a connection listener}
      dspCLListen   = 249;  {post a listener request}
      dspCLDeny     = 248;  {deny an open-connection request}
      dspStatus     = 247;  {get status of connection end}
      dspRead       = 246;  {read data from the connection}
      dspWrite      = 245;  {write data on the connection}
      dspAttention  = 244;  {send an attention message}
      dspOptions    = 243;  {set connection end options}
      dspReset      = 242;  {forward reset the connection}
      dspNewCID     = 241;  {generate a cid for a connection end}
```

The qStatus field is reserved for use by ADSP. The ccbRefNum field is the reference number of the CCB. The CCB reference number is returned by ADSP in response to the dspInit routine. You must specify this number as a parameter to every .DSP driver routine you call subsequently.

The remaining fields are used only for specific routines; each of these fields is described in ".DSP Driver Routines" later in this chapter.

Opening and Maintaining an ADSP Connection

To use the AppleTalk Data Stream Protocol (ADSP) to establish and maintain a connection between a socket on your local node and a remote socket, use the following procedure:

1. Use the MPPOpen function to open the .MPP driver, and then use the OpenDriver function to open the .DSP driver. The OpenDriver function returns the reference number for the .DSP driver. You must supply this reference number each time you call the .DSP driver.

2. Allocate nonrelocatable memory for a connection control block (CCB), send and receive queues, and an attention-message buffer. If you need to allocate the memory dynamically while the program is running, use the NewPtr routine. Otherwise, the way in which you allocate the memory depends on the compiler you are using. (Listing 32-4 at the end of this section shows how it's done in Pascal.) The memory that you allocate becomes the property of ADSP when you call the dspInit routine to establish a connection end. You cannot write any data to this memory except by calling ADSP, and you must ensure that the memory remains locked until you call the dspRemove routine to eliminate the connection end.

   The CCB is 242 bytes. The attention-message buffer must be 570 bytes. When you send bytes to a remote connection end, ADSP stores the bytes in a buffer called the *send queue.* Until the remote connection end acknowledges their receipt, ADSP keeps the bytes you sent in the send queue so that they are available to be retransmitted if necessary. When the local connection end receives bytes, it stores them in a buffer, called the *receive queue,* until you read them. The sizes you need for the send and receive queues depend on the lengths of the messages being sent.

   ADSP does not transmit data from the remote connection end until there is room for it in your receive queue. If your send or receive queues are too small, they limit the speed with which you can transmit and receive data. A queue size of 600 bytes should work well for most applications. If you are using ADSP to send a continuous flow of data, a larger data buffer improves performance. If your application is sending or receiving the user's keystrokes, a smaller buffer should be adequate. The constant minDSPQueueSize indicates the minimum queue size that you can use.

   If you are using a version of the .DSP driver prior to version 1.5, you must allocate send and receive queues that are 12 percent larger than the actual buffer sizes you need. You must do this in order to provide some extra space for use by the .DSP driver. Version 1.5 and later versions of the .DSP driver use a much smaller, and variable, portion of buffer space for overhead. The .DSP driver version number is stored in the low byte of the qFlags field, which is the first field in the dCtlQHdr field in the driver's device control entry (DCE) data structure. Version 1.5 of the .DSP driver has a version number of 4 in the DCE. The DCE is described in the Device Manager chapters of Volumes II and V.

3. Use the dspInit routine to establish a connection end. You must provide pointers to the CCB, send queue, receive queue, and attention-message buffer. You may also provide a pointer to the user routine that ADSP calls when your connection end receives an unsolicited connection event. User routines are discussed in "Writing a User Routine for Connection Events" later in this chapter.

   If there is a specific socket that you want to use for the connection end, you can specify the socket number in the localSocket parameter. If you want ADSP to assign the socket for you, specify 0 for the localSocket parameter. ADSP returns the socket number when the dspInit routine completes execution.

4. If you wish, you can use the NBPRegister function to add the name and address of your connection end to the node's names table. The NBPRegister function is described in the AppleTalk Manager chapter of Volume II.

5. You can use the dspOptions routine to set several parameters that control the behavior of the connection end. Because every parameter has a default value, the use of the dspOptions routine is optional. You can specify values for the following parameters:

   - The sendBlocking parameter, which sets the maximum number of bytes that may accumulate in the send queue before ADSP sends a packet to the remote connection end. You can experiment with different values of the sendBlocking parameter to determine which provides the best performance. Under most circumstances, the default value of 16 bytes gives good performance.

   - The badSeqMax parameter, which sets the maximum number of out-of sequence data packets that the local connection end can receive before requesting the remote connection end to retransmit the missing data. Under most circumstances, the default value of 3 provides good performance.

   - The useCheckSum parameter, which determines whether the Datagram Delivery Protocol (DDP) should compute a checksum and include it in each packet that it sends to the remote connection end. Using checksums slows communications slightly. Normally ADSP and DDP perform enough error checking to ensure safe delivery of all data. Set the useCheckSum parameter to 1 only if you feel that the network is highly unreliable.

6. Call the dspOpen routine to open the connection. The dspOpen routine has four possible modes of operation: ocAccept, ocEstablish, ocRequest, and ocPassive. Normally you use either the ocRequest or ocPassive mode. You must specify one of these four modes for the ocMode parameter when you call the dspOpen routine.

   The ocAccept mode is used only by connection servers. The ocEstablish mode is used by routines that determine their connection-opening parameters and establish a connection independently of ADSP, but use ADSP to transmit and receive data.

   Use the ocRequest mode when you want to establish communications with a specific socket on the internet. When you execute the dspOpen routine in the ocRequest mode, ADSP sends an open-connection request to the address you specify.

   If the socket to which you send the open-connection request is a connection listener, the connection server that operates that connection listener can choose any socket on the internet to be the connection end that responds to the open-connection request. To restrict the socket from which you will accept a response to your open-connection request, specify a value for the filterAddress parameter to the dspOpen routine. When your connection end receives a response from a socket that meets the restrictions of the filterAddress parameter, it acknowledges the response and ADSP completes the connection.

   To use the ocRequest mode, you must know the complete internet address of the remote socket, and the ADSP client at that address must either be a connection listener or have executed the dspOpen routine in the ocPassive mode. You can use the PLookupName function to obtain a list of names of objects on the internet and to determine the internet address of a socket when you know its name. The PLookupName function is the preferred interface version of the NBPLookup function. The NBPLookup function is described in the AppleTalk Manager chapter of Volume II. The preferred interface is described in the AppleTalk Manager chapter of Volume V. Enhancements to the wildcard-lookup feature of the Name-Binding Protocol (NBP) are discussed in "A New NBP Wildcard Character" earlier in this chapter.

Use the ocPassive mode when you expect to receive an open-connection request from a remote socket. You can specify a value for the filterAddress parameter to restrict the network number, node ID, or socket number from which you will accept an open-connection request. When your connection end receives an open-connection request that meets the restrictions of the filterAddress parameter, it acknowledges the request and ADSP completes the connection.

You can poll the state field in the CCB to determine when the connection end is waiting to receive an open-connection request, when the connection end is waiting to receive an acknowledgment of an open-connection request, and when the connection is open. (The CCB is described in "The ADSP Connection Control Block" earlier in this chapter.) Alternatively, you can check the result code for the dspOpen routine when the routine completes execution. If the routine returns the noErr result code, then the connection is open.

7. Use the dspRead routine to read data that your connection end has received from the remote connection end. Use the dspWrite routine to send data to the remote connection end. Use the dspAttention routine to send attention messages to the remote connection end.

   The dspWrite routine places data in the send queue. ADSP is a full-duplex, symmetric communications protocol. You can send data at any time, and your connection end can receive data at any time, even at the same time as you are sending data. ADSP transmits the data in the send queue when one of the following conditions occurs:

   - You call the dspWrite routine with the flush parameter set to a nonzero number.
   - The number of bytes in the send queue equals or exceeds the blocking factor that you set with the dspOptions routine.
   - The send timer expires. The send timer sets the maximum amount of time that can pass before ADSP sends all unsent data in the send queue to the remote connection end. ADSP calculates the best value to use for this timer and sets it automatically.
   - A connection event requires that the local connection end send an acknowledgment packet to the remote connection end.

   If you send more data to the send queue than it can hold, the dspWrite routine does not complete execution until it has written all the data to the send queue. If you execute the dspWrite routine asynchronously, ADSP returns control to your program and writes the data to the send queue as quickly as it can. This technique provides the most efficient use of the send queue by your program and by ADSP. Because ADSP does not remove data from the send queue until that data has not only been sent but also acknowledged by the remote connection end, using the flush parameter to the dspWrite routine does not guarantee that the send queue is empty. You can use the dspStatus routine to determine how much free buffer space is available in the send queue.

   The dspRead routine reads data from the receive queue into your application's private data buffer. ADSP does not transmit data until there is space available in the other end's receive queue to accept it. Because a full receive queue slows the communications rate, you should read data from the receive queue as often as necessary to keep sufficient buffer space available for new data. You can use either of two techniques to do this:

- Allocate a small receive queue (about 600 bytes) and call the dspRead routine asynchronously. Your completion routine for the dspRead routine should then call the dspRead routine again.
- Allocate a large receive queue and call the dspRead routine less frequently.

If there is less data in the receive queue than the amount you specify with the reqCount parameter to the dspRead command, the command does not complete execution until there is enough data available to satisfy the request. There are three exceptions to this rule:

- If the end-of-message bit in the ADSP packet header is set, the dspRead command reads the data in the receive queue, returns the actual amount of data read in the actCount parameter, and returns the eom parameter set to 1.
- If you have closed the connection end before calling the dspRead routine (that is, the connection is half open), the command reads whatever data is available and returns the actual amount of data read in the actCount parameter.
- If ADSP has closed the connection before you call the dspRead routine and there is no data in the receive queue, the routine returns the noErr result code with the actCount parameter set to 0 and the eom parameter set to 0.

In addition to the byte-stream data format implemented by the dspRead and dspWrite routines, ADSP provides a mechanism for sending and receiving control signals or information separate from the byte stream. You use the dspAttention routine to send an attention code and an attention message to the remote connection end. When your connection end receives an attention message, ADSP's interrupt handler sets the eAttention flag in the userFlags field of the CCB and calls your user routine. Your user routine must first clear the userFlags field. Then your routine can read the attention code and attention message and take whatever action you deem appropriate.

Because ADSP is often used by terminal emulation programs and other applications that pass the data they receive on to the user without processing it, attention messages provide a mechanism for the applications that are clients of the connection ends to communicate with each other. For example, you could use attention messages to implement a handshaking and data-checking protocol for a program that transfers disk files between two applications, neither one of which is a file server. Or a database server on a mainframe computer that uses ADSP to communicate with Macintosh computer workstations could use the attention mechanism to inform the workstations when the database is about to be closed down for maintenance.

8. When you are ready to close the ADSP connection, you can use the dspClose or dspRemove routine to close the connection end. Use the dspClose routine if you intend to use that connection end to open another connection and do not want to release the memory you allocated for the connection end. Use the dspRemove routine if you are completely finished with the connection end and want to release the memory.

You can continue to read data from the receive queue after you have called the dspClose routine, but not after you have called the dspRemove routine. You can use the dspStatus routine to determine whether any data is remaining in the receive queue, or you can read data from the receive queue until both the actCount and eom fields of the dspRead parameter block return 0.

If you set the abort parameter for the dspClose or dspRemove routine to 0, then ADSP does not close the connection or the connection end until it has sent—and received acknowledgment for—all data in the send queue and any pending attention messages. If you set the abort parameter to 1, then ADSP discards any data in the send queue and any attention messages that have not already been sent.

After you have executed the dspRemove routine, you can release the memory you allocated for the CCB and data buffers.

Listing 32-4 illustrates the use of ADSP. This routine opens the .MPP and .DSP drivers and allocates memory for its internal data buffers, for the CCB, and for the send, receive, and attention-message buffers. Then the routine uses the dspInit routine to establish a connection end and uses NBP to register the name of the connection end on the internet. (The user routine specified by the userRoutine parameter to the dspInit function is shown in Listing 32-6.) Next, Listing 32-4 uses the dspOptions routine to set the blocking factor to 24 bytes. The routine uses NBP to determine the address of a socket whose name was chosen by the user and sends an open-connection request (dspOpen) to that socket. When the dspOpen routine completes execution, the routine sends data and an attention message to the remote connection end and reads data from its receive queue. Finally, the routine closes the connection end with the dspRemove routine and releases the memory it allocated.

Listing 32-4. Using ADSP to establish and use a connection

```
PROCEDURE MyADSP;

CONST
   qSize =  600;          {queue space}
   myDataSize =   128;    {size of internal read/write buffers}
   blockFact = 24;        {blocking factor}

TYPE
{modify the connection control block to add storage for A5}
myTRCCB =
   RECORD
      myA5: LongInt;
      u: TRCCB
   END;

VAR
   dspSendQPtr:        Ptr;
   dspRecvQPtr:        Ptr;
   dspAttnBufPtr:      Ptr;
   myData2ReadPtr:     Ptr;
   myData2WritePtr:    Ptr;
   myAttnMsgPtr:       Ptr;
   dspCCB:             myTRCCB;
```

```
   myDSPPBPtr:        DSPPBPtr;
   myMPPPBPtr:        MPPPBPtr;
   myNTEName:         NamesTableEntry;
   myAddrBlk:         AddrBlock;
   drvrRefNum:        Integer;
   mppRefNum:         Integer;
   connRefNum:        Integer;
   gReceivedAnEvent:  Boolean;
   myAttnCode:        Integer;
   tempFlag:          Byte;
   tempCFlag:         Integer;
   myErr:             OSErr;

BEGIN
   myErr := OpenDriver('.MPP', mppRefNum);    {open .MPP driver}
   IF myErr <> noErr THEN DoErr(myErr);       {check and handle error}
   myErr := OpenDriver('.DSP', drvrRefNum);   {open .DSP driver}
   IF myErr <> noErr THEN DoErr(myErr);       {check and handle error}

   {allocate memory for data buffers}
   dspSendQPtr := NewPtr(qSize);              {ADSP use only}
   dspRecvQPtr := NewPtr(qSize);              {ADSP use only}
   dspAttnBufPtr := NewPtr(attnBufSize);      {ADSP use only}
   myData2ReadPtr := NewPtr(myDataSize);
   myData2WritePtr := NewPtr(myDataSize);
   myAttnMsgPtr := NewPtr(myDataSize);
   myDSPPBPtr := DSPPBPtr(NewPtr(SizeOf(DSPParamBlock)));
   myMPPPBPtr := MPPPBPtr(NewPtr(SizeOf(MPPParamBlock)));

   WITH myDSPPBPtr^ DO          {set up dspInit parameters}
   BEGIN
      ioCRefNum := drvrRefNum;   {ADSP driver ref num}
      csCode := dspInit;
      ccbPtr := @dspCCB;         {pointer to CCB}
      userRoutine := @myConnectionEvtUserRoutine;
                                 {see Listing 32-6}
      sendQSize := qSize;        {size of send queue}
      sendQueue := dspSendQPtr;  {send-queue buffer}
      recvQSize := qSize;        {size of receive queue}
      recvQueue := dspRecvQPtr;  {receive-queue buffer}
      attnPtr := dspAttnBufPtr;  {receive-attention buffer}
      localSocket := 0           {let ADSP assign socket}
   END;

   gReceivedAnEvent := FALSE;
   dspCCB.myA5 := SetCurrentA5;  {save A5 for the user routine}
   {establish a connection end}
   myErr := PBControl(ParmBlkPtr(myDSPPBPtr), FALSE);
   IF myErr <> noErr THEN DoErr(myErr);  {check and handle error}
   connRefNum := myDSPPBPtr^.ccbRefNum;  {save CCB ref num for later}
```

(Continued)

Listing 32-4. Using ADSP to establish and use a connection (Continued)

```
NBPSetNTE(@myNTEName, 'The Object', 'The Type',
          '*', myDSPPBPtr^.localSocket);
                                       {set up NBP names table entry}
WITH myMPPPBPtr^ DO                    {set up PRegisterName }
                                       { parameters}
BEGIN
   interval := 7;                      {retransmit every 7*8=56 ticks}
   count := 3;                         {and retry 3 times}
   entityPtr := @myNTEName;            {name to register}
   verifyFlag := 0                     {don't verify this name}
END;
{register this socket}
myErr := PRegisterName(myMPPPBPtr, FALSE);
                                       {register this socket}
IF myErr <> noErr THEN DoErr(myErr);   {check and handle error}

WITH myDSPPBPtr^ DO                    {set up dspOptions parameters}
BEGIN
   ioCRefNum := drvrRefNum;            {ADSP driver ref num}
   csCode := dspOptions;
   ccbRefNum := connRefNum;            {connection ref num}
   sendBlocking := blockFact;          {quantum for data packet}
   badSeqMax := 0:                     {use default}
   useCheckSum := 0                    {don't calculate checksum}
END;
myErr := PBControl(ParmBlkPtr(myDSPPBPtr), FALSE);
                                       {set options}
IF myErr <> noErr THEN DoErr(myErr);   {check and handle error}

PickASocket(myAddrBlk);
   {routine using the PLookupName function to pick a socket }
   { that will be used to establish an open connection}

{open a connection with the chosen socket}
WITH myDSPPBPtr^ DO                  {set up dspOpen parameters}
BEGIN
   ioCRefNum := drvrRefNum;          {ADSP driver ref num}
   csCode := dspOpen;
   ccbRefNum := connRefNum;          {connection ref num}
   remoteAddress := myAddrBlk;       {address of remote socket }
                                     { from PLookupName function}
   filterAddress := myAddrBlk;       {address filter, specified }
                                     { socket address only}
   ocMode := ocRequest;              {open connection mode}
   ocInterval := 0;                  {use default retry interval}
   ocMaximum := 0                    {use default retry maximum}
END;
myErr := PBControl(ParmBlkPtr(myDSPPBPtr), FALSE);
                                     {open a connection}
IF myErr <> noErr THEN DoErr(myErr);{check and handle error}
```

```
{the connection with the chosen socket is open, so now send to }
{ the send queue exactly myDataSize number of bytes}
WITH myDSPPBPtr^ DO                  {set up dspWrite parameters}
BEGIN
   ioCRefNum := drvrRefNum;          {ADSP driver ref num}
   csCode := dspWrite;
   ccbRefNum := connRefNum;          {connection ref num}
   reqCount := myDataSize;           {write this number of bytes}
   dataPtr := myData2WritePtr;       {pointer to send queue}
   eom := 1;                         {1 means last byte is logical }
                                     { end-of-message}
   flush := 1                        {1 means send data now}
END;
myErr := PBControl(ParmBlkPtr(myDSPPBPtr), FALSE);
                                     {send data to the remote }
                                     { connection}
IF myErr <> noErr THEN DoErr(myErr);{check and handle error}

{now send an attention message to the remote connection end}
WITH myDSPPBPtr^ DO                  {set up dspAttention parameters}
BEGIN
   ioCRefNum := drvrRefNum;          {ADSP driver ref num}
   csCode := dspAttention;
   ccbRefNum := connRefNum;          {connection ref num}
   attnCode := 0;                    {user-defined attention code}
   attnSize := myDataSize;           {length of attention message}
   attnData := myAttnMsgPtr          {attention message}
END;
myErr := PBControl(ParmBlkPtr(myDSPPBPtr), FALSE);
IF myErr <> noErr THEN DoErr(myErr);{check and handle error}

{Now read from the receive queue exactly myDataSize number }
{ of bytes.}
WITH myDSPPBPtr^ DO                  {set up dspRead parameters}
BEGIN
   ioCRefNum := drvrRefNum;          {ADSP driver ref num}
   csCode := dspRead;
   ccbRefNum := connRefNum;          {connection ref num}
   reqCount := myDataSize;           {read this number of bytes}
   dataPtr := myData2ReadPtr         {pointer to read buffer}
END;
myErr := PBControl(ParmBlkPtr(myDSPPBPtr), FALSE);
                                     {read data from the remote }
                                     { connection}
IF myErr <> noErr THEN DoErr(myErr);{check and handle error}

{we're done with the connection, so remove it}
WITH myDSPPBPtr^ DO                  {set up dspRemove parameters}
BEGIN
   ioCRefNum := drvrRefNum;          {ADSP driver ref num}
   csCode := dspRemove;
```

(Continued)

Listing 32-4. Using ADSP to establish and use a connection (Continued)

```
        ccbRefNum := connRefNum;            {connection ref num}
        abort := 0                          {don't close until everything }
                                            { is sent and received}
    END;
    myErr := PBControl(ParmBlkPtr(myDSPPBPtr), FALSE);
                                            {close and remove the connection}
    IF myErr <> noErr THEN DOErr(myErr);{check and handle error}

    {you're done with this connection, so give back the memory}
    DisposPtr(dspSendQPtr);
    DisposPtr(dspRecvQPtr);
    DisposPtr(dspAttnBufPtr);
    DisposPtr(myData2ReadPtr);
    DisposPtr(myData2WritePtr);
    DisposPtr(myAttnMsgPtr);
    DisposPtr(Ptr(myDSPPBPtr));
    DisposPtr(Ptr(myMPPPBPtr))

END;        {MyADSP}
```

Creating and Using a Connection Listener

A connection listener is a special sort of AppleTalk Data Stream Protocol (ADSP) connection end that cannot receive or transmit data streams or attention messages. The sole function of a connection listener is to wait passively to receive an open-connection request and to inform its client, the connection server, when it receives one. The connection server can then accept or deny the open-connection request. If it accepts the request, the connection server selects a socket to use as a connection end, establishes a connection end on that socket, and sends an acknowledgment and connection request back to the requesting connection end. The connection server can use the same socket as it used for the connection listener or can select a different socket as the connection end.

Use the following procedure to establish a connection listener and to use that connection listener to open a connection with a remote connection end:

1. Use the MPPOpen function to open the .MPP driver and then use the OpenDriver function to open the .DSP driver. The OpenDriver function returns the reference number for the .DSP driver. You must supply this reference number each time you call the .DSP driver.

2. Allocate nonrelocatable memory for a connection control block (CCB). (The CCB is described in "The ADSP Connection Control Block" earlier in this chapter.) A connection listener does not need send and receive queues or an attention-message buffer. The memory that you allocate becomes the property of ADSP when you call the dspCLInit routine to establish a connection listener. You cannot write any data to this memory except by calling ADSP, and you must ensure that the memory remains locked until you call the dspRemove routine to eliminate the connection end. The CCB is 242 bytes.

3. Call the dspCLInit routine to establish a connection listener. You must provide a pointer to the CCB.

If there is a specific socket that you want to use for the connection listener, you can specify the socket number in the localSocket parameter. If you want ADSP to assign the socket for you, specify 0 for the localSocket parameter. ADSP returns the socket number when the dspCLInit routine completes execution.

4. If you wish, you can use the NBPRegister function to add the name and address of your connection listener to the node's names table. The NBPRegister function is described in the AppleTalk Manager chapter of Volume II.

5. Use the dspCLListen routine to cause the connection listener to wait for an open-connection request. Because the dspCLListen routine does not complete execution until it receives a connection request, you should call this routine asynchronously. You can specify a value for the filterAddress parameter to restrict the network number, node ID, or socket number from which you will accept an open-connection request.

   When the dspCLListen routine receives an open-connection request that meets the restrictions of the filterAddress parameter, it returns a noErr result code (if you executed the routine asynchronously, it places a noErr result code in the ioResult parameter) and places values in the parameter block for the remoteCID, remoteAddress, sendSeq, sendWindow, and attnSendSeq parameters.

6. If you want to open the connection, call the dspInit routine to establish a connection end. You can use any available socket on the node for the connection end, including the socket that you used for the connection listener. Because a single socket can have more than one CCB connected with it, the socket can function simultaneously as a connection end and a connection listener.

   You can check the address of the remote socket to determine if it meets your criteria for a connection end. Although the filterAddress parameter to the dspCLListen routine provides some screening of socket addresses, it cannot check for network number ranges, for example, or for a specific set of socket numbers. If for some reason you want to deny the connection request, call the dspDeny routine, specifying the CCB of the connection listener in the ccbRefNum parameter. Because the dspCLListen routine completes execution when it receives an open-connection request, you must return to step 5 to wait for another connection request.

7. Call the dspOpen routine to open the connection. Specify the value ocAccept for the ocMode parameter and specify in the ccbRefNum parameter the reference number of the CCB for the connection end that you want to use. When you call the dspOpen routine, you must provide the values returned by the dspCLListen routine for the remoteCID, remoteAddress, sendSeq, sendWindow, and attnSendSeq parameters.

   You can poll the state field in the CCB to determine when the connection is open. Alternatively, you can check the result code for the dspOpen routine when the routine completes execution. If the routine returns the noErr result code, then the connection is open.

8. You can now send and receive data and attention messages over the connection, as described in the preceding section, "Opening and Maintaining an ADSP Connection." When you are ready to close the connection, you can use the dspClose or dspRemove routines, which are also described in the preceding section.

9. When you are finished using the connection listener, you can use the dspCLRemove routine to eliminate it. Once you have called the dspCLRemove routine, you can release the memory you allocated for the connection listener's CCB.

Listing 32-5 illustrates the use of ADSP to establish and use a connection listener. It opens the .MPP and .DSP drivers and allocates memory for the CCB. Then it uses the dspCLInit routine to establish a connection listener, uses the Name-Binding Protocol (NBP) to register the name of the connection end on the internet, and uses the dspCLListen routine to wait for a connection request. When the routine receives a connection request, it calls the dspOpen routine to complete the connection.

Listing 32-5. Using ADSP to establish and use a connection listener

```
VAR
   dspCCBPtr:      TPCCB;
   myDSPPBPtr:     DSPPBPtr;
   myMPPPBPtr:     MPPPBPtr;
   myNTEName:      NamesTableEntry;
   drvrRefNum:     Integer;
   mppRefNum:      Integer;
   connRefNum:     Integer;
   myErr:          OSErr;

BEGIN
   myErr := OpenDriver('.MPP', mppRefNum);    { open .MPP driver }
   IF myErr <> noErr THEN DoErr(myErr);       {check and handle error}
   myErr := OpenDriver('.DSP', drvrRefNum);   {open .DSP driver}
   IF myErr <> noErr THEN DoErr(myErr);       {check and handle error}

   {allocate memory for data buffers}
   dspCCBPtr := TPCCB(NewPtr(SizeOf(TRCCB)));
   myDSPPBPtr := DSPPBPtr(NewPtr(SizeOf(DSPParamBlock)));
   myMPPPBPtr := MPPPBPtr(NewPtr(SizeOf(MPPParamBlock)));

   WITH myDSPPBPtr^ DO                  {set up dspCLInit parameters}
   BEGIN
      ioCRefNum := drvrRefNum;          {ADSP driver ref num}
      csCode := dspCLInit;
      ccbPtr := dspCCBPtr;              {pointer to CCB}
      localSocket := 0                  {local socket number}
   END;
   myErr := PBControl(ParmBlkPtr(myDSPPBPtr), FALSE);
                                        {establish a connection listener}
   IF myErr <> noErr THEN DoErr(myErr);{check and handle error}
   connRefNum := myDSPPBPtr^.ccbRefNum;{save CCB ref num for later}

   NBPSetNTE(@myNTEName, 'The Object', 'The Type',
             '*', myDSPPBPtr^.localSocket);
                                        {set up NBP names table entry}
   WITH myMPPPBPtr^ DO                  {set up PRegisterName parameters}
```

```
    BEGIN
      interval := 7;                   {retransmit every 7*8=56 ticks}
      count := 3;                      {and retry 3 times}
      entityPtr := @myNTEname;         {name to register}
      verifyFlag := 0                  {don't verify this name}
    END;
    myErr := PRegisterName(myMPPPBPtr, FALSE);
                                       {register this name}
    IF myErr <> noErr THEN DoErr(myErr);{check and handle error}

    WITH myDSPPBPtr^ DO                {set up dspCLListen parameters}
    BEGIN
      ioCRefNum := drvrRefNum;         {ADSP driver ref num}
      csCode := dspCLListen;
      ccbRefNum := connRefNum;         {connection ref num}
      filterAddress := AddrBlock(0)    {connect with anybody}
    END;
    myErr := PBControl(ParmBlkPtr(myDSPPBPtr), TRUE);
                                       {listen for connection requests}
    WHILE myDSPPBPtr^.ioResult = 1 DO
    BEGIN
      {return control to user while waiting for }
      { a connection request}
      GoDoSomething;
    END;
    IF myErr <> noErr THEN DoErr(myErr);{check and handle error}

    {You received a connection request; now open a connection. }
    { The dspCLListen call has returned values into the }
    { remoteCID, remoteAddress, sendSeq, sendWindow, }
    { and attnSendSeq fields of the parameter block.}

    WITH myDSPPBPtr^ DO                {set up dspOpen parameters}
    BEGIN
      ioCRefNum := drvrRefNum;         {ADSP driver ref num}
      csCode := dspOpen;
      ccbRefNum := connRefNum;         {connection ref num}
      ocMode := ocAccept;              {open connection mode}
      ocInterval := 0;                 {use default retry interval}
      ocMaximum := 0                   {use default retry maximum}
    END;
    myErr := PBControl(ParmBlkPtr(myDSPPBPtr), FALSE);
                                       {open a connection}
    IF myErr <> noErr THEN DoErr(myErr) {check and handle error}

    {Listing 32-4 shows how to use ADSP to maintain a connection.}

END;        {MyCLADSP}
```

Writing a User Routine for Connection Events

When you execute the dspInit routine, you can specify a pointer to a routine that you provide (referred to as the *user routine*). Whenever an unsolicited connection event occurs, the AppleTalk Data Stream Protocol (ADSP) sets a flag in the connection control block (CCB) and calls the user routine. The user routine must clear the flag to acknowledge that it has read the flag field, and then can respond to the event in any manner you deem appropriate. The CCB flags are described in "The ADSP Connection Control Block" earlier in this chapter. The four following types of unsolicited connection events set flags in the CCB:

- ADSP has been informed by the remote connection end that the remote connection end is about to close the connection. An appropriate reponse might be to store a flag indicating that the connection end is about to close. When your application regains control, it can then display a dialog box informing the user of this event and asking whether the application should attempt to reconnect later.
- ADSP has determined that the remote connection end is not responding and so has closed the connection. Your user routine can attempt to open a new connection immediately. Alternatively, you can store a flag indicating that the connection has closed, and when your application regains control, it can display a dialog box asking the user whether to attempt to reconnect.
- ADSP has received an attention message from the remote connection end. Depending on what you are using the attention-message mechanism for, you might want to read the attention code in the attnCode field of the CCB and the attention message pointed to by the attnPtr field of the CCB.
- ADSP has received a forward reset command from the remote client end, has discarded all ADSP data not yet delivered, including the data in the receive queue of the local client end, and has resynchronized the connection. Your response to this event depends on the purpose for which you are using the forward reset mechanism. You might want to resend the last data you have sent or inform the user of the event.

When ADSP calls your user routine, the CPU is in interrupt-processing mode and register A1 contains a pointer to the CCB of the connection end that generated the event. You can examine the userFlags field of the CCB to determine what event caused the interrupt, and you can examine the state field of the CCB to determine the current state of the connection.

Because the CPU is set to interrupt-processing mode, your user routine must preserve all registers other than A0, A1, D0, D1, and D2. Your routine must not make any direct or indirect calls to the Memory Manager and can't depend on handles to unlocked blocks being valid. If you want to use any of your application's global variables, you must save the contents of the A5 register before using the variables, and you must restore the A5 register before your routine terminates. Listings 32-4 and 32-6 illustrate the use of the CCB to store the pointer to your application's global variables.

If you want to execute a routine each time an unsolicited connection event occurs but the interrupt environment is too restrictive, you can specify a NIL pointer to the user routine and periodically poll the userFlags field of the CCB.

▲ **Warning:** When an unsolicited connection event occurs, you must clear the bit in the userFlags field to 0 or the connection will hang. To ensure that you do not lose any attention messages, you must read any attention messages into an internal buffer before you clear the bit in the userFlags field. ▲

Listing 32-6 is the user routine called by Listing 32-4. When this routine is called, it first checks the CCB to determine the source of the interrupt and then clears the bit in the userFlags field of the CCB. If the routine has received an attention message, the user routine reads the message into an internal buffer before it clears the flag bit. The definitions of procedures PushA5, GetMyTRCCBA5, and PopA5 are shown in Listing 32-6 for your convenience. In a complete application these procedures would be defined in the calling routine (Listing 32-4).

Listing 32-6. An ADSP user routine

```
PROCEDURE PushA5;        {moves current value of A5 onto stack}
   INLINE $2F0D;         {MOVE.L A5,-(SP)}

PROCEDURE GetMyTRCCBA5; {Retrieves A5 from the head of the TRCCB }
                         { (pointed to by A1) and sticks it in A5.}
   INLINE $2A69, $FFFC; {MOVE.L -4(A1), A5}

PROCEDURE PopA5;         {restores A5 from stack}
   INLINE $2A5F;         {MOVE.L (SP)+, A5}

PROCEDURE myConnectionEvtUserRoutine;

BEGIN
{The connection received an unexpected connection event.  Find out }
{ what kind and process accordingly.}

   PushA5;               {save the current A5}
   GetMyTRCCBA5;         {set up A5 to point to your application's }
                         { global variables}

   WITH dspCCB.u DO
   BEGIN
      IF BAND(userFlags, eClosed) <> 0 THEN TellUserItsClosed;
      IF BAND(userFlags, eTearDown) <> 0 THEN TellUserItsBroken;
      IF BAND(userFlags, eFwdReset) <> 0 THEN TellUserItsReset;
      IF BAND(userFlags, eAttention) <> 0 THEN
      BEGIN       {the event is an attention message}
         myAttnCode := AttnCode;            {Get the attention code.}
         CopyAttnMsg(AttnPtr, AttnSize, @myAttnData);
                                            {copy the attention }
                                            { message into our buffer}
         tempFlag := userFlags;
         tempCFlag := eAttention;
         BClr(LongInt(tempFlag), tempCFlag); {clear the flag}
         userFlags := tempFlag
         {do something with the message}
      END;
      gReceivedAnEvent := TRUE
   END;
   PopA5                                    {restore the current A5}
END;
```

.DSP Driver Routines

The .DSP driver implements the AppleTalk Data Stream Protocol (ADSP). You send commands to ADSP and obtain information about ADSP by executing the .DSP driver routines described in this section. Each routine is implemented as a call to the Device Manager's PBControl function, as follows:

```
FUNCTION PBControl (paramBlock: ParmBlkPtr; async: Boolean) : OSErr;
```

The paramBlock parameter is a pointer to the parameter block used by the PBControl function for .DSP routines, and the async parameter is a Boolean that specifies whether the function is to execute synchronously or asynchronously. Set the async parameter to TRUE to execute the function asynchronously.

The parameter block is shown in "The .DSP Parameter Block" earlier in this chapter. The parameters used with each function are described in this section.

For a general discussion of the use of ADSP, see "Using ADSP" earlier in this chapter.

Establishing and Terminating an ADSP Connection

You can use the routines described in this section to

- establish a connection end
- set the values for parameters that control the behavior of a connection end
- open a connection
- assign an identification number to a connection end
- close a connection end
- eliminate a connection end

dspInit

Parameter block

←	16	ioResult	word	result code
→	24	ioCRefNum	word	driver reference number
→	26	csCode	word	always dspInit
←	32	ccbRefNum	word	reference number of CCB
→	34	ccbPtr	long	pointer to CCB
→	38	userRoutine	long	pointer to routine to call on connection events
→	42	sendQSize	word	size in bytes of the send queue
→	44	sendQueue	long	pointer to send queue

→	48	recvQSize	word	size in bytes of the receive queue
→	50	recvQueue	long	pointer to receive queue
→	54	attnPtr	long	pointer to buffer for incoming attention messages
↔	58	localSocket	byte	DDP socket number for this connection end

The dspInit routine establishes a connection end; that is, it assigns a specific socket for use by ADSP and initializes the variables that ADSP uses to maintain the connection. The dspInit routine does not open the connection end or establish a connection with a remote connection end; you must follow the dspInit routine with the dspOpen routine to perform those tasks. Use the dspCLInit routine to establish a connection listener. Use the dspRemove routine to eliminate a connection end.

When you send bytes to a remote connection end, ADSP stores the bytes in a buffer called the *send queue.* Until the remote connection end acknowledges their receipt, ADSP keeps the bytes you sent in the send queue so that they are available to be retransmitted if necessary. When the local connection end receives bytes, it stores them in a buffer called the *receive queue* until you read them.

You must allocate memory for the send and receive queues and for a buffer that holds incoming attention messages. You must also allocate a nonrelocatable block of memory for the CCB for this connection end.

> **Note:** When you call the dspInit routine, the memory that you allocate becomes the property of ADSP. You cannot write any data to this memory except by calling ADSP routines, and you must ensure that the memory remains locked until you call the dspRemove routine to eliminate the connection end.

Field descriptions

ioResult — The result of the routine. When you execute the routine asynchronously, the routine sets this parameter to 1 and returns a routine result of noErr as soon as the routine begins execution. When the routine completes execution, it sets the ioResult parameter to the actual result code.

ioCRefNum — The driver reference number. This parameter is returned by the OpenDriver function. You must specify this number every time you call the .DSP driver.

csCode — The routine selector, always equal to dspInit for this routine.

ccbRefNum — The CCB reference number. The dspInit routine returns this number. You must provide this number in all subsequent calls to this connection end.

ccbPtr — A pointer to the CCB that you allocated. The CCB is 242 bytes in size and is described in "The ADSP Connection Control Block" earlier in this chapter.

userRoutine	A pointer to a routine that is to be called each time the connection end receives an unsolicited connection event. Specify NIL for this parameter if you do not want to supply a user routine. Connection events and user routines are discussed in "Writing a User Routine for Connection Events" earlier in this chapter.
sendQSize	The size in bytes of the send queue. A queue size of 600 bytes should work well for most applications. If you are using ADSP to send a continuous flow of data, a larger data buffer improves performance. If your application is sending the user's keystrokes, a smaller buffer should be adequate. The constant minDSPQucueSize indicates the minimum queue size that you can use.
sendQueue	A pointer to the send queue that you allocated.
recvQSize	The size in bytes of the receive queue. A queue size of 600 bytes should work well for most applications. If you are using ADSP to receive a continuous flow of data, a larger data buffer improves performance. If your application is receiving a user's keystrokes, a smaller buffer should be adequate. The constant minDSPQueueSize indicates the minimum queue size that you can use.
recvQueue	A pointer to the receive queue that you allocated.
attnPtr	A pointer to the attention-message buffer that you allocated. The attention-message buffer must be the size of the constant attnBufSize.
localSocket	The DDP socket number of the socket that you want ADSP to use for this connection end. Specify 0 for this parameter to cause ADSP to assign the socket. In the latter case, ADSP returns the socket number when the dspInit routine completes execution.

Result codes

noErr	0	No error
ddpSktErr	–91	Error opening socket
errDSPQueueSize	–1274	Send or receive queue is too small

dspOptions

Parameter block

←	16	ioResult	word	result code
→	24	ioCRefNum	word	driver reference number
→	26	csCode	word	always dspOptions
→	32	ccbRefNum	word	reference number of CCB
→	34	sendBlocking	word	send-blocking threshold
→	38	badSeqMax	byte	threshold to send retransmit advice
→	39	useCheckSum	byte	DDP checksum flag

The dspOptions routine allows you to set values for several parameters that affect the behavior of the local connection end. You can set the options for any established connection end, whether open or not.

Field descriptions

ioResult — The result of the routine. When you execute the routine asynchronously, the routine sets this parameter to 1 and returns a routine result of noErr as soon as the routine begins execution. When the routine completes execution, it sets the ioResult parameter to the actual result code.

ioCRefNum — The driver reference number. This parameter is returned by the OpenDriver function. You must specify this number every time you call the .DSP driver.

csCode — The routine selector, always equal to dspOptions for this routine.

ccbRefNum — The CCB reference number that was returned by the dspInit routine.

sendBlocking — The maximum number of bytes that may accumulate in the send queue before ADSP sends a packet to the remote connection end. ADSP sends a packet before the maximum number of bytes accumulates if the period specified by the send timer expires, if you execute the dspWrite routine with the flush parameter set to 1, or if a connection event requires that the local connection end send an acknowledgment packet to the remote connection end.

You can set the sendBlocking parameter to any value from 1 byte to the maximum size of a packet (572 bytes). If you set the sendBlocking parameter to 0, the current value for this parameter is not changed. The default value for the sendBlocking parameter is 16 bytes.

badSeqMax — The maximum number of out-of-sequence data packets that the local connection end can receive before requesting the remote connection end to retransmit the missing data. Because a connection end does not acknowledge the receipt of a data packet received out of sequence, the retransmit timer of the remote connection end will expire eventually and the connection end will retransmit the data. The badSeqMax parameter allows you to cause the data to be retransmitted before the retransmit timer of the remote connection end has expired.

You can set the badSeqMax parameter to any value from 1 to 255. If you set the badSeqMax parameter to 0, the current value for this parameter is not changed. The default value for the badSeqMax parameter is 3.

useCheckSum — A flag specifying whether DDP should compute a checksum and include it in each packet that it sends to the remote connection end. Set this parameter to 1 if you want DDP to use checksums or to 0 if you do not want DDP to use checksums. The default value for useCheckSum is 0.

ADSP cannot include a checksum in a packet that has a short DDP header—that is, a packet being sent over LocalTalk to a remote socket that is on the same cable as the local socket. Note that the useCheckSum parameter affects only whether ADSP includes a checksum in a packet that it is sending. If ADSP receives a packet that includes a checksum, it validates the checksum regardless of the setting of the useCheckSum parameter.

Result codes

noErr	0	No error
errRefNum	–1280	Bad connection reference number

dspOpen

Parameter block

←	16	ioResult	word	result code
→	24	ioCRefNum	word	driver reference number
→	26	csCode	word	always dspOpen
→	32	ccbRefNum	word	reference number of CCB
←	34	localCID	word	ID of this connection end
↔	36	remoteCID	word	ID of remote connection end
↔	38	remoteAddress	long	remote internet address
→	42	filterAddress	long	filter for open-connection requests
↔	46	sendSeq	long	initial send sequence number
↔	50	sendWindow	word	initial size of remote receive queue
→	52	recvSeq	long	initial receive sequence number
↔	56	attnSendSeq	long	attention send sequence number
→	60	attnRecvSeq	long	attention receive sequence number
→	64	ocMode	byte	connection-opening mode
→	65	ocInterval	byte	interval between open requests
→	66	ocMaximum	byte	retries of open-connection request

You use the ocMode field of the parameter block to specify the opening mode that the dspOpen routine is to use. The dspOpen routine puts a connection end into one of the four following opening modes:

- The ocRequest mode, in which ADSP attempts to open a connection with the socket at the internet address you specify with the remoteAddress parameter. If the socket you specify as a remote address is a connection listener, it is possible that your application will receive a connection acknowledgment and request from a different address than the one to which you sent the open-connection request. You can use the filterAddress parameter to restrict the addresses with which you will accept a connection.

  The dspOpen routine completes execution in the ocRequest mode when one of the following occurs: ADSP establishes a connection, your connection end receives a connection denial from the remote connection end, your connection end denies the connection request returned by a connection listener, or ADSP cannot complete the connection within the maximum number of retries that you specified with the ocMaximum parameter.

- The ocPassive mode, in which the connection end waits to receive an open-connection request from a remote connection end. You can use the filterAddress parameter to restrict the addresses from which you will accept a connection request.

  The dspOpen routine completes execution in the ocPassive mode when ADSP establishes a connection or when either connection end receives a connection denial.

- The ocAccept mode, used by connection servers to complete an open-connection dialog. When a connection server is informed by its connection listener that the connection listener has received an open-connection request, the connection server calls the dspInit routine to establish a connection end and then calls the dspOpen routine in ocAccept mode to complete the connection. You must obtain the following parameters from the dspCLListen routine and provide them to the dspOpen routine: remoteAddress, remoteCID, sendSeq, sendWindow, and attnSendSeq. Connection listeners and connection servers are described in "Creating and Using a Connection Listener" earlier in this chapter and in "Establishing and Terminating an ADSP Connection" later in this chapter.

  The dspOpen routine completes execution in the ocAccept mode when ADSP establishes a connection or when either connection end receives a connection denial.

- The ocEstablish mode, in which ADSP considers the connection end established and the connection state open. This mode is for use by clients that determine their connection-opening parameters without using ADSP or the .DSP driver to do so.

  You must first use the dspInit routine to establish a connection end and then execute the dspNewCID routine to obtain an identification number (ID) for the local connection end. You must then communicate with the remote connection end to send it the local connection ID and to determine the values of the following parameters: remoteAddress, remoteCID, sendSeq, sendWindow, recvSeq, attnSendSeq, and attnRecvSeq. Only then can you execute the dspOpen routine in the ocEstablish mode.

  The dspOpen routine completes execution in the ocEstablish mode immediately.

The use of parameters by the dspOpen routine depends on the mode in which the routine is executed, as follows:

ocRequest	**ocPassive**	**ocAccept**	**ocEstablish**
← ioResult	← ioResult	← ioResult	← ioResult
→ ioCRefNum	→ ioCRefNum	→ ioCRefNum	→ ioCRefNum
→ csCode	→ csCode	→ csCode	→ csCode
→ ccbRefNum	→ ccbRefNum	→ ccbRefNum	→ ccbRefNum
← localCID	← localCID	← localCID	— localCID
← remoteCID	← remoteCID	→ remoteCID	→ remoteCID
→ remoteAddress	← remoteAddress	→ remoteAddress	→ remoteAddress
→ filterAddress	→ filterAddress	— filterAddress	— filterAddress
← sendSeq	← sendSeq	→ sendSeq	→ sendSeq
← sendWindow	← sendWindow	→ sendWindow	→ sendWindow
— recvSeq	— recvSeq	— recvSeq	→ recvSeq
← attnSendSeq	← attnSendSeq	→ attnSendSeq	→ attnSendSeq
— attnRecvSeq	— attnRecvSeq	— attnRecvSeq	→ attnRecvSeq
→ ocMode	→ ocMode	→ ocMode	→ ocMode
→ ocInterval	→ ocInterval	→ ocInterval	— ocInterval
→ ocMaximum	→ ocMaximum	→ ocMaximum	— ocMaximum

Key: → input ← output — not used

Field descriptions

ioResult — The result of the routine. When you execute the routine asynchronously, the routine sets this parameter to 1 and returns a routine result of noErr as soon as the routine begins execution. When the routine completes execution, it sets the ioResult parameter to the actual result code.

ioCRefNum — The driver reference number. This parameter is returned by the OpenDriver function. You must specify this number every time you call the .DSP driver.

csCode — The routine selector, always equal to dspOpen for this routine.

ccbRefNum — The CCB reference number that was returned by the dspInit routine for the connection end that you want to use.

localCID — The identification number of the local connection end. This number is assigned by ADSP when the connection is opened. ADSP includes this number in every packet sent to a remote connection end. Before you call the dspOpen routine in ocEstablish mode, you must call the dspNewCID routine to cause ADSP to assign this value.

remoteCID — The identification number of the remote connection end. This parameter is returned by the dspOpen routine in the ocRequest and ocPassive modes. A connection server must provide this number to the dspOpen routine when the server executes the routine in ocAccept mode; in this case, the connection server obtains the remoteCID value from the dspCLListen routine. You must provide the remoteCID value to the dspOpen routine when you use the routine in ocEstablish mode.

remoteAddress — The internet address of the remote socket with which you wish to establish communications. This address consists of a 2-byte network number, a 1-byte node ID, and a 1-byte socket number. You must provide this parameter when you call the dspOpen routine in the ocRequest or ocEstablish mode. This parameter is returned by the dspOpen routine when you call the routine in the ocPassive mode. When you call the dspOpen routine in the ocAccept mode, you must use the value for the remoteAddress parameter that was returned by the dspCLListen routine.

filterAddress — The internet address of the socket from which you will accept a connection request. The address consists of three fields: a 2-byte network number, a 1-byte node ID, and a 1-byte socket number. Specify 0 for any of these fields for which you wish to impose no restrictions. If you specify a filter address of $00082500, for example, the connection end accepts a connection request from any socket at node $25 of network $0008. Set the filterAddress parameter equal to the remoteAddress parameter to accept a connection only with the socket to which you sent a connection request.

When you execute the dspOpen routine in the ocPassive mode, you can receive a connection request from any ADSP connection end on the internet. When you execute the dspOpen routine in the ocRequest mode, your connection end can receive a connection request acknowledgment from an address different from the one you specified in the remoteAddress parameter only if the remote address you specified was that of a connection listener. In either case, you can use the filterAddress parameter to avoid acknowledging unwanted connection requests.

When you execute the dspOpen routine in the ocAccept mode, your connection listener has already received and decided to accept the connection request. You can specify a filter address for a connection listener with the dspCLListen routine. A connection server can use the dspCLDeny routine to deny a connection request that was accepted by its connection listener.

You cannot use the filter address when you execute the dspOpen routine in ocEstablish mode.

sendSeq — The sequence number of the first byte that the local connection end will send to the remote connection end. ADSP uses this number to coordinate communications and to check for errors. ADSP returns a value for the sendSeq parameter when you execute the dspOpen routine in the ocRequest or ocPassive mode. When you execute the dspOpen routine in the ocAccept mode, you must specify the value for the sendSeq parameter that was returned by the dspCLListen routine. You must provide the value for this parameter when you execute the dspOpen routine in the ocEstablish mode.

sendWindow — The sequence number of the last byte that the remote connection end has buffer space to receive. ADSP uses this number to coordinate communications and to check for errors. ADSP returns a value for the sendWindow parameter when you execute the dspOpen routine in the ocRequest or ocPassive mode. When you execute the dspOpen routine in the ocAccept mode, you must specify the value for the sendWindow parameter that was returned by the dspCLListen routine. You must provide the value for this parameter when you execute the dspOpen routine in the ocEstablish mode.

recvSeq — The sequence number of the next byte that the local connection end expects to receive. ADSP uses this number to coordinate communications and to check for errors. You must provide the value for this parameter when you execute the dspOpen routine in the ocEstablish mode. The dspOpen routine does not use this parameter when you execute it in any other mode.

attnSendSeq — The sequence number of the next attention packet that the local connection end will transmit. ADSP uses this number to coordinate communications and to check for errors. ADSP returns a value for the attnSendSeq parameter when you execute the dspOpen routine in the ocRequest or ocPassive mode. When you execute the dspOpen routine in the ocAccept mode, you must specify the value for the attnSendSeq parameter that was returned by the dspCLListen routine. You must provide the value for this parameter when you execute the dspOpen routine in the ocEstablish mode.

attnRecvSeq — The sequence number of the next attention packet that the local connection end expects to receive. ADSP uses this number to coordinate communications and to check for errors. You must provide the value for this parameter when you execute the dspOpen routine in the ocEstablish mode. The dspOpen routine does not use this parameter when you execute it in any other mode.

ocMode — The mode in which the dspOpen routine is to operate, as follows:

Mode	Value	Meaning
ocRequest	1	ADSP attempts to open a connection with the socket you specify.
ocPassive	2	The connection end waits to receive a connection request.
ocAccept	3	The connection server accepts and acknowledges receipt of a connection request.
ocEstablish	4	ADSP considers the connection established and open; you are responsible for setting up and synchronizing both connection ends.

ocInterval — The period between transmissions of open-connection requests. If the remote connection end does not acknowledge or deny an open-connection request, ADSP retransmits the request after a time period specified by this parameter. The time period used by ADSP is (ocInterval × 10) ticks, or (ocInterval / 6) seconds. For example, if you set the ocInterval parameter to 3, the time period between retransmissions is 30 ticks (1/2 second). You can set the ocInterval parameter to any value from 1 (1/6 second) to 180 (30 seconds). If you specify 0 for the ocInterval parameter, ADSP uses the default value of 6 (1 second).

You must provide a value for the ocInterval parameter when you execute the dspOpen routine in the ocRequest, ocPassive, or ocAccept mode. The dspOpen routine does not use this parameter when you execute it in the ocEstablish mode.

ocMaximum — The maximum number of times to retransmit an open-connection request before ADSP terminates execution of the dspOpen routine. If you specify 0 for the ocMaximum parameter, ADSP uses the default value of 3. If you specify 255 for the ocMaximum parameter, ADSP retransmits the open-connection request indefinitely until the remote connection end either acknowledges or denies the request.

You must provide a value for the ocMaximum parameter when you execute the dspOpen routine in the ocRequest, ocPassive, or ocAccept mode. The dspOpen routine does not use this parameter when you execute it in the ocEstablish mode.

Result codes

noErr	0	No error
errOpenDenied	–1273	Open request denied by recipient
errOpening	–1277	Attempt to open connection failed
errState	–1278	Connection end must be closed
errAborted	–1279	Request aborted by dspRemove or dspClose routine
errRefNum	–1280	Bad connection reference number

dspNewCID

Parameter block

←	16	ioResult	word	result code
→	24	ioCRefNum	word	driver reference number
→	26	csCode	word	always dspNewCID
→	32	ccbRefNum	word	reference number of CCB
←	34	newCID	word	ID of new connection

The dspNewCID routine causes ADSP to assign an ID to a connection end without opening the connection end or attempting to establish a connection with a remote connection end. Use this routine only if you implement your own protocol to establish communication with a remote connection end. You must first use the dspInit routine to establish a connection end. Next, you must call the dspNewCID routine to obtain a connection-end ID. Then you must establish communication with a remote connection end and pass the ID to the remote connection end. Finally, you must call the dspOpen routine in ocEstablish mode to cause ADSP to open the connection. See the description of the dspOpen routine for more information on establishing a connection in this fashion.

The ioResult parameter returns the result of the routine. If you call the routine asynchronously, the routine sets this field to 1 as soon as it begins execution, and it changes the field to the actual result code when it completes execution. The ioCRefNum parameter is the driver reference number returned by the OpenDriver function. You must specify this number every time you call the .DSP driver. The csCode parameter is the routine selector; it is always dspNewCID for this routine. The ccbRefNum parameter is the CCB reference number that was returned by the dspInit routine. The newCID parameter is the connection-end ID returned by this routine. You must provide this number to the client of the remote connection end so that it can use it for the remoteCID parameter when it calls the dspOpen routine.

Result codes

noErr	0	No error
errState	–1278	Connection is not closed
errRefNum	–1280	Bad connection reference number

dspClose

Parameter block

←	16	ioResult	word	result code
→	24	ioCRefNum	word	driver reference number
→	26	csCode	word	always dspClose
→	32	ccbRefNum	word	reference number of CCB
→	34	abort	byte	abort send requests if not 0

The dspClose routine closes the connection end. The connection end is still established; that is, ADSP retains ownership of the CCB, send queue, receive queue, and attention-message buffer. You can continue to read bytes from the receive queue after you have called the dspClose routine. Use the dspRemove routine instead of the dspClose routine if you are through reading bytes from the receive queue and want to release the memory associated with the connection end. The dspClose routine does not return an error if you call it for a connection end that is already closed.

The ioResult parameter returns the result of the routine. If you call the routine asynchronously, the routine sets this field to 1 as soon as it begins execution, and it changes the field to the actual result code when it completes execution. The ioCRefNum parameter is the driver reference number returned by the OpenDriver function. You must specify this number every time you call the .DSP driver. The csCode parameter is the routine selector; it is always dspClose for this routine. The ccbRefNum parameter is the CCB reference number that was returned by the dspInit routine. If the abort parameter is nonzero, ADSP cancels any outstanding requests to send data packets (such as the dspAttention routine) and discards all data in the send queue. If the abort parameter is 0, ADSP does not close the connection end until all of the data in the send queue and all outstanding attention messages have been sent and acknowledged.

Result codes

noErr	0	No error
errRefNum	–1280	Bad connection reference number

dspRemove

Parameter block

←	16	ioResult	word	result code
→	24	ioCRefNum	word	driver reference number
→	26	csCode	word	always dspRemove
→	32	ccbRefNum	word	reference number of CCB
→	34	abort	byte	abort connection if not 0

The dspRemove routine closes any open connection and eliminates the connection end; that is, ADSP no longer retains control of the CCB, send queue, receive queue, and attention-message buffer. You cannot continue to read bytes from the receive queue after you have called the dspRemove routine. After you call the dspRemove routine, you can release all of the memory you allocated for the connection end if you do not intend to reopen the connection end.

The ioResult parameter returns the result of the routine. If you call the routine asynchronously, the routine sets this field to 1 as soon as it begins execution, and it changes the field to the actual result code when it completes execution. The ioCRefNum parameter is the driver reference number returned by the OpenDriver function. You must specify this number every time you call the .DSP driver. The csCode parameter is the routine selector, always dspRemove for this routine. The ccbRefNum parameter is the CCB reference number that was returned by the dspInit routine. If the abort parameter is nonzero, ADSP cancels any outstanding requests to send data packets (such as the dspAttention routine) and discards all data in the send queue. If the abort parameter is 0, ADSP does not close the connection end until all of the data in the send queue has been sent and acknowledged.

Result codes

noErr	0	No error
errRefNum	–1280	Bad connection reference number

Establishing and Terminating an ADSP Connection Listener

A connection listener is a special kind of connection end that listens for open-connection requests from remote connection ends. Connection listeners are used by **connection servers**—that is, programs that assign a socket for the local connection end only after they receive a connection request from a remote connection end. A single connection listener can receive connection requests from any number of remote connection ends.

You can use the routines in this section to

- establish a connection listener
- cause the connection listener to wait for a connection request
- deny a connection request
- close and eliminate a connection listener

dspCLInit

Parameter block

←	16	ioResult	word	result code
→	24	ioCRefNum	word	driver reference number
→	26	csCode	word	always dspCLInit
←	32	ccbRefNum	word	reference number of CCB
→	34	ccbPtr	long	pointer to CCB
↔	58	localSocket	byte	local DDP socket number

The dspCLInit routine establishes a connection listener; that is, it assigns a specific socket for use by ADSP and initializes the variables that ADSP uses to maintain a connection listener. The dspCLInit routine does not cause the connection listener to listen for connection requests; you must follow the dspCLInit routine with the dspCLListen routine to activate the connection listener. Use the dspInit routine to establish a connection end that is not a connection listener. Use the dspCLRemove routine to eliminate a connection listener.

The ioResult parameter returns the result of the routine. If you call the routine asynchronously, the routine sets this field to 1 as soon as it begins execution, and it changes the field to the actual result code when it completes execution. The ioCRefNum parameter is the driver reference number returned by the OpenDriver function. You must specify this number every time you call the .DSP driver. The csCode parameter is the routine selector, always dspCLInit for this routine. The dspCLInit routine returns the ccbRefNum parameter, which is the CCB reference number. You must provide this number in all subsequent dspCLListen and dspCLRemove calls to this connection listener.

You must allocate memory for a CCB before you call the dspCLInit routine. The ccbPtr parameter is a pointer to the CCB that you allocated. The CCB is 242 bytes in size and is described in "The ADSP Connection Control Block" earlier in this chapter.

The localSocket parameter is the DDP socket number of the socket that you want ADSP to use for this connection end. Specify 0 for this parameter to cause ADSP to assign the socket. In the latter case, ADSP returns the socket number when the dspCLInit routine completes execution.

Result codes

noErr	0	No error
ddpSktErr	–91	Error opening socket

dspCLListen

Parameter block

←	16	ioResult	word	result code
→	24	ioCRefNum	word	driver reference number
→	26	csCode	word	always dspCLListen
→	32	ccbRefNum	word	reference number of CCB
←	36	remoteCID	word	ID of remote connection end
←	38	remoteAddress	long	remote internet address
→	42	filterAddress	long	filter for open-connection requests
←	46	sendSeq	long	initial send sequence number
←	50	sendWindow	word	initial size of remote receive queue
←	56	attnSendSeq	long	attention send sequence number

The dspCLListen routine causes a connection listener to listen for connection requests. You must have already used the dspCLInit routine to establish a connection listener before using the dspCLListen routine. The dspCLListen routine is used only by connection servers.

When ADSP receives an open-connection request from a socket that satisfies the address requirements of the filterAddress parameter, it returns values for the remoteCID, remoteAddress, sendSeq, sendWindow, and attnSendSeq parameters and completes execution of the dspCLListen routine. You must then either accept the open-connection request by calling the dspOpen routine in the ocAccept mode or deny the request by calling the dspCLDeny routine.

You can call the dspCLListen routine several times, specifying the same connection listener. For example, if you wanted to accept connections from any or all of three different addresses, you could call the dspCLListen routine three times with a different value for the filterAddress parameter each time. Note that you must execute the dspCLListen routine asynchronously to take advantage of this feature.

Field descriptions

ioResult	The result of the routine. When you execute the routine asynchronously, the routine sets this parameter to 1 and returns a routine result of noErr as soon as the routine begins execution. When the routine completes execution, it sets the ioResult parameter to the actual result code.
ioCRefNum	The driver reference number. This parameter is returned by the OpenDriver function. You must specify this number every time you call the .DSP driver.
csCode	The routine selector, always dspCLListen for this routine.
ccbRefNum	The CCB reference number that was returned by the dspCLInit routine.
remoteCID	The identification number of the remote connection end. You must pass this value to the dspOpen routine when you open the connection or to the dspCLDeny routine when you deny the connection request.
remoteAddress	The internet address of the remote socket that sent a request to open a connection. This address consists of a 2-byte network number, a 1-byte node ID, and a 1-byte socket number. You must pass this value to the dspOpen routine when you open the connection or to the dspCLDeny routine when you deny the connection request.
filterAddress	The internet address of the socket from which you will accept a connection request. The address consists of three fields: a 2-byte network number, a 1-byte node ID, and a 1-byte socket number. Specify 0 for any of these fields for which you wish to impose no restrictions. If you specify a filter address of $00082500, for example, the connection listener accepts a connection request from any socket at node $25 of network $0008.
sendSeq	The sequence number of the first byte that the local connection end will send to the remote connection end. ADSP uses this number to coordinate communications and to check for errors. You must pass this value to the dspOpen routine when you open the connection.
sendWindow	The sequence number of the last byte that the remote connection end has buffer space to receive. ADSP uses this number to coordinate communications and to check for errors. You must pass this value to the dspOpen routine when you open the connection.
attnSendSeq	The sequence number of the next attention packet that the local connection end will transmit. ADSP uses this number to coordinate communications and to check for errors. You must pass this value to the dspOpen routine when you open the connection.

Result codes

noErr	0	No error
errState	–1278	Not a connection listener
errAborted	–1279	Request aborted by the dspRemove routine
errRefNum	–1280	Bad connection reference number

dspCLDeny

Parameter block

←	16	ioResult	word	result code
→	24	ioCRefNum	word	driver reference number
→	26	csCode	word	always dspCLDeny
→	32	ccbRefNum	word	reference number of CCB
→	36	remoteCID	word	ID of remote connection end
→	38	remoteAddress	long	remote internet address

The dspCLDeny routine is used by a connection server to inform a remote connection end that its request to open a connection cannot be honored.

The ioResult parameter returns the result of the routine. If you call the routine asynchronously, the routine sets this field to 1 as soon as it begins execution, and it changes the field to the actual result code when it completes execution. The ioCRefNum parameter is the driver reference number returned by the OpenDriver function. You must specify this number every time you call the .DSP driver. The csCode parameter is the routine selector; it is always dspCLDeny for this routine. The ccbRefNum parameter is the CCB reference number for the connection listener that received the connection request. This number is returned by the dspCLInit routine when you establish a connection listener. The remoteCID and remoteAddress parameters specify the address and ID of the remote connection end. These parameters are returned by the dspCLListen routine.

Result codes

noErr	0	No error
errState	–1278	Not a connection listener
errAborted	–1279	Request aborted by the dspRemove routine
errRefNum	–1280	Bad connection reference number

dspCLRemove

Parameter block

←	16	ioResult	word	result code
→	24	ioCRefNum	word	driver reference number
→	26	csCode	word	always dspCLRemove
→	32	ccbRefNum	word	reference number of CCB
→	34	abort	byte	abort connection listener if not 0

The dspCLRemove routine closes a connection end used as a connection listener. You can release the memory you allocated for the CCB if you do not intend to reopen the connection end.

The ioResult parameter returns the result of the routine. If you call the routine asynchronously, the routine sets this field to 1 as soon as it begins execution, and it changes the field to the actual result code when it completes execution. The ioCRefNum parameter is the driver reference number returned by the OpenDriver function. You must specify this number every time you call the .DSP driver. The csCode parameter is the routine selector, always dspCLRemove for this routine. The ccbRefNum parameter is the CCB reference number that was returned by the dspCLInit routine. If the abort parameter is nonzero, ADSP cancels any outstanding requests to send packets (such as the dspCLDeny routine).

Result codes

noErr	0	No error
errRefNum	–1280	Bad connection reference number

Maintaining an ADSP Connection

Once you have established a connection end and opened a connection, you must be able to send and receive data over the connection. You can use the routines in this section to

- determine the status of a connection
- read bytes from the connection end's receive queue
- write bytes to the connection end's send queue and transmit them to the remote connection end
- send an attention message to the remote connection end
- discard all data that has been sent but not yet delivered, and reset the connection

dspStatus

Parameter block

←	16	ioResult	word	result code
→	24	ioCRefNum	word	driver reference number
→	26	csCode	word	always dspStatus
→	32	ccbRefNum	word	reference number of CCB
←	34	statusCCB	long	pointer to CCB
←	38	sendQPending	word	bytes waiting to be sent or acknowledged
←	40	sendQFree	word	available send queue in bytes
←	42	recvQPending	word	bytes waiting to be read from queue
←	44	recvQFree	word	available receive queue in bytes

The dspStatus routine returns the number of bytes waiting to be read and sent and the space available in the send and receive queues. This routine also returns a pointer to the CCB, which contains information about the state of the connection end and about connection events received by the connection end. The CCB is described in "The ADSP Connection Control Block" earlier in this chapter.

The ioResult parameter returns the result of the routine. If you call the routine asynchronously, the routine sets this field to 1 as soon as it begins execution, and it changes the field to the actual result code when it completes execution. The ioCRefNum parameter is the driver reference number returned by the OpenDriver function. You must specify this number every time you call the .DSP driver. The csCode parameter is the routine selector; it is always dspStatus for this routine. The ccbRefNum parameter is the CCB reference number that was returned by the dspInit routine. The statusCCB parameter returns a pointer to the CCB.

The sendQPending parameter indicates the number of bytes of data in the send queue, including 1 byte for each end-of-message (EOM) indicator in the send queue. (ADSP counts 1 byte for each EOM, even though no actual data corresponds to the EOM indicator.) The send queue contains all data that has been sent to ADSP for transmission and that has not yet been acknowledged. Some of the data in the send queue might have already been transmitted, but ADSP retains it in the send queue until the remote connection end acknowledges its receipt in case the data has to be retransmitted. The sendQFree parameter indicates the number of bytes available in the send queue for additional data.

The recvQPending parameter indicates the number of bytes in the receive queue, including 1 byte for each EOM if the EOM bit is set in an ADSP packet header. The receive queue contains all of the data that has been received by the connection end but not yet read by the connection end's client. The recvQFree parameter indicates the number of bytes available in the receive queue for additional data.

Result codes

noErr	0	No error
errRefNum	–1280	Bad connection reference number

dspRead

Parameter block

←	16	ioResult	word	result code
→	24	ioCRefNum	word	driver reference number
→	26	csCode	word	always dspRead
→	32	ccbRefNum	word	reference number of CCB
→	34	reqCount	word	requested number of bytes
←	36	actCount	word	actual number of bytes read
→	38	dataPtr	long	pointer to data buffer
←	42	eom	byte	1 if end-of-message; 0 otherwise

The dspRead routine reads bytes from the connection end's receive queue and places them in a buffer that you specify. You can continue to read bytes as long as data is in the receive queue, even after you have called the dspClose routine or after the remote connection end has called the dspClose or dspRemove routine. The dspRead routine completes execution when it has read the number of bytes you specify or when it encounters an end-of-message (that is, the last byte of data in an ADSP packet that has the EOM bit set in the packet header).

You can call the dspStatus routine to determine the number of bytes remaining to be read from the read queue, or you can continue to call the dspRead routine until the actCount and eom parameters both return 0.

The ioResult parameter returns the result of the routine. If you call the routine asynchronously, the routine sets this field to 1 as soon as it begins execution, and it changes the field to the actual result code when it completes execution. The ioCRefNum parameter is the driver reference number returned by the OpenDriver function. You must specify this number every time you call the .DSP driver. The csCode parameter is the routine selector; it is always dspRead for this routine. The ccbRefNum parameter is the CCB reference number that was returned by the dspInit routine.

You specify the number of bytes to read with the reqCount parameter, and you use the dataPtr parameter to provide a pointer to the buffer into which ADSP should place the data. ADSP returns the actual number of bytes read in the actCount parameter. If the last byte read constitutes an EOM, ADSP sets the eom parameter to 1.

If either end closes the connection before you call the dspRead routine, the command reads whatever data is available and returns the actual amount of data read in the actCount parameter. If the connection is closed and there is no data in the receive queue, the dspRead routine returns the noErr result code with the actCount parameter set to 0 and the eom parameter set to 0.

Result codes

noErr	0	No error
errFwdReset	–1275	Read terminated by forward reset
errState	–1278	State isn't open, closing, or closed
errAborted	–1279	Request aborted by dspRemove or dspClose routine
errRefNum	–1280	Bad connection reference number

dspWrite

Parameter block

←	16	ioResult	word	result code
→	24	ioCRefNum	word	driver reference number
→	26	csCode	word	always dspWrite
→	32	ccbRefNum	word	reference number of CCB
→	34	reqCount	word	requested number of bytes
←	36	actCount	word	actual number of bytes written
→	38	dataPtr	long	pointer to data buffer
→	42	eom	byte	1 if end-of-message; 0 otherwise
→	43	flush	byte	1 to send data now; 0 otherwise

The dspWrite routine writes bytes into the connection end's send queue. The send queue contains all data that has been sent to ADSP for transmission and that has not yet been acknowledged. Some of the data in the send queue might have already been transmitted, but ADSP retains it in the send queue until the remote connection end acknowledges its receipt in case the data has to be retransmitted. The dspWrite routine completes execution when it has copied all of the data from the data buffer into the ADSP send queue.

ADSP transmits the data in the send queue when the remote connection end has room to accept the data and one of the following conditions occurs:

- You call the dspWrite routine with the flush parameter set to a nonzero number.
- The number of bytes in the send queue equals or exceeds the blocking factor. (You use the sendBlocking parameter to the dspOptions routine to set the blocking factor.)
- The send timer expires.
- A connection event requires that the local connection end send an acknowledgment packet to the remote connection end.

The ioResult parameter returns the result of the routine. If you call the routine asynchronously, the routine sets this field to 1 as soon as it begins execution, and it changes the field to the actual result code when it completes execution. The ioCRefNum parameter is the driver reference number returned by the OpenDriver function. You must specify this number every time you call the .DSP driver. The csCode parameter is the routine selector; it is always dspWrite for this routine. The ccbRefNum parameter is the CCB reference number that was returned by the dspInit routine.

You specify the number of bytes to write with the reqCount parameter, and you use the dataPtr parameter to provide a pointer to the buffer from which ADSP should read the data. The dspWrite routine returns the actual number of bytes written in the actCount parameter. If the last byte written constitutes an EOM, set the eom parameter to 1. You can also set the reqCount parameter to 0 and the eom parameter to 1 to indicate that the last byte you sent the previous time you called the dspWrite routine was the end of the message. The high-order bits of the eom parameter are reserved for use by ADSP; you must leave these bits equal to 0.

You can set the reqCount parameter to a value larger than the size of the send queue. If you do so, the dspWrite routine writes as much data as it can into the send queue, sends the data and waits for acknowledgment, and then writes more data into the send queue until it has written the amount of data you requested. In this case, the routine does not complete execution until it has finished writing all of the data into the send queue.

Set the flush parameter to 1 to cause ADSP to immediately transmit any data in the send queue that has not already been transmitted. Set the flush parameter to 0 to allow data to accumulate in the send queue until another condition occurs that causes data to be transmitted. The high-order bits of the flush parameter are reserved for use by ADSP; you must leave these bits equal to 0.

Result codes

noErr	0	No error
errState	–1278	Connection is not open
errAborted	–1279	Request aborted by dspRemove or dspClose routine
errRefNum	–1280	Bad connection reference number

dspAttention

Parameter block

←	16	ioResult	word	result code
→	24	ioCRefNum	word	driver reference number
→	26	csCode	word	always dspAttention
→	32	ccbRefNum	word	reference number of CCB
→	34	attnCode	word	client attention code
→	36	attnSize	word	size of attention data in bytes
→	38	attnData	long	pointer to attention data

The dspAttention routine sends an attention code and an attention message to the remote connection end. Attention codes and attention messages can have any meaning that your application and the application at the remote connection end both recognize. The purpose of attention codes and messages is to allow clients of ADSP to send messages outside the normal data stream. For example, if a connection end on a mainframe computer is connected to several connection ends in Macintosh computers being used as remote terminals, the mainframe computer might wish to inform the remote terminals that all connections will be terminated in ten minutes. The mainframe application could send an attention message to each of the remote terminals informing them of this fact, and the terminal emulation programs in the Macintosh computers could then display an alert message on the screen so that the users could prepare to shut down.

The ioResult parameter returns the result of the routine. If you call the routine asynchronously, the routine sets this field to 1 as soon as it begins execution, and it changes the field to the actual result code when it completes execution. The ioCRefNum parameter is the driver reference number returned by the OpenDriver function. You must specify this number every time you call the .DSP driver. The csCode parameter is the routine selector; it is always dspAttention for this routine. The ccbRefNum parameter is the CCB reference number that was returned by the dspInit routine.

The attnCode parameter is the attention code that you wish to send to the remote connection end. You can use any value from $0000 through $EFFF for the attention code. The values $F000 through $FFFF are reserved for use by ADSP. The attnSize parameter is the size in bytes of the attention message you wish to send, and the attnData parameter provides a pointer to the attention message. The attention message can be any size from 0 through 570 bytes. There are no restrictions on the content of the attention message.

Result codes

noErr	0	No error
errAttention	–1276	Attention message too long
errState	–1278	Connection is not open
errAborted	–1279	Request aborted by dspRemove or dspClose routine
errRefNum	–1280	Bad connection reference number

dspReset

Parameter block

←	16	ioResult	word	result code
→	24	ioCRefNum	word	driver reference number
→	26	csCode	word	always dspReset
→	32	ccbRefNum	word	reference number of CCB

The dspReset routine causes ADSP to discard all data in the send queue, all data in transit to the remote connection end, and all data in the remote connection end's receive queue that the client has not yet read. This process is known as a *forward reset*. ADSP then resynchronizes the connection. You can determine that your connection end has received a forward reset and has discarded all data in the receive queue by checking the eFwdReset flag in the userFlags field of the CCB. The CCB is described in "The ADSP Connection Control Block" earlier in this chapter.

The ioResult parameter returns the result of the routine. If you call the routine asynchronously, the routine sets this field to 1 as soon as it begins execution, and it changes the field to the actual result code when it completes execution. The ioCRefNum parameter is the driver reference number returned by the OpenDriver function. You must specify this number every time you call the .DSP driver. The csCode parameter is the routine selector; it is always dspReset for this routine. The ccbRefNum parameter is the CCB reference number that was returned by the dspInit routine.

Result codes

noErr	0	No error
errState	–1278	Connection is not open
errAborted	–1279	Request aborted by dspRemove or dspClose routine
errRefNum	–1280	Bad connection reference number

THE .ENET DRIVER

The .ENET driver is normally called by the AppleTalk Manager through the AppleTalk connection file for EtherTalk when the user has selected EtherTalk from the Network control panel. You can write your own protocol stack or application that uses the .ENET driver directly, rather than through AppleTalk. This section describes how to open the .ENET driver, how to send data to it directly for transmission over the Ethernet network, and how to write a protocol handler to receive data from the network.

The system .ENET driver locates and opens the drivers for installed NuBus™ Ethernet cards. For each Ethernet NuBus card, the .ENET driver searches the open resource files for a driver with a resource type of 'enet' and a resource ID equal to the board ID of the NuBus card. If it doesn't find such a driver resource, it then looks for a driver named .ENET in the slot resources in the ROM of the NuBus card. See *Designing Cards and Drivers for the Macintosh Family,* second edition, for discussions of NuBus board IDs and slot resources.

Providing Your Own Ethernet Driver

If you write an Ethernet driver for use with your own Ethernet NuBus card, you should provide the features and functions described in this chapter. You can store the driver in the firmware of the NuBus card as described in *Designing Cards and Drivers for the Macintosh Family,* second edition, and in the Device Manager chapter of *Inside Macintosh,* Volume V, or you can provide a RAM-based driver as described in the Device Manager chapter of *Inside Macintosh,* Volume II. If you place your Ethernet driver in the ROM of the NuBus card, you must name the driver .ENET. If you provide a RAM-based driver, you must give it a resource type of 'enet' and a resource ID equal to the board ID of your NuBus card. The 'enet' resource type is identical to the 'DRVR' resource type described in the Device Manager chapter of Volume II.

> **Note:** You must *not* name a RAM-based driver .ENET, because doing so would replace the system .ENET driver.

If you write an Ethernet driver for use with a non-NuBus network interface (such as an Ethernet card for the Macintosh SE/30 or an Ethernet connection through the SCSI port), you should provide the features and functions described in this chapter for the .ENET driver and should name your driver .ENET0. If you do so, any software written to use the .ENET driver should work with your driver.

Changing the Ethernet Hardware Address

Each Ethernet NuBus card or other Ethernet hardware interface device contains a unique 6-byte hardware address assigned by the manufacturer of the device. The .ENET driver normally uses this address to determine whether to receive a packet. To change the hardware address for your node, place in the System file a resource of type 'eadr' with a resource ID equal to the slot number of the Ethernet NuBus card. If the Ethernet device is not a NuBus card (it might be a slot card in a Macintosh SE/30, for example), use a resource ID of 0.

The 'eadr' resource consists only of a 6-byte number. Do not use the broadcast address or a multicast address for this number. (The **broadcast address** is $FF-FF-FF-FF-FF-FF. A multicast address is any Ethernet address in which the low-order bit of the high-order byte is set to 1.) When you open the .ENET driver, it looks for an 'eadr' resource. If it finds one, the driver substitutes the number in this resource for the Ethernet hardware address and uses it until the driver is closed or reset.

> **Note:** To avoid address collisions, you should never arbitrarily change the Ethernet hardware address. This feature should be used only by a system administrator who can keep track of all the Ethernet addresses in the system.

Opening the .ENET Driver

Before you use the OpenSlot function to open the .ENET driver, you must determine which NuBus slots contain EtherTalk cards. The OpenSlot function is described in the Device Manager chapter of Volume V. Use the SGetTypeSRsrc function described in the Slot Manager chapter of this volume to determine which NuBus slots contain EtherTalk cards. To find EtherTalk

NuBus cards, use the value catNetwork in the field spCategory of the GetTypeSRsrc function parameter block, and use the value typeEtherNet in the field spCType. If you cannot find any EtherTalk NuBus cards, you should also attempt to open the .ENET0 driver in case a non-NuBus EtherTalk card is attached to the system. You should provide a user interface that allows the user to select a specific EtherTalk card in the case that more than one is present.

Listing 32-7 illustrates the use of the GetTypeSRsrc function and the OpenSlot function to open the .ENET driver.

Listing 32-7. Finding an EtherTalk card and opening the .ENET driver

```
VAR
   mySBlk:      SpBlock;
   myPBRec:     ParamBlockRec;
   myErr:       OSErr;
   Found:       Integer;
   EnetStr:     Str15;
   Enet0Str:    Str15;
   myRefNum:    Integer;

BEGIN
   Found := 0;                {assume no sResource found}
   EnetStr := '.ENET';
   Enet0Str := '.ENET0';

   WITH mySBlk DO
   BEGIN
      spParamData := 1; {include search of disabled resources. }
                        { Start searching from spSlot and search }
                        { the slots above it as well.}
      spCategory := catNetwork;
      spCType := typeEtherNet;
      spDrvrSW := 0;
      spDrvrHW := 0;
      spTBMask := 3;    {match only Category and CType fields}
      spSlot := 0;      {start search from here}
      spID := 0;        {start search from here}
      spExtDev := 0     {ID of the external device}
   END;
   REPEAT
      myErr := SGetTypeSRsrc(@mySBlk);
      IF myErr = noErr THEN
      {You found an sResource match; save it for later.}
      BEGIN
         Found := Found + 1;
         SaveSInfo(@mySBlk)
      END;
   UNTIL myErr = smNoMoresRsrcs;
```

```
   IF Found > 1 THEN
   BEGIN
      {If you found more than one sResource, put up a dialog box }
      { and let the user choose one. If any of the sResources you }
      { found were disabled, let the user know they are not available.}
      DisplaySInfo(@mySBLk)
   END;


   IF Found <> 0 THEN
   BEGIN
      WITH myPBRec DO
      BEGIN
         ioCompletion := NIL;
         ioNamePtr := @EnetStr;
         ioMix := NIL;          {reserved}
         ioFlags := 0;          {single device sResource}
         ioSlot := mySBlk.spSlot;
         ioID := mySBlk.spID
      END;
      myErr := OpenSlot(@myPBRec, FALSE)      {go open this}
   END
   ELSE myErr := OpenDriver(Enet0Str, myRefNum);
   IF myErr <> NoErr THEN DoError(myErr)
END;
```


Using a Write-Data Structure to Transmit Ethernet Data

When you use the EWrite function to send data to the .ENET driver for transmission over the Ethernet network, you provide a pointer to a write-data structure (Figure 32-5). A write-data structure contains a series of pairs of length words and pointers. Each pair indicates the length and location of a portion of the data that constitutes the packet to be sent over the network. The first length-pointer pair points to a 14-byte header block, which starts with the destination node hardware address. Note that this is not the AppleTalk address, but is the hardware address of the destination node. If you are calling the .ENET driver directly, you must obtain the Ethernet address of the destination node yourself; AppleTalk cannot provide it.

The next 6 bytes of the header block are reserved for use by the .ENET driver. These bytes are followed by the 2-byte Ethernet protocol type. Data may follow the header block; all other length-pointer pairs point to data. The write-data structure terminates with a 0 word.

When you first open the .ENET driver, it allocates a 768-byte buffer that it uses for transmitting data packets. This buffer is large enough to hold the largest EtherTalk packet, which is 621 bytes in size. If you want to transmit data packets larger than 768 bytes, call the ESetGeneral function. The .ENET driver then allocates a large enough data buffer to send packets up to 1514 bytes in size.

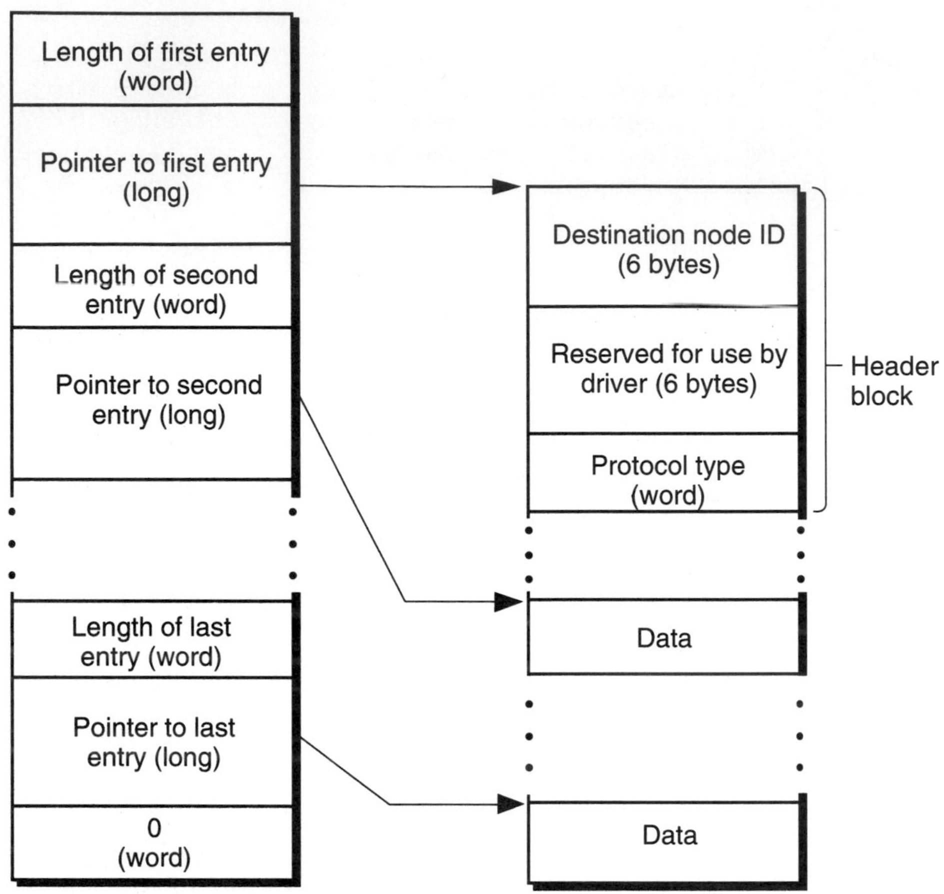

Figure 32-5. An Ethernet write-data structure

Listing 32-8 defines an Ethernet write-data structure and then calls the EWrite function to send a data packet over Ethernet.

Listing 32-8. Sending a data packet over Ethernet

```
CONST
   size1 =  100;
   size2 =  333;

TYPE
   WDS   =  RECORD                    {write-data structure}
            length: Integer;          {length of nth entry}
            aptr: Ptr                 {pointer to nth entry}
         END;

VAR
   myWDS:    ARRAY[1..4] OF WDS;
   myPB:     EParamBlock;             {.ENET parameter block}
   wheader: ARRAY[1..14] OF Byte;
   stuff1:   ARRAY[1..size1] OF Byte;
   stuff2:   ARRAY[1..size2] OF Byte;
   myErr:    OSErr;
```

```
BEGIN
   {set up the write header}
   wheader[1]  := $02;                {dest node ID}
   wheader[2]  := $60;
   wheader[3]  := $8C;
   wheader[4]  := $04;
   wheader[5]  := $05;
   wheader[6]  := $06;
                                      {bytes 7-12 are reserved}
   wheader[13]  := $08;               {protocol type}
   wheader[14]  :   $00;

   myWDS[1].length := 14;             {the write header is always 14 bytes}
   myWDS[1].aptr := @wheader;
   myWDS[2].length := size1;
   myWDS[2].aptr := @stuff1;
   myWDS[3].length := size2;
   myWDS[3].aptr := @stuff2;
   myWDS[4].length := 0;              {terminator}

   myPB.ePointer := @myWDS;           {pointer to write-data structure}
   myErr := EWrite(@myPB, FALSE);     {send something}
   IF myErr <> NoErr THEN DoError(myErr)
END;
```


Using the Default Ethernet Protocol Handler to Read Data

When the EtherTalk NuBus card or other Ethernet hardware receives a data packet, it generates an interrupt to the CPU. The interrupt handler in ROM determines the source of the interrupt and calls the .ENET driver. The .ENET driver reads the packet header to determine the protocol type of the data packet and checks to see if any client has specified that protocol type in a call to the EAttachPH function. If so, the client either specified a NIL pointer to a protocol handler, or the client provided its own protocol handler. If the client specified a NIL pointer, the .ENET driver uses its default protocol handler to read the data. If no one has specified that protocol type in a call to the EAttachPH function, the .ENET driver discards the data. The EAttachPH function is described in "Attaching and Detaching an Ethernet Protocol Handler" later in this chapter.

The default protocol handler checks for an ERead function pending execution and places the entire packet—including the packet header—into the buffer specified by that function. The function returns the number of bytes actually read. If the packet is larger than the data buffer, the ERead function places as much of the packet as will fit into the buffer and returns the buf2SmallErr result code.

Call the ERead function asynchronously to await the next data packet. When the .ENET driver receives the data packet, it completes execution of the ERead function and calls your completion routine. Your completion routine should call the ERead function again so that an ERead function is always pending execution. If the .ENET driver receives a data packet with a protocol type for which you specified the default protocol handler while no ERead function is pending, the .ENET driver discards the packet.

You can have several asynchronous calls to the ERead function pending execution simultaneously as long as you use different buffers and a different parameter block for each call.

Listing 32-9 calls the EAttachPH function to specify that the .ENET driver should use the default protocol handler to process protocol type eProtType. The listing includes a completion routine that processes a received data packet and then makes an asynchronous call to the ERead function to await the next incoming data packet.

In practice, you should call the EAttachPH function very early, during your program initialization sequence, if possible. As soon as the connection is established and you are expecting data, you should call the ERead function asynchronously. When the .ENET driver receives a packet, it then calls your completion routine, which should process the packet and queue another asynchronous call to the ERead function to await the next packet.

Listing 32-9. Using the default Ethernet protocol handler to read data

```
CONST
   BigBytes = 8888;

VAR
   myPB:     EParamBlock;
   EPBPtr:   EParamBlkPtr;
   APtr:     Ptr;
   myErr:    OSErr;

   PROCEDURE MyCompRoutine;

   VAR
      myErr:    OSErr;

   BEGIN
   {If this gets called, an incoming packet with the specified protocol }
   { type is here.}

      ProcessData(BigBytes, APtr);         {do something with the data}
      IF EPBPtr^.ioResult <> noErr THEN DoError(myErr);

      {call ERead again}
      WITH EPBPtr^ DO                      {set up ERead parameters}
      BEGIN
         ioCompletion := @MyCompRoutine;   {pointer to completion routine}
         eProtType := 77;                  {protocol type}
         ePointer := APtr;                 {pointer to read-data area}
         eBuffSize := BigBytes             {size of read-data area}
      END;
      myErr := ERead(EPBPtr, TRUE);        {call ERead to wait for }
                                           { the next packet}
      IF myErr <> noErr THEN DoError(myErr)
   END;
```

```
BEGIN {main}
   EPBPtr := @myPB;
   WITH EPBPtr^ DO                     {set up EAttachPH parameters}
   BEGIN
      eProtType := 77;                 {protocol type}
      ePointer := NIL                  {use default protocol handler}
   END;
   myErr := EAttachPH(EPBPtr, FALSE);  {tell .ENET about this }
                                       { protocol handler}
   IF myErr <> NoErr THEN DoError(myErr);

   APtr := NewPtr(BigBytes);
   WITH EPBPtr^ DO                     {set up ERead parameters}
   BEGIN
      ioCompletion := @MyCompRoutine;  {pointer to completion routine}
      eProtType := 77;                 {protocol type}
      ePointer := APtr;                {pointer to read-data area}
      eBuffSize := BigBytes            {size of read-data area}
   END;
   myErr := ERead(EPBPtr, TRUE);       {wait for your packet and }
                                       { then read it}
   IF myErr <> noErr THEN DoError(myErr)

   {application-defined tasks}

END;  {main}
```


Using Your Own Ethernet Protocol Handler to Read Data

If a client of the .ENET driver has used the EAttachPH function to provide a pointer to its own protocol handler, the .ENET driver calls that protocol handler, which must in turn call the .ENET driver's ReadPacket and ReadRest routines to read the data. Your protocol handler calls the .ENET driver's ReadPacket and ReadRest routines in essentially the same way as you call the .MPP driver's ReadPacket and ReadRest routines (see the AppleTalk Manager chapter of Volume II). The following sections describe how the .ENET driver calls a custom protocol handler and the ReadPacket and ReadRest routines.

Note: Because an Ethernet protocol handler must read from and write to the CPU's registers, you cannot write a protocol handler in Pascal.

How the .ENET Driver Calls Your Protocol Handler

You can provide an Ethernet protocol handler for a particular protocol type and use the EAttachPH function to attach it to the .ENET driver. When the driver receives an Ethernet packet, it reads the packet header into an internal buffer, reads the protocol type, and calls the protocol handler for that protocol type. The CPU is in interrupt mode, and the registers are used as follows:

Registers on call to Ethernet protocol handler

A0	Reserved for internal use by the .ENET driver. You must preserve this register until after the ReadRest routine has completed execution.
A1	Reserved for internal use by the .ENET driver. You must preserve this register until after the ReadRest routine has completed execution.
A2	Free for your use.
A3	Pointer to first byte past data-link header bytes (the first byte after the 2-byte protocol-type field).
A4	Pointer to the ReadPacket routine. The ReadRest routine starts 2 bytes after the start of the ReadPacket routine.
A5	Free for your use until after the ReadRest routine has completed execution.
D0	Free for your use.
D1	Number of bytes in the Ethernet packet left to be read (that is, the number of bytes following the Ethernet header).
D2	Free for your use.
D3	Free for your use.

If your protocol handler processes more than one protocol type, you can read the protocol-type field in the data-link header to determine the protocol type of the packet. The protocol-type field starts 2 bytes before the address pointed to by the A3 register.

> **Note:** The source address starts 8 bytes before the address pointed to by the A3 register, and the destination address starts 14 bytes before the address pointed to by the A3 register.

If you know that the packet contains pad bytes and you know the actual size of the data, you can reduce the number in the D1 register by the number of pad bytes so that the .ENET driver can keep accurate track of the number of bytes remaining to be read. In all other circumstances, you should not change the value in the D1 register.

After you have called the ReadRest routine, you can use registers A0 through A3 and D0 through D3 for your own use, but you must preserve all other registers. You cannot depend on having access to your application global variables.

How Your Protocol Handler Calls the .ENET Driver

Your protocol handler must call the .ENET driver routines ReadPacket and ReadRest to read the incoming data packet. You may call the ReadPacket routine as many times as you like to read the data piece by piece into one or more data buffers, but you must always use the ReadRest routine to read the final piece of the data packet. The ReadRest routine restores the machine state (the stack pointers, status register, and so forth) and checks for error conditions.

Before you call the ReadPacket routine, you must allocate memory for a data buffer and place a pointer to the buffer in the A3 register. You place the number of bytes you want to read in the D3 register. You must not request more bytes than remain in the data packet.

To call the ReadPacket routine, execute a JSR instruction to the address in the A4 register. The ReadPacket routine uses the registers as follows:

Registers on entry to the ReadPacket routine

A3	Pointer to a buffer to hold the data you want to read
D3	Number of bytes to read; must be nonzero

Registers on exit from the ReadPacket routine

A0	Unchanged
A1	Unchanged
A2	Unchanged
A3	First byte after the last byte read into buffer
D0	Changed
D1	Number of bytes left to be read
D2	Unchanged
D3	Equals 0 if requested number of bytes were read, nonzero if error

The ReadPacket routine indicates an error by clearing to 0 the zero (z) flag in the status register. If the ReadPacket routine returns an error, you must terminate execution of your protocol handler with an RTS instruction without calling ReadPacket again or calling ReadRest at all.

Call the ReadRest routine to read the last portion of the data packet, or call it after you have read all the data with ReadPacket routines and before you do any other processing or terminate execution. You must provide in the A3 register a pointer to a data buffer and must indicate in the D3 register the size of the data buffer. If you have already read all of the data with calls to the ReadPacket routine, you can specify a buffer of size 0.

▲ **Warning:** If you do not call the ReadRest routine after your last call to the ReadPacket routine, the system will crash. ▲

To call the ReadRest routine, execute a JSR instruction to an address 2 bytes past the address in the A4 register. The ReadRest routine uses the registers as follows:

Registers on entry to the ReadRest routine

A3	Pointer to a buffer to hold the data you want to read
D3	Size of the buffer (word length); may be 0

Registers on exit from the ReadRest routine

A0	Unchanged
A1	Unchanged
A2	Unchanged
A3	Pointer to first byte after the last byte read into buffer
D0	Changed
D1	Changed
D2	Unchanged
D3	Equals 0 if requested number of bytes were read; less than 0 if more data was left than would fit in buffer (extra data equals –D3 bytes); greater than 0 if less data was left than the size of the buffer (extra buffer space equals D3 bytes)

The ReadRest routine indicates an error by clearing to 0 the zero (z) flag in the status register.

You must terminate execution of your protocol handler with an RTS instruction whether or not the ReadRest routine returns an error.

.ENET Driver Routines

An application that uses AppleTalk Manager routines for network communication can talk to whatever AppleTalk network the user has selected through the Network Setup control panel. However, you can choose to write an application that talks only to Ethernet; in this case, your application has to address the Ethernet driver directly. This section describes the functions that you can use to control the .ENET driver, the Ethernet driver provided with system software version 7.0. Each .ENET driver function is of the following form:

```
FUNCTION EFunc (thePBptr: EParamBlkPtr; async: Boolean) : OSErr;
```

The thePBptr parameter is a pointer to the .ENET parameter block and the async parameter is a Boolean that specifies whether the function is to be executed synchronously or asynchronously. Set the async parameter to TRUE to execute the function asynchronously.

The .ENET parameter block is defined as follows:

```
TYPE EParamBlock =
     PACKED RECORD
        qLink:        QElemPtr;          {next queue entry}
        qType:        Integer;           {queue type}
        ioTrap:       Integer;           {routine trap}
        ioCmdAddr:    Ptr;               {routine address}
        ioCompletion: ProcPtr;           {completion routine}
        ioResult:     OSErr;             {result code}
        ioNamePtr:    StringPtr;         {driver name}
        ioVRefNum:    Integer;           {volume reference number}
        ioRefNum:     Integer;           {driver reference number}
        csCode:       Integer;           {primary command code}
```

```
        CASE Integer OF
        ENetWrite,
        ENetAttachPH,
        ENetDetachPH,
        ENetRead,
        ENetRdCancel,
        ENetGetInfo,
        ENetSetGeneral:
        (
        eProtType:    Integer;                 {Ethernet protocol type}
        ePointer:     Ptr;                     {pointer; use depends on }
                                               { function}
        eBuffSize:    Integer;                 {buffer size}
        eDataSize:    Integer                  {number of bytes read}
        );

        ENetAddMulti,
        ENetDelMulti:
        (
        eMultiAddr:   ARRAY[0..5] of Char      {multicast address}
        )
    END;
```

The qLink, qType, ioTrap, ioCmdAddr, ioNamePtr, and ioVRefNum fields are filled in by the Device Manager; your application should not have to set or read these fields. The ioResult field returns the result of the function. If you call the function asynchronously, the function sets this field to 1 as soon as it begins execution, and it changes the field to the actual result code when it completes execution. The ioCompletion field is a pointer to a completion routine that you can provide; the Device Manager calls your completion routine when it completes execution of the function. If you are not providing a completion routine, specify NIL for this field. You must obtain the driver reference number from the OpenDriver function and use it for the ioRefNum field.

The csCode field specifies the command to be executed; the MPW Pascal interface fills in this field for you. The .ENET driver accepts the following constants as routine selectors:

```
CONST {.ENET driver routine selectors}
      ENetSetGeneral   = 253;  {set "general" mode}
      ENetGetInfo      = 252;  {get info}
      ENetRdCancel     = 251;  {cancel read}
      ENetRead         = 250;  {read}
      ENetWrite        = 249;  {write}
      ENetDetachPH     = 248;  {detach protocol handler}
      ENetAttachPH     = 247;  {attach protocol handler}
      ENetAddMulti     = 246;  {add a multicast address}
      ENetDelMulti     = 245;  {delete a multicast address}
```

The remaining parameters are used only for specific functions; all of these parameters are described in the following sections.

For a general discussion of the use of the Ethernet driver, see “The .ENET Driver” earlier in this chapter.

Attaching and Detaching an Ethernet Protocol Handler

The functions in this section allow you to attach a protocol handler to the .ENET driver, to specify which protocol handler the .ENET driver is to use for each protocol type, and to detach a protocol handler that you previously attached. The section "Using Your Own Ethernet Protocol Handler to Read Data" earlier in this chapter describes how to write and use Ethernet protocol handlers.

```
FUNCTION EAttachPH (thePBptr: EParamBlkPtr; async: Boolean) : OSErr;
```

Parameter block

←	16	ioResult	word	result code
→	26	csCode	word	always ENetAttachPH
→	28	eProtType	word	Ethernet protocol type
→	30	ePointer	long	pointer to protocol handler

The EAttachPH function serves two purposes: you can use it to attach to the .ENET driver your own protocol handler for a specific protocol type, or you can use it to specify that the .ENET driver should use the default protocol handler for a particular protocol type. If you attach your own protocol handler, the .ENET driver calls that protocol handler each time it receives a packet with the protocol type you specified. If you specify that the .ENET driver should use the default protocol handler, then you can use the ERead command to read packets with that protocol type.

The ioResult parameter returns the result of the function. If you call the function asynchronously, the function sets this field to 1 as soon as it begins execution, and it changes the field to the actual result code when it completes execution. The csCode parameter is a routine selector; it is always equal to ENetAttachPH for this function.

You specify the protocol type in the eProtType parameter and provide a pointer to the protocol handler in the ePointer parameter. If you specify NIL for the ePointer parameter, then the .ENET driver uses the default protocol handler for that protocol type. Specify 0 for the eProtType parameter to attach a protocol handler for the IEEE 802.3 protocol, which uses protocol types 0 through $5DC.

Note: The LAP Manager calls the EAttachPH function with a protocol type of 0 and thus receives all 802.3 protocol packets. Instead of using the EAttachPH function to install a protocol handler for an 802.3 Ethernet protocol type, you should use the L802Attach routine. In the case of an 802.3 protocol packet, the .ENET driver passes the packet to the LAP Manager 802.2 protocol handler. If the packet has the protocol type you specified with the L802Attach routine, the 802.2 protocol handler passes the packet on to your protocol handler. For more information about IEEE 802.2 and 802.3 protocols, see "The LAP Manager 802.2 Protocol" earlier in this chapter.

Result codes

noErr	0	No error
LAPProtErr	–94	Protocol handler is already attached or node's protocol table is full

```
FUNCTION EDetachPH (thePBptr: EParamBlkPtr; async: Boolean) : OSErr;
```

Parameter block

←	16	ioResult	word	result code
→	26	csCode	word	always ENetDetachPH
→	28	eProtType	word	Ethernet protocol type

The EDetachPH function detaches a protocol handler from the .ENET driver. Once you have removed a protocol type from the node's protocol table with this function, the .ENET driver no longer delivers packets with that protocol type. You specify the protocol type in the eProtType parameter.

The ioResult parameter returns the result of the function. If you call the function asynchronously, the function sets this field to 1 as soon as it begins execution, and it changes the field to the actual result code when it completes execution. The csCode parameter is a routine selector that is set automatically for you by the MPW interface; it is always equal to ENetDetachPH for this function.

When you call the EDetachPH function, any pending calls to the ERead function terminate with the reqAborted result code.

Result codes

noErr	0	No error
LAPProtErr	–94	No protocol handler is attached

Writing and Reading Ethernet Packets

The functions in this section send and read Ethernet packets, cancel execution of a read operation, return information about the .ENET driver, and switch the .ENET driver from limited-transmission mode to general-transmission mode.

```
FUNCTION EWrite (thePBptr: EParamBlkPtr; async: Boolean) : OSErr;
```

Parameter block

←	16	ioResult	word	result code
→	26	csCode	word	always ENetWrite
→	30	ePointer	long	pointer to write-data structure

The EWrite function uses the .ENET driver to send a data packet over Ethernet. You must first prepare a write-data structure that specifies the destination address and the protocol type and contains the data that you want to send. You place a pointer to the write-data structure in the ePointer parameter. If you want to send a packet larger than 768 bytes, you must first call the ESetGeneral function to put the .ENET driver in general-transmission mode. If the size of the packet you provide is less than 60 bytes, the driver adds pad bytes to the packet. Write-data structures are described in "Using a Write-Data Structure to Transmit Ethernet Data" earlier in this chapter.

The ioResult parameter returns the result of the function. If you call the function asynchronously, the function sets this field to 1 as soon as it begins execution, and it changes the field to the actual result code when it completes execution. The csCode parameter is a routine selector that is set automatically for you by the MPW interface; it is always equal to ENetWrite for this function.

Result codes

noErr	0	No error
eLenErr	–92	Packet too large or first entry of the write-data structure did not contain the full 14-byte header
excessCollsns	–95	Hardware error

```
FUNCTION ERead (thePBptr: EParamBlkPtr; async: Boolean) : OSErr;
```

Parameter block

←	16	ioResult	word	result code
→	26	csCode	word	always ENetRead
→	28	eProtType	word	Ethernet protocol type
→	30	ePointer	long	pointer to data buffer
→	34	eBuffSize	word	size of data buffer
←	36	eDataSize	word	number of bytes read

The ERead function uses the default protocol handler to read a data packet and place it in a data buffer. You can use the ERead function to read packets of a particular protocol type only after you have used the EAttachPH function to specify a NIL pointer to the protocol handler for that protocol type.

The ioResult parameter returns the result of the function. If you call the function asynchronously, the function sets this field to 1 as soon as it begins execution, and it changes the field to the actual result code when it completes execution. The csCode parameter is the routine selector, automatically set by the MPW interface. It is always ENetRead for this function.

The eProtType parameter specifies the protocol type of the packet you want to read. The ePointer parameter is a pointer to the data buffer into which you want to read data, and the eBuffSize parameter indicates the size of the data buffer. If you are expecting EtherTalk data packets, the buffer should be at least 621 bytes in size; if you are expecting general Ethernet data packets, the buffer should be at least 1514 bytes in size.

The ERead function places the entire packet, including the packet header, into your buffer. The function returns in the eDataSize parameter the number of bytes actually read. If the packet is larger than the data buffer, the ERead function places as much of the packet as will fit into the buffer and returns the buf2SmallErr result code.

Call the ERead function asynchronously to await the next data packet. When the .ENET driver receives the data packet, it completes execution of the ERead function and calls your completion routine. If the .ENET driver receives a data packet with a protocol type for which you specified the default protocol handler while no ERead command is pending, the driver discards the data packet.

You can have several asynchronous calls to the ERead function pending execution simultaneously, as long as you use a different parameter block for each call.

Result codes

noErr	0	No error
LAPProtErr	–94	No protocol is attached or protocol handler pointer was not 0
reqAborted	–1105	ERdCancel or EDetachPH function called
buf2SmallErr	–3101	Packet too large for buffer; partial data returned

```
FUNCTION ERdCancel (thePBptr: EParamBlkPtr; async: Boolean) : OSErr;
```

Parameter block

←	16	ioResult	word	result code
→	26	csCode	word	always ENetRdCancel
→	30	ePointer	long	pointer to ERead parameter block

The ERdCancel function cancels execution of a specific call to the ERead function. You must have called the ERead function asynchronously to use the ERdCancel function. You specify in the ePointer parameter a pointer to the parameter block that you used when you called the ERead function.

The ioResult parameter returns the result of the function. If you call the function asynchronously, the function sets this field to 1 as soon as it begins execution, and it changes the field to the actual result code when it completes execution. The csCode parameter is the routine selector, automatically set by the MPW interface. It is always ENetRdCancel for this function.

When you call the ERdCancel function, the pending ERead function that you cancel receives the reqAborted result code.

Result codes

noErr	0	No error
cbNotFound	–1102	ERead not active

```
FUNCTION EGetInfo (thePBptr: EParamBlkPtr; async: Boolean) : OSErr;
```

Parameter block

←	16	ioResult	word	result code
→	26	csCode	word	always ENetGetInfo
→	30	ePointer	long	pointer to buffer
→	34	eBuffSize	word	size of buffer

The EGetInfo function returns information about the .ENET driver. Before calling this function, you must allocate a data buffer of at least 18 bytes. Put a pointer to the buffer in the ePointer parameter and the size of the buffer in the eBuffSize parameter.

The EGetInfo function places the following information in the data buffer:

Bytes	**Information**
1–6	Ethernet address of the node on which the driver is installed
7–10	Number of times the receive queue has overflowed
11–14	Number of data transmission operations that have timed out
15–18	Number of packets received that contain an incorrect address

An incorrect Ethernet address is one that is neither the broadcast address, a multicast address for which this node is registered, nor the node's data link address. A node could receive an incorrect Ethernet address due to a hardware or software error.

The ioResult parameter returns the result of the function. If you call the function asynchronously, the function sets this field to 1 as soon as it begins execution, and it changes the field to the actual result code when it completes execution. The csCode parameter is the routine selector, automatically set by the MPW interface. It is always ENetGetInfo for this function.

Result code

noErr	0	No error

```
FUNCTION ESetGeneral (thePBptr: EParamBlkPtr; async: Boolean) : OSErr;
```

Parameter block

←	16	ioResult	word	result code
→	26	csCode	word	always ENetSetGeneral

The ESetGeneral function switches the .ENET driver from limited-transmission mode to general-transmission mode. In limited-transmission mode, the .ENET driver allocates a write-data buffer of 768 bytes. This buffer size is more than sufficient to hold an EtherTalk data packet, which can be no larger than 621 bytes. In general-transmission mode, the .ENET driver can transmit an Ethernet data packet of up to 1514 bytes.

The ioResult parameter returns the result of the function. If you call the function asynchronously, the function sets this field to 1 as soon as it begins execution, and it changes the field to the actual result code when it completes execution. The csCode parameter is the routine selector, automatically set by the MPW interface. It is always ENetSetGeneral for this function.

There is no command to switch the .ENET driver from general-transmission mode to limited-transmission mode. To switch back to limited-transmission mode, you have to reset the driver by restarting the computer.

Result codes

noErr	0	No error
memFullErr	–108	Insufficient memory in heap

Adding and Removing Ethernet Multicast Addresses

The functions in this section add or delete Ethernet multicast addresses for a particular node. A **multicast address** is an Ethernet address for which the node accepts packets just as it does for its permanently assigned Ethernet hardware address. In a multicast address, the low-order bit of the high-order byte is set to 1. Each node can have any number of multicast addresses, and any number of nodes can have the same multicast address. The purpose of a multicast address is to allow a group of Ethernet nodes to receive the same transmission simultaneously, in a fashion similar to the AppleTalk broadcast service.

```
FUNCTION EAddMulti (thePBptr: EParamBlkPtr; async: Boolean) : OSErr;
```

Parameter block

←	16	ioResult	word	result code
→	26	csCode	word	always ENetAddMulti
→	28	eMultiAddr	6 bytes	multicast address

The EAddMulti function adds a multicast address to the node on which the .ENET driver is running.

You must provide (in the eMultiAddr parameter) the multicast address that you want to use. Each time a client of the .ENET driver calls the EAddMulti function for a particular multicast address, the driver increments a counter for that multicast address. Each time a client of the .ENET driver calls the EDelMulti function, the driver decrements the counter for that address. As long as the count for a multicast address is equal to or greater than 1, the .ENET driver accepts packets directed to that multicast address. Therefore, if any client of the .ENET driver in the node has called the EAddMulti function for a particular multicast address, the driver receives packets delivered to that address.

The ioResult parameter returns the result of the function. If you call the function asynchronously, the function sets this field to 1 as soon as it begins execution, and it changes the field to the actual result code when it completes execution. The csCode parameter is the routine selector, automatically set by the MPW interface. It is always ENetAddMulti for this function.

Result codes

noErr	0	No error
eMultiErr	–91	Invalid address or table is full

```
FUNCTION EDelMulti (thePBptr: EParamBlkPtr; async: Boolean) : OSErr;
```

Parameter block

←	16	ioResult	word	result code
→	26	csCode	word	always ENetDelMulti
→	28	eMultiAddr	6 bytes	multicast address

The EDelMulti function decrements the counter kept by the .ENET driver for a particular multicast address. Each time a client of the .ENET driver calls the EAddMulti function, the driver increments a counter for the multicast address specified by the eMultiAddr parameter. Each time a client of the .ENET driver calls the EDelMulti function, the driver decrements the counter for the address specified by the eMultiAddr parameter. As long as the count for a multicast address is equal to or greater than 1, the .ENET driver accepts packets directed to that multicast address. When the count for an address equals 0, the driver removes that address from the list of multicast addresses that it accepts.

> **Note:** Because more than one client of the .ENET driver might be using a particular multicast address, you should call the EDelMulti function only once for each time you called the EAddMulti function.

The ioResult parameter returns the result of the function. If you call the function asynchronously, the function sets this field to 1 as soon as it begins execution, and it changes the field to the actual result code when it completes execution. The csCode parameter is the routine selector automatically set by the MPW interface. It is always ENetDelMulti for this function.

Result codes

noErr	0	No error
eMultiErr	–91	Address not found

SUMMARY OF THE APPLETALK MANAGER

Constants

```
CONST
      {AppleTalk transitions}
      ATTransOpen        = 0;    {open transition}
      ATTransClose       = 2;    {prepare-to-close transition}
      ATTransClosePrep   = 3;    {permission-to-close transition}
      ATTransCancelClose = 4;    {cancel-close transition}

      {.XPP driver routine selector}
      xCall              = 246;

      {.XPP driver routine selector subcodes}
      zipGetLocalZones   = 5;
      zipGetZoneList     = 6;
      zipGetMyZone       = 7;

      {ADSP routine selectors}
      dspInit            = 255;  {create a new connection end}
      dspRemove          = 254;  {remove a connection end}
      dspOpen            = 253;  {open a connection}
      dspClose           = 252;  {close a connection}
      dspCLInit          = 251;  {create a connection listener}
      dspCLRemove        = 250;  {remove a connection listener}
      dspCLListen        = 249;  {post a listener request}
      dspCLDeny          = 248;  {deny an open-connection request}
      dspStatus          = 247;  {get status of connection end}
      dspRead            = 246;  {read data from the connection}
      dspWrite           = 245;  {write data on the connection}
      dspAttention       = 244;  {send an attention message}
      dspOptions         = 243;  {set connection end options}
      dspReset           = 242;  {forward reset the connection}
      dspNewCID          = 241;  {generate a cid for a connection end}

      {ADSP connection-opening modes}
      ocRequest          = 1;    {request a connection with remote}
      ocPassive          = 2;    {wait for a connection request from }
                                 { remote connection end}
      ocAccept           = 3;    {accept request as delivered by listener}
      ocEstablish        = 4;    {consider connection to be open}

      {ADSP connection end states}
      sListening         = 1;    {for connection listeners}
      sPassive           = 2;    {waiting for a connection request from }
                                 { remote connection end}
      sOpening           = 3;    {requesting a connection with remote}
      sOpen              = 4;    {connection is open}
```

```
sClosing            = 5;    {connection is being torn down}
sClosed             = 6;    {connection end state is closed}

{ADSP client event flags}
eClosed             = $80;  {received connection-closed advice}
eTearDown           = $40;  {closed due to broken connection}
eAttention          = $20;  {received attention message}
eFwdReset           = $10;  {received forward reset advice}

{miscellaneous ADSP constants}
attnBufSize         = 570;  {size of client attention buffer}
minDSPQueueSize     = 100;  {minimum size of receive or send queue}

{.ENET driver values}
catNetwork          = 4;    {spCategory for EtherTalk NB card}
typeEtherNet        = 1;    {spCType for EtherTalk NB card}

{LAP Manager values}
LAPMgrCall          = 2;    {offset to LAP routines}
LAddAEQ             = 23;   {LAPAddATQ routine selector}
LRmvAEQ             = 24;   {LAPRmvATQ routine selector}

{.ENET driver routine selectors}
ENetSetGeneral      = 253;  {set "general" mode}
ENetGetInfo         = 252;  {get info}
ENetRdCancel        = 251;  {cancel read}
ENetRead            = 250;  {read}
ENetWrite           = 249;  {write}
ENetDetachPH        = 248;  {detach protocol handler}
ENetAttachPH        = 247;  {attach protocol handler}
ENetAddMulti        = 246;  {add a multicast address}
ENetDelMulti        = 245;  {delete a multicast address}
```

Data Types

```
TYPE ATQEntry =
     RECORD
        qLink:              ATQEntryPtr;   {next queue entry}
        qType:              Integer;       {reserved}
        CallAddr:           ProcPtr        {pointer to your routine}
     END;
     ATQentryptr = ^ATQEntry;


     ATPParamBlock =
     PACKED RECORD                        {extended parameter block for }
                                          { PSendRequest and PNSendRequest}
        qLink:            QElemPtr;       {next queue entry}
        qType:            Integer;        {queue type}
        ioTrap:           Integer;        {routine trap}
```

```
   ioCmdAddr:        Ptr;          {routine address}
   ioCompletion:     ProcPtr;      {completion routine}
   ioResult:         OSErr;        {result code}
   userData:         LongInt;      {ATP user bytes}
   reqTID:           Integer;      {request transaction ID}
   ioRefNum:         Integer;      {driver reference number}
   csCode:           Integer;      {primary command code}
   atpSocket:        Byte;         {currBitMap or socket number}
   atpFlags:         Byte;         {control information - set bit 2 }
                                   { for extended parameter block}
   addrBlock:        AddrBlock;    {source socket address}
   reqLength:        Integer;      {request size in bytes}
   reqPointer:       Ptr;          {pointer to request data}
   bdsPointer:       Ptr;          {pointer to response buffer }
                                   { data structure}
   numOfBuffs:       Byte;         {number of responses expected}
   timeOutVal:       Byte;         {timeout interval}
   numOfResps:       Byte;         {number of responses }
                                   { actually received}
   retryCount:       Byte;         {number of retries}
   intBuff:          Integer;      {used internally for NSendRequest}
   TRelTime:         Byte          {release timer setting}

END;


XPPParamBlock =
PACKED RECORD
   qLink:               QElemPtr;      {next queue entry}
   qType:               Integer;       {queue type}
   ioTrap:              Integer;       {routine trap}
   ioCmdAddr:           Ptr;           {routine address}
   ioCompletion:        ProcPtr;       {completion routine}
   ioResult:            OSErr;         {result code}
   cmdResult:           LongInt;       {command result}
   ioVRefNum:           Integer;       {volume reference number}
   ioRefNum:            Integer;       {driver reference number}
   csCode:              Integer;       {primary command code}
   CASE XPPPrmBlkType OF
     xCallParam
       xppSubCode:      Integer;       {secondary command code}
       xppTimeOut:      Byte;          {timeout period for .XPP}
       xppRetry:        Byte;          {retry count}
       filler1:         Integer;       {reserved}
       zipBuffPtr:      Ptr;           {returned zone names}
       zipNumZones:     Integer;       {number of zones returned}
       zipLastFlag:     Byte;          {nonzero when all zone }
                                       { names have been returned}
       filler2:         Byte;          {reserved}
       zipInfoField: PACKED ARRAY[1..70] OF Byte
                                       {reserved for use by .XPP}
END;
XPPParmBlkPtr = ^XPPParamBlock;
```

```
TRCCB =
PACKED RECORD
   ccbLink:             TPCCB;        {link to next CCB}
   refNum:              Integer;      {reference number}
   state:               Integer;      {state of the connection end}
   userFlags:           Byte;         {user flags for connection}
   localSocket:         Byte;         {local socket number}
   remoteAddress:       AddrBlock;    {remote end internet address}
   attnCode:            Integer;      {attention code received}
   attnSize:            Integer;      {size of attention data}
   attnPtr:             Ptr;          {pointer to attention data}
   reserved:            PACKED ARRAY[1..220] OF Byte
                                      {reserved for use by ADSP}
END;

AddrBlock =
PACKED RECORD
   aNet:                Integer;      {network number}
   aNode:               Byte;         {node ID}
   aSocket:             Byte          {socket number}
END;

DSPParamBlock =
PACKED RECORD
   qLink:               QElemPtr;     {next queue entry}
   qType:               Integer;      {queue type}
   ioTrap:              Integer;      {routine trap}
   ioCmdAddr:           Ptr;          {routine address}
   ioCompletion:        ProcPtr;      {completion routine}
   ioResult:            OSErr;        {result code}
   ioNamePtr:           StringPtr;    {reserved}
   ioVRefNum:           Integer;      {reserved}
   ioCRefNum:           Integer;      {driver reference number}
   csCode:              Integer;      {primary command code}
   qStatus:             LongInt;      {reserved for ADSP}
   ccbRefNum:           Integer;      {CCB reference number}

   CASE Integer OF
   dspInit,
   dspCLInit:
   (
     ccbPtr:            TPCCB;        {pointer to CCB}
     userRoutine:       ProcPtr;      {pointer to user routine}
     sendQSize:         Integer;      {size of send queue}
     sendQueue:         Ptr;          {pointer to send queue}
     recvQSize:         Integer;      {size of receive queue}
     recvQueue:         Ptr;          {pointer to receive queue}
     attnPtr:           Ptr;          {pointer to attention- }
                                      { message buffer}
     localSocket:       Byte;         {local socket number}
     filler1:           Byte;         {filler for proper alignment}
   );
```

```
dspOpen,
dspCLListen,
dspCLDeny:
(
  localCID:          Integer;      {local connection ID}
  remoteCID:         Integer;      {remote connection ID}
  remoteAddress:     AddrBlock;    {remote internet address}
  filterAddress:     AddrBlock;    {address filter}
  sendSeq:           LongInt;      {send sequence number}
  sendWindow:        Integer;      {size of remote buffer}
  recvSeq:           LongInt;      {receive sequence number}
  attnSendSeq:       LongInt;      {attention send seq number}
  attnRecvSeq:       LongInt;      {attention receive seq num}
  ocMode:            Byte;         {connection-opening mode}
  ocInterval:        Byte;         {interval bet open requests}
  ocMaximum:         Byte;         {retries of open-conn req}
  filler2:           Byte;         {filler for proper alignment}
);

dspClose,
dspRemove:
(
  abort:             Byte;         {abort send requests}
  filler3:           Byte;         {filler for proper alignment}
);

dspStatus:
(
  statusCCB:         TPCCB;        {pointer to CCB}
  sendQPending:      Integer;      {bytes waiting in send queue}
  sendQFree:         Integer;      {available send-queue buffer}
  recvQPending:      Integer;      {bytes in receive queue}
  recvQFree:         Integer;      {avail receive-queue buffer}
)

dspRead,
dspWrite:
(
  reqCount:          Integer;      {requested number of bytes}
  actCount:          Integer;      {actual number of bytes}
  dataPtr:           Ptr;          {pointer to data buffer}
  eom:               Byte;         {1 if end of message}
  flush:             Byte;         {1 to send data now}
)

dspAttention:
(
  attnCode:          Integer;      {client attention code}
  attnSize:          Integer;      {size of attention data}
  attnData:          Ptr;          {pointer to attention data}
  attnInterval:      Byte;         {reserved}
  filler4:           Byte;         {filler for proper alignment}
)
```

```
    dspOptions:
    (
      sendBlocking:       Integer;      {send-blocking threshold}
      sendTimer:          Byte;         {reserved}
      rtmtTimer:          Byte;         {reserved}
      badSeqMax:          Byte;         {retransmit advice threshold}
      useCheckSum:        Byte;         {DDP checksum for packets}
    )

    dspNewCID:
    (
      newCID:             Integer       {new connection ID}
    )
  END;


  EParamBlock =
  PACKED RECORD
    qLink:                QElemPtr;     {next queue entry}
    qType:                Integer;      {queue type}
    ioTrap:               Integer;      {routine trap}
    ioCmdAddr:            Ptr;          {routine address}
    ioCompletion:         ProcPtr;      {completion routine}
    ioResult:             OSErr;        {result code}
    ioNamePtr:            StringPtr;    {driver name}
    ioVRefNum:            Integer;      {volume reference number}
    ioRefNum:             Integer;      {driver reference number}
    csCode:               Integer;      {primary command code}

    CASE Integer OF
    ENetWrite,
    ENetAttachPH,
    ENetDetachPH,
    ENetRead,
    ENetRdCancel,
    ENetGetInfo,
    ENetSetGeneral:
    (
    eProtType:            Integer;      {Ethernet protocol type}
    ePointer:             Ptr;          {pointer; use depends on }
                                        { function}
    eBuffSize:            Integer;      {buffer size}
    eDataSize:            Integer       {number of bytes read}
    );


    ENetAddMulti,
    ENetDelMulti:
    (
    eMultiAddr:     ARRAY[0..5] of Char   {multicast address}
    )
  END;
  EParamBlkPtr = ^EParamBlock;
```

Routines

Getting Information About the .MPP Driver

```
FUNCTION PGetAppleTalkInfo  (thePBptr: MPPPBPtr; async: Boolean) : OSErr;
```

Adding and Removing AppleTalk Transition Queue Entries

```
FUNCTION LAPAddATQ          (theATQEntry: ATQEntryPtr) : OSErr;
FUNCTION LAPRmvATQ          (theATQEntry: ATQEntryPtr) : OSErr;
```

Sending Messages to the AppleTalk Transition Queue

```
FUNCTION PATalkClosePrep    (thePBptr: MPPPBPtr; async: Boolean) : OSErr;
```

Defining Your Own AppleTalk Transition

```
PROCEDURE ATEvent           (event: LongInt; infoPtr: Ptr);
FUNCTION ATPreFlightEvent   (event,cancel: LongInt; infoPtr: Ptr) : OSErr;
```

Canceling All Calls to the ATPGetRequest Function

```
FUNCTION ATPKillAllGetReq   (thePBptr: ATPPBPtr; async: Boolean) : OSErr;
```

Obtaining Zone Information

```
FUNCTION GetMyZone          (thePBptr: XPPParmBlkPtr; async: Boolean) :
                             OSErr;
FUNCTION GetLocalZones      (thePBptr: XPPParmBlkPtr; async: Boolean) :
                             OSErr;
FUNCTION GetZoneList        (thePBptr: XPPParmBlkPtr; async: Boolean) :
                             OSErr;
```

Attaching and Detaching an Ethernet Protocol Handler

```
FUNCTION EAttachPH          (thePBptr: EParamBlkPtr; async: Boolean) :
                             OSErr;
FUNCTION EDetachPH          (thePBptr: EParamBlkPtr; async: Boolean) :
                             OSErr;
```

Writing and Reading Ethernet Packets

```
FUNCTION EWrite          (thePBptr: EParamBlkPtr; async: Boolean) :
                          OSErr;
FUNCTION ERead           (thePBptr: EParamBlkPtr; async: Boolean) :
                          OSErr;
FUNCTION ERdCancel       (thePBptr: EParamBlkPtr; async: Boolean) :
                          OSErr;
FUNCTION EGetInfo        (thePBptr: EParamBlkPtr; async: Boolean) :
                          OSErr;
FUNCTION ESetGeneral     (thePBptr: EParamBlkPtr; async: Boolean) :
                          OSErr;
```

Adding and Removing Ethernet Multicast Addresses

```
FUNCTION EAddMulti       (thePBptr: EParamBlkPtr; async: Boolean) :
                          OSErr;
FUNCTION EDelMulti       (thePBptr: EParamBlkPtr; async: Boolean) :
                          OSErr;
```

Global Variable

LapMgrPtr	The start of the LAP Manager

Result Codes

noErr	0	No error or unrecognized event code
qErr	–1	Queue element not found
closeErr	–24	Permission to close .MPP driver was denied
paramErr	–50	Version number is too high
ddpSktErr	–91	Error opening socket
eMultiErr	–91	Invalid address, address not found, or table is full
eLenErr	–92	Packet too large or first entry of the write-data structure did not contain the full 14-byte header
noBridgeErr	–93	No router is available
LAPProtErr	–94	Protocol handler is already attached, node's protocol table is full, no protocol handler is attached, or protocol handler pointer was not 0
excessCollsns	–95	Hardware error
memFullErr	–108	Insufficient memory in heap

reqFailed	–1096	Request to contact router failed; retry count exceeded
tooManyReqs	–1097	Too may concurrent requests
cbNotFound	–1102	Control block not found, no pending asynchronous calls, or ERead not active
noDataArea	–1104	Too may outstanding ATP calls
reqAborted	–1105	ERdCancel or EDetachPH function called
errOpenDenied	–1273	Open request denied by recipient
errDSPQueueSize	–1274	Send or receive queue is too small
errFwdReset	–1275	Read terminated by forward reset
errAttention	–1276	Attention message too long
errOpening	–1277	Attempt to open connection failed
errState	–1278	Bad connection state for this operation
errAborted	–1279	Request aborted by dspRemove or dspClose routine
errRefNum	–1280	Bad connection reference number
buf2SmallErr	–3101	Packet too large for buffer; partial data returned

Assembly-Language Information

Constants

```
;ADSP queue element equates & size
csQStatus       EQU     CSParam     ;adsp internal use
csCCBRef        EQU     csQStatus+4 ;refnum of ccb
```

AppleTalk Transition Queue Entry Data Structure

AeQQLink	long	next queue entry
AeQQType	word	reserved
AeQCallAddr	long	pointer to your routine

ADSP Connection Control Block Data Structure

ccbLink	long	link to next CCB
refNum	word	reference number
state	word	state of the connection end
userFlags	byte	user flags for connection
localSocket	byte	local socket number
remoteAddress	long	internet address of remote end
attnCode	word	attention code received
attnSize	word	size of received attention data
attnPtr	long	pointer to received attention data
reserved	220 bytes	reserved

XPP Parameter Block xCallParam Variant

←	16	ioResult	word	result code
→	26	csCode	word	routine selector; always xCall
→	28	xppSubCode	word	routine selector subcode
→	30	xppTimeOut	byte	retry interval in seconds
→	31	xppRetry	byte	retry count
→	34	zipBuffPtr	long	pointer to data buffer
←	38	zipNumZones	word	number of names returned
←	40	zipLastFlag	byte	nonzero if no more names
→	42	zipInfoField	70 bytes	for use by ZIP; first word set to 0

Parameter Block for dspInit and dspCLInit

←	16	ioResult	word	result code
→	24	ioCRefNum	word	driver reference number
→	26	csCode	word	dspInit or dspCLInit
←	32	ccbRefNum	word	reference number of CCB
→	34	ccbPtr	long	pointer to CCB
→	38	userRoutine	long	pointer to routine to call on connection events
→	42	sendQSize	word	size in bytes of the send queue
→	44	sendQueue	long	pointer to send queue
→	48	recvQSize	word	size in bytes of the receive queue
→	50	recvQueue	long	pointer to receive queue
→	54	attnPtr	long	pointer to buffer for incoming attention messages
↔	58	localSocket	byte	DDP socket number for this connection end

Parameter Block for dspOptions

←	16	ioResult	word	result code
→	24	ioCRefNum	word	driver reference number
→	26	csCode	word	always dspOptions

→	32	ccbRefNum	word	reference number of CCB
→	34	sendBlocking	word	send-blocking threshold
→	38	badSeqMax	byte	threshold to send retransmit advice
→	39	useCheckSum	byte	DDP checksum flag

Parameter Block for dspOpen, dspCLListen, and dspCLDeny

←	16	ioResult	word	result code
→	24	ioCRefNum	word	driver reference number
→	26	csCode	word	dspOpen, dspCLListen, or dspCLDeny
→	32	ccbRefNum	word	reference number of CCB
←	34	localCID	word	ID of this connection end
↔	36	remoteCID	word	ID of remote connection end
↔	38	remoteAddress	long	remote internet address
→	42	filterAddress	long	filter for open-connection requests
↔	46	sendSeq	long	initial send sequence number
↔	50	sendWindow	word	initial size of remote receive queue
→	52	recvSeq	long	initial receive sequence number
↔	56	attnSendSeq	long	attention send sequence number
→	60	attnRecvSeq	long	attention receive sequence number
→	64	ocMode	byte	connection-opening mode
→	65	ocInterval	byte	interval between open requests
→	66	ocMaximum	byte	retries of open-connection request

Parameter Block for dspNewCID

←	16	ioResult	word	result code
→	24	ioCRefNum	word	driver reference number
→	26	csCode	word	always dspNewCID
→	32	ccbRefNum	word	reference number of CCB
←	34	newCID	word	ID of new connection

Parameter Block for dspClose, dspRemove, and dspCLRemove

←	16	ioResult	word	result code
→	24	ioCRefNum	word	driver reference number
→	26	csCode	word	dspClose, dspRemove, or dspCLRemove
→	32	ccbRefNum	word	reference number of CCB
→	34	abort	byte	abort send requests or connection listener if not 0

Parameter Block for dspStatus

←	16	ioResult	word	result code
→	24	ioCRefNum	word	driver reference number
→	26	csCode	word	always dspStatus
→	32	ccbRefNum	word	reference number of CCB
←	34	statusCCB	pointer	pointer to CCB
←	38	sendQPending	word	bytes waiting to be sent or acknowledged
←	40	sendQFree	word	available send queue in bytes
←	42	recvQPending	word	bytes waiting to be read from queue
←	44	recvQFree	word	available receive queue in bytes

Parameter Block for dspRead and dspWrite

←	16	ioResult	word	result code
→	24	ioCRefNum	word	driver reference number
→	26	csCode	word	dspRead or dspWrite
→	32	ccbRefNum	word	reference number of CCB
→	34	reqCount	word	requested number of bytes
←	36	actCount	word	actual number of bytes read or written
→	38	dataPtr	pointer	pointer to data buffer
←	42	eom	byte	1 if end-of-message; 0 otherwise
→	43	flush	byte	1 to send data now; 0 otherwise

Parameter Block for dspAttention and dspReset

←	16	ioResult	word	result code
→	24	ioCRefNum	word	driver reference number
→	26	csCode	word	dspAttention or dspReset
→	32	ccbRefNum	word	reference number of CCB
→	34	attnCode	word	client attention code
→	36	attnSize	word	size of attention data in bytes
→	38	attnData	pointer	pointer to attention data

.ENET Driver Parameter Block

←	16	ioResult	word	result code
→	26	csCode	word	routine selector
→	28	eMultiAddr	6 bytes	multicast address
→	28	eProtType	word	Ethernet protocol type
→	30	ePointer	long	pointer
→	34	eBuffSize	word	size of buffer
←	36	eDataSize	word	number of bytes read

APPENDIX A: RESULT CODES

This appendix lists the result codes returned by functions described in this volume of *Inside Macintosh*. They are ordered by value, for convenience when debugging. The names and meanings of the result codes are also listed.

Some result codes are returned by more than one manager and therefore have more than one meaning. This appendix lists each meaning for these result codes.

For a list of result codes returned by each manager, see the summary at the end of the corresponding chapter.

Table A-1. Result codes

Value	Name	Meaning
0	noErr	No error
0	smNotTruncated	No truncation necessary
–1	smTruncErr	Truncation indicator alone is wider than the specified width
–1	qErr	Not in queue
–24	closeErr	Permission to close .MPP driver was denied
–27	abortErr	Publisher has written a new edition
–33	dirFulErr	Directory full
–34	dskFulErr	Disk full
–35	nsvErr	Volume not found
–36	ioErr	I/O error
–37	bdNamErr	Bad file name
–39	eofErr	No additional data in the format
–42	tmfoErr	Too many files open
–43	fnfErr	File not found; Folder not found; Edition container not found; Target not found
–44	wPrErr	Volume is locked through hardware
–45	fLckdErr	File locked
–45	flLckedErr	Publisher writing to an edition
–46	vLckdErr	Volume is locked through software
–47	fBsyErr	Section doing I/O
–48	dupFNErr	File found instead of folder
–49	opWrErr	File already open for writing

(Continued)

Table A-1. Result codes (Continued)

Value	Name	Meaning
–50	paramErr	Error in parameter list
–51	rfNumErr	Reference number invalid
–53	volOfflinErr	Volume is off line
–54	permErr	Not a subscriber; Software lock on file
–58	extFSErr	External file system—file system identifier is nonzero
–61	wrPermErr	Not a publisher
–91	ddpSktErr	Error opening socket
–91	eMultiErr	Invalid address or table is full
–92	eLenErr	Packet too large or first entry of the write-data structure did not contain the full 14-byte header
–93	noBridgeErr	No router is available
–94	LAPProtErr	Protocol handler is already attached, node's protocol table is full, protocol not attached, or protocol handler pointer was not 0
–95	excessCollsns	Hardware error
–102	noTypeErr	Format not available
–108	memFullErr	Ran out of memory
–109	nilHandleErr	GetHandleSize fails on baseText or substitutionText; NIL master pointer
–111	memWZErr	Attempt to operate on a free block; GetHandleSize fails on baseText or substitutionText
–120	dirNFErr	Directory not found
–123	wrgVolTypeErr	Not an HFS volume
–128	userCanceledErr	User canceled an operation
–147	regionTooBigError	Region too big or complex
–148	pixmapTooDeepErr	Pixel map record is deeper than 1 bit per pixel
–149	mfStackErr	Insufficient stack
–157	cDepthErr	Invalid pixel depth
–188	resourceInMemory	Resource already in memory
–189	writingPastEnd	Writing past end of file
–190	inputOutOfBounds	Offset or count out of bounds
–192	resNotFound	Resource not found
–199	mapReadErr	Map inconsistent with operation
–200	noHardwareErr	Required sound hardware not available

Table A-1. Result codes (Continued)

Value	Name	Meaning
–201	notEnoughHardwareErr	Insufficient hardware available
–203	queueFull	No room in the queue
–204	resProblem	Problem loading the resource
–205	badChannel	Channel is corrupt or unusable
–206	badFormat	Resource is corrupt or unusable
–207	notEnoughBufferSpace	Insufficient memory available
–208	badFileFormat	File is corrupt or unusable, or not AIFF or AIFF-C
–209	channelBusy	Channel is busy
–210	buffersTooSmall	Buffer is too small
–211	channelNotBusy	Channel not currently used
–212	noMoreRealTime	Not enough CPU time available
–213	badParam	A parameter is incorrect
–220	siNoSoundInHardware	No sound input hardware available
–221	siBadSoundInDevice	Invalid sound input device
–222	siNoBufferSpecified	No buffer specified
–223	siInvalidCompression	Invalid compression type
–224	siHardDiskTooSlow	Hard drive too slow to record
–225	siInvalidSampleRate	Invalid sample rate
–226	siInvalidSampleSize	Invalid sample size
–227	siDeviceBusyErr	Sound input device is busy
–228	siBadDeviceName	Invalid device name
–229	siBadRefNum	Invalid reference number
–230	siInputDeviceErr	Input device hardware failure
–231	siUnknownInfoType	Unknown type of information
–232	siUnknownQuality	Unknown quality
–299	nmTypErr	Invalid qType—must be ORD(nmType)
–308	smUnExBusErr	Unexpected bus error
–330	smBadRefId	Reference ID not found in list
–331	smBadsList	Bad sResource structure: ID1 < ID2 < ID3 . . .
–332	smReservedErr	Reserved field not zero
–338	smSelOOBErr	Selector out of bounds; function not implemented
–344	smNoMoresResources	Specified sResource data structure not found

(Continued)

Appendixes

Table A-1. Result codes (Continued)

Value	Name	Meaning
–346	smBadsPtrErr	Bad pointer was passed to sCaldSPointer function
–347	smByteLanesErr	ByteLanes field in card's format block was determined to be zero
–450	editionMgrInitErr	Manager not initialized or could not load package
–451	badSectionErr	Not a valid section type
–452	notRegisteredSectionErr	Not registered
–454	badSubPartErr	Bad edition container spec or invalid edition container
–460	multiplePublisherWrn	Already is a publisher
–461	containerNotFoundWrn	Alias was not resolved
–463	notThePublisherWrn	Not the publisher
–500	rgnTooBigErr	Bitmap would convert into a region greater than 64 KB
–600	procNotFound	No eligible process with specified process serial number
–601	memFragErr	Not enough room to launch application with special requirements
–602	appModeErr	Memory mode is 32-bit, but application is not 32-bit clean
–605	appMemFullErr	Partition size specified in 'SIZE' resource is not big enough for launch
–606	appIsDaemon	Application is background-only
–607	bufferIsSmall	Buffer is too small
–608	noOutstandingHLE	No outstanding high-level event
–609	connectionInvalid	Connection is invalid
–610	noUserInteractionAllowed	Attempted PostHighLevelEvent from background and no session yet established
–620	notEnoughMemoryErr	Insufficient physical memory
–621	notHeldErr	Specified range of memory is not held
–622	cannotMakeContiguousErr	Cannot make specified range contiguous
–623	notLockedErr	Specified range of memory is not locked
–624	interruptsMaskedErr	Called with interrupts masked
–625	cannotDeferErr	Unable to defer additional user functions
–800	rcDBNull	The data item was NULL
–801	rcDBValue	Data available or successfully retrieved
–802	rcDBError	Error executing function
–803	rcDBBadType	Next data item not of requested data type

Table A-1. Result codes (Continued)

Value	Name	Meaning
–804	rcDBBreak	Function timed out
–805	rcDBExec	Query currently executing
–806	rcDBBadSessID	Session ID is invalid
–807	rcDBBadSessNum	Invalid session number
–808	rcDBBadDDev	Couldn't find the specified database extension, or error occurred in opening database extension
–809	rcDBAsyncNotSupp	The database extension does not support asynchronous calls
–810	rcDBBadAsynchPB	Invalid parameter block specified
–811	rcDBNoHandler	There is no handler for this data type installed for the current application
–812	rcDBWrongVersion	Wrong version number
–813	rcDBPackNotInited	The InitDBPack function has not yet been called
–850	hmHelpDisabled	Help balloons are not enabled
–853	hmBalloonAborted	Because of constant cursor movement, the help balloon wasn't displayed
–854	hmSameAsLastBalloon	Menu and item are same as previous menu and item
–855	hmHelpManagerNotInited	Help menu not set up
–857	hmSkippedBalloon	No ballon content to fill in
–858	hmWrongVersion	Wrong version of Help Manager resource
–859	hmUnknownHelpType	Help message record contained a bad type
–861	hmOperationUnsupported	Bad method parameter
–862	hmNoBalloonUp	No balloon showing
–863	hmCloseViewActive	User using Close View won't let you remove balloon
–900	notInitErr	PPC Toolbox has not been initialized yet
–902	nameTypeErr	Invalid or inappropriate locationKindSelector in location name
–903	noPortErr	Invalid port name; Unable to open port or bad port reference number
–904	noGlobalsErr	System unable to allocate memory, critical error
–905	localOnlyErr	Network activity is currently disabled
–906	destPortErr	Port does not exist at destination
–907	sessTableErr	PPC Toolbox is unable to create a session
–908	noSessionErr	Invalid session reference number

(Continued)

Appendixes

Table A-1. Result codes (Continued)

Value	Name	Meaning
–909	badReqErr	Bad parameter or invalid state for this operation
–910	portNameExistsErr	Another port is already open with this name
–911	noUserNameErr	User name unknown on destination machine
–912	userRejectErr	Destination rejected the session request
–915	noResponseErr	Unable to contact application
–916	portClosedErr	The port was closed
–917	sessClosedErr	The session has closed
–919	badPortNameErr	PPC port record is invalid
–922	noDefaultUserErr	User has not specified owner name in Sharing Setup control panel
–923	notLoggedInErr	Default user reference number does not yet exist
–924	noUserRefErr	Unable to create a new user reference number
–925	networkErr	An error has occurred in the network
–926	noInformErr	PPCStart failed because target application did not have an inform pending
–927	authFailErr	User's password is wrong
–928	noUserRecErr	Invalid user reference number
–930	badServiceMethodErr	Service method is other than ppcServiceRealTime
–931	badLocNameErr	Location name is invalid
–932	guestNotAllowedErr	Destination port requires authentication
–1027	nbpDuplicate	Duplicate name exists already
–1096	reqFailed	Request to contact router failed; retry count exceeded
–1102	cbNotFound	Control block not found; no pending asynchronous calls
–1105	reqAborted	ERdCancel function called for this ERead
–1273	errOpenDenied	Open request denied by recipient
–1274	errDSPQueueSize	Send or receive queue is too small
–1275	errFwdReset	Read terminated by forward reset
–1276	errAttention	Attention message too long
–1277	errOpening	Attempt to open connection failed
–1278	errState	Bad connection state for this operation
–1279	errAborted	Request aborted by dspRemove or dspClose function
–1280	errRefNum	Bad connection reference number
–1300	fidNotFoundErr	File ID not found

Table A-1. Result codes (Continued)

Value	Name	Meaning
–1302	notAFileErr	Specified file is a directory
–1303	diffVolErr	Files on different volumes
–1304	catalogChangedErr	Catalog has changed and CatPosition may be invalid
–1305	desktopDamagedErr	The desktop database has become corrupted—the Finder will fix this, but if your application is not running with the Finder, use DTReset or DTDelete
–1700	errAECoercionFail	Data could not be coerced to the requested descriptor type
–1701	errAEDescNotFound	Descriptor record was not found
–1702	errAECorruptData	Data in an Apple event could not be read
–1703	errAEWrongDataType	Wrong descriptor type
–1704	errAENotAEDesc	Not a valid descriptor record
–1705	errAEBadListItem	Operation involving a list item failed
–1706	errAENewerVersion	Need a newer version of the Apple Event Manager
–1707	errAENotAppleEvent	Event is not an Apple event
–1708	errAEEventNotHandled	Event wasn't handled by an Apple event handler
–1709	errAEReplyNotValid	AEResetTimer was passed an invalid reply
–1710	errAEUnknownSendMode	Invalid sending mode was passed
–1711	errAEWaitCanceled	User canceled out of wait loop for reply or receipt
–1712	errAETimeout	Apple event timed out
–1713	errAENoUserInteraction	No user interaction allowed
–1714	errAENotASpecialFunction	Wrong keyword for a special function
–1715	errAEParamMissed	Handler did not get all required parameters
–1716	errAEUnknownAddressType	Unknown Apple event address type
–1717	errAEHandlerNotFound	No handler found for an Apple event or a coercion
–1718	errAEReplyNotArrived	Reply has not yet arrived
–1719	errAEIllegalIndex	Not a valid list index
–3101	buf2SmallErr	Packet too large for buffer; partial data returned
–5012	afpItemNotFound	Information not found
–5030	afpIconTypeError	Size of new icon and one it replaces don't match
–5550	gestaltUnknownErr	Could not obtain the response
–5551	gestaltUndefSelectorErr	Undefined selector
–5552	gestaltDupSelectorErr	Selector already exists

(Continued)

Appendixes

Table A-1. Result codes (Continued)

Value	Name	Meaning
–5553	gestaltLocationErr	Function not in system heap
–11000	pictInfoVersionErr	Version number not zero
–11001	pictInfoIDErr	Invalid PictInfo ID
–11002	pictInfoVerbErr	Invalid verb combination specified
–11003	cantLoadPickMethodErr	Custom pick method not in resource chain
–11004	colorsRequestedErr	Number out of range or greater than passed to NewPictInfo
–11005	pictureDataErr	Invalid picture data
–13000	pmBusyErr	Power Manager IC stuck busy
–13001	pmReplyTOErr	Timed out waiting to begin reply handshake
–13002	pmSendStartErr	Power Manager IC did not start handshake
–13003	pmSendEndErr	During send, Power Manager did not finish handshake
–13004	pmRecvStartErr	During receive, Power Manager did not start handshake
–13005	pmRecvEndErr	During receive, Power Manager did not finish handshake

APPENDIX B: ROUTINES AND THEIR MEMORY BEHAVIOR

This appendix lists the routines described in this volume of *Inside Macintosh* according to their reentrancy and memory behavior.

Table B-1 includes routines that may move or purge memory. You should not call these routines from within an interrupt, such as in a completion routine or a VBL task.

Table B-2 includes routines that do not move or purge memory, but that for some other reason you should not call from within an interrupt. For example, these routines may examine movable memory, or they might not be reentrant.

Table B-3 includes routines that you may call from within an interrupt.

Some routines exhibit different memory behavior when executed synchronously than when executed asynchronously. These routines are included in more than one list: a single dagger (†) indicates a synchronous execution of the routine, and a double dagger (‡) indicates an asynchronous execution.

Table B-1. Routines that may move or purge memory

AcceptHighLevelEvent
ActivatePalette
AECoerceDesc
AECoercePtr
AECreateAppleEvent
AECreateDesc
AEGetAttributeDesc
AECreateList
AEDeleteItem
AEDeleteKeyDesc
AEDeleteParam
AEDisposeDesc
AEDuplicateDesc
AEGetArray
AEGetAttributePtr
AEGetCoercionHandler
AEGetEventHandler
AEGetKeyDesc
AEGetKeyPtr
AEGetNthDesc
AEGetNthPtr
AEGetParamDesc
AEGetParamPtr
AEGetSpecialHandler
AEInstallCoercionHandler
AEInstallEventHandler
AEInstallSpecialHandler
AEInteractWithUser
AEProcessAppleEvent
AEPutArray
AEPutAttributeDesc
AEPutAttributePtr
AEPutDesc
AEPutKeyDesc
AEPutKeyPtr
AEPutParamDesc
AEPutParamPtr
AEPutPtr
AERemoveCoercionHandler
AERemoveEventHandler
AERemoveSpecialHandler
AEResetTimer

(Continued)

Table B-1. Routines that may move or purge memory (Continued)

AEResumeTheCurrentEvent
AESend
AESetInteractionAllowed
AESizeOfAttribute
AESizeOfKeyDesc
AESizeOfNthItem
AESizeOfParam
AnimateEntry
AnimatePalette
AppendDITL
AssociateSection
ATPreFlightEvent
BitMapToRegion
CallEditionOpenerProc
CallFormatIOProc
CloseEdition
CMY2RGB
Comp3to1
Comp6to1
CopyDeepMask
CountDITL
CopyPalette
CreateEditionContainerFile
CTab2Palette
CustomGetFile
CustomPutFile
DBBreak
DBDisposeQuery
DBEnd
DBExec
DBGetConnInfo
DBGetErr
DBGetItem
DBGetNewQuery
DBGetQueryResults
DBGetResultHandler
DBGetSessionNum
DBInit
DBInstallResultHandler
DBKill
DBRemoveResultHandler
DBResultsToText
DBSend
DBSendItem
DBStartQuery
DBState
DBUnGetItem
DeleteEditionContainerFile
DeleteUserIdentity
DeviceLoop
DisposePalette
EditionHasFormat
Exp1to3
Exp1to6
FindFolder
FindScriptRun
Fix2SmallFract
FlushFonts
FSpCreateResFile
FSpOpenDF
FSpOpenResFile
FSpOpenRF
GetColor
GetCTable
GetDefaultUser
GetEditionFormatMark
GetEditionInfo
GetEditionOpenerProc
GetFormatOrder
GetGray
GetLastEditionContainerUsed
GetNewPalette
GetPalette
GetPictInfo
GetPixMapInfo
GetProcessInformation
GetSpecificHighLevelEvent
GetStandardFormats
GoToPublisherSection
HasDepth
HCreateResFile
HiliteText

Table B-1. Routines that may move or purge memory (Continued)

HMBalloonPict
HMBalloonRect
HMExtractHelpMsg
HMGetBalloonWindow
HMGetDialogResID
HMGetFont
HMGetFontSizc
HMGetHelpMenuHandle
HMGetIndHelpMsg
HMGetMenuResID
HMIsBalloon
HMRemoveBalloon
HMScanTemplateItems
HMSetBalloons
HMSetDialogResID
HMSetFont
HMSetFontSize
HMSetMenuResID
HMShowBalloon
HMShowMenuBalloon
HOpen
HOpenDF
HOpenResFile
HOpenRF
HSL2RGB
HSV2RGB
InitDateCache
InitDBPack
InitEditionPack
InitGDevice
InitPalettes
InsertSRTRec
IntlTokenize
IPCListPorts †
IsOutline
IsRegisteredSection
IsSpecialFont
IUClearCache
IUCompPString
IUEqualPString
IUGetItlTable
IULangOrder
IULDateString
IULTimeString
IUMagIDPString
IUMagPString
IUScriptOrder
IUStringOrder
IUTextOrder
LaunchApplication
LaunchDeskAccessory
LowerText
MatchAlias
NChar2Pixel
NDrawJust
NewAlias
NewAliasMinimal
NewAliasMinimalFromFullpath
NewGDevice
NewGestalt
NewGWorld
NewPalette
NewPictInfo
NewPublisherDialog
NewPublisherExpDialog
NewScreenBuffer
NewSection
NewSubscriberDialog
NewSubscriberExpDialog
NewTempScreenBuffer
NFindWord
NMeasureJust
NPixel2Char
NPortionText
NSetPalette
OpenCPicture
OpenDF
OpenEdition
OpenNewEdition
OpenWD

(Continued)

Table B-1. Routines that may move or purge memory (Continued)

OutlineMetrics	RGB2HSV
Palette2CTab	SaveBack
PBDTCloseDown	SaveFore
PBDTDelete †	SectionOptionsDialog
PBDTGetPath	SectionOptionsExpDialog
PBDTOpenInform	SctDepth
PBDTReset †	SetEditionFormatMark
PBHOpenDF †	SetEditionOpenerProc
PBOpenDF	SetPalette
PBVolumeMount	SetResourceSize
PmBackColor	SetStylScrap
PmForeColor	SGetBlock
PostHighLevelEvent	SGetCString
PPCAccept †	SGetDriver
PPCBrowser	ShortenDITL
PPCClose †	SmallFract2Fix
PPCEnd †	SndAddModifier
PPCInform †	SndChannelStatus
PPCOpen †	SndControl
PPCRead †	SndDoCommand
PPCReject †	SndDoImmediate
PPCStart †	SndNewChannel
PPCWrite †	SndPlay
RawPrinterValues	SndPlayDoubleBuffer
ReadEdition	SndRecord
ReadPartialResource	SndRecordToFile
RecordColors	SndStartFilePlay
RecordPictInfo	SndStopFilePlay
RecordPixMapInfo	SPBBytesToMilliseconds
RegisterSection	SPBCloseDevice
ReplaceGestalt	SPBGetDeviceInfo
ReplaceText	SPBGetIndexedDevice
ResizePalette	SPBMillisecondsToBytes
ResolveAlias	SPBOpenDevice
ResolveAliasFile	SPBRecord
RestoreBack	SPBRecordToFile
RestoreDeviceClut	SPBSetDeviceInfo
RestoreFore	SPBSignInDevice
RetrievePictInfo	SPBSignOutDevice
RGB2CMY	StandardGetFile
RGB2HSL	StandardPutFile

Table B-1. Routines that may move or purge memory (Continued)

StartSecureSession	TESetStyle
Str2Format	TruncString
String2Date	TruncText
String2Time	UnRegisterSection
StripText	UpdateAlias
StripUpperText	UpdateGWorld
StyledLineBreak	UpperText
SysBeep	VisibleLength
TEGetPoint	WaitNextEvent
TEKey	WriteEdition
TempMaxMem	WritePartialResource
TempNewHandle	

Table B-2. Routines that do not move or purge memory but may not be called at interrupt time

AECountItems	FSpExchangeFiles
AEGetInteractionAllowed	FSpGetFInfo
AEGetTheCurrentEvent	FSpRename
AESetTheCurrentEvent	FSpRstFLock
AESuspendTheCurrentEvent	FSpSetFInfo
AllocContig	FSpSetFLock
AllowPurgePixels	GDeviceChanged
AOff	GetAliasInfo
AOn	GetCurrentProcess
AOnIgnoreModem	GetDeviceList
BOff	GetEntryColor
BOn	GetEntryUsage
CatMove	GetGDevice
CloseWD	GetGWorld
CTabChanged	GetGWorldDevice
DirCreate	GetLocalZones †
DisposeGWorld	GetMainDevice
DisposPictInfo	GetMaxDevice
DisposeScreenBuffer	GetMyZone †
DisposGDevice	GetNextDevice
FSMakeFSSpec	GetOutlinePreferred
FSpCatMove	GetPixBaseAddr
FSpCreate	GetPixelsState
FSpDelete	GetPortNameFromProcessSerialNumber
FSpDirCreate	GetPreserveGlyph

(Continued)

Table B-2. Routines that do not move or purge memory but may not be called at interrupt time (Continued)

GetProcessSerialNumberFromPortName
GetZoneList †
HCreate
HDelete
HGetFInfo
HGetVol
HMGetBalloons
HoldMemory
HRename
HRstFLock
HSetFInfo
HSetFLock
HSetVol
LAPAddATQ
LAPRmvATQ
LockPixels
ModemStatus
NoPurgePixels
ParseTable
PATalkClosePrep †
PBCatSearch †
PBCreateFileIDRef †
PBDeleteFileIDRef †
PBDTAddAPPL †
PBDTAddIcon †
PBDTFlush †
PBDTGetAPPL †
PBDTGetComment †
PBDTGetIcon †
PBDTGetIconInfo †
PBDTGetInfo †
PBDTRemoveAPPL †
PBDTRemoveComment †
PBDTSetComment †
PBExchangeFiles †
PBHGetVolParms †
PBMakeFSSpec †
PBResolveFileIDRef †
PBSetForeignPriv †
PGetAppleTalkInfo †
PixPatChanged
ReadLocation
SetCurrentA5
SetDeviceAttribute
SetEntryColor
SetEntryUsage
SetFrontProcess
SetGDevice
SetGWorld
SetOutlinePreferred
SetPixelsState
SetPreserveGlyph
SndDisposeChannel
TEContinuousStyle
TECustomHook
TEFeatureFlag
TempDisposHandle
TempFreeMem
TempHLock
TempHUnlock
TENumStyles
TestDeviceAttribute
ToggleDate
UnlockPixels
ValidDate
WriteLocation

Table B-3. Routines that may be called at interrupt time

ATPKillAllGetReq	InsXTime
BatteryStatus	IPCListPorts ‡
DebuggerEnter	LockMemory
DebuggerExit	LockMemoryContiguous
DebuggerGetMax	LongDate2Secs
DebuggerLockMemory	LongSecs2Date
DebuggerPoll	MACEVersion
DebuggerUnlockMemory	NMInstall
DeferUserFn	NMRemove
DisableIdle	OffscreenVersion
DisableWUTime	PageFaultFatal
EAddMulti	PATalkClosePrep ‡
EAttachPH	PBCatSearch ‡
EDelMulti	PBCreateFileIDRef ‡
EDetachPH	PBDeleteFileIDRef ‡
EGetInfo	PBDTAddAPPL ‡
EnableIdle	PBDTAddIcon ‡
EnterSupervisorMode	PBDTDelete ‡
ERdCancel	PBDTFlush ‡
ERead	PBDTGetAPPL ‡
ESetGeneral	PBDTGetComment ‡
EWrite	PBDTGetIcon ‡
Format2Str	PBDTGetIconInfo ‡
FormatStr2X	PBDTGetInfo ‡
FormatX2Str	PBDTRemoveAPPL ‡
Gestalt	PBDTRemoveComment ‡
GetCPUSpeed	PBDTReset ‡
GetFrontProcess	PBDTSetComment ‡
GetLocalZones ‡	PBExchangeFiles ‡
GetMyZone ‡	PBGetForeignPrivs
GetNextProcess	PBGetVolMountInfo
GetPageState	PBGetVolMountInfoSize
GetPaletteUpdates	PBHGetVolParms ‡
GetPhysical	PBMakeFSSpec ‡
GetWDInfo	PBResolveFileIDRef ‡
GetWUTime	PBSetForeignPriv ‡
GetZoneList ‡	PGetAppleTalkInfo ‡
IdleUpdate	PMgrVersion
InsTime	PortChanged

(Continued)

Appendixes

Table B-3. Routines that may be called at interrupt time (Continued)

PortionText
PPCAccept ‡
PPCClose ‡
PPCEnd ‡
PPCInform ‡
PPCOpcn ‡
PPCRead ‡
PPCReject ‡
PPCStart ‡
PPCWrite ‡
PrimeTime
QDDone
QDError
RmvTime
SameProcess
SCalcSPointer
SCalcStep
SCardChanged
SCkCardStatus
SDeleteSRTRec
SetA5
SetPaletteUpdates
SetSRsrcState
SetupAIFFHeader
SetupSndHeader
SetWUTime
SExec
SFindDevBase
SFindSInfoRecPtr
SFindSRsrcPtr
SFindStruct
SGetSRsrc
SGetTypeSRsrc
SleepQInstall
SleepQRemove
SndGetSysBeepState
SndManagerStatus
SndPauseFilePlay
SndSetSysBeepState
SndSoundManagerVersion
SNextRsrc
SNextTypeSRsrc
SOffsetData
SPBGetRecordingStatus
SPBPauseRecording
SPBResumeRecording
SPBStopRecording
SPBVersion
SPtrToSlot
SPutPRAMRec
SReadByte
SReadDrvrName
SReadFHeader
SReadInfo
SReadLong
SReadPBSize
SReadPRAMRec
SReadStruct
SReadWord
SRsrcInfo
SSearchSRT
StripAddress
SVersion
Translate24To32
UnholdMemory
UnlockMemory
WakeUpProcess

APPENDIX C: SYSTEM TRAPS

This appendix includes four tables listing the system traps and routines described in this volume of *Inside Macintosh.*

The first two tables list all of the system traps. Table C-1 lists them in alphabetical order by trap name and Table C-2 lists them in numerical order by trap word. If the name of the equivalent Pascal routine is different from the trap name, these tables list the Pascal name in parentheses under trap name.

The next two tables list the system traps that take selectors and the routines selected from them.

Table C-3 lists the traps that take selectors in alphabetical order by trap name. For each system trap, the Routine column lists the routines selected from the trap and the Selector column lists the corresponding selector. The routines are listed in numerical order by their selector value.

Table C-4 lists the routines from Table C-3 in alphabetical order by routine name. For each routine, the Trap name column lists the corresponding trap name and the Selector column lists the routine's selector.

Table C-1. System traps by trap name

Trap name	Trap word	Trap name	Trap word
_ActivatePalette	$AA94	_FontDispatch	$A854
_AliasDispatch	$A823	_Gestalt	$A1AD
_AllocContig	$A210	_GetCTable	$AA18
_AnimateEntry	$AA99	_GetDeviceList	$AA29
_AnimatePalette	$AA9A	_GetEntryColor	$AA9B
_BitMapToRegion	$A8D7	_GetEntryUsage	$AA9D
_CommToolboxDispatch	$A08B	_GetGDevice	$AA32
_CopyDeepMask	$AA51	_GetMainDevice	$AA2A
_CopyPalette	$AAA1	_GetMaxDevice	$AA27
_CTab2Palette	$AA9F	_GetNewPalette	$AA92
_DebugUtil	$A08D	_GetNextDevice	$AA2B
_DeferUserFn	$A08F	_GetPalette	$AA96
_DeviceLoop	$ABCA	_HCreate	$A208
_DisposePalette	$AA93	_HCreateResFile	$A81B
_DisposGDevice	$AA30	_HDelete	$A209

(Continued)

Table C-1. System traps by trap name (Continued)

Trap name	Trap word	Trap name	Trap word
_HFSDispatch	$A060	_Pack11	$A82D
_HGetVol	$A214	_Pack12	$A82E
_HighLevelFSDispatch	$AA52	_Pack13	$A82F
_HOpen	$A200	_Pack14	$A830
_HOpenResFile	$A81A	_Pack15	$A831
_HOpenRF	$A20A	_Palette2CTab	$AAA0
_HRename	$A20B	_PaletteDispatch	$AAA2
_HRstFLock	$A242	_PmBackColor	$AA98
_HSetFLock	$A241	_PmForeColor	$AA97
_HSetVol	$A215	_PPC	$A0DD
_IdleState	$A485	_PrimeTime	$A05A
_IdleUpdate	$A285	_QDError	$AA40
_InitGDevice	$AA2E	_QDExtensions	$AB1D
_InitPalettes	$AA90	_ReadXPRam	$A051
_InsTime	$A058	_ReplaceGestalt	$A5AD
_InsXTime	$A458	_ResourceDispatch	$A822
_LaunchApplication	$A9F2	_RmvTime	$A059
_LowerText	$A056	_ScriptUtil	$A8B5
_MemoryDispatch	$A05C	_SerialPower	$A685
_MemoryDispatchA0Result	$A15C	_SetDeviceAttribute	$AA2D
_NewGDevice	$AA2F	_SetEntryColor	$AA9C
_NewGestalt	$A3AD	_SetEntryUsage	$AA9E
_NewPalette	$AA91	_SetGDevice	$AA31
_NMInstall	$A05E	_SetPalette	$AA95
_NMRemove	$A05F	_SlpQInstall (SleepQInstall)	$A28A
_NSetPalette	$AA95	_SlpQRemove (SleepQRemove)	$A48A
_OpenCPicture	$AA20	_SlotManager	$A06E
_OSDispatch	$A88F	_SndAddModifier	$A802
_Pack3	$A9EA	_SndControl	$A806
_Pack6	$A9ED	_SndDisposeChannel	$A801
_Pack8	$A816	_SndDoCommand	$A803
_Pack9	$A82B		

Table C-1. System traps by trap name (Continued)

Trap name	Trap word	Trap name	Trap word
_SndDoImmediate	$A804	_TEDispatch	$A83D
_SndNewChannel	$A807	_TEKey	$A9DC
_SndPlay	$A805	_TestDeviceAttribute	$AA2C
_SoundDispatch	$A800	_Translate24To32	$A191
_StripAddress	$A055	_UpperText	$A456
_StripText	$A256	_WaitNextEvent	$A860
_StripUpperText	$A656	_WriteXPRam	$A052
_SysBeep	$A9C8		

Table C-2. System traps by trap word

Trap word	Trap name	Trap word	Trap name
$A051	_ReadXPRam	$A209	_HDelete
$A052	_WriteXPRam	$A20A	_HOpenRF
$A055	_StripAddress	$A20B	_HRename
$A056	_LowerText	$A210	_AllocContig
$A058	_InsTime	$A214	_HGetVol
$A059	_RmvTime	$A215	_HSetVol
$A05A	_PrimeTime	$A241	_HSetFLock
$A05C	_MemoryDispatch	$A242	_HRstFLock
$A05E	_NMInstall	$A256	_StripText
$A05F	_NMRemove	$A285	_IdleUpdate
$A060	_HFSDispatch	$A28A	_SlpQInstall (SleepQInstall)
$A06E	_SlotManager	$A3AD	_NewGestalt
$A08B	_CommToolboxDispatch	$A456	_UpperText
$A08D	_DebugUtil	$A458	_InsXTime
$A08F	_DeferUserFn	$A485	_IdleState
$A0DD	_PPC	$A48A	_SlpQRemove (SleepQRemove)
$A15C	_MemoryDispatchA0Result	$A5AD	_ReplaceGestalt
$A191	_Translate24To32	$A656	_StripUpperText
$A1AD	_Gestalt		
$A200	_HOpen		
$A208	_HCreate		

(Continued)

Appendixes

Table C-2. System traps by trap word (Continued)

Trap word	Trap name	Trap word	Trap name
$A685	_SerialPower	$AA2A	_GetMainDevice
$A800	_SoundDispatch	$AA2B	_GetNextDevice
$A801	_SndDisposeChannel	$AA2C	_TestDeviceAttribute
$A802	_SndAddModifier	$AA2D	_SetDeviceAttribute
$A803	_SndDoCommand	$AA2E	_InitGDevice
$A804	_SndDoImmediate	$AA2F	_NewGDevice
$A805	_SndPlay	$AA30	_DisposGDevice
$A806	_SndControl	$AA31	_SetGDevice
$A807	_SndNewChannel	$AA32	_GetGDevice
$A816	_Pack8	$AA40	_QDError
$A81A	_HOpenResFile	$AA51	_CopyDeepMask
$A81B	_HCreateResFile	$AA52	_HighLevelFSDispatch
$A823	_AliasDispatch	$AA90	_InitPalettes
$A82B	_Pack9	$AA91	_NewPalette
$A82D	_Pack11	$AA92	_GetNewPalette
$A82E	_Pack12	$AA93	_DisposePalette
$A82F	_Pack13	$AA94	_ActivatePalette
$A830	_Pack14	$AA95	_NSetPalette
$A831	_Pack15	$AA95	_SetPalette
$A83D	_TEDispatch	$AA96	_GetPalette
$A854	_FontDispatch	$AA97	_PmForeColor
$A860	_WaitNextEvent	$AA98	_PmBackColor
$A88F	_OSDispatch	$AA99	_AnimateEntry
$A8B5	_ScriptUtil	$AA9A	_AnimatePalette
$A8D7	_BitMapToRegion	$AA9B	_GetEntryColor
$A9C8	_SysBeep	$AA9C	_SetEntryColor
$A9DC	_TEKey	$AA9D	_GetEntryUsage
$A9EA	_Pack3	$AA9E	_SetEntryUsage
$A9ED	_Pack6	$AA9F	_CTab2Palette
$A9F2	_LaunchApplication	$AAA0	_Palette2CTab
$AA18	_GetCTable	$AAA1	_CopyPalette
$AA20	_OpenCPicture	$AAA2	_PaletteDispatch
$AA27	_GetMaxDevice	$AB1D	_QDExtensions
$AA29	_GetDeviceList	$ABCA	_DeviceLoop

Table C-3. System traps that take selectors

System trap	Selector	Routine
_AliasDispatch	$0000	FindFolder
$A823	$0002	NewAlias
	$0003	ResolveAlias
	$0005	MatchAlias
	$0006	UpdateAlias
	$0007	GetAliasInfo
	$0008	NewAliasMinimal
	$0009	NewAliasMinimalFromFullpath
	$000C	ResolveAliasFile
_CommToolboxDispatch	$0402	AppendDITL
$A08B	$0403	CountDITL
	$0404	ShortenDITL
_DebugUtil	$0000	DebuggerGetMax
$A08D	$0001	DebuggerEnter
	$0002	DebuggerExit
	$0003	DebuggerPoll
	$0004	GetPageState
	$0005	PageFaultFatal
	$0006	DebuggerLockMemory
	$0007	DebuggerUnlockMemory
	$0008	EnterSupervisorMode
_FontDispatch	$0000	IsOutline
$A854	$0001	SetOutlinePreferred
	$0008	OutlineMetrics
	$0009	GetOutlinePreferred
	$000A	SetPreserveGlyph
	$000B	GetPreserveGlyph
	$000C	FlushFonts
_HFSDispatch	$0001	OpenWD
$A060	$0002	CloseWD
	$0005	CatMove
	$0006	DirCreate
	$0007	GetWDInfo
	$0014	PBCreateFileIDRef
	$0015	PBDeleteFileIDRef

(Continued)

Table C-3. System traps that take selectors (Continued)

System trap	Selector	Routine
_HFSDispatch *(Continued)*	$0016	PBResolveFileIDRef
$A060	$0017	PBExchangeFiles
	$0018	PBCatSearch
	$001A	OpenDF
	$001A	PBHOpenDF
	$001A	PBOpenDF
	$001B	PBMakeFSSpec
	$0020	PBDTGetPath
	$0021	PBDTCloseDown
	$0022	PBDTAddIcon
	$0023	PBDTGetIcon
	$0024	PBDTGetIconInfo
	$0025	PBDTAddAPPL
	$0026	PBDTRemoveAPPL
	$0027	PBDTGetAPPL
	$0028	PBDTSetComment
	$0029	PBDTRemoveComment
	$002A	PBDTGetComment
	$002B	PBDTFlush
	$002C	PBDTReset
	$002D	PBDTGetInfo
	$002E	PBDTOpenInform
	$002F	PBDTDelete
	$0030	PBHGetVolParms
	$003F	PBGetVolMountInfoSize
	$0040	PBGetVolMountInfo
	$0041	PBVolumeMount
	$0060	PBGetForeignPrivs
	$0061	PBSetForeignPrivs
_HighLevelFSDispatch	$0001	FSMakeFSSpec
$AA52	$0002	FSpOpenDF
	$0003	FSpOpenRF
	$0004	FSpCreate
	$0005	FSpDirCreate
	$0006	FSpDelete
	$0007	FSpGetFInfo
	$0008	FSpSetFInfo
	$0009	FSpSetFLock
	$000A	FSpRstFLock

Table C-3. System traps that take selectors (Continued)

System trap	Selector	Routine
_HighLevelFSDispatch *(Continued)*	$000B	FSpRename
$AA52	$000C	FSpCatMove
	$000D	FSpOpenResFile
	$000E	FSpCreateResFile
	$000F	FSpExchangeFiles
_IdleState	$FFFF	GetCPUSpeed
$A485	$0000	EnableIdle
	$0001	DisableIdle
_MemoryDispatch	$0000	HoldMemory
$A05C	$0001	UnholdMemory
	$0002	LockMemory
	$0003	UnlockMemory
	$0004	LockMemoryContiguous
_MemoryDispatchA0Result	$0005	GetPhysical
$A15C		
_OSDispatch	$0015	TempMaxMem
$A88F	$0016	TempTopMem
	$0018	TempFreeMem
	$001D	TempNewHandle
	$001E	TempHLock
	$001F	TempHUnlock
	$0020	TempDisposeHandle
	$0033	AcceptHighLevelEvent
	$0034	PostHighLevelEvent
	$0035	GetProcessSerialNumberFromPortName
	$0036	LaunchDeskAccessory
	$0037	GetCurrentProcess
	$0038	GetNextProcess
	$0039	GetFrontProcess
	$003A	GetProcessInformation
	$003B	SetFrontProcess
	$003C	WakeUpProcess
	$003D	SameProcess
	$0045	GetSpecificHighLevelEvent
	$0046	GetPortNameFromProcessSerialNumber

(Continued)

Appendixes

Table C-3. System traps that take selectors (Continued)

System trap	Selector	Routine
_Pack3	$0005	StandardPutFile
$A9EA	$0006	StandardGetFile
	$0007	CustomPutFile
	$0008	CustomGetFile
_Pack6	$0014	IULDateString
$A9ED	$0016	IULTimeString
	$0018	IUClearCache
	$001A	IUMagPString
	$001C	IUMagIDPString
	$001E	IUScriptOrder
	$0020	IULangOrder
	$0022	IUTextOrder
	$0024	IUGetItlTable
_Pack8	$011E	AESetInteractionAllowed
$A816	$0204	AEDisposeDesc
	$0219	AEResetTimer
	$021A	AEGetTheCurrentEvent
	$021B	AEProcessAppleEvent
	$021D	AEGetInteractionAllowed
	$022B	AESuspendTheCurrentEvent
	$022C	AESetTheCurrentEvent
	$0405	AEDuplicateDesc
	$0407	AECountItems
	$040E	AEDeleteItem
	$0413	AEDeleteKeyDesc
	$0413	AEDeleteParam
	$0500	AEInstallSpecialHandler
	$0501	AERemoveSpecialHandler
	$052D	AEGetSpecialHandler
	$0603	AECoerceDesc
	$0609	AEPutDesc
	$0610	AEPutKeyDesc
	$0610	AEPutParamDesc
	$061C	AEInteractWithUser
	$0627	AEPutAttributeDesc
	$0706	AECreateList
	$0720	AERemoveEventHandler
	$0723	AERemoveCoercionHandler

Table C-3. System traps that take selectors (Continued)

System trap	Selector	Routine
_Pack8 *(Continued)*	$0812	AEGetKeyDesc
$A816	$0812	AEGetParamDesc
	$0818	AEResumeTheCurrentEvent
	$0825	AECreateDesc
	$0826	AEGetAttributeDesc
	$0828	AESizeOfAttribute
	$0829	AESizeOfKeyDesc
	$0829	AESizeOfParam
	$082A	AESizeOfNthItem
	$091F	AEInstallEventHandler
	$0921	AEGetEventHandler
	$0A02	AECoercePtr
	$0A08	AEPutPtr
	$0A16	AEPutAttributePtr
	$0A22	AEInstallCoercionHandler
	$0A0B	AEGetNthDesc
	$0A0F	AEPutKeyPtr
	$0A0F	AEPutParamPtr
	$0B0D	AEPutArray
	$0B14	AECreateAppleEvent
	$0B24	AEGetCoercionHandler
	$0D0C	AEGetArray
	$0D17	AESend
	$0E11	AEGetKeyPtr
	$0E11	AEGetParamPtr
	$0E15	AEGetAttributePtr
	$100A	AEGetNthPtr
_Pack9	$0D00	PPCBrowser
$A82B		
_Pack11	$0100	InitEditionPack
$A82D	$0206	UnRegisterSection
	$0208	IsRegisteredSection
	$0210	DeleteEditionContainerFile
	$0224	GoToPublisherSection
	$0226	GetLastEditionContainerUsed
	$022A	GetEditionOpenerProc
	$022C	SetEditionOpenerProc

(Continued)

Table C-3. System traps that take selectors (Continued)

System trap	Selector	Routine
_Pack11 *(Continued)*	$0232	NewSubscriberDialog
$A82D	$0236	NewPublisherDialog
	$023A	SectionOptionsDialog
	$0316	CloseEdition
	$040C	AssociateSection
	$0412	OpenEdition
	$0422	GetEditionInfo
	$050E	CreateEditionContainerFile
	$052E	CallEditionOpenerProc
	$0530	CallFormatIOProc
	$0604	RegisterSection
	$0618	EditionHasFormat
	$061E	GetEditionFormatMark
	$0620	SetEditionFormatMark
	$0814	OpenNewEdition
	$081A	ReadEdition
	$081C	WriteEdition
	$0A02	NewSection
	$0A28	GetStandardFormats
	$0B34	NewSubscriberExpDialog
	$0B38	NewPublisherExpDialog
	$0B3C	SectionOptionsExpDialog
_Pack12	$0001	Fix2SmallFract
$A82E	$0002	SmallFract2Fix
	$0003	CMY2RGB
	$0004	RGB2CMY
	$0005	HSL2RGB
	$0006	RGB2HSL
	$0007	HSV2RGB
	$0008	RGB2HSV
	$0009	GetColor
_Pack13	$0100	InitDBPack
$A82F	$020E	DBKill
	$0210	DBDisposeQuery
	$0215	DBRemoveResultHandler
	$030F	DBGetNewQuery
	$0403	DBEnd
	$0408	DBExec

Table C-3. System traps that take selectors (Continued)

System trap	Selector	Routine
_Pack13 *(Continued)*	$0409	DBState
$A82F	$040D	DBUnGetItem
	$0413	DBResultsToText
	$050B	DBBreak
	$0514	DBInstallResultHandler
	$0516	DBGetResultHandler
	$0605	DBGetSessionNum
	$0706	DBSend
	$0811	DBStartQuery
	$0A12	DBGetQueryResults
	$0B07	DBSendItem
	$0E02	DBInit
	$0E0A	DBGetErr
	$100C	DBGetItem
	$1704	DBGetConnInfo
_Pack14	$0002	HMRemoveBalloon
$A830	$0003	HMGetBalloons
	$0007	HMIsBalloon
	$0104	HMSetBalloons
	$0108	HMSetFont
	$0109	HMSetFontSize
	$010C	HMSetDialogResID
	$0200	HMGetHelpMenuHandle
	$020A	HMGetFont
	$020B	HMGetFontSize
	$020D	HMSetMenuResID
	$0213	HMGetDialogResID
	$0215	HMGetBalloonWindow
	$0314	HMGetMenuResID
	$040E	HMBalloonRect
	$040F	HMBalloonPict
	$0410	HMScanTemplateItems
	$0711	HMExtractHelpMsg
	$0B01	HMShowBalloon
	$0E05	HMShowMenuBalloon
	$1306	HMGetIndHelpMsg

(Continued)

Appendixes

Table C-3. System traps that take selectors (Continued)

System trap	Selector	Routine
_Pack15	$0206	DisposPictInfo
$A831	$0403	RecordPictInfo
	$0404	RecordPixMapInfo
	$0505	RetrievePictInfo
	$0602	NewPictInfo
	$0800	GetPictInfo
	$0801	GetPixMapInfo
_PaletteDispatch	$0002	RestoreDeviceClut
$AAA2	$0003	ResizePalette
	$0015	PMgrVersion
	$040D	SaveFore
	$040E	SaveBack
	$040F	RestoreFore
	$0410	RestoreBack
	$0417	GetPaletteUpdates
	$0616	SetPaletteUpdates
	$0A13	SetDepth
	$0A14	HasDepth
	$1219	GetGray
_PPC	$0000	PPCInit
$A0DD	$0001	PPCOpen
	$0002	PPCStart
	$0003	PPCInform
	$0004	PPCAccept
	$0005	PPCReject
	$0006	PPCWrite
	$0007	PPCRead
	$0008	PPCEnd
	$0009	PPCClose
	$000A	IPCListPorts
	$000C	DeleteUserIdentity
	$000D	GetDefaultUser
	$000E	StartSecureSession
_QDExtensions	$0000	NewGWorld
$AB1D	$0001	LockPixels
	$0002	UnlockPixels
	$0003	UpdateGWorld
	$0004	DisposeGWorld

Table C-3. System traps that take selectors (Continued)

System trap	Selector	Routine
_QDExtensions *(Continued)*	$0005	GetGWorld
$AB1D	$0006	SetGWorld
	$0007	CTabChanged
	$0008	PixPatChanged
	$0009	PortChanged
	$000A	GDeviceChanged
	$000B	AllowPurgePixels
	$000C	NoPurgePixels
	$000D	GetPixelsState
	$000E	SetPixelsState
	$000F	GetPixBaseAddr
	$0010	NewScreenBuffer
	$0011	DisposeScreenBuffer
	$0012	GetGWorldDevice
	$0013	QDDone
	$0014	OffscreenVersion
	$0015	NewTempScreenBuffer
_ResourceDispatch	$0001	ReadPartialResource
$A822	$0002	WritePartialResource
	$0003	SetResourceSize
_ScriptUtil	$8008FFF0	LongSecs2Date
$A8B5	$8008FFF2	LongDate2Secs
	$800E001C	HiliteText
	$8012FFE2	NFindWord
	$8012FFFC	GetFormatOrder
	$80160032	NDrawJust
	$801A0034	NMeasureJust
	$8202002A	IsSpecialFont
	$82040022	ParseTable
	$8204FFF8	InitDateCache
	$8204FFFA	IntlTokenize
	$8208FFE0	TruncString
	$820C0026	FindScriptRun
	$820CFFDC	ReplaceText
	$820CFFDE	TruncText
	$820CFFE4	ValidDate
	$820CFFEC	Str2Format

(Continued)

Appendixes

Table C-3. System traps that take selectors (Continued)

System trap	Selector	Routine
_ScriptUtil *(Continued)*	$820EFFEE	ToggleDate
$A8B5	$8210FFE6	FormatStr2X
	$8210FFE8	FormatX2Str
	$8210FFEA	Format2Str
	$8214FFF4	String2Time
	$8214FFF6	String2Date
	$8216002C	RawPrinterValues
	$821C0030	NChar2Pixel
	$821CFFFE	StyledLineBreak
	$8222002E	NPixel2Char
	$84080024	PortionText
	$84080028	VisibleLength
	$84120036	NPortionText
_SerialPower	$0000	BOn
$A685	$0004	AOn
	$0005	AOnIgnoreModem
	$0080	BOff
	$0084	AOff
_SlotManager	$0000	SReadByte
$A06E	$0001	SReadWord
	$0002	SReadLong
	$0003	SGetCString
	$0005	SGetBlock
	$0006	SFindStruct
	$0007	SReadStruct
	$0008	SVersion
	$0009	SetSRsrcState
	$000A	InsertSRTRec
	$000B	SGetSRsrc
	$000C	SGetTypeSRsrc
	$0010	SReadInfo
	$0011	SReadPRAMRec
	$0012	SPutPRAMRec
	$0013	SReadFHeader
	$0014	SNextRsrc
	$0015	SNextTypeSRsrc
	$0016	SRsrcInfo
	$0018	SCkCardStatus

Table C-3. System traps that take selectors (Continued)

System trap	Selector	Routine
_SlotManager *(Continued)*	$0019	SReadDrvrName
$A06E	$001B	SFindDevBase
	$0022	SCardChanged
	$0023	SExec
	$0024	SOffsetData
	$0026	SReadPBSize
	$0028	SCalcStep
	$002A	SSearchSRT
	$002B	SUpdateSRT
	$002C	SCalcsPointer
	$002D	SGetDriver
	$002E	SPtrToSlot
	$002F	SFindSInfoRecPtr
	$0030	SFindSRsrcPtr
	$0031	SDeleteSRTRec
_SoundDispatch	$00000010	MACEVersion
$A800	$00000014	SPBVersion
	$00040010	Comp3to1
	$00080010	Exp1to3
	$00100008	SndChannelStatus
	$00100010	Exp1to6
	$000C0008	SndSoundManagerVersion
	$000C0010	Comp6to1
	$00140008	SndManagerStatus
	$00180008	SndGetSysBeepState
	$001C0008	SndSetSysBeepState
	$00200008	SndPlayDoubleBuffer
	$01100014	SPBSignOutDevice
	$02040008	SndPauseFilePlay
	$021C0014	SPBCloseDevice
	$02280014	SPBPauseRecording
	$022C0014	SPBResumeRecording
	$02300014	SPBStopRecording
	$03080008	SndStopFilePlay
	$030C0014	SPBSignInDevice
	$03200014	SPBRecord
	$04240014	SPBRecordToFile
	$04400014	SPBMillisecondsToBytes

(Continued)

Appendixes

Table C-3. System traps that take selectors (Continued)

System trap	Selector	Routine
_SoundDispatch *(Continued)*	$04440014	SPBBytesToMilliseconds
$A800	$05140014	SPBGetIndexedDevice
	$05180014	SPBOpenDevice
	$06380014	SPBGetDeviceInfo
	$063C0014	SPBSetDeviceInfo
	$07080014	SndRecordToFile
	$08040014	SndRecord
	$0B4C0014	SetupAIFFHeader
	$0D000008	SndStartFilePlay
	$0D480014	SetupSndHeader
	$0E340014	SPBGetRecordingStatus
_TEDispatch	$0001	TESetStyle
$A83D	$0008	TEGetPoint
	$000A	TEContinuousStyle
	$000B	SetStylScrap
	$000C	TECustomHook
	$000D	TENumStyles
	$000E	TEFeatureFlag

Table C-4. Routines selected from system traps

Routine name	Trap name	Selector
AcceptHighLevelEvent	_OSDispatch	$0033
AECoerceDesc	_Pack8	$0603
AECoercePtr	_Pack8	$0A02
AECountItems	_Pack8	$0407
AECreateAppleEvent	_Pack8	$0B14
AECreateDesc	_Pack8	$0825
AECreateList	_Pack8	$0706
AEDeleteItem	_Pack8	$040E
AEDeleteKeyDesc	_Pack8	$0413
AEDeleteParam	_Pack8	$0413
AEDisposeDesc	_Pack8	$0204
AEDuplicateDesc	_Pack8	$0405
AEGetArray	_Pack8	$0D0C
AEGetAttributeDesc	_Pack8	$0826
AEGetAttributePtr	_Pack8	$0E15
AEGetCoercionHandler	_Pack8	$0B24
AEGetEventHandler	_Pack8	$0921

Table C-4. Routines selected from system traps (Continued)

Routine name	Trap name	Selector
AEGetInteractionAllowed	_Pack8	$021D
AEGetKeyDesc	_Pack8	$0812
AEGetKeyPtr	_Pack8	$0E11
AEGetNthDesc	_Pack8	$0A0B
AEGetNthPtr	_Pack8	$100A
AEGetParamDesc	_Pack8	$0812
AEGetParamPtr	_Pack8	$0E11
AEGetSpecialHandler	_Pack8	$052D
AEGetTheCurrentEvent	_Pack8	$021A
AEInstallCoercionHandler	_Pack8	$0A22
AEInstallEventHandler	_Pack8	$091F
AEInstallSpecialHandler	_Pack8	$0500
AEInteractWithUser	_Pack8	$061C
AEProcessAppleEvent	_Pack8	$021B
AEPutArray	_Pack8	$0B0D
AEPutAttributeDesc	_Pack8	$0627
AEPutAttributePtr	_Pack8	$0A16
AEPutDesc	_Pack8	$0609
AEPutKeyDesc	_Pack8	$0610
AEPutKeyPtr	_Pack8	$0A0F
AEPutParamDesc	_Pack8	$0610
AEPutParamPtr	_Pack8	$0A0F
AEPutPtr	_Pack8	$0A08
AERemoveCoercionHandler	_Pack8	$0723
AERemoveEventHandler	_Pack8	$0720
AERemoveSpecialHandler	_Pack8	$0501
AEResetTimer	_Pack8	$0219
AEResumeTheCurrentEvent	_Pack8	$0818
AESend	_Pack8	$0D17
AESetInteractionAllowed	_Pack8	$011E
AESetTheCurrentEvent	_Pack8	$022C
AESizeOfAttribute	_Pack8	$0828
AESizeOfKeyDesc	_Pack8	$0829
AESizeOfNthItem	_Pack8	$082A
AESizeOfParam	_Pack8	$0829
AESuspendTheCurrentEvent	_Pack8	$022B
AllowPurgePixels	_QDExtensions	$000B
AOff	_SerialPower	$0084

(Continued)

Appendixes

Table C-4. Routines selected from system traps (Continued)

Routine name	Trap name	Selector
AOn	_SerialPower	$0004
AOnIgnoreModem	_SerialPower	$0005
AppendDITL	_CommToolboxDispatch	$0402
AssociateSection	_Pack11	$040C
BOff	_SerialPower	$0080
BOn	_SerialPower	$0000
CallEditionOpenerProc	_Pack11	$052E
CallFormatIOProc	_Pack11	$0530
CatMove	_HFSDispatch	$0005
CloseEdition	_Pack11	$0316
CloseWD	_HFSDispatch	$0002
CMY2RGB	_Pack12	$0003
Comp3to1	_SoundDispatch	$00040010
Comp6to1	_SoundDispatch	$000C0010
CountDITL	_CommToolboxDispatch	$0403
CreateEditionContainerFile	_Pack11	$050E
CTabChanged	_QDExtensions	$0007
CustomGetFile	_Pack3	$0008
CustomPutFile	_Pack3	$0007
DBBreak	_Pack13	$050B
DBDisposeQuery	_Pack13	$0210
DBEnd	_Pack13	$0403
DBExec	_Pack13	$0408
DBGetConnInfo	_Pack13	$1704
DBGetErr	_Pack13	$0E0A
DBGetItem	_Pack13	$100C
DBGetNewQuery	_Pack13	$030F
DBGetQueryResults	_Pack13	$0A12
DBGetResultHandler	_Pack13	$0516
DBGetSessionNum	_Pack13	$0605
DBInit	_Pack13	$0E02
DBInstallResultHandler	_Pack13	$0514
DBKill	_Pack13	$020E
DBRemoveResultHandler	_Pack13	$0215
DBResultsToText	_Pack13	$0413
DBSend	_Pack13	$0706
DBSendItem	_Pack13	$0B07
DBStartQuery	_Pack13	$0811
DBState	_Pack13	$0409

Table C-4. Routines selected from system traps (Continued)

Routine name	Trap name	Selector
DBUnGetItem	_Pack13	$040D
DebuggerEnter	_DebugUtil	$0001
DebuggerExit	_DebugUtil	$0002
DebuggerGetMax	_DebugUtil	$0000
DebuggerLockMemory	_DebugUtil	$0006
DebuggerPoll	_DebugUtil	$0003
DebuggerUnlockMemory	_DebugUtil	$0007
DeleteEditionContainerFile	_Pack11	$0210
DeleteUserIdentity	_PPC	$000C
DirCreate	_HFSDispatch	$0006
DisableIdle	_IdleState	$0001
DisposeGWorld	_QDExtensions	$0004
DisposPictInfo	_Pack15	$0206
DisposeScreenBuffer	_QDExtensions	$0011
EditionHasFormat	_Pack11	$0618
EnableIdle	_IdleState	$0000
EnterSupervisorMode	_DebugUtil	$0008
Exp1to3	_SoundDispatch	$00080010
Exp1to6	_SoundDispatch	$00100010
FindFolder	_AliasDispatch	$0000
FindScriptRun	_ScriptUtil	$820C0026
Fix2SmallFract	_Pack12	$0001
FlushFonts	_FontDispatch	$000C
Format2Str	_ScriptUtil	$8210FFEA
FormatStr2X	_ScriptUtil	$8210FFE6
FormatX2Str	_ScriptUtil	$8210FFE8
FSMakeFSSpec	_HighLevelFSDispatch	$0001
FSpCatMove	_HighLevelFSDispatch	$000C
FSpCreate	_HighLevelFSDispatch	$0004
FSpCreateResFile	_HighLevelFSDispatch	$000E
FSpDelete	_HighLevelFSDispatch	$0006
FSpDirCreate	_HighLevelFSDispatch	$0005
FSpExchangeFiles	_HighLevelFSDispatch	$000F
FSpGetFInfo	_HighLevelFSDispatch	$0007
FSpOpenDF	_HighLevelFSDispatch	$0002
FSpOpenResFile	_HighLevelFSDispatch	$000D
FSpOpenRF	_HighLevelFSDispatch	$0003
FSpRename	_HighLevelFSDispatch	$000B

(Continued)

Appendixes

Table C-4. Routines selected from system traps (Continued)

Routine name	Trap name	Selector
FSpRstFLock	_HighLevelFSDispatch	$000A
FSpSetFInfo	_HighLevelFSDispatch	$0008
FSpSetFLock	_HighLevelFSDispatch	$0009
GDeviceChanged	_QDExtensions	$000A
GetAliasInfo	_AliasDispatch	$0007
GetColor	_Pack12	$0009
GetCPUSpeed	_IdleState	$FFFF
GetCurrentProcess	_OSDispatch	$0037
GetDefaultUser	_PPC	$000D
GetEditionFormatMark	_Pack11	$061E
GetEditionInfo	_Pack11	$0422
GetEditionOpenerProc	_Pack11	$022A
GetFormatOrder	_ScriptUtil	$8012FFFC
GetFrontProcess	_OSDispatch	$0039
GetGray	_PaletteDispatch	$1219
GetGWorld	_QDExtensions	$0005
GetGWorldDevice	_QDExtensions	$0012
GetLastEditionContainerUsed	_Pack11	$0226
GetNextProcess	_OSDispatch	$0038
GetOutlinePreferred	_FontDispatch	$0009
GetPageState	_DebugUtil	$0004
GetPaletteUpdates	_PaletteDispatch	$0417
GetPhysical	_MemoryDispatchA0Result	$0005
GetPictInfo	_Pack15	$0800
GetPixBaseAddr	_QDExtensions	$000F
GetPixelsState	_QDExtensions	$000D
GetPixMapInfo	_Pack15	$0801
GetPortNameFromProcessSerialNumber	_OSDispatch	$0046
GetPreserveGlyph	_FontDispatch	$000B
GetProcessInformation	_OSDispatch	$003A
GetProcessSerialNumberFromPortName	_OSDispatch	$0035
GetSpecificHighLevelEvent	_OSDispatch	$0045
GetStandardFormats	_Pack11	$0A28
GetWDInfo	_HFSDispatch	$0007
GoToPublisherSection	_Pack11	$0224
HasDepth	_PaletteDispatch	$0A14
HiliteText	_ScriptUtil	$800E001C
HMBalloonPict	_Pack14	$040F

Table C-4. Routines selected from system traps (Continued)

Routine name	Trap name	Selector
HMBalloonRect	_Pack14	$040E
HMExtractHelpMsg	_Pack14	$0711
HMGetBalloons	_Pack14	$0003
HMGetBalloonWindow	_Pack14	$0215
HMGetDialogResID	_Pack14	$0213
HMGetFont	_Pack14	$020A
HMGetFontSize	_Pack14	$020B
HMGetHelpMenuHandle	_Pack14	$0200
HMGetIndHelpMsg	_Pack14	$1306
HMGetMenuResID	_Pack14	$0314
HMIsBalloon	_Pack14	$0007
HMRemoveBalloon	_Pack14	$0002
HMScanTemplateItems	_Pack14	$0410
HMSetBalloons	_Pack14	$0104
HMSetDialogResID	_Pack14	$010C
HMSetFont	_Pack14	$0108
HMSetFontSize	_Pack14	$0109
HMSetMenuResID	_Pack14	$020D
HMShowBalloon	_Pack14	$0B01
HMShowMenuBalloon	_Pack14	$0E05
HoldMemory	_MemoryDispatch	$0000
HSL2RGB	_Pack12	$0005
HSV2RGB	_Pack12	$0007
InitDateCache	_ScriptUtil	$8204FFF8
InitDBPack	_Pack13	$0100
InitEditionPack	_Pack11	$0100
InsertSRTRec	_SlotManager	$000A
IntlTokenize	_ScriptUtil	$8204FFFA
IPCListPorts	_PPC	$000A
IsOutline	_FontDispatch	$0000
IsRegisteredSection	_Pack11	$0208
IsSpecialFont	_ScriptUtil	$8202002A
IUClearCache	_Pack6	$0018
IUGetItlTable	_Pack6	$0024
IULangOrder	_Pack6	$0020
IULDateString	_Pack6	$0014
IULTimeString	_Pack6	$0016
IUMagIDPString	_Pack6	$001C

(Continued)

Appendixes

Table C-4. Routines selected from system traps (Continued)

Routine name	Trap name	Selector
IUMagPString	_Pack6	$001A
IUScriptOrder	_Pack6	$001E
IUTextOrder	_Pack6	$0022
LaunchDeskAccessory	_OSDispatch	$0036
LockMemory	_MemoryDispatch	$0002
LockMemoryContiguous	_MemoryDispatch	$0004
LockPixels	_QDExtensions	$0001
LongDate2Secs	_ScriptUtil	$8008FFF2
LongSecs2Date	_ScriptUtil	$8008FFF0
MACEVersion	_SoundDispatch	$00000010
MatchAlias	_AliasDispatch	$0005
NChar2Pixel	_ScriptUtil	$821C0030
NDrawJust	_ScriptUtil	$80160032
NewAlias	_AliasDispatch	$0002
NewAliasMinimal	_AliasDispatch	$0008
NewAliasMinimalFromFullpath	_AliasDispatch	$0009
NewGWorld	_QDExtensions	$0000
NewPictInfo	_Pack15	$0602
NewPublisherDialog	_Pack11	$0236
NewPublisherExpDialog	_Pack11	$0B38
NewScreenBuffer	_QDExtensions	$0010
NewSection	_Pack11	$0A02
NewSubscriberDialog	_Pack11	$0232
NewSubscriberExpDialog	_Pack11	$0B34
NewTempScreenBuffer	_QDExtensions	$0015
NFindWord	_ScriptUtil	$8012FFE2
NMeasureJust	_ScriptUtil	$801A0034
NoPurgePixels	_QDExtensions	$000C
NPixel2Char	_ScriptUtil	$8222002E
NPortionText	_ScriptUtil	$84120036
OffscreenVersion	_QDExtensions	$0014
OpenDF	_HFSDispatch	$001A
OpenEdition	_Pack11	$0412
OpenNewEdition	_Pack11	$0814
OpenWD	_HFSDispatch	$0001
OutlineMetrics	_FontDispatch	$0008
PageFaultFatal	_DebugUtil	$0005
ParseTable	_ScriptUtil	$82040022
PBCatSearch	_HFSDispatch	$0018

Table C-4. Routines selected from system traps (Continued)

Routine name	Trap name	Selector
PBCreateFileIDRef	_HFSDispatch	$0014
PBDeleteFileIDRef	_HFSDispatch	$0015
PBDTAddAPPL	_HFSDispatch	$0025
PBDTAddIcon	_HFSDispatch	$0022
PBDTCloseDown	_HFSDispatch	$0021
PBDTDelete	_HFSDispatch	$002F
PBDTFlush	_HFSDispatch	$002B
PBDTGetAPPL	_HFSDispatch	$0027
PBDTGetComment	_HFSDispatch	$002A
PBDTGetIcon	_HFSDispatch	$0023
PBDTGetIconInfo	_HFSDispatch	$0024
PBDTGetInfo	_HFSDispatch	$002D
PBDTGetPath	_HFSDispatch	$0020
PBDTOpenInform	_HFSDispatch	$002E
PBDTRemoveAPPL	_HFSDispatch	$0026
PBDTRemoveComment	_HFSDispatch	$0029
PBDTReset	_HFSDispatch	$002C
PBDTSetComment	_HFSDispatch	$0028
PBExchangeFiles	_HFSDispatch	$0017
PBGetForeignPrivs	_HFSDispatch	$0060
PBGetVolMountInfo	_HFSDispatch	$0040
PBGetVolMountInfoSize	_HFSDispatch	$003F
PBHGetVolParms	_HFSDispatch	$0030
PBHOpenDF	_HFSDispatch	$001A
PBMakeFSSpec	_HFSDispatch	$001B
PBOpenDF	_HFSDispatch	$001A
PBResolveFileIDRef	_HFSDispatch	$0016
PBSetForeignPrivs	_HFSDispatch	$0061
PBVolumeMount	_HFSDispatch	$0041
PixPatChanged	_QDExtensions	$0008
PMgrVersion	_PaletteDispatch	$0015
PortChanged	_QDExtensions	$0009
PortionText	_ScriptUtil	$84080024
PostHighLevelEvent	_OSDispatch	$0034
PPCAccept	_PPC	$0004
PPCBrowser	_Pack9	$0D00
PPCClose	_PPC	$0009
PPCEnd	_PPC	$0008

(Continued)

Appendixes

Table C-4. Routines selected from system traps (Continued)

Routine name	Trap name	Selector
PPCInform	_PPC	$0003
PPCInit	_PPC	$0000
PPCOpen	_PPC	$0001
PPCRead	_PPC	$0007
PPCReject	_PPC	$0005
PPCStart	_PPC	$0002
PPCWrite	_PPC	$0006
QDDone	_QDExtensions	$0013
RawPrinterValues	_ScriptUtil	$8216002C
ReadEdition	_Pack11	$081A
ReadPartialResource	_ResourceDispatch	$0001
RecordPictInfo	_Pack15	$0403
RecordPixMapInfo	_Pack15	$0404
RegisterSection	_Pack11	$0604
ReplaceText	_ScriptUtil	$820CFFDC
ResizePalette	_PaletteDispatch	$0003
ResolveAlias	_AliasDispatch	$0003
ResolveAliasFile	_AliasDispatch	$000C
RestoreBack	_PaletteDispatch	$0410
RestoreDeviceClut	_PaletteDispatch	$0002
RestoreFore	_PaletteDispatch	$040F
RetrievePictInfo	_Pack15	$0505
RGB2CMY	_Pack12	$0004
RGB2HSL	_Pack12	$0006
RGB2HSV	_Pack12	$0008
SameProcess	_OSDispatch	$003D
SaveBack	_PaletteDispatch	$040E
SaveFore	_PaletteDispatch	$040D
SCalcsPointer	_SlotManager	$002C
SCalcStep	_SlotManager	$0028
SCardChanged	_SlotManager	$0022
SCkCardStatus	_SlotManager	$0018
SDeleteSRTRec	_SlotManager	$0031
SectionOptionsDialog	_Pack11	$023A
SectionOptionsExpDialog	_Pack11	$0B3C
SetDepth	_PaletteDispatch	$0A13
SetEditionFormatMark	_Pack11	$0620
SetEditionOpenerProc	_Pack11	$022C
SetFrontProcess	_OSDispatch	$003B

Table C-4. Routines selected from system traps (Continued)

Routine name	Trap name	Selector
SetGWorld	_QDExtensions	$0006
SetOutlinePreferred	_FontDispatch	$0001
SetPaletteUpdates	_PaletteDispatch	$0616
SetPixelsState	_QDExtensions	$000E
SetPreserveGlyph	_FontDispatch	$000A
SetResourceSize	_ResourceDispatch	$0003
SetSRsrcState	_SlotManager	$0009
SetStylScrap	_TEDispatch	$000B
SetupAIFFHeader	_SoundDispatch	$0B4C0014
SetupSndHeader	_SoundDispatch	$0D480014
SExec	_SlotManager	$0023
SFindDevBase	_SlotManager	$001B
SFindSInfoRecPtr	_SlotManager	$002F
SFindSRsrcPtr	_SlotManager	$0030
SFindStruct	_SlotManager	$0006
SGetBlock	_SlotManager	$0005
SGetCString	_SlotManager	$0003
SGetDriver	_SlotManager	$002D
SGetSRsrc	_SlotManager	$000B
SGetTypeSRsrc	_SlotManager	$000C
ShortenDITL	_CommToolboxDispatch	$0404
SmallFract2Fix	_Pack12	$0002
SndChannelStatus	_SoundDispatch	$00100008
SndGetSysBeepState	_SoundDispatch	$00180008
SndManagerStatus	_SoundDispatch	$00140008
SndPauseFilePlay	_SoundDispatch	$02040008
SndPlayDoubleBuffer	_SoundDispatch	$00200008
SndRecord	_SoundDispatch	$08040014
SndRecordToFile	_SoundDispatch	$07080014
SndSetSysBeepState	_SoundDispatch	$001C0008
SndSoundManagerVersion	_SoundDispatch	$000C0008
SndStartFilePlay	_SoundDispatch	$0D000008
SndStopFilePlay	_SoundDispatch	$03080008
SNextRsrc	_SlotManager	$0014
SNextTypeSRsrc	_SlotManager	$0015
SOffsetData	_SlotManager	$0024
SPBBytesToMilliseconds	_SoundDispatch	$04440014
SPBCloseDevice	_SoundDispatch	$021C0014

(Continued)

Table C-4. Routines selected from system traps (Continued)

Routine name	Trap name	Selector
SPBGetDeviceInfo	_SoundDispatch	$06380014
SPBGetIndexedDevice	_SoundDispatch	$05140014
SPBGetRecordingStatus	_SoundDispatch	$0E340014
SPBMillisecondsToBytes	_SoundDispatch	$04400014
SPBOpenDevice	_SoundDispatch	$05180014
SPBPauseRecording	_SoundDispatch	$02280014
SPBRecord	_SoundDispatch	$03200014
SPBRecordToFile	_SoundDispatch	$04240014
SPBResumeRecording	_SoundDispatch	$022C0014
SPBSetDeviceInfo	_SoundDispatch	$063C0014
SPBSignInDevice	_SoundDispatch	$030C0014
SPBSignOutDevice	_SoundDispatch	$01100014
SPBStopRecording	_SoundDispatch	$02300014
SPBVersion	_SoundDispatch	$00000014
SPtrToSlot	_SlotManager	$002E
SPutPRAMRec	_SlotManager	$0012
SReadByte	_SlotManager	$0000
SReadDrvrName	_SlotManager	$0019
SReadFHeader	_SlotManager	$0013
SReadInfo	_SlotManager	$0010
SReadLong	_SlotManager	$0002
SReadPBSize	_SlotManager	$0026
SReadPRAMRec	_SlotManager	$0011
SReadStruct	_SlotManager	$0007
SReadWord	_SlotManager	$0001
SRsrcInfo	_SlotManager	$0016
SSearchSRT	_SlotManager	$002A
StandardGetFile	_Pack3	$0006
StandardPutFile	_Pack3	$0005
StartSecureSession	_PPC	$000E
Str2Format	_ScriptUtil	$820CFFEC
String2Date	_ScriptUtil	$8214FFF6
String2Time	_ScriptUtil	$8214FFF4
StyledLineBreak	_ScriptUtil	$821CFFFE
SUpdateSRT	_SlotManager	$002B
SVersion	_SlotManager	$0008
TEContinuousStyle	_TEDispatch	$000A
TECustomHook	_TEDispatch	$000C
TEFeatureFlag	_TEDispatch	$000E

Table C-4. Routines selected from system traps (Continued)

Routine name	Trap name	Selector
TEGetPoint	_TEDispatch	$0008
TempDisposeHandle	_OSDispatch	$0020
TempFreeMem	_OSDispatch	$0018
TempHLock	_OSDispatch	$001E
TempHUnlock	_OSDispatch	$001F
TempMaxMem	_OSDispatch	$0015
TempNewHandle	_OSDispatch	$001D
TempTopMem	_OSDispatch	$0016
TENumStyles	_TEDispatch	$000D
TESetStyle	_TEDispatch	$0001
ToggleDate	_ScriptUtil	$820EFFEE
TruncString	_ScriptUtil	$8208FFE0
TruncText	_ScriptUtil	$820CFFDE
UnholdMemory	_MemoryDispatch	$0001
UnlockMemory	_MemoryDispatch	$0003
UnlockPixels	_QDExtensions	$0002
UnRegisterSection	_Pack11	$0206
UpdateAlias	_AliasDispatch	$0006
UpdateGWorld	_QDExtensions	$0003
ValidDate	_ScriptUtil	$820CFFE4
VisibleLength	_ScriptUtil	$84080028
WakeUpProcess	_OSDispatch	$003C
WriteEdition	_Pack11	$081C
WritePartialResource	_ResourceDispatch	$0002

Appendixes

APPENDIX D: GLOBAL VARIABLES

This appendix gives an alphabetical list of all system global variables described in this volume of *Inside Macintosh,* along with their locations in memory and a brief description of their contents.

Table D-1. Global variables

Name	**Location**	**Contents**
DeviceList	$8A8	Handle to the first element in the device list
GrayRgn	$9EE	Size and shape of current desktop
LapMgrPtr	$B18	Start of the LAP Manager
MainDevice	$8A4	Handle to the current main device
TEFindWord	$7F8	The low-memory address for TextEdit's word-breaking routine
TESysJust	$BAC	The system alignment whose default value is set by the last installed script
TheGDevice	$CC8	Handle to current active device
WordRedraw	$BA5	Value that indicates how much of a line must be redrawn after a character is entered

APPENDIX E: THE STANDARD ROMAN CHARACTER SET

This appendix lists the standard Roman character set in Table E-1. The Glyph column displays a glyph example or “np” for nonprinting characters. The Hex column lists the hexadecimal code for the character and the Dec column lists the decimal code. The fourth column lists the characters’ PostScript® names; characters that do not have PostScript names are listed in square brackets.

Table E-2 at the end of this appendix lists the standard PostScript characters that are not encoded in the standard Roman character set but which are in a standard TrueType 'sfnt' resource. You can access these glyphs using PostScript. See the *PostScript Language Reference Manual* for more information.

Table E-1. The standard Roman character set

Glyph	Hex	Dec	PostScript name
np	0	0	.null
np	1	1	[Start of heading]
np	2	2	[Start of text]
np	3	3	[End of text]
np	4	4	[End of transmission]
np	5	5	[Enquiry]
np	6	6	[Acknowledge]
np	7	7	[Bell]
np	8	8	[Backspace]
np	9	9	[Horizontal tabulation]
np	A	10	[Line feed]
np	B	11	[Vertical tabulation]
np	C	12	[Form feed]
np	D	13	nonmarkingreturn
np	E	14	[Shift out]
np	F	15	[Shift in]
np	10	16	[Data link escape]
np	11	17	[Device control 1]
np	12	18	[Device control 2]
np	13	19	[Device control 3]
np	14	20	[Device control 4]
np	15	21	[Negative acknowledge]
np	16	22	[Synchronous idle]
np	17	23	[End of transmission block]
np	18	24	[Cancel]
np	19	25	[End of medium]
np	1A	26	[Substitute]
np	1B	27	[Escape]
np	1C	28	[File separator]
np	1D	29	[Group separator]
np	1E	30	[Record separator]
np	1F	31	[Unit separator]
	20	32	space
!	21	33	exclam
"	22	34	quotedbl

(Continued)

Table E-1. The standard Roman character set (Continued)

Glyph	Hex	Dec	PostScript name
#	23	35	numbersign
$	24	36	dollar
%	25	37	percent
&	26	38	ampersand
'	27	39	quotesingle
(	28	40	parenleft
)	29	41	parenright
*	2A	42	asterisk
+	2B	43	plus
,	2C	44	comma
-	2D	45	hyphen
.	2E	46	period
/	2F	47	slash
0	30	48	zero
1	31	49	one
2	32	50	two
3	33	51	three
4	34	52	four
5	35	53	five
6	36	54	six
7	37	55	seven
8	38	56	eight
9	39	57	nine
:	3A	58	colon
;	3B	59	semicolon
<	3C	60	less
=	3D	61	equal
>	3E	62	greater
?	3F	63	question
@	40	64	at
A	41	65	A
B	42	66	B
C	43	67	C
D	44	68	D
E	45	69	E
F	46	70	F
G	47	71	G
H	48	72	H
I	49	73	I
J	4A	74	J
K	4B	75	K
L	4C	76	L
M	4D	77	M
N	4E	78	N
O	4F	79	O
P	50	80	P
Q	51	81	Q
R	52	82	R
S	53	83	S
T	54	84	T
U	55	85	U
V	56	86	V
W	57	87	W
X	58	88	X
Y	59	89	Y
Z	5A	90	Z
[	5B	91	bracketleft
\	5C	92	backslash
]	5D	93	bracketright
^	5E	94	asciicircum
_	5F	95	underscore

Table E-1. The standard Roman character set (Continued)

Glyph	Hex	Dec	PostScript name	Glyph	Hex	Dec	PostScript name
`	60	96	grave	np	7F	127	[Delete]
a	61	97	a	Ä	80	128	Adieresis
b	62	98	b	Å	81	129	Aring
c	63	99	c	Ç	82	130	Ccedilla
d	64	100	d	É	83	131	Eacute
e	65	101	e	Ñ	84	132	Ntilde
f	66	102	f	Ö	85	133	Odieresis
g	67	103	g	Ü	86	134	Udieresis
h	68	104	h	á	87	135	aacute
i	69	105	i	à	88	136	agrave
j	6A	106	j	â	89	137	acircumflex
k	6B	107	k	ä	8A	138	adieresis
l	6C	108	l	ã	8B	139	atilde
m	6D	109	m	å	8C	140	aring
n	6E	110	n	ç	8D	141	ccedilla
o	6F	111	o	é	8E	142	eacute
p	70	112	p	è	8F	143	egrave
q	71	113	q	ê	90	144	ecircumflex
r	72	114	r	ë	91	145	edieresis
s	73	115	s	í	92	146	iacute
t	74	116	t	ì	93	147	igrave
u	75	117	u	î	94	148	icircumflex
v	76	118	v	ï	95	149	idieresis
w	77	119	w	ñ	96	150	ntilde
x	78	120	x	ó	97	151	oacute
y	79	121	y	ò	98	152	ograve
z	8A	122	z	ô	99	153	ocircumflex
{	7B	123	braceleft	ö	9A	154	odieresis
|	7C	124	bar	õ	9B	155	otilde
}	7D	125	braceright	ú	9C	156	uacute
~	7E	126	asciitilde	ù	9D	157	ugrave

(Continued)

Table E-1. The standard Roman character set (Continued)

Glyph	Hex	Dec	PostScript name	Glyph	Hex	Dec	PostScript name
û	9E	158	ucircumflex	æ	BE	190	ae
ü	9F	159	udieresis	ø	BF	191	oslash
†	A0	160	dagger	¿	C0	192	questiondown
°	A1	161	degree	¡	C1	193	exclamdown
¢	A2	162	cent	¬	C2	194	logicalnot
£	A3	163	sterling	√	C3	195	radical
§	A4	164	section	*f*	C4	196	florin
•	A5	165	bullet	≈	C5	197	approxequal
¶	A6	166	paragraph	∆	C6	198	Delta
ß	A7	167	germandbls	«	C7	199	guillemotleft
®	A8	168	registered	»	C8	200	guillemotright
©	A9	169	copyright	…	C9	201	ellipsis
™	AA	170	trademark		CA	202	[No-break space]
´	AB	171	acute	À	CB	203	Agrave
¨	AC	172	dieresis	Ã	CC	204	Atilde
≠	AD	173	notequal	Õ	CD	205	Otilde
Æ	AE	174	AE	Œ	CE	206	OE
Ø	AF	175	Oslash	œ	CF	207	oe
∞	B0	176	infinity	–	D0	208	endash
±	B1	177	plusminus	—	D1	209	emdash
≤	B2	178	lessequal	“	D2	210	quotedblleft
≥	B3	179	greaterequal	”	D3	211	quotedblright
¥	B4	180	yen	‘	D4	212	quoteleft
µ	B5	181	mu	’	D5	213	quoteright
∂	B6	182	partialdiff	÷	D6	214	divide
∑	B7	183	summation	◊	D7	215	lozenge
∏	B8	184	product	ÿ	D8	216	ydieresis
π	B9	185	pi	Ÿ	D9	217	Ydieresis
∫	BA	186	integral	⁄	DA	218	fraction
ª	BB	187	ordfeminine	¤	DB	219	currency
º	BC	188	ordmasculine	‹	DC	220	guilsinglleft
Ω	BD	189	Omega	›	DD	221	guilsinglright

Table E-1. The standard Roman character set (Continued)

Glyph	Hex	Dec	PostScript name	Glyph	Hex	Dec	PostScript name
ﬁ	DE	222	fi	Ô	EF	239	Ocircumflex
ﬂ	DF	223	fl		F0	240	apple
‡	EO	224	daggerdbl	Ò	F1	241	Ograve
·	E1	225	periodcentered	Ú	F2	242	Uacute
‚	E2	226	quotesinglbase	Û	F3	243	Ucircumflex
„	E3	227	quotedblbase	Ù	F4	244	Ugrave
‰	E4	228	perthousand	ı	F5	245	dotlessi
Â	E5	229	Acircumflex	ˆ	F6	246	circumflex
Ê	E6	230	Ecircumflex	˜	F7	247	tilde
Á	E7	231	Aacute	¯	F8	248	macron
Ë	E8	232	Edieresis	˘	F9	249	breve
È	E9	233	Egrave	˙	FA	250	dotaccent
Í	EA	234	Iacute	˚	FB	251	ring
Î	EB	235	Icircumflex	¸	FC	252	cedilla
Ï	EC	236	Idieresis	˝	FD	253	hungarumlaut
Ì	ED	237	Igrave	˛	FE	254	ogonek
Ó	EE	238	Oacute	ˇ	FF	255	caron

The PostScript characters in Table E-2 do not have character codes in the standard Roman character set but are found in a standard TrueType 'sfnt' resource.

Table E-2. Unencoded PostScript characters

Cacute	lslash	brokenbar
cacute	Scaron	franc
Ccaron	scaron	minus
ccaron	Scedilla	multiply
dmacron	scedilla	onesuperior
Eth	Thorn	twosuperior
eth	thorn	threesuperior
Gbreve	Yacute	onequarter
gbreve	yacute	onehalf
Idot	Zcaron	threequarters
Lslash	zcaron	

GLOSSARY

activation procedure: A procedure supplied by your application for highlighting customized dialog box items that can be the target of keyboard input in a standard file dialog box.

active application: The application currently interacting with the user. Its icon appears on the right side of the menu bar. See also **current process, foreground process.**

active field: The target of keyboard input in a dialog box.

additional parameter: A keyword-specified descriptor record that the server application uses in addition to the data specified in the direct parameter. For example, an Apple event for arithmetic operations may include additional parameters that specify operands in an equation. Additional parameters may be required, or they may be optional.

address descriptor record: A descriptor record that contains the address of the target or source of an Apple event.

ADSP: See **AppleTalk Data Stream Protocol.**

advance width: The full width of a glyph, measured from the glyph origin to the other side of the glyph, including any white space on either side. See also **glyph origin.**

AEIMP: See **Apple Event Interprocess Messaging Protocol.**

AEP: See **AppleTalk Echo Protocol.**

AE record: A record of data type AERecord that contains a list of parameters for an Apple event. See also **Apple event parameter.**

A5 world: An area of memory in the application's partition that contains QuickDraw global variables and the application's global variables, parameters, and jump table—all of which are accessed through the A5 register.

AFP: See **AppleTalk Filing Protocol.**

AIFF: See **Audio Interchange File Format.**

alert sound: See **system alert sound.**

alias: An object on the desktop that represents another file, directory, or volume. An alias looks like the icon of its **target,** but its name is displayed in a different font style. The style depends on the **system script;** for Roman and most other scripts, alias names are displayed in italic. Aliases give users more flexibility in organizing their desktops and offer a convenient way to store local copies of large or dynamic files that reside on file servers.

alias file: A file that contains a record that points to another file, directory, or volume. An alias file is displayed by the Finder as an **alias.**

alias record: A data structure created by the Alias Manager to identify a file, folder, or volume.

alignment: The horizontal placement of lines of text with respect to the left and right edges of the destination rectangle. Alignment can be flush left, flush right, centered, or justified (that is, flush on both the left and right edges of the destination rectangle). TextEdit supports text alignment that is flush left, centered, flush right, and flush according to the line direction of the script. TextEdit does not support fully justified alignment. The Script Manager supplies routines you can use to provide support for fully justified text in your applications. See also **justification.**

alphabetic: Used to describe a type of character representation in which characters symbolize, more or less, the discrete phonemic elements in the languages represented by the script. For example, Roman script letters are alphabetic.

alternate rectangle: A rectangle used by the Help Manager (under some circumstances) for transposing a help balloon's **tip** when trying to fit the balloon on screen. For all help resources except the 'hdlg' resource, the Help Manager moves the tip to different sides of the hot rectangle. For 'hdlg' resources, however, the Help Manager allows you to specify alternate rectangles for transposing balloon tips. You can also specify alternate rectangles when you use the HMShowBalloon and HMShowMenuBalloon functions. Compare **hot rectangle.**

animated color: A usage category for colors in a palette. It specifies that a palette entry is to be used for color animation effects.

Apple event: A high-level event that adheres to the **Apple Event Interprocess Messaging Protocol.** An Apple event consists of attributes (including the event class and event ID, which identify the event and its task) and, usually, parameters (which contain data used by the target application of the event). See also **Apple event attribute, Apple event parameter.**

Apple event attribute: A **keyword-specified descriptor record** that identifies the event class, event ID, target application, or some other characteristic of an Apple event. Taken together, the attributes of an Apple event identify the event and denote the task to be performed on the data specified in the Apple event's parameters. Compared to parameters (which contain data used only by the target application of the Apple event), attributes contain information that can be used by both the Apple Event Manager and the target application. See also **Apple event parameter.**

Apple event dispatch table: A table that the Apple Event Manager uses to map Apple events to application-defined functions called **Apple event handlers.**

Apple event handler: An application-defined function that extracts pertinent data from an Apple event, performs the action requested by the Apple event, and returns a result.

Apple Event Interprocess Messaging Protocol (AEIMP): A standard defined by Apple Computer, Inc., for communication and data sharing among applications. High-level events that adhere to this protocol are called **Apple events.**

Apple event parameter: A keyword-specified descriptor record that contains data which the target application of an Apple event must use. Compared to attributes (which contain information that can be used by both the Apple Event Manager and the target application), parameters contain data used only by the target application of the Apple event. See also **Apple event attribute, direct parameter, optional parameter, required parameter.**

Apple event record: A record of data type AppleEvent that contains a list of **keyword-specified descriptor records.** These descriptor records describe—at least—the attributes necessary for an Apple event; they may also describe parameters for the Apple event. Apple Event Manager functions are used to add parameters to an Apple event record.

Apple Menu Items folder: A directory located in the System Folder for storing desk accessories, applications, folders, and aliases that the user wants to display in and access from the Apple menu.

AppleTalk connection file: A file of file type 'adev' that contains a **link access protocol** implementation for a data link (ELAP for EtherTalk, for example).

AppleTalk Data Stream Protocol (ADSP): An AppleTalk protocol that appears to its clients to maintain an open pipeline between two entities on the internet. Either entity can write a stream of bytes to the pipeline or read data bytes from the pipeline. ADSP is a symmetrical protocol.

AppleTalk Echo Protocol (AEP): An AppleTalk protocol that listens for special packets sent by other nodes and that, when it receives such a packet, echoes it back to the sender.

AppleTalk Filing Protocol (AFP): An AppleTalk protocol that provides an interface between an application and a file server. AFP is a client of ASP and is used to access AppleShare file servers on Macintosh computer workstations. See also **AppleTalk Session Protocol.**

AppleTalk Phase 2: The changes to AppleTalk, other than ADSP and the LAP Manager, included as part of system software version 7.0.

AppleTalk Session Protocol (ASP): An AppleTalk protocol that sets up and maintains sessions between a workstation and a server. ASP is a nonsymmetrical protocol—that is, only one of the two entities involved in the session (the workstation) can send commands. The other entity (the server) is restricted to responding to the commands.

AppleTalk Transaction Protocol (ATP): An AppleTalk protocol that provides loss-free communications by retransmitting any data packets that are lost. ATP is a transaction-based protocol.

AppleTalk transition: A message sent by the AppleTalk Manager or by an application to all of the entries in the **AppleTalk Transition Queue.** AppleTalk transitions indicate such occurrences as the opening or closing of the .MPP driver.

AppleTalk Transition Queue: An operating-system queue maintained by the **LAP Manager.** Each of the entries in the AppleTalk Transition Queue is called each time one of a set of predefined AppleTalk transitions occurs. An application can also use LAP Manager routines to call the elements in the AppleTalk Transition Queue.

application heap: An area of memory in the application **partition** that contains the application's 'CODE' segment 1, data structures, resources, and other code segments as needed.

application result handler: A **result handler** that is associated with a particular application. Compare **system result handler.**

Arabic calendar: The lunar calendar used in much of the Arabic world.

ascent line: An imaginary horizontal line that usually marks the tops of the tallest glyphs in a font.

ASP: See **AppleTalk Session Protocol.**

ATP: See **AppleTalk Transaction Protocol.**

Audio Interchange File Format (AIFF): A sound storage file format designed to allow easy exchange of audio data among applications.

authentication: The process of establishing the identity of a user. The authentication mechanism of the PPC Toolbox identifies each user through an assigned name and password.

A/UX Toolbox: A library that enables a program running under the A/UX operating system to call Macintosh User Interface Toolbox routines and Macintosh Operating System routines.

background-only application: An application that does not have a user interface. A background-only application does not call the InitWindows procedure and is identified by having the onlyBackground flag set in its 'SIZE' resource.

background process: A process that isn't currently interacting with the user. Compare **foreground process.**

backing-store file: The file that **virtual memory** uses to store the contents of unneeded pages of memory.

backing-store order: The order in which character codes are stored in memory.

backing volume: See **paging device.**

balloon definition function: An implementation of a window definition function that defines the general appearance of a **help balloon.**

base line: An imaginary line on which the glyphs in a line of text appear to sit.

Bézier curve: A curve defined by three outline points: two on-curve points that serve as endpoints, and one off-curve point that determines the degree of curvature.

bidirectional script system: A script system in which text is generally flush right and most characters are written from right to left, but some text is written left to right as well. Arabic and Hebrew are examples of bidirectional script systems. See also **script system.**

bitmap: A set of bits that represents the positions and states of a corresponding set of items, such as pixels.

bitmapped font: A collection of bitmapped glyphs in a particular typeface, size, and style.

bitmapped glyph: A **glyph** in a bitmapped font that exists in a computer file or in memory as a bitmap, is drawn as a pixel pattern on the display screen, and is sent to the printer as graphics data.

bounding box: The smallest rectangle that encloses the bitmap of a glyph.

brightness: A measurement of the amount of black in a color—the less black, the brighter the color. Brightness is equivalent to lightness in the HLS color system, and it is equivalent to value in the HSV color system.

broadcast address: The Ethernet address for which all nodes accept packets just as they do for their permanently assigned Ethernet hardware addresses. The broadcast address is $FF-FF-FF-FF-FF-FF. See also **multicast address.**

bundle bit: A flag in a file's FInfo record that informs the Finder that a 'BNDL' resource exists for the file. A file's FInfo record is stored in a volume's **catalog.** The Finder uses the information in the 'BNDL' resource to associate icons with the file.

canonical number format: A private, internal format that specifies how a number is written in a way that is independent of country, language, and other cultural considerations.

caret position: A location on the screen corresponding to a leading or trailing edge of a displayed character. In **mixed-directional text,** one **character offset** may correspond to two character positions, and one caret position may correspond to two character offsets.

catalog: A list of all files and folders stored on a volume.

CCB: See **connection control block.**

character: A symbol standing for a sound, syllable, or concept used in a script; one of the simple elements of a human language. A character may represent the concept of, for example, a lowercase "b", the number "2", or the arithmetic operator "+". Characters that can be displayed or printed—such as letters, numbers, and punctuation—are represented by glyphs. See also **glyph.**

character code: A hexadecimal number from $00 through $FF that represents the character that a key or key combination stands for.

character offsets: Byte offsets of the characters in the text buffer. The values of the character offsets correspond to the **backing-store order** of characters.

character representation: The ways in which scripts use symbols in relationship to sounds, concepts, letters, and one another to create words as the basic components of language. Scripts may use **alphabetic, syllabic,** or **ideographic** methods of character representation.

character set encoding: The numeric codes that represent the characters of a script in memory.

client: In AppleTalk, a protocol that uses services of another protocol in order to carry out some functions.

client application: An application that uses the **Apple Event Interprocess Messaging Protocol** to request a service—for example, printing a list of files, spell-checking a list of words, or performing a numerical calculation—from another application (called a **server application**). These applications can reside on the same local computer or on remote computers connected to a network.

closed connection: The state of a connection when both connection ends terminate the link and dispose of the connection information each maintains. Compare **half-open connection, open connection.**

coercion handler: A routine that coerces data from one **descriptor type** to another.

color grafPort: A data structure that describes a window's portion of the color graphics environment, including its pixel map, the graphics pen position, and the foreground and background colors. It is defined by a record of data type CGrafPort. See also **pixel map.**

colorizing: The process of substituting a color for black or white in an image.

color table: A data structure containing a number of RGB color records. Many color tables are used for color look-up, notably the color look-up table (CLUT) that is associated with a screen device and describes the colors the device can display.

common parent: The lowest-level directory that appears in the pathnames of multiple files or directories on the same volume.

compatibility: The ability of an application program to execute properly in different operating environments.

connection control block (CCB): A data structure that is used by ADSP to store state information about the connection end. See also **AppleTalk Data Stream Protocol.**

connection end: The combination of an AppleTalk socket and the ADSP information maintained by the socket client.

connection listener: A connection end that waits passively to receive a connection request and then passes the connection request on to its client, the connection server.

connection listening socket: A socket that accepts ADSP requests to open connections and passes them on to a socket client. Such sockets are normally used only by connection servers.

connection server: A routine that accepts an open-connection request passed to it by a connection listener and selects a socket to respond to the request.

context: The information about a **process** maintained by the Process Manager. This information includes the current state of the process, the address and size of its **partition,** its type, its creator, a copy of its low-memory globals, information about its 'SIZE' resource, and a **process serial number.**

context dependence: In text, when the glyph corresponding to a character may be modified depending on the preceding and following characters.

contextual script system: A script system in which the displayed glyph for a character depends on the adjacent characters—for example, Arabic. See also **script system.**

continuous play from disk: See **play from disk.**

contour: One closed loop in a TrueType outline glyph, defined by a group of **outline points.**

control panel: A dialog box defined by a file of file type 'cdev'. A control panel allows the user to set or control some feature of hardware or software, such as the volume of the speaker or the number of colors displayed on screen.

control panel file: A file of file type 'cdev'. See also **control panel.**

Control Panels folder: A directory located in the System Folder for storing control panels, which allow users to modify the work environment of their Macintosh computer.

core Apple event: An Apple event that nearly all applications can use to communicate. The suite of core Apple events is described in the *Apple Event Registry;* Apple Computer, Inc., recommends that all applications support the core Apple events.

courteous color: A usage category for colors in a palette. It denotes the color as not demanding a close match when the color is displayed.

current process: The process that is currently executing and whose **A5 world** is valid; this process can be in the background or foreground.

custom Apple event: An Apple event defined by you for use by your own applications. You should register all of your custom Apple events with Macintosh Developer Technical Support. You can choose to publish your Apple events in the *Apple Event Registry* so that other applications can share them, or you may choose to keep them unpublished for exclusive use by your own applications.

customized icon: An icon created by the user or by an application and stored with a resource ID of –16455 in the resource fork of a file. A file with a customized icon has the hasCustomIcon bit set in its Finder flags field.

database extension: The interface between the Data Access Manager and a data server.

Datagram Delivery Protocol (DDP): A protocol that provides socket-to-socket delivery of data packets within an AppleTalk internet.

data link: A physical communications connection and the protocol that implements it, including the cabling and the encoding or modulation of data.

data server: An application that acts as an interface between a database extension on a Macintosh computer and a data source, which can be on the Macintosh computer or on a remote host computer. A data server can be a database server program that can provide an interface to a variety of different databases, or it can be the data source itself, such as a Macintosh application.

DDP: See **Datagram Delivery Protocol.**

dead key: A specially designated key or modifier-and-key combination that usually produces no immediate effect when pressed, but instead affects the character or characters produced when the next key (called the *completer key*) is pressed. For example, Option-E has no effect; however, when you press E after pressing Option-E, "é" appears.

descent line: An imaginary line that usually marks the furthest distance below the base line of the descenders of glyphs in a particular font.

descriptor list: A record of data type AEDescList that contains a list of **descriptor records.**

descriptor record: A record of data type AEDesc that consists of a handle to data and a **descriptor type** that identifies the type of the data referred to by the handle. Descriptor records are the fundamental structures from which Apple events are constructed.

descriptor type: An identifier for the type of data referred to by the handle in a **descriptor record.**

desktop database: A database of icons, file types, applications, and comments maintained by the Finder for all volumes over 2 MB.

Desktop Folder: A directory, located at the root level of each volume, used by the Finder for storing information about the icons that appear on the desktop area of the screen. The Desktop Folder is invisible to the user. What the user sees on screen is the union of the contents of Desktop Folders for all mounted volumes.

diacritical mark: A sign that modifies the implicit sound or value of the character with which it is associated.

dialog hook function: A function supplied by your application for handling item hits in a dialog box.

direction run: A contiguous (in memory) sequence of characters all written in the same direction—for example, left to right or right to left.

directory: A subdivision of a volume, available in the Hierarchical File System (HFS). A directory can contain files and other directories.

direct parameter: The parameter in an Apple event that contains the data to be used by the server application. For example, a list of documents to be opened is specified in the direct parameter of the Open Documents event. See also **Apple event parameter.**

direct pixel: A pixel whose value directly specifies an RGB color.

disk cache: A part of RAM that acts as an intermediate buffer when data is read from and written to file systems on secondary storage devices.

display list: In a standard file dialog box, the list of the files, folders, and volumes at one level of the display hierarchy, from which the user can select items.

display order: The left-to-right order in which glyphs are drawn on a screen by QuickDraw. The Script Manager handles differences between **backing-store order** and QuickDraw display order. For example, Hebrew characters appear on the screen so that the glyph corresponding to the first character in the string actually appears on the right of the string.

dithering: The process of mixing colors to create the effect of additional colors.

dpi: Dots-per-inch; used to measure the resolution of a screen or printer.

dual caret: A primary caret and a secondary caret, each measuring half the line's height. The high (primary) caret is displayed at the primary caret position for the character offset in the primary line direction. The low (secondary) caret is displayed at the secondary caret position for the character offset. When the caret position is unambiguous (for example, not on a direction boundary), the primary and secondary carets are at the same position, so the user sees one caret. See also **primary caret, primary caret position, secondary caret, secondary caret position.**

dynamic window: A window that may change its title or reposition any of the objects within its content area.

edition: The data written to an edition container by a publisher. A publisher writes data to an edition whenever a user saves a document that contains a publisher, and subscribers in other documents may read the data from the edition whenever it is updated. See also **publisher, subscriber.**

edition container: A file that holds edition data, represented on the desktop by an edition icon. An edition container obtains its data from a publisher within a document. See also **edition, publisher.**

environmental selector: A selector code that returns information about the operating environment that can be used by the requesting application to guide its actions. Compare **informational selector.**

event class: An attribute that identifies a group of related Apple events. The event class appears in the message field of the Apple event's event record. In conjunction with the event ID attribute, the event class specifies what action an Apple event performs. See also **Apple event attribute.**

event ID: An attribute that identifies a particular Apple event within a group of related Apple events. The event class appears in the where field of the Apple event's event record. In conjunction with the event class attribute, the event ID specifies what action an Apple event performs. See also **Apple event attribute.**

explicit color: A usage category for colors in a palette. It specifies that the color table index corresponding to that palette entry is to determine the color to display.

extended network: A network of a type that allows a range of network numbers. Each node in an extended network must be specified by both its 16-bit network number and its 8-bit node ID.

Extensions folder: A directory located in the System Folder for storing system extension files such as printer and network drivers and files of types 'INIT', 'scri', and 'appe'.

file filter function: A function supplied by your application for determining which files the user can open through a standard file dialog box.

file ID: An unchanging number assigned by the File Manager to identify a file on a volume. When it establishes a file ID, the File Manager records the filename and parent directory ID of the file. The Alias Manager records a file's ID to help identify it if it is moved or renamed.

file system specification (FSSpec) record: A record that identifies a stored file or directory by volume reference number, parent directory ID, and name. The file system specification record is the file-identification convention adopted by system software version 7.0.

Finder flags: Bits in the fdFlags field of a file's FInfo record; these bits are used by the Finder and by applications for setting and reading certain information about the file, such as whether the file is an alias file, whether it has a bundle resource, whether it is a stationery pad, and whether it has a customized icon.

font: (1) For bitmapped fonts, a complete set of characters in one typeface, size, and style. (2) For outline fonts, a complete set of characters in one typeface and style. See also **bitmapped font, outline font.**

font family: A complete set of glyphs for one typeface, including all available styles and sizes of the glyphs in that font. A font family may include both bitmapped and outline fonts. For example, the Geneva font family includes 9-point to 36-point glyphs in italic, bold, underline, and other styles.

font scaling: The process of changing a glyph from one size or shape to another. The Font Manager can scale bitmapped and outline fonts in three ways: changing a glyph's point size on the same display device, modifying the glyph but keeping the point size constant when using a different display device, and altering the shape of a glyph.

font script: The script that corresponds to the font of the current grafPort.

font size: The size of the glyphs in a font in points, measured from the base line of one line of text to the base line of the next line of single-spaced text.

font style: Stylistic variations in the appearance of a typeface, such as italic, bold, and underline.

foreground process: The process currently interacting with the user; it appears to the user as the active application. The foreground process displays its menu bar, and its windows are in front of the windows of all other applications. Compare **background process**.

functional-area Apple event: An Apple event supported by applications with related features—for example, an Apple event related to text manipulation for word-processing applications, or an Apple event related to graphics manipulation for drawing applications. Functional-area Apple events are defined by Apple Computer, Inc., in consultation with interested developers, and they are published in the *Apple Event Registry*.

gamma table: A table used by a video card driver to correct for the fact that the intensity of each color on a video display is not linearly proportional to the intensity of the electron beam. The gamma table helps the video driver to provide the most accurate colors possible for a video display. Because the user might prefer a nonstandard color correction, many developers of video cards provide more than one gamma table for a given card.

Gestalt function: See **selector function.**

glyph: A distinct visual representation of a **character** that a display device, such as a monitor or printer, can display. One glyph can represent a single character, such as a lowercase "a"; more than one character, such as the "fi" ligature, which is two characters but only one glyph; or a nonprinting character, such as the space character.

glyph origin: A point on the **base line** where QuickDraw begins drawing a glyph. The glyph origin may not represent a visible point on the glyph, since white space to the left of the glyph may be specified. See also **bounding box, left-side bearing.**

graphics device record: A data structure that describes the characteristics of a display device, such as a video card.

graphics environment: The combination of one or more grafPorts, which contain information about windows, and graphics device records, which contain information about display devices attached to a computer system.

gray region: The region that defines the desktop, or the display area of all active devices, excluding the menu bar on the main screen and the rounded corners on the outermost screens. It is the area in which windows can be moved. See also **main screen.**

Gregorian calendar: The calendar used in Europe and America. It is not universally accepted—for example, entirely different calendar systems are often used in Japan, China, and the Middle East.

half-open connection: The state of a connection when one connection end is established, but the other connection end is unreachable or has disposed of its connection information. No communication can occur over a half-open connection. Compare **closed connection, open connection.**

help balloon: A rounded-rectangle window that contains explanatory information for the user. With tips pointing at the objects they annotate, help balloons look like the bubbles used for dialog in comic strips. Help balloons are turned on by the user from the Help menu; when Balloon Help assistance is on, a help balloon appears whenever the user moves the cursor over its **hot rectangle.** See also **alternate rectangle.**

hicharge counter: A counter in the Macintosh Portable computer that measures the time required to raise the battery voltage to 7.2 volts.

high-level event: An event that your application can send to another application to transmit some information, to receive from it some information, or to have it perform some action.

hot rectangle: An area defined to display a help balloon whenever the user moves the cursor over it. Compare **alternate rectangle.**

hue: An arbitrary assignment of numbers to colors as used in the HLS and HSV color systems.

icon family: The set of icons that represent an object, such as an application or document, on the desktop. An entire icon family consists of large (32-by-32 pixel) and small (16-by-16 pixel) icons, each with a mask, and each available in three different versions of color: black and white, 4 bits of color data per pixel, and 8 bits of color data per pixel.

ideographic: Used to describe a type of character representation in which characters do not represent pronunciation alone, but are also related to the component meanings of words. For example, Japanese Kanji, Chinese Hanzi, and Korean Hanja are ideographic.

idle state: A state in which the Macintosh Portable computer slows from its normal 16 MHz clock speed to a 1 MHz clock speed. The Power Manager puts the Macintosh Portable in the idle state when the system has been inactive for 15 seconds.

informational selector: A selector code that only provides information and should never be used as an indication of some feature's existence. Compare **environmental selector.**

inhibited color: A usage category for colors in a palette. It specifies the devices on which the color should not be displayed.

inline input: A keyboard input method (often used for double-byte script systems) in which conversion from a phonetic to an ideographic representation of a character takes place at the current line position where the text is intended to appear rather than in a separate window. This allows the user to type text directly in the line instead of in a special conversion window.

instructions: Commands that a font manufacturer includes with a TrueType font that instruct the Font Manager how to improve the appearance of outline glyphs under various conditions, such as low resolution or small point size.

interapplication communication (IAC): A collection of features, provided by the Edition Manager, Apple Event Manager, Event Manager, and PPC Toolbox, that help applications work together. You can use these managers to share data, send and receive events, or exchange low-level message blocks.

international resources: Resources that are used specifically by the Macintosh Script Management System, including the International Utilities Package. The international resources contain information specific to language or region, such as date and time formats. You can use multiple formats for different languages or regions with the same script system by adding multiple versions of the international resources. Each installed script has one or more 'itl0', 'itl1', 'itl2', 'itl4', and optional 'itl5' resources, and the resource IDs are generally in the range used for that script's fonts.

internet address: An AppleTalk address that includes the socket number, node ID, and network number.

jump table: An area of memory in the application partition that contains one entry for every externally referenced routine in every code segment of your application. The jump table is the means by which the loading and unloading of segments is implemented.

justification: A type of alignment that involves the spreading or compressing of printed text to fit into a given line width—so that it is flush on both the left and right edges of the destination rectangle. Also called *full justification*. See also **alignment.**

keyboard icon: A small icon associated with each keyboard layout ('KCHR' resource). Before system software version 7.0, the keyboard icon was of type 'SICN'; in version 7.0, the keyboard icon includes an icon family with types 'kcs#', 'kcs4', and 'kcs8'. These icons are used in the new Keyboard menu and the Keyboard control panel.

keyboard resources: A category of files that are stored in a resource file by the Resource Manager and are used by the Macintosh Script Management System, including the International Utilities Package. The keyboard resources include some localizable information such as keyboard layouts ('KCHR' resources) as well as hardware-specific information (for example, the 'KMAP' and 'KCAP' resources).

keyboard script: The script for keyboard input. It determines the character input method and the keyboard mapping—that is, what character codes are produced when a sequence of keys is pressed.

keyword: A four character code used to uniquely identify the **descriptor record** for either an attribute or a parameter in an Apple event. In Apple Event Manager functions, constants are typically used to represent the four-character codes.

keyword-specified descriptor record: A record of data type AEKeyDesc that consists of a **keyword** and a **descriptor record.** Keyword-specified descriptor records are used to describe the attributes and parameters of an Apple event.

language: On the Macintosh computer, the graphic representation of words and methods of combining words, as opposed to the spoken representation of words. This has implications for the treatment of languages, including the numeric codes assigned to represent each language. A spoken language that may be written in more than one script is treated on the Macintosh as several languages: one for each script in which the language is written. See also **language code, natural language, programming language, script, script code.**

language code: A number used to indicate a particular written version of a language on the Macintosh. In system software version 7.0, constants for these numbers are defined in the MPW files Language.p, LanguageEqu.a, and Language.h.

LAP Manager: A set of operating-system utilities that provide a standard interface between the AppleTalk protocols and the various **link access protocols,** such as LocalTalk (LLAP), EtherTalk (ELAP), and TokenTalk (TLAP).

leading: Pronounced "LED-ing"; the amount of blank vertical space between the **descent line** of one line of text and the **ascent line** of the next line of single-spaced text.

left-side bearing: The offset from the **glyph origin** to the left edge of the **bounding box.**

line spacing: The leading of a font plus the distance from the **ascent line** to the **descent line.**

link access protocol: An AppleTalk protocol that controls the access of a node to the network hardware. A link access protocol makes it possible for many nodes to share the same communications hardware.

localization: The process of adapting software to a particular region, language, and culture. Script and language adaptations are necessary but not sufficient for this process. Localization also includes date and time formats, keyboard resources, and fonts.

localized system software: Macintosh system software that has been adapted to a particular region, language, and culture. Japanese system software is the combination of the U.S. system software (including the Roman Script System, the Macintosh Operating System, the Toolbox, and so forth) and the Japanese Script System, all of which are adapted for use in Japan. The French and Turkish versions of the Macintosh system software are examples of localized variations of the U.S. system software that do not include a second script system.

location name: An identifier for the network location of the computer on which a port resides. The PPC Toolbox provides the location name. It contains an object string, a type string, and a zone. An application can specify an **alias** for its location name by modifying its type string. See also **port.**

luminance: The intensity of light in a color. Color QuickDraw uses a color's luminance to convert the color to an appropriate gray-scale color.

MACE: See **Macintosh Audio Compression and Expansion.**

Macintosh Audio Compression and Expansion (MACE): A set of Sound Manager routines that allow your application to compress and expand audio data.

Macintosh Script Management System: The Script Manager and one or more Macintosh script systems.

main screen: The screen on which the menu bar appears. QuickDraw uses it to determine global coordinates.

major switch: The Process Manager switches the context of the **foreground process** with the context of a **background process** (including the A5 worlds and low-memory globals) and brings the background process to the front, sending the previous foreground process to the background. See also **context.**

message block: A byte stream that an open application uses to send data to and receive data from another open application (which can be located on the same computer or across a network). The PPC Toolbox delivers message blocks to an application in the same sequence in which they were sent.

minimum partition size: The actual partition size limit below which your application cannot run.

minor switch: The Process Manager switches the **context** of a process to give time to a **background process** without bringing the background process to the front.

mixed-directional text: The combination of scripts with left-to-right and right-to-left directional text—within a single line.

modal-dialog filter function: A function supplied by your application for handling events received from the Event Manager while a dialog box is displayed.

mouse-down region: The region between the caret position and the middle of an adjacent character mapped unambiguously to a single character offset.

multibyte script system: A script system that represents exceedingly large character sets and requires comprehensive procedures for character input. Examples of multibyte script systems are Japanese, Chinese, and Korean. See also **script system.**

multicast address: An Ethernet address for which the node accepts packets just as it does for its permanently assigned Ethernet hardware address. In a multicast address, the low-order bit of the high-order byte is set to 1. Each node can have any number of multicast addresses, and any number of nodes can have the same multicast address. The purpose of a multicast address is to allow a group of Ethernet nodes to receive the same transmission simultaneously, in a fashion similar to the AppleTalk broadcast service. See also **broadcast address.**

name: In AppleTalk, consists of three fields: the object, type, and zone.

Name-Binding Protocol (NBP): An AppleTalk protocol that maintains a table that contains the internet address and name of each entity in the node that is visible to other entities on the internet (that is, each entity that has registered a name with NBP).

natural language: The whole body of words and methods of combining words used by a particular group of people.

NBP: See **Name-Binding Protocol.**

notification: An audible or visible indication that your application (or other software) requires the user's attention.

notification queue: The Notification Manager's list of pending notification requests.

notification record: The internal representation of a notification request, through which you specify how a **notification** is to occur.

notification request: A request to the Notification Manager to create a notification.

notification response procedure: A procedure that the Notification Manager can execute as the final step in a notification.

object: The first field in the name of an AppleTalk entity. The object is assigned by the entity itself and can be anything the user or application assigns. See also **name, type, zone.**

offscreen graphics world: A graphics environment created by the offscreen graphics routines of the Graphics Devices Manager.

Open Application event: An Apple event that asks an application to perform the tasks—such as displaying untitled windows—associated with opening itself; one of the four required Apple events.

open connection: The state of a connection when the two connection ends have established communication. Compare **closed connection, half-open connection.**

Open Documents event: An Apple event that requests an application to open one or more documents specified in a list; one of the four required Apple events.

optional parameter: A supplemental parameter in an Apple event used to specify data that the server application should use in addition to the data specified in the **direct parameter.** Optional parameters are listed in the attribute identified by the keyOptionalKeywordAttr keyword. Applications use this attribute to specify or determine whether data exists in the form of optional parameters. Optional parameters need not be included in an Apple event; default values for optional parameters are part of the event definition. It is the responsibility of the server application that handles the event to supply values if optional parameters are omitted. See also **Apple event attribute, Apple event parameter.**

outline: The mathematical description of the **Bézier curves** that make up an outline glyph.

outline font: A collection of outline glyphs in a particular typeface and style with no size restriction. The Font Manager can generate thousands of point sizes from the same TrueType font.

outline glyph: The model of a **glyph** in an outline font, described mathematically by lines and arcs between points.

outline point: A point used by the Font Manager to calculate the lines and curves that constitute an **outline glyph.** See also **Bézier curve.**

page: The basic unit of memory used in **virtual memory.**

paging: The process of moving data between physical memory and the **backing-store file.**

paging device: The volume that contains the **backing-store file.**

palette: A collection of color records, each containing an RGB color and its usage category.

partition: A contiguous block of memory that the Process Manager allocates for an application's use. The partition is divided into specific areas: **application heap, A5 world,** and **stack.**

phonetic order: The order in which characters are pronounced.

pixel: Short for *picture element;* the smallest dot you can draw on the screen.

pixel map: A data structure that contains information about an image's pixels, including their arrangement for display, the number of bits per pixel (its depth), and the colors the image requires.

play from disk: The ability of the Sound Manager to play sampled sounds stored on disk (either in a file or in a resource) continuously without audible gaps.

point: (1) A unit of measurement for type. Twelve points equal 1 pica, and 6 picas equal 1 inch; thus, 1 point equals approximately 1/72 inch. (2) The intersection of a horizontal grid line and a vertical grid line on the coordinate plane, defined by a horizontal and a vertical coordinate. See also **outline point.**

port: (1) A portal through which an open application can exchange information with another open application using the PPC Toolbox. A port is designated by a **port name** and a **location name.** An application can open as many ports as it requires so long as each port name is unique within a particular computer. (2) A connection between the CPU and main memory or a device (such as a terminal) for transferring data. (3) A socket on the back panel of a computer where you plug in a cable for connection to a network or a peripheral device.

port name: A unique identifier for a particular application within a computer. The port name contains a name string, a type string, and a **script code.** An application can specify any number of port names for a single port so long as each name is unique. See also **port.**

Power Manager: The firmware that provides an interface to the power management hardware in the Macintosh Portable computer. The Power Manager also provides some services unique to the Macintosh Portable—such as reading the current clock speed—that are not directly related to power control. See also **Power Manager IC.**

Power Manager IC: The 50753 microprocessor in the Macintosh Portable computer. The Power Manager IC (along with other circuits) controls power to the various subsystems of the Macintosh Portable. See also **Power Manager.**

Preferences folder: A directory located in the System Folder for holding files that record users' configuration settings for applications on a particular Macintosh computer.

preferred partition size: The partition size at which your application can run most effectively and which the Operating System attempts to secure upon launch of the application.

primary caret: The high caret that is displayed at the primary caret position for the character offset in the primary line direction. See also **dual caret.**

primary caret position: The screen location (denoted by a primary caret) associated with the character that has the same direction as the primary line direction.

PrimaryInit record: A data structure in the declaration ROM of a NuBus card that contains initialization code. The Slot Manager executes the code in the PrimaryInit record when it first locates a declaration ROM during system startup. See also **SecondaryInit record.**

primary line direction: The dominant line direction of the current script system, specified by the value of the system alignment global variable, TESysJust.

Print Documents event: An Apple event that requests that an application print a list of documents; one of the four required Apple events.

PrintMonitor Documents folder: A directory located in the System Folder for storing spooled documents waiting to be printed.

privilege model: A set of conventions for controlling access to stored files.

process: An open application or, in some cases, an open desk accessory. (Only desk accessories that are not opened in the context of another application are considered processes.)

process serial number: A number assigned by the Process Manager to identify a particular instance of an application during a single boot of the local machine.

programming language: A set of symbols and associated rules or conventions for writing programs. For example, BASIC, Logo, and Pascal are programming languages.

publish: To make data available to other documents and applications through a publisher. When a user creates or edits the data in the publisher and then saves it, the current version of the data is stored in an edition. See also **edition, publisher, subscribe.**

publisher: A portion of a document that makes its data available to other documents or applications. A publisher stores its data in an edition whenever a user creates or edits the data in the publisher and then saves it. See also **edition, section, subscriber.**

query: A string of commands and data sent to a database or other data source. A query does not necessarily extract data from a data source; it might only send data or commands to a database or other application.

query definition function: A function contained in a **query document** that prompts the user for information and modifies the query before the Data Access Manager sends it to the data server.

query document: A file of file type 'qery' containing commands and data in a format appropriate for a database or other data source. An application uses high-level Data Access Manager routines to open a query document.

query record: A data structure in memory containing information provided by a 'qrsc' resource. The query record includes a pointer to a **query.**

Quit Application event: An Apple event that requests that an application perform the tasks—such as releasing memory, asking the user to save documents, and so on—associated with quitting; one of the four required Apple events. The Finder sends this event to an application immediately after sending it a Print Documents event or if the user chooses Restart or Shut Down from the Finder's Special menu.

region: (1) An arbitrary area or set of areas on the QuickDraw coordinate plane. The outline of a region should be one or more closed loops. (2) A linguistic or cultural entity that does not necessarily correspond to a province or nation and is associated with a number, called a **region code,** that indicates a specific localized version of Macintosh system software.

region code: A number used to indicate a particular localized version of Macintosh system software. Constants for region codes are defined in the MPW files PackMacs.a, Packages.h, and Packages.p.

relative path: The path through a volume's hierarchy from one file or directory to another.

required Apple event: One of four core Apple events that the Finder sends to applications. These events are called Open Documents, Open Application, Print Documents, and Quit Application. They are a subset of the **core Apple events.**

required parameter: A keyword-specified descriptor record in an Apple event that must be specified. For example, a list of documents to open is a required parameter for the Open Documents event. **Direct parameters** are often required, and other **additional parameters** may be required. **Optional parameters** are never required.

Rescued Items from *volume name* folder: A directory located in the Trash directory that is created by the Finder at system startup, restart, or shutdown only when it finds items in the Temporary Items folder, usually after a system crash. The Rescued Items from *volume name* directory is named for the volume on which the Temporary Items folder exists. When a user empties the Trash, all Rescued Items folders disappear.

result handler: A routine that the Data Access Manager calls to convert a data item to a character string.

routing table: A table, maintained by RTMP, that specifies the shortest path to each possible destination network number. See also **Routing Table Maintenance Protocol.**

Routing Table Maintenance Protocol (RTMP): A protocol used by routers on an AppleTalk internet to determine how to forward a data packet to the network number to which it is addressed. See also **routing table, RTMP stub.**

RTMP: See **Routing Table Maintenance Protocol.**

RTMP stub: The portion of the Routing Table Maintenance Protocol contained in an AppleTalk node other than a router. DDP uses the RTMP stub to determine the network number (or range of network numbers) of the network cable to which the node is connected and to determine the network number and node ID of one router on that network cable. See also **Datagram Delivery Protocol.**

run: A sequence of text that is contiguous in memory and that has the same attributes, such as font, size, style, script, color, and direction. See also **direction run, script run, style run.**

sampled sound synthesizer: A **sound synthesizer** that generates digitally recorded or computed sounds.

saturation: A measurement of how much white a color contains—the less white, the more saturated the color.

script: A writing system for a human language, which may include characters that are **alphabetic, syllabic,** or **ideographic.** Scripts may differ in the direction in which their characters and lines are written sequentially, the size of the character set used to represent the script, and context dependence. Examples of scripts include Roman, Japanese, Arabic, and Hebrew. Many scripts—like Japanese, Chinese, and Korean—have more than one **subscript.**

script code: A number indicating a particular script system on the Macintosh. Constants for these numbers are defined in the MPW interface files ScriptEqu.a, Script.h, and Script.p.

script run: A sequence of text that is contiguous in memory and that is all in the same script.

script system: A collection of software facilities that provides for basic differences between writing systems, such as character sets, fonts, keyboards, text collation, and word breaks. Examples of script systems are Roman, Japanese, Arabic, Traditional Chinese, Simplified Chinese, Hebrew, Greek, Thai, and Korean. See also **script, subscript.**

secondary caret: The low caret that is displayed at the secondary caret position for the character offset. See also **dual caret**.

secondary caret position: The screen location (denoted by the secondary caret) associated with the character that has an opposing direction from the primary line direction.

SecondaryInit record: A data structure in the declaration ROM of a NuBus card that contains initialization code. The Slot Manager executes the code in the SecondaryInit record after RAM patches to the Operating System have been loaded from disk during system startup. See also **PrimaryInit record.**

secondary script: An auxiliary writing system that can be used in documents but does not control the default behavior of the script system.

section: A document or portion of a document that shares its contents with other documents. The Edition Manager supports two types of sections: publishers and subscribers. A publisher makes its data available to share and a subscriber subscribes to available data. See also **publisher, subscriber.**

selector: See **selector code.**

selector code: A parameter passed to the Gestalt function indicating what information about the operating environment the application currently requires.

selector function: The function called by the Gestalt function when an application has called Gestalt to determine information about the operating environment.

server application: An application that, using the **Apple Event Interprocess Messaging Protocol,** offers a service (for example, printing files, spell-checking words, or performing numerical calculations) to other applications (called **client applications**). Apple event servers and clients can reside on the same local computer or on remote computers connected to a network.

session: (1) A logical (as opposed to physical) connection between two entities (such as a Macintosh program and a database server) that facilitates the transmission of information between the two entities. (2) In the PPC Toolbox, an exchange of information between one open application with a port and another open application with a port. Sessions can occur between applications that are located on the same computer or across a network. An application has the option to accept or reject a session request. Authentication of the requesting user may be required before a session can commence. See also **authentication, message block, port.**

session ID: A number that uniquely identifies a **session.**

7.0-compatible: Said of an application that runs without problems in system software version 7.0.

7.0-dependent: Said of an application that requires the existence of features that are present only in system software version 7.0.

7.0-friendly: Said of an application that is 7.0-compatible and takes advantage of some of the special features of system software version 7.0, but is still able to perform all its principal functions when operating in version 6.0.

signature: A resource whose type is defined by a four-character sequence that uniquely identifies an application to the Finder. A signature is located in an application's resource fork.

simple script system: A script system that represents scripts with small character sets, requires only single-byte characters, has a text direction of left to right, and is not context-dependent. Examples of simple script systems are Roman and Cyrillic. See also **script system.**

sleep demand: A message from the Power Manager that informs a sleep queue routine that the Power Manager is about to put the Macintosh Portable into the sleep state. When a routine in the sleep queue receives a sleep demand, it must prepare for the sleep state as quickly as possible and return control to the Power Manager. See also **sleep request, sleep-request revocation, wakeup demand.**

sleep queue: An operating-system queue that contains pointers to all of the routines that the Power Manager must call before it puts the Macintosh Portable computer into the sleep state or returns it to the operating state.

sleep request: A message from the Power Manager that informs a sleep queue routine that the Power Manager would like to put the Macintosh Portable computer into the sleep state. The routine then has the option of denying the sleep request. See also **sleep demand, sleep-request revocation, wakeup demand.**

sleep-request revocation: A message from the Power Manager that informs a sleep queue routine that the Power Manager has canceled a sleep request. The routine then can reverse any changes it made in response to the sleep request. See also **sleep demand, sleep request, wakeup demand.**

sleep state: A low–power-consumption state of the Macintosh Portable computer. In the sleep state, the Power Manager and the various device drivers shut off power or remove clocks from the computer's various subsystems, including the CPU, RAM, ROM, and I/O ports.

slop value: The difference between the desired width and actual width before justification of a line of text or of a **style run.** The Script Manager justification routines assume the slop value for a line is to be distributed among the style runs on a line and among the words and characters within a style run.

slot: A connector into which a card can be installed to expand the capabilities of a computer.

slot resource: See **sResource data structure.**

Slot Resource Table: A table maintained by the Slot Manager that lists all of the sResource data structures currently available to the system.

sound channel: A queue of **sound commands** created by the Sound Manager and linked to a sound synthesizer.

sound-channel initialization parameter: A parameter passed to the SndNewChannel function indicating the type of sound characteristics the specified sound channel should have.

sound command: An instruction to a synthesizer to produce sound, modify sound, or otherwise assist in the overall process of sound production.

sound file: A file of file type 'AIFF' or 'AIFC' that can be used to store sound commands and sound data. See also **sound resource.**

sound resource: A resource of resource type 'snd ' that can be used to store sound commands and sound data. See also **sound file.**

sound synthesizer: The executable code (stored in a resource of resource type 'snth') that is linked to a sound channel and manages all communication between the Sound Manager and the available sound hardware. See also **sampled sound synthesizer, square-wave synthesizer, wave-table synthesizer.**

source application: The application that sends a particular Apple event to another application or to itself. Typically, an Apple event client sends an Apple event requesting a service from an Apple event server; in this case, the client is the source application for the Apple event. The Apple event server may return a different Apple event as a reply—in which case, the server is the source for the reply Apple event.

square-wave synthesizer: A sound synthesizer that generates sounds described by a square wave.

sResource data structure: A data structure in the declaration ROM of a NuBus card that defines a function or capability of the card. There is one sResource data structure for each function the card can perform plus one sResource data structure that identifies the card. Sometimes called a *slot resource.*

stack: An area of memory in the application **partition** that is used to store temporary variables.

Startup Items folder: A directory located in the System Folder for storing applications and desk accessories that the user wants started up every time the Finder starts up.

static window: A window that doesn't change its title or reposition any of the objects within its content area.

stationery pad: A document that a user creates to serve as a template for other documents. The Finder tags a document as a stationery pad by setting the isStationery bit in the Finder flags field of the file's FInfo record. An application that is asked to open a stationery pad should copy the template's contents into a new document and open the document in an untitled window.

status routine: A routine provided by a developer that can update windows, check the results of the low-level calls made by the Data Access Manager's DBStartQuery and DBGetQueryResults functions, and cancel execution of these functions when appropriate to do so.

style run: A sequence of text that is contiguous in memory and in which all the characters are in the same typeface, size, style, color, and script. Also called *format run.*

subscribe: To obtain data that a publisher makes available in an edition. A user subscribes to a publisher by choosing Subscribe To from the Edit menu and selecting the desired edition. See also **edition, publish.**

subscriber: A portion of a document that automatically obtains current data from other documents and applications. A subscriber reads data from an edition. See also **edition, section.**

subscript: A distinguishable subset of characters included within a script. For example, the subscripts of the Japanese Script System include Hiragana and Katakana (syllabic), Kanji (ideographic), and Romaji (alphabetic).

syllabic: Used to describe a type of character representation in which the characters stand for syllables in the language—for example, Japanese Katakana.

symmetrical protocol: A communications protocol in which the two clients at either end of the connection are equal and can perform exactly the same operations.

synthesizer: See **sound synthesizer.**

system alert sound: A sound resource stored in the System file that is played whenever an application or other executable code calls the SysBeep procedure.

system Apple event dispatch table: A table in the system heap that the Apple Event Manager uses to map Apple events to those Apple event handlers that are available to all applications and processes running on the same computer.

system coercion table: A table in the system heap that contains **coercion handlers** available to all applications and processes running on the same computer.

System file: A file, located in the System Folder, that contains the basic system software plus some system resources, such as font and sound resources. In system software version 7.0, the System file behaves like a folder in this regard: although it looks like a suitcase icon, double-clicking it opens a window that reveals movable resource files (such as fonts, sounds, keyboard layouts, and script system resource collections) stored in the System file.

system menu: A menu that is used to provide access to system features such as application switching, Balloon Help, keyboard script systems, and so forth. All system menus use icons as titles.

system result handler: A **result handler** that is available to all applications that use the Operating System. Compare **application result handler.**

system script: The primary **script system** specified in the 'itlc' resource that is used by various parts of the Operating System—in dialog boxes and menu bars, for example. The system script affects system defaults, such as the default font, line direction, and so forth. All other scripts are secondary or auxiliary to the system script. Also called *primary script.*

target: The file, directory, or volume described by an alias record.

target address: An application signature, a process serial number, a session ID, a target ID record, or some other application-defined type that identifies the target of an Apple event.

target application: The application addressed to receive an Apple event. Typically, an Apple event client sends an Apple event requesting a service from an Apple event server; in this case, the server is the target application of the Apple event. The Apple event server may return a different Apple event as a reply—in which case, the client is the target of the reply Apple event.

Temporary Items folder: A directory located at the root level of a volume for storing temporary buffer files created by applications. The Temporary Items folder is invisible to the user.

temporary memory: Memory allocated outside of an application's heap zone that may be available for occasional short-term use.

text rendering: The process of displaying characters that are stored in memory.

32-bit addressing: The ability to use all 32 bits of a pointer or handle in determining memory addresses.

32-bit clean: Said of an application that is able to run in an environment where all 32 bits of a memory address are used for addressing.

tip: For a help balloon, the point at the side of the rounded rectangle that indicates what object or area is explained in the help balloon. See also **help balloon, variation code.**

token: An abstract category (represented by sequences of characters) that stands for a variable name, symbol, or quoted literal. A token may have more than one representation—for example, less than or equal to can be represented as <= or ≤.

tolerant color: A usage category for colors in a palette. It specifies how closely the RGB color needs to be matched when the color is displayed.

transaction: A sequence of Apple events sent back and forth between a client and a server application, beginning with the client's initial request for a service. All Apple events that are part of one transaction must have the same transaction ID.

transaction-based protocol: A communications protocol in which one socket client transmits a request for some action and the other socket client carries out the action and transmits a response.

Trash folder: A directory at the root level of a volume for storing files that the user has moved to the Trash icon. After opening the Trash icon, the user sees the collection of all items that the user has moved to the Trash icon—that is, the union of appropriate Trash directories from all mounted volumes. A Macintosh set up to share files among users in a network environment maintains separate Trash subdirectories for remote users within its shared, network Trash directory. The Finder for system software version 7.0 empties a Trash directory (or, in the case of a file server, a Trash subdirectory) only when the user of that directory chooses the Empty Trash command.

type: The second field in the name of an AppleTalk entity. The type is assigned by the entity itself and can be anything the user or application assigns. See also **name, object, zone.**

typeface: A distinctly designed collection of glyphs for a particular character set. Each typeface has its own name, such as New York or Symbol. Compare **font.**

unsolicited connection event: An event initiated by ADSP or the remote connection end that is not in response to any .DSP routine that you executed. See also **AppleTalk Data Stream Protocol.**

usage category: A specification of how colors in a palette are to be displayed. Categories are animated, courteous, explicit, inhibited, tolerant, pmWhite, and pmBlack.

variation code: In the header component of a help resource, an integer that specifies the preferred position of a help balloon relative to its hot rectangle. The balloon definition function draws the frame of the help balloon based on its variation code.

verb: An integer constant that controls the function of a multipurpose routine.

virtual memory: The part of the Operating System that allows any properly configured Macintosh computer with an MMU (or PMMU) to extend the available amount of memory beyond the limits of physical RAM.

wakeup demand: A message from the Power Manager that informs a sleep queue routine that it must reverse whatever steps it followed when it prepared for the sleep state. See also **sleep demand, sleep request, sleep-request revocation.**

wakeup timer: A timer that the Power Manager uses to return the Macintosh Portable computer from the sleep state to the operating state at a specific time.

wave table: A sequence of wave amplitudes measured at fixed intervals.

wave-table synthesizer: A sound synthesizer that generates sounds described by a wave table.

word: (1) In natural languages, a representation of a sound or a combination of sounds meaning a certain object, feeling, or idea; one of the basic components of language. A word comprises one or more characters whose visual representations are called **glyphs.** (2) Prior to system software version 6.0.4, as defined by TextEdit, any series of printing characters, excluding spaces (ASCII code $20) and including nonbreaking spaces (ASCII code $CA). In system software version 7.0, TextEdit also depends on the Script Manager's FindWord procedure, so TextEdit's definition of a word has been extended. The way TextEdit uses the Script Manager's FindWord procedure to calculate word breaks has a significant impact on word selection. For example, in the system software that is localized for the United States, parentheses and other punctuation marks are no longer included as part of a word selection. However, this behavior may vary on other localized versions of the U.S. system software. Furthermore, when a user double-clicks a series of spaces, that series of spaces is selected as a word.

word wrap: The automatic continuation of text from the end of one line to the beginning of the next without breaking in the middle of a word.

working directory: A temporary directory reference that the File Manager uses to specify both a directory and the volume it resides on. The File Manager assigns a reference number to each working directory.

worldwide system software: The system software that enables you to create versions of your applications that run in other regions or work with different scripts and languages. Worldwide software includes the **Macintosh Script Management System** and related components, such as the International Utilities Package, the international resources, the keyboard resources, the Macintosh script systems, and certain keyboard-handling routines.

ZIP: See **Zone Information Protocol.**

zone: A logical grouping of a subset of the nodes on the internet. The zone is the third field in the name of an AppleTalk entity. See also **name, object, type.**

Zone Information Protocol (ZIP): An AppleTalk protocol that maintains a table in each router, called the *zone information table,* that lists the relationships between zone names and networks.

INDEX

A

Index

Index

Index

Index

C

D

Index

E

F

G

Index

H

Index

Index

L

N

Index

Index

S

Index

T

Index

U

Index

V

X, Y

Z

THE APPLE PUBLISHING SYSTEM

This Apple manual was written, edited, and composed on a desktop publishing system using Apple Macintosh® computers and Microsoft Word software. Proof pages were created on an Apple LaserWriter® IINTX printer. Final page negatives were output directly from text files on an Agfa ProSet 9800 imagesetter. Line art was created using Adobe Illustrator. PostScript®, the page-description language for the LaserWriter, was developed by Adobe Systems Incorporated.

Text type is Times and display type is Helvetica Bold. Bullets are ITC Zapf Dingbats®. Some elements, such as program listings, are set in Apple Courier.

Lead Writer: Sharon Everson

Writers: Paul Black, Patria Brown, Rob Dearborn, Tony Francis, Mitchell Gass, Lori E. Kaplan, Marq Laube, Sue Luttner, Tim Monroe, Diane Patterson, Laine Rapin

Lead Developmental Editor: Sue Factor

Developmental Editors: Stella Hackell, Antonio Padial, Anne Szabla, George Truett

Indexing Specialist: Laurel Rezeau

Editorial Advisor: Lorraine Aochi

Lead Illustrator: Deb Dennis

Art staff: Tim Hughan, Sandee Karr, Peggy Kunz, Dave Olmos

Programmer: Ray Chiang

Technical Advisor: Sharon Everson

Production: Rex Wolf, Gerri Gray

Formatter: Roy Zitting

Proofreaders: Beverly Zegarski, Wendy Krafft

Inside Macintosh Manager: Trish Eastman

Special thanks to the Macintosh system software engineering team, for creating the system software of the 1990s, and Macintosh Developer Technical Support, for being there.